AGING in AMERICA

AGING in AMERICA

Second Edition
2016

Edited by Robert L. Scardamalia

FOR REFERENCE
Not to be taken
from this room

LOS ALAMOS COUNTY LIBRARY
MESA PUBLIC LIBRARY
2400 CENTRAL AVENUE
LOS ALAMOS, NM 87544

Bernan Press

Lanham, MD

REF
305.26
Ag 471
2016

Published in the United States of America
by Bernan Press, a wholly owned subsidiary of
The Rowman & Littlefield Publishing Group, Inc.
4501 Forbes Boulevard, Suite 200
Lanham, Maryland 20706

800-462-6420; info@bernan.com
www.rowman.com

Copyright © 2016 by Bernan Press

All rights reserved. No part of this publication may be reproduced, stored in
a retrieval system, or transmitted in any form or by any means, electronic,
mechanical, photocopying, recording, or otherwise, without the prior
permission of the publisher. Bernan Press does not claim copyright in
U.S. government information

ISBN-13: 978-1-59888-863-8
eISBN-13: 978-1-59888-864-5

∞™ The paper used in this publication meets the minimum requirements
of American National Standard for Information Sciences—Permanence of
Paper for Printed Library Materials, ANSI/NISO Z39.48-1992.
Manufactured in the United States of America.

Contents

Preface

The 2010 census was different from any census in recent memory. All American households answered a simple questionnaire with ten questions. No longer did some people get the "long form" which included dozens of detailed questions about employment, education, income, previous residence, housing characteristics, and more. The data gleaned from these important questions have long been used by federal, state, and local governments to evaluate their populations and program needs; by large and small businesses and nonprofit organizations for a variety of planning and location purposes; and by academic researchers to study trends in social and economic conditions. However, the cost, timeliness, and quality of the traditional long form data made it necessary to develop a new data collection strategy for gathering economic and demographic characteristics of the nation.

The "long form" has been replaced by the American Community Survey (ACS). Under development for more than a decade, the ACS is an ongoing survey of the American people that ushered in a new era in social and economic data analysis. The census "long form" provided detailed estimates of social and economic characteristics every ten years. The ACS collects this same information on a rolling basis. It takes 5 years of ACS responses to accumulate a sample almost as large as the census "long form" collected at a single point in time. But data users now have the ability to study these characteristics and trends throughout the decade—annually for some areas.

Because the ACS is a sample survey, large numbers of sample cases are needed before reliable estimates can be made for small populations. Each year's sample is large enough to produce estimates for the nation, all the states, most metropolitan areas, and many counties and cities. The tables in this volume include single year estimates for 2014 (the most current year available) for the United States, all states and congressional districts, as well as, metropolitan and micropolitan areas, counties, and cities of 65,000 or more population.

The richness of the ACS data can be accessed in varying degrees. Much more subject matter detail is available for large geographic areas partly because reliable estimates for large areas can be produced with smaller samples, and partly because more data must be suppressed for the smaller areas to protect the confidentiality of the respondents.

This second edition is designed to include a sampling of key information about the older population but also help users understand the survey data and resources to access more detailed data available from the Census Bureau and the ACS. The ten subject area tables in this book include 130 data items for each geographic area. This is a small sampling of the detailed data available.

One of the most notable differences between the census "long form" and the ACS is the time frame of the estimates. We are accustomed to the census data that give us specific information every ten years, a snapshot of the country on April 1. The ACS multiyear estimates are different as the Census Bureau surveys nearly 300,000 households every month. The data in this book are from the ACS 1-year 2014 estimates which are produced from the 12 calendar months of survey data collection. The estimates reported here represent an "average" population profile over the 12 months of 2014. The sample cases are spread evenly throughout the year rather than the "point in time" decennial census estimates reported as of April 1.

To help in the understanding of these estimates, we have included a measure of population change for each geographic area. These are from the 2010 census and the 2014 estimates, showing the actual population growth or decline in each geographic area. Each table shows population characteristics as estimated for 2014. It should be remembered that the decennial census and the Census Bureau's Population Estimates Program provide the official population counts that underlie the ACS sample. If an area experienced unusually large population growth or decline, we should understand that these short-term population impacts may not be reflected in the ACS period estimates. Changes due to a city annexing a large tract of land, many people moving into a new development, or many people leaving the area because of a plant closing may be hidden in the short-term.

With the ACS, there is always a trade-off between data currency and data reliability. More current 1-year estimates come from smaller samples and therefore have larger margins of error. Estimates from the 5-year data are based on five times the sample size and have smaller margins of error—but of course, they do not represent as current a period. The first edition of Aging in American relied on the Census Bureau's 3-year (2010–2012) estimates because of the larger sample size and smaller margins of error inherent in the longer period estimates. Due to the elimination of the 3-year data series, the current volume reports the results of the 1-year 2014 data. Users may want to compare data between the two editions but should use caution as there will be more sample variability in the 2014 data and small differences may not be meaningful. Users will also notice that there are a number of geographic areas where the estimates not reported due to the Census Bureau's data disclosure rules.

Finally, it is always critical to remember that all estimates are subject to sampling error. On the Census Bureau's website, every ACS number is accompanied by its margin of error. In the interests of space and simplicity, this book does not include the margins of error, but all users are encouraged to consult the Census Bureau's website and to understand some basics: small differences are very likely to represent no difference at all; do not draw conclusions from small numbers; use these numbers as a starting point to explore the wealth of information from the ACS.

Introduction

The American Community Survey (ACS) has ushered in the most substantial change in the decennial census in more than 60 years. It replaced the decennial census long form in 2010, providing more current data throughout the decade by collecting long-form-type information annually rather than only once every 10 years. The ACS provides annual data for states, metropolitan areas, and large cities and counties, and combines multiple years of survey responses to produce data for midsize communities. Very small communities (under 65,000 population) and statistical areas like census tracts and zip code tabulation areas require 5 years of survey responses to yield characteristic estimates.

The ACS gathers demographic, social, economic, housing, and financial information about the nation's people and communities on a continuous basis. The ACS is an ongoing survey conducted by the U.S. Census Bureau in every county, American Indian and Alaska Native Area, and Hawaiian Home Land in the United States. The ACS is also conducted as the Puerto Rico Community Survey in every municipality in Puerto Rico. As the largest survey in the United States, it is the only source of small-area data on a wide range of important social and economic characteristics for all communities in the country. After years of planning, development, and a demonstration period, the ACS began nationwide full implementation in 2005.

Information about the ACS are available on the Census Bureau's website. The ACS main page is http://www.census.gov/acs/www. Data from the ACS is available from American FactFinder at http://factfinder.census.gov.

A vast amount of information is collected in the ACS. In this publication, selections of these data have been assembled in various tables by subject and geographic type.

VOLUME ORGANIZATION

The data tables in this book pertain to the older population, generally those 60 years of age and over and include a selection of population and housing characteristics from the ACS in ten subject areas:

- Population summary
- Age structure
- Race and ethnicity
- Household relationships and living arrangements
- Educational attainment and veteran status
- Employment and labor force status
- Income and poverty status
- Disability status
- Health insurance
- Housing summary

The 1-year estimates from the American Community Survey provide data for all areas of 65,000 population or more. Each subject area includes data for the United States, the 50 states and the District of Columbia and the following:

- 800+ counties, listed alphabetically within state,
- 500+ metropolitan and micropolitan statistical areas, listed alphabetically,
- 500+ cities, listed alphabetically within state,
- All 435 Congressional districts, listed numerically by state.

In addition, each part is preceded by highlights, maps and/or summary tables that show how areas diverge from the national norm, as well as the differences among areas. These research aids are invaluable for helping people understand what the census data tell us about who we are, what we do, and where we live.

In the following sections, information about the ACS and how to use the data is included, much of it excerpted from the wealth of information available on the Census Bureau's website. Especially helpful are the instructions, definitions, and guidelines on using the data in the section on "Guidance for Data Users." Readers are encouraged to explore the Census Bureau's website to expand on the information contained here and to keep up to date with this constantly changing dataset.

Robert Scardamalia is President of RLS Demographics, Inc. a firm providing data and analysis to private organizations, government agencies, and not-for-profits, especially in the areas of aging services and business development. He is an adjunct professor in the Sociology Department of the State University of New York at Albany. Prior to forming RLS Demographics, he was Chief Demographer of New York State and directed the Center for Research and Information Analysis in the New York Department of Economic Development. He also directed the New York State Data Center for more than 20 years. Mr. Scardamalia serves on the Board of the Association of Public Data Users and is a past President. He has chaired the national State Data Center Steering Committee and served on numerous Census Bureau committees. He holds a Master of Arts in Demography from Georgetown University and Bachelor of Arts in Sociology from Penn State University.

Understanding the American Community Survey

Every 10 years since 1790, as required by the U.S. Constitution, Congress has authorized funds to conduct a national census of the U.S. population. From 1960 through 2000, censuses have consisted of:

- a "short form," which included basic questions about age, sex, race, Hispanic origin (since 1980), household relationship, and owner/renter status, and

- a "long form" used for a sample of approximately one of every six households that included not only the basic short-form questions but also detailed questions about socioeconomic and housing characteristics.

Beginning with the 2010 census, the American Community Survey (ACS) replaced the decennial census long form by collecting long-form-type information annually rather than only once every 10 years, providing more current data throughout the decade. The 2010 Census counted the population to support the constitutional mandate—to provide population counts needed to apportion the seats in the U.S. House of Representatives. The ACS data now provide, for the first time, a regular stream of updated information for states and local areas, revolutionizing the way we use data to understand our communities. It produces social, housing, and economic characteristics for demographic groups, even for geographic areas as small as census tracts and block groups.

SOME KEY FACTS ABOUT THE ACS

- The ACS annually provides the same kind of detailed information previously available only every 10 years from the census. The ACS is conducted under the authority of Title 13, United States Code, Sections 141 and 193.

- All answers are confidential. Any Census Bureau employee who violates that confidentiality is subject to a jail term, a fine, or both.

- The Census Bureau may use the information it collects only for statistical purposes.

- Addresses are selected at random from the Master Address File to represent similar households in the area. Approximately 290,000 addresses are selected each month and the survey is conducted by mail, telephone, and personal visit. Response to this survey is required by federal statute Section 221 of Title 13.

- Approximately 2.9 percent of U.S. households are surveyed each year. A sample of group quarters (nursing homes, college dormitories, etc.) is included in the ACS as well.

- While the ACS sample size approximates the traditional long-form census sample, it is a smaller sample resulting in somewhat larger margins of error.

The traditional long-form census taken once a decade provided the socio-economic portrait of the nation and communities but that portrait was fixed in time for 10 years. Data from the ACS provides a regular update to that portrait which is used for a variety of purposes that include: monitoring the well-being of America's older population, children and families, tracking trends in disability, analyzing the growth in the number of grandparents responsible for their grandchildren, determining the economic well-being of the elderly and working-poor families, or tracking social, economic, and demographic changes in the general U.S. population.

The ACS provides critical information for communities on a current basis, when they need it most. But the ACS is still a relatively new data collection instrument and a different measure of the characteristics of the population and households. Researchers are still working to understand the differences from the traditional census data so it is good to be cautious in the interpretation of differences between areas and across time. Small differences may not be meaningful. On the other hand, the ACS provides annual estimates and the frequency of updates and currency of the data far outweighs waiting 10 years for new results.

NEW OPPORTUNITIES

The main benefits of the ACS are timeliness and access to annual data for states, local areas, and small population subgroups. The ACS will deliver useful, relevant data, similar to data from previous census long forms, but updated every year rather than every 10 years. The ACS provides comparable information across and within states for program evaluation and use in funding formulas.

- ACS information is often used to determine the placement of new schools, senior residential services, hospitals, and highways.

- ACS provides information for tracking the well-being of children, families, and the elderly allowing service providers to better target populations in need.

- The data will improve the distribution of aid through federal, state, and local governments. More than $400 billion in federal program funds are distributed each year based, in whole or in part, on census and ACS data.

- The data are used by community programs, such as those for the elderly, libraries, hospitals, banks, and other organizations.

- The data are used by transportation planners to evaluate peak volumes of traffic in order to reduce congestion, plan for parking, and develop plans for carpooling and flexible work schedules.

- Corporations, small businesses, and individuals use these data to develop business plans, to set strategies for expansion or starting a business, and to determine trends in their service areas to meet current and future needs.

- Small towns and rural communities have much to gain from the ACS. Lacking the staff and resources to conduct their own research, many local communities have relied on decennial census information that became increasingly outdated throughout the decade, or used local administrative records that are not comparable with information collected in neighboring areas.

- The ACS also provides tools for those who want to conduct their own research. The ACS includes a Public Use Microdata Sample (PUMS) file each year that enables researchers to create custom universes and tabulations from individual ACS records that have been stripped of personally identifiable information.

- Because the ACS data collection occurs every month, the Census Bureau uses professional, highly trained, permanent interviewers which have improved the accuracy of ACS data compared with those from the decennial census long-form sample. This strategy has effectively reduced the number of refusals to complete the ACS questionnaire and allows interviewers to obtain more complete information than decennial census interviewers.

NEW CHALLENGES

The main challenges for ACS data users are understanding and using multiyear estimates and the relatively large margins of error associated with ACS data for smaller geographic areas and subgroups of the population.

- ACS data will be produced every year, but the sample size of the ACS is smaller than that of the Census 2000 long form sample. Data users need to pay more attention to the margin of error.

- Data users have access to 5-year estimates of ACS data. The sample size based on 5-year period estimates of ACS data is still smaller than the long-form sample in the decennial census, resulting in larger margins of error in the ACS 5-year estimates.

- Prior to the current 2014 data release, the ACS produced 1-year, 3-year, and 5-year estimates so areas of 65,000 population or more received three separate estimates of the same characteristic every year. For example, a large city would receive 1-year, 3-year and 5-year estimates of the number of persons 65 and over in poverty. Data users will have to decide which datasets were appropriate for their needs.

- As of 2014, the Census Bureau eliminated all 3-year estimates products as a cost saving measure. Areas of 65,000 or more will still receive annual estimates but all other areas below 65,000 will only receive estimates based on five years of data collection. Large areas of 65,000 or more will now only have two separate estimates rather than three. The historical 3-year data is still available.

- Data users will need to be aware of the implications of multiyear estimates, particularly in analyzing employment and income data that will span a full year or even a 5-year period.

- Multiyear estimates, especially the 5-year estimates will not reflect short-term changes in the population or economy of an area. The recent recession is a good example because the 5-year ACS estimates span both the fall into recession and the resulting growth coming out.

The ACS includes several questions that are very similar to those collected in other federal surveys—especially the Current Population Survey (CPS), the American Housing Survey, and the Survey of Income and Program Participation. In some cases, there are clear guidelines about which data to use. For example, the CPS is the official source of income and poverty data. It includes detailed questions on these topics and should be used in reporting national trends in these subject areas. The Census Bureau recommends that ACS information on income and poverty be used to supplement CPS data for areas below the state level and for population subgroups (such as age, sex, race, Hispanic origin, type of household) at the state level. For an explanation of various income and poverty data sources, see the Census Bureau's guidelines at http://www.census.gov/hhes/www/poverty/about/data-sources/description.html. For states, generally the Census Bureau recommends using the ACS, though the CPS is still valuable as a source for examining historical state income and poverty trends.

DATA COLLECTION VERSUS DATA REPORTING

Results from the ACS are reported each year which is a major advantage over the traditional long-form data from the decennial census. But unlike the release of data only once every 10 years in the decennial census, the annual release of data from the ACS can be quite confusing. The ACS sample size is such that the reliability of the data is greatly affected by the length of the data collection period and the size of geographic reporting areas. In survey sampling, it is well understood that larger samples yield more reliable estimates with smaller margins of error. In order to produce reliable estimates from the ACS, it is necessary to collect the data over differing periods of time in order to provide estimates for all areas, including small areas like census tracts.

Each set of period estimates is released each year, generally between September and December, and reflect data collection ending in the previous calendar year. Thus, the collection year 2014 1-year estimates for areas of 65,000 or more were released in September of 2014 while the 2010–2014 5-year estimates followed with a December 2014 release.

THE ACS SAMPLE

The ACS is sent each month to a sample of roughly 290,000 addresses in the United States and Puerto Rico, or about 3.5 million a year, resulting in more than 2.3 million final interviews. The sample represents all housing units and group quarters in the United States and Puerto Rico. (Group quarters include places such as college dormitories, prisons, military barracks, and nursing homes.) The addresses are selected from the Census Bureau's Master Address File (MAF), which is also the basis for the decennial census.

The annual ACS sample is smaller than that of the Census 2000 long-form sample, which included about 18 million housing units. As a result, the ACS needs to combine population or housing data from multiple years to produce reliable numbers for small counties, neighborhoods, and other local areas. To provide information for communities each year, the ACS will provide 1- and 5-year estimates.

The ACS sample is not spread evenly across all areas but includes a larger proportion of addresses in sparsely populated rural communities and American Indian reservations and a lower proportion in densely populated areas. Over a 5-year period, the ACS will sample more than 15 million addresses and complete interviews for about 11 million. This sample is sufficient to produce estimates for small geographic areas, such as neighborhoods and sparsely-populated rural counties though the estimates will have larger margins of error than the census long-form data. In a 5-year period no address will be selected for the ACS more than once, and many addresses will never be selected for the survey. It's important to remember that the sample is address based so while a given address will not be in sample again for at least five years, it is possible that individuals who move or have a second home could be surveyed more than once.

GEOGRAPHY

The ACS data are tabulated for a variety of geographic areas ranging in size from broad geographic regions (Northeast, Midwest, South, and West) to cities, towns, neighborhoods, and census block groups. Before December 2008, the ACS data were only available for geographic areas with at least 65,000 people, including regions, divisions, states, the District of Columbia, Puerto Rico, congressional districts, Public Use Microdata Areas (PUMAs)—census-constructed geographic areas, each with approximately a population of 100,000—and many large counties, metropolitan areas, cities, school districts, and American Indian areas. Starting in December 2008, 3-year estimates became available for all areas with at least 20,000 residents, and in 2010, 5-year estimates for geographic areas down to the block group level became available. One-, three-, and five-year estimates—three

Data Product	Population Threshold	Year of Data Release							
		2008	**2009**	**2010**	**2011**	**2012**	**2013**	**2014**	**2015**
		Year(s) of Data Collection							
1-year Estimates	65,000+	2007	2008	2009	2010	2011	2012	2013	2014
5-year Estimates	All Areas			2005–2009	2006–2010	2007–2011	2008–2012	2009–2013	

sets of numbers—were available and were refreshed every year up until the 2014 data release. Less populous areas will receive only 5-year estimates. The vast majority of areas will receive only 5-year estimates.

The data tables in this book contain data from the 1-year 2014 estimates. These tables are based on the 2010 tabulation geography for political and statistical areas, the same definitions as the 2010 Census. Changes in area boundaries can occur as a result of annexation, new incorporation or disincorporation of cities, towns, and places. For multiyear estimates, the Census Bureau reports the data based on the most current geographic boundaries incorporating any changes occurring in the multiyear period.

DATA COMPARABILITY

Since the ACS data are collected continuously, they are not always comparable with data collected from the decennial census. For example, both surveys ask about employment status during the week prior to the survey. However, data from the decennial census are typically collected between March and July with a reference date of April 1, whereas data from the ACS are collected nearly every day and reflect employment throughout the year. Other factors that may also have an impact on the data include seasonal variation in population and minor differences in question wording and question order.

While the categories of income by source are comparable with the decennial long-form data, the monthly collection of ACS data results in a significant difference in concept. In the decennial census, income refers to the previous calendar year whereas the ACS it refers to the previous 12-month period. Most people have a better understanding of what their calendar year income is, especially since the census is taken around tax time. With the ACS, individuals have to report income for a different period each month. A response to the survey in October of the year will report income from October of the previous year through September of the current year. This may require respondents to actually compute their 12-month income.

In 2006, the ACS began including samples of the population living in group quarters (e.g., jails, college dormitories, and nursing homes) for the first time. As a result, the ACS data from 2008 through 2010 may not be comparable with data from earlier ACS surveys. This is especially true for estimates of young adults and the elderly, who are more likely than other groups to be living in group quarters facilities.

One of the most important uses of the ACS estimates is to make comparisons between estimates—over time or across areas. Several key types of comparisons are of general interest to users:

- Comparisons of estimates from different geographic areas within the same time period (e.g., comparing the proportion of seniors below the poverty level in two counties).

- Comparisons of estimates for the same geographic area across time periods (e.g., comparing the proportion of people below the poverty level in a metropolitan area for 2011 and 2012).

- Comparisons of ACS estimates with the corresponding estimates from past decennial census samples (e.g., comparing the proportion of people below the poverty level in a county in 2014 compared to 2010 and 2000).

A number of conditions must be met when comparing survey estimates.

- When comparing data for different geographic areas, always use the same period estimates. When comparing data for an area which only have 5-year estimates to an area with 1-, 3-, and 5-year estimates, it is important to compare only the 5-year estimates.

- When comparing over time for the same geographic area, again, only compare like-year period estimates. For example, it is not appropriate to compare a 1-year estimate for 2014 to a 5-year estimate for 2010–2014.

- Of primary importance is that the comparison takes into account the sampling error associated with each estimate, thus determining whether the observed differences between estimates are statistically significant. Statistical significance means that there is statistical evidence that a true difference exists within the full population, and that the observed difference is unlikely to have occurred by chance due to sampling. A method for determining statistical significance when making comparisons, as well as considerations associated with the various types of comparisons, can be found in Appendix 4 of the *ACS General Handbook*: https://www.census.gov/library/publications/2008/acs/general.html.

- The statistical properties of survey samples like the ACS are dependent upon independence of samples. In the ACS multiyear period estimates, the estimates are based on the sampled households for each year. That means that when comparing estimates for the period 2009–2011 to 2010–2012, two thirds of the sample cases are the same households—those surveyed in 2010 and 2011. The only different (independent) households are those taken in 2009 and 2012. When comparisons over time are made, it is best to compare non-overlapping samples. That is, compare estimates for 2007–2009 to the period 2010–1012 because both periods contain independent household samples. To meet this criteria for the use of 5-year estimates, data users should wait for the 2011–2015 data to make time series comparisons.

Finally, the decennial census and the ACS have different residency rules. In the decennial census, population in tabulated by their "usual place of residence" typically where they spend six months or more of the year. This is subject to some seasonal variation due to persons with dual residences. In the ACS, there is a 2-month residency rule. That is, if the respondent has been in the sampled housing unit for 2 months or expects to be resident there for 2 months they are captured in the survey. This can have an impact on communities with highly seasonal populations and college communities.

SUBJECTS COVERED

The topics covered by the ACS focus on demographic, social, economic, and housing characteristics. These topics are virtually the same as those covered by the 2000 census long-form sample data.

Demographic Characteristics
Age, Sex, Hispanic Origin, Race, and Relationship to Householder (e.g., spouse)

Social Characteristics
Marital Status and Marital History; Fertility; Grandparents as Caregivers; Ancestry Place of Birth; Citizenship and Year of Entry; Language Spoken at Home; Educational Attainment and School Enrollment; Residence One Year Ago; Veteran Status, Period of Military Service, and VA Service-Connected Disability Rating; and Disability

Economic Characteristics
Income, Food Stamps Benefit, Labor Force Status, Industry, Occupation, Class of Worker, Place of Work and Journey to Work, Work Status Last Year, Vehicles Available, and Health Insurance Coverage

Housing Characteristics
Year Structure Built, Units in Structure, Year Moved Into Unit, Rooms, Bedrooms, Kitchen Facilities, Plumbing Facilities, House Heating Fuel, Telephone Service Available, and Farm Residence

Financial Characteristics
Tenure (Owner/Renter), Housing Value, Rent, and Selected Monthly Owner Costs

AVAILABILITY OF ACS ESTIMATES

The ACS began in 1996 and has expanded each subsequent year. From 2000 through 2004, the sample included between 740,000 and 900,000 addresses annually. In 2005, the ACS shifted from a demonstration program to the full sample size and design. It became the largest household survey in the United States, with an annual sample size of about 3 million addresses. Beginning with 2005, the ACS single-year estimates are available for geographic areas with a population of 65,000 or more. Three-year period estimates for areas of 20,000 or more were first released for the 2005–2007 time period and there are annual 3-year estimates through the 2011–2013 period. 5-year estimates for all areas were first released in 2010 and are available for every subsequent year with 2014 being the most current as of this writing. The ACS will continue to accumulate samples over 5-year intervals to produce estimates for smaller geographic areas, including census tracts and block groups.

Annually, the ACS produces updated, single-year estimates of demographic, housing, social, and economic characteristics for all states, as well as for larger counties, cities, metropolitan and urban areas, and congressional districts. Geographic areas must have a minimum population of 65,000 to qualify for estimates based on a single year's sample. Every congressional district meets this threshold and therefore new single year estimates are released each year for every congressional district. Some school districts, townships, and American Indian and Alaska Native areas also meet this population threshold.

For areas with populations of at least 20,000, the Census Bureau produced estimates using data collected over a 3-year period. The 3-year estimates are available through the 2011–2013 collection period (released in 2014), however the Census Bureau is no longer producing the 3-year data products. For rural areas and city neighborhoods (including census tracts and block groups) with fewer than 20,000 people, the Census Bureau produces estimates using data collected over a 5-year period and updates these multiyear estimates every year. ACS data are released annually, about nine months after the end of each calendar year of data collection.

For most geographic areas—including three-quarters of all counties, most school districts, and most cities, towns, and American Indian reservations—only 5-year estimates are available because of their population size. Because some federal grant programs allocate funds directly to these areas, Congress can use the 5-year estimates to evaluate needs at the relevant geographic level, compare characteristics between areas within and among states, and analyze how various formulas distribute funds. The vast majority of areas will receive only 5-year estimates. In partnership with the states, the Census Bureau created *Public Use Microdata Areas (PUMAs)*, which are special, non-overlapping areas within a state, each with a population of about 100,000. These areas will have annual 1-year estimates.

Definitions of these geographic areas are at: https://www.census.gov/programs-surveys/acs/geography-acs/concepts-definitions.html.

Using the ACS

DIFFERENCES BETWEEN THE ACS AND THE DECENNIAL CENSUS

While the main function of the decennial census is to provide *counts* of people for the purpose of congressional apportionment and legislative redistricting, the primary purpose of the ACS is to measure the changing social and economic *characteristics* of the U.S. population. As a result, the ACS does not provide official counts of the population though users of the data will report the estimate results as though they were counts. In non-decennial census years, the Census Bureau's Population Estimates Program continues to be the official source for annual population totals, by age, race, Hispanic origin, and sex. The ACS sample estimates are controlled to match the decennial census and the Census Bureau's annual population estimates by selected age, sex, race, and Hispanic origin categories. For more information about population estimates, visit the Census Bureau's website at http://www.census.gov/popest/estimates.html.

There are many similarities between the methods used in the traditional decennial census sample and the ACS but there are also a number of differences in collection method and concepts. Response to both the ACS and decennial census is required by law, a factor that helps improve overall response. Both the ACS and the decennial census sample data are based on information from a sample of the population. The data from the Census 2000 sample of about one-sixth of the population were collected using a "long-form" questionnaire, whose content was the model for the ACS. The sample for the ACS is somewhat smaller, approximately 1 in 7 households, resulting in larger margins of error.

While some differences exist in the specific Census 2000 long-form question wording and that of the ACS, most questions are identical or nearly identical. Differences in the design and implementation of the two surveys are noted below with references provided to a series of evaluation studies that assess the degree to which these differences are likely to impact the estimates. The ACS produces period estimates (covering one or five years of data collection) so these estimates do not measure characteristics for the same time frame as the decennial census estimates, which are interpreted to be a snapshot as of April 1 of the census year.

Some data items were collected by both the ACS and the Census 2000 long form with slightly different definitions or reference periods that could affect the comparability of the estimates for these items. One example is annual costs for a mobile home. Census 2000 included installment loan costs in the total annual costs but the ACS does not. In this example, the ACS could be expected to yield smaller estimates than Census 2000.

While some differences were a part of the census and survey design objectives, other differences observed between ACS and census results were not by design, but due to nonsampling error—differences related to how well the surveys were conducted. The ACS and the census experience different levels and types of coverage error, different levels and treatment of housing unit and questionnaire item nonresponse, and different instances of measurement and processing error. Both Census 2000 and the ACS had similar high levels of survey coverage and low levels of unit nonresponse. Higher levels of unit nonresponse were found in the nonresponse follow-up stage of Census 2000 while lower levels of item nonresponse were found in the ACS due to a permanent staff of trained interviewers.

Census Bureau analysts have compared sample estimates from Census 2000 with 1-year ACS estimates based on data collected in 2000 and 3-year ACS estimates based on data collected in 1999–2001 in selected counties. In general, ACS estimates were found to be quite similar to those produced from decennial census data.

Detailed information about the ACS methodology can be found at:
http://www.census.gov/programs-surveys/acs/methodology.html

RESIDENCE RULES

The fundamentally different purposes of the ACS and the census, and their timing, led to important differences in the choice of data collection methods. For example, the residence rules for a census or survey determine the sample unit's occupancy status and household membership at the time of collection. Defining the rules in a dissimilar way can affect those two very important estimates. The 2010 census residence rules, which determined where people should be counted, were based on the principle of "usual residence" on April 1, 2010, in keeping with the focus of the census on the requirements of congressional apportionment and state redistricting. To accomplish this, the decennial census attempts to restrict and determine a principal place of residence on one specific date for everyone enumerated. The ACS residence rules are based on a "current residence" concept since data are collected continuously throughout the entire year with responses provided relative to the continuously changing survey interview dates. Under this concept, anyone who is living or staying at an address for two months or more is considered a resident of that address. This method is consistent with the goal of the ACS to produce estimates that reflect annual averages of the characteristics of all areas.

Residence rules determine which individuals are considered to be residents of a particular housing unit or group quarters. While many people have definite ties to a single housing unit or group quarters, some people may stay in different places for significant periods of time over the course of the year. For example, "snow birds" can maintain residences in different states and do not live in any one location for the entire year. In the decennial census, it is their residence on April 1, or their interpretation of their "usual place of residence," that is the basis for their location. College students are another example. Students are enumerated at the college in the decennial census but may be counted at home if sampled during their summer break. Differences in treatment of these populations in the census and ACS can lead to differences in estimates of the characteristics of some areas.

For the past several censuses, decennial census residence rules were designed to produce an accurate count of the population as of Census Day, April 1, while the ACS residence rules were designed to collect representative information to produce annual average estimates of the characteristics of all types of areas. The residence rules governing the census enumerations of people in group quarters depend on the type of group quarter and, where permitted, whether people claim a "usual residence" elsewhere. The ACS applies a straight de facto residence rule to every type of group quarter. Everyone living or staying in a group quarter on the day it is visited by an ACS interviewer is eligible to be sampled and interviewed for the survey.

Further information on residence rules can be found in Chapter 6 of the Design and Methodology report at: http://www.census.gov/programs-surveys/acs/methodology/design-and-methodology.html.

The differences in the ACS and census data, as a consequence of the different residence rules, are most likely minimal for most areas and most characteristics. However, for certain segments of the population the usual and current residence concepts could result in different residence decisions. The older population is one of those segments as many retired and active seniors maintain dual residences. Appreciable differences may occur in areas where large proportions of the total population spend several months of the year in what would not be considered their residence under decennial census rules. In particular, data for areas that include large beach, lake, or mountain vacation areas may differ appreciably between the census and the ACS if populations live there for more than two months. In addition, college students are to be counted at the location of the college rather than their parent's home. However, during summer months, college students can meet the two month residency rule for the ACS and be counted along with their parents rather than at the college.

REFERENCE PERIODS

Estimates produced by the ACS are not measuring exactly what decennial samples have been measuring. The ACS yearly samples, spread over 12 months, collect information that is anchored to the day on which the sampled unit was interviewed, whether it is the day that a mail questionnaire is completed or the day that an interview is conducted by telephone or personal visit. Individual questions with time references such as "last week" or "the last 12 months" all begin the reference period as of this interview date. Even the information on types and amounts of income refers to the 12 months prior to the day the question is answered. ACS interviews are conducted just about every day of the year, and all of the estimates that the survey releases are considered to be averages for a specific time period. The 1-year estimates reflect the full calendar year; 3-year and 5-year estimates reflect the full 36- or 60-month period.

Most decennial census sample estimates are anchored in this same way to the reference date of April 1. The most obvious difference between the ACS and the census is the overall time frame in which they are conducted. The census enumeration time period is less than half the time period used to collect data for each single-year ACS estimate. But a more important difference is that the distribution of census enumeration dates are highly clustered in March and April (when most census mail returns were received) with additional, smaller clusters seen in May and June (when nonresponse follow-up activities took place).

This means that the data from the decennial census, intended to reflect the characteristics of the population and housing on April 1, tend to describe the characteristics in the March through June time period (with an over-representation of March/April). The ACS data describe the characteristics nearly every day over the full calendar year. For employment and income estimates, the decennial census referred to the prior calendar year for all respondents, while the ACS asks about the 12 months preceding the interview.

Those who are interested in more information about differences in reference periods should refer to the Census Bureau's guidance on comparisons that contrasts for each question the specific reference periods used in Census 2000 with those used in the ACS: https://www.census.gov/acs/www/guidance/comparing-acs-data/acs-census-table-lookup/. Individual tables can be compared with the table comparison tool or you can download the entire comparison table.

Some specific differences in reference periods between the ACS and the decennial census are described below. Users should consider the potential impact these different reference periods could have on distributions when comparing ACS estimates with Census 2000. As we get further and further away from use of the 2000 data, and compare current ACS data to prior years ACS data, these differences will become less important.

Income Data

To estimate annual income, the Census 2000 long-form sample used the calendar year prior to Census Day as the reference period, and the ACS uses the 12 months prior to the interview date as the reference period. Thus, while Census 2000 collected income information for calendar year 1999, the ACS collects income information for the 12 months preceding the interview date. The responses are a mixture of 12 reference periods ranging from, in the case of the 2014 ACS single-year estimates, the full calendar year 2013 through November 2014. The ACS income responses for each of these reference periods are individually inflation-adjusted to represent dollar values for the ACS collection year. Further inflation adjustments are made to the 3- and 5-year estimates to reflect dollar values of the final year of the estimate. It's important to note that the rotating reference period for income can result in misreporting. The calendar year reference period of the decennial census coincides with an individual's annual salary and is also collected around tax time. Respondents will have a good idea of what their annual salary is. In the ACS, the respondent has to calculate their income for the previous 12 months, a figure which can vary considerably throughout the year.

School Enrollment

The school enrollment question on the ACS asks if a person had "at any time in the last 3 months attended a school or college." A consistent 3-month reference period is used for all interviews. In contrast, Census 2000 asked if a person had "at any time since February 1 attended a school or college." Since Census 2000 data were collected from mid-March to late-August, the reference period could have been as short as about six weeks or as long as seven months.

Utility Costs

The reference periods for two utility cost questions—gas and electricity—differ between Census 2000 and the ACS. The census asked for annual costs, while the ACS asks for the utility costs in the previous month.

PERIOD ESTIMATES

The ACS produces period estimates of socioeconomic and housing characteristics. It is designed to provide estimates that describe the average characteristics of an area over a specific time period. In the case of ACS single-year estimates, the period is the calendar year (e.g., the 2014 ACS covers January through December 2014). In the case of ACS multiyear estimates, the period is either 3 or 5 calendar years (e.g., the 2011–2013 ACS 3-year estimates cover January 2011 through December 2012, and the 2010–2014 ACS 5-year estimates cover January 2010 through December 2014). The ACS multiyear estimates are similar in many ways to the ACS single-year estimates, but they encompass a longer time period.

The differences in time periods between single-year and multiyear ACS estimates affect decisions about which set of estimates should be used for a particular analysis. While one may think of these estimates as representing average characteristics over a single calendar year or multiple calendar years, it must be remembered that the 1-year estimates are not calculated as an average of 12 monthly values and the multiyear estimates are not calculated as the average of either 36 or 60 monthly values, nor are the multiyear estimates calculated as the average of 3 or 5 single-year estimates. Rather, the ACS collects survey information continuously nearly every day of the year and then aggregates the results over a specific time period—1 year, 3 years, or 5 years. The data collection is spread evenly across the entire period represented so as not to over-represent any particular month or year within the period.

Because ACS estimates provide information about the characteristics of the population and housing for areas over an entire time frame, ACS single-year and multiyear estimates contrast with "point-in-time" estimates, such as those from the decennial census long-form samples or monthly employment estimates from the Current Population Survey (CPS), which are designed to measure characteristics as of a certain date or narrow time period. For example, Census 2000 was designed to measure the characteristics of the population and housing in the United States based upon data collected around April 1, 2000, and thus its data reflect a narrower time frame than ACS data. The monthly CPS collects data for an even narrower time frame, the week containing the 12th of each month.

Most areas have consistent population characteristics throughout the calendar year, and their period estimates may not look much different from estimates that would be obtained from a "point-in-time" survey design. However, some areas may experience changes in the estimated characteristics of the population, depending on when in the calendar year the measurement occurred. For these areas, the ACS period estimates (even for a single-year) may noticeably differ from "point-in-time" estimates. The impact will be more noticeable in smaller areas where changes such as a factory closing can have a large impact on population characteristics, and in areas with a large natural event such as Hurricane Katrina's impact on the New Orleans area.

This logic can be extended to better interpret 3- and 5-year estimates where the periods involved are much longer. If, over the full period of time there have been major or consistent changes in certain population or housing characteristics for an area, a period estimate for that area could differ markedly from estimates based on a "point-in-time" survey. For example, the 5-year estimates for 2010–2014 will be affected by the volatility in the economy and the housing market during those years and may mask shorter term fluctuations such as the continued recessionary period in 2010 compared to more normal economic conditions by 2014.

The tables in this book were prepared from the 1-year 2014 survey results. Some areas will have experienced a more rapid recovery from the recession while others still struggle and haven't returned to previous levels of growth. Strong growth between the 2000 and 2010 censuses may be replaced by a slowdown in the most recent years.

The important thing to keep in mind is that ACS single-year estimates describe the population and characteristics of an area for the full year, not for any specific day or period within the year. The ACS multiyear estimates describe the population and characteristics of an area for the full 3- or 5-year period, not for any specific day, period, or year within the multiyear time period.

Single-year estimates provide more current information

Single-year estimates provide more current information about areas that have changing population and/or housing characteristics because they are based on the most current data—survey responses from the past calendar year. In contrast, multiyear estimates provide less current information because they are based on both survey responses from the previous year and responses that are up to 5 years old. As noted earlier, for many areas with minimal change taking place, using the "less current" sample used to produce the multiyear estimates may not have a substantial influence on the estimates. However, in areas experiencing major changes over a given time period, the multiyear estimates may be quite different from the single-year estimates for any of the individual years. Single-year and multiyear estimates are not expected to be the same because they are based on data from two different time periods. This will be true even if the ACS single year is the midyear of the ACS multiyear period (e.g., 2012 single year, 2010–2014 multiyear).

Multiyear estimates are based on larger sample sizes and are therefore more reliable

The 5-year estimates are based on five times as many sample cases as the 1-year estimates. For some characteristics this increased sample is needed for the estimates to be reliable enough for use in certain applications. For other characteristics the increased sample may not be necessary.

Multiyear estimates are the only type of estimates available for geographic areas with populations of less than 65,000. Users may think that they only need to use multiyear estimates when they are working with small areas, but this isn't the case. Estimates for large geographic areas benefit from the increased sample, resulting in more precise estimates of population and housing characteristics, especially for subpopulations within those areas. In addition, users may determine that they want to use single-year estimates, despite their reduced reliability, as building blocks to produce estimates for meaningful higher levels of geography. These aggregations will similarly benefit from the increased sample sizes and gain reliability.

Currency	Reliability
1-year estimates provide information based on the most current year	Sample sizes producing estimates may be small and impact statistical reliability
3-year estimates provide information based on the last year and the 2 years before that	3-year estimates are based on 3 times as many sample cases as 1-year estimates
5-year estimates provide information based on the last year and the 4 years before that	5-year estimates are based on 5 times as many sample cases as 1-year estimates

DECIDING WHICH ACS ESTIMATE TO USE

Three primary uses of ACS estimates are:

- to understand the characteristics of the population of an area for local planning needs,

- to make comparisons across areas, and

- to assess change over time in an area.

Local planning could include making local decisions such as where to place schools or hospitals, determining the need for senior services or transportation, and carrying out other infrastructure analysis. In the past, decennial census sample data provided the most comprehensive information. However, the currency of those data suffered through the intercensal period, and the ability to assess change over time was limited. ACS estimates greatly improve the currency of data for understanding the characteristics of housing and population and enhance the ability to assess change over time. At the same time, small differences between ACS estimates can lead to misinterpretation due to larger margins of error.

Several key factors can help users decide whether to use single-year or multiyear ACS estimates for areas where both are available:

- intended use of the estimates

- required precision, or reliability, of the estimates

- currency of the estimates

All of these factors, along with an understanding of the differences between single-year and multiyear ACS estimates, should be taken into consideration when deciding which set of estimates to use.

For users analyzing estimates for areas of different size and for different time periods, it is important to recognize that 3-year estimates for areas of any size were eliminated in the 2014 ACS product release. Three year estimates had been available for areas of 20,000 or more so it is still possible to analyze the 3-year data for time periods prior to 2014. For the smallest of geographic areas (under 20,000 population), the only option is to use the 5-year ACS estimates. When comparing areas of different size it is critical that users only make comparisons between similar period estimates. Even if the study area has 1-year estimates, it is not appropriate to compare the 1-year estimate to a 5-year estimate from a different area.

The key trade-off to be made in deciding whether to use single-year or multiyear estimates is between currency and precision. In general, the single-year estimates are preferred, as they will be more relevant to the current conditions. However, the user must take into account the level of uncertainty present in the single-year estimates, which may be large for small subpopulation groups and rare characteristics. While single-year estimates offer more current estimates, they also have higher sampling variability. One measure, the coefficient of variation (CV) can help you determine the fitness for use of a single-year estimate in order to assess if you should opt instead to use the multiyear estimate (or if you should use a 5-year estimate rather than a 3-year estimate). The CV is calculated as the ratio of the standard error of the estimate to the estimate, times 100. A single-year estimate with a small CV is usually preferable to a multiyear estimate as it is more up to date. However, multiyear estimates are an alternative option when a single-year estimate has an unacceptably high CV. Single-year estimates for small subpopulations (e.g., grandparents 65 and over who are responsible for grandchildren) will typically have larger CVs. In general, multiyear estimates are preferable to single-year estimates when looking at estimates for small subpopulations.

For the complete discussion on deciding which estimates to use and on calculating the CV, see Appendix 1 of the *ACS General Handbook*: http://www.census.gov/acs/www/Downloads/handbooks/ACSGeneralHandbook.pdf.

Often users want to compare the characteristics of one area to those of another area. These comparisons can be in the form of rankings or of specific pairs of comparisons. Whenever you want to make a comparison between two different geographic areas you need to take the type of estimate into account. It is important that comparisons be made within the same estimate type. That is, 1-year estimates should only be compared with other 1-year estimates, 3-year estimates should only be compared with other 3-year estimates, and 5-year estimates should only be compared with other 5-year estimates.

You certainly can compare characteristics for areas with populations of 30,000 to areas with populations of 100,000 but you should use the data set that they have in common. In this example you could use the 3- or the 5-year estimates because they are available for areas of 30,000 and areas of 100,000. You should NOT compare the single year estimate for the area of 100,000 to the 3-year estimate for the area of 30,000.

Users are encouraged to make comparisons between sequential single-year estimates. In American FactFinder (AFF), comparison profiles are available beginning with the 2007 single-year data. These profiles identify statistically significant differences between each year from 2007 through the most recently released year.

Caution is needed when using multiyear estimates for estimating year-to-year change in a particular characteristic. This is because roughly two-thirds of the respondents in a 3-year estimate overlap with the respondents in the next year's 3-year estimate period (the overlap is roughly four-fifths for 5-year estimates). When comparing 3-year estimates from 2009–2011 with those from 2010–2012, the differences in overlapping multiyear estimates are driven by differences in the non-overlapping years (i.e. 2009 and 2012). A more appropriate comparison of change over time would be comparing the 2007–2009 3-year estimate to the 2010–2012 3-year estimate because they include responses from total independent samples. Comparison of overlapping periods should be made with caution.

Users who are interested in comparing overlapping multiyear period estimates should refer to Appendix 4 of the *ACS General Handbook* for more information: http://www.census.gov/acs/www/Downloads/handbooks/ACS-GeneralHandbook.pdf.

Multiyear estimates are likely to confuse some data users, in part because of their statistical properties, and in part because this is a new product from the Census Bureau. The ACS will provide all states and communities that have at least 65,000 residents with single-year estimates of demographic, housing, social, and economic characteristics—a boon to government agencies that need to budget and plan for public services like transportation, medical care, and schools. For geographic areas with smaller populations, the ACS samples too few households to provide reliable single-year estimates. For these communities, several years of data will be pooled together to create reliable 3- or 5-year estimates.

Single-year, 3- and 5-year estimates from the ACS are all "period" estimates that represent data collected over a period of time as opposed to "point-in-time" estimates, such as the decennial census. While a single-year estimate includes information collected over a 12-month period, a 3-year estimate represents data collected over a 36-month period, and a 5-year estimate includes data collected over a 60-month period. Therefore, ACS estimates based on data collected from 2010–2012 should not be called "2011" or "2012" estimates. Nor should 2008–2012 period estimates be labeled "2010" estimates, even though that is the midpoint of the 5-year period. Multiyear estimates should be labeled to indicate clearly the full period of time (e.g., "The poverty rate for persons 65 and over in 2010–2012 was X percent"). The primary advantage of using multiyear estimates is the increased statistical reliability of the data for less populated areas and small population subgroups.

Multiyear estimates should, in general, be used when single-year estimates have large CVs or when the precision of the estimates is more important than the currency of the data. Multiyear estimates should also be used when analyzing data for smaller geographies and smaller population subgroups in larger geographies. Multiyear estimates are also of value when examining change over non-overlapping time periods and for smoothing data trends over time.

Single-year estimates should, in general, be used for larger geographies and populations when currency is more important than the precision of the estimates. Single-year estimates should be used to examine year-to-year change for estimates with small CVs. Given the availability of a single-year estimate, calculating the CV provides useful information to determine if the single-year estimate should be used. For areas believed to be experiencing rapid changes in a characteristic, single-year estimates should generally be used rather than multiyear estimates as long as the CV for the single-year estimate is reasonable for the specific usage.

Local area variations may occur due to rapidly occurring changes. Multiyear estimates will tend to be insensitive to such changes when they first occur. Single-year estimates, if associated with sufficiently small CVs, can be very valuable in identifying and studying such phenomena.

Data users also need to use caution in looking at trends involving income or other measures that are adjusted for inflation, such as rental costs, home values, and energy costs. Note that inflation adjustment is based on a national-level consumer price index: it does not adjust for differences in costs of living across different geographic areas.

Appendix 5 of the *ACS General Handbook* provides information on the adjustment of single-year and multi-year ACS estimates for inflation: http://www.census.gov/library/publications/2008/acs/general.html.

MARGIN OF ERROR

All data that are based on samples, such as the ACS and the census long-form samples, include a range of uncertainty. Two broad types of error can occur: sampling error and nonsampling error. Nonsampling errors can result from mistakes in how the data are reported or coded, problems in the sampling frame or survey questionnaires, or problems related to nonresponse or interviewer bias. The Census Bureau tries to minimize nonsampling errors by using trained interviewers and by carefully reviewing the survey's sampling methods, data processing techniques, and questionnaire design.

Appendix 6 of the *ACS General Handbook* includes a more detailed description of different types of errors in the ACS and other measures of ACS quality: http://www.census.gov/library/publications/2008/acs/general.html.

Sampling error occurs when data are based on a sample of a population rather than the full population. Sampling error is easier to measure than nonsampling error and can be used to assess the statistical reliability of survey data. For any given area, the larger the sample and the more months included in the data, the greater the confidence in the estimate. The Census Bureau reports the 90-percent confidence interval on all ACS estimates produced since 2005. Beginning with the release of the 2006 ACS data, *margins of error (MOE)* are now provided for every ACS estimate. Ninety percent confidence intervals define a range expected to contain the

true value of an estimate with a level of confidence of 90 percent. Margins of error are easily converted into these confidence ranges. By adding and subtracting the margin of error from the point estimate, we can calculate the 90-percent confidence interval for an estimate. Therefore, we can be 90 percent confident that the true number falls between the lower-bound interval and the upper-bound interval.

Detailed information about sampling error and instructions for calculating confidence intervals and margins of error are included in Appendix 3 of the *ACS General Handbook*: http://www.census.gov/library/publications/2008/acs/general.html.

The margin of error around an estimate is important because it helps one draw conclusions about the data. Small differences between two estimates may not be statistically significant if the confidence intervals of those estimates overlap. However, the Census Bureau cautions data users not to rely on overlapping confidence intervals as a test for statistical significance, because this method will not always produce accurate results. Instead, the Census Bureau recommends following the detailed instructions for conducting statistical significance tests in Appendix 4 of the *ACS General Handbook*.

In some cases, data users will need to construct custom ACS estimates by combining data across multiple geographic areas or population subgroups or it may be necessary to derive a new percentage, proportion, or ratio from published ACS data. In such cases, additional calculations are needed to produce confidence intervals and margins of error for the derived estimates. Appendix 3 of the *ACS General Handbook* provides detailed instructions on how to make these calculations. Note that these error measures do not tell us about the magnitude of nonsampling errors.

Some advanced data users will also want to construct custom ACS estimates from the Census Bureau's Public Use Microdata Samples (PUMS). There are separate instructions for conducting significance tests for PUMS estimates, available on the Census Bureau's American FactFinder (AFF) website at: http://www2.census.gov/programs-surveys/acs/tech_docs/accuracy/ACS_Accuracy_of_Data_2014.pdf.

Accessing ACS Data Online

All ACS data are available through the Census Bureau's American FactFinder (AFF) website at http://factfinder.census.gov. From the AFF home page, there are three paths to accessing the data:

- Community Facts – this will provide summary data profiles for a single geographic area such as a state, county, town or zip code. The table links include data from the 2010 Census as well as the most current ACS dataset. It will be important to check the table titles to verify that the ACS is the source of the data presented.

- Guided Search – this path is a "wizard" leads the user through six steps to select the characteristics and geography of interest. Guided Search is available for all Census datasets so it can return a large number of "Search Results." It only displays the first 25 tables however and there may be thousands more results available. It is also still important to verify that the ACS is the desired source.

- Advanced Search – this path provides the most flexibility for data selection by the user but also requires a basic level of knowledge about Census datasets and characteristics. Clicking on the "Topics" button will allow the user to view and select "Datasets." For each year of available ACS data there are three datasets shown—the 1-year estimates (based on the 2014 ACS), the 3-year estimates (based on the 2011–2013 ACS, though 3-year estimates have been eliminated by the Census Bureau), and the 5-year estimates (based on the 2010–2014 ACS). The tables in this book were produced from the 1-year estimates for 2014. It is important for all users to understand that once a data set is selected, the accessed tables will all correspond to this specific data set. All tables are clearly labeled, identifying the data set.

Basic information on using the functions and features of American FactFinder can be found at http://factfinder.census.gov/faccs/nav/jsf/pages/index.xhtml. The American FactFinder main page provides information about available data and guidance on using FactFinder, under the tabs Using American FactFinder and What We Provide. Additional assistance can be found at FactFinder Help (online help, census data information, glossary, and tutorial): http://factfinder.census.gov/help/en/index.htm#.

The various ACS data products are described below.

- **Data profiles, quick tables and ranking tables.** The *data profiles, quick tables* and *ranking tables* are good places to start for novice data users. *Data profiles and quick tables* provide separate fact sheets on the social, economic, demographic, and housing characteristics for different geographic areas, while *ranking tables* provide state-level rankings of key ACS variables.

- **Geographic comparison tables.** Those interested in geographic comparisons for areas other than states may be interested in the *geographic comparison tables*, which allow comparison of ACS data across a variety of geographic areas, including metropolitan areas, cities, counties, and congressional districts.

- **Subject tables.** These are similar to *data profiles* but are specific to a more detailed characteristic or topic (e.g., employment, education, and income). *Subject tables* provide pre-tabulated numbers and percentages for a wide variety of topics, often available separately by age (60 and over and 65 and over), gender, or race/ethnicity.

- **Selected population profiles.** The most detailed race/ethnic data are available through the *selected population profiles*, which provide summary tables separately for more than 400 detailed race, ethnic, tribal, ancestry, and country of birth groups.

- **Comparison profiles.** The *comparison profiles* show data side-by-side from multiple years, indicating where there is a statistically significant difference between the two sets of estimates. Comparison profiles are only available for 1-year estimates.

- **Detailed tables and summary files.** The *detailed tables* are the best source for advanced data users or those who want access to the most comprehensive ACS tables. The tables in this book were developed through this option. For more advanced users, *detailed tables* are also available for download through the ACS *Summary File*: http://www.census.gov/programs-surveys/acs/technical-documentation/summary-file-documentation.html.

- **Thematic maps.** The *thematic maps* provide graphic displays of the data available through the various tables. Different shades of color are used to display variations in the data across geographic areas. Data users can also highlight areas with statistically different values from a selected state, county, or metropolitan area of interest. If a mapping option is available, it will display as an option when you view a table.

- **Public Use Microdata Sample files.** Those with expertise in using SAS, SPSS, or STATA may also be interested in the *Public Use Microdata Sample (PUMS) files*, which contain a sample of individual records of people and households that responded to the survey (stripped of all identifying information). The PUMS files permit analysis of specific population groups and custom variables that are not available through the summary tables in American FactFinder. For example, PUMS data users can look at the proportion of persons 60 to 69 with a disability by whether they own or rent their home or employment status and occupation of the 55 to 69 population. This flexibility is not provided by the pre-tabulated summary tables provided in American FactFinder. Data users can also combine multiple years of PUMS data to produce data for relatively small population subgroups (e.g., female physicians over age 55). More information about the PUMS is available at http://www.census.gov/programs-surveys/acs/technical-documentation/pums.html.

For readers who are used to data from the traditional decennial census long-form, it is important to note that there are many conceptual and data collection differences in the ACS. The following is a summary of some of these differences which are described more fully in the chapter Using the ACS.

The ACS data are complex and cover a broad range of topics and geographic areas. Because this is a relatively new survey, many people do not fully understand how to interpret and use the ACS data. The key points are summarized below.

- Use caution in comparing ACS data with data from the decennial census or other sources. Every survey uses different methods, which could affect the comparability of the numbers. Some characteristics in the ACS, such as income, reflect a different reference period from the traditional long-form census.

- The ACS was designed to provide estimates of the characteristics of the population, not to provide counts of the population in different geographic areas or population subgroups. However, counts of the population are often what is required by grant applications and researchers and is primarily what is provided in this publication.

- Be careful in drawing conclusions about small differences between two estimates because they may not be statistically different. Statistical testing should always be considered based on the sensitivity of conclusions to differences in the data results.

- Data users need to be careful not to interpret annual fluctuations in the data as long-term trends. Again, statistical testing is necessary to determine if annual fluctuations are real or merely a result of the sample.

- Use caution in comparing data from 2006 and later surveys with data from the 2000–2005 surveys. Unlike earlier surveys, the 2006 and later ACS surveys include samples of the population living in group quarters (e.g., college dorms and nursing homes), so the data may not be comparable, especially for young adults and the elderly, who are more likely than other age groups to be living in group quarters facilities.

- The questionnaire series to define disability changed in 2008 making it impossible to compare disability status for periods before that date.

- Data users should not interpret or refer to multi-year period estimates as estimates of the middle year or last year in the series. For example, a 2010–2014 estimate is not a "2012 average."

- Data users should always be consistent in comparing similar period estimates over time or between geographic areas. Compare 1-year to 1-year, 3-year to 3-year and 5-year to 5-year estimates. Since geographic areas of different population size have different period estimates available, always compare make comparisons using the same period estimate. Do not compare a 1-year estimate for a large population size are to a 5-year estimate for a small area or census tract.

- Due to reductions in funding authorization for data products, the Census Bureau has eliminated the 3-year ACS estimates. The last set of 3-year estimates covered the period 2011–2013.

- Data users should *not* rely on overlapping confidence intervals as a test for statistical significance because this method will not always provide an accurate result.

More ACS Resources

There is a wealth of information about the ACS on the Web with new information available on a regular basis. Each year, the ACS data release represents a new stage in the proccss. Consequently, many new documents are required to explain the survey, year-to-year changes, and how to use it. These resources cover many of the topics discussed in this book, but in greater detail.

The best place to start is the Census Bureau's ACS main page: http://www.census.gov/programs-surveys/acs.

BACKGROUND AND OVERVIEW INFORMATION

The American Community Survey home page provides an overview of the links and materials that are available online, including numerous reference documents.

The site map corresponds to the menu headings on the ACS main page and provides much more detail than the "drop-down" categories displayed.

About the Survey provides background and general information about the importance of the ACS, how sampled households are selected, response options, privacy protections and questionnaire information. It also includes information about how any individual household is selcected for the survey.
http://www.census.gov/programs-surveys/acs/about.html

Data provides information about data updates and new releases. Links to data tables and tools are provided, as well as, other options for accessing data such as the Census Bureau's API source for developers.
http://www.census.gov/programs-surveys/acs/data.html

Guidance for Data Users provides detailed information that helps users understand the geographic coverage of the survey data, the subjects include, how and when to use the multi-year estimates and handbooks for users of various types.
http://www.census.gov/programs-surveys/acs/guidance.html

Geography and the ACS describes geographic concepts and definitions. This is where users will find information on the geographic areas with published data and if there have been geographic boundary changes to be aware of.

http://www.census.gov/programs-surveys/acs/geography-acs.html

Technical Documentation is critical for users who need to understand the details of the data that's available, research and detailed documentation for the various data file products.
http://www.census.gov/programs-surveys/acs/technical-documentation.html

Methodology provides the most detailed information about the survey sample size, response rates and data quality.
http://www.census.gov/programs-surveys/acs/methodology.html

Library is a link to volumes of research and papers describing aspects of survey methodology, research, and analytical reports categorized by year.
http://www.census.gov/programs-surveys/acs/library.html

Accuracy of the Data (2014)
Provides a basic understanding of the sample design, estimation methodology, and accuracy of the ACS data.
http://www2.census.gov/programs-surveys/acs/tech_docs/accuracy/ACS_Accuracy_of_Data_2014.pdf

ACS Sample Size
Provides sample size information for each state for each year of the ACS. The initial sample size, coverage measures and response rates are provided for individual states and the nation. Sample sizes for all published geographic entities starting with the 2007 ACS are available in the B98 series of detailed tables on American FactFinder.
http://www.census.gov/acs/www/methodology/sample-size-and-data-quality/

ACS Quality Measures
Multi-Year Estimate Study Quality Measures Definitions: Includes information about the steps taken by the Census Bureau to improve the accuracy of ACS data. Four indicators of survey quality are described and measures are provided at the national and state level.
http://www2.census.gov/programs-surveys/acs/data/archive/multiyear_estimates_study/Quality_Measures_Documentation_MYE.pdf

xxx AGING IN AMERICA (BERNAN PRESS)

GUIDANCE ON DATA PRODUCTS AND USING THE DATA

How to Use the Data
Includes links to many documents and materials that explain the ACS data products.
http://www.census.gov/programs-surveys/acs/guidance.html

Comparing ACS Data to Other Sources
Guidance on comparing the ACS data products to other years of ACS data and to Census 2000 long-form data.
https://www.census.gov/programs-surveys/acs/guidance/comparing-acs-data.html

When to Use 1-year, 3-year, or 5-year Estimates
The availability of multiple characteristic estimates for a given geographic area for different period estimates can be confusing for users of ACS data. Guidance on comparing across geographies and time periods.
https://www.census.gov/programs-surveys/acs/guidance/estimates.html

Information on Using Different Sources of Data for Income and Poverty
Highlights the sources that should be used for data on income and poverty, focusing on comparing the ACS and the Current Population Survey (CPS).
http://www.census.gov/hhes/www/poverty/about/data-sources/description.html

Poverty: 2012 and 2013. American Community Survey Brief on poverty.
http://www.census.gov/content/dam/Census/library/publications/2014/acs/acsbr13-01.pdf

Public Use Microdata Sample (PUMS)
Provides guidance on accessing ACS microdata.
https://www.census.gov/programs-surveys/acs/technical-documentation/pums.html

Other Data Resources

- FactFinder Help (online help, census data information, glossary, and tutorial): http://factfinder.census.gov/help/en/index.htm#

- Guide to the Data Products (Web page): https://www.census.gov/acs/www/data/data-tables-and-tools/index.php

- *A Compass for Understanding and Using American Community Survey Data: What General Data Users Need to Know* provides a complete overview: https://www.census.gov/library/publications/2008/acs/general.html

- Other Compass handbooks are available for the business community, media, Congress and many other user groups at: https://www.census.gov/programs-surveys/acs/guidance/handbooks.html

- *Using the American Community Survey: Benefits and Challenges*, edited by Constance F. Citro and Graham Kalton (The National Academies Press, 2007). An excellent overview of the ACS, complete with several chapters of useful information for data users. The book is available for purchase and is also available to read online at no charge. http://www.nap.edu/catalog/11901/using-the-american-community-survey-benefits-and-challenges

PART A
POPULATION SUMMARY

POPULATION SUMMARY

In 1950, at the early stage of the Baby Boom generation, the nation's population stood at 179,323,000. More than 30 percent of the population was under the age of 15 while less than 10 percent was age 65 or older. The median age in 1950 was 29.5 years. By 2010, less than 20 percent of the population was under the age of 15 and 13 percent was 65 or older with a median age of 37.2 years. Based on the Census Bureau's latest projections, by 2030 when the youngest of the Baby Boom generation passes the age of 65, fully one out of every five residents (20.3 percent) will be over the age of 65 while less than 19 percent are under 15 years of age resulting in a median age of 39.6 years.

While the aging of the Baby Boom generation captures a lot of national attention, it's important to note that change is not uniform. As the geographic level of analysis gets smaller, the variation across our communities grows with some areas following national trends while others outpace or lag the nation. Analyzing population change is like telling a story of our communities. It's important to look at population change over time, the varying demographic composition of our communities, and how each compares to other areas. The text and tables in this volume are intended to provide the basic demographic portrait of the nation's older population at the state, county, city, metropolitan area, and congressional district levels and allow planners, researchers, and interested individuals to tell their own stories.

The tables in this book are from the Census Bureau's 2014 American Community Survey for geographic areas of at least 65,000 population. The one exception is Table A which presents a population summary and includes the population change from the 2010 Census. *It is important to note that the April 1, 2010, Census figures reported here represent various revisions to the originally published Census counts. These populations are labeled "April 1, 2010 Census Population Estimates Base."* Most of these revisions represent the correction of small geographic misallocations.

POPULATION CHANGE

In the few short years from the 2010 Census, the nation's population has grown by over 10 million people, or 3.3 percent and totals 318.9 million people. California remains in the largest state with a population of 38.8 million, followed by Texas, Florida, New York, and Illinois as the remaining top five states. Florida has recently taken over New York as the third largest state in the nation. More than a third (37.1 percent) of the nation's total population lives in these five largest states and they have about the same proportion (35.8 percent) of the population age 65 years or more. The smallest five states (Wyoming, the District of Columbia, Vermont, North Dakota, and Alaska) total 3.3 million in population, slightly over one percent of the nation's total. Their share of the 65 and over population is just less than one percent.

North Dakota grew the fastest at 9.9 percent followed by the District of Columbia at 9.5 percent and Texas increasing by 7.2 percent. Numerically, the North Dakota increased by about 66,900 while Texas added more than 1.8 million people. West Virginia was the only state to show a population loss between 2010 and the 2014 estimates of just under 3,000 people. Rhode Island, Vermont, and Maine were the slowest growth states, each increasing but less than 3,000.

One third of the nation's population (109.5 million people) lives in cities of over 65,000 population. New York City remains the largest city with a population of 8.5 million followed by Los Angeles with 3.9 million, Chicago with 2.7 million, and Houston with 2.2 million residents. The data presented here is limited to 533 cities of 65,000 or more in population. The smallest city in this group is Youngstown City in Ohio with a population of 65,051. Of the 20 fastest growing cities, only two, Irvine City, CA and Austin City, TX are in the top 100 of population size. Frisco City, TX had the fastest rate of growth at 23.9 percent, but it is the 178th largest city. Ten cities have populations of over 1 million and 34 are over 500,000. There are 239 cities with populations between 65,000 and 100,000. California has the most cities over 65,000 with 132 while Alaska, Delaware, Hawaii, and Maine have only one each.

The 508 Metropolitan and Micropolitan Statistical Areas over 65,000 shown here total 284.0 million in population or 89.1 percent of the U.S. total. The New York-Northern New Jersey-Long Island metro area is the largest at 20.1 million followed by Los Angeles-Long Beach-Anaheim

Percent of Householders 65 Years and Over Who are Living Alone

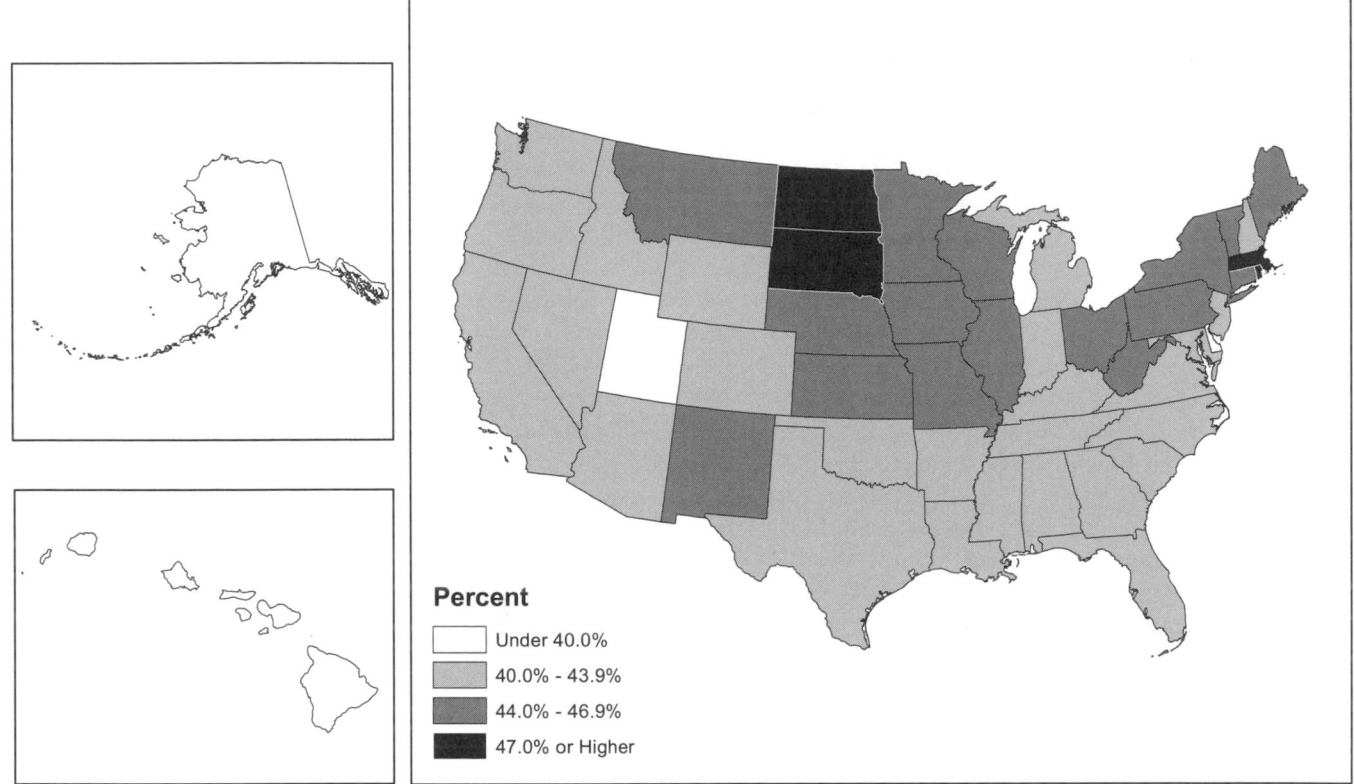

Percent

☐ Under 40.0%
☐ 40.0% - 43.9%
☐ 44.0% - 46.9%
■ 47.0% or Higher

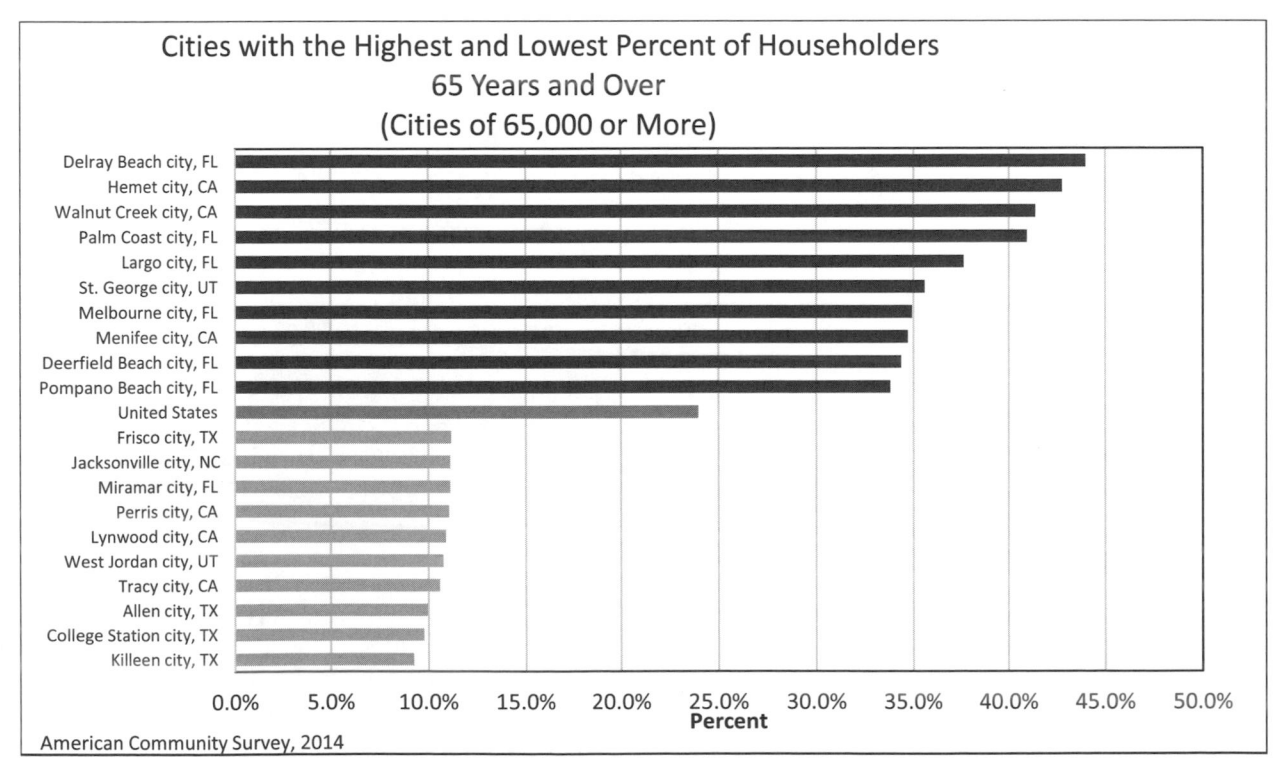

Cities with the Highest and Lowest Percent of Householders 65 Years and Over (Cities of 65,000 or More)

American Community Survey, 2014

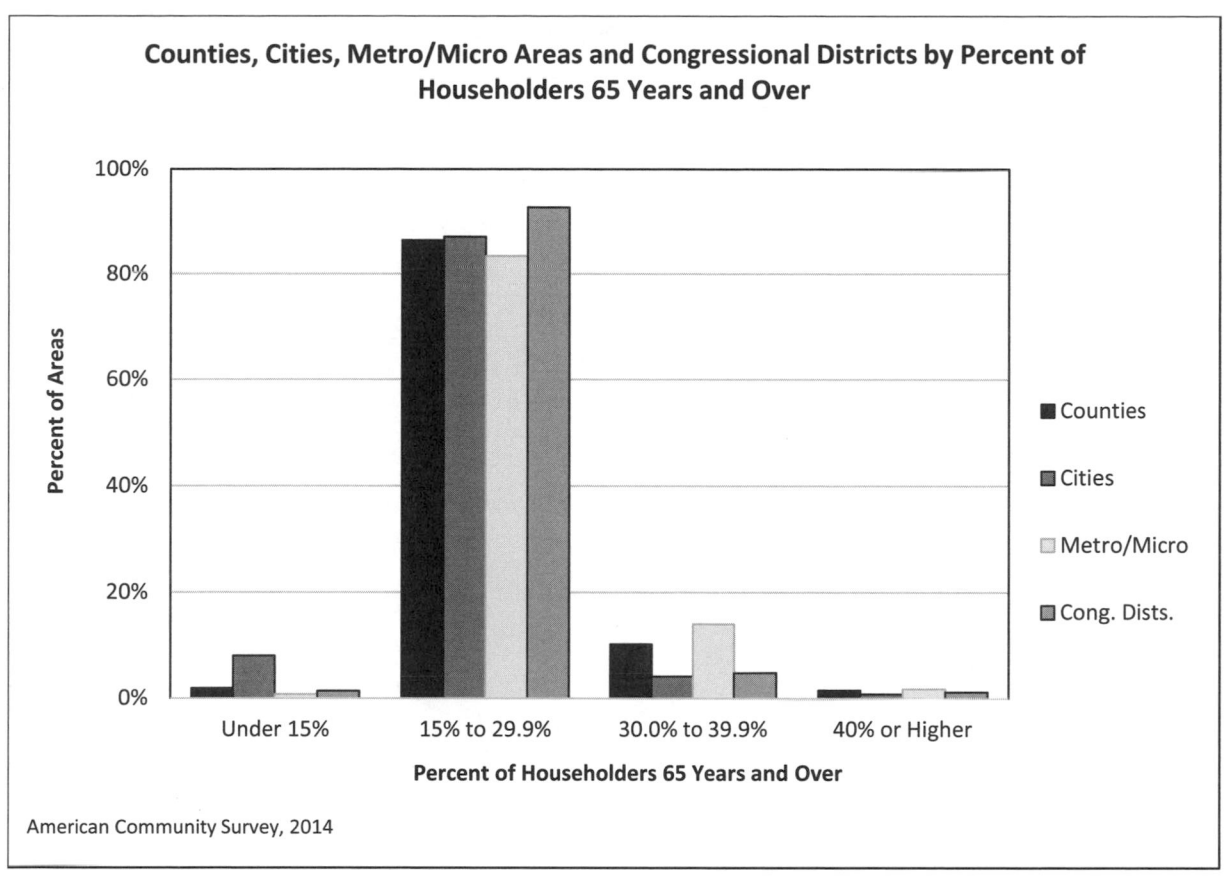

Counties, Cities, Metro/Micro Areas and Congressional Districts by Percent of Householders 65 Years and Over

American Community Survey, 2014

at 13.3 million. Fifty three metropolitan areas have more than 1 million population while twice that number have populations of 500,000 or more. While the New York-Northern New Jersey-Long Island area is the largest, its growth rate ranked only 202nd. The Villages, FL metropolitan area was the fastest growing at a rate of 22.4 percent but with 114,350 residents, it is the 349th largest area. Pine Bluff, AR metropolitan area, the 398th largest area declined by 5.1 percent while the Clarksburg, WV micropolitan area declined by 5.6 percent.

Nationwide, excluding the District of Columbia, the average population of the 435 congressional districts is 731,490. California has the largest congressional delegation with 53 seats while Alaska, Delaware, Montana, North Dakota, South Dakota, Vermont, and Wyoming all have 1 seat each. Wyoming has the smallest population per representative at 584,000 while Montana's single representative represents more than 1 million residents. Sixty congressional districts are estimated to have lost population between the 2010 Census count and the 2014 American Community Survey estimates. Congressional District 22 in Texas had the fastest growth rate at 16.6 percent and six other districts growing by more than 10 percent. Congressional District 11 in Ohio had the greatest decline in population at 3.0 percent.

Selected State Rankings

State	Total Population 2014	Population Rank	Percent Change 2010 to 2014	Percent Change Rank	Total Households 2014	Households Rank	Total Population 65 And Over	Population 65 and Over Rank
Alabama	4,849,377	23	1.4%	37	1,841,217	23	746,512	23
Alaska	736,732	48	3.7%	19	249,659	50	69,899	51
Arizona	6,731,484	15	5.3%	7	2,428,743	17	1,070,757	13
Arkansas	2,966,369	32	1.7%	34	1,131,288	31	465,012	31
California	38,802,500	1	4.2%	17	12,758,648	1	4,990,092	1
Colorado	5,355,866	22	6.5%	4	2,039,592	22	679,572	24
Connecticut	3,596,677	29	0.6%	44	1,355,817	29	555,528	29
Delaware	935,614	45	4.2%	16	349,743	45	153,759	45
District of Columbia	658,893	49	9.5%	2	277,378	48	74,465	50
Florida	19,893,297	3	5.8%	6	7,328,046	3	3,790,954	2
Georgia	10,097,343	8	4.2%	15	3,587,521	10	1,248,870	11
Hawaii	1,419,561	40	4.4%	12	450,769	42	228,061	41
Idaho	1,634,464	39	4.3%	14	591,587	39	234,979	40
Illinois	12,880,580	5	0.4%	46	4,772,421	6	1,787,854	7
Indiana	6,596,855	16	1.7%	33	2,502,739	16	941,494	17
Iowa	3,107,126	30	2.0%	30	1,241,471	30	490,628	30
Kansas	2,904,021	34	1.8%	32	1,109,280	32	417,533	33
Kentucky	4,413,457	26	1.7%	35	1,712,094	26	653,022	25
Louisiana	4,649,676	25	2.6%	29	1,718,194	25	631,170	27
Maine	1,330,089	41	0.1%	50	549,841	40	242,564	39
Maryland	5,976,407	19	3.5%	22	2,165,438	20	822,171	20
Massachusetts	6,745,408	14	3.0%	27	2,549,336	14	1,015,577	14
Michigan	9,909,877	10	0.3%	47	3,834,574	8	1,531,067	8
Minnesota	5,457,173	21	2.9%	28	2,129,195	21	777,833	21
Mississippi	2,994,079	31	0.9%	41	1,095,823	33	427,313	32
Missouri	6,063,589	18	1.2%	39	2,354,809	18	931,890	18
Montana	1,023,579	44	3.5%	23	410,962	43	170,153	43
Nebraska	1,881,503	37	3.0%	26	740,765	37	270,677	38
Nevada	2,839,099	35	5.1%	8	1,021,519	34	400,514	34
New Hampshire	1,326,813	42	0.8%	42	519,756	41	209,447	42
New Jersey	8,938,175	11	1.7%	36	3,194,844	11	1,312,125	10
New Mexico	2,085,572	36	1.3%	38	760,916	36	318,086	36
New York	19,746,227	4	1.9%	31	7,282,398	4	2,895,680	4
North Carolina	9,943,964	9	4.3%	13	3,790,620	9	1,461,149	9
North Dakota	739,482	47	9.9%	1	305,431	47	104,679	48
Ohio	11,594,163	7	0.5%	45	4,593,172	7	1,796,868	6
Oklahoma	3,878,051	28	3.4%	24	1,459,759	28	561,568	28
Oregon	3,970,239	27	3.6%	20	1,535,511	27	634,226	26
Pennsylvania	12,787,209	6	0.7%	43	4,945,972	5	2,134,099	5
Rhode Island	1,055,173	43	0.2%	48	409,654	44	167,180	44
South Carolina	4,832,482	24	4.5%	11	1,826,914	24	761,583	22
South Dakota	853,175	46	4.8%	10	334,475	46	129,354	46
Tennessee	6,549,352	17	3.2%	25	2,509,665	15	986,813	16
Texas	26,956,958	2	7.2%	3	9,277,197	2	3,096,013	3
Utah	2,942,902	33	6.5%	5	918,370	35	294,979	37
Vermont	626,562	50	0.1%	49	257,229	49	106,655	47
Virginia	8,326,289	12	4.1%	18	3,083,820	12	1,146,846	12
Washington	7,061,530	13	5.0%	9	2,679,601	13	992,516	15
West Virginia	1,850,326	38	-0.1%	51	735,375	38	329,055	35
Wisconsin	5,757,564	20	1.2%	40	2,307,685	19	875,720	19
Wyoming	584,153	51	3.6%	21	232,594	51	80,332	49

Table A-1: States—Summary Population Characteristics

	April 1, 2010 Census Population Estimates Base	2014 ACS Population	2010-2014 Population Change	2010-2014 Percent Change	Total Households	2014 ACS			
						Population 65 and Over	Population 85 and Over	Householders 65 and Over	Persons 65 and Over Living Alone
United States..............	308,758,105	318,857,056	10,098,951	3.3%	117,259,127	46,214,893	6,045,970	28,146,157	12,122,226
Alabama.....................	4,780,127	4,849,377	69,250	1.4%	1,841,217	746,512	83,549	472,668	203,126
Alaska.......................	710,249	736,732	26,483	3.7%	249,659	69,899	6,237	40,996	16,214
Arizona......................	6,392,307	6,731,484	339,177	5.3%	2,428,743	1,070,757	119,594	647,612	258,575
Arkansas....................	2,915,958	2,966,369	50,411	1.7%	1,131,288	465,012	55,496	289,802	123,406
California...................	37,254,503	38,802,500	1,547,997	4.2%	12,758,648	4,990,092	666,819	2,830,348	1,137,891
Colorado....................	5,029,324	5,355,866	326,542	6.5%	2,039,592	679,572	80,024	418,629	176,111
Connecticut................	3,574,118	3,596,677	22,559	0.6%	1,355,817	555,528	86,328	339,658	155,034
Delaware...................	897,936	935,614	37,678	4.2%	349,743	153,759	17,141	92,377	36,371
District of Columbia......	601,767	658,893	57,126	9.5%	277,378	74,465	10,144	50,463	28,337
Florida......................	18,804,623	19,893,297	1,088,674	5.8%	7,328,046	3,790,954	524,256	2,223,738	911,506
Georgia.....................	9,688,681	10,097,343	408,662	4.2%	3,587,521	1,248,870	129,202	750,454	308,458
Hawaii.......................	1,360,301	1,419,561	59,260	4.4%	450,769	228,061	38,946	122,744	41,222
Idaho........................	1,567,652	1,634,464	66,812	4.3%	591,587	234,979	26,441	144,224	59,400
Illinois......................	12,831,549	12,880,580	49,031	0.4%	4,772,421	1,787,854	245,215	1,105,546	502,666
Indiana......................	6,484,229	6,596,855	112,626	1.7%	2,502,739	941,494	126,695	585,693	251,716
Iowa.........................	3,046,869	3,107,126	60,257	2.0%	1,241,471	490,628	74,948	310,729	144,436
Kansas......................	2,853,132	2,904,021	50,889	1.8%	1,109,280	417,533	62,108	260,361	116,958
Kentucky....................	4,339,349	4,413,457	74,108	1.7%	1,712,094	653,022	78,264	413,817	181,255
Louisiana...................	4,533,479	4,649,676	116,197	2.6%	1,718,194	631,170	72,202	395,166	170,438
Maine........................	1,328,361	1,330,089	1,728	0.1%	549,841	242,564	31,360	151,281	68,638
Maryland....................	5,773,785	5,976,407	202,622	3.5%	2,165,438	822,171	109,919	495,982	208,317
Massachusetts............	6,547,817	6,745,408	197,591	3.0%	2,549,336	1,015,577	151,610	624,797	295,297
Michigan....................	9,884,129	9,909,877	25,748	0.3%	3,834,574	1,531,067	203,730	969,176	424,384
Minnesota..................	5,303,925	5,457,173	153,248	2.9%	2,129,195	777,833	114,331	486,149	219,424
Mississippi.................	2,968,103	2,994,079	25,976	0.9%	1,095,823	427,313	49,517	273,148	119,270
Missouri....................	5,988,927	6,063,589	74,662	1.2%	2,354,809	931,890	119,446	584,979	257,368
Montana....................	989,417	1,023,579	34,162	3.5%	410,962	170,153	20,899	106,654	49,228
Nebraska...................	1,826,341	1,881,503	55,162	3.0%	740,765	270,677	40,376	173,986	81,488
Nevada......................	2,700,691	2,839,099	138,408	5.1%	1,021,519	400,514	36,432	235,135	95,089
New Hampshire...........	1,316,466	1,326,813	10,347	0.8%	519,756	209,447	27,521	123,515	53,106
New Jersey.................	8,791,936	8,938,175	146,239	1.7%	3,194,844	1,312,125	193,988	783,199	341,714
New Mexico................	2,059,192	2,085,572	26,380	1.3%	760,916	318,086	33,080	199,105	88,566
New York....................	19,378,087	19,746,227	368,140	1.9%	7,282,398	2,895,680	424,809	1,776,118	828,896
North Carolina............	9,535,692	9,943,964	408,272	4.3%	3,790,620	1,461,149	164,331	908,096	388,901
North Dakota..............	672,591	739,482	66,891	9.9%	305,431	104,679	17,350	67,092	33,093
Ohio.........................	11,536,725	11,594,163	57,438	0.5%	4,593,172	1,796,868	248,579	1,142,958	523,164
Oklahoma...................	3,751,616	3,878,051	126,435	3.4%	1,459,759	561,568	66,463	351,005	150,479
Oregon......................	3,831,073	3,970,239	139,166	3.6%	1,535,511	634,226	85,176	392,764	169,904
Pennsylvania..............	12,702,887	12,787,209	84,322	0.7%	4,945,972	2,134,099	325,029	1,321,941	597,309
Rhode Island..............	1,052,931	1,055,173	2,242	0.2%	409,654	167,180	28,782	102,237	48,183
South Carolina............	4,625,401	4,832,482	207,081	4.5%	1,826,914	761,583	81,660	475,305	193,272
South Dakota..............	814,191	853,175	38,984	4.8%	334,475	129,354	20,888	82,186	39,065
Tennessee..................	6,346,275	6,549,352	203,077	3.2%	2,509,665	986,813	106,368	613,436	258,347
Texas.......................	25,146,105	26,956,958	1,810,853	7.2%	9,277,197	3,096,013	346,631	1,843,597	743,872
Utah.........................	2,763,888	2,942,902	179,014	6.5%	918,370	294,979	32,769	175,745	62,212
Vermont.....................	625,745	626,562	817	0.1%	257,229	106,655	13,354	67,260	31,115
Virginia.....................	8,001,045	8,326,289	325,244	4.1%	3,083,820	1,146,846	141,634	702,308	299,166
Washington.................	6,724,543	7,061,530	336,987	5.0%	2,679,601	992,516	130,093	605,828	263,373
West Virginia..............	1,853,011	1,850,326	-2,685	-0.1%	735,375	329,055	38,813	211,788	93,966
Wisconsin..................	5,687,289	5,757,564	70,275	1.2%	2,307,685	875,720	129,317	552,031	250,397
Wyoming...................	563,767	584,153	20,386	3.6%	232,594	80,332	8,106	51,531	22,503

Table A-2: Counties—Summary Population Characteristics

	April 1, 2010 Census Population Estimates Base	2014 ACS Population	2010-2014 Population Change	2010-2014 Percent Change	Total Households	2014 ACS			
						Population 65 and Over	Population 85 and Over	Householders 65 and Over	Persons 65 and Over Living Alone
Alabama									
Baldwin County	182,265	200,111	17,846	9.8%	71,307	37,782	3,808	23,509	10,002
Calhoun County	118,586	115,916	-2,670	-2.3%	46,087	18,543	1,655	11,702	5,215
Cullman County	80,410	81,289	879	1.1%	30,424	14,266	1,310	8,705	4,261
DeKalb County	71,115	71,065	-50	-0.1%	24,720	11,063	958	7,047	2,855
Elmore County	79,296	80,977	1,681	2.1%	28,352	11,214	1,392	7,218	3,331
Etowah County	104,427	103,531	-896	-0.9%	39,714	18,077	2,294	11,562	5,198
Houston County	101,547	104,193	2,646	2.6%	38,825	16,677	1,981	10,400	4,833
Jefferson County	658,350	660,793	2,443	0.4%	261,980	94,503	12,770	62,053	27,317
Lauderdale County	92,709	93,096	387	0.4%	38,093	17,085	2,035	11,076	5,202
Lee County	140,296	154,255	13,959	9.9%	57,880	15,875	1,057	10,631	4,815
Limestone County	82,782	90,787	8,005	9.7%	31,638	12,511	1,106	7,272	2,132
Madison County	334,811	350,299	15,488	4.6%	140,771	48,332	5,702	30,351	12,991
Marshall County	93,019	94,636	1,617	1.7%	34,872	15,298	1,510	8,968	4,500
Mobile County	413,143	415,123	1,980	0.5%	153,450	60,050	8,299	37,513	15,114
Montgomery County	229,363	226,189	-3,174	-1.4%	89,415	30,656	2,624	20,165	8,838
Morgan County	119,486	119,607	121	0.1%	45,016	18,376	1,871	11,989	6,145
Shelby County	195,218	206,655	11,437	5.9%	75,714	27,380	2,670	16,635	6,069
St. Clair County	83,593	86,697	3,104	3.7%	32,267	13,385	1,340	8,466	2,615
Talladega County	82,291	81,322	-969	-1.2%	30,649	13,005	1,595	7,759	3,329
Tuscaloosa County	194,653	202,212	7,559	3.9%	68,320	23,922	3,775	14,352	6,343
Walker County	67,023	65,471	-1,552	-2.3%	25,211	11,863	853	7,720	3,298
Alaska									
Anchorage Municipality	291,826	301,010	9,184	3.1%	104,683	26,906	2,469	14,870	5,216
Fairbanks North Star Borough	97,581	99,357	1,776	1.8%	35,692	7,884	865	5,189	2,009
Matanuska-Susitna Borough	88,995	97,882	8,887	10.0%	30,766	9,457	525	5,232	2,019
Arizona									
Apache County	71,518	71,828	310	0.4%	18,766	9,430	1,187	5,612	2,229
Cochise County	131,357	127,448	-3,909	-3.0%	47,653	25,160	3,151	15,100	6,212
Coconino County	134,437	137,682	3,245	2.4%	46,919	15,520	1,173	9,700	3,514
Maricopa County	3,817,357	4,087,191	269,834	7.1%	1,458,064	565,983	69,695	337,926	139,515
Mohave County	200,186	203,361	3,175	1.6%	81,292	55,039	4,626	32,387	10,922
Navajo County	107,494	108,101	607	0.6%	33,236	17,129	1,339	10,706	3,276
Pima County	980,263	1,004,516	24,253	2.5%	389,737	178,045	20,248	112,162	47,908
Pinal County	375,770	401,918	26,148	7.0%	132,176	71,896	5,497	41,068	12,886
Yavapai County	211,015	218,844	7,829	3.7%	90,584	61,708	7,413	38,908	15,845
Yuma County	195,750	203,247	7,497	3.8%	70,593	35,937	2,445	22,044	7,789
Arkansas									
Benton County	221,344	242,321	20,977	9.5%	86,232	31,400	3,923	18,489	6,546
Craighead County	96,443	102,518	6,075	6.3%	38,548	13,613	1,205	8,000	3,390
Faulkner County	113,237	120,768	7,531	6.7%	42,782	13,216	1,467	7,644	2,901
Garland County	96,024	97,322	1,298	1.4%	39,045	20,953	2,310	13,006	5,567
Jefferson County	77,435	72,297	-5,138	-6.6%	28,494	10,791	1,254	6,951	3,273
Lonoke County	68,354	71,557	3,203	4.7%	26,688	8,950	706	5,881	2,136
Pulaski County	382,796	392,702	9,906	2.6%	152,045	52,923	7,357	33,031	15,162
Saline County	107,118	115,719	8,601	8.0%	41,587	19,377	1,790	11,194	3,413
Sebastian County	125,744	126,776	1,032	0.8%	48,779	17,984	2,613	12,077	5,649
Washington County	203,060	220,792	17,732	8.7%	81,600	24,137	3,021	15,798	7,502
White County	77,076	78,592	1,516	2.0%	29,146	11,920	1,233	7,197	2,642
California									
Alameda County	1,510,261	1,610,921	100,660	6.7%	563,601	200,925	28,257	115,959	48,528
Butte County	220,000	224,241	4,241	1.9%	85,366	38,055	5,627	22,765	10,623
Contra Costa County	1,049,197	1,111,339	62,142	5.9%	387,936	157,940	21,135	90,887	35,074
El Dorado County	181,057	183,087	2,030	1.1%	65,804	32,972	2,723	19,247	7,714
Fresno County	930,452	965,974	35,522	3.8%	297,993	108,445	14,835	61,609	24,646
Humboldt County	134,623	134,809	186	0.1%	53,195	20,327	2,155	12,469	5,368
Imperial County	174,528	179,091	4,563	2.6%	43,635	21,684	2,884	10,308	4,219
Kern County	839,631	874,589	34,958	4.2%	261,135	86,486	9,115	49,947	20,268
Kings County	152,982	150,269	-2,713	-1.8%	41,596	13,331	1,080	7,781	2,581
Lake County	64,665	64,184	-481	-0.7%	27,636	12,703	1,205	8,588	4,309
Los Angeles County	9,818,664	10,116,705	298,041	3.0%	3,269,112	1,233,009	170,916	676,487	271,934
Madera County	150,865	154,548	3,683	2.4%	42,895	19,640	2,663	10,815	3,722
Marin County	252,409	260,750	8,341	3.3%	103,509	49,955	7,301	32,293	16,215
Mendocino County	87,840	87,869	29	0.0%	33,464	16,976	2,172	10,713	4,854
Merced County	255,798	266,353	10,555	4.1%	79,255	28,299	3,565	16,007	6,520
Monterey County	415,057	431,344	16,287	3.9%	123,920	51,152	7,658	30,238	11,543
Napa County	136,530	141,667	5,137	3.8%	50,516	24,631	3,589	14,395	5,623
Nevada County	98,748	98,893	145	0.1%	40,186	23,122	2,911	13,350	4,483
Orange County	3,010,269	3,145,515	135,246	4.5%	1,018,862	413,352	55,151	233,783	87,736
Placer County	348,494	371,694	23,200	6.7%	136,239	66,706	8,318	39,994	16,089
Riverside County	2,189,757	2,329,271	139,514	6.4%	700,584	307,476	40,381	171,808	66,173
Sacramento County	1,418,742	1,482,026	63,284	4.5%	523,353	189,271	24,596	111,627	46,221
San Bernardino County	2,035,215	2,112,619	77,404	3.8%	617,066	217,869	24,755	116,634	43,631
San Diego County	3,095,308	3,263,431	168,123	5.4%	1,100,858	414,632	56,136	234,218	94,278
San Francisco County	805,195	852,469	47,274	5.9%	353,406	122,906	18,704	73,562	34,970
San Joaquin County	685,308	715,597	30,289	4.4%	221,874	84,298	10,225	44,199	17,606
San Luis Obispo County	269,593	279,083	9,490	3.5%	102,645	49,252	5,523	29,273	12,439
San Mateo County	718,498	758,581	40,083	5.6%	257,473	111,339	14,891	62,142	25,649

Table A-2: Counties—Summary Population Characteristics—*Continued*

	April 1, 2010 Census Population Estimates Base	2014 ACS Population	2010-2014 Population Change	2010-2014 Percent Change	Total Households	2014 ACS			
						Population 65 and Over	Population 85 and Over	Householders 65 and Over	Persons 65 and Over Living Alone
California—Cont.									
Santa Barbara County	423,939	440,668	16,729	3.9%	142,912	61,405	10,704	37,459	16,155
Santa Clara County	1,781,672	1,894,605	112,933	6.3%	622,068	231,475	29,172	123,457	47,627
Santa Cruz County	262,362	271,804	9,442	3.6%	96,127	36,267	4,187	22,945	9,828
Shasta County	177,223	179,804	2,581	1.5%	68,542	34,665	4,885	21,110	8,847
Solano County	413,344	431,131	17,787	4.3%	145,313	58,204	5,866	33,203	13,130
Sonoma County	483,880	500,292	16,412	3.4%	190,875	82,536	13,079	51,802	23,254
Stanislaus County	514,451	531,997	17,546	3.4%	169,038	64,448	8,466	37,075	14,763
Sutter County	94,737	95,847	1,110	1.2%	31,634	14,050	1,501	8,132	3,497
Tulare County	442,182	458,198	16,016	3.6%	132,742	47,336	6,886	25,327	7,859
Ventura County	823,420	846,178	22,758	2.8%	269,869	114,954	17,233	68,153	26,075
Yolo County	200,850	207,590	6,740	3.4%	72,228	23,782	3,506	14,516	6,944
Yuba County	72,155	73,966	1,811	2.5%	25,732	8,658	1,272	5,227	2,014
Colorado									
Adams County	441,687	480,718	39,031	8.8%	159,422	46,424	5,130	27,741	10,084
Arapahoe County	572,158	618,821	46,663	8.2%	232,763	73,558	8,619	43,824	17,907
Boulder County	294,571	313,333	18,762	6.4%	123,690	37,931	4,638	23,881	11,309
Denver County	600,025	663,862	63,837	10.6%	281,928	72,266	10,549	47,806	26,219
Douglas County	285,465	314,638	29,173	10.2%	108,135	31,423	3,171	18,561	6,910
El Paso County	622,261	663,519	41,258	6.6%	245,158	75,841	8,302	46,007	18,496
Jefferson County	534,583	558,503	23,920	4.5%	224,502	81,753	10,288	50,496	20,953
Larimer County	299,630	324,122	24,492	8.2%	125,165	45,151	5,178	27,063	12,042
Mesa County	146,723	148,255	1,532	1.0%	59,703	24,742	3,212	15,207	5,367
Pueblo County	159,063	161,875	2,812	1.8%	63,385	27,960	3,506	17,236	7,811
Weld County	252,837	277,670	24,833	9.8%	96,803	30,841	2,938	19,316	7,394
Connecticut									
Fairfield County	916,828	945,438	28,610	3.1%	338,421	135,852	20,186	84,643	37,012
Hartford County	894,029	897,985	3,956	0.4%	346,525	140,399	24,261	86,024	41,136
Litchfield County	189,927	184,993	-4,934	-2.6%	73,572	34,102	5,055	20,304	8,802
Middlesex County	165,676	164,943	-733	-0.4%	67,106	28,763	4,392	17,518	7,358
New Haven County	862,474	861,277	-1,197	-0.1%	326,050	134,334	22,801	82,837	41,386
New London County	274,046	273,676	-370	-0.1%	105,504	44,057	5,971	26,286	11,210
Tolland County	152,682	151,367	-1,315	-0.9%	53,984	21,085	1,463	12,396	4,555
Windham County	118,434	116,998	-1,436	-1.2%	44,655	16,936	2,199	9,650	3,575
Delaware									
Kent County	162,344	171,987	9,643	5.9%	61,270	26,587	2,685	15,895	5,969
New Castle County	538,477	552,778	14,301	2.7%	202,204	75,966	9,580	45,586	20,217
Sussex County	197,115	210,849	13,734	7.0%	86,269	51,206	4,876	30,896	10,185
Florida									
Alachua County	247,335	256,380	9,045	3.7%	97,215	31,565	4,390	19,828	8,989
Bay County	168,852	178,985	10,133	6.0%	66,024	29,182	3,242	16,999	6,609
Brevard County	543,378	556,885	13,507	2.5%	225,226	126,012	17,681	76,243	29,395
Broward County	1,748,148	1,869,235	121,087	6.9%	665,192	286,827	45,554	168,076	81,208
Charlotte County	159,989	168,474	8,485	5.3%	75,234	63,386	7,724	38,266	14,681
Citrus County	141,236	139,377	-1,859	-1.3%	60,315	49,006	5,730	29,294	10,819
Clay County	190,865	199,798	8,933	4.7%	70,307	28,648	2,972	16,153	5,779
Collier County	321,520	348,777	27,257	8.5%	133,162	102,262	11,201	59,575	21,109
Columbia County	67,532	67,857	325	0.5%	23,825	11,980	1,642	7,095	3,083
Duval County	864,263	897,698	33,435	3.9%	340,985	114,700	14,613	72,122	33,693
Escambia County	297,619	310,659	13,040	4.4%	115,094	49,205	5,761	30,783	12,203
Flagler County	95,696	102,408	6,712	7.0%	36,798	29,218	4,057	15,366	4,024
Hernando County	172,777	175,855	3,078	1.8%	70,558	48,302	6,960	30,147	11,978
Highlands County	98,786	98,236	-550	-0.6%	39,288	33,181	3,933	19,624	7,306
Hillsborough County	1,229,224	1,316,298	87,074	7.1%	489,603	172,521	23,897	102,060	41,405
Indian River County	138,028	144,755	6,727	4.9%	55,618	43,896	7,638	26,256	10,372
Lake County	297,047	315,690	18,643	6.3%	117,696	82,699	8,119	46,585	16,370
Lee County	618,754	679,513	60,759	9.8%	263,295	178,227	22,013	102,374	38,161
Leon County	275,480	283,988	8,508	3.1%	112,145	31,731	4,092	20,891	9,768
Manatee County	322,833	351,746	28,913	9.0%	137,695	90,209	11,030	53,715	19,759
Marion County	331,303	339,167	7,864	2.4%	132,275	94,207	11,070	57,018	21,705
Martin County	146,850	153,392	6,542	4.5%	62,518	44,627	7,354	27,796	12,467
Miami-Dade County	2,498,017	2,662,874	164,857	6.6%	843,887	404,713	60,615	202,456	80,448
Monroe County	73,090	77,136	4,046	5.5%	28,065	15,903	2,037	8,836	3,645
Nassau County	73,314	76,619	3,305	4.5%	28,336	15,340	1,845	9,257	3,350
Okaloosa County	180,822	196,512	15,690	8.7%	73,277	30,098	3,749	19,161	7,915
Orange County	1,145,954	1,253,001	107,047	9.3%	444,543	135,067	17,620	75,328	29,078
Osceola County	268,687	310,211	41,524	15.5%	89,328	39,980	5,823	18,816	6,100
Palm Beach County	1,320,134	1,397,710	77,576	5.9%	538,246	317,632	56,528	196,495	90,638
Pasco County	464,701	485,331	20,630	4.4%	186,999	109,037	14,413	65,438	26,514
Pinellas County	916,812	938,098	21,286	2.3%	402,575	215,292	34,313	134,967	67,551
Polk County	602,095	634,638	32,543	5.4%	218,286	124,198	14,528	74,155	26,525
Putnam County	74,364	72,143	-2,221	-3.0%	26,580	14,899	952	10,067	4,826
Santa Rosa County	151,372	163,422	12,050	8.0%	56,085	23,713	1,967	14,143	5,195
Sarasota County	379,437	396,962	17,525	4.6%	175,881	134,564	19,906	82,974	32,730
Seminole County	422,718	442,516	19,798	4.7%	148,732	63,415	9,355	33,408	14,192
St. Johns County	190,039	217,919	27,880	14.7%	81,309	39,637	4,858	23,395	8,084
St. Lucie County	277,257	291,028	13,771	5.0%	108,771	65,273	9,183	39,460	16,126

Table A-2: Counties—Summary Population Characteristics—*Continued*

	April 1, 2010 Census Population Estimates Base	2014 ACS Population	2010-2014 Population Change	2010-2014 Percent Change	Total Households	2014 ACS			
						Population 65 and Over	Population 85 and Over	Householders 65 and Over	Persons 65 and Over Living Alone
Florida—Cont.									
Sumter County	93,420	114,350	20,930	22.4%	50,209	60,225	4,423	34,307	8,031
Volusia County	494,597	507,531	12,934	2.6%	200,729	117,711	18,119	70,258	29,430
Georgia									
Barrow County	69,367	73,240	3,873	5.6%	22,508	8,674	343	4,604	1,814
Bartow County	100,157	101,736	1,579	1.6%	37,742	12,527	1,120	6,989	2,623
Bibb County	155,510	153,905	-1,605	-1.0%	56,135	21,544	3,037	13,579	6,820
Bulloch County	70,217	72,087	1,870	2.7%	25,844	7,492	760	4,989	2,147
Carroll County	110,591	114,093	3,502	3.2%	38,875	13,565	1,549	8,925	4,077
Catoosa County	63,940	65,621	1,681	2.6%	23,476	10,263	659	6,525	2,554
Chatham County	265,133	283,379	18,246	6.9%	106,188	38,466	5,290	23,779	10,241
Cherokee County	214,346	230,985	16,639	7.8%	81,991	27,286	1,821	16,062	5,337
Clarke County	116,707	120,938	4,231	3.6%	44,016	11,912	1,798	7,604	3,355
Clayton County	259,467	267,542	8,075	3.1%	88,538	23,355	2,289	12,424	4,782
Cobb County	688,076	730,981	42,905	6.2%	271,686	77,458	8,035	45,973	17,377
Columbia County	124,053	139,257	15,204	12.3%	45,371	16,285	2,118	7,910	2,574
Coweta County	127,317	135,571	8,254	6.5%	49,546	16,433	1,399	9,871	3,731
DeKalb County	691,894	722,161	30,267	4.4%	266,307	74,670	7,420	45,984	21,248
Dougherty County	94,565	92,407	-2,158	-2.3%	35,539	12,545	1,699	8,532	4,510
Douglas County	132,339	138,776	6,437	4.9%	47,687	14,007	1,122	8,231	3,612
Fayette County	106,566	109,664	3,098	2.9%	38,945	17,936	1,610	10,184	3,248
Floyd County	96,317	96,063	-254	-0.3%	36,177	14,678	2,121	9,055	3,938
Forsyth County	175,511	204,302	28,791	16.4%	66,429	22,319	2,337	12,083	3,789
Fulton County	920,579	996,319	75,740	8.2%	381,990	103,801	14,598	65,170	34,536
Glynn County	79,626	82,175	2,549	3.2%	32,361	14,449	1,301	8,667	3,880
Gwinnett County	805,324	877,922	72,598	9.0%	278,652	75,405	7,159	38,128	13,110
Hall County	179,684	190,761	11,077	6.2%	63,383	26,142	2,623	15,730	5,494
Henry County	203,879	213,869	9,990	4.9%	68,524	22,003	1,214	12,818	5,062
Houston County	139,910	149,111	9,201	6.6%	53,519	16,680	1,801	10,261	3,359
Liberty County	63,469	65,198	1,729	2.7%	22,096	4,882	260	2,672	1,717
Lowndes County	109,233	113,523	4,290	3.9%	38,547	12,418	844	7,928	3,672
Muscogee County	190,545	200,887	10,342	5.4%	74,339	23,945	2,973	15,599	6,115
Newton County	99,958	103,675	3,717	3.7%	35,923	12,379	821	7,833	2,990
Paulding County	142,324	148,987	6,663	4.7%	50,248	13,848	540	8,128	2,356
Richmond County	200,549	201,368	819	0.4%	71,031	25,432	3,355	14,911	6,469
Rockdale County	85,215	87,754	2,539	3.0%	29,707	11,021	930	5,825	1,779
Troup County	67,044	69,469	2,425	3.6%	23,942	9,657	810	6,242	2,673
Walker County	68,756	68,218	-538	-0.8%	25,458	11,566	1,199	7,319	2,576
Walton County	83,768	87,615	3,847	4.6%	30,355	12,412	1,069	7,324	2,544
Whitfield County	102,599	103,542	943	0.9%	36,388	13,037	965	7,666	3,300
Hawaii									
Hawaii County	185,079	194,190	9,111	4.9%	65,178	34,298	5,231	19,257	6,837
Honolulu County	953,207	991,788	38,581	4.0%	309,002	156,728	27,910	83,122	27,905
Kauai County	67,090	70,475	3,385	5.0%	22,234	12,381	1,886	6,749	2,364
Maui County	154,835	163,046	8,211	5.3%	54,303	24,652	3,919	13,616	4,116
Idaho									
Ada County	392,365	426,236	33,871	8.6%	159,896	53,994	6,852	32,075	12,539
Bannock County	82,839	83,347	508	0.6%	30,240	10,666	888	6,874	3,152
Bonneville County	104,304	108,623	4,319	4.1%	36,420	12,855	1,486	8,348	3,056
Canyon County	188,923	203,143	14,220	7.5%	66,791	25,064	2,637	14,309	4,971
Kootenai County	138,494	147,326	8,832	6.4%	56,177	25,326	2,971	15,029	6,235
Twin Falls County	77,230	80,914	3,684	4.8%	29,482	12,084	1,623	7,574	3,755
Illinois									
Adams County	67,103	66,988	-115	-0.2%	27,657	12,490	2,314	8,049	3,652
Champaign County	201,081	207,133	6,052	3.0%	81,347	22,939	2,574	14,942	7,429
Cook County	5,195,060	5,246,456	51,396	1.0%	1,938,055	679,084	96,449	420,247	201,213
DeKalb County	105,160	105,462	302	0.3%	36,965	11,929	2,097	7,023	2,585
DuPage County	916,896	932,708	15,812	1.7%	338,548	125,510	15,970	74,062	30,245
Kane County	515,302	527,306	12,004	2.3%	172,350	62,171	7,528	37,775	15,490
Kankakee County	113,449	111,375	-2,074	-1.8%	40,732	16,517	2,053	9,376	3,629
Kendall County	114,735	121,350	6,615	5.8%	39,923	10,270	772	6,322	2,503
Lake County	703,409	705,186	1,777	0.3%	240,673	85,888	12,027	49,803	20,876
LaSalle County	113,922	111,241	-2,681	-2.4%	42,956	19,377	3,596	11,879	4,990
Macon County	110,768	108,350	-2,418	-2.2%	44,063	19,253	2,331	12,440	5,436
Madison County	269,328	266,560	-2,768	-1.0%	106,253	42,283	5,915	28,067	13,016
McHenry County	308,826	307,283	-1,543	-0.5%	109,417	37,130	3,621	21,959	7,926
McLean County	169,572	174,061	4,489	2.6%	66,361	19,826	3,195	12,445	5,978
Peoria County	186,494	187,319	825	0.4%	74,982	27,686	3,613	18,183	8,476
Rock Island County	147,546	146,063	-1,483	-1.0%	59,384	25,613	3,786	17,268	8,631
Sangamon County	197,465	198,997	1,532	0.8%	83,286	31,382	4,318	20,192	9,567
St. Clair County	270,063	265,729	-4,334	-1.6%	99,917	36,959	4,628	24,017	10,700
Tazewell County	135,394	135,707	313	0.2%	53,763	23,021	3,528	14,198	5,863
Vermilion County	81,625	79,728	-1,897	-2.3%	31,338	14,058	1,387	8,761	4,225
Will County	677,560	685,419	7,859	1.2%	224,012	76,398	8,391	43,516	16,591
Williamson County	66,362	67,008	646	1.0%	27,211	11,713	1,287	6,946	2,613
Winnebago County	295,264	288,542	-6,722	-2.3%	114,034	45,002	5,685	28,626	13,924

Table A-2: Counties—Summary Population Characteristics—*Continued*

	April 1, 2010 Census Population Estimates Base	2014 ACS Population	2010-2014 Population Change	2010-2014 Percent Change	Total Households	2014 ACS			
						Population 65 and Over	Population 85 and Over	Householders 65 and Over	Persons 65 and Over Living Alone
Indiana									
Allen County	355,327	365,918	10,591	3.0%	138,980	48,080	6,908	30,075	13,721
Bartholomew County	76,786	80,217	3,431	4.5%	31,827	11,824	1,234	7,952	3,610
Clark County	110,232	114,262	4,030	3.7%	42,686	16,379	1,957	10,542	4,745
Delaware County	117,671	117,074	-597	-0.5%	45,207	18,735	2,883	11,571	4,323
Elkhart County	197,561	201,971	4,410	2.2%	70,636	26,148	3,952	16,374	7,010
Floyd County	74,580	76,179	1,599	2.1%	29,679	10,796	1,723	6,805	3,077
Grant County	70,063	68,569	-1,494	-2.1%	25,600	12,016	1,690	8,091	3,745
Hamilton County	274,569	302,623	28,054	10.2%	110,844	31,734	3,880	19,298	7,583
Hancock County	70,045	71,978	1,933	2.8%	26,700	10,861	1,101	6,836	2,664
Hendricks County	145,412	156,056	10,644	7.3%	56,010	18,949	2,166	11,731	4,828
Howard County	82,752	82,982	230	0.3%	34,026	14,846	1,972	9,929	4,491
Johnson County	139,867	147,538	7,671	5.5%	53,015	20,379	2,996	11,811	4,432
Kosciusko County	77,356	78,564	1,208	1.6%	29,741	11,763	1,062	7,172	2,765
Lake County	496,031	490,228	-5,803	-1.2%	182,108	71,219	11,367	43,006	18,176
LaPorte County	111,467	111,444	-23	-0.0%	42,068	17,551	2,100	11,239	5,178
Madison County	131,636	130,069	-1,567	-1.2%	52,650	22,437	2,262	14,579	6,031
Marion County	903,389	934,243	30,854	3.4%	360,783	105,602	14,109	66,134	33,121
Monroe County	137,959	143,339	5,380	3.9%	54,003	15,923	1,781	9,958	3,794
Morgan County	68,939	69,693	754	1.1%	25,255	10,417	1,001	6,023	2,054
Porter County	164,347	167,076	2,729	1.7%	61,797	24,218	2,453	14,662	4,964
St. Joseph County	266,929	267,618	689	0.3%	101,296	38,008	6,183	24,329	11,452
Tippecanoe County	172,780	183,074	10,294	6.0%	65,834	19,830	3,044	11,272	4,609
Vanderburgh County	179,703	182,006	2,303	1.3%	73,663	27,816	4,923	17,998	8,789
Vigo County	107,848	108,175	327	0.3%	41,395	15,835	2,721	10,262	4,987
Wayne County	69,003	67,671	-1,332	-1.9%	26,937	12,325	1,278	7,721	2,908
Iowa									
Black Hawk County	131,090	132,897	1,807	1.4%	53,204	19,547	2,297	12,981	6,754
Dallas County	66,137	77,400	11,263	17.0%	27,718	8,524	1,382	5,192	2,279
Dubuque County	93,653	96,370	2,717	2.9%	38,824	15,598	2,103	9,597	3,732
Johnson County	130,882	142,287	11,405	8.7%	55,574	13,874	1,634	8,573	3,983
Linn County	211,226	217,751	6,525	3.1%	88,216	30,974	3,960	20,002	8,770
Polk County	430,635	459,862	29,227	6.8%	179,188	53,735	7,688	34,468	16,649
Pottawattamie County	93,149	93,128	-21	-0.0%	37,321	14,453	2,438	9,357	4,572
Scott County	165,224	171,387	6,163	3.7%	67,822	24,748	3,102	15,479	7,394
Story County	89,542	94,073	4,531	5.1%	35,880	10,136	1,101	6,087	2,201
Woodbury County	102,177	102,271	94	0.1%	38,898	13,869	1,736	8,423	4,047
Kansas									
Butler County	65,880	66,227	347	0.5%	23,088	9,354	1,223	6,286	2,911
Douglas County	110,826	116,585	5,759	5.2%	45,224	12,127	1,714	7,496	3,216
Johnson County	544,179	574,272	30,093	5.5%	220,587	73,158	10,910	45,448	19,650
Leavenworth County	76,227	78,797	2,570	3.4%	26,305	10,075	991	5,373	1,964
Riley County	71,131	75,194	4,063	5.7%	26,265	6,131	967	3,835	1,350
Sedgwick County	498,365	508,803	10,438	2.1%	191,636	65,078	7,801	41,124	18,824
Shawnee County	177,934	178,406	472	0.3%	70,857	28,205	4,520	18,107	7,817
Wyandotte County	157,505	161,636	4,131	2.6%	60,106	18,222	2,780	11,729	5,831
Kentucky									
Boone County	118,811	126,413	7,602	6.4%	44,988	14,280	1,985	8,586	3,929
Bullitt County	74,319	77,955	3,636	4.9%	28,682	10,492	835	6,786	2,157
Campbell County	90,336	91,833	1,497	1.7%	35,602	12,646	1,729	7,975	3,702
Christian County	73,939	74,250	311	0.4%	25,855	8,044	969	5,274	2,827
Daviess County	96,659	98,275	1,616	1.7%	39,638	15,623	1,877	9,745	4,105
Fayette County	295,803	310,797	14,994	5.1%	127,412	35,972	5,596	22,793	10,733
Hardin County	105,549	108,266	2,717	2.6%	39,314	13,354	1,716	8,860	3,969
Jefferson County	741,096	760,026	18,930	2.6%	307,676	110,272	16,039	71,392	33,950
Kenton County	159,721	163,929	4,208	2.6%	62,900	20,884	3,427	13,193	5,967
Madison County	82,916	87,340	4,424	5.3%	33,257	10,913	1,166	7,004	2,458
McCracken County	65,565	65,316	-249	-0.4%	28,659	11,968	2,152	7,522	3,367
Pike County	65,024	63,034	-1,990	-3.1%	26,477	10,263	1,332	6,768	2,719
Warren County	113,781	120,460	6,679	5.9%	44,846	13,937	1,203	9,565	4,637
Louisiana									
Ascension Parish	107,194	117,029	9,835	9.2%	41,433	12,045	926	6,832	2,425
Bossier Parish	116,979	125,064	8,085	6.9%	47,072	15,826	1,733	9,661	4,692
Caddo Parish	254,969	252,603	-2,366	-0.9%	94,854	37,649	5,279	23,269	10,181
Calcasieu Parish	192,770	197,204	4,434	2.3%	73,873	27,229	3,501	16,874	7,411
East Baton Rouge Parish	440,178	446,042	5,864	1.3%	170,572	54,755	6,330	34,864	15,118
Iberia Parish	73,240	73,913	673	0.9%	25,855	9,547	1,084	6,093	2,370
Jefferson Parish	432,552	435,716	3,164	0.7%	169,033	65,885	8,405	42,086	18,204
Lafayette Parish	221,578	235,644	14,066	6.3%	88,611	26,429	3,123	16,922	7,587
Lafourche Parish	96,592	98,020	1,428	1.5%	34,564	13,082	1,545	7,759	2,894
Livingston Parish	128,040	135,751	7,711	6.0%	48,943	15,006	913	9,362	3,461
Orleans Parish	343,829	384,320	40,491	11.8%	152,788	46,481	5,761	30,343	14,954
Ouachita Parish	153,720	156,325	2,605	1.7%	57,766	20,720	2,376	13,274	5,636
Rapides Parish	131,613	132,488	875	0.7%	46,738	19,756	2,378	12,179	5,062
St. Landry Parish	83,384	83,709	325	0.4%	28,739	12,313	1,937	7,856	3,567
St. Tammany Parish	233,737	245,829	12,092	5.2%	88,123	37,110	4,287	21,728	7,731

Table A-2: Counties—Summary Population Characteristics—*Continued*

	April 1, 2010 Census Population Estimates Base	2014 ACS Population	2010-2014 Population Change	2010-2014 Percent Change	Total Households	2014 ACS			
						Population 65 and Over	Population 85 and Over	Householders 65 and Over	Persons 65 and Over Living Alone
Louisiana—Cont.									
Tangipahoa Parish..........	121,101	127,049	5,948	4.9%	45,786	16,233	1,453	9,280	4,428
Terrebonne Parish..........	111,584	113,328	1,744	1.6%	39,975	13,901	1,659	8,103	3,115
Maine									
Androscoggin County	107,702	107,440	-262	-0.2%	44,267	17,336	1,850	11,311	5,892
Aroostook County	71,871	69,447	-2,424	-3.4%	30,146	14,791	2,280	9,323	4,464
Cumberland County	281,673	287,797	6,124	2.2%	117,186	47,191	7,190	29,244	13,805
Kennebec County............	122,151	121,112	-1,039	-0.9%	50,219	21,422	2,384	13,203	5,858
Penobscot County...........	153,920	153,414	-506	-0.3%	61,218	25,127	3,416	16,041	7,676
York County	197,134	200,710	3,576	1.8%	83,504	35,962	4,570	22,173	8,991
Maryland									
Allegany County..............	75,087	72,952	-2,135	-2.8%	29,348	13,871	1,822	8,621	3,821
Anne Arundel County	537,656	560,133	22,477	4.2%	203,775	75,050	8,810	46,746	17,829
Baltimore County	804,973	826,925	21,952	2.7%	311,099	130,772	20,733	80,304	36,425
Calvert County...............	88,737	90,613	1,876	2.1%	31,200	11,616	1,539	7,333	2,642
Carroll County	167,138	167,830	692	0.4%	59,430	25,952	3,064	15,953	7,435
Cecil County	101,108	102,383	1,275	1.3%	36,857	14,187	1,689	8,804	3,374
Charles County...............	146,551	154,747	8,196	5.6%	54,600	17,429	1,750	10,298	3,628
Frederick County	233,385	243,675	10,290	4.4%	89,084	31,824	4,165	18,569	6,816
Harford County	244,826	250,105	5,279	2.2%	92,304	36,565	4,584	20,953	7,947
Howard County	287,085	309,284	22,199	7.7%	109,651	37,630	4,292	19,963	7,927
Montgomery County	971,806	1,030,447	58,641	6.0%	364,854	140,966	24,064	81,009	33,935
Prince George's County.....	863,519	904,430	40,911	4.7%	307,022	102,118	10,346	59,365	22,220
St. Mary's County...........	105,151	110,382	5,231	5.0%	39,179	13,166	1,302	7,889	2,894
Washington County..........	147,430	149,573	2,143	1.5%	54,722	23,264	3,546	14,529	6,891
Wicomico County............	98,733	101,539	2,806	2.8%	37,036	14,520	2,084	8,973	3,501
Massachusetts									
Barnstable County...........	215,888	214,914	-974	-0.5%	95,697	59,991	7,498	38,887	18,267
Berkshire County............	131,272	128,715	-2,557	-1.9%	54,706	26,665	4,323	17,764	8,852
Bristol County	548,285	554,194	5,909	1.1%	212,901	87,043	13,289	53,030	24,204
Essex County	743,175	769,091	25,916	3.5%	287,808	119,375	18,724	72,038	33,572
Franklin County	71,372	70,862	-510	-0.7%	29,859	12,876	1,995	8,174	4,196
Hampden County	463,625	468,161	4,536	1.0%	176,742	71,053	12,260	44,605	21,145
Hampshire County	158,080	160,939	2,859	1.8%	58,332	24,070	3,322	15,614	7,875
Middlesex County............	1,503,126	1,570,315	67,189	4.5%	585,634	219,875	32,141	135,519	63,318
Norfolk County................	670,743	692,254	21,511	3.2%	260,058	108,372	18,186	65,417	30,153
Plymouth County	494,915	507,022	12,107	2.4%	183,251	82,295	9,189	47,601	20,109
Suffolk County	722,087	767,254	45,167	6.3%	295,187	84,187	12,077	54,064	30,672
Worcester County	798,542	813,475	14,933	1.9%	299,841	114,883	18,217	69,289	31,508
Michigan									
Allegan County...............	111,408	113,847	2,439	2.2%	41,779	17,109	1,920	10,476	3,855
Bay County....................	107,771	106,179	-1,592	-1.5%	42,706	19,487	2,221	12,621	5,848
Berrien County	156,817	155,233	-1,584	-1.0%	62,984	27,218	3,430	17,528	7,677
Calhoun County..............	136,148	134,878	-1,270	-0.9%	52,385	21,797	3,110	13,899	6,091
Clinton County	75,382	77,297	1,915	2.5%	28,448	11,770	1,262	6,754	2,453
Eaton County.................	107,759	108,579	820	0.8%	44,115	18,189	2,295	11,184	4,582
Genesee County.............	425,790	412,895	-12,895	-3.0%	167,096	64,986	7,341	42,588	17,534
Grand Traverse County......	86,986	90,782	3,796	4.4%	35,935	15,466	1,858	10,196	4,876
Ingham County	280,891	284,582	3,691	1.3%	110,794	34,000	4,689	21,687	10,847
Isabella County	70,311	70,616	305	0.4%	24,999	7,589	999	4,940	2,274
Jackson County..............	160,248	159,741	-507	-0.3%	61,686	25,771	3,238	16,640	8,329
Kalamazoo County	250,331	258,818	8,487	3.4%	100,171	34,798	4,778	21,548	9,114
Kent County	602,622	629,237	26,615	4.4%	231,986	77,090	14,316	47,846	20,017
Lapeer County................	88,316	88,153	-163	-0.2%	31,395	14,338	1,637	8,529	3,130
Lenawee County.............	99,892	99,047	-845	-0.8%	38,483	16,465	1,745	10,605	3,877
Livingston County...........	180,967	185,596	4,629	2.6%	69,272	27,436	2,274	16,676	5,844
Macomb County..............	840,987	860,112	19,125	2.3%	337,712	133,886	20,210	84,860	37,903
Marquette County............	67,077	67,676	599	0.9%	26,250	11,257	1,324	6,904	3,186
Midland County..............	83,629	83,427	-202	-0.2%	33,579	13,835	1,902	8,858	3,516
Monroe County	152,021	149,824	-2,197	-1.4%	57,879	23,690	3,255	13,962	6,240
Muskegon County............	172,188	172,344	156	0.1%	64,646	25,849	3,289	17,066	7,244
Oakland County..............	1,202,362	1,237,868	35,506	3.0%	492,063	186,242	26,325	119,199	57,272
Ottawa County...............	263,801	276,292	12,491	4.7%	97,198	36,445	4,816	22,645	9,019
Saginaw County.............	200,169	195,012	-5,157	-2.6%	78,000	33,397	3,726	21,226	8,190
Shiawassee County.........	70,648	68,933	-1,715	-2.4%	27,285	11,593	1,745	6,935	2,678
St. Clair County..............	163,040	160,078	-2,962	-1.8%	62,728	26,930	2,962	17,313	7,333
Van Buren County	76,265	75,199	-1,066	-1.4%	28,584	12,303	1,157	7,044	2,664
Washtenaw County	345,066	356,874	11,808	3.4%	137,240	43,044	5,441	27,312	11,673
Wayne County................	1,820,641	1,764,804	-55,837	-3.1%	661,414	243,710	35,546	159,506	75,548
Minnesota									
Anoka County................	330,844	341,864	11,020	3.3%	124,579	40,207	4,550	23,879	8,717
Blue Earth County...........	64,013	65,385	1,372	2.1%	24,986	8,415	1,490	5,028	2,402
Carver County	91,079	97,338	6,259	6.9%	34,298	9,447	1,598	6,245	2,917
Dakota County................	398,552	412,529	13,977	3.5%	157,153	50,260	5,251	31,239	13,953
Hennepin County............	1,152,388	1,212,064	59,676	5.2%	493,219	151,476	23,578	97,368	48,720
Olmsted County..............	144,260	150,287	6,027	4.2%	58,607	20,755	2,994	12,547	5,077

Table A-2: Counties—Summary Population Characteristics—*Continued*

	April 1, 2010 Census Population Estimates Base	2014 ACS Population	2010-2014 Population Change	2010-2014 Percent Change	Total Households	2014 ACS			
						Population 65 and Over	Population 85 and Over	Householders 65 and Over	Persons 65 and Over Living Alone
Minnesota—Cont.									
Ramsey County	508,640	532,655	24,015	4.7%	207,243	69,060	11,408	44,594	21,844
Rice County	64,144	65,151	1,007	1.6%	22,933	9,149	816	6,214	3,624
Scott County	129,928	139,672	9,744	7.5%	46,741	12,957	1,297	7,874	3,226
Sherburne County	88,499	91,126	2,627	3.0%	30,571	9,253	1,284	5,370	2,046
St. Louis County	200,226	200,949	723	0.4%	85,475	34,521	5,352	22,900	11,330
Stearns County	150,642	152,912	2,270	1.5%	57,226	20,344	3,228	12,262	4,953
Washington County	238,134	249,283	11,149	4.7%	91,281	31,752	4,474	18,287	6,346
Wright County	124,700	129,918	5,218	4.2%	44,435	14,492	1,569	8,544	3,278
Mississippi									
DeSoto County	161,264	170,913	9,649	6.0%	60,534	20,399	2,059	12,206	4,380
Forrest County	74,932	76,330	1,398	1.9%	26,683	9,407	1,096	5,532	2,177
Harrison County	187,105	199,058	11,953	6.4%	78,512	26,479	2,419	18,357	8,238
Hinds County	245,365	243,729	-1,636	-0.7%	88,660	29,705	4,485	19,283	8,974
Jackson County	139,668	141,137	1,469	1.1%	49,410	19,968	2,408	11,759	4,322
Jones County	67,761	68,290	529	0.8%	24,132	10,600	1,292	6,516	2,482
Lauderdale County	80,261	79,739	-522	-0.7%	28,683	11,959	1,614	7,202	3,662
Lee County	82,910	85,246	2,336	2.8%	31,006	12,149	1,737	6,963	2,914
Madison County	95,203	101,688	6,485	6.8%	36,629	12,642	1,428	7,871	3,445
Rankin County	142,061	148,070	6,009	4.2%	54,093	19,456	2,069	11,985	4,802
Missouri									
Boone County	162,642	172,717	10,075	6.2%	67,198	18,413	2,293	11,871	5,623
Buchanan County	89,201	89,486	285	0.3%	33,015	12,961	1,818	8,952	4,805
Cape Girardeau County	75,674	78,043	2,369	3.1%	29,949	12,093	1,997	7,147	3,024
Cass County	99,478	100,889	1,411	1.4%	38,241	15,445	1,388	9,240	3,780
Christian County	77,422	82,101	4,679	6.0%	30,525	11,973	1,822	7,253	2,710
Clay County	221,939	233,682	11,743	5.3%	88,345	29,743	3,229	19,267	8,050
Cole County	75,983	76,557	574	0.8%	29,184	10,815	1,141	6,748	2,621
Franklin County	101,491	102,084	593	0.6%	40,748	16,058	2,003	9,697	2,993
Greene County	275,174	285,865	10,691	3.9%	117,910	43,776	5,826	28,854	13,406
Jackson County	674,158	683,191	9,033	1.3%	272,945	92,284	11,139	59,505	28,692
Jasper County	117,404	117,543	139	0.1%	44,377	16,015	2,476	9,867	4,467
Jefferson County	218,728	222,716	3,988	1.8%	83,045	30,156	2,823	17,812	6,572
Platte County	89,322	94,788	5,466	6.1%	36,951	11,976	1,675	7,048	3,079
St. Charles County	360,485	379,493	19,008	5.3%	140,043	51,031	5,903	31,721	13,429
St. Francois County	65,364	65,960	596	0.9%	24,915	10,095	1,468	6,200	2,697
St. Louis County	998,883	1,001,876	2,993	0.3%	398,531	164,829	24,306	105,403	45,467
Montana									
Cascade County	81,327	82,344	1,017	1.3%	34,018	13,756	1,424	9,011	4,313
Flathead County	90,928	94,924	3,996	4.4%	36,820	16,537	1,186	9,898	3,688
Gallatin County	89,510	97,308	7,798	8.7%	39,067	10,707	978	6,915	3,153
Lewis and Clark County	63,395	65,856	2,461	3.9%	26,593	10,680	1,361	6,192	2,879
Missoula County	109,299	112,684	3,385	3.1%	46,407	15,155	2,649	10,170	4,984
Yellowstone County	147,975	155,634	7,659	5.2%	61,936	23,672	3,029	14,746	7,614
Nebraska									
Douglas County	517,110	543,244	26,134	5.1%	209,520	62,609	10,377	41,021	20,208
Lancaster County	285,407	301,795	16,388	5.7%	119,205	36,338	4,779	23,688	10,534
Sarpy County	158,840	172,193	13,353	8.4%	63,029	17,499	2,147	10,850	4,337
Nevada									
Clark County	1,951,269	2,069,681	118,412	6.1%	731,322	274,915	24,386	156,767	61,513
Washoe County	421,427	440,078	18,651	4.4%	166,641	64,426	6,546	40,668	18,141
New Hampshire									
Cheshire County	77,117	76,115	-1,002	-1.3%	31,305	12,998	1,918	8,186	3,300
Grafton County	89,114	89,658	544	0.6%	35,436	15,896	2,275	9,339	3,902
Hillsborough County	400,721	405,184	4,463	1.1%	153,482	56,374	7,581	31,803	13,660
Merrimack County	146,442	147,171	729	0.5%	57,023	23,480	2,888	13,787	5,999
Rockingham County	295,220	300,621	5,401	1.8%	119,020	45,788	6,138	27,957	12,349
Strafford County	123,146	125,604	2,458	2.0%	46,859	16,887	1,887	9,910	4,685
New Jersey									
Atlantic County	274,549	275,209	660	0.2%	101,937	43,435	4,347	26,503	12,711
Bergen County	905,117	933,572	28,455	3.1%	337,469	149,621	23,126	84,279	32,144
Burlington County	448,728	449,722	994	0.2%	165,424	70,099	9,185	43,499	18,859
Camden County	513,678	511,038	-2,640	-0.5%	188,064	72,754	10,516	47,093	21,099
Cape May County	97,265	95,344	-1,921	-2.0%	40,779	22,927	2,659	14,468	5,814
Cumberland County	156,898	157,389	491	0.3%	50,593	21,282	2,994	13,024	5,311
Essex County	783,987	795,723	11,736	1.5%	277,735	98,173	15,119	61,017	31,603
Gloucester County	288,288	290,951	2,663	0.9%	104,305	41,094	6,459	25,692	11,001
Hudson County	634,277	669,115	34,838	5.5%	253,300	72,052	9,084	43,207	20,093
Hunterdon County	127,351	126,067	-1,284	-1.0%	47,387	19,613	2,830	11,952	5,019
Mercer County	367,508	371,537	4,029	1.1%	131,564	51,229	6,863	30,427	12,582
Middlesex County	809,860	836,297	26,437	3.3%	282,860	111,947	17,308	63,356	26,550
Monmouth County	630,378	629,279	-1,099	-0.2%	230,391	98,218	15,704	59,863	26,221
Morris County	492,279	499,727	7,448	1.5%	179,654	77,287	11,426	45,402	18,421
Ocean County	576,565	586,301	9,736	1.7%	220,941	128,434	21,904	81,638	36,490
Passaic County	501,624	508,856	7,232	1.4%	159,309	66,620	10,040	35,641	15,288

Table A-2: Counties—Summary Population Characteristics—*Continued*

	April 1, 2010 Census Population Estimates Base	2014 ACS Population	2010-2014 Population Change	2010-2014 Percent Change	Total Households	2014 ACS Population 65 and Over	2014 ACS Population 85 and Over	2014 ACS Householders 65 and Over	2014 ACS Persons 65 and Over Living Alone
New Jersey—Cont.									
Salem County	66,083	64,715	-1,368	-2.1%	23,832	10,977	1,759	7,136	3,014
Somerset County	323,441	332,568	9,127	2.8%	117,482	45,848	6,577	24,819	10,704
Sussex County	148,869	144,909	-3,960	-2.7%	54,174	21,232	2,243	12,312	4,851
Union County	536,499	552,939	16,440	3.1%	186,037	72,050	10,755	41,557	19,500
Warren County	108,692	106,917	-1,775	-1.6%	41,607	17,233	3,090	10,314	4,439
New Mexico									
Bernalillo County	662,555	675,551	12,996	2.0%	261,279	95,769	11,046	59,692	28,554
Chaves County	65,645	65,878	233	0.4%	23,747	9,807	711	6,495	3,024
Doña Ana County	0	213,676	0	0.0%	75,530	30,057	3,322	17,799	6,850
Lea County	64,727	69,999	5,272	8.1%	21,805	7,340	656	4,381	1,731
McKinley County	71,491	74,098	2,607	3.6%	18,148	7,509	566	4,880	1,671
Otero County	63,799	65,082	1,283	2.0%	23,190	10,366	942	6,074	1,796
San Juan County	130,045	123,785	-6,260	-4.8%	40,378	15,809	2,028	9,919	3,502
Sandoval County	131,563	137,608	6,045	4.6%	49,357	20,986	1,994	13,613	5,818
Santa Fe County	144,171	148,164	3,993	2.8%	60,565	29,029	2,639	18,581	8,610
Valencia County	76,574	75,817	-757	-1.0%	26,595	11,626	596	7,783	3,410
New York									
Albany County	304,208	308,171	3,963	1.3%	124,716	47,327	6,170	29,822	13,676
Bronx County	1,385,108	1,438,159	53,051	3.8%	492,481	161,753	20,245	98,671	52,395
Broome County	200,600	197,349	-3,251	-1.6%	78,810	34,371	5,355	21,537	10,088
Cattaraugus County	80,317	78,600	-1,717	-2.1%	30,735	13,428	1,680	8,548	4,118
Cayuga County	80,025	78,823	-1,202	-1.5%	31,290	13,146	1,955	8,338	4,113
Chautauqua County	134,905	132,053	-2,852	-2.1%	52,916	23,641	3,616	14,768	6,728
Chemung County	88,830	87,770	-1,060	-1.2%	34,617	14,901	2,414	8,995	3,784
Clinton County	82,128	81,632	-496	-0.6%	31,426	12,286	1,290	7,776	3,495
Dutchess County	297,448	296,579	-869	-0.3%	104,190	45,496	6,648	25,920	11,161
Erie County	919,064	922,835	3,771	0.4%	383,657	152,661	24,864	101,398	50,575
Jefferson County	116,229	119,103	2,874	2.5%	43,516	14,632	1,566	8,616	3,588
Kings County	2,504,709	2,621,793	117,084	4.7%	942,402	317,536	47,342	196,991	96,660
Livingston County	65,250	64,586	-664	-1.0%	25,334	10,556	1,623	7,095	3,299
Madison County	73,440	72,369	-1,071	-1.5%	25,932	11,386	1,562	6,308	2,417
Monroe County	744,340	749,857	5,517	0.7%	298,271	115,998	18,948	74,052	37,537
Nassau County	1,339,710	1,358,627	18,917	1.4%	440,168	222,921	37,327	126,595	47,589
New York County	1,585,873	1,636,268	50,395	3.2%	762,228	234,962	35,425	167,700	100,802
Niagara County	216,477	213,525	-2,952	-1.4%	86,907	36,927	6,032	24,133	12,530
Oneida County	234,879	232,871	-2,008	-0.9%	90,583	40,694	6,483	24,683	11,261
Onondaga County	467,031	468,196	1,165	0.2%	185,474	71,672	11,833	45,806	22,376
Ontario County	108,105	109,707	1,602	1.5%	43,581	19,592	3,264	12,487	6,236
Orange County	372,813	376,099	3,286	0.9%	124,587	47,416	5,505	27,498	12,060
Oswego County	122,107	120,913	-1,194	-1.0%	45,646	17,363	2,225	10,409	4,589
Putnam County	99,750	99,487	-263	-0.3%	34,234	14,355	1,741	8,294	2,623
Queens County	2,230,539	2,321,580	91,041	4.1%	785,985	315,879	45,379	176,063	74,065
Rensselaer County	159,427	159,774	347	0.2%	63,289	24,080	3,292	15,633	6,988
Richmond County	468,730	473,279	4,549	1.0%	164,971	68,263	9,281	38,825	14,766
Rockland County	311,687	323,866	12,179	3.9%	98,873	48,111	7,153	25,950	9,387
Saratoga County	219,613	224,921	5,308	2.4%	90,964	35,222	4,949	22,418	9,456
Schenectady County	154,725	155,735	1,010	0.7%	56,255	24,058	4,543	14,354	6,958
St. Lawrence County	111,944	111,400	-544	-0.5%	40,286	16,993	2,445	9,894	5,223
Steuben County	98,988	98,394	-594	-0.6%	41,046	17,344	2,461	11,088	5,269
Suffolk County	1,493,346	1,502,968	9,622	0.6%	493,287	228,758	28,677	135,519	55,160
Sullivan County	77,545	75,943	-1,602	-2.1%	27,524	12,838	873	7,204	3,729
Tompkins County	101,595	104,691	3,096	3.0%	38,120	12,325	2,319	7,857	3,303
Ulster County	182,494	180,445	-2,049	-1.1%	69,522	31,737	4,110	21,122	10,569
Warren County	65,705	64,973	-732	-1.1%	26,193	12,805	2,024	7,527	3,311
Wayne County	93,762	92,051	-1,711	-1.8%	35,577	15,341	2,336	9,442	4,913
Westchester County	949,114	972,634	23,520	2.5%	342,557	152,223	25,886	91,882	41,180
North Carolina									
Alamance County	151,241	155,792	4,551	3.0%	62,799	25,110	3,301	16,058	7,572
Brunswick County	107,431	118,836	11,405	10.6%	49,842	31,946	2,271	18,313	6,177
Buncombe County	238,307	250,539	12,232	5.1%	103,299	45,118	5,676	27,853	13,485
Burke County	90,914	89,486	-1,428	-1.6%	33,214	16,362	2,140	9,454	4,595
Cabarrus County	178,182	192,103	13,921	7.8%	69,144	23,827	3,027	15,055	6,519
Caldwell County	83,029	81,484	-1,545	-1.9%	30,458	14,740	1,509	9,454	4,232
Carteret County	66,469	68,811	2,342	3.5%	28,773	15,294	1,462	9,697	4,098
Catawba County	154,356	154,534	178	0.1%	56,304	24,813	2,016	14,624	4,735
Chatham County	63,494	68,698	5,204	8.2%	28,264	16,084	2,375	10,205	4,250
Cleveland County	98,083	97,076	-1,007	-1.0%	37,038	16,837	1,817	11,438	4,501
Craven County	103,505	104,510	1,005	1.0%	40,109	17,610	2,535	11,320	4,793
Cumberland County	319,431	326,328	6,897	2.2%	122,359	35,286	3,066	22,057	9,757
Davidson County	162,878	164,072	1,194	0.7%	61,896	27,021	1,653	17,710	7,707
Durham County	269,974	294,460	24,486	9.1%	118,565	32,356	4,598	20,075	9,384
Forsyth County	350,670	365,298	14,628	4.2%	146,198	52,193	7,633	33,763	16,072
Gaston County	206,083	211,127	5,044	2.4%	76,610	32,006	4,349	18,971	8,484
Guilford County	488,406	512,119	23,713	4.9%	198,860	70,308	9,221	44,306	22,535
Harnett County	114,678	126,666	11,988	10.5%	44,153	13,669	1,431	8,883	3,898
Henderson County	106,742	111,149	4,407	4.1%	45,597	27,505	3,906	16,786	7,448
Iredell County	159,440	166,675	7,235	4.5%	61,911	24,123	1,869	13,802	4,380

Table A-2: Counties—Summary Population Characteristics—*Continued*

	April 1, 2010 Census Population Estimates Base	2014 ACS Population	2010-2014 Population Change	2010-2014 Percent Change	Total Households	2014 ACS			
						Population 65 and Over	Population 85 and Over	Householders 65 and Over	Persons 65 and Over Living Alone
North Carolina—Cont.									
Johnston County	168,878	181,423	12,545	7.4%	63,831	22,004	2,215	13,892	5,136
Lincoln County	78,265	79,829	1,564	2.0%	30,327	12,894	1,130	7,702	1,993
Mecklenburg County	919,666	1,012,539	92,873	10.1%	389,047	101,554	11,895	62,064	28,506
Moore County	88,247	93,077	4,830	5.5%	37,179	22,340	4,339	13,871	5,835
Nash County	95,837	94,357	-1,480	-1.5%	36,957	15,441	1,552	10,013	5,195
New Hanover County	202,683	216,298	13,615	6.7%	90,106	34,104	4,277	21,442	8,305
Onslow County	177,772	187,589	9,817	5.5%	61,873	15,988	1,085	9,938	4,455
Orange County	133,702	140,420	6,718	5.0%	51,325	15,716	1,637	9,772	4,212
Pitt County	168,148	175,354	7,206	4.3%	68,412	19,820	2,417	12,463	5,098
Randolph County	141,752	142,778	1,026	0.7%	53,711	23,187	2,442	15,552	6,963
Robeson County	134,168	134,760	592	0.4%	46,484	17,379	1,812	11,080	4,770
Rockingham County	93,640	91,696	-1,944	-2.1%	36,879	16,633	2,235	10,672	4,482
Rowan County	138,442	138,630	188	0.1%	52,294	22,566	1,903	14,616	5,366
Rutherford County	67,809	66,600	-1,209	-1.8%	25,805	13,004	2,213	8,116	4,244
Surry County	73,673	72,968	-705	-1.0%	27,632	13,770	1,826	8,171	3,373
Union County	201,307	218,568	17,261	8.6%	71,569	25,231	2,421	14,167	6,192
Wake County	901,018	998,691	97,673	10.8%	370,061	99,924	9,873	59,068	24,264
Wayne County	122,623	124,456	1,833	1.5%	46,281	18,027	1,903	11,015	4,734
Wilkes County	69,340	68,838	-502	-0.7%	27,257	13,662	1,405	8,517	3,978
Wilson County	81,234	81,401	167	0.2%	32,691	13,432	1,473	8,299	3,485
North Dakota									
Burleigh County	81,308	90,503	9,195	11.3%	38,892	13,056	2,440	8,176	3,232
Cass County	149,778	167,005	17,227	11.5%	69,621	17,715	2,648	11,545	5,988
Grand Forks County	66,861	70,138	3,277	4.9%	29,217	7,808	1,245	5,261	2,726
Ward County	61,675	69,384	7,709	12.5%	26,091	7,888	1,550	5,001	2,443
Ohio									
Allen County	106,331	105,040	-1,291	-1.2%	39,412	16,543	1,998	10,595	4,495
Ashtabula County	101,497	99,175	-2,322	-2.3%	38,891	17,004	2,391	10,195	4,183
Belmont County	70,400	69,461	-939	-1.3%	27,205	13,196	2,149	7,957	3,554
Butler County	368,130	374,158	6,028	1.6%	134,613	49,424	6,196	29,611	11,521
Clark County	138,333	136,554	-1,779	-1.3%	55,199	24,356	3,393	15,290	6,659
Clermont County	197,363	201,560	4,197	2.1%	75,561	28,320	2,230	17,922	7,162
Columbiana County	107,841	105,686	-2,155	-2.0%	42,107	19,192	2,592	12,009	5,358
Cuyahoga County	1,280,109	1,259,828	-20,281	-1.6%	535,295	207,350	32,684	136,488	69,519
Delaware County	174,189	189,113	14,924	8.6%	66,615	21,322	2,566	12,304	4,452
Erie County	77,079	75,828	-1,251	-1.6%	31,492	14,639	1,942	9,653	4,411
Fairfield County	146,152	150,381	4,229	2.9%	55,316	21,807	2,107	13,321	5,713
Franklin County	1,163,543	1,231,393	67,850	5.8%	486,877	133,707	17,500	83,709	39,867
Geauga County	93,410	94,295	885	0.9%	35,450	16,626	2,757	9,686	2,619
Greene County	161,569	163,820	2,251	1.4%	64,527	25,607	3,196	15,735	7,068
Hamilton County	802,374	806,631	4,257	0.5%	335,137	114,493	18,600	76,287	39,740
Hancock County	74,782	75,337	555	0.7%	31,747	11,946	2,007	7,754	3,692
Jefferson County	69,709	67,694	-2,015	-2.9%	27,447	13,255	2,043	8,680	3,911
Lake County	230,038	229,230	-808	-0.4%	95,116	40,970	5,353	26,291	11,824
Licking County	166,482	169,390	2,908	1.7%	65,290	25,955	3,143	16,224	6,758
Lorain County	301,356	304,216	2,860	0.9%	116,551	49,382	7,526	31,749	14,539
Lucas County	441,815	435,286	-6,529	-1.5%	176,302	63,203	10,326	41,777	21,200
Mahoning County	238,823	233,204	-5,619	-2.4%	96,868	44,554	8,686	29,231	13,965
Marion County	66,501	65,720	-781	-1.2%	24,346	11,007	1,613	7,518	3,183
Medina County	172,333	176,029	3,696	2.1%	66,081	27,114	3,566	16,367	6,659
Miami County	102,506	103,900	1,394	1.4%	41,339	17,781	1,733	11,088	5,306
Montgomery County	535,141	533,116	-2,025	-0.4%	221,744	88,739	10,750	57,759	27,995
Muskingum County	86,074	85,818	-256	-0.3%	33,921	14,224	2,018	9,403	4,324
Portage County	161,421	161,882	461	0.3%	61,796	23,895	3,299	15,282	6,621
Richland County	124,475	121,942	-2,533	-2.0%	47,378	22,015	2,710	15,369	7,499
Ross County	78,064	77,159	-905	-1.2%	27,569	11,396	916	7,322	3,511
Scioto County	79,499	77,258	-2,241	-2.8%	30,790	12,766	1,687	7,877	3,455
Stark County	375,584	375,736	152	0.0%	149,011	66,181	9,107	41,136	17,712
Summit County	541,786	541,943	157	0.0%	221,568	87,526	13,667	56,247	26,640
Trumbull County	210,307	205,175	-5,132	-2.4%	86,855	39,588	6,389	25,474	11,555
Tuscarawas County	92,582	92,788	206	0.2%	37,516	16,746	2,740	10,625	5,366
Warren County	212,868	221,659	8,791	4.1%	79,096	28,959	2,472	16,994	5,834
Wayne County	114,514	115,537	1,023	0.9%	42,830	18,369	2,491	10,626	4,037
Wood County	125,488	129,590	4,102	3.3%	50,731	18,045	2,352	11,081	4,582
Oklahoma									
Canadian County	115,541	129,582	14,041	12.2%	44,093	15,628	1,935	9,226	3,547
Cleveland County	255,761	269,908	14,147	5.5%	100,767	32,134	3,086	19,193	7,639
Comanche County	124,098	125,033	935	0.8%	41,156	13,777	1,238	8,367	3,880
Creek County	69,967	70,632	665	1.0%	26,529	11,860	993	7,083	2,793
Muskogee County	70,988	69,966	-1,022	-1.4%	26,016	11,148	1,696	6,952	3,083
Oklahoma County	718,627	766,215	47,588	6.6%	293,079	95,721	12,163	60,997	27,280
Payne County	77,350	80,264	2,914	3.8%	29,934	8,789	1,339	5,632	2,557
Pottawatomie County	69,442	71,811	2,369	3.4%	25,733	11,228	1,390	6,475	2,581
Rogers County	86,904	89,815	2,911	3.3%	33,586	13,877	1,471	8,787	3,677
Tulsa County	603,442	629,598	26,156	4.3%	248,907	82,093	11,171	51,474	23,361
Wagoner County	73,087	75,702	2,615	3.6%	27,368	11,210	1,040	6,775	2,008

Table A-2: Counties—Summary Population Characteristics—*Continued*

	April 1, 2010 Census Population Estimates Base	2014 ACS Population	2010-2014 Population Change	2010-2014 Percent Change	Total Households	2014 ACS			
						Population 65 and Over	Population 85 and Over	Householders 65 and Over	Persons 65 and Over Living Alone
Oregon									
Benton County	85,581	86,316	735	0.9%	33,904	12,373	2,159	7,923	3,367
Clackamas County	375,992	394,972	18,980	5.0%	149,910	63,969	7,640	38,693	15,273
Deschutes County	157,733	170,388	12,655	8.0%	66,218	30,318	3,703	18,070	6,678
Douglas County	107,667	106,972	-695	-0.6%	43,290	25,170	3,680	15,674	6,690
Jackson County	203,206	210,287	7,081	3.5%	83,131	42,200	5,864	26,718	11,568
Josephine County	82,713	83,599	886	1.1%	33,486	20,667	2,077	12,767	4,729
Klamath County	66,380	65,455	-925	-1.4%	26,377	12,304	1,962	8,131	3,880
Lane County	351,715	358,337	6,622	1.9%	145,732	62,237	8,754	39,122	16,431
Linn County	116,672	119,356	2,684	2.3%	45,907	20,720	2,558	12,694	5,116
Marion County	315,335	326,110	10,775	3.4%	114,484	47,186	6,015	30,083	13,145
Multnomah County	735,332	776,712	41,380	5.6%	313,812	92,620	13,285	57,511	27,773
Polk County	75,403	77,916	2,513	3.3%	27,487	13,601	1,949	8,211	3,570
Umatilla County	75,889	76,705	816	1.1%	26,895	11,533	1,448	5,823	2,702
Washington County	529,712	562,998	33,286	6.3%	209,426	66,871	9,984	41,521	18,233
Yamhill County	99,193	101,758	2,565	2.6%	34,072	15,549	2,235	9,461	4,181
Pennsylvania									
Adams County	101,413	101,714	301	0.3%	38,748	18,272	1,894	10,910	4,099
Allegheny County	1,223,348	1,231,255	7,907	0.6%	530,977	213,668	36,759	142,538	72,521
Armstrong County	68,940	67,785	-1,155	-1.7%	28,351	13,655	2,470	9,063	4,238
Beaver County	170,539	169,392	-1,147	-0.7%	68,555	33,446	4,883	21,820	9,771
Berks County	411,587	413,691	2,104	0.5%	152,908	66,449	9,085	40,172	16,546
Blair County	127,078	125,955	-1,123	-0.9%	49,678	24,112	4,143	14,864	7,538
Bucks County	625,255	626,685	1,430	0.2%	232,629	104,583	14,754	61,999	25,616
Butler County	183,862	185,943	2,081	1.1%	76,410	31,328	4,708	20,090	9,178
Cambria County	143,674	137,732	-5,942	-4.1%	57,004	28,088	4,887	18,477	8,804
Carbon County	65,250	64,441	-809	-1.2%	26,015	12,729	1,096	7,877	3,106
Centre County	153,981	158,742	4,761	3.1%	57,583	19,873	2,417	12,199	4,872
Chester County	499,146	512,784	13,638	2.7%	186,144	74,034	10,445	44,264	17,082
Clearfield County	81,644	81,191	-453	-0.6%	31,784	15,340	2,219	9,947	4,981
Columbia County	67,296	67,122	-174	-0.3%	26,261	11,417	1,390	7,303	3,023
Crawford County	88,765	87,175	-1,590	-1.8%	34,834	15,919	1,617	10,082	4,075
Cumberland County	235,408	243,762	8,354	3.5%	96,906	41,459	5,882	26,592	11,685
Dauphin County	268,100	271,453	3,353	1.3%	111,364	40,893	6,315	25,789	12,726
Delaware County	558,726	562,960	4,234	0.8%	204,574	85,104	13,937	52,263	23,966
Erie County	280,566	278,443	-2,123	-0.8%	108,655	44,087	6,442	27,024	11,655
Fayette County	136,607	134,086	-2,521	-1.8%	53,900	26,078	4,169	15,564	7,481
Franklin County	149,618	152,892	3,274	2.2%	58,565	27,775	4,037	16,463	6,669
Indiana County	88,891	87,706	-1,185	-1.3%	34,536	14,868	2,054	9,335	3,511
Lackawanna County	214,436	212,719	-1,717	-0.8%	84,280	40,198	7,617	24,720	12,713
Lancaster County	519,448	533,320	13,872	2.7%	194,764	87,648	13,077	50,614	19,589
Lawrence County	91,140	88,771	-2,369	-2.6%	35,935	17,555	3,075	11,449	4,809
Lebanon County	133,573	136,359	2,786	2.1%	51,234	24,696	3,161	14,125	5,685
Lehigh County	349,626	357,823	8,197	2.3%	134,442	57,247	9,530	34,260	15,447
Luzerne County	320,918	318,829	-2,089	-0.7%	125,235	60,268	10,955	36,645	18,340
Lycoming County	116,108	116,508	400	0.3%	45,742	20,476	3,224	12,944	5,969
Mercer County	116,674	114,884	-1,790	-1.5%	45,074	22,912	3,239	14,146	6,662
Monroe County	169,842	166,314	-3,528	-2.1%	54,404	25,516	3,255	12,922	4,970
Montgomery County	799,873	816,857	16,984	2.1%	308,912	133,682	22,393	81,685	35,530
Northampton County	297,735	300,654	2,919	1.0%	113,312	52,208	9,327	30,546	13,170
Northumberland County	94,517	93,944	-573	-0.6%	38,712	18,608	2,721	11,777	4,792
Philadelphia County	1,526,006	1,560,297	34,291	2.2%	577,862	195,574	29,379	124,800	65,727
Schuylkill County	148,289	145,797	-2,492	-1.7%	58,061	28,211	4,590	17,799	8,715
Somerset County	77,748	76,218	-1,530	-2.0%	29,481	15,608	2,400	9,658	4,393
Washington County	207,820	208,187	367	0.2%	82,396	39,617	6,144	24,643	10,370
Westmoreland County	365,169	359,320	-5,849	-1.6%	151,362	74,350	12,542	47,595	20,503
York County	435,002	440,755	5,753	1.3%	169,212	70,222	7,480	41,712	16,430
Rhode Island									
Kent County	166,158	165,128	-1,030	-0.6%	67,432	29,210	5,675	18,266	8,861
Newport County	83,141	82,358	-783	-0.9%	35,825	15,977	2,107	10,345	4,808
Providence County	626,663	631,974	5,311	0.8%	237,787	89,958	16,025	54,243	26,185
Washington County	127,094	126,653	-441	-0.3%	48,898	22,813	3,315	13,918	5,658
South Carolina									
Aiken County	160,106	164,753	4,647	2.9%	63,518	28,801	2,883	17,610	7,471
Anderson County	187,123	192,810	5,687	3.0%	74,333	32,602	3,732	20,200	8,891
Beaufort County	162,233	175,852	13,619	8.4%	66,191	42,529	4,469	25,981	9,738
Berkeley County	177,850	198,205	20,355	11.4%	69,821	24,245	2,376	13,756	4,349
Charleston County	350,204	381,015	30,811	8.8%	153,179	55,147	6,772	34,760	14,156
Darlington County	68,683	67,799	-884	-1.3%	25,099	11,134	856	7,554	3,162
Dorchester County	136,589	148,469	11,880	8.7%	53,509	17,563	1,468	10,319	3,637
Florence County	136,888	139,231	2,343	1.7%	52,716	20,638	2,292	12,482	5,529
Greenville County	451,219	482,752	31,533	7.0%	181,092	69,257	8,484	42,834	17,452
Greenwood County	69,661	69,520	-141	-0.2%	27,151	11,827	2,217	7,829	3,431
Horry County	269,291	298,832	29,541	11.0%	125,157	61,159	4,919	38,767	15,805
Lancaster County	76,652	83,160	6,508	8.5%	28,903	15,542	1,412	9,146	3,998
Laurens County	66,539	66,533	-6	-0.0%	24,998	11,023	1,444	7,067	2,875

Table A-2: Counties—Summary Population Characteristics—*Continued*

	April 1, 2010 Census Population Estimates Base	2014 ACS Population	2010-2014 Population Change	2010-2014 Percent Change	Total Households	2014 ACS			
						Population 65 and Over	Population 85 and Over	Householders 65 and Over	Persons 65 and Over Living Alone
South Carolina—Cont.									
Lexington County	262,396	277,888	15,492	5.9%	107,408	39,324	4,473	25,022	10,961
Oconee County	74,275	75,192	917	1.2%	32,113	15,950	1,271	9,788	3,876
Orangeburg County	92,495	90,090	-2,405	-2.6%	31,350	15,222	2,064	9,240	4,609
Pickens County	119,226	120,368	1,142	1.0%	43,859	18,410	1,674	11,532	5,144
Richland County	384,507	401,566	17,059	4.4%	146,458	45,259	4,257	29,698	12,788
Spartanburg County	284,305	293,542	9,237	3.2%	110,179	44,399	4,478	27,831	10,979
Sumter County	107,463	107,919	456	0.4%	39,936	15,488	1,882	9,981	4,077
York County	226,071	245,346	19,275	8.5%	91,868	32,506	2,592	19,598	7,390
South Dakota									
Minnehaha County	169,471	182,882	13,411	7.9%	71,099	22,532	3,479	14,087	7,171
Pennington County	100,937	108,242	7,305	7.2%	42,161	16,239	2,148	10,370	5,045
Tennessee									
Anderson County	75,126	75,528	402	0.5%	30,183	14,394	1,514	8,798	4,015
Blount County	123,016	126,339	3,323	2.7%	47,871	23,362	2,644	13,469	5,206
Bradley County	98,963	102,975	4,012	4.1%	37,741	16,557	1,825	10,286	4,640
Davidson County	626,663	668,347	41,684	6.7%	267,952	74,165	9,077	47,229	23,019
Greene County	68,831	68,335	-496	-0.7%	27,296	13,573	1,475	7,564	2,836
Hamilton County	336,465	351,220	14,755	4.4%	136,427	55,747	6,920	35,090	14,170
Knox County	432,234	448,644	16,410	3.8%	177,479	65,185	8,430	41,265	20,268
Madison County	98,294	98,178	-116	-0.1%	38,009	14,667	1,921	9,190	3,390
Maury County	80,959	85,515	4,556	5.6%	31,472	12,658	880	7,418	2,807
Montgomery County	172,337	189,961	17,624	10.2%	65,474	16,531	977	9,301	3,050
Putnam County	72,328	74,165	1,837	2.5%	29,705	11,902	1,058	8,106	3,921
Robertson County	66,293	68,079	1,786	2.7%	24,867	9,020	932	5,423	2,031
Rutherford County	262,604	288,906	26,302	10.0%	103,456	28,048	2,435	16,979	6,971
Sevier County	89,876	95,110	5,234	5.8%	35,072	16,976	1,475	10,950	4,455
Shelby County	927,640	938,803	11,163	1.2%	347,377	108,912	14,641	67,957	29,531
Sullivan County	156,823	157,047	224	0.1%	66,956	31,833	3,838	20,462	9,330
Sumner County	160,645	172,706	12,061	7.5%	62,455	25,540	2,708	14,283	4,994
Washington County	122,979	126,242	3,263	2.7%	52,788	21,323	2,126	13,840	5,872
Williamson County	183,180	205,226	22,046	12.0%	71,407	23,299	2,806	13,046	4,103
Wilson County	114,011	125,376	11,365	10.0%	46,768	17,938	1,269	10,626	4,320
Texas									
Angelina County	86,771	87,750	979	1.1%	30,344	13,926	2,710	7,889	3,505
Bastrop County	74,169	78,069	3,900	5.3%	25,974	9,679	1,222	5,639	2,005
Bell County	310,233	329,140	18,907	6.1%	114,953	32,479	4,954	19,437	7,746
Bexar County	1,714,774	1,855,866	141,092	8.2%	625,260	209,599	25,716	124,741	50,802
Bowie County	92,565	93,275	710	0.8%	32,915	14,144	1,713	8,827	3,516
Brazoria County	313,127	338,124	24,997	8.0%	114,265	36,573	2,847	20,884	7,205
Brazos County	194,851	209,152	14,301	7.3%	77,806	17,275	1,878	11,057	4,867
Cameron County	406,220	420,392	14,172	3.5%	121,009	52,048	7,032	30,043	11,397
Collin County	782,351	885,241	102,890	13.2%	312,298	85,836	8,772	48,511	19,127
Comal County	108,477	123,694	15,217	14.0%	44,382	21,355	1,850	13,048	4,735
Coryell County	75,388	75,562	174	0.2%	22,380	6,308	700	4,034	1,697
Dallas County	2,367,636	2,518,638	151,002	6.4%	891,554	243,900	28,715	146,790	63,720
Denton County	662,604	753,363	90,759	13.7%	265,729	65,810	4,236	37,253	13,859
Ector County	137,133	153,904	16,771	12.2%	50,724	14,664	1,798	9,158	3,976
El Paso County	800,647	833,487	32,840	4.1%	255,736	93,883	10,849	52,580	19,961
Ellis County	149,610	159,317	9,707	6.5%	53,454	18,787	1,649	11,745	3,838
Fort Bend County	584,897	685,345	100,448	17.2%	214,215	64,750	6,004	33,770	9,763
Galveston County	291,304	314,198	22,894	7.9%	117,452	40,306	4,078	25,568	9,619
Grayson County	120,877	123,534	2,657	2.2%	46,621	20,866	2,202	12,404	5,359
Gregg County	121,724	123,204	1,480	1.2%	46,314	17,781	2,227	10,987	5,269
Guadalupe County	131,537	147,250	15,713	11.9%	50,383	19,064	1,947	11,530	4,270
Harris County	4,093,011	4,441,370	348,359	8.5%	1,538,072	409,017	43,480	244,310	102,680
Harrison County	65,632	67,336	1,704	2.6%	22,997	10,152	1,653	7,012	2,698
Hays County	157,127	185,025	27,898	17.8%	63,497	18,519	1,507	10,742	3,935
Henderson County	78,536	79,290	754	1.0%	30,422	16,737	1,600	10,304	3,633
Hidalgo County	774,773	831,073	56,300	7.3%	226,000	86,414	10,077	44,905	13,426
Hunt County	86,129	88,493	2,364	2.7%	30,698	13,915	1,293	7,898	3,359
Jefferson County	252,273	252,235	-38	-0.0%	94,400	33,724	4,796	22,367	11,222
Johnson County	150,943	157,456	6,513	4.3%	55,458	20,175	2,200	12,410	4,087
Kaufman County	103,346	111,236	7,890	7.6%	35,725	12,804	1,082	7,131	2,542
Liberty County	75,643	78,117	2,474	3.3%	24,886	9,949	892	5,944	2,900
Lubbock County	278,831	293,974	15,143	5.4%	110,867	34,686	4,137	23,469	10,410
McLennan County	234,906	243,441	8,535	3.6%	87,345	32,752	3,945	21,145	8,672
Midland County	136,875	155,830	18,955	13.8%	53,655	15,092	2,206	9,061	4,248
Montgomery County	455,764	518,947	63,183	13.9%	179,867	62,494	6,365	38,397	14,996
Nacogdoches County	64,524	65,301	777	1.2%	24,734	8,511	1,127	5,704	2,562
Nueces County	340,223	356,221	15,998	4.7%	129,264	46,078	5,264	28,983	11,060
Orange County	81,837	83,433	1,596	2.0%	32,952	12,665	1,570	7,803	3,513
Parker County	116,927	123,164	6,237	5.3%	42,629	18,412	2,151	11,109	3,671
Potter County	121,073	121,627	554	0.5%	42,467	14,321	1,841	9,261	4,249
Randall County	120,725	128,220	7,495	6.2%	49,310	17,425	2,221	11,006	4,246
Rockwall County	78,337	87,809	9,472	12.1%	29,401	10,610	957	5,014	1,046
San Patricio County	64,807	66,915	2,108	3.3%	23,156	9,365	1,009	6,278	2,516

Table A-2: Counties—Summary Population Characteristics—*Continued*

	April 1, 2010 Census Population Estimates Base	2014 ACS Population	2010-2014 Population Change	2010-2014 Percent Change	Total Households	2014 ACS Population 65 and Over	Population 85 and Over	Householders 65 and Over	Persons 65 and Over Living Alone
Texas—Cont.									
Smith County	209,714	218,842	9,128	4.4%	77,469	33,899	4,075	20,300	8,347
Tarrant County	1,809,537	1,945,360	135,823	7.5%	681,915	198,798	20,030	119,389	48,679
Taylor County	131,510	135,143	3,633	2.8%	48,997	18,559	3,009	10,911	3,854
Tom Green County	110,224	116,608	6,384	5.8%	42,501	17,225	2,460	10,470	5,709
Travis County	1,024,301	1,151,145	126,844	12.4%	437,375	97,149	11,553	58,269	26,060
Victoria County	86,793	91,081	4,288	4.9%	32,572	12,935	1,844	7,916	3,105
Walker County	67,861	69,789	1,928	2.8%	20,097	7,295	943	4,737	2,704
Webb County	250,304	266,673	16,369	6.5%	70,418	22,508	2,496	12,074	4,307
Wichita County	131,669	132,355	686	0.5%	46,671	17,988	2,422	11,817	5,891
Williamson County	422,649	489,250	66,601	15.8%	164,805	53,303	5,719	28,309	9,621
Utah									
Cache County	112,656	118,343	5,687	5.0%	35,895	10,038	1,428	6,400	2,331
Davis County	306,479	329,692	23,213	7.6%	99,117	30,044	2,858	17,527	5,267
Salt Lake County	1,029,655	1,091,742	62,087	6.0%	358,269	105,306	12,889	64,084	25,511
Utah County	516,564	560,974	44,410	8.6%	151,010	40,147	3,253	21,905	5,421
Washington County	138,115	151,948	13,833	10.0%	49,468	30,065	3,932	17,020	4,760
Weber County	231,236	240,475	9,239	4.0%	80,956	26,781	3,701	15,863	6,789
Vermont									
Chittenden County	156,540	160,531	3,991	2.5%	63,887	21,038	2,863	13,660	6,911
Virginia									
Albemarle County	98,998	104,489	5,491	5.5%	39,568	17,466	3,124	9,918	3,631
Arlington County	207,676	226,908	19,232	9.3%	100,732	20,220	2,920	13,054	7,022
Augusta County	73,736	73,862	126	0.2%	28,533	14,115	641	8,167	2,520
Bedford County	74,866	76,583	1,717	2.3%	30,259	14,783	986	8,680	2,733
Chesterfield County	316,231	332,499	16,268	5.1%	119,732	42,771	5,165	25,786	9,424
Fairfax County	1,081,685	1,137,538	55,853	5.2%	391,479	130,422	15,957	74,927	28,691
Fauquier County	65,275	68,248	2,973	4.6%	23,334	10,906	936	5,663	1,922
Frederick County	78,306	82,377	4,071	5.2%	29,505	12,551	1,748	6,926	2,478
Hanover County	99,852	101,918	2,066	2.1%	37,481	16,069	1,864	10,084	3,771
Henrico County	306,906	321,924	15,018	4.9%	124,447	44,427	6,764	26,909	12,924
James City County	67,401	72,583	5,182	7.7%	29,312	16,500	2,076	10,401	3,828
Loudoun County	312,316	363,050	50,734	16.2%	117,946	28,721	3,002	13,846	5,501
Montgomery County	94,412	97,244	2,832	3.0%	34,549	10,902	1,447	6,191	3,420
Prince William County	401,972	446,094	44,122	11.0%	137,434	36,882	3,519	19,265	6,616
Roanoke County	92,439	93,785	1,346	1.5%	38,879	18,197	2,873	12,015	5,365
Rockingham County	76,310	78,171	1,861	2.4%	30,333	14,310	2,160	8,823	3,157
Spotsylvania County	122,660	129,188	6,528	5.3%	43,049	15,592	1,788	9,065	2,998
Stafford County	128,952	139,992	11,040	8.6%	44,246	12,875	1,468	6,419	1,560
York County	65,186	66,342	1,156	1.8%	23,533	9,880	1,286	6,077	1,779
Washington									
Benton County	175,177	186,486	11,309	6.5%	67,815	25,253	3,603	15,174	6,585
Chelan County	72,456	74,588	2,132	2.9%	27,087	12,926	1,824	7,680	3,450
Clallam County	71,404	72,715	1,311	1.8%	31,361	19,479	3,167	12,052	5,542
Clark County	425,363	451,008	25,645	6.0%	165,133	62,019	6,200	37,639	16,231
Cowlitz County	102,410	102,133	-277	-0.3%	40,036	18,254	2,370	11,975	5,710
Franklin County	78,163	87,809	9,646	12.3%	25,542	6,911	668	3,904	1,394
Grant County	89,120	93,147	4,027	4.5%	29,758	11,740	1,346	7,129	3,208
Grays Harbor County	72,797	70,818	-1,979	-2.7%	27,401	13,420	1,384	8,568	3,533
Island County	78,506	79,275	769	1.0%	32,464	18,182	1,979	10,375	3,594
King County	1,931,256	2,079,967	148,711	7.7%	825,188	253,331	37,733	154,794	71,106
Kitsap County	251,133	254,183	3,050	1.2%	95,249	40,852	4,994	25,250	10,320
Lewis County	75,455	75,128	-327	-0.4%	29,969	14,747	2,331	9,400	3,647
Pierce County	795,229	831,928	36,699	4.6%	302,388	105,354	14,243	63,751	27,293
Skagit County	116,901	120,365	3,464	3.0%	45,447	22,864	2,862	13,628	5,625
Snohomish County	713,330	759,583	46,253	6.5%	278,683	91,291	11,830	53,519	23,263
Spokane County	471,221	484,318	13,097	2.8%	187,603	72,217	10,425	45,346	20,427
Thurston County	252,264	265,851	13,587	5.4%	103,319	40,285	4,593	24,728	10,607
Whatcom County	201,140	208,351	7,211	3.6%	81,973	31,955	4,198	20,850	9,879
Yakima County	243,231	247,687	4,456	1.8%	79,700	31,605	3,816	18,654	7,886
West Virginia									
Berkeley County	104,172	110,497	6,325	6.1%	41,198	14,531	1,335	8,312	3,277
Cabell County	96,317	97,109	792	0.8%	41,147	16,577	2,605	10,872	5,085
Harrison County	69,102	68,761	-341	-0.5%	27,787	12,288	1,771	8,001	3,533
Kanawha County	193,058	190,223	-2,835	-1.5%	80,762	34,402	4,208	23,441	10,198
Monongalia County	96,189	103,463	7,274	7.6%	37,575	11,012	1,367	6,989	3,330
Raleigh County	78,862	78,241	-621	-0.8%	30,469	14,207	1,883	9,425	4,209
Wood County	86,956	86,237	-719	-0.8%	36,214	16,073	1,895	11,022	5,506
Wisconsin									
Brown County	248,007	256,670	8,663	3.5%	101,533	33,744	4,511	21,159	8,768
Dane County	488,075	516,284	28,209	5.8%	211,842	61,507	8,977	38,868	16,968
Dodge County	88,761	88,574	-187	-0.2%	33,273	14,291	1,716	8,850	3,972
Eau Claire County	98,885	101,564	2,679	2.7%	40,277	14,040	2,146	8,825	4,252
Fond du Lac County	101,633	101,759	126	0.1%	41,938	16,906	3,137	10,414	4,762
Jefferson County	83,681	84,395	714	0.9%	31,607	12,488	1,512	7,994	3,767
Kenosha County	166,426	168,068	1,642	1.0%	61,593	21,557	3,417	14,242	6,641

Table A-2: Counties—Summary Population Characteristics—*Continued*

	April 1, 2010 Census Population Estimates Base	2014 ACS Population	2010-2014 Population Change	2010-2014 Percent Change	Total Households	2014 ACS			
						Population 65 and Over	Population 85 and Over	Householders 65 and Over	Persons 65 and Over Living Alone
Wisconsin—Cont.									
La Crosse County	114,638	118,011	3,373	2.9%	46,846	17,198	2,555	10,519	4,222
Manitowoc County	81,442	80,160	-1,282	-1.6%	33,272	15,034	2,685	9,744	4,909
Marathon County	134,063	135,780	1,717	1.3%	54,739	21,426	3,386	13,355	5,654
Milwaukee County	947,736	956,406	8,670	0.9%	382,382	115,947	20,818	74,007	39,971
Outagamie County	176,695	182,006	5,311	3.0%	71,492	23,546	2,604	14,650	5,375
Ozaukee County	86,395	87,470	1,075	1.2%	34,913	15,269	2,211	10,031	4,426
Portage County	70,019	70,482	463	0.7%	27,360	10,224	1,110	6,738	2,830
Racine County	195,428	195,163	-265	-0.1%	75,876	29,486	4,309	19,041	9,100
Rock County	160,331	161,188	857	0.5%	63,037	24,180	4,347	15,033	7,330
Sheboygan County	115,507	115,290	-217	-0.2%	46,504	18,520	2,826	11,782	5,817
St. Croix County	84,345	86,759	2,414	2.9%	32,583	10,514	1,457	5,858	1,930
Walworth County	102,228	103,527	1,299	1.3%	39,679	15,610	1,950	9,925	4,794
Washington County	131,885	133,251	1,366	1.0%	53,983	20,984	3,071	13,671	6,178
Waukesha County	389,938	395,118	5,180	1.3%	154,970	65,276	8,648	40,660	16,433
Winnebago County	166,994	169,511	2,517	1.5%	69,417	25,191	3,315	16,060	7,494
Wood County	74,749	73,608	-1,141	-1.5%	32,383	13,822	2,581	9,251	4,436
Wyoming									
Laramie County	91,881	96,389	4,508	4.9%	38,705	13,897	1,343	8,768	2,881
Natrona County	75,450	81,624	6,174	8.2%	33,323	9,975	1,147	7,213	3,938

Table A-3: Places—Summary Population Characteristics

	April 1, 2010 Census Population Estimates Base	2014 ACS Population	2010-2014 Population Change	2010-2014 Percent Change	Total Households	2014 ACS			
						Population 65 and Over	Population 85 and Over	Householders 65 and Over	Persons 65 and Over Living Alone
Alabama									
Birmingham city	212,193	212,653	460	0.2%	88,556	26,897	3,440	18,584	8,563
Dothan city	65,916	69,400	3,484	5.3%	25,760	11,055	1,308	6,879	3,162
Hoover city	81,024	84,352	3,328	4.1%	35,528	15,063	2,012	9,713	5,038
Huntsville city	180,241	187,592	7,351	4.1%	79,383	29,432	3,803	18,606	9,221
Mobile city	195,243	194,670	-573	-0.3%	75,594	28,402	4,536	18,539	8,982
Montgomery city	205,595	200,486	-5,109	-2.5%	79,190	26,425	2,330	17,248	7,739
Tuscaloosa city	90,524	96,116	5,592	6.2%	33,487	11,678	1,480	7,595	na
Alaska									
Anchorage municipality	291,826	301,010	9,184	3.1%	104,683	26,906	2,469	14,870	5,216
Arizona									
Avondale city	76,130	79,621	3,491	4.6%	24,046	6,002	85	2,820	824
Chandler city	236,167	254,275	18,108	7.7%	88,216	24,905	2,099	13,500	4,550
Flagstaff city	66,067	68,786	2,719	4.1%	22,669	6,705	511	3,897	na
Glendale city	226,437	237,529	11,092	4.9%	77,424	25,288	3,143	14,813	7,202
Goodyear city	65,225	75,676	10,451	16.0%	24,655	10,226	436	6,045	na
Mesa city	439,865	464,682	24,817	5.6%	170,193	73,374	11,007	43,735	19,070
Peoria city	154,083	166,955	12,872	8.4%	61,466	27,895	3,653	15,825	5,991
Phoenix city	1,447,617	1,537,045	89,428	6.2%	532,210	150,296	16,922	90,321	39,081
Scottsdale city	217,434	230,502	13,068	6.0%	102,535	50,844	7,809	31,511	13,923
Surprise city	117,517	126,278	8,761	7.5%	45,919	25,319	2,444	15,018	4,963
Tempe city	161,781	172,836	11,055	6.8%	65,078	18,549	2,282	11,278	5,182
Tucson city	520,561	527,948	7,387	1.4%	204,262	70,275	9,461	46,294	24,291
Yuma city	90,702	93,399	2,697	3.0%	33,115	13,333	940	8,707	3,811
Arkansas									
Fayetteville city	73,581	80,614	7,033	9.6%	33,016	6,733	1,217	5,021	na
Fort Smith city	86,261	87,362	1,101	1.3%	34,200	11,061	1,837	7,690	4,392
Jonesboro city	67,388	72,214	4,826	7.2%	27,567	9,775	984	5,829	na
Little Rock city	193,524	197,701	4,177	2.2%	77,081	26,160	3,883	16,457	7,966
North Little Rock city	62,368	66,813	4,445	7.1%	26,439	8,783	871	5,156	2,203
Springdale city	70,747	78,122	7,375	10.4%	25,425	7,398	929	4,332	2,107
California									
Alameda city	73,812	77,661	3,849	5.2%	30,574	9,619	1,321	6,453	2,535
Alhambra city	83,089	85,585	2,496	3.0%	27,880	12,235	1,202	6,209	2,657
Anaheim city	336,440	346,961	10,521	3.1%	99,402	34,669	4,219	18,062	6,193
Antioch city	102,365	108,953	6,588	6.4%	34,536	11,932	1,111	6,234	2,173
Bakersfield city	347,587	368,748	21,161	6.1%	114,774	33,824	4,676	19,005	8,089
Baldwin Park city	75,390	77,134	1,744	2.3%	19,153	8,110	728	3,402	927
Bellflower city	76,610	78,246	1,636	2.1%	23,975	8,481	1,180	4,540	1,671
Berkeley city	112,489	118,851	6,362	5.7%	43,322	15,015	1,911	9,722	4,132
Buena Park city	80,613	83,114	2,501	3.1%	24,001	9,043	1,512	4,647	1,194
Burbank city	103,340	105,366	2,026	2.0%	42,396	15,294	1,998	8,929	4,011
Camarillo city	65,221	66,932	1,711	2.6%	23,784	12,444	1,736	7,459	3,176
Carlsbad city	105,459	112,310	6,851	6.5%	43,234	16,869	2,549	10,215	4,323
Carson city	91,714	93,272	1,558	1.7%	25,325	12,575	1,157	6,846	2,272
Chico city	86,198	89,187	2,989	3.5%	35,657	10,403	1,874	6,668	3,722
Chino city	77,972	84,743	6,771	8.7%	18,218	6,974	531	2,674	637
Chino Hills city	74,799	77,005	2,206	2.9%	21,940	6,110	1,217	3,086	916
Chula Vista city	243,916	260,977	17,061	7.0%	78,058	33,568	4,097	17,558	6,361
Citrus Heights city	83,255	86,147	2,892	3.5%	33,709	14,073	1,974	9,454	4,317
Clovis city	95,633	102,190	6,557	6.9%	34,358	10,583	1,538	6,658	3,101
Compton city	96,412	98,596	2,184	2.3%	23,763	6,538	1,290	4,086	
Concord city	122,282	127,511	5,229	4.3%	45,111	16,893	2,543	10,031	4,615
Corona city	152,374	161,498	9,124	6.0%	50,041	15,605	1,707	8,019	3,358
Costa Mesa city	109,929	112,793	2,864	2.6%	38,510	10,517	1,527	6,368	2,002
Daly City city	101,146	106,099	4,953	4.9%	29,834	17,945	1,934	7,380	2,066
Davis city	65,611	66,733	1,122	1.7%	25,702	6,433	1,043	4,224	na
Downey city	111,791	114,168	2,377	2.1%	34,629	12,619	1,923	6,453	2,403
El Cajon city	99,476	103,075	3,599	3.6%	31,028	12,444	1,570	5,369	1,626
El Monte city	113,475	116,617	3,142	2.8%	30,516	14,300	2,029	5,961	1,914
Elk Grove city	153,015	163,560	10,545	6.9%	50,142	17,702	1,725	7,958	3,112
Escondido city	143,913	150,252	6,339	4.4%	44,612	17,178	3,646	9,541	3,979
Fairfield city	105,318	111,139	5,821	5.5%	35,360	13,189	1,800	6,986	2,582
Folsom city	72,199	75,366	3,167	4.4%	25,980	10,645	1,587	5,957	2,812
Fontana city	196,074	204,953	8,879	4.5%	51,347	16,304	1,361	5,801	1,976
Fremont city	214,079	228,760	14,681	6.9%	73,007	25,269	3,400	12,648	4,323
Fresno city	496,080	515,985	19,905	4.0%	163,875	55,505	7,297	31,243	13,539
Fullerton city	135,235	139,663	4,428	3.3%	44,648	16,126	2,994	8,868	3,648
Garden Grove city	170,964	175,085	4,121	2.4%	46,959	22,427	2,619	10,083	3,711
Glendale city	191,713	200,161	8,448	4.4%	72,163	33,011	4,233	17,427	6,849
Hawthorne city	84,293	87,591	3,298	3.9%	31,391	8,383	822	4,333	1,963
Hayward city	144,369	154,633	10,264	7.1%	49,031	17,297	2,827	9,324	3,860
Hemet city	78,658	83,040	4,382	5.6%	31,058	19,601	4,771	13,288	7,766
Hesperia city	90,173	92,744	2,571	2.9%	26,853	8,420	1,067	5,155	1,772
Huntington Beach city	191,037	200,814	9,777	5.1%	76,357	31,412	3,000	19,057	7,886
Indio city	79,116	85,639	6,523	8.2%	27,184	12,082	1,150	7,007	2,797

Table A-3: Places—Summary Population Characteristics—*Continued*

	April 1, 2010 Census Population Estimates Base	2014 ACS Population	2010-2014 Population Change	2010-2014 Percent Change	Total Households	2014 ACS			
						Population 65 and Over	Population 85 and Over	Householders 65 and Over	Persons 65 and Over Living Alone
California—Cont.									
Inglewood city	109,673	111,901	2,228	2.0%	36,439	11,530	1,444	6,571	3,263
Irvine city	211,906	248,521	36,615	17.3%	90,513	25,264	2,268	13,548	5,422
Jurupa Valley city	95,004	98,843	3,839	4.0%	23,734	8,579	1,050	4,127	1,429
Laguna Niguel city	62,985	65,435	2,450	3.9%	25,916	10,169	1,043	6,069	1,566
Lake Forest city	77,448	80,125	2,677	3.5%	25,428	8,556	990	4,433	na
Lakewood city	80,048	81,641	1,593	2.0%	25,755	10,332	741	5,521	2,239
Lancaster city	156,633	161,036	4,403	2.8%	47,527	16,676	1,654	8,632	2,618
Livermore city	81,108	86,856	5,748	7.1%	30,976	11,143	1,247	6,443	2,338
Long Beach city	462,257	473,605	11,348	2.5%	161,870	47,506	5,359	27,282	12,641
Los Angeles city	3,792,657	3,928,827	136,170	3.6%	1,343,084	455,128	66,466	261,218	117,216
Lynwood city	69,772	71,846	2,074	3.0%	15,577	5,231	842	1,698	na
Manteca city	67,276	73,477	6,201	9.2%	23,295	9,233	713	5,354	2,098
Menifee city	77,519	85,201	7,682	9.9%	27,000	16,342	2,344	9,373	3,435
Merced city	78,957	81,739	2,782	3.5%	26,930	9,253	1,218	5,246	2,523
Milpitas city	66,815	73,679	6,864	10.3%	21,145	7,522	584	3,546	1,014
Mission Viejo city	93,105	97,231	4,126	4.4%	32,761	15,883	2,766	9,116	2,785
Modesto city	203,116	209,308	6,192	3.0%	71,759	28,774	4,152	17,326	7,168
Moreno Valley city	193,365	202,978	9,613	5.0%	50,308	17,528	1,717	7,677	2,016
Mountain View city	74,020	79,374	5,354	7.2%	33,647	8,321	1,273	5,265	2,845
Murrieta city	103,429	108,371	4,942	4.8%	32,617	10,643	1,432	5,796	2,037
Napa city	76,989	80,009	3,020	3.9%	29,117	11,133	2,129	7,078	3,228
Newport Beach city	85,199	87,242	2,043	2.4%	39,212	18,500	3,143	12,641	5,954
Norwalk city	105,549	107,111	1,562	1.5%	26,336	11,581	1,548	5,729	1,655
Oakland city	390,905	413,782	22,877	5.9%	156,724	49,051	5,923	31,156	15,384
Oceanside city	167,086	174,552	7,466	4.5%	62,000	27,682	3,391	16,383	7,573
Ontario city	163,924	169,085	5,161	3.1%	47,375	13,332	1,708	6,587	2,850
Orange city	136,419	139,826	3,407	2.5%	41,868	14,699	1,767	7,669	2,993
Oxnard city	197,899	205,434	7,535	3.8%	51,646	19,138	2,417	9,871	3,228
Palmdale city	152,750	158,274	5,524	3.6%	43,658	12,560	750	6,429	2,482
Palo Alto city	64,409	66,968	2,559	4.0%	26,288	11,899	1,885	7,784	3,554
Pasadena city	137,122	140,860	3,738	2.7%	53,100	19,189	2,491	11,297	5,235
Perris city	68,383	73,751	5,368	7.8%	16,481	4,546	66	1,826	na
Pittsburg city	63,260	68,122	4,862	7.7%	20,071	7,481	1,097	3,844	1,374
Pleasanton city	70,317	77,676	7,359	10.5%	26,340	10,367	1,098	5,929	2,282
Pomona city	149,058	153,381	4,323	2.9%	39,439	14,158	1,879	6,313	1,930
Rancho Cordova city	64,805	69,727	4,922	7.6%	24,395	8,295	884	4,927	1,717
Rancho Cucamonga city	165,350	174,302	8,952	5.4%	58,305	17,388	1,872	8,841	3,711
Redding city	89,861	91,588	1,727	1.9%	33,424	16,762	2,935	10,201	4,955
Redlands city	68,667	70,618	1,951	2.8%	21,806	8,868	1,023	4,848	1,697
Redondo Beach city	66,748	68,146	1,398	2.1%	26,069	7,350	947	4,948	2,071
Redwood City city	76,802	82,868	6,066	7.9%	29,245	10,409	1,287	5,999	3,049
Rialto city	99,150	102,740	3,590	3.6%	25,834	8,635	1,135	4,629	1,644
Richmond city	103,671	108,562	4,891	4.7%	39,235	12,367	1,324	7,086	2,725
Riverside city	303,987	319,519	15,532	5.1%	90,204	30,344	4,544	15,524	5,746
Roseville city	118,660	128,593	9,933	8.4%	48,152	21,745	3,491	13,779	6,575
Sacramento city	466,488	485,193	18,705	4.0%	177,553	56,425	7,676	35,122	16,147
Salinas city	150,498	156,678	6,180	4.1%	39,390	12,458	1,839	6,480	2,099
San Bernardino city	209,961	215,227	5,266	2.5%	54,615	18,120	2,054	9,306	3,998
San Buenaventura (Ventura) city	107,231	109,478	2,247	2.1%	42,233	17,456	3,122	11,652	5,601
San Clemente city	63,497	65,342	1,845	2.9%	24,678	12,132	2,008	7,847	na
San Diego city	1,301,621	1,381,083	79,462	6.1%	493,446	157,889	21,752	89,228	38,095
San Francisco city	805,195	852,469	47,274	5.9%	353,406	122,906	18,704	73,562	34,970
San Jose city	952,560	1,015,796	63,236	6.6%	312,227	118,855	13,722	59,611	21,732
San Leandro city	84,950	89,347	4,397	5.2%	33,134	12,775	2,775	7,478	3,411
San Marcos city	83,650	92,910	9,260	11.1%	28,337	11,153	1,230	6,690	2,796
San Mateo city	97,207	102,885	5,678	5.8%	39,763	16,356	2,184	10,570	5,112
San Ramon city	72,211	75,319	3,108	4.3%	24,199	7,824	396	3,454	878
Santa Ana city	324,782	334,924	10,142	3.1%	78,068	27,767	3,737	12,454	4,100
Santa Barbara city	88,411	91,208	2,797	3.2%	35,786	15,502	3,128	9,968	5,399
Santa Clara city	116,497	122,198	5,701	4.9%	44,068	14,903	2,291	7,717	2,701
Santa Clarita city	176,313	181,559	5,246	3.0%	58,505	20,680	2,851	11,788	4,796
Santa Maria city	99,597	103,414	3,817	3.8%	26,846	9,259	1,626	5,153	1,690
Santa Monica city	89,736	92,989	3,253	3.6%	46,474	16,165	2,461	10,231	5,783
Santa Rosa city	167,834	174,166	6,332	3.8%	65,282	25,327	4,259	16,477	8,514
Simi Valley city	124,239	126,873	2,634	2.1%	42,595	17,559	2,299	10,587	4,362
South Gate city	94,396	96,299	1,903	2.0%	23,254	8,373	1,143	3,870	1,575
South San Francisco city	63,664	67,011	3,347	5.3%	22,319	9,033	1,175	5,175	2,023
Stockton city	291,731	302,405	10,674	3.7%	95,166	34,220	4,639	17,432	7,461
Sunnyvale city	140,058	149,984	9,926	7.1%	54,473	16,587	2,095	9,250	4,705
Temecula city	100,156	109,446	9,290	9.3%	33,643	12,439	1,091	6,339	1,712
Thousand Oaks city	126,555	129,344	2,789	2.2%	45,863	22,071	3,759	13,740	4,350
Torrance city	145,438	148,483	3,045	2.1%	53,971	25,099	5,004	15,122	6,339
Tracy city	83,101	85,835	2,734	3.3%	23,424	5,816	528	2,481	916
Turlock city	68,549	71,246	2,697	3.9%	24,667	9,352	1,505	5,810	2,805
Tustin city	75,314	80,617	5,303	7.0%	26,426	7,666	844	4,296	1,521
Union City city	69,524	73,608	4,084	5.9%	20,605	11,828	1,793	4,994	1,308

Table A-3: Places—Summary Population Characteristics—*Continued*

	April 1, 2010 Census Population Estimates Base	2014 ACS Population	2010-2014 Population Change	2010-2014 Percent Change	Total Households	2014 ACS			
						Population 65 and Over	Population 85 and Over	Householders 65 and Over	Persons 65 and Over Living Alone
California—Cont.									
Upland city	73,732	76,039	2,307	3.1%	28,151	11,441	1,314	6,692	2,354
Vacaville city	92,422	95,863	3,441	3.7%	32,430	10,733	1,058	7,162	3,601
Vallejo city	115,940	120,210	4,270	3.7%	41,802	16,929	1,802	9,711	4,014
Victorville city	115,921	121,911	5,990	5.2%	31,716	10,085	588	4,916	1,480
Visalia city	124,457	129,280	4,823	3.9%	41,367	16,303	2,466	8,783	2,899
Vista city	93,854	98,086	4,232	4.5%	29,165	7,915	917	4,268	1,536
Walnut Creek city	64,174	67,664	3,490	5.4%	31,515	19,791	4,300	13,048	7,103
West Covina city	106,098	108,445	2,347	2.2%	30,607	15,430	2,046	7,108	2,036
Westminster city	89,614	92,062	2,448	2.7%	28,260	16,388	1,888	8,163	2,575
Whittier city	85,328	87,348	2,020	2.4%	26,240	10,996	1,331	6,065	2,068
Yorba Linda city	64,193	67,824	3,631	5.7%	21,052	10,198	907	5,981	1,551
Yuba City city	64,925	65,775	850	1.3%	22,264	8,590	712	4,994	2,344
Colorado									
Arvada city	106,474	113,775	7,301	6.9%	43,588	16,182	2,075	10,289	4,316
Aurora city	324,688	353,381	28,693	8.8%	126,677	36,720	4,649	21,898	9,727
Boulder city	97,468	105,101	7,633	7.8%	44,059	10,674	1,536	7,086	3,988
Centennial city	100,547	107,193	6,646	6.6%	39,055	16,073	1,472	9,307	2,837
Colorado Springs city	417,341	445,820	28,479	6.8%	174,943	55,830	7,273	34,450	14,936
Denver city	600,025	663,862	63,837	10.6%	281,928	72,266	10,549	47,806	26,219
Fort Collins city	144,073	156,473	12,400	8.6%	57,064	14,455	1,924	8,830	4,587
Greeley city	92,881	98,593	5,712	6.1%	33,714	12,632	1,455	8,073	3,447
Lakewood city	142,995	149,650	6,655	4.7%	65,127	23,200	3,995	14,660	7,590
Longmont city	86,303	90,189	3,886	4.5%	33,314	11,832	1,778	7,205	3,448
Loveland city	66,824	72,647	5,823	8.7%	31,579	14,439	1,861	9,494	na
Pueblo city	106,544	108,439	1,895	1.8%	42,859	18,118	2,697	11,571	5,942
Thornton city	118,792	130,309	11,517	9.7%	42,725	11,035	1,140	6,686	2,136
Westminster city	106,129	112,099	5,970	5.6%	43,731	14,592	1,077	9,185	3,597
Connecticut									
Bridgeport city	144,236	147,608	3,372	2.3%	49,779	14,575	2,093	9,660	4,981
Danbury city	80,897	83,795	2,898	3.6%	28,524	10,659	1,272	6,217	3,161
Hartford city	124,775	124,721	-54	-0.0%	44,740	11,160	1,738	7,453	4,483
New Britain city	73,202	72,889	-313	-0.4%	27,764	7,898	2,164	4,729	2,706
New Haven city	129,890	130,285	395	0.3%	49,281	13,338	1,463	9,275	6,143
Norwalk city	85,621	88,144	2,523	2.9%	33,461	12,926	1,540	7,780	2,504
Stamford city	122,630	128,283	5,653	4.6%	49,377	16,521	2,342	11,163	5,227
Waterbury city	110,331	109,311	-1,020	-0.9%	39,608	12,970	2,365	8,338	4,582
Delaware									
Wilmington city	70,852	71,808	956	1.3%	29,969	9,181	711	6,632	4,265
District of Columbia									
Washington city	601,767	658,893	57,126	9.5%	277,378	74,465	10,144	50,463	28,337
Florida									
Boca Raton city	84,401	91,321	6,920	8.2%	35,995	17,798	2,705	11,644	5,658
Boynton Beach city	68,215	73,121	4,906	7.2%	28,361	14,940	3,236	8,263	3,700
Cape Coral city	154,301	169,855	15,554	10.1%	64,329	38,214	5,367	21,305	7,184
Clearwater city	108,334	110,709	2,375	2.2%	46,053	23,304	2,903	15,507	8,241
Coral Springs city	121,098	127,963	6,865	5.7%	40,278	13,479	1,455	6,081	1,889
Deerfield Beach city	75,018	78,898	3,880	5.2%	30,923	15,824	3,152	10,628	6,012
Delray Beach city	60,601	65,054	4,453	7.3%	26,774	16,140	3,550	11,781	7,049
Deltona city	85,182	86,907	1,725	2.0%	29,801	12,123	1,025	6,813	2,584
Fort Lauderdale city	165,578	176,018	10,440	6.3%	75,205	31,632	4,082	20,346	10,884
Fort Myers city	62,202	70,916	8,714	14.0%	26,571	11,842	1,367	6,835	3,173
Gainesville city	124,486	128,474	3,988	3.2%	49,098	13,043	2,188	8,820	4,169
Hialeah city	224,667	235,566	10,899	4.9%	68,027	42,948	6,469	20,395	8,283
Hollywood city	140,769	148,040	7,271	5.2%	56,965	23,942	3,212	14,733	7,586
Homestead city	60,509	65,514	5,005	8.3%	19,025	5,590	677	2,201	na
Jacksonville city	821,784	853,376	31,592	3.8%	320,809	107,837	13,892	67,188	31,326
Kissimmee city	59,620	66,729	7,109	11.9%	20,172	6,670	1,305	2,939	na
Lakeland city	97,433	102,335	4,902	5.0%	38,052	20,960	2,597	12,712	5,393
Largo city	78,135	79,028	893	1.1%	36,179	20,582	2,608	13,624	6,892
Lauderhill city	66,954	70,636	3,682	5.5%	23,073	11,822	1,444	6,029	2,025
Melbourne city	76,196	78,486	2,290	3.0%	33,573	17,488	1,960	11,725	6,307
Miami Beach city	87,784	91,721	3,937	4.5%	41,959	15,254	2,347	9,107	5,123
Miami city	399,508	430,341	30,833	7.7%	158,039	68,412	11,586	37,894	19,203
Miami Gardens city	107,163	112,270	5,107	4.8%	30,786	14,569	1,794	8,286	2,955
Miramar city	122,041	134,991	12,950	10.6%	36,377	13,811	1,585	4,054	828
Orlando city	238,834	262,396	23,562	9.9%	109,685	26,234	3,446	16,912	8,797
Palm Bay city	103,203	105,845	2,642	2.6%	37,241	17,667	2,313	9,804	3,101
Palm Coast city	75,197	82,388	7,191	9.6%	28,925	23,381	3,424	11,851	3,328
Pembroke Pines city	154,019	164,625	10,606	6.9%	54,927	26,703	4,641	15,395	7,943
Plantation city	84,877	91,454	6,577	7.7%	34,058	12,276	1,569	7,511	na
Pompano Beach city	99,844	106,115	6,271	6.3%	43,307	22,233	5,114	14,641	8,368
Port St. Lucie city	164,716	174,093	9,377	5.7%	63,557	35,685	5,333	21,129	8,953
St. Petersburg city	245,193	253,682	8,489	3.5%	103,519	43,252	6,335	25,780	12,433
Sunrise city	84,381	91,256	6,875	8.1%	30,491	13,310	2,421	8,022	5,121

Table A-3: Places—Summary Population Characteristics—Continued

	April 1, 2010 Census Population Estimates Base	2014 ACS Population	2010-2014 Population Change	2010-2014 Percent Change	Total Households	2014 ACS			
						Population 65 and Over	Population 85 and Over	Householders 65 and Over	Persons 65 and Over Living Alone
Florida—Cont.									
Tallahassee city	181,383	188,106	6,723	3.7%	75,056	16,884	2,408	12,043	6,625
Tampa city	335,715	358,684	22,969	6.8%	140,429	43,961	6,116	26,403	12,737
West Palm Beach city	100,347	104,017	3,670	3.7%	42,349	17,866	2,165	11,322	6,330
Weston city	65,333	69,091	3,758	5.8%	22,030	7,040	1,272	4,270	na
Georgia									
Albany city	77,434	73,016	-4,418	-5.7%	28,248	9,515	1,513	6,494	3,723
Athens-Clarke County unified govt (bal)	115,453	119,841	4,388	3.8%	43,568	11,791	1,798	7,501	3,299
Atlanta city	420,256	456,012	35,756	8.5%	189,431	51,783	5,915	35,365	20,874
Augusta-Richmond County consolidated govt (bal)	195,844	197,465	1,621	0.8%	69,436	24,669	3,285	14,469	6,274
Columbus city	190,545	200,887	10,342	5.4%	74,339	23,945	2,973	15,599	6,115
Johns Creek city	76,727	83,108	6,381	8.3%	28,014	6,042	919	3,735	na
Macon-Bibb County	155,292	153,633	-1,659	-1.1%	56,052	21,544	3,037	13,579	6,820
Roswell city	88,347	94,073	5,726	6.5%	34,288	10,700	2,360	5,898	na
Sandy Springs city	93,852	101,914	8,062	8.6%	44,822	13,767	2,394	8,023	na
Savannah city	136,340	144,355	8,015	5.9%	54,628	19,380	3,196	12,670	6,086
Warner Robins city	68,618	73,060	4,442	6.5%	27,331	7,209	721	5,042	na
Hawaii									
Urban Honolulu CDP	337,256	350,403	13,147	3.9%	127,394	66,002	13,377	37,927	15,695
Idaho									
Boise City city	206,105	216,280	10,175	4.9%	84,511	26,987	4,175	17,197	7,822
Meridian city	75,130	87,739	12,609	16.8%	31,969	10,068	899	6,095	na
Nampa city	81,748	88,208	6,460	7.9%	29,806	10,088	1,183	6,283	2,957
Illinois									
Aurora city	197,952	200,708	2,756	1.4%	59,547	15,369	2,076	8,469	3,039
Bloomington city	76,616	78,743	2,127	2.8%	31,373	9,031	1,612	5,832	3,092
Champaign city	81,072	84,520	3,448	4.3%	33,606	7,732	832	5,174	2,665
Chicago city	2,695,598	2,722,407	26,809	1.0%	1,031,672	309,874	39,534	196,065	97,334
Decatur city	76,126	73,081	-3,045	-4.0%	30,237	12,346	1,480	8,194	na
Elgin city	108,146	116,548	8,402	7.8%	37,537	14,203	1,228	7,503	3,011
Evanston city	74,486	75,657	1,171	1.6%	28,577	10,067	1,797	6,153	2,747
Joliet city	147,459	146,578	-881	-0.6%	47,219	12,951	1,946	7,714	3,726
Naperville city	142,087	145,396	3,309	2.3%	51,165	14,553	1,549	8,329	3,277
Peoria city	115,021	117,288	2,267	2.0%	47,432	15,847	2,276	10,416	5,365
Rockford city	153,054	148,996	-4,058	-2.7%	59,772	22,275	3,806	14,526	7,661
Springfield city	116,365	116,649	284	0.2%	50,157	18,896	2,510	12,632	7,134
Waukegan city	89,099	88,998	-101	-0.1%	28,445	8,417	1,223	4,373	1,365
Indiana									
Bloomington city	80,307	83,423	3,116	3.9%	29,984	5,853	1,058	3,598	1,607
Carmel city	79,191	87,015	7,824	9.9%	32,573	13,390	1,766	8,080	2,692
Evansville city	120,081	121,299	1,218	1.0%	51,287	18,824	3,699	12,499	6,222
Fort Wayne city	253,700	256,023	2,323	0.9%	100,239	31,931	4,569	21,156	10,699
Gary city	80,314	71,180	-9,134	-11.4%	28,078	11,909	2,077	7,700	3,810
Hammond city	80,823	78,383	-2,440	-3.0%	28,168	8,129	1,153	5,055	2,277
Indianapolis city (bal)	820,441	851,353	30,912	3.8%	328,526	94,476	12,980	59,437	29,636
Lafayette city	68,867	67,012	-1,855	-2.7%	27,331	8,951	1,044	4,974	na
Muncie city	70,201	70,580	379	0.5%	26,981	10,772	1,818	6,377	2,428
South Bend city	101,046	103,019	1,973	2.0%	40,677	12,990	2,338	8,925	4,600
Iowa									
Cedar Rapids city	126,326	129,183	2,857	2.3%	53,672	17,136	2,554	11,580	5,895
Davenport city	99,687	102,431	2,744	2.8%	40,657	12,702	1,959	8,170	4,087
Des Moines city	204,186	209,064	4,878	2.4%	81,779	23,627	3,786	15,788	8,968
Iowa City city	67,894	73,424	5,530	8.1%	29,824	6,150	1,161	4,080	na
Sioux City city	82,684	81,392	-1,292	-1.6%	31,220	11,202	1,473	6,786	3,265
Waterloo city	68,406	68,365	-41	-0.1%	29,169	9,874	1,314	6,873	na
Kansas									
Kansas City city	145,786	148,323	2,537	1.7%	55,680	16,791	2,497	10,753	5,428
Lawrence city	87,643	91,282	3,639	4.2%	36,264	8,606	1,328	5,439	na
Olathe city	125,875	133,059	7,184	5.7%	45,063	11,970	1,466	7,151	2,713
Overland Park city	173,333	184,524	11,191	6.5%	75,459	26,969	4,144	16,657	7,822
Topeka city	127,474	127,223	-251	-0.2%	51,318	18,625	3,334	11,974	6,089
Wichita city	382,386	388,413	6,027	1.6%	149,920	49,811	6,114	31,417	15,196
Kentucky									
Lexington-Fayette urban county	295,803	310,797	14,994	5.1%	127,412	35,972	5,596	22,793	10,733
Louisville/Jefferson County metro govt (bal)	597,265	612,775	15,510	2.6%	244,583	81,870	11,987	53,042	25,539
Louisiana									
Baton Rouge city	229,447	228,909	-538	-0.2%	91,034	29,500	4,016	19,560	9,578
Bossier City city	61,631	67,453	5,822	9.4%	24,869	8,844	1,345	5,211	2,858
Kenner city	66,705	67,058	353	0.5%	25,553	12,129	1,103	7,390	2,824
Lafayette city	121,131	126,068	4,937	4.1%	49,939	14,463	1,558	10,215	na
Lake Charles city	72,033	74,875	2,842	3.9%	30,751	12,692	1,808	8,354	4,284
New Orleans city	343,829	384,320	40,491	11.8%	152,788	46,481	5,761	30,343	14,954

Table A-3: Places—Summary Population Characteristics—*Continued*

	April 1, 2010 Census Population Estimates Base	2014 ACS Population	2010-2014 Population Change	2010-2014 Percent Change	Total Households	2014 ACS			
						Population 65 and Over	Population 85 and Over	Householders 65 and Over	Persons 65 and Over Living Alone
Louisiana—Cont.									
Shreveport city	200,410	197,979	-2,431	-1.2%	74,512	30,000	4,232	18,496	8,418
Maine									
Portland city	66,194	66,669	475	0.7%	30,023	7,924	1,267	5,751	na
Maryland									
Baltimore city	621,121	622,793	1,672	0.3%	238,897	76,707	8,753	52,216	27,022
Frederick city	65,287	68,404	3,117	4.8%	27,209	7,802	929	4,645	2,257
Gaithersburg city	59,897	66,807	6,910	11.5%	22,988	7,819	1,155	3,665	1,722
Rockville city	61,285	65,941	4,656	7.6%	25,545	10,613	1,830	6,438	3,323
Massachusetts									
Boston city	617,680	656,051	38,371	6.2%	253,749	67,857	9,733	43,696	25,079
Brockton city	93,810	94,780	970	1.0%	33,006	11,872	1,958	7,102	3,773
Cambridge city	105,201	109,699	4,498	4.3%	43,058	10,703	1,426	7,644	4,609
Fall River city	88,857	88,705	-152	-0.2%	39,121	14,379	2,250	9,414	5,206
Lawrence city	76,377	78,192	1,815	2.4%	25,613	6,670	1,015	4,104	2,099
Lowell city	106,519	109,931	3,412	3.2%	38,173	11,569	2,408	7,275	3,950
Lynn city	90,329	92,137	1,808	2.0%	32,235	10,329	2,004	6,378	3,110
New Bedford city	95,072	94,855	-217	-0.2%	38,046	12,283	2,597	7,776	3,911
Newton city	85,174	88,298	3,124	3.7%	31,595	16,501	2,693	10,070	4,401
Quincy city	92,271	93,391	1,120	1.2%	40,083	14,295	1,849	9,321	5,364
Somerville city	75,635	78,903	3,268	4.3%	31,566	7,829	1,055	5,097	2,953
Springfield city	153,195	153,994	799	0.5%	55,816	16,792	2,466	11,472	5,919
Worcester city	181,041	183,033	1,992	1.1%	64,923	19,664	4,363	12,197	5,976
Michigan									
Ann Arbor city	113,947	117,759	3,812	3.3%	46,326	12,203	2,103	8,228	4,136
Dearborn city	98,146	95,546	-2,600	-2.6%	31,827	12,618	2,156	7,987	4,317
Detroit city	713,862	680,281	-33,581	-4.7%	253,490	85,166	10,927	59,257	28,936
Farmington Hills city	79,740	81,440	1,700	2.1%	34,613	17,713	2,013	11,077	5,066
Flint city	102,400	98,990	-3,410	-3.3%	39,125	11,588	1,529	8,369	3,423
Grand Rapids city	188,051	193,793	5,742	3.1%	72,388	22,351	5,643	14,506	7,718
Kalamazoo city	74,262	75,909	1,647	2.2%	28,996	7,437	1,280	4,700	2,325
Lansing city	114,299	113,659	-640	-0.6%	47,908	13,160	1,690	8,827	5,253
Livonia city	96,942	94,959	-1,983	-2.0%	35,937	17,322	2,038	10,299	4,463
Rochester Hills city	70,995	73,120	2,125	3.0%	27,668	12,074	2,204	7,676	3,906
Southfield city	71,739	73,001	1,262	1.8%	33,860	13,608	1,570	9,558	5,812
Sterling Heights city	129,699	131,729	2,030	1.6%	49,635	21,835	3,174	13,641	5,266
Troy city	80,980	83,120	2,140	2.6%	30,597	13,147	1,490	7,929	3,215
Warren city	134,056	135,099	1,043	0.8%	53,403	19,648	3,886	12,733	6,288
Westland city	84,097	82,318	-1,779	-2.1%	34,251	14,419	2,434	9,447	5,282
Wyoming city	72,122	74,820	2,698	3.7%	27,786	7,675	1,436	4,965	2,337
Minnesota									
Bloomington city	82,893	86,319	3,426	4.1%	37,593	16,884	3,106	10,509	4,785
Brooklyn Park city	75,784	78,741	2,957	3.9%	26,544	7,704	662	4,945	na
Duluth city	86,266	86,242	-24	-0.0%	36,307	13,031	2,648	8,747	4,722
Eagan city	64,205	66,087	1,882	2.9%	27,007	7,732	885	4,723	2,194
Maple Grove city	61,569	66,949	5,380	8.7%	27,457	7,557	797	4,932	na
Minneapolis city	382,599	407,181	24,582	6.4%	169,306	33,790	4,272	23,005	13,924
Plymouth city	70,561	75,065	4,504	6.4%	29,678	11,581	1,612	7,280	3,091
Rochester city	106,748	111,398	4,650	4.4%	44,661	16,110	2,516	9,817	4,172
St. Cloud city	65,946	64,221	-1,725	-2.6%	25,421	7,652	1,228	4,491	2,054
St. Paul city	285,068	297,644	12,576	4.4%	110,978	26,550	4,634	17,553	9,629
Woodbury city	61,965	66,799	4,834	7.8%	26,101	7,465	809	4,388	
Mississippi									
Gulfport city	67,786	71,747	3,961	5.8%	30,048	10,039	909	7,242	4,266
Jackson city	173,593	171,146	-2,447	-1.4%	62,679	19,917	3,281	12,952	6,205
Missouri									
Columbia city	108,835	116,892	8,057	7.4%	45,405	10,872	1,470	7,080	na
Independence city	116,828	117,503	675	0.6%	47,145	20,505	1,584	12,769	5,354
Kansas City city	459,787	470,816	11,029	2.4%	195,125	56,470	7,536	37,862	19,042
Lee's Summit city	91,388	94,627	3,239	3.5%	34,259	13,248	1,984	7,931	na
O'Fallon city	79,588	83,999	4,411	5.5%	29,689	8,590	1,236	5,357	na
Springfield city	159,500	165,399	5,899	3.7%	69,761	25,710	4,629	17,249	8,843
St. Charles city	65,846	68,087	2,241	3.4%	27,104	10,132	1,325	6,498	2,684
St. Joseph city	76,807	76,529	-278	-0.4%	28,421	10,575	1,693	7,418	4,274
St. Louis city	319,365	317,419	-1,946	-0.6%	137,784	36,162	5,001	24,010	13,179
Montana									
Billings city	104,224	108,870	4,646	4.5%	43,498	15,956	2,496	10,379	6,024
Missoula city	66,877	69,824	2,947	4.4%	30,054	8,420	2,085	5,797	na
Nebraska									
Lincoln city	258,468	273,002	14,534	5.6%	108,954	32,090	4,556	21,278	9,785
Omaha city	423,327	446,618	23,291	5.5%	174,747	53,390	8,813	35,064	17,557
Nevada									
Henderson city	257,354	277,458	20,104	7.8%	107,007	49,751	4,914	28,217	10,088

Table A-3: Places—Summary Population Characteristics—*Continued*

	April 1, 2010 Census Population Estimates Base	2014 ACS Population	2010-2014 Population Change	2010-2014 Percent Change	Total Households	2014 ACS Population 65 and Over	Population 85 and Over	Householders 65 and Over	Persons 65 and Over Living Alone
Nevada—Cont.									
Las Vegas city	584,240	613,590	29,350	5.0%	212,742	79,751	7,160	46,224	18,630
North Las Vegas city	216,700	230,793	14,093	6.5%	72,412	24,712	1,494	12,277	4,253
Reno city	226,012	236,995	10,983	4.9%	92,608	31,675	3,516	21,629	12,064
Sparks city	90,258	94,704	4,446	4.9%	35,785	14,039	1,946	8,455	3,326
New Hampshire									
Manchester city	109,571	110,451	880	0.8%	44,156	14,073	2,484	8,171	4,333
Nashua city	86,494	87,258	764	0.9%	34,864	11,430	1,540	6,403	2,750
New Jersey									
Bayonne city	63,010	65,984	2,974	4.7%	24,733	7,910	1,118	4,357	2,037
Camden city	77,346	77,317	-29	-0.0%	26,396	7,619	673	6,042	2,904
Clifton city	84,136	85,920	1,784	2.1%	29,065	9,438	1,565	5,859	3,347
East Orange city	64,107	65,095	988	1.5%	25,913	8,621	1,285	5,998	3,628
Elizabeth city	124,969	128,695	3,726	3.0%	39,546	11,545	1,134	6,042	2,615
Jersey City city	247,643	262,146	14,503	5.9%	98,873	24,928	2,310	15,824	6,673
Newark city	277,149	280,577	3,428	1.2%	89,182	23,518	2,663	15,434	8,342
Passaic city	69,781	71,517	1,736	2.5%	18,813	6,034	865	3,548	1,649
Paterson city	146,199	146,746	547	0.4%	42,318	16,361	2,400	8,388	4,014
Trenton city	84,910	84,047	-863	-1.0%	28,185	8,747	903	5,591	2,775
Union City city	66,439	68,673	2,234	3.4%	24,707	7,621	1,079	4,553	2,322
New Mexico									
Albuquerque city	546,360	557,172	10,812	2.0%	219,867	74,936	8,503	48,418	24,244
Las Cruces city	97,636	101,405	3,769	3.9%	40,668	14,506	2,179	9,355	4,039
Rio Rancho city	87,394	93,011	5,617	6.4%	33,530	11,832	1,595	7,725	3,400
Santa Fe city	67,968	70,291	2,323	3.4%	31,001	14,310	1,400	10,284	5,554
New York									
Albany city	97,856	98,566	710	0.7%	41,262	12,346	2,242	7,767	4,224
Buffalo city	261,325	258,699	-2,626	-1.0%	110,070	33,059	4,006	23,277	13,185
Mount Vernon city	67,290	68,455	1,165	1.7%	24,538	9,606	1,566	5,949	2,995
New Rochelle city	77,062	79,630	2,568	3.3%	27,841	11,070	2,075	7,137	3,333
New York city	8,174,959	8,491,079	316,120	3.9%	3,148,067	1,098,393	157,672	678,250	338,688
Rochester city	210,512	209,974	-538	-0.3%	83,944	22,664	2,542	15,228	8,658
Schenectady city	66,134	65,930	-204	-0.3%	24,127	8,751	1,938	5,189	3,177
Syracuse city	145,196	144,263	-933	-0.6%	54,712	18,153	3,895	11,056	6,001
Yonkers city	195,979	200,665	4,686	2.4%	74,187	33,294	5,508	20,776	10,626
North Carolina									
Asheville city	83,417	87,884	4,467	5.4%	39,930	15,727	2,273	9,967	5,710
Charlotte city	735,758	809,974	74,216	10.1%	310,106	75,902	9,207	47,756	23,367
Concord city	79,195	85,571	6,376	8.1%	30,591	9,684	1,571	6,519	3,424
Durham city	228,404	251,872	23,468	10.3%	104,830	26,993	3,992	17,276	8,729
Fayetteville city	200,582	203,939	3,357	1.7%	79,637	23,862	2,173	14,543	6,454
Gastonia city	71,741	73,696	1,955	2.7%	28,187	11,703	1,644	6,574	3,322
Greensboro city	268,877	282,558	13,681	5.1%	113,350	35,286	4,534	23,393	13,237
Greenville city	84,573	89,850	5,277	6.2%	37,752	9,292	1,629	5,777	2,606
High Point city	104,387	107,957	3,570	3.4%	38,948	13,385	1,139	8,256	4,188
Jacksonville city	70,145	69,031	-1,114	-1.6%	20,741	4,110	311	2,312	na
Raleigh city	403,971	439,884	35,913	8.9%	173,456	41,216	4,737	26,544	12,929
Wilmington city	106,478	113,676	7,198	6.8%	49,459	15,529	3,209	10,603	4,585
Winston-Salem city	229,634	239,273	9,639	4.2%	95,771	32,080	5,257	21,394	10,941
North Dakota									
Bismarck city	61,264	67,666	6,402	10.4%	30,704	10,762	2,203	6,789	2,860
Fargo city	105,549	116,572	11,023	10.4%	50,430	11,939	2,401	8,362	4,807
Ohio									
Akron city	199,092	197,846	-1,246	-0.6%	83,604	26,314	4,247	18,210	9,898
Canton city	73,017	72,274	-743	-1.0%	29,075	9,468	1,660	6,344	3,639
Cincinnati city	296,950	298,162	1,212	0.4%	137,197	34,872	5,989	25,463	15,531
Cleveland city	396,697	389,524	-7,173	-1.8%	165,984	47,362	7,229	33,681	19,442
Columbus city	788,654	836,293	47,639	6.0%	339,145	76,657	10,554	50,131	26,278
Dayton city	141,761	140,995	-766	-0.5%	56,251	16,179	1,827	11,354	6,310
Lorain city	64,097	63,774	-323	-0.5%	24,321	9,809	1,459	6,090	3,281
Parma city	81,601	80,023	-1,578	-1.9%	33,940	14,266	2,303	9,382	5,049
Toledo city	287,206	281,014	-6,192	-2.2%	116,450	37,846	6,842	26,214	14,581
Youngstown city	66,982	65,051	-1,931	-2.9%	26,934	10,860	2,602	7,604	4,413
Oklahoma									
Broken Arrow city	98,832	106,226	7,394	7.5%	37,813	11,644	1,054	6,656	2,116
Edmond city	81,399	88,594	7,195	8.8%	32,977	10,894	1,284	6,752	2,942
Lawton city	96,867	97,017	150	0.2%	32,315	10,103	936	6,211	3,264
Norman city	110,925	118,046	7,121	6.4%	45,454	13,781	1,439	8,245	3,355
Oklahoma City city	580,008	620,553	40,545	7.0%	237,213	75,118	9,403	46,993	20,399
Tulsa city	391,922	399,274	7,352	1.9%	165,817	53,425	7,925	34,775	17,464
Oregon									
Beaverton city	89,779	95,113	5,334	5.9%	38,807	10,175	1,427	6,292	3,229
Bend city	76,639	84,075	7,436	9.7%	33,526	12,154	2,014	7,517	3,587
Eugene city	156,358	160,552	4,194	2.7%	64,345	21,967	4,067	14,864	7,614
Gresham city	105,590	109,877	4,287	4.1%	38,393	14,968	2,195	9,217	3,779

Table A-3: Places—Summary Population Characteristics—*Continued*

	April 1, 2010 Census Population Estimates Base	2014 ACS Population	2010-2014 Population Change	2010-2014 Percent Change	Total Households	2014 ACS Population 65 and Over	Population 85 and Over	Householders 65 and Over	Persons 65 and Over Living Alone
Oregon—Cont.									
Hillsboro city	92,149	99,374	7,225	7.8%	37,134	10,448	1,169	6,631	2,064
Medford city	74,943	78,560	3,617	4.8%	30,122	14,200	2,235	8,593	4,006
Portland city	583,789	619,445	35,656	6.1%	257,267	71,073	10,290	44,071	22,134
Salem city	154,742	161,648	6,906	4.5%	58,793	22,415	3,574	14,193	7,254
Pennsylvania									
Allentown city	118,161	119,105	944	0.8%	40,275	14,455	2,863	8,774	4,303
Bethlehem city	74,982	78,759	3,777	5.0%	30,474	11,760	2,238	7,843	4,246
Erie city	101,784	99,466	-2,318	-2.3%	40,433	13,807	2,362	9,063	4,585
Philadelphia city	1,526,006	1,560,297	34,291	2.2%	577,862	195,574	29,379	124,800	65,727
Pittsburgh city	305,702	305,434	-268	-0.1%	131,112	41,145	8,574	28,274	16,258
Reading city	88,080	87,809	-271	-0.3%	29,942	9,265	1,250	6,525	na
Scranton city	76,089	75,278	-811	-1.1%	27,886	13,797	2,692	8,401	4,537
Rhode Island									
Cranston city	80,386	81,029	643	0.8%	31,653	14,551	3,014	8,849	3,905
Pawtucket city	71,141	71,490	349	0.5%	26,336	7,647	1,187	5,034	2,428
Providence city	178,038	179,142	1,104	0.6%	62,020	16,432	2,865	10,316	5,772
Warwick city	82,670	81,964	-706	-0.9%	33,887	15,793	3,322	9,995	4,899
South Carolina									
Charleston city	120,246	130,750	10,504	8.7%	54,144	16,944	2,670	10,952	5,104
Columbia city	130,065	131,758	1,693	1.3%	45,297	12,099	1,675	7,894	4,333
North Charleston city	97,601	107,972	10,371	10.6%	40,977	11,024	1,350	6,844	2,947
Rock Hill city	66,474	69,967	3,493	5.3%	26,841	9,547	825	5,886	2,792
South Dakota									
Rapid City city	67,964	72,642	4,678	6.9%	28,494	11,017	1,864	7,146	na
Sioux Falls city	153,897	168,604	14,707	9.6%	67,005	20,658	2,778	12,944	6,490
Tennessee									
Chattanooga city	168,828	173,778	4,950	2.9%	70,382	26,147	3,506	17,375	8,691
Clarksville city	132,963	146,814	13,851	10.4%	51,617	11,876	565	7,033	2,584
Franklin city	62,601	70,613	8,012	12.8%	25,725	7,496	1,085	4,514	na
Jackson city	66,929	67,308	379	0.6%	25,948	8,303	1,442	5,098	2,183
Johnson City city	63,476	65,820	2,344	3.7%	28,059	11,053	1,263	7,325	3,431
Knoxville city	178,764	184,292	5,528	3.1%	77,502	25,128	3,781	16,720	9,973
Memphis city	651,858	656,876	5,018	0.8%	250,553	73,617	10,207	48,707	22,983
Murfreesboro city	109,046	120,960	11,914	10.9%	46,058	11,371	1,056	7,449	3,550
Nashville-Davidson metropolitan govt (bal)	603,506	644,008	40,502	6.7%	258,263	69,971	8,959	44,768	22,265
Texas									
Abilene city	117,463	120,176	2,713	2.3%	41,710	15,677	2,702	9,239	3,353
Allen city	84,290	94,170	9,880	11.7%	30,341	5,619	679	3,027	na
Amarillo city	190,672	200,246	9,574	5.0%	74,709	25,416	2,923	16,390	7,066
Arlington city	365,361	383,202	17,841	4.9%	135,093	37,142	3,337	21,203	8,407
Austin city	811,458	912,798	101,340	12.5%	360,996	72,705	8,402	44,806	21,359
Baytown city	72,024	75,670	3,646	5.1%	27,073	10,382	1,086	5,810	2,730
Beaumont city	117,267	117,576	309	0.3%	45,669	15,056	2,570	10,045	5,646
Brownsville city	174,982	183,016	8,034	4.6%	50,340	20,524	3,572	10,856	3,967
Bryan city	76,218	80,916	4,698	6.2%	29,718	7,875	749	5,373	na
Carrollton city	119,100	128,342	9,242	7.8%	45,936	11,673	706	6,565	2,437
College Station city	94,061	103,486	9,425	10.0%	38,725	6,147	760	3,785	na
Conroe city	56,992	65,873	8,881	15.6%	23,105	7,327	848	3,691	1,445
Corpus Christi city	305,215	320,431	15,216	5.0%	117,685	40,850	4,933	25,209	9,669
Dallas city	1,197,792	1,281,031	83,239	6.9%	484,335	120,778	14,669	76,474	35,387
Denton city	116,207	128,200	11,993	10.3%	46,295	12,089	876	7,434	4,053
Edinburg city	74,565	83,017	8,452	11.3%	23,471	6,351	1,252	3,625	na
El Paso city	649,133	679,024	29,891	4.6%	218,127	82,640	9,499	46,798	18,093
Fort Worth city	742,060	812,553	70,493	9.5%	281,924	72,845	8,709	45,983	21,643
Frisco city	117,084	145,038	27,954	23.9%	47,880	10,158	448	5,359	na
Garland city	226,871	235,597	8,726	3.8%	75,775	27,813	2,786	15,697	5,970
Grand Prairie city	175,468	185,415	9,947	5.7%	58,703	13,791	1,598	7,664	2,735
Harlingen city	64,918	65,914	996	1.5%	20,831	9,098	1,194	5,593	2,375
Houston city	2,096,661	2,240,796	144,135	6.9%	834,204	219,325	26,022	137,392	63,332
Irving city	216,287	232,413	16,126	7.5%	84,734	17,776	2,110	10,332	4,562
Killeen city	127,911	138,143	10,232	8.0%	48,652	7,035	950	4,504	na
Laredo city	236,058	253,747	17,689	7.5%	66,985	21,333	2,478	11,300	4,132
League City city	83,560	94,287	10,727	12.8%	32,128	8,623	602	4,608	1,468
Lewisville city	95,309	102,283	6,974	7.3%	39,017	9,395	813	5,954	2,766
Longview city	80,455	84,313	3,858	4.8%	31,082	12,222	1,861	7,631	3,893
Lubbock city	229,399	243,843	14,444	6.3%	94,682	28,571	3,741	19,168	8,766
McAllen city	130,289	138,584	8,295	6.4%	41,458	13,983	1,230	6,779	1,504
McKinney city	131,025	156,753	25,728	19.6%	53,943	13,788	1,800	7,938	3,898
Mesquite city	139,629	144,289	4,660	3.3%	47,715	13,811	1,553	8,169	3,383
Midland city	111,127	128,037	16,910	15.2%	43,086	12,862	2,033	7,439	3,834
Mission city	77,665	82,429	4,764	6.1%	22,849	9,343	1,085	4,875	1,632
Missouri City city	66,825	75,128	8,303	12.4%	23,115	7,224	724	3,521	1,013
New Braunfels city	57,727	65,714	7,987	13.8%	21,463	8,269	1,009	5,151	2,061
North Richland Hills city	63,343	68,527	5,184	8.2%	24,849	9,624	1,150	5,889	2,302

Table A-3: Places—Summary Population Characteristics—*Continued*

	April 1, 2010 Census Population Estimates Base	2014 ACS Population	2010-2014 Population Change	2010-2014 Percent Change	Total Households	2014 ACS			
						Population 65 and Over	Population 85 and Over	Householders 65 and Over	Persons 65 and Over Living Alone
Texas—Cont.									
Odessa city	99,880	116,394	16,514	16.5%	40,556	12,199	1,666	7,892	3,568
Pasadena city	149,300	153,914	4,614	3.1%	49,719	14,549	1,655	8,727	3,338
Pearland city	89,891	104,759	14,868	16.5%	35,128	9,586	715	5,052	na
Pharr city	70,470	75,381	4,911	7.0%	20,333	8,186	1,318	4,146	na
Plano city	259,041	277,910	18,069	7.0%	104,535	33,323	2,823	18,614	6,832
Richardson city	99,223	108,609	9,386	9.5%	43,569	15,066	2,552	9,583	4,185
Round Rock city	99,990	112,196	12,206	12.2%	36,034	8,908	995	4,471	1,951
San Angelo city	93,227	97,207	3,980	4.3%	36,051	14,383	2,121	8,818	4,799
San Antonio city	1,327,556	1,436,723	109,167	8.2%	492,940	166,030	21,122	100,110	41,274
Sugar Land city	78,592	86,775	8,183	10.4%	28,213	11,818	1,324	6,371	1,946
Temple city	66,315	70,785	4,470	6.7%	25,732	11,634	2,312	6,643	2,730
Tyler city	96,945	101,436	4,491	4.6%	35,901	15,307	2,432	9,397	4,973
Victoria city	62,601	66,098	3,497	5.6%	24,195	9,631	1,566	5,640	2,340
Waco city	124,810	130,191	5,381	4.3%	46,843	15,128	2,071	10,158	5,072
Wichita Falls city	104,724	105,107	383	0.4%	34,845	12,507	1,823	8,025	3,719
Utah									
Layton city	67,297	72,223	4,926	7.3%	22,863	6,404	448	4,170	na
Ogden city	82,827	84,325	1,498	1.8%	29,689	8,994	1,124	5,607	2,800
Orem city	88,323	91,781	3,458	3.9%	25,216	7,255	647	4,276	na
Provo city	112,494	114,807	2,313	2.1%	32,916	7,309	897	4,063	1,183
Salt Lake City city	186,452	190,873	4,421	2.4%	75,923	18,190	2,661	13,227	7,552
Sandy city	87,720	91,135	3,415	3.9%	27,007	8,992	488	4,911	1,467
St. George city	72,763	78,509	5,746	7.9%	26,640	16,989	2,672	9,483	2,644
West Jordan city	103,708	110,917	7,209	7.0%	32,100	6,297	666	3,460	na
West Valley City city	129,475	134,492	5,017	3.9%	35,717	9,160	350	5,200	1,971
Virginia									
Alexandria city	140,006	150,575	10,569	7.5%	68,796	15,315	1,834	9,620	5,046
Chesapeake city	222,209	233,371	11,162	5.0%	83,904	27,540	3,491	16,451	5,896
Hampton city	137,508	136,879	-629	-0.5%	53,420	18,550	1,930	11,850	5,061
Lynchburg city	75,613	79,047	3,434	4.5%	27,870	11,355	2,438	7,509	3,646
Newport News city	180,918	182,965	2,047	1.1%	68,768	21,258	2,889	12,876	6,305
Norfolk city	242,831	245,428	2,597	1.1%	87,760	24,165	4,507	15,883	8,516
Portsmouth city	95,535	96,004	469	0.5%	37,123	13,009	1,601	8,758	4,005
Richmond city	204,246	217,853	13,607	6.7%	88,421	24,862	4,068	17,129	10,485
Roanoke city	96,919	99,428	2,509	2.6%	42,636	15,237	3,042	10,367	4,985
Suffolk city	84,596	86,806	2,210	2.6%	30,689	11,260	1,417	7,248	2,840
Virginia Beach city	437,966	450,980	13,014	3.0%	167,008	55,306	6,634	34,442	14,156
Washington									
Auburn city	70,172	78,769	8,597	12.3%	27,524	8,735	1,577	4,890	1,995
Bellevue city	127,887	136,426	8,539	6.7%	53,945	20,529	3,468	12,331	5,677
Bellingham city	80,867	83,363	2,496	3.1%	34,963	11,342	2,259	7,944	na
Everett city	103,022	106,741	3,719	3.6%	40,895	9,645	1,738	6,673	4,306
Federal Way city	89,306	93,428	4,122	4.6%	35,121	12,408	1,417	7,765	3,353
Kennewick city	73,874	77,424	3,550	4.8%	27,028	9,649	1,397	5,914	2,819
Kent city	118,593	125,547	6,954	5.9%	41,586	11,917	1,622	6,863	3,534
Kirkland city	80,585	85,778	5,193	6.4%	34,240	11,208	1,163	6,571	2,623
Marysville city	60,024	65,088	5,064	8.4%	24,298	9,593	1,582	5,333	2,408
Pasco city	61,083	69,807	8,724	14.3%	20,549	4,245	394	2,613	na
Renton city	91,819	98,382	6,563	7.1%	36,913	8,936	1,596	5,388	2,277
Seattle city	608,658	668,337	59,679	9.8%	304,564	81,461	13,398	52,142	26,649
Spokane city	209,440	212,067	2,627	1.3%	85,300	29,815	4,718	19,774	10,564
Spokane Valley city	89,745	91,733	1,988	2.2%	36,986	13,454	1,677	9,147	4,489
Tacoma city	198,397	205,153	6,756	3.4%	78,717	25,667	3,949	16,417	7,931
Vancouver city	161,849	169,303	7,454	4.6%	67,721	23,457	2,983	14,948	7,698
Yakima city	91,276	93,355	2,079	2.3%	33,212	12,977	1,895	8,154	
Wisconsin									
Appleton city	72,628	72,654	26	0.0%	28,648	7,878	1,335	4,767	2,073
Eau Claire city	66,190	68,207	2,017	3.0%	27,180	8,532	1,154	5,565	na
Green Bay city	103,913	104,893	980	0.9%	42,292	12,815	2,139	8,151	4,183
Kenosha city	99,228	99,898	670	0.7%	36,471	12,472	1,822	8,318	3,733
Madison city	233,059	245,674	12,615	5.4%	103,771	26,967	4,180	17,553	8,355
Milwaukee city	594,738	599,653	4,915	0.8%	233,161	60,278	9,854	38,497	21,058
Oshkosh city	66,083	66,631	548	0.8%	26,698	9,331	2,058	6,269	3,762
Racine city	78,860	78,054	-806	-1.0%	29,646	9,217	1,638	6,207	3,291
Waukesha city	70,706	71,482	776	1.1%	28,137	7,556	1,053	4,989	na

Table A-4: Metropolitan/Micropolitan Statistical Areas—Summary Population Characteristics

	April 1, 2010 Census Population Estimates Base	2014 ACS Population	2010-2014 Population Change	2010-2014 Percent Change	Total Households	2014 ACS			
						Population 65 and Over	Population 85 and Over	Householders 65 and Over	Persons 65 and Over Living Alone
Aberdeen, WA Micro Area	72,797	70,818	-1,979	-2.7%	27,401	13,420	1,384	8,568	3,533
Abilene, TX Metro Area	165,252	166,900	1,648	1.0%	59,932	24,261	3,466	14,504	5,458
Adrian, MI Micro Area	99,892	99,047	-845	-0.8%	38,483	16,465	1,745	10,605	3,877
Akron, OH Metro Area	703,207	703,825	618	0.1%	283,364	111,421	16,966	71,529	33,261
Alamogordo, NM Micro Area	63,799	65,082	1,283	2.0%	23,190	10,366	942	6,074	1,796
Albany, GA Metro Area	157,500	152,596	-4,904	-3.1%	57,795	21,658	2,549	14,031	5,959
Albany, OR Metro Area	116,672	119,356	2,684	2.3%	45,907	20,720	2,558	12,694	5,116
Albany-Schenectady-Troy, NY Metro Area	870,720	880,167	9,447	1.1%	347,291	136,420	19,741	86,243	39,014
Albertville, AL Micro Area	93,019	94,636	1,617	1.7%	34,872	15,298	1,510	8,968	4,500
Albuquerque, NM Metro Area	887,075	905,213	18,138	2.0%	342,552	131,492	13,715	82,564	38,135
Alexandria, LA Metro Area	153,922	154,872	950	0.6%	53,802	22,841	2,952	14,007	5,791
Allentown-Bethlehem-Easton, PA-NJ Metro Area	821,303	829,835	8,532	1.0%	315,376	139,417	23,043	82,997	36,162
Altoona, PA Metro Area	127,078	125,955	-1,123	-0.9%	49,678	24,112	4,143	14,864	7,538
Amarillo, TX Metro Area	251,933	261,752	9,819	3.9%	95,667	33,463	4,272	21,264	8,746
Ames, IA Metro Area	89,542	94,073	4,531	5.1%	35,880	10,136	1,101	6,087	na
Anchorage, AK Metro Area	380,821	398,892	18,071	4.7%	135,449	36,363	2,994	20,102	7,235
Ann Arbor, MI Metro Area	345,066	356,874	11,808	3.4%	137,240	43,044	5,441	27,312	11,673
Anniston-Oxford-Jacksonville, AL Metro Area	118,586	115,916	-2,670	-2.3%	46,087	18,543	1,655	11,702	5,215
Appleton, WI Metro Area	225,666	231,497	5,831	2.6%	90,046	30,003	3,461	18,685	6,915
Asheville, NC Metro Area	424,859	442,316	17,457	4.1%	182,129	90,920	11,935	55,387	25,124
Ashtabula, OH Micro Area	101,497	99,175	-2,322	-2.3%	38,891	17,004	2,391	10,195	4,183
Athens, TX Micro Area	78,536	79,290	754	1.0%	30,422	16,737	1,600	10,304	3,633
Athens-Clarke County, GA Metro Area	192,541	197,268	4,727	2.5%	71,814	23,192	3,009	14,195	5,447
Atlanta-Sandy Springs-Roswell, GA Metro Area	5,286,727	5,611,829	325,102	6.1%	1,981,447	604,850	59,110	353,875	143,483
Atlantic City-Hammonton, NJ Metro Area	274,549	275,209	660	0.2%	101,937	43,435	4,347	26,503	12,711
Auburn, NY Micro Area	80,025	78,823	-1,202	-1.5%	31,290	13,146	1,955	8,338	4,113
Auburn-Opelika, AL Metro Area	140,296	154,255	13,959	9.9%	57,880	15,875	1,057	10,631	4,815
Augusta-Richmond County, GA-SC Metro Area	564,873	583,010	18,137	3.2%	208,479	84,309	9,425	49,028	20,095
Augusta-Waterville, ME Micro Area	122,151	121,112	-1,039	-0.9%	50,219	21,422	2,384	13,203	5,858
Austin-Round Rock, TX Metro Area	1,716,303	1,943,299	226,996	13.2%	703,976	183,274	20,759	105,797	42,784
Bakersfield, CA Metro Area	839,631	874,589	34,958	4.2%	261,135	86,486	9,115	49,947	20,268
Baltimore-Columbia-Towson, MD Metro Area	2,710,597	2,785,874	75,277	2.8%	1,032,604	390,577	51,512	240,780	106,173
Bangor, ME Metro Area	153,920	153,414	-506	-0.3%	61,218	25,127	3,416	16,041	7,676
Barnstable Town, MA Metro Area	215,888	214,914	-974	-0.5%	95,697	59,991	7,498	38,887	18,267
Baton Rouge, LA Metro Area	802,500	825,478	22,978	2.9%	305,096	100,331	9,714	61,930	25,569
Battle Creek, MI Metro Area	136,148	134,878	-1,270	-0.9%	52,385	21,797	3,110	13,899	6,091
Bay City, MI Metro Area	107,771	106,179	-1,592	-1.5%	42,706	19,487	2,221	12,621	5,848
Beaumont-Port Arthur, TX Metro Area	403,190	403,958	768	0.2%	152,806	59,554	7,404	37,765	18,092
Beaver Dam, WI Micro Area	88,761	88,574	-187	-0.2%	33,273	14,291	1,716	8,850	3,972
Beckley, WV Metro Area	124,901	123,373	-1,528	-1.2%	49,335	22,492	2,999	14,622	6,169
Bellingham, WA Metro Area	201,140	208,351	7,211	3.6%	81,973	31,955	4,198	20,850	9,879
Bend-Redmond, OR Metro Area	157,733	170,388	12,655	8.0%	66,218	30,318	3,703	18,070	6,678
Billings, MT Metro Area	158,934	167,521	8,587	5.4%	66,824	26,193	3,355	16,291	8,348
Binghamton, NY Metro Area	251,725	247,219	-4,506	-1.8%	99,298	43,574	6,857	27,324	12,312
Birmingham-Hoover, AL Metro Area	1,128,056	1,143,772	15,716	1.4%	439,531	168,322	18,791	107,765	44,374
Bismarck, ND Metro Area	114,778	126,526	11,748	10.2%	53,813	18,261	3,159	11,754	5,448
Blacksburg-Christiansburg-Radford, VA Metro Area	178,254	181,249	2,995	1.7%	67,185	26,047	3,005	15,631	7,652
Bloomington, IL Metro Area	186,133	188,917	2,784	1.5%	72,551	22,817	3,753	14,146	6,644
Bloomington, IN Metro Area	159,542	164,308	4,766	3.0%	61,929	19,346	2,160	11,974	4,675
Bloomsburg-Berwick, PA Metro Area	85,563	85,763	200	0.2%	33,873	15,046	1,950	9,142	3,818
Bluefield, WV-VA Micro Area	107,344	105,237	-2,107	-2.0%	42,039	20,550	2,376	13,568	6,686
Boise City, ID Metro Area	616,561	666,144	49,583	8.0%	240,402	86,909	10,248	51,350	19,551
Boston-Cambridge-Newton, MA-NH Metro Area	4,552,412	4,732,161	179,749	3.9%	1,777,817	676,779	98,342	412,506	194,858
Boulder, CO Metro Area	294,571	313,333	18,762	6.4%	123,690	37,931	4,638	23,881	11,309
Bowling Green, KY Metro Area	158,599	165,928	7,329	4.6%	61,834	21,206	1,812	14,024	6,809
Bozeman, MT Micro Area	89,510	97,308	7,798	8.7%	39,067	10,707	978	6,915	3,153
Brainerd, MN Micro Area	91,067	91,824	757	0.8%	39,920	20,088	2,475	12,583	5,188
Branson, MO Micro Area	83,877	85,334	1,457	1.7%	35,340	19,163	1,601	12,253	4,608
Bremerton-Silverdale, WA Metro Area	251,133	254,183	3,050	1.2%	95,249	40,852	4,994	25,250	10,320
Bridgeport-Stamford-Norwalk, CT Metro Area	916,828	945,438	28,610	3.1%	338,421	135,852	20,186	84,643	37,012
Brownsville-Harlingen, TX Metro Area	406,220	420,392	14,172	3.5%	121,009	52,048	7,032	30,043	11,397
Brunswick, GA Metro Area	112,368	112,663	295	0.3%	43,618	19,945	1,750	12,140	5,408
Buffalo-Cheektowaga-Niagara Falls, NY Metro Area	1,135,541	1,136,360	819	0.1%	470,564	189,588	30,896	125,531	63,105
Burlington, NC Metro Area	151,241	155,792	4,551	3.0%	62,799	25,110	3,301	16,058	7,572
Burlington-South Burlington, VT Metro Area	211,262	215,824	4,562	2.2%	85,222	28,601	3,739	18,342	8,993
California-Lexington Park, MD Metro Area	105,151	110,382	5,231	5.0%	39,179	13,166	1,302	7,889	na
Canton-Massillon, OH Metro Area	404,420	403,923	-497	-0.1%	159,604	71,654	9,552	44,574	19,247
Cape Coral-Fort Myers, FL Metro Area	618,754	679,513	60,759	9.8%	263,295	178,227	22,013	102,374	38,161
Cape Girardeau, MO-IL Metro Area	96,275	97,612	1,337	1.4%	37,842	16,275	2,169	9,954	4,081
Carbondale-Marion, IL Metro Area	126,580	126,685	105	0.1%	50,423	19,486	2,295	11,887	4,323
Carson City, NV Metro Area	55,274	54,522	-752	-1.4%	21,228	10,141	1,737	6,651	3,782
Casper, WY Metro Area	75,450	81,624	6,174	8.2%	33,323	9,975	1,147	7,213	3,938
Cedar Rapids, IA Metro Area	257,940	263,885	5,945	2.3%	106,799	39,042	5,330	25,107	11,095
Centralia, WA Micro Area	75,455	75,128	-327	-0.4%	29,969	14,747	2,331	9,400	3,647
Chambersburg-Waynesboro, PA Metro Area	149,618	152,892	3,274	2.2%	58,565	27,775	4,037	16,463	6,669
Champaign-Urbana, IL Metro Area	231,889	238,680	6,791	2.9%	94,306	28,580	3,333	18,635	9,181
Charleston, WV Metro Area	227,071	223,371	-3,700	-1.6%	93,385	40,079	4,471	27,136	11,861
Charleston-Mattoon, IL Micro Area	64,921	63,148	-1,773	-2.7%	25,076	9,546	1,882	6,127	na

Table A-4: Metropolitan/Micropolitan Statistical Areas—Summary Population Characteristics—*Continued*

	April 1, 2010 Census Population Estimates Base	2014 ACS Population	2010-2014 Population Change	2010-2014 Percent Change	Total Households	2014 ACS Population 65 and Over	Population 85 and Over	Householders 65 and Over	Persons 65 and Over Living Alone
Charleston-North Charleston, SC Metro Area	664,643	727,689	63,046	9.5%	276,509	96,955	10,616	58,835	22,142
Charlotte-Concord-Gastonia, NC-SC Metro Area	2,217,248	2,380,314	163,066	7.4%	883,281	295,401	31,392	178,503	73,994
Charlottesville, VA Metro Area	218,710	227,738	9,028	4.1%	87,139	35,028	5,358	20,925	8,348
Chattanooga, TN-GA Metro Area	528,145	543,153	15,008	2.8%	207,829	87,927	10,032	56,504	21,956
Cheyenne, WY Metro Area	91,881	96,389	4,508	4.9%	38,705	13,897	1,343	8,768	2,881
Chicago Naperville-Elgin, IL-IN-WI Metro Area	9,461,537	9,553,810	92,273	1.0%	3,442,174	1,219,572	165,526	741,292	330,344
Chico, CA Metro Area	220,000	224,241	4,241	1.9%	85,366	38,055	5,627	22,765	10,623
Chillicothe, OH Micro Area	78,064	77,159	-905	-1.2%	27,569	11,396	916	7,322	3,511
Cincinnati, OH-KY-IN Metro Area	2,114,755	2,149,971	35,216	1.7%	829,142	293,931	39,067	185,564	83,312
Claremont-Lebanon, NH-VT Micro Area	218,458	217,634	-824	-0.4%	89,665	40,841	5,072	24,525	10,742
Clarksburg, WV Micro Area	94,196	88,953	-5,243	-5.6%	36,004	16,597	2,167	10,942	4,958
Clarksville, TN-KY Metro Area	260,610	279,593	18,983	7.3%	97,747	27,999	2,095	16,860	6,582
Clearlake, CA Micro Area	64,665	64,184	-481	-0.7%	27,636	12,703	1,205	8,588	4,309
Cleveland, TN Metro Area	115,788	118,959	3,171	2.7%	44,048	19,852	1,979	12,406	5,413
Cleveland-Elyria, OH Metro Area	2,077,246	2,063,598	-13,648	-0.7%	848,493	341,442	51,886	220,581	105,160
Coeur d'Alene, ID Metro Area	138,494	147,326	8,832	6.4%	56,177	25,326	2,971	15,029	6,235
College Station-Bryan, TX Metro Area	228,660	239,953	11,293	4.9%	89,858	24,299	2,629	15,260	6,728
Colorado Springs, CO Metro Area	645,611	686,908	41,297	6.4%	255,330	80,400	8,825	48,830	19,525
Columbia, MO Metro Area	162,642	172,717	10,075	6.2%	67,198	18,413	2,293	11,871	5,623
Columbia, SC Metro Area	767,477	800,752	33,275	4.3%	298,600	105,378	10,785	67,284	27,441
Columbus, GA-AL Metro Area	295,529	312,731	17,202	5.8%	113,195	38,507	4,865	23,640	8,855
Columbus, IN Metro Area	76,786	80,217	3,431	4.5%	31,827	11,824	1,234	7,952	3,610
Columbus, OH Metro Area	1,902,015	1,994,536	92,521	4.9%	764,395	238,980	29,637	147,766	66,233
Concord, NH Micro Area	146,442	147,171	729	0.5%	57,023	23,480	2,888	13,787	5,999
Cookeville, TN Micro Area	106,050	108,189	2,139	2.0%	42,778	18,846	1,310	12,176	5,414
Coos Bay, OR Micro Area	63,043	62,475	-568	-0.9%	25,160	15,170	2,101	9,135	4,166
Corning, NY Micro Area	98,988	98,394	-594	-0.6%	41,046	17,344	2,461	11,088	5,269
Corpus Christi, TX Metro Area	428,188	443,480	15,292	3.6%	160,869	62,197	6,618	38,942	14,835
Corvallis, OR Metro Area	85,581	86,316	735	0.9%	33,904	12,373	2,159	7,923	3,367
Crestview-Fort Walton Beach-Destin, FL Metro Area	235,865	258,042	22,177	9.4%	95,662	41,399	4,890	26,949	11,081
Cullman, AL Micro Area	80,410	81,289	879	1.1%	30,424	14,266	1,310	8,705	4,261
Cumberland, MD-WV Metro Area	103,299	100,530	-2,769	-2.7%	40,318	19,362	2,517	11,770	5,500
Dallas-Fort Worth-Arlington, TX Metro Area	6,426,210	6,954,003	527,793	8.2%	2,445,239	712,091	73,597	420,736	168,970
Dalton, GA Metro Area	142,227	142,952	725	0.5%	50,238	18,120	1,266	10,758	4,711
Danville, IL Metro Area	81,625	79,728	-1,897	-2.3%	31,338	14,058	1,387	8,761	4,225
Danville, VA Micro Area	106,558	104,827	-1,731	-1.6%	45,370	20,717	2,044	13,851	5,848
Daphne-Fairhope-Foley, AL Metro Area	182,265	200,111	17,846	9.8%	71,307	37,782	3,808	23,509	10,002
Davenport-Moline-Rock Island, IA-IL Metro Area	379,689	382,382	2,693	0.7%	153,602	62,773	8,377	40,792	19,797
Dayton, OH Metro Area	799,216	800,836	1,620	0.2%	327,610	132,127	15,679	84,582	40,369
Decatur, AL Metro Area	153,825	153,084	-741	-0.5%	58,351	23,704	2,340	15,624	7,488
Decatur, IL Metro Area	110,768	108,350	-2,418	-2.2%	44,063	19,253	2,331	12,440	5,436
Deltona-Daytona Beach-Ormond Beach, FL Metro Area	590,293	609,939	19,646	3.3%	237,527	146,929	22,176	85,624	33,454
Denver-Aurora-Lakewood, CO Metro Area	2,543,594	2,754,258	210,664	8.3%	1,054,371	321,678	38,956	198,278	85,539
Des Moines-West Des Moines, IA Metro Area	569,633	611,549	41,916	7.4%	235,515	74,232	10,637	47,347	22,879
Detroit-Warren-Dearborn, MI Metro Area	4,296,313	4,296,611	298	0.0%	1,654,584	632,542	88,954	406,083	187,030
Dothan, AL Metro Area	145,639	148,095	2,456	1.7%	55,998	25,311	2,480	15,885	6,680
Dover, DE Metro Area	162,344	171,987	9,643	5.9%	61,270	26,587	2,685	15,895	5,969
DuBois, PA Micro Area	81,644	81,191	-453	-0.6%	31,784	15,340	2,219	9,947	4,981
Dubuque, IA Metro Area	93,653	96,370	2,717	2.9%	38,824	15,598	2,103	9,597	3,732
Duluth, MN-WI Metro Area	279,771	280,218	447	0.2%	116,768	47,561	7,589	30,770	14,638
Dunn, NC Micro Area	114,678	126,666	11,988	10.5%	44,153	13,669	1,431	8,883	3,898
Durham-Chapel Hill, NC Metro Area	506,634	542,710	36,076	7.1%	213,163	70,926	9,579	43,911	18,948
East Stroudsburg, PA Metro Area	169,842	166,314	-3,528	-2.1%	54,404	25,516	3,255	12,922	4,970
Eau Claire, WI Metro Area	161,390	165,024	3,634	2.3%	65,392	24,234	3,170	15,310	7,156
El Centro, CA Metro Area	174,528	179,091	4,563	2.6%	43,635	21,684	2,884	10,308	4,219
El Paso, TX Metro Area	804,123	836,444	32,321	4.0%	256,548	94,367	10,874	52,864	19,997
Elizabeth City, NC Micro Area	64,094	63,015	-1,079	-1.7%	23,930	10,688	904	6,264	na
Elizabethtown-Fort Knox, KY Metro Area	148,339	151,491	3,152	2.1%	54,612	19,612	2,266	13,028	5,557
Elkhart-Goshen, IN Metro Area	197,561	201,971	4,410	2.2%	70,636	26,148	3,952	16,374	7,010
Elmira, NY Metro Area	88,830	87,770	-1,060	-1.2%	34,617	14,901	2,414	8,995	3,784
Erie, PA Metro Area	280,566	278,443	-2,123	-0.8%	108,655	44,087	6,442	27,024	11,655
Eugene, OR Metro Area	351,715	358,337	6,622	1.9%	145,732	62,237	8,754	39,122	16,431
Eureka-Arcata-Fortuna, CA Micro Area	134,623	134,809	186	0.1%	53,195	20,327	2,155	12,469	5,368
Evansville, IN-KY Metro Area	311,552	315,162	3,610	1.2%	125,439	49,114	7,087	30,371	13,965
Fairbanks, AK Metro Area	97,581	99,357	1,776	1.8%	35,692	7,884	865	5,189	na
Fargo, ND-MN Metro Area	208,777	228,291	19,514	9.3%	92,345	25,605	4,172	16,843	8,898
Faribault-Northfield, MN Micro Area	64,144	65,151	1,007	1.6%	22,933	9,149	816	6,214	3,624
Farmington, MO Micro Area	65,364	65,960	596	0.9%	24,915	10,095	1,468	6,200	2,697
Farmington, NM Micro Area	130,045	123,785	-6,260	-4.8%	40,378	15,809	2,028	9,919	3,502
Fayetteville, NC Metro Area	366,383	377,939	11,556	3.2%	140,204	39,654	3,809	24,426	10,774
Fayetteville-Springdale-Rogers, AR-MO Metro Area	463,207	503,046	39,839	8.6%	182,570	61,691	7,541	38,246	15,855
Findlay, OH Metro Area	74,782	75,337	555	0.7%	31,747	11,946	2,007	7,754	3,692
Flagstaff, AZ Metro Area	134,437	137,682	3,245	2.4%	46,919	15,520	1,173	9,700	3,514
Flint, MI Metro Area	425,790	412,895	-12,895	-3.0%	167,096	64,986	7,341	42,588	17,534
Florence, SC Metro Area	205,571	207,030	1,459	0.7%	77,815	31,772	3,148	20,036	8,691
Florence-Muscle Shoals, AL Metro Area	147,137	147,639	502	0.3%	61,239	27,452	3,180	17,403	7,615
Fond du Lac, WI Metro Area	101,633	101,759	126	0.1%	41,938	16,906	3,137	10,414	4,762

Table A-4: Metropolitan/Micropolitan Statistical Areas—Summary Population Characteristics—*Continued*

	April 1, 2010 Census Population Estimates Base	2014 ACS Population	2010-2014 Population Change	2010-2014 Percent Change	Total Households	2014 ACS			
						Population 65 and Over	Population 85 and Over	Householders 65 and Over	Persons 65 and Over Living Alone
Forest City, NC Micro Area	67,809	66,600	-1,209	-1.8%	25,805	13,004	2,213	8,116	4,244
Fort Collins, CO Metro Area	299,630	324,122	24,492	8.2%	125,165	45,151	5,178	27,063	12,042
Fort Smith, AR-OK Metro Area	280,515	279,592	-923	-0.3%	106,099	43,062	4,708	28,526	12,556
Fort Wayne, IN Metro Area	416,255	427,183	10,928	2.6%	163,139	58,375	8,055	36,659	16,443
Frankfort, KY Micro Area	70,706	72,880	2,174	3.1%	29,797	10,932	1,204	6,903	na
Fresno, CA Metro Area	930,452	965,974	35,522	3.8%	297,993	108,445	14,835	61,609	24,646
Gadsden, AL Metro Area	104,427	103,531	-896	-0.9%	39,714	18,077	2,294	11,562	5,198
Gainesville, FL Metro Area	264,274	272,994	8,720	3.3%	103,619	35,087	4,724	22,119	9,652
Gainesville, GA Metro Area	179,684	190,761	11,077	6.2%	63,383	26,142	2,623	15,730	5,494
Gallup, NM Micro Area	71,491	74,098	2,607	3.6%	18,148	7,509	566	4,880	1,671
Gettysburg, PA Metro Area	101,413	101,714	301	0.3%	38,748	18,272	1,894	10,910	4,099
Glens Falls, NY Metro Area	128,921	127,345	-1,576	-1.2%	49,937	23,426	2,852	13,564	5,507
Glenwood Springs, CO Micro Area	73,537	76,724	3,187	4.3%	26,927	8,578	551	5,544	2,013
Goldsboro, NC Metro Area	122,623	124,456	1,833	1.5%	46,281	18,027	1,903	11,015	4,734
Grand Forks, ND-MN Metro Area	98,461	101,842	3,381	3.4%	41,882	13,204	1,757	8,567	4,434
Grand Island, NE Metro Area	81,850	84,467	2,617	3.2%	32,187	13,522	1,523	8,353	3,963
Grand Junction, CO Metro Area	146,723	148,255	1,532	1.0%	59,703	24,742	3,212	15,207	5,367
Grand Rapids-Wyoming, MI Metro Area	988,940	1,027,703	38,763	3.9%	375,683	133,763	21,499	82,744	34,036
Grants Pass, OR Metro Area	82,713	83,599	886	1.1%	33,486	20,667	2,077	12,767	4,729
Great Falls, MT Metro Area	81,327	82,344	1,017	1.3%	34,018	13,756	1,424	9,011	4,313
Greeley, CO Metro Area	252,837	277,670	24,833	9.8%	96,803	30,841	2,938	19,316	7,394
Green Bay, WI Metro Area	306,241	314,531	8,290	2.7%	124,899	44,505	5,942	27,801	11,232
Greeneville, TN Micro Area	68,831	68,335	-496	-0.7%	27,296	13,573	1,475	7,564	2,836
Greenfield Town, MA Micro Area	71,372	70,862	-510	-0.7%	29,859	12,876	1,995	8,174	4,196
Greensboro-High Point, NC Metro Area	723,798	746,593	22,795	3.1%	289,450	110,128	13,898	70,530	33,980
Greenville, NC Metro Area	168,148	175,354	7,206	4.3%	68,412	19,820	2,417	12,463	5,098
Greenville-Anderson-Mauldin, SC Metro Area	824,107	862,463	38,356	4.7%	324,282	131,292	15,334	81,633	34,362
Greenwood, SC Micro Area	95,077	93,954	-1,123	-1.2%	36,573	16,542	2,910	10,887	4,400
Gulfport-Biloxi-Pascagoula, MS Metro Area	370,787	386,144	15,357	4.1%	146,693	54,589	5,216	35,579	14,058
Hagerstown-Martinsburg, MD-WV Metro Area	251,602	260,070	8,468	3.4%	95,920	37,795	4,881	22,841	10,168
Hammond, LA Metro Area	121,101	127,049	5,948	4.9%	45,786	16,233	1,453	9,280	4,428
Hanford-Corcoran, CA Metro Area	152,982	150,269	-2,713	-1.8%	41,596	13,331	1,080	7,781	2,581
Harrisburg-Carlisle, PA Metro Area	549,473	560,849	11,376	2.1%	226,058	89,485	13,336	56,876	26,476
Harrisonburg, VA Metro Area	125,217	130,649	5,432	4.3%	47,052	18,348	2,735	11,181	4,472
Hartford-West Hartford-East Hartford, CT Metro Area	1,212,387	1,214,295	1,908	0.2%	467,615	190,247	30,116	115,938	53,049
Hattiesburg, MS Metro Area	142,857	149,312	6,455	4.5%	52,610	18,066	2,251	11,282	4,764
Helena, MT Micro Area	74,801	77,424	2,623	3.5%	31,152	12,962	1,435	7,564	3,250
Hermiston-Pendleton, OR Micro Area	87,062	86,147	-915	-1.1%	30,573	13,168	1,524	7,109	3,498
Hickory-Lenoir-Morganton, NC Metro Area	365,492	362,896	-2,596	-0.7%	131,741	62,984	6,202	38,170	15,516
Hilo, HI Micro Area	185,079	194,190	9,111	4.9%	65,178	34,298	5,231	19,257	6,837
Hilton Head Island-Bluffton-Beaufort, SC Metro Area	187,010	203,022	16,012	8.6%	74,717	47,365	5,107	28,322	10,420
Hinesville, GA Metro Area	77,917	82,768	4,851	6.2%	28,069	6,257	323	3,679	na
Hobbs, NM Micro Area	64,727	69,999	5,272	8.1%	21,805	7,340	656	4,381	na
Holland, MI Micro Area	111,408	113,847	2,439	2.2%	41,779	17,109	1,920	10,476	3,855
Homosassa Springs, FL Metro Area	141,236	139,377	-1,859	-1.3%	60,315	49,006	5,730	29,294	10,819
Hot Springs, AR Metro Area	96,024	97,322	1,298	1.4%	39,045	20,953	2,310	13,006	5,567
Houma-Thibodaux, LA Metro Area	208,176	211,348	3,172	1.5%	74,539	26,983	3,204	15,862	6,009
Houston-The Woodlands-Sugar Land, TX Metro Area	5,920,490	6,490,180	569,690	9.6%	2,226,123	638,592	64,725	377,793	150,746
Huntington-Ashland, WV-KY-OH Metro Area	364,930	363,325	-1,605	-0.4%	146,108	64,359	7,828	41,916	19,348
Huntsville, AL Metro Area	417,593	441,086	23,493	5.6%	172,409	60,843	6,808	37,623	15,123
Huntsville, TX Micro Area	82,536	84,289	1,753	2.1%	25,219	11,417	1,131	7,210	3,700
Hutchinson, KS Micro Area	64,511	63,794	-717	-1.1%	24,076	11,796	1,904	7,134	na
Idaho Falls, ID Metro Area	133,337	138,403	5,066	3.8%	45,712	16,370	1,922	10,672	3,916
Indiana, PA Micro Area	88,891	87,706	-1,185	-1.3%	34,536	14,868	2,054	9,335	3,511
Indianapolis-Carmel-Anderson, IN Metro Area	1,888,082	1,972,241	84,159	4.5%	744,765	244,434	30,310	150,796	66,359
Iowa City, IA Metro Area	152,586	164,357	11,771	7.7%	64,409	18,116	2,180	11,302	5,152
Ithaca, NY Metro Area	101,595	104,691	3,096	3.0%	38,120	12,325	2,319	7,857	3,303
Jackson, MI Metro Area	160,248	159,741	-507	-0.3%	61,686	25,771	3,238	16,640	8,329
Jackson, MS Metro Area	567,645	576,246	8,601	1.5%	206,952	72,747	9,917	46,494	20,494
Jackson, TN Metro Area	130,009	130,225	216	0.2%	49,095	19,908	2,390	12,029	4,960
Jacksonville, FL Metro Area	1,345,596	1,419,127	73,531	5.5%	528,993	201,996	24,576	122,887	51,384
Jacksonville, NC Metro Area	177,772	187,589	9,817	5.5%	61,873	15,988	1,085	9,938	4,455
Jamestown-Dunkirk-Fredonia, NY Micro Area	134,905	132,053	-2,852	-2.1%	52,916	23,641	3,616	14,768	6,728
Janesville-Beloit, WI Metro Area	160,331	161,188	857	0.5%	63,037	24,180	4,347	15,033	7,330
Jefferson City, MO Metro Area	149,807	150,131	324	0.2%	55,887	21,761	2,337	13,240	5,515
Johnson City, TN Metro Area	198,716	201,750	3,034	1.5%	84,847	36,440	3,445	23,000	9,640
Johnstown, PA Metro Area	143,674	137,732	-5,942	-4.1%	57,004	28,088	4,887	18,477	8,804
Jonesboro, AR Metro Area	121,026	126,764	5,738	4.7%	48,043	17,879	1,621	10,678	4,489
Joplin, MO Metro Area	175,516	176,141	625	0.4%	66,564	26,049	3,265	16,199	6,485
Kahului-Wailuku-Lahaina, HI Micro Area	154,925	163,108	8,183	5.3%	54,355	24,654	3,919	13,616	4,116
Kalamazoo-Portage, MI Metro Area	326,596	334,017	7,421	2.3%	128,755	47,101	5,935	28,592	11,778
Kalispell, MT Micro Area	90,928	94,924	3,996	4.4%	36,820	16,537	1,186	9,898	3,688
Kankakee, IL Metro Area	113,449	111,375	-2,074	-1.8%	40,732	16,517	2,053	9,376	3,629
Kansas City, MO-KS Metro Area	2,009,338	2,070,221	60,883	3.0%	800,035	275,867	35,931	172,768	78,084
Kapaa, HI Micro Area	67,090	70,475	3,385	5.0%	22,234	12,381	1,886	6,749	2,364
Keene, NH Micro Area	77,117	76,115	-1,002	-1.3%	31,305	12,998	1,918	8,186	3,300
Kennewick-Richland, WA Metro Area	253,340	274,295	20,955	8.3%	93,357	32,164	4,271	19,078	7,979

Table A-4: Metropolitan/Micropolitan Statistical Areas—Summary Population Characteristics—*Continued*

	April 1, 2010 Census Population Estimates Base	2014 ACS Population	2010-2014 Population Change	2010-2014 Percent Change	Total Households	2014 ACS			
						Population 65 and Over	Population 85 and Over	Householders 65 and Over	Persons 65 and Over Living Alone
Key West, FL Micro Area	73,090	77,136	4,046	5.5%	28,065	15,903	2,037	8,836	3,645
Killeen-Temple, TX Metro Area	405,298	425,230	19,941	4.9%	145,055	42,572	6,239	25,887	10,248
Kingsport-Bristol-Bristol, TN-VA Metro Area	309,542	308,590	-952	-0.3%	130,044	61,544	6,989	40,278	16,800
Kingston, NY Metro Area	182,494	180,445	-2,049	-1.1%	69,522	31,737	4,110	21,122	10,569
Klamath Falls, OR Micro Area	66,380	65,455	-925	-1.4%	26,377	12,304	1,962	8,131	3,880
Knoxville, TN Metro Area	837,579	857,385	19,806	2.4%	336,174	144,988	17,082	89,830	40,667
Kokomo, IN Metro Area	82,752	82,982	230	0.3%	34,026	14,846	1,972	9,929	4,491
La Crosse-Onalaska, WI-MN Metro Area	133,665	136,749	3,084	2.3%	54,762	20,808	3,288	12,824	5,290
Lafayette, LA Metro Area	466,750	484,974	18,224	3.9%	178,319	59,820	6,291	38,161	15,959
Lafayette-West Lafayette, IN Metro Area	201,789	211,515	9,726	4.8%	77,266	25,239	3,973	14,598	6,082
LaGrange, GA Micro Area	67,044	69,469	2,425	3.6%	23,942	9,657	810	6,242	2,673
Lake Charles, LA Metro Area	199,629	204,059	4,430	2.2%	76,395	28,372	3,620	17,517	7,411
Lake City, FL Micro Area	67,532	67,857	325	0.5%	23,825	11,980	1,642	7,095	3,083
Lake Havasu City-Kingman, AZ Metro Area	200,186	203,361	3,175	1.6%	81,292	55,039	4,626	32,387	10,922
Lakeland-Winter Haven, FL Metro Area	602,095	634,638	32,543	5.4%	218,286	124,198	14,528	74,155	26,525
Lancaster, PA Metro Area	519,448	533,320	13,872	2.7%	194,764	87,648	13,077	50,614	19,589
Lansing-East Lansing, MI Metro Area	464,032	470,458	6,426	1.4%	183,357	63,959	8,246	39,625	17,882
Laredo, TX Metro Area	250,304	266,673	16,369	6.5%	70,418	22,508	2,496	12,074	4,307
Las Cruces, NM Metro Area	209,241	213,676	4,435	2.1%	75,530	30,057	3,322	17,799	6,850
Las Vegas-Henderson-Paradise, NV Metro Area	1,951,269	2,069,681	118,412	6.1%	731,322	274,915	24,386	156,767	61,513
Laurel, MS Micro Area	84,823	84,836	13	0.0%	31,075	14,171	1,364	8,738	3,220
Lawrence, KS Metro Area	110,826	116,585	5,759	5.2%	45,224	12,127	1,714	7,496	na
Lawton, OK Metro Area	130,291	131,395	1,104	0.8%	43,648	15,157	1,325	9,147	4,071
Lebanon, PA Metro Area	133,573	136,359	2,786	2.1%	51,234	24,696	3,161	14,125	5,685
Lewiston, ID-WA Metro Area	60,888	62,196	1,308	2.1%	25,932	12,040	1,963	8,152	3,923
Lewiston-Auburn, ME Metro Area	107,702	107,440	-262	-0.2%	44,267	17,336	1,850	11,311	5,892
Lexington-Fayette, KY Metro Area	472,099	494,189	22,090	4.7%	196,716	62,177	8,799	39,175	16,904
Lima, OH Metro Area	106,331	105,040	-1,291	-1.2%	39,412	16,543	1,998	10,595	4,495
Lincoln, NE Metro Area	302,157	320,227	18,070	6.0%	125,923	39,384	5,181	25,476	11,144
Little Rock-North Little Rock-Conway, AR Metro Area	699,799	727,777	27,978	4.0%	273,841	98,729	12,027	60,596	24,667
Logan, UT-ID Metro Area	125,442	130,934	5,492	4.4%	40,017	11,813	1,509	7,340	na
London, KY Micro Area	126,369	127,315	946	0.7%	47,472	19,863	1,953	12,112	5,517
Longview, TX Metro Area	214,378	217,481	3,103	1.4%	78,567	32,254	3,906	19,425	8,646
Longview, WA Metro Area	102,410	102,133	-277	-0.3%	40,036	18,254	2,370	11,975	5,710
Los Angeles-Long Beach-Anaheim, CA Metro Area	12,828,933	13,262,220	433,287	3.4%	4,287,974	1,646,361	226,067	910,270	359,670
Louisville/Jefferson County, KY-IN Metro Area	1,235,710	1,265,210	29,500	2.4%	493,973	182,428	24,565	115,701	51,037
Lubbock, TX Metro Area	290,805	305,262	14,457	5.0%	115,322	36,837	4,413	24,877	10,937
Lufkin, TX Micro Area	86,771	87,750	979	1.1%	30,344	13,926	2,710	7,889	3,505
Lumberton, NC Micro Area	134,168	134,760	592	0.4%	46,484	17,379	1,812	11,080	4,770
Lynchburg, VA Metro Area	252,656	257,570	4,914	1.9%	98,399	45,279	5,501	28,161	11,649
Macon, GA Metro Area	232,293	233,212	919	0.4%	84,688	33,763	4,264	20,490	8,996
Madera, CA Metro Area	150,865	154,548	3,683	2.4%	42,895	19,640	2,663	10,815	3,722
Madison, WI Metro Area	605,437	633,787	28,350	4.7%	259,371	80,723	11,396	50,608	21,829
Manchester-Nashua, NH Metro Area	400,721	405,184	4,463	1.1%	153,482	56,374	7,581	31,803	13,660
Manhattan, KS Metro Area	92,735	98,091	5,356	5.8%	34,452	9,055	1,158	5,683	na
Manitowoc, WI Micro Area	81,442	80,160	-1,282	-1.6%	33,272	15,034	2,685	9,744	4,909
Mankato-North Mankato, MN Metro Area	96,740	98,478	1,738	1.8%	37,736	12,905	2,212	7,626	3,390
Mansfield, OH Metro Area	124,475	121,942	-2,533	-2.0%	47,378	22,015	2,710	15,369	7,499
Marinette, WI-MI Micro Area	65,778	65,012	-766	-1.2%	30,183	14,023	2,053	8,992	4,380
Marion, IN Micro Area	70,063	68,569	-1,494	-2.1%	25,600	12,016	1,690	8,091	3,745
Marion, OH Micro Area	66,501	65,720	-781	-1.2%	24,346	11,007	1,613	7,518	3,183
Marquette, MI Micro Area	67,077	67,676	599	0.9%	26,250	11,257	1,324	6,904	3,186
Marshall, TX Micro Area	65,632	67,336	1,704	2.6%	22,997	10,152	1,653	7,012	2,698
Martinsville, VA Micro Area	67,964	65,878	-2,086	-3.1%	27,434	14,229	1,790	9,167	3,992
McAllen-Edinburg-Mission, TX Metro Area	774,773	831,073	56,300	7.3%	226,000	86,414	10,077	44,905	13,426
Meadville, PA Micro Area	88,765	87,175	-1,590	-1.8%	34,834	15,919	1,617	10,082	4,075
Medford, OR Metro Area	203,206	210,287	7,081	3.5%	83,131	42,200	5,864	26,718	11,568
Memphis, TN-MS-AR Metro Area	1,324,829	1,344,121	19,292	1.5%	493,329	162,772	19,998	100,887	41,625
Merced, CA Metro Area	255,798	266,353	10,555	4.1%	79,255	28,299	3,565	16,007	6,520
Meridian, MS Micro Area	107,454	105,464	-1,990	-1.9%	39,485	16,019	2,136	10,037	5,132
Miami-Fort Lauderdale-West Palm Beach, FL Metro Area	5,566,299	5,929,819	363,520	6.5%	2,047,325	1,009,172	162,697	567,027	252,294
Michigan City-La Porte, IN Metro Area	111,467	111,444	-23	-0.0%	42,068	17,551	2,100	11,239	5,178
Midland, MI Metro Area	83,629	83,427	-202	-0.2%	33,579	13,835	1,902	8,858	3,516
Midland, TX Metro Area	141,674	163,470	21,796	15.4%	55,814	15,795	2,217	9,395	4,316
Milwaukee-Waukesha-West Allis, WI Metro Area	1,555,954	1,572,245	16,291	1.0%	626,248	217,476	34,748	138,369	67,008
Minneapolis-St. Paul-Bloomington, MN-WI Metro Area	3,348,857	3,495,176	146,319	4.4%	1,337,263	429,252	60,948	267,566	120,331
Minot, ND Micro Area	69,540	79,188	9,648	13.9%	30,112	9,354	1,801	5,950	na
Missoula, MT Metro Area	109,299	112,684	3,385	3.1%	46,407	15,155	2,649	10,170	4,084
Mobile, AL Metro Area	413,143	415,123	1,980	0.5%	153,450	60,050	8,299	37,513	15,114
Modesto, CA Metro Area	514,451	531,997	17,546	3.4%	169,038	64,448	8,466	37,075	14,763
Monroe, LA Metro Area	176,502	178,864	2,362	1.3%	66,596	24,659	2,628	15,804	6,299
Monroe, MI Metro Area	152,021	149,824	-2,197	-1.4%	57,879	23,690	3,255	13,962	6,240
Montgomery, AL Metro Area	374,529	374,430	-99	-0.0%	142,432	51,069	4,777	32,901	14,376
Morehead City, NC Micro Area	66,469	68,811	2,342	3.5%	28,773	15,294	1,462	9,697	4,098
Morgantown, WV Metro Area	129,709	137,251	7,542	5.8%	49,804	16,881	2,073	10,484	4,691
Morristown, TN Metro Area	114,111	115,713	1,602	1.4%	45,581	21,165	1,795	12,957	4,853
Moses Lake, WA Micro Area	89,120	93,147	4,027	4.5%	29,758	11,740	1,346	7,129	3,208

Table A-4: Metropolitan/Micropolitan Statistical Areas—Summary Population Characteristics—*Continued*

	April 1, 2010 Census Population Estimates Base	2014 ACS Population	2010-2014 Population Change	2010-2014 Percent Change	Total Households	2014 ACS Population 65 and Over	Population 85 and Over	Householders 65 and Over	Persons 65 and Over Living Alone
Mount Airy, NC Micro Area	73,673	72,968	-705	-1.0%	27,632	13,770	1,826	8,171	3,373
Mount Pleasant, MI Micro Area	70,311	70,616	305	0.4%	24,999	7,589	999	4,940	2,274
Mount Vernon-Anacortes, WA Metro Area	116,901	120,365	3,464	3.0%	45,447	22,864	2,862	13,628	5,625
Muncie, IN Metro Area	117,671	117,074	-597	-0.5%	45,207	18,735	2,883	11,571	4,323
Muskegon, MI Metro Area	172,188	172,344	156	0.1%	64,646	25,849	3,289	17,066	7,244
Muskogee, OK Micro Area	70,988	69,966	-1,022	-1.4%	26,016	11,148	1,696	6,952	3,083
Myrtle Beach-Conway-North Myrtle Beach, SC-NC Metro Area	376,722	417,668	40,946	10.9%	174,999	93,105	7,190	57,080	21,982
Nacogdoches, TX Micro Area	64,524	65,301	777	1.2%	24,734	8,511	1,127	5,704	na
Napa, CA Metro Area	136,530	141,667	5,137	3.8%	50,516	24,631	3,589	14,395	5,623
Naples-Immokalee-Marco Island, FL Metro Area	321,520	348,777	27,257	8.5%	133,162	102,262	11,201	59,575	21,109
Nashville-Davidson–Murfreesboro–Franklin, TN Metro Area	1,670,900	1,792,468	121,568	7.3%	674,665	218,527	22,545	132,276	55,432
New Bern, NC Metro Area	126,802	127,886	1,084	0.9%	49,335	23,613	3,152	15,137	6,107
New Castle, PA Micro Area	91,140	88,771	-2,369	-2.6%	35,935	17,555	3,075	11,449	4,809
New Haven-Milford, CT Metro Area	862,474	861,277	-1,197	-0.1%	326,050	134,334	22,801	82,837	41,386
New Orleans-Metairie, LA Metro Area	1,189,863	1,251,849	61,986	5.2%	474,715	171,538	20,088	107,714	44,804
New Philadelphia-Dover, OH Micro Area	92,582	92,788	206	0.2%	37,516	16,746	2,740	10,625	5,366
New York-Newark-Jersey City, NY-NJ-PA Metro Area	19,566,440	20,092,883	526,443	2.7%	7,152,760	2,829,805	417,907	1,691,688	767,324
Niles-Benton Harbor, MI Metro Area	156,817	155,233	-1,584	-1.0%	62,984	27,218	3,430	17,528	7,677
North Port-Sarasota-Bradenton, FL Metro Area	702,270	748,708	46,438	6.6%	313,576	224,773	30,936	136,689	52,489
North Wilkesboro, NC Micro Area	69,340	68,838	-502	-0.7%	27,257	13,662	1,405	8,517	3,978
Norwich-New London, CT Metro Area	274,046	273,676	-370	-0.1%	105,504	44,057	5,971	26,286	11,210
Oak Harbor, WA Micro Area	78,506	79,275	769	1.0%	32,464	18,182	1,979	10,375	3,594
Ocala, FL Metro Area	331,303	339,167	7,864	2.4%	132,275	94,207	11,070	57,018	21,705
Ocean City, NJ Metro Area	97,265	95,344	-1,921	-2.0%	40,779	22,927	2,659	14,468	5,814
Odessa, TX Metro Area	137,133	153,904	16,771	12.2%	50,724	14,664	1,798	9,158	3,976
Ogden-Clearfield, UT Metro Area	597,159	631,146	33,987	5.7%	199,206	63,949	7,310	37,737	13,484
Ogdensburg-Massena, NY Micro Area	111,944	111,400	-544	-0.5%	40,286	16,993	2,445	9,894	5,223
Oklahoma City, OK Metro Area	1,252,992	1,336,767	83,775	6.7%	499,878	169,740	19,844	105,072	44,031
Olean, NY Micro Area	80,317	78,600	-1,717	-2.1%	30,735	13,428	1,680	8,548	4,118
Olympia-Tumwater, WA Metro Area	252,264	265,851	13,587	5.4%	103,319	40,285	4,593	24,728	10,607
Omaha-Council Bluffs, NE-IA Metro Area	865,350	904,491	39,141	4.5%	346,283	110,526	16,822	71,113	33,284
Opelousas, LA Micro Area	83,384	83,709	325	0.4%	28,739	12,313	1,937	7,856	3,567
Orangeburg, SC Micro Area	92,495	90,090	-2,405	-2.6%	31,350	15,222	2,064	9,240	4,609
Orlando-Kissimmee-Sanford, FL Metro Area	2,134,406	2,321,418	187,012	8.8%	800,299	321,161	40,917	174,137	65,740
Oshkosh-Neenah, WI Metro Area	166,994	169,511	2,517	1.5%	69,417	25,191	3,315	16,060	7,494
Ottawa-Peru, IL Micro Area	154,906	151,415	-3,491	-2.3%	59,853	27,752	4,693	17,048	7,065
Owensboro, KY Metro Area	114,755	116,170	1,415	1.2%	46,540	19,370	2,088	12,013	4,866
Owosso, MI Micro Area	70,648	68,933	-1,715	-2.4%	27,285	11,593	1,745	6,935	2,678
Oxnard-Thousand Oaks-Ventura, CA Metro Area	823,420	846,178	22,758	2.8%	269,869	114,954	17,233	68,153	26,075
Paducah, KY-IL Micro Area	98,760	97,953	-807	-0.8%	41,394	17,976	2,744	10,957	4,667
Palatka, FL Micro Area	74,364	72,143	-2,221	-3.0%	26,580	14,899	952	10,067	4,826
Palm Bay-Melbourne-Titusville, FL Metro Area	543,378	556,885	13,507	2.5%	225,226	126,012	17,681	76,243	29,395
Panama City, FL Metro Area	184,715	192,406	7,691	4.2%	71,161	31,924	3,634	18,635	7,295
Parkersburg-Vienna, WV Metro Area	92,673	92,684	11	0.0%	38,667	17,292	2,048	11,881	5,970
Pensacola-Ferry Pass-Brent, FL Metro Area	448,991	474,081	25,090	5.6%	171,179	72,918	7,728	44,926	17,398
Peoria, IL Metro Area	379,186	379,520	334	0.1%	149,515	60,638	9,073	38,761	17,460
Philadelphia-Camden-Wilmington, PA-NJ-DE-MD Metro Area	5,965,368	6,051,170	85,802	1.4%	2,230,807	878,054	130,096	542,821	245,485
Phoenix-Mesa-Scottsdale, AZ Metro Area	4,193,127	4,489,109	295,982	7.1%	1,590,240	637,879	75,192	378,994	152,401
Pine Bluff, AR Metro Area	100,258	95,127	-5,131	-5.1%	35,978	14,658	1,609	9,236	4,029
Pinehurst-Southern Pines, NC Micro Area	88,247	93,077	4,830	5.5%	37,179	22,340	4,339	13,871	5,835
Pittsburgh, PA Metro Area	2,356,285	2,355,968	-317	-0.0%	991,951	432,142	71,675	281,313	134,062
Pittsfield, MA Metro Area	131,272	128,715	-2,557	-1.9%	54,706	26,665	4,323	17,764	8,852
Plattsburgh, NY Micro Area	82,128	81,632	-496	-0.6%	31,426	12,286	1,290	7,776	3,495
Pocatello, ID Metro Area	82,839	83,347	508	0.6%	30,240	10,666	888	6,874	3,152
Port Angeles, WA Micro Area	71,404	72,715	1,311	1.8%	31,361	19,479	3,167	12,052	5,542
Port St. Lucie, FL Metro Area	424,107	444,420	20,313	4.8%	171,289	109,900	16,537	67,256	28,593
Portland-South Portland, ME Metro Area	514,100	523,552	9,452	1.8%	215,232	89,941	12,407	56,005	24,408
Portland-Vancouver-Hillsboro, OR-WA Metro Area	2,226,011	2,347,127	121,116	5.4%	894,801	311,095	40,494	190,816	84,137
Portsmouth, OH Micro Area	79,499	77,258	-2,241	-2.8%	30,790	12,766	1,687	7,877	3,455
Pottsville, PA Micro Area	148,289	145,797	-2,492	-1.7%	58,061	28,211	4,590	17,799	8,715
Prescott, AZ Metro Area	211,015	218,844	7,829	3.7%	90,584	61,708	7,413	38,908	15,845
Providence-Warwick, RI-MA Metro Area	1,601,216	1,609,367	8,151	0.5%	622,555	254,223	42,071	155,267	72,387
Provo-Orem, UT Metro Area	526,810	572,798	45,988	8.7%	154,567	41,046	3,300	22,346	5,533
Pueblo, CO Metro Area	159,063	161,875	2,812	1.8%	63,385	27,960	3,506	17,236	7,811
Punta Gorda, FL Metro Area	159,989	168,474	8,485	5.3%	75,234	63,386	7,724	38,266	14,681
Quincy, IL-MO Micro Area	77,314	76,618	-696	-0.9%	31,347	14,137	2,567	9,020	4,306
Racine, WI Metro Area	195,428	195,163	-265	-0.1%	75,876	29,486	4,309	19,041	9,100
Raleigh, NC Metro Area	1,130,490	1,242,974	112,484	10.0%	457,547	132,215	12,671	79,654	31,843
Rapid City, SD Metro Area	134,609	143,867	9,258	6.9%	56,274	21,760	3,100	13,423	6,108
Reading, PA Metro Area	411,587	413,691	2,104	0.5%	152,908	66,449	9,085	40,172	16,546
Redding, CA Metro Area	177,223	179,804	2,581	1.5%	68,542	34,665	4,885	21,110	8,847
Reno, NV Metro Area	425,437	444,487	19,050	4.5%	168,863	65,768	6,619	41,425	18,412
Richmond, IN Micro Area	69,003	67,671	-1,332	-1.9%	26,937	12,325	1,278	7,721	2,908
Richmond, VA Metro Area	1,208,080	1,260,668	52,588	4.4%	474,003	171,447	23,009	107,795	48,989

Table A-4: Metropolitan/Micropolitan Statistical Areas—Summary Population Characteristics—*Continued*

	April 1, 2010 Census Population Estimates Base	2014 ACS Population	2010-2014 Population Change	2010-2014 Percent Change	Total Households	2014 ACS			
						Population 65 and Over	Population 85 and Over	Householders 65 and Over	Persons 65 and Over Living Alone
Richmond-Berea, KY Micro Area	99,972	103,645	3,673	3.7%	39,682	14,076	1,428	8,709	3,089
Riverside-San Bernardino-Ontario, CA Metro Area	4,224,972	4,441,890	216,918	5.1%	1,317,650	525,345	65,136	288,442	109,804
Roanoke Rapids, NC Micro Area	76,789	73,433	-3,356	-4.4%	28,010	14,119	1,689	9,066	4,569
Roanoke, VA Metro Area	308,693	312,837	4,144	1.3%	129,528	57,681	8,392	36,891	16,214
Rochester, MN Metro Area	206,877	212,778	5,901	2.9%	83,812	31,746	4,782	19,359	7,885
Rochester, NY Metro Area	1,079,692	1,083,393	3,701	0.3%	428,750	173,008	27,164	110,552	55,187
Rockford, IL Metro Area	349,431	342,411	-7,020	-2.0%	133,136	52,810	6,727	33,441	16,285
Rocky Mount, NC Metro Area	152,388	149,290	-3,098	-2.0%	58,714	24,752	2,592	16,555	8,389
Rome, GA Metro Area	96,317	96,063	-254	-0.3%	36,177	14,678	2,121	9,055	3,938
Roseburg, OR Micro Area	107,667	106,972	-695	-0.6%	43,290	25,170	3,680	15,674	6,690
Roswell, NM Micro Area	65,645	65,878	233	0.4%	23,747	9,807	711	6,495	3,024
Russellville, AR Micro Area	83,939	85,152	1,213	1.4%	30,488	13,147	1,342	7,902	3,512
Sacramento–Roseville–Arden-Arcade, CA Metro Area	2,149,143	2,244,397	95,254	4.4%	797,624	312,731	39,143	185,384	76,968
Saginaw, MI Metro Area	200,169	195,012	-5,157	-2.6%	78,000	33,397	3,726	21,226	8,190
Salem, OH Micro Area	107,841	105,686	-2,155	-2.0%	42,107	19,192	2,592	12,009	5,358
Salem, OR Metro Area	390,738	404,026	13,288	3.4%	141,971	60,787	7,964	38,294	16,715
Salinas, CA Metro Area	415,057	431,344	16,287	3.9%	123,920	51,152	7,658	30,238	11,543
Salisbury, MD-DE Metro Area	373,769	389,922	16,153	4.3%	151,227	81,658	9,044	49,882	18,301
Salt Lake City, UT Metro Area	1,087,873	1,153,340	65,467	6.0%	376,913	110,379	13,081	67,200	26,953
San Angelo, TX Metro Area	111,823	118,296	6,473	5.8%	43,143	17,528	2,505	10,610	5,748
San Antonio-New Braunfels, TX Metro Area	2,142,518	2,326,665	184,147	8.6%	786,460	281,067	33,675	166,825	66,290
San Diego-Carlsbad, CA Metro Area	3,095,308	3,263,431	168,123	5.4%	1,100,858	414,632	56,136	234,218	94,278
San Francisco-Oakland-Hayward, CA Metro Area	4,335,560	4,594,060	258,500	6.0%	1,665,925	643,065	90,288	374,843	160,436
San Jose-Sunnyvale-Santa Clara, CA Metro Area	1,836,941	1,952,872	115,931	6.3%	639,301	237,813	29,742	127,012	48,703
San Luis Obispo-Paso Robles-Arroyo Grande, CA Metro Area	269,593	279,083	9,490	3.5%	102,645	49,252	5,523	29,273	12,439
Sandusky, OH Micro Area	77,079	75,828	-1,251	-1.6%	31,492	14,039	1,942	9,653	4,411
Santa Cruz-Watsonville, CA Metro Area	262,362	271,804	9,442	3.6%	96,127	36,267	4,187	22,945	9,828
Santa Fe, NM Metro Area	144,171	148,164	3,993	2.8%	60,565	29,029	2,639	18,581	8,610
Santa Maria-Santa Barbara, CA Metro Area	423,939	440,668	16,729	3.9%	142,912	61,405	10,704	37,459	16,155
Santa Rosa, CA Metro Area	483,880	500,292	16,412	3.4%	190,875	82,536	13,079	51,802	23,254
Savannah, GA Metro Area	347,621	372,708	25,087	7.2%	135,708	47,695	6,232	28,809	12,041
Scranton–Wilkes-Barre–Hazleton, PA Metro Area	563,630	559,679	-3,951	-0.7%	220,225	105,588	19,015	64,628	32,472
Searcy, AR Micro Area	77,076	78,592	1,516	2.0%	29,146	11,920	1,233	7,197	2,642
Seattle-Tacoma-Bellevue, WA Metro Area	3,439,815	3,671,478	231,663	6.7%	1,406,259	449,976	63,806	272,064	121,662
Sebastian-Vero Beach, FL Metro Area	138,028	144,755	6,727	4.9%	55,618	43,896	7,638	26,256	10,372
Sebring, FL Metro Area	98,786	98,236	-550	-0.6%	39,288	33,181	3,933	19,624	7,306
Seneca, SC Micro Area	74,275	75,192	917	1.2%	32,113	15,950	1,271	9,788	na
Sevierville, TN Micro Area	89,876	95,110	5,234	5.8%	35,072	16,976	1,475	10,950	4,455
Shawnee, OK Micro Area	69,442	71,811	2,369	3.4%	25,733	11,228	1,390	6,475	2,581
Sheboygan, WI Metro Area	115,507	115,290	-217	-0.2%	46,504	18,520	2,826	11,782	5,817
Shelby, NC Micro Area	98,083	97,076	-1,007	-1.0%	37,038	16,837	1,817	11,438	4,501
Sherman-Denison, TX Metro Area	120,877	123,534	2,657	2.2%	46,621	20,866	2,202	12,404	5,359
Show Low, AZ Micro Area	107,494	108,101	607	0.6%	33,236	17,129	1,339	10,706	3,276
Shreveport-Bossier City, LA Metro Area	439,811	445,142	5,331	1.2%	167,018	65,150	8,423	40,247	18,554
Sierra Vista-Douglas, AZ Metro Area	131,357	127,448	-3,909	-3.0%	47,653	25,160	3,151	15,100	6,212
Sioux City, IA-NE-SD Metro Area	168,563	169,058	495	0.3%	64,369	24,983	3,696	15,558	7,346
Sioux Falls, SD Metro Area	228,264	248,252	19,988	8.8%	94,764	30,550	4,488	18,872	8,977
Somerset, PA Micro Area	77,748	76,218	-1,530	-2.0%	29,481	15,608	2,400	9,658	4,393
South Bend-Mishawaka, IN-MI Metro Area	319,215	319,226	11	0.0%	121,857	47,979	7,211	30,275	13,277
Spartanburg, SC Metro Area	313,268	321,418	8,150	2.6%	121,860	49,559	4,979	31,274	12,489
Spokane-Spokane Valley, WA Metro Area	527,753	542,073	14,320	2.7%	209,867	83,901	11,625	52,153	22,812
Springfield, IL Metro Area	210,170	211,311	1,141	0.5%	88,468	33,942	4,697	21,883	10,529
Springfield, MA Metro Area	621,705	629,100	7,395	1.2%	235,074	95,123	15,582	60,219	29,020
Springfield, MO Metro Area	436,712	450,619	13,907	3.2%	179,069	69,605	9,635	44,305	19,149
Springfield, OH Metro Area	138,333	136,554	-1,779	-1.3%	55,199	24,356	3,393	15,290	6,659
St. Cloud, MN Metro Area	189,093	192,418	3,325	1.8%	72,884	25,714	3,779	15,334	6,197
St. George, UT Metro Area	138,115	151,948	13,833	10.0%	49,468	30,065	3,932	17,020	4,760
St. Joseph, MO-KS Metro Area	127,329	127,671	342	0.3%	46,526	19,344	2,570	12,920	6,613
St. Louis, MO-IL Metro Area	2,787,747	2,805,856	18,109	0.6%	1,096,200	417,428	55,504	265,178	116,235
State College, PA Metro Area	153,981	158,742	4,761	3.1%	57,583	19,873	2,417	12,199	4,872
Statesboro, GA Micro Area	70,217	72,087	1,870	2.7%	25,844	7,492	760	4,989	2,147
Staunton-Waynesboro, VA Metro Area	118,502	119,766	1,264	1.1%	48,754	22,989	1,478	14,271	5,266
Stevens Point, WI Micro Area	70,019	70,482	463	0.7%	27,360	10,224	1,110	6,738	2,830
Stillwater, OK Micro Area	77,350	80,264	2,914	3.8%	29,934	8,789	1,339	5,632	2,557
Stockton-Lodi, CA Metro Area	685,308	715,597	30,289	4.4%	221,874	84,298	10,225	44,199	17,606
Sumter, SC Metro Area	107,463	107,919	456	0.4%	39,936	15,488	1,882	9,981	4,077
Sunbury, PA Micro Area	94,517	93,944	-573	-0.6%	38,712	18,608	2,721	11,777	4,792
Syracuse, NY Metro Area	662,578	661,478	-1,100	-0.2%	257,052	100,421	15,620	62,523	29,382
Talladega-Sylacauga, AL Micro Area	94,049	91,507	-2,542	-2.7%	34,375	15,341	1,752	9,339	3,896
Tallahassee, FL Metro Area	368,770	374,890	6,120	1.7%	144,333	45,738	5,566	30,156	13,640
Tampa-St. Petersburg-Clearwater, FL Metro Area	2,783,514	2,915,582	132,068	4.7%	1,149,735	545,152	79,583	332,612	147,448
Terre Haute, IN Metro Area	172,422	171,555	-867	-0.5%	65,313	26,056	4,249	16,481	7,195
Texarkana, TX-AR Metro Area	149,195	147,740	-1,455	-1.0%	54,860	23,048	2,784	14,570	6,265
The Villages, FL Metro Area	93,420	114,350	20,930	22.4%	50,209	60,225	4,423	34,307	8,031
Toledo, OH Metro Area	610,001	607,456	-2,545	-0.4%	242,952	88,188	13,882	56,992	27,343
Topeka, KS Metro Area	233,868	233,758	-110	-0.0%	92,799	38,126	5,675	24,175	10,181
Torrington, CT Micro Area	189,927	184,993	-4,934	-2.6%	73,572	34,102	5,055	20,304	8,802

Table A-4: Metropolitan/Micropolitan Statistical Areas—Summary Population Characteristics—*Continued*

	April 1, 2010 Census Population Estimates Base	2014 ACS Population	2010-2014 Population Change	2010-2014 Percent Change	Total Households	2014 ACS			
						Population 65 and Over	Population 85 and Over	Householders 65 and Over	Persons 65 and Over Living Alone
Traverse City, MI Micro Area	143,372	147,610	4,238	3.0%	58,898	29,046	3,001	18,300	7,583
Trenton, NJ Metro Area	367,508	371,537	4,029	1.1%	131,564	51,229	6,863	30,427	12,582
Truckee-Grass Valley, CA Micro Area	98,748	98,893	145	0.1%	40,186	23,122	2,911	13,350	4,483
Tucson, AZ Metro Area	980,263	1,004,516	24,253	2.5%	389,737	178,045	20,248	112,162	47,908
Tullahoma-Manchester, TN Micro Area	100,209	102,651	2,442	2.4%	40,421	18,288	1,521	12,022	5,016
Tulsa, OK Metro Area	937,528	970,391	32,863	3.5%	375,790	137,415	16,548	85,626	36,502
Tupelo, MS Micro Area	136,268	139,723	3,455	2.5%	50,641	20,215	3,008	12,350	5,525
Tuscaloosa, AL Metro Area	230,159	235,954	5,795	2.5%	80,582	30,054	4,896	18,044	8,032
Twin Falls, ID Micro Area	99,604	105,226	5,622	5.6%	37,258	15,304	1,728	9,351	4,088
Tyler, TX Metro Area	209,714	218,842	9,128	4.4%	77,469	33,899	4,075	20,300	8,347
Ukiah, CA Micro Area	87,840	87,869	29	0.0%	33,464	16,976	2,172	10,713	4,854
Urban Honolulu, HI Metro Area	953,207	991,788	38,581	4.0%	309,002	156,728	27,910	83,122	27,905
Utica-Rome, NY Metro Area	299,382	296,615	-2,767	-0.9%	116,231	52,755	8,393	31,917	14,491
Valdosta, GA Metro Area	139,665	143,140	3,475	2.5%	49,067	17,171	1,065	11,392	5,099
Vallejo-Fairfield, CA Metro Area	413,344	431,131	17,787	4.3%	145,313	58,204	5,866	33,203	13,130
Victoria, TX Metro Area	94,003	99,536	5,533	5.9%	35,523	14,742	1,954	9,079	3,393
Vineland-Bridgeton, NJ Metro Area	156,898	157,389	491	0.3%	50,593	21,282	2,994	13,024	5,311
Virginia Beach-Norfolk-Newport News, VA-NC Metro Area	1,676,817	1,717,387	40,570	2.4%	637,189	222,256	28,249	139,331	58,701
Visalia-Porterville, CA Metro Area	442,182	458,198	16,016	3.6%	132,742	47,336	6,886	25,327	7,859
Waco, TX Metro Area	252,772	261,958	9,186	3.6%	93,166	35,065	4,429	22,603	9,355
Walla Walla, WA Metro Area	62,859	63,706	847	1.3%	23,296	10,261	1,645	6,214	na
Warner Robins, GA Metro Area	179,605	186,675	7,070	3.9%	67,667	22,239	2,484	13,927	5,136
Warsaw, IN Micro Area	77,356	78,564	1,208	1.6%	29,741	11,763	1,062	7,172	2,765
Washington-Arlington-Alexandria, DC-VA-MD-WV Metro Area	5,636,406	6,032,744	396,338	7.0%	2,154,147	687,817	87,227	402,152	166,386
Waterloo-Cedar Falls, IA Metro Area	167,819	169,993	2,174	1.3%	67,957	26,495	3,349	17,443	8,694
Watertown-Fort Atkinson, WI Micro Area	83,681	84,395	714	0.9%	31,607	12,488	1,512	7,994	3,767
Watertown-Fort Drum, NY Metro Area	116,229	119,103	2,874	2.5%	43,516	14,632	1,566	8,616	3,588
Wausau, WI Metro Area	134,063	135,780	1,717	1.3%	54,739	21,426	3,386	13,355	5,654
Weirton-Steubenville, WV-OH Metro Area	124,454	125,467	1,013	0.8%	51,058	24,105	3,271	15,436	6,789
Wenatchee, WA Metro Area	110,887	114,392	3,505	3.2%	41,500	19,406	2,660	11,579	4,664
Wheeling, WV-OH Metro Area	147,950	145,205	-2,745	-1.9%	58,775	27,773	3,756	17,770	7,854
Whitewater-Elkhorn, WI Micro Area	102,228	103,527	1,299	1.3%	39,679	15,610	1,950	9,925	4,794
Wichita Falls, TX Metro Area	151,476	151,536	60	0.0%	54,196	21,784	3,035	14,242	6,957
Wichita, KS Metro Area	630,919	641,225	10,306	1.6%	240,230	86,458	11,172	54,312	24,353
Williamsport, PA Metro Area	116,108	116,508	400	0.3%	45,742	20,476	3,224	12,944	5,969
Wilmington, NC Metro Area	254,884	272,548	17,664	6.9%	110,993	43,583	5,031	26,961	10,640
Wilson, NC Micro Area	81,234	81,401	167	0.2%	32,691	13,432	1,473	8,299	3,485
Winchester, VA-WV Metro Area	128,473	134,221	5,748	4.5%	51,140	21,556	3,148	13,121	5,710
Winston-Salem, NC Metro Area	640,577	655,015	14,438	2.3%	256,999	102,715	11,775	66,793	29,748
Wisconsin Rapids-Marshfield, WI Micro Area	74,749	73,608	-1,141	-1.5%	32,383	13,822	2,581	9,251	4,436
Wooster, OH Micro Area	114,514	115,537	1,023	0.9%	42,830	18,369	2,491	10,626	4,037
Worcester, MA-CT Metro Area	916,976	930,473	13,497	1.5%	344,496	131,819	20,416	78,939	35,083
Yakima, WA Metro Area	243,231	247,687	4,456	1.8%	79,700	31,605	3,816	18,654	7,886
York-Hanover, PA Metro Area	435,002	440,755	5,753	1.3%	169,212	70,222	7,480	41,712	16,430
Youngstown-Warren-Boardman, OH-PA Metro Area	565,804	553,263	-12,541	-2.2%	228,797	107,054	18,314	68,851	32,182
Yuba City, CA Metro Area	166,892	169,813	2,921	1.8%	57,366	22,708	2,773	13,359	5,511
Yuma, AZ Metro Area	195,750	203,247	7,497	3.8%	70,593	35,937	2,445	22,044	7,789
Zanesville, OH Micro Area	86,074	85,818	-256	-0.3%	33,921	14,224	2,018	9,403	4,324

Table A-5: 114th Congressional Districts—Summary Population Characteristics

	April 1, 2010 Census Population	2014 ACS Population	2010-2014 Population Change	2010-2014 Percent Change	Total Households	2014 ACS			
						Population 65 and Over	Population 85 and Over	Householders 65 and Over	Persons 65 and Over Living Alone
Alabama									
Congressional District 1	682,820	696,783	13,963	2.0%	255,303	113,016	13,300	71,277	29,600
Congressional District 2	682,820	678,622	-4,198	-0.6%	258,138	105,469	11,163	67,200	30,080
Congressional District 3	682,819	706,574	23,755	3.5%	270,971	105,875	11,081	67,169	28,268
Congressional District 4	682,819	683,372	553	0.1%	259,439	117,390	12,520	73,422	32,303
Congressional District 5	682,819	706,373	23,554	3.4%	274,891	106,010	11,626	66,956	29,381
Congressional District 6	682,819	696,788	13,969	2.0%	265,000	106,530	11,608	66,627	27,098
Congressional District 7	682,820	680,865	-1,955	-0.3%	257,475	92,222	12,251	60,017	26,396
Alaska									
Congressional District (at Large)	710,231	736,732	26,501	3.7%	249,659	69,899	6,237	40,996	16,214
Arizona									
Congressional District 1	710,224	739,373	29,149	4.1%	249,074	120,886	10,185	75,218	26,032
Congressional District 2	710,224	713,036	2,812	0.4%	292,370	139,664	18,057	89,098	39,806
Congressional District 3	710,224	757,119	46,895	6.6%	234,874	81,001	5,649	46,538	18,110
Congressional District 4	710,224	734,258	24,034	3.4%	282,598	191,506	17,400	113,071	39,986
Congressional District 5	710,224	781,441	71,217	10.0%	269,256	121,024	16,338	70,872	27,833
Congressional District 6	710,224	737,185	26,961	3.8%	299,053	123,006	14,650	76,013	30,735
Congressional District 7	710,224	763,089	52,865	7.4%	224,388	53,047	4,980	30,263	13,681
Congressional District 8	710,225	760,904	50,679	7.1%	284,913	154,715	20,239	94,086	37,929
Congressional District 9	710,224	745,079	34,855	4.9%	292,217	85,908	12,096	52,453	24,463
Arkansas									
Congressional District 1	728,765	723,492	-5,273	-0.7%	282,699	125,713	14,206	79,867	35,227
Congressional District 2	729,192	756,326	27,134	3.7%	285,873	107,177	13,832	65,456	26,755
Congressional District 3	728,959	767,904	38,945	5.3%	283,989	104,556	12,609	65,607	28,500
Congressional District 4	729,002	718,647	-10,355	-1.4%	278,727	127,566	14,849	78,872	32,924
California									
Congressional District 1	702,905	710,428	7,523	1.1%	273,795	139,511	19,970	84,018	35,203
Congressional District 2	702,905	720,049	17,144	2.4%	280,016	129,623	17,235	81,683	37,615
Congressional District 3	702,906	720,104	17,198	2.4%	245,160	93,212	10,917	55,847	24,154
Congressional District 4	702,906	719,688	16,782	2.4%	267,604	137,704	14,064	84,023	33,349
Congressional District 5	702,905	722,814	19,909	2.8%	265,421	115,118	16,164	69,937	29,738
Congressional District 6	702,905	737,671	34,766	4.9%	264,422	83,495	10,614	50,970	22,299
Congressional District 7	702,904	736,555	33,651	4.8%	258,041	104,127	13,894	59,781	24,014
Congressional District 8	702,905	715,953	13,048	1.9%	231,229	91,372	9,438	54,549	20,670
Congressional District 9	702,904	738,320	35,416	5.0%	230,743	90,961	11,453	47,782	17,213
Congressional District 10	702,905	732,084	29,179	4.2%	228,743	83,750	10,199	47,092	18,877
Congressional District 11	702,906	739,693	36,787	5.2%	268,357	111,746	16,435	66,857	27,821
Congressional District 12	702,905	736,123	33,218	4.7%	318,240	106,978	16,350	65,252	32,444
Congressional District 13	702,906	743,310	40,404	5.7%	282,191	92,962	13,273	59,551	27,928
Congressional District 14	702,905	753,002	50,097	7.1%	249,842	108,974	13,556	59,497	23,616
Congressional District 15	702,904	753,911	51,007	7.3%	245,929	94,419	12,964	49,013	17,944
Congressional District 16	702,904	718,849	15,945	2.3%	207,675	73,473	10,000	40,628	16,364
Congressional District 17	702,904	756,995	54,091	7.7%	248,336	86,689	10,288	43,857	15,722
Congressional District 18	702,906	734,378	31,472	4.5%	269,816	105,697	15,079	61,855	23,903
Congressional District 19	702,904	746,211	43,307	6.2%	221,998	86,993	10,483	44,725	17,239
Congressional District 20	702,906	732,074	29,168	4.1%	222,810	86,320	11,972	52,030	21,464
Congressional District 21	702,904	712,295	9,391	1.3%	181,929	56,320	5,847	30,001	9,887
Congressional District 22	702,905	739,418	36,513	5.2%	235,530	85,553	12,587	48,857	18,738
Congressional District 23	702,904	747,914	45,010	6.4%	240,106	86,903	10,797	50,468	20,185
Congressional District 24	702,904	726,519	23,615	3.4%	248,895	111,451	16,266	67,270	28,943
Congressional District 25	702,904	718,796	15,892	2.3%	220,969	75,750	8,088	40,984	14,814
Congressional District 26	702,905	725,795	22,890	3.3%	228,883	98,519	15,675	58,450	22,200
Congressional District 27	702,905	714,911	12,006	1.7%	239,911	116,157	17,998	60,320	23,239
Congressional District 28	702,904	721,435	18,531	2.6%	292,855	103,760	13,225	58,539	25,887
Congressional District 29	702,905	718,633	15,728	2.2%	201,576	72,146	8,077	35,620	13,629
Congressional District 30	702,904	754,331	51,427	7.3%	276,791	110,173	17,095	63,729	27,769
Congressional District 31	702,905	738,321	35,416	5.0%	217,372	72,239	9,375	36,874	14,171
Congressional District 32	702,905	735,945	33,040	4.7%	198,676	95,253	11,770	45,765	15,248
Congressional District 33	702,904	714,411	11,507	1.6%	297,852	118,886	19,516	75,283	33,962
Congressional District 34	702,904	720,406	17,502	2.5%	239,711	78,323	10,933	43,055	20,014
Congressional District 35	702,905	732,845	29,940	4.3%	185,910	60,573	6,612	27,614	9,556
Congressional District 36	702,905	746,522	43,617	6.2%	261,820	145,615	21,061	90,719	40,167
Congressional District 37	702,904	723,724	20,820	3.0%	271,981	88,926	14,896	56,344	27,989
Congressional District 38	702,905	720,208	17,303	2.5%	203,362	96,491	12,851	51,026	16,722
Congressional District 39	702,905	716,854	13,949	2.0%	219,406	96,278	14,506	51,356	15,704
Congressional District 40	702,904	713,940	11,036	1.6%	179,453	55,925	7,104	26,284	8,359
Congressional District 41	702,904	739,287	36,383	5.2%	191,499	66,896	8,405	32,241	10,216
Congressional District 42	702,906	754,191	51,285	7.3%	219,885	85,783	10,172	44,085	14,631
Congressional District 43	702,904	731,916	29,012	4.1%	240,996	82,190	10,657	47,677	18,823
Congressional District 44	702,904	726,147	23,243	3.3%	184,112	61,865	7,262	32,690	11,432
Congressional District 45	702,906	763,368	60,462	8.6%	265,906	102,060	14,165	58,224	22,482
Congressional District 46	702,906	730,783	27,877	4.0%	187,247	64,460	8,210	30,943	11,519
Congressional District 47	702,905	718,747	15,842	2.3%	242,825	89,115	10,915	49,151	20,351
Congressional District 48	702,906	726,491	23,585	3.4%	268,779	115,597	14,474	70,006	27,245
Congressional District 49	702,906	728,456	25,550	3.6%	251,417	103,754	13,808	62,730	25,153
Congressional District 50	702,905	737,332	34,427	4.9%	239,592	102,746	12,967	58,738	21,509

Table A-5: 114th Congressional Districts—Summary Population Characteristics—*Continued*

	April 1, 2010 Census Population	2014 ACS Population	2010-2014 Population Change	2010-2014 Percent Change	Total Households	2014 ACS			
						Population 65 and Over	Population 85 and Over	Householders 65 and Over	Persons 65 and Over Living Alone
California—Cont.									
Congressional District 51	702,906	720,935	18,029	2.6%	194,825	76,301	10,279	39,205	15,251
Congressional District 52	702,904	759,602	56,698	8.1%	282,394	96,469	13,728	55,711	23,941
Congressional District 53	702,904	753,810	50,906	7.2%	265,815	94,491	13,150	51,442	20,578
Colorado									
Congressional District 1	718,457	788,694	70,237	9.8%	332,241	87,451	12,059	56,915	29,727
Congressional District 2	718,457	765,721	47,264	6.6%	300,661	100,906	9,976	61,254	25,597
Congressional District 3	718,457	729,368	10,911	1.5%	282,857	115,912	13,408	71,846	28,756
Congressional District 4	718,456	768,242	49,786	6.9%	272,870	96,036	11,126	58,798	22,966
Congressional District 5	718,457	759,664	41,207	5.7%	283,910	96,351	10,495	58,669	23,043
Congressional District 6	718,456	772,966	54,510	7.6%	277,454	85,399	10,260	50,915	20,810
Congressional District 7	718,456	771,211	52,755	7.3%	289,599	97,517	12,700	60,232	25,212
Connecticut									
Congressional District 1	714,820	711,205	-3,615	-0.5%	279,974	114,464	19,424	71,138	34,848
Congressional District 2	714,819	710,798	-4,021	-0.6%	267,479	114,850	13,384	67,409	26,480
Congressional District 3	714,819	720,986	6,167	0.9%	278,098	112,824	19,000	69,849	34,625
Congressional District 4	714,819	740,215	25,396	3.6%	262,907	102,522	15,211	63,660	26,748
Congressional District 5	714,820	713,473	-1,347	-0.2%	267,359	110,868	19,309	67,602	32,333
Delaware									
Congressional District (at Large)	897,934	935,614	37,680	4.2%	349,743	153,759	17,141	92,377	36,371
District of Columbia									
Delegate District (at Large)	601,723	658,893	57,170	9.5%	277,378	74,465	10,144	50,463	28,337
Florida									
Congressional District 1	696,345	743,897	47,552	6.8%	271,005	116,518	12,977	73,410	28,850
Congressional District 2	696,345	711,296	14,951	2.1%	262,789	103,379	11,706	64,479	27,304
Congressional District 3	696,345	716,034	19,689	2.8%	261,176	122,179	15,081	72,526	29,527
Congressional District 4	696,345	714,880	18,535	2.7%	272,496	102,171	12,581	62,922	27,881
Congressional District 5	696,345	742,217	45,872	6.6%	260,285	85,080	10,597	52,304	23,721
Congressional District 6	696,345	736,069	39,724	5.7%	286,085	173,836	23,635	102,474	38,716
Congressional District 7	696,345	735,643	39,298	5.6%	256,554	103,551	16,768	58,004	25,307
Congressional District 8	696,344	715,672	19,328	2.8%	285,836	171,342	25,527	103,216	40,072
Congressional District 9	696,345	769,993	73,648	10.6%	245,209	88,291	10,648	44,691	14,561
Congressional District 10	696,345	758,350	62,005	8.9%	280,952	143,887	15,549	80,880	27,879
Congressional District 11	696,345	728,133	31,788	4.6%	297,719	239,116	25,753	142,838	49,969
Congressional District 12	696,344	729,937	33,593	4.8%	281,737	157,114	24,937	92,508	38,449
Congressional District 13	696,345	707,503	11,158	1.6%	310,672	167,042	24,013	107,006	53,657
Congressional District 14	696,345	757,963	61,618	8.8%	290,566	96,569	13,755	57,456	26,108
Congressional District 15	696,345	724,176	27,831	4.0%	255,190	105,177	11,416	62,657	22,934
Congressional District 16	696,345	744,076	47,731	6.9%	311,660	223,476	30,936	136,033	52,375
Congressional District 17	696,344	725,251	28,907	4.2%	275,502	193,295	24,894	114,554	43,805
Congressional District 18	696,344	731,704	35,360	5.1%	292,179	177,066	26,218	110,320	47,916
Congressional District 19	696,345	753,542	57,197	8.2%	303,652	220,177	27,672	128,026	48,024
Congressional District 20	696,345	745,656	49,311	7.1%	244,629	104,708	16,921	59,018	26,099
Congressional District 21	696,345	742,664	46,319	6.7%	275,199	172,588	31,538	103,633	46,586
Congressional District 22	696,345	731,165	34,820	5.0%	307,349	156,483	28,742	100,876	52,624
Congressional District 23	696,345	730,033	33,688	4.8%	278,160	119,038	18,322	71,549	35,539
Congressional District 24	696,345	741,950	45,605	6.5%	230,890	89,089	11,178	48,511	21,036
Congressional District 25	696,344	745,358	49,014	7.0%	223,881	117,022	14,454	57,967	19,741
Congressional District 26	696,345	749,692	53,347	7.7%	218,812	118,445	16,931	54,237	17,785
Congressional District 27	696,345	760,443	64,098	9.2%	247,862	124,315	21,507	61,643	25,041
Georgia									
Congressional District 1	691,974	729,328	37,354	5.4%	264,770	95,698	11,222	57,508	24,817
Congressional District 2	691,976	685,342	-6,634	-1.0%	245,947	94,595	10,787	60,723	27,341
Congressional District 3	691,974	725,530	33,556	4.8%	257,294	98,916	9,587	60,882	24,020
Congressional District 4	691,976	728,367	36,391	5.3%	251,970	74,242	7,079	43,299	17,839
Congressional District 5	691,976	738,016	46,040	6.7%	287,587	77,417	7,801	50,505	28,147
Congressional District 6	691,975	732,089	40,114	5.8%	275,326	80,113	11,276	46,602	19,204
Congressional District 7	691,975	752,996	61,021	8.8%	242,595	67,003	5,978	34,875	11,730
Congressional District 8	691,976	705,698	13,722	2.0%	254,286	100,371	10,356	62,890	25,464
Congressional District 9	691,975	717,371	25,396	3.7%	251,634	123,737	11,515	74,286	28,181
Congressional District 10	691,976	713,570	21,594	3.1%	243,617	98,899	9,729	57,195	21,192
Congressional District 11	691,975	725,169	33,194	4.8%	270,931	79,383	6,900	47,502	17,643
Congressional District 12	691,975	701,628	9,653	1.4%	244,477	92,884	10,336	56,063	24,381
Congressional District 13	691,976	741,383	49,407	7.1%	248,292	70,861	7,951	40,043	16,338
Congressional District 14	691,974	700,856	8,882	1.3%	248,795	94,751	8,685	58,081	22,161
Hawaii									
Congressional District 1	680,496	707,541	27,045	4.0%	231,099	121,155	22,293	63,780	22,874
Congressional District 2	679,805	712,020	32,215	4.7%	219,670	106,906	16,653	58,964	18,348
Idaho									
Congressional District 1	784,132	834,295	50,163	6.4%	304,513	129,721	13,790	77,362	30,698
Congressional District 2	783,450	800,169	16,719	2.1%	287,074	105,258	12,651	66,862	28,702
Illinois									
Congressional District 2	712,813	707,817	-4,996	-0.7%	258,513	97,870	12,752	61,057	27,024

Table A-5: 114th Congressional Districts—Summary Population Characteristics—*Continued*

	April 1, 2010 Census Population	2014 ACS Population	2010-2014 Population Change	2010-2014 Percent Change	Total Households	2014 ACS			
						Population 65 and Over	Population 85 and Over	Householders 65 and Over	Persons 65 and Over Living Alone
Illinois—Cont.									
Congressional District 3	712,813	730,269	17,456	2.4%	245,112	99,695	14,281	59,770	26,502
Congressional District 4	712,813	725,616	12,803	1.8%	223,752	64,015	8,143	34,683	15,337
Congressional District 5	712,813	717,666	4,853	0.7%	294,812	84,881	12,104	53,721	25,448
Congressional District 6	712,813	734,700	21,887	3.1%	265,609	102,513	12,183	60,986	24,437
Congressional District 7	712,812	727,478	14,666	2.1%	286,948	83,693	9,039	56,109	28,603
Congressional District 8	712,812	725,320	12,508	1.8%	253,238	87,525	9,352	49,012	21,367
Congressional District 9	712,813	710,295	-2,518	-0.4%	280,810	112,944	19,433	68,205	35,282
Congressional District 10	712,813	711,698	-1,115	-0.2%	244,599	94,581	16,689	54,782	23,657
Congressional District 11	712,813	712,657	-156	-0.0%	236,716	69,102	8,420	40,276	16,147
Congressional District 12	712,813	701,698	-11,115	-1.6%	273,446	108,711	14,170	70,647	33,054
Congressional District 13	712,813	715,374	2,561	0.4%	285,134	107,646	14,964	69,702	32,771
Congressional District 14	712,813	725,522	12,709	1.8%	252,091	90,878	9,988	54,959	22,270
Congressional District 15	712,813	705,504	-7,309	-1.0%	274,400	122,508	17,647	76,931	35,608
Congressional District 16	712,813	699,582	-13,231	-1.9%	268,332	115,902	16,709	72,216	32,400
Congressional District 17	712,813	701,014	-11,799	-1.7%	280,965	120,998	15,929	78,897	37,831
Congressional District 18	712,813	710,629	-2,184	-0.3%	282,923	119,333	18,594	74,612	32,904
Indiana									
Congressional District 1	720,422	718,064	-2,358	-0.3%	265,908	105,429	15,272	63,780	25,824
Congressional District 2	720,423	721,627	1,204	0.2%	268,091	106,025	15,319	66,436	30,014
Congressional District 3	720,423	734,384	13,961	1.9%	278,743	104,775	13,654	65,510	27,769
Congressional District 4	720,422	742,958	22,536	3.1%	277,447	105,754	14,425	65,949	27,726
Congressional District 5	720,423	743,454	23,031	3.2%	290,210	100,486	12,395	63,514	27,428
Congressional District 6	720,422	720,106	-316	-0.0%	280,605	116,610	15,189	73,490	29,725
Congressional District 7	720,423	756,223	35,800	5.0%	282,965	80,135	10,209	49,583	24,350
Congressional District 8	720,422	723,064	2,642	0.4%	281,213	114,920	17,067	72,470	32,278
Congressional District 9	720,422	736,975	16,553	2.3%	277,557	107,360	13,165	64,961	26,602
Iowa									
Congressional District 1	761,548	770,612	9,064	1.2%	311,138	126,918	19,231	80,762	36,875
Congressional District 2	761,624	776,785	15,161	2.0%	308,412	122,458	17,074	77,746	35,406
Congressional District 3	761,612	801,039	39,427	5.2%	312,956	108,317	16,270	69,055	33,074
Congressional District 4	761,571	758,690	-2,881	-0.4%	308,965	132,935	22,373	83,166	39,081
Kansas									
Congressional District 1	713,278	718,346	5,068	0.7%	274,215	111,280	18,559	68,107	30,925
Congressional District 2	713,272	715,446	2,174	0.3%	277,280	111,015	15,873	69,590	30,844
Congressional District 3	713,287	749,250	35,963	5.0%	285,307	92,995	13,942	58,168	25,894
Congressional District 4	713,281	720,979	7,698	1.1%	272,478	102,243	13,734	64,496	29,295
Kentucky									
Congressional District 1	723,178	724,041	863	0.1%	282,156	120,648	13,391	77,242	34,022
Congressional District 2	723,137	742,858	19,721	2.7%	277,832	107,519	11,803	67,302	27,822
Congressional District 3	723,171	736,532	13,361	1.8%	300,489	107,350	15,929	70,239	33,868
Congressional District 4	723,450	748,191	24,741	3.4%	275,723	103,184	12,855	62,197	26,114
Congressional District 5	723,228	712,274	-10,954	-1.5%	278,624	115,986	11,897	74,642	33,347
Congressional District 6	723,203	749,561	26,358	3.6%	297,270	98,335	12,389	62,195	26,082
Louisiana									
Congressional District 1	755,445	796,858	41,413	5.5%	294,038	113,868	15,232	68,554	27,210
Congressional District 2	755,538	775,807	20,269	2.7%	292,635	94,688	9,253	62,129	28,002
Congressional District 3	755,596	777,665	22,069	2.9%	286,954	101,238	11,499	64,299	27,222
Congressional District 4	755,605	756,663	1,058	0.1%	276,860	111,255	13,715	68,931	31,513
Congressional District 5	755,581	750,819	-4,762	-0.6%	271,296	112,164	13,093	71,150	32,702
Congressional District 6	755,007	791,864	36,257	4.8%	296,411	97,957	9,410	60,103	23,789
Maine									
Congressional District 1	664,180	673,835	9,655	1.5%	279,939	120,918	15,687	75,384	32,976
Congressional District 2	664,181	656,254	-7,927	-1.2%	269,902	121,646	15,673	75,897	35,662
Maryland									
Congressional District 1	722,650	728,405	5,755	0.8%	268,746	125,329	16,169	75,955	30,570
Congressional District 2	723,447	743,321	19,874	2.7%	273,842	93,242	11,505	56,987	25,682
Congressional District 3	720,094	768,378	48,284	6.7%	290,531	106,972	16,022	65,092	30,878
Congressional District 4	720,065	742,761	22,696	3.2%	263,670	89,693	10,398	54,092	21,062
Congressional District 5	720,472	753,079	32,607	4.5%	255,049	91,039	9,006	53,079	18,302
Congressional District 6	728,448	755,369	26,921	3.7%	269,094	98,470	13,669	56,961	23,809
Congressional District 7	716,862	738,431	21,569	3.0%	270,119	101,979	13,159	63,904	28,188
Congressional District 8	721,514	746,663	25,149	3.5%	274,387	115,447	19,991	69,912	29,826
Massachusetts									
Congressional District 1	727,515	733,426	5,911	0.8%	285,689	120,509	20,003	77,027	36,955
Congressional District 2	727,514	736,475	8,961	1.2%	271,530	104,634	16,418	63,503	30,521
Congressional District 3	727,514	755,778	28,264	3.9%	270,944	101,327	12,869	61,551	28,583
Congressional District 4	727,514	748,190	20,676	2.8%	273,453	108,530	16,595	64,533	27,503
Congressional District 5	727,515	755,944	28,429	3.9%	291,331	112,437	17,222	70,670	33,763
Congressional District 6	727,515	757,309	29,794	4.1%	286,188	123,052	20,223	73,451	33,210
Congressional District 7	727,514	769,929	42,415	5.8%	281,429	74,933	10,808	48,348	26,891
Congressional District 8	727,514	751,768	24,254	3.3%	294,978	121,501	18,847	73,309	36,611
Congressional District 9	727,514	736,589	9,075	1.2%	293,794	148,654	18,625	92,405	41,260
Michigan									
Congressional District 1	705,974	703,687	-2,287	-0.3%	287,370	147,970	18,552	92,775	40,854

Table A-5: 114th Congressional Districts—Summary Population Characteristics—*Continued*

	April 1, 2010 Census Population	2014 ACS Population	2010-2014 Population Change	2010-2014 Percent Change	Total Households	2014 ACS			
						Population 65 and Over	Population 85 and Over	Householders 65 and Over	Persons 65 and Over Living Alone
Michigan—Cont.									
Congressional District 2..............	705,975	724,843	18,868	2.7%	268,751	102,443	14,033	64,455	26,167
Congressional District 3..............	705,974	725,487	19,513	2.8%	267,811	99,236	15,968	61,839	25,900
Congressional District 4..............	705,974	702,630	-3,344	-0.5%	269,433	122,134	15,052	75,303	30,597
Congressional District 5..............	705,975	687,292	-18,683	-2.6%	281,383	116,369	12,585	75,937	31,826
Congressional District 6..............	705,974	712,100	6,126	0.9%	276,704	111,036	13,301	68,168	27,018
Congressional District 7..............	705,974	702,894	-3,080	-0.4%	272,507	114,367	13,690	70,855	29,948
Congressional District 8..............	705,975	725,201	19,226	2.7%	272,435	93,893	11,925	58,139	24,509
Congressional District 9..............	705,975	720,485	14,510	2.1%	298,688	112,643	18,129	75,302	37,491
Congressional District 10..............	705,974	706,525	551	0.1%	269,546	117,268	14,040	71,246	28,293
Congressional District 11..............	705,974	718,435	12,461	1.8%	274,567	103,432	14,648	64,684	30,601
Congressional District 12..............	705,974	705,207	-767	-0.1%	269,662	94,924	14,387	60,740	28,396
Congressional District 13..............	705,974	687,170	-18,804	-2.7%	257,008	88,274	12,942	59,444	29,178
Congressional District 14..............	705,974	687,921	-18,053	-2.6%	268,709	107,078	14,478	70,289	33,606
Minnesota									
Congressional District 1..............	662,991	666,946	3,955	0.6%	261,328	107,149	18,471	66,836	31,110
Congressional District 2..............	662,991	689,759	26,768	4.0%	254,262	83,333	8,771	51,713	22,380
Congressional District 3..............	662,990	685,736	22,746	3.4%	268,815	96,580	13,619	60,336	26,600
Congressional District 4..............	662,990	695,920	32,930	5.0%	267,760	91,498	14,492	57,315	26,140
Congressional District 5..............	662,991	706,584	43,593	6.6%	293,412	78,468	13,282	51,551	28,403
Congressional District 6..............	662,990	684,784	21,794	3.3%	242,232	74,673	9,063	44,534	16,767
Congressional District 7..............	662,991	662,682	-309	-0.0%	267,071	122,176	20,666	76,384	34,480
Congressional District 8..............	662,991	664,762	1,771	0.3%	274,315	123,956	15,967	77,480	33,544
Mississippi									
Congressional District 1..............	741,837	760,275	18,438	2.5%	282,173	111,512	11,171	70,107	28,826
Congressional District 2..............	741,862	722,640	-19,222	-2.6%	255,841	96,434	12,085	63,779	30,226
Congressional District 3..............	741,822	749,430	7,608	1.0%	280,938	112,016	14,479	72,252	33,246
Congressional District 4..............	741,776	761,734	19,958	2.7%	276,871	107,351	11,782	67,010	26,972
Missouri									
Congressional District 1..............	748,616	744,782	-3,834	-0.5%	307,630	92,404	12,512	60,997	30,069
Congressional District 2..............	748,616	758,288	9,672	1.3%	297,764	132,448	19,422	83,030	34,814
Congressional District 3..............	748,615	766,993	18,378	2.5%	283,399	111,362	12,639	67,252	26,500
Congressional District 4..............	748,616	763,003	14,387	1.9%	283,862	116,009	13,913	71,976	30,456
Congressional District 5..............	748,616	758,442	9,826	1.3%	307,730	107,562	14,101	70,105	35,050
Congressional District 6..............	748,616	760,291	11,675	1.6%	285,617	114,924	14,807	71,255	30,957
Congressional District 7..............	748,616	765,669	17,053	2.3%	299,852	124,610	16,266	78,366	33,131
Congressional District 8..............	748,616	746,121	-2,495	-0.3%	288,955	132,571	15,786	81,998	36,391
Montana									
Congressional District (at Large)	989,415	1,023,579	34,164	3.5%	410,962	170,153	20,899	106,654	49,228
Nebraska									
Congressional District 1..............	608,780	634,290	25,510	4.2%	249,406	88,161	11,561	56,407	25,010
Congressional District 2..............	608,781	641,045	32,264	5.3%	243,695	71,659	11,466	46,308	21,940
Congressional District 3..............	608,780	606,168	-2,612	-0.4%	247,664	110,857	17,349	71,271	34,538
Nevada									
Congressional District 1..............	675,138	693,623	18,485	2.7%	245,248	88,117	8,789	54,073	25,050
Congressional District 2..............	675,138	697,426	22,288	3.3%	262,993	108,256	10,313	67,849	29,500
Congressional District 3..............	675,138	734,973	59,835	8.9%	274,521	105,942	9,485	59,400	21,614
Congressional District 4..............	675,137	713,077	37,940	5.6%	238,757	98,199	7,845	53,813	18,925
New Hampshire									
Congressional District 1..............	658,233	665,612	7,379	1.1%	262,564	103,178	13,673	62,176	27,715
Congressional District 2..............	658,237	661,201	2,964	0.5%	257,192	106,269	13,848	61,339	25,391
New Jersey									
Congressional District 1..............	732,658	732,232	-426	-0.1%	271,572	106,412	15,980	68,271	30,688
Congressional District 2..............	732,658	733,973	1,315	0.2%	268,122	122,069	14,478	75,481	32,444
Congressional District 3..............	732,658	734,551	1,893	0.3%	274,785	134,369	20,034	82,952	34,763
Congressional District 4..............	732,657	748,864	16,207	2.2%	270,829	132,163	23,528	82,620	38,502
Congressional District 5..............	732,658	745,147	12,489	1.7%	264,036	117,829	16,978	65,224	23,627
Congressional District 6..............	732,657	748,924	16,267	2.2%	250,583	93,531	13,978	54,830	23,027
Congressional District 7..............	732,658	748,182	15,524	2.1%	264,239	108,930	16,592	62,766	28,466
Congressional District 8..............	732,658	762,249	29,591	4.0%	276,592	77,019	10,500	44,930	22,250
Congressional District 9..............	732,658	759,352	26,694	3.6%	261,555	103,614	15,566	59,278	25,562
Congressional District 10..............	732,658	742,855	10,197	1.4%	263,010	82,245	10,166	54,385	27,294
Congressional District 11..............	732,658	739,014	6,356	0.9%	263,467	126,601	20,992	71,126	29,173
Congressional District 12..............	732,658	742,832	10,174	1.4%	266,054	107,343	15,196	61,336	25,918
New Mexico									
Congressional District 1..............	686,393	699,493	13,100	1.9%	270,360	103,680	11,144	64,389	30,496
Congressional District 2..............	686,393	699,424	13,031	1.9%	248,398	109,869	9,963	68,238	28,401
Congressional District 3..............	686,393	686,655	262	0.0%	242,158	104,537	11,973	66,478	29,669
New York									
Congressional District 1..............	717,707	725,932	8,225	1.1%	249,690	119,218	14,306	72,206	31,149
Congressional District 2..............	717,708	724,171	6,463	0.9%	225,524	98,722	13,859	58,967	21,901
Congressional District 3..............	717,707	718,780	1,073	0.1%	247,359	132,656	23,144	73,784	28,911
Congressional District 4..............	717,708	721,920	4,212	0.6%	231,363	113,509	18,343	65,338	24,624

Table A-5: 114th Congressional Districts—Summary Population Characteristics—*Continued*

	April 1, 2010 Census Population	2014 ACS Population	2010-2014 Population Change	2010-2014 Percent Change	Total Households	2014 ACS			
						Population 65 and Over	Population 85 and Over	Householders 65 and Over	Persons 65 and Over Living Alone
New York—Cont.									
Congressional District 5	717,708	760,487	42,779	6.0%	227,580	100,133	13,082	53,390	20,082
Congressional District 6	717,707	733,419	15,712	2.2%	269,779	116,114	17,442	66,597	29,351
Congressional District 7	717,708	732,079	14,371	2.0%	254,793	70,783	9,788	43,626	21,807
Congressional District 8	717,708	758,543	40,835	5.7%	281,396	102,895	16,182	64,981	32,431
Congressional District 9	717,708	755,073	37,365	5.2%	280,103	97,627	13,611	61,570	29,454
Congressional District 10	717,707	736,997	19,290	2.7%	310,947	101,748	15,279	67,272	37,531
Congressional District 11	717,708	726,893	9,185	1.3%	258,510	108,150	15,385	63,069	26,297
Congressional District 12	717,707	729,253	11,546	1.6%	367,878	103,067	13,934	74,429	46,250
Congressional District 13	717,707	782,199	64,492	9.0%	291,316	85,515	14,547	55,969	31,513
Congressional District 14	717,708	752,344	34,636	4.8%	249,345	90,710	11,639	49,001	22,790
Congressional District 15	717,708	750,915	33,207	4.6%	247,735	69,554	7,230	46,280	25,145
Congressional District 16	717,707	732,521	14,814	2.1%	263,056	114,006	19,101	70,132	34,717
Congressional District 17	717,708	739,263	21,555	3.0%	242,676	112,076	18,143	63,796	25,656
Congressional District 18	717,707	720,115	2,408	0.3%	244,301	102,127	12,829	58,508	23,955
Congressional District 19	717,708	708,116	-9,592	-1.3%	268,269	127,561	15,580	79,439	35,378
Congressional District 20	717,708	727,913	10,205	1.4%	287,521	111,662	16,654	69,952	33,577
Congressional District 21	717,707	713,276	-4,431	-0.6%	271,972	114,268	15,025	69,707	30,637
Congressional District 22	717,708	709,851	-7,857	-1.1%	275,383	121,362	18,515	73,982	33,816
Congressional District 23	717,707	715,663	-2,044	-0.3%	281,202	120,189	17,891	75,608	33,940
Congressional District 24	717,707	715,188	-2,519	-0.4%	280,593	110,781	17,685	69,822	34,181
Congressional District 25	717,707	721,227	3,520	0.5%	287,527	112,161	18,834	71,712	36,854
Congressional District 26	717,707	717,332	-375	-0.1%	306,964	119,748	20,412	81,837	43,397
Congressional District 27	717,707	716,757	-950	-0.1%	279,616	119,338	16,369	75,144	33,552
North Carolina									
Congressional District 1	733,499	742,851	9,352	1.3%	286,254	114,038	15,910	74,055	36,738
Congressional District 2	733,499	774,723	41,224	5.6%	283,123	104,162	12,596	64,947	27,667
Congressional District 3	733,499	759,653	26,154	3.6%	286,013	110,189	10,141	69,395	27,978
Congressional District 4	733,498	795,798	62,300	8.5%	308,881	84,421	9,342	53,434	24,171
Congressional District 5	733,499	750,233	16,734	2.3%	291,365	121,854	14,252	77,817	34,637
Congressional District 6	733,499	755,280	21,781	3.0%	297,049	125,799	16,944	77,737	33,761
Congressional District 7	733,498	772,311	38,813	5.3%	297,924	132,834	12,838	82,751	32,506
Congressional District 8	733,499	746,671	13,172	1.8%	273,964	111,591	10,829	71,074	29,232
Congressional District 9	733,498	805,960	72,462	9.9%	303,975	96,630	10,834	56,843	24,417
Congressional District 10	733,499	744,808	11,309	1.5%	283,641	128,002	15,091	78,257	32,186
Congressional District 11	733,499	744,956	11,457	1.6%	296,292	157,833	19,349	94,233	39,394
Congressional District 12	733,499	778,251	44,752	6.1%	292,966	73,967	7,433	48,212	23,117
Congressional District 13	733,498	772,469	38,971	5.3%	289,173	99,829	8,772	59,341	23,097
North Dakota									
Congressional District (at Large)	672,591	739,482	66,891	9.9%	305,431	104,679	17,350	67,092	33,093
Ohio									
Congressional District 1	721,032	729,726	8,694	1.2%	285,010	96,760	13,289	62,140	29,007
Congressional District 2	721,031	724,587	3,556	0.5%	291,964	111,135	14,414	72,544	33,985
Congressional District 3	721,031	755,499	34,468	4.8%	296,151	72,237	8,844	46,478	23,744
Congressional District 4	721,032	709,882	-11,150	-1.5%	277,572	116,092	16,291	76,550	33,953
Congressional District 5	721,031	730,503	9,472	1.3%	288,070	115,792	16,755	73,459	33,195
Congressional District 6	721,032	713,457	-7,575	-1.1%	278,327	128,957	17,060	79,648	35,125
Congressional District 7	721,031	725,548	4,517	0.6%	277,654	125,165	16,628	77,403	32,463
Congressional District 8	721,032	722,889	1,857	0.3%	273,993	111,346	14,253	68,145	28,811
Congressional District 9	721,032	709,813	-11,219	-1.6%	293,191	102,832	15,454	69,370	36,444
Congressional District 10	721,032	720,794	-238	-0.0%	295,834	118,210	14,277	75,909	36,168
Congressional District 11	721,032	699,736	-21,296	-3.0%	298,796	105,744	17,354	71,354	37,977
Congressional District 12	721,031	755,978	34,947	4.8%	285,099	101,287	13,585	63,629	28,365
Congressional District 13	721,031	707,940	-13,091	-1.8%	297,444	125,239	21,082	81,590	40,069
Congressional District 14	721,032	722,474	1,442	0.2%	287,411	130,710	19,457	81,678	34,172
Congressional District 15	721,031	740,854	19,823	2.7%	280,269	105,960	11,099	64,398	26,782
Congressional District 16	721,031	724,483	3,452	0.5%	286,387	129,402	18,737	78,663	32,904
Oklahoma									
Congressional District 1	750,270	781,067	30,797	4.1%	305,903	105,061	14,264	65,940	28,575
Congressional District 2	750,270	749,768	-502	-0.1%	280,477	133,127	14,672	84,298	36,504
Congressional District 3	750,270	776,896	26,626	3.5%	285,371	116,023	13,842	71,857	29,875
Congressional District 4	750,270	773,994	23,724	3.2%	284,755	104,745	10,923	64,333	26,799
Congressional District 5	750,271	796,326	46,055	6.1%	303,253	102,612	12,762	64,577	28,726
Oregon									
Congressional District 1	766,216	805,943	39,727	5.2%	305,696	105,267	15,208	65,156	28,742
Congressional District 2	766,215	784,114	17,899	2.3%	302,941	149,828	19,707	91,423	38,665
Congressional District 3	766,215	806,382	40,167	5.2%	317,520	101,549	13,564	62,500	28,983
Congressional District 4	766,214	775,615	9,401	1.2%	313,058	148,967	20,217	93,134	39,054
Congressional District 5	766,214	798,185	31,971	4.2%	296,296	128,615	16,390	80,551	34,460
Pennsylvania									
Congressional District 1	705,688	716,072	10,384	1.5%	266,461	82,621	11,101	52,194	26,463
Congressional District 2	705,688	716,892	11,204	1.6%	269,128	95,283	14,681	64,690	34,768
Congressional District 3	705,688	702,323	-3,365	-0.5%	283,310	125,010	18,911	79,461	35,896
Congressional District 4	705,687	719,504	13,817	2.0%	280,428	115,119	13,595	70,561	29,166
Congressional District 5	705,688	700,531	-5,157	-0.7%	269,986	121,399	17,190	76,241	33,841

Table A-5: 114th Congressional Districts—Summary Population Characteristics—*Continued*

	April 1, 2010 Census Population	2014 ACS Population	2010-2014 Population Change	2010-2014 Percent Change	Total Households	2014 ACS			
						Population 65 and Over	Population 85 and Over	Householders 65 and Over	Persons 65 and Over Living Alone
Pennsylvania—Cont.									
Congressional District 6	705,688	716,612	10,924	1.5%	267,004	111,627	16,782	66,895	27,463
Congressional District 7	705,688	714,577	8,889	1.3%	260,127	120,105	19,558	72,192	30,993
Congressional District 8	705,688	713,387	7,699	1.1%	263,799	118,481	17,173	69,837	28,566
Congressional District 9	705,688	694,973	-10,715	-1.5%	275,792	132,680	20,645	82,081	36,641
Congressional District 10	705,687	696,416	-9,271	-1.3%	265,081	128,612	17,557	78,768	34,015
Congressional District 11	705,688	700,342	-5,346	-0.8%	279,363	125,779	18,519	77,826	34,819
Congressional District 12	705,688	704,560	-1,128	-0.2%	287,682	141,111	21,854	91,695	40,691
Congressional District 13	705,687	725,185	19,498	2.8%	269,264	110,466	17,450	65,577	29,763
Congressional District 14	705,688	701,362	-4,326	-0.6%	311,663	114,220	21,187	78,109	43,101
Congressional District 15	705,687	722,560	16,873	2.4%	273,061	118,883	19,033	71,594	30,830
Congressional District 16	705,688	722,837	17,149	2.4%	262,000	109,404	16,662	64,185	26,325
Congressional District 17	705,687	707,062	1,375	0.2%	268,401	128,427	21,454	75,051	36,303
Congressional District 18	705,688	712,014	6,326	0.9%	293,422	134,872	21,677	84,984	37,665
Rhode Island									
Congressional District 1	526,283	532,145	5,862	1.1%	205,292	80,585	13,801	48,914	23,762
Congressional District 2	526,284	523,028	-3,256	-0.6%	204,362	86,595	14,981	53,323	24,421
South Carolina									
Congressional District 1	660,766	728,626	67,860	10.3%	279,589	119,021	12,435	71,036	25,887
Congressional District 2	660,766	686,952	26,186	4.0%	260,687	97,024	10,622	61,668	26,400
Congressional District 3	660,767	666,489	5,722	0.9%	254,391	115,243	12,908	72,226	29,385
Congressional District 4	660,766	703,720	42,954	6.5%	264,315	103,101	12,015	64,297	26,321
Congressional District 5	660,766	684,083	23,317	3.5%	255,114	105,685	10,183	66,373	26,183
Congressional District 6	660,766	673,637	12,871	1.9%	242,578	95,020	11,150	60,294	26,490
Congressional District 7	660,767	688,975	28,208	4.3%	270,240	126,489	12,347	79,411	32,606
South Dakota									
Congressional District (at Large)	814,180	853,175	38,995	4.8%	334,475	129,354	20,888	82,186	39,065
Tennessee									
Congressional District 1	705,123	713,317	8,194	1.2%	292,994	134,354	13,193	84,988	35,042
Congressional District 2	705,123	726,315	21,192	3.0%	284,921	120,832	14,197	73,990	32,724
Congressional District 3	705,122	716,365	11,243	1.6%	277,570	121,801	13,621	76,832	32,656
Congressional District 4	705,123	747,195	42,072	6.0%	277,263	106,790	10,182	66,528	28,099
Congressional District 5	705,123	751,222	46,099	6.5%	297,372	85,432	10,335	53,893	26,036
Congressional District 6	705,123	733,467	28,344	4.0%	280,870	126,505	10,937	78,575	30,632
Congressional District 7	705,123	743,173	38,050	5.4%	268,304	103,331	10,128	61,094	22,734
Congressional District 8	705,122	710,910	5,788	0.8%	265,181	112,416	13,921	68,914	27,640
Congressional District 9	705,123	707,388	2,265	0.3%	265,190	75,352	9,854	48,622	22,784
Texas									
Congressional District 1	698,488	712,779	14,291	2.0%	255,970	114,330	15,134	69,577	29,275
Congressional District 2	698,488	737,492	39,004	5.6%	269,587	73,480	7,126	43,804	16,712
Congressional District 3	698,488	792,608	94,120	13.5%	283,000	76,813	7,511	43,498	17,113
Congressional District 4	698,488	719,372	20,884	3.0%	255,142	115,687	12,700	68,369	26,878
Congressional District 5	698,488	734,553	36,065	5.2%	249,636	94,271	8,586	56,327	22,130
Congressional District 6	698,498	737,480	38,982	5.6%	255,443	76,511	7,349	44,972	16,306
Congressional District 7	698,488	770,950	72,462	10.4%	293,681	74,322	10,717	45,707	20,370
Congressional District 8	698,488	767,431	68,943	9.9%	257,776	97,110	9,807	60,442	24,201
Congressional District 9	698,488	772,152	73,664	10.5%	261,388	67,645	6,782	38,572	15,506
Congressional District 10	698,487	771,009	72,522	10.4%	271,381	88,856	11,290	51,065	20,998
Congressional District 11	698,488	741,069	42,581	6.1%	267,234	113,614	13,772	69,340	30,497
Congressional District 12	698,488	750,952	52,464	7.5%	271,290	93,197	10,566	55,966	23,728
Congressional District 13	698,488	707,803	9,315	1.3%	256,294	100,604	12,453	63,080	27,637
Congressional District 14	698,472	724,881	26,409	3.8%	266,576	94,635	10,534	60,139	25,059
Congressional District 15	698,488	764,850	66,362	9.5%	217,726	81,411	9,226	44,688	14,132
Congressional District 16	698,488	735,246	36,758	5.3%	229,932	83,823	9,787	47,385	18,449
Congressional District 17	698,487	740,151	41,664	6.0%	273,445	83,714	9,211	52,613	22,610
Congressional District 18	698,488	750,812	52,324	7.5%	260,178	65,930	7,413	42,364	21,040
Congressional District 19	698,487	719,594	21,107	3.0%	257,049	95,153	12,360	59,989	24,928
Congressional District 20	698,488	762,801	64,313	9.2%	248,715	78,464	10,033	45,644	16,576
Congressional District 21	698,488	766,190	67,702	9.7%	306,367	116,742	13,391	73,292	33,080
Congressional District 22	698,504	814,594	116,090	16.6%	263,321	79,169	7,062	42,330	13,628
Congressional District 23	698,488	743,201	44,713	6.4%	226,174	91,511	9,333	51,174	18,189
Congressional District 24	698,488	759,022	60,534	8.7%	304,192	76,576	7,595	45,655	18,060
Congressional District 25	698,478	748,022	49,544	7.1%	266,438	93,544	10,331	55,791	19,950
Congressional District 26	698,488	783,257	84,769	12.1%	266,038	71,165	4,313	40,455	15,367
Congressional District 27	698,487	726,394	27,907	4.0%	259,534	104,188	12,685	64,415	25,391
Congressional District 28	698,488	725,977	27,489	3.9%	208,891	77,861	9,133	42,688	14,864
Congressional District 29	698,488	749,098	50,610	7.2%	224,503	57,825	5,137	32,967	13,078
Congressional District 30	698,487	744,247	45,760	6.6%	249,315	68,243	7,321	40,286	17,508
Congressional District 31	698,487	776,518	78,031	11.2%	267,991	85,284	10,673	47,520	17,293
Congressional District 32	698,488	747,437	48,949	7.0%	286,216	88,132	11,087	52,931	22,305
Congressional District 33	698,488	742,701	44,213	6.3%	223,616	56,098	6,681	35,769	16,074
Congressional District 34	698,487	717,582	19,095	2.7%	211,742	94,905	12,577	55,273	21,307
Congressional District 35	698,488	767,436	68,948	9.9%	254,107	67,067	7,444	41,117	18,788
Congressional District 36	698,488	731,297	32,809	4.7%	257,309	98,133	9,511	58,393	24,845

Table A-5: 114th Congressional Districts—Summary Population Characteristics—*Continued*

	April 1, 2010 Census Population	2014 ACS Population	2010-2014 Population Change	2010-2014 Percent Change	Total Households	2014 ACS			
						Population 65 and Over	Population 85 and Over	Householders 65 and Over	Persons 65 and Over Living Alone
Utah									
Congressional District 1....................	690,971	727,828	36,857	5.3%	232,907	72,667	8,240	43,547	15,917
Congressional District 2....................	690,971	729,552	38,581	5.6%	236,700	85,165	9,672	52,140	19,530
Congressional District 3....................	690,972	721,048	30,076	4.4%	213,752	68,462	7,161	39,088	11,491
Congressional District 4....................	690,971	764,474	73,503	10.6%	235,011	68,685	7,696	40,970	15,274
Vermont									
Congressional District (at Large)	625,741	626,562	821	0.1%	257,229	106,655	13,354	67,260	31,115
Virginia									
Congressional District 1....................	727,366	770,044	42,678	5.9%	268,803	105,884	13,013	61,991	22,618
Congressional District 2....................	708,087	732,346	24,259	3.4%	274,587	93,506	11,814	59,210	26,512
Congressional District 3....................	746,645	753,380	6,735	0.9%	286,632	89,370	12,709	57,552	28,836
Congressional District 4....................	727,366	746,976	19,610	2.7%	265,513	97,959	11,826	60,850	24,715
Congressional District 5....................	727,365	733,330	5,965	0.8%	289,733	136,227	15,412	84,852	35,404
Congressional District 6....................	727,366	746,357	18,991	2.6%	290,076	127,885	17,509	81,215	35,023
Congressional District 7....................	727,366	769,995	42,629	5.9%	286,332	113,948	13,133	69,449	28,364
Congressional District 8....................	727,366	774,065	46,699	6.4%	308,510	80,302	10,974	49,403	24,235
Congressional District 9....................	727,366	715,465	-11,901	-1.6%	284,490	132,919	16,350	85,129	39,814
Congressional District 10.................	727,365	802,127	74,762	10.3%	263,798	87,999	9,385	46,709	16,744
Congressional District 11.................	727,366	782,204	54,838	7.5%	265,346	80,847	9,509	45,948	16,901
Washington									
Congressional District 1....................	672,444	713,399	40,955	6.1%	259,859	87,321	10,306	51,723	20,470
Congressional District 2....................	672,454	708,323	35,869	5.3%	275,308	106,599	14,612	65,104	29,241
Congressional District 3....................	672,448	697,884	25,436	3.8%	264,592	111,563	12,038	69,054	29,081
Congressional District 4....................	672,456	704,219	31,763	4.7%	235,617	90,733	10,778	54,375	22,542
Congressional District 5....................	672,455	690,518	18,063	2.7%	267,126	106,584	14,792	66,503	29,628
Congressional District 6....................	672,448	676,910	4,462	0.7%	265,236	122,055	15,377	75,550	31,130
Congressional District 7....................	672,457	732,733	60,276	9.0%	328,789	93,936	14,447	59,863	30,524
Congressional District 8....................	672,463	711,629	39,166	5.8%	254,292	84,687	10,094	50,179	20,125
Congressional District 9....................	672,460	711,466	39,006	5.8%	267,150	93,388	14,579	55,278	24,784
Congressional District 10.................	672,455	714,449	41,994	6.2%	261,632	95,650	13,070	58,199	25,848
West Virginia									
Congressional District 1....................	615,991	616,232	241	0.0%	242,233	107,899	13,444	69,426	31,314
Congressional District 2....................	620,862	628,276	7,414	1.2%	247,865	108,800	12,138	69,289	30,191
Congressional District 3....................	616,141	605,818	-10,323	-1.7%	245,277	112,356	13,231	73,073	32,461
Wisconsin									
Congressional District 1....................	710,874	712,072	1,198	0.2%	272,387	104,861	15,748	67,267	30,504
Congressional District 2....................	710,874	740,988	30,114	4.2%	302,685	97,881	14,770	61,641	27,561
Congressional District 3....................	710,873	718,518	7,645	1.1%	282,399	115,652	16,834	72,525	32,495
Congressional District 4....................	710,873	717,657	6,784	1.0%	281,593	78,044	13,763	49,461	26,650
Congressional District 5....................	710,873	722,537	11,664	1.6%	291,080	117,422	17,214	74,606	34,747
Congressional District 6....................	710,873	712,031	1,158	0.2%	287,900	118,610	18,022	75,390	35,566
Congressional District 7....................	710,873	711,006	133	0.0%	298,690	131,630	17,830	82,287	34,470
Congressional District 8....................	710,873	722,755	11,882	1.7%	290,951	111,620	15,136	69,654	28,404
Wyoming									
Congressional District (at Large)	563,626	584,153	20,527	3.6%	232,594	80,332	8,106	51,531	22,503

PART B
AGE STRUCTURE

AGE STRUCTURE

Based on the 2014 American Community Survey, 14.5 percent of the national population is age 65 years old or over while 1.9 percent was age 85 and over. This is a slight but growing change from the 2010 Census results where the 65 and over population was 13.0 percent and the 85 and over percent was 1.8 percent of the total. Though these are relatively small changes in the proportion of the older population, it indicates the coming growth in this segment as the oldest of the Baby Boom generation (age 68 in 2014) has passed this threshold and the numbers will continue to grow quickly. The youngest Boomers are just passing age 50.

There are 46.2 million people in the United States over the age of 65 and 6.0 million of them are over the age of 85. The proportion of the population that is over 65 is higher than the national average in 29 states while 26 states have a higher proportion of the 85 and over population. As one might expect, Florida leads the nation with the largest proportion of population over 65 but Hawaii has the highest proportion of population over age 85 at 2.7 percent. States with older populations aren't all retirement destinations. Among the states with the highest percentage of population 65 and over, most are a result of the existing age structure rather than being a retirement destination as is the case in Maine, Pennsylvania, Vermont, and West Virginia. Those states with the lowest

Percent of the Population 65 Years and Over

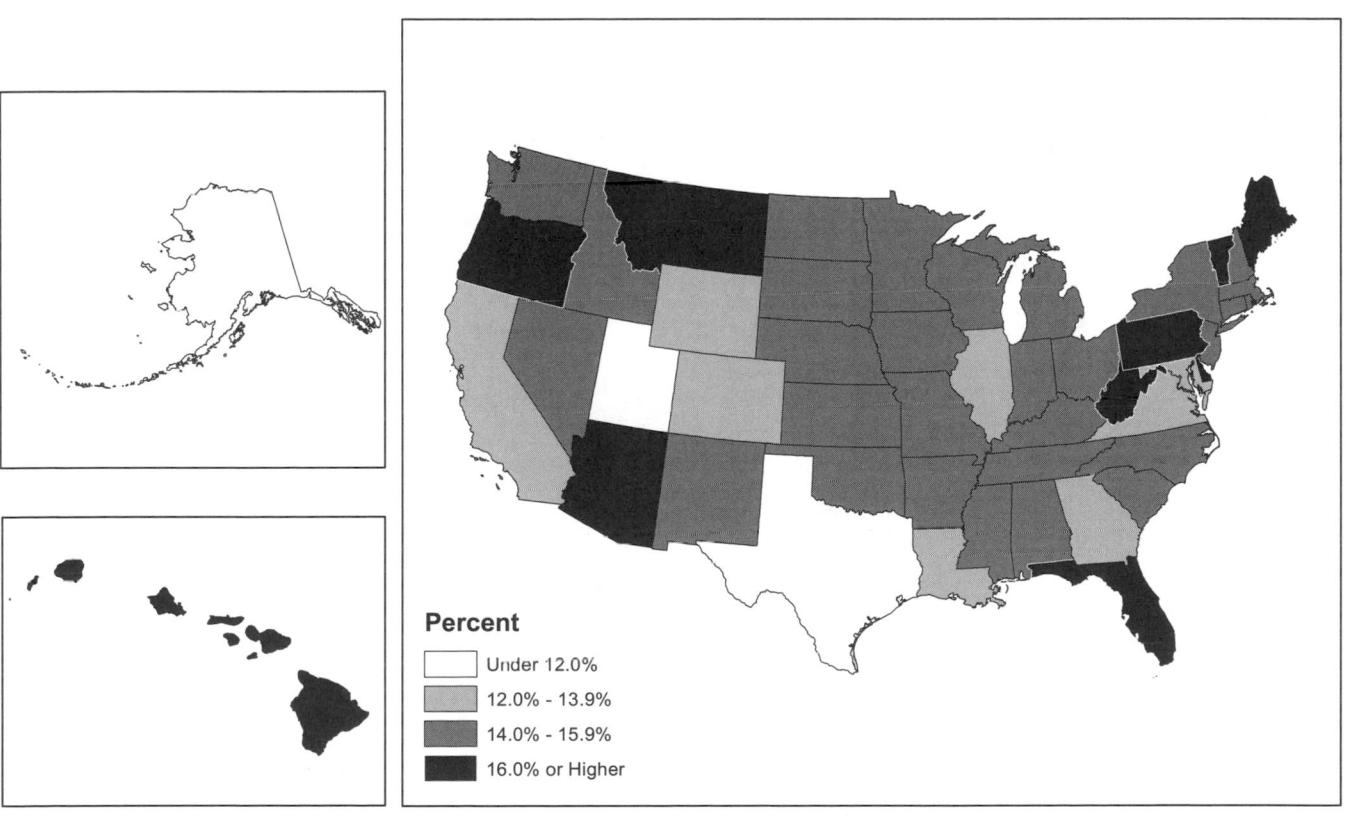

Percent
- Under 12.0%
- 12.0% - 13.9%
- 14.0% - 15.9%
- 16.0% or Higher

proportion of population 65 and over include Alaska, Utah, the District of Columbia, and Texas. The younger population in Texas likely reflects its high in-migration status rather than attraction as a retirement destination.

65 Years and Over – Top 10		65 Years and Over – Bottom 10	
Florida	19.1%	Maryland	13.8%
Maine	18.2%	Wyoming	13.8%
West Virginia	17.8%	Louisiana	13.6%
Vermont	17.0%	California	12.9%
Pennsylvania	16.7%	Colorado	12.7%
Montana	16.6%	Georgia	12.4%
Delaware	16.4%	Texas	11.5%
Hawaii	16.1%	District of Columbia	11.3%
Oregon	16.0%	Utah	10.0%
Arizona	15.9%	Alaska	9.5%

Only four of the states in the 65 and over top 10 are also among the 85 and over top 10. Florida, Hawaii, Maine, and Pennsylvania join the list. But eight of the states in the 65 and over bottom 10 are also in the 85 and over bottom 10.

85 Years and Over – Top 10		85 Years and Over – Bottom 10	
Hawaii	2.7%	New Mexico	1.6%
Rhode Island	2.7%	Louisiana	1.6%
Florida	2.6%	District of Columbia	1.5%
Pennsylvania	2.5%	Colorado	1.5%
South Dakota	2.4%	Wyoming	1.4%
Iowa	2.4%	Texas	1.3%
Connecticut	2.4%	Nevada	1.3%
Maine	2.4%	Georgia	1.3%
North Dakota	2.3%	Utah	1.1%
Massachusetts	2.2%	Alaska	0.8%

Los Angeles County, California (1.2 million) and Cook County, Illinois (679,000) have the largest number of people age 65 and over but rank 624th and 563rd, respectively, of the 802 counties in terms of the percent of their total population. Liberty County, Georgia has the fewest number of persons 65 and over at almost 4,900 but Utah County, Utah has the lowest percentage at 7.2 percent. The ten counties with the largest 65 and over population account for 11.0 percent of the nation's 46.2 million population or a total of 5.1 million people. The smallest ten counties have only 69,265 people over

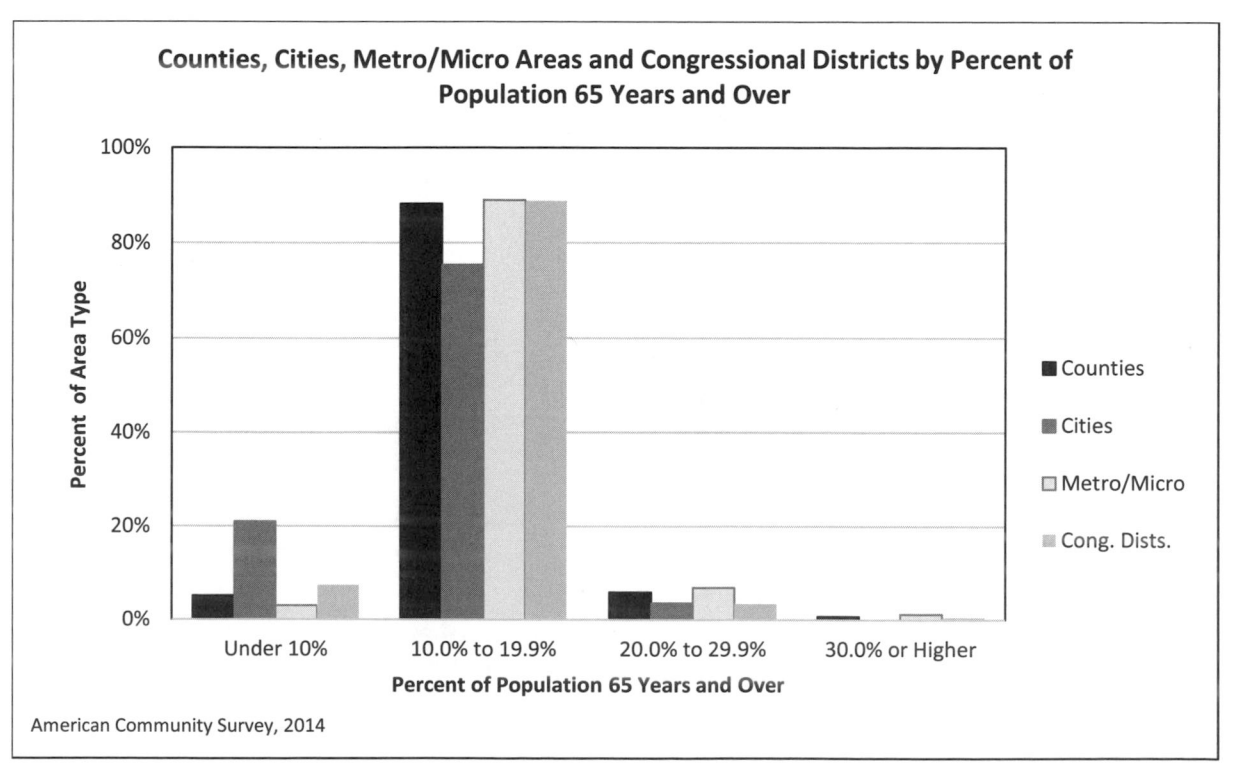

American Community Survey, 2014

Rank	Counties		Cities		Metropolitan/Micropolitan Areas		Congressional Districts	
					Top 20 Areas—Percent 85 and Over			
1	Indian River County, FL	5.3%	Walnut Creek city, CA	6.4%	Sebastian-Vero Beach, FL Metro Area	5.3%	Congressional District 21, FL	4.2%
2	Sarasota County, FL	5.0%	Hemet city, CA	5.7%	Pinehurst-Southern Pines, NC Micro Area	4.7%	Congressional District 16, FL	4.2%
3	Martin County, FL	4.8%	Delray Beach city, FL	5.5%	Punta Gorda, FL Metro Area	4.6%	Congressional District 22, FL	3.9%
4	Moore County, NC	4.7%	Pompano Beach city, FL	4.8%	Port Angeles, WA Micro Area	4.4%	Congressional District 19, FL	3.7%
5	Charlotte County, FL	4.6%	Boynton Beach city, FL	4.4%	North Port-Sarasota-Bradenton, FL Metro Area	4.1%	Congressional District 18, FL	3.6%
6	Clallam County, WA	4.4%	Palm Coast city, FL	4.2%	Homosassa Springs, FL Metro Area	4.1%	Congressional District 8, FL	3.6%
7	Citrus County, FL	4.1%	Warwick city, RI	4.1%	Sebring, FL Metro Area	4.0%	Congressional District 11, FL	3.5%
8	Palm Beach County, FL	4.0%	Youngstown city, OH	4.0%	The Villages, FL Metro Area	3.9%	Congressional District 17, FL	3.4%
9	Highlands County, FL	4.0%	Deerfield Beach city, FL	4.0%	Port St. Lucie, FL Metro Area	3.7%	Congressional District 12, FL	3.4%
10	Flagler County, FL	4.0%	Urban Honolulu CDP, HI	3.8%	Deltona-Daytona Beach-Ormond Beach, FL Metro Area	3.6%	Congressional District 13, FL	3.4%
11	Hernando County, FL	4.0%	Cranston city, RI	3.7%	Johnstown, PA Metro Area	3.5%	Congressional District 3, NY	3.2%
12	Sumter County, FL	3.9%	Newport Beach city, CA	3.6%	Wisconsin Rapids-Marshfield, WI Micro Area	3.5%	Congressional District 6, FL	3.2%
13	Ocean County, NJ	3.7%	Bloomington city, MN	3.6%	Barnstable Town, MA Metro Area	3.5%	Congressional District 1, HI	3.2%
14	Mahoning County, OH	3.7%	Scranton city, PA	3.6%	New Castle, PA Metro Area	3.5%	Congressional District 4, NJ	3.1%
15	Pinellas County, FL	3.7%	Santa Barbara city, CA	3.4%	Roseburg, OR Micro Area	3.4%	Congressional District 7, MN	3.1%
16	Armstrong County, PA	3.6%	St. George city, UT	3.4%	Scranton–Wilkes-Barre–Hazleton, PA Metro Area	3.4%	Congressional District 12, PA	3.1%
17	Lackawanna County, PA	3.6%	Scottsdale city, AZ	3.4%	Prescott, AZ Metro Area	3.4%	Congressional District 18, PA	3.0%
18	Volusia County, FL	3.6%	Torrance city, CA	3.4%	Coos Bay, OR Micro Area	3.4%	Congressional District 17, PA	3.0%
19	Cambria County, PA	3.5%	Largo city, FL	3.3%	Pittsfield, MA Metro Area	3.4%	Congressional District 14, PA	3.0%
20	Henderson County	3.5%	Temple city, TX	3.3%	Quincy, IL-MO Micro Area	3.4%	Congressional District 13, OH	3.0%

age 65 and represent only 0.15 percent of the total. More than 420 counties have a larger proportion of their population over the age of 65 and the national average of 14.5 percent.

While cities make up a third of the total population, they contain only 28.5 percent of the 65 and over population, indicating that a relatively larger proportion of the population live outside of the densest urban centers. More almost 3 million (6.5 percent of all 65 and over) people age 65 and over live in the top 10 cities. About the same proportion (6.4 percent) of the 85 and over population lives in the top 10 cities. Only 53,000 people 65 and over live in the bottom 10 cities and, like counties, account for only 0.11 percent of the total. New York City, Los Angeles, and Chicago have the largest populations over age 65 but all rank low in terms of their percent of total population. New York ranks 216th while Los Angeles and Chicago rank 310th and 329th, respectively. Jacksonville City, Wisconsin has the smallest population 65 and over at 4,110. Of the 531 cities reported here, 126 are above the national percentage of 65 and over.

More than four out of every five people age 65 and over lives in a metropolitan or micropolitan area. This is almost 40 million people or 86.5 percent of the nation's 46.5 million population age 65 and over. A slightly higher proportion, 87.1 percent of the nation's 85 and over population lives in metropolitan and micropolitan areas numbering 5.3 million. As with the city populations, the New York, Los Angeles, Chicago, and Miami metropolitan areas have the largest 65 and over populations, all numbering more than 1 million. Just these four areas account for 16.8 percent of the national total or 6.7 million people. The Hinesville, Georgia metropolitan area has the lowest number of people 65 and over at 6,257 which is 7.6 percent of the metropolitan area total population.

Congressional District 11 in Florida has the largest number of persons 65 and over at 239,116. That district also has the largest proportion of its total population over the age of 65 at 32.8 percent, almost one out of every three people in the district. However, the district includes the city of Tampa and surrounding area which ranks 52nd in total size of the 65 and over population but only 266th in its proportion of the total. More than 1.9 million persons 65 and over reside in the 10 congressional districts with the largest older population while 596,000 reside in the 10 districts with the smallest population. Congressional District 7 in Arizona has the fewest residents age 65 and over at 53,000 and also the lowest percentage of the total population at 7.0 percent. This district includes the city of Phoenix and surrounding area.

Table B-1: States—Older Population by Age

	Total Population	60 to 61 Years	62 to 64 Years	65 to 66 Years	67 to 69 Years	70 to 74 Years	75 to 79 Years	80 to 84 Years	85 Years and Over	65 Years and Over
United States	318,857,056	7,931,266	10,837,042	6,789,780	8,469,781	11,158,643	7,942,125	5,808,594	6,045,970	46,214,893
Alabama	4,849,377	128,234	169,388	109,345	139,719	185,180	135,284	93,435	83,549	746,512
Alaska	736,732	18,394	22,666	13,355	15,108	17,764	10,904	6,531	6,237	69,899
Arizona	6,731,484	156,127	226,722	150,070	199,807	272,639	194,775	133,872	119,594	1,070,757
Arkansas	2,966,369	72,422	104,838	65,991	87,948	114,824	82,422	58,331	55,496	465,012
California	38,802,500	895,484	1,203,882	739,710	917,650	1,179,238	851,362	635,313	666,819	4,990,092
Colorado	5,355,866	132,391	186,861	112,689	131,368	165,838	114,416	75,237	80,024	679,572
Connecticut	3,596,677	95,078	124,934	78,563	99,801	126,347	93,632	70,857	86,328	555,528
Delaware	935,614	23,699	32,114	23,426	29,258	38,894	26,808	18,232	17,141	153,759
District of Columbia	658,893	13,563	19,134	10,045	12,426	19,475	13,624	8,751	10,144	74,465
Florida	19,893,297	515,057	724,323	490,363	667,736	925,791	688,788	494,020	524,256	3,790,954
Georgia	10,097,343	235,163	319,095	199,533	248,309	321,121	209,424	141,281	129,202	1,248,870
Hawaii	1,419,561	37,432	51,062	35,519	42,656	48,825	34,107	28,008	38,946	228,061
Idaho	1,634,464	42,061	57,682	35,650	45,011	60,307	41,035	26,535	26,441	234,979
Illinois	12,880,580	320,725	425,563	257,972	318,689	426,258	307,860	231,860	245,215	1,787,854
Indiana	6,596,855	165,007	224,139	145,320	168,846	221,289	157,256	122,088	126,695	941,494
Iowa	3,107,126	83,896	108,004	67,258	82,224	109,614	89,393	67,191	74,948	490,628
Kansas	2,904,021	71,779	100,591	60,059	71,229	95,467	72,899	55,771	62,108	417,533
Kentucky	4,413,457	110,892	157,752	101,209	121,512	162,657	114,673	74,707	78,264	653,022
Louisiana	4,649,676	114,032	159,613	100,509	114,299	157,521	111,285	75,354	72,202	631,170
Maine	1,330,089	42,718	55,870	36,163	46,524	57,504	39,249	31,764	31,360	242,564
Maryland	5,976,407	145,185	204,485	127,917	152,416	198,684	136,809	96,426	109,919	822,171
Massachusetts	6,745,408	177,357	236,120	146,033	177,292	240,081	166,837	133,724	151,610	1,015,577
Michigan	9,909,877	271,234	371,463	224,736	270,482	378,341	260,140	193,638	203,730	1,531,067
Minnesota	5,457,173	134,714	192,676	112,195	136,706	181,274	133,685	99,642	114,331	777,833
Mississippi	2,994,079	74,412	97,303	62,704	78,644	106,304	77,724	52,420	49,517	427,313
Missouri	6,063,589	150,959	220,217	133,592	162,409	231,188	165,638	119,617	119,446	931,890
Montana	1,023,579	28,066	43,424	25,398	32,264	41,797	29,953	19,842	20,899	170,153
Nebraska	1,881,503	46,933	60,959	37,206	45,666	62,361	48,003	37,065	40,376	270,677
Nevada	2,839,099	70,252	95,186	63,981	79,382	106,825	67,097	46,797	36,432	400,514
New Hampshire	1,326,813	41,198	52,708	31,689	41,710	49,452	33,694	25,381	27,521	209,447
New Jersey	8,938,175	224,916	306,561	185,821	232,855	310,844	217,778	170,839	193,988	1,312,125
New Mexico	2,085,572	54,576	76,476	47,670	60,919	77,235	57,785	41,397	33,080	318,086
New York	19,746,227	491,211	667,198	413,441	516,067	674,223	489,433	377,707	424,809	2,895,680
North Carolina	9,943,964	245,642	328,407	225,250	286,255	357,831	248,212	179,270	164,331	1,461,149
North Dakota	739,482	17,671	25,073	14,296	17,213	22,741	18,649	14,430	17,350	104,679
Ohio	11,594,163	311,079	418,147	262,662	315,284	425,723	322,474	222,146	248,579	1,796,868
Oklahoma	3,878,051	94,525	126,793	79,883	106,189	136,857	100,849	71,327	66,463	561,568
Oregon	3,970,239	112,960	160,370	96,490	122,596	156,931	101,270	71,763	85,176	634,226
Pennsylvania	12,787,209	355,505	472,749	295,945	375,166	482,696	365,004	290,259	325,029	2,134,099
Rhode Island	1,055,173	25,407	41,209	22,499	30,215	37,215	25,384	23,085	28,782	167,180
South Carolina	4,832,482	127,000	181,600	116,029	158,126	194,810	125,468	85,490	81,660	761,583
South Dakota	853,175	21,317	31,033	19,941	23,402	25,601	21,463	18,059	20,888	129,354
Tennessee	6,549,352	166,253	233,131	154,018	188,046	247,330	168,442	122,609	106,368	986,813
Texas	26,956,958	582,431	774,278	470,140	588,553	774,959	531,980	383,750	346,631	3,096,013
Utah	2,942,902	53,627	77,907	46,798	52,320	73,400	54,657	35,035	32,769	294,979
Vermont	626,562	19,531	25,175	15,977	19,912	26,774	16,493	14,145	13,354	106,655
Virginia	8,326,289	206,090	281,011	176,353	212,395	290,178	193,014	133,272	141,634	1,146,846
Washington	7,061,530	180,979	249,328	156,706	193,618	241,881	154,894	115,324	130,093	992,516
West Virginia	1,850,326	53,330	77,406	51,349	62,447	76,777	59,425	40,244	38,813	329,055
Wisconsin	5,757,564	155,417	211,501	126,338	155,001	202,821	148,420	113,823	129,317	875,720
Wyoming	584,153	17,335	22,915	13,974	16,111	18,956	12,255	10,930	8,106	80,332

Table B-2: Counties—Older Population by Age

	Total Population	60 to 61 Years	62 to 64 Years	65 to 66 Years	67 to 69 Years	70 to 74 Years	75 to 79 Years	80 to 84 Years	85 Years and Over	65 Years and Over
Alabama										
Baldwin County	200,111	5,538	8,487	5,601	6,164	10,630	6,178	5,401	3,808	37,782
Calhoun County	115,916	4,789	3,858	2,163	4,281	4,470	2,915	3,059	1,655	18,543
Cullman County	81,289	1,628	2,650	2,155	1,958	4,270	2,667	1,906	1,310	14,266
DeKalb County	71,065	813	3,159	1,090	2,484	3,222	2,392	917	958	11,063
Elmore County	80,977	2,396	2,179	1,719	2,648	2,424	1,896	1,135	1,392	11,214
Etowah County	103,531	2,182	4,520	2,732	3,466	4,353	2,924	2,308	2,294	18,077
Houston County	104,193	2,791	3,656	2,235	3,373	4,028	3,284	1,776	1,981	16,677
Jefferson County	660,793	17,606	22,274	14,553	16,277	21,723	16,763	12,417	12,770	94,503
Lauderdale County	93,096	2,843	3,220	1,713	2,825	5,242	3,202	2,068	2,035	17,085
Lee County	154,255	3,227	4,970	2,806	3,048	4,111	3,012	1,841	1,057	15,875
Limestone County	90,787	2,062	2,847	1,816	2,679	2,999	2,707	1,204	1,106	12,511
Madison County	350,299	9,043	11,349	6,897	7,368	12,482	8,293	7,590	5,702	48,332
Marshall County	94,636	2,920	3,326	1,927	3,042	4,099	2,824	1,896	1,510	15,298
Mobile County	415,123	10,228	14,084	8,796	11,577	14,649	9,940	6,789	8,299	60,050
Montgomery County	226,189	5,926	7,061	4,761	5,975	6,419	6,739	4,138	2,624	30,656
Morgan County	119,607	3,355	4,687	3,092	3,204	4,435	2,821	2,953	1,871	18,376
Shelby County	206,655	4,883	8,004	4,433	5,786	6,858	5,548	2,085	2,670	27,380
St. Clair County	86,697	2,546	2,847	1,854	3,473	2,718	2,536	1,464	1,340	13,385
Talladega County	81,322	2,744	2,826	1,841	2,722	3,254	2,144	1,449	1,595	13,005
Tuscaloosa County	202,212	3,980	7,096	3,928	4,094	5,849	3,483	2,793	3,775	23,922
Walker County	65,471	1,487	2,579	1,636	2,040	3,271	2,596	1,467	853	11,863
Alaska										
Anchorage Municipality	301,010	6,302	7,491	4,494	5,346	6,788	4,877	2,932	2,469	26,906
Fairbanks North Star Borough	99,357	2,278	2,757	1,761	1,860	1,572	1,279	547	865	7,884
Matanuska-Susitna Borough	97,882	2,317	3,974	1,886	1,916	2,834	1,541	755	525	9,457
Arizona										
Apache County	71,828	1,630	2,530	1,159	1,809	2,775	1,450	1,050	1,187	9,430
Cochise County	127,448	3,859	5,963	3,781	5,059	5,499	4,961	2,709	3,151	25,160
Coconino County	137,682	3,805	4,319	2,825	3,649	3,495	2,510	1,868	1,173	15,520
Maricopa County	4,087,191	85,250	126,478	82,448	104,982	140,112	97,933	70,813	69,695	565,983
Mohave County	203,361	5,427	10,012	5,880	10,309	15,957	11,256	7,011	4,626	55,039
Navajo County	108,101	2,452	3,470	2,190	3,728	4,906	3,322	1,644	1,339	17,129
Pima County	1,004,516	26,119	35,873	25,582	31,073	43,829	32,639	24,674	20,248	178,045
Pinal County	401,918	10,915	14,260	9,430	15,825	20,725	13,056	7,363	5,497	71,896
Yavapai County	218,844	8,578	12,723	7,555	13,077	16,105	10,882	6,676	7,413	61,708
Yuma County	203,247	3,545	5,188	4,600	4,887	9,079	9,579	5,347	2,445	35,937
Arkansas										
Benton County	242,321	5,363	6,087	3,817	6,356	7,985	4,649	4,670	3,923	31,400
Craighead County	102,518	1,833	3,373	2,159	1,868	3,633	2,604	2,144	1,205	13,613
Faulkner County	120,768	2,750	3,575	2,108	2,470	3,475	2,120	1,576	1,467	13,216
Garland County	97,322	2,353	3,908	3,117	2,579	5,928	4,393	2,626	2,310	20,953
Jefferson County	72,297	1,439	2,956	1,498	2,243	2,508	2,135	1,153	1,254	10,791
Lonoke County	71,557	1,239	2,911	1,632	1,967	1,817	1,656	1,172	706	8,950
Pulaski County	392,702	9,615	14,883	9,125	10,847	10,472	8,591	6,531	7,357	52,923
Saline County	115,719	2,851	3,976	3,259	4,103	4,544	4,076	1,605	1,790	19,377
Sebastian County	126,776	3,051	4,382	2,570	3,817	4,084	2,915	1,985	2,613	17,984
Washington County	220,792	5,018	5,667	3,895	4,140	6,189	4,719	2,173	3,021	24,137
White County	78,592	1,950	2,057	1,298	2,462	2,882	2,709	1,336	1,233	11,920
California										
Alameda County	1,610,921	36,984	53,942	30,892	39,985	44,940	30,850	26,001	28,257	200,925
Butte County	224,241	6,557	8,032	3,930	6,869	10,566	6,849	4,214	5,627	38,055
Contra Costa County	1,111,339	27,376	39,670	23,836	28,860	38,883	26,959	18,267	21,135	157,940
El Dorado County	183,087	6,179	9,524	5,537	6,047	8,958	5,711	3,996	2,723	32,972
Fresno County	965,974	21,749	25,594	16,270	19,912	25,649	19,559	12,220	14,835	108,445
Humboldt County	134,809	5,024	5,783	3,399	3,272	5,731	3,334	2,436	2,155	20,327
Imperial County	179,091	2,658	4,845	2,940	3,134	5,527	3,987	3,212	2,884	21,684
Kern County	874,589	17,253	22,382	11,648	15,371	24,627	16,896	8,829	9,115	86,486
Kings County	150,269	3,137	2,777	2,522	2,076	3,215	3,093	1,345	1,080	13,331
Lake County	64,184	2,817	3,140	1,620	2,809	3,251	2,520	1,298	1,205	12,703
Los Angeles County	10,116,705	223,129	295,744	181,519	221,915	284,892	214,723	159,044	170,916	1,233,009
Madera County	154,548	3,566	4,462	3,188	3,039	5,268	3,155	2,327	2,663	19,640
Marin County	260,750	8,769	10,780	8,083	9,420	12,080	7,138	5,933	7,301	49,955
Mendocino County	87,869	2,830	4,455	2,241	4,231	4,273	2,102	1,957	2,172	16,976
Merced County	266,353	4,690	4,937	3,590	5,633	6,994	5,234	3,283	3,565	28,299
Monterey County	431,344	10,834	11,937	7,610	10,210	10,915	7,373	7,386	7,658	51,152
Napa County	141,667	4,486	5,755	3,662	4,758	6,055	2,924	3,643	3,589	24,631
Nevada County	98,893	3,969	6,516	2,916	4,727	6,069	2,581	3,918	2,911	23,122
Orange County	3,145,515	69,001	93,323	60,041	75,313	96,937	73,013	52,897	55,151	413,352
Placer County	371,694	8,444	14,338	9,256	11,483	16,961	11,575	9,113	8,318	66,706
Riverside County	2,320,271	49,573	68,020	41,603	58,213	74,259	51,011	42,009	40,381	307,476
Sacramento County	1,482,026	34,341	48,985	31,682	33,815	42,168	32,317	24,693	24,596	189,271
San Bernardino County	2,112,619	42,188	56,540	36,564	43,697	50,192	37,361	25,300	24,755	217,869
San Diego County	3,263,431	77,684	97,454	57,015	76,631	97,793	70,421	56,636	56,136	414,632
San Francisco County	852,469	19,711	32,177	19,179	22,088	23,806	21,439	17,690	18,704	122,906
San Joaquin County	715,597	14,897	20,279	13,080	14,693	21,211	14,882	10,207	10,225	84,298
San Luis Obispo County	279,083	8,289	9,910	6,968	9,203	12,462	7,673	7,423	5,523	49,252
San Mateo County	758,581	19,369	27,434	15,695	19,365	26,946	20,698	13,744	14,891	111,339
Santa Barbara County	440,668	10,173	13,772	8,636	10,160	13,114	9,627	9,164	10,704	61,405
Santa Clara County	1,894,605	42,554	55,237	32,776	39,231	57,180	43,351	29,765	29,172	231,475

Table B-2: Counties—Older Population by Age—*Continued*

	Total Population	60 to 61 Years	62 to 64 Years	65 to 66 Years	67 to 69 Years	70 to 74 Years	75 to 79 Years	80 to 84 Years	85 Years and Over	65 Years and Over
California—Cont.										
Santa Cruz County	271,804	7,516	11,057	7,592	6,693	8,416	5,931	3,448	4,187	36,267
Shasta County	179,804	5,175	8,742	5,335	5,628	9,265	5,148	4,404	4,885	34,665
Solano County	431,131	13,348	16,296	9,515	10,874	14,306	11,826	5,817	5,866	58,204
Sonoma County	500,292	15,666	21,214	12,792	16,619	20,283	9,885	9,878	13,079	82,536
Stanislaus County	531,997	11,088	14,729	11,005	11,141	14,681	11,132	8,023	8,466	64,448
Sutter County	95,847	2,817	2,498	1,673	3,000	3,297	2,863	1,716	1,501	14,050
Tulare County	458,198	8,425	11,179	7,647	9,499	10,197	7,595	5,512	6,886	47,336
Ventura County	846,178	22,722	25,054	17,022	22,511	26,064	18,409	13,715	17,233	114,954
Yolo County	207,590	3,943	7,342	3,685	5,091	5,116	3,706	2,678	3,506	23,782
Yuba County	73,966	1,050	1,988	1,231	1,648	2,115	1,320	1,072	1,272	8,658
Colorado										
Adams County	480,718	8,602	14,833	7,175	9,346	12,016	8,402	4,355	5,130	46,424
Arapahoe County	618,821	15,166	19,980	12,293	14,750	17,722	12,369	7,805	8,619	73,558
Boulder County	313,333	8,337	12,004	5,986	7,260	9,558	5,593	4,896	4,638	37,931
Denver County	663,862	13,072	19,422	11,176	13,547	17,491	11,865	7,638	10,549	72,266
Douglas County	314,638	6,124	9,914	7,647	6,138	7,081	3,532	3,854	3,171	31,423
El Paso County	663,519	15,335	21,490	12,326	14,327	18,911	13,246	8,729	8,302	75,841
Jefferson County	558,503	16,483	23,231	12,350	16,340	19,669	14,759	8,347	10,288	81,753
Larimer County	324,122	7,572	10,755	7,376	7,310	12,228	7,587	5,472	5,178	45,151
Mesa County	148,255	4,188	5,844	3,787	4,299	5,912	5,138	2,394	3,212	24,742
Pueblo County	161,875	4,036	7,073	3,544	5,365	6,493	5,438	3,614	3,506	27,960
Weld County	277,670	6,711	7,291	5,389	6,254	7,080	5,256	3,924	2,938	30,841
Connecticut										
Fairfield County	945,438	25,327	29,112	18,297	25,174	29,800	24,408	17,987	20,186	135,852
Hartford County	897,985	19,995	31,923	19,688	24,607	31,109	23,089	17,645	24,261	140,399
Litchfield County	184,993	5,298	7,952	4,003	7,022	8,695	5,421	3,906	5,055	34,102
Middlesex County	164,943	4,993	6,216	4,714	5,230	6,225	4,394	3,808	4,392	28,763
New Haven County	861,277	24,946	30,317	19,721	22,822	30,563	22,283	16,144	22,801	134,334
New London County	273,676	7,675	9,623	6,306	7,523	10,797	7,307	6,153	5,971	44,057
Tolland County	151,367	3,703	5,743	3,552	4,454	4,659	3,929	3,028	1,463	21,085
Windham County	116,998	3,141	4,048	2,282	2,969	4,499	2,801	2,186	2,199	16,936
Delaware										
Kent County	171,987	3,413	5,007	4,158	4,568	7,334	4,767	3,075	2,685	26,587
New Castle County	552,778	13,513	16,886	11,879	13,922	17,753	13,697	9,135	9,580	75,966
Sussex County	210,849	6,773	10,221	7,389	10,768	13,807	8,344	6,022	4,876	51,206
Florida										
Alachua County	256,380	5,505	8,891	5,005	5,621	7,873	4,682	3,994	4,390	31,565
Bay County	178,985	5,053	5,671	4,608	5,327	7,152	4,750	4,103	3,242	29,182
Brevard County	556,885	16,432	22,715	15,722	22,375	29,310	24,130	16,794	17,681	126,012
Broward County	1,869,235	48,025	60,788	35,665	51,316	69,404	47,811	37,077	45,554	286,827
Charlotte County	168,474	4,734	8,198	8,167	10,992	14,926	12,282	9,295	7,724	63,386
Citrus County	139,377	4,080	6,585	5,206	8,393	12,900	10,000	6,777	5,730	49,006
Clay County	199,798	6,139	5,267	4,211	5,524	8,269	4,224	3,448	2,972	28,648
Collier County	348,777	10,033	14,825	10,263	16,903	26,074	22,449	15,372	11,201	102,262
Columbia County	67,857	1,952	2,672	2,038	2,150	2,983	1,648	1,519	1,642	11,980
Duval County	897,698	23,906	27,317	18,954	22,461	26,800	18,163	13,709	14,613	114,700
Escambia County	310,659	7,124	10,926	7,980	8,111	12,108	9,162	6,083	5,761	49,205
Flagler County	102,408	3,764	4,923	3,974	5,964	6,930	4,962	3,331	4,057	29,218
Hernando County	175,855	5,286	7,460	5,829	8,447	11,947	8,590	6,529	6,960	48,302
Highlands County	98,236	2,654	3,969	3,756	5,155	7,954	7,322	5,061	3,933	33,181
Hillsborough County	1,316,298	30,708	40,079	26,347	32,881	41,028	29,013	19,355	23,897	172,521
Indian River County	144,755	4,999	7,351	5,067	7,278	9,713	7,479	6,721	7,638	43,896
Lake County	315,690	8,971	11,686	9,189	14,625	22,264	16,823	11,679	8,119	82,699
Lee County	679,513	19,935	29,360	21,011	35,704	45,060	32,517	21,922	22,013	178,227
Leon County	283,988	7,558	8,268	4,207	6,577	8,182	5,172	3,501	4,092	31,731
Manatee County	351,746	10,551	14,508	12,327	16,384	20,745	18,718	11,005	11,030	90,209
Marion County	339,167	9,850	14,885	10,661	16,936	25,410	16,548	13,582	11,070	94,207
Martin County	153,392	5,016	7,215	4,937	6,502	10,863	7,208	7,763	7,354	44,627
Miami-Dade County	2,662,874	60,375	87,507	51,467	69,227	94,241	74,189	54,974	60,615	404,713
Monroe County	77,136	2,536	3,482	1,749	3,627	4,616	2,557	1,317	2,037	15,903
Nassau County	76,619	2,074	3,545	2,516	3,574	3,435	2,758	1,212	1,845	15,340
Okaloosa County	196,512	4,240	6,354	4,628	5,549	6,829	5,061	4,282	3,749	30,098
Orange County	1,253,001	28,092	33,322	19,702	25,566	34,152	23,641	14,386	17,620	135,067
Osceola County	310,211	4,769	11,495	6,307	7,519	9,878	5,699	4,754	5,823	39,980
Palm Beach County	1,397,710	34,405	50,999	36,690	48,253	68,151	58,129	49,881	56,528	317,632
Pasco County	485,331	12,642	19,351	14,910	18,434	26,928	20,154	14,198	14,413	109,037
Pinellas County	938,098	28,989	39,402	26,135	34,923	52,097	38,086	29,738	34,313	215,292
Polk County	634,638	17,310	23,828	16,159	22,571	31,698	23,500	15,742	14,528	124,198
Putnam County	72,143	2,111	2,921	1,970	2,176	4,438	2,955	2,408	952	14,899
Santa Rosa County	163,422	3,636	5,287	2,971	4,992	6,758	4,416	2,609	1,967	23,713
Sarasota County	396,962	11,054	19,564	15,473	21,664	32,052	28,078	17,391	19,906	134,564
Seminole County	442,516	10,604	16,187	9,984	10,306	16,983	10,042	6,745	9,355	63,415
St. Johns County	217,919	6,504	7,587	5,652	7,980	10,464	6,235	4,448	4,858	39,637
St. Lucie County	291,028	6,375	11,656	8,922	10,481	15,580	12,037	9,070	9,183	65,273
Sumter County	114,350	3,484	8,800	7,176	11,969	19,449	11,793	5,415	4,423	60,225
Volusia County	507,531	15,297	22,320	15,395	20,117	28,700	22,369	13,011	18,119	117,711
Georgia										
Barrow County	73,240	1,587	2,278	1,141	1,840	2,511	1,778	1,061	343	8,674
Bartow County	101,736	3,136	3,375	2,533	1,816	3,721	2,576	761	1,120	12,527

Table B-2: Counties—Older Population by Age—*Continued*

	Total Population	60 to 61 Years	62 to 64 Years	65 to 66 Years	67 to 69 Years	70 to 74 Years	75 to 79 Years	80 to 84 Years	85 Years and Over	65 Years and Over
Georgia—Cont.										
Bibb County	153,905	4,736	4,814	2,830	5,026	4,601	3,588	2,462	3,037	21,544
Bulloch County	72,087	1,792	1,818	1,019	1,492	1,985	1,296	940	760	7,492
Carroll County	114,093	2,421	3,754	1,864	2,225	3,993	2,887	1,047	1,549	13,565
Catoosa County	65,621	1,702	2,769	1,400	1,537	3,149	2,402	1,116	659	10,263
Chatham County	283,379	5,455	8,874	5,866	6,784	9,755	5,593	5,178	5,290	38,466
Cherokee County	230,985	3,981	8,421	6,625	5,043	6,871	4,324	2,602	1,821	27,286
Clarke County	120,938	2,489	2,628	2,481	2,182	2,709	1,844	898	1,798	11,912
Clayton County	267,542	5,584	6,928	3,849	5,679	6,377	3,327	1,834	2,289	23,355
Cobb County	730,981	15,333	23,256	14,068	16,776	18,044	10,740	9,795	8,035	77,458
Columbia County	139,257	3,751	6,006	3,119	3,091	3,270	2,957	1,730	2,118	16,285
Coweta County	135,571	4,157	4,344	2,775	3,921	3,696	2,886	1,756	1,399	16,433
DeKalb County	722,161	16,861	21,660	12,002	14,580	19,782	12,515	8,371	7,420	74,670
Dougherty County	92,407	3,144	3,503	1,999	1,793	3,459	1,879	1,716	1,699	12,545
Douglas County	138,776	3,105	3,227	2,803	2,242	4,184	2,065	1,591	1,122	14,007
Fayette County	109,664	2,749	4,455	2,800	3,202	4,786	3,003	2,535	1,610	17,936
Floyd County	96,063	1,892	2,961	1,812	2,352	3,823	2,549	2,021	2,121	14,678
Forsyth County	204,302	3,551	6,626	2,954	5,663	5,760	3,217	2,388	2,337	22,319
Fulton County	996,319	19,294	30,854	15,360	19,089	26,978	16,202	11,574	14,598	103,801
Glynn County	82,175	2,328	3,319	2,199	2,566	3,383	2,756	2,244	1,301	14,449
Gwinnett County	877,922	16,814	25,094	14,272	16,991	17,916	12,128	6,939	7,159	75,405
Hall County	190,761	3,651	5,985	3,311	4,944	7,073	4,294	3,897	2,623	26,142
Henry County	213,869	6,220	5,460	2,825	6,602	5,573	2,795	2,994	1,214	22,003
Houston County	149,111	3,722	4,231	2,640	3,891	3,214	3,984	1,150	1,801	16,680
Liberty County	65,198	1,399	1,025	857	1,031	1,538	969	227	260	4,882
Lowndes County	113,523	1,627	3,275	1,302	3,055	3,453	2,416	1,348	844	12,418
Muscogee County	200,887	5,226	4,652	3,396	4,815	5,366	3,378	4,017	2,973	23,945
Newton County	103,675	2,283	3,790	2,107	2,789	3,344	1,928	1,390	821	12,379
Paulding County	148,987	2,807	3,527	2,303	3,132	3,574	2,835	1,464	540	13,848
Richmond County	201,368	4,954	7,307	4,431	5,218	5,201	4,080	3,147	3,355	25,432
Rockdale County	87,754	1,894	3,190	2,740	2,359	2,688	1,781	523	930	11,021
Troup County	69,469	1,697	2,502	1,367	1,414	2,541	1,951	1,574	810	9,657
Walker County	68,218	1,800	1,856	2,133	2,347	2,569	2,121	1,197	1,199	11,566
Walton County	87,615	2,201	2,198	1,524	2,675	3,426	2,400	1,318	1,069	12,412
Whitfield County	103,542	1,919	2,263	1,542	2,318	3,466	3,346	1,400	965	13,037
Hawaii										
Hawaii County	194,190	6,905	8,368	5,117	7,249	9,328	4,155	3,218	5,231	34,298
Honolulu County	991,788	23,779	32,501	23,611	28,153	31,469	24,737	20,848	27,910	156,728
Kauai County	70,475	2,083	3,470	2,498	2,069	2,721	1,529	1,678	1,886	12,381
Maui County	163,046	4,665	6,723	4,293	5,185	5,307	3,684	2,264	3,919	24,652
Idaho										
Ada County	426,236	11,203	13,324	9,582	9,186	13,772	9,081	5,521	6,852	53,994
Bannock County	83,347	2,792	2,429	1,553	2,322	2,467	2,105	1,331	888	10,666
Bonneville County	108,623	2,777	3,816	1,879	2,645	2,922	2,192	1,731	1,486	12,855
Canyon County	203,143	3,296	7,018	3,229	5,729	6,500	4,015	2,954	2,637	25,064
Kootenai County	147,326	3,631	6,617	3,133	4,752	7,155	5,025	2,290	2,971	25,326
Twin Falls County	80,914	1,722	2,488	1,662	2,055	3,083	1,835	1,826	1,623	12,084
Illinois										
Adams County	66,988	1,315	3,287	2,077	2,194	2,126	2,071	1,708	2,314	12,490
Champaign County	207,133	4,142	6,427	3,857	3,350	4,895	4,968	3,295	2,574	22,939
Cook County	5,246,456	126,335	164,203	96,599	123,821	157,682	115,528	89,005	96,449	679,084
DeKalb County	105,462	2,270	2,771	1,659	2,398	2,562	1,915	1,298	2,097	11,929
DuPage County	932,708	24,548	33,376	19,923	21,582	31,681	20,330	16,024	15,970	125,510
Kane County	527,306	12,145	16,626	10,017	12,569	15,123	9,606	7,328	7,528	62,171
Kankakee County	111,375	3,456	3,025	1,753	3,441	3,918	2,891	2,461	2,053	16,517
Kendall County	121,350	2,545	3,154	2,327	2,139	2,096	2,134	802	772	10,270
Lake County	705,186	16,757	21,632	12,601	15,337	22,216	13,563	10,144	12,027	85,888
LaSalle County	111,241	3,715	4,919	2,140	3,066	4,726	3,405	2,444	3,596	19,377
Macon County	108,350	3,451	3,811	3,107	3,050	4,252	3,419	3,094	2,331	19,253
Madison County	266,560	6,242	9,750	6,167	6,385	10,402	8,620	4,794	5,915	42,283
McHenry County	307,283	8,307	8,195	6,353	6,480	10,255	7,125	3,296	3,621	37,130
McLean County	174,061	4,336	4,197	2,505	3,447	5,056	2,788	2,835	3,195	19,826
Peoria County	187,319	5,091	7,082	3,623	5,018	6,833	5,151	3,448	3,613	27,686
Rock Island County	146,063	3,971	5,418	2,886	4,806	6,389	3,742	4,004	3,786	25,613
Sangamon County	198,997	5,702	6,975	4,314	5,294	7,552	6,517	3,387	4,318	31,382
St. Clair County	265,729	7,406	9,159	4,339	7,020	9,004	5,768	6,200	4,628	36,959
Tazewell County	135,707	4,489	4,127	3,896	3,808	4,589	4,133	3,067	3,528	23,021
Vermilion County	79,728	2,369	3,258	2,064	2,178	3,652	2,009	2,768	1,387	14,058
Will County	685,419	15,235	20,093	13,501	13,779	19,340	12,250	9,137	8,391	76,398
Williamson County	67,008	804	2,955	1,184	1,933	3,529	1,874	1,906	1,287	11,713
Winnebago County	288,542	7,000	10,524	5,464	8,799	11,275	7,834	5,945	5,685	45,002
Indiana										
Allen County	365,918	8,944	10,836	7,649	9,141	10,461	8,752	5,169	6,908	48,080
Bartholomew County	80,217	1,783	3,152	2,091	2,131	2,523	2,144	1,701	1,234	11,824
Clark County	114,262	2,116	5,128	2,292	4,774	2,921	2,390	2,045	1,957	16,379
Delaware County	117,074	2,578	3,721	2,941	3,163	4,278	3,547	1,923	2,883	18,735
Elkhart County	201,971	5,190	5,895	3,395	4,590	5,980	4,548	3,683	3,952	26,148
Floyd County	76,179	2,074	3,102	1,712	1,479	3,118	1,791	973	1,723	10,796
Grant County	68,569	2,534	2,778	1,512	2,077	3,188	2,039	1,510	1,690	12,016

Table B-2: Counties—Older Population by Age—*Continued*

	Total Population	60 to 61 Years	62 to 64 Years	65 to 66 Years	67 to 69 Years	70 to 74 Years	75 to 79 Years	80 to 84 Years	85 Years and Over	65 Years and Over
Indiana—Cont.										
Hamilton County	302,623	6,913	7,027	5,044	5,880	8,441	4,743	3,746	3,880	31,734
Hancock County	71,978	2,286	2,183	2,428	2,304	1,989	1,643	1,396	1,101	10,861
Hendricks County	156,056	3,966	4,872	3,535	3,239	4,448	3,095	2,466	2,166	18,949
Howard County	82,982	2,360	3,914	2,772	2,952	2,509	2,735	1,906	1,972	14,846
Johnson County	147,538	3,087	5,248	3,321	3,337	5,352	3,562	1,811	2,996	20,379
Kosciusko County	78,564	1,903	3,281	1,872	2,034	2,951	2,109	1,735	1,062	11,763
Lake County	490,228	12,536	17,709	10,944	12,245	16,611	10,692	9,360	11,367	71,219
LaPorte County	111,444	3,111	4,181	2,891	3,250	4,337	2,918	2,055	2,100	17,551
Madison County	130,069	3,113	4,353	3,771	4,127	4,891	3,707	3,679	2,262	22,437
Marion County	934,243	21,577	27,721	17,028	17,326	25,010	17,468	14,661	14,109	105,602
Monroe County	143,339	3,112	3,496	2,856	3,003	2,970	3,206	2,107	1,781	15,923
Morgan County	69,693	2,361	2,664	1,979	1,931	2,415	1,898	1,193	1,001	10,417
Porter County	167,076	4,298	6,285	3,563	4,123	6,441	4,554	3,084	2,453	24,218
St. Joseph County	267,618	6,901	9,938	5,157	6,483	8,629	5,609	5,947	6,183	38,008
Tippecanoe County	183,074	3,698	3,623	2,936	4,244	4,131	3,064	2,411	3,044	19,830
Vanderburgh County	182,006	4,996	6,515	4,449	4,286	5,936	4,504	3,718	4,923	27,816
Vigo County	108,175	2,655	3,261	2,187	3,282	3,549	2,072	2,024	2,721	15,835
Wayne County	67,671	1,247	2,708	1,686	1,719	3,349	2,544	1,749	1,278	12,325
Iowa										
Black Hawk County	132,897	3,331	4,661	2,538	3,861	3,708	4,333	2,810	2,297	19,547
Dallas County	77,400	1,491	1,868	1,249	1,864	1,772	1,700	557	1,382	8,524
Dubuque County	96,370	2,297	3,828	2,599	2,124	3,373	3,076	2,323	2,103	15,598
Johnson County	142,287	3,526	4,342	2,168	3,026	2,758	2,149	2,139	1,634	13,874
Linn County	217,751	4,968	7,620	4,197	5,016	7,765	5,540	4,496	3,960	30,974
Polk County	459,862	11,087	13,528	8,923	10,094	11,921	8,175	6,934	7,688	53,735
Pottawattamie County	93,128	2,267	3,523	2,360	2,788	2,749	2,360	1,758	2,438	14,453
Scott County	171,387	4,495	5,885	3,650	4,200	6,200	4,758	2,838	3,102	24,748
Story County	94,073	1,832	2,551	1,246	1,927	2,307	2,273	1,282	1,101	10,136
Woodbury County	102,271	2,862	3,337	2,162	2,648	2,934	2,200	2,189	1,736	13,869
Kansas										
Butler County	66,227	1,891	1,890	1,344	1,630	1,913	2,055	1,189	1,223	9,354
Douglas County	116,585	2,437	3,808	1,805	1,835	3,298	2,072	1,403	1,714	12,127
Johnson County	574,272	13,654	20,312	11,693	12,858	17,084	11,074	9,539	10,910	73,158
Leavenworth County	78,797	1,417	3,491	1,637	1,567	2,483	1,985	1,412	991	10,075
Riley County	75,194	918	1,055	752	984	1,279	1,157	992	967	6,131
Sedgwick County	508,803	13,118	17,498	9,575	11,887	14,982	11,046	9,787	7,801	65,078
Shawnee County	178,406	4,077	6,838	3,577	5,301	6,650	5,123	3,034	4,520	28,205
Wyandotte County	161,636	4,024	4,357	2,862	3,897	3,926	2,923	1,834	2,780	18,222
Kentucky										
Boone County	126,413	3,159	4,039	2,388	1,986	4,349	2,114	1,458	1,985	14,280
Bullitt County	77,955	1,605	3,246	1,499	2,221	3,136	1,673	1,128	835	10,492
Campbell County	91,833	2,813	3,142	1,821	2,359	3,163	2,261	1,313	1,729	12,646
Christian County	74,250	1,011	2,182	1,442	1,117	1,764	1,294	1,458	969	8,044
Daviess County	98,275	2,192	3,151	1,851	2,503	4,226	3,113	2,053	1,877	15,623
Fayette County	310,797	7,915	9,646	4,045	8,818	7,969	6,302	3,242	5,596	35,972
Hardin County	108,266	2,272	3,205	1,891	2,691	3,406	1,953	1,697	1,716	13,354
Jefferson County	760,026	17,043	27,150	17,052	18,564	26,323	19,195	13,099	16,039	110,272
Kenton County	163,929	4,192	5,136	4,676	2,881	4,682	3,634	1,584	3,427	20,884
Madison County	87,340	1,381	2,939	1,658	2,382	2,545	2,034	1,128	1,166	10,913
McCracken County	65,316	1,154	3,692	1,541	1,762	3,554	1,463	1,496	2,152	11,968
Pike County	63,034	1,458	2,685	1,683	2,668	1,937	1,438	1,205	1,332	10,263
Warren County	120,460	2,650	3,358	1,850	2,746	3,634	2,758	1,746	1,203	13,937
Louisiana										
Ascension Parish	117,029	2,700	2,321	1,797	2,778	3,187	2,271	1,086	926	12,045
Bossier Parish	125,064	3,401	3,940	2,224	3,608	3,291	2,548	2,422	1,733	15,826
Caddo Parish	252,603	6,486	7,875	5,011	6,313	9,867	7,057	4,122	5,279	37,649
Calcasieu Parish	197,204	4,891	7,603	3,983	5,007	7,008	4,217	3,513	3,501	27,229
East Baton Rouge Parish	446,042	9,611	15,606	10,843	8,790	12,860	8,569	7,363	6,330	54,755
Iberia Parish	73,913	2,708	1,565	928	1,135	3,173	1,973	1,254	1,084	9,547
Jefferson Parish	435,716	11,346	16,328	10,039	12,243	16,131	10,835	8,232	8,405	65,885
Lafayette Parish	235,644	5,252	6,980	4,065	3,573	7,673	5,375	2,620	3,123	26,429
Lafourche Parish	98,020	2,888	3,129	2,298	1,963	3,278	2,645	1,353	1,545	13,082
Livingston Parish	135,751	2,382	4,510	2,228	3,270	4,092	3,164	1,339	913	15,006
Orleans Parish	384,320	8,287	14,884	7,611	8,388	11,302	8,576	4,843	5,761	46,481
Ouachita Parish	156,325	4,639	4,879	2,843	4,237	4,523	3,774	2,967	2,376	20,720
Rapides Parish	132,488	3,200	4,024	3,738	3,294	4,556	3,699	2,091	2,378	19,756
St. Landry Parish	83,709	2,077	2,854	1,805	2,249	2,821	2,028	1,473	1,937	12,313
St. Tammany Parish	245,829	6,086	9,797	6,087	7,533	9,574	5,358	4,271	4,287	37,110
Tangipahoa Parish	127,049	3,177	3,788	2,890	3,077	4,447	2,443	1,923	1,453	16,233
Terrebonne Parish	113,328	2,786	3,120	2,316	2,050	3,623	2,129	2,124	1,659	13,901
Maine										
Androscoggin County	107,440	2,906	3,532	2,426	2,808	4,773	2,830	2,649	1,850	17,336
Aroostook County	69,447	2,514	3,158	2,531	2,995	2,735	2,706	1,544	2,280	14,791
Cumberland County	287,797	8,918	11,106	6,516	9,660	10,595	7,194	6,036	7,190	47,191
Kennebec County	121,112	3,409	5,406	2,484	4,294	5,548	3,628	3,084	2,384	21,422
Penobscot County	153,414	5,004	5,713	3,670	4,131	6,328	3,663	3,919	3,416	25,127
York County	200,710	6,843	8,596	6,334	6,371	8,051	6,016	4,620	4,570	35,962

Table B-2: Counties—Older Population by Age—*Continued*

	Total Population	60 to 61 Years	62 to 64 Years	65 to 66 Years	67 to 69 Years	70 to 74 Years	75 to 79 Years	80 to 84 Years	85 Years and Over	65 Years and Over
Maryland										
Allegany County	72,952	1,444	2,757	1,941	2,652	2,848	2,617	1,991	1,822	13,871
Anne Arundel County	560,133	13,978	18,919	11,937	14,262	19,630	11,262	9,149	8,810	75,050
Baltimore County	826,925	20,472	29,480	20,230	22,352	27,462	24,093	15,902	20,733	130,772
Calvert County	90,613	2,440	2,826	1,839	1,726	3,449	1,567	1,496	1,539	11,616
Carroll County	167,830	4,573	5,210	4,332	4,789	5,994	4,983	2,790	3,064	25,952
Cecil County	102,383	2,726	3,030	2,779	2,552	3,507	2,482	1,178	1,689	14,187
Charles County	154,747	3,586	4,267	2,420	3,194	4,881	2,896	2,288	1,750	17,429
Frederick County	243,675	5,864	8,219	4,920	5,790	7,719	5,535	3,695	4,165	31,024
Harford County	250,105	6,466	9,998	5,666	6,862	9,703	5,465	4,285	4,584	36,565
Howard County	309,284	7,832	10,172	5,844	7,462	10,393	5,950	3,689	4,292	37,630
Montgomery County	1,030,447	24,589	34,386	20,694	25,444	32,695	22,098	15,971	24,064	140,966
Prince George's County	904,430	20,684	29,882	18,409	21,685	24,347	16,250	11,081	10,346	102,118
St. Mary's County	110,382	3,356	3,304	1,749	2,780	3,935	2,238	1,162	1,302	13,166
Washington County	149,573	3,183	4,969	3,117	4,180	5,705	3,861	2,855	3,546	23,264
Wicomico County	101,539	2,565	4,470	1,908	2,747	3,909	2,183	1,689	2,084	14,520
Massachusetts										
Barnstable County	214,914	6,915	12,350	6,694	10,332	15,543	11,796	8,128	7,498	59,991
Berkshire County	128,715	3,554	6,323	3,660	4,516	6,375	4,718	3,073	4,323	26,665
Bristol County	554,194	16,604	18,665	10,017	15,872	22,779	14,436	10,650	13,289	87,043
Essex County	769,091	20,708	27,100	18,915	20,082	27,289	18,322	16,043	18,724	119,375
Franklin County	70,862	2,770	3,678	2,351	2,909	2,544	1,504	1,573	1,995	12,876
Hampden County	468,161	14,681	15,478	11,281	11,018	16,409	11,362	8,723	12,260	71,053
Hampshire County	160,939	3,583	5,989	4,705	3,868	5,379	3,906	2,890	3,322	24,070
Middlesex County	1,570,315	35,945	50,859	32,169	37,661	50,732	37,926	29,246	32,141	219,875
Norfolk County	692,254	20,010	23,183	15,045	20,426	22,544	16,664	15,507	18,186	108,372
Plymouth County	507,022	14,521	21,084	11,640	15,370	21,506	14,553	10,037	9,189	82,295
Suffolk County	767,254	16,573	20,848	11,598	14,372	20,828	14,030	11,282	12,077	84,187
Worcester County	813,475	20,512	29,103	17,194	19,809	26,990	16,660	16,013	18,217	114,883
Michigan										
Allegan County	113,847	3,788	3,851	2,208	3,689	4,501	3,446	1,345	1,920	17,109
Bay County	106,179	2,764	3,960	2,799	3,688	4,263	3,446	3,070	2,221	19,487
Berrien County	155,233	4,912	5,977	4,045	4,478	6,541	5,135	3,589	3,430	27,218
Calhoun County	134,878	4,574	5,103	3,341	3,667	5,260	4,204	2,215	3,110	21,797
Clinton County	77,297	1,990	3,192	1,564	2,270	3,120	2,301	1,253	1,262	11,770
Eaton County	108,579	2,969	3,880	2,665	3,716	4,280	2,998	2,235	2,295	18,189
Genesee County	412,895	10,632	15,796	9,630	12,015	15,047	12,334	8,619	7,341	64,986
Grand Traverse County	90,782	2,691	3,685	2,522	3,223	3,137	2,338	2,388	1,858	15,466
Ingham County	284,582	6,761	9,509	5,703	7,420	7,127	4,905	4,156	4,689	34,000
Isabella County	70,616	1,520	1,907	992	1,157	2,182	1,276	983	999	7,589
Jackson County	159,741	3,907	6,067	2,806	4,974	6,708	4,708	3,337	3,238	25,771
Kalamazoo County	258,818	5,397	10,020	5,097	6,424	7,945	5,310	5,244	4,778	34,798
Kent County	629,237	14,892	19,355	11,772	12,780	18,162	11,433	8,627	14,316	77,090
Lapeer County	88,153	2,269	3,818	2,168	2,485	4,103	2,154	1,791	1,637	14,338
Lenawee County	99,047	2,522	3,801	2,255	2,914	4,489	3,174	1,888	1,745	16,465
Livingston County	185,596	5,281	6,658	4,452	5,395	7,482	5,033	2,800	2,274	27,436
Macomb County	860,112	25,987	30,330	17,597	22,526	33,708	23,256	16,589	20,210	133,886
Marquette County	67,676	1,835	3,104	1,222	2,083	3,036	2,389	1,203	1,324	11,257
Midland County	83,427	2,161	2,714	1,668	2,149	3,726	2,218	2,172	1,902	13,835
Monroe County	149,824	4,118	6,022	3,530	3,973	6,116	4,424	2,392	3,255	23,690
Muskegon County	172,344	4,742	5,378	4,232	4,552	5,910	4,396	3,470	3,289	25,849
Oakland County	1,237,868	36,148	45,750	29,035	30,552	47,575	28,246	24,509	26,325	186,242
Ottawa County	276,292	6,252	8,288	5,994	6,139	8,791	5,518	5,187	4,816	36,445
Saginaw County	195,012	4,780	8,173	4,488	5,294	8,547	6,464	4,878	3,726	33,397
Shiawassee County	68,933	2,012	2,936	1,989	1,937	2,640	1,938	1,344	1,745	11,593
St. Clair County	160,078	4,329	7,038	3,738	5,303	6,548	4,658	3,721	2,962	26,930
Van Buren County	75,199	2,358	3,469	1,793	2,023	3,402	2,371	1,557	1,157	12,303
Washtenaw County	356,874	8,466	12,432	6,370	8,422	11,448	6,890	4,473	5,441	43,044
Wayne County	1,764,804	45,513	61,625	36,987	42,680	56,672	39,514	32,311	35,546	243,710
Minnesota										
Anoka County	341,864	7,028	11,875	7,611	6,911	10,448	6,794	3,893	4,550	40,207
Blue Earth County	65,385	1,567	1,683	1,177	1,282	1,961	1,519	986	1,490	8,415
Carver County	97,338	2,653	2,811	1,487	1,677	2,296	1,302	1,087	1,598	9,447
Dakota County	412,529	10,333	12,182	7,379	10,010	12,137	9,323	6,160	5,251	50,260
Hennepin County	1,212,064	28,725	40,306	22,462	28,341	33,641	24,114	19,340	23,578	151,476
Olmsted County	150,287	3,345	5,372	3,046	3,246	4,700	3,855	2,914	2,994	20,755
Ramsey County	532,655	13,832	18,425	10,007	12,633	14,823	11,779	8,410	11,408	69,060
Rice County	65,151	1,254	2,405	1,566	1,572	1,768	2,138	1,289	816	9,149
Scott County	139,672	2,121	3,872	1,827	2,795	3,290	1,959	1,789	1,297	12,957
Sherburne County	91,126	1,954	2,203	1,124	1,819	2,741	1,454	831	1,284	9,253
St. Louis County	200,949	6,288	8,799	4,451	5,773	8,697	5,952	4,296	5,352	34,521
Stearns County	152,912	3,227	4,239	2,845	3,691	4,256	3,598	2,726	3,228	20,344
Washington County	249,283	5,591	8,486	4,816	5,768	8,346	4,543	3,805	4,474	31,752
Wright County	129,918	2,514	4,318	2,522	2,544	3,656	2,575	1,626	1,569	14,492
Mississippi										
DeSoto County	170,913	4,295	4,398	3,322	3,621	5,652	3,258	2,487	2,059	20,399
Forrest County	76,330	2,423	2,433	1,630	1,752	2,271	1,396	1,262	1,096	9,407
Harrison County	199,058	4,443	6,885	3,406	5,759	6,306	4,573	4,016	2,419	26,479
Hinds County	243,729	5,339	7,472	4,772	4,489	7,761	4,709	3,489	4,485	29,705

Table B-2: Counties—Older Population by Age—*Continued*

	Total Population	60 to 61 Years	62 to 64 Years	65 to 66 Years	67 to 69 Years	70 to 74 Years	75 to 79 Years	80 to 84 Years	85 Years and Over	65 Years and Over
Mississippi—Cont.										
Jackson County	141,137	2,957	4,637	3,068	4,354	4,918	3,736	1,484	2,408	19,968
Jones County	68,290	1,293	2,174	1,595	1,941	2,673	1,677	1,422	1,292	10,600
Lauderdale County	79,739	1,766	2,863	1,333	2,103	2,991	2,430	1,488	1,614	11,959
Lee County	85,246	1,946	1,849	2,064	2,767	2,294	1,887	1,400	1,737	12,149
Madison County	101,688	2,950	3,743	2,088	2,707	2,959	1,806	1,654	1,428	12,642
Rankin County	148,070	3,020	4,860	2,842	3,706	4,736	3,431	2,672	2,069	19,456
Missouri										
Boone County	172,717	4,114	5,596	2,838	2,655	5,465	3,181	1,981	2,293	18,413
Buchanan County	89,486	2,202	2,528	2,170	2,201	2,827	2,106	1,839	1,818	12,961
Cape Girardeau County	78,043	2,278	3,003	1,447	2,456	2,540	2,029	1,624	1,997	12,093
Cass County	100,889	2,945	3,521	2,212	3,288	3,399	2,871	2,287	1,388	15,445
Christian County	82,101	1,517	3,571	1,658	2,672	2,974	1,787	1,060	1,822	11,973
Clay County	233,682	5,411	7,703	4,555	4,906	7,990	5,388	3,675	3,229	29,743
Cole County	76,557	2,140	2,800	1,173	1,606	3,453	2,032	1,410	1,141	10,815
Franklin County	102,084	2,596	3,568	2,462	2,026	4,735	2,524	2,308	2,003	16,058
Greene County	285,865	5,907	9,307	5,500	7,801	10,211	8,207	6,231	5,826	43,776
Jackson County	683,191	15,072	23,000	12,804	16,238	22,309	17,406	12,388	11,139	92,284
Jasper County	117,543	2,301	3,993	1,878	3,275	3,773	2,671	1,942	2,476	16,015
Jefferson County	222,716	6,094	8,218	5,379	6,557	7,117	4,667	3,613	2,823	30,156
Platte County	94,788	2,159	3,274	2,343	2,630	2,544	1,252	1,532	1,675	11,976
St. Charles County	379,493	9,952	10,654	7,225	9,666	12,853	9,385	5,999	5,903	51,031
St. Francois County	65,960	2,845	2,660	1,761	1,164	2,838	1,326	1,538	1,468	10,095
St. Louis County	1,001,876	24,843	40,164	23,351	27,548	37,176	29,581	22,867	24,306	164,829
Montana										
Cascade County	82,344	1,870	3,408	1,879	2,331	3,403	2,704	2,015	1,424	13,756
Flathead County	94,924	3,529	3,754	2,461	2,930	4,578	3,718	1,664	1,186	16,537
Gallatin County	97,308	2,315	2,940	1,591	1,772	3,143	1,789	1,434	978	10,707
Lewis and Clark County	65,856	2,131	3,045	1,518	2,020	2,893	1,567	1,321	1,361	10,680
Missoula County	112,684	2,295	4,110	2,660	3,078	3,577	1,633	1,558	2,649	15,155
Yellowstone County	155,634	4,534	5,435	3,185	4,518	5,217	4,337	3,386	3,029	23,672
Nebraska										
Douglas County	543,244	12,225	16,727	8,541	11,389	15,355	9,757	7,190	10,377	62,609
Lancaster County	301,795	7,155	8,560	5,111	6,755	8,902	5,732	5,059	4,779	36,338
Sarpy County	172,193	3,793	4,128	3,249	3,392	4,018	2,269	2,424	2,147	17,499
Nevada										
Clark County	2,069,681	47,540	65,899	44,595	53,513	73,584	46,875	31,962	24,386	274,915
Washoe County	440,078	12,138	16,555	10,550	13,863	16,108	8,940	8,419	6,546	64,426
New Hampshire										
Cheshire County	76,115	2,673	3,692	1,708	2,767	3,131	2,064	1,410	1,918	12,998
Grafton County	89,658	3,178	4,362	1,807	3,496	3,934	2,402	1,982	2,275	15,896
Hillsborough County	405,184	10,745	13,594	8,678	10,427	13,493	9,085	7,110	7,581	56,374
Merrimack County	147,171	4,539	5,805	3,185	4,328	6,040	4,137	2,902	2,888	23,480
Rockingham County	300,621	10,426	11,835	8,043	9,332	10,364	7,207	4,704	6,138	45,788
Strafford County	125,604	2,991	4,509	2,442	2,750	4,462	3,193	2,153	1,887	16,887
New Jersey										
Atlantic County	275,209	7,217	11,374	5,814	8,369	11,435	8,044	5,426	4,347	43,435
Bergen County	933,572	25,123	32,100	18,873	26,108	35,018	26,919	19,577	23,126	149,621
Burlington County	449,722	12,667	13,146	9,213	12,260	17,179	12,089	10,173	9,185	70,099
Camden County	511,038	12,720	18,271	10,265	14,044	16,758	11,113	10,058	10,516	72,754
Cape May County	95,344	3,749	4,422	3,190	4,149	5,571	4,463	2,895	2,659	22,927
Cumberland County	157,389	3,855	4,111	3,913	3,293	4,882	3,467	2,733	2,994	21,282
Essex County	795,723	19,373	24,011	14,209	16,935	23,826	16,806	11,278	15,119	98,173
Gloucester County	290,951	7,497	10,570	6,502	7,534	10,088	5,536	4,975	6,459	41,094
Hudson County	669,115	13,766	21,739	9,873	13,414	17,683	14,068	7,930	9,084	72,052
Hunterdon County	126,067	3,615	5,075	3,004	4,268	4,593	2,796	2,122	2,830	19,613
Mercer County	371,537	8,585	13,017	8,104	8,856	11,361	8,782	7,263	6,863	51,229
Middlesex County	836,297	21,590	26,178	17,165	20,644	24,592	17,743	14,495	17,308	111,947
Monmouth County	629,279	16,970	23,366	14,663	16,386	24,060	14,862	12,543	15,704	98,218
Morris County	499,727	13,618	17,120	12,042	14,351	17,524	11,965	9,979	11,426	77,287
Ocean County	586,301	14,381	21,979	14,821	20,542	31,223	23,485	16,459	21,904	128,434
Passaic County	508,856	12,176	16,496	9,924	11,983	15,634	11,605	7,434	10,040	66,620
Salem County	64,715	1,546	2,651	1,418	1,691	2,989	1,660	1,460	1,759	10,977
Somerset County	332,568	7,708	13,644	5,672	8,085	10,751	7,103	7,660	6,577	45,848
Sussex County	144,909	4,186	6,237	4,076	4,182	5,065	3,650	2,016	2,243	21,232
Union County	552,939	11,979	16,709	10,111	12,401	16,943	9,766	12,074	10,755	72,050
Warren County	106,917	2,595	4,345	2,969	3,360	3,669	1,856	2,289	3,090	17,233
New Mexico										
Bernalillo County	675,551	18,163	23,997	13,951	19,503	21,674	16,733	12,862	11,046	95,769
Chaves County	65,878	1,557	2,994	1,528	1,655	2,461	1,952	1,500	711	9,807
Doña Ana County	213,676	4,029	7,830	4,414	5,122	7,776	5,053	4,370	3,322	30,057
Lea County	69,999	1,755	1,546	844	1,572	1,326	1,842	1,100	656	7,340
McKinley County	74,098	2,077	2,102	847	1,206	2,162	1,334	1,394	566	7,509
Otero County	65,082	1,699	2,185	1,566	2,019	2,551	2,359	929	942	10,366
San Juan County	123,785	2,744	4,063	2,370	2,645	3,934	2,835	1,997	2,028	15,809
Sandoval County	137,608	3,362	4,974	3,003	4,373	5,783	3,618	2,215	1,994	20,986
Santa Fe County	148,164	4,170	8,250	4,673	6,533	7,461	4,643	3,080	2,639	29,029
Valencia County	75,817	1,571	3,549	1,430	1,867	3,868	2,575	1,290	596	11,626

Table B-2: Counties—Older Population by Age—*Continued*

	Total Population	60 to 61 Years	62 to 64 Years	65 to 66 Years	67 to 69 Years	70 to 74 Years	75 to 79 Years	80 to 84 Years	85 Years and Over	65 Years and Over
New York										
Albany County	308,171	6,457	11,311	7,798	7,549	10,769	8,536	6,505	6,170	47,327
Bronx County	1,438,159	29,996	37,480	23,065	26,182	41,706	30,268	20,287	20,245	161,753
Broome County	197,349	5,216	9,295	4,854	6,174	6,710	6,120	5,158	5,355	34,371
Cattaraugus County	78,600	2,710	3,053	1,546	2,478	3,582	2,218	1,924	1,680	13,428
Cayuga County	78,823	2,205	3,030	2,007	2,535	2,731	2,413	1,505	1,955	13,146
Chautauqua County	132,053	3,560	4,777	3,198	4,184	5,321	3,900	3,422	3,616	23,641
Chemung County	87,770	2,653	3,775	2,529	2,665	3,012	2,127	2,154	2,414	14,901
Clinton County	81,632	2,510	2,611	1,694	2,124	3,177	2,297	1,704	1,290	12,286
Dutchess County	296,579	8,531	10,984	7,650	7,807	10,630	7,490	5,271	6,648	45,496
Erie County	922,835	24,607	35,157	21,640	26,607	32,688	24,595	22,267	24,864	152,661
Jefferson County	119,103	2,780	3,033	2,081	2,159	4,075	2,890	1,861	1,566	14,632
Kings County	2,621,793	55,771	79,937	49,197	58,207	69,377	51,785	41,628	47,342	317,536
Livingston County	64,586	2,697	2,210	1,440	1,509	2,887	1,789	1,308	1,623	10,556
Madison County	72,369	2,003	3,251	1,118	2,108	3,352	2,234	1,012	1,562	11,386
Monroe County	749,857	18,476	29,205	14,843	21,988	27,531	19,900	12,788	18,948	115,998
Nassau County	1,358,627	36,805	47,058	29,473	40,353	47,266	37,152	31,350	37,327	222,921
New York County	1,636,268	41,440	49,496	33,473	40,810	55,923	39,028	30,303	35,425	234,962
Niagara County	213,525	6,790	8,556	5,147	6,231	8,707	6,393	4,417	6,032	36,927
Oneida County	232,871	7,632	7,957	5,559	7,190	9,141	7,627	4,694	6,483	40,694
Onondaga County	468,196	11,968	17,446	10,008	11,475	17,004	11,873	9,479	11,833	71,672
Ontario County	109,707	2,850	4,890	2,731	4,432	4,196	2,591	2,378	3,264	19,592
Orange County	376,099	8,295	11,628	7,148	8,273	11,767	8,321	6,402	5,505	47,416
Oswego County	120,913	2,813	4,112	2,129	3,283	4,968	2,614	2,144	2,225	17,363
Putnam County	99,487	2,673	4,115	2,072	3,485	3,367	2,011	1,679	1,741	14,355
Queens County	2,321,580	56,999	69,865	45,224	56,102	73,149	56,344	39,681	45,379	315,879
Rensselaer County	159,774	4,661	6,672	3,984	4,563	5,388	4,375	2,478	3,292	24,080
Richmond County	473,279	12,821	16,864	9,923	12,393	17,801	11,073	7,792	9,281	68,263
Rockland County	323,866	7,283	10,295	6,658	9,374	10,827	7,224	6,875	7,153	48,111
Saratoga County	224,921	5,946	9,097	6,137	7,410	7,447	5,619	3,660	4,949	35,222
Schenectady County	155,735	3,355	6,564	3,530	3,408	5,179	3,204	4,194	4,543	24,058
St. Lawrence County	111,400	2,803	4,402	2,296	3,214	4,184	2,823	2,031	2,445	16,993
Steuben County	98,394	3,071	3,417	2,512	3,500	3,702	3,417	1,752	2,461	17,344
Suffolk County	1,502,968	35,917	50,113	33,157	40,324	55,139	39,962	31,499	28,677	228,758
Sullivan County	75,943	1,881	3,337	1,757	2,263	4,203	2,162	1,580	873	12,838
Tompkins County	104,691	2,868	3,411	1,905	1,381	3,880	1,648	1,192	2,319	12,325
Ulster County	180,445	4,610	7,958	4,802	6,216	7,401	3,930	5,278	4,110	31,737
Warren County	64,973	2,151	3,057	1,704	2,099	3,572	1,864	1,542	2,024	12,805
Wayne County	92,051	2,328	4,154	1,653	3,229	4,326	2,204	1,593	2,336	15,341
Westchester County	972,634	24,316	32,591	19,650	26,520	34,201	25,493	20,473	25,886	152,223
North Carolina										
Alamance County	155,792	3,617	5,035	4,043	4,791	5,371	4,364	3,240	3,301	25,110
Brunswick County	118,836	4,503	5,974	4,142	7,932	9,733	4,734	3,134	2,271	31,946
Buncombe County	250,539	6,605	10,605	6,380	8,659	10,456	8,088	5,859	5,676	45,118
Burke County	89,486	2,376	3,663	2,345	2,960	4,145	2,684	2,088	2,140	16,362
Cabarrus County	192,103	4,047	5,371	3,011	4,595	6,546	3,564	3,084	3,027	23,827
Caldwell County	81,484	2,800	3,206	2,408	3,217	3,345	2,126	2,135	1,509	14,740
Carteret County	68,811	2,350	2,670	2,374	3,397	3,626	2,840	1,595	1,462	15,294
Catawba County	154,534	3,911	4,773	3,552	5,133	5,706	5,385	3,021	2,016	24,813
Chatham County	68,698	1,466	2,630	1,944	3,047	4,294	2,211	2,213	2,375	16,084
Cleveland County	97,076	3,727	3,722	1,904	3,390	4,604	3,217	1,905	1,817	16,837
Craven County	104,510	2,476	3,958	1,589	3,521	4,986	2,631	2,348	2,535	17,610
Cumberland County	326,328	7,173	8,351	3,414	7,551	10,059	6,672	4,524	3,066	35,286
Davidson County	164,072	4,386	5,300	4,473	4,636	7,020	5,205	4,034	1,653	27,021
Durham County	294,460	7,077	8,966	5,884	4,763	8,320	5,677	3,114	4,598	32,356
Forsyth County	365,298	8,992	12,679	8,981	10,246	10,432	8,125	6,776	7,633	52,193
Gaston County	211,127	5,534	6,547	5,126	6,600	7,533	4,491	3,907	4,349	32,006
Guilford County	512,119	11,795	14,839	9,027	12,542	18,898	10,769	9,851	9,221	70,308
Harnett County	126,666	2,784	2,760	1,810	2,926	3,765	2,333	1,404	1,431	13,669
Henderson County	111,149	2,343	4,508	3,491	4,739	7,288	4,366	3,715	3,906	27,505
Iredell County	166,675	4,960	4,594	4,459	4,443	5,726	4,335	3,291	1,869	24,123
Johnston County	181,423	3,680	7,154	3,250	5,311	5,468	2,969	2,791	2,215	22,004
Lincoln County	79,829	2,006	3,448	2,618	2,434	3,051	2,200	1,461	1,130	12,894
Mecklenburg County	1,012,539	20,633	25,779	16,709	21,488	23,356	16,278	11,828	11,895	101,554
Moore County	93,077	1,599	3,430	3,224	3,146	5,692	3,169	2,770	4,339	22,340
Nash County	94,357	2,855	4,402	1,967	3,165	3,900	2,220	2,637	1,552	15,441
New Hanover County	216,298	5,417	7,852	6,315	6,302	7,540	5,601	4,069	4,277	34,104
Onslow County	187,589	1,718	3,472	3,358	2,919	3,392	3,211	2,023	1,085	15,988
Orange County	140,420	3,511	4,931	2,269	3,675	3,814	2,635	1,686	1,637	15,716
Pitt County	175,354	3,743	4,222	4,522	3,416	4,190	2,801	2,474	2,417	19,820
Randolph County	142,778	4,670	5,144	4,003	4,616	5,442	3,981	2,703	2,442	23,187
Robeson County	134,760	2,780	4,671	2,611	3,608	4,479	2,804	2,065	1,812	17,379
Rockingham County	91,696	2,895	4,083	2,394	2,510	4,595	3,427	1,472	2,235	16,633
Rowan County	138,630	3,292	4,305	4,567	4,108	4,480	4,436	3,072	1,903	22,566
Rutherford County	66,600	2,029	2,753	1,924	2,858	2,718	1,918	1,373	2,213	13,004
Surry County	72,968	2,042	2,267	2,040	2,096	3,562	2,637	1,609	1,826	13,770
Union County	218,568	3,893	6,310	3,930	5,154	7,632	3,545	2,549	2,421	25,231
Wake County	998,691	22,406	27,033	16,222	22,318	22,962	16,810	11,739	9,873	99,924
Wayne County	124,456	2,959	3,085	2,438	3,711	4,216	3,955	1,804	1,903	18,027
Wilkes County	68,838	1,830	2,672	1,992	3,010	3,010	2,674	1,571	1,405	13,662
Wilson County	81,401	1,991	3,188	1,349	2,264	4,010	3,277	1,059	1,473	13,432

Table B-2: Counties—Older Population by Age—*Continued*

	Total Population	60 to 61 Years	62 to 64 Years	65 to 66 Years	67 to 69 Years	70 to 74 Years	75 to 79 Years	80 to 84 Years	85 Years and Over	65 Years and Over
North Dakota										
Burleigh County	90,503	1,580	3,494	1,753	1,779	3,366	1,973	1,745	2,440	13,056
Cass County	167,005	2,939	5,662	2,585	3,317	3,493	3,255	2,417	2,648	17,715
Grand Forks County	70,138	1,288	2,172	1,038	1,527	1,694	1,409	895	1,245	7,808
Ward County	69,384	1,535	1,525	973	1,425	1,633	1,445	862	1,550	7,888
Ohio										
Allen County	105,040	3,010	4,098	1,971	3,309	3,843	2,395	3,027	1,998	16,543
Ashtabula County	99,175	3,291	4,158	2,898	2,170	4,745	3,300	1,500	2,391	17,004
Belmont County	69,461	1,536	3,515	1,950	2,440	2,763	2,338	1,556	2,149	13,196
Butler County	374,158	7,660	10,910	9,106	8,107	11,208	9,886	4,921	6,196	49,424
Clark County	136,554	3,602	5,430	3,289	4,084	6,286	3,910	3,394	3,393	24,356
Clermont County	201,560	6,313	7,138	4,563	5,844	6,859	5,057	3,767	2,230	28,320
Columbiana County	105,686	3,477	4,083	2,615	3,289	4,801	3,375	2,520	2,592	19,192
Cuyahoga County	1,259,828	34,106	46,945	27,524	35,796	45,310	38,982	27,054	32,684	207,350
Delaware County	189,113	3,734	5,859	3,446	4,557	5,285	3,625	1,843	2,566	21,322
Erie County	75,828	2,159	2,380	1,773	2,213	4,249	2,252	2,210	1,942	14,639
Fairfield County	150,381	4,247	5,941	3,168	4,504	5,163	4,190	2,675	2,107	21,807
Franklin County	1,231,393	25,882	38,163	20,503	25,638	31,899	24,011	14,156	17,500	133,707
Geauga County	94,295	2,726	3,790	3,117	2,756	3,738	2,855	1,403	2,757	16,626
Greene County	163,820	4,672	6,030	3,661	4,156	6,944	4,287	3,363	3,196	25,607
Hamilton County	806,631	22,753	28,332	15,579	18,886	26,934	19,473	15,021	18,600	114,493
Hancock County	75,337	2,107	2,080	1,456	2,159	3,010	1,688	1,626	2,007	11,946
Jefferson County	67,694	2,256	2,521	1,862	2,113	3,044	2,124	2,069	2,043	13,255
Lake County	229,230	6,937	7,682	5,882	7,489	9,814	7,533	4,899	5,353	40,970
Licking County	169,390	4,048	6,349	4,853	4,406	6,253	3,953	3,347	3,143	25,955
Lorain County	304,216	8,004	11,516	6,925	8,635	12,840	7,865	5,591	7,526	49,382
Lucas County	435,286	12,402	15,629	10,170	11,475	13,479	10,571	7,182	10,326	63,203
Mahoning County	233,204	7,340	9,316	7,376	5,324	10,313	7,577	5,278	8,686	44,554
Marion County	65,720	1,963	1,587	2,113	1,700	2,300	1,902	1,379	1,613	11,007
Medina County	176,029	5,278	6,087	3,822	5,131	7,290	4,936	2,369	3,566	27,114
Miami County	103,900	3,097	3,959	2,618	2,995	4,707	3,545	2,183	1,733	17,781
Montgomery County	533,116	13,882	19,743	10,447	17,508	20,016	16,944	13,074	10,750	88,739
Muskingum County	85,818	2,022	3,588	2,587	2,386	2,852	2,247	2,134	2,018	14,224
Portage County	161,882	4,694	6,381	2,768	3,793	7,288	3,710	3,037	3,299	23,895
Richland County	121,942	3,603	4,618	2,843	4,334	4,916	4,526	2,686	2,710	22,015
Ross County	77,159	1,878	3,580	1,283	1,770	3,491	2,368	1,568	916	11,396
Scioto County	77,258	2,108	2,914	1,861	2,310	2,820	2,334	1,754	1,687	12,766
Stark County	375,736	12,057	14,699	9,861	11,087	15,619	12,830	7,677	9,107	66,181
Summit County	541,943	14,866	20,239	13,195	16,712	18,227	15,219	10,506	13,667	87,526
Trumbull County	205,175	5,862	8,085	4,563	6,439	10,800	5,975	5,422	6,389	39,588
Tuscarawas County	92,788	2,807	3,293	1,945	2,381	4,609	3,146	1,925	2,740	16,746
Warren County	221,659	5,433	7,990	5,916	5,756	5,245	5,987	3,583	2,472	28,959
Wayne County	115,537	2,725	4,234	2,676	3,113	4,407	3,275	2,407	2,491	18,369
Wood County	129,590	2,871	4,947	2,901	2,982	4,235	2,895	2,680	2,352	18,045
Oklahoma										
Canadian County	129,582	2,332	4,420	2,841	3,024	3,576	2,167	2,085	1,935	15,628
Cleveland County	269,908	5,673	9,050	5,003	7,005	7,342	5,610	4,088	3,086	32,134
Comanche County	125,033	2,616	3,210	2,214	1,754	3,725	2,662	2,184	1,238	13,777
Creek County	70,632	2,221	2,496	1,558	2,167	3,272	2,418	1,452	993	11,860
Muskogee County	69,966	1,598	2,462	1,852	1,912	2,606	1,306	1,776	1,696	11,148
Oklahoma County	766,215	16,940	22,627	13,309	18,752	22,356	17,035	12,106	12,163	95,721
Payne County	80,264	1,756	1,947	1,406	1,149	2,440	1,617	838	1,339	8,789
Pottawatomie County	71,811	1,949	2,553	1,581	2,190	2,739	1,862	1,466	1,390	11,228
Rogers County	89,815	2,526	2,717	1,901	2,932	3,341	2,624	1,608	1,471	13,877
Tulsa County	629,598	16,530	19,440	12,516	15,292	18,620	13,203	11,291	11,171	82,093
Wagoner County	75,702	1,749	2,646	1,661	2,877	2,696	1,639	1,297	1,040	11,210
Oregon										
Benton County	86,316	2,422	2,914	1,576	2,097	3,457	1,370	1,714	2,159	12,373
Clackamas County	394,972	11,446	16,254	11,074	12,067	15,318	11,080	6,790	7,640	63,969
Deschutes County	170,388	6,390	6,837	4,395	5,812	8,563	5,094	2,751	3,703	30,318
Douglas County	106,972	4,021	5,831	3,828	4,033	6,255	4,540	2,834	3,680	25,170
Jackson County	210,287	7,032	10,596	5,376	7,380	11,979	6,611	4,990	5,864	42,200
Josephine County	83,599	3,112	4,708	3,993	4,040	4,164	4,425	1,968	2,077	20,667
Klamath County	65,455	2,256	3,094	1,377	2,219	3,877	1,825	1,044	1,962	12,304
Lane County	358,337	9,879	15,059	8,960	12,509	15,270	9,504	7,240	8,754	62,237
Linn County	119,356	3,773	4,302	2,096	3,700	6,557	2,968	2,841	2,558	20,720
Marion County	326,110	8,903	11,832	7,766	8,009	11,722	7,999	5,675	6,015	47,186
Multnomah County	776,712	18,568	28,909	15,980	18,698	21,305	13,616	9,736	13,285	92,620
Polk County	77,916	2,226	2,630	2,263	1,900	3,857	1,674	1,958	1,949	13,601
Umatilla County	76,705	1,671	2,586	1,408	2,067	2,797	2,168	1,645	1,448	11,533
Washington County	562,998	13,571	17,211	10,292	14,867	14,923	9,590	7,215	9,984	66,871
Yamhill County	101,758	2,244	3,743	3,044	2,638	3,189	2,098	2,345	2,235	15,549
Pennsylvania										
Adams County	101,714	2,603	4,432	2,836	3,250	4,098	3,683	2,511	1,894	18,272
Allegheny County	1,231,255	35,036	48,390	28,598	36,876	44,592	35,735	31,108	36,759	213,668
Armstrong County	67,785	1,669	3,152	1,850	2,494	3,063	2,278	1,500	2,470	13,655
Beaver County	169,392	5,199	6,702	4,072	5,833	7,456	5,856	5,346	4,883	33,446
Berks County	413,691	10,930	15,363	9,307	11,123	15,466	11,650	9,818	9,085	66,449
Blair County	125,955	4,141	4,887	3,492	3,787	5,430	3,820	3,440	4,143	24,112

Table B-2: Counties—Older Population by Age—*Continued*

	Total Population	60 to 61 Years	62 to 64 Years	65 to 66 Years	67 to 69 Years	70 to 74 Years	75 to 79 Years	80 to 84 Years	85 Years and Over	65 Years and Over
Pennsylvania—Cont.										
Bucks County	626,685	18,678	22,946	14,644	19,976	23,313	·18,531	13,365	14,754	104,583
Butler County	185,943	5,451	6,740	4,516	5,424	7,101	5,256	4,323	4,708	31,328
Cambria County	137,732	4,049	6,248	4,595	4,029	5,937	4,578	4,062	4,887	28,088
Carbon County	64,441	1,870	2,241	2,238	2,317	2,706	2,243	2,129	1,096	12,729
Centre County	158,742	3,546	4,789	3,235	3,254	4,495	4,198	2,274	2,417	19,873
Chester County	512,784	13,810	16,422	10,562	13,424	18,240	12,337	9,026	10,445	74,034
Clearfield County	81,191	2,191	3,693	1,829	3,072	3,412	2,939	1,869	2,219	15,340
Columbia County	67,122	2,308	2,196	1,474	2,192	2,598	2,182	1,581	1,390	11,417
Crawford County	87,175	2,701	4,637	1,782	3,240	4,302	2,951	2,027	1,617	15,919
Cumberland County	243,762	6,534	9,520	5,924	6,512	10,188	7,706	5,247	5,882	41,459
Dauphin County	271,453	8,232	9,876	6,926	7,855	8,159	6,566	5,072	6,315	40,893
Delaware County	562,960	14,696	20,932	11,079	16,059	17,163	13,822	13,044	13,937	85,104
Erie County	278,443	8,353	9,073	5,835	8,071	10,052	7,757	5,930	6,442	44,087
Fayette County	134,086	4,101	6,254	3,581	4,678	5,815	4,230	3,605	4,169	26,078
Franklin County	152,892	4,412	5,456	3,757	5,140	6,335	4,641	3,865	4,037	27,775
Indiana County	87,706	2,342	3,246	2,345	2,671	3,131	2,434	2,233	2,054	14,868
Lackawanna County	212,719	5,582	9,391	4,631	6,908	9,763	6,043	5,236	7,617	40,198
Lancaster County	533,320	14,709	17,167	13,603	14,635	17,753	16,986	11,594	13,077	87,648
Lawrence County	88,771	2,782	3,441	1,810	3,192	3,887	3,084	2,507	3,075	17,555
Lebanon County	136,359	3,693	5,004	3,394	4,527	5,122	4,441	4,051	3,161	24,696
Lehigh County	357,823	9,486	13,173	8,515	8,715	13,210	9,776	7,501	9,530	57,247
Luzerne County	318,829	9,001	12,796	7,956	9,556	14,155	9,824	7,822	10,955	60,268
Lycoming County	116,508	4,214	5,075	2,964	3,330	4,847	2,883	3,228	3,224	20,476
Mercer County	114,884	3,798	4,506	2,420	4,304	5,232	4,541	3,176	3,239	22,912
Monroe County	166,314	3,537	7,157	3,860	4,340	7,015	3,567	3,479	3,255	25,516
Montgomery County	816,857	21,624	29,414	17,090	21,496	31,757	22,489	18,457	22,393	133,682
Northampton County	300,654	9,069	11,361	6,531	9,142	11,942	8,817	6,449	9,327	52,208
Northumberland County	93,944	2,463	3,744	2,651	3,367	3,888	3,531	2,450	2,721	18,608
Philadelphia County	1,560,297	36,317	45,147	27,735	36,238	43,893	32,513	25,816	29,379	195,574
Schuylkill County	145,797	4,638	6,455	3,600	4,507	6,905	4,425	4,184	4,590	28,211
Somerset County	76,218	2,914	2,670	1,823	2,552	3,916	2,784	2,133	2,400	15,608
Washington County	208,187	5,643	9,314	5,541	7,537	8,261	7,503	4,631	6,144	39,617
Westmoreland County	359,320	12,215	14,997	11,121	12,392	16,513	12,607	9,175	12,542	74,350
York County	440,755	12,583	14,797	10,374	12,531	17,244	12,517	10,076	7,480	70,222
Rhode Island										
Kent County	165,128	3,850	6,500	3,999	5,525	6,350	3,800	3,861	5,675	29,210
Newport County	82,358	2,361	4,221	2,231	3,432	3,472	3,091	1,644	2,107	15,977
Providence County	631,974	15,371	22,691	11,523	15,432	20,412	14,333	12,233	16,025	89,958
Washington County	126,653	2,668	6,607	3,261	4,113	5,461	3,211	3,452	3,315	22,813
South Carolina										
Aiken County	164,753	5,232	6,714	3,730	5,506	7,963	3,915	4,804	2,883	28,801
Anderson County	192,810	4,077	7,731	3,607	6,555	9,000	6,169	3,539	3,732	32,602
Beaufort County	175,852	4,774	7,059	5,776	8,595	12,058	7,234	4,397	4,469	42,529
Berkeley County	198,205	5,077	6,231	3,951	5,925	6,213	3,471	2,309	2,376	24,245
Charleston County	381,015	10,664	14,111	9,431	12,068	12,003	8,782	6,091	6,772	55,147
Darlington County	67,799	2,394	2,841	2,142	1,943	2,646	2,153	1,394	856	11,134
Dorchester County	148,469	3,569	4,163	3,307	3,584	4,299	3,012	1,893	1,468	17,563
Florence County	139,231	4,451	6,257	3,047	4,354	5,116	3,754	2,075	2,292	20,638
Greenville County	482,752	10,905	17,133	10,134	13,880	17,283	10,920	8,556	8,484	69,257
Greenwood County	69,520	1,517	2,409	1,836	1,959	2,847	2,009	959	2,217	11,827
Horry County	298,832	9,043	14,086	8,991	12,260	18,253	10,575	6,161	4,919	61,159
Lancaster County	83,160	2,298	2,991	2,942	3,060	3,599	2,390	2,139	1,412	15,542
Laurens County	66,533	1,449	2,761	1,389	2,760	2,306	1,195	1,929	1,444	11,023
Lexington County	277,888	6,700	9,054	5,424	8,043	10,733	6,411	4,240	4,473	39,324
Oconee County	75,192	2,310	4,045	1,984	4,127	3,677	2,862	2,029	1,271	15,950
Orangeburg County	90,090	3,321	3,097	2,042	2,740	4,240	2,959	1,177	2,064	15,222
Pickens County	120,368	3,155	3,898	3,355	3,274	4,671	3,232	2,204	1,674	18,410
Richland County	401,566	7,853	12,842	6,911	9,555	11,138	7,404	5,994	4,257	45,259
Spartanburg County	293,542	7,529	8,485	6,076	10,047	10,509	7,530	5,759	4,478	44,399
Sumter County	107,919	2,532	3,581	1,857	3,290	3,706	3,416	1,337	1,882	15,488
York County	245,346	5,814	8,355	6,718	5,783	7,929	6,322	3,162	2,592	32,506
South Dakota										
Minnehaha County	182,882	3,069	5,308	3,584	4,322	4,785	3,047	3,315	3,479	22,532
Pennington County	108,242	2,891	3,583	2,740	2,544	3,873	2,865	2,069	2,148	16,239
Tennessee										
Anderson County	75,528	1,952	3,830	2,105	3,066	2,930	3,224	1,555	1,514	14,394
Blount County	126,339	3,761	4,199	3,792	4,219	6,024	4,307	2,376	2,644	23,362
Bradley County	102,975	2,767	3,831	2,184	3,022	4,593	3,124	1,809	1,825	16,557
Davidson County	668,347	17,920	17,560	11,301	13,724	17,988	12,481	9,534	9,077	74,165
Greene County	68,335	1,891	2,946	1,977	2,540	3,736	2,636	1,209	1,475	13,573
Hamilton County	351,220	8,954	14,402	8,838	10,533	12,219	8,681	8,556	6,920	55,747
Knox County	448,644	10,700	17,199	10,888	11,712	15,048	11,371	7,736	8,430	65,185
Madison County	98,178	2,011	3,549	2,151	2,993	3,468	2,256	1,878	1,921	14,667
Maury County	85,515	1,738	3,502	1,954	2,345	3,403	2,621	1,455	880	12,658
Montgomery County	189,961	3,641	4,596	3,239	3,347	3,785	4,030	1,153	977	16,531
Putnam County	74,165	1,778	2,645	1,574	2,151	3,142	2,430	1,547	1,058	11,902
Robertson County	68,079	1,967	1,219	1,469	1,676	2,244	1,525	1,174	932	9,020
Rutherford County	288,906	4,680	8,230	4,148	5,252	8,076	4,994	3,143	2,435	28,048

Table B-2: Counties—Older Population by Age—*Continued*

	Total Population	60 to 61 Years	62 to 64 Years	65 to 66 Years	67 to 69 Years	70 to 74 Years	75 to 79 Years	80 to 84 Years	85 Years and Over	65 Years and Over
Tennessee—Cont.										
Sevier County	95,110	2,747	3,537	2,277	2,942	5,573	2,914	1,795	1,475	16,976
Shelby County	938,803	22,918	30,073	18,491	20,422	25,728	15,440	14,190	14,641	108,912
Sullivan County	157,047	4,285	6,227	3,972	6,484	7,800	5,814	3,925	3,838	31,833
Sumner County	172,706	4,438	5,572	4,155	4,562	7,016	3,817	3,282	2,708	25,540
Washington County	126,242	3,320	5,634	3,122	4,339	5,053	4,535	2,148	2,126	21,323
Williamson County	205,226	5,039	5,529	4,603	4,412	5,117	3,048	3,313	2,806	23,299
Wilson County	125,376	2,515	5,342	2,900	4,329	4,121	3,403	1,916	1,269	17,938
Texas										
Angelina County	87,750	2,034	2,396	2,145	2,322	3,233	2,324	1,192	2,710	13,926
Bastrop County	78,069	2,774	3,863	1,066	2,446	2,742	1,485	718	1,222	9,679
Bell County	329,140	5,692	8,771	4,943	6,537	7,893	3,769	4,383	4,954	32,479
Bexar County	1,855,866	35,752	53,035	31,599	40,285	49,507	35,130	27,362	25,716	209,599
Bowie County	93,275	2,349	2,742	1,533	2,930	3,699	2,339	1,930	1,713	14,144
Brazoria County	338,124	7,513	10,043	6,863	5,350	10,613	7,545	3,355	2,847	36,573
Brazos County	209,152	3,876	4,602	2,774	3,073	4,294	2,777	2,479	1,878	17,275
Cameron County	420,392	7,271	11,302	9,361	8,755	10,844	9,636	6,420	7,032	52,048
Collin County	885,241	19,331	23,831	13,214	18,729	24,163	13,153	7,805	8,772	85,836
Comal County	123,694	3,804	6,591	2,976	4,453	5,609	3,609	2,858	1,850	21,355
Coryell County	75,562	964	1,188	1,622	999	1,196	1,223	568	700	6,308
Dallas County	2,518,638	52,546	67,381	37,263	45,557	61,612	41,527	29,226	28,715	243,900
Denton County	753,363	12,629	17,609	11,238	15,369	17,232	10,765	6,970	4,236	65,810
Ector County	153,904	3,263	3,536	2,663	3,021	2,492	2,363	2,327	1,798	14,664
El Paso County	833,487	14,986	22,335	12,137	14,975	24,531	18,335	13,056	10,849	93,883
Ellis County	159,317	3,907	4,916	3,319	3,644	4,976	3,336	1,863	1,649	18,787
Fort Bend County	685,345	14,565	19,365	11,134	14,121	17,099	10,348	6,044	6,004	64,750
Galveston County	314,198	9,128	10,244	6,377	7,271	10,855	5,902	5,823	4,078	40,306
Grayson County	123,534	3,991	4,924	2,924	3,365	5,836	3,630	2,909	2,202	20,866
Gregg County	123,204	2,357	4,684	2,044	4,119	3,628	3,227	2,536	2,227	17,781
Guadalupe County	147,250	3,489	3,882	2,929	3,572	4,948	3,536	2,132	1,947	19,064
Harris County	4,441,370	92,782	119,363	67,981	80,367	104,311	65,474	47,404	43,480	409,017
Harrison County	67,336	1,555	2,687	1,961	1,530	2,276	1,277	1,455	1,653	10,152
Hays County	185,025	3,726	5,057	3,146	3,756	5,261	2,796	2,053	1,507	18,519
Henderson County	79,290	3,151	2,224	2,033	3,630	3,922	2,998	2,554	1,600	16,737
Hidalgo County	831,073	10,532	17,645	12,225	15,083	21,418	15,752	11,859	10,077	86,414
Hunt County	88,493	1,920	3,706	1,805	2,391	3,838	2,672	1,916	1,293	13,915
Jefferson County	252,235	5,864	8,144	5,334	6,671	5,871	6,426	4,626	4,796	33,724
Johnson County	157,456	4,530	4,285	3,327	4,224	4,904	3,963	1,557	2,200	20,175
Kaufman County	111,236	1,991	3,278	2,019	3,008	3,123	2,507	1,065	1,082	12,804
Liberty County	78,117	1,967	3,121	1,934	819	3,460	1,399	1,445	892	9,949
Lubbock County	293,974	5,334	7,401	5,528	6,405	7,632	5,939	5,045	4,137	34,686
McLennan County	243,441	6,171	5,698	4,520	6,378	7,131	5,869	4,909	3,945	32,752
Midland County	155,830	4,947	4,157	2,632	2,956	2,543	2,116	2,640	2,205	15,092
Montgomery County	518,947	12,389	17,744	9,527	13,370	16,385	8,891	7,956	6,365	62,494
Nacogdoches County	65,301	1,281	2,301	1,153	1,779	1,728	2,001	723	1,127	8,511
Nueces County	356,221	9,621	11,714	7,334	8,291	11,071	7,820	6,298	5,264	46,078
Orange County	83,433	1,680	2,834	2,103	2,001	3,359	1,931	1,701	1,570	12,665
Parker County	123,164	3,605	5,005	2,974	3,702	4,608	3,352	1,625	2,151	18,412
Potter County	121,627	2,261	2,800	1,731	2,912	3,441	2,692	1,704	1,841	14,321
Randall County	128,220	3,154	4,227	2,212	3,180	4,663	2,842	2,307	2,221	17,425
Rockwall County	87,809	1,365	2,673	1,863	1,666	2,914	2,450	760	957	10,610
San Patricio County	66,915	1,311	1,423	1,939	1,963	2,121	1,343	990	1,009	9,365
Smith County	218,842	6,404	7,416	3,534	5,871	9,804	6,044	4,571	4,075	33,899
Tarrant County	1,945,360	38,813	50,610	31,662	39,938	48,150	35,165	23,853	20,030	198,798
Taylor County	135,143	2,985	3,764	2,206	3,501	4,155	3,416	2,272	3,009	18,559
Tom Green County	116,608	2,513	3,524	1,867	2,744	4,215	3,348	2,591	2,460	17,225
Travis County	1,151,145	22,371	31,406	16,037	19,570	24,476	13,798	11,715	11,553	97,149
Victoria County	91,081	1,981	3,892	1,357	2,605	3,358	1,643	2,128	1,844	12,935
Walker County	69,789	1,498	2,158	1,538	724	1,880	1,463	747	943	7,295
Webb County	266,673	3,783	6,266	3,229	4,294	5,729	3,955	2,805	2,496	22,508
Wichita County	132,355	3,304	4,172	2,101	3,172	4,158	2,605	3,530	2,422	17,988
Williamson County	489,250	10,048	14,903	7,929	10,556	14,188	8,771	6,140	5,719	53,303
Utah										
Cache County	118,343	1,839	2,645	1,631	1,838	2,131	1,876	1,134	1,428	10,038
Davis County	329,692	5,358	8,306	4,771	5,776	6,994	6,438	3,207	2,858	30,044
Salt Lake County	1,091,742	21,626	32,484	16,287	19,301	26,651	17,954	12,224	12,889	105,306
Utah County	560,974	6,774	9,998	5,679	8,428	9,273	7,703	5,811	3,253	40,147
Washington County	151,948	3,532	4,356	4,037	4,262	8,174	5,577	4,083	3,932	30,065
Weber County	240,475	5,417	6,262	5,297	4,112	6,192	4,806	2,673	3,701	26,781
Vermont										
Chittenden County	160,531	4,569	5,718	3,287	3,787	4,921	2,751	3,429	2,863	21,038
Virginia										
Albemarle County	104,489	2,741	4,674	3,135	2,617	3,705	2,963	1,922	3,124	17,466
Arlington County	226,908	4,787	6,058	2,941	4,189	5,028	2,964	2,178	2,920	20,220
Augusta County	73,862	2,273	3,054	1,556	3,215	3,675	3,196	1,832	641	14,115
Bedford County	76,583	3,035	2,983	2,161	2,960	3,908	2,793	1,975	986	14,783
Chesterfield County	332,499	8,008	12,967	7,816	8,689	11,065	5,892	4,144	5,165	42,771
Fairfax County	1,137,538	25,247	37,478	20,861	27,472	32,122	21,345	12,665	15,957	130,422
Fauquier County	68,248	1,168	3,536	1,677	2,354	2,846	1,764	1,329	936	10,906

Table B-2: Counties—Older Population by Age—*Continued*

	Total Population	60 to 61 Years	62 to 64 Years	65 to 66 Years	67 to 69 Years	70 to 74 Years	75 to 79 Years	80 to 84 Years	85 Years and Over	65 Years and Over
Virginia—Cont.										
Frederick County	82,377	1,863	2,751	1,810	2,173	3,549	2,142	1,129	1,748	12,551
Hanover County	101,918	3,371	4,362	2,376	2,522	4,639	2,366	2,302	1,864	16,069
Henrico County	321,924	9,281	9,250	6,662	7,452	10,854	7,880	4,815	6,764	44,427
James City County	72,583	1,769	3,212	1,611	2,790	4,997	2,908	2,118	2,076	16,500
Loudoun County	363,050	7,892	8,953	5,559	5,482	6,836	4,646	3,196	3,002	28,721
Montgomery County	97,244	1,369	2,504	1,349	2,334	2,587	1,683	1,502	1,447	10,902
Prince William County	446,094	7,741	11,459	7,162	7,019	9,887	5,393	3,902	3,519	36,882
Roanoke County	93,785	3,558	4,671	2,193	3,620	4,335	3,343	1,833	2,873	18,197
Rockingham County	78,171	2,096	2,305	2,368	2,012	3,583	2,569	1,618	2,160	14,310
Spotsylvania County	129,188	3,036	3,582	2,746	2,869	4,080	2,430	1,679	1,788	15,592
Stafford County	139,992	2,934	3,534	1,797	2,936	3,229	2,252	1,193	1,468	12,875
York County	66,342	1,360	1,801	1,650	2,050	2,298	1,435	1,161	1,286	9,880
Washington										
Benton County	186,486	5,161	6,978	3,426	5,197	6,127	3,446	3,454	3,603	25,253
Chelan County	74,588	1,847	3,408	2,038	2,731	2,607	2,426	1,300	1,824	12,926
Clallam County	72,715	3,136	3,620	3,202	3,408	4,388	3,104	2,210	3,167	19,479
Clark County	451,008	10,363	16,601	10,359	13,546	14,676	9,890	7,348	6,200	62,019
Cowlitz County	102,133	3,363	3,771	2,233	3,791	4,821	3,025	2,014	2,370	18,254
Franklin County	87,809	1,414	2,289	1,585	1,391	1,750	912	605	668	6,911
Grant County	93,147	2,353	3,332	1,645	2,833	2,507	1,475	1,934	1,346	11,740
Grays Harbor County	70,818	1,990	3,054	2,568	2,140	3,582	2,228	1,518	1,384	13,420
Island County	79,275	2,408	3,321	3,432	3,309	4,408	2,769	2,285	1,979	18,182
King County	2,079,967	49,740	68,566	39,858	48,449	59,308	39,549	28,434	37,733	253,331
Kitsap County	254,183	6,410	9,724	6,846	8,280	10,463	6,790	3,479	4,994	40,852
Lewis County	75,128	1,764	2,790	1,581	2,503	4,404	2,086	1,842	2,331	14,747
Pierce County	831,928	19,438	24,754	16,559	21,773	24,540	16,091	12,148	14,243	105,354
Skagit County	120,365	3,438	4,804	2,951	4,520	5,934	3,582	3,015	2,862	22,864
Snohomish County	759,583	21,045	26,118	15,895	19,194	20,401	12,810	11,161	11,830	91,291
Spokane County	484,318	12,129	16,202	11,791	13,169	17,896	9,553	9,383	10,425	72,217
Thurston County	265,851	7,864	10,386	7,167	7,783	9,216	6,300	5,226	4,593	40,285
Whatcom County	208,351	5,305	8,683	5,278	4,989	9,218	5,693	2,579	4,198	31,955
Yakima County	247,687	4,096	7,784	4,650	4,725	8,730	5,549	4,135	3,816	31,605
West Virginia										
Berkeley County	110,497	2,889	3,500	3,033	1,860	4,225	2,298	1,780	1,335	14,531
Cabell County	97,109	3,177	3,689	2,672	2,670	3,854	3,298	1,478	2,605	16,577
Harrison County	68,761	1,910	2,775	1,819	2,762	2,366	2,305	1,265	1,771	12,288
Kanawha County	190,223	5,315	7,843	4,951	5,958	8,689	6,495	4,101	4,208	34,402
Monongalia County	103,463	2,498	2,305	1,975	2,417	1,970	1,833	1,450	1,367	11,012
Raleigh County	78,241	2,015	3,496	1,959	2,792	3,340	2,753	1,480	1,883	14,207
Wood County	86,237	2,594	2,843	2,156	3,053	4,015	3,406	1,548	1,895	16,073
Wisconsin										
Brown County	256,670	5,624	9,236	4,782	7,071	7,354	5,846	4,180	4,511	33,744
Dane County	516,284	12,990	17,368	9,653	12,374	14,046	9,231	7,226	8,977	61,507
Dodge County	88,574	2,512	3,440	1,932	2,258	3,241	2,862	2,282	1,716	14,291
Eau Claire County	101,564	2,281	2,898	1,682	2,624	3,511	2,034	2,043	2,146	14,040
Fond du Lac County	101,759	3,606	3,839	2,161	2,589	4,351	2,474	2,194	3,137	16,906
Jefferson County	84,395	2,451	2,863	1,696	2,457	3,059	2,460	1,304	1,512	12,488
Kenosha County	168,068	4,600	5,409	3,244	3,285	5,967	3,158	2,486	3,417	21,557
La Crosse County	118,011	3,542	3,856	2,679	3,168	3,425	3,139	2,232	2,555	17,198
Manitowoc County	80,160	2,412	3,040	2,011	2,506	3,482	2,481	1,869	2,685	15,034
Marathon County	135,780	3,610	5,056	3,646	3,759	4,123	3,512	3,000	3,386	21,426
Milwaukee County	956,406	23,489	30,680	17,826	18,440	25,206	16,980	16,677	20,818	115,947
Outagamie County	182,006	3,893	6,317	3,249	4,377	5,430	4,492	3,394	2,604	23,546
Ozaukee County	87,470	3,062	3,604	2,149	2,950	3,525	2,538	1,896	2,211	15,269
Portage County	70,482	1,853	2,338	1,398	1,845	2,520	1,959	1,392	1,110	10,224
Racine County	195,163	4,723	7,483	4,261	5,078	7,128	4,792	3,918	4,309	29,486
Rock County	161,188	4,505	5,006	2,820	5,119	5,353	3,941	2,600	4,347	24,180
Sheboygan County	115,290	2,359	4,831	2,293	2,715	4,826	3,283	2,577	2,826	18,520
St. Croix County	86,759	1,982	3,194	1,869	1,943	2,431	1,394	1,420	1,457	10,514
Walworth County	103,527	3,147	2,996	1,898	3,094	3,866	2,792	2,010	1,950	15,610
Washington County	133,251	3,475	4,832	2,841	3,855	5,047	4,155	2,015	3,071	20,984
Waukesha County	395,118	12,350	15,092	9,321	11,977	14,428	11,993	8,909	8,648	65,276
Winnebago County	169,511	3,726	6,017	3,345	4,754	5,221	4,667	3,889	3,315	25,191
Wood County	73,608	1,925	2,267	1,424	2,210	3,642	2,059	1,906	2,581	13,822
Wyoming										
Laramie County	96,389	2,287	3,916	1,825	3,109	3,400	2,183	2,037	1,343	13,897
Natrona County	81,624	2,147	3,197	1,740	1,717	2,089	2,020	1,262	1,147	9,975

Table B-3: Places—Older Population by Age

	Total Population	60 to 61 Years	62 to 64 Years	65 to 66 Years	67 to 69 Years	70 to 74 Years	75 to 79 Years	80 to 84 Years	85 Years and Over	65 Years and Over
Alabama										
Birmingham city	212,653	6,282	7,314	4,224	4,929	5,740	5,256	3,308	3,440	26,897
Dothan city	69,400	2,050	2,273	1,568	2,097	2,556	2,236	1,290	1,308	11,055
Hoover city	84,352	1,670	3,209	2,509	2,484	3,472	3,055	1,531	2,012	15,063
Huntsville city	187,592	3,908	5,644	3,141	3,394	7,567	6,292	5,235	3,803	29,432
Mobile city	194,670	4,208	6,545	4,246	5,189	6,242	4,698	3,491	4,536	28,402
Montgomery city	200,486	5,230	5,594	4,066	5,121	5,554	5,791	3,563	2,330	26,425
Tuscaloosa city	96,116	1,466	3,209	1,573	2,102	3,044	1,707	1,772	1,480	11,678
Alaska										
Anchorage municipality	301,010	6,302	7,491	4,494	5,346	6,788	4,877	2,932	2,469	26,906
Arizona										
Avondale city	79,621	716	1,590	956	1,378	1,811	1,055	717	85	6,002
Chandler city	254,275	5,340	6,195	4,850	5,161	5,571	4,599	2,625	2,099	24,905
Flagstaff city	68,786	1,447	1,667	1,304	1,842	1,259	1,021	768	511	6,705
Glendale city	237,529	4,136	7,763	4,965	5,297	5,446	3,973	2,464	3,143	25,288
Goodyear city	75,676	3,124	2,945	1,587	2,436	2,376	2,070	1,321	436	10,226
Mesa city	464,682	9,512	15,062	8,516	12,191	18,903	12,799	9,958	11,007	73,374
Peoria city	166,955	4,786	5,533	3,760	5,226	6,535	5,036	3,685	3,653	27,895
Phoenix city	1,537,045	30,295	43,502	25,657	30,344	37,087	23,229	17,057	16,922	150,296
Scottsdale city	230,502	6,089	9,471	6,747	9,226	11,811	9,639	5,612	7,809	50,844
Surprise city	126,278	3,062	4,514	3,605	4,278	7,164	4,421	3,407	2,444	25,319
Tempe city	172,836	2,831	4,347	3,458	3,576	3,970	3,080	2,183	2,282	18,549
Tucson city	527,948	13,460	17,511	9,936	12,871	15,709	12,589	9,709	9,461	70,275
Yuma city	93,399	1,495	2,391	1,787	1,484	3,701	3,161	2,260	940	13,333
Arkansas										
Fayetteville city	80,614	1,402	1,885	764	1,141	1,140	1,519	952	1,217	6,733
Fort Smith city	87,362	1,945	2,573	1,200	1,991	2,526	1,906	1,601	1,837	11,061
Jonesboro city	72,214	1,016	2,338	1,542	1,329	2,225	1,923	1,772	984	9,775
Little Rock city	197,701	5,209	7,309	4,303	5,106	5,316	4,341	3,211	3,883	26,160
North Little Rock city	66,813	1,338	2,007	1,811	2,232	1,504	1,137	1,228	871	8,783
Springdale city	78,122	1,528	1,637	1,244	1,396	1,665	1,657	507	929	7,398
California										
Alameda city	77,661	2,697	3,419	1,622	1,622	2,758	1,271	1,025	1,321	9,619
Alhambra city	85,585	2,077	3,460	2,135	2,415	2,234	1,664	2,585	1,202	12,235
Anaheim city	346,961	8,591	9,529	6,545	5,557	8,127	6,572	3,649	4,219	34,669
Antioch city	108,953	2,786	3,907	1,861	2,077	2,816	2,367	1,700	1,111	11,932
Bakersfield city	368,748	7,710	10,863	5,205	4,735	9,071	6,527	3,610	4,676	33,824
Baldwin Park city	77,134	1,563	2,164	1,142	2,206	1,442	1,361	1,231	728	8,110
Bellflower city	78,246	1,843	2,037	1,230	1,296	2,732	1,448	595	1,180	8,481
Berkeley city	118,851	2,439	4,530	2,376	3,600	3,306	2,189	1,633	1,911	15,015
Buena Park city	83,114	1,265	2,774	1,029	1,446	2,396	1,324	1,336	1,512	9,043
Burbank city	105,366	2,152	3,118	1,627	2,435	3,608	2,850	2,776	1,998	15,294
Camarillo city	66,932	1,994	1,661	1,596	2,259	3,055	2,119	1,679	1,736	12,444
Carlsbad city	112,310	2,982	4,705	1,472	3,995	4,115	2,918	1,820	2,549	16,869
Carson city	93,272	1,751	2,537	1,736	1,964	3,467	2,375	1,876	1,157	12,575
Chico city	89,187	1,580	2,289	904	2,539	2,341	1,520	1,225	1,874	10,403
Chino city	84,743	908	1,464	1,554	1,648	1,572	1,137	532	531	6,974
Chino Hills city	77,005	2,107	2,385	1,224	974	741	1,362	592	1,217	6,110
Chula Vista city	260,977	4,472	5,323	3,268	5,625	9,449	6,858	4,271	4,097	33,568
Citrus Heights city	86,147	1,572	3,417	2,258	2,446	2,829	3,117	1,449	1,974	14,073
Clovis city	102,190	2,036	3,456	1,503	1,743	2,790	1,847	1,162	1,538	10,583
Compton city	98,596	1,491	2,372	775	1,343	1,242	1,050	838	1,290	6,538
Concord city	127,511	2,716	4,058	2,936	3,694	4,117	2,447	1,156	2,543	16,893
Corona city	161,498	4,208	5,636	2,340	3,665	4,046	2,548	1,299	1,707	15,605
Costa Mesa city	112,793	2,109	2,495	1,605	2,162	2,121	1,933	1,169	1,527	10,517
Daly City city	106,099	2,340	3,247	2,307	3,906	3,962	3,206	2,630	1,934	17,945
Davis city	66,733	1,319	1,367	896	1,381	1,042	1,336	735	1,043	6,433
Downey city	114,168	3,031	2,811	1,540	2,572	2,622	2,398	1,564	1,923	12,619
El Cajon city	103,075	1,717	2,389	2,090	2,553	3,136	1,547	1,548	1,570	12,444
El Monte city	116,617	1,837	3,849	2,536	2,561	2,613	2,735	1,826	2,029	14,300
Elk Grove city	163,560	3,522	4,654	2,666	2,738	4,851	2,709	3,013	1,725	17,702
Escondido city	150,252	3,680	3,706	2,075	2,732	4,001	2,679	2,045	3,646	17,178
Fairfield city	111,139	2,808	3,783	1,770	2,448	3,265	2,819	1,087	1,800	13,189
Folsom city	75,366	1,109	2,646	1,109	1,997	2,614	2,363	975	1,587	10,645
Fontana city	204,953	3,050	4,177	2,219	3,672	4,585	2,918	1,549	1,361	16,304
Fremont city	228,760	5,120	6,544	4,317	4,535	5,961	3,420	3,636	3,400	25,269
Fresno city	515,985	12,497	13,515	9,016	10,391	12,922	9,861	6,018	7,297	55,505
Fullerton city	139,663	2,314	3,080	1,714	2,501	3,006	3,214	2,697	2,994	16,126
Garden Grove city	175,085	3,499	5,366	2,723	4,050	5,525	4,471	3,039	2,619	22,427
Glendale city	200,161	5,215	6,891	4,377	6,034	7,606	6,803	3,958	4,233	33,011
Hawthorne city	87,591	1,980	1,840	1,573	743	1,779	2,380	1,086	822	8,383
Hayward city	154,633	3,681	4,353	2,592	3,981	2,684	2,933	2,280	2,827	17,297
Hemet city	83,040	2,038	3,012	2,061	3,749	3,785	2,556	2,679	4,771	19,601
Hesperia city	92,744	2,016	2,957	1,279	2,111	1,851	915	1,197	1,067	8,420
Huntington Beach city	200,814	4,728	5,583	4,157	7,461	6,751	5,207	4,836	3,000	31,412
Indio city	85,639	1,601	2,238	1,620	2,376	3,877	1,718	1,341	1,150	12,082
Inglewood city	111,901	2,269	3,002	2,198	1,683	3,318	1,484	1,403	1,444	11,530
Irvine city	248,521	4,743	5,282	3,818	5,186	6,403	4,350	3,239	2,268	25,264
Jurupa Valley city	98,843	2,115	1,570	994	1,842	2,310	1,247	1,136	1,050	8,579

Table B-3: Places—Older Population by Age—*Continued*

	Total Population	60 to 61 Years	62 to 64 Years	65 to 66 Years	67 to 69 Years	70 to 74 Years	75 to 79 Years	80 to 84 Years	85 Years and Over	65 Years and Over
California—Cont.										
Laguna Niguel city	65,435	1,825	3,215	1,355	2,512	3,119	1,048	1,092	1,043	10,169
Lake Forest city	80,125	1,875	2,122	1,212	2,359	1,536	1,226	1,233	990	8,556
Lakewood city	81,641	2,177	2,557	1,707	1,962	2,824	1,692	1,406	741	10,332
Lancaster city	161,036	3,146	3,671	2,436	3,416	4,429	2,752	1,989	1,654	16,676
Livermore city	86,856	1,601	3,050	1,700	2,400	2,947	1,685	1,164	1,247	11,143
Long Beach city	473,605	10,789	12,909	7,757	10,161	10,971	6,558	6,700	5,359	47,506
Los Angeles city	3,928,827	83,920	109,814	69,501	78,990	103,389	77,294	59,488	66,466	455,128
Lynwood city	71,846	1,691	1,727	816	960	944	1,506	163	842	5,231
Manteca city	73,477	1,359	2,215	1,802	1,856	2,243	1,827	792	713	9,233
Menifee city	85,201	1,938	3,205	1,818	2,865	3,307	3,450	2,558	2,344	16,342
Merced city	81,739	1,472	1,254	1,459	1,775	2,152	1,351	1,298	1,218	9,253
Milpitas city	73,679	1,617	2,459	1,081	1,246	1,910	1,707	994	584	7,522
Mission Viejo city	97,231	2,313	2,903	1,747	3,021	3,118	3,649	1,582	2,766	15,883
Modesto city	209,308	4,724	6,639	4,169	4,152	7,316	5,360	3,625	4,152	28,774
Moreno Valley city	202,978	3,263	5,744	2,951	3,733	5,034	2,731	1,362	1,717	17,528
Mountain View city	79,374	1,170	2,158	1,138	1,523	2,299	1,335	753	1,273	8,321
Murrieta city	108,371	2,328	1,999	996	1,535	2,366	1,735	2,579	1,432	10,643
Napa city	80,009	2,591	2,997	1,744	1,469	3,005	1,173	1,613	2,129	11,133
Newport Beach city	87,242	2,271	3,231	3,110	4,104	3,989	2,160	1,994	3,143	18,500
Norwalk city	107,111	2,345	3,420	1,242	2,370	2,796	2,208	1,417	1,548	11,581
Oakland city	413,782	8,678	14,345	6,887	9,566	11,798	7,116	7,761	5,923	49,051
Oceanside city	174,552	3,697	4,896	3,188	4,205	6,185	5,659	5,054	3,391	27,682
Ontario city	169,085	2,115	4,547	1,792	2,108	3,875	2,094	1,755	1,708	13,332
Orange city	139,826	2,678	3,440	1,885	2,672	4,002	2,524	1,849	1,767	14,699
Oxnard city	205,434	3,957	4,415	2,709	4,293	4,537	2,654	2,528	2,417	19,138
Palmdale city	158,274	3,748	3,820	1,721	2,374	3,316	2,971	1,428	750	12,560
Palo Alto city	66,968	1,640	1,652	1,474	1,892	2,829	1,960	1,859	1,885	11,899
Pasadena city	140,860	3,430	3,983	2,491	3,567	4,179	3,855	2,606	2,491	19,189
Perris city	73,751	1,003	1,119	995	1,302	1,112	501	570	66	4,546
Pittsburg city	68,122	1,314	2,039	823	1,215	2,478	965	903	1,097	7,481
Pleasanton city	77,676	2,020	1,706	1,327	1,726	2,661	1,758	1,797	1,098	10,367
Pomona city	153,381	3,359	3,045	1,365	2,563	3,210	3,094	2,047	1,879	14,158
Rancho Cordova city	69,727	1,543	1,966	1,620	1,369	2,060	1,455	907	884	8,295
Rancho Cucamonga city	174,302	4,703	4,397	4,003	4,000	3,578	2,331	1,604	1,872	17,388
Redding city	91,588	2,391	3,788	2,728	2,528	3,734	2,516	2,321	2,935	16,762
Redlands city	70,618	1,265	2,076	1,787	1,051	2,022	1,585	1,400	1,023	8,868
Redondo Beach city	68,146	1,487	2,125	796	1,599	2,120	854	1,034	947	7,350
Redwood City city	82,868	2,419	2,143	1,310	2,353	2,866	1,510	1,083	1,287	10,409
Rialto city	102,740	1,849	2,333	1,323	1,688	2,207	1,193	1,089	1,135	8,635
Richmond city	108,562	2,645	4,690	2,401	2,143	2,792	2,252	1,455	1,324	12,367
Riverside city	319,519	6,018	10,395	4,385	5,995	6,296	4,803	4,321	4,544	30,344
Roseville city	128,593	1,855	3,885	3,375	3,728	4,962	3,126	3,063	3,491	21,745
Sacramento city	485,193	11,489	15,257	10,189	10,418	11,569	9,241	7,332	7,676	56,425
Salinas city	156,678	4,387	3,504	2,300	1,559	2,697	2,002	2,061	1,839	12,458
San Bernardino city	215,227	3,697	4,180	2,835	3,789	4,640	2,717	2,085	2,054	18,120
San Buenaventura (Ventura) city	109,478	3,612	4,267	2,257	3,080	3,151	3,269	2,577	3,122	17,456
San Clemente city	65,342	1,518	2,262	1,604	2,168	2,725	2,783	844	2,008	12,132
San Diego city	1,381,083	31,912	39,569	20,707	28,999	38,648	25,361	22,422	21,752	157,889
San Francisco city	852,469	19,711	32,177	19,179	22,088	23,806	21,439	17,690	18,704	122,906
San Jose city	1,015,796	21,949	29,045	18,375	20,642	29,779	21,429	14,908	13,722	118,855
San Leandro city	89,347	2,371	3,778	2,445	2,351	2,114	1,636	1,454	2,775	12,775
San Marcos city	92,910	1,140	2,939	1,895	2,598	2,161	1,644	1,625	1,230	11,153
San Mateo city	102,885	2,081	4,063	2,548	1,888	3,885	2,724	3,127	2,184	16,356
San Ramon city	75,319	1,088	1,350	1,210	1,763	1,808	1,559	1,088	396	7,824
Santa Ana city	334,924	4,802	7,386	4,610	4,669	7,342	4,272	3,137	3,737	27,767
Santa Barbara city	91,208	2,656	2,572	2,877	2,828	2,656	2,161	1,852	3,128	15,502
Santa Clara city	122,198	2,232	3,695	2,695	1,709	3,692	2,733	1,783	2,291	14,903
Santa Clarita city	181,559	3,087	5,438	3,257	4,248	4,752	3,250	2,322	2,851	20,680
Santa Maria city	103,414	1,512	2,303	1,596	1,074	2,151	1,620	1,192	1,626	9,259
Santa Monica city	92,989	2,364	3,294	1,493	3,839	3,505	3,015	1,852	2,461	16,165
Santa Rosa city	174,166	4,834	5,380	4,358	4,397	6,190	3,132	2,991	4,259	25,327
Simi Valley city	126,873	2,390	4,571	3,103	3,337	4,411	2,568	1,841	2,299	17,559
South Gate city	96,299	2,671	2,294	1,305	1,529	2,428	1,435	533	1,143	8,373
South San Francisco city	67,011	2,442	3,179	1,655	1,243	2,046	2,793	721	1,175	9,633
Stockton city	302,405	6,288	9,532	5,835	5,239	8,594	6,055	3,858	4,639	34,220
Sunnyvale city	149,984	2,744	2,804	2,159	3,301	3,719	3,295	2,018	2,095	16,587
Temecula city	109,446	1,909	2,897	2,451	2,247	2,862	1,914	1,874	1,091	12,439
Thousand Oaks city	129,344	4,252	4,883	3,053	4,124	5,518	3,660	1,957	3,759	22,071
Torrance city	148,483	3,393	5,130	2,857	4,468	5,031	4,048	3,691	5,004	25,099
Tracy city	85,835	1,861	2,164	505	1,458	1,381	1,459	485	528	5,816
Turlock city	71,246	1,349	1,951	1,737	1,893	1,512	1,542	1,163	1,505	9,352
Tustin city	80,617	2,174	1,981	1,183	1,300	1,836	1,678	825	844	7,666
Union City city	73,608	1,395	1,781	2,176	2,738	2,173	1,669	1,279	1,793	11,828
Upland city	76,039	1,428	2,079	2,243	1,805	2,098	2,506	1,475	1,314	11,441
Vacaville city	95,863	3,320	2,634	1,606	2,111	2,276	2,348	1,334	1,058	10,733
Vallejo city	120,210	4,490	5,860	2,320	3,278	4,746	3,446	1,337	1,802	16,929
Victorville city	121,911	2,282	3,852	2,292	2,190	2,654	1,498	863	588	10,085
Visalia city	129,280	2,829	3,247	2,748	2,776	3,972	2,389	1,952	2,466	16,303
Vista city	98,086	2,089	1,955	1,280	1,905	1,189	1,267	1,357	917	7,915

Table B-3: Places—Older Population by Age—*Continued*

	Total Population	60 to 61 Years	62 to 64 Years	65 to 66 Years	67 to 69 Years	70 to 74 Years	75 to 79 Years	80 to 84 Years	85 Years and Over	65 Years and Over
California—Cont.										
Walnut Creek city	67,664	1,679	2,071	2,310	2,502	3,957	3,353	3,369	4,300	19,791
West Covina city	108,445	3,296	3,694	2,607	3,719	3,184	2,099	1,775	2,046	15,430
Westminster city	92,062	2,641	3,513	2,031	2,561	4,413	2,947	2,548	1,888	16,388
Whittier city	87,348	1,950	1,722	1,897	1,816	2,333	2,192	1,427	1,331	10,996
Yorba Linda city	67,824	1,696	2,102	2,086	2,141	2,585	1,550	929	907	10,198
Yuba City city	65,775	1,798	1,435	1,087	1,605	2,225	1,922	1,039	712	8,590
Colorado										
Arvada city	113,775	3,387	4,225	2,038	3,514	3,171	3,615	1,769	2,075	16,182
Aurora city	353,381	6,776	9,937	6,237	7,330	9,119	5,298	4,087	4,649	36,720
Boulder city	105,101	1,881	3,247	1,599	2,379	2,711	1,223	1,226	1,536	10,674
Centennial city	107,193	3,366	3,965	2,574	3,203	4,459	2,926	1,439	1,472	16,073
Colorado Springs city	445,820	10,766	14,856	8,625	10,606	12,583	9,746	6,997	7,273	55,830
Denver city	663,862	13,072	19,422	11,176	13,547	17,491	11,865	7,638	10,549	72,266
Fort Collins city	156,473	2,885	3,845	2,846	2,415	3,180	2,327	1,763	1,924	14,455
Greeley city	98,593	2,134	2,127	1,627	2,395	2,466	2,468	2,221	1,455	12,632
Lakewood city	149,650	4,118	6,193	3,031	3,636	5,115	4,051	3,372	3,995	23,200
Longmont city	90,189	2,430	2,698	1,290	1,784	3,503	1,787	1,690	1,778	11,832
Loveland city	72,647	1,503	2,461	1,879	1,963	3,744	2,845	2,147	1,861	14,439
Pueblo city	108,439	2,068	4,339	2,166	3,362	3,725	3,506	2,662	2,697	18,118
Thornton city	130,309	2,402	3,825	2,551	2,033	2,618	1,943	750	1,140	11,035
Westminster city	112,099	1,987	4,919	1,890	3,241	4,729	2,334	1,321	1,077	14,592
Connecticut										
Bridgeport city	147,608	3,247	3,982	2,015	2,635	3,400	2,622	1,810	2,093	14,575
Danbury city	83,795	1,728	2,123	1,431	2,105	2,781	2,074	996	1,272	10,659
Hartford city	124,721	1,562	3,037	1,451	2,089	2,482	1,956	1,444	1,738	11,160
New Britain city	72,889	1,236	2,776	1,187	1,019	1,531	1,178	819	2,164	7,898
New Haven city	130,285	2,428	3,196	2,342	2,809	3,051	2,236	1,437	1,463	13,338
Norwalk city	88,144	2,062	2,854	1,766	1,771	3,126	2,269	2,454	1,540	12,926
Stamford city	128,283	4,042	3,763	2,331	3,202	3,549	2,415	2,682	2,342	16,521
Waterbury city	109,311	3,698	2,991	1,670	2,545	3,463	1,556	1,371	2,365	12,970
Delaware										
Wilmington city	71,808	1,432	1,294	1,915	1,300	1,923	1,397	1,935	711	9,181
District of Columbia										
Washington city	658,893	13,563	19,134	10,045	12,426	19,475	13,624	8,751	10,144	74,465
Florida										
Boca Raton city	91,321	3,036	4,395	2,950	2,848	4,043	2,895	2,357	2,705	17,798
Boynton Beach city	73,121	1,199	3,429	1,677	1,079	3,517	3,621	1,810	3,236	14,940
Cape Coral city	169,855	5,414	7,145	4,315	8,679	9,158	6,197	4,498	5,367	38,214
Clearwater city	110,709	3,411	3,975	3,621	3,386	5,618	4,456	3,320	2,903	23,304
Coral Springs city	127,963	3,176	4,871	2,837	3,243	3,342	1,682	920	1,455	13,479
Deerfield Beach city	78,898	1,686	3,099	1,581	1,929	3,703	2,852	2,607	3,152	15,824
Delray Beach city	65,054	2,321	2,885	2,952	2,463	3,099	2,185	1,891	3,550	16,140
Deltona city	86,907	2,164	2,521	2,691	2,639	2,637	1,947	1,184	1,025	12,123
Fort Lauderdale city	176,018	4,347	7,215	4,916	5,382	8,763	5,232	3,257	4,082	31,632
Fort Myers city	70,916	1,485	2,483	1,728	2,692	3,159	1,651	1,245	1,367	11,842
Gainesville city	128,474	2,485	3,228	1,928	1,795	3,441	2,334	1,357	2,188	13,043
Hialeah city	235,566	5,817	6,359	4,928	4,063	11,477	9,574	6,437	6,469	42,948
Hollywood city	148,040	4,442	4,039	3,321	3,551	6,320	4,200	3,338	3,212	23,942
Homestead city	65,514	1,800	1,472	745	2,165	867	279	857	677	5,590
Jacksonville city	853,376	22,197	25,634	17,592	21,381	25,433	16,656	12,883	13,892	107,837
Kissimmee city	66,729	722	2,660	1,189	1,222	1,779	988	187	1,305	6,670
Lakeland city	102,335	2,587	2,937	2,373	3,834	3,909	4,637	3,610	2,597	20,960
Largo city	79,028	2,535	3,714	2,350	4,021	4,607	3,597	3,399	2,608	20,582
Lauderhill city	70,636	1,943	2,184	1,800	1,633	3,408	2,028	1,509	1,444	11,822
Melbourne city	78,486	2,082	2,897	2,053	3,223	4,256	3,194	2,802	1,960	17,488
Miami Beach city	91,721	1,226	3,721	1,876	2,518	3,300	2,800	2,413	2,347	15,254
Miami city	430,341	9,739	16,030	8,428	12,481	17,588	10,250	8,079	11,586	68,412
Miami Gardens city	112,270	2,621	3,803	2,482	2,579	3,578	2,138	1,998	1,794	14,569
Miramar city	134,991	3,391	3,261	1,673	3,414	2,958	2,547	1,634	1,585	13,811
Orlando city	262,396	3,787	6,235	4,403	4,696	6,035	3,971	3,683	3,446	26,234
Palm Bay city	105,845	2,982	4,243	2,518	3,535	4,024	3,210	2,067	2,313	17,667
Palm Coast city	82,388	2,366	3,433	3,021	4,693	5,919	3,798	2,526	3,424	23,381
Pembroke Pines city	164,625	3,893	5,287	2,805	4,032	7,196	3,971	4,058	4,641	26,703
Plantation city	91,454	3,281	3,442	1,704	2,903	2,587	2,190	1,323	1,569	12,276
Pompano Beach city	106,115	1,763	4,430	1,797	3,355	4,070	4,186	3,711	5,114	22,233
Port St. Lucie city	174,093	3,739	7,481	4,977	4,975	8,304	6,079	6,017	5,333	35,685
St. Petersburg city	253,682	7,995	9,150	6,622	8,231	10,487	6,664	4,913	6,335	43,252
Sunrise city	91,256	2,445	2,388	1,288	2,976	2,701	1,777	2,147	2,421	13,310
Tallahassee city	188,106	3,985	3,983	2,188	3,532	3,784	3,072	1,900	2,408	16,884
Tampa city	358,684	8,544	8,766	6,242	7,832	10,317	7,645	5,809	6,116	43,961
West Palm Beach city	104,017	2,432	3,855	2,123	4,868	3,612	2,833	2,265	2,165	17,866
Weston city	69,091	2,268	2,324	826	1,348	1,229	1,786	579	1,272	7,040
Georgia										
Albany city	73,016	2,007	2,639	1,367	1,134	2,535	1,443	1,523	1,513	9,515
Athens-Clarke County unified govt (bal)	119,841	2,408	2,617	2,440	2,135	2,692	1,844	882	1,798	11,791

Table B-3: Places—Older Population by Age—*Continued*

	Total Population	60 to 61 Years	62 to 64 Years	65 to 66 Years	67 to 69 Years	70 to 74 Years	75 to 79 Years	80 to 84 Years	85 Years and Over	65 Years and Over
Georgia—Cont.										
Atlanta city	456,012	7,770	13,270	7,152	9,792	15,185	8,606	5,133	5,915	51,783
Augusta-Richmond County consolidated govt (bal)	197,465	4,922	7,219	4,378	5,025	4,965	3,949	3,067	3,285	24,669
Columbus city	200,887	5,226	4,652	3,396	4,815	5,366	3,378	4,017	2,973	23,945
Johns Creek city	83,108	2,652	3,030	1,275	1,368	1,191	438	851	919	6,042
Macon-Bibb County	153,633	4,695	4,809	2,830	5,026	4,601	3,588	2,462	3,037	21,544
Roswell city	94,073	1,771	2,911	1,694	2,393	2,041	1,339	873	2,360	10,700
Sandy Springs city	101,914	2,220	3,076	2,250	2,629	3,774	1,679	1,041	2,394	13,767
Savannah city	144,355	2,885	3,719	3,244	2,816	4,245	3,051	2,828	3,196	19,380
Warner Robins city	73,060	1,584	1,848	790	1,457	1,528	2,274	439	721	7,209
Hawaii										
Urban Honolulu CDP	350,403	9,432	12,114	9,617	11,076	11,991	10,248	9,693	13,377	66,002
Idaho										
Boise City city	216,280	6,052	6,564	2,865	4,642	7,602	4,724	2,979	4,175	26,987
Meridian city	87,739	2,261	2,412	3,301	1,121	3,189	969	589	899	10,068
Nampa city	88,208	1,217	3,100	1,553	2,264	1,526	1,565	1,997	1,183	10,088
Illinois										
Aurora city	200,708	3,245	5,005	3,210	3,015	4,047	1,495	1,526	2,076	15,369
Bloomington city	78,743	1,639	2,180	1,129	1,438	2,216	1,112	1,524	1,612	9,031
Champaign city	84,520	1,662	2,029	1,119	1,265	1,603	1,973	940	832	7,732
Chicago city	2,722,407	57,364	75,261	47,509	55,540	73,128	53,424	40,739	39,534	309,874
Decatur city	73,081	1,591	2,641	2,343	1,766	2,584	2,118	2,055	1,480	12,346
Elgin city	116,548	3,075	3,256	1,963	3,113	3,829	2,482	1,588	1,228	14,203
Evanston city	75,657	1,188	2,928	1,262	2,022	2,202	1,489	1,295	1,797	10,067
Joliet city	146,578	2,357	2,713	2,106	2,297	2,918	1,864	1,820	1,946	12,951
Naperville city	145,396	4,085	5,849	3,067	2,900	2,678	2,356	2,003	1,549	14,553
Peoria city	117,288	3,558	3,927	2,153	3,149	3,489	2,728	2,052	2,276	15,847
Rockford city	148,996	3,495	6,100	2,128	4,102	5,294	4,016	2,929	3,806	22,275
Springfield city	116,649	3,694	3,574	2,378	2,856	4,803	3,966	2,383	2,510	18,896
Waukegan city	88,998	1,739	2,825	986	1,794	2,268	1,347	799	1,223	8,417
Indiana										
Bloomington city	83,423	1,572	1,287	917	927	867	1,167	917	1,058	5,853
Carmel city	87,015	2,291	2,555	2,581	2,053	3,320	1,808	1,862	1,766	13,390
Evansville city	121,299	2,920	3,426	3,036	2,816	3,703	3,137	2,433	3,699	18,824
Fort Wayne city	256,023	6,297	7,364	4,860	6,808	6,899	5,742	3,053	4,569	31,931
Gary city	71,180	1,933	2,838	1,879	1,699	3,183	1,617	1,454	2,077	11,909
Hammond city	78,383	1,917	2,182	1,140	1,165	2,453	1,084	1,134	1,153	8,129
Indianapolis city (bal)	851,353	19,764	25,156	15,321	15,392	22,030	15,559	13,194	12,980	94,476
Lafayette city	67,012	1,204	1,440	1,686	1,459	2,030	1,717	1,015	1,044	8,951
Muncie city	70,580	1,226	1,927	1,730	1,813	2,221	1,920	1,270	1,818	10,772
South Bend city	103,019	1,767	3,890	1,770	2,558	2,570	1,958	1,796	2,338	12,990
Iowa										
Cedar Rapids city	129,183	2,525	3,832	2,331	2,549	4,328	2,910	2,464	2,554	17,136
Davenport city	102,431	2,469	3,124	1,606	2,157	2,872	2,379	1,729	1,959	12,702
Des Moines city	209,064	3,806	5,941	3,802	4,849	4,340	3,685	3,165	3,786	23,627
Iowa City city	73,424	1,910	2,163	486	1,119	1,043	1,103	1,238	1,161	6,150
Sioux City city	81,392	1,984	2,391	1,771	2,177	2,280	1,827	1,674	1,473	11,202
Waterloo city	68,365	2,047	2,597	1,429	1,917	1,844	2,094	1,276	1,314	9,874
Kansas										
Kansas City city	148,323	3,921	4,235	2,718	3,623	3,579	2,638	1,736	2,497	16,791
Lawrence city	91,282	1,847	2,365	1,072	1,595	1,867	1,744	1,000	1,328	8,606
Olathe city	133,059	1,998	3,775	2,227	2,565	3,174	1,518	1,020	1,466	11,970
Overland Park city	184,524	4,999	6,319	4,309	4,211	5,551	4,486	4,268	4,144	26,969
Topeka city	127,223	2,641	5,120	2,547	3,258	4,359	3,174	1,953	3,334	18,625
Wichita city	388,413	9,442	12,291	7,265	9,099	10,810	8,404	8,119	6,114	49,811
Kentucky										
Lexington-Fayette urban county	310,797	7,915	9,646	4,045	8,818	7,969	6,302	3,242	5,596	35,972
Louisville/Jefferson County metro govt (bal)	612,775	12,989	21,780	13,438	13,141	19,700	14,160	9,444	11,987	81,870
Louisiana										
Baton Rouge city	228,909	5,234	7,325	5,518	4,601	5,614	5,137	4,614	4,016	29,500
Bossier City city	67,453	1,651	1,977	954	1,879	2,075	1,150	1,441	1,345	8,844
Kenner city	67,058	1,626	3,345	2,068	2,386	3,457	1,696	1,419	1,103	12,129
Lafayette city	126,068	3,677	4,863	2,629	2,157	4,265	2,904	950	1,558	14,463
Lake Charles city	74,875	1,671	2,472	963	1,773	3,818	2,452	1,878	1,808	12,692
New Orleans city	384,320	8,287	14,884	7,611	8,388	11,302	8,576	4,843	5,761	46,481
Shreveport city	197,979	5,317	5,275	4,152	4,785	7,362	5,750	3,719	4,232	30,000
Maine										
Portland city	66,669	1,840	1,922	1,089	1,207	2,006	1,549	806	1,267	7,924
Maryland										
Baltimore city	622,793	13,687	20,224	12,969	12,931	18,308	13,233	10,513	8,753	76,707
Frederick city	68,404	1,440	1,941	1,134	1,278	2,284	1,250	927	929	7,802
Gaithersburg city	66,807	1,293	1,559	919	1,203	2,211	1,288	1,043	1,155	7,819
Rockville city	65,941	1,552	2,172	1,368	1,715	2,029	1,797	1,874	1,830	10,613

Table B-3: Places—Older Population by Age—*Continued*

	Total Population	60 to 61 Years	62 to 64 Years	65 to 66 Years	67 to 69 Years	70 to 74 Years	75 to 79 Years	80 to 84 Years	85 Years and Over	65 Years and Over
Massachusetts										
Boston city	656,051	13,188	17,794	9,927	11,523	16,102	11,491	9,081	9,733	67,857
Brockton city	94,780	2,322	3,516	1,879	1,600	3,711	1,461	1,263	1,958	11,872
Cambridge city	109,699	1,421	3,362	2,142	1,874	2,342	1,411	1,508	1,426	10,703
Fall River city	88,705	2,557	2,497	1,159	2,845	3,739	2,052	2,334	2,250	14,379
Lawrence city	78,192	1,319	1,642	1,462	1,358	1,441	961	433	1,015	6,670
Lowell city	109,931	2,322	2,607	2,253	1,884	2,045	1,638	1,341	2,408	11,569
Lynn city	92,137	2,298	2,565	1,406	1,403	2,507	1,616	1,393	2,004	10,329
New Bedford city	94,855	2,470	2,750	1,717	1,614	2,579	2,121	1,655	2,597	12,283
Newton city	88,298	2,426	3,458	2,438	3,373	3,124	2,356	2,517	2,693	16,501
Quincy city	93,391	3,048	2,613	2,699	2,063	2,809	2,148	2,727	1,849	14,295
Somerville city	78,903	908	1,956	1,924	919	1,620	982	1,329	1,055	7,829
Springfield city	153,994	3,783	4,142	2,905	2,109	4,087	3,018	2,207	2,466	16,792
Worcester city	183,033	3,772	6,373	2,921	2,541	3,687	3,474	2,678	4,363	19,664
Michigan										
Ann Arbor city	117,759	2,546	3,334	1,401	1,974	3,071	1,985	1,669	2,103	12,203
Dearborn city	95,546	1,405	3,548	1,845	2,181	2,784	2,194	1,458	2,156	12,618
Detroit city	680,281	16,671	23,784	14,369	14,707	20,064	13,800	11,299	10,927	85,166
Farmington Hills city	81,440	2,292	3,329	2,845	2,679	4,343	3,566	2,267	2,013	17,713
Flint city	98,990	2,582	2,746	2,084	1,486	2,808	1,917	1,764	1,529	11,588
Grand Rapids city	193,793	3,157	5,266	3,051	2,972	4,828	2,963	2,894	5,643	22,351
Kalamazoo city	75,909	1,273	1,607	1,389	1,424	1,031	1,000	1,313	1,280	7,437
Lansing city	113,659	2,152	3,163	1,885	3,428	2,911	1,567	1,679	1,690	13,160
Livonia city	94,959	3,111	4,268	2,792	3,196	3,246	3,039	3,011	2,038	17,322
Rochester Hills city	73,120	2,239	2,702	1,913	1,901	2,965	1,788	1,303	2,204	12,074
Southfield city	73,001	1,591	3,346	2,304	2,363	3,512	2,058	1,801	1,570	13,608
Sterling Heights city	131,729	3,463	4,606	2,464	3,076	4,913	4,839	3,369	3,174	21,835
Troy city	83,120	2,592	3,279	2,616	1,441	3,213	2,587	1,800	1,490	13,147
Warren city	135,099	4,493	4,269	2,661	3,228	3,925	3,123	2,825	3,886	19,648
Westland city	82,318	2,055	2,932	1,509	2,416	3,518	2,875	1,667	2,434	14,419
Wyoming city	74,820	1,933	2,147	1,430	1,067	1,488	1,233	1,021	1,436	7,675
Minnesota										
Bloomington city	86,319	2,588	3,550	1,359	3,421	3,344	2,184	3,470	3,106	16,884
Brooklyn Park city	78,741	1,298	1,840	1,315	1,611	1,996	1,494	626	662	7,704
Duluth city	86,242	2,683	3,039	1,419	2,042	3,155	1,869	1,898	2,648	13,031
Eagan city	66,087	1,618	1,682	1,151	1,535	1,904	906	1,351	885	7,732
Maple Grove city	66,949	1,653	3,199	1,759	1,496	2,337	525	643	797	7,557
Minneapolis city	407,181	8,149	10,738	6,414	7,066	8,037	4,555	3,446	4,272	33,790
Plymouth city	75,065	2,189	2,331	1,977	2,278	3,281	1,486	947	1,612	11,581
Rochester city	111,398	1,704	4,190	2,188	2,435	3,305	3,203	2,463	2,516	16,110
St. Cloud city	64,221	1,560	1,316	968	1,456	2,270	1,006	724	1,228	7,652
St. Paul city	297,644	7,789	8,996	4,131	4,988	6,057	3,911	2,829	4,634	26,550
Woodbury city	66,799	1,895	1,753	579	1,472	2,668	1,206	731	809	7,465
Mississippi										
Gulfport city	71,747	1,880	2,709	1,341	2,308	1,749	1,801	1,931	909	10,039
Jackson city	171,146	3,756	5,607	3,141	3,289	5,118	2,813	2,275	3,281	19,917
Missouri										
Columbia city	116,892	2,729	2,496	1,689	1,514	3,768	1,547	884	1,470	10,872
Independence city	117,503	2,936	5,055	3,086	3,464	4,630	4,438	3,303	1,584	20,505
Kansas City city	470,816	9,295	14,533	7,622	9,997	14,120	10,203	6,992	7,536	56,470
Lee's Summit city	94,627	1,959	4,156	2,432	2,166	3,256	1,925	1,485	1,984	13,248
O'Fallon city	83,999	1,724	1,162	1,614	975	1,745	1,868	1,152	1,236	8,590
Springfield city	165,399	2,481	4,671	2,530	4,033	6,051	4,774	3,693	4,629	25,710
St. Charles city	68,087	2,015	2,539	1,080	1,399	2,805	1,646	1,877	1,325	10,132
St. Joseph city	76,529	1,838	2,090	1,809	1,476	2,162	1,756	1,679	1,693	10,575
St. Louis city	317,419	8,304	10,983	5,131	7,605	7,537	5,946	4,942	5,001	36,162
Montana										
Billings city	108,870	2,809	3,302	1,730	2,727	3,159	3,126	2,718	2,496	15,956
Missoula city	69,824	1,227	2,843	1,262	1,424	1,554	1,108	987	2,085	8,420
Nebraska										
Lincoln city	273,002	6,239	7,587	4,639	6,184	7,363	5,090	4,258	4,556	32,090
Omaha city	446,618	9,951	14,091	7,341	9,401	13,145	8,385	6,305	8,813	53,390
Nevada										
Henderson city	277,458	9,103	9,582	7,308	8,099	14,825	9,124	5,481	4,914	49,751
Las Vegas city	613,590	11,523	18,141	11,343	15,854	21,736	14,606	9,052	7,160	79,751
North Las Vegas city	230,793	4,699	4,742	4,310	5,694	7,087	2,983	3,144	1,494	24,712
Reno city	236,995	6,018	7,267	5,261	5,852	7,476	4,985	4,585	3,516	31,675
Sparks city	94,704	2,557	3,671	2,531	3,265	3,380	1,746	1,171	1,946	14,039
New Hampshire										
Manchester city	110,451	3,032	2,875	2,390	2,399	3,453	1,581	1,766	2,484	14,073
Nashua city	87,258	2,085	3,937	1,230	2,019	2,921	1,774	1,946	1,540	11,430
New Jersey										
Bayonne city	65,984	1,870	2,126	1,319	1,755	1,616	1,399	703	1,118	7,910
Camden city	77,317	1,299	2,077	1,568	1,345	2,040	579	1,414	673	7,619
Clifton city	85,920	1,816	3,618	1,026	2,320	2,012	1,470	1,045	1,565	9,438
East Orange city	65,095	1,741	2,054	1,767	1,378	1,958	1,685	548	1,285	8,621
Elizabeth city	128,695	2,107	2,368	1,531	1,871	3,208	1,773	2,028	1,134	11,545

Table B-3: Places—Older Population by Age—*Continued*

	Total Population	60 to 61 Years	62 to 64 Years	65 to 66 Years	67 to 69 Years	70 to 74 Years	75 to 79 Years	80 to 84 Years	85 Years and Over	65 Years and Over
New Jersey—Cont.										
Jersey City city	262,146	4,839	8,813	4,004	4,965	6,225	5,263	2,161	2,310	24,928
Newark city	280,577	5,686	6,622	4,109	4,439	6,391	3,943	1,973	2,663	23,518
Passaic city	71,517	1,110	1,889	859	919	1,976	708	707	865	6,034
Paterson city	146,746	2,724	3,628	2,704	2,587	3,407	3,434	1,829	2,400	16,361
Trenton city	84,047	1,373	2,619	1,259	1,416	2,354	1,966	849	903	8,747
Union City city	68,673	1,138	2,351	509	1,638	1,683	1,432	1,280	1,079	7,621
New Mexico										
Albuquerque city	557,172	14,203	18,919	11,024	14,924	16,631	13,008	10,846	8,503	74,936
Las Cruces city	101,405	2,660	4,084	1,333	2,314	4,036	2,181	2,463	2,179	14,506
Rio Rancho city	93,011	1,982	3,364	1,747	2,039	3,418	1,931	1,102	1,595	11,832
Santa Fe city	70,291	1,518	4,221	2,290	3,082	3,679	2,556	1,303	1,400	14,310
New York										
Albany city	98,566	1,901	3,311	2,070	1,793	3,259	1,495	1,487	2,242	12,346
Buffalo city	258,699	5,763	7,649	3,931	6,542	7,345	5,652	5,583	4,006	33,059
Mount Vernon city	68,455	1,125	2,331	1,137	1,699	2,418	1,735	1,051	1,566	9,606
New Rochelle city	79,630	1,780	2,816	1,631	1,634	1,893	2,172	1,665	2,075	11,070
New York city	8,491,079	197,027	253,642	160,882	193,694	257,956	188,498	139,691	157,672	1,098,393
Rochester city	209,974	4,510	6,323	2,810	5,801	6,247	3,011	2,253	2,542	22,664
Schenectady city	65,930	1,253	3,110	1,103	1,308	1,659	1,123	1,620	1,938	8,751
Syracuse city	144,263	2,510	4,187	2,843	2,675	3,771	2,892	2,077	3,895	18,153
Yonkers city	200,665	4,128	6,413	4,382	6,846	8,002	4,986	3,570	5,508	33,294
North Carolina										
Asheville city	87,884	2,268	3,011	2,059	2,975	2,838	3,137	2,445	2,273	15,727
Cary town	155,724	3,402	5,297	2,756	4,411	4,625	2,708	2,086	1,860	18,446
Charlotte city	809,974	15,790	19,547	12,118	16,303	17,090	12,021	9,163	9,207	75,902
Concord city	85,571	1,826	2,070	853	2,148	2,748	1,459	905	1,571	9,684
Durham city	251,872	6,577	7,787	4,846	4,030	6,766	4,721	2,638	3,992	26,993
Fayetteville city	203,939	4,077	5,428	2,223	4,799	6,553	4,779	3,335	2,173	23,862
Gastonia city	73,696	1,668	2,056	1,483	2,355	3,026	1,835	1,360	1,644	11,703
Greensboro city	282,558	5,713	8,136	4,602	6,381	9,607	5,986	4,176	4,534	35,286
Greenville city	89,850	1,549	1,793	1,780	1,623	1,972	1,298	990	1,629	9,292
High Point city	107,957	2,367	2,371	1,778	2,339	3,652	2,047	2,430	1,139	13,385
Jacksonville city	69,031	551	710	1,214	542	525	907	611	311	4,110
Raleigh city	439,884	8,284	10,017	7,212	8,348	8,257	6,949	5,713	4,737	41,216
Wilmington city	113,676	1,993	4,524	2,494	2,605	3,139	2,415	1,667	3,209	15,529
Winston-Salem city	239,273	5,654	6,407	5,038	5,931	6,098	5,247	4,509	5,257	32,080
North Dakota										
Bismarck city	67,666	1,267	1,811	1,329	1,225	2,866	1,627	1,512	2,203	10,762
Fargo city	116,572	1,799	4,205	1,690	1,838	1,888	2,448	1,674	2,401	11,939
Ohio										
Akron city	197,846	5,670	8,367	3,796	6,163	4,983	4,203	2,922	4,247	26,314
Canton city	72,274	2,421	2,609	1,207	1,699	1,448	2,065	1,389	1,660	9,468
Cincinnati city	298,162	8,022	9,195	5,510	6,020	7,173	5,555	4,625	5,989	34,872
Cleveland city	389,524	9,782	13,483	7,425	8,684	10,039	7,999	5,986	7,229	47,362
Columbus city	836,293	15,638	23,869	11,932	14,055	17,832	14,011	8,273	10,554	76,657
Dayton city	140,995	3,151	4,193	2,302	3,488	3,437	2,633	2,492	1,827	16,179
Lorain city	63,774	1,229	1,549	1,392	1,814	2,589	1,567	988	1,459	9,809
Parma city	80,023	2,182	2,816	1,337	2,074	3,342	3,210	2,000	2,303	14,266
Toledo city	281,014	7,469	8,726	6,175	6,381	7,798	6,529	4,121	6,842	37,846
Youngstown city	65,051	1,475	2,316	1,452	1,238	2,203	1,588	1,777	2,602	10,860
Oklahoma										
Broken Arrow city	106,226	2,833	3,184	2,259	2,407	2,766	1,725	1,433	1,054	11,644
Edmond city	88,594	2,688	3,271	1,898	2,033	2,567	2,112	1,000	1,284	10,894
Lawton city	97,017	1,786	2,648	1,862	1,023	2,784	1,788	1,710	936	10,103
Norman city	118,046	2,303	4,060	1,482	3,159	3,283	2,481	1,937	1,439	13,781
Oklahoma City city	620,553	12,380	18,664	10,953	15,593	18,055	12,390	8,724	9,403	75,118
Tulsa city	399,274	10,841	13,810	7,641	9,421	12,349	8,038	8,051	7,925	53,425
Oregon										
Beaverton city	95,113	2,547	3,309	1,748	2,185	2,757	885	1,173	1,427	10,175
Bend city	84,075	2,942	2,472	1,924	1,871	2,922	1,883	1,540	2,014	12,154
Eugene city	160,552	3,996	5,583	3,564	4,014	4,761	2,604	2,957	4,067	21,967
Gresham city	109,877	2,762	3,685	2,759	2,881	3,421	2,497	1,215	2,195	14,968
Hillsboro city	99,374	2,266	2,338	2,190	2,150	2,424	1,363	1,152	1,169	10,448
Medford city	78,560	2,079	3,367	1,828	2,582	3,293	2,366	1,896	2,235	14,200
Portland city	619,445	14,300	22,233	11,740	13,927	16,593	10,541	7,982	10,290	71,073
Salem city	161,648	4,486	5,823	3,738	3,585	5,470	4,052	1,996	3,574	22,415
Pennsylvania										
Allentown city	119,105	2,455	3,145	2,396	2,357	2,594	2,804	1,441	2,863	14,455
Bethlehem city	78,759	1,629	3,114	1,633	1,559	2,739	2,076	1,515	2,238	11,760
Erie city	99,466	2,284	2,865	1,905	1,942	2,577	2,943	2,078	2,362	13,807
Philadelphia city	1,560,297	36,317	45,147	27,735	36,238	43,893	32,513	25,816	29,379	195,574
Pittsburgh city	305,434	6,966	10,352	4,823	6,853	8,215	6,880	5,800	8,574	41,145
Reading city	87,809	1,221	2,287	1,597	1,741	1,733	1,517	1,427	1,250	9,265
Scranton city	75,278	1,138	2,752	1,453	2,266	3,003	2,413	1,970	2,692	13,797
Rhode Island										
Cranston city	81,029	2,062	4,326	1,893	3,036	2,376	2,210	2,022	3,014	14,551
Pawtucket city	71,490	1,388	1,786	1,166	1,348	1,781	1,212	953	1,187	7,647

Table B-3: Places—Older Population by Age—*Continued*

	Total Population	60 to 61 Years	62 to 64 Years	65 to 66 Years	67 to 69 Years	70 to 74 Years	75 to 79 Years	80 to 84 Years	85 Years and Over	65 Years and Over
Rhode Island—Cont.										
Providence city	179,142	2,569	4,009	1,467	2,879	3,858	3,385	1,978	2,865	16,432
Warwick city	81,964	2,541	3,109	2,110	3,057	3,116	2,105	2,083	3,322	15,793
South Carolina										
Charleston city	130,750	2,621	5,193	3,146	4,333	3,083	2,013	1,699	2,670	16,944
Columbia city	131,758	2,457	3,147	2,140	2,162	2,934	1,382	1,806	1,675	12,099
Mount Pleasant town	77,787	2,482	2,872	2,191	1,610	2,155	1,981	2,063	1,171	11,171
North Charleston city	107,972	2,901	2,081	1,587	2,283	3,198	1,848	758	1,350	11,024
Rock Hill city	69,967	965	1,841	1,240	1,525	2,565	2,340	1,052	825	9,547
South Dakota										
Rapid City city	72,642	1,416	2,365	1,524	1,532	2,116	2,348	1,633	1,864	11,017
Sioux Falls city	168,604	3,102	5,148	3,243	4,026	4,634	2,987	2,990	2,778	20,658
Tennessee										
Chattanooga city	173,778	4,566	7,285	3,909	4,384	5,789	4,189	4,370	3,506	26,147
Clarksville city	146,814	2,518	3,077	2,164	2,604	2,530	3,180	833	565	11,876
Franklin city	70,613	1,339	2,413	1,180	1,180	1,610	934	1,507	1,085	7,496
Jackson city	67,308	1,438	2,147	1,183	1,785	1,594	1,350	949	1,442	8,303
Johnson City city	65,820	1,559	2,205	1,574	1,821	2,615	2,245	1,535	1,263	11,053
Knoxville city	184,292	3,563	5,312	4,088	4,396	5,548	4,270	3,045	3,781	25,128
Memphis city	656,876	15,576	21,311	11,234	13,271	17,806	11,059	10,040	10,207	73,617
Murfreesboro city	120,960	2,365	2,509	2,012	1,706	3,178	1,532	1,887	1,056	11,371
Nashville-Davidson metropolitan govt (bal)	644,008	17,044	16,589	10,857	12,673	16,726	11,671	9,085	8,959	69,971
Texas										
Abilene city	120,176	2,464	3,199	1,932	2,351	3,723	3,080	1,889	2,702	15,677
Allen city	94,170	1,675	1,851	953	1,305	1,297	1,237	148	679	5,619
Amarillo city	200,246	3,706	5,055	3,309	4,908	6,498	4,751	3,027	2,923	25,416
Arlington city	383,202	8,771	10,255	6,804	7,701	9,571	5,420	4,309	3,337	37,142
Austin city	912,798	16,501	23,433	12,190	14,575	18,482	10,394	8,662	8,402	72,705
Baytown city	75,670	1,854	2,727	1,503	1,964	2,651	1,764	1,414	1,086	10,382
Beaumont city	117,576	2,475	3,744	2,273	3,203	2,560	2,683	1,767	2,570	15,056
Brownsville city	183,016	2,447	4,209	3,236	4,313	3,793	3,714	1,896	3,572	20,524
Bryan city	80,916	1,295	1,772	1,439	1,386	2,132	1,081	1,088	749	7,875
Carrollton city	128,342	3,759	4,349	1,871	2,400	3,067	1,951	1,678	706	11,673
College Station city	103,486	1,771	1,807	748	1,036	1,543	1,201	859	760	6,147
Conroe city	65,873	1,078	1,002	947	563	1,757	1,200	2,012	848	7,327
Corpus Christi city	320,431	9,225	10,919	6,730	7,249	9,842	6,482	5,614	4,933	40,850
Dallas city	1,281,031	24,239	32,738	17,259	22,198	30,838	21,268	14,546	14,669	120,778
Denton city	128,200	2,623	2,881	2,719	2,381	3,324	1,596	1,193	876	12,089
Edinburg city	83,017	1,351	1,208	1,269	1,088	897	933	912	1,252	6,351
El Paso city	679,024	12,865	18,728	10,883	12,577	21,044	16,758	11,879	9,499	82,640
Flower Mound town	69,419	1,255	1,349	827	1,715	1,981	1,227	428	398	6,576
Fort Worth city	812,553	12,553	18,623	10,564	14,425	16,713	13,455	8,979	8,709	72,845
Frisco city	145,038	1,944	2,870	1,071	3,103	3,454	1,463	619	448	10,158
Garland city	235,597	4,498	7,623	5,156	5,223	7,101	4,773	2,774	2,786	27,813
Grand Prairie city	185,415	3,992	4,921	2,566	2,631	3,619	2,417	960	1,598	13,791
Harlingen city	65,914	1,136	1,480	1,695	1,109	2,005	1,438	1,657	1,194	9,098
Houston city	2,240,796	44,603	54,079	34,821	39,990	54,275	36,229	27,988	26,022	219,325
Irving city	232,413	3,038	4,784	3,769	2,100	5,256	2,709	1,832	2,110	17,776
Killeen city	138,143	1,845	3,232	1,212	1,404	1,609	740	1,120	950	7,035
Laredo city	253,747	3,537	5,981	3,154	4,018	5,504	3,587	2,592	2,478	21,333
League City city	94,287	2,040	2,425	1,637	1,943	1,745	1,611	1,085	602	8,623
Lewisville city	102,283	1,321	2,185	1,590	1,718	2,288	1,673	1,313	813	9,395
Longview city	84,313	1,037	2,560	1,306	2,111	2,644	2,350	1,950	1,861	12,222
Lubbock city	243,843	4,324	6,130	4,227	4,831	6,366	5,036	4,370	3,741	28,571
McAllen city	138,584	2,384	3,422	3,337	2,184	3,146	2,511	1,575	1,230	13,983
McKinney city	156,753	2,203	3,453	1,968	2,851	3,466	1,792	1,911	1,800	13,788
Mesquite city	144,289	4,667	4,108	1,781	3,019	3,076	2,322	2,060	1,553	13,811
Midland city	128,037	3,953	3,128	2,056	2,615	1,760	1,845	2,553	2,033	12,862
Mission city	82,429	800	2,126	1,043	1,178	3,315	1,700	1,022	1,085	9,343
Missouri City city	75,128	2,027	3,514	996	2,134	1,859	1,028	483	724	7,224
New Braunfels city	65,714	1,089	2,781	995	1,530	2,187	1,332	1,216	1,009	8,269
North Richland Hills city	68,527	1,498	2,032	1,667	1,636	2,056	1,723	1,392	1,150	9,624
Odessa city	116,394	2,542	3,121	2,323	2,527	2,012	1,926	1,745	1,666	12,199
Pasadena city	153,914	3,786	5,185	1,746	2,423	4,222	2,261	2,242	1,655	14,549
Pearland city	104,759	2,392	2,941	1,623	873	2,534	2,756	1,085	715	9,586
Pharr city	75,381	755	1,980	878	1,600	1,669	1,707	1,014	1,318	8,186
Plano city	277,910	7,438	8,586	5,624	6,738	9,096	5,948	3,094	2,823	33,323
Richardson city	108,609	2,807	3,881	2,131	2,890	3,769	1,933	1,791	2,552	15,066
Round Rock city	112,196	2,504	2,686	1,566	2,241	2,106	1,128	872	995	8,908
San Angelo city	97,207	1,912	2,472	1,329	2,219	3,615	2,537	2,562	2,121	14,383
San Antonio city	1,436,723	28,239	43,032	25,216	30,511	38,645	28,302	22,234	21,122	166,030
Sugar Land city	86,775	2,886	2,848	1,872	2,717	2,792	1,649	1,464	1,324	11,818
Temple city	70,785	1,473	2,038	2,694	2,005	2,491	647	1,485	2,312	11,634
Tyler city	101,436	2,867	3,077	1,190	2,762	3,870	2,861	2,192	2,432	15,307
Victoria city	66,098	1,617	1,952	1,117	1,886	2,376	1,234	1,452	1,566	9,631
Waco city	130,191	3,005	2,780	2,329	3,230	2,448	2,500	2,550	2,071	15,128
Wichita Falls city	105,107	2,677	3,410	1,777	2,245	2,350	1,769	2,543	1,823	12,507

Table B-3: Places—Older Population by Age—*Continued*

	Total Population	60 to 61 Years	62 to 64 Years	65 to 66 Years	67 to 69 Years	70 to 74 Years	75 to 79 Years	80 to 84 Years	85 Years and Over	65 Years and Over
Utah										
Layton city	72,223	1,401	2,009	1,136	1,040	1,629	1,509	642	448	6,404
Ogden city	84,325	1,774	1,315	2,060	1,296	1,994	1,511	1,009	1,124	8,994
Orem city	91,781	1,215	1,897	1,012	1,506	1,615	1,373	1,102	647	7,255
Provo city	114,007	1,281	1,535	549	1,582	1,780	1,584	917	897	7,309
Salt Lake City city	190,873	3,614	5,623	2,993	3,673	4,641	2,407	1,815	2,661	18,190
Sandy city	91,135	2,886	4,048	1,303	1,650	3,125	1,397	1,029	488	8,992
St. George city	78,509	1,865	2,186	2,149	1,609	4,433	3,604	2,522	2,672	16,989
West Jordan city	110,917	2,164	3,135	1,468	1,166	1,366	825	806	666	6,297
West Valley City city	134,492	2,139	2,294	2,017	1,840	2,308	1,907	738	350	9,160
Virginia										
Alexandria city	150,575	2,988	4,238	2,333	3,303	3,950	2,494	1,401	1,834	15,315
Chesapeake city	233,371	5,144	6,441	4,596	4,330	8,392	4,684	2,047	3,491	27,540
Hampton city	136,879	3,122	4,818	2,393	3,406	4,933	3,467	2,421	1,930	18,550
Lynchburg city	79,047	1,763	1,689	1,456	1,493	2,364	2,087	1,517	2,438	11,355
Newport News city	182,965	4,952	4,452	4,053	3,333	4,633	4,003	2,347	2,889	21,258
Norfolk city	245,428	4,630	6,697	4,141	4,500	4,885	3,301	2,831	4,507	24,165
Portsmouth city	96,004	2,701	2,644	1,636	2,664	2,816	2,490	1,802	1,601	13,009
Richmond city	217,853	5,424	7,326	3,740	4,766	5,251	4,416	2,621	4,068	24,862
Roanoke city	99,428	3,331	3,523	2,207	3,201	2,615	2,438	1,734	3,042	15,237
Suffolk city	86,806	2,213	3,110	1,715	2,530	2,641	2,001	956	1,417	11,260
Virginia Beach city	450,980	10,643	13,288	8,585	10,199	13,432	8,727	7,729	6,634	55,306
Washington										
Auburn city	78,769	1,500	2,037	1,411	1,165	1,702	1,463	1,417	1,577	8,735
Bellevue city	136,426	1,900	5,163	2,553	3,337	3,862	3,593	3,716	3,468	20,529
Bellingham city	83,363	1,608	3,129	2,032	1,686	2,754	1,628	983	2,259	11,342
Everett city	106,741	2,502	2,897	1,071	1,726	2,139	1,187	1,784	1,738	9,645
Federal Way city	93,428	1,865	3,306	2,276	2,097	2,919	2,012	1,687	1,417	12,408
Kennewick city	77,424	1,922	2,870	1,673	1,847	1,632	1,494	1,606	1,397	9,649
Kent city	125,547	2,385	4,331	2,274	2,251	2,971	1,802	997	1,622	11,917
Kirkland city	85,778	1,963	2,930	1,804	2,100	2,805	2,664	672	1,163	11,208
Marysville city	65,088	1,943	1,638	1,337	1,591	2,806	1,399	878	1,582	9,593
Pasco city	69,807	1,263	1,798	594	1,304	1,055	386	512	394	4,245
Renton city	98,382	1,798	3,230	1,021	1,463	1,745	1,954	1,157	1,596	8,936
Seattle city	668,337	16,725	20,674	13,628	16,049	18,873	11,050	8,463	13,398	81,461
Spokane city	212,067	4,724	7,039	4,763	5,689	7,035	3,990	3,620	4,718	29,815
Spokane Valley city	91,733	1,905	2,937	1,809	2,465	3,048	2,015	2,440	1,677	13,454
Tacoma city	205,153	4,023	6,210	4,740	5,071	5,581	3,662	2,664	3,949	25,667
Vancouver city	169,303	4,357	5,699	3,813	4,134	5,479	3,951	3,097	2,983	23,457
Yakima city	93,355	1,530	2,775	1,637	2,063	2,811	2,663	1,908	1,895	12,977
Wisconsin										
Appleton city	72,654	2,364	2,132	889	1,190	1,675	1,256	1,533	1,335	7,878
Eau Claire city	68,207	1,102	1,884	1,122	1,709	1,953	1,138	1,456	1,154	8,532
Green Bay city	104,893	2,137	3,563	1,886	2,535	2,293	2,501	1,461	2,139	12,815
Kenosha city	99,898	2,653	3,109	1,976	1,746	3,731	1,820	1,377	1,822	12,472
Madison city	245,674	6,344	6,801	4,521	5,760	5,657	3,802	3,047	4,180	26,967
Milwaukee city	599,653	13,795	16,608	9,536	9,788	13,904	9,931	7,265	9,854	60,278
Oshkosh city	66,631	1,050	2,454	732	1,812	1,321	1,484	1,924	2,058	9,331
Racine city	78,054	1,777	2,701	1,443	1,565	1,809	1,756	1,006	1,638	9,217
Waukesha city	71,482	2,060	2,305	806	1,436	1,840	1,394	1,027	1,053	7,556

Table B-4: Metropolitan/Micropolitan Statistical Areas—Older Population by Age

	Total Population	60 to 61 Years	62 to 64 Years	65 to 66 Years	67 to 69 Years	70 to 74 Years	75 to 79 Years	80 to 84 Years	85 Years and Over	65 Years and Over
Aberdeen, WA Micro Area	70,818	1,990	3,054	2,568	2,140	3,582	2,228	1,518	1,384	13,420
Abilene, TX Metro Area	166,900	3,877	4,671	2,815	4,359	5,913	4,914	2,794	3,466	24,261
Adrian, MI Micro Area	99,047	2,522	3,801	2,255	2,914	4,489	3,174	1,888	1,745	16,465
Akron, OH Metro Area	703,825	19,560	26,620	15,963	20,505	25,515	18,929	13,543	16,966	111,421
Alamogordo, NM Micro Area	65,082	1,699	2,185	1,566	2,019	2,551	2,359	929	942	10,366
Albany, GA Metro Area	152,596	5,110	5,472	3,377	3,744	6,121	3,190	2,677	2,549	21,658
Albany, OR Metro Area	119,356	3,773	4,302	2,096	3,700	6,557	2,968	2,841	2,558	20,720
Albany-Schenectady-Troy, NY Metro Area	880,167	21,386	34,923	22,320	24,073	30,152	22,462	17,672	19,741	136,420
Albertville, AL Micro Area	94,636	2,920	3,326	1,927	3,042	4,099	2,824	1,896	1,510	15,298
Albuquerque, NM Metro Area	905,213	24,065	33,136	19,095	25,964	31,979	24,194	16,545	13,715	131,492
Alexandria, LA Metro Area	154,872	4,015	4,747	4,580	3,991	5,017	3,979	2,322	2,952	22,841
Allentown-Bethlehem-Easton, PA-NJ Metro Area	829,835	23,020	31,120	20,253	23,534	31,527	22,692	18,368	23,043	139,417
Altoona, PA Metro Area	125,955	4,141	4,887	3,492	3,787	5,430	3,820	3,440	4,143	24,112
Amarillo, TX Metro Area	261,752	5,571	7,347	4,112	6,380	8,699	5,847	4,153	4,272	33,463
Ames, IA Metro Area	94,073	1,832	2,551	1,246	1,927	2,307	2,273	1,282	1,101	10,136
Anchorage, AK Metro Area	398,892	8,619	11,465	6,380	7,262	9,622	6,418	3,687	2,994	36,363
Ann Arbor, MI Metro Area	356,874	8,466	12,432	6,370	8,422	11,448	6,890	4,473	5,441	43,044
Anniston-Oxford-Jacksonville, AL Metro Area	115,916	4,789	3,858	2,163	4,281	4,470	2,915	3,059	1,655	18,543
Appleton, WI Metro Area	231,497	5,043	7,988	3,954	5,889	6,885	5,748	4,066	3,461	30,003
Asheville, NC Metro Area	442,316	10,950	18,141	12,577	16,193	22,616	15,848	11,751	11,935	90,920
Ashtabula, OH Micro Area	99,175	3,291	4,158	2,898	2,170	4,745	3,300	1,500	2,391	17,004
Athens, TX Micro Area	79,290	3,151	2,224	2,033	3,630	3,922	2,998	2,554	1,600	16,737
Athens-Clarke County, GA Metro Area	197,268	4,393	6,052	4,142	4,641	5,783	3,876	1,741	3,009	23,192
Atlanta-Sandy Springs-Roswell, GA Metro Area	5,611,829	120,980	172,575	102,637	124,999	155,363	98,581	64,160	59,110	604,850
Atlantic City-Hammonton, NJ Metro Area	275,209	7,217	11,374	5,814	8,369	11,445	8,044	5,426	4,347	43,435
Auburn, NY Micro Area	78,823	2,205	3,030	2,007	2,535	2,731	2,413	1,505	1,955	13,146
Auburn-Opelika, AL Metro Area	154,255	3,227	4,970	2,806	3,048	4,111	3,012	1,841	1,057	15,875
Augusta-Richmond County, GA-SC Metro Area	583,010	15,823	23,653	13,556	16,603	19,853	13,996	10,876	9,425	84,309
Augusta-Waterville, ME Micro Area	121,112	3,409	5,406	2,484	4,294	5,548	3,628	3,084	2,384	21,422
Austin-Round Rock, TX Metro Area	1,943,299	39,689	56,422	28,838	36,950	48,080	27,353	21,294	20,759	183,274
Bakersfield, CA Metro Area	874,589	17,253	22,382	11,648	15,371	24,627	16,896	8,829	9,115	86,486
Baltimore-Columbia-Towson, MD Metro Area	2,785,874	68,514	96,080	61,844	70,731	93,458	65,946	47,086	51,512	390,577
Bangor, ME Metro Area	153,414	5,004	5,713	3,670	4,131	6,328	3,663	3,919	3,416	25,127
Barnstable Town, MA Metro Area	214,914	6,915	12,350	6,694	10,332	15,543	11,796	8,128	7,498	59,991
Baton Rouge, LA Metro Area	825,478	17,838	27,296	17,095	17,954	25,825	17,890	11,853	9,714	100,331
Battle Creek, MI Metro Area	134,878	4,574	5,103	3,341	3,667	5,260	4,204	2,215	3,110	21,797
Bay City, MI Metro Area	106,179	2,764	3,960	2,799	3,688	4,263	3,446	3,070	2,221	19,487
Beaumont-Port Arthur, TX Metro Area	403,958	8,992	14,474	9,607	12,161	12,278	10,712	7,392	7,404	59,554
Beaver Dam, WI Micro Area	88,574	2,512	3,440	1,932	2,258	3,241	2,862	2,282	1,716	14,291
Beckley, WV Metro Area	123,373	3,682	5,223	3,613	4,459	4,731	4,199	2,491	2,999	22,492
Bellingham, WA Metro Area	208,351	5,305	8,683	5,278	4,989	9,218	5,693	2,579	4,198	31,955
Bend-Redmond, OR Metro Area	170,388	6,390	6,837	4,395	5,812	8,563	5,094	2,751	3,703	30,318
Billings, MT Metro Area	167,521	4,892	6,183	3,652	5,060	5,825	4,654	3,647	3,355	26,193
Binghamton, NY Metro Area	247,219	6,786	11,184	6,175	8,414	8,396	7,290	6,442	6,857	43,574
Birmingham-Hoover, AL Metro Area	1,143,772	30,090	39,374	25,672	31,534	40,251	31,712	20,362	18,791	168,322
Bismarck, ND Metro Area	126,526	2,754	4,392	2,822	2,728	4,258	2,985	2,309	3,159	18,261
Blacksburg-Christiansburg-Radford, VA Metro Area	181,249	3,933	5,245	3,407	5,415	6,838	4,049	3,333	3,005	26,047
Bloomington, IL Metro Area	188,917	4,712	4,740	2,935	3,951	5,824	3,231	3,123	3,753	22,817
Bloomington, IN Metro Area	164,308	3,617	4,573	3,150	3,927	4,129	3,540	2,440	2,160	19,346
Bloomsburg-Berwick, PA Metro Area	85,763	2,869	2,928	1,815	2,932	3,326	2,683	2,340	1,950	15,046
Bluefield, WV-VA Micro Area	105,237	2,763	5,924	2,467	3,589	5,408	3,702	3,008	2,376	20,550
Boise City, ID Metro Area	666,144	15,210	22,160	14,110	16,275	22,583	14,393	9,240	10,248	86,909
Boston-Cambridge-Newton, MA-NH Metro Area	4,732,161	121,174	159,418	99,852	119,993	157,725	111,895	88,972	98,342	676,779
Boulder, CO Metro Area	313,333	8,337	12,004	5,986	7,260	9,558	5,593	4,896	4,638	37,931
Bowling Green, KY Metro Area	165,928	3,758	5,325	2,739	3,939	5,960	4,134	2,622	1,812	21,206
Bozeman, MT Micro Area	97,308	2,315	2,940	1,591	1,772	3,143	1,789	1,434	978	10,707
Brainerd, MN Micro Area	91,824	2,601	4,140	2,901	3,504	5,234	3,424	2,550	2,475	20,088
Branson, MO Micro Area	85,334	2,395	4,485	2,476	3,645	5,496	4,180	1,765	1,601	19,163
Bremerton-Silverdale, WA Metro Area	254,183	6,410	9,724	6,846	8,280	10,463	6,790	3,479	4,994	40,852
Bridgeport-Stamford-Norwalk, CT Metro Area	945,438	25,327	29,112	18,297	25,174	29,800	24,408	17,987	20,186	135,852
Brownsville-Harlingen, TX Metro Area	420,392	7,271	11,302	9,361	8,755	10,844	9,636	6,420	7,032	52,048
Brunswick, GA Metro Area	112,663	2,998	4,926	2,853	4,387	4,301	3,981	2,673	1,750	19,945
Buffalo-Cheektowaga-Niagara Falls, NY Metro Area	1,136,360	31,397	43,713	26,787	32,838	41,395	30,988	26,684	30,896	189,588
Burlington, NC Metro Area	155,792	3,617	5,035	4,043	4,791	5,371	4,364	3,240	3,301	25,110
Burlington-South Burlington, VT Metro Area	215,824	5,891	7,750	4,279	5,123	7,056	3,936	4,468	3,739	28,601
California-Lexington Park, MD Metro Area	110,382	3,356	3,304	1,749	2,780	3,935	2,238	1,162	1,302	13,166
Canton-Massillon, OH Metro Area	403,923	12,833	15,903	10,608	12,517	16,594	14,154	8,229	9,552	71,654
Cape Coral-Fort Myers, FL Metro Area	679,513	19,935	29,360	21,011	35,704	45,060	32,517	21,922	22,013	178,227
Cape Girardeau, MO-IL Metro Area	97,612	2,844	3,748	2,354	2,974	3,928	2,713	2,137	2,169	16,275
Carbondale-Marion, IL Metro Area	126,685	2,158	4,781	2,485	3,560	4,964	3,498	2,684	2,295	19,486
Carson City, NV Metro Area	54,522	1,397	1,707	1,317	1,728	2,661	1,873	825	1,737	10,141
Casper, WY Metro Area	81,624	2,147	3,197	1,740	1,717	2,089	2,020	1,262	1,147	9,975
Cedar Rapids, IA Metro Area	263,885	6,333	9,302	5,415	6,064	9,757	7,026	5,450	5,330	39,042
Centralia, WA Micro Area	75,128	1,764	2,790	1,581	2,503	4,404	2,086	1,842	2,331	14,747
Chambersburg-Waynesboro, PA Metro Area	152,892	4,412	5,456	3,757	5,140	6,335	4,641	3,865	4,037	27,775
Champaign-Urbana, IL Metro Area	238,680	5,034	7,237	4,448	4,252	6,317	6,357	3,873	3,333	28,580
Charleston, WV Metro Area	223,371	6,508	9,302	5,576	7,205	9,919	7,909	4,999	4,471	40,079
Charleston-Mattoon, IL Micro Area	63,148	1,832	2,443	827	1,911	2,300	1,607	1,019	1,882	9,546
Charleston-North Charleston, SC Metro Area	727,689	19,310	24,505	16,689	21,577	22,515	15,265	10,293	10,616	96,955
Charlotte-Concord-Gastonia, NC-SC Metro Area	2,380,314	53,324	69,382	50,786	58,491	71,586	48,470	34,676	31,392	295,401

Table B-4: Metropolitan/Micropolitan Statistical Areas—Older Population by Age—*Continued*

	Total Population	60 to 61 Years	62 to 64 Years	65 to 66 Years	67 to 69 Years	70 to 74 Years	75 to 79 Years	80 to 84 Years	85 Years and Over	65 Years and Over
Charlottesville, VA Metro Area	227,738	5,880	9,269	6,276	5,290	7,535	6,330	4,239	5,358	35,028
Chattanooga, TN-GA Metro Area	543,153	14,636	20,966	14,045	16,202	20,115	15,487	12,046	10,032	87,927
Cheyenne, WY Metro Area	96,389	2,287	3,916	1,825	3,109	3,400	2,183	2,037	1,343	13,897
Chicago-Naperville-Elgin, IL.-IN-WI Metro Area	9,553,810	232,047	302,202	183,045	221,228	292,585	203,305	153,883	165,526	1,219,572
Chico, CA Metro Area	224,241	6,557	8,032	3,930	6,869	10,566	6,849	4,214	5,627	38,055
Chillicothe, OH Micro Area	77,159	1,878	3,580	1,283	1,770	3,491	2,368	1,568	916	11,396
Cincinnati, OH-KY-IN Metro Area	2,149,971	56,775	72,804	48,163	50,921	68,097	52,692	34,991	39,067	293,931
Claremont-Lebanon, NH-VT Micro Area	217,634	7,457	10,714	6,211	8,653	9,442	6,495	4,968	5,072	40,841
Clarksburg, WV Micro Area	88,953	2,638	3,895	2,738	3,473	3,643	2,791	1,785	2,167	16,597
Clarksville, TN-KY Metro Area	279,593	5,031	7,403	5,538	5,256	6,507	5,704	2,899	2,095	27,999
Clearlake, CA Micro Area	64,184	2,817	3,140	1,620	2,809	3,251	2,520	1,298	1,205	12,703
Cleveland, TN Metro Area	118,959	3,478	4,373	2,689	3,626	5,280	3,842	2,436	1,979	19,852
Cleveland-Elyria, OH Metro Area	2,063,598	57,051	76,020	47,270	59,807	78,992	62,171	41,316	51,886	341,442
Coeur d'Alene, ID Metro Area	147,326	3,631	6,617	3,133	4,752	7,155	5,025	2,290	2,971	25,326
College Station-Bryan, TX Metro Area	239,953	5,063	5,370	3,594	4,106	6,157	4,329	3,484	2,629	24,299
Colorado Springs, CO Metro Area	686,908	16,141	22,405	13,256	15,653	19,731	14,033	8,902	8,825	80,400
Columbia, MO Metro Area	172,717	4,114	5,596	2,838	2,655	5,465	3,181	1,981	2,293	18,413
Columbia, SC Metro Area	800,752	18,019	27,894	16,064	22,251	26,985	16,917	12,376	10,785	105,378
Columbus, GA-AL Metro Area	312,731	8,269	8,758	6,100	7,896	8,693	5,407	5,546	4,865	38,507
Columbus, IN Metro Area	80,217	1,783	3,152	2,091	2,131	2,523	2,144	1,701	1,234	11,824
Columbus, OH Metro Area	1,994,536	43,483	65,261	36,967	46,037	58,309	42,002	26,028	29,637	238,980
Concord, NH Micro Area	147,171	4,539	5,805	3,185	4,328	6,040	4,137	2,902	2,888	23,480
Cookeville, TN Micro Area	108,189	2,588	4,650	2,777	3,280	4,924	4,385	2,170	1,310	18,846
Coos Bay, OR Micro Area	62,475	2,404	3,979	1,637	2,695	4,393	2,796	1,548	2,101	15,170
Corning, NY Micro Area	98,394	3,071	3,417	2,512	3,500	3,702	3,417	1,752	2,461	17,344
Corpus Christi, TX Metro Area	443,480	11,469	14,662	10,461	11,677	15,139	10,299	8,003	6,618	62,197
Corvallis, OR Metro Area	86,316	2,422	2,914	1,576	2,097	3,457	1,370	1,714	2,159	12,373
Crestview-Fort Walton Beach-Destin, FL Metro Area	258,042	6,259	8,780	6,806	7,686	9,540	7,119	5,358	4,890	41,399
Cullman, AL Micro Area	81,289	1,628	2,650	2,155	1,958	4,270	2,667	1,906	1,310	14,266
Cumberland, MD-WV Metro Area	100,530	2,122	4,185	3,223	3,380	4,065	3,329	2,848	2,517	19,362
Dallas-Fort Worth-Arlington, TX Metro Area	6,954,003	143,724	188,403	112,890	142,483	180,970	123,862	78,289	73,597	712,091
Dalton, GA Metro Area	142,952	3,281	3,176	2,071	3,345	5,185	4,111	2,142	1,266	18,120
Danville, IL Metro Area	79,728	2,369	3,258	2,064	2,178	3,652	2,009	2,768	1,387	14,058
Danville, VA Micro Area	104,827	2,770	4,604	3,451	3,207	4,693	4,051	3,271	2,044	20,717
Daphne-Fairhope-Foley, AL Metro Area	200,111	5,538	8,487	5,601	6,164	10,630	6,178	5,401	3,808	37,782
Davenport-Moline-Rock Island, IA-IL Metro Area	382,382	10,310	14,149	8,548	10,570	15,835	10,469	8,974	8,377	62,773
Dayton, OH Metro Area	800,836	21,651	29,732	16,726	24,659	31,667	24,776	18,620	15,679	132,127
Decatur, AL Metro Area	153,084	4,215	6,247	3,613	4,502	5,694	3,884	3,671	2,340	23,704
Decatur, IL Metro Area	108,350	3,451	3,811	3,107	3,050	4,252	3,419	3,094	2,331	19,253
Deltona-Daytona Beach-Ormond Beach, FL Metro Area	609,939	19,061	27,243	19,369	26,081	35,630	27,331	16,342	22,176	146,929
Denver-Aurora-Lakewood, CO Metro Area	2,754,258	63,197	91,872	53,575	64,050	78,433	52,978	33,686	38,956	321,678
Des Moines-West Des Moines, IA Metro Area	611,549	14,944	17,653	11,741	14,730	16,012	11,891	9,221	10,637	74,232
Detroit-Warren-Dearborn, MI Metro Area	4,296,611	119,527	155,219	93,977	108,941	156,088	102,861	81,721	88,954	632,542
Dothan, AL Metro Area	148,095	4,028	5,019	3,427	4,773	6,589	5,202	2,840	2,480	25,311
Dover, DE Metro Area	171,987	3,413	5,007	4,158	4,568	7,334	4,767	3,075	2,685	26,587
DuBois, PA Micro Area	81,191	2,191	3,693	1,829	3,072	3,412	2,939	1,869	2,219	15,340
Dubuque, IA Metro Area	96,370	2,297	3,828	2,599	2,124	3,373	3,076	2,323	2,103	15,598
Duluth, MN-WI Metro Area	280,218	8,116	11,782	6,285	8,140	11,767	7,951	5,829	7,589	47,561
Dunn, NC Micro Area	126,666	2,784	2,760	1,810	2,926	3,765	2,333	1,404	1,431	13,669
Durham-Chapel Hill, NC Metro Area	542,710	14,093	18,130	11,065	12,423	18,625	11,651	7,583	9,579	70,926
East Stroudsburg, PA Metro Area	166,314	3,537	7,157	3,860	4,340	7,015	3,567	3,479	3,255	25,516
Eau Claire, WI Metro Area	165,024	4,467	5,231	3,448	4,647	5,404	3,539	4,026	3,170	24,234
El Centro, CA Metro Area	179,091	2,658	4,845	2,940	3,134	5,527	3,987	3,212	2,884	21,684
El Paso, TX Metro Area	836,444	15,084	22,401	12,319	15,045	24,634	18,439	13,056	10,874	94,367
Elizabeth City, NC Micro Area	63,015	1,356	2,267	1,380	1,807	3,139	2,274	1,184	904	10,688
Elizabethtown-Fort Knox, KY Metro Area	151,491	2,883	4,348	2,732	3,953	5,295	2,831	2,535	2,266	19,612
Elkhart-Goshen, IN Metro Area	201,971	5,190	5,895	3,395	4,590	5,980	4,548	3,683	3,952	26,148
Elmira, NY Metro Area	87,770	2,653	3,775	2,529	2,665	3,012	2,127	2,154	2,414	14,901
Erie, PA Metro Area	278,443	8,353	9,073	5,835	8,071	10,052	7,757	5,930	6,442	44,087
Eugene, OR Metro Area	358,337	9,879	15,059	8,960	12,509	15,270	9,504	7,240	8,754	62,237
Eureka-Arcata-Fortuna, CA Micro Area	134,809	5,024	5,783	3,399	3,272	5,731	3,334	2,436	2,155	20,327
Evansville, IN-KY Metro Area	315,162	8,210	12,471	7,655	8,708	10,932	8,230	6,502	7,087	49,114
Fairbanks, AK Metro Area	99,357	2,278	2,757	1,761	1,860	1,572	1,279	547	865	7,884
Fargo, ND-MN Metro Area	228,291	4,464	7,738	3,710	4,644	5,048	4,771	3,260	4,172	25,605
Faribault-Northfield, MN Micro Area	65,151	1,254	2,405	1,566	1,572	1,768	2,138	1,289	816	9,149
Farmington, MO Micro Area	65,960	2,845	2,660	1,761	1,164	2,838	1,326	1,538	1,468	10,095
Farmington, NM Metro Area	123,785	2,744	4,063	2,370	2,645	3,934	2,835	1,997	2,028	15,809
Fayetteville, NC Metro Area	377,939	8,024	9,358	4,467	8,093	10,880	7,421	4,984	3,809	39,654
Fayetteville-Springdale-Rogers, AR-MO Metro Area	503,046	11,803	13,154	8,328	11,581	16,437	10,643	7,161	7,541	61,691
Findlay, OH Micro Area	75,337	2,107	2,080	1,456	2,159	3,010	1,688	1,623	2,007	11,946
Flagstaff, AZ Metro Area	137,682	3,805	4,319	2,825	3,649	3,495	2,510	1,868	1,173	15,520
Flint, MI Metro Area	412,895	10,632	15,796	9,630	12,015	15,047	12,334	8,619	7,341	64,986
Florence, SC Metro Area	207,030	6,845	9,098	5,189	6,297	7,762	5,907	3,469	3,148	31,772
Florence-Muscle Shoals, AL Metro Area	147,639	4,086	5,268	2,975	4,611	8,117	5,167	3,402	3,180	27,452
Fond du Lac, WI Metro Area	101,759	3,606	3,839	2,161	2,589	4,351	2,474	2,194	3,137	16,906
Forest City, NC Micro Area	66,600	2,029	2,753	1,924	2,858	2,718	1,918	1,373	2,213	13,004
Fort Collins, CO Metro Area	324,122	7,572	10,755	7,376	7,310	12,228	7,587	5,472	5,178	45,151
Fort Smith, AR-OK Metro Area	279,592	6,617	9,967	5,859	9,153	10,693	7,529	5,120	4,708	43,062
Fort Wayne, IN Metro Area	427,183	10,847	12,072	9,463	11,129	12,502	10,706	6,520	8,055	58,375
Frankfort, KY Micro Area	72,880	2,500	2,394	1,658	2,022	2,708	2,188	1,152	1,204	10,932

Table B-4: Metropolitan/Micropolitan Statistical Areas—Older Population by Age—*Continued*

	Total Population	60 to 61 Years	62 to 64 Years	65 to 66 Years	67 to 69 Years	70 to 74 Years	75 to 79 Years	80 to 84 Years	85 Years and Over	65 Years and Over
Fresno, CA Metro Area	965,974	21,749	25,594	16,270	19,912	25,649	19,559	12,220	14,835	108,445
Gadsden, AL Metro Area	103,531	2,182	4,520	2,732	3,466	4,353	2,924	2,308	2,294	18,077
Gainesville, FL Metro Area	272,994	5,826	9,461	5,558	6,175	8,869	5,549	4,212	4,724	35,087
Gainesville, GA Metro Area	190,761	3,651	5,985	3,311	4,944	7,073	4,294	3,897	2,623	26,142
Gallup, NM Micro Area	74,098	2,077	2,102	847	1,206	2,162	1,334	1,394	566	7,509
Gettysburg, PA Metro Area	101,714	2,603	4,432	2,836	3,250	4,098	3,683	2,511	1,894	18,272
Glens Falls, NY Metro Area	127,345	3,885	6,235	3,174	4,091	6,281	4,041	2,987	2,852	23,426
Glenwood Springs, CO Micro Area	76,724	1,744	2,868	1,937	1,465	1,993	1,827	805	551	8,578
Goldsboro, NC Metro Area	124,456	2,959	3,085	2,438	3,711	4,216	3,955	1,804	1,903	18,027
Grand Forks, ND-MN Metro Area	101,842	2,156	3,634	1,864	2,400	2,761	2,617	1,805	1,757	13,204
Grand Island, NE Metro Area	84,467	1,574	2,917	1,609	2,399	3,000	3,276	1,715	1,523	13,522
Grand Junction, CO Metro Area	148,255	4,188	5,844	3,787	4,299	5,912	5,138	2,394	3,212	24,742
Grand Rapids-Wyoming, MI Metro Area	1,027,703	24,358	33,114	21,000	21,745	32,660	20,136	16,633	21,499	133,763
Grants Pass, OR Metro Area	83,599	3,112	4,708	3,993	4,040	4,164	4,425	1,968	2,077	20,667
Great Falls, MT Metro Area	82,344	1,870	3,408	1,879	2,331	3,403	2,704	2,015	1,424	13,756
Greeley, CO Metro Area	277,670	6,711	7,291	5,389	6,254	7,080	5,256	3,924	2,938	30,841
Green Bay, WI Metro Area	314,531	7,322	11,846	6,386	8,760	10,157	7,765	5,495	5,942	44,505
Greeneville, TN Micro Area	68,335	1,891	2,946	1,977	2,540	3,736	2,636	1,209	1,475	13,573
Greenfield Town, MA Micro Area	70,862	2,770	3,678	2,351	2,909	2,544	1,504	1,573	1,995	12,876
Greensboro-High Point, NC Metro Area	746,593	19,360	24,066	15,424	19,668	28,935	18,177	14,026	13,898	110,128
Greenville, NC Metro Area	175,354	3,743	4,222	4,522	3,416	4,190	2,801	2,474	2,417	19,820
Greenville-Anderson-Mauldin, SC Metro Area	862,463	19,586	31,523	18,485	26,469	33,260	21,516	16,228	15,334	131,292
Greenwood, SC Micro Area	93,954	2,109	3,884	2,440	2,939	4,102	2,544	1,607	2,910	16,542
Gulfport-Biloxi-Pascagoula, MS Metro Area	386,144	8,608	13,304	7,759	11,888	13,024	10,588	6,114	5,216	54,589
Hagerstown-Martinsburg, MD-WV Metro Area	260,070	6,072	8,469	6,150	6,040	9,930	6,159	4,635	4,881	37,795
Hammond, LA Metro Area	127,049	3,177	3,788	2,890	3,077	4,447	2,443	1,923	1,453	16,233
Hanford-Corcoran, CA Metro Area	150,269	3,137	2,777	2,522	2,076	3,215	3,093	1,345	1,080	13,331
Harrisburg-Carlisle, PA Metro Area	560,849	16,252	21,383	13,933	15,990	20,038	15,272	10,916	13,336	89,485
Harrisonburg, VA Metro Area	130,649	2,973	2,830	2,900	2,633	4,366	3,522	2,192	2,735	18,348
Hartford-West Hartford-East Hartford, CT Metro Area	1,214,295	28,691	43,882	27,954	34,291	41,993	31,412	24,481	30,116	190,247
Hattiesburg, MS Metro Area	149,312	3,890	4,589	2,939	3,637	4,290	2,868	2,081	2,251	18,066
Helena, MT Micro Area	77,424	2,450	3,909	1,879	2,493	3,905	1,808	1,442	1,435	12,962
Hermiston-Pendleton, OR Micro Area	86,147	1,951	2,909	1,645	2,408	3,480	2,411	1,700	1,524	13,168
Hickory-Lenoir-Morganton, NC Metro Area	362,896	9,948	13,231	9,924	12,508	14,672	11,308	8,370	6,202	62,984
Hilo, HI Micro Area	194,190	6,905	8,368	5,117	7,249	9,328	4,155	3,218	5,231	34,298
Hilton Head Island-Bluffton-Beaufort, SC Metro Area	203,022	5,432	7,920	6,551	10,136	13,319	7,779	4,473	5,107	47,365
Hinesville, GA Metro Area	82,768	2,003	1,387	1,188	1,419	1,707	1,202	418	323	6,257
Hobbs, NM Micro Area	69,999	1,755	1,546	844	1,572	1,326	1,842	1,100	656	7,340
Holland, MI Micro Area	113,847	3,788	3,851	2,208	3,689	4,501	3,446	1,345	1,920	17,109
Homosassa Springs, FL Metro Area	139,377	4,080	6,585	5,206	8,393	12,900	10,000	6,777	5,730	49,006
Hot Springs, AR Metro Area	97,322	2,353	3,908	3,117	2,579	5,928	4,393	2,626	2,310	20,953
Houma-Thibodaux, LA Metro Area	211,348	5,674	6,249	4,614	4,013	6,901	4,774	3,477	3,204	26,983
Houston-The Woodlands-Sugar Land, TX Metro Area	6,490,180	140,700	183,140	106,068	124,884	167,420	101,347	74,148	64,725	638,592
Huntington-Ashland, WV-KY-OH Metro Area	363,325	10,640	14,476	10,952	10,321	15,848	11,965	7,445	7,828	64,359
Huntsville, AL Metro Area	441,086	11,105	14,196	8,713	10,047	15,481	11,000	8,794	6,808	60,843
Huntsville, TX Micro Area	84,289	1,581	2,921	1,883	1,208	3,205	2,733	1,257	1,131	11,417
Hutchinson, KS Micro Area	63,794	1,892	2,187	1,835	2,020	2,154	2,229	1,654	1,904	11,796
Idaho Falls, ID Metro Area	138,403	3,293	4,565	2,504	3,127	3,890	2,639	2,288	1,922	16,370
Indiana, PA Micro Area	87,706	2,342	3,246	2,345	2,671	3,131	2,434	2,233	2,054	14,868
Indianapolis-Carmel-Anderson, IN Metro Area	1,972,241	46,430	60,789	40,639	41,578	59,184	40,788	31,935	30,310	244,434
Iowa City, IA Metro Area	164,357	3,861	5,176	2,716	3,649	3,639	2,972	2,960	2,180	18,116
Ithaca, NY Metro Area	104,691	2,868	3,411	1,905	1,381	3,880	1,648	1,192	2,319	12,325
Jackson, MI Metro Area	159,741	3,907	6,067	2,806	4,974	6,708	4,708	3,337	3,238	25,771
Jackson, MS Metro Area	576,246	13,014	17,810	10,710	12,743	18,392	12,047	8,938	9,917	72,747
Jackson, TN Metro Area	130,225	3,096	4,594	2,754	4,125	4,616	3,195	2,828	2,390	19,908
Jacksonville, FL Metro Area	1,419,127	38,891	44,326	31,526	40,265	50,228	32,045	23,356	24,576	201,996
Jacksonville, NC Metro Area	187,589	1,718	3,472	3,358	2,919	3,392	3,211	2,023	1,085	15,988
Jamestown-Dunkirk-Fredonia, NY Micro Area	132,053	3,560	4,777	3,198	4,184	5,321	3,900	3,422	3,616	23,641
Janesville-Beloit, WI Metro Area	161,188	4,505	5,006	2,820	5,119	5,353	3,941	2,600	4,347	24,180
Jefferson City, MO Metro Area	150,131	3,939	5,832	3,217	3,264	6,788	4,097	2,058	2,337	21,761
Johnson City, TN Metro Area	201,750	5,610	9,492	5,960	6,399	9,144	7,611	3,881	3,445	36,440
Johnstown, PA Metro Area	137,732	4,049	6,248	4,595	4,029	5,937	4,578	4,062	4,887	28,088
Jonesboro, AR Metro Area	126,764	2,488	4,319	2,438	2,487	5,324	3,374	2,635	1,621	17,879
Joplin, MO Metro Area	176,141	3,771	6,180	3,448	4,859	6,341	4,236	3,900	3,265	26,049
Kahului-Wailuku-Lahaina, HI Metro Area	163,108	4,665	6,723	4,293	5,185	5,307	3,686	2,264	3,919	24,654
Kalamazoo-Portage, MI Metro Area	334,017	7,755	13,489	6,890	8,447	11,347	7,681	6,801	5,935	47,101
Kalispell, MT Micro Area	94,924	3,529	3,754	2,461	2,930	4,578	3,718	1,664	1,186	16,537
Kankakee, IL Metro Area	111,375	3,456	3,025	1,753	3,441	3,918	2,891	2,461	2,053	16,517
Kansas City, MO-KS Metro Area	2,070,221	48,833	70,703	42,317	49,101	65,992	46,708	35,818	35,931	275,867
Kapaa, HI Micro Area	70,475	2,083	3,470	2,498	2,069	2,721	1,529	1,678	1,886	12,381
Keene, NH Micro Area	76,115	2,673	3,692	1,708	2,767	3,131	2,064	1,410	1,918	12,998
Kennewick-Richland, WA Metro Area	274,295	6,575	9,267	5,011	6,588	7,877	4,358	4,059	4,271	32,164
Key West, FL Micro Area	77,136	2,536	3,482	1,749	3,627	4,616	2,557	1,317	2,037	15,903
Killeen-Temple, TX Metro Area	425,239	7,257	11,204	6,871	8,604	9,903	5,782	5,173	6,239	42,572
Kingsport-Bristol-Bristol, TN-VA Metro Area	308,590	8,719	12,833	8,414	12,024	15,386	11,596	7,135	6,989	61,544
Kingston, NY Metro Area	180,445	4,610	7,958	4,802	6,216	7,401	3,930	5,278	4,110	31,737
Klamath Falls, OR Micro Area	65,455	2,256	3,094	1,377	2,219	3,877	1,825	1,044	1,962	12,304
Knoxville, TN Metro Area	857,385	22,798	34,217	22,543	28,038	35,067	25,766	16,492	17,082	144,988
Kokomo, IN Metro Area	82,982	2,360	3,914	2,772	2,952	2,509	2,735	1,906	1,972	14,846
La Crosse-Onalaska, WI-MN Metro Area	136,749	4,246	4,518	3,042	3,942	4,149	3,790	2,597	3,288	20,808

Table B-4: Metropolitan/Micropolitan Statistical Areas—Older Population by Age—*Continued*

	Total Population	60 to 61 Years	62 to 64 Years	65 to 66 Years	67 to 69 Years	70 to 74 Years	75 to 79 Years	80 to 84 Years	85 Years and Over	65 Years and Over
Lafayette, LA Metro Area	484,974	11,915	13,841	8,330	9,092	17,333	12,671	6,103	6,291	59,820
Lafayette-West Lafayette, IN Metro Area	211,515	4,718	5,232	3,752	5,215	5,094	4,110	3,095	3,973	25,239
LaGrange, GA Micro Area	69,469	1,697	2,502	1,367	1,414	2,541	1,951	1,574	810	9,657
Lake Charles, LA Metro Area	204,059	5,038	7,899	4,363	5,214	7,099	4,435	3,641	3,620	28,372
Lake City, FL Micro Area	67,857	1,952	2,672	2,038	2,150	2,983	1,648	1,519	1,642	11,980
Lake Havasu City-Kingman, AZ Metro Area	203,361	5,427	10,012	5,880	10,309	15,957	11,256	7,011	4,626	55,039
Lakeland-Winter Haven, FL Metro Area	634,638	17,310	23,828	16,159	22,571	31,698	23,500	15,742	14,528	124,198
Lancaster, PA Metro Area	533,320	14,709	17,167	13,603	14,635	17,753	16,986	11,594	13,077	87,648
Lansing-East Lansing, MI Metro Area	470,458	11,720	16,581	9,932	13,406	14,527	10,204	7,644	8,246	63,959
Laredo, TX Metro Area	266,673	3,783	6,266	3,229	4,294	5,729	3,955	2,805	2,496	22,508
Las Cruces, NM Metro Area	213,676	4,029	7,830	4,414	5,122	7,776	5,053	4,370	3,322	30,057
Las Vegas-Henderson-Paradise, NV Metro Area	2,069,681	47,540	65,899	44,595	53,513	73,584	46,875	31,962	24,386	274,915
Laurel, MS Micro Area	84,836	1,558	3,063	2,111	2,577	3,657	2,422	2,040	1,364	14,171
Lawrence, KS Metro Area	116,585	2,437	3,808	1,805	1,835	3,298	2,072	1,403	1,714	12,127
Lawton, OK Metro Area	131,395	2,921	3,345	2,433	2,036	3,894	3,046	2,423	1,325	15,157
Lebanon, PA Metro Area	136,359	3,693	5,004	3,394	4,527	5,122	4,441	4,051	3,161	24,696
Lewiston, ID-WA Metro Area	62,196	1,784	2,010	1,495	1,399	3,535	2,162	1,486	1,963	12,040
Lewiston-Auburn, ME Metro Area	107,440	2,906	3,532	2,426	2,808	4,773	2,830	2,649	1,850	17,336
Lexington-Fayette, KY Metro Area	494,189	13,232	15,342	9,345	13,481	14,191	10,368	5,993	8,799	62,177
Lima, OH Metro Area	105,040	3,010	4,098	1,971	3,309	3,843	2,395	3,027	1,998	16,543
Lincoln, NE Metro Area	320,227	7,707	9,237	5,721	7,446	9,459	6,283	5,294	5,181	39,384
Little Rock-North Little Rock-Conway, AR Metro Area	727,777	17,193	26,039	16,739	19,796	21,725	17,164	11,278	12,027	98,729
Logan, UT-ID Metro Area	130,934	2,045	3,062	1,922	2,183	2,547	2,258	1,394	1,509	11,813
London, KY Micro Area	127,315	3,657	3,781	2,182	4,105	5,951	3,327	2,345	1,953	19,863
Longview, TX Metro Area	217,481	5,457	7,548	3,907	6,690	7,651	5,428	4,672	3,906	32,254
Longview, WA Metro Area	102,133	3,363	3,771	2,233	3,791	4,821	3,025	2,014	2,370	18,254
Los Angeles-Long Beach-Anaheim, CA Metro Area	13,262,220	292,130	389,067	241,560	297,228	381,829	287,736	211,941	226,067	1,646,361
Louisville/Jefferson County, KY-IN Metro Area	1,265,210	28,961	45,867	29,293	34,393	43,880	30,061	20,236	24,565	182,428
Lubbock, TX Metro Area	305,262	5,496	7,901	5,921	6,770	8,110	6,378	5,245	4,413	36,837
Lufkin, TX Micro Area	87,750	2,034	2,396	2,145	2,322	3,233	2,324	1,192	2,710	13,926
Lumberton, NC Micro Area	134,760	2,780	4,671	2,611	3,608	4,479	2,804	2,065	1,812	17,379
Lynchburg, VA Metro Area	257,570	7,613	8,771	6,580	7,713	11,258	7,564	6,663	5,501	45,279
Macon, GA Metro Area	233,212	7,332	7,079	4,859	7,174	8,296	5,536	3,634	4,264	33,763
Madera, CA Metro Area	154,548	3,566	4,462	3,188	3,039	5,268	3,155	2,327	2,663	19,640
Madison, WI Metro Area	633,787	16,402	22,606	13,671	15,469	17,808	12,557	9,822	11,396	80,723
Manchester-Nashua, NH Metro Area	405,184	10,745	13,594	8,678	10,427	13,493	9,085	7,110	7,581	56,374
Manhattan, KS Metro Area	98,091	1,726	1,974	1,200	1,318	2,114	1,813	1,452	1,158	9,055
Manitowoc, WI Micro Area	80,160	2,412	3,040	2,011	2,506	3,482	2,481	1,869	2,685	15,034
Mankato-North Mankato, MN Metro Area	98,478	2,193	2,978	1,713	2,253	2,904	2,210	1,613	2,212	12,905
Mansfield, OH Metro Area	121,942	3,603	4,618	2,843	4,334	4,916	4,526	2,686	2,710	22,015
Marinette, WI-MI Micro Area	65,012	2,028	3,398	2,184	2,305	3,240	2,725	1,516	2,053	14,023
Marion, IN Micro Area	68,569	2,534	2,778	1,512	2,077	3,188	2,039	1,510	1,690	12,016
Marion, OH Micro Area	65,720	1,963	1,587	2,113	1,700	2,300	1,902	1,379	1,613	11,007
Marquette, MI Micro Area	67,676	1,835	3,104	1,222	2,083	3,036	2,389	1,203	1,324	11,257
Marshall, TX Micro Area	67,336	1,555	2,687	1,961	1,530	2,276	1,277	1,455	1,653	10,152
Martinsville, VA Micro Area	65,878	1,970	3,581	1,315	2,337	4,360	2,831	1,596	1,790	14,229
McAllen-Edinburg-Mission, TX Metro Area	831,073	10,532	17,645	12,225	15,083	21,418	15,752	11,859	10,077	86,414
Meadville, PA Micro Area	87,175	2,701	4,637	1,782	3,240	4,302	2,951	2,027	1,617	15,919
Medford, OR Metro Area	210,287	7,032	10,596	5,376	7,380	11,979	6,611	4,990	5,864	42,200
Memphis, TN-MS-AR Metro Area	1,344,121	33,979	42,783	28,732	30,580	38,659	24,247	20,556	19,998	162,772
Merced, CA Metro Area	266,353	4,690	4,937	3,590	5,633	6,994	5,234	3,283	3,565	28,299
Meridian, MS Micro Area	105,464	2,311	4,100	2,206	2,606	4,151	3,158	1,762	2,136	16,019
Miami-Fort Lauderdale-West Palm Beach, FL Metro Area	5,929,819	142,805	199,294	123,822	168,796	231,796	180,129	141,932	162,697	1,009,172
Michigan City-La Porte, IN Metro Area	111,444	3,111	4,181	2,891	3,250	4,337	2,918	2,055	2,100	17,551
Midland, MI Metro Area	83,427	2,161	2,714	1,668	2,149	3,726	2,218	2,172	1,902	13,835
Midland, TX Metro Area	163,470	5,353	4,350	2,690	3,355	2,671	2,200	2,662	2,217	15,795
Milwaukee-Waukesha-West Allis, WI Metro Area	1,572,245	42,376	54,208	32,137	37,222	48,206	35,666	29,497	34,748	217,476
Minneapolis-St. Paul-Bloomington, MN-WI Metro Area	3,495,176	81,659	115,046	65,947	80,092	100,313	70,163	51,789	60,948	429,252
Minot, ND Micro Area	79,188	1,890	1,762	1,139	1,659	1,916	1,656	1,183	1,801	9,354
Missoula, MT Metro Area	112,684	2,295	4,110	2,660	3,078	3,577	1,633	1,558	2,649	15,155
Mobile, AL Metro Area	415,123	10,228	14,084	8,796	11,577	14,649	9,940	6,789	8,299	60,050
Modesto, CA Metro Area	531,997	11,088	14,729	11,005	11,141	14,681	11,132	8,023	8,466	64,448
Monroe, LA Metro Area	178,864	5,595	5,936	3,565	4,841	5,635	4,520	3,470	2,628	24,659
Monroe, MI Metro Area	149,824	4,118	6,022	3,530	3,973	6,116	4,424	2,392	3,255	23,690
Montgomery, AL Metro Area	374,430	10,127	11,015	7,618	10,192	11,307	10,376	6,799	4,777	51,069
Morehead City, NC Micro Area	68,811	2,350	2,670	2,374	3,397	3,626	2,840	1,595	1,462	15,294
Morgantown, WV Metro Area	137,251	3,414	4,441	3,308	3,186	3,329	3,090	1,895	2,073	16,881
Morristown, TN Metro Area	115,713	3,384	4,247	3,068	4,130	5,723	3,659	2,790	1,795	21,165
Moses Lake, WA Micro Area	93,147	2,353	3,332	1,645	2,833	2,507	1,475	1,934	1,346	11,740
Mount Airy, NC Micro Area	72,968	2,042	2,267	2,040	2,096	3,562	2,637	1,609	1,826	13,770
Mount Pleasant, MI Micro Area	70,616	1,520	1,907	992	1,157	2,182	1,276	983	999	7,589
Mount Vernon-Anacortes, WA Metro Area	120,365	3,438	4,804	2,951	4,520	5,934	3,582	3,015	2,862	22,864
Muncie, IN Metro Area	117,074	2,578	3,721	2,941	3,163	4,278	3,547	1,923	2,883	18,735
Muskegon, MI Metro Area	172,344	4,742	5,378	4,232	4,552	5,910	4,396	3,470	3,289	25,849
Muskogee, OK Micro Area	69,966	1,598	2,462	1,852	1,912	2,606	1,306	1,776	1,696	11,148
Myrtle Beach-Conway-North Myrtle Beach, SC-NC Metro Area	417,668	13,546	20,060	13,133	20,192	27,986	15,309	9,295	7,190	93,105
Nacogdoches, TX Micro Area	65,301	1,281	2,301	1,153	1,779	1,728	2,001	723	1,127	8,511
Napa, CA Metro Area	141,667	4,486	5,755	3,662	4,758	6,055	2,924	3,643	3,589	24,631
Naples-Immokalee-Marco Island, FL Metro Area	348,777	10,033	14,825	10,263	16,903	26,074	22,440	15,372	11,201	102,202

Table B-4: Metropolitan/Micropolitan Statistical Areas—Older Population by Age—*Continued*

	Total Population	60 to 61 Years	62 to 64 Years	65 to 66 Years	67 to 69 Years	70 to 74 Years	75 to 79 Years	80 to 84 Years	85 Years and Over	65 Years and Over
Nashville-Davidson–Murfreesboro–Franklin, TN Metro Area	1,792,468	43,498	53,439	35,619	41,882	55,044	36,196	27,241	22,545	218,527
New Bern, NC Metro Area	127,886	3,162	4,958	2,717	4,628	6,248	3,433	3,435	3,152	23,613
New Castle, PA Micro Area	88,771	2,782	3,441	1,810	3,192	3,887	3,084	2,507	3,075	17,555
New Haven-Milford, CT Metro Area	861,277	24,946	30,317	19,721	22,822	30,563	22,283	16,144	22,801	134,334
New Orleans-Metairie, LA Metro Area	1,251,849	29,947	47,124	27,273	33,587	42,340	27,842	20,408	20,088	171,538
New Philadelphia-Dover, OH Micro Area	92,788	2,807	3,293	1,945	2,381	4,609	3,146	1,925	2,740	16,746
New York-Newark-Jersey City, NY-NJ-PA Metro Area	20,092,883	486,988	648,005	402,242	501,830	661,011	478,727	368,088	417,907	2,829,805
Niles-Benton Harbor, MI Metro Area	155,233	4,912	5,977	4,045	4,478	6,541	5,135	3,589	3,430	27,218
North Port-Sarasota-Bradenton, FL Metro Area	748,708	21,605	34,072	27,800	38,048	52,797	46,796	28,396	30,936	224,773
North Wilkesboro, NC Micro Area	68,838	1,830	2,672	1,992	3,010	3,010	2,674	1,571	1,405	13,662
Norwich-New London, CT Metro Area	273,676	7,675	9,623	6,306	7,523	10,797	7,307	6,153	5,971	44,057
Oak Harbor, WA Micro Area	79,275	2,408	3,321	3,432	3,309	4,408	2,769	2,285	1,979	18,182
Ocala, FL Metro Area	339,167	9,850	14,885	10,661	16,936	25,410	16,548	13,582	11,070	94,207
Ocean City, NJ Metro Area	95,344	3,749	4,422	3,190	4,149	5,571	4,463	2,895	2,659	22,927
Odessa, TX Metro Area	153,904	3,263	3,536	2,663	3,021	2,492	2,363	2,327	1,798	14,664
Ogden-Clearfield, UT Metro Area	631,146	12,024	16,095	10,984	11,069	15,041	12,862	6,683	7,310	63,949
Ogdensburg-Massena, NY Micro Area	111,400	2,803	4,402	2,296	3,214	4,184	2,823	2,031	2,445	16,993
Oklahoma City, OK Metro Area	1,336,767	29,670	42,105	25,005	34,026	39,563	29,588	21,714	19,844	169,740
Olean, NY Micro Area	78,600	2,710	3,053	1,546	2,478	3,582	2,218	1,924	1,680	13,428
Olympia-Tumwater, WA Metro Area	265,851	7,864	10,386	7,167	7,783	9,216	6,300	5,226	4,593	40,285
Omaha-Council Bluffs, NE-IA Metro Area	904,491	20,830	28,410	16,491	20,683	25,697	17,320	13,513	16,822	110,526
Opelousas, LA Micro Area	83,709	2,077	2,854	1,805	2,249	2,821	2,028	1,473	1,937	12,313
Orangeburg, SC Micro Area	90,090	3,321	3,097	2,042	2,740	4,240	2,959	1,177	2,064	15,222
Orlando-Kissimmee-Sanford, FL Metro Area	2,321,418	52,436	72,690	45,182	58,016	83,277	56,205	37,564	40,917	321,161
Oshkosh-Neenah, WI Metro Area	169,511	3,726	6,017	3,345	4,754	5,221	4,667	3,889	3,315	25,191
Ottawa-Peru, IL Micro Area	151,415	5,037	6,476	2,942	4,740	6,708	4,841	3,828	4,693	27,752
Owensboro, KY Metro Area	116,170	2,608	3,766	2,832	3,153	4,935	3,729	2,633	2,088	19,370
Owosso, MI Micro Area	68,933	2,012	2,936	1,989	1,937	2,640	1,938	1,344	1,745	11,593
Oxnard-Thousand Oaks-Ventura, CA Metro Area	846,178	22,722	25,054	17,022	22,511	26,064	18,409	13,715	17,233	114,954
Paducah, KY-IL Micro Area	97,953	2,437	4,734	2,307	2,751	5,383	2,617	2,174	2,744	17,976
Palatka, FL Micro Area	72,143	2,111	2,921	1,970	2,176	4,438	2,955	2,408	952	14,899
Palm Bay-Melbourne-Titusville, FL Metro Area	556,885	16,432	22,715	15,722	22,375	29,310	24,130	16,794	17,681	126,012
Panama City, FL Metro Area	192,406	5,669	6,173	4,796	5,978	7,768	4,995	4,753	3,634	31,924
Parkersburg-Vienna, WV Metro Area	92,684	2,594	3,103	2,480	3,398	4,101	3,432	1,833	2,048	17,292
Pensacola-Ferry Pass-Brent, FL Metro Area	474,081	10,760	16,213	10,951	13,103	18,866	13,578	8,692	7,728	72,918
Peoria, IL Metro Area	379,520	10,886	13,523	8,705	10,564	13,624	10,753	7,919	9,073	60,638
Philadelphia-Camden-Wilmington, PA-NJ-DE-MD Metro Area	6,051,170	155,794	199,415	123,166	159,196	202,640	146,269	116,687	130,096	878,054
Phoenix-Mesa-Scottsdale, AZ Metro Area	4,489,109	96,165	140,738	91,878	120,807	160,837	110,989	78,176	75,192	637,879
Pine Bluff, AR Metro Area	95,121	2,076	4,052	2,053	2,723	3,536	3,034	1,703	1,609	14,658
Pinehurst-Southern Pines, NC Micro Area	93,077	1,599	3,430	3,224	3,146	5,692	3,169	2,770	4,339	22,340
Pittsburgh, PA Metro Area	2,355,968	69,314	95,549	59,279	75,234	92,801	73,465	59,688	71,675	432,142
Pittsfield, MA Metro Area	128,715	3,554	6,323	3,660	4,516	6,375	4,718	3,073	4,323	26,665
Plattsburgh, NY Micro Area	81,632	2,510	2,611	1,694	2,124	3,177	2,297	1,704	1,290	12,286
Pocatello, ID Metro Area	83,347	2,792	2,429	1,553	2,322	2,467	2,105	1,331	888	10,666
Port Angeles, WA Micro Area	72,715	3,136	3,620	3,202	3,408	4,388	3,104	2,210	3,167	19,479
Port St. Lucie, FL Metro Area	444,420	11,391	18,871	13,859	16,983	26,443	19,245	16,833	16,537	109,900
Portland-South Portland, ME Metro Area	523,552	16,593	20,631	13,710	16,869	20,896	14,503	11,556	12,407	89,941
Portland-Vancouver-Hillsboro, OR-WA Metro Area	2,347,127	58,483	85,841	52,274	64,472	71,682	47,610	34,563	40,494	311,095
Portsmouth, OH Micro Area	77,258	2,108	2,914	1,861	2,310	2,820	2,334	1,754	1,687	12,766
Pottsville, PA Micro Area	145,797	4,638	6,455	3,600	4,507	6,905	4,425	4,184	4,590	28,211
Prescott, AZ Metro Area	218,844	8,578	12,723	7,555	13,077	16,105	10,882	6,676	7,413	61,708
Providence-Warwick, RI-MA Metro Area	1,609,367	42,011	59,874	32,516	46,087	59,994	39,820	33,735	42,071	254,223
Provo-Orem, UT Metro Area	572,798	6,920	10,405	6,036	8,510	9,575	7,763	5,862	3,300	41,046
Pueblo, CO Metro Area	161,875	4,036	7,073	3,544	5,365	6,493	5,438	3,614	3,506	27,960
Punta Gorda, FL Metro Area	168,474	4,734	8,198	8,167	10,992	14,926	12,282	9,295	7,724	63,386
Quincy, IL-MO Micro Area	76,618	1,513	3,730	2,208	2,447	2,557	2,496	1,862	2,567	14,137
Racine, WI Metro Area	195,163	4,723	7,483	4,261	5,078	7,128	4,792	3,918	4,309	29,486
Raleigh, NC Metro Area	1,242,974	27,081	36,351	21,141	30,215	30,707	21,672	15,809	12,671	132,215
Rapid City, SD Metro Area	143,867	3,878	5,577	3,631	4,038	4,642	3,611	2,738	3,100	21,760
Reading, PA Metro Area	413,691	10,930	15,363	9,307	11,123	15,466	11,650	9,818	9,085	66,449
Redding, CA Metro Area	179,804	5,175	8,742	5,335	5,628	9,265	5,148	4,404	4,885	34,665
Reno, NV Metro Area	444,487	12,318	16,696	10,788	14,039	16,419	9,031	8,872	6,619	65,768
Richmond, IN Micro Area	67,671	1,247	2,708	1,686	1,719	3,349	2,544	1,749	1,278	12,325
Richmond, VA Metro Area	1,260,668	34,399	44,309	27,695	32,484	42,249	27,397	18,613	23,009	171,447
Richmond-Berea, KY Micro Area	103,645	1,741	3,678	1,718	2,987	3,856	2,534	1,553	1,428	14,076
Riverside-San Bernardino-Ontario, CA Metro Area	4,441,890	91,761	124,560	78,167	101,910	124,451	88,372	67,309	65,136	525,345
Roanoke Rapids, NC Micro Area	73,433	1,758	2,983	2,261	2,166	3,106	2,637	2,260	1,689	14,119
Roanoke, VA Metro Area	312,837	10,007	13,344	7,195	11,553	14,044	10,465	6,032	8,392	57,681
Rochester, MN Metro Area	212,778	5,005	8,008	4,609	5,102	7,127	5,620	4,506	4,782	31,746
Rochester, NY Metro Area	1,083,393	28,296	42,664	22,517	33,159	41,738	28,482	19,948	27,164	173,008
Rockford, IL Metro Area	342,411	8,721	11,880	6,691	10,486	13,351	8,815	6,740	6,727	52,810
Rocky Mount, NC Metro Area	149,290	4,216	6,342	3,572	4,899	6,133	3,906	3,650	2,592	24,752
Rome, GA Metro Area	96,063	1,892	2,961	1,812	2,352	3,823	2,549	2,021	2,121	14,678
Roseburg, OR Micro Area	106,972	4,021	5,831	3,828	4,033	6,255	4,540	2,834	3,680	25,170
Roswell, NM Micro Area	65,878	1,557	2,994	1,528	1,655	2,461	1,952	1,500	711	9,807
Russellville, AR Micro Area	85,152	1,494	2,160	1,665	2,468	3,238	2,198	2,236	1,342	13,147
Sacramento–Roseville–Arden-Arcade, CA Metro Area	2,244,397	52,907	80,189	50,160	56,436	73,203	53,309	40,480	39,143	312,731
Saginaw, MI Metro Area	195,012	4,780	8,173	4,488	5,294	8,547	6,464	4,878	3,726	33,397

Table B-4: Metropolitan/Micropolitan Statistical Areas—Older Population by Age—*Continued*

	Total Population	60 to 61 Years	62 to 64 Years	65 to 66 Years	67 to 69 Years	70 to 74 Years	75 to 79 Years	80 to 84 Years	85 Years and Over	65 Years and Over
Salem, OH Micro Area	105,686	3,477	4,083	2,615	3,289	4,801	3,375	2,520	2,592	19,192
Salem, OR Metro Area	404,026	11,129	14,462	10,029	9,909	15,579	9,673	7,633	7,964	60,787
Salinas, CA Metro Area	431,344	10,834	11,937	7,610	10,210	10,915	7,373	7,386	7,658	51,152
Salisbury, MD-DE Metro Area	389,922	11,254	17,785	11,797	16,465	21,396	13,424	9,532	9,044	81,658
Salt Lake City, UT Metro Area	1,153,340	22,938	34,017	17,051	20,231	28,112	19,182	12,722	13,081	110,379
San Angelo, TX Metro Area	118,296	2,577	3,687	1,867	2,814	4,259	3,376	2,707	2,505	17,528
San Antonio-New Braunfels, TX Metro Area	2,326,665	49,514	69,951	41,852	54,944	67,063	47,533	36,000	33,675	281,067
San Diego-Carlsbad, CA Metro Area	3,263,431	77,684	97,454	57,015	76,631	97,793	70,421	56,636	56,136	414,632
San Francisco-Oakland-Hayward, CA Metro Area	4,594,060	112,209	164,003	97,685	119,718	146,655	107,084	81,635	90,288	643,065
San Jose-Sunnyvale-Santa Clara, CA Metro Area	1,952,872	44,210	57,078	34,541	40,380	58,523	44,330	30,297	29,742	237,813
San Luis Obispo-Paso Robles-Arroyo Grande, CA Metro Area	279,083	8,289	9,910	6,968	9,203	12,462	7,673	7,423	5,523	49,252
Sandusky, OH Micro Area	75,828	2,159	2,380	1,773	2,213	4,249	2,252	2,210	1,942	14,639
Santa Cruz-Watsonville, CA Metro Area	271,804	7,516	11,057	7,592	6,693	8,416	5,931	3,448	4,187	36,267
Santa Fe, NM Metro Area	148,164	4,170	8,250	4,673	6,533	7,461	4,643	3,080	2,639	29,029
Santa Maria-Santa Barbara, CA Metro Area	440,668	10,173	13,772	8,636	10,160	13,114	9,627	9,164	10,704	61,405
Santa Rosa, CA Metro Area	500,292	15,666	21,214	12,792	16,619	20,283	9,885	9,878	13,079	82,536
Savannah, GA Metro Area	372,708	7,406	11,507	7,555	8,653	12,695	6,853	5,707	6,232	47,695
Scranton–Wilkes-Barre–Hazleton, PA Metro Area	559,679	15,459	23,125	13,353	17,492	25,284	16,740	13,704	19,015	105,588
Searcy, AR Micro Area	78,592	1,950	2,057	1,298	2,462	2,882	2,709	1,336	1,233	11,920
Seattle-Tacoma-Bellevue, WA Metro Area	3,671,478	90,223	119,438	72,312	89,416	104,249	68,450	51,743	63,806	449,976
Sebastian-Vero Beach, FL Metro Area	144,755	4,999	7,351	5,067	7,278	9,713	7,479	6,721	7,638	43,896
Sebring, FL Metro Area	98,236	2,654	3,969	3,756	5,155	7,954	7,322	5,061	3,933	33,181
Seneca, SC Micro Area	75,192	2,310	4,045	1,984	4,127	3,677	2,862	2,029	1,271	15,950
Sevierville, TN Micro Area	95,110	2,747	3,537	2,277	2,942	5,573	2,914	1,795	1,475	16,976
Shawnee, OK Micro Area	71,811	1,949	2,553	1,581	2,190	2,739	1,862	1,466	1,390	11,228
Sheboygan, WI Metro Area	115,290	2,359	4,831	2,293	2,715	4,826	3,283	2,577	2,826	18,520
Shelby, NC Micro Area	97,076	3,727	3,722	1,904	3,390	4,604	3,217	1,905	1,817	16,837
Sherman-Denison, TX Metro Area	123,534	3,991	4,924	2,924	3,365	5,836	3,630	2,909	2,202	20,866
Show Low, AZ Micro Area	108,101	2,452	3,470	2,190	3,728	4,906	3,322	1,644	1,339	17,129
Shreveport-Bossier City, LA Metro Area	445,142	12,083	14,760	9,071	11,965	16,292	11,570	7,829	8,423	65,150
Sierra Vista-Douglas, AZ Metro Area	127,448	3,859	5,963	3,781	5,059	5,499	4,961	2,709	3,151	25,160
Sioux City, IA-NE-SD Metro Area	169,058	4,530	5,329	3,884	4,899	4,919	3,721	3,864	3,696	24,983
Sioux Falls, SD Metro Area	248,252	4,240	7,917	4,585	5,956	6,685	4,361	4,475	4,488	30,550
Somerset, PA Micro Area	76,218	2,914	2,670	1,823	2,552	3,916	2,784	2,133	2,400	15,608
South Bend-Mishawaka, IN-MI Metro Area	319,226	8,505	12,046	7,072	8,275	11,125	7,512	6,784	7,211	47,979
Spartanburg, SC Metro Area	321,418	8,690	9,440	6,762	11,046	11,733	8,230	6,809	4,979	49,559
Spokane-Spokane Valley, WA Metro Area	542,073	14,207	19,257	13,479	15,449	21,486	11,382	10,480	11,625	83,901
Springfield, IL Metro Area	211,311	6,079	7,391	4,570	5,830	8,102	7,062	3,681	4,697	33,942
Springfield, MA Metro Area	629,100	18,264	21,467	15,986	14,886	21,788	15,268	11,613	15,582	95,123
Springfield, MO Metro Area	450,619	8,904	15,834	9,273	12,942	16,431	12,474	8,850	9,635	69,605
Springfield, OH Metro Area	136,554	3,602	5,430	3,289	4,084	6,286	3,910	3,394	3,393	24,356
St. Cloud, MN Metro Area	192,418	4,170	5,122	3,537	4,434	5,618	4,768	3,578	3,779	25,714
St. George, UT Metro Area	151,948	3,532	4,356	4,037	4,262	8,174	5,577	4,083	3,932	30,065
St. Joseph, MO-KS Metro Area	127,671	2,997	4,221	2,739	3,034	5,045	3,261	2,695	2,570	19,344
St. Louis, MO-IL Metro Area	2,805,856	70,988	102,811	59,831	73,744	98,066	74,180	56,103	55,504	417,428
State College, PA Metro Area	158,742	3,546	4,789	3,235	3,254	4,495	4,198	2,274	2,417	19,873
Statesboro, GA Micro Area	72,087	1,792	1,818	1,019	1,492	1,985	1,296	940	760	7,492
Staunton-Waynesboro, VA Metro Area	119,766	3,736	4,336	2,740	4,797	6,130	4,767	3,077	1,478	22,989
Stevens Point, WI Micro Area	70,482	1,853	2,338	1,398	1,845	2,520	1,959	1,392	1,110	10,224
Stillwater, OK Micro Area	80,264	1,756	1,947	1,406	1,149	2,440	1,617	838	1,339	8,789
Stockton-Lodi, CA Metro Area	715,597	14,897	20,279	13,080	14,693	21,211	14,882	10,207	10,225	84,298
Sumter, SC Metro Area	107,919	2,532	3,581	1,857	3,290	3,706	3,416	1,337	1,882	15,400
Sunbury, PA Micro Area	93,944	2,463	3,744	2,651	3,367	3,888	3,531	2,450	2,721	18,608
Syracuse, NY Metro Area	661,478	16,784	24,809	13,255	16,866	25,324	16,721	12,635	15,620	100,421
Talladega-Sylacauga, AL Micro Area	91,507	2,954	3,470	2,209	3,296	4,024	2,384	1,676	1,752	15,341
Tallahassee, FL Metro Area	374,890	10,610	12,323	5,836	9,506	12,237	7,558	5,035	5,566	45,738
Tampa-St. Petersburg-Clearwater, FL Metro Area	2,915,582	77,625	106,292	73,221	94,685	132,000	95,843	69,820	79,583	545,152
Terre Haute, IN Metro Area	171,555	4,158	6,078	3,153	5,408	6,387	3,692	3,167	4,249	26,056
Texarkana, TX-AR Metro Area	147,740	3,743	5,327	2,571	4,722	6,013	3,612	3,346	2,784	23,048
The Villages, FL Metro Area	114,350	3,484	8,800	7,176	11,969	19,449	11,793	5,415	4,423	60,225
Toledo, OH Metro Area	607,456	16,346	22,264	14,171	15,676	19,287	14,687	10,485	13,882	88,188
Topeka, KS Metro Area	233,758	5,062	8,911	5,353	6,940	8,874	7,419	3,865	5,675	38,126
Torrington, CT Micro Area	184,993	5,298	7,952	4,003	7,022	8,695	5,421	3,906	5,055	34,102
Traverse City, MI Micro Area	147,610	4,264	6,842	4,210	6,208	6,383	5,114	4,130	3,001	29,046
Trenton, NJ Metro Area	371,537	8,585	13,017	8,104	8,856	11,361	8,782	7,263	6,863	51,229
Truckee-Grass Valley, CA Micro Area	98,893	3,969	6,516	2,916	4,727	6,069	2,581	3,918	2,911	23,122
Tucson, AZ Metro Area	1,004,516	26,119	35,873	25,582	31,073	43,829	32,639	24,674	20,248	178,045
Tullahoma-Manchester, TN Micro Area	102,651	2,343	3,789	2,487	2,843	5,648	3,306	2,483	1,521	18,288
Tulsa, OK Metro Area	970,391	25,947	31,832	20,336	26,454	33,205	22,948	17,924	16,548	137,415
Tupelo, MS Micro Area	139,723	3,680	3,013	3,233	4,164	4,100	3,058	2,652	3,008	20,215
Tuscaloosa, AL Metro Area	235,954	5,219	8,752	4,604	5,443	7,162	4,287	3,662	4,896	30,054
Twin Falls, ID Micro Area	105,226	2,586	3,591	2,143	2,570	4,045	2,446	2,372	1,728	15,304
Tyler, TX Metro Area	218,842	6,404	7,416	3,534	5,871	9,804	6,044	4,571	4,075	33,899
Ukiah, CA Micro Area	87,869	2,830	4,455	2,241	4,231	4,273	2,102	1,957	2,172	16,976
Urban Honolulu, HI Metro Area	991,788	23,779	32,501	23,611	28,153	31,469	24,737	20,848	27,910	156,728
Utica-Rome, NY Metro Area	296,615	9,236	10,268	6,769	9,499	12,208	9,734	6,152	8,393	52,755
Valdosta, GA Metro Area	143,140	2,864	4,351	1,819	3,980	5,040	3,308	1,959	1,065	17,171
Vallejo-Fairfield, CA Metro Area	431,131	13,348	16,296	9,515	10,874	14,306	11,826	5,817	5,866	58,204
Victoria, TX Metro Area	99,536	2,041	4,097	1,621	3,012	3,665	1,971	2,519	1,954	14,742

Table B-4: Metropolitan/Micropolitan Statistical Areas—Older Population by Age—*Continued*

	Total Population	60 to 61 Years	62 to 64 Years	65 to 66 Years	67 to 69 Years	70 to 74 Years	75 to 79 Years	80 to 84 Years	85 Years and Over	65 Years and Over
Vineland-Bridgeton, NJ Metro Area	157,389	3,855	4,111	3,913	3,293	4,882	3,467	2,733	2,994	21,282
Virginia Beach-Norfolk-Newport News, VA-NC Metro Area	1,717,387	40,824	53,227	34,678	39,039	57,027	37,163	26,100	28,249	222,256
Visalia-Porterville, CA Metro Area	458,198	8,425	11,179	7,647	9,499	10,197	7,595	5,512	6,886	47,336
Waco, TX Metro Area	261,958	6,414	6,579	4,806	6,927	7,720	6,047	5,136	4,429	35,065
Walla Walla, WA Metro Area	63,706	2,159	2,496	1,232	2,121	2,194	1,652	1,417	1,645	10,261
Warner Robins, GA Metro Area	186,675	4,495	5,000	3,282	4,595	4,734	4,922	2,222	2,484	22,239
Warsaw, IN Micro Area	78,564	1,903	3,281	1,872	2,034	2,951	2,109	1,735	1,062	11,763
Washington-Arlington-Alexandria, DC-VA-MD-WV Metro Area	6,032,744	132,834	188,178	110,591	133,853	169,489	110,934	75,723	87,227	687,817
Waterloo-Cedar Falls, IA Metro Area	169,993	4,227	6,082	3,341	5,103	5,253	5,740	3,709	3,349	26,495
Watertown-Fort Atkinson, WI Micro Area	84,395	2,451	2,863	1,696	2,457	3,059	2,460	1,304	1,512	12,488
Watertown-Fort Drum, NY Metro Area	119,103	2,780	3,033	2,081	2,159	4,075	2,890	1,861	1,566	14,632
Wausau, WI Metro Area	135,780	3,610	5,056	3,646	3,759	4,123	3,512	3,000	3,386	21,426
Weirton-Steubenville, WV-OH Metro Area	125,467	4,025	4,304	3,017	4,106	5,504	4,634	3,573	3,271	24,105
Wenatchee, WA Metro Area	114,392	3,083	4,702	2,930	3,944	4,282	3,445	2,145	2,660	19,406
Wheeling, WV-OH Metro Area	145,205	3,850	7,975	3,793	5,373	5,829	5,827	3,195	3,756	27,773
Whitewater-Elkhorn, WI Micro Area	103,527	3,147	2,996	1,898	3,094	3,866	2,792	2,010	1,950	15,610
Wichita Falls, TX Metro Area	151,536	3,806	5,288	2,806	3,752	5,024	3,203	3,964	3,035	21,784
Wichita, KS Metro Area	641,225	16,373	22,202	12,558	15,406	19,595	15,127	12,600	11,172	86,458
Williamsport, PA Metro Area	116,508	4,214	5,075	2,964	3,330	4,847	2,883	3,228	3,224	20,476
Wilmington, NC Metro Area	272,548	6,725	9,608	7,763	8,179	10,130	7,068	5,412	5,031	43,583
Wilson, NC Micro Area	81,401	1,991	3,188	1,349	2,264	4,010	3,277	1,059	1,473	13,432
Winchester, VA-WV Metro Area	134,221	3,365	5,757	2,909	3,881	5,678	4,129	1,811	3,148	21,556
Winston-Salem, NC Metro Area	655,015	17,336	23,112	16,673	19,448	23,194	17,675	13,950	11,775	102,715
Wisconsin Rapids-Marshfield, WI Micro Area	73,608	1,925	2,267	1,424	2,210	3,642	2,059	1,906	2,581	13,822
Wooster, OH Micro Area	115,537	2,725	4,234	2,676	3,113	4,407	3,275	2,407	2,491	18,369
Worcester, MA-CT Metro Area	930,473	23,653	33,151	19,476	22,778	31,489	19,461	18,199	20,416	131,819
Yakima, WA Metro Area	247,687	4,096	7,784	4,650	4,725	8,730	5,549	4,135	3,816	31,605
York-Hanover, PA Metro Area	440,755	12,583	14,797	10,374	12,531	17,244	12,517	10,076	7,480	70,222
Youngstown-Warren-Boardman, OH-PA Metro Area	553,263	17,000	21,907	14,359	16,067	26,345	18,093	13,876	18,314	107,054
Yuba City, CA Metro Area	169,813	3,867	4,486	2,904	4,648	5,412	4,183	2,788	2,773	22,708
Yuma, AZ Metro Area	203,247	3,545	5,188	4,600	4,887	9,079	9,579	5,347	2,445	35,937
Zanesville, OH Micro Area	85,818	2,022	3,588	2,587	2,386	2,852	2,247	2,134	2,018	14,224

Table B-5: 114th Congressional Districts—Older Population by Age

	Total Population	60 to 61 Years	62 to 64 Years	65 to 66 Years	67 to 69 Years	70 to 74 Years	75 to 79 Years	80 to 84 Years	85 Years and Over	65 Years and Over
Alabama										
Congressional District 1	696,783	18,093	25,378	16,572	19,970	29,693	19,047	14,434	13,300	113,016
Congressional District 2	678,622	19,275	20,675	14,157	20,390	25,923	21,061	12,775	11,163	105,469
Congressional District 3	706,574	20,468	24,055	16,077	23,003	24,369	17,992	13,353	11,081	105,875
Congressional District 4	683,372	15,710	27,108	15,328	21,591	31,716	22,371	13,864	12,520	117,390
Congressional District 5	706,373	19,901	23,626	15,616	17,943	27,005	18,982	14,838	11,626	106,010
Congressional District 6	696,788	18,099	24,572	16,141	19,716	26,639	19,531	12,895	11,608	106,530
Congressional District 7	680,865	16,688	23,974	15,454	17,106	19,835	16,300	11,276	12,251	92,222
Alaska										
Congressional District (at Large)	736,732	18,394	22,666	13,355	15,108	17,764	10,904	6,531	6,237	69,899
Arizona										
Congressional District 1	739,373	19,604	26,261	17,021	26,440	31,590	21,982	13,668	10,185	120,886
Congressional District 2	713,036	20,788	28,389	21,096	24,629	32,721	24,565	18,596	18,057	139,664
Congressional District 3	757,119	13,309	19,907	11,514	14,895	22,487	15,453	11,003	5,649	81,001
Congressional District 4	734,258	21,693	33,324	22,900	35,947	52,497	40,185	22,577	17,400	191,506
Congressional District 5	781,441	15,475	22,298	15,634	20,943	31,009	21,758	15,342	16,338	121,024
Congressional District 6	737,185	19,100	28,046	19,303	23,097	31,982	20,105	13,869	14,650	123,006
Congressional District 7	763,089	11,679	16,538	9,902	11,698	13,025	7,925	5,517	4,980	53,047
Congressional District 8	760,904	19,124	30,271	19,865	27,075	37,277	27,621	22,638	20,239	154,715
Congressional District 9	745,079	15,355	21,688	12,835	15,083	20,051	15,181	10,662	12,096	85,908
Arkansas										
Congressional District 1	723,492	18,184	28,067	15,558	23,233	33,440	22,615	16,661	14,206	125,713
Congressional District 2	756,326	18,705	26,288	17,074	21,541	23,796	19,054	11,880	13,832	107,177
Congressional District 3	767,904	17,103	23,049	13,743	20,815	25,944	18,030	13,415	12,609	104,556
Congressional District 4	718,647	18,430	27,434	19,616	22,359	31,644	22,723	16,375	14,849	127,566
California										
Congressional District 1	710,428	22,257	34,085	17,874	25,657	37,063	21,871	17,076	19,970	139,511
Congressional District 2	720,049	24,746	33,926	19,698	25,911	33,335	17,903	15,541	17,235	129,623
Congressional District 3	720,104	18,267	24,533	14,853	18,620	20,477	17,465	10,880	10,917	93,212
Congressional District 4	719,688	20,196	34,120	20,764	23,986	37,479	23,107	18,304	14,064	137,704
Congressional District 5	722,814	22,759	27,787	17,941	21,327	29,125	17,061	13,500	16,164	115,118
Congressional District 6	737,671	16,716	22,111	13,933	15,888	18,181	14,509	10,370	10,614	83,495
Congressional District 7	736,555	17,268	26,188	17,400	17,576	23,544	17,807	13,906	13,894	104,127
Congressional District 8	715,953	17,489	24,714	14,996	18,910	21,123	15,968	10,937	9,438	91,372
Congressional District 9	738,320	15,588	22,624	13,191	15,097	24,226	16,090	10,904	11,453	90,961
Congressional District 10	732,084	15,463	20,001	14,127	15,089	19,220	15,148	9,967	10,199	83,750
Congressional District 11	739,693	18,516	28,026	17,421	20,731	26,208	17,704	13,247	16,435	111,746
Congressional District 12	736,123	16,304	27,899	16,016	19,857	20,385	18,937	15,433	16,350	106,978
Congressional District 13	743,310	16,811	27,734	14,478	18,661	21,066	13,002	12,482	13,273	92,962
Congressional District 14	753,002	19,060	27,295	16,258	19,254	25,809	20,578	13,519	13,556	108,974
Congressional District 15	753,911	17,395	22,522	13,676	19,591	21,292	15,717	11,179	12,964	94,419
Congressional District 16	718,849	14,616	15,559	10,033	14,836	17,637	12,551	8,416	10,000	73,473
Congressional District 17	756,995	15,964	19,913	13,411	14,712	21,415	15,822	11,041	10,288	86,689
Congressional District 18	734,378	18,901	23,460	14,791	16,680	25,489	19,034	14,624	15,079	105,697
Congressional District 19	746,211	16,654	23,031	12,922	15,074	22,450	15,779	10,285	10,483	86,993
Congressional District 20	732,074	18,763	23,430	15,167	16,736	17,844	13,436	11,165	11,972	86,320
Congressional District 21	712,295	12,003	13,847	8,445	10,722	13,882	11,077	6,347	5,847	56,320
Congressional District 22	739,418	16,502	20,284	14,190	15,250	20,224	14,474	8,828	12,587	85,553
Congressional District 23	747,914	16,987	21,889	11,628	15,279	22,588	16,848	9,763	10,797	86,903
Congressional District 24	726,519	18,628	24,098	15,893	19,451	25,798	17,317	16,726	16,266	111,451
Congressional District 25	718,796	14,429	20,187	11,764	15,464	19,825	12,566	8,043	8,088	75,750
Congressional District 26	725,795	20,356	20,453	13,837	19,160	21,597	16,148	12,102	15,675	98,519
Congressional District 27	714,911	17,300	25,171	15,606	20,347	27,375	18,981	15,850	17,998	116,157
Congressional District 28	721,435	15,653	24,024	15,693	18,080	24,522	18,580	13,660	13,225	103,760
Congressional District 29	718,633	15,305	16,233	12,730	12,597	16,330	13,557	8,855	8,077	72,146
Congressional District 30	754,331	19,719	26,602	15,245	20,592	22,867	17,850	16,524	17,095	110,173
Congressional District 31	738,321	14,210	17,136	12,951	14,669	16,320	10,995	7,929	9,375	72,239
Congressional District 32	735,945	16,855	24,093	14,819	20,205	20,658	16,769	11,032	11,770	95,253
Congressional District 33	714,411	17,301	23,913	15,079	22,035	26,098	20,102	16,056	19,516	118,886
Congressional District 34	720,406	15,208	19,078	11,995	12,546	17,957	13,750	11,142	10,933	78,323
Congressional District 35	732,845	11,825	15,310	8,409	12,269	14,903	11,362	7,018	6,612	60,573
Congressional District 36	746,522	18,243	25,765	16,383	25,641	36,294	25,098	21,138	21,061	145,615
Congressional District 37	723,724	15,990	22,080	14,086	15,332	19,496	14,896	10,220	14,896	88,926
Congressional District 38	720,208	16,260	21,225	12,552	15,618	24,005	19,136	12,329	12,851	96,491
Congressional District 39	716,854	16,426	22,757	13,723	16,128	21,986	17,818	12,117	14,506	96,278
Congressional District 40	713,940	11,970	16,679	8,319	10,491	13,108	10,163	6,740	7,104	55,925
Congressional District 41	739,287	13,705	19,689	10,339	14,282	15,939	10,110	7,821	8,405	66,896
Congressional District 42	754,191	15,934	20,104	13,204	16,489	20,006	14,174	11,738	10,172	85,783
Congressional District 43	731,916	14,390	19,616	13,241	13,023	20,557	13,896	10,816	10,657	82,190
Congressional District 44	726,147	13,891	16,884	9,432	11,074	15,583	11,192	7,322	7,262	61,865
Congressional District 45	763,388	18,301	22,419	14,280	18,131	23,726	18,243	13,515	14,165	102,060
Congressional District 46	730,783	12,675	17,067	11,070	10,370	16,709	10,523	7,578	8,210	64,460
Congressional District 47	718,747	17,200	22,604	13,565	16,635	19,982	15,897	12,121	10,915	89,115
Congressional District 48	726,491	18,466	24,592	16,586	24,609	26,168	18,710	15,050	14,474	115,597
Congressional District 49	728,456	15,759	23,288	13,009	20,795	23,216	19,629	13,297	13,808	103,754
Congressional District 50	737,332	19,946	24,935	16,866	19,130	24,079	16,554	13,150	12,967	102,746
Congressional District 51	720,935	11,915	20,096	10,841	13,097	18,555	13,202	10,327	10,279	76,301
Congressional District 52	759,602	19,205	23,041	13,149	17,332	23,411	14,884	13,965	13,728	96,469
Congressional District 53	753,810	19,194	19,765	11,831	16,614	22,106	17,372	13,418	13,150	94,491

Table B-5: 114th Congressional Districts—Older Population by Age—*Continued*

	Total Population	60 to 61 Years	62 to 64 Years	65 to 66 Years	67 to 69 Years	70 to 74 Years	75 to 79 Years	80 to 84 Years	85 Years and Over	65 Years and Over
Colorado										
Congressional District 1	788,694	16,821	24,392	13,757	16,271	21,684	14,641	9,039	12,059	87,451
Congressional District 2	765,721	21,065	30,215	18,272	19,736	26,830	15,376	10,716	9,976	100,906
Congressional District 3	729,368	21,767	30,641	19,228	23,062	26,883	20,578	12,753	13,408	115,912
Congressional District 4	768,242	18,978	25,133	16,889	18,333	22,251	15,348	12,089	11,126	96,036
Congressional District 5	759,664	18,799	25,227	15,790	18,204	24,480	16,554	10,828	10,495	96,351
Congressional District 6	772,966	16,806	22,720	15,091	16,777	20,536	14,007	8,728	10,260	85,399
Congressional District 7	771,211	18,155	28,533	13,662	18,985	23,174	17,912	11,084	12,700	97,517
Connecticut										
Congressional District 1	711,205	16,428	25,273	15,636	19,579	26,415	18,748	14,662	19,424	114,464
Congressional District 2	710,798	19,254	25,489	17,330	21,036	27,252	20,202	15,646	13,384	114,850
Congressional District 3	720,986	20,239	25,925	17,177	18,940	24,365	19,684	13,658	19,000	112,824
Congressional District 4	740,215	20,049	23,298	13,727	18,905	22,409	18,008	14,262	15,211	102,522
Congressional District 5	713,473	19,108	24,949	14,693	21,341	25,906	16,990	12,629	19,309	110,868
Delaware										
Congressional District (at Large)	935,614	23,699	32,114	23,426	29,258	38,894	26,808	18,232	17,141	153,759
District of Columbia										
Delegate District (at Large)	658,893	13,563	19,134	10,045	12,426	19,475	13,624	8,751	10,144	74,465
Florida										
Congressional District 1	743,897	17,277	25,547	18,077	21,111	28,926	21,037	14,390	12,977	116,518
Congressional District 2	711,296	19,787	24,269	15,686	19,803	26,356	17,761	12,067	11,706	103,379
Congressional District 3	716,034	18,083	24,921	17,253	23,585	32,439	19,253	14,568	15,081	122,179
Congressional District 4	714,880	19,032	22,404	16,234	20,772	24,274	16,645	11,665	12,581	102,171
Congressional District 5	742,217	19,050	21,405	12,766	15,092	20,118	15,222	11,285	10,597	85,080
Congressional District 6	736,069	23,961	32,543	22,622	31,055	43,898	32,476	20,150	23,635	173,836
Congressional District 7	735,643	17,048	26,115	16,198	17,218	26,465	15,941	10,961	16,768	103,551
Congressional District 8	715,672	22,069	30,384	21,326	29,940	39,205	31,725	23,619	25,527	171,342
Congressional District 9	769,993	13,787	23,199	12,544	18,141	22,378	16,305	8,275	10,648	88,291
Congressional District 10	758,350	19,971	25,373	18,778	26,555	40,475	25,617	16,913	15,549	143,887
Congressional District 11	728,133	21,583	35,836	26,857	43,445	65,485	45,871	31,705	25,753	239,116
Congressional District 12	729,937	18,649	29,723	21,009	26,272	36,567	27,643	20,686	24,937	157,114
Congressional District 13	707,503	22,320	29,789	21,512	26,739	41,836	30,000	22,942	24,013	167,042
Congressional District 14	757,963	18,158	21,818	13,405	17,967	23,578	16,891	10,973	13,755	96,569
Congressional District 15	724,176	18,741	22,508	15,451	20,428	25,891	18,933	13,058	11,416	105,177
Congressional District 16	744,076	21,496	33,609	27,470	38,012	52,150	46,644	28,264	30,936	223,476
Congressional District 17	725,251	18,702	31,460	24,487	32,891	45,645	37,996	27,382	24,894	193,295
Congressional District 18	731,704	18,840	31,379	20,894	27,875	42,403	32,404	27,272	26,218	177,066
Congressional District 19	753,542	22,775	34,938	24,656	42,277	55,394	39,365	30,813	27,672	220,177
Congressional District 20	745,656	19,343	22,679	12,984	17,341	25,460	17,829	14,173	16,921	104,708
Congressional District 21	742,664	15,309	25,211	18,256	27,451	34,695	32,104	28,544	31,538	172,588
Congressional District 22	731,165	20,890	28,650	20,935	25,171	34,788	25,924	20,923	28,742	156,483
Congressional District 23	730,033	17,755	24,788	14,125	20,379	28,993	21,604	15,615	18,322	119,038
Congressional District 24	741,950	18,614	23,653	14,017	16,527	21,403	14,929	11,035	11,178	89,089
Congressional District 25	745,358	15,922	21,361	13,174	17,779	31,721	25,910	13,984	14,454	117,022
Congressional District 26	749,692	18,918	26,468	14,597	22,596	27,207	22,008	15,106	16,931	118,445
Congressional District 27	760,443	16,977	24,293	15,050	21,314	28,041	20,751	17,652	21,507	124,315
Georgia										
Congressional District 1	729,328	15,973	22,821	15,091	19,047	23,814	15,271	11,253	11,222	95,698
Congressional District 2	685,342	19,513	21,533	14,705	18,569	23,756	15,403	11,375	10,787	94,595
Congressional District 3	725,530	18,479	22,679	15,300	19,753	26,293	16,116	11,867	9,587	98,916
Congressional District 4	728,367	18,248	22,783	13,071	16,101	19,763	11,137	7,091	7,079	74,242
Congressional District 5	738,016	14,362	22,760	11,492	15,099	22,213	12,437	8,375	7,801	77,417
Congressional District 6	732,089	15,343	23,310	12,606	16,332	18,253	12,531	9,115	11,276	80,113
Congressional District 7	752,996	14,217	22,034	12,375	14,402	16,629	11,108	6,511	5,978	67,003
Congressional District 8	705,698	18,539	21,797	14,016	20,159	25,921	18,869	11,050	10,356	100,371
Congressional District 9	717,371	18,457	27,011	18,081	23,534	34,511	21,444	14,652	11,515	123,737
Congressional District 10	713,570	18,096	23,984	15,402	20,962	24,323	17,633	10,850	9,729	98,899
Congressional District 11	725,169	15,500	23,599	16,054	15,943	18,986	13,138	8,362	6,900	79,383
Congressional District 12	701,628	17,517	24,233	15,477	17,706	22,208	15,619	11,538	10,336	92,884
Congressional District 13	741,383	14,372	20,306	11,997	13,855	18,354	10,121	8,583	7,951	70,861
Congressional District 14	700,856	16,547	20,245	13,866	16,847	26,097	18,597	10,659	8,685	94,751
Hawaii										
Congressional District 1	707,541	17,859	24,054	18,057	20,844	24,601	18,928	16,432	22,293	121,155
Congressional District 2	712,020	19,573	27,008	17,462	21,812	24,224	15,179	11,576	16,653	106,906
Idaho										
Congressional District 1	834,295	21,315	32,551	21,732	25,437	33,296	22,524	12,942	13,790	129,721
Congressional District 2	800,169	20,746	25,131	13,918	19,574	27,011	18,511	13,593	12,651	105,258
Illinois										
Congressional District 1	717,741	20,280	23,829	15,353	18,069	25,158	17,442	14,219	14,818	105,059
Congressional District 2	707,817	18,417	24,689	16,050	18,231	21,570	16,309	12,958	12,752	97,870
Congressional District 3	730,269	16,944	23,024	14,116	19,764	23,340	15,561	12,633	14,281	99,695
Congressional District 4	725,616	15,789	17,475	10,389	11,639	13,896	12,180	7,768	8,143	64,015
Congressional District 5	717,666	14,121	19,340	10,385	15,122	18,988	13,875	14,407	12,104	84,881
Congressional District 6	734,700	21,598	24,739	16,694	17,418	27,199	16,799	12,220	12,183	102,513
Congressional District 7	727,478	15,191	21,039	14,260	16,304	19,972	14,287	9,831	9,039	83,693
Congressional District 8	725,320	18,275	22,173	11,935	17,163	23,243	14,271	11,561	9,352	87,525

Table B-5: 114th Congressional Districts—Older Population by Age—*Continued*

	Total Population	60 to 61 Years	62 to 64 Years	65 to 66 Years	67 to 69 Years	70 to 74 Years	75 to 79 Years	80 to 84 Years	85 Years and Over	65 Years and Over
Illinois—Cont.										
Congressional District 9	710,295	17,168	27,205	14,107	18,686	25,547	21,072	14,099	19,433	112,944
Congressional District 10	711,698	17,667	22,849	13,087	16,751	22,160	14,790	11,104	16,689	94,581
Congressional District 11	712,657	16,471	20,951	11,282	12,209	17,061	11,658	8,472	8,420	69,102
Congressional District 12	701,698	16,534	24,929	13,544	19,424	26,470	19,195	15,908	14,170	108,711
Congressional District 13	715,374	16,850	24,727	16,625	17,240	24,770	20,485	13,562	14,964	107,646
Congressional District 14	725,522	17,917	22,364	15,056	17,810	23,852	15,417	8,755	9,988	90,878
Congressional District 15	705,504	19,027	26,328	16,828	20,117	28,309	22,965	16,642	17,647	122,508
Congressional District 16	699,582	18,942	25,427	15,380	21,823	27,126	20,043	14,821	16,709	115,902
Congressional District 17	701,014	19,283	27,749	16,114	21,273	29,640	20,532	17,510	15,929	120,998
Congressional District 18	710,629	20,251	26,726	16,767	19,646	27,957	20,979	15,390	18,594	119,333
Indiana										
Congressional District 1	718,064	18,291	25,989	16,531	17,857	25,460	16,767	13,542	15,272	105,429
Congressional District 2	721,627	20,230	25,346	14,818	18,651	25,091	16,736	15,410	15,319	106,025
Congressional District 3	734,384	18,341	24,074	17,659	18,603	23,092	18,937	12,830	13,654	104,775
Congressional District 4	742,958	17,666	24,757	15,727	19,395	24,279	18,902	13,026	14,425	105,754
Congressional District 5	743,454	18,107	23,482	15,087	17,749	24,219	15,608	15,428	12,395	100,486
Congressional District 6	720,106	18,832	25,241	19,409	20,883	26,464	20,538	14,127	15,189	116,610
Congressional District 7	756,223	17,398	20,445	13,150	13,589	19,761	13,785	9,641	10,209	80,135
Congressional District 8	723,064	18,095	27,676	15,180	21,095	28,591	17,724	15,263	17,067	114,920
Congressional District 9	736,975	18,047	27,129	17,759	21,024	24,332	18,259	12,821	13,165	107,360
Iowa										
Congressional District 1	770,612	20,399	28,312	15,848	20,216	30,189	23,985	17,449	19,231	126,918
Congressional District 2	776,785	22,466	27,634	17,078	21,054	28,726	22,111	16,415	17,074	122,458
Congressional District 3	801,039	20,730	24,369	16,545	20,581	23,220	18,010	13,691	16,270	108,317
Congressional District 4	758,690	20,301	27,689	17,787	20,373	27,479	25,287	19,636	22,373	132,935
Kansas										
Congressional District 1	718,346	17,991	23,546	14,362	17,617	24,791	20,483	15,468	18,559	111,280
Congressional District 2	715,446	17,004	27,255	16,455	18,990	26,024	19,888	13,785	15,873	111,015
Congressional District 3	749,250	18,118	24,802	14,893	16,880	21,385	14,275	11,620	13,942	92,995
Congressional District 4	720,979	18,666	24,988	14,349	17,742	23,267	18,253	14,898	13,734	102,243
Kentucky										
Congressional District 1	724,041	18,379	28,876	18,154	20,020	31,133	22,320	15,630	13,391	120,648
Congressional District 2	742,858	16,639	24,985	15,223	19,719	28,925	18,581	13,268	11,803	107,519
Congressional District 3	736,532	16,179	26,533	16,440	18,014	25,706	18,415	12,846	15,929	107,350
Congressional District 4	748,191	21,256	24,234	18,391	18,443	25,687	17,849	9,959	12,855	103,184
Congressional District 5	712,274	17,954	28,794	17,853	23,668	29,014	20,438	13,116	11,897	115,986
Congressional District 6	749,561	20,485	24,330	15,148	21,648	22,192	17,070	9,888	12,389	98,335
Louisiana										
Congressional District 1	796,858	19,523	28,688	18,176	21,850	27,482	16,908	14,220	15,232	113,868
Congressional District 2	775,807	17,824	26,860	14,416	17,985	25,531	16,509	10,994	9,253	94,688
Congressional District 3	777,665	19,064	24,904	14,744	16,617	27,733	19,627	11,018	11,499	101,238
Congressional District 4	756,663	19,854	26,338	16,346	20,565	27,310	19,744	13,575	13,715	111,255
Congressional District 5	750,819	20,090	25,067	19,582	19,761	25,291	20,646	13,791	13,093	112,164
Congressional District 6	791,864	17,677	27,756	17,245	17,521	24,174	17,851	11,756	9,410	97,957
Maine										
Congressional District 1	673,835	20,189	28,207	17,196	23,374	28,950	20,079	15,632	15,687	120,918
Congressional District 2	656,254	22,529	27,663	18,967	23,150	28,554	19,170	16,132	15,673	121,646
Maryland										
Congressional District 1	728,405	19,251	29,566	18,631	24,615	31,039	20,825	14,050	16,169	125,329
Congressional District 2	743,321	18,676	22,712	14,609	16,189	23,763	16,472	10,704	11,505	93,242
Congressional District 3	768,378	16,484	27,528	16,303	20,122	23,289	16,283	14,953	16,022	106,972
Congressional District 4	742,761	16,761	23,287	15,572	17,603	20,895	14,145	11,080	10,398	89,693
Congressional District 5	753,079	19,907	25,078	14,783	18,393	24,798	14,761	9,298	9,006	91,039
Congressional District 6	755,369	15,391	24,658	14,735	18,901	23,115	16,157	11,893	13,669	98,470
Congressional District 7	738,431	18,302	25,253	16,701	17,058	24,601	18,910	11,550	13,159	101,979
Congressional District 8	746,663	20,413	26,403	16,583	19,535	27,184	19,256	12,898	19,991	115,447
Massachusetts										
Congressional District 1	733,426	22,087	27,632	18,919	19,923	28,640	19,066	13,958	20,003	120,509
Congressional District 2	736,475	19,460	26,954	16,818	17,593	23,528	15,845	14,432	16,418	104,634
Congressional District 3	755,778	17,801	24,009	15,918	19,521	24,285	17,428	11,306	12,869	101,327
Congressional District 4	748,190	21,589	27,539	14,802	21,190	25,857	16,575	13,511	16,595	108,530
Congressional District 5	755,944	16,961	23,544	15,084	18,691	26,145	20,004	15,291	17,222	112,437
Congressional District 6	757,309	22,296	28,648	17,564	19,484	28,816	18,880	18,085	20,223	123,052
Congressional District 7	769,929	14,689	20,069	12,369	13,081	16,765	11,598	10,312	10,808	74,933
Congressional District 8	751,768	19,820	24,582	16,869	20,707	28,747	19,623	16,708	18,847	121,501
Congressional District 9	736,589	22,654	33,143	17,690	27,102	37,298	27,818	20,121	18,625	148,654
Michigan										
Congressional District 1	703,687	21,609	34,649	20,424	26,456	36,989	26,099	19,450	18,552	147,970
Congressional District 2	724,843	19,324	24,010	16,084	17,662	24,184	16,848	13,632	14,033	102,443
Congressional District 3	725,487	18,346	24,563	15,149	17,249	24,320	15,648	10,902	15,968	99,236
Congressional District 4	702,630	19,439	28,140	17,482	20,251	32,529	21,312	15,508	15,052	122,134
Congressional District 5	687,292	18,319	27,109	16,547	21,010	27,799	22,481	15,947	12,585	116,369
Congressional District 6	712,100	19,898	27,545	16,553	20,583	26,909	20,255	13,435	13,301	111,036
Congressional District 7	702,894	18,407	28,104	15,796	21,780	29,365	21,136	12,600	13,690	114,367
Congressional District 8	725,201	19,373	25,249	15,943	18,510	23,418	13,984	10,113	11,925	93,893
Congressional District 9	720,485	21,925	25,576	16,235	17,759	26,654	18,550	15,316	18,129	112,643
Congressional District 10	706,525	20,714	27,922	15,171	21,831	31,982	19,491	14,753	14,040	117,268

Table B-5: 114th Congressional Districts—Older Population by Age—*Continued*

	Total Population	60 to 61 Years	62 to 64 Years	65 to 66 Years	67 to 69 Years	70 to 74 Years	75 to 79 Years	80 to 84 Years	85 Years and Over	65 Years and Over
Michigan—Cont.										
Congressional District 11	718,435	21,516	26,741	14,909	18,079	25,602	16,096	14,098	14,648	103,432
Congressional District 12	705,207	16,457	24,281	13,819	15,930	23,180	15,671	11,937	14,387	94,924
Congressional District 13	687,170	17,254	22,158	13,851	15,795	19,732	14,375	11,579	12,942	88,274
Congressional District 14	687,921	18,653	25,416	16,773	17,587	25,678	18,194	14,368	14,478	107,078
Minnesota										
Congressional District 1	666,946	16,357	24,484	14,673	15,757	24,166	18,588	15,494	18,471	107,149
Congressional District 2	689,759	16,042	21,116	12,326	16,740	19,912	15,204	10,380	8,771	83,333
Congressional District 3	685,736	16,958	25,997	14,328	18,202	22,212	15,358	12,861	13,619	96,580
Congressional District 4	695,920	17,872	23,819	13,157	16,909	20,769	15,027	11,144	14,492	91,498
Congressional District 5	706,584	15,881	21,184	12,003	14,093	16,922	12,900	9,268	13,282	78,468
Congressional District 6	684,784	14,283	19,905	12,234	13,553	19,467	12,283	8,073	9,063	74,673
Congressional District 7	662,682	18,007	26,224	15,605	19,270	27,858	22,107	16,670	20,666	122,176
Congressional District 8	664,762	19,314	29,947	17,869	22,182	29,968	22,218	15,752	15,967	123,956
Mississippi										
Congressional District 1	760,275	19,175	23,304	17,112	19,698	28,220	19,247	16,064	11,171	111,512
Congressional District 2	722,640	17,009	23,060	14,159	17,930	23,148	18,147	10,965	12,085	96,434
Congressional District 3	749,430	19,099	26,854	15,185	19,828	28,569	20,089	13,866	14,479	112,016
Congressional District 4	761,734	19,129	24,085	16,248	21,188	26,367	20,241	11,525	11,782	107,351
Missouri										
Congressional District 1	744,782	18,751	26,385	14,321	17,679	20,088	16,574	11,230	12,512	92,404
Congressional District 2	758,288	19,385	30,257	17,879	21,326	31,065	23,762	18,994	19,422	132,448
Congressional District 3	766,993	20,123	26,622	16,250	20,062	30,338	18,953	13,120	12,639	111,362
Congressional District 4	763,003	19,215	26,949	16,716	19,564	31,267	20,382	14,167	13,913	116,009
Congressional District 5	758,442	18,235	24,157	14,681	18,199	25,802	19,648	15,131	14,101	107,562
Congressional District 6	760,291	17,027	27,296	17,429	20,026	28,348	19,754	14,560	14,807	114,924
Congressional District 7	765,669	17,313	28,313	16,662	22,947	30,898	22,667	15,170	16,266	124,610
Congressional District 8	746,121	20,910	30,238	19,654	22,606	33,382	23,898	17,245	15,786	132,571
Montana										
Congressional District (at Large)	1,023,579	28,066	43,424	25,398	32,264	41,797	29,953	19,842	20,899	170,153
Nebraska										
Congressional District 1	634,290	15,497	20,114	13,210	15,469	20,154	15,251	12,516	11,561	88,161
Congressional District 2	641,045	14,464	19,220	10,297	13,069	17,355	11,173	8,299	11,466	71,659
Congressional District 3	606,168	16,972	21,625	13,699	17,128	24,852	21,579	16,250	17,349	110,857
Nevada										
Congressional District 1	693,623	13,363	22,445	16,036	15,547	21,984	13,591	12,170	8,789	88,117
Congressional District 2	697,426	20,576	25,642	17,128	22,758	28,420	16,919	12,718	10,313	108,256
Congressional District 3	734,973	19,845	24,913	16,265	20,525	28,694	19,684	11,289	9,485	105,942
Congressional District 4	713,077	16,468	22,186	14,552	20,552	27,727	16,903	10,620	7,845	98,199
New Hampshire										
Congressional District 1	665,612	21,580	24,996	16,363	21,028	23,391	15,999	12,724	13,673	103,178
Congressional District 2	661,201	19,618	27,712	15,326	20,682	26,061	17,695	12,657	13,848	106,269
New Jersey										
Congressional District 1	732,232	18,980	26,880	15,626	19,656	24,763	16,007	14,380	15,980	106,412
Congressional District 2	733,973	20,097	28,143	17,783	22,309	30,690	21,380	15,429	14,478	122,069
Congressional District 3	734,551	19,732	25,263	17,581	23,188	31,501	23,473	18,592	20,034	134,369
Congressional District 4	748,864	18,321	26,908	16,733	20,510	32,053	22,726	16,613	23,528	132,163
Congressional District 5	745,147	20,443	27,276	18,034	21,757	27,036	19,591	14,433	16,978	117,829
Congressional District 6	748,924	18,584	23,288	14,843	17,499	22,707	13,970	10,534	13,978	93,531
Congressional District 7	748,182	18,699	27,757	15,957	20,621	25,580	14,727	15,453	16,592	108,930
Congressional District 8	762,249	14,483	20,151	11,154	13,329	18,805	13,051	10,180	10,500	77,019
Congressional District 9	759,352	17,812	25,740	12,530	18,467	25,698	19,131	12,222	15,566	103,614
Congressional District 10	742,855	17,389	25,466	13,407	14,832	19,734	15,091	9,015	10,166	82,245
Congressional District 11	739,014	20,684	24,517	16,570	22,064	28,850	21,293	16,832	20,992	126,601
Congressional District 12	742,832	19,692	25,172	15,603	18,623	23,427	17,338	17,156	15,196	107,343
New Mexico										
Congressional District 1	699,493	19,592	25,461	14,900	21,196	24,209	19,016	13,215	11,144	103,680
Congressional District 2	699,424	17,633	25,455	17,302	20,014	26,759	21,735	14,096	9,963	109,869
Congressional District 3	686,655	17,351	25,560	15,468	19,709	26,267	17,034	14,086	11,973	104,537
New York										
Congressional District 1	725,932	19,266	24,798	17,478	22,435	29,286	19,864	15,849	14,306	119,218
Congressional District 2	724,171	17,044	23,363	13,572	17,909	23,541	16,839	13,002	13,859	98,722
Congressional District 3	718,780	18,135	27,204	17,183	20,873	27,970	22,489	20,997	23,144	132,656
Congressional District 4	721,920	20,095	25,361	15,056	20,240	25,231	19,409	15,230	18,343	113,509
Congressional District 5	760,487	18,511	21,218	15,456	18,950	23,141	17,964	11,540	13,082	100,133
Congressional District 6	733,419	21,489	25,888	16,361	21,305	25,020	19,395	16,591	17,442	116,114
Congressional District 7	732,079	14,661	18,219	11,770	9,959	16,088	13,875	9,303	9,788	70,783
Congressional District 8	758,543	16,053	25,490	15,386	18,610	24,089	16,145	12,483	16,182	102,895
Congressional District 9	755,073	17,145	24,213	15,192	19,813	20,922	15,412	12,677	13,611	97,627
Congressional District 10	736,997	17,454	23,586	15,329	21,126	24,237	14,411	11,366	15,279	101,748
Congressional District 11	726,893	19,513	26,466	15,427	19,209	25,857	18,355	13,917	15,385	108,150
Congressional District 12	729,253	16,431	18,771	15,585	17,740	22,309	19,421	14,078	13,934	103,067
Congressional District 13	782,199	19,841	21,764	11,734	14,024	20,944	14,010	10,256	14,547	85,515
Congressional District 14	752,344	15,321	19,715	13,209	14,584	22,390	17,393	11,445	11,639	90,710
Congressional District 15	750,915	12,584	16,646	9,849	12,351	19,501	12,317	8,306	7,230	69,554
Congressional District 16	732,521	16,487	23,425	14,312	17,996	26,234	21,063	15,300	19,101	114,006

Table B-5: 114th Congressional Districts—Older Population by Age—*Continued*

	Total Population	60 to 61 Years	62 to 64 Years	65 to 66 Years	67 to 69 Years	70 to 74 Years	75 to 79 Years	80 to 84 Years	85 Years and Over	65 Years and Over
New York—Cont.										
Congressional District 17	739,263	18,907	25,512	15,272	21,116	24,604	17,471	15,470	18,143	112,076
Congressional District 18	720,115	18,414	23,530	15,651	17,800	25,547	17,194	13,106	12,829	102,127
Congressional District 19	708,116	20,680	30,621	18,978	24,301	31,281	19,674	17,747	15,580	127,561
Congressional District 20	727,913	17,185	29,253	17,682	19,526	24,949	17,923	14,928	16,654	111,662
Congressional District 21	713,276	19,439	28,898	16,611	19,959	27,890	20,307	14,476	15,025	114,268
Congressional District 22	709,851	19,565	27,206	16,168	21,791	28,032	22,275	14,581	18,515	121,362
Congressional District 23	715,663	20,689	25,909	16,866	21,776	28,249	19,420	15,987	17,891	120,189
Congressional District 24	715,188	18,221	27,059	14,968	19,251	27,106	17,721	14,050	17,685	110,781
Congressional District 25	721,227	17,679	27,508	14,151	21,377	26,170	19,152	12,477	18,834	112,161
Congressional District 26	717,332	19,967	25,252	16,869	21,092	24,873	18,461	18,041	20,412	119,748
Congressional District 27	716,757	20,435	30,323	17,326	20,954	28,762	21,473	14,454	16,369	119,338
North Carolina										
Congressional District 1	742,851	20,621	26,569	17,835	20,719	26,845	20,213	12,516	15,910	114,038
Congressional District 2	774,723	15,522	22,666	15,337	19,593	27,605	17,265	11,766	12,596	104,162
Congressional District 3	759,653	15,597	24,355	18,747	21,646	25,535	19,864	14,256	10,141	110,189
Congressional District 4	795,798	15,505	20,020	12,620	17,223	19,915	13,928	11,393	9,342	84,421
Congressional District 5	750,233	20,816	27,263	19,622	23,997	27,231	20,865	15,887	14,252	121,854
Congressional District 6	755,280	20,965	28,575	18,398	21,276	31,467	22,193	15,521	16,944	125,799
Congressional District 7	772,311	22,677	29,391	20,734	27,963	34,627	20,694	15,978	12,838	132,834
Congressional District 8	746,671	18,790	23,186	17,680	21,416	28,408	18,348	14,910	10,829	111,591
Congressional District 9	805,960	18,668	23,636	15,592	19,373	24,111	15,318	11,402	10,834	96,630
Congressional District 10	744,808	20,963	27,818	19,002	26,009	29,832	22,229	15,839	15,091	128,002
Congressional District 11	744,956	20,452	31,336	23,698	28,773	39,747	26,475	19,791	19,349	157,833
Congressional District 12	778,251	14,645	17,960	11,898	14,735	18,628	12,355	8,918	7,433	73,967
Congressional District 13	772,469	20,421	25,632	14,087	23,532	23,880	18,465	11,093	8,772	99,829
North Dakota										
Congressional District (at Large)	739,482	17,671	25,073	14,296	17,213	22,741	18,649	14,430	17,350	104,679
Ohio										
Congressional District 1	729,726	18,895	24,804	14,607	17,540	20,956	18,097	12,271	13,289	96,760
Congressional District 2	724,587	20,979	28,487	16,098	19,940	26,442	18,910	15,331	14,414	111,135
Congressional District 3	755,499	13,188	22,479	12,540	13,588	16,771	12,784	7,710	8,844	72,237
Congressional District 4	709,882	21,002	24,948	16,580	18,815	28,188	20,046	16,172	16,291	116,092
Congressional District 5	730,503	20,229	28,337	17,469	20,683	27,440	19,374	14,071	16,755	115,792
Congressional District 6	713,457	22,442	28,534	19,279	21,415	32,387	23,540	15,276	17,060	128,957
Congressional District 7	725,548	21,349	27,079	18,593	21,796	30,803	22,963	14,382	16,628	125,165
Congressional District 8	722,889	18,029	24,087	17,976	18,467	26,895	21,296	12,459	14,253	111,346
Congressional District 9	709,813	18,047	21,891	15,022	17,743	22,916	18,737	12,960	15,454	102,832
Congressional District 10	720,794	19,071	27,090	14,751	22,318	27,920	22,069	16,875	14,277	118,210
Congressional District 11	699,736	18,434	28,304	14,267	19,538	21,921	18,098	14,566	17,354	105,744
Congressional District 12	755,978	17,580	26,999	16,093	19,855	23,744	16,746	11,264	13,585	101,287
Congressional District 13	707,940	19,659	26,341	18,512	19,221	29,032	21,305	16,087	21,082	125,239
Congressional District 14	722,474	21,769	26,459	19,285	22,185	30,938	23,328	15,517	19,457	130,710
Congressional District 15	740,854	19,012	25,702	14,827	20,112	26,845	20,442	12,635	11,099	105,960
Congressional District 16	724,483	21,394	26,606	16,763	22,068	32,525	24,739	14,570	18,737	129,402
Oklahoma										
Congressional District 1	781,067	19,919	24,253	15,983	20,308	23,659	17,274	13,573	14,264	105,061
Congressional District 2	749,768	20,291	27,550	17,521	26,073	35,227	23,213	16,421	14,672	133,127
Congressional District 3	776,896	18,501	26,056	16,286	20,132	28,775	22,206	14,782	13,842	116,023
Congressional District 4	773,994	18,186	25,149	16,020	18,806	25,080	19,763	14,153	10,923	104,745
Congressional District 5	796,326	17,628	23,785	14,073	20,870	24,116	18,393	12,398	12,762	102,612
Oregon										
Congressional District 1	805,943	20,232	28,028	17,199	23,281	22,954	14,749	11,876	15,208	105,267
Congressional District 2	784,114	24,924	34,705	19,107	28,105	39,714	26,828	16,277	19,797	149,828
Congressional District 3	806,382	19,023	29,740	17,532	19,694	24,326	15,584	10,849	13,564	101,549
Congressional District 4	775,615	25,102	35,463	21,770	27,948	38,623	23,136	17,273	20,217	148,967
Congressional District 5	798,185	23,679	32,434	20,882	23,568	31,314	20,973	15,488	16,390	128,615
Pennsylvania										
Congressional District 1	716,072	16,603	21,276	12,701	15,657	18,479	13,450	11,233	11,101	82,621
Congressional District 2	716,892	16,925	21,714	14,141	16,969	21,919	15,688	11,885	14,681	95,283
Congressional District 3	702,323	20,751	26,810	15,566	22,393	28,535	22,587	17,018	18,911	125,010
Congressional District 4	719,504	19,217	26,352	16,723	19,863	27,617	20,662	16,659	13,595	115,119
Congressional District 5	700,531	19,355	27,372	16,841	21,810	28,785	21,396	15,377	17,190	121,399
Congressional District 6	716,612	19,503	23,380	13,802	20,340	25,069	18,950	16,684	16,782	111,627
Congressional District 7	714,577	19,878	26,094	14,353	22,578	26,279	19,990	17,347	19,558	120,105
Congressional District 8	713,387	20,713	26,336	16,574	22,245	26,607	20,539	15,343	17,173	118,481
Congressional District 9	694,973	21,204	27,373	19,046	23,383	29,233	22,260	18,113	20,645	132,680
Congressional District 10	696,416	19,968	29,710	17,359	23,987	30,498	21,614	17,597	17,557	128,612
Congressional District 11	700,342	21,031	26,980	19,447	22,834	27,849	20,904	16,226	18,519	125,779
Congressional District 12	704,560	22,073	29,866	20,678	23,865	30,154	23,920	20,640	21,854	141,111
Congressional District 13	725,185	18,416	25,760	14,767	17,965	25,238	19,988	15,058	17,450	110,466
Congressional District 14	701,362	19,606	27,024	14,597	18,051	23,757	20,056	16,572	21,187	114,220
Congressional District 15	722,560	22,546	26,626	17,954	18,635	28,078	20,460	14,723	19,033	118,883
Congressional District 16	722,837	18,225	22,682	16,956	18,124	23,081	19,968	14,613	16,662	109,404
Congressional District 17	707,062	17,971	28,005	16,051	21,624	31,567	20,128	17,603	21,454	128,427
Congressional District 18	712,014	21,520	29,389	18,389	24,843	29,951	22,444	17,568	21,677	134,872

Table B-5: 114th Congressional Districts—Older Population by Age—*Continued*

	Total Population	60 to 61 Years	62 to 64 Years	65 to 66 Years	67 to 69 Years	70 to 74 Years	75 to 79 Years	80 to 84 Years	85 Years and Over	65 Years and Over
Rhode Island										
Congressional District 1	532,145	12,590	19,809	10,763	13,770	17,426	14,084	10,741	13,801	80,585
Congressional District 2	523,028	12,817	21,400	11,736	16,445	19,789	11,300	12,344	14,981	86,595
South Carolina										
Congressional District 1	728,626	19,260	25,886	18,935	26,235	29,734	19,498	12,184	12,435	119,021
Congressional District 2	686,952	16,834	24,285	13,324	19,470	25,968	15,020	12,620	10,622	97,024
Congressional District 3	666,489	16,381	28,074	16,837	24,170	28,847	19,012	13,469	12,908	115,243
Congressional District 4	703,720	16,401	23,048	14,158	21,255	25,398	16,927	13,348	12,015	103,101
Congressional District 5	684,083	18,308	24,792	18,025	21,564	26,332	18,383	11,198	10,183	105,685
Congressional District 6	673,637	18,351	23,081	14,406	19,716	24,426	15,045	10,277	11,150	95,020
Congressional District 7	688,975	21,465	32,434	20,344	25,716	34,105	21,583	12,394	12,347	126,489
South Dakota										
Congressional District (at Large)	853,175	21,317	31,033	19,941	23,402	25,601	21,463	18,059	20,888	129,354
Tennessee										
Congressional District 1	713,317	19,882	30,859	19,328	24,838	36,116	26,240	14,639	13,193	134,354
Congressional District 2	726,315	18,632	27,409	18,702	23,285	29,778	21,174	13,696	14,197	120,832
Congressional District 3	716,365	20,411	30,364	19,032	24,562	27,428	20,033	17,125	13,621	121,801
Congressional District 4	747,195	15,186	25,385	16,521	20,582	27,763	18,232	13,510	10,182	106,790
Congressional District 5	751,222	20,109	20,411	13,898	15,694	20,537	14,209	10,759	10,335	85,432
Congressional District 6	733,467	17,983	27,019	18,586	23,753	35,008	22,880	15,341	10,937	126,505
Congressional District 7	743,173	18,688	24,488	16,234	20,906	25,685	17,746	12,632	10,128	103,331
Congressional District 8	710,910	19,263	24,097	19,209	21,186	26,332	16,725	15,043	13,921	112,416
Congressional District 9	707,388	16,099	23,099	12,508	13,240	18,683	11,203	9,864	9,854	75,352
Texas										
Congressional District 1	712,779	18,516	24,779	14,309	20,918	29,013	21,100	13,856	15,134	114,330
Congressional District 2	737,492	18,221	23,944	13,549	14,180	19,283	11,453	7,889	7,126	73,480
Congressional District 3	792,608	17,165	22,233	12,439	17,051	20,617	11,876	7,319	7,511	76,813
Congressional District 4	719,372	18,237	24,714	14,617	20,640	31,676	20,911	15,143	12,700	115,687
Congressional District 5	734,553	18,653	20,869	13,847	19,897	21,965	15,960	14,016	8,586	94,271
Congressional District 6	737,480	16,102	20,463	12,918	14,899	19,492	12,338	9,515	7,349	76,511
Congressional District 7	770,950	15,707	22,161	10,900	13,591	17,725	11,422	9,967	10,717	74,322
Congressional District 8	767,431	18,467	25,953	15,323	18,141	25,862	16,003	11,974	9,807	97,110
Congressional District 9	772,152	14,509	20,618	11,631	14,105	18,063	10,752	6,312	6,782	67,645
Congressional District 10	771,009	19,034	23,302	13,426	17,483	24,327	11,927	10,403	11,290	88,856
Congressional District 11	741,069	20,504	23,889	17,001	19,903	25,541	21,110	16,287	13,772	113,614
Congressional District 12	750,952	16,673	21,175	13,672	18,600	22,540	17,515	10,304	10,566	93,197
Congressional District 13	707,803	16,742	23,746	12,961	18,209	24,951	17,892	14,138	12,453	100,604
Congressional District 14	724,881	18,355	24,266	15,225	17,327	22,929	15,962	12,658	10,534	94,635
Congressional District 15	764,850	12,430	16,006	12,397	15,350	19,997	14,972	9,469	9,226	81,411
Congressional District 16	735,246	13,104	19,180	10,320	12,823	21,594	17,375	11,924	9,787	83,823
Congressional District 17	740,151	16,857	18,901	12,233	16,480	19,751	14,590	11,449	9,211	83,714
Congressional District 18	750,812	14,970	17,297	12,427	11,098	15,978	10,396	8,618	7,413	65,930
Congressional District 19	719,594	15,637	20,204	13,512	17,375	21,268	17,827	12,811	12,360	95,153
Congressional District 20	762,801	14,918	19,877	11,890	14,730	17,936	12,911	10,964	10,033	78,464
Congressional District 21	766,190	19,378	29,011	16,569	23,356	28,320	20,348	14,758	13,391	116,742
Congressional District 22	814,594	16,923	20,603	13,697	14,906	21,237	15,181	7,086	7,062	79,169
Congressional District 23	743,201	14,173	19,740	13,912	18,580	23,165	14,821	11,700	9,333	91,511
Congressional District 24	759,022	17,158	20,020	12,359	14,907	19,564	12,991	9,160	7,595	76,576
Congressional District 25	748,022	17,717	26,222	15,868	17,446	23,457	15,222	11,220	10,331	93,544
Congressional District 26	783,257	13,003	17,193	11,907	17,023	18,500	11,978	7,444	4,313	71,165
Congressional District 27	726,394	19,207	26,389	14,644	19,028	26,887	17,051	13,893	12,685	104,188
Congressional District 28	725,977	12,571	19,357	10,885	13,776	20,532	14,639	8,896	9,133	77,861
Congressional District 29	749,098	12,885	14,426	9,037	12,161	14,477	9,248	7,765	5,137	57,825
Congressional District 30	744,247	16,748	20,741	10,672	13,399	16,688	11,807	8,356	7,321	68,243
Congressional District 31	776,518	15,224	22,964	12,713	16,953	21,995	12,453	10,497	10,673	85,284
Congressional District 32	747,437	15,879	21,543	12,316	16,173	23,436	15,652	9,468	11,087	88,132
Congressional District 33	742,701	10,478	17,449	9,895	9,640	13,660	10,715	5,507	6,681	56,098
Congressional District 34	717,582	13,594	17,708	14,878	16,833	19,660	17,604	13,353	12,577	94,905
Congressional District 35	767,436	11,740	20,315	10,352	12,397	16,434	11,567	8,873	7,444	67,067
Congressional District 36	731,297	20,952	27,020	15,839	19,175	26,439	16,411	10,758	9,511	98,133
Utah										
Congressional District 1	727,828	14,478	18,395	13,330	11,990	17,171	14,413	7,523	8,240	72,667
Congressional District 2	729,552	13,553	19,562	13,016	14,895	22,352	15,214	10,016	9,672	85,165
Congressional District 3	721,048	13,352	19,852	9,721	12,860	16,899	12,609	9,212	7,161	68,462
Congressional District 4	764,474	12,244	20,098	10,731	12,575	16,978	12,421	8,284	7,696	68,685
Vermont										
Congressional District (at Large)	626,562	19,531	25,175	15,977	19,912	26,774	16,493	14,145	13,354	106,655
Virginia										
Congressional District 1	770,044	16,613	24,640	15,805	19,220	28,286	17,009	12,551	13,013	105,884
Congressional District 2	732,346	17,739	22,670	14,961	17,081	22,245	14,964	12,441	11,814	93,506
Congressional District 3	753,380	16,963	22,613	13,484	16,600	20,505	15,771	10,301	12,709	89,370
Congressional District 4	746,976	20,330	25,369	15,328	19,168	27,321	14,889	9,427	11,826	97,959
Congressional District 5	733,330	20,852	31,631	21,895	22,989	33,834	24,199	17,898	15,412	136,227
Congressional District 6	746,357	20,818	26,897	16,770	22,750	31,836	23,039	15,981	17,509	127,885
Congressional District 7	769,995	21,075	27,425	19,298	21,521	27,165	19,040	13,791	13,133	113,948
Congressional District 8	774,065	14,963	21,699	12,141	16,405	20,114	12,563	8,105	10,974	80,302
Congressional District 9	715,465	21,304	28,705	17,826	22,131	36,659	23,651	16,302	16,350	132,919
Congressional District 10	802,127	18,588	24,704	15,673	17,638	23,300	13,780	8,223	9,385	87,999

Table B-5: 114th Congressional Districts—Older Population by Age—*Continued*

	Total Population	60 to 61 Years	62 to 64 Years	65 to 66 Years	67 to 69 Years	70 to 74 Years	75 to 79 Years	80 to 84 Years	85 Years and Over	65 Years and Over
Virginia—Cont.										
Congressional District 11	782,204	16,845	24,658	13,172	16,892	18,913	14,109	8,252	9,509	80,847
Washington										
Congressional District 1	713,399	19,190	25,569	13,994	19,090	22,185	13,679	8,067	10,306	87,321
Congressional District 2	708,323	19,059	24,887	18,097	19,881	25,483	15,344	13,182	14,612	106,599
Congressional District 3	697,884	18,149	26,439	16,313	23,021	28,754	19,025	12,412	12,038	111,563
Congressional District 4	704,219	15,284	24,204	13,941	17,332	23,328	13,195	12,159	10,778	90,733
Congressional District 5	690,518	10,681	24,648	16,740	19,614	26,644	15,711	13,083	14,792	106,584
Congressional District 6	676,910	19,949	27,521	19,037	25,061	30,143	19,425	13,012	15,377	122,055
Congressional District 7	732,733	20,949	25,499	14,204	19,024	21,788	13,993	10,480	14,447	93,936
Congressional District 8	711,629	18,015	22,411	14,407	16,870	19,590	14,433	9,293	10,094	84,687
Congressional District 9	711,466	14,064	23,704	14,154	15,949	20,963	16,203	11,540	14,579	93,388
Congressional District 10	714,449	17,639	24,446	15,819	17,776	23,003	13,886	12,096	13,070	95,650
West Virginia										
Congressional District 1	616,232	18,209	24,834	17,020	20,926	23,859	19,613	13,037	13,444	107,899
Congressional District 2	628,276	17,439	25,202	17,782	19,172	26,727	19,230	13,751	12,138	108,800
Congressional District 3	605,818	17,682	27,370	16,547	22,349	26,191	20,582	13,456	13,231	112,356
Wisconsin										
Congressional District 1	712,072	19,682	25,386	14,689	19,332	25,402	16,052	13,638	15,748	104,861
Congressional District 2	740,988	19,769	25,900	15,215	19,609	21,459	15,577	11,251	14,770	97,881
Congressional District 3	718,518	19,953	25,762	16,466	20,180	26,902	19,989	15,281	16,834	115,652
Congressional District 4	717,657	17,057	20,953	12,547	13,042	16,760	12,072	9,860	13,763	78,044
Congressional District 5	722,537	20,206	26,543	16,090	19,381	26,778	21,490	16,469	17,214	117,422
Congressional District 6	712,031	20,027	27,518	16,561	19,600	27,673	20,555	16,199	18,022	118,610
Congressional District 7	711,006	20,654	30,821	18,653	22,804	32,094	23,155	17,094	17,830	131,630
Congressional District 8	722,755	18,069	28,618	16,117	21,053	25,753	19,530	14,031	15,136	111,620
Wyoming										
Congressional District (at Large)	584,153	17,335	22,915	13,974	16,111	18,956	12,255	10,930	8,106	80,332

PART C
RACE AND ETHNICITY

RACE AND ETHNICITY

While it is clear that the nation's population continues to grow more diverse, these tables show how diversity is not uniform across the country and how large differences occur at smaller geographic levels. Racial and ethnic identification in the Census is obtained in a number of different ways including direct questions on race and Hispanic Origin. Other questions obtain data on ancestry, language spoken at home, and place of birth. The Census and American Community Survey also allow for respondents to identify with more than one racial group. The term race "Alone" means the respondent identifies with that single racial group. Those who identify with two or more racial groups are identified here as "Multi-race." Hispanic Origin is obtained in a separate question. The tables in this section present only selected major response categories—White, Non-Hispanic; Black Alone; Asian Alone; Multi-race; and Hispanic. A relatively small number of individuals identify themselves as "some other race" and are not included here. The American Indian

and Alaskan Native population is also a relatively small population but very important in specific areas. Summary data for this population is included in a separate table.

Unlike many other tables in this volume, the ACS sample population counts by race and Hispanic Origin are often too small to be reported. As a result, the Census files do not report results for these categories and they are indicated here by "na." It is important to also note that the age structure of many minority populations are younger than the White population due to historic immigration and fertility patterns. Part C—Race and Ethnicity presents data only for the population age 65 and over and therefore may exhibit different distributions of the racial and Hispanic Origin population than that for the general population. For example, in the White Non-Hispanic population, 18.3 percent are age 65 and over but among the Hispanic population, only 7.0 percent are 65 and over. Those who identify as Multi-race are even lower at 5.1 percent, which may result from a larger number of mixed-race children.

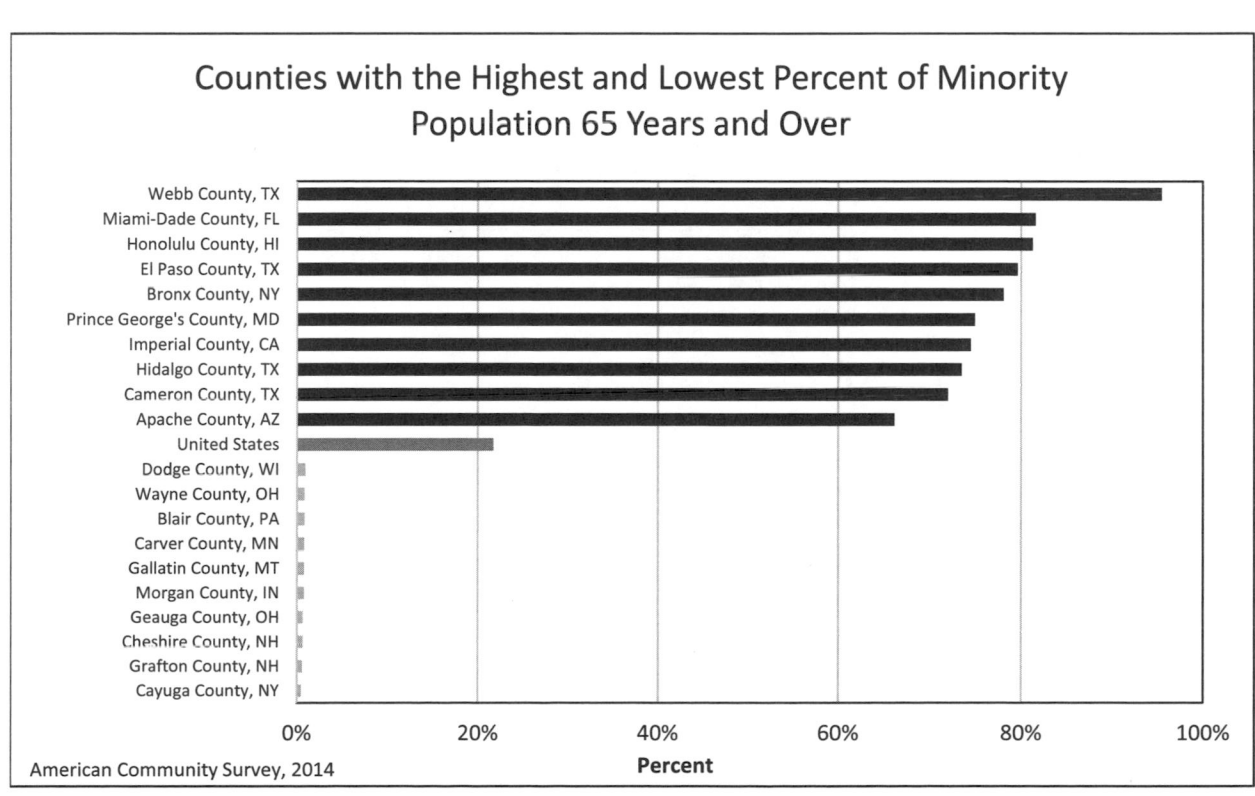

In the nation as a whole, 78.3 percent of the population age 65 and over is White, Non-Hispanic which means that more than one out of every five (21.7 percent) over age 65 identifies with some minority group. Across states, the proportion of the 65 and over population that is White, Non-Hispanic population ranges from a low of 26.2 percent in the state of Hawaii to a high of 98.0 percent in the state of Maine. Thirty-four states have a higher proportion of White, Non-Hispanic population than the national average. Among the 65 year and over population, Hawaii and the District of Columbia are both "majority minority" which means their proportion of minority populations is actually greater than 50 percent. In Hawaii, 73.8 percent of the population identifies with a minority group (mostly Asian Alone and Multi-race) while in the District of Columbia, 67.2 percent of the 65 and over population is minority and mostly Black Alone.

Nine states have less than one-half of one percent of their 65 and over population that is Black Alone while in twelve states, more than one of every five people is Black Alone. Not surprising, Hawaii has the largest Asian Alone population at 55.2 percent with California a distant second at 14.7 percent. Every other state is less than 8 percent Asian Alone and 15 states are less than 1 percent. Hawaii is also the state with the highest Multi-race population at 11.0 percent but Oklahoma has the second highest proportion at 3.6 percent. At 32.1 percent, New

Mexico has the highest proportion of Hispanic population age 65 and over followed by Texas (21.7 percent) and California (19.0 percent). Twelve states are less than 1 percent Hispanic but nine states have more than the U.S. average of 7.6 percent.

Black Alone

For the age 65 and over population, the District of Columbia (60.7 percent), Georgia (22.1 percent), Louisiana (23.4 percent), Maryland (22.7 percent) and Mississippi (25.0 percent) are the only states with proportions over 20 percent. Among the 443 counties with reported populations, 73 are greater than 20 percent Black Alone with Prince George's County, Maryland having the highest proportion at 63.3 percent. There are 134 counties with at least some Black Alone population over age 65 but less than 5.0 percent. East Orange, New Jersey is the city with the highest proportion of Black Alone population at 90.0 percent followed closely by Detroit, Michigan at 83.3 percent and Gary, Indiana at 77.4 percent. In 21 cities the Black Alone population is a majority of the total 65 and over population. The Orangeburg, South Carolina metropolitan area has the highest proportion of Black Alone population at 50.5 percent. More than one out of every five people age 65 and over are Black Alone in 47 metropolitan areas. Congressional District 5 in Georgia has the largest proportion of Black Alone at 63.3 percent followed by District 2 in

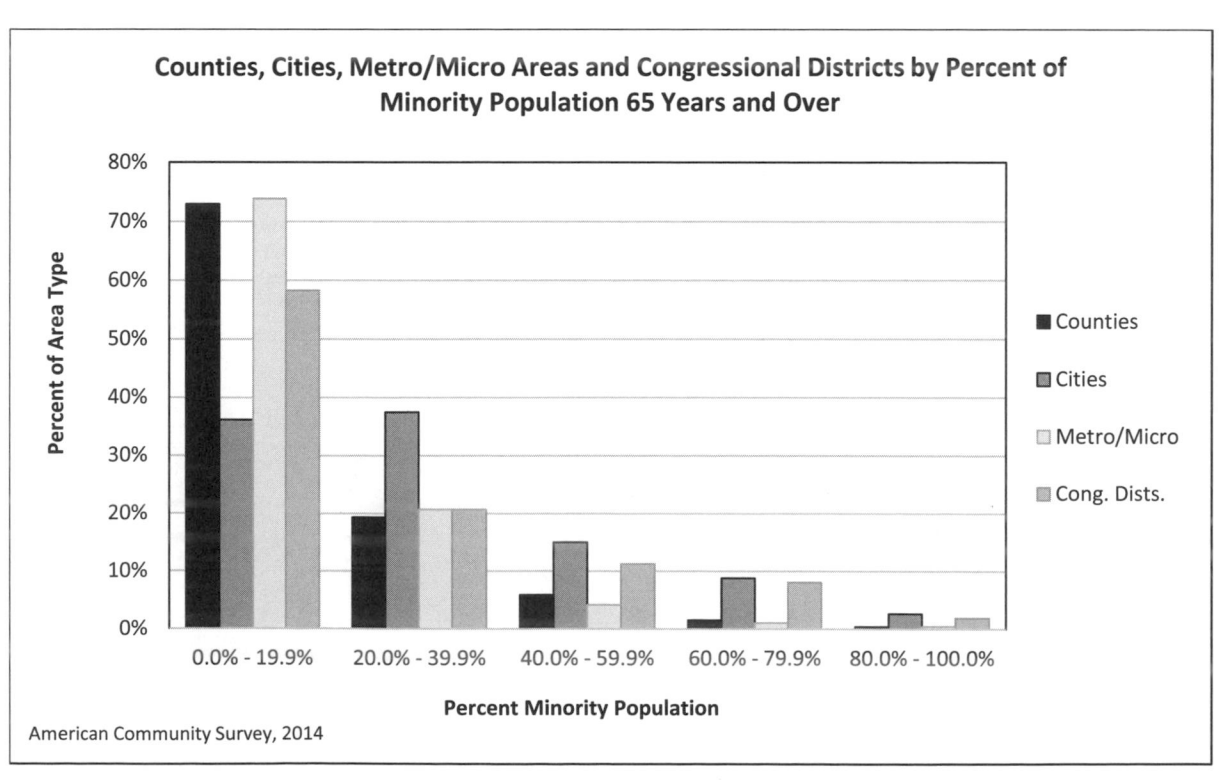

American Community Survey, 2014

Pennsylvania at 61.8 percent. Seventeen districts are a majority Black Alone.

Asian Alone

Nationally, 4.0 percent of the 65 and over population is Asian Alone. Of the 803 counties reported here, only 255 have large enough Asian Alone populations to be reported in the 2014 ACS. Ninety-one counties exceed that average, with Honolulu, Hawaii having the highest proportion at 64.6 percent. Eight other counties have at least 25 percent Asian Alone including the California counties of Alameda (26.7 percent), San Francisco (43.9 percent), San Mateo (25.3 percent) and Santa Clara (30.5 percent) and the Hawaiian counties of Hawaii (29.7 percent), Honolulu (64.6 percent), Kauai (40.8 percent) and Maui (38.2 percent). The Honolulu Census Designated Place has the highest proportion of 65 and over that is Asian Alone at 70.2 percent. In addition to Honolulu, three California cities have more than 50 percent Asian Alone population and 93 cities are well above the national average at over 10 percent. Only three metropolitan areas have greater than 30 percent Asian Alone population—all in Hawaii—Honolulu (64.6 percent), Kahului-Wailuku-Lahaina (38.2 percent) and the Kapaa, Hawaii micropolitan area (40.8 percent). Congressional District 1 in Hawaii has the highest proportion at 70.5 followed by Hawaii's 2nd Congressional District at 37.8 percent. Eighteen other districts have

more than 20 percent Asian Alone: 13 of which are in California with two in New York and one in Washington State.

Multi-race

The four Hawaiian counties also have the largest proportion of Multi-race 65 and over population: Hawaii at 15.9 percent; Honolulu at 9.9 percent, Kauai at 9.8 percent and Maui at 12.0 percent. Yuba County, California and Creek County, Oklahoma have proportions of Multi-race population over 65 greater than 5 percent each. Nationally, about 1 percent of the 65 and over population identifies as Multi-race and 124 counties exceed that level.

Hispanic

The Hispanic population has grown to more than 53 million people in the United States or 16.9 percent of the total population. Among those 65 years and over, 7.6 percent are Hispanic. California has the largest Hispanic population over 65 at nearly 946,000 followed by Texas at almost 672,000 and Florida at nearly 532,000. However, New Mexico has the largest proportion of Hispanic population over the age of 65 at 32.1 percent. North Dakota has the smallest absolute number and proportion of Hispanic population. Webb County, Texas has the largest proportion of its Hispanic population in

Percent Native American for Areas with 5 Percent or More Native American Population

	Percent of Total Population	Percent of Population 65 Years or Over		Percent of Total Population	Percent of Population 65 Years or Over
Counties					
Anchorage Municipality, Alaska	7.0%	7.0%	Otero County, New Mexico	7.0%	2.0%
Apache County, Arizona	72.2%	11.4%	Pennington County, South Dakota	7.9%	4.8%
Coconino County, Arizona	26.2%	8.8%	Pinal County, Arizona	5.2%	5.9%
Comanche County, Oklahoma	5.6%	10.5%	Pottawatomie County, Oklahoma	15.3%	7.1%
Creek County, Oklahoma	11.3%	6.3%	Robeson County, North Carolina	37.7%	11.6%
Humboldt County, California	5.5%	8.5%	Rogers County, Oklahoma	12.1%	7.5%
Matanuska-Susitna Borough, Alaska	5.0%	10.0%	San Juan County, New Mexico	38.7%	9.0%
McKinley County, New Mexico	76.6%	8.8%	Sandoval County, New Mexico	12.4%	9.7%
Muskogee County, Oklahoma	18.2%	9.8%	Wagoner County, Oklahoma	8.1%	9.1%
Navajo County, Arizona	45.0%	9.2%			
Places					
Anchorage municipality, Alaska	7.0%	7.0%	Rapid City city, South Dakota	10.4%	5.5%
Metropolitan Statistical Areas					
Alamogordo, NM Micro Area	7.0%	2.0%	Gallup, NM Micro Area	76.6%	8.8%
Albuquerque, NM Metro Area	5.9%	8.7%	Lawton, OK Metro Area	6.0%	11.0%
Anchorage, AK Metro Area	6.5%	7.6%	Lumberton, NC Micro Area	37.7%	11.6%
Bismarck, ND Metro Area	7.0%	4.1%	Muskogee, OK Micro Area	18.2%	9.8%
Eureka-Arcata-Fortuna, CA Micro Area	5.5%	8.5%	Rapid City, SD Metro Area	7.0%	4.9%
Farmington, NM Metro Area	38.7%	9.0%	Shawnee, OK Micro Area	15.3%	7.1%
Flagstaff, AZ Metro Area	26.2%	8.8%	Show Low, AZ Micro Area	45.0%	9.2%
Fort Smith, AR-OK Metro Area	6.1%	0.6%	Tulsa, OK Metro Area	6.9%	7.8%
113th Congressional Districts					
Congressional District (at Large) (114th Congress), Alaska	14.0%	8.1%	Congressional District 2 (114th Congress), New Mexico	5.7%	9.3%
Congressional District 1 (114th Congress), Arizona	23.5%	9.5%	Congressional District 2 (114th Congress), Oklahoma	17.3%	9.7%
Congressional District (at Large) (114th Congress), Montana	6.8%	7.2%	Congressional District 3 (114th Congress), Oklahoma	6.0%	6.6%
Congressional District 8 (114th Congress), North Carolina	7.0%	12.4%	Congressional District 1 (114th Congress), Oklahoma	5.4%	7.7%
Congressional District (at Large) (114th Congress), North Dakota	5.4%	5.9%	Congressional District (at Large) (114th Congress), South Dakota	8.4%	6.1%
Congressional District 3 (114th Congress), New Mexico	18.5%	9.1%			

the 65 and over age group at 94.7 percent followed by El Paso County, Texas at 76.0 percent. The 65 and over population is more than 25 percent Hispanic in 28 counties, most of which are in California, New Mexico and Texas. Hialeah City, Florida has the largest proportion of Hispanic 65 and over at 97.2 percent. In 25 cities the 65 and over population is a majority Hispanic and 79 cities are more than 25 percent Hispanic 65 and over. At the metropolitan area level, Laredo, Texas is the largest proportion with 94.4 percent Hispanic 65 and over. El Paso, Texas is the next largest with 76.1 percent. Five metropolitan areas are over 50 percent. Florida's 27th Congressional District has the largest proportion at 79.3 percent and five of Florida's districts are over 30 percent. California has 19 districts more than 20 percent of the 65 and over population is Hispanic.

Native American

The American Indian and Alaska Native population is a small proportion of the nation's total and is not included in the data tables because most of the areas would have no data reported. However, the American Indian and Alaska Native population is also concentrated in specific areas and represents an important segment of those communities. Many of these areas are in states with federal or state reservations but not all. Included in the following table are areas where at least five percent of the total population is Native American. This includes 19 counties, 2 cities, 16 metropolitan and micropolitan areas and 11 congressional districts. Within these areas, McKinley County, New Mexico which is the Gallup, New Mexico micropolitan area (76.6 percent) has the largest proportion of American Indian and Alaska Native population that is 65 and over while Matanuska-Susitna Borough, Alaska (5.0 percent) has the lowest. Apache County and Navajo County, Arizona, Robeson County, North Carolina, and San Juan County, New Mexico are all more than 30 percent Native American. Additionally, the Farmington, New Mexico metropolitan area and the Lumberton, North Carolina micropolitan area are above 30 percent Native American.

Percent of the Population 65 Years and Over Who are Minority (Not - White, Non-Hispanic)

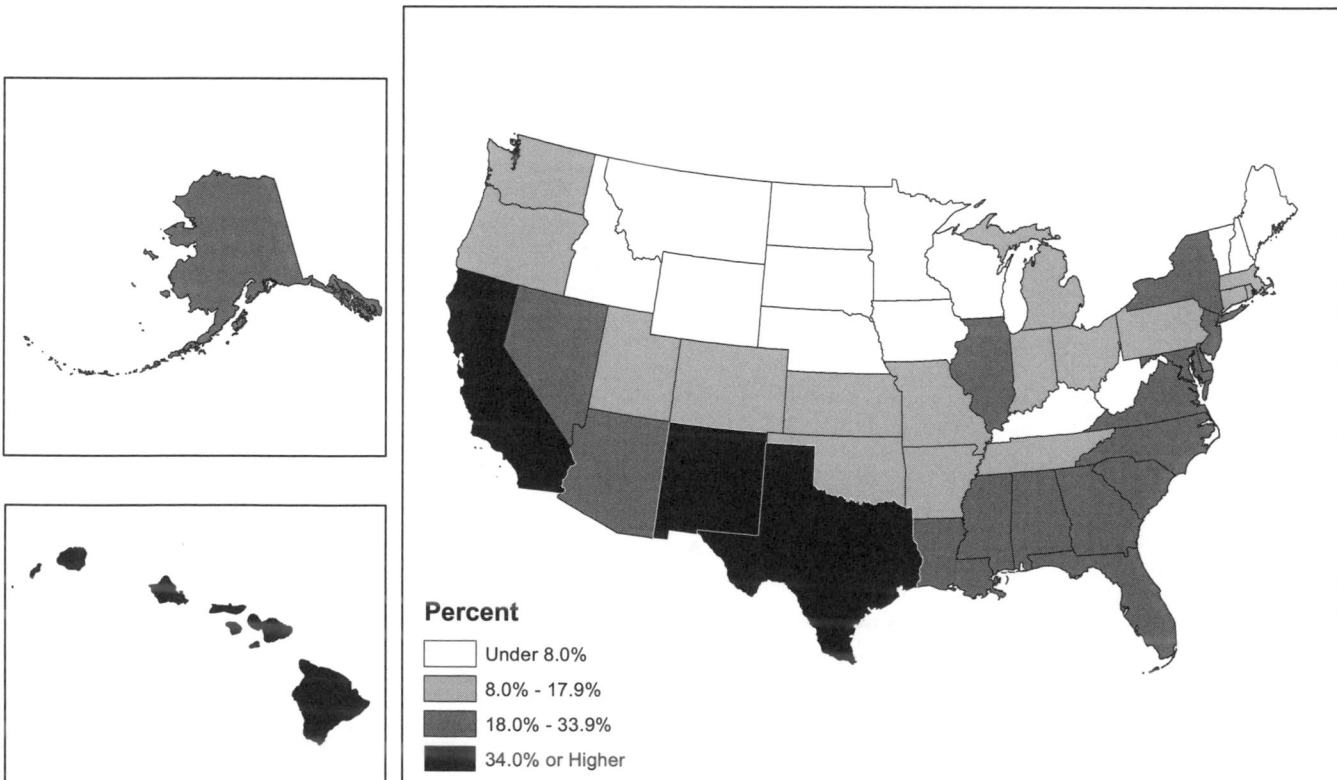

Percent

- Under 8.0%
- 8.0% - 17.9%
- 18.0% - 33.9%
- 34.0% or Higher

Table C-1: States—Older Population by Race and Hispanic Origin

	Total Population		White, Non-Hispanic		Black, Alone		Asian, Alone		Multi-race		Hispanic	
	65 Years and Over	85 Years and Over	65 Years and Over	85 Years and Over	65 Years and Over	85 Years and Over	65 Years and Over	85 Years and Over	65 Years and Over	85 Years and Over	65 Years and Over	85 Years and Over
United States........................	46,214,893	6,045,970	36,170,542	4,989,845	4,085,597	443,742	1,862,495	198,488	472,717	43,593	3,522,782	366,938
Alabama	746,512	83,549	588,698	67,198	137,416	14,361	5,134	263	6,192	591	7,343	774
Alaska	69,899	6,237	51,628	4,658	2,297	229	3,508	625	1,719	54	2,161	42
Arizona	1,070,757	119,594	870,293	104,343	23,517	2,106	21,833	1,569	10,141	644	126,604	9,041
Arkansas	465,012	55,496	406,973	49,809	43,398	4,996	2,204	90	4,835	268	6,758	137
California	4,990,092	666,819	2,961,393	439,627	258,353	26,849	734,268	89,125	91,909	9,399	945,640	103,277
Colorado	679,572	80,024	570,284	70,417	17,505	1,689	14,603	1,288	8,085	870	68,303	5,943
Connecticut	555,528	86,328	475,691	79,438	36,308	4,784	11,037	339	4,121	31	29,242	1,640
Delaware	153,759	17,141	124,696	14,343	21,311	2,049	3,403	266	905	41	3,233	360
District of Columbia	74,465	10,144	24,433	3,106	45,190	6,615	1,607	291	559	23	3,598	207
Florida	3,790,954	524,256	2,858,541	412,202	319,520	36,481	64,529	4,749	25,676	2,337	531,658	69,515
Georgia	1,248,870	129,202	909,949	99,008	275,996	26,095	29,280	1,562	8,388	635	25,920	2,102
Hawaii	228,061	38,946	59,771	6,858	1,452	79	125,849	27,552	25,148	3,148	6,567	455
Idaho	234,979	26,441	218,657	25,206	664	54	2,305	200	2,850	243	8,534	602
Illinois	1,787,854	245,215	1,393,142	206,222	202,997	22,467	70,115	5,251	12,461	1,160	109,876	10,589
Indiana	941,494	126,695	854,067	115,709	56,091	7,344	7,174	330	5,749	521	16,589	2,505
Iowa	490,628	74,948	474,240	73,179	5,490	543	3,389	273	1,351	262	5,371	608
Kansas	417,533	62,108	375,783	58,231	15,701	1,615	5,354	272	5,156	496	13,991	1,173
Kentucky	653,022	78,264	607,039	73,078	32,823	4,020	3,575	459	4,359	327	4,554	269
Louisiana	631,170	72,202	455,894	55,981	147,484	13,593	6,854	440	4,922	484	13,573	1,739
Maine	242,564	31,360	237,633	31,184	395	0	877	0	1,688	130	953	46
Maryland	822,171	109,919	561,654	84,475	186,398	18,506	40,024	3,564	10,199	1,310	24,262	2,374
Massachusetts	1,015,577	151,610	894,099	140,193	43,331	4,469	33,681	3,288	8,162	1,107	37,670	2,730
Michigan	1,531,067	203,730	1,312,329	181,061	154,228	18,081	22,752	1,291	12,203	986	24,799	2,186
Minnesota	777,833	114,331	735,723	110,511	13,867	1,331	13,201	1,393	3,848	462	7,655	749
Mississippi	427,313	49,517	312,218	37,658	106,830	11,233	3,266	280	1,937	125	2,852	288
Missouri	931,890	119,446	831,608	110,263	72,519	6,731	7,537	291	7,488	933	10,383	1,058
Montana	170,153	20,899	162,011	20,210	na	na	537	72	1,164	25	1,460	344
Nebraska	270,677	40,376	253,539	37,979	5,881	730	2,431	567	1,244	114	6,570	870
Nevada	400,514	36,432	295,826	28,367	24,195	1,890	31,551	1,679	5,747	577	40,850	3,953
New Hampshire	209,447	27,521	204,113	27,317	787	0	2,129	35	893	4	1,440	149
New Jersey	1,312,125	193,988	972,976	161,535	131,997	14,813	80,925	6,089	11,027	1,449	119,919	11,554
New Mexico	318,086	33,080	189,859	22,001	4,964	516	3,408	93	4,252	222	102,233	8,849
New York	2,895,680	424,809	2,049,516	330,136	363,347	44,989	172,409	16,600	33,695	2,719	302,833	32,717
North Carolina	1,461,149	164,331	1,163,998	136,374	236,761	23,801	14,535	681	8,306	487	25,313	1,841
North Dakota	104,679	17,350	101,022	17,216	112	0	326	0	404	0	462	57
Ohio	1,796,868	248,579	1,591,681	224,434	154,771	19,578	18,322	1,595	11,168	1,309	20,295	1,544
Oklahoma	561,568	66,463	472,973	57,964	24,935	3,038	6,338	384	20,013	1,955	12,302	864
Oregon	634,226	85,176	580,359	80,503	6,139	522	15,350	1,559	9,291	1,077	18,814	1,377
Pennsylvania	2,134,099	325,029	1,900,559	298,927	149,126	19,280	33,732	2,087	12,636	958	41,045	3,909
Rhode Island	167,180	28,782	149,623	26,643	4,753	549	3,023	447	2,243	581	7,274	581
South Carolina	761,583	81,660	588,011	65,128	151,244	14,750	7,111	565	4,775	351	8,966	751
South Dakota	129,354	20,888	122,579	20,185	197	0	379	0	992	72	1,071	4
Tennessee	986,813	106,368	855,679	94,410	101,945	10,496	9,600	709	8,054	473	9,680	238
Texas	3,096,013	346,631	2,019,908	244,283	274,727	26,080	97,937	6,961	34,089	2,251	671,887	67,685
Utah	294,979	32,769	269,366	30,208	1,438	378	4,907	541	1,886	53	14,350	1,491
Vermont	106,655	13,354	102,896	13,111	164	0	638	0	1,712	60	899	107
Virginia	1,146,846	141,634	887,389	112,528	172,937	20,958	47,632	4,176	9,922	1,063	28,255	2,900
Washington	992,516	130,093	858,756	118,619	20,238	1,532	62,220	6,967	12,337	604	30,264	2,128
West Virginia	329,055	38,813	315,440	37,630	8,775	794	907	108	1,763	52	1,594	229
Wisconsin	875,720	129,317	821,240	122,457	24,752	2,728	7,936	1,432	4,056	494	14,332	2,124
Wyoming	80,332	8,106	74,787	7,722	na	na	na	na	917	56	2,585	263

Table C-2: Counties—Older Population by Race and Hispanic Origin

	Total Population		White, Non-Hispanic		Black, Alone		Asian, Alone		Multi-race		Hispanic	
	65 Years and Over	85 Years and Over	65 Years and Over	85 Years and Over	65 Years and Over	85 Years and Over	65 Years and Over	85 Years and Over	65 Years and Over	85 Years and Over	65 Years and Over	85 Years and Over
Alabama												
Baldwin County	37,782	3,808	34,542	3,441	2,017	91	na	na	na	na	na	na
Calhoun County	18,543	1,655	15,656	1,316	2,481	339	na	na	na	na	na	na
Cullman County	14,266	1,310	13,857	1,234	na	na	na	na	na	na	na	na
DeKalb County	11,063	958	10,604	958	na	na	na	na	na	na	na	na
Elmore County	11,214	1,392	9,918	1,295	1,121	97	na	na	na	na	na	na
Etowah County	18,077	2,294	15,859	2,135	1,696	80	na	na	na	na	na	na
Houston County	16,677	1,981	13,617	1,780	2,843	190	na	na	na	na	88	0
Jefferson County	94,503	12,770	62,210	9,452	30,213	3,161	282	0	645	43	1,190	84
Lauderdale County	17,085	2,035	15,560	1,846	na	na	na	na	na	na	na	na
Lee County	15,875	1,057	12,357	953	2,917	104	na	na	na	na	na	na
Limestone County	12,511	1,106	11,066	1,106	na	na	na	na	na	na	na	na
Madison County	48,332	5,702	38,552	4,569	7,152	916	na	na	557	0	649	126
Marshall County	15,298	1,510	14,784	1,424	na	na	na	na	na	na	99	64
Mobile County	60,050	8,299	42,344	5,781	15,620	2,310	735	0	na	na	719	0
Montgomery County	30,656	2,624	17,792	1,727	11,869	897	na	na	na	na	332	0
Morgan County	18,376	1,871	17,251	1,796	881	75	na	na	na	na	na	na
Shelby County	27,380	2,670	24,428	2,407	1,516	170	na	na	na	na	307	0
St. Clair County	13,385	1,340	12,274	1,296	na	na	na	na	na	na	na	na
Talladega County	13,005	1,595	10,040	1,374	2,726	221	na	na	na	na	na	na
Tuscaloosa County	23,922	3,775	18,116	2,914	5,008	464	na	na	na	na	na	na
Walker County	11,863	853	11,243	776	na	na	na	na	na	na	na	na
Alaska												
Anchorage Municipality	26,906	2,469	19,621	1,649	1,812	137	2,400	440	559	0	932	42
Fairbanks North Star Borough	7,884	865	6,594	739	na	na	na	na	na	na	na	na
Matanuska-Susitna Borough	9,457	525	8,355	502	na	na	na	na	183	0	224	0
Arizona												
Apache County	9,430	1,187	3,189	306	na	na	na	na	na	na	na	na
Cochise County	25,160	3,151	19,429	2,602	na	na	na	na	798	0	4,629	358
Coconino County	15,520	1,173	10,599	714	na	na	na	na	na	na	1,059	127
Maricopa County	565,983	69,695	469,235	62,610	16,467	1,878	15,011	916	5,041	508	58,891	3,648
Mohave County	55,039	4,626	49,554	4,284	na	na	na	na	na	na	3,311	125
Navajo County	17,129	1,339	10,975	908	na	na	na	na	na	na	1,156	0
Pima County	178,045	20,248	139,683	16,904	3,422	0	3,247	389	1,534	40	28,900	2,899
Pinal County	71,896	5,497	60,774	4,724	896	32	na	na	603	0	7,698	725
Yavapai County	61,708	7,413	57,284	7,257	na	na	na	na	na	na	2,766	150
Yuma County	35,937	2,445	24,793	1,839	na	na	na	na	na	na	9,445	510
Arkansas												
Benton County	31,400	3,923	29,454	3,923	na	na	235	0	469	0	1,094	0
Craighead County	13,613	1,205	12,560	1,205	376	0	na	na	na	na	na	na
Faulkner County	13,216	1,467	12,594	1,467	408	0	na	na	na	na	na	na
Garland County	20,953	2,310	19,746	2,158	876	152	na	na	na	na	na	na
Jefferson County	10,791	1,254	6,399	869	4,303	355	na	na	na	na	na	na
Lonoke County	8,950	706	8,256	665	na	na	na	na	na	na	na	na
Pulaski County	52,923	7,357	39,954	5,896	11,112	1,379	na	na	743	0	937	82
Saline County	19,377	1,790	18,808	1,790	na	na	na	na	na	na	na	na
Sebastian County	17,984	2,613	16,273	2,281	555	89	na	na	na	na	117	0
Washington County	24,137	3,021	21,967	2,967	na	na	na	na	na	na	1,076	0
White County	11,920	1,233	11,385	1,233	na	na	na	na	na	na	na	na
California												
Alameda County	200,925	28,257	95,669	16,610	23,780	2,745	53,744	5,976	4,420	184	21,872	2,738
Butte County	38,055	5,627	33,923	5,168	na	na	963	42	733	160	2,132	257
Contra Costa County	157,940	21,135	103,329	15,771	11,535	1,017	23,173	2,305	3,767	620	16,762	1,620
El Dorado County	32,972	2,723	29,384	2,644	na	na	na	na	na	na	1,658	79
Fresno County	108,445	14,835	61,273	9,625	3,777	356	9,591	1,471	2,058	244	30,582	3,118
Humboldt County	20,327	2,155	18,657	1,982	na	na	na	na	209	9	622	116
Imperial County	21,684	2,884	5,524	755	na	na	na	na	660	121	14,866	1,862
Kern County	86,486	9,115	54,808	6,429	3,536	200	5,080	535	1,783	108	21,362	1,819
Kings County	13,331	1,080	7,723	795	600	16	na	na	na	na	4,330	269
Lake County	12,703	1,205	11,376	1,160	na	na	na	na	na	na	776	29
Los Angeles County	1,233,009	170,916	527,726	85,965	111,221	13,256	228,489	30,781	23,941	2,486	346,913	39,328
Madera County	19,640	2,663	13,390	1,502	na	na	na	na	na	na	4,805	994
Marin County	49,955	7,301	44,833	6,653	na	na	2,010	399	245	0	2,014	249
Mendocino County	16,976	2,172	14,556	2,081	na	na	na	na	na	na	1,455	0
Merced County	28,299	3,565	15,543	1,584	1,119	271	1,885	503	1,208	176	8,765	1,109
Monterey County	51,152	7,658	32,424	5,737	1,241	291	4,361	629	1,079	219	12,296	782
Napa County	24,631	3,589	19,146	3,125	na	na	1,911	72	na	na	2,531	392
Nevada County	23,122	2,911	21,572	2,593	na	na	na	na	na	na	744	0
Orange County	413,352	55,151	263,247	40,618	4,372	69	80,255	8,154	5,359	386	59,473	5,946
Placer County	66,706	8,318	57,353	7,497	na	na	3,466	362	308	0	3,979	459
Riverside County	307,476	40,381	205,238	28,874	15,196	1,253	18,238	2,054	5,299	583	63,516	7,801
Sacramento County	189,271	24,596	124,123	17,657	14,565	1,261	28,406	3,385	3,159	337	18,938	2,105
San Bernardino County	217,869	24,755	115,700	14,347	16,166	1,302	18,097	2,022	4,861	577	63,477	6,561
San Diego County	414,632	56,136	278,674	41,271	13,844	1,592	46,981	5,554	6,754	680	68,126	7,356
San Francisco County	122,906	18,704	48,942	6,951	7,050	981	53,895	8,751	2,125	208	11,144	1,863
San Joaquin County	84,298	10,225	48,285	7,185	4,755	258	12,594	902	3,656	379	16,734	1,554
San Luis Obispo County	49,252	5,523	42,952	5,193	na	na	na	na	na	na	3,759	263
San Mateo County	111,339	14,891	63,772	10,779	3,756	246	28,138	2,452	1,781	95	13,626	1,335

Table C-2: Counties—Older Population by Race and Hispanic Origin—*Continued*

	Total Population		White, Non-Hispanic		Black, Alone		Asian, Alone		Multi-race		Hispanic	
	65 Years and Over	85 Years and Over	65 Years and Over	85 Years and Over	65 Years and Over	85 Years and Over	65 Years and Over	85 Years and Over	65 Years and Over	85 Years and Over	65 Years and Over	85 Years and Over
California—Cont.												
Santa Barbara County	61,405	10,704	45,811	8,758	739	117	2,454	379	992	232	11,495	998
Santa Clara County	231,475	29,172	121,274	16,490	4,679	338	70,650	8,526	3,506	586	31,321	3,308
Santa Cruz County	36,267	4,187	29,633	3,495	na	na	1,532	205	199	0	4,797	487
Shasta County	34,665	4,885	31,742	4,755	na	na	na	na	806	39	1,413	60
Solano County	58,204	5,866	32,267	4,031	7,167	371	10,849	920	1,364	80	6,502	484
Sonoma County	82,536	13,079	72,200	11,918	na	na	2,657	156	1,173	57	6,377	885
Stanislaus County	64,448	8,466	44,730	6,240	1,368	404	3,106	228	1,880	344	13,492	1,385
Sutter County	14,050	1,501	9,254	1,049	na	na	2,009	60	na	na	1,729	346
Tulare County	47,336	6,886	28,507	4,879	na	na	2,108	304	807	48	15,804	1,546
Ventura County	114,954	17,233	80,131	13,250	1,581	86	8,872	1,009	1,881	109	22,783	2,804
Yolo County	23,782	3,506	16,703	2,742	518	63	2,134	56	524	77	4,119	568
Yuba County	8,658	1,272	6,556	727	na	na	na	na	458	0	696	111
Colorado												
Adams County	46,424	5,130	33,290	3,941	1,347	0	1,670	215	121	54	9,634	920
Arapahoe County	73,558	8,619	60,012	8,070	4,451	299	3,280	197	916	0	4,786	53
Boulder County	37,931	4,638	34,771	4,409	na	na	808	80	433	68	2,056	149
Denver County	72,266	10,549	48,538	8,128	7,622	862	2,386	251	1,007	0	12,603	1,308
Douglas County	31,423	3,171	28,720	2,713	na	na	943	0	78	0	1,434	415
El Paso County	75,841	8,302	64,435	7,606	2,697	147	2,111	294	1,095	105	5,334	150
Jefferson County	81,753	10,288	73,532	9,326	na	na	1,652	64	483	199	5,630	806
Larimer County	45,151	5,178	42,265	4,967	na	na	501	77	443	0	1,854	38
Mesa County	24,742	3,212	23,147	3,097	na	na	na	na	na	na	1,246	85
Pueblo County	27,960	3,506	19,065	2,529	na	na	na	na	850	226	7,728	621
Weld County	30,841	2,938	25,861	2,650	na	na	na	na	343	0	4,340	247
Connecticut												
Fairfield County	135,852	20,186	110,504	18,124	11,011	1,568	3,957	138	644	31	9,905	325
Hartford County	140,399	24,261	115,422	22,050	12,081	1,182	3,054	67	1,026	0	9,124	873
Litchfield County	34,102	5,055	32,879	4,917	na	na	na	na	na	na	427	0
Middlesex County	28,763	4,392	27,356	4,216	na	na	na	na	na	na	347	0
New Haven County	134,334	22,801	113,470	20,969	10,572	1,289	2,344	134	1,094	0	7,251	409
New London County	44,057	5,971	39,739	5,533	1,076	438	1,045	0	924	0	1,253	0
Tolland County	21,085	1,463	20,135	1,463	na	na	0	0	na	na	na	na
Windham County	16,936	2,199	16,186	2,166	na	na	na	na	na	na	545	33
Delaware												
Kent County	26,587	2,685	20,351	1,991	4,784	551	na	na	na	na	438	109
New Castle County	75,966	9,580	57,829	7,717	13,430	1,288	2,326	266	648	41	2,157	220
Sussex County	51,206	4,876	46,516	4,635	3,097	210	na	na	na	na	638	31
Florida												
Alachua County	31,565	4,390	25,009	3,723	4,599	378	592	71	73	61	1,272	157
Bay County	29,182	3,242	25,545	2,950	1,871	168	na	na	na	na	743	53
Brevard County	126,012	17,681	109,071	15,619	7,917	954	1,919	207	1,001	180	6,051	842
Broward County	286,827	45,554	178,852	33,259	48,104	5,798	7,418	635	3,333	349	50,649	5,645
Charlotte County	63,386	7,724	59,060	7,064	na	na	na	na	na	na	1,371	119
Citrus County	49,006	5,730	45,799	5,359	na	na	na	na	na	na	na	na
Clay County	28,648	2,972	24,714	2,839	1,477	93	na	na	na	na	1,216	0
Collier County	102,262	11,201	92,960	9,837	2,150	243	na	na	na	na	6,062	1,121
Columbia County	11,980	1,642	9,922	1,386	1,378	168	na	na	na	na	na	na
Duval County	114,700	14,613	80,861	10,628	23,298	2,791	4,675	422	723	129	5,032	700
Escambia County	49,205	5,761	38,497	4,547	7,495	925	1,274	140	928	45	1,241	104
Flagler County	29,218	4,057	23,818	3,138	3,241	567	na	na	na	na	1,602	352
Hernando County	48,302	6,960	43,339	6,068	1,370	421	na	na	na	na	2,955	505
Highlands County	33,181	3,933	29,445	3,604	na	na	na	na	na	na	1,894	226
Hillsborough County	172,521	23,897	119,477	18,456	17,907	1,740	5,365	375	1,324	79	29,276	3,274
Indian River County	43,896	7,638	40,245	7,153	na	na	na	na	na	na	1,391	42
Lake County	82,699	8,119	72,935	7,578	3,803	242	na	na	684	31	3,887	283
Lee County	178,227	22,013	161,612	20,555	5,626	568	na	na	684	31	9,272	587
Leon County	31,731	4,092	24,259	3,464	6,348	351	585	0	na	na	430	284
Manatee County	90,209	11,030	82,238	10,513	2,837	400	na	na	na	na	3,094	85
Marion County	94,207	11,070	82,157	10,227	5,862	680	na	na	na	na	4,570	163
Martin County	44,627	7,354	42,544	7,306	881	14	na	na	na	na	1,202	34
Miami-Dade County	404,713	60,615	74,384	12,663	55,624	6,675	5,021	515	3,735	495	274,129	41,283
Monroe County	15,903	2,037	13,137	1,763	na	na	na	na	na	na	2,165	274
Nassau County	15,340	1,845	14,023	1,506	na	na	na	na	na	na	na	na
Okaloosa County	30,098	3,749	26,227	3,304	2,074	385	na	na	190	31	465	0
Orange County	135,067	17,620	77,348	11,461	21,087	2,026	6,944	501	1,734	204	28,992	3,586
Osceola County	39,980	5,823	20,387	3,052	3,870	661	1,667	117	na	na	13,994	2,017
Palm Beach County	317,632	56,528	263,149	50,870	23,211	2,384	3,840	141	1,644	247	25,802	2,743
Pasco County	109,037	14,413	98,691	13,818	2,311	78	1,435	0	716	46	5,942	506
Pinellas County	215,292	34,313	191,929	31,893	10,452	867	4,033	404	1,022	0	7,627	924
Polk County	124,198	14,528	103,173	12,328	9,799	1,443	na	na	591	59	8,377	542
Putnam County	14,899	952	13,129	944	1,178	8	na	na	na	na	na	na
Santa Rosa County	23,713	1,967	21,842	1,877	560	90	na	na	na	na	na	na
Sarasota County	134,564	19,906	127,318	19,643	2,206	117	na	na	na	na	3,309	77
Seminole County	63,415	9,355	48,111	8,097	5,159	496	1,858	117	779	37	7,460	647
St. Johns County	39,637	4,858	36,235	4,622	1,458	82	na	na	na	na	1,318	0
St. Lucie County	65,273	9,183	52,722	7,166	6,962	1,113	na	na	na	na	4,850	904

Table C-2: Counties—Older Population by Race and Hispanic Origin—*Continued*

	Total Population		White, Non-Hispanic		Black, Alone		Asian, Alone		Multi-race		Hispanic	
	65 Years and Over	85 Years and Over	65 Years and Over	85 Years and Over	65 Years and Over	85 Years and Over	65 Years and Over	85 Years and Over	65 Years and Over	85 Years and Over	65 Years and Over	85 Years and Over
Florida—Cont.												
Sumter County	60,225	4,423	57,995	4,375	na	na	na	na	na	na	na	na
Volusia County	117,711	18,119	103,243	16,150	5,704	1,238	na	na	na	na	6,855	583
Georgia												
Barrow County	8,674	343	7,034	343	1,114	0	na	na	na	na	na	na
Bartow County	12,527	1,120	11,679	1,083	663	37	na	na	na	na	na	na
Bibb County	21,544	3,037	12,710	2,314	8,243	723	na	na	na	na	na	na
Bulloch County	7,492	760	5,808	615	1,457	145	na	na	na	na	na	na
Carroll County	13,565	1,549	12,118	1,143	1,447	406	na	na	na	na	na	na
Catoosa County	10,263	659	10,067	605	na	na	na	na	na	na	na	na
Chatham County	38,466	5,290	25,665	3,790	11,386	1,350	543	0	na	na	626	114
Cherokee County	27,286	1,821	25,383	1,763	886	0	na	na	na	na	570	58
Clarke County	11,912	1,798	8,338	1,414	2,826	384	na	na	na	na	na	na
Clayton County	23,355	2,289	8,681	930	10,873	1,129	2,331	59	na	na	1,351	171
Cobb County	77,458	8,035	61,302	6,387	9,785	1,392	2,335	131	1,405	0	2,889	215
Columbia County	16,285	2,118	13,358	1,594	1,895	442	na	na	na	na	na	na
Coweta County	16,433	1,399	13,775	1,191	2,071	208	na	na	na	na	na	na
DeKalb County	74,670	7,420	34,795	5,184	34,460	1,932	3,095	0	373	0	2,021	304
Dougherty County	12,545	1,699	6,390	1,024	5,931	675	na	na	na	na	na	na
Douglas County	14,007	1,122	10,356	833	3,263	289	na	na	na	na	na	na
Fayette County	17,936	1,610	14,035	1,369	2,788	184	na	na	na	na	na	na
Floyd County	14,678	2,121	13,146	1,512	1,271	609	na	na	na	na	na	na
Forsyth County	22,319	2,337	20,199	2,256	na	na	1,023	58	na	na	470	0
Fulton County	103,801	14,598	54,769	9,720	43,537	3,880	3,191	499	538	158	2,477	341
Glynn County	14,449	1,301	11,927	1,003	2,228	248	na	na	na	na	na	na
Gwinnett County	75,405	7,159	50,313	5,535	10,742	899	8,712	595	497	0	5,205	43
Hall County	26,142	2,623	22,911	2,427	1,696	196	na	na	na	na	1,117	0
Henry County	22,003	1,214	15,089	983	5,860	231	na	na	na	na	na	na
Houston County	16,680	1,801	13,350	1,663	2,291	138	na	na	na	na	na	na
Liberty County	4,882	260	2,675	145	1,824	74	na	na	na	na	na	na
Lowndes County	12,418	844	8,767	770	3,196	74	na	na	na	na	na	na
Muscogee County	23,945	2,973	13,952	2,420	8,993	514	na	na	na	na	327	39
Newton County	12,379	821	8,515	458	3,575	363	na	na	na	na	na	na
Paulding County	13,848	540	11,923	540	1,353	0	na	na	na	na	na	na
Richmond County	25,432	3,355	13,261	1,977	10,766	868	na	na	na	na	na	na
Rockdale County	11,021	930	7,209	848	3,556	82	na	na	na	na	282	82
Troup County	9,657	810	7,129	607	2,353	203	na	na	na	na	na	na
Walker County	11,566	1,199	10,788	1,101	na	na	na	na	na	na	na	na
Walton County	12,412	1,069	10,687	984	1,504	85	na	na	na	na	na	na
Whitfield County	13,037	965	11,614	965	na	na	na	na	na	na	714	0
Hawaii												
Hawaii County	34,298	5,231	15,394	1,056	na	na	10,175	3,141	5,459	565	1,472	84
Honolulu County	156,728	27,910	29,311	4,026	683	0	101,202	21,336	15,527	1,913	3,997	239
Kauai County	12,381	1,886	4,719	499	na	na	5,049	1,096	1,209	189	426	53
Maui County	24,652	3,919	10,347	1,277	na	na	9,423	1,979	2,953	481	672	79
Idaho												
Ada County	53,994	6,852	50,385	6,723	na	na	998	103	445	0	1,063	0
Bannock County	10,666	888	9,902	888	na	na	na	na	na	na	561	0
Bonneville County	12,855	1,486	12,487	1,486	na	na	na	na	na	na	153	0
Canyon County	25,064	2,637	22,787	2,426	na	na	na	na	na	na	2,057	211
Kootenai County	25,326	2,971	24,153	2,713	na	na	na	na	na	na	na	na
Twin Falls County	12,084	1,623	11,217	1,489	na	na	na	na	na	na	543	61
Illinois												
Adams County	12,490	2,314	12,151	2,314	na	na	na	na	na	na	na	na
Champaign County	22,939	2,574	20,016	2,541	1,698	33	767	0	407	0	146	0
Cook County	679,084	96,449	398,898	66,209	158,378	19,055	42,400	3,547	5,587	663	74,965	7,445
DeKalb County	11,929	2,097	11,102	2,049	na	na	na	na	na	na	605	0
DuPage County	125,510	15,970	104,088	14,135	2,835	304	12,243	841	620	76	5,730	614
Kane County	62,171	7,528	50,553	6,633	2,296	59	2,036	37	254	0	6,786	799
Kankakee County	16,517	2,053	14,392	1,845	1,677	105	na	na	na	na	222	0
Kendall County	10,270	772	9,435	766	na	na	na	na	na	na	287	6
Lake County	85,888	12,027	71,699	11,209	3,836	353	4,555	225	329	37	5,453	203
LaSalle County	19,377	3,596	18,784	3,389	na	na	na	na	na	na	410	135
Macon County	19,253	2,331	17,288	2,298	1,420	33	na	na	461	0	na	na
Madison County	42,283	5,915	38,935	5,347	1,674	230	na	na	na	na	na	na
McHenry County	37,130	3,621	34,816	3,432	na	na	na	na	na	na	1,183	53
McLean County	19,826	3,195	18,709	3,180	439	15	375	0	na	na	269	0
Peoria County	27,686	3,613	24,700	3,523	2,177	90	na	na	na	na	259	0
Rock Island County	25,613	3,786	22,913	3,438	1,291	173	na	na	256	30	1,207	175
Sangamon County	31,382	4,318	28,423	4,051	1,954	216	na	na	na	na	na	na
St. Clair County	36,959	4,628	27,390	3,837	8,208	668	na	na	na	na	880	123
Tazewell County	23,021	3,528	22,684	3,528	na	na	na	na	na	na	na	na
Vermilion County	14,058	1,387	12,728	1,292	994	40	na	na	na	na	na	na
Will County	76,398	8,391	61,985	7,362	6,022	537	3,389	111	450	0	4,653	381
Williamson County	11,713	1,287	11,382	1,176	na	na	na	na	na	na	na	na
Winnebago County	45,002	5,685	39,777	5,138	3,014	172	na	na	428	51	1,394	83

Table C-2: Counties—Older Population by Race and Hispanic Origin—*Continued*

	Total Population		White, Non-Hispanic		Black, Alone		Asian, Alone		Multi-race		Hispanic	
	65 Years and Over	85 Years and Over	65 Years and Over	85 Years and Over	65 Years and Over	85 Years and Over	65 Years and Over	85 Years and Over	65 Years and Over	85 Years and Over	65 Years and Over	85 Years and Over
Indiana												
Allen County	48,080	6,908	42,336	6,600	3,624	150	715	56	139	0	1,077	102
Bartholomew County	11,824	1,234	11,510	1,197	na	na	na	na	na	na	na	na
Clark County	16,379	1,957	15,258	1,798	1,077	159	na	na	na	na	na	na
Delaware County	18,735	2,883	17,552	2,693	816	190	na	na	na	na	na	na
Elkhart County	26,148	3,952	25,019	3,563	587	255	na	na	na	na	311	97
Floyd County	10,796	1,723	10,475	1,698	na	na	na	na	na	na	na	na
Grant County	12,016	1,690	11,168	1,690	na	na	na	na	na	na	na	na
Hamilton County	31,734	3,880	29,358	3,439	na	na	1,157	0	na	na	265	158
Hancock County	10,861	1,101	10,564	1,101	na	na	na	na	na	na	na	na
Hendricks County	18,949	2,166	18,169	2,166	na	na	na	na	na	na	na	na
Howard County	14,846	1,972	13,923	1,790	na	na	na	na	na	na	na	na
Johnson County	20,379	2,996	19,824	2,996	na	na	na	na	na	na	na	na
Kosciusko County	11,763	1,062	11,418	1,062	na	na	na	na	na	na	na	na
Lake County	71,219	11,367	48,991	8,118	14,595	2,212	604	100	507	49	6,475	888
LaPorte County	17,551	2,100	16,196	2,014	1,085	86	na	na	na	na	85	0
Madison County	22,437	2,262	20,597	2,075	1,402	131	na	na	na	na	na	na
Marion County	105,602	14,109	78,828	11,180	21,996	2,623	1,537	0	792	30	2,016	130
Monroe County	15,923	1,781	15,597	1,737	na	na	na	na	na	na	na	na
Morgan County	10,417	1,001	10,338	1,001	na	na	na	na	na	na	na	na
Porter County	24,218	2,453	22,380	2,372	na	na	na	na	na	na	1,281	81
St. Joseph County	38,008	6,183	34,053	5,482	2,778	417	na	na	171	53	592	193
Tippecanoe County	19,830	3,044	17,887	2,603	na	na	666	0	na	na	647	441
Vanderburgh County	27,816	4,923	25,598	4,460	1,493	351	na	na	na	na	na	na
Vigo County	15,835	2,721	14,839	2,529	423	109	na	na	na	na	na	na
Wayne County	12,325	1,278	11,371	1,278	na	na	na	na	na	na	na	na
Iowa												
Black Hawk County	19,547	2,297	18,294	2,137	895	139	na	na	na	na	40	21
Dallas County	8,524	1,382	8,312	1,382	na	na	na	na	na	na	na	na
Dubuque County	15,598	2,103	15,410	2,103	na	na	na	na	na	na	na	na
Johnson County	13,874	1,634	13,305	1,628	na	na	na	na	na	na	76	0
Linn County	30,974	3,960	30,130	3,783	na	na	na	na	na	na	na	na
Polk County	53,735	7,688	49,618	7,385	1,709	152	1,046	151	101	0	1,285	0
Pottawattamie County	14,453	2,438	14,069	2,378	na	na	na	na	na	na	203	25
Scott County	24,748	3,102	22,903	2,954	939	129	na	na	na	na	451	19
Story County	10,136	1,101	9,677	1,101	na	na	na	na	na	na	na	na
Woodbury County	13,869	1,736	13,175	1,726	na	na	na	na	na	na	489	0
Kansas												
Butler County	9,354	1,223	8,872	1,080	na	na	na	na	na	na	na	na
Douglas County	12,127	1,714	11,068	1,714	na	na	na	na	na	na	na	na
Johnson County	73,158	10,910	67,401	10,293	1,437	160	1,545	145	1,190	110	2,288	202
Leavenworth County	10,075	991	9,003	792	na	na	na	na	na	na	na	na
Riley County	6,131	967	5,457	967	na	na	na	na	na	na	na	na
Sedgwick County	65,078	7,801	55,470	7,030	4,057	295	1,836	47	667	89	2,721	234
Shawnee County	28,205	4,520	25,347	4,071	1,247	240	na	na	467	58	978	107
Wyandotte County	18,222	2,780	11,131	2,059	4,628	416	395	0	na	na	1,538	257
Kentucky												
Boone County	14,280	1,985	13,570	1,722	na	na	na	na	na	na	na	na
Bullitt County	10,492	835	10,305	835	na	na	na	na	na	na	na	na
Campbell County	12,646	1,729	12,294	1,729	na	na	na	na	na	na	na	na
Christian County	8,044	969	6,760	707	1,132	262	na	na	na	na	na	na
Daviess County	15,623	1,877	15,070	1,751	na	na	na	na	na	na	na	na
Fayette County	35,972	5,596	30,919	5,232	3,945	290	652	0	280	0	102	0
Hardin County	13,354	1,716	11,699	1,479	899	30	na	na	na	na	na	na
Jefferson County	110,272	16,039	91,660	14,093	15,055	1,682	1,354	156	906	68	1,390	40
Kenton County	20,884	3,427	19,947	3,224	493	203	na	na	na	na	na	na
Madison County	10,913	1,166	10,542	1,166	na	na	na	na	na	na	na	na
McCracken County	11,968	2,152	10,898	2,056	na	na	na	na	na	na	na	na
Pike County	10,263	1,332	9,855	1,276	na	na	na	na	na	na	na	na
Warren County	13,937	1,203	13,186	1,045	566	158	na	na	na	na	na	na
Louisiana												
Ascension Parish	12,045	926	9,351	521	2,044	288	na	na	na	na	na	na
Bossier Parish	15,826	1,733	13,025	1,519	2,382	167	na	na	na	na	na	na
Caddo Parish	37,649	5,279	23,460	4,125	12,877	997	na	na	na	na	na	na
Calcasieu Parish	27,229	3,501	21,060	2,989	5,137	432	na	na	na	na	na	na
East Baton Rouge Parish	54,755	6,330	35,231	4,859	17,515	1,240	987	0	na	na	501	99
Iberia Parish	9,547	1,084	7,164	677	2,181	407	na	na	na	na	na	na
Jefferson Parish	65,885	8,405	48,546	7,031	9,741	905	1,687	0	643	99	5,179	370
Lafayette Parish	26,429	3,123	20,966	2,585	4,615	425	na	na	na	na	na	na
Lafourche Parish	13,082	1,545	11,782	1,340	881	205	na	na	na	na	na	na
Livingston Parish	15,006	913	14,729	743	na	na	na	na	na	na	na	na
Orleans Parish	46,481	5,761	16,682	2,537	26,851	2,754	934	177	161	34	1,647	272
Ouachita Parish	20,720	2,376	15,833	2,106	4,267	270	na	na	na	na	na	na
Rapides Parish	19,756	2,378	14,720	2,067	4,332	311	na	na	na	na	na	na
St. Landry Parish	12,313	1,937	8,156	1,320	4,068	617	na	na	na	na	na	na
St. Tammany Parish	37,110	4,287	32,116	4,042	2,602	0	na	na	na	na	955	245

Table C-2: Counties—Older Population by Race and Hispanic Origin—*Continued*

	Total Population		White, Non-Hispanic		Black, Alone		Asian, Alone		Multi-race		Hispanic	
	65 Years and Over	85 Years and Over	65 Years and Over	85 Years and Over	65 Years and Over	85 Years and Over	65 Years and Over	85 Years and Over	65 Years and Over	85 Years and Over	65 Years and Over	85 Years and Over
Louisiana—Cont.												
Tangipahoa Parish	16,233	1,453	12,857	1,177	2,850	218	na	na	na	na	na	na
Terrebonne Parish	13,901	1,659	11,451	1,457	1,820	0	na	na	na	na	na	na
Maine												
Androscoggin County	17,336	1,850	16,648	1,850	na	na	na	na	289	0	na	na
Aroostook County	14,791	2,280	14,483	2,240	na	na	na	na	na	na	na	na
Cumberland County	47,191	7,190	45,787	7,190	182	0	na	na	369	0	na	na
Kennebec County	21,422	2,384	20,987	2,384	na	na	na	na	na	na	na	na
Penobscot County	25,127	3,416	24,746	3,416	na	na	na	na	na	na	na	na
York County	35,962	4,570	35,322	4,499	na	na	na	na	na	na	na	na
Maryland												
Allegany County	13,871	1,822	13,446	1,783	na	na	na	na	na	na	na	na
Anne Arundel County	75,050	8,810	63,169	7,536	8,151	938	1,633	0	851	135	1,529	201
Baltimore County	130,772	20,733	101,392	18,165	22,409	2,028	4,349	334	769	75	1,839	119
Calvert County	11,616	1,539	9,817	1,219	1,336	320	na	na	na	na	na	na
Carroll County	25,952	3,064	24,396	2,913	na	na	na	na	na	na	na	na
Cecil County	14,187	1,689	13,134	1,510	na	na	na	na	na	na	na	na
Charles County	17,429	1,750	10,977	1,144	5,026	518	na	na	220	0	310	58
Frederick County	31,824	4,165	27,986	3,660	1,832	432	998	73	520	0	907	169
Harford County	36,565	4,584	32,120	4,305	2,662	124	967	40	na	na	562	115
Howard County	37,630	4,292	26,543	3,205	5,302	702	4,332	94	617	167	786	124
Montgomery County	140,966	24,064	91,588	17,754	16,151	2,368	19,472	2,553	3,603	559	10,822	859
Prince George's County	102,118	10,346	25,547	4,166	64,631	5,134	4,644	440	1,967	228	4,665	424
St. Mary's County	13,166	1,302	10,881	1,213	1,573	62	na	na	na	na	na	na
Washington County	23,264	3,546	22,257	3,498	504	48	na	na	na	na	na	na
Wicomico County	14,520	2,084	11,451	1,720	2,570	364	na	na	na	na	na	na
Massachusetts												
Barnstable County	59,991	7,498	58,035	7,390	na	na	na	na	na	na	na	na
Berkshire County	26,665	4,323	26,010	4,302	na	na	na	na	na	na	na	na
Bristol County	87,043	13,289	81,030	12,982	1,619	75	999	0	577	53	1,752	0
Essex County	119,375	18,724	107,610	17,740	1,624	0	2,140	236	907	177	7,977	748
Franklin County	12,876	1,995	12,502	1,921	na	na	na	na	na	na	na	na
Hampden County	71,053	12,260	60,217	11,194	3,994	602	631	41	517	86	5,927	337
Hampshire County	24,070	3,322	22,590	3,322	na	na	527	0	na	na	323	0
Middlesex County	219,875	32,141	194,954	29,623	6,219	647	12,268	1,373	1,608	42	5,478	456
Norfolk County	108,372	18,186	96,523	16,823	3,845	624	5,905	685	585	54	1,439	0
Plymouth County	82,295	9,189	75,017	8,509	4,287	477	na	na	590	43	891	7
Suffolk County	84,187	12,077	49,511	8,270	18,321	1,911	6,809	748	1,886	361	9,048	992
Worcester County	114,883	18,217	105,707	17,728	1,916	25	2,714	90	919	291	4,074	95
Michigan												
Allegan County	17,109	1,920	16,353	1,914	na	na	na	na	na	na	492	0
Bay County	19,487	2,221	18,677	2,221	na	na	na	na	na	na	na	na
Berrien County	27,218	3,430	24,290	3,226	2,494	165	na	na	na	na	99	0
Calhoun County	21,797	3,110	19,490	2,921	1,824	146	na	na	na	na	239	0
Clinton County	11,770	1,262	11,438	1,262	na	na	na	na	na	na	na	na
Eaton County	18,189	2,295	16,338	1,948	1,052	302	na	na	na	na	na	na
Genesee County	64,986	7,341	52,523	6,687	9,945	476	na	na	602	0	943	71
Grand Traverse County	15,466	1,858	15,198	1,858	na	na	na	na	na	na	na	na
Ingham County	34,000	4,689	28,896	4,366	2,600	271	655	0	616	0	1,225	44
Isabella County	7,589	999	7,328	952	na	na	na	na	na	na	na	na
Jackson County	25,771	3,238	23,864	3,094	959	144	na	na	na	na	na	na
Kalamazoo County	34,798	4,778	31,609	4,689	2,101	50	300	0	449	6	353	0
Kent County	77,090	14,316	68,508	13,288	4,360	555	1,366	66	628	115	2,260	374
Lapeer County	14,338	1,637	13,613	1,637	na	na	na	na	na	na	na	na
Lenawee County	16,465	1,745	15,690	1,653	na	na	na	na	na	na	583	76
Livingston County	27,436	2,274	26,467	2,274	na	na	na	na	na	na	363	0
Macomb County	133,886	20,210	122,722	19,527	6,018	263	3,153	220	631	25	1,312	175
Marquette County	11,257	1,324	10,898	1,288	na	na	na	na	na	na	na	na
Midland County	13,835	1,902	13,211	1,902	na	na	na	na	na	na	na	na
Monroe County	23,690	3,255	22,727	3,126	na	na	na	na	na	na	na	na
Muskegon County	25,849	3,289	22,953	3,020	2,120	200	na	na	363	69	402	0
Oakland County	186,242	26,325	152,645	23,097	22,387	2,460	6,849	457	1,709	53	2,489	295
Ottawa County	36,445	4,816	34,674	4,816	na	na	na	na	na	na	1,162	0
Saginaw County	33,397	3,726	27,380	3,117	4,361	399	na	na	na	na	1,499	210
Shiawassee County	11,593	1,745	10,988	1,573	na	na	na	na	na	na	na	na
St. Clair County	26,930	2,962	25,532	2,927	na	na	na	na	na	na	na	na
Van Buren County	12,303	1,157	11,040	959	na	na	na	na	na	na	165	0
Washtenaw County	43,044	5,441	35,881	4,909	4,086	408	1,972	124	346	0	764	0
Wayne County	243,710	35,546	146,145	23,157	84,494	11,204	4,987	284	2,069	177	5,395	628
Minnesota												
Anoka County	40,207	4,550	38,476	4,293	415	0	256	58	471	167	544	199
Blue Earth County	8,415	1,490	8,258	1,490	na	na	na	na	na	na	na	na
Carver County	9,447	1,598	9,372	1,566	na	na	na	na	na	na	na	na
Dakota County	50,260	5,251	46,658	4,783	1,050	0	1,292	307	81	0	1,022	98
Hennepin County	151,476	23,578	135,309	22,283	8,006	838	4,792	375	806	0	1,981	44
Olmsted County	20,755	2,994	19,742	2,994	na	na	766	0	na	na	na	na

Table C-2: Counties—Older Population by Race and Hispanic Origin—*Continued*

	Total Population		White, Non-Hispanic		Black, Alone		Asian, Alone		Multi-race		Hispanic	
	65 Years and Over	85 Years and Over	65 Years and Over	85 Years and Over	65 Years and Over	85 Years and Over	65 Years and Over	85 Years and Over	65 Years and Over	85 Years and Over	65 Years and Over	85 Years and Over
Minnesota—Cont.												
Ramsey County	69,060	11,408	60,280	10,131	2,726	407	3,645	584	818	43	1,475	243
Rice County	9,149	816	8,926	816	na	na	na	na	na	na	na	na
Scott County	12,957	1,297	12,059	1,297	na	na	457	0	na	na	na	na
Sherburne County	9,253	1,284	9,044	1,284	na	na	na	na	na	na	na	na
St. Louis County	34,521	5,352	33,712	5,352	na	na	na	na	172	0	na	na
Stearns County	20,344	3,228	20,047	3,228	44	0	na	na	na	na	na	na
Washington County	31,752	4,474	30,291	4,421	573	0	682	0	na	na	206	53
Wright County	14,492	1,569	14,263	1,569	na	na	na	na	na	na	na	na
Mississippi												
DeSoto County	20,399	2,059	16,991	1,747	2,680	312	na	na	na	na	135	0
Forrest County	9,407	1,096	7,384	1,026	1,954	70	na	na	na	na	na	na
Harrison County	26,479	2,419	21,162	2,028	3,846	185	na	na	na	na	525	36
Hinds County	29,705	4,485	13,973	2,290	14,983	1,963	na	na	na	na	na	na
Jackson County	19,968	2,408	16,440	2,273	2,904	115	na	na	na	na	191	0
Jones County	10,600	1,292	8,468	812	2,018	480	na	na	na	na	na	na
Lauderdale County	11,959	1,614	8,472	1,181	2,945	433	na	na	na	na	na	na
Lee County	12,149	1,737	10,154	1,677	1,995	60	na	na	na	na	na	na
Madison County	12,642	1,428	8,943	991	3,369	437	na	na	na	na	na	na
Rankin County	19,456	2,069	17,046	1,590	2,002	319	na	na	na	na	na	na
Missouri												
Boone County	18,413	2,293	16,538	2,255	1,203	0	na	na	na	na	na	na
Buchanan County	12,961	1,818	12,352	1,782	na	na	na	na	na	na	na	na
Cape Girardeau County	12,093	1,997	11,504	1,967	na	na	na	na	na	na	na	na
Cass County	15,445	1,388	14,866	1,388	na	na	na	na	na	na	na	na
Christian County	11,973	1,822	11,411	1,614	na	na	na	na	na	na	na	na
Clay County	29,743	3,229	27,697	3,050	936	0	na	na	80	0	701	179
Cole County	10,815	1,141	10,128	1,104	642	37	na	na	na	na	na	na
Franklin County	16,058	2,003	15,478	2,003	na	na	na	na	na	na	na	na
Greene County	43,776	5,826	42,047	5,493	708	54	na	na	418	94	na	na
Jackson County	92,284	11,139	70,335	9,330	17,352	1,523	740	70	898	149	2,996	0
Jasper County	16,015	2,476	15,519	2,394	na	na	na	na	na	na	na	na
Jefferson County	30,156	2,823	28,910	2,784	na	na	na	na	na	na	na	na
Platte County	11,976	1,675	11,351	1,675	na	na	na	na	na	na	na	na
St. Charles County	51,031	5,903	47,511	5,640	1,970	141	609	75	345	23	693	24
St. Francois County	10,095	1,468	9,883	1,468	na	na	na	na	na	na	na	na
St. Louis County	164,829	24,306	133,243	21,756	26,051	2,073	3,422	0	1,149	234	1,250	230
Montana												
Cascade County	13,756	1,424	13,201	1,424	na	na	na	na	na	na	na	na
Flathead County	16,537	1,186	15,750	950	na	na	na	na	na	na	na	na
Gallatin County	10,707	978	10,625	978	na	na	na	na	na	na	na	na
Lewis and Clark County	10,680	1,361	10,288	1,354	na	na	na	na	na	na	na	na
Missoula County	15,155	2,649	14,779	2,604	na	na	na	na	na	na	na	na
Yellowstone County	23,672	3,029	22,789	2,914	na	na	na	na	na	na	na	na
Nebraska												
Douglas County	62,609	10,377	54,227	8,878	4,965	689	876	355	377	25	1,969	430
Lancaster County	36,338	4,779	34,459	4,633	279	0	662	0	na	na	728	107
Sarpy County	17,499	2,147	16,117	1,935	431	41	na	na	na	na	368	29
Nevada												
Clark County	274,915	24,386	187,340	18,247	22,823	1,643	28,302	1,510	4,119	413	31,659	2,787
Washoe County	64,426	6,546	53,977	5,398	1,163	227	3,063	152	939	117	4,929	654
New Hampshire												
Cheshire County	12,998	1,918	12,918	1,918	na	na	na	na	na	na	na	na
Grafton County	15,896	2,275	15,800	2,271	na	na	na	na	na	na	na	na
Hillsborough County	56,374	7,581	53,266	7,547	341	0	1,455	0	331	0	981	34
Merrimack County	23,480	2,888	23,121	2,888	na	na	na	na	na	na	na	na
Rockingham County	45,788	6,138	44,607	6,023	na	na	na	na	96	0	na	na
Strafford County	16,887	1,887	16,670	1,852	na	na	na	na	na	na	na	na
New Jersey												
Atlantic County	43,435	4,347	32,666	3,497	5,106	747	2,485	57	604	37	2,783	37
Bergen County	149,621	23,126	112,450	19,351	7,087	739	16,571	1,692	623	43	13,033	1,336
Burlington County	70,099	9,185	55,929	7,881	8,683	739	2,086	183	1,608	361	1,831	56
Camden County	72,754	10,516	54,053	9,194	10,451	764	3,524	189	490	69	4,248	369
Cape May County	22,927	2,659	21,677	2,616	na	na	na	na	na	na	na	na
Cumberland County	21,282	2,994	15,796	2,344	2,589	393	na	na	na	na	2,550	241
Essex County	98,173	15,119	47,495	9,314	34,253	4,458	4,519	211	897	119	11,912	1,195
Gloucester County	41,094	6,459	35,765	5,880	3,418	446	1,122	0	221	0	564	133
Hudson County	72,052	9,084	27,826	5,340	7,732	408	7,896	298	593	0	28,712	3,159
Hunterdon County	19,613	2,830	18,561	2,785	na	na	na	na	na	na	na	na
Mercer County	51,229	6,863	36,761	6,101	8,275	496	3,048	266	na	na	2,735	0
Middlesex County	111,947	17,308	76,800	14,054	7,816	889	16,576	1,732	857	87	10,097	699
Monmouth County	98,218	15,704	84,301	14,459	5,952	865	3,758	107	727	68	3,714	205
Morris County	77,287	11,426	65,688	10,400	2,398	163	5,429	585	na	na	3,663	278
Ocean County	128,434	21,904	120,631	20,345	2,476	532	1,481	413	481	52	3,709	969
Passaic County	66,620	10,040	42,072	7,624	6,465	702	3,059	214	1,549	364	14,863	1,438

Table C-2: Counties—Older Population by Race and Hispanic Origin—*Continued*

	Total Population		White, Non-Hispanic		Black, Alone		Asian, Alone		Multi-race		Hispanic	
	65 Years and Over	85 Years and Over	65 Years and Over	85 Years and Over	65 Years and Over	85 Years and Over	65 Years and Over	85 Years and Over	65 Years and Over	85 Years and Over	65 Years and Over	85 Years and Over
New Jersey—Cont.												
Salem County	10,977	1,759	9,476	1,602	1,369	157	na	na	na	na	na	na
Somerset County	45,848	6,577	35,893	5,701	2,522	325	5,162	142	na	na	2,178	409
Sussex County	21,232	2,243	20,076	2,232	na	na	na	na	na	na	490	11
Union County	72,050	10,755	43,138	7,725	13,964	1,954	2,822	0	891	29	11,493	981
Warren County	17,233	3,090	15,922	3,090	361	0	na	na	na	na	634	0
New Mexico												
Bernalillo County	95,769	11,046	58,312	7,762	2,027	225	1,920	93	1,646	106	31,225	2,895
Chaves County	9,807	711	6,354	648	na	na	na	na	na	na	3,048	63
Doña Ana County	30,057	3,322	15,703	2,044	na	na	na	na	na	na	13,699	1,278
Lea County	7,340	656	4,865	531	na	na	na	na	na	na	2,036	54
McKinley County	7,509	566	na	na	na	na	na	na	na	na	na	na
Otero County	10,366	942	7,639	927	na	na	na	na	na	na	2,260	0
San Juan County	15,809	2,028	9,772	1,320	na	na	na	na	na	na	1,572	100
Sandoval County	20,986	1,994	13,513	1,418	na	na	na	na	na	na	4,621	442
Santa Fe County	29,029	2,639	19,217	1,846	na	na	na	na	na	na	8,887	746
Valencia County	11,626	596	6,136	154	na	na	na	na	na	na	5,043	348
New York												
Albany County	47,327	6,170	41,540	5,823	3,337	80	1,155	161	306	0	1,090	106
Bronx County	161,753	20,245	35,423	7,780	53,413	4,821	5,752	415	3,459	93	70,087	7,612
Broome County	34,371	5,355	32,854	5,267	437	64	515	24	na	na	385	0
Cattaraugus County	13,428	1,680	12,886	1,646	na	na	na	na	na	na	na	na
Cayuga County	13,146	1,955	13,086	1,955	na	na	na	na	na	na	na	na
Chautauqua County	23,641	3,616	23,018	3,531	na	na	na	na	na	na	367	0
Chemung County	14,901	2,414	14,115	2,414	na	na	na	na	na	na	na	na
Clinton County	12,286	1,290	12,020	1,284	na	na	na	na	na	na	na	na
Dutchess County	45,496	6,648	39,340	6,083	2,981	264	901	148	374	90	1,995	99
Erie County	152,661	24,864	133,586	23,392	13,163	1,151	1,940	109	514	22	2,697	138
Jefferson County	14,632	1,566	14,079	1,522	na	na	na	na	na	na	236	0
Kings County	317,536	47,342	136,045	26,873	109,941	13,762	29,495	2,584	3,855	544	46,267	4,279
Livingston County	10,556	1,623	9,876	1,541	na	na	na	na	na	na	na	na
Madison County	11,386	1,562	11,213	1,562	na	na	na	na	na	na	na	na
Monroe County	115,998	18,948	99,226	17,256	10,087	689	2,083	165	561	95	3,421	472
Nassau County	222,921	37,327	174,164	32,180	18,975	1,903	14,090	1,204	2,563	241	14,738	1,895
New York County	234,962	35,425	124,192	17,262	35,248	7,455	23,923	3,888	5,865	188	53,720	8,075
Niagara County	36,927	6,032	34,712	5,860	1,431	83	na	na	na	na	na	na
Oneida County	40,694	6,483	38,269	6,420	1,089	48	631	15	na	na	425	0
Onondaga County	71,672	11,833	64,742	11,029	4,183	547	1,455	178	236	59	976	40
Ontario County	19,592	3,264	18,740	3,209	na	na	na	na	na	na	na	na
Orange County	47,416	5,505	38,508	4,725	3,395	319	1,094	115	351	0	4,201	346
Oswego County	17,363	2,225	17,125	2,225	na	na	na	na	na	na	na	na
Putnam County	14,355	1,741	13,518	1,668	na	na	na	na	na	na	569	73
Queens County	315,879	45,379	131,032	25,199	57,969	8,219	64,093	5,637	7,775	649	56,546	5,682
Rensselaer County	24,080	3,292	22,973	3,209	688	0	na	na	21	0	359	83
Richmond County	68,263	9,281	53,978	7,726	3,227	443	5,150	535	750	0	5,278	648
Rockland County	48,111	7,153	36,397	5,809	5,019	757	3,284	278	430	0	3,283	188
Saratoga County	35,222	4,949	34,435	4,899	na	na	275	0	na	na	225	0
Schenectady County	24,058	4,543	21,853	3,947	1,310	410	324	0	na	na	223	0
St. Lawrence County	16,993	2,445	16,428	2,445	na	na	na	na	na	na	na	na
Steuben County	17,344	2,461	16,589	2,461	na	na	na	na	na	na	na	na
Suffolk County	228,758	28,677	195,343	26,126	11,526	1,088	6,282	350	1,762	212	15,429	985
Sullivan County	12,838	873	11,024	852	na	na	na	na	na	na	672	21
Tompkins County	12,325	2,319	11,969	2,259	na	na	na	na	na	na	na	na
Ulster County	31,737	4,110	28,596	4,071	1,186	0	na	na	616	0	1,364	0
Warren County	12,805	2,024	12,542	1,978	na	na	na	na	na	na	na	na
Wayne County	15,341	2,336	14,484	2,248	na	na	na	na	na	na	na	na
Westchester County	152,223	25,886	111,589	21,602	18,699	2,028	6,686	700	950	80	14,940	1,571
North Carolina												
Alamance County	25,110	3,301	20,433	2,733	3,904	554	na	na	na	na	793	0
Brunswick County	31,946	2,271	29,376	2,021	2,040	250	na	na	na	na	na	na
Buncombe County	45,118	5,676	41,998	5,177	1,744	128	na	na	na	na	764	172
Burke County	16,362	2,140	15,108	1,936	na	na	na	na	na	na	na	na
Cabarrus County	23,827	3,027	20,279	2,592	2,679	413	na	na	na	na	647	22
Caldwell County	14,740	1,509	13,495	1,246	na	na	na	na	na	na	na	na
Carteret County	15,294	1,462	14,135	1,347	na	na	na	na	na	na	na	na
Catawba County	24,813	2,016	22,721	1,923	1,612	93	na	na	na	na	393	0
Chatham County	16,084	2,375	13,794	2,052	na	na	na	na	na	na	na	na
Cleveland County	16,837	1,817	13,766	1,443	2,586	374	na	na	na	na	na	na
Craven County	17,610	2,535	14,451	1,928	2,986	508	na	na	na	na	173	99
Cumberland County	35,286	3,066	20,170	2,051	11,610	894	1,205	12	710	0	1,269	62
Davidson County	27,021	1,653	24,976	1,634	1,621	0	na	na	na	na	276	0
Durham County	32,356	4,598	19,996	3,098	10,682	1,395	1,023	0	na	na	486	105
Forsyth County	52,193	7,633	40,498	6,707	10,239	869	339	0	na	na	1,023	57
Gaston County	32,006	4,349	27,570	3,927	3,333	338	na	na	na	na	518	84
Guilford County	70,308	9,221	51,896	7,488	15,693	1,503	1,355	175	303	0	980	55
Harnett County	13,669	1,431	10,991	1,031	2,444	369	na	na	na	na	0	0
Henderson County	27,505	3,906	26,033	3,833	na	na	na	na	na	na	na	na
Iredell County	24,123	1,869	21,308	1,813	2,305	56	na	na	na	na	325	0

Table C-2: Counties—Older Population by Race and Hispanic Origin—*Continued*

	Total Population		White, Non-Hispanic		Black, Alone		Asian, Alone		Multi-race		Hispanic	
	65 Years and Over	85 Years and Over	65 Years and Over	85 Years and Over	65 Years and Over	85 Years and Over	65 Years and Over	85 Years and Over	65 Years and Over	85 Years and Over	65 Years and Over	85 Years and Over
North Carolina—Cont.												
Johnston County	22,004	2,215	18,438	1,712	2,948	503	na	na	na	na	510	0
Lincoln County	12,894	1,130	11,790	1,068	na	na	na	na	na	na	na	na
Mecklenburg County	101,554	11,895	69,778	10,420	23,867	1,097	2,869	97	1,410	30	3,827	251
Moore County	22,340	4,339	19,812	4,046	2,398	260	na	na	na	na	na	na
Nash County	15,441	1,552	10,572	946	4,140	503	na	na	na	na	12	0
New Hanover County	34,104	4,277	29,574	3,687	3,941	590	na	na	na	na	427	0
Unslow County	15,988	1,085	12,469	859	2,740	188	na	na	na	na	718	38
Orange County	15,716	1,637	12,972	1,410	1,896	227	316	0	na	na	510	0
Pitt County	19,820	2,417	13,624	1,585	5,822	832	na	na	na	na	289	0
Randolph County	23,187	2,442	21,256	2,372	1,095	23	na	na	na	na	523	0
Robeson County	17,379	1,812	7,332	817	3,918	393	na	na	na	na	100	0
Rockingham County	16,633	2,235	13,856	1,796	2,719	439	na	na	na	na	na	na
Rowan County	22,566	1,903	19,397	1,582	2,691	165	na	na	na	na	402	145
Rutherford County	13,004	2,213	11,815	1,999	na	na	na	na	na	na	na	na
Surry County	13,770	1,826	13,068	1,815	na	na	na	na	na	na	0	0
Union County	25,231	2,421	20,937	2,147	2,372	274	na	na	na	na	1,070	0
Wake County	99,924	9,873	76,663	8,138	15,324	1,247	4,037	162	822	83	2,741	243
Wayne County	18,027	1,903	12,201	1,358	5,207	545	na	na	na	na	342	0
Wilkes County	13,662	1,405	12,914	1,333	na	na	na	na	na	na	na	na
Wilson County	13,432	1,473	8,777	889	4,240	459	na	na	na	na	na	na
North Dakota												
Burleigh County	13,056	2,440	12,808	2,440	na	na	na	na	na	na	na	na
Cass County	17,715	2,648	17,501	2,591	na	na	na	na	na	na	na	na
Grand Forks County	7,808	1,245	7,566	1,245	na	na	na	na	na	na	na	na
Ward County	7,888	1,550	7,733	1,550	na	na	na	na	na	na	na	na
Ohio												
Allen County	16,543	1,998	15,018	1,784	1,326	214	na	na	na	na	na	na
Ashtabula County	17,004	2,391	16,473	2,391	na	na	na	na	na	na	199	0
Belmont County	13,196	2,149	12,795	2,065	na	na	na	na	na	na	na	na
Butler County	49,424	6,196	45,397	5,774	2,245	260	1,131	64	326	98	325	0
Clark County	24,356	3,393	22,249	3,182	1,663	211	na	na	na	na	na	na
Clermont County	28,320	2,230	27,408	2,230	na	na	na	na	na	na	na	na
Columbiana County	19,192	2,592	18,879	2,487	na	na	na	na	na	na	na	na
Cuyahoga County	207,350	32,604	149,710	25,068	48,441	6,790	3,805	274	1,471	314	3,917	252
Delaware County	21,322	2,566	20,336	2,566	362	0	473	0	na	na	na	na
Erie County	14,639	1,942	13,774	1,685	na	na	na	na	na	na	na	na
Fairfield County	21,807	2,107	20,759	2,004	na	na	na	na	na	na	na	na
Franklin County	133,707	17,500	105,747	14,723	21,811	2,299	3,356	162	939	125	1,635	191
Geauga County	16,626	2,757	16,523	2,757	na	na	na	na	na	na	na	na
Greene County	25,607	3,196	23,454	2,855	988	269	na	na	na	na	na	na
Hamilton County	114,493	18,600	89,231	15,209	22,100	2,754	1,271	386	551	161	1,352	90
Hancock County	11,946	2,007	11,637	2,007	na	na	na	na	na	na	na	na
Jefferson County	13,255	2,043	12,387	1,859	na	na	na	na	na	na	na	na
Lake County	40,970	5,353	39,430	5,353	na	na	na	na	na	na	27	0
Licking County	25,955	3,143	24,809	3,143	na	na	na	na	na	na	na	na
Lorain County	49,382	7,526	44,369	7,038	2,396	366	na	na	427	58	2,027	64
Lucas County	63,203	10,326	52,181	8,989	8,498	902	584	79	619	172	1,554	184
Mahoning County	44,554	8,686	38,557	7,788	4,736	842	na	na	na	na	752	56
Marion County	11,007	1,613	10,065	1,613	na	na	na	na	na	na	na	na
Medina County	27,114	3,566	26,499	3,519	na	na	na	na	na	na	na	na
Miami County	17,781	1,733	17,367	1,704	na	na	na	na	na	na	na	na
Montgomery County	88,739	10,750	71,817	9,142	14,582	1,419	1,146	56	464	45	797	140
Muskingum County	14,224	2,018	13,644	1,832	na	na	na	na	na	na	na	na
Portage County	23,895	3,299	22,749	2,992	na	na	na	na	na	na	na	na
Richland County	22,015	2,710	20,427	2,558	na	na	na	na	na	na	na	na
Ross County	11,396	916	10,987	774	na	na	na	na	na	na	na	na
Scioto County	12,766	1,687	12,539	1,670	na	na	na	na	na	na	na	na
Stark County	66,181	9,107	61,902	8,624	3,149	275	na	na	501	90	504	118
Summit County	87,526	13,667	76,471	12,800	8,912	639	1,295	96	405	12	189	0
Trumbull County	39,588	6,389	36,901	5,957	2,295	290	na	na	na	na	na	na
Tuscarawas County	16,746	2,740	16,297	2,531	na	na	na	na	na	na	na	na
Warren County	28,959	2,472	27,546	2,293	na	na	650	56	na	na	na	na
Wayne County	18,369	2,491	18,212	2,491	na	na	na	na	na	na	na	na
Wood County	18,045	2,352	17,303	2,304	na	na	na	na	na	na	na	na
Oklahoma												
Canadian County	15,628	1,935	14,129	1,741	na	na	na	na	276	57	263	0
Cleveland County	32,134	3,086	28,376	2,951	465	59	858	0	879	0	679	0
Comanche County	13,777	1,238	10,538	1,158	1,307	80	na	na	488	0	380	U
Creek County	11,860	993	10,555	897	na	na	na	na	530	0	na	na
Muskogee County	11,148	1,696	8,453	1,451	1,010	106	na	na	308	33	na	na
Oklahoma County	95,721	12,163	75,432	10,152	10,125	1,227	2,245	29	2,014	145	3,784	362
Payne County	8,789	1,339	8,212	1,283	na	na	na	na	na	na	na	na
Pottawatomie County	11,228	1,390	9,891	1,156	na	na	na	na	na	na	205	26
Rogers County	13,877	1,471	11,982	1,325	na	na	na	na	811	90	108	0
Tulsa County	82,093	11,171	68,409	9,430	5,129	640	1,327	229	2,886	506	2,151	200
Wagoner County	11,210	1,040	9,715	959	na	na	na	na	475	0	246	0

Table C-2: Counties—Older Population by Race and Hispanic Origin—*Continued*

	Total Population		White, Non-Hispanic		Black, Alone		Asian, Alone		Multi-race		Hispanic	
	65 Years and Over	85 Years and Over	65 Years and Over	85 Years and Over	65 Years and Over	85 Years and Over	65 Years and Over	85 Years and Over	65 Years and Over	85 Years and Over	65 Years and Over	85 Years and Over
Oregon												
Benton County	12,373	2,159	11,650	2,045	na	na	na	na	na	na	na	na
Clackamas County	63,969	7,640	59,659	7,410	na	na	1,736	163	596	0	1,546	67
Deschutes County	30,318	3,703	29,814	3,695	na	na	na	na	na	na	na	na
Douglas County	25,170	3,680	23,894	3,498	na	na	na	na	na	na	na	na
Jackson County	42,200	5,864	39,806	5,848	na	na	na	na	na	na	1,209	0
Josephine County	20,667	2,077	19,540	2,069	na	na	na	na	na	na	na	na
Klamath County	12,304	1,962	11,559	1,909	na	na	na	na	na	na	272	9
Lane County	62,237	8,754	58,734	8,285	na	na	729	251	832	0	1,342	150
Linn County	20,720	2,558	19,620	2,456	na	na	na	na	na	na	na	na
Marion County	47,186	6,015	42,564	5,848	na	na	na	na	899	65	2,575	78
Multnomah County	92,620	13,285	78,261	11,793	4,037	471	5,738	566	955	223	2,599	111
Polk County	13,601	1,949	12,397	1,949	na	na	na	na	na	na	513	0
Umatilla County	11,533	1,448	9,649	1,284	na	na	na	na	na	na	1,406	144
Washington County	66,871	9,984	58,459	9,335	437	0	4,402	256	752	184	2,607	209
Yamhill County	15,549	2,235	14,761	2,134	na	na	na	na	na	na	556	89
Pennsylvania												
Adams County	18,272	1,894	18,014	1,894	na	na	na	na	na	na	206	0
Allegheny County	213,668	36,759	189,073	33,664	19,394	2,809	2,738	49	987	141	1,394	96
Armstrong County	13,655	2,470	13,442	2,413	na	na	na	na	na	na	na	na
Beaver County	33,446	4,883	31,589	4,812	1,459	38	na	na	na	na	na	na
Berks County	66,449	9,085	59,945	8,516	2,122	115	439	93	1,747	109	3,450	361
Blair County	24,112	4,143	23,909	4,104	na	na	na	na	na	na	na	na
Bucks County	104,583	14,754	97,303	14,317	2,224	240	3,137	103	261	76	1,636	18
Butler County	31,328	4,708	30,935	4,658	na	na	na	na	na	na	na	na
Cambria County	28,088	4,887	27,314	4,755	566	132	na	na	na	na	na	na
Carbon County	12,729	1,096	12,292	1,096	na	na	na	na	na	na	na	na
Centre County	19,873	2,417	19,159	2,417	na	na	na	na	na	na	na	na
Chester County	74,034	10,445	67,823	9,692	3,476	681	871	72	841	0	1,120	0
Clearfield County	15,340	2,219	15,147	2,219	na	na	na	na	na	na	na	na
Columbia County	11,417	1,390	11,283	1,390	na	na	na	na	na	na	na	na
Crawford County	15,919	1,617	15,631	1,582	na	na	na	na	na	na	na	na
Cumberland County	41,459	5,882	39,847	5,732	418	23	671	91	na	na	306	36
Dauphin County	40,893	6,315	34,438	5,534	5,161	781	594	0	199	0	664	0
Delaware County	85,104	13,937	70,880	12,662	10,084	1,008	2,741	163	162	44	1,344	60
Erie County	44,087	6,442	41,623	6,125	1,642	196	454	68	51	0	461	53
Fayette County	26,078	4,169	24,951	4,132	na	na	na	na	na	na	na	na
Franklin County	27,775	4,037	26,794	3,862	na	na	na	na	na	na	na	na
Indiana County	14,868	2,054	14,713	2,054	na	na	na	na	na	na	na	na
Lackawanna County	40,198	7,617	38,492	7,579	294	0	na	na	na	na	470	38
Lancaster County	87,648	13,077	82,175	12,284	1,519	212	1,100	84	181	62	2,535	435
Lawrence County	17,555	3,075	17,068	2,958	na	na	na	na	na	na	na	na
Lebanon County	24,696	3,161	23,815	3,065	na	na	na	na	na	na	628	0
Lehigh County	57,247	9,530	51,184	9,134	1,045	61	1,255	0	564	28	3,636	294
Luzerne County	60,268	10,955	58,289	10,888	762	11	na	na	na	na	1,114	56
Lycoming County	20,476	3,224	19,917	3,224	na	na	na	na	na	na	na	na
Mercer County	22,912	3,239	21,795	3,179	na	na	na	na	na	na	na	na
Monroe County	25,516	3,255	20,893	2,277	1,912	290	na	na	na	na	1,950	444
Montgomery County	133,682	22,393	117,213	21,128	8,924	962	5,650	226	349	0	1,675	122
Northampton County	52,208	9,327	48,024	8,274	924	266	839	0	778	270	2,091	625
Northumberland County	18,608	2,721	18,196	2,721	na	na	na	na	na	na	na	na
Philadelphia County	195,574	29,379	94,703	17,122	78,216	10,811	9,015	409	2,890	154	11,353	762
Schuylkill County	28,211	4,590	27,723	4,528	na	na	na	na	na	na	323	62
Somerset County	15,608	2,400	15,312	2,357	na	na	na	na	na	na	na	na
Washington County	39,617	6,144	37,975	5,809	1,133	223	na	na	na	na	na	na
Westmoreland County	74,350	12,542	72,399	12,377	1,047	65	na	na	na	na	na	na
York County	70,222	7,480	66,347	7,344	1,852	0	na	na	370	0	1,101	16
Rhode Island												
Kent County	29,210	5,675	27,621	5,356	na	na	na	na	na	na	na	na
Newport County	15,977	2,107	15,068	2,073	na	na	na	na	na	na	na	na
Providence County	89,958	16,025	76,066	14,907	3,931	279	2,022	157	1,461	236	6,392	465
Washington County	22,813	3,315	21,908	2,771	na	na	na	na	na	na	na	na
South Carolina												
Aiken County	28,801	2,883	23,199	2,626	4,852	91	na	na	na	na	na	na
Anderson County	32,602	3,732	28,471	3,656	3,781	4	na	na	na	na	na	na
Beaufort County	42,529	4,469	37,436	4,095	3,896	288	na	na	na	na	734	66
Berkeley County	24,245	2,376	17,675	1,801	5,001	495	914	74	na	na	105	0
Charleston County	55,147	6,772	39,619	4,843	14,033	1,929	na	na	na	na	626	0
Darlington County	11,134	856	7,533	442	3,540	414	na	na	na	na	na	na
Dorchester County	17,563	1,468	13,230	1,210	3,457	258	na	na	na	na	na	na
Florence County	20,638	2,292	13,631	1,788	6,766	477	na	na	na	na	na	na
Greenville County	69,257	8,484	57,867	7,369	8,090	653	1,007	189	528	141	1,699	86
Greenwood County	11,827	2,217	9,139	1,780	2,506	437	na	na	na	na	na	na
Horry County	61,159	4,919	55,441	4,493	4,169	401	na	na	na	na	733	25
Lancaster County	15,542	1,412	13,241	1,195	1,854	217	na	na	na	na	na	na
Laurens County	11,023	1,444	8,727	1,180	2,262	264	na	na	na	na	na	na
Lexington County	39,324	4,473	35,385	4,010	2,976	268	584	122	138	0	159	58

Table C-2: Counties—Older Population by Race and Hispanic Origin—*Continued*

	Total Population		White, Non-Hispanic		Black, Alone		Asian, Alone		Multi-race		Hispanic	
	65 Years and Over	85 Years and Over	65 Years and Over	85 Years and Over	65 Years and Over	85 Years and Over	65 Years and Over	85 Years and Over	65 Years and Over	85 Years and Over	65 Years and Over	85 Years and Over
South Carolina—Cont.												
Oconee County	15,950	1,271	15,148	986	na	na	na	na	na	na	na	na
Orangeburg County	15,222	2,064	7,341	774	7,684	1,205	na	na	na	na	na	na
Pickens County	18,410	1,674	17,085	1,612	na	na	na	na	na	na	na	na
Richland County	45,259	4,257	26,897	3,410	16,093	810	989	0	695	0	645	37
Spartanburg County	44,399	4,478	36,486	4,017	6,339	228	na	na	na	na	562	53
Sumter County	15,488	1,882	8,650	1,195	6,534	687	na	na	na	na	na	na
York County	32,506	2,592	26,621	2,216	4,254	376	na	na	312	0	670	0
South Dakota												
Minnehaha County	22,532	3,479	21,423	3,430	107	0	na	na	na	na	na	na
Pennington County	16,239	2,148	15,501	2,059	na	na	na	na	na	na	na	na
Tennessee												
Anderson County	14,394	1,514	13,579	1,514	na	na	na	na	na	na	na	na
Blount County	23,362	2,644	22,387	2,543	na	na	na	na	na	na	na	na
Bradley County	16,557	1,825	15,388	1,733	na	na	na	na	na	na	na	na
Davidson County	74,165	9,077	55,291	7,803	15,179	1,057	1,588	105	400	33	1,790	79
Greene County	13,573	1,475	13,271	1,475	na	na	na	na	na	na	na	na
Hamilton County	55,747	6,920	46,560	6,174	7,849	504	712	227	na	na	154	0
Knox County	65,185	8,430	59,221	7,608	3,849	588	872	169	538	65	760	0
Madison County	14,667	1,921	11,043	1,439	3,324	482	na	na	na	na	na	na
Maury County	12,658	880	11,283	765	na	na	na	na	na	na	na	na
Montgomery County	16,531	977	13,005	861	1,854	116	na	na	114	0	725	0
Putnam County	11,902	1,058	11,516	1,014	na	na	na	na	na	na	na	na
Robertson County	9,020	932	8,319	808	na	na	na	na	na	na	na	na
Rutherford County	28,048	2,435	24,421	2,261	2,101	115	850	36	na	na	505	23
Sevier County	16,976	1,475	16,340	1,475	na	na	na	na	na	na	na	na
Shelby County	108,912	14,641	60,913	9,839	43,651	4,802	1,525	0	1,325	0	1,238	0
Sullivan County	31,833	3,838	31,032	3,766	na	na	na	na	na	na	na	na
Sumner County	25,540	2,708	23,570	2,596	1,079	33	na	na	na	na	na	na
Washington County	21,323	2,126	20,444	1,950	na	na	na	na	na	na	na	na
Williamson County	23,299	2,806	22,008	2,586	na	na	455	81	na	na	na	na
Wilson County	17,938	1,269	16,832	1,148	794	103	na	na	na	na	na	na
Texas												
Angelina County	13,926	2,710	10,761	2,494	1,872	216	na	na	na	na	1,068	0
Bastrop County	9,679	1,222	8,271	1,102	na	na	na	na	na	na	864	87
Bell County	32,479	4,954	23,469	3,812	3,763	444	1,049	0	497	111	3,531	610
Bexar County	209,599	25,716	95,139	13,303	13,218	1,578	4,764	405	3,195	510	95,099	10,272
Bowie County	14,144	1,713	11,574	1,428	2,200	240	na	na	na	na	na	na
Brazoria County	36,573	2,847	25,989	2,579	2,575	61	1,884	0	na	na	5,284	207
Brazos County	17,275	1,878	13,374	1,422	1,770	119	199	0	na	na	1,885	337
Cameron County	52,048	7,032	14,545	1,604	na	na	na	na	na	na	36,859	5,306
Collin County	85,836	8,772	68,161	7,950	4,027	203	7,393	201	1,162	49	5,245	369
Comal County	21,355	1,850	18,171	1,591	na	na	na	na	na	na	2,723	259
Coryell County	6,308	700	5,468	604	358	72	na	na	na	na	374	0
Dallas County	243,900	28,715	143,532	21,597	47,708	3,642	11,507	673	2,847	0	38,343	2,711
Denton County	65,810	4,236	53,436	3,287	2,901	314	3,521	138	871	153	4,999	389
Ector County	14,664	1,798	9,039	974	na	na	na	na	na	na	4,848	679
El Paso County	93,883	10,849	19,122	2,460	2,168	103	1,060	99	891	36	71,380	8,123
Ellis County	18,787	1,649	15,454	1,424	1,380	197	na	na	na	na	1,796	0
Fort Bend County	64,750	6,004	31,847	3,149	10,112	982	12,042	1,356	1,133	0	9,411	517
Galveston County	40,306	4,078	28,917	2,797	4,581	505	1,254	0	869	0	4,844	746
Grayson County	20,866	2,202	19,075	2,202	na	na	na	na	na	na	410	0
Gregg County	17,781	2,227	14,169	2,104	2,414	123	na	na	na	na	1,079	0
Guadalupe County	19,064	1,947	13,448	1,348	871	64	na	na	na	na	4,234	535
Harris County	409,017	43,480	219,826	27,171	71,101	6,811	29,568	2,190	4,474	107	84,835	7,296
Harrison County	10,152	1,653	7,582	1,249	1,831	324	na	na	na	na	352	0
Hays County	18,519	1,507	14,142	1,180	na	na	na	na	na	na	3,554	327
Henderson County	16,737	1,600	15,100	1,514	na	na	na	na	na	na	754	0
Hidalgo County	86,414	10,077	22,877	3,032	na	na	na	na	na	na	62,263	7,045
Hunt County	13,915	1,293	12,098	1,129	655	88	na	na	na	na	817	0
Jefferson County	33,724	4,796	21,128	3,188	9,301	1,236	618	140	na	na	2,362	178
Johnson County	20,175	2,200	18,464	2,037	na	na	na	na	na	na	739	55
Kaufman County	12,804	1,082	10,936	1,082	1,236	0	na	na	na	na	353	0
Liberty County	9,949	892	8,339	708	na	na	na	na	na	na	780	44
Lubbock County	34,686	4,137	26,017	3,687	1,931	10	na	na	522	76	6,134	440
McLennan County	32,752	3,945	25,235	3,477	3,544	148	na	na	na	na	3,151	277
Midland County	15,092	2,205	11,448	1,732	694	115	na	na	na	na	2,495	358
Montgomery County	62,494	6,365	54,323	5,348	1,152	0	1,404	608	na	na	4,537	409
Nacogdoches County	8,511	1,127	6,955	970	1,340	81	na	na	na	na	101	0
Nueces County	46,078	5,264	20,971	2,804	1,529	94	617	36	na	na	22,728	2,330
Orange County	12,665	1,570	11,175	1,468	na	na	na	na	na	na	na	na
Parker County	18,412	2,151	17,082	2,008	na	na	na	na	na	na	994	143
Potter County	14,321	1,841	10,420	1,662	1,067	148	476	0	na	na	2,177	31
Randall County	17,425	2,221	15,971	2,221	na	na	na	na	na	na	817	0
Rockwall County	10,610	957	9,134	789	na	na	na	na	na	na	843	168
San Patricio County	9,365	1,009	5,431	955	na	na	na	na	na	na	3,792	19
Smith County	33,899	4,075	27,558	3,327	4,372	669	na	na	na	na	1,752	79

Table C-2: Counties—Older Population by Race and Hispanic Origin—*Continued*

	Total Population		White, Non-Hispanic		Black, Alone		Asian, Alone		Multi-race		Hispanic	
	65 Years and Over	85 Years and Over	65 Years and Over	85 Years and Over	65 Years and Over	85 Years and Over	65 Years and Over	85 Years and Over	65 Years and Over	85 Years and Over	65 Years and Over	85 Years and Over
Texas—Cont.												
Tarrant County	198,798	20,030	146,236	15,320	20,321	2,118	8,245	600	1,902	125	21,891	1,776
Taylor County	18,559	3,009	15,643	2,877	662	2	na	na	na	na	1,957	62
Tom Green County	17,225	2,460	12,623	1,732	na	na	na	na	na	na	3,403	639
Travis County	97,149	11,553	67,512	9,324	7,635	699	4,259	222	965	56	16,376	1,252
Victoria County	12,935	1,844	8,741	1,133	na	na	na	na	na	na	3,652	595
Walker County	7,295	943	6,351	803	na	na	na	na	na	na	na	na
Webb County	22,508	2,496	1,020	58	na	na	na	na	na	na	21,309	2,438
Wichita County	17,988	2,422	15,233	1,937	1,182	92	na	na	na	na	1,307	252
Williamson County	53,303	5,719	44,313	5,353	1,686	27	1,834	0	201	30	5,101	309
Utah												
Cache County	10,038	1,428	9,678	1,407	na	na	na	na	na	na	188	0
Davis County	30,044	2,858	27,822	2,636	na	na	522	0	284	0	1,268	222
Salt Lake County	105,306	12,889	92,464	11,239	876	304	3,259	502	304	53	7,109	791
Utah County	40,147	3,253	37,356	3,214	na	na	352	0	240	0	1,981	39
Washington County	30,065	3,932	28,410	3,847	na	na	na	na	na	na	711	39
Weber County	26,781	3,701	23,992	3,520	na	na	na	na	na	na	1,886	153
Vermont												
Chittenden County	21,038	2,863	20,401	2,737	na	na	na	na	na	na	na	na
Virginia												
Albemarle County	17,466	3,124	15,495	2,781	1,208	206	335	85	na	na	na	na
Arlington County	20,220	2,920	15,321	1,736	1,800	147	1,625	549	na	na	1,624	488
Augusta County	14,115	641	13,746	564	na	na	na	na	na	na	na	na
Bedford County	14,783	986	13,828	877	na	na	na	na	na	na	na	na
Chesterfield County	42,771	5,165	34,379	4,032	5,954	865	1,415	268	245	0	934	0
Fairfax County	130,422	15,957	90,927	12,834	8,258	756	20,580	1,587	1,933	96	8,687	684
Fauquier County	10,906	936	8,911	731	na	na	na	na	na	na	na	na
Frederick County	12,551	1,748	11,803	1,740	na	na	na	na	na	na	na	na
Hanover County	16,069	1,864	14,084	1,647	1,606	217	na	na	na	na	na	na
Henrico County	44,427	6,764	32,006	5,002	9,365	1,363	1,216	102	616	138	1,062	122
James City County	16,500	2,076	14,752	1,822	na	na	na	na	na	na	na	na
Loudoun County	28,721	3,002	20,609	2,556	1,724	58	3,845	167	451	0	1,948	168
Montgomery County	10,902	1,447	10,073	1,447	na	na	na	na	na	na	na	na
Prince William County	36,882	3,519	24,953	2,588	5,137	393	3,030	135	879	293	2,941	200
Roanoke County	18,197	2,873	17,343	2,795	na	na	na	na	na	na	na	na
Rockingham County	14,310	2,160	13,653	2,152	na	na	na	na	na	na	na	na
Spotsylvania County	15,592	1,788	13,051	1,321	1,955	350	na	na	na	na	304	69
Stafford County	12,875	1,468	10,310	952	1,431	366	na	na	221	0	462	150
York County	9,880	1,286	7,937	1,204	na	na	na	na	na	na	na	na
Washington												
Benton County	25,253	3,603	22,460	3,271	na	na	na	na	na	na	1,170	0
Chelan County	12,926	1,824	12,047	1,685	na	na	na	na	na	na	580	18
Clallam County	19,479	3,167	18,394	3,069	na	na	na	na	na	na	na	na
Clark County	62,019	6,200	56,721	5,894	na	na	1,949	116	528	84	1,503	0
Cowlitz County	18,254	2,370	17,524	2,341	na	na	na	na	na	na	232	29
Franklin County	6,911	668	5,240	668	na	na	na	na	na	na	1,321	0
Grant County	11,740	1,346	9,978	1,310	na	na	na	na	na	na	1,117	0
Grays Harbor County	13,420	1,384	12,415	1,370	na	na	na	na	na	na	na	na
Island County	18,182	1,979	16,615	1,904	na	na	na	na	na	na	na	na
King County	253,331	37,733	196,752	31,970	10,783	900	35,001	3,968	2,644	109	6,784	768
Kitsap County	40,852	4,994	36,493	4,818	na	na	2,047	176	815	0	806	0
Lewis County	14,747	2,331	14,124	2,254	na	na	na	na	na	na	na	na
Pierce County	105,354	14,243	88,256	12,133	4,603	405	7,386	1,394	1,474	91	2,694	252
Skagit County	22,864	2,862	21,008	2,762	na	na	na	na	na	na	1,143	0
Snohomish County	91,291	11,830	79,135	10,997	839	51	7,371	487	1,133	17	2,258	278
Spokane County	72,217	10,425	67,420	10,304	882	0	1,592	91	835	0	897	30
Thurston County	40,285	4,593	36,308	4,168	552	69	1,841	52	191	0	752	304
Whatcom County	31,955	4,198	29,511	4,144	na	na	na	na	na	na	765	0
Yakima County	31,605	3,816	24,883	3,416	na	na	na	na	287	0	5,111	206
West Virginia												
Berkeley County	14,531	1,335	13,374	1,238	na	na	na	na	na	na	na	na
Cabell County	16,577	2,605	15,678	2,493	na	na	na	na	na	na	na	na
Harrison County	12,288	1,771	11,919	1,771	na	na	na	na	na	na	na	na
Kanawha County	34,402	4,208	32,239	4,131	1,745	69	na	na	na	na	na	na
Monongalia County	11,012	1,367	10,652	1,331	na	na	na	na	na	na	na	na
Raleigh County	14,207	1,883	13,127	1,699	na	na	na	na	na	na	na	na
Wood County	16,073	1,895	15,710	1,853	na	na	na	na	na	na	na	na
Wisconsin												
Brown County	33,744	4,511	31,966	4,511	na	na	753	0	92	0	517	0
Dane County	61,507	8,977	57,857	8,758	1,055	27	1,270	94	663	98	793	98
Dodge County	14,291	1,716	14,158	1,716	na	na	na	na	na	na	na	na
Eau Claire County	14,040	2,146	13,832	2,146	na	na	na	na	na	na	na	na
Fond du Lac County	16,906	3,137	16,508	3,137	na	na	na	na	na	na	na	na
Jefferson County	12,488	1,512	12,350	1,512	na	na	na	na	na	na	na	na
Kenosha County	21,557	3,417	19,318	3,292	460	44	na	na	na	na	1,373	0
La Crosse County	17,198	2,555	16,970	2,555	na	na	na	na	na	na	na	na

Table C-2: Counties—Older Population by Race and Hispanic Origin—*Continued*

	Total Population		White, Non-Hispanic		Black, Alone		Asian, Alone		Multi-race		Hispanic	
	65 Years and Over	85 Years and Over	65 Years and Over	85 Years and Over	65 Years and Over	85 Years and Over	65 Years and Over	85 Years and Over	65 Years and Over	85 Years and Over	65 Years and Over	85 Years and Over
Wisconsin—Cont.												
Manitowoc County	15,034	2,685	14,655	2,617	na	na	na	na	na	na	na	na
Marathon County	21,426	3,386	21,143	3,254	na	na	215	132	na	na	na	na
Milwaukee County	115,947	20,818	88,137	17,057	19,505	2,102	2,173	540	531	136	5,333	1,006
Outagamie County	23,546	2,604	23,007	2,526	na	na	96	0	na	na	103	41
Ozaukee County	15,269	2,211	14,821	2,211	na	na	na	na	na	na	na	na
Portage County	10,224	1,110	10,039	1,110	na	na	na	na	na	na	na	na
Racine County	29,486	4,309	25,550	3,441	1,907	437	na	na	na	na	1,867	493
Rock County	24,180	4,347	22,928	4,090	497	29	na	na	na	na	503	105
Sheboygan County	18,520	2,826	18,091	2,801	na	na	na	na	na	na	121	0
St. Croix County	10,514	1,457	10,407	1,457	na	na	na	na	na	na	na	na
Walworth County	15,610	1,950	15,293	1,950	na	na	na	na	na	na	207	0
Washington County	20,984	3,071	20,527	2,915	na	na	na	na	na	na	na	na
Waukesha County	65,276	8,648	62,748	8,486	na	na	856	125	na	na	926	0
Winnebago County	25,191	3,315	24,332	3,135	na	na	na	na	na	na	191	20
Wood County	13,822	2,581	13,402	2,552	na	na	na	na	na	na	na	na
Wyoming												
Laramie County	13,897	1,343	11,914	1,150	na	na	na	na	na	na	1,146	103
Natrona County	9,975	1,147	9,703	1,147	na	na	na	na	na	na	na	na

Table C-3: Places—Older Population by Race and Hispanic Origin

	Total Population		White, Non-Hispanic		Black, Alone		Asian, Alone		Multi-race		Hispanic	
	65 Years and Over	85 Years and Over	65 Years and Over	85 Years and Over	65 Years and Over	85 Years and Over	65 Years and Over	85 Years and Over	65 Years and Over	85 Years and Over	65 Years and Over	85 Years and Over
Alabama												
Birmingham city	26,897	3,440	6,954	1,401	19,565	2,039	na	na	na	na	na	na
Dothan city	11,055	1,308	8,781	1,127	2,162	170	na	na	na	na	na	na
Hoover city	15,063	2,012	13,767	1,835	na	na	na	na	na	na	na	na
Huntsville city	29,432	3,803	22,790	2,950	5,479	762	na	na	na	na	452	0
Mobile city	28,402	4,536	16,218	2,881	11,655	1,618	na	na	na	na	na	na
Montgomery city	26,425	2,330	15,012	1,637	10,418	693	na	na	na	na	332	0
Tuscaloosa city	11,678	1,480	7,888	1,068	3,391	118	na	na	na	na	na	na
Alaska												
Anchorage municipality	26,906	2,469	19,621	1,649	1,812	137	2,400	440	559	0	932	42
Arizona												
Avondale city	6,002	85	3,004	85	439	0	na	na	na	na	2,080	0
Chandler city	24,905	2,099	17,820	1,633	1,174	0	1,875	25	417	31	3,735	410
Flagstaff city	6,705	511	4,909	384	na	na	na	na	na	na	1,059	127
Glendale city	25,288	3,143	19,597	2,854	845	0	1,442	52	378	0	3,051	237
Goodyear city	10,226	436	8,778	359	na	na	na	na	na	na	723	77
Mesa city	73,374	11,007	63,483	9,344	1,599	547	545	48	366	0	7,140	1,032
Peoria city	27,895	3,653	24,041	3,284	na	na	na	na	na	na	1,155	120
Phoenix city	150,296	16,922	109,289	14,333	6,719	909	4,382	300	1,754	236	27,641	1,162
Scottsdale city	50,844	7,809	48,137	7,488	na	na	813	175	na	na	941	41
Surprise city	25,319	2,444	22,377	2,329	na	na	na	na	na	na	1,729	36
Tempe city	18,549	2,282	14,998	2,085	na	na	503	0	na	na	2,083	118
Tucson city	70,275	9,461	47,542	7,292	2,363	0	1,605	389	567	0	17,689	1,780
Yuma city	13,333	940	8,618	724	na	na	na	na	na	na	4,092	164
Arkansas												
Fayetteville city	6,733	1,217	6,408	1,217	na	na	na	na	na	na	na	na
Fort Smith city	11,061	1,837	9,558	1,505	555	89	na	na	na	na	0	0
Jonesboro city	9,775	984	8,820	984	376	0	na	na	na	na	na	na
Little Rock city	26,160	3,883	18,706	3,124	6,511	677	na	na	na	na	na	na
North Little Rock city	8,783	871	6,167	604	2,595	267	na	na	na	na	na	na
Springdale city	7,398	929	5,989	929	na	na	na	na	na	na	570	0
California												
Alameda city	9,619	1,321	5,473	1,020	na	na	2,705	194	na	na	na	na
Alhambra city	12,235	1,202	2,117	329	na	na	6,378	773	na	na	3,256	100
Anaheim city	34,669	4,219	16,136	2,739	na	na	9,113	891	829	43	7,978	495
Antioch city	11,932	1,111	5,596	444	2,128	119	na	na	241	0	2,478	256
Bakersfield city	33,824	4,676	20,344	3,099	2,761	160	2,550	409	604	37	7,447	947
Baldwin Park city	8,110	728	na	na	na	na	2,428	200	na	na	4,715	342
Bellflower city	8,481	1,180	3,110	393	829	248	2,430	276	na	na	1,889	205
Berkeley city	15,015	1,911	10,753	1,440	2,014	159	1,340	267	426	45	477	45
Buena Park city	9,043	1,512	3,609	544	na	na	3,077	730	na	na	2,181	243
Burbank city	15,294	1,998	10,816	1,334	na	na	964	0	na	na	3,361	664
Camarillo city	12,444	1,736	9,583	1,311	na	na	na	na	na	na	1,202	174
Carlsbad city	16,869	2,549	13,308	2,335	na	na	na	na	na	na	1,811	95
Carson city	12,575	1,157	1,511	144	3,942	450	3,389	322	na	na	3,378	343
Chico city	10,403	1,874	9,690	1,753	na	na	na	na	na	na	379	79
Chino city	6,974	531	2,510	203	na	na	439	88	546	0	3,133	240
Chino Hills city	6,110	1,217	2,204	536	na	na	2,573	623	na	na	1,192	58
Chula Vista city	33,568	4,097	11,609	1,894	na	na	6,986	774	473	177	13,309	1,239
Citrus Heights city	14,073	1,974	12,679	1,815	na	na	na	na	na	na	339	0
Clovis city	10,583	1,538	7,882	1,232	na	na	575	70	na	na	1,222	33
Compton city	6,538	1,290	na	na	4,323	995	na	na	na	na	1,955	179
Concord city	16,893	2,543	11,580	1,748	na	na	1,661	78	na	na	2,643	519
Corona city	15,605	1,707	7,668	932	921	0	2,265	394	412	138	4,614	381
Costa Mesa city	10,517	1,527	8,287	1,307	na	na	1,064	111	na	na	932	109
Daly City city	17,945	1,934	2,981	543	na	na	12,035	1,020	na	na	2,013	371
Davis city	6,433	1,043	4,833	960	na	na	1,044	0	na	na	na	na
Downey city	12,619	1,923	4,082	690	na	na	1,785	194	na	na	6,219	1,013
El Cajon city	12,444	1,570	10,219	1,468	na	na	na	na	na	na	1,333	102
El Monte city	14,300	2,029	na	na	na	na	6,476	657	na	na	5,702	1,016
Elk Grove city	17,702	1,725	8,657	868	1,888	67	4,725	469	351	0	2,226	321
Escondido city	17,178	3,646	12,057	2,879	na	na	824	133	na	na	3,199	380
Fairfield city	13,189	1,800	6,261	1,201	1,633	42	2,931	400	372	0	1,976	157
Folsom city	10,645	1,587	7,967	1,578	na	na	1,026	0	na	na	920	9
Fontana city	16,304	1,361	3,245	379	1,585	217	2,132	282	692	0	9,106	483
Fremont city	25,269	3,400	11,319	2,011	na	na	11,616	952	570	105	1,014	288
Fresno city	55,505	7,297	28,984	4,501	3,107	55	6,613	1,106	950	206	15,416	1,480
Fullerton city	16,126	2,994	10,016	1,827	na	na	2,422	523	na	na	3,202	508
Garden Grove city	22,427	2,619	8,837	1,519	na	na	10,142	677	na	na	3,187	423
Glendale city	33,011	4,233	24,502	3,294	na	na	3,992	318	na	na	4,050	561
Hawthorne city	8,383	822	1,399	384	2,075	114	na	na	1,222	0	3,229	75
Hayward city	17,297	2,827	6,716	1,594	1,400	184	4,705	519	371	0	3,868	523
Hemet city	19,601	4,771	14,682	3,323	na	na	na	na	na	na	3,175	980
Hesperia city	8,420	1,067	5,886	726	na	na	na	na	na	na	2,024	341
Huntington Beach city	31,412	3,000	22,765	2,464	na	na	5,064	375	179	0	3,037	161
Indio city	12,082	1,150	7,611	611	na	na	na	na	na	na	4,110	492
Inglewood city	11,530	1,444	na	na	6,144	836	na	na	na	na	3,606	351

Table C-3: Places—Older Population by Race and Hispanic Origin—*Continued*

	Total Population		White, Non-Hispanic		Black, Alone		Asian, Alone		Multi-race		Hispanic	
	65 Years and Over	85 Years and Over	65 Years and Over	85 Years and Over	65 Years and Over	85 Years and Over	65 Years and Over	85 Years and Over	65 Years and Over	85 Years and Over	65 Years and Over	85 Years and Over
California—Cont.												
Irvine city	25,264	2,268	16,149	1,791	na	na	6,612	163	191	42	2,065	272
Jurupa Valley city	8,579	1,050	3,804	516	na	na	na	na	na	na	3,745	534
Laguna Niguel city	10,169	1,043	8,520	898	na	na	na	na	na	na	na	na
Lake Forest city	8,556	990	6,311	575	na	na	1,269	223	na	na	894	192
Lakewood city	10,332	741	6,258	659	na	na	1,455	0	na	na	1,740	82
Lancaster city	16,676	1,654	8,759	829	2,419	260	na	na	462	0	4,273	435
Livermore city	11,143	1,247	7,942	806	na	na	1,554	59	na	na	1,472	382
Long Beach city	47,506	5,359	24,859	3,409	4,991	187	7,318	565	1,229	52	9,244	1,124
Los Angeles city	455,128	66,466	204,006	36,393	50,520	7,133	73,807	9,651	8,014	1,020	120,850	12,827
Lynwood city	5,231	842	na	na	739	134	na	na	na	na	4,039	480
Manteca city	9,233	713	6,136	496	na	na	na	na	na	na	1,929	157
Menifee city	16,342	2,344	11,336	1,728	na	na	na	na	na	na	2,678	322
Merced city	9,253	1,218	5,271	700	na	na	915	272	na	na	2,490	246
Milpitas city	7,522	584	1,712	253	na	na	4,595	211	na	na	616	92
Mission Viejo city	15,883	2,766	13,166	2,403	na	na	910	57	na	na	1,269	306
Modesto city	28,774	4,152	20,181	3,115	998	404	2,016	113	904	77	4,781	520
Moreno Valley city	17,528	1,717	5,575	657	3,751	259	2,964	371	383	27	4,944	403
Mountain View city	8,321	1,273	5,542	626	na	na	1,813	324	na	na	855	208
Murrieta city	10,643	1,432	8,203	1,290	839	0	na	na	na	na	1,142	69
Napa city	11,133	2,129	8,946	1,852	na	na	na	na	na	na	1,325	241
Newport Beach city	18,500	3,143	16,045	2,930	na	na	na	na	na	na	na	na
Norwalk city	11,581	1,548	2,490	496	na	na	2,625	448	na	na	5,894	604
Oakland city	49,051	5,923	15,642	2,083	15,502	1,977	11,456	1,498	889	0	5,129	411
Oceanside city	27,682	3,391	20,586	2,757	na	na	1,892	158	104	0	4,282	476
Ontario city	13,332	1,708	4,602	837	663	6	848	112	na	na	6,997	710
Orange city	14,699	1,767	8,974	1,127	na	na	2,899	339	na	na	2,547	349
Oxnard city	19,138	2,417	7,052	1,067	na	na	2,681	254	na	na	8,853	1,096
Palmdale city	12,560	750	5,862	539	1,457	42	752	0	200	47	4,386	169
Palo Alto city	11,899	1,885	9,629	1,635	na	na	1,569	203	na	na	na	na
Pasadena city	19,189	2,491	10,567	1,464	2,102	153	3,054	440	na	na	3,103	335
Perris city	4,546	66	na	na	na	na	na	na	na	na	2,511	13
Pittsburg city	7,481	1,097	2,992	303	745	87	2,175	333	na	na	997	139
Pleasanton city	10,367	1,098	7,723	1,098	na	na	1,628	0	na	na	303	0
Pomona city	14,158	1,879	3,485	516	1,341	74	2,087	292	na	na	6,930	997
Rancho Cordova city	8,295	884	6,076	712	na	na	899	61	na	na	444	74
Rancho Cucamonga city	17,388	1,872	10,227	1,479	1,373	101	1,843	0	476	47	3,543	245
Redding city	16,762	2,935	15,911	2,875	na	na	na	na	na	na	389	60
Redlands city	8,868	1,023	5,613	757	na	na	na	na	na	na	2,273	248
Redondo Beach city	7,350	947	5,612	814	na	na	na	na	na	na	800	94
Redwood City city	10,409	1,287	6,603	1,092	na	na	1,085	0	na	na	1,764	63
Rialto city	8,635	1,135	2,579	386	1,743	321	na	na	na	na	3,793	400
Richmond city	12,367	1,324	3,663	746	3,844	245	2,860	205	na	na	1,396	171
Riverside city	30,344	4,544	17,219	2,647	1,374	134	1,761	414	800	130	9,132	1,293
Roseville city	21,745	3,491	17,981	3,108	na	na	1,852	281	na	na	1,286	102
Sacramento city	56,425	7,676	27,098	4,046	6,905	545	12,951	1,931	755	211	8,707	1,092
Salinas city	12,458	1,839	4,812	1,107	na	na	1,562	301	na	na	5,851	364
San Bernardino city	18,120	2,054	6,271	736	2,687	198	1,111	99	411	91	7,772	884
San Buenaventura (Ventura) city	17,456	3,122	14,570	3,059	na	na	na	na	na	na	1,999	63
San Clemente city	12,132	2,008	10,635	2,008	na	na	na	na	na	na	na	na
San Diego city	157,889	21,752	96,113	14,190	8,460	1,056	25,425	3,367	2,564	108	25,241	3,056
San Francisco city	122,906	18,704	48,942	6,951	7,050	901	53,895	8,751	2,125	208	11,144	1,863
San Jose city	118,855	13,722	51,229	6,428	2,576	150	41,290	5,171	2,560	301	21,172	1,748
San Leandro city	12,775	2,775	5,588	1,907	800	52	4,341	364	na	na	1,780	388
San Marcos city	11,153	1,230	7,823	1,031	na	na	1,088	108	na	na	1,405	91
San Mateo city	16,356	2,184	12,068	1,872	na	na	2,145	168	na	na	1,466	97
San Ramon city	7,824	396	4,386	262	na	na	2,873	105	na	na	na	na
Santa Ana city	27,767	3,737	7,075	1,183	na	na	6,068	1,105	na	na	14,071	1,449
Santa Barbara city	15,502	3,128	11,843	2,420	na	na	na	na	na	na	2,863	313
Santa Clara city	14,903	2,291	7,653	1,397	na	na	5,428	525	95	58	1,489	311
Santa Clarita city	20,680	2,851	14,314	2,077	na	na	2,335	161	380	0	3,227	572
Santa Maria city	9,259	1,626	4,344	1,100	na	na	na	na	na	na	3,913	328
Santa Monica city	16,165	2,461	12,748	2,229	na	na	na	na	na	na	2,176	122
Santa Rosa city	25,327	4,259	21,449	4,079	na	na	1,351	0	449	0	1,925	117
Simi Valley city	17,559	2,299	13,353	1,842	na	na	1,852	147	na	na	1,986	310
South Gate city	8,373	1,143	na	na	na	na	na	na	na	na	7,399	1,000
South San Francisco city	9,633	1,175	3,792	764	na	na	2,763	213	na	na	2,510	198
Stockton city	34,220	4,639	15,528	3,026	3,670	215	7,473	815	1,131	0	6,812	583
Sunnyvale city	16,587	2,095	8,909	1,417	na	na	5,892	389	na	na	1,434	289
Temecula city	12,439	1,091	8,148	872	na	na	941	0	na	na	2,798	178
Thousand Oaks city	22,071	3,759	19,077	3,538	na	na	727	69	na	na	1,457	85
Torrance city	25,099	5,004	15,598	3,116	na	na	6,046	1,410	771	130	1,913	347
Tracy city	5,816	528	3,217	429	na	na	924	10	na	na	1,321	89
Turlock city	9,352	1,505	7,221	1,172	na	na	na	na	na	na	1,744	143
Tustin city	7,666	844	3,846	730	na	na	1,742	114	na	na	959	0
Union City city	11,828	1,793	2,749	487	na	na	5,803	1,128	na	na	1,804	120
Upland city	11,441	1,314	7,894	1,002	na	na	na	na	na	na	1,746	94
Vacaville city	10,733	1,058	7,460	811	na	na	1,031	0	321	0	927	247

Table C-3: Places—Older Population by Race and Hispanic Origin—*Continued*

	Total Population		White, Non-Hispanic		Black, Alone		Asian, Alone		Multi-race		Hispanic	
	65 Years and Over	85 Years and Over	65 Years and Over	85 Years and Over	65 Years and Over	85 Years and Over	65 Years and Over	85 Years and Over	65 Years and Over	85 Years and Over	65 Years and Over	85 Years and Over
California—Cont.												
Vallejo city	16,929	1,802	6,882	1,204	2,820	267	4,994	251	468	80	1,912	80
Victorville city	10,085	588	3,692	365	1,780	0	na	na	na	na	3,528	34
Visalia city	16,303	2,466	11,837	2,291	na	na	na	na	na	na	3,374	84
Vista city	7,915	917	5,685	811	na	na	na	na	na	na	1,846	66
Walnut Creek city	19,791	4,300	16,832	4,156	na	na	1,324	100	na	na	na	na
West Covina city	15,430	2,046	3,888	828	na	na	5,981	617	na	na	4,109	529
Westminster city	16,388	1,888	6,451	656	na	na	8,428	1,033	na	na	1,083	88
Whittier city	10,996	1,331	4,675	702	na	na	na	na	na	na	4,968	253
Yorba Linda city	10,198	907	8,020	700	na	na	949	115	na	na	803	92
Yuba City city	8,590	712	5,452	494	na	na	1,699	60	na	na	442	112
Colorado												
Arvada city	16,182	2,075	14,724	1,844	na	na	na	na	na	na	1,052	180
Aurora city	36,720	4,649	27,562	4,397	3,773	235	1,643	0	391	0	3,163	17
Boulder city	10,674	1,536	9,965	1,493	na	na	na	na	na	na	467	0
Centennial city	16,073	1,472	14,201	1,211	na	na	na	na	na	na	427	0
Colorado Springs city	55,830	7,273	47,414	6,761	1,236	147	1,678	110	883	105	4,477	150
Denver city	72,266	10,549	48,538	8,128	7,622	862	2,386	251	1,007	0	12,603	1,308
Fort Collins city	14,455	1,924	13,157	1,803	na	na	na	na	na	na	822	38
Greeley city	12,632	1,455	10,177	1,257	na	na	na	na	na	na	2,304	157
Lakewood city	23,200	3,995	19,936	3,692	na	na	na	na	na	na	2,185	303
Longmont city	11,832	1,778	10,380	1,629	na	na	na	na	na	na	1,152	149
Loveland city	14,439	1,861	13,535	1,813	na	na	na	na	na	na	na	na
Pueblo city	18,118	2,697	11,027	1,890	na	na	na	na	na	na	6,239	483
Thornton city	11,035	1,140	9,004	1,140	na	na	na	na	na	na	1,862	0
Westminster city	14,592	1,077	11,595	1,035	na	na	na	na	na	na	1,574	42
Connecticut												
Bridgeport city	14,575	2,093	6,406	1,490	4,230	560	na	na	na	na	3,687	25
Danbury city	10,659	1,272	8,488	1,172	na	na	na	na	na	na	895	0
Hartford city	11,160	1,738	2,580	640	4,179	548	na	na	359	0	4,194	505
New Britain city	7,898	2,164	5,720	2,045	611	0	na	na	na	na	1,245	119
New Haven city	13,338	1,463	6,750	1,100	5,231	333	na	na	na	na	1,091	30
Norwalk city	12,926	1,540	9,825	1,157	2,003	296	na	na	na	na	883	87
Stamford city	16,521	2,342	12,044	1,833	1,754	509	847	0	na	na	1,754	0
Waterbury city	12,970	2,365	9,686	1,908	1,354	229	na	na	na	na	1,893	228
Delaware												
Wilmington city	9,181	711	4,345	516	4,171	195	na	na	na	na	362	0
District of Columbia												
Washington city	74,465	10,144	24,433	3,106	45,190	6,615	1,607	291	559	23	3,598	207
Florida												
Boca Raton city	17,798	2,705	16,395	2,620	na	na	na	na	na	na	na	na
Boynton Beach city	14,940	3,236	11,019	2,837	1,402	65	na	na	na	na	2,373	334
Cape Coral city	38,214	5,367	34,303	5,018	na	na	na	na	na	na	2,608	349
Clearwater city	23,304	2,903	21,014	2,751	1,229	0	na	na	na	na	799	99
Coral Springs city	13,479	1,455	9,440	1,039	2,125	327	na	na	na	na	1,405	89
Deerfield Beach city	15,824	3,152	12,529	2,473	1,386	164	na	na	na	na	1,647	366
Delray Beach city	16,140	3,550	12,277	3,096	2,821	161	na	na	na	na	na	na
Deltona city	12,123	1,025	8,052	670	980	290	na	na	na	na	2,819	145
Fort Lauderdale city	31,632	4,082	21,517	2,907	5,239	688	na	na	na	na	3,959	483
Fort Myers city	11,842	1,367	9,288	1,207	1,767	129	na	na	na	na	886	0
Gainesville city	13,043	2,188	9,774	1,706	2,581	378	na	na	na	na	na	na
Hialeah city	42,948	6,469	868	347	na	na	na	na	na	na	41,753	6,122
Hollywood city	23,942	3,212	15,089	2,682	2,452	0	na	na	na	na	5,168	435
Homestead city	5,590	677	na	na	na	na	na	na	na	na	3,424	451
Jacksonville city	107,837	13,892	74,838	9,907	23,101	2,791	4,469	422	702	129	4,663	700
Kissimmee city	6,670	1,305	2,431	326	na	na	na	na	na	na	3,346	825
Lakeland city	20,960	2,597	16,580	2,394	2,283	168	na	na	na	na	1,560	35
Largo city	20,582	2,608	19,208	2,456	na	na	na	na	na	na	716	152
Lauderhill city	11,822	1,444	na	na	6,098	399	na	na	na	na	na	na
Melbourne city	17,488	1,960	14,659	1,648	na	na	na	na	na	na	988	121
Miami Beach city	15,254	2,347	7,631	1,266	na	na	na	na	na	na	7,295	1,081
Miami city	68,412	11,586	5,488	878	10,340	1,591	na	na	na	na	53,771	9,631
Miami Gardens city	14,569	1,794	na	na	10,843	1,415	na	na	na	na	3,742	174
Miramar city	13,811	1,585	na	na	4,807	1,050	na	na	na	na	4,972	222
Orlando city	26,234	3,446	13,945	2,250	5,776	565	na	na	na	na	5,762	723
Palm Bay city	17,667	2,313	13,333	1,825	2,683	360	na	na	na	na	1,576	128
Palm Coast city	23,381	3,424	18,222	2,516	na	na	na	na	na	na	1,565	352
Pembroke Pines city	26,703	4,641	12,315	3,226	4,813	541	769	0	na	na	9,048	874
Plantation city	12,276	1,569	9,350	1,425	1,184	87	na	na	na	na	1,516	57
Pompano Beach city	22,233	5,114	17,325	4,896	2,984	30	na	na	na	na	1,502	92
Port St. Lucie city	35,685	5,333	27,683	3,900	4,170	788	na	na	na	na	3,364	645
St. Petersburg city	43,252	6,335	33,380	5,291	6,742	755	na	na	na	na	1,108	0
Sunrise city	13,310	2,421	6,970	1,796	3,366	371	na	na	na	na	2,424	185
Tallahassee city	16,884	2,408	12,058	2,104	4,243	304	395	0	na	na	136	0
Tampa city	43,961	6,116	24,377	3,999	8,663	928	1,604	153	264	0	9,462	1,075
West Palm Beach city	17,866	2,165	10,664	1,461	3,766	397	na	na	na	na	2,814	279

Table C-3: Places—Older Population by Race and Hispanic Origin—*Continued*

	Total Population		White, Non-Hispanic		Black, Alone		Asian, Alone		Multi-race		Hispanic	
	65 Years and Over	85 Years and Over	65 Years and Over	85 Years and Over	65 Years and Over	85 Years and Over	65 Years and Over	85 Years and Over	65 Years and Over	85 Years and Over	65 Years and Over	85 Years and Over
Florida—Cont.												
Weston city	7,040	1,272	4,325	883	na	na	na	na	na	na	2,399	389
Georgia												
Albany city	9,515	1,513	4,460	906	4,831	607	na	na	na	na	na	na
Athens-Clarke County unified govt (bal)	11,791	1,798	8,267	1,414	2,776	384	na	na	na	na	na	na
Atlanta city	51,783	5,915	18,569	2,530	31,642	3,291	547	0	286	32	697	62
Augusta-Richmond County consolidated govt (bal)	24,669	3,285	12,657	1,907	10,607	868	na	na	na	na	na	na
Columbus city	23,945	2,973	13,952	2,420	8,993	514	na	na	na	na	327	39
Johns Creek city	6,042	919	5,290	811	na	na	295	0	na	na	na	na
Macon-Bibb County	21,544	3,037	12,710	2,314	8,243	723	na	na	na	na	na	na
Roswell city	10,700	2,360	9,369	1,758	na	na	na	na	na	na	na	na
Sandy Springs city	13,767	2,394	12,202	2,310	874	84	na	na	na	na	na	na
Savannah city	19,380	3,196	9,764	2,017	9,119	1,096	na	na	na	na	na	na
Warner Robins city	7,209	721	5,694	583	1,403	138	na	na	na	na	na	na
Hawaii												
Urban Honolulu CDP	66,002	13,377	10,839	1,744	na	na	46,342	10,710	4,631	493	949	111
Idaho												
Boise City city	26,987	4,175	24,498	4,149	na	na	488	0	na	na	804	0
Meridian city	10,068	899	9,861	857	na	na	na	na	na	na	na	na
Nampa city	10,088	1,183	9,185	1,183	na	na	na	na	na	na	903	0
Illinois												
Aurora city	15,369	2,076	8,927	1,870	2,251	59	1,359	43	na	na	2,731	104
Bloomington city	9,031	1,612	8,077	1,612	373	0	na	na	na	na	na	na
Champaign city	7,732	832	6,014	799	922	33	697	0	na	na	na	na
Chicago city	309,874	39,534	123,111	18,054	114,279	14,854	16,761	1,429	3,281	349	53,403	5,181
Decatur city	12,346	1,480	10,794	1,447	1,344	33	na	na	na	na	na	na
Elgin city	14,203	1,228	10,043	933	na	na	1,029	0	na	na	2,870	295
Evanston city	10,067	1,797	7,429	1,351	1,841	272	na	na	na	na	na	na
Joliet city	12,951	1,946	8,956	1,631	2,107	240	na	na	na	na	1,545	75
Naperville city	14,553	1,549	12,291	1,506	na	na	1,517	43	na	na	101	0
Peoria city	15,847	2,276	13,055	2,186	2,079	90	na	na	na	na	259	0
Rockford city	22,275	3,806	18,039	3,293	2,542	138	na	na	na	na	1,073	83
Springfield city	18,896	2,510	16,276	2,310	1,778	155	na	na	na	na	na	na
Waukegan city	8,417	1,223	4,923	1,183	1,264	40	na	na	na	na	1,823	0
Indiana												
Bloomington city	5,853	1,058	5,661	1,014	na	na	na	na	na	na	na	na
Carmel city	13,390	1,766	12,625	1,691	na	na	554	0	na	na	na	na
Evansville city	18,824	3,699	16,762	3,348	1,493	351	na	na	na	na	na	na
Fort Wayne city	31,931	4,569	27,729	4,317	2,835	150	599	0	139	0	559	102
Gary city	11,909	2,077	2,181	373	9,219	1,655	na	na	na	na	na	na
Hammond city	8,129	1,153	5,476	790	937	8	na	na	na	na	1,633	315
Indianapolis city (bal)	94,476	12,980	69,239	10,061	20,586	2,613	1,499	0	792	30	1,933	130
Lafayette city	8,951	1,044	7,763	959	na	na	na	na	na	na	na	na
Muncie city	10,772	1,818	9,589	1,628	816	190	na	na	na	na	na	na
South Bend city	12,990	2,338	10,134	1,800	2,297	402	na	na	na	na	155	45
Iowa												
Cedar Rapids city	17,136	2,554	16,687	2,508	na	na	na	na	na	na	na	na
Davenport city	12,702	1,959	11,291	1,830	810	129	na	na	na	na	432	0
Des Moines city	23,627	3,786	20,255	3,483	1,496	152	814	151	na	na	958	0
Iowa City city	6,150	1,161	5,798	1,155	na	na	na	na	na	na	na	na
Sioux City city	11,202	1,473	10,550	1,463	na	na	na	na	na	na	481	0
Waterloo city	9,874	1,314	8,799	1,175	895	139	na	na	na	na	na	na
Kansas												
Kansas City city	16,791	2,497	9,896	1,828	4,490	369	395	0	na	na	1,538	257
Lawrence city	8,606	1,328	7,547	1,328	na	na	na	na	na	na	na	na
Olathe city	11,970	1,466	11,196	1,306	468	160	na	na	na	na	98	0
Overland Park city	26,969	4,144	24,989	3,999	371	0	952	145	na	na	379	0
Topeka city	18,625	3,334	16,598	2,943	1,114	240	na	na	219	0	528	107
Wichita city	49,811	6,114	40,931	5,371	3,965	272	1,760	47	569	89	2,320	229
Kentucky												
Lexington-Fayette urban county	35,972	5,596	30,919	5,232	3,945	290	652	0	280	0	102	0
Louisville/Jefferson County metro govt (bal)	81,870	11,987	66,380	10,257	13,150	1,499	856	136	567	55	965	40
Louisiana												
Baton Rouge city	29,500	4,016	16,363	2,875	12,178	910	na	na	na	na	284	33
Bossier City city	8,844	1,345	7,235	1,200	1,234	98	na	na	na	na	na	na
Kenner city	12,129	1,103	8,460	885	1,223	206	na	na	na	na	2,155	12
Lafayette city	14,463	1,558	11,060	1,251	2,734	255	na	na	na	na	na	na
Lake Charles city	12,692	1,808	7,820	1,366	4,203	432	na	na	na	na	na	na
New Orleans city	46,481	5,761	16,682	2,537	26,851	2,754	934	177	161	34	1,647	272
Shreveport city	30,000	4,232	17,210	3,183	11,871	892	na	na	na	na	na	na
Maine												
Portland city	7,924	1,267	7,397	1,267	na	na	na	na	na	na	na	na

Table C-3: Places—Older Population by Race and Hispanic Origin—*Continued*

	Total Population		White, Non-Hispanic		Black, Alone		Asian, Alone		Multi-race		Hispanic	
	65 Years and Over	85 Years and Over	65 Years and Over	85 Years and Over	65 Years and Over	85 Years and Over	65 Years and Over	85 Years and Over	65 Years and Over	85 Years and Over	65 Years and Over	85 Years and Over
Maryland												
Baltimore city	76,707	8,753	26,426	3,877	47,248	4,761	1,368	0	739	32	993	88
Frederick city	7,802	929	6,403	821	863	108	na	na	na	na	na	na
Gaithersburg city	7,819	1,155	4,709	1,046	169	0	1,451	81	na	na	1,162	28
Rockville city	10,613	1,830	7,102	1,244	na	na	1,938	196	na	na	492	83
Massachusetts												
Boston city	67,857	9,733	35,890	6,175	17,955	1,911	6,421	739	1,394	278	7,028	752
Brockton city	11,872	1,958	7,836	1,508	3,211	443	na	na	na	na	579	7
Cambridge city	10,703	1,426	8,145	1,268	1,174	126	630	0	na	na	637	32
Fall River city	14,379	2,250	13,242	2,197	na	na	na	na	na	na	238	0
Lawrence city	6,670	1,015	2,988	731	na	na	na	na	na	na	3,424	259
Lowell city	11,569	2,408	8,841	2,011	na	na	1,074	203	na	na	1,325	146
Lynn city	10,329	2,004	6,626	1,523	475	0	759	0	na	na	2,506	481
New Bedford city	12,283	2,597	10,018	2,418	670	0	na	na	na	na	679	0
Newton city	16,501	2,693	13,317	2,640	na	na	1,896	27	na	na	na	na
Quincy city	14,295	1,849	12,206	1,772	na	na	1,616	77	na	na	na	na
Somerville city	7,829	1,055	6,411	994	na	na	na	na	na	na	na	na
Springfield city	16,792	2,466	10,095	1,676	3,635	602	na	na	na	na	2,811	102
Worcester city	19,664	4,363	16,063	3,929	1,037	25	763	90	274	236	1,484	40
Michigan												
Ann Arbor city	12,203	2,103	9,773	1,929	877	127	1,163	47	na	na	372	0
Dearborn city	12,618	2,156	11,232	1,935	na	na	na	na	na	na	na	na
Detroit city	85,166	10,927	10,776	1,716	70,942	8,979	450	0	1,095	103	1,535	76
Farmington Hills city	17,713	2,013	13,725	1,822	2,345	191	1,031	0	na	na	na	na
Flint city	11,588	1,529	4,762	1,123	6,138	355	na	na	na	na	na	na
Grand Rapids city	22,351	5,643	17,696	4,941	3,472	555	na	na	na	na	592	114
Kalamazoo city	7,437	1,280	5,385	1,224	1,577	50	na	na	na	na	na	na
Lansing city	13,160	1,690	9,437	1,462	2,211	184	na	na	488	0	884	44
Livonia city	17,322	2,038	15,777	1,809	na	na	na	na	na	na	na	na
Rochester Hills city	12,074	2,204	10,836	2,112	na	na	613	0	na	na	na	na
Southfield city	13,608	1,570	4,653	780	8,336	690	na	na	na	na	na	na
Sterling Heights city	21,835	3,174	20,495	2,975	na	na	846	117	na	na	na	na
Troy city	13,147	1,490	11,560	1,406	na	na	1,014	0	na	na	na	na
Warren city	19,648	3,886	17,491	3,786	1,264	20	669	80	na	na	na	na
Westland city	14,419	2,434	12,280	2,305	1,580	129	na	na	na	na	na	na
Wyoming city	7,675	1,436	6,841	1,297	na	na	na	na	na	na	706	139
Minnesota												
Bloomington city	16,884	3,106	15,648	3,062	na	na	na	na	na	na	na	na
Brooklyn Park city	7,704	662	5,896	552	1,148	110	523	0	na	na	na	na
Duluth city	13,031	2,648	12,628	2,648	na	na	na	na	na	na	na	na
Eagan city	7,732	885	6,822	592	na	na	616	230	na	na	na	na
Maple Grove city	7,557	797	7,022	797	na	na	na	na	na	na	na	na
Minneapolis city	33,790	4,272	26,301	3,692	5,229	373	995	169	431	0	614	0
Plymouth city	11,581	1,612	10,626	1,452	na	na	373	102	na	na	na	na
Rochester city	16,110	2,516	15,147	2,516	na	na	716	0	na	na	na	na
St. Cloud city	7,652	1,228	7,323	1,228	102	0	na	na	na	na	na	na
St. Paul city	26,550	4,634	21,008	3,824	1,726	305	2,384	263	584	43	834	199
Woodbury city	7,465	809	6,855	809	na	na	na	na	na	na	na	na
Mississippi												
Gulfport city	10,039	909	7,718	670	2,057	185	na	na	na	na	na	na
Jackson city	19,917	3,281	7,117	1,537	12,378	1,652	na	na	na	na	na	na
Missouri												
Columbia city	10,872	1,470	9,760	1,432	827	0	na	na	na	na	na	na
Independence city	20,505	1,584	19,109	1,584	na	na	na	na	na	na	742	0
Kansas City city	56,470	7,536	37,207	5,956	15,844	1,371	638	70	373	72	2,427	0
Lee's Summit city	13,248	1,984	12,213	1,984	na	na	na	na	na	na	na	na
O'Fallon city	8,590	1,236	7,942	1,212	na	na	na	na	na	na	na	na
Springfield city	25,710	4,629	24,328	4,305	631	54	na	na	na	na	na	na
St. Charles city	10,132	1,325	9,567	1,325	na	na	na	na	na	na	na	na
St. Joseph city	10,575	1,693	10,039	1,657	na	na	na	na	na	na	na	na
St. Louis city	36,162	5,001	17,399	2,555	16,875	2,402	1,062	44	205	0	412	0
Montana												
Billings city	15,956	2,496	15,243	2,381	na	na	na	na	na	na	na	na
Missoula city	8,420	2,085	8,269	2,040	na	na	na	na	na	na	na	na
Nebraska												
Lincoln city	32,090	4,556	30,211	4,410	279	0	662	0	na	na	728	107
Omaha city	53,390	8,813	45,238	7,314	4,942	689	850	355	355	25	1,865	430
Nevada												
Henderson city	49,751	4,914	39,995	3,873	2,139	55	3,941	286	512	65	3,071	635
Las Vegas city	79,751	7,160	53,100	5,693	8,140	349	7,369	364	1,135	34	9,939	656
North Las Vegas city	24,712	1,494	12,370	395	4,925	696	2,867	136	505	0	4,076	336
Reno city	31,675	3,516	25,702	3,016	709	101	1,908	125	478	36	2,721	274
Sparks city	14,039	1,946	11,981	1,537	na	na	na	na	na	na	940	283

Table C-3: Places—Older Population by Race and Hispanic Origin—*Continued*

	Total Population		White, Non-Hispanic		Black, Alone		Asian, Alone		Multi-race		Hispanic	
	65 Years and Over	85 Years and Over	65 Years and Over	85 Years and Over	65 Years and Over	85 Years and Over	65 Years and Over	85 Years and Over	65 Years and Over	85 Years and Over	65 Years and Over	85 Years and Over
New Hampshire												
Manchester city	14,073	2,484	12,685	2,450	na	na	na	na	na	na	626	34
Nashua city	11,430	1,540	10,913	1,540	na	na	na	na	na	na	0	0
New Jersey												
Bayonne city	7,910	1,118	5,817	990	na	na	na	na	na	na	389	0
Camden city	7,619	673	na	na	3,670	322	na	na	na	na	2,851	192
Clifton city	9,438	1,565	7,296	1,317	na	na	1,137	177	na	na	981	71
East Orange city	8,621	1,285	na	na	7,756	882	na	na	na	na	na	na
Elizabeth city	11,545	1,134	3,130	271	1,895	200	na	na	na	na	6,272	597
Jersey City city	24,928	2,310	7,309	1,556	6,141	41	4,684	103	na	na	6,875	610
Newark city	23,518	2,663	3,168	399	12,789	1,601	na	na	na	na	6,943	636
Passaic city	6,034	865	1,490	608	na	na	na	na	na	na	3,465	78
Paterson city	16,361	2,400	3,573	1,025	4,766	414	na	na	na	na	7,966	899
Trenton city	8,747	903	2,579	556	4,813	297	na	na	na	na	1,293	0
Union City city	7,621	1,079	1,423	381	na	na	na	na	na	na	6,058	698
New Mexico												
Albuquerque city	74,936	8,503	46,817	6,090	1,836	160	1,636	93	1,565	106	23,105	2,153
Las Cruces city	14,506	2,179	9,290	1,751	na	na	na	na	na	na	4,656	428
Rio Rancho city	11,832	1,595	8,765	1,338	na	na	na	na	na	na	2,048	201
Santa Fe city	14,310	1,400	10,046	1,025	na	na	na	na	na	na	3,827	352
New York												
Albany city	12,346	2,242	8,575	2,015	2,634	66	na	na	na	na	627	0
Buffalo city	33,059	4,006	19,119	2,851	11,149	1,017	788	0	431	0	1,527	138
Mount Vernon city	9,606	1,566	3,511	992	5,469	568	na	na	na	na	343	0
New Rochelle city	11,070	2,075	7,127	1,817	2,183	200	na	na	na	na	799	58
New York city	1,098,393	157,672	480,720	84,840	259,798	34,700	128,413	13,059	21,704	1,474	231,898	26,296
Rochester city	22,664	2,542	12,629	1,693	7,497	557	530	0	165	0	1,860	292
Schenectady city	8,751	1,938	7,489	1,503	1,106	410	na	na	na	na	na	na
Syracuse city	18,153	3,895	13,071	3,137	3,538	547	805	132	207	59	497	40
Yonkers city	33,294	5,508	22,118	4,594	4,058	281	2,155	197	na	na	5,105	490
North Carolina												
Asheville city	15,727	2,273	13,586	1,958	1,533	81	na	na	na	na	na	na
Charlotte city	75,902	9,207	47,375	7,787	22,155	1,042	2,522	97	876	30	3,353	251
Concord city	9,684	1,571	8,255	1,158	1,279	413	na	na	na	na	80	0
Durham city	26,993	3,992	15,214	2,536	10,235	1,395	933	0	na	na	442	61
Fayetteville city	23,862	2,173	12,743	1,305	8,759	794	1,174	12	410	0	844	62
Gastonia city	11,703	1,644	9,078	1,545	2,159	99	na	na	na	na	na	na
Greensboro city	35,286	4,534	23,307	3,354	10,621	1,042	957	138	na	na	277	0
Greenville city	9,292	1,629	6,049	808	3,016	821	na	na	na	na	na	na
High Point city	13,385	1,139	9,776	870	2,571	177	na	na	na	na	574	55
Jacksonville city	4,110	311	2,395	176	1,598	97	na	na	na	na	na	na
Raleigh city	41,216	4,737	28,984	3,938	9,215	759	1,417	40	613	0	964	0
Wilmington city	15,529	3,209	12,744	2,690	2,542	519	na	na	na	na	na	na
Winston-Salem city	32,080	5,257	21,742	4,487	9,315	770	na	na	na	na	790	0
North Dakota												
Bismarck city	10,762	2,203	10,567	2,203	na	na	na	na	na	na	na	na
Fargo city	11,939	2,401	11,783	2,344	na	na	na	na	na	na	na	na
Ohio												
Akron city	26,314	4,247	18,909	3,767	6,446	468	na	na	na	na	na	na
Canton city	9,468	1,660	7,499	1,318	1,641	193	na	na	na	na	na	na
Cincinnati city	34,872	5,989	20,960	4,229	13,219	1,569	na	na	195	67	296	0
Cleveland city	47,362	7,229	18,569	3,021	25,429	4,073	538	0	614	89	2,335	60
Columbus city	76,657	10,554	51,817	8,177	20,043	2,078	2,785	66	484	42	1,365	191
Dayton city	16,179	1,827	8,706	1,162	7,138	665	na	na	na	na	na	na
Lorain city	9,809	1,459	6,987	1,289	1,210	145	na	na	na	na	1,544	25
Parma city	14,266	2,303	13,711	2,177	na	na	na	na	na	na	na	na
Toledo city	37,846	6,842	28,416	5,813	7,608	673	na	na	476	172	1,353	184
Youngstown city	10,860	2,602	6,692	1,842	3,548	704	na	na	na	na	389	56
Oklahoma												
Broken Arrow city	11,644	1,054	10,162	870	na	na	na	na	513	0	282	0
Edmond city	10,894	1,284	10,152	1,236	na	na	na	na	229	0	na	na
Lawton city	10,103	936	7,475	856	1,307	80	na	na	325	0	274	0
Norman city	13,781	1,439	12,691	1,368	na	na	na	na	358	0	59	0
Oklahoma City city	75,118	9,403	57,528	7,474	8,037	1,081	2,509	99	1,467	145	3,645	362
Tulsa city	53,425	7,925	42,123	6,370	5,474	668	1,020	145	1,692	450	1,580	200
Oregon												
Beaverton city	10,175	1,427	8,883	1,366	na	na	575	61	na	na	498	0
Bend city	12,154	2,014	11,762	2,014	na	na	na	na	na	na	na	na
Eugene city	21,967	4,067	20,625	3,939	na	na	na	na	240	0	305	0
Gresham city	14,968	2,195	13,676	1,869	na	na	na	na	na	na	267	74
Hillsboro city	10,448	1,169	9,377	1,070	na	na	na	na	na	na	237	0
Medford city	14,200	2,235	13,502	2,235	na	na	na	na	na	na	466	0
Portland city	71,073	10,290	58,458	9,124	3,702	260	4,940	525	829	223	2,160	37
Salem city	22,415	3,574	20,067	3,485	na	na	na	na	496	46	1,241	0
Pennsylvania												
Allentown city	14,455	2,863	11,207	2,540	636	39	na	na	na	na	2,272	243

Table C-3: Places—Older Population by Race and Hispanic Origin—*Continued*

	Total Population		White, Non-Hispanic		Black, Alone		Asian, Alone		Multi-race		Hispanic	
	65 Years and Over	85 Years and Over	65 Years and Over	85 Years and Over	65 Years and Over	85 Years and Over	65 Years and Over	85 Years and Over	65 Years and Over	85 Years and Over	65 Years and Over	85 Years and Over
Pennsylvania—Cont.												
Bethlehem city	11,760	2,238	9,390	1,772	na	na	na	na	na	na	1,810	312
Erie city	13,807	2,362	11,919	2,113	1,463	196	na	na	na	na	461	53
Philadelphia city	195,574	29,379	94,703	17,122	78,216	10,811	9,015	409	2,890	154	11,353	762
Pittsburgh city	41,145	8,574	31,183	7,232	8,898	1,305	579	0	196	37	304	0
Reading city	9,265	1,250	4,711	951	1,622	68	na	na	1,339	109	2,827	231
Scranton city	13,797	2,692	12,561	2,692	246	0	na	na	na	na	343	0
Rhode Island												
Cranston city	14,551	3,014	12,992	2,881	na	na	na	na	na	na	na	na
Pawtucket city	7,647	1,187	5,512	1,187	421	0	na	na	na	na	1,045	0
Providence city	16,432	2,865	9,925	2,272	2,704	146	583	48	na	na	3,115	345
Warwick city	15,793	3,322	14,869	3,176	na	na	na	na	na	na	na	na
South Carolina												
Charleston city	16,944	2,670	12,767	2,134	3,719	536	na	na	na	na	na	na
Columbia city	12,099	1,675	7,031	1,345	4,689	330	na	na	na	na	na	na
North Charleston city	11,024	1,350	5,974	566	4,373	784	na	na	na	na	189	0
Rock Hill city	9,547	825	6,364	654	2,374	171	na	na	na	na	na	na
South Dakota												
Rapid City city	11,017	1,864	10,313	1,790	na	na	na	na	na	na	na	na
Sioux Falls city	20,658	2,778	19,624	2,778	107	0	na	na	na	na	na	na
Tennessee												
Chattanooga city	26,147	3,506	18,129	2,787	7,258	492	na	na	na	na	na	na
Clarksville city	11,876	565	9,213	449	1,332	116	na	na	na	na	436	0
Franklin city	7,496	1,085	7,388	1,039	na	na	na	na	na	na	na	na
Jackson city	8,303	1,442	5,611	1,050	2,415	392	na	na	na	na	na	na
Johnson City city	11,053	1,263	10,329	1,174	na	na	na	na	na	na	na	na
Knoxville city	25,128	3,781	21,292	3,213	3,165	451	na	na	na	na	247	0
Memphis city	73,617	10,207	31,466	5,732	39,112	4,475	865	0	1,168	0	829	0
Murfreesboro city	11,371	1,056	9,260	1,056	1,342	0	na	na	na	na	na	na
Nashville-Davidson metropolitan govt (bal)	69,971	8,959	51,209	7,685	15,082	1,057	1,588	105	385	33	1,790	79
Texas												
Abilene city	15,677	2,702	13,153	2,570	594	2	na	na	na	na	1,717	62
Allen city	5,619	679	4,588	679	na	na	na	na	na	na	na	na
Amarillo city	25,416	2,923	20,560	2,744	1,142	148	685	0	na	na	2,567	31
Arlington city	37,142	3,337	27,036	2,822	3,200	113	2,444	0	474	31	3,712	361
Austin city	72,705	8,402	48,263	6,566	5,979	522	4,142	131	664	0	13,685	1,183
Baytown city	10,382	1,086	6,355	773	1,131	29	na	na	na	na	2,558	284
Beaumont city	15,056	2,570	8,159	1,581	6,193	989	na	na	na	na	466	0
Brownsville city	20,524	3,572	na	na	na	na	na	na	na	na	17,715	3,442
Bryan city	7,875	749	5,104	590	1,277	27	na	na	na	na	1,494	132
Carrollton city	11,673	706	7,819	450	756	95	1,299	69	na	na	1,496	92
College Station city	6,147	760	5,598	668	na	na	199	0	na	na	58	0
Conroe city	7,327	848	6,322	848	na	na	na	na	na	na	702	0
Corpus Christi city	40,850	4,933	19,059	2,527	1,508	94	613	36	na	na	19,451	2,276
Dallas city	120,778	14,669	62,588	10,685	31,808	2,342	3,842	230	1,758	0	21,178	1,371
Denton city	12,089	876	10,015	757	689	119	na	na	na	na	1,192	0
Edinburg city	6,351	1,252	na	na	na	na	na	na	na	na	5,171	1,018
El Paso city	82,640	9,499	18,018	2,212	2,081	103	1,038	90	784	36	61,359	7,021
Fort Worth city	72,845	8,709	45,682	5,816	13,429	1,710	1,373	0	1,154	94	11,495	1,019
Frisco city	10,158	448	7,743	310	586	37	565	0	na	na	1,125	101
Garland city	27,813	2,786	17,487	2,162	3,110	239	2,871	0	na	na	4,203	385
Grand Prairie city	13,791	1,598	7,388	1,160	2,079	108	721	126	na	na	3,185	204
Harlingen city	9,098	1,194	3,752	538	na	na	na	na	na	na	5,215	576
Houston city	219,325	26,022	103,416	15,797	54,740	5,946	14,331	1,225	1,846	42	45,846	3,051
Irving city	17,776	2,110	10,901	1,641	1,219	163	2,537	141	118	0	3,018	165
Killeen city	7,035	950	2,726	237	1,498	347	na	na	na	na	1,794	278
Laredo city	21,333	2,478	883	58	na	na	na	na	na	na	20,271	2,420
League City city	8,623	602	6,768	375	na	na	na	na	na	na	909	227
Lewisville city	9,395	813	7,259	475	411	0	359	0	na	na	1,294	338
Longview city	12,222	1,861	9,826	1,778	1,632	83	na	na	na	na	683	0
Lubbock city	28,571	3,741	21,203	3,312	1,865	10	na	na	na	na	4,953	419
McAllen city	13,983	1,230	2,724	245	na	na	na	na	na	na	10,954	985
McKinney city	13,788	1,800	11,624	1,754	188	0	na	na	na	na	1,049	46
Mesquite city	13,811	1,553	10,161	1,455	1,062	0	na	na	na	na	2,075	98
Midland city	12,862	2,033	9,665	1,619	635	56	na	na	na	na	2,267	358
Mission city	9,343	1,085	na	na	na	na	na	na	na	na	5,350	298
Missouri City city	7,224	724	2,380	246	1,988	282	1,465	196	na	na	na	na
New Braunfels city	8,269	1,009	6,587	840	na	na	na	na	na	na	1,579	169
North Richland Hills city	9,624	1,150	8,840	1,150	na	na	na	na	na	na	128	0
Odessa city	12,199	1,666	7,392	974	na	na	na	na	na	na	4,101	547
Pasadena city	14,549	1,655	9,132	1,056	na	na	na	na	na	na	4,739	599
Pearland city	9,586	715	6,038	464	na	na	na	na	na	na	549	169
Pharr city	8,186	1,318	na	na	na	na	na	na	na	na	5,518	830
Plano city	33,323	2,823	25,785	2,527	1,668	113	3,789	82	305	49	1,852	52
Richardson city	15,066	2,552	12,149	2,331	na	na	1,235	163	na	na	722	0
Round Rock city	8,908	995	6,072	939	834	0	291	0	na	na	1,619	56

Table C-3: Places—Older Population by Race and Hispanic Origin—*Continued*

	Total Population		White, Non-Hispanic		Black, Alone		Asian, Alone		Multi-race		Hispanic	
	65 Years and Over	85 Years and Over	65 Years and Over	85 Years and Over	65 Years and Over	85 Years and Over	65 Years and Over	85 Years and Over	65 Years and Over	85 Years and Over	65 Years and Over	85 Years and Over
Texas—Cont.												
San Angelo city	14,383	2,121	10,287	1,467	na	na	na	na	na	na	3,158	565
San Antonio city	166,030	21,122	67,924	10,404	9,979	1,373	3,430	405	2,576	400	83,960	8,928
Sugar Land city	11,818	1,324	6,422	751	na	na	3,969	391	na	na	na	na
Temple city	11,634	2,312	8,938	2,119	1,603	97	na	na	na	na	880	96
Tyler city	15,307	2,432	11,509	1,878	2,871	475	na	na	na	na	767	79
Victoria city	9,631	1,566	6,171	888	na	na	na	na	na	na	2,951	595
Waco city	15,128	2,071	10,149	1,759	2,772	76	na	na	na	na	1,848	236
Wichita Falls city	12,507	1,823	9,971	1,446	1,158	92	na	na	na	na	1,261	252
Utah												
Layton city	6,404	448	5,433	448	na	na	na	na	na	na	415	0
Ogden city	8,994	1,124	6,746	1,022	na	na	na	na	na	na	1,717	74
Orem city	7,255	647	6,637	608	na	na	na	na	na	na	446	39
Provo city	7,309	897	6,886	897	na	na	na	na	na	na	232	0
Salt Lake City city	18,190	2,661	15,645	2,422	na	na	619	0	62	0	1,532	239
Sandy city	8,992	488	8,340	488	na	na	na	na	na	na	512	0
St. George city	16,989	2,672	15,890	2,595	na	na	na	na	na	na	na	na
West Jordan city	6,297	666	5,316	417	na	na	na	na	na	na	630	190
West Valley City city	9,160	350	6,128	267	na	na	983	30	na	na	1,173	0
Virginia												
Alexandria city	15,315	1,834	10,583	1,241	2,411	185	1,351	0	na	na	857	408
Chesapeake city	27,540	3,491	18,678	2,295	7,429	1,108	873	88	na	na	464	0
Hampton city	18,550	1,930	9,378	1,067	8,276	863	na	na	na	na	361	0
Lynchburg city	11,355	2,438	8,236	1,817	2,496	387	na	na	na	na	na	na
Newport News city	21,258	2,889	13,436	1,790	6,229	785	na	na	na	na	384	70
Norfolk city	24,165	4,507	13,600	3,035	8,924	1,258	915	71	350	90	415	53
Portsmouth city	13,009	1,601	6,962	908	5,925	646	na	na	na	na	na	na
Richmond city	24,862	4,068	11,611	1,927	12,277	2,108	na	na	na	na	213	0
Roanoke city	15,237	3,042	11,109	2,337	3,196	568	na	na	na	na	na	na
Suffolk city	11,260	1,417	7,037	868	3,838	549	na	na	na	na	na	na
Virginia Beach city	55,306	6,634	42,194	5,554	6,882	650	4,577	300	505	37	1,408	131
Washington												
Auburn city	8,735	1,577	6,557	1,168	na	na	na	na	na	na	642	165
Bellevue city	20,529	3,468	16,301	3,109	na	na	3,767	359	na	na	0	0
Bellingham city	11,342	2,259	10,142	2,223	na	na	na	na	na	na	na	na
Everett city	9,645	1,738	8,104	1,738	na	na	na	na	na	na	187	0
Federal Way city	12,408	1,417	10,062	1,358	na	na	1,412	59	na	na	470	0
Kennewick city	9,649	1,397	8,492	1,397	na	na	na	na	na	na	539	0
Kent city	11,917	1,622	8,136	1,386	718	77	2,203	159	107	0	607	0
Kirkland city	11,208	1,163	9,051	1,113	na	na	1,567	50	na	na	na	na
Marysville city	9,593	1,582	8,643	1,582	na	na	na	na	na	na	na	na
Pasco city	4,245	394	2,992	394	na	na	na	na	na	na	1,053	0
Renton city	8,936	1,596	6,181	1,275	na	na	1,687	167	152	0	482	154
Seattle city	81,461	13,398	59,112	10,524	6,523	657	12,680	2,081	997	0	1,574	187
Spokane city	29,815	4,718	27,491	4,718	na	na	na	na	231	0	372	0
Spokane Valley city	13,454	1,677	12,980	1,677	na	na	na	na	na	na	na	na
Tacoma city	25,667	3,949	19,619	3,341	1,972	191	2,485	279	266	0	958	170
Vancouver city	23,457	2,983	20,876	2,801	na	na	722	0	373	84	875	0
Yakima city	12,977	1,895	11,195	1,895	na	na	na	na	na	na	1,471	0
Wisconsin												
Appleton city	7,878	1,335	7,705	1,294	na	na	na	na	na	na	na	na
Eau Claire city	8,532	1,154	8,425	1,154	na	na	na	na	na	na	na	na
Green Bay city	12,815	2,139	11,898	2,139	na	na	na	na	na	na	312	0
Kenosha city	12,472	1,822	10,861	1,778	379	44	na	na	na	na	969	0
Madison city	26,967	4,180	24,566	4,055	819	27	840	0	328	98	516	98
Milwaukee city	60,278	9,854	36,808	7,084	17,919	1,779	635	0	254	23	4,399	991
Oshkosh city	9,331	2,058	9,087	1,898	na	na	na	na	na	na	na	na
Racine city	9,217	1,638	6,230	897	1,512	370	na	na	na	na	1,391	371
Waukesha city	7,556	1,053	7,071	1,053	na	na	na	na	na	na	279	0

Table C-4: Metropolitan/Micropolitan Statistical Areas—Older Population by Race and Hispanic Origin

	Total Population		White, Non-Hispanic		Black, Alone		Asian, Alone		Multi-race		Hispanic	
	65 Years and Over	85 Years and Over	65 Years and Over	85 Years and Over	65 Years and Over	85 Years and Over	65 Years and Over	85 Years and Over	65 Years and Over	85 Years and Over	65 Years and Over	85 Years and Over
Aberdeen, WA Micro Area	13,420	1,384	12,415	1,370	na	na	na	na	na	na	na	na
Abilene, TX Metro Area	24,261	3,466	20,997	3,285	741	2	na	na	na	na	2,185	111
Adrian, MI Micro Area	16,465	1,745	15,690	1,653	na	na	na	na	na	na	583	76
Akron, OH Metro Area	111,421	16,966	99,220	15,792	9,763	946	1,504	96	405	12	275	0
Alamogordo, NM Micro Area	10,366	942	7,639	927	na	na	na	na	na	na	2,260	0
Albany, GA Metro Area	21,658	2,549	13,013	1,762	8,283	741	na	na	na	na	na	na
Albany, OR Metro Area	20,720	2,558	19,620	2,456	na	na	na	na	na	na	na	na
Albany-Schenectady-Troy, NY Metro Area	136,420	19,741	126,476	18,665	5,582	540	1,771	161	808	186	1,940	189
Albertville, AL Micro Area	15,298	1,510	14,784	1,424	na	na	na	na	na	na	99	64
Albuquerque, NM Metro Area	131,492	13,715	80,199	9,413	2,454	281	2,364	93	1,933	106	41,762	3,685
Alexandria, LA Metro Area	22,841	2,952	17,411	2,641	4,566	311	na	na	na	na	na	na
Allentown-Bethlehem-Easton, PA-NJ Metro Area	139,417	23,043	127,422	21,594	2,490	327	2,390	0	1,562	298	6,438	919
Altoona, PA Metro Area	24,112	4,143	23,909	4,104	na	na	na	na	na	na	na	na
Amarillo, TX Metro Area	33,463	4,272	27,943	4,065	1,142	148	693	0	432	0	3,151	59
Ames, IA Metro Area	10,136	1,101	9,677	1,101	na	na	na	na	na	na	na	na
Anchorage, AK Metro Area	36,363	2,994	27,976	2,151	1,852	137	2,551	440	742	0	1,156	42
Ann Arbor, MI Metro Area	43,044	5,441	35,881	4,909	4,086	408	1,972	124	346	0	764	0
Anniston-Oxford-Jacksonville, AL Metro Area	18,543	1,655	15,656	1,316	2,481	339	na	na	na	na	na	na
Appleton, WI Metro Area	30,003	3,461	29,392	3,383	na	na	96	0	na	na	118	41
Asheville, NC Metro Area	90,920	11,935	86,042	11,295	2,439	188	na	na	669	157	1,483	185
Ashtabula, OH Micro Area	17,004	2,391	16,473	2,391	na	na	na	na	na	na	199	0
Athens, TX Micro Area	16,737	1,600	15,100	1,514	na	na	na	na	na	na	754	0
Athens-Clarke County, GA Metro Area	23,192	3,009	18,946	2,503	3,487	506	na	na	na	na	456	0
Atlanta-Sandy Springs-Roswell, GA Metro Area	604,850	59,110	416,072	44,339	144,811	12,062	22,564	1,342	4,307	352	17,839	1,271
Atlantic City-Hammonton, NJ Metro Area	43,435	4,347	32,666	3,497	5,106	747	2,485	57	604	37	2,783	37
Auburn, NY Micro Area	13,146	1,955	13,086	1,955	na	na	na	na	na	na	na	na
Auburn-Opelika, AL Metro Area	15,875	1,057	12,357	953	2,917	104	na	na	na	na	na	na
Augusta-Richmond County, GA-SC Metro Area	84,309	9,425	59,479	7,044	21,365	1,623	1,633	179	354	143	1,466	436
Augusta-Waterville, ME Micro Area	21,422	2,384	20,987	2,384	na	na	na	na	na	na	na	na
Austin-Round Rock, TX Metro Area	183,274	20,759	137,595	17,658	10,259	759	6,427	222	1,669	144	26,943	2,034
Bakersfield, CA Metro Area	86,486	9,115	54,808	6,429	3,536	200	5,080	535	1,783	108	21,362	1,819
Baltimore-Columbia-Towson, MD Metro Area	390,577	51,512	281,732	41,236	86,996	8,707	12,982	468	3,252	482	5,923	685
Bangor, ME Metro Area	25,127	3,416	24,746	3,416	na	na	na	na	na	na	na	na
Barnstable Town, MA Metro Area	59,991	7,498	58,035	7,390	na	na	na	na	na	na	na	na
Baton Rouge, LA Metro Area	100,331	9,714	71,271	6,986	25,964	2,154	1,194	0	734	300	980	272
Battle Creek, MI Metro Area	21,797	3,110	19,490	2,921	1,824	146	na	na	na	na	239	0
Bay City, MI Metro Area	19,487	2,221	18,677	2,221	na	na	na	na	na	na	na	na
Beaumont-Port Arthur, TX Metro Area	59,554	7,404	42,372	5,581	12,663	1,451	744	140	na	na	2,876	178
Beaver Dam, WI Micro Area	14,291	1,716	14,158	1,716	na	na	na	na	na	na	na	na
Beckley, WV Metro Area	22,492	2,999	21,040	2,771	1,179	140	na	na	na	na	na	na
Bellingham, WA Metro Area	31,955	4,198	29,511	4,144	na	na	na	na	na	na	765	0
Bend-Redmond, OR Metro Area	30,318	3,703	29,814	3,695	na	na	na	na	na	na	na	na
Billings, MT Metro Area	26,193	3,355	25,195	3,240	na	na	na	na	na	na	517	115
Binghamton, NY Metro Area	43,574	6,857	41,594	6,725	481	108	615	24	na	na	490	0
Birmingham-Hoover, AL Metro Area	168,322	18,791	129,039	14,944	34,428	3,496	754	93	1,794	95	2,216	90
Bismarck, ND Metro Area	18,261	3,159	17,707	3,148	na	na	na	na	na	na	na	na
Blacksburg-Christiansburg-Radford, VA Metro Area	26,047	3,005	24,553	2,931	929	74	na	na	na	na	na	na
Bloomington, IL Metro Area	22,817	3,753	21,690	3,738	439	15	375	0	na	na	269	0
Bloomington, IN Metro Area	19,346	2,160	19,020	2,116	na	na	na	na	na	na	na	na
Bloomsburg-Berwick, PA Metro Area	15,046	1,950	14,870	1,950	na	na	na	na	na	na	na	na
Bluefield, WV-VA Micro Area	20,550	2,376	19,296	2,160	na	na	na	na	na	na	na	na
Boise City, ID Metro Area	86,909	10,248	80,104	9,835	na	na	1,132	103	794	0	3,616	284
Boston-Cambridge-Newton, MA-NH Metro Area	676,779	98,342	584,892	88,840	34,699	3,659	28,426	3,192	5,722	677	25,250	2,318
Boulder, CO Metro Area	37,931	4,638	34,771	4,409	na	na	808	80	433	68	2,056	149
Bowling Green, KY Metro Area	21,206	1,812	20,455	1,654	566	158	na	na	na	na	51	0
Bozeman, MT Micro Area	10,707	978	10,625	978	na	na	na	na	na	na	na	na
Brainerd, MN Micro Area	20,088	2,475	19,304	2,431	na	na	na	na	na	na	na	na
Branson, MO Micro Area	19,163	1,601	18,632	1,458	na	na	na	na	na	na	na	na
Bremerton-Silverdale, WA Metro Area	40,852	4,994	36,493	4,818	na	na	2,047	176	815	0	806	0
Bridgeport-Stamford-Norwalk, CT Metro Area	135,852	20,186	110,504	18,124	11,011	1,568	3,957	138	644	31	9,905	325
Brownsville-Harlingen, TX Metro Area	52,048	7,032	14,545	1,604	na	na	na	na	na	na	36,859	5,306
Brunswick, GA Metro Area	19,945	1,750	16,851	1,343	2,578	357	na	na	na	na	na	na
Buffalo-Cheektowaga-Niagara Falls, NY Metro Area	189,588	30,896	168,298	29,252	14,594	1,234	2,085	109	601	22	2,942	174
Burlington, NC Metro Area	25,110	3,301	20,433	2,733	3,904	554	na	na	na	na	793	0
Burlington-South Burlington, VT Metro Area	28,601	3,739	27,759	3,574	na	na	na	na	na	na	na	na
California-Lexington Park, MD Metro Area	13,166	1,302	10,881	1,213	1,573	62	na	na	na	na	na	na
Canton-Massillon, OH Metro Area	71,654	9,552	67,225	9,069	3,179	275	na	na	501	90	504	118
Cape Coral-Fort Myers, FL Metro Area	178,227	22,013	161,612	20,555	5,626	568	na	na	684	31	9,272	587
Cape Girardeau, MO-IL Metro Area	16,275	2,169	15,420	2,139	657	0	na	na	na	na	na	na
Carbondale-Marion, IL Metro Area	19,486	2,295	18,337	2,184	875	111	na	na	na	na	na	na
Carson City, NV Metro Area	10,141	1,737	9,200	1,465	na	na	na	na	na	na	731	225
Casper, WY Metro Area	9,975	1,147	9,703	1,147	na	na	na	na	na	na	na	na
Cedar Rapids, IA Metro Area	39,042	5,330	38,160	5,153	378	46	na	na	na	na	204	62
Centralia, WA Micro Area	14,747	2,331	14,124	2,254	na	na	na	na	na	na	na	na
Chambersburg-Waynesboro, PA Metro Area	27,775	4,037	26,794	3,862	na	na	na	na	na	na	na	na
Champaign-Urbana, IL Metro Area	28,580	3,333	25,542	3,300	1,708	33	767	0	473	0	185	0
Charleston, WV Metro Area	40,079	4,471	37,660	4,394	1,872	69	na	na	na	na	na	na
Charleston-Mattoon, IL Micro Area	9,546	1,882	9,454	1,882	na	na	na	na	na	na	na	na

Table C-4: Metropolitan/Micropolitan Statistical Areas—Older Population by Race and Hispanic Origin—*Continued*

	Total Population		White, Non-Hispanic		Black, Alone		Asian, Alone		Multi-race		Hispanic	
	65 Years and Over	85 Years and Over	65 Years and Over	85 Years and Over	65 Years and Over	85 Years and Over	65 Years and Over	85 Years and Over	65 Years and Over	85 Years and Over	65 Years and Over	85 Years and Over
Charleston-North Charleston, SC Metro Area.............	96,955	10,616	70,524	7,854	22,491	2,682	1,603	74	1,052	6	1,154	0
Charlotte-Concord-Gastonia, NC-SC Metro Area........	295,401	31,392	234,754	27,680	45,515	3,010	4,119	97	2,373	41	8,010	564
Charlottesville, VA Metro Area.............	35,028	5,358	30,863	4,922	3,307	299	382	85	na	na	44	0
Chattanooga, TN-GA Metro Area.............	87,927	10,032	76,842	9,134	8,766	656	801	227	1,152	15	278	0
Cheyenne, WY Metro Area.............	13,897	1,343	11,914	1,150	na	na	na	na	na	na	1,146	103
Chicago-Naperville-Elgin, IL-IN-WI Metro Area...........	1,219,572	165,526	847,027	126,783	189,635	22,597	66,186	4,963	8,597	1,008	109,035	10,608
Chico, CA Metro Area.............	38,055	5,627	33,923	5,168	na	na	963	42	733	160	2,132	257
Chillicothe, OH Micro Area.............	11,396	916	10,907	774	na	na	na	na	na	na	na	na
Cincinnati, OH-KY-IN Metro Area.............	293,931	39,067	260,017	34,568	25,911	3,381	3,660	769	1,741	259	2,706	90
Claremont-Lebanon, NH-VT Micro Area.............	40,841	5,072	40,127	5,068	na	na	na	na	na	na	na	na
Clarksburg, WV Micro Area.............	16,597	2,167	16,046	2,167	na	na	na	na	na	na	na	na
Clarksville, TN-KY Metro Area.............	27,999	2,095	22,789	1,717	3,363	378	na	na	177	0	748	0
Clearlake, CA Micro Area.............	12,703	1,205	11,376	1,160	na	na	na	na	na	na	776	29
Cleveland, TN Metro Area.............	19,852	1,979	18,668	1,887	na	na	na	na	na	na	na	na
Cleveland-Elyria, OH Metro Area.............	341,442	51,886	276,531	43,735	51,921	7,156	4,602	321	2,101	372	6,200	316
Coeur d'Alene, ID Metro Area.............	25,326	2,971	24,153	2,713	na	na	na	na	na	na	na	na
College Station-Bryan, TX Metro Area.............	24,299	2,629	18,523	2,041	2,721	251	238	0	na	na	2,623	337
Colorado Springs, CO Metro Area.............	80,400	8,825	68,500	7,972	2,697	147	2,308	294	1,221	105	5,505	307
Columbia, MO Metro Area.............	18,413	2,293	16,538	2,255	1,203	0	na	na	na	na	na	na
Columbia, SC Metro Area.............	105,378	10,785	76,681	8,841	24,934	1,617	1,605	122	857	0	1,279	190
Columbus, GA-AL Metro Area.............	38,507	4,865	24,709	3,720	12,632	1,106	na	na	119	0	360	39
Columbus, IN Metro Area.............	11,824	1,234	11,510	1,197	na	na	na	na	na	na	na	na
Columbus, OH Metro Area.............	238,980	29,637	206,996	26,668	23,633	2,377	4,516	205	1,362	125	2,268	262
Concord, NH Micro Area.............	23,480	2,888	23,121	2,888	na	na	na	na	na	na	na	na
Cookeville, TN Micro Area.............	18,846	1,310	18,399	1,266	na	na	na	na	na	na	na	na
Coos Bay, OR Micro Area.............	15,170	2,101	13,988	1,870	na	na	na	na	na	na	na	na
Corning, NY Micro Area.............	17,344	2,461	16,589	2,461	na	na	na	na	na	na	na	na
Corpus Christi, TX Metro Area.............	62,197	6,618	32,628	4,088	1,740	94	617	36	380	0	26,946	2,365
Corvallis, OR Metro Area.............	12,373	2,159	11,650	2,045	na	na	na	na	na	na	na	na
Crestview-Fort Walton Beach-Destin, FL Metro Area...	41,399	4,890	36,887	4,218	2,488	385	na	na	190	31	465	0
Cullman, AL Micro Area.............	14,266	1,310	13,857	1,234	na	na	na	na	na	na	na	na
Cumberland, MD-WV Metro Area.............	19,362	2,517	18,712	2,478	317	25	na	na	na	na	na	na
Dallas-Fort Worth-Arlington, TX Metro Area.............	712,091	73,597	516,278	58,936	79,153	6,618	31,629	1,612	7,701	498	76,523	5,795
Dalton, GA Metro Area.............	18,120	1,266	16,595	1,219	na	na	na	na	na	na	740	0
Danville, IL Metro Area.............	14,058	1,387	12,728	1,292	994	40	na	na	na	na	na	na
Danville, VA Micro Area.............	20,717	2,044	15,419	1,426	5,139	500	na	na	na	na	na	na
Daphne-Fairhope-Foley, AL Metro Area.............	37,782	3,808	34,542	3,441	2,017	91	na	na	na	na	na	na
Davenport-Moline-Rock Island, IA-IL Metro Area.......	62,773	8,377	57,860	7,881	2,230	302	na	na	327	30	1,874	194
Dayton, OH Metro Area.............	132,127	15,679	112,638	13,701	15,881	1,703	1,753	86	849	101	1,073	140
Decatur, AL Metro Area.............	23,704	2,340	21,944	2,164	1,410	176	na	na	na	na	na	na
Decatur, IL Metro Area.............	19,253	2,331	17,288	2,298	1,420	33	na	na	461	0	na	na
Deltona-Daytona Beach-Ormond Beach, FL Metro Area.............	146,929	22,176	127,061	19,288	8,945	1,805	1,964	228	na	na	8,457	935
Denver-Aurora-Lakewood, CO Metro Area.............	321,678	38,956	258,639	33,246	13,999	1,204	10,263	776	3,136	317	34,904	3,520
Des Moines-West Des Moines, IA Metro Area.............	74,232	10,637	69,751	10,334	1,866	152	1,104	151	116	0	1,373	0
Detroit-Warren-Dearborn, MI Metro Area.............	632,542	88,954	487,124	72,619	113,413	13,956	15,229	961	5,259	255	10,283	1,104
Dothan, AL Metro Area.............	25,311	2,480	20,920	2,220	3,865	249	na	na	na	na	88	0
Dover, DE Metro Area.............	26,587	2,685	20,351	1,991	4,784	551	na	na	na	na	438	109
DuBois, PA Micro Area.............	15,340	2,219	15,147	2,219	na	na	na	na	na	na	na	na
Dubuque, IA Micro Area.............	15,598	2,103	15,410	2,103	na	na	na	na	na	na	na	na
Duluth, MN-WI Metro Area.............	47,561	7,589	46,167	7,396	na	na	na	na	314	0	149	62
Dunn, NC Micro Area.............	13,669	1,431	10,991	1,031	2,444	369	na	na	na	na	0	0
Durham-Chapel Hill, NC Metro Area.............	70,926	9,579	51,869	7,259	16,339	2,215	1,339	0	71	0	1,060	105
East Stroudsburg, PA Metro Area.............	25,516	3,255	20,893	2,277	1,912	290	na	na	na	na	1,950	444
Eau Claire, WI Metro Area.............	24,234	3,170	23,981	3,170	na	na	10	0	na	na	na	na
El Centro, CA Metro Area.............	21,684	2,884	5,524	755	na	na	na	na	660	121	14,866	1,862
El Paso, TX Metro Area.............	94,367	10,874	19,178	2,460	2,168	103	1,060	99	891	36	71,808	8,148
Elizabeth City, NC Micro Area.............	10,688	904	7,862	709	2,613	195	na	na	na	na	na	na
Elizabethtown-Fort Knox, KY Metro Area.............	19,612	2,266	17,472	2,005	1,270	54	na	na	na	na	367	207
Elkhart-Goshen, IN Metro Area.............	26,148	3,952	25,019	3,563	587	255	na	na	na	na	311	97
Elmira, NY Metro Area.............	14,901	2,414	14,115	2,414	na	na	na	na	na	na	na	na
Erie, PA Metro Area.............	44,087	6,442	41,623	6,125	1,642	196	454	68	51	0	461	53
Eugene, OR Metro Area.............	62,237	8,754	58,734	8,285	na	na	729	251	832	0	1,342	150
Eureka-Arcata-Fortuna, CA Micro Area.............	20,327	2,155	18,657	1,982	na	na	na	na	209	9	622	116
Evansville, IN-KY Metro Area.............	49,114	7,087	45,972	6,557	2,264	418	na	na	na	na	na	na
Fairbanks, AK Metro Area.............	7,884	865	6,594	739	na	na	na	na	na	na	na	na
Fargo, ND-MN Metro Area.............	25,605	4,172	24,974	4,071	na	na	na	na	na	na	na	na
Faribault-Northfield, MN Micro Area.............	9,149	816	8,926	816	na	na	na	na	na	na	na	na
Farmington, MO Micro Area.............	10,095	1,468	9,883	1,468	na	na	na	na	na	na	na	na
Farmington, NM Metro Area.............	15,809	2,028	9,772	1,320	na	na	na	na	na	na	1,572	100
Fayetteville, NC Metro Area.............	39,654	3,800	22,218	2,187	13,297	1,352	1,205	12	729	0	1,469	171
Fayetteville-Springdale-Rogers, AR-MO Metro Area ...	61,691	7,541	57,234	7,479	515	0	424	0	750	54	2,198	0
Findlay, OH Micro Area.............	11,946	2,007	11,637	2,007	na	na	na	na	na	na	na	na
Flagstaff, AZ Metro Area.............	15,520	1,173	10,599	714	na	na	na	na	na	na	1,059	127
Flint, MI Metro Area.............	64,986	7,341	52,523	6,687	9,945	476	na	na	602	0	943	71
Florence, SC Metro Area.............	31,772	3,148	21,164	2,230	10,306	891	na	na	na	na	na	na
Florence-Muscle Shoals, AL Metro Area.............	27,452	3,180	24,119	2,826	2,834	222	na	na	na	na	na	na

Table C-4: Metropolitan/Micropolitan Statistical Areas—Older Population by Race and Hispanic Origin—*Continued*

	Total Population		White, Non-Hispanic		Black, Alone		Asian, Alone		Multi-race		Hispanic	
	65 Years and Over	85 Years and Over	65 Years and Over	85 Years and Over	65 Years and Over	85 Years and Over	65 Years and Over	85 Years and Over	65 Years and Over	85 Years and Over	65 Years and Over	85 Years and Over
Fond du Lac, WI Metro Area	16,906	3,137	16,508	3,137	na	na	na	na	na	na	na	na
Forest City, NC Micro Area	13,004	2,213	11,815	1,999	na	na	na	na	na	na	na	na
Fort Collins, CO Metro Area	45,151	5,178	42,265	4,967	na	na	501	77	443	0	1,854	38
Fort Smith, AR-OK Metro Area	43,062	4,708	37,861	4,175	1,091	98	na	na	1,124	153	412	0
Fort Wayne, IN Metro Area	58,375	8,055	52,251	7,747	3,624	150	786	56	271	0	1,254	102
Frankfort, KY Micro Area	10,932	1,204	10,594	1,118	na	na	na	na	na	na	na	na
Fresno, CA Metro Area	108,445	14,835	61,273	9,625	3,777	356	9,591	1,471	2,058	244	30,582	3,118
Gadsden, AL Metro Area	18,077	2,294	15,859	2,135	1,696	80	na	na	na	na	na	na
Gainesville, FL Metro Area	35,087	4,724	28,099	4,019	4,830	416	592	71	73	61	1,473	157
Gainesville, GA Metro Area	26,142	2,623	22,911	2,427	1,696	196	na	na	na	na	1,117	0
Gallup, NM Micro Area	7,509	566	na	na	na	na	na	na	na	na	na	na
Gettysburg, PA Metro Area	18,272	1,894	18,014	1,894	na	na	na	na	na	na	206	0
Glens Falls, NY Metro Area	23,426	2,852	23,075	2,778	na	na	na	na	na	na	na	na
Glenwood Springs, CO Micro Area	8,578	551	7,753	478	na	na	na	na	na	na	567	0
Goldsboro, NC Metro Area	18,027	1,903	12,201	1,358	5,207	545	na	na	na	na	342	0
Grand Forks, ND-MN Metro Area	13,204	1,757	12,826	1,757	na	na	na	na	na	na	na	na
Grand Island, NE Metro Area	13,522	1,523	12,552	1,393	na	na	na	na	na	na	621	14
Grand Junction, CO Metro Area	24,742	3,212	23,147	3,097	na	na	na	na	na	na	1,246	85
Grand Rapids-Wyoming, MI Metro Area	133,763	21,499	122,828	20,346	4,616	575	1,660	77	857	209	3,676	374
Grants Pass, OR Metro Area	20,667	2,077	19,540	2,069	na	na	na	na	na	na	na	na
Great Falls, MT Metro Area	13,756	1,424	13,201	1,424	na	na	na	na	na	na	na	na
Greeley, CO Metro Area	30,841	2,938	25,861	2,650	na	na	na	na	343	0	4,340	247
Green Bay, WI Metro Area	44,505	5,942	42,566	5,850	na	na	753	0	121	0	638	92
Greeneville, TN Metro Area	13,573	1,475	13,271	1,475	na	na	na	na	na	na	na	na
Greenfield Town, MA Micro Area	12,876	1,995	12,502	1,921	na	na	na	na	na	na	na	na
Greensboro-High Point, NC Metro Area	110,128	13,898	87,008	11,656	19,507	1,965	1,429	175	332	0	1,503	55
Greenville, NC Metro Area	19,820	2,417	13,624	1,585	5,822	832	na	na	na	na	289	0
Greenville-Anderson-Mauldin, SC Metro Area	131,292	15,334	112,150	13,817	14,910	983	1,328	189	761	213	1,962	86
Greenwood, SC Micro Area	16,542	2,910	12,573	2,225	3,755	685	na	na	na	na	na	na
Gulfport-Biloxi-Pascagoula, MS Metro Area	54,589	5,216	44,896	4,654	7,332	336	na	na	na	na	890	36
Hagerstown-Martinsburg, MD-WV Metro Area	37,795	4,881	35,631	4,736	1,101	81	na	na	393	0	na	na
Hammond, LA Metro Area	16,233	1,453	12,857	1,177	2,850	218	na	na	na	na	na	na
Hanford-Corcoran, CA Metro Area	13,331	1,080	7,723	795	600	16	na	na	na	na	4,330	269
Harrisburg-Carlisle, PA Metro Area	89,485	13,336	81,418	12,405	5,579	804	1,265	91	416	0	970	36
Harrisonburg, VA Metro Area	18,348	2,735	17,431	2,683	na	na	na	na	na	na	279	8
Hartford-West Hartford-East Hartford, CT Metro Area	190,247	30,116	162,913	27,729	13,080	1,351	3,123	67	1,396	0	9,861	873
Hattiesburg, MS Metro Area	18,066	2,251	14,820	1,901	3,177	350	na	na	na	na	na	na
Helena, MT Micro Area	12,962	1,435	12,504	1,428	na	na	na	na	na	na	na	na
Hermiston-Pendleton, OR Micro Area	13,168	1,524	11,284	1,360	na	na	na	na	na	na	1,406	144
Hickory-Lenoir-Morganton, NC Metro Area	62,984	6,202	57,890	5,555	3,475	438	10	0	na	na	808	0
Hilo, HI Micro Area	34,298	5,231	15,394	1,056	na	na	10,175	3,141	5,459	565	1,472	84
Hilton Head Island-Bluffton-Beaufort, SC Metro Area	47,365	5,107	40,088	4,358	6,080	663	na	na	na	na	734	66
Hinesville, GA Metro Area	6,257	323	3,615	208	2,140	74	na	na	na	na	236	0
Hobbs, NM Micro Area	7,340	656	4,865	531	na	na	na	na	na	na	2,036	54
Holland, MI Micro Area	17,109	1,920	16,353	1,914	na	na	na	na	na	na	492	0
Homosassa Springs, FL Metro Area	49,006	5,730	45,799	5,359	na	na	na	na	na	na	na	na
Hot Springs, AR Metro Area	20,953	2,310	19,746	2,158	876	152	na	na	na	na	na	na
Houma-Thibodaux, LA Metro Area	26,983	3,204	23,233	2,797	2,701	205	na	na	na	na	na	na
Houston-The Woodlands-Sugar Land, TX Metro Area	638,592	64,725	380,523	42,694	92,556	8,390	46,320	4,154	9,380	236	111,079	9,316
Huntington-Ashland, WV-KY-OH Metro Area	64,359	7,828	62,242	7,595	1,142	198	na	na	na	na	na	na
Huntsville, AL Metro Area	60,843	6,808	49,618	5,675	8,255	916	1,295	91	557	0	886	126
Huntsville, TX Micro Area	11,417	1,131	10,085	991	na	na	na	na	na	na	217	113
Hutchinson, KS Micro Area	11,796	1,904	10,871	1,791	na	na	na	na	na	na	na	na
Idaho Falls, ID Metro Area	16,370	1,922	15,984	1,922	na	na	na	na	na	na	171	0
Indiana, PA Micro Area	14,868	2,054	14,713	2,054	na	na	na	na	na	na	na	na
Indianapolis-Carmel-Anderson, IN Metro Area	244,434	30,310	211,253	26,722	24,565	2,965	3,361	0	2,021	61	2,540	319
Iowa City, IA Metro Area	18,116	2,180	17,301	2,174	na	na	333	0	na	na	106	0
Ithaca, NY Metro Area	12,325	2,319	11,969	2,259	na	na	na	na	na	na	na	na
Jackson, MI Metro Area	25,771	3,238	23,864	3,094	959	144	na	na	na	na	na	na
Jackson, MS Metro Area	72,747	9,917	47,414	6,466	23,810	3,059	na	na	na	na	576	252
Jackson, TN Metro Area	19,908	2,390	15,919	1,908	3,689	482	na	na	na	na	na	na
Jacksonville, FL Metro Area	201,996	24,576	159,010	19,883	27,068	3,028	6,130	532	1,278	173	8,223	912
Jacksonville, NC Metro Area	15,988	1,085	12,469	859	2,740	188	na	na	na	na	718	38
Jamestown-Dunkirk-Fredonia, NY Micro Area	23,641	3,616	23,018	3,531	na	na	na	na	na	na	367	0
Janesville-Beloit, WI Metro Area	24,180	4,347	22,928	4,090	497	29	na	na	na	na	503	105
Jefferson City, MO Metro Area	21,761	2,337	20,743	2,300	736	37	na	na	na	na	na	na
Johnson City, TN Metro Area	36,440	3,445	35,345	3,248	681	176	na	na	na	na	na	na
Johnstown, PA Metro Area	28,088	4,887	27,314	4,755	566	132	na	na	na	na	na	na
Jonesboro, AR Metro Area	17,879	1,621	16,462	1,606	450	15	na	na	na	na	na	na
Joplin, MO Metro Area	26,049	3,265	25,087	3,183	na	na	na	na	na	na	220	0
Kahului-Wailuku-Lahaina, HI Metro Area	24,654	3,919	10,347	1,277	na	na	9,423	1,979	2,953	481	672	79
Kalamazoo-Portage, MI Metro Area	47,101	5,935	42,649	5,648	2,858	248	359	0	725	6	518	0
Kalispell, MT Micro Area	16,537	1,186	15,750	950	na	na	na	na	na	na	na	na
Kankakee, IL Metro Area	16,517	2,053	14,392	1,845	1,677	105	na	na	na	na	222	0
Kansas City, MO-KS Metro Area	275,867	35,931	236,162	32,406	25,732	2,234	3,029	274	2,932	264	8,181	643
Kapaa, HI Micro Area	12,381	1,886	4,719	499	na	na	5,049	1,096	1,209	189	426	53
Keene, NH Micro Area	12,998	1,918	12,918	1,918	na	na	na	na	na	na	na	na

Table C-4: Metropolitan/Micropolitan Statistical Areas—Older Population by Race and Hispanic Origin—*Continued*

	Total Population		White, Non-Hispanic		Black, Alone		Asian, Alone		Multi-race		Hispanic	
	65 Years and Over	85 Years and Over	65 Years and Over	85 Years and Over	65 Years and Over	85 Years and Over	65 Years and Over	85 Years and Over	65 Years and Over	85 Years and Over	65 Years and Over	85 Years and Over
Kennewick-Richland, WA Metro Area	32,164	4,271	27,700	3,939	na	na	na	na	563	29	2,491	0
Key West, FL Micro Area	15,903	2,037	13,137	1,763	na	na	na	na	na	na	2,165	274
Killeen-Temple, TX Metro Area	42,572	6,239	32,491	5,001	4,121	516	1,073	24	623	111	4,136	610
Kingsport-Bristol-Bristol, TN-VA Metro Area	61,544	6,989	60,125	6,762	na	na	na	na	na	na	287	0
Kingston, NY Metro Area	31,737	4,110	28,596	4,071	1,186	0	na	na	616	0	1,364	0
Klamath Falls, OR Micro Area	12,304	1,962	11,559	1,909	na	na	na	na	na	na	272	9
Knoxville, TN Metro Area	144,988	17,082	135,975	15,983	5,299	825	1,428	209	911	65	1,330	0
Kokomo, IN Metro Area	14,846	1,972	13,923	1,790	na	na	na	na	na	na	na	na
La Crosse-Onalaska, WI-MN Metro Area	20,808	3,288	20,580	3,288	na	na	na	na	na	na	na	na
Lafayette, LA Metro Area	59,820	6,291	47,616	4,898	10,656	1,258	na	na	na	na	776	135
Lafayette-West Lafayette, IN Metro Area	25,239	3,973	23,156	3,532	na	na	806	0	na	na	647	441
LaGrange, GA Micro Area	9,657	810	7,129	607	2,353	203	na	na	na	na	na	na
Lake Charles, LA Metro Area	28,372	3,620	22,203	3,108	5,137	432	na	na	na	na	na	na
Lake City, FL Micro Area	11,980	1,642	9,922	1,386	1,378	168	na	na	na	na	na	na
Lake Havasu City-Kingman, AZ Metro Area	55,039	4,626	49,554	4,284	na	na	na	na	na	na	3,311	125
Lakeland-Winter Haven, FL Metro Area	124,198	14,528	103,173	12,328	9,799	1,443	na	na	591	59	8,377	542
Lancaster, PA Metro Area	87,648	13,077	82,175	12,284	1,519	212	1,100	84	181	62	2,535	435
Lansing-East Lansing, MI Metro Area	63,959	8,246	56,672	7,576	3,652	573	924	0	968	45	1,823	44
Laredo, TX Metro Area	22,508	2,496	1,020	58	na	na	na	na	na	na	21,309	2,438
Las Cruces, NM Metro Area	30,057	3,322	15,703	2,044	na	na	na	na	na	na	13,699	1,278
Las Vegas-Henderson-Paradise, NV Metro Area	274,915	24,386	187,340	18,247	22,823	1,643	28,302	1,510	4,119	413	31,659	2,787
Laurel, MS Micro Area	14,171	1,364	10,864	884	3,193	480	na	na	na	na	na	na
Lawrence, KS Metro Area	12,127	1,714	11,068	1,714	na	na	na	na	na	na	na	na
Lawton, OK Metro Area	15,157	1,325	11,681	1,245	1,376	80	na	na	532	0	380	0
Lebanon, PA Metro Area	24,696	3,161	23,815	3,065	na	na	na	na	na	na	628	0
Lewiston, ID-WA Metro Area	12,040	1,963	11,433	1,879	na	na	na	na	na	na	na	na
Lewiston-Auburn, ME Metro Area	17,336	1,850	16,648	1,850	na	na	na	na	289	0	na	na
Lexington-Fayette, KY Metro Area	62,177	8,799	54,862	8,294	5,230	404	682	0	831	27	432	0
Lima, OH Metro Area	16,543	1,998	15,018	1,784	1,326	214	na	na	na	na	na	na
Lincoln, NE Metro Area	39,384	5,181	37,505	5,035	279	0	662	0	na	na	728	107
Little Rock-North Little Rock-Conway, AR Metro Area	98,729	12,027	83,801	10,525	12,573	1,420	335	0	990	0	1,199	82
Logan, UT-ID Metro Area	11,813	1,509	11,396	1,488	na	na	na	na	na	na	188	0
London, KY Micro Area	19,863	1,953	19,437	1,890	na	na	na	na	na	na	na	na
Longview, TX Metro Area	32,254	3,906	26,809	3,532	3,973	328	na	na	na	na	1,272	46
Longview, WA Metro Area	18,254	2,370	17,524	2,341	na	na	na	na	na	na	232	29
Los Angeles-Long Beach-Anaheim, CA Metro Area	1,646,361	226,067	790,973	126,583	115,593	13,325	308,744	38,935	29,300	2,872	406,386	45,274
Louisville/Jefferson County, KY-IN Metro Area	182,428	24,565	159,907	22,165	17,439	2,011	1,471	156	1,035	68	2,566	128
Lubbock, TX Metro Area	36,837	4,413	27,787	3,908	1,951	10	na	na	546	76	6,471	495
Lufkin, TX Micro Area	13,926	2,710	10,761	2,494	1,872	216	na	na	na	na	1,068	0
Lumberton, NC Micro Area	17,379	1,812	7,332	817	3,918	393	na	na	na	na	100	0
Lynchburg, VA Metro Area	45,279	5,501	38,448	4,452	5,714	815	na	na	na	na	na	na
Macon, GA Metro Area	33,763	4,264	21,918	3,260	11,164	1,004	na	na	na	na	na	na
Madera, CA Metro Area	19,640	2,663	13,390	1,502	na	na	na	na	na	na	4,805	994
Madison, WI Metro Area	80,723	11,396	76,945	11,177	1,089	27	1,277	94	728	98	808	98
Manchester-Nashua, NH Metro Area	56,374	7,581	53,266	7,547	341	0	1,455	0	331	0	981	34
Manhattan, KS Metro Area	9,055	1,158	8,371	1,158	na	na	na	na	na	na	na	na
Manitowoc, WI Micro Area	15,034	2,685	14,655	2,617	na	na	na	na	na	na	na	na
Mankato-North Mankato, MN Metro Area	12,905	2,212	12,742	2,212	na	na	na	na	na	na	na	na
Mansfield, OH Metro Area	22,015	2,710	20,427	2,558	na	na	na	na	na	na	na	na
Marinette, WI-MI Micro Area	14,023	2,053	13,822	1,996	na	na	na	na	na	na	na	na
Marion, IN Micro Area	12,016	1,690	11,168	1,690	na	na	na	na	na	na	na	na
Marion, OH Micro Area	11,007	1,613	10,065	1,613	na	na	na	na	na	na	na	na
Marquette, MI Micro Area	11,257	1,324	10,898	1,288	na	na	na	na	na	na	na	na
Marshall, TX Micro Area	10,152	1,653	7,582	1,249	1,831	324	na	na	na	na	352	0
Martinsville, VA Micro Area	14,229	1,790	10,550	1,643	3,246	147	na	na	na	na	na	na
McAllen-Edinburg-Mission, TX Metro Area	86,414	10,077	22,877	3,032	na	na	na	na	na	na	62,263	7,045
Meadville, PA Micro Area	15,919	1,617	15,631	1,582	na	na	na	na	na	na	na	na
Medford, OR Metro Area	42,200	5,864	39,806	5,848	na	na	na	na	na	na	1,209	0
Memphis, TN-MS-AR Metro Area	162,772	19,998	102,465	14,201	54,525	5,759	2,108	0	1,768	0	1,611	38
Merced, CA Metro Area	28,299	3,565	15,543	1,584	1,119	271	1,885	503	1,208	176	8,765	1,109
Meridian, MS Micro Area	16,019	2,136	11,315	1,578	4,162	558	na	na	na	na	na	na
Miami-Fort Lauderdale-West Palm Beach, FL Metro Area	1,009,172	162,697	516,385	96,792	126,939	14,857	16,279	1,291	8,712	1,091	350,580	49,671
Michigan City-La Porte, IN Metro Area	17,551	2,100	16,196	2,014	1,085	86	na	na	na	na	85	0
Midland, MI Metro Area	13,835	1,902	13,211	1,902	na	na	na	na	na	na	na	na
Midland, TX Metro Area	15,795	2,217	11,695	1,738	731	115	na	na	na	na	2,914	364
Milwaukee-Waukesha-West Allis, WI Metro Area	217,476	34,748	186,233	30,669	20,279	2,102	3,224	665	990	136	6,415	1,162
Minneapolis-St. Paul-Bloomington, MN-WI Metro Area	429,252	60,948	395,519	57,550	13,124	1,245	11,413	1,356	2,358	263	5,642	653
Minot, ND Micro Area	9,354	1,801	9,159	1,801	na	na	na	na	na	na	na	na
Missoula, MT Metro Area	15,155	2,649	14,779	2,604	na	na	na	na	na	na	na	na
Mobile, AL Metro Area	60,050	8,299	42,344	5,781	15,620	2,310	735	0	na	na	719	0
Modesto, CA Metro Area	64,448	8,466	44,730	6,240	1,368	404	3,106	228	1,880	344	13,492	1,385
Monroe, LA Metro Area	24,659	2,628	19,138	2,261	4,886	367	na	na	na	na	na	na
Monroe, MI Metro Area	23,690	3,255	22,727	3,126	na	na	na	na	na	na	na	na
Montgomery, AL Metro Area	51,069	4,777	34,824	3,624	14,990	1,153	na	na	na	na	432	0
Morehead City, NC Micro Area	15,294	1,462	14,135	1,347	na	na	na	na	na	na	na	na
Morgantown, WV Metro Area	16,881	2,073	16,505	2,037	na	na	na	na	na	na	na	na

Table C-4: Metropolitan/Micropolitan Statistical Areas—Older Population by Race and Hispanic Origin—*Continued*

	Total Population		White, Non-Hispanic		Black, Alone		Asian, Alone		Multi-race		Hispanic	
	65 Years and Over	85 Years and Over	65 Years and Over	85 Years and Over	65 Years and Over	85 Years and Over	65 Years and Over	85 Years and Over	65 Years and Over	85 Years and Over	65 Years and Over	85 Years and Over
Morristown, TN Metro Area	21,165	1,795	20,112	1,678	na	na	na	na	na	na	na	na
Moses Lake, WA Micro Area	11,740	1,346	9,978	1,310	na	na	na	na	na	na	1,117	0
Mount Airy, NC Micro Area	13,770	1,826	13,068	1,815	na	na	na	na	na	na	0	0
Mount Pleasant, MI Micro Area	7,589	999	7,328	952	na	na	na	na	na	na	na	na
Mount Vernon-Anacortes, WA Metro Area	22,864	2,862	21,008	2,762	na	na	na	na	na	na	1,143	0
Muncie, IN Metro Area	18,735	2,883	17,552	2,693	816	190	na	na	na	na	na	na
Muskegon, MI Metro Area	25,849	3,289	22,953	3,020	2,120	200	na	na	363	69	402	0
Muskogee, OK Micro Area	11,148	1,696	8,453	1,451	1,010	106	na	na	308	33	na	na
Myrtle Beach-Conway-North Myrtle Beach, SC-NC Metro Area	93,105	7,190	84,817	6,514	6,209	651	na	na	na	na	1,016	25
Nacogdoches, TX Micro Area	8,511	1,127	6,955	970	1,340	81	na	na	na	na	101	0
Napa, CA Metro Area	24,631	3,589	19,146	3,125	na	na	1,911	72	na	na	2,531	392
Naples-Immokalee-Marco Island, FL Metro Area	102,262	11,201	92,960	9,837	2,150	243	na	na	na	na	6,062	1,121
Nashville-Davidson–Murfreesboro–Franklin, TN Metro Area	218,527	22,545	187,655	20,120	22,602	1,898	3,454	222	1,396	203	3,398	102
New Bern, NC Metro Area	23,613	3,152	18,329	2,204	5,065	849	na	na	na	na	173	99
New Castle, PA Metro Area	17,555	3,075	17,068	2,958	na	na	na	na	na	na	na	na
New Haven-Milford, CT Metro Area	134,334	22,801	113,470	20,969	10,572	1,289	2,344	134	1,094	0	7,251	409
New Orleans-Metairie, LA Metro Area	171,538	20,088	112,143	14,751	45,320	4,095	3,800	177	1,178	173	8,529	945
New Philadelphia-Dover, OH Micro Area	16,746	2,740	16,297	2,531	na	na	na	na	na	na	na	na
New York-Newark-Jersey City, NY-NJ-PA Metro Area	2,829,805	417,907	1,794,897	303,545	411,952	52,101	229,006	21,248	35,637	3,079	391,438	42,171
Niles-Benton Harbor, MI Metro Area	27,218	3,430	24,290	3,226	2,494	165	na	na	na	na	99	0
North Port-Sarasota-Bradenton, FL Metro Area	224,773	30,936	209,556	30,156	5,043	517	2,598	32	na	na	6,403	162
North Wilkesboro, NC Micro Area	13,662	1,405	12,914	1,333	na	na	na	na	na	na	na	na
Norwich-New London, CT Metro Area	44,057	5,971	39,739	5,533	1,076	438	1,045	0	924	0	1,253	0
Oak Harbor, WA Micro Area	18,182	1,979	16,615	1,904	na	na	na	na	na	na	na	na
Ocala, FL Metro Area	94,207	11,070	82,157	10,227	5,862	680	na	na	na	na	4,570	163
Ocean City, NJ Metro Area	22,927	2,659	21,677	2,616	na	na	na	na	na	na	na	na
Odessa, TX Metro Area	14,664	1,798	9,039	974	na	na	na	na	na	na	4,848	679
Ogden-Clearfield, UT Metro Area	63,949	7,310	58,702	6,776	na	na	834	18	910	0	3,372	488
Ogdensburg-Massena, NY Micro Area	16,993	2,445	16,428	2,445	na	na	na	na	na	na	na	na
Oklahoma City, OK Metro Area	169,740	19,844	141,504	17,036	11,654	1,600	3,649	124	4,133	271	5,065	362
Olean, NY Micro Area	13,428	1,680	12,886	1,646	na	na	na	na	na	na	na	na
Olympia-Tumwater, WA Metro Area	40,285	4,593	36,308	4,168	552	69	1,841	52	191	0	752	304
Omaha-Council Bluffs, NE-IA Metro Area	110,526	16,822	100,318	15,030	5,431	765	1,331	406	560	25	2,579	484
Opelousas, LA Micro Area	12,313	1,937	8,156	1,320	4,068	617	na	na	na	na	na	na
Orangeburg, SC Micro Area	15,222	2,064	7,341	774	7,684	1,205	na	na	na	na	na	na
Orlando-Kissimmee-Sanford, FL Metro Area	321,161	40,917	218,781	30,188	33,919	3,425	12,328	735	3,439	309	54,333	6,533
Oshkosh-Neenah, WI Metro Area	25,191	3,315	24,332	3,135	na	na	na	na	na	na	191	20
Ottawa-Peru, IL Micro Area	27,752	4,693	26,911	4,486	na	na	na	na	na	na	575	135
Owensboro, KY Metro Area	19,370	2,088	18,806	1,951	na	na	na	na	na	na	569	0
Owosso, MI Micro Area	11,593	1,745	10,988	1,573	na	na	na	na	na	na	na	na
Oxnard-Thousand Oaks-Ventura, CA Metro Area	114,954	17,233	80,131	13,250	1,581	86	8,872	1,009	1,881	109	22,783	2,804
Paducah, KY-IL Micro Area	17,976	2,744	16,635	2,638	1,107	96	na	na	na	na	na	na
Palatka, FL Micro Area	14,899	952	13,129	944	1,178	8	na	na	na	na	na	na
Palm Bay-Melbourne-Titusville, FL Metro Area	126,012	17,681	109,071	15,619	7,917	954	1,919	207	1,001	180	6,051	842
Panama City, FL Metro Area	31,924	3,634	27,587	3,253	2,159	245	na	na	na	na	886	65
Parkersburg-Vienna, WV Metro Area	17,292	2,048	16,929	2,006	na	na	na	na	na	na	na	na
Pensacola-Ferry Pass-Brent, FL Metro Area	72,918	7,728	60,339	6,424	8,055	1,015	1,808	140	1,335	45	1,558	104
Peoria, IL Metro Area	60,638	9,073	57,175	8,983	2,177	90	203	0	506	0	569	0
Philadelphia-Camden-Wilmington, PA-NJ-DE-MD Metro Area	878,054	130,096	674,108	108,705	140,684	17,096	30,472	1,611	7,511	745	26,652	1,919
Phoenix-Mesa-Scottsdale, AZ Metro Area	637,879	75,192	530,009	67,334	17,363	1,910	15,965	916	5,644	508	66,589	4,373
Pine Bluff, AR Metro Area	14,658	1,609	9,681	1,171	4,866	408	na	na	na	na	na	na
Pinehurst-Southern Pines, NC Micro Area	22,340	4,339	19,812	4,046	2,398	260	na	na	na	na	na	na
Pittsburgh, PA Metro Area	432,142	71,675	400,364	67,865	24,103	3,229	3,564	173	1,639	149	2,286	291
Pittsfield, MA Metro Area	26,665	4,323	26,010	4,302	na	na	na	na	na	na	na	na
Plattsburgh, NY Micro Area	12,286	1,290	12,020	1,284	na	na	na	na	na	na	na	na
Pocatello, ID Metro Area	10,666	888	9,902	888	na	na	na	na	na	na	561	0
Port Angeles, WA Micro Area	19,479	3,167	18,394	3,069	na	na	na	na	na	na	na	na
Port St. Lucie, FL Metro Area	109,900	16,537	95,266	14,472	7,843	1,127	na	na	na	na	6,052	938
Portland-South Portland, ME Metro Area	89,941	12,407	87,755	12,336	182	0	658	0	597	71	425	0
Portland-Vancouver-Hillsboro, OR-WA Metro Area	311,095	40,494	277,561	37,716	5,578	560	13,847	1,101	3,041	498	8,844	476
Portsmouth, OH Micro Area	12,766	1,687	12,539	1,670	na	na	na	na	na	na	na	na
Pottsville, PA Micro Area	28,211	4,590	27,723	4,528	na	na	na	na	na	na	323	62
Prescott, AZ Metro Area	61,708	7,413	57,284	7,257	na	na	na	na	na	na	2,766	150
Providence-Warwick, RI-MA Metro Area	254,223	42,071	230,653	39,625	6,372	624	4,022	447	2,820	634	9,026	581
Provo-Orem, UT Metro Area	41,046	3,300	38,255	3,261	na	na	352	0	240	0	1,981	39
Pueblo, CO Metro Area	27,960	3,506	19,065	2,529	na	na	na	na	850	226	7,728	621
Punta Gorda, FL Metro Area	63,386	7,724	59,060	7,064	na	na	na	na	na	na	1,371	119
Quincy, IL-MO Micro Area	14,137	2,567	13,774	2,567	na	na	na	na	na	na	na	na
Racine, WI Metro Area	29,486	4,309	25,550	3,441	1,907	437	na	na	na	na	1,867	493
Raleigh, NC Metro Area	132,215	12,671	101,868	10,203	21,329	1,946	4,185	162	945	83	3,455	243
Rapid City, SD Metro Area	21,760	3,100	20,937	3,011	na	na	na	na	na	na	na	na
Reading, PA Metro Area	66,449	9,085	59,945	8,516	2,122	115	439	93	1,747	109	3,450	361
Redding, CA Metro Area	34,665	4,885	31,742	4,755	na	na	na	na	806	39	1,413	60
Reno, NV Metro Area	65,768	6,619	55,193	5,471	1,163	227	3,105	152	939	117	4,929	654

Table C-4: Metropolitan/Micropolitan Statistical Areas—Older Population by Race and Hispanic Origin—*Continued*

	Total Population		White, Non-Hispanic		Black, Alone		Asian, Alone		Multi-race		Hispanic	
	65 Years and Over	85 Years and Over	65 Years and Over	85 Years and Over	65 Years and Over	85 Years and Over	65 Years and Over	85 Years and Over	65 Years and Over	85 Years and Over	65 Years and Over	85 Years and Over
Richmond, IN Micro Area	12,325	1,278	11,371	1,278	na	na	na	na	na	na	na	na
Richmond, VA Metro Area	171,447	23,009	121,526	15,957	41,326	6,027	3,368	555	1,520	202	3,330	184
Richmond-Berea, KY Micro Area	14,076	1,428	13,658	1,428	na	na	na	na	na	na	na	na
Riverside-San Bernardino-Ontario, CA Metro Area	525,345	65,136	320,938	43,221	31,362	2,555	36,335	4,076	10,160	1,160	126,993	14,362
Roanoke Rapids, NC Micro Area	14,119	1,689	6,947	1,245	6,768	404	na	na	na	na	na	na
Roanoke, VA Metro Area	57,681	8,392	50,965	7,410	4,915	629	na	na	na	na	765	182
Rochester, MN Metro Area	31,746	4,782	30,511	4,753	na	na	800	18	na	na	256	10
Rochester, NY Metro Area	173,008	27,164	153,298	25,193	11,651	792	2,525	224	881	127	4,048	557
Rockford, IL Metro Area	52,810	6,727	46,728	6,180	3,057	172	na	na	502	51	2,084	83
Rocky Mount, NC Metro Area	24,752	2,592	15,188	1,673	8,678	805	na	na	na	na	99	11
Rome, GA Metro Area	14,678	2,121	13,146	1,512	1,271	609	na	na	na	na	na	na
Roseburg, OR Micro Area	25,170	3,680	23,894	3,498	na	na	na	na	na	na	na	na
Roswell, NM Micro Area	9,807	711	6,354	648	na	na	na	na	na	na	3,048	63
Russellville, AR Micro Area	13,147	1,342	12,500	1,296	na	na	na	na	na	na	258	0
Sacramento–Roseville–Arden-Arcade, CA Metro Area	312,731	39,143	227,563	30,540	16,135	1,324	35,275	3,803	4,293	414	28,694	3,211
Saginaw, MI Metro Area	33,397	3,726	27,380	3,117	4,361	399	na	na	na	na	1,499	210
Salem, OH Micro Area	19,192	2,592	18,879	2,487	na	na	na	na	na	na	na	na
Salem, OR Metro Area	60,787	7,964	54,961	7,797	na	na	945	0	1,101	65	3,088	78
Salinas, CA Metro Area	51,152	7,658	32,424	5,737	1,241	291	4,361	629	1,079	219	12,296	782
Salisbury, MD-DE Metro Area	81,658	9,044	71,440	8,203	7,809	810	800	0	na	na	789	31
Salt Lake City, UT Metro Area	110,379	13,081	97,193	11,431	876	304	3,259	502	418	53	7,339	791
San Angelo, TX Metro Area	17,528	2,505	12,891	1,742	na	na	na	na	na	na	3,438	674
San Antonio-New Braunfels, TX Metro Area	281,067	33,675	149,301	19,190	14,652	1,642	5,100	405	3,824	594	110,010	12,280
San Diego-Carlsbad, CA Metro Area	414,632	56,136	278,674	41,271	13,844	1,592	46,981	5,554	6,754	680	68,126	7,356
San Francisco-Oakland-Hayward, CA Metro Area	643,065	90,288	356,545	56,764	46,891	4,989	160,960	19,883	12,338	1,107	65,418	7,805
San Jose-Sunnyvale-Santa Clara, CA Metro Area	237,813	29,742	125,118	17,027	4,729	338	70,666	8,542	3,539	586	33,742	3,325
San Luis Obispo-Paso Robles-Arroyo Grande, CA Metro Area	49,252	5,523	42,952	5,193	na	na	na	na	na	na	3,759	263
Sandusky, OH Micro Area	14,639	1,942	13,774	1,685	na	na	na	na	na	na	na	na
Santa Cruz-Watsonville, CA Metro Area	36,267	4,187	29,633	3,495	na	na	1,532	205	199	0	4,797	487
Santa Fe, NM Metro Area	29,029	2,639	19,217	1,846	na	na	na	na	na	na	8,887	746
Santa Maria-Santa Barbara, CA Metro Area	61,405	10,704	45,811	8,758	739	117	2,454	379	992	232	11,495	998
Santa Rosa, CA Metro Area	82,536	13,079	72,200	11,918	na	na	2,657	156	1,173	57	6,377	885
Savannah, GA Metro Area	47,695	6,232	33,392	4,689	12,764	1,393	667	0	251	36	626	114
Scranton–Wilkes-Barre–Hazleton, PA Metro Area	105,588	19,015	101,870	18,910	1,056	11	1,037	0	177	0	1,591	94
Searcy, AR Micro Area	11,920	1,233	11,385	1,233	na	na	na	na	na	na	na	na
Seattle-Tacoma-Bellevue, WA Metro Area	449,976	63,806	364,143	55,100	16,225	1,356	49,758	5,849	5,251	217	11,736	1,298
Sebastian-Vero Beach, FL Metro Area	43,896	7,638	40,245	7,153	na	na	na	na	na	na	1,391	42
Sebring, FL Metro Area	33,181	3,933	29,445	3,604	na	na	na	na	na	na	1,894	226
Seneca, SC Micro Area	15,950	1,271	15,148	986	na	na	na	na	na	na	na	na
Sevierville, TN Micro Area	16,976	1,475	16,340	1,475	na	na	na	na	na	na	na	na
Shawnee, OK Micro Area	11,228	1,390	9,891	1,156	na	na	na	na	na	na	205	26
Sheboygan, WI Metro Area	18,520	2,826	18,091	2,801	na	na	na	na	na	na	121	0
Shelby, NC Micro Area	16,837	1,817	13,766	1,443	2,586	374	na	na	na	na	na	na
Sherman-Denison, TX Metro Area	20,866	2,202	19,075	2,202	na	na	na	na	na	na	410	0
Show Low, AZ Micro Area	17,129	1,339	10,975	908	na	na	na	na	na	na	1,156	0
Shreveport-Bossier City, LA Metro Area	65,150	8,423	44,472	6,792	18,586	1,427	na	na	na	na	695	47
Sierra Vista-Douglas, AZ Metro Area	25,160	3,151	19,429	2,602	na	na	na	na	798	0	4,629	358
Sioux City, IA-NE-SD Metro Area	24,983	3,696	23,694	3,457	na	na	na	na	na	na	790	229
Sioux Falls, SD Metro Area	30,550	4,488	29,386	4,403	107	0	na	na	na	na	418	0
Somerset, PA Micro Area	15,608	2,400	15,312	2,357	na	na	na	na	na	na	na	na
South Bend-Mishawaka, IN-MI Metro Area	47,979	7,211	43,189	6,385	3,408	542	na	na	255	53	592	193
Spartanburg, SC Metro Area	49,559	4,979	40,353	4,350	7,535	396	na	na	na	na	585	53
Spokane-Spokane Valley, WA Metro Area	83,901	11,625	78,564	11,492	927	0	1,632	91	977	0	945	30
Springfield, IL Metro Area	33,942	4,697	30,983	4,430	1,954	216	na	na	na	na	na	na
Springfield, MA Metro Area	95,123	15,582	82,807	14,516	4,335	602	1,158	41	696	86	6,250	337
Springfield, MO Metro Area	69,605	9,635	67,101	9,061	747	54	na	na	506	127	683	393
Springfield, OH Metro Area	24,356	3,393	22,249	3,182	1,663	211	na	na	na	na	na	na
St. Cloud, MN Metro Area	25,714	3,779	25,298	3,771	44	0	na	na	na	na	30	8
St. George, UT Metro Area	30,065	3,932	28,410	3,847	na	na	na	na	na	na	711	39
St. Joseph, MO-KS Metro Area	19,344	2,570	18,401	2,534	na	na	na	na	na	na	na	na
St. Louis, MO-IL Metro Area	417,428	55,504	348,147	48,799	55,270	5,562	6,653	279	2,680	257	4,681	594
State College, PA Metro Area	19,873	2,417	19,159	2,417	na	na	na	na	na	na	na	na
Statesboro, GA Micro Area	7,492	760	5,808	615	1,457	145	na	na	na	na	na	na
Staunton-Waynesboro, VA Metro Area	22,989	1,478	21,425	1,287	na	na	na	na	na	na	na	na
Stevens Point, WI Micro Area	10,224	1,110	10,039	1,110	na	na	na	na	na	na	na	na
Stillwater, OK Micro Area	8,789	1,339	8,212	1,283	na	na	na	na	na	na	na	na
Stockton-Lodi, CA Metro Area	84,298	10,225	48,285	7,185	4,755	258	12,594	902	3,656	379	16,734	1,554
Sumter, SC Metro Area	15,488	1,882	8,650	1,195	6,534	687	na	na	na	na	na	na
Sunbury, PA Micro Area	18,608	2,721	18,196	2,721	na	na	na	na	na	na	na	na
Syracuse, NY Metro Area	100,421	15,620	93,080	14,816	4,183	547	1,596	178	339	59	1,129	40
Talladega-Sylacauga, AL Micro Area	15,341	1,752	11,969	1,501	3,133	251	na	na	na	na	na	na
Tallahassee, FL Metro Area	45,738	5,566	33,684	4,588	10,645	701	585	0	na	na	562	284
Tampa-St. Petersburg-Clearwater, FL Metro Area	545,152	79,583	453,436	70,235	32,040	3,106	11,053	779	3,285	175	45,800	5,209
Terre Haute, IN Metro Area	26,056	4,249	24,822	3,929	471	157	na	na	na	na	na	na
Texarkana, TX-AR Metro Area	23,048	2,784	19,146	2,435	3,408	304	na	na	na	na	na	na
The Villages, FL Metro Area	60,225	4,423	57,995	4,375	na	na	na	na	na	na	na	na

Table C-4: Metropolitan/Micropolitan Statistical Areas—Older Population by Race and Hispanic Origin—*Continued*

	Total Population		White, Non-Hispanic		Black, Alone		Asian, Alone		Multi-race		Hispanic	
	65 Years and Over	85 Years and Over	65 Years and Over	85 Years and Over	65 Years and Over	85 Years and Over	65 Years and Over	85 Years and Over	65 Years and Over	85 Years and Over	65 Years and Over	85 Years and Over
Toledo, OH Metro Area	88,188	13,882	75,997	12,444	8,835	966	711	79	666	203	2,177	184
Topeka, KS Metro Area	38,126	5,675	34,716	5,226	1,300	240	na	na	581	58	1,192	107
Torrington, CT Micro Area	34,102	5,055	32,879	4,917	na	na	na	na	na	na	427	0
Traverse City, MI Micro Area	29,046	3,001	28,415	3,001	na	na	na	na	na	na	na	na
Trenton, NJ Metro Area	51,229	6,863	36,761	6,101	8,275	496	3,048	266	na	na	2,735	0
Truckee-Grass Valley, CA Micro Area	23,122	2,911	21,572	2,593	na	na	na	na	na	na	744	0
Tucson, AZ Metro Area	178,045	20,248	139,683	16,904	3,422	0	3,247	389	1,534	40	28,900	2,899
Tullahoma-Manchester, TN Micro Area	18,288	1,521	17,688	1,490	na	na	na	na	na	na	na	na
Tulsa, OK Metro Area	137,415	16,548	115,127	14,174	7,183	922	1,554	247	5,681	652	2,591	200
Tupelo, MS Micro Area	20,215	3,008	17,396	2,789	2,676	219	na	na	na	na	na	na
Tuscaloosa, AL Metro Area	30,054	4,896	21,649	3,289	7,599	1,210	na	na	na	na	na	na
Twin Falls, ID Micro Area	15,304	1,728	13,997	1,594	na	na	na	na	na	na	913	61
Tyler, TX Metro Area	33,899	4,075	27,558	3,327	4,372	669	na	na	na	na	1,752	79
Ukiah, CA Micro Area	16,976	2,172	14,556	2,081	na	na	na	na	na	na	1,455	0
Urban Honolulu, HI Metro Area	156,728	27,910	29,311	4,026	683	0	101,202	21,336	15,527	1,913	3,997	239
Utica-Rome, NY Metro Area	52,755	8,393	50,029	8,319	1,089	48	682	15	na	na	425	0
Valdosta, GA Metro Area	17,171	1,065	12,140	957	4,539	108	na	na	na	na	97	0
Vallejo-Fairfield, CA Metro Area	58,204	5,866	32,267	4,031	7,167	371	10,849	920	1,364	80	6,502	484
Victoria, TX Metro Area	14,742	1,954	10,090	1,163	na	na	na	na	na	na	4,061	675
Vineland-Bridgeton, NJ Metro Area	21,282	2,994	15,796	2,344	2,589	393	na	na	na	na	2,550	241
Virginia Beach-Norfolk-Newport News, VA-NC Metro Area	222,256	28,249	154,425	20,830	53,945	6,302	8,277	624	1,702	230	3,746	301
Visalia-Porterville, CA Metro Area	47,336	6,886	28,507	4,879	na	na	2,108	304	807	48	15,804	1,546
Waco, TX Metro Area	35,065	4,429	27,249	3,961	3,843	148	na	na	na	na	3,151	277
Walla Walla, WA Metro Area	10,261	1,645	9,815	1,590	na	na	na	na	na	na	322	55
Warner Robins, GA Metro Area	22,239	2,484	17,722	2,337	3,372	147	na	na	na	na	na	na
Warsaw, IN Micro Area	11,763	1,062	11,418	1,062	na	na	na	na	na	na	na	na
Washington-Arlington-Alexandria, DC-VA-MD-WV Metro Area	687,817	87,227	418,277	58,575	160,642	17,948	60,159	5,870	11,331	1,309	38,831	3,904
Waterloo-Cedar Falls, IA Metro Area	26,495	3,349	25,236	3,189	895	139	na	na	na	na	46	21
Watertown-Fort Atkinson, WI Micro Area	12,488	1,512	12,350	1,512	na	na	na	na	na	na	na	na
Watertown-Fort Drum, NY Metro Area	14,632	1,566	14,079	1,522	na	na	na	na	na	na	236	0
Wausau, WI Metro Area	21,426	3,386	21,143	3,254	na	na	215	132	na	na	na	na
Weirton-Steubenville, WV-OH Metro Area	24,105	3,271	22,643	3,025	na	na	na	na	na	na	na	na
Wenatchee, WA Metro Area	19,406	2,660	17,834	2,440	na	na	na	na	na	na	1,107	99
Wheeling, WV-OH Metro Area	27,773	3,756	27,127	3,615	na	na	na	na	na	na	na	na
Whitewater-Elkhorn, WI Micro Area	15,610	1,950	15,293	1,950	na	na	na	na	na	na	207	0
Wichita Falls, TX Metro Area	21,784	3,035	18,753	2,535	1,182	92	na	na	na	na	1,405	252
Wichita, KS Metro Area	86,458	11,172	75,383	10,017	4,331	427	1,841	47	930	167	3,415	292
Williamsport, PA Metro Area	20,476	3,224	19,917	3,224	na	na	na	na	na	na	na	na
Wilmington, NC Metro Area	43,583	5,031	37,315	4,288	5,679	743	na	na	na	na	427	0
Wilson, NC Micro Area	13,432	1,473	8,777	889	4,240	459	na	na	na	na	na	na
Winchester, VA-WV Metro Area	21,556	3,148	19,961	2,952	na	na	na	na	na	na	na	na
Winston-Salem, NC Metro Area	102,715	11,775	87,874	10,645	12,715	1,054	339	0	399	57	1,419	57
Wisconsin Rapids-Marshfield, WI Micro Area	13,822	2,581	13,402	2,552	na	na	na	na	na	na	na	na
Wooster, OH Micro Area	18,369	2,491	18,212	2,491	na	na	na	na	na	na	na	na
Worcester, MA-CT Metro Area	131,819	20,416	121,893	19,894	1,942	25	2,871	90	941	291	4,619	128
Yakima, WA Metro Area	31,605	3,816	24,883	3,416	na	na	na	na	287	0	5,111	206
York-Hanover, PA Metro Area	70,222	7,480	66,347	7,344	1,852	0	na	na	370	0	1,101	16
Youngstown-Warren-Boardman, OH-PA Metro Area	107,054	18,314	97,253	16,924	7,658	1,132	na	na	465	88	1,193	116
Yuba City, CA Metro Area	22,708	2,773	15,810	1,776	na	na	2,500	425	1,174	0	2,425	457
Yuma, AZ Metro Area	35,937	2,445	24,793	1,839	na	na	na	na	na	na	9,445	510
Zanesville, OH Micro Area	14,224	2,018	13,644	1,832	na	na	na	na	na	na	na	na

Table C-5: 114th Congressional Districts—Older Population by Race and Hispanic Origin

	Total Population		White, Non-Hispanic		Black, Alone		Asian, Alone		Multi-race		Hispanic	
	65 Years and Over	85 Years and Over	65 Years and Over	85 Years and Over	65 Years and Over	85 Years and Over	65 Years and Over	85 Years and Over	65 Years and Over	85 Years and Over	65 Years and Over	85 Years and Over
Alabama												
Congressional District 1	113,016	13,300	87,421	10,210	21,501	2,530	1,379	41	na	na	1,251	92
Congressional District 2	105,469	11,163	83,972	9,417	18,988	1,556	na	na	817	22	515	62
Congressional District 3	105,875	11,081	83,274	8,768	20,282	2,313	na	na	733	0	904	0
Congressional District 4	117,390	12,520	108,198	11,733	6,278	557	na	na	1,401	52	742	143
Congressional District 5	106,010	11,626	91,544	10,113	10,731	1,199	1,295	91	956	97	1,342	126
Congressional District 6	106,530	11,608	95,897	10,839	7,330	513	738	93	1,176	0	1,307	90
Congressional District 7	92,222	12,251	38,392	6,118	52,306	5,693	na	na	400	179	1,282	261
Alaska												
Congressional District (at Large)	69,899	6,237	51,628	4,658	2,297	229	3,508	625	1,719	54	2,161	42
Arizona												
Congressional District 1	120,886	10,185	88,314	7,239	1,720	90	1,886	0	955	0	11,811	1,092
Congressional District 2	139,664	18,057	116,943	15,783	2,416	138	2,894	442	1,676	40	15,728	1,654
Congressional District 3	81,001	5,649	40,560	3,184	2,950	0	1,280	52	763	35	34,603	2,397
Congressional District 4	191,506	17,400	175,103	16,802	1,311	0	na	na	1,873	61	11,361	367
Congressional District 5	121,024	16,338	105,415	14,121	2,272	342	3,190	197	910	162	8,565	1,417
Congressional District 6	123,006	14,650	110,991	13,565	1,536	377	3,085	327	903	82	6,152	339
Congressional District 7	53,047	4,980	23,380	3,170	5,016	520	1,729	96	995	114	21,416	1,058
Congressional District 8	154,715	20,239	139,677	19,291	3,466	317	4,095	190	1,018	87	6,750	277
Congressional District 9	85,908	12,096	69,910	11,188	2,830	322	2,255	106	1,048	63	10,218	440
Arkansas												
Congressional District 1	125,713	14,206	109,127	12,627	13,385	1,544	na	na	1,736	0	1,505	0
Congressional District 2	107,177	13,832	91,912	12,294	12,692	1,456	335	0	1,132	0	1,143	82
Congressional District 3	104,556	12,609	97,564	12,101	1,249	135	1,377	90	1,147	217	2,597	0
Congressional District 4	127,566	14,849	108,370	12,787	16,072	1,861	na	na	820	51	1,513	55
California												
Congressional District 1	139,511	19,970	126,411	18,508	208	0	2,261	311	2,627	379	6,478	587
Congressional District 2	129,623	17,235	115,843	15,592	936	0	3,295	555	1,193	130	6,961	819
Congressional District 3	93,212	10,917	63,838	8,083	4,967	240	9,881	1,080	2,440	137	11,737	1,301
Congressional District 4	137,704	14,064	121,408	13,009	1,129	0	4,735	374	1,517	0	7,364	575
Congressional District 5	115,118	16,164	83,274	13,750	5,523	420	12,610	727	2,498	80	11,464	1,204
Congressional District 6	83,495	10,614	44,639	6,150	9,684	797	15,628	2,080	1,544	273	12,068	1,463
Congressional District 7	104,127	13,894	78,549	11,604	5,175	506	11,821	1,042	1,682	15	6,910	727
Congressional District 8	91,372	9,438	63,258	6,739	5,540	344	4,647	313	1,147	61	16,068	1,893
Congressional District 9	90,961	11,453	51,981	7,761	6,628	377	14,180	1,461	3,173	319	17,032	1,588
Congressional District 10	83,750	10,199	57,415	7,609	1,806	404	4,702	238	2,807	404	17,312	1,679
Congressional District 11	111,746	16,435	76,643	12,689	7,583	716	14,565	1,545	2,789	620	10,088	1,063
Congressional District 12	106,978	16,350	43,900	6,014	5,970	772	46,196	8,059	1,831	161	9,260	1,394
Congressional District 13	92,962	13,273	41,943	7,536	19,250	2,406	21,145	2,456	1,679	45	8,206	857
Congressional District 14	108,974	13,556	53,977	8,411	4,670	455	34,707	3,029	1,908	142	13,727	1,586
Congressional District 15	94,419	12,964	48,768	8,029	4,181	368	27,009	2,927	2,501	139	11,679	1,470
Congressional District 16	73,473	10,000	34,731	4,927	4,079	503	6,483	1,153	2,350	260	26,529	3,235
Congressional District 17	86,689	10,288	36,838	5,919	1,945	0	38,669	2,993	948	165	7,859	1,250
Congressional District 18	105,697	15,079	80,190	10,863	1,201	202	15,877	3,027	1,245	135	7,327	801
Congressional District 19	86,993	10,483	36,459	4,937	2,196	136	26,228	3,369	2,049	286	19,740	1,792
Congressional District 20	86,320	11,972	58,492	9,232	1,544	291	5,561	850	1,184	219	19,927	1,380
Congressional District 21	56,320	5,847	23,481	2,839	2,012	117	3,065	332	851	82	26,883	2,493
Congressional District 22	85,553	12,587	57,619	9,550	1,304	192	5,581	832	1,192	159	18,935	1,836
Congressional District 23	86,903	10,797	61,784	7,921	3,641	280	4,907	732	1,852	75	14,455	1,705
Congressional District 24	111,451	16,266	89,474	13,990	1,139	117	3,944	379	1,616	232	15,254	1,261
Congressional District 25	75,750	8,088	47,602	5,684	4,537	277	7,020	825	1,308	114	14,912	1,235
Congressional District 26	98,519	15,675	67,636	12,145	1,452	86	7,007	818	1,811	109	20,917	2,542
Congressional District 27	116,157	17,998	45,427	7,747	5,496	500	44,159	7,313	1,617	291	18,927	2,029
Congressional District 28	103,760	13,225	68,892	9,871	1,280	75	14,117	968	1,622	221	18,263	2,213
Congressional District 29	72,146	8,077	26,036	3,621	3,146	233	8,995	1,056	1,101	150	32,919	3,062
Congressional District 30	110,173	17,095	80,984	13,981	3,074	532	11,752	946	1,826	82	12,710	1,509
Congressional District 31	72,239	9,375	33,299	5,093	7,432	803	7,893	696	1,873	397	21,864	2,362
Congressional District 32	95,253	11,770	27,535	4,859	4,370	403	22,903	2,177	1,554	55	39,526	4,444
Congressional District 33	118,886	19,516	94,826	16,709	1,799	343	11,748	686	3,264	573	7,223	1,337
Congressional District 34	78,323	10,933	9,421	2,116	2,826	291	30,731	4,263	1,200	246	34,932	4,184
Congressional District 35	60,573	6,612	18,633	2,599	4,317	192	4,729	533	1,754	145	31,633	3,245
Congressional District 36	145,615	21,061	112,237	16,482	3,533	723	4,903	296	1,935	247	22,912	3,383
Congressional District 37	88,926	14,896	31,541	6,503	30,226	4,929	9,664	1,825	1,734	179	16,521	1,604
Congressional District 38	96,491	12,851	28,712	4,504	3,446	428	20,109	2,197	2,177	285	42,625	5,438
Congressional District 39	96,278	14,506	48,613	7,359	1,290	69	26,757	5,033	1,362	106	18,537	1,939
Congressional District 40	55,925	7,104	7,780	986	4,632	710	3,869	500	910	83	39,368	4,825
Congressional District 41	66,896	8,405	31,062	4,619	7,321	530	5,408	785	1,453	157	21,698	2,337
Congressional District 42	85,783	10,172	55,737	7,137	4,108	0	7,200	973	1,736	130	17,117	2,015
Congressional District 43	82,190	10,667	22,294	3,338	23,578	1,941	15,085	3,867	2,774	76	19,283	1,488
Congressional District 44	61,865	7,262	9,625	1,399	15,852	2,220	5,893	739	1,248	53	29,657	3,030
Congressional District 45	102,060	14,165	73,447	11,808	1,171	0	17,152	1,321	1,194	42	8,692	1,042
Congressional District 46	64,460	8,210	25,097	4,189	935	0	15,171	1,883	1,318	88	22,307	2,044
Congressional District 47	89,115	10,915	47,486	6,709	4,601	156	21,408	1,896	1,599	154	14,177	1,958
Congressional District 48	115,597	14,474	81,486	11,812	811	0	22,762	1,981	1,276	48	8,769	633
Congressional District 49	103,754	13,808	83,874	12,609	1,107	0	6,833	336	316	0	11,252	837
Congressional District 50	102,746	12,967	82,947	10,768	1,802	244	4,037	410	2,069	345	11,695	1,354

Table C-5: 114th Congressional Districts—Older Population by Race and Hispanic Origin—*Continued*

	Total Population		White, Non-Hispanic		Black, Alone		Asian, Alone		Multi-race		Hispanic	
	65 Years and Over	85 Years and Over	65 Years and Over	85 Years and Over	65 Years and Over	85 Years and Over	65 Years and Over	85 Years and Over	65 Years and Over	85 Years and Over	65 Years and Over	85 Years and Over
California—Cont.												
Congressional District 51	76,301	10,279	21,452	3,706	4,971	845	8,868	1,372	2,104	256	39,803	4,298
Congressional District 52	96,469	13,728	71,827	11,172	1,791	0	14,327	1,927	1,508	118	7,036	551
Congressional District 53	94,491	13,150	54,970	8,440	5,138	676	15,271	1,639	1,723	123	17,102	2,380
Colorado												
Congressional District 1	87,451	12,059	62,102	9,507	7,922	862	2,624	290	1,053	0	13,640	1,400
Congressional District 2	100,906	9,976	93,953	9,394	213	96	1,676	206	1,214	130	3,921	150
Congressional District 3	115,912	13,408	98,772	11,745	476	183	na	na	1,905	330	14,433	1,138
Congressional District 4	96,036	11,126	82,466	9,708	176	102	1,217	41	978	118	11,082	1,225
Congressional District 5	96,351	10,495	83,172	9,512	2,782	147	2,308	294	1,638	105	6,296	437
Congressional District 6	85,399	10,260	69,682	9,453	4,806	299	3,919	260	834	0	6,045	248
Congressional District 7	97,517	12,700	80,137	11,098	1,130	0	2,512	177	463	187	12,886	1,345
Connecticut												
Congressional District 1	114,464	19,424	92,483	17,375	11,253	1,182	2,495	67	803	0	7,716	711
Congressional District 2	114,850	13,384	107,757	12,913	1,830	438	1,318	0	1,343	0	2,407	33
Congressional District 3	112,824	19,000	94,331	17,273	10,287	1,372	1,936	134	800	0	5,767	214
Congressional District 4	102,522	15,211	82,320	13,497	9,094	1,365	3,231	48	385	31	7,463	270
Congressional District 5	110,868	19,309	98,800	18,380	3,844	427	2,057	90	790	0	5,889	412
Delaware												
Congressional District (at Large)	153,759	17,141	124,696	14,343	21,311	2,049	3,403	266	905	41	3,233	360
District of Columbia												
Delegate District (at Large)	74,465	10,144	24,433	3,106	45,190	6,615	1,607	291	559	23	3,598	207
Florida												
Congressional District 1	116,518	12,977	99,235	10,989	10,607	1,400	2,721	169	1,634	76	2,035	116
Congressional District 2	103,379	11,706	83,027	10,134	15,916	1,156	1,348	0	952	0	1,737	352
Congressional District 3	122,179	15,081	107,021	13,610	8,313	946	1,448	71	1,258	99	3,947	270
Congressional District 4	102,171	12,581	87,962	10,858	5,120	475	3,445	398	612	42	4,884	743
Congressional District 5	85,080	10,597	36,063	4,836	37,565	4,039	2,446	24	791	87	8,611	1,737
Congressional District 6	173,836	23,635	155,505	21,284	9,522	1,605	2,040	196	455	44	6,055	506
Congressional District 7	103,551	16,768	79,711	13,906	6,779	741	2,483	324	935	98	13,617	1,805
Congressional District 8	171,342	25,527	150,320	22,837	9,454	1,322	2,708	207	1,274	398	7,605	884
Congressional District 9	88,291	10,648	47,128	6,145	8,297	1,346	3,438	117	1,356	52	29,234	3,166
Congressional District 10	143,887	15,549	116,073	13,653	8,939	695	6,570	465	706	16	11,519	720
Congressional District 11	239,116	25,753	217,801	23,727	8,817	1,208	na	na	824	50	8,954	852
Congressional District 12	157,114	24,937	140,514	23,314	4,096	134	2,211	145	1,028	84	9,324	1,295
Congressional District 13	167,042	24,013	152,932	22,940	4,142	185	3,047	108	871	0	6,142	555
Congressional District 14	96,569	13,755	53,278	9,227	18,743	1,940	3,127	442	877	0	20,960	2,185
Congressional District 15	105,177	11,416	85,010	9,463	7,727	1,129	2,945	193	563	59	8,790	567
Congressional District 16	223,476	30,936	208,305	30,156	5,043	517	2,598	32	na	na	6,357	162
Congressional District 17	193,295	24,894	174,101	22,624	8,029	981	1,722	422	467	41	8,860	858
Congressional District 18	177,066	26,218	155,734	23,701	10,242	1,165	898	25	653	134	9,334	1,193
Congressional District 19	220,177	27,672	204,358	26,106	5,133	457	na	na	949	31	8,982	933
Congressional District 20	104,708	16,921	47,780	10,644	38,046	4,571	1,856	361	1,101	83	15,991	1,293
Congressional District 21	172,588	31,538	146,915	28,516	8,539	898	2,646	200	1,079	178	13,357	1,650
Congressional District 22	156,483	28,742	130,232	25,686	7,610	639	2,488	18	884	153	15,730	2,246
Congressional District 23	119,038	18,322	73,087	12,700	8,275	416	2,717	172	1,491	48	34,352	4,986
Congressional District 24	89,089	11,178	13,921	2,917	45,333	5,281	1,208	0	1,145	41	30,218	3,161
Congressional District 25	117,022	14,454	41,951	4,541	6,083	1,297	1,532	0	344	0	68,764	8,654
Congressional District 26	118,445	16,931	30,052	4,420	7,974	815	2,797	0	1,546	274	77,684	11,528
Congressional District 27	124,315	21,507	20,525	3,268	5,176	1,123	1,309	515	1,192	180	98,615	17,098
Georgia												
Congressional District 1	95,698	11,222	71,608	8,668	20,942	2,221	930	41	667	80	1,255	164
Congressional District 2	94,595	10,787	54,508	7,360	37,768	3,244	749	0	702	106	1,094	115
Congressional District 3	98,916	9,587	80,314	7,571	16,044	1,959	1,030	0	360	0	1,184	57
Congressional District 4	74,242	7,079	36,525	4,804	32,610	2,026	3,088	0	346	0	2,198	331
Congressional District 5	77,417	7,801	24,150	3,381	48,999	4,326	1,979	0	580	32	1,672	62
Congressional District 6	80,113	11,276	67,352	9,860	4,865	326	5,278	630	644	126	2,565	334
Congressional District 7	67,003	5,978	47,593	4,874	6,264	298	8,105	653	542	23	4,537	43
Congressional District 8	100,371	10,356	76,167	8,401	21,724	1,850	na	na	789	59	663	46
Congressional District 9	123,737	11,515	112,209	10,566	7,017	808	na	na	705	0	2,411	95
Congressional District 10	98,899	9,729	76,555	7,347	19,613	2,360	467	0	175	0	1,779	22
Congressional District 11	79,383	6,900	70,254	6,316	4,844	441	1,394	0	1,127	0	1,926	143
Congressional District 12	92,884	10,336	65,016	6,885	24,544	2,845	1,751	179	336	38	1,293	389
Congressional District 13	70,861	7,951	40,356	5,222	26,231	2,459	1,735	59	617	171	2,451	301
Congressional District 14	94,751	8,685	87,342	7,753	4,531	932	na	na	na	na	892	0
Hawaii												
Congressional District 1	121,155	22,293	19,280	2,429	548	0	85,467	18,180	9,149	1,175	2,646	210
Congressional District 2	106,906	16,653	40,491	4,429	904	79	40,382	9,372	15,999	1,973	3,921	245
Idaho												
Congressional District 1	129,721	13,790	121,033	13,040	na	na	1,183	116	1,789	167	4,578	363
Congressional District 2	105,258	12,651	97,624	12,166	na	na	1,122	84	1,061	76	3,956	239
Illinois												
Congressional District 1	105,059	14,818	44,436	6,408	55,748	8,183	844	0	760	95	3,441	132

Table C-5: 114th Congressional Districts—Older Population by Race and Hispanic Origin—*Continued*

	Total Population		White, Non-Hispanic		Black, Alone		Asian, Alone		Multi-race		Hispanic	
	65 Years and Over	85 Years and Over	65 Years and Over	85 Years and Over	65 Years and Over	85 Years and Over	65 Years and Over	85 Years and Over	65 Years and Over	85 Years and Over	65 Years and Over	85 Years and Over
Illinois—Cont.												
Congressional District 2	97,870	12,752	46,120	7,826	44,215	3,844	na	na	719	133	6,230	934
Congressional District 3	99,695	14,281	78,341	12,154	3,109	464	3,993	209	540	102	13,927	1,472
Congressional District 4	64,015	8,143	25,937	4,450	2,659	407	3,328	291	895	82	31,975	3,021
Congressional District 5	84,881	12,104	68,364	10,472	1,669	189	5,110	508	816	65	9,212	1,024
Congressional District 6	102,513	12,183	89,234	10,712	1,781	254	8,148	647	294	76	2,827	494
Congressional District 7	83,693	9,039	27,599	3,340	45,750	5,126	4,685	326	453	0	5,101	247
Congressional District 8	87,525	9,352	67,310	7,653	1,133	21	11,257	769	411	65	7,323	844
Congressional District 9	112,944	19,433	88,602	17,011	8,020	1,118	11,056	838	1,160	121	4,015	345
Congressional District 10	94,581	16,689	75,245	15,288	3,666	136	9,048	904	788	37	5,818	324
Congressional District 11	69,102	8,420	52,202	7,713	6,590	405	4,311	123	288	0	5,763	179
Congressional District 12	108,711	14,170	94,688	12,949	10,969	977	924	41	615	80	1,402	123
Congressional District 13	107,646	14,964	98,851	14,414	5,525	360	1,355	80	1,152	0	757	103
Congressional District 14	90,878	9,988	81,773	8,907	1,333	299	2,891	167	684	183	4,152	485
Congressional District 15	122,508	17,647	118,521	17,258	1,803	207	na	na	373	7	974	171
Congressional District 16	115,902	16,709	111,532	16,208	1,347	66	446	0	669	0	2,206	363
Congressional District 17	120,998	15,929	108,928	15,031	5,962	316	608	241	1,458	93	4,034	278
Congressional District 18	119,333	18,594	115,459	18,428	1,718	95	1,071	0	386	21	719	50
Indiana												
Congressional District 1	105,429	15,272	80,224	11,893	15,844	2,261	717	100	651	49	7,841	969
Congressional District 2	106,025	15,319	99,095	14,088	3,905	709	456	75	608	77	1,834	370
Congressional District 3	104,775	13,654	97,153	13,110	3,778	150	879	56	671	169	2,060	169
Congressional District 4	105,754	14,425	101,220	13,697	1,912	218	928	0	419	31	1,059	510
Congressional District 5	100,486	12,395	91,291	11,418	5,653	691	1,829	0	699	0	791	158
Congressional District 6	116,610	15,189	112,570	14,776	2,229	330	na	na	878	37	506	83
Congressional District 7	80,135	10,209	57,342	7,629	19,088	2,274	977	0	792	30	1,598	130
Congressional District 8	114,920	17,067	110,664	16,221	2,392	519	390	55	757	128	522	64
Congressional District 9	107,360	13,165	104,508	12,877	1,290	192	779	44	274	0	378	52
Iowa												
Congressional District 1	126,918	19,231	123,637	18,602	1,347	185	406	37	409	129	816	257
Congressional District 2	122,458	17,074	117,168	16,880	1,816	129	1,129	3	342	6	1,682	19
Congressional District 3	108,317	16,270	103,207	15,822	2,032	187	1,294	211	132	0	1,586	25
Congressional District 4	132,935	22,373	130,228	21,875	295	42	560	22	468	127	1,287	307
Kansas												
Congressional District 1	111,280	18,560	102,293	18,098	1,739	137	1,308	21	1,273	87	4,330	253
Congressional District 2	111,015	15,873	102,811	14,998	3,497	460	na	na	1,278	127	2,230	136
Congressional District 3	92,995	13,942	80,147	12,604	6,065	576	1,940	145	1,535	115	3,826	459
Congressional District 4	102,243	13,734	90,532	12,531	4,400	442	1,902	47	1,070	167	3,605	325
Kentucky												
Congressional District 1	120,648	13,391	113,948	12,693	5,486	688	na	na	281	0	430	10
Congressional District 2	107,519	11,803	102,798	11,100	2,798	367	492	0	673	129	666	207
Congressional District 3	107,350	15,929	88,886	13,983	15,055	1,682	1,325	156	787	68	1,390	40
Congressional District 4	103,184	12,855	97,971	11,937	2,727	578	na	na	569	0	1,068	0
Congressional District 5	115,986	11,897	113,752	11,645	718	162	na	na	na	na	469	12
Congressional District 6	98,335	12,389	89,684	11,720	6,039	543	682	0	1,139	52	531	0
Louisiana												
Congressional District 1	113,868	15,232	97,325	13,766	7,214	495	2,435	106	920	40	5,398	865
Congressional District 2	94,688	9,253	35,588	3,927	52,862	4,679	1,627	177	595	168	3,565	315
Congressional District 3	101,238	11,499	79,451	9,457	18,661	1,800	427	0	774	11	1,728	215
Congressional District 4	111,255	13,715	79,455	10,654	28,123	2,799	na	na	1,148	0	1,108	105
Congressional District 5	112,164	13,093	83,044	10,500	26,779	2,550	na	na	839	0	721	43
Congressional District 6	97,957	9,410	81,031	7,677	13,845	1,270	1,194	0	646	265	1,053	196
Maine												
Congressional District 1	120,918	15,687	118,252	15,616	225	0	691	0	797	71	543	0
Congressional District 2	121,646	15,673	119,381	15,568	na	na	na	na	891	59	410	46
Maryland												
Congressional District 1	125,329	16,169	111,918	14,786	9,561	1,107	1,904	0	285	0	1,587	276
Congressional District 2	93,242	11,505	69,233	9,712	18,381	1,438	3,980	183	695	148	947	73
Congressional District 3	106,972	16,022	82,612	13,354	15,428	1,464	4,161	204	2,114	402	3,435	623
Congressional District 4	89,693	10,398	37,239	5,357	45,432	4,335	2,360	137	1,691	297	2,500	318
Congressional District 5	91,039	9,006	53,720	6,297	28,628	2,131	4,104	333	1,378	27	2,825	218
Congressional District 6	98,470	13,669	78,484	11,562	4,858	648	8,830	1,124	1,545	179	4,959	156
Congressional District 7	101,979	13,159	41,508	7,414	53,441	5,415	4,106	99	1,046	104	1,706	119
Congressional District 8	115,447	19,991	86,940	15,993	10,669	1,968	10,579	1,484	1,445	153	6,303	591
Massachusetts												
Congressional District 1	120,509	20,003	108,127	18,910	4,490	602	885	41	583	86	6,630	364
Congressional District 2	104,634	16,418	95,987	15,907	1,763	25	2,887	90	1,052	245	3,142	117
Congressional District 3	101,327	12,869	88,771	12,039	1,236	48	3,610	323	885	99	7,729	459
Congressional District 4	108,530	16,595	98,775	15,960	2,512	140	4,628	400	657	95	1,916	0
Congressional District 5	112,437	17,222	100,649	15,556	2,856	347	5,948	919	626	42	2,458	358
Congressional District 6	123,052	20,223	115,528	19,265	1,191	100	2,567	288	707	124	3,570	570
Congressional District 7	74,933	10,808	38,519	7,105	20,646	2,250	7,050	757	2,258	361	8,132	540
Congressional District 8	121,501	18,847	107,536	17,320	5,789	784	4,769	409	522	19	2,767	322
Congressional District 9	148,654	18,625	140,207	18,131	2,848	173	1,337	61	872	36	1,326	0

Table C-5: 114th Congressional Districts—Older Population by Race and Hispanic Origin—*Continued*

	Total Population		White, Non-Hispanic		Black, Alone		Asian, Alone		Multi-race		Hispanic	
	65 Years and Over	85 Years and Over	65 Years and Over	85 Years and Over	65 Years and Over	85 Years and Over	65 Years and Over	85 Years and Over	65 Years and Over	85 Years and Over	65 Years and Over	85 Years and Over
Michigan												
Congressional District 1	147,970	18,552	143,333	17,942	544	307	363	13	927	94	442	89
Congressional District 2	102,443	14,033	94,792	13,371	3,070	306	735	9	712	87	2,908	260
Congressional District 3	99,236	15,968	89,549	14,991	6,086	721	1,026	66	724	158	1,770	114
Congressional District 4	122,134	15,052	118,362	14,495	838	78	403	11	654	286	1,586	182
Congressional District 5	116,369	12,585	97,176	11,412	14,353	847	945	107	1,086	0	2,619	219
Congressional District 6	111,036	13,301	101,752	12,663	6,249	544	470	0	1,051	61	1,173	0
Congressional District 7	114,367	13,690	108,082	12,968	2,880	601	na	na	783	45	1,917	76
Congressional District 8	93,893	11,925	85,383	11,482	3,794	341	1,680	0	1,055	38	1,849	44
Congressional District 9	112,643	18,129	101,773	17,163	6,287	461	3,004	266	420	25	974	175
Congressional District 10	117,268	14,040	111,491	13,855	1,384	81	1,290	0	1,209	0	1,727	104
Congressional District 11	103,432	14,648	92,206	13,225	3,940	671	5,571	443	715	0	1,089	307
Congressional District 12	94,924	14,387	81,923	13,099	7,241	871	2,676	124	517	74	2,263	266
Congressional District 13	88,274	12,942	39,074	6,639	44,969	6,005	887	36	839	60	2,241	178
Congressional District 14	107,078	14,478	47,433	7,756	52,593	6,247	2,856	216	1,511	58	2,241	172
Minnesota												
Congressional District 1	107,149	18,471	104,705	18,337	211	0	1,131	18	265	74	740	60
Congressional District 2	83,333	8,771	78,412	8,303	1,384	0	1,883	307	123	0	1,303	98
Congressional District 3	96,580	13,619	90,476	13,208	2,001	228	3,009	102	236	37	683	81
Congressional District 4	91,498	14,492	81,483	13,162	3,151	407	4,249	584	871	96	1,681	296
Congressional District 5	78,468	13,282	67,210	12,199	6,248	610	1,981	273	910	130	1,800	162
Congressional District 6	74,673	9,063	73,207	8,965	330	0	443	90	156	0	193	8
Congressional District 7	122,176	20,666	119,478	20,454	283	86	192	0	679	105	683	44
Congressional District 8	123,956	15,967	120,752	15,883	259	0	313	19	608	20	572	0
Mississippi												
Congressional District 1	111,512	11,171	90,226	9,881	19,377	1,289	na	na	533	1	679	0
Congressional District 2	96,434	12,085	50,036	7,246	44,964	4,692	na	na	na	na	349	85
Congressional District 3	112,016	14,479	82,857	10,471	26,959	3,756	767	0	na	na	744	167
Congressional District 4	107,351	11,782	89,099	10,060	15,530	1,496	na	na	418	20	1,080	36
Missouri												
Congressional District 1	92,404	12,512	48,326	7,995	40,320	4,089	1,778	44	779	212	1,030	159
Congressional District 2	132,448	19,422	123,871	18,880	3,653	386	3,185	39	812	22	1,161	95
Congressional District 3	111,362	12,639	107,209	12,343	1,982	198	na	na	788	23	1,031	0
Congressional District 4	116,009	13,913	110,954	13,663	2,628	132	356	38	840	80	939	0
Congressional District 5	107,562	14,101	84,353	12,297	18,067	1,523	704	70	832	72	3,436	72
Congressional District 6	114,924	14,807	110,646	14,479	1,840	88	461	0	860	118	939	122
Congressional District 7	124,610	16,266	120,309	15,438	896	54	311	25	1,262	266	931	393
Congressional District 8	132,571	15,786	125,940	15,168	3,133	261	na	na	1,315	140	916	217
Montana												
Congressional District (at Large)	170,153	20,899	162,011	20,210	na	na	537	72	1,164	25	1,460	344
Nebraska												
Congressional District 1	88,161	11,561	84,443	11,157	689	41	891	96	373	0	1,471	228
Congressional District 2	71,659	11,466	62,821	9,876	4,986	689	1,017	355	453	25	2,096	430
Congressional District 3	110,857	17,349	106,275	16,946	na	na	na	na	418	89	3,003	212
Nevada												
Congressional District 1	88,117	8,789	55,517	6,662	7,350	455	9,124	344	1,213	209	14,729	1,328
Congressional District 2	108,256	10,313	93,080	8,732	1,364	247	3,178	152	1,326	164	7,910	938
Congressional District 3	105,942	9,485	79,137	7,427	5,055	284	11,992	826	1,538	170	7,824	778
Congressional District 4	98,199	7,845	68,092	5,546	10,426	904	7,257	357	1,670	34	10,387	909
New Hampshire												
Congressional District 1	103,178	13,673	100,469	13,489	538	0	854	35	316	0	973	149
Congressional District 2	106,269	13,848	103,644	13,828	249	0	1,275	0	577	4	467	0
New Jersey												
Congressional District 1	106,412	15,980	82,695	14,020	13,816	1,320	4,493	207	602	0	4,745	433
Congressional District 2	122,069	14,478	101,368	12,578	10,572	1,326	3,142	137	1,149	106	6,071	398
Congressional District 3	134,369	20,034	117,593	18,198	8,526	678	2,952	417	1,837	413	3,436	363
Congressional District 4	132,163	23,528	116,311	21,584	7,336	1,366	3,084	230	675	9	5,344	746
Congressional District 5	117,829	16,978	97,283	14,801	4,598	631	8,583	699	598	43	6,869	839
Congressional District 6	93,531	13,978	66,617	11,455	6,890	823	11,077	1,049	533	59	8,673	745
Congressional District 7	108,930	16,592	93,793	15,533	3,165	724	7,028	0	379	0	4,705	335
Congressional District 8	77,019	10,500	27,717	5,257	5,951	890	4,630	135	1,112	0	39,158	4,273
Congressional District 9	103,614	15,566	63,532	11,840	8,883	696	10,619	1,267	1,442	291	20,376	1,701
Congressional District 10	82,245	10,166	25,663	5,183	42,369	4,474	5,374	145	906	119	8,239	245
Congressional District 11	126,601	20,992	106,750	18,442	4,561	1,038	8,880	754	409	73	6,186	936
Congressional District 12	107,343	15,196	73,654	12,644	15,330	847	11,063	1,049	1,385	336	6,117	540
New Mexico												
Congressional District 1	103,680	11,144	63,679	7,729	2,027	225	1,829	93	1,838	106	33,738	3,090
Congressional District 2	109,869	9,963	65,740	6,850	1,726	98	na	na	1,222	110	37,714	2,648
Congressional District 3	104,537	11,973	60,440	7,422	na	na	820	0	1,192	6	30,781	3,111
New York												
Congressional District 1	119,218	14,306	107,250	13,262	3,639	615	2,627	174	739	0	5,882	255
Congressional District 2	98,722	13,859	80,164	12,461	6,996	438	2,057	137	871	138	9,343	840
Congressional District 3	132,656	23,144	110,735	20,123	2,600	476	11,984	1,501	930	74	6,289	875

Table C-5: 114th Congressional Districts—Older Population by Race and Hispanic Origin—*Continued*

	Total Population		White, Non-Hispanic		Black, Alone		Asian, Alone		Multi-race		Hispanic	
	65 Years and Over	85 Years and Over	65 Years and Over	85 Years and Over	65 Years and Over	85 Years and Over	65 Years and Over	85 Years and Over	65 Years and Over	85 Years and Over	65 Years and Over	85 Years and Over
New York—Cont.												
Congressional District 4	113,509	18,343	84,739	15,557	14,063	1,371	6,945	401	1,761	241	7,573	893
Congressional District 5	100,133	13,082	21,003	4,394	50,581	6,387	9,588	248	3,741	94	14,020	1,649
Congressional District 6	116,114	17,442	60,578	11,877	3,859	400	36,257	3,475	2,464	304	13,602	1,350
Congressional District 7	70,783	9,788	18,911	3,882	9,233	1,039	18,225	2,907	964	75	26,898	2,056
Congressional District 8	102,895	16,182	39,304	7,895	47,944	6,209	2,892	290	2,078	601	13,060	1,548
Congressional District 9	97,627	13,611	32,173	6,552	52,734	6,196	6,014	728	922	0	8,639	507
Congressional District 10	101,748	15,279	71,271	10,919	6,460	1,535	11,863	796	1,217	0	11,383	2,351
Congressional District 11	108,150	15,385	84,791	12,922	3,965	567	11,184	1,042	916	0	7,592	950
Congressional District 12	103,067	13,934	78,368	11,232	3,827	565	9,178	1,097	867	77	11,697	1,128
Congressional District 13	85,515	14,547	10,794	2,633	30,031	6,174	5,264	457	5,097	157	42,461	6,097
Congressional District 14	90,710	11,639	35,280	5,690	10,716	1,700	12,278	1,092	1,381	73	32,836	3,262
Congressional District 15	69,554	7,230	1,809	542	24,388	2,077	1,415	227	1,745	93	44,840	4,759
Congressional District 16	114,006	19,101	63,899	14,263	31,852	3,247	5,225	343	766	80	12,827	1,241
Congressional District 17	112,076	18,143	84,231	14,653	10,897	1,480	5,490	676	950	0	11,061	1,174
Congressional District 18	102,127	12,829	86,326	11,489	6,232	517	2,064	263	739	90	6,791	506
Congressional District 19	127,561	15,580	119,131	14,886	3,572	516	1,388	15	981	64	2,935	75
Congressional District 20	111,662	16,654	101,393	15,578	5,468	540	1,876	161	772	186	2,332	189
Congressional District 21	114,268	15,025	111,385	14,681	699	52	512	20	327	44	684	108
Congressional District 22	121,362	18,515	116,554	18,271	1,572	112	1,365	39	762	11	980	82
Congressional District 23	120,189	17,891	115,753	17,584	1,305	203	634	0	983	20	1,234	70
Congressional District 24	110,781	17,685	102,791	16,793	4,720	611	1,548	178	343	68	1,304	55
Congressional District 25	112,161	18,834	95,389	17,142	10,087	689	2,083	165	561	95	3,421	472
Congressional District 26	119,748	20,412	101,044	18,976	13,606	1,187	1,567	66	493	22	2,669	161
Congressional District 27	119,338	16,369	114,450	15,879	2,301	86	886	102	325	112	480	64
North Carolina												
Congressional District 1	114,038	15,910	54,954	8,840	55,675	6,672	1,046	131	750	48	853	127
Congressional District 2	104,162	12,596	85,367	10,813	13,191	1,267	2,114	154	433	0	2,035	257
Congressional District 3	110,189	10,141	90,205	8,364	17,486	1,611	na	na	311	0	1,810	82
Congressional District 4	84,421	9,342	55,991	7,170	22,493	2,000	2,739	40	977	0	1,978	118
Congressional District 5	121,854	14,252	109,533	13,349	9,856	660	339	0	364	98	1,708	202
Congressional District 6	125,799	16,944	109,105	14,754	13,831	1,960	1,186	175	134	0	1,343	55
Congressional District 7	132,834	12,838	110,833	10,134	18,614	2,553	na	na	702	13	1,116	42
Congressional District 8	111,591	10,829	87,553	8,671	15,392	1,504	190	0	362	47	1,718	22
Congressional District 9	96,630	10,834	82,493	9,927	7,805	671	2,248	97	833	0	3,248	139
Congressional District 10	128,002	15,091	113,691	13,532	10,664	1,103	303	0	788	89	2,322	318
Congressional District 11	157,833	19,349	149,283	18,515	2,543	383	458	0	971	68	2,767	154
Congressional District 12	73,967	7,433	33,011	4,974	36,244	2,306	1,724	0	1,101	41	2,163	112
Congressional District 13	99,829	8,772	81,979	7,331	12,967	1,111	1,631	0	580	83	2,252	213
North Dakota												
Congressional District (at Large)	104,679	17,350	101,022	17,216	112	0	326	0	404	0	462	57
Ohio												
Congressional District 1	96,760	13,289	78,968	10,731	14,392	2,008	1,515	342	595	118	1,328	90
Congressional District 2	111,135	14,414	100,319	13,136	8,870	1,118	556	100	704	43	763	0
Congressional District 3	72,237	8,844	48,298	6,417	20,476	2,067	1,572	153	569	83	1,159	124
Congressional District 4	116,092	16,291	109,229	15,689	3,418	457	na	na	1,443	58	1,519	87
Congressional District 5	115,792	16,755	110,071	15,834	1,942	466	661	79	676	203	2,528	167
Congressional District 6	128,957	17,060	125,468	16,643	2,154	382	na	na	530	0	na	na
Congressional District 7	125,165	16,628	120,175	15,774	2,711	283	na	na	825	125	668	148
Congressional District 8	111,346	14,253	104,256	13,570	4,306	486	1,363	64	658	133	708	0
Congressional District 9	102,832	15,454	86,591	13,926	10,459	1,233	805	39	473	0	4,706	256
Congressional District 10	118,210	14,277	98,909	12,253	15,645	1,763	1,724	86	874	87	1,074	140
Congressional District 11	105,744	17,354	51,124	10,234	50,711	6,804	1,311	53	1,152	200	1,576	77
Congressional District 12	101,287	13,585	95,632	13,072	3,440	472	1,159	0	702	41	420	0
Congressional District 13	125,239	21,082	112,692	19,126	9,861	1,626	909	54	486	62	1,017	94
Congressional District 14	130,710	19,457	124,078	19,123	3,777	181	1,774	0	411	66	596	87
Congressional District 15	105,960	11,099	101,159	10,754	1,269	113	1,906	52	641	42	868	138
Congressional District 16	129,402	18,737	124,712	18,152	1,340	119	1,711	317	429	48	1,125	101
Oklahoma												
Congressional District 1	105,061	14,264	88,654	12,249	5,321	676	1,419	229	3,866	594	2,483	208
Congressional District 2	133,127	14,672	108,392	12,458	3,150	295	444	31	7,144	641	1,509	103
Congressional District 3	116,023	13,842	103,161	12,592	3,407	489	876	95	3,428	373	2,413	165
Congressional District 4	104,745	10,923	90,917	10,009	3,488	326	1,504	0	3,339	113	2,139	0
Congressional District 5	102,612	12,762	81,849	10,576	9,569	1,252	2,095	29	2,236	234	3,758	388
Oregon												
Congressional District 1	105,267	15,208	94,186	14,296	561	0	5,019	256	1,529	353	3,600	298
Congressional District 2	149,828	19,797	140,546	19,114	na	na	na	na	2,361	180	4,838	396
Congressional District 3	101,549	13,564	87,353	12,020	3,935	471	5,497	618	902	223	2,778	111
Congressional District 4	148,967	20,217	139,846	19,119	na	na	1,344	338	2,721	256	3,178	427
Congressional District 5	128,615	16,390	118,429	15,954	596	43	2,714	202	1,778	65	4,420	145
Pennsylvania												
Congressional District 1	82,621	11,101	48,013	8,122	23,187	2,232	4,186	351	1,246	80	6,171	199
Congressional District 2	95,283	14,681	31,367	5,226	58,856	9,054	1,832	0	948	118	2,574	279
Congressional District 3	125,010	18,911	120,241	18,343	2,969	370	498	0	461	52	966	146
Congressional District 4	115,119	13,595	107,000	13,082	4,455	250	1,404	211	692	0	1,682	52

Table C-5: 114th Congressional Districts—Older Population by Race and Hispanic Origin—*Continued*

	Total Population		White, Non-Hispanic		Black, Alone		Asian, Alone		Multi-race		Hispanic	
	65 Years and Over	85 Years and Over	65 Years and Over	85 Years and Over	65 Years and Over	85 Years and Over	65 Years and Over	85 Years and Over	65 Years and Over	85 Years and Over	65 Years and Over	85 Years and Over
Pennsylvania—Cont.												
Congressional District 5	121,399	17,190	119,376	17,110	671	0	490	68	425	0	335	12
Congressional District 6	111,627	16,782	105,414	16,121	2,404	464	1,131	138	1,035	0	1,761	59
Congressional District 7	120,105	19,558	112,552	18,784	3,263	531	2,790	107	134	0	1,199	136
Congressional District 8	118,481	17,173	110,055	16,705	2,324	240	3,947	134	300	76	1,798	18
Congressional District 9	132,680	20,645	129,072	20,183	1,889	163	na	na	523	0	827	131
Congressional District 10	128,612	17,557	124,581	17,121	1,747	352	422	0	581	14	1,258	65
Congressional District 11	125,779	18,519	120,270	17,898	3,396	565	397	0	323	0	1,536	56
Congressional District 12	141,111	21,854	134,549	20,988	4,157	584	827	25	719	85	874	172
Congressional District 13	110,466	17,450	85,838	15,855	11,788	905	7,868	334	1,061	0	4,293	401
Congressional District 14	114,220	21,187	95,007	18,689	16,755	2,434	972	0	574	64	869	0
Congressional District 15	118,883	19,033	109,608	17,963	1,855	61	1,581	0	1,198	290	5,506	814
Congressional District 16	109,404	16,662	97,059	15,149	4,712	603	1,295	182	1,747	171	5,909	666
Congressional District 17	128,427	21,454	120,616	20,345	2,248	266	2,028	244	536	8	2,928	591
Congressional District 18	134,872	21,677	129,941	21,243	2,450	206	1,681	148	133	0	559	112
Rhode Island												
Congressional District 1	80,585	13,801	71,011	12,991	2,960	313	1,010	76	1,122	78	4,282	281
Congressional District 2	86,595	14,981	78,612	13,652	1,793	236	2,013	371	1,121	503	2,992	300
South Carolina												
Congressional District 1	119,021	12,435	99,375	10,988	15,217	1,281	1,694	74	807	6	1,777	66
Congressional District 2	97,024	10,622	81,836	9,279	12,392	860	1,525	122	336	105	835	241
Congressional District 3	115,243	12,908	97,910	11,215	15,375	1,557	na	na	385	72	829	0
Congressional District 4	103,101	12,015	85,400	10,546	12,943	774	1,646	369	689	141	2,168	139
Congressional District 5	105,685	10,183	80,834	7,866	21,895	2,317	na	na	679	0	1,325	30
Congressional District 6	95,020	11,150	43,376	5,382	48,691	5,656	na	na	1,320	0	945	112
Congressional District 7	126,489	12,347	99,280	9,852	24,731	2,305	na	na	559	27	1,087	163
South Dakota												
Congressional District (at Large)	129,354	20,888	122,579	20,185	127	0	379	0	992	72	1,071	4
Tennessee												
Congressional District 1	134,354	13,193	130,470	12,791	1,571	319	na	na	833	62	856	21
Congressional District 2	120,832	14,197	112,770	13,098	5,028	825	1,311	209	698	65	1,030	0
Congressional District 3	121,801	13,621	110,068	12,833	8,989	546	883	227	780	15	661	0
Congressional District 4	106,790	10,182	96,368	9,440	5,963	671	896	36	1,934	12	1,432	23
Congressional District 5	85,432	10,335	65,409	9,047	16,005	1,071	1,588	105	600	33	1,913	79
Congressional District 6	126,505	10,937	119,528	10,105	3,433	534	na	na	598	170	1,104	77
Congressional District 7	103,331	10,128	93,518	9,348	6,279	584	1,275	81	827	73	976	0
Congressional District 8	112,416	13,921	97,040	12,453	13,051	1,387	451	0	664	43	1,055	38
Congressional District 9	75,352	9,854	30,508	5,295	41,626	4,559	1,268	0	1,120	0	653	0
Texas												
Congressional District 1	114,330	15,134	92,485	12,327	15,796	2,302	287	0	596	76	4,913	349
Congressional District 2	73,480	7,126	53,525	5,346	3,591	199	4,523	577	1,707	0	10,380	1,004
Congressional District 3	76,813	7,511	60,831	6,779	2,762	113	7,262	201	1,162	49	4,948	369
Congressional District 4	115,687	12,700	100,868	11,324	9,010	924	754	101	1,184	76	3,351	275
Congressional District 5	94,271	8,586	79,316	8,007	6,118	351	1,278	0	974	53	6,831	175
Congressional District 6	76,511	7,349	60,102	6,412	6,742	441	2,693	0	970	59	5,555	378
Congressional District 7	74,322	10,717	55,943	8,889	4,172	805	4,375	161	771	42	8,792	859
Congressional District 8	97,110	9,807	83,414	8,038	4,002	457	2,027	608	1,843	3	6,228	701
Congressional District 9	67,645	6,782	16,729	3,006	25,506	1,805	13,301	1,152	576	0	12,176	819
Congressional District 10	88,856	11,290	68,698	9,953	6,891	473	2,737	0	633	65	9,586	855
Congressional District 11	113,614	13,772	92,223	10,960	2,375	357	na	na	1,218	68	16,512	2,433
Congressional District 12	93,197	10,566	77,826	9,272	4,740	406	2,484	172	588	15	7,095	639
Congressional District 13	100,604	12,453	86,915	11,318	3,013	247	965	108	964	25	8,574	732
Congressional District 14	94,635	10,534	65,304	7,578	15,187	1,770	2,059	140	1,358	0	10,887	962
Congressional District 15	81,411	9,226	26,947	3,228	1,270	126	na	na	na	na	52,056	5,872
Congressional District 16	83,823	9,787	18,583	2,242	2,168	103	1,038	90	792	36	61,867	7,279
Congressional District 17	83,714	9,211	64,441	7,930	8,970	552	1,900	0	928	107	7,621	663
Congressional District 18	65,930	7,413	18,987	2,513	32,965	4,038	3,093	41	643	0	10,693	821
Congressional District 19	95,153	12,360	73,445	10,622	4,370	155	593	0	1,175	156	16,002	1,494
Congressional District 20	78,464	10,033	25,805	4,283	3,038	639	2,426	154	2,001	471	46,436	4,798
Congressional District 21	116,742	13,391	95,437	11,779	2,012	81	1,297	190	1,282	0	16,901	1,341
Congressional District 22	79,169	7,062	47,103	4,350	6,825	538	13,752	1,456	2,122	0	9,505	718
Congressional District 23	91,511	9,333	37,496	4,633	2,608	233	na	na	547	0	51,053	4,575
Congressional District 24	76,576	7,595	58,569	6,234	2,838	229	6,030	699	1,079	45	7,840	392
Congressional District 25	93,544	10,331	81,023	8,893	4,548	560	1,509	115	1,025	166	5,288	655
Congressional District 26	71,165	4,313	59,833	3,419	2,534	261	2,824	69	774	161	5,222	403
Congressional District 27	104,188	12,685	64,342	8,398	4,547	455	904	36	793	0	33,871	3,761
Congressional District 28	77,861	9,133	26,738	3,509	3,126	167	na	na	755	73	46,901	5,332
Congressional District 29	57,825	5,137	17,964	2,248	5,566	287	na	na	103	0	33,172	2,602
Congressional District 30	68,243	7,321	21,867	4,147	33,944	2,666	1,156	171	425	0	10,698	337
Congressional District 31	85,284	10,673	67,621	9,165	5,449	471	2,883	0	539	141	8,454	919
Congressional District 32	88,132	11,087	67,054	9,814	7,056	365	5,411	223	738	0	7,790	634
Congressional District 33	56,098	6,681	19,161	2,537	14,178	1,903	1,856	77	914	41	20,341	2,104
Congressional District 34	94,905	12,577	31,017	4,075	1,589	269	na	na	na	na	62,146	8,245
Congressional District 35	67,067	7,444	25,521	3,111	6,447	834	1,313	121	730	123	33,328	3,415
Congressional District 36	98,133	9,511	76,775	7,944	8,774	498	1,743	159	1,567	129	8,874	775

Table C-5: 114th Congressional Districts—Older Population by Race and Hispanic Origin—*Continued*

	Total Population		White, Non-Hispanic		Black, Alone		Asian, Alone		Multi-race		Hispanic	
	65 Years and Over	85 Years and Over	65 Years and Over	85 Years and Over	65 Years and Over	85 Years and Over	65 Years and Over	85 Years and Over	65 Years and Over	85 Years and Over	65 Years and Over	85 Years and Over
Utah												
Congressional District 1	72,667	8,240	66,880	7,736	na	na	906	39	1,165	0	3,307	437
Congressional District 2	85,165	9,672	78,408	9,273	368	46	1,380	0	239	0	3,853	353
Congressional District 3	68,462	7,161	63,684	6,632	na	na	826	219	301	0	2,368	158
Congressional District 4	68,685	7,696	60,394	6,567	471	250	1,795	283	181	53	4,822	543
Vermont												
Congressional District (at Large)	106,655	13,354	102,896	13,111	164	0	638	0	1,712	60	899	107
Virginia												
Congressional District 1	105,884	13,013	85,384	10,976	14,669	1,615	2,577	62	768	100	2,302	322
Congressional District 2	93,506	11,814	72,083	9,794	12,894	1,279	5,990	499	967	79	1,830	201
Congressional District 3	89,370	12,709	37,563	5,068	47,724	7,027	1,108	138	1,212	313	1,456	100
Congressional District 4	97,959	11,826	68,158	8,270	25,662	3,238	1,780	265	280	0	1,887	0
Congressional District 5	136,227	15,412	109,845	12,479	23,705	2,553	632	85	959	132	1,078	163
Congressional District 6	127,885	17,509	114,768	15,617	9,986	1,513	1,532	314	531	0	1,123	65
Congressional District 7	113,948	13,133	95,161	11,074	13,842	1,550	2,425	226	757	62	1,596	191
Congressional District 8	80,302	10,974	55,720	8,194	8,463	797	9,784	899	894	0	5,739	1,084
Congressional District 9	132,919	16,350	125,420	15,596	4,759	650	na	na	775	0	769	0
Congressional District 10	87,999	9,385	68,716	8,130	4,535	349	9,413	398	1,299	287	3,864	168
Congressional District 11	80,847	9,509	54,571	7,330	6,698	387	11,440	1,186	1,480	90	6,611	606
Washington												
Congressional District 1	87,321	10,306	78,016	9,670	na	na	4,631	297	1,465	11	2,625	275
Congressional District 2	106,599	14,612	93,542	13,868	1,027	25	7,612	611	1,066	0	2,349	72
Congressional District 3	111,563	12,038	104,160	11,608	898	89	2,082	116	1,317	113	2,134	124
Congressional District 4	90,733	10,778	75,643	9,952	583	0	1,636	397	1,289	29	9,962	206
Congressional District 5	106,584	14,792	100,121	14,604	948	0	2,036	91	1,168	0	1,354	85
Congressional District 6	122,055	15,377	110,846	14,669	2,135	191	4,602	499	1,947	0	1,759	79
Congressional District 7	93,936	14,447	80,816	13,169	2,354	13	6,738	992	1,315	54	2,402	150
Congressional District 8	84,687	10,094	74,519	9,163	1,490	159	5,003	375	1,005	121	2,076	276
Congressional District 9	93,388	14,579	60,529	10,820	7,218	803	21,301	2,562	664	61	2,839	384
Congressional District 10	95,650	13,070	80,564	11,096	3,031	208	6,579	1,027	1,101	215	2,764	477
West Virginia												
Congressional District 1	107,899	13,444	104,789	13,199	1,687	87	na	na	433	0	696	122
Congressional District 2	108,800	12,138	104,025	11,878	3,094	188	na	na	684	0	237	0
Congressional District 3	112,356	13,231	106,626	12,553	3,994	519	na	na	na	na	na	na
Wisconsin												
Congressional District 1	104,861	15,748	96,781	14,366	2,458	481	1,371	442	113	11	4,031	510
Congressional District 2	97,881	14,770	92,752	14,398	1,620	90	1,365	94	875	100	1,359	186
Congressional District 3	115,652	16,834	113,904	16,738	125	0	138	39	486	16	447	41
Congressional District 4	78,044	13,763	52,466	10,325	19,039	2,057	1,338	277	367	136	4,522	991
Congressional District 5	117,422	17,214	113,336	16,824	771	45	1,053	137	619	0	1,587	171
Congressional District 6	118,610	18,022	115,707	17,749	533	0	855	93	523	160	878	20
Congressional District 7	131,630	17,830	128,348	17,141	113	55	808	350	721	71	514	62
Congressional District 8	111,620	15,136	107,946	14,916	93	0	1,008	0	352	0	994	143
Wyoming												
Congressional District (at Large)	80,332	8,106	74,787	7,722	na	na	na	na	917	56	2,585	263

PART D
HOUSEHOLD RELATIONSHIP

HOUSEHOLD RELATIONSHIP

Though people live in a multitude of different living arrangements, the Census classifies everyone as living in either households or group quarters facilities. Those living in households live in either family or non-family households. A family household is comprised of two or more individuals related by blood, marriage, or adoption to the householder. Non-family households are ones where all of the individuals are unrelated or it is occupied by a single person living alone. There are no other household types. All households have a single householder which is generally the person who owns or rents the unit. Group quarters facilities can be either institutional or non-institutional. Examples of institutional facilities include correctional facilities, nursing homes,

and other institutional health facilities. Non-institutional group quarters include college student housing, military, and other group home situations. For the older population described here, the group quarters total will be predominantly nursing home facilities.

A slight majority (54.3 percent) of U.S. households, where the householder is age 65 or over, are family households—those that include related family members leaving 45.7 percent who live in non-family households. Householders age 65 and over make up 94.2 percent of all non-family households. About 3.2 percent of the 65 and over population lives in group quarters, a total of 1.5 million people. The percent of 65 and over living alone ranges from a low of 18.1 percent in Hawaii to a high of 63.3 percent in Utah. The totals for family householders

Percent of Grandparents 60 Years and Over Who are Responsible for Grandchildren

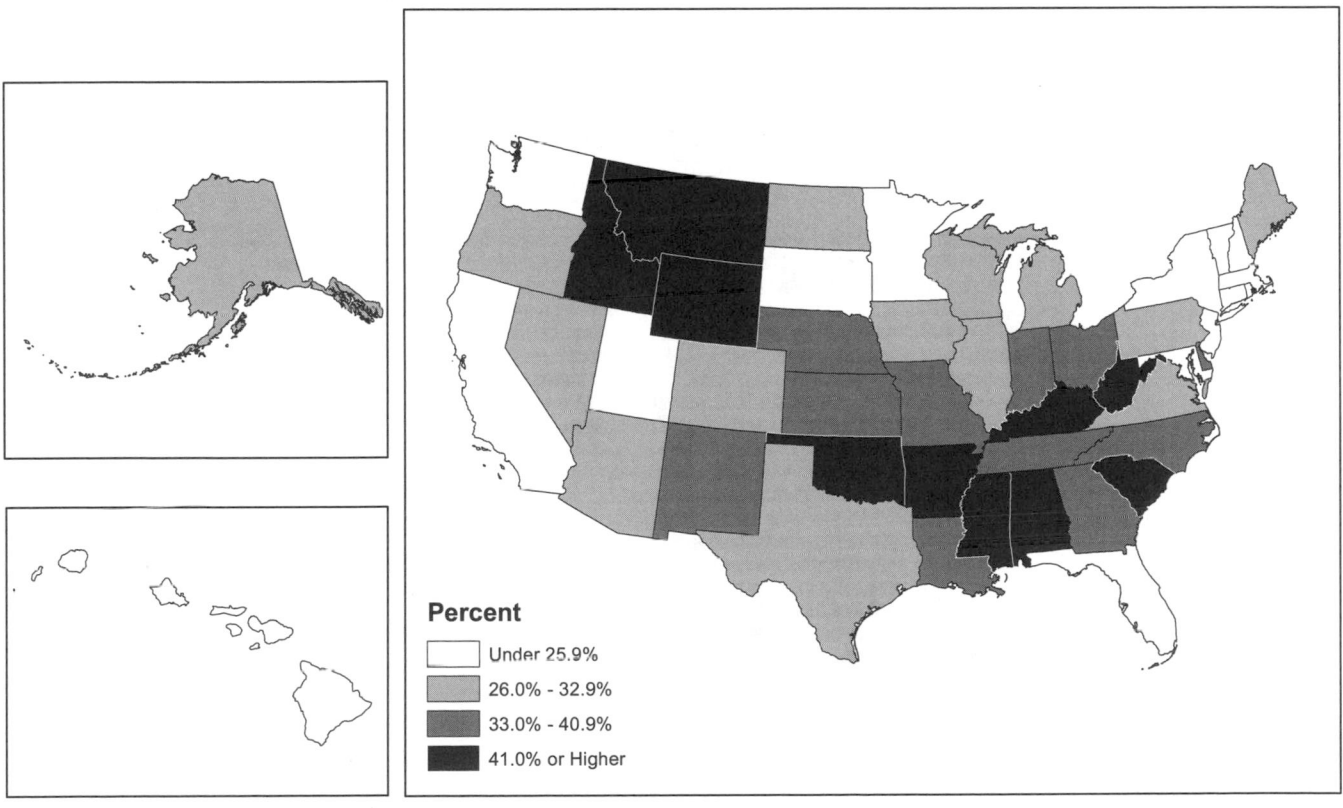

Percent

☐	Under 25.9%
☐	26.0% - 32.9%
☐	33.0% - 40.9%
■	41.0% or Higher

show the District of Columbia having the lowest percent at 40.4 and Utah with the highest at 63.5 percent. Hawaii is a close second at 61.5 percent. North Dakota has the highest percent population 65 and over living in group quarters at 5.8 percent while at 1.3 percent, Utah is the lowest.

The aging Baby Boom population is faced with care of older parents as well as care for younger grandchildren. Nationally, 3.6 million people over the age of 65 are grandparents living with their grandchildren. Not only are they living with their grandchildren but an increasingly important responsibility is care for their grandchildren. In the Census data, a "responsible grandparent" is defined as being financially responsible for such needs as food, shelter, clothing, day care, etc. More than a million grandparents (28.6 percent) 65 and over are responsible for their grandchildren. That percent varies from a low of 18.3 percent in Massachusetts to 50.9 percent in South Dakota. Of those responsible, many have incomes below the poverty level. Nationwide, 17.6 percent of grandparents responsible for grandchildren are in poverty. Vermont has the lowest percent at 2.5 while Maine is the highest at 28.4 percent. Twelve states have 20 percent or more of responsible grandparents below the poverty level. While mortality and divorce take a toll on couple's relationships, more than half (56.6 percent) of the population 65 and over are currently married. The District of Columbia has the lowest percent (35.8 percent) while Utah is highest at 67.0 percent.

More than half of the 803 counties have a higher percent of the 65 and over population that are family householders than the U.S. average. Rockwall County, Texas has the highest percent (75.3 percent) while New York County (Manhattan), New York has the lowest at 37.5 percent. The percentage of persons 65 and over living alone varies from a low of 9.9 percent to a high of 42.9 percent with 426 counties above the national average. More than 68 percent of all counties have a higher percentage of grandparents responsible for their grandchildren than the U.S. as a whole. Buchanan County, Missouri is the highest at 89.1 percent while the lowest (3.1 percent) is Kaufman County, Texas. More than 90 percent of the grandparents responsible for grandchildren are in poverty in Lincoln County, North Carolina which is the nation's highest rate and 190 counties are above the national rate. At 73.4 percent, Utah County, Utah has the highest percentage of those 65 and over who are now married. Thirty-seven counties have less than 50 percent who are married and Bronx County, New York has the lowest percent at 37.8 percent. Denver County, Colorado has the highest percentage of 65 and over who are divorced at 23.4 percent.

Miramar City, Florida has the highest percentage of family households among the 65 and over population and consequently the lowest percent of persons living alone. Everett City, Washington has the lowest percent of family households with only about one out of three (31.3 percent) households occupied by a family. Wilmington, Delaware

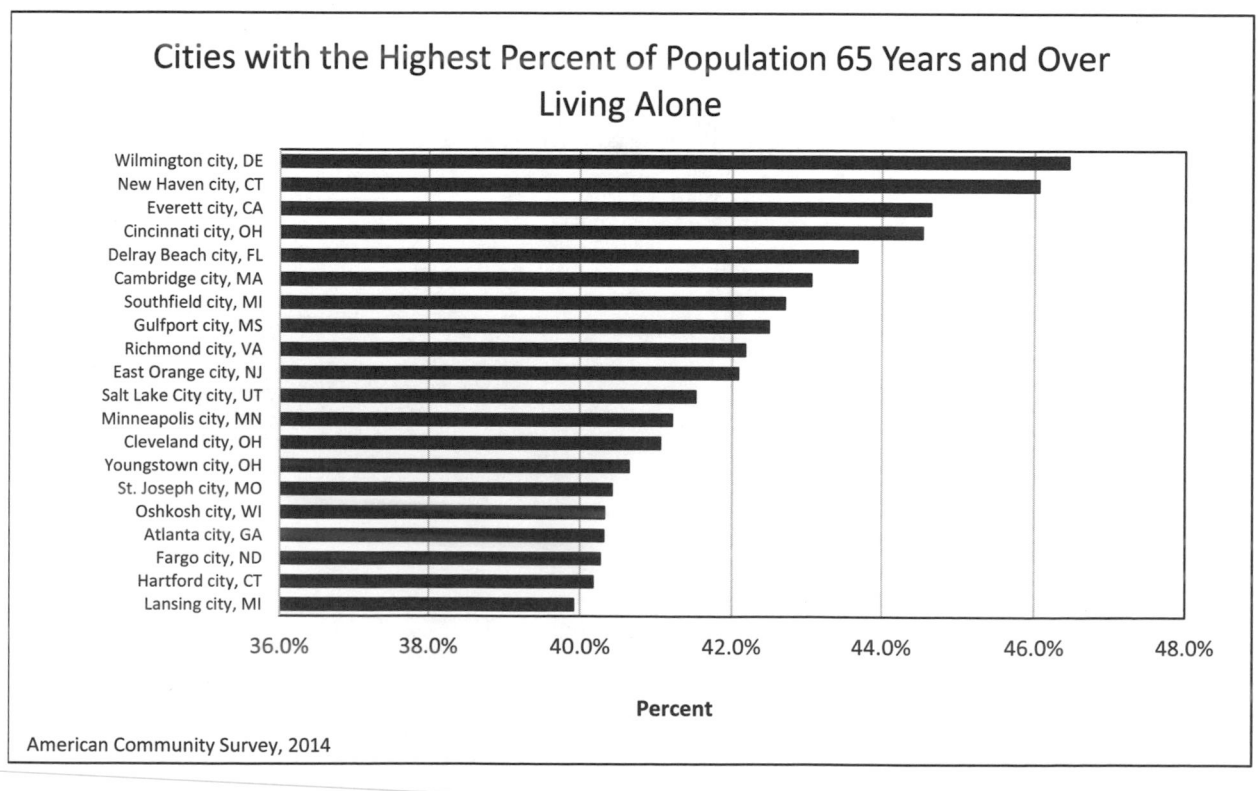

Cities with the Highest Percent of Population 65 Years and Over Living Alone

American Community Survey, 2014

is the city with the highest percentage of persons 65 and over living alone at 46.5 percent while Miramar City, Florida is lowest at 6.0 percent. There are 353 cities where the percent of persons living alone is above the national average of 26.2 percent. In St. Joseph City, Missouri the percentage of grandparents responsible for grandchildren is highest at 92.3 percent while the national average is only 28.6 percent. 398 cities exceed the national rate while Lorain City, Ohio (4.3 percent) is the lowest in the nation. In Huntsville, Alabama, 59.2 percent of grandparents who are responsible for their grandchildren are in poverty—the highest in the nation. With 14.2 percent of the 65 and over population in group quarters, the city of Chino, California has the highest proportion.

Householders over the age of 65 that head family households ranges from a low of 40.6 percent in the Faribault-Northfield, Minnesota micropolitan area to a high of 74.7 percent in the Provo-Orem, Utah metro area. Other metropolitan areas with high percentages of family households include: St. George, Utah metro (71.8 percent), The Villages, Florida metro (69.0 percent), the McAllen-Edinburg-Mission, Texas metro (67.7 percent) and the Alamogordo, New Mexico micropolitan area (67.0 percent). As expected, those metros with high percentages of family households have low percentages of persons 65 and over living alone. More than 85 percent of grandparents in the St. Joseph, Missouri-Kansas metropolitan area are responsible for their grandchildren and 16.4 percent of them have incomes below the poverty level. The Wilson, North Carolina micropolitan area has the highest percent of poverty grandparents responsible for grandchildren at 63.9 percent, almost four times the national rate of 17.6 percent. It's one of 148 metro areas above the national average.

Congressional District 3 in Utah has the highest percentage of family households (70.0 percent) but District 40 in California the lowest percent of persons living alone (14.9 percent). New York's 12th Congressional District has the highest percentage of persons living alone and the lowest percent of 65 and over householders of family households at 36.2 percent. The percent of grandparents responsible for grandchildren is highest in Arkansas' 1st Congressional District at 61.3 percent and 16.3 percent are poverty households. The district with the highest poverty percentage is Kentucky's 5th Congressional District at 44.9 percent. Congressional districts with a higher percentage of responsible grandparents in poverty than the national average number 182. Nearly three-quarters (73.4 percent) of persons 65 and older are married in Utah's 3rd Congressional District.

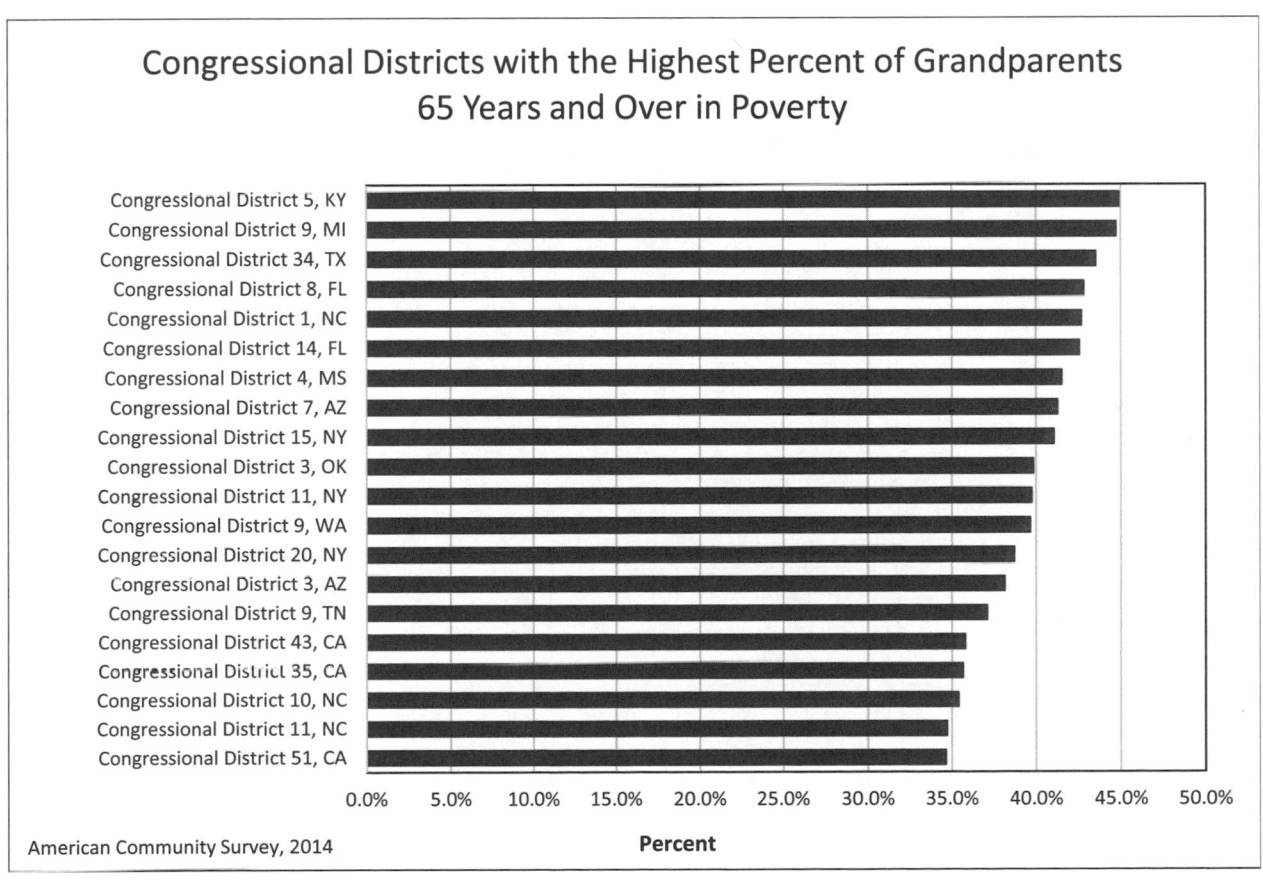

Congressional Districts with the Highest Percent of Grandparents 65 Years and Over in Poverty

American Community Survey, 2014

Percent

Table D-1: States—Household Relationship, Grandparents, and Marital Status

	Total Householders 65 Years and Over	Family Householders 65 Years and Over	Non-Family Householders 65 Years and Over		Persons 65 Years and Over Living in Group Quarters	Grandparents 60 Years and Over Living with Grandchildren			Marital Status - Persons 60 Years and Over		
			Male Living Alone	Female Living Alone		Total	Responsible for Grandchildren	Responsible for Grandchildren and In Poverty	Now Married	Widowed	Divorced
United States.................	28,146,157	15,279,428	3,721,036	8,401,190	1,486,585	3,585,360	1,023,625	180,604	36,782,702	12,993,722	9,391,697
Alabama.........................	472,668	262,736	61,116	142,010	22,260	50,889	24,821	5,120	586,511	238,466	150,960
Alaska...........................	40,996	22,734	7,032	9,182	2,229	7,814	2,505	208	62,030	16,406	19,943
Arizona..........................	647,612	367,175	87,750	170,825	18,400	77,137	23,172	5,934	842,661	260,300	235,587
Arkansas........................	289,802	160,937	38,204	85,202	17,370	28,698	13,709	2,118	375,171	137,355	85,659
California.......................	2,830,348	1,578,982	359,366	778,525	124,554	643,853	122,260	17,570	3,860,958	1,342,859	1,085,561
Colorado........................	418,629	232,611	57,468	118,643	16,499	43,040	12,913	1,749	597,663	153,630	175,436
Connecticut....................	339,658	175,974	43,709	111,325	25,038	33,104	7,240	1,093	431,897	148,743	114,734
Delaware........................	92,377	53,529	12,387	23,984	4,382	10,804	3,588	495	122,223	39,773	29,737
District of Columbia	50,463	20,372	9,095	19,242	3,745	5,033	1,808	335	38,382	21,217	20,667
Florida..........................	2,223,738	1,228,119	290,172	621,334	74,797	270,183	65,393	12,109	2,792,900	1,032,449	783,069
Georgia.........................	750,454	425,089	93,214	215,244	33,681	122,099	43,303	7,781	1,012,566	374,719	270,276
Hawaii...........................	122,744	75,527	14,350	26,872	7,792	36,901	7,568	497	169,397	65,233	41,863
Idaho............................	144,224	81,787	19,301	40,099	3,926	13,047	5,789	1,027	212,236	55,614	48,966
Illinois..........................	1,105,546	579,646	150,755	351,911	70,007	128,967	34,033	5,933	1,412,381	528,347	335,561
Indiana..........................	585,693	320,915	73,907	177,809	38,440	49,629	18,400	2,301	778,305	267,859	194,920
Iowa.............................	310,729	160,668	41,787	102,649	25,797	14,934	4,568	467	415,369	139,696	78,827
Kansas..........................	260,361	138,658	34,869	82,089	19,834	23,534	9,294	1,537	350,790	116,469	82,785
Kentucky........................	413,817	223,405	54,210	127,045	22,987	41,778	19,143	4,080	527,377	200,458	135,249
Louisiana.......................	395,166	215,749	53,502	116,936	21,688	50,759	20,500	5,269	495,085	203,046	131,872
Maine............................	151,281	77,120	21,538	47,100	7,268	9,801	2,912	826	196,887	62,099	55,401
Maryland........................	495,982	273,372	60,658	147,659	28,516	77,983	19,523	1,801	654,174	235,218	160,653
Massachusetts.................	624,797	311,517	87,419	207,878	42,624	72,034	13,208	1,852	774,632	283,185	194,792
Michigan........................	969,176	522,868	128,725	295,659	48,899	83,010	24,521	3,531	1,250,336	427,719	317,858
Minnesota......................	486,149	256,236	64,445	154,979	34,286	29,913	6,778	677	670,803	198,127	144,420
Mississippi.....................	273,148	150,539	36,326	82,944	13,881	36,633	17,526	4,628	329,770	142,790	81,516
Missouri.........................	584,979	314,350	75,945	181,423	39,698	52,776	20,707	3,793	754,753	264,835	192,337
Montana.........................	106,654	55,588	18,282	30,946	5,434	6,573	3,266	441	144,259	44,960	35,607
Nebraska........................	173,986	89,799	24,263	57,225	11,471	9,053	3,604	454	229,409	76,606	44,794
Nevada..........................	235,135	128,149	39,718	55,371	6,013	32,283	10,119	1,333	303,391	95,126	111,793
New Hampshire................	123,515	66,003	17,071	36,035	8,126	12,324	2,837	110	180,727	53,358	45,833
New Jersey......................	783,199	420,810	98,299	243,415	45,565	117,560	23,570	2,770	1,019,366	390,973	225,593
New Mexico.....................	199,105	104,443	29,654	58,912	7,798	23,865	9,708	1,674	247,055	84,343	74,733
New York........................	1,776,118	900,887	245,146	583,750	119,980	245,590	56,521	11,210	2,116,169	860,022	524,034
North Carolina.................	908,096	501,390	113,322	275,579	43,755	93,887	36,845	9,609	1,184,660	427,105	281,243
North Dakota...................	67,092	33,093	10,188	22,905	6,114	2,910	919	52	89,978	30,375	15,600
Ohio..............................	1,142,958	593,798	160,572	362,592	73,907	94,640	35,026	6,325	1,418,171	529,642	379,886
Oklahoma.......................	351,005	193,892	45,811	104,668	20,303	39,796	19,094	3,680	454,953	163,852	118,080
Oregon..........................	392,764	207,229	54,906	114,998	15,540	37,950	10,713	1,449	516,716	156,377	165,802
Pennsylvania...................	1,321,941	693,727	174,880	422,429	87,615	113,368	31,041	3,870	1,681,354	635,823	363,270
Rhode Island...................	102,237	51,592	13,462	34,721	8,072	11,128	2,727	480	123,960	49,406	35,549
South Carolina.................	475,305	273,452	58,504	134,768	18,233	57,359	26,126	6,046	631,150	222,576	136,885
South Dakota...................	82,186	41,420	12,518	26,547	7,228	6,192	3,150	632	108,533	37,772	21,431
Tennessee......................	613,436	344,215	79,068	179,279	30,412	70,105	27,653	6,026	802,004	286,402	205,459
Texas............................	1,843,597	1,062,749	232,645	511,227	90,381	339,216	102,274	21,496	2,575,287	878,393	655,324
Utah..............................	175,745	111,304	20,280	41,932	3,830	32,666	7,803	902	285,594	66,264	53,831
Vermont.........................	67,260	33,640	9,855	21,260	3,983	5,129	1,059	26	89,313	25,398	23,205
Virginia..........................	702,308	387,247	90,874	208,292	26,913	96,419	27,066	3,084	950,864	325,810	219,548
Washington.....................	605,828	322,970	80,710	182,663	30,362	68,236	16,705	2,608	835,142	240,263	237,681
West Virginia...................	211,788	113,018	28,925	65,041	9,840	20,421	9,805	2,104	263,332	102,291	62,497
Wisconsin.......................	552,831	290,128	77,056	173,341	34,699	31,048	9,214	1,266	743,450	233,685	164,184
Wyoming	51,531	28,270	7,777	14,726	2,413	3,284	1,598	226	72,608	20,288	21,186

Table D-2: Counties—Household Relationship, Grandparents, and Marital Status

	Total Householders 65 Years and Over	Family Householders 65 Years and Over	Non-Family Householders 65 Years and Over		Persons 65 Years and Over Living in Group Quarters	Grandparents 60 Years and Over Living with Grandchildren			Marital Status - Persons 60 Years and Over		
			Male Living Alone	Female Living Alone		Total	Responsible for Grandchildren	Responsible for Grandchildren and In Poverty	Now Married	Widowed	Divorced
Alabama											
Baldwin County	23,509	12,706	3,020	6,982	550	951	501	na	na	na	na
Calhoun County	11,702	6,329	1,159	4,056	470	1,376	824	275	na	na	na
Cullman County	8,705	4,382	958	3,303	475	na	na	na	na	na	na
DeKalb County	7,047	4,165	877	1,978	472	na	na	0	na	na	na
Elmore County	7,218	3,673	1,320	2,011	361	na	na	na	na	na	na
Etowah County	11,562	6,134	1,408	3,790	741	923	700	53	na	na	na
Houston County	10,400	5,376	1,533	3,300	186	1,176	316	32	12,205	5,409	3,973
Jefferson County	62,053	34,064	7,826	19,491	2,847	6,828	3,494	973	68,767	32,008	21,378
Lauderdale County	11,076	5,741	1,917	3,285	523	na	na	na	na	na	na
Lee County	10,631	5,816	1,619	3,196	323	na	na	186	na	na	na
Limestone County	7,272	4,943	289	1,843	369	na	na	na	na	na	na
Madison County	30,351	17,099	4,755	8,236	1,284	3,168	1,031	339	39,703	14,482	10,001
Marshall County	8,968	4,371	1,317	3,183	479	813	342	158	na	na	na
Mobile County	37,513	21,576	4,090	11,024	1,527	4,542	2,121	371	47,918	18,173	12,848
Montgomery County	20,165	11,098	2,434	6,404	1,188	2,706	1,258	229	21,861	9,090	9,470
Morgan County	11,989	5,792	2,042	4,103	616	na	na	na	na	na	na
Shelby County	16,635	10,291	1,746	4,323	520	2,410	1,037	22	na	na	na
St. Clair County	na	na	na	na	na	na	na	na	na	na	na
Talladega County	7,759	4,430	999	2,330	500	971	482	185	na	na	na
Tuscaloosa County	14,352	7,877	1,652	4,691	798	1,902	1,027	172	na	na	na
Walker County	7,720	4,292	810	2,488	387	1,359	836	304	na	na	na
Alaska											
Anchorage Municipality	14,870	8,885	1,963	3,253	633	2,711	739	31	22,348	6,431	7,155
Fairbanks North Star Borough	na	na	na	na	na	na	na	na	na	na	na
Matanuska-Susitna Borough	5,232	2,931	971	1,048	287	1,270	368	21	na	na	na
Arizona											
Apache County	5,612	3,266	866	1,363	68	2,325	963	127	7,233	2,037	1,560
Cochise County	15,100	8,406	2,016	4,196	477	1,725	996	448	na	na	na
Coconino County	9,700	5,898	1,422	2,092	234	1,558	597	144	na	na	na
Maricopa County	337,926	187,339	45,548	93,967	9,997	42,533	10,459	2,548	442,171	142,235	129,013
Mohave County	32,387	20,217	4,583	6,339	510	2,707	577	309	44,156	12,762	10,630
Navajo County	10,706	7,099	1,144	2,132	277	2,438	1,343	473	13,813	4,023	2,950
Pima County	112,162	59,877	15,429	32,479	4,113	10,208	3,008	556	135,145	41,777	42,406
Pinal County	41,068	27,126	4,956	7,930	1,296	5,710	1,456	314	60,963	15,443	14,359
Yavapai County	38,908	21,762	5,533	10,312	745	1,738	893	214	48,240	15,230	14,671
Yuma County	22,044	13,460	3,095	4,694	275	3,347	1,633	715	30,295	7,858	4,150
Arkansas											
Benton County	18,489	11,514	2,054	4,492	730	2,204	481	81	27,902	7,560	4,475
Craighead County	8,000	4,465	741	2,649	602	na	na	na	na	na	na
Faulkner County	7,644	4,709	815	2,086	424	1,115	701	86	na	na	na
Garland County	13,006	7,124	2,316	3,251	439	na	na	na	na	na	na
Jefferson County	6,951	3,583	1,214	2,059	619	1,066	443	309	na	na	na
Lonoke County	5,881	3,716	490	1,646	405	na	na	na	na	na	na
Pulaski County	33,031	17,116	4,231	10,931	1,808	2,915	850	43	41,187	15,584	13,289
Saline County	11,194	7,620	990	2,423	708	1,016	485	0	na	na	na
Sebastian County	12,077	6,246	1,423	4,226	648	1,370	685	63	na	na	na
Washington County	15,798	8,042	2,152	5,350	887	1,067	357	146	na	na	na
White County	7,197	4,371	746	1,896	402	823	343	93	na	na	na
California											
Alameda County	115,959	62,465	14,996	33,532	5,693	32,125	5,192	242	152,930	58,129	45,715
Butte County	22,765	10,900	3,605	7,018	1,088	2,531	1,401	441	28,840	10,305	8,510
Contra Costa County	90,887	52,700	10,134	24,940	3,256	18,834	3,509	249	129,609	37,712	34,639
El Dorado County	19,247	10,883	3,166	4,548	34	3,407	917	78	na	. na	na
Fresno County	61,609	34,531	8,239	16,407	2,795	18,331	4,077	857	87,516	26,677	24,128
Humboldt County	12,469	6,621	1,943	3,425	507	993	291	6	na	na	na
Imperial County	10,308	5,799	1,159	3,060	338	3,881	655	218	14,670	7,452	3,543
Kern County	49,947	27,693	7,294	12,974	2,050	12,956	4,197	1,393	70,019	24,493	20,705
Kings County	7,781	4,946	696	1,885	317	2,183	322	0	11,474	3,525	2,841
Lake County	8,588	3,867	1,728	2,581	127	na	na	na	na	na	na
Los Angeles County	676,487	376,999	86,009	185,925	32,812	184,145	34,152	4,805	894,169	348,228	247,357
Madera County	10,815	6,643	1,175	2,547	562	1,485	420	90	na	na	na
Marin County	32,293	14,325	4,813	11,402	1,240	na	na	na	34,564	11,158	14,641
Mendocino County	10,713	5,383	1,287	3,567	518	1,826	639	9	na	na	na
Merced County	16,007	8,737	2,529	3,991	399	4,318	1,028	110	20,815	7,860	6,196
Monterey County	30,238	17,357	4,045	7,498	1,679	7,573	1,527	63	40,757	15,382	9,686
Napa County	14,395	8,071	1,452	4,171	1,119	2,741	419	na	20,475	5,789	5,496
Nevada County	13,350	8,385	1,253	3,230	433	na	na	na	na	na	na
Orange County	233,783	137,306	24,388	63,348	10,556	49,046	6,744	1,023	330,849	105,247	83,169
Placer County	39,994	22,286	4,619	11,470	1,137	3,009	691	23	54,151	15,565	13,482
Riverside County	171,808	97,184	22,572	43,601	5,753	41,624	7,897	1,546	239,695	84,128	65,411
Sacramento County	111,627	61,776	12,334	33,887	5,816	23,522	5,612	442	145,488	53,274	48,010
San Bernardino County	116,634	68,643	15,716	27,915	5,483	38,668	6,926	1,546	174,631	60,035	52,474
San Diego County	234,218	132,201	28,574	65,704	8,991	49,760	9,545	1,906	321,912	114,672	98,643
San Francisco County	73,562	35,100	13,253	21,717	3,109	12,890	1,878	298	78,030	31,945	24,331
San Joaquin County	44,199	24,265	5,365	12,241	3,545	13,581	2,463	376	62,894	25,104	18,580
San Luis Obispo County	29,273	15,466	4,499	7,940	1,218	2,943	432	na	39,603	13,451	9,545

Table D-2: Counties—Household Relationship, Grandparents, and Marital Status—*Continued*

	Total Householders 65 Years and Over	Family Householders 65 Years and Over	Non-Family Householders 65 Years and Over		Persons 65 Years and Over Living in Group Quarters	Grandparents 60 Years and Over Living with Grandchildren			Marital Status - Persons 60 Years and Over		
			Male Living Alone	Female Living Alone		Total	Responsible for Grandchildren	Responsible for Grandchildren and In Poverty	Now Married	Widowed	Divorced
California—Cont.											
San Mateo County	62,142	33,848	8,546	17,103	2,855	11,498	2,706	243	86,875	30,232	22,283
Santa Barbara County	37,459	19,938	5,115	11,040	1,798	6,218	1,221	0	46,730	15,131	15,513
Santa Clara County	123,457	71,659	14,034	33,593	6,390	32,362	3,551	371	184,523	59,982	44,837
Santa Cruz County	22,945	11,607	2,967	6,861	591	2,448	549	0	30,415	7,749	11,167
Shasta County	21,110	11,520	3,189	5,658	1,122	1,615	504	0	26,364	9,767	9,171
Solano County	33,203	19,020	4,595	8,535	965	8,719	2,261	105	50,308	14,436	14,797
Sonoma County	51,802	25,762	6,691	16,563	1,827	5,333	1,196	0	64,325	19,457	22,970
Stanislaus County	37,075	20,980	4,549	10,214	2,095	9,269	2,098	211	50,838	17,464	14,046
Sutter County	8,132	4,409	950	2,547	265	na	na	na	na	na	na
Tulare County	25,327	16,631	2,035	5,824	1,715	7,189	1,792	637	40,151	14,533	7,764
Ventura County	68,153	39,209	7,450	18,625	2,100	13,287	2,106	114	95,505	27,935	25,684
Yolo County	14,516	6,934	2,475	4,469	587	2,321	269	0	20,367	6,326	6,097
Yuba County	5,227	3,023	557	1,457	116	709	317	na	na	na	na
Colorado											
Adams County	27,741	16,986	3,695	6,389	1,094	5,867	1,777	66	38,170	13,854	12,822
Arapahoe County	43,824	24,545	5,098	12,809	1,817	6,079	1,851	47	62,645	15,428	21,322
Boulder County	23,881	11,900	3,301	8,008	973	na	na	na	33,446	8,621	10,946
Denver County	47,806	20,295	8,925	17,294	2,345	4,648	1,301	418	49,484	17,266	24,467
Douglas County	18,561	11,417	2,039	4,871	202	2,935	535	na	na	na	na
El Paso County	46,007	26,565	6,390	12,106	1,090	4,818	1,328	40	72,130	16,323	19,733
Jefferson County	50,496	28,266	5,955	14,998	1,957	4,927	908	222	74,922	18,612	20,870
Larimer County	27,063	14,703	3,748	8,294	898	1,382	218	na	40,892	8,717	10,316
Mesa County	15,207	9,431	1,478	3,889	518	1,009	644	na	na	na	na
Pueblo County	17,236	8,905	2,442	5,369	1,559	1,566	1,044	58	21,164	8,034	6,314
Weld County	19,316	11,367	2,307	5,087	368	2,866	780	41	27,144	8,348	6,359
Connecticut											
Fairfield County	84,643	45,371	9,618	27,394	5,059	8,666	1,782	434	105,000	37,427	27,960
Hartford County	86,024	42,714	11,321	29,815	6,860	9,365	2,646	622	102,834	39,016	29,331
Litchfield County	20,304	10,897	2,703	6,099	1,318	1,618	187	na	na	na	na
Middlesex County	17,518	9,751	1,876	5,482	1,442	na	na	na	na	na	na
New Haven County	82,837	39,655	12,619	28,767	6,659	8,281	1,515	37	100,957	37,255	29,328
New London County	26,286	14,663	3,260	7,950	1,760	2,559	331	0	36,781	11,429	8,887
Tolland County	12,396	7,010	1,380	3,175	864	na	na	na	na	na	na
Windham County	9,650	5,913	932	2,643	1,076	na	na	na	na	na	na
Delaware											
Kent County	15,895	9,731	2,255	3,714	745	2,035	620	37	na	na	na
New Castle County	45,586	24,024	6,259	13,958	2,448	6,343	1,839	90	55,564	22,509	17,586
Sussex County	30,896	19,774	3,873	6,312	1,189	2,426	1,129	368	45,425	10,706	7,575
Florida											
Alachua County	19,828	10,111	3,044	5,945	879	1,512	704	0	24,827	7,938	8,366
Bay County	16,999	9,901	2,112	4,497	740	2,169	786	0	22,787	8,049	6,744
Brevard County	76,243	43,486	9,335	20,060	1,969	5,833	2,087	743	94,012	31,480	29,017
Broward County	168,076	80,092	25,913	55,295	3,931	32,348	5,397	747	190,450	87,831	72,217
Charlotte County	38,266	22,112	4,526	10,155	1,366	1,566	750	200	na	na	na
Citrus County	29,294	17,494	4,000	6,819	653	2,323	827	114	na	na	na
Clay County	16,153	9,745	2,327	3,452	615	3,332	1,634	156	na	na	na
Collier County	59,575	36,193	6,347	14,762	1,017	4,637	975	538	86,600	19,944	12,297
Columbia County	7,095	3,932	1,479	1,604	612	na	na	na	na	na	na
Duval County	72,122	36,472	10,515	23,178	2,968	11,144	4,579	949	82,688	36,915	33,314
Escambia County	30,783	17,865	4,094	8,109	1,837	2,143	715	81	35,446	17,618	9,629
Flagler County	15,366	10,872	1,621	2,403	207	na	na	na	na	na	na
Hernando County	30,147	16,257	4,449	7,529	770	2,079	381	136	36,946	12,908	8,231
Highlands County	19,624	11,523	2,606	4,700	609	na	na	na	na	na	na
Hillsborough County	102,060	57,196	12,802	28,603	2,949	15,665	4,590	1,102	133,381	44,978	42,303
Indian River County	26,256	15,013	3,666	6,706	507	na	na	na	na	na	na
Lake County	46,585	29,104	5,704	10,666	923	3,867	1,094	415	66,268	19,351	11,187
Lee County	102,374	60,535	11,715	26,446	1,705	6,107	1,270	242	139,106	43,307	30,094
Leon County	20,891	10,521	2,130	7,638	998	2,220	1,172	316	24,298	9,492	10,552
Manatee County	53,715	31,605	6,129	13,630	1,076	3,111	1,564	0	73,679	21,772	13,515
Marion County	57,018	33,317	7,597	14,108	1,240	3,149	516	44	70,942	24,747	17,025
Martin County	27,796	14,279	4,589	7,878	813	1,337	152	na	na	na	na
Miami-Dade County	202,456	114,406	25,673	54,775	8,094	62,283	7,432	1,372	258,732	116,280	96,814
Monroe County	8,836	4,533	1,634	2,011	202	na	na	na	na	na	na
Nassau County	9,257	5,777	698	2,652	460	889	388	na	na	na	na
Okaloosa County	19,161	10,693	2,724	5,191	779	1,328	678	69	23,516	9,858	4,805
Orange County	75,328	44,182	7,971	21,107	2,787	14,185	3,238	377	105,637	37,610	35,885
Osceola County	18,816	11,782	1,856	4,244	1,021	5,692	654	161	29,372	11,225	7,577
Palm Beach County	196,495	97,634	26,675	63,963	5,710	18,899	4,281	770	213,041	90,054	64,620
Pasco County	65,438	36,514	8,371	18,143	2,427	5,881	1,672	353	82,939	29,102	20,846
Pinellas County	134,967	60,852	21,771	45,780	6,664	7,821	2,482	423	140,130	65,126	52,021
Polk County	74,155	45,246	7,743	18,782	2,567	10,646	2,355	149	99,020	34,073	20,092
Putnam County	10,067	4,885	1,530	3,296	466	na	na	na	na	na	na
Santa Rosa County	14,143	8,692	2,177	3,018	502	1,811	1,220	119	na	na	na
Sarasota County	82,974	46,306	9,232	23,498	2,463	3,660	2,057	205	104,010	30,788	20,100
Seminole County	33,408	18,576	3,951	10,241	2,257	4,957	741	112	49,097	18,825	14,757

Table D-2: Counties—Household Relationship, Grandparents, and Marital Status—*Continued*

| | Total Householders 65 Years and Over | Family Householders 65 Years and Over | Non-Family Householders 65 Years and Over | | Persons 65 Years and Over Living in Group Quarters | Grandparents 60 Years and Over Living with Grandchildren | | | Marital Status - Persons 60 Years and Over | | |
			Male Living Alone	Female Living Alone		Total	Responsible for Grandchildren	Responsible for Grandchildren and In Poverty	Now Married	Widowed	Divorced
Florida—Cont.											
St. Johns County	23,395	14,352	2,824	5,260	440	1,363	193	na	na	na	na
St. Lucie County	39,460	21,617	6,329	9,797	622	3,183	577	110	48,749	17,431	12,684
Sumter County	34,307	23,684	2,627	5,404	632	912	572	na	na	na	na
Volusia County	70,258	38,105	9,249	20,181	2,725	7,404	1,657	547	85,163	35,046	24,526
Georgia											
Barrow County	4,604	2,687	587	1,227	104	1,021	322	na	na	na	na
Bartow County	6,989	4,310	1,166	1,457	291	1,402	1,094	73	na	na	na
Bibb County	13,579	6,316	2,286	4,534	833	1,908	384	191	14,070	7,826	5,975
Bulloch County	4,989	2,756	866	1,281	312	na	na	na	na	na	na
Carroll County	8,925	4,575	856	3,221	152	599	398	na	na	na	na
Catoosa County	na	na	na	na	na	na	na	na	na	na	na
Chatham County	23,779	12,893	2,570	7,671	1,139	3,643	1,436	166	28,150	11,359	9,153
Cherokee County	16,062	9,989	1,572	3,765	349	na	na	na	na	na	na
Clarke County	7,604	3,905	790	2,565	325	na	na	na	na	na	na
Clayton County	12,424	7,472	1,862	2,920	549	3,529	1,581	613	17,183	8,030	7,678
Cobb County	45,973	26,960	4,817	12,560	1,485	6,131	1,578	230	70,117	21,043	16,853
Columbia County	7,910	4,996	899	1,675	345	1,769	500	na	na	na	na
Coweta County	9,871	5,873	724	3,007	155	na	na	na	na	na	na
DeKalb County	45,984	23,718	5,384	15,864	2,544	8,682	3,566	552	54,377	23,259	22,521
Dougherty County	8,532	3,956	1,003	3,507	556	750	439	90	na	na	na
Douglas County	8,231	4,475	1,249	2,363	245	2,700	1,115	108	na	na	na
Fayette County	10,184	6,664	863	2,385	258	1,148	396	na	na	na	na
Floyd County	9,055	4,845	1,234	2,704	501	999	716	0	na	na	na
Forsyth County	12,083	8,078	1,032	2,757	263	2,262	441	na	na	na	na
Fulton County	65,170	29,075	11,308	23,228	2,920	9,193	2,467	302	72,645	34,459	26,605
Glynn County	8,667	4,598	1,477	2,403	542	na	na	na	na	na	na
Gwinnett County	38,128	24,621	3,445	9,665	1,234	15,711	2,682	0	67,968	20,734	18,487
Hall County	15,730	9,786	1,225	4,269	483	2,798	589	108	22,193	6,896	4,339
Henry County	12,818	7,368	1,965	3,097	198	2,753	625	377	na	na	na
Houston County	10,261	6,745	1,141	2,218	448	2,380	950	195	na	na	na
Liberty County	na	na	na	na	na	na	na	na	na	na	na
Lowndes County	7,928	4,057	1,028	2,644	227	1,510	1,015	145	na	na	na
Muscogee County	15,599	9,219	1,573	4,542	729	1,732	974	297	17,284	8,766	5,038
Newton County	7,833	4,644	681	2,309	241	na	na	na	na	na	na
Paulding County	8,128	5,276	524	1,832	100	2,232	247	na	na	na	na
Richmond County	14,911	8,198	2,403	4,066	1,484	3,235	1,276	49	16,156	10,122	7,493
Rockdale County	5,825	3,892	373	1,406	329	1,050	180	na	na	na	na
Troup County	6,242	3,513	578	2,095	386	1,242	615	0	na	na	na
Walker County	7,319	4,559	832	1,744	437	819	474	0	na	na	na
Walton County	7,324	4,299	769	1,775	195	814	439	189	na	na	na
Whitfield County	7,666	4,234	868	2,432	412	1,226	457	0	na	na	na
Hawaii											
Hawaii County	19,257	11,033	2,444	4,393	880	4,240	1,733	68	27,876	9,104	7,083
Honolulu County	83,122	52,576	9,502	18,403	6,019	26,686	4,632	276	112,758	45,124	26,851
Kauai County	6,749	3,828	593	1,771	311	1,890	260	0	na	na	na
Maui County	13,616	8,090	1,811	2,305	580	4,085	943	153	18,904	7,142	5,830
Idaho											
Ada County	32,075	19,218	3,075	9,464	837	3,018	1,668	72	53,121	11,359	10,288
Bannock County	6,874	3,486	1,074	2,078	203	768	291	na	na	na	na
Bonneville County	na	na	na	na	na	na	na	na	na	na	na
Canyon County	14,309	9,083	1,398	3,573	391	2,355	902	na	na	na	na
Kootenai County	15,029	8,194	1,809	4,426	416	na	na	na	na	na	na
Twin Falls County	7,574	3,684	1,254	2,501	324	na	na	na	na	na	na
Illinois											
Adams County	8,049	4,251	923	2,729	927	na	na	na	na	na	na
Champaign County	14,942	7,362	2,268	5,161	1,004	1,378	456	na	na	na	na
Cook County	420,247	209,248	59,515	141,698	23,654	66,416	14,743	2,756	480,173	216,178	134,123
DeKalb County	7,023	4,165	647	1,938	519	na	na	na	na	na	na
DuPage County	74,062	42,686	8,199	22,046	4,544	9,784	1,829	183	115,800	32,230	20,212
Kane County	37,775	21,813	4,080	11,410	1,461	6,557	1,042	260	56,105	15,476	11,325
Kankakee County	9,376	5,331	1,042	2,587	1,403	666	109	na	na	na	na
Kendall County	na	na	na	na	na	na	na	na	na	na	na
Lake County	49,803	27,586	6,113	14,763	2,810	7,028	2,205	298	75,684	23,013	15,578
LaSalle County	11,879	6,660	1,386	3,604	1,230	636	261	0	na	na	na
Macon County	12,440	6,697	1,453	3,983	987	865	408	61	na	na	na
Madison County	28,067	14,618	4,412	8,604	1,287	1,753	920	341	32,374	12,437	8,724
McHenry County	21,959	13,400	1,821	6,105	922	2,433	244	0	35,283	7,621	6,880
McLean County	12,445	6,161	1,983	3,995	688	590	158	0	na	na	na
Peoria County	18,183	9,185	2,227	6,249	1,025	1,085	450	233	na	na	na
Rock Island County	17,268	8,315	2,685	5,946	847	1,324	785	na	na	na	na
Sangamon County	20,192	10,069	3,030	6,537	1,363	792	584	190	25,613	8,419	6,891
St. Clair County	24,017	12,717	3,695	7,005	1,344	3,225	795	52	26,983	12,731	8,286
Tazewell County	14,198	7,956	1,425	4,438	1,117	na	na	na	na	na	na
Vermilion County	8,761	4,446	1,459	2,766	577	na	na	na	na	na	na

Table D-2: Counties—Household Relationship, Grandparents, and Marital Status—*Continued*

	Total Householders 65 Years and Over	Family Householders 65 Years and Over	Non-Family Householders 65 Years and Over		Persons 65 Years and Over Living in Group Quarters	Grandparents 60 Years and Over Living with Grandchildren			Marital Status - Persons 60 Years and Over		
			Male Living Alone	Female Living Alone		Total	Responsible for Grandchildren	Responsible for Grandchildren and In Poverty	Now Married	Widowed	Divorced
Illinois—Cont.											
Will County	43,516	26,209	5,106	11,485	2,341	7,747	2,496	112	70,057	20,936	11,607
Williamson County	6,946	4,089	806	1,807	510	578	351	45	na	na	na
Winnebago County	28,626	14,255	5,243	8,681	1,317	2,498	679	239	34,028	13,664	9,712
Indiana											
Allen County	30,075	15,739	4,086	9,635	2,143	2,275	898	241	39,203	14,643	8,945
Bartholomew County	7,952	4,227	991	2,619	425	na	na	na	na	na	na
Clark County	10,542	5,797	1,303	3,442	550	na	na	0	na	na	na
Delaware County	11,571	7,064	860	3,463	958	918	160	0	na	na	na
Elkhart County	16,374	9,027	1,794	5,216	1,210	1,488	785	202	na	na	na
Floyd County	6,805	3,651	941	2,136	654	709	376	na	na	na	na
Grant County	8,091	4,214	1,337	2,408	501	na	na	na	na	na	na
Hamilton County	19,298	11,620	2,216	5,367	904	na	na	na	na	na	na
Hancock County	na	na	na	na	na	na	na	na	na	na	na
Hendricks County	11,731	6,680	977	3,851	683	525	181	na	na	na	na
Howard County	9,929	5,128	1,151	3,340	400	1,109	576	0	na	na	na
Johnson County	11,811	7,321	1,366	3,066	1,034	929	409	na	na	na	na
Kosciusko County	7,172	4,332	828	1,937	234	na	na	na	na	na	na
Lake County	43,006	23,720	5,295	12,881	2,310	5,439	1,684	291	56,234	21,840	14,276
LaPorte County	11,239	5,911	1,896	3,282	721	583	289	na	na	na	na
Madison County	14,579	8,247	1,726	4,305	886	1,083	608	57	17,632	5,713	4,988
Marion County	66,134	30,964	11,348	21,773	4,041	6,205	2,339	188	73,511	31,099	32,514
Monroe County	9,958	5,413	724	3,070	613	na	na	na	na	na	na
Morgan County	6,023	3,873	624	1,430	265	na	na	na	na	na	na
Porter County	14,662	9,110	1,516	3,448	887	1,280	282	na	na	na	na
St. Joseph County	24,329	12,298	3,442	8,010	1,051	1,245	494	111	30,563	11,171	9,288
Tippecanoe County	11,272	6,416	1,679	2,930	786	792	291	na	na	na	na
Vanderburgh County	17,998	8,744	2,713	6,076	1,609	1,273	535	135	20,885	8,209	7,497
Vigo County	10,262	4,986	1,737	3,250	1,019	1,381	255	0	na	na	na
Wayne County	7,721	4,634	481	2,427	566	708	423	na	na	na	na
Iowa											
Black Hawk County	12,981	5,993	2,033	4,721	685	949	476	0	na	na	na
Dallas County	na	na	na	na	na	na	na	na	na	na	na
Dubuque County	9,597	5,782	1,113	2,619	1,428	na	na	na	na	na	na
Johnson County	8,573	4,435	1,371	2,612	331	na	na	na	na	na	na
Linn County	20,002	10,756	2,581	6,189	1,162	796	265	na	26,300	6,995	6,488
Polk County	34,468	17,054	5,437	11,212	2,021	3,514	897	86	44,076	15,843	11,486
Pottawattamie County	9,357	4,657	1,274	3,298	399	595	138	63	na	na	na
Scott County	15,479	7,631	2,367	5,027	1,056	1,121	274	na	na	na	na
Story County	na	na	na	na	na	na	na	na	na	na	na
Woodbury County	8,423	4,161	1,306	2,741	508	na	na	na	na	na	na
Kansas											
Butler County	6,286	3,312	900	2,011	468	na	na	na	na	na	na
Douglas County	na	na	na	na	na	na	na	na	na	na	na
Johnson County	45,448	25,114	4,583	15,067	2,642	4,322	1,846	226	66,716	17,606	16,138
Leavenworth County	5,373	3,317	656	1,308	448	na	na	na	na	na	na
Riley County	na	na	na	na	na	na	na	na	na	na	na
Sedgwick County	41,124	21,584	6,596	12,228	2,200	5,444	1,245	216	56,360	17,896	15,073
Shawnee County	18,107	9,844	1,635	6,182	1,250	1,859	806	80	na	na	na
Wyandotte County	11,729	5,532	1,957	3,874	650	1,594	404	31	13,867	5,668	4,794
Kentucky											
Boone County	na	na	na	na	na	1,011	436	na	na	na	na
Bullitt County	na	na	na	na	na	1,207	291	na	na	na	na
Campbell County	7,975	4,098	1,124	2,578	559	1,006	344	na	na	na	na
Christian County	5,274	2,268	691	2,136	431	na	na	na	na	na	na
Daviess County	9,745	5,462	906	3,199	860	957	302	45	na	na	na
Fayette County	22,793	11,244	2,805	7,928	1,240	1,542	532	152	27,313	10,289	11,566
Hardin County	8,860	4,447	1,476	2,493	385	1,123	257	0	na	na	na
Jefferson County	71,392	35,511	9,273	24,677	4,076	6,957	2,798	293	80,974	32,508	29,033
Kenton County	13,193	6,820	1,737	4,230	970	1,549	925	0	na	na	na
Madison County	7,004	4,111	542	1,916	314	na	na	na	na	na	na
McCracken County	7,522	3,940	1,298	2,069	435	na	na	na	na	na	na
Pike County	6,768	3,998	692	2,027	417	1,152	871	626	na	na	na
Warren County	na	na	na	na	na	na	na	na	na	na	na
Louisiana											
Ascension Parish	6,832	4,342	776	1,649	248	na	na	na	na	na	na
Bossier Parish	9,661	4,825	1,568	3,124	634	1,737	950	29	na	na	na
Caddo Parish	23,269	12,262	3,405	6,776	1,918	3,845	1,718	487	25,911	13,903	7,629
Calcasieu Parish	16,874	9,082	1,774	5,637	843	1,989	824	375	23,010	8,741	5,761
East Baton Rouge Parish	34,864	18,788	4,696	10,422	1,247	3,157	1,022	209	42,773	19,071	12,233
Iberia Parish	6,093	3,574	789	1,581	356	na	na	na	na	na	na
Jefferson Parish	42,086	23,258	5,720	12,484	1,142	5,203	1,599	298	50,175	20,870	14,533
Lafayette Parish	16,922	9,031	2,482	5,105	1,040	1,132	312	0	21,844	7,540	6,149
Lafourche Parish	7,759	4,780	889	2,005	345	na	na	na	na	na	na
Livingston Parish	na	na	na	na	na	2,263	1,215	na	na	na	na

Table D-2: Counties—Household Relationship, Grandparents, and Marital Status—*Continued*

	Total Householders 65 Years and Over	Family Householders 65 Years and Over	Non-Family Householders 65 Years and Over — Male Living Alone	Non-Family Householders 65 Years and Over — Female Living Alone	Persons 65 Years and Over Living in Group Quarters	Grandparents 60 Years and Over Living with Grandchildren — Total	Grandparents 60 Years and Over Living with Grandchildren — Responsible for Grandchildren	Grandparents 60 Years and Over Living with Grandchildren — Responsible for Grandchildren and In Poverty	Marital Status - Persons 60 Years and Over — Now Married	Marital Status - Persons 60 Years and Over — Widowed	Marital Status - Persons 60 Years and Over — Divorced
Louisiana—Cont.											
Orleans Parish	30,343	14,724	5,231	9,723	1,224	3,050	793	414	29,738	16,279	13,092
Ouachita Parish	13,274	7,453	1,555	4,081	999	1,040	619	129	17,914	6,167	4,429
Rapides Parish	12,179	6,813	923	4,139	1,197	1,448	833	312	na	na	na
St. Landry Parish	7,856	4,155	1,020	2,547	683	na	na	175	na	na	na
St. Tammany Parish	21,728	13,312	2,301	5,430	699	2,742	1,076	200	na	na	na
Tangipahoa Parish	9,280	4,654	1,473	2,955	363	1,918	488	305	na	na	na
Terrebonne Parish	8,103	4,829	864	2,251	427	970	266	0	na	na	na
Maine											
Androscoggin County	11,311	4,991	2,018	3,874	619	na	na	na	na	na	na
Aroostook County	9,323	4,774	1,460	3,004	726	508	235	na	na	na	na
Cumberland County	29,244	14,655	3,620	10,185	1,493	1,967	616	na	38,545	11,299	11,442
Kennebec County	13,203	6,893	1,762	4,096	797	919	110	na	na	na	na
Penobscot County	16,041	7,983	1,799	5,877	897	1,232	371	na	na	na	na
York County	22,173	12,030	2,727	6,264	1,155	na	na	na	30,382	8,121	9,354
Maryland											
Allegany County	8,621	4,643	977	2,844	1,044	470	181	58	na	na	na
Anne Arundel County	46,746	27,454	5,323	12,506	1,433	4,918	2,013	0	63,757	20,494	14,973
Baltimore County	80,304	41,916	10,604	25,821	5,270	10,583	2,717	0	95,922	42,782	25,611
Calvert County	7,333	4,383	656	1,986	249	na	na	na	na	na	na
Carroll County	15,953	8,369	2,153	5,282	1,042	2,458	291	na	na	na	na
Cecil County	8,804	5,160	1,051	2,323	718	1,147	543	0	na	na	na
Charles County	10,298	6,238	906	2,722	617	2,511	594	0	na	na	na
Frederick County	18,569	11,053	2,147	4,669	1,281	2,475	783	88	27,182	8,863	6,173
Harford County	20,953	12,732	2,004	5,943	833	3,323	328	na	32,961	8,776	7,983
Howard County	19,963	11,623	2,324	5,603	767	3,738	413	85	35,373	9,315	6,641
Montgomery County	81,009	44,068	8,240	25,695	5,285	15,896	2,606	221	115,903	36,073	24,410
Prince George's County	59,365	35,598	6,846	15,374	2,157	16,154	3,745	644	79,980	28,415	23,191
St. Mary's County	na	na	na	na	na	1,552	516	na	na	na	na
Washington County	14,529	7,296	2,410	4,481	1,425	848	543	153	17,715	7,381	4,333
Wicomico County	8,973	5,301	794	2,707	552	na	na	na	na	na	na
Massachusetts											
Barnstable County	38,887	19,546	5,315	12,952	1,633	1,442	427	na	46,965	14,698	10,408
Berkshire County	17,764	8,500	3,154	5,698	1,468	na	na	na	na	na	na
Bristol County	53,030	27,139	6,340	17,864	4,277	7,563	1,618	207	68,508	26,141	15,580
Essex County	72,038	36,485	10,072	23,500	4,219	8,987	1,474	62	92,416	34,898	22,456
Franklin County	8,174	3,669	1,172	3,024	404	460	76	na	na	na	na
Hampden County	44,605	22,050	5,921	15,224	3,253	3,989	1,423	471	52,936	20,241	15,338
Hampshire County	15,614	7,578	2,615	5,260	948	1,302	242	41	na	na	na
Middlesex County	135,519	67,968	18,122	45,196	8,634	16,391	2,593	149	166,898	58,303	40,102
Norfolk County	65,417	33,394	8,334	21,819	4,634	9,567	1,248	125	82,077	31,581	18,993
Plymouth County	47,601	26,326	5,659	14,450	3,207	6,598	821	0	68,682	23,035	15,118
Suffolk County	54,064	21,353	10,579	20,093	3,808	6,590	922	155	50,487	24,175	20,257
Worcester County	69,289	36,254	9,543	21,965	6,045	8,614	2,312	532	92,819	31,792	21,523
Michigan											
Allegan County	10,476	6,444	1,228	2,627	674	na	na	0	na	na	na
Bay County	12,621	6,285	1,492	4,356	1,012	na	na	na	na	na	na
Berrien County	17,528	9,384	2,180	5,497	734	1,158	442	107	22,550	7,677	5,133
Calhoun County	13,899	7,457	2,183	3,908	1,016	1,133	491	0	na	na	na
Clinton County	6,754	4,260	804	1,649	382	na	na	na	na	na	na
Eaton County	11,184	6,110	1,180	3,402	540	468	61	na	na	na	na
Genesee County	42,588	24,261	5,262	12,272	1,559	3,645	928	61	52,384	17,955	14,982
Grand Traverse County	na	na	na	na	na	854	226	na	na	na	na
Ingham County	21,687	10,486	3,463	7,384	1,228	2,291	732	0	28,003	8,834	8,176
Isabella County	4,940	2,470	599	1,675	488	289	42	na	na	na	na
Jackson County	16,640	7,702	2,735	5,594	854	1,424	733	69	19,615	8,629	4,891
Kalamazoo County	21,548	11,893	2,464	6,650	1,168	1,796	663	0	29,961	9,132	6,765
Kent County	47,846	26,788	5,424	14,593	3,535	5,074	1,227	248	64,944	21,850	14,642
Lapeer County	8,529	5,322	1,130	2,000	325	1,003	395	na	na	na	na
Lenawee County	10,605	6,317	972	2,905	619	702	240	na	na	na	na
Livingston County	16,676	10,515	1,986	3,858	477	1,773	577	na	na	na	na
Macomb County	84,860	45,049	10,861	27,042	4,133	8,104	2,068	807	107,485	39,522	27,659
Marquette County	6,904	3,584	906	2,280	717	na	na	na	na	na	na
Midland County	8,858	5,223	1,144	2,372	392	na	na	na	na	na	na
Monroe County	13,962	7,491	1,438	4,802	750	1,049	572	na	na	na	na
Muskegon County	17,066	9,409	2,035	5,209	862	1,640	714	57	20,197	7,468	5,471
Oakland County	119,199	59,307	16,912	40,360	4,328	9,927	2,810	296	153,215	51,759	41,741
Ottawa County	22,645	13,195	2,360	6,659	1,101	1,611	366	na	na	na	na
Saginaw County	21,226	12,627	2,454	5,736	1,380	2,060	967	127	27,825	8,884	5,776
Shiawassee County	6,935	4,121	730	1,948	202	na	na	na	na	na	na
St. Clair County	17,313	9,726	2,186	5,147	675	1,450	199	25	23,500	7,250	5,351
Van Buren County	7,044	4,217	716	1,948	310	593	222	102	na	na	na
Washtenaw County	27,312	14,719	2,951	8,722	1,356	2,693	692	72	37,510	10,088	10,872
Wayne County	159,506	80,782	23,312	52,236	7,137	18,618	4,531	584	160,066	80,285	64,321

Table D-2: Counties—Household Relationship, Grandparents, and Marital Status—*Continued*

	Total Householders 65 Years and Over	Family Householders 65 Years and Over	Non-Family Householders 65 Years and Over Male Living Alone	Female Living Alone	Persons 65 Years and Over Living in Group Quarters	Grandparents 60 Years and Over Living with Grandchildren Total	Responsible for Grandchildren	Responsible for Grandchildren and In Poverty	Marital Status - Persons 60 Years and Over Now Married	Widowed	Divorced
Minnesota											
Anoka County	23,879	14,408	2,840	5,877	690	2,697	634	0	36,931	11,353	7,395
Blue Earth County	5,028	2,524	677	1,725	792	na	na	na	na	na	na
Carver County	na	na	na	na	na	na	na	na	na	na	na
Dakota County	31,239	16,579	3,663	10,290	1,181	2,244	251	0	44,369	13,598	10,392
Hennepin County	97,368	45,351	13,781	34,939	5,646	6,662	1,075	279	122,248	37,590	36,632
Olmsted County	12,547	7,137	1,247	3,830	890	954	329	na	na	na	na
Ramsey County	44,594	21,937	6,181	15,663	3,316	4,563	753	68	53,465	17,886	16,855
Rice County	6,214	2,524	960	2,664	365	na	na	na	na	na	na
Scott County	7,874	4,580	890	2,336	406	na	na	na	na	na	na
Sherburne County	5,370	3,211	481	1,565	509	781	181	na	na	na	na
St. Louis County	22,900	11,184	3,325	8,005	1,614	617	171	38	29,072	9,334	7,287
Stearns County	12,262	7,123	1,455	3,498	1,265	482	117	na	16,795	5,457	2,663
Washington County	18,287	11,615	1,626	4,720	1,747	na	na	na	30,615	6,275	5,832
Wright County	8,544	5,205	1,205	2,073	520	na	na	na	na	na	na
Mississippi											
DeSoto County	12,206	7,625	1,355	3,025	219	2,138	1,233	69	na	na	na
Forrest County	na	na	na	na	na	1,334	509	423	na	na	na
Harrison County	18,357	9,909	2,848	5,390	632	2,567	675	133	19,962	8,172	6,955
Hinds County	19,283	10,189	2,700	6,274	1,613	2,626	905	181	21,519	10,194	6,714
Jackson County	11,759	7,243	1,317	3,005	318	1,839	661	0	na	na	na
Jones County	6,516	4,034	393	2,089	443	na	na	na	na	na	na
Lauderdale County	7,202	3,529	598	3,064	236	1,329	798	28	na	na	na
Lee County	6,963	3,905	523	2,391	604	873	385	72	na	na	na
Madison County	7,871	4,355	1,091	2,354	450	893	745	na	na	na	na
Rankin County	11,985	7,063	1,211	3,591	576	1,523	453	na	na	na	na
Missouri											
Boone County	11,871	5,927	1,516	4,107	742	na	na	na	na	na	na
Buchanan County	8,952	3,947	1,215	3,590	433	613	546	116	na	na	na
Cape Girardeau County	7,147	4,123	792	2,232	795	na	na	na	na	na	na
Cass County	9,240	5,198	1,128	2,652	663	na	na	na	na	na	na
Christian County	7,253	4,491	810	1,900	212	576	342	na	na	na	na
Clay County	19,267	10,709	2,103	5,947	817	2,270	1,000	149	na	na	na
Cole County	na	na	na	na	na	na	na	na	na	na	na
Franklin County	9,697	6,457	560	2,433	452	na	na	na	na	na	na
Greene County	28,854	14,941	2,951	10,455	1,639	1,639	971	152	34,463	12,519	8,894
Jackson County	59,505	29,476	8,753	19,939	3,719	5,263	1,470	152	67,007	25,258	25,937
Jasper County	9,867	5,098	1,749	2,718	664	2,196	525	290	na	na	na
Jefferson County	17,812	10,459	1,415	5,157	913	2,214	983	228	na	na	na
Platte County	7,048	3,826	1,096	1,983	405	na	na	na	na	na	na
St. Charles County	31,721	17,744	3,856	9,573	1,145	3,479	803	0	45,422	13,203	9,155
St. Francois County	6,200	3,503	773	1,924	579	na	na	na	na	na	na
St. Louis County	105,403	57,639	11,342	34,125	8,471	9,200	3,206	397	128,929	47,827	33,411
Montana											
Cascade County	9,011	4,544	1,700	2,613	329	607	269	na	na	na	na
Flathead County	9,898	5,932	1,344	2,344	320	na	na	na	na	na	na
Gallatin County	6,915	3,645	1,125	2,028	217	na	na	na	na	na	na
Lewis and Clark County	6,192	3,286	1,253	1,626	562	na	na	na	na	na	na
Missoula County	10,170	5,033	1,831	3,153	349	na	na	na	na	na	na
Yellowstone County	14,746	7,016	2,438	5,176	859	804	451	na	na	na	na
Nebraska											
Douglas County	41,021	19,732	6,020	14,188	2,092	2,216	494	45	49,963	19,684	13,501
Lancaster County	23,688	12,850	3,191	7,343	689	1,503	581	220	32,224	8,750	7,388
Sarpy County	10,850	6,362	1,368	2,969	526	898	387	0	na	na	na
Nevada											
Clark County	156,767	86,409	25,109	36,404	3,486	25,825	7,854	1,060	203,387	65,360	76,019
Washoe County	40,668	20,530	7,633	10,508	1,132	4,200	1,216	51	50,570	15,109	19,798
New Hampshire											
Cheshire County	8,186	4,615	1,098	2,202	581	na	na	na	na	na	na
Grafton County	9,339	5,112	1,449	2,453	568	na	na	na	na	na	na
Hillsborough County	31,803	16,985	4,690	8,970	2,668	5,568	837	0	45,955	15,440	12,361
Merrimack County	13,787	7,174	1,841	4,158	1,080	825	93	na	19,739	6,527	4,666
Rockingham County	27,957	15,006	3,827	8,522	1,097	2,998	796	na	43,126	10,428	10,820
Strafford County	9,910	4,475	1,455	3,230	443	na	na	na	na	na	na
New Jersey											
Atlantic County	26,503	13,062	3,975	8,736	1,542	4,830	1,676	101	32,122	13,352	10,066
Bergen County	84,279	49,762	8,081	24,063	4,566	12,536	1,220	275	122,956	41,445	21,787
Burlington County	43,499	23,508	5,342	13,517	2,356	5,424	1,571	106	56,833	19,552	11,689
Camden County	47,093	25,335	6,776	14,323	2,646	6,772	2,394	233	55,509	23,774	14,015
Cape May County	14,468	8,081	2,185	3,629	993	na	na	na	na	na	na
Cumberland County	13,024	7,241	1,758	3,553	1,149	1,780	826	174	14,418	6,359	4,518
Essex County	61,017	26,816	10,024	21,579	3,994	11,559	2,238	463	63,187	33,209	21,670
Gloucester County	25,692	13,645	3,027	7,974	865	4,990	1,153	72	33,212	14,154	6,982
Hudson County	43,207	21,472	7,120	12,973	2,228	8,943	1,882	425	49,032	23,011	15,494
Hunterdon County	11,952	6,563	1,810	3,209	453	na	na	na	na	na	na

Table D-2: Counties—Household Relationship, Grandparents, and Marital Status—*Continued*

| | Total Householders 65 Years and Over | Family Householders 65 Years and Over | Non-Family Householders 65 Years and Over | | Persons 65 Years and Over Living in Group Quarters | Grandparents 60 Years and Over Living with Grandchildren | | | Marital Status - Persons 60 Years and Over | | |
			Male Living Alone	Female Living Alone		Total	Responsible for Grandchildren	Responsible for Grandchildren and In Poverty	Now Married	Widowed	Divorced
New Jersey—Cont.											
Mercer County	30,427	17,017	3,413	9,169	1,924	3,813	1,102	216	40,494	14,784	9,554
Middlesex County	63,356	35,982	7,622	18,928	3,524	12,811	1,998	112	89,652	34,549	16,863
Monmouth County	59,863	32,118	7,916	18,305	2,675	8,294	1,358	146	78,800	30,345	17,891
Morris County	45,402	25,578	5,061	13,360	2,966	5,364	486	na	66,031	18,973	12,523
Ocean County	81,638	42,911	9,385	27,105	3,139	4,705	957	58	98,238	34,651	19,072
Passaic County	35,641	19,886	3,918	11,370	2,530	8,330	1,369	100	49,998	21,215	9,860
Salem County	7,136	3,937	737	2,277	549	1,172	599	na	na	na	na
Somerset County	24,819	13,677	1,884	8,820	2,395	5,861	479	44	40,207	14,092	7,367
Sussex County	12,312	7,206	1,137	3,714	789	1,217	323	0	na	na	na
Union County	41,557	21,392	5,698	13,802	3,357	7,306	1,468	85	50,971	21,422	10,583
Warren County	10,314	5,621	1,430	3,009	925	na	na	na	na	na	na
New Mexico											
Bernalillo County	59,692	29,733	8,468	20,086	2,249	6,126	1,909	538	71,351	27,068	25,574
Chaves County	6,495	3,326	973	2,051	423	793	520	20	na	na	na
Doña Ana County	17,799	10,709	1,715	5,135	779	2,364	565	107	na	na	na
Lea County	na	na	na	na	na	na	na	na	na	na	na
McKinley County	4,880	3,157	614	1,057	153	1,462	689	210	5,568	2,187	1,225
Otero County	6,074	4,068	514	1,282	350	703	579	na	na	na	na
San Juan County	9,919	5,863	1,114	2,388	546	2,712	932	378	na	na	na
Sandoval County	13,613	7,095	2,034	3,784	338	2,169	831	57	na	na	na
Santa Fe County	18,581	8,925	2,931	5,679	441	1,463	492	na	22,751	5,160	9,337
Valencia County	na	na	na	na	na	na	na	na	na	na	na
New York											
Albany County	29,822	14,762	3,909	9,767	3,040	1,927	308	na	33,195	13,662	8,613
Bronx County	98,671	43,609	16,512	35,883	9,598	21,436	4,296	1,813	86,537	52,112	36,255
Broome County	21,537	11,152	3,064	7,024	1,951	1,483	652	159	26,002	9,944	8,261
Cattaraugus County	8,548	4,181	1,498	2,620	814	518	223	na	na	na	na
Cayuga County	8,338	3,970	1,472	2,641	424	na	na	na	10,441	4,344	1,936
Chautauqua County	14,768	7,746	2,072	4,656	1,229	774	216	53	17,660	6,836	4,663
Chemung County	8,995	4,718	733	3,051	773	427	276	16	na	na	na
Clinton County	7,776	3,851	1,196	2,299	544	na	na	na	na	na	na
Dutchess County	25,920	13,901	3,826	7,335	2,883	4,341	354	na	36,843	12,656	8,944
Erie County	101,398	48,727	14,439	36,136	6,665	5,373	1,522	85	109,113	49,296	29,499
Jefferson County	8,616	4,581	769	2,819	486	1,090	465	na	12,113	4,349	2,572
Kings County	196,991	96,750	27,737	68,923	11,787	38,973	9,879	1,984	213,942	97,920	59,135
Livingston County	7,095	3,606	1,147	2,152	533	na	na	na	na	na	na
Madison County	6,308	3,737	710	1,707	379	na	na	na	na	na	na
Monroe County	74,052	34,807	11,982	25,555	4,323	4,035	1,810	147	86,052	36,667	23,466
Nassau County	126,595	74,719	10,969	36,620	6,531	25,438	3,237	75	184,468	66,066	29,748
New York County	167,700	62,952	32,086	68,716	7,493	13,402	5,407	1,573	133,547	61,463	51,191
Niagara County	24,133	11,175	3,757	8,773	1,367	1,595	610	247	29,556	10,794	6,858
Oneida County	24,683	12,869	3,516	7,745	3,310	1,519	504	196	30,563	11,739	8,115
Onondaga County	45,806	22,559	6,854	15,522	3,095	4,197	1,431	408	54,828	21,641	13,402
Ontario County	12,487	5,818	1,692	4,544	763	na	na	na	na	na	na
Orange County	27,498	14,691	3,305	8,755	1,910	5,291	1,452	0	36,280	14,405	8,076
Oswego County	10,409	5,096	1,545	3,044	411	844	270	na	na	na	na
Putnam County	8,294	5,448	711	1,912	239	na	na	na	na	na	na
Queens County	176,063	97,043	20,288	53,777	11,494	44,473	10,097	2,055	215,083	99,175	54,290
Rensselaer County	15,633	8,365	1,313	5,675	1,078	1,238	408	na	19,279	6,577	5,259
Richmond County	38,825	23,628	3,632	11,134	3,064	6,799	606	177	56,589	21,654	8,939
Rockland County	25,950	16,345	2,484	6,903	1,933	6,493	668	na	41,628	12,779	5,118
Saratoga County	22,418	12,293	3,517	5,939	982	2,056	262	na	31,345	8,645	6,701
Schenectady County	14,354	6,998	2,049	4,909	1,327	na	na	na	na	na	na
St. Lawrence County	9,894	4,154	1,545	3,678	1,067	na	na	na	12,718	5,806	3,380
Steuben County	11,088	5,496	1,201	4,068	963	426	192	0	12,432	5,110	3,780
Suffolk County	135,519	76,551	15,647	39,513	8,967	21,532	3,019	336	182,331	69,274	36,100
Sullivan County	7,204	3,341	1,397	2,332	1,000	na	na	na	na	na	na
Tompkins County	7,857	4,272	973	2,330	297	na	na	na	na	na	na
Ulster County	21,122	9,980	3,510	7,059	1,848	1,104	552	na	21,933	10,128	6,312
Warren County	7,527	4,143	1,161	2,150	330	na	na	na	na	na	na
Wayne County	9,442	4,473	1,803	3,110	645	304	132	na	na	na	na
Westchester County	91,882	48,225	11,168	30,012	6,424	13,755	3,442	791	115,436	41,581	25,316
North Carolina											
Alamance County	16,058	8,229	2,148	5,424	1,016	1,179	661	257	19,315	7,344	5,227
Brunswick County	18,313	11,780	2,292	3,885	530	888	463	229	na	na	na
Buncombe County	27,853	13,548	3,623	9,862	1,775	1,934	937	73	35,435	11,852	9,611
Burke County	9,454	4,668	1,472	3,123	643	na	na	na	na	na	na
Cabarrus County	15,055	7,985	2,029	4,490	563	1,523	325	144	na	na	na
Caldwell County	9,454	4,983	1,062	3,170	404	1,244	707	284	na	na	na
Carteret County	9,697	5,450	1,339	2,759	346	958	580	na	na	na	na
Catawba County	14,624	9,513	1,352	3,383	900	1,959	1,330	745	na	na	na
Chatham County	10,205	5,641	1,225	3,025	465	524	131	na	na	na	na
Cleveland County	11,438	6,540	1,277	3,224	225	1,158	781	89	na	na	na
Craven County	11,320	6,434	1,354	3,439	254	1,040	542	37	na	na	na
Cumberland County	22,057	12,074	2,814	6,943	890	3,749	1,214	295	28,672	11,134	6,599
Davidson County	17,710	9,793	1,890	5,817	927	1,646	433	23	na	na	na

Table D-2: Counties—Household Relationship, Grandparents, and Marital Status—*Continued*

	Total Householders 65 Years and Over	Family Householders 65 Years and Over	Non-Family Householders 65 Years and Over — Male Living Alone	Non-Family Householders 65 Years and Over — Female Living Alone	Persons 65 Years and Over Living in Group Quarters	Grandparents 60 Years and Over Living with Grandchildren — Total	Grandparents — Responsible for Grandchildren	Grandparents — Responsible for Grandchildren and In Poverty	Marital Status - Persons 60 Years and Over — Now Married	Marital Status — Widowed	Marital Status — Divorced
North Carolina—Cont.											
Durham County	20,075	10,431	2,435	6,949	1,480	2,006	840	38	26,046	9,773	8,204
Forsyth County	33,763	16,987	4,577	11,495	1,231	3,127	993	92	40,711	15,447	11,683
Gaston County	18,971	10,214	3,035	5,449	1,342	2,484	959	177	23,178	11,090	6,325
Guilford County	44,306	20,941	6,704	15,831	2,289	4,145	1,308	128	49,632	21,983	16,973
Harnett County	8,883	4,785	1,247	2,651	480	1,384	768	30	10,821	4,656	2,394
Henderson County	16,786	9,159	1,787	5,661	338	1,308	423	na	na	na	na
Iredell County	13,802	9,155	1,068	3,312	630	1,110	239	0	22,495	6,107	3,312
Johnston County	13,892	8,373	1,283	3,853	576	2,380	290	41	na	na	na
Lincoln County	7,702	5,405	552	1,441	299	1,215	690	633	na	na	na
Mecklenburg County	62,064	32,437	7,693	20,813	2,556	7,570	2,447	645	82,990	28,142	25,103
Moore County	13,871	7,785	1,872	3,963	928	524	250	na	na	na	na
Nash County	10,013	4,651	1,399	3,796	415	na	na	53	na	na	na
New Hanover County	21,442	12,493	1,964	6,341	922	1,239	254	na	30,402	7,404	7,346
Onslow County	9,938	5,153	1,510	2,945	285	na	na	na	na	na	na
Orange County	na	na	na	na	na	na	na	na	na	na	na
Pitt County	12,463	6,895	1,659	3,439	545	1,902	733	364	na	na	na
Randolph County	15,552	8,386	2,471	4,492	660	1,815	387	251	na	na	na
Robeson County	11,080	6,205	1,514	3,256	681	1,623	790	315	13,099	6,108	4,026
Rockingham County	na	na	na	na	na	984	612	0	na	na	na
Rowan County	14,616	8,906	1,509	3,857	1,034	1,849	1,457	346	na	na	na
Rutherford County	8,116	3,744	1,746	2,498	443	na	na	na	na	na	na
Surry County	8,171	4,601	891	2,482	557	na	na	na	na	na	na
Union County	14,167	7,928	2,579	3,613	480	2,000	629	0	na	na	na
Wake County	59,068	34,134	5,597	18,667	2,817	8,909	2,551	683	87,926	28,855	20,843
Wayne County	11,015	6,170	978	3,756	408	na	na	na	na	na	na
Wilkes County	8,517	4,539	1,377	2,601	377	na	na	na	na	na	na
Wilson County	8,299	4,561	993	2,492	746	690	302	193	na	na	na
North Dakota											
Burleigh County	8,176	4,767	603	2,629	703	na	na	na	na	na	na
Cass County	11,545	5,289	1,445	4,543	718	na	na	na	na	na	na
Grand Forks County	5,261	2,489	743	1,983	371	na	na	na	na	na	na
Ward County	na	na	na	na	na	na	na	na	na	na	na
Ohio											
Allen County	10,595	5,779	1,172	3,323	550	1,111	211	41	na	na	na
Ashtabula County	10,195	5,847	1,379	2,804	1,346	1,377	746	450	na	na	na
Belmont County	7,957	4,171	1,087	2,467	840	na	na	na	na	na	na
Butler County	29,611	17,333	4,097	7,424	1,937	3,232	1,255	218	42,319	12,910	9,971
Clark County	15,290	8,408	1,810	4,849	1,428	714	355	159	na	na	na
Clermont County	17,922	10,492	2,013	5,149	659	1,396	380	137	26,988	6,394	5,726
Columbiana County	12,009	6,544	1,813	3,545	975	958	373	114	na	na	na
Cuyahoga County	136,488	64,200	22,236	47,283	9,377	10,379	4,057	1,122	138,710	63,030	51,417
Delaware County	12,304	7,271	1,272	3,180	376	na	na	na	na	na	na
Erie County	9,653	4,738	1,408	3,003	670	na	na	na	na	na	na
Fairfield County	13,321	7,412	1,851	3,862	670	2,106	464	12	na	na	na
Franklin County	83,709	41,566	12,119	27,748	3,928	10,886	3,754	712	104,791	38,584	34,366
Geauga County	9,686	6,624	591	2,028	650	705	196	na	na	na	na
Greene County	15,735	8,441	2,059	5,009	704	929	324	na	na	na	na
Hamilton County	76,287	34,963	12,775	26,965	5,733	5,329	1,745	460	80,615	36,559	29,690
Hancock County	7,754	4,062	1,082	2,610	578	na	na	na	na	na	na
Jefferson County	8,680	4,477	982	2,929	634	462	173	7	na	na	na
Lake County	26,291	13,797	3,320	8,504	1,425	2,377	310	41	na	na	na
Licking County	16,224	9,122	2,065	4,693	881	1,521	455	0	na	na	na
Lorain County	31,749	16,496	4,473	10,066	1,876	3,541	785	0	39,650	14,432	10,241
Lucas County	41,777	19,617	6,293	14,907	2,533	3,287	1,051	117	46,289	20,092	16,770
Mahoning County	29,231	14,428	4,019	9,946	2,176	1,380	463	51	32,694	15,197	9,112
Marion County	7,518	4,180	1,054	2,129	322	na	na	na	na	na	na
Medina County	16,367	9,519	1,826	4,833	896	1,432	490	0	na	na	na
Miami County	11,088	5,579	1,777	3,529	464	na	na	na	na	na	na
Montgomery County	57,759	28,412	9,346	18,649	3,973	4,985	2,766	631	62,342	26,886	19,622
Muskingum County	9,403	4,828	1,555	2,769	344	na	na	na	na	na	na
Portage County	15,282	8,243	2,070	4,551	46	na	na	na	na	na	na
Richland County	15,369	7,413	2,126	5,373	648	na	na	na	na	na	na
Ross County	7,322	3,805	1,556	1,955	441	na	na	na	na	na	na
Scioto County	7,877	4,181	874	2,581	777	704	371	na	na	na	na
Stark County	41,136	22,159	4,840	12,872	3,598	3,356	1,097	76	54,234	17,295	15,214
Summit County	56,247	28,593	8,050	18,590	3,438	3,895	1,685	217	67,356	25,352	19,582
Trumbull County	25,474	13,191	4,051	7,504	1,443	2,318	732	54	30,286	11,761	8,445
Tuscarawas County	10,625	5,017	1,963	3,403	771	476	215	38	na	na	na
Warren County	16,994	10,572	1,144	4,690	667	1,826	692	na	na	na	na
Wayne County	10,626	6,472	1,285	2,752	979	na	na	43	na	na	na
Wood County	11,081	6,188	1,475	3,107	857	935	374	na	na	na	na
Oklahoma											
Canadian County	9,226	5,534	591	2,956	539	838	80	16	na	na	na
Cleveland County	19,193	11,248	1,982	5,657	893	1,917	415	0	28,399	8,227	7,225
Comanche County	8,367	4,209	1,345	2,535	769	1,439	875	44	na	na	na

Table D-2: Counties—Household Relationship, Grandparents, and Marital Status—*Continued*

	Total Householders 65 Years and Over	Family Householders 65 Years and Over	Non-Family Householders 65 Years and Over		Persons 65 Years and Over Living in Group Quarters	Grandparents 60 Years and Over Living with Grandchildren			Marital Status - Persons 60 Years and Over		
			Male Living Alone	Female Living Alone		Total	Responsible for Grandchildren	Responsible for Grandchildren and In Poverty	Now Married	Widowed	Divorced
Oklahoma—Cont.											
Creek County	7,083	4,290	847	1,946	520	1,200	384	276	na	na	na
Muskogee County	6,952	3,618	1,111	1,972	762	913	511	143	na	na	na
Oklahoma County	60,997	32,038	8,456	18,824	3,074	5,676	3,198	363	73,096	27,931	24,563
Payne County	5,632	3,018	634	1,923	132	na	na	na	na	na	na
Pottawatomie County	6,475	3,843	738	1,843	199	637	297	6	9,510	3,384	2,342
Rogers County	8,787	5,087	1,055	2,622	737	1,749	653	39	na	na	na
Tulsa County	51,474	26,842	5,930	17,431	2,177	5,268	1,948	93	66,842	21,855	20,808
Wagoner County	6,775	4,488	693	1,315	146	642	219	0	na	na	na
Oregon											
Benton County	7,923	4,193	1,203	2,164	107	na	na	na	na	na	na
Clackamas County	38,693	22,301	4,385	10,888	1,120	3,677	747	0	55,179	14,501	16,721
Deschutes County	18,070	10,641	1,826	4,852	617	na	na	na	na	na	na
Douglas County	15,674	8,246	3,104	3,586	475	1,490	523	14	na	na	na
Jackson County	26,718	13,950	4,086	7,482	674	1,387	698	397	34,369	10,004	11,920
Josephine County	12,767	6,869	1,541	3,188	532	na	na	na	na	na	na
Klamath County	8,131	3,916	1,352	2,528	210	na	na	na	na	na	na
Lane County	39,122	20,813	5,116	11,315	1,310	3,181	1,089	54	49,571	14,677	17,796
Linn County	12,694	7,188	1,390	3,726	584	1,060	469	na	na	na	na
Marion County	30,083	16,101	3,753	9,392	1,457	3,070	990	161	36,983	13,690	12,164
Multnomah County	57,511	27,110	8,419	19,354	3,622	7,797	1,878	219	68,819	23,549	28,687
Polk County	8,211	4,518	1,555	2,015	197	982	96	na	na	na	na
Umatilla County	5,823	3,109	778	1,924	797	na	na	na	na	na	na
Washington County	41,521	21,989	5,168	13,065	1,523	5,135	1,061	0	56,106	16,514	17,368
Yamhill County	9,461	4,957	1,061	3,120	189	na	na	na	na	na	na
Pennsylvania											
Adams County	10,910	6,617	1,288	2,811	829	726	169	0	na	na	na
Allegheny County	142,538	66,647	20,896	51,625	8,183	7,362	1,880	113	154,478	69,645	36,588
Armstrong County	9,063	4,710	1,080	3,158	52	na	na	na	na	na	na
Beaver County	21,820	11,664	3,189	6,582	733	1,638	529	0	26,455	10,140	5,227
Berks County	40,172	22,630	5,898	10,648	2,571	3,441	1,017	276	57,209	17,248	11,887
Blair County	14,864	7,062	1,734	5,804	1,493	1,003	372	43	na	na	na
Bucks County	61,999	36,015	6,975	18,641	2,756	6,787	1,096	39	92,296	27,677	15,405
Butler County	20,090	10,235	2,358	6,820	928	852	447	13	25,999	8,677	5,972
Cambria County	18,477	9,504	2,581	6,223	1,125	1,425	579	16	22,376	9,251	3,653
Carbon County	7,877	4,576	1,161	1,945	404	1,253	597	na	na	na	na
Centre County	12,199	7,128	1,533	3,339	733	na	na	na	na	na	na
Chester County	44,264	26,030	4,908	12,174	2,744	4,474	1,123	115	64,810	18,979	12,157
Clearfield County	9,947	4,895	1,312	3,669	732	789	451	15	na	na	na
Columbia County	7,303	4,088	913	2,110	530	517	219	na	na	na	na
Crawford County	10,082	5,702	1,548	2,527	335	700	184	29	na	na	na
Cumberland County	26,592	14,481	2,777	8,908	1,836	2,056	525	na	35,001	11,920	6,584
Dauphin County	25,789	12,476	3,036	9,690	1,494	2,258	709	0	31,931	12,850	7,936
Delaware County	52,263	27,296	6,961	17,005	3,459	6,450	1,761	213	64,789	27,343	13,976
Erie County	27,024	14,444	3,187	8,468	2,253	2,712	1,013	256	35,265	13,942	7,339
Fayette County	15,564	7,568	2,364	5,117	1,531	1,047	148	90	18,201	8,573	4,823
Franklin County	16,463	9,616	2,146	4,523	898	1,161	283	na	na	na	na
Indiana County	9,335	5,638	895	2,616	471	na	na	na	na	na	na
Lackawanna County	24,720	11,549	2,770	9,943	2,276	1,973	436	na	28,654	12,889	5,714
Lancaster County	50,614	29,287	4,007	14,782	4,327	3,806	752	64	75,612	21,816	11,984
Lawrence County	11,449	6,573	1,586	3,223	864	850	327	na	na	na	na
Lebanon County	14,125	8,012	1,595	4,090	1,181	na	na	16	na	na	na
Lehigh County	34,260	18,112	4,899	10,548	2,711	3,453	672	93	45,545	16,485	12,027
Luzerne County	36,645	17,453	5,080	13,260	2,766	3,551	987	103	42,185	18,975	11,074
Lycoming County	12,944	6,642	1,841	4,128	943	685	328	na	16,673	6,374	4,251
Mercer County	14,146	7,299	2,324	4,338	1,302	1,422	382	0	18,506	6,941	4,117
Monroe County	12,922	7,361	1,495	3,475	506	2,547	560	0	na	na	na
Montgomery County	81,685	43,584	9,245	26,285	6,661	7,224	1,223	0	107,770	37,784	21,172
Northampton County	30,546	16,943	3,521	9,649	2,688	3,604	1,157	156	45,342	14,593	7,151
Northumberland County	11,777	6,272	1,372	3,420	977	550	212	38	na	na	na
Philadelphia County	124,800	56,451	20,648	45,079	8,075	17,058	4,959	1,314	112,064	66,630	48,622
Schuylkill County	17,799	8,710	2,781	5,934	1,575	1,220	595	75	21,214	9,377	4,666
Somerset County	9,658	5,106	1,316	3,077	901	473	236	62	na	na	na
Washington County	24,643	13,305	2,945	7,425	1,396	1,547	239	0	31,927	12,054	7,285
Westmoreland County	47,595	26,128	5,598	14,905	2,188	2,918	598	86	62,338	22,048	10,246
York County	41,712	24,027	5,073	11,357	2,099	4,051	719	132	63,603	17,887	10,922
Rhode Island											
Kent County	18,266	8,879	2,677	6,184	1,176	1,596	247	na	na	na	na
Newport County	10,345	5,158	1,539	3,269	533	na	na	na	na	na	na
Providence County	54,243	27,033	7,240	18,945	5,281	8,247	2,089	386	62,797	28,681	19,789
Washington County	13,918	7,804	1,581	4,077	477	na	na	na	na	na	na
South Carolina											
Aiken County	17,610	10,114	2,573	4,898	624	2,115	916	290	na	na	na
Anderson County	20,200	10,783	2,445	6,446	981	1,886	1,030	47	27,235	9,726	4,511
Beaufort County	25,981	15,408	2,912	6,826	404	1,564	403	na	na	na	na
Berkeley County	13,756	9,209	1,714	2,635	116	3,633	2,056	621	21,734	6,201	5,584

Table D-2: Counties—Household Relationship, Grandparents, and Marital Status—*Continued*

	Total Householders 65 Years and Over	Family Householders 65 Years and Over	Non-Family Householders 65 Years and Over		Persons 65 Years and Over Living in Group Quarters	Grandparents 60 Years and Over Living with Grandchildren			Marital Status - Persons 60 Years and Over		
			Male Living Alone	Female Living Alone		Total	Responsible for Grandchildren	Responsible for Grandchildren and In Poverty	Now Married	Widowed	Divorced
South Carolina—Cont.											
Charleston County	34,760	20,161	4,035	10,121	1,177	3,429	1,714	248	47,541	15,992	10,720
Darlington County	7,554	4,192	1,099	2,063	271	na	na	na	na	na	na
Dorchester County	10,319	6,585	1,207	2,430	204	1,019	389	na	na	na	na
Florence County	12,482	6,833	1,808	3,721	848	2,275	1,781	510	na	na	na
Greenville County	42,834	24,889	4,427	13,025	1,511	4,904	1,488	308	57,171	19,775	13,025
Greenwood County	7,829	4,323	821	2,610	469	618	254	86	na	na	na
Horry County	38,767	21,816	5,298	10,507	580	4,143	2,468	668	51,724	15,653	12,074
Lancaster County	9,146	5,050	1,248	2,750	372	2,655	1,838	287	na	na	na
Laurens County	7,067	4,137	807	2,068	763	1,078	566	42	na	na	na
Lexington County	25,022	13,608	3,095	7,866	1,069	3,068	1,605	241	33,056	11,977	7,441
Oconee County	na	na	na	na	na	na	na	na	na	na	na
Orangeburg County	9,240	4,479	1,526	3,083	304	850	357	55	na	na	na
Pickens County	11,532	6,161	1,339	3,805	486	1,045	320	na	na	na	na
Richland County	29,698	16,323	3,193	9,595	1,680	3,815	1,080	543	33,562	13,763	11,267
Spartanburg County	27,831	16,199	3,375	7,604	1,269	3,681	1,180	450	36,574	13,023	7,224
Sumter County	9,981	5,812	1,255	2,822	529	1,528	880	81	na	na	na
York County	19,598	11,664	2,279	5,111	595	2,399	532	12	29,700	8,142	6,088
South Dakota											
Minnehaha County	14,087	6,634	2,452	4,719	1,186	1,376	329	na	na	na	na
Pennington County	10,370	5,026	2,113	2,932	557	828	181	na	na	na	na
Tennessee											
Anderson County	8,798	4,542	1,378	2,637	588	na	na	na	na	na	na
Blount County	13,469	8,047	1,631	3,575	538	1,777	611	104	na	na	na
Bradley County	10,286	5,459	1,513	3,127	438	na	na	na	na	na	na
Davidson County	47,229	23,001	6,787	16,232	1,696	7,282	2,334	290	55,605	20,872	21,117
Greene County	7,564	4,381	1,295	1,541	403	693	182	na	na	na	na
Hamilton County	35,090	20,383	4,201	9,969	1,652	4,115	1,788	266	44,176	16,301	12,019
Knox County	41,265	20,130	6,124	14,144	1,960	4,053	1,486	469	51,717	18,297	16,650
Madison County	9,190	5,712	748	2,642	578	1,088	538	24	na	na	na
Maury County	7,418	4,571	807	2,000	336	1,213	704	178	na	na	na
Montgomery County	9,301	5,751	560	2,490	587	1,223	440	na	na	na	na
Putnam County	8,106	4,185	1,026	2,895	331	na	na	na	na	na	na
Robertson County	5,423	3,333	690	1,341	344	na	na	na	na	na	na
Rutherford County	16,979	9,784	2,198	4,773	755	3,480	934	0	na	na	na
Sevier County	10,950	6,075	1,414	3,041	285	1,184	328	na	na	na	na
Shelby County	67,957	37,174	9,462	20,069	3,375	8,223	2,315	771	79,033	37,432	28,845
Sullivan County	20,462	11,016	2,659	6,671	524	1,205	424	na	na	na	na
Sumner County	14,283	9,030	1,558	3,436	656	1,536	692	74	na	na	na
Washington County	13,840	7,645	1,700	4,172	907	na	na	na	na	na	na
Williamson County	13,046	8,511	841	3,262	217	2,267	438	na	na	na	na
Wilson County	10,626	6,221	1,762	2,558	539	1,233	409	45	na	na	na
Texas											
Angelina County	7,889	4,370	1,095	2,410	1,202	845	186	na	na	na	na
Bastrop County	5,639	3,573	963	1,042	404	na	na	na	na	na	na
Bell County	19,437	11,452	2,593	5,153	1,320	3,016	1,313	217	26,099	8,023	8,599
Bexar County	124,741	70,582	16,353	34,449	5,698	25,637	6,789	1,269	157,431	62,445	50,433
Bowie County	8,827	5,311	1,079	2,437	703	1,075	517	31	na	na	na
Brazoria County	20,884	13,103	2,503	4,702	1,368	4,117	1,335	116	32,986	9,231	6,658
Brazos County	11,057	5,998	1,673	3,194	603	2,112	989	103	na	na	na
Cameron County	30,043	18,263	3,235	8,162	1,158	8,672	2,066	706	39,320	16,081	8,582
Collin County	48,511	28,409	5,123	14,004	935	10,623	1,271	251	81,345	19,688	20,220
Comal County	13,048	8,142	1,401	3,334	495	na	na	na	na	na	na
Coryell County	4,034	2,337	456	1,241	225	na	na	na	na	na	na
Dallas County	146,790	79,239	19,102	44,618	6,733	32,676	10,355	2,392	189,052	69,637	66,526
Denton County	37,253	22,181	3,632	10,227	1,215	7,504	1,763	0	60,358	14,750	15,989
Ector County	9,158	4,931	1,111	2,865	255	1,454	456	50	na	na	na
El Paso County	52,580	31,900	5,575	14,386	1,811	16,063	3,999	1,607	72,761	30,058	17,073
Ellis County	11,745	7,728	784	3,054	556	1,781	653	78	na	na	na
Fort Bend County	33,770	23,559	2,435	7,328	870	14,064	1,408	448	65,315	14,870	11,143
Galveston County	25,568	15,225	3,667	5,952	960	4,568	1,560	358	34,840	10,871	10,541
Grayson County	12,404	6,975	2,042	3,317	881	2,050	542	86	na	na	na
Gregg County	10,987	5,633	1,240	4,029	1,017	1,692	545	46	na	na	na
Guadalupe County	11,530	7,001	1,404	2,866	619	2,762	1,283	100	na	na	na
Harris County	244,310	136,555	32,858	69,822	6,780	54,062	14,632	2,719	342,355	123,629	92,922
Harrison County	7,012	4,085	479	2,219	311	na	na	na	na	na	na
Hays County	10,742	6,687	705	3,230	495	2,033	601	0	na	na	na
Henderson County	10,304	6,451	1,347	2,286	611	1,067	396	73	na	na	na
Hidalgo County	44,905	30,406	4,672	8,754	2,053	13,895	3,153	1,317	68,669	25,571	9,330
Hunt County	7,898	4,317	1,423	1,936	511	1,610	813	256	na	na	na
Jefferson County	22,367	10,755	3,725	7,497	1,575	3,758	1,401	470	21,456	11,332	9,548
Johnson County	12,410	7,940	1,412	2,675	845	1,798	771	71	na	na	na
Kaufman County	7,131	4,264	941	1,601	567	1,355	24	0	na	na	na
Liberty County	5,944	3,039	921	1,979	195	na	na	na	na	na	na
Lubbock County	23,469	12,586	2,979	7,431	840	1,847	1,141	88	27,870	11,030	5,959
McLennan County	21,145	11,860	2,725	5,947	1,376	1,488	560	156	24,249	9,009	8,613

Table D-2: Counties—Household Relationship, Grandparents, and Marital Status—*Continued*

	Total Householders 65 Years and Over	Family Householders 65 Years and Over	Non-Family Householders 65 Years and Over — Male Living Alone	Non-Family Householders 65 Years and Over — Female Living Alone	Persons 65 Years and Over Living in Group Quarters	Grandparents 60 Years and Over Living with Grandchildren — Total	Grandparents 60 Years and Over Living with Grandchildren — Responsible for Grandchildren	Grandparents 60 Years and Over Living with Grandchildren — Responsible for Grandchildren and In Poverty	Marital Status - Persons 60 Years and Over — Now Married	Marital Status - Persons 60 Years and Over — Widowed	Marital Status - Persons 60 Years and Over — Divorced
Texas—Cont.											
Midland County	9,061	4,813	1,429	2,819	344	1,279	547	0	na	na	na
Montgomery County	38,397	22,043	3,817	11,179	1,053	5,780	829	na	61,097	14,334	12,950
Nacogdoches County	na	na	na	na	na	na	na	na	na	na	na
Nueces County	28,983	17,217	3,585	7,475	1,274	4,640	1,199	633	36,956	15,294	10,278
Orange County	7,803	4,205	1,112	2,401	443	1,083	611	0	na	na	na
Parker County	11,109	7,273	1,256	2,415	293	1,425	317	na	na	na	na
Potter County	9,261	4,878	1,309	2,940	468	1,681	674	184	na	na	na
Randall County	11,006	6,631	1,034	3,212	146	1,611	629	147	na	na	na
Rockwall County	5,014	3,777	124	922	379	na	na	na	na	na	na
San Patricio County	na	na	na	na	na	956	616	371	na	na	na
Smith County	20,300	11,927	2,592	5,755	1,053	3,105	1,275	358	28,348	9,328	6,876
Tarrant County	119,389	68,258	13,695	34,984	5,369	20,526	6,268	915	165,740	56,425	46,996
Taylor County	10,911	6,941	842	3,012	865	1,044	478	41	na	na	na
Tom Green County	10,470	4,536	1,877	3,832	759	1,485	1,124	108	na	na	na
Travis County	58,269	30,553	7,418	18,642	2,654	7,906	3,041	413	81,765	23,850	29,852
Victoria County	7,916	4,663	808	2,297	539	na	na	na	na	na	na
Walker County	na	na	na	na	na	na	na	na	na	na	na
Webb County	12,074	7,720	1,530	2,777	415	6,464	1,053	420	16,658	8,517	3,345
Wichita County	11,817	5,880	1,816	4,075	1,172	1,102	848	273	na	na	na
Williamson County	28,309	18,296	2,671	6,950	964	6,440	1,243	0	50,124	12,462	11,612
Utah											
Cache County	na	na	na	na	na	na	na	na	na	na	na
Davis County	17,527	11,917	1,367	3,900	117	3,333	1,186	172	29,707	6,822	5,891
Salt Lake County	64,084	37,330	8,436	17,075	1,826	14,236	2,570	158	99,566	26,354	23,352
Utah County	21,905	16,362	1,592	3,829	166	5,846	1,211	27	41,783	7,456	5,584
Washington County	17,020	12,223	1,381	3,379	343	na	na	na	na	na	na
Weber County	15,863	8,937	1,963	4,826	530	3,108	1,210	258	24,869	5,399	6,471
Vermont											
Chittenden County	13,660	6,555	1,746	5,165	858	na	na	na	na	na	na
Virginia											
Albemarle County	9,918	6,034	1,289	2,342	1,459	na	na	na	na	na	na
Arlington County	13,054	5,614	2,237	4,785	662	na	na	na	14,848	4,822	5,093
Augusta County	8,167	5,330	1,014	1,506	334	na	na	na	na	na	na
Bedford County	8,680	5,752	618	2,115	180	na	na	na	na	na	na
Chesterfield County	25,786	15,963	2,631	6,793	262	3,614	525	27	43,161	9,717	6,902
Fairfax County	74,927	43,893	8,607	20,084	1,983	16,119	3,014	46	120,742	29,743	23,856
Fauquier County	5,663	3,576	589	1,333	215	na	na	na	na	na	na
Frederick County	6,926	4,224	955	1,523	99	1,366	394	na	na	na	na
Hanover County	na	na	na	na	na	na	na	na	na	na	na
Henrico County	26,909	13,622	3,231	9,693	984	4,087	981	na	33,162	13,693	9,991
James City County	na	na	na	na	na	na	na	na	na	na	na
Loudoun County	13,846	8,149	1,448	4,053	290	na	na	na	28,829	8,038	4,888
Montgomery County	6,191	2,443	873	2,547	257	na	na	na	na	na	na
Prince William County	19,265	12,018	2,083	4,533	440	7,127	652	62	33,790	9,403	7,088
Roanoke County	12,015	6,553	1,661	3,704	556	725	211	na	na	na	na
Rockingham County	8,823	5,436	910	2,247	206	404	93	na	na	na	na
Spotsylvania County	9,065	5,796	792	2,206	186	2,156	697	na	na	na	na
Stafford County	6,419	4,777	323	1,237	134	1,987	224	na	na	na	na
York County	6,077	4,298	424	1,355	130	na	na	na	na	na	na
Washington											
Benton County	15,174	8,190	2,059	4,526	387	1,068	395	na	na	na	na
Chelan County	7,680	3,900	1,413	2,037	334	na	na	na	na	na	na
Clallam County	12,052	6,302	1,889	3,653	556	na	na	na	na	na	na
Clark County	37,639	20,332	5,208	11,023	1,359	5,268	1,265	183	53,878	14,809	14,913
Cowlitz County	11,975	5,967	2,146	3,564	369	566	320	na	na	na	na
Franklin County	3,904	2,510	466	928	433	827	329	na	na	na	na
Grant County	7,129	3,873	1,132	2,076	317	na	na	na	na	na	na
Grays Harbor County	8,568	4,627	1,175	2,358	444	na	na	na	na	na	na
Island County	10,375	6,597	832	2,762	298	na	na	na	na	na	na
King County	154,794	79,139	20,663	50,443	9,477	22,169	3,447	854	207,513	62,800	64,034
Kitsap County	25,250	14,524	3,154	7,166	1,272	2,317	372	na	34,758	9,777	9,571
Lewis County	9,400	5,583	937	2,710	330	639	375	na	na	na	na
Pierce County	63,751	33,730	8,324	18,969	3,339	8,244	2,254	211	83,836	27,722	26,200
Skagit County	13,628	7,456	1,458	4,167	620	na	na	na	na	na	na
Snohomish County	53,519	28,011	7,019	16,244	2,432	7,761	1,857	353	80,079	22,512	24,970
Spokane County	45,346	23,682	5,866	14,561	1,931	3,018	663	78	59,072	17,492	17,327
Thurston County	24,728	12,956	3,189	7,418	1,550	2,201	811	0	32,290	9,873	10,593
Whatcom County	20,850	10,555	2,968	6,911	1,058	1,807	625	na	na	na	na
Yakima County	18,654	10,420	2,288	5,598	1,469	2,983	927	0	25,683	8,006	6,269
West Virginia											
Berkeley County	8,312	4,919	1,015	2,262	198	na	na	na	na	na	na
Cabell County	10,872	5,516	1,322	3,763	696	na	na	91	na	na	na
Harrison County	8,001	4,271	1,184	2,349	537	960	429	184	na	na	na
Kanawha County	23,441	13,023	3,147	7,051	854	2,000	1,012	46	26,481	11,019	6,085

Table D-2: Counties—Household Relationship, Grandparents, and Marital Status—*Continued*

	Total Householders 65 Years and Over	Family Householders 65 Years and Over	Non-Family Householders 65 Years and Over — Male Living Alone	Non-Family Householders 65 Years and Over — Female Living Alone	Persons 65 Years and Over Living in Group Quarters	Grandparents 60 Years and Over Living with Grandchildren — Total	Grandparents 60 Years and Over Living with Grandchildren — Responsible for Grandchildren	Grandparents 60 Years and Over Living with Grandchildren — Responsible for Grandchildren and In Poverty	Marital Status - Persons 60 Years and Over — Now Married	Marital Status - Persons 60 Years and Over — Widowed	Marital Status - Persons 60 Years and Over — Divorced
West Virginia—Cont.											
Monongalia County	6,989	3,588	1,024	2,306	321	na	na	105	na	na	na
Raleigh County	9,425	5,113	1,543	2,666	499	na	na	na	na	na	na
Wood County	11,022	5,285	1,300	4,206	333	na	na	na	na	na	na
Wisconsin											
Brown County	21,159	11,678	2,589	6,179	1,182	1,824	690	45	29,975	8,545	6,318
Dane County	38,868	20,450	4,966	12,002	1,687	2,312	525	na	55,538	13,954	13,902
Dodge County	8,850	4,716	1,077	2,895	1,070	na	na	na	na	na	na
Eau Claire County	8,825	4,537	1,254	2,998	600	na	na	na	na	na	na
Fond du Lac County	10,414	5,501	1,437	3,325	873	na	na	na	na	na	na
Jefferson County	7,994	4,101	1,233	2,534	307	na	na	na	na	na	na
Kenosha County	14,242	7,235	2,108	4,533	844	na	na	na	na	na	na
La Crosse County	10,519	5,744	1,114	3,108	1,100	na	na	na	na	na	na
Manitowoc County	9,744	4,640	1,750	3,159	912	273	100	na	na	na	na
Marathon County	13,355	7,577	1,650	4,004	762	na	na	na	na	na	na
Milwaukee County	74,007	32,108	12,740	27,231	4,694	7,679	2,368	349	77,648	36,760	30,857
Outagamie County	14,650	9,211	1,287	4,088	1,110	508	82	na	na	na	na
Ozaukee County	10,031	5,500	1,113	3,313	347	na	na	na	na	na	na
Portage County	6,738	3,749	727	2,103	268	na	na	na	na	na	na
Racine County	19,041	9,521	3,217	5,883	518	1,671	594	na	24,430	7,086	6,906
Rock County	15,033	7,508	2,079	5,251	920	1,515	201	50	na	na	na
Sheboygan County	11,782	5,881	1,903	3,914	794	na	na	na	na	na	na
St. Croix County	5,858	3,851	642	1,288	485	na	na	na	na	na	na
Walworth County	9,925	4,963	1,533	3,261	623	546	62	na	na	na	na
Washington County	13,671	7,367	1,376	4,802	600	na	na	na	na	na	na
Waukesha County	40,660	23,653	4,927	11,506	1,966	1,357	233	na	60,914	16,062	9,932
Winnebago County	16,060	8,188	1,819	5,675	999	570	261	na	na	na	na
Wood County	9,251	4,585	1,024	3,412	203	na	na	na	na	na	na
Wyoming											
Laramie County	8,768	5,850	713	2,168	319	na	na	na	na	na	na
Natrona County	7,213	3,256	1,078	2,860	390	na	na	na	na	na	na

Table D-3: Places—Household Relationship, Grandparents, and Marital Status

	Total Householders 65 Years and Over	Family Householders 65 Years and Over	Non-Family Householders 65 Years and Over		Persons 65 Years and Over Living in Group Quarters	Grandparents 60 Years and Over Living with Grandchildren			Marital Status - Persons 60 Years and Over		
			Male Living Alone	Female Living Alone		Total	Responsible for Grandchildren	Responsible for Grandchildren and In Poverty	Now Married	Widowed	Divorced
Alabama											
Birmingham city	18,584	9,726	2,915	5,648	1,276	2,643	1,410	459	15,854	10,891	8,694
Dothan city	6,879	3,572	888	2,274	179	762	90	32	7,833	3,603	2,732
Hoover city	9,713	4,675	1,757	3,281	279	na	na	na	na	na	na
Huntsville city	18,606	9,164	3,415	5,806	840	1,502	534	316	20,047	8,849	6,879
Mobile city	18,539	9,188	2,349	6,633	1,126	1,913	731	79	19,726	8,809	7,240
Montgomery city	17,248	9,280	2,170	5,569	1,188	2,298	1,119	229	17,836	7,922	8,718
Tuscaloosa city	na	na	na	na	na	na	na	na	na	na	na
Alaska											
Anchorage municipality	14,870	8,885	1,963	3,253	633	2,711	739	31	22,348	6,431	7,155
Arizona											
Avondale city	2,820	1,849	270	554	167	441	121	na	na	na	na
Chandler city	13,500	8,490	990	3,560	361	2,244	355	na	na	na	na
Flagstaff city	na	na	na	na	na	na	na	na	na	na	na
Glendale city	14,813	7,229	1,888	5,314	1,161	3,320	1,175	292	18,915	7,232	7,711
Goodyear city	na	na	na	na	na	na	na	na	na	na	na
Mesa city	43,735	23,645	5,533	13,537	1,224	4,282	1,221	463	54,455	20,657	14,592
Peoria city	15,825	9,481	2,072	3,919	990	2,628	721	106	na	na	na
Phoenix city	90,321	47,489	14,772	24,309	3,058	17,095	4,234	1,118	113,225	37,763	47,472
Scottsdale city	31,511	16,372	3,925	9,998	962	na	na	na	37,970	11,759	11,267
Surprise city	15,018	9,773	1,298	3,665	150	na	na	na	na	na	na
Tempe city	11,278	5,837	2,460	2,722	447	na	na	na	na	na	na
Tucson city	46,294	20,506	8,361	15,930	3,166	5,047	1,309	318	44,538	19,920	24,753
Yuma city	8,707	4,487	1,298	2,513	251	2,078	947	245	na	na	na
Arkansas											
Fayetteville city	na	na	na	na	na	na	na	na	na	na	na
Fort Smith city	7,690	3,153	800	3,592	456	1,226	638	na	na	na	na
Jonesboro city	na	na	na	na	na	na	na	na	na	na	na
Little Rock city	16,457	7,921	1,882	6,084	931	1,451	599	43	18,749	7,750	7,271
North Little Rock city	5,156	2,823	696	1,507	422	na	na	na	na	na	na
Springdale city	4,332	2,195	885	1,222	505	na	na	na	na	na	na
California											
Alameda city	6,453	3,710	852	1,683	520	na	na	na	na	na	na
Alhambra city	6,209	3,466	763	1,894	298	3,362	320	na	na	na	na
Anaheim city	18,062	11,386	2,019	4,174	1,923	6,549	553	91	29,272	9,772	8,511
Antioch city	6,234	3,955	1,154	1,019	255	2,648	481	132	na	na	na
Bakersfield city	19,005	10,415	1,946	6,143	1,247	5,972	1,630	583	29,328	10,670	7,895
Baldwin Park city	3,402	2,335	268	659	259	1,234	411	0	na	na	na
Bellflower city	4,540	2,639	559	1,112	317	1,422	464	na	na	na	na
Berkeley city	9,722	5,094	1,240	2,892	327	na	na	na	na	na	na
Buena Park city	4,647	3,282	441	753	292	na	na	na	na	na	na
Burbank city	8,929	4,777	1,044	2,967	124	na	na	na	na	na	na
Camarillo city	7,459	4,146	935	2,241	277	na	na	na	na	na	na
Carlsbad city	10,215	5,767	904	3,419	323	na	na	na	na	na	na
Carson city	6,846	4,420	711	1,561	119	na	na	na	na	na	na
Chico city	6,668	2,636	748	2,974	346	na	na	na	na	na	na
Chino city	2,674	1,972	242	395	989	na	na	na	na	na	na
Chino Hills city	3,086	1,844	256	660	0	na	na	na	na	na	na
Chula Vista city	17,558	10,585	2,180	4,181	482	6,398	1,022	167	24,333	8,777	6,414
Citrus Heights city	9,454	4,993	647	3,670	282	na	na	na	na	na	na
Clovis city	6,658	3,426	920	2,181	114	1,456	345	na	na	na	na
Compton city	na	na	na	na	na	1,700	279	127	na	na	na
Concord city	10,031	5,039	1,701	2,914	507	na	na	na	na	na	na
Corona city	8,019	4,622	937	2,421	368	3,566	991	66	na	na	na
Costa Mesa city	6,368	4,051	954	1,048	353	1,353	497	na	na	na	na
Daly City city	7,380	5,099	680	1,386	622	3,494	1,007	na	na	na	na
Davis city	na	na	na	na	na	na	na	na	na	na	na
Downey city	6,453	4,050	924	1,479	365	na	na	na	na	na	na
El Cajon city	5,369	3,197	589	1,037	1,041	na	na	na	na	na	na
El Monte city	5,961	4,001	609	1,305	448	2,962	727	176	na	na	na
Elk Grove city	7,958	4,846	959	2,153	196	3,916	970	na	na	na	na
Escondido city	9,541	5,487	1,051	2,928	905	1,850	174	71	na	na	na
Fairfield city	6,986	4,209	942	1,640	169	2,680	350	0	na	na	na
Folsom city	5,957	3,064	615	2,197	584	na	na	na	na	na	na
Fontana city	5,801	3,698	599	1,377	149	5,982	297	0	na	na	na
Fremont city	12,648	7,552	986	3,337	834	6,621	1,122	30	20,060	7,040	4,895
Fresno city	31,243	16,098	4,971	8,568	1,897	10,497	2,062	564	42,169	13,847	14,968
Fullerton city	8,868	4,813	997	2,651	872	na	na	na	na	na	na
Garden Grove city	10,083	6,170	1,508	2,203	1,011	na	na	0	16,361	6,308	4,028
Glendale city	17,427	10,119	1,971	4,878	1,093	2,343	737	219	24,404	10,130	4,617
Hawthorne city	4,333	2,209	895	1,068	290	na	na	na	na	na	na
Hayward city	9,324	5,208	1,297	2,563	840	na	na	na	12,087	6,419	3,567
Hemet city	13,288	4,865	3,505	4,261	449	na	na	na	na	na	na
Hesperia city	5,155	3,383	803	969	10	2,203	1,017	148	na	na	na
Huntington Beach city	19,057	10,421	2,822	5,064	567	na	na	na	na	na	na

Table D-3: Places—Household Relationship, Grandparents, and Marital Status—*Continued*

	Total Householders 65 Years and Over	Family Householders 65 Years and Over	Non-Family Householders 65 Years and Over		Persons 65 Years and Over Living in Group Quarters	Grandparents 60 Years and Over Living with Grandchildren			Marital Status - Persons 60 Years and Over		
			Male Living Alone	Female Living Alone		Total	Responsible for Grandchildren	Responsible for Grandchildren and In Poverty	Now Married	Widowed	Divorced
California—Cont.											
Indio city	7,007	3,777	1,099	1,698	296	na	na	na	na	na	na
Inglewood city	6,571	3,171	734	2,529	416	1,949	530	50	na	na	na
Irvine city	13,548	7,513	911	4,511	377	na	na	na	na	na	na
Jurupa Valley city	4,127	2,390	579	850	443	1,926	273	0	na	na	na
Laguna Niguel city	6,069	3,915	344	1,222	68	na	na	na	na	na	na
Lake Forest city	na	na	na	na	na	na	na	na	na	na	na
Lakewood city	5,521	2,735	925	1,314	20	1,742	358	na	na	na	na
Lancaster city	8,632	5,852	809	1,809	607	2,994	592	42	12,254	3,773	3,164
Livermore city	6,443	3,966	671	1,667	151	na	na	na	na	na	na
Long Beach city	27,282	12,757	4,694	7,947	2,147	7,052	1,476	191	30,240	13,530	13,717
Los Angeles city	261,218	131,612	38,330	78,886	13,234	57,990	10,082	1,765	303,438	132,366	96,593
Lynwood city	na	na	na	na	na	1,920	211	0	na	na	na
Manteca city	5,354	3,087	752	1,346	397	na	na	na	na	na	na
Menifee city	9,373	5,296	1,133	2,302	122	na	na	na	na	na	na
Merced city	5,246	2,315	874	1,649	175	na	na	na	na	na	na
Milpitas city	3,546	2,385	308	706	100	2,021	230	na	na	na	na
Mission Viejo city	9,116	5,834	576	2,209	821	na	na	na	na	na	na
Modesto city	17,326	9,261	2,795	4,373	1,263	3,076	502	0	21,388	7,420	7,192
Moreno Valley city	7,677	5,504	464	1,552	312	5,564	692	171	13,768	5,861	4,129
Mountain View city	5,265	2,242	1,152	1,693	149	na	na	na	na	na	na
Murrieta city	5,796	3,694	412	1,625	159	na	na	na	na	na	na
Napa city	7,078	3,599	854	2,374	399	1,089	214	na	na	na	na
Newport Beach city	12,641	6,082	2,057	3,897	136	na	na	na	na	na	na
Norwalk city	5,729	4,035	413	1,242	359	3,137	255	0	na	na	na
Oakland city	31,156	13,948	4,858	10,526	1,094	7,451	1,231	139	30,439	14,539	15,683
Oceanside city	16,383	8,423	2,722	4,851	157	2,359	525	na	na	na	na
Ontario city	6,587	3,319	1,147	1,703	333	4,061	559	253	9,661	4,652	3,162
Orange city	7,669	4,301	576	2,417	717	2,564	361	na	na	na	na
Oxnard city	9,871	6,359	981	2,247	431	4,320	379	79	15,754	5,192	3,058
Palmdale city	6,429	3,679	923	1,559	13	3,339	329	34	na	na	na
Palo Alto city	7,784	4,085	649	2,905	407	na	na	na	na	na	na
Pasadena city	11,297	5,280	1,018	4,217	872	2,372	307	107	13,497	4,735	3,966
Perris city	na	na	na	na	na	na	na	na	na	na	na
Pittsburg city	3,844	2,237	172	1,202	231	2,016	640	0	na	na	na
Pleasanton city	5,929	3,316	589	1,693	180	na	na	na	na	na	na
Pomona city	6,313	4,210	616	1,314	897	3,683	390	185	10,967	4,343	2,417
Rancho Cordova city	4,927	3,132	695	1,022	342	na	na	na	na	na	na
Rancho Cucamonga city	8,841	4,556	815	2,896	74	3,131	881	0	na	na	na
Redding city	10,201	4,966	1,525	3,430	878	na	na	na	na	na	na
Redlands city	4,848	3,025	222	1,475	529	na	na	na	na	na	na
Redondo Beach city	4,948	2,366	701	1,370	75	na	na	na	na	na	na
Redwood City city	5,999	2,756	1,082	1,967	204	na	na	na	na	na	na
Rialto city	4,629	2,919	510	1,134	96	3,474	769	150	na	na	na
Richmond city	7,086	3,905	779	1,946	157	na	na	na	na	na	na
Riverside city	15,524	9,149	1,016	4,730	1,614	6,645	935	0	25,983	9,097	7,956
Roseville city	13,779	6,793	1,483	5,092	463	na	na	na	na	na	na
Sacramento city	35,122	17,422	4,977	11,170	1,808	6,443	1,254	43	39,477	17,971	14,056
Salinas city	6,480	4,121	824	1,275	767	2,963	455	0	na	na	na
San Bernardino city	9,306	4,896	1,216	2,782	1,295	3,976	497	226	11,972	5,158	4,776
San Buenaventura (Ventura) city	11,652	5,299	1,899	3,702	539	na	na	na	na	na	na
San Clemente city	na	na	na	na	na	na	na	na	na	na	na
San Diego city	89,228	47,554	11,293	26,802	3,069	19,449	3,364	952	121,507	43,073	39,714
San Francisco city	73,562	35,100	13,253	21,717	3,109	12,890	1,878	298	78,030	31,945	24,331
San Jose city	59,611	36,225	7,193	14,539	3,165	20,987	2,408	330	93,339	31,120	23,262
San Leandro city	7,478	3,910	1,376	2,035	264	na	na	na	na	na	na
San Marcos city	na	na	na	na	na	1,221	248	na	na	na	na
San Mateo city	10,570	5,225	1,844	3,268	388	na	na	na	na	na	na
San Ramon city	3,454	2,410	278	600	8	na	na	na	na	na	na
Santa Ana city	12,454	7,945	1,781	2,319	1,150	7,020	707	162	20,373	7,317	5,292
Santa Barbara city	9,968	4,223	1,969	3,430	514	na	na	na	na	na	na
Santa Clara city	7,717	4,559	650	2,051	486	na	na	na	na	na	na
Santa Clarita city	11,788	6,824	1,097	3,699	144	2,749	746	na	na	na	na
Santa Maria city	5,153	3,145	527	1,163	604	1,678	425	na	na	na	na
Santa Monica city	10,231	3,945	2,491	3,292	655	na	na	na	na	na	na
Santa Rosa city	16,477	7,354	2,244	6,270	739	na	na	na	na	na	na
Simi Valley city	10,587	5,751	1,318	3,044	143	na	na	na	na	na	na
South Gate city	3,870	2,126	602	973	74	3,103	275	0	na	na	na
South San Francisco city	5,175	3,048	511	1,512	114	na	na	na	na	na	na
Stockton city	17,432	8,841	1,972	5,489	1,927	6,458	1,313	308	23,633	11,485	8,452
Sunnyvale city	9,250	4,342	1,171	3,534	487	na	na	na	na	na	na
Temecula city	6,339	4,475	523	1,189	40	1,763	408	na	na	na	na
Thousand Oaks city	13,740	9,015	828	3,522	269	na	na	na	na	na	na
Torrance city	15,122	8,380	1,599	4,740	678	2,262	258	na	na	na	na
Tracy city	2,481	1,498	258	658	157	na	na	na	na	na	na
Turlock city	5,810	2,875	549	2,256	460	1,588	694	211	na	na	na
Tustin city	4,296	2,493	499	1,022	255	na	na	na	na	na	na

Table D-3: Places—Household Relationship, Grandparents, and Marital Status—*Continued*

	Total Householders 65 Years and Over	Family Householders 65 Years and Over	Non-Family Householders 65 Years and Over		Persons 65 Years and Over Living in Group Quarters	Grandparents 60 Years and Over Living with Grandchildren			Marital Status - Persons 60 Years and Over		
			Male Living Alone	Female Living Alone		Total	Responsible for Grandchildren	Responsible for Grandchildren and In Poverty	Now Married	Widowed	Divorced
California—Cont.											
Union City city	4,994	3,520	359	949	197	2,449	604	na	na	na	na
Upland city	6,692	4,092	1,112	1,242	303	na	na	na	na	na	na
Vacaville city	7,162	3,347	988	2,613	348	na	na	na	na	na	na
Vallejo city	9,711	5,216	1,404	2,610	403	3,365	1,147	40	na	na	na
Victorville city	4,916	3,274	782	698	165	2,249	729	328	na	na	na
Visalia city	8,783	5,573	798	2,101	471	2,326	859	na	na	na	na
Vista city	4,268	2,596	347	1,189	427	na	na	na	na	na	na
Walnut Creek city	13,048	5,597	1,522	5,581	547	na	na	na	na	na	na
West Covina city	7,108	4,989	666	1,370	348	3,174	903	186	na	na	na
Westminster city	8,163	5,189	835	1,740	241	na	na	na	na	na	na
Whittier city	6,065	3,959	564	1,504	445	1,236	329	20	na	na	na
Yorba Linda city	5,981	4,277	392	1,159	79	na	na	na	na	na	na
Yuba City city	4,994	2,594	595	1,749	156	na	na	na	na	na	na
Colorado											
Arvada city	10,289	5,583	1,000	3,316	332	na	na	na	na	na	na
Aurora city	21,898	11,258	2,255	7,472	1,033	3,634	1,023	0	26,994	8,925	12,052
Boulder city	7,086	2,917	953	3,035	467	na	na	na	na	na	na
Centennial city	9,307	6,302	967	1,870	266	na	na	na	na	na	na
Colorado Springs city	34,450	18,819	4,791	10,145	1,081	3,684	1,035	0	49,475	13,434	15,051
Denver city	47,806	20,295	8,925	17,294	2,345	4,648	1,301	418	49,484	17,266	24,467
Fort Collins city	8,830	4,176	1,375	3,212	432	na	na	na	na	na	na
Greeley city	8,073	4,305	825	2,622	318	1,326	406	41	na	na	na
Lakewood city	14,660	6,587	2,289	5,301	1,017	na	na	na	na	na	na
Longmont city	7,205	3,641	814	2,634	387	na	na	na	na	na	na
Loveland city	na	na	na	na	na	na	na	na	na	na	na
Pueblo city	11,571	5,193	1,622	4,320	1,527	807	559	58	na	na	na
Thornton city	6,686	4,510	665	1,471	250	na	na	na	na	na	na
Westminster city	9,185	5,491	1,167	2,430	245	1,191	539	na	na	na	na
Connecticut											
Bridgeport city	9,660	4,402	2,060	2,921	514	1,753	494	207	8,549	4,922	3,966
Danbury city	6,217	2,837	428	2,733	564	na	na	na	na	na	na
Hartford city	7,453	2,725	978	3,505	733	1,737	1,090	520	4,240	3,785	3,731
New Britain city	4,729	1,874	847	1,859	775	na	na	0	na	na	na
New Haven city	9,275	2,913	2,082	4,061	815	1,211	503	37	na	na	na
Norwalk city	7,780	5,170	495	2,009	389	na	na	na	na	na	na
Stamford city	11,163	5,444	1,598	3,629	575	na	na	na	na	na	na
Waterbury city	8,338	3,431	1,627	2,955	840	na	na	na	na	na	na
Delaware											
Wilmington city	6,632	2,166	1,054	3,211	569	na	na	na	na	na	na
District of Columbia											
Washington city	50,463	20,372	9,095	19,242	3,745	5,033	1,808	335	38,382	21,217	20,667
Florida											
Boca Raton city	11,644	5,494	1,666	3,992	450	na	na	na	na	na	na
Boynton Beach city	8,263	4,304	1,361	2,339	667	na	na	na	na	na	na
Cape Coral city	21,305	13,038	1,983	5,201	314	na	na	na	na	na	na
Clearwater city	15,507	6,942	3,260	4,981	682	na	na	na	na	na	na
Coral Springs city	6,081	4,119	527	1,362	36	na	na	na	na	na	na
Deerfield Beach city	10,628	4,442	2,347	3,665	414	na	na	na	na	na	na
Delray Beach city	11,781	4,286	1,970	5,079	285	na	na	na	na	na	na
Deltona city	6,813	3,856	667	1,917	69	na	na	na	na	na	na
Fort Lauderdale city	20,346	8,204	4,917	5,967	330	1,954	390	na	18,743	8,756	8,872
Fort Myers city	6,835	3,475	1,048	2,125	395	na	na	na	na	na	na
Gainesville city	8,820	4,305	1,328	2,841	591	952	281	na	na	na	na
Hialeah city	20,395	11,550	2,183	6,100	666	5,725	629	121	25,881	13,007	6,599
Hollywood city	14,733	6,497	3,107	4,479	538	1,207	261	na	14,386	7,125	7,017
Homestead city	na	na	na	na	na	na	na	na	na	na	na
Jacksonville city	67,188	34,034	9,888	21,438	2,883	10,783	4,483	949	77,070	34,340	31,927
Kissimmee city	na	na	na	na	na	na	na	na	na	na	na
Lakeland city	12,712	7,048	1,242	4,151	1,172	738	221	77	na	na	na
Largo city	13,624	5,793	2,395	4,497	643	na	na	na	na	na	na
Lauderhill city	6,029	3,468	505	1,520	160	na	na	na	na	na	na
Melbourne city	11,725	4,985	1,847	4,460	608	na	na	na	na	na	na
Miami Beach city	9,107	3,649	2,096	3,027	430	na	na	na	na	na	na
Miami city	37,894	17,163	7,772	11,431	1,924	5,253	705	368	34,967	19,505	19,737
Miami Gardens city	8,286	5,092	543	2,412	99	3,116	882	76	na	na	na
Miramar city	4,054	3,226	310	518	21	6,260	1,930	203	na	na	na
Orlando city	16,912	7,579	2,620	6,177	926	1,343	325	43	15,204	7,951	8,855
Palm Bay city	9,804	6,262	933	2,168	393	na	na	na	na	na	na
Palm Coast city	11,851	8,113	1,281	2,047	90	na	na	na	na	na	na
Pembroke Pines city	15,395	7,319	911	7,032	146	na	na	na	na	na	na
Plantation city	na	na	na	na	na	na	na	na	na	na	na
Pompano Beach city	14,641	5,307	3,328	5,040	465	1,810	289	na	na	na	na

Table D-3: Places—Household Relationship, Grandparents, and Marital Status—*Continued*

	Total Householders 65 Years and Over	Family Householders 65 Years and Over	Non-Family Householders 65 Years and Over — Male Living Alone	Non-Family Householders 65 Years and Over — Female Living Alone	Persons 65 Years and Over Living in Group Quarters	Grandparents 60 Years and Over Living with Grandchildren — Total	Grandparents 60 Years and Over Living with Grandchildren — Responsible for Grandchildren	Grandparents 60 Years and Over Living with Grandchildren — Responsible for Grandchildren and In Poverty	Marital Status - Persons 60 Years and Over — Now Married	Marital Status - Persons 60 Years and Over — Widowed	Marital Status - Persons 60 Years and Over — Divorced
Florida—Cont.											
Port St. Lucie city	21,129	11,274	3,487	5,466	424	na	na	na	na	na	na
St. Petersburg city	25,780	12,161	4,571	7,862	2,094	2,211	822	273	28,850	14,753	10,981
Sunrise city	8,022	2,651	1,001	4,120	419	na	na	na	na	na	na
Tallahassee city	12,043	5,110	1,437	5,188	783	na	na	na	na	na	na
Tampa city	26,403	13,057	4,014	8,723	682	3,156	630	162	28,403	11,207	13,817
West Palm Beach city	11,322	4,515	1,791	4,539	999	na	na	na	na	na	na
Weston city	na	na	na	na	na	na	na	na	na	na	na
Georgia											
Albany city	6,494	2,739	774	2,949	556	463	198	35	na	na	na
Athens-Clarke County unified govt (bal)	7,501	3,858	763	2,536	325	na	na	na	na	na	na
Atlanta city	35,365	13,424	7,244	13,630	2,076	3,257	1,532	247	25,785	19,981	14,876
Augusta-Richmond County consolidated govt (bal)	14,469	7,973	2,289	3,985	1,484	3,235	1,276	49	15,532	9,976	7,389
Columbus city	15,599	9,219	1,573	4,542	729	1,732	974	297	17,284	8,766	5,038
Johns Creek city	na	na	na	na	na	na	na	na	na	na	na
Macon-Bibb County	13,579	6,316	2,286	4,534	833	1,903	379	186	14,070	7,780	5,975
Roswell city	na	na	na	na	na	na	na	na	na	na	na
Sandy Springs city	na	na	na	na	na	na	na	na	na	na	na
Savannah city	12,670	6,409	1,603	4,483	587	1,263	373	52	11,786	6,496	5,110
Warner Robins city	na	na	na	na	na	na	na	na	na	na	na
Hawaii											
Urban Honolulu CDP	37,927	20,749	5,658	10,037	2,894	7,769	1,641	276	41,744	18,840	13,173
Idaho											
Boise City city	17,197	9,152	1,656	6,166	547	na	na	na	na	na	na
Meridian city	na	na	na	na	na	na	na	na	na	na	na
Nampa city	6,283	3,151	739	2,218	301	na	na	na	na	na	na
Illinois											
Aurora city	8,469	5,205	897	2,142	497	3,057	813	209	na	na	na
Bloomington city	5,832	2,639	1,170	1,922	262	na	na	na	na	na	na
Champaign city	5,174	2,382	980	1,685	359	na	na	na	na	na	na
Chicago city	196,065	93,382	31,733	65,601	10,095	33,332	8,728	2,063	188,386	100,861	70,005
Decatur city	na	na	na	na	na	na	na	61	na	na	na
Elgin city	7,503	4,468	720	2,291	488	2,014	178	51	na	na	na
Evanston city	6,153	3,134	452	2,295	1,045	na	na	na	na	na	na
Joliet city	7,714	3,810	1,244	2,482	1,156	1,535	303	0	na	na	na
Naperville city	8,329	4,951	1,009	2,268	907	na	na	na	na	na	na
Peoria city	10,416	4,777	1,266	4,099	626	825	364	204	na	na	na
Rockford city	14,526	6,547	3,094	4,567	1,142	960	405	239	13,736	7,865	6,493
Springfield city	12,632	5,242	2,281	4,853	957	na	na	146	na	na	na
Waukegan city	4,373	3,008	437	928	562	na	na	na	na	na	na
Indiana											
Bloomington city	3,598	1,628	241	1,366	335	na	na	na	na	na	na
Carmel city	8,080	5,293	761	1,931	367	na	na	na	na	na	na
Evansville city	12,499	5,924	1,889	4,333	1,295	1,007	460	135	na	na	na
Fort Wayne city	21,156	9,901	3,189	7,510	1,260	1,378	470	117	23,587	10,759	7,245
Gary city	7,700	3,659	1,298	2,512	402	871	318	50	na	na	na
Hammond city	5,055	2,597	786	1,491	124	na	na	0	na	na	na
Indianapolis city (bal)	59,437	27,958	10,675	18,961	3,682	5,875	2,339	188	65,356	28,262	29,539
Lafayette city	na	na	na	na	na	na	na	na	na	na	na
Muncie city	6,377	3,848	634	1,794	675	na	na	na	na	na	na
South Bend city	8,925	4,166	1,329	3,271	510	432	292	111	na	na	na
Iowa											
Cedar Rapids city	11,580	5,434	1,675	4,220	694	na	na	na	na	na	na
Davenport city	8,170	3,800	1,293	2,794	838	na	na	na	na	na	na
Des Moines city	15,788	6,556	2,715	6,253	1,142	2,264	604	86	14,814	8,109	6,262
Iowa City city	na	na	na	na	na	na	na	na	na	na	na
Sioux City city	6,786	3,359	1,109	2,156	434	na	na	na	na	na	na
Waterloo city	na	na	na	na	na	472	201	na	na	na	na
Kansas											
Kansas City city	10,753	4,983	1,909	3,519	478	1,594	404	31	13,130	5,329	4,384
Lawrence city	na	na	na	na	na	na	na	na	na	na	na
Olathe city	7,151	4,231	344	2,369	629	947	358	na	na	na	na
Overland Park city	16,657	8,623	1,862	5,960	967	na	na	na	na	na	na
Topeka city	11,974	5,530	1,276	4,813	963	1,277	621	na	na	na	na
Wichita city	31,417	15,599	5,783	9,413	1,834	3,862	752	216	40,020	13,842	12,390
Kentucky											
Lexington-Fayette urban county	22,793	11,244	2,805	7,928	1,240	1,542	532	152	27,313	10,289	11,566
Louisville/Jefferson County metro govt (bal)	53,042	25,792	7,014	18,525	2,859	4,818	2,192	263	59,627	24,705	22,719
Louisiana											
Baton Rouge city	19,560	9,463	2,871	6,707	797	1,202	460	67	19,877	11,281	7,164
Bossier City city	5,211	2,353	796	2,062	555	na	na	na	na	na	na

Table D-3: Places—Household Relationship, Grandparents, and Marital Status—*Continued*

	Total Householders 65 Years and Over	Family Householders 65 Years and Over	Non-Family Householders 65 Years and Over		Persons 65 Years and Over Living in Group Quarters	Grandparents 60 Years and Over Living with Grandchildren			Marital Status - Persons 60 Years and Over		
			Male Living Alone	Female Living Alone		Total	Responsible for Grandchildren	Responsible for Grandchildren and In Poverty	Now Married	Widowed	Divorced
Louisiana—Cont.											
Kenner city	7,390	4,566	846	1,978	271	na	na	na	na	na	na
Lafayette city	na	na	na	na	na	590	266	na	na	na	na
Lake Charles city	8,354	4,014	1,139	3,145	511	na	na	na	na	na	na
New Orleans city	30,343	14,724	5,231	9,723	1,224	3,050	793	414	29,738	16,279	13,092
Shreveport city	18,496	9,420	2,830	5,588	1,918	2,652	1,233	287	18,406	11,450	6,413
Maine											
Portland city	na	na	na	na	na	na	na	na	na	na	na
Maryland											
Baltimore city	52,216	23,107	9,452	17,570	3,069	6,945	2,449	326	43,648	25,569	19,862
Frederick city	4,645	2,122	700	1,557	788	na	na	na	na	na	na
Gaithersburg city	3,665	1,811	450	1,272	317	na	na	na	na	na	na
Rockville city	6,438	2,932	900	2,423	637	na	na	na	na	na	na
Massachusetts											
Boston city	43,696	17,053	9,027	16,052	3,241	5,446	899	155	39,308	20,247	16,466
Brockton city	7,102	3,068	1,130	2,643	797	1,725	186	0	na	na	na
Cambridge city	7,644	2,743	1,257	3,352	364	na	na	na	na	na	na
Fall River city	9,414	3,963	1,134	4,072	953	na	na	na	na	na	na
Lawrence city	4,104	1,974	915	1,184	312	na	na	na	na	na	na
Lowell city	7,275	3,083	1,153	2,797	1,060	934	472	na	na	na	na
Lynn city	6,378	3,127	1,107	2,003	249	1,360	385	0	na	na	na
New Bedford city	7,776	3,692	776	3,135	1,251	858	272	na	na	na	na
Newton city	10,070	5,307	937	3,464	561	na	na	na	na	na	na
Quincy city	9,321	3,753	2,267	3,097	428	na	na	na	na	na	na
Somerville city	5,097	2,100	1,350	1,603	243	na	na	na	na	na	na
Springfield city	11,472	5,288	1,600	4,319	303	977	519	276	na	na	na
Worcester city	12,197	5,899	1,777	4,199	1,846	1,993	706	415	13,043	6,376	5,338
Michigan											
Ann Arbor city	8,228	3,780	971	3,165	267	na	na	na	na	na	na
Dearborn city	7,987	3,670	1,746	2,571	177	1,264	280	38	na	na	na
Detroit city	59,257	28,594	10,187	18,749	2,910	7,940	2,473	509	41,046	29,845	30,106
Farmington Hills city	11,077	5,738	1,604	3,462	387	1,466	422	na	na	na	na
Flint city	8,369	4,557	1,220	2,203	197	1,159	396	61	na	na	na
Grand Rapids city	14,506	6,132	2,154	5,564	2,209	1,367	152	0	13,065	7,961	5,096
Kalamazoo city	4,700	2,233	598	1,727	643	na	na	na	na	na	na
Lansing city	8,827	3,463	1,728	3,525	506	1,422	282	0	na	na	na
Livonia city	10,299	5,757	972	3,491	801	na	na	na	na	na	na
Rochester Hills city	7,676	3,743	1,078	2,828	332	na	na	na	na	na	na
Southfield city	9,558	3,610	1,681	4,131	547	na	na	na	na	na	na
Sterling Heights city	13,641	8,247	954	4,312	619	na	na	na	na	na	na
Troy city	7,929	4,676	824	2,391	147	na	na	na	na	na	na
Warren city	12,733	6,112	2,045	4,243	1,042	1,837	544	na	na	na	na
Westland city	9,447	4,047	1,471	3,811	484	na	na	na	na	na	na
Wyoming city	4,965	2,628	548	1,789	191	na	na	na	na	na	na
Minnesota											
Bloomington city	10,509	5,451	1,128	3,657	484	na	na	na	na	na	na
Brooklyn Park city	na	na	na	na	na	na	na	na	na	na	na
Duluth city	8,747	3,896	1,450	3,272	910	na	na	na	na	na	na
Eagan city	4,723	2,422	344	1,850	77	na	na	na	na	na	na
Maple Grove city	na	na	na	na	na	na	na	na	na	na	na
Minneapolis city	23,005	8,150	5,604	8,320	2,335	1,461	340	72	23,167	8,040	10,198
Plymouth city	7,280	4,081	398	2,693	254	na	na	na	na	na	na
Rochester city	9,817	5,415	815	3,357	796	na	na	na	na	na	na
St. Cloud city	4,491	2,281	555	1,499	736	na	na	na	na	na	na
St. Paul city	17,553	7,400	2,960	6,669	1,603	2,821	683	68	20,230	7,066	8,247
Woodbury city	na	na	na	na	na	na	na	na	na	na	na
Mississippi											
Gulfport city	7,242	2,845	1,502	2,764	300	886	194	na	na	na	na
Jackson city	12,952	6,627	2,309	3,896	1,383	1,815	649	181	13,559	7,891	4,551
Missouri											
Columbia city	na	na	na	na	na	na	na	na	na	na	na
Independence city	12,769	7,174	1,688	3,666	781	na	na	na	na	na	na
Kansas City city	37,862	17,787	5,518	13,524	1,908	3,155	1,018	301	37,292	17,157	16,900
Lee's Summit city	na	na	na	na	na	na	na	na	na	na	na
O'Fallon city	na	na	na	na	na	895	160	na	na	na	na
Springfield city	17,249	7,997	1,711	7,132	1,262	954	676	53	16,271	8,182	5,928
St. Charles city	6,498	3,686	653	2,031	476	na	na	na	na	na	na
St. Joseph city	7,418	2,965	950	3,324	433	521	482	na	na	na	na
St. Louis city	24,010	9,859	4,566	8,613	1,423	2,744	797	185	21,806	12,553	12,100
Montana											
Billings city	10,379	4,251	2,017	4,007	786	na	na	na	na	na	na
Missoula city	na	na	na	na	na	na	na	na	na	na	na

Table D-3: Places—Household Relationship, Grandparents, and Marital Status—*Continued*

	Total Householders 65 Years and Over	Family Householders 65 Years and Over	Non-Family Householders 65 Years and Over		Persons 65 Years and Over Living in Group Quarters	Grandparents 60 Years and Over Living with Grandchildren			Marital Status - Persons 60 Years and Over		
			Male Living Alone	Female Living Alone		Total	Responsible for Grandchildren	Responsible for Grandchildren and In Poverty	Now Married	Widowed	Divorced
Nebraska											
Lincoln city	21,278	11,189	2,743	7,042	593	1,495	581	220	27,445	8,195	6,828
Omaha city	35,064	16,814	5,495	12,062	1,953	1,900	460	45	41,179	17,040	11,289
Nevada											
Henderson city	28,217	16,908	3,100	6,988	611	2,700	411	69	38,975	12,058	11,111
Las Vegas city	46,224	25,324	8,340	10,290	1,716	7,118	2,639	219	55,913	18,803	21,444
North Las Vegas city	12,277	7,134	1,100	3,153	341	3,887	1,114	106	16,632	6,439	7,711
Reno city	21,629	8,250	4,896	7,168	801	2,024	494	38	18,619	8,529	12,802
Sparks city	8,455	5,027	1,121	2,205	224	1,069	329	na	na	na	na
New Hampshire											
Manchester city	8,171	3,617	1,601	2,732	776	1,890	553	na	na	na	na
Nashua city	6,403	3,388	971	1,779	455	715	164	na	na	na	na
New Jersey											
Bayonne city	4,357	2,230	603	1,434	0	na	na	na	na	na	na
Camden city	6,042	2,882	1,061	1,843	227	na	na	0	na	na	na
Clifton city	5,859	2,465	806	2,541	240	na	na	na	na	na	na
East Orange city	5,998	2,140	1,499	2,129	558	na	na	na	na	na	na
Elizabeth city	6,042	3,324	716	1,899	758	1,672	319	85	na	na	na
Jersey City city	15,824	8,032	2,009	4,664	1,041	3,748	768	166	17,306	8,336	4,932
Newark city	15,434	6,192	2,424	5,918	968	4,119	1,096	228	13,714	8,385	5,887
Passaic city	3,548	1,854	612	1,037	118	na	na	na	na	na	na
Paterson city	8,388	4,154	716	3,298	328	2,556	998	100	na	na	na
Trenton city	5,591	2,575	925	1,850	408	595	300	na	na	na	na
Union City city	4,553	1,928	1,054	1,268	272	na	na	na	na	na	na
New Mexico											
Albuquerque city	48,418	22,887	7,231	17,013	1,979	4,859	1,562	473	53,016	22,857	21,670
Las Cruces city	9,355	5,217	1,110	2,929	441	na	na	na	na	na	na
Rio Rancho city	7,725	3,928	1,054	2,346	271	na	na	na	na	na	na
Santa Fe city	10,284	4,082	2,070	3,484	432	na	na	na	na	na	na
New York											
Albany city	7,767	3,012	1,194	3,030	1,340	na	na	na	na	na	na
Buffalo city	23,277	9,423	4,212	8,973	1,707	1,803	285	0	15,567	11,151	9,017
Mount Vernon city	5,949	2,893	689	2,306	502	1,182	277	na	na	na	na
New Rochelle city	7,137	3,591	722	2,611	979	na	na	na	na	na	na
New York city	678,250	323,982	100,255	238,433	43,436	125,083	30,285	7,602	705,698	332,324	209,810
Rochester city	15,228	6,239	3,550	5,108	1,391	1,593	1,184	105	12,903	8,758	5,128
Schenectady city	5,189	1,806	1,026	2,151	363	na	na	na	na	na	na
Syracuse city	11,056	4,840	2,015	3,986	1,684	1,616	796	355	9,846	6,147	4,197
Yonkers city	20,776	9,682	3,416	7,210	710	3,875	452	94	20,643	10,029	6,223
North Carolina											
Asheville city	9,967	3,776	1,219	4,491	920	na	na	na	na	na	na
Charlotte city	47,756	23,440	6,252	17,115	1,889	6,667	2,099	645	57,681	23,409	20,168
Concord city	6,519	3,011	848	2,576	393	na	na	na	na	na	na
Durham city	17,276	8,287	2,435	6,294	1,239	1,611	647	38	20,569	8,430	7,551
Fayetteville city	14,543	7,911	1,698	4,756	604	1,754	577	59	19,315	6,969	4,088
Gastonia city	6,574	3,228	1,270	2,052	746	856	310	na	na	na	na
Greensboro city	23,393	9,876	3,570	9,667	1,660	1,942	487	66	23,911	11,071	9,858
Greenville city	5,777	2,843	899	1,707	398	na	na	na	na	na	na
High Point city	8,256	3,889	977	3,211	397	663	191	62	na	na	na
Jacksonville city	na	na	na	na	na	na	na	na	na	na	na
Raleigh city	26,544	13,364	3,447	9,482	1,896	2,224	1,010	269	28,569	14,359	11,100
Wilmington city	10,603	5,656	1,293	3,292	271	na	na	na	na	na	na
Winston-Salem city	21,394	10,148	3,391	7,550	1,024	2,898	819	92	21,253	11,187	7,065
North Dakota											
Bismarck city	6,789	3,759	466	2,394	633	na	na	na	na	na	na
Fargo city	8,362	3,329	1,027	3,780	691	na	na	na	na	na	na
Ohio											
Akron city	18,210	7,937	3,643	6,255	801	1,446	775	102	18,231	8,494	9,000
Canton city	6,344	2,545	980	2,659	762	744	316	0	na	na	na
Cincinnati city	25,463	9,206	5,357	10,174	2,150	1,209	383	161	18,202	11,631	12,721
Cleveland city	33,681	13,674	8,215	11,227	2,412	2,983	1,340	576	23,897	17,017	16,565
Columbus city	50,131	22,402	7,339	18,939	2,353	6,837	2,350	641	54,426	24,308	24,001
Dayton city	11,354	4,713	2,404	3,906	783	1,217	567	209	7,418	5,144	5,729
Lorain city	6,090	2,702	1,313	1,968	451	996	43	na	na	na	na
Parma city	9,382	4,179	1,307	3,742	765	na	na	na	na	na	na
Toledo city	26,214	10,820	4,479	10,102	1,301	1,953	543	71	22,511	13,917	11,094
Youngstown city	7,604	3,042	1,290	3,123	694	567	257	51	na	na	na
Oklahoma											
Broken Arrow city	6,656	4,436	768	1,348	387	1,085	533	0	na	na	na
Edmond city	6,752	3,762	951	1,991	130	na	na	na	na	na	na
Lawton city	6,211	2,679	965	2,299	700	939	522	29	na	na	na
Norman city	8,245	4,763	790	2,565	519	na	na	na	na	na	na
Oklahoma City city	46,993	25,109	6,544	13,855	2,248	5,253	2,467	328	57,399	21,111	20,107
Tulsa city	34,775	16,251	4,525	12,939	1,476	2,810	738	60	40,274	14,800	16,362

Table D-3: Places—Household Relationship, Grandparents, and Marital Status—*Continued*

	Total Householders 65 Years and Over	Family Householders 65 Years and Over	Non-Family Householders 65 Years and Over		Persons 65 Years and Over Living in Group Quarters	Grandparents 60 Years and Over Living with Grandchildren			Marital Status - Persons 60 Years and Over		
			Male Living Alone	Female Living Alone		Total	Responsible for Grandchildren	Responsible for Grandchildren and In Poverty	Now Married	Widowed	Divorced
Oregon											
Beaverton city	6,292	2,911	1,314	1,915	334	na	na	na	na	na	na
Bend city	7,517	3,571	1,002	2,585	327	na	na	na	na	na	na
Eugene city	14,864	6,681	2,231	5,383	695	na	na	na	na	na	na
Gresham city	9,217	4,862	630	3,149	686	1,326	432	na	na	na	na
Hillsboro city	6,631	4,388	457	1,607	388	903	410	0	na	na	na
Medford city	8,593	4,228	1,331	2,675	604	na	na	na	na	na	na
Portland city	44,071	20,003	6,953	15,181	2,878	5,702	1,215	106	51,267	17,958	23,124
Salem city	14,193	6,658	2,268	4,986	1,063	na	na	na	na	na	na
Pennsylvania											
Allentown city	8,774	4,270	1,131	3,172	857	932	353	30	na	na	na
Bethlehem city	7,843	3,448	1,386	2,860	632	na	na	na	na	na	na
Erie city	9,063	4,306	1,207	3,378	830	1,024	246	100	8,271	5,264	3,110
Philadelphia city	124,800	56,451	20,648	45,079	8,075	17,058	4,959	1,314	112,064	66,630	48,622
Pittsburgh city	28,274	11,352	4,803	11,455	2,647	1,778	488	70	23,731	14,384	9,860
Reading city	na	na	na	na	na	1,039	420	238	na	na	na
Scranton city	8,401	3,593	1,106	3,431	1,313	768	342	na	na	na	na
Rhode Island											
Cranston city	8,849	4,904	565	3,340	393	na	na	na	na	na	na
Pawtucket city	5,034	2,606	622	1,806	428	na	na	na	na	na	na
Providence city	10,316	4,239	2,163	3,609	1,146	1,722	418	233	8,941	4,966	3,611
Warwick city	9,995	4,842	1,594	3,305	555	na	na	na	na	na	na
South Carolina											
Charleston city	10,952	5,764	1,194	3,910	332	na	na	na	na	na	na
Columbia city	7,894	3,504	1,005	3,328	1,030	na	na	na	7,491	3,732	3,344
North Charleston city	6,844	3,694	1,145	1,802	395	908	491	51	na	na	na
Rock Hill city	5,886	2,923	882	1,910	344	na	na	na	na	na	na
South Dakota											
Rapid City city	na	na	na	na	na	398	85	na	na	na	na
Sioux Falls city	12,944	6,210	1,883	4,607	1,069	1,227	384	0	na	na	na
Tennessee											
Chattanooga city	17,375	8,428	3,028	5,663	1,044	2,415	1,349	104	17,436	8,844	7,373
Clarksville city	7,033	3,949	535	2,049	535	691	162	na	na	na	na
Franklin city	na	na	na	na	na	na	na	na	na	na	na
Jackson city	5,098	2,887	366	1,817	578	na	na	na	na	na	na
Johnson City city	7,325	3,653	765	2,666	690	na	na	na	na	na	na
Knoxville city	16,720	6,131	2,989	6,984	1,250	1,782	669	255	13,668	8,851	8,086
Memphis city	48,707	24,594	7,475	15,508	2,652	5,509	1,753	771	46,331	28,218	21,775
Murfreesboro city	7,449	3,854	1,042	2,508	447	na	na	na	na	na	na
Nashville-Davidson metropolitan govt (bal)	44,768	21,462	6,561	15,704	1,601	7,200	2,252	290	51,579	20,123	20,166
Texas											
Abilene city	9,239	5,770	703	2,650	826	710	277	0	na	na	na
Allen city	na	na	na	na	na	na	na	na	na	na	na
Amarillo city	16,390	9,061	1,843	5,223	402	2,233	639	184	19,492	7,293	5,305
Arlington city	21,203	12,266	1,647	6,760	960	3,877	1,025	20	34,417	9,662	9,190
Austin city	44,806	22,241	6,194	15,165	2,073	5,802	1,681	413	57,611	18,546	24,433
Baytown city	5,810	3,080	1,203	1,527	348	na	na	na	na	na	na
Beaumont city	10,045	4,244	1,645	4,001	637	1,510	418	119	na	na	na
Brownsville city	10,856	6,800	1,352	2,615	690	4,156	1,196	458	14,227	7,061	2,910
Bryan city	na	na	na	na	na	na	na	na	na	na	na
Carrollton city	6,565	3,825	735	1,702	419	1,921	586	156	na	na	na
College Station city	na	na	na	na	na	na	na	na	na	na	na
Conroe city	3,691	2,207	309	1,136	307	na	na	na	na	na	na
Corpus Christi city	25,209	14,834	3,029	6,640	1,200	4,020	842	372	33,873	13,084	9,473
Dallas city	76,474	38,779	10,697	24,690	3,453	12,446	4,020	1,010	84,025	36,306	35,279
Denton city	7,434	3,311	1,011	3,042	293	na	na	na	na	na	na
Edinburg city	na	na	na	na	na	1,207	778	na	na	na	na
El Paso city	46,798	27,986	5,142	12,951	1,659	12,252	3,261	959	61,856	26,581	14,944
Fort Worth city	45,983	23,633	6,999	14,644	2,230	8,878	3,099	711	49,577	24,488	20,662
Frisco city	na	na	na	na	na	na	na	na	na	na	na
Garland city	15,697	9,461	1,890	4,080	541	4,876	1,371	72	23,085	7,064	6,414
Grand Prairie city	7,664	4,885	719	2,016	126	2,989	585	267	na	na	na
Harlingen city	5,593	3,023	878	1,497	457	na	na	na	na	na	na
Houston city	137,392	70,925	20,195	43,137	4,207	22,993	6,694	1,627	153,288	69,623	54,102
Irving city	10,332	5,397	1,398	3,164	347	2,838	933	0	12,224	5,181	5,034
Killeen city	na	na	na	na	na	1,271	533	na	na	na	na
Laredo city	11,300	7,121	1,403	2,729	415	6,226	932	363	15,299	8,418	3,194
League City city	4,608	3,140	547	921	314	1,559	445	na	na	na	na
Lewisville city	5,954	2,693	688	2,078	280	na	na	na	na	na	na
Longview city	7,631	3,653	821	3,072	795	740	198	46	na	na	na
Lubbock city	19,168	9,956	2,478	6,288	724	1,137	601	88	22,181	9,475	4,916
McAllen city	6,779	5,275	333	1,171	984	na	na	138	na	na	na
McKinney city	7,938	3,921	585	3,313	338	na	na	na	na	na	na

Table D-3: Places—Household Relationship, Grandparents, and Marital Status—*Continued*

	Total Householders 65 Years and Over	Family Householders 65 Years and Over	Non-Family Householders 65 Years and Over		Persons 65 Years and Over Living in Group Quarters	Grandparents 60 Years and Over Living with Grandchildren			Marital Status - Persons 60 Years and Over		
			Male Living Alone	Female Living Alone		Total	Responsible for Grandchildren	Responsible for Grandchildren and In Poverty	Now Married	Widowed	Divorced
Texas—Cont.											
Mesquite city	8,169	4,625	635	2,748	321	2,863	715	119	na	na	na
Midland city	7,439	3,605	1,368	2,466	344	1,111	379	0	na	na	na
Mission city	4,875	3,131	314	1,318	129	1,264	148	na	na	na	na
Missouri City city	3,521	2,508	312	701	148	na	na	na	na	na	na
New Braunfels city	5,151	3,012	382	1,679	486	na	na	na	na	na	na
North Richland Hills city	5,889	3,587	641	1,661	261	na	na	na	na	na	na
Odessa city	7,892	4,169	912	2,656	255	913	343	na	na	na	na
Pasadena city	8,727	5,118	1,213	2,125	471	3,118	511	0	13,485	4,602	3,402
Pearland city	na	na	na	na	na	na	na	na	na	na	na
Pharr city	na	na	na	na	na	na	na	na	na	na	na
Plano city	18,614	11,224	1,850	4,982	359	3,556	197	na	32,090	7,271	7,064
Richardson city	9,583	5,214	1,373	2,812	454	na	na	na	na	na	na
Round Rock city	4,471	2,482	509	1,442	232	na	na	na	na	na	na
San Angelo city	8,818	3,836	1,338	3,461	759	1,137	832	108	na	na	na
San Antonio city	100,110	55,968	13,353	27,921	5,225	20,809	5,168	909	121,587	50,561	40,707
Sugar Land city	6,371	4,425	387	1,559	245	na	na	na	na	na	na
Temple city	6,643	3,862	911	1,819	815	na	na	na	na	na	na
Tyler city	9,397	4,398	1,246	3,727	788	na	na	na	na	na	na
Victoria city	5,640	3,187	639	1,701	539	na	na	na	na	na	na
Waco city	10,158	4,891	1,657	3,415	1,017	na	na	na	na	na	na
Wichita Falls city	8,025	4,271	1,389	2,330	1,073	679	614	273	na	na	na
Utah											
Layton city	na	na	na	na	na	na	na	na	na	na	na
Ogden city	5,607	2,738	946	1,854	247	na	na	na	na	na	na
Orem city	na	na	na	na	na	1,119	131	0	na	na	na
Provo city	4,063	2,821	505	678	92	na	na	na	na	na	na
Salt Lake City city	13,227	5,555	2,609	4,943	491	na	na	na	na	na	na
Sandy city	4,911	3,342	386	1,081	228	na	na	na	na	na	na
St. George city	9,483	6,802	555	2,089	285	na	na	na	na	na	na
West Jordan city	na	na	na	na	na	na	na	na	na	na	na
West Valley City city	5,200	3,152	542	1,429	62	2,614	783	0	na	na	na
Virginia											
Alexandria city	9,620	4,220	1,404	3,642	436	1,050	274	0	na	na	na
Chesapeake city	16,451	10,156	1,610	4,286	733	3,112	1,707	44	24,147	7,991	4,630
Hampton city	11,850	6,420	1,905	3,156	100	1,266	471	70	14,162	6,335	3,604
Lynchburg city	7,509	3,596	909	2,737	753	na	na	na	na	na	na
Newport News city	12,876	6,343	2,053	4,252	559	1,920	797	84	16,368	6,213	5,886
Norfolk city	15,883	6,756	2,979	5,537	816	1,800	673	205	15,407	8,231	6,923
Portsmouth city	8,758	4,611	1,231	2,774	311	1,391	409	220	na	na	na
Richmond city	17,129	6,127	3,294	7,191	579	2,268	1,436	306	12,637	8,962	9,239
Roanoke city	10,367	5,097	1,400	3,585	466	na	na	na	na	na	na
Suffolk city	7,248	4,305	865	1,975	196	1,502	417	45	na	na	na
Virginia Beach city	34,442	19,399	3,979	10,177	1,103	4,730	1,465	121	45,277	15,282	13,258
Washington											
Auburn city	4,890	2,630	566	1,429	316	na	na	na	na	na	na
Bellevue city	12,331	6,592	1,291	4,386	653	na	na	na	na	na	na
Bellingham city	na	na	na	na	na	na	na	na	na	na	na
Everett city	6,673	2,091	1,624	2,682	627	na	na	na	na	na	na
Federal Way city	7,765	4,250	1,010	2,343	564	na	na	na	na	na	na
Kennewick city	5,914	2,893	1,001	1,818	240	na	na	na	na	na	na
Kent city	6,863	3,061	994	2,540	394	na	na	na	na	na	na
Kirkland city	6,571	3,875	823	1,800	422	na	na	na	na	na	na
Marysville city	5,333	2,751	636	1,772	208	na	na	na	na	na	na
Pasco city	na	na	na	na	na	779	329	na	na	na	na
Renton city	5,388	3,111	773	1,504	434	na	na	na	na	na	na
Seattle city	52,142	23,665	8,165	18,484	3,686	5,286	820	338	59,749	20,118	22,534
Spokane city	19,774	8,637	2,875	7,689	1,277	1,112	376	78	21,073	8,333	8,194
Spokane Valley city	9,147	4,300	1,409	3,080	232	na	na	na	na	na	na
Tacoma city	16,417	7,606	2,607	5,324	1,266	2,119	723	211	16,460	6,928	8,445
Vancouver city	14,948	7,126	2,241	5,457	883	1,438	439	57	na	na	na
Yakima city	na	na	na	na	na	na	na	0	na	na	na
Wisconsin											
Appleton city	4,767	2,662	673	1,400	568	728	128	0	na	na	na
Eau Claire city	na	na	na	na	na	na	na	na	na	na	na
Green Bay city	8,151	3,899	1,429	2,754	644	1,144	530	na	na	na	na
Kenosha city	8,318	4,232	1,119	2,614	581	na	na	na	na	na	na
Madison city	17,553	8,340	2,391	5,964	820	na	na	na	na	na	na
Milwaukee city	38,497	16,369	6,981	14,077	2,316	5,251	1,816	272	37,018	19,200	18,688
Oshkosh city	6,269	2,227	862	2,900	659	na	na	na	na	na	na
Racine city	6,207	2,624	1,116	2,175	161	na	na	na	na	na	na
Waukesha city	na	na	na	na	na	na	na	na	na	na	na

Table D-4: Metropolitan/Micropolitan Statistical Areas—Household Relationship, Grandparents, and Marital Status

	Total Householders 65 Years and Over	Family Householders 65 Years and Over	Non-Family Householders 65 Years and Over		Persons 65 Years and Over Living in Group Quarters	Grandparents 60 Years and Over Living with Grandchildren			Marital Status - Persons 60 Years and Over		
			Male Living Alone	Female Living Alone		Total	Responsible for Grandchildren	Responsible for Grandchildren and In Poverty	Now Married	Widowed	Divorced
Aberdeen, WA Micro Area	8,568	4,627	1,175	2,358	444	na	na	na	na	na	na
Abilene, TX Metro Area	14,504	8,906	1,551	3,907	1,110	1,456	796	107	21,557	6,147	3,752
Adrian, MI Micro Area	10,605	6,317	972	2,905	619	702	240	na	na	na	na
Akron, OH Metro Area	71,529	36,836	10,120	23,141	3,484	5,199	2,055	217	88,265	31,829	25,826
Alamogordo, NM Micro Area	6,074	4,068	514	1,282	350	703	579	na	na	na	na
Albany, GA Metro Area	14,031	7,939	1,213	4,746	831	1,398	605	90	18,660	6,589	4,335
Albany, OR Metro Area	12,694	7,188	1,390	3,726	584	1,060	469	na	na	na	na
Albany-Schenectady-Troy, NY Metro Area	86,243	44,338	11,611	27,403	6,448	6,870	1,155	353	105,463	38,826	26,440
Albertville, AL Micro Area	8,968	4,371	1,317	3,183	479	813	342	158	na	na	na
Albuquerque, NM Metro Area	82,564	42,090	11,689	26,446	2,720	9,494	3,233	632	100,630	36,250	33,334
Alexandria, LA Metro Area	14,007	7,905	1,167	4,624	1,385	1,526	897	344	na	na	na
Allentown-Bethlehem-Easton, PA-NJ Metro Area	82,997	45,252	11,011	25,151	6,728	9,198	2,678	249	115,654	39,463	23,931
Altoona, PA Metro Area	14,864	7,062	1,734	5,804	1,493	1,003	372	43	na	na	na
Amarillo, TX Metro Area	21,264	12,203	2,391	6,355	718	3,292	1,303	331	27,311	10,210	6,248
Ames, IA Metro Area	na	na	na	na	na	na	na	na	na	na	na
Anchorage, AK Metro Area	20,102	11,816	2,934	4,301	920	3,981	1,107	52	31,527	8,731	10,182
Ann Arbor, MI Metro Area	27,312	14,719	2,951	8,722	1,356	2,693	692	72	37,510	10,088	10,872
Anniston-Oxford-Jacksonville, AL Metro Area	11,702	6,329	1,159	4,056	470	1,376	824	275	na	na	na
Appleton, WI Metro Area	18,685	11,635	1,758	5,157	1,286	1,095	264	70	28,542	7,709	4,447
Asheville, NC Metro Area	55,387	28,964	6,561	18,563	2,501	3,794	1,521	114	71,375	23,804	15,891
Ashtabula, OH Micro Area	10,195	5,847	1,379	2,804	1,346	1,377	746	450	na	na	na
Athens, TX Micro Area	10,304	6,451	1,347	2,286	611	1,067	396	73	na	na	na
Athens-Clarke County, GA Metro Area	14,195	8,302	1,265	4,182	504	1,731	523	301	na	na	na
Atlanta-Sandy Springs-Roswell, GA Metro Area	353,875	201,278	42,105	101,378	13,095	68,517	20,307	3,117	507,548	172,832	142,142
Atlantic City-Hammonton, NJ Metro Area	26,503	13,062	3,975	8,736	1,542	4,830	1,676	101	32,122	13,352	10,066
Auburn, NY Micro Area	8,338	3,970	1,472	2,641	424	na	na	na	10,441	4,344	1,936
Auburn-Opelika, AL Metro Area	10,631	5,816	1,619	3,196	323	na	na	186	na	na	na
Augusta-Richmond County, GA-SC Metro Area	49,028	28,266	7,253	12,842	2,886	8,243	3,407	446	69,327	26,165	17,808
Augusta-Waterville, ME Micro Area	13,203	6,893	1,762	4,096	797	919	110	na	na	na	na
Austin-Round Rock, TX Metro Area	105,797	60,784	11,913	30,871	4,748	18,644	6,058	489	162,897	44,195	48,517
Bakersfield, CA Metro Area	49,947	27,693	7,294	12,974	2,050	12,956	4,197	1,393	70,019	24,493	20,705
Baltimore-Columbia-Towson, MD Metro Area	240,780	128,158	32,214	73,959	12,495	32,416	8,253	504	301,487	116,156	80,423
Bangor, ME Metro Area	16,041	7,983	1,799	5,877	897	1,232	371	na	na	na	na
Barnstable Town, MA Metro Area	38,887	19,546	5,315	12,952	1,633	1,442	427	na	46,965	14,698	10,408
Baton Rouge, LA Metro Area	61,930	35,161	7,792	17,777	2,967	7,962	3,344	400	80,984	33,015	20,887
Battle Creek, MI Metro Area	13,899	7,457	2,183	3,908	1,016	1,133	491	0	na	na	na
Bay City, MI Metro Area	12,621	6,285	1,492	4,356	1,012	na	na	na	na	na	na
Beaumont-Port Arthur, TX Metro Area	37,765	19,121	6,424	11,668	2,431	5,533	2,304	509	42,243	18,152	15,444
Beaver Dam, WI Micro Area	8,850	4,716	1,077	2,895	1,070	na	na	na	na	na	na
Beckley, WV Metro Area	14,622	8,194	1,897	4,272	803	1,842	1,288	305	na	na	na
Bellingham, WA Metro Area	20,850	10,555	2,968	6,911	1,058	1,807	625	na	na	na	na
Bend-Redmond, OR Metro Area	18,070	10,641	1,826	4,852	617	na	na	na	na	na	na
Billings, MT Metro Area	16,291	7,805	2,862	5,486	901	956	535	na	na	na	na
Binghamton, NY Metro Area	27,324	14,566	3,837	8,475	2,302	2,254	896	159	34,081	12,224	9,824
Birmingham-Hoover, AL Metro Area	107,765	62,122	12,874	31,500	4,747	12,806	6,303	1,486	134,991	52,694	33,819
Bismarck, ND Metro Area	11,754	6,055	1,592	3,856	854	413	111	0	na	na	na
Blacksburg-Christiansburg-Radford, VA Metro Area	15,631	7,393	2,356	5,296	594	1,575	582	0	na	na	na
Bloomington, IL Metro Area	14,146	7,196	2,075	4,569	853	697	237	0	na	na	na
Bloomington, IN Metro Area	11,974	6,348	892	3,783	770	785	331	0	na	na	na
Bloomsburg-Berwick, PA Metro Area	9,142	5,113	1,141	2,677	934	577	219	na	na	na	na
Bluefield, WV-VA Micro Area	13,568	6,381	2,003	4,683	558	1,335	366	50	na	na	na
Boise City, ID Metro Area	51,350	30,862	5,587	13,964	1,292	5,607	2,727	296	79,883	20,348	17,393
Boston-Cambridge-Newton, MA-NH Metro Area	412,506	205,007	58,048	136,810	26,042	51,654	8,055	601	517,313	186,961	131,282
Boulder, CO Metro Area	23,881	11,900	3,301	8,008	973	na	na	na	33,446	8,621	10,946
Bowling Green, KY Metro Area	14,024	7,167	1,911	4,898	418	757	217	60	na	na	na
Bozeman, MT Micro Area	6,915	3,645	1,125	2,028	217	na	na	na	na	na	na
Brainerd, MN Micro Area	12,583	7,125	1,946	3,242	635	326	178	71	17,909	4,407	2,872
Branson, MO Micro Area	12,253	7,174	1,638	2,970	415	na	na	na	na	na	na
Bremerton-Silverdale, WA Metro Area	25,250	14,524	3,154	7,166	1,272	2,317	372	na	34,758	9,777	9,571
Bridgeport-Stamford-Norwalk, CT Metro Area	84,643	45,371	9,618	27,394	5,059	8,666	1,782	434	105,000	37,427	27,960
Brownsville-Harlingen, TX Metro Area	30,043	18,263	3,235	8,162	1,158	8,672	2,066	706	39,320	16,081	8,582
Brunswick, GA Metro Area	12,140	6,378	1,825	3,583	601	1,858	1,075	108	na	na	na
Buffalo-Cheektowaga-Niagara Falls, NY Metro Area	125,531	59,902	18,196	44,909	8,032	6,968	2,132	332	138,669	60,090	36,357
Burlington, NC Metro Area	16,058	8,229	2,148	5,424	1,016	1,179	661	257	19,315	7,344	5,227
Burlington-South Burlington, VT Metro Area	18,342	8,921	2,620	6,373	1,148	1,883	270	0	25,168	7,387	6,153
California-Lexington Park, MD Metro Area	na	na	na	na	na	1,552	516	na	na	na	na
Canton-Massillon, OH Metro Area	44,574	24,001	5,475	13,772	3,899	3,454	1,179	76	58,796	18,869	16,012
Cape Coral-Fort Myers, FL Metro Area	102,374	60,535	11,715	26,446	1,705	6,107	1,270	242	139,106	43,307	30,094
Cape Girardeau, MO-IL Metro Area	9,954	5,873	1,150	2,931	870	649	439	234	na	na	na
Carbondale-Marion, IL Metro Area	11,887	7,167	1,264	3,059	888	871	351	45	na	na	na
Carson City, NV Metro Area	6,651	2,720	1,294	2,488	634	na	na	na	na	na	na
Casper, WY Metro Area	7,213	3,256	1,078	2,860	390	na	na	na	na	na	na
Cedar Rapids, IA Metro Area	25,107	13,441	3,260	7,835	1,714	1,115	265	na	33,284	9,775	7,275

Table D-4: Metropolitan/Micropolitan Statistical Areas—Household Relationship, Grandparents, and Marital Status—*Continued*

	Total Householders 65 Years and Over	Family Householders 65 Years and Over	Non-Family Householders 65 Years and Over Male Living Alone	Non-Family Householders 65 Years and Over Female Living Alone	Persons 65 Years and Over Living in Group Quarters	Grandparents 60 Years and Over Living with Grandchildren Total	Grandparents 60 Years and Over Living with Grandchildren Responsible for Grandchildren	Grandparents 60 Years and Over Living with Grandchildren Responsible for Grandchildren and In Poverty	Marital Status - Persons 60 Years and Over Now Married	Widowed	Divorced
Centralia, WA Micro Area	9,400	5,583	937	2,710	330	639	375	na	na	na	na
Chambersburg-Waynesboro, PA Metro Area	16,463	9,616	2,146	4,523	898	1,161	283	na	na	na	na
Champaign-Urbana, IL Metro Area	18,635	9,193	2,656	6,525	1,414	1,436	514	40	22,898	7,617	7,305
Charleston, WV Metro Area	27,136	14,981	3,747	8,114	955	2,356	1,275	155	31,323	12,906	7,204
Charleston-Mattoon, IL Micro Area	na	na	na	na	na	na	na	na	na	na	na
Charleston-North Charleston, SC Metro Area	58,835	35,955	6,956	15,186	1,497	8,081	4,159	992	85,092	26,404	19,869
Charlotte-Concord-Gastonia, NC-SC Metro Area	178,503	100,798	22,297	51,697	7,942	22,975	9,183	2,244	245,568	86,075	58,591
Charlottesville, VA Metro Area	20,925	11,945	2,454	5,894	1,945	2,411	669	55	29,630	9,331	6,827
Chattanooga, TN-GA Metro Area	56,504	33,709	6,225	15,731	2,564	6,554	2,751	573	70,507	26,639	17,711
Cheyenne, WY Metro Area	8,768	5,850	713	2,168	319	na	na	na	na	na	na
Chicago-Naperville-Elgin, IL-IN-WI Metro Area	741,292	394,382	96,190	234,154	40,804	109,463	25,231	3,938	962,453	359,733	229,154
Chico, CA Metro Area	22,765	10,900	3,605	7,018	1,088	2,531	1,401	441	28,840	10,305	8,510
Chillicothe, OH Micro Area	7,322	3,805	1,556	1,955	441	na	na	na	na	na	na
Cincinnati, OH-KY-IN Metro Area	185,564	97,863	25,770	57,542	11,612	17,536	6,528	929	239,251	85,287	67,118
Claremont-Lebanon, NH-VT Micro Area	24,525	13,010	3,428	7,314	1,261	1,300	283	26	35,052	10,271	9,093
Clarksburg, WV Micro Area	10,942	5,738	2,006	2,952	669	1,163	594	196	na	na	na
Clarksville, TN-KY Metro Area	16,860	9,557	1,446	5,136	1,068	2,101	951	44	23,690	8,698	5,404
Clearlake, CA Micro Area	8,588	3,867	1,728	2,581	127	na	na	na	na	na	na
Cleveland, TN Metro Area	12,406	6,709	1,712	3,701	543	1,184	521	248	na	na	na
Cleveland-Elyria, OH Metro Area	220,581	110,636	32,446	72,714	14,224	18,434	5,838	1,163	252,402	101,285	75,066
Coeur d'Alene, ID Metro Area	15,029	8,194	1,809	4,426	416	na	na	na	na	na	na
College Station-Bryan, TX Metro Area	15,260	8,196	2,458	4,270	816	2,322	1,028	116	20,117	8,170	4,130
Colorado Springs, CO Metro Area	48,830	28,359	7,124	12,401	1,142	5,503	1,493	40	76,287	16,993	20,718
Columbia, MO Metro Area	11,871	5,927	1,516	4,107	742	na	na	na	na	na	na
Columbia, SC Metro Area	67,284	38,660	7,555	19,886	3,364	8,301	3,117	784	85,339	30,795	21,823
Columbus, GA-AL Metro Area	23,640	14,267	2,341	6,514	1,011	3,481	1,738	503	30,110	13,007	8,851
Columbus, IN Metro Area	7,952	4,227	991	2,619	425	na	na	na	na	na	na
Columbus, OH Metro Area	147,766	77,627	20,041	46,192	7,518	17,714	5,569	802	197,873	66,877	54,048
Concord, NH Micro Area	13,787	7,174	1,841	4,158	1,080	825	93	na	19,739	6,527	4,666
Cookeville, TN Micro Area	12,176	6,607	1,526	3,888	495	1,718	721	147	na	na	na
Coos Bay, OR Micro Area	9,135	4,548	1,578	2,588	271	na	na	na	na	na	na
Corning, NY Micro Area	11,088	5,496	1,201	4,068	963	426	192	0	12,432	5,110	3,780
Corpus Christi, TX Metro Area	38,942	22,621	5,011	9,824	1,883	5,800	1,945	1,004	48,577	19,977	13,742
Corvallis, OR Metro Area	7,923	4,193	1,203	2,164	107	na	na	na	na	na	na
Crestview-Fort Walton Beach-Destin, FL Metro Area	26,949	15,239	3,870	7,211	991	1,943	1,201	69	33,619	12,296	6,779
Cullman, AL Micro Area	8,705	4,382	958	3,303	475	na	na	na	na	na	na
Cumberland, MD-WV Metro Area	11,770	5,938	1,587	3,913	1,235	571	221	58	na	na	na
Dallas-Fort Worth-Arlington, TX Metro Area	420,736	241,457	49,224	119,746	18,173	81,769	23,287	3,990	605,616	190,517	170,659
Dalton, GA Metro Area	10,758	5,880	1,486	3,225	506	1,761	703	0	na	na	na
Danville, IL Metro Area	8,761	4,446	1,459	2,766	577	na	na	na	na	na	na
Danville, VA Micro Area	13,851	7,847	1,633	4,215	605	755	310	na	na	na	na
Daphne-Fairhope-Foley, AL Metro Area	23,509	12,706	3,020	6,982	550	951	501	na	na	na	na
Davenport-Moline-Rock Island, IA-IL Metro Area	40,792	20,023	5,954	13,843	2,349	2,744	1,120	349	50,264	18,458	12,189
Dayton, OH Metro Area	84,582	42,432	13,182	27,187	5,141	6,246	3,266	758	99,448	38,453	28,011
Decatur, AL Metro Area	15,624	8,057	2,490	4,998	727	1,456	474	23	na	na	na
Decatur, IL Metro Area	12,440	6,697	1,453	3,983	987	865	408	61	na	na	na
Deltona-Daytona Beach-Ormond Beach, FL Metro Area	85,624	48,977	10,870	22,584	2,932	8,757	1,946	634	111,001	41,665	28,483
Denver-Aurora-Lakewood, CO Metro Area	198,278	107,805	27,024	58,515	7,633	25,303	6,562	753	274,850	73,855	89,042
Des Moines-West Des Moines, IA Metro Area	47,347	23,397	7,372	15,507	3,138	3,947	1,182	86	61,432	21,255	15,437
Detroit-Warren-Dearborn, MI Metro Area	406,083	210,701	56,387	130,643	17,075	40,875	10,580	1,838	483,817	189,916	145,754
Dothan, AL Metro Area	15,885	8,897	2,045	4,635	493	1,849	830	98	19,097	7,699	5,557
Dover, DE Metro Area	15,895	9,731	2,255	3,714	745	2,035	620	37	na	na	na
DuBois, PA Micro Area	9,947	4,895	1,312	3,669	732	789	451	15	na	na	na
Dubuque, IA Metro Area	9,597	5,782	1,113	2,619	1,428	na	na	na	na	na	na
Duluth, MN-WI Metro Area	30,770	15,569	4,347	10,291	2,426	1,195	268	68	39,699	13,134	9,449
Dunn, NC Micro Area	8,883	4,785	1,247	2,651	480	1,384	768	30	10,821	4,656	2,394
Durham-Chapel Hill, NC Metro Area	43,911	24,066	5,093	13,855	2,414	3,846	1,263	127	58,664	19,846	15,693
East Stroudsburg, PA Metro Area	12,922	7,361	1,495	3,475	506	2,547	560	0	na	na	na
Eau Claire, WI Metro Area	15,310	8,003	2,187	4,969	794	431	278	83	na	na	na
El Centro, CA Metro Area	10,308	5,799	1,159	3,060	338	3,881	655	218	14,670	7,452	3,543
El Paso, TX Metro Area	52,864	32,148	5,575	14,422	1,811	16,063	3,999	1,607	73,237	30,193	17,085
Elizabeth City, NC Micro Area	na	na	na	na	na	na	na	na	na	na	na
Elizabethtown-Fort Knox, KY Metro Area	13,028	7,027	2,110	3,447	580	1,347	290	18	na	na	na
Elkhart-Goshen, IN Metro Area	16,374	9,027	1,794	5,216	1,210	1,488	785	202	na	na	na
Elmira, NY Metro Area	8,995	4,718	733	3,051	773	427	276	16	na	na	na
Erie, PA Metro Area	27,024	14,444	3,187	8,468	2,253	2,712	1,013	256	35,265	13,942	7,339
Eugene, OR Metro Area	39,122	20,813	5,116	11,315	1,310	3,181	1,089	54	49,571	14,677	17,796
Eureka-Arcata-Fortuna, CA Micro Area	12,469	6,621	1,943	3,425	507	993	291	6	na	na	na
Evansville, IN-KY Metro Area	30,371	15,855	3,944	10,021	2,539	2,174	985	135	40,516	13,457	11,689
Fairbanks, AK Metro Area	na	na	na	na	na	na	na	na	na	na	na
Fargo, ND-MN Metro Area	16,843	7,549	2,363	6,535	1,071	na	na	na	na	na	na
Faribault-Northfield, MN Micro Area	6,214	2,524	960	2,664	365	na	na	na	na	na	na

Table D-4: Metropolitan/Micropolitan Statistical Areas—Household Relationship, Grandparents, and Marital Status—*Continued*

	Total Householders 65 Years and Over	Family Householders 65 Years and Over	Non-Family Householders 65 Years and Over		Persons 65 Years and Over Living in Group Quarters	Grandparents 60 Years and Over Living with Grandchildren			Marital Status - Persons 60 Years and Over		
			Male Living Alone	Female Living Alone		Total	Responsible for Grandchildren	Responsible for Grandchildren and In Poverty	Now Married	Widowed	Divorced
Farmington, MO Micro Area	6,200	3,503	773	1,924	579	na	na	na	na	na	na
Farmington, NM Metro Area	9,919	5,863	1,114	2,388	546	2,712	932	378	na	na	na
Fayetteville, NC Metro Area	24,426	13,352	3,246	7,528	1,017	4,422	1,504	386	31,716	12,527	7,808
Fayetteville-Springdale-Rogers, AR-MO Metro Area	38,246	21,668	5,227	10,628	1,729	3,886	966	227	52,915	16,497	11,127
Findlay, OH Micro Area	7,754	4,062	1,082	2,610	578	na	na	na	na	na	na
Flagstaff, AZ Metro Area	9,700	5,898	1,422	2,092	234	1,558	597	144	na	na	na
Flint, MI Metro Area	42,588	24,261	5,262	12,272	1,559	3,645	928	61	52,384	17,955	14,982
Florence, SC Metro Area	20,036	11,025	2,907	5,784	1,119	4,135	2,415	574	28,242	10,724	5,003
Florence-Muscle Shoals, AL Metro Area	17,403	9,599	2,653	4,962	826	884	395	21	na	na	na
Fond du Lac, WI Metro Area	10,414	5,501	1,437	3,325	873	na	na	na	na	na	na
Forest City, NC Micro Area	8,116	3,744	1,746	2,498	443	na	na	na	na	na	na
Fort Collins, CO Metro Area	27,063	14,703	3,748	8,294	898	1,382	218	na	40,892	8,717	10,316
Fort Smith, AR-OK Metro Area	28,526	15,602	3,707	8,849	1,615	3,282	1,616	422	35,810	13,660	7,241
Fort Wayne, IN Metro Area	36,659	19,468	4,782	11,661	2,639	2,674	1,155	241	48,164	17,037	10,495
Frankfort, KY Micro Area	na	na	na	na	na	603	228	na	na	na	na
Fresno, CA Metro Area	61,609	34,531	8,239	16,407	2,795	18,331	4,077	857	87,516	26,677	24,128
Gadsden, AL Metro Area	11,562	6,134	1,408	3,790	741	923	700	53	na	na	na
Gainesville, FL Metro Area	22,119	11,709	3,262	6,390	1,036	1,673	828	0	27,686	8,639	9,113
Gainesville, GA Metro Area	15,730	9,786	1,225	4,269	483	2,798	589	108	22,193	6,896	4,339
Gallup, NM Micro Area	4,880	3,157	614	1,057	153	1,462	689	210	5,568	2,187	1,225
Gettysburg, PA Metro Area	10,910	6,617	1,288	2,811	829	726	169	0	na	na	na
Glens Falls, NY Metro Area	13,564	7,861	1,945	3,562	683	785	369	na	21,150	5,919	3,820
Glenwood Springs, CO Micro Area	5,544	3,373	660	1,353	216	na	na	na	na	na	na
Goldsboro, NC Metro Area	11,015	6,170	978	3,756	408	na	na	na	na	na	na
Grand Forks, ND-MN Metro Area	8,567	4,066	1,254	3,180	833	na	na	na	na	na	na
Grand Island, NE Metro Area	8,353	4,291	1,005	2,958	709	na	na	na	na	na	na
Grand Junction, CO Metro Area	15,207	9,431	1,478	3,889	518	1,009	644	na	na	na	na
Grand Rapids-Wyoming, MI Metro Area	82,744	47,012	9,081	24,955	5,165	8,155	1,930	338	118,255	35,390	23,398
Grants Pass, OR Metro Area	12,767	6,869	1,541	3,188	532	na	na	na	na	na	na
Great Falls, MT Metro Area	9,011	4,544	1,700	2,613	329	607	269	na	na	na	na
Greeley, CO Metro Area	19,316	11,367	2,307	5,087	368	2,866	780	41	27,144	8,348	6,359
Green Bay, WI Metro Area	27,801	15,738	3,388	7,844	1,516	2,085	774	77	39,461	11,570	7,640
Greeneville, TN Micro Area	7,564	4,381	1,295	1,541	403	693	182	na	na	na	na
Greenfield Town, MA Micro Area	8,174	3,669	1,172	3,024	404	460	76	na	na	na	na
Greensboro-High Point, NC Metro Area	70,530	35,419	10,908	23,072	3,499	6,944	2,307	379	83,406	34,169	24,239
Greenville, NC Metro Area	12,463	6,895	1,659	3,439	545	1,902	733	364	na	na	na
Greenville-Anderson-Mauldin, SC Metro Area	81,633	45,970	9,018	25,344	3,741	8,913	3,404	397	106,607	38,788	24,020
Greenwood, SC Micro Area	10,887	6,380	1,105	3,295	612	1,042	487	86	na	na	na
Gulfport-Biloxi-Pascagoula, MS Metro Area	35,579	20,902	4,546	9,512	986	4,875	1,731	436	43,568	16,534	11,245
Hagerstown-Martinsburg, MD-WV Metro Area	22,841	12,215	3,425	6,743	1,623	2,046	812	153	29,900	11,090	7,967
Hammond, LA Metro Area	9,280	4,654	1,473	2,955	363	1,918	488	305	na	na	na
Hanford-Corcoran, CA Metro Area	7,781	4,946	696	1,885	317	2,183	322	0	11,474	3,525	2,841
Harrisburg-Carlisle, PA Metro Area	56,876	29,345	6,614	19,862	3,628	4,828	1,494	0	73,555	26,906	15,935
Harrisonburg, VA Metro Area	11,181	6,428	1,127	3,345	586	500	130	na	na	na	na
Hartford-West Hartford-East Hartford, CT Metro Area	115,938	59,475	14,577	38,472	9,166	11,121	3,340	622	146,971	50,893	37,855
Hattiesburg, MS Metro Area	11,282	6,312	1,194	3,570	788	2,079	927	446	na	na	na
Helena, MT Micro Area	7,564	4,287	1,415	1,835	617	na	na	na	na	na	na
Hermiston-Pendleton, OR Micro Area	7,109	3,553	1,026	2,472	805	na	na	na	na	na	na
Hickory-Lenoir-Morganton, NC Metro Area	38,170	21,759	4,368	11,148	2,099	4,291	2,370	1,144	50,681	17,596	12,118
Hilo, HI Micro Area	19,257	11,033	2,444	4,393	880	4,240	1,733	68	27,876	9,104	7,083
Hilton Head Island-Bluffton-Beaufort, SC Metro Area	28,322	17,067	3,314	7,106	540	1,795	634	34	40,544	11,406	5,722
Hinesville, GA Metro Area	na	na	na	na	na	na	na	na	na	na	na
Hobbs, NM Micro Area	na	na	na	na	na	na	na	na	na	na	na
Holland, MI Micro Area	10,476	6,444	1,228	2,627	674	na	na	na	0	na	na
Homosassa Springs, FL Metro Area	29,294	17,494	4,000	6,819	653	2,323	827	114	na	na	na
Hot Springs, AR Metro Area	13,006	7,124	2,316	3,251	439	na	na	na	na	na	na
Houma-Thibodaux, LA Metro Area	15,862	9,609	1,753	4,256	772	1,708	476	123	22,772	8,707	4,479
Houston-The Woodlands-Sugar Land, TX Metro Area	377,793	218,782	47,806	102,940	11,560	85,334	20,966	3,862	557,311	180,283	140,094
Huntington-Ashland, WV-KY-OH Metro Area	41,916	21,701	5,288	14,060	2,004	5,258	2,828	405	51,441	20,870	12,589
Huntsville, AL Metro Area	37,623	22,042	5,044	10,079	1,653	3,874	1,412	339	51,202	17,657	12,208
Huntsville, TX Micro Area	7,210	3,395	1,444	2,256	564	na	na	na	na	na	na
Hutchinson, KS Micro Area	na	na	na	na	na	na	na	na	na	na	na
Idaho Falls, ID Metro Area	10,672	6,571	1,007	2,909	194	1,119	429	77	na	na	na
Indiana, PA Micro Area	9,335	5,638	895	2,616	471	na	na	na	na	na	na
Indianapolis-Carmel-Anderson, IN Metro Area	150,796	80,981	21,318	45,041	9,197	14,130	4,844	375	199,798	66,230	59,063
Iowa City, IA Metro Area	11,302	5,982	1,763	3,389	614	na	na	na	na	na	na
Ithaca, NY Metro Area	7,857	4,272	973	2,330	297	na	na	na	na	na	na
Jackson, MI Metro Area	16,640	7,702	2,735	5,594	854	1,424	733	69	19,615	8,629	4,891
Jackson, MS Metro Area	46,494	25,573	5,897	14,597	3,136	6,240	2,180	568	55,513	25,113	14,789
Jackson, TN Metro Area	12,029	6,931	1,049	3,911	732	1,546	579	55	na	na	na
Jacksonville, FL Metro Area	122,887	67,828	16,618	34,766	5,069	17,500	7,036	1,220	158,942	58,612	48,287

Table D-4: Metropolitan/Micropolitan Statistical Areas—Household Relationship, Grandparents, and Marital Status—*Continued*

	Total Householders 65 Years and Over	Family Householders 65 Years and Over	Non-Family Householders 65 Years and Over — Male Living Alone	Non-Family Householders 65 Years and Over — Female Living Alone	Persons 65 Years and Over Living in Group Quarters	Grandparents 60 Years and Over Living with Grandchildren — Total	Responsible for Grandchildren	Responsible for Grandchildren and In Poverty	Marital Status - Persons 60 Years and Over — Now Married	Widowed	Divorced
Jacksonville, NC Metro Area	9,938	5,153	1,510	2,945	285	na	na	na	na	na	na
Jamestown-Dunkirk-Fredonia, NY Micro Area	14,768	7,746	2,072	4,656	1,229	774	216	53	17,660	6,836	4,663
Janesville-Beloit, WI Metro Area	15,033	7,508	2,079	5,251	920	1,515	201	50	na	na	na
Jefferson City, MO Metro Area	13,240	7,267	1,554	3,961	809	1,145	774	171	na	na	na
Johnson City, TN Metro Area	23,000	12,987	2,701	6,939	1,674	1,874	768	201	30,277	10,089	7,773
Johnstown, PA Metro Area	18,477	9,504	2,581	6,223	1,125	1,425	579	16	22,376	9,251	3,653
Jonesboro, AR Metro Area	10,678	6,024	1,137	3,352	795	993	331	na	na	na	na
Joplin, MO Metro Area	16,199	9,192	2,149	4,336	889	2,488	619	290	na	na	na
Kahului-Wailuku-Lahaina, HI Metro Area	13,616	8,090	1,811	2,305	582	4,085	943	153	18,904	7,144	5,830
Kalamazoo-Portage, MI Metro Area	28,592	16,110	3,180	8,598	1,478	2,389	885	102	41,313	12,296	9,084
Kalispell, MT Micro Area	9,898	5,932	1,344	2,344	320	na	na	na	na	na	na
Kankakee, IL Metro Area	9,376	5,331	1,042	2,587	1,403	666	109	na	na	na	na
Kansas City, MO-KS Metro Area	172,768	90,957	22,715	55,369	10,846	17,236	5,725	712	228,183	73,903	64,710
Kapaa, HI Micro Area	6,749	3,828	593	1,771	311	1,890	260	0	na	na	na
Keene, NH Micro Area	8,186	4,615	1,098	2,202	581	na	na	na	na	na	na
Kennewick-Richland, WA Metro Area	19,078	10,700	2,525	5,454	820	1,895	724	0	30,030	8,577	6,412
Key West, FL Micro Area	8,836	4,533	1,634	2,011	202	na	na	na	na	na	na
Killeen-Temple, TX Metro Area	25,887	15,359	3,397	6,851	1,707	3,417	1,571	237	35,438	10,925	9,930
Kingsport-Bristol-Bristol, TN-VA Metro Area	40,278	23,139	5,154	11,646	962	2,624	1,242	293	50,495	17,247	11,072
Kingston, NY Metro Area	21,122	9,980	3,510	7,059	1,848	1,104	552	na	21,933	10,128	6,312
Klamath Falls, OR Micro Area	8,131	3,916	1,352	2,528	210	na	na	na	na	na	na
Knoxville, TN Metro Area	89,830	47,343	13,058	27,609	4,314	9,779	4,001	707	118,276	39,452	31,727
Kokomo, IN Metro Area	9,929	5,128	1,151	3,340	400	1,109	576	0	na	na	na
La Crosse-Onalaska, WI-MN Metro Area	12,824	6,952	1,413	3,877	1,282	na	na	na	na	na	na
Lafayette, LA Metro Area	38,161	21,312	5,632	10,327	2,349	4,042	1,294	253	47,353	17,496	13,285
Lafayette-West Lafayette, IN Metro Area	14,598	8,269	2,186	3,896	880	1,101	291	0	na	na	na
LaGrange, GA Micro Area	6,242	3,513	578	2,095	386	1,242	615	0	na	na	na
Lake Charles, LA Metro Area	17,517	9,630	1,774	5,637	843	1,989	824	375	24,379	8,741	5,978
Lake City, FL Micro Area	7,095	3,932	1,479	1,604	612	na	na	na	na	na	na
Lake Havasu City-Kingman, AZ Metro Area	32,387	20,217	4,583	6,339	510	2,707	577	309	44,156	12,762	10,630
Lakeland-Winter Haven, FL Metro Area	74,155	45,246	7,743	18,782	2,567	10,646	2,355	149	99,020	34,073	20,092
Lancaster, PA Metro Area	50,614	29,287	4,807	14,782	4,327	3,806	752	64	75,612	21,816	11,984
Lansing-East Lansing, MI Metro Area	39,625	20,856	5,447	12,435	2,150	3,101	857	34	55,240	16,202	12,493
Laredo, TX Metro Area	12,074	7,720	1,530	2,777	415	6,464	1,053	420	16,658	8,517	3,345
Las Cruces, NM Metro Area	17,799	10,709	1,715	5,135	779	2,364	565	107	na	na	na
Las Vegas-Henderson-Paradise, NV Metro Area	156,767	86,409	25,109	36,404	3,486	25,825	7,854	1,060	203,387	65,360	76,019
Laurel, MS Micro Area	8,738	5,518	707	2,513	443	1,022	187	na	na	na	na
Lawrence, KS Metro Area	na	na	na	na	na	na	na	na	na	na	na
Lawton, OK Metro Area	9,147	4,798	1,431	2,640	827	1,511	893	44	11,545	5,784	3,225
Lebanon, PA Metro Area	14,125	8,012	1,595	4,090	1,181	na	na	16	na	na	na
Lewiston, ID-WA Metro Area	8,152	4,036	1,025	2,898	518	1,064	652	na	na	na	na
Lewiston-Auburn, ME Metro Area	11,311	4,991	2,018	3,874	619	na	na	na	na	na	na
Lexington-Fayette, KY Metro Area	39,175	21,104	4,659	12,245	2,034	3,136	1,389	353	51,844	17,010	15,855
Lima, OH Metro Area	10,595	5,779	1,172	3,323	550	1,111	211	41	na	na	na
Lincoln, NE Metro Area	25,476	14,013	3,371	7,773	881	1,539	581	220	35,249	9,491	7,680
Little Rock-North Little Rock-Conway, AR Metro Area	60,596	34,952	6,736	17,931	3,494	5,914	2,369	129	80,612	28,535	21,116
Logan, UT-ID Metro Area	na	na	na	na	na	na	na	na	na	na	na
London, KY Micro Area	12,112	6,449	2,148	3,369	825	1,712	499	99	na	na	na
Longview, TX Metro Area	19,425	10,496	2,266	6,380	1,757	2,784	1,504	113	26,985	10,191	5,611
Longview, WA Metro Area	11,975	5,967	2,146	3,564	369	566	320	na	na	na	na
Los Angeles-Long Beach-Anaheim, CA Metro Area	910,270	514,305	110,397	249,273	43,368	233,191	40,896	5,828	1,225,018	453,475	330,526
Louisville/Jefferson County, KY-IN Metro Area	115,701	62,207	14,813	36,224	6,374	12,523	5,265	439	143,111	52,965	43,373
Lubbock, TX Metro Area	24,877	13,467	3,166	7,771	906	1,931	1,157	88	29,858	11,485	6,160
Lufkin, TX Micro Area	7,889	4,370	1,095	2,410	1,202	845	186	na	na	na	na
Lumberton, NC Micro Area	11,080	6,205	1,514	3,256	681	1,623	790	315	13,099	6,108	4,026
Lynchburg, VA Metro Area	28,161	15,874	3,239	8,410	1,192	1,798	675	0	37,575	12,739	7,238
Macon, GA Metro Area	20,490	10,936	2,908	6,088	1,409	3,063	871	442	24,311	11,038	8,305
Madera, CA Metro Area	10,815	6,643	1,175	2,547	562	1,485	420	90	na	na	na
Madison, WI Metro Area	50,608	27,004	6,646	15,183	2,522	2,921	766	0	73,219	18,306	17,569
Manchester-Nashua, NH Metro Area	31,803	16,985	4,690	8,970	2,668	5,568	837	0	45,955	15,440	12,361
Manhattan, KS Metro Area	na	na	na	na	na	na	na	na	na	na	na
Manitowoc, WI Micro Area	9,744	4,640	1,750	3,159	912	273	100	na	na	na	na
Mankato-North Mankato, MN Metro Area	7,626	4,105	800	2,590	1,121	na	na	na	na	na	na
Mansfield, OH Metro Area	15,369	7,413	2,126	5,373	648	na	na	na	na	na	na
Marinette, WI-MI Micro Area	8,992	4,456	1,608	2,772	761	na	na	na	na	na	na
Marion, IN Micro Area	8,091	4,214	1,337	2,408	501	na	na	na	na	na	na
Marion, OH Micro Area	7,518	4,180	1,054	2,129	322	na	na	na	na	na	na
Marquette, MI Micro Area	6,904	3,584	906	2,280	717	na	na	na	na	na	na
Marshall, TX Micro Area	7,012	4,085	479	2,219	311	na	na	na	na	na	na
Martinsville, VA Micro Area	9,167	5,001	962	3,030	313	na	na	na	na	na	na
McAllen-Edinburg-Mission, TX Metro Area	44,905	30,406	4,672	8,754	2,053	13,895	3,153	1,317	68,669	25,571	9,330
Meadville, PA Micro Area	10,082	5,702	1,548	2,527	335	700	184	29	na	na	na
Medford, OR Metro Area	26,718	13,950	4,086	7,482	674	1,387	698	397	34,369	10,004	11,920

Table D-4: Metropolitan/Micropolitan Statistical Areas—Household Relationship, Grandparents, and Marital Status—*Continued*

	Total Householders 65 Years and Over	Family Householders 65 Years and Over	Non-Family Householders 65 Years and Over		Persons 65 Years and Over Living in Group Quarters	Grandparents 60 Years and Over Living with Grandchildren			Marital Status - Persons 60 Years and Over		
			Male Living Alone	Female Living Alone		Total	Responsible for Grandchildren	Responsible for Grandchildren and In Poverty	Now Married	Widowed	Divorced
Memphis, TN-MS-AR Metro Area	100,887	57,423	13,243	28,382	4,574	14,183	5,370	1,161	128,013	51,858	38,575
Merced, CA Metro Area	16,007	8,737	2,529	3,991	399	4,318	1,028	110	20,815	7,860	6,196
Meridian, MS Micro Area	10,037	4,866	1,314	3,818	236	1,729	843	28	na	na	na
Miami-Fort Lauderdale-West Palm Beach, FL Metro Area	567,027	292,132	78,261	174,033	17,735	113,530	17,110	2,889	662,223	294,165	233,651
Michigan City-La Porte, IN Metro Area	11,239	5,911	1,896	3,282	721	583	289	na	na	na	na
Midland, MI Metro Area	8,858	5,223	1,144	2,372	392	na	na	na	na	na	na
Midland, TX Metro Area	9,395	5,079	1,456	2,860	379	1,642	885	0	na	na	na
Milwaukee-Waukesha-West Allis, WI Metro Area	138,369	68,628	20,156	46,852	7,607	10,121	2,623	349	171,154	63,395	45,797
Minneapolis-St. Paul-Bloomington, MN-WI Metro Area	267,566	140,387	35,039	85,292	16,182	22,277	4,432	384	371,288	107,978	90,954
Minot, ND Micro Area	na	na	na	na	na	na	na	na	na	na	na
Missoula, MT Metro Area	10,170	5,033	1,831	3,153	349	na	na	na	na	na	na
Mobile, AL Metro Area	37,513	21,576	4,090	11,024	1,527	4,542	2,121	371	47,918	18,173	12,848
Modesto, CA Metro Area	37,075	20,980	4,549	10,214	2,095	9,269	2,098	211	50,838	17,464	14,046
Monroe, LA Metro Area	15,804	9,208	1,859	4,440	1,075	1,212	756	139	22,130	7,193	4,823
Monroe, MI Metro Area	13,962	7,491	1,438	4,802	750	1,049	572	na	na	na	na
Montgomery, AL Metro Area	32,901	17,889	4,309	10,067	1,750	4,286	1,772	229	37,450	15,476	13,416
Morehead City, NC Micro Area	9,697	5,450	1,339	2,759	346	958	580	na	na	na	na
Morgantown, WV Metro Area	10,484	5,548	1,437	3,254	514	1,671	741	105	na	na	na
Morristown, TN Metro Area	12,957	7,935	1,539	3,314	708	1,195	539	89	na	na	na
Moses Lake, WA Micro Area	7,129	3,873	1,132	2,076	317	na	na	na	na	na	na
Mount Airy, NC Micro Area	8,171	4,601	891	2,482	557	na	na	na	na	na	na
Mount Pleasant, MI Micro Area	4,940	2,470	599	1,675	488	289	42	0	na	na	na
Mount Vernon-Anacortes, WA Metro Area	13,628	7,456	1,458	4,167	620	na	na	na	na	na	na
Muncie, IN Metro Area	11,571	7,064	860	3,463	958	918	160	0	na	na	na
Muskegon, MI Metro Area	17,066	9,489	2,035	5,209	862	1,640	714	57	20,197	7,468	5,471
Muskogee, OK Micro Area	6,952	3,618	1,111	1,972	762	913	511	143	na	na	na
Myrtle Beach-Conway-North Myrtle Beach, SC-NC Metro Area	57,080	33,596	7,590	14,392	1,110	5,031	2,931	897	80,595	22,417	17,129
Nacogdoches, TX Micro Area	na	na	na	na	na	na	na	na	na	na	na
Napa, CA Metro Area	14,395	8,071	1,452	4,171	1,119	2,741	419	na	20,475	5,789	5,496
Naples-Immokalee-Marco Island, FL Metro Area	59,575	36,193	6,347	14,762	1,017	4,637	975	538	86,600	19,944	12,297
Nashville-Davidson–Murfreesboro–Franklin, TN Metro Area	132,276	74,094	16,740	38,692	5,390	18,561	6,105	631	182,397	62,457	48,647
New Bern, NC Metro Area	15,137	8,929	1,808	4,299	319	1,130	593	51	20,020	6,387	3,303
New Castle, PA Micro Area	11,449	6,573	1,586	3,223	864	850	327	na	na	na	na
New Haven-Milford, CT Metro Area	82,837	39,655	12,619	28,767	6,659	8,281	1,515	37	100,957	37,255	29,328
New Orleans-Metairie, LA Metro Area	107,714	60,791	14,185	30,619	3,488	14,362	4,202	1,042	136,100	51,354	38,721
New Philadelphia-Dover, OH Micro Area	10,625	5,017	1,963	3,403	771	476	215	38	na	na	na
New York-Newark-Jersey City, NY-NJ-PA Metro Area	1,691,688	881,164	219,095	548,229	105,072	291,143	56,658	10,699	2,070,344	840,475	487,788
Niles-Benton Harbor, MI Metro Area	17,528	9,384	2,180	5,497	734	1,158	442	107	22,550	7,677	5,133
North Port-Sarasota-Bradenton, FL Metro Area	136,689	77,911	15,361	37,128	3,539	6,771	3,621	205	177,689	52,560	33,615
North Wilkesboro, NC Micro Area	8,517	4,539	1,377	2,601	377	na	na	na	na	na	na
Norwich-New London, CT Metro Area	26,286	14,663	3,260	7,950	1,760	2,559	331	0	36,781	11,429	8,887
Oak Harbor, WA Micro Area	10,375	6,597	832	2,762	298	na	na	na	na	na	na
Ocala, FL Metro Area	57,018	33,317	7,597	14,108	1,240	3,149	516	44	70,942	24,747	17,025
Ocean City, NJ Metro Area	14,468	8,081	2,185	3,629	993	na	na	na	na	na	na
Odessa, TX Metro Area	9,158	4,931	1,111	2,865	255	1,454	456	50	na	na	na
Ogden-Clearfield, UT Metro Area	37,737	23,763	3,827	9,657	735	6,615	2,492	459	62,061	13,728	13,012
Ogdensburg-Massena, NY Micro Area	9,894	4,154	1,545	3,678	1,067	na	na	na	12,718	5,806	3,380
Oklahoma City, OK Metro Area	105,072	58,730	12,467	31,564	5,292	10,746	4,508	452	141,565	47,648	37,682
Olean, NY Micro Area	8,548	4,181	1,498	2,620	814	518	223	na	na	na	na
Olympia-Tumwater, WA Metro Area	24,728	12,956	3,189	7,418	1,550	2,201	811	0	32,290	9,873	10,593
Omaha-Council Bluffs, NE-IA Metro Area	71,113	36,365	9,917	23,367	3,905	4,462	1,242	108	93,073	32,710	21,668
Opelousas, LA Micro Area	7,856	4,155	1,020	2,547	683	na	na	175	na	na	na
Orangeburg, SC Micro Area	9,240	4,479	1,526	3,083	304	850	357	55	na	na	na
Orlando-Kissimmee-Sanford, FL Metro Area	174,137	103,644	19,482	46,258	6,988	28,701	5,727	1,065	250,374	87,011	69,406
Oshkosh-Neenah, WI Metro Area	16,060	8,188	1,819	5,675	999	570	261	na	na	na	na
Ottawa-Peru, IL Micro Area	17,048	9,698	2,080	4,985	1,588	972	373	0	na	na	na
Owensboro, KY Metro Area	12,013	6,943	1,163	3,703	937	1,395	368	45	na	na	na
Owosso, MI Micro Area	6,935	4,121	730	1,948	202	na	na	na	na	na	na
Oxnard-Thousand Oaks-Ventura, CA Metro Area	68,153	39,209	7,450	18,625	2,100	13,287	2,106	114	95,505	27,935	25,684
Paducah, KY-IL Micro Area	10,957	5,858	1,715	2,952	703	848	537	0	na	na	na
Palatka, FL Micro Area	10,067	4,885	1,530	3,296	466	na	na	na	na	na	na
Palm Bay-Melbourne-Titusville, FL Metro Area	76,243	43,486	9,335	20,060	1,969	5,833	2,087	743	94,012	31,480	29,017
Panama City, FL Metro Area	18,635	10,851	2,296	4,999	995	2,287	846	0	25,247	8,802	7,233
Parkersburg-Vienna, WV Metro Area	11,881	5,680	1,540	4,430	333	na	na	na	na	na	na
Pensacola-Ferry Pass-Brent, FL Metro Area	44,926	26,557	6,271	11,127	2,339	3,954	1,935	200	56,063	23,619	13,822
Peoria, IL Metro Area	38,761	20,344	4,379	13,081	2,967	2,046	803	233	50,785	18,075	10,359
Philadelphia-Camden-Wilmington, PA-NJ-DE-MD Metro Area	542,821	283,985	71,929	173,556	33,277	67,841	18,261	2,242	662,562	266,427	166,092
Phoenix-Mesa-Scottsdale, AZ Metro Area	378,994	214,465	50,504	101,897	11,293	48,243	11,915	2,862	503,134	157,678	143,372
Pine Bluff, AR Metro Area	9,236	5,092	1,412	2,617	859	1,499	854	331	na	na	na

Table D-4: Metropolitan/Micropolitan Statistical Areas—Household Relationship, Grandparents, and Marital Status—Continued

	Total Householders 65 Years and Over	Family Householders 65 Years and Over	Non-Family Householders 65 Years and Over		Persons 65 Years and Over Living in Group Quarters	Grandparents 60 Years and Over Living with Grandchildren			Marital Status - Persons 60 Years and Over		
			Male Living Alone	Female Living Alone		Total	Responsible for Grandchildren	Responsible for Grandchildren and In Poverty	Now Married	Widowed	Divorced
Pinehurst-Southern Pines, NC Micro Area	13,871	7,785	1,872	3,963	928	524	250	na	na	na	na
Pittsburgh, PA Metro Area	281,313	140,257	38,430	95,632	15,011	15,782	4,034	302	330,662	135,505	71,902
Pittsfield, MA Metro Area	17,764	8,500	3,154	5,698	1,468	na	na	na	na	na	na
Plattsburgh, NY Micro Area	7,776	3,851	1,196	2,299	544	na	na	na	na	na	na
Pocatello, ID Metro Area	6,874	3,486	1,074	2,078	203	768	291	na	na	na	na
Port Angeles, WA Micro Area	12,052	6,302	1,889	3,653	556	na	na	na	na	na	na
Port St. Lucie, FL Metro Area	67,256	35,896	10,918	17,675	1,435	4,520	729	110	82,146	29,048	21,202
Portland-South Portland, ME Metro Area	56,005	29,609	6,865	17,543	2,752	3,358	900	124	74,777	20,645	21,829
Portland-Vancouver-Hillsboro, OR-WA Metro Area	190,816	100,129	25,274	58,863	7,878	23,053	5,238	420	255,844	75,300	84,716
Portsmouth, OH Micro Area	7,877	4,181	874	2,581	777	704	371	na	na	na	na
Pottsville, PA Micro Area	17,799	8,710	2,781	5,934	1,575	1,220	595	75	21,214	9,377	4,666
Prescott, AZ Metro Area	38,908	21,762	5,533	10,312	745	1,738	893	214	48,240	15,230	14,671
Providence-Warwick, RI-MA Metro Area	155,267	78,731	19,802	52,585	12,349	18,691	4,345	687	192,468	75,547	51,129
Provo-Orem, UT Metro Area	22,346	16,691	1,613	3,920	166	5,971	1,211	27	42,887	7,707	5,681
Pueblo, CO Metro Area	17,236	8,905	2,442	5,369	1,559	1,566	1,044	58	21,164	8,034	6,314
Punta Gorda, FL Metro Area	38,266	22,112	4,526	10,155	1,366	1,566	750	200	na	na	na
Quincy, IL-MO Micro Area	9,020	4,546	1,102	3,204	1,106	na	na	na	na	na	na
Racine, WI Metro Area	19,041	9,521	3,217	5,883	518	1,671	594	na	24,430	7,086	6,906
Raleigh, NC Metro Area	79,654	46,645	7,610	24,233	3,781	11,735	3,163	797	117,360	38,862	25,981
Rapid City, SD Metro Area	13,423	6,920	2,466	3,642	782	1,292	421	na	na	na	na
Reading, PA Metro Area	40,172	22,630	5,898	10,648	2,571	3,441	1,017	276	57,209	17,248	11,887
Redding, CA Metro Area	21,110	11,520	3,189	5,658	1,122	1,615	504	0	26,364	9,767	9,171
Reno, NV Metro Area	41,425	21,016	7,767	10,645	1,132	4,200	1,216	51	51,603	15,507	19,890
Richmond, IN Micro Area	7,721	4,634	481	2,427	566	708	423	na	na	na	na
Richmond, VA Metro Area	107,795	57,227	14,726	34,263	3,140	14,181	4,405	704	140,255	49,804	36,103
Richmond-Berea, KY Micro Area	8,709	5,135	880	2,209	509	440	192	67	na	na	na
Riverside-San Bernardino-Ontario, CA Metro Area	288,442	165,827	38,288	71,516	11,236	80,292	14,823	3,092	414,326	144,163	117,885
Roanoke Rapids, NC Micro Area	9,066	4,234	1,464	3,105	593	1,254	600	214	na	na	na
Roanoke, VA Metro Area	36,891	20,178	5,031	11,183	1,667	2,809	1,166	97	46,185	16,979	11,697
Rochester, MN Metro Area	19,359	11,033	2,052	5,833	1,389	1,224	387	0	30,017	6,632	4,957
Rochester, NY Metro Area	110,552	52,584	17,884	37,303	6,831	5,968	2,081	186	132,175	53,377	34,069
Rockford, IL Metro Area	33,441	16,589	6,292	9,993	1,520	3,006	792	352	40,744	15,741	11,305
Rocky Mount, NC Metro Area	16,555	7,757	2,669	5,720	785	1,658	605	238	na	na	na
Rome, GA Metro Area	9,055	4,845	1,234	2,704	501	999	716	0	na	na	na
Roseburg, OR Micro Area	15,674	8,246	3,104	3,586	475	1,490	523	14	na	na	na
Roswell, NM Micro Area	6,495	3,326	973	2,051	423	793	520	20	na	na	na
Russellville, AR Micro Area	7,902	4,135	1,324	2,188	550	722	333	104	na	na	na
Sacramento–Roseville–Arden-Arcade, CA Metro Area	185,384	101,879	22,594	54,374	7,574	32,259	7,489	543	250,858	83,391	73,943
Saginaw, MI Metro Area	21,226	12,627	2,454	5,736	1,380	2,060	967	127	27,825	8,884	5,776
Salem, OH Micro Area	12,009	6,544	1,813	3,545	975	958	373	114	na	na	na
Salem, OR Metro Area	38,294	20,619	5,308	11,407	1,654	4,052	1,086	161	48,220	16,958	14,513
Salinas, CA Metro Area	30,238	17,357	4,045	7,498	1,679	7,573	1,527	63	40,757	15,382	9,686
Salisbury, MD-DE Metro Area	49,882	30,228	5,934	12,367	2,393	4,077	1,501	445	71,338	19,320	12,333
Salt Lake City, UT Metro Area	67,200	38,941	9,390	17,563	1,826	14,606	2,670	158	104,107	28,118	24,468
San Angelo, TX Metro Area	10,610	4,637	1,896	3,852	759	1,485	1,124	108	na	na	na
San Antonio-New Braunfels, TX Metro Area	166,825	96,343	22,034	44,256	8,381	32,269	8,480	1,428	220,756	80,596	64,402
San Diego-Carlsbad, CA Metro Area	234,218	132,201	28,574	65,704	8,991	49,760	9,545	1,906	321,912	114,672	98,643
San Francisco-Oakland-Hayward, CA Metro Area	374,843	198,438	51,742	108,694	16,153	76,526	13,512	1,032	482,008	169,176	141,609
San Jose-Sunnyvale-Santa Clara, CA Metro Area	127,012	73,952	14,359	34,344	6,497	33,912	3,905	371	191,225	61,405	46,154
San Luis Obispo-Paso Robles-Arroyo Grande, CA Metro Area	29,273	15,466	4,499	7,940	1,218	2,943	432	na	39,603	13,451	9,545
Sandusky, OH Micro Area	9,653	4,738	1,408	3,003	670	na	na	na	na	na	na
Santa Cruz-Watsonville, CA Metro Area	22,945	11,607	2,967	6,861	591	2,448	549	0	30,415	7,749	11,167
Santa Fe, NM Metro Area	18,581	8,925	2,931	5,679	441	1,463	492	na	22,751	5,160	9,337
Santa Maria-Santa Barbara, CA Metro Area	37,459	19,938	5,115	11,040	1,798	6,218	1,221	0	46,730	15,131	15,513
Santa Rosa, CA Metro Area	51,802	25,762	6,691	16,563	1,827	5,333	1,196	0	64,325	19,457	22,970
Savannah, GA Metro Area	28,809	16,069	3,095	8,946	1,279	4,310	1,756	166	36,448	13,905	11,755
Scranton–Wilkes-Barre–Hazleton, PA Metro Area	64,628	30,783	8,436	24,036	5,176	5,914	1,562	251	74,992	33,055	17,939
Searcy, AR Micro Area	7,197	4,371	746	1,896	402	823	343	93	na	na	na
Seattle-Tacoma-Bellevue, WA Metro Area	272,064	140,910	36,006	85,656	15,248	38,174	7,558	1,418	371,428	113,034	115,212
Sebastian-Vero Beach, FL Metro Area	26,256	15,013	3,666	6,706	507	na	na	na	na	na	na
Sebring, FL Metro Area	19,624	11,523	2,606	4,700	609	na	na	na	na	na	na
Seneca, SC Micro Area	na	na	na	na	na	na	na	na	na	na	na
Sevierville, TN Micro Area	10,950	6,075	1,414	3,041	285	1,184	328	na	na	na	na
Shawnee, OK Micro Area	6,475	3,843	738	1,843	199	637	297	6	9,510	3,384	2,342
Sheboygan, WI Metro Area	11,782	5,881	1,903	3,914	794	na	na	na	na	na	na
Shelby, NC Micro Area	11,438	6,540	1,277	3,224	225	1,158	781	89	na	na	na
Sherman-Denison, TX Metro Area	12,404	6,975	2,042	3,317	881	2,050	542	86	na	na	na
Show Low, AZ Micro Area	10,706	7,099	1,144	2,132	277	2,438	1,343	473	13,813	4,023	2,950
Shreveport-Bossier City, LA Metro Area	40,247	20,507	6,116	12,438	2,925	6,386	2,927	516	47,919	22,581	12,936
Sierra Vista-Douglas, AZ Metro Area	15,100	8,406	2,016	4,196	477	1,725	996	448	na	na	na
Sioux City, IA-NE-SD Metro Area	15,558	7,776	1,784	5,562	1,016	606	194	na	21,520	6,784	4,435

Table D-4: Metropolitan/Micropolitan Statistical Areas—Household Relationship, Grandparents, and Marital Status—*Continued*

	Total Householders 65 Years and Over	Family Householders 65 Years and Over	Non-Family Householders 65 Years and Over		Persons 65 Years and Over Living in Group Quarters	Grandparents 60 Years and Over Living with Grandchildren			Marital Status - Persons 60 Years and Over		
			Male Living Alone	Female Living Alone		Total	Responsible for Grandchildren	Responsible for Grandchildren and In Poverty	Now Married	Widowed	Divorced
Sioux Falls, SD Metro Area	18,872	9,487	2,867	6,110	1,618	1,487	401	0	24,735	9,204	4,955
Somerset, PA Micro Area	9,658	5,106	1,316	3,077	901	473	236	62	na	na	na
South Bend-Mishawaka, IN-MI Metro Area	30,275	16,091	4,269	9,008	1,175	2,123	952	149	39,318	13,204	10,959
Spartanburg, SC Metro Area	31,274	18,087	3,657	8,832	1,464	4,131	1,382	450	40,758	15,073	7,793
Spokane-Spokane Valley, WA Metro Area	52,153	27,962	6,512	16,300	2,230	3,873	1,346	336	70,610	19,839	19,561
Springfield, IL Metro Area	21,883	10,722	3,232	7,297	1,467	806	598	190	27,257	9,233	7,486
Springfield, MA Metro Area	60,219	29,628	8,536	20,484	4,201	5,291	1,665	512	71,280	27,186	20,100
Springfield, MO Metro Area	44,305	24,393	4,758	14,391	2,283	2,759	1,582	327	57,464	18,281	13,800
Springfield, OH Metro Area	15,290	8,408	1,810	4,849	1,428	714	355	159	na	na	na
St. Cloud, MN Metro Area	15,334	8,839	1,851	4,346	1,778	590	202	na	21,521	6,572	3,263
St. George, UT Metro Area	17,020	12,223	1,381	3,379	343	na	na	na	na	na	na
St. Joseph, MO-KS Metro Area	12,920	6,041	1,709	4,904	953	826	709	116	na	na	na
St. Louis, MO-IL Metro Area	265,178	142,672	32,855	83,380	16,755	25,853	8,092	1,225	330,966	124,374	85,462
State College, PA Metro Area	12,199	7,128	1,533	3,339	733	na	na	na	na	na	na
Statesboro, GA Micro Area	4,989	2,756	866	1,281	312	na	na	na	na	na	na
Staunton-Waynesboro, VA Metro Area	14,271	8,550	1,582	3,684	684	1,141	524	na	na	na	na
Stevens Point, WI Micro Area	6,738	3,749	727	2,103	268	na	na	na	na	na	na
Stillwater, OK Micro Area	5,632	3,018	634	1,923	132	na	na	na	na	na	na
Stockton-Lodi, CA Metro Area	44,199	24,265	5,365	12,241	3,545	13,581	2,463	376	62,894	25,104	18,580
Sumter, SC Metro Area	9,981	5,812	1,255	2,822	529	1,528	880	81	na	na	na
Sunbury, PA Micro Area	11,777	6,272	1,372	3,420	977	550	212	38	na	na	na
Syracuse, NY Metro Area	62,523	31,392	9,109	20,273	3,885	5,369	1,755	453	79,178	29,137	19,473
Talladega-Sylacauga, AL Micro Area	9,339	5,443	1,237	2,659	545	1,100	504	207	na	na	na
Tallahassee, FL Metro Area	30,156	15,883	3,170	10,470	1,446	3,209	1,507	316	36,033	13,559	14,160
Tampa-St. Petersburg-Clearwater, FL Metro Area	332,612	170,819	47,393	100,055	12,810	31,446	9,125	2,014	393,396	152,114	123,401
Terre Haute, IN Metro Area	16,481	8,750	2,264	4,931	1,438	1,905	518	28	21,048	7,350	6,144
Texarkana, TX-AR Metro Area	14,570	8,270	1,932	4,333	1,019	1,351	517	31	18,754	7,125	3,766
The Villages, FL Metro Area	34,307	23,684	2,627	5,404	632	912	572	na	na	na	na
Toledo, OH Metro Area	56,992	28,271	8,196	19,147	3,737	4,592	1,529	200	69,386	26,547	20,775
Topeka, KS Metro Area	24,175	13,544	2,215	7,966	1,613	2,425	1,168	230	31,959	10,377	7,074
Torrington, CT Micro Area	20,304	10,897	2,703	6,099	1,318	1,618	187	na	na	na	na
Traverse City, MI Micro Area	18,300	10,219	2,628	4,955	778	1,146	341	0	na	na	na
Trenton, NJ Metro Area	30,427	17,017	3,413	9,169	1,924	3,813	1,102	216	40,494	14,784	9,554
Truckee-Grass Valley, CA Micro Area	13,350	8,385	1,253	3,230	433	na	na	na	na	na	na
Tucson, AZ Metro Area	112,162	59,877	15,429	32,479	4,113	10,208	3,008	556	135,145	41,777	42,406
Tullahoma-Manchester, TN Micro Area	12,022	7,006	1,370	3,646	397	1,400	573	na	na	na	na
Tulsa, OK Metro Area	85,626	47,318	10,461	26,041	4,186	10,213	4,149	579	112,648	37,365	33,139
Tupelo, MS Micro Area	12,350	6,640	1,029	4,496	914	1,414	549	72	na	na	na
Tuscaloosa, AL Metro Area	18,044	9,880	2,014	6,018	1,041	2,647	1,330	309	23,170	10,707	6,663
Twin Falls, ID Micro Area	9,351	5,128	1,309	2,779	324	980	313	na	na	na	na
Tyler, TX Metro Area	20,300	11,927	2,592	5,755	1,053	3,105	1,275	358	28,348	9,328	6,876
Ukiah, CA Micro Area	10,713	5,383	1,287	3,567	518	1,826	639	9	na	na	na
Urban Honolulu, HI Metro Area	83,122	52,576	9,502	18,403	6,019	26,686	4,632	276	112,758	45,124	26,851
Utica-Rome, NY Metro Area	31,917	16,817	4,618	9,873	3,849	1,788	559	196	40,112	15,021	9,793
Valdosta, GA Metro Area	11,392	6,094	1,322	3,777	236	2,098	1,249	183	na	na	na
Vallejo-Fairfield, CA Metro Area	33,203	19,020	4,595	8,535	965	8,719	2,261	105	50,308	14,436	14,797
Victoria, TX Metro Area	9,079	5,538	878	2,515	539	na	na	na	na	na	na
Vineland-Bridgeton, NJ Metro Area	13,024	7,241	1,758	3,553	1,149	1,780	826	174	14,418	6,359	4,518
Virginia Beach-Norfolk-Newport News, VA-NC Metro Area	139,331	77,611	18,234	40,467	5,004	18,190	6,255	856	180,052	65,609	46,525
Visalia-Porterville, CA Metro Area	25,327	16,631	2,035	5,824	1,715	7,189	1,792	637	40,151	14,533	7,764
Waco, TX Metro Area	22,603	12,635	2,884	6,471	1,467	1,754	578	156	26,028	9,811	9,352
Walla Walla, WA Metro Area	na	na	na	na	na	na	na	na	na	na	na
Warner Robins, GA Metro Area	13,927	8,634	1,650	3,486	554	2,727	1,173	320	na	na	na
Warsaw, IN Micro Area	7,172	4,332	828	1,937	234	na	na	na	na	na	na
Washington-Arlington-Alexandria, DC-VA-MD-WV Metro Area	402,152	222,525	48,262	118,124	18,683	82,861	16,696	1,512	566,258	179,221	138,411
Waterloo-Cedar Falls, IA Metro Area	17,443	8,492	2,576	6,118	1,058	982	509	0	22,136	7,671	4,192
Watertown-Fort Atkinson, WI Micro Area	7,994	4,101	1,233	2,534	307	na	na	na	na	na	na
Watertown-Fort Drum, NY Metro Area	8,616	4,581	769	2,819	486	1,090	465	na	12,113	4,349	2,572
Wausau, WI Metro Area	13,355	7,577	1,650	4,004	762	na	na	na	na	na	na
Weirton-Steubenville, WV-OH Metro Area	15,436	8,327	1,761	5,028	1,007	972	375	130	na	na	na
Wenatchee, WA Metro Area	11,579	6,465	1,899	2,765	459	na	na	na	na	na	na
Wheeling, WV-OH Metro Area	17,770	9,527	1,894	5,960	1,313	843	548	na	22,884	7,829	5,358
Whitewater-Elkhorn, WI Micro Area	9,925	4,963	1,533	3,261	623	546	62	na	na	na	na
Wichita Falls, TX Metro Area	14,242	7,208	2,173	4,784	1,270	1,334	915	273	16,048	6,905	5,770
Wichita, KS Metro Area	54,312	29,006	8,396	15,957	3,530	6,542	1,879	315	74,844	24,536	17,626
Williamsport, PA Metro Area	12,944	6,642	1,841	4,128	943	685	328	na	16,673	6,374	4,251
Wilmington, NC Metro Area	26,961	15,481	2,882	7,758	1,306	1,621	398	63	37,601	10,347	8,952
Wilson, NC Micro Area	8,299	4,561	993	2,492	746	690	302	193	na	na	na
Winchester, VA-WV Metro Area	13,121	7,113	2,302	3,408	287	1,722	523	67	na	na	na
Winston-Salem, NC Metro Area	66,793	36,004	8,381	21,367	2,923	6,100	1,913	115	82,311	30,400	20,928
Wisconsin Rapids-Marshfield, WI Micro Area	9,251	4,585	1,024	3,412	203	na	na	na	na	na	na
Wooster, OH Micro Area	10,626	6,472	1,285	2,752	979	na	na	43	na	na	na

Table D-4: Metropolitan/Micropolitan Statistical Areas—Household Relationship, Grandparents, and Marital Status—*Continued*

	Total Householders 65 Years and Over	Family Householders 65 Years and Over	Non-Family Householders 65 Years and Over		Persons 65 Years and Over Living in Group Quarters	Grandparents 60 Years and Over Living with Grandchildren			Marital Status - Persons 60 Years and Over		
			Male Living Alone	Female Living Alone		Total	Responsible for Grandchildren	Responsible for Grandchildren and In Poverty	Now Married	Widowed	Divorced
Worcester, MA-CT Metro Area	78,939	42,167	10,475	24,608	7,121	9,473	2,397	532	106,668	35,842	24,999
Yakima, WA Metro Area	18,654	10,420	2,288	5,598	1,469	2,983	927	0	25,683	8,006	6,269
York-Hanover, PA Metro Area..............................	41,712	24,027	5,073	11,357	2,099	4,051	719	132	63,603	17,887	10,922
Youngstown-Warren-Boardman, OH-PA Metro Area	68,851	34,918	10,394	21,788	4,921	5,120	1,577	105	81,486	33,899	21,674
Yuba City, CA Metro Area	13,359	7,432	1,507	4,004	381	3,711	519	54	17,236	5,980	5,450
Yuma, AZ Metro Area	22,044	13,460	3,095	4,694	275	3,347	1,633	715	30,295	7,858	4,150
Zanesville, OH Micro Area	9,403	4,828	1,555	2,769	344	na	na	na	na	na	na

Table D-5: 114th Congressional Districts—Household Relationship, Grandparents, and Marital Status

	Total Householders 65 Years and Over	Family Householders 65 Years and Over	Non-Family Householders 65 Years and Over		Persons 65 Years and Over Living in Group Quarters	Grandparents 60 Years and Over Living with Grandchildren			Marital Status - Persons 60 Years and Over		
			Male Living Alone	Female Living Alone		Total	Responsible for Grandchildren	Responsible for Grandchildren and In Poverty	Now Married	Widowed	Divorced
Alabama											
Congressional District 1	71,277	39,982	8,277	21,323	2,366	6,601	3,383	411	91,096	34,439	22,318
Congressional District 2	67,200	35,749	9,553	20,527	3,495	6,638	2,936	474	77,063	34,562	22,622
Congressional District 3	67,169	38,132	8,081	20,187	3,058	7,896	4,372	943	85,968	33,802	21,528
Congressional District 4	73,422	40,217	9,395	22,908	4,020	6,989	3,588	1,009	94,158	36,576	21,321
Congressional District 5	66,956	36,906	9,832	19,549	3,006	6,190	2,199	339	87,196	32,707	21,117
Congressional District 6	66,627	38,796	7,863	19,235	2,595	7,159	3,406	576	91,004	31,469	18,416
Congressional District 7	60,017	32,954	8,115	18,281	3,720	9,416	4,937	1,368	60,026	34,911	23,638
Alaska											
Congressional District (at Large)	40,996	22,734	7,032	9,182	2,229	7,814	2,505	208	62,030	16,406	19,943
Arizona											
Congressional District 1	75,218	46,874	9,823	16,209	1,268	11,264	5,521	1,016	103,956	25,744	21,748
Congressional District 2	89,098	46,314	12,443	27,363	3,805	6,160	2,138	551	105,257	34,280	34,514
Congressional District 3	46,538	26,370	6,207	11,903	1,157	11,429	3,158	1,204	62,528	21,298	18,695
Congressional District 4	113,071	69,063	15,692	24,294	2,412	9,134	2,594	876	151,798	44,146	37,770
Congressional District 5	70,872	41,310	7,269	20,564	1,513	7,273	1,543	465	96,028	29,482	22,013
Congressional District 6	76,013	42,577	9,569	21,166	2,095	7,182	2,027	349	99,262	28,130	30,620
Congressional District 7	30,263	15,094	5,695	7,986	939	9,950	2,397	989	35,362	14,592	19,306
Congressional District 8	94,086	53,386	11,478	26,451	3,093	9,397	2,533	261	128,437	38,165	26,202
Congressional District 9	52,453	26,187	9,574	14,889	2,118	5,348	1,261	223	60,033	24,463	24,719
Arkansas											
Congressional District 1	79,867	43,032	11,131	24,096	5,538	7,919	4,856	810	98,820	40,104	22,410
Congressional District 2	65,456	37,413	7,618	19,137	3,628	6,445	2,624	222	86,760	30,530	22,405
Congressional District 3	65,607	35,812	8,037	20,463	3,548	6,097	2,101	450	87,421	29,960	17,997
Congressional District 4	78,872	44,680	11,418	21,506	4,656	8,237	4,128	636	102,170	36,761	22,847
California											
Congressional District 1	84,018	45,609	12,098	23,105	3,430	6,499	3,069	475	114,936	35,290	32,053
Congressional District 2	81,683	39,914	11,944	25,671	3,120	6,477	1,932	15	99,260	29,143	36,540
Congressional District 3	55,847	29,931	7,818	16,336	1,645	11,331	2,147	119	77,018	24,758	23,908
Congressional District 4	84,023	47,442	11,738	21,611	1,641	8,367	2,353	225	119,895	32,727	26,476
Congressional District 5	69,937	37,262	8,292	21,446	2,958	13,631	2,702	40	91,313	29,563	29,125
Congressional District 6	50,970	26,340	6,389	15,910	2,594	9,897	2,240	254	59,513	26,685	21,222
Congressional District 7	59,781	34,381	6,241	17,773	3,133	13,075	2,915	188	83,205	26,425	26,757
Congressional District 8	54,549	32,170	8,609	12,061	1,015	9,218	2,494	553	75,343	26,130	22,249
Congressional District 9	47,782	28,149	5,049	12,164	2,951	14,396	2,843	354	72,103	24,861	19,076
Congressional District 10	47,092	26,577	5,958	12,919	3,106	12,452	2,635	279	66,906	23,612	18,251
Congressional District 11	66,857	36,611	8,231	19,590	2,664	10,096	2,114	203	88,487	26,357	26,107
Congressional District 12	65,252	29,708	12,550	19,894	2,931	10,615	1,336	298	66,445	27,617	21,251
Congressional District 13	59,551	28,900	9,053	18,875	2,241	12,364	1,909	139	66,249	26,111	25,680
Congressional District 14	59,497	33,658	7,785	15,831	2,519	12,555	3,248	243	83,162	30,643	21,703
Congressional District 15	49,013	29,273	5,466	12,478	2,768	15,738	2,084	73	77,106	26,813	17,082
Congressional District 16	40,628	21,973	6,627	9,737	2,161	12,891	2,905	674	53,836	19,384	17,977
Congressional District 17	43,857	26,458	4,260	11,462	2,474	16,644	2,928	229	69,079	23,498	14,610
Congressional District 18	61,855	34,607	6,592	17,311	3,137	7,324	377	0	87,123	24,624	20,898
Congressional District 19	44,725	26,241	5,895	11,344	1,908	15,625	1,868	172	67,969	22,861	19,326
Congressional District 20	52,030	28,201	6,843	14,621	2,454	11,451	2,396	63	70,692	23,947	20,078
Congressional District 21	30,001	19,160	3,358	6,529	1,694	11,109	2,553	761	48,629	14,808	9,831
Congressional District 22	48,857	28,745	5,175	13,563	1,706	11,834	2,741	520	74,043	23,335	15,929
Congressional District 23	50,468	28,171	6,529	13,656	2,667	10,671	3,507	1,081	68,998	24,815	21,586
Congressional District 24	67,270	35,547	9,773	19,170	3,163	9,161	1,653	39	86,942	28,701	25,403
Congressional District 25	40,984	24,594	4,719	10,095	527	14,577	2,353	34	62,593	20,058	18,089
Congressional District 26	58,450	33,859	6,146	16,054	1,845	10,307	1,679	114	81,978	23,901	21,569
Congressional District 27	60,320	34,743	7,561	15,678	3,376	17,687	2,985	244	84,412	32,125	20,515
Congressional District 28	58,539	29,447	7,620	18,267	3,101	7,161	1,518	479	71,034	28,884	19,769
Congressional District 29	35,620	20,733	4,091	9,538	2,629	14,479	2,206	312	50,945	20,020	13,588
Congressional District 30	63,729	33,359	8,946	18,823	3,267	9,678	2,009	43	81,253	33,691	21,886
Congressional District 31	36,874	21,062	3,591	10,580	2,833	14,528	2,841	519	56,400	17,470	18,663
Congressional District 32	45,765	29,299	4,447	10,801	2,374	19,474	5,436	869	72,654	28,261	17,580
Congressional District 33	75,283	38,070	10,992	22,970	1,818	5,677	997	132	89,923	25,131	25,577
Congressional District 34	43,055	21,191	7,470	12,544	2,716	11,905	1,352	412	51,884	23,272	13,869
Congressional District 35	27,614	17,170	3,374	6,182	2,695	16,862	1,877	669	45,404	18,932	12,446
Congressional District 36	90,719	45,441	15,313	24,854	2,291	9,522	2,935	953	103,862	38,580	30,504
Congressional District 37	56,344	25,587	8,864	19,125	1,915	8,741	2,169	224	52,236	25,429	24,339
Congressional District 38	51,026	32,867	4,433	12,289	2,342	19,070	4,313	420	76,062	29,006	14,144
Congressional District 39	51,356	33,665	3,911	11,793	1,700	14,666	2,283	421	85,488	25,114	13,750
Congressional District 40	26,284	16,690	2,692	5,667	1,279	14,314	2,290	211	40,314	18,663	9,741
Congressional District 41	32,241	20,803	2,660	7,556	2,532	17,051	2,126	313	53,383	21,318	16,281
Congressional District 42	44,085	27,336	4,483	10,148	896	13,911	2,660	239	73,289	22,502	16,789
Congressional District 43	47,677	27,692	6,256	12,567	2,315	11,518	2,460	880	57,755	23,142	18,265
Congressional District 44	32,690	19,770	3,762	7,670	1,838	17,495	1,971	212	44,877	17,955	14,213
Congressional District 45	58,224	33,381	4,365	18,117	2,053	9,463	1,130	0	84,130	25,609	20,494
Congressional District 46	30,943	18,458	3,826	7,693	3,971	14,776	1,169	290	47,649	18,809	14,648
Congressional District 47	49,151	26,467	6,863	13,488	2,843	12,526	2,121	106	61,489	24,865	22,767
Congressional District 48	70,006	39,381	8,898	18,347	1,581	8,332	1,430	255	92,028	27,211	25,002
Congressional District 49	62,730	36,102	7,228	17,925	1,581	8,137	1,578	225	87,032	26,423	19,189
Congressional District 50	58,738	35,497	7,181	14,328	2,193	10,803	2,382	172	84,406	28,563	24,339

Table D-5: 114th Congressional Districts—Household Relationship, Grandparents, and Marital Status—*Continued*

	Total Householders 65 Years and Over	Family Householders 65 Years and Over	Non-Family Householders 65 Years and Over		Persons 65 Years and Over Living in Group Quarters	Grandparents 60 Years and Over Living with Grandchildren			Marital Status - Persons 60 Years and Over		
			Male Living Alone	Female Living Alone		Total	Responsible for Grandchildren	Responsible for Grandchildren and In Poverty	Now Married	Widowed	Divorced
California—Cont.											
Congressional District 51	39,205	22,442	4,635	10,616	1,303	14,801	3,126	1,083	53,057	24,518	17,940
Congressional District 52	55,711	29,943	6,966	16,975	1,768	8,563	1,549	409	77,464	24,404	23,885
Congressional District 53	51,442	28,905	5,800	14,778	2,892	14,408	2,366	333	69,705	26,295	22,602
Colorado											
Congressional District 1	56,915	25,721	9,842	19,885	2,503	5,743	1,503	457	64,038	20,576	29,027
Congressional District 2	61,254	34,571	7,877	17,720	1,900	4,086	530	64	99,124	17,801	23,900
Congressional District 3	71,846	41,178	10,308	18,448	3,390	4,582	2,467	472	102,838	26,505	28,151
Congressional District 4	58,798	34,567	7,115	15,851	2,342	7,062	2,154	194	85,778	24,803	21,045
Congressional District 5	58,669	34,511	8,626	14,417	1,870	6,236	2,096	266	91,064	19,201	23,000
Congressional District 6	50,915	28,631	5,719	15,091	2,025	7,078	2,000	47	74,011	18,528	23,211
Congressional District 7	60,232	33,432	7,981	17,231	2,469	8,253	2,163	249	80,810	26,216	27,102
Connecticut											
Congressional District 1	71,138	34,689	9,019	25,829	5,570	6,922	2,031	580	82,376	32,739	23,549
Congressional District 2	67,409	39,133	7,634	18,846	4,834	5,879	1,344	0	98,727	26,330	21,946
Congressional District 3	69,849	33,725	9,348	25,277	4,931	7,302	1,585	37	82,826	32,545	25,372
Congressional District 4	63,660	35,156	7,507	19,241	3,896	7,265	1,432	434	81,614	26,700	22,597
Congressional District 5	67,602	33,271	10,201	22,132	5,807	5,736	848	42	86,354	30,429	21,270
Delaware											
Congressional District (at Large)	92,377	53,529	12,387	23,984	4,382	10,804	3,588	495	122,223	39,773	29,737
District of Columbia											
Delegate District (at Large)	50,463	20,372	9,095	19,242	3,745	5,033	1,808	335	38,382	21,217	20,667
Florida											
Congressional District 1	73,410	42,892	10,153	18,697	3,330	6,013	3,136	269	91,368	36,810	21,027
Congressional District 2	64,479	35,958	7,393	19,911	4,098	7,599	3,766	757	81,554	30,305	25,348
Congressional District 3	72,526	40,029	10,687	18,840	4,225	6,295	3,477	408	91,894	34,726	26,199
Congressional District 4	62,922	33,456	8,587	19,294	2,978	8,616	3,092	347	79,909	30,721	23,679
Congressional District 5	52,304	26,882	7,527	16,194	2,252	9,374	4,342	1,053	56,167	28,277	27,799
Congressional District 6	102,474	59,951	12,877	25,839	3,014	8,476	1,728	406	138,367	46,431	31,514
Congressional District 7	58,004	31,161	7,336	17,971	3,419	7,751	1,569	344	78,725	30,547	25,937
Congressional District 8	103,216	58,911	13,118	26,954	2,476	8,072	2,350	1,006	127,634	43,276	38,536
Congressional District 9	44,691	28,727	3,565	10,996	1,811	12,787	1,858	409	69,919	22,847	18,820
Congressional District 10	80,880	50,587	8,937	18,942	1,851	10,283	2,146	462	117,345	34,216	24,085
Congressional District 11	142,838	86,047	18,081	31,888	3,176	8,333	2,296	348	190,202	55,439	37,507
Congressional District 12	92,508	50,392	11,372	27,077	3,296	8,165	2,009	353	118,177	41,044	32,708
Congressional District 13	107,006	48,158	18,063	35,594	5,102	5,783	1,808	150	109,600	51,613	38,345
Congressional District 14	57,456	29,267	8,191	17,917	2,458	8,675	2,926	1,245	63,571	27,625	28,520
Congressional District 15	62,657	38,163	6,632	16,302	2,320	9,706	2,612	207	87,273	27,742	20,533
Congressional District 16	136,033	77,369	15,313	37,062	3,539	6,771	3,621	205	176,210	52,458	33,327
Congressional District 17	114,554	66,309	14,342	29,463	3,322	8,910	2,403	361	146,256	52,064	30,065
Congressional District 18	110,320	58,111	15,986	31,930	1,851	7,212	1,592	110	130,378	47,754	35,389
Congressional District 19	128,026	75,560	13,966	34,058	2,553	7,095	1,757	567	175,235	51,407	33,620
Congressional District 20	59,018	29,968	9,021	17,078	3,701	14,862	2,772	335	63,953	35,053	25,699
Congressional District 21	103,633	52,719	12,782	33,804	1,249	9,572	1,556	409	118,694	49,315	30,397
Congressional District 22	100,876	43,785	17,907	34,717	3,471	8,604	1,211	182	100,962	42,390	38,960
Congressional District 23	71,549	33,195	11,223	24,316	1,349	8,706	1,338	347	77,517	34,237	32,394
Congressional District 24	48,511	25,640	7,014	14,022	2,603	16,894	3,406	827	50,701	28,537	26,186
Congressional District 25	57,967	36,070	6,083	13,658	1,153	17,753	3,766	555	85,644	30,488	20,752
Congressional District 26	54,237	34,508	5,853	11,932	1,710	23,621	1,796	162	87,778	31,911	27,197
Congressional District 27	61,643	34,304	8,163	16,878	2,490	14,255	1,060	285	77,867	35,216	28,526
Georgia											
Congressional District 1	57,508	31,133	7,430	17,387	2,971	7,826	3,507	528	75,032	28,062	21,362
Congressional District 2	60,723	32,317	7,426	19,915	3,589	7,247	3,068	1,022	65,740	34,104	21,379
Congressional District 3	60,882	35,421	6,061	17,959	2,429	8,300	3,180	502	82,858	29,400	20,691
Congressional District 4	43,299	24,482	4,979	12,860	1,772	9,155	3,199	240	61,587	20,689	19,472
Congressional District 5	50,505	21,083	9,093	19,054	3,400	7,429	3,656	927	41,785	30,243	24,887
Congressional District 6	46,602	26,192	5,448	13,756	1,166	6,412	777	194	72,661	20,837	16,157
Congressional District 7	34,875	22,758	2,603	9,127	1,293	13,932	2,648	0	62,345	17,815	15,199
Congressional District 8	62,890	36,683	8,527	16,937	3,188	9,065	4,427	1,307	81,333	31,306	16,876
Congressional District 9	74,286	44,306	9,224	18,957	2,200	9,142	3,687	714	104,583	33,362	19,677
Congressional District 10	57,195	34,499	6,434	14,758	2,222	9,465	2,981	986	80,465	28,245	22,450
Congressional District 11	47,502	28,220	5,321	12,322	1,535	6,924	2,460	125	77,084	18,660	15,266
Congressional District 12	56,063	30,393	8,575	15,806	4,039	9,119	3,317	278	69,399	32,709	20,886
Congressional District 13	40,043	23,025	5,602	10,736	1,284	9,667	3,323	632	57,234	21,579	18,592
Congressional District 14	58,081	34,577	6,491	15,670	2,593	8,416	3,073	326	80,460	27,708	17,382
Hawaii											
Congressional District 1	63,780	39,060	7,946	14,928	4,937	19,567	2,988	276	86,144	34,498	19,653
Congressional District 2	58,964	36,467	6,404	11,944	2,855	17,334	4,580	221	83,253	30,735	22,210
Idaho											
Congressional District 1	77,362	44,779	10,811	19,887	2,125	7,439	4,186	534	116,107	30,626	27,304
Congressional District 2	66,862	37,008	8,490	20,212	1,801	5,608	1,603	493	96,129	24,988	21,662

Table D-5: 114th Congressional Districts—Household Relationship, Grandparents, and Marital Status—*Continued*

	Total Householders 65 Years and Over	Family Householders 65 Years and Over	Non-Family Householders 65 Years and Over		Persons 65 Years and Over Living in Group Quarters	Grandparents 60 Years and Over Living with Grandchildren			Marital Status - Persons 60 Years and Over		
			Male Living Alone	Female Living Alone		Total	Responsible for Grandchildren	Responsible for Grandchildren and In Poverty	Now Married	Widowed	Divorced
Illinois											
Congressional District 1	68,981	35,689	8,867	23,157	2,697	10,912	3,539	372	67,631	36,942	25,247
Congressional District 2	61,057	33,003	8,733	18,291	3,724	9,605	3,473	560	69,129	32,062	21,385
Congressional District 3	59,770	31,736	8,136	18,366	2,810	9,374	1,680	323	75,349	32,810	16,671
Congressional District 4	34,683	17,968	5,070	10,267	1,222	11,100	1,926	387	47,905	19,836	10,421
Congressional District 5	53,721	26,950	8,205	17,243	3,120	4,612	528	0	61,085	23,698	15,580
Congressional District 6	60,986	35,757	6,545	17,892	3,616	7,577	1,141	0	96,590	23,940	16,982
Congressional District 7	56,109	25,968	9,864	18,739	2,055	8,124	2,435	820	49,325	28,049	18,637
Congressional District 8	49,012	26,869	5,299	16,068	2,341	10,077	1,541	273	74,446	26,297	15,452
Congressional District 9	68,205	31,323	8,680	26,602	6,888	7,643	1,055	189	83,773	32,366	20,233
Congressional District 10	54,782	29,892	6,875	16,782	4,598	8,661	2,193	298	81,102	26,327	15,166
Congressional District 11	40,276	23,288	4,535	11,612	2,664	7,727	1,835	351	65,792	18,758	12,905
Congressional District 12	70,647	36,111	11,184	21,870	4,665	6,261	2,369	521	79,576	35,147	21,894
Congressional District 13	69,702	35,472	9,884	22,887	5,390	4,517	1,791	420	84,288	29,192	23,549
Congressional District 14	54,959	31,469	5,380	16,890	1,513	5,842	1,283	0	85,163	21,899	15,301
Congressional District 15	76,931	40,169	11,602	24,006	5,936	4,214	2,272	342	97,262	37,028	21,920
Congressional District 16	72,216	38,465	11,005	21,395	5,498	5,036	1,596	303	95,473	34,013	19,502
Congressional District 17	78,897	39,533	11,706	26,125	5,004	4,067	2,042	589	95,868	35,240	25,083
Congressional District 18	74,612	39,984	9,185	23,719	6,266	3,530	1,334	185	102,624	34,743	19,633
Indiana											
Congressional District 1	63,780	36,193	7,463	18,361	3,672	6,997	2,124	291	85,999	31,070	20,371
Congressional District 2	66,436	35,197	9,226	20,788	3,713	5,153	2,153	382	88,464	30,699	22,423
Congressional District 3	65,510	36,442	8,173	19,596	4,647	4,714	1,567	505	90,706	30,243	17,285
Congressional District 4	65,949	36,474	7,810	19,916	3,810	4,846	2,050	24	89,105	29,951	21,359
Congressional District 5	63,514	35,184	9,231	18,197	4,109	5,050	1,674	57	85,448	25,208	21,850
Congressional District 6	73,490	42,166	7,723	22,002	5,184	5,978	1,857	284	97,122	32,773	21,164
Congressional District 7	49,583	23,558	7,848	16,502	2,628	5,365	2,295	188	54,570	24,232	25,208
Congressional District 8	72,470	38,525	9,193	23,085	6,057	5,702	1,958	235	94,582	34,569	22,910
Congressional District 9	64,961	37,176	7,240	19,362	4,620	5,824	2,722	335	92,309	29,114	22,350
Iowa											
Congressional District 1	80,762	42,468	10,942	25,933	7,214	3,849	1,328	41	108,708	35,014	18,553
Congressional District 2	77,746	40,744	9,980	25,426	5,360	3,503	1,085	130	103,855	35,213	21,754
Congressional District 3	69,055	34,567	10,043	23,031	4,855	4,948	1,392	149	90,339	31,355	20,437
Congressional District 4	83,166	42,889	10,822	28,259	8,368	2,634	763	147	112,467	38,114	18,083
Kansas											
Congressional District 1	68,107	35,721	9,307	21,618	6,700	4,424	1,834	282	89,890	33,071	19,314
Congressional District 2	69,590	37,657	8,876	21,968	5,222	6,091	2,968	573	92,499	30,395	21,563
Congressional District 3	58,168	31,187	6,708	19,186	3,380	5,984	2,318	257	81,759	23,663	21,467
Congressional District 4	64,496	34,093	9,978	19,317	4,532	7,035	2,174	425	86,642	29,340	20,441
Kentucky											
Congressional District 1	77,242	41,311	9,914	24,108	4,609	5,890	3,271	457	99,767	36,976	21,402
Congressional District 2	67,302	38,496	8,538	19,284	3,781	6,317	1,970	224	89,393	32,263	19,411
Congressional District 3	70,239	34,440	9,191	24,677	4,000	6,719	2,711	293	77,306	32,114	28,650
Congressional District 4	62,197	34,681	8,793	17,321	3,576	8,765	3,713	223	86,506	29,809	23,088
Congressional District 5	74,642	40,278	10,409	22,938	3,988	9,013	5,169	2,320	91,473	41,242	19,439
Congressional District 6	62,195	34,199	7,365	18,717	3,033	5,074	2,309	563	82,852	28,054	23,259
Louisiana											
Congressional District 1	68,554	39,706	8,380	18,830	2,654	8,605	2,386	550	97,261	30,842	23,764
Congressional District 2	62,129	32,944	9,094	18,908	2,648	8,719	2,839	638	62,695	35,833	23,658
Congressional District 3	64,299	35,308	8,853	18,369	3,721	7,740	2,858	783	80,892	31,063	22,268
Congressional District 4	68,931	35,250	10,310	21,203	4,942	9,659	4,810	1,121	84,743	37,663	21,467
Congressional District 5	71,150	37,167	9,594	23,108	5,846	8,194	4,163	1,411	82,124	38,538	22,453
Congressional District 6	60,103	35,374	7,271	16,518	1,877	7,842	3,444	766	87,370	29,107	18,262
Maine											
Congressional District 1	75,384	39,588	9,844	23,132	3,538	4,500	1,213	312	99,613	27,781	28,718
Congressional District 2	75,897	37,532	11,694	23,968	3,730	5,301	1,699	514	97,274	34,318	26,683
Maryland											
Congressional District 1	75,955	43,807	8,469	22,101	3,870	8,925	2,674	123	109,692	34,686	19,413
Congressional District 2	56,987	29,635	8,675	17,007	3,608	8,894	2,098	59	66,943	30,832	22,549
Congressional District 3	65,092	32,528	8,728	22,150	3,330	7,688	2,057	137	83,767	31,415	20,419
Congressional District 4	54,092	31,838	6,283	14,779	1,954	10,477	2,389	519	69,390	25,446	19,766
Congressional District 5	53,079	32,730	5,419	12,883	2,393	12,801	3,440	125	79,728	24,059	17,828
Congressional District 6	56,961	31,535	7,554	16,255	4,495	9,350	1,822	244	79,384	27,276	19,244
Congressional District 7	63,904	33,391	8,492	19,696	4,082	10,032	2,790	274	70,464	30,717	22,207
Congressional District 8	69,912	37,908	7,038	22,788	4,784	9,816	2,253	320	94,806	30,787	19,227
Massachusetts											
Congressional District 1	77,027	37,879	11,317	25,638	5,182	5,789	1,792	517	91,943	33,360	25,557
Congressional District 2	63,503	31,398	9,115	21,406	5,855	8,136	1,986	527	83,787	28,882	21,038
Congressional District 3	61,551	31,487	9,527	19,056	3,977	7,978	1,450	106	79,059	26,425	21,276
Congressional District 4	64,533	35,054	7,358	20,145	4,890	8,868	1,973	172	95,365	27,973	18,450
Congressional District 5	70,670	34,115	9,277	24,486	4,445	7,034	534	43	80,331	29,780	19,454
Congressional District 6	73,451	38,205	9,215	23,995	4,585	9,186	1,882	62	98,326	36,777	22,077
Congressional District 7	48,348	20,365	9,145	17,746	2,712	7,382	1,345	82	43,854	23,133	17,999
Congressional District 8	73,309	34,388	11,011	25,600	6,120	10,441	1,146	198	82,152	36,035	23,808
Congressional District 9	92,405	48,626	11,454	29,806	4,858	7,220	1,100	145	119,815	40,820	25,133

Table D-5: 114th Congressional Districts—Household Relationship, Grandparents, and Marital Status—*Continued*

	Total Householders 65 Years and Over	Family Householders 65 Years and Over	Non-Family Householders 65 Years and Over		Persons 65 Years and Over Living in Group Quarters	Grandparents 60 Years and Over Living with Grandchildren			Marital Status - Persons 60 Years and Over		
			Male Living Alone	Female Living Alone		Total	Responsible for Grandchildren	Responsible for Grandchildren and In Poverty	Now Married	Widowed	Divorced
Michigan											
Congressional District 1	92,775	49,537	14,134	26,720	5,439	4,068	1,323	55	123,756	38,146	29,124
Congressional District 2	64,455	37,093	7,356	18,811	3,503	5,707	1,685	129	90,907	27,359	18,142
Congressional District 3	61,839	34,380	7,896	18,004	4,320	6,009	1,652	284	85,676	26,944	17,437
Congressional District 4	75,303	43,282	10,010	20,587	4,454	4,557	1,486	372	108,570	30,954	20,220
Congressional District 5	75,937	42,329	9,575	22,251	3,554	6,458	1,906	298	91,782	33,085	24,677
Congressional District 6	68,168	39,375	8,043	18,975	3,197	5,535	2,366	247	97,293	27,959	21,488
Congressional District 7	70,855	38,536	7,956	21,992	3,812	4,771	2,087	236	98,437	31,881	20,721
Congressional District 8	58,139	32,700	7,327	17,182	2,445	5,510	2,053	42	87,231	23,807	18,640
Congressional District 9	75,302	35,792	10,550	26,941	3,616	5,817	1,693	757	82,436	35,883	27,035
Congressional District 10	71,246	41,888	8,810	19,483	3,431	6,055	1,185	319	105,575	29,539	20,719
Congressional District 11	64,684	33,145	8,420	22,181	2,727	6,399	1,233	72	90,603	29,577	20,180
Congressional District 12	60,740	31,259	8,687	19,709	2,496	7,201	1,871	110	72,485	27,344	22,440
Congressional District 13	59,444	28,717	9,479	19,699	2,716	6,859	1,773	321	48,889	32,031	26,403
Congressional District 14	70,289	34,835	10,482	23,124	3,189	8,064	2,208	289	66,696	33,210	30,632
Minnesota											
Congressional District 1	66,836	34,796	8,485	22,625	5,707	2,511	711	8	93,203	27,660	16,534
Congressional District 2	51,713	28,243	5,986	16,394	2,048	4,324	686	0	76,092	22,250	15,389
Congressional District 3	60,336	32,058	5,914	20,686	1,713	4,062	735	180	87,772	23,624	20,128
Congressional District 4	57,315	30,043	7,460	18,680	4,824	5,456	875	68	75,158	21,782	20,919
Congressional District 5	51,551	21,122	9,704	18,699	4,388	3,213	488	99	54,727	21,286	21,020
Congressional District 6	44,534	26,934	5,434	11,333	3,120	3,815	988	0	70,523	18,571	12,018
Congressional District 7	76,384	40,665	9,932	24,548	7,054	2,917	871	130	102,653	32,960	17,072
Congressional District 8	77,480	42,375	11,530	22,014	5,432	3,615	1,424	192	110,675	29,994	21,340
Mississippi											
Congressional District 1	70,107	40,665	7,610	21,216	2,754	8,629	4,913	611	91,040	33,180	20,302
Congressional District 2	63,779	32,887	9,844	20,382	3,550	9,956	5,081	1,310	67,973	36,636	16,763
Congressional District 3	72,252	38,005	10,312	22,934	4,463	7,961	3,795	1,156	85,574	40,185	21,345
Congressional District 4	67,010	38,982	8,560	18,412	3,114	10,087	3,737	1,551	85,183	32,789	23,106
Missouri											
Congressional District 1	60,997	29,178	9,817	20,252	4,028	8,214	2,676	582	61,883	30,812	27,368
Congressional District 2	83,030	46,464	7,143	27,671	6,805	5,861	1,908	98	109,740	36,711	22,546
Congressional District 3	67,252	39,041	7,873	18,627	3,043	6,468	2,205	218	99,837	29,464	20,267
Congressional District 4	71,976	39,242	9,952	20,504	4,798	6,575	2,571	459	99,168	30,340	22,674
Congressional District 5	70,105	33,225	11,049	24,001	4,260	5,726	1,987	212	74,408	31,827	29,509
Congressional District 6	71,255	39,395	9,172	21,785	6,073	6,248	2,789	371	99,738	31,202	19,602
Congressional District 7	78,366	43,632	9,905	23,226	4,046	7,076	3,097	794	101,067	33,662	27,345
Congressional District 8	81,998	44,173	11,034	25,357	6,645	6,608	3,474	1,059	108,912	40,817	23,026
Montana											
Congressional District (at Large)	106,654	55,588	18,282	30,946	5,434	6,578	3,266	441	144,259	44,960	35,607
Nebraska											
Congressional District 1	56,407	30,683	7,519	17,491	3,112	3,269	1,344	312	77,626	23,325	14,908
Congressional District 2	46,308	23,264	6,580	15,360	2,592	2,789	724	45	59,441	21,872	14,713
Congressional District 3	71,271	35,852	10,164	24,374	5,767	2,995	1,536	97	92,342	31,409	15,173
Nevada											
Congressional District 1	54,073	25,845	11,910	13,140	1,277	7,487	3,160	754	55,502	21,625	28,935
Congressional District 2	67,849	35,739	12,803	16,697	2,197	6,104	2,017	273	86,481	25,035	31,639
Congressional District 3	59,400	34,830	7,913	13,701	1,069	8,624	1,941	69	86,151	24,149	25,591
Congressional District 4	53,813	31,735	7,092	11,833	1,470	10,068	3,001	237	75,257	24,317	25,628
New Hampshire											
Congressional District 1	62,176	32,234	8,060	19,655	4,071	5,623	1,530	110	89,410	25,941	22,779
Congressional District 2	61,339	33,769	9,011	16,380	4,055	6,701	1,307	0	91,317	27,417	23,054
New Jersey											
Congressional District 1	68,271	36,334	9,284	21,404	3,584	10,277	3,132	233	82,308	34,997	20,265
Congressional District 2	75,481	40,436	10,224	22,220	4,653	10,661	3,803	407	94,966	35,884	23,185
Congressional District 3	82,952	45,960	10,455	24,308	3,939	8,261	2,030	164	107,812	35,147	21,456
Congressional District 4	82,620	41,605	9,988	28,514	3,814	8,139	1,320	82	99,880	41,535	22,072
Congressional District 5	65,224	40,071	6,845	16,782	5,661	9,657	944	165	101,502	31,720	16,432
Congressional District 6	54,830	31,044	6,871	16,156	2,980	10,773	1,958	102	73,507	31,064	15,456
Congressional District 7	62,766	33,297	7,496	20,970	4,314	8,398	1,074	44	94,478	30,956	16,203
Congressional District 8	44,930	21,102	7,704	14,546	2,848	8,695	1,261	365	49,156	24,721	16,436
Congressional District 9	59,278	32,062	5,724	19,838	1,202	10,842	2,224	266	78,871	31,627	16,365
Congressional District 10	54,385	24,503	9,050	18,244	2,728	11,586	3,099	552	51,004	28,347	19,346
Congressional District 11	71,126	40,180	8,060	21,113	6,041	10,320	1,056	100	99,357	35,155	19,562
Congressional District 12	61,336	34,216	6,598	19,320	3,801	9,951	1,669	290	86,525	29,820	18,815
New Mexico											
Congressional District 1	64,389	32,003	9,127	21,369	2,261	7,097	2,109	521	77,537	28,136	27,555
Congressional District 2	68,238	38,242	10,063	18,338	3,397	7,446	3,572	514	90,582	28,986	21,706
Congressional District 3	66,478	34,198	10,464	19,205	2,140	9,322	4,027	639	78,936	27,221	25,472
New York											
Congressional District 1	72,206	39,040	9,262	21,887	4,635	10,327	1,970	296	97,497	33,473	19,983

Table D-5: 114th Congressional Districts—Household Relationship, Grandparents, and Marital Status—*Continued*

	Total Householders 65 Years and Over	Family Householders 65 Years and Over	Non-Family Householders 65 Years and Over		Persons 65 Years and Over Living in Group Quarters	Grandparents 60 Years and Over Living with Grandchildren			Marital Status - Persons 60 Years and Over		
			Male Living Alone	Female Living Alone		Total	Responsible for Grandchildren	Responsible for Grandchildren and In Poverty	Now Married	Widowed	Divorced
New York—Cont.											
Congressional District 2	58,967	35,631	5,627	16,274	2,858	11,115	1,324	65	77,423	33,808	14,916
Congressional District 3	73,784	42,522	7,382	21,529	5,686	10,699	1,461	11	109,565	38,507	15,084
Congressional District 4	65,338	38,333	5,112	19,512	3,432	13,299	1,211	0	92,792	33,860	17,227
Congressional District 5	53,390	31,673	5,657	14,425	1,726	19,002	3,092	392	67,280	29,906	17,956
Congressional District 6	66,597	35,405	7,601	21,750	3,422	12,344	3,012	517	81,459	37,887	17,168
Congressional District 7	43,626	20,841	6,434	15,373	2,435	10,613	2,939	1,005	47,605	22,249	13,486
Congressional District 8	64,981	31,426	9,346	23,085	5,033	10,616	2,164	484	60,835	34,206	22,617
Congressional District 9	61,570	30,940	9,220	20,234	2,585	11,416	2,576	118	64,143	27,882	18,281
Congressional District 10	67,272	27,779	12,358	25,173	2,555	7,748	2,660	384	71,982	23,298	17,317
Congressional District 11	63,069	36,137	6,354	19,943	4,016	10,920	1,839	731	86,590	34,832	14,683
Congressional District 12	74,429	26,920	14,616	31,634	2,744	2,655	942	183	59,389	24,723	22,962
Congressional District 13	55,969	22,979	9,438	22,075	4,795	11,941	3,537	1,064	45,327	30,150	20,312
Congressional District 14	49,001	24,925	6,315	16,475	4,797	14,388	4,381	1,439	53,023	29,184	18,583
Congressional District 15	46,280	20,002	8,315	16,830	1,652	11,227	2,767	1,136	34,711	20,472	17,981
Congressional District 16	70,132	33,353	10,020	24,697	6,552	10,581	1,949	282	72,863	35,413	20,366
Congressional District 17	63,796	36,832	6,720	18,936	4,922	12,803	2,512	784	94,339	28,770	16,090
Congressional District 18	58,508	32,635	7,228	16,727	4,215	10,023	2,174	0	82,249	29,628	17,193
Congressional District 19	79,439	41,852	12,144	23,234	6,529	5,509	1,927	108	100,410	35,580	22,222
Congressional District 20	69,952	33,954	9,779	23,798	6,365	5,099	664	257	83,817	32,017	22,896
Congressional District 21	69,707	36,681	9,526	21,111	4,189	5,733	2,151	362	96,061	33,552	19,695
Congressional District 22	73,982	38,494	11,367	22,449	6,920	4,233	1,351	355	92,858	33,693	25,593
Congressional District 23	75,608	39,207	9,944	23,996	6,133	4,555	1,835	130	95,155	33,524	23,633
Congressional District 24	69,822	34,010	10,993	23,188	4,554	5,583	1,883	453	85,620	34,049	20,304
Congressional District 25	71,712	33,207	11,777	25,077	4,301	4,035	1,810	147	81,477	36,127	22,584
Congressional District 26	81,837	36,839	13,164	30,233	4,235	4,374	1,228	280	79,645	39,256	24,219
Congressional District 27	75,144	39,270	9,447	24,105	5,695	4,672	1,162	227	102,054	33,976	20,683
North Carolina											
Congressional District 1	74,055	35,588	10,964	25,774	5,626	8,335	3,884	1,657	78,048	41,370	24,574
Congressional District 2	64,947	36,222	8,457	19,210	3,268	9,428	3,025	764	83,367	30,674	18,385
Congressional District 3	69,395	40,052	8,948	19,030	2,232	7,050	2,625	693	90,795	30,157	20,877
Congressional District 4	53,434	28,356	6,516	17,655	2,735	5,287	2,043	466	64,311	24,868	19,488
Congressional District 5	77,817	41,778	9,022	25,615	3,401	5,969	2,710	239	102,316	33,467	23,557
Congressional District 6	77,737	42,461	10,085	23,676	4,123	5,999	2,616	243	104,729	37,140	23,307
Congressional District 7	82,751	48,408	9,455	23,051	3,358	7,917	2,451	406	116,670	34,584	23,817
Congressional District 8	71,074	40,569	9,058	20,174	3,650	10,431	4,503	1,026	88,769	37,067	18,836
Congressional District 9	56,843	31,803	6,563	17,854	1,631	5,591	1,416	217	87,850	24,423	19,078
Congressional District 10	78,257	44,024	10,566	21,620	4,792	8,927	4,874	1,724	99,721	40,455	23,190
Congressional District 11	94,233	52,615	10,882	28,512	3,539	7,237	2,748	954	127,071	40,465	27,318
Congressional District 12	48,212	24,008	7,318	15,799	3,102	5,563	1,917	533	48,122	24,734	21,810
Congressional District 13	59,341	35,506	5,488	17,609	2,298	6,153	2,033	687	92,891	27,701	17,006
North Dakota											
Congressional District (at Large)	67,092	33,093	10,188	22,905	6,114	2,910	919	52	89,978	30,375	15,600
Ohio											
Congressional District 1	62,140	31,587	9,204	19,803	4,064	5,495	1,833	376	74,472	31,035	22,676
Congressional District 2	72,544	37,407	9,753	24,232	4,875	5,015	2,042	567	89,966	31,893	25,224
Congressional District 3	46,478	21,426	6,922	16,822	2,181	7,842	2,472	532	50,405	21,625	23,416
Congressional District 4	76,550	40,736	9,885	24,068	4,429	6,421	2,266	400	93,277	36,788	22,321
Congressional District 5	73,459	38,797	9,074	24,121	5,005	5,545	2,308	234	99,066	33,948	20,565
Congressional District 6	79,648	42,911	11,135	23,990	6,275	6,227	2,803	383	105,517	39,623	23,773
Congressional District 7	77,403	42,605	9,702	22,761	5,710	6,306	2,430	174	104,405	35,575	23,546
Congressional District 8	68,145	38,094	9,313	19,498	4,786	5,121	1,987	464	92,145	31,575	20,888
Congressional District 9	69,370	31,043	11,990	24,454	4,046	5,032	1,733	367	68,476	32,747	26,282
Congressional District 10	75,909	38,157	11,685	24,483	5,027	6,212	3,242	671	89,154	33,449	25,677
Congressional District 11	71,354	32,082	12,637	25,340	5,763	6,716	2,979	928	63,483	34,866	30,762
Congressional District 12	63,629	33,364	9,059	19,306	3,067	5,142	1,786	67	87,357	27,852	21,086
Congressional District 13	81,590	39,285	12,502	27,567	4,701	5,138	1,747	227	89,593	39,537	30,417
Congressional District 14	81,678	45,492	9,375	24,797	4,881	7,124	2,029	560	109,924	37,317	20,575
Congressional District 15	64,398	36,248	8,911	17,871	3,385	6,073	1,893	332	91,446	29,415	18,489
Congressional District 16	78,663	44,564	9,425	23,479	5,712	5,231	1,476	43	109,485	32,397	24,189
Oklahoma											
Congressional District 1	65,940	35,815	7,348	21,227	2,606	6,788	2,412	93	85,995	28,342	25,184
Congressional District 2	84,298	46,303	12,494	24,010	5,685	11,602	6,165	1,492	104,965	39,376	25,935
Congressional District 3	71,857	41,103	9,023	20,852	4,853	7,643	3,127	1,246	96,851	34,449	21,267
Congressional District 4	64,333	36,409	7,977	18,822	3,868	7,788	4,061	420	87,888	31,875	20,309
Congressional District 5	64,577	34,262	8,969	10,757	3,291	5,975	3,329	429	79,254	29,810	25,305
Oregon											
Congressional District 1	65,156	34,254	8,396	20,346	2,089	7,114	1,526	18	87,578	25,755	28,290
Congressional District 2	91,423	48,732	12,585	26,080	4,167	7,039	2,225	528	123,158	35,372	38,639
Congressional District 3	62,500	31,142	9,213	19,770	3,456	8,759	2,192	219	77,675	24,212	30,071
Congressional District 4	93,134	49,599	14,400	24,654	2,850	8,324	3,282	523	121,484	36,961	38,254
Congressional District 5	80,551	43,502	10,312	24,148	2,978	6,714	1,488	161	106,821	34,077	30,548
Pennsylvania											
Congressional District 1	52,194	24,555	8,706	17,757	2,344	8,932	2,593	881	49,418	30,635	20,790

Table D-5: 114th Congressional Districts—Household Relationship, Grandparents, and Marital Status—*Continued*

	Total Householders 65 Years and Over	Family Householders 65 Years and Over	Non-Family Householders 65 Years and Over		Persons 65 Years and Over Living in Group Quarters	Grandparents 60 Years and Over Living with Grandchildren			Marital Status - Persons 60 Years and Over		
			Male Living Alone	Female Living Alone		Total	Responsible for Grandchildren	Responsible for Grandchildren and In Poverty	Now Married	Widowed	Divorced
Pennsylvania—Cont.											
Congressional District 2	64,690	28,044	10,464	24,304	4,558	6,309	2,058	438	51,522	29,922	25,322
Congressional District 3	79,461	41,714	10,595	25,301	5,126	5,630	2,042	237	100,370	38,275	22,126
Congressional District 4	70,561	39,376	8,194	20,972	3,856	5,607	1,205	132	101,166	31,165	18,504
Congressional District 5	76,241	40,945	10,481	23,360	5,145	4,339	1,523	228	102,064	35,307	19,207
Congressional District 6	66,895	37,756	8,196	19,267	4,644	5,203	1,031	29	95,957	28,900	17,611
Congressional District 7	72,192	39,461	8,811	22,182	4,499	6,778	1,911	44	97,748	35,416	17,647
Congressional District 8	69,837	39,594	7,728	20,838	2,968	7,754	1,441	39	104,797	31,718	16,768
Congressional District 9	82,081	43,922	11,079	25,562	5,554	5,628	1,987	195	104,498	39,895	21,101
Congressional District 10	78,768	42,775	10,833	23,182	5,336	5,357	1,527	204	106,634	39,001	19,165
Congressional District 11	77,826	41,308	10,009	24,810	5,882	7,090	2,524	118	100,501	36,857	21,506
Congressional District 12	91,695	49,080	13,102	27,589	4,281	5,290	1,883	101	113,689	44,011	19,975
Congressional District 13	65,577	34,364	8,155	21,608	6,556	8,235	1,341	208	83,076	33,075	19,787
Congressional District 14	78,109	33,580	12,944	30,157	4,518	4,693	1,038	113	73,494	38,823	23,472
Congressional District 15	71,594	39,490	9,578	21,252	4,976	6,957	1,625	131	100,826	33,725	20,974
Congressional District 16	64,185	35,895	7,471	18,854	5,205	6,346	1,666	360	89,919	28,398	18,658
Congressional District 17	75,051	37,092	9,572	26,731	6,845	8,266	2,645	387	94,089	39,405	21,196
Congressional District 18	84,984	44,776	8,962	28,703	5,322	4,954	1,001	25	111,586	41,295	19,461
Rhode Island											
Congressional District 1	48,914	24,002	6,053	17,709	4,989	5,439	1,270	285	57,466	22,846	19,301
Congressional District 2	53,323	27,590	7,409	17,012	3,083	5,689	1,457	195	66,494	26,560	16,248
South Carolina											
Congressional District 1	71,036	43,872	7,731	18,156	1,406	7,221	3,114	313	107,288	29,249	19,405
Congressional District 2	61,668	34,527	7,642	18,758	2,138	7,468	3,392	963	83,319	27,816	18,304
Congressional District 3	72,226	41,750	8,236	21,149	3,565	6,867	3,718	264	96,750	33,687	19,037
Congressional District 4	64,297	36,830	7,020	19,301	2,565	8,027	2,312	678	84,257	30,016	18,130
Congressional District 5	66,373	38,768	8,454	17,729	2,277	8,680	3,907	536	87,820	30,768	18,595
Congressional District 6	60,294	32,788	8,133	18,357	3,577	8,066	3,820	1,273	64,401	34,214	20,179
Congressional District 7	79,411	44,917	11,288	21,318	2,705	11,030	5,863	2,019	107,315	36,826	23,235
South Dakota											
Congressional District (at Large)	82,186	41,420	12,518	26,547	7,228	6,192	3,150	632	108,533	37,772	21,431
Tennessee											
Congressional District 1	84,988	48,425	11,371	23,671	3,740	7,318	3,262	787	108,947	38,892	26,302
Congressional District 2	73,990	39,869	10,012	22,712	3,611	7,141	2,774	709	99,423	32,531	25,554
Congressional District 3	76,832	42,876	10,134	22,522	3,932	9,874	4,124	758	99,386	35,725	25,248
Congressional District 4	66,528	37,580	8,727	19,372	3,407	9,284	3,498	845	86,620	29,479	22,316
Congressional District 5	53,893	26,590	7,691	18,345	1,977	7,781	2,537	290	64,478	25,220	23,839
Congressional District 6	78,575	46,750	9,860	20,772	3,574	8,086	3,942	869	106,107	36,385	21,235
Congressional District 7	61,094	36,882	6,121	16,613	3,270	6,859	2,539	522	92,118	28,078	17,428
Congressional District 8	68,914	40,577	7,521	20,119	4,172	7,419	2,899	475	96,802	30,959	20,472
Congressional District 9	48,622	24,666	7,631	15,153	2,729	6,343	2,078	771	48,123	29,133	23,065
Texas											
Congressional District 1	69,577	39,637	8,847	20,428	5,204	8,003	3,912	794	92,039	34,375	21,067
Congressional District 2	43,804	25,975	5,104	11,608	1,473	7,999	2,414	539	68,512	19,046	16,998
Congressional District 3	43,498	25,449	4,620	12,493	807	9,285	1,132	251	74,062	16,867	18,466
Congressional District 4	68,369	40,197	9,298	17,580	5,285	9,078	4,364	995	96,931	31,647	20,891
Congressional District 5	56,327	33,105	6,569	15,561	3,790	10,113	3,358	969	78,000	25,472	20,330
Congressional District 6	44,972	27,590	3,665	12,641	2,283	7,263	1,863	98	72,333	19,039	15,783
Congressional District 7	45,707	24,796	5,964	14,406	726	5,409	1,336	0	68,181	19,017	14,367
Congressional District 8	60,442	34,453	7,807	16,394	2,610	7,091	955	139	89,576	25,005	19,302
Congressional District 9	38,572	22,585	4,241	11,265	1,419	12,337	3,248	735	51,707	21,712	16,345
Congressional District 10	51,065	29,392	6,043	14,955	3,001	8,731	3,208	166	78,327	22,759	20,241
Congressional District 11	69,340	37,840	9,820	20,677	3,613	7,510	3,667	314	94,797	32,973	20,729
Congressional District 12	55,966	31,546	7,277	16,451	3,077	8,313	1,971	44	76,539	25,230	21,489
Congressional District 13	63,080	34,675	8,593	19,044	3,685	6,530	2,757	645	84,527	29,247	20,101
Congressional District 14	60,139	33,490	8,804	16,255	3,590	9,150	3,124	828	74,326	27,912	23,514
Congressional District 15	44,688	29,779	4,934	9,198	2,162	12,299	3,835	1,275	66,102	24,342	10,647
Congressional District 16	47,385	28,217	5,146	13,303	1,811	12,933	2,945	922	62,972	27,309	15,353
Congressional District 17	52,613	28,725	7,705	14,905	3,368	6,586	2,909	410	66,559	24,663	19,971
Congressional District 18	42,364	20,334	7,577	13,463	1,101	7,194	2,452	741	40,763	24,670	19,261
Congressional District 19	59,989	34,095	7,446	17,482	3,667	6,255	3,381	605	80,859	28,699	15,198
Congressional District 20	45,644	27,396	4,414	12,162	2,032	12,485	3,427	533	60,408	24,413	18,480
Congressional District 21	73,292	38,805	10,447	22,633	3,128	5,581	1,162	149	98,961	27,960	25,226
Congressional District 22	42,330	28,085	3,579	10,049	1,208	15,833	2,434	483	75,649	18,107	13,266
Congressional District 23	51,174	32,461	5,713	12,476	1,940	14,092	5,404	1,805	76,023	26,764	14,377
Congressional District 24	45,655	26,120	4,502	13,558	1,621	7,151	2,036	296	68,224	17,752	18,372
Congressional District 25	55,791	34,425	5,893	14,057	3,489	5,761	1,805	273	87,502	23,577	17,415
Congressional District 26	40,455	23,531	4,263	11,104	1,381	7,784	1,649	0	61,901	18,018	16,876
Congressional District 27	64,415	37,191	7,916	17,475	3,960	10,647	3,204	778	86,151	31,451	21,781
Congressional District 28	42,688	26,792	4,842	10,022	1,952	14,726	2,824	826	61,784	25,156	13,318
Congressional District 29	32,967	19,070	5,408	7,670	867	12,474	2,223	637	44,541	20,625	11,593
Congressional District 30	40,286	21,873	5,661	11,047	2,519	10,591	3,083	940	49,538	21,855	21,870
Congressional District 31	47,520	29,596	5,264	12,029	2,284	8,905	2,556	217	75,352	20,485	19,854
Congressional District 32	52,931	29,284	6,830	15,475	1,838	10,158	3,189	529	72,283	21,468	20,497
Congressional District 33	35,769	18,963	5,308	10,766	1,254	10,404	4,555	1,083	38,007	21,659	15,360

Table D-5: 114th Congressional Districts—Household Relationship, Grandparents, and Marital Status—*Continued*

	Total Householders 65 Years and Over	Family Householders 65 Years and Over	Non-Family Householders 65 Years and Over		Persons 65 Years and Over Living in Group Quarters	Grandparents 60 Years and Over Living with Grandchildren			Marital Status - Persons 60 Years and Over		
			Male Living Alone	Female Living Alone		Total	Responsible for Grandchildren	Responsible for Grandchildren and In Poverty	Now Married	Widowed	Divorced
Texas—Cont.											
Congressional District 34	55,273	33,227	6,846	14,461	2,950	13,788	4,036	1,756	69,310	29,603	14,372
Congressional District 35	41,117	21,395	6,671	12,117	2,624	7,302	2,182	491	44,761	21,789	20,619
Congressional District 36	58,393	32,655	9,628	15,217	2,662	9,455	3,674	230	87,780	27,727	21,995
Utah											
Congressional District 1	43,547	27,182	4,645	11,272	947	6,992	2,652	417	71,416	15,664	14,421
Congressional District 2	52,140	32,020	7,134	12,396	1,237	7,135	1,734	331	77,575	19,134	14,534
Congressional District 3	39,088	27,386	3,548	7,943	589	8,534	1,774	27	74,660	14,035	9,662
Congressional District 4	40,970	24,716	4,953	10,321	1,057	10,005	1,643	127	61,943	17,431	15,214
Vermont											
Congressional District (at Large)	67,260	33,640	9,855	21,260	3,983	5,129	1,059	26	89,313	25,398	23,205
Virginia											
Congressional District 1	61,991	38,300	7,100	15,518	1,964	10,266	1,918	129	92,754	27,750	16,420
Congressional District 2	59,210	31,348	8,308	18,204	1,959	7,481	2,745	169	75,901	26,729	21,922
Congressional District 3	57,552	27,268	9,703	19,133	1,808	8,202	3,424	1,158	57,263	30,631	24,622
Congressional District 4	60,850	35,298	7,685	17,030	3,011	9,391	3,624	197	86,050	29,948	17,247
Congressional District 5	84,852	47,425	11,206	24,198	4,368	6,988	2,261	433	111,163	39,522	23,182
Congressional District 6	81,215	44,104	10,730	24,293	3,870	5,813	2,269	101	100,422	36,276	25,759
Congressional District 7	69,449	39,926	7,458	20,906	1,882	9,576	2,363	108	100,461	30,479	19,776
Congressional District 8	49,403	23,350	7,709	16,526	2,283	7,382	1,983	46	61,494	19,723	17,623
Congressional District 9	85,129	43,728	11,154	28,660	3,665	7,834	3,023	658	104,737	43,390	23,129
Congressional District 10	46,709	28,912	5,306	11,438	724	13,368	1,814	85	85,606	22,596	13,343
Congressional District 11	45,948	27,588	4,515	12,386	1,379	10,118	1,642	0	75,013	18,766	16,525
Washington											
Congressional District 1	51,723	29,795	5,574	14,896	2,142	7,560	2,514	331	84,917	17,467	21,277
Congressional District 2	65,104	33,506	8,829	20,412	2,939	6,722	962	191	87,342	26,319	25,623
Congressional District 3	69,054	37,168	9,711	19,370	2,368	6,976	2,104	345	94,201	26,082	25,630
Congressional District 4	54,375	30,424	7,289	15,253	2,996	6,575	2,285	90	79,722	22,747	18,314
Congressional District 5	66,503	35,334	8,763	20,865	3,049	4,795	1,893	422	90,348	25,083	25,359
Congressional District 6	75,550	42,245	10,430	20,700	3,535	6,703	1,913	309	101,581	27,497	29,560
Congressional District 7	59,863	26,950	8,929	21,595	3,945	4,545	1,155	329	71,700	23,766	26,794
Congressional District 8	50,179	28,175	6,574	13,551	1,937	6,717	879	25	77,116	20,871	18,780
Congressional District 9	55,278	29,411	7,084	17,700	3,983	10,805	1,039	412	73,801	24,062	20,789
Congressional District 10	58,199	29,962	7,527	18,321	3,468	6,838	1,961	154	74,414	26,369	25,555
West Virginia											
Congressional District 1	69,426	36,390	8,956	22,358	3,607	5,625	2,559	652	87,112	32,925	20,688
Congressional District 2	69,289	37,576	10,268	19,923	2,704	6,754	2,772	267	85,941	31,880	21,867
Congressional District 3	73,073	39,052	9,701	22,760	3,529	8,042	4,474	1,185	90,279	37,486	19,942
Wisconsin											
Congressional District 1	67,267	35,464	9,893	20,611	2,759	4,406	1,000	304	89,420	27,034	21,872
Congressional District 2	61,641	32,005	8,497	19,064	3,103	3,808	847	61	86,807	23,855	20,562
Congressional District 3	72,525	38,014	9,849	22,646	5,418	2,988	1,281	117	99,201	30,513	20,739
Congressional District 4	49,461	21,315	8,846	17,804	2,991	6,166	1,978	272	50,823	24,071	22,515
Congressional District 5	74,606	38,767	9,256	25,491	4,774	3,274	679	77	99,066	32,477	19,578
Congressional District 6	75,390	38,554	10,582	24,984	5,310	2,911	894	149	99,208	35,208	19,287
Congressional District 7	82,287	46,175	11,742	22,728	5,200	3,056	1,297	72	119,093	31,259	21,392
Congressional District 8	69,654	39,834	8,391	20,013	5,144	4,439	1,238	214	99,832	29,268	18,239
Wyoming											
Congressional District (at Large)	51,531	28,270	7,777	14,726	2,413	3,284	1,598	226	72,608	20,288	21,186

PART E

EDUCATIONAL ATTAINMENT AND VETERAN STATUS

EDUCATIONAL ATTAINMENT AND VETERAN STATUS

Today's population age 65 and over was born before 1950. It includes generations born at a time when college, and even high school educations, weren't as universally accepted or expected as they are today. This factor is reflected in the educational attainment levels of the older population and also across geographic areas. In 1944, the Servicemen's Readjustment Act—known as the GI Bill—was enacted giving a broad array of benefits to returning World War II veterans. More than 9.3 million veterans are age 65 and over and almost 300,000 of them are women. Many of those veterans would have used education and training benefits from the GI Bill.

Education

Nationally, 32.7 percent of the population over 65 years has a high school or equivalent education but about one in four (24.8 percent) have a bachelor's degree or higher. Among the states, California has the lowest percent of people with only a high school education at 22.0 percent while nearly two-thirds of Utah's older population (65.6 percent) have not gone beyond high school. In the District of Columbia, 39.2 percent of residents 65 and over have a bachelor's degree or higher (the nation's highest) compared to only 13.7 percent in West Virginia. Colorado is the only other state where one-third or more of its older residents have a college education. In 471 of the 803 counties, the percent of 65 and over with a high school education exceeds that of the nation and in 25 counties it's greater than 50 percent. Northumberland County, Pennsylvania has the highest rate of persons with only a high school education at 59.7 percent while at 11.9 percent James City County, Virginia is lowest. More than 60 percent (62.0) of Riley County, Kansas residents 65 and over have bachelor's degrees which is two and a half times the national rate of 24.8 percent. More than 320 counties are above the national average but in 21 counties, less than

Percent of the Population 65 Years and Over With a Bachelor's Degree or Greater

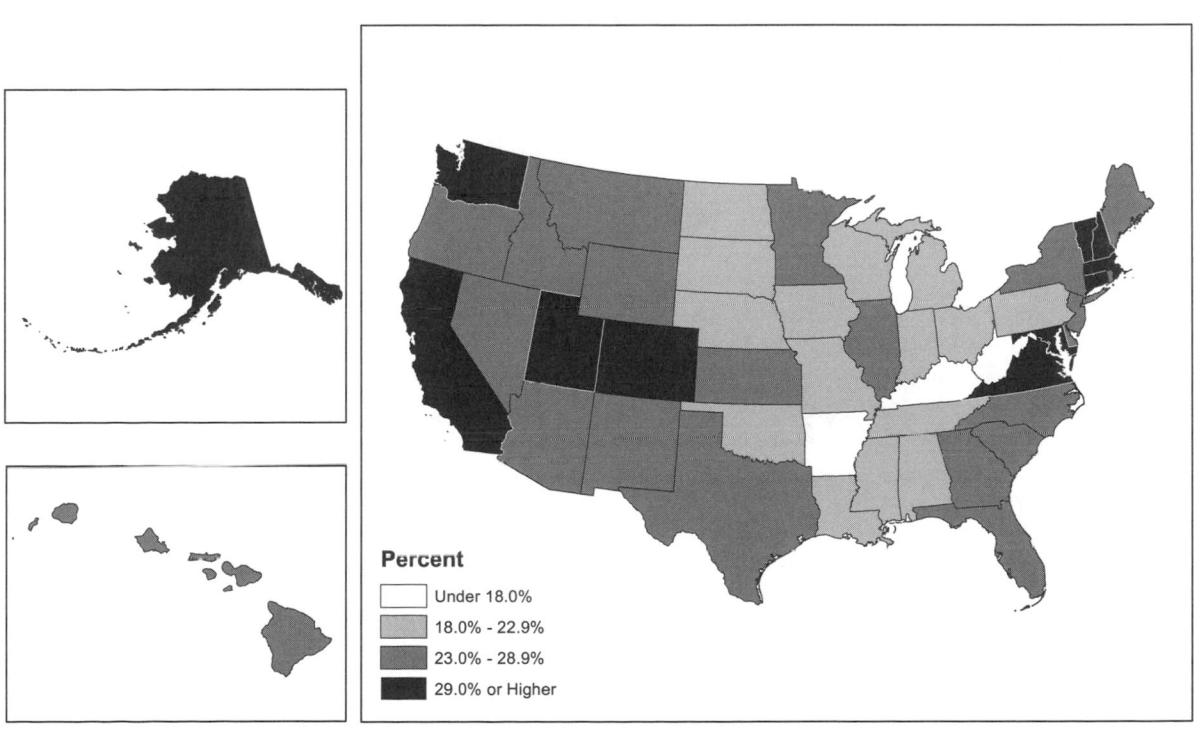

Percent
- Under 18.0%
- 18.0% - 22.9%
- 23.0% - 28.9%
- 29.0% or Higher

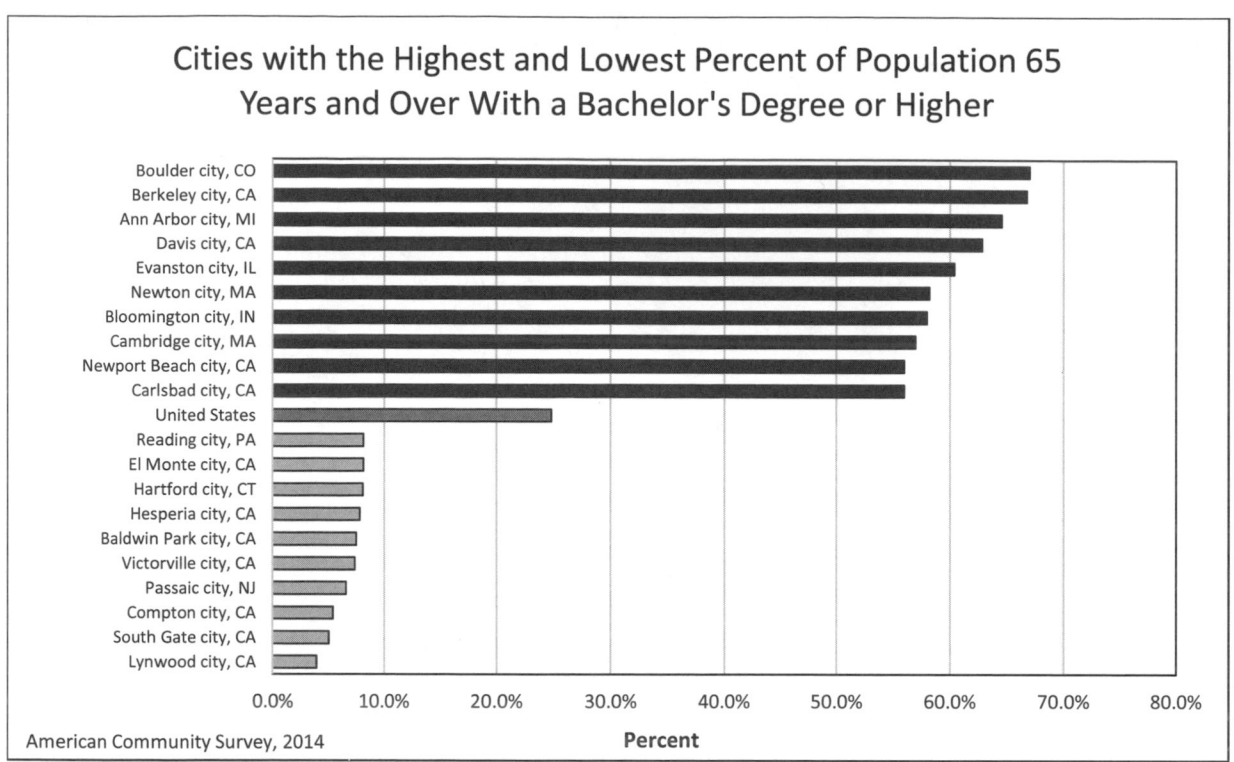

Cities with the Highest and Lowest Percent of Population 65 Years and Over With a Bachelor's Degree or Higher

American Community Survey, 2014

Percent

10 percent of the population has a college education. The lowest is Liberty County, Texas with 3.1 percent.

In 140 cities, the percent of older residents with only a high school education is above the national rate and Bayonne City, New Jersey at 56.6 percent is the highest. Newport Beach City, California is the city with the lowest percent of persons with only a high school education at 6.9 percent. Boulder City, Colorado as the highest percent (67.0 percent) of residents with a bachelor's degree or higher. In 28 cities the percent of older residents with a bachelor's degree over 50 percent. Linwood City, California is the lowest at 3.9 percent. In 22 cities the percent of persons 65 and over with a bachelor's degree is less than 10 percent. The Sunbury, Pennsylvania micropolitan area has the highest percent (59.7 percent) of persons with only a high school education and, while not the lowest, only 7.5 percent have a bachelor's degree or higher. The El Centro, California metro area has the lowest percent of high school diploma holders at 15.0 percent. The Boulder, Colorado metro area has the highest percent of residents with a bachelor's degree or higher at 52.5 percent. The Talladega-Sylacauga, Alabama micropolitan area is lowest at 5.3 percent. In four congressional districts more than 50 percent of the residents 65 and over have only a high school education. These are in Districts 6 and 7 in Ohio and Districts 3 and 9 in Pennsylvania. There are also four congressional districts where more than 50 percent of the residents have a bachelor's degree or higher: Districts 18 and 33 in California, District 12 in New York, and District 8 in Virginia. Residents of Congressional District 40 in California have the lowest percent of bachelor's degree holders at 7.4 percent and in 144 districts fewer than 20 percent of residents have bachelor's degrees or higher.

Veteran Status

As of 2014, all veterans currently 55 and over would have been born before 1960 which means that those who served in the Second World War would be among the oldest living veterans. Nationwide there are more than 13 million veterans age 55 and older and nearly 9.4 million of them are age 65 and older. Not surprising, most veterans are male (95.4 percent) but more than 600,000 are females and 47 percent of them are age 65 and over.

Veterans by Age and Period of Service		
Age in 2014	Period of Birth	Primary Service Era
55 to 64	1950 to 1959	Gulf War
65 to 74	1940 to 1949	Vietnam Era
75 and Over	Before 1940	World War II

Alaska has the highest percent of persons 65 and over who are veterans at 30.3 percent while New York has the lowest percentage at 15.1 percent. In 38 states the percent of veterans who are 65 and over is greater than the

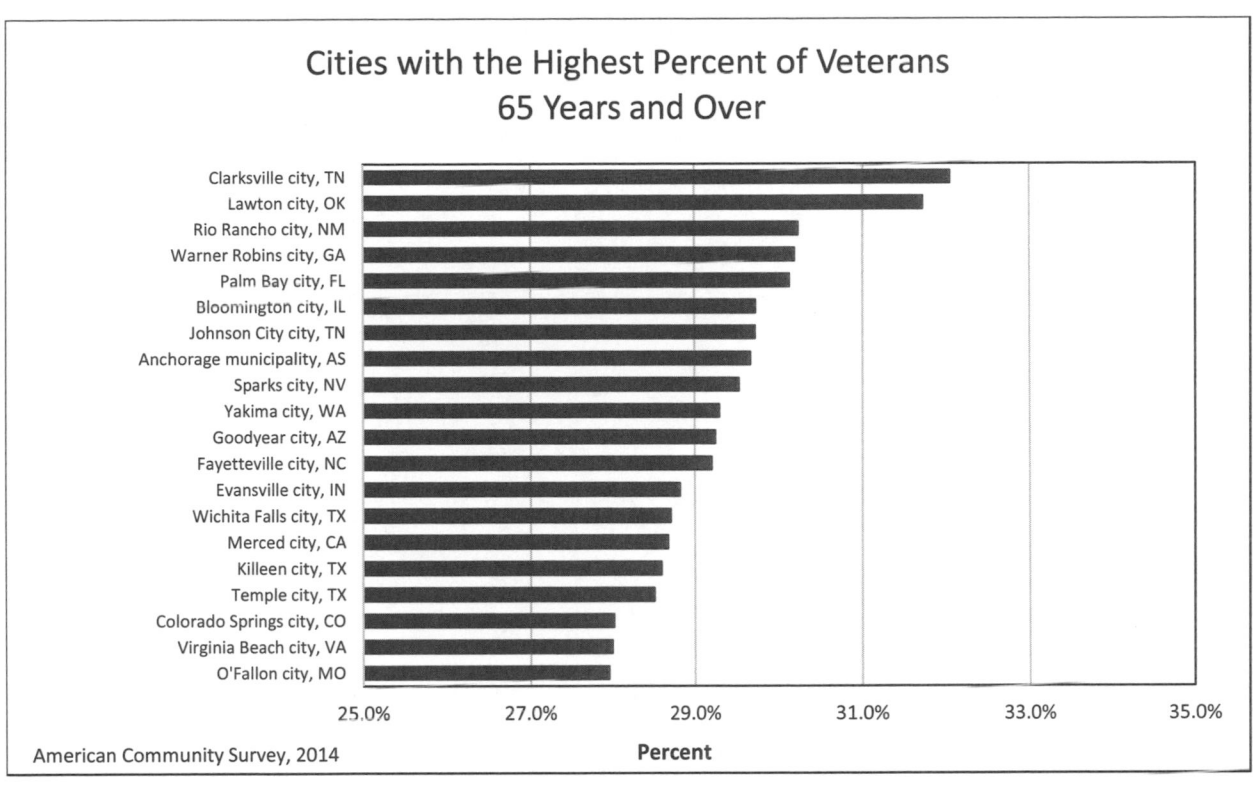

Cities with the Highest Percent of Veterans 65 Years and Over

Clarksville city, TN
Lawton city, OK
Rio Rancho city, NM
Warner Robins city, GA
Palm Bay city, FL
Bloomington city, IL
Johnson City city, TN
Anchorage municipality, AS
Sparks city, NV
Yakima city, WA
Goodyear city, AZ
Fayetteville city, NC
Evansville city, IN
Wichita Falls city, TX
Merced city, CA
Killeen city, TX
Temple city, TX
Colorado Springs city, CO
Virginia Beach city, VA
O'Fallon city, MO

25.0%   27.0%   29.0%   31.0%   33.0%   35.0%

American Community Survey, 2014

Percent

national average of 20.3 percent. Female veterans age 65 and over make up the largest percentage in the District of Columbia at 8.7 percent while Missouri and Montana are tied for is lowest at 1.9 percent. Los Angeles County, California has the largest number of veterans 65 and over with almost 150,000 and that is 12.1 percent of the total 65 and over population. Maricopa County, Arizona is the next closest with 130,500 veterans which makes up 23.1 percent of the total population age 65 and over. Grays Harbor County in Washington State has the highest percentage of older population who are veterans at 35.7 percent while Miami-Dade County, Florida is lowest at 5.4 percent. Female veterans age 65 and over make up the largest percentage Comanche County, Oklahoma at 17.0 percent. In 12 counties the percentage of veterans who are female exceeds 10 percent but in 473 counties this group makes up less than 3 percent of veterans age 65 and over.

New York City is the city location for the most veterans age 65 and over with more than 92,000 and that's 8.4 percent of the total population that is at least 65 years old. It's the only city with more than 50,000 veterans. Seven other cities have over 30,000 vets including Phoenix, Arizona (33,505), Los Angeles, California (47,828), San Diego, California (33,324), Chicago, Illinois (38,202), Philadelphia, Pennsylvania (31,760), Houston, Texas (31,354) and San Antonio, Texas (38,919). In Lawton City, Oklahoma nearly one out of every four

(24.3 percent) veterans over the age of 65 is female. In 21 cities female veterans make up more than 10 percent of those over the age of 65.

With New York City having the highest number of veterans age 65 and over it's not surprising that the New York-Newark-Jersey City metropolitan area is largest with more than 375,000 older veterans. It's the largest but not in percentage terms. The percentage is only 13.3 compared to the highest area, the Aberdeen, Washington micropolitan area at 35.7 percent. In 80 metropolitan and micropolitan areas more than 25 percent of the 65 and over population are veterans. The Laredo, Texas metro area is lowest at 10.3 percent. Women make up 15.9 percent of older veterans in the Lawton, Oklahoma metro area but in 441 metro areas the proportion of female vets is less than 5 percent. Eleven congressional districts have greater than 40,000 veterans age 65 and over. Congressional District 12 in Florida is the largest at almost 63,000. New York's 7th Congressional District is the smallest at just over 3,300. Alaska's At-large Congressional District has the highest percentage of vets age 65 and over at 30.3 percent while New York's 7th District is lowest at 4.8 percent. In 28 congressional districts the percentage of older female veterans is greater than 5 percent and the District of Columbia's Delegate District is highest at 8.7 percent. Ten districts have less than 10 percent female veterans with New York's 17th District being the lowest at 0.5 percent.

Table E-1: States—Educational Attainment and Veteran Status, Persons 55 and Over

	High School or Equivalent	Some College or Associates Degree	Bachelor's Degree or Higher	Veterans by Age and Gender					
				Male			Female		
				55 to 64 Years	65 to 74 Years	75 Years and Over	55 to 64 Years	65 to 74 Years	75 Years and Over
United States	15,114,320	11,282,365	11,469,158	3,324,271	4,758,119	4,320,081	318,373	138,536	143,680
Alabama	262,193	174,336	142,151	69,672	81,952	67,597	5,730	3,003	2,173
Alaska	18,377	20,339	21,230	11,306	13,371	6,362	1,624	745	726
Arizona	289,561	336,572	291,943	78,728	127,215	116,315	9,008	4,165	3,838
Arkansas	172,610	108,020	82,093	40,129	51,422	44,197	2,974	1,858	1,014
California	1,095,939	1,372,127	1,471,488	276,693	418,489	406,968	23,999	10,453	16,386
Colorado	179,791	192,820	230,965	68,314	86,538	68,859	8,896	2,929	2,918
Connecticut	185,905	113,503	168,984	31,262	51,128	55,243	2,622	897	2,242
Delaware	57,810	35,145	39,540	14,279	18,941	13,922	1,538	433	279
District of Columbia	18,227	14,766	29,198	4,970	5,613	6,224	526	498	629
Florida	1,202,276	982,914	971,376	234,105	365,246	396,814	25,860	10,713	12,524
Georgia	413,292	286,338	290,133	118,349	147,360	105,514	12,297	4,131	3,937
Hawaii	70,908	57,658	63,468	17,671	22,325	21,290	1,592	719	473
Idaho	75,193	79,145	54,380	22,568	32,518	24,491	1,717	1,056	596
Illinois	617,366	420,073	431,983	103,791	165,608	162,250	7,594	2,975	4,399
Indiana	400,876	210,881	177,545	74,996	104,013	91,376	6,131	2,252	2,507
Iowa	212,387	120,784	98,408	32,980	50,741	50,086	2,828	1,500	1,330
Kansas	141,683	115,436	108,508	33,007	43,988	45,132	3,097	1,500	1,461
Kentucky	238,230	135,536	111,963	53,740	66,389	57,342	4,344	1,705	1,681
Louisiana	230,394	130,128	128,179	43,956	63,487	51,858	3,334	1,621	1,601
Maine	87,118	56,101	63,945	18,521	31,765	25,213	1,614	592	853
Maryland	259,372	177,008	262,180	63,617	78,131	75,365	9,464	3,255	3,832
Massachusetts	321,604	217,032	304,615	50,966	88,801	98,106	3,691	1,952	3,488
Michigan	559,651	402,135	334,256	109,027	162,339	141,204	7,924	4,088	4,023
Minnesota	280,437	198,207	204,105	57,339	85,220	84,084	4,511	2,025	2,882
Mississippi	131,492	104,961	81,784	33,852	42,639	36,109	2,807	751	1,274
Missouri	362,151	226,588	189,243	83,173	111,498	94,708	7,925	1,988	2,054
Montana	60,703	46,883	44,354	17,702	21,464	18,849	1,148	437	358
Nebraska	108,941	72,909	55,985	18,029	30,854	30,365	1,563	1,076	594
Nevada	114,867	132,052	94,448	34,992	56,549	39,156	4,599	2,441	1,161
New Hampshire	68,557	48,161	63,694	18,108	26,613	23,919	977	514	934
New Jersey	470,750	243,288	360,644	54,039	101,070	114,375	4,081	2,016	3,194
New Mexico	82,146	82,440	91,542	27,653	39,534	32,082	3,854	1,280	973
New York	959,960	563,493	743,795	120,977	203,355	222,425	9,144	5,266	5,850
North Carolina	472,414	371,216	339,325	123,143	161,394	126,577	13,630	5,739	3,271
North Dakota	36,906	28,966	21,256	8,684	11,306	9,734	398	154	270
Ohio	753,283	397,676	353,895	135,788	193,325	175,258	9,579	6,065	5,387
Oklahoma	199,927	153,287	119,362	51,363	66,684	54,816	4,746	2,607	1,857
Oregon	179,737	201,861	179,353	49,719	84,337	64,899	5,873	4,059	2,811
Pennsylvania	957,692	386,872	431,939	132,393	217,812	225,679	9,768	5,286	8,628
Rhode Island	53,862	32,423	42,497	10,283	16,299	18,400	837	263	509
South Carolina	249,428	183,408	181,667	65,201	94,471	67,460	6,662	2,262	1,786
South Dakota	49,265	33,627	26,562	11,920	14,462	13,801	1,120	529	559
Tennessee	349,441	213,105	197,466	86,827	113,892	87,370	8,529	2,901	3,209
Texas	828,254	797,356	752,064	264,591	329,548	265,209	29,196	11,897	9,141
Utah	75,254	103,594	89,785	22,939	30,288	30,959	1,314	1,067	939
Vermont	34,586	24,180	33,948	7,928	10,995	10,847	722	490	657
Virginia	326,856	272,108	331,555	113,290	140,005	108,252	16,247	5,273	3,369
Washington	262,458	316,025	301,763	102,001	130,059	105,036	12,546	5,622	5,367
West Virginia	140,749	62,407	45,142	26,092	38,399	29,736	1,553	1,160	788
Wisconsin	368,569	199,803	192,591	65,042	97,397	90,661	5,795	1,887	2,520
Wyoming	24,872	26,672	20,863	8,556	11,270	7,587	845	441	428

Table E-2: Counties—Educational Attainment and Veteran Status, Persons 55 and Over

| | High School or Equivalent | Some College or Associates Degree | Bachelor's Degree or Higher | Veterans by Age and Gender | | | | | |
| | | | | Male | | | Female | | |
				55 to 64 Years	65 to 74 Years	75 Years and Over	55 to 64 Years	65 to 74 Years	75 Years and Over
Alabama									
Baldwin County	10,484	9,992	11,060	1,992	5,098	4,667	389	166	353
Calhoun County	5,827	4,978	2,531	1,945	2,920	1,386	139	155	127
Cullman County	6,086	3,116	1,749	1,429	1,275	1,182	88	58	0
DeKalb County	4,411	2,089	921	494	1,488	864	42	65	0
Elmore County	4,629	2,062	2,334	1,804	1,713	948	410	0	113
Etowah County	5,980	5,095	2,728	1,339	2,051	1,739	160	0	32
Houston County	6,560	4,003	2,567	1,583	1,998	1,694	128	140	106
Jefferson County	32,195	26,177	22,210	8,002	9,793	8,961	680	205	271
Lauderdale County	7,243	3,165	3,343	874	1,675	1,880	0	33	51
Lee County	4,626	4,235	4,119	1,047	2,120	1,324	260	33	87
Limestone County	4,942	2,676	2,128	1,278	1,593	741	58	67	38
Madison County	12,232	13,494	14,048	6,964	5,866	5,353	623	287	175
Marshall County	6,209	3,123	2,072	1,471	1,698	1,118	125	21	52
Mobile County	21,139	14,227	10,888	6,593	6,651	5,128	635	44	274
Montgomery County	8,637	7,695	7,846	3,565	3,042	2,494	71	370	35
Morgan County	6,443	4,800	3,948	2,102	1,971	2,010	140	0	0
Shelby County	8,390	6,772	8,724	2,014	3,170	2,851	128	130	0
St. Clair County	4,792	3,099	1,814	1,849	1,347	1,097	0	82	0
Talladega County	4,940	3,427	579	1,618	1,452	1,106	90	137	0
Tuscaloosa County	8,847	5,032	5,162	2,744	2,609	1,800	80	0	50
Walker County	4,337	2,557	1,457	1,176	1,238	1,186	0	172	0
Alaska									
Anchorage Municipality	7,099	7,451	8,806	3,973	4,613	2,677	1,239	383	310
Fairbanks North Star Borough	1,578	1,988	3,100	1,797	1,102	872	84	59	227
Matanuska-Susitna Borough	2,438	3,254	2,530	1,907	2,014	819	150	93	0
Arizona									
Apache County	2,203	2,096	911	710	1,073	494	43	0	0
Cochise County	6,557	8,195	6,179	3,383	3,443	3,340	993	332	37
Coconino County	2,720	3,227	7,193	1,534	1,743	1,077	85	126	0
Maricopa County	152,148	179,543	164,388	40,044	64,999	61,539	4,733	2,090	1,872
Mohave County	18,176	20,944	6,835	3,800	8,477	7,213	173	80	26
Navajo County	4,131	5,902	3,134	1,257	2,342	1,497	14	42	84
Pima County	41,537	53,047	59,727	13,856	19,564	19,867	1,675	885	1,149
Pinal County	23,262	24,289	13,599	5,599	9,704	7,260	363	169	210
Yavapai County	18,292	21,081	17,405	4,771	9,487	6,931	446	70	280
Yuma County	11,379	8,452	5,168	2,185	2,844	3,607	292	214	95
Arkansas									
Benton County	11,325	9,325	6,582	2,243	4,034	3,939	261	0	90
Craighead County	3,478	4,820	2,927	447	1,309	1,220	36	76	127
Faulkner County	4,982	3,099	3,223	1,347	1,898	1,113	0	127	133
Garland County	5,724	6,545	5,917	1,562	3,146	2,432	0	54	0
Jefferson County	3,987	2,429	1,943	804	1,141	866	160	0	0
Lonoke County	3,213	2,298	1,123	1,243	1,297	932	21	66	0
Pulaski County	16,318	11,851	17,787	6,295	5,079	4,987	553	410	0
Saline County	8,255	4,576	3,030	1,071	2,240	1,747	183	77	59
Sebastian County	6,743	4,674	2,676	1,856	1,768	1,725	0	135	0
Washington County	7,741	5,482	4,843	1,720	2,977	2,184	251	66	89
White County	5,201	1,666	2,010	1,375	1,143	1,190	0	132	47
California									
Alameda County	46,657	49,745	67,185	10,003	13,354	13,475	693	292	849
Butte County	10,332	11,138	10,841	2,957	4,563	3,609	170	214	335
Contra Costa County	32,527	46,564	61,066	8,322	13,282	14,101	492	353	776
El Dorado County	8,493	11,798	9,236	2,497	3,768	3,634	378	163	76
Fresno County	23,038	29,392	22,812	5,976	11,005	8,287	179	244	549
Humboldt County	5,017	6,302	6,348	1,557	2,737	2,047	191	110	147
Imperial County	3,256	2,835	2,158	1,216	1,100	1,230	0	51	0
Kern County	21,933	26,238	14,270	6,045	9,335	7,099	648	144	286
Kings County	2,938	3,983	1,942	2,339	1,757	1,234	64	29	51
Lake County	3,271	4,508	3,069	1,256	1,135	1,470	53	0	159
Los Angeles County	260,856	284,117	331,561	42,680	68,894	76,315	3,601	1,611	2,713
Madera County	5,322	6,201	3,309	1,496	2,137	1,703	38	0	0
Marin County	5,924	12,988	27,989	1,469	3,777	4,614	415	0	0
Mendocino County	3,220	5,274	5,881	818	2,225	1,436	27	292	50
Merced County	7,425	8,136	4,111	1,245	3,256	2,905	310	228	0
Monterey County	8,914	13,115	17,488	3,174	4,634	4,443	524	122	0
Napa County	6,221	7,370	8,772	1,311	2,274	2,494	83	107	100
Nevada County	5,531	9,228	7,552	1,757	2,465	2,914	78	39	81
Orange County	84,663	119,486	142,804	16,775	31,739	33,766	1,867	589	1,432
Placer County	14,778	26,762	20,951	4,106	7,218	8,499	481	152	202
Riverside County	74,958	97,803	74,452	21,234	28,682	30,229	1,300	506	1,906
Sacramento County	46,047	57,897	53,300	16,201	20,672	18,809	1,378	789	1,281
San Bernardino County	56,346	66,300	40,134	17,156	23,830	16,035	1,881	669	690
San Diego County	85,144	116,963	141,589	34,950	46,364	40,822	3,533	1,479	1,820
San Francisco County	22,140	25,492	42,471	3,575	6,012	7,535	305	0	107
San Joaquin County	22,262	23,400	16,728	6,637	7,456	6,501	557	116	177
San Luis Obispo County	9,600	16,264	18,890	2,850	5,387	5,671	469	143	135

Table E-2: Counties—Educational Attainment and Veteran Status, Persons 55 and Over—*Continued*

	High School or Equivalent	Some College or Associates Degree	Bachelor's Degree or Higher	Veterans by Age and Gender					
				Male			Female		
				55 to 64 Years	65 to 74 Years	75 Years and Over	55 to 64 Years	65 to 74 Years	75 Years and Over
California—Cont.									
San Mateo County	24,355	26,341	43,808	3,179	7,220	7,226	79	33	251
Santa Barbara County	12,497	17,928	22,466	3,178	5,531	7,226	43	248	355
Santa Clara County	45,558	53,178	89,311	8,645	14,722	17,115	827	298	441
Santa Cruz County	5,750	9,747	16,956	2,139	3,140	2,591	115	94	85
Shasta County	8,773	13,924	7,062	2,943	4,819	3,643	220	234	105
Solano County	14,587	20,039	14,858	6,627	7,159	5,683	707	350	350
Sonoma County	16,472	27,229	31,496	5,330	9,174	7,834	519	260	240
Stanislaus County	15,966	18,944	12,097	4,242	6,144	5,382	315	68	0
Sutter County	3,250	4,223	2,539	998	1,199	1,493	99	99	51
Tulare County	12,676	11,574	6,802	2,769	3,024	3,715	50	47	8
Ventura County	25,003	35,750	35,252	7,432	10,997	11,505	468	61	150
Yolo County	5,780	6,194	7,288	895	2,747	2,034	127	111	0
Yuba County	1,370	3,634	2,021	641	1,427	604	27	50	39
Colorado									
Adams County	14,896	12,908	7,747	5,453	5,462	4,278	515	51	111
Arapahoe County	17,479	21,476	27,586	6,803	8,446	6,651	1,007	347	436
Boulder County	7,315	8,165	19,929	1,751	4,091	4,085	462	22	76
Denver County	15,974	16,942	26,285	5,582	7,807	6,866	377	274	154
Douglas County	6,928	8,512	14,693	2,701	4,868	2,806	295	115	70
El Paso County	19,471	23,963	25,820	14,034	12,434	9,052	2,757	611	510
Jefferson County	22,932	23,287	29,215	7,774	9,989	8,625	715	468	373
Larimer County	10,747	13,946	18,250	2,779	5,522	4,679	215	279	280
Mesa County	8,116	7,833	6,434	2,240	3,083	2,330	534	0	329
Pueblo County	8,679	8,776	5,848	2,507	2,683	3,490	554	126	142
Weld County	9,635	9,084	6,885	2,529	4,763	3,015	165	233	245
Connecticut									
Fairfield County	39,105	25,748	49,257	4,872	10,381	12,192	461	99	409
Hartford County	47,186	29,405	39,180	7,702	11,078	14,000	605	364	1,003
Litchfield County	11,256	8,367	10,531	2,547	3,921	3,773	91	44	46
Middlesex County	9,226	6,783	9,551	1,846	3,361	3,219	96	0	0
New Haven County	49,511	26,104	35,638	7,002	11,167	13,095	855	84	588
New London County	15,751	9,512	14,037	4,072	6,141	5,630	338	306	87
Tolland County	8,211	3,865	6,402	1,649	2,621	1,959	176	0	10
Windham County	5,659	3,719	4,388	1,572	2,458	1,375	0	0	99
Delaware									
Kent County	9,785	6,114	6,089	4,378	4,039	2,714	390	77	0
New Castle County	28,865	16,744	21,168	6,776	8,386	6,564	719	211	184
Sussex County	19,160	12,287	12,283	3,125	6,516	4,644	429	145	95
Florida									
Alachua County	7,913	8,277	11,514	3,238	3,612	3,031	291	22	221
Bay County	9,014	9,620	5,937	2,719	4,726	3,808	849	117	37
Brevard County	43,210	37,542	30,696	12,039	15,013	18,186	1,281	458	1,212
Broward County	94,872	67,533	72,773	13,324	18,490	22,392	781	465	470
Charlotte County	20,836	17,989	16,248	2,407	6,265	8,664	161	411	120
Citrus County	16,729	14,594	9,774	3,090	5,149	6,536	237	188	264
Clay County	10,230	7,838	6,213	3,611	5,264	3,578	504	174	274
Collier County	25,460	24,879	41,641	2,427	8,360	12,273	0	262	466
Columbia County	4,590	3,252	2,419	1,465	1,946	1,404	113	59	0
Duval County	37,568	32,451	28,228	16,518	14,380	11,280	2,348	442	365
Escambia County	16,507	16,399	10,161	6,205	6,906	6,294	1,074	231	113
Flagler County	10,265	7,239	7,225	2,659	3,541	3,418	158	105	73
Hernando County	18,780	12,755	7,412	3,017	5,758	6,615	152	95	132
Highlands County	10,754	9,550	7,113	1,133	3,368	4,517	132	147	22
Hillsborough County	57,952	44,287	38,545	15,648	20,250	16,190	2,023	389	655
Indian River County	14,628	11,580	13,476	1,577	4,503	6,652	192	151	173
Lake County	29,770	24,879	18,089	4,615	9,117	10,488	987	226	294
Lee County	55,275	47,465	52,503	8,430	16,781	21,876	619	256	387
Leon County	7,508	8,317	12,412	3,369	3,184	3,108	146	144	236
Manatee County	27,275	23,201	30,671	4,615	9,485	11,508	184	230	201
Marion County	31,605	29,550	17,428	4,331	11,013	12,421	259	378	494
Martin County	12,825	14,442	13,636	1,197	4,161	7,196	82	0	0
Miami-Dade County	104,085	72,991	78,773	9,285	12,604	8,772	1,225	202	297
Monroe County	3,505	4,132	6,111	988	1,888	995	248	317	103
Nassau County	3,783	3,623	5,347	1,560	2,486	1,854	102	85	0
Okaloosa County	8,598	9,163	8,872	5,870	5,851	3,686	797	0	374
Orange County	40,969	30,697	34,741	11,205	11,045	10,999	1,276	599	614
Osceola County	14,780	8,208	5,324	2,326	3,684	2,377	224	75	90
Palm Beach County	90,543	81,645	106,843	9,873	20,432	37,669	1,037	937	652
Pasco County	41,745	30,397	19,620	6,458	11,640	14,046	1,137	441	630
Pinellas County	68,658	61,589	58,197	13,394	22,670	26,711	2,404	500	879
Polk County	47,433	32,696	21,878	8,258	13,944	13,400	513	268	507
Putnam County	5,793	3,340	2,494	1,965	1,868	1,672	395	0	190
Santa Rosa County	8,686	6,645	6,600	4,206	4,464	2,897	374	47	38
Sarasota County	36,764	36,704	51,039	5,788	11,910	18,061	807	365	352
Seminole County	21,327	18,169	15,912	5,243	7,743	4,569	531	128	0

Table E-2: Counties—Educational Attainment and Veteran Status, Persons 55 and Over—*Continued*

| | High School or Equivalent | Some College or Associates Degree | Bachelor's Degree or Higher | Veterans by Age and Gender | | | | | |
| | | | | Male | | | Female | | |
				55 to 64 Years	65 to 74 Years	75 Years and Over	55 to 64 Years	65 to 74 Years	75 Years and Over
Florida—Cont.									
St. Johns County	10,698	9,599	16,842	3,934	6,082	4,675	143	382	488
St. Lucie County	26,525	18,116	11,938	3,058	6,729	8,479	368	213	125
Sumter County	19,252	18,003	18,433	1,306	8,674	7,856	38	264	46
Volusia County	42,695	32,112	26,935	10,125	13,914	14,042	364	598	560
Georgia									
Barrow County	3,530	1,941	868	929	797	633	31	0	0
Bartow County	4,548	3,377	2,149	2,207	1,782	1,264	48	0	0
Bibb County	7,245	3,435	5,005	1,915	2,642	1,728	164	102	92
Bulloch County	2,949	1,096	1,548	356	908	535	85	0	0
Carroll County	4,272	2,983	2,162	1,434	1,689	883	65	248	0
Catoosa County	4,227	2,943	1,011	701	1,241	966	0	105	0
Chatham County	9,253	9,055	13,354	3,337	4,209	4,104	512	91	213
Cherokee County	9,070	8,271	6,559	2,232	4,595	2,344	66	0	403
Clarke County	2,414	2,114	4,960	996	683	980	61	88	0
Clayton County	8,466	5,909	3,261	3,233	3,286	1,466	549	65	22
Cobb County	25,195	19,970	24,042	7,571	10,468	7,945	575	231	175
Columbia County	5,629	3,577	4,069	2,579	1,984	1,660	651	108	0
Coweta County	5,962	4,205	3,742	1,794	2,759	1,393	199	96	0
DeKalb County	18,463	16,805	27,568	7,022	6,821	5,441	1,298	109	91
Dougherty County	2,813	2,730	2,160	1,188	1,282	832	131	34	0
Douglas County	6,803	2,185	1,670	1,407	1,665	1,366	259	0	86
Fayette County	5,444	4,425	6,370	2,769	2,514	1,333	329	148	0
Floyd County	5,684	2,869	2,738	1,210	1,941	1,592	130	76	102
Forsyth County	7,111	5,658	6,781	1,502	2,549	2,249	262	0	68
Fulton County	24,702	24,750	40,685	8,825	9,154	8,572	1,266	312	97
Glynn County	3,510	4,525	4,680	1,054	1,881	1,186	99	0	117
Gwinnett County	22,810	19,659	21,194	6,374	8,662	3,847	802	68	748
Hall County	7,736	6,145	7,415	1,389	3,535	3,070	162	99	116
Henry County	7,713	6,667	2,594	2,418	3,762	1,910	182	275	0
Houston County	6,397	3,760	3,552	3,274	2,862	1,845	253	80	252
Liberty County	2,038	1,091	709	1,348	1,038	145	58	56	0
Lowndes County	3,486	3,226	2,548	1,271	1,161	1,071	0	76	77
Muscogee County	7,436	5,376	6,331	4,466	3,283	2,897	398	162	226
Newton County	4,916	2,921	1,622	1,186	1,716	872	187	0	0
Paulding County	5,466	3,351	2,387	1,056	1,996	1,308	70	86	0
Richmond County	8,685	6,407	4,282	3,730	3,167	2,291	728	331	92
Rockdale County	4,996	2,535	1,702	1,429	1,315	674	155	97	0
Troup County	3,627	1,981	1,856	1,514	1,062	817	0	0	0
Walker County	4,393	2,540	1,124	993	765	1,138	0	0	0
Walton County	5,534	3,417	1,596	771	1,763	978	35	0	0
Whitfield County	5,106	2,059	1,710	337	1,270	1,288	0	0	0
Hawaii									
Hawaii County	10,820	10,549	9,100	3,034	4,231	3,294	22	157	0
Honolulu County	50,257	37,579	43,039	11,741	14,545	15,832	1,421	412	473
Kauai County	2,841	3,020	4,352	988	1,103	804	28	0	0
Maui County	6,988	6,510	6,977	1,908	2,446	1,360	121	150	0
Idaho									
Ada County	14,425	19,464	16,260	5,505	7,768	5,632	618	290	59
Bannock County	2,970	3,446	2,498	1,034	1,257	968	51	80	0
Bonneville County	4,715	4,273	2,986	1,323	1,232	1,346	0	150	132
Canyon County	10,079	6,663	5,653	2,946	3,553	2,113	251	92	0
Kootenai County	6,240	9,671	6,890	2,487	3,415	2,718	342	99	46
Twin Falls County	3,831	4,323	2,516	1,375	1,143	1,462	102	86	38
Illinois									
Adams County	5,125	3,446	1,766	1,096	1,363	1,410	65	0	0
Champaign County	7,648	6,200	6,814	1,889	2,486	2,397	395	7	38
Cook County	199,492	149,679	179,360	25,408	45,831	51,153	1,617	749	1,627
DeKalb County	4,948	1,876	3,456	618	943	1,526	33	29	0
DuPage County	34,150	29,963	45,566	4,724	10,639	10,109	248	189	427
Kane County	18,803	14,241	17,020	4,241	6,738	5,149	132	287	143
Kankakee County	7,029	3,947	2,660	1,266	1,666	1,987	184	0	49
Kendall County	3,770	3,153	1,993	543	1,646	670	0	0	0
Lake County	24,799	17,513	33,971	5,574	7,668	7,660	272	160	430
LaSalle County	8,652	4,741	2,822	1,312	2,151	2,025	82	0	29
Macon County	8,742	4,052	3,484	1,240	1,772	2,073	29	0	15
Madison County	17,324	10,121	8,843	4,584	5,768	4,823	542	339	23
McHenry County	13,138	11,046	8,968	2,396	4,464	3,505	85	43	245
McLean County	6,853	4,284	6,583	1,240	2,625	2,178	55	244	0
Peoria County	10,578	7,255	5,566	2,363	3,613	2,781	36	0	38
Rock Island County	10,340	7,238	4,221	1,942	2,328	2,506	220	123	43
Sangamon County	11,725	7,730	7,544	2,160	3,675	2,944	158	144	141
St. Clair County	14,867	8,766	7,651	4,914	5,065	4,406	1,076	0	151
Tazewell County	9,600	6,666	4,134	1,179	2,407	2,607	30	13	0
Vermilion County	6,084	3,564	1,522	1,438	1,551	1,346	54	0	8

Table E-2: Counties—Educational Attainment and Veteran Status, Persons 55 and Over—*Continued*

	High School or Equivalent	Some College or Associates Degree	Bachelor's Degree or Higher	Veterans by Age and Gender					
				Male			Female		
				55 to 64 Years	65 to 74 Years	75 Years and Over	55 to 64 Years	65 to 74 Years	75 Years and Over
Illinois—Cont.									
Will County	27,101	21,046	17,603	5,016	8,121	7,266	581	23	311
Williamson County	4,446	3,418	1,700	722	1,399	794	52	13	0
Winnebago County	17,563	10,445	9,191	3,123	4,821	4,353	291	43	24
Indiana									
Allen County	19,063	12,817	10,178	4,190	5,225	4,896	62	65	0
Bartholomew County	5,833	2,368	2,113	999	1,514	1,255	0	51	0
Clark County	7,070	3,805	2,718	1,683	2,520	1,154	212	0	0
Delaware County	8,251	3,340	4,259	825	1,763	2,215	49	96	40
Elkhart County	12,262	5,825	4,308	1,277	2,846	2,292	292	0	201
Floyd County	3,698	2,465	2,604	1,192	1,353	1,024	54	62	0
Grant County	5,291	2,224	1,308	902	1,355	1,392	0	43	0
Hamilton County	9,119	8,919	11,946	2,075	2,973	2,935	134	0	16
Hancock County	3,918	3,546	2,208	1,483	1,837	980	0	0	74
Hendricks County	8,457	5,781	2,838	1,323	2,868	2,438	162	6	80
Howard County	6,421	3,608	2,799	1,510	1,511	1,874	33	0	36
Johnson County	8,286	5,217	4,641	1,335	2,238	2,127	231	0	86
Kosciusko County	4,554	2,465	2,165	933	1,034	1,306	34	0	0
Lake County	28,677	16,843	10,945	5,809	7,215	6,957	420	83	179
LaPorte County	7,088	4,813	3,040	1,564	2,356	1,608	58	90	35
Madison County	9,474	5,697	3,577	1,416	2,366	2,191	106	0	146
Marion County	37,608	25,666	23,731	10,625	9,784	10,066	1,127	279	148
Monroe County	5,368	2,368	6,569	926	1,141	1,047	45	72	0
Morgan County	5,476	1,872	1,853	1,245	1,373	865	93	0	0
Porter County	9,778	5,408	5,857	1,773	2,833	2,602	139	105	0
St. Joseph County	15,276	8,485	8,692	2,859	4,694	3,435	375	193	51
Tippecanoe County	5,925	3,996	6,699	1,101	1,536	1,634	146	21	0
Vanderburgh County	12,279	6,693	5,211	1,865	3,398	3,456	79	103	307
Vigo County	6,775	2,955	3,156	1,356	1,299	1,257	23	0	69
Wayne County	4,677	3,086	2,017	1,276	1,420	984	0	116	145
Iowa									
Black Hawk County	8,573	4,791	3,995	1,393	2,324	2,049	121	73	13
Dallas County	3,502	1,812	2,855	460	929	650	55	0	9
Dubuque County	7,108	2,712	3,388	947	1,546	1,702	48	36	45
Johnson County	4,070	3,401	5,646	1,151	1,197	1,427	75	59	0
Linn County	12,135	8,360	7,676	2,680	3,598	3,254	144	85	137
Polk County	19,819	13,680	13,852	3,617	5,800	4,827	485	238	227
Pottawattamie County	6,288	4,561	1,995	1,354	1,766	1,473	114	62	145
Scott County	9,203	6,559	6,253	1,848	2,556	2,185	105	244	0
Story County	3,129	2,215	4,412	337	651	1,074	14	0	97
Woodbury County	6,127	3,531	2,334	1,201	1,710	1,573	234	5	0
Kansas									
Butler County	3,981	2,969	1,263	601	1,105	1,150	23	91	60
Douglas County	3,804	2,388	5,288	1,104	1,295	1,516	221	0	91
Johnson County	16,380	20,202	31,679	4,383	7,472	7,969	221	152	150
Leavenworth County	4,133	1,940	2,630	2,172	1,326	890	79	121	0
Riley County	1,237	796	3,804	655	571	586	97	149	72
Sedgwick County	21,271	18,620	16,088	5,457	7,700	7,005	870	107	271
Shawnee County	11,535	7,263	6,892	2,966	2,961	3,414	380	123	145
Wyandotte County	5,541	5,638	2,770	1,808	2,355	2,006	71	30	0
Kentucky									
Boone County	4,661	3,779	3,248	1,698	1,419	1,279	144	72	65
Bullitt County	4,717	1,687	925	1,211	1,310	754	13	0	24
Campbell County	5,971	2,875	1,511	1,094	1,531	1,279	30	0	0
Christian County	3,115	2,357	679	811	603	991	6	0	60
Daviess County	5,957	3,885	2,773	1,534	1,297	1,547	0	52	192
Fayette County	12,191	8,586	11,043	2,979	3,551	2,928	756	235	81
Hardin County	4,168	3,093	2,869	3,061	1,734	1,147	245	69	0
Jefferson County	37,772	26,488	27,933	8,017	10,943	10,858	501	160	333
Kenton County	7,379	5,287	4,473	2,539	1,984	1,966	41	107	79
Madison County	3,358	1,994	2,534	1,497	1,451	852	117	0	0
McCracken County	3,468	4,495	1,821	1,078	1,217	1,630	83	59	30
Pike County	3,339	1,083	1,180	465	1,085	638	0	0	44
Warren County	4,774	3,117	3,218	1,028	1,733	1,473	0	0	0
Louisiana									
Ascension Parish	5,437	1,235	2,045	1,006	1,354	1,085	0	0	0
Bossier Parish	5,962	4,472	3,312	1,825	1,588	1,890	250	0	0
Caddo Parish	13,709	8,285	8,615	3,459	3,857	2,915	155	144	267
Calcasieu Parish	8,706	6,751	5,947	1,817	3,187	2,261	129	0	49
East Baton Rouge Parish	17,342	12,396	16,316	3,909	4,999	4,746	281	32	99
Iberia Parish	3,548	1,814	1,567	1,088	510	1,187	32	0	0
Jefferson Parish	25,633	14,224	11,651	2,887	6,002	5,394	180	109	168
Lafayette Parish	8,084	5,612	6,936	1,841	2,102	1,974	274	154	156
Lafourche Parish	5,149	2,238	1,450	437	976	889	326	0	0
Livingston Parish	6,427	2,787	1,959	1,378	1,741	1,246	34	0	78

Table E-2: Counties—Educational Attainment and Veteran Status, Persons 55 and Over—*Continued*

	High School or Equivalent	Some College or Associates Degree	Bachelor's Degree or Higher	Male 55 to 64 Years	Male 65 to 74 Years	Male 75 Years and Over	Female 55 to 64 Years	Female 65 to 74 Years	Female 75 Years and Over
Louisiana—Cont.									
Orleans Parish	13,147	9,155	14,019	3,118	4,059	3,331	41	396	116
Ouachita Parish	7,372	4,627	5,079	2,095	2,525	1,910	76	0	0
Rapides Parish	7,544	4,746	4,003	1,674	2,273	1,757	66	140	10
St. Landry Parish	4,174	1,907	1,359	472	688	850	268	0	0
St. Tammany Parish	12,081	9,746	11,561	2,831	3,919	3,167	343	46	100
Tangipahoa Parish	7,508	2,495	3,132	1,021	1,828	1,828	98	0	0
Terrebonne Parish	5,592	2,709	1,659	310	1,059	1,225	302	0	0
Maine									
Androscoggin County	7,013	4,140	3,072	1,377	2,361	1,762	189	0	0
Aroostook County	6,379	2,596	2,011	1,344	2,035	1,401	79	7	18
Cumberland County	13,603	11,310	17,799	2,654	5,232	4,886	470	148	169
Kennebec County	8,063	5,166	4,804	1,762	3,093	2,456	165	26	136
Penobscot County	9,640	6,105	4,098	1,690	3,428	2,455	66	80	127
York County	12,469	8,347	9,162	2,800	4,444	3,508	269	96	169
Maryland									
Allegany County	6,767	2,735	2,035	1,365	1,380	1,640	0	73	100
Anne Arundel County	23,290	17,038	24,867	7,588	10,206	7,089	1,061	94	276
Baltimore County	45,255	26,832	38,622	6,713	10,171	13,729	916	475	316
Calvert County	3,859	2,903	3,296	1,278	1,855	1,031	413	51	0
Carroll County	10,468	5,968	5,464	1,651	3,548	2,315	632	52	0
Cecil County	6,730	2,510	1,865	1,328	2,030	1,228	359	0	72
Charles County	6,423	4,106	4,230	2,580	2,211	2,051	369	176	54
Frederick County	11,119	7,252	8,935	2,449	3,769	2,972	365	242	191
Harford County	12,992	10,427	8,563	5,093	4,048	4,053	299	200	110
Howard County	10,131	6,997	17,646	1,685	3,404	3,119	531	94	483
Montgomery County	22,884	26,090	76,958	5,205	8,155	11,791	1,076	398	724
Prince George's County	31,705	26,171	26,995	11,174	9,926	7,433	1,919	918	419
St. Mary's County	5,471	3,173	2,411	1,980	1,646	1,323	316	72	141
Washington County	10,411	4,828	3,984	2,212	2,159	2,495	0	23	112
Wicomico County	5,389	3,259	4,300	946	2,286	1,529	127	66	378
Massachusetts									
Barnstable County	13,312	16,442	28,160	2,187	6,122	7,926	239	163	367
Berkshire County	8,541	5,616	9,148	1,753	2,509	2,850	72	0	87
Bristol County	28,490	17,295	14,352	5,265	8,225	7,610	261	75	383
Essex County	36,639	27,669	34,444	5,805	9,361	12,213	666	264	756
Franklin County	4,191	2,503	4,435	935	1,488	1,432	146	54	12
Hampden County	24,141	15,367	16,544	5,333	7,352	7,246	450	39	211
Hampshire County	7,247	5,061	8,807	1,276	2,322	2,474	0	60	0
Middlesex County	66,782	43,384	78,267	9,353	16,944	19,958	785	475	687
Norfolk County	33,702	23,526	38,255	3,628	9,218	11,158	64	98	228
Plymouth County	27,683	21,742	22,318	5,455	9,222	8,380	396	230	385
Suffolk County	25,159	13,077	20,695	2,669	4,395	4,633	204	76	135
Worcester County	44,675	24,193	26,613	6,662	11,301	11,955	408	389	237
Michigan									
Allegan County	7,156	3,576	3,738	883	1,886	1,165	157	30	13
Bay County	7,801	4,990	2,893	1,591	2,802	1,944	129	0	0
Berrien County	10,572	7,133	6,382	1,178	3,216	2,769	143	88	322
Calhoun County	8,636	5,216	4,555	2,225	2,748	2,205	32	38	31
Clinton County	4,946	2,783	2,423	947	1,018	1,045	14	0	113
Eaton County	7,668	5,096	3,188	1,371	2,406	1,726	161	0	100
Genesee County	26,765	19,297	9,342	4,803	6,431	5,386	372	58	46
Grand Traverse County	4,003	4,157	6,092	1,729	1,974	1,457	306	114	93
Ingham County	9,420	8,834	10,820	2,763	3,749	2,630	121	146	131
Isabella County	3,482	1,288	1,603	832	673	472	18	0	0
Jackson County	9,904	7,208	5,040	2,006	3,061	2,513	49	346	175
Kalamazoo County	10,458	10,776	10,244	2,350	2,998	3,605	292	92	0
Kent County	24,144	21,149	19,914	6,068	7,180	7,838	370	178	179
Lapeer County	6,090	4,152	1,907	904	1,906	1,243	50	0	0
Lenawee County	7,489	3,780	2,379	1,058	1,752	1,335	100	0	0
Livingston County	10,357	8,327	6,616	2,068	3,476	2,167	88	0	96
Macomb County	51,944	36,377	21,533	8,630	12,870	12,819	907	202	112
Marquette County	4,140	3,630	2,757	1,206	1,995	1,234	34	48	31
Midland County	5,726	4,137	2,801	693	1,211	1,645	169	39	0
Monroe County	10,193	6,336	2,746	2,667	2,797	2,497	65	133	101
Muskegon County	9,745	7,289	5,023	2,160	3,444	3,151	259	298	174
Oakland County	49,818	49,412	65,879	9,793	16,567	15,358	796	559	345
Ottawa County	13,515	11,520	7,300	2,211	3,683	3,447	68	164	121
Saginaw County	14,357	7,211	5,525	2,540	2,831	2,754	72	57	112
Shiawassee County	5,563	2,875	1,608	1,101	1,260	1,207	0	0	14
St. Clair County	11,060	7,009	4,784	1,565	3,036	2,466	43	0	161
Van Buren County	4,552	3,469	1,793	1,450	1,402	930	39	0	0
Washtenaw County	9,147	10,057	19,573	2,108	3,848	3,012	186	207	15
Wayne County	88,155	59,120	43,827	17,881	23,406	21,381	1,130	409	693

Table E-2: Counties—Educational Attainment and Veteran Status, Persons 55 and Over—*Continued*

	High School or Equivalent	Some College or Associates Degree	Bachelor's Degree or Higher	Veterans by Age and Gender					
				Male			Female		
				55 to 64 Years	65 to 74 Years	75 Years and Over	55 to 64 Years	65 to 74 Years	75 Years and Over
Minnesota									
Anoka County	15,398	11,976	8,708	4,592	5,421	3,425	507	189	122
Blue Earth County	3,535	1,886	2,045	519	844	946	12	37	0
Carver County	3,321	2,738	2,436	755	1,492	757	0	13	0
Dakota County	16,414	14,133	15,069	3,861	5,746	5,151	353	158	579
Hennepin County	40,547	41,449	55,536	8,133	12,976	16,638	983	413	767
Olmsted County	5,476	6,017	7,162	1,387	1,822	2,532	104	0	38
Ramsey County	21,330	14,167	26,023	4,640	6,357	7,276	266	79	354
Rice County	3,156	2,457	2,403	535	1,101	1,161	0	0	0
Scott County	4,582	3,288	3,269	1,114	1,698	1,071	193	23	0
Sherburne County	3,451	2,507	2,172	894	1,328	900	80	0	17
St. Louis County	13,532	8,693	8,092	3,342	4,030	3,900	110	147	213
Stearns County	8,303	4,422	4,742	1,733	2,482	2,250	18	0	89
Washington County	10,333	8,328	10,488	2,204	4,442	3,442	237	92	0
Wright County	5,896	3,692	3,240	1,412	2,041	1,432	0	14	0
Mississippi									
DeSoto County	7,970	5,456	2,931	2,382	2,111	1,953	340	36	104
Forrest County	2,985	2,321	2,681	762	936	1,089	135	0	0
Harrison County	7,387	8,600	5,722	2,756	3,582	3,045	415	0	55
Hinds County	7,015	7,231	7,847	2,589	2,650	2,644	188	221	146
Jackson County	6,414	6,062	5,429	3,061	2,729	2,407	186	23	53
Jones County	3,143	2,059	2,566	577	1,226	1,121	0	0	0
Lauderdale County	4,949	3,565	1,102	1,446	1,387	1,128	0	65	0
Lee County	3,054	3,514	3,416	475	1,031	1,035	0	0	0
Madison County	2,792	3,600	4,188	1,141	957	905	61	0	0
Rankin County	5,301	7,006	3,706	1,914	2,599	2,284	321	76	46
Missouri									
Boone County	6,023	4,384	6,397	1,619	2,075	1,805	207	55	86
Buchanan County	5,462	3,742	1,866	715	1,166	1,415	38	0	36
Cape Girardeau County	4,817	2,003	3,203	644	1,210	1,528	0	0	23
Cass County	6,938	5,182	1,945	1,665	2,249	1,656	0	80	47
Christian County	5,084	3,175	1,923	1,094	1,968	852	179	0	0
Clay County	10,784	7,950	6,786	2,834	3,797	2,904	73	0	205
Cole County	3,730	2,513	3,094	1,046	1,211	1,149	63	5	0
Franklin County	6,800	3,187	1,750	1,229	2,463	1,965	420	0	0
Greene County	16,406	12,324	10,271	3,450	4,138	4,776	216	75	173
Jackson County	35,596	24,250	20,487	8,776	10,118	9,206	1,032	302	78
Jasper County	7,937	3,591	2,236	1,255	2,274	1,435	223	9	33
Jefferson County	12,786	6,861	4,521	4,067	5,071	2,641	325	85	86
Platte County	4,055	3,622	3,101	1,299	1,903	984	97	0	0
St. Charles County	19,200	13,613	12,759	4,669	6,847	5,791	357	138	172
St. Francois County	4,069	2,927	1,174	1,765	1,212	1,357	0	0	0
St. Louis County	50,282	42,319	53,551	10,368	15,792	16,886	1,108	399	390
Montana									
Cascade County	5,807	3,951	2,568	1,751	1,987	1,574	0	65	0
Flathead County	5,254	5,059	4,558	2,621	2,466	1,706	61	0	0
Gallatin County	3,459	2,013	4,759	491	1,296	1,206	87	95	46
Lewis and Clark County	3,956	2,129	3,887	1,486	1,239	1,327	116	79	0
Missoula County	3,104	4,136	6,669	1,684	1,887	1,488	64	14	68
Yellowstone County	8,702	6,193	5,457	2,334	2,920	2,431	80	0	0
Nebraska									
Douglas County	23,027	15,409	16,301	4,765	7,179	6,417	339	328	74
Lancaster County	12,911	10,469	9,839	1,813	4,248	3,378	255	151	136
Sarpy County	6,020	4,991	4,837	2,855	3,600	2,206	427	93	214
Nevada									
Clark County	79,951	85,895	64,214	24,388	37,199	25,946	3,268	1,601	841
Washoe County	16,044	22,657	18,590	4,175	8,825	7,002	707	676	105
New Hampshire									
Cheshire County	5,421	2,758	3,033	1,010	1,409	1,720	204	62	154
Grafton County	4,723	3,329	6,002	878	1,806	1,606	62	108	70
Hillsborough County	16,985	12,621	16,426	5,410	6,842	5,856	178	118	201
Merrimack County	8,734	4,592	7,550	1,857	3,322	2,715	41	112	123
Rockingham County	13,892	11,317	14,573	4,277	6,201	5,196	257	38	290
Strafford County	5,662	3,783	4,810	1,466	1,999	2,135	143	64	0
New Jersey									
Atlantic County	16,675	8,262	10,217	1,772	3,755	3,723	229	0	171
Bergen County	49,241	26,657	48,494	2,811	7,878	13,658	118	258	253
Burlington County	25,707	15,983	19,213	5,281	7,191	7,783	888	377	144
Camden County	28,047	13,708	16,766	5,424	7,022	7,329	345	12	307
Cape May County	8,652	5,193	5,219	650	2,129	2,629	56	116	117
Cumberland County	8,077	3,360	3,116	1,000	1,876	1,485	80	0	112
Essex County	31,362	15,400	26,806	3,466	4,112	5,974	169	210	134
Gloucester County	17,197	9,121	7,836	3,239	4,692	3,664	111	126	154
Hudson County	25,253	9,477	13,238	1,743	2,663	2,955	103	0	43
Hunterdon County	6,416	3,536	7,318	623	1,780	1,919	0	0	134

Table E-2: Counties—Educational Attainment and Veteran Status, Persons 55 and Over—*Continued*

| | High School or Equivalent | Some College or Associates Degree | Bachelor's Degree or Higher | Veterans by Age and Gender | | | | | |
| | | | | Male | | | Female | | |
				55 to 64 Years	65 to 74 Years	75 Years and Over	55 to 64 Years	65 to 74 Years	75 Years and Over
New Jersey—Cont.									
Mercer County	14,486	9,388	18,504	2,172	3,306	4,218	83	62	102
Middlesex County	40,559	18,361	31,851	3,799	7,573	8,191	119	91	110
Monmouth County	32,806	21,610	32,393	5,489	8,969	8,821	46	259	164
Morris County	23,548	14,103	29,247	1,919	6,597	7,056	0	131	217
Ocean County	52,869	29,826	30,469	4,494	12,292	15,911	955	137	530
Passaic County	25,285	9,120	15,050	2,331	3,863	4,980	188	219	113
Salem County	5,305	2,445	1,188	807	1,156	1,434	21	18	12
Somerset County	15,882	7,620	17,558	1,412	4,213	3,651	0	0	283
Sussex County	7,663	4,580	5,788	1,125	2,810	2,078	153	0	32
Union County	28,007	12,470	17,057	3,297	5,265	5,359	337	0	0
Warren County	7,713	3,068	3,316	1,185	1,928	1,557	80	0	62
New Mexico									
Bernalillo County	24,011	25,990	31,231	8,779	12,476	10,264	1,049	435	491
Chaves County	2,562	2,799	2,005	732	1,077	698	197	0	0
Doña Ana County	5,348	5,435	10,140	1,970	3,808	2,923	66	0	78
Lea County	1,301	1,697	1,011	486	610	445	0	0	0
McKinley County	1,342	1,729	539	609	301	688	183	47	76
Otero County	2,729	3,168	2,659	1,487	2,007	1,503	265	51	58
San Juan County	4,239	5,116	2,757	1,262	1,906	1,361	274	82	0
Sandoval County	6,084	6,111	6,706	2,563	2,817	2,354	771	161	45
Santa Fe County	6,034	6,905	13,408	1,722	3,235	2,245	112	55	44
Valencia County	3,871	3,735	2,048	1,046	1,861	1,063	156	25	0
New York									
Albany County	16,969	10,859	14,183	2,921	3,444	3,598	75	235	259
Bronx County	45,786	23,122	21,786	5,604	5,910	7,350	214	184	203
Broome County	13,629	9,156	6,966	2,481	2,706	4,006	116	135	53
Cattaraugus County	5,543	3,414	2,463	1,419	1,902	1,454	129	50	7
Cayuga County	4,676	3,414	2,275	966	1,520	1,539	0	19	0
Chautauqua County	9,797	5,782	5,190	1,669	2,084	2,269	104	54	36
Chemung County	6,201	3,261	3,582	1,072	1,863	1,556	52	0	17
Clinton County	5,110	2,221	2,308	1,631	1,057	993	62	0	47
Dutchess County	14,197	10,422	13,582	2,791	3,900	4,677	76	75	22
Erie County	57,528	34,689	35,717	8,934	14,704	15,656	1,040	545	537
Jefferson County	6,352	3,642	2,216	1,177	2,093	1,647	488	0	33
Kings County	98,887	46,306	64,886	6,862	8,919	9,175	498	378	210
Livingston County	4,482	2,380	1,989	662	1,216	1,257	19	39	293
Madison County	4,223	2,515	2,547	1,100	888	1,184	218	27	30
Monroe County	39,443	26,937	31,587	5,198	8,939	11,844	291	440	326
Nassau County	80,867	42,733	69,496	4,894	16,242	20,267	402	225	459
New York County	36,083	32,435	107,845	3,765	9,338	12,934	205	253	351
Niagara County	17,508	7,333	5,805	2,555	3,582	3,867	163	210	0
Oneida County	15,046	10,998	8,063	3,227	4,233	4,615	242	131	261
Onondaga County	24,284	17,599	19,325	5,469	6,836	6,894	357	241	228
Ontario County	7,408	4,775	5,200	1,402	2,044	1,912	196	0	199
Orange County	17,976	11,131	10,130	3,328	4,859	4,237	280	210	200
Oswego County	7,752	3,654	2,057	1,543	2,840	1,878	307	9	25
Putnam County	4,955	3,408	3,969	745	1,517	1,249	0	0	0
Queens County	97,469	53,566	64,790	6,617	10,972	15,019	428	399	139
Rensselaer County	8,531	6,334	5,557	1,566	2,647	2,222	124	0	12
Richmond County	27,803	12,914	13,661	2,504	5,411	4,985	180	97	217
Rockland County	11,321	10,381	17,998	1,130	2,912	3,410	33	0	0
Saratoga County	11,690	8,434	11,481	2,334	4,405	3,003	182	71	121
Schenectady County	8,770	6,032	6,553	1,335	1,639	2,606	44	31	254
St. Lawrence County	6,986	3,917	2,850	1,509	1,659	1,787	8	251	0
Steuben County	6,205	3,975	3,757	1,843	1,828	1,814	101	57	28
Suffolk County	85,776	50,147	60,326	8,783	20,361	23,796	858	238	310
Sullivan County	5,334	2,650	2,591	898	1,424	1,233	0	0	0
Tompkins County	2,981	2,985	5,183	419	1,276	1,009	10	64	0
Ulster County	11,404	6,728	8,720	2,072	2,785	3,010	320	99	27
Warren County	4,476	2,916	3,177	1,160	1,342	1,095	88	0	30
Wayne County	6,854	3,296	2,300	1,141	1,464	1,131	41	0	146
Westchester County	43,892	25,040	55,140	3,177	9,747	11,539	200	124	184
North Carolina									
Alamance County	8,772	6,828	5,195	2,270	1,676	2,201	354	0	97
Brunswick County	9,362	9,280	9,859	2,767	5,578	2,914	212	327	59
Buncombe County	11,986	11,222	16,055	3,804	5,162	4,253	111	71	49
Burke County	5,153	4,069	2,776	1,559	2,645	1,077	0	0	0
Cabarrus County	8,133	6,918	4,200	2,236	2,514	2,348	584	0	57
Caldwell County	4,679	3,564	2,527	1,161	1,481	1,600	21	0	0
Carteret County	4,676	4,171	4,477	888	2,092	1,796	163	74	43
Catawba County	8,527	6,137	3,741	1,873	2,199	2,117	193	207	0
Chatham County	4,776	3,278	6,467	624	1,461	1,719	60	0	55
Cleveland County	5,515	4,809	2,852	825	1,621	1,102	290	342	40
Craven County	5,263	5,124	4,337	1,683	2,841	2,505	225	76	64
Cumberland County	11,626	10,029	6,370	8,443	5,244	3,123	1,274	561	244
Davidson County	11,524	6,069	3,821	2,046	2,545	2,077	126	199	44

Table E-2: Counties—Educational Attainment and Veteran Status, Persons 55 and Over—*Continued*

	High School or Equivalent	Some College or Associates Degree	Bachelor's Degree or Higher	Veterans by Age and Gender					
				Male			Female		
				55 to 64 Years	65 to 74 Years	75 Years and Over	55 to 64 Years	65 to 74 Years	75 Years and Over
North Carolina—Cont.									
Durham County	8,862	5,994	13,901	3,215	3,298	2,255	843	256	151
Forsyth County	17,067	12,623	14,134	5,105	5,477	5,030	766	148	91
Gaston County	10,209	9,983	4,445	2,228	3,704	2,868	88	41	135
Guilford County	23,912	17,405	18,363	5,185	6,790	6,285	778	0	172
Harnett County	5,145	3,546	1,732	1,489	1,707	1,096	241	71	93
Henderson County	7,712	8,457	8,587	1,264	2,998	3,827	77	258	0
Iredell County	8,278	7,143	4,905	1,366	3,196	2,115	233	0	0
Johnston County	7,798	6,209	3,062	2,292	2,599	1,722	68	59	42
Lincoln County	4,446	2,266	1,435	1,288	1,486	858	43	0	0
Mecklenburg County	26,330	28,519	33,584	8,569	10,122	8,332	1,341	370	203
Moore County	5,052	5,194	9,311	1,293	2,298	1,968	94	135	14
Nash County	6,087	3,756	1,756	1,180	1,417	1,392	102	125	0
New Hanover County	9,867	9,273	12,021	2,729	4,821	3,552	142	112	0
Onslow County	5,554	4,504	2,928	2,796	2,873	2,039	146	242	67
Orange County	3,648	3,292	7,648	1,020	1,885	1,398	7	40	70
Pitt County	7,133	5,083	4,407	1,173	1,874	1,530	173	156	0
Randolph County	8,495	4,856	2,658	1,498	3,172	1,893	98	68	88
Robeson County	6,702	2,842	1,717	1,487	1,422	956	136	171	37
Rockingham County	6,251	4,165	2,010	2,049	1,269	1,153	43	202	69
Rowan County	8,382	6,483	4,086	2,211	2,873	2,318	86	0	134
Rutherford County	3,903	3,394	2,461	983	1,431	730	115	0	0
Surry County	4,227	3,779	1,395	489	1,615	1,109	15	44	82
Union County	9,132	6,601	6,072	2,095	3,071	1,733	154	25	0
Wake County	24,650	27,779	36,970	8,581	10,609	8,632	1,375	377	411
Wayne County	7,312	4,401	2,773	2,349	2,037	1,833	466	51	0
Wilkes County	5,793	2,454	1,397	1,120	1,533	843	68	0	82
Wilson County	5,234	1,908	2,979	970	831	1,276	0	41	0
North Dakota									
Burleigh County	3,369	3,928	3,787	880	1,348	1,306	68	35	0
Cass County	6,690	4,334	4,948	1,640	2,154	1,705	44	8	40
Grand Forks County	2,835	2,285	1,753	924	1,078	815	49	0	0
Ward County	2,934	2,365	1,447	811	1,020	955	163	0	83
Ohio									
Allen County	7,825	4,066	1,916	1,364	1,473	1,869	151	20	41
Ashtabula County	8,473	3,728	1,738	1,482	2,336	1,956	82	24	257
Belmont County	7,510	2,425	1,913	997	1,642	1,274	33	62	38
Butler County	19,428	11,477	10,949	3,403	5,525	4,057	129	216	142
Clark County	10,781	6,226	3,627	2,058	3,134	2,769	120	119	0
Clermont County	10,758	7,466	5,455	3,546	3,683	2,393	294	0	23
Columbiana County	10,329	2,960	2,079	1,721	2,947	2,017	95	115	0
Cuyahoga County	74,964	47,711	47,769	13,085	18,438	20,518	695	562	912
Delaware County	7,936	4,694	7,606	1,931	2,662	1,838	86	0	0
Erie County	6,593	3,280	2,742	939	1,287	1,784	0	117	0
Fairfield County	9,311	5,422	4,617	1,624	2,799	2,155	80	72	49
Franklin County	47,156	29,859	37,376	11,943	14,771	12,037	1,831	392	320
Geauga County	5,514	4,043	5,366	680	1,749	1,538	66	248	17
Greene County	8,997	5,899	7,962	2,908	2,827	2,561	565	299	226
Hamilton County	36,194	28,123	33,391	7,292	9,590	11,667	300	238	297
Hancock County	5,220	2,952	1,744	869	759	1,143	8	0	0
Jefferson County	7,124	2,055	1,403	1,062	1,259	872	0	17	0
Lake County	16,866	10,158	8,049	2,458	4,953	3,919	0	47	99
Licking County	10,149	5,920	5,693	3,084	3,774	2,616	214	64	139
Lorain County	20,227	12,110	8,831	4,062	5,424	4,301	483	115	240
Lucas County	23,373	16,062	13,064	3,633	6,612	6,462	375	214	396
Mahoning County	20,673	10,007	6,951	3,474	4,915	5,433	40	136	369
Marion County	4,996	2,519	1,446	1,225	1,245	1,085	65	23	0
Medina County	11,185	7,474	5,040	1,973	3,434	2,844	77	0	0
Miami County	6,896	3,542	3,357	1,436	2,387	1,402	0	0	55
Montgomery County	32,015	25,108	18,473	6,951	9,961	9,141	782	488	361
Muskingum County	6,706	2,413	1,915	1,451	1,299	1,054	229	0	0
Portage County	9,906	4,601	4,532	2,113	2,956	2,548	170	44	36
Richland County	9,923	4,503	3,527	1,720	2,456	2,350	367	0	39
Ross County	5,911	1,491	1,416	1,262	1,587	998	184	44	0
Scioto County	5,668	2,013	2,030	1,187	1,342	1,022	28	0	0
Stark County	32,878	14,522	8,885	5,267	7,260	7,262	197	300	272
Summit County	35,566	19,956	20,595	5,600	8,039	8,725	201	213	25
Trumbull County	19,093	7,965	4,841	2,195	4,398	4,099	78	27	0
Tuscarawas County	9,776	2,013	1,574	1,428	1,967	1,619	219	67	0
Warren County	10,501	6,684	8,621	2,635	2,449	2,819	172	180	55
Wayne County	7,850	3,559	3,027	1,374	2,048	1,789	7	71	46
Wood County	7,932	3,684	4,418	1,111	1,834	1,969	38	127	83
Oklahoma									
Canadian County	4,809	5,736	3,344	1,231	1,451	1,221	349	197	84
Cleveland County	10,060	9,606	9,081	3,594	4,197	3,085	549	71	142
Comanche County	4,546	3,952	2,700	3,274	2,047	1,756	255	585	193

Table E-2: Counties—Educational Attainment and Veteran Status, Persons 55 and Over—*Continued*

	High School or Equivalent	Some College or Associates Degree	Bachelor's Degree or Higher	Veterans by Age and Gender					
				Male			Female		
				55 to 64 Years	65 to 74 Years	75 Years and Over	55 to 64 Years	65 to 74 Years	75 Years and Over
Oklahoma—Cont.									
Creek County	5,891	2,599	967	1,234	1,345	1,072	149	21	19
Muskogee County	4,099	3,092	2,317	984	1,990	1,264	71	17	0
Oklahoma County	26,705	28,484	28,933	10,322	10,844	9,243	851	455	204
Payne County	2,928	2,446	2,189	681	834	740	13	0	0
Pottawatomie County	4,325	3,043	2,201	1,502	1,360	1,214	24	0	94
Rogers County	6,614	3,190	1,825	1,255	2,012	1,423	151	0	0
Tulsa County	26,285	23,461	21,619	6,081	8,679	7,573	381	257	214
Wagoner County	4,564	3,251	1,703	1,437	2,102	1,092	70	0	0
Oregon									
Benton County	2,381	3,060	6,018	778	1,343	1,482	58	59	163
Clackamas County	17,004	22,802	19,444	4,979	8,141	6,120	578	244	482
Deschutes County	8,066	9,651	10,483	2,189	4,307	2,567	113	118	154
Douglas County	7,943	8,855	3,595	2,659	4,155	3,580	38	386	0
Jackson County	11,951	11,474	13,592	3,435	5,544	4,672	510	465	105
Josephine County	5,990	7,958	3,431	1,667	2,649	1,923	199	298	0
Klamath County	4,155	4,165	1,910	1,498	1,933	1,404	82	0	8
Lane County	17,012	19,823	18,739	5,126	8,623	6,914	792	575	202
Linn County	7,462	6,775	3,572	1,625	2,926	2,015	260	110	73
Marion County	13,405	15,427	12,350	3,154	5,619	5,322	545	353	98
Multnomah County	23,413	28,276	29,509	6,565	10,885	7,739	652	287	479
Polk County	3,789	4,134	3,965	947	1,406	1,750	177	59	90
Umatilla County	4,206	3,427	1,865	1,379	1,851	1,243	0	130	0
Washington County	16,783	19,508	25,910	5,000	8,307	5,586	954	147	127
Yamhill County	4,308	3,850	4,428	1,113	1,786	1,460	124	34	57
Pennsylvania									
Adams County	7,609	3,217	3,800	1,267	1,867	2,033	78	0	13
Allegheny County	94,981	42,009	53,180	13,268	19,788	24,438	775	274	1,011
Armstrong County	7,961	1,916	1,092	902	1,623	1,824	0	15	52
Beaver County	16,172	7,292	5,013	2,133	3,519	3,759	38	119	54
Berks County	30,026	10,932	11,104	4,603	7,001	7,968	251	161	198
Blair County	13,025	3,208	4,155	2,532	2,240	3,233	124	82	134
Bucks County	43,624	22,568	26,692	6,063	10,702	10,618	485	169	310
Butler County	15,874	6,676	5,287	2,064	3,524	3,715	49	141	14
Cambria County	15,752	4,413	3,155	1,778	3,016	3,678	94	79	29
Carbon County	7,004	3,323	1,023	1,013	1,698	1,211	0	0	21
Centre County	7,739	3,411	6,251	1,430	2,105	1,678	137	0	0
Chester County	22,894	15,671	27,659	2,745	8,208	7,652	219	155	205
Clearfield County	8,033	2,775	1,326	535	1,588	1,610	64	39	0
Columbia County	5,920	1,827	1,622	460	1,132	1,038	17	50	52
Crawford County	8,302	2,975	2,267	1,542	2,327	1,823	63	88	112
Cumberland County	18,059	7,279	10,222	3,298	4,197	5,250	280	87	46
Dauphin County	16,500	8,479	9,000	2,244	3,813	4,296	485	292	173
Delaware County	34,720	16,430	22,481	4,901	7,541	8,895	643	129	143
Erie County	20,399	8,661	9,031	3,596	5,193	4,677	185	94	271
Fayette County	15,188	3,275	2,913	1,481	3,335	3,409	0	102	0
Franklin County	11,610	4,925	4,975	1,887	2,923	2,872	107	0	140
Indiana County	7,099	2,260	3,007	880	1,521	1,363	298	239	32
Lackawanna County	19,532	8,189	7,624	2,278	3,600	4,898	148	151	424
Lancaster County	37,638	12,910	18,161	4,737	8,750	8,833	233	254	554
Lawrence County	9,026	2,841	2,106	562	1,723	2,048	110	0	112
Lebanon County	12,777	3,402	3,940	2,095	2,884	3,074	73	118	0
Lehigh County	24,457	10,070	11,398	3,594	4,813	5,613	295	91	92
Luzerne County	28,639	12,293	9,427	3,347	6,352	6,254	342	325	240
Lycoming County	9,455	4,400	2,999	1,956	2,192	2,179	194	38	35
Mercer County	12,765	3,362	3,434	1,479	2,965	2,127	108	21	0
Monroe County	9,728	5,286	6,107	1,820	3,526	2,049	59	64	241
Montgomery County	44,858	26,056	45,574	5,619	12,329	13,764	552	103	886
Northampton County	23,293	9,304	9,713	3,591	5,476	5,704	281	72	159
Northumberland County	11,106	2,488	1,398	1,509	2,104	1,960	106	0	16
Philadelphia County	77,766	33,354	31,760	11,678	14,260	15,675	942	789	1,036
Schuylkill County	15,883	3,497	2,623	1,738	3,167	3,344	74	43	230
Somerset County	8,507	2,092	1,722	928	1,843	1,482	0	82	37
Washington County	19,293	6,603	7,471	2,921	4,534	4,195	21	128	13
Westmoreland County	37,413	14,151	13,139	3,521	8,497	8,713	329	41	316
York County	33,009	12,788	10,440	5,084	7,612	6,785	415	176	411
Rhode Island									
Kent County	10,629	5,528	8,270	1,993	3,517	3,689	134	0	50
Newport County	3,962	3,764	6,333	1,394	1,908	2,023	500	30	73
Providence County	30,050	15,854	16,890	5,513	7,181	9,059	182	144	340
Washington County	5,706	5,714	8,113	880	2,941	2,219	21	89	46
South Carolina									
Aiken County	7,403	6,147	10,374	2,012	2,633	3,426	386	127	179
Anderson County	11,886	8,240	5,233	2,526	4,729	2,343	0	75	134
Beaufort County	7,417	11,681	21,194	2,594	4,469	4,807	325	223	0
Berkeley County	8,589	7,063	3,912	4,513	4,210	1,799	504	128	104

Table E-2: Counties—Educational Attainment and Veteran Status, Persons 55 and Over—*Continued*

	High School or Equivalent	Some College or Associates Degree	Bachelor's Degree or Higher	Veterans by Age and Gender					
				Male			Female		
				55 to 64 Years	65 to 74 Years	75 Years and Over	55 to 64 Years	65 to 74 Years	75 Years and Over
South Carolina—Cont.									
Charleston County	14,378	14,950	19,148	4,711	6,524	4,834	370	147	63
Darlington County	4,375	1,897	1,470	1,252	1,642	1,043	43	0	62
Dorchester County	6,294	4,943	3,738	3,515	2,971	1,210	267	40	0
Florence County	7,386	4,553	3,841	1,723	2,529	1,861	357	0	0
Greenville County	24,521	16,691	16,938	4,971	9,154	6,450	175	102	254
Greenwood County	4,137	2,637	2,028	496	1,203	1,198	0	23	54
Horry County	24,065	17,765	11,568	4,670	8,995	6,178	416	222	72
Lancaster County	5,740	3,987	4,222	1,584	1,340	1,707	0	34	56
Laurens County	5,061	1,718	1,659	772	1,309	1,202	0	49	7
Lexington County	12,999	10,270	9,904	3,166	5,042	3,454	321	147	95
Oconee County	4,893	3,471	4,835	1,262	2,322	1,668	0	34	76
Orangeburg County	4,531	3,737	1,848	1,656	1,265	988	762	0	26
Pickens County	6,409	4,196	4,048	473	2,274	1,566	0	41	0
Richland County	11,541	12,362	14,960	5,379	5,335	4,692	1,211	324	0
Spartanburg County	14,407	10,399	9,278	3,885	4,878	4,074	189	138	54
Sumter County	4,294	2,965	2,287	1,983	1,947	1,423	216	0	55
York County	9,640	9,033	6,897	3,105	4,335	2,308	345	99	146
South Dakota									
Minnehaha County	9,760	5,131	4,764	1,608	2,267	2,285	143	50	155
Pennington County	5,651	5,231	3,884	2,094	2,550	1,973	394	0	104
Tennessee									
Anderson County	5,322	2,884	3,320	1,667	1,495	1,769	77	71	255
Blount County	9,688	6,306	3,858	1,863	2,669	2,106	169	0	158
Bradley County	6,148	3,001	3,336	817	2,260	805	78	69	0
Davidson County	22,434	17,488	20,902	6,591	7,538	6,627	1,336	253	120
Greene County	5,580	2,757	1,506	847	1,686	1,193	85	0	0
Hamilton County	18,870	13,852	14,578	5,087	6,165	5,744	536	54	226
Knox County	20,990	15,403	18,048	5,461	7,129	7,047	369	359	573
Madison County	5,424	2,534	3,892	1,044	1,396	1,015	68	40	0
Maury County	4,732	2,739	2,519	847	1,533	612	0	0	48
Montgomery County	5,558	4,898	2,769	4,305	3,219	1,630	896	73	27
Putnam County	2,970	2,760	2,862	966	1,422	1,365	97	0	47
Robertson County	3,981	1,858	1,105	711	1,274	729	122	27	0
Rutherford County	11,180	5,769	4,742	3,080	4,070	2,601	198	0	99
Sevier County	5,585	3,711	2,757	817	1,858	1,098	153	0	58
Shelby County	32,663	28,803	27,254	11,710	12,399	8,447	1,111	355	373
Sullivan County	11,770	6,072	6,491	2,244	3,838	3,297	203	72	137
Sumner County	10,920	5,368	5,381	1,924	2,728	2,195	0	90	0
Washington County	6,737	4,019	5,970	2,760	3,076	2,275	130	282	70
Williamson County	6,265	5,697	9,424	1,433	2,342	2,063	40	0	63
Wilson County	6,659	3,960	3,316	1,749	2,082	1,606	75	0	0
Texas									
Angelina County	5,455	2,915	2,212	884	1,450	1,635	42	0	0
Bastrop County	2,676	3,550	1,778	1,676	1,667	915	72	70	0
Bell County	9,545	10,146	7,070	7,316	4,608	3,554	1,401	259	151
Bexar County	52,379	54,374	51,887	25,364	26,694	21,406	5,579	1,346	1,202
Bowie County	4,324	4,468	2,535	1,649	2,026	1,405	145	11	138
Brazoria County	13,256	10,022	6,644	2,794	4,481	2,576	217	101	0
Brazos County	4,587	4,094	5,736	1,598	1,943	1,803	180	0	0
Cameron County	10,562	9,014	7,340	3,481	3,624	3,832	8	53	109
Collin County	18,572	24,861	33,781	7,639	10,455	6,290	573	486	46
Comal County	6,439	6,392	6,821	2,122	3,638	2,130	462	93	0
Coryell County	2,127	2,179	1,208	1,742	1,182	685	173	0	240
Dallas County	58,189	60,760	69,188	19,340	21,580	19,501	2,377	866	462
Denton County	17,502	19,124	21,684	7,572	8,513	4,955	594	279	76
Ector County	3,267	3,818	2,021	1,272	1,410	1,356	50	53	0
El Paso County	19,158	16,675	12,908	7,904	6,890	5,634	768	175	354
Ellis County	7,665	4,562	3,867	2,241	2,888	1,575	226	71	16
Fort Bend County	11,845	14,048	24,713	4,024	5,501	3,190	857	69	67
Galveston County	11,697	11,546	10,475	3,128	4,489	3,026	553	151	26
Grayson County	7,780	5,541	4,634	2,618	3,081	2,227	277	62	39
Gregg County	5,378	5,489	4,132	1,367	2,081	2,095	86	71	176
Guadalupe County	6,740	5,116	4,524	2,782	3,469	1,937	858	66	0
Harris County	92,551	106,475	112,793	27,299	35,385	27,609	2,362	1,347	513
Harrison County	3,402	3,123	2,008	639	1,044	979	83	0	47
Hays County	4,079	5,283	6,712	1,557	2,613	1,667	285	73	56
Henderson County	5,595	4,656	3,786	1,294	1,467	1,695	0	127	27
Hidalgo County	16,270	12,979	9,490	3,184	4,547	4,597	265	252	102
Hunt County	5,576	3,058	1,963	946	1,671	1,434	104	0	0
Jefferson County	13,445	8,598	4,509	4,231	3,449	3,227	342	105	40
Johnson County	6,317	6,659	3,578	1,392	2,801	2,026	209	0	198
Kaufman County	5,283	2,931	2,233	1,654	1,352	1,121	70	179	36
Liberty County	4,254	2,813	312	946	1,136	954	0	76	0
Lubbock County	9,414	9,462	8,508	2,298	3,512	3,013	90	68	42
McLennan County	8,559	9,809	7,489	3,546	4,033	3,884	223	68	231

Table E-2: Counties—Educational Attainment and Veteran Status, Persons 55 and Over—*Continued*

	High School or Equivalent	Some College or Associates Degree	Bachelor's Degree or Higher	Veterans by Age and Gender					
				Male			Female		
				55 to 64 Years	65 to 74 Years	75 Years and Over	55 to 64 Years	65 to 74 Years	75 Years and Over
Texas—Cont.									
Midland County	4,086	4,828	3,636	1,169	1,322	1,217	100	142	0
Montgomery County	16,350	19,435	18,530	7,295	8,209	5,402	282	229	100
Nacogdoches County	3,229	2,350	1,843	644	864	1,035	20	0	185
Nueces County	11,366	10,786	9,663	5,947	6,787	3,821	366	68	105
Orange County	5,277	2,847	2,223	566	1,370	1,180	0	0	34
Parker County	6,088	5,315	3,861	2,734	3,233	1,914	176	15	73
Potter County	4,150	4,038	2,572	1,764	1,484	1,541	0	93	148
Randall County	4,146	5,402	5,689	1,400	1,768	2,224	225	74	25
Rockwall County	2,699	3,776	3,227	773	1,185	669	145	0	0
San Patricio County	2,819	2,464	1,430	661	1,128	749	11	12	44
Smith County	9,881	9,937	8,925	1,338	2,129	3,356	57	0	107
Tarrant County	50,336	57,646	55,766	20,998	23,094	17,427	2,028	1,106	625
Taylor County	5,530	4,665	4,938	1,252	2,127	2,205	142	43	45
Tom Green County	4,890	4,730	3,942	1,863	2,011	2,032	59	87	48
Travis County	18,811	22,939	42,066	7,372	10,360	8,449	1,293	553	299
Victoria County	3,076	3,479	2,123	959	1,257	1,204	114	61	31
Walker County	3,276	1,811	1,154	1,265	604	1,036	173	22	54
Webb County	4,204	2,626	2,348	732	1,416	901	0	0	0
Wichita County	6,018	5,588	3,483	1,957	2,211	2,197	164	20	96
Williamson County	13,277	15,566	18,346	4,940	7,421	5,194	792	274	178
Utah									
Cache County	2,565	3,191	3,875	431	956	1,164	32	0	11
Davis County	7,657	11,425	9,051	2,884	3,277	3,366	244	76	150
Salt Lake County	27,988	34,425	32,737	8,027	10,324	10,020	426	237	398
Utah County	8,224	13,495	15,546	2,735	3,664	3,887	201	130	47
Washington County	6,751	12,358	8,448	1,283	3,133	4,310	0	78	51
Weber County	6,199	10,141	7,122	2,773	2,959	3,280	211	446	192
Vermont									
Chittenden County	5,463	5,310	8,435	1,617	1,608	2,229	274	178	169
Virginia									
Albemarle County	4,073	3,344	7,450	1,316	2,155	1,427	24	0	18
Arlington County	2,859	3,747	11,188	1,436	2,594	1,743	347	64	285
Augusta County	4,545	4,426	2,863	1,006	2,074	1,504	74	141	0
Bedford County	4,750	3,875	3,762	1,027	1,782	1,276	0	0	39
Chesterfield County	10,313	13,801	13,405	3,539	6,326	4,085	587	222	97
Fairfax County	20,589	24,441	70,895	12,194	15,815	11,882	3,085	877	530
Fauquier County	3,903	2,032	3,098	1,395	1,427	1,112	102	0	0
Frederick County	3,915	2,967	2,901	1,542	1,592	1,629	127	0	0
Hanover County	5,741	4,303	3,349	1,042	1,579	1,391	43	150	88
Henrico County	13,805	10,317	13,294	2,273	4,323	4,540	378	117	88
James City County	1,968	4,136	9,280	1,671	2,116	2,271	137	66	89
Loudoun County	4,851	6,242	12,864	4,139	2,781	2,203	410	9	82
Montgomery County	3,144	1,870	4,247	499	843	1,090	0	90	0
Prince William County	10,011	9,480	13,316	5,899	5,861	3,386	1,100	428	129
Roanoke County	7,218	4,193	4,336	1,305	1,708	1,858	105	173	0
Rockingham County	5,418	3,208	2,436	1,083	1,432	1,490	101	0	0
Spotsylvania County	4,911	3,367	4,391	2,575	2,215	1,521	376	207	95
Stafford County	3,884	3,123	3,776	2,926	1,751	1,306	305	114	0
York County	2,188	3,390	3,536	1,917	1,817	1,189	0	97	38
Washington									
Benton County	7,039	8,611	7,198	2,474	2,947	2,705	353	126	0
Chelan County	3,572	4,697	3,306	861	1,306	1,515	96	0	211
Clallam County	5,410	6,566	5,867	1,391	3,145	1,880	160	179	0
Clark County	16,128	22,450	17,377	6,834	7,571	6,089	633	343	268
Cowlitz County	6,071	7,339	2,541	1,535	3,328	2,150	0	159	128
Franklin County	2,091	2,236	1,071	883	1,121	341	133	0	54
Grant County	3,831	2,989	1,979	1,331	1,519	1,077	107	135	0
Grays Harbor County	4,362	5,403	2,060	1,105	2,940	1,572	102	0	282
Island County	4,344	5,391	7,305	2,202	3,130	2,107	304	42	0
King County	52,192	70,559	103,041	18,937	25,145	25,032	2,683	1,201	1,656
Kitsap County	10,755	12,893	14,238	6,230	7,050	4,460	762	271	201
Lewis County	4,337	5,949	2,026	1,503	2,287	1,805	106	99	108
Pierce County	30,859	34,998	26,488	15,537	16,420	11,658	2,125	1,204	439
Skagit County	5,806	7,540	7,309	1,747	3,252	2,638	99	173	11
Snohomish County	27,976	31,300	22,432	10,989	11,428	8,714	1,155	331	210
Spokane County	20,882	22,286	20,903	8,570	9,592	8,606	1,020	158	281
Thurston County	10,589	13,603	13,483	5,383	5,252	5,157	829	139	25
Whatcom County	8,735	10,159	10,251	2,204	3,713	2,909	63	75	445
Yakima County	8,634	8,855	5,268	2,142	4,058	3,363	399	0	148
West Virginia									
Berkeley County	5,791	3,448	2,610	1,644	2,836	1,373	209	72	0
Cabell County	5,931	3,399	2,802	1,277	1,926	1,595	83	0	0
Harrison County	5,212	3,631	931	694	1,735	1,308	25	0	109
Kanawha County	14,338	7,449	6,292	2,609	3,121	3,210	0	0	20

Table E-2: Counties—Educational Attainment and Veteran Status, Persons 55 and Over—*Continued*

	High School or Equivalent	Some College or Associates Degree	Bachelor's Degree or Higher	Veterans by Age and Gender					
				Male			Female		
				55 to 64 Years	65 to 74 Years	75 Years and Over	55 to 64 Years	65 to 74 Years	75 Years and Over
West Virginia—Cont.									
Monongalia County	3,621	1,537	3,387	1,225	1,352	848	76	75	0
Raleigh County	4,742	3,500	1,798	1,114	878	1,072	70	35	0
Wood County	7,280	3,949	2,195	1,809	1,615	1,781	160	394	44
Wisconsin									
Brown County	14,491	7,915	7,158	2,945	3,984	3,572	153	0	128
Dane County	17,781	15,631	23,446	4,102	6,621	5,792	349	76	244
Dodge County	7,471	2,912	1,332	1,204	1,264	1,581	350	19	43
Eau Claire County	5,979	3,303	3,166	1,027	1,673	1,546	45	0	0
Fond du Lac County	8,318	3,613	2,501	1,409	1,718	1,354	178	24	0
Jefferson County	6,163	2,924	1,863	713	1,759	1,486	20	0	94
Kenosha County	9,026	4,998	4,084	1,725	2,684	2,053	183	0	174
La Crosse County	7,391	3,453	4,277	2,210	1,988	2,144	122	90	77
Manitowoc County	7,809	2,646	1,986	1,111	1,900	1,726	98	22	48
Marathon County	10,095	3,626	4,416	1,361	2,327	2,725	83	0	18
Milwaukee County	42,645	26,357	26,362	9,020	10,634	11,529	1,209	291	162
Outagamie County	11,687	4,455	4,307	1,488	2,686	2,297	40	0	0
Ozaukee County	4,683	3,234	6,419	916	1,406	1,724	0	0	57
Portage County	4,121	2,315	2,540	581	1,247	1,003	64	0	58
Racine County	10,995	7,336	5,149	2,397	2,831	3,086	356	40	0
Rock County	10,771	5,878	5,337	2,127	2,672	2,403	178	0	80
Sheboygan County	9,294	3,782	3,504	1,181	1,994	2,292	0	0	114
St. Croix County	4,463	2,356	3,087	1,162	1,673	808	77	32	0
Walworth County	5,288	3,927	4,625	1,007	1,650	1,380	32	294	83
Washington County	8,588	5,284	4,331	1,316	2,084	2,072	208	0	84
Waukesha County	23,743	16,698	19,605	3,196	6,910	6,986	157	380	78
Winnebago County	10,915	6,789	5,241	1,768	3,070	2,900	117	0	40
Wood County	6,782	2,613	2,360	608	1,746	1,491	80	10	0
Wyoming									
Laramie County	4,361	3,534	4,349	2,098	2,147	1,284	273	0	58
Natrona County	3,209	3,895	1,949	1,058	924	1,295	60	42	166

Table E-3: Places—Educational Attainment and Veteran Status, Persons 55 and Over

	High School or Equivalent	Some College or Associates Degree	Bachelor's Degree or Higher	Veterans by Age and Gender Male 55 to 64 Years	Male 65 to 74 Years	Male 75 Years and Over	Female 55 to 64 Years	Female 65 to 74 Years	Female 75 Years and Over
Alabama									
Birmingham city	8,520	7,886	5,446	3,322	2,938	2,449	76	172	0
Dothan city	3,938	3,008	2,211	990	1,265	1,028	112	127	71
Hoover city	2,356	4,416	7,660	535	1,780	2,109	0	0	140
Huntsville city	7,180	7,668	8,997	3,362	2,460	3,498	349	219	136
Mobile city	8,386	7,954	7,340	2,873	2,907	2,473	378	44	127
Montgomery city	7,585	6,623	6,949	2,857	2,619	2,097	71	337	35
Tuscaloosa city	4,377	2,530	3,387	834	1,108	928	18	0	50
Alaska									
Anchorage municipality	7,099	7,451	8,806	3,973	4,613	2,677	1,239	383	310
Arizona									
Avondale city	1,792	1,775	655	540	842	427	36	0	0
Chandler city	6,265	8,016	8,031	2,186	2,598	1,969	69	80	38
Flagstaff city	1,377	1,214	3,526	421	1,028	546	0	61	0
Glendale city	8,019	8,577	4,970	3,537	3,215	2,108	319	238	116
Goodyear city	2,071	3,402	4,048	1,489	1,498	1,287	238	77	129
Mesa city	24,477	23,533	16,575	5,480	8,169	7,961	669	163	317
Peoria city	7,757	9,376	7,816	2,306	3,599	2,904	291	124	113
Phoenix city	38,492	45,311	38,832	12,558	18,998	13,660	1,767	430	417
Scottsdale city	8,860	16,935	22,596	1,555	4,319	6,235	263	142	79
Surprise city	5,783	8,779	8,396	1,298	3,107	3,495	225	123	44
Tempe city	3,924	6,003	6,770	938	2,533	1,701	219	105	0
Tucson city	15,953	22,220	18,656	7,344	7,417	7,424	987	455	555
Yuma city	3,734	3,319	2,133	1,151	1,275	890	192	137	40
Arkansas									
Fayetteville city	1,893	1,411	2,328	664	855	741	138	0	89
Fort Smith city	3,984	3,182	1,758	862	1,080	1,089	0	38	0
Jonesboro city	1,881	3,996	2,471	275	1,035	868	0	0	127
Little Rock city	6,985	6,229	10,430	2,319	2,372	2,316	56	315	0
North Little Rock city	2,454	1,704	2,815	1,460	1,075	902	76	62	0
Springdale city	2,155	1,457	1,657	299	760	840	72	0	0
California									
Alameda city	1,561	3,028	3,817	768	1,027	552	42	0	0
Alhambra city	2,430	2,990	2,524	160	396	540	0	0	0
Anaheim city	8,824	9,386	8,335	1,596	2,213	2,533	37	0	36
Antioch city	3,504	3,114	3,300	1,584	919	1,170	77	0	0
Bakersfield city	7,952	10,590	6,878	2,543	3,344	2,808	230	144	286
Baldwin Park city	2,460	1,232	607	170	292	236	0	0	0
Bellflower city	2,257	1,610	1,538	470	414	457	0	0	11
Berkeley city	1,722	2,982	10,026	356	919	1,153	156	0	0
Buena Park city	2,861	2,516	1,716	377	435	1,148	0	0	0
Burbank city	4,568	3,798	2,831	239	815	975	0	0	38
Camarillo city	2,384	4,799	4,220	487	1,140	1,412	0	22	0
Carlsbad city	2,196	4,859	9,445	474	1,617	1,980	242	0	0
Carson city	2,871	4,119	2,502	319	621	1,232	0	0	0
Chico city	2,510	2,220	4,772	524	1,080	970	170	0	0
Chino city	1,525	2,589	933	766	953	468	33	0	0
Chino Hills city	1,649	1,767	1,806	468	286	224	0	0	0
Chula Vista city	6,382	8,982	6,352	2,628	2,872	2,698	449	115	235
Citrus Heights city	4,290	5,536	2,945	1,109	1,266	1,094	45	87	333
Clovis city	3,197	3,634	2,182	701	1,098	748	0	153	241
Compton city	1,036	1,931	352	221	0	570	0	0	0
Concord city	3,775	4,920	6,329	661	1,580	1,497	39	0	133
Corona city	3,931	4,656	3,947	556	1,439	998	0	0	0
Costa Mesa city	2,459	3,145	3,435	442	591	873	35	35	0
Daly City city	4,615	3,451	5,428	220	553	594	13	0	0
Davis city	774	918	4,042	123	418	439	0	0	0
Downey city	3,953	1,866	2,523	139	410	802	0	0	46
El Cajon city	2,738	3,804	2,916	631	1,638	801	66	37	0
El Monte city	2,382	2,277	1,164	265	571	617	0	0	0
Elk Grove city	4,655	4,878	4,276	1,445	2,185	1,168	105	0	0
Escondido city	4,419	4,589	5,412	1,057	1,602	1,811	0	41	41
Fairfield city	3,893	4,209	2,269	1,330	1,525	1,628	75	150	150
Folsom city	3,385	2,752	3,565	805	1,039	1,035	0	182	107
Fontana city	3,376	3,469	1,816	392	710	609	0	64	0
Fremont city	6,327	6,906	8,124	1,036	1,183	1,360	0	61	64
Fresno city	11,404	15,722	11,711	3,103	6,412	4,315	111	46	183
Fullerton city	2,772	4,364	5,431	441	1,124	1,516	0	0	140
Garden Grove city	6,527	6,078	3,604	748	1,074	1,165	37	64	62
Glendale city	6,953	4,844	9,353	558	1,352	1,438	11	38	0
Hawthorne city	1,363	1,633	1,950	120	210	364	0	43	0
Hayward city	4,586	3,955	3,856	1,161	631	1,095	73	0	134
Hemet city	5,560	6,983	2,931	990	1,954	3,101	73	0	303
Hesperia city	2,508	3,314	657	1,680	985	752	0	79	40
Huntington Beach city	5,233	8,961	14,506	896	2,881	3,020	42	41	59

Table E-3: Places—Educational Attainment and Veteran Status, Persons 55 and Over—*Continued*

	High School or Equivalent	Some College or Associates Degree	Bachelor's Degree or Higher	Veterans by Age and Gender Male 55 to 64 Years	Male 65 to 74 Years	Male 75 Years and Over	Female 55 to 64 Years	Female 65 to 74 Years	Female 75 Years and Over
California—Cont.									
Indio city..............................	2,934	3,113	2,726	281	832	992	74	23	0
Inglewood city.......................	1,903	3,593	1,752	830	772	749	0	71	0
Irvine city.............................	3,837	5,772	13,099	878	1,373	1,668	0	0	0
Jurupa Valley city..................	1,879	2,382	767	794	846	577	78	0	0
Laguna Niguel city.................	2,292	2,762	4,714	592	1,568	924	0	0	0
Lake Forest city.....................	2,103	2,779	2,600	456	1,345	583	0	0	0
Lakewood city........................	2,538	3,735	2,294	400	1,175	635	43	49	0
Lancaster city........................	5,681	4,200	2,031	1,799	1,988	927	186	72	39
Livermore city........................	2,204	3,583	3,676	919	1,134	626	57	0	129
Long Beach city......................	10,671	14,234	12,170	3,214	5,336	3,283	146	40	176
Los Angeles city.....................	91,512	99,679	132,631	12,858	20,033	26,066	1,610	411	1,318
Lynwood city..........................	1,203	211	205	0	192	0	85	0	0
Manteca city..........................	2,978	2,801	1,065	1,143	1,068	660	0	0	43
Menifee city...........................	4,315	5,710	2,834	1,145	1,655	1,638	0	0	161
Merced city............................	2,480	3,025	1,453	430	1,639	987	41	27	0
Milpitas city..........................	2,010	1,737	2,053	546	240	544	0	0	147
Mission Viejo city...................	3,588	4,997	6,183	594	1,582	1,163	0	0	130
Modesto city..........................	6,430	9,622	6,972	1,850	2,176	2,586	198	68	0
Moreno Valley city..................	5,096	4,762	2,692	2,296	1,661	1,061	354	67	52
Mountain View city..................	1,272	2,207	4,258	526	601	433	43	42	0
Murrieta city..........................	2,150	3,062	3,622	1,131	965	1,485	40	0	62
Napa city...............................	3,199	3,146	3,312	867	1,039	1,142	83	82	100
Newport Beach city.................	1,270	6,372	10,360	226	2,249	1,572	0	0	201
Norwalk city...........................	2,088	2,685	1,102	315	839	656	0	37	48
Oakland city...........................	7,944	11,171	16,667	2,164	3,549	3,332	187	101	280
Oceanside city........................	5,429	8,784	9,975	2,893	2,797	3,721	158	114	318
Ontario city...........................	2,435	3,576	1,901	997	1,196	704	0	41	0
Orange city............................	3,386	4,450	4,411	1,218	1,258	1,238	68	0	0
Oxnard city............................	3,061	3,981	4,604	1,576	2,177	1,550	0	0	0
Palmdale city.........................	2,360	3,759	1,635	2,390	1,105	788	72	0	0
Palo Alto city.........................	na	na	na	216	858	936	0	0	67
Pasadena city........................	3,917	3,421	8,510	754	1,293	942	0	38	73
Perris city..............................	798	1,311	402	343	364	73	0	33	4
Pittsburg city.........................	2,427	2,366	1,386	542	543	618	0	66	0
Pleasanton city.......................	2,617	3,148	3,792	258	759	864	0	0	0
Pomona city...........................	3,577	2,516	2,276	789	677	1,083	0	0	36
Rancho Cordova city................	2,274	3,692	1,587	852	1,134	860	101	40	38
Rancho Cucamonga city...........	4,528	6,340	4,255	1,254	2,254	840	60	56	0
Redding city...........................	3,645	6,697	4,230	855	1,665	2,019	220	77	38
Redlands city.........................	2,930	2,236	2,413	460	920	390	129	0	101
Redondo Beach city.................	820	3,048	3,027	206	373	402	60	0	0
Redwood City city...................	2,517	3,318	3,803	394	920	865	0	0	0
Rialto city.............................	2,055	2,331	1,391	465	996	559	0	37	132
Richmond city........................	2,877	3,886	3,192	775	1,566	777	0	77	187
Riverside city.........................	8,330	9,064	6,288	2,077	2,758	1,854	202	0	456
Roseville city.........................	5,011	8,929	6,319	906	2,239	2,627	118	66	162
Sacramento city......................	11,794	14,934	17,310	5,096	4,509	5,874	513	77	402
Salinas city...........................	2,678	2,693	2,032	790	730	826	142	0	0
San Bernardino city.................	4,420	4,688	2,294	1,718	1,339	1,395	33	34	31
San Buenaventura (Ventura) city.......	3,973	6,755	5,275	1,419	1,364	2,406	86	0	113
San Clemente city..................	1,532	5,215	5,070	202	1,078	1,271	146	0	0
San Diego city........................	31,516	39,187	57,814	14,025	17,181	14,774	1,132	858	511
San Francisco city..................	22,140	25,492	42,471	3,575	6,012	7,535	305	0	107
San Jose city..........................	24,244	26,939	38,494	4,959	7,880	7,056	311	129	117
San Leandro city....................	5,202	2,228	2,521	694	868	1,219	0	0	70
San Marcos city.....................	2,325	3,710	3,340	499	1,382	898	48	0	82
San Mateo city.......................	3,561	3,908	6,823	497	1,295	1,332	0	0	0
San Ramon city......................	1,470	2,402	3,661	57	541	285	24	41	159
Santa Ana city.......................	4,456	5,104	3,414	892	738	914	369	65	72
Santa Barbara city..................	2,606	3,443	7,521	362	1,002	1,661	0	74	153
Santa Clara city.....................	4,363	3,418	4,390	502	974	1,624	81	0	39
Santa Clarita city...................	5,438	6,679	5,833	1,312	1,871	1,934	211	41	36
Santa Maria city.....................	2,836	2,254	1,115	837	496	697	0	0	5
Santa Monica city...................	2,433	5,010	6,872	402	526	2,007	239	0	0
Santa Rosa city......................	4,677	8,307	9,801	1,660	2,295	2,341	274	119	50
Simi Valley city......................	5,890	5,708	4,079	1,210	1,587	1,515	23	0	0
South Gate city......................	594	1,365	419	218	502	135	0	0	0
South San Francisco city..........	2,931	1,906	2,499	465	539	642	0	0	0
Stockton city..........................	7,891	9,229	7,884	2,604	2,683	2,101	338	102	73
Sunnyvale city........................	2,897	4,906	6,393	722	908	1,172	81	0	0
Temecula city.........................	2,953	4,435	2,787	1,485	1,896	1,389	0	0	0
Thousand Oaks city.................	3,943	7,112	9,358	759	1,970	1,930	0	0	0
Torrance city..........................	7,136	7,072	8,288	972	2,182	2,971	37	56	52
Tracy city..............................	1,516	1,270	887	708	539	448	148	0	0
Turlock city...........................	1,991	3,382	1,361	624	1,157	570	117	0	0
Tustin city.............................	1,299	2,636	2,527	266	549	740	0	0	131

Table E-3: Places—Educational Attainment and Veteran Status, Persons 55 and Over—*Continued*

	High School or Equivalent	Some College or Associates Degree	Bachelor's Degree or Higher	Veterans by Age and Gender					
				Male			Female		
				55 to 64 Years	65 to 74 Years	75 Years and Over	55 to 64 Years	65 to 74 Years	75 Years and Over
California—Cont.									
Union City city	4,335	2,325	3,407	322	732	469	0	32	19
Upland city	2,840	3,503	3,838	580	1,133	1,088	101	48	0
Vacaville city	2,874	4,283	2,524	1,846	1,538	1,274	300	39	62
Vallejo city	4,198	4,920	4,878	1,075	1,738	1,523	244	38	0
Victorville city	3,128	3,893	742	786	1,722	606	159	0	0
Visalia city	5,440	4,514	3,194	745	706	1,576	0	0	0
Vista city	1,728	2,601	2,022	864	680	1,007	181	0	0
Walnut Creek city	3,200	5,787	10,346	366	1,123	2,873	0	107	95
West Covina city	4,151	3,552	4,245	333	1,444	932	24	37	0
Westminster city	4,538	4,144	2,936	599	1,297	1,008	52	55	41
Whittier city	2,444	3,028	2,028	447	868	973	0	0	0
Yorba Linda city	1,540	3,596	4,562	920	1,130	1,097	0	40	39
Yuba City city	1,701	2,698	1,697	838	894	1,043	70	33	35
Colorado									
Arvada city	4,586	5,252	4,666	1,535	2,321	1,695	0	82	39
Aurora city	10,344	11,624	9,991	4,414	4,637	2,631	574	166	364
Boulder city	1,266	1,695	7,155	98	1,214	667	0	0	0
Centennial city	2,808	4,078	8,728	1,265	1,945	1,642	299	136	72
Colorado Springs city	13,365	17,129	19,709	8,194	7,644	7,210	1,510	354	426
Denver city	15,974	16,942	26,285	5,582	7,807	6,866	377	274	154
Fort Collins city	2,511	4,507	6,918	832	1,870	1,485	59	22	196
Greeley city	2,967	4,043	3,042	893	951	1,633	109	164	145
Lakewood city	7,130	6,194	7,540	2,035	2,327	3,082	134	99	115
Longmont city	3,643	3,172	3,657	675	1,348	1,324	334	0	76
Loveland city	3,312	5,461	5,044	789	1,645	1,554	0	159	45
Pueblo city	5,804	5,617	3,010	1,228	1,299	2,547	427	44	91
Thornton city	4,221	3,113	1,933	988	1,678	933	82	0	0
Westminster city	3,682	4,190	4,239	1,943	1,489	1,375	151	90	0
Connecticut									
Bridgeport city	3,983	2,886	1,809	618	912	1,027	125	0	0
Danbury city	4,433	1,292	2,743	189	980	581	0	0	0
Hartford city	3,555	1,008	901	584	307	443	0	0	0
New Britain city	3,276	916	1,378	651	331	719	28	58	0
New Haven city	3,888	1,507	3,657	333	989	595	0	0	113
Norwalk city	4,165	2,265	4,233	742	591	1,286	41	0	79
Stamford city	4,987	2,389	6,934	553	950	1,579	87	63	0
Waterbury city	4,275	2,680	2,007	1,362	1,038	719	38	22	42
Delaware									
Wilmington city	3,393	1,560	2,306	673	560	421	0	0	0
District of Columbia									
Washington city	18,227	14,766	29,198	4,970	5,613	6,224	526	498	629
Florida									
Boca Raton city	3,651	3,987	9,191	307	1,253	1,645	0	69	0
Boynton Beach city	4,839	4,082	3,023	732	665	1,580	119	0	0
Cape Coral city	13,946	12,468	6,647	2,467	3,943	4,611	263	51	0
Clearwater city	6,328	7,894	5,981	1,195	1,767	2,928	237	35	62
Coral Springs city	3,561	3,137	4,628	819	1,105	560	245	0	92
Deerfield Beach city	6,462	2,932	3,929	312	754	1,837	111	0	0
Delray Beach city	4,740	3,491	5,135	188	963	2,268	0	29	48
Deltona city	5,446	2,781	1,701	1,885	1,155	985	0	0	0
Fort Lauderdale city	7,715	8,909	9,651	1,384	3,548	2,496	82	155	29
Fort Myers city	3,453	2,087	4,341	934	962	1,105	0	0	0
Gainesville city	2,711	3,591	5,170	1,366	1,085	1,341	83	0	111
Hialeah city	10,313	4,550	4,021	508	326	246	0	38	0
Hollywood city	8,073	5,146	5,258	963	1,048	1,947	98	72	43
Homestead city	527	1,921	997	1,083	543	127	0	0	0
Jacksonville city	35,455	31,027	25,328	15,495	13,494	10,413	2,022	428	305
Kissimmee city	2,265	1,080	932	230	362	199	0	0	0
Lakeland city	6,730	6,334	4,407	1,030	2,348	2,368	143	0	43
Largo city	6,120	7,232	4,527	1,887	2,648	2,724	541	0	149
Lauderhill city	4,639	2,342	2,185	640	404	1,026	0	74	0
Melbourne city	6,869	5,274	3,437	1,528	1,374	2,238	82	37	221
Miami Beach city	3,431	3,904	4,604	280	993	392	205	47	63
Miami city	17,322	9,607	10,829	1,378	1,625	723	64	36	38
Miami Gardens city	5,775	2,248	1,511	573	515	470	36	40	0
Miramar city	4,176	2,588	3,980	442	704	251	0	0	0
Orlando city	8,239	5,625	7,107	1,252	1,821	2,325	249	259	44
Palm Bay city	6,373	4,960	2,666	1,595	3,265	1,987	248	0	73
Palm Coast city	8,739	5,836	4,845	1,731	3,051	2,467	158	66	73
Pembroke Pines city	10,596	7,102	4,694	911	1,395	1,943	105	42	0
Plantation city	3,301	2,819	4,892	824	702	796	0	0	0
Pompano Beach city	6,230	4,995	6,425	1,086	1,120	3,036	26	0	0

Table E-3: Places—Educational Attainment and Veteran Status, Persons 55 and Over—*Continued*

	High School or Equivalent	Some College or Associates Degree	Bachelor's Degree or Higher	Veterans by Age and Gender					
				Male			Female		
				55 to 64 Years	65 to 74 Years	75 Years and Over	55 to 64 Years	65 to 74 Years	75 Years and Over
Florida—Cont.									
Port St. Lucie city	16,046	9,923	5,166	1,392	3,207	4,988	295	128	0
St. Petersburg city	13,787	12,093	11,183	3,560	4,923	4,841	640	132	82
Sunrise city	5,264	3,442	2,272	514	687	646	72	0	0
Tallahassee city	3,423	4,343	7,160	1,931	1,297	1,839	43	144	236
Tampa city	13,120	11,157	8,921	4,291	4,248	3,353	379	79	310
West Palm Beach city	3,281	3,785	6,584	898	1,125	1,117	44	67	16
Weston city	2,263	1,812	2,533	357	606	599	0	75	0
Georgia									
Albany city	2,023	1,829	1,417	719	777	686	131	0	0
Athens-Clarke County unified govt (bal)	2,399	2,041	4,960	985	641	980	61	88	0
Atlanta city	11,407	12,144	18,403	3,817	5,463	3,698	399	195	97
Augusta-Richmond County consolidated govt (bal)	8,201	6,259	4,256	3,648	3,006	2,225	728	331	92
Columbus city	7,436	5,376	6,331	4,466	3,283	2,897	398	162	226
Johns Creek city	1,225	1,707	2,760	368	364	272	70	0	0
Macon-Bibb County	7,245	3,435	5,005	1,915	2,642	1,728	164	102	92
Roswell city	2,663	2,192	5,592	421	866	985	0	68	0
Sandy Springs city	2,362	3,322	7,652	202	968	1,200	243	74	0
Savannah city	4,891	4,115	5,512	1,835	1,456	2,217	244	0	41
Warner Robins city	2,673	2,153	1,100	1,284	1,165	932	195	80	0
Hawaii									
Urban Honolulu CDP	19,800	14,793	19,476	2,708	4,320	6,214	162	126	249
Idaho									
Boise City city	6,110	9,546	8,860	3,060	3,284	3,104	329	173	59
Meridian city	3,895	3,574	2,265	803	2,145	363	162	79	0
Nampa city	4,145	2,588	2,190	1,377	1,653	670	162	70	0
Illinois									
Aurora city	4,425	3,094	3,149	1,209	1,516	1,011	68	26	0
Bloomington city	2,851	1,882	3,302	583	1,266	1,225	36	194	0
Champaign city	1,398	1,781	3,262	1,090	818	847	0	0	0
Chicago city	89,593	57,889	71,661	11,195	19,037	18,192	608	319	654
Decatur city	5,476	2,490	2,197	871	989	1,381	29	0	0
Elgin city	4,286	2,573	4,012	774	273	1,030	106	118	45
Evanston city	1,811	1,339	6,077	262	425	659	0	0	0
Joliet city	5,194	2,990	1,886	1,072	1,140	1,350	196	0	84
Naperville city	3,120	3,249	7,207	595	1,608	931	59	77	47
Peoria city	5,922	3,594	3,732	1,558	2,017	1,269	0	0	38
Rockford city	7,772	4,770	5,336	1,783	1,945	2,224	149	43	0
Springfield city	6,456	4,783	4,629	1,193	1,736	1,730	140	93	124
Waukegan city	3,618	840	1,335	344	622	674	0	53	31
Indiana									
Bloomington city	1,198	810	3,393	307	476	447	0	0	0
Carmel city	3,212	3,270	6,553	414	1,507	1,537	0	0	16
Evansville city	8,037	4,482	3,242	928	2,673	2,466	79	103	182
Fort Wayne city	12,887	7,906	7,183	3,156	3,512	3,068	0	0	0
Gary city	3,954	3,220	1,708	843	865	1,006	0	0	0
Hammond city	3,369	1,690	702	877	881	609	39	41	0
Indianapolis city (bal)	33,624	22,753	21,775	9,342	8,864	9,070	1,072	267	142
Lafayette city	2,874	2,206	2,099	637	864	531	136	21	0
Muncie city	4,043	2,211	2,695	453	1,163	1,400	49	30	40
South Bend city	4,425	2,932	3,041	1,136	1,510	821	183	35	51
Iowa									
Cedar Rapids city	6,161	4,620	4,609	1,398	1,561	1,639	120	0	86
Davenport city	4,756	3,096	3,091	613	1,392	1,069	97	124	0
Des Moines city	8,704	5,728	4,978	1,973	2,419	2,156	356	85	108
Iowa City city	1,596	1,725	2,732	471	414	664	52	0	0
Sioux City city	4,748	2,643	2,118	632	1,337	1,297	234	0	0
Waterloo city	4,334	2,814	1,495	889	1,054	1,243	96	0	0
Kansas									
Kansas City city	5,141	5,124	2,457	1,759	2,128	1,816	71	30	0
Lawrence city	2,630	1,487	3,985	863	746	1,060	221	0	91
Olathe city	2,746	4,235	4,191	1,047	1,350	775	160	0	41
Overland Park city	5,899	7,374	11,624	928	2,590	3,444	0	114	24
Topeka city	7,567	4,808	4,567	1,413	1,940	2,240	341	20	129
Wichita city	15,492	14,073	12,747	4,042	5,788	5,146	525	71	235
Kentucky									
Lexington-Fayette urban county	12,191	8,586	11,043	2,979	3,551	2,928	756	235	81
Louisville/Jefferson County metro govt (bal)	29,911	19,254	17,777	6,030	8,048	8,042	357	85	231
Louisiana									
Baton Rouge city	8,736	6,077	9,544	1,594	1,896	2,612	136	0	37
Bossier City city	3,691	2,450	1,735	1,164	915	1,262	250	0	0

Table E-3: Places—Educational Attainment and Veteran Status, Persons 55 and Over—*Continued*

	High School or Equivalent	Some College or Associates Degree	Bachelor's Degree or Higher	Veterans by Age and Gender					
				Male			Female		
				55 to 64 Years	65 to 74 Years	75 Years and Over	55 to 64 Years	65 to 74 Years	75 Years and Over
Louisiana—Cont.									
Kenner city	5,737	2,595	1,817	158	1,213	718	57	0	68
Lafayette city	3,662	3,461	4,840	1,456	1,477	877	69	154	110
Lake Charles city	3,626	3,003	3,165	834	1,050	1,308	55	0	0
New Orleans city	13,147	9,155	14,019	3,118	4,059	3,331	41	396	116
Shreveport city	10,850	6,361	7,169	2,498	2,798	2,468	155	41	267
Maine									
Portland city	2,000	1,808	3,311	582	768	511	151	0	55
Maryland									
Baltimore city	26,710	14,112	16,267	6,746	6,007	5,417	724	276	122
Frederick city	2,020	2,353	2,514	556	1,181	366	180	194	86
Gaithersburg city	1,621	1,342	3,937	634	240	675	39	0	0
Rockville city	1,707	2,228	5,462	228	609	884	0	0	0
Massachusetts									
Boston city	18,519	10,214	18,453	2,187	3,548	3,461	204	76	135
Brockton city	4,224	2,499	1,404	798	1,092	755	84	110	0
Cambridge city	2,168	1,079	6,097	206	316	774	0	68	82
Fall River city	4,130	2,365	1,187	637	1,073	929	85	0	0
Lawrence city	2,151	708	729	143	208	296	0	62	0
Lowell city	4,074	1,785	1,718	652	1,038	631	40	74	77
Lynn city	4,078	1,845	1,204	810	776	673	196	0	39
New Bedford city	3,481	1,815	1,486	505	785	1,108	33	0	34
Newton city	2,716	2,593	9,605	338	904	1,190	0	0	0
Quincy city	5,095	3,239	3,609	466	1,704	1,612	43	0	14
Somerville city	3,188	743	1,762	413	360	383	67	0	0
Springfield city	5,718	3,503	2,385	1,237	1,341	1,304	103	0	59
Worcester city	7,223	2,881	4,887	789	1,101	2,259	107	0	88
Michigan									
Ann Arbor city	1,181	2,221	7,874	285	569	1,187	56	62	0
Dearborn city	3,188	2,761	3,579	433	676	936	0	0	0
Detroit city	27,434	22,087	12,643	6,687	7,118	6,224	449	200	143
Farmington Hills city	3,025	4,750	8,094	469	1,172	1,820	73	148	0
Flint city	4,627	2,855	1,880	1,008	1,213	725	0	0	0
Grand Rapids city	6,652	5,919	5,903	2,029	1,774	2,977	203	36	110
Kalamazoo city	2,045	1,379	3,005	375	621	743	50	40	0
Lansing city	3,925	3,559	2,901	936	1,546	609	34	43	131
Livonia city	6,865	4,340	4,129	1,268	1,640	1,733	156	0	0
Rochester Hills city	2,808	3,109	5,291	857	757	1,112	0	0	43
Southfield city	3,811	4,146	4,241	688	1,471	707	217	90	0
Sterling Heights city	8,305	6,799	3,510	944	1,107	2,357	0	0	0
Troy city	3,329	2,211	5,974	426	1,066	819	0	0	0
Warren city	8,187	4,236	2,833	1,509	1,925	1,706	45	40	0
Westland city	6,794	3,563	1,542	1,641	1,439	1,269	0	0	75
Wyoming city	2,448	1,890	1,130	972	428	666	67	0	0
Minnesota									
Bloomington city	4,512	4,900	5,844	1,019	1,662	2,501	107	92	291
Brooklyn Park city	2,923	2,237	1,533	314	909	156	0	0	0
Duluth city	4,224	3,281	3,682	1,107	1,273	1,558	22	66	110
Eagan city	1,925	2,304	2,725	463	965	710	47	34	0
Maple Grove city	2,075	2,476	2,466	469	821	726	100	0	0
Minneapolis city	8,449	6,567	13,319	2,005	2,648	3,299	428	62	195
Plymouth city	1,960	3,523	5,326	434	1,417	883	275	68	0
Rochester city	3,870	4,655	5,804	923	1,137	2,134	44	0	38
St. Cloud city	2,331	2,024	2,617	809	980	765	0	0	89
St. Paul city	8,115	5,248	9,231	2,471	2,280	2,417	138	0	199
Woodbury city	2,231	2,041	2,838	193	1,199	532	0	0	0
Mississippi									
Gulfport city	3,140	3,269	1,672	730	1,237	1,331	74	0	55
Jackson city	4,592	3,902	5,584	1,975	1,861	2,178	122	126	111
Missouri									
Columbia city	2,816	2,394	4,986	758	1,342	1,110	167	55	0
Independence city	8,909	5,593	3,344	2,282	2,140	2,174	117	192	7
Kansas City city	19,802	14,644	13,055	5,183	5,189	5,267	482	110	245
Lee's Summit city	4,509	3,151	4,904	1,273	2,073	1,587	110	0	0
O'Fallon city	3,207	2,795	1,879	520	1,289	902	0	138	71
Springfield city	9,605	6,978	5,776	1,818	2,347	2,993	139	0	124
St. Charles city	4,032	2,842	2,153	877	1,030	1,670	168	0	83
St. Joseph city	4,615	3,278	1,117	633	674	1,263	38	0	36
St. Louis city	10,474	8,606	7,271	4,260	3,606	3,280	522	67	50
Montana									
Billings city	5,469	4,653	3,966	1,620	1,577	1,998	62	0	0
Missoula city	1,459	2,163	4,072	1,092	982	664	64	0	68

Table E-3: Places—Educational Attainment and Veteran Status, Persons 55 and Over—*Continued*

	High School or Equivalent	Some College or Associates Degree	Bachelor's Degree or Higher	Veterans by Age and Gender					
				Male			Female		
				55 to 64 Years	65 to 74 Years	75 Years and Over	55 to 64 Years	65 to 74 Years	75 Years and Over
Nebraska									
Lincoln city	11,188	9,089	8,838	1,620	3,892	3,160	241	142	136
Omaha city	20,081	12,821	13,181	3,760	5,704	5,374	244	178	74
Nevada									
Henderson city	14,005	16,180	14,458	4,489	7,339	5,356	738	470	247
Las Vegas city	23,606	25,318	19,368	7,750	10,077	7,349	430	492	227
North Las Vegas city	5,770	8,268	4,163	2,399	3,725	936	296	38	0
Reno city	7,015	11,526	9,031	1,721	4,091	2,998	215	332	81
Sparks city	3,996	5,295	3,724	726	2,122	1,751	100	273	0
New Hampshire									
Manchester city	4,325	2,905	2,795	1,665	1,463	1,424	0	43	0
Nashua city	2,942	2,563	3,628	1,060	1,395	1,256	40	46	0
New Jersey									
Bayonne city	4,478	715	1,451	200	391	185	0	0	0
Camden city	1,506	917	1,041	825	776	302	63	0	0
Clifton city	4,520	1,261	1,878	268	396	727	49	0	0
East Orange city	3,058	2,131	1,605	353	609	506	0	123	0
Elizabeth city	4,507	1,925	1,218	314	396	367	182	0	0
Jersey City city	6,774	3,380	5,572	455	711	972	44	0	43
Newark city	7,979	3,685	2,098	1,520	738	818	30	0	56
Passaic city	2,390	511	397	211	261	126	0	0	0
Paterson city	5,021	2,062	1,582	621	608	915	42	70	78
Trenton city	2,891	1,729	747	557	660	221	38	0	35
Union City city	2,925	903	741	42	0	104	0	0	0
New Mexico									
Albuquerque city	18,170	21,988	24,385	6,586	9,536	8,182	813	289	491
Las Cruces city	2,745	3,179	6,180	1,236	1,703	2,067	0	0	78
Rio Rancho city	4,135	3,503	3,249	2,004	1,988	1,527	721	63	0
Santa Fe city	2,979	3,136	7,419	802	1,539	1,234	112	48	44
New York									
Albany city	4,365	3,094	3,081	515	828	759	43	132	133
Buffalo city	10,546	6,799	6,250	2,628	2,458	3,200	340	264	93
Mount Vernon city	3,503	1,028	1,811	252	642	320	19	0	0
New Rochelle city	3,015	1,370	3,762	385	370	917	0	0	0
New York city	306,028	168,343	272,908	25,352	40,550	49,463	1,525	1,311	1,120
Rochester city	7,968	3,104	4,600	1,013	1,825	1,236	93	263	0
Schenectady city	3,857	2,075	1,848	341	525	730	0	0	183
Syracuse city	5,910	3,385	3,624	1,130	1,129	1,627	200	0	104
Yonkers city	10,669	5,709	8,130	558	2,229	1,877	69	0	102
North Carolina									
Asheville city	3,632	4,144	5,933	1,258	1,284	1,428	37	0	49
Charlotte city	19,698	22,033	22,944	6,241	7,547	5,828	1,140	296	203
Concord city	3,872	2,366	1,883	1,018	940	935	482	0	0
Durham city	6,992	5,102	12,068	2,347	2,781	1,851	782	256	73
Fayetteville city	7,308	7,142	5,269	5,853	3,837	2,442	997	446	244
Gastonia city	3,461	3,500	2,190	1,072	990	923	47	41	65
Greensboro city	10,244	8,972	10,775	2,501	3,847	2,776	648	0	32
Greenville city	3,320	2,237	2,940	454	636	742	56	0	0
High Point city	4,373	3,534	3,255	905	1,132	1,522	37	0	29
Jacksonville city	1,109	1,402	887	796	379	550	55	49	0
Raleigh city	8,555	11,941	16,463	2,816	3,855	3,523	687	94	236
Wilmington city	5,048	3,643	5,061	1,112	1,961	1,862	82	64	0
Winston-Salem city	9,087	8,114	9,385	2,741	2,920	2,727	355	60	37
North Dakota									
Bismarck city	2,838	2,991	3,175	600	1,078	1,137	48	35	0
Fargo city	4,057	2,851	3,759	1,078	1,186	1,481	0	0	0
Ohio									
Akron city	11,698	5,343	4,441	2,670	2,634	2,729	65	126	25
Canton city	4,716	1,501	1,261	801	751	766	43	171	69
Cincinnati city	9,811	8,523	9,982	2,831	2,332	3,474	27	108	220
Cleveland city	17,211	9,876	4,712	5,034	4,504	4,071	106	112	308
Columbus city	26,582	16,509	19,295	7,095	7,912	6,396	1,427	392	241
Dayton city	5,560	4,347	2,269	1,164	1,522	1,358	255	84	59
Lorain city	3,953	2,568	1,031	711	1,228	532	107	0	81
Parma city	7,466	3,277	1,442	896	1,202	1,668	62	42	40
Toledo city	14,431	8,984	6,349	2,569	3,680	3,969	85	0	396
Youngstown city	4,952	2,113	1,404	1,199	815	1,352	25	70	96
Oklahoma									
Broken Arrow city	3,658	3,475	3,727	1,242	1,392	1,250	52	38	0
Edmond city	1,983	3,624	4,916	1,147	1,301	1,363	44	0	81
Lawton city	3,441	2,860	1,783	2,797	1,369	1,057	240	585	193
Norman city	2,980	3,633	5,933	1,122	1,564	1,636	154	71	0
Oklahoma City city	21,323	22,793	20,355	8,171	9,228	6,534	934	611	278
Tulsa city	15,676	16,213	15,272	4,099	5,217	4,862	177	219	214

Table E-3: Places—Educational Attainment and Veteran Status, Persons 55 and Over—*Continued*

| | High School or Equivalent | Some College or Associates Degree | Bachelor's Degree or Higher | Veterans by Age and Gender | | | | | |
| | | | | Male | | | Female | | |
				55 to 64 Years	65 to 74 Years	75 Years and Over	55 to 64 Years	65 to 74 Years	75 Years and Over
Oregon									
Beaverton city	1,854	2,991	4,708	719	1,533	765	182	0	72
Bend city	2,442	3,353	5,399	975	1,837	865	113	0	87
Eugene city	4,932	5,849	10,023	1,331	2,723	2,432	176	153	49
Gresham city	5,058	4,834	2,790	830	2,012	1,322	0	63	74
Hillsboro city	2,912	3,127	3,678	1,011	1,403	947	271	0	0
Medford city	5,095	3,447	4,109	1,019	1,543	1,683	0	163	58
Portland city	16,634	21,112	24,775	5,159	7,566	5,929	638	224	405
Salem city	5,253	6,969	7,544	1,448	2,731	3,038	502	205	0
Pennsylvania									
Allentown city	5,108	2,913	2,385	715	836	1,147	149	56	42
Bethlehem city	4,594	1,668	2,163	778	1,056	1,109	71	35	0
Erie city	6,479	1,790	2,877	956	676	1,688	68	77	164
Philadelphia city	77,766	33,354	31,760	11,678	14,260	15,675	942	789	1,036
Pittsburgh city	17,805	7,257	9,847	2,991	3,773	4,505	146	43	252
Reading city	4,099	856	755	647	562	796	26	0	37
Scranton city	6,676	2,366	2,379	689	1,034	2,066	25	24	55
Rhode Island									
Cranston city	4,808	2,732	2,916	760	1,065	1,593	0	81	0
Pawtucket city	2,453	1,291	938	583	542	640	0	0	0
Providence city	3,399	2,899	4,060	771	723	1,651	0	0	213
Warwick city	5,043	3,125	5,621	751	2,061	1,987	84	0	0
South Carolina									
Charleston city	3,831	4,767	6,555	1,742	2,253	1,208	195	27	23
Columbia city	2,881	2,518	4,672	1,351	1,296	1,174	337	86	0
North Charleston city	3,449	2,926	2,088	1,466	1,727	777	39	0	0
Rock Hill city	2,471	2,840	1,938	282	993	652	49	99	0
South Dakota									
Rapid City city	4,025	2,966	2,848	1,248	1,221	1,462	213	0	104
Sioux Falls city	8,473	4,237	5,327	1,470	2,003	2,032	143	50	101
Tennessee									
Chattanooga city	8,957	6,205	5,900	2,744	2,457	3,027	150	0	148
Clarksville city	3,842	4,081	1,770	2,748	2,571	1,134	569	73	27
Franklin city	1,871	1,939	3,239	375	453	934	0	0	0
Jackson city	2,801	1,754	2,254	773	740	532	30	40	0
Johnson City city	2,548	1,990	3,942	1,229	1,530	1,480	74	206	70
Knoxville city	8,333	5,316	6,214	2,545	2,356	2,320	244	213	362
Memphis city	21,382	18,347	17,187	7,023	7,334	4,878	904	221	197
Murfreesboro city	3,635	2,714	2,823	898	1,449	935	0	0	0
Nashville-Davidson metropolitan govt (bal)	21,706	16,425	18,760	6,260	7,075	6,384	1,336	253	120
Texas									
Abilene city	4,474	4,020	4,189	1,315	1,700	1,919	72	43	45
Allen city	749	1,704	2,204	342	865	284	83	0	0
Amarillo city	6,914	7,208	6,506	1,963	2,514	2,494	155	93	173
Arlington city	8,454	10,669	11,968	4,327	4,725	3,203	231	339	0
Austin city	14,389	16,349	31,223	5,147	7,608	5,779	1,055	624	264
Baytown city	2,710	3,312	1,588	519	1,368	972	79	82	0
Beaumont city	5,384	3,638	2,487	1,634	1,131	1,297	37	41	40
Brownsville city	3,102	3,453	2,100	1,079	1,042	1,134	0	53	0
Bryan city	1,709	1,839	1,953	230	910	770	63	0	0
Carrollton city	2,669	3,875	3,602	945	1,251	767	34	73	37
College Station city	1,872	1,273	2,759	861	678	398	89	0	0
Conroe city	1,649	2,582	1,667	1,364	576	1,166	0	0	0
Corpus Christi city	10,019	9,804	9,054	5,562	6,245	3,363	272	68	105
Dallas city	25,432	27,785	37,280	8,017	9,897	9,865	787	459	378
Denton city	2,304	3,538	4,618	1,043	1,426	750	44	40	0
Edinburg city	898	902	936	525	357	208	0	0	0
El Paso city	17,793	15,720	12,606	7,364	6,429	5,257	747	175	354
Fort Worth city	17,475	19,305	19,273	8,077	7,567	5,442	1,125	205	391
Frisco city	2,601	2,678	4,579	1,067	1,057	658	45	39	0
Garland city	7,748	8,375	5,629	2,115	2,651	1,910	48	91	0
Grand Prairie city	4,289	2,704	3,232	2,065	1,265	1,135	256	0	0
Harlingen city	2,883	1,075	1,912	898	1,351	739	0	0	0
Houston city	47,590	50,453	64,468	9,896	15,560	14,777	1,568	681	336
Irving city	3,857	4,524	4,707	1,158	1,488	1,208	0	51	58
Killeen city	2,116	2,080	1,261	3,220	1,052	769	603	39	151
Laredo city	4,070	2,504	2,288	645	1,294	869	0	0	0
League City city	2,763	2,358	2,794	101	1,393	565	128	70	0
Lewisville city	2,341	3,332	1,682	698	978	373	43	38	39
Longview city	3,776	3,812	2,489	831	1,195	1,554	86	71	176
Lubbock city	7,121	7,862	7,654	1,738	2,678	2,542	73	68	42
McAllen city	3,020	2,278	1,986	712	874	924	80	28	0
McKinney city	2,801	5,729	4,001	1,404	1,518	1,054	0	195	0

Table E-3: Places—Educational Attainment and Veteran Status, Persons 55 and Over—*Continued*

	High School or Equivalent	Some College or Associates Degree	Bachelor's Degree or Higher	Veterans by Age and Gender					
				Male			Female		
				55 to 64 Years	65 to 74 Years	75 Years and Over	55 to 64 Years	65 to 74 Years	75 Years and Over
Texas—Cont.									
Mesquite city	4,764	3,167	2,238	1,531	1,673	1,309	81	41	47
Midland city	3,049	4,285	3,415	1,169	754	1,217	100	142	0
Mission city	2,669	1,923	1,720	109	570	906	0	0	0
Missouri City city	1,482	1,274	2,974	501	795	580	150	0	0
New Braunfels city	2,939	2,692	1,568	963	1,010	693	40	0	0
North Richland Hills city	2,903	3,466	2,534	413	710	1,260	121	40	0
Odessa city	2,820	3,631	1,837	1,107	1,098	1,168	0	53	0
Pasadena city	2,948	3,929	3,160	1,658	1,306	1,448	45	0	0
Pearland city	2,788	2,510	3,133	361	708	740	0	0	0
Pharr city	1,797	1,187	687	233	523	350	0	0	102
Plano city	6,019	9,261	14,771	3,134	3,576	3,194	368	164	0
Richardson city	2,776	3,604	7,809	1,153	1,743	1,694	118	55	0
Round Rock city	1,883	3,148	2,348	981	1,253	515	112	0	84
San Angelo city	4,103	3,777	3,561	1,369	1,632	1,728	59	87	48
San Antonio city	41,018	42,686	39,160	18,523	20,494	16,382	3,730	1,026	1,017
Sugar Land city	1,458	3,030	6,231	291	837	210	0	63	67
Temple city	3,384	3,374	2,775	1,487	1,957	1,263	394	96	0
Tyler city	3,920	3,811	4,936	448	847	1,192	57	0	41
Victoria city	2,097	2,446	1,656	418	707	938	62	61	31
Waco city	4,133	3,627	3,634	1,681	1,785	1,548	95	68	138
Wichita Falls city	3,662	3,779	3,037	1,469	1,733	1,741	81	20	96
Utah									
Layton city	1,345	2,368	1,883	903	914	446	97	0	60
Ogden city	1,864	2,616	2,365	1,083	571	968	114	0	8
Orem city	1,121	2,520	3,026	388	614	839	0	40	0
Provo city	1,103	1,717	3,998	236	465	694	0	0	47
Salt Lake City city	4,003	5,110	7,585	1,881	1,853	1,379	68	0	0
Sandy city	2,364	2,586	3,228	913	995	815	0	39	43
St. George city	4,048	6,936	4,570	741	1,148	2,614	0	78	0
West Jordan city	1,879	2,138	1,373	875	968	538	0	81	0
West Valley City city	3,658	2,317	1,405	743	926	429	37	40	0
Virginia									
Alexandria city	2,575	2,554	8,125	798	1,945	806	255	0	0
Chesapeake city	9,119	10,136	4,536	5,304	3,644	2,311	563	219	229
Hampton city	5,131	5,618	3,792	2,369	2,244	2,039	756	273	0
Lynchburg city	3,185	2,475	3,836	823	1,142	1,112	150	0	67
Newport News city	7,085	5,835	4,291	4,128	3,252	2,022	694	107	218
Norfolk city	7,698	5,558	5,796	4,353	3,767	2,372	438	105	60
Portsmouth city	3,619	3,766	2,815	2,035	1,775	1,562	196	0	58
Richmond city	6,687	5,518	6,924	2,037	2,269	2,103	630	88	86
Roanoke city	5,228	4,495	2,614	1,067	1,658	1,619	55	0	0
Suffolk city	3,045	3,330	2,440	1,415	1,539	832	184	114	98
Virginia Beach city	15,396	15,916	18,398	9,429	8,311	6,424	1,630	458	284
Washington									
Auburn city	2,683	2,281	2,188	1,182	803	1,053	196	0	89
Bellevue city	3,186	5,534	10,557	784	1,117	2,178	132	118	211
Bellingham city	3,258	2,462	4,363	464	1,073	920	63	21	124
Everett city	3,108	3,277	2,085	1,495	857	1,070	208	0	97
Federal Way city	3,879	3,175	4,034	1,749	1,639	1,341	123	145	147
Kennewick city	2,996	3,803	1,901	1,008	886	1,173	234	0	0
Kent city	3,713	3,463	2,648	939	1,201	1,333	63	132	178
Kirkland city	1,694	3,685	5,407	616	1,513	1,030	0	0	93
Marysville city	3,501	3,532	1,205	1,241	1,121	1,037	194	0	9
Pasco city	1,453	856	799	604	580	134	133	0	54
Renton city	2,477	3,396	1,972	1,133	1,066	1,022	67	60	0
Seattle city	12,330	19,982	38,180	4,979	6,951	6,899	1,500	236	685
Spokane city	7,887	9,297	9,053	3,197	3,576	3,492	398	158	186
Spokane Valley city	4,037	5,082	2,390	1,149	1,424	1,804	214	0	95
Tacoma city	7,480	7,559	5,881	3,306	3,264	2,568	316	224	209
Vancouver city	6,233	7,793	7,478	2,724	2,449	2,676	262	163	71
Yakima city	3,636	3,879	2,556	828	1,904	1,750	163	0	148
Wisconsin									
Appleton city	3,231	1,731	2,013	818	599	977	0	0	0
Eau Claire city	3,401	2,077	2,328	775	1,000	793	0	0	0
Green Bay city	5,287	2,739	3,181	1,217	1,161	1,506	153	0	60
Kenosha city	5,015	2,970	2,370	799	1,771	1,133	68	0	42
Madison city	6,531	6,070	12,405	1,962	2,462	2,273	182	30	228
Milwaukee city	21,774	13,905	10,656	5,420	4,889	5,358	559	209	113
Oshkosh city	3,738	2,955	1,726	620	921	1,251	0	0	40
Racine city	2,921	1,746	1,571	645	931	877	79	0	0
Waukesha city	2,907	1,797	1,765	1,013	880	788	0	56	37

Table E-4: Metropolitan/Micropolitan Statistical Areas—Educational Attainment and Veteran Status, Persons 55 and Over

	High School or Equivalent	Some College or Associates Degree	Bachelor's Degree or Higher	Veterans by Age and Gender					
				Male			Female		
				55 to 64 Years	65 to 74 Years	75 Years and Over	55 to 64 Years	65 to 74 Years	75 Years and Over
Aberdeen, WA Micro Area	4,362	5,403	2,060	1,105	2,940	1,572	102	0	282
Abilene, TX Metro Area	8,145	6,603	5,473	1,717	2,811	3,004	142	43	45
Adrian, MI Micro Area	7,489	3,780	2,379	1,058	1,752	1,335	100	0	U
Akron, OH Metro Area	45,472	24,557	25,127	7,713	10,995	11,273	371	257	61
Alamogordo, NM Micro Area	2,729	3,168	2,659	1,487	2,007	1,503	265	51	58
Albany, GA Metro Area	6,447	4,646	3,672	1,863	2,081	1,502	151	34	0
Albany, OR Metro Area	7,462	6,775	3,572	1,625	2,926	2,015	260	110	73
Albany-Schenectady-Troy, NY Metro Area	48,805	32,837	38,777	8,604	12,521	12,259	425	373	646
Albertville, AL Micro Area	6,209	3,123	2,072	1,471	1,698	1,118	125	21	52
Albuquerque, NM Metro Area	35,032	36,952	40,412	12,988	17,510	13,747	2,113	725	536
Alexandria, LA Metro Area	8,497	5,891	4,364	1,953	2,363	1,951	72	152	10
Allentown-Bethlehem-Easton, PA-NJ Metro Area	62,467	25,765	25,450	9,383	13,915	14,085	656	163	334
Altoona, PA Metro Area	13,025	3,208	4,155	2,532	2,240	3,233	124	82	134
Amarillo, TX Metro Area	8,817	9,974	8,699	3,349	3,512	3,877	232	167	173
Ames, IA Metro Area	3,129	2,215	4,412	337	651	1,074	14	0	97
Anchorage, AK Metro Area	9,537	10,705	11,336	5,880	6,627	3,496	1,389	476	310
Ann Arbor, MI Metro Area	9,147	10,057	19,573	2,108	3,848	3,012	186	207	15
Anniston-Oxford-Jacksonville, AL Metro Area	5,827	4,978	2,531	1,945	2,920	1,386	139	155	127
Appleton, WI Metro Area	14,608	5,672	5,640	2,106	3,398	2,865	40	15	0
Asheville, NC Metro Area	24,329	24,925	29,010	6,512	10,834	9,979	201	442	49
Ashtabula, OH Micro Area	8,473	3,728	1,738	1,482	2,336	1,956	82	24	257
Athens, TX Micro Area	5,595	4,656	3,786	1,294	1,467	1,695	0	127	27
Athens-Clarke County, GA Metro Area	6,877	4,080	7,557	1,902	2,308	2,101	69	88	9
Atlanta-Sandy Springs-Roswell, GA Metro Area	189,692	149,742	165,070	57,290	73,333	47,789	6,638	1,902	1,719
Atlantic City-Hammonton, NJ Metro Area	16,675	8,262	10,217	1,772	3,755	3,723	229	0	171
Auburn, NY Micro Area	4,676	3,414	2,275	966	1,520	1,539	0	19	0
Auburn-Opelika, AL Metro Area	4,626	4,235	4,119	1,047	2,120	1,324	260	33	87
Augusta-Richmond County, GA-SC Metro Area	26,543	18,501	20,680	9,452	9,768	8,541	1,990	664	271
Augusta-Waterville, ME Micro Area	8,063	5,166	4,804	1,762	3,093	2,456	165	26	136
Austin-Round Rock, TX Metro Area	40,379	48,356	69,661	15,882	22,655	16,520	2,498	970	656
Bakersfield, CA Metro Area	21,933	26,238	14,270	6,045	9,335	7,099	648	144	286
Baltimore-Columbia-Towson, MD Metro Area	131,432	83,087	114,129	30,188	38,059	36,618	4,163	1,198	1,307
Bangor, ME Metro Area	9,640	6,105	4,098	1,690	3,428	2,455	66	80	127
Barnstable Town, MA Metro Area	13,312	16,442	28,160	2,187	6,122	7,926	239	163	367
Baton Rouge, LA Metro Area	37,172	19,986	22,895	7,771	9,645	8,458	328	121	204
Battle Creek, MI Metro Area	8,636	5,216	4,555	2,225	2,748	2,265	32	38	31
Bay City, MI Metro Area	7,801	4,990	2,893	1,591	2,802	1,944	129	0	0
Beaumont-Port Arthur, TX Metro Area	24,667	15,340	7,500	5,403	6,589	5,570	342	158	105
Beaver Dam, WI Micro Area	7,471	2,912	1,332	1,204	1,264	1,581	350	19	43
Beckley, WV Metro Area	8,554	4,995	2,303	2,042	2,025	1,973	70	74	50
Bellingham, WA Metro Area	8,735	10,159	10,251	2,204	3,713	2,909	63	75	445
Bend-Redmond, OR Metro Area	8,066	9,651	10,483	2,189	4,307	2,567	113	118	154
Billings, MT Metro Area	9,399	7,178	6,177	2,470	3,438	2,756	98	0	0
Binghamton, NY Metro Area	17,333	11,504	8,682	3,389	4,286	5,181	127	221	53
Birmingham-Hoover, AL Metro Area	58,456	43,360	36,503	14,450	17,976	15,979	891	670	271
Bismarck, ND Metro Area	4,941	5,764	4,362	1,211	1,943	1,873	92	35	5
Blacksburg-Christiansburg-Radford, VA Metro Area	7,454	5,356	7,041	1,347	3,005	2,494	85	90	33
Bloomington, IL Metro Area	8,057	5,149	7,128	1,366	2,957	2,491	55	244	0
Bloomington, IN Metro Area	6,770	3,063	6,969	1,174	1,623	1,188	161	121	0
Bloomsburg-Berwick, PA Metro Area	7,804	2,245	2,324	641	1,693	1,440	17	63	52
Bluefield, WV-VA Micro Area	7,468	3,793	2,741	1,595	2,496	1,262	162	0	7
Boise City, ID Metro Area	26,846	28,420	23,275	9,023	12,738	8,783	891	420	124
Boston-Cambridge-Newton, MA-NH Metro Area	209,519	144,498	213,362	32,653	57,340	63,673	2,515	1,245	2,481
Boulder, CO Metro Area	7,315	8,165	19,929	1,751	4,091	4,085	462	22	76
Bowling Green, KY Metro Area	7,826	4,006	3,618	1,434	2,170	1,930	0	0	0
Bozeman, MT Micro Area	3,459	2,013	4,759	491	1,296	1,206	87	95	46
Brainerd, MN Micro Area	8,083	5,560	4,270	1,332	2,582	2,301	207	66	50
Branson, MO Micro Area	6,729	5,767	3,620	1,431	2,716	1,527	41	42	70
Bremerton-Silverdale, WA Metro Area	10,755	12,893	14,238	6,230	7,050	4,460	762	271	201
Bridgeport-Stamford-Norwalk, CT Metro Area	39,105	25,748	49,257	4,872	10,381	12,192	461	99	409
Brownsville-Harlingen, TX Metro Area	10,562	9,014	7,340	3,481	3,624	3,832	8	53	109
Brunswick, GA Metro Area	5,741	5,979	5,233	1,507	2,259	1,861	222	0	117
Buffalo-Cheektowaga-Niagara Falls, NY Metro Area	75,036	42,022	41,522	11,489	18,286	19,523	1,203	755	537
Burlington, NC Metro Area	8,772	6,828	5,195	2,270	1,676	2,201	354	0	97
Burlington-South Burlington, VT Metro Area	9,050	6,702	9,363	2,382	2,160	2,761	301	178	169
California-Lexington Park, MD Metro Area	5,471	3,173	2,411	1,980	1,646	1,323	316	72	141
Canton-Massillon, OH Metro Area	35,331	15,752	9,570	5,766	7,939	7,835	197	300	272
Cape Coral-Fort Myers, FL Metro Area	55,275	47,465	52,503	8,430	16,781	21,876	619	256	387
Cape Girardeau, MO-IL Metro Area	6,354	2,957	3,692	863	1,718	1,751	0	23	23
Carbondale-Marion, IL Metro Area	6,620	5,635	4,377	1,097	2,184	1,707	82	123	0
Carson City, NV Metro Area	2,888	3,742	2,446	473	1,626	1,208	0	0	64
Casper, WY Metro Area	3,209	3,895	1,949	1,058	924	1,295	60	42	166
Cedar Rapids, IA Metro Area	16,498	10,508	8,365	3,375	4,493	3,813	219	129	178
Centralia, WA Micro Area	4,337	5,949	2,026	1,503	2,287	1,805	106	99	108
Chambersburg-Waynesboro, PA Metro Area	11,610	4,925	4,975	1,887	2,923	2,872	107	0	140

Table E-4: Metropolitan/Micropolitan Statistical Areas—Educational Attainment and Veteran Status, Persons 55 and Over—*Continued*

	High School or Equivalent	Some College or Associates Degree	Bachelor's Degree or Higher	Veterans by Age and Gender					
				Male			Female		
				55 to 64 Years	65 to 74 Years	75 Years and Over	55 to 64 Years	65 to 74 Years	75 Years and Over
Champaign-Urbana, IL Metro Area....................	10,165	7,726	7,964	2,271	3,240	3,177	402	7	38
Charleston, WV Metro Area...............................	16,501	8,139	6,834	3,040	3,596	3,731	0	96	20
Charleston-Mattoon, IL Micro Area..................	3,373	2,329	1,922	935	990	982	0	0	12
Charleston-North Charleston, SC Metro Area...	29,261	26,956	26,798	12,739	13,705	7,843	1,141	315	167
Charlotte-Concord-Gastonia, NC-SC Metro Area....	92,627	81,950	70,328	24,908	32,943	24,945	2,874	569	731
Charlottesville, VA Metro Area..........................	9,029	6,679	12,225	2,477	3,814	3,408	249	0	18
Chattanooga, TN-GA Metro Area.......................	31,869	20,895	17,795	7,408	9,403	8,995	583	203	353
Cheyenne, WY Metro Area.................................	4,361	3,534	4,349	2,098	2,147	1,284	273	0	58
Chicago-Naperville-Elgin, IL-IN-WI Metro Area...........	379,925	279,401	330,890	58,725	100,801	100,288	3,858	1,668	3,550
Chico, CA Metro Area.......................................	10,332	11,138	10,841	2,957	4,563	3,609	170	214	335
Chillicothe, OH Micro Area...............................	5,911	1,491	1,416	1,262	1,587	998	184	44	0
Cincinnati, OH-KY-IN Metro Area......................	107,943	69,805	70,154	23,831	30,113	27,293	1,319	860	661
Claremont-Lebanon, NH-VT Micro Area............	12,729	9,357	14,381	2,897	4,761	4,611	94	185	131
Clarksburg, WV Micro Area..............................	6,795	4,655	1,478	840	2,255	1,710	25	91	116
Clarksville, TN-KY Metro Area..........................	9,380	8,071	4,631	5,701	4,474	2,794	956	73	87
Clearlake, CA Micro Area.................................	3,271	4,508	3,069	1,256	1,135	1,470	53	0	159
Cleveland, TN Metro Area.................................	7,342	3,636	3,509	1,013	2,575	1,082	78	69	0
Cleveland-Elyria, OH Metro Area......................	128,756	81,496	75,055	22,258	33,998	33,120	1,321	972	1,268
Coeur d'Alene, ID Metro Area..........................	6,240	9,671	6,890	2,487	3,415	2,718	342	99	46
College Station-Bryan, TX Metro Area..............	6,879	6,037	6,918	1,944	2,593	2,732	180	22	0
Colorado Springs, CO Metro Area.....................	20,281	25,603	27,529	14,609	13,288	9,320	2,799	678	510
Columbia, MO Metro Area................................	6,023	4,384	6,397	1,619	2,075	1,805	207	55	86
Columbia, SC Metro Area.................................	32,176	26,501	28,485	10,708	13,012	9,438	1,794	619	138
Columbus, GA-AL Metro Area..........................	12,824	7,786	8,784	6,719	4,937	3,901	495	207	226
Columbus, IN Metro Area.................................	5,833	2,368	2,113	999	1,514	1,255	0	51	0
Columbus, OH Metro Area................................	91,384	52,813	59,168	21,934	28,569	21,651	2,563	743	656
Concord, NH Micro Area..................................	8,734	4,592	7,550	1,857	3,322	2,715	41	112	123
Cookeville, TN Micro Area...............................	5,365	4,136	3,772	1,445	2,368	2,032	97	0	78
Coos Bay, OR Micro Area.................................	5,268	5,376	2,901	1,182	2,255	1,952	125	133	229
Corning, NY Micro Area...................................	6,205	3,975	3,757	1,843	1,828	1,814	101	57	28
Corpus Christi, TX Metro Area.........................	16,051	15,779	12,843	7,266	9,064	5,056	377	80	149
Corvallis, OR Metro Area.................................	2,381	3,060	6,018	778	1,343	1,482	58	59	163
Crestview-Fort Walton Beach-Destin, FL Metro Area.....	10,941	13,295	11,888	6,861	7,105	4,895	797	44	528
Cullman, AL Micro Area...................................	6,086	3,116	1,749	1,429	1,275	1,182	88	58	0
Cumberland, MD-WV Metro Area......................	9,779	3,323	2,371	1,623	1,760	1,993	80	73	217
Dallas-Fort Worth-Arlington, TX Metro Area	185,265	196,086	204,533	67,543	79,887	59,060	6,672	3,049	1,632
Dalton, GA Metro Area.....................................	6,830	2,740	2,348	867	1,851	1,561	122	0	47
Danville, IL Metro Area....................................	6,084	3,564	1,522	1,438	1,551	1,346	54	0	8
Danville, VA Micro Area...................................	7,767	4,557	2,483	1,434	2,225	1,906	0	46	92
Daphne-Fairhope-Foley, AL Metro Area............	10,484	9,992	11,060	1,992	5,098	4,667	389	166	353
Davenport-Moline-Rock Island, IA-IL Metro Area	25,208	16,681	11,896	4,570	6,331	5,955	325	447	80
Dayton, OH Metro Area....................................	47,908	34,549	29,792	11,295	15,175	13,104	1,347	787	642
Decatur, AL Metro Area....................................	9,022	5,769	4,169	2,542	2,477	2,348	140	0	0
Decatur, IL Metro Area.....................................	8,742	4,052	3,484	1,240	1,772	2,073	29	0	15
Deltona-Daytona Beach-Ormond Beach, FL Metro Area	52,960	39,351	34,160	12,784	17,455	17,460	522	703	633
Denver-Aurora-Lakewood, CO Metro Area	82,508	88,424	110,792	30,384	39,237	30,496	3,194	1,379	1,144
Des Moines-West Des Moines, IA Metro Area	28,607	18,809	19,191	5,123	7,992	6,546	549	416	263
Detroit-Warren-Dearborn, MI Metro Area.........	217,424	164,397	144,546	40,841	61,261	55,434	3,014	1,170	1,407
Dothan, AL Metro Area.....................................	10,440	5,770	3,448	2,175	3,005	2,246	243	140	143
Dover, DE Metro Area......................................	9,785	6,114	6,089	4,378	4,039	2,714	390	77	0
DuBois, PA Micro Area.....................................	8,033	2,775	1,326	535	1,588	1,610	64	39	0
Dubuque, IA Metro Area...................................	7,108	2,712	3,388	947	1,546	1,702	48	36	45
Duluth, MN-WI Metro Area...............................	18,937	11,785	10,959	4,876	5,760	5,206	172	202	334
Dunn, NC Micro Area.......................................	5,145	3,546	1,732	1,489	1,707	1,096	241	71	93
Durham-Chapel Hill, NC Metro Area.................	20,330	13,623	28,340	5,259	6,924	5,862	910	296	276
East Stroudsburg, PA Metro Area	9,728	5,286	6,107	1,820	3,526	2,049	59	64	241
Eau Claire, WI Metro Area...............................	10,956	5,498	5,055	1,725	2,635	2,526	63	23	77
El Centro, CA Metro Area.................................	3,256	2,835	2,158	1,216	1,100	1,230	0	51	0
El Paso, TX Metro Area....................................	19,228	16,687	12,908	7,939	6,916	5,634	768	175	354
Elizabeth City, NC Micro Area..........................	3,718	2,605	1,328	1,305	1,013	1,153	175	0	85
Elizabethtown-Fort Knox, KY Metro Area	6,992	3,968	3,488	4,209	2,634	1,963	353	69	0
Elkhart-Goshen, IN Metro Area........................	12,262	5,825	4,308	1,277	2,846	2,292	292	0	201
Elmira, NY Metro Area.....................................	6,201	3,261	3,582	1,072	1,863	1,556	52	0	17
Erie, PA Metro Area...	20,399	8,661	9,031	3,596	5,193	4,677	185	94	271
Eugene, OR Metro Area....................................	17,012	19,823	18,739	5,126	8,623	6,914	792	575	202
Eureka-Arcata-Fortuna, CA Micro Area............	5,017	6,302	6,348	1,557	2,737	2,047	191	110	147
Evansville, IN-KY Metro Area...........................	22,598	11,536	9,037	3,456	6,349	5,393	156	133	307
Fairbanks, AK Metro Area................................	1,578	1,988	3,100	1,797	1,102	872	84	59	227
Fargo, ND-MN Metro Area................................	10,250	6,356	6,292	1,972	2,565	2,511	172	178	110
Faribault-Northfield, MN Micro Area.................	3,156	2,457	2,403	535	1,101	1,161	0	0	0
Farmington, MO Micro Area.............................	4,069	2,927	1,174	1,765	1,212	1,357	0	0	0
Farmington, NM Metro Area.............................	4,239	5,116	2,757	1,262	1,906	1,361	274	82	0
Fayetteville, NC Metro Area.............................	12,647	11,148	6,721	9,096	5,678	3,336	1,309	561	244
Fayetteville-Springdale-Rogers, AR-MO Metro Area	21,713	15,797	12,161	4,777	7,815	6,488	635	66	192
Findlay, OH Micro Area....................................	5,220	2,952	1,744	869	759	1,143	8	0	0

Table E-4: Metropolitan/Micropolitan Statistical Areas—Educational Attainment and Veteran Status, Persons 55 and Over—Continued

| | | | | Veterans by Age and Gender | | | | | |
| | | | | Male | | | Female | | |
	High School or Equivalent	Some College or Associates Degree	Bachelor's Degree or Higher	55 to 64 Years	65 to 74 Years	75 Years and Over	55 to 64 Years	65 to 74 Years	75 Years and Over
Flagstaff, AZ Metro Area	2,720	3,227	7,193	1,534	1,743	1,077	85	126	0
Flint, MI Metro Area	26,765	19,297	9,342	4,803	6,431	5,386	372	58	46
Florence, SC Metro Area	11,761	6,450	5,311	2,975	4,171	2,904	400	0	62
Florence-Muscle Shoals, AL Metro Area	11,011	5,182	5,001	1,198	2,547	2,971	59	131	51
Fond du Lac, WI Metro Area	8,318	3,613	2,501	1,409	1,718	1,354	178	24	0
Forest City, NC Micro Area	3,903	3,394	2,461	983	1,431	730	115	0	0
Fort Collins, CO Metro Area	10,747	13,946	18,250	2,779	5,522	4,679	215	279	280
Fort Smith, AR-OK Metro Area	15,855	10,502	6,088	3,930	4,649	4,248	166	153	0
Fort Wayne, IN Metro Area	24,212	15,025	11,434	4,703	6,010	5,777	147	136	0
Frankfort, KY Micro Area	2,798	2,551	3,783	965	870	684	0	263	0
Fresno, CA Metro Area	23,038	29,392	22,812	5,976	11,005	8,287	179	244	549
Gadsden, AL Metro Area	5,980	5,095	2,728	1,339	2,051	1,739	160	0	32
Gainesville, FL Metro Area	9,299	9,269	11,839	3,413	4,015	3,344	323	29	262
Gainesville, GA Metro Area	7,736	6,145	7,415	1,389	3,535	3,070	162	99	116
Gallup, NM Micro Area	1,342	1,729	539	609	301	688	183	47	76
Gettysburg, PA Metro Area	7,609	3,217	3,800	1,267	1,867	2,033	78	0	13
Glens Falls, NY Metro Area	9,408	4,972	5,464	2,080	2,548	2,332	88	0	158
Glenwood Springs, CO Micro Area	2,438	1,753	3,462	540	1,066	602	0	0	0
Goldsboro, NC Metro Area	7,312	4,401	2,773	2,349	2,037	1,833	466	51	0
Grand Forks, ND-MN Metro Area	5,219	3,486	2,643	1,384	1,670	1,285	49	0	16
Grand Island, NE Metro Area	5,439	4,286	1,907	1,072	1,534	1,863	64	26	0
Grand Junction, CO Metro Area	8,116	7,833	6,434	2,240	3,083	2,330	534	0	329
Grand Rapids-Wyoming, MI Metro Area	46,296	38,395	30,585	10,221	13,634	13,266	438	466	520
Grants Pass, OR Metro Area	5,990	7,958	3,431	1,667	2,649	1,923	199	298	0
Great Falls, MT Metro Area	5,807	3,951	2,568	1,751	1,987	1,574	0	65	0
Greeley, CO Metro Area	9,635	9,084	6,885	2,529	4,763	3,015	165	233	245
Green Bay, WI Metro Area	20,456	9,864	8,343	3,829	5,318	4,646	236	64	155
Greeneville, TN Micro Area	5,580	2,757	1,506	847	1,686	1,193	85	0	0
Greenfield Town, MA Micro Area	4,191	2,503	4,435	935	1,488	1,432	146	54	12
Greensboro-High Point, NC Metro Area	38,658	26,426	23,031	8,732	11,231	9,331	919	270	329
Greenville, NC Metro Area	7,133	5,083	4,407	1,173	1,874	1,530	173	156	0
Greenville-Anderson-Mauldin, SC Metro Area	47,877	30,845	27,878	8,742	17,466	11,561	175	267	395
Greenwood, SC Micro Area	5,776	3,285	2,937	1,102	1,695	1,719	0	23	77
Gulfport-Biloxi-Pascagoula, MS Metro Area	15,458	17,740	13,341	5,894	7,462	6,218	601	23	108
Hagerstown-Martinsburg, MD-WV Metro Area	16,202	8,276	6,594	3,856	4,995	3,868	209	95	112
Hammond, LA Metro Area	7,508	2,495	3,132	1,021	1,828	1,828	98	0	0
Hanford-Corcoran, CA Metro Area	2,938	3,983	1,942	2,339	1,757	1,234	64	29	51
Harrisburg-Carlisle, PA Metro Area	37,995	16,985	20,192	6,397	8,981	10,102	773	425	219
Harrisonburg, VA Metro Area	7,055	3,817	3,666	1,409	1,644	1,791	101	0	26
Hartford-West Hartford-East Hartford, CT Metro Area	64,623	40,053	55,133	11,197	17,060	19,178	877	364	1,013
Hattiesburg, MS Metro Area	6,137	4,421	4,692	1,292	2,274	1,737	135	0	43
Helena, MT Micro Area	4,721	2,796	4,517	1,865	1,697	1,427	139	79	0
Hermiston-Pendleton, OR Micro Area	4,798	3,919	2,082	1,406	2,146	1,344	0	184	0
Hickory-Lenoir-Morganton, NC Metro Area	20,844	15,329	10,479	4,924	7,646	5,032	309	207	0
Hilo, HI Micro Area	10,820	10,549	9,100	3,034	4,231	3,294	22	157	0
Hilton Head Island-Bluffton-Beaufort, SC Metro Area	9,150	12,169	22,596	2,621	5,313	5,068	421	223	0
Hinesville, GA Metro Area	2,513	1,374	830	1,657	1,142	181	178	56	0
Hobbs, NM Micro Area	1,301	1,697	1,011	486	610	445	0	0	0
Holland, MI Micro Area	7,156	3,576	3,738	883	1,886	1,165	157	30	13
Homosassa Springs, FL Metro Area	16,729	14,594	9,774	3,090	5,149	6,536	237	188	264
Hot Springs, AR Metro Area	5,724	6,545	5,917	1,562	3,146	2,432	0	54	0
Houma-Thibodaux, LA Metro Area	10,741	4,947	3,109	747	2,035	2,114	628	0	0
Houston-The Woodlands-Sugar Land, TX Metro Area	155,873	168,678	175,906	46,385	61,071	44,380	4,306	2,215	706
Huntington-Ashland, WV-KY-OH Metro Area	27,046	13,109	8,872	4,471	7,240	5,465	367	210	44
Huntsville, AL Metro Area	17,174	16,170	16,176	8,242	7,459	6,094	681	354	213
Huntsville, TX Micro Area	4,970	3,227	1,735	1,477	1,248	1,433	173	49	89
Hutchinson, KS Micro Area	3,662	3,856	2,656	373	1,261	1,197	66	0	69
Idaho Falls, ID Metro Area	6,356	5,182	3,622	1,491	1,751	1,881	0	150	132
Indiana, PA Micro Area	7,099	2,260	3,007	880	1,521	1,363	298	239	32
Indianapolis-Carmel-Anderson, IN Metro Area	93,300	61,577	55,776	22,049	26,052	24,548	1,968	383	626
Iowa City, IA Metro Area	5,893	4,562	6,307	1,295	1,587	1,874	121	81	0
Ithaca, NY Metro Area	2,981	2,985	5,183	419	1,276	1,009	10	64	0
Jackson, MI Metro Area	9,904	7,208	5,040	2,006	3,061	2,513	49	346	175
Jackson, MS Metro Area	18,972	19,767	17,754	6,121	7,200	6,594	778	297	192
Jackson, TN Metro Area	7,453	3,755	4,360	1,285	1,644	1,743	115	142	0
Jacksonville, FL Metro Area	63,702	54,057	57,120	25,899	29,077	21,726	3,097	1,092	1,127
Jacksonville, NC Metro Area	5,554	4,504	2,928	2,796	2,873	2,039	146	242	67
Jamestown-Dunkirk-Fredonia, NY Micro Area	9,797	5,782	5,190	1,669	2,084	2,269	104	54	36
Janesville-Beloit, WI Metro Area	10,771	5,878	5,337	2,127	2,672	2,403	178	0	80
Jefferson City, MO Metro Area	9,288	4,602	4,399	2,421	2,834	1,837	69	157	0
Johnson City, TN Metro Area	11,690	7,577	7,888	3,618	5,110	3,518	130	324	70
Johnstown, PA Metro Area	15,752	4,413	3,155	1,778	3,016	3,678	94	79	29
Jonesboro, AR Metro Area	5,172	5,567	3,125	798	1,839	1,343	36	76	127
Joplin, MO Metro Area	12,197	6,281	3,922	2,087	3,492	2,372	268	43	33

Table E-4: Metropolitan/Micropolitan Statistical Areas—Educational Attainment and Veteran Status, Persons 55 and Over—*Continued*

	High School or Equivalent	Some College or Associates Degree	Bachelor's Degree or Higher	Veterans by Age and Gender					
				Male			Female		
				55 to 64 Years	65 to 74 Years	75 Years and Over	55 to 64 Years	65 to 74 Years	75 Years and Over
Kahului-Wailuku-Lahaina, HI Metro Area	6,990	6,510	6,977	1,908	2,446	1,360	121	150	0
Kalamazoo-Portage, MI Metro Area	15,010	14,245	12,037	3,800	4,400	4,535	331	92	0
Kalispell, MT Micro Area	5,254	5,059	4,558	2,621	2,466	1,706	61	0	0
Kankakee, IL Metro Area	7,029	3,947	2,660	1,266	1,666	1,987	184	0	49
Kansas City, MO-KS Metro Area	94,508	75,140	72,554	25,599	32,634	28,279	1,955	730	480
Kapaa, HI Micro Area	2,841	3,020	4,352	988	1,103	804	28	0	0
Keene, NH Micro Area	5,421	2,758	3,033	1,010	1,409	1,720	204	62	154
Kennewick-Richland, WA Metro Area	9,130	10,847	8,269	3,357	4,068	3,046	486	126	54
Key West, FL Micro Area	3,505	4,132	6,111	988	1,888	995	248	317	103
Killeen-Temple, TX Metro Area	12,504	13,773	9,226	9,787	6,092	4,771	1,591	259	391
Kingsport-Bristol-Bristol, TN-VA Metro Area	21,860	12,327	11,895	3,866	6,742	6,022	283	122	262
Kingston, NY Metro Area	11,404	6,728	8,720	2,072	2,785	3,010	320	99	27
Klamath Falls, OR Micro Area	4,155	4,165	1,910	1,498	1,933	1,404	82	0	8
Knoxville, TN Metro Area	50,669	32,395	33,337	13,433	16,173	15,037	909	430	1,152
Kokomo, IN Metro Area	6,421	3,608	2,799	1,510	1,511	1,874	33	0	36
La Crosse-Onalaska, WI-MN Metro Area	8,679	4,519	4,941	2,342	2,421	2,610	122	104	77
Lafayette, LA Metro Area	21,137	11,401	11,323	4,470	5,062	4,619	306	154	212
Lafayette-West Lafayette, IN Metro Area	8,713	5,215	7,503	1,584	2,236	2,147	155	21	79
LaGrange, GA Micro Area	3,627	1,981	1,856	1,514	1,062	817	0	0	0
Lake Charles, LA Metro Area	9,080	6,896	6,132	1,873	3,279	2,430	171	0	49
Lake City, FL Micro Area	4,590	3,252	2,419	1,465	1,946	1,404	113	59	0
Lake Havasu City-Kingman, AZ Metro Area	18,176	20,944	6,835	3,800	8,477	7,213	173	80	26
Lakeland-Winter Haven, FL Metro Area	47,433	32,696	21,878	8,258	13,944	13,400	513	268	507
Lancaster, PA Metro Area	37,638	12,910	18,161	4,737	8,750	8,833	233	254	554
Lansing-East Lansing, MI Metro Area	22,034	16,713	16,431	5,081	7,173	5,401	296	146	344
Laredo, TX Metro Area	4,204	2,626	2,348	732	1,416	901	0	0	0
Las Cruces, NM Metro Area	5,348	5,435	10,140	1,970	3,808	2,923	66	0	78
Las Vegas-Henderson-Paradise, NV Metro Area	79,951	85,895	64,214	24,388	37,199	25,946	3,268	1,601	841
Laurel, MS Micro Area	4,639	2,932	3,017	833	1,598	1,350	7	0	0
Lawrence, KS Metro Area	3,804	2,388	5,288	1,104	1,295	1,516	221	0	91
Lawton, OK Metro Area	5,018	4,368	2,925	3,421	2,179	1,921	255	585	193
Lebanon, PA Metro Area	12,777	3,402	3,940	2,095	2,884	3,074	73	118	0
Lewiston, ID-WA Metro Area	4,453	3,622	2,756	857	1,678	1,311	5	139	160
Lewiston-Auburn, ME Metro Area	7,013	4,140	3,072	1,377	2,361	1,762	189	0	0
Lexington-Fayette, KY Metro Area	20,269	16,188	16,497	4,952	5,958	5,662	932	336	169
Lima, OH Metro Area	7,825	4,066	1,916	1,364	1,473	1,869	151	20	41
Lincoln, NE Metro Area	13,974	11,270	10,744	1,980	4,589	3,552	272	151	136
Little Rock-North Little Rock-Conway, AR Metro Area	34,812	22,678	25,670	10,467	10,764	9,082	757	680	192
Logan, UT-ID Micro Area	2,941	3,699	4,470	607	1,097	1,306	32	0	11
London, KY Micro Area	8,142	1,987	1,982	855	2,470	1,149	206	76	0
Longview, TX Metro Area	10,474	10,206	5,758	2,876	3,457	3,459	232	71	176
Longview, WA Metro Area	6,071	7,339	2,541	1,535	3,328	2,150	0	159	128
Los Angeles-Long Beach-Anaheim, CA Metro Area	345,519	403,603	474,365	59,455	100,633	110,081	5,468	2,200	4,145
Louisville/Jefferson County, KY-IN Metro Area	68,567	42,031	39,373	15,181	20,517	16,525	1,677	222	357
Lubbock, TX Metro Area	10,038	9,910	9,047	2,441	3,666	3,283	90	68	42
Lufkin, TX Micro Area	5,455	2,915	2,212	884	1,450	1,635	42	0	0
Lumberton, NC Micro Area	6,702	2,842	1,717	1,487	1,422	956	136	171	37
Lynchburg, VA Metro Area	15,593	9,874	10,460	3,279	4,370	4,479	150	0	106
Macon, GA Metro Area	11,195	6,206	6,759	2,673	4,165	2,690	426	102	92
Madera, CA Metro Area	5,322	6,201	3,309	1,496	2,137	1,703	38	0	0
Madison, WI Metro Area	27,180	19,878	26,963	5,057	8,667	7,696	434	107	255
Manchester-Nashua, NH Metro Area	16,985	12,621	16,426	5,410	6,842	5,856	178	118	201
Manhattan, KS Metro Area	2,508	1,881	4,216	1,137	794	905	97	149	72
Manitowoc, WI Micro Area	7,809	2,646	1,986	1,111	1,900	1,726	98	22	48
Mankato-North Mankato, MN Metro Area	5,331	3,105	3,067	752	1,380	1,463	29	70	43
Mansfield, OH Metro Area	9,923	4,503	3,527	1,720	2,456	2,350	367	0	39
Marinette, WI-MI Micro Area	7,244	3,320	1,288	1,400	2,330	1,257	47	111	40
Marion, IN Micro Area	5,291	2,224	1,308	902	1,355	1,392	0	43	0
Marion, OH Micro Area	4,996	2,519	1,446	1,225	1,245	1,085	65	23	0
Marquette, MI Micro Area	4,140	3,630	2,757	1,206	1,995	1,234	34	48	31
Marshall, TX Micro Area	3,402	3,123	2,008	639	1,044	979	83	0	47
Martinsville, VA Micro Area	4,756	3,606	1,410	853	1,729	1,103	28	0	0
McAllen-Edinburg-Mission, TX Metro Area	16,270	12,979	9,490	3,184	4,547	4,597	265	252	102
Meadville, PA Micro Area	8,302	2,975	2,267	1,542	2,327	1,823	63	88	112
Medford, OR Metro Area	11,951	11,474	13,592	3,435	5,544	4,672	510	465	105
Memphis, TN-MS-AR Metro Area	52,277	42,082	35,815	17,215	17,908	13,192	1,839	391	604
Merced, CA Metro Area	7,425	8,136	4,111	1,245	3,256	2,905	310	228	0
Meridian, MS Micro Area	6,413	4,449	1,628	1,827	1,809	1,433	47	65	0
Miami-Fort Lauderdale-West Palm Beach, FL Metro Area	289,500	222,169	258,389	32,482	51,526	68,833	3,043	1,604	1,419
Michigan City-La Porte, IN Metro Area	7,088	4,813	3,040	1,564	2,356	1,608	58	90	35
Midland, MI Metro Area	5,726	4,137	2,801	693	1,211	1,645	169	39	0
Midland, TX Metro Area	4,332	4,963	3,743	1,220	1,349	1,301	107	142	0
Milwaukee-Waukesha-West Allis, WI Metro Area	79,659	51,573	56,717	14,448	21,034	22,311	1,574	671	381
Minneapolis-St. Paul-Bloomington, MN-WI Metro Area	138,549	111,877	134,464	31,334	46,759	44,024	2,928	1,075	1,903

Table E-4: Metropolitan/Micropolitan Statistical Areas—Educational Attainment and Veteran Status, Persons 55 and Over—*Continued*

	High School or Equivalent	Some College or Associates Degree	Bachelor's Degree or Higher	Veterans by Age and Gender					
				Male			Female		
				55 to 64 Years	65 to 74 Years	75 Years and Over	55 to 64 Years	65 to 74 Years	75 Years and Over
Minot, ND Micro Area	3,473	2,701	1,761	884	1,133	1,070	163	0	83
Missoula, MT Metro Area	3,104	4,136	6,669	1,684	1,887	1,488	64	14	68
Mobile, AL Metro Area	21,139	14,227	10,888	6,593	6,651	5,128	635	44	274
Modesto, CA Metro Area	15,966	18,944	12,097	4,242	6,144	5,382	315	68	0
Monroe, LA Metro Area	9,314	5,618	5,538	2,277	3,304	2,073	118	0	58
Monroe, MI Metro Area	10,193	6,336	2,746	2,667	2,797	2,497	65	133	101
Montgomery, AL Metro Area	16,536	12,408	11,681	6,709	5,466	4,675	481	425	234
Morehead City, NC Micro Area	4,676	4,171	4,477	888	2,092	1,796	163	74	43
Morgantown, WV Metro Area	6,710	2,414	3,940	2,000	2,105	1,345	76	75	9
Morristown, TN Metro Area	7,284	4,459	4,668	2,222	2,401	1,927	256	59	0
Moses Lake, WA Micro Area	3,831	2,989	1,979	1,331	1,519	1,077	107	135	0
Mount Airy, NC Micro Area	4,227	3,779	1,395	489	1,615	1,109	15	44	82
Mount Pleasant, MI Micro Area	3,482	1,288	1,603	832	673	472	18	0	0
Mount Vernon-Anacortes, WA Metro Area	5,806	7,540	7,309	1,747	3,252	2,638	99	173	11
Muncie, IN Metro Area	8,251	3,340	4,259	825	1,763	2,215	49	96	40
Muskegon, MI Metro Area	9,745	7,289	5,023	2,160	3,444	3,151	259	298	174
Muskogee, OK Micro Area	4,099	3,092	2,317	984	1,990	1,264	71	17	0
Myrtle Beach-Conway-North Myrtle Beach, SC-NC Metro Area	33,427	27,045	21,427	7,437	14,573	9,092	628	549	131
Nacogdoches, TX Micro Area	3,229	2,350	1,843	644	864	1,035	20	0	185
Napa, CA Metro Area	6,221	7,370	8,772	1,311	2,274	2,494	83	107	100
Naples-Immokalee-Marco Island, FL Metro Area	25,460	24,879	41,641	2,427	8,360	12,273	0	262	466
Nashville-Davidson—Murfreesboro—Franklin, TN Metro Area	76,915	47,463	50,263	18,710	25,059	18,590	2,212	370	343
New Bern, NC Metro Area	6,756	6,820	5,542	2,025	3,556	3,156	232	76	76
New Castle, PA Micro Area	9,026	2,841	2,106	562	1,723	2,048	110	0	112
New Haven-Milford, CT Metro Area	49,511	26,104	35,638	7,002	11,167	13,095	855	84	588
New Orleans-Metairie, LA Metro Area	60,925	37,110	40,613	10,663	17,192	13,096	564	551	448
New Philadelphia-Dover, OH Micro Area	9,776	2,013	1,574	1,428	1,967	1,619	219	67	0
New York-Newark-Jersey City, NY-NJ-PA Metro Area	908,009	496,961	781,739	83,178	169,625	200,134	5,635	3,488	4,427
Niles-Benton Harbor, MI Metro Area	10,572	7,133	6,382	1,178	3,216	2,769	143	88	322
North Port-Sarasota-Bradenton, FL Metro Area	64,039	59,905	81,710	10,403	21,395	29,569	991	595	553
North Wilkesboro, NC Micro Area	5,793	2,454	1,397	1,120	1,533	843	68	0	82
Norwich-New London, CT Metro Area	15,751	9,512	14,037	4,072	6,141	5,630	338	306	87
Oak Harbor, WA Micro Area	4,344	5,391	7,305	2,202	3,130	2,107	304	42	0
Ocala, FL Metro Area	31,605	29,550	17,428	4,331	11,013	12,421	259	378	494
Ocean City, NJ Metro Area	8,652	5,193	5,219	650	2,129	2,629	56	116	117
Odessa, TX Metro Area	3,267	3,818	2,021	1,272	1,410	1,356	50	53	0
Ogden-Clearfield, UT Metro Area	16,506	23,488	18,145	6,287	7,270	7,147	455	540	354
Ogdensburg-Massena, NY Micro Area	6,986	3,917	2,850	1,509	1,659	1,787	8	251	0
Oklahoma City, OK Metro Area	52,244	50,077	45,381	17,385	20,321	15,713	2,083	801	530
Olean, NY Micro Area	5,543	3,414	2,463	1,419	1,902	1,454	129	50	7
Olympia-Tumwater, WA Metro Area	10,589	13,603	13,483	5,383	5,252	5,157	829	139	25
Omaha-Council Bluffs, NE-IA Metro Area	42,590	29,292	26,109	10,962	14,469	11,851	1,018	523	464
Opelousas, LA Micro Area	4,174	1,907	1,359	472	688	850	268	0	0
Orangeburg, SC Micro Area	4,531	3,737	1,848	1,656	1,265	988	762	0	26
Orlando-Kissimmee-Sanford, FL Metro Area	106,846	81,953	74,066	23,389	31,589	28,433	3,018	1,028	998
Oshkosh-Neenah, WI Metro Area	10,915	6,789	5,241	1,768	3,070	2,900	117	0	40
Ottawa-Peru, IL Micro Area	13,311	6,491	3,970	1,765	3,086	2,868	123	0	39
Owensboro, KY Metro Area	7,556	4,643	3,075	1,781	1,722	1,708	141	61	239
Owosso, MI Micro Area	5,563	2,875	1,608	1,101	1,260	1,207	0	0	14
Oxnard-Thousand Oaks-Ventura, CA Metro Area	25,003	35,750	35,252	7,432	10,997	11,505	468	61	150
Paducah, KY-IL Micro Area	6,065	5,276	2,263	1,333	1,923	2,345	112	60	30
Palatka, FL Micro Area	5,793	3,340	2,494	1,965	1,868	1,672	395	0	190
Palm Bay-Melbourne-Titusville, FL Metro Area	43,210	37,542	30,696	12,039	15,013	18,186	1,281	458	1,212
Panama City, FL Metro Area	9,352	10,429	6,570	3,019	5,315	4,084	890	212	37
Parkersburg-Vienna, WV Metro Area	8,027	4,270	2,257	1,924	1,798	2,030	160	394	44
Pensacola-Ferry Pass-Brent, FL Metro Area	25,193	23,044	16,761	10,411	11,370	9,191	1,448	278	151
Peoria, IL Metro Area	24,950	16,703	11,231	3,950	7,053	6,629	141	13	38
Philadelphia-Camden-Wilmington, PA-NJ-DE-MD Metro Area	335,713	174,590	222,202	53,761	83,517	84,606	5,284	2,089	3,453
Phoenix-Mesa-Scottsdale, AZ Metro Area	175,410	203,832	177,987	45,643	74,703	68,799	5,096	2,259	2,082
Pine Bluff, AR Metro Area	5,585	3,265	2,376	1,002	1,298	1,153	182	0	0
Pinehurst-Southern Pines, NC Micro Area	5,052	5,194	9,311	1,293	2,298	1,968	94	135	14
Pittsburgh, PA Metro Area	206,882	81,922	88,095	26,290	44,820	50,053	1,212	820	1,460
Pittsfield, MA Metro Area	8,541	5,616	9,148	1,753	2,509	2,850	72	0	87
Plattsburgh, NY Micro Area	5,110	2,221	2,308	1,631	1,057	993	62	0	47
Pocatello, ID Metro Area	2,970	3,446	2,498	1,034	1,257	968	51	80	0
Port Angeles, WA Micro Area	5,410	6,566	5,867	1,391	3,145	1,880	160	179	0
Port St. Lucie, FL Metro Area	39,350	32,558	25,574	4,255	10,890	15,675	450	213	125
Portland-South Portland, ME Metro Area	28,203	21,339	29,388	6,359	10,834	9,076	739	328	338
Portland-Vancouver-Hillsboro, OR-WA Metro Area	81,320	100,415	98,189	26,146	38,237	27,569	2,966	1,060	1,413
Portsmouth, OH Micro Area	5,668	2,013	2,030	1,187	1,342	1,022	28	0	0
Pottsville, PA Micro Area	15,883	3,497	2,623	1,738	3,167	3,344	74	43	230
Prescott, AZ Metro Area	18,292	21,081	17,405	4,771	9,487	6,931	446	70	280

Table E-4: Metropolitan/Micropolitan Statistical Areas—Educational Attainment and Veteran Status, Persons 55 and Over—*Continued*

	High School or Equivalent	Some College or Associates Degree	Bachelor's Degree or Higher	Veterans by Age and Gender					
				Male			Female		
				55 to 64 Years	65 to 74 Years	75 Years and Over	55 to 64 Years	65 to 74 Years	75 Years and Over
Providence-Warwick, RI-MA Metro Area	82,352	49,718	56,849	15,548	24,524	26,010	1,098	338	892
Provo-Orem, UT Metro Area	8,532	13,896	15,736	2,921	3,677	3,935	201	130	47
Pueblo, CO Metro Area	8,679	8,776	5,848	2,507	2,683	3,490	554	126	142
Punta Gorda, FL Metro Area	20,836	17,989	16,248	2,407	6,265	8,664	161	411	120
Quincy, IL-MO Micro Area	6,042	3,734	1,875	1,278	1,568	1,671	65	0	0
Racine, WI Metro Area	10,995	7,336	5,149	2,397	2,831	3,086	356	40	0
Raleigh, NC Metro Area	35,941	36,151	41,009	11,537	13,825	10,828	1,511	436	476
Rapid City, SD Metro Area	7,801	6,704	4,929	3,259	2,999	2,576	394	0	272
Reading, PA Metro Area	30,026	10,932	11,104	4,603	7,001	7,968	251	161	198
Redding, CA Metro Area	8,773	13,924	7,062	2,943	4,819	3,643	220	234	105
Reno, NV Metro Area	16,255	23,348	18,952	4,236	8,921	7,273	707	676	105
Richmond, IN Micro Area	4,677	3,086	2,017	1,276	1,420	984	0	116	145
Richmond, VA Metro Area	51,536	43,781	44,622	14,096	19,996	15,429	2,552	870	359
Richmond-Berea, KY Micro Area	4,641	2,512	2,629	1,607	1,756	1,132	117	0	0
Riverside-San Bernardino-Ontario, CA Metro Area	131,304	164,103	114,586	38,390	52,512	46,264	3,181	1,175	2,596
Roanoke Rapids, NC Micro Area	6,143	1,957	1,325	723	766	1,064	43	14	18
Roanoke, VA Metro Area	21,733	15,491	10,908	3,861	6,227	5,802	266	378	0
Rochester, MN Metro Area	10,573	8,779	8,772	2,202	3,403	3,889	157	60	38
Rochester, NY Metro Area	62,946	39,802	43,628	9,491	15,024	17,298	581	491	964
Rockford, IL Metro Area	21,106	11,648	10,830	4,278	5,572	5,176	309	43	24
Rocky Mount, NC Metro Area	9,075	5,699	2,724	2,236	2,306	1,871	102	160	0
Rome, GA Metro Area	5,684	2,869	2,738	1,210	1,941	1,592	130	76	102
Roseburg, OR Micro Area	7,943	8,855	3,595	2,659	4,155	3,580	38	386	0
Roswell, NM Micro Area	2,562	2,799	2,005	732	1,077	698	197	0	0
Russellville, AR Micro Area	5,859	2,495	1,539	1,029	1,777	1,303	14	0	14
Sacramento–Roseville–Arden-Arcade, CA Metro Area	75,098	102,651	90,775	23,699	34,405	32,976	2,364	1,215	1,559
Saginaw, MI Metro Area	14,357	7,211	5,525	2,540	2,831	2,754	72	57	112
Salem, OH Micro Area	10,329	2,960	2,079	1,721	2,947	2,017	95	115	0
Salem, OR Metro Area	17,194	19,561	16,315	4,101	7,025	7,072	722	412	188
Salinas, CA Metro Area	8,914	13,115	17,488	3,174	4,634	4,443	524	122	0
Salisbury, MD-DE Metro Area	29,697	20,046	20,590	5,410	9,842	7,776	817	249	587
Salt Lake City, UT Metro Area	29,955	36,099	33,509	9,410	11,077	10,593	426	237	398
San Angelo, TX Metro Area	4,987	4,848	3,995	1,863	2,011	2,072	59	87	48
San Antonio-New Braunfels, TX Metro Area	75,125	72,598	69,244	33,145	37,986	29,416	7,428	1,932	1,472
San Diego-Carlsbad, CA Metro Area	85,144	116,963	141,589	34,950	46,364	40,822	3,533	1,479	1,820
San Francisco-Oakland-Hayward, CA Metro Area	131,603	161,130	242,519	26,548	43,645	46,951	1,984	678	1,983
San Jose-Sunnyvale-Santa Clara, CA Metro Area	46,866	55,129	90,784	8,957	15,410	17,465	1,006	356	464
San Luis Obispo-Paso Robles-Arroyo Grande, CA Metro Area	9,600	16,264	18,890	2,850	5,387	5,671	469	143	135
Sandusky, OH Micro Area	6,593	3,280	2,742	939	1,287	1,784	0	117	0
Santa Cruz-Watsonville, CA Metro Area	5,750	9,747	16,956	2,139	3,140	2,591	115	94	85
Santa Fe, NM Metro Area	6,034	6,905	13,408	1,722	3,235	2,245	112	55	44
Santa Maria-Santa Barbara, CA Metro Area	12,497	17,928	22,466	3,178	5,531	7,226	43	248	355
Santa Rosa, CA Metro Area	16,472	27,229	31,496	5,330	9,174	7,834	519	260	240
Savannah, GA Metro Area	13,647	10,526	14,928	4,813	5,964	4,740	565	128	213
Scranton–Wilkes-Barre–Hazleton, PA Metro Area	51,071	21,391	17,802	5,969	10,733	11,599	500	476	664
Searcy, AR Micro Area	5,201	1,666	2,010	1,375	1,143	1,190	0	132	47
Seattle-Tacoma-Bellevue, WA Metro Area	111,027	136,857	151,961	45,463	52,993	45,404	5,963	2,736	2,305
Sebastian-Vero Beach, FL Metro Area	14,628	11,580	13,476	1,577	4,503	6,652	192	151	173
Sebring, FL Metro Area	10,754	9,550	7,113	1,133	3,368	4,517	132	147	22
Seneca, SC Micro Area	4,893	3,471	4,835	1,262	2,322	1,668	0	34	76
Sevierville, TN Micro Area	5,585	3,711	2,757	817	1,858	1,098	153	0	58
Shawnee, OK Micro Area	4,325	3,043	2,201	1,502	1,360	1,214	24	0	94
Sheboygan, WI Metro Area	9,294	3,782	3,504	1,181	1,994	2,292	0	0	114
Shelby, NC Micro Area	5,515	4,809	2,852	825	1,621	1,102	290	342	40
Sherman-Denison, TX Metro Area	7,780	5,541	4,634	2,618	3,081	2,227	277	62	39
Show Low, AZ Micro Area	4,131	5,902	3,134	1,257	2,342	1,497	14	42	84
Shreveport-Bossier City, LA Metro Area	24,206	15,160	14,041	6,287	6,908	5,590	413	178	287
Sierra Vista-Douglas, AZ Metro Area	6,557	8,195	6,179	3,383	3,443	3,340	993	332	37
Sioux City, IA-NE-SD Metro Area	10,797	6,004	4,126	1,479	2,997	2,748	295	145	23
Sioux Falls, SD Metro Area	12,462	7,039	7,157	2,301	2,876	3,217	191	65	155
Somerset, PA Micro Area	8,507	2,092	1,722	928	1,843	1,482	0	82	37
South Bend-Mishawaka, IN-MI Metro Area	19,311	11,101	10,233	3,624	6,172	4,528	406	301	51
Spartanburg, SC Metro Area	16,493	11,648	9,924	4,243	5,118	4,563	215	138	54
Spokane-Spokane Valley, WA Metro Area	24,953	26,449	22,854	9,805	11,844	9,994	1,247	298	397
Springfield, IL Metro Area	12,761	8,449	7,762	2,340	4,066	3,211	158	157	155
Springfield, MA Metro Area	31,388	20,428	25,351	6,609	9,674	9,720	450	99	211
Springfield, MO Metro Area	27,984	18,150	14,260	6,323	7,602	6,898	767	128	267
Springfield, OH Metro Area	10,781	6,226	3,627	2,058	3,134	2,769	120	119	0
St. Cloud, MN Metro Area	10,467	6,050	5,638	2,153	3,184	3,065	100	0	97
St. George, UT Metro Area	6,751	12,358	8,448	1,283	3,133	4,310	0	78	51
St. Joseph, MO-KS Metro Area	8,301	5,308	2,713	1,527	1,757	1,871	85	14	119
St. Louis, MO-IL Metro Area	150,182	102,676	100,771	37,667	49,901	43,555	5,044	1,258	985
State College, PA Metro Area	7,739	3,411	6,251	1,430	2,105	1,678	137	0	0

Table E-4: Metropolitan/Micropolitan Statistical Areas—Educational Attainment and Veteran Status, Persons 55 and Over—Continued

	High School or Equivalent	Some College or Associates Degree	Bachelor's Degree or Higher	Veterans by Age and Gender					
				Male			Female		
				55 to 64 Years	65 to 74 Years	75 Years and Over	55 to 64 Years	65 to 74 Years	75 Years and Over
Statesboro, GA Micro Area	2,949	1,096	1,548	356	908	535	85	0	0
Staunton-Waynesboro, VA Metro Area	6,978	6,983	4,771	1,555	2,717	1,822	137	141	0
Stevens Point, WI Micro Area	4,121	2,315	2,540	581	1,247	1,003	64	0	58
Stillwater, OK Micro Area	2,928	2,446	2,189	681	834	740	13	0	0
Stockton-Lodi, CA Metro Area	22,262	23,400	16,728	6,637	7,456	6,501	557	116	177
Sumter, SC Metro Area	4,294	2,965	2,287	1,983	1,947	1,423	216	0	55
Sunbury, PA Micro Area	11,106	2,488	1,398	1,509	2,104	1,960	106	0	16
Syracuse, NY Metro Area	36,259	23,768	23,929	8,112	10,564	9,956	882	277	283
Talladega-Sylacauga, AL Micro Area	5,768	4,012	818	1,840	1,824	1,106	129	137	0
Tallahassee, FL Metro Area	12,121	12,289	14,846	5,463	5,050	4,352	296	193	236
Tampa-St. Petersburg-Clearwater, FL Metro Area	187,135	149,028	123,774	38,517	60,318	63,562	5,716	1,425	2,296
Terre Haute, IN Metro Area	12,247	5,226	4,029	1,967	2,545	2,207	156	0	82
Texarkana, TX-AR Metro Area	8,116	7,108	3,657	2,575	2,960	2,257	145	98	181
The Villages, FL Metro Area	19,252	18,003	18,433	1,306	8,674	7,856	38	264	46
Toledo, OH Metro Area	34,403	21,408	18,633	5,011	9,264	9,024	413	341	479
Topeka, KS Metro Area	16,145	10,089	8,482	4,261	4,131	4,332	587	135	179
Torrington, CT Micro Area	11,256	8,367	10,531	2,547	3,921	3,773	91	44	46
Traverse City, MI Micro Area	7,417	8,504	10,364	2,597	3,541	2,574	473	153	125
Trenton, NJ Metro Area	14,486	9,388	18,504	2,172	3,306	4,218	83	62	102
Truckee-Grass Valley, CA Micro Area	5,531	9,228	7,552	1,757	2,465	2,914	78	39	81
Tucson, AZ Metro Area	41,537	53,047	59,727	13,856	19,564	19,867	1,675	885	1,149
Tullahoma-Manchester, TN Micro Area	7,098	3,794	3,534	1,750	2,523	1,355	241	233	85
Tulsa, OK Metro Area	50,663	37,679	28,582	11,440	16,356	12,881	836	402	334
Tupelo, MS Micro Area	6,576	5,516	3,747	1,173	1,356	1,689	33	59	0
Tuscaloosa, AL Metro Area	11,338	5,961	5,840	3,473	3,091	2,170	80	0	50
Twin Falls, ID Micro Area	5,129	5,210	2,850	1,694	1,563	1,665	102	145	38
Tyler, TX Metro Area	9,881	9,937	8,925	1,338	2,129	3,356	57	0	107
Ukiah, CA Micro Area	3,220	5,274	5,881	818	2,225	1,436	27	292	50
Urban Honolulu, HI Metro Area	50,257	37,579	43,039	11,741	14,545	15,832	1,421	412	473
Utica-Rome, NY Metro Area	19,979	14,423	10,260	3,797	5,797	6,103	308	158	291
Valdosta, GA Metro Area	5,108	4,144	3,101	1,805	1,621	1,495	21	76	77
Vallejo-Fairfield, CA Metro Area	14,587	20,039	14,858	6,627	7,159	5,683	707	350	350
Victoria, TX Metro Area	3,923	3,894	2,346	1,044	1,381	1,475	114	61	31
Vineland-Bridgeton, NJ Metro Area	8,077	3,360	3,116	1,000	1,876	1,485	80	0	112
Virginia Beach-Norfolk-Newport News, VA-NC Metro Area	62,509	63,634	62,206	35,097	32,384	23,080	4,729	1,640	1,111
Visalia-Porterville, CA Metro Area	12,676	11,574	6,802	2,769	3,024	3,715	50	47	8
Waco, TX Metro Area	9,274	10,563	7,826	3,644	4,318	4,018	223	108	231
Walla Walla, WA Metro Area	2,986	2,957	3,222	1,107	995	1,311	286	71	139
Warner Robins, GA Metro Area	8,982	5,490	4,359	3,937	3,501	2,326	253	109	252
Warsaw, IN Micro Area	4,554	2,465	2,165	933	1,034	1,306	34	0	0
Washington-Arlington-Alexandria, DC-VA-MD-WV Metro Area	159,283	145,464	288,917	62,861	71,104	59,055	11,270	4,310	3,415
Waterloo-Cedar Falls, IA Metro Area	11,480	6,758	5,213	1,734	2,992	2,638	154	80	13
Watertown-Fort Atkinson, WI Micro Area	6,163	2,924	1,863	713	1,759	1,486	20	0	94
Watertown-Fort Drum, NY Metro Area	6,352	3,642	2,216	1,177	2,093	1,647	488	0	33
Wausau, WI Metro Area	10,095	3,626	4,416	1,361	2,327	2,725	83	0	18
Weirton-Steubenville, WV-OH Metro Area	13,255	3,673	2,807	1,613	2,487	1,875	9	80	76
Wenatchee, WA Metro Area	5,706	6,742	4,521	1,542	2,245	2,171	96	0	255
Wheeling, WV-OH Metro Area	14,693	5,555	4,338	1,808	3,728	2,700	83	62	49
Whitewater-Elkhorn, WI Micro Area	5,288	3,927	4,625	1,007	1,650	1,380	32	294	83
Wichita Falls, TX Metro Area	7,713	6,668	4,009	2,361	2,668	2,734	164	20	153
Wichita, KS Metro Area	29,933	25,668	19,832	6,646	9,845	9,169	904	198	360
Williamsport, PA Metro Area	9,455	4,400	2,999	1,956	2,192	2,179	194	38	35
Wilmington, NC Metro Area	13,609	11,860	13,502	4,042	6,199	4,666	217	112	0
Wilson, NC Micro Area	5,234	1,908	2,979	970	831	1,276	0	41	0
Winchester, VA-WV Metro Area	7,615	4,311	4,220	2,136	2,096	2,864	156	0	0
Winston-Salem, NC Metro Area	38,156	23,657	20,783	8,743	10,287	9,141	892	397	194
Wisconsin Rapids-Marshfield, WI Micro Area	6,782	2,613	2,360	608	1,746	1,491	80	10	0
Wooster, OH Micro Area	7,850	3,559	3,027	1,374	2,048	1,789	7	71	46
Worcester, MA-CT Metro Area	50,334	27,912	31,001	8,231	13,759	13,330	408	389	336
Yakima, WA Metro Area	8,634	8,855	5,268	2,142	4,058	3,363	399	0	148
York-Hanover, PA Metro Area	33,009	12,788	10,440	5,084	7,612	6,785	415	176	411
Youngstown-Warren-Boardman, OH-PA Metro Area	52,531	21,334	15,226	7,148	12,278	11,659	226	184	369
Yuba City, CA Metro Area	4,620	7,857	4,560	1,639	2,626	2,097	126	149	90
Yuma, AZ Metro Area	11,379	8,452	5,168	2,185	2,044	3,607	292	214	95
Zanesville, OH Micro Area	6,706	2,413	1,915	1,451	1,299	1,054	229	0	0

Table E-5: 114th Congressional Districts—Educational Attainment and Veteran Status, Persons 55 and Over

	High School or Equivalent	Some College or Associates Degree	Bachelor's Degree or Higher	Veterans by Age and Gender					
				Male			Female		
				55 to 64 Years	65 to 74 Years	75 Years and Over	55 to 64 Years	65 to 74 Years	75 Years and Over
Alabama									
Congressional District 1	37,672	26,904	24,860	9,382	13,075	10,881	1,086	237	684
Congressional District 2	37,198	24,213	18,810	12,118	12,557	10,539	1,402	655	530
Congressional District 3	36,695	24,878	16,172	10,358	12,623	8,967	776	689	214
Congressional District 4	44,601	25,072	16,128	8,794	11,715	10,151	605	490	147
Congressional District 5	34,416	25,772	24,743	11,761	12,198	10,464	821	387	264
Congressional District 6	37,224	26,492	27,225	7,526	10,807	10,240	597	211	212
Congressional District 7	34,387	21,005	14,213	9,733	8,977	6,355	443	334	122
Alaska									
Congressional District (at Large)	18,377	20,339	21,230	11,306	13,371	6,362	1,624	745	726
Arizona									
Congressional District 1	30,731	35,250	34,776	8,545	16,092	11,972	1,005	397	299
Congressional District 2	32,392	43,436	50,210	12,973	15,945	16,421	2,097	932	876
Congressional District 3	19,617	19,670	12,060	6,440	8,904	6,159	501	327	95
Congressional District 4	62,875	67,505	35,374	13,559	25,574	23,354	856	497	927
Congressional District 5	38,370	38,445	32,742	8,255	13,769	13,412	854	328	316
Congressional District 6	27,746	39,248	47,874	5,869	12,885	13,178	1,016	256	194
Congressional District 7	15,018	13,333	7,058	5,897	5,667	3,347	452	102	76
Congressional District 8	43,647	51,949	44,378	10,588	18,130	19,278	1,575	941	571
Congressional District 9	19,165	27,736	27,471	6,602	10,249	9,194	652	385	484
Arkansas									
Congressional District 1	45,398	27,194	16,342	9,996	13,562	11,754	747	544	317
Congressional District 2	39,153	23,204	27,714	10,804	11,236	10,010	809	746	276
Congressional District 3	37,493	28,787	17,755	8,610	12,397	10,693	749	312	227
Congressional District 4	50,566	28,835	20,282	10,719	14,227	11,740	669	256	194
California									
Congressional District 1	36,996	50,454	35,847	11,213	17,193	15,378	836	487	579
Congressional District 2	22,906	38,835	55,687	6,521	13,837	11,824	878	469	246
Congressional District 3	23,640	29,884	22,799	8,637	11,122	9,034	734	461	520
Congressional District 4	34,048	52,580	39,734	10,168	16,539	15,792	1,018	360	475
Congressional District 5	25,696	37,600	38,478	8,021	11,282	10,917	683	338	547
Congressional District 6	18,296	24,311	22,453	7,026	8,034	8,560	748	264	510
Congressional District 7	26,566	33,663	30,428	8,398	12,419	10,160	665	636	750
Congressional District 8	25,956	31,616	15,421	8,431	12,842	8,927	1,439	306	197
Congressional District 9	23,440	26,285	20,670	7,175	7,639	6,898	648	102	173
Congressional District 10	21,917	24,352	14,712	6,388	8,693	7,025	463	82	43
Congressional District 11	21,611	30,902	47,500	5,295	9,217	10,800	147	312	533
Congressional District 12	19,125	22,233	36,196	3,538	5,400	6,458	305	0	82
Congressional District 13	17,110	20,755	36,930	4,060	6,512	6,721	409	101	391
Congressional District 14	24,341	25,049	41,057	2,816	6,542	6,927	79	0	79
Congressional District 15	25,108	26,505	27,303	5,153	6,163	6,210	200	232	617
Congressional District 16	17,063	18,573	10,458	3,690	7,522	6,363	334	228	201
Congressional District 17	20,629	20,365	30,384	3,217	5,040	5,338	313	0	186
Congressional District 18	17,242	25,430	54,726	3,777	6,867	9,869	241	202	375
Congressional District 19	17,516	19,607	24,333	3,604	6,120	4,651	381	129	77
Congressional District 20	15,310	22,232	31,744	5,056	7,667	6,993	818	274	108
Congressional District 21	11,463	11,498	4,856	4,616	4,497	3,486	169	29	160
Congressional District 22	20,573	26,041	19,281	5,007	8,097	6,892	107	246	312
Congressional District 23	24,917	28,089	16,952	6,652	9,691	7,840	806	144	260
Congressional District 24	22,265	34,416	41,638	6,239	10,994	12,968	512	391	490
Congressional District 25	20,732	23,265	16,819	7,516	8,246	5,594	642	176	105
Congressional District 26	19,366	29,988	32,062	5,965	9,274	10,396	445	61	150
Congressional District 27	24,863	25,221	38,515	3,104	6,150	7,246	78	176	186
Congressional District 28	22,804	21,509	33,153	2,028	4,620	5,331	232	113	164
Congressional District 29	15,796	14,384	12,038	2,978	3,292	2,645	439	0	59
Congressional District 30	22,758	28,085	41,885	3,083	5,661	7,988	227	84	557
Congressional District 31	18,059	20,559	15,812	5,467	7,174	4,085	323	173	493
Congressional District 32	21,066	22,044	17,923	3,020	5,742	5,326	66	73	261
Congressional District 33	16,544	30,172	63,657	2,078	6,997	11,657	425	155	267
Congressional District 34	14,334	12,167	15,099	1,478	2,069	2,519	136	0	285
Congressional District 35	14,413	14,394	7,508	3,533	4,493	3,572	119	142	36
Congressional District 36	33,427	46,998	42,733	7,089	12,081	17,238	461	276	672
Congressional District 37	18,930	22,181	26,643	2,543	4,069	6,536	359	203	111
Congressional District 38	23,566	22,080	16,068	3,500	6,509	5,663	137	127	100
Congressional District 39	22,282	27,762	31,428	4,042	6,672	7,813	181	190	258
Congressional District 40	10,738	7,014	4,166	1,331	1,109	2,410	118	75	177
Congressional District 41	17,589	19,042	11,311	5,596	6,136	4,257	711	100	553
Congressional District 42	21,423	28,533	18,184	7,246	9,102	7,803	128	130	681
Congressional District 43	19,987	23,015	16,784	3,527	5,790	5,156	209	283	150
Congressional District 44	11,341	14,341	7,319	2,262	2,918	3,310	127	46	61
Congressional District 45	19,638	29,652	43,651	4,885	8,143	8,387	312	0	356
Congressional District 46	15,342	14,725	11,317	2,582	3,133	3,774	535	65	42
Congressional District 47	23,036	26,069	21,240	4,980	7,812	6,491	439	146	258
Congressional District 48	19,883	34,789	46,984	3,966	10,171	9,207	438	279	510
Congressional District 49	16,213	33,012	46,255	5,994	9,653	12,181	1,054	171	481
Congressional District 50	25,496	32,719	31,252	8,389	14,241	10,087	658	264	706

Table E-5: 114th Congressional Districts—Educational Attainment and Veteran Status, Persons 55 and Over—*Continued*

	High School or Equivalent	Some College or Associates Degree	Bachelor's Degree or Higher	Veterans by Age and Gender					
				Male			Female		
				55 to 64 Years	65 to 74 Years	75 Years and Over	55 to 64 Years	65 to 74 Years	75 Years and Over
California—Cont.									
Congressional District 51	15,741	15,862	9,078	6,946	5,907	5,447	457	162	234
Congressional District 52	17,149	24,717	46,297	8,310	11,288	9,464	633	674	515
Congressional District 53	19,689	26,553	26,720	8,557	10,108	9,354	977	316	47
Colorado									
Congressional District 1	20,081	21,349	31,786	6,866	9,535	8,691	655	327	194
Congressional District 2	20,298	27,189	48,570	6,360	12,923	10,042	787	417	280
Congressional District 3	33,087	33,812	36,185	11,353	14,165	11,889	1,539	231	559
Congressional District 4	29,820	28,308	25,048	9,517	13,399	9,262	1,101	533	405
Congressional District 5	26,096	30,030	31,821	16,433	15,333	11,445	3,086	678	600
Congressional District 6	20,237	24,553	32,258	8,299	10,239	7,399	1,078	393	436
Congressional District 7	30,172	27,579	25,297	9,486	10,944	10,131	650	350	444
Connecticut									
Congressional District 1	38,833	24,182	29,885	6,115	9,021	11,577	418	66	908
Congressional District 2	39,971	25,961	35,676	9,143	15,005	12,868	619	370	250
Congressional District 3	41,949	22,201	29,385	5,028	9,981	10,218	802	62	491
Congressional District 4	27,661	19,106	40,135	4,079	6,824	9,709	461	99	312
Congressional District 5	37,491	22,053	33,903	6,897	10,297	10,871	322	300	281
Delaware									
Congressional District (at Large)	57,810	35,145	39,540	14,279	18,941	13,922	1,538	433	279
District of Columbia									
Delegate District (at Large)	18,227	14,766	29,198	4,970	5,613	6,224	526	498	629
Florida									
Congressional District 1	36,732	36,850	28,927	17,458	18,774	14,394	2,245	322	679
Congressional District 2	30,929	28,905	25,940	11,325	13,710	11,095	1,584	438	387
Congressional District 3	39,489	33,720	30,313	11,473	17,611	13,411	1,415	441	814
Congressional District 4	32,725	27,418	29,944	13,096	14,777	10,889	1,072	536	326
Congressional District 5	28,510	19,802	14,648	9,242	6,999	7,722	1,247	108	207
Congressional District 6	58,652	45,650	48,253	15,986	22,212	20,805	1,060	1,040	1,039
Congressional District 7	33,582	28,776	27,171	9,319	12,422	9,246	787	233	589
Congressional District 8	58,256	49,526	44,521	13,971	19,938	24,942	1,543	609	1,385
Congressional District 9	30,712	20,225	14,649	6,162	7,746	5,791	565	581	228
Congressional District 10	49,479	39,543	33,200	9,483	14,538	14,434	1,283	276	471
Congressional District 11	83,054	70,665	50,415	11,150	28,557	32,563	612	813	764
Congressional District 12	58,499	42,843	34,358	9,121	16,720	19,715	1,439	525	717
Congressional District 13	51,556	50,512	44,227	9,593	18,693	21,088	2,230	459	796
Congressional District 14	33,110	21,730	18,549	8,919	10,365	7,476	1,065	120	398
Congressional District 15	37,710	27,968	22,223	10,005	12,192	11,906	815	367	223
Congressional District 16	63,613	59,677	81,143	10,318	21,349	29,513	991	595	553
Congressional District 17	69,039	52,486	41,619	9,689	20,651	24,670	871	598	641
Congressional District 18	55,750	51,447	50,123	7,655	16,106	23,660	828	624	209
Congressional District 19	60,352	58,506	77,354	7,979	20,805	26,662	495	444	495
Congressional District 20	36,142	21,341	18,790	5,430	6,588	7,660	297	178	82
Congressional District 21	56,948	44,087	55,023	3,871	9,217	21,536	568	299	432
Congressional District 22	39,957	40,638	56,762	5,926	11,946	16,003	330	296	402
Congressional District 23	36,690	29,048	32,766	4,230	6,601	7,929	489	265	262
Congressional District 24	25,884	17,199	11,265	2,580	3,089	2,292	235	40	62
Congressional District 25	32,776	20,954	24,996	2,991	4,274	5,584	60	112	165
Congressional District 26	31,331	23,792	26,743	4,887	5,516	3,204	566	358	198
Congressional District 27	30,799	19,606	27,454	2,246	3,850	2,624	368	36	0
Georgia									
Congressional District 1	30,984	23,082	24,028	10,618	12,591	9,165	1,361	249	362
Congressional District 2	30,885	19,268	15,691	10,411	10,352	7,511	609	601	205
Congressional District 3	33,270	23,049	20,833	10,402	14,091	7,484	539	766	162
Congressional District 4	23,482	18,941	19,218	8,479	7,623	4,449	1,481	160	705
Congressional District 5	19,782	19,196	22,123	8,016	7,845	5,388	635	225	129
Congressional District 6	17,215	19,703	39,148	4,266	7,282	7,510	666	187	59
Congressional District 7	20,029	16,984	19,303	4,753	7,971	4,255	766	68	111
Congressional District 8	35,645	22,374	17,704	9,782	11,219	8,581	747	268	643
Congressional District 9	41,574	29,100	28,733	7,609	15,461	12,754	564	321	439
Congressional District 10	33,518	20,733	20,315	7,564	10,328	7,661	535	111	0
Congressional District 11	25,264	21,237	23,945	8,797	11,844	7,386	580	113	495
Congressional District 12	35,933	18,032	14,737	11,158	10,655	7,634	1,933	521	164
Congressional District 13	29,652	14,488	11,975	9,742	9,032	6,867	1,512	274	101
Congressional District 14	36,050	20,151	12,380	6,752	11,066	8,869	369	267	272
Hawaii									
Congressional District 1	38,863	28,647	32,964	8,333	10,344	11,447	940	255	339
Congressional District 2	32,045	29,011	30,504	9,338	11,981	9,843	652	464	134
Idaho									
Congressional District 1	42,346	44,667	28,537	13,514	20,539	13,120	1,105	463	367
Congressional District 2	32,847	34,478	25,843	9,054	11,979	11,371	612	593	229

Table E-5: 114th Congressional Districts—Educational Attainment and Veteran Status, Persons 55 and Over—*Continued*

	High School or Equivalent	Some College or Associates Degree	Bachelor's Degree or Higher	Veterans by Age and Gender					
				Male			Female		
				55 to 64 Years	65 to 74 Years	75 Years and Over	55 to 64 Years	65 to 74 Years	75 Years and Over
Illinois									
Congressional District 1	34,380	27,394	22,035	4,886	9,727	8,498	223	91	163
Congressional District 2	32,212	26,578	19,366	5,552	9,547	9,625	347	131	223
Congressional District 3	37,025	21,650	17,319	3,140	7,562	8,038	113	234	140
Congressional District 4	16,466	9,719	9,078	1,933	3,293	3,222	375	23	251
Congressional District 5	25,891	16,280	27,400	2,414	4,878	6,624	162	118	136
Congressional District 6	26,764	25,219	40,881	4,318	9,307	8,677	46	92	373
Congressional District 7	19,590	15,960	23,146	4,608	5,570	5,141	501	131	216
Congressional District 8	29,164	20,753	21,265	3,751	7,245	6,869	279	216	281
Congressional District 9	29,198	23,643	47,806	3,121	5,873	8,957	130	7	454
Congressional District 10	25,292	20,258	37,369	4,489	6,731	8,799	192	160	386
Congressional District 11	21,159	17,979	16,471	4,405	5,562	5,847	521	103	328
Congressional District 12	43,783	27,219	18,428	11,145	13,234	11,656	1,559	248	219
Congressional District 13	42,581	25,325	23,659	8,145	11,581	11,588	1,031	585	286
Congressional District 14	31,001	24,487	25,505	6,428	11,183	7,234	230	174	281
Congressional District 15	52,379	30,219	16,668	10,315	14,125	13,322	662	83	159
Congressional District 16	50,253	27,229	21,919	8,333	12,544	12,706	442	90	116
Congressional District 17	51,560	29,876	17,888	8,895	13,064	12,932	475	319	261
Congressional District 18	48,668	30,285	25,780	7,913	14,582	12,515	306	170	126
Indiana									
Congressional District 1	43,283	24,817	18,300	8,408	10,994	10,645	617	278	214
Congressional District 2	45,849	23,083	19,109	7,108	13,397	9,474	905	218	439
Congressional District 3	44,679	26,167	17,873	8,113	10,789	9,757	343	346	69
Congressional District 4	46,018	24,484	20,748	8,308	12,090	11,043	753	231	297
Congressional District 5	33,495	24,357	29,784	6,571	9,169	9,948	395	150	258
Congressional District 6	53,418	24,143	18,955	9,456	13,693	11,999	383	353	450
Congressional District 7	32,089	19,641	12,488	8,767	7,942	7,438	972	172	52
Congressional District 8	55,618	22,751	17,582	8,851	13,730	11,783	601	321	599
Congressional District 9	46,427	21,438	22,706	9,414	12,209	9,289	1,162	183	129
Iowa									
Congressional District 1	58,282	29,274	23,763	8,862	13,659	13,346	584	280	427
Congressional District 2	51,479	29,777	25,230	8,320	12,477	11,731	937	521	150
Congressional District 3	44,943	27,955	23,533	7,602	11,583	10,157	796	558	476
Congressional District 4	57,683	33,778	25,882	8,196	13,022	14,852	511	141	277
Kansas									
Congressional District 1	39,877	30,367	25,165	7,132	10,754	11,091	556	619	431
Congressional District 2	43,869	28,045	25,411	12,021	12,276	12,752	1,272	400	469
Congressional District 3	22,289	26,421	34,811	6,221	10,040	10,182	328	182	150
Congressional District 4	35,648	30,603	23,121	7,633	10,918	11,107	941	299	411
Kentucky									
Congressional District 1	47,300	25,858	15,601	9,101	10,867	11,196	585	192	284
Congressional District 2	40,361	22,050	17,495	11,862	11,321	9,787	857	202	501
Congressional District 3	37,006	25,521	26,946	7,804	10,555	10,559	457	160	333
Congressional District 4	41,179	23,660	17,494	10,081	11,958	9,123	856	257	144
Congressional District 5	39,424	16,466	11,069	6,247	12,233	8,912	358	270	137
Congressional District 6	32,960	21,981	23,358	8,645	9,455	7,765	1,231	624	282
Louisiana									
Congressional District 1	42,501	26,689	27,386	5,924	10,301	10,176	628	106	339
Congressional District 2	33,580	16,350	17,797	6,554	9,079	5,816	275	445	109
Congressional District 3	35,273	19,625	18,962	7,084	9,449	7,947	562	154	301
Congressional District 4	40,990	25,516	20,360	9,570	12,028	9,500	681	493	526
Congressional District 5	41,874	22,265	21,056	7,975	12,218	10,136	486	338	122
Congressional District 6	36,176	19,683	22,618	6,849	10,412	8,283	702	85	204
Maine									
Congressional District 1	38,477	28,390	39,527	8,189	14,596	12,859	971	354	548
Congressional District 2	48,641	27,711	24,418	10,332	17,169	12,354	643	238	305
Maryland									
Congressional District 1	46,017	29,360	31,838	8,509	13,835	12,621	1,217	181	780
Congressional District 2	35,677	20,917	18,828	8,931	9,275	9,523	1,269	408	271
Congressional District 3	31,421	19,172	41,375	6,897	8,059	9,724	1,616	381	550
Congressional District 4	27,800	23,789	24,519	8,606	8,902	7,942	1,260	510	202
Congressional District 5	30,099	21,431	26,618	11,748	11,413	7,700	1,957	765	412
Congressional District 6	31,846	19,477	33,885	6,638	9,039	9,144	590	510	545
Congressional District 7	32,122	20,723	30,477	6,701	9,308	8,086	642	264	519
Congressional District 8	24,390	22,139	54,640	5,587	8,300	10,625	913	236	553
Massachusetts									
Congressional District 1	41,245	25,629	31,960	8,123	12,324	12,175	645	46	342
Congressional District 2	38,638	21,577	27,525	6,317	10,057	11,131	353	204	164
Congressional District 3	31,104	22,769	26,523	5,717	9,387	8,894	577	289	281
Congressional District 4	31,307	22,025	38,320	5,800	10,355	9,817	64	392	482
Congressional District 5	34,740	20,869	42,539	3,782	7,944	10,332	306	168	459
Congressional District 6	40,854	29,253	36,077	6,260	9,951	13,618	579	324	744
Congressional District 7	21,505	10,756	18,420	2,344	3,322	3,864	185	76	36
Congressional District 8	40,828	27,366	34,316	4,961	10,552	11,029	278	141	294
Congressional District 9	41,383	36,788	48,935	7,662	14,909	17,246	704	312	686

Table E-5: 114th Congressional Districts—Educational Attainment and Veteran Status, Persons 55 and Over—*Continued*

	High School or Equivalent	Some College or Associates Degree	Bachelor's Degree or Higher	Veterans by Age and Gender					
				Male			Female		
				55 to 64 Years	65 to 74 Years	75 Years and Over	55 to 64 Years	65 to 74 Years	75 Years and Over
Michigan									
Congressional District 1	55,467	38,427	36,537	12,062	18,955	16,677	1,274	380	378
Congressional District 2	38,344	29,311	19,603	7,763	11,216	9,951	653	462	337
Congressional District 3	34,873	27,148	23,705	7,845	11,110	10,407	346	415	528
Congressional District 4	54,073	31,116	18,901	9,052	13,530	11,270	380	171	242
Congressional District 5	47,400	31,601	17,107	9,776	12,321	10,190	664	158	121
Congressional District 6	40,981	29,244	25,313	7,309	11,742	10,025	711	335	383
Congressional District 7	46,000	30,336	20,687	8,990	13,950	10,219	518	703	431
Congressional District 8	29,338	27,127	28,035	7,518	10,836	7,585	338	146	270
Congressional District 9	39,448	28,471	24,855	6,442	10,106	10,969	659	224	277
Congressional District 10	48,290	32,027	18,052	7,341	13,454	9,995	655	199	253
Congressional District 11	32,493	25,838	33,952	6,339	8,860	9,407	451	128	158
Congressional District 12	31,644	22,529	24,556	6,365	9,145	8,664	270	156	353
Congressional District 13	33,737	22,353	9,941	7,206	8,538	7,317	486	211	176
Congressional District 14	27,563	26,607	33,012	5,019	8,576	8,528	519	400	116
Minnesota									
Congressional District 1	41,824	27,558	21,390	7,660	11,036	12,435	435	167	223
Congressional District 2	29,018	21,688	23,938	6,318	10,173	8,603	731	270	579
Congressional District 3	24,073	29,289	36,497	5,457	9,900	9,733	489	355	516
Congressional District 4	28,498	20,293	33,619	5,871	9,546	9,573	353	120	354
Congressional District 5	24,060	18,894	25,655	4,714	5,735	8,935	670	104	333
Congressional District 6	30,091	19,981	16,363	7,870	10,873	7,831	535	170	154
Congressional District 7	52,592	29,674	21,051	8,163	12,608	13,202	558	325	353
Congressional District 8	50,281	30,830	25,592	11,286	15,349	13,772	740	514	370
Mississippi									
Congressional District 1	36,680	27,094	19,183	8,332	10,211	9,604	715	259	405
Congressional District 2	26,842	19,628	18,437	7,255	7,723	6,697	237	278	285
Congressional District 3	35,100	27,854	21,423	9,057	11,852	8,747	962	141	301
Congressional District 4	32,870	30,385	22,741	9,208	12,853	11,061	893	73	283
Missouri									
Congressional District 1	30,945	22,097	19,563	10,215	10,208	8,914	1,211	213	195
Congressional District 2	37,959	35,502	47,274	6,815	12,553	13,623	497	338	316
Congressional District 3	46,365	26,591	19,176	10,967	15,523	11,450	1,302	345	134
Congressional District 4	51,993	28,152	19,002	11,360	15,313	12,096	1,047	271	322
Congressional District 5	42,546	27,887	21,112	10,290	11,087	11,217	1,123	225	210
Congressional District 6	50,118	27,840	20,961	10,097	14,647	11,404	974	155	263
Congressional District 7	50,799	32,339	23,410	10,848	15,174	11,822	1,101	218	320
Congressional District 8	51,426	26,180	18,745	12,581	16,993	14,182	670	223	294
Montana									
Congressional District (at Large)	60,703	46,883	44,354	17,702	21,464	18,849	1,148	437	358
Nebraska									
Congressional District 1	35,636	23,477	19,489	6,759	10,733	9,077	631	357	318
Congressional District 2	26,227	18,551	18,275	5,959	8,876	7,648	582	372	173
Congressional District 3	47,078	30,881	18,221	5,311	11,245	13,640	350	347	103
Nevada									
Congressional District 1	28,478	26,738	15,367	7,185	10,618	8,218	1,012	457	124
Congressional District 2	28,753	39,431	28,189	8,895	16,593	11,492	1,237	772	214
Congressional District 3	30,524	32,193	29,502	8,479	14,329	11,774	1,468	774	474
Congressional District 4	27,112	33,690	21,390	10,433	15,009	7,672	882	438	349
New Hampshire									
Congressional District 1	32,513	24,908	31,095	10,095	12,657	11,161	423	283	323
Congressional District 2	36,044	23,253	32,599	8,013	13,956	12,758	554	231	611
New Jersey									
Congressional District 1	41,939	20,734	23,291	8,189	10,275	10,667	430	180	461
Congressional District 2	47,974	24,983	25,225	5,770	11,382	11,140	678	134	439
Congressional District 3	51,925	31,342	34,737	7,570	14,406	16,921	1,200	472	506
Congressional District 4	50,198	28,528	37,852	5,938	10,938	13,384	468	62	305
Congressional District 5	42,496	20,762	38,602	3,639	9,565	11,761	302	191	164
Congressional District 6	35,601	15,744	24,264	3,960	7,892	6,334	42	307	0
Congressional District 7	39,146	19,040	37,824	3,770	9,787	8,963	80	42	576
Congressional District 8	25,217	10,466	11,777	1,915	3,408	2,743	182	0	164
Congressional District 9	35,085	17,205	23,941	2,442	4,675	7,122	150	137	182
Congressional District 10	30,759	15,110	15,629	3,964	4,249	4,796	239	169	78
Congressional District 11	38,869	20,168	40,092	3,147	7,441	11,755	164	279	35
Congressional District 12	31,541	19,206	38,410	3,735	7,052	8,789	146	43	284
New Mexico									
Congressional District 1	25,985	28,646	33,320	9,417	13,179	10,559	1,169	583	491
Congressional District 2	29,189	26,398	26,088	8,815	14,516	11,421	913	192	195
Congressional District 3	26,972	27,396	32,134	9,421	11,839	10,102	1,772	505	287
New York									
Congressional District 1	40,655	30,473	33,204	3,996	11,637	12,460	406	119	154

Table E-5: 114th Congressional Districts—Educational Attainment and Veteran Status, Persons 55 and Over—*Continued*

	High School or Equivalent	Some College or Associates Degree	Bachelor's Degree or Higher	Veterans by Age and Gender					
				Male			Female		
				55 to 64 Years	65 to 74 Years	75 Years and Over	55 to 64 Years	65 to 74 Years	75 Years and Over
New York—Cont.									
Congressional District 2	46,415	18,769	16,191	4,448	9,476	9,107	494	119	174
Congressional District 3	42,001	23,182	50,980	2,976	7,955	14,756	0	84	225
Congressional District 4	41,445	22,190	34,963	2,430	8,266	9,520	288	180	216
Congressional District 5	34,403	18,748	16,591	3,462	4,247	4,985	433	126	69
Congressional District 6	34,358	21,439	30,130	1,473	3,805	4,696	0	95	70
Congressional District 7	17,439	6,615	10,333	1,258	1,225	2,057	0	47	39
Congressional District 8	34,270	16,981	19,885	2,767	3,154	3,023	254	29	89
Congressional District 9	31,952	16,868	20,464	1,621	3,328	2,856	285	266	36
Congressional District 10	18,124	11,967	49,042	651	4,824	5,640	146	161	258
Congressional District 11	40,713	17,604	23,816	3,411	6,837	6,391	180	133	263
Congressional District 12	15,358	17,484	57,835	1,785	3,739	6,208	0	80	93
Congressional District 13	19,705	10,569	12,957	2,605	2,144	3,735	148	161	127
Congressional District 14	26,809	11,608	12,471	2,012	3,293	3,063	125	122	0
Congressional District 15	16,578	8,134	5,413	2,958	1,197	2,155	26	0	44
Congressional District 16	34,292	20,010	33,312	2,684	6,485	7,599	88	176	134
Congressional District 17	30,200	20,892	41,454	2,543	6,802	8,445	145	0	82
Congressional District 18	34,567	22,901	29,618	5,640	9,618	9,799	342	285	222
Congressional District 19	47,682	28,796	30,758	9,009	13,164	12,588	741	174	127
Congressional District 20	38,445	26,940	33,186	6,663	9,321	9,510	216	337	613
Congressional District 21	46,048	25,309	22,877	9,688	12,947	11,406	944	310	450
Congressional District 22	47,469	31,052	23,349	8,596	11,985	13,545	868	394	441
Congressional District 23	47,881	28,306	26,762	9,714	13,879	12,514	747	365	201
Congressional District 24	40,793	26,610	25,234	8,752	11,663	10,634	603	269	399
Congressional District 25	38,216	25,660	30,499	5,001	8,434	11,624	291	440	252
Congressional District 26	44,396	27,267	26,435	6,825	10,203	12,782	862	734	179
Congressional District 27	49,746	27,119	26,036	8,009	13,727	11,327	512	60	893
North Carolina									
Congressional District 1	41,974	22,017	17,733	10,199	9,589	7,125	1,292	527	302
Congressional District 2	32,245	24,901	25,266	10,040	11,420	8,649	1,161	476	288
Congressional District 3	37,138	30,299	24,385	10,358	14,447	12,405	1,068	610	376
Congressional District 4	20,323	22,558	31,625	9,655	9,009	7,872	1,637	641	396
Congressional District 5	43,018	28,952	26,941	9,748	13,424	10,287	978	185	273
Congressional District 6	44,499	31,307	27,061	9,671	11,588	11,073	820	424	479
Congressional District 7	42,701	36,203	30,363	12,123	18,295	11,347	953	656	196
Congressional District 8	42,353	28,180	14,598	8,444	12,277	9,625	825	395	185
Congressional District 9	24,500	27,504	34,288	7,200	10,843	7,970	816	123	157
Congressional District 10	38,836	33,197	26,412	9,436	13,911	10,583	831	611	259
Congressional District 11	48,116	43,147	37,831	10,816	18,022	15,542	567	442	0
Congressional District 12	24,898	18,691	13,600	7,997	6,962	5,234	1,733	247	46
Congressional District 13	31,813	24,260	29,222	7,456	11,607	8,865	949	402	314
North Dakota									
Congressional District (at Large)	36,906	28,966	21,256	8,684	11,306	9,734	398	154	270
Ohio									
Congressional District 1	34,304	22,760	25,118	7,422	8,728	9,696	316	418	227
Congressional District 2	40,521	25,818	26,676	8,768	11,526	10,418	734	178	214
Congressional District 3	29,103	16,051	12,398	7,712	8,479	5,639	1,257	245	278
Congressional District 4	56,453	25,027	13,745	9,694	10,862	11,090	832	451	301
Congressional District 5	52,927	26,955	21,532	7,203	12,568	11,066	438	428	221
Congressional District 6	66,992	22,200	15,584	10,635	16,502	11,864	312	458	120
Congressional District 7	63,610	23,307	16,900	9,375	14,494	12,516	439	534	241
Congressional District 8	48,460	24,060	19,892	8,279	12,540	10,210	249	335	269
Congressional District 9	41,396	23,691	17,348	7,160	10,066	11,040	363	231	774
Congressional District 10	43,164	31,366	26,962	10,192	13,259	12,035	1,347	839	587
Congressional District 11	37,100	24,035	21,212	8,128	9,165	9,162	511	278	428
Congressional District 12	36,301	21,962	29,536	9,149	11,858	10,036	1,083	244	282
Congressional District 13	57,424	26,985	19,265	8,621	12,933	13,941	327	387	463
Congressional District 14	51,128	30,410	32,255	7,428	13,433	13,375	202	433	488
Congressional District 15	43,232	21,882	24,734	8,505	12,736	9,688	805	308	140
Congressional District 16	51,168	31,167	30,738	7,517	14,176	13,482	364	298	354
Oklahoma									
Congressional District 1	35,520	29,701	26,025	8,744	11,943	10,284	624	306	214
Congressional District 2	51,292	33,765	20,846	10,940	17,327	13,526	1,029	569	414
Congressional District 3	46,018	31,635	20,756	8,465	12,527	11,332	979	521	252
Congressional District 4	36,983	28,349	21,828	12,240	13,227	9,887	1,333	801	679
Congressional District 5	30,114	29,837	29,907	10,974	11,660	9,787	781	410	298
Oregon									
Congressional District 1	26,733	30,515	37,733	8,543	13,233	8,555	1,116	342	260
Congressional District 2	47,388	45,066	38,294	12,359	20,874	15,945	1,100	1,028	528
Congressional District 3	27,302	33,426	28,271	7,936	12,503	8,667	696	476	581
Congressional District 4	43,215	49,959	37,103	12,225	21,439	17,584	1,511	1,561	667
Congressional District 5	35,099	42,895	37,952	8,656	16,288	14,148	1,450	652	775
Pennsylvania									
Congressional District 1	33,208	12,962	13,378	5,310	6,503	6,288	638	514	253

Table E-5: 114th Congressional Districts—Educational Attainment and Veteran Status, Persons 55 and Over—*Continued*

	High School or Equivalent	Some College or Associates Degree	Bachelor's Degree or Higher	Veterans by Age and Gender					
				Male			Female		
				55 to 64 Years	65 to 74 Years	75 Years and Over	55 to 64 Years	65 to 74 Years	75 Years and Over
Pennsylvania—Cont.									
Congressional District 2	33,339	17,590	23,689	5,406	7,441	7,426	455	175	604
Congressional District 3	65,196	21,710	19,166	8,336	14,235	14,231	388	310	458
Congressional District 4	51,871	20,330	21,632	8,419	11,547	11,796	776	176	447
Congressional District 5	58,845	21,869	20,484	8,533	14,857	12,434	828	183	313
Congressional District 6	42,325	22,898	31,281	6,263	12,987	13,534	536	160	276
Congressional District 7	45,937	22,144	36,516	5,376	10,930	13,225	341	149	463
Congressional District 8	50,296	24,980	29,607	6,397	12,579	12,020	554	208	310
Congressional District 9	67,283	19,420	20,089	9,579	14,434	15,025	561	526	373
Congressional District 10	62,398	23,798	20,972	9,774	14,488	14,047	847	349	789
Congressional District 11	59,478	24,996	20,915	7,550	15,096	12,935	752	661	387
Congressional District 12	66,586	26,253	28,844	7,568	14,637	16,640	301	288	588
Congressional District 13	40,925	20,200	26,478	5,416	7,835	10,325	509	207	835
Congressional District 14	54,551	21,820	22,750	8,598	11,192	13,808	576	207	414
Congressional District 15	52,220	20,755	23,409	8,096	11,169	13,046	603	402	174
Congressional District 16	46,787	16,748	22,378	6,258	10,586	11,278	259	254	591
Congressional District 17	63,353	22,343	19,812	8,307	13,665	13,173	442	311	821
Congressional District 18	63,094	26,056	30,539	7,207	13,631	14,448	402	206	532
Rhode Island									
Congressional District 1	26,047	15,240	19,273	5,314	6,930	8,906	682	30	200
Congressional District 2	27,815	17,183	23,224	4,969	9,369	9,494	155	233	309
South Carolina									
Congressional District 1	29,726	33,976	45,039	12,295	15,955	11,333	1,162	511	167
Congressional District 2	27,068	24,275	30,483	9,088	10,442	9,526	925	411	394
Congressional District 3	41,654	25,081	22,403	7,681	15,556	9,676	203	342	337
Congressional District 4	34,515	24,048	25,116	8,100	12,454	9,784	364	181	308
Congressional District 5	36,542	25,058	19,599	10,137	12,282	8,447	787	318	231
Congressional District 6	31,685	20,329	16,525	8,911	10,503	6,952	2,357	277	144
Congressional District 7	48,238	30,641	22,502	8,989	17,279	11,742	864	222	205
South Dakota									
Congressional District (at Large)	49,265	33,627	26,562	11,920	14,462	13,801	1,120	529	559
Tennessee									
Congressional District 1	47,235	26,816	24,500	10,633	16,346	11,874	787	426	329
Congressional District 2	41,893	27,921	28,311	10,120	13,982	11,637	832	522	902
Congressional District 3	42,554	25,849	24,910	11,258	13,790	12,693	878	125	526
Congressional District 4	41,238	20,868	17,260	8,711	13,191	8,372	908	340	345
Congressional District 5	25,931	19,940	22,040	7,797	8,677	7,442	1,559	253	120
Congressional District 6	48,374	25,434	23,081	9,586	15,792	10,812	652	288	243
Congressional District 7	37,391	22,724	18,492	10,856	11,866	9,417	1,265	462	206
Congressional District 8	41,442	24,321	24,750	9,331	11,861	10,099	588	264	341
Congressional District 9	23,383	19,232	14,122	8,535	8,387	5,024	1,060	221	197
Texas									
Congressional District 1	38,406	32,398	23,230	6,913	11,025	11,964	662	240	549
Congressional District 2	15,867	21,529	24,255	5,365	7,764	5,646	283	343	0
Congressional District 3	14,947	22,693	31,882	6,536	9,477	5,749	573	414	46
Congressional District 4	40,694	32,301	20,888	10,497	14,341	10,939	977	241	291
Congressional District 5	29,914	23,484	21,242	8,461	9,255	8,200	334	527	196
Congressional District 6	23,690	21,089	22,441	8,348	9,972	7,489	740	492	145
Congressional District 7	12,268	20,498	34,227	5,314	6,027	6,835	560	320	137
Congressional District 8	28,559	27,615	25,957	10,472	11,690	9,260	649	486	289
Congressional District 9	13,792	16,023	18,154	3,546	4,370	3,680	845	60	145
Congressional District 10	23,930	24,601	27,572	7,118	9,946	7,715	866	568	112
Congressional District 11	33,093	32,236	24,721	7,651	11,716	11,505	583	379	420
Congressional District 12	24,805	27,261	25,530	11,057	11,225	9,214	919	276	530
Congressional District 13	30,639	30,400	21,061	9,486	11,465	10,941	547	203	485
Congressional District 14	32,397	26,377	17,650	9,257	10,671	7,838	1,063	357	66
Congressional District 15	18,312	14,512	10,411	4,506	6,589	5,126	347	400	158
Congressional District 16	17,415	15,754	12,612	7,242	6,331	5,364	768	175	290
Congressional District 17	23,738	23,138	19,818	8,226	9,522	8,811	486	222	485
Congressional District 18	19,978	14,482	12,594	4,847	5,244	3,664	592	219	67
Congressional District 19	28,170	24,370	19,934	6,253	8,876	8,932	422	226	385
Congressional District 20	21,709	19,285	15,269	9,567	9,911	6,924	1,533	391	468
Congressional District 21	24,444	30,417	50,568	8,709	15,694	13,939	1,989	879	1,023
Congressional District 22	18,809	18,822	27,640	3,633	6,962	4,140	643	173	67
Congressional District 23	20,240	18,263	16,256	7,336	8,946	6,921	1,126	449	373
Congressional District 24	16,503	25,675	26,437	6,832	7,902	6,452	477	448	134
Congressional District 25	25,070	25,588	30,145	9,325	11,193	9,781	990	265	523
Congressional District 26	19,779	20,150	22,716	7,660	9,552	4,930	904	299	39
Congressional District 27	28,088	27,914	19,854	11,338	13,595	9,241	865	175	338
Congressional District 28	20,366	14,790	9,342	5,401	7,281	6,014	1,179	364	120
Congressional District 29	11,949	9,358	5,379	2,801	3,739	2,786	145	0	54
Congressional District 30	19,806	17,106	10,754	7,186	5,382	4,592	938	41	145
Congressional District 31	22,756	25,392	25,330	11,479	11,943	8,748	2,193	533	329
Congressional District 32	17,844	22,632	35,719	6,003	8,637	8,047	1,114	438	145
Congressional District 33	14,677	10,323	5,263	4,676	5,181	3,200	406	78	25

Table E-5: 114th Congressional Districts—Educational Attainment and Veteran Status, Persons 55 and Over—*Continued*

	High School or Equivalent	Some College or Associates Degree	Bachelor's Degree or Higher	Veterans by Age and Gender					
				Male			Female		
				55 to 64 Years	65 to 74 Years	75 Years and Over	55 to 64 Years	65 to 74 Years	75 Years and Over
Texas—Cont.									
Congressional District 34..................	21,291	15,372	12,146	6,572	7,447	6,832	198	161	199
Congressional District 35..................	19,014	17,578	8,361	7,868	8,322	4,902	2,098	412	188
Congressional District 36..................	35,295	27,930	16,706	7,110	12,355	8,888	182	643	175
Utah									
Congressional District 1..................	19,630	25,368	20,875	7,226	8,632	7,820	559	546	302
Congressional District 2..................	22,075	31,118	24,965	5,982	8,524	9,445	293	194	163
Congressional District 3..................	14,453	23,661	25,017	5,150	6,560	7,229	165	169	242
Congressional District 4..................	19,096	23,447	18,928	4,581	6,572	6,465	297	158	232
Vermont									
Congressional District (at Large)	34,586	24,180	33,948	7,928	10,995	10,847	722	490	657
Virginia									
Congressional District 1..................	28,138	26,113	36,414	14,519	14,202	11,570	2,198	533	319
Congressional District 2..................	27,776	26,218	27,467	14,686	13,832	10,436	2,868	722	470
Congressional District 3..................	27,230	22,536	15,736	11,991	10,805	7,963	1,759	490	236
Congressional District 4..................	31,204	28,461	19,498	13,112	14,236	7,856	1,394	572	424
Congressional District 5..................	43,591	30,058	29,088	9,923	15,254	12,158	488	110	194
Congressional District 6..................	45,632	31,752	26,364	8,426	13,136	12,159	888	296	198
Congressional District 7..................	33,174	28,362	36,429	8,296	13,355	11,441	1,182	673	316
Congressional District 8..................	13,943	14,284	41,407	5,679	9,329	7,027	2,115	505	489
Congressional District 9..................	44,285	27,901	20,030	7,588	14,046	12,085	548	517	175
Congressional District 10..................	17,353	17,919	40,798	10,875	11,506	8,078	1,564	134	259
Congressional District 11..................	14,530	18,504	38,324	8,195	10,304	7,479	1,243	721	289
Washington									
Congressional District 1..................	21,258	28,807	30,905	8,475	10,791	8,315	486	474	340
Congressional District 2..................	30,039	33,938	32,136	10,427	14,160	10,260	1,333	382	526
Congressional District 3..................	32,513	40,817	25,478	11,638	15,578	11,638	990	606	617
Congressional District 4..................	26,079	27,625	18,415	8,466	11,726	8,920	1,091	545	226
Congressional District 5..................	31,698	33,692	29,355	12,191	14,787	12,661	1,589	544	728
Congressional District 6..................	32,549	39,425	39,069	14,744	20,200	14,072	1,526	914	822
Congressional District 7..................	16,665	25,690	44,204	5,350	8,867	8,682	1,608	289	654
Congressional District 8..................	23,961	28,246	23,973	9,091	11,013	8,891	1,327	585	607
Congressional District 9..................	20,829	24,668	32,848	7,391	8,610	10,232	562	508	715
Congressional District 10..................	26,867	33,117	25,380	14,228	14,327	11,365	2,034	775	132
West Virginia									
Congressional District 1..................	50,267	20,795	15,616	8,310	13,199	10,214	620	652	440
Congressional District 2..................	47,059	21,343	17,066	9,561	14,122	10,504	346	217	172
Congressional District 3..................	43,423	20,269	12,460	8,221	11,078	9,018	587	291	176
Wisconsin									
Congressional District 1..................	42,540	25,626	22,879	7,926	11,899	10,331	878	337	274
Congressional District 2..................	34,017	23,330	30,980	6,536	10,830	9,315	486	145	302
Congressional District 3..................	52,817	24,667	22,971	9,803	13,403	12,045	1,083	141	382
Congressional District 4..................	26,808	17,479	17,554	6,380	6,877	7,191	675	252	113
Congressional District 5..................	46,736	28,658	28,605	6,409	11,617	12,994	776	435	315
Congressional District 6..................	53,564	26,252	24,133	8,525	12,997	12,849	795	119	365
Congressional District 7..................	58,433	30,584	25,249	10,567	15,861	14,317	604	241	395
Congressional District 8..................	53,654	23,207	20,220	8,896	13,913	11,619	498	217	374
Wyoming									
Congressional District (at Large)	24,872	26,672	20,863	8,556	11,270	7,587	845	441	428

PART F
EMPLOYMENT AND LABOR FORCE STATUS

EMPLOYMENT AND LABOR FORCE STATUS

U.S. Bureau of Labor Statistics employment data show that between 1980 and 2015, the employment of people age 65 and over nearly tripled (from 3.0 million to 8.3 million) while employment for the civilian non-institutional population 16 and over increased by nearly 50 percent. The labor force participation rate for seniors was 12.7 in 1980 and increased to 18.9 in 2015.[1] This is only starting to be impacted by the Baby Boom generation as the oldest of that age cohort had not entered the 65 and over population until about 2010. The older population has been working more and working longer in life and that trend can be expected to continue as those numbers swell with the Baby Boomers.

The absolute number of employed persons is important but equally important is the rate at which the population participates in the labor force. Not everyone wants to work, so the older labor force is comprised of only those who are employed or unemployed and looking for work. Nationally, of the 65.0 million persons age 60 and over, 18.3 million or 28.2 percent are actively participating in the labor force. Even by age 70 more than 10 percent of the older population is participating in the labor force. Among the 60 and over population, Alaska has the highest participation rate at 38.6 percent while West Virginia (22.0 percent) has the lowest. There's a more narrow range between the highest (Alaska at 15.8 percent) and lowest (Oregon at 8.0 percent) state for the 70 and over population. In 10 states, more than one-third of the 60 and over labor force population is participating in the labor force (either employed or unemployed and looking for work). The unemployment rate for both the 60 and over and the 70 years and over is around 4 percent but varies from a low of 0.5 percent in Montana to a high of 10.1 percent in Nevada.

Los Angeles County, California has the largest 60 and over labor force with more than 550,000 people and the participation rate is 31.6 percent. Midland County, Texas has the highest participation rate at 46.7 percent and

1. U.S. Department of Labor, Bureau of Labor Statistics, Labor Force Statistics from the Current Population Survey, 1st quarter data, http://data.bls.gov.

Citrus County, Florida the lowest at 14.7 percent. The 60 and over labor force participation rate is higher than the national average of 28.2 percent in 482 counties greater than 40 percent in 80 counties. Unemployment is highest in Kootenai County, Idaho where more than 13.5 percent of the 60 and over population are unemployed and looking for work. The unemployment rate for persons 70 and over is low with the highest rate in Schenectady County, New York at only 3.5 percent. The unemployment rate for the 70 and over population is higher than the national average in only 67 counties but among the 60 and over, 316 counties are above the national average.

Among cities, more than half (50.2 percent) of the Stamford, Connecticut population 60 and over participates in the labor force and, while not the highest, 25.7 percent of the 70 and over population is still participating. Schenectady, New York has the highest percent of the 70 and over population participating in the labor force at 30.0 percent. Lawrence, Massachusetts has the highest unemployment rate for persons 60 and over at 20.6 percent and 131 cities have unemployment rates greater than 10 percent for the 70 and over population.

The New York-Northern New Jersey-Long Island metropolitan area has the largest 60 and over labor force with a population over 1.3 million and its participation rate at 32.8 percent is higher than the national rate of 28.2 percent. The Midland, Texas metropolitan area has the highest participation rate at 47.1 percent while the Homosassa Springs, Florida metro area is lowest at 14.7 percent. Labor force participation among the 60 and over population is above the national rate in 253 metropolitan and micropolitan areas and in 254 areas it's above the national rate for the 70 and over population. The Coeur d'Alene, Idaho metropolitan area has the highest unemployment rate among the 60 and over population at 13.5 percent but the Modesto, California metro area and the Eureka-Arcata-Fortuna, California micropolitan area are both over 10 percent. 185 metropolitan and micropolitan areas have higher unemployment rates than the nation for the 60 and over population and 26 are above the 70 and over rate.

Virginia's 10th Congressional District has the highest labor force participation for the 60 and over population

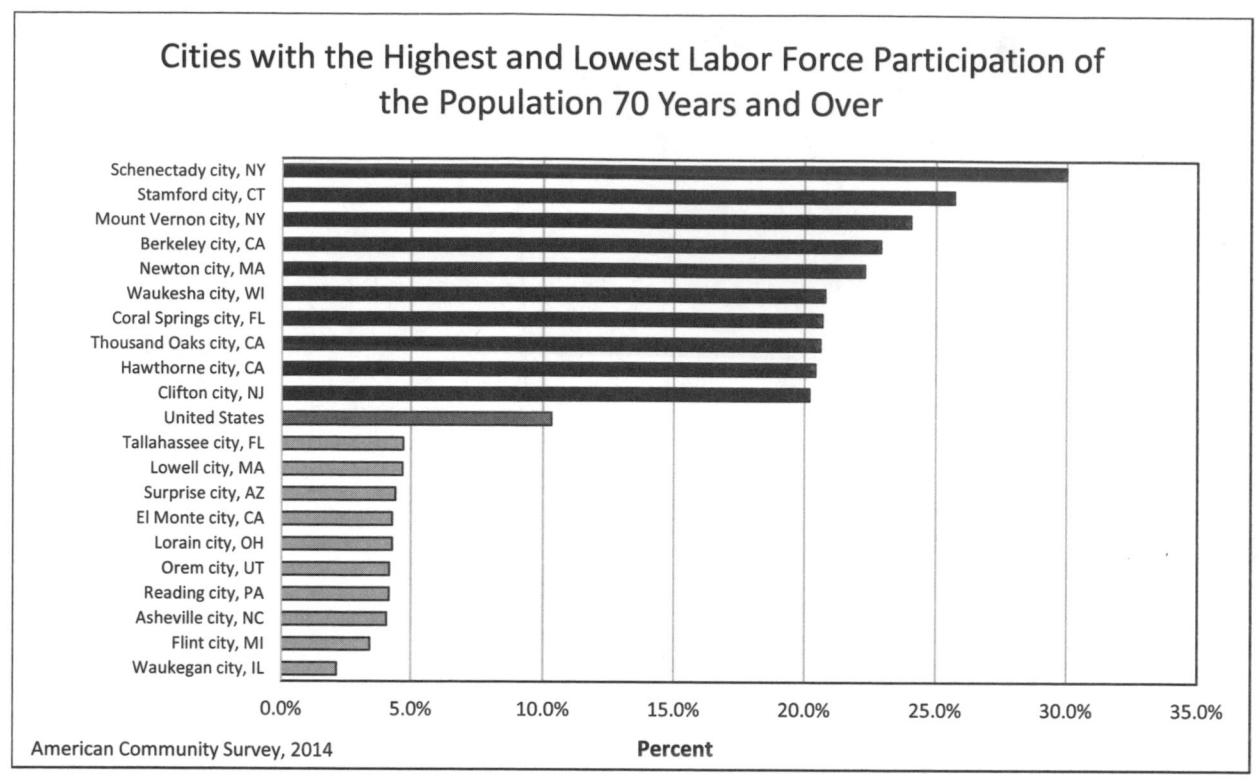

Cities with the Highest and Lowest Labor Force Participation of the Population 70 Years and Over

American Community Survey, 2014

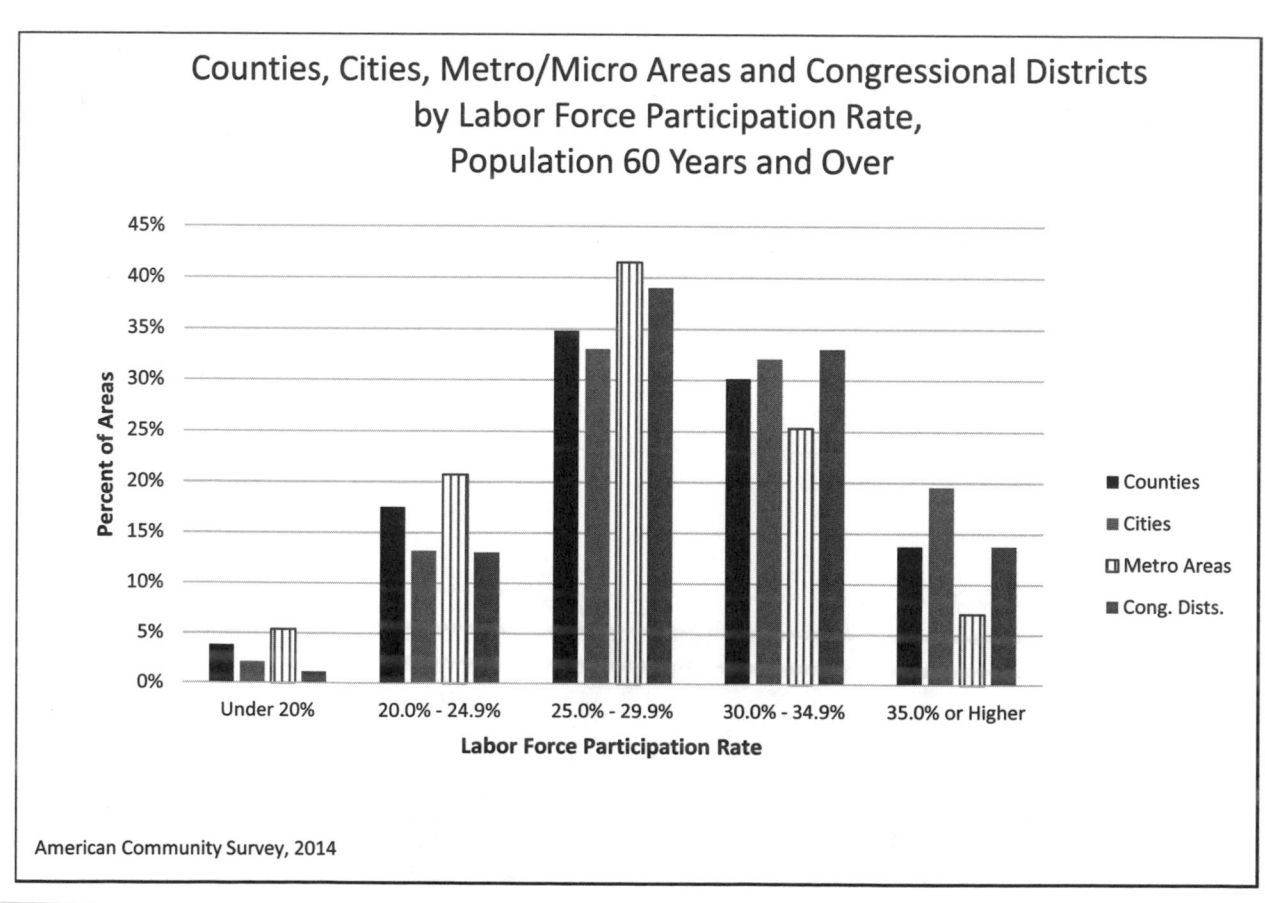

Counties, Cities, Metro/Micro Areas and Congressional Districts by Labor Force Participation Rate, Population 60 Years and Over

American Community Survey, 2014

at 41.3 percent while Kentucky's 5th District has the lowest rate at 15.6 percent. More than half of all congressional districts (265) have participation rates above the national average for the 60 and over population and nine districts have participation over 40 percent. In 241 districts the rate is above the national rate for the population 70 and over. At 11.2 percent New York's 13th District has the highest unemployment among the 60 and over while Connecticut's 4th District is highest among the 70 and over population but still only 2.4 percent.

Percent of the Population 60 Years and Over Participating in the Labor Force

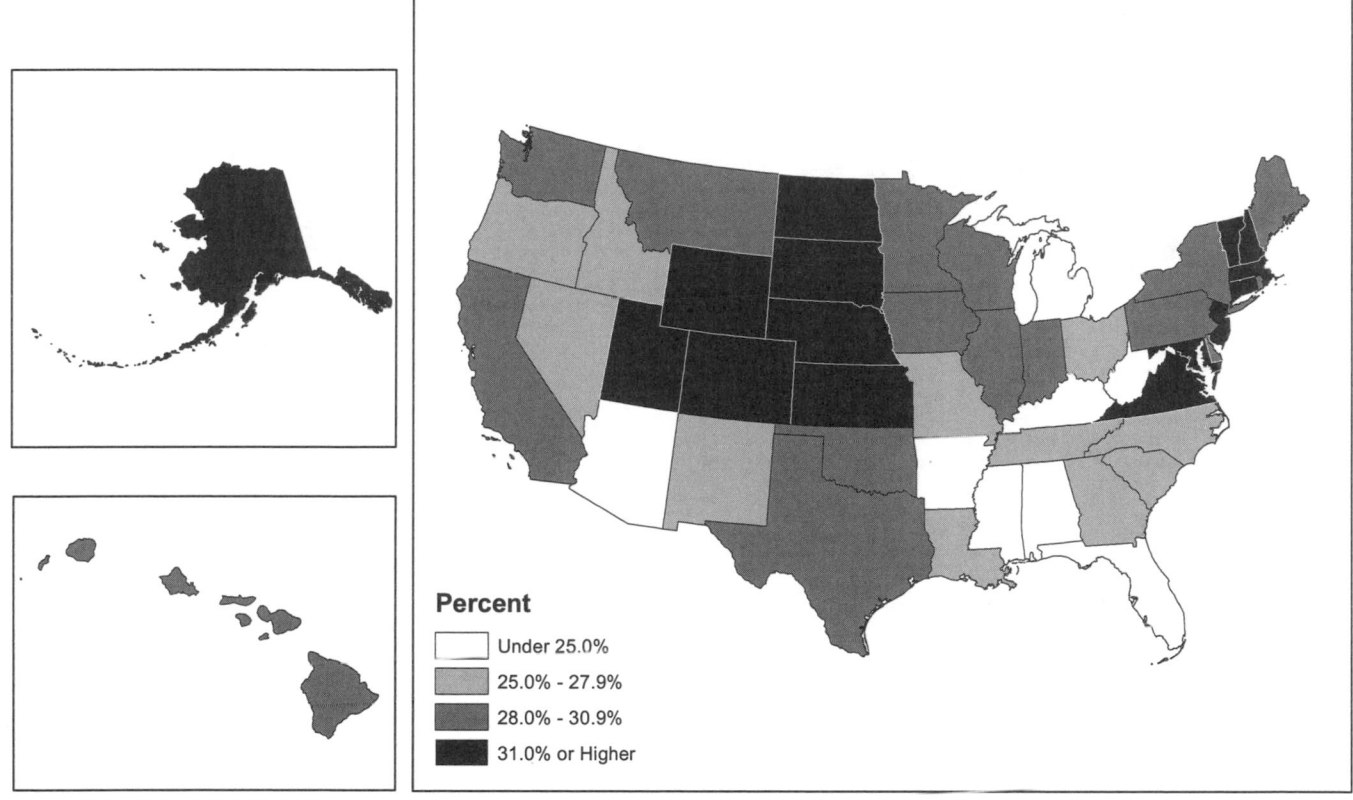

Percent

	Under 25.0%
	25.0% - 27.9%
	28.0% - 30.9%
	31.0% or Higher

Table F-1: States—Employment and Labor Force Status, Civilian Labor Force

	60 to 61 Years		62 to 64 Years		65 to 69 Years		70 Years and Over		60 Years and Over Not in the Labor Force
	Employed	Unemployed	Employed	Unemployed	Employed	Unemployed	Employed	Unemployed	
United States	4,726,274	252,975	5,181,475	235,094	4,545,218	198,926	3,051,978	131,609	46,659,339
Alabama	65,877	3,641	69,694	2,084	62,500	2,443	43,148	1,530	793,217
Alaska	12,265	478	11,847	683	10,620	362	6,230	300	68,151
Arizona	86,925	6,016	92,356	6,671	84,634	4,089	58,423	2,993	1,111,499
Arkansas	38,312	1,953	45,891	823	40,599	742	30,127	715	483,110
California	513,900	35,991	575,534	37,841	501,896	30,822	320,025	16,884	5,056,565
Colorado	83,291	4,172	99,150	3,416	83,418	3,835	44,638	2,033	674,871
Connecticut	66,947	3,949	70,091	3,519	67,833	3,386	45,339	3,412	511,064
Delaware	14,424	1,029	14,866	687	16,260	604	10,166	478	151,058
District of Columbia	7,696	593	8,093	787	8,849	356	7,727	277	72,784
Florida	291,537	22,382	324,846	16,632	308,987	15,430	224,973	11,987	3,813,560
Georgia	135,596	6,316	138,961	5,782	118,146	4,887	73,065	3,477	1,316,898
Hawaii	24,631	804	25,969	690	27,023	825	16,616	273	219,724
Idaho	24,614	1,045	27,321	1,609	19,334	1,100	13,861	642	245,163
Illinois	194,069	12,644	211,006	10,892	176,500	8,418	117,592	4,501	1,798,520
Indiana	100,254	4,687	105,858	3,902	93,172	4,486	64,954	1,997	951,330
Iowa	58,076	1,598	58,716	1,628	51,746	1,016	37,178	938	471,632
Kansas	47,566	1,319	55,000	1,240	46,336	1,515	32,742	866	403,319
Kentucky	56,188	2,313	59,680	2,417	54,737	2,296	38,307	1,347	704,381
Louisiana	60,635	2,529	68,382	2,071	60,050	2,003	45,750	1,387	662,008
Maine	27,608	1,138	27,973	1,002	26,807	734	15,583	507	239,800
Maryland	93,221	4,684	113,006	5,353	104,031	4,185	64,068	2,850	780,402
Massachusetts	117,719	6,414	135,420	7,085	120,104	6,131	80,133	3,588	952,460
Michigan	146,380	7,182	152,237	6,484	116,664	5,117	80,604	3,664	1,655,432
Minnesota	92,295	3,124	104,012	2,695	79,081	2,588	52,055	1,346	768,027
Mississippi	37,877	1,890	39,359	1,656	31,987	1,081	25,862	1,472	457,844
Missouri	88,930	2,912	98,625	3,259	87,792	3,018	59,408	1,398	957,724
Montana	16,432	356	20,767	748	18,260	871	14,291	77	169,841
Nebraska	33,660	684	37,563	654	32,763	326	25,358	370	247,191
Nevada	41,452	2,950	42,009	3,210	34,621	2,935	23,947	2,704	412,124
New Hampshire	28,987	1,298	31,038	931	25,555	959	16,561	457	197,567
New Jersey	146,335	9,848	166,944	9,972	150,671	9,383	98,293	6,955	1,245,201
New Mexico	30,154	1,707	31,975	1,363	28,435	1,787	21,196	1,094	331,427
New York	295,616	17,886	325,010	16,913	288,838	14,251	204,479	10,103	2,880,993
North Carolina	137,953	7,541	146,022	7,253	131,835	6,049	86,362	3,903	1,508,280
North Dakota	12,277	139	15,598	233	12,173	199	9,320	141	97,343
Ohio	187,342	8,172	201,288	6,899	169,623	5,176	113,048	4,817	1,829,729
Oklahoma	55,245	1,305	58,033	1,150	56,004	1,474	44,352	1,417	563,906
Oregon	66,551	3,258	70,580	2,762	57,453	2,792	31,626	1,408	671,126
Pennsylvania	223,074	10,754	231,419	10,617	208,126	8,851	144,662	7,350	2,117,500
Rhode Island	15,827	1,370	21,509	645	17,771	708	10,815	1,065	164,086
South Carolina	72,226	3,620	77,007	3,531	70,016	2,534	42,992	1,136	797,048
South Dakota	15,458	274	18,282	139	16,571	277	12,065	144	118,494
Tennessee	90,459	4,262	101,159	4,521	91,966	4,184	63,480	2,269	1,023,897
Texas	348,434	16,418	375,136	16,340	337,585	12,326	227,968	7,256	3,111,158
Utah	35,170	1,360	42,866	1,462	31,293	421	21,162	561	292,218
Vermont	13,345	848	14,213	571	14,014	421	10,624	297	97,028
Virginia	129,060	6,347	150,896	5,746	125,672	4,393	85,406	3,064	1,123,321
Washington	108,879	5,556	122,624	5,016	106,377	3,439	55,200	1,728	1,014,004
West Virginia	24,549	1,568	29,204	555	25,524	883	18,269	482	358,757
Wisconsin	99,474	4,267	103,992	2,780	84,059	2,716	55,719	1,649	887,982
Wyoming	11,482	384	12,448	175	10,907	102	6,209	300	78,575

Table F-2: Counties—Employment and Labor Force Status, Civilian Labor Force

	60 to 61 Years		62 to 64 Years		65 to 69 Years		70 Years and Over		60 Years and Over Not in the Labor Force
	Employed	Unemployed	Employed	Unemployed	Employed	Unemployed	Employed	Unemployed	
Alabama									
Baldwin County	3,661	133	4,626	0	3,243	174	2,150	0	38,127
Calhoun County	2,453	251	1,502	0	1,626	0	1,474	121	20,135
Cullman County	na	na	na	na	na	na	na	na	na
DeKalb County	na	na	na	na	na	na	na	na	na
Elmore County	779	0	717	0	1,293	94	657	0	12,343
Etowah County	1,080	0	2,270	23	1,585	0	1,573	43	18,271
Houston County	1,579	123	1,759	32	1,265	75	950	10	17,571
Jefferson County	9,141	473	10,528	98	9,033	392	6,630	116	99,051
Lauderdale County	1,431	85	1,143	17	1,110	44	1,127	110	18,337
Lee County	1,541	0	1,854	151	1,764	172	870	0	18,043
Limestone County	1,081	0	1,281	79	956	43	1,019	0	13,083
Madison County	6,290	457	5,689	250	4,095	248	4,416	258	48,234
Marshall County	1,601	10	1,097	47	706	33	1,105	5	17,035
Mobile County	5,636	224	5,838	274	5,870	167	3,175	44	63,843
Montgomery County	4,046	172	3,550	99	3,812	93	2,146	191	30,089
Morgan County	1,356	56	2,418	153	1,677	64	612	0	20,355
Shelby County	3,355	77	3,893	150	3,436	74	1,703	0	27,880
St. Clair County	na	na	na	na	na	na	na	na	na
Talladega County	1,057	65	1,625	204	1,240	51	1,217	179	13,436
Tuscaloosa County	2,339	173	3,054	43	2,202	46	1,759	37	25,644
Walker County	726	75	768	0	878	0	836	0	12,721
Alaska									
Anchorage Municipality	4,319	0	4,490	85	3,909	45	2,794	137	25,187
Fairbanks North Star Borough	1,581	139	1,387	79	1,480	0	636	0	7,812
Matanuska-Susitna Borough	1,659	108	2,109	239	1,368	129	1,065	126	9,547
Arizona									
Apache County	877	11	762	0	475	0	233	0	11,243
Cochise County	2,244	140	2,361	107	1,346	0	1,326	82	27,705
Coconino County	2,500	0	2,324	51	1,966	0	857	0	15,997
Maricopa County	52,853	3,765	59,035	3,251	54,140	1,894	35,402	2,122	576,281
Mohave County	2,224	287	2,907	211	2,696	140	2,086	119	60,565
Navajo County	968	143	1,483	129	905	164	765	0	18,930
Pima County	15,656	787	15,257	1,235	14,514	754	9,768	312	184,842
Pinal County	5,756	103	5,556	731	4,153	192	3,461	301	78,145
Yavapai County	5,311	406	4,754	742	4,278	644	2,777	0	65,889
Yuma County	2,484	338	1,890	127	2,563	222	1,897	57	35,836
Arkansas									
Benton County	3,303	82	3,213	76	2,599	36	2,219	43	31,516
Craighead County	1,030	0	1,322	0	1,769	0	843	0	13,855
Faulkner County	1,874	43	1,775	39	837	0	801	38	14,254
Garland County	1,515	227	1,375	46	1,369	153	1,720	98	21,235
Jefferson County	803	21	1,473	0	1,022	51	548	0	11,340
Lonoke County	na	na	na	na	na	na	na	na	na
Pulaski County	4,992	62	8,363	0	7,844	250	3,634	98	52,588
Saline County	1,464	130	1,613	71	1,103	47	1,364	0	20,660
Sebastian County	1,756	13	1,888	134	1,959	27	929	31	18,885
Washington County	3,010	105	2,921	0	2,538	13	1,702	68	24,651
White County	777	0	803	46	570	0	1,198	99	12,579
California									
Alameda County	23,394	1,556	28,218	1,467	24,711	1,396	14,090	996	201,438
Butte County	3,604	274	4,279	298	2,916	256	2,857	70	30,908
Contra Costa County	17,777	915	21,376	584	18,409	1,314	10,670	357	156,754
El Dorado County	3,548	185	3,864	225	3,214	499	2,613	29	35,436
Fresno County	11,958	1,239	13,168	820	10,061	452	6,618	38	113,983
Humboldt County	2,517	691	2,388	149	1,852	105	1,322	58	23,055
Imperial County	1,472	35	2,451	436	1,591	34	1,087	114	22,586
Kern County	9,228	604	7,886	301	5,990	369	5,044	140	97,973
Kings County	1,546	111	934	160	1,137	0	760	0	14,868
Lake County	na	na	na	na	na	na	na	na	na
Los Angeles County	140,998	10,687	156,970	9,431	137,807	8,643	85,004	4,864	1,231,103
Madera County	1,494	107	1,890	262	1,473	57	1,319	28	21,492
Marin County	6,366	241	7,906	479	9,194	325	6,423	71	39,615
Mendocino County	1,549	63	2,953	0	2,035	0	1,414	0	16,310
Merced County	2,387	103	2,301	67	2,803	165	1,658	0	28,777
Monterey County	6,983	283	6,317	277	5,216	24	3,606	80	51,801
Napa County	2,724	53	3,326	84	2,905	166	1,915	200	24,002
Nevada County	2,426	0	2,954	199	2,694	273	1,927	27	23,606
Orange County	45,973	2,706	53,226	4,268	48,844	2,070	31,448	1,740	396,185
Placer County	4,973	466	6,173	141	5,515	302	3,931	103	68,896
Riverside County	28,070	2,112	30,227	2,282	24,699	1,083	19,013	1,283	323,060
Sacramento County	18,770	906	21,917	1,794	16,435	1,120	10,569	634	204,906
San Bernardino County	24,009	1,340	23,769	1,172	20,020	1,491	11,757	758	237,042
San Diego County	51,103	3,309	53,794	3,460	42,684	2,670	25,768	1,348	416,421
San Francisco County	12,791	1,026	18,436	1,604	14,220	623	8,542	126	120,805
San Joaquin County	8,462	879	9,055	793	8,366	350	4,834	78	88,757
San Luis Obispo County	4,809	247	4,948	244	4,967	571	2,867	77	49,860
San Mateo County	12,689	276	14,642	917	13,446	544	9,095	540	108,270
Santa Barbara County	7,684	251	7,457	406	6,574	317	5,019	282	58,616
Santa Clara County	26,641	1,824	30,244	2,162	25,347	1,309	16,048	524	230,086

Table F-2: Counties—Employment and Labor Force Status, Civilian Labor Force—*Continued*

	60 to 61 Years		62 to 64 Years		65 to 69 Years		70 Years and Over		60 Years and Over Not in the Labor Force
	Employed	Unemployed	Employed	Unemployed	Employed	Unemployed	Employed	Unemployed	
California—Cont.									
Santa Cruz County	5,075	452	6,235	471	6,595	335	2,423	52	34,512
Shasta County	2,793	162	2,872	166	2,526	125	2,513	202	37,878
Solano County	7,778	459	7,783	318	6,296	263	3,842	101	62,149
Sonoma County	9,383	646	11,439	441	11,250	382	6,185	282	81,159
Stanislaus County	6,087	289	5,889	801	6,829	1,112	3,452	270	68,008
Sutter County	1,855	74	1,051	115	1,275	0	967	61	14,217
Tulare County	5,152	310	4,632	181	4,871	417	3,033	151	49,252
Ventura County	13,145	588	13,921	284	14,883	830	8,879	561	111,902
Yolo County	2,619	84	3,750	157	2,239	126	1,095	115	25,364
Yuba County	718	22	930	25	1,054	0	209	0	8,785
Colorado									
Adams County	5,433	151	7,994	85	5,729	193	2,799	289	47,904
Arapahoe County	10,105	375	12,005	200	10,586	202	6,761	119	69,247
Boulder County	6,182	357	8,256	133	5,095	171	2,358	55	36,381
Denver County	7,716	366	9,868	719	9,109	504	4,856	39	73,211
Douglas County	4,125	198	5,439	188	5,514	255	1,844	142	30,539
El Paso County	9,182	368	10,905	535	7,803	688	4,062	329	80,714
Jefferson County	12,176	253	13,554	667	10,568	364	5,763	124	79,406
Larimer County	5,253	465	6,125	327	4,995	242	3,167	317	43,938
Mesa County	2,681	668	3,049	0	2,277	161	1,492	82	25,275
Pueblo County	2,611	174	2,887	43	2,188	234	1,363	0	30,020
Weld County	4,958	83	3,901	0	4,403	54	2,484	262	29,097
Connecticut									
Fairfield County	19,233	869	18,463	692	19,326	882	14,297	1,890	118,972
Hartford County	14,164	649	17,081	866	16,133	632	10,313	570	134,626
Litchfield County	4,475	218	4,108	93	4,144	131	3,549	70	31,076
Middlesex County	4,470	149	3,691	199	4,550	171	2,448	0	24,813
New Haven County	17,208	962	18,897	1,061	16,778	1,110	11,463	882	125,251
New London County	5,657	614	5,922	342	5,933	199	3,667	0	40,176
Tolland County	3,032	0	3,714	195	3,172	162	1,912	0	18,701
Windham County	2,657	488	1,734	71	1,183	99	1,102	0	17,449
Delaware									
Kent County	2,532	159	2,778	0	2,377	27	1,261	41	26,059
New Castle County	8,760	603	8,521	490	8,754	121	5,177	116	75,153
Sussex County	4,161	267	4,254	197	5,733	456	4,206	321	49,846
Florida									
Alachua County	4,018	137	4,481	57	3,276	0	2,124	101	32,062
Bay County	2,654	121	3,254	116	2,437	0	1,290	74	30,271
Brevard County	8,219	492	8,291	444	10,417	415	7,855	722	130,377
Broward County	32,494	3,206	34,675	3,198	31,508	2,428	22,831	1,967	274,132
Charlotte County	2,320	90	3,646	346	4,876	146	3,889	420	61,587
Citrus County	2,337	100	1,781	39	1,774	80	2,451	181	51,328
Clay County	3,244	398	2,843	112	2,688	244	1,510	42	29,769
Collier County	6,060	249	7,694	439	6,512	111	6,978	616	99,876
Columbia County	na	na	na	na	na	na	na	na	na
Duval County	14,241	770	12,797	491	10,966	320	6,806	335	121,113
Escambia County	3,577	173	5,887	78	3,706	262	2,952	21	51,133
Flagler County	2,002	107	2,026	35	2,188	66	1,099	134	30,590
Hernando County	2,564	316	1,916	63	3,309	169	2,070	0	51,189
Highlands County	910	175	1,411	240	1,209	25	2,275	123	33,999
Hillsborough County	18,918	921	20,901	708	16,997	1,307	10,794	185	175,698
Indian River County	3,297	478	2,974	91	3,145	0	2,366	103	44,464
Lake County	4,352	60	4,942	28	5,530	95	3,986	234	84,546
Lee County	12,511	597	11,879	734	14,036	593	11,908	674	177,188
Leon County	4,917	521	5,406	126	3,907	77	1,610	0	31,717
Manatee County	6,126	608	6,460	412	6,611	215	4,873	302	91,198
Marion County	6,680	937	5,711	341	6,779	459	5,154	166	94,618
Martin County	3,026	157	3,390	438	4,184	623	3,792	177	42,466
Miami-Dade County	40,351	3,202	44,779	2,011	40,632	1,899	26,401	985	400,432
Monroe County	na	na	na	na	na	na	na	na	na
Nassau County	na	na	na	na	na	na	na	na	na
Okaloosa County	2,713	78	3,591	39	3,079	137	2,097	46	29,212
Orange County	18,574	817	17,157	1,000	13,041	791	9,906	189	137,803
Osceola County	2,211	228	5,017	63	3,285	447	1,755	190	43,976
Palm Beach County	24,634	1,741	28,407	1,287	28,564	1,128	24,295	706	297,136
Pasco County	7,141	781	6,984	502	6,461	366	5,128	287	115,316
Pinellas County	17,670	990	19,134	610	19,469	793	12,944	337	214,466
Polk County	9,016	603	11,701	895	10,130	519	6,723	160	127,766
Putnam County	na	na	na	na	na	na	na	na	na
Santa Rosa County	1,707	63	1,852	63	2,386	0	1,569	40	25,122
Sarasota County	6,611	272	8,233	141	9,367	239	6,904	491	134,067
Seminole County	7,561	460	8,104	350	6,814	268	3,702	161	64,025
St. Johns County	3,685	77	3,849	109	4,400	82	2,827	265	38,967
St. Lucie County	3,812	152	4,197	189	5,152	191	3,543	504	66,600
Sumter County	na	na	na	na	na	na	na	na	na
Volusia County	8,558	218	8,680	249	9,328	470	5,944	425	122,818
Georgia									
Barrow County	513	0	890	0	703	0	604	76	9,829

Table F-2: Counties—Employment and Labor Force Status, Civilian Labor Force—*Continued*

	60 to 61 Years		62 to 64 Years		65 to 69 Years		70 Years and Over		60 Years and Over Not in the Labor Force
	Employed	Unemployed	Employed	Unemployed	Employed	Unemployed	Employed	Unemployed	
Georgia—Cont.									
Bartow County	2,174	82	1,704	0	946	0	655	108	13,559
Bibb County	2,434	114	2,578	127	1,237	62	804	70	24,041
Bulloch County	na	na	na	na	na	na	na	na	na
Carroll County	1,130	0	1,727	0	1,126	47	611	0	15,146
Catoosa County	na	na	na	na	na	na	na	na	na
Chatham County	3,637	129	4,035	157	4,250	84	2,050	271	38,823
Cherokee County	2,609	72	3,678	101	3,105	275	2,255	111	28,041
Clarke County	1,382	0	1,312	107	1,997	86	534	0	11,804
Clayton County	2,809	46	2,758	44	2,743	221	1,065	0	26,492
Cobb County	11,723	724	14,583	544	10,569	600	5,647	124	73,525
Columbia County	2,116	0	2,557	0	1,865	57	990	0	18,514
Coweta County	2,894	87	2,140	7	1,938	78	1,558	0	16,404
DeKalb County	11,006	479	10,490	405	9,357	254	4,918	317	77,420
Dougherty County	1,228	54	1,442	106	1,087	167	869	120	14,566
Douglas County	2,103	326	1,265	193	1,729	61	324	0	14,918
Fayette County	2,179	289	1,845	0	1,920	113	1,416	136	17,780
Floyd County	1,229	32	1,486	0	630	105	1,066	0	15,120
Forsyth County	2,342	48	3,872	151	2,076	176	878	0	23,328
Fulton County	11,586	417	15,027	854	11,968	881	7,151	216	108,217
Glynn County	na	na	na	na	na	na	na	na	na
Gwinnett County	10,593	628	13,795	924	11,004	305	4,857	33	77,064
Hall County	2,566	0	2,887	48	2,406	0	1,951	105	25,968
Henry County	3,617	407	1,999	50	2,529	64	991	0	24,547
Houston County	2,049	0	1,541	178	1,242	47	763	57	19,038
Liberty County	831	0	287	52	265	0	170	92	5,753
Lowndes County	988	0	1,143	0	1,374	70	744	0	13,071
Muscogee County	2,867	35	1,943	59	1,990	78	1,505	0	25,518
Newton County	na	na	na	na	na	na	na	na	na
Paulding County	na	na	na	na	na	na	na	na	na
Richmond County	2,506	55	3,669	99	2,262	134	1,246	0	28,010
Rockdale County	na	na	na	na	na	na	na	na	na
Troup County	653	0	1,134	136	712	0	713	178	10,644
Walker County	na	na	na	na	na	na	na	na	na
Walton County	1,545	235	691	0	749	97	478	72	13,348
Whitfield County	na	na	na	na	na	na	na	na	na
Hawaii									
Hawaii County	3,909	191	3,507	68	3,992	60	2,111	12	36,052
Honolulu County	16,781	459	18,120	557	18,684	674	11,081	84	148,342
Kauai County	1,420	49	1,456	4	1,995	0	908	177	12,155
Maui County	3,325	105	3,576	61	3,177	91	2,789	0	23,173
Idaho									
Ada County	7,183	349	7,141	274	4,167	184	3,752	143	56,278
Bannock County	1,907	178	1,291	75	1,072	33	569	0	11,048
Bonneville County	1,920	42	2,058	24	1,004	0	758	12	13,708
Canyon County	1,645	45	3,536	159	2,222	0	1,677	0	26,298
Kootenai County	2,279	240	3,470	545	1,942	356	1,075	226	26,808
Twin Falls County	na	na	na	na	na	na	na	na	na
Illinois									
Adams County	1,146	75	1,800	30	1,316	46	1,008	0	11,822
Champaign County	2,810	313	3,069	261	2,979	0	2,211	42	22,439
Cook County	79,985	7,012	86,363	5,030	72,573	3,848	44,344	2,456	686,357
DeKalb County	1,508	65	1,310	219	1,423	0	1,000	60	11,729
DuPage County	17,162	822	20,461	793	17,451	658	10,365	245	117,995
Kane County	8,411	122	9,685	270	7,651	207	5,375	46	59,820
Kankakee County	2,056	44	1,625	95	1,557	0	787	0	16,973
Kendall County	na	na	na	na	na	na	na	na	na
Lake County	11,984	207	13,229	495	10,556	992	7,132	450	81,376
LaSalle County	1,975	76	2,009	57	1,107	6	882	0	22,038
Macon County	2,333	36	2,111	138	1,786	189	955	13	19,330
Madison County	3,982	75	4,743	158	3,642	368	2,813	108	43,095
McHenry County	5,737	159	4,649	274	4,158	203	2,728	52	36,360
McLean County	2,477	11	2,127	65	2,037	52	1,809	0	19,909
Peoria County	3,390	288	3,317	346	2,549	281	1,668	37	28,935
Rock Island County	2,269	164	2,824	223	1,820	68	1,390	0	26,699
Sangamon County	3,427	229	3,594	102	2,924	0	2,019	99	32,095
St. Clair County	5,132	277	3,855	38	3,754	89	2,401	0	38,382
Tazewell County	2,234	82	1,843	76	2,179	62	1,543	40	23,838
Vermilion County	1,219	198	1,477	0	966	65	844	0	15,179
Will County	10,422	385	10,901	742	8,303	564	5,032	90	77,068
Williamson County	416	13	1,026	48	1,154	56	884	0	11,992
Winnebago County	4,644	268	6,012	160	4,203	226	2,590	235	45,077
Indiana									
Allen County	5,815	46	5,173	504	4,785	279	4,274	65	47,813
Bartholomew County	na	na	na	na	na	na	na	na	na
Clark County	1,686	122	2,146	82	2,431	0	715	44	16,645
Delaware County	1,492	0	1,813	49	1,608	0	1,428	97	18,693
Elkhart County	2,875	0	3,316	37	2,516	107	2,264	100	26,262

Table F-2: Counties—Employment and Labor Force Status, Civilian Labor Force—*Continued*

	60 to 61 Years		62 to 64 Years		65 to 69 Years		70 Years and Over		60 Years and Over Not in the Labor Force
	Employed	Unemployed	Employed	Unemployed	Employed	Unemployed	Employed	Unemployed	
Indiana—Cont.									
Floyd County	1,146	0	849	44	892	0	1,283	0	11,802
Grant County	na	na	na	na	na	na	na	na	na
Hamilton County	5,131	375	5,119	125	4,498	168	3,474	57	27,452
Hancock County	na	na	na	na	na	na	na	na	na
Hendricks County	2,918	103	2,754	0	2,270	219	1,558	0	18,287
Howard County	1,367	69	1,148	40	1,991	114	629	37	15,985
Johnson County	1,848	0	2,647	118	2,709	46	1,380	0	20,130
Kosciusko County	1,405	79	1,616	14	1,370	0	955	0	11,601
Lake County	7,485	420	7,600	397	7,040	460	4,009	174	75,330
LaPorte County	2,164	72	2,141	13	1,810	182	1,148	19	17,580
Madison County	1,301	0	1,819	144	1,905	17	1,146	151	23,732
Marion County	13,462	1,039	14,378	887	11,166	1,071	7,161	419	108,733
Monroe County	2,073	0	2,126	70	3,054	0	1,412	64	13,866
Morgan County	na	na	na	na	na	na	na	na	na
Porter County	2,797	0	2,831	172	2,524	79	2,077	74	24,572
St. Joseph County	4,666	414	5,125	206	4,280	260	3,030	97	37,746
Tippecanoe County	2,435	81	1,712	0	2,160	0	1,158	0	19,686
Vanderburgh County	3,398	331	3,213	0	2,601	101	1,841	131	28,274
Vigo County	1,509	301	1,512	0	2,071	200	923	15	15,736
Wayne County	708	0	1,580	0	1,098	39	781	0	12,113
Iowa									
Black Hawk County	2,427	54	2,151	23	1,639	0	1,361	128	19,961
Dallas County	na	na	na	na	na	na	na	na	na
Dubuque County	1,821	0	2,031	0	1,735	37	1,310	0	14,826
Johnson County	2,500	0	2,494	92	2,766	136	1,032	0	12,950
Linn County	3,477	130	4,263	83	3,578	68	2,320	0	29,924
Polk County	7,783	253	8,665	328	5,984	161	4,214	219	51,704
Pottawattamie County	1,774	0	2,064	0	1,127	58	1,098	40	14,180
Scott County	3,069	159	3,132	294	2,688	15	1,674	0	24,565
Story County	1,269	0	1,412	0	1,104	29	716	0	10,018
Woodbury County	1,857	0	2,163	7	1,775	14	813	13	13,460
Kansas									
Butler County	1,349	0	1,157	0	1,006	0	502	0	9,121
Douglas County	2,024	76	2,472	0	1,312	0	1,297	0	11,267
Johnson County	9,720	314	11,647	315	10,164	422	5,095	0	70,498
Leavenworth County	870	29	1,725	0	771	0	707	0	10,910
Riley County	510	36	637	0	1,175	58	482	0	5,300
Sedgwick County	8,809	104	8,935	398	6,556	200	4,442	273	66,952
Shawnee County	2,531	64	3,370	149	3,062	162	1,179	75	28,978
Wyandotte County	1,896	179	1,742	138	2,470	186	891	78	19,604
Kentucky									
Boone County	1,892	0	2,378	127	1,569	191	1,087	111	14,552
Bullitt County	987	50	1,431	28	431	33	426	0	12,068
Campbell County	2,306	37	1,418	90	1,351	18	535	0	12,991
Christian County	443	0	852	30	584	0	323	0	9,035
Daviess County	1,027	0	1,518	72	665	0	1,346	0	16,410
Fayette County	5,578	446	4,576	488	4,150	60	2,235	117	36,994
Hardin County	1,020	0	1,858	122	1,628	0	580	0	13,745
Jefferson County	10,513	374	12,337	402	12,061	673	8,397	187	111,157
Kenton County	2,463	249	2,010	0	2,921	89	1,803	208	21,015
Madison County	698	55	1,410	0	925	0	592	79	11,608
McCracken County	na	na	na	na	na	na	na	na	na
Pike County	528	0	498	48	550	0	417	84	12,413
Warren County	1,311	49	1,626	79	1,379	8	1,164	0	14,465
Louisiana									
Ascension Parish	na	na	na	na	na	na	na	na	na
Bossier Parish	2,623	189	2,029	0	1,937	0	1,358	61	15,220
Caddo Parish	3,777	162	3,599	0	3,781	191	2,803	72	38,050
Calcasieu Parish	2,282	26	2,819	96	3,129	112	1,863	0	29,630
East Baton Rouge Parish	6,060	376	7,493	262	6,667	376	3,937	35	55,815
Iberia Parish	na	na	na	na	na	na	na	na	na
Jefferson Parish	6,787	388	8,509	362	7,774	334	5,749	264	64,740
Lafayette Parish	2,750	0	3,753	31	2,742	0	3,225	138	26,191
Lafourche Parish	1,723	104	1,002	29	1,277	0	903	45	14,194
Livingston Parish	na	na	na	na	na	na	na	na	na
Orleans Parish	4,862	313	6,399	255	4,501	264	2,986	220	50,904
Ouachita Parish	2,654	0	2,882	38	2,068	65	1,673	0	20,961
Rapides Parish	1,897	68	1,594	32	2,054	84	727	12	20,708
St. Landry Parish	710	33	862	0	1,207	0	549	0	13,916
St. Tammany Parish	4,381	163	4,920	73	4,376	124	3,409	105	35,907
Tangipahoa Parish	1,473	0	976	0	1,172	7	990	0	18,587
Terrebonne Parish	na	na	na	na	na	na	na	na	na
Maine									
Androscoggin County	1,848	70	2,250	0	1,696	35	1,180	28	16,800
Aroostook County	1,401	42	1,190	6	1,298	8	1,009	0	15,565
Cumberland County	6,695	290	7,155	202	6,224	131	3,479	22	43,662
Kennebec County	2,431	74	2,517	99	2,184	112	1,211	47	21,894

Table F-2: Counties—Employment and Labor Force Status, Civilian Labor Force—Continued

	60 to 61 Years		62 to 64 Years		65 to 69 Years		70 Years and Over		60 Years and Over Not in the Labor Force
	Employed	Unemployed	Employed	Unemployed	Employed	Unemployed	Employed	Unemployed	
Maine—Cont.									
Penobscot County	3,031	0	2,745	168	2,726	93	1,456	50	25,886
York County	4,790	118	4,273	168	5,214	84	2,492	108	34,632
Maryland									
Allegany County	831	58	1,624	38	1,125	59	380	0	14,112
Anne Arundel County	8,886	150	10,895	586	11,091	248	6,802	224	70,273
Baltimore County	13,949	588	17,164	883	16,900	641	10,249	306	122,462
Calvert County	1,290	133	1,489	0	963	0	650	0	12,490
Carroll County	3,574	49	2,806	50	3,030	142	1,915	88	24,410
Cecil County	1,618	0	1,548	0	1,240	52	652	48	14,885
Charles County	2,318	139	1,552	40	1,646	39	1,074	0	18,692
Frederick County	4,144	270	4,934	298	3,840	79	2,310	43	30,679
Harford County	3,812	139	4,872	215	4,702	252	2,645	173	36,998
Howard County	6,356	45	7,440	114	5,584	109	3,222	80	33,032
Montgomery County	18,277	891	23,816	883	22,289	421	13,959	680	121,600
Prince George's County	13,913	843	16,704	1,045	17,113	1,093	8,712	515	96,201
St. Mary's County	2,108	0	2,045	0	979	0	838	0	13,856
Washington County	2,098	446	2,406	60	2,150	109	1,334	0	23,428
Wicomico County	1,545	0	2,689	0	1,798	213	1,118	12	14,405
Massachusetts									
Barnstable County	4,338	231	7,997	233	7,158	587	5,542	153	54,221
Berkshire County	2,105	133	3,695	277	3,269	168	2,265	150	25,208
Bristol County	11,269	445	10,048	321	8,213	173	5,185	51	87,597
Essex County	13,863	1,104	17,658	763	15,741	961	8,827	414	111,094
Franklin County	2,079	0	2,123	156	1,965	0	1,072	0	12,085
Hampden County	10,298	584	7,260	183	7,197	251	4,338	165	72,119
Hampshire County	2,585	161	4,340	176	3,176	13	1,487	0	22,054
Middlesex County	27,087	737	31,359	1,960	30,388	1,757	21,874	675	195,971
Norfolk County	15,381	829	15,995	522	15,462	1,027	10,004	340	94,723
Plymouth County	10,765	945	12,159	568	10,213	249	7,277	624	77,486
Suffolk County	8,483	479	11,882	1,262	9,060	289	5,311	501	86,872
Worcester County	15,229	713	16,790	664	13,482	625	10,203	510	108,794
Michigan									
Allegan County	2,208	30	1,787	16	1,315	24	1,230	0	18,208
Bay County	1,648	36	902	60	1,484	15	593	0	21,584
Berrien County	3,018	188	3,266	0	2,944	91	1,723	20	27,156
Calhoun County	2,482	73	1,836	0	1,156	139	882	85	25,118
Clinton County	1,196	384	1,418	43	883	32	521	0	12,934
Eaton County	1,529	13	1,338	40	1,402	37	1,096	36	19,673
Genesee County	4,258	140	5,724	399	3,582	112	2,418	150	75,432
Grand Traverse County	1,675	0	1,328	73	1,539	0	852	0	16,448
Ingham County	4,257	166	4,663	180	3,019	151	1,905	53	36,426
Isabella County	978	0	644	44	680	73	514	13	8,200
Jackson County	2,051	107	2,675	0	2,056	22	1,158	0	27,805
Kalamazoo County	3,325	183	4,713	255	3,323	110	1,807	16	37,047
Kent County	9,876	333	9,586	153	7,648	403	4,752	193	79,475
Lapeer County	1,326	114	1,354	46	519	45	406	23	16,820
Lenawee County	2,007	95	1,647	0	1,096	14	938	0	17,100
Livingston County	3,168	24	3,105	44	2,219	34	1,747	190	29,136
Macomb County	14,372	1,013	14,984	785	9,011	149	6,355	343	145,481
Marquette County	959	15	1,028	66	310	0	338	75	13,561
Midland County	1,235	0	1,022	0	719	0	735	18	14,999
Monroe County	2,373	0	2,752	0	1,862	94	599	0	26,244
Muskegon County	2,114	169	2,338	91	2,401	56	1,191	72	27,925
Oakland County	23,132	993	24,835	919	18,082	905	14,274	442	187,817
Ottawa County	4,847	192	4,783	151	4,074	86	2,526	342	34,755
Saginaw County	1,945	71	2,343	93	2,098	53	2,455	75	37,509
Shiawassee County	1,371	268	1,200	12	727	91	702	0	12,541
St. Clair County	2,235	133	2,426	167	1,972	32	1,332	92	30,332
Van Buren County	1,309	0	1,370	18	871	0	785	12	13,795
Washtenaw County	5,359	282	6,574	179	5,396	417	3,584	0	43,029
Wayne County	22,781	997	22,518	1,623	17,676	889	12,167	1,020	275,706
Minnesota									
Anoka County	5,235	73	6,574	515	4,774	130	2,407	41	40,120
Blue Earth County	1,152	15	674	18	617	0	479	90	8,743
Carver County	2,068	70	1,204	47	1,291	14	924	0	9,424
Dakota County	6,634	203	6,741	50	6,493	434	4,052	25	48,855
Hennepin County	20,837	684	23,392	621	19,562	839	11,110	137	145,606
Olmsted County	2,768	65	3,753	8	1,934	64	1,364	40	19,653
Ramsey County	9,022	371	10,490	220	7,218	74	4,193	92	70,394
Rice County	948	14	1,634	0	1,335	30	683	0	8,208
Scott County	1,617	0	2,286	0	1,630	53	799	0	12,618
Sherburne County	1,082	32	1,445	110	985	0	608	0	9,290
St. Louis County	3,856	97	3,993	152	2,527	147	1,838	84	37,394
Stearns County	2,502	97	2,804	86	2,051	30	1,543	127	18,910
Washington County	3,569	302	4,264	111	3,344	110	2,041	59	32,611
Wright County	2,077	15	2,423	0	1,625	26	1,050	0	14,149

Table F-2: Counties—Employment and Labor Force Status, Civilian Labor Force—*Continued*

	60 to 61 Years		62 to 64 Years		65 to 69 Years		70 Years and Over		60 Years and Over Not in the Labor Force
	Employed	Unemployed	Employed	Unemployed	Employed	Unemployed	Employed	Unemployed	
Mississippi									
DeSoto County	3,722	43	2,394	78	1,872	35	1,673	61	19,431
Forrest County	1,310	240	256	0	732	0	1,233	99	10,732
Harrison County	2,520	195	3,579	386	2,653	75	1,376	359	27,679
Hinds County	2,849	123	3,306	61	1,949	0	2,860	0	31,552
Jackson County	1,400	71	1,903	169	1,398	0	630	0	22,231
Jones County	na	na	na	na	na	na	na	na	na
Lauderdale County	na	na	na	na	na	na	na	na	na
Lee County	na	na	na	na	na	na	na	na	na
Madison County	1,903	34	2,753	0	1,179	0	733	0	12,767
Rankin County	1,678	29	2,069	0	2,020	0	1,901	45	19,668
Missouri									
Boone County	2,933	29	3,405	283	2,036	0	1,837	96	17,912
Buchanan County	1,522	69	1,148	0	1,551	0	728	66	12,742
Cape Girardeau County	1,772	0	1,229	98	1,404	0	844	113	12,125
Cass County	1,530	261	1,260	52	1,607	105	753	0	16,761
Christian County	na	na	na	na	na	na	na	na	na
Clay County	4,123	0	4,529	65	2,470	0	2,598	107	29,137
Cole County	1,375	0	952	12	945	61	565	0	11,918
Franklin County	1,563	0	1,340	0	1,134	53	1,048	0	17,137
Greene County	3,789	206	4,373	155	4,666	169	2,613	0	43,549
Jackson County	9,507	238	9,406	175	10,076	254	6,337	96	95,030
Jasper County	1,071	0	2,215	77	2,482	37	1,130	0	15,411
Jefferson County	3,640	45	3,353	101	3,152	0	1,567	71	32,756
Platte County	1,415	117	1,911	0	1,618	0	420	0	12,045
St. Charles County	6,738	276	6,137	189	6,262	274	3,277	293	49,223
St. Francois County	na	na	na	na	na	na	na	na	na
St. Louis County	15,953	631	22,166	1,002	17,886	620	11,205	69	162,626
Montana									
Cascade County	1,118	0	1,753	0	1,766	94	1,076	0	13,321
Flathead County	na	na	na	na	na	na	na	na	na
Gallatin County	1,658	0	1,362	0	1,182	24	729	33	11,031
Lewis and Clark County	na	na	na	na	na	na	na	na	na
Missoula County	1,578	0	1,616	0	2,013	231	1,072	0	15,281
Yellowstone County	2,618	149	2,816	61	2,990	90	2,524	18	22,693
Nebraska									
Douglas County	8,364	191	10,283	96	7,257	105	5,428	18	60,229
Lancaster County	5,298	145	5,259	55	4,741	23	2,638	56	34,117
Sarpy County	2,784	0	2,763	46	2,452	0	1,110	0	16,311
Nevada									
Clark County	29,930	2,451	30,395	2,347	25,498	1,939	19,224	2,146	283,307
Washoe County	7,446	152	8,672	505	7,069	528	3,782	332	66,150
New Hampshire									
Cheshire County	na	na	na	na	na	na	na	na	na
Grafton County	2,393	86	2,102	0	2,105	31	1,748	0	15,088
Hillsborough County	8,297	394	8,760	194	7,305	563	4,018	100	52,333
Merrimack County	3,064	75	3,728	51	2,277	24	2,304	137	22,451
Rockingham County	8,073	397	7,738	218	5,729	52	4,094	43	42,415
Strafford County	2,158	78	2,594	0	1,879	35	1,411	0	16,345
New Jersey									
Atlantic County	5,093	543	6,125	675	4,377	438	3,142	334	43,289
Bergen County	17,263	1,055	20,173	798	20,293	1,301	13,496	635	135,619
Burlington County	8,775	271	7,387	249	8,728	503	6,433	232	64,589
Camden County	8,357	451	11,421	599	8,430	264	5,577	344	69,960
Cape May County	2,685	99	2,119	0	2,345	193	1,902	142	22,047
Cumberland County	2,294	272	1,417	26	2,251	268	1,638	80	21,648
Essex County	14,118	953	13,555	697	12,389	744	7,765	540	93,730
Gloucester County	4,925	272	5,798	598	5,294	233	3,129	178	40,015
Hudson County	9,259	638	11,577	891	6,925	292	5,003	254	74,793
Hunterdon County	2,967	36	3,737	177	3,183	193	1,907	186	16,509
Mercer County	5,613	0	7,436	442	6,508	313	4,661	191	48,613
Middlesex County	15,518	1,089	16,060	1,613	14,118	702	7,969	415	106,050
Monmouth County	11,226	713	14,449	604	12,252	774	9,377	667	91,250
Morris County	10,836	365	10,921	610	12,212	800	5,909	397	68,147
Ocean County	9,221	904	11,062	659	11,683	983	8,488	837	124,340
Passaic County	8,221	482	9,983	394	8,232	409	5,254	617	63,602
Salem County	844	159	1,153	148	1,012	0	892	36	11,273
Somerset County	5,633	188	8,186	277	5,418	53	4,695	324	43,268
Sussex County	3,038	203	3,360	0	3,173	27	1,784	33	20,300
Union County	8,384	1,028	9,159	413	8,865	633	5,304	458	69,026
Warren County	1,913	127	1,838	102	2,366	260	923	55	17,133
New Mexico									
Bernalillo County	11,110	763	10,991	952	9,041	566	5,981	406	100,806
Chaves County	806	0	1,198	0	1,007	0	674	59	10,673
Doña Ana County	2,163	317	3,488	71	2,492	0	2,346	82	31,427
Lea County	1,070	41	689	0	876	0	719	0	7,287
McKinley County	1,111	17	877	0	400	63	1,069	0	8,231
Otero County	1,190	0	850	8	641	86	444	30	11,125

Table F-2: Counties—Employment and Labor Force Status, Civilian Labor Force—*Continued*

	60 to 61 Years		62 to 64 Years		65 to 69 Years		70 Years and Over		60 Years and Over Not in the Labor Force
	Employed	Unemployed	Employed	Unemployed	Employed	Unemployed	Employed	Unemployed	
New Mexico—Cont.									
San Juan County	1,553	42	1,743	34	2,115	202	1,477	0	15,728
Sandoval County	1,906	170	2,364	0	2,162	318	1,275	291	21,615
Santa Fe County	3,146	209	3,818	89	4,161	168	2,479	37	27,845
Valencia County	742	0	885	0	660	0	1,421	118	13,038
New York									
Albany County	4,031	194	5,339	138	5,319	299	3,325	104	47,081
Bronx County	15,419	1,787	17,928	1,249	11,893	964	7,207	497	176,782
Broome County	3,092	61	3,794	212	3,081	130	1,909	0	37,006
Cattaraugus County	1,729	104	1,353	54	936	32	832	0	14,341
Cayuga County	1,394	99	1,309	18	1,353	0	1,137	0	13,188
Chautauqua County	2,061	58	2,160	46	1,460	26	1,221	116	25,076
Chemung County	1,463	0	1,461	75	1,294	93	865	37	16,246
Clinton County	1,307	0	731	0	1,195	0	720	0	13,454
Dutchess County	5,672	301	6,509	318	5,095	41	3,594	219	44,141
Erie County	15,615	390	16,800	655	13,782	653	9,515	401	156,713
Jefferson County	1,749	8	1,170	89	897	81	1,385	0	15,244
Kings County	33,641	2,729	40,394	2,677	35,095	1,688	16,201	813	327,913
Livingston County	1,414	119	1,098	0	738	0	634	34	11,579
Madison County	930	0	2,080	79	873	85	663	0	12,094
Monroe County	12,095	631	14,507	481	10,724	540	8,631	276	117,722
Nassau County	24,930	923	28,206	1,596	27,806	946	21,024	666	204,818
New York County	27,490	2,992	26,548	1,710	30,748	1,967	28,530	1,323	212,582
Niagara County	4,493	123	3,884	34	3,554	347	2,025	44	38,317
Oneida County	4,385	55	4,075	196	3,025	165	3,123	190	41,675
Onondaga County	8,086	376	8,599	370	6,308	244	4,972	549	73,121
Ontario County	2,091	0	2,130	98	1,779	257	1,269	54	20,063
Orange County	6,537	98	6,164	318	5,454	87	3,315	186	45,869
Oswego County	1,728	0	1,316	47	1,087	45	847	59	19,310
Putnam County	1,961	59	1,998	44	2,416	74	875	0	13,893
Queens County	35,947	2,048	35,356	1,980	31,345	1,706	18,769	785	321,326
Rensselaer County	2,881	76	3,479	88	2,691	74	1,936	62	24,426
Richmond County	8,140	271	7,283	46	6,313	201	3,441	253	72,771
Rockland County	5,699	210	6,169	200	6,975	231	4,647	137	42,199
Saratoga County	3,928	105	4,934	243	3,474	143	1,090	14	36,239
Schenectady County	1,826	163	3,055	184	2,054	79	2,255	592	24,787
St. Lawrence County	1,257	29	1,296	74	1,069	23	684	102	19,892
Steuben County	2,068	153	1,355	73	1,493	38	1,012	63	17,904
Suffolk County	25,019	1,056	27,023	885	26,058	1,487	21,007	1,020	215,681
Sullivan County	924	105	1,605	46	1,592	22	1,275	30	12,660
Tompkins County	2,102	171	1,964	0	1,398	0	1,505	0	11,635
Ulster County	2,710	132	4,282	450	3,915	263	2,431	136	30,967
Warren County	1,239	0	1,503	0	874	76	1,403	58	12,994
Wayne County	1,360	85	1,609	35	922	37	848	0	17,084
Westchester County	18,027	1,027	21,182	980	19,009	601	15,066	917	135,846
North Carolina									
Alamance County	2,279	216	2,308	164	2,798	56	1,667	88	24,710
Brunswick County	2,865	219	2,657	117	3,420	109	1,397	0	32,084
Buncombe County	3,853	44	5,295	0	3,795	129	2,136	111	47,249
Burke County	1,136	38	1,258	0	1,614	155	1,115	16	17,278
Cabarrus County	2,563	222	2,826	600	2,077	74	1,714	72	24,065
Caldwell County	1,333	89	1,189	38	1,177	108	893	0	16,154
Carteret County	1,433	49	1,071	30	1,507	0	879	81	15,424
Catawba County	2,522	230	2,151	0	2,580	183	1,415	35	24,829
Chatham County	na	na	na	na	na	na	na	na	na
Cleveland County	2,085	184	1,962	0	1,019	109	903	0	18,317
Craven County	1,655	0	1,754	50	1,271	184	993	62	18,371
Cumberland County	3,332	92	3,401	127	3,098	56	2,276	54	38,703
Davidson County	2,585	339	2,034	64	2,556	0	1,183	51	28,349
Durham County	4,208	422	4,689	328	4,330	72	2,440	0	33,532
Forsyth County	5,892	327	5,785	138	5,217	389	2,759	53	54,211
Gaston County	3,159	288	2,774	203	2,986	152	1,803	35	33,365
Guilford County	7,514	546	8,284	201	6,739	355	5,504	206	68,901
Harnett County	1,582	0	896	0	917	10	728	0	15,090
Henderson County	1,403	87	1,653	0	1,697	68	942	0	28,661
Iredell County	3,341	219	2,209	301	1,878	32	1,718	0	24,531
Johnston County	2,601	140	2,984	0	1,448	0	1,137	164	24,668
Lincoln County	1,542	46	1,397	78	752	0	473	7	14,184
Mecklenburg County	13,740	419	14,656	1,439	12,560	793	7,436	310	99,574
Moore County	na	na	na	na	na	na	na	na	na
Nash County	2,016	84	2,712	250	975	69	713	0	16,282
New Hanover County	3,308	56	4,544	60	3,422	94	1,999	0	34,100
Onslow County	722	46	1,575	0	1,474	117	1,240	0	16,167
Orange County	2,492	0	3,296	0	2,143	120	1,344	0	14,883
Pitt County	2,210	126	1,539	0	2,914	157	1,515	0	19,607
Randolph County	2,576	49	1,821	41	2,220	122	1,606	84	24,778
Robeson County	975	102	1,543	0	872	42	447	5	20,993
Rockingham County	1,653	67	1,628	0	1,422	79	1,826	0	17,082
Rowan County	1,875	42	2,190	34	2,666	146	1,215	43	22,217

Table F-2: Counties—Employment and Labor Force Status, Civilian Labor Force—*Continued*

	60 to 61 Years		62 to 64 Years		65 to 69 Years		70 Years and Over		60 Years and Over Not in the Labor Force
	Employed	Unemployed	Employed	Unemployed	Employed	Unemployed	Employed	Unemployed	
North Carolina—Cont.									
Rutherford County	na	na	na	na	na	na	na	na	na
Surry County	1,007	0	1,182	0	1,090	0	659	42	14,141
Union County	2,335	278	3,326	309	2,439	389	1,996	42	25,338
Wake County	15,340	710	15,172	1,197	13,545	332	7,467	256	97,839
Wayne County	1,239	126	1,410	119	1,375	79	1,174	67	18,873
Wilkes County	na	na	na	na	na	na	na	na	na
Wilson County	1,221	0	1,690	0	1,289	0	942	162	13,469
North Dakota									
Burleigh County	985	67	2,134	9	1,480	0	1,523	0	12,008
Cass County	2,290	0	3,737	117	2,414	86	1,753	141	16,122
Grand Forks County	898	12	1,428	6	944	51	607	0	7,391
Ward County	1,189	0	869	0	1,214	22	524	0	7,152
Ohio									
Allen County	1,700	90	2,289	220	1,176	17	567	32	17,919
Ashtabula County	2,139	40	1,872	95	1,037	153	784	0	18,621
Belmont County	782	0	1,610	42	853	0	793	0	14,209
Butler County	5,518	183	5,117	39	5,722	336	2,860	0	48,777
Clark County	2,058	90	2,492	156	2,608	102	1,826	89	24,404
Clermont County	3,764	71	2,881	191	4,234	325	1,787	273	29,105
Columbiana County	1,775	102	2,145	5	1,869	115	2,036	0	18,927
Cuyahoga County	21,941	1,658	25,076	909	20,386	669	13,378	635	207,620
Delaware County	2,750	77	3,956	40	2,719	0	1,417	0	20,073
Erie County	1,361	171	1,229	203	998	0	807	37	14,783
Fairfield County	2,381	0	2,761	30	2,311	37	1,293	0	23,249
Franklin County	17,412	922	21,671	525	16,980	363	9,938	710	131,751
Geauga County	na	na	na	na	na	na	na	na	na
Greene County	2,578	73	3,093	0	2,221	114	2,147	0	26,270
Hamilton County	14,151	592	14,351	482	12,089	284	9,104	358	115,883
Hancock County	1,297	0	1,013	45	754	80	1,131	0	11,938
Jefferson County	1,339	59	1,025	34	886	0	539	9	14,243
Lake County	4,938	240	4,396	91	4,675	116	3,103	150	38,477
Licking County	2,853	129	3,285	0	2,503	63	1,502	0	26,209
Lorain County	5,188	296	5,154	51	4,717	173	2,156	78	51,687
Lucas County	7,683	321	8,165	514	6,511	207	3,595	44	65,280
Mahoning County	4,662	118	4,170	70	4,252	20	2,786	173	45,340
Marion County	980	96	903	144	1,315	50	816	33	10,543
Medina County	3,821	194	2,742	165	2,980	92	2,106	216	26,830
Miami County	na	na	na	na	na	na	na	na	na
Montgomery County	8,995	402	10,375	522	8,484	140	6,299	141	88,211
Muskingum County	1,090	7	1,721	44	761	0	757	190	15,505
Portage County	3,531	116	3,759	320	2,073	0	2,268	259	23,339
Richland County	2,019	63	2,020	55	1,531	188	756	0	23,910
Ross County	814	52	1,254	0	687	15	595	0	13,504
Scioto County	746	0	1,139	0	622	0	806	0	14,475
Stark County	6,976	542	7,136	86	6,563	127	4,354	331	67,908
Summit County	10,496	224	11,078	149	9,449	421	5,597	465	86,011
Trumbull County	2,883	50	3,561	159	2,584	0	1,576	80	42,931
Tuscarawas County	2,016	0	1,753	76	1,342	0	1,104	0	16,631
Warren County	3,501	159	4,152	44	3,583	58	2,413	30	28,733
Wayne County	1,996	7	1,843	39	1,538	43	1,262	25	18,689
Wood County	1,694	274	2,083	59	2,216	133	1,529	0	18,341
Oklahoma									
Canadian County	1,838	69	2,528	34	1,859	0	1,011	0	15,144
Cleveland County	3,718	87	4,632	179	4,789	176	2,152	0	31,566
Comanche County	1,717	0	1,371	0	924	84	923	84	14,668
Creek County	1,090	31	1,099	106	1,033	17	1,038	0	12,317
Muskogee County	990	74	973	0	547	0	989	73	11,709
Oklahoma County	10,674	273	10,750	185	10,755	241	9,604	428	93,505
Payne County	1,202	35	919	0	723	0	464	0	9,184
Pottawatomie County	938	0	989	19	1,310	108	607	0	11,886
Rogers County	1,729	0	1,117	0	1,766	23	955	0	13,553
Tulsa County	10,892	300	11,025	224	10,303	301	8,015	353	77,828
Wagoner County	1,372	26	1,240	91	1,660	66	796	20	10,537
Oregon									
Benton County	1,555	88	1,568	51	1,099	167	910	0	12,577
Clackamas County	8,160	109	8,908	631	8,318	450	3,093	220	63,190
Deschutes County	4,082	0	3,554	228	2,533	355	1,258	140	32,118
Douglas County	2,348	64	1,626	0	1,396	0	735	0	28,917
Jackson County	3,736	489	4,176	91	3,144	161	2,422	124	46,350
Josephine County	na	na	na	na	na	na	na	na	na
Klamath County	1,356	0	1,106	143	941	0	429	29	13,822
Lane County	5,990	369	6,810	366	6,829	137	2,853	138	64,693
Linn County	2,035	190	1,606	85	1,534	64	1,068	49	22,552
Marion County	5,082	192	6,630	61	4,346	245	2,893	39	48,970
Multnomah County	12,564	772	13,618	459	10,256	195	5,171	200	98,488
Polk County	1,293	265	1,398	0	1,034	0	612	0	14,120
Umatilla County	1,012	12	994	0	938	0	603	0	12,243
Washington County	9,169	139	8,638	88	7,958	239	3,899	130	67,989

Table F-2: Counties—Employment and Labor Force Status, Civilian Labor Force—*Continued*

	60 to 61 Years		62 to 64 Years		65 to 69 Years		70 Years and Over		60 Years and Over Not in the Labor Force
	Employed	Unemployed	Employed	Unemployed	Employed	Unemployed	Employed	Unemployed	
Oregon—Cont.									
Yamhill County	948	84	1,516	25	844	33	1,077	0	17,151
Pennsylvania									
Adams County	1,881	68	2,511	55	1,791	71	947	0	18,177
Allegheny County	24,618	941	26,822	1,164	22,075	838	15,573	601	208,006
Armstrong County	910	14	1,057	22	953	51	500	26	15,056
Beaver County	3,532	213	3,666	172	3,561	147	2,141	65	32,447
Berks County	8,056	460	8,964	452	7,112	225	4,527	140	64,083
Blair County	2,272	53	2,120	41	1,993	54	1,673	49	25,082
Bucks County	13,593	493	13,925	760	14,811	384	8,106	558	95,772
Butler County	3,270	174	3,300	120	3,343	92	1,830	66	31,776
Cambria County	2,186	176	2,967	117	2,380	22	1,426	23	29,426
Carbon County	na	na	na	na	na	na	na	na	na
Centre County	2,335	220	2,324	294	1,845	0	905	0	20,799
Chester County	10,443	466	10,413	483	9,886	400	7,426	440	66,098
Clearfield County	1,305	166	1,334	202	1,347	34	1,029	55	16,209
Columbia County	1,574	22	819	53	631	0	622	19	12,275
Crawford County	1,723	205	2,034	140	1,328	69	1,243	21	16,929
Cumberland County	4,738	107	5,298	82	3,534	140	3,046	61	40,897
Dauphin County	5,383	138	4,315	122	4,287	27	2,515	79	42,501
Delaware County	10,035	380	11,283	562	10,159	212	7,079	464	82,176
Erie County	5,134	184	4,502	158	3,496	251	2,424	175	45,957
Fayette County	2,333	233	2,390	60	1,903	32	2,142	36	27,665
Franklin County	2,895	0	2,601	50	2,659	142	1,787	70	27,701
Indiana County	1,227	39	1,363	59	1,581	162	811	44	15,474
Lackawanna County	3,091	281	4,107	231	3,060	25	3,316	42	41,597
Lancaster County	10,219	266	9,688	259	11,214	202	7,923	348	80,480
Lawrence County	1,802	69	1,833	19	1,314	77	807	0	18,022
Lebanon County	2,190	105	2,661	66	2,127	0	1,530	43	24,885
Lehigh County	6,446	599	7,471	538	6,213	509	3,499	86	56,277
Luzerne County	5,547	420	5,991	564	5,302	417	4,117	393	61,108
Lycoming County	2,548	30	2,360	133	2,278	105	1,231	107	21,348
Mercer County	2,553	111	2,408	114	1,638	131	1,352	9	23,265
Monroe County	2,465	104	3,749	158	2,622	457	1,951	408	25,423
Montgomery County	16,969	836	17,900	622	18,053	593	14,787	825	117,011
Northampton County	5,987	321	6,138	40	4,428	397	4,136	194	51,949
Northumberland County	1,430	98	1,524	0	1,710	63	951	62	19,200
Philadelphia County	19,300	965	20,252	1,034	16,677	1,004	11,508	662	209,301
Schuylkill County	2,664	18	2,757	77	2,484	0	2,053	65	29,346
Somerset County	1,725	93	1,275	148	882	29	1,125	85	16,185
Washington County	3,189	44	3,779	187	4,057	51	1,899	45	41,650
Westmoreland County	8,551	330	7,726	198	7,761	416	5,454	150	72,070
York County	9,000	349	8,090	506	8,111	39	4,408	240	67,993
Rhode Island									
Kent County	2,988	230	3,391	24	3,742	104	2,092	292	27,347
Newport County	1,380	278	2,574	38	2,441	150	1,436	188	14,728
Providence County	10,134	741	11,982	552	8,398	127	6,324	464	91,182
Washington County	1,884	121	3,317	31	2,567	327	1,725	121	22,595
South Carolina									
Aiken County	2,967	284	3,065	67	2,091	62	1,548	0	31,076
Anderson County	2,420	246	3,494	308	3,048	52	2,222	61	33,226
Beaufort County	2,688	131	3,345	46	3,917	69	2,486	116	41,926
Berkeley County	2,849	68	2,578	152	1,908	123	1,035	36	27,183
Charleston County	6,858	482	6,817	479	5,944	91	4,026	126	56,277
Darlington County	1,533	74	870	0	1,204	35	472	0	12,290
Dorchester County	2,527	183	2,018	38	1,581	97	758	0	18,411
Florence County	2,638	95	3,051	281	2,179	0	1,604	21	21,874
Greenville County	7,071	202	7,875	250	6,716	161	4,021	71	71,612
Greenwood County	na	na	na	na	na	na	na	na	na
Horry County	5,411	342	4,903	96	5,086	158	3,253	51	65,635
Lancaster County	1,003	183	1,187	0	1,667	0	1,006	0	15,968
Laurens County	946	0	1,029	100	1,019	0	648	0	11,591
Lexington County	4,619	47	4,374	95	4,643	109	2,432	120	39,010
Oconee County	1,123	39	1,281	53	1,158	104	887	0	17,856
Orangeburg County	1,867	0	1,112	0	1,436	55	729	0	16,496
Pickens County	1,425	111	1,633	0	1,443	111	960	132	20,002
Richland County	4,865	204	6,484	158	5,893	450	3,243	79	45,396
Spartanburg County	5,061	128	3,675	7	4,292	0	2,579	55	44,806
Sumter County	1,039	79	1,050	0	1,300	113	609	45	10,131
York County	3,925	303	3,847	45	3,813	272	2,220	0	32,870
South Dakota									
Minnehaha County	1,890	40	3,392	0	3,511	74	2,757	116	19,359
Pennington County	2,200	0	2,069	21	1,556	86	1,487	0	15,401
Tennessee									
Anderson County	1,075	32	1,934	0	1,427	116	1,112	0	14,628
Blount County	1,845	11	1,875	274	2,420	85	1,871	69	23,311
Bradley County	1,352	56	1,542	0	974	0	1,222	85	18,065
Davidson County	11,281	283	10,226	163	9,867	476	6,744	269	71,536

Table F-2: Counties—Employment and Labor Force Status, Civilian Labor Force—*Continued*

	60 to 61 Years		62 to 64 Years		65 to 69 Years		70 Years and Over		60 Years and Over Not in the Labor Force
	Employed	Unemployed	Employed	Unemployed	Employed	Unemployed	Employed	Unemployed	
Tennessee—Cont.									
Greene County	1,118	232	1,200	0	1,733	198	935	0	13,424
Hamilton County	5,282	220	7,258	478	6,430	216	3,832	143	56,301
Knox County	6,468	288	7,444	120	5,996	319	4,218	0	68,958
Madison County	1,297	32	1,812	19	2,137	0	865	0	14,116
Maury County	1,318	153	1,738	0	894	61	1,378	99	12,570
Montgomery County	1,715	0	2,045	180	1,657	0	804	0	18,547
Putnam County	na	na	na	na	na	na	na	na	na
Robertson County	na	na	na	na	na	na	na	na	na
Rutherford County	2,720	227	4,652	259	3,394	188	1,653	46	28,539
Sevier County	1,442	81	1,495	0	1,661	198	1,860	81	16,802
Shelby County	13,699	827	15,296	714	12,911	725	9,432	200	110,565
Sullivan County	2,386	76	2,960	0	2,826	0	1,970	78	32,203
Sumner County	2,938	80	3,204	284	2,721	115	2,455	43	24,232
Washington County	1,576	112	1,825	258	1,655	0	1,233	148	23,988
Williamson County	3,255	0	2,680	0	3,691	23	2,241	0	22,000
Wilson County	1,644	0	2,829	132	2,877	0	811	87	17,634
Texas									
Angelina County	719	12	840	61	750	32	1,121	0	14,926
Bastrop County	na	na	na	na	na	na	na	na	na
Bell County	3,441	104	4,913	164	3,399	273	1,670	0	33,474
Bexar County	22,471	1,444	24,345	1,097	21,712	915	14,729	721	215,129
Bowie County	1,770	21	1,181	85	976	8	499	0	14,809
Brazoria County	5,145	240	5,057	94	4,279	192	2,311	65	37,337
Brazos County	2,843	386	2,025	0	1,916	0	1,205	78	17,764
Cameron County	4,395	178	4,001	154	3,317	182	2,901	262	56,007
Collin County	13,379	762	14,843	931	12,140	502	7,796	153	80,840
Comal County	2,455	0	3,469	45	1,998	0	1,868	0	21,960
Coryell County	506	59	387	0	645	0	264	0	6,658
Dallas County	34,073	1,060	35,766	1,555	31,225	1,347	21,427	957	241,336
Denton County	9,666	568	9,980	478	10,983	604	4,490	160	60,929
Ector County	1,905	39	1,890	68	2,210	115	1,006	0	14,452
El Paso County	9,385	601	9,492	405	6,378	161	6,243	314	99,706
Ellis County	2,557	0	2,057	13	2,523	14	1,537	16	18,936
Fort Bend County	9,888	206	10,217	290	8,744	442	5,694	337	64,137
Galveston County	5,530	26	5,612	356	4,442	0	2,419	79	41,675
Grayson County	2,316	338	2,302	0	2,014	22	1,506	53	21,643
Gregg County	1,185	203	2,672	0	1,892	0	1,353	41	17,720
Guadalupe County	2,227	92	1,801	33	2,323	36	1,744	82	18,340
Harris County	58,080	2,652	68,721	3,730	55,270	2,347	36,222	1,014	402,869
Harrison County	na	na	na	na	na	na	na	na	na
Hays County	2,583	210	2,750	407	2,066	61	1,531	29	18,372
Henderson County	1,458	266	719	0	770	28	1,178	0	17,987
Hidalgo County	6,270	796	7,794	630	6,159	303	3,483	282	90,885
Hunt County	1,254	0	1,267	0	832	0	1,009	0	15,179
Jefferson County	3,568	94	3,741	106	2,766	34	1,760	44	35,897
Johnson County	3,080	196	2,009	112	2,704	62	957	55	20,240
Kaufman County	937	6	1,817	350	1,568	128	837	73	12,914
Liberty County	544	0	1,040	0	1,206	78	970	0	11,277
Lubbock County	2,935	149	3,583	28	4,960	39	3,216	28	32,727
McLennan County	3,687	233	2,684	144	2,916	189	2,239	31	33,095
Midland County	3,895	0	2,628	0	2,657	112	1,900	98	13,116
Montgomery County	8,137	255	10,794	87	8,184	70	5,186	474	60,326
Nacogdoches County	na	na	na	na	na	na	na	na	na
Nueces County	5,945	373	6,126	484	4,477	43	3,316	70	47,549
Orange County	1,148	88	792	38	1,003	45	1,211	13	13,025
Parker County	2,193	66	2,500	113	1,724	52	1,736	0	18,869
Potter County	1,269	0	1,274	89	1,670	41	1,073	0	14,096
Randall County	na	na	na	na	na	na	na	na	na
Rockwall County	na	na	na	na	na	na	na	na	na
San Patricio County	na	na	na	na	na	na	na	na	na
Smith County	3,532	41	4,363	237	3,605	79	2,367	137	33,852
Tarrant County	26,688	992	25,743	1,178	25,900	735	15,251	331	194,639
Taylor County	2,025	0	2,183	111	2,227	18	1,669	0	17,204
Tom Green County	1,491	26	1,329	68	1,143	0	1,913	0	17,386
Travis County	15,541	609	16,676	901	13,961	715	8,340	26	96,408
Victoria County	na	na	na	na	na	na	na	na	na
Walker County	na	na	na	na	na	na	na	na	na
Webb County	1,988	75	2,254	22	1,968	0	1,179	0	25,168
Wichita County	2,266	74	1,897	37	1,844	0	1,769	44	17,688
Williamson County	7,235	393	7,069	538	6,638	67	2,607	195	54,705
Utah									
Cache County	1,187	24	1,453	0	1,092	0	655	0	10,135
Davis County	3,254	40	4,764	70	2,685	0	2,353	0	30,652
Salt Lake County	16,073	735	19,776	318	12,386	192	9,144	245	102,037
Utah County	4,376	70	5,725	285	5,498	98	2,868	152	38,452
Washington County	2,012	34	1,592	125	1,673	0	1,114	0	31,562
Weber County	3,803	191	3,739	341	2,359	65	1,542	64	27,017

Table F-2: Counties—Employment and Labor Force Status, Civilian Labor Force—*Continued*

	60 to 61 Years		62 to 64 Years		65 to 69 Years		70 Years and Over		60 Years and Over Not in the Labor Force
	Employed	Unemployed	Employed	Unemployed	Employed	Unemployed	Employed	Unemployed	
Vermont									
Chittenden County	3,506	88	3,709	291	3,181	13	2,137	173	18,792
Virginia									
Albemarle County	1,822	0	2,097	130	2,154	159	1,592	123	17,216
Arlington County	3,209	63	3,501	0	2,759	125	1,688	37	19,908
Augusta County	na	na	na	na	na	na	na	na	na
Bedford County	na	na	na	na	na	na	na	na	na
Chesterfield County	5,274	184	7,303	46	5,984	34	4,021	204	41,164
Fairfax County	18,974	1,727	26,627	1,036	21,055	554	11,740	248	114,751
Fauquier County	na	na	na	na	na	na	na	na	na
Frederick County	na	na	na	na	na	na	na	na	na
Hanover County	2,599	193	2,604	0	1,713	48	1,530	0	15,356
Henrico County	6,610	377	5,375	252	5,160	432	4,042	202	41,771
James City County	na	na	na	na	na	na	na	na	na
Loudoun County	6,164	452	5,917	304	4,096	171	2,551	40	26,838
Montgomery County	873	0	1,209	0	1,043	0	827	0	10,823
Prince William County	5,540	98	6,742	214	5,178	45	2,640	157	35,982
Roanoke County	2,656	0	2,273	277	1,751	0	2,002	84	17,744
Rockingham County	1,202	65	1,264	24	1,792	0	1,383	55	13,070
Spotsylvania County	1,939	0	2,143	134	1,712	53	1,252	0	15,122
Stafford County	1,967	148	1,949	85	1,394	97	1,151	122	12,882
York County	na	na	na	na	na	na	na	na	na
Washington									
Benton County	3,020	288	3,156	27	2,684	105	996	88	27,536
Chelan County	na	na	na	na	na	na	na	na	na
Clallam County	1,998	85	1,696	90	1,533	35	973	22	20,035
Clark County	6,667	358	8,079	502	7,156	156	2,928	39	64,153
Cowlitz County	1,877	47	1,262	63	1,189	239	1,065	41	19,995
Franklin County	na	na	na	na	na	na	na	na	na
Grant County	1,753	0	2,235	0	1,000	0	544	0	11,893
Grays Harbor County	1,014	49	1,577	0	1,608	68	546	0	13,719
Island County	1,524	41	1,652	107	2,162	100	999	0	17,574
King County	34,843	1,549	38,503	1,291	33,598	993	17,815	476	246,878
Kitsap County	3,576	85	3,874	165	4,166	220	2,944	139	42,426
Lewis County	874	0	1,390	120	828	0	656	0	15,553
Pierce County	10,662	777	12,557	280	11,898	578	5,878	201	108,551
Skagit County	2,092	112	2,493	187	1,996	46	1,592	104	22,933
Snohomish County	14,172	534	14,414	593	10,391	134	4,217	292	95,260
Spokane County	6,811	185	8,546	381	8,248	189	3,303	0	73,640
Thurston County	5,007	37	5,120	383	3,761	0	2,170	65	42,477
Whatcom County	3,610	290	4,238	139	3,264	53	2,042	20	32,789
Yakima County	2,614	39	4,331	160	2,730	170	1,707	0	32,103
West Virginia									
Berkeley County	1,104	373	1,608	51	1,419	0	1,332	231	15,457
Cabell County	1,880	93	1,494	0	1,632	0	944	0	17,493
Harrison County	689	0	1,811	0	899	28	525	28	13,049
Kanawha County	2,964	150	3,344	0	2,997	337	2,103	0	36,152
Monongalia County	1,637	150	872	0	1,237	62	866	0	11,203
Raleigh County	na	na	na	na	na	na	na	na	na
Wood County	1,084	81	986	0	1,099	0	1,143	0	17,198
Wisconsin									
Brown County	3,753	207	4,132	77	4,142	74	2,048	0	34,529
Dane County	9,872	824	9,979	388	7,405	510	4,460	85	60,149
Dodge County	1,546	25	1,925	65	1,556	15	1,227	0	13,989
Eau Claire County	1,189	15	1,440	57	1,717	57	1,082	0	13,791
Fond du Lac County	2,436	32	1,936	17	1,440	21	1,152	0	17,387
Jefferson County	1,856	59	1,583	36	1,231	0	850	0	12,282
Kenosha County	2,763	242	2,057	41	1,444	0	1,248	0	24,054
La Crosse County	2,343	29	2,431	15	1,824	0	472	0	17,526
Manitowoc County	1,465	14	1,604	22	1,178	0	1,171	51	15,068
Marathon County	2,744	50	2,778	77	2,347	186	919	12	21,304
Milwaukee County	13,943	585	13,980	541	11,151	453	7,205	335	123,837
Outagamie County	2,742	120	3,454	0	1,834	0	1,186	23	24,540
Ozaukee County	2,218	117	2,337	74	1,738	22	1,582	0	14,060
Portage County	1,263	38	1,124	20	787	0	577	10	10,664
Racine County	2,830	106	3,750	56	2,598	119	1,988	77	30,526
Rock County	2,677	130	2,181	20	2,392	70	1,657	141	24,784
Sheboygan County	1,709	0	2,670	24	1,617	58	1,213	0	18,501
St. Croix County	na	na	na	na	na	na	na	na	na
Walworth County	2,380	108	1,836	88	2,164	69	1,607	50	13,766
Washington County	2,492	135	2,668	0	2,151	189	1,912	89	20,068
Waukesha County	8,322	264	8,829	260	7,684	219	5,001	231	62,882
Winnebago County	2,620	242	3,279	27	2,010	0	1,274	106	25,751
Wood County	1,179	26	621	0	1,190	0	635	11	14,389
Wyoming									
Laramie County	1,559	67	2,197	53	1,343	0	1,247	91	13,754
Natrona County	1,752	0	1,486	0	1,367	0	857	68	9,857

Table F-3: Places—Employment and Labor Force Status, Civilian Labor Force

	60 to 61 Years		62 to 64 Years		65 to 69 Years		70 Years and Over		60 Years and Over Not in the Labor Force
	Employed	Unemployed	Employed	Unemployed	Employed	Unemployed	Employed	Unemployed	
Alabama									
Birmingham city	2,849	259	2,764	98	2,569	79	1,434	44	30,877
Dothan city	1,173	111	1,085	19	909	63	797	10	11,414
Hoover city	na	na	na	na	na	na	na	na	na
Huntsville city	2,930	164	2,954	78	2,203	248	2,849	258	28,048
Mobile city	2,720	24	2,973	75	2,744	38	1,232	44	29,486
Montgomery city	3,490	0	3,055	99	3,384	93	1,483	96	25,837
Tuscaloosa city	1,024	46	1,434	43	1,145	46	1,203	0	11,547
Alaska									
Anchorage municipality	4,319	0	4,490	85	3,909	45	2,794	137	25,187
Arizona									
Avondale city	412	0	535	0	542	0	583	0	6,236
Chandler city	3,647	99	3,451	243	3,205	136	1,365	88	24,772
Flagstaff city	1,021	0	825	0	1,189	0	216	0	6,568
Glendale city	2,214	416	3,191	188	2,421	171	1,909	159	27,452
Goodyear city	na	na	na	na	na	na	na	na	na
Mesa city	5,901	395	5,974	412	5,334	77	4,130	379	76,609
Peoria city	2,670	0	2,856	86	2,151	160	2,208	179	28,329
Phoenix city	19,439	1,427	20,228	1,277	17,220	513	10,318	543	156,888
Scottsdale city	4,828	310	5,892	43	5,983	268	4,111	124	45,590
Surprise city	1,398	27	1,850	341	1,490	72	727	43	27,430
Tempe city	1,770	65	2,454	33	2,512	114	1,462	80	17,529
Tucson city	7,238	274	7,125	692	6,120	324	3,629	43	77,134
Yuma city	855	0	820	0	1,224	0	821	0	13,499
Arkansas									
Fayetteville city	na	na	na	na	na	na	na	na	na
Fort Smith city	1,158	13	1,121	78	900	27	832	31	11,568
Jonesboro city	na	na	na	na	na	na	na	na	na
Little Rock city	3,149	36	4,352	0	3,518	50	2,005	34	25,654
North Little Rock city	na	na	na	na	na	na	na	na	na
Springdale city	na	na	na	na	na	na	na	na	na
California									
Alameda city	1,737	298	2,177	121	830	0	894	0	10,097
Alhambra city	1,143	0	928	43	1,213	130	721	0	13,767
Anaheim city	4,748	578	5,850	449	3,277	146	2,386	165	36,528
Antioch city	1,406	0	2,164	0	1,615	172	732	72	12,708
Bakersfield city	4,886	318	4,494	186	2,828	78	2,640	140	37,549
Baldwin Park city	na	na	na	na	na	na	na	na	na
Bellflower city	na	na	na	na	na	na	na	na	na
Berkeley city	1,337	208	2,306	122	2,480	41	2,031	39	13,830
Buena Park city	na	na	na	na	na	na	na	na	na
Burbank city	1,496	139	2,115	39	1,582	78	1,096	0	14,275
Camarillo city	na	na	na	na	na	na	na	na	na
Carlsbad city	na	na	na	na	na	na	na	na	na
Carson city	1,293	64	1,465	113	1,232	0	685	0	12,188
Chico city	897	0	956	0	1,242	0	921	0	10,256
Chino city	507	0	566	103	468	36	193	0	7,612
Chino Hills city	na	na	na	na	na	na	na	na	na
Chula Vista city	3,774	319	3,102	117	2,942	104	2,609	166	30,936
Citrus Heights city	833	24	1,974	279	1,185	110	1,097	81	13,973
Clovis city	1,015	41	2,566	246	991	0	849	0	10,654
Compton city	565	0	1,254	166	528	0	251	40	7,803
Concord city	1,916	166	2,483	162	2,267	172	1,235	0	15,766
Corona city	2,693	188	2,648	39	2,034	70	1,110	0	16,964
Costa Mesa city	1,365	39	1,525	114	1,385	172	729	41	10,117
Daly City city	1,417	0	1,608	81	1,874	201	1,136	83	17,497
Davis city	na	na	na	na	na	na	na	na	na
Downey city	1,985	337	1,265	0	1,052	195	463	74	13,696
El Cajon city	753	54	1,186	0	837	122	538	0	13,236
El Monte city	1,200	0	1,710	76	757	72	395	0	15,924
Elk Grove city	2,063	39	2,028	84	1,143	0	1,025	24	19,619
Escondido city	2,219	0	2,249	134	1,651	105	812	0	17,633
Fairfield city	1,849	0	1,628	93	1,305	0	928	0	14,070
Folsom city	na	na	na	na	na	na	na	na	na
Fontana city	1,329	0	1,589	92	1,353	181	429	65	18,831
Fremont city	3,026	221	3,325	156	3,476	174	1,248	0	25,858
Fresno city	6,789	621	6,547	311	5,809	337	2,206	38	60,166
Fullerton city	1,632	71	1,814	119	1,513	0	900	69	15,661
Garden Grove city	1,881	278	2,310	231	1,761	24	1,202	0	24,138
Glendale city	3,244	264	3,417	129	3,054	332	1,842	0	33,560
Hawthorne city	1,150	41	1,135	0	1,084	0	1,100	138	7,734
Hayward city	2,531	201	1,572	179	2,088	214	701	0	18,439
Hemet city	na	na	na	na	na	na	na	na	na
Hesperia city	1,167	0	1,316	145	838	81	237	61	9,835
Huntington Beach city	3,590	185	2,572	40	4,277	83	2,688	47	28,596
Indio city	895	102	975	63	592	101	886	71	12,573
Inglewood city	999	138	2,031	104	1,192	0	660	93	11,919
Irvine city	3,517	47	3,400	43	3,186	310	1,940	295	23,246

Table F-3: Places—Employment and Labor Force Status, Civilian Labor Force—*Continued*

	60 to 61 Years		62 to 64 Years		65 to 69 Years		70 Years and Over		60 Years and Over Not in the Labor Force
	Employed	Unemployed	Employed	Unemployed	Employed	Unemployed	Employed	Unemployed	
California—Cont.									
Jurupa Valley city	1,266	41	592	0	648	43	396	48	9,362
Laguna Niguel city	na	na	na	na	na	na	na	na	na
Lake Forest city	895	0	1,233	238	1,771	114	672	83	7,982
Lakewood city	1,327	195	1,175	0	1,621	0	634	44	10,309
Lancaster city	1,454	185	1,318	103	1,565	0	772	0	18,384
Livermore city	na	na	na	na	na	na	na	na	na
Long Beach city	6,534	794	6,215	153	5,469	455	3,401	280	49,585
Los Angeles city	55,721	3,839	60,664	4,494	56,661	3,905	38,233	2,477	437,583
Lynwood city	na	na	na	na	na	na	na	na	na
Manteca city	na	na	na	na	na	na	na	na	na
Menifee city	1,063	92	1,145	59	756	39	862	136	17,659
Merced city	674	40	636	34	766	33	482	0	9,421
Milpitas city	696	0	1,090	28	638	0	607	0	8,567
Mission Viejo city	1,258	81	1,890	73	1,892	155	2,020	43	14,039
Modesto city	2,821	47	3,095	657	2,228	459	1,404	38	30,589
Moreno Valley city	1,900	113	2,485	280	1,414	169	884	100	19,852
Mountain View city	na	na	na	na	na	na	na	na	na
Murrieta city	1,173	36	1,369	125	612	0	467	38	11,349
Napa city	1,377	28	1,615	0	958	129	723	179	12,048
Newport Beach city	na	na	na	na	na	na	na	na	na
Norwalk city	1,560	191	1,716	73	754	94	558	189	12,758
Oakland city	5,209	436	7,714	521	6,611	736	3,929	502	48,611
Oceanside city	1,701	254	2,097	160	2,103	143	1,753	342	28,621
Ontario city	1,220	0	2,000	55	1,105	58	1,006	80	14,663
Orange city	1,705	0	2,239	147	1,708	0	1,195	84	13,970
Oxnard city	1,905	40	2,277	80	2,495	215	655	65	20,178
Palmdale city	2,098	64	1,516	0	1,079	103	421	0	15,014
Palo Alto city	na	na	na	na	na	na	na	na	na
Pasadena city	2,143	42	1,895	156	1,459	65	1,269	51	19,836
Perris city	na	na	na	na	na	na	na	na	na
Pittsburg city	977	0	879	39	537	81	671	39	7,770
Pleasanton city	na	na	na	na	na	na	na	na	na
Pomona city	1,571	39	1,264	181	948	40	635	0	16,144
Rancho Cordova city	773	0	1,210	226	578	0	781	44	8,462
Rancho Cucamonga city	3,600	106	2,023	40	2,181	114	1,251	0	17,433
Redding city	1,231	37	1,451	23	1,351	72	1,124	154	17,784
Redlands city	na	na	na	na	na	na	na	na	na
Redondo Beach city	na	na	na	na	na	na	na	na	na
Redwood City city	1,757	44	1,551	47	1,199	0	1,019	0	9,445
Rialto city	1,055	166	1,080	48	687	0	322	0	9,673
Richmond city	1,737	147	2,825	94	1,700	0	937	0	12,503
Riverside city	4,016	400	5,075	195	3,093	39	1,740	108	32,833
Roseville city	1,234	167	1,695	104	2,123	56	1,624	0	20,809
Sacramento city	6,411	415	5,799	428	5,539	412	2,930	297	62,492
Salinas city	2,430	84	1,799	0	1,140	24	1,023	67	13,957
San Bernardino city	1,850	104	1,378	35	1,515	122	1,378	248	19,876
San Buenaventura (Ventura) city	2,108	33	2,365	90	1,750	46	1,127	82	17,985
San Clemente city	na	na	na	na	na	na	na	na	na
San Diego city	21,529	1,307	23,064	1,376	16,246	1,051	10,470	523	158,061
San Francisco city	12,791	1,026	18,436	1,604	14,220	623	8,542	126	120,805
San Jose city	13,555	1,103	16,012	955	13,050	757	7,685	291	119,547
San Leandro city	na	na	na	na	na	na	na	na	na
San Marcos city	na	na	na	na	na	na	na	na	na
San Mateo city	1,534	0	2,088	300	2,199	155	1,925	164	14,754
San Ramon city	na	na	na	na	na	na	na	na	na
Santa Ana city	3,089	103	3,833	185	2,333	66	1,881	55	28,819
Santa Barbara city	1,994	76	1,632	79	1,879	81	961	0	14,264
Santa Clara city	1,470	145	1,355	114	2,020	0	643	45	15,342
Santa Clarita city	2,366	124	2,827	160	2,304	182	1,568	24	20,140
Santa Maria city	1,119	0	813	44	1,199	165	422	0	9,521
Santa Monica city	1,397	257	2,354	227	2,462	363	1,938	77	13,672
Santa Rosa city	2,560	113	2,389	138	2,501	217	1,782	117	26,309
Simi Valley city	1,480	228	2,666	0	2,512	131	1,325	296	16,545
South Gate city	1,159	74	1,138	139	1,097	24	376	0	9,568
South San Francisco city	na	na	na	na	na	na	na	na	na
Stockton city	3,550	676	4,237	450	3,452	174	1,955	43	36,846
Sunnyvale city	1,702	74	1,847	166	1,694	44	946	0	15,946
Temecula city	1,202	101	1,356	0	1,793	134	1,031	0	11,003
Thousand Oaks city	2,796	155	3,253	57	3,541	312	2,955	112	18,661
Torrance city	2,189	112	2,940	0	2,158	0	1,567	0	24,768
Tracy city	1,168	86	1,029	0	612	0	418	35	6,614
Turlock city	877	242	655	0	1,140	132	325	0	9,655
Tustin city	na	na	na	na	na	na	na	na	na
Union City city	972	83	675	125	953	49	465	0	11,939
Upland city	570	0	1,002	85	1,654	217	503	0	11,219
Vacaville city	1,305	230	1,061	0	1,024	57	776	0	12,521
Vallejo city	2,826	0	3,131	0	1,670	51	965	62	18,687
Victorville city	1,383	253	1,243	0	1,317	0	422	153	11,824

Table F-3: Places—Employment and Labor Force Status, Civilian Labor Force—*Continued*

	60 to 61 Years		62 to 64 Years		65 to 69 Years		70 Years and Over		60 Years and Over Not in the Labor Force
	Employed	Unemployed	Employed	Unemployed	Employed	Unemployed	Employed	Unemployed	
California—Cont.									
Visalia city	1,830	46	939	100	1,776	0	1,148	42	16,686
Vista city	1,651	59	825	123	609	26	357	0	8,517
Walnut Creek city	na	na	na	na	na	na	na	na	na
West Covina city	2,177	95	2,063	137	1,989	109	481	68	15,710
Westminster city	1,916	208	1,803	133	1,172	0	828	0	16,823
Whittier city	1,197	69	882	212	1,026	57	695	0	10,868
Yorba Linda city	1,242	117	1,163	300	2,324	71	784	41	8,483
Yuba City city	1,270	37	494	97	605	0	624	61	8,830
Colorado									
Arvada city	2,498	86	2,393	286	2,537	137	1,093	0	15,273
Aurora city	4,332	183	5,778	26	4,875	73	3,215	0	35,233
Boulder city	1,353	0	2,273	61	1,562	0	447	0	10,167
Centennial city	2,217	114	2,424	35	2,503	160	1,618	0	14,642
Colorado Springs city	6,441	326	7,033	464	5,573	431	2,729	213	59,676
Denver city	7,716	366	9,868	719	9,109	504	4,856	39	73,211
Fort Collins city	2,200	196	2,327	167	2,298	67	901	38	13,459
Greeley city	1,298	83	1,172	0	1,500	54	1,037	0	11,886
Lakewood city	3,070	42	3,467	41	2,340	39	1,233	85	23,401
Longmont city	1,928	357	1,556	0	1,267	65	988	55	11,221
Loveland city	na	na	na	na	na	na	na	na	na
Pueblo city	1,381	93	1,668	43	1,142	157	627	0	19,707
Thornton city	1,768	0	2,208	65	1,697	72	713	117	10,876
Westminster city	1,315	44	2,612	44	1,780	120	1,034	131	14,757
Connecticut									
Bridgeport city	2,291	0	2,197	207	1,745	0	998	239	14,573
Danbury city	1,384	0	1,377	0	1,402	0	642	32	9,705
Hartford city	692	20	1,625	60	720	30	656	28	12,066
New Britain city	521	0	959	75	1,122	77	579	39	8,729
New Haven city	1,725	227	1,962	37	1,696	322	1,245	224	12,334
Norwalk city	1,527	112	2,143	43	1,698	36	1,820	0	10,654
Stamford city	3,169	254	2,624	73	2,984	283	2,370	453	13,179
Waterbury city	2,221	172	1,668	44	1,673	148	960	67	13,137
Delaware									
Wilmington city	797	133	544	29	1,476	0	761	0	8,329
District of Columbia									
Washington city	8,289	593	8,880	787	9,205	356	8,004	277	72,784
Florida									
Boca Raton city	2,062	0	2,751	61	2,208	75	1,626	0	16,582
Boynton Beach city	na	na	na	na	na	na	na	na	na
Cape Coral city	3,682	67	2,671	36	3,238	49	2,386	179	38,796
Clearwater city	2,406	40	1,778	0	2,324	130	2,076	0	22,106
Coral Springs city	2,088	41	2,954	97	2,081	329	1,435	94	12,968
Deerfield Beach city	na	na	na	na	na	na	na	na	na
Delray Beach city	1,562	36	1,158	99	2,677	207	1,430	0	14,519
Deltona city	na	na	na	na	na	na	na	na	na
Fort Lauderdale city	2,820	583	3,855	253	3,912	386	1,967	202	30,640
Fort Myers city	na	na	na	na	na	na	na	na	na
Gainesville city	2,024	29	1,768	0	1,637	0	767	31	12,560
Hialeah city	3,802	71	2,893	102	1,990	133	2,521	229	43,918
Hollywood city	2,856	103	2,018	252	2,534	74	2,154	406	22,861
Homestead city	na	na	na	na	na	na	na	na	na
Jacksonville city	13,128	722	11,926	491	10,233	277	6,558	335	113,823
Kissimmee city	na	na	na	na	na	na	na	na	na
Lakeland city	1,530	130	1,484	73	2,105	0	1,198	89	20,167
Largo city	na	na	na	na	na	na	na	na	na
Lauderhill city	na	na	na	na	na	na	na	na	na
Melbourne city	na	na	na	na	na	na	na	na	na
Miami Beach city	971	113	1,899	0	1,354	0	717	0	15,260
Miami city	6,034	832	8,602	372	7,598	405	5,585	327	66,362
Miami Gardens city	1,537	40	2,499	203	1,916	136	458	0	14,583
Miramar city	2,713	171	2,450	476	1,450	192	1,625	0	12,225
Orlando city	2,196	166	3,266	170	2,619	43	2,099	0	26,076
Palm Bay city	1,211	0	1,074	0	1,176	0	1,087	100	20,344
Palm Coast city	na	na	na	na	na	na	na	na	na
Pembroke Pines city	2,635	45	2,482	0	2,746	87	1,694	0	26,326
Plantation city	na	na	na	na	na	na	na	na	na
Pompano Beach city	630	0	2,236	335	1,208	91	1,286	318	23,066
Port St. Lucie city	2,554	152	2,648	143	2,341	0	2,039	399	37,323
St. Petersburg city	4,348	225	4,325	130	4,855	198	2,786	132	44,083
Sunrise city	1,796	387	1,266	97	1,541	41	932	51	12,608
Tallahassee city	2,412	418	2,505	74	2,357	0	525	0	17,053
Tampa city	5,048	75	4,345	63	3,777	158	2,445	39	45,656
West Palm Beach city	2,148	75	1,915	73	2,271	42	985	90	16,834
Weston city	na	na	na	na	na	na	na	na	na

Table F-3: Places—Employment and Labor Force Status, Civilian Labor Force—*Continued*

	60 to 61 Years		62 to 64 Years		65 to 69 Years		70 Years and Over		60 Years and Over Not in the Labor Force
	Employed	Unemployed	Employed	Unemployed	Employed	Unemployed	Employed	Unemployed	
Georgia									
Albany city	848	30	972	73	730	112	584	120	11,027
Athens-Clarke County unified govt (bal)	1,368	0	1,301	107	1,969	86	534	0	11,644
Atlanta city	3,698	141	6,067	297	4,399	454	2,830	102	55,829
Augusta-Richmond County consolidated govt (bal)	2,474	55	3,624	99	2,232	134	1,201	0	27,279
Columbus city	2,867	35	1,943	59	1,990	78	1,505	0	25,518
Johns Creek city	na	na	na	na	na	na	na	na	na
Macon-Bibb County	2,393	114	2,578	127	1,237	62	804	70	24,036
Roswell city	na	na	na	na	na	na	na	na	na
Sandy Springs city	na	na	na	na	na	na	na	na	na
Savannah city	1,871	129	1,672	157	2,241	49	1,168	108	19,032
Warner Robins city	na	na	na	na	na	na	na	na	na
Hawaii									
Urban Honolulu CDP	6,643	115	5,959	43	7,482	213	5,154	18	62,310
Idaho									
Boise City city	3,897	259	3,265	227	1,632	101	2,936	43	27,873
Meridian city	na	na	na	na	na	na	na	na	na
Nampa city	na	na	na	na	na	na	na	na	na
Illinois									
Aurora city	2,474	43	2,714	0	2,397	115	938	122	15,096
Bloomington city	872	0	856	42	957	0	463	0	9,702
Champaign city	927	150	1,081	0	862	0	981	42	7,572
Chicago city	34,259	4,085	35,634	2,625	29,557	1,668	17,858	1,247	325,191
Decatur city	906	20	1,314	138	1,077	85	604	0	12,677
Elgin city	2,184	0	1,729	84	1,616	0	1,056	0	13,949
Evanston city	625	77	1,985	38	1,689	124	1,040	109	8,844
Joliet city	1,635	0	1,428	0	900	0	847	0	13,211
Naperville city	3,243	229	3,894	63	2,424	34	687	0	14,239
Peoria city	2,378	225	2,009	306	1,959	281	513	0	16,473
Rockford city	2,165	128	3,593	160	1,753	109	1,140	123	23,219
Springfield city	2,190	0	1,721	33	1,566	0	1,462	71	19,225
Waukegan city	756	41	1,358	34	1,075	122	121	0	9,671
Indiana									
Bloomington city	1,244	0	544	0	746	0	594	0	5,584
Carmel city	na	na	na	na	na	na	na	na	na
Evansville city	2,034	331	1,444	0	1,586	101	1,141	53	18,965
Fort Wayne city	3,711	0	3,506	416	3,630	188	2,507	65	32,238
Gary city	916	28	1,156	85	1,036	112	681	81	12,891
Hammond city	1,223	0	1,196	67	785	92	442	0	8,582
Indianapolis city (bal)	12,229	842	12,985	861	10,209	945	6,362	348	97,611
Lafayette city	964	0	749	0	851	0	550	0	8,481
Muncie city	691	0	1,189	49	897	0	675	72	10,473
South Bend city	1,111	158	1,872	82	1,322	46	988	0	13,354
Iowa									
Cedar Rapids city	1,638	130	2,318	0	1,784	52	1,295	0	16,458
Davenport city	1,530	159	1,755	0	1,390	0	1,007	0	12,613
Des Moines city	2,845	209	3,203	173	2,624	161	1,662	0	23,040
Iowa City city	1,453	0	991	0	899	0	240	0	6,640
Sioux City city	1,270	0	1,611	0	1,379	0	589	0	10,728
Waterloo city	1,559	45	1,147	23	857	0	701	128	10,254
Kansas									
Kansas City city	1,875	179	1,742	138	2,412	186	829	78	18,089
Lawrence city	1,500	0	1,419	0	721	0	836	0	8,342
Olathe city	1,431	43	2,292	105	1,583	120	519	0	11,918
Overland Park city	3,490	44	3,753	173	3,698	120	2,150	0	25,196
Topeka city	1,340	0	2,571	94	2,103	162	763	75	19,609
Wichita city	6,227	104	6,166	329	4,809	114	2,913	236	51,429
Kentucky									
Lexington-Fayette urban county	5,578	446	4,576	488	4,150	60	2,235	117	36,994
Louisville/Jefferson County metro govt (bal)	7,778	152	9,397	141	8,747	662	5,536	130	85,181
Louisiana									
Baton Rouge city	3,282	33	3,927	187	3,164	246	1,592	35	30,094
Bossier City city	na	na	na	na	na	na	na	na	na
Kenner city	882	104	2,018	101	1,576	101	891	0	11,733
Lafayette city	1,718	0	2,678	31	1,706	0	1,782	82	15,119
Lake Charles city	800	0	827	62	1,059	112	1,196	0	12,953
New Orleans city	4,862	313	6,399	255	4,501	264	2,986	220	50,904
Shreveport city	3,264	88	2,474	0	3,473	122	2,401	72	28,980
Maine									
Portland city	na	na	na	na	na	na	na	na	na
Maryland									
Baltimore city	7,550	837	9,253	805	7,754	258	6,081	549	79,980
Frederick city	na	na	na	na	na	na	na	na	na

Table F-3: Places—Employment and Labor Force Status, Civilian Labor Force—*Continued*

	60 to 61 Years		62 to 64 Years		65 to 69 Years		70 Years and Over		60 Years and Over Not in the Labor Force
	Employed	Unemployed	Employed	Unemployed	Employed	Unemployed	Employed	Unemployed	
Maryland—Cont.									
Gaithersburg city	na	na	na	na	na	na	na	na	na
Rockville city	na	na	na	na	na	na	na	na	na
Massachusetts									
Boston city	6,747	336	10,170	1,192	7,866	244	4,322	501	69,734
Brockton city	1,560	76	1,561	149	1,704	101	1,455	0	11,430
Cambridge city	1,186	0	2,161	133	2,357	130	1,317	0	8,465
Fall River city	1,194	0	967	0	700	0	575	0	15,997
Lawrence city	681	129	702	237	984	341	351	0	6,913
Lowell city	837	78	1,594	158	1,662	572	348	0	12,057
Lynn city	1,010	365	1,374	37	794	41	435	0	11,579
New Bedford city	1,673	50	1,371	213	1,013	70	523	0	12,923
Newton city	1,814	0	2,375	128	2,972	178	2,343	40	12,881
Quincy city	2,047	73	1,775	148	1,593	283	782	0	13,759
Somerville city	653	79	996	51	824	0	610	0	7,610
Springfield city	2,084	261	1,267	0	1,254	104	956	79	19,156
Worcester city	2,071	193	3,451	201	2,071	146	1,464	60	20,752
Michigan									
Ann Arbor city	1,725	118	2,264	0	1,606	44	1,019	0	11,469
Dearborn city	723	0	1,224	77	1,420	24	1,112	0	13,092
Detroit city	6,025	499	7,058	677	5,338	606	3,604	739	103,596
Farmington Hills city	1,700	46	2,129	73	2,080	46	1,792	0	15,633
Flint city	820	39	944	60	338	0	194	81	14,620
Grand Rapids city	1,996	36	2,388	0	1,841	39	1,176	117	23,373
Kalamazoo city	795	39	507	0	787	45	525	0	7,703
Lansing city	1,168	42	1,450	80	582	109	911	0	14,364
Livonia city	1,940	0	2,177	111	1,852	43	617	0	18,115
Rochester Hills city	1,377	80	1,746	68	1,570	38	1,312	36	11,010
Southfield city	1,116	114	1,881	110	967	51	741	28	13,840
Sterling Heights city	2,181	88	2,684	83	1,415	76	870	0	22,754
Troy city	1,527	66	1,931	129	1,202	0	691	39	13,667
Warren city	2,132	39	1,610	141	1,218	0	679	0	22,771
Westland city	1,032	286	1,208	85	980	0	1,054	139	15,132
Wyoming city	na	na	na	na	na	na	na	na	na
Minnesota									
Bloomington city	na	na	na	na	na	na	na	na	na
Brooklyn Park city	na	na	na	na	na	na	na	na	na
Duluth city	1,802	20	1,549	63	781	109	567	21	14,054
Eagan city	na	na	na	na	na	na	na	na	na
Maple Grove city	na	na	na	na	na	na	na	na	na
Minneapolis city	5,123	224	5,558	38	5,439	40	3,027	36	33,530
Plymouth city	na	na	na	na	na	na	na	na	na
Rochester city	1,509	51	2,917	0	1,477	64	824	0	15,277
St. Cloud city	855	0	888	48	841	0	677	46	7,267
St. Paul city	4,900	188	5,425	220	3,181	0	1,704	0	28,125
Woodbury city	na	na	na	na	na	na	na	na	na
Mississippi									
Gulfport city	na	na	na	na	na	na	na	na	na
Jackson city	1,851	123	2,524	61	1,420	0	1,530	0	21,955
Missouri									
Columbia city	2,207	18	1,453	0	1,336	0	1,335	96	9,766
Independence city	1,528	39	1,628	0	1,874	0	1,123	34	22,343
Kansas City city	5,560	199	6,675	65	5,876	181	4,092	69	58,095
Lee's Summit city	na	na	na	na	na	na	na	na	na
O'Fallon city	na	na	na	na	na	na	na	na	na
Springfield city	1,644	67	2,364	82	2,497	102	1,808	0	24,549
St. Charles city	903	34	1,090	0	565	118	647	51	11,481
St. Joseph city	1,293	61	940	0	1,092	0	705	66	10,473
St. Louis city	4,816	282	5,019	406	3,385	212	1,702	179	40,527
Montana									
Billings city	1,525	81	1,703	61	1,768	90	1,612	0	15,459
Missoula city	na	na	na	na	na	na	na	na	na
Nebraska									
Lincoln city	4,484	125	4,551	55	4,459	23	2,249	56	30,173
Omaha city	7,119	153	8,466	72	5,967	105	4,487	18	51,393
Nevada									
Henderson city	6,371	426	3,826	405	4,502	192	3,295	286	50,442
Las Vegas city	7,096	691	9,127	786	8,252	824	5,033	609	79,907
North Las Vegas city	2,751	442	1,671	101	1,180	116	1,811	39	26,740
Reno city	3,763	46	4,101	256	3,561	231	1,606	221	31,929
Sparks city	1,506	0	1,657	78	1,551	59	791	36	14,762
New Hampshire									
Manchester city	2,258	73	1,825	43	1,607	252	718	0	13,572
Nashua city	1,673	136	2,187	125	993	45	934	84	11,665

Table F-3: Places—Employment and Labor Force Status, Civilian Labor Force—*Continued*

	60 to 61 Years		62 to 64 Years		65 to 69 Years		70 Years and Over		60 Years and Over Not in the Labor Force
	Employed	Unemployed	Employed	Unemployed	Employed	Unemployed	Employed	Unemployed	
New Jersey									
Bayonne city	na	na	na	na	na	na	na	na	na
Camden city	689	44	1,072	0	570	0	237	0	8,427
Clifton city	1,282	73	2,363	101	1,297	51	1,072	157	8,858
East Orange city	1,009	355	1,257	66	1,353	170	714	34	8,083
Elizabeth city	1,551	252	1,237	40	1,304	201	875	137	11,053
Jersey City city	2,655	110	5,059	162	3,232	187	1,647	0	25,987
Newark city	3,701	245	2,918	358	2,300	155	1,522	44	25,385
Passaic city	na	na	na	na	na	na	na	na	na
Paterson city	1,600	188	1,374	0	1,524	229	582	0	17,633
Trenton city	642	0	766	0	763	110	526	127	10,042
Union City city	na	na	na	na	na	na	na	na	na
New Mexico									
Albuquerque city	8,369	704	8,660	837	6,872	481	4,951	328	79,206
Las Cruces city	1,497	201	1,512	0	1,069	0	1,216	0	15,956
Rio Rancho city	1,087	80	1,679	0	1,434	68	653	215	12,325
Santa Fe city	na	na	na	na	na	na	na	na	na
New York									
Albany city	928	112	1,355	65	1,200	62	805	80	13,270
Buffalo city	3,206	145	2,665	200	2,778	353	2,116	123	35,706
Mount Vernon city	985	39	1,282	0	978	0	1,598	30	8,219
New Rochelle city	1,051	84	1,887	119	1,326	84	788	0	10,614
New York city	120,637	9,827	127,509	7,662	115,394	6,526	74,148	3,671	1,111,374
Rochester city	2,461	240	2,186	135	1,887	256	1,288	66	25,675
Schenectady city	579	0	1,307	58	930	79	1,310	592	8,988
Syracuse city	1,375	112	1,847	204	1,591	34	1,347	118	18,690
Yonkers city	2,730	27	3,324	92	4,335	153	2,386	229	31,060
North Carolina									
Asheville city	1,412	44	1,854	0	1,107	72	435	0	16,198
Charlotte city	10,161	419	10,775	1,103	9,989	632	5,400	205	74,914
Concord city	1,459	139	1,228	109	1,015	74	746	0	9,132
Durham city	3,468	422	4,229	254	3,846	72	2,042	0	27,772
Fayetteville city	2,239	92	2,262	74	2,095	56	1,651	54	25,120
Gastonia city	na	na	na	na	na	na	na	na	na
Greensboro city	3,565	100	4,865	201	3,335	249	2,988	127	34,382
Greenville city	1,101	0	711	0	1,793	102	773	0	8,256
High Point city	1,686	376	1,259	0	1,213	62	1,403	79	12,562
Jacksonville city	na	na	na	na	na	na	na	na	na
Raleigh city	6,358	74	5,461	238	6,152	168	3,400	101	38,146
Wilmington city	1,090	56	2,550	0	1,533	94	1,005	0	15,868
Winston-Salem city	3,500	59	2,759	100	3,217	389	1,863	0	32,802
North Dakota									
Bismarck city	818	67	957	0	1,181	0	1,311	0	9,573
Fargo city	1,221	0	2,860	117	1,484	86	1,266	141	11,112
Ohio									
Akron city	4,000	98	3,934	0	3,022	46	1,432	281	27,963
Canton city	1,104	201	1,029	86	823	0	860	290	10,682
Cincinnati city	4,234	161	4,114	201	4,044	21	2,554	125	37,143
Cleveland city	4,813	789	5,325	520	3,193	231	2,272	81	55,024
Columbus city	9,963	626	13,728	123	9,375	228	4,942	473	78,156
Dayton city	1,662	112	1,966	161	2,036	45	626	40	17,233
Lorain city	507	0	516	51	710	52	283	0	10,571
Parma city	na	na	na	na	na	na	na	na	na
Toledo city	3,901	214	4,640	193	3,052	142	1,534	0	40,914
Youngstown city	768	0	397	0	684	20	597	27	12,205
Oklahoma									
Broken Arrow city	2,071	83	1,703	40	1,993	187	1,051	0	10,843
Edmond city	2,012	41	1,990	0	1,497	0	1,061	0	10,293
Lawton city	1,133	0	1,014	0	702	66	695	84	10,993
Norman city	1,545	63	2,414	0	1,971	79	983	0	13,231
Oklahoma City city	8,153	230	9,730	260	9,379	241	7,869	295	71,031
Tulsa city	6,671	171	7,799	146	6,143	44	5,219	353	52,244
Oregon									
Beaverton city	1,502	59	1,504	47	1,108	0	875	0	11,042
Bend city	na	na	na	na	na	na	na	na	na
Eugene city	2,613	148	2,636	166	2,645	65	1,021	0	22,631
Gresham city	1,919	173	1,500	0	1,343	0	779	90	15,874
Hillsboro city	1,870	0	976	0	973	0	478	0	10,755
Medford city	1,793	317	1,256	91	1,113	148	465	53	15,019
Portland city	9,588	549	10,676	459	7,649	119	4,061	71	75,632
Salem city	2,992	181	3,680	61	2,385	205	1,411	39	22,256
Pennsylvania									
Allentown city	1,536	138	1,197	0	1,792	322	1,124	65	14,406
Bethlehem city	1,319	136	1,300	0	616	43	1,018	0	12,250
Erie city	1,410	123	1,458	53	1,227	68	579	67	14,282
Philadelphia city	19,300	965	20,252	1,034	16,677	1,004	11,508	662	209,301
Pittsburgh city	4,235	90	5,070	100	3,929	107	2,973	23	42,256
Reading city	677	32	764	199	923	40	247	0	10,162

Table F-3: Places—Employment and Labor Force Status, Civilian Labor Force—*Continued*

	60 to 61 Years		62 to 64 Years		65 to 69 Years		70 Years and Over		60 Years and Over Not in the Labor Force
	Employed	Unemployed	Employed	Unemployed	Employed	Unemployed	Employed	Unemployed	
Pennsylvania—Cont.									
Scranton city	636	43	1,297	112	1,164	0	740	0	13,850
Rhode Island									
Cranston city	1,474	100	2,437	91	1,283	0	1,242	115	14,503
Pawtucket city	809	105	671	0	504	73	355	42	8,482
Providence city	1,759	107	2,336	34	1,617	0	1,483	238	15,815
Warwick city	2,037	143	1,489	24	2,050	32	1,085	106	14,782
South Carolina									
Charleston city	1,877	208	2,680	77	2,066	0	1,061	74	17,074
Columbia city	1,405	28	1,542	90	1,607	147	908	0	12,241
North Charleston city	1,488	75	997	128	1,153	20	860	38	11,508
Rock Hill city	na	na	na	na	na	na	na	na	na
South Dakota									
Rapid City city	na	na	na	na	na	na	na	na	na
Sioux Falls city	2,022	40	3,393	0	3,367	25	2,540	116	17,586
Tennessee									
Chattanooga city	2,397	112	3,425	0	2,615	0	2,198	0	27,363
Clarksville city	1,176	0	1,404	137	1,024	0	653	0	13,214
Franklin city	na	na	na	na	na	na	na	na	na
Jackson city	799	0	943	0	1,112	0	600	0	8,434
Johnson City city	731	112	855	128	1,137	0	761	95	11,333
Knoxville city	1,697	0	1,968	34	2,440	226	1,555	0	26,343
Memphis city	8,660	624	9,548	187	8,046	468	6,040	126	78,210
Murfreesboro city	1,256	227	1,676	0	1,282	137	745	46	11,286
Nashville-Davidson metropolitan govt (bal)	10,480	283	9,496	163	9,338	461	5,937	269	68,353
Texas									
Abilene city	1,712	0	1,856	50	1,616	0	1,465	0	14,691
Allen city	na	na	na	na	na	na	na	na	na
Amarillo city	2,577	21	2,813	84	3,087	41	2,178	0	23,522
Arlington city	5,875	0	4,631	186	5,430	76	3,217	0	37,015
Austin city	12,422	695	12,955	974	10,258	451	6,426	26	70,578
Baytown city	na	na	na	na	na	na	na	na	16,169
Beaumont city	1,543	0	1,505	54	1,136	34	922	0	16,169
Brownsville city	1,083	0	1,633	35	1,514	93	748	59	22,202
Bryan city	na	na	na	na	na	na	na	na	na
Carrollton city	2,764	81	2,636	33	1,526	0	1,190	0	11,665
College Station city	na	na	na	na	na	na	na	na	na
Conroe city	na	na	na	na	na	na	na	na	na
Corpus Christi city	5,706	373	5,725	394	3,841	0	3,074	70	42,648
Dallas city	14,625	349	16,024	955	14,964	631	10,983	567	121,159
Denton city	1,902	299	1,509	166	2,293	162	510	0	11,379
Edinburg city	na	na	na	na	na	na	na	na	na
El Paso city	8,060	409	7,872	258	6,151	142	5,813	314	86,337
Fort Worth city	8,095	611	8,572	141	8,077	307	4,978	177	74,299
Frisco city	1,476	138	1,823	384	1,155	0	512	31	10,006
Garland city	3,015	234	4,383	116	3,765	0	1,867	228	26,904
Grand Prairie city	2,899	130	2,618	0	2,181	101	974	0	14,032
Harlingen city	na	na	na	na	na	na	na	na	na
Houston city	27,082	1,211	32,938	2,670	26,979	1,288	19,834	538	211,174
Irving city	2,176	115	2,760	105	2,782	70	1,420	37	16,460
Killeen city	822	44	1,663	20	949	116	398	0	8,235
Laredo city	1,895	60	2,041	22	1,771	0	1,179	0	23,965
League City city	na	na	na	na	na	na	na	na	na
Lewisville city	na	na	na	na	na	na	na	na	na
Longview city	547	203	1,528	0	1,569	0	1,237	41	10,938
Lubbock city	2,361	70	3,008	28	3,761	0	2,534	28	27,361
McAllen city	1,956	257	1,464	188	1,753	0	827	0	13,789
McKinney city	na	na	na	na	na	na	na	na	na
Mesquite city	3,804	0	2,452	85	1,707	175	910	0	13,713
Midland city	na	na	na	na	na	na	na	na	na
Mission city	na	na	na	na	na	na	na	na	na
Missouri City city	na	na	na	na	na	na	na	na	na
New Braunfels city	na	na	na	na	na	na	na	na	na
North Richland Hills city	na	na	na	na	na	na	na	na	na
Odessa city	1,519	39	1,797	68	2,021	115	819	0	11,706
Pasadena city	2,577	282	2,509	0	1,646	0	1,310	50	15,478
Pearland city	na	na	na	na	na	na	na	na	na
Pharr city	na	na	na	na	na	na	na	na	na
Plano city	5,408	474	5,662	292	5,294	395	3,029	113	29,954
Richardson city	2,176	42	2,536	82	1,923	77	1,548	0	13,571
Round Rock city	1,957	235	904	129	1,812	34	601	90	8,824
San Angelo city	1,150	26	939	68	855	0	1,598	0	14,225
San Antonio city	17,880	1,127	19,891	769	16,778	871	11,545	518	171,207
Sugar Land city	na	na	na	na	na	na	na	na	na
Temple city	na	na	na	na	na	na	na	na	na
Tyler city	1,818	41	1,625	0	1,052	79	1,329	137	15,427

Table F-3: Places—Employment and Labor Force Status, Civilian Labor Force—*Continued*

	60 to 61 Years		62 to 64 Years		65 to 69 Years		70 Years and Over		60 Years and Over Not in the Labor Force
	Employed	Unemployed	Employed	Unemployed	Employed	Unemployed	Employed	Unemployed	
Texas—Cont.									
Victoria city	na	na	na	na	na	na	na	na	na
Waco city	1,950	169	1,058	144	1,166	143	926	31	15,813
Wichita Falls city	1,992	74	1,614	37	1,631	0	1,074	44	12,283
Utah									
Layton city	na	na	na	na	na	na	na	na	na
Ogden city	1,193	119	460	33	1,159	65	568	0	8,703
Orem city	907	0	1,112	150	872	0	198	0	7,278
Provo city	617	0	784	0	854	0	559	46	7,311
Salt Lake City city	2,618	246	2,711	0	2,623	116	1,570	95	17,905
Sandy city	na	na	na	na	na	na	na	na	na
St. George city	na	na	na	na	na	na	na	na	na
West Jordan city	1,463	0	1,889	0	930	0	644	35	6,670
West Valley City city	1,459	264	1,252	105	1,225	0	989	0	8,668
Virginia									
Alexandria city	2,700	151	3,424	169	2,459	40	1,402	46	12,556
Chesapeake city	3,310	25	2,855	86	2,770	37	1,953	49	28,237
Hampton city	2,109	309	2,983	188	1,691	101	1,599	37	18,108
Lynchburg city	1,283	51	855	0	1,062	0	721	0	10,886
Newport News city	3,571	215	2,420	138	2,350	139	1,080	0	21,241
Norfolk city	2,838	301	3,490	88	2,466	177	1,316	0	25,382
Portsmouth city	2,003	88	1,260	16	1,054	66	928	72	13,109
Richmond city	3,480	117	3,997	500	2,643	118	2,198	0	25,294
Roanoke city	2,004	0	2,113	127	1,894	0	955	0	15,125
Suffolk city	1,488	140	1,691	83	1,513	58	1,230	17	10,661
Virginia Beach city	7,180	353	8,109	359	6,324	255	3,963	237	53,661
Washington									
Auburn city	na	na	na	na	na	na	na	na	na
Bellevue city	1,576	98	2,968	243	2,678	113	1,886	72	18,484
Bellingham city	1,099	58	1,442	64	1,452	0	769	0	11,317
Everett city	1,747	97	1,297	137	471	0	548	0	10,981
Federal Way city	1,445	0	1,525	64	1,628	0	504	0	12,477
Kennewick city	na	na	na	na	na	na	na	na	na
Kent city	1,642	0	2,123	124	1,373	0	1,048	0	12,447
Kirkland city	na	na	na	na	na	na	na	na	na
Marysville city	na	na	na	na	na	na	na	na	na
Pasco city	na	na	na	na	na	na	na	na	na
Renton city	1,136	58	1,849	101	705	53	330	0	9,944
Seattle city	11,101	719	12,184	122	11,946	670	6,443	177	77,186
Spokane city	2,513	59	3,523	123	3,303	48	974	0	31,265
Spokane Valley city	1,066	0	1,532	95	1,285	98	584	0	13,829
Tacoma city	1,989	282	3,599	165	3,474	374	1,492	123	25,346
Vancouver city	2,457	199	3,017	118	2,437	46	1,034	0	24,568
Yakima city	1,000	0	1,847	0	1,234	121	543	0	12,658
Wisconsin									
Appleton city	1,767	0	1,155	0	639	0	477	23	8,336
Eau Claire city	na	na	na	na	na	na	na	na	na
Green Bay city	1,451	112	1,451	35	1,801	61	690	0	13,122
Kenosha city	1,370	0	1,284	1	812	0	475	0	14,293
Madison city	4,721	572	3,762	228	3,403	128	1,684	0	26,542
Milwaukee city	7,377	400	7,081	207	5,432	344	4,111	291	66,680
Oshkosh city	na	na	na	na	na	na	na	na	na
Racine city	938	66	1,020	0	786	0	398	0	10,553
Waukesha city	1,446	41	1,234	0	747	40	936	168	7,558

Table F-4: Metropolitan/Micropolitan Statistical Areas—Employment and Labor Force Status, Civilian Labor Force

	60 to 61 Years		62 to 64 Years		65 to 69 Years		70 Years and Over		60 Years and Over Not in the Labor Force
	Employed	Unemployed	Employed	Unemployed	Employed	Unemployed	Employed	Unemployed	
Aberdeen, WA Micro Area	1,014	49	1,577	0	1,608	68	546	0	13,719
Abilene, TX Metro Area	2,406	19	2,655	111	2,544	18	2,285	0	22,919
Adrian, MI Micro Area	2,007	95	1,647	0	1,096	14	938	0	17,100
Akron, OH Metro Area	14,027	340	14,837	469	11,522	421	7,865	724	109,350
Alamogordo, NM Micro Area	1,190	0	850	8	641	86	444	30	11,125
Albany, GA Metro Area	2,699	196	2,467	106	2,004	167	1,665	190	23,405
Albany, OR Metro Area	2,035	190	1,606	85	1,534	64	1,068	49	22,552
Albany-Schenectady-Troy, NY Metro Area	13,289	598	17,494	653	14,033	613	9,719	792	138,194
Albertville, AL Micro Area	1,601	10	1,097	47	706	33	1,105	5	17,035
Albuquerque, NM Metro Area	14,296	933	14,394	952	12,045	884	8,938	815	139,020
Alexandria, LA Metro Area	2,304	68	1,894	32	2,222	84	804	12	24,379
Allentown-Bethlehem-Easton, PA-NJ Metro Area	15,685	1,047	16,757	717	14,084	1,475	9,496	335	137,535
Altoona, PA Metro Area	2,272	53	2,120	41	1,993	54	1,673	49	25,082
Amarillo, TX Metro Area	3,669	21	3,816	89	3,880	290	2,718	0	32,298
Ames, IA Metro Area	1,269	0	1,412	0	1,104	29	716	0	10,018
Anchorage, AK Metro Area	5,978	108	6,599	324	5,277	174	3,859	263	34,734
Ann Arbor, MI Metro Area	5,359	282	6,574	179	5,396	417	3,584	0	43,029
Anniston-Oxford-Jacksonville, AL Metro Area	2,453	251	1,502	0	1,626	0	1,474	121	20,135
Appleton, WI Metro Area	3,738	120	4,072	0	2,388	0	1,521	23	31,315
Asheville, NC Metro Area	6,328	175	8,655	43	6,732	197	3,804	161	94,492
Ashtabula, OH Micro Area	2,139	40	1,872	95	1,037	153	784	0	18,621
Athens, TX Micro Area	1,458	266	719	0	770	28	1,178	0	17,987
Athens-Clarke County, GA Metro Area	2,761	190	2,658	144	3,441	125	891	6	23,886
Atlanta-Sandy Springs-Roswell, GA Metro Area	76,667	4,323	84,445	3,854	71,017	3,387	37,872	1,557	628,404
Atlantic City-Hammonton, NJ Metro Area	5,093	543	6,125	675	4,377	438	3,142	334	43,289
Auburn, NY Micro Area	1,394	99	1,309	18	1,353	0	1,137	0	13,188
Auburn-Opelika, AL Metro Area	1,541	0	1,854	151	1,764	172	870	0	18,043
Augusta-Richmond County, GA-SC Metro Area	8,516	477	11,357	300	7,732	483	4,561	27	91,619
Augusta-Waterville, ME Micro Area	2,431	74	2,517	99	2,184	112	1,211	47	21,894
Austin-Round Rock, TX Metro Area	27,372	1,632	28,707	1,923	23,953	919	13,988	250	185,365
Bakersfield, CA Metro Area	9,228	604	7,886	301	5,990	369	5,044	140	97,973
Baltimore-Columbia-Towson, MD Metro Area	45,331	1,817	53,695	2,653	50,216	1,730	31,575	1,420	374,354
Bangor, ME Metro Area	3,031	0	2,745	168	2,726	93	1,456	50	25,886
Barnstable Town, MA Metro Area	4,338	231	7,997	233	7,158	587	5,542	153	54,221
Baton Rouge, LA Metro Area	10,577	386	12,173	601	10,490	376	7,327	95	104,898
Battle Creek, MI Metro Area	2,482	73	1,836	0	1,156	139	882	85	25,118
Bay City, MI Metro Area	1,648	36	902	60	1,484	15	593	0	21,584
Beaumont-Port Arthur, TX Metro Area	5,635	366	5,706	144	4,473	116	3,548	57	63,658
Beaver Dam, WI Micro Area	1,546	25	1,925	65	1,556	15	1,227	0	13,989
Beckley, WV Metro Area	1,565	199	1,719	106	1,664	0	1,093	0	25,356
Bellingham, WA Metro Area	3,610	290	4,238	139	3,264	53	2,042	20	32,789
Bend-Redmond, OR Metro Area	4,082	0	3,554	228	2,533	355	1,258	140	32,118
Billings, MT Metro Area	2,803	149	3,269	89	3,146	90	2,592	18	25,458
Binghamton, NY Metro Area	4,296	61	4,855	351	4,424	130	2,265	0	45,704
Birmingham-Hoover, AL Metro Area	16,625	810	17,289	248	17,298	508	11,184	227	175,390
Bismarck, ND Metro Area	1,626	67	2,459	71	1,864	0	1,789	0	17,669
Blacksburg-Christiansburg-Radford, VA Metro Area	2,255	42	2,720	0	2,448	0	1,655	124	26,147
Bloomington, IL Metro Area	2,787	11	2,367	65	2,372	52	2,034	0	22,709
Bloomington, IN Metro Area	2,329	0	2,455	70	3,368	0	1,580	64	17,804
Bloomsburg-Berwick, PA Metro Area	1,897	22	1,290	64	898	0	849	19	15,909
Bluefield, WV-VA Micro Area	1,106	62	2,461	0	1,709	0	1,043	73	22,918
Boise City, ID Metro Area	9,153	409	11,265	489	6,719	184	5,548	143	91,594
Boston-Cambridge-Newton, MA-NH Metro Area	85,810	4,569	99,385	5,293	88,472	4,370	58,798	2,597	624,906
Boulder, CO Metro Area	6,182	357	8,256	133	5,095	171	2,358	55	36,381
Bowling Green, KY Metro Area	2,048	49	2,098	79	1,846	8	1,620	78	22,677
Bozeman, MT Micro Area	1,658	0	1,362	0	1,182	24	729	33	11,031
Brainerd, MN Micro Area	1,682	45	1,757	68	1,464	16	1,365	9	20,561
Branson, MO Micro Area	1,226	187	1,640	216	1,174	75	1,177	81	20,826
Bremerton-Silverdale, WA Metro Area	3,576	85	3,874	165	4,166	220	2,944	139	42,426
Bridgeport-Stamford-Norwalk, CT Metro Area	19,233	869	18,463	692	19,326	882	14,297	1,890	118,972
Brownsville-Harlingen, TX Metro Area	4,395	178	4,001	154	3,317	182	2,901	262	56,007
Brunswick, GA Metro Area	1,464	0	1,877	69	2,111	0	995	0	21,422
Buffalo-Cheektowaga-Niagara Falls, NY Metro Area	20,108	513	20,684	689	17,336	1,000	11,540	445	195,030
Burlington, NC Metro Area	2,279	216	2,308	164	2,798	56	1,667	88	24,710
Burlington-South Burlington, VT Metro Area	4,574	150	4,686	308	3,919	13	2,818	173	26,245
California-Lexington Park, MD Metro Area	2,108	0	2,045	0	979	0	838	0	13,856
Canton-Massillon, OH Metro Area	7,468	542	7,485	131	7,308	127	4,435	331	73,694
Cape Coral-Fort Myers, FL Metro Area	12,511	597	11,879	734	14,036	593	11,908	674	177,188
Cape Girardeau, MO-IL Metro Area	2,046	0	1,357	98	1,630	0	943	130	16,891
Carbondale-Marion, IL Metro Area	1,137	229	1,760	48	1,675	56	1,131	0	20,722
Carson City, NV Metro Area	na	na	na	na	na	na	na	na	na
Casper, WY Metro Area	1,752	0	1,486	0	1,367	0	857	68	9,857
Cedar Rapids, IA Metro Area	4,506	173	5,198	108	4,307	120	3,184	0	37,482
Centralia, WA Micro Area	874	0	1,390	120	828	0	656	0	15,553
Chambersburg-Waynesboro, PA Metro Area	2,895	0	2,601	50	2,659	142	1,787	70	27,701
Champaign-Urbana, IL Metro Area	3,569	471	3,486	261	3,450	0	2,799	42	27,547
Charleston, WV Metro Area	3,313	150	3,439	0	3,084	337	2,158	0	43,895
Charleston-Mattoon, IL Micro Area	1,050	70	1,260	0	779	0	515	0	10,217

Table F-4: Metropolitan/Micropolitan Statistical Areas—Employment and Labor Force Status, Civilian Labor Force—*Continued*

	60 to 61 Years		62 to 64 Years		65 to 69 Years		70 Years and Over		60 Years and Over Not in the Labor Force
	Employed	Unemployed	Employed	Unemployed	Employed	Unemployed	Employed	Unemployed	
Charleston-North Charleston, SC Metro Area	12,234	733	11,413	669	9,433	311	5,819	162	101,871
Charlotte-Concord-Gastonia, NC-SC Metro Area	33,854	2,036	35,215	3,048	31,380	1,858	19,980	509	297,678
Charlottesville, VA Metro Area	3,958	151	4,640	213	4,200	159	2,758	174	34,621
Chattanooga, TN-GA Metro Area	9,217	326	9,754	478	8,978	430	6,351	213	89,229
Cheyenne, WY Metro Area	1,559	67	2,197	53	1,343	0	1,247	91	13,754
Chicago-Naperville-Elgin, IL-IN-WI Metro Area	150,803	9,721	161,924	8,710	136,970	7,011	85,252	3,779	1,218,872
Chico, CA Metro Area	3,604	274	4,279	298	2,916	256	2,857	70	38,988
Chillicothe, OH Micro Area	814	52	1,254	0	687	15	595	0	13,504
Cincinnati, OH-KY-IN Metro Area	35,753	1,348	35,548	988	34,048	1,393	20,993	1,007	297,168
Claremont-Lebanon, NH-VT Micro Area	5,513	217	6,489	295	6,462	165	4,637	13	35,911
Clarksburg, WV Micro Area	1,057	0	2,238	0	1,305	28	955	28	17,575
Clarksville, TN-KY Metro Area	2,347	64	3,063	210	2,964	418	1,252	0	30,807
Clearlake, CA Micro Area	na	na	na	na	na	na	na	na	na
Cleveland, TN Metro Area	1,784	56	1,674	0	1,117	0	1,379	85	21,749
Cleveland-Elyria, OH Metro Area	37,839	2,418	39,834	1,216	35,014	1,050	21,728	1,079	340,098
Coeur d'Alene, ID Metro Area	2,279	240	3,470	545	1,942	356	1,075	226	26,808
College Station-Bryan, TX Metro Area	3,581	386	2,443	0	2,381	36	1,851	78	24,476
Colorado Springs, CO Metro Area	9,619	434	11,322	610	8,610	688	4,442	329	84,953
Columbia, MO Metro Area	2,933	29	3,405	283	2,036	0	1,837	96	17,912
Columbia, SC Metro Area	11,130	251	13,997	670	13,277	653	6,648	262	106,166
Columbus, GA-AL Metro Area	4,593	245	4,072	106	3,436	78	2,388	18	41,045
Columbus, IN Metro Area	na	na	na	na	na	na	na	na	na
Columbus, OH Metro Area	28,115	1,174	35,519	662	27,285	520	17,138	710	239,667
Concord, NH Micro Area	3,064	75	3,728	51	2,277	24	2,304	137	22,451
Cookeville, TN Micro Area	957	0	1,709	0	1,509	21	619	0	21,290
Coos Bay, OR Micro Area	na	na	na	na	na	na	na	na	na
Corning, NY Micro Area	2,068	153	1,355	73	1,493	38	1,012	63	17,904
Corpus Christi, TX Metro Area	7,129	530	7,464	484	6,190	71	4,507	70	63,038
Corvallis, OR Metro Area	1,555	88	1,568	51	1,099	167	910	0	12,577
Crestview-Fort Walton Beach-Destin, FL Metro Area	3,659	136	4,572	39	4,163	137	3,332	46	40,712
Cullman, AL Micro Area	na	na	na	na	na	na	na	na	na
Cumberland, MD-WV Metro Area	1,244	58	2,242	38	1,438	68	589	55	20,156
Dallas-Fort Worth-Arlington, TX Metro Area	96,323	3,650	100,209	4,769	93,946	3,479	57,836	1,760	695,904
Dalton, GA Metro Area	2,097	254	1,144	139	1,263	98	1,366	0	18,707
Danville, IL Metro Area	1,219	198	1,477	0	966	65	844	0	15,179
Danville, VA Micro Area	1,565	0	1,895	145	1,985	0	1,440	60	21,206
Daphne-Fairhope-Foley, AL Metro Area	3,661	133	4,626	0	3,243	174	2,150	0	38,127
Davenport-Moline-Rock Island, IA-IL Metro Area	6,457	335	7,049	517	5,185	167	3,890	18	64,651
Dayton, OH Metro Area	13,680	475	15,841	709	11,893	254	10,519	141	131,577
Decatur, AL Metro Area	1,822	56	2,994	165	1,793	99	700	0	26,857
Decatur, IL Metro Area	2,333	36	2,111	138	1,786	189	955	13	19,330
Deltona-Daytona Beach-Ormond Beach, FL Metro Area	10,560	325	10,706	284	11,516	536	7,043	559	153,408
Denver-Aurora-Lakewood, CO Metro Area	42,210	1,414	51,425	1,973	44,102	1,613	23,153	713	315,857
Des Moines-West Des Moines, IA Metro Area	10,752	416	11,099	402	9,208	262	5,814	219	69,956
Detroit-Warren-Dearborn, MI Metro Area	67,014	3,274	69,222	3,584	49,479	2,054	36,281	2,110	685,292
Dothan, AL Metro Area	2,396	123	2,226	32	1,890	75	1,384	10	26,462
Dover, DE Metro Area	2,532	159	2,778	0	2,377	27	1,261	41	26,059
DuBois, PA Micro Area	1,305	166	1,334	202	1,347	34	1,029	55	16,209
Dubuque, IA Metro Area	1,821	0	2,031	0	1,735	37	1,310	0	14,826
Duluth, MN-WI Metro Area	4,733	114	5,217	152	3,814	172	2,363	97	51,332
Dunn, NC Micro Area	1,582	0	896	0	917	10	728	0	15,090
Durham-Chapel Hill, NC Metro Area	8,491	422	9,642	368	7,513	192	5,277	6	72,226
East Stroudsburg, PA Metro Area	2,465	104	3,749	158	2,622	457	1,951	408	25,423
Eau Claire, WI Metro Area	2,601	81	2,546	94	2,833	57	1,715	87	24,237
El Centro, CA Metro Area	1,472	35	2,451	436	1,591	34	1,087	114	22,586
El Paso, TX Metro Area	9,400	616	9,492	405	6,401	161	6,243	314	100,316
Elizabeth City, NC Micro Area	691	0	789	36	1,145	172	816	23	10,870
Elizabethtown-Fort Knox, KY Metro Area	1,274	38	2,261	122	2,005	0	881	75	20,422
Elkhart-Goshen, IN Metro Area	2,875	0	3,316	37	2,516	107	2,264	100	26,262
Elmira, NY Metro Area	1,463	0	1,461	75	1,294	93	865	37	16,246
Erie, PA Metro Area	5,134	184	4,502	158	3,496	251	2,424	175	45,957
Eugene, OR Metro Area	5,990	369	6,810	366	6,829	137	2,853	138	64,693
Eureka-Arcata-Fortuna, CA Micro Area	2,517	691	2,388	149	1,852	105	1,322	58	23,055
Evansville, IN-KY Metro Area	5,356	413	5,960	84	4,930	117	2,952	131	50,597
Fairbanks, AK Metro Area	1,581	139	1,387	79	1,480	0	636	0	7,812
Fargo, ND-MN Metro Area	3,293	5	5,140	130	3,439	86	2,184	141	23,751
Faribault-Northfield, MN Micro Area	948	14	1,634	0	1,335	30	683	0	8,208
Farmington, MO Micro Area	na	na	na	na	na	na	na	na	na
Farmington, NM Metro Area	1,553	42	1,743	34	2,115	202	1,477	0	15,728
Fayetteville, NC Metro Area	3,732	92	3,816	127	3,405	56	2,276	54	43,807
Fayetteville-Springdale-Rogers, AR-MO Metro Area	7,133	187	6,910	76	5,473	49	4,540	111	62,592
Findlay, OH Micro Area	1,297	0	1,013	45	754	80	1,131	0	11,938
Flagstaff, AZ Metro Area	2,500	0	2,324	51	1,966	0	857	0	15,997
Flint, MI Metro Area	4,258	140	5,724	399	3,582	112	2,418	150	75,432
Florence, SC Metro Area	4,171	169	3,921	281	3,383	35	2,076	21	34,164
Florence-Muscle Shoals, AL Metro Area	1,998	194	2,036	17	1,875	44	1,469	159	29,428
Fond du Lac, WI Metro Area	2,436	32	1,936	17	1,440	21	1,152	0	17,387

Table F-4: Metropolitan/Micropolitan Statistical Areas—Employment and Labor Force Status, Civilian Labor Force—*Continued*

	60 to 61 Years		62 to 64 Years		65 to 69 Years		70 Years and Over		60 Years and Over Not in the Labor Force
	Employed	Unemployed	Employed	Unemployed	Employed	Unemployed	Employed	Unemployed	
Forest City, NC Micro Area...	na	na	na	na	na	na	na	na	na
Fort Collins, CO Metro Area...	5,253	465	6,125	327	4,995	242	3,167	317	43,938
Fort Smith, AR-OK Metro Area..	3,402	228	4,005	167	3,654	73	2,359	112	46,226
Fort Wayne, IN Metro Area...	6,894	76	5,650	504	5,942	326	4,877	65	57,931
Frankfort, KY Micro Area..	na	na	na	na	na	na	na	na	na
Fresno, CA Metro Area...	11,958	1,239	13,168	820	10,061	452	6,618	38	113,983
Gadsden, AL Metro Area...	1,080	0	2,270	23	1,585	0	1,573	43	18,271
Gainesville, FL Metro Area...	4,192	228	4,639	57	3,615	33	2,221	101	35,707
Gainesville, GA Metro Area..	2,566	0	2,887	48	2,406	0	1,951	105	25,968
Gallup, NM Micro Area..	1,111	17	877	0	400	63	1,069	0	8,231
Gettysburg, PA Metro Area...	1,881	68	2,511	55	1,791	71	947	0	18,177
Glens Falls, NY Metro Area..	2,428	34	2,781	114	1,789	102	2,001	58	24,547
Glenwood Springs, CO Micro Area.................................	na	na	na	na	na	na	na	na	na
Goldsboro, NC Metro Area...	1,239	126	1,410	119	1,375	79	1,174	67	18,873
Grand Forks, ND-MN Metro Area....................................	1,511	231	2,164	13	1,432	57	910	12	12,977
Grand Island, NE Metro Area..	na	na	na	na	na	na	na	na	na
Grand Junction, CO Metro Area......................................	2,681	668	3,049	0	2,277	161	1,492	82	25,275
Grand Rapids-Wyoming, MI Metro Area...........................	16,665	616	16,219	361	13,049	590	7,964	535	137,338
Grants Pass, OR Metro Area...	na	na	na	na	na	na	na	na	na
Great Falls, MT Metro Area..	1,118	0	1,753	0	1,766	94	1,076	0	13,321
Greeley, CO Metro Area..	4,958	83	3,901	0	4,403	54	2,484	262	29,097
Green Bay, WI Metro Area..	4,832	207	5,455	103	4,910	118	2,489	0	45,987
Greeneville, TN Micro Area..	1,118	232	1,200	0	1,733	198	935	0	13,424
Greenfield Town, MA Micro Area.....................................	2,079	0	2,123	156	1,965	0	1,072	0	12,085
Greensboro-High Point, NC Metro Area...........................	11,743	662	11,733	242	10,381	556	8,936	290	110,761
Greenville, NC Metro Area..	2,210	126	1,539	0	2,914	157	1,515	0	19,607
Greenville-Anderson-Mauldin, SC Metro Area..................	11,862	559	14,031	658	12,226	324	7,851	264	136,431
Greenwood, SC Micro Area..	1,369	81	1,746	148	1,321	34	907	0	17,192
Gulfport-Biloxi-Pascagoula, MS Metro Area....................	4,767	266	6,465	555	4,767	75	2,315	359	58,187
Hagerstown-Martinsburg, MD-WV Metro Area.................	3,202	819	4,014	111	3,569	109	2,666	231	38,885
Hammond, LA Metro Area...	1,473	0	976	0	1,172	7	990	0	18,587
Hanford-Corcoran, CA Metro Area..................................	1,546	111	934	160	1,137	0	760	0	14,868
Harrisburg-Carlisle, PA Metro Area................................	10,982	282	10,744	278	8,538	202	5,982	155	90,874
Harrisonburg, VA Metro Area..	1,694	65	1,505	24	2,291	0	1,730	55	16,931
Hartford-West Hartford-East Hartford, CT Metro Area ..	21,666	798	24,486	1,260	23,855	965	14,673	570	178,140
Hattiesburg, MS Metro Area...	1,907	267	843	0	1,410	75	1,756	99	20,629
Helena, MT Micro Area...	1,630	37	2,229	74	1,257	53	1,085	0	13,120
Hermiston-Pendleton, OR Micro Area..............................	1,238	12	1,159	0	1,142	0	680	0	13,809
Hickory-Lenoir-Morganton, NC Metro Area.....................	5,554	357	5,049	38	6,176	446	3,795	136	65,589
Hilo, HI Micro Area..	3,909	191	3,507	68	3,992	60	2,111	12	36,052
Hilton Head Island-Bluffton-Beaufort, SC Metro Area ...	3,251	131	3,637	155	4,053	69	2,900	162	46,876
Hinesville, GA Metro Area..	969	0	287	52	265	0	243	92	7,883
Hobbs, NM Micro Area...	1,070	41	689	0	876	0	719	0	7,287
Holland, MI Micro Area...	2,208	30	1,787	16	1,315	24	1,230	0	18,208
Homosassa Springs, FL Metro Area...............................	2,337	100	1,781	39	1,774	80	2,451	181	51,328
Hot Springs, AR Metro Area...	1,515	227	1,375	46	1,369	153	1,720	98	21,235
Houma-Thibodaux, LA Metro Area..................................	3,148	104	2,850	77	2,485	71	1,650	133	28,773
Houston-The Woodlands-Sugar Land, TX Metro Area ..	88,518	3,393	103,341	4,696	84,030	3,129	54,155	1,969	632,388
Huntington-Ashland, WV-KY-OH Metro Area	5,624	276	5,076	106	5,438	133	3,666	71	69,671
Huntsville, AL Metro Area..	7,371	457	6,970	329	5,051	291	5,435	258	61,317
Huntsville, TX Micro Area..	763	9	670	10	1,051	43	924	153	12,511
Hutchinson, KS Micro Area..	1,224	39	1,014	50	1,334	0	1,065	0	11,238
Idaho Falls, ID Metro Area..	2,284	42	2,363	24	1,268	0	1,146	12	17,167
Indiana, PA Micro Area..	1,227	39	1,363	59	1,581	162	811	44	15,474
Indianapolis-Carmel-Anderson, IN Metro Area................	30,486	1,532	32,091	1,348	27,462	1,630	18,806	681	242,808
Iowa City, IA Metro Area..	2,750	0	2,836	92	3,459	161	1,573	61	16,535
Ithaca, NY Metro Area..	2,102	171	1,964	0	1,398	0	1,505	0	11,635
Jackson, MI Metro Area..	2,051	107	2,675	0	2,056	22	1,158	0	27,805
Jackson, MS Metro Area...	7,330	283	8,884	158	5,960	14	6,206	45	75,191
Jackson, TN Metro Area...	2,071	68	2,106	61	2,433	0	1,018	50	19,970
Jacksonville, FL Metro Area...	22,485	1,609	21,022	712	19,979	662	12,378	693	209,349
Jacksonville, NC Metro Area..	722	46	1,575	0	1,474	117	1,240	0	16,167
Jamestown-Dunkirk-Fredonia, NY Micro Area.................	2,061	58	2,160	46	1,460	26	1,221	116	25,076
Janesville-Beloit, WI Metro Area....................................	2,677	130	2,181	20	2,392	70	1,657	141	24,784
Jefferson City, MO Metro Area.......................................	2,483	0	2,495	12	1,944	159	1,483	0	23,127
Johnson City, TN Metro Area..	2,787	184	3,119	282	2,531	0	2,407	153	40,698
Johnstown, PA Metro Area...	2,186	176	2,967	117	2,380	22	1,426	23	29,426
Jonesboro, AR Metro Area...	1,399	0	1,760	0	2,041	0	1,008	0	18,478
Joplin, MO Metro Area..	1,992	45	3,227	77	3,185	127	1,358	0	26,238
Kahului-Wailuku-Lahaina, HI Metro Area........................	3,325	105	3,576	61	3,177	91	2,789	0	23,175
Kalamazoo-Portage, MI Metro Area................................	4,634	183	6,083	273	4,194	110	2,592	28	50,842
Kalispell, MT Micro Area..	na	na	na	na	na	na	na	na	na
Kankakee, IL Metro Area..	2,056	44	1,625	95	1,557	0	787	0	16,973
Kansas City, MO-KS Metro Area.....................................	31,067	1,227	34,882	745	31,514	967	19,143	384	278,797
Kapaa, HI Micro Area...	1,420	49	1,456	4	1,995	0	908	177	12,155
Keene, NH Micro Area..	na	na	na	na	na	na	na	na	na
Kennewick-Richland, WA Metro Area..............................	3,950	321	4,212	27	3,510	105	1,296	173	35,038

Table F-4: Metropolitan/Micropolitan Statistical Areas—Employment and Labor Force Status, Civilian Labor Force—*Continued*

	60 to 61 Years		62 to 64 Years		65 to 69 Years		70 Years and Over		60 Years and Over Not in the Labor Force
	Employed	Unemployed	Employed	Unemployed	Employed	Unemployed	Employed	Unemployed	
Key West, FL Micro Area	na	na	na	na	na	na	na	na	na
Killeen-Temple, TX Metro Area	4,371	163	6,242	164	4,622	273	2,200	0	43,497
Kingsport-Bristol-Bristol, TN-VA Metro Area	4,589	224	5,150	87	5,310	39	3,200	78	64,847
Kingston, NY Metro Area	2,710	132	4,282	450	3,915	263	2,431	136	30,967
Klamath Falls, OR Micro Area	1,356	0	1,106	143	941	0	429	29	13,822
Knoxville, TN Metro Area	13,058	500	14,165	623	13,393	720	9,262	98	152,125
Kokomo, IN Metro Area	1,367	69	1,148	40	1,991	114	629	37	15,985
La Crosse-Onalaska, WI-MN Metro Area	2,903	43	2,922	15	2,228	0	697	0	20,822
Lafayette, LA Metro Area	6,338	106	6,492	117	5,014	0	7,072	138	60,660
Lafayette-West Lafayette, IN Metro Area	3,104	128	2,547	21	2,787	0	1,364	36	25,387
LaGrange, GA Micro Area	653	0	1,134	136	712	0	713	178	10,644
Lake Charles, LA Metro Area	2,372	26	2,911	96	3,292	112	1,863	0	30,871
Lake City, FL Micro Area	na	na	na	na	na	na	na	na	na
Lake Havasu City-Kingman, AZ Metro Area	2,224	287	2,907	211	2,696	140	2,086	119	60,565
Lakeland-Winter Haven, FL Metro Area	9,016	603	11,701	895	10,130	519	6,723	160	127,766
Lancaster, PA Metro Area	10,219	266	9,688	259	11,214	202	7,923	348	80,480
Lansing-East Lansing, MI Metro Area	6,982	563	7,419	263	5,304	220	3,522	89	69,033
Laredo, TX Metro Area	1,988	75	2,254	22	1,968	0	1,179	0	25,168
Las Cruces, NM Metro Area	2,163	317	3,488	71	2,492	0	2,346	82	31,427
Las Vegas-Henderson-Paradise, NV Metro Area	29,930	2,451	30,395	2,347	25,498	1,939	19,224	2,146	283,307
Laurel, MS Micro Area	973	0	1,327	139	1,388	0	1,083	18	14,021
Lawrence, KS Metro Area	2,024	76	2,472	0	1,312	0	1,297	0	11,267
Lawton, OK Metro Area	1,961	0	1,425	0	987	84	1,081	84	15,969
Lebanon, PA Metro Area	2,190	105	2,661	66	2,127	0	1,530	43	24,885
Lewiston, ID-WA Metro Area	na	na	na	na	na	na	na	na	na
Lewiston-Auburn, ME Metro Area	1,848	70	2,250	0	1,696	35	1,180	28	16,800
Lexington-Fayette, KY Metro Area	8,325	567	7,400	488	7,520	240	4,442	159	63,064
Lima, OH Metro Area	1,700	90	2,289	220	1,176	17	567	32	17,919
Lincoln, NE Metro Area	5,635	145	5,574	55	5,278	23	2,778	56	37,063
Little Rock-North Little Rock-Conway, AR Metro Area	9,609	253	13,090	118	11,177	297	6,546	136	101,539
Logan, UT-ID Metro Area	1,280	24	1,716	8	1,150	0	858	0	11,916
London, KY Micro Area	1,175	87	1,111	0	1,166	65	758	0	23,091
Longview, TX Metro Area	2,508	203	4,138	0	2,897	0	2,196	41	33,520
Longview, WA Metro Area	1,877	47	1,262	63	1,189	239	1,065	41	19,995
Los Angeles-Long Beach-Anaheim, CA Metro Area	186,971	13,393	210,196	13,699	186,651	10,713	116,452	6,604	1,627,288
Louisville/Jefferson County, KY-IN Metro Area	18,041	604	20,177	818	19,758	776	13,685	253	185,595
Lubbock, TX Metro Area	2,987	149	3,820	28	5,374	39	3,417	28	34,636
Lufkin, TX Micro Area	719	12	840	61	750	32	1,121	0	14,926
Lumberton, NC Micro Area	975	102	1,543	0	872	42	447	5	20,993
Lynchburg, VA Metro Area	4,814	96	3,861	81	3,719	156	2,545	40	46,724
Macon, GA Metro Area	4,181	114	3,468	127	2,206	62	1,543	105	36,776
Madera, CA Metro Area	1,494	107	1,890	262	1,473	57	1,319	28	21,492
Madison, WI Metro Area	12,354	833	12,897	479	10,242	599	5,832	101	78,406
Manchester-Nashua, NH Metro Area	8,297	394	8,760	194	7,305	563	4,018	100	52,333
Manhattan, KS Metro Area	987	36	1,259	0	1,588	148	895	0	8,026
Manitowoc, WI Micro Area	1,465	14	1,604	22	1,178	0	1,171	51	15,068
Mankato-North Mankato, MN Metro Area	1,723	15	1,556	18	821	0	995	90	12,981
Mansfield, OH Metro Area	2,019	63	2,020	55	1,531	188	756	0	23,910
Marinette, WI-MI Micro Area	1,343	106	1,230	0	1,010	45	666	9	15,200
Marion, IN Micro Area	na	na	na	na	na	na	na	na	na
Marion, OH Micro Area	980	96	903	144	1,315	50	816	33	10,543
Marquette, MI Micro Area	959	15	1,028	66	310	0	338	75	13,561
Marshall, TX Micro Area	na	na	na	na	na	na	na	na	na
Martinsville, VA Micro Area	na	na	na	na	na	na	na	na	na
McAllen-Edinburg-Mission, TX Metro Area	6,270	796	7,794	630	6,159	303	3,483	282	90,885
Meadville, PA Micro Area	1,723	205	2,034	140	1,328	69	1,243	21	16,929
Medford, OR Metro Area	3,736	489	4,176	91	3,144	161	2,422	124	46,350
Memphis, TN-MS-AR Metro Area	21,851	1,464	21,515	875	18,216	910	12,546	333	165,406
Merced, CA Metro Area	2,387	103	2,301	67	2,803	165	1,658	0	28,777
Meridian, MS Micro Area	962	0	1,583	0	1,188	0	656	0	18,041
Miami-Fort Lauderdale-West Palm Beach, FL Metro Area	97,479	8,149	107,861	6,496	100,704	5,455	73,527	3,658	971,700
Michigan City-La Porte, IN Metro Area	2,164	72	2,141	13	1,810	182	1,148	19	17,580
Midland, MI Metro Area	1,235	0	1,022	0	719	0	735	18	14,999
Midland, TX Metro Area	4,259	0	2,733	0	2,715	112	2,101	98	13,690
Milwaukee-Waukesha-West Allis, WI Metro Area	26,975	1,101	27,814	875	22,724	883	15,700	655	220,847
Minneapolis-St. Paul-Bloomington, MN-WI Metro Area	57,421	2,065	64,504	1,854	50,846	1,767	29,614	354	423,572
Minot, ND Micro Area	1,364	0	1,017	0	1,362	30	633	0	6,030
Missoula, MT Metro Area	1,578	0	1,616	0	2,013	231	1,072	0	15,281
Mobile, AL Metro Area	5,636	224	5,838	274	5,870	167	3,175	44	63,843
Modesto, CA Metro Area	6,087	289	5,889	801	6,829	1,112	3,452	270	68,008
Monroe, LA Metro Area	3,336	92	3,308	38	2,336	79	1,964	42	25,246
Monroe, MI Metro Area	2,373	0	2,752	0	1,862	94	599	0	26,244
Montgomery, AL Metro Area	6,074	172	4,934	99	5,469	227	3,597	191	52,137
Morehead City, NC Micro Area	1,433	49	1,071	30	1,507	0	879	81	15,424
Morgantown, WV Metro Area	2,275	150	2,162	0	1,735	62	1,225	0	17,339
Morristown, TN Metro Area	1,393	96	2,526	178	1,769	55	1,348	45	21,760
Moses Lake, WA Micro Area	1,753	0	2,235	0	1,000	0	544	0	11,893

Table F-4: Metropolitan/Micropolitan Statistical Areas—Employment and Labor Force Status, Civilian Labor Force—*Continued*

	60 to 61 Years		62 to 64 Years		65 to 69 Years		70 Years and Over		60 Years and Over Not in the Labor Force
	Employed	Unemployed	Employed	Unemployed	Employed	Unemployed	Employed	Unemployed	
Mount Airy, NC Micro Area	1,007	0	1,182	0	1,090	0	659	42	14,141
Mount Pleasant, MI Micro Area	978	0	644	44	680	73	514	13	8,200
Mount Vernon-Anacortes, WA Metro Area	2,092	112	2,493	187	1,996	46	1,592	104	22,933
Muncie, IN Metro Area	1,492	0	1,813	49	1,608	0	1,428	97	18,693
Muskegon, MI Metro Area	2,114	169	2,338	91	2,401	56	1,191	72	27,925
Muskogee, OK Micro Area	990	74	973	0	547	0	989	73	11,709
Myrtle Beach-Conway-North Myrtle Beach, SC-NC Metro Area	8,276	561	7,560	213	8,506	267	4,650	51	97,719
Nacogdoches, TX Micro Area	na	na	na	na	na	na	na	na	na
Napa, CA Metro Area	2,724	53	3,326	84	2,905	166	1,915	200	24,002
Naples-Immokalee-Marco Island, FL Metro Area	6,060	249	7,694	439	6,512	111	6,978	616	99,876
Nashville-Davidson–Murfreesboro–Franklin, TN Metro Area	26,515	935	28,544	904	26,691	1,021	17,594	577	216,120
New Bern, NC Metro Area	2,146	59	2,270	50	1,820	319	1,398	92	24,099
New Castle, PA Micro Area	1,802	69	1,833	19	1,314	77	807	0	18,022
New Haven-Milford, CT Metro Area	17,208	962	18,897	1,061	16,778	1,110	11,463	882	125,251
New Orleans-Metairie, LA Metro Area	18,082	937	22,635	751	19,177	841	13,867	649	174,848
New Philadelphia-Dover, OH Micro Area	2,016	0	1,753	76	1,342	0	1,104	0	16,631
New York-Newark-Jersey City, NY-NJ-PA Metro Area	325,242	21,193	357,903	19,192	327,959	16,904	221,215	12,270	2,732,479
Niles-Benton Harbor, MI Metro Area	3,018	188	3,266	0	2,944	91	1,723	20	27,156
North Port-Sarasota-Bradenton, FL Metro Area	12,737	880	14,693	553	15,978	454	11,777	793	225,265
North Wilkesboro, NC Micro Area	na	na	na	na	na	na	na	na	na
Norwich-New London, CT Metro Area	5,657	614	5,922	342	5,933	199	3,667	0	40,176
Oak Harbor, WA Micro Area	1,524	41	1,652	107	2,162	100	999	0	17,574
Ocala, FL Metro Area	6,680	937	5,711	341	6,779	459	5,154	166	94,618
Ocean City, NJ Metro Area	2,685	99	2,119	0	2,345	193	1,902	142	22,047
Odessa, TX Metro Area	1,905	39	1,890	68	2,210	115	1,006	0	14,452
Ogden-Clearfield, UT Metro Area	7,782	294	9,264	439	5,710	65	4,302	64	65,010
Ogdensburg-Massena, NY Micro Area	1,257	29	1,296	74	1,069	23	684	102	19,892
Oklahoma City, OK Metro Area	19,474	437	20,231	407	19,718	443	14,483	428	167,609
Olean, NY Micro Area	1,729	104	1,353	54	936	32	832	0	14,341
Olympia-Tumwater, WA Metro Area	5,007	37	5,120	383	3,761	0	2,170	65	42,477
Omaha-Council Bluffs, NE-IA Metro Area	14,693	217	17,288	142	12,761	163	9,019	58	106,005
Opelousas, LA Micro Area	710	33	862	0	1,207	0	549	0	13,916
Orangeburg, SC Micro Area	1,867	0	1,112	0	1,436	55	729	0	16,496
Orlando-Kissimmee-Sanford, FL Metro Area	32,698	1,565	35,220	1,441	28,670	1,601	19,349	774	330,350
Oshkosh-Neenah, WI Metro Area	2,620	242	3,279	27	2,010	0	1,274	106	25,751
Ottawa-Peru, IL Micro Area	2,999	107	2,997	140	1,780	6	1,746	110	29,743
Owensboro, KY Metro Area	1,237	6	1,734	72	1,120	0	1,494	0	20,159
Owosso, MI Micro Area	1,371	268	1,200	12	727	91	702	0	12,541
Oxnard-Thousand Oaks-Ventura, CA Metro Area	13,145	588	13,921	284	14,883	830	8,879	561	111,902
Paducah, KY-IL Micro Area	1,165	0	2,059	216	1,238	14	879	28	19,806
Palatka, FL Micro Area	na	na	na	na	na	na	na	na	na
Palm Bay-Melbourne-Titusville, FL Metro Area	8,219	492	8,291	444	10,417	415	7,855	722	130,377
Panama City, FL Metro Area	3,061	163	3,481	165	2,625	0	1,435	74	33,164
Parkersburg-Vienna, WV Metro Area	1,084	81	1,033	0	1,134	0	1,143	0	18,595
Pensacola-Ferry Pass-Brent, FL Metro Area	5,284	236	7,739	141	6,092	262	4,521	61	76,255
Peoria, IL Metro Area	6,597	370	6,117	422	5,293	377	3,915	85	63,125
Philadelphia-Camden-Wilmington, PA-NJ-DE-MD Metro Area	103,619	4,896	109,601	5,545	103,044	3,766	70,766	3,903	846,233
Phoenix-Mesa-Scottsdale, AZ Metro Area	58,609	3,868	64,591	3,982	58,293	2,086	38,863	2,423	654,426
Pine Bluff, AR Metro Area	1,100	33	1,816	0	1,274	51	961	66	15,635
Pinehurst-Southern Pines, NC Micro Area	na	na	na	na	na	na	na	na	na
Pittsburgh, PA Metro Area	46,403	1,949	48,740	1,923	43,653	1,627	29,539	989	428,670
Pittsfield, MA Metro Area	2,105	133	3,695	277	3,269	168	2,265	150	25,208
Plattsburgh, NY Micro Area	1,307	0	731	0	1,195	0	720	0	13,454
Pocatello, ID Metro Area	1,907	178	1,291	75	1,072	33	569	0	11,048
Port Angeles, WA Micro Area	1,998	85	1,696	90	1,533	35	973	22	20,035
Port St. Lucie, FL Metro Area	6,838	309	7,587	627	9,336	814	7,335	681	109,066
Portland-South Portland, ME Metro Area	12,074	467	12,111	421	11,995	215	6,760	130	84,225
Portland-Vancouver-Hillsboro, OR-WA Metro Area	38,484	1,582	41,857	1,847	35,296	1,146	16,570	589	323,212
Portsmouth, OH Micro Area	746	0	1,139	0	622	0	806	0	14,475
Pottsville, PA Micro Area	2,664	18	2,757	77	2,484	0	2,053	65	29,346
Prescott, AZ Metro Area	5,311	406	4,754	742	4,278	644	2,777	0	65,889
Providence-Warwick, RI-MA Metro Area	28,466	1,815	32,202	966	26,692	881	17,065	1,116	251,683
Provo-Orem, UT Metro Area	4,495	70	6,024	285	5,671	98	2,914	152	39,267
Pueblo, CO Metro Area	2,611	174	2,887	43	2,188	234	1,363	0	30,020
Punta Gorda, FL Metro Area	2,320	90	3,646	346	4,876	146	3,889	420	61,587
Quincy, IL-MO Micro Area	1,285	75	1,987	30	1,479	46	1,098	0	13,531
Racine, WI Metro Area	2,830	106	3,750	56	2,598	119	1,988	77	30,526
Raleigh, NC Metro Area	18,597	850	19,537	1,197	15,798	332	9,231	420	132,484
Rapid City, SD Metro Area	2,957	0	3,199	64	2,593	86	1,809	0	20,657
Reading, PA Metro Area	8,056	460	8,964	452	7,112	225	4,527	140	64,083
Redding, CA Metro Area	2,793	162	2,872	166	2,526	125	2,513	202	37,878
Reno, NV Metro Area	7,567	152	8,813	505	7,159	528	3,916	332	67,327
Richmond, IN Micro Area	708	0	1,580	0	1,098	39	781	0	12,113
Richmond, VA Metro Area	21,914	931	24,532	851	21,456	882	14,972	483	167,281

Table F-4: Metropolitan/Micropolitan Statistical Areas—Employment and Labor Force Status, Civilian Labor Force—*Continued*

	60 to 61 Years		62 to 64 Years		65 to 69 Years		70 Years and Over		60 Years and Over Not in the Labor Force
	Employed	Unemployed	Employed	Unemployed	Employed	Unemployed	Employed	Unemployed	
Richmond-Berea, KY Micro Area	698	55	1,671	0	1,023	0	1,024	79	15,079
Riverside-San Bernardino-Ontario, CA Metro Area	52,079	3,452	53,996	3,454	44,719	2,574	30,770	2,041	560,102
Roanoke Rapids, NC Micro Area	883	77	686	69	689	9	561	15	16,041
Roanoke, VA Metro Area	7,094	42	6,856	520	5,817	46	5,046	111	56,219
Rochester, MN Metro Area	4,095	108	5,294	46	2,907	82	2,146	40	30,317
Rochester, NY Metro Area	18,157	835	20,621	646	15,538	834	12,337	414	177,315
Rockford, IL Metro Area	5,856	627	6,670	160	5,000	226	2,877	235	53,008
Rocky Mount, NC Metro Area	2,902	84	3,408	250	1,569	69	1,327	0	26,104
Rome, GA Metro Area	1,229	32	1,486	0	630	105	1,066	0	15,120
Roseburg, OR Micro Area	2,348	64	1,626	0	1,396	0	735	0	28,917
Roswell, NM Micro Area	806	0	1,198	0	1,007	0	674	59	10,673
Russellville, AR Micro Area	717	0	759	0	1,004	0	676	0	13,645
Sacramento–Roseville–Arden-Arcade, CA Metro Area	29,910	1,641	35,704	2,317	27,403	2,047	18,208	881	334,602
Saginaw, MI Metro Area	1,945	71	2,343	93	2,098	53	2,455	75	37,509
Salem, OH Micro Area	1,775	102	2,145	5	1,869	115	2,036	0	18,927
Salem, OR Metro Area	6,375	457	8,028	61	5,380	245	3,505	39	63,090
Salinas, CA Metro Area	6,983	283	6,317	277	5,216	24	3,606	80	51,801
Salisbury, MD-DE Metro Area	6,953	267	8,851	403	9,399	925	6,535	399	78,959
Salt Lake City, UT Metro Area	16,796	789	20,544	502	12,820	192	9,292	245	107,882
San Angelo, TX Metro Area	1,515	26	1,419	68	1,179	0	1,936	0	17,743
San Antonio-New Braunfels, TX Metro Area	30,439	1,559	32,322	1,175	29,334	951	20,758	900	287,679
San Diego-Carlsbad, CA Metro Area	51,103	3,309	53,794	3,460	42,684	2,670	25,768	1,348	416,421
San Francisco-Oakland-Hayward, CA Metro Area	73,017	4,014	90,578	5,051	79,980	4,202	48,820	2,090	626,882
San Jose-Sunnyvale-Santa Clara, CA Metro Area	27,623	1,902	31,237	2,250	26,698	1,497	16,429	524	237,114
San Luis Obispo-Paso Robles-Arroyo Grande, CA Metro Area	4,809	247	4,948	244	4,967	571	2,867	77	49,860
Sandusky, OH Micro Area	1,361	171	1,229	203	998	0	807	37	14,783
Santa Cruz-Watsonville, CA Metro Area	5,075	452	6,235	471	6,595	335	2,423	52	34,512
Santa Fe, NM Metro Area	3,146	209	3,818	89	4,161	168	2,479	37	27,845
Santa Maria-Santa Barbara, CA Metro Area	7,684	251	7,457	406	6,574	317	5,019	282	58,616
Santa Rosa, CA Metro Area	9,383	646	11,439	441	11,250	382	6,185	282	81,159
Savannah, GA Metro Area	5,039	269	5,395	182	5,258	84	2,864	496	48,052
Scranton–Wilkes-Barre–Hazleton, PA Metro Area	9,275	733	10,469	795	8,864	442	7,737	442	107,827
Searcy, AR Micro Area	777	0	803	46	570	0	1,198	99	12,579
Seattle-Tacoma-Bellevue, WA Metro Area	59,677	2,860	65,474	2,164	55,887	1,705	27,910	969	450,689
Sebastian-Vero Beach, FL Metro Area	3,297	478	2,974	91	3,145	0	2,366	103	44,464
Sebring, FL Metro Area	910	175	1,411	240	1,209	25	2,275	123	33,999
Seneca, SC Micro Area	1,123	39	1,281	53	1,158	104	887	0	17,856
Sevierville, TN Micro Area	1,442	81	1,495	0	1,661	198	1,860	81	16,802
Shawnee, OK Micro Area	938	0	989	19	1,310	108	607	0	11,886
Sheboygan, WI Metro Area	1,709	0	2,670	24	1,617	58	1,213	0	18,501
Shelby, NC Micro Area	2,085	184	1,962	0	1,019	109	903	0	18,317
Sherman-Denison, TX Metro Area	2,316	338	2,302	0	2,014	22	1,506	53	21,643
Show Low, AZ Micro Area	968	143	1,483	129	905	164	765	0	18,930
Shreveport-Bossier City, LA Metro Area	7,284	517	6,783	47	6,417	221	5,070	209	66,439
Sierra Vista-Douglas, AZ Metro Area	2,244	140	2,361	107	1,346	0	1,326	82	27,705
Sioux City, IA-NE-SD Metro Area	3,246	0	3,600	37	3,482	21	1,644	13	22,870
Sioux Falls, SD Metro Area	2,857	40	5,108	23	4,677	80	3,660	116	26,405
Somerset, PA Micro Area	1,725	93	1,275	148	882	29	1,125	85	16,185
South Bend-Mishawaka, IN-MI Metro Area	5,964	428	6,249	264	5,238	260	3,323	97	47,756
Spartanburg, SC Metro Area	5,867	197	4,108	7	4,575	23	3,105	55	50,034
Spokane-Spokane Valley, WA Metro Area	7,967	208	9,581	398	9,113	194	3,792	0	86,912
Springfield, IL Metro Area	3,727	229	3,717	102	3,032	33	2,101	99	34,835
Springfield, MA Metro Area	12,883	745	11,600	359	10,373	264	5,825	165	94,173
Springfield, MO Metro Area	5,287	289	7,318	155	6,579	169	4,003	43	71,156
Springfield, OH Metro Area	2,058	90	2,492	156	2,608	102	1,826	89	24,404
St. Cloud, MN Metro Area	3,285	97	3,363	131	2,446	30	1,735	127	24,177
St. George, UT Metro Area	2,012	34	1,592	125	1,673	0	1,114	0	31,562
St. Joseph, MO-KS Metro Area	1,902	69	2,066	0	1,906	0	1,046	66	19,642
St. Louis, MO-IL Metro Area	45,702	1,642	51,439	1,894	43,104	1,622	26,367	720	424,615
State College, PA Metro Area	2,335	220	2,324	294	1,845	0	905	0	20,799
Statesboro, GA Micro Area	na	na	na	na	na	na	na	na	na
Staunton-Waynesboro, VA Metro Area	2,093	0	2,264	0	3,006	50	1,902	119	21,796
Stevens Point, WI Micro Area	1,263	38	1,124	20	787	0	577	10	10,664
Stillwater, OK Micro Area	1,202	35	919	0	723	0	464	0	9,184
Stockton-Lodi, CA Metro Area	8,462	879	9,055	793	8,366	350	4,834	78	88,757
Sumter, SC Metro Area	1,839	79	1,656	0	1,306	113	669	45	16,131
Sunbury, PA Micro Area	1,430	98	1,524	0	1,710	63	951	62	19,200
Syracuse, NY Metro Area	10,744	376	11,995	496	8,268	374	6,482	608	104,525
Talladega-Sylacauga, AL Micro Area	1,123	65	1,808	204	1,636	141	1,217	179	15,981
Tallahassee, FL Metro Area	6,604	858	7,291	201	4,994	138	2,116	0	47,666
Tampa-St. Petersburg-Clearwater, FL Metro Area	46,293	3,008	48,935	1,883	46,236	2,635	30,936	809	556,669
Terre Haute, IN Metro Area	2,418	301	2,771	0	2,501	220	1,285	15	27,317
Texarkana, TX-AR Metro Area	2,375	143	1,932	85	1,724	8	1,314	0	24,773
The Villages, FL Metro Area	na	na	na	na	na	na	na	na	na
Toledo, OH Metro Area	10,231	595	11,270	640	9,321	340	5,561	44	90,415
Topeka, KS Metro Area	3,734	104	4,258	209	4,465	214	2,182	89	38,260
Torrington, CT Micro Area	4,475	218	4,108	93	4,144	131	3,549	70	31,076

Table F-4: Metropolitan/Micropolitan Statistical Areas—Employment and Labor Force Status, Civilian Labor Force—*Continued*

	60 to 61 Years		62 to 64 Years		65 to 69 Years		70 Years and Over		60 Years and Over Not in the Labor Force
	Employed	Unemployed	Employed	Unemployed	Employed	Unemployed	Employed	Unemployed	
Traverse City, MI Micro Area	2,404	20	3,011	127	2,998	82	1,575	9	30,164
Trenton, NJ Metro Area	5,613	0	7,436	442	6,508	313	4,661	191	48,613
Truckee-Grass Valley, CA Micro Area	2,426	0	2,954	199	2,694	273	1,927	27	23,606
Tucson, AZ Metro Area	15,656	787	15,257	1,235	14,514	754	9,768	312	184,842
Tullahoma-Manchester, TN Micro Area	1,556	0	1,515	0	1,045	0	594	0	19,710
Tulsa, OK Metro Area	16,603	411	16,241	421	16,504	428	11,867	391	133,979
Tupelo, MS Micro Area	2,348	76	1,202	0	1,878	46	778	0	20,702
Tuscaloosa, AL Metro Area	2,780	234	3,412	70	2,707	46	1,943	37	33,183
Twin Falls, ID Micro Area	1,723	20	1,561	65	1,359	102	1,299	141	15,539
Tyler, TX Metro Area	3,532	41	4,363	237	3,605	79	2,367	137	33,852
Ukiah, CA Micro Area	1,549	63	2,953	0	2,035	0	1,414	0	16,310
Urban Honolulu, HI Metro Area	16,781	459	18,120	557	18,684	674	11,081	84	148,342
Utica-Rome, NY Metro Area	5,254	92	5,316	229	4,083	268	3,627	190	53,979
Valdosta, GA Metro Area	1,545	0	1,721	0	1,659	70	1,196	0	18,265
Vallejo-Fairfield, CA Metro Area	7,778	459	7,783	318	6,296	263	3,842	101	62,149
Victoria, TX Metro Area	na	na	na	na	na	na	na	na	na
Vineland-Bridgeton, NJ Metro Area	2,294	272	1,417	26	2,251	268	1,638	80	21,648
Virginia Beach-Norfolk-Newport News, VA-NC Metro Area	27,883	1,894	29,204	1,115	22,493	990	16,167	412	220,560
Visalia-Porterville, CA Metro Area	5,152	310	4,632	181	4,871	417	3,033	151	49,252
Waco, TX Metro Area	3,877	248	2,795	144	3,035	189	2,366	31	35,985
Walla Walla, WA Metro Area	1,673	384	1,347	0	1,170	0	678	0	10,048
Warner Robins, GA Metro Area	2,548	0	2,079	214	1,619	47	1,372	86	24,116
Warsaw, IN Micro Area	1,405	79	1,616	14	1,370	0	955	0	11,601
Washington-Arlington-Alexandria, DC-VA-MD-WV Metro Area	93,488	5,681	115,557	5,066	101,491	3,566	61,345	2,235	636,865
Waterloo-Cedar Falls, IA Metro Area	3,149	54	2,989	23	2,261	28	1,749	128	26,656
Watertown-Fort Atkinson, WI Micro Area	1,856	59	1,583	36	1,231	0	850	0	12,282
Watertown-Fort Drum, NY Metro Area	1,749	8	1,170	89	897	81	1,385	0	15,244
Wausau, WI Metro Area	2,744	50	2,778	77	2,347	186	919	12	21,304
Weirton-Steubenville, WV-OH Metro Area	2,246	197	1,686	34	1,593	0	1,575	9	25,334
Wenatchee, WA Metro Area	1,883	128	2,379	144	1,772	0	1,351	0	19,806
Wheeling, WV-OH Metro Area	2,007	0	3,648	42	2,575	115	1,949	0	29,419
Whitewater-Elkhorn, WI Micro Area	2,380	108	1,836	88	2,164	69	1,607	50	13,766
Wichita Falls, TX Metro Area	2,509	74	2,222	37	2,415	0	1,957	44	21,775
Wichita, KS Metro Area	10,943	104	11,647	398	8,820	200	5,791	285	87,832
Williamsport, PA Metro Area	2,548	30	2,360	133	2,278	105	1,231	107	21,348
Wilmington, NC Metro Area	3,934	166	5,438	89	4,203	124	2,429	5	43,912
Wilson, NC Micro Area	1,221	0	1,690	0	1,289	0	942	162	13,469
Winchester, VA-WV Metro Area	2,171	65	2,912	136	1,735	210	2,182	124	21,678
Winston-Salem, NC Metro Area	11,432	666	9,835	267	9,683	626	4,827	104	107,386
Wisconsin Rapids-Marshfield, WI Micro Area	1,179	26	621	0	1,190	0	635	11	14,389
Wooster, OH Micro Area	1,996	7	1,843	39	1,538	43	1,262	25	18,689
Worcester, MA-CT Metro Area	17,886	1,201	18,524	735	14,665	724	11,305	510	126,243
Yakima, WA Metro Area	2,614	39	4,331	160	2,730	170	1,707	0	32,103
York-Hanover, PA Metro Area	9,000	349	8,090	506	8,111	39	4,408	240	67,993
Youngstown-Warren-Boardman, OH-PA Metro Area	10,098	279	10,139	343	8,474	151	5,714	262	111,536
Yuba City, CA Metro Area	2,573	96	1,981	140	2,329	0	1,176	61	23,000
Yuma, AZ Metro Area	2,484	338	1,890	127	2,563	222	1,897	57	35,836
Zanesville, OH Micro Area	1,090	7	1,721	44	761	0	757	190	15,505

Table F-5: 114th Congressional Districts—Employment and Labor Force Status, Civilian Labor Force

	60 to 61 Years		62 to 64 Years		65 to 69 Years		70 Years and Over		60 Years and Over Not in the Labor Force
	Employed	Unemployed	Employed	Unemployed	Employed	Unemployed	Employed	Unemployed	
Alabama									
Congressional District 1	10,112	416	11,390	291	9,824	341	5,854	44	119,307
Congressional District 2	10,562	372	8,000	168	8,390	332	6,091	102	112,376
Congressional District 3	10,196	631	10,024	560	10,327	451	6,426	483	113,425
Congressional District 4	8,086	324	10,599	248	7,687	186	6,905	126	126,931
Congressional District 5	11,559	852	11,137	499	8,772	451	7,358	368	110,711
Congressional District 6	10,841	571	11,654	150	12,242	427	7,538	183	106,926
Congressional District 7	8,162	475	8,974	168	7,701	255	4,506	224	103,541
Alaska									
Congressional District (at Large)	12,743	478	12,530	683	10,982	362	6,530	300	68,151
Arizona									
Congressional District 1	10,854	464	11,380	607	8,667	584	6,329	113	129,521
Congressional District 2	12,389	669	11,809	563	11,607	331	7,498	200	145,538
Congressional District 3	7,962	443	8,976	936	7,180	614	4,425	198	85,674
Congressional District 4	11,262	817	11,104	1,533	10,135	860	9,068	401	204,954
Congressional District 5	9,259	721	11,108	713	10,644	278	6,965	476	120,821
Congressional District 6	13,802	1,149	14,651	335	15,065	352	10,277	522	116,357
Congressional District 7	6,292	655	6,162	823	4,278	327	2,890	150	61,642
Congressional District 8	10,684	553	12,725	677	11,704	482	8,043	613	160,954
Congressional District 9	10,437	545	11,112	484	9,443	261	5,921	320	86,038
Arkansas									
Congressional District 1	10,043	654	11,470	319	10,778	84	7,915	205	131,758
Congressional District 2	10,055	270	13,324	156	10,792	309	7,210	235	110,789
Congressional District 3	9,974	470	11,072	188	9,457	76	6,874	177	107,331
Congressional District 4	10,193	559	10,848	160	10,314	273	8,843	98	133,232
California									
Congressional District 1	12,452	514	14,749	893	10,772	646	10,047	394	147,833
Congressional District 2	15,313	1,330	20,352	807	19,183	591	13,069	179	120,378
Congressional District 3	10,549	643	11,018	566	9,390	292	5,153	161	99,902
Congressional District 4	11,230	1,054	13,979	751	12,017	1,029	9,291	219	145,503
Congressional District 5	13,404	484	13,902	395	13,364	849	8,028	894	116,966
Congressional District 6	9,136	502	8,896	563	7,362	599	3,990	412	92,938
Congressional District 7	9,451	404	12,980	1,231	8,576	466	6,870	277	109,706
Congressional District 8	9,398	658	9,880	599	7,719	524	4,286	378	102,292
Congressional District 9	9,659	884	9,698	957	8,260	643	4,977	103	96,579
Congressional District 10	8,337	375	8,209	817	8,855	1,112	4,399	305	89,414
Congressional District 11	11,952	621	16,226	369	14,358	889	8,234	225	107,518
Congressional District 12	10,122	727	15,924	1,063	12,562	521	7,230	126	105,343
Congressional District 13	10,122	942	15,175	878	12,943	818	8,279	582	90,988
Congressional District 14	12,804	531	14,461	1,385	12,876	646	8,274	436	106,914
Congressional District 15	12,216	508	11,495	468	10,231	561	5,423	414	94,971
Congressional District 16	6,938	451	6,851	140	6,934	438	3,399	66	79,526
Congressional District 17	9,455	652	9,997	886	9,530	363	4,455	85	89,129
Congressional District 18	12,424	571	14,044	726	12,658	855	9,345	422	99,587
Congressional District 19	10,083	878	12,307	849	9,163	400	5,770	121	89,355
Congressional District 20	12,248	801	12,574	766	12,059	353	5,963	132	85,669
Congressional District 21	6,276	577	5,319	481	3,993	227	3,074	21	63,508
Congressional District 22	9,687	658	10,858	655	8,861	349	5,790	105	87,143
Congressional District 23	9,480	702	7,953	274	6,929	446	5,403	165	96,014
Congressional District 24	12,628	498	12,444	650	11,687	888	7,886	359	109,532
Congressional District 25	8,832	956	9,978	535	8,091	390	4,838	473	78,627
Congressional District 26	11,657	419	11,323	284	12,428	809	7,710	265	96,210
Congressional District 27	10,895	495	12,022	522	11,329	672	7,015	230	117,367
Congressional District 28	10,753	979	13,186	619	12,562	1,206	7,890	509	99,046
Congressional District 29	9,994	488	8,643	337	9,726	1,424	4,700	95	70,621
Congressional District 30	13,188	707	16,553	1,159	14,418	831	9,992	862	102,343
Congressional District 31	8,830	495	7,917	342	8,369	712	4,465	248	74,004
Congressional District 32	9,623	688	12,271	702	9,386	441	3,206	248	101,715
Congressional District 33	12,966	884	15,030	734	18,057	1,062	13,998	443	100,049
Congressional District 34	9,031	684	9,483	781	8,115	382	4,633	305	81,347
Congressional District 35	5,965	211	5,940	412	4,342	315	2,864	145	68,597
Congressional District 36	9,339	434	10,350	1,086	9,326	310	10,860	757	149,748
Congressional District 37	10,683	787	13,080	1,607	11,497	591	7,457	305	84,279
Congressional District 38	10,154	828	10,332	657	7,982	376	5,307	379	100,201
Congressional District 39	12,385	514	12,673	699	10,135	192	5,942	217	94,326
Congressional District 40	6,793	1,018	8,187	253	4,121	536	2,087	389	63,386
Congressional District 41	8,493	744	9,013	533	6,652	251	3,283	256	72,849
Congressional District 42	9,211	833	9,669	663	7,241	388	4,147	270	91,553
Congressional District 43	8,315	767	10,389	414	8,546	0	5,765	423	83,181
Congressional District 44	7,471	803	8,106	556	6,324	294	3,145	185	67,594
Congressional District 45	11,495	357	14,652	1,192	13,578	807	9,297	502	93,758
Congressional District 46	7,578	639	8,992	618	5,533	179	4,383	292	67,716
Congressional District 47	10,751	928	11,660	470	8,743	419	5,862	373	91,903
Congressional District 48	13,117	863	13,498	1,168	16,878	667	9,689	566	105,473
Congressional District 49	11,109	898	12,386	1,211	10,637	587	7,192	446	101,477
Congressional District 50	12,685	655	13,639	532	12,483	655	6,235	185	102,585
Congressional District 51	6,843	606	9,829	833	6,227	423	3,423	236	81,990
Congressional District 52	13,990	689	14,740	786	10,882	762	6,808	403	92,295

Table F-5: 114th Congressional Districts—Employment and Labor Force Status, Civilian Labor Force—*Continued*

	60 to 61 Years		62 to 64 Years		65 to 69 Years		70 Years and Over		60 Years and Over Not in the Labor Force
	Employed	Unemployed	Employed	Unemployed	Employed	Unemployed	Employed	Unemployed	
California—Cont.									
Congressional District 53................	12,381	657	10,543	967	8,828	636	6,081	296	95,617
Colorado									
Congressional District 1...................	10,188	366	12,965	831	10,840	544	6,593	116	88,078
Congressional District 2...................	14,691	617	19,017	558	13,399	392	6,765	317	98,314
Congressional District 3...................	14,346	1,240	15,410	126	14,027	885	7,270	315	117,267
Congressional District 4...................	12,589	726	13,198	298	13,931	457	7,432	493	92,997
Congressional District 5...................	11,151	434	12,801	802	10,673	784	5,674	337	100,078
Congressional District 6...................	11,661	493	13,571	227	11,931	324	7,376	158	80,386
Congressional District 7...................	12,837	296	15,604	574	12,452	449	5,561	297	97,751
Connecticut									
Congressional District 1...................	11,844	710	12,817	765	12,825	238	7,936	397	110,743
Congressional District 2...................	15,294	1,245	15,108	750	14,619	631	10,025	162	104,547
Congressional District 3...................	14,914	815	16,927	811	14,694	1,138	9,717	610	102,736
Congressional District 4...................	15,494	822	14,955	650	14,964	749	11,838	1,710	88,618
Congressional District 5...................	13,350	357	13,803	543	14,117	630	9,235	533	104,420
Delaware									
Congressional District (at Large)	15,453	1,029	15,553	687	16,864	604	10,644	478	151,058
District of Columbia									
Delegate District (at Large)	8,289	593	8,880	787	9,205	356	8,004	277	72,784
Florida									
Congressional District 1...................	9,022	372	12,530	180	10,255	399	7,943	107	119,592
Congressional District 2...................	11,428	1,152	13,182	631	9,443	170	5,214	165	108,168
Congressional District 3...................	9,752	958	10,965	212	9,652	541	6,105	164	128,709
Congressional District 4...................	11,734	1,060	10,490	364	10,377	131	6,559	172	104,447
Congressional District 5...................	10,577	645	10,832	415	7,484	599	5,265	243	91,377
Congressional District 6...................	13,219	421	13,749	509	14,386	251	9,761	727	179,225
Congressional District 7...................	12,247	679	12,350	421	10,459	673	5,874	334	105,784
Congressional District 8...................	12,154	970	11,397	535	13,787	415	10,221	825	176,236
Congressional District 9...................	8,062	768	10,869	329	6,609	558	4,602	224	95,135
Congressional District 10.................	11,246	96	11,597	882	12,325	512	8,822	361	145,241
Congressional District 11.................	12,232	1,329	10,857	471	13,482	578	12,194	649	247,770
Congressional District 12.................	11,421	851	12,860	785	10,631	456	8,341	367	162,233
Congressional District 13.................	13,696	920	14,542	522	15,392	632	9,613	217	165,908
Congressional District 14.................	10,500	456	10,638	355	8,849	656	5,969	119	100,589
Congressional District 15.................	11,439	963	11,895	262	10,881	486	6,676	167	105,535
Congressional District 16.................	12,657	880	14,342	553	15,942	454	11,661	793	223,979
Congressional District 17.................	8,828	541	12,584	910	13,598	933	10,818	664	197,629
Congressional District 18.................	12,515	623	14,995	1,266	15,633	1,019	13,444	911	170,698
Congressional District 19.................	14,053	612	15,452	778	16,443	573	14,736	816	217,206
Congressional District 20.................	12,619	1,993	12,143	657	10,569	963	6,722	668	104,677
Congressional District 21.................	10,691	504	14,693	519	14,610	876	13,419	630	159,695
Congressional District 22.................	14,682	1,353	16,298	989	16,280	849	12,096	658	146,667
Congressional District 23.................	12,263	891	12,362	1,205	13,524	428	9,242	487	114,190
Congressional District 24.................	12,739	1,371	11,683	1,163	9,872	847	3,852	56	93,210
Congressional District 25.................	10,538	601	11,310	981	7,831	521	8,935	544	115,691
Congressional District 26.................	12,461	714	13,422	185	12,654	540	8,624	392	116,670
Congressional District 27.................	11,144	659	13,441	553	13,449	370	10,252	527	117,299
Georgia									
Congressional District 1...................	9,268	337	9,302	310	9,097	84	4,586	363	102,239
Congressional District 2...................	9,091	359	9,158	322	7,738	307	5,958	409	103,696
Congressional District 3...................	10,789	529	9,782	296	8,885	277	7,416	314	103,202
Congressional District 4...................	12,740	767	10,372	832	9,590	152	5,318	413	77,253
Congressional District 5...................	7,368	243	10,389	494	7,159	743	4,144	102	85,479
Congressional District 6...................	11,163	523	14,595	741	12,014	469	6,600	263	74,394
Congressional District 7...................	8,426	518	11,914	727	8,758	108	3,516	0	70,640
Congressional District 8...................	11,014	0	8,740	178	7,751	271	6,061	136	107,141
Congressional District 9...................	11,637	352	11,866	514	10,655	547	6,961	641	128,086
Congressional District 10.................	9,614	967	9,538	330	8,467	463	4,637	272	108,723
Congressional District 11.................	10,783	388	12,089	342	10,516	786	6,220	219	78,874
Congressional District 12.................	10,035	191	10,086	161	7,483	191	6,000	225	101,030
Congressional District 13.................	8,977	604	8,672	396	7,751	206	2,593	50	77,546
Congressional District 14.................	11,007	538	8,240	139	7,169	283	6,532	70	98,595
Hawaii									
Congressional District 1...................	12,591	391	13,600	339	13,987	490	8,568	18	114,322
Congressional District 2...................	12,844	413	13,059	351	13,861	335	8,321	255	105,402
Idaho									
Congressional District 1...................	11,482	403	15,705	1,065	11,324	630	6,431	305	138,645
Congressional District 2...................	14,177	642	13,225	544	9,110	470	8,072	337	106,518
Illinois									
Congressional District 1...................	12,401	1,240	11,271	669	8,759	643	7,307	595	109,430
Congressional District 2...................	9,570	807	11,426	953	9,876	393	4,922	330	105,182
Congressional District 3...................	10,555	932	11,612	1,015	9,623	275	5,248	226	102,625
Congressional District 4...................	9,100	891	9,132	650	6,132	141	3,505	34	69,410
Congressional District 5...................	8,671	651	11,507	656	10,207	264	5,773	571	82,184

Table F-5: 114th Congressional Districts—Employment and Labor Force Status, Civilian Labor Force—*Continued*

	60 to 61 Years		62 to 64 Years		65 to 69 Years		70 Years and Over		60 Years and Over Not in the Labor Force
	Employed	Unemployed	Employed	Unemployed	Employed	Unemployed	Employed	Unemployed	
Illinois—Cont.									
Congressional District 6	14,175	284	16,158	471	14,382	397	8,477	162	95,658
Congressional District 7	9,845	853	9,801	867	9,437	929	5,484	251	85,356
Congressional District 8	13,844	824	12,899	536	10,997	594	7,082	22	83,151
Congressional District 9	12,151	1,124	16,931	768	12,846	942	8,734	333	106,655
Congressional District 10	12,931	402	13,186	464	12,450	966	7,957	410	88,573
Congressional District 11	11,539	509	11,479	87	8,187	505	4,614	139	70,705
Congressional District 12	10,251	781	9,516	170	9,084	299	6,933	133	114,390
Congressional District 13	10,458	207	11,965	581	10,842	438	7,545	126	108,413
Congressional District 14	13,069	482	13,044	831	11,291	423	7,425	243	86,330
Congressional District 15	11,703	729	12,464	339	10,233	264	7,107	123	126,356
Congressional District 16	11,619	668	12,700	639	11,064	218	7,727	408	117,161
Congressional District 17	11,681	637	13,146	402	9,263	332	8,205	202	125,735
Congressional District 18	13,150	623	13,661	794	10,245	395	8,048	193	121,206
Indiana									
Congressional District 1	11,230	420	11,287	582	10,608	721	7,042	267	109,542
Congressional District 2	13,120	511	13,797	352	10,554	486	8,066	211	106,064
Congressional District 3	11,894	476	10,892	590	10,913	389	7,852	187	105,639
Congressional District 4	11,873	424	11,342	171	11,638	756	7,663	73	105,661
Congressional District 5	11,541	586	14,317	563	10,417	185	8,165	358	97,635
Congressional District 6	11,834	320	12,158	283	11,509	207	7,212	271	117,970
Congressional District 7	10,842	930	9,525	679	8,462	1,071	5,067	314	84,082
Congressional District 8	11,354	814	14,283	198	10,648	445	7,203	164	117,203
Congressional District 9	11,253	206	12,159	484	12,909	226	8,681	152	107,534
Iowa									
Congressional District 1	14,956	382	15,221	212	12,048	334	9,960	196	123,444
Congressional District 2	15,707	318	14,022	832	14,225	205	10,290	173	118,314
Congressional District 3	14,776	561	14,753	402	12,663	320	8,448	285	102,776
Congressional District 4	14,235	337	16,348	182	13,826	157	9,418	284	127,098
Kansas									
Congressional District 1	13,195	319	14,520	90	13,067	293	11,478	160	100,557
Congressional District 2	11,343	336	14,820	260	11,564	413	8,715	343	108,832
Congressional District 3	11,814	493	13,443	453	12,772	608	6,025	78	91,861
Congressional District 4	12,533	171	13,457	437	10,448	201	7,390	285	102,069
Kentucky									
Congressional District 1	9,852	290	9,917	350	9,828	568	7,381	155	130,925
Congressional District 2	8,790	272	10,534	342	8,431	179	6,698	111	114,690
Congressional District 3	10,079	374	12,103	402	11,714	673	7,975	144	108,191
Congressional District 4	11,855	435	10,501	421	10,738	453	7,183	442	108,397
Congressional District 5	5,782	225	8,114	414	5,805	183	4,652	243	138,381
Congressional District 6	12,143	717	10,928	488	10,517	240	5,765	252	103,797
Louisiana									
Congressional District 1	12,870	441	13,999	385	13,985	451	9,876	459	111,349
Congressional District 2	9,499	534	12,119	601	8,282	537	5,744	300	103,728
Congressional District 3	10,023	179	10,726	266	9,527	222	9,927	138	105,003
Congressional District 4	11,081	855	10,658	80	9,949	235	7,738	264	118,021
Congressional District 5	9,151	68	9,921	296	9,779	226	6,410	108	122,060
Congressional District 6	10,540	452	13,030	443	10,531	332	7,442	118	101,847
Maine									
Congressional District 1	14,618	642	15,667	450	15,566	382	9,232	177	114,231
Congressional District 2	14,128	496	13,308	552	11,975	352	6,858	330	125,569
Maryland									
Congressional District 1	13,481	239	16,848	515	14,882	794	9,868	299	119,067
Congressional District 2	10,719	484	11,721	713	10,550	504	7,085	237	94,555
Congressional District 3	12,248	302	16,949	803	16,722	365	9,213	669	95,852
Congressional District 4	11,796	688	13,639	819	14,109	766	7,311	253	82,886
Congressional District 5	12,507	515	13,021	523	11,801	366	7,294	262	91,360
Congressional District 6	10,410	883	15,694	676	13,244	504	6,241	110	92,930
Congressional District 7	11,439	823	13,381	651	11,222	504	8,282	432	101,210
Congressional District 8	15,305	750	17,106	653	15,686	382	11,624	588	102,542
Massachusetts									
Congressional District 1	14,695	815	13,984	680	13,246	432	8,605	315	119,698
Congressional District 2	14,740	551	17,083	784	12,425	516	9,004	510	97,796
Congressional District 3	12,861	616	13,954	718	15,297	1,407	7,102	257	93,923
Congressional District 4	16,258	509	17,388	518	15,497	397	11,291	253	97,224
Congressional District 5	12,299	365	14,874	791	14,341	662	11,633	334	99,795
Congressional District 6	15,683	1,149	18,759	817	14,229	437	10,720	458	114,605
Congressional District 7	7,430	450	11,063	1,409	8,966	422	4,228	251	77,996
Congressional District 8	15,101	1,147	16,292	681	15,961	1,032	9,713	641	108,836
Congressional District 9	15,058	812	19,108	687	16,273	826	11,425	569	142,587
Michigan									
Congressional District 1	11,640	232	13,124	499	10,804	541	7,729	337	160,931
Congressional District 2	12,379	576	11,712	368	9,957	384	5,103	464	106,626
Congressional District 3	11,057	419	10,665	217	8,186	402	5,603	278	106,634
Congressional District 4	10,528	837	9,767	432	7,912	498	6,744	31	134,762
Congressional District 5	7,889	436	8,413	475	6,803	155	4,858	250	133,834
Congressional District 6	12,185	448	13,252	347	10,740	267	6,390	48	115,912

Table F-5: 114th Congressional Districts—Employment and Labor Force Status, Civilian Labor Force—*Continued*

	60 to 61 Years		62 to 64 Years		65 to 69 Years		70 Years and Over		60 Years and Over Not in the Labor Force
	Employed	Unemployed	Employed	Unemployed	Employed	Unemployed	Employed	Unemployed	
Michigan—Cont.									
Congressional District 7	10,693	309	12,105	93	9,581	429	5,664	49	122,835
Congressional District 8	11,858	410	12,520	337	8,702	223	5,754	279	99,681
Congressional District 9	12,626	1,012	12,407	622	8,920	164	6,115	234	120,076
Congressional District 10	11,163	664	12,237	670	7,538	177	6,027	402	128,939
Congressional District 11	13,595	426	13,585	408	9,487	387	6,949	244	108,073
Congressional District 12	9,729	296	10,264	442	8,690	350	6,230	0	100,749
Congressional District 13	7,934	681	7,626	381	5,527	436	3,613	542	102,986
Congressional District 14	10,286	436	11,044	1,193	8,934	704	7,489	506	113,394
Minnesota									
Congressional District 1	12,526	237	14,807	143	9,112	187	7,815	326	103,730
Congressional District 2	11,067	481	11,592	81	10,293	534	6,531	76	81,008
Congressional District 3	12,557	326	15,283	550	12,725	697	6,360	101	92,610
Congressional District 4	11,457	412	13,340	307	9,844	172	5,350	140	93,198
Congressional District 5	11,278	487	11,790	189	10,176	203	6,115	36	76,174
Congressional District 6	10,884	181	11,259	686	7,571	151	5,581	179	73,566
Congressional District 7	13,406	511	15,158	296	12,040	306	9,020	248	116,783
Congressional District 8	12,244	489	13,478	443	9,908	338	6,629	240	130,958
Mississippi									
Congressional District 1	11,542	244	10,311	94	9,030	432	7,163	554	115,945
Congressional District 2	8,497	724	9,487	531	7,011	336	6,303	277	105,205
Congressional District 3	9,835	221	11,590	228	8,640	66	7,559	101	120,345
Congressional District 4	9,893	701	9,627	803	8,387	247	6,309	540	116,349
Missouri									
Congressional District 1	10,474	423	14,109	1,097	10,382	386	4,425	179	98,150
Congressional District 2	13,957	611	16,589	400	13,355	522	9,849	311	128,340
Congressional District 3	12,192	222	12,051	231	11,775	539	7,163	208	114,926
Congressional District 4	11,554	570	11,717	399	9,917	343	8,417	159	120,568
Congressional District 5	11,111	238	10,182	201	11,549	254	8,088	203	109,024
Congressional District 6	11,841	243	13,907	148	11,682	196	8,415	85	113,402
Congressional District 7	10,158	438	12,458	448	12,199	371	7,287	81	128,134
Congressional District 8	10,555	167	10,871	335	9,951	407	7,162	172	145,180
Montana									
Congressional District (at Large)	16,788	356	21,515	748	19,131	871	14,368	77	169,841
Nebraska									
Congressional District 1	11,353	197	12,677	101	11,174	71	7,423	69	81,145
Congressional District 2	10,138	191	11,732	96	8,910	105	6,157	18	68,406
Congressional District 3	12,853	296	13,808	457	13,005	150	12,148	283	97,640
Nevada									
Congressional District 1	8,041	715	11,409	714	9,094	988	6,346	714	89,035
Congressional District 2	13,141	366	13,357	863	10,830	896	6,619	548	110,527
Congressional District 3	13,853	650	11,488	965	10,394	509	7,554	1,002	107,411
Congressional District 4	9,367	1,219	8,965	668	7,238	542	6,132	440	105,151
New Hampshire									
Congressional District 1	15,935	715	15,621	442	13,648	460	7,990	201	96,560
Congressional District 2	14,350	583	16,348	489	12,866	499	9,028	256	101,007
New Jersey									
Congressional District 1	12,390	636	16,382	992	12,599	457	8,183	522	102,718
Congressional District 2	13,643	1,282	13,607	1,096	12,796	1,006	9,194	592	121,069
Congressional District 3	13,567	868	13,653	789	15,107	1,147	10,479	686	126,558
Congressional District 4	11,783	720	15,771	911	13,861	1,007	10,883	728	125,094
Congressional District 5	15,249	972	15,998	538	17,328	740	10,157	521	106,816
Congressional District 6	12,121	482	13,720	764	11,504	619	7,123	587	90,935
Congressional District 7	14,212	782	17,029	723	15,953	422	9,770	483	98,422
Congressional District 8	10,271	647	11,068	972	8,009	389	5,566	364	76,739
Congressional District 9	11,371	842	14,764	562	12,315	1,147	8,278	425	100,438
Congressional District 10	11,173	983	13,747	796	10,165	948	4,916	319	85,099
Congressional District 11	15,649	657	16,058	614	16,876	806	11,333	1,068	111,886
Congressional District 12	14,754	977	15,119	1,215	13,541	695	9,366	660	99,427
New Mexico									
Congressional District 1	11,864	626	11,248	887	9,766	763	6,486	492	109,369
Congressional District 2	9,211	457	10,160	235	8,960	403	7,696	314	116,930
Congressional District 3	10,786	624	11,930	241	11,496	621	8,108	288	105,128
New York									
Congressional District 1	13,876	680	12,854	418	14,525	1,035	10,625	307	111,402
Congressional District 2	11,176	452	12,784	335	9,794	413	8,635	689	96,740
Congressional District 3	12,596	181	16,224	800	16,538	615	13,380	453	119,257
Congressional District 4	13,650	630	15,696	751	13,845	335	10,103	237	105,671
Congressional District 5	11,713	790	11,106	868	10,839	731	5,476	227	100,728
Congressional District 6	13,547	603	12,469	644	12,064	1,000	6,982	362	118,429
Congressional District 7	8,737	607	7,424	407	5,907	158	3,294	105	78,301
Congressional District 8	9,806	656	12,302	643	11,226	558	6,132	253	104,972
Congressional District 9	10,157	918	14,011	1,171	11,886	577	5,201	322	97,730
Congressional District 10	12,220	936	13,302	393	14,437	1,080	13,050	753	89,779

Table F-5: 114th Congressional Districts—Employment and Labor Force Status, Civilian Labor Force—*Continued*

	60 to 61 Years		62 to 64 Years		65 to 69 Years		70 Years and Over		60 Years and Over Not in the Labor Force
	Employed	Unemployed	Employed	Unemployed	Employed	Unemployed	Employed	Unemployed	
New York—Cont.									
Congressional District 11	12,755	688	12,124	465	10,437	389	4,684	386	114,129
Congressional District 12	11,209	833	10,655	735	10,090	517	15,850	310	84,465
Congressional District 13	10,364	2,133	10,445	916	6,996	587	3,283	320	96,032
Congressional District 14	9,147	713	9,819	596	6,551	153	4,322	276	95,907
Congressional District 15	5,568	733	6,805	338	5,021	407	1,787	161	79,603
Congressional District 16	11,554	564	13,698	1,196	11,691	688	10,518	538	106,457
Congressional District 17	14,358	745	17,076	647	15,379	483	10,033	712	99,049
Congressional District 18	13,592	639	12,934	411	12,642	267	8,114	236	96,789
Congressional District 19	12,208	760	16,364	988	12,862	369	9,726	613	127,702
Congressional District 20	10,593	410	14,693	551	11,992	595	8,729	758	112,093
Congressional District 21	10,717	537	11,236	585	9,323	275	7,421	197	123,908
Congressional District 22	11,022	188	13,549	692	10,483	511	8,067	190	125,012
Congressional District 23	13,027	618	12,029	497	10,671	225	8,018	335	123,042
Congressional District 24	12,135	560	12,170	470	9,215	326	7,426	608	115,115
Congressional District 25	11,411	588	13,617	481	10,513	540	8,304	276	113,503
Congressional District 26	11,918	168	11,713	451	10,653	753	7,412	301	123,271
Congressional District 27	14,446	556	14,824	464	11,509	664	7,410	178	121,907
North Carolina									
Congressional District 1	9,822	874	10,229	576	10,063	322	6,789	288	124,325
Congressional District 2	8,323	263	9,672	601	9,705	188	6,724	171	107,926
Congressional District 3	8,942	458	10,192	124	11,006	701	7,396	514	112,605
Congressional District 4	10,118	222	10,643	457	10,624	178	5,624	159	82,937
Congressional District 5	13,821	707	12,264	249	12,086	622	6,049	223	125,713
Congressional District 6	13,657	361	13,888	405	11,914	322	9,500	247	126,380
Congressional District 7	13,613	726	13,640	354	12,640	314	7,439	551	137,570
Congressional District 8	9,338	953	10,380	644	9,875	584	6,179	217	117,795
Congressional District 9	13,281	517	13,246	1,207	10,579	660	8,144	352	93,684
Congressional District 10	12,192	625	12,379	336	10,905	580	6,923	306	134,384
Congressional District 11	10,789	405	13,289	240	11,287	494	8,038	444	166,218
Congressional District 12	8,280	797	8,817	909	6,673	671	4,401	134	78,401
Congressional District 13	13,318	633	14,636	1,151	10,527	413	7,059	297	100,342
North Dakota									
Congressional District (at Large)	12,416	139	15,831	233	12,372	199	9,461	141	97,343
Ohio									
Congressional District 1	11,605	600	11,733	510	10,081	172	7,496	281	99,544
Congressional District 2	12,127	331	13,332	286	12,409	510	7,774	380	114,959
Congressional District 3	8,604	482	12,948	266	8,140	237	4,306	173	73,906
Congressional District 4	12,689	661	11,762	796	9,399	324	5,891	126	122,301
Congressional District 5	13,099	570	14,753	580	11,421	430	8,175	152	116,910
Congressional District 6	12,735	216	12,225	309	10,630	357	7,718	99	136,625
Congressional District 7	12,369	548	11,868	206	11,625	287	6,930	634	130,801
Congressional District 8	11,834	330	11,869	382	11,101	472	8,334	151	110,324
Congressional District 9	9,950	601	10,952	714	8,597	227	5,767	116	107,504
Congressional District 10	11,968	512	13,844	522	11,050	254	8,914	141	118,595
Congressional District 11	10,800	1,175	13,224	538	9,991	339	6,232	418	112,235
Congressional District 12	12,530	265	14,618	444	11,721	262	7,121	276	99,876
Congressional District 13	12,423	379	12,409	293	10,892	66	7,354	585	128,161
Congressional District 14	15,829	449	15,383	385	15,169	607	9,205	520	123,352
Congressional District 15	10,873	460	12,262	104	10,234	205	7,559	458	109,746
Congressional District 16	16,079	593	15,005	564	12,339	427	9,089	307	124,890
Oklahoma									
Congressional District 1	13,152	326	13,365	351	13,229	390	9,807	373	99,680
Congressional District 2	10,373	320	10,405	150	9,788	234	9,303	284	141,099
Congressional District 3	10,916	188	12,371	234	11,677	204	9,514	204	116,102
Congressional District 4	11,284	198	12,051	202	10,703	285	7,465	261	106,577
Congressional District 5	10,825	273	10,991	213	12,081	361	9,680	295	100,448
Oregon									
Congressional District 1	12,754	413	13,211	255	11,849	523	6,395	168	109,318
Congressional District 2	14,177	682	14,735	711	11,380	884	7,330	457	161,835
Congressional District 3	12,854	702	14,217	597	10,582	195	5,206	200	107,453
Congressional District 4	15,150	832	13,579	502	12,748	368	7,242	324	160,813
Congressional District 5	14,874	629	17,600	697	13,686	822	6,861	259	131,707
Pennsylvania									
Congressional District 1	8,830	334	10,134	375	7,091	364	5,796	474	88,649
Congressional District 2	9,128	352	9,435	684	8,941	530	7,326	310	99,092
Congressional District 3	12,920	600	12,627	356	10,514	617	6,908	288	129,602
Congressional District 4	13,346	524	13,834	643	12,125	235	7,053	278	114,330
Congressional District 5	12,310	1,028	11,902	866	10,025	360	6,591	302	127,298
Congressional District 6	14,181	826	15,317	557	13,040	413	10,613	500	101,359
Congressional District 7	15,023	771	14,456	934	15,687	488	9,263	478	111,648
Congressional District 8	15,314	756	15,677	785	16,683	425	9,388	603	108,468
Congressional District 9	12,256	440	11,653	231	11,380	507	8,927	279	137,041
Congressional District 10	11,818	513	12,983	564	11,379	487	8,952	678	133,158
Congressional District 11	13,957	534	13,111	483	11,498	419	8,047	435	127,177
Congressional District 12	14,301	800	16,273	993	14,873	687	8,992	233	138,611
Congressional District 13	12,658	474	14,987	371	12,752	534	9,620	695	104,625

Table F-5: 114th Congressional Districts—Employment and Labor Force Status, Civilian Labor Force—*Continued*

	60 to 61 Years		62 to 64 Years		65 to 69 Years		70 Years and Over		60 Years and Over Not in the Labor Force
	Employed	Unemployed	Employed	Unemployed	Employed	Unemployed	Employed	Unemployed	
Pennsylvania—Cont.									
Congressional District 14..............	13,187	602	14,738	474	9,747	486	8,939	437	114,239
Congressional District 15..............	15,712	908	15,221	651	12,561	735	7,727	276	116,834
Congressional District 16..............	12,714	385	11,732	532	13,117	232	9,288	420	103,460
Congressional District 17..............	10,814	565	13,677	544	10,576	983	9,514	376	129,822
Congressional District 18..............	15,359	342	14,279	574	14,988	349	9,068	288	132,087
Rhode Island									
Congressional District 1................	7,421	875	11,039	268	8,591	277	5,244	292	80,689
Congressional District 2................	9,776	495	11,115	377	9,888	431	6,636	773	83,397
South Carolina									
Congressional District 1................	12,712	799	13,111	435	11,817	170	7,268	240	119,259
Congressional District 2................	11,034	400	11,474	205	10,477	264	5,803	120	99,282
Congressional District 3................	9,191	520	11,896	833	10,193	531	6,760	220	121,658
Congressional District 4................	10,784	330	10,443	211	10,061	161	6,040	126	105,222
Congressional District 5................	10,384	670	11,415	566	11,228	464	6,158	101	109,600
Congressional District 6................	9,527	284	9,837	560	7,570	705	5,427	226	104,091
Congressional District 7................	12,214	617	12,362	721	11,204	239	6,672	103	137,936
South Dakota									
Congressional District (at Large)	15,732	274	18,421	139	16,848	277	12,209	144	118,494
Tennessee									
Congressional District 1................	10,176	757	11,839	282	10,999	451	9,435	357	142,646
Congressional District 2................	10,778	316	11,726	670	11,115	490	7,418	69	125,836
Congressional District 3................	11,413	460	12,866	609	11,659	603	7,058	323	129,580
Congressional District 4................	7,998	287	12,135	329	9,512	670	7,313	485	110,403
Congressional District 5................	12,179	283	11,229	163	10,694	529	7,251	269	84,599
Congressional District 6................	9,607	310	12,753	541	11,206	428	7,442	295	130,499
Congressional District 7................	10,870	387	9,898	667	10,286	67	5,966	168	109,487
Congressional District 8................	12,782	838	12,500	863	12,826	397	7,884	127	109,784
Congressional District 9................	8,918	624	10,734	397	7,853	549	5,982	176	81,063
Texas									
Congressional District 1................	9,330	256	13,035	333	10,422	385	7,970	178	116,868
Congressional District 2................	12,151	773	15,489	745	11,397	295	7,059	119	69,549
Congressional District 3................	11,882	762	13,973	931	11,570	395	6,879	153	71,907
Congressional District 4................	10,807	468	10,640	156	8,909	450	8,453	323	119,829
Congressional District 5................	10,227	395	10,644	594	9,081	506	6,553	114	97,288
Congressional District 6................	10,603	42	10,518	171	11,125	300	6,495	16	74,335
Congressional District 7................	10,659	192	13,559	757	11,321	452	8,707	42	67,944
Congressional District 8................	11,572	264	13,589	148	12,068	134	8,055	663	96,246
Congressional District 9................	8,858	163	12,428	1,235	8,562	493	6,738	429	66,186
Congressional District 10..............	12,480	628	12,849	582	10,241	498	7,061	105	88,561
Congressional District 11..............	12,999	322	12,299	320	13,320	438	11,148	120	108,241
Congressional District 12..............	11,240	541	10,443	628	10,693	222	6,881	15	91,788
Congressional District 13..............	10,539	231	11,519	243	11,600	308	8,353	44	99,081
Congressional District 14..............	11,318	264	12,400	556	9,112	34	5,670	188	98,756
Congressional District 15..............	7,623	706	7,081	624	7,932	109	4,677	364	82,534
Congressional District 16..............	8,360	446	8,052	331	6,075	142	5,869	245	87,751
Congressional District 17..............	11,405	976	9,077	274	8,029	225	6,136	109	84,825
Congressional District 18..............	7,967	745	10,636	812	6,132	221	4,402	113	69,060
Congressional District 19..............	9,903	265	10,636	195	11,944	118	8,479	97	90,032
Congressional District 20..............	8,806	617	8,294	293	6,515	251	4,933	320	84,711
Congressional District 21..............	13,558	504	14,617	779	14,974	466	8,923	428	113,059
Congressional District 22..............	11,551	219	9,712	65	10,678	639	7,104	303	77,650
Congressional District 23..............	8,083	572	9,371	304	9,988	550	6,268	158	91,714
Congressional District 24..............	13,016	302	12,948	503	11,650	248	7,875	390	68,265
Congressional District 25..............	10,320	608	12,731	288	12,434	397	6,683	110	95,259
Congressional District 26..............	9,846	703	9,438	550	11,304	678	4,647	247	66,126
Congressional District 27..............	11,491	784	13,300	696	9,233	328	7,814	193	107,946
Congressional District 28..............	6,392	265	7,715	235	6,221	230	3,982	23	85,479
Congressional District 29..............	8,266	753	6,482	139	7,529	471	3,431	36	59,428
Congressional District 30..............	8,767	517	9,320	493	7,850	572	4,761	407	75,034
Congressional District 31..............	10,613	497	11,584	702	10,037	340	4,191	195	87,002
Congressional District 32..............	11,704	352	12,657	449	12,233	256	9,097	326	79,863
Congressional District 33..............	6,264	229	6,714	351	5,476	202	3,439	37	62,132
Congressional District 34..............	7,433	435	7,143	169	6,225	290	5,146	262	100,260
Congressional District 35..............	6,945	195	8,910	357	6,905	317	4,807	136	71,555
Congressional District 36..............	11,874	427	11,673	332	11,126	366	6,538	248	104,894
Utah									
Congressional District 1................	9,358	343	10,636	453	7,386	93	4,729	101	73,431
Congressional District 2................	8,856	521	9,248	396	7,822	154	5,871	158	86,483
Congressional District 3................	9,369	207	12,141	413	8,784	98	5,392	165	65,980
Congressional District 4................	8,947	289	12,303	200	7,722	76	5,731	137	66,324
Vermont									
Congressional District (at Large)	14,193	848	14,784	571	14,435	421	10,921	297	97,028
Virginia									
Congressional District 1................	11,740	498	13,906	431	11,070	381	7,136	156	103,285
Congressional District 2................	11,980	919	12,626	738	10,156	407	6,208	279	92,945

Table F-5: 114th Congressional Districts—Employment and Labor Force Status, Civilian Labor Force—*Continued*

	60 to 61 Years		62 to 64 Years		65 to 69 Years		70 Years and Over		60 Years and Over Not in the Labor Force
	Employed	Unemployed	Employed	Unemployed	Employed	Unemployed	Employed	Unemployed	
Virginia—Cont.									
Congressional District 3	10,925	510	11,175	570	9,008	858	6,616	109	91,222
Congressional District 4	12,450	510	11,994	169	11,489	213	7,984	278	99,741
Congressional District 5	13,343	239	14,889	595	13,662	519	10,668	383	136,148
Congressional District 6	12,667	268	14,567	524	13,380	237	10,356	431	124,630
Congressional District 7	14,266	671	17,079	485	13,916	332	10,179	271	106,966
Congressional District 8	11,303	383	15,079	237	11,403	323	6,931	167	72,248
Congressional District 9	10,533	210	12,260	457	9,847	75	6,923	469	143,365
Congressional District 10	13,688	750	16,779	851	13,246	817	8,804	281	78,774
Congressional District 11	12,512	1,389	16,288	689	12,888	231	6,665	240	73,997
Washington									
Congressional District 1	13,402	673	14,226	849	11,501	140	5,110	137	87,841
Congressional District 2	12,764	536	12,737	562	11,454	241	5,824	287	107,766
Congressional District 3	10,554	477	11,535	786	10,301	468	5,470	166	118,291
Congressional District 4	9,773	403	12,649	268	8,776	285	4,489	173	94,534
Congressional District 5	11,242	619	12,233	457	11,555	194	5,441	105	109,442
Congressional District 6	11,256	791	12,932	497	12,598	823	6,519	325	126,220
Congressional District 7	14,577	693	14,508	122	13,407	515	7,299	177	90,593
Congressional District 8	10,869	376	13,132	307	10,507	261	5,217	227	85,388
Congressional District 9	9,769	439	12,536	670	10,373	354	6,676	72	91,802
Congressional District 10	10,229	549	11,152	498	9,344	158	4,883	59	102,127
West Virginia									
Congressional District 1	9,334	417	10,985	76	8,788	271	6,889	83	114,946
Congressional District 2	8,756	690	10,160	139	9,808	485	7,079	368	115,638
Congressional District 3	8,027	461	8,614	340	7,811	127	4,783	31	128,173
Wisconsin									
Congressional District 1	12,678	565	12,105	409	10,177	310	7,198	184	107,771
Congressional District 2	14,152	930	14,454	430	11,915	658	7,591	264	95,438
Congressional District 3	13,577	208	12,256	259	11,918	168	6,421	108	117,195
Congressional District 4	9,955	478	9,456	207	7,473	417	4,871	291	84,299
Congressional District 5	13,769	487	14,902	491	12,543	397	9,211	307	113,746
Congressional District 6	13,617	505	14,887	278	11,128	136	7,705	165	118,818
Congressional District 7	13,489	573	15,110	509	11,258	418	7,970	298	135,278
Congressional District 8	12,504	521	13,602	197	10,363	212	6,401	32	115,437
Wyoming									
Congressional District (at Large)	11,866	384	12,623	175	11,009	102	6,509	300	78,575

PART G

INCOME AND POVERTY

INCOME AND POVERTY

The Census Bureau reports that real median household income (adjusted for inflation) for all households in 2014 was statistically unchanged from the 2013 median income.[1] At the same time, inflation pushes prices higher which disproportionately affects persons on fixed incomes, a group which includes many seniors. The Census definition of income includes sources of cash income: wages and salary, social security, retirement, interest, dividends and rent, for example. It does not include measures of assets and may not be a good measure of overall wealth. However, it still illustrates the wide variation across states and sub-state areas in income distributions and poverty. Most importantly poverty because that population likely has very little in assets to offset their limited money income.

This historical data indicates that the median household income of householders age 65 and over is considerably below that of all householders. However, it also shows that the gap has narrowed in the last 5 years—until 2014 which shows a slight increase. This may be an indication of greater income grow among all households as the impact of the recession fades while seniors don't see as large a benefit.

Median Household Income, Adjusted for Inflation

	Householder 65 Years and Over	All Households	Gap
2008	$33,787	$52,029	$18,242
2009	$33,712	$50,221	$16,509
2010	$34,381	$50,046	$15,665
2011	$35,107	$50,502	$15,395
2012	$36,743	$51,371	$14,628
2013	$37,847	$52,250	$14,403
2014	$39,186	$53,657	$14,471

U.S. Census Bureau, American Community Survey 1-year Estimates, Table B19049.

---

1. U.S. Census Bureau, Current Population Reports, P60-245, *Income, Poverty, and Health Insurance Coverage in the United States: 2012*, U.S. Government Printing Office, Washington, DC, 2013.

Median Income

There are 22 states above the national median income of householders age 65 and over. Alaska has the highest median income at $58,311 followed closely by Hawaii with $58,150. Mississippi has the lowest at $30,254 followed by West Virginia ($32,219), Kentucky ($32,870) and Arkansas ($32,897).

The county with the highest median income, with nearly $86,000, is Fairfax County, Virginia followed by Montgomery County, Maryland at $77,934. In 389 counties, householders age 65 and over have median incomes greater than the national average and 105 counties have a median income over $50,000 while the median in 60 counties is below $30,000. Each of the counties in the states of Alaska (3), Connecticut (8), Delaware (3), Hawaii (4), Nevada (2), Utah (6), Vermont (1), and Virginia (20) have median incomes above the national median. Among householders 65 and over, Berkeley, California is the city with the highest median income at $92,475 and at $16,292, Passaic, New Jersey has the lowest median income, less than one half the national figure. In 260 cities the median income is less than the national median and in 71 cities it is below $30,000. More than 100 cities (105) have median incomes above $50,000. New York City, the city with the largest number of householders 65 and over had a median income of $32,041, more than seven thousand dollars below the national figure.

The Fairbanks, Alaska metro area has the highest median for householders age 65 and over at $69,669 followed by the Washington-Arlington-Alexandria MSA with a median of $67,969. Only five other areas, Anchorage, Alaska; Urban Honolulu, Hawaii; Kahului-Wailuku-Lahaina, Hawaii; Trenton, New Jersey; and Boulder, Colorado have medians above $60,000. The Hinesville, Georgia metro area has the lowest median at $21,993 and 46 metropolitan and micropolitan areas have median incomes below $30,000. Congressional districts with median incomes above the national figure number 205. The highest median ($80,744) is in Virginia's 11th Congressional District while the lowest is New York's 15th Congressional District at only $15,975. Thirty-seven congressional districts have median incomes that are less than $30,000 while 58 districts have medians above $50,000.

Median Household Income of Householders 65 Years and Over

Percent
- Under $34,000
- $34,000 - $36,999
- $37,000 - $39,999
- $40,000 - $45,999
- $46,000 or Higher

Percent of the Population 75 Years and Over With Income Below the Poverty Level

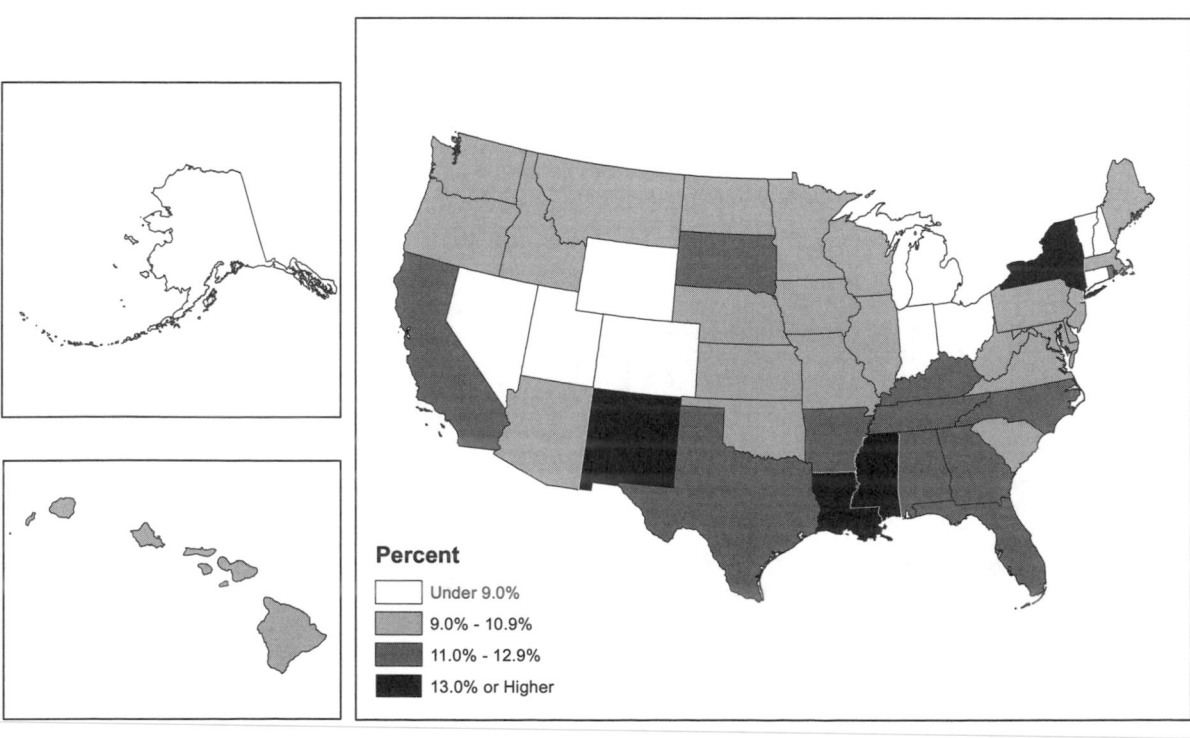

Percent
- Under 9.0%
- 9.0% - 10.9%
- 11.0% - 12.9%
- 13.0% or Higher

Poverty Status and Receipt of Food Stamps

Poverty status is determined by comparing total family or unrelated individual income to the established national poverty thresholds which vary by size and type of household and number of children. When a family or single person household is determined to be in poverty, every member of the family is so defined. The national poverty rate of persons age 55 to 64 years is 11.1 percent, for persons 65 to 74 years it declines to 8.6 percent then increases again to 10.7 percent for the 75 and over population. This pattern of decline to the 65 to 74 population followed by an increase in the 75 and over holds for every state except North and South Dakota where the poverty rate increases across each age. The pattern does not hold for other sub-state areas.

The poverty rate for the 55 to 64 population is higher than the national rate in 23 states and the highest rate (19.2 percent) is in the District of Columbia. The District of Columbia is also the highest for the 75 and over population at 16.7 percent. New Hampshire has the lowest rate among the 55 to 64 age category at 6.0 percent but Alaska has the lowest rate (3.6 percent) for the 75 and over population. While the District of Columbia has the highest 75 and over rate, the next closest is Arkansas at 12.7 percent. Seventeen states are above the national rate for the 75 and over population. Food stamp recipient households are those containing one or more people

age 60 and over. The District of Columbia (16.0 percent) and the State of New York (16.1 percent) have the highest percentages of food stamp recipient households. Wyoming has the lowest rate of food stamp recipients at 4.6 percent. Twenty-five states are above the national rate of 9.5 percent.

McKinley County, New Mexico has the highest rate of poverty among the 55 to 64 population at 33.7 percent and 25.8 percent of the 75 and over population is also in poverty. Both measures are more than two and a half times the national rates for their respective age groups. McKinley County is not the highest rate among the 75 and over population however. That distinction belongs to Webb County, Texas at 33.9 percent. Carver County, Minnesota has the lowest poverty rate for the 55 to 64 population at only 1.6 percent. In five counties, Hancock County, Indiana; Fairbanks North Star Borough, Alaska; Riley County, Kansas; Platte County, Missouri; and Hancock County, Ohio all have less than 1 percent of their 75 and over population in poverty. There are 328 counties with poverty rates above the national figure for the 55 to 64 population and 253 are above the nation for the 75 and over population. Bronx County, New York has the highest food stamp recipient rate at 36.8 percent while Delaware County, Ohio is lowest at 1.5 percent. Ten percent or more households with a person 60 years or over receive food stamps in 310 counties and in 17 counties more than 20 percent are recipient households.

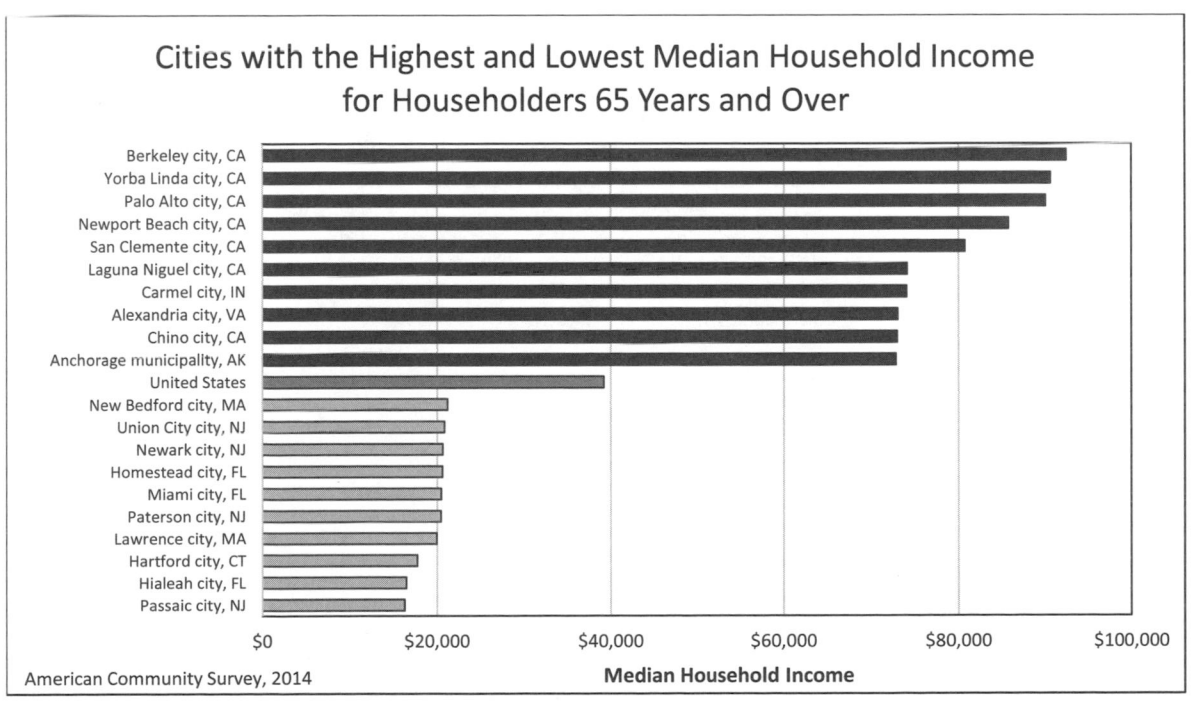

American Community Survey, 2014

In 19 cities, more than 25 percent of the 55 to 64 population is in poverty and the 75 and over poverty rate is over 25 percent in only 17 cities. More than half of the 75 and over population (52.5 percent) of Pasco, Washington is in poverty followed closely by Homestead, Florida. In 20 cities the poverty rate for persons 75 and over is less than 3 percent. The poverty rate for persons 55 to 64 is over 30 percent in six cities: Flint, Michigan; Youngstown, Ohio; Brownsville, Texas; Passaic and Trenton, New Jersey; and Lawrence, Massachusetts. Just over half (52.6 percent) of the households with a member 60 or over in Hialeah, Florida is receiving food stamps. In 38 cities, at least 25 percent of the households are receiving food stamps. San Clemente, California has the lowest rate at only 0.4 percent.

The Gallup, New Mexico micropolitan area has the highest rate of poverty (33.7 percent) among the 55 to 64 population while the Faribault-Northfield, Minnesota micropolitan area is lowest at 3.3 percent. Five other metropolitan areas are below 5 percent in the rate of poverty for 55 to 64 year olds. Among the 75 and over population, the Laredo, Texas metropolitan area has the highest rate (33.9 percent) and the Fairbanks, Alaska metro has the lowest rate which, along with the Findlay, Ohio micropolitan area are both below one percent.

Only three areas have more than 25 percent of households receiving food stamps with the highest being the Laredo, Texas metro at 33.5 percent. The Faribault-Northfield, Minnesota micropolitan area has the lowest percent receiving food stamps at 1.7 percent and in 40 metropolitan or micropolitan areas, less than 5 percent of the households receive food stamps.

New York's 15th Congressional District has the highest poverty rate (34.8 percent) among the 55 to 64 population, well above the next highest in Arizona's 7th Congressional District at 27.1 percent. Virginia's 11th District is the lowest at 3.4 percent and 8 other districts have a poverty rate under 5 percent. Among the 75 and over population, seven congressional districts have poverty rates over 25 percent, led again by New York's 15th District at 38.8 percent. New York's 7th, 8th, and 13th Districts have the next highest rates with all of them over 29 percent. Alaska's At-large Congressional District is the lowest at 3.6 percent. New York's 15th District also has the highest percent (51.7 percent) of households with members over 60 receiving food stamps. Three additional districts have more than a third of the households receiving food stamps: Florida's 27th District and New York's 7th and 13th Districts.

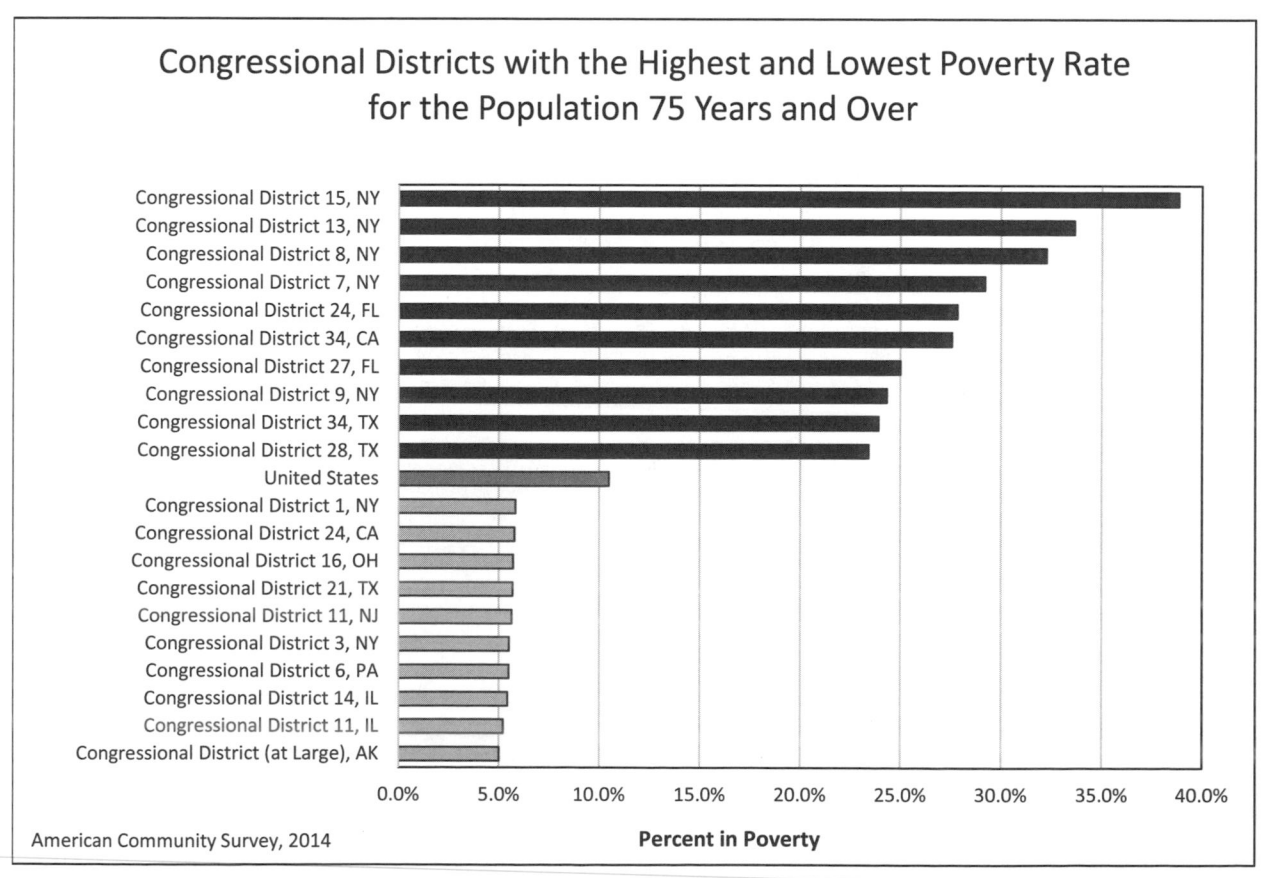

Congressional Districts with the Highest and Lowest Poverty Rate for the Population 75 Years and Over

American Community Survey, 2014

Percent in Poverty

Table G-1: States—Income, Poverty Status and Receipt of Food Stamps (SNAP)

	Income of Households with Householder 65 Years and Over					Poverty Rate of Persons			Households with 1 or More Persons 60 Years and Over	
	Total Households	Less Than $25,000	$25,000 - $49,999	$50,000 - $99,999	$100,000 or More	Median Household Income	55 to 64 Years	65 to 74 Years	75 Years and Over	Receiving SNAP	Not Receiving SNAP
United States	28,146,157	8,995,856	8,049,002	7,138,673	3,962,626	2,025,047	11.1%	8.6%	10.7%	4,498,585	39,197,516
Alabama	472,668	176,256	142,603	108,484	45,325	33,375	13.8%	10.5%	12.2%	74,279	634,840
Alaska	40,996	8,930	8,811	12,601	10,654	58,311	8.7%	4.7%	3.6%	6,139	67,293
Arizona	647,612	192,039	199,102	175,897	80,574	40,195	14.0%	9.4%	9.5%	89,208	873,830
Arkansas	289,802	112,893	86,485	64,441	25,983	32,897	13.0%	9.1%	12.7%	41,020	389,931
California	2,830,348	817,758	692,929	739,870	579,791	45,732	11.9%	9.7%	11.8%	292,343	4,414,247
Colorado	418,629	112,926	116,144	120,253	69,306	45,093	8.7%	6.4%	8.1%	48,698	633,696
Connecticut	339,658	91,995	89,619	91,546	66,498	46,216	7.4%	6.9%	8.8%	54,710	465,367
Delaware	92,377	23,080	27,297	28,116	13,884	45,510	9.3%	6.5%	9.0%	12,337	127,198
District of Columbia	50,463	16,060	9,803	12,302	12,298	47,906	19.2%	12.9%	16.7%	12,596	66,366
Florida	2,223,738	713,016	651,881	559,950	298,891	38,425	13.7%	9.7%	11.4%	385,518	2,860,560
Georgia	750,454	256,226	215,910	182,901	95,417	36,859	13.0%	9.4%	12.1%	152,866	1,053,335
Hawaii	122,744	26,818	27,185	35,994	32,747	58,150	11.3%	7.0%	9.8%	20,987	177,083
Idaho	144,224	49,495	44,905	36,966	12,858	36,048	9.1%	8.8%	10.4%	15,976	205,667
Illinois	1,105,546	345,798	315,230	281,510	163,008	39,898	10.2%	7.9%	10.1%	184,494	1,535,917
Indiana	585,693	182,005	198,452	148,771	56,465	37,521	9.8%	6.1%	8.2%	72,246	820,586
Iowa	310,729	102,137	96,962	79,007	32,623	37,099	7.5%	5.7%	9.4%	31,319	425,870
Kansas	260,361	80,144	78,414	69,477	32,326	39,009	8.3%	7.0%	9.0%	24,150	369,692
Kentucky	413,817	156,903	131,196	90,741	34,977	33,041	14.4%	10.5%	12.5%	77,905	551,216
Louisiana	395,166	154,307	114,286	81,852	44,721	32,870	15.4%	12.3%	13.6%	76,823	540,907
Maine	151,281	52,211	47,853	36,262	14,955	35,498	10.0%	7.8%	10.5%	28,778	202,415
Maryland	495,982	121,140	116,250	143,061	115,531	52,458	7.5%	6.1%	9.3%	72,983	721,093
Massachusetts	624,797	198,745	156,247	157,293	112,512	41,489	9.1%	8.4%	10.3%	125,838	847,423
Michigan	969,176	295,856	319,965	252,230	101,125	38,373	10.8%	7.8%	8.7%	172,269	1,308,308
Minnesota	486,149	147,600	143,988	136,428	58,133	40,041	8.0%	5.6%	9.9%	48,639	690,872
Mississippi	273,148	113,957	79,438	57,046	22,707	30,254	16.9%	12.3%	14.5%	53,813	360,607
Missouri	584,979	198,380	182,573	146,007	58,019	36,059	11.1%	8.0%	10.6%	78,751	798,371
Montana	106,654	36,784	33,479	25,192	11,199	35,710	11.5%	7.8%	9.0%	11,082	151,815
Nebraska	173,986	58,275	51,424	44,662	19,625	37,174	7.2%	5.7%	10.6%	16,509	240,766
Nevada	235,135	71,960	68,077	65,513	29,585	40,482	12.1%	8.1%	8.5%	37,923	338,375
New Hampshire	123,515	33,555	37,054	33,280	19,626	43,069	6.0%	4.0%	6.9%	12,018	190,612
New Jersey	783,199	223,291	190,872	205,251	163,785	46,170	7.9%	7.6%	9.9%	105,002	1,139,630
New Mexico	199,105	72,176	53,500	48,521	24,908	36,740	15.5%	13.0%	13.4%	34,049	272,130
New York	1,776,118	601,356	450,154	429,462	295,146	39,278	12.0%	10.5%	13.3%	447,398	2,338,176
North Carolina	908,096	314,020	272,307	221,846	99,923	36,252	12.4%	8.7%	11.1%	154,215	1,222,608
North Dakota	67,092	21,153	20,290	17,335	8,314	37,196	6.1%	6.9%	10.9%	6,248	93,978
Ohio	1,142,958	375,799	371,090	282,177	113,892	36,574	10.7%	7.7%	8.6%	182,459	1,548,627
Oklahoma	351,005	117,725	106,845	87,875	38,560	36,820	13.1%	7.8%	9.6%	48,779	479,905
Oregon	392,764	121,810	118,880	104,200	47,874	39,337	11.4%	8.4%	9.5%	86,034	525,876
Pennsylvania	1,321,941	446,802	404,319	320,989	149,831	36,415	9.4%	7.2%	9.1%	201,082	1,793,851
Rhode Island	102,237	34,420	27,902	23,088	16,827	38,391	10.6%	7.9%	11.9%	23,341	136,334
South Carolina	475,305	157,829	146,717	116,077	54,682	36,694	14.0%	8.6%	10.3%	76,557	640,645
South Dakota	82,186	28,821	25,745	18,808	8,812	35,240	8.6%	8.9%	12.7%	8,951	113,563
Tennessee	613,436	223,941	184,945	143,704	60,846	34,224	13.0%	9.1%	11.7%	122,165	818,138
Texas	1,843,597	608,049	502,306	460,869	272,373	39,202	11.1%	10.0%	12.4%	329,172	2,660,896
Utah	175,745	44,155	50,222	55,601	25,767	45,738	7.8%	5.5%	8.3%	16,770	265,302
Vermont	67,260	21,903	20,753	17,122	7,482	36,346	9.6%	6.0%	8.7%	12,460	91,838
Virginia	702,308	197,021	176,221	192,551	136,515	45,966	8.0%	6.7%	9.5%	88,233	1,022,671
Washington	605,828	163,974	175,544	171,289	95,021	44,104	9.4%	7.6%	9.8%	112,924	844,241
West Virginia	211,788	81,808	68,963	47,532	13,485	32,219	13.5%	8.6%	10.3%	33,246	280,517
Wisconsin	552,831	177,103	183,075	141,970	50,683	36,606	8.5%	5.7%	9.0%	73,514	765,465
Wyoming	51,531	15,451	14,790	14,753	6,537	40,773	9.0%	4.7%	8.7%	3,769	78,867

Table G-2: Counties—Income, Poverty Status and Receipt of Food Stamps (SNAP)

	Income of Households with Householder 65 Years and Over					Poverty Rate of Persons			Households with 1 or More Persons 60 Years and Over	
	Total Households	Less Than $25,000	$25,000 - $49,999	$50,000 - $99,999	$100,000 or More	Median Household Income	55 to 64 Years	65 to 74 Years	75 Years and Over	Receiving SNAP	Not Receiving SNAP
Alabama											
Baldwin County	23,509	7,320	7,164	6,654	2,371	39,143	9.6%	11.1%	10.8%	1,650	31,792
Calhoun County	11,702	4,567	3,508	2,689	938	32,658	14.9%	17.0%	10.3%	1,465	17,382
Cullman County	8,705	3,871	2,842	1,640	352	26,835	10.5%	12.6%	5.8%	1,153	11,175
DeKalb County	7,047	2,821	1,728	1,671	827	28,831	27.7%	11.7%	12.2%	1,081	8,711
Elmore County	7,218	2,424	1,766	2,112	916	40,800	9.5%	4.8%	7.7%	906	9,763
Etowah County	11,562	4,931	3,078	2,792	761	32,024	12.9%	5.9%	14.9%	1,516	14,903
Houston County	10,400	4,111	3,358	2,055	876	31,822	15.4%	9.8%	11.6%	1,372	14,471
Jefferson County	62,053	20,323	18,555	16,674	6,501	36,863	15.5%	9.2%	10.7%	10,550	84,567
Lauderdale County	11,076	4,276	3,544	2,393	863	31,786	14.1%	9.7%	7.8%	1,721	14,219
Lee County	10,631	3,862	2,820	2,416	1,533	37,990	12.5%	6.9%	12.2%	1,561	15,318
Limestone County	7,272	2,174	2,264	2,139	695	39,375	10.9%	8.6%	4.0%	817	10,432
Madison County	30,351	9,131	6,799	8,979	5,442	46,171	9.4%	13.2%	8.9%	3,302	43,738
Marshall County	8,968	4,010	2,812	1,260	886	26,955	15.7%	8.3%	16.3%	1,561	12,664
Mobile County	37,513	13,698	11,285	8,705	3,825	35,086	13.5%	10.6%	12.8%	7,306	49,854
Montgomery County	20,165	6,815	5,752	4,734	2,864	35,209	11.2%	8.6%	12.2%	4,355	26,171
Morgan County	11,989	4,528	4,066	2,335	1,060	34,187	10.2%	9.4%	5.0%	1,310	16,511
Shelby County	16,635	4,475	5,536	3,507	3,117	42,742	9.9%	6.2%	8.1%	1,376	24,774
St. Clair County	8,466	2,597	2,622	2,443	804	36,742	9.7%	5.3%	24.9%	1,105	10,964
Talladega County	7,759	3,447	2,412	1,579	321	29,272	16.6%	12.0%	16.0%	2,045	10,318
Tuscaloosa County	14,352	4,781	3,757	3,983	1,831	37,385	11.6%	9.4%	7.3%	1,454	21,634
Walker County	7,720	3,293	2,302	1,309	816	30,628	21.2%	11.7%	12.4%	1,205	9,920
Alaska											
Anchorage Municipality	14,870	2,408	2,865	5,097	4,500	72,850	7.4%	4.6%	3.2%	1,876	24,902
Fairbanks North Star Borough	5,189	942	1,058	1,605	1,584	69,668	6.0%	4.1%	0.0%	472	8,274
Matanuska-Susitna Borough	5,232	1,407	1,389	1,297	1,139	44,913	9.6%	6.1%	6.7%	941	8,760
Arizona											
Apache County	5,612	2,744	1,342	1,259	267	25,767	26.2%	17.8%	19.8%	1,474	7,269
Cochise County	15,100	6,025	4,473	3,389	1,213	30,976	18.1%	14.9%	12.2%	2,599	19,974
Coconino County	9,700	2,185	3,242	2,349	1,924	42,437	12.6%	8.8%	17.6%	1,644	14,623
Maricopa County	337,926	93,721	100,176	94,425	49,604	42,266	12.5%	8.3%	8.8%	41,352	473,395
Mohave County	32,387	10,834	11,898	7,832	1,823	34,866	19.8%	9.4%	7.2%	4,406	41,309
Navajo County	10,706	4,895	2,670	2,656	485	28,168	26.0%	18.3%	15.9%	3,031	12,075
Pima County	112,162	30,744	34,269	31,700	15,449	41,719	14.3%	9.5%	8.3%	16,600	147,750
Pinal County	41,068	11,430	13,652	12,548	3,438	42,288	12.5%	11.0%	7.8%	5,687	55,382
Yavapai County	38,908	12,118	13,657	10,081	3,052	36,586	14.6%	6.6%	11.3%	4,245	49,477
Yuma County	22,044	9,230	6,477	4,369	1,968	31,587	19.7%	15.5%	16.9%	4,389	25,335
Arkansas											
Benton County	18,489	6,041	5,279	5,107	2,062	37,755	9.5%	5.9%	9.7%	1,165	26,753
Craighead County	8,000	2,552	2,248	2,146	1,054	41,337	5.9%	9.3%	5.5%	1,226	10,895
Faulkner County	7,644	2,084	2,266	2,333	961	43,057	11.4%	2.2%	8.2%	926	12,117
Garland County	13,006	4,009	4,398	3,071	1,528	37,088	16.2%	5.1%	8.9%	1,247	16,142
Jefferson County	6,951	2,775	2,199	1,355	622	30,337	16.8%	5.6%	10.7%	1,183	9,008
Lonoke County	5,881	1,390	2,460	1,567	464	39,164	7.8%	4.8%	13.0%	484	8,367
Pulaski County	33,031	10,204	8,427	9,194	5,206	43,122	11.2%	6.6%	5.5%	4,166	48,005
Saline County	11,194	3,093	3,774	3,222	1,105	41,073	7.4%	3.8%	3.9%	1,069	15,201
Sebastian County	12,077	4,898	3,282	2,569	1,328	31,905	13.7%	8.9%	15.1%	1,647	16,187
Washington County	15,798	7,067	4,021	2,576	2,134	28,474	10.7%	11.0%	21.2%	1,633	23,067
White County	7,197	3,344	2,151	1,041	661	26,860	17.9%	15.7%	12.4%	1,681	9,436
California											
Alameda County	115,959	33,552	24,404	29,200	28,803	50,033	10.7%	8.8%	13.5%	10,512	187,879
Butte County	22,765	8,032	6,146	5,110	3,477	38,334	19.0%	5.5%	13.7%	2,163	32,520
Contra Costa County	90,887	17,980	20,809	26,665	25,433	59,860	8.9%	5.2%	7.0%	6,346	144,292
El Dorado County	19,247	4,818	4,812	6,039	3,578	49,975	12.6%	5.0%	5.4%	2,507	29,138
Fresno County	61,609	20,720	17,356	15,268	8,265	37,086	15.7%	14.3%	14.6%	11,666	92,035
Humboldt County	12,469	3,368	4,155	3,248	1,698	42,566	18.9%	8.3%	4.2%	1,475	19,629
Imperial County	10,308	5,531	2,481	1,515	781	23,950	14.9%	19.1%	15.1%	1,889	15,282
Kern County	49,947	16,945	14,711	11,738	6,553	36,209	15.6%	12.8%	15.3%	8,934	76,396
Kings County	7,781	2,503	2,214	2,200	864	38,911	23.0%	11.0%	13.1%	1,699	11,321
Lake County	8,588	3,122	2,753	1,886	827	35,953	18.9%	8.4%	3.8%	390	13,105
Los Angeles County	676,487	228,107	154,494	159,266	134,620	41,279	14.0%	12.7%	15.5%	69,815	1,094,766
Madera County	10,815	3,632	2,167	3,374	1,642	41,847	15.6%	10.1%	13.7%	1,516	14,990
Marin County	32,293	5,778	6,609	7,620	12,286	68,628	6.7%	4.4%	6.2%	2,003	46,818
Mendocino County	10,713	3,159	2,770	3,047	1,737	44,619	14.7%	7.3%	7.2%	1,142	14,963
Merced County	16,007	5,801	4,016	4,445	1,745	34,363	11.9%	8.7%	13.1%	2,755	22,549
Monterey County	30,238	6,899	7,569	8,046	7,724	54,108	8.2%	8.4%	11.5%	1,860	46,360
Napa County	14,395	3,325	2,987	4,466	3,617	58,662	7.6%	6.0%	8.9%	673	22,685
Nevada County	13,350	2,686	3,896	4,382	2,386	50,322	10.7%	4.8%	2.4%	1,057	19,976
Orange County	233,783	55,336	53,795	64,277	60,375	54,426	9.1%	7.5%	10.5%	17,210	364,755
Placer County	39,994	8,665	10,381	12,551	8,397	52,385	8.0%	6.8%	6.5%	1,375	55,615
Riverside County	171,808	50,269	48,599	43,531	29,409	41,106	12.1%	10.2%	11.0%	19,855	253,925
Sacramento County	111,627	29,701	30,189	33,286	18,451	45,799	13.2%	8.9%	12.7%	12,953	173,278
San Bernardino County	116,634	39,146	31,480	30,442	15,566	38,942	15.0%	10.6%	12.4%	23,350	183,863
San Diego County	234,218	63,502	56,850	63,418	50,448	48,504	10.6%	9.1%	9.9%	22,720	366,722
San Francisco County	73,564	23,861	16,997	16,401	16,303	44,457	12.0%	10.9%	14.1%	5,977	114,886
San Joaquin County	44,199	14,794	11,673	11,267	6,465	38,148	14.2%	10.5%	9.6%	6,579	70,499
San Luis Obispo County	29,273	6,480	7,880	7,925	6,988	51,292	7.3%	8.2%	2.9%	1,755	43,217

Table G-2: Counties—Income, Poverty Status and Receipt of Food Stamps (SNAP)—*Continued*

	Income of Households with Householder 65 Years and Over					Poverty Rate of Persons			Households with 1 or More Persons 60 Years and Over	
	Total Households	Less Than $25,000	$25,000 - $49,999	$50,000 - $99,999	$100,000 or More	Median Household Income	55 to 64 Years	65 to 74 Years	75 Years and Over	Receiving SNAP	Not Receiving SNAP
California—Cont.											
San Mateo County	62,142	13,490	13,384	15,926	19,342	60,656	7.2%	5.4%	7.2%	3,324	99,455
Santa Barbara County	37,459	9,749	8,905	9,422	9,383	50,173	10.6%	5.6%	7.4%	2,257	54,795
Santa Clara County	123,457	29,959	28,508	32,469	32,521	53,425	7.7%	8.6%	10.0%	10,536	203,044
Santa Cruz County	22,945	5,531	5,571	6,512	5,331	51,380	12.4%	6.5%	9.0%	2,494	36,307
Shasta County	21,110	6,670	6,023	6,423	1,994	40,627	13.6%	5.8%	8.3%	1,529	30,020
Solano County	33,203	7,280	8,798	10,625	6,500	51,913	9.7%	5.8%	6.6%	3,511	56,681
Sonoma County	51,802	12,613	11,844	16,593	10,752	54,320	9.4%	7.3%	8.7%	3,910	78,559
Stanislaus County	37,075	11,805	10,065	10,260	4,945	41,335	13.8%	8.5%	14.1%	5,711	54,265
Sutter County	8,132	2,470	1,848	2,901	913	46,472	9.8%	8.7%	17.5%	658	12,600
Tulare County	25,327	8,597	6,951	7,124	2,655	38,816	14.8%	17.6%	11.0%	5,480	37,751
Ventura County	68,153	15,804	16,722	20,044	15,583	53,139	7.2%	7.1%	10.5%	4,510	102,875
Yolo County	14,516	4,819	3,284	2,830	3,583	42,011	12.9%	10.4%	11.7%	1,365	23,270
Yuba County	5,227	2,524	1,247	851	605	25,932	9.0%	15.0%	26.7%	971	7,297
Colorado											
Adams County	27,741	6,849	8,355	8,344	4,193	45,315	8.7%	6.9%	6.8%	5,083	41,899
Arapahoe County	43,824	9,532	11,502	13,791	8,999	53,133	8.3%	4.8%	9.2%	4,483	69,548
Boulder County	23,881	5,590	4,284	8,163	5,844	60,057	7.6%	5.2%	9.9%	1,595	38,023
Denver County	47,806	16,511	12,079	11,663	7,553	39,017	16.2%	10.6%	10.8%	8,739	68,318
Douglas County	18,561	3,009	4,772	6,248	4,532	60,294	2.5%	2.0%	5.1%	742	30,485
El Paso County	46,007	12,160	12,453	13,246	8,148	46,912	8.1%	6.3%	6.6%	6,365	70,318
Jefferson County	50,496	11,349	14,324	15,488	9,335	49,112	4.0%	6.0%	6.1%	3,696	79,208
Larimer County	27,063	7,269	7,880	8,078	3,836	42,247	7.4%	5.6%	6.8%	1,725	41,207
Mesa County	15,207	4,006	5,518	3,952	1,731	35,413	11.8%	8.1%	6.7%	2,028	21,014
Pueblo County	17,236	6,445	5,801	3,794	1,196	33,119	14.0%	10.4%	12.0%	2,576	24,380
Weld County	19,316	5,740	5,113	5,665	2,798	44,771	8.5%	5.8%	5.5%	2,227	29,386
Connecticut											
Fairfield County	84,643	21,299	19,221	20,900	23,223	53,372	6.0%	8.1%	7.0%	10,998	118,119
Hartford County	86,024	24,762	24,609	22,044	14,609	41,646	7.7%	8.2%	10.4%	16,990	113,982
Litchfield County	20,304	5,152	5,117	5,878	4,157	49,636	8.3%	4.0%	8.9%	1,730	29,984
Middlesex County	17,518	3,457	5,065	4,813	4,183	51,209	7.3%	3.6%	5.2%	1,849	24,986
New Haven County	82,837	26,235	23,032	21,411	12,159	39,820	9.0%	7.4%	9.9%	16,014	110,246
New London County	26,286	6,002	6,059	8,763	4,862	51,729	8.2%	5.8%	7.1%	4,143	36,115
Tolland County	12,396	2,253	2,879	5,067	2,197	58,182	5.3%	2.9%	8.4%	1,160	17,847
Windham County	9,650	2,835	3,037	2,670	1,108	41,063	5.3%	5.2%	13.2%	1,826	14,088
Delaware											
Kent County	15,895	3,764	5,257	5,356	1,518	42,761	11.4%	7.5%	7.8%	2,072	20,488
New Castle County	45,586	12,784	12,654	12,920	7,228	44,433	8.0%	7.2%	9.8%	6,717	66,176
Sussex County	30,896	6,532	9,386	9,840	5,138	48,120	10.8%	5.1%	8.2%	3,548	40,534
Florida											
Alachua County	19,828	5,957	5,094	5,753	3,024	40,813	13.5%	10.9%	8.8%	2,630	28,906
Bay County	16,999	4,874	5,517	4,236	2,372	37,837	14.2%	9.9%	13.3%	2,835	22,992
Brevard County	76,243	20,911	25,224	22,031	8,077	41,247	11.8%	9.3%	5.8%	8,375	100,024
Broward County	168,076	62,598	45,079	39,054	21,345	35,217	13.0%	11.5%	12.5%	36,431	225,277
Charlotte County	38,266	11,041	12,239	10,154	4,832	39,421	11.0%	5.7%	8.1%	2,497	46,773
Citrus County	29,294	10,192	10,513	6,181	2,408	33,951	21.1%	9.1%	12.0%	3,146	34,144
Clay County	16,153	3,353	5,054	5,365	2,381	48,192	12.0%	6.5%	8.7%	2,698	24,307
Collier County	59,575	10,497	15,879	16,301	16,898	57,191	10.0%	4.5%	7.6%	3,799	74,536
Columbia County	7,095	2,925	1,725	1,954	491	33,242	10.6%	15.5%	15.0%	1,191	9,046
Duval County	72,122	23,908	23,032	17,127	8,055	36,159	15.3%	12.2%	10.8%	14,739	100,045
Escambia County	30,783	8,461	10,085	9,706	2,531	40,248	10.0%	6.7%	7.1%	4,975	41,151
Flagler County	15,366	3,474	5,148	4,981	1,763	44,801	8.1%	8.0%	7.9%	1,432	20,494
Hernando County	30,147	10,039	11,849	6,539	1,720	35,332	12.4%	8.9%	9.5%	4,093	35,929
Highlands County	19,624	6,427	6,399	5,398	1,400	36,280	15.2%	9.2%	10.1%	1,874	21,877
Hillsborough County	102,060	34,880	29,802	23,871	13,507	37,204	13.6%	10.3%	13.5%	24,481	138,912
Indian River County	26,256	7,298	7,725	6,893	4,340	41,981	9.4%	9.2%	8.2%	2,555	32,498
Lake County	46,585	14,121	14,389	13,410	4,665	40,881	11.1%	7.8%	8.3%	4,239	58,408
Lee County	102,374	27,116	29,881	29,276	16,101	44,442	12.7%	6.8%	8.9%	8,311	132,108
Leon County	20,891	5,372	5,548	5,572	4,399	47,919	12.7%	9.6%	10.2%	4,412	30,072
Manatee County	53,715	15,273	14,684	16,305	7,453	42,737	12.3%	9.0%	7.2%	4,494	69,083
Marion County	57,018	16,057	22,046	14,581	4,334	36,542	15.9%	7.5%	9.2%	7,474	67,781
Martin County	27,796	7,964	7,478	7,973	4,381	45,429	10.4%	3.8%	4.1%	1,761	35,284
Miami-Dade County	202,456	94,316	44,221	38,473	25,446	27,242	18.4%	18.8%	23.3%	105,541	235,447
Monroe County	8,836	2,554	1,961	2,551	1,770	48,415	16.9%	11.6%	13.9%	682	12,696
Nassau County	9,257	2,123	3,295	2,291	1,548	43,939	11.9%	3.3%	13.0%	1,144	13,118
Okaloosa County	19,161	3,787	5,192	6,368	3,814	53,256	10.6%	7.4%	3.5%	1,841	24,966
Orange County	75,328	24,650	21,678	18,193	10,807	37,683	12.5%	9.6%	13.6%	20,290	109,556
Osceola County	18,816	8,146	4,483	4,486	1,701	33,271	17.5%	14.7%	11.6%	6,715	26,764
Palm Beach County	196,495	60,081	51,558	48,114	36,742	41,238	13.2%	9.2%	9.9%	21,557	244,922
Pasco County	65,438	22,779	22,084	16,109	4,466	33,830	14.0%	8.3%	10.3%	8,557	81,758
Pinellas County	134,967	49,232	38,147	30,974	16,614	34,551	14.0%	8.9%	12.3%	15,759	174,109
Polk County	74,155	25,323	23,661	17,873	7,298	35,185	14.8%	8.8%	13.8%	11,173	93,407
Putnam County	10,067	4,430	3,339	1,479	819	29,331	17.6%	10.9%	17.6%	1,993	11,973
Santa Rosa County	14,143	3,116	4,522	4,330	2,175	48,472	8.3%	5.5%	4.3%	1,782	19,963
Sarasota County	82,974	19,966	23,917	23,328	15,763	47,108	8.8%	5.7%	5.6%	4,499	102,591
Seminole County	33,408	10,417	9,651	8,484	4,856	39,341	8.4%	7.7%	10.4%	3,959	51,205

Table G-2: Counties—Income, Poverty Status and Receipt of Food Stamps (SNAP)—*Continued*

	Income of Households with Householder 65 Years and Over					Poverty Rate of Persons			Households with 1 or More Persons 60 Years and Over	
	Total Households	Less Than $25,000	$25,000 - $49,999	$50,000 - $99,999	$100,000 or More	Median Household Income	55 to 64 Years	65 to 74 Years	75 Years and Over	Receiving SNAP	Not Receiving SNAP
Florida—Cont.											
St. Johns County	23,395	3,415	7,217	7,727	5,036	56,582	5.4%	3.3%	4.5%	1,128	33,047
St. Lucie County	39,460	11,356	13,320	10,704	4,080	36,997	12.1%	7.2%	9.5%	5,121	49,829
Sumter County	34,307	6,719	11,234	10,465	5,889	48,678	11.9%	5.0%	4.4%	1,182	40,752
Volusia County	70,258	21,439	23,098	18,730	6,991	37,724	15.3%	7.5%	9.5%	8,498	91,497
Georgia											
Barrow County	4,604	1,652	1,855	847	250	32,828	15.3%	6.6%	4.7%	1,112	6,648
Bartow County	6,989	1,779	2,584	1,532	1,094	37,592	14.3%	9.0%	4.3%	1,159	11,128
Bibb County	13,579	5,415	3,912	2,831	1,421	31,937	15.9%	15.0%	10.8%	2,745	19,213
Bulloch County	4,989	2,082	1,464	1,084	359	31,374	18.1%	5.2%	14.2%	1,063	6,903
Carroll County	8,925	3,937	2,903	1,252	833	30,340	10.0%	12.6%	15.8%	1,346	12,320
Catoosa County						33,879	7.6%	5.8%	4.8%	1,080	8,536
Chatham County	23,779	7,009	6,393	5,932	4,445	40,364	8.0%	6.2%	9.1%	4,789	30,905
Cherokee County	16,062	3,498	4,399	5,668	2,497	50,277	7.2%	2.7%	11.0%	1,796	24,072
Clarke County	7,604	2,097	2,135	1,629	1,743	40,357	23.3%	12.6%	10.9%	1,833	10,122
Clayton County	12,424	3,950	4,210	3,116	1,148	35,652	13.9%	10.4%	11.6%	4,814	18,859
Cobb County	45,973	10,530	11,866	13,306	10,271	51,336	7.0%	5.7%	7.2%	5,855	72,854
Columbia County	7,910	1,470	2,577	2,504	1,359	49,385	5.4%	4.8%	2.1%	653	15,029
Coweta County	9,871	2,277	2,597	3,441	1,556	52,106	12.9%	3.3%	11.1%	913	15,385
DeKalb County	45,984	13,033	13,882	13,203	5,866	41,998	13.1%	9.9%	11.5%	11,873	65,688
Dougherty County	8,532	3,998	1,936	1,837	761	26,343	18.5%	25.9%	13.0%	3,058	10,576
Douglas County	8,231	2,871	2,436	2,160	764	34,803	12.0%	12.6%	24.6%	2,557	12,233
Fayette County	10,184	1,757	2,716	3,523	2,188	58,854	5.2%	4.8%	3.9%	1,053	15,679
Floyd County	9,055	3,116	3,287	1,714	938	36,414	12.6%	10.8%	12.7%	1,173	12,123
Forsyth County	12,083	3,212	3,508	3,320	2,043	45,571	7.7%	6.0%	6.1%	782	19,124
Fulton County	65,170	25,093	16,027	12,744	11,306	34,513	12.7%	12.1%	10.4%	14,253	92,960
Glynn County	8,667	1,943	1,994	3,683	1,047	52,394	14.5%	3.8%	8.4%	1,263	12,238
Gwinnett County	38,128	9,700	9,712	11,547	7,169	48,757	8.3%	6.2%	10.0%	6,670	67,035
Hall County	15,730	4,360	3,906	4,929	2,535	47,573	10.0%	8.3%	11.6%	2,281	21,630
Henry County	12,818	3,109	4,234	4,256	1,219	42,850	9.4%	8.7%	19.7%	2,219	19,222
Houston County	10,261	2,558	3,246	3,263	1,194	45,242	18.9%	4.9%	11.0%	2,428	14,461
Liberty County	2,672	1,345	685	592	50	24,643	13.5%	11.0%	19.6%	819	4,692
Lowndes County	7,928	2,949	2,415	1,666	898	32,004	11.3%	4.1%	19.6%	1,972	10,536
Muscogee County	15,599	5,100	4,185	4,583	1,731	38,733	20.7%	12.1%	14.7%	3,555	19,753
Newton County	7,833	2,773	2,663	1,512	885	36,550	18.2%	11.7%	9.6%	1,967	10,814
Paulding County	8,128	1,876	2,868	2,400	984	44,725	9.3%	6.8%	9.4%	1,076	12,786
Richmond County	14,911	5,446	4,677	3,428	1,360	30,860	18.4%	13.1%	8.0%	4,757	20,399
Rockdale County	5,825	1,287	2,005	1,857	676	45,794	11.4%	8.1%	6.0%	1,150	9,134
Troup County	6,242	2,795	1,700	1,152	595	27,315	22.8%	11.1%	14.4%	1,669	7,809
Walker County	7,319	3,065	2,442	1,323	489	27,976	16.6%	4.6%	10.5%	743	9,754
Walton County	7,324	2,619	2,580	1,374	751	34,721	7.9%	8.7%	18.9%	1,703	9,146
Whitfield County	7,666	2,819	2,018	1,673	1,156	32,999	12.5%	12.1%	14.2%	1,756	10,578
Hawaii											
Hawaii County	19,257	5,411	4,987	5,001	3,858	45,982	15.9%	12.4%	5.8%	4,479	27,216
Honolulu County	83,122	16,777	17,419	25,078	23,848	63,491	8.7%	5.5%	9.8%	13,734	117,274
Kauai County	6,749	1,858	1,762	1,670	1,459	45,158	18.5%	8.2%	9.6%	825	10,487
Maui County	13,616	2,772	3,017	4,245	3,582	61,960	14.3%	6.9%	14.7%	1,949	22,106
Idaho											
Ada County	32,075	8,834	8,857	10,204	4,180	43,376	5.8%	5.6%	10.4%	3,812	48,113
Bannock County	6,874	2,439	2,315	1,261	859	33,260	8.5%	7.1%	3.6%	513	10,573
Bonneville County	8,348	2,658	2,951	2,121	618	37,223	11.2%	8.2%	8.6%	833	12,476
Canyon County	14,309	4,403	5,050	4,249	607	38,712	13.9%	9.0%	13.5%	2,316	19,771
Kootenai County	15,029	4,552	5,125	3,711	1,641	36,911	7.3%	9.8%	6.3%	1,228	21,679
Twin Falls County	7,574	3,130	2,464	1,494	486	30,598	5.6%	8.4%	19.2%	738	10,209
Illinois											
Adams County	8,049	2,879	2,606	2,020	544	32,825	8.8%	4.3%	11.3%	910	10,399
Champaign County	14,942	3,939	4,225	4,500	2,278	44,181	11.6%	5.7%	8.1%	1,385	21,705
Cook County	420,247	146,159	109,444	100,735	63,909	37,606	13.1%	10.7%	12.5%	103,278	569,508
DeKalb County	7,023	1,608	1,800	2,229	1,386	50,819	6.7%	4.3%	7.6%	972	10,215
DuPage County	74,062	16,402	19,841	21,390	16,429	51,261	6.5%	5.4%	6.5%	7,179	113,802
Kane County	37,775	9,462	10,884	9,095	8,334	44,992	7.3%	3.9%	4.5%	4,644	55,273
Kankakee County	9,376	2,973	2,765	2,452	1,186	42,124	9.0%	9.9%	12.3%	2,420	12,369
Kendall County	na	na	na	na	na	49,955	7.0%	6.4%	4.1%	801	9,864
Lake County	49,803	11,734	11,212	13,560	13,297	52,926	6.6%	5.7%	7.8%	6,915	74,945
LaSalle County	11,879	3,760	4,022	2,979	1,118	38,676	11.5%	7.0%	12.7%	1,372	16,761
Macon County	12,440	3,749	4,710	2,911	1,070	37,491	17.4%	6.1%	8.5%	1,197	16,554
Madison County	28,067	8,244	9,281	7,617	2,925	36,771	8.0%	6.2%	7.0%	3,243	37,104
McHenry County	21,959	4,714	6,978	6,235	4,032	46,458	6.7%	2.2%	5.5%	2,107	34,167
McLean County	12,445	3,032	3,749	3,833	1,831	45,695	10.8%	5.1%	10.2%	1,234	18,220
Peoria County	18,183	6,177	4,397	5,338	2,271	41,124	11.6%	10.3%	10.0%	2,338	25,508
Rock Island County	17,268	6,462	5,255	4,058	1,493	32,442	10.8%	13.4%	14.0%	1,595	23,470
Sangamon County	20,192	5,781	4,897	6,361	3,153	46,400	9.6%	6.3%	5.5%	2,162	28,608
St. Clair County	24,017	7,181	7,188	6,118	3,530	38,931	12.8%	6.7%	13.0%	3,221	33,729
Tazewell County	14,198	3,711	4,185	4,688	1,614	46,783	4.3%	2.1%	6.8%	1,174	19,489
Vermilion County	8,761	2,930	2,781	2,284	766	38,370	8.5%	8.8%	3.8%	1,280	12,037

Table G-2: Counties—Income, Poverty Status and Receipt of Food Stamps (SNAP)—*Continued*

	Income of Households with Householder 65 Years and Over						Poverty Rate of Persons			Households with 1 or More Persons 60 Years and Over	
	Total Households	Less Than $25,000	$25,000 - $49,999	$50,000 - $99,999	$100,000 or More	Median Household Income	55 to 64 Years	65 to 74 Years	75 Years and Over	Receiving SNAP	Not Receiving SNAP
Illinois—Cont.											
Will County	43,516	9,493	13,606	13,866	6,551	46,851	4.6%	4.2%	4.2%	5,913	67,977
Williamson County	6,946	2,522	1,913	1,963	548	33,232	13.6%	6.4%	5.8%	1,212	8,913
Winnebago County	28,626	10,433	9,722	6,143	2,328	33,153	11.8%	5.5%	10.6%	4,322	39,720
Indiana											
Allen County	30,075	8,957	9,669	8,602	2,847	37,147	9.9%	5.1%	7.4%	3,559	42,121
Bartholomew County	7,952	2,383	2,552	2,079	938	39,129	7.6%	10.3%	1.5%	722	10,890
Clark County	10,542	4,066	2,991	2,728	757	38,002	11.2%	8.4%	5.9%	1,541	14,743
Delaware County	11,571	3,120	4,021	3,054	1,376	39,118	9.7%	6.8%	11.7%	671	15,418
Elkhart County	16,374	5,061	6,639	3,525	1,149	36,766	11.6%	2.1%	6.6%	1,552	23,219
Floyd County	6,805	2,274	1,962	1,986	583	38,474	7.8%	9.8%	9.8%	701	10,082
Grant County	8,091	3,109	3,225	1,376	381	30,319	9.8%	12.0%	13.2%	937	11,015
Hamilton County	19,298	3,949	4,604	6,403	4,342	53,693	4.3%	2.4%	2.2%	2,087	28,685
Hancock County	6,836	1,378	2,187	2,333	938	48,024	3.1%	1.9%	0.0%	390	9,594
Hendricks County	11,731	2,557	4,743	3,470	961	43,164	8.2%	3.8%	4.9%	530	17,493
Howard County	9,929	2,951	3,070	3,012	896	39,221	15.3%	9.0%	3.6%	865	13,324
Johnson County	11,811	2,424	4,607	3,542	1,238	45,330	11.7%	3.9%	3.7%	1,283	17,355
Kosciusko County	7,172	1,606	2,731	2,238	597	44,538	11.2%	7.2%	2.3%	249	10,554
Lake County	43,006	12,908	13,922	11,274	4,902	39,096	10.5%	7.4%	8.4%	7,956	61,507
LaPorte County	11,239	3,327	3,877	2,991	1,044	37,243	7.1%	9.1%	6.0%	1,280	15,651
Madison County	14,579	4,460	5,538	3,624	957	36,959	12.9%	3.9%	11.4%	2,264	18,276
Marion County	66,134	20,937	23,030	16,156	6,011	36,387	12.6%	8.5%	8.5%	13,603	93,279
Monroe County	9,958	1,681	3,278	2,383	2,616	50,340	7.7%	6.3%	1.3%	948	14,383
Morgan County	6,023	1,713	2,157	1,829	324	42,355	6.4%	0.2%	8.1%	746	9,125
Porter County	14,662	3,923	4,235	4,603	1,901	44,198	4.9%	3.6%	4.6%	1,188	21,519
St. Joseph County	24,329	8,715	8,205	5,280	2,129	34,160	11.5%	3.6%	9.8%	3,277	34,196
Tippecanoe County	11,272	2,912	3,212	3,450	1,698	46,052	11.0%	2.8%	4.2%	1,099	16,184
Vanderburgh County	17,998	5,924	6,321	3,878	1,875	33,988	9.8%	4.0%	12.5%	2,111	24,565
Vigo County	10,262	3,934	3,801	1,821	706	31,076	15.5%	6.0%	12.5%	1,376	13,605
Wayne County	7,721	2,689	2,186	2,295	551	37,293	14.2%	6.2%	13.3%	852	10,073
Iowa											
Black Hawk County	12,901	3,980	4,421	3,230	1,350	36,022	8.8%	4.1%	6.0%	895	18,047
Dallas County	5,192	1,392	1,451	1,574	775	44,713	5.2%	2.4%	5.8%	621	7,392
Dubuque County	9,597	2,535	3,523	2,757	782	41,353	7.5%	2.0%	25.5%	947	12,889
Johnson County	8,573	2,321	1,281	2,883	2,088	59,390	9.4%	7.4%	5.8%	941	14,287
Linn County	20,002	5,295	5,765	6,000	2,942	43,964	4.8%	3.1%	6.0%	1,475	27,871
Polk County	34,468	10,366	10,125	10,191	3,786	39,329	6.5%	6.3%	11.2%	5,067	49,412
Pottawattamie County	9,357	3,408	2,787	2,264	898	35,946	6.6%	4.1%	8.2%	1,136	12,945
Scott County	15,479	4,506	4,643	4,845	1,485	40,574	8.8%	5.0%	6.3%	2,033	21,766
Story County	6,087	733	2,051	1,594	1,709	54,447	5.8%	0.2%	5.0%	193	8,833
Woodbury County	8,423	2,979	3,275	1,625	544	29,738	10.8%	4.1%	11.1%	1,374	11,969
Kansas											
Butler County	6,286	1,912	1,382	2,558	434	45,603	5.5%	4.9%	10.0%	279	8,353
Douglas County	7,496	1,751	2,044	2,334	1,367	48,433	7.6%	3.4%	8.8%	681	11,544
Johnson County	45,448	10,357	11,890	13,685	9,516	51,116	4.6%	4.7%	6.8%	1,989	69,986
Leavenworth County	5,373	1,140	1,439	2,119	675	51,609	5.8%	6.9%	16.6%	387	8,945
Riley County	3,835	848	478	1,308	1,201	64,393	5.1%	2.2%	0.2%	239	4,942
Sedgwick County	41,124	12,270	13,712	9,960	5,182	36,790	8.5%	9.5%	8.3%	4,623	59,584
Shawnee County	18,107	5,071	5,615	5,164	2,257	40,612	10.1%	8.4%	8.8%	1,248	24,957
Wyandotte County	11,729	4,943	3,110	2,410	1,266	32,509	16.4%	9.4%	10.9%	2,118	16,900
Kentucky											
Boone County	8,586	2,771	2,891	2,364	560	35,151	4.5%	7.3%	16.1%	638	14,309
Bullitt County	6,786	2,161	2,255	1,928	442	37,014	5.7%	11.3%	9.2%	890	9,550
Campbell County	7,975	2,898	2,419	1,951	707	33,400	7.7%	11.8%	8.5%	845	11,788
Christian County	5,274	1,974	2,144	898	258	33,165	11.1%	7.6%	11.9%	885	6,965
Daviess County	9,745	3,614	3,110	2,508	513	33,594	7.8%	13.3%	5.3%	1,069	13,566
Fayette County	22,793	7,208	6,750	5,924	2,911	37,379	14.1%	9.0%	9.4%	3,446	34,371
Hardin County	8,860	2,519	3,124	2,168	1,049	38,429	6.2%	6.5%	13.2%	1,131	11,471
Jefferson County	71,392	22,763	24,099	15,924	8,606	38,132	13.0%	7.1%	10.1%	11,219	96,664
Kenton County	13,193	4,282	3,862	3,589	1,460	36,945	15.5%	6.6%	10.4%	2,643	18,517
Madison County	7,004	3,166	1,581	1,634	623	32,028	14.9%	11.6%	1.4%	1,343	9,671
McCracken County	7,522	3,135	2,611	1,040	736	28,497	18.4%	9.7%	5.3%	974	10,454
Pike County	6,768	3,688	2,002	828	250	22,995	17.2%	25.2%	24.9%	1,273	9,250
Warren County	9,565	3,031	2,609	2,987	938	40,042	11.2%	7.0%	6.9%	1,083	12,876
Louisiana											
Ascension Parish	6,832	2,445	2,361	1,188	838	37,522	13.4%	13.9%	12.5%	1,059	10,787
Bossier Parish	9,661	2,768	3,742	2,092	1,059	40,257	12.0%	8.0%	5.6%	1,133	14,767
Caddo Parish	23,269	8,820	6,649	4,991	2,809	33,313	20.7%	9.3%	12.8%	4,028	31,447
Calcasieu Parish	16,874	6,135	4,382	3,862	2,495	32,686	13.1%	12.2%	9.2%	4,494	22,247
East Baton Rouge Parish	34,864	11,143	9,967	8,464	5,290	38,874	10.8%	6.7%	12.3%	6,937	49,096
Iberia Parish	6,093	2,578	2,121	763	631	31,784	8.5%	17.6%	9.2%	1,417	8,365
Jefferson Parish	42,086	15,149	12,946	8,139	5,852	34,035	12.9%	9.2%	11.6%	6,512	58,547
Lafayette Parish	16,922	5,884	4,766	4,195	2,077	39,762	10.1%	8.2%	9.9%	2,832	23,176
Lafourche Parish	7,759	3,211	1,856	1,959	733	32,888	10.2%	10.9%	12.9%	521	11,114
Livingston Parish	9,362	3,030	3,210	2,176	946	35,998	7.0%	8.0%	10.5%	2,218	13,432

Table G-2: Counties—Income, Poverty Status and Receipt of Food Stamps (SNAP)—*Continued*

	Income of Households with Householder 65 Years and Over					Poverty Rate of Persons			Households with 1 or More Persons 60 Years and Over	
	Total Households	Less Than $25,000	$25,000 - $49,999	$50,000 - $99,999	$100,000 or More	Median Household Income	55 to 64 Years	65 to 74 Years	75 Years and Over	Receiving SNAP	Not Receiving SNAP
Louisiana—Cont.											
Orleans Parish	30,343	13,432	7,840	4,573	4,498	28,790	23.8%	20.0%	18.1%	8,417	41,263
Ouachita Parish	13,274	5,657	3,442	2,917	1,258	31,750	10.6%	12.5%	13.9%	1,621	19,614
Rapides Parish	12,179	4,998	3,734	2,035	1,412	31,106	17.4%	12.4%	11.8%	2,944	15,420
St. Landry Parish	7,856	4,683	1,980	671	522	22,766	25.3%	23.5%	16.0%	1,436	10,740
St. Tammany Parish	21,728	5,640	5,827	7,022	3,239	48,072	10.6%	5.2%	10.7%	2,206	31,615
Tangipahoa Parish	9,280	4,330	2,695	1,829	426	27,034	12.5%	12.7%	21.5%	2,641	13,157
Terrebonne Parish	8,103	2,586	2,498	2,116	903	35,142	17.9%	4.4%	6.2%	1,049	11,764
Maine											
Androscoggin County	11,311	4,159	3,991	2,523	638	34,263	11.6%	9.6%	11.2%	2,546	14,246
Aroostook County	9,323	4,336	2,843	1,783	361	27,076	15.7%	12.3%	13.7%	2,707	11,181
Cumberland County	29,244	9,422	7,518	7,752	4,552	39,263	7.5%	7.2%	7.6%	3,282	42,968
Kennebec County	13,203	4,489	4,703	2,815	1,196	33,280	7.8%	8.7%	11.6%	2,287	17,943
Penobscot County	16,041	6,403	4,943	3,760	935	31,124	10.3%	6.5%	10.6%	3,802	20,607
York County	22,173	6,635	6,974	6,048	2,516	39,815	7.2%	7.6%	7.7%	3,581	31,204
Maryland											
Allegany County	8,621	3,247	2,927	1,898	549	33,228	15.7%	7.1%	7.6%	1,487	10,770
Anne Arundel County	46,746	8,156	10,246	15,501	12,843	66,313	4.7%	3.3%	5.0%	3,892	69,039
Baltimore County	80,304	19,952	22,513	23,222	14,617	46,370	7.4%	5.6%	9.5%	10,531	112,526
Calvert County	7,333	1,474	1,216	2,717	1,926	60,838	3.4%	11.2%	13.7%	1,507	10,298
Carroll County	15,953	4,224	4,236	4,565	2,928	47,568	4.9%	3.2%	5.5%	1,022	22,705
Cecil County	8,804	2,669	2,444	2,273	1,418	42,361	9.2%	7.2%	11.3%	1,180	12,332
Charles County	10,298	2,350	2,267	2,649	3,032	58,097	6.2%	5.8%	8.8%	1,741	16,107
Frederick County	18,569	3,966	4,766	5,767	4,070	52,373	6.4%	5.0%	8.1%	1,883	28,627
Harford County	20,953	6,194	4,368	6,908	3,483	49,455	7.0%	6.2%	7.6%	1,877	34,271
Howard County	19,963	3,348	2,613	7,145	6,857	73,804	2.6%	3.5%	10.6%	1,025	34,981
Montgomery County	81,009	14,532	12,486	22,516	31,475	77,934	4.5%	4.6%	9.0%	9,275	124,209
Prince George's County	59,365	10,333	14,663	18,250	16,119	61,023	6.2%	5.1%	7.5%	10,302	93,954
St. Mary's County	7,889	2,205	1,954	2,084	1,646	46,791	4.9%	4.4%	10.9%	1,193	12,276
Washington County	14,529	5,624	4,099	3,633	1,173	32,725	7.5%	9.6%	4.9%	1,757	19,072
Wicomico County	8,973	2,851	2,006	2,642	1,474	42,407	14.2%	6.1%	9.5%	1,227	13,243
Massachusetts											
Barnstable County	38,887	9,796	10,053	11,072	7,966	48,516	7.8%	6.1%	4.9%	3,269	49,896
Berkshire County	17,764	5,692	4,500	4,360	3,212	41,554	7.9%	6.4%	8.1%	2,718	22,505
Bristol County	53,030	20,849	14,847	11,959	5,375	33,801	9.5%	8.6%	14.4%	13,254	70,355
Essex County	72,038	24,036	17,953	17,495	12,554	40,706	8.7%	8.8%	11.5%	15,706	98,445
Franklin County	8,174	2,924	2,084	2,096	1,070	36,604	7.5%	4.5%	8.0%	1,888	11,449
Hampden County	44,605	15,938	13,428	10,876	4,363	34,038	15.3%	12.2%	9.2%	11,918	57,422
Hampshire County	15,614	4,128	4,772	4,194	2,520	42,070	11.4%	5.8%	12.0%	2,652	21,440
Middlesex County	135,519	37,678	29,372	36,849	31,620	50,568	6.9%	8.1%	8.4%	18,435	189,119
Norfolk County	65,417	16,773	15,976	16,880	15,788	49,925	4.6%	5.6%	9.3%	9,255	93,420
Plymouth County	47,601	11,406	12,944	14,034	9,217	48,173	7.8%	4.1%	5.3%	8,552	69,041
Suffolk County	54,064	25,595	10,650	10,155	7,664	28,532	16.7%	17.8%	19.3%	24,114	63,129
Worcester County	69,289	23,119	19,040	16,821	10,309	36,149	9.4%	7.8%	11.9%	13,998	96,643
Michigan											
Allegan County	10,476	3,187	3,659	2,596	1,034	37,086	9.9%	4.3%	14.5%	1,283	14,621
Bay County	12,621	3,976	4,925	2,570	1,150	35,086	10.9%	8.5%	9.9%	1,544	16,479
Berrien County	17,528	5,569	5,726	4,408	1,825	38,680	12.8%	6.8%	9.1%	2,335	24,367
Calhoun County	13,899	4,586	5,740	2,745	828	32,818	12.6%	7.7%	7.6%	2,404	18,648
Clinton County	6,754	1,175	2,722	2,013	844	43,387	6.9%	3.4%	1.8%	469	10,197
Eaton County	11,184	2,706	4,172	3,453	853	41,055	6.3%	6.4%	8.5%	1,412	15,317
Genesee County	42,588	12,465	15,168	11,955	3,000	37,890	13.6%	5.8%	9.4%	9,506	54,922
Grand Traverse County	10,196	2,817	3,806	2,518	1,055	38,349	7.8%	6.7%	6.3%	965	13,552
Ingham County	21,687	6,130	7,203	4,992	3,362	40,844	9.2%	7.8%	6.7%	4,758	29,832
Isabella County	4,940	1,500	1,613	1,252	575	38,154	11.4%	7.1%	6.9%	859	6,764
Jackson County	16,640	5,563	6,165	3,710	1,202	34,788	6.5%	7.3%	5.6%	2,460	22,347
Kalamazoo County	21,548	6,010	7,099	5,880	2,559	39,282	11.2%	7.9%	5.7%	3,278	30,600
Kent County	47,846	13,823	15,787	12,931	5,305	40,104	10.3%	7.4%	7.2%	7,380	67,227
Lapeer County	8,529	2,420	3,333	2,109	667	39,334	7.9%	9.2%	6.6%	764	12,235
Lenawee County	10,605	2,892	4,005	3,008	700	37,938	9.2%	2.6%	6.5%	1,734	13,502
Livingston County	16,676	3,095	5,209	6,056	2,316	50,143	4.1%	4.0%	6.4%	1,299	24,634
Macomb County	84,860	25,888	27,198	24,421	7,353	39,437	8.1%	7.2%	6.3%	14,960	116,340
Marquette County	6,904	2,533	2,116	1,768	487	38,868	10.7%	8.8%	9.7%	1,342	9,656
Midland County	8,858	2,443	3,413	2,310	692	37,344	7.6%	7.1%	8.5%	811	11,746
Monroe County	13,962	3,635	5,207	4,133	987	36,305	8.0%	4.2%	3.0%	1,845	20,160
Muskegon County	17,066	5,283	6,350	3,937	1,496	36,777	13.8%	7.2%	8.5%	4,014	20,636
Oakland County	119,199	28,796	33,698	34,882	21,823	47,238	6.6%	7.2%	7.8%	14,460	171,342
Ottawa County	22,645	6,980	7,606	6,061	1,998	37,677	5.3%	5.3%	8.5%	1,534	31,969
Saginaw County	21,226	5,935	7,984	5,601	1,706	40,449	8.9%	4.4%	9.7%	4,391	26,752
Shiawassee County	6,935	2,087	2,491	1,765	592	35,993	9.5%	7.3%	10.2%	741	9,913
St. Clair County	17,313	5,555	5,812	4,218	1,728	37,011	10.4%	6.9%	7.6%	3,896	21,961
Van Buren County	7,044	2,031	2,211	2,163	639	37,344	7.7%	8.2%	8.1%	1,647	9,901
Washtenaw County	27,312	4,978	7,943	7,224	7,167	53,338	7.9%	4.8%	7.3%	3,790	40,456
Wayne County	159,506	59,115	49,618	36,727	14,046	34,064	17.1%	12.9%	11.7%	48,727	201,280

Table G-2: Counties—Income, Poverty Status and Receipt of Food Stamps (SNAP)—*Continued*

	Income of Households with Householder 65 Years and Over						Poverty Rate of Persons			Households with 1 or More Persons 60 Years and Over	
	Total Households	Less Than $25,000	$25,000 - $49,999	$50,000 - $99,999	$100,000 or More	Median Household Income	55 to 64 Years	65 to 74 Years	75 Years and Over	Receiving SNAP	Not Receiving SNAP
Minnesota											
Anoka County	23,879	5,501	7,980	7,131	3,267	43,308	4.9%	4.1%	7.2%	2,399	36,776
Blue Earth County	5,028	1,725	1,624	1,202	477	34,453	8.7%	6.3%	4.5%	435	7,298
Carver County	6,245	1,791	2,057	1,716	681	35,857	1.6%	2.8%	5.6%	322	9,772
Dakota County	31,239	7,455	8,600	10,813	4,371	47,708	6.4%	5.6%	4.5%	1,967	47,492
Hennepin County	97,368	29,132	26,471	27,779	13,986	42,755	10.3%	7.0%	8.0%	13,300	140,652
Olmsted County	12,547	2,803	2,845	4,737	2,162	53,745	4.7%	2.7%	5.7%	516	18,396
Ramsey County	44,594	12,289	12,983	12,517	6,805	41,259	9.4%	5.3%	9.5%	8,126	61,265
Rice County	6,214	2,508	1,750	1,455	501	32,743	3.3%	5.1%	18.7%	156	8,846
Scott County	7,874	2,274	1,718	2,564	1,318	49,309	5.7%	6.3%	14.9%	910	11,426
Sherburne County	5,370	1,175	1,795	1,680	720	47,617	6.4%	1.9%	7.4%	413	8,133
St. Louis County	22,900	7,124	7,850	5,978	1,948	36,848	12.7%	5.8%	5.3%	2,234	31,832
Stearns County	12,262	3,994	4,030	3,293	945	34,979	8.6%	9.6%	17.2%	1,184	16,577
Washington County	18,287	3,913	4,904	5,823	3,647	51,600	4.5%	4.0%	8.5%	1,140	28,171
Wright County	8,544	2,224	2,815	2,547	958	40,833	11.2%	4.5%	8.9%	763	12,797
Mississippi											
DeSoto County	12,206	2,950	5,162	3,414	680	39,708	7.9%	4.3%	4.0%	1,705	18,783
Forrest County	5,532	1,762	1,863	1,387	520	32,132	24.1%	7.4%	5.2%	1,115	8,384
Harrison County	18,357	5,592	5,985	4,805	1,975	39,669	20.0%	12.3%	11.6%	3,945	24,136
Hinds County	19,283	7,774	5,914	3,429	2,166	33,253	17.5%	13.6%	16.9%	4,744	24,953
Jackson County	11,759	3,317	4,376	3,143	923	36,792	8.0%	9.3%	2.4%	1,324	16,147
Jones County	6,516	2,510	2,701	1,134	171	31,336	20.3%	11.1%	9.8%	508	9,227
Lauderdale County	7,202	3,505	1,392	1,760	545	25,863	11.4%	18.1%	20.6%	1,185	9,853
Lee County	6,963	2,490	1,967	1,328	1,178	37,848	11.9%	9.4%	7.2%	976	9,113
Madison County	7,871	2,660	1,244	2,373	1,594	50,256	6.0%	11.5%	12.5%	502	12,407
Rankin County	11,985	3,861	3,403	3,452	1,269	37,411	10.9%	4.4%	10.9%	1,653	17,212
Missouri											
Boone County	11,871	2,940	3,748	3,942	1,241	43,817	10.1%	7.1%	5.2%	1,694	17,889
Buchanan County	8,952	2,974	2,640	2,946	392	37,665	11.9%	5.8%	10.9%	1,094	11,501
Cape Girardeau County	7,147	2,771	1,846	1,724	806	38,608	11.2%	5.7%	14.1%	761	10,543
Cass County	9,240	2,030	4,092	2,305	813	37,655	9.8%	4.5%	4.8%	1,519	13,005
Christian County	7,253	2,758	2,324	1,365	806	30,909	4.6%	4.0%	6.5%	566	10,435
Clay County	19,267	5,188	6,466	5,603	2,010	41,416	5.3%	4.8%	4.2%	1,634	27,384
Cole County	6,748	1,712	1,730	2,523	783	48,692	9.2%	4.4%	4.9%	281	10,348
Franklin County	9,697	2,880	3,724	2,465	628	33,592	9.4%	6.7%	7.6%	1,186	13,819
Greene County	28,854	11,309	8,453	6,617	2,475	33,088	10.9%	4.6%	14.1%	2,461	38,432
Jackson County	59,505	20,699	17,318	15,920	5,568	36,078	12.5%	9.7%	9.0%	8,804	81,277
Jasper County	9,867	3,438	3,020	2,720	689	33,909	14.5%	7.7%	16.0%	2,376	13,303
Jefferson County	17,812	5,109	6,097	4,989	1,617	38,890	6.0%	5.2%	5.6%	2,880	26,361
Platte County	7,048	1,390	2,285	1,949	1,424	48,427	5.0%	8.4%	0.2%	825	10,952
St. Charles County	31,721	7,063	10,232	10,102	4,324	45,930	4.1%	4.2%	6.2%	1,816	46,385
St. Francois County	6,200	2,414	2,418	1,106	262	30,020	12.4%	11.8%	12.7%	1,176	9,340
St. Louis County	105,403	27,151	30,399	29,143	18,710	44,180	7.4%	5.2%	7.0%	9,475	145,096
Montana											
Cascade County	9,011	3,341	2,808	2,247	615	35,155	11.0%	5.6%	8.7%	556	12,654
Flathead County	9,898	2,920	3,492	2,739	747	38,979	13.3%	10.7%	8.5%	531	14,723
Gallatin County	6,915	2,171	1,836	1,899	1,009	38,449	9.6%	4.6%	8.7%	573	10,651
Lewis and Clark County	6,192	1,757	1,933	1,924	578	40,511	10.4%	3.6%	8.5%	1,342	9,360
Missoula County	10,170	3,080	3,233	1,877	1,980	38,121	8.8%	7.5%	8.0%	1,834	13,156
Yellowstone County	14,746	4,922	4,825	3,480	1,519	38,633	11.5%	8.4%	7.0%	1,494	21,674
Nebraska											
Douglas County	41,021	13,573	11,775	10,141	5,532	37,769	10.4%	5.2%	10.5%	5,208	59,191
Lancaster County	23,688	5,902	7,819	7,387	2,580	43,804	5.9%	3.5%	5.7%	1,449	34,000
Sarpy County	10,850	1,909	3,198	4,041	1,702	52,520	4.1%	3.1%	6.8%	582	16,642
Nevada											
Clark County	156,767	48,238	45,099	43,251	20,179	40,332	12.1%	8.4%	9.2%	28,055	229,394
Washoe County	40,668	13,244	10,881	10,975	5,568	41,771	13.0%	8.0%	6.9%	5,210	57,760
New Hampshire											
Cheshire County	8,186	2,437	2,887	1,900	962	37,494	8.5%	8.4%	13.2%	1,077	11,443
Grafton County	9,339	2,127	3,018	2,705	1,489	46,174	7.9%	4.7%	7.8%	1,146	14,573
Hillsborough County	31,803	8,362	9,576	8,888	4,977	44,838	4.5%	4.4%	7.5%	3,472	50,118
Merrimack County	13,787	4,417	4,133	3,582	1,655	38,854	6.9%	3.8%	3.4%	965	21,805
Rockingham County	27,957	6,310	8,154	7,974	5,519	47,353	4.2%	2.2%	3.9%	1,659	44,705
Strafford County	9,910	3,218	2,292	2,893	1,507	40,188	8.4%	3.3%	6.6%	1,534	14,706
New Jersey											
Atlantic County	26,503	8,868	6,416	6,918	4,301	42,911	10.2%	7.8%	7.2%	4,547	38,329
Bergen County	84,279	20,678	19,316	21,606	22,679	53,419	6.4%	6.3%	11.4%	8,160	127,284
Burlington County	43,499	10,318	11,868	13,198	8,115	48,493	6.1%	5.2%	7.0%	3,370	61,226
Camden County	47,093	15,470	12,079	11,660	7,884	40,163	9.7%	9.6%	11.7%	7,318	65,729
Cape May County	14,468	4,398	3,812	3,622	2,636	41,250	8.2%	10.0%	10.4%	1,088	20,200
Cumberland County	13,024	4,675	3,842	3,227	1,280	37,523	20.1%	6.1%	8.3%	2,629	17,316
Essex County	61,017	23,307	14,148	11,038	12,524	34,660	10.8%	14.1%	14.1%	12,666	85,471
Gloucester County	25,692	6,285	7,481	6,957	4,969	46,457	5.4%	4.1%	7.8%	3,922	36,996
Hudson County	43,207	18,924	9,773	8,225	6,285	30,482	14.8%	15.2%	16.8%	14,511	61,884
Hunterdon County	11,952	2,210	3,117	3,263	3,362	56,374	4.4%	3.6%	4.4%	495	19,395

Table G-2: Counties—Income, Poverty Status and Receipt of Food Stamps (SNAP)—*Continued*

	Income of Households with Householder 65 Years and Over					Poverty Rate of Persons			Households with 1 or More Persons 60 Years and Over	
	Total Households	Less Than $25,000	$25,000 - $49,999	$50,000 - $99,999	$100,000 or More	Median Household Income	55 to 64 Years	65 to 74 Years	75 Years and Over	Receiving SNAP	Not Receiving SNAP
New Jersey—Cont.											
Mercer County	30,427	7,671	5,878	8,235	8,643	60,196	10.0%	8.4%	11.3%	3,801	45,156
Middlesex County	63,356	15,669	15,880	16,997	14,810	50,236	5.9%	6.1%	8.2%	6,948	99,773
Monmouth County	59,863	15,637	12,124	17,042	15,060	54,217	4.9%	5.4%	8.7%	5,540	88,247
Morris County	45,402	9,850	9,700	14,024	11,828	60,498	4.0%	4.9%	6.6%	2,601	68,222
Ocean County	81,638	21,906	23,681	24,145	11,906	43,005	7.2%	5.7%	7.4%	6,886	103,790
Passaic County	35,641	12,552	8,086	7,925	7,078	39,545	11.7%	13.4%	13.5%	9,923	51,752
Salem County	7,136	2,370	1,811	1,974	981	39,689	11.6%	7.9%	5.1%	1,448	8,961
Somerset County	24,819	5,034	6,746	6,539	6,500	54,302	4.3%	2.9%	8.3%	1,535	41,793
Sussex County	12,312	2,546	2,565	4,514	2,687	58,288	6.1%	4.1%	6.4%	866	20,755
Union County	41,557	11,987	9,443	11,535	8,592	47,457	7.2%	6.8%	11.4%	5,616	61,987
Warren County	10,314	2,936	3,106	2,607	1,665	43,938	8.7%	3.3%	7.6%	1,132	15,364
New Mexico											
Bernalillo County	59,692	20,283	15,456	15,181	8,772	40,685	13.8%	12.5%	11.4%	9,640	87,001
Chaves County	6,495	2,852	1,809	1,355	479	27,828	9.9%	15.8%	21.0%	1,397	8,711
Doña Ana County	17,799	5,259	5,457	4,290	2,793	44,600	16.7%	14.2%	13.2%	3,186	24,209
Lea County	4,381	1,601	1,260	1,035	485	34,281	11.2%	9.7%	10.1%	597	6,241
McKinley County	4,880	2,514	901	965	500	23,918	33.7%	25.5%	25.8%	2,342	5,796
Otero County	6,074	1,697	2,033	1,935	409	42,896	11.2%	17.6%	5.7%	856	7,808
San Juan County	9,919	3,563	2,301	2,554	1,501	40,483	14.7%	10.4%	11.4%	1,918	13,267
Sandoval County	13,613	4,468	3,631	4,019	1,495	38,037	9.2%	14.3%	16.7%	1,623	18,683
Santa Fe County	18,581	5,319	4,546	4,530	4,186	48,046	12.2%	5.4%	8.0%	1,189	27,469
Valencia County	7,783	2,648	2,835	1,590	710	35,279	20.7%	11.9%	16.4%	1,375	9,672
New York											
Albany County	29,822	7,708	8,249	8,660	5,205	45,194	10.2%	7.4%	7.9%	4,772	39,638
Bronx County	98,671	53,082	19,636	18,001	7,952	22,118	25.4%	25.8%	26.0%	60,680	104,244
Broome County	21,537	6,120	8,202	5,379	1,836	38,135	13.4%	7.8%	8.4%	4,327	29,361
Cattaraugus County	8,548	3,463	2,528	1,739	818	31,408	11.1%	8.4%	13.4%	1,812	11,612
Cayuga County	8,338	2,739	2,629	2,273	697	37,563	7.5%	4.5%	8.7%	1,737	10,867
Chautauqua County	14,768	5,179	4,941	3,313	1,335	36,538	13.2%	10.3%	8.8%	2,616	18,757
Chemung County	8,995	2,926	3,320	1,984	765	34,625	6.5%	11.5%	13.0%	1,019	12,908
Clinton County	7,776	2,615	1,950	2,404	807	36,237	11.5%	6.5%	8.3%	1,848	10,092
Dutchess County	25,920	5,820	7,404	7,513	5,183	49,034	10.2%	5.1%	7.3%	2,673	38,707
Erie County	101,398	34,873	31,584	23,718	11,223	35,858	10.6%	8.1%	9.8%	20,628	129,916
Jefferson County	8,616	2,613	2,532	2,621	850	40,851	14.0%	4.6%	7.7%	1,959	11,361
Kings County	196,991	97,553	40,807	36,844	21,787	25,418	17.6%	19.9%	28.5%	102,390	221,937
Livingston County	7,095	2,318	2,265	1,959	553	35,368	12.3%	3.8%	10.8%	1,330	9,141
Madison County	6,308	1,939	2,330	1,557	482	36,404	5.8%	8.6%	2.3%	1,169	9,252
Monroe County	74,052	21,854	27,115	17,679	7,404	36,377	9.0%	5.2%	7.4%	13,626	99,834
Nassau County	126,595	25,487	28,204	36,319	36,585	62,171	4.7%	4.2%	6.1%	10,613	189,878
New York County	167,700	63,922	29,294	33,855	40,629	39,197	18.9%	15.1%	21.1%	53,028	193,899
Niagara County	24,133	9,490	7,586	5,321	1,736	31,131	9.3%	9.0%	11.6%	3,647	32,279
Oneida County	24,683	8,105	7,538	6,520	2,520	35,625	11.0%	8.1%	6.1%	5,141	31,464
Onondaga County	45,806	14,617	13,735	12,269	5,185	37,860	8.6%	6.9%	9.9%	7,817	61,942
Ontario County	12,487	4,064	4,025	2,943	1,455	35,984	7.1%	4.7%	10.9%	1,693	16,455
Orange County	27,498	7,853	6,729	7,731	5,185	46,293	9.6%	5.2%	10.6%	3,246	40,827
Oswego County	10,409	3,796	3,259	2,597	757	37,594	9.9%	6.4%	11.9%	2,011	14,399
Putnam County	8,294	1,458	2,515	2,330	1,991	54,566	3.3%	2.3%	7.1%	639	13,380
Queens County	176,063	65,645	39,343	42,834	28,241	37,607	13.2%	13.0%	16.4%	57,133	243,565
Rensselaer County	15,633	3,575	4,629	4,964	2,465	47,876	7.9%	5.1%	4.1%	2,238	22,283
Richmond County	38,825	11,926	9,230	10,580	7,089	43,578	11.8%	10.5%	11.6%	9,015	58,010
Rockland County	25,950	4,956	6,408	5,565	9,021	60,160	5.1%	3.4%	8.6%	3,341	38,318
Saratoga County	22,418	5,154	6,761	5,549	4,954	47,894	3.8%	4.4%	5.5%	2,716	31,155
Schenectady County	14,354	3,658	4,024	4,658	2,014	45,040	7.9%	4.9%	5.2%	2,735	19,209
St. Lawrence County	9,894	3,559	3,108	2,734	493	30,000	9.0%	12.9%	5.9%	2,137	13,982
Steuben County	11,088	4,348	3,389	2,338	1,013	32,537	15.3%	9.2%	3.9%	2,186	14,316
Suffolk County	135,519	31,636	30,903	39,785	33,195	54,690	6.3%	4.8%	6.3%	15,478	194,399
Sullivan County	7,204	2,315	2,411	1,734	744	35,960	15.7%	8.0%	9.4%	1,227	10,448
Tompkins County	7,857	1,581	2,342	2,148	1,786	50,299	12.1%	3.5%	4.3%	1,081	11,702
Ulster County	21,122	6,950	5,805	5,061	3,306	38,553	9.3%	10.8%	10.0%	3,390	27,357
Warren County	7,527	2,012	1,901	2,181	1,433	46,658	11.2%	8.0%	5.9%	1,176	10,674
Wayne County	9,442	2,289	4,599	1,908	646	32,736	13.0%	5.0%	6.9%	1,426	13,109
Westchester County	91,882	22,746	20,593	22,616	25,927	53,829	8.5%	7.8%	10.2%	11,731	128,062
North Carolina											
Alamance County	16,058	6,114	5,026	3,312	1,606	30,729	14.1%	10.5%	12.6%	2,608	20,626
Brunswick County	18,313	4,368	5,832	5,347	2,766	44,666	8.7%	7.6%	6.4%	2,066	24,606
Buncombe County	27,853	9,031	8,473	6,437	3,912	37,884	9.7%	4.4%	8.9%	3,843	37,897
Burke County	9,454	4,161	2,586	2,027	680	29,090	14.5%	14.0%	14.2%	2,142	12,288
Cabarrus County	15,055	5,211	5,292	3,390	1,162	37,092	7.9%	11.2%	11.8%	2,157	20,614
Caldwell County	9,454	4,275	2,838	1,828	513	27,510	14.7%	15.1%	21.2%	1,727	11,775
Carteret County	9,697	2,966	2,403	3,056	1,272	44,144	10.0%	6.1%	8.4%	1,091	12,637
Catawba County	14,624	4,584	5,848	3,031	1,161	33,708	13.5%	6.9%	10.8%	2,262	20,018
Chatham County	10,205	2,520	2,514	3,047	2,124	52,378	10.4%	7.8%	7.1%	563	12,493
Cleveland County	11,438	4,874	3,197	2,853	514	29,814	18.4%	9.1%	14.1%	2,455	14,209
Craven County	11,320	3,505	3,850	3,295	670	38,164	12.7%	7.4%	7.5%	1,971	14,397
Cumberland County	22,057	7,174	6,608	5,700	2,575	39,058	10.7%	9.6%	10.5%	4,779	30,075
Davidson County	17,710	7,410	5,028	3,957	1,315	31,624	14.9%	8.6%	10.3%	2,453	22,728

Table G-2: Counties—Income, Poverty Status and Receipt of Food Stamps (SNAP)—*Continued*

	Income of Households with Householder 65 Years and Over						Poverty Rate of Persons			Households with 1 or More Persons 60 Years and Over	
	Total Households	Less Than $25,000	$25,000 - $49,999	$50,000 - $99,999	$100,000 or More	Median Household Income	55 to 64 Years	65 to 74 Years	75 Years and Over	Receiving SNAP	Not Receiving SNAP
North Carolina—Cont.											
Durham County	20,075	5,267	5,314	4,937	4,557	47,951	13.6%	6.5%	10.3%	3,539	29,941
Forsyth County	33,763	10,469	9,725	9,295	4,274	39,954	14.6%	8.0%	9.1%	4,054	47,280
Gaston County	18,971	6,773	6,906	4,081	1,211	32,587	10.9%	9.1%	10.9%	3,786	25,268
Guilford County	44,306	15,374	14,021	10,691	4,220	35,418	9.9%	8.1%	9.4%	8,116	58,606
Harnett County	8,883	3,593	2,299	2,303	688	32,956	9.3%	15.2%	12.2%	1,977	11,394
Henderson County	16,786	4,948	5,279	4,540	2,019	37,280	8.1%	5.6%	8.5%	1,440	20,950
Iredell County	13,802	3,465	4,067	5,008	1,262	44,830	8.9%	8.2%	8.0%	1,835	20,367
Johnston County	13,892	4,968	4,447	2,974	1,503	35,247	7.8%	9.3%	12.3%	2,665	18,645
Lincoln County	7,702	2,801	2,572	1,767	562	32,039	11.4%	10.9%	22.7%	2,010	10,533
Mecklenburg County	62,064	19,384	17,291	15,768	9,621	39,671	11.7%	9.4%	8.8%	10,247	92,081
Moore County	13,871	3,717	3,423	4,316	2,415	48,255	13.3%	7.9%	6.3%	1,584	15,898
Nash County	10,013	4,791	2,745	2,226	251	27,273	11.2%	6.1%	16.3%	2,095	14,434
New Hanover County	21,442	5,328	5,869	5,944	4,301	48,049	8.5%	4.2%	6.9%	2,624	29,602
Onslow County	9,938	2,968	2,671	3,246	1,053	43,723	15.4%	6.0%	8.1%	1,727	13,760
Orange County	9,772	2,371	2,487	2,110	2,804	51,458	7.8%	3.0%	8.2%	1,027	16,013
Pitt County	12,463	3,985	3,517	3,335	1,626	36,331	14.1%	11.0%	8.4%	2,907	16,578
Randolph County	15,552	6,643	4,902	3,078	929	32,611	8.2%	14.2%	6.6%	3,025	19,491
Robeson County	11,080	5,642	3,261	1,689	488	24,536	20.8%	19.3%	17.5%	3,730	13,475
Rockingham County	10,672	4,233	3,224	2,141	1,074	33,193	13.4%	6.6%	6.0%	1,802	14,315
Rowan County	14,616	5,023	4,390	4,334	869	35,532	10.1%	7.3%	8.8%	2,426	18,262
Rutherford County	8,116	3,498	3,026	1,097	495	29,615	17.9%	6.3%	8.2%	753	11,516
Surry County	8,171	3,597	2,470	1,708	396	28,804	22.7%	13.4%	13.2%	1,961	10,026
Union County	14,167	4,006	4,379	4,429	1,353	38,400	10.4%	3.9%	4.9%	1,777	21,615
Wake County	59,068	13,228	15,451	18,080	12,309	51,138	9.1%	4.7%	8.3%	6,194	92,810
Wayne County	11,015	4,041	3,581	2,294	1,099	31,994	14.6%	10.9%	14.0%	2,317	14,532
Wilkes County	8,517	4,536	2,390	1,290	301	22,074	22.5%	20.5%	24.0%	1,611	10,685
Wilson County	8,299	3,059	3,071	1,713	456	32,961	15.7%	11.7%	6.8%	1,365	11,569
North Dakota											
Burleigh County	8,176	2,214	2,087	2,882	993	46,075	3.9%	2.9%	10.3%	527	11,677
Cass County	11,545	2,719	4,954	2,982	890	36,105	8.5%	6.7%	8.0%	933	17,368
Grand Forks County	5,261	1,640	1,206	1,837	578	42,119	8.9%	3.0%	3.6%	499	7,267
Ward County	5,001	1,189	1,720	1,182	910	42,555	5.5%	3.0%	4.7%	178	7,110
Ohio											
Allen County	10,595	4,081	3,232	2,784	498	33,109	13.3%	6.7%	10.9%	1,783	14,190
Ashtabula County	10,195	4,775	3,156	1,972	292	26,390	16.7%	18.9%	8.2%	2,982	13,318
Belmont County	7,957	2,947	2,675	1,852	483	32,081	13.8%	2.8%	7.4%	1,468	10,101
Butler County	29,611	7,123	9,923	8,550	4,015	42,364	7.2%	1.9%	6.8%	3,595	41,403
Clark County	15,290	5,209	5,681	3,081	1,319	35,707	16.2%	6.8%	7.4%	2,522	20,292
Clermont County	17,922	5,118	5,032	5,198	2,574	41,897	6.6%	6.6%	6.8%	2,032	25,727
Columbiana County	12,009	4,571	3,689	2,750	999	32,450	12.9%	8.1%	10.9%	2,885	15,536
Cuyahoga County	136,488	51,374	40,132	31,134	13,848	33,748	13.6%	12.3%	8.6%	27,556	177,846
Delaware County	12,304	2,374	3,479	3,521	2,930	55,310	4.4%	6.8%	6.8%	292	19,584
Erie County	9,653	2,503	3,948	2,335	867	37,938	7.5%	10.2%	3.0%	1,197	12,299
Fairfield County	13,321	4,306	3,859	3,291	1,865	38,472	9.1%	4.9%	7.7%	2,609	19,216
Franklin County	83,709	25,819	23,879	22,495	11,516	40,012	10.5%	8.8%	8.2%	16,397	121,592
Geauga County	9,686	1,856	2,635	3,297	1,898	58,319	6.2%	1.4%	4.8%	655	14,123
Greene County	15,735	4,137	4,511	4,160	2,927	46,444	5.0%	4.6%	8.6%	937	23,209
Hamilton County	76,287	26,012	20,746	18,261	11,268	36,892	14.1%	8.0%	10.2%	12,168	105,473
Hancock County	7,754	2,000	2,913	1,931	910	40,069	6.9%	14.5%	0.7%	633	10,391
Jefferson County	8,680	3,635	2,775	1,747	523	30,559	16.5%	7.4%	7.9%	1,309	10,963
Lake County	26,291	6,549	9,427	7,485	2,830	40,515	6.4%	4.3%	6.1%	3,172	35,519
Licking County	16,224	4,143	5,756	4,256	2,069	41,572	6.3%	6.2%	6.2%	2,246	21,687
Lorain County	31,749	11,034	10,852	7,491	2,372	35,355	9.5%	7.0%	13.3%	4,414	43,028
Lucas County	41,777	15,656	12,597	9,436	4,088	33,118	11.3%	8.7%	10.0%	7,988	56,175
Mahoning County	29,231	11,142	10,304	6,541	1,244	33,100	13.9%	6.8%	8.4%	5,377	36,347
Marion County	7,518	2,158	2,617	1,961	782	36,126	14.3%	11.4%	8.6%	1,355	8,980
Medina County	16,367	4,004	5,512	5,257	1,594	43,799	3.7%	3.6%	6.3%	1,131	24,265
Miami County	11,088	3,906	3,647	2,489	1,046	37,810	6.2%	7.7%	6.2%	1,274	15,215
Montgomery County	57,759	18,996	17,473	16,075	5,215	37,479	13.9%	6.8%	13.3%	9,073	74,799
Muskingum County	9,403	4,230	3,310	1,552	311	26,965	14.8%	9.4%	13.7%	2,514	11,207
Portage County	15,282	4,212	5,038	4,216	1,816	40,998	8.3%	4.4%	6.3%	2,350	22,204
Richland County	15,369	5,842	5,905	2,843	779	29,978	10.5%	9.3%	8.9%	2,566	19,027
Ross County	7,322	2,979	2,591	1,244	508	29,676	13.1%	8.8%	15.5%	1,571	9,693
Scioto County	7,877	3,421	2,083	1,548	825	30,137	16.9%	9.0%	14.9%	1,980	9,994
Stark County	41,136	12,960	15,311	9,837	3,028	35,707	10.0%	8.2%	10.0%	6,430	55,699
Summit County	56,247	17,001	19,248	13,682	6,336	38,822	9.6%	6.7%	6.7%	9,141	76,176
Trumbull County	25,474	8,086	8,733	6,583	2,072	36,762	11.2%	5.3%	9.3%	2,976	33,840
Tuscarawas County	10,625	4,096	3,377	2,664	488	32,825	13.0%	10.0%	4.5%	1,885	13,681
Warren County	16,994	4,246	4,691	5,561	2,496	46,011	3.7%	2.8%	3.8%	1,085	27,271
Wayne County	10,626	3,015	3,953	2,868	790	37,701	7.9%	4.3%	4.5%	935	15,756
Wood County	11,081	2,978	3,361	2,986	1,756	41,332	6.9%	5.0%	5.5%	1,051	16,077
Oklahoma											
Canadian County	9,226	2,069	2,495	3,077	1,585	50,542	6.8%	5.4%	6.0%	774	13,804
Cleveland County	19,193	4,768	5,561	6,118	2,746	43,337	8.2%	4.2%	8.5%	1,784	29,915
Comanche County	8,367	2,734	2,777	1,891	965	37,191	9.5%	8.2%	14.8%	1,301	11,681

Table G-2: Counties—Income, Poverty Status and Receipt of Food Stamps (SNAP)—*Continued*

	Income of Households with Householder 65 Years and Over						Poverty Rate of Persons			Households with 1 or More Persons 60 Years and Over	
	Total Households	Less Than $25,000	$25,000 - $49,999	$50,000 - $99,999	$100,000 or More	Median Household Income	55 to 64 Years	65 to 74 Years	75 Years and Over	Receiving SNAP	Not Receiving SNAP
Oklahoma—Cont.											
Creek County	7,083	2,849	2,278	1,654	302	28,836	12.6%	12.5%	9.2%	1,252	10,127
Muskogee County	6,952	2,428	2,021	1,942	561	36,326	10.9%	6.8%	9.5%	1,045	8,914
Oklahoma County	60,997	16,499	18,670	17,128	8,700	42,189	14.0%	6.2%	7.1%	8,486	85,462
Payne County	5,632	2,178	1,552	1,462	440	33,409	9.3%	3.3%	8.6%	667	7,867
Pottawatomie County	6,475	1,790	2,153	1,994	538	38,763	11.4%	6.4%	8.8%	1,243	8,821
Rogers County	8,787	2,509	3,200	2,046	1,032	38,492	9.9%	5.7%	5.5%	753	11,748
Tulsa County	51,474	14,767	15,812	13,724	7,171	42,039	10.9%	7.5%	7.8%	6,467	74,834
Wagoner County	6,775	1,603	2,075	1,981	1,116	45,157	7.0%	4.3%	6.9%	864	9,416
Oregon											
Benton County	7,923	2,042	1,734	2,929	1,218	52,510	7.5%	5.7%	7.9%	1,123	10,723
Clackamas County	38,693	9,107	12,371	11,896	5,319	45,570	7.8%	5.8%	9.9%	6,540	54,915
Deschutes County	18,070	5,096	6,189	4,241	2,544	38,048	12.1%	9.1%	9.1%	2,932	23,986
Douglas County	15,674	5,376	4,817	4,311	1,170	37,550	11.0%	10.5%	6.6%	2,718	20,121
Jackson County	26,718	7,924	8,652	7,103	3,039	38,703	14.0%	7.4%	7.4%	4,983	35,121
Josephine County	12,767	4,318	4,285	2,936	1,228	36,973	18.0%	7.3%	4.7%	2,672	15,673
Klamath County	8,131	3,044	3,086	1,452	549	33,123	14.9%	3.4%	9.4%	1,807	9,824
Lane County	39,122	12,328	12,316	10,199	4,279	38,890	13.0%	7.1%	12.5%	9,164	50,540
Linn County	12,694	3,698	4,618	3,603	775	39,205	13.1%	9.6%	4.9%	2,830	16,100
Marion County	30,083	9,820	7,843	8,701	3,719	38,228	7.9%	7.2%	13.8%	7,851	39,177
Multnomah County	57,511	20,240	14,971	13,802	8,498	37,480	15.6%	11.6%	13.0%	18,633	80,286
Polk County	8,211	2,424	1,984	2,499	1,304	46,567	8.0%	7.9%	4.7%	866	11,071
Umatilla County	5,823	2,141	1,955	1,183	544	32,813	5.7%	6.1%	5.2%	2,017	8,066
Washington County	41,521	9,628	12,339	12,428	7,126	46,411	7.1%	5.2%	8.3%	6,817	60,411
Yamhill County	9,461	2,771	2,890	2,529	1,271	43,639	10.5%	10.1%	5.7%	1,548	12,549
Pennsylvania											
Adams County	10,910	2,593	3,370	3,341	1,606	45,969	7.5%	2.8%	6.0%	677	15,380
Allegheny County	142,538	49,684	43,259	32,347	17,248	35,335	8.6%	7.2%	8.6%	19,635	188,821
Armstrong County	9,063	3,753	3,245	1,609	456	29,915	8.4%	5.0%	10.7%	1,221	11,507
Beaver County	21,820	7,466	7,415	5,122	1,817	35,262	7.7%	5.5%	8.6%	3,376	27,693
Berks County	40,172	12,872	12,313	10,251	4,736	37,652	7.2%	7.8%	7.9%	6,096	55,053
Blair County	14,864	5,968	4,691	3,510	695	29,389	8.4%	7.9%	13.6%	1,912	20,719
Bucks County	61,999	15,358	16,520	18,600	11,521	47,970	5.2%	4.4%	5.2%	5,860	91,333
Butler County	20,090	5,832	6,885	5,500	1,873	36,837	8.0%	3.5%	8.6%	2,231	28,236
Cambria County	18,477	7,439	6,525	3,274	1,239	30,437	8.9%	5.6%	11.5%	2,281	23,885
Carbon County	7,877	2,577	2,630	2,336	334	37,557	9.3%	6.5%	7.4%	892	10,537
Centre County	12,199	3,244	3,649	3,322	1,984	41,752	5.0%	6.7%	5.8%	905	18,010
Chester County	44,264	9,541	11,364	12,669	10,690	52,880	5.0%	4.4%	4.0%	2,302	66,915
Clearfield County	9,947	4,333	3,311	1,878	425	27,288	16.9%	8.5%	9.7%	2,326	12,149
Columbia County	7,303	2,772	2,548	1,406	577	32,613	6.1%	2.3%	8.4%	1,053	9,669
Crawford County	10,082	3,261	3,995	2,194	632	35,332	8.9%	7.2%	3.2%	1,432	14,296
Cumberland County	26,592	6,671	7,519	8,603	3,799	44,646	5.1%	1.9%	5.3%	2,143	37,699
Dauphin County	25,789	8,213	7,587	6,637	3,352	37,726	9.1%	7.8%	5.9%	3,649	36,891
Delaware County	52,263	14,168	14,636	14,854	8,605	44,044	7.9%	7.0%	9.1%	6,881	75,133
Erie County	27,024	9,723	9,045	5,709	2,547	34,258	11.2%	7.9%	9.6%	4,760	36,447
Fayette County	15,564	6,424	5,269	2,979	892	30,626	16.0%	14.0%	12.7%	3,654	20,281
Franklin County	16,463	4,377	6,186	4,106	1,794	39,407	11.6%	6.9%	8.8%	1,716	22,535
Indiana County	9,335	3,060	2,770	2,618	887	35,257	7.9%	4.4%	10.9%	867	12,679
Lackawanna County	24,720	9,557	7,771	5,581	1,811	32,652	13.0%	7.7%	9.0%	4,493	33,106
Lancaster County	50,614	14,812	16,755	13,446	5,601	38,747	5.5%	6.0%	8.8%	5,461	70,628
Lawrence County	11,449	4,502	3,787	2,253	907	30,291	12.6%	6.1%	7.7%	2,272	13,953
Lebanon County	14,125	3,850	5,019	4,441	815	41,268	6.3%	7.1%	4.1%	2,123	19,623
Lehigh County	34,260	11,314	10,753	8,312	3,881	36,274	7.5%	8.4%	6.8%	5,186	48,744
Luzerne County	36,645	13,700	13,978	6,987	1,980	31,716	13.0%	6.2%	11.9%	7,790	47,314
Lycoming County	12,944	4,979	4,575	2,494	896	32,136	11.0%	6.4%	8.8%	1,447	18,086
Mercer County	14,146	5,003	4,758	3,677	708	33,834	9.9%	6.7%	5.0%	1,665	19,102
Monroe County	12,922	3,030	5,051	3,642	1,199	38,424	7.7%	6.4%	6.8%	1,033	20,982
Montgomery County	81,685	19,127	22,134	21,902	18,522	49,408	5.6%	5.3%	7.8%	5,940	116,167
Northampton County	30,546	9,937	8,838	8,289	3,482	39,074	7.4%	4.8%	7.6%	4,167	42,999
Northumberland County	11,777	4,997	3,688	2,610	482	29,441	13.7%	9.6%	14.6%	2,202	15,388
Philadelphia County	124,800	58,422	31,354	23,636	11,388	27,423	22.3%	16.0%	17.1%	47,424	147,062
Schuylkill County	17,799	7,664	5,826	3,336	973	30,076	10.5%	4.3%	15.9%	2,948	23,697
Somerset County	9,658	4,000	3,641	1,547	470	28,796	10.3%	6.7%	11.1%	1,331	12,542
Washington County	24,643	8,722	7,805	5,797	2,319	36,185	8.2%	7.6%	6.7%	3,995	32,262
Westmoreland County	47,595	17,266	14,731	11,598	4,000	34,353	6.4%	5.5%	9.6%	5,630	63,365
York County	41,712	13,728	12,879	11,123	3,982	36,807	6.8%	6.5%	8.7%	4,795	60,067
Rhode Island											
Kent County	18,266	5,826	4,727	4,564	3,149	42,646	6.7%	6.4%	6.5%	2,625	24,763
Newport County	10,345	2,079	2,689	2,713	2,864	56,421	9.2%	4.8%	7.0%	1,733	13,800
Providence County	54,243	20,665	15,693	10,991	6,894	33,691	13.9%	10.0%	14.7%	16,401	71,156
Washington County	13,918	3,940	3,352	3,892	2,734	48,013	6.0%	6.4%	10.3%	1,607	19,801
South Carolina											
Aiken County	17,610	5,472	5,133	4,816	2,189	38,321	12.7%	10.1%	4.8%	2,516	24,502
Anderson County	20,200	8,105	6,911	3,883	1,301	31,645	15.6%	6.3%	9.7%	3,111	26,192
Beaufort County	25,981	4,575	6,204	9,760	5,442	58,022	9.4%	5.0%	5.3%	1,444	33,000
Berkeley County	13,756	3,769	4,753	3,746	1,488	38,393	10.5%	8.5%	11.3%	2,033	20,697

Table G-2: Counties—Income, Poverty Status and Receipt of Food Stamps (SNAP)—*Continued*

	Income of Households with Householder 65 Years and Over						Poverty Rate of Persons			Households with 1 or More Persons 60 Years and Over	
	Total Households	Less Than $25,000	$25,000 - $49,999	$50,000 - $99,999	$100,000 or More	Median Household Income	55 to 64 Years	65 to 74 Years	75 Years and Over	Receiving SNAP	Not Receiving SNAP
South Carolina—Cont.											
Charleston County	34,760	8,803	10,390	8,292	7,275	43,252	12.6%	6.0%	8.8%	5,127	48,237
Darlington County	7,554	3,556	2,097	1,207	694	27,613	13.5%	15.4%	21.6%	1,737	9,812
Dorchester County	10,319	3,118	3,184	2,568	1,449	39,056	12.2%	8.4%	11.1%	1,897	15,029
Florence County	12,482	5,363	3,170	3,057	892	28,541	17.1%	10.9%	16.9%	3,117	18,185
Greenville County	42,834	14,890	12,218	10,928	4,798	34,655	11.0%	6.0%	8.4%	4,860	59,442
Greenwood County	7,829	3,102	2,512	1,415	800	35,585	13.7%	11.8%	9.0%	1,066	9,646
Horry County	38,767	10,591	14,151	11,208	2,817	41,229	13.0%	7.5%	7.9%	4,611	52,341
Lancaster County	9,146	2,446	2,852	2,763	1,085	41,460	17.1%	9.4%	9.8%	1,273	12,587
Laurens County	7,067	2,285	2,644	1,696	442	36,960	23.6%	13.0%	6.5%	1,240	8,639
Lexington County	25,022	7,648	7,335	7,061	2,978	39,216	9.6%	5.7%	8.9%	3,007	34,437
Oconee County	9,788	3,718	2,483	2,384	1,203	34,251	15.0%	4.5%	8.0%	1,273	14,195
Orangeburg County	9,240	4,319	2,645	1,468	808	28,585	25.3%	21.2%	16.0%	2,674	11,690
Pickens County	11,532	4,866	3,895	1,516	1,255	28,112	13.8%	8.5%	7.7%	1,241	16,038
Richland County	29,698	7,760	9,615	7,009	5,314	43,944	10.3%	6.5%	8.1%	5,141	40,949
Spartanburg County	27,831	8,949	9,445	7,294	2,143	36,061	14.3%	8.9%	9.5%	4,450	37,344
Sumter County	9,981	4,521	2,580	2,069	811	29,297	20.3%	16.6%	20.8%	2,913	12,347
York County	19,598	5,722	6,371	4,633	2,872	38,946	8.4%	6.7%	9.6%	2,513	28,134
South Dakota											
Minnehaha County	14,087	4,270	4,728	3,446	1,643	39,854	8.2%	11.3%	8.8%	2,151	18,858
Pennington County	10,370	3,434	4,116	2,012	808	35,774	10.1%	7.8%	5.7%	998	14,530
Tennessee											
Anderson County	8,798	3,509	2,290	1,459	1,540	32,417	11.4%	8.6%	7.5%	1,229	11,552
Blount County	13,469	4,614	4,538	3,043	1,274	37,611	9.9%	7.7%	9.9%	2,202	18,256
Bradley County	10,286	4,107	3,455	2,108	616	31,333	12.9%	3.7%	14.9%	1,638	13,591
Davidson County	47,229	14,897	11,688	13,353	7,291	42,417	14.2%	8.2%	10.5%	9,325	67,418
Greene County	7,564	2,950	2,537	1,664	413	31,987	17.7%	9.6%	11.5%	1,264	11,313
Hamilton County	35,090	11,617	9,976	9,122	4,375	40,454	11.5%	8.1%	8.7%	5,693	47,814
Knox County	41,265	14,763	12,521	9,625	4,356	34,785	11.6%	9.5%	8.2%	6,921	57,633
Madison County	9,190	3,080	2,229	2,680	1,201	37,374	13.9%	6.7%	9.2%	1,533	12,268
Maury County	7,418	2,667	2,363	1,595	793	38,946	12.3%	4.6%	14.2%	1,224	10,799
Montgomery County	9,301	2,764	2,452	2,888	1,197	45,564	10.5%	7.5%	5.0%	1,847	14,310
Putnam County	8,106	3,564	2,510	1,341	691	28,798	9.1%	14.0%	19.5%	2,076	9,251
Robertson County	5,423	1,718	1,409	1,731	565	39,322	15.9%	10.5%	9.7%	1,006	7,005
Rutherford County	16,979	5,519	5,532	4,484	1,444	37,072	6.8%	6.4%	18.4%	2,432	25,178
Sevier County	10,950	3,871	3,111	2,830	1,138	36,347	17.5%	6.8%	7.2%	1,951	13,613
Shelby County	67,957	22,845	18,602	16,320	10,190	37,256	14.3%	9.2%	12.7%	20,566	93,866
Sullivan County	20,462	7,566	6,741	4,415	1,740	31,994	10.7%	7.6%	9.7%	3,183	25,918
Sumner County	14,283	4,426	4,056	4,403	1,398	37,901	7.5%	5.8%	8.9%	1,950	20,652
Washington County	13,840	3,982	5,282	3,373	1,203	38,082	8.9%	3.7%	6.1%	2,136	18,932
Williamson County	13,046	2,031	3,802	3,790	3,423	56,298	4.9%	2.9%	2.1%	624	20,767
Wilson County	10,626	2,713	3,610	2,844	1,459	42,027	5.5%	4.5%	7.8%	894	16,338
Texas											
Angelina County	7,889	2,866	2,847	1,903	273	32,015	10.7%	6.1%	13.9%	1,091	9,816
Bastrop County	5,639	1,427	1,797	1,304	1,111	41,872	10.4%	8.7%	15.8%	1,298	9,373
Bell County	19,437	6,089	5,462	5,193	2,693	41,462	10.7%	6.7%	7.1%	2,798	28,862
Bexar County	124,741	39,237	33,651	30,944	20,909	41,248	13.5%	10.4%	12.2%	25,154	175,532
Bowie County	8,827	2,890	2,503	2,363	1,071	36,095	9.6%	6.7%	12.8%	965	11,730
Brazoria County	20,884	6,304	5,688	6,214	2,678	39,989	8.0%	8.1%	10.4%	2,632	32,737
Brazos County	11,057	3,116	2,850	3,056	2,035	43,020	10.5%	7.3%	17.0%	1,311	16,677
Cameron County	30,043	15,102	6,804	4,941	3,196	24,874	25.9%	23.4%	23.0%	9,998	36,576
Collin County	48,511	9,942	12,837	13,808	11,924	53,261	4.6%	4.4%	7.6%	2,619	82,586
Comal County	13,048	2,528	4,013	4,166	2,341	49,882	13.8%	4.9%	3.0%	407	20,092
Coryell County	4,034	1,325	1,135	1,170	404	34,740	2.0%	4.6%	10.4%	340	5,641
Dallas County	146,790	47,062	40,374	36,893	22,461	39,026	12.9%	10.6%	10.6%	30,260	221,732
Denton County	37,253	7,820	10,690	10,290	8,453	50,358	5.2%	4.0%	8.1%	3,430	61,162
Ector County	9,158	3,765	1,966	1,818	1,609	32,297	5.3%	11.9%	16.9%	1,918	12,978
El Paso County	52,580	22,802	15,521	10,269	3,988	28,925	16.6%	18.1%	23.3%	20,450	67,375
Ellis County	11,745	2,886	4,021	3,403	1,435	42,769	6.9%	5.0%	10.9%	1,078	17,066
Fort Bend County	33,770	7,654	7,276	10,331	8,509	54,397	3.9%	7.5%	8.9%	6,526	58,845
Galveston County	25,568	6,684	7,789	5,846	5,249	42,341	11.9%	6.0%	9.6%	3,559	38,013
Grayson County	12,404	4,782	3,700	2,905	1,017	36,953	14.2%	7.6%	9.1%	1,950	18,355
Gregg County	10,987	3,497	2,515	3,457	1,518	45,023	9.9%	9.6%	10.4%	1,371	15,842
Guadalupe County	11,530	2,742	3,590	3,428	1,770	46,073	6.2%	6.4%	1.8%	1,068	16,794
Harris County	244,310	79,161	62,179	59,224	43,746	40,458	10.8%	10.7%	12.8%	49,652	382,188
Harrison County	7,012	3,197	1,729	1,541	545	33,399	26.4%	11.2%	25.8%	643	9,118
Hays County	10,742	2,571	2,817	3,256	2,098	49,900	8.2%	4.4%	4.2%	1,296	17,775
Henderson County	10,304	3,178	3,589	2,666	871	38,657	17.9%	9.4%	10.7%	1,503	13,024
Hidalgo County	44,905	22,140	11,044	9,085	2,636	25,410	20.4%	24.0%	24.7%	21,227	52,945
Hunt County	7,898	3,267	1,438	2,627	566	33,768	14.2%	11.8%	6.8%	1,961	11,070
Jefferson County	22,367	9,062	7,161	4,357	1,787	30,908	16.0%	12.1%	11.2%	3,883	30,370
Johnson County	12,410	3,112	3,904	3,812	1,582	42,380	8.1%	5.3%	3.1%	1,257	17,947
Kaufman County	7,131	2,061	2,230	2,110	730	41,709	14.7%	6.2%	10.5%	895	11,190
Liberty County	5,944	2,785	1,771	813	575	27,595	14.8%	9.8%	13.9%	1,488	8,484
Lubbock County	23,469	7,215	6,837	6,709	2,708	40,731	10.6%	8.8%	11.6%	3,064	29,886
McLennan County	21,145	6,341	6,571	5,712	2,521	42,465	9.7%	4.8%	7.5%	3,126	27,319

Table G-2: Counties—Income, Poverty Status and Receipt of Food Stamps (SNAP)—*Continued*

	Income of Households with Householder 65 Years and Over					Poverty Rate of Persons			Households with 1 or More Persons 60 Years and Over	
	Total Households	Less Than $25,000	$25,000 - $49,999	$50,000 - $99,999	$100,000 or More	Median Household Income	55 to 64 Years	65 to 74 Years	75 Years and Over	Receiving SNAP	Not Receiving SNAP
Texas—Cont.											
Midland County	9,061	3,024	2,298	1,695	2,044	43,395	8.9%	5.9%	6.4%	427	15,699
Montgomery County	38,397	10,205	9,687	10,515	7,990	47,279	4.7%	8.6%	9.5%	3,766	58,569
Nacogdoches County	5,704	2,517	1,462	1,267	458	34,799	11.5%	10.4%	8.0%	906	7,785
Nueces County	28,983	10,303	7,992	6,654	4,034	36,558	12.8%	16.7%	11.6%	7,538	39,356
Orange County	7,803	3,230	2,498	1,497	578	30,902	14.2%	7.6%	8.7%	1,919	10,302
Parker County	11,109	2,471	3,837	3,348	1,453	43,159	5.3%	7.0%	7.8%	747	16,291
Potter County	9,261	3,661	3,138	1,547	915	33,621	16.5%	9.6%	14.4%	1,332	12,307
Randall County	11,006	2,903	2,863	3,350	1,890	42,386	7.7%	5.1%	5.1%	581	16,284
Rockwall County	5,014	1,198	1,337	1,122	1,357	49,271	4.7%	13.7%	3.9%	458	8,281
San Patricio County	6,278	2,154	1,812	1,631	681	41,348	5.1%	8.0%	10.9%	1,065	7,533
Smith County	20,300	7,660	5,215	4,838	2,587	36,164	11.8%	9.1%	12.6%	2,523	28,423
Tarrant County	119,389	34,844	31,086	33,555	19,904	42,745	8.8%	7.4%	8.7%	17,721	175,841
Taylor County	10,911	2,897	3,447	2,913	1,654	42,335	10.1%	8.6%	13.7%	1,083	15,471
Tom Green County	10,470	4,159	2,997	2,299	1,015	33,819	11.7%	12.3%	12.3%	1,621	14,351
Travis County	58,269	13,440	14,013	17,512	13,304	53,718	10.4%	7.7%	8.7%	9,240	94,762
Victoria County	7,916	2,433	2,240	2,496	747	38,497	8.5%	8.2%	10.9%	966	11,273
Walker County	na	na	na	na	na	37,550	10.3%	4.5%	8.4%	294	6,484
Webb County	12,074	6,258	2,872	1,971	973	23,336	25.2%	26.8%	33.9%	7,501	14,892
Wichita County	11,817	4,474	3,030	3,034	1,279	36,349	12.9%	5.1%	15.8%	1,364	16,748
Williamson County	28,309	5,445	6,822	10,175	5,867	55,803	6.5%	4.9%	5.6%	1,831	47,106
Utah											
Cache County	6,400	1,517	1,945	2,167	771	44,850	5.1%	5.0%	8.2%	401	9,494
Davis County	17,527	3,822	4,855	5,822	3,028	50,372	3.6%	4.3%	4.7%	1,337	27,949
Salt Lake County	64,084	15,601	18,155	19,362	10,966	47,154	7.8%	4.6%	9.5%	6,741	100,442
Utah County	21,905	4,669	5,907	7,335	3,994	51,598	7.4%	4.8%	4.9%	2,467	33,732
Washington County	17,020	4,270	5,720	5,654	1,376	41,630	10.7%	5.7%	8.8%	542	21,975
Weber County	15,863	4,858	4,017	5,549	1,439	43,311	7.8%	8.5%	9.6%	2,224	24,214
Vermont											
Chittenden County	13,660	3,568	3,928	3,839	2,325	43,418	6.3%	5.3%	6.9%	1,955	20,244
Virginia											
Albemarle County	9,918	1,834	2,220	3,527	2,337	60,189	13.2%	3.9%	9.4%	990	15,251
Arlington County	13,054	2,454	2,317	3,131	5,152	72,316	6.0%	8.2%	3.5%	1,328	20,892
Augusta County	8,167	2,310	1,993	2,510	1,354	48,201	7.1%	1.8%	11.5%	972	11,672
Bedford County	8,680	2,420	2,408	2,970	882	46,050	6.9%	9.0%	5.3%	979	12,606
Chesterfield County	25,786	4,900	6,228	8,624	6,034	57,412	3.5%	2.0%	5.7%	1,515	40,740
Fairfax County	74,927	10,816	10,664	20,827	32,620	85,662	4.0%	4.7%	6.5%	5,708	122,158
Fauquier County	5,663	921	1,100	1,537	2,105	69,933	3.3%	5.1%	6.9%	585	8,656
Frederick County	6,926	1,570	2,040	2,073	1,243	48,216	9.8%	3.7%	11.8%	695	10,836
Hanover County	10,084	1,992	2,441	3,194	2,457	53,714	3.8%	4.3%	7.3%	644	15,205
Henrico County	26,909	7,079	7,509	7,935	4,386	46,562	5.7%	4.5%	8.1%	2,401	41,254
James City County	10,401	1,412	1,857	3,591	3,541	74,283	5.5%	0.0%	2.4%	347	14,012
Loudoun County	13,846	2,579	2,211	3,821	5,235	72,752	2.7%	4.7%	5.0%	1,428	28,566
Montgomery County	6,191	2,149	1,486	1,289	1,267	42,172	18.5%	7.8%	10.5%	599	8,803
Prince William County	19,265	3,058	3,154	6,492	6,561	73,652	4.5%	4.2%	7.5%	3,234	35,554
Roanoke County	12,015	3,156	3,436	4,210	1,213	43,048	7.1%	5.3%	5.2%	811	17,211
Rockingham County	8,823	2,523	2,918	2,223	1,159	41,043	7.3%	6.6%	9.0%	670	12,011
Spotsylvania County	9,065	1,812	2,616	2,250	2,387	51,643	8.9%	4.9%	8.9%	1,073	13,389
Stafford County	6,419	935	1,402	2,323	1,759	65,011	2.9%	3.1%	8.2%	725	11,420
York County	6,077	968	1,552	2,046	1,511	59,929	2.5%	2.9%	10.3%	300	8,140
Washington											
Benton County	15,174	3,869	4,420	4,410	2,475	46,060	11.3%	4.2%	9.4%	3,285	21,331
Chelan County	7,680	2,764	1,845	1,971	1,100	42,122	16.2%	13.0%	14.5%	1,077	10,833
Clallam County	12,052	2,938	3,665	4,051	1,398	42,239	10.6%	5.7%	7.1%	999	16,268
Clark County	37,639	10,463	10,258	11,275	5,643	45,136	6.6%	6.2%	6.0%	6,701	53,649
Cowlitz County	11,975	3,577	4,276	3,226	896	38,341	13.4%	9.6%	13.2%	2,206	15,393
Franklin County	3,904	1,625	535	1,037	707	36,012	7.4%	7.2%	33.8%	894	6,302
Grant County	7,129	2,374	2,362	1,661	732	33,937	7.9%	10.0%	15.1%	1,690	10,067
Grays Harbor County	8,568	2,465	3,161	1,965	977	38,154	12.2%	5.7%	14.2%	1,815	10,668
Island County	10,375	2,311	2,752	3,348	1,964	52,358	7.4%	2.2%	7.6%	1,203	13,852
King County	154,794	37,898	39,799	43,260	33,837	49,822	8.8%	8.4%	10.5%	29,350	225,141
Kitsap County	25,250	6,015	7,716	7,035	4,484	45,568	7.6%	8.3%	11.9%	3,532	34,606
Lewis County	9,400	2,714	3,293	2,622	771	38,010	11.5%	6.2%	4.3%	1,668	11,161
Pierce County	63,751	16,416	18,269	19,510	9,556	45,811	10.4%	7.7%	9.0%	13,519	86,515
Skagit County	13,628	3,937	3,601	4,151	1,939	44,839	12.6%	6.1%	9.2%	2,084	18,314
Snohomish County	53,519	15,413	16,487	13,642	7,977	42,740	7.9%	7.6%	8.7%	11,640	82,216
Spokane County	45,346	13,008	14,265	12,522	5,551	40,514	12.2%	8.0%	9.6%	9,364	58,151
Thurston County	24,728	6,056	7,434	7,311	3,927	45,611	7.7%	6.8%	14.7%	3,707	35,316
Whatcom County	20,850	6,080	5,715	6,076	2,979	41,847	8.3%	6.8%	11.7%	3,565	27,869
Yakima County	18,654	6,374	6,666	4,159	1,455	36,482	9.3%	9.9%	7.5%	4,180	24,432
West Virginia											
Berkeley County	8,312	2,461	2,279	2,927	645	44,670	13.6%	4.5%	11.1%	864	13,171
Cabell County	10,872	3,880	3,868	2,105	1,019	33,509	16.8%	7.5%	9.4%	1,704	14,403
Harrison County	8,001	3,166	2,846	1,649	340	29,901	9.3%	6.1%	9.8%	1,191	10,374
Kanawha County	23,441	7,071	8,509	5,903	1,958	36,630	12.3%	7.5%	6.5%	2,942	31,144

Table G-2: Counties—Income, Poverty Status and Receipt of Food Stamps (SNAP)—*Continued*

	Income of Households with Householder 65 Years and Over					Poverty Rate of Persons			Households with 1 or More Persons 60 Years and Over	
	Total Households	Less Than $25,000	$25,000 - $49,999	$50,000 - $99,999	$100,000 or More	Median Household Income	55 to 64 Years	65 to 74 Years	75 Years and Over	Receiving SNAP	Not Receiving SNAP
West Virginia—Cont.											
Monongalia County	6,989	2,210	2,122	1,710	947	38,768	11.9%	7.2%	12.8%	881	10,224
Raleigh County	9,425	3,811	3,379	1,740	495	31,930	9.4%	6.9%	9.0%	1,561	11,905
Wood County	11,022	4,188	3,658	2,412	764	33,660	7.8%	8.5%	10.2%	1,020	14,466
Wisconsin											
Brown County	21,159	5,494	7,919	6,045	1,701	40,231	6.8%	6.5%	5.6%	2,229	30,057
Dane County	38,868	9,438	10,779	12,085	6,566	47,232	7.2%	3.6%	9.1%	5,162	57,457
Dodge County	8,850	3,042	3,046	2,265	497	34,014	9.2%	6.4%	9.1%	1,205	11,915
Eau Claire County	8,825	2,963	2,909	2,395	558	34,252	8.3%	4.0%	12.0%	1,406	11,367
Fond du Lac County	10,414	3,282	3,930	2,339	863	35,868	8.4%	4.8%	7.5%	1,000	15,180
Jefferson County	7,994	2,182	3,150	2,256	406	37,352	6.0%	2.9%	7.0%	701	11,365
Kenosha County	14,242	5,146	4,224	3,722	1,150	34,961	13.3%	3.7%	5.8%	2,097	19,749
La Crosse County	10,519	2,649	3,802	2,752	1,316	39,757	4.1%	2.7%	9.3%	1,309	14,733
Manitowoc County	9,744	3,367	4,140	1,799	438	31,535	8.6%	2.5%	11.3%	859	12,564
Marathon County	13,355	4,769	5,039	2,941	606	35,479	5.6%	1.4%	6.1%	1,256	18,582
Milwaukee County	74,007	28,886	21,816	16,132	7,173	32,413	15.6%	10.4%	11.2%	19,721	101,278
Outagamie County	14,650	3,714	5,493	4,168	1,275	40,129	6.0%	2.5%	6.2%	1,768	20,593
Ozaukee County	10,031	2,291	3,107	2,468	2,165	46,085	5.0%	1.9%	5.9%	256	14,898
Portage County	6,738	1,902	2,346	2,173	317	39,777	8.2%	3.5%	15.3%	637	8,835
Racine County	19,041	6,112	6,664	4,756	1,509	33,663	13.4%	9.8%	5.7%	3,680	25,711
Rock County	15,033	3,693	6,089	3,982	1,269	40,099	10.2%	4.7%	9.6%	2,026	20,487
Sheboygan County	11,782	3,940	4,147	2,548	1,147	35,025	5.4%	1.2%	8.0%	1,042	15,995
St. Croix County	5,858	1,394	1,542	2,452	470	49,913	1.9%	4.3%	3.9%	183	9,173
Walworth County	9,925	2,919	3,522	2,435	1,049	38,401	9.1%	6.4%	7.1%	1,101	13,795
Washington County	13,671	3,518	4,927	3,809	1,417	38,331	3.4%	7.7%	2.7%	1,161	19,114
Waukesha County	40,660	8,637	12,241	13,336	6,446	48,975	3.0%	3.2%	7.0%	1,711	59,034
Winnebago County	16,060	5,846	4,737	4,450	1,027	33,570	5.3%	4.1%	10.1%	1,839	22,368
Wood County	9,251	3,521	2,962	1,986	782	32,570	6.3%	5.3%	9.9%	1,051	11,795
Wyoming											
Laramie County	8,768	2,110	2,185	3,223	1,250	50,484	9.6%	1.6%	8.5%	924	12,846
Natrona County	7,213	2,503	1,379	2,466	865	41,005	8.0%	2.9%	7.4%	1,036	9,914

Table G-3: Places—Income, Poverty Status and Receipt of Food Stamps (SNAP)

	Income of Households with Householder 65 Years and Over						Poverty Rate of Persons			Households with 1 or More Persons 60 Years and Over	
	Total Households	Less Than $25,000	$25,000 - $49,999	$50,000 - $99,999	$100,000 or More	Median Household Income	55 to 64 Years	65 to 74 Years	75 Years and Over	Receiving SNAP	Not Receiving SNAP
Alabama											
Birmingham city	18,584	7,751	5,268	4,128	1,437	30,932	26.3%	15.0%	12.4%	6,098	24,390
Dothan city	6,879	2,738	2,003	1,536	602	31,700	13.4%	11.4%	12.9%	1,013	9,647
Hoover city	9,713	2,315	2,707	2,869	1,822	48,290	7.5%	1.5%	9.7%	117	13,515
Huntsville city	18,606	5,727	4,261	5,506	3,112	43,826	11.9%	12.4%	10.0%	2,107	25,092
Mobile city	18,539	7,662	4,925	4,013	1,939	32,688	12.0%	14.8%	14.2%	4,194	23,268
Montgomery city	17,248	5,760	4,996	3,848	2,644	34,702	12.1%	8.5%	13.4%	3,720	22,374
Tuscaloosa city	7,595	2,660	1,707	2,076	1,152	41,057	15.4%	8.6%	7.2%	992	10,680
Alaska											
Anchorage municipality	14,870	2,408	2,865	5,097	4,500	72,850	7.4%	4.6%	3.2%	1,876	24,902
Arizona											
Avondale city	2,820	848	666	993	313	45,592	12.6%	16.9%	22.1%	915	4,578
Chandler city	13,500	2,566	4,032	4,710	2,192	50,974	7.4%	5.9%	5.6%	1,006	22,639
Flagstaff city	3,897	881	1,211	728	1,077	46,466	7.9%	8.5%	20.3%	439	6,168
Glendale city	14,813	5,730	4,282	2,866	1,935	32,174	15.5%	10.0%	7.8%	3,756	21,147
Goodyear city	6,045	576	1,476	2,954	1,039	71,790	14.2%	3.5%	9.3%	148	9,535
Mesa city	43,735	13,707	12,870	12,724	4,434	38,763	12.0%	9.3%	10.0%	4,179	60,182
Peoria city	15,825	3,416	5,233	5,572	1,604	45,393	10.8%	4.5%	3.8%	1,779	22,733
Phoenix city	90,321	29,629	25,784	21,625	13,283	38,961	16.9%	12.9%	11.4%	19,696	133,234
Scottsdale city	31,511	5,875	9,248	8,996	7,392	51,632	5.8%	5.0%	3.6%	1,259	43,510
Surprise city	15,018	3,249	4,345	5,060	2,364	49,663	14.4%	3.5%	12.5%	1,213	19,640
Tempe city	11,278	2,868	3,098	3,233	2,079	43,846	8.7%	8.0%	11.0%	1,444	16,289
Tucson city	46,294	16,918	14,926	10,539	3,911	32,396	18.3%	14.6%	12.1%	10,834	61,884
Yuma city	8,707	3,704	1,944	2,140	919	35,466	18.1%	13.1%	23.6%	1,370	10,475
Arkansas											
Fayetteville city	5,021	1,835	1,531	804	851	33,120	3.1%	7.3%	13.2%	218	7,266
Fort Smith city	7,690	3,616	1,868	1,399	807	27,922	15.3%	10.0%	15.1%	1,219	10,154
Jonesboro city	5,829	1,775	1,561	1,570	923	43,094	6.7%	9.2%	3.6%	808	7,586
Little Rock city	16,457	4,813	4,174	4,430	3,040	46,425	10.3%	5.9%	4.5%	1,560	24,750
North Little Rock city	5,156	1,762	1,201	1,259	934	40,472	23.5%	8.8%	5.2%	990	6,978
Springdale city	4,332	2,315	815	719	483	21,333	17.8%	20.3%	24.5%	781	6,420
California											
Alameda city	6,453	1,600	1,260	1,793	1,800	55,215	11.2%	7.6%	10.1%	207	10,770
Alhambra city	6,209	2,278	1,773	1,372	786	33,849	13.7%	8.8%	20.0%	512	11,309
Anaheim city	18,062	5,772	3,459	4,962	3,869	46,125	11.0%	11.8%	11.7%	2,913	31,783
Antioch city	6,234	1,355	1,515	2,289	1,075	51,664	8.0%	2.0%	8.6%	1,166	11,146
Bakersfield city	19,005	5,792	5,058	4,994	3,161	42,495	12.5%	13.0%	15.6%	3,178	32,092
Baldwin Park city	3,402	1,271	625	1,179	327	38,486	12.6%	15.3%	20.3%	339	7,099
Bellflower city	4,540	1,525	1,215	1,231	569	43,302	14.1%	11.9%	11.3%	917	7,637
Berkeley city	9,722	2,298	919	1,986	4,519	92,475	9.0%	11.5%	9.9%	725	14,026
Buena Park city	4,647	1,455	1,387	1,174	631	41,583	15.4%	16.3%	14.7%	506	7,907
Burbank city	8,929	3,439	1,723	2,087	1,680	37,824	8.4%	4.9%	13.3%	204	14,299
Camarillo city	7,459	1,633	1,996	2,274	1,556	51,978	4.2%	1.8%	10.1%	354	10,387
Carlsbad city	10,215	1,495	2,176	2,816	3,728	72,318	4.9%	2.1%	2.3%	232	16,815
Carson city	6,846	1,794	1,701	2,400	951	48,302	12.4%	15.0%	9.9%	894	10,380
Chico city	6,668	2,478	1,604	1,506	1,080	40,134	11.8%	2.7%	8.4%	340	9,861
Chino city	2,674	459	385	1,036	794	73,010	12.2%	3.9%	4.7%	298	4,860
Chino Hills city	na	na	na	na	na	44,606	5.2%	2.0%	0.0%	68	6,891
Chula Vista city	17,558	5,774	3,813	5,180	2,791	43,718	8.4%	13.7%	8.1%	1,849	26,059
Citrus Heights city	9,454	2,452	3,390	2,481	1,131	39,827	11.5%	4.1%	7.6%	1,537	12,140
Clovis city	6,658	2,065	2,176	1,365	1,052	35,801	7.7%	5.0%	4.9%	633	10,634
Compton city	4,086	1,775	960	796	555	34,392	18.0%	22.2%	21.9%	635	6,877
Concord city	10,031	2,403	3,502	1,908	2,218	44,747	12.9%	8.8%	15.7%	834	15,164
Corona city	8,019	2,048	1,960	2,144	1,867	50,013	7.9%	6.1%	14.0%	1,157	15,164
Costa Mesa city	6,368	1,712	1,556	1,646	1,454	46,289	10.4%	8.9%	16.3%	589	9,169
Daly City city	7,380	1,893	1,308	2,274	1,905	60,151	12.0%	9.4%	11.5%	936	12,378
Davis city	4,224	1,169	855	720	1,480	55,304	7.1%	9.1%	5.8%	55	6,640
Downey city	6,453	1,729	1,936	2,104	684	43,250	10.4%	21.1%	5.7%	1,099	11,116
El Cajon city	5,369	1,965	1,112	1,325	967	37,359	16.7%	7.5%	6.9%	1,554	8,390
El Monte city	5,961	3,321	1,041	810	789	23,238	17.1%	20.2%	14.0%	914	11,261
Elk Grove city	7,958	2,103	1,662	2,378	1,815	54,674	7.4%	6.0%	4.0%	1,409	15,937
Escondido city	9,541	2,918	2,480	2,597	1,546	43,249	13.2%	13.1%	10.2%	1,112	14,767
Fairfield city	6,986	1,201	1,972	2,393	1,420	54,196	11.9%	6.9%	3.4%	760	13,024
Folsom city	5,957	1,688	1,350	2,000	919	48,093	6.2%	6.1%	8.2%	46	9,306
Fontana city	5,801	2,100	1,415	1,829	457	36,465	16.4%	11.0%	14.0%	1,901	13,233
Fremont city	12,648	3,536	2,647	2,886	3,579	51,179	5.6%	7.7%	13.2%	1,069	22,814
Fresno city	31,243	11,557	8,696	7,279	3,711	34,138	18.2%	17.2%	19.2%	6,679	49,014
Fullerton city	8,868	2,463	2,338	2,314	1,753	45,500	14.7%	6.9%	9.9%	848	13,073
Garden Grove city	10,083	3,895	1,742	2,869	1,577	41,897	13.7%	12.3%	15.9%	1,912	17,902
Glendale city	17,427	7,769	3,845	2,790	3,023	30,234	12.7%	11.1%	15.3%	2,170	27,677
Hawthorne city	4,333	1,041	1,319	1,358	615	46,404	21.8%	20.4%	10.7%	413	7,958
Hayward city	9,324	2,724	2,630	2,515	1,455	38,476	10.3%	7.4%	15.1%	1,406	16,039
Hemet city	13,288	5,269	4,847	2,733	439	31,186	20.7%	8.0%	13.2%	1,595	15,060
Hesperia city	5,155	1,963	1,668	1,147	377	32,892	15.6%	6.0%	10.0%	1,671	7,666
Huntington Beach city	19,057	3,719	4,519	5,384	5,435	57,769	7.1%	3.8%	9.3%	653	27,585

Table G-3: Places—Income, Poverty Status and Receipt of Food Stamps (SNAP)—*Continued*

	Income of Households with Householder 65 Years and Over					Poverty Rate of Persons			Households with 1 or More Persons 60 Years and Over	
	Total Households	Less Than $25,000	$25,000 - $49,999	$50,000 - $99,999	$100,000 or More	Median Household Income	55 to 64 Years	65 to 74 Years	75 Years and Over	Receiving SNAP	Not Receiving SNAP
California—Cont.											
Indio city	7,007	2,559	1,465	2,288	695	37,671	16.8%	16.5%	8.5%	470	9,832
Inglewood city	6,571	2,443	2,135	1,401	592	33,473	15.6%	13.6%	16.1%	951	10,639
Irvine city	13,548	3,088	2,268	3,395	4,797	67,672	8.6%	3.8%	11.1%	208	23,999
Jurupa Valley city	4,127	1,419	1,250	979	479	34,776	9.2%	18.7%	14.2%	1,057	6,960
Laguna Niguel city	na	na	na	na	na	74,164	7.4%	0.0%	4.5%	389	9,326
Lake Forest city	4,433	750	755	1,773	1,155	66,130	8.7%	2.2%	4.9%	130	8,007
Lakewood city	5,521	1,219	1,950	1,385	967	41,582	6.8%	13.9%	3.6%	368	9,810
Lancaster city	8,632	3,435	2,027	2,317	853	36,699	20.9%	18.3%	19.7%	1,505	13,776
Livermore city	6,443	1,549	1,299	1,732	1,863	60,625	5.0%	9.5%	13.9%	226	10,393
Long Beach city	27,282	8,470	6,825	6,463	5,524	41,938	15.9%	11.6%	12.3%	3,551	46,213
Los Angeles city	261,218	97,754	55,343	55,554	52,567	37,728	16.4%	15.4%	18.4%	29,109	411,049
Lynwood city	1,698	858	251	498	91	24,679	29.4%	24.6%	23.8%	738	4,052
Manteca city	5,354	1,917	1,362	1,403	672	43,067	5.0%	5.0%	6.7%	813	8,085
Menifee city	9,373	2,620	3,955	2,334	464	35,855	9.0%	11.0%	13.3%	549	13,419
Merced city	5,246	2,019	1,462	1,163	602	35,149	15.8%	14.5%	8.7%	935	7,175
Milpitas city	na	na	na	na	na	54,112	2.7%	12.0%	12.8%	373	6,862
Mission Viejo city	9,116	966	2,219	3,428	2,503	62,154	2.5%	2.4%	4.5%	199	13,356
Modesto city	17,326	5,325	4,333	5,411	2,257	43,611	15.5%	8.1%	12.1%	2,314	24,344
Moreno Valley city	7,677	2,116	2,205	2,409	947	42,110	15.0%	14.9%	10.2%	2,045	15,068
Mountain View city	5,265	1,651	1,426	1,428	760	40,812	11.2%	2.9%	13.5%	233	8,248
Murrieta city	5,796	1,188	1,527	1,724	1,357	54,228	4.5%	1.2%	9.3%	602	8,592
Napa city	7,078	1,990	1,454	2,060	1,574	53,035	7.7%	7.7%	6.8%	546	11,318
Newport Beach city	12,641	2,613	2,160	2,173	5,695	85,726	5.4%	5.5%	8.4%	375	17,239
Norwalk city	5,729	1,977	1,627	1,822	303	36,164	7.7%	4.2%	18.5%	742	9,878
Oakland city	31,156	11,402	6,395	7,201	6,158	39,044	17.6%	12.5%	21.0%	3,872	48,415
Oceanside city	16,383	5,004	4,309	5,100	1,970	44,507	21.2%	12.1%	6.5%	863	23,738
Ontario city	6,587	2,618	1,453	1,879	637	37,306	10.1%	12.6%	20.5%	1,457	11,512
Orange city	7,669	2,082	1,426	2,569	1,592	54,618	5.6%	10.9%	16.8%	752	13,377
Oxnard city	9,871	2,621	2,400	2,717	2,133	49,288	10.6%	9.4%	14.1%	1,026	16,328
Palmdale city	6,429	2,302	1,766	1,515	846	34,953	12.3%	9.9%	20.3%	1,442	12,368
Palo Alto city	na	na	na	na	na	90,042	5.4%	2.0%	10.6%	181	9,986
Pasadena city	11,297	3,518	2,026	2,723	3,030	52,442	15.2%	16.2%	14.7%	552	16,825
Perris city	na	na	na	na	na	57,201	22.5%	20.9%	16.0%	892	3,625
Pittsburg city	3,844	1,291	618	1,287	648	50,378	8.8%	11.7%	3.3%	845	6,679
Pleasanton city	na	na	na	na	na	42,618	1.7%	7.0%	7.4%	176	9,200
Pomona city	6,313	2,074	1,504	1,719	1,016	42,009	21.1%	10.8%	10.7%	1,280	11,281
Rancho Cordova city	4,927	972	1,358	1,805	792	51,531	7.8%	3.3%	14.7%	354	7,655
Rancho Cucamonga city	8,841	2,450	2,595	2,277	1,519	43,307	10.6%	10.0%	2.6%	970	16,208
Redding city	10,201	3,571	2,411	3,248	971	39,789	10.7%	5.3%	8.8%	732	14,150
Redlands city	4,848	1,639	807	1,368	1,034	49,682	9.9%	12.0%	19.9%	856	7,142
Redondo Beach city	na	na	na	na	na	61,714	10.2%	9.1%	15.8%	39	7,842
Redwood City city	5,999	1,778	1,158	1,421	1,642	56,194	7.4%	7.6%	8.2%	365	9,818
Rialto city	4,629	1,068	1,647	1,436	478	41,373	20.7%	14.0%	10.5%	1,820	6,508
Richmond city	7,086	1,753	1,282	2,452	1,599	58,465	17.0%	5.4%	7.5%	988	13,452
Riverside city	15,524	4,026	4,485	3,944	3,069	46,317	9.2%	11.4%	9.3%	2,268	27,944
Roseville city	13,779	3,798	3,504	3,298	3,179	44,735	7.1%	8.3%	5.6%	238	17,841
Sacramento city	35,122	10,589	9,158	9,876	5,499	42,526	18.7%	10.5%	15.3%	4,878	53,861
Salinas city	6,480	1,606	1,675	1,946	1,253	49,764	10.3%	7.9%	10.0%	691	12,620
San Bernardino city	9,306	3,642	2,402	2,345	917	32,987	24.8%	11.7%	15.2%	3,078	13,571
San Buenaventura (Ventura) city	11,652	2,944	3,005	3,377	2,326	49,042	5.2%	9.4%	13.0%	819	16,851
San Clemente city	na	na	na	na	na	80,728	5.3%	2.8%	2.7%	42	10,298
San Diego city	89,228	25,587	21,681	20,869	21,091	46,377	10.8%	10.4%	12.7%	9,646	143,733
San Francisco city	73,562	23,861	16,997	16,401	16,303	44,457	12.0%	10.9%	14.1%	5,977	114,886
San Jose city	59,611	15,909	13,864	15,490	14,348	50,059	8.8%	10.0%	10.2%	7,764	101,338
San Leandro city	7,478	2,566	1,703	1,495	1,714	38,554	11.2%	6.4%	12.8%	1,046	12,190
San Marcos city	6,690	1,980	1,554	2,000	1,156	45,250	3.9%	4.2%	13.3%	402	9,345
San Mateo city	10,570	2,141	2,653	2,459	3,317	58,414	6.7%	6.4%	7.7%	618	15,009
San Ramon city	na	na	na	na	na	65,253	0.0%	2.3%	0.3%	278	6,124
Santa Ana city	12,454	3,742	3,234	3,692	1,786	39,489	15.7%	12.7%	15.4%	3,067	22,710
Santa Barbara city	9,968	2,735	2,038	2,334	2,861	51,561	13.2%	3.9%	9.8%	311	14,180
Santa Clara city	7,717	2,406	2,110	1,571	1,630	40,570	8.3%	9.4%	5.6%	393	12,407
Santa Clarita city	11,788	3,069	2,746	3,760	2,213	52,568	6.2%	4.2%	6.1%	752	19,589
Santa Maria city	5,153	1,845	1,293	1,392	623	38,345	15.2%	9.8%	8.0%	913	7,351
Santa Monica city	10,231	3,766	1,721	1,555	3,189	47,198	16.8%	5.6%	19.8%	152	14,838
Santa Rosa city	16,477	4,445	3,468	5,358	3,206	53,376	9.9%	6.5%	6.2%	1,816	23,828
Simi Valley city	10,587	2,676	2,719	3,377	1,815	48,725	7.0%	8.9%	10.9%	493	16,279
South Gate city	3,870	1,253	1,539	863	215	34,284	15.8%	17.1%	23.7%	1,065	7,335
South San Francisco city	na	na	na	na	na	39,113	0.0%	0.0%	0.0%	247	9,587
Stockton city	17,432	6,485	4,052	3,774	3,121	36,475	19.1%	13.4%	11.1%	3,773	28,470
Sunnyvale city	9,250	2,428	2,399	2,708	1,715	47,869	9.8%	6.7%	9.7%	502	14,181
Temecula city	6,339	1,324	1,655	2,035	1,325	61,168	3.6%	4.7%	16.7%	233	10,699
Thousand Oaks city	13,740	2,398	3,273	3,829	4,240	64,990	4.6%	5.3%	4.9%	527	19,862
Torrance city	15,122	3,898	4,191	3,852	3,181	46,523	3.9%	8.3%	11.7%	380	22,234
Tracy city	2,481	719	538	927	297	49,531	5.7%	7.9%	8.3%	490	5,927
Turlock city	5,810	2,503	1,434	1,121	752	31,366	9.0%	10.6%	31.8%	809	7,927
Tustin city	4,296	998	1,128	1,020	1,150	52,814	7.8%	9.3%	10.9%	506	7,520

Table G-3: Places—Income, Poverty Status and Receipt of Food Stamps (SNAP)—*Continued*

	Income of Households with Householder 65 Years and Over					Poverty Rate of Persons			Households with 1 or More Persons 60 Years and Over	
	Total Households	Less Than $25,000	$25,000 - $49,999	$50,000 - $99,999	$100,000 or More	Median Household Income	55 to 64 Years	65 to 74 Years	75 Years and Over	Receiving SNAP	Not Receiving SNAP
California—Cont.											
Union City city	4,994	1,209	1,076	1,627	1,082	57,788	11.2%	5.2%	9.2%	151	8,675
Upland city	6,692	1,716	1,548	1,890	1,538	50,903	10.9%	6.4%	8.2%	437	9,566
Vacaville city	7,162	1,891	2,211	2,245	815	45,762	5.0%	6.3%	10.7%	471	11,276
Vallejo city	9,711	2,457	2,916	2,625	1,713	44,399	13.3%	8.2%	8.1%	1,458	17,188
Victorville city	4,916	2,533	855	1,223	305	24,460	11.3%	11.0%	14.2%	1,605	7,919
Visalia city	8,783	2,677	2,619	2,521	966	43,444	10.9%	13.5%	5.2%	1,726	12,653
Vista city	4,268	1,312	1,420	1,132	404	43,400	8.3%	8.6%	8.2%	767	7,513
Walnut Creek city	13,048	2,594	2,999	4,373	3,082	56,585	5.9%	2.8%	6.8%	210	15,701
West Covina city	7,108	1,440	2,226	1,906	1,536	48,750	10.1%	10.1%	5.7%	767	12,669
Westminster city	8,163	3,505	1,973	1,594	1,091	28,125	16.9%	17.7%	18.1%	1,324	12,601
Whittier city	6,065	2,166	1,291	985	1,623	39,154	18.2%	11.7%	10.7%	395	9,219
Yorba Linda city	na	na	na	na	na	90,660	1.9%	2.8%	6.1%	170	8,451
Yuba City city	4,994	1,448	1,401	1,734	411	43,226	11.6%	6.0%	11.6%	450	7,962
Colorado											
Arvada city	10,289	2,507	2,980	3,239	1,563	45,648	3.4%	5.7%	7.6%	778	15,569
Aurora city	21,898	5,712	6,007	6,600	3,579	47,457	10.4%	7.0%	11.0%	3,473	33,863
Boulder city	7,086	1,928	1,007	2,369	1,782	61,027	10.4%	4.9%	11.2%	514	10,465
Centennial city	9,307	1,030	2,215	3,505	2,557	62,760	3.0%	2.7%	6.7%	152	14,726
Colorado Springs city	34,450	9,325	9,818	9,609	5,698	44,159	8.5%	6.2%	6.4%	5,092	50,543
Denver city	47,806	16,511	12,079	11,663	7,553	39,017	16.2%	10.6%	10.8%	8,739	68,318
Fort Collins city	8,830	2,227	2,372	2,715	1,516	46,398	10.1%	5.8%	9.6%	936	13,737
Greeley city	8,073	2,840	1,981	2,127	1,125	41,985	13.1%	9.2%	7.2%	1,282	10,564
Lakewood city	14,660	4,142	4,420	4,129	1,969	42,415	4.1%	8.5%	6.9%	1,815	21,490
Longmont city	7,205	2,398	1,659	2,069	1,079	40,462	7.0%	4.6%	16.9%	876	10,737
Loveland city	9,494	3,375	3,269	2,291	559	31,851	5.6%	7.8%	4.3%	360	12,267
Pueblo city	11,571	4,810	3,915	2,145	701	29,664	17.8%	13.7%	11.8%	2,261	15,182
Thornton city	6,686	920	2,283	2,477	1,006	52,706	5.4%	0.0%	2.3%	1,404	10,127
Westminster city	9,185	1,909	2,607	3,054	1,615	50,315	6.0%	4.5%	4.8%	1,103	13,827
Connecticut											
Bridgeport city	9,660	4,251	2,213	1,818	1,378	31,209	12.8%	18.8%	9.4%	4,688	11,392
Danbury city	6,217	2,040	1,164	1,726	1,287	44,682	4.7%	12.1%	11.7%	1,013	8,856
Hartford city	7,453	4,959	1,341	860	293	17,712	28.5%	35.7%	39.7%	5,421	6,835
New Britain city	4,729	2,042	1,368	787	532	31,778	19.1%	7.9%	23.0%	2,299	5,879
New Haven city	9,275	4,566	2,434	1,427	848	25,301	18.4%	21.1%	13.4%	3,913	10,020
Norwalk city	7,780	1,709	1,853	2,479	1,739	54,256	4.0%	6.3%	14.5%	678	11,333
Stamford city	11,163	2,239	2,770	2,049	4,105	60,142	6.5%	16.9%	5.5%	2,002	15,578
Waterbury city	8,338	3,687	2,369	1,458	824	29,433	16.5%	11.5%	17.0%	3,194	10,706
Delaware											
Wilmington city	6,632	3,533	1,047	1,077	975	22,099	21.4%	22.4%	22.3%	2,044	6,991
District of Columbia											
Washington city	50,463	16,060	9,803	12,302	12,298	47,906	19.2%	12.9%	16.7%	12,596	66,366
Florida											
Boca Raton city	11,644	2,946	2,569	2,510	3,619	52,649	4.9%	3.0%	4.8%	362	16,539
Boynton Beach city	8,263	3,188	2,453	1,429	1,193	32,389	11.1%	21.2%	17.6%	1,424	10,515
Cape Coral city	21,305	6,410	6,798	6,324	1,773	39,194	9.0%	7.0%	10.3%	2,650	28,457
Clearwater city	15,507	5,571	4,528	3,482	1,926	36,144	14.1%	6.5%	11.6%	1,989	19,789
Coral Springs city	6,081	1,446	1,667	1,604	1,364	46,953	3.5%	5.7%	3.8%	1,112	11,792
Deerfield Beach city	10,628	5,191	2,237	2,353	847	25,686	12.3%	24.5%	16.3%	1,821	12,788
Delray Beach city	11,781	3,617	4,241	2,134	1,789	33,247	19.1%	15.9%	11.0%	1,629	13,568
Deltona city	6,813	2,465	2,396	1,841	111	31,487	13.9%	10.9%	21.2%	1,008	9,850
Fort Lauderdale city	20,346	6,227	5,706	5,106	3,307	41,672	19.9%	16.0%	11.6%	5,098	24,394
Fort Myers city	6,835	2,023	1,839	1,989	984	43,881	21.7%	5.4%	17.9%	1,305	8,745
Gainesville city	8,820	2,574	1,999	3,009	1,238	46,835	18.0%	8.5%	7.2%	1,537	11,747
Hialeah city	20,395	13,442	3,514	2,663	776	16,474	25.2%	34.1%	31.4%	17,112	15,396
Hollywood city	14,733	5,414	4,773	2,929	1,617	33,669	16.5%	11.2%	17.7%	4,136	17,943
Homestead city	na	na	na	na	na	20,625	18.6%	24.4%	49.1%	2,202	3,727
Jacksonville city	67,188	22,354	22,304	15,855	6,675	35,509	16.1%	12.4%	11.2%	13,793	93,356
Kissimmee city	na	na	na	na	na	39,635	22.5%	9.5%	16.3%	1,383	4,687
Lakeland city	12,712	4,965	3,538	2,294	1,915	32,355	22.3%	6.9%	16.6%	1,875	15,548
Largo city	13,624	4,902	4,565	2,712	1,445	33,101	9.3%	7.9%	11.2%	2,017	16,061
Lauderhill city	6,029	2,563	1,222	1,575	669	36,903	24.1%	9.8%	14.7%	1,950	7,794
Melbourne city	11,725	4,434	3,998	2,474	819	33,506	16.0%	18.0%	3.9%	1,348	14,590
Miami Beach city	9,107	4,451	1,428	1,496	1,732	26,432	19.8%	16.8%	25.9%	3,860	9,691
Miami city	37,894	22,312	7,408	4,613	3,561	20,484	23.2%	21.1%	30.9%	24,933	36,416
Miami Gardens city	8,286	3,289	2,133	1,914	950	35,402	14.1%	16.1%	25.5%	4,886	9,183
Miramar city	4,054	767	697	1,370	1,220	64,133	12.2%	3.4%	7.0%	2,509	9,616
Orlando city	16,912	7,954	4,169	2,758	2,031	27,621	14.9%	14.3%	24.3%	5,475	20,251
Palm Bay city	9,804	3,254	3,035	2,605	910	37,574	12.6%	7.7%	7.1%	1,038	14,289
Palm Coast city	11,851	2,892	3,821	4,129	1,009	43,174	8.4%	8.8%	5.3%	1,284	15,614
Pembroke Pines city	15,395	6,674	4,062	3,034	1,625	29,395	13.2%	10.6%	13.6%	3,577	19,737
Plantation city	7,511	2,030	2,067	1,780	1,634	47,943	8.8%	2.9%	6.3%	796	11,545
Pompano Beach city	14,641	6,419	3,229	3,190	1,803	28,978	22.9%	13.0%	13.0%	2,307	17,191

Table G-3: Places—Income, Poverty Status and Receipt of Food Stamps (SNAP)—*Continued*

	Income of Households with Householder 65 Years and Over					Poverty Rate of Persons			Households with 1 or More Persons 60 Years and Over	
	Total Households	Less Than $25,000	$25,000 - $49,999	$50,000 - $99,999	$100,000 or More	Median Household Income	55 to 64 Years	65 to 74 Years	75 Years and Over	Receiving SNAP	Not Receiving SNAP
Florida—Cont.											
Port St. Lucie city	21,129	5,831	7,722	5,714	1,862	35,861	6.8%	4.7%	9.7%	2,695	27,929
St. Petersburg city	25,780	9,261	6,319	6,798	3,402	36,378	16.4%	10.5%	13.5%	4,011	36,432
Sunrise city	8,022	3,553	2,555	1,204	710	26,893	9.6%	16.7%	11.3%	2,013	10,425
Tallahassee city	12,043	3,300	3,264	2,942	2,537	45,726	16.2%	12.8%	10.5%	2,313	16,156
Tampa city	26,403	11,340	6,309	5,547	3,207	31,421	18.1%	15.8%	17.4%	9,157	34,608
West Palm Beach city	11,322	4,863	2,679	2,430	1,350	31,195	21.1%	13.8%	14.2%	2,864	13,756
Weston city	na	na	na	na	na	72,045	5.9%	1.4%	10.0%	618	7,101
Georgia											
Albany city	6,494	3,427	1,389	1,301	377	22,032	22.2%	33.0%	13.4%	2,269	7,766
Athens-Clarke County unified govt (bal)	7,501	2,068	2,107	1,583	1,743	40,095	23.1%	12.7%	10.9%	1,833	9,938
Atlanta city	35,365	16,024	8,599	6,486	4,256	29,112	18.2%	19.3%	12.9%	10,964	41,791
Augusta-Richmond County consolidated govt (bal)	14,469	5,294	4,503	3,329	1,343	30,905	18.7%	13.3%	8.2%	4,720	19,790
Columbus city	15,599	5,100	4,185	4,583	1,731	38,733	20.7%	12.1%	14.7%	3,555	19,753
Johns Creek city	na	na	na	na	na	44,013	10.3%	3.4%	12.1%	72	7,996
Macon-Bibb County	13,579	5,415	3,912	2,831	1,421	31,937	15.9%	15.0%	10.8%	2,699	19,213
Roswell city	5,898	794	1,719	1,469	1,916	63,125	4.9%	5.9%	5.3%	335	9,580
Sandy Springs city	8,023	2,257	1,991	1,521	2,254	43,031	3.7%	2.5%	17.5%	498	12,509
Savannah city	12,670	4,850	3,508	2,454	1,858	33,375	12.9%	10.0%	11.0%	3,722	14,546
Warner Robins city	5,042	1,248	1,887	1,574	333	41,894	23.1%	4.6%	14.6%	1,584	6,321
Hawaii											
Urban Honolulu CDP	37,927	9,872	8,271	11,004	8,780	53,017	10.3%	8.4%	12.4%	6,258	49,715
Idaho											
Boise City city	17,197	5,501	4,327	4,475	2,894	42,139	6.8%	9.3%	8.1%	2,486	24,433
Meridian city	na	na	na	na	na	43,877	6.7%	1.2%	16.8%	193	9,403
Nampa city	6,283	1,991	2,524	1,690	78	37,040	15.3%	12.7%	17.3%	611	8,570
Illinois											
Aurora city	8,469	2,168	2,872	1,968	1,461	41,595	11.7%	10.7%	2.5%	2,146	13,504
Bloomington city	5,832	1,988	1,755	1,237	852	36,208	16.4%	9.0%	17.4%	934	8,412
Champaign city	5,174	1,528	1,399	1,390	857	43,598	12.9%	8.9%	12.1%	609	7,336
Chicago city	196,065	82,025	47,299	40,915	25,826	31,885	18.8%	15.2%	18.3%	70,184	245,224
Decatur city	8,194	2,914	3,173	1,602	505	33,742	25.2%	9.1%	11.4%	945	10,567
Elgin city	7,503	2,311	2,209	924	2,059	36,361	6.8%	4.1%	10.2%	1,283	12,432
Evanston city	6,153	1,007	1,416	1,438	2,292	72,071	12.7%	8.0%	4.3%	480	9,056
Joliet city	7,714	2,416	2,428	2,143	727	37,316	9.1%	11.7%	8.5%	1,661	10,618
Naperville city	8,329	1,163	2,440	2,220	2,506	61,782	3.5%	3.4%	3.2%	633	14,727
Peoria city	10,416	4,047	2,143	2,749	1,477	38,984	13.6%	15.4%	15.2%	1,772	14,525
Rockford city	14,526	6,219	4,298	3,111	898	29,795	18.2%	8.9%	13.0%	2,958	20,356
Springfield city	12,632	4,208	2,862	4,129	1,433	42,281	12.5%	9.1%	6.1%	1,445	17,583
Waukegan city	4,373	1,615	969	1,285	504	40,279	12.2%	15.9%	9.2%	1,730	6,889
Indiana											
Bloomington city	3,598	539	1,028	745	1,286	62,041	13.0%	7.2%	3.1%	372	5,592
Carmel city	8,080	1,363	1,354	2,441	2,922	74,092	2.9%	1.6%	2.0%	309	11,416
Evansville city	12,499	4,492	4,508	2,403	1,096	32,103	14.3%	4.3%	10.9%	1,956	15,350
Fort Wayne city	21,156	6,958	6,365	5,978	1,855	35,326	13.3%	5.3%	8.3%	3,041	28,987
Gary city	7,700	3,389	1,779	2,025	507	28,662	25.5%	14.6%	16.9%	3,208	8,889
Hammond city	5,055	1,360	1,959	1,300	436	38,436	11.4%	6.1%	5.0%	985	8,035
Indianapolis city (bal)	59,437	18,799	20,666	14,358	5,614	36,328	13.7%	8.1%	8.5%	12,580	83,943
Lafayette city	4,974	1,617	1,396	1,519	442	40,286	12.7%	1.7%	1.4%	797	6,485
Muncie city	6,377	1,755	2,164	1,753	705	38,012	7.5%	7.4%	13.7%	574	8,542
South Bend city	8,925	3,185	3,439	1,729	572	34,248	18.4%	4.0%	9.4%	1,784	11,940
Iowa											
Cedar Rapids city	11,580	3,467	3,383	3,148	1,582	39,334	5.6%	3.7%	6.4%	897	15,448
Davenport city	8,170	2,780	2,256	2,401	733	36,833	12.9%	7.4%	8.5%	1,455	11,086
Des Moines city	15,788	6,010	3,929	4,280	1,569	34,339	11.0%	9.7%	14.6%	3,586	20,978
Iowa City city	4,080	1,342	686	1,174	878	50,385	7.8%	12.3%	7.5%	303	6,897
Sioux City city	6,786	2,309	2,726	1,366	385	29,931	12.3%	4.0%	10.5%	1,271	9,175
Waterloo city	6,873	2,235	2,338	1,821	479	33,313	11.6%	5.3%	7.2%	627	9,821
Kansas											
Kansas City city	10,753	4,537	2,910	2,149	1,157	32,631	16.8%	9.7%	11.1%	2,071	15,832
Lawrence city	5,439	1,441	1,363	1,731	904	46,620	7.6%	5.3%	9.0%	558	8,317
Olathe city	7,151	1,843	1,716	1,783	1,809	50,236	4.4%	1.6%	7.9%	655	10,787
Overland Park city	16,657	3,938	4,733	5,024	2,962	47,906	5.3%	4.6%	6.3%	477	25,835
Topeka city	11,974	4,128	3,939	2,722	1,185	36,179	13.6%	11.3%	10.8%	1,053	16,851
Wichita city	31,417	10,171	10,378	7,330	3,538	34,228	10.5%	10.3%	9.0%	4,301	44,208
Kentucky											
Lexington-Fayette urban county	22,793	7,208	6,750	5,924	2,911	37,379	14.1%	9.0%	9.4%	3,446	34,371
Louisville/Jefferson County metro govt (bal)	53,042	18,301	17,716	11,635	5,390	35,724	15.4%	8.6%	11.8%	10,135	71,864
Louisiana											
Baton Rouge city	19,560	7,646	4,809	4,590	2,515	35,456	11.7%	11.2%	14.0%	5,193	25,159
Bossier City city	5,211	1,331	2,491	1,025	364	37,478	11.6%	6.7%	5.2%	676	7,656

Table G-3: Places—Income, Poverty Status and Receipt of Food Stamps (SNAP)—*Continued*

	Income of Households with Householder 65 Years and Over						Poverty Rate of Persons			Households with 1 or More Persons 60 Years and Over	
	Total Households	Less Than $25,000	$25,000 - $49,999	$50,000 - $99,999	$100,000 or More	Median Household Income	55 to 64 Years	65 to 74 Years	75 Years and Over	Receiving SNAP	Not Receiving SNAP
Louisiana—Cont.											
Kenner city	7,390	1,949	2,611	2,148	682	38,418	13.2%	10.9%	6.4%	1,166	10,326
Lafayette city	10,215	3,468	2,810	2,448	1,489	41,442	9.8%	8.5%	5.6%	1,690	14,756
Lake Charles city	8,354	3,445	1,751	2,056	1,102	28,963	16.3%	13.0%	10.0%	2,252	9,481
New Orleans city	30,343	13,432	7,840	4,573	4,498	28,790	23.8%	20.0%	18.1%	8,417	41,263
Shreveport city	18,496	7,167	5,049	4,115	2,165	33,253	22.1%	10.9%	12.5%	3,496	24,066
Maine											
Portland city	5,751	2,651	1,271	1,222	607	29,604	13.0%	17.0%	9.9%	981	7,954
Maryland											
Baltimore city	52,216	20,483	13,963	11,985	5,785	33,205	20.3%	15.1%	18.9%	17,479	62,060
Frederick city	4,645	819	1,605	1,549	672	48,033	10.0%	2.6%	10.4%	820	7,027
Gaithersburg city	3,665	555	1,039	1,175	896	62,679	4.9%	2.9%	5.4%	825	6,368
Rockville city	6,438	1,702	957	1,729	2,050	66,875	1.9%	13.5%	13.4%	996	8,947
Massachusetts											
Boston city	43,696	21,422	7,728	8,015	6,531	26,352	17.7%	18.6%	21.0%	20,755	50,747
Brockton city	7,102	2,802	1,989	1,679	632	33,169	17.0%	11.5%	10.7%	3,799	8,734
Cambridge city	7,644	2,591	1,318	1,232	2,503	46,040	6.4%	9.7%	19.2%	1,652	10,336
Fall River city	9,414	4,954	2,523	1,549	388	23,787	18.7%	15.8%	16.2%	3,442	10,382
Lawrence city	4,104	2,336	1,181	395	192	19,946	33.4%	24.7%	34.7%	3,392	3,682
Lowell city	7,275	3,683	1,614	1,550	428	24,689	22.8%	18.0%	20.8%	3,104	8,243
Lynn city	6,378	3,113	1,408	1,318	539	25,757	8.6%	24.5%	17.3%	3,836	7,499
New Bedford city	7,776	4,236	1,530	1,678	332	21,198	17.4%	17.6%	23.5%	3,104	9,190
Newton city	10,070	2,110	2,199	2,785	2,976	59,805	1.7%	4.9%	4.2%	826	13,823
Quincy city	9,321	3,761	2,392	2,038	1,130	34,139	6.6%	14.2%	13.1%	2,339	11,885
Somerville city	5,097	2,123	1,290	735	949	32,706	9.4%	13.7%	21.4%	1,749	5,874
Springfield city	11,472	4,842	3,271	2,127	1,232	30,163	29.3%	15.5%	12.3%	4,913	13,649
Worcester city	12,197	4,527	2,786	2,999	1,885	32,477	23.2%	11.3%	15.7%	4,960	15,880
Michigan											
Ann Arbor city	8,228	1,529	1,686	2,032	2,981	69,107	7.9%	6.7%	6.9%	1,067	11,865
Dearborn city	7,987	2,649	2,439	1,895	1,004	35,170	11.2%	11.0%	7.7%	2,180	10,544
Detroit city	59,257	27,041	18,550	9,737	3,929	28,050	28.8%	19.2%	20.3%	29,781	63,661
Farmington Hills city	11,077	1,994	2,137	4,443	2,503	62,994	5.3%	5.0%	7.3%	525	15,212
Flint city	8,369	2,692	2,802	2,418	457	38,260	30.2%	12.8%	8.7%	3,482	9,779
Grand Rapids city	14,506	5,941	4,333	3,206	1,026	30,303	17.2%	13.6%	9.4%	3,157	18,185
Kalamazoo city	4,700	1,409	1,409	1,347	535	33,303	22.9%	15.2%	5.8%	1,541	5,766
Lansing city	8,827	3,192	3,207	1,730	698	33,579	20.3%	13.0%	8.6%	3,467	10,298
Livonia city	10,299	2,877	2,736	3,718	968	45,162	5.3%	4.9%	4.6%	1,075	15,549
Rochester Hills city	7,676	1,478	1,833	2,403	1,962	60,528	4.3%	2.5%	6.9%	590	11,139
Southfield city	9,558	2,990	2,739	2,735	1,094	40,531	12.2%	9.0%	14.1%	1,535	12,438
Sterling Heights city	13,641	3,276	4,952	3,876	1,537	42,110	8.4%	5.9%	7.5%	2,351	18,259
Troy city	7,929	1,488	1,989	2,381	2,071	60,836	4.0%	1.4%	6.5%	986	11,561
Warren city	12,733	4,891	4,095	3,100	647	33,684	13.8%	8.4%	10.1%	3,501	16,664
Westland city	9,447	3,606	3,536	1,734	571	31,359	15.5%	11.6%	7.6%	2,330	11,781
Wyoming city	4,965	1,625	1,971	1,138	231	34,519	15.8%	9.4%	5.2%	1,294	7,226
Minnesota											
Bloomington city	10,509	2,296	3,506	3,097	1,610	45,443	5.0%	2.5%	4.3%	768	14,584
Brooklyn Park city	4,945	1,489	1,494	1,676	286	39,683	13.0%	7.9%	7.0%	918	7,096
Duluth city	8,747	2,897	2,982	1,986	882	35,038	13.7%	9.8%	7.8%	1,230	11,654
Eagan city	4,723	1,189	1,179	1,661	694	49,786	2.9%	7.0%	1.6%	349	7,401
Maple Grove city	na	na	na	na	na	55,763	4.1%	10.4%	15.4%	538	7,487
Minneapolis city	23,005	8,875	6,125	5,165	2,840	34,062	17.7%	12.1%	14.8%	6,782	32,635
Plymouth city	7,280	1,535	1,983	2,202	1,560	51,495	3.6%	1.2%	4.6%	396	10,357
Rochester city	9,817	2,081	2,323	3,896	1,517	52,987	6.0%	2.3%	5.4%	356	13,807
St. Cloud city	4,491	850	1,689	1,502	450	41,028	9.5%	6.0%	5.4%	484	6,165
St. Paul city	17,553	6,468	4,353	4,447	2,285	34,404	14.1%	10.7%	18.0%	5,861	24,756
Woodbury city	na	na	na	na	na	70,800	6.7%	4.4%	2.2%	176	7,009
Mississippi											
Gulfport city	7,242	2,478	2,608	1,641	515	37,440	23.1%	21.3%	7.4%	2,158	9,467
Jackson city	12,952	5,763	3,759	1,937	1,493	28,664	20.9%	17.0%	22.3%	3,981	16,809
Missouri											
Columbia city	7,080	1,124	2,736	2,171	1,049	48,516	13.3%	4.0%	1.6%	1,185	10,088
Independence city	12,769	4,183	4,276	3,508	802	35,653	12.8%	9.9%	4.3%	2,422	16,511
Kansas City city	37,862	13,226	11,464	9,328	3,844	35,671	15.2%	10.9%	8.5%	6,508	50,748
Lee's Summit city	7,931	2,045	1,765	2,792	1,329	52,559	3.3%	3.1%	4.7%	119	12,737
O'Fallon city	5,357	1,406	1,591	1,922	438	43,838	3.4%	6.0%	6.7%	235	7,521
Springfield city	17,249	7,339	5,078	3,663	1,169	30,710	18.8%	8.2%	12.3%	2,082	21,097
St. Charles city	6,498	1,521	2,042	1,949	986	44,732	7.9%	4.1%	6.2%	565	9,275
St. Joseph city	7,418	2,656	2,256	2,228	278	34,195	12.6%	7.1%	12.2%	1,033	9,420
St. Louis city	24,010	11,446	6,305	4,692	1,567	26,511	22.8%	15.5%	20.0%	8,530	31,879
Montana											
Billings city	10,379	3,719	3,000	2,479	1,181	38,653	11.1%	5.9%	8.3%	1,152	14,615
Missoula city	5,797	2,362	1,673	668	1,094	33,655	11.3%	14.3%	7.5%	1,144	7,600

Table G-3: Places—Income, Poverty Status and Receipt of Food Stamps (SNAP)—*Continued*

	Income of Households with Householder 65 Years and Over						Poverty Rate of Persons			Households with 1 or More Persons 60 Years and Over	
	Total Households	Less Than $25,000	$25,000 - $49,999	$50,000 - $99,999	$100,000 or More	Median Household Income	55 to 64 Years	65 to 74 Years	75 Years and Over	Receiving SNAP	Not Receiving SNAP
Nebraska											
Lincoln city	21,278	5,210	7,054	6,832	2,182	43,947	6.2%	3.9%	6.4%	1,408	30,009
Omaha city	35,064	11,952	10,237	8,378	4,497	36,440	11.1%	5.2%	11.1%	4,955	50,082
Nevada											
Henderson city	28,217	6,745	8,831	8,583	4,058	44,010	10.1%	3.5%	5.3%	2,318	41,184
Las Vegas city	46,224	15,294	10,743	13,734	6,453	41,726	14.3%	9.8%	10.0%	8,858	64,456
North Las Vegas city	12,277	3,956	3,631	3,512	1,178	36,722	10.0%	10.0%	9.9%	3,460	19,048
Reno city	21,629	8,124	6,176	5,004	2,325	33,778	12.3%	12.4%	7.7%	3,295	29,288
Sparks city	8,455	2,413	2,516	2,565	961	44,484	14.0%	2.6%	8.7%	1,159	11,967
New Hampshire											
Manchester city	8,171	2,637	2,761	2,072	701	39,453	7.9%	6.5%	6.9%	1,916	12,011
Nashua city	6,403	1,608	1,793	1,827	1,175	44,544	3.2%	3.1%	14.3%	567	11,033
New Jersey											
Bayonne city	4,357	1,799	1,049	735	774	31,782	9.3%	7.9%	13.1%	735	7,728
Camden city	6,042	2,667	1,907	1,231	237	27,354	28.7%	22.7%	37.0%	3,057	5,643
Clifton city	5,859	2,259	1,598	939	1,063	33,335	8.3%	5.5%	20.9%	291	10,213
East Orange city	5,998	2,688	1,223	1,193	894	28,214	17.3%	18.9%	21.0%	2,116	7,164
Elizabeth city	6,042	2,294	1,364	1,839	545	34,873	13.0%	13.7%	28.5%	1,813	9,118
Jersey City city	15,824	6,508	3,823	2,800	2,693	32,322	18.3%	15.1%	22.1%	5,444	21,974
Newark city	15,434	8,979	3,176	1,968	1,311	20,651	19.0%	23.9%	26.2%	6,249	19,743
Passaic city	3,548	2,180	719	367	282	16,292	31.6%	39.9%	27.3%	2,207	4,280
Paterson city	8,388	4,711	1,979	1,211	487	20,454	21.0%	29.1%	20.9%	5,777	8,941
Trenton city	5,591	2,812	1,066	1,176	537	24,792	32.3%	22.8%	21.0%	1,602	7,647
Union City city	4,553	2,752	1,142	435	224	20,849	15.5%	36.4%	10.5%	2,604	5,508
New Mexico											
Albuquerque city	48,418	16,964	12,113	12,391	6,950	40,538	14.5%	14.9%	11.6%	7,715	69,895
Las Cruces city	9,355	1,927	3,457	2,533	1,438	47,509	11.4%	3.2%	3.7%	1,639	12,595
Rio Rancho city	7,725	2,131	2,650	2,068	876	38,873	3.7%	11.0%	13.6%	711	11,201
Santa Fe city	10,284	2,649	2,611	2,544	2,480	49,414	16.7%	5.8%	7.5%	864	13,849
New York											
Albany city	7,767	2,870	1,651	1,978	1,268	39,339	23.2%	11.3%	12.5%	2,568	10,080
Buffalo city	23,277	9,929	7,159	4,550	1,639	29,777	24.8%	17.6%	16.9%	11,197	24,490
Mount Vernon city	5,949	2,263	1,276	1,510	900	36,353	8.9%	9.5%	16.1%	1,355	8,060
New Rochelle city	7,137	2,049	2,320	1,140	1,628	37,938	12.4%	10.5%	10.5%	1,405	8,943
New York city	678,250	292,128	138,310	142,114	105,698	32,041	17.4%	17.2%	22.1%	282,246	821,655
Rochester city	15,228	6,698	5,015	2,555	960	26,883	23.7%	10.3%	13.5%	8,355	16,258
Schenectady city	5,189	1,935	1,238	1,503	513	35,502	13.3%	11.2%	4.9%	1,999	6,709
Syracuse city	11,056	5,109	2,662	2,158	1,127	26,737	21.5%	17.1%	16.8%	4,672	12,738
Yonkers city	20,776	6,247	5,132	5,532	3,865	45,973	14.7%	10.8%	15.1%	4,452	25,786
North Carolina											
Asheville city	9,967	3,336	2,870	2,295	1,466	39,348	8.3%	5.5%	8.6%	1,515	12,892
Charlotte city	47,756	15,995	13,573	11,076	7,112	37,089	13.1%	10.8%	8.3%	9,307	69,564
Concord city	6,519	2,448	2,365	1,007	699	35,323	10.3%	12.0%	9.8%	529	9,403
Durham city	17,276	4,680	4,584	4,315	3,697	46,814	14.4%	7.5%	12.2%	3,370	25,523
Fayetteville city	14,543	4,412	4,128	3,874	2,129	41,129	9.9%	9.9%	9.1%	2,925	19,544
Gastonia city	6,574	1,855	2,572	1,676	471	37,372	11.2%	6.4%	11.1%	1,502	8,696
Greensboro city	23,393	8,745	6,906	5,286	2,456	35,107	11.7%	9.2%	8.2%	4,861	30,529
Greenville city	5,777	1,722	1,856	1,368	831	36,813	11.4%	9.6%	9.1%	1,383	7,457
High Point city	8,256	2,654	2,629	2,391	582	34,115	14.5%	7.1%	13.0%	1,782	10,610
Jacksonville city	na	na	na	na	na	47,045	12.8%	7.7%	9.0%	538	3,491
Raleigh city	26,544	6,654	6,925	7,282	5,683	48,832	12.8%	6.6%	11.7%	4,022	38,268
Wilmington city	10,603	3,201	2,890	2,456	2,056	44,197	8.6%	4.7%	10.1%	1,711	13,760
Winston-Salem city	21,394	7,292	5,621	5,303	3,178	38,933	16.7%	11.3%	8.2%	3,335	28,153
North Dakota											
Bismarck city	6,789	1,917	1,863	2,168	841	43,653	5.1%	2.5%	9.4%	487	9,057
Fargo city	8,362	2,062	3,831	2,039	430	34,387	11.7%	6.6%	7.7%	770	11,835
Ohio											
Akron city	18,210	7,366	5,884	3,753	1,207	29,846	14.5%	13.8%	8.4%	5,876	24,115
Canton city	6,344	3,028	2,052	1,163	101	26,369	22.1%	19.8%	18.7%	2,411	8,144
Cincinnati city	25,463	11,109	6,289	4,547	3,518	30,360	26.5%	14.8%	15.1%	8,125	32,224
Cleveland city	33,681	19,053	8,380	4,758	1,490	22,118	27.6%	28.4%	16.1%	16,663	37,316
Columbus city	50,131	18,712	14,431	11,959	5,029	34,077	13.8%	13.7%	10.9%	13,256	71,126
Dayton city	11,354	5,436	3,018	2,448	452	26,154	28.1%	12.7%	17.5%	3,770	13,671
Lorain city	6,090	2,683	1,925	1,198	284	30,091	18.9%	9.9%	19.2%	1,609	7,574
Parma city	9,382	3,610	3,205	2,265	302	31,622	7.1%	6.8%	8.4%	860	12,701
Toledo city	26,214	12,082	7,616	5,144	1,372	26,040	16.4%	12.3%	13.1%	6,846	33,025
Youngstown city	7,604	4,246	2,181	1,016	181	22,566	30.9%	21.4%	13.8%	2,784	7,969
Oklahoma											
Broken Arrow city	6,656	1,308	1,580	2,583	1,185	56,028	3.9%	2.9%	9.2%	558	10,887
Edmond city	6,752	1,369	1,785	2,099	1,499	53,686	2.2%	5.4%	4.0%	88	10,720
Lawton city	6,211	2,177	2,237	1,348	449	33,999	10.0%	9.0%	17.1%	1,196	8,601
Norman city	8,245	1,876	1,945	2,856	1,568	55,760	11.3%	2.1%	11.4%	434	13,302
Oklahoma City city	46,993	12,693	13,916	13,590	6,794	43,496	15.5%	6.2%	7.8%	6,681	67,398
Tulsa city	34,775	10,521	11,269	8,387	4,598	40,074	14.3%	9.8%	8.4%	5,322	50,204

Table G-3: Places—Income, Poverty Status and Receipt of Food Stamps (SNAP)—*Continued*

	Income of Households with Householder 65 Years and Over					Poverty Rate of Persons			Households with 1 or More Persons 60 Years and Over	
	Total Households	Less Than $25,000	$25,000 - $49,999	$50,000 - $99,999	$100,000 or More	Median Household Income	55 to 64 Years	65 to 74 Years	75 Years and Over	Receiving SNAP	Not Receiving SNAP
Oregon											
Beaverton city	6,292	1,616	2,034	1,611	1,031	43,228	9.1%	4.4%	6.6%	862	10,155
Bend city	7,517	2,089	2,613	1,571	1,244	36,695	8.2%	8.1%	7.9%	1,241	9,957
Eugene city	14,864	4,610	4,249	3,873	2,132	41,184	11.8%	6.7%	15.2%	3,079	19,527
Gresham city	9,217	2,873	3,045	2,249	1,050	38,705	11.7%	9.3%	13.7%	2,740	11,786
Hillsboro city	6,631	1,068	2,448	2,180	935	43,807	9.9%	5.8%	8.2%	1,600	8,565
Medford city	8,593	2,312	2,968	2,074	1,239	39,599	15.5%	10.3%	8.2%	2,135	10,877
Portland city	44,071	16,111	11,007	10,298	6,655	37,053	16.4%	12.9%	12.7%	15,201	61,663
Salem city	14,193	4,413	3,420	4,311	2,049	41,636	7.7%	6.7%	5.8%	3,672	19,422
Pennsylvania											
Allentown city	8,774	3,527	2,594	1,883	770	31,775	18.1%	18.0%	8.9%	2,881	11,106
Bethlehem city	7,843	3,489	1,933	1,522	899	28,799	11.5%	13.2%	11.2%	1,843	9,733
Erie city	9,063	4,145	3,083	1,302	533	27,021	15.9%	17.1%	11.9%	3,134	10,628
Philadelphia city	124,800	58,422	31,354	23,636	11,388	27,423	22.3%	16.0%	17.1%	47,424	147,062
Pittsburgh city	28,274	12,384	7,319	5,445	3,126	28,609	14.0%	11.2%	11.7%	6,911	35,773
Reading city	6,525	3,248	2,088	710	479	25,075	23.2%	22.4%	24.0%	3,587	6,103
Scranton city	8,401	3,671	2,429	1,830	471	29,017	16.8%	10.0%	13.0%	2,064	9,687
Rhode Island											
Cranston city	8,849	2,578	3,482	1,776	1,013	36,848	8.5%	8.7%	9.9%	1,808	11,902
Pawtucket city	5,034	2,139	1,673	990	232	29,844	22.2%	7.6%	19.3%	2,131	5,725
Providence city	10,316	5,460	1,581	1,612	1,663	23,562	21.2%	22.1%	23.8%	5,049	11,110
Warwick city	9,995	3,336	2,457	2,379	1,823	41,052	4.0%	3.8%	7.5%	1,396	13,636
South Carolina											
Charleston city	10,952	2,048	3,581	2,832	2,491	47,910	8.0%	3.6%	6.9%	1,213	15,752
Columbia city	7,894	3,223	1,909	1,585	1,177	34,823	17.7%	13.1%	14.7%	1,636	10,771
North Charleston city	6,844	3,009	1,607	1,602	626	30,209	20.7%	11.5%	11.0%	2,183	9,100
Rock Hill city	5,886	2,089	1,919	1,255	623	33,935	7.4%	10.3%	13.4%	860	7,402
South Dakota											
Rapid City city	7,146	2,607	2,791	1,118	630	32,415	12.8%	8.3%	7.0%	608	9,516
Sioux Falls city	12,944	3,981	4,254	3,094	1,615	38,104	8.5%	12.1%	8.8%	1,975	17,858
Tennessee											
Chattanooga city	17,375	6,917	4,532	4,098	1,828	36,200	14.6%	13.9%	12.0%	4,221	22,743
Clarksville city	7,033	2,126	1,724	2,179	1,004	47,078	10.8%	10.1%	4.5%	1,429	10,342
Franklin city	4,514	689	1,400	1,631	794	54,300	2.0%	0.0%	2.3%	327	6,990
Jackson city	5,098	1,923	1,186	1,167	822	35,716	17.5%	9.8%	9.3%	1,067	7,197
Johnson City city	7,325	1,931	2,587	1,798	1,009	41,852	9.1%	5.7%	4.2%	1,017	9,100
Knoxville city	16,720	6,684	5,171	3,707	1,158	29,401	24.6%	11.7%	13.1%	4,112	20,785
Memphis city	48,707	18,882	13,862	10,591	5,372	31,734	18.2%	13.1%	16.5%	18,257	62,621
Murfreesboro city	7,449	2,992	1,950	2,037	470	35,307	8.6%	8.1%	24.2%	936	10,086
Nashville-Davidson metropolitan govt (bal)	44,768	14,666	11,182	12,878	6,042	40,134	14.8%	8.4%	11.0%	9,108	63,746
Texas											
Abilene city	9,239	2,456	3,042	2,482	1,259	41,843	9.6%	7.7%	12.5%	944	12,790
Allen city	na	na	na	na	na	58,649	5.3%	1.5%	9.6%	194	5,801
Amarillo city	16,390	5,212	4,722	4,134	2,322	40,000	11.8%	6.8%	11.3%	1,806	22,035
Arlington city	21,203	6,398	4,618	5,852	4,335	48,573	7.6%	5.6%	10.4%	3,408	33,505
Austin city	44,806	10,687	10,704	14,674	8,741	52,651	10.0%	9.0%	7.8%	7,463	71,802
Baytown city	5,810	1,861	1,545	1,497	907	36,051	14.5%	0.7%	17.3%	1,003	8,679
Beaumont city	10,045	3,948	3,343	1,849	905	32,925	16.0%	13.4%	10.3%	2,060	13,869
Brownsville city	10,856	5,894	2,618	1,302	1,042	22,755	31.5%	25.1%	26.8%	4,458	13,290
Bryan city	5,373	1,829	1,808	1,146	590	34,117	10.6%	13.4%	31.0%	738	7,304
Carrollton city	6,565	1,713	1,408	2,111	1,333	52,795	4.1%	7.1%	10.8%	1,002	11,876
College Station city	3,785	911	516	1,413	945	62,217	10.5%	1.7%	10.2%	416	6,365
Conroe city	3,691	1,121	1,011	945	614	36,283	9.9%	3.5%	9.5%	418	5,600
Corpus Christi city	25,209	8,819	6,732	5,942	3,716	38,467	11.8%	16.6%	11.2%	6,306	35,655
Dallas city	76,474	26,778	19,917	17,433	12,346	36,342	17.9%	13.5%	14.5%	19,000	107,455
Denton city	7,434	1,977	2,595	1,844	1,018	43,037	9.4%	8.6%	9.6%	439	11,538
Edinburg city	na	na	na	na	na	37,026	26.7%	33.4%	24.3%	1,779	4,298
El Paso city	46,798	19,524	14,223	9,167	3,884	29,943	15.0%	16.6%	22.5%	17,116	59,381
Fort Worth city	45,983	16,230	11,923	11,987	5,843	37,018	12.1%	12.8%	10.4%	9,961	63,514
Frisco city	5,359	640	1,860	1,135	1,724	62,118	0.9%	6.9%	3.5%	204	9,110
Garland city	15,697	4,812	4,960	4,304	1,621	40,567	11.7%	9.1%	4.9%	3,074	23,563
Grand Prairie city	7,664	2,226	1,799	2,669	970	44,654	9.4%	9.0%	7.0%	1,322	14,265
Harlingen city	5,593	2,966	1,092	842	693	23,885	22.6%	18.6%	14.3%	1,304	6,353
Houston city	137,392	51,834	32,009	30,450	23,099	36,902	14.2%	13.8%	15.3%	31,404	197,403
Irving city	10,332	3,091	2,714	2,887	1,640	40,353	10.8%	9.9%	11.0%	1,658	16,290
Killeen city	4,504	1,197	874	1,658	775	58,283	10.1%	5.9%	0.0%	702	8,086
Laredo city	11,300	5,804	2,698	1,885	913	23,840	24.8%	26.9%	33.8%	7,115	14,063
League City city	na	na	na	na	na	64,630	5.0%	1.8%	0.0%	183	8,334
Lewisville city	5,954	1,777	2,073	1,116	988	36,254	5.8%	5.1%	14.8%	420	8,524
Longview city	7,631	2,683	1,735	2,238	975	42,649	15.3%	13.0%	10.3%	852	9,950
Lubbock city	19,168	6,203	5,610	5,204	2,151	39,398	11.3%	8.7%	10.9%	2,680	24,534
McAllen city	6,779	3,015	1,239	1,778	747	31,689	9.5%	18.0%	20.3%	3,270	9,446
McKinney city	7,938	1,705	2,126	2,763	1,344	50,846	6.2%	1.1%	2.4%	395	12,826

Table G-3: Places—Income, Poverty Status and Receipt of Food Stamps (SNAP)—*Continued*

		Income of Households with Householder 65 Years and Over					Poverty Rate of Persons			Households with 1 or More Persons 60 Years and Over	
	Total Households	Less Than $25,000	$25,000 - $49,999	$50,000 - $99,999	$100,000 or More	Median Household Income	55 to 64 Years	65 to 74 Years	75 Years and Over	Receiving SNAP	Not Receiving SNAP
Texas—Cont.											
Mesquite city	8,169	2,488	2,625	2,438	618	39,530	3.1%	3.5%	2.6%	860	14,889
Midland city	7,439	2,605	1,782	1,424	1,628	43,177	9.5%	5.3%	4.3%	427	12,708
Mission city	4,875	1,947	1,234	1,512	182	38,947	20.3%	16.6%	12.8%	1,381	6,440
Missouri City city	na	na	na	na	na	54,624	8.2%	3.4%	8.5%	540	7,753
New Braunfels city	5,151	1,401	1,695	1,679	376	42,811	9.2%	6.7%	4.2%	182	7,835
North Richland Hills city	5,889	1,164	2,089	2,095	541	41,682	5.9%	3.7%	4.0%	152	8,342
Odessa city	7,892	3,185	1,734	1,636	1,337	34,592	1.7%	12.8%	17.9%	1,595	10,951
Pasadena city	8,727	2,791	2,470	2,211	1,255	37,321	11.1%	5.8%	16.8%	1,951	13,549
Pearland city	na	na	na	na	na	50,402	1.4%	1.2%	1.7%	518	9,298
Pharr city	na	na	na	na	na	30,940	15.1%	19.9%	29.0%	2,207	4,938
Plano city	18,614	3,824	4,238	5,652	4,900	55,569	6.5%	4.9%	12.6%	1,168	32,223
Richardson city	9,583	2,080	3,330	2,312	1,861	45,515	4.4%	4.5%	6.8%	808	13,431
Round Rock city	4,471	959	917	1,442	1,153	59,776	3.4%	4.1%	10.1%	276	8,606
San Angelo city	8,818	3,856	2,454	1,681	827	31,750	12.3%	14.7%	14.3%	1,411	11,540
San Antonio city	100,110	32,914	27,334	24,602	15,260	39,744	14.8%	11.2%	12.9%	21,996	138,243
Sugar Land city	6,371	1,023	1,760	1,326	2,262	63,072	3.4%	1.5%	12.2%	413	10,822
Temple city	6,643	2,134	2,598	880	1,031	36,730	14.3%	5.6%	7.5%	861	9,016
Tyler city	9,397	3,382	3,193	2,034	788	33,343	13.9%	9.7%	13.6%	1,350	12,670
Victoria city	5,640	1,907	1,421	1,612	700	37,403	10.0%	8.9%	10.4%	695	8,021
Waco city	10,158	3,555	3,046	2,549	1,008	37,407	12.5%	4.3%	12.0%	1,797	12,660
Wichita Falls city	8,025	2,306	2,345	2,210	1,164	42,271	15.7%	6.5%	13.8%	1,089	12,067
Utah											
Layton city	4,170	774	1,044	1,388	964	56,081	1.4%	5.1%	2.3%	552	6,124
Ogden city	5,607	2,057	1,539	1,688	323	36,716	18.5%	12.9%	17.5%	1,487	7,415
Orem city	4,276	1,080	958	1,294	944	54,551	7.9%	4.7%	5.6%	405	6,240
Provo city	4,063	789	1,079	1,278	917	52,140	15.1%	3.5%	5.4%	568	6,137
Salt Lake City city	13,227	4,668	3,838	3,065	1,656	37,258	13.4%	10.3%	9.7%	1,996	18,239
Sandy city	4,911	846	954	1,747	1,364	64,647	3.5%	1.0%	3.4%	212	9,830
St. George city	9,483	2,474	3,008	3,336	665	44,178	12.2%	4.2%	9.9%	176	12,032
West Jordan city	3,460	383	1,007	1,421	649	66,151	7.4%	0.0%	18.6%	316	6,973
West Valley City city	5,200	1,322	1,503	1,718	657	46,336	5.5%	7.7%	12.8%	1,458	7,672
Virginia											
Alexandria city	9,620	1,916	1,479	2,529	3,696	73,055	5.8%	8.8%	12.2%	652	15,276
Chesapeake city	16,451	4,092	4,165	5,567	2,627	49,706	5.9%	7.6%	5.7%	1,737	25,133
Hampton city	11,850	3,729	2,731	3,708	1,682	42,070	10.9%	9.8%	13.7%	1,289	17,271
Lynchburg city	7,509	3,237	1,602	1,933	737	29,512	9.8%	3.8%	11.9%	1,392	8,764
Newport News city	12,876	3,414	4,163	3,194	2,105	42,144	10.4%	7.7%	10.3%	2,493	19,681
Norfolk city	15,883	5,879	4,413	3,823	1,768	35,378	15.4%	18.7%	13.5%	3,693	21,145
Portsmouth city	8,758	3,267	1,935	2,786	770	36,295	12.8%	14.8%	9.0%	1,675	11,938
Richmond city	17,129	6,259	5,079	3,697	2,094	34,480	17.6%	10.2%	18.1%	4,223	23,232
Roanoke city	10,367	3,483	3,475	2,259	1,150	38,675	15.5%	9.1%	10.4%	1,888	13,797
Suffolk city	7,248	2,072	2,131	2,008	1,037	45,533	8.4%	12.4%	12.7%	2,065	10,087
Virginia Beach city	34,442	7,980	8,674	10,682	7,106	52,218	5.0%	6.5%	6.8%	3,452	51,359
Washington											
Auburn city	4,890	1,012	1,319	1,919	640	55,263	8.4%	9.7%	7.5%	1,365	6,675
Bellevue city	12,331	2,194	3,445	2,961	3,731	54,380	4.7%	3.3%	7.7%	1,285	17,766
Bellingham city	7,944	3,256	2,166	1,450	1,072	30,857	3.5%	10.8%	18.1%	1,620	9,998
Everett city	6,673	3,153	1,713	1,381	426	26,778	15.7%	13.1%	10.0%	2,428	9,049
Federal Way city	7,765	2,153	2,594	1,701	1,317	40,987	5.2%	5.7%	5.8%	1,387	10,439
Kennewick city	5,914	1,605	2,078	1,738	493	39,378	16.9%	5.4%	5.6%	2,297	7,422
Kent city	6,863	1,950	2,369	1,824	720	40,176	11.5%	10.6%	12.0%	2,966	10,231
Kirkland city	6,571	1,770	1,380	1,923	1,498	52,860	7.6%	5.5%	7.7%	784	10,144
Marysville city	5,333	1,479	2,626	1,062	166	38,236	5.7%	1.5%	8.2%	1,054	8,300
Pasco city	na	na	na	na	na	31,359	7.5%	8.7%	52.5%	764	4,495
Renton city	5,388	1,501	1,389	1,414	1,084	41,000	8.9%	7.3%	16.0%	1,298	8,760
Seattle city	52,142	14,036	12,381	14,692	11,033	49,452	12.8%	10.8%	14.9%	11,725	70,612
Spokane city	19,774	7,207	5,210	4,886	2,471	36,503	14.9%	9.5%	14.4%	5,751	23,333
Spokane Valley city	9,147	2,973	3,875	1,913	386	34,867	13.0%	10.8%	4.8%	1,611	10,977
Tacoma city	16,417	5,726	4,272	4,019	2,400	35,633	14.6%	17.2%	17.2%	5,473	19,179
Vancouver city	14,948	4,500	4,253	3,911	2,284	40,320	8.1%	9.3%	6.9%	3,569	20,338
Yakima city	8,154	3,162	2,879	1,452	661	30,402	10.2%	11.0%	7.8%	1,900	10,243
Wisconsin											
Appleton city	4,767	1,320	1,545	1,466	436	40,512	7.7%	1.1%	5.1%	870	8,032
Eau Claire city	5,565	1,804	1,986	1,321	454	34,320	8.5%	3.7%	6.0%	1,181	6,697
Green Bay city	8,151	2,340	3,090	2,260	461	37,025	10.3%	11.9%	4.9%	1,792	11,352
Kenosha city	8,318	2,865	2,388	2,235	830	35,554	15.1%	4.6%	4.3%	1,405	11,240
Madison city	17,553	3,744	5,069	5,668	3,072	49,666	8.5%	3.6%	8.6%	2,240	25,906
Milwaukee city	38,497	16,430	11,776	6,889	3,402	29,121	20.6%	14.8%	13.8%	15,065	51,051
Oshkosh city	6,269	2,869	1,720	1,317	363	27,788	7.1%	8.8%	7.2%	694	8,652
Racine city	6,207	2,847	1,921	1,258	181	27,949	22.4%	16.2%	12.6%	2,414	7,962
Waukesha city	4,989	1,334	1,770	1,433	452	41,227	3.1%	2.4%	9.1%	584	7,627

Table G-4: Metropolitan/Micropolitan Statistical Areas—Income, Poverty Status and Receipt of Food Stamps (SNAP)

	Income of Households with Householder 65 Years and Over					Poverty Rate of Persons			Households with 1 or More Persons 60 Years and Over	
	Total Households	Less Than $25,000	$25,000 - $49,999	$50,000 - $99,999	$100,000 or More	Median Household Income	55 to 64 Years	65 to 74 Years	75 Years and Over	Receiving SNAP	Not Receiving SNAP
Aberdeen, WA Micro Area	8,568	2,465	3,161	1,965	977	38,154	12.2%	5.7%	14.2%	1,815	10,668
Abilene, TX Metro Area	14,504	4,389	4,783	3,508	1,824	40,184	10.8%	11.1%	13.8%	1,301	20,097
Adrian, MI Micro Area	10,605	2,892	4,005	3,008	700	37,938	9.2%	2.6%	6.5%	1,734	13,502
Akron, OH Metro Area	71,529	21,213	24,286	17,878	8,152	39,385	9.4%	6.1%	6.6%	11,491	98,380
Alamogordo, NM Micro Area	6,074	1,697	2,033	1,935	409	42,896	11.2%	17.6%	5.7%	856	7,808
Albany, GA Metro Area	14,031	5,457	3,422	4,002	1,150	31,814	14.1%	16.1%	12.4%	4,496	17,768
Albany, OR Metro Area	12,694	3,698	4,618	3,603	775	39,205	13.1%	9.6%	4.9%	2,830	16,100
Albany-Schenectady-Troy, NY Metro Area	86,243	21,618	24,765	24,970	14,890	45,827	7.9%	5.8%	6.2%	13,168	117,407
Albertville, AL Micro Area	8,968	4,010	2,812	1,260	886	26,955	15.7%	8.3%	16.3%	1,561	12,664
Albuquerque, NM Metro Area	82,564	27,883	22,608	21,042	11,031	39,233	14.0%	12.9%	13.7%	13,262	117,238
Alexandria, LA Metro Area	14,007	5,814	4,223	2,403	1,567	30,863	17.8%	13.7%	15.5%	3,308	17,808
Allentown-Bethlehem-Easton, PA-NJ Metro Area	82,997	26,764	25,327	21,544	9,362	38,049	7.5%	6.2%	7.2%	11,377	117,644
Altoona, PA Metro Area	14,864	5,968	4,691	3,510	695	29,389	8.4%	7.9%	13.6%	1,912	20,719
Amarillo, TX Metro Area	21,264	6,813	6,274	5,096	3,081	38,987	11.5%	6.9%	9.3%	1,967	29,761
Ames, IA Metro Area	6,087	733	2,051	1,594	1,709	54,447	5.8%	0.2%	5.0%	193	8,833
Anchorage, AK Metro Area	20,102	3,815	4,254	6,394	5,639	65,435	8.0%	5.0%	4.0%	2,817	33,662
Ann Arbor, MI Metro Area	27,312	4,978	7,943	7,224	7,167	53,338	7.9%	4.8%	7.3%	3,790	40,456
Anniston-Oxford-Jacksonville, AL Metro Area	11,702	4,567	3,508	2,689	938	32,658	14.9%	17.0%	10.3%	1,465	17,382
Appleton, WI Metro Area	18,685	4,861	6,865	5,321	1,638	40,246	5.9%	2.6%	6.7%	2,060	26,595
Asheville, NC Metro Area	55,387	17,660	17,226	13,802	6,699	37,319	9.6%	4.7%	8.9%	6,134	72,847
Ashtabula, OH Micro Area	10,195	4,775	3,156	1,972	292	26,390	16.7%	18.9%	8.2%	2,982	13,318
Athens, TX Micro Area	10,304	3,178	3,589	2,666	871	38,657	17.9%	9.4%	10.7%	1,503	13,024
Athens-Clarke County, GA Metro Area	14,195	3,718	3,877	3,969	2,631	43,814	16.9%	8.4%	12.1%	2,617	19,954
Atlanta-Sandy Springs-Roswell, GA Metro Area	353,875	105,522	101,833	92,420	54,100	41,384	10.6%	8.4%	10.8%	67,378	530,340
Atlantic City-Hammonton, NJ Metro Area	26,503	8,868	6,416	6,918	4,301	42,911	10.2%	7.8%	7.2%	4,547	38,329
Auburn, NY Micro Area	8,338	2,739	2,629	2,273	697	37,563	7.5%	4.5%	8.7%	1,737	10,867
Auburn-Opelika, AL Metro Area	10,631	3,862	2,820	2,416	1,533	37,990	12.5%	6.9%	12.2%	1,561	15,318
Augusta-Richmond County, GA-SC Metro Area	49,028	15,906	14,552	12,454	6,116	37,095	13.1%	11.0%	6.5%	9,770	70,869
Augusta-Waterville, ME Micro Area	13,203	4,489	4,703	2,815	1,196	33,280	7.8%	8.7%	11.6%	2,287	17,943
Austin-Round Rock, TX Metro Area	105,797	23,945	26,068	33,114	22,670	52,792	9.2%	6.7%	7.8%	14,085	172,649
Bakersfield, CA Metro Area	49,947	16,945	14,711	11,738	6,553	36,209	15.6%	12.8%	15.3%	8,934	76,396
Baltimore-Columbia-Towson, MD Metro Area	240,780	63,471	59,360	70,176	47,773	48,732	8.7%	6.6%	10.2%	36,286	342,774
Bangor, ME Metro Area	16,041	6,403	4,943	3,760	935	31,124	10.3%	6.5%	10.6%	3,802	20,607
Barnstable Town, MA Metro Area	38,887	9,796	10,053	11,072	7,966	48,516	7.8%	6.1%	4.9%	3,269	49,896
Baton Rouge, LA Metro Area	61,930	21,184	18,651	14,105	7,990	36,824	11.2%	10.7%	12.6%	11,875	88,871
Battle Creek, MI Metro Area	13,899	4,586	5,740	2,745	828	32,818	12.6%	7.7%	7.6%	2,404	18,648
Bay City, MI Metro Area	12,621	3,976	4,925	2,570	1,150	35,086	10.9%	8.5%	9.9%	1,544	16,479
Beaumont-Port Arthur, TX Metro Area	37,765	16,109	11,784	7,167	2,705	30,024	15.1%	10.1%	11.5%	6,432	51,604
Beaver Dam, WI Micro Area	8,850	3,042	3,046	2,265	497	34,014	9.2%	6.4%	9.1%	1,205	11,915
Beckley, WV Metro Area	14,622	6,166	4,984	2,689	783	31,084	10.3%	6.2%	8.2%	3,121	18,515
Bellingham, WA Metro Area	20,850	6,080	5,715	6,076	2,979	41,847	8.3%	6.8%	11.7%	3,565	27,869
Bend-Redmond, OR Metro Area	18,070	5,096	6,189	4,241	2,544	38,048	12.1%	9.1%	9.1%	2,932	23,986
Billings, MT Metro Area	16,291	5,525	5,329	3,881	1,556	38,117	10.9%	8.6%	7.6%	1,650	23,770
Binghamton, NY Metro Area	27,324	7,931	10,029	6,832	2,532	38,470	12.5%	6.3%	7.9%	5,473	36,568
Birmingham-Hoover, AL Metro Area	107,765	35,017	34,032	26,228	12,488	36,390	14.2%	8.7%	12.3%	15,935	147,053
Bismarck, ND Metro Area	11,754	3,739	3,340	3,504	1,171	39,432	4.5%	8.1%	10.4%	974	16,464
Blacksburg-Christiansburg-Radford, VA Metro Area	15,631	5,468	4,372	3,949	1,842	40,012	13.0%	7.1%	12.3%	1,591	21,652
Bloomington, IL Metro Area	14,146	3,426	4,333	4,339	2,048	45,364	10.6%	4.7%	9.5%	1,289	20,578
Bloomington, IN Metro Area	11,974	2,400	3,938	2,930	2,706	46,873	9.2%	6.7%	3.0%	1,079	17,482
Bloomsburg-Berwick, PA Metro Area	9,142	3,325	3,134	1,893	790	34,002	7.1%	3.0%	8.3%	1,299	12,437
Bluefield, WV-VA Micro Area	13,568	6,209	3,570	3,183	606	28,401	13.6%	10.7%	11.0%	2,757	17,302
Boise City, ID Metro Area	51,350	15,265	15,557	15,507	5,021	41,449	9.0%	7.6%	10.9%	6,997	73,893
Boston-Cambridge-Newton, MA-NH Metro Area	412,506	125,016	97,341	106,280	83,869	44,732	8.0%	8.0%	9.8%	79,255	572,565
Boulder, CO Metro Area	23,881	5,590	4,284	8,163	5,844	60,057	7.6%	5.2%	9.9%	1,595	38,023
Bowling Green, KY Metro Area	14,024	5,298	4,034	3,596	1,096	34,555	12.0%	10.1%	10.9%	2,049	18,949
Bozeman, MT Micro Area	6,915	2,171	1,836	1,899	1,009	38,449	9.6%	4.6%	8.7%	573	10,651
Brainerd, MN Micro Area	12,583	4,080	4,236	3,135	1,132	36,179	9.8%	6.6%	11.9%	897	16,822
Branson, MO Micro Area	12,253	3,871	4,621	2,957	804	34,693	16.9%	8.8%	6.3%	2,281	16,212
Bremerton-Silverdale, WA Metro Area	25,250	6,015	7,716	7,035	4,484	45,568	7.6%	8.3%	11.9%	3,532	34,606
Bridgeport-Stamford-Norwalk, CT Metro Area	84,643	21,299	19,221	20,900	23,223	53,372	6.0%	8.1%	7.0%	10,998	118,119
Brownsville-Harlingen, TX Metro Area	30,043	15,102	6,804	4,941	3,196	24,874	25.9%	23.4%	23.0%	9,998	36,576
Brunswick, GA Metro Area	12,140	3,530	2,887	4,293	1,430	46,343	17.6%	7.6%	7.3%	2,268	16,416
Buffalo-Cheektowaga-Niagara Falls, NY Metro Area	125,531	44,363	39,170	29,039	12,959	34,679	10.3%	8.3%	10.1%	24,275	162,195
Burlington, NC Metro Area	16,058	6,114	5,026	3,312	1,606	30,729	14.1%	10.5%	12.6%	2,608	20,626
Burlington-South Burlington, VT Metro Area	18,342	5,292	5,536	4,921	2,593	39,078	6.4%	4.7%	7.0%	2,780	26,753
California-Lexington Park, MD Metro Area	7,889	2,205	1,954	2,084	1,646	46,791	4.9%	4.4%	10.9%	1,193	12,276
Canton-Massillon, OH Metro Area	44,574	13,939	16,554	10,656	3,425	35,813	9.7%	8.1%	9.7%	6,859	60,010
Cape Coral-Fort Myers, FL Metro Area	102,374	27,116	29,881	29,276	16,101	44,442	12.7%	6.8%	8.9%	8,311	132,108
Cape Girardeau, MO-IL Metro Area	9,954	3,627	2,836	2,442	1,049	38,050	15.7%	6.2%	15.3%	1,160	13,769
Carbondale-Marion, IL Metro Area	11,887	3,907	3,269	3,306	1,405	34,610	13.7%	8.2%	11.1%	1,959	15,167
Carson City, NV Metro Area	6,651	2,123	2,320	1,586	622	34,002	6.4%	11.0%	10.4%	1,160	8,312
Casper, WY Metro Area	7,213	2,503	1,379	2,466	865	41,005	8.0%	2.9%	7.4%	1,036	9,914
Cedar Rapids, IA Metro Area	25,107	7,229	7,173	7,216	3,489	42,564	5.6%	3.1%	7.5%	1,733	35,072
Centralia, WA Micro Area	9,400	2,714	3,293	2,622	771	38,010	11.5%	6.2%	4.3%	1,668	11,161
Chambersburg-Waynesboro, PA Metro Area	16,463	4,377	6,186	4,106	1,794	39,407	11.6%	6.9%	8.8%	1,716	22,535

Table G-4: Metropolitan/Micropolitan Statistical Areas—Income, Poverty Status and Receipt of Food Stamps (SNAP)—Continued

	Income of Households with Householder 65 Years and Over					Poverty Rate of Persons			Households with 1 or More Persons 60 Years and Over	
	Total Households	Less Than $25,000	$25,000 - $49,999	$50,000 - $99,999	$100,000 or More	Median Household Income	55 to 64 Years	65 to 74 Years	75 Years and Over	Receiving SNAP	Not Receiving SNAP
Champaign-Urbana, IL Metro Area...............	18,635	4,891	5,640	5,402	2,702	42,357	10.3%	5.1%	9.3%	1,642	26,354
Charleston, WV Metro Area.......................	27,136	8,864	9,578	6,593	2,101	35,601	13.1%	8.6%	6.6%	4,029	35,877
Charleston-Mattoon, IL Micro Area............	6,127	1,872	1,799	1,843	613	40,181	10.3%	6.9%	6.4%	904	8,154
Charleston-North Charleston, SC Metro Area..	58,835	15,690	18,327	14,606	10,212	41,136	12.0%	7.1%	9.8%	9,057	83,963
Charlotte-Concord-Gastonia, NC-SC Metro Area.........	178,503	56,533	54,876	46,882	20,212	37,812	10.9%	8.7%	9.7%	28,485	254,059
Charlottesville, VA Metro Area....................	20,925	5,719	5,043	6,351	3,812	48,128	9.9%	6.1%	10.9%	2,563	31,063
Chattanooga, TN-GA Metro Area................	56,504	19,921	17,098	13,830	5,655	36,745	11.8%	8.1%	8.1%	9,821	74,071
Cheyenne, WY Metro Area	8,768	2,110	2,185	3,223	1,250	50,484	9.6%	1.6%	8.5%	924	12,846
Chicago-Naperville-Elgin, IL-IN-WI Metro Area..	741,292	224,984	201,378	190,455	124,475	41,845	10.3%	8.1%	9.9%	143,931	1,051,099
Chico, CA Metro Area..............................	22,765	8,032	6,146	5,110	3,477	38,334	19.0%	5.5%	13.7%	2,163	32,520
Chillicothe, OH Micro Area.......................	7,322	2,979	2,591	1,244	508	29,676	13.1%	8.8%	15.5%	1,571	9,693
Cincinnati, OH-KY-IN Metro Area...............	185,564	57,203	55,017	49,209	24,135	38,915	10.2%	6.6%	9.0%	25,428	265,293
Claremont-Lebanon, NH-VT Micro Area.......	24,525	7,354	7,377	6,783	3,011	40,052	7.6%	5.1%	7.3%	3,492	36,623
Clarksburg, WV Micro Area.......................	10,942	4,134	3,868	2,355	585	30,920	14.2%	7.1%	8.8%	1,557	14,177
Clarksville, TN-KY Metro Area..................	16,860	5,232	5,164	4,801	1,663	40,310	10.4%	7.0%	7.9%	2,919	24,117
Clearlake, CA Micro Area.........................	8,588	3,122	2,753	1,886	827	35,953	18.9%	8.4%	3.8%	390	13,105
Cleveland, TN Metro Area........................	12,406	5,130	4,267	2,367	642	29,686	14.5%	5.8%	18.0%	2,011	16,251
Cleveland-Elyria, OH Metro Area...............	220,581	74,817	68,558	54,664	22,542	36,747	11.0%	9.1%	8.7%	36,928	294,781
Coeur d'Alene, ID Metro Area...................	15,029	4,552	5,125	3,711	1,641	36,911	7.3%	9.8%	6.3%	1,228	21,679
College Station-Bryan, TX Metro Area.........	15,260	4,529	4,109	4,225	2,397	41,039	10.2%	6.7%	15.5%	1,951	21,951
Colorado Springs, CO Metro Area..............	48,830	12,918	13,292	14,223	8,397	47,445	8.7%	6.6%	6.7%	6,698	74,147
Columbia, MO Metro Area........................	11,871	2,940	3,748	3,942	1,241	43,817	10.1%	7.1%	5.2%	1,694	17,889
Columbia, SC Metro Area........................	67,284	18,768	21,608	17,327	9,581	41,048	11.6%	6.1%	8.9%	9,714	93,153
Columbus, GA-AL Metro Area...................	23,640	8,033	6,323	7,016	2,268	37,630	16.5%	10.2%	12.2%	5,131	31,796
Columbus, IN Metro Area.........................	7,952	2,383	2,552	2,079	938	39,129	7.6%	10.3%	1.5%	722	10,890
Columbus, OH Metro Area........................	147,766	43,691	45,163	39,091	19,821	40,239	9.1%	7.8%	7.5%	25,539	211,968
Concord, NH Micro Area...........................	13,787	4,417	4,133	3,582	1,655	38,854	6.9%	3.8%	3.4%	965	21,805
Cookeville, TN Micro Area........................	12,176	5,139	4,238	1,942	857	28,139	12.5%	14.0%	20.8%	2,728	14,965
Coos Bay, OR Micro Area.........................	9,135	3,119	3,371	2,049	596	35,906	10.9%	15.8%	7.9%	2,104	11,947
Corning, NY Micro Area...........................	11,088	4,348	3,389	2,338	1,013	32,537	15.3%	9.2%	3.9%	2,186	14,316
Corpus Christi, TX Metro Area..................	38,942	13,208	10,903	9,232	5,599	37,860	11.6%	15.4%	10.7%	8,992	51,731
Corvallis, OR Metro Area.........................	7,923	2,042	1,734	2,929	1,218	52,510	7.5%	5.7%	7.9%	1,123	10,723
Crestview-Fort Walton Beach-Destin, FL Metro Area.....	26,949	6,015	8,146	7,661	5,127	46,867	10.0%	7.0%	7.3%	2,555	34,743
Cullman, AL Micro Area...........................	8,705	3,871	2,842	1,640	352	26,835	10.5%	12.6%	5.8%	1,153	11,175
Cumberland, MD-WV Metro Area...............	11,770	4,628	4,214	2,352	576	30,995	17.9%	11.9%	7.5%	1,860	15,512
Dallas-Fort Worth-Arlington, TX Metro Area	420,736	117,957	115,473	115,589	71,717	43,688	9.4%	7.6%	9.0%	61,861	641,726
Dalton, GA Metro Area............................	10,758	4,130	2,734	2,552	1,342	32,632	14.0%	11.5%	12.1%	2,697	14,749
Danville, IL Metro Area............................	8,761	2,930	2,781	2,284	766	38,370	8.5%	8.8%	3.8%	1,280	12,037
Danville, VA Micro Area...........................	13,851	5,806	4,125	3,221	699	32,462	12.9%	10.9%	12.8%	3,157	16,811
Daphne-Fairhope-Foley, AL Metro Area......	23,509	7,320	7,164	6,654	2,371	39,143	9.6%	11.1%	10.8%	1,650	31,792
Davenport-Moline-Rock Island, IA-IL Metro Area.........	40,792	13,570	12,593	10,960	3,669	36,528	9.4%	9.1%	9.8%	4,658	55,845
Dayton, OH Metro Area...........................	84,582	27,039	25,631	22,724	9,188	39,263	11.1%	6.5%	11.5%	11,284	113,223
Decatur, AL Metro Area...........................	15,624	6,010	5,382	3,172	1,060	32,633	10.4%	9.8%	8.0%	1,823	21,318
Decatur, IL Metro Area............................	12,440	3,749	4,710	2,911	1,070	37,491	17.4%	6.1%	8.5%	1,197	16,554
Deltona-Daytona Beach-Ormond Beach, FL Metro Area	85,624	24,913	28,246	23,711	8,754	39,506	14.1%	7.6%	9.2%	9,930	111,991
Denver-Aurora-Lakewood, CO Metro Area	198,278	48,830	54,205	58,997	36,246	47,780	8.0%	6.2%	7.9%	23,684	305,005
Des Moines-West Des Moines, IA Metro Area	47,347	13,956	14,286	14,059	5,046	39,806	6.3%	5.5%	10.6%	6,623	67,021
Detroit-Warren-Dearborn, MI Metro Area	406,083	124,869	124,868	108,413	47,933	39,612	11.1%	9.3%	8.9%	84,106	547,792
Dothan, AL Metro Area............................	15,885	6,568	5,334	2,852	1,131	30,234	14.2%	9.4%	12.0%	2,161	21,552
Dover, DE Metro Area.............................	15,895	3,764	5,257	5,356	1,518	42,761	11.4%	7.5%	7.8%	2,072	20,488
DuBois, PA Micro Area............................	9,947	4,333	3,311	1,878	425	27,288	16.9%	8.5%	9.7%	2,326	12,149
Dubuque, IA Metro Area..........................	9,597	2,535	3,523	2,757	782	41,353	7.5%	2.0%	25.5%	947	12,889
Duluth, MN-WI Metro Area	30,770	9,521	10,332	8,240	2,677	37,383	12.0%	7.1%	6.9%	2,976	42,833
Dunn, NC Micro Area..............................	8,883	3,593	2,299	2,303	688	32,956	9.3%	15.2%	12.2%	1,977	11,394
Durham-Chapel Hill, NC Metro Area..........	43,911	11,662	11,744	10,878	9,627	47,146	11.6%	6.1%	11.4%	6,216	63,552
East Stroudsburg, PA Metro Area	12,922	3,030	5,051	3,642	1,199	38,424	7.7%	6.4%	6.8%	1,033	20,982
Eau Claire, WI Metro Area.......................	15,310	5,407	4,909	4,171	823	34,476	7.9%	4.6%	8.7%	2,252	20,402
El Centro, CA Metro Area........................	10,308	5,531	2,481	1,515	781	23,950	14.9%	19.1%	15.1%	1,889	15,282
El Paso, TX Metro Area...........................	52,864	22,961	15,600	10,315	3,988	28,889	16.6%	18.4%	23.2%	20,573	67,657
Elizabeth City, NC Micro Area..................	6,264	1,909	1,739	1,917	699	41,678	14.5%	10.0%	15.4%	1,381	7,761
Elizabethtown-Fort Knox, KY Metro Area	13,028	3,770	5,195	2,891	1,172	34,982	8.5%	6.8%	15.3%	1,953	16,050
Elkhart-Goshen, IN Metro Area	16,374	5,061	6,639	3,525	1,149	36,766	11.6%	2.1%	6.6%	1,552	23,219
Elmira, NY Metro Area	8,995	2,926	3,320	1,984	765	34,625	6.5%	11.5%	13.0%	1,019	12,908
Erie, PA Metro Area................................	27,024	9,723	9,045	5,709	2,547	34,258	11.2%	7.9%	9.6%	4,760	36,447
Eugene, OR Metro Area...........................	39,122	12,328	12,316	10,199	4,279	38,890	13.0%	7.1%	12.5%	9,164	50,540
Eureka-Arcata-Fortuna, CA Micro Area.......	12,469	3,368	4,155	3,248	1,698	42,566	18.9%	8.3%	4.2%	1,475	19,629
Evansville, IN-KY Metro Area...................	30,371	10,388	10,695	5,996	3,292	34,451	9.7%	4.6%	13.5%	3,902	43,120
Fairbanks, AK Metro Area........................	5,189	942	1,058	1,605	1,584	69,668	6.0%	4.1%	0.0%	472	8,274
Fargo, ND-MN Metro Area........................	16,843	4,917	6,405	3,965	1,556	35,386	7.5%	6.4%	8.5%	1,255	25,294
Faribault-Northfield, MN Micro Area	6,214	2,508	1,750	1,455	501	32,743	3.3%	5.1%	18.7%	156	8,846
Farmington, MO Micro Area......................	6,200	2,414	2,418	1,106	262	30,020	12.4%	11.8%	12.7%	1,176	9,340
Farmington, NM Metro Area	9,919	3,563	2,301	2,554	1,501	40,483	14.7%	10.4%	11.4%	1,918	13,267
Fayetteville, NC Metro Area.....................	24,426	8,348	7,336	6,099	2,643	35,734	12.4%	9.7%	12.3%	5,938	33,309
Fayetteville-Springdale-Rogers, AR-MO Metro Area	38,246	15,097	9,989	8,848	4,312	32,372	10.2%	8.2%	15.4%	3,419	55,499
Findlay, OH Micro Area............................	7,754	2,000	2,913	1,931	910	40,069	6.9%	14.5%	0.7%	633	10,391

Table G-4: Metropolitan/Micropolitan Statistical Areas—Income, Poverty Status and Receipt of Food Stamps (SNAP)—*Continued*

	Income of Households with Householder 65 Years and Over					Poverty Rate of Persons			Households with 1 or More Persons 60 Years and Over	
	Total Households	Less Than $25,000	$25,000 - $49,999	$50,000 - $99,999	$100,000 or More	Median Household Income	55 to 64 Years	65 to 74 Years	75 Years and Over	Receiving SNAP	Not Receiving SNAP
Flagstaff, AZ Metro Area	9,700	2,185	3,242	2,349	1,924	42,437	12.6%	8.8%	17.6%	1,644	14,623
Flint, MI Metro Area	42,588	12,465	15,168	11,955	3,000	37,890	13.6%	5.8%	9.4%	9,506	54,922
Florence, SC Metro Area	20,036	8,919	5,267	4,264	1,586	28,051	15.9%	12.5%	18.6%	4,854	27,997
Florence-Muscle Shoals, AL Metro Area	17,403	6,039	6,139	3,996	1,229	33,777	11.3%	8.3%	10.7%	2,627	22,642
Fond du Lac, WI Metro Area	10,414	3,282	3,930	2,339	863	35,868	8.4%	4.8%	7.5%	1,000	15,180
Forest City, NC Micro Area	8,116	3,498	3,026	1,097	495	29,615	17.9%	6.3%	8.2%	753	11,516
Fort Collins, CO Metro Area	27,063	7,269	7,880	8,078	3,836	42,247	7.4%	5.6%	6.8%	1,725	41,207
Fort Smith, AR-OK Metro Area	28,526	12,221	8,615	5,377	2,313	29,766	16.1%	9.5%	16.9%	3,884	37,441
Fort Wayne, IN Metro Area	36,659	11,138	12,075	10,058	3,388	36,045	8.9%	4.9%	8.2%	4,060	50,305
Frankfort, KY Micro Area	6,903	1,457	1,650	2,189	1,607	56,656	8.6%	4.0%	12.8%	429	9,905
Fresno, CA Metro Area	61,609	20,720	17,356	15,268	8,265	37,086	15.7%	14.3%	14.6%	11,666	92,035
Gadsden, AL Metro Area	11,562	4,931	3,078	2,792	761	32,024	12.9%	5.9%	14.9%	1,516	14,903
Gainesville, FL Metro Area	22,119	6,545	6,000	6,394	3,180	39,991	13.5%	10.1%	8.9%	2,987	31,728
Gainesville, GA Metro Area	15,730	4,360	3,906	4,929	2,535	47,573	10.0%	8.3%	11.6%	2,281	21,630
Gallup, NM Micro Area	4,880	2,514	901	965	500	23,918	33.7%	25.5%	25.8%	2,342	5,796
Gettysburg, PA Metro Area	10,910	2,593	3,370	3,341	1,606	45,969	7.5%	2.8%	6.0%	677	15,380
Glens Falls, NY Metro Area	13,564	3,823	4,122	3,536	2,083	42,826	11.9%	7.8%	5.1%	2,518	19,106
Glenwood Springs, CO Micro Area	5,544	1,325	1,384	1,492	1,343	53,133	7.4%	5.9%	12.5%	520	8,864
Goldsboro, NC Metro Area	11,015	4,041	3,581	2,294	1,099	31,994	14.6%	10.9%	14.0%	2,317	14,532
Grand Forks, ND-MN Metro Area	8,567	3,132	1,923	2,638	874	37,031	9.4%	4.1%	10.1%	874	11,992
Grand Island, NE Metro Area	8,353	3,003	2,473	2,163	714	36,233	6.3%	8.2%	18.4%	666	11,417
Grand Junction, CO Metro Area	15,207	4,006	5,518	3,952	1,731	35,413	11.8%	8.1%	6.7%	2,028	21,014
Grand Rapids-Wyoming, MI Metro Area	82,744	24,701	27,146	22,417	8,480	38,855	8.7%	6.6%	7.7%	10,799	116,386
Grants Pass, OR Metro Area	12,767	4,318	4,285	2,936	1,228	36,973	18.0%	7.3%	4.7%	2,672	15,673
Great Falls, MT Metro Area	9,011	3,341	2,808	2,247	615	35,155	11.0%	5.6%	8.7%	556	12,654
Greeley, CO Metro Area	19,316	5,740	5,113	5,665	2,798	44,771	8.5%	5.8%	5.5%	2,227	29,386
Green Bay, WI Metro Area	27,801	8,190	10,018	7,593	2,000	38,179	6.8%	7.2%	8.0%	2,907	39,467
Greeneville, TN Micro Area	7,564	2,950	2,537	1,664	413	31,987	17.7%	9.6%	11.5%	1,264	11,313
Greenfield Town, MA Micro Area	8,174	2,924	2,084	2,096	1,070	36,604	7.5%	4.5%	8.0%	1,888	11,449
Greensboro-High Point, NC Metro Area	70,530	26,250	22,147	15,910	6,223	34,353	10.1%	9.2%	8.3%	12,943	92,412
Greenville, NC Metro Area	12,463	3,985	3,517	3,335	1,626	36,331	14.1%	11.0%	8.4%	2,907	16,578
Greenville-Anderson-Mauldin, SC Metro Area	81,633	30,146	25,668	18,023	7,796	33,004	13.5%	7.0%	8.5%	10,452	110,311
Greenwood, SC Micro Area	10,887	4,323	3,635	1,951	978	33,805	14.1%	11.6%	10.0%	2,015	13,517
Gulfport-Biloxi-Pascagoula, MS Metro Area	35,579	10,101	12,046	9,620	3,812	39,622	13.8%	10.9%	9.0%	5,644	47,451
Hagerstown-Martinsburg, MD-WV Metro Area	22,841	8,085	6,378	6,560	1,818	38,064	10.1%	7.4%	7.2%	2,621	32,243
Hammond, LA Metro Area	9,280	4,330	2,695	1,829	426	27,034	12.5%	12.7%	21.5%	2,641	13,157
Hanford-Corcoran, CA Metro Area	7,781	2,503	2,214	2,200	864	38,911	23.0%	11.0%	13.1%	1,699	11,321
Harrisburg-Carlisle, PA Metro Area	56,876	16,299	16,299	16,729	7,549	40,924	7.1%	4.8%	5.5%	6,297	81,390
Harrisonburg, VA Metro Area	11,181	3,444	3,516	2,855	1,366	40,074	8.7%	7.9%	8.6%	1,114	15,217
Hartford-West Hartford-East Hartford, CT Metro Area ..	115,938	30,472	32,553	31,924	20,989	45,311	7.3%	6.8%	9.4%	19,999	156,815
Hattiesburg, MS Metro Area	11,282	4,112	3,239	2,718	1,213	31,127	23.8%	6.9%	7.3%	2,198	15,699
Helena, MT Micro Area	7,564	1,935	2,588	2,375	666	41,102	10.4%	2.8%	8.4%	1,370	11,507
Hermiston-Pendleton, OR Micro Area	7,109	2,780	2,203	1,435	691	30,810	5.5%	8.6%	6.1%	2,442	9,443
Hickory-Lenoir-Morganton, NC Metro Area	38,170	14,759	12,367	8,478	2,566	31,089	15.5%	11.0%	14.7%	6,857	49,442
Hilo, HI Micro Area	19,257	5,411	4,987	5,001	3,858	45,982	15.9%	12.4%	5.8%	4,479	27,216
Hilton Head Island-Bluffton-Beaufort, SC Metro Area ...	28,322	5,585	6,786	10,353	5,598	55,910	9.8%	4.9%	5.6%	1,597	36,253
Hinesville, GA Metro Area	3,679	2,040	770	746	123	21,993	11.3%	8.7%	17.9%	1,156	5,908
Hobbs, NM Micro Area	4,381	1,601	1,260	1,035	485	34,281	11.2%	9.7%	10.1%	597	6,241
Holland, MI Micro Area	10,476	3,187	3,659	2,596	1,034	37,086	9.9%	4.3%	14.5%	1,283	14,621
Homosassa Springs, FL Metro Area	29,294	10,192	10,513	6,181	2,408	33,951	21.1%	9.1%	12.0%	3,146	34,144
Hot Springs, AR Metro Area	13,006	4,009	4,398	3,071	1,528	37,088	16.2%	5.1%	8.9%	1,247	16,142
Houma-Thibodaux, LA Metro Area	15,862	5,797	4,354	4,075	1,636	34,494	14.1%	7.6%	9.5%	1,570	22,878
Houston-The Woodlands-Sugar Land, TX Metro Area ..	377,793	115,190	96,741	95,390	70,472	42,329	9.4%	9.6%	11.7%	68,614	591,197
Huntington-Ashland, WV-KY-OH Metro Area	41,916	15,451	14,577	9,181	2,707	33,164	13.2%	10.8%	8.5%	6,975	53,382
Huntsville, AL Metro Area	37,623	11,305	9,063	11,118	6,137	43,901	9.7%	12.2%	8.0%	4,119	54,170
Huntsville, TX Micro Area	7,210	2,713	1,993	1,681	823	33,969	11.4%	3.1%	6.5%	625	9,340
Hutchinson, KS Micro Area	7,134	2,276	2,079	2,373	406	38,439	9.1%	8.0%	9.6%	1,149	9,473
Idaho Falls, ID Metro Area	10,672	3,604	3,552	2,502	1,014	35,668	9.2%	7.4%	9.4%	1,008	15,339
Indiana, PA Micro Area	9,335	3,060	2,770	2,618	887	35,257	7.9%	4.4%	10.9%	867	12,679
Indianapolis-Carmel-Anderson, IN Metro Area	150,796	41,342	51,320	41,782	16,352	41,312	10.0%	5.3%	7.0%	22,235	214,385
Iowa City, IA Metro Area	11,302	2,940	2,363	3,721	2,278	52,339	9.4%	7.2%	7.4%	971	17,895
Ithaca, NY Metro Area	7,857	1,581	2,342	2,148	1,786	50,299	12.1%	3.5%	4.3%	1,081	11,702
Jackson, MI Metro Area	16,640	5,563	6,165	3,710	1,202	34,788	6.5%	7.3%	5.6%	2,460	22,347
Jackson, MS Metro Area	46,494	17,699	12,731	10,600	5,464	33,936	14.3%	11.1%	15.1%	8,379	63,046
Jackson, TN Metro Area	12,029	4,640	3,166	2,978	1,245	32,245	14.3%	7.9%	10.7%	2,043	16,557
Jacksonville, FL Metro Area	122,887	33,335	39,133	32,921	17,498	41,377	12.8%	8.9%	9.4%	20,224	172,425
Jacksonville, NC Metro Area	9,938	2,968	2,671	3,246	1,053	43,723	15.4%	6.0%	8.1%	1,727	13,760
Jamestown-Dunkirk-Fredonia, NY Micro Area	14,768	5,179	4,941	3,313	1,335	36,538	13.2%	10.3%	8.8%	2,616	18,757
Janesville-Beloit, WI Metro Area	15,033	3,693	6,089	3,982	1,269	40,099	10.2%	4.7%	9.6%	2,026	20,487
Jefferson City, MO Metro Area	13,240	3,821	3,922	4,206	1,291	37,656	7.2%	7.9%	5.8%	1,160	19,673
Johnson City, TN Metro Area	23,000	8,074	7,857	5,164	1,905	33,844	11.7%	8.3%	10.7%	4,159	31,116
Johnstown, PA Metro Area	18,477	7,439	6,525	3,274	1,239	30,437	8.9%	5.6%	11.5%	2,281	23,885
Jonesboro, AR Metro Area	10,678	3,702	3,162	2,709	1,105	36,436	7.7%	9.0%	6.5%	1,843	14,333
Joplin, MO Metro Area	16,199	5,647	5,579	3,733	1,240	32,634	11.8%	8.2%	14.9%	2,766	21,853

Table G-4: Metropolitan/Micropolitan Statistical Areas—Income, Poverty Status and Receipt of Food Stamps (SNAP)—Continued

	Income of Households with Householder 65 Years and Over					Poverty Rate of Persons			Households with 1 or More Persons 60 Years and Over	
	Total Households	Less Than $25,000	$25,000 - $49,999	$50,000 - $99,999	$100,000 or More	Median Household Income	55 to 64 Years	65 to 74 Years	75 Years and Over	Receiving SNAP	Not Receiving SNAP
Kahului-Wailuku-Lahaina, HI Metro Area	13,616	2,772	3,017	4,245	3,582	61,960	14.4%	6.9%	14.7%	1,949	22,106
Kalamazoo-Portage, MI Metro Area	28,592	8,041	9,310	8,043	3,198	38,974	10.3%	8.0%	6.3%	4,925	40,501
Kalispell, MT Micro Area	9,898	2,920	3,492	2,739	747	38,979	13.3%	10.7%	8.5%	531	14,723
Kankakee, IL Metro Area	9,376	2,973	2,765	2,452	1,186	42,124	9.0%	9.9%	12.3%	2,420	12,369
Kansas City, MO-KS Metro Area	172,768	50,781	51,909	47,537	22,541	40,460	8.9%	7.3%	8.2%	19,046	249,456
Kapaa, HI Micro Area	6,749	1,858	1,762	1,670	1,459	45,158	18.5%	8.2%	9.6%	825	10,487
Keene, NH Micro Area	8,186	2,437	2,887	1,900	962	37,494	8.5%	8.4%	13.2%	1,077	11,443
Kennewick-Richland, WA Metro Area	19,078	5,494	4,955	5,447	3,182	45,012	10.4%	4.9%	13.7%	4,179	27,633
Key West, FL Micro Area	8,836	2,554	1,961	2,551	1,770	48,415	16.9%	11.6%	13.9%	682	12,696
Killeen-Temple, TX Metro Area	25,887	7,934	7,903	6,827	3,223	40,662	9.0%	6.1%	7.4%	3,219	37,963
Kingsport-Bristol-Bristol, TN-VA Metro Area	40,278	15,542	13,317	8,066	3,353	31,676	10.8%	9.0%	13.0%	7,341	49,401
Kingston, NY Metro Area	21,122	6,950	5,805	5,061	3,306	38,553	9.3%	10.8%	10.0%	3,390	27,357
Klamath Falls, OR Micro Area	8,131	3,044	3,086	1,452	549	33,123	14.9%	3.4%	9.4%	1,807	9,824
Knoxville, TN Metro Area	89,830	32,371	28,062	19,683	9,714	34,579	11.8%	9.6%	9.2%	15,489	121,394
Kokomo, IN Metro Area	9,929	2,951	3,070	3,012	896	39,221	15.3%	9.0%	3.6%	865	13,324
La Crosse-Onalaska, WI-MN Metro Area	12,824	3,333	4,480	3,624	1,387	40,290	4.5%	2.8%	10.3%	1,457	17,903
Lafayette, LA Metro Area	38,161	14,886	11,197	7,800	4,278	33,071	13.1%	11.7%	11.6%	8,315	49,919
Lafayette-West Lafayette, IN Metro Area	14,598	4,055	4,288	4,189	2,066	43,668	11.0%	4.1%	5.4%	1,529	21,023
LaGrange, GA Micro Area	6,242	2,795	1,700	1,152	595	27,315	22.8%	11.1%	14.4%	1,669	7,809
Lake Charles, LA Metro Area	17,517	6,313	4,598	4,068	2,538	33,160	13.0%	11.7%	10.6%	4,494	23,133
Lake City, FL Micro Area	7,095	2,925	1,725	1,954	491	33,242	10.6%	15.5%	15.8%	1,191	9,046
Lake Havasu City-Kingman, AZ Metro Area	32,387	10,834	11,898	7,832	1,823	34,866	19.8%	9.4%	7.2%	4,406	41,309
Lakeland-Winter Haven, FL Metro Area	74,155	25,323	23,661	17,873	7,298	35,185	14.8%	8.8%	13.8%	11,173	93,407
Lancaster, PA Metro Area	50,614	14,812	16,755	13,446	5,601	38,747	5.5%	6.0%	8.8%	5,461	70,628
Lansing-East Lansing, MI Metro Area	39,625	10,011	14,097	10,458	5,059	41,472	8.0%	6.6%	6.3%	6,639	55,346
Laredo, TX Metro Area	12,074	6,258	2,872	1,971	973	23,336	25.2%	26.8%	33.9%	7,501	14,892
Las Cruces, NM Metro Area	17,799	5,259	5,457	4,290	2,793	44,600	16.7%	14.2%	13.2%	3,186	24,209
Las Vegas-Henderson-Paradise, NV Metro Area	156,767	48,238	45,099	43,251	20,179	40,332	12.1%	8.4%	9.2%	28,055	229,394
Laurel, MS Micro Area	8,738	3,526	3,325	1,546	341	29,692	17.7%	11.9%	11.4%	945	12,034
Lawrence, KS Metro Area	7,496	1,751	2,044	2,334	1,367	48,433	7.6%	3.4%	8.8%	681	11,544
Lawton, OK Metro Area	9,147	2,973	2,930	2,206	1,038	37,574	10.1%	9.4%	13.2%	1,362	12,795
Lebanon, PA Metro Area	14,125	3,850	5,019	4,441	815	41,268	6.3%	7.1%	4.1%	2,123	19,623
Lewiston, ID-WA Metro Area	8,152	2,997	2,339	1,879	937	31,481	11.2%	10.9%	8.2%	1,618	9,493
Lewiston-Auburn, ME Metro Area	11,311	4,159	3,991	2,523	638	34,263	11.6%	9.6%	11.2%	2,546	14,246
Lexington-Fayette, KY Metro Area	39,175	11,686	11,699	10,343	5,447	40,014	12.6%	7.3%	8.1%	6,049	56,425
Lima, OH Metro Area	10,595	4,081	3,232	2,784	498	33,109	13.3%	6.7%	10.9%	1,783	14,190
Lincoln, NE Metro Area	25,476	6,274	8,494	7,984	2,724	43,531	5.7%	3.2%	5.8%	1,465	36,606
Little Rock-North Little Rock-Conway, AR Metro Area	60,596	17,872	17,870	16,926	7,928	42,125	10.5%	5.4%	6.4%	7,001	87,360
Logan, UT-ID Metro Area	7,340	1,590	2,173	2,732	845	47,300	5.2%	5.3%	7.1%	408	11,058
London, KY Micro Area	12,112	5,641	3,561	2,512	398	27,067	25.0%	19.5%	14.2%	3,510	14,800
Longview, TX Metro Area	19,425	7,164	4,883	5,269	2,109	36,437	10.3%	9.2%	9.0%	2,857	26,927
Longview, WA Metro Area	11,975	3,577	4,276	3,226	896	38,341	13.4%	9.6%	13.2%	2,206	15,393
Los Angeles-Long Beach-Anaheim, CA Metro Area	910,270	283,443	208,289	223,543	194,995	44,396	12.8%	11.4%	14.2%	87,025	1,459,521
Louisville/Jefferson County, KY-IN Metro Area	115,701	36,884	37,525	28,460	12,832	38,699	11.3%	8.0%	9.4%	17,108	159,044
Lubbock, TX Metro Area	24,877	7,668	7,169	7,041	2,999	41,008	10.6%	8.7%	11.5%	3,271	31,518
Lufkin, TX Micro Area	7,889	2,866	2,847	1,903	273	32,015	10.7%	6.1%	13.9%	1,091	9,816
Lumberton, NC Micro Area	11,080	5,642	3,261	1,689	488	24,536	20.8%	19.3%	17.5%	3,730	13,475
Lynchburg, VA Metro Area	28,161	9,998	8,241	7,077	2,845	35,081	8.9%	5.9%	10.1%	3,671	37,736
Macon, GA Metro Area	20,490	7,477	6,563	4,355	2,095	33,148	14.8%	15.9%	11.2%	4,234	28,566
Madera, CA Metro Area	10,815	3,632	2,167	3,374	1,642	41,847	15.6%	10.1%	13.7%	1,516	14,990
Madison, WI Metro Area	50,608	13,123	14,616	15,291	7,578	44,409	6.8%	3.8%	9.2%	6,528	74,536
Manchester-Nashua, NH Metro Area	31,803	8,362	9,576	8,888	4,977	44,838	4.5%	4.4%	7.5%	3,472	50,118
Manhattan, KS Metro Area	5,683	1,400	853	1,903	1,527	58,724	9.7%	5.9%	2.5%	731	7,450
Manitowoc, WI Micro Area	9,744	3,367	4,140	1,799	438	31,535	8.6%	2.5%	11.3%	859	12,564
Mankato-North Mankato, MN Metro Area	7,626	2,391	2,515	1,944	776	35,512	6.9%	8.3%	7.3%	472	11,076
Mansfield, OH Metro Area	15,369	5,842	5,905	2,843	779	29,978	10.5%	9.3%	8.9%	2,566	19,027
Marinette, WI-MI Micro Area	8,992	3,863	2,997	1,801	331	28,066	12.2%	6.7%	19.2%	1,399	11,833
Marion, IN Micro Area	8,091	3,109	3,225	1,376	381	30,319	9.8%	12.0%	13.2%	937	11,015
Marion, OH Micro Area	7,518	2,158	2,617	1,961	782	36,126	14.3%	11.4%	8.6%	1,355	8,980
Marquette, MI Micro Area	6,904	2,533	2,116	1,768	487	38,868	10.7%	8.8%	9.7%	1,342	9,656
Marshall, TX Micro Area	7,012	3,197	1,729	1,541	545	33,399	26.4%	11.2%	25.8%	643	9,118
Martinsville, VA Micro Area	9,167	4,205	3,006	1,327	629	26,483	14.1%	7.8%	8.5%	1,963	11,951
McAllen-Edinburg-Mission, TX Metro Area	44,905	22,140	11,044	9,085	2,636	25,410	20.4%	24.0%	24.7%	21,227	52,945
Meadville, PA Micro Area	10,082	3,261	3,995	2,194	632	35,332	8.9%	7.2%	3.2%	1,432	14,296
Medford, OR Metro Area	26,718	7,924	8,652	7,103	3,039	38,703	14.0%	7.4%	7.4%	4,983	35,121
Memphis, TN-MS-AR Metro Area	100,887	34,376	29,826	24,251	12,434	36,932	13.3%	9.5%	12.5%	27,855	140,249
Merced, CA Metro Area	16,007	5,801	4,016	4,445	1,745	34,363	11.9%	8.7%	13.1%	2,755	22,549
Meridian, MS Micro Area	10,037	4,911	2,302	2,122	702	25,604	13.9%	17.8%	19.8%	2,038	13,708
Miami-Fort Lauderdale-West Palm Beach, FL Metro Area	567,027	216,995	140,858	125,641	83,533	34,488	15.3%	13.8%	15.9%	163,529	705,646
Michigan City-La Porte, IN Metro Area	11,239	3,327	3,877	2,991	1,044	37,243	7.1%	9.1%	6.0%	1,280	15,651
Midland, MI Micro Area	8,858	2,443	3,413	2,310	692	37,344	7.6%	7.1%	8.5%	811	11,746
Midland, TX Metro Area	9,395	3,065	2,325	1,834	2,171	43,996	8.6%	5.5%	6.3%	427	16,327
Milwaukee-Waukesha-West Allis, WI Metro Area	138,369	43,332	42,091	35,745	17,201	38,170	10.1%	7.3%	8.8%	22,849	194,324
Minneapolis-St. Paul-Bloomington, MN-WI Metro Area	267,566	73,417	76,030	79,694	38,425	43,768	7.8%	5.5%	8.1%	31,167	391,890

Table G-4: Metropolitan/Micropolitan Statistical Areas—Income, Poverty Status and Receipt of Food Stamps (SNAP)—Continued

	Income of Households with Householder 65 Years and Over					Poverty Rate of Persons			Households with 1 or More Persons 60 Years and Over	
	Total Households	Less Than $25,000	$25,000 - $49,999	$50,000 - $99,999	$100,000 or More	Median Household Income	55 to 64 Years	65 to 74 Years	75 Years and Over	Receiving SNAP	Not Receiving SNAP
Minot, ND Micro Area	5,950	1,538	1,967	1,381	1,064	41,667	5.9%	4.4%	7.3%	255	8,421
Missoula, MT Metro Area	10,170	3,080	3,233	1,877	1,980	38,121	8.8%	7.5%	8.0%	1,834	13,156
Mobile, AL Metro Area	37,513	13,698	11,285	8,705	3,825	35,086	13.5%	10.6%	12.8%	7,306	49,854
Modesto, CA Metro Area	37,075	11,805	10,065	10,260	4,945	41,335	13.8%	8.5%	14.1%	5,711	54,265
Monroe, LA Metro Area	15,804	6,242	4,034	4,017	1,511	34,000	11.4%	11.8%	14.3%	2,095	22,881
Monroe, MI Metro Area	13,962	3,635	5,207	4,133	987	36,305	8.0%	4.2%	3.0%	1,845	20,160
Montgomery, AL Metro Area	32,901	11,142	8,974	8,789	3,996	35,862	11.4%	8.7%	10.0%	6,137	43,470
Morehead City, NC Micro Area	9,697	2,966	2,403	3,056	1,272	44,144	10.0%	6.1%	8.4%	1,091	12,637
Morgantown, WV Metro Area	10,484	3,346	3,473	2,610	1,055	38,530	10.6%	6.2%	10.7%	1,591	15,321
Morristown, TN Metro Area	12,957	4,883	3,784	3,240	1,050	32,990	16.7%	10.7%	8.3%	2,151	17,102
Moses Lake, WA Micro Area	7,129	2,374	2,362	1,661	732	33,937	7.9%	10.0%	15.1%	1,690	10,067
Mount Airy, NC Micro Area	8,171	3,597	2,470	1,708	396	28,804	22.7%	13.4%	13.2%	1,961	10,026
Mount Pleasant, MI Micro Area	4,940	1,500	1,613	1,252	575	38,154	11.4%	7.1%	6.9%	859	6,764
Mount Vernon-Anacortes, WA Metro Area	13,628	3,937	3,601	4,151	1,939	44,839	12.6%	6.1%	9.2%	2,084	18,314
Muncie, IN Metro Area	11,571	3,120	4,021	3,054	1,376	39,118	9.7%	6.8%	11.7%	671	15,418
Muskegon, MI Metro Area	17,066	5,283	6,350	3,937	1,496	36,777	13.8%	7.2%	8.5%	4,014	20,636
Muskogee, OK Micro Area	6,952	2,428	2,021	1,942	561	36,326	10.9%	6.8%	9.5%	1,045	8,914
Myrtle Beach-Conway-North Myrtle Beach, SC-NC Metro Area	57,080	14,959	19,983	16,555	5,583	42,222	11.7%	7.5%	7.4%	6,677	76,947
Nacogdoches, TX Micro Area	5,704	2,517	1,462	1,267	458	34,799	11.5%	10.4%	8.0%	906	7,785
Napa, CA Metro Area	14,395	3,325	2,987	4,466	3,617	58,662	7.6%	6.0%	8.9%	673	22,685
Naples-Immokalee-Marco Island, FL Metro Area	59,575	10,497	15,879	16,301	16,898	57,191	10.0%	4.5%	7.6%	3,799	74,536
Nashville-Davidson–Murfreesboro–Franklin, TN Metro Area	132,276	41,232	37,099	36,598	17,347	40,157	10.8%	6.8%	10.8%	21,227	191,132
New Bern, NC Metro Area	15,137	4,974	5,020	4,131	1,012	36,988	13.4%	6.6%	8.7%	2,487	18,907
New Castle, PA Micro Area	11,449	4,502	3,787	2,253	907	30,291	12.6%	6.1%	7.7%	2,272	13,953
New Haven-Milford, CT Metro Area	82,837	26,235	23,032	21,411	12,159	39,820	9.0%	7.4%	9.9%	16,014	110,246
New Orleans-Metairie, LA Metro Area	107,714	39,106	30,213	22,701	15,694	36,174	15.6%	11.8%	13.3%	19,205	150,459
New Philadelphia-Dover, OH Micro Area	10,625	4,096	3,377	2,664	488	32,825	13.0%	10.0%	4.5%	1,885	13,681
New York-Newark-Jersey City, NY-NJ-PA Metro Area	1,691,688	554,306	377,593	412,834	346,955	42,963	11.2%	10.7%	14.0%	406,239	2,304,871
Niles-Benton Harbor, MI Metro Area	17,528	5,569	5,726	4,408	1,825	38,680	12.8%	6.8%	9.1%	2,335	24,367
North Port-Sarasota-Bradenton, FL Metro Area	136,689	35,239	38,601	39,633	23,216	45,535	10.4%	7.1%	6.2%	8,993	171,674
North Wilkesboro, NC Micro Area	8,517	4,536	2,390	1,290	301	22,074	22.5%	20.5%	24.0%	1,611	10,685
Norwich-New London, CT Metro Area	26,286	6,002	6,659	8,763	4,862	51,729	8.2%	5.8%	7.1%	4,143	36,115
Oak Harbor, WA Micro Area	10,375	2,311	2,752	3,348	1,964	52,358	7.4%	2.2%	7.6%	1,203	13,852
Ocala, FL Metro Area	57,018	16,057	22,046	14,581	4,334	36,542	15.9%	7.5%	9.2%	7,474	67,781
Ocean City, NJ Metro Area	14,468	4,398	3,812	3,622	2,636	41,250	8.2%	10.0%	10.4%	1,088	20,200
Odessa, TX Metro Area	9,158	3,765	1,966	1,818	1,609	32,297	5.3%	11.9%	16.9%	1,918	12,978
Ogden-Clearfield, UT Metro Area	37,737	9,824	10,055	12,858	5,000	45,727	5.5%	6.7%	6.7%	3,707	58,552
Ogdensburg-Massena, NY Micro Area	9,894	3,559	3,108	2,734	493	30,000	9.0%	12.9%	5.9%	2,137	13,982
Oklahoma City, OK Metro Area	105,072	28,401	31,480	30,181	15,010	41,875	11.9%	5.4%	7.1%	12,821	151,208
Olean, NY Micro Area	8,548	3,463	2,528	1,739	818	31,408	11.1%	8.4%	13.4%	1,812	11,612
Olympia-Tumwater, WA Metro Area	24,728	6,056	7,434	7,311	3,927	45,611	7.7%	6.8%	14.7%	3,707	35,316
Omaha-Council Bluffs, NE-IA Metro Area	71,113	21,787	20,347	19,839	9,140	40,430	8.4%	4.7%	9.5%	7,822	102,711
Opelousas, LA Micro Area	7,856	4,683	1,980	671	522	22,766	25.3%	23.5%	16.0%	1,436	10,740
Orangeburg, SC Micro Area	9,240	4,319	2,645	1,468	808	28,585	25.3%	21.2%	16.0%	2,674	11,690
Orlando-Kissimmee-Sanford, FL Metro Area	174,137	57,334	50,201	44,573	22,029	38,440	12.0%	9.4%	11.3%	35,203	245,933
Oshkosh-Neenah, WI Metro Area	16,060	5,846	4,737	4,450	1,027	33,570	5.3%	4.1%	10.1%	1,839	22,368
Ottawa-Peru, IL Micro Area	17,048	5,270	5,704	4,415	1,659	38,064	10.5%	5.9%	10.1%	1,822	23,702
Owensboro, KY Metro Area	12,013	4,228	4,173	2,976	636	34,816	8.2%	10.4%	6.6%	1,393	16,307
Owosso, MI Micro Area	6,935	2,087	2,491	1,765	592	35,993	9.5%	7.3%	10.2%	741	9,913
Oxnard-Thousand Oaks-Ventura, CA Metro Area	68,153	15,804	16,722	20,044	15,583	53,139	7.2%	7.1%	10.5%	4,510	102,875
Paducah, KY-IL Micro Area	10,957	4,313	3,881	1,741	1,022	29,985	16.7%	10.0%	12.6%	1,730	15,127
Palatka, FL Micro Area	10,067	4,430	3,339	1,479	819	29,331	17.6%	10.9%	17.6%	1,993	11,973
Palm Bay-Melbourne-Titusville, FL Metro Area	76,243	20,911	25,224	22,031	8,077	41,247	11.8%	9.3%	5.8%	8,375	100,024
Panama City, FL Metro Area	18,635	5,574	5,869	4,714	2,478	37,449	14.1%	9.3%	12.4%	2,900	25,411
Parkersburg-Vienna, WV Metro Area	11,881	4,560	4,030	2,527	764	33,080	8.6%	8.2%	9.5%	1,126	15,385
Pensacola-Ferry Pass-Brent, FL Metro Area	44,926	11,577	14,607	14,036	4,706	42,957	9.4%	6.3%	6.3%	6,757	61,114
Peoria, IL Metro Area	38,761	11,547	11,213	11,424	4,577	43,267	8.0%	6.4%	7.9%	3,773	53,502
Philadelphia-Camden-Wilmington, PA-NJ-DE-MD Metro Area	542,821	166,512	144,345	140,643	91,321	41,946	10.2%	8.2%	9.8%	92,362	748,030
Phoenix-Mesa-Scottsdale, AZ Metro Area	378,994	105,151	113,828	106,973	53,042	42,269	12.5%	8.6%	8.7%	47,039	528,777
Pine Bluff, AR Metro Area	9,236	3,715	2,910	1,775	836	30,031	15.6%	7.0%	11.4%	1,529	12,007
Pinehurst-Southern Pines, NC Micro Area	13,871	3,717	3,423	4,316	2,415	48,255	13.3%	7.9%	6.3%	1,584	15,898
Pittsburgh, PA Metro Area	281,313	99,147	88,609	64,952	28,605	34,795	8.5%	6.9%	8.9%	39,742	372,165
Pittsfield, MA Metro Area	17,764	5,692	4,500	4,360	3,212	41,554	7.9%	6.4%	8.1%	2,718	22,505
Plattsburgh, NY Micro Area	7,776	2,615	1,950	2,404	807	36,237	11.5%	6.5%	8.3%	1,848	10,092
Pocatello, ID Metro Area	6,874	2,439	2,315	1,261	859	33,260	8.5%	7.1%	3.6%	513	10,573
Port Angeles, WA Micro Area	12,052	2,938	3,665	4,051	1,398	42,239	10.6%	5.7%	7.1%	999	16,268
Port St. Lucie, FL Metro Area	67,256	19,320	20,798	18,677	8,461	40,403	11.5%	5.9%	7.2%	6,882	85,113
Portland-South Portland, ME Metro Area	56,005	16,990	15,842	15,176	7,997	40,297	7.2%	7.1%	7.7%	7,429	79,399
Portland-Vancouver-Hillsboro, OR-WA Metro Area	190,816	54,111	54,771	53,864	28,064	42,954	10.1%	7.7%	9.3%	41,519	270,660
Portsmouth, OH Micro Area	7,877	3,421	2,083	1,548	825	30,137	16.9%	9.0%	14.9%	1,980	9,994
Pottsville, PA Micro Area	17,799	7,664	5,826	3,336	973	30,076	10.5%	4.3%	15.9%	2,948	23,697
Prescott, AZ Metro Area	38,908	12,118	13,657	10,081	3,052	36,586	14.6%	6.6%	11.3%	4,245	49,477

Table G-4: Metropolitan/Micropolitan Statistical Areas—Income, Poverty Status and Receipt of Food Stamps (SNAP)—*Continued*

	Income of Households with Householder 65 Years and Over					Poverty Rate of Persons			Households with 1 or More Persons 60 Years and Over	
	Total Households	Less Than $25,000	$25,000 - $49,999	$50,000 - $99,999	$100,000 or More	Median Household Income	55 to 64 Years	65 to 74 Years	75 Years and Over	Receiving SNAP	Not Receiving SNAP
Providence-Warwick, RI-MA Metro Area	155,267	55,269	42,749	35,047	22,202	36,646	10.2%	8.1%	12.8%	36,595	206,689
Provo-Orem, UT Metro Area	22,346	4,719	6,156	7,414	4,057	51,265	7.4%	4.7%	4.9%	2,475	34,639
Pueblo, CO Metro Area	17,236	6,445	5,801	3,794	1,196	33,119	14.0%	10.4%	12.0%	2,576	24,380
Punta Gorda, FL Metro Area	38,266	11,041	12,239	10,154	4,832	39,421	11.0%	5.7%	8.1%	2,497	46,773
Quincy, IL-MO Micro Area	9,020	3,189	3,054	2,149	628	32,038	9.3%	5.2%	10.7%	963	11,929
Racine, WI Metro Area	19,041	6,112	6,664	4,756	1,509	33,663	13.4%	9.8%	5.7%	3,680	25,711
Raleigh, NC Metro Area	79,654	20,306	22,520	22,578	14,250	46,827	8.7%	5.8%	9.4%	9,896	119,829
Rapid City, SD Metro Area	13,423	4,368	4,846	2,970	1,239	36,319	8.6%	8.6%	6.3%	1,241	19,742
Reading, PA Metro Area	40,172	12,872	12,313	10,251	4,736	37,652	7.2%	7.8%	7.9%	6,096	55,053
Redding, CA Metro Area	21,110	6,670	6,023	6,423	1,994	40,627	13.6%	5.8%	8.3%	1,529	30,020
Reno, NV Metro Area	41,425	13,423	11,183	11,212	5,607	41,763	12.8%	8.1%	6.8%	5,210	58,873
Richmond, IN Micro Area	7,721	2,689	2,186	2,295	551	37,293	14.2%	6.2%	13.3%	852	10,073
Richmond, VA Metro Area	107,795	27,465	29,661	31,487	19,182	46,707	7.1%	5.0%	8.7%	12,480	159,383
Richmond-Berea, KY Micro Area	8,709	4,023	2,110	1,796	780	30,885	16.6%	10.5%	6.0%	1,714	11,940
Riverside-San Bernardino-Ontario, CA Metro Area	288,442	89,415	80,079	73,973	44,975	40,183	13.4%	10.4%	11.6%	43,205	437,788
Roanoke Rapids, NC Micro Area	9,066	4,804	2,355	1,551	356	22,356	21.3%	13.5%	15.1%	2,394	10,712
Roanoke, VA Metro Area	36,891	11,225	11,234	10,683	3,749	39,798	8.5%	5.9%	9.8%	3,731	51,633
Rochester, MN Metro Area	19,359	4,796	4,894	6,643	3,026	49,902	4.2%	4.3%	7.7%	989	27,810
Rochester, NY Metro Area	110,552	32,406	40,861	26,604	10,681	35,876	9.7%	5.0%	8.0%	19,053	148,105
Rockford, IL Metro Area	33,441	12,213	11,280	7,176	2,772	32,946	11.6%	5.1%	11.5%	4,935	46,304
Rocky Mount, NC Metro Area	16,555	7,981	4,530	3,494	550	26,744	14.5%	7.0%	18.1%	3,878	22,132
Rome, GA Metro Area	9,055	3,116	3,287	1,714	938	36,414	12.6%	10.8%	12.7%	1,173	12,123
Roseburg, OR Micro Area	15,674	5,376	4,817	4,311	1,170	37,550	11.0%	10.5%	6.6%	2,718	20,121
Roswell, NM Micro Area	6,495	2,852	1,809	1,355	479	27,828	9.9%	15.8%	21.0%	1,397	8,711
Russellville, AR Micro Area	7,902	3,561	2,299	1,795	247	27,886	15.3%	12.0%	7.4%	1,078	9,939
Sacramento–Roseville–Arden-Arcade, CA Metro Area	185,384	48,003	48,666	54,706	34,009	47,167	12.2%	8.1%	10.6%	18,200	281,301
Saginaw, MI Micro Area	21,226	5,935	7,984	5,601	1,706	40,449	8.9%	4.4%	9.7%	4,391	26,752
Salem, OH Micro Area	12,009	4,571	3,689	2,750	999	32,450	12.9%	8.1%	10.9%	2,885	15,536
Salem, OR Metro Area	38,294	12,244	9,827	11,200	5,023	39,918	7.9%	7.4%	11.7%	8,717	50,248
Salinas, CA Metro Area	30,238	6,899	7,569	8,046	7,724	54,108	8.2%	8.4%	11.5%	1,860	46,360
Salisbury, MD-DE Metro Area	49,882	12,005	14,359	15,632	7,886	46,379	11.2%	5.5%	9.2%	6,070	66,281
Salt Lake City, UT Metro Area	67,200	16,439	19,436	20,090	11,235	46,302	8.0%	4.7%	10.2%	7,647	105,132
San Angelo, TX Metro Area	10,610	4,177	3,048	2,336	1,049	34,058	11.8%	12.1%	12.0%	1,621	14,672
San Antonio-New Braunfels, TX Metro Area	166,825	49,727	46,164	43,674	27,260	42,334	12.9%	9.2%	10.8%	29,225	237,929
San Diego-Carlsbad, CA Metro Area	234,218	63,502	56,850	63,418	50,448	48,504	10.6%	9.1%	9.9%	22,720	366,722
San Francisco-Oakland-Hayward, CA Metro Area	374,843	94,661	82,203	95,812	102,167	54,029	9.6%	7.3%	10.4%	28,162	593,330
San Jose-Sunnyvale-Santa Clara, CA Metro Area	127,012	30,767	29,290	33,610	33,345	53,400	7.7%	8.6%	10.1%	11,233	209,162
San Luis Obispo-Paso Robles-Arroyo Grande, CA Metro Area	29,273	6,480	7,880	7,925	6,988	51,292	7.3%	8.2%	2.9%	1,755	43,217
Sandusky, OH Micro Area	9,653	2,503	3,948	2,335	867	37,938	7.5%	10.2%	3.0%	1,197	12,299
Santa Cruz-Watsonville, CA Metro Area	22,945	5,531	5,571	6,512	5,331	51,380	12.4%	6.5%	9.0%	2,494	36,307
Santa Fe, NM Metro Area	18,581	5,319	4,546	4,530	4,186	48,046	12.2%	5.4%	8.0%	1,189	27,469
Santa Maria-Santa Barbara, CA Metro Area	37,459	9,749	8,905	9,422	9,383	50,173	10.6%	5.6%	7.4%	2,257	54,795
Santa Rosa, CA Metro Area	51,802	12,613	11,844	16,593	10,752	54,320	9.4%	7.3%	8.7%	3,910	78,559
Savannah, GA Metro Area	28,809	8,608	8,003	7,172	5,026	39,718	7.5%	5.8%	9.9%	5,651	39,283
Scranton–Wilkes-Barre–Hazleton, PA Metro Area	64,628	24,441	22,565	13,280	4,342	32,230	12.6%	6.9%	10.8%	12,568	84,786
Searcy, AR Micro Area	7,197	3,344	2,151	1,041	661	26,860	17.9%	15.7%	12.4%	1,681	9,436
Seattle-Tacoma-Bellevue, WA Metro Area	272,064	69,727	74,555	76,412	51,370	47,260	8.9%	8.0%	9.8%	54,509	393,872
Sebastian-Vero Beach, FL Metro Area	26,256	7,298	7,725	6,893	4,340	41,981	9.4%	9.2%	8.2%	2,555	32,498
Sebring, FL Metro Area	19,624	6,427	6,399	5,398	1,400	36,280	15.2%	9.2%	10.1%	1,874	21,877
Seneca, SC Micro Area	9,788	3,718	2,483	2,384	1,203	34,251	15.0%	4.5%	8.0%	1,273	14,195
Sevierville, TN Micro Area	10,950	3,871	3,111	2,830	1,138	36,347	17.5%	6.8%	7.2%	1,951	13,613
Shawnee, OK Micro Area	6,475	1,790	2,153	1,994	538	38,763	11.4%	6.4%	8.8%	1,243	8,821
Sheboygan, WI Metro Area	11,782	3,940	4,147	2,548	1,147	35,025	5.4%	1.2%	8.0%	1,042	15,995
Shelby, NC Micro Area	11,438	4,874	3,197	2,853	514	29,814	18.4%	9.1%	14.1%	2,455	14,209
Sherman-Denison, TX Metro Area	12,404	4,782	3,700	2,905	1,017	36,953	14.2%	7.6%	9.1%	1,950	18,355
Show Low, AZ Micro Area	10,706	4,895	2,670	2,656	485	28,168	26.0%	18.3%	15.9%	3,031	12,075
Shreveport-Bossier City, LA Metro Area	40,247	14,555	12,868	8,434	4,390	34,551	19.6%	10.2%	10.9%	6,353	55,641
Sierra Vista-Douglas, AZ Metro Area	15,100	6,025	4,473	3,389	1,213	30,976	18.1%	14.9%	12.2%	2,599	19,974
Sioux City, IA-NE-SD Metro Area	15,558	5,390	5,675	3,115	1,378	32,647	7.0%	6.1%	11.6%	2,141	21,260
Sioux Falls, SD Metro Area	18,872	5,483	6,520	4,514	2,355	39,423	7.9%	9.9%	9.1%	2,306	26,209
Somerset, PA Micro Area	9,658	4,000	3,641	1,547	470	28,796	10.3%	6.7%	11.1%	1,331	12,542
South Bend-Mishawaka, IN-MI Metro Area	30,275	10,246	10,425	7,196	2,408	35,580	11.2%	4.4%	9.7%	3,806	42,390
Spartanburg, SC Metro Area	31,274	10,580	10,536	7,938	2,220	35,378	14.2%	8.7%	10.7%	5,183	41,649
Spokane-Spokane Valley, WA Metro Area	52,153	15,402	16,295	14,687	5,769	39,978	12.4%	8.6%	10.1%	10,949	67,140
Springfield, IL Metro Area	21,883	6,461	5,382	6,859	3,181	45,546	10.1%	5.8%	6.2%	2,302	30,846
Springfield, MA Metro Area	60,219	20,066	18,200	15,070	6,883	36,043	14.3%	10.5%	9.9%	14,570	78,862
Springfield, MO Metro Area	44,305	17,236	13,462	9,814	3,793	32,216	12.0%	4.7%	12.7%	4,291	59,021
Springfield, OH Metro Area	15,290	5,209	5,681	3,081	1,319	35,707	16.2%	6.8%	7.4%	2,522	20,292
St. Cloud, MN Metro Area	15,334	5,186	4,880	4,214	1,054	34,788	9.4%	8.2%	16.9%	1,644	20,533
St. George, UT Metro Area	17,020	4,270	5,720	5,654	1,376	41,630	10.7%	5.7%	8.8%	542	21,975
St. Joseph, MO-KS Metro Area	12,920	4,537	3,857	3,795	731	34,547	11.2%	7.6%	13.0%	1,671	16,557
St. Louis, MO-IL Metro Area	265,178	76,612	81,834	70,724	36,008	40,266	9.0%	6.5%	8.7%	32,748	368,896
State College, PA Metro Area	12,199	3,244	3,649	3,322	1,984	41,752	5.0%	6.7%	5.8%	905	18,010

Table G-4: Metropolitan/Micropolitan Statistical Areas—Income, Poverty Status and Receipt of Food Stamps (SNAP)—Continued

	Income of Households with Householder 65 Years and Over					Poverty Rate of Persons			Households with 1 or More Persons 60 Years and Over	
	Total Households	Less Than $25,000	$25,000 - $49,999	$50,000 - $99,999	$100,000 or More	Median Household Income	55 to 64 Years	65 to 74 Years	75 Years and Over	Receiving SNAP	Not Receiving SNAP
Statesboro, GA Micro Area	4,989	2,082	1,464	1,084	359	31,374	18.1%	5.2%	14.2%	1,063	6,903
Staunton-Waynesboro, VA Metro Area	14,271	4,603	3,894	4,058	1,716	41,766	7.5%	2.7%	12.8%	2,049	18,854
Stevens Point, WI Micro Area	6,738	1,902	2,346	2,173	317	39,777	8.2%	3.5%	15.3%	637	8,835
Stillwater, OK Micro Area	5,632	2,178	1,552	1,462	440	33,409	9.3%	3.3%	8.6%	667	7,867
Stockton-Lodi, CA Metro Area	44,199	14,794	11,673	11,267	6,465	38,148	14.2%	10.5%	9.6%	6,579	70,499
Sumter, SC Metro Area	9,981	4,521	2,580	2,069	811	29,297	20.3%	16.6%	20.8%	2,913	12,347
Sunbury, PA Micro Area	11,777	4,997	3,688	2,610	482	29,441	13.7%	9.6%	14.6%	2,202	15,388
Syracuse, NY Metro Area	62,523	20,352	19,324	16,423	6,424	37,653	8.5%	7.0%	9.4%	10,997	85,593
Talladega-Sylacauga, AL Micro Area	9,339	3,891	3,239	1,888	321	31,460	16.6%	10.7%	18.6%	2,124	12,389
Tallahassee, FL Metro Area	30,156	8,382	8,948	8,006	4,820	43,076	12.9%	9.2%	15.0%	6,270	42,902
Tampa-St. Petersburg-Clearwater, FL Metro Area	332,612	116,930	101,882	77,493	36,307	35,326	13.7%	9.2%	12.0%	52,890	430,708
Terre Haute, IN Metro Area	16,481	6,311	6,253	3,017	900	31,505	14.5%	6.4%	10.4%	2,122	22,160
Texarkana, TX-AR Metro Area	14,570	5,015	4,130	3,828	1,597	36,127	14.0%	5.7%	13.5%	1,653	19,642
The Villages, FL Metro Area	34,307	6,719	11,234	10,465	5,889	48,678	11.9%	5.0%	4.4%	1,182	40,752
Toledo, OH Metro Area	56,992	19,673	17,404	14,000	5,915	35,371	9.8%	7.5%	9.2%	9,290	78,334
Topeka, KS Metro Area	24,175	6,632	7,461	7,418	2,664	40,813	10.0%	6.9%	9.0%	1,508	33,759
Torrington, CT Micro Area	20,304	5,152	5,117	5,878	4,157	49,636	8.3%	4.0%	8.9%	1,730	29,984
Traverse City, MI Micro Area	18,300	4,677	6,338	5,166	2,119	41,582	9.2%	5.4%	5.4%	1,670	24,378
Trenton, NJ Metro Area	30,427	7,671	5,878	8,235	8,643	60,196	10.0%	8.4%	11.3%	3,801	45,156
Truckee-Grass Valley, CA Micro Area	13,350	2,686	3,896	4,382	2,386	50,322	10.7%	4.8%	2.4%	1,057	19,976
Tucson, AZ Metro Area	112,162	30,744	34,269	31,700	15,449	41,719	14.3%	9.5%	8.3%	16,600	147,750
Tullahoma-Manchester, TN Micro Area	12,022	4,507	3,708	2,882	925	37,783	8.5%	7.1%	10.8%	1,902	14,953
Tulsa, OK Metro Area	85,626	26,377	26,972	22,143	10,134	39,644	11.4%	7.6%	8.1%	11,101	121,265
Tupelo, MS Micro Area	12,350	5,322	3,639	1,907	1,482	30,020	14.3%	12.1%	13.2%	2,116	15,930
Tuscaloosa, AL Metro Area	18,044	6,645	4,607	4,888	1,904	32,471	12.7%	12.6%	9.8%	2,647	26,463
Twin Falls, ID Micro Area	9,351	3,724	2,961	2,136	530	31,525	5.7%	7.0%	17.6%	964	13,473
Tyler, TX Metro Area	20,300	7,660	5,215	4,838	2,587	36,164	11.8%	9.1%	12.6%	2,523	28,423
Ukiah, CA Micro Area	10,713	3,159	2,770	3,047	1,737	44,619	14.7%	7.3%	7.2%	1,142	14,963
Urban Honolulu, HI Metro Area	83,122	16,777	17,419	25,078	23,848	63,491	8.7%	5.5%	9.8%	13,734	117,274
Utica-Rome, NY Metro Area	31,917	11,026	9,887	8,036	2,968	34,163	11.7%	8.0%	5.6%	6,846	40,180
Valdosta, GA Metro Area	11,392	4,557	3,542	2,315	978	29,898	11.8%	6.7%	18.6%	2,835	14,663
Vallejo-Fairfield, CA Metro Area	33,203	7,280	8,798	10,625	6,500	51,913	9.7%	5.8%	6.6%	3,511	56,681
Victoria, TX Metro Area	9,079	2,869	2,635	2,765	810	37,615	8.3%	7.2%	10.7%	984	12,798
Vineland-Bridgeton, NJ Metro Area	13,024	4,675	3,842	3,227	1,280	37,523	20.1%	6.1%	8.3%	2,629	17,316
Virginia Beach-Norfolk-Newport News, VA-NC Metro Area	139,331	36,336	35,384	41,922	25,689	48,308	8.0%	8.3%	8.7%	18,988	199,948
Visalia-Porterville, CA Metro Area	25,327	8,597	6,951	7,124	2,655	38,816	14.8%	17.6%	11.0%	5,480	37,751
Waco, TX Metro Area	22,603	6,907	7,109	5,890	2,697	40,290	10.2%	5.4%	7.2%	3,647	29,148
Walla Walla, WA Metro Area	6,214	1,581	2,086	1,971	576	41,791	12.6%	6.0%	7.2%	1,472	8,484
Warner Robins, GA Metro Area	13,927	3,634	5,126	3,725	1,442	39,154	17.0%	5.1%	8.6%	2,962	19,074
Warsaw, IN Micro Area	7,172	1,606	2,731	2,238	597	44,538	11.2%	7.2%	2.3%	249	10,554
Washington-Arlington-Alexandria, DC-VA-MD-WV Metro Area	402,152	78,228	75,754	114,163	134,007	67,969	6.4%	5.9%	8.9%	54,731	630,217
Waterloo-Cedar Falls, IA Metro Area	17,443	5,265	5,766	4,594	1,818	36,755	8.0%	3.6%	5.9%	1,105	24,036
Watertown-Fort Atkinson, WI Micro Area	7,994	2,182	3,150	2,256	406	37,352	6.0%	2.9%	7.0%	701	11,365
Watertown-Fort Drum, NY Metro Area	8,616	2,613	2,532	2,621	850	40,851	14.0%	4.6%	7.7%	1,959	11,361
Wausau, WI Metro Area	13,355	4,769	5,039	2,941	606	35,479	5.6%	1.4%	6.1%	1,256	18,582
Weirton-Steubenville, WV-OH Metro Area	15,436	6,262	4,672	3,541	961	32,158	11.9%	6.0%	8.2%	2,236	19,635
Wenatchee, WA Metro Area	11,579	3,554	3,679	2,947	1,399	41,145	11.8%	11.8%	12.1%	1,772	15,704
Wheeling, WV-OH Metro Area	17,770	6,976	5,600	3,980	1,214	31,709	13.4%	5.5%	10.8%	2,928	23,049
Whitewater-Elkhorn, WI Micro Area	9,925	2,919	3,522	2,435	1,049	38,401	9.1%	6.4%	7.1%	1,101	13,795
Wichita Falls, TX Metro Area	14,242	5,407	3,861	3,434	1,540	35,690	12.6%	4.6%	14.7%	1,532	20,214
Wichita, KS Metro Area	54,312	15,778	17,590	14,749	6,195	38,869	8.8%	8.1%	7.7%	5,432	77,267
Williamsport, PA Metro Area	12,944	4,979	4,575	2,494	896	32,136	11.0%	6.4%	8.8%	1,447	18,086
Wilmington, NC Metro Area	26,961	7,015	7,636	7,552	4,758	46,063	9.3%	4.4%	9.0%	3,339	37,081
Wilson, NC Micro Area	8,299	3,059	3,071	1,713	456	32,961	15.7%	11.7%	6.8%	1,365	11,569
Winchester, VA-WV Metro Area	13,121	4,505	3,606	3,223	1,787	38,592	14.7%	7.9%	12.8%	1,477	19,612
Winston-Salem, NC Metro Area	66,793	24,009	19,411	16,918	6,455	36,635	13.6%	8.2%	9.4%	8,917	90,027
Wisconsin Rapids-Marshfield, WI Micro Area	9,251	3,521	2,962	1,986	782	32,570	6.3%	5.3%	9.9%	1,051	11,795
Wooster, OH Micro Area	10,626	3,015	3,953	2,868	790	37,701	7.9%	4.3%	4.5%	935	15,756
Worcester, MA-CT Metro Area	78,939	25,954	22,077	19,491	11,417	37,063	8.9%	7.5%	12.1%	15,824	110,731
Yakima, WA Metro Area	18,654	6,374	6,666	4,159	1,455	36,482	9.3%	9.9%	7.5%	4,180	24,432
York-Hanover, PA Metro Area	41,712	13,728	12,879	11,123	3,982	36,807	6.8%	6.5%	8.7%	4,795	60,067
Youngstown-Warren-Boardman, OH-PA Metro Area	68,851	24,231	23,795	16,801	4,024	35,052	12.1%	6.2%	8.0%	10,018	89,289
Yuba City, CA Metro Area	13,359	4,994	3,095	3,752	1,518	38,055	9.5%	11.1%	20.9%	1,629	19,897
Yuma, AZ Metro Area	22,044	9,230	6,477	4,369	1,968	31,587	19.7%	15.5%	16.9%	4,389	25,335
Zanesville, OH Micro Area	9,403	4,230	3,310	1,552	311	26,965	14.8%	9.4%	13.7%	2,514	11,207

Table G-5: 114th Congressional Districts—Income, Poverty Status and Receipt of Food Stamps (SNAP)

	Income of Households with Householder 65 Years and Over					Poverty Rate of Persons			Households with 1 or More Persons 60 Years and Over	
	Total Households	Less Than $25,000	$25,000 - $49,999	$50,000 - $99,999	$100,000 or More	Median Household Income	55 to 64 Years	65 to 74 Years	75 Years and Over	Receiving SNAP	Not Receiving SNAP
Alabama											
Congressional District 1	71,277	26,247	21,331	17,078	6,621	35,238	12.9%	11.8%	12.3%	10,873	93,775
Congressional District 2	67,200	25,688	20,656	14,805	6,051	32,388	13.5%	9.5%	12.4%	11,182	80,069
Congressional District 3	67,169	25,953	20,183	15,225	5,808	33,072	14.6%	10.5%	14.0%	11,598	91,083
Congressional District 4	73,422	30,580	22,421	15,235	5,186	29,238	14.2%	9.4%	12.7%	9,702	98,043
Congressional District 5	66,956	23,143	18,857	16,642	8,314	36,858	10.7%	11.6%	8.0%	8,243	92,973
Congressional District 6	66,627	18,889	22,031	16,952	8,755	39,075	10.3%	6.8%	11.8%	5,525	94,706
Congressional District 7	60,017	25,756	17,124	12,547	4,590	30,164	20.8%	14.7%	14.6%	17,156	76,191
Alaska											
Congressional District (at Large)	40,996	8,930	8,811	12,601	10,654	58,311	8.7%	4.7%	3.6%	6,139	67,293
Arizona											
Congressional District 1	75,218	22,816	22,268	21,662	8,472	40,659	16.6%	9.5%	13.0%	11,572	98,755
Congressional District 2	89,098	24,865	27,753	23,685	12,795	41,011	13.5%	9.6%	7.8%	10,398	117,721
Congressional District 3	46,538	19,460	12,932	11,204	2,942	29,981	20.1%	17.3%	17.8%	15,911	62,743
Congressional District 4	113,071	35,780	40,001	29,256	8,034	36,490	14.3%	10.1%	7.8%	13,110	143,931
Congressional District 5	70,872	19,607	21,497	21,023	8,745	41,894	7.3%	7.3%	9.1%	5,269	97,287
Congressional District 6	76,013	16,320	22,345	20,737	16,611	48,626	9.3%	6.4%	6.3%	6,608	106,806
Congressional District 7	30,263	14,837	7,845	4,812	2,769	25,579	27.1%	21.3%	13.2%	13,767	42,737
Congressional District 8	94,086	23,465	30,292	28,013	12,316	42,718	10.9%	3.9%	8.1%	6,419	125,491
Congressional District 9	52,453	14,889	14,169	15,505	7,890	43,392	11.8%	7.5%	10.6%	6,154	78,359
Arkansas											
Congressional District 1	79,867	34,322	24,505	15,936	5,104	29,500	13.3%	11.4%	14.8%	14,007	102,080
Congressional District 2	65,456	21,160	18,777	17,167	8,352	39,966	11.4%	6.3%	8.1%	8,531	92,953
Congressional District 3	65,607	25,949	18,223	14,895	6,540	32,301	12.6%	8.8%	13.0%	7,058	91,141
Congressional District 4	78,872	31,462	24,980	16,443	5,987	31,084	14.7%	9.4%	14.1%	11,424	103,757
California											
Congressional District 1	84,018	25,726	23,956	23,749	10,587	41,016	14.5%	6.0%	9.4%	7,454	119,771
Congressional District 2	81,683	18,835	19,721	21,973	21,154	53,756	11.2%	6.6%	7.4%	5,902	122,516
Congressional District 3	55,847	16,441	14,414	15,514	9,478	45,033	10.7%	7.5%	10.8%	5,232	88,850
Congressional District 4	84,023	21,338	21,496	26,107	15,082	48,484	9.8%	7.0%	6.8%	6,006	118,541
Congressional District 5	69,937	17,613	16,406	21,301	14,617	52,538	9.7%	6.3%	7.9%	5,757	108,983
Congressional District 6	50,970	15,992	13,735	14,165	7,078	41,229	18.9%	13.9%	15.0%	7,439	78,762
Congressional District 7	59,781	13,649	16,165	18,721	11,246	50,149	8.8%	4.9%	10.5%	5,243	93,647
Congressional District 8	54,549	20,194	14,700	13,614	6,041	34,655	15.5%	11.6%	12.8%	10,316	79,203
Congressional District 9	47,782	13,594	13,472	12,662	8,054	41,549	13.8%	10.2%	10.2%	6,912	75,019
Congressional District 10	47,092	15,056	12,534	13,420	6,082	41,927	11.7%	7.8%	12.6%	7,061	72,498
Congressional District 11	66,857	13,964	14,271	19,246	19,376	60,030	10.1%	5.8%	7.2%	4,339	103,055
Congressional District 12	65,252	21,999	15,220	13,765	14,268	42,831	13.0%	11.6%	15.0%	5,487	100,230
Congressional District 13	59,551	18,892	11,091	13,782	15,786	49,297	14.2%	10.4%	16.4%	6,157	91,809
Congressional District 14	59,497	13,378	13,280	16,024	16,815	56,378	7.2%	6.3%	7.3%	3,471	97,007
Congressional District 15	49,013	11,768	12,310	13,274	11,661	51,991	8.0%	7.1%	9.4%	3,513	83,700
Congressional District 16	40,628	15,775	10,940	9,571	4,342	32,020	19.5%	15.1%	14.6%	9,674	58,833
Congressional District 17	43,857	11,769	9,929	11,376	10,783	50,729	6.5%	8.0%	10.4%	3,233	74,858
Congressional District 18	61,855	11,849	12,519	17,580	19,907	63,698	6.9%	5.3%	7.3%	2,798	94,387
Congressional District 19	44,725	12,657	10,770	10,551	10,747	47,423	9.4%	10.9%	13.2%	6,056	77,099
Congressional District 20	52,030	12,218	13,208	14,112	12,492	51,570	9.4%	7.5%	11.1%	4,963	81,864
Congressional District 21	30,001	12,360	8,699	6,450	2,492	31,228	22.2%	18.1%	17.7%	6,919	45,857
Congressional District 22	48,857	14,415	13,045	14,046	7,351	44,221	9.9%	11.6%	12.1%	7,786	73,641
Congressional District 23	50,468	15,584	14,785	13,106	6,993	38,257	14.6%	12.3%	14.1%	7,939	76,902
Congressional District 24	67,270	16,286	16,956	17,552	16,476	50,604	9.1%	7.0%	5.5%	4,012	99,018
Congressional District 25	40,984	11,400	10,329	12,391	6,864	47,075	8.6%	7.9%	11.9%	4,500	70,043
Congressional District 26	58,450	13,355	14,474	16,332	14,289	53,541	7.8%	6.7%	10.3%	4,059	87,506
Congressional District 27	60,320	17,520	13,446	14,831	14,523	48,393	12.5%	10.3%	13.4%	3,386	98,433
Congressional District 28	58,539	24,330	11,585	11,210	11,414	32,047	13.1%	13.5%	20.4%	5,159	91,503
Congressional District 29	35,620	13,803	8,732	7,875	5,210	33,991	15.5%	14.7%	16.3%	5,361	61,489
Congressional District 30	63,729	18,592	13,710	16,094	15,333	49,006	8.7%	9.7%	11.8%	4,558	99,288
Congressional District 31	36,874	10,914	10,510	10,083	5,367	42,556	15.6%	9.9%	12.0%	7,499	58,854
Congressional District 32	45,765	14,480	12,189	11,594	7,502	41,490	11.4%	10.6%	10.6%	4,639	81,166
Congressional District 33	75,283	17,494	11,833	14,845	31,111	71,825	8.4%	6.9%	12.6%	904	109,666
Congressional District 34	43,055	23,492	8,500	7,355	3,708	21,603	25.1%	24.4%	27.6%	7,060	68,651
Congressional District 35	27,614	9,631	6,559	7,839	3,585	39,697	16.7%	12.0%	13.9%	6,948	48,973
Congressional District 36	90,719	29,612	25,062	20,618	15,427	30,108	15.2%	10.2%	10.6%	8,539	116,468
Congressional District 37	56,344	21,076	12,455	12,696	10,117	37,091	17.3%	15.9%	20.6%	5,129	85,982
Congressional District 38	51,026	16,962	12,907	13,632	7,525	40,080	9.9%	10.0%	12.1%	5,922	79,573
Congressional District 39	51,356	11,236	12,323	14,733	13,064	55,074	9.1%	6.4%	9.2%	2,674	83,095
Congressional District 40	26,284	10,822	7,718	5,766	1,978	31,773	19.7%	21.1%	17.8%	6,648	48,833
Congressional District 41	32,241	8,905	9,106	9,008	5,222	43,754	12.2%	14.3%	10.7%	6,500	57,751
Congressional District 42	44,085	10,992	13,021	12,271	7,801	45,232	9.6%	7.8%	12.0%	4,728	71,348
Congressional District 43	47,677	14,397	13,397	13,138	6,745	41,087	15.1%	14.0%	14.2%	4,995	74,498
Congressional District 44	32,690	11,705	9,072	7,868	4,045	34,334	17.4%	15.3%	20.0%	6,143	55,607
Congressional District 45	58,224	11,396	13,135	16,954	16,739	61,074	6.2%	4.4%	7.3%	1,816	93,455
Congressional District 46	30,943	10,575	6,358	9,094	4,916	40,290	13.5%	13.2%	15.3%	6,115	55,590
Congressional District 47	49,151	15,972	11,613	12,215	9,351	41,505	13.7%	13.1%	13.8%	6,484	81,515
Congressional District 48	70,006	15,464	16,214	18,219	20,109	56,698	8.0%	5.7%	11.0%	3,911	102,940
Congressional District 49	62,730	12,844	14,354	18,224	17,308	57,896	10.3%	6.3%	5.8%	2,428	93,572
Congressional District 50	58,738	14,984	15,320	17,130	11,304	48,209	10.0%	5.4%	9.8%	5,362	90,210

Table G-5: 114th Congressional Districts—Income, Poverty Status and Receipt of Food Stamps (SNAP)—*Continued*

	Income of Households with Householder 65 Years and Over						Poverty Rate of Persons			Households with 1 or More Persons 60 Years and Over	
	Total Households	Less Than $25,000	$25,000 - $49,999	$50,000 - $99,999	$100,000 or More	Median Household Income	55 to 64 Years	65 to 74 Years	75 Years and Over	Receiving SNAP	Not Receiving SNAP
California—Cont.											
Congressional District 51	39,205	17,528	10,370	7,477	3,830	28,934	16.1%	18.5%	17.6%	8,084	60,633
Congressional District 52	55,711	12,837	12,439	14,015	16,420	54,979	7.6%	6.8%	8.0%	2,375	89,950
Congressional District 53	51,442	14,088	12,576	14,702	10,076	47,103	9.4%	11.1%	10.5%	6,748	81,605
Colorado											
Congressional District 1	56,915	18,016	14,814	14,524	9,561	42,368	14.6%	8.9%	9.6%	9,818	83,895
Congressional District 2	61,254	13,315	14,682	20,225	13,032	54,151	6.2%	4.9%	6.4%	4,014	98,331
Congressional District 3	71,846	22,628	22,230	17,875	9,113	37,692	11.3%	8.0%	9.9%	9,471	104,884
Congressional District 4	58,798	17,017	17,005	16,042	8,734	43,127	7.4%	4.7%	8.8%	5,903	88,714
Congressional District 5	58,669	15,751	16,684	17,026	9,208	45,060	9.0%	6.5%	6.3%	7,413	86,940
Congressional District 6	50,915	10,908	12,772	16,637	10,598	54,766	6.8%	5.2%	8.5%	4,862	79,549
Congressional District 7	60,232	15,291	17,957	17,924	9,060	44,752	6.3%	7.0%	7.1%	7,217	91,383
Connecticut											
Congressional District 1	71,138	21,220	20,400	18,319	11,199	41,206	7.6%	8.6%	10.3%	14,380	93,443
Congressional District 2	67,409	14,334	18,351	22,532	12,192	51,420	6.3%	4.8%	7.5%	8,522	94,910
Congressional District 3	69,849	22,538	19,088	17,208	11,015	39,960	8.3%	7.9%	9.7%	12,011	94,528
Congressional District 4	63,660	14,786	14,010	15,383	19,481	57,572	5.8%	7.8%	6.9%	8,911	89,990
Congressional District 5	67,602	19,117	17,770	18,104	12,611	45,703	9.1%	5.8%	9.5%	10,886	92,496
Delaware											
Congressional District (at Large)	92,377	23,080	27,297	28,116	13,884	45,510	9.3%	6.5%	9.0%	12,337	127,198
District of Columbia											
Delegate District (at Large)	50,463	16,060	9,803	12,302	12,298	47,906	19.2%	12.9%	16.7%	12,596	66,366
Florida											
Congressional District 1	73,410	18,295	23,093	22,120	9,902	44,365	10.1%	6.9%	6.9%	9,764	97,488
Congressional District 2	64,479	19,963	19,991	15,893	8,632	38,695	14.2%	10.3%	12.8%	12,492	88,155
Congressional District 3	72,526	22,888	22,718	18,765	8,155	38,209	14.3%	8.9%	8.9%	11,966	95,977
Congressional District 4	62,922	17,600	19,812	16,032	9,478	41,117	9.9%	8.4%	6.7%	9,171	88,798
Congressional District 5	52,304	22,502	14,849	10,992	3,961	29,434	22.1%	16.3%	17.5%	18,409	67,243
Congressional District 6	102,474	26,585	33,968	28,735	13,186	41,823	12.1%	5.6%	7.9%	10,741	135,509
Congressional District 7	58,004	18,179	17,393	14,383	8,049	37,586	9.1%	9.4%	12.5%	7,239	86,201
Congressional District 8	103,216	28,388	33,260	29,044	12,524	41,405	11.6%	9.2%	6.4%	11,119	133,909
Congressional District 9	44,691	17,206	12,060	10,712	4,713	33,931	12.8%	13.8%	14.1%	14,007	64,391
Congressional District 10	80,880	24,896	23,739	22,860	9,385	40,274	12.5%	7.9%	9.9%	10,291	107,233
Congressional District 11	142,838	40,258	52,593	36,628	13,359	37,638	15.2%	7.4%	8.9%	14,664	170,147
Congressional District 12	92,508	31,437	29,558	22,159	9,354	34,866	11.7%	7.5%	10.6%	10,948	118,810
Congressional District 13	107,006	38,582	31,117	24,789	12,518	34,675	13.5%	8.6%	12.0%	12,147	137,290
Congressional District 14	57,456	23,409	15,894	11,923	6,230	32,625	19.3%	14.6%	18.1%	18,919	74,545
Congressional District 15	62,657	20,020	18,750	15,403	8,484	38,066	12.8%	7.7%	12.4%	9,893	85,790
Congressional District 16	136,033	35,131	38,304	39,435	23,163	45,594	10.4%	7.1%	6.2%	8,857	170,672
Congressional District 17	114,554	34,358	38,019	31,072	11,105	38,653	14.4%	6.8%	9.8%	11,923	140,467
Congressional District 18	110,320	31,153	31,283	28,702	19,182	42,505	10.7%	5.6%	7.6%	9,485	142,331
Congressional District 19	128,026	30,397	35,670	34,514	27,445	48,385	11.9%	6.2%	7.9%	9,065	162,957
Congressional District 20	59,018	25,609	16,824	12,443	4,142	29,527	18.0%	16.8%	13.9%	18,873	74,646
Congressional District 21	103,633	31,051	29,026	27,481	16,075	40,684	8.6%	8.0%	9.3%	9,876	128,262
Congressional District 22	100,876	32,318	25,383	23,865	19,310	41,122	14.2%	10.3%	10.5%	11,658	128,235
Congressional District 23	71,549	27,428	16,755	15,906	11,460	35,716	14.1%	12.3%	16.6%	16,300	91,987
Congressional District 24	48,511	23,632	11,985	8,467	4,427	25,843	23.9%	21.7%	27.8%	26,053	58,315
Congressional District 25	57,967	21,941	14,146	13,473	8,407	35,810	15.5%	15.0%	18.2%	24,617	69,975
Congressional District 26	54,237	20,934	12,995	13,742	6,566	33,575	13.3%	13.2%	17.1%	21,582	74,406
Congressional District 27	61,643	28,856	12,696	10,412	9,679	27,607	17.7%	18.4%	25.0%	35,459	66,821
Georgia											
Congressional District 1	57,508	19,576	15,236	14,856	7,840	37,485	12.5%	8.2%	10.5%	10,967	79,547
Congressional District 2	60,723	25,300	16,929	13,420	5,074	30,614	21.6%	15.1%	16.0%	18,114	75,648
Congressional District 3	60,882	19,753	18,685	15,890	6,554	39,120	11.9%	8.8%	13.5%	9,624	84,526
Congressional District 4	43,299	12,862	13,271	12,274	4,892	40,765	13.0%	9.1%	10.7%	11,627	66,288
Congressional District 5	50,505	21,976	14,094	9,763	4,672	29,733	18.3%	18.1%	11.7%	16,927	63,691
Congressional District 6	46,602	9,016	12,634	12,886	12,066	53,538	5.2%	3.4%	8.7%	3,284	75,355
Congressional District 7	34,875	9,224	8,933	10,200	6,518	47,275	8.1%	6.4%	9.0%	5,969	59,341
Congressional District 8	62,890	24,310	18,822	13,730	6,028	32,287	16.2%	9.6%	14.1%	14,388	81,329
Congressional District 9	74,286	26,152	22,136	16,934	9,064	35,527	14.4%	8.5%	11.6%	11,502	97,565
Congressional District 10	57,195	19,475	17,189	13,811	6,720	36,794	13.4%	9.5%	12.9%	11,911	78,178
Congressional District 11	47,502	10,742	12,376	14,389	9,995	50,764	8.3%	4.1%	8.6%	6,053	73,203
Congressional District 12	56,063	23,071	16,411	11,466	5,115	30,238	15.7%	11.8%	13.5%	13,053	77,151
Congressional District 13	40,043	13,347	10,856	10,373	5,467	37,152	11.2%	9.9%	13.7%	9,995	61,813
Congressional District 14	58,081	21,422	18,338	12,909	5,412	33,973	12.5%	8.7%	12.2%	9,452	79,700
Hawaii											
Congressional District 1	63,780	13,796	13,559	18,860	17,565	60,690	7.8%	5.9%	10.5%	9,715	90,444
Congressional District 2	58,964	13,022	13,626	17,134	15,182	56,486	14.3%	8.0%	8.9%	11,272	86,639
Idaho											
Congressional District 1	77,362	25,192	25,854	20,006	6,310	36,147	10.5%	8.7%	11.4%	9,567	110,035
Congressional District 2	66,862	24,303	19,051	16,960	6,548	35,864	7.6%	8.9%	9.4%	6,409	95,632

Table G-5: 114th Congressional Districts—Income, Poverty Status and Receipt of Food Stamps (SNAP)—*Continued*

	Income of Households with Householder 65 Years and Over						Poverty Rate of Persons			Households with 1 or More Persons 60 Years and Over	
	Total Households	Less Than $25,000	$25,000 - $49,999	$50,000 - $99,999	$100,000 or More	Median Household Income	55 to 64 Years	65 to 74 Years	75 Years and Over	Receiving SNAP	Not Receiving SNAP
Illinois											
Congressional District 1	68,981	24,277	19,315	18,151	7,238	36,311	15.7%	9.7%	13.3%	19,772	85,634
Congressional District 2	61,057	21,412	16,474	16,350	6,821	37,280	15.7%	8.8%	9.6%	15,758	83,360
Congressional District 3	59,770	18,909	17,293	16,638	6,930	37,187	8.0%	7.7%	8.9%	10,349	85,133
Congressional District 4	34,683	14,630	9,740	6,523	3,790	30,783	15.8%	15.8%	14.5%	12,882	52,884
Congressional District 5	53,721	16,180	14,036	13,675	9,830	42,046	7.9%	7.4%	12.8%	7,337	74,184
Congressional District 6	60,986	10,915	17,424	16,569	16,078	54,902	5.7%	3.1%	7.1%	5,068	93,096
Congressional District 7	56,109	24,611	11,602	8,977	10,919	31,055	20.5%	18.0%	22.1%	23,349	64,409
Congressional District 8	49,012	13,502	13,308	13,840	8,362	44,957	7.5%	6.2%	6.1%	6,993	78,931
Congressional District 9	68,205	21,651	16,474	16,523	13,557	43,392	10.1%	10.4%	11.6%	11,765	94,250
Congressional District 10	54,782	13,438	13,029	14,117	14,198	51,537	6.3%	7.4%	6.8%	8,167	79,851
Congressional District 11	40,276	10,075	12,622	10,982	6,597	44,148	6.9%	7.4%	4.1%	6,751	64,020
Congressional District 12	70,647	23,876	22,193	17,466	7,112	35,101	12.7%	9.1%	10.7%	10,451	92,680
Congressional District 13	69,702	21,893	21,774	17,822	8,213	38,106	12.8%	6.9%	9.2%	7,585	93,940
Congressional District 14	54,959	12,051	15,165	16,545	11,198	50,457	5.7%	2.5%	4.7%	4,987	81,895
Congressional District 15	76,931	26,257	23,686	18,973	8,015	36,365	7.7%	7.7%	10.1%	9,236	102,817
Congressional District 16	72,216	22,346	23,111	18,784	7,975	38,813	9.0%	4.7%	10.7%	7,177	99,664
Congressional District 17	78,897	28,895	25,517	17,999	6,486	33,615	11.2%	9.5%	10.8%	10,671	105,141
Congressional District 18	74,612	20,880	22,467	21,576	9,689	41,642	7.2%	4.9%	7.7%	6,196	104,020
Indiana											
Congressional District 1	63,780	18,654	20,333	17,471	7,322	40,116	9.1%	6.7%	7.4%	10,135	91,038
Congressional District 2	66,436	22,053	24,478	15,005	4,900	35,619	9.7%	5.0%	8.6%	7,920	93,825
Congressional District 3	65,510	20,594	21,809	17,447	5,660	35,999	8.8%	6.0%	8.5%	6,521	91,394
Congressional District 4	65,949	19,893	22,279	17,749	6,028	38,671	9.5%	5.1%	6.9%	5,984	92,202
Congressional District 5	63,514	16,964	19,220	18,234	9,096	44,097	8.2%	5.1%	7.2%	6,849	89,353
Congressional District 6	73,490	23,171	23,842	19,528	6,949	37,351	8.7%	7.3%	9.1%	7,558	99,079
Congressional District 7	49,583	16,333	19,087	11,027	3,136	33,916	13.2%	8.5%	9.1%	12,309	69,268
Congressional District 8	72,470	25,458	26,003	15,059	5,950	33,430	10.9%	5.7%	10.5%	6,952	100,965
Congressional District 9	64,961	18,885	21,401	17,251	7,424	41,792	9.9%	6.0%	6.1%	8,018	93,462
Iowa											
Congressional District 1	80,762	25,397	25,688	21,331	8,346	37,988	6.3%	4.5%	10.2%	6,229	110,293
Congressional District 2	77,746	26,396	23,578	20,226	7,546	36,693	9.7%	7.4%	9.6%	8,677	108,073
Congressional District 3	69,055	22,161	20,960	19,015	6,919	38,237	6.2%	5.6%	10.3%	9,348	95,774
Congressional District 4	83,166	28,183	26,736	18,435	9,812	35,744	7.5%	5.3%	7.8%	7,065	111,730
Kansas											
Congressional District 1	68,107	23,002	20,639	17,199	7,267	36,452	7.9%	6.8%	9.5%	7,236	93,979
Congressional District 2	69,590	22,282	21,100	19,248	6,960	37,821	9.3%	7.6%	10.3%	6,583	96,659
Congressional District 3	58,168	15,515	15,467	16,286	10,900	45,747	7.1%	5.5%	7.8%	4,107	88,467
Congressional District 4	64,496	19,345	21,208	16,744	7,199	37,867	8.9%	8.1%	8.1%	6,224	90,587
Kentucky											
Congressional District 1	77,242	31,494	25,220	15,228	5,300	31,647	14.6%	8.7%	14.2%	13,985	99,795
Congressional District 2	67,302	23,634	21,110	17,025	5,533	34,820	10.6%	8.9%	11.8%	10,828	89,025
Congressional District 3	70,239	22,683	23,966	15,500	8,090	37,689	12.9%	7.2%	10.3%	11,219	94,238
Congressional District 4	62,197	20,976	19,495	15,985	5,741	35,791	11.7%	9.8%	12.6%	10,154	89,571
Congressional District 5	74,642	36,431	23,379	11,983	2,849	25,578	22.9%	19.0%	15.9%	21,218	90,648
Congressional District 6	62,195	21,685	18,026	15,020	7,464	36,619	13.5%	8.1%	9.4%	10,501	87,939
Louisiana											
Congressional District 1	68,554	21,355	19,901	16,930	10,368	40,517	11.5%	7.9%	9.4%	7,257	98,956
Congressional District 2	62,129	28,174	16,991	10,127	6,837	27,662	20.1%	17.0%	20.9%	18,474	81,993
Congressional District 3	64,299	25,549	18,013	13,265	7,472	31,351	13.4%	12.6%	11.6%	15,133	83,485
Congressional District 4	68,931	27,265	21,282	14,013	6,371	32,390	19.7%	12.9%	12.8%	12,388	93,395
Congressional District 5	71,150	32,943	19,961	12,793	5,453	27,353	18.8%	15.1%	18.7%	15,425	94,651
Congressional District 6	60,103	19,021	18,138	14,724	8,220	38,341	9.7%	8.9%	9.0%	8,146	88,427
Maine											
Congressional District 1	75,384	22,789	22,544	19,467	10,584	39,510	7.7%	7.0%	8.3%	10,250	105,066
Congressional District 2	75,897	29,422	25,309	16,795	4,371	31,912	12.2%	8.6%	12.6%	18,528	97,349
Maryland											
Congressional District 1	75,955	21,351	18,792	21,538	14,274	45,813	7.8%	6.2%	9.1%	8,613	107,080
Congressional District 2	56,987	16,339	16,875	15,234	8,539	41,469	10.5%	6.6%	10.1%	11,013	81,918
Congressional District 3	65,092	15,608	13,486	18,891	17,107	55,984	5.6%	6.0%	10.2%	10,013	93,005
Congressional District 4	54,092	9,402	14,378	16,473	13,839	56,608	5.7%	5.1%	7.7%	7,077	82,015
Congressional District 5	53,079	9,681	10,817	16,864	15,717	66,284	5.2%	4.8%	7.7%	8,191	84,446
Congressional District 6	56,961	15,323	14,501	14,715	12,422	47,181	6.8%	4.6%	8.3%	8,841	83,241
Congressional District 7	63,904	19,080	15,027	19,548	10,249	45,553	13.7%	9.7%	12.8%	13,613	86,229
Congressional District 8	69,912	14,356	12,374	19,798	23,384	67,206	5.4%	5.7%	8.2%	5,622	103,159
Massachusetts											
Congressional District 1	77,027	25,705	23,303	18,758	9,261	35,599	12.6%	9.6%	9.0%	17,261	100,182
Congressional District 2	63,503	21,302	16,578	16,101	9,522	37,410	9.4%	7.9%	10.8%	13,521	89,314
Congressional District 3	61,551	20,282	14,951	15,653	10,665	39,925	10.7%	9.9%	12.2%	13,226	84,575
Congressional District 4	64,533	17,713	15,934	16,060	14,826	47,410	5.2%	5.3%	11.4%	10,430	93,795
Congressional District 5	70,670	19,655	16,089	18,012	16,914	49,101	7.2%	8.6%	8.1%	9,356	94,712
Congressional District 6	73,451	22,059	17,384	20,061	13,947	45,740	6.4%	6.9%	9.9%	11,419	105,134
Congressional District 7	48,348	23,511	8,537	9,062	7,238	26,568	15.4%	17.4%	20.4%	22,705	57,007
Congressional District 8	73,309	21,698	19,015	18,779	13,817	44,063	8.1%	7.4%	9.7%	14,510	99,808
Congressional District 9	92,405	26,820	24,456	24,807	16,322	43,151	8.5%	6.5%	7.0%	13,410	122,896

Table G-5: 114th Congressional Districts—Income, Poverty Status and Receipt of Food Stamps (SNAP)—*Continued*

	Income of Households with Householder 65 Years and Over						Poverty Rate of Persons			Households with 1 or More Persons 60 Years and Over	
	Total Households	Less Than $25,000	$25,000 - $49,999	$50,000 - $99,999	$100,000 or More	Median Household Income	55 to 64 Years	65 to 74 Years	75 Years and Over	Receiving SNAP	Not Receiving SNAP
Michigan											
Congressional District 1	92,775	31,345	30,998	22,695	7,737	35,338	11.6%	6.7%	9.8%	12,943	122,686
Congressional District 2	64,455	20,933	23,073	15,475	4,974	35,463	10.4%	7.4%	8.8%	10,712	86,295
Congressional District 3	61,839	18,388	20,590	16,429	6,432	38,398	10.0%	7.3%	7.5%	9,024	85,815
Congressional District 4	75,303	23,859	27,317	18,409	5,718	36,167	10.3%	6.8%	9.3%	10,213	100,378
Congressional District 5	75,937	22,521	27,719	20,467	5,230	37,406	13.7%	6.4%	9.3%	16,055	96,583
Congressional District 6	68,168	19,865	23,039	18,372	6,892	38,712	10.9%	6.9%	8.4%	9,773	96,003
Congressional District 7	70,855	19,736	24,953	19,450	6,716	38,325	7.2%	5.5%	5.8%	9,200	98,133
Congressional District 8	58,139	13,194	17,352	17,628	9,965	47,965	5.9%	5.5%	7.3%	8,034	84,726
Congressional District 9	75,302	25,368	23,420	18,180	8,334	37,131	9.2%	10.0%	7.9%	15,698	98,344
Congressional District 10	71,246	19,888	24,081	20,659	6,618	40,947	8.3%	6.1%	6.4%	9,939	99,361
Congressional District 11	64,684	15,191	19,210	19,428	10,855	46,379	5.0%	5.4%	6.0%	6,237	97,882
Congressional District 12	60,740	16,697	19,453	15,948	8,642	41,637	9.8%	7.2%	7.3%	10,572	84,330
Congressional District 13	59,444	26,073	19,086	10,861	3,424	29,352	23.6%	17.9%	15.7%	25,712	68,002
Congressional District 14	70,289	22,798	19,674	18,229	9,588	40,095	17.7%	12.2%	12.2%	18,157	89,770
Minnesota											
Congressional District 1	66,836	21,723	19,674	18,721	6,718	38,761	6.1%	5.6%	9.7%	4,055	92,908
Congressional District 2	51,713	13,239	14,266	17,127	7,081	46,478	5.5%	5.3%	6.7%	3,499	77,560
Congressional District 3	60,336	14,592	17,224	18,185	10,335	47,574	4.7%	4.6%	6.7%	4,963	89,409
Congressional District 4	57,315	14,903	16,130	16,700	9,582	45,359	8.4%	4.8%	10.1%	8,871	80,408
Congressional District 5	51,551	18,654	13,841	13,213	5,843	35,859	16.1%	9.0%	9.3%	9,756	73,466
Congressional District 6	44,534	11,206	14,705	13,665	4,958	41,625	6.4%	4.5%	9.9%	4,108	65,890
Congressional District 7	76,384	27,740	22,808	18,968	6,868	34,742	6.9%	5.8%	13.4%	6,287	103,415
Congressional District 8	77,480	25,543	25,340	19,849	6,748	36,597	10.8%	5.8%	11.1%	7,100	107,816
Mississippi											
Congressional District 1	70,107	28,286	21,253	15,123	5,445	32,132	14.5%	10.1%	11.8%	11,676	94,727
Congressional District 2	63,779	30,124	18,259	10,805	4,591	26,407	21.5%	17.4%	18.0%	17,898	78,311
Congressional District 3	72,252	32,165	18,165	14,949	6,973	29,111	15.3%	12.3%	18.1%	12,002	97,628
Congressional District 4	67,010	23,382	21,761	16,169	5,698	34,335	16.4%	10.2%	10.0%	12,237	89,941
Missouri											
Congressional District 1	60,997	22,658	18,573	14,038	5,728	33,959	15.6%	11.4%	12.3%	14,820	84,054
Congressional District 2	83,030	18,992	23,208	24,329	16,501	48,647	5.0%	3.5%	6.8%	4,538	114,700
Congressional District 3	67,252	18,840	22,620	19,307	6,485	40,000	7.3%	5.8%	7.3%	6,284	98,156
Congressional District 4	71,976	25,905	23,191	17,621	5,259	33,539	13.6%	8.5%	13.0%	8,916	97,781
Congressional District 5	70,105	25,213	21,955	17,185	5,752	34,476	12.6%	10.3%	9.2%	10,805	93,862
Congressional District 6	71,255	22,019	22,161	19,610	7,465	38,105	8.6%	6.9%	9.0%	7,038	97,855
Congressional District 7	78,366	29,033	25,418	17,852	6,063	32,582	12.4%	7.0%	12.0%	10,037	105,255
Congressional District 8	81,998	35,720	25,447	16,065	4,766	28,746	14.5%	11.2%	15.2%	16,313	106,708
Montana											
Congressional District (at Large)	106,654	36,784	33,479	25,192	11,199	35,710	11.5%	7.8%	9.0%	11,082	151,815
Nebraska											
Congressional District 1	56,407	16,612	17,438	16,632	5,725	40,574	5.8%	4.4%	8.1%	4,208	78,451
Congressional District 2	46,308	14,250	13,325	12,177	6,556	39,992	9.6%	4.8%	10.3%	5,505	67,918
Congressional District 3	71,271	27,413	20,661	15,853	7,344	32,674	6.5%	7.4%	12.6%	6,796	94,397
Nevada											
Congressional District 1	54,073	21,223	15,023	13,217	4,610	32,790	17.2%	13.8%	13.1%	14,562	71,545
Congressional District 2	67,849	20,390	19,616	18,859	8,984	41,567	12.2%	7.8%	6.6%	8,691	95,647
Congressional District 3	59,400	14,716	17,983	16,919	9,782	44,349	8.0%	4.8%	7.2%	5,152	91,857
Congressional District 4	53,813	15,631	15,455	16,518	6,209	41,310	11.2%	6.9%	7.8%	9,518	79,326
New Hampshire											
Congressional District 1	62,176	16,878	17,482	16,909	10,907	44,614	6.2%	3.3%	5.7%	6,523	94,499
Congressional District 2	61,339	16,677	19,572	16,371	8,719	41,900	5.8%	4.6%	8.0%	5,495	96,113
New Jersey											
Congressional District 1	68,271	21,188	18,017	17,282	11,784	41,680	8.7%	8.0%	9.8%	10,599	96,169
Congressional District 2	75,481	23,648	20,261	19,508	12,064	42,146	10.3%	7.2%	7.8%	11,458	104,450
Congressional District 3	82,952	19,844	22,636	25,999	14,473	48,429	6.0%	5.2%	7.5%	6,450	113,556
Congressional District 4	82,620	22,236	21,093	22,198	17,093	46,370	6.3%	5.5%	8.2%	6,305	113,607
Congressional District 5	65,224	12,826	14,926	18,603	18,869	59,721	5.0%	3.7%	6.7%	5,030	101,885
Congressional District 6	54,830	14,991	12,527	15,637	11,675	49,708	6.8%	6.4%	9.0%	7,382	84,506
Congressional District 7	62,766	13,055	16,120	16,526	17,065	55,584	3.6%	3.9%	7.9%	4,074	98,333
Congressional District 8	44,930	21,424	9,177	9,373	4,956	26,897	12.2%	15.5%	22.7%	15,490	63,486
Congressional District 9	59,278	21,323	14,012	12,724	11,219	37,461	12.3%	14.1%	17.1%	12,846	85,976
Congressional District 10	54,385	23,821	12,951	9,825	7,788	30,928	15.7%	17.3%	16.7%	14,779	75,522
Congressional District 11	71,126	14,572	15,798	20,077	20,679	60,827	4.2%	3.7%	5.0%	3,710	107,333
Congressional District 12	61,336	14,363	13,354	17,499	16,120	56,621	6.8%	6.5%	8.4%	6,879	94,807
New Mexico											
Congressional District 1	64,389	22,199	16,596	16,554	9,040	39,762	14.3%	13.0%	13.1%	10,763	92,298
Congressional District 2	68,238	25,408	20,863	15,730	6,237	33,965	17.6%	15.3%	13.6%	12,840	88,796
Congressional District 3	66,478	24,569	16,041	16,237	9,631	37,309	14.9%	10.7%	13.6%	10,446	91,036
New York											
Congressional District 1	72,206	18,113	16,052	20,769	17,272	52,238	6.2%	3.7%	5.6%	7,557	101,427

Table G-5: 114th Congressional Districts—Income, Poverty Status and Receipt of Food Stamps (SNAP)—*Continued*

		Income of Households with Householder 65 Years and Over					Poverty Rate of Persons			Households with 1 or More Persons 60 Years and Over	
	Total Households	Less Than $25,000	$25,000 - $49,999	$50,000 - $99,999	$100,000 or More	Median Household Income	55 to 64 Years	65 to 74 Years	75 Years and Over	Receiving SNAP	Not Receiving SNAP
New York—Cont.											
Congressional District 2	58,967	13,653	13,937	18,077	13,300	54,188	5.6%	5.7%	7.7%	7,644	86,321
Congressional District 3	73,784	14,021	15,912	19,938	23,913	65,471	5.1%	5.4%	5.0%	4,423	109,048
Congressional District 4	65,338	13,784	14,852	19,522	17,180	60,395	5.7%	3.8%	6.9%	6,040	98,355
Congressional District 5	53,390	17,738	12,316	13,348	9,988	43,464	10.6%	10.0%	13.4%	19,341	76,291
Congressional District 6	66,597	25,860	13,929	16,308	10,500	36,349	15.2%	14.6%	20.0%	19,406	90,581
Congressional District 7	43,626	25,491	8,940	5,869	3,326	20,814	22.1%	25.1%	29.2%	28,231	46,089
Congressional District 8	64,981	34,179	12,772	11,693	6,337	23,240	19.4%	18.5%	32.3%	34,313	70,580
Congressional District 9	61,570	27,251	12,634	13,252	8,433	31,090	14.4%	20.6%	24.3%	29,491	71,777
Congressional District 10	67,272	22,497	12,560	15,195	17,020	46,119	14.5%	10.6%	18.5%	18,759	83,415
Congressional District 11	63,069	23,721	13,974	15,144	10,230	37,088	12.1%	11.9%	16.5%	18,740	87,308
Congressional District 12	74,429	22,086	11,448	16,681	24,214	59,443	13.2%	10.2%	14.0%	10,581	93,616
Congressional District 13	55,969	31,425	12,578	9,093	2,873	20,970	26.3%	29.4%	33.7%	39,181	56,661
Congressional District 14	49,001	20,266	12,238	10,941	5,556	31,489	14.9%	15.3%	19.4%	19,382	67,150
Congressional District 15	46,280	31,901	7,739	4,847	1,793	15,975	34.8%	36.4%	38.8%	39,240	36,716
Congressional District 16	70,132	20,086	16,741	18,730	14,575	46,849	12.4%	9.5%	12.1%	14,188	90,683
Congressional District 17	63,796	14,430	14,050	14,836	20,480	59,184	6.2%	5.9%	9.1%	6,892	94,853
Congressional District 18	58,508	13,507	15,457	15,994	13,550	50,672	8.7%	4.7%	8.2%	5,782	87,750
Congressional District 19	79,439	23,259	23,421	22,360	10,399	40,724	10.0%	7.1%	7.5%	10,570	108,618
Congressional District 20	69,952	18,016	19,654	19,982	12,300	45,213	8.2%	6.3%	6.5%	11,415	95,257
Congressional District 21	69,707	22,969	20,529	18,794	7,415	37,980	9.8%	7.7%	7.3%	13,816	93,852
Congressional District 22	73,982	23,932	25,643	18,092	6,315	35,846	11.5%	7.6%	7.0%	14,875	97,203
Congressional District 23	75,608	25,556	24,451	17,611	7,990	35,659	11.2%	7.8%	8.3%	12,925	99,648
Congressional District 24	69,822	21,715	22,750	18,308	7,049	37,032	8.9%	6.2%	9.6%	12,097	94,503
Congressional District 25	71,712	21,378	26,085	17,073	7,176	36,075	8.9%	5.3%	7.4%	13,473	95,720
Congressional District 26	81,837	31,141	26,075	17,734	6,887	32,300	13.5%	10.0%	10.4%	19,926	100,277
Congressional District 27	75,144	23,381	23,417	19,271	9,075	38,232	7.4%	6.1%	10.0%	9,110	104,477
North Carolina											
Congressional District 1	74,055	33,282	21,798	14,267	4,708	28,099	19.9%	12.9%	18.7%	22,715	90,506
Congressional District 2	64,947	22,078	18,784	16,819	7,266	37,902	10.5%	10.2%	9.2%	11,386	84,674
Congressional District 3	69,395	21,643	19,564	20,757	7,431	40,257	11.1%	6.0%	10.5%	11,279	92,051
Congressional District 4	53,434	14,028	14,471	13,865	11,070	46,584	11.7%	9.3%	10.1%	8,915	73,913
Congressional District 5	77,817	26,831	22,662	20,498	7,826	37,540	13.6%	8.6%	11.8%	8,509	106,552
Congressional District 6	77,737	26,694	24,701	17,850	8,492	36,109	9.6%	6.1%	9.8%	10,829	107,397
Congressional District 7	82,751	27,261	25,579	19,025	10,886	37,251	10.7%	9.2%	8.8%	13,074	110,099
Congressional District 8	71,074	27,829	23,726	14,769	4,750	32,285	14.2%	11.5%	11.0%	14,277	90,749
Congressional District 9	56,843	14,603	15,287	17,232	9,721	46,075	8.3%	5.4%	6.1%	4,969	87,939
Congressional District 10	78,257	27,632	26,696	16,947	6,982	33,414	12.6%	7.5%	12.1%	13,217	104,310
Congressional District 11	94,233	34,329	29,247	22,097	8,560	34,111	12.8%	8.4%	12.1%	14,070	121,909
Congressional District 12	48,212	21,477	13,697	10,234	2,804	28,487	18.6%	15.7%	14.9%	15,919	61,417
Congressional District 13	59,341	16,333	16,095	17,486	9,427	46,457	8.3%	4.4%	9.1%	5,056	91,092
North Dakota											
Congressional District (at Large)	67,092	21,153	20,290	17,335	8,314	37,196	6.1%	6.9%	10.9%	6,248	93,978
Ohio											
Congressional District 1	62,140	20,528	17,187	16,233	8,192	37,957	12.9%	7.6%	9.7%	8,779	89,824
Congressional District 2	72,544	24,256	20,843	17,335	10,110	36,779	11.0%	8.5%	8.7%	13,560	97,281
Congressional District 3	46,478	18,730	13,549	10,339	3,860	31,430	14.5%	12.5%	12.1%	14,431	63,700
Congressional District 4	76,550	26,753	27,604	17,883	4,230	33,154	9.3%	8.0%	8.4%	10,244	102,461
Congressional District 5	73,459	21,316	25,462	18,636	8,045	38,754	6.8%	6.1%	5.8%	6,918	103,898
Congressional District 6	79,648	29,779	26,525	17,911	5,433	32,217	13.1%	7.6%	10.4%	15,880	103,380
Congressional District 7	77,403	24,719	28,936	18,495	5,253	35,330	9.9%	7.6%	10.0%	10,509	104,434
Congressional District 8	68,145	20,569	23,122	17,228	7,226	38,468	9.8%	4.0%	7.5%	8,735	93,488
Congressional District 9	69,370	28,811	22,228	13,916	4,415	30,173	14.2%	12.5%	10.3%	15,000	88,175
Congressional District 10	75,909	23,787	22,936	20,926	8,260	39,735	11.9%	6.2%	12.3%	10,219	101,606
Congressional District 11	71,354	29,610	20,015	15,255	6,474	31,495	19.5%	16.6%	10.1%	22,735	88,249
Congressional District 12	63,629	17,563	19,923	16,311	9,832	42,056	7.2%	6.6%	6.3%	7,401	90,544
Congressional District 13	81,590	28,476	28,389	18,655	6,070	34,672	12.2%	7.2%	8.1%	13,487	106,268
Congressional District 14	81,678	24,048	25,414	21,904	10,312	39,916	7.2%	5.7%	7.0%	9,316	111,573
Congressional District 15	64,398	17,834	21,357	17,742	7,465	39,774	8.9%	6.3%	6.6%	9,556	91,084
Congressional District 16	78,663	19,020	27,520	23,408	8,715	42,936	5.4%	4.4%	5.4%	5,689	112,662
Oklahoma											
Congressional District 1	65,940	19,054	20,227	17,272	9,387	41,866	10.6%	7.2%	7.3%	7,776	94,660
Congressional District 2	84,298	34,220	26,961	17,384	5,733	30,346	17.8%	9.7%	11.8%	14,474	107,101
Congressional District 3	71,857	25,727	21,079	18,068	6,983	35,730	11.8%	7.7%	10.2%	9,365	97,209
Congressional District 4	64,333	20,319	19,090	17,246	7,678	37,643	10.5%	7.0%	10.2%	7,744	91,436
Congressional District 5	64,577	18,405	19,488	17,905	8,779	41,272	14.5%	6.7%	7.7%	9,420	89,499
Oregon											
Congressional District 1	65,156	16,700	19,308	19,264	9,884	44,722	8.2%	5.9%	7.9%	11,255	93,446
Congressional District 2	91,423	29,587	30,728	21,829	9,279	36,246	12.3%	8.8%	8.1%	19,395	117,820
Congressional District 3	62,500	21,353	17,715	15,213	8,219	37,173	14.9%	11.0%	11.8%	19,315	86,189
Congressional District 4	93,134	29,988	29,208	24,760	9,178	38,768	12.5%	8.9%	8.9%	19,778	119,829
Congressional District 5	80,551	24,182	21,921	23,134	11,314	41,281	8.8%	7.4%	11.2%	16,291	108,592
Pennsylvania											
Congressional District 1	52,194	22,565	13,737	11,050	4,042	29,793	22.2%	15.1%	17.4%	20,333	65,397

Table G-5: 114th Congressional Districts—Income, Poverty Status and Receipt of Food Stamps (SNAP)—*Continued*

	Income of Households with Householder 65 Years and Over						Poverty Rate of Persons			Households with 1 or More Persons 60 Years and Over	
	Total Households	Less Than $25,000	$25,000 - $49,999	$50,000 - $99,999	$100,000 or More	Median Household Income	55 to 64 Years	65 to 74 Years	75 Years and Over	Receiving SNAP	Not Receiving SNAP
Pennsylvania—Cont.											
Congressional District 2	64,690	28,997	14,651	12,312	8,730	30,167	21.2%	16.0%	15.2%	22,403	73,053
Congressional District 3	79,461	28,031	27,275	18,236	5,919	33,640	10.2%	6.4%	7.7%	12,130	105,796
Congressional District 4	70,561	21,333	21,866	19,201	8,161	38,670	7.9%	6.0%	7.0%	7,732	100,514
Congressional District 5	76,241	28,188	25,394	16,757	5,902	32,760	9.2%	6.8%	7.5%	10,021	102,717
Congressional District 6	66,895	16,153	19,711	18,684	12,347	46,412	5.8%	4.5%	5.0%	5,428	96,573
Congressional District 7	72,192	17,924	19,380	21,237	13,651	47,580	5.1%	4.6%	7.4%	4,896	104,528
Congressional District 8	69,837	17,383	18,500	21,109	12,845	48,085	5.0%	4.8%	5.8%	6,289	103,255
Congressional District 9	82,081	30,364	26,967	18,712	6,038	33,017	10.9%	8.7%	11.1%	12,581	108,336
Congressional District 10	78,768	27,646	25,460	19,279	6,383	34,991	9.5%	5.8%	8.3%	9,113	107,219
Congressional District 11	77,826	26,669	24,503	19,764	6,890	35,531	8.6%	4.8%	10.1%	11,611	106,099
Congressional District 12	91,695	30,598	29,098	22,182	9,817	36,289	5.8%	4.5%	9.4%	9,779	121,018
Congressional District 13	65,577	21,185	18,779	14,743	10,870	38,054	10.6%	8.8%	12.3%	11,476	90,710
Congressional District 14	78,109	33,605	23,385	14,570	6,549	29,588	12.7%	10.8%	10.4%	16,680	100,491
Congressional District 15	71,594	21,446	22,329	19,010	8,809	39,009	6.6%	6.8%	5.7%	9,718	101,816
Congressional District 16	64,185	20,373	20,462	16,140	7,210	36,773	7.2%	8.4%	9.3%	9,778	88,168
Congressional District 17	75,051	28,233	25,283	17,069	4,466	32,382	10.8%	6.6%	11.4%	12,471	102,552
Congressional District 18	84,984	26,109	27,539	20,934	10,402	37,884	5.8%	5.6%	6.9%	8,643	115,609
Rhode Island											
Congressional District 1	48,914	17,159	13,887	10,288	7,580	35,284	13.2%	7.7%	13.8%	13,658	64,376
Congressional District 2	53,323	17,261	14,015	12,800	9,247	40,979	8.1%	8.1%	10.2%	9,683	71,958
South Carolina											
Congressional District 1	71,036	13,807	20,570	21,774	14,885	51,797	9.2%	5.0%	6.3%	5,467	100,125
Congressional District 2	61,668	17,702	18,386	16,183	9,397	41,124	10.8%	7.1%	7.1%	7,244	86,670
Congressional District 3	72,226	27,312	23,282	14,643	6,989	33,231	14.9%	7.7%	8.6%	10,757	95,272
Congressional District 4	64,297	21,805	19,975	16,067	6,450	34,928	12.5%	7.8%	9.3%	8,928	87,606
Congressional District 5	66,373	22,324	21,584	15,571	6,894	35,608	14.9%	9.3%	12.9%	10,542	88,767
Congressional District 6	60,294	26,855	17,758	11,495	4,186	29,412	19.4%	13.7%	15.5%	17,435	75,970
Congressional District 7	79,411	28,024	25,162	20,344	5,881	35,488	16.4%	10.3%	13.1%	16,184	106,235
South Dakota											
Congressional District (at Large)	82,186	28,821	25,745	18,808	8,812	35,240	8.6%	8.9%	12.7%	8,951	113,563
Tennessee											
Congressional District 1	84,988	32,331	26,890	19,235	6,532	32,331	13.7%	9.2%	12.1%	16,335	110,343
Congressional District 2	73,990	26,417	22,778	17,383	7,412	34,952	11.0%	9.6%	8.7%	12,115	100,216
Congressional District 3	76,832	29,605	22,609	16,902	7,716	34,094	13.8%	10.3%	11.2%	14,859	101,541
Congressional District 4	66,528	25,449	22,215	14,073	4,791	32,533	12.1%	7.1%	14.1%	13,146	86,602
Congressional District 5	53,893	17,634	13,236	15,391	7,632	41,132	14.1%	8.5%	11.6%	10,599	77,182
Congressional District 6	78,575	27,839	24,789	19,308	6,639	34,404	11.7%	8.7%	11.6%	13,673	100,415
Congressional District 7	61,094	21,637	18,783	14,629	6,045	34,174	12.9%	8.6%	9.4%	10,246	84,743
Congressional District 8	68,914	23,820	19,004	16,119	9,971	36,297	10.4%	7.8%	11.4%	11,775	92,940
Congressional District 9	48,622	19,209	14,641	10,664	4,108	31,306	18.3%	12.8%	17.3%	19,417	64,156
Texas											
Congressional District 1	69,577	26,990	18,391	17,294	6,902	35,382	12.8%	9.3%	12.5%	9,017	93,467
Congressional District 2	43,804	10,447	11,325	12,455	9,577	50,366	7.1%	6.9%	10.1%	4,028	74,398
Congressional District 3	43,498	8,381	11,253	12,653	11,211	55,061	5.0%	4.7%	8.1%	2,440	74,455
Congressional District 4	68,369	25,778	19,927	16,121	6,543	33,868	12.1%	9.3%	9.8%	10,249	93,450
Congressional District 5	56,327	18,151	17,847	14,005	6,324	38,128	13.2%	8.8%	9.6%	8,331	80,378
Congressional District 6	44,972	11,194	11,775	13,634	8,369	48,966	6.1%	5.9%	8.8%	5,109	68,785
Congressional District 7	45,707	11,825	9,931	10,085	13,866	53,266	6.7%	6.7%	7.9%	2,969	75,470
Congressional District 8	60,442	18,222	15,565	15,876	10,779	42,446	6.1%	8.3%	11.8%	6,844	86,494
Congressional District 9	38,572	14,753	9,169	9,187	5,463	35,778	15.0%	13.3%	16.6%	14,005	59,330
Congressional District 10	51,065	12,254	13,723	14,647	10,441	48,586	7.8%	4.6%	9.6%	6,336	80,108
Congressional District 11	69,340	24,979	19,501	14,971	9,889	36,033	9.8%	9.5%	12.1%	7,710	96,963
Congressional District 12	55,966	14,160	17,065	16,308	8,433	43,106	8.2%	6.9%	6.4%	6,328	80,635
Congressional District 13	63,080	22,709	17,027	15,947	7,397	36,757	10.5%	7.3%	10.3%	6,712	89,323
Congressional District 14	60,139	19,462	18,707	13,533	8,437	36,928	13.1%	9.2%	10.5%	8,970	85,935
Congressional District 15	44,688	19,607	12,025	8,775	4,281	29,786	17.5%	21.4%	20.9%	17,934	54,478
Congressional District 16	47,385	19,774	14,163	9,570	3,878	29,853	15.6%	16.6%	22.4%	17,020	60,737
Congressional District 17	52,613	16,183	15,180	13,833	7,417	40,031	8.7%	6.9%	11.0%	8,548	73,241
Congressional District 18	42,364	19,181	9,849	9,424	3,910	28,577	14.5%	17.9%	17.0%	13,092	58,461
Congressional District 19	59,989	19,698	17,894	14,382	8,015	38,652	9.4%	10.7%	12.1%	7,844	79,779
Congressional District 20	45,644	15,973	13,411	11,047	5,213	37,500	16.4%	11.4%	16.5%	12,480	62,487
Congressional District 21	73,292	15,825	20,507	20,656	16,304	50,948	8.9%	5.3%	5.0%	5,075	105,427
Congressional District 22	42,330	9,993	9,786	12,943	9,608	53,185	4.2%	6.9%	9.1%	6,426	70,451
Congressional District 23	51,174	20,366	11,911	11,031	7,866	34,244	13.7%	13.8%	19.4%	14,299	67,503
Congressional District 24	45,655	10,617	11,337	13,609	10,092	51,996	4.9%	4.8%	7.5%	3,128	73,786
Congressional District 25	55,791	14,109	15,430	15,973	10,279	47,126	10.4%	4.4%	8.7%	5,705	84,187
Congressional District 26	40,455	9,024	12,216	10,877	8,338	46,966	5.2%	4.9%	6.6%	4,347	64,108
Congressional District 27	64,415	21,693	18,864	15,933	7,925	37,602	11.3%	13.4%	13.0%	12,732	87,934
Congressional District 28	42,688	18,036	10,926	10,006	3,720	31,224	18.9%	17.1%	23.4%	16,161	56,261
Congressional District 29	32,967	14,493	9,301	6,587	2,586	27,672	15.2%	17.8%	19.0%	11,647	48,079
Congressional District 30	40,286	16,615	11,670	8,550	3,451	31,425	21.8%	14.4%	15.5%	13,536	60,451
Congressional District 31	47,520	11,534	12,284	15,216	8,486	49,894	8.2%	5.6%	6.2%	4,629	74,839
Congressional District 32	52,931	12,879	13,947	14,856	11,249	49,300	7.5%	6.5%	6.8%	6,389	78,876
Congressional District 33	35,769	17,457	9,166	7,541	1,605	25,865	18.1%	17.9%	19.4%	11,679	47,756

Table G-5: 114th Congressional Districts—Income, Poverty Status and Receipt of Food Stamps (SNAP)—*Continued*

		Income of Households with Householder 65 Years and Over					Poverty Rate of Persons			Households with 1 or More Persons 60 Years and Over	
	Total Households	Less Than $25,000	$25,000 - $49,999	$50,000 - $99,999	$100,000 or More	Median Household Income	55 to 64 Years	65 to 74 Years	75 Years and Over	Receiving SNAP	Not Receiving SNAP
Texas—Cont.											
Congressional District 34	55,273	27,950	12,753	9,378	5,192	24,732	20.8%	20.2%	23.9%	17,429	65,721
Congressional District 35	41,117	16,577	11,176	10,595	2,769	31,544	16.3%	17.2%	11.6%	11,003	58,694
Congressional District 36	58,393	21,160	17,304	13,371	6,558	35,056	10.8%	7.5%	10.6%	9,021	88,449
Utah											
Congressional District 1	43,547	11,689	11,478	14,370	6,010	45,283	6.4%	6.9%	8.2%	4,009	68,114
Congressional District 2	52,140	14,676	15,550	16,405	5,509	41,526	10.4%	6.6%	9.1%	5,133	71,870
Congressional District 3	39,088	8,762	11,040	10,895	8,391	49,166	6.7%	4.5%	6.8%	3,649	61,729
Congressional District 4	40,970	9,028	12,154	13,931	5,857	48,451	7.8%	3.6%	9.1%	3,979	63,589
Vermont											
Congressional District (at Large)	67,260	21,903	20,753	17,122	7,482	36,346	9.6%	6.0%	8.7%	12,460	91,838
Virginia											
Congressional District 1	61,991	12,173	15,274	19,214	15,330	56,005	5.8%	3.2%	5.9%	5,846	91,563
Congressional District 2	59,210	14,728	15,826	18,237	10,419	48,286	6.9%	7.1%	8.1%	6,008	86,700
Congressional District 3	57,552	22,670	14,939	13,852	6,091	33,175	15.3%	12.5%	15.4%	13,396	79,311
Congressional District 4	60,850	15,908	17,159	18,658	9,125	45,266	7.1%	7.0%	7.9%	8,354	89,346
Congressional District 5	84,852	29,025	24,055	21,407	10,365	37,412	10.4%	8.1%	13.3%	13,380	114,853
Congressional District 6	81,215	27,669	24,013	21,082	8,451	37,547	9.0%	5.9%	10.0%	9,335	109,415
Congressional District 7	69,449	14,031	16,963	22,427	16,028	54,852	4.7%	4.6%	6.0%	5,084	103,326
Congressional District 8	49,403	9,714	8,338	12,683	18,668	72,215	5.2%	8.3%	8.8%	4,127	77,604
Congressional District 9	85,129	36,666	24,896	17,728	5,839	29,257	14.8%	9.6%	12.8%	13,865	111,265
Congressional District 10	46,709	7,862	8,560	12,552	17,735	71,681	4.7%	4.1%	5.9%	3,658	82,385
Congressional District 11	45,948	6,575	6,198	14,711	18,464	80,744	3.4%	3.9%	6.1%	5,180	76,903
Washington											
Congressional District 1	51,723	12,072	14,217	14,445	10,989	49,259	7.2%	5.5%	7.1%	7,507	80,056
Congressional District 2	65,104	19,658	18,828	18,075	8,543	41,927	8.8%	7.6%	10.7%	12,389	90,248
Congressional District 3	69,054	19,276	22,030	19,821	7,927	41,043	8.8%	6.8%	7.2%	12,134	93,352
Congressional District 4	54,375	17,717	16,732	13,623	6,303	38,104	10.3%	8.1%	11.3%	12,065	74,214
Congressional District 5	66,503	20,030	20,317	18,979	7,177	40,001	12.2%	8.4%	10.2%	13,664	86,546
Congressional District 6	75,550	19,212	22,973	21,595	11,770	43,794	10.5%	8.0%	10.0%	12,158	100,799
Congressional District 7	59,863	14,658	15,030	17,168	13,007	50,848	11.0%	7.6%	9.7%	8,713	88,515
Congressional District 8	50,179	11,506	13,220	16,195	9,258	50,640	7.7%	5.9%	6.5%	7,525	76,357
Congressional District 9	55,278	14,957	14,841	13,770	11,710	45,902	8.2%	10.2%	13.6%	15,242	73,987
Congressional District 10	58,199	14,888	17,356	17,618	8,337	45,007	9.7%	7.6%	10.4%	11,527	80,167
West Virginia											
Congressional District 1	69,426	26,763	22,757	15,651	4,255	32,210	12.6%	8.1%	11.3%	9,041	93,364
Congressional District 2	69,289	23,008	23,231	17,483	5,567	36,219	13.5%	7.4%	10.7%	9,159	94,431
Congressional District 3	73,073	32,037	22,975	14,398	3,663	29,383	14.6%	10.3%	8.8%	15,046	92,722
Wisconsin											
Congressional District 1	67,267	19,739	22,002	18,535	6,991	40,305	9.5%	5.5%	5.8%	8,648	94,215
Congressional District 2	61,641	16,878	18,892	17,784	8,087	42,151	7.7%	3.8%	9.6%	8,382	88,663
Congressional District 3	72,525	24,618	24,539	18,138	5,230	35,211	6.9%	5.2%	10.2%	9,400	97,717
Congressional District 4	49,461	19,768	14,996	9,808	4,889	31,583	18.3%	12.4%	12.8%	16,685	66,809
Congressional District 5	74,606	20,744	24,334	21,178	8,350	40,018	5.4%	5.2%	7.3%	6,068	104,276
Congressional District 6	75,390	24,990	25,862	17,900	6,638	35,165	7.0%	3.6%	8.7%	7,361	104,826
Congressional District 7	82,287	28,905	27,523	20,628	5,231	34,524	7.7%	6.1%	9.4%	9,543	111,720
Congressional District 8	69,654	21,461	24,927	17,999	5,267	36,499	7.3%	6.0%	9.4%	7,427	97,239
Wyoming											
Congressional District (at Large)	51,531	15,451	14,790	14,753	6,537	40,773	9.0%	4.7%	8.7%	3,769	78,867

PART H
DISABILITY STATUS AND TYPE

DISABILITY STATUS AND TYPE

Life expectancy at birth in the United States has steadily increased and the latest data from the National Center for Health Statistics says women's life expectancy has increased from 77.4 years in 1980 to 81.2 years in 2013. Male life expectancy has also increased from 70.0 years in 1980 to 76.4 years in 2013.[1] Both were unchanged from 2012 and the gap between male and female life expectancy remained at 4.8 years even though it has declined from its peak in the 1970's. It is unclear whether the increasing life span will bring increased incidence of disability or if medical advances will ease the process of aging. Part of the uncertainty lies in the data. While life

expectancy can be calculated based on detailed mortality data, measuring basic functions of activity that are defined as disabilities is much more difficult.

The Census Bureau's American Community Survey asks a series of questions about activities of daily living to measure the extent of identified disabilities. These are not clinical measures but the respondent's identification of difficulties they experience. These include difficulties in: vision, hearing, cognitive ability, ambulatory ability, and self-care ability.

In the United States, just over 25 percent of the population age 65 to 74 indicated that they experience some disability but that percentage doubles for those age 75 and over where 50.3 percent have a disability. Ambulatory difficulty is most prevalent at 33.1 percent followed by hearing difficulty (22.9 percent), cognitive difficulty (14.2 percent), self-care difficulty (13.9 percent)

1. U.S. Department of Health and Human Services, Centers for Disease Control and Prevention, National Center for Health Statistics, National Vital Statistics Reports, Vol. 62, No. 2, *Deaths: Final Data for 2013*.

Percent of the Population 75 Years and Over With a Disability

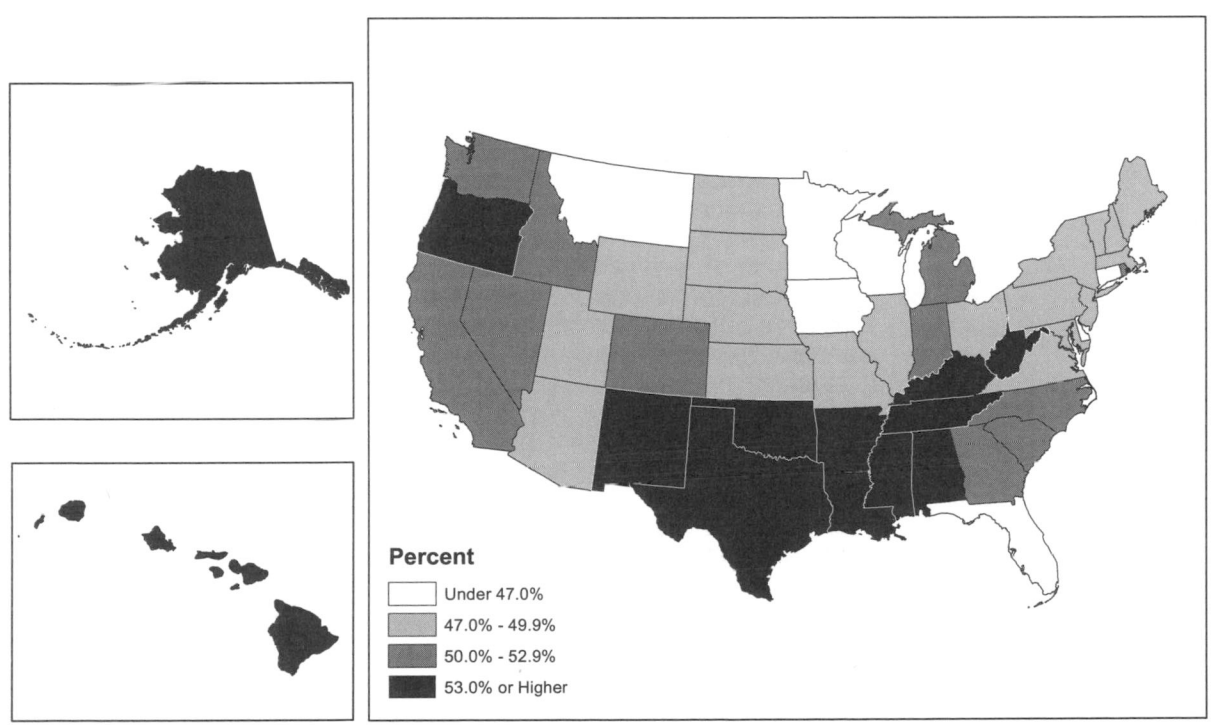

Percent
- Under 47.0%
- 47.0% - 49.9%
- 50.0% - 52.9%
- 53.0% or Higher

and vision difficult at 10.0 percent. Among the states, Mississippi has the highest percent of 75 and over population (57.6 percent) indicating that they have a disability and Mississippi is also the highest for those with ambulatory disabilities at (41.2 percent). Hawaii has the highest percentage of those with cognitive disabilities at 21.2 percent while Alaskans have the highest for self-care (22.9 percent) and vision (14.9 percent) difficulties. Residents of Idaho who are 75 and over have the highest percentage for hearing difficulties (31.1 percent). Delaware has the lowest percent for disabilities overall at 41.8 percent. The states with the lowest percent of persons 75 and over experiencing difficulties are: the District of Columbia for hearing difficulty at 13.2 percent; North Dakota for vision difficulty at 6.5 percent; Iowa for cognitive (9.3 percent) and ambulatory difficulty (26.4 percent); and North Dakota for self-care difficulty at 7.0 percent.

There is wide variation across the nation's counties in the percentage of 75 and over population with a disability or experiencing difficulty. Ward County, North Dakota has the lowest experience of any county with only 0.3 percent of the population experiencing vision difficulties while Hardin County, Kentucky has the highest percentage of persons experiencing ambulatory

difficulties at 62.8 percent. Overall, Hardin County, Kentucky also has the highest percent reporting any disability at 76.1 percent. In 429 counties, greater than 50 percent of the population 75 and over report some disability and only five counties have less than one-third of the population reporting any disability.

In Homestead, Florida 88.2 percent of the 75 and over population (the highest of all cities) reports some disability while Laguna Niguel, California is the lowest at 24.5 percent indicating that at least one-quarter of the population in each city reports some disability. Among all cities, ambulatory difficulty is most common and reported by 38.2 percent of the 75 and over population. Vision difficulty is the least often reported at 10.1 percent. Homestead, Florida has the highest percent reporting for each category of disability: hearing difficulty (59.4 percent); vision difficulty (42.8 percent); cognitive difficulty (44.8 percent); ambulatory difficulty (62.7 percent); and self-care difficulty at 43.0 percent. Nearly 300 counties report that at least one-third of the 75 and over population have ambulatory difficulty.

Across all metropolitan areas, half (50.0 percent) of the 75 and over population report some form of disability. The Hinesville, Georgia metro area is highest, where

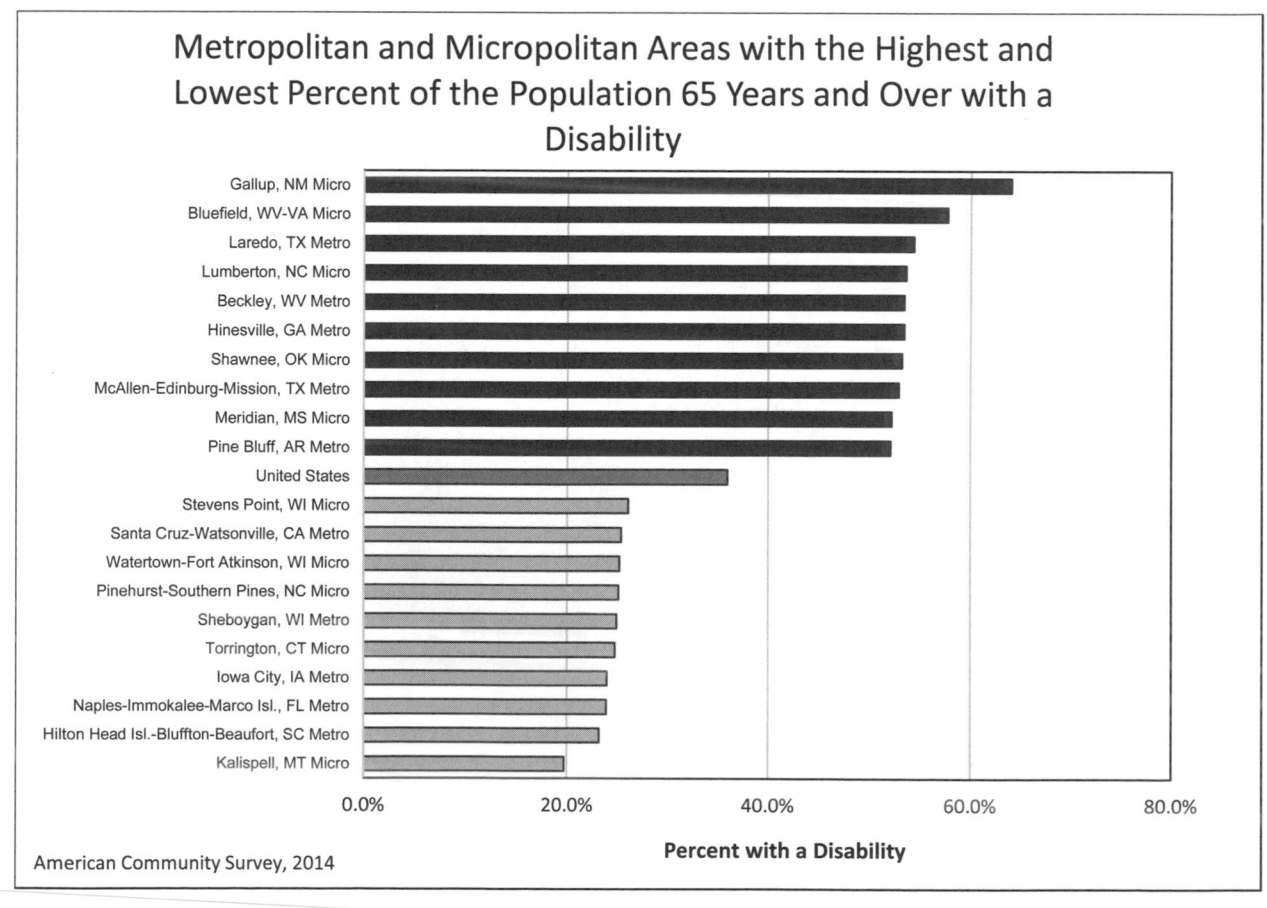

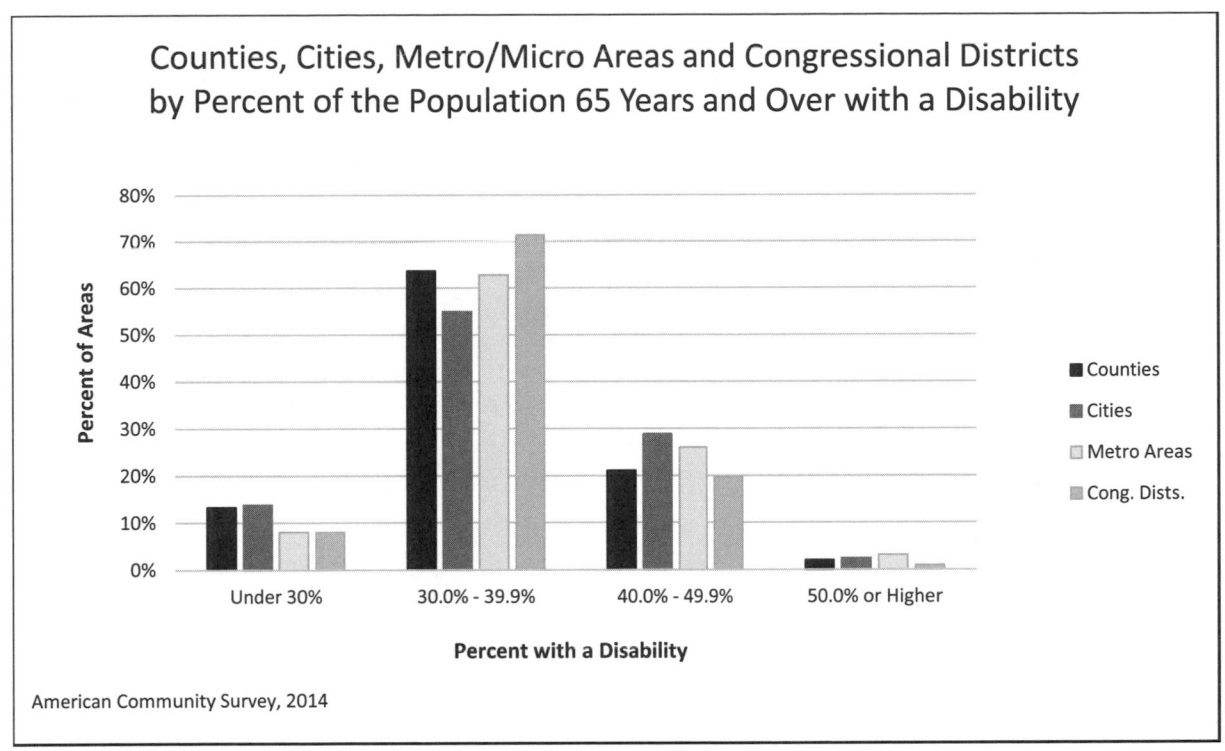

Counties, Cities, Metro/Micro Areas and Congressional Districts by Percent of the Population 65 Years and Over with a Disability

American Community Survey, 2014

three of every four people 75 and over (76.8 percent) report a disability. The Hinesville area also has the highest rate for cognitive difficulty at 35.4 percent. The Kalispell, Montana micropolitan area is lowest in overall reporting of some disability at 30.4 percent. The Minot, North Dakota micropolitan area has the lowest percentage of any disability category at 0.4 percent experiencing vision difficulties. The area experiencing the highest percent of a disability is the Gallup, New Mexico micropolitan area where 57.4 percent report ambulatory difficulties. The Portsmouth, Ohio micropolitan area has the highest reporting of hearing difficulty (43.3 percent) while self-care difficulties are reported the most in the Fairbanks, Alaska metro area (36.8 percent). In nearly 286 metropolitan or micropolitan areas, more than 50 percent of the 75 and over population report some type of disability.

Nearly two-thirds (65.4 percent) of the 75 and over population report some type of disability West Virginia's 3rd Congressional District, the highest of all districts but 19 districts have more than 60 of residents reporting some disability. In more than half of all districts (236) over 50 percent of the population reports a disability. Even in Pennsylvania's 6th District, the lowest, 39.4 percent have some type of disability. West Virginia's 3rd District has the highest percent of persons with a hearing difficulty (37.3 percent) as well as a vision difficulty (21.4 percent). Nearly one-third (32.2 percent) of New York's 8th District population 75 and over has self-care difficulties. New York's 13th District is highest for cognitive difficulties at 27.2 percent and the 15th District is highest with more than one-half of older residents (52.6 percent) reporting ambulatory difficulties.

Table H-1: States—Disability Status and Type of Disability

	Total Population		With a Disability		With a Hearing Disability		With a Vision Disability		With a Cognitive Disability		With an Ambulatory Disability		With a Self-Care Disability	
	65 to 74 Years	75 Years and Over	65 to 74 Years	75 Years and Over	65 to 74 Years	75 Years and Over	65 to 74 Years	75 Years and Over	65 to 74 Years	75 Years and Over	65 to 74 Years	75 Years and Over	65 to 74 Years	75 Years and Over
United States...................	26,123,154	18,789,782	6,701,559	9,458,954	2,442,225	4,299,567	1,129,029	1,870,450	1,424,069	2,676,241	4,136,854	6,214,256	1,173,525	2,611,858
Alabama...........................	430,263	294,906	138,295	165,151	50,062	71,204	22,386	35,740	33,317	49,627	89,362	114,846	24,414	50,158
Alaska..............................	46,028	22,990	15,155	13,206	8,119	6,812	2,663	3,417	2,491	4,318	7,992	8,153	2,527	5,276
Arizona............................	618,033	439,973	159,744	210,522	67,099	109,446	29,175	46,072	33,307	58,913	93,580	136,109	25,432	53,373
Arkansas..........................	264,336	183,994	88,036	102,947	36,573	49,554	16,363	21,355	20,080	27,287	55,579	70,405	16,368	25,921
California.........................	2,812,162	2,085,653	671,663	1,075,059	221,384	481,255	117,015	211,136	160,426	338,235	415,494	718,579	140,875	353,718
Colorado..........................	406,478	257,802	91,076	129,089	39,722	68,593	13,712	25,670	17,796	33,968	50,340	77,540	13,282	28,421
Connecticut......................	300,007	233,518	61,600	108,413	22,200	46,145	8,144	18,141	14,245	26,232	37,257	69,442	12,487	33,122
Delaware..........................	90,743	58,983	20,915	24,662	7,646	11,141	3,282	4,097	4,771	6,638	12,241	16,951	3,531	6,817
District of Columbia..........	40,997	30,983	10,513	15,807	2,349	4,081	2,678	3,543	2,831	5,260	7,990	10,892	2,931	5,505
Florida............................	2,065,459	1,658,040	479,760	776,839	166,609	352,652	79,607	144,069	101,478	226,884	290,470	508,677	76,696	212,523
Georgia...........................	760,426	457,560	218,740	241,764	75,388	102,660	42,312	50,936	51,583	74,160	136,649	164,055	38,874	68,866
Hawaii.............................	126,012	97,671	27,377	53,143	9,436	27,269	3,690	8,091	6,451	20,753	16,106	35,040	4,409	16,345
Idaho..............................	139,923	91,410	37,888	48,097	17,531	28,446	5,554	10,754	8,827	13,951	20,447	28,372	4,905	10,705
Illinois............................	988,260	734,862	239,245	366,325	75,637	155,043	39,438	70,455	46,214	92,607	156,779	247,045	42,793	98,059
Indiana............................	527,846	377,694	144,067	195,731	54,365	92,107	22,665	40,151	30,588	52,550	89,666	127,959	23,849	46,849
Iowa...............................	255,429	211,979	56,838	91,612	24,935	43,850	6,730	14,853	9,818	19,756	31,660	55,874	8,299	18,959
Kansas............................	223,440	175,902	57,503	85,396	22,907	39,877	9,315	15,269	10,653	20,213	35,145	54,102	10,000	21,051
Kentucky..........................	380,142	250,941	129,991	142,047	50,948	64,782	25,851	29,474	30,415	39,701	83,782	96,477	22,039	38,564
Louisiana.........................	366,682	243,620	115,474	130,350	38,099	52,764	21,920	27,441	25,762	41,266	75,406	90,512	24,666	40,692
Maine..............................	139,305	96,472	31,591	47,282	13,551	23,338	3,788	9,090	6,319	10,313	17,721	28,893	5,655	10,733
Maryland..........................	472,598	326,048	99,708	155,784	31,183	63,683	13,599	30,122	20,226	44,735	62,398	103,566	16,061	42,061
Massachusetts.................	556,990	420,039	115,558	202,894	42,002	96,718	18,704	39,019	27,219	56,383	66,447	129,077	20,656	58,082
Michigan..........................	865,317	626,098	224,259	314,132	84,234	140,332	34,398	58,788	47,244	83,375	136,713	202,084	38,697	80,533
Minnesota........................	425,055	322,353	90,352	147,403	40,085	70,222	11,622	25,860	17,312	36,146	47,060	88,696	13,490	35,886
Mississippi.......................	244,198	170,944	86,156	98,391	29,742	41,718	16,084	23,840	20,297	34,628	57,427	70,427	15,852	30,782
Missouri...........................	520,120	373,486	142,967	184,872	55,695	84,328	23,691	36,835	26,383	48,504	85,918	118,836	22,069	40,828
Montana...........................	98,311	67,203	24,581	31,476	11,923	15,832	3,016	5,699	4,778	6,803	12,905	19,205	3,631	6,285
Nebraska..........................	143,281	116,010	35,649	55,231	16,398	28,303	5,109	10,521	5,757	13,187	19,835	30,759	4,901	10,627
Nevada............................	248,566	147,449	71,263	74,226	25,724	35,927	13,370	14,900	15,993	19,944	47,353	48,907	11,691	17,519
New Hampshire.................	121,773	79,771	25,945	39,604	11,142	19,429	3,843	6,697	4,119	9,648	15,458	24,257	4,191	8,273
New Jersey.......................	720,881	551,228	154,332	266,640	42,667	110,982	24,700	49,976	30,618	73,189	101,296	180,233	24,343	77,755
New Mexico......................	184,341	128,822	56,333	71,115	24,098	36,511	10,394	16,901	14,192	22,657	32,678	46,039	9,912	18,097
New York..........................	1,582,444	1,214,356	367,611	603,016	112,483	240,288	67,880	118,412	77,080	174,612	240,523	415,193	68,394	192,177
North Carolina.................	860,279	559,996	235,776	291,135	83,003	133,869	42,335	56,816	47,735	84,109	150,207	191,152	44,421	83,114
North Dakota....................	53,675	45,217	12,409	21,273	5,569	10,461	1,562	2,949	2,299	4,257	5,889	13,256	1,302	3,145
Ohio................................	989,862	738,329	252,982	358,220	88,898	160,466	41,499	69,907	50,090	92,452	159,380	230,020	47,597	90,139
Oklahoma.........................	317,698	225,101	105,496	124,518	43,963	63,326	20,113	26,199	19,870	33,908	65,761	86,391	17,079	33,000
Oregon.............................	372,763	251,832	100,693	136,500	43,861	72,468	13,892	27,132	21,696	41,305	57,422	85,259	16,697	34,746
Pennsylvania....................	1,138,280	917,602	268,240	443,891	99,381	198,043	36,396	80,305	50,761	116,320	160,923	279,835	40,486	107,698
Rhode Island....................	88,813	71,150	21,932	36,147	7,419	16,086	3,674	6,986	4,443	8,155	13,512	24,068	3,353	8,303
South Carolina.................	464,574	279,753	131,025	146,277	46,237	66,984	22,928	31,677	31,876	44,224	83,357	96,342	22,489	42,847
South Dakota....................	68,243	54,412	16,257	26,041	7,134	13,838	1,503	5,774	2,914	7,105	9,850	16,759	2,690	4,939
Tennessee........................	582,581	375,499	174,205	202,984	63,720	91,689	33,382	42,285	39,138	60,238	112,771	135,328	32,753	56,764
Texas..............................	1,810,564	1,201,553	537,171	649,906	197,176	291,609	107,337	143,454	113,273	189,726	341,285	436,509	101,231	185,304
Utah...............................	170,842	120,335	40,664	59,004	19,178	30,940	6,527	11,867	8,277	14,541	21,918	36,719	5,198	14,033
Vermont...........................	61,836	41,295	15,048	20,504	6,251	10,686	2,315	3,832	3,582	5,251	8,603	13,212	2,308	5,043
Virginia............................	673,544	446,954	161,193	221,130	52,086	99,111	22,237	43,843	29,604	61,572	99,871	145,015	26,167	59,154
Washington......................	586,661	384,653	155,102	199,980	66,899	101,394	21,764	40,009	36,031	62,997	90,915	126,224	23,705	57,089
West Virginia....................	188,910	131,023	68,421	73,386	29,774	38,368	13,472	19,072	14,820	20,782	43,128	47,790	11,444	19,948
Wisconsin........................	479,739	366,722	101,882	165,386	43,721	78,191	13,156	28,302	16,548	39,094	55,592	104,798	14,467	39,523
Wyoming..........................	48,444	29,596	12,878	14,446	6,019	6,746	2,239	2,717	2,522	3,762	6,793	8,377	2,218	2,507

Table H-2: Counties—Disability Status and Type of Disability

	Total Population		With a Disability		With a Hearing Disability		With a Vision Disability		With a Cognitive Disability		With an Ambulatory Disability		With a Self-Care Disability	
	65 to 74 Years	75 Years and Over	65 to 74 Years	75 Years and Over	65 to 74 Years	75 Years and Over	65 to 74 Years	75 Years and Over	65 to 74 Years	75 Years and Over	65 to 74 Years	75 Years and Over	65 to 74 Years	75 Years and Over
Alabama														
Baldwin County	22,261	14,992	5,127	8,011	2,340	3,375	290	1,097	539	1,908	3,298	5,560	878	1,458
Calhoun County	10,914	7,167	3,612	4,116	1,220	2,013	571	1,111	907	1,332	2,735	3,255	667	1,222
Cullman County	8,344	5,539	3,236	3,083	1,394	2,130	567	889	652	1,099	1,615	1,697	779	868
DeKalb County	6,728	3,863	2,615	2,516	1,084	1,354	544	604	538	935	1,807	1,984	518	1,184
Elmore County	6,558	4,295	2,098	2,391	948	1,088	212	395	320	725	1,339	1,712	374	946
Etowah County	10,533	6,846	3,623	4,468	911	1,905	682	1,156	1,281	1,360	2,691	3,356	964	1,537
Houston County	9,636	6,862	3,334	4,043	1,263	1,683	452	906	710	1,100	2,229	3,060	515	1,194
Jefferson County	52,143	39,649	13,652	20,944	4,802	7,615	2,456	3,878	3,340	6,680	8,732	15,332	2,480	7,625
Lauderdale County	9,681	6,881	2,696	3,512	695	1,658	412	438	918	850	1,678	2,314	846	1,123
Lee County	9,921	5,647	3,281	2,772	1,459	1,356	567	674	620	525	2,301	1,594	623	438
Limestone County	7,416	4,726	2,722	2,318	846	1,126	122	510	607	406	1,847	1,479	280	452
Madison County	26,521	20,560	8,169	10,149	3,862	4,514	1,388	2,213	2,069	2,494	4,517	5,260	1,545	2,329
Marshall County	8,858	5,961	3,495	4,023	916	1,760	615	820	1,457	945	2,462	3,103	543	1,610
Mobile County	34,746	23,799	9,526	13,058	3,468	4,773	1,355	2,463	2,331	4,378	6,113	9,705	1,251	4,822
Montgomery County	16,791	12,715	4,924	6,254	1,158	2,409	654	1,563	847	2,039	3,368	5,114	966	2,083
Morgan County	10,664	7,096	3,758	5,020	1,433	2,685	834	1,340	960	1,696	2,050	3,368	522	1,412
Shelby County	17,021	9,839	4,472	5,711	1,882	2,065	847	801	846	1,627	2,317	4,337	905	1,939
St. Clair County	8,045	5,214	2,529	2,887	811	1,312	658	534	555	660	1,582	2,178	307	763
Talladega County	7,786	4,719	2,815	2,602	1,056	1,013	661	745	273	670	2,077	1,750	604	712
Tuscaloosa County	13,794	9,349	4,520	5,021	1,473	1,864	530	1,076	713	1,743	3,259	3,617	622	1,712
Walker County	6,851	4,636	3,028	2,664	1,110	1,404	645	505	1,104	843	2,209	1,682	403	413
Alaska														
Anchorage Municipality	16,514	9,913	4,073	5,403	2,264	2,335	273	1,099	701	2,110	2,155	2,708	533	2,310
Fairbanks North Star Borough	5,193	2,657	1,916	1,690	1,220	606	657	393	318	376	743	1,246	283	978
Matanuska-Susitna Borough	6,616	2,776	2,274	1,347	1,060	618	152	296	463	376	1,546	925	192	510
Arizona														
Apache County	5,743	3,630	1,953	2,333	1,019	1,708	634	420	804	920	1,015	1,378	398	643
Cochise County	14,323	10,482	4,469	5,652	2,189	3,441	1,107	1,561	1,162	2,216	2,584	3,164	1,009	1,770
Coconino County	9,962	5,412	2,647	2,868	1,186	1,794	521	654	312	957	1,579	2,011	376	757
Maricopa County	325,173	234,408	78,593	112,075	32,068	56,937	13,858	25,064	15,589	31,414	46,458	73,860	11,495	29,459
Mohave County	32,061	22,488	10,808	11,022	5,290	6,312	1,461	2,235	1,868	2,933	6,295	5,979	1,643	2,531
Navajo County	10,768	6,118	3,893	3,703	1,791	2,432	1,340	1,180	847	1,504	2,368	2,434	534	970
Pima County	99,643	75,661	27,713	35,477	11,846	17,988	4,770	6,354	5,710	8,635	14,296	23,969	4,171	9,532
Pinal County	45,061	25,702	10,068	11,630	4,681	5,855	1,885	3,090	1,817	4,198	6,338	7,077	1,694	3,038
Yavapai County	36,601	24,362	7,511	11,473	2,866	5,571	1,567	2,672	2,503	2,608	4,314	7,362	1,024	1,914
Yuma County	18,552	17,185	5,682	7,745	1,664	4,022	712	1,436	939	1,856	3,844	4,903	1,217	1,397
Arkansas														
Benton County	18,158	12,512	4,050	5,296	1,684	2,719	641	793	709	1,114	2,344	3,171	502	1,308
Craighead County	7,345	5,721	2,524	2,772	776	937	1,074	414	521	1,029	1,707	2,193	765	1,052
Faulkner County	7,785	5,042	2,711	2,882	1,250	1,646	144	879	665	867	1,683	1,829	410	642
Garland County	11,482	9,047	2,845	4,423	1,308	2,375	222	809	610	1,184	1,448	2,425	399	973
Jefferson County	5,986	4,186	2,419	2,742	912	1,450	567	397	252	614	1,418	2,008	189	647
Lonoke County	5,416	3,141	2,079	1,735	830	899	728	398	499	189	1,318	941	268	595
Pulaski County	30,037	21,138	8,766	11,190	2,479	4,656	1,666	1,648	3,071	2,348	6,239	8,317	1,527	2,501
Saline County	11,889	6,780	4,108	3,270	1,909	1,097	622	498	964	735	2,186	2,415	1,256	883
Sebastian County	10,261	7,153	2,932	3,861	1,302	2,327	549	1,076	713	1,581	1,681	2,376	549	917
Washington County	13,914	9,336	4,177	4,781	1,717	2,516	516	1,365	622	1,319	2,580	2,908	1,142	932
White County	6,547	5,018	2,379	2,647	843	1,483	508	392	635	811	1,463	1,799	574	670
California														
Alameda County	115,342	81,455	23,784	41,344	6,779	18,684	4,334	7,060	5,021	12,478	15,428	27,311	5,087	13,895
Butte County	21,032	15,990	6,896	8,034	2,265	3,976	1,189	993	1,516	2,425	5,063	5,375	1,319	1,789
Contra Costa County	91,058	64,352	18,698	32,971	6,391	15,901	3,728	5,609	4,044	10,771	10,622	22,865	2,546	10,886
El Dorado County	20,542	12,396	4,054	6,729	1,875	3,991	709	1,615	1,165	2,064	2,265	3,730	682	1,452
Fresno County	61,200	44,776	18,288	25,893	6,285	12,791	3,047	5,367	4,329	8,096	11,927	18,394	3,856	8,086
Humboldt County	12,402	7,725	3,695	3,779	2,093	1,722	633	754	712	1,361	1,999	2,401	500	840
Imperial County	11,601	9,835	4,671	5,664	1,564	2,596	1,215	1,055	608	2,105	2,616	3,692	596	2,256
Kern County	51,079	33,812	14,754	17,310	5,091	6,880	2,198	4,587	3,156	4,528	10,119	11,644	2,822	5,236
Kings County	7,604	5,435	2,929	3,344	1,748	1,375	504	330	773	1,491	1,754	2,265	337	792
Lake County	7,662	4,925	2,806	2,414	1,014	1,190	319	544	1,278	869	1,509	1,485	795	757
Los Angeles County	681,212	524,752	167,647	273,529	44,097	110,656	31,129	56,099	40,365	97,245	109,651	192,081	43,221	107,065
Madera County	11,258	7,834	4,351	4,470	1,909	2,842	1,688	1,784	837	1,505	3,205	3,086	1,044	1,623
Marin County	29,451	19,478	4,065	7,741	2,230	2,968	714	1,316	627	1,591	1,750	5,448	909	2,251
Mendocino County	10,701	5,949	3,845	3,176	1,680	1,935	811	699	853	1,413	2,094	2,034	937	924
Merced County	16,204	11,786	6,853	6,816	2,182	3,882	2,083	2,206	1,943	1,966	4,520	4,205	1,114	2,177
Monterey County	28,351	21,486	5,907	12,461	1,876	5,675	1,002	2,124	1,397	4,794	3,840	8,375	895	4,233
Napa County	14,295	9,433	2,310	5,279	930	3,039	218	710	297	1,145	1,389	3,230	258	1,255
Nevada County	13,697	9,047	3,233	3,544	1,780	1,728	388	607	544	886	1,517	2,634	588	1,425
Orange County	230,547	177,303	41,631	83,798	13,828	36,655	7,664	14,702	9,115	24,692	23,607	54,836	7,558	26,328
Placer County	37,483	28,536	6,867	13,516	2,874	7,744	788	1,965	941	3,468	3,332	7,878	763	2,559
Riverside County	173,157	131,133	42,172	64,603	15,217	29,484	8,136	13,042	8,858	17,737	26,618	42,232	8,700	20,262
Sacramento County	106,486	79,440	28,566	44,636	9,808	20,789	4,593	8,621	7,290	14,271	16,504	29,936	5,629	15,445
San Bernardino County	128,816	84,545	37,597	46,000	13,342	20,816	5,913	9,986	9,793	14,120	24,353	31,658	8,669	14,773
San Diego County	229,799	178,670	53,272	91,864	16,140	41,786	10,275	18,555	15,792	29,963	31,431	60,462	10,909	27,799
San Francisco County	64,318	55,979	13,794	28,090	4,671	10,418	3,319	7,383	3,645	9,801	8,408	18,160	2,319	9,427
San Joaquin County	48,091	33,253	12,940	18,702	4,437	8,523	1,535	3,282	3,309	4,801	8,957	11,522	2,673	5,243
San Luis Obispo County	28,506	19,858	6,063	10,267	2,871	5,531	748	1,683	1,384	3,010	3,732	6,228	1,426	2,298

Table H-2: Counties—Disability Status and Type of Disability—*Continued*

	Total Population		With a Disability		With a Hearing Disability		With a Vision Disability		With a Cognitive Disability		With an Ambulatory Disability		With a Self-Care Disability	
	65 to 74 Years	75 Years and Over	65 to 74 Years	75 Years and Over	65 to 74 Years	75 Years and Over	65 to 74 Years	75 Years and Over	65 to 74 Years	75 Years and Over	65 to 74 Years	75 Years and Over	65 to 74 Years	75 Years and Over
California—Cont.														
San Mateo County	61,519	48,278	10,079	23,670	3,011	8,994	1,486	2,962	2,140	7,086	6,250	15,128	2,366	7,631
Santa Barbara County	31,781	28,290	6,434	14,368	2,516	7,555	728	3,528	1,408	4,214	3,763	7,899	785	3,435
Santa Clara County	128,324	98,724	25,409	50,596	8,036	20,949	3,486	8,882	6,011	14,594	14,207	34,116	5,216	17,504
Santa Cruz County	22,519	13,273	3,997	5,092	1,487	2,337	449	830	782	1,242	2,184	3,397	496	1,002
Shasta County	20,036	14,021	6,272	7,794	2,606	4,560	888	2,421	1,793	2,528	3,664	5,197	1,360	2,181
Solano County	34,155	23,187	8,011	10,692	2,857	4,847	666	1,930	1,710	3,290	5,372	6,384	1,246	3,211
Sonoma County	49,600	31,352	10,168	15,849	3,707	8,234	1,226	2,849	2,062	3,871	5,788	10,465	1,995	3,982
Stanislaus County	36,565	26,014	11,722	15,667	4,468	7,878	2,781	2,670	2,913	4,530	6,938	10,776	1,324	5,147
Sutter County	7,854	5,962	2,291	2,961	818	1,416	414	494	764	1,002	1,398	1,745	562	763
Tulare County	26,920	18,842	7,695	9,691	2,221	4,280	680	1,592	2,251	2,362	5,615	6,801	1,358	2,579
Ventura County	65,271	48,253	14,759	24,848	5,182	11,678	1,896	4,232	3,726	7,085	8,630	17,002	2,801	8,392
Yolo County	13,520	9,675	3,159	5,512	1,347	2,849	713	995	631	1,895	1,740	3,362	336	1,589
Yuba County	4,994	3,579	1,815	1,850	986	763	304	490	533	256	910	1,384	357	789
Colorado														
Adams County	28,161	17,388	9,396	9,248	4,429	4,412	1,766	1,786	2,074	2,800	5,671	4,868	1,817	1,693
Arapahoe County	44,313	27,466	8,331	12,545	2,977	6,784	577	2,122	969	3,324	5,027	7,215	1,292	2,535
Boulder County	22,580	14,510	3,898	7,608	1,801	3,464	753	1,760	790	1,560	1,899	4,489	1,081	977
Denver County	41,696	28,721	9,864	15,793	3,321	7,328	2,253	3,373	2,376	4,112	6,207	9,573	1,597	4,271
Douglas County	20,802	10,419	3,860	5,284	1,462	2,796	184	877	366	1,444	1,745	2,757	166	1,466
El Paso County	45,084	29,683	9,840	13,940	4,414	6,904	1,314	2,609	1,665	4,319	5,561	9,083	984	3,458
Jefferson County	48,219	31,700	9,538	15,964	4,601	8,053	1,344	2,803	1,848	3,729	4,572	10,043	1,099	3,046
Larimer County	26,875	17,392	5,073	7,677	2,397	4,325	531	826	1,177	1,387	2,224	4,230	512	2,064
Mesa County	13,998	10,226	3,430	5,003	1,422	2,730	376	1,596	519	1,197	2,117	3,003	610	707
Pueblo County	15,107	11,332	5,191	5,584	1,922	3,381	1,163	1,175	1,313	1,599	3,112	3,547	951	1,230
Weld County	18,723	11,759	4,102	6,245	2,016	4,269	833	1,655	1,345	1,235	2,391	3,592	609	1,688
Connecticut														
Fairfield County	72,006	59,112	13,328	26,482	4,333	9,842	2,015	4,288	3,068	7,246	8,000	17,235	2,644	7,954
Hartford County	73,859	60,591	17,067	29,976	6,247	12,452	2,567	5,221	4,783	6,995	10,387	19,573	3,406	10,256
Litchfield County	19,469	13,602	3,080	5,121	951	2,775	133	884	416	1,634	1,781	2,594	433	1,362
Middlesex County	16,065	11,545	2,890	5,109	1,409	2,420	310	926	664	639	1,432	3,035	317	1,667
New Haven County	72,282	56,291	15,537	26,930	5,582	11,612	1,905	4,804	3,638	6,040	9,375	17,558	3,836	7,757
New London County	24,393	18,052	4,585	8,698	1,738	3,884	821	1,262	952	2,078	3,198	6,109	1,152	2,729
Tolland County	12,405	7,917	2,662	2,814	870	1,421	143	413	410	848	1,699	1,721	374	722
Windham County	9,528	6,408	2,451	3,283	1,070	1,739	250	343	314	752	1,385	1,617	325	675
Delaware														
Kent County	15,869	10,121	4,443	4,568	1,610	1,727	464	440	882	1,395	3,147	3,029	947	1,365
New Castle County	42,980	30,670	10,078	12,143	3,308	5,419	1,975	2,171	2,416	3,449	5,940	8,467	1,982	3,574
Sussex County	31,894	18,192	6,394	7,951	2,728	3,995	843	1,486	1,473	1,794	3,154	5,455	602	1,878
Florida														
Alachua County	18,472	12,442	5,173	5,812	1,844	3,168	721	979	607	1,487	2,923	3,641	589	1,173
Bay County	16,784	11,676	6,741	7,646	2,324	4,019	1,236	1,631	2,047	2,606	5,179	5,437	2,097	1,824
Brevard County	66,810	57,233	16,515	26,676	6,499	12,982	1,813	4,626	3,540	6,555	9,084	17,241	2,646	6,485
Broward County	155,452	127,626	38,196	66,452	11,404	27,476	8,646	13,470	7,758	20,185	24,740	42,463	7,023	18,005
Charlotte County	33,584	28,446	7,099	13,477	2,705	7,449	1,249	1,380	1,213	4,264	3,970	7,082	953	2,222
Citrus County	26,335	22,032	6,493	10,711	2,074	5,947	631	3,040	1,224	3,605	4,192	6,875	546	3,804
Clay County	17,879	10,334	5,471	5,121	1,891	2,481	511	855	1,236	1,650	3,506	3,987	1,718	1,502
Collier County	53,154	48,118	8,132	16,107	2,985	8,061	1,377	1,917	1,058	3,918	4,303	8,659	610	2,870
Columbia County	6,885	4,483	2,633	2,694	924	1,757	233	793	447	1,250	1,923	1,959	226	356
Duval County	67,800	44,094	21,438	23,420	5,689	10,142	3,302	4,976	4,788	6,698	13,942	16,040	4,106	6,744
Escambia County	27,181	20,364	5,707	11,775	1,854	5,257	664	2,339	1,570	3,227	3,423	9,024	922	3,017
Flagler County	16,868	12,155	3,939	5,934	1,097	2,236	400	1,081	991	2,342	2,661	4,533	971	2,400
Hernando County	26,143	21,411	7,496	9,071	2,973	4,786	940	1,250	1,525	2,240	4,943	6,160	962	1,895
Highlands County	16,690	15,910	4,624	7,302	1,120	3,775	678	953	1,042	1,763	2,830	4,520	392	1,315
Hillsborough County	99,265	70,619	22,958	37,865	8,111	15,714	4,045	8,321	3,621	11,570	14,901	25,803	4,648	11,563
Indian River County	21,964	21,445	4,379	8,650	1,910	4,069	605	1,664	797	2,378	2,207	4,791	707	2,039
Lake County	46,029	35,758	11,159	14,374	4,966	7,850	1,550	3,489	2,128	3,966	5,888	9,013	802	3,240
Lee County	101,580	75,149	19,039	32,273	9,601	17,619	2,799	5,063	3,122	9,411	8,911	19,454	3,010	6,327
Leon County	18,749	12,132	5,012	6,982	1,752	3,375	763	1,207	678	1,732	3,128	4,492	640	1,420
Manatee County	49,191	40,006	9,392	16,155	4,118	8,853	1,458	2,299	1,575	3,252	4,986	9,840	970	4,517
Marion County	52,703	40,301	13,718	17,409	4,206	8,775	1,622	4,209	2,400	5,073	9,865	12,405	2,062	4,091
Martin County	22,175	21,639	4,342	8,630	2,191	4,647	935	1,153	1,161	1,363	1,956	4,403	426	1,550
Miami-Dade County	213,084	185,106	45,469	90,412	10,649	28,054	8,507	17,766	12,527	37,521	28,146	63,904	7,573	35,116
Monroe County	9,992	5,754	2,302	2,029	821	1,082	474	517	99	673	1,206	669	238	484
Nassau County	9,400	5,642	2,798	2,553	1,455	1,682	384	591	259	839	1,773	1,374	766	634
Okaloosa County	16,627	12,708	3,805	6,583	1,721	2,896	551	1,217	399	2,116	2,153	4,177	310	1,366
Orange County	78,626	53,659	20,009	28,896	4,791	11,308	4,373	5,751	4,808	8,777	13,081	20,692	3,032	7,823
Osceola County	23,565	15,493	7,431	8,628	2,056	2,877	2,770	1,324	2,036	3,856	4,025	6,896	673	2,268
Palm Beach County	151,816	160,654	29,003	66,476	9,007	29,682	5,645	12,366	6,164	15,219	17,532	42,267	4,723	19,843
Pasco County	59,750	47,187	15,300	22,162	5,710	11,164	1,646	2,930	4,118	6,130	8,906	13,650	3,453	5,411
Pinellas County	111,954	96,828	24,636	42,727	9,437	19,417	2,975	7,710	4,988	11,343	15,121	28,984	3,962	11,136
Polk County	69,955	52,266	16,382	23,395	6,115	11,676	2,273	4,362	3,074	6,742	10,212	16,350	2,293	5,672
Putnam County	8,515	6,075	2,171	2,896	980	1,109	304	673	651	811	1,471	1,568	719	708
Santa Rosa County	14,543	8,682	4,921	4,501	2,417	2,044	521	752	1,484	1,312	2,853	2,799	1,201	1,422
Sarasota County	68,785	63,426	12,814	26,639	4,652	13,645	1,150	3,389	2,111	7,339	8,247	16,013	1,438	7,037
Seminole County	37,069	25,238	6,913	11,490	1,866	5,060	1,002	2,615	1,889	3,820	4,086	8,648	1,175	3,419
St. Johns County	23,988	15,223	4,168	7,220	1,546	3,604	950	2,069	619	1,605	1,839	3,888	550	1,771

Table H-2: Counties—Disability Status and Type of Disability—*Continued*

	Total Population		With a Disability		With a Hearing Disability		With a Vision Disability		With a Cognitive Disability		With an Ambulatory Disability		With a Self-Care Disability	
	65 to 74 Years	75 Years and Over	65 to 74 Years	75 Years and Over	65 to 74 Years	75 Years and Over	65 to 74 Years	75 Years and Over	65 to 74 Years	75 Years and Over	65 to 74 Years	75 Years and Over	65 to 74 Years	75 Years and Over
Florida—Cont.														
St. Lucie County	34,946	29,835	9,145	15,594	2,274	7,982	1,851	2,031	2,340	3,243	6,611	11,119	1,795	4,784
Sumter County	38,317	21,276	5,651	10,340	3,315	6,154	1,262	1,094	942	772	2,015	4,579	583	908
Volusia County	63,430	51,811	14,231	23,634	5,447	10,671	1,680	4,022	2,659	5,832	8,522	15,898	1,722	6,771
Georgia														
Barrow County	5,447	3,123	2,017	1,702	676	401	494	222	404	421	1,393	1,300	147	409
Bartow County	7,934	4,328	2,898	2,385	1,265	1,333	381	626	263	406	1,840	1,980	125	751
Bibb County	12,104	8,628	4,607	4,822	1,134	2,102	974	597	1,548	1,609	3,344	3,231	1,289	1,173
Bulloch County	4,455	2,786	1,477	1,280	412	623	377	278	513	463	863	1,011	284	394
Carroll County	8,082	5,347	2,239	2,543	815	1,549	171	431	398	651	1,390	1,691	431	932
Catoosa County	6,005	4,083	1,293	1,958	750	802	137	199	403	53	771	1,262	81	182
Chatham County	22,062	15,280	5,446	9,023	2,049	3,477	1,061	1,681	765	2,500	3,601	6,413	1,409	2,576
Cherokee County	18,468	8,514	4,569	4,453	2,052	2,225	737	932	1,101	1,000	2,959	2,732	712	949
Clarke County	7,240	4,347	1,527	2,133	240	882	378	568	139	853	1,109	1,299	33	868
Clayton County	15,690	7,265	5,521	3,390	1,803	1,831	1,506	735	1,222	499	3,627	2,270	1,163	431
Cobb County	48,742	27,288	11,208	14,882	4,001	6,492	1,665	2,424	2,536	3,434	6,362	9,502	2,489	2,518
Columbia County	9,465	6,516	2,021	3,076	516	870	228	578	311	915	1,433	2,454	68	686
Coweta County	10,383	5,895	2,081	3,689	1,042	1,426	155	618	251	791	1,185	2,627	303	986
DeKalb County	45,931	26,531	10,320	12,293	1,852	5,122	1,602	2,117	2,199	4,704	6,933	8,287	2,216	3,688
Dougherty County	7,139	5,020	2,046	2,943	585	853	512	468	562	893	1,410	1,863	387	710
Douglas County	9,174	4,593	2,288	3,047	653	990	533	662	193	542	1,865	2,150	447	414
Fayette County	10,765	6,913	2,593	2,901	977	1,608	269	726	698	1,164	1,301	1,991	473	867
Floyd County	7,827	6,350	2,863	3,576	1,432	1,409	844	360	485	949	1,644	2,700	386	1,353
Forsyth County	14,285	7,771	2,739	3,767	1,292	1,729	416	781	684	1,229	1,569	2,827	731	1,358
Fulton County	60,418	40,819	15,217	21,227	3,374	7,340	2,394	4,491	3,756	6,986	9,635	15,236	1,859	7,748
Glynn County	8,130	5,793	2,360	2,444	432	1,167	146	497	881	660	1,796	1,432	188	855
Gwinnett County	48,869	25,561	10,537	14,032	3,271	4,740	1,500	2,788	2,826	4,578	5,398	10,156	1,267	4,071
Hall County	15,306	10,386	3,905	5,149	1,607	2,118	504	1,043	783	1,816	2,276	3,124	512	860
Henry County	15,000	6,805	4,769	3,819	1,380	1,358	931	704	1,533	1,126	3,282	2,215	1,530	584
Houston County	9,729	6,529	2,196	3,416	870	1,493	326	701	456	1,207	1,514	2,490	295	892
Liberty County	3,367	1,403	1,328	1,001	278	578	644	270	225	607	837	849	385	521
Lowndes County	7,801	4,403	2,703	1,817	736	1,137	615	235	197	591	2,098	1,234	181	487
Muscogee County	13,287	9,959	4,575	5,385	1,203	2,587	923	1,145	772	1,976	3,507	4,222	807	2,156
Newton County	8,167	3,985	2,706	2,038	1,054	813	679	490	889	653	1,356	1,595	399	641
Paulding County	8,966	4,796	2,059	1,386	1,067	461	93	45	272	382	1,132	1,166	315	383
Richmond County	14,404	9,731	5,247	5,255	1,924	2,533	995	1,596	2,065	1,964	3,031	3,838	1,014	1,291
Rockdale County	7,654	3,096	1,678	1,337	444	588	409	277	433	318	972	908	327	442
Troup County	5,246	4,029	2,320	2,088	1,060	660	664	588	658	737	1,151	1,637	162	684
Walker County	7,038	4,091	1,587	2,728	430	1,622	0	648	336	893	1,097	1,024	79	427
Walton County	7,536	4,681	1,845	1,767	921	653	162	433	531	283	1,028	1,472	182	624
Whitfield County	7,203	5,555	1,585	2,703	518	1,230	233	231	421	1,122	990	1,669	110	1,068
Hawaii														
Hawaii County	21,588	12,225	4,728	6,749	1,889	4,846	842	1,817	622	3,211	2,161	4,491	388	2,865
Honolulu County	82,586	71,000	17,034	38,023	5,319	18,225	2,310	4,878	4,615	13,610	10,939	25,488	3,393	10,803
Kauai County	7,138	4,943	1,934	3,040	662	1,768	159	479	423	1,720	1,275	2,012	346	1,314
Maui County	14,700	9,503	3,681	5,331	1,566	2,430	379	917	791	2,212	1,731	3,049	282	1,363
Idaho														
Ada County	32,308	20,977	6,534	10,917	2,659	5,859	634	2,988	1,469	2,510	3,447	6,012	395	3,276
Bannock County	6,222	4,246	1,625	2,186	902	1,467	206	432	565	552	650	1,104	66	526
Bonneville County	7,347	5,369	2,370	2,864	884	1,954	259	523	269	1,049	1,388	1,496	198	435
Canyon County	15,458	9,306	3,435	4,916	2,096	2,830	502	947	876	1,577	1,757	2,766	631	742
Kootenai County	14,826	10,084	3,897	4,714	2,039	3,557	514	1,158	1,052	1,734	1,928	2,296	874	868
Twin Falls County	6,777	4,983	1,780	2,414	685	1,127	416	563	348	795	748	1,625	190	545
Illinois														
Adams County	6,397	5,166	1,133	2,607	462	863	112	476	262	223	875	1,545	212	349
Champaign County	11,639	10,322	2,728	4,563	916	1,984	503	794	454	1,235	1,599	2,926	506	1,161
Cook County	371,889	285,404	90,309	149,196	21,998	56,636	17,178	30,968	19,189	43,160	62,641	106,103	17,745	46,882
DeKalb County	6,568	4,843	1,220	2,405	489	1,281	115	378	71	700	734	1,617	45	861
DuPage County	72,376	49,033	13,153	22,373	4,209	9,529	1,716	3,023	2,776	5,408	7,419	14,808	2,234	5,827
Kane County	37,325	23,448	7,932	9,917	2,314	5,476	1,291	3,083	1,403	2,916	5,846	6,427	1,336	3,033
Kankakee County	8,904	6,416	2,919	2,911	964	1,326	451	501	792	329	1,958	2,256	627	267
Kendall County	6,528	3,624	1,488	1,483	839	765	88	334	21	100	743	786	191	444
Lake County	49,261	33,943	9,793	16,895	2,895	6,952	716	2,926	1,450	4,513	6,807	12,185	2,187	5,438
LaSalle County	9,904	8,270	2,820	3,577	922	1,494	225	510	572	667	1,710	2,142	429	931
Macon County	10,039	8,268	2,294	4,421	574	2,353	446	1,115	339	1,472	1,554	2,763	352	1,233
Madison County	22,817	18,189	5,761	7,272	2,130	2,665	717	907	1,476	2,317	3,755	4,427	1,050	1,475
McHenry County	23,088	13,255	5,860	6,288	2,362	3,245	923	970	1,240	1,246	3,959	4,122	980	1,390
McLean County	10,846	8,301	2,364	4,807	465	2,182	224	895	372	1,224	1,692	3,047	472	1,223
Peoria County	15,144	11,542	3,951	5,052	1,526	2,232	464	820	962	1,132	2,227	2,917	723	1,119
Rock Island County	14,081	10,767	3,081	5,301	1,005	2,279	374	1,118	448	1,101	1,987	3,767	277	1,422
Sangamon County	16,937	13,417	4,394	6,491	1,731	2,801	719	1,465	658	1,203	2,718	4,191	881	979
St. Clair County	20,272	15,362	5,734	7,461	2,175	2,754	885	1,504	1,161	2,166	4,344	4,711	690	2,355
Tazewell County	12,205	9,754	2,790	4,965	839	2,098	408	795	544	350	1,526	3,193	452	587
Vermilion County	7,855	5,708	1,950	3,091	662	1,405	596	480	596	687	1,330	2,108	734	545
Will County	46,047	28,111	10,141	13,963	3,878	5,317	2,337	3,213	1,760	2,939	6,850	8,622	1,667	3,621
Williamson County	6,526	4,677	1,683	1,797	680	810	263	341	392	531	1,176	1,304	475	512

Table H-2: Counties—Disability Status and Type of Disability—*Continued*

	Total Population		With a Disability		With a Hearing Disability		With a Vision Disability		With a Cognitive Disability		With an Ambulatory Disability		With a Self-Care Disability	
	65 to 74 Years	75 Years and Over	65 to 74 Years	75 Years and Over	65 to 74 Years	75 Years and Over	65 to 74 Years	75 Years and Over	65 to 74 Years	75 Years and Over	65 to 74 Years	75 Years and Over	65 to 74 Years	75 Years and Over
Illinois—Cont.														
Winnebago County	25,345	18,365	7,229	10,051	2,266	4,545	773	1,537	1,182	2,228	4,623	6,411	1,079	2,182
Indiana														
Allen County	26,835	19,112	6,376	9,461	2,007	3,827	674	1,696	1,791	2,305	3,979	6,688	985	2,520
Bartholomew County	6,738	4,661	2,704	1,998	925	787	305	336	694	580	1,562	1,318	375	526
Clark County	9,759	6,086	3,255	3,350	975	1,750	269	510	298	721	2,278	2,061	350	500
Delaware County	10,350	7,523	2,450	4,372	1,254	2,724	689	836	463	1,738	1,446	2,548	660	1,085
Elkhart County	13,812	11,159	4,022	5,548	1,675	2,793	550	1,224	646	1,703	2,275	3,462	655	1,353
Floyd County	6,255	3,887	1,648	1,737	697	737	402	536	470	767	1,199	1,170	265	637
Grant County	6,720	4,871	2,236	2,364	1,073	1,233	475	240	694	581	1,542	1,848	637	646
Hamilton County	19,365	11,470	2,892	4,981	1,252	1,948	101	598	507	1,650	1,773	3,193	522	1,683
Hancock County	6,520	4,019	1,648	2,842	386	1,481	245	494	317	589	980	2,015	137	291
Hendricks County	11,040	7,226	2,374	4,422	900	2,375	94	1,083	299	1,845	1,390	3,387	647	1,203
Howard County	8,152	6,303	2,509	3,137	798	1,753	355	537	471	673	1,380	1,791	264	327
Johnson County	12,010	7,369	2,487	4,232	1,247	1,498	187	634	385	725	1,215	2,791	486	979
Kosciusko County	6,851	4,678	1,801	1,999	844	584	221	389	265	497	879	1,307	122	499
Lake County	39,465	29,685	11,189	16,394	3,094	5,750	1,715	3,466	2,352	4,821	7,227	11,493	2,260	4,470
LaPorte County	10,262	6,568	2,751	2,798	1,106	1,118	421	426	465	468	1,413	2,047	537	435
Madison County	12,396	9,155	3,681	5,023	1,919	2,330	678	1,082	890	1,343	2,405	3,432	821	1,003
Marion County	57,502	44,413	18,708	24,490	6,570	11,157	3,702	6,640	4,950	8,736	12,710	17,680	3,601	8,707
Monroe County	8,726	6,590	1,827	3,232	744	1,420	342	520	270	659	904	1,841	256	494
Morgan County	6,231	3,921	1,772	2,243	319	1,317	152	446	453	330	1,352	1,323	399	261
Porter County	13,874	9,457	3,330	4,232	747	1,975	274	835	1,038	1,054	2,321	2,523	458	806
St. Joseph County	19,879	17,176	5,083	8,459	1,860	4,261	592	1,348	832	1,644	3,068	5,558	478	1,712
Tippecanoe County	11,157	7,952	3,152	3,870	955	1,611	348	719	645	917	2,206	2,138	493	736
Vanderburgh County	14,407	11,977	4,769	6,011	1,680	3,371	1,027	1,557	692	2,198	3,355	3,527	804	1,457
Vigo County	8,893	6,076	2,455	4,035	815	1,817	392	615	544	725	1,675	2,091	645	464
Wayne County	6,619	5,172	1,858	2,741	910	1,167	379	701	625	638	1,083	2,062	173	658
Iowa														
Black Hawk County	10,008	8,925	2,674	3,454	1,178	1,240	309	837	327	412	1,577	2,400	306	832
Dallas County	4,834	3,334	644	1,388	381	474	57	113	48	121	303	882	11	174
Dubuque County	7,964	6,799	1,544	2,501	512	1,202	168	333	458	724	795	1,663	210	428
Johnson County	7,943	5,607	1,088	2,068	461	857	63	472	175	414	640	1,420	115	652
Linn County	16,634	13,312	3,797	4,569	1,297	2,517	592	1,034	366	1,495	2,327	2,313	346	957
Polk County	30,743	21,332	6,910	9,128	2,586	5,261	870	1,840	2,126	2,435	4,087	5,820	1,210	2,509
Pottawattamie County	7,845	6,209	1,708	3,443	946	1,940	462	511	303	766	1,004	2,008	420	623
Scott County	13,968	9,936	3,814	4,084	1,554	1,983	551	478	692	1,200	2,152	2,571	954	1,067
Story County	5,416	4,262	917	1,646	708	962	10	174	16	300	280	826	77	222
Woodbury County	7,710	5,703	1,791	3,062	594	1,142	139	388	326	475	1,290	2,245	436	585
Kansas														
Butler County	4,733	4,153	1,088	1,617	381	670	85	205	93	351	721	895	166	397
Douglas County	6,850	4,985	1,177	2,159	414	1,172	197	209	42	523	755	1,338	211	605
Johnson County	40,929	29,796	7,883	14,545	3,388	6,285	1,020	2,315	1,313	3,855	4,761	9,499	1,047	3,858
Leavenworth County	5,592	4,163	1,718	2,725	863	789	133	356	119	319	903	1,754	234	853
Riley County	3,015	2,906	328	1,239	154	649	0	132	35	305	209	632	15	407
Sedgwick County	36,048	27,217	9,520	11,998	3,513	5,380	1,575	2,250	2,136	4,271	6,012	7,507	1,735	3,175
Shawnee County	15,161	11,965	5,068	5,401	2,073	2,629	667	986	1,051	1,230	2,598	3,466	802	1,714
Wyandotte County	10,567	7,042	3,867	3,728	1,367	1,389	497	793	614	759	2,671	2,526	749	1,068
Kentucky														
Boone County	8,660	5,449	3,421	2,800	1,753	1,614	162	480	697	1,508	1,970	1,592	564	863
Bullitt County	6,856	3,551	2,083	1,483	1,034	645	386	260	236	255	1,338	1,023	242	432
Campbell County	7,079	5,220	1,681	3,014	672	1,571	233	1,264	278	497	884	1,861	348	996
Christian County	4,189	3,424	1,558	1,821	501	822	351	291	255	462	1,076	1,582	443	637
Daviess County	8,331	6,432	2,590	3,357	530	1,639	337	375	964	937	1,716	2,710	379	896
Fayette County	20,678	14,057	5,405	7,508	2,047	2,937	698	1,473	706	1,999	3,561	4,267	1,204	1,829
Hardin County	7,758	5,211	2,644	3,965	803	1,735	965	657	810	1,244	1,836	3,275	394	1,338
Jefferson County	61,012	45,387	16,830	24,435	5,487	9,583	2,529	4,157	3,953	6,456	10,876	16,431	3,192	6,998
Kenton County	12,111	7,963	3,585	4,009	1,005	2,262	899	904	773	797	2,352	2,559	609	1,322
Madison County	6,523	4,076	1,837	2,338	894	1,144	514	348	506	769	819	1,385	122	760
McCracken County	6,742	4,791	2,116	2,460	898	1,141	498	274	476	316	1,343	1,774	46	658
Pike County	6,205	3,641	3,081	2,524	911	1,680	378	1,177	1,051	1,304	2,216	1,503	587	699
Warren County	8,174	5,642	1,746	2,898	955	593	421	491	397	710	1,168	1,966	338	515
Louisiana														
Ascension Parish	7,690	4,107	2,602	1,861	608	833	1,003	207	775	879	1,128	1,483	296	897
Bossier Parish	9,123	6,069	2,404	3,108	835	1,160	174	531	605	723	1,770	2,008	480	970
Caddo Parish	20,653	15,088	6,940	7,970	2,369	3,579	1,891	1,155	1,757	2,671	4,563	5,876	1,299	3,187
Calcasieu Parish	15,870	10,556	4,609	5,302	1,654	2,524	830	1,209	624	1,427	2,900	3,658	935	1,235
East Baton Rouge Parish	32,324	21,212	11,931	11,565	3,276	4,025	1,840	2,595	2,519	3,666	9,401	8,958	1,740	3,146
Iberia Parish	5,210	3,981	1,068	2,233	336	793	212	236	259	855	787	1,210	329	354
Jefferson Parish	37,919	26,879	10,187	13,126	3,376	4,574	2,135	1,940	2,297	3,032	5,321	9,506	2,025	4,254
Lafayette Parish	15,159	10,255	4,180	5,707	1,578	1,606	1,034	1,334	943	2,028	2,451	3,856	698	1,688
Lafourche Parish	7,434	5,315	2,140	3,019	722	1,695	471	521	146	791	1,255	2,065	565	863
Livingston Parish	9,561	5,134	2,601	3,257	1,057	1,859	279	552	565	935	1,675	1,703	647	738
Orleans Parish	26,746	18,699	8,159	9,806	1,994	3,014	1,506	2,627	1,879	3,214	5,502	6,643	1,818	2,911
Ouachita Parish	11,229	8,561	2,955	4,089	737	1,937	461	689	611	1,005	1,931	3,031	387	1,473
Rapides Parish	11,311	7,370	4,513	4,222	1,458	1,875	1,090	960	1,578	1,268	3,251	3,070	1,652	1,444

Table H-2: Counties—Disability Status and Type of Disability—*Continued*

	Total Population		With a Disability		With a Hearing Disability		With a Vision Disability		With a Cognitive Disability		With an Ambulatory Disability		With a Self-Care Disability	
	65 to 74 Years	75 Years and Over	65 to 74 Years	75 Years and Over	65 to 74 Years	75 Years and Over	65 to 74 Years	75 Years and Over	65 to 74 Years	75 Years and Over	65 to 74 Years	75 Years and Over	65 to 74 Years	75 Years and Over
Louisiana—Cont.														
St. Landry Parish...............	6,875	4,822	1,791	2,583	549	708	214	631	326	815	890	1,862	334	1,233
St. Tammany Parish.............	22,971	13,495	5,628	6,987	2,415	2,828	667	1,976	808	2,646	3,240	4,970	431	2,567
Tangipahoa Parish...............	10,345	5,554	4,286	3,678	1,373	754	673	420	997	1,880	3,209	2,058	1,622	1,213
Terrebonne Parish...............	7,912	5,607	2,265	3,341	588	1,525	738	517	347	1,602	1,788	2,119	399	857
Maine														
Androscoggin County	9,907	6,843	2,244	3,486	474	1,503	237	430	296	520	1,429	2,070	318	709
Aroostook County	8,164	5,901	2,756	3,084	1,177	1,783	826	549	791	505	1,841	1,766	697	802
Cumberland County	26,583	19,115	4,703	9,617	2,110	4,810	512	2,341	1,132	3,065	2,132	6,598	875	2,925
Kennebec County................	12,236	8,520	1,955	3,556	690	2,161	209	265	392	610	1,206	1,808	378	778
Penobscot County...............	13,957	10,273	4,192	5,325	2,603	2,669	569	775	956	791	1,965	3,316	976	960
York County	20,656	14,348	5,251	7,067	1,650	3,200	650	1,403	614	1,198	3,804	4,533	993	855
Maryland														
Allegany County	7,293	5,552	1,790	2,641	522	1,557	35	567	462	940	1,130	1,563	155	663
Anne Arundel County	44,894	28,771	9,295	12,365	2,933	5,240	805	2,867	1,335	2,620	5,732	7,357	707	3,117
Baltimore County	68,846	57,323	13,225	28,162	4,974	11,428	2,260	5,445	2,507	8,629	7,889	20,076	2,447	8,531
Calvert County....................	6,913	4,481	1,762	1,968	608	814	181	499	391	316	1,032	1,441	313	606
Carroll County	14,771	10,178	3,080	4,633	1,318	1,936	266	518	304	1,271	1,655	2,477	206	757
Cecil County.......................	8,838	4,774	2,566	1,987	1,187	814	467	186	564	473	1,568	1,463	576	561
Charles County....................	10,314	6,658	2,628	3,001	728	1,254	138	677	292	784	1,953	1,870	496	629
Frederick County.................	18,393	12,309	4,551	5,337	1,965	2,644	1,092	1,334	496	1,195	2,602	3,462	681	1,270
Harford County	22,062	13,692	3,838	6,283	1,459	2,710	304	939	1,074	1,666	2,371	3,552	951	1,826
Howard County	23,699	13,522	4,150	6,733	1,227	2,937	334	1,151	931	1,730	2,380	3,748	1,240	1,761
Montgomery County............	78,311	59,377	11,439	26,983	3,380	10,867	1,281	5,193	2,456	8,713	6,673	17,024	1,729	7,083
Prince George's County........	63,698	36,620	13,939	17,231	2,783	6,109	1,922	2,839	2,364	5,547	9,669	12,143	2,173	5,666
St. Mary's County.................	8,247	4,257	2,907	2,641	699	1,307	392	628	1,164	789	1,481	1,901	367	622
Washington County..............	12,537	9,383	3,024	4,843	1,094	2,375	356	783	622	1,036	2,249	3,204	189	1,289
Wicomico County.................	8,564	5,469	1,842	2,942	951	1,493	313	907	412	682	983	2,131	303	483
Massachusetts														
Barnstable County................	32,495	26,050	5,159	10,701	2,138	5,656	1,123	1,557	1,303	1,924	2,053	6,346	736	2,575
Berkshire County.................	14,310	10,887	2,594	4,483	1,180	1,888	514	826	602	827	1,377	3,133	453	1,494
Bristol County	47,718	35,169	11,563	17,945	3,962	8,176	2,362	2,880	2,851	5,812	7,078	11,905	2,616	6,220
Essex County	65,383	49,861	13,683	25,053	5,648	11,681	1,881	5,392	2,411	7,135	7,427	15,013	1,283	6,331
Franklin County	7,791	4,681	1,380	2,177	529	1,362	262	365	165	861	873	1,399	177	925
Hampden County	38,229	29,714	9,573	15,210	3,330	6,288	1,520	2,583	1,918	4,466	5,351	9,222	2,082	4,762
Hampshire County	13,773	9,355	2,876	4,871	1,253	1,918	374	460	418	1,750	1,578	3,362	488	1,509
Middlesex County	119,458	93,006	21,703	42,548	7,153	21,486	2,727	7,429	5,097	11,183	11,943	26,734	4,121	11,333
Norfolk County....................	57,436	46,409	10,683	21,471	4,327	11,676	1,330	4,286	2,630	5,249	6,018	13,158	1,356	5,352
Plymouth County	47,935	31,563	9,544	14,116	3,450	6,605	726	2,707	2,196	3,339	5,682	9,371	1,757	4,138
Suffolk County	46,309	34,601	13,890	19,420	4,527	8,045	3,969	5,686	4,487	7,415	9,361	13,995	2,789	6,559
Worcester County	63,169	46,929	12,636	24,267	4,462	11,611	1,805	4,731	3,047	6,422	7,571	15,046	2,798	6,856
Michigan														
Allegan County....................	10,362	6,315	2,224	3,064	915	1,704	147	711	262	991	1,180	1,937	265	1,007
Bay County.........................	10,750	8,155	1,809	4,554	643	2,107	86	819	466	776	1,018	3,199	255	1,593
Berrien County	14,994	11,590	3,299	5,236	1,559	2,198	472	758	694	1,269	1,520	3,278	391	893
Calhoun County...................	12,135	8,865	3,495	4,544	1,147	2,292	517	860	868	1,242	2,126	2,174	696	1,055
Clinton County	6,922	4,506	1,337	2,117	493	1,213	284	304	187	240	871	982	107	220
Eaton County......................	10,449	7,348	2,569	3,603	1,458	1,779	486	746	500	1,190	1,220	2,036	323	959
Genesee County	36,404	27,510	9,350	14,141	3,011	6,579	1,346	2,534	1,951	4,205	5,882	9,668	1,178	3,027
Grand Traverse County.........	8,719	6,359	1,197	2,623	377	1,066	30	308	242	146	702	1,573	252	610
Ingham County	20,207	12,902	5,427	6,339	1,820	3,030	905	1,165	1,416	2,175	3,180	3,965	1,171	1,534
Isabella County	4,309	2,959	1,171	1,849	771	1,079	43	293	511	345	479	1,138	132	492
Jackson County....................	14,388	10,678	3,598	5,614	1,374	2,063	185	1,136	677	1,912	2,076	3,629	436	1,363
Kalamazoo County	19,061	14,660	4,080	7,374	1,560	3,120	601	1,006	917	1,406	1,967	4,862	322	1,374
Kent County	42,093	31,999	9,756	16,189	3,682	6,814	1,460	2,605	1,950	4,311	5,578	9,641	1,721	3,704
Lapeer County	8,703	5,310	3,193	3,050	1,233	1,443	516	987	569	724	1,951	1,797	654	986
Lenawee County	9,522	6,421	3,115	2,870	1,102	1,433	594	434	799	689	2,217	1,535	488	575
Livingston County	17,234	9,815	3,363	4,088	1,330	2,194	383	656	679	1,371	1,727	2,163	515	1,073
Macomb County	73,243	57,429	19,316	30,339	6,332	12,493	2,656	5,373	4,180	7,635	13,929	20,433	3,787	7,898
Marquette County	6,112	4,520	1,712	2,037	746	1,001	194	511	301	769	810	1,239	239	828
Midland County....................	7,504	6,021	2,130	2,645	928	1,184	228	275	590	507	1,227	1,458	266	534
Monroe County	13,508	9,547	2,492	4,338	946	2,196	464	964	515	934	1,574	2,897	312	1,127
Muskegon County	14,540	10,585	3,568	5,349	1,013	2,376	323	904	893	930	2,359	3,041	518	946
Oakland County...................	106,565	76,035	26,303	37,090	9,688	14,471	4,230	7,905	5,690	11,185	16,136	24,515	3,591	10,800
Ottawa County....................	20,812	14,709	4,597	6,524	2,086	3,331	162	1,009	1,105	1,067	2,290	4,211	270	719
Saginaw County	18,096	14,139	5,097	6,605	2,413	2,841	1,026	1,310	1,104	2,273	3,141	4,337	899	1,567
Shiawassee County	6,482	4,909	1,655	2,451	627	1,121	276	600	135	667	1,073	1,421	168	782
St. Clair County...................	15,395	10,933	4,784	5,885	2,009	2,705	1,023	909	947	911	2,795	3,741	975	1,062
Van Buren County	7,189	4,804	2,021	2,426	975	1,169	224	436	254	793	1,045	1,570	208	646
Washtenaw County	25,988	16,037	5,046	7,140	2,136	3,414	952	1,126	849	2,250	2,896	4,144	605	1,395
Wayne County.....................	134,878	102,771	41,369	55,130	11,580	22,245	7,858	12,532	9,318	15,060	28,608	38,103	10,709	16,814
Minnesota														
Anoka County	24,729	14,797	4,691	6,619	2,175	3,367	272	1,233	636	1,913	2,306	3,841	547	1,620
Blue Earth County	4,383	3,607	768	1,653	206	890	194	191	223	296	566	1,112	209	511
Carver County	5,460	3,795	828	1,616	539	692	116	143	277	588	143	1,078	30	179
Dakota County....................	29,171	20,114	6,230	8,131	2,890	3,260	792	1,010	1,251	2,047	3,425	5,346	1,007	2,543

Table H-2: Counties—Disability Status and Type of Disability—*Continued*

	Total Population		With a Disability		With a Hearing Disability		With a Vision Disability		With a Cognitive Disability		With an Ambulatory Disability		With a Self-Care Disability	
	65 to 74 Years	75 Years and Over	65 to 74 Years	75 Years and Over	65 to 74 Years	75 Years and Over	65 to 74 Years	75 Years and Over	65 to 74 Years	75 Years and Over	65 to 74 Years	75 Years and Over	65 to 74 Years	75 Years and Over
Minnesota—Cont.														
Hennepin County	83,649	62,535	17,108	28,004	6,639	12,784	2,691	4,970	4,059	6,946	8,766	17,210	3,253	6,334
Olmsted County	10,602	9,263	2,042	3,777	665	2,010	261	562	407	666	1,250	1,981	371	587
Ramsey County	36,950	29,529	8,538	15,356	2,989	6,435	1,414	3,465	1,917	4,452	5,212	9,585	1,868	3,859
Rice County	4,738	4,046	834	1,492	439	569	281	175	181	295	145	743	39	699
Scott County	7,909	4,667	1,333	1,991	625	903	90	284	201	468	571	1,307	115	420
Sherburne County	5,548	3,230	1,109	1,421	696	704	37	17	182	327	536	566	186	482
St. Louis County	18,753	14,267	4,078	6,889	1,871	3,395	491	1,468	863	1,570	2,025	4,327	503	1,468
Stearns County	10,510	8,921	1,802	3,667	1,025	1,927	289	656	537	724	1,105	1,909	361	654
Washington County	18,676	11,434	4,132	6,192	2,437	2,447	757	635	573	1,845	1,314	3,825	485	1,917
Wright County	8,667	5,340	1,698	2,136	656	1,095	150	271	443	330	908	1,254	303	457
Mississippi														
DeSoto County	12,556	7,624	4,039	4,302	1,707	1,452	778	546	1,294	1,590	2,424	3,348	958	1,564
Forrest County	5,605	3,562	2,465	2,199	997	928	127	538	1,101	706	1,488	1,845	614	717
Harrison County	15,325	10,566	4,983	5,940	1,480	2,741	725	1,215	720	2,149	3,694	4,146	785	2,047
Hinds County	16,727	11,956	4,549	6,535	700	2,547	826	1,238	620	2,213	2,939	4,801	803	2,430
Jackson County	12,081	7,569	3,798	5,133	1,566	3,352	559	2,155	1,038	2,371	2,965	3,719	830	2,259
Jones County	6,122	4,035	1,813	2,233	729	995	319	292	271	615	1,043	1,577	456	508
Lauderdale County	6,278	5,451	2,730	3,286	1,146	1,306	705	788	1,215	1,316	2,073	1,745	622	693
Lee County	7,071	4,508	2,253	2,857	884	1,415	405	759	541	961	1,236	2,087	358	928
Madison County	7,703	4,525	2,438	2,270	849	804	446	422	204	964	1,442	1,433	241	1,047
Rankin County	10,922	8,026	3,656	4,793	983	2,253	43	1,229	987	1,574	2,568	3,620	365	1,568
Missouri														
Boone County	10,958	6,746	2,367	3,281	877	1,351	161	293	265	939	1,330	2,170	318	649
Buchanan County	7,010	5,518	1,698	2,543	696	1,082	432	399	142	452	823	1,668	73	554
Cape Girardeau County	6,395	4,903	1,500	2,012	647	837	220	464	519	492	1,039	1,184	251	93
Cass County	8,684	6,098	2,622	3,394	1,000	2,171	68	373	367	611	1,637	2,195	379	421
Christian County	7,202	4,559	2,515	1,676	1,041	709	533	666	322	483	1,201	1,111	173	55
Clay County	17,334	11,653	4,049	5,535	1,573	3,194	752	1,111	658	1,201	2,204	2,645	94	620
Cole County	6,076	4,173	2,183	1,757	1,066	959	732	405	401	602	1,479	1,010	289	450
Franklin County	9,212	6,409	1,993	2,874	704	1,221	80	313	450	1,145	1,307	2,040	338	724
Greene County	23,195	18,965	5,816	8,460	2,352	4,130	582	734	1,020	2,456	3,051	5,645	744	2,189
Jackson County	50,562	38,142	12,500	18,465	3,885	7,786	2,236	3,010	2,554	6,069	7,198	12,274	2,153	3,868
Jasper County	8,887	6,483	2,849	3,604	1,158	2,123	387	1,101	392	565	2,259	2,323	467	668
Jefferson County	18,845	10,438	4,906	5,707	2,496	2,582	1,129	1,627	815	1,548	2,051	3,751	619	1,356
Platte County	7,517	4,071	1,202	2,652	552	1,247	178	288	118	574	590	1,659	288	633
St. Charles County	29,646	20,288	7,239	9,026	3,348	3,986	1,692	1,625	1,821	1,971	3,492	5,735	857	1,853
St. Francois County	5,555	3,961	1,940	2,611	656	712	606	675	99	704	1,201	1,955	286	560
St. Louis County	86,565	69,820	17,252	31,309	5,721	12,970	1,997	6,923	2,753	7,790	10,575	19,541	2,948	7,434
Montana														
Cascade County	7,545	5,922	2,592	2,954	1,088	1,491	218	568	278	703	1,223	1,555	563	512
Flathead County	9,892	6,341	1,275	1,925	616	928	0	189	121	297	574	963	192	389
Gallatin County	6,506	4,011	1,814	1,686	1,289	967	539	331	487	626	699	1,052	418	493
Lewis and Clark County	6,392	4,071	1,311	2,222	808	1,100	235	229	406	500	764	1,365	313	673
Missoula County	9,235	5,571	2,330	3,459	1,363	2,168	153	1,289	241	920	1,101	2,452	109	762
Yellowstone County	12,765	10,099	3,257	3,749	861	1,861	624	647	503	1,014	1,995	2,339	263	691
Nebraska														
Douglas County	34,752	25,803	7,778	13,008	2,869	6,154	1,080	3,058	1,781	3,949	4,806	7,251	1,110	3,494
Lancaster County	20,609	15,049	5,181	7,286	2,782	3,705	448	1,034	518	1,948	2,496	4,423	673	1,565
Sarpy County	10,586	6,387	1,744	3,123	781	1,689	225	333	81	954	1,158	1,944	172	927
Nevada														
Clark County	170,882	101,562	47,951	51,872	16,380	24,500	10,136	10,880	11,110	14,832	32,582	35,366	8,723	13,430
Washoe County	40,145	23,545	9,798	11,495	3,883	5,672	1,457	2,446	2,415	2,656	5,848	6,901	976	1,912
New Hampshire														
Cheshire County	7,482	5,034	2,479	2,761	1,130	1,665	217	352	157	462	1,444	1,476	379	645
Grafton County	9,237	6,127	2,181	3,198	1,206	1,715	284	569	539	854	1,101	2,219	322	591
Hillsborough County	32,137	21,583	6,082	10,813	2,800	4,908	1,018	1,814	987	2,998	4,041	6,565	1,394	3,080
Merrimack County	13,365	9,035	2,780	5,243	1,149	1,837	325	882	578	1,279	1,353	3,510	593	1,372
Rockingham County	27,607	17,135	4,793	7,809	1,718	3,915	580	1,302	783	1,901	2,936	4,698	806	1,548
Strafford County	9,598	6,852	2,849	3,287	1,082	1,617	364	822	354	960	1,727	2,467	174	281
New Jersey														
Atlantic County	25,226	16,739	6,980	8,042	1,993	3,193	514	1,473	1,167	1,955	5,449	5,103	1,205	1,652
Bergen County	79,394	66,059	11,969	27,986	3,641	11,498	1,109	3,496	2,290	7,122	7,351	19,663	1,552	9,779
Burlington County	37,918	29,968	8,441	14,099	2,697	6,665	1,277	2,717	1,344	4,151	5,036	9,577	1,368	3,004
Camden County	40,305	30,118	10,736	15,551	3,254	6,289	2,794	2,569	2,582	4,224	6,921	10,417	2,380	3,611
Cape May County	12,859	9,354	2,410	4,721	778	1,845	411	722	674	1,020	1,540	3,195	660	1,020
Cumberland County	11,839	8,471	3,117	4,326	710	1,995	379	534	373	846	2,379	2,792	579	1,274
Essex County	54,235	40,753	15,196	21,109	2,349	8,272	3,376	5,254	2,484	5,458	11,190	14,460	2,642	6,802
Gloucester County	24,099	16,130	5,844	8,724	1,686	4,408	1,192	1,472	1,297	2,589	4,269	5,365	584	1,853
Hudson County	40,414	29,433	10,929	15,269	2,286	5,235	1,898	3,608	2,982	5,055	8,210	12,405	2,080	5,492
Hunterdon County	11,865	7,339	2,147	3,628	917	2,080	113	1,018	198	1,178	1,160	2,547	283	1,025
Mercer County	28,054	21,527	5,284	9,972	1,153	3,625	770	1,601	1,459	2,514	3,343	6,604	898	3,127
Middlesex County	61,497	47,165	12,694	21,488	3,028	9,985	1,878	4,653	2,167	7,005	8,644	15,368	1,898	6,582
Monmouth County	54,787	41,042	10,316	19,658	3,082	7,675	1,564	2,907	1,836	6,044	6,149	12,101	1,196	5,727
Morris County	43,085	31,931	6,650	15,126	2,185	6,349	302	2,501	1,154	3,379	4,169	9,237	725	4,353

Table H-2: Counties—Disability Status and Type of Disability—*Continued*

	Total Population		With a Disability		With a Hearing Disability		With a Vision Disability		With a Cognitive Disability		With an Ambulatory Disability		With a Self-Care Disability	
	65 to 74 Years	75 Years and Over	65 to 74 Years	75 Years and Over	65 to 74 Years	75 Years and Over	65 to 74 Years	75 Years and Over	65 to 74 Years	75 Years and Over	65 to 74 Years	75 Years and Over	65 to 74 Years	75 Years and Over
New Jersey—Cont.														
Ocean County	66,288	59,057	13,486	29,342	4,168	13,485	2,000	5,900	2,587	6,642	8,286	18,863	1,376	5,887
Passaic County	37,113	27,207	8,354	13,099	1,771	4,777	2,302	2,624	1,641	3,250	5,814	8,981	1,943	4,964
Salem County	6,024	4,411	1,791	1,969	911	976	343	729	435	566	1,067	1,001	209	572
Somerset County	23,928	20,327	4,768	10,451	1,579	3,416	87	1,675	1,253	3,103	3,042	7,369	1,112	3,476
Sussex County	12,975	7,532	3,408	3,385	1,285	1,475	722	392	505	1,298	1,789	2,219	411	1,191
Union County	39,050	30,078	6,647	15,161	2,069	6,228	1,273	3,528	1,375	4,880	3,306	10,530	1,034	5,211
Warren County	9,926	6,587	3,165	3,534	1,125	1,511	396	603	815	910	2,182	2,436	208	1,153
New Mexico														
Bernalillo County	54,755	39,748	15,162	20,765	5,794	10,342	3,421	4,332	4,581	6,867	9,356	14,004	3,808	5,676
Chaves County	5,559	4,092	2,620	2,201	912	1,152	295	821	966	756	1,799	1,052	417	489
Doña Ana County	17,066	12,450	5,205	7,042	1,913	2,724	633	1,641	642	1,754	3,093	5,189	790	1,909
Lea County	3,742	3,460	1,441	2,076	408	1,359	336	731	305	635	867	1,247	200	770
McKinley County	4,215	3,186	2,419	2,318	1,097	1,160	591	639	586	870	1,344	1,830	291	713
Otero County	6,031	4,052	1,456	2,122	647	1,269	85	443	282	513	859	1,330	90	658
San Juan County	8,830	6,533	2,794	3,569	1,173	2,148	325	501	658	1,186	1,747	2,222	304	734
Sandoval County	13,111	7,672	3,296	3,726	1,449	1,397	511	548	699	1,144	1,239	2,644	396	1,084
Santa Fe County	18,667	10,198	4,213	4,667	2,261	2,449	634	1,286	1,178	1,013	1,883	2,494	656	665
Valencia County	7,128	4,433	1,779	2,594	1,160	1,940	345	503	619	377	722	1,272	233	422
New York														
Albany County	25,841	19,093	5,351	7,952	1,653	2,887	705	789	1,083	1,852	3,162	5,835	741	1,883
Bronx County	88,432	64,061	29,945	38,003	7,950	13,707	7,495	10,280	9,162	13,960	21,603	27,663	7,401	13,247
Broome County	17,241	15,336	4,780	8,008	1,810	3,167	812	848	1,171	2,080	3,001	4,344	772	2,078
Cattaraugus County	7,487	5,373	2,161	2,804	721	1,630	198	461	546	825	1,452	1,275	334	334
Cayuga County	6,919	5,859	1,339	3,367	541	1,558	158	704	215	1,057	791	2,308	251	1,282
Chautauqua County	12,533	10,024	3,061	4,566	1,159	2,431	566	833	309	1,390	2,123	3,016	441	1,141
Chemung County	8,118	6,012	2,297	2,484	730	1,004	553	415	591	639	1,432	1,773	244	757
Clinton County	6,876	4,929	1,917	2,126	863	874	398	591	199	656	1,011	1,207	296	730
Dutchess County	25,462	18,190	6,016	8,835	2,744	4,729	695	2,694	842	2,420	3,473	6,480	1,175	2,447
Erie County	79,581	67,216	17,386	33,375	5,096	13,965	2,492	5,010	2,684	8,040	11,836	21,568	2,863	8,137
Jefferson County	8,315	5,998	2,206	3,016	1,062	1,320	670	461	511	497	1,500	1,637	632	683
Kings County	174,987	136,931	46,047	78,351	9,455	25,370	11,134	20,854	11,369	28,591	32,991	63,301	9,835	35,812
Livingston County	5,667	4,446	1,153	2,148	677	904	137	436	220	515	538	1,366	166	509
Madison County	6,537	4,485	2,213	2,161	660	1,346	404	349	465	456	1,060	1,332	185	471
Monroe County	63,511	48,428	15,888	22,983	6,598	8,955	2,782	3,205	3,013	6,640	10,040	15,581	2,132	4,982
Nassau County	115,750	101,031	17,659	43,825	5,813	16,459	2,392	8,420	3,459	12,040	9,928	29,101	2,916	14,881
New York County	129,102	100,411	29,978	52,272	8,458	18,936	6,991	9,962	7,979	18,642	21,102	40,026	6,024	22,286
Niagara County	19,877	15,813	4,473	7,044	1,548	2,926	559	772	740	1,739	2,812	4,610	468	1,240
Oneida County	21,362	16,401	6,617	9,084	2,043	3,764	1,465	1,784	1,690	2,279	4,475	5,303	1,097	2,155
Onondaga County	37,847	30,888	7,657	13,639	3,107	6,209	1,550	3,146	1,411	4,017	4,014	8,527	1,301	3,650
Ontario County	11,246	7,890	1,979	4,114	898	2,056	170	621	369	1,223	883	2,499	162	1,089
Orange County	26,902	19,107	6,109	10,411	2,442	5,280	1,179	2,600	1,250	2,581	3,880	6,386	1,163	3,405
Oswego County	10,325	6,673	2,530	3,778	958	2,195	345	631	308	863	1,682	2,725	612	1,285
Putnam County	8,924	5,307	1,750	2,796	840	955	231	579	99	702	738	1,681	159	704
Queens County	172,201	133,523	37,874	66,833	8,050	21,641	8,140	13,644	8,052	19,988	26,861	49,255	7,520	22,601
Rensselaer County	13,834	9,192	3,641	4,803	1,523	2,071	411	590	595	647	2,554	2,793	420	1,336
Richmond County	39,195	26,406	8,509	12,451	2,564	3,921	1,211	2,229	1,967	3,342	5,903	8,903	1,873	3,231
Rockland County	26,708	20,086	4,220	9,654	1,055	5,755	552	2,184	647	2,435	2,677	5,498	868	2,491
Saratoga County	20,878	13,365	3,700	6,940	2,002	2,979	1,047	735	200	1,573	1,943	4,873	503	2,316
Schenectady County	11,889	10,907	2,705	4,720	622	2,189	394	1,075	265	1,384	1,619	3,576	265	1,654
St. Lawrence County	9,694	6,345	3,736	3,380	1,418	1,959	712	1,013	756	928	2,470	1,835	446	1,024
Steuben County	9,450	7,126	2,673	3,742	896	1,736	510	1,154	449	810	1,859	2,445	376	961
Suffolk County	127,044	93,550	26,021	39,061	7,700	17,095	3,811	6,123	3,669	8,724	16,481	24,254	3,832	10,441
Sullivan County	8,164	4,200	2,697	2,135	1,072	1,066	120	254	552	413	1,535	1,066	776	565
Tompkins County	7,039	4,996	1,166	1,993	543	1,521	36	167	147	107	512	936	313	536
Ulster County	18,217	12,305	4,351	6,079	1,187	3,096	497	785	1,044	1,735	3,128	3,768	958	1,375
Warren County	7,333	5,177	993	3,096	328	1,504	155	664	249	764	627	1,752	181	517
Wayne County	9,042	5,788	2,540	3,235	1,149	1,469	337	218	486	758	1,186	2,076	396	552
Westchester County	79,461	67,073	14,883	30,059	4,424	10,980	2,353	5,260	3,430	8,626	8,664	20,215	3,255	9,025
North Carolina														
Alamance County	14,040	10,262	3,179	5,132	1,171	2,470	544	894	715	1,300	1,876	3,702	223	1,160
Brunswick County	21,775	9,641	5,172	5,279	2,471	3,006	1,087	1,134	1,395	1,278	2,913	3,501	946	1,395
Buncombe County	25,251	18,107	5,180	9,553	2,227	4,349	517	2,225	846	2,678	2,913	5,987	1,240	3,182
Burke County	9,450	6,302	2,583	3,696	365	1,881	583	892	443	1,555	1,913	2,306	248	1,015
Cabarrus County	14,057	9,306	3,766	5,986	1,474	2,418	547	794	788	2,068	2,582	4,455	704	2,517
Caldwell County	8,892	5,451	3,358	3,224	975	1,582	707	502	798	727	2,572	1,898	480	899
Carteret County	9,206	5,765	2,800	2,901	985	1,335	148	982	374	537	1,833	1,924	492	493
Catawba County	14,144	9,782	3,774	5,239	1,367	1,629	160	706	645	1,420	2,301	4,015	522	1,627
Chatham County	9,108	6,511	1,822	2,761	850	1,796	296	560	422	689	1,091	1,371	309	470
Cleveland County	9,822	6,830	3,801	3,545	1,777	1,882	1,478	881	466	1,117	2,342	2,438	1,199	1,279
Craven County	9,970	7,386	3,060	4,073	1,542	2,024	409	424	222	982	1,701	2,830	245	1,133
Cumberland County	20,892	13,590	6,860	8,246	2,518	3,856	1,364	1,776	1,395	2,400	4,463	5,544	1,483	2,469
Davidson County	15,780	10,314	4,192	4,839	1,385	2,317	858	626	884	918	2,308	2,994	524	941
Durham County	18,472	12,470	4,935	6,795	1,754	3,311	556	994	1,191	1,799	3,096	4,353	862	1,266
Forsyth County	29,221	21,743	7,075	10,462	1,964	4,251	1,647	1,582	1,527	2,844	4,325	6,622	1,145	2,880
Gaston County	19,237	11,493	6,494	7,258	2,604	3,518	482	1,690	1,933	2,441	3,791	4,956	587	2,089
Guilford County	39,955	28,436	8,778	14,810	2,501	5,845	1,170	1,885	1,746	4,668	5,696	10,057	1,875	5,238
Harnett County	8,402	4,794	2,557	2,117	1,071	1,001	403	480	778	693	1,563	1,605	250	809

Table H-2: Counties—Disability Status and Type of Disability—*Continued*

	Total Population		With a Disability		With a Hearing Disability		With a Vision Disability		With a Cognitive Disability		With an Ambulatory Disability		With a Self-Care Disability	
	65 to 74 Years	75 Years and Over	65 to 74 Years	75 Years and Over	65 to 74 Years	75 Years and Over	65 to 74 Years	75 Years and Over	65 to 74 Years	75 Years and Over	65 to 74 Years	75 Years and Over	65 to 74 Years	75 Years and Over
North Carolina—Cont.														
Henderson County	15,395	11,781	3,371	5,582	1,602	3,233	858	674	620	930	1,697	3,358	519	1,287
Iredell County	14,628	8,867	3,473	3,300	1,395	1,574	669	578	809	1,205	2,141	1,952	473	935
Johnston County	13,917	7,516	5,580	4,485	1,395	1,707	1,014	778	1,027	768	3,818	2,586	932	1,128
Lincoln County	7,947	4,659	2,696	1,917	1,006	600	645	127	502	420	1,595	1,492	398	528
Mecklenburg County	61,226	38,332	14,573	20,427	4,742	9,297	2,802	4,196	2,801	6,014	8,521	11,835	2,479	4,810
Moore County	12,001	9,451	2,135	3,261	988	1,623	229	213	357	408	1,115	1,934	695	907
Nash County	8,896	6,130	2,653	3,672	1,241	1,720	174	519	561	744	1,596	2,645	303	625
New Hanover County	19,943	13,239	3,568	6,541	1,286	3,850	447	1,877	595	2,402	2,099	3,767	359	2,234
Onslow County	9,634	6,104	4,076	3,831	1,472	2,629	527	1,005	864	654	3,040	1,936	612	801
Orange County	9,735	5,796	1,254	2,396	311	911	205	522	64	622	598	1,557	290	371
Pitt County	11,930	7,376	3,228	4,596	704	2,205	615	1,463	530	1,323	2,143	3,286	1,018	1,556
Randolph County	13,948	8,622	4,506	4,098	1,725	1,886	1,224	1,116	646	1,416	2,703	3,100	517	1,054
Robeson County	10,634	6,073	5,342	3,612	1,754	1,510	1,288	1,212	1,618	1,462	3,704	2,818	610	1,666
Rockingham County	9,493	6,613	2,545	2,640	1,137	1,299	774	645	623	688	1,694	1,944	540	750
Rowan County	12,569	8,974	3,360	3,895	1,282	1,840	603	640	668	1,065	1,946	2,628	615	1,472
Rutherford County	7,492	5,179	2,026	2,939	851	1,545	154	736	266	1,056	1,395	1,477	483	469
Surry County	7,643	5,570	2,785	2,732	1,017	1,196	690	474	542	943	2,031	2,032	400	935
Union County	16,704	8,077	4,458	3,511	1,416	1,377	488	584	1,261	906	3,093	2,750	1,053	1,406
Wake County	60,819	36,460	12,038	17,207	3,998	8,132	2,661	3,581	2,491	5,501	7,151	11,657	2,272	5,245
Wayne County	10,280	7,339	2,604	4,543	693	2,198	628	575	670	1,257	2,202	3,143	261	1,242
Wilkes County	7,942	5,359	2,070	3,095	738	1,334	501	603	459	893	1,458	2,425	412	1,237
Wilson County	7,623	5,072	2,096	2,809	617	1,354	194	414	603	641	1,499	1,404	759	586
North Dakota														
Burleigh County	6,879	5,559	1,246	2,523	675	1,004	7	468	535	491	504	1,647	96	351
Cass County	9,294	7,807	2,945	4,327	1,088	2,536	640	315	713	1,136	1,332	2,771	254	753
Grand Forks County	4,185	3,262	1,327	1,685	644	577	172	320	193	246	670	1,147	273	265
Ward County	3,953	3,549	736	1,846	524	841	52	9	38	127	242	1,027	45	135
Ohio														
Allen County	8,884	7,123	1,688	3,644	541	1,932	254	844	294	1,105	1,284	1,996	138	540
Ashtabula County	9,621	6,201	2,710	3,563	920	1,655	261	722	508	823	1,682	1,956	421	497
Belmont County	6,976	5,393	1,934	2,427	819	1,408	564	930	161	427	1,215	1,362	204	664
Butler County	28,092	19,395	6,743	9,759	3,104	3,875	1,331	1,659	1,256	2,010	4,260	5,562	1,462	2,181
Clark County	13,645	9,361	3,483	4,129	1,697	2,334	880	821	855	1,408	2,011	3,147	659	1,025
Clermont County	17,096	10,777	4,648	5,020	2,118	2,406	912	913	1,010	1,219	2,724	3,321	824	1,317
Columbiana County	10,628	7,600	2,706	3,596	1,152	2,184	579	819	531	649	1,463	1,987	207	836
Cuyahoga County	107,546	91,743	27,725	45,212	7,175	17,315	4,423	8,975	6,332	13,995	18,883	30,244	6,300	14,565
Delaware County	13,201	7,745	2,743	3,679	1,223	1,011	161	562	245	1,138	1,806	2,634	595	704
Erie County	8,216	5,836	1,970	2,832	894	1,057	482	673	192	688	981	1,458	69	770
Fairfield County	12,631	8,552	2,936	4,580	705	1,807	346	769	379	1,472	2,188	2,749	502	831
Franklin County	77,018	52,932	18,498	25,465	5,140	10,391	2,950	4,654	4,820	8,518	12,109	15,609	4,134	7,367
Geauga County	9,611	6,379	1,896	2,025	1,166	1,069	255	390	437	376	511	1,103	96	491
Greene County	14,670	10,233	4,508	4,927	1,576	2,440	624	654	531	879	2,786	3,341	567	1,041
Hamilton County	60,290	48,612	13,771	22,467	4,061	8,241	2,600	3,526	2,573	6,220	8,334	14,614	1,936	5,424
Hancock County	6,508	4,860	1,757	2,490	598	962	254	274	120	444	1,277	1,419	528	438
Jefferson County	6,969	5,748	2,226	3,217	1,102	1,613	401	796	202	937	1,577	2,232	339	671
Lake County	22,994	16,628	4,779	7,419	1,854	3,408	187	1,719	624	2,344	2,812	4,751	785	1,903
Licking County	15,210	9,885	3,610	5,525	926	2,535	434	829	517	1,198	2,250	3,372	295	595
Lorain County	27,592	20,061	7,584	10,459	2,149	5,291	1,141	1,927	1,304	2,177	5,525	6,909	1,762	2,173
Lucas County	34,741	26,453	9,617	13,425	4,160	6,491	1,686	1,964	2,037	3,003	6,119	8,186	2,418	3,440
Mahoning County	22,504	19,916	5,543	9,582	2,319	4,137	1,054	1,723	1,262	2,737	3,078	6,735	403	3,291
Marion County	5,918	4,777	1,428	2,845	758	1,854	129	520	212	507	1,083	1,695	194	624
Medina County	16,181	10,170	4,254	4,974	1,856	2,548	551	728	424	1,234	2,362	3,362	832	1,135
Miami County	10,218	7,099	2,807	3,088	1,422	1,387	510	687	871	533	1,943	2,122	431	381
Montgomery County	47,104	37,863	12,321	17,251	4,301	7,233	2,350	4,021	2,583	5,026	7,903	11,216	2,500	4,409
Muskingum County	7,809	6,071	2,816	3,706	878	2,185	766	943	745	847	1,454	2,660	681	1,436
Portage County	13,849	10,046	2,918	6,313	1,235	2,998	537	1,849	696	1,721	1,775	3,912	629	1,256
Richland County	11,868	9,508	2,979	4,392	904	1,988	659	622	590	1,187	1,960	2,950	438	1,095
Ross County	6,458	4,497	2,043	3,032	900	1,482	647	386	506	775	1,129	1,960	514	667
Scioto County	6,839	5,158	2,559	3,160	1,123	2,231	286	682	358	992	1,377	1,887	346	1,151
Stark County	36,259	26,633	8,440	12,045	2,794	5,361	1,194	2,513	1,648	3,067	5,438	7,461	1,507	2,917
Summit County	47,428	36,994	10,405	14,824	3,423	6,311	1,631	2,956	2,280	2,462	6,243	9,889	2,623	3,633
Trumbull County	21,654	16,555	5,181	7,988	1,898	3,739	677	1,097	827	2,104	2,872	5,688	712	1,853
Tuscarawas County	8,735	7,240	2,263	3,430	1,052	2,015	499	811	451	635	1,131	2,189	603	490
Warren County	16,721	11,595	3,715	5,021	1,321	2,202	1,025	770	642	872	1,913	3,655	644	963
Wayne County	10,188	7,341	2,229	2,911	867	1,242	370	494	487	565	1,193	1,401	188	413
Wood County	10,104	7,133	2,220	3,262	808	1,550	202	705	350	678	1,048	2,184	343	898
Oklahoma														
Canadian County	9,391	5,951	2,315	3,277	744	1,536	212	731	451	759	1,718	2,344	358	1,092
Cleveland County	19,088	12,157	5,234	6,066	2,116	2,821	692	924	570	1,972	3,350	4,459	801	1,484
Comanche County	7,517	5,614	2,839	3,063	922	1,351	923	882	414	1,026	1,949	2,109	415	766
Creek County	6,831	4,509	2,095	2,559	1,046	1,417	291	561	249	419	1,077	1,641	310	448
Muskogee County	6,066	4,379	2,244	2,575	984	1,079	350	495	435	490	1,405	2,036	489	988
Oklahoma County	53,931	39,015	17,097	21,113	6,291	10,064	2,519	4,716	3,152	6,901	11,095	15,276	2,349	6,849
Payne County	4,995	3,671	949	2,450	211	1,107	304	634	101	371	677	1,681	18	669
Pottawatomie County	6,368	4,661	2,868	2,997	1,503	1,356	317	325	431	507	1,636	1,924	508	407
Rogers County	7,977	5,163	2,380	2,903	1,142	1,801	698	597	413	542	1,131	2,188	291	657

Table H-2: Counties—Disability Status and Type of Disability—*Continued*

	Total Population		With a Disability		With a Hearing Disability		With a Vision Disability		With a Cognitive Disability		With an Ambulatory Disability		With a Self-Care Disability	
	65 to 74 Years	75 Years and Over	65 to 74 Years	75 Years and Over	65 to 74 Years	75 Years and Over	65 to 74 Years	75 Years and Over	65 to 74 Years	75 Years and Over	65 to 74 Years	75 Years and Over	65 to 74 Years	75 Years and Over
Oklahoma—Cont.														
Tulsa County	45,749	34,298	12,515	17,804	4,579	9,156	2,228	3,181	3,077	4,752	7,362	11,554	2,378	4,641
Wagoner County	7,192	3,872	2,224	1,786	1,211	1,140	481	266	709	301	1,404	995	533	366
Oregon														
Benton County	7,089	5,182	1,211	2,590	665	1,127	142	336	169	614	605	1,662	151	579
Clackamas County	38,251	24,959	8,649	12,514	4,160	7,159	1,035	1,902	1,753	3,293	4,558	7,920	932	3,287
Deschutes County	18,744	11,415	5,215	5,076	3,144	2,478	816	814	1,176	1,705	1,914	2,801	592	1,388
Douglas County	13,949	10,914	3,561	6,442	1,503	3,342	285	1,057	1,179	1,679	1,944	3,830	731	993
Jackson County	24,721	17,123	6,839	9,013	3,398	4,636	744	2,102	1,472	2,417	3,691	5,504	843	1,459
Josephine County	12,197	8,232	2,717	4,356	1,400	2,362	539	855	399	1,068	1,357	2,672	225	811
Klamath County	7,455	4,676	2,373	2,603	1,070	1,292	288	611	349	655	1,458	1,578	514	818
Lane County	36,615	24,888	10,006	14,159	3,595	7,070	1,461	2,582	2,472	3,593	6,032	8,666	1,732	3,198
Linn County	12,251	8,231	3,791	4,464	1,814	2,394	290	477	1,347	1,552	2,049	2,795	804	1,029
Marion County	27,223	18,921	6,154	10,169	1,952	4,652	787	2,540	1,391	3,848	3,818	5,985	953	2,672
Multnomah County	54,854	35,697	15,708	20,721	5,702	11,193	3,186	5,064	3,506	6,534	9,016	13,634	2,948	5,371
Polk County	8,007	5,522	2,416	3,636	1,101	2,362	200	76	393	1,022	1,395	2,386	411	1,263
Umatilla County	5,872	5,051	2,057	3,073	968	1,440	232	1,217	480	1,776	1,244	2,356	724	1,832
Washington County	39,752	26,273	9,182	12,985	4,286	6,394	1,185	3,004	1,500	4,448	5,065	8,244	1,513	3,617
Yamhill County	8,828	6,532	2,687	3,790	1,266	2,370	557	814	413	1,012	1,225	2,035	407	860
Pennsylvania														
Adams County	9,951	7,503	1,956	3,258	962	1,573	215	460	445	793	949	1,981	254	661
Allegheny County	108,994	97,600	23,933	46,319	8,378	21,368	2,161	7,348	5,704	12,218	14,904	28,923	4,022	10,716
Armstrong County	7,395	6,211	2,155	3,189	1,012	1,612	139	924	435	521	1,029	1,792	207	685
Beaver County	17,166	15,689	3,116	7,118	1,317	3,875	342	1,232	510	1,498	1,813	4,240	361	1,036
Berks County	35,492	28,417	7,849	13,079	2,319	6,101	884	2,375	1,087	3,746	4,654	8,318	942	3,092
Blair County	12,438	10,450	3,456	5,650	1,165	2,191	334	857	334	1,641	2,116	3,886	747	1,178
Bucks County	57,469	44,447	11,670	21,000	4,051	8,681	1,760	3,781	1,818	5,461	7,103	14,123	1,537	5,645
Butler County	16,640	13,795	3,780	6,368	1,528	2,666	443	784	734	1,202	1,988	3,745	364	989
Cambria County	14,503	12,543	3,690	7,320	1,337	2,906	628	1,876	774	1,950	2,266	4,478	746	1,898
Carbon County	7,240	5,100	1,860	1,891	998	924	231	430	475	352	1,136	1,000	400	513
Centre County	10,721	8,446	2,626	4,200	987	1,922	236	838	490	1,256	1,414	2,670	419	1,359
Chester County	41,614	30,002	6,984	11,446	2,722	5,680	1,071	2,201	1,092	3,457	3,766	7,048	1,148	2,246
Clearfield County	8,168	6,456	2,961	3,090	1,090	1,343	610	919	532	533	1,580	2,029	385	741
Columbia County	6,167	4,730	1,390	1,830	619	735	173	245	87	571	748	1,170	184	584
Crawford County	9,255	6,371	2,723	2,863	1,397	1,711	514	426	510	348	1,275	1,388	120	579
Cumberland County	22,220	17,421	4,440	9,301	1,286	3,600	823	1,688	364	2,206	2,894	6,369	274	2,249
Dauphin County	22,445	17,062	6,009	7,665	1,559	3,356	1,022	1,263	923	1,982	3,520	5,747	680	2,181
Delaware County	43,899	38,133	9,273	18,839	2,864	8,367	1,366	2,658	1,849	6,098	6,173	11,902	1,578	4,693
Erie County	23,659	18,613	5,211	9,375	2,691	4,194	549	1,410	731	3,024	2,617	5,370	672	1,994
Fayette County	13,967	11,254	3,446	5,955	1,173	2,324	264	985	576	2,140	1,972	4,008	593	1,904
Franklin County	14,897	12,108	3,052	5,544	1,021	2,192	545	780	522	1,813	1,810	3,350	630	1,467
Indiana County	8,121	6,276	1,943	3,128	1,183	1,620	484	486	402	1,046	850	1,908	169	795
Lackawanna County	20,810	17,451	5,694	9,415	1,801	4,434	732	1,431	1,147	1,678	3,590	5,646	708	2,412
Lancaster County	45,428	38,145	9,225	16,825	4,893	8,184	1,039	2,515	1,168	3,047	4,995	8,504	880	3,026
Lawrence County	8,889	7,945	2,091	3,596	1,101	1,993	253	479	239	584	1,053	2,315	195	1,063
Lebanon County	12,861	10,665	3,004	4,693	1,090	1,779	187	1,131	618	1,528	1,798	2,985	179	1,018
Lehigh County	30,071	24,529	6,730	10,940	2,019	4,526	516	1,633	1,341	3,742	4,138	6,245	1,077	2,309
Luzerne County	30,860	26,724	7,525	15,351	3,140	6,865	996	3,792	1,162	4,157	4,613	10,708	1,315	4,234
Lycoming County	11,027	8,518	3,190	4,895	1,499	2,180	293	852	615	939	1,568	2,995	491	1,097
Mercer County	11,627	10,039	2,526	5,414	814	2,696	280	1,490	429	1,357	1,742	3,369	433	1,386
Monroe County	15,062	10,039	3,917	6,551	1,456	3,545	381	2,129	803	1,976	2,710	3,738	857	1,287
Montgomery County	69,134	58,517	13,339	23,821	4,157	10,617	1,659	3,494	2,591	5,777	8,046	14,737	2,036	5,991
Northampton County	27,058	22,787	6,272	11,743	2,340	4,337	779	1,646	2,061	3,436	3,442	7,167	1,133	2,752
Northumberland County	9,738	7,943	1,790	4,692	758	2,271	328	1,240	150	915	832	2,848	73	1,250
Philadelphia County	106,536	82,649	32,036	44,449	7,296	14,985	6,309	8,276	7,772	13,127	22,762	32,327	6,724	12,583
Schuylkill County	14,739	12,189	4,483	6,184	1,830	2,791	758	1,134	694	1,652	2,621	3,709	339	1,750
Somerset County	8,172	6,630	2,154	2,957	1,012	1,437	269	501	445	565	1,087	1,777	180	605
Washington County	21,297	17,102	4,754	8,805	1,790	3,975	548	1,481	755	2,579	3,219	5,734	888	2,711
Westmoreland County	39,514	32,796	9,108	15,926	3,783	8,636	1,185	3,791	1,685	4,538	5,511	9,831	1,257	3,856
York County	39,976	28,343	10,108	12,121	4,804	5,311	1,122	1,895	1,966	2,432	6,560	7,860	1,701	2,960
Rhode Island														
Kent County	15,736	12,342	5,017	6,815	2,055	3,304	702	1,695	929	1,057	2,896	4,065	661	880
Newport County	9,135	6,353	1,961	2,757	428	1,046	138	418	205	616	1,243	1,898	340	556
Providence County	46,576	38,764	11,421	19,709	3,549	8,776	2,211	3,383	2,573	5,198	7,389	13,733	1,811	5,484
Washington County	12,757	9,657	2,911	4,619	1,307	2,248	509	1,088	576	528	1,483	2,323	443	596
South Carolina														
Aiken County	17,189	10,994	4,941	5,440	2,417	2,555	892	1,103	667	1,333	2,816	3,593	811	1,890
Anderson County	19,162	12,459	5,662	7,037	1,622	2,956	1,061	1,257	1,889	2,435	3,558	4,725	575	1,992
Beaufort County	26,267	15,867	3,728	5,441	1,491	2,775	527	1,059	825	1,550	1,912	2,648	312	1,231
Berkeley County	16,089	8,040	4,923	4,518	1,708	2,129	1,167	1,084	754	1,720	2,655	3,577	546	1,975
Charleston County	33,205	20,932	8,044	9,654	2,921	4,434	1,157	1,854	2,186	2,687	5,718	5,335	1,758	2,342
Darlington County	6,641	4,250	2,153	2,200	569	760	570	380	1,420	797	1,586	1,223	321	244
Dorchester County	11,076	6,343	3,267	3,296	731	1,539	377	795	1,039	1,090	1,906	2,068	706	1,006
Florence County	12,503	7,287	3,394	4,559	1,092	2,580	908	1,445	1,480	1,966	1,964	3,427	600	1,354
Greenville County	41,029	26,811	9,091	14,143	2,796	6,080	1,008	3,410	1,563	4,266	5,526	10,272	1,836	4,073
Greenwood County	6,491	4,867	1,820	2,702	826	1,584	293	740	45	858	1,225	1,988	165	725

Table H-2: Counties—Disability Status and Type of Disability—*Continued*

	Total Population		With a Disability		With a Hearing Disability		With a Vision Disability		With a Cognitive Disability		With an Ambulatory Disability		With a Self-Care Disability	
	65 to 74 Years	75 Years and Over	65 to 74 Years	75 Years and Over	65 to 74 Years	75 Years and Over	65 to 74 Years	75 Years and Over	65 to 74 Years	75 Years and Over	65 to 74 Years	75 Years and Over	65 to 74 Years	75 Years and Over
South Carolina—Cont.														
Horry County	39,406	21,176	11,883	10,772	4,266	5,179	1,812	1,826	2,352	2,804	7,830	7,227	2,653	3,383
Lancaster County	9,507	5,687	2,258	2,835	870	1,373	504	429	421	470	1,455	1,517	471	1,103
Laurens County	6,352	3,908	2,280	2,266	1,064	1,051	308	382	525	836	1,588	1,771	202	649
Lexington County	23,930	14,381	6,502	7,780	2,435	3,508	1,054	1,937	1,124	1,619	4,264	5,721	959	2,123
Oconee County	9,788	6,029	3,296	3,665	1,609	1,310	502	596	585	1,230	1,946	2,129	318	883
Orangeburg County	8,971	5,953	3,548	3,951	1,124	1,256	1,286	892	1,056	1,559	2,619	3,193	1,078	1,638
Pickens County	11,264	6,758	3,736	2,781	872	1,280	205	263	1,009	905	2,489	1,879	795	706
Richland County	26,837	16,880	7,298	8,488	2,442	3,572	1,385	2,071	2,134	2,343	4,168	5,585	1,431	2,548
Spartanburg County	26,287	16,893	7,815	9,748	2,638	4,370	965	1,922	1,826	2,041	5,151	5,801	579	2,550
Sumter County	8,764	6,195	3,803	3,568	1,407	1,539	893	1,041	1,428	1,365	2,356	2,323	919	1,372
York County	20,095	11,841	4,801	4,774	1,800	3,156	644	547	983	1,530	3,043	2,553	681	1,105
South Dakota														
Minnehaha County	12,609	8,998	2,380	4,301	846	1,941	171	795	363	1,591	1,434	2,648	675	970
Pennington County	9,100	6,582	2,261	2,861	930	1,321	0	363	364	549	1,539	1,971	409	345
Tennessee														
Anderson County	8,101	5,765	2,393	3,358	779	1,813	430	919	485	858	1,397	2,252	852	1,213
Blount County	14,035	8,896	3,407	5,242	1,022	2,580	905	516	244	1,764	2,014	3,580	401	1,038
Bradley County	9,632	6,543	3,401	3,436	1,626	1,856	966	289	394	982	1,869	1,995	250	393
Davidson County	42,417	30,082	10,220	15,532	2,902	5,552	1,583	2,684	1,683	4,014	6,612	10,712	1,101	3,556
Greene County	8,241	4,929	2,955	3,233	762	1,855	1,226	844	585	689	1,963	2,113	535	1,093
Hamilton County	31,267	23,115	7,221	9,866	3,135	4,262	919	2,270	1,868	3,108	4,325	6,389	1,120	2,921
Knox County	37,339	25,933	9,638	13,709	4,228	6,132	1,427	2,230	2,812	4,366	5,934	9,035	1,677	4,036
Madison County	8,472	5,705	2,434	3,952	913	1,814	521	1,450	432	1,144	1,334	2,736	544	2,036
Maury County	7,564	4,771	1,916	2,086	725	902	517	611	568	546	1,255	1,658	329	377
Montgomery County	10,101	5,852	4,405	2,211	1,151	757	1,031	178	684	529	3,347	1,668	1,095	635
Putnam County	6,687	4,884	1,561	2,620	516	1,386	246	637	427	616	1,103	1,637	458	646
Robertson County	5,376	3,300	1,574	1,734	760	820	140	162	108	397	886	1,191	141	442
Rutherford County	17,349	9,955	3,940	4,246	1,746	2,181	1,078	1,004	1,226	1,579	2,823	3,111	835	1,515
Sevier County	10,732	5,959	3,116	2,750	862	1,465	356	733	271	576	2,298	1,406	758	725
Shelby County	63,710	42,233	17,011	21,854	4,268	6,785	3,202	3,886	2,980	7,050	11,198	14,481	3,175	7,076
Sullivan County	17,994	13,321	5,245	7,754	1,777	3,969	1,053	2,081	903	2,069	3,657	5,092	935	2,239
Sumner County	15,579	9,319	4,737	5,323	2,214	2,431	1,322	1,617	942	1,701	2,701	4,233	941	2,295
Washington County	12,201	8,257	5,224	4,666	2,426	2,360	1,099	1,139	1,292	1,312	3,611	3,625	1,672	1,394
Williamson County	14,130	8,952	2,403	4,333	1,221	2,707	460	424	975	1,195	1,273	2,513	177	1,030
Wilson County	11,343	6,119	2,480	3,583	1,092	1,552	239	792	493	1,382	1,249	2,290	486	1,118
Texas														
Angelina County	7,207	5,609	2,875	3,319	988	1,617	273	907	300	1,488	1,918	2,207	403	1,419
Bastrop County	6,024	3,251	1,401	1,789	1,065	706	76	291	56	392	742	1,387	0	360
Bell County	19,207	11,952	7,287	7,304	2,478	3,289	1,683	1,325	1,327	1,836	4,898	5,590	1,486	2,055
Bexar County	120,532	84,362	39,770	48,491	15,333	22,135	6,398	11,436	9,515	14,160	25,615	31,183	7,325	13,782
Bowie County	8,003	5,455	2,410	2,856	906	1,083	643	444	759	1,103	1,509	2,073	706	1,293
Brazoria County	22,028	13,225	6,760	5,825	3,135	3,084	370	1,196	1,938	1,761	4,558	4,353	1,505	1,141
Brazos County	10,039	6,719	3,234	3,492	1,013	1,290	585	637	910	522	2,213	2,380	683	671
Cameron County	28,679	22,328	10,884	12,906	4,250	5,528	3,016	3,434	2,741	3,174	6,582	9,177	2,297	4,501
Collin County	55,807	29,110	11,065	14,002	3,970	6,579	1,751	2,726	2,358	3,705	7,172	8,232	2,425	3,638
Comal County	12,880	7,989	2,736	4,055	1,017	1,988	361	810	841	1,240	1,893	2,390	661	1,223
Coryell County	3,746	2,337	972	1,187	143	480	178	448	51	295	791	789	132	306
Dallas County	142,978	95,078	39,818	46,248	10,656	18,975	7,508	11,112	8,526	14,519	26,258	31,386	8,332	13,674
Denton County	43,586	21,149	10,487	10,911	4,017	4,282	1,389	971	1,862	3,202	6,776	7,222	1,622	2,766
Ector County	8,175	6,234	2,916	3,574	880	1,859	932	673	495	1,102	1,683	2,125	181	867
El Paso County	51,143	40,953	17,618	25,188	7,088	10,886	5,262	6,638	4,762	8,845	10,927	17,482	3,318	9,432
Ellis County	11,713	6,518	3,541	3,570	2,108	1,383	443	601	324	1,401	1,917	2,377	683	634
Fort Bend County	42,032	22,199	8,433	11,573	2,265	3,748	1,382	2,038	1,426	2,742	5,092	8,811	1,527	3,670
Galveston County	24,146	15,207	7,502	7,623	2,648	2,704	763	934	1,056	2,292	5,108	4,830	1,233	2,093
Grayson County	12,009	8,026	3,363	4,096	1,623	2,567	832	654	1,094	1,071	2,069	2,462	703	838
Gregg County	9,434	7,360	3,095	4,236	944	1,917	210	947	588	977	2,158	2,855	727	1,278
Guadalupe County	11,176	7,269	2,978	3,365	1,450	1,324	336	404	553	982	1,345	2,609	615	1,185
Harris County	251,676	151,584	67,563	80,567	21,098	31,640	13,187	16,630	15,950	25,281	43,027	54,767	12,372	25,990
Harrison County	5,767	4,074	1,602	1,966	360	1,021	76	632	473	359	956	1,302	281	535
Hays County	11,967	6,083	2,847	3,378	954	1,613	127	399	365	1,013	1,663	2,061	457	554
Henderson County	9,585	6,541	2,597	3,130	877	1,494	282	346	399	394	1,981	1,798	289	346
Hidalgo County	48,330	36,031	22,264	22,338	7,592	11,109	7,799	6,332	5,152	7,665	13,964	15,664	7,127	9,578
Hunt County	7,742	5,728	2,734	3,703	1,016	1,388	540	684	447	826	2,171	2,479	717	968
Jefferson County	17,443	14,783	5,730	8,390	2,040	4,294	1,168	1,888	1,265	2,211	3,949	5,649	957	2,464
Johnson County	12,211	7,131	3,681	3,733	1,408	1,973	793	1,183	530	601	2,381	2,269	505	413
Kaufman County	8,141	4,096	1,594	2,209	403	884	344	362	501	577	1,379	1,420	351	374
Liberty County	6,169	3,585	2,127	2,582	1,072	1,765	195	756	195	788	1,214	1,798	186	730
Lubbock County	19,295	14,685	6,205	7,691	2,883	3,717	864	2,220	1,161	2,109	4,007	4,873	1,174	1,815
McLennan County	17,693	13,714	5,098	7,310	2,415	3,615	1,051	1,501	729	1,968	3,391	4,790	1,057	1,621
Midland County	7,940	6,844	1,965	2,958	980	1,159	570	438	344	924	1,210	2,082	240	1,136
Montgomery County	39,254	22,197	13,165	11,603	5,971	6,180	2,882	1,943	1,453	2,822	7,532	7,452	1,772	3,122
Nacogdoches County	4,421	3,633	1,502	1,948	528	645	169	502	361	626	1,161	1,347	309	614
Nueces County	26,255	18,675	8,691	10,991	3,194	4,741	2,043	2,959	1,150	2,855	5,334	7,083	1,796	2,200
Orange County	7,418	4,804	1,553	3,281	524	1,151	319	894	135	707	917	2,319	82	482
Parker County	11,284	6,835	2,280	4,092	1,180	1,969	509	1,153	321	1,695	1,108	3,063	375	1,146
Potter County	7,879	6,002	2,317	2,783	1,023	1,234	407	544	154	534	1,438	1,816	206	767

Table H-2: Counties—Disability Status and Type of Disability—*Continued*

	Total Population		With a Disability		With a Hearing Disability		With a Vision Disability		With a Cognitive Disability		With an Ambulatory Disability		With a Self-Care Disability	
	65 to 74 Years	75 Years and Over	65 to 74 Years	75 Years and Over	65 to 74 Years	75 Years and Over	65 to 74 Years	75 Years and Over	65 to 74 Years	75 Years and Over	65 to 74 Years	75 Years and Over	65 to 74 Years	75 Years and Over
Texas—Cont.														
Randall County	9,988	7,318	2,730	4,046	746	1,946	570	552	707	1,215	1,680	3,032	376	1,187
Rockwall County	6,382	3,849	1,801	1,139	486	598	459	314	562	177	1,393	703	378	180
San Patricio County	5,973	3,058	2,397	1,491	1,124	460	685	352	723	803	1,587	1,164	459	614
Smith County	18,908	14,074	4,755	7,243	1,201	3,112	989	989	1,126	1,533	2,709	4,771	750	2,051
Tarrant County	117,006	75,786	30,251	39,584	9,947	17,783	6,306	7,420	5,961	11,218	19,821	28,022	5,381	10,067
Taylor County	9,787	7,928	3,564	4,032	1,626	2,283	1,340	752	1,197	1,366	2,328	2,765	409	1,733
Tom Green County	8,772	7,905	2,614	5,002	1,172	2,246	648	1,283	452	1,266	1,449	3,757	353	1,598
Travis County	59,327	35,418	13,038	18,721	3,820	8,254	2,377	4,718	2,452	4,299	8,029	12,709	2,222	4,369
Victoria County	7,160	5,236	2,459	3,001	1,085	2,023	379	578	775	786	1,509	1,566	585	480
Walker County	3,801	2,979	475	1,556	262	648	49	480	0	417	332	1,150	52	326
Webb County	13,215	8,878	5,758	6,251	1,711	2,355	1,384	1,622	1,812	2,294	3,828	4,583	1,553	2,775
Wichita County	9,011	8,024	2,848	4,326	796	2,296	686	1,079	399	1,633	2,242	3,324	647	1,115
Williamson County	32,652	19,825	6,399	10,737	2,486	5,227	701	2,245	679	3,691	3,921	6,609	684	2,882
Utah														
Cache County	5,550	4,327	1,184	1,732	491	1,175	156	325	245	421	666	715	93	483
Davis County	17,434	12,493	3,430	6,273	1,516	3,350	410	1,185	775	1,312	1,798	3,745	453	1,252
Salt Lake County	61,489	41,991	14,477	21,093	6,582	11,008	2,007	3,773	2,618	5,436	7,719	13,107	1,895	5,320
Utah County	23,286	16,723	5,523	7,188	2,897	3,625	1,021	1,602	1,311	1,893	3,310	4,244	880	1,566
Washington County	16,266	13,456	4,652	7,107	2,287	3,251	1,011	1,542	1,019	1,770	2,438	4,713	492	1,431
Weber County	15,396	10,855	3,830	5,669	1,730	2,693	744	1,188	353	1,048	1,907	4,025	537	1,565
Vermont														
Chittenden County	11,822	8,369	2,149	3,974	806	2,060	397	714	548	1,299	1,475	2,532	238	945
Virginia														
Albemarle County	9,329	6,775	1,565	3,062	282	1,553	193	615	186	818	1,174	1,887	126	501
Arlington County	12,041	7,538	2,165	3,670	615	1,291	141	749	341	1,440	1,225	2,301	430	1,219
Augusta County	8,280	5,501	1,866	1,436	779	588	299	352	228	274	1,085	863	179	471
Bedford County	8,987	5,616	2,262	2,365	414	1,204	324	536	769	662	1,219	1,285	225	592
Chesterfield County	27,550	14,973	5,562	6,658	1,505	2,815	732	1,257	766	1,736	4,079	5,488	1,038	2,080
Fairfax County	80,312	48,262	13,681	21,986	4,914	9,829	1,841	3,080	1,806	4,770	8,086	14,333	1,918	4,875
Fauquier County	6,866	3,834	1,786	1,558	539	678	138	228	456	385	1,087	925	356	347
Frederick County	7,532	4,920	1,138	2,702	319	1,214	103	905	259	1,030	557	1,986	244	953
Hanover County	9,518	6,286	1,956	2,632	869	945	100	560	522	878	1,006	1,920	257	866
Henrico County	24,877	18,579	5,004	8,449	1,372	3,486	346	1,682	525	2,139	2,776	5,969	836	2,924
James City County	9,346	6,819	1,719	2,913	628	1,280	111	254	186	1,050	1,166	1,887	541	655
Loudoun County	17,781	10,650	3,304	5,219	1,106	2,162	362	1,177	461	1,347	2,045	3,422	343	1,475
Montgomery County	6,270	4,375	1,495	1,692	242	1,075	391	144	107	237	977	975	176	407
Prince William County	24,056	12,425	5,363	5,824	1,633	1,832	539	901	1,230	1,863	3,728	4,015	917	1,459
Roanoke County	10,035	7,606	1,710	3,944	624	1,998	119	905	337	691	778	2,288	304	665
Rockingham County	7,947	6,173	1,696	3,190	610	1,484	181	1,011	436	900	1,101	1,814	612	871
Spotsylvania County	9,608	5,798	1,773	2,967	758	1,216	110	485	294	1,047	997	2,060	163	703
Stafford County	7,872	4,869	1,478	2,334	451	795	182	323	197	913	965	1,229	180	1,104
York County	5,929	3,821	1,038	1,954	355	1,187	166	341	406	509	527	1,368	438	270
Washington														
Benton County	14,669	10,361	3,782	5,340	1,833	2,279	455	915	791	1,634	2,141	3,779	755	1,470
Chelan County	7,325	5,414	1,451	2,536	559	1,767	242	696	361	1,178	895	1,747	287	653
Clallam County	10,929	8,132	2,982	4,263	1,154	2,024	127	1,248	215	1,316	1,987	2,828	160	712
Clark County	38,474	22,744	9,513	10,684	3,896	5,170	655	2,028	2,761	3,329	6,267	7,108	1,274	3,146
Cowlitz County	10,828	7,094	4,562	3,764	2,249	1,813	358	766	1,005	937	2,541	1,982	549	998
Franklin County	4,387	2,185	1,428	1,363	766	894	94	655	6	575	896	982	86	473
Grant County	6,920	4,518	1,673	2,763	547	1,377	98	444	327	793	831	1,743	214	578
Grays Harbor County	8,018	4,983	3,196	2,418	1,714	1,475	284	645	625	503	2,067	1,323	354	644
Island County	11,059	6,858	2,313	3,484	1,160	1,914	426	539	493	871	1,437	2,143	465	955
King County	146,578	100,955	33,025	51,213	13,216	23,960	5,040	9,500	9,378	17,107	18,134	33,378	5,586	16,887
Kitsap County	25,356	14,341	6,017	7,296	2,729	3,761	771	1,893	913	2,551	3,839	4,570	423	2,302
Lewis County	8,366	6,141	3,020	3,944	1,579	2,407	502	862	1,126	1,561	1,531	2,304	504	1,302
Pierce County	61,867	40,966	17,807	22,113	6,971	11,484	3,227	4,272	3,936	5,677	11,044	13,864	2,451	6,079
Skagit County	13,349	9,036	3,240	4,452	1,545	2,259	627	559	944	1,599	1,749	2,849	610	981
Snohomish County	55,024	34,436	13,935	17,258	5,781	8,585	2,787	2,822	3,113	5,362	8,035	10,309	2,437	4,610
Spokane County	42,341	28,462	11,427	15,845	5,743	8,272	1,484	3,141	2,205	5,615	6,066	10,010	1,032	5,189
Thurston County	24,010	15,525	5,657	8,164	2,616	4,342	577	2,039	620	2,960	3,141	5,332	547	2,361
Whatcom County	19,338	11,882	4,749	5,990	1,778	3,108	486	1,355	1,125	1,864	3,367	3,570	923	1,449
Yakima County	17,924	12,721	5,882	7,405	1,910	3,700	236	1,439	1,279	1,903	4,020	4,982	1,283	1,886
West Virginia														
Berkeley County	9,116	5,345	3,274	2,560	1,249	1,317	677	458	620	645	1,625	1,264	402	381
Cabell County	9,058	6,990	3,137	4,210	1,221	2,507	524	1,287	223	1,144	2,068	2,964	288	1,273
Harrison County	6,858	4,933	2,533	2,759	945	1,567	377	759	668	792	1,798	1,630	669	849
Kanawha County	19,438	14,120	7,664	7,618	3,642	3,435	1,070	1,691	1,780	1,780	4,296	4,988	1,475	1,998
Monongalia County	6,214	4,499	1,768	2,348	783	1,046	233	397	399	781	1,275	1,607	363	565
Raleigh County	7,965	5,868	3,484	3,804	1,832	2,426	658	1,444	1,005	1,553	1,909	2,337	453	1,263
Wood County	9,173	6,586	2,084	3,808	1,016	1,590	263	371	269	1,246	1,309	2,161	496	672
Wisconsin														
Brown County	19,061	13,597	3,416	6,611	1,235	3,014	398	1,024	468	1,663	2,085	4,556	427	1,248
Dane County	35,930	23,954	6,732	11,289	2,889	4,302	773	2,189	1,204	2,758	2,978	6,161	793	2,444
Dodge County	7,251	5,995	1,474	2,497	574	1,088	151	137	371	765	802	1,825	235	498
Eau Claire County	7,811	5,854	1,808	2,714	651	1,507	121	471	333	1,027	1,138	1,559	282	703

Table H-2: Counties—Disability Status and Type of Disability—*Continued*

	Total Population		With a Disability		With a Hearing Disability		With a Vision Disability		With a Cognitive Disability		With an Ambulatory Disability		With a Self-Care Disability	
	65 to 74 Years	75 Years and Over	65 to 74 Years	75 Years and Over	65 to 74 Years	75 Years and Over	65 to 74 Years	75 Years and Over	65 to 74 Years	75 Years and Over	65 to 74 Years	75 Years and Over	65 to 74 Years	75 Years and Over
Wisconsin—Cont.														
Fond du Lac County	9,097	7,215	2,023	3,525	840	1,922	305	405	277	1,012	1,214	2,219	276	1,134
Jefferson County	7,137	5,044	1,287	1,788	560	734	0	126	191	77	758	1,218	180	410
Kenosha County	12,159	8,743	3,250	3,959	1,029	2,330	358	387	544	1,044	2,189	2,467	367	895
La Crosse County	9,259	7,130	2,248	2,386	907	1,087	378	282	376	426	1,229	1,522	290	616
Manitowoc County	7,999	6,593	923	3,131	449	1,804	104	736	96	472	560	1,859	201	1,004
Marathon County	11,414	9,286	2,307	4,331	1,262	2,319	431	542	156	834	1,077	3,116	206	1,311
Milwaukee County	60,893	51,242	15,527	26,820	5,253	11,343	2,342	5,510	3,077	7,472	10,061	17,944	3,352	8,137
Outagamie County	12,978	9,693	2,446	3,591	1,268	2,091	580	453	430	1,354	1,320	2,486	565	789
Ozaukee County	8,624	6,331	1,412	2,985	387	1,641	118	521	117	323	841	1,711	86	720
Portage County	5,763	4,301	785	1,841	369	1,051	62	185	67	434	448	913	83	307
Racine County	16,348	12,651	4,143	5,470	2,032	2,127	171	776	441	1,088	2,216	3,145	592	1,433
Rock County	13,255	10,105	3,497	4,954	1,620	1,883	438	904	302	1,207	1,883	3,348	558	1,357
Sheboygan County	9,723	8,047	1,533	2,899	662	1,255	343	528	301	566	859	1,633	212	558
St. Croix County	6,098	3,984	724	2,048	425	707	67	243	143	517	289	1,556	144	568
Walworth County	8,858	6,239	1,833	2,912	1,179	1,755	119	323	208	1,081	862	1,949	88	730
Washington County	11,743	8,727	2,202	3,019	1,206	993	278	83	256	297	1,345	2,321	331	518
Waukesha County	35,477	28,310	5,717	12,236	2,555	5,803	663	2,266	990	2,566	2,865	8,468	601	2,362
Winnebago County	13,225	11,074	3,630	4,861	1,442	2,183	822	1,007	853	1,506	1,878	3,091	382	970
Wood County	7,198	6,546	1,201	2,660	554	1,130	69	456	224	553	472	1,884	180	932
Wyoming														
Laramie County	8,255	5,323	2,232	2,770	848	1,244	229	323	608	1,053	1,432	1,757	432	734
Natrona County	5,416	4,169	1,436	2,244	564	1,105	349	593	392	201	755	1,074	233	243

Table H-3: Places—Disability Status and Type of Disability

	Total Population		With a Disability		With a Hearing Disability		With a Vision Disability		With a Cognitive Disability		With an Ambulatory Disability		With a Self-Care Disability	
	65 to 74 Years	75 Years and Over	65 to 74 Years	75 Years and Over	65 to 74 Years	75 Years and Over	65 to 74 Years	75 Years and Over	65 to 74 Years	75 Years and Over	65 to 74 Years	75 Years and Over	65 to 74 Years	75 Years and Over
Alabama														
Birmingham city	14,720	11,014	4,968	5,702	1,137	1,657	792	1,112	1,197	1,752	3,883	4,207	1,225	2,262
Dothan city	6,221	4,655	2,108	2,614	800	919	256	360	485	500	1,398	1,872	362	539
Hoover city	8,416	6,368	1,591	2,843	995	805	127	182	281	1,191	351	2,402	133	1,151
Huntsville city	13,951	14,674	4,125	6,986	1,808	2,518	506	1,724	737	1,856	2,166	3,553	576	1,450
Mobile city	15,490	11,808	3,965	6,014	1,423	2,333	533	1,377	917	2,235	2,297	4,358	452	1,914
Montgomery city	14,377	10,898	4,292	5,507	898	2,192	541	1,439	668	1,850	3,088	4,470	825	2,031
Tuscaloosa city	6,680	4,820	2,647	2,403	850	807	446	510	280	803	1,837	1,668	238	715
Alaska														
Anchorage municipality	16,514	9,913	4,073	5,403	2,264	2,335	273	1,099	701	2,110	2,155	2,708	533	2,310
Arizona														
Avondale city	4,091	1,748	1,511	665	534	301	48	149	416	122	1,199	446	262	230
Chandler city	15,563	9,307	3,930	5,022	2,252	2,622	711	1,028	871	1,800	2,215	3,633	691	1,831
Flagstaff city	4,398	2,161	1,551	1,087	766	745	262	222	50	354	898	725	238	280
Glendale city	15,577	9,273	5,095	4,298	1,786	2,138	950	1,355	1,422	1,781	3,449	3,363	646	1,720
Goodyear city	6,362	3,611	1,179	1,409	654	894	210	483	59	338	332	522	88	297
Mesa city	39,254	33,313	10,460	16,633	4,352	9,325	1,875	3,122	1,551	4,984	5,649	10,735	935	4,589
Peoria city	15,192	11,952	3,273	6,052	1,264	2,920	358	1,057	568	1,263	1,859	4,187	351	1,441
Phoenix city	92,181	56,184	23,525	28,954	8,098	13,417	4,883	7,535	4,958	8,434	14,851	20,307	4,660	7,885
Scottsdale city	27,448	22,559	4,742	10,694	2,182	5,330	1,196	2,593	859	2,909	2,528	6,610	835	2,639
Surprise city	15,042	10,272	3,093	3,612	1,661	2,096	410	775	335	786	1,543	2,349	534	567
Tempe city	10,990	7,269	2,689	4,462	1,013	2,402	422	1,022	900	1,174	1,719	3,247	503	1,422
Tucson city	37,826	30,396	11,899	15,664	5,160	7,930	2,442	2,791	2,711	4,365	5,916	10,540	1,976	5,724
Yuma city	6,958	6,175	2,573	2,736	689	1,405	539	387	771	770	1,800	1,790	448	519
Arkansas														
Fayetteville city	2,881	3,432	694	1,522	299	703	53	389	0	432	410	612	109	143
Fort Smith city	5,542	5,063	1,260	2,615	356	1,474	49	565	384	1,265	870	1,550	291	702
Jonesboro city	4,904	4,530	1,708	2,190	519	651	641	293	401	736	1,217	1,681	469	805
Little Rock city	14,520	10,769	3,636	5,871	1,359	2,553	770	1,159	1,652	1,381	2,498	4,100	554	1,041
North Little Rock city	5,525	2,836	2,016	1,602	185	559	415	125	574	188	1,595	1,322	253	531
Springdale city	4,159	2,734	1,152	1,544	360	1,178	129	626	181	404	708	912	176	373
California														
Alameda city	5,979	3,120	1,218	1,562	567	804	243	525	257	425	841	954	306	403
Alhambra city	6,712	5,231	1,235	1,643	349	736	238	220	131	458	755	1,021	212	503
Anaheim city	19,735	13,476	4,307	6,080	1,158	1,821	1,147	708	1,273	1,588	3,040	4,100	1,822	1,485
Antioch city	6,721	5,076	1,728	3,172	432	1,578	233	825	54	964	1,355	2,133	102	1,413
Bakersfield city	18,870	14,092	6,062	7,465	2,386	2,585	644	1,866	1,249	2,382	3,697	5,275	943	2,759
Baldwin Park city	4,735	3,124	854	1,267	177	587	238	144	417	641	470	970	62	677
Bellflower city	5,158	3,017	1,268	1,403	263	649	225	261	173	681	894	1,310	433	700
Berkeley city	9,244	5,573	1,943	2,237	431	903	205	446	647	1,094	1,363	1,509	718	1,107
Buena Park city	4,827	4,096	1,297	2,066	319	1,159	168	584	331	522	842	1,485	323	515
Burbank city	7,622	7,548	998	3,585	288	1,016	175	1,133	39	1,729	646	2,678	198	2,033
Camarillo city	6,853	5,400	1,674	2,971	778	1,346	133	479	320	649	1,058	1,919	549	775
Carlsbad city	9,497	7,083	1,541	3,326	596	1,307	203	240	88	555	816	1,996	138	678
Carson city	7,157	5,393	1,904	2,437	416	1,035	341	407	505	963	1,361	1,502	468	1,182
Chico city	5,629	4,428	1,975	2,057	640	1,124	294	347	364	679	1,626	1,470	499	227
Chino city	3,939	2,061	1,437	1,141	293	434	165	160	522	215	1,033	716	371	94
Chino Hills city	2,939	3,171	449	1,501	120	704	35	87	39	731	308	1,174	39	1,079
Chula Vista city	18,293	14,992	3,969	8,193	815	3,232	663	1,281	983	3,056	2,579	5,512	879	2,519
Citrus Heights city	7,489	6,453	2,094	3,300	474	1,748	281	533	810	1,062	1,147	1,877	506	706
Clovis city	5,987	4,482	1,529	2,570	307	1,389	70	472	129	797	1,204	1,616	267	712
Compton city	3,315	3,133	930	1,699	286	563	179	100	248	772	603	1,333	145	623
Concord city	10,648	5,836	2,873	3,152	1,339	1,833	364	535	825	988	1,528	2,439	438	995
Corona city	9,989	5,352	2,051	2,714	316	1,297	529	559	718	669	1,287	1,946	530	800
Costa Mesa city	5,888	4,511	669	2,639	323	901	42	609	143	1,224	371	2,162	42	963
Daly City city	10,006	7,487	1,845	3,831	688	1,157	374	363	333	1,289	899	2,295	223	963
Davis city	3,166	3,059	402	1,398	128	848	143	243	95	336	187	656	0	142
Downey city	6,684	5,576	1,831	2,982	218	1,040	117	589	701	1,308	934	2,500	463	899
El Cajon city	7,425	4,107	3,249	2,489	304	1,367	542	890	1,316	910	1,927	1,652	1,250	1,586
El Monte city	7,529	6,331	1,822	4,012	568	1,730	281	951	426	1,398	1,075	2,946	441	1,121
Elk Grove city	10,173	7,438	2,979	4,640	1,105	2,671	918	1,391	703	1,214	1,523	3,511	277	1,940
Escondido city	8,799	7,846	2,914	4,723	910	1,880	402	1,588	1,547	1,738	2,107	3,519	996	1,728
Fairfield city	7,418	5,622	1,496	3,008	498	1,266	34	401	567	921	1,303	2,082	377	937
Folsom city	5,315	4,825	1,060	2,222	497	1,628	46	201	183	580	428	1,471	236	439
Fontana city	10,382	5,795	2,807	2,722	715	1,046	755	920	1,066	1,003	1,788	1,949	828	471
Fremont city	14,736	10,057	2,211	4,947	719	2,580	550	400	509	1,631	1,255	3,518	504	2,181
Fresno city	31,915	21,892	9,956	13,500	3,004	7,104	1,783	2,462	2,686	3,843	6,846	9,400	2,467	4,601
Fullerton city	6,933	8,564	1,958	4,104	451	1,781	458	636	556	725	1,068	2,909	389	808
Garden Grove city	12,192	9,896	2,936	5,320	852	2,100	624	657	856	2,448	1,640	4,157	592	2,390
Glendale city	17,541	14,377	6,374	8,984	817	2,187	529	1,045	2,531	3,698	2,788	5,462	3,058	5,369
Hawthorne city	4,068	4,040	937	1,400	57	1,071	92	484	460	297	897	547	490	276
Hayward city	9,179	7,499	2,200	4,811	414	2,268	319	834	643	1,638	1,638	3,642	830	1,693
Hemet city	9,356	9,830	2,825	6,077	811	3,091	766	1,258	752	2,138	2,070	3,927	611	1,753
Hesperia city	5,241	3,179	1,848	2,217	840	1,087	243	682	144	679	1,445	1,264	447	418
Huntington Beach city	18,289	12,757	2,615	5,843	1,031	2,697	264	1,112	526	1,796	1,086	4,331	121	1,918
Indio city	7,873	4,086	2,591	1,816	977	793	496	341	162	579	1,495	1,002	336	562

Table H-3: Places—Disability Status and Type of Disability—*Continued*

	Total Population		With a Disability		With a Hearing Disability		With a Vision Disability		With a Cognitive Disability		With an Ambulatory Disability		With a Self-Care Disability	
	65 to 74 Years	75 Years and Over	65 to 74 Years	75 Years and Over	65 to 74 Years	75 Years and Over	65 to 74 Years	75 Years and Over	65 to 74 Years	75 Years and Over	65 to 74 Years	75 Years and Over	65 to 74 Years	75 Years and Over
California—Cont.														
Inglewood city	7,129	4,158	2,520	2,177	783	973	671	529	811	908	1,619	1,408	475	1,169
Irvine city	15,406	9,803	1,992	4,263	677	1,587	0	317	296	1,351	1,322	3,210	538	2,242
Jurupa Valley city	5,132	3,079	1,274	1,967	534	725	301	293	164	523	772	1,434	333	811
Laguna Niguel city	6,986	3,183	853	781	418	545	72	104	10	181	417	304	59	166
Lake Forest city	5,098	3,395	803	1,383	344	824	261	130	82	314	428	835	0	389
Lakewood city	6,493	3,839	1,631	2,450	489	1,143	237	291	70	723	825	1,284	216	720
Lancaster city	10,108	6,159	2,666	2,254	788	949	544	520	742	1,026	1,931	1,655	778	797
Livermore city	7,047	3,988	1,002	1,794	551	971	232	429	278	293	517	1,297	62	353
Long Beach city	28,355	17,368	8,084	8,185	1,930	3,682	1,885	2,075	1,727	3,337	5,538	5,229	2,340	2,861
Los Angeles city	249,515	195,384	64,558	106,292	16,698	43,415	12,949	25,564	16,011	38,194	45,421	76,034	16,326	41,492
Lynwood city	2,517	2,358	688	1,723	94	484	194	300	77	671	454	1,148	225	497
Manteca city	5,873	3,008	1,563	1,530	715	877	179	187	404	288	1,178	864	53	242
Menifee city	7,990	8,263	2,359	4,152	828	2,031	283	796	611	947	1,375	2,486	489	1,248
Merced city	5,373	3,705	2,647	2,095	616	1,594	806	1,074	458	1,150	1,677	1,633	274	1,067
Milpitas city	4,193	3,248	1,043	1,405	315	657	269	92	257	457	587	990	115	410
Mission Viejo city	7,831	7,906	1,589	3,627	573	1,626	178	412	297	952	860	2,231	209	1,214
Modesto city	15,420	12,243	4,347	7,467	1,855	3,962	1,150	811	1,218	2,122	2,502	5,238	373	2,789
Moreno Valley city	11,714	5,790	3,777	2,963	922	1,267	970	404	1,053	776	2,926	2,150	964	1,363
Mountain View city	4,960	3,289	773	2,050	252	809	68	167	206	430	322	1,403	279	647
Murrieta city	4,897	5,692	1,680	2,478	733	860	358	398	220	562	884	1,571	485	690
Napa city	6,205	4,553	897	2,798	314	1,840	127	435	180	565	544	1,725	119	771
Newport Beach city	11,167	7,261	811	3,935	265	1,877	142	1,215	50	1,407	364	2,752	50	1,304
Norwalk city	6,222	5,052	1,879	2,652	675	1,095	304	507	506	1,257	977	2,057	490	898
Oakland city	28,179	20,052	7,739	11,505	2,149	4,533	1,532	1,962	1,464	3,916	5,063	8,054	1,312	4,252
Oceanside city	13,542	14,058	2,974	7,133	902	3,748	746	1,928	762	2,710	1,407	3,769	353	1,323
Ontario city	7,769	5,299	2,090	3,327	577	1,330	243	530	359	902	1,427	2,507	364	1,543
Orange city	8,487	5,957	1,246	3,036	673	1,109	113	411	268	624	850	1,628	305	618
Oxnard city	11,407	7,425	3,012	4,555	867	1,743	618	1,038	1,031	1,412	1,825	3,132	950	2,176
Palmdale city	7,411	5,149	2,386	2,564	525	935	174	579	595	733	1,605	1,781	712	913
Palo Alto city	6,080	5,423	641	2,234	404	827	43	556	191	745	176	1,598	0	705
Pasadena city	10,116	8,279	2,339	4,340	414	1,087	382	552	802	1,545	1,756	3,366	996	2,354
Perris city	3,350	1,108	1,116	769	292	161	178	43	428	0	805	674	432	285
Pittsburg city	4,471	2,867	2,278	1,900	804	819	892	138	823	915	1,085	1,224	573	645
Pleasanton city	5,700	4,522	873	2,081	88	897	98	433	54	393	487	1,079	222	200
Pomona city	6,938	6,393	1,732	3,101	339	1,129	285	478	323	1,589	1,159	1,914	255	1,597
Rancho Cordova city	5,044	3,234	1,852	1,954	533	956	200	281	499	501	1,405	1,173	651	670
Rancho Cucamonga city	11,523	5,799	2,633	3,088	788	1,690	194	784	980	810	1,758	2,314	687	1,055
Redding city	8,808	7,428	2,008	4,314	521	2,504	59	1,174	889	1,334	1,131	2,963	516	1,335
Redlands city	4,780	3,644	845	2,024	336	904	0	430	296	350	421	1,083	60	174
Redondo Beach city	4,515	2,767	447	1,521	279	598	0	362	0	146	130	914	0	402
Redwood City city	6,508	3,834	1,027	1,878	263	492	40	251	345	806	414	1,458	277	596
Rialto city	5,204	3,367	2,100	1,911	589	725	499	553	511	547	1,186	1,269	260	446
Richmond city	7,332	4,920	1,694	2,862	428	1,437	693	628	203	751	888	2,213	284	1,006
Riverside city	16,401	13,057	3,339	6,321	963	2,355	717	1,372	698	2,424	2,359	4,701	1,081	2,964
Roseville city	11,925	9,479	2,433	4,475	955	2,714	365	761	296	1,381	1,046	3,202	233	1,158
Sacramento city	31,872	23,323	8,251	13,567	2,465	5,919	1,524	2,279	1,956	5,154	5,261	9,308	1,865	4,496
Salinas city	6,406	5,536	1,195	3,441	479	936	162	454	291	1,255	800	2,478	130	1,288
San Bernardino city	11,047	6,212	3,590	3,547	1,219	1,516	318	549	845	937	2,647	2,442	755	1,230
San Buenaventura (Ventura) city	8,390	8,729	2,209	4,187	361	2,187	162	622	442	1,009	1,732	2,916	248	1,078
San Clemente city	6,497	5,635	590	2,579	327	1,064	112	137	118	896	218	1,178	73	1,080
San Diego city	87,855	68,273	19,442	32,486	6,010	14,010	4,506	5,586	5,770	10,149	11,127	21,900	3,895	9,878
San Francisco city	64,318	55,979	13,794	28,090	4,671	10,418	3,319	7,383	3,645	9,801	8,408	18,160	2,319	9,427
San Jose city	68,567	48,384	14,842	26,176	4,623	10,734	1,987	5,403	3,172	9,001	9,000	18,230	3,159	9,977
San Leandro city	6,858	5,714	1,605	3,059	247	1,707	186	282	306	547	934	1,725	121	652
San Marcos city	6,654	4,499	1,112	2,498	551	1,217	165	892	335	569	404	1,404	162	612
San Mateo city	8,316	7,908	1,027	4,334	134	1,558	85	531	252	1,274	822	2,692	268	1,750
San Ramon city	4,781	3,043	685	922	281	483	147	203	50	232	374	527	69	188
Santa Ana city	16,296	10,616	4,577	5,803	1,386	2,567	1,425	1,298	1,465	2,156	2,445	3,090	1,167	1,508
Santa Barbara city	8,361	6,726	1,260	3,107	880	1,565	78	763	429	1,078	420	1,639	40	719
Santa Clara city	8,096	6,710	1,991	3,638	481	1,193	290	437	716	838	878	2,534	637	1,231
Santa Clarita city	12,207	8,373	2,935	4,640	1,382	2,455	297	1,098	488	1,631	1,675	3,048	472	1,482
Santa Maria city	4,815	4,142	1,486	2,087	695	1,205	236	519	450	555	808	1,081	289	519
Santa Monica city	8,654	6,920	2,059	2,987	657	1,606	295	279	749	1,241	1,300	2,234	486	1,405
Santa Rosa city	14,883	9,766	3,585	4,493	893	2,622	402	1,400	911	1,185	2,561	2,974	1,208	1,546
Simi Valley city	10,841	6,624	2,169	3,128	752	1,383	315	492	471	1,123	1,327	2,282	169	1,147
South Gate city	5,225	3,074	1,754	2,220	444	622	149	321	458	1,017	1,355	1,712	578	1,110
South San Francisco city	4,944	4,689	1,432	2,231	423	877	456	296	432	482	1,146	1,405	494	848
Stockton city	19,175	13,520	6,190	8,158	1,522	3,131	842	1,415	2,253	2,344	4,523	5,849	1,452	2,945
Sunnyvale city	9,103	7,004	1,331	3,525	271	1,468	476	900	358	761	890	2,491	332	1,280
Temecula city	7,551	4,871	1,462	1,839	859	791	0	713	159	491	527	1,171	37	517
Thousand Oaks city	12,675	9,201	2,134	3,825	657	2,399	106	602	714	1,447	924	1,895	114	1,070
Torrance city	12,285	12,240	2,525	6,595	928	3,181	285	1,691	624	2,425	1,445	4,162	580	2,209
Tracy city	3,335	2,324	631	1,240	139	500	200	54	55	142	366	542	224	111
Turlock city	5,113	3,787	1,622	2,493	431	903	339	596	379	924	771	1,841	197	797
Tustin city	4,319	3,189	582	1,812	167	972	58	245	80	428	402	1,010	118	500
Union City city	7,079	4,727	1,299	2,210	551	987	123	317	152	590	822	1,640	366	1,106

Table H-3: Places—Disability Status and Type of Disability—*Continued*

	Total Population		With a Disability		With a Hearing Disability		With a Vision Disability		With a Cognitive Disability		With an Ambulatory Disability		With a Self-Care Disability	
	65 to 74 Years	75 Years and Over	65 to 74 Years	75 Years and Over	65 to 74 Years	75 Years and Over	65 to 74 Years	75 Years and Over	65 to 74 Years	75 Years and Over	65 to 74 Years	75 Years and Over	65 to 74 Years	75 Years and Over
California—Cont.														
Upland city	6,146	5,041	1,164	2,242	292	999	79	510	37	785	727	1,418	222	680
Vacaville city	5,653	4,732	1,283	2,196	543	742	96	680	314	736	944	1,646	195	590
Vallejo city	10,209	6,365	3,144	3,035	834	1,481	254	600	342	889	2,060	1,646	453	913
Victorville city	7,028	2,892	2,330	1,654	688	871	551	647	460	461	1,530	926	546	363
Visalia city	9,457	6,413	3,036	3,174	1,056	1,740	23	471	702	620	2,207	1,800	359	736
Vista city	4,273	3,335	1,240	1,858	418	670	30	554	403	991	603	664	227	218
Walnut Creek city	8,718	10,526	1,697	4,859	486	2,631	290	944	504	1,457	856	3,302	107	1,558
West Covina city	9,459	5,657	1,666	3,098	461	947	251	447	180	1,208	1,166	2,084	366	1,273
Westminster city	8,993	7,289	2,939	4,142	664	1,483	346	973	705	1,583	1,676	2,926	356	1,708
Whittier city	5,946	4,667	1,474	2,093	334	767	175	333	371	763	1,116	1,450	496	653
Yorba Linda city	6,799	3,332	862	1,668	317	824	178	453	116	501	396	886	0	441
Yuba City city	4,851	3,606	1,518	1,649	384	1,015	210	214	656	496	1,129	986	514	484
Colorado														
Arvada city	8,723	7,197	1,959	3,715	956	1,910	148	761	302	974	889	2,106	318	512
Aurora city	22,471	13,238	5,672	6,709	1,741	4,005	292	1,479	776	1,825	3,913	3,918	905	1,304
Boulder city	6,593	3,715	1,211	2,258	439	760	287	396	190	262	824	1,505	429	309
Centennial city	10,184	5,623	1,117	2,118	549	1,035	45	139	196	503	494	1,169	193	237
Colorado Springs city	31,334	23,422	6,790	11,096	3,024	5,501	1,054	1,998	1,250	3,334	3,401	7,269	542	2,620
Denver city	41,696	28,721	9,864	15,793	3,321	7,328	2,253	3,373	2,376	4,112	6,207	9,573	1,597	4,271
Fort Collins city	8,441	5,586	1,713	2,623	689	1,525	154	201	595	331	845	1,448	187	378
Greeley city	6,488	5,835	1,610	3,038	712	2,157	435	764	628	306	820	1,667	301	818
Lakewood city	11,698	10,504	2,351	5,694	1,199	2,684	495	1,127	603	1,685	1,299	4,090	361	1,465
Longmont city	6,484	4,972	1,151	2,982	743	1,656	232	819	265	812	396	1,704	412	468
Loveland city	7,547	6,515	1,371	2,574	557	1,360	252	344	177	596	641	1,286	82	964
Pueblo city	8,958	7,639	3,591	3,942	1,243	2,429	885	887	940	1,222	2,178	2,735	775	1,060
Thornton city	7,135	3,657	2,416	1,933	1,019	1,088	327	497	685	494	1,539	852	469	301
Westminster city	9,761	4,586	2,938	2,334	1,669	1,115	746	115	519	677	1,200	1,151	500	414
Connecticut														
Bridgeport city	7,977	6,114	2,697	2,850	572	922	630	992	995	927	1,984	1,994	405	687
Danbury city	6,269	3,896	1,812	1,845	671	615	108	159	243	521	1,017	1,305	598	590
Hartford city	5,879	4,853	2,483	2,773	586	512	452	482	838	766	1,576	2,228	523	1,025
New Britain city	3,670	3,810	987	2,232	230	623	0	281	289	873	844	1,452	339	1,066
New Haven city	8,067	4,690	2,674	2,032	519	771	210	501	563	630	1,785	1,821	743	970
Norwalk city	6,507	6,064	821	2,602	285	952	103	508	30	573	414	1,962	72	604
Stamford city	8,788	7,232	2,313	3,326	990	1,063	755	221	744	943	1,369	2,378	427	1,509
Waterbury city	7,547	4,640	1,818	2,564	659	1,022	288	413	282	406	1,382	1,638	535	707
Delaware														
Wilmington city	5,051	3,665	1,500	1,678	524	304	92	398	244	613	1,078	1,146	175	482
District of Columbia														
Washington city	40,997	30,983	10,513	15,807	2,349	4,081	2,678	3,543	2,831	5,260	7,990	10,892	2,931	5,505
Florida														
Boca Raton city	9,641	7,711	1,858	3,422	552	1,568	198	698	108	985	1,339	1,996	734	1,233
Boynton Beach city	6,143	8,142	1,665	4,231	836	2,126	550	858	700	1,391	920	2,634	156	1,174
Cape Coral city	22,089	15,822	4,960	8,486	2,719	5,005	765	1,500	750	2,035	2,506	5,766	438	1,918
Clearwater city	12,396	10,308	2,636	4,888	1,016	2,653	257	1,279	528	1,940	1,725	3,542	319	1,478
Coral Springs city	9,422	4,021	2,233	2,400	954	1,156	433	867	642	627	1,743	1,562	314	689
Deerfield Beach city	7,158	8,252	1,238	3,977	394	1,639	392	572	207	1,826	577	2,930	196	1,634
Delray Beach city	8,504	7,481	850	3,674	286	1,916	143	1,113	82	1,621	285	2,372	39	1,699
Deltona city	7,925	4,156	2,487	1,526	998	665	118	199	490	587	1,616	1,032	442	196
Fort Lauderdale city	19,011	12,330	6,101	6,752	2,428	2,795	1,153	1,354	1,909	1,628	3,763	4,023	1,333	1,774
Fort Myers city	7,490	4,053	623	1,866	376	928	63	287	125	587	167	1,151	101	591
Gainesville city	7,137	5,372	1,691	2,489	461	1,337	298	187	39	896	971	1,463	464	483
Hialeah city	20,418	22,146	3,558	8,879	880	3,123	813	1,971	1,609	4,315	2,102	6,162	748	3,625
Hollywood city	13,032	10,372	3,671	4,874	831	2,004	1,502	931	536	1,524	2,509	3,294	505	1,540
Homestead city	3,777	1,700	2,574	1,500	946	1,010	950	727	1,158	761	1,235	1,066	451	731
Jacksonville city	63,991	41,090	20,583	22,091	5,392	9,694	3,050	4,623	4,732	6,487	13,480	15,335	3,834	6,451
Kissimmee city	4,179	2,361	1,152	1,493	0	410	276	258	283	918	914	1,283	120	305
Lakeland city	9,909	10,046	2,816	4,820	1,177	2,448	414	735	554	1,197	1,451	3,398	338	1,153
Largo city	10,853	9,111	3,389	3,852	1,334	2,111	242	637	441	1,282	1,781	2,343	885	769
Lauderhill city	6,841	4,841	2,806	2,737	776	1,369	852	547	288	693	1,533	1,814	482	376
Melbourne city	9,256	7,624	1,672	3,038	557	1,223	249	209	281	766	1,150	1,664	321	517
Miami Beach city	7,552	7,292	1,202	4,255	289	1,594	189	1,012	342	1,751	821	3,128	451	1,445
Miami city	37,943	28,719	9,509	15,570	1,944	3,858	1,894	2,790	3,226	5,861	6,175	11,964	1,899	6,149
Miami Gardens city	8,639	5,920	1,598	3,349	71	931	313	690	372	803	1,255	2,340	287	1,107
Miramar city	8,045	5,754	1,034	2,982	206	1,000	205	539	293	1,720	801	1,849	103	207
Orlando city	14,812	10,496	4,654	5,844	536	2,102	715	780	891	1,650	3,265	4,074	446	1,142
Palm Bay city	9,992	7,282	2,634	3,473	1,314	1,644	170	604	344	725	1,313	2,578	493	1,163
Palm Coast city	13,633	9,670	3,355	4,602	875	1,727	251	755	923	1,791	2,475	3,648	931	2,124
Pembroke Pines city	14,003	12,554	3,216	7,298	905	2,362	565	2,161	474	2,373	1,955	5,184	512	2,398
Plantation city	7,141	4,916	1,008	2,368	680	1,147	132	79	182	481	241	1,597	0	253
Pompano Beach city	9,172	12,596	1,756	5,944	305	2,941	367	1,121	570	1,972	1,359	3,892	199	1,973
Port St. Lucie city	18,256	17,116	4,806	10,392	1,142	5,110	1,126	1,057	1,284	1,924	3,303	8,178	1,120	3,432
St. Petersburg city	25,077	16,119	4,510	7,398	1,270	2,739	774	1,174	1,132	1,829	3,320	4,563	954	2,361
Sunrise city	6,833	6,058	1,535	3,596	550	1,302	261	764	295	1,153	1,036	1,770	349	674

Table H-3: Places—Disability Status and Type of Disability—*Continued*

	Total Population		With a Disability		With a Hearing Disability		With a Vision Disability		With a Cognitive Disability		With an Ambulatory Disability		With a Self-Care Disability	
	65 to 74 Years	75 Years and Over	65 to 74 Years	75 Years and Over	65 to 74 Years	75 Years and Over	65 to 74 Years	75 Years and Over	65 to 74 Years	75 Years and Over	65 to 74 Years	75 Years and Over	65 to 74 Years	75 Years and Over
Florida—Cont.														
Tallahassee city	9,365	6,862	2,725	3,844	734	1,885	608	824	441	1,096	1,819	2,323	391	741
Tampa city	24,085	19,238	5,937	9,943	1,262	3,366	1,293	2,091	1,146	2,930	4,508	6,545	965	3,199
West Palm Beach city	10,435	6,458	2,452	2,716	193	560	181	673	802	888	1,845	2,028	648	1,192
Weston city	3,403	3,637	291	1,581	171	445	0	247	0	361	120	824	0	373
Georgia														
Albany city	4,924	4,205	1,495	2,564	389	719	331	436	444	815	986	1,656	309	632
Athens-Clarke County unified govt (bal)	7,135	4,331	1,482	2,133	195	882	378	568	139	853	1,078	1,299	33	868
Atlanta city	31,403	18,660	10,201	10,276	1,785	3,013	1,987	2,578	2,317	3,169	7,066	7,809	1,667	3,670
Augusta-Richmond County consolidated govt (bal)	13,922	9,450	5,158	5,199	1,914	2,493	995	1,596	2,055	1,948	2,942	3,822	962	1,275
Columbus city	13,287	9,959	4,575	5,385	1,203	2,587	923	1,145	772	1,976	3,507	4,222	807	2,156
Johns Creek city	3,834	2,208	809	1,234	398	853	313	89	271	173	72	621	139	311
Macon-Bibb County	12,104	8,628	4,607	4,822	1,134	2,102	974	597	1,548	1,609	3,344	3,231	1,289	1,173
Roswell city	5,984	4,396	1,373	2,306	538	726	0	311	278	965	949	1,651	0	895
Sandy Springs city	8,568	5,030	1,234	1,972	378	1,095	0	179	498	361	448	1,240	0	883
Savannah city	10,093	8,715	3,241	5,108	1,282	1,853	535	924	562	1,170	2,089	3,731	812	1,094
Warner Robins city	3,775	3,221	1,174	1,776	364	554	255	239	273	379	814	1,388	135	368
Hawaii														
Urban Honolulu CDP	32,294	31,857	6,001	15,537	1,383	7,211	817	1,832	1,932	5,103	3,924	11,240	1,271	4,720
Idaho														
Boise City city	15,047	11,432	2,828	5,916	1,217	2,555	444	1,319	637	1,600	1,321	3,563	270	1,764
Meridian city	7,560	2,457	1,397	919	576	449	84	224	7	169	891	630	7	335
Nampa city	5,343	4,484	1,474	2,450	895	1,477	331	311	268	684	836	1,291	270	453
Illinois														
Aurora city	10,130	4,753	2,544	2,335	432	1,026	166	490	1,020	223	1,804	1,719	487	573
Bloomington city	4,677	4,092	1,327	2,458	257	1,386	166	663	127	791	1,067	1,577	147	924
Champaign city	3,821	3,568	729	1,681	329	1,062	244	534	237	232	405	813	164	319
Chicago city	173,157	127,707	47,452	73,920	10,636	24,721	9,951	15,883	10,999	23,518	34,633	54,044	9,008	24,636
Decatur city	6,424	5,077	1,386	2,480	289	1,206	310	891	115	804	983	1,414	64	740
Elgin city	8,692	5,043	2,242	1,841	361	856	456	431	431	312	1,333	1,660	321	831
Evanston city	5,215	3,815	618	1,671	65	896	37	576	233	183	443	1,071	185	444
Joliet city	7,087	4,751	2,083	2,167	919	861	1,040	486	576	502	1,348	1,437	343	585
Naperville city	8,350	5,333	1,282	2,677	325	1,205	349	357	312	551	666	1,960	297	811
Peoria city	8,526	6,717	2,258	2,805	528	1,323	321	573	744	997	1,487	1,580	512	613
Rockford city	11,408	9,734	4,130	5,682	1,124	2,425	604	896	894	1,225	2,490	3,852	789	1,232
Springfield city	9,873	8,327	2,748	4,038	940	1,290	387	951	530	1,063	1,833	2,847	778	687
Waukegan city	4,789	3,071	1,452	1,851	280	895	107	279	51	343	1,166	1,515	515	578
Indiana														
Bloomington city	2,684	2,834	864	1,228	140	363	301	51	244	185	565	677	42	216
Carmel city	7,954	5,069	750	2,006	449	623	79	151	134	853	408	987	41	510
Evansville city	9,344	8,314	3,462	4,587	1,050	2,468	872	1,224	647	1,464	2,664	2,768	694	1,266
Fort Wayne city	18,378	12,303	4,303	6,336	1,219	2,594	388	1,301	1,097	1,430	3,084	4,638	675	1,724
Gary city	6,685	4,916	2,541	2,640	244	884	856	562	766	800	1,682	1,988	594	1,057
Hammond city	4,758	3,303	1,636	1,802	427	854	251	322	187	703	1,089	1,383	369	776
Indianapolis city (bal)	51,067	40,081	16,829	22,003	6,131	9,708	3,108	5,661	4,296	7,480	11,461	15,678	2,971	7,625
Lafayette city	5,087	3,534	1,736	1,818	475	914	315	96	363	345	1,282	729	242	312
Muncie city	5,732	4,416	1,661	2,600	782	1,599	613	630	340	1,281	989	1,802	537	707
South Bend city	6,654	5,836	1,917	3,428	599	1,646	217	570	208	736	1,379	2,093	115	668
Iowa														
Cedar Rapids city	8,962	7,614	2,109	2,551	803	1,180	280	569	219	704	1,305	1,289	164	426
Davenport city	6,579	5,485	1,941	2,534	710	1,071	247	332	444	699	1,073	1,670	466	605
Des Moines city	12,864	9,884	2,748	4,544	1,110	2,695	500	927	739	1,286	1,983	3,098	629	1,099
Iowa City city	2,639	3,328	441	1,387	124	445	63	334	118	294	310	1,005	85	436
Sioux City city	6,198	4,622	1,499	2,543	395	916	139	349	294	417	1,194	1,926	409	571
Waterloo city	5,104	4,541	1,066	2,135	300	626	133	509	227	218	712	1,650	222	295
Kansas														
Kansas City city	9,828	6,522	3,427	3,321	1,119	1,259	453	666	586	602	2,528	2,256	697	881
Lawrence city	4,485	3,927	1,024	1,718	261	918	197	179	42	412	755	1,195	211	605
Olathe city	7,833	3,564	1,626	2,016	848	663	255	147	147	512	826	1,421	148	368
Overland Park city	13,739	12,348	1,802	6,791	711	2,309	281	1,457	171	1,948	1,007	4,738	49	1,831
Topeka city	9,835	7,998	3,821	3,545	1,439	1,537	490	478	922	900	2,121	2,268	624	1,213
Wichita city	26,797	21,567	7,371	9,856	2,670	4,707	1,326	1,803	1,821	3,477	4,654	6,158	1,463	2,386
Kentucky														
Lexington-Fayette urban county	20,678	14,057	5,405	7,508	2,047	2,937	698	1,473	706	1,999	3,561	4,267	1,204	1,829
Louisville/Jefferson County metro govt (bal)	45,722	33,480	13,197	18,588	3,972	7,483	1,984	3,486	3,181	5,020	9,048	12,476	2,790	5,800
Louisiana														
Baton Rouge city	15,605	13,126	6,154	7,872	1,120	2,605	772	1,990	1,153	2,871	5,061	6,507	994	2,209
Bossier City city	4,908	3,381	1,290	2,086	439	1,043	125	421	147	365	912	1,316	260	643
Kenner city	7,858	4,000	2,190	1,607	544	585	663	204	896	363	578	1,214	420	623
Lafayette city	8,938	5,161	2,455	2,905	906	555	576	697	432	817	1,396	1,928	439	557
Lake Charles city	6,513	5,708	2,073	2,833	781	1,187	148	764	405	715	1,169	2,159	499	646

Table H-3: Places—Disability Status and Type of Disability—*Continued*

	Total Population		With a Disability		With a Hearing Disability		With a Vision Disability		With a Cognitive Disability		With an Ambulatory Disability		With a Self-Care Disability	
	65 to 74 Years	75 Years and Over	65 to 74 Years	75 Years and Over	65 to 74 Years	75 Years and Over	65 to 74 Years	75 Years and Over	65 to 74 Years	75 Years and Over	65 to 74 Years	75 Years and Over	65 to 74 Years	75 Years and Over
Louisiana—Cont.														
New Orleans city	26,746	18,699	8,159	9,806	1,994	3,014	1,506	2,627	1,879	3,214	5,502	6,643	1,818	2,911
Shreveport city	15,761	12,331	5,516	6,520	1,585	2,999	1,565	996	1,399	2,302	3,678	4,745	1,093	2,503
Maine														
Portland city	4,273	3,236	880	1,578	305	691	56	421	372	178	530	1,152	218	383
Maryland														
Baltimore city	43,066	30,985	12,975	17,197	2,736	4,886	2,572	3,775	3,453	5,351	9,383	13,302	2,466	5,400
Frederick city	4,660	2,367	1,476	1,212	590	504	368	389	94	320	1,043	487	452	271
Gaithersburg city	4,333	3,230	676	1,647	193	385	77	197	73	506	423	1,315	148	414
Rockville city	5,061	5,164	830	2,237	187	516	138	336	214	913	569	1,844	133	690
Massachusetts														
Boston city	37,123	27,997	11,699	15,740	3,761	5,936	3,143	4,289	3,700	6,115	7,505	11,257	2,359	5,891
Brockton city	7,079	4,146	2,217	2,687	892	1,125	0	410	351	475	1,225	1,880	729	1,185
Cambridge city	6,294	4,098	837	1,936	235	1,078	75	401	491	667	594	1,114	353	601
Fall River city	7,548	5,896	2,603	4,283	483	1,907	774	818	611	1,282	2,412	2,911	720	1,691
Lawrence city	4,261	2,104	901	1,211	320	585	274	621	376	749	433	876	122	254
Lowell city	5,937	4,667	1,516	2,828	404	1,394	328	327	518	793	1,011	1,499	340	879
Lynn city	5,275	4,811	2,132	3,053	630	1,322	321	897	604	1,001	1,301	2,059	370	1,426
New Bedford city	5,642	5,477	2,194	2,840	1,042	862	341	274	893	969	1,168	2,047	672	1,391
Newton city	8,839	7,218	1,696	3,268	440	1,806	311	442	206	1,294	1,008	2,226	449	1,149
Quincy city	7,571	6,297	1,816	3,544	725	2,021	336	996	829	838	1,014	2,189	200	889
Somerville city	4,463	3,343	804	2,098	256	708	7	441	205	899	509	1,411	7	659
Springfield city	9,101	7,416	2,989	4,050	797	1,416	666	400	710	1,571	1,729	2,643	1,104	1,780
Worcester city	8,960	9,210	2,454	4,401	676	1,900	509	1,149	735	1,324	1,802	2,768	549	1,441
Michigan														
Ann Arbor city	6,402	5,634	988	2,361	474	1,453	141	218	164	698	626	938	203	361
Dearborn city	6,810	5,644	1,544	3,304	755	1,368	368	851	251	1,156	944	1,854	400	1,222
Detroit city	48,329	34,339	16,963	19,388	2,600	6,631	3,909	5,406	5,103	6,411	12,979	14,846	6,161	6,558
Farmington Hills city	9,867	7,653	2,351	3,090	1,008	1,381	330	506	399	984	1,311	1,963	565	560
Flint city	6,336	5,210	2,283	2,342	424	1,030	192	579	438	655	1,689	1,575	258	651
Grand Rapids city	10,404	9,951	3,239	5,363	1,250	1,750	568	721	733	1,495	1,959	3,466	679	1,204
Kalamazoo city	3,565	3,320	607	1,847	247	691	87	331	188	194	358	1,151	38	304
Lansing city	8,189	4,698	2,793	2,506	507	1,133	475	244	873	928	2,149	1,619	702	812
Livonia city	9,140	7,572	1,739	3,703	479	1,480	292	768	170	902	1,112	2,494	236	1,005
Rochester Hills city	6,632	5,110	934	2,431	552	931	137	557	199	544	361	1,702	0	878
Southfield city	8,072	5,027	2,538	2,798	597	1,192	248	556	375	989	1,380	1,742	372	1,117
Sterling Heights city	10,439	10,884	2,311	5,234	472	2,545	268	391	662	1,342	2,007	3,335	608	1,323
Troy city	7,253	5,755	1,168	2,700	406	1,114	96	509	317	1,043	735	1,429	207	984
Warren city	9,556	9,182	2,762	4,522	860	2,022	172	1,264	670	782	2,135	3,017	635	1,243
Westland city	7,380	6,563	2,771	3,711	944	1,894	239	1,197	621	1,106	1,721	2,687	452	1,385
Wyoming city	3,979	3,570	1,054	1,890	336	514	240	348	92	1,049	693	1,267	212	515
Minnesota														
Bloomington city	8,056	8,357	1,190	3,839	534	1,556	149	758	309	665	693	1,936	457	552
Brooklyn Park city	4,914	2,775	1,040	1,950	552	787	143	99	198	1,063	220	1,324	44	606
Duluth city	6,507	5,718	1,850	2,701	802	1,420	352	836	528	329	1,140	1,819	374	457
Eagan city	4,590	3,083	998	1,065	545	368	114	194	208	597	601	944	92	594
Maple Grove city	5,584	1,965	927	703	484	306	0	187	259	339	202	334	18	120
Minneapolis city	21,250	10,347	6,325	4,986	2,032	2,871	1,247	1,229	1,921	1,198	3,700	3,369	1,638	1,121
Plymouth city	7,488	3,889	465	1,205	84	698	219	221	5	82	242	445	5	80
Rochester city	7,546	7,768	1,349	3,028	284	1,469	227	414	221	605	844	1,778	331	550
St. Cloud city	4,497	2,442	764	1,061	426	449	43	218	394	353	650	565	216	349
St. Paul city	15,000	10,401	4,628	6,550	1,456	2,921	906	1,761	1,282	1,689	2,650	4,320	1,275	1,908
Woodbury city	4,702	2,586	771	1,730	567	490	203	235	47	198	106	1,169	99	348
Mississippi														
Gulfport city	5,330	4,448	1,690	2,709	528	1,214	430	426	262	1,130	1,385	1,855	188	1,065
Jackson city	11,325	7,783	3,175	4,493	454	1,413	734	1,089	367	1,436	1,956	3,455	522	1,916
Missouri														
Columbia city	6,971	3,334	1,306	1,581	540	581	46	110	71	495	788	1,080	266	474
Independence city	11,180	8,565	2,722	3,874	1,063	2,367	305	391	528	1,225	1,503	2,638	601	656
Kansas City city	31,218	23,444	7,045	12,603	1,902	4,179	1,846	2,473	1,383	4,138	3,933	7,788	782	2,910
Lee's Summit city	7,804	4,944	1,569	2,620	472	1,772	450	113	163	933	823	1,567	0	458
O'Fallon city	4,334	3,921	1,430	2,143	975	832	595	350	101	503	464	1,204	103	315
Springfield city	12,305	12,159	3,521	5,651	1,244	2,646	264	513	629	1,954	2,096	3,918	560	1,773
St. Charles city	5,197	4,490	1,206	1,689	368	1,005	33	256	433	460	859	1,149	199	422
St. Joseph city	5,259	4,883	1,161	2,268	410	978	228	352	100	326	642	1,471	31	429
St. Louis city	19,949	14,890	6,383	8,866	1,938	2,932	1,574	1,919	1,235	2,760	4,691	5,866	1,169	2,629
Montana														
Billings city	7,476	7,745	1,853	3,011	477	1,421	202	533	466	993	1,209	2,151	192	603
Missoula city	4,160	3,911	1,376	2,691	691	1,644	113	1,200	228	890	780	2,022	96	660
Nebraska														
Lincoln city	18,027	13,479	4,454	6,791	2,407	3,359	413	906	491	1,867	2,079	4,297	584	1,491
Omaha city	29,395	22,080	6,735	11,559	2,471	5,446	1,000	2,743	1,531	3,595	4,132	6,490	1,001	3,152

Table H-3: Places—Disability Status and Type of Disability—*Continued*

	Total Population		With a Disability		With a Hearing Disability		With a Vision Disability		With a Cognitive Disability		With an Ambulatory Disability		With a Self-Care Disability	
	65 to 74 Years	75 Years and Over	65 to 74 Years	75 Years and Over	65 to 74 Years	75 Years and Over	65 to 74 Years	75 Years and Over	65 to 74 Years	75 Years and Over	65 to 74 Years	75 Years and Over	65 to 74 Years	75 Years and Over
Nevada														
Henderson city	30,046	19,173	5,918	8,877	1,982	4,933	620	1,638	1,352	1,992	3,950	5,353	1,429	2,438
Las Vegas city	48,586	29,917	13,916	14,740	4,597	7,377	3,300	2,966	3,774	4,368	9,691	9,867	3,483	4,039
North Las Vegas city	16,907	7,522	6,655	5,076	1,775	1,547	1,624	628	1,921	1,721	4,691	4,057	1,244	1,269
Reno city	18,327	12,871	5,055	6,894	1,841	3,051	773	1,437	1,299	1,902	2,777	3,783	456	1,169
Sparks city	9,062	4,764	2,430	2,658	811	1,490	430	527	637	387	1,679	1,932	198	429
New Hampshire														
Manchester city	8,067	5,244	2,417	3,107	1,114	1,313	401	457	453	912	1,672	2,194	347	865
Nashua city	6,042	4,933	574	2,784	427	1,155	45	740	132	925	312	1,638	267	988
New Jersey														
Bayonne city	4,690	3,220	736	1,747	124	645	49	438	138	344	646	1,501	186	612
Camden city	4,875	2,543	1,975	1,696	498	423	785	285	697	656	1,370	1,458	503	464
Clifton city	5,269	3,947	836	1,789	56	565	280	311	50	268	453	987	89	362
East Orange city	4,977	3,093	1,021	1,774	49	374	237	298	402	230	916	1,520	91	267
Elizabeth city	6,584	4,349	1,417	2,051	118	736	478	237	262	719	724	1,574	74	1,058
Jersey City city	14,872	9,031	3,982	4,647	723	1,367	576	1,473	812	1,525	2,893	3,660	724	1,081
Newark city	14,726	8,455	6,733	4,863	1,116	1,803	2,121	1,841	1,408	1,067	4,877	3,459	1,284	1,750
Passaic city	3,741	2,184	830	1,364	182	199	227	69	463	560	706	1,191	84	399
Paterson city	8,608	7,523	2,739	3,276	323	1,049	701	705	246	876	2,179	2,528	731	1,688
Trenton city	4,850	3,566	1,169	1,573	247	434	180	312	505	548	873	1,115	341	379
Union City city	3,785	3,566	1,180	1,927	343	551	447	630	318	638	834	1,776	56	817
New Mexico														
Albuquerque city	42,291	31,464	11,816	16,300	4,342	8,250	2,759	3,933	3,618	5,717	7,426	10,696	3,342	4,662
Las Cruces city	7,600	6,636	2,395	3,680	995	1,428	304	1,094	341	718	1,384	2,651	347	917
Rio Rancho city	7,156	4,473	1,376	2,191	630	845	238	424	220	684	423	1,511	211	538
Santa Fe city	9,051	5,095	2,291	2,416	1,193	1,195	450	576	817	382	876	1,539	317	304
New York														
Albany city	7,006	4,318	1,591	2,352	557	895	237	261	271	593	814	1,448	224	438
Buffalo city	17,325	14,468	5,409	8,609	1,058	3,292	737	1,171	1,195	2,760	4,135	5,418	798	1,639
Mount Vernon city	5,214	3,938	1,590	2,180	363	758	454	498	613	815	936	1,593	368	740
New Rochelle city	5,013	5,142	1,062	2,147	225	584	278	247	65	301	704	1,571	145	651
New York city	603,917	461,332	152,353	247,910	36,477	83,575	34,971	56,969	38,529	84,523	108,460	189,148	32,653	97,177
Rochester city	14,441	6,843	5,098	4,351	1,832	1,562	833	769	1,744	1,456	3,478	3,277	637	1,591
Schenectady city	4,018	4,400	1,166	2,130	88	1,017	250	433	99	791	697	1,687	153	1,040
Syracuse city	8,958	7,617	2,617	3,795	1,066	1,591	652	1,138	463	1,457	1,395	2,485	363	1,182
Yonkers city	19,087	13,627	3,775	7,705	1,226	3,061	342	1,715	829	2,752	2,153	5,347	795	2,480
North Carolina														
Asheville city	7,742	7,073	1,445	4,136	660	2,111	25	1,456	209	1,223	1,089	2,223	476	1,223
Charlotte city	45,296	29,269	10,868	15,763	3,335	6,826	2,105	3,019	2,111	4,766	6,686	8,995	1,939	3,759
Concord city	5,737	3,653	1,528	2,446	390	989	102	265	246	929	1,151	1,912	351	1,206
Durham city	15,272	10,548	4,097	5,825	1,217	2,608	466	994	1,071	1,691	2,665	3,859	810	1,105
Fayetteville city	13,467	9,837	4,329	6,112	1,520	2,717	905	1,147	762	1,539	2,553	4,098	1,074	1,539
Gastonia city	6,842	4,137	2,054	2,389	664	1,340	189	502	1,121	1,088	1,132	1,706	25	650
Greensboro city	20,196	13,691	4,954	6,843	1,017	2,833	526	460	590	1,169	3,577	4,366	1,088	1,719
Greenville city	5,280	3,645	1,125	2,539	345	870	104	1,038	129	763	665	1,898	316	1,051
High Point city	7,733	5,333	1,775	2,557	743	675	559	483	820	689	977	1,937	413	818
Jacksonville city	2,281	1,614	1,164	1,143	240	692	114	333	322	172	908	433	257	325
Raleigh city	23,351	16,104	4,547	7,333	1,048	3,640	1,114	1,403	781	2,209	2,743	5,108	493	2,208
Wilmington city	8,189	7,069	1,644	3,771	552	2,355	332	1,161	336	1,333	824	1,944	195	978
Winston-Salem city	16,669	14,387	4,977	7,069	1,494	2,737	1,304	938	1,084	1,866	3,147	4,598	756	1,969
North Dakota														
Bismarck city	5,401	4,743	1,026	2,140	538	827	0	452	502	411	443	1,372	96	274
Fargo city	5,315	6,037	1,629	3,222	623	1,884	610	194	184	998	469	2,340	174	745
Ohio														
Akron city	14,839	10,790	4,376	4,453	1,045	1,634	827	518	1,248	674	2,637	2,731	867	897
Canton city	4,301	4,478	1,258	2,583	465	790	294	205	144	580	873	1,648	354	529
Cincinnati city	18,277	14,504	5,003	7,681	1,582	3,269	897	1,540	800	2,353	3,405	5,106	821	1,812
Cleveland city	25,902	19,563	9,943	11,541	1,998	3,781	2,382	2,382	2,385	3,155	7,278	8,095	2,764	4,018
Columbus city	43,122	31,252	11,602	16,522	2,707	6,146	2,050	3,348	3,224	5,987	7,946	11,058	2,606	4,818
Dayton city	9,038	6,505	3,470	3,356	855	1,326	954	833	324	1,196	2,726	2,518	799	1,034
Lorain city	5,530	3,852	1,786	2,084	341	1,323	301	334	169	430	1,383	989	387	669
Parma city	6,700	6,857	1,259	3,293	201	1,304	162	324	396	794	927	1,496	450	640
Toledo city	20,220	16,820	5,936	9,408	2,385	4,164	1,462	1,327	1,652	2,423	4,376	5,774	1,906	2,577
Youngstown city	4,714	5,467	1,574	2,960	530	1,108	589	615	181	907	1,035	1,975	279	1,164
Oklahoma														
Broken Arrow city	7,297	3,984	1,609	1,372	936	700	121	280	234	387	662	776	219	298
Edmond city	6,498	4,266	912	2,287	356	1,383	206	605	209	937	522	2,018	162	1,282
Lawton city	5,493	3,964	2,371	2,012	671	770	808	659	326	496	1,651	1,474	349	495
Norman city	7,818	5,448	1,844	2,508	636	1,090	140	306	111	760	1,180	2,132	114	377
Oklahoma City city	44,274	28,895	14,568	16,090	5,731	7,879	1,772	3,439	2,365	4,742	8,890	11,468	1,706	5,002
Tulsa city	28,948	23,097	8,441	12,301	2,382	6,028	1,959	1,854	2,224	2,920	5,346	7,856	1,539	2,959
Oregon														
Beaverton city	6,641	3,327	1,009	1,477	553	756	144	380	170	462	315	859	70	325
Bend city	6,691	5,344	1,532	2,211	876	755	364	510	412	514	490	1,342	303	501
Eugene city	12,215	9,224	2,568	5,044	912	2,438	731	734	645	1,656	1,667	3,091	376	1,375

Table H-3: Places—Disability Status and Type of Disability—*Continued*

	Total Population		With a Disability		With a Hearing Disability		With a Vision Disability		With a Cognitive Disability		With an Ambulatory Disability		With a Self-Care Disability	
	65 to 74 Years	75 Years and Over	65 to 74 Years	75 Years and Over	65 to 74 Years	75 Years and Over	65 to 74 Years	75 Years and Over	65 to 74 Years	75 Years and Over	65 to 74 Years	75 Years and Over	65 to 74 Years	75 Years and Over
Oregon—Cont.														
Gresham city	8,706	5,715	3,202	3,476	1,268	1,575	406	924	326	1,520	2,189	2,281	605	942
Hillsboro city	6,561	3,633	2,163	1,676	922	877	169	343	316	620	1,201	1,342	503	403
Medford city	7,703	6,199	2,571	2,927	1,208	1,782	252	651	744	924	1,590	1,756	359	717
Portland city	41,495	28,065	11,057	16,048	4,112	8,901	2,650	3,620	2,893	4,610	5,872	10,569	2,318	4,193
Salem city	12,628	9,055	3,449	4,992	1,118	2,496	397	1,139	1,199	1,641	2,158	2,925	356	1,577
Pennsylvania														
Allentown city	7,279	6,352	2,270	2,945	637	1,320	228	550	318	1,114	1,438	1,795	573	713
Bethlehem city	5,776	5,402	1,457	2,423	387	1,112	300	250	690	318	985	981	389	294
Erie city	6,424	6,839	1,597	3,911	730	1,380	171	792	360	1,369	904	2,431	225	1,084
Philadelphia city	106,536	82,649	32,036	44,449	7,296	14,985	6,309	8,276	7,772	13,127	22,762	32,327	6,724	12,583
Pittsburgh city	19,648	19,158	5,050	9,694	1,522	4,309	710	1,550	1,225	1,929	3,460	5,822	901	1,312
Reading city	5,071	4,085	2,359	2,295	278	761	388	1,047	359	571	1,760	1,361	275	445
Scranton city	6,421	6,079	1,780	3,416	526	1,521	34	670	367	454	1,416	1,968	203	514
Rhode Island														
Cranston city	7,219	7,034	1,740	3,315	634	1,115	441	366	471	893	1,222	2,315	427	1,325
Pawtucket city	4,183	3,160	946	1,572	276	906	288	129	218	489	423	1,092	66	334
Providence city	7,952	7,593	2,592	3,741	469	1,810	405	1,020	752	1,309	1,788	2,229	493	892
Warwick city	8,189	7,064	1,977	3,931	1,017	2,257	249	1,106	353	430	720	1,871	72	260
South Carolina														
Charleston city	10,498	6,160	1,939	2,820	669	1,161	110	514	724	712	1,411	1,670	387	512
Columbia city	6,712	4,449	1,863	2,188	489	869	132	503	560	594	1,122	1,367	222	676
North Charleston city	6,948	3,773	2,423	2,142	636	687	507	283	801	620	1,885	1,250	644	406
Rock Hill city	5,078	4,135	895	1,198	380	716	141	152	263	333	621	570	185	355
South Dakota														
Rapid City city	5,163	5,345	1,294	2,423	495	1,102	0	316	139	320	734	1,751	166	265
Sioux Falls city	11,821	8,029	2,580	3,581	726	1,780	162	631	495	1,545	1,717	2,324	762	996
Tennessee														
Chattanooga city	13,858	11,509	3,504	5,142	1,141	1,603	442	963	1,091	1,542	2,203	3,390	627	1,518
Clarksville city	7,028	4,322	3,181	1,797	901	645	614	118	531	432	2,585	1,351	915	515
Franklin city	3,968	3,347	345	1,888	196	1,163	0	115	97	391	101	1,341	101	469
Jackson city	4,422	3,391	1,348	2,228	545	920	364	848	217	550	447	1,684	155	1,347
Johnson City city	5,797	4,602	2,220	2,882	1,165	1,675	369	991	648	934	1,498	2,078	648	976
Knoxville city	13,876	10,049	4,241	5,772	1,394	2,210	822	979	1,508	2,117	2,669	3,781	1,213	2,121
Memphis city	41,574	29,777	11,893	15,681	2,607	4,577	2,352	2,920	2,393	5,084	8,072	10,857	2,658	4,948
Murfreesboro city	6,811	4,124	1,307	1,770	749	787	209	278	387	694	763	1,134	163	720
Nashville-Davidson metropolitan govt (bal)	39,647	28,753	9,857	14,923	2,842	5,160	1,515	2,616	1,683	3,863	6,377	10,397	1,073	3,451
Texas														
Abilene city	7,911	6,961	2,931	3,646	1,320	2,143	1,157	712	992	1,355	1,795	2,584	389	1,576
Allen city	3,506	2,015	935	1,176	289	579	172	215	68	69	619	573	168	152
Amarillo city	14,619	10,450	4,427	5,047	1,525	2,491	884	770	798	894	2,676	3,193	489	1,244
Arlington city	23,638	12,560	5,447	6,269	2,230	2,836	1,020	759	1,323	1,927	3,327	4,125	985	1,225
Austin city	44,629	26,237	9,581	13,794	2,702	6,732	1,668	3,422	1,768	3,133	5,710	9,575	1,601	3,480
Baytown city	6,090	3,944	2,789	1,675	1,415	584	751	683	768	553	1,624	874	264	610
Beaumont city	7,954	6,523	2,354	3,613	908	2,137	424	1,271	447	1,032	1,578	2,397	492	1,040
Brownsville city	11,190	8,670	3,738	5,505	1,821	2,431	818	1,152	1,005	1,744	2,279	4,049	1,127	2,475
Bryan city	4,877	2,624	1,839	1,546	497	654	437	379	471	122	1,335	800	357	170
Carrollton city	7,284	3,995	1,738	2,114	822	893	60	126	232	553	923	1,488	381	435
College Station city	3,305	2,699	872	1,251	396	240	143	225	228	353	455	1,017	173	410
Conroe city	3,267	3,763	1,246	1,632	488	684	361	589	38	500	904	1,269	176	545
Corpus Christi city	23,380	16,392	7,753	9,199	2,589	3,979	1,918	2,286	928	2,184	4,693	6,146	1,537	1,733
Dallas city	69,595	48,440	19,937	23,482	5,179	9,227	3,634	6,139	4,991	8,280	12,790	16,302	4,966	8,062
Denton city	8,340	3,483	2,367	1,689	847	613	354	212	703	474	1,511	1,017	502	206
Edinburg city	3,254	2,912	1,128	1,920	396	1,068	365	157	218	1,300	609	1,488	384	1,079
El Paso city	44,156	36,849	14,963	21,655	5,745	9,628	3,864	5,060	3,796	7,646	9,607	15,833	2,869	8,405
Fort Worth city	41,044	29,704	11,975	15,682	2,961	6,671	2,900	2,867	2,391	4,627	8,240	11,175	2,145	4,107
Frisco city	7,570	2,373	1,478	833	685	424	72	27	62	107	767	523	418	145
Garland city	17,328	9,978	5,814	5,757	1,866	2,433	1,478	1,123	894	1,407	3,497	3,130	851	1,120
Grand Prairie city	8,753	4,912	2,137	2,133	225	824	468	607	613	559	1,394	1,691	338	537
Harlingen city	4,680	4,041	2,075	2,098	574	940	274	743	317	297	1,514	1,287	91	726
Houston city	128,460	87,528	35,845	45,777	10,091	18,376	7,488	9,475	8,469	12,795	22,935	32,357	6,825	14,969
Irving city	11,063	6,392	2,963	2,616	850	1,060	686	682	713	659	1,884	2,077	334	1,018
Killeen city	4,225	2,743	1,326	1,774	440	808	295	179	135	466	810	1,352	187	413
Laredo city	12,639	8,279	5,429	5,709	1,610	2,171	1,342	1,526	1,745	2,198	3,586	4,190	1,392	2,527
League City city	5,179	3,130	1,226	941	282	325	289	207	0	421	944	575	0	390
Lewisville city	5,573	3,649	1,584	2,038	498	626	181	192	494	604	1,071	1,310	293	498
Longview city	5,762	5,695	1,577	3,140	411	1,399	199	573	513	700	930	2,131	438	721
Lubbock city	15,202	12,760	4,903	6,631	2,277	3,251	825	1,981	1,066	1,819	3,013	4,433	1,006	1,651
McAllen city	8,421	4,578	2,889	2,006	1,485	1,240	1,086	616	137	676	1,119	1,666	664	928
McKinney city	8,184	5,266	1,418	2,931	389	1,049	0	370	184	816	991	1,759	201	704
Mesquite city	7,767	5,733	2,033	2,968	496	1,395	830	396	166	392	1,673	1,937	578	480
Midland city	6,240	6,314	1,450	2,786	626	1,159	436	379	295	811	1,013	2,082	191	964
Mission city	5,536	3,678	2,369	2,414	1,052	1,405	589	779	1,170	246	1,364	1,082	337	291
Missouri City city	4,931	2,235	812	842	107	408	82	373	0	366	577	762	85	439
New Braunfels city	4,554	3,229	1,435	1,665	615	522	304	282	499	707	1,023	1,357	389	758

Table H-3: Places—Disability Status and Type of Disability—*Continued*

	Total Population		With a Disability		With a Hearing Disability		With a Vision Disability		With a Cognitive Disability		With an Ambulatory Disability		With a Self-Care Disability	
	65 to 74 Years	75 Years and Over	65 to 74 Years	75 Years and Over	65 to 74 Years	75 Years and Over	65 to 74 Years	75 Years and Over	65 to 74 Years	75 Years and Over	65 to 74 Years	75 Years and Over	65 to 74 Years	75 Years and Over
Texas—Cont.														
North Richland Hills city	5,305	4,058	862	2,575	381	1,356	0	526	117	789	586	2,106	77	730
Odessa city	6,861	5,083	2,204	2,835	763	1,315	547	390	495	881	1,388	1,783	181	778
Pasadena city	8,330	5,801	2,314	3,459	862	1,527	533	432	541	1,362	1,682	1,957	546	1,030
Pearland city	4,914	4,359	1,063	1,615	393	725	0	569	420	908	670	1,380	420	677
Pharr city	4,147	4,039	1,611	2,348	835	1,159	406	623	334	865	1,267	1,291	373	563
Plano city	21,344	11,633	3,596	4,870	1,324	2,296	354	791	715	1,061	2,272	2,777	594	1,193
Richardson city	8,583	6,045	1,070	3,017	93	1,377	145	612	154	780	923	1,960	247	651
Round Rock city	5,913	2,877	1,269	2,108	479	1,105	174	516	229	1,137	727	1,555	246	855
San Angelo city	7,109	6,726	1,904	4,162	837	1,857	490	1,038	417	923	1,079	2,927	291	1,296
San Antonio city	93,529	68,246	32,307	39,205	11,571	17,688	5,304	9,262	8,127	11,293	20,689	24,761	6,266	10,625
Sugar Land city	7,295	4,437	1,190	2,225	492	708	447	756	293	797	642	1,456	133	599
Temple city	7,082	3,737	3,344	2,369	1,158	1,013	671	347	534	495	2,547	1,877	927	997
Tyler city	7,566	6,957	1,797	3,065	408	1,336	233	552	463	570	1,066	2,087	402	1,063
Victoria city	5,219	3,873	1,963	2,247	921	1,375	327	563	695	589	1,152	1,360	457	348
Waco city	7,742	6,400	2,290	3,625	1,002	1,779	467	414	286	849	1,679	2,588	804	894
Wichita Falls city	5,995	5,658	1,785	3,147	467	1,761	497	1,048	342	1,238	1,415	2,604	399	1,073
Utah														
Layton city	3,805	2,599	968	1,172	392	494	44	267	178	251	490	568	168	218
Ogden city	5,242	3,505	1,451	1,807	373	1,042	370	376	76	139	822	999	231	405
Orem city	4,114	3,122	1,015	1,789	616	987	346	240	300	456	740	941	42	203
Provo city	3,873	3,372	756	1,214	480	580	0	188	137	117	428	728	320	265
Salt Lake City city	11,175	6,524	3,268	3,517	1,536	1,822	557	868	593	587	1,691	2,420	348	685
Sandy city	6,016	2,748	1,376	1,258	641	563	119	218	334	334	855	889	386	454
St. George city	8,005	8,699	2,622	4,016	1,153	1,962	398	680	585	984	1,439	2,542	124	796
West Jordan city	4,000	2,208	796	1,155	221	571	259	156	85	380	575	668	267	486
West Valley City city	6,103	2,995	1,667	1,242	763	621	254	35	358	452	1,054	684	245	174
Virginia														
Alexandria city	9,453	5,426	1,923	2,735	510	1,368	331	702	51	964	1,086	1,486	40	663
Chesapeake city	17,318	9,489	3,058	4,820	980	2,034	178	873	546	1,389	1,760	2,731	140	1,266
Hampton city	10,632	7,818	2,815	3,834	1,092	1,656	120	615	513	883	1,937	2,644	527	743
Lynchburg city	5,313	5,299	1,528	2,358	411	1,266	301	317	420	263	1,115	1,415	274	797
Newport News city	11,893	8,806	2,770	5,527	468	1,458	335	724	860	2,123	1,936	4,316	702	2,032
Norfolk city	13,335	10,098	3,879	5,290	576	1,878	693	1,042	888	1,603	3,293	3,946	871	2,147
Portsmouth city	6,997	5,701	1,656	3,523	534	1,772	138	414	271	742	1,082	2,379	337	761
Richmond city	13,484	10,811	3,169	4,625	554	1,376	425	1,267	512	1,291	2,263	3,419	639	1,472
Roanoke city	7,914	6,857	2,927	3,352	522	1,169	465	677	617	1,387	1,613	2,110	613	732
Suffolk city	6,839	4,225	1,888	1,955	509	642	42	353	186	545	1,526	1,314	177	448
Virginia Beach city	32,055	22,148	7,571	9,709	1,871	3,932	1,247	2,088	747	2,524	4,365	6,007	1,162	1,824
Washington														
Auburn city	4,265	4,177	1,105	2,114	384	923	140	265	396	618	760	1,556	204	722
Bellevue city	9,752	10,581	1,556	5,064	680	2,861	239	732	226	1,885	525	3,073	257	1,334
Bellingham city	6,373	4,428	1,502	2,668	419	1,181	145	992	491	903	1,125	1,941	532	869
Everett city	4,846	4,257	1,403	2,413	527	1,061	203	388	213	868	770	1,302	293	652
Federal Way city	7,186	4,745	2,104	1,994	830	1,364	384	325	645	423	1,212	1,347	395	845
Kennewick city	5,091	4,436	1,615	2,567	636	974	379	527	355	623	1,215	2,104	430	839
Kent city	7,422	4,333	2,163	2,225	635	1,222	579	587	601	1,128	1,419	1,796	757	1,069
Kirkland city	6,657	4,366	1,245	1,998	499	897	80	185	483	648	730	1,293	414	670
Marysville city	5,697	3,723	1,759	1,836	374	1,123	373	227	279	630	1,267	999	193	674
Pasco city	2,842	1,292	1,023	956	565	624	94	537	0	524	521	802	0	394
Renton city	4,199	4,540	1,552	2,685	426	1,254	107	529	694	759	1,213	1,751	391	715
Seattle city	48,216	30,884	10,313	15,914	3,427	6,518	1,405	2,935	2,655	5,686	5,432	11,249	1,330	5,489
Spokane city	17,196	11,578	5,164	6,230	2,274	2,721	672	1,370	830	2,297	3,168	4,353	506	2,339
Spokane Valley city	7,322	6,001	1,509	3,318	708	1,788	195	410	299	873	738	1,869	6	814
Tacoma city	14,847	9,717	5,062	5,776	1,452	2,850	1,092	1,422	1,359	1,785	3,870	3,918	1,053	1,831
Vancouver city	13,328	9,573	3,348	4,942	1,100	2,269	463	1,128	969	1,527	2,285	3,156	558	1,363
Yakima city	6,433	5,987	2,488	3,795	522	2,041	81	796	415	868	2,050	2,698	356	1,062
Wisconsin														
Appleton city	3,744	3,640	657	1,469	381	706	71	270	171	429	139	1,087	36	275
Eau Claire city	4,784	3,478	1,011	1,746	311	1,083	121	404	145	494	595	1,114	59	508
Green Bay city	6,685	5,536	1,471	2,391	557	1,276	309	515	287	482	886	1,424	191	362
Kenosha city	7,166	4,751	1,889	2,057	443	939	138	273	177	442	1,447	1,420	222	492
Madison city	15,852	10,359	3,407	5,009	1,414	1,658	314	722	723	1,323	1,535	3,028	487	952
Milwaukee city	33,043	25,516	9,527	13,386	3,080	5,127	1,966	2,577	1,778	3,947	6,661	9,226	2,520	4,399
Oshkosh city	3,779	4,966	1,083	2,017	296	717	190	632	328	729	722	1,459	190	486
Racine city	4,791	4,265	1,239	2,370	468	754	62	299	16	655	912	1,427	271	794
Waukesha city	4,049	3,254	826	1,709	411	844	187	481	154	410	408	1,307	77	454

Table H-4: Metropolitan/Micropolitan Statistical Areas—Disability Status and Type of Disability

	Total Population		With a Disability		With a Hearing Disability		With a Vision Disability		With a Cognitive Disability		With an Ambulatory Disability		With a Self-Care Disability	
	65 to 74 Years	75 Years and Over	65 to 74 Years	75 Years and Over	65 to 74 Years	75 Years and Over	65 to 74 Years	75 Years and Over	65 to 74 Years	75 Years and Over	65 to 74 Years	75 Years and Over	65 to 74 Years	75 Years and Over
Aberdeen, WA Micro Area	8,018	4,983	3,196	2,418	1,714	1,475	284	645	625	503	2,067	1,323	354	644
Abilene, TX Metro Area	12,958	10,219	4,738	5,197	1,887	2,873	1,380	964	1,499	1,583	2,992	3,628	589	1,966
Adrian, MI Micro Area	9,522	6,421	3,115	2,870	1,102	1,433	594	434	799	689	2,217	1,535	488	575
Akron, OH Metro Area	61,277	47,040	13,323	21,137	4,658	9,309	2,168	4,805	2,976	4,183	8,018	13,801	3,252	4,889
Alamogordo, NM Micro Area	6,031	4,052	1,456	2,122	647	1,269	85	443	282	513	859	1,330	90	658
Albany, GA Metro Area	13,052	7,945	3,812	4,654	1,267	1,398	798	864	816	1,589	2,418	2,951	808	1,020
Albany, OR Metro Area	12,251	8,231	3,791	4,464	1,814	2,394	290	477	1,347	1,552	2,049	2,795	804	1,029
Albany-Schenectady-Troy, NY Metro Area	75,825	54,907	16,357	25,518	6,114	10,604	2,777	3,271	2,305	5,575	9,698	17,772	2,065	7,365
Albertville, AL Micro Area	8,858	5,961	3,495	4,023	916	1,760	615	820	1,457	945	2,462	3,103	543	1,610
Albuquerque, NM Metro Area	76,580	53,378	20,656	28,416	8,457	13,818	4,296	5,471	5,899	9,588	11,433	18,724	4,482	7,248
Alexandria, LA Metro Area	13,165	8,413	5,182	4,936	1,826	2,287	1,104	1,201	1,992	1,596	3,863	3,527	1,967	1,783
Allentown-Bethlehem-Easton, PA-NJ Metro Area..	74,295	59,003	18,027	28,108	6,482	11,298	1,922	4,312	4,692	8,440	10,898	16,848	2,818	6,727
Altoona, PA Metro Area	12,438	10,450	3,456	5,650	1,165	2,191	334	857	334	1,641	2,116	3,886	747	1,178
Amarillo, TX Metro Area	18,859	13,982	5,288	7,193	1,927	3,392	1,017	1,153	901	1,827	3,206	5,090	660	2,013
Ames, IA Metro Area	5,416	4,262	917	1,646	708	962	10	174	16	300	280	826	77	222
Anchorage, AK Metro Area	23,130	12,689	6,347	6,750	3,324	2,953	425	1,395	1,164	2,486	3,701	3,633	725	2,820
Ann Arbor, MI Metro Area	25,988	16,037	5,046	7,140	2,136	3,414	952	1,126	849	2,250	2,896	4,144	605	1,395
Anniston-Oxford-Jacksonville, AL Metro Area	10,914	7,167	3,612	4,116	1,220	2,013	571	1,111	907	1,332	2,735	3,255	667	1,222
Appleton, WI Metro Area	16,630	12,378	3,019	4,814	1,578	2,402	595	634	592	1,613	1,599	3,328	680	1,019
Asheville, NC Metro Area	50,991	37,458	11,264	18,757	4,817	9,537	1,835	3,893	1,722	4,633	6,302	11,868	2,317	5,426
Ashtabula, OH Micro Area	9,621	6,201	2,710	3,563	920	1,655	261	722	508	823	1,682	1,956	421	497
Athens, TX Micro Area	9,585	6,541	2,597	3,130	877	1,494	282	346	399	394	1,981	1,798	289	346
Athens-Clarke County, GA Metro Area	14,428	8,260	2,737	4,333	759	1,867	505	1,018	260	1,509	1,753	2,727	285	1,564
Atlanta-Sandy Springs-Roswell, GA Metro Area	379,795	213,512	96,339	109,353	32,286	44,892	15,925	21,296	22,034	32,256	57,708	74,899	16,694	30,148
Atlantic City-Hammonton, NJ Metro Area	25,226	16,739	6,980	8,042	1,993	3,193	514	1,473	1,167	1,955	5,449	5,103	1,205	1,652
Auburn, NY Micro Area	6,919	5,859	1,339	3,367	541	1,558	158	704	215	1,057	791	2,308	251	1,282
Auburn-Opelika, AL Metro Area	9,921	5,647	3,281	2,772	1,459	1,356	567	674	620	525	2,301	1,594	623	438
Augusta-Richmond County, GA-SC Metro Area	49,320	32,366	15,144	16,437	5,537	6,894	2,778	4,537	3,408	5,254	9,283	11,660	2,414	4,632
Augusta-Waterville, ME Micro Area	12,236	8,520	1,955	3,556	690	2,161	209	265	392	610	1,206	1,808	378	778
Austin-Round Rock, TX Metro Area	112,580	66,360	24,423	35,775	8,514	16,636	3,281	8,180	3,667	9,040	14,952	23,389	3,499	8,534
Bakersfield, CA Metro Area	51,079	33,812	14,754	17,310	5,091	6,880	2,198	4,587	3,156	4,528	10,119	11,644	2,822	5,236
Baltimore-Columbia-Towson, MD Metro Area	222,245	157,396	47,471	76,580	15,143	30,024	6,677	14,813	9,781	21,549	29,848	51,340	8,254	21,548
Bangor, ME Metro Area	13,957	10,273	4,192	5,325	2,603	2,669	569	775	956	791	1,965	3,316	976	960
Barnstable Town, MA Metro Area	32,495	26,050	5,159	10,701	2,138	5,656	1,123	1,557	1,303	1,924	2,053	6,346	736	2,575
Baton Rouge, LA Metro Area	59,928	37,466	21,471	20,797	6,138	8,807	3,688	4,321	4,815	7,147	15,021	15,183	3,858	6,388
Battle Creek, MI Metro Area	12,135	8,865	3,495	4,544	1,147	2,292	517	860	868	1,242	2,126	2,174	696	1,055
Bay City, MI Metro Area	10,750	8,155	1,809	4,554	643	2,107	86	819	466	776	1,018	3,199	255	1,593
Beaumont-Port Arthur, TX Metro Area	33,379	23,843	11,184	14,435	3,490	7,254	3,430	3,451	3,314	3,711	7,821	9,631	1,645	3,575
Beaver Dam, WI Micro Area	7,251	5,995	1,474	2,497	574	1,088	151	137	371	765	802	1,825	235	498
Beckley, WV Metro Area	12,677	9,137	5,667	5,983	2,962	3,360	1,228	2,012	1,649	2,021	3,667	3,808	1,055	2,036
Bellingham, WA Metro Area	19,338	11,882	4,749	5,990	1,778	3,108	486	1,355	1,125	1,864	3,367	3,570	923	1,449
Bend-Redmond, OR Metro Area	18,744	11,415	5,215	5,076	3,144	2,478	816	814	1,176	1,705	1,914	2,801	592	1,388
Billings, MT Metro Area	14,377	10,966	3,742	4,216	1,151	2,004	745	740	657	1,072	2,229	2,641	435	871
Binghamton, NY Metro Area	22,430	19,053	5,889	10,007	2,431	4,183	1,075	1,080	1,213	2,671	3,771	5,786	943	2,744
Birmingham-Hoover, AL Metro Area	96,697	67,330	27,771	36,260	9,763	14,130	5,196	6,585	6,894	11,260	17,340	26,076	4,794	11,820
Bismarck, ND Metro Area	9,741	7,751	1,831	3,488	963	1,464	254	610	685	543	981	2,298	109	482
Blacksburg-Christiansburg-Radford, VA Metro Area	15,614	9,861	4,437	4,623	1,594	2,686	878	1,047	825	1,370	2,680	2,639	634	1,325
Bloomington, IL Metro Area	12,492	9,481	2,620	5,405	529	2,621	295	1,032	385	1,453	1,878	3,419	497	1,331
Bloomington, IN Metro Area	11,062	7,542	2,491	3,704	1,087	1,638	495	703	296	673	1,330	2,026	282	545
Bloomsburg-Berwick, PA Metro Area	7,915	6,326	1,981	2,467	893	999	258	408	175	860	1,052	1,491	276	681
Bluefield, WV-VA Micro Area	11,274	8,726	5,398	6,142	1,890	3,355	1,085	1,904	1,439	2,272	3,649	4,390	831	2,636
Boise City, ID Metro Area	52,783	33,053	11,879	17,694	5,804	9,614	1,586	4,121	2,824	4,547	6,214	9,858	1,411	4,335
Boston-Cambridge-Newton, MA-NH Metro Area..	373,726	279,427	77,145	133,704	27,905	65,025	11,577	27,624	17,958	37,182	45,094	85,436	12,286	35,542
Boulder, CO Metro Area	22,580	14,510	3,898	7,608	1,801	3,464	753	1,760	790	1,560	1,099	4,489	1,081	977
Bowling Green, KY Metro Area	12,551	8,262	3,875	4,778	1,761	1,595	918	922	1,057	1,084	2,543	3,119	847	762
Bozeman, MT Metro Area	6,506	4,011	1,814	1,686	1,289	967	539	331	487	626	699	1,052	418	493
Brainerd, MN Micro Area	11,584	7,947	2,875	3,928	1,357	2,138	629	684	401	822	1,509	2,212	251	873
Branson, MO Micro Area	11,447	7,305	2,891	4,406	1,313	1,936	365	1,061	507	812	2,163	2,916	586	563
Bremerton-Silverdale, WA Metro Area	25,356	14,341	6,017	7,296	2,729	3,761	771	1,893	913	2,551	3,839	4,570	423	2,302
Bridgeport-Stamford-Norwalk, CT Metro Area	72,006	59,112	13,328	26,482	4,333	9,842	2,015	4,288	3,068	7,246	8,000	17,235	2,644	7,954
Brownsville-Harlingen, TX Metro Area	28,679	22,328	10,884	12,906	4,250	5,528	3,016	3,434	2,741	3,174	6,582	9,177	2,297	4,501
Brunswick, GA Metro Area	11,523	7,837	4,011	3,345	561	1,811	469	597	1,408	753	3,146	1,881	791	993
Buffalo-Cheektowaga-Niagara Falls, NY Metro Area	99,458	83,029	21,859	40,419	6,644	16,891	3,051	5,782	3,424	9,779	14,648	26,178	3,331	9,377
Burlington, NC Metro Area	14,040	10,262	3,179	5,132	1,171	2,470	544	894	715	1,300	1,876	3,702	223	1,160
Burlington-South Burlington, VT Metro Area	16,200	11,296	3,292	5,460	1,173	2,943	614	1,161	750	1,476	2,321	3,538	354	1,360
California-Lexington Park, MD Metro Area	8,247	4,257	2,907	2,641	699	1,307	392	628	1,164	789	1,481	1,901	367	622
Canton-Massillon, OH Metro Area	39,340	28,755	9,060	13,114	2,965	5,877	1,306	2,974	1,881	3,193	5,768	8,372	1,617	3,224
Cape Coral-Fort Myers, FL Metro Area	101,580	75,149	19,039	32,273	9,601	17,619	2,799	5,063	3,122	9,411	8,911	19,454	3,010	6,327
Cape Girardeau, MO-IL Metro Area	9,174	6,239	2,267	2,839	1,135	1,125	241	706	689	759	1,244	1,679	439	242
Carbondale-Marion, IL Metro Area	10,835	7,810	2,591	3,217	1,050	1,590	370	586	500	971	1,775	2,179	687	576
Carson City, NV Metro Area	5,431	4,076	1,747	2,478	692	1,361	97	570	214	759	950	1,645	151	1,020
Casper, WY Metro Area	5,416	4,169	1,436	2,244	564	1,105	349	593	392	201	755	1,074	233	243
Cedar Rapids, IA Metro Area	20,794	16,871	4,509	6,179	1,482	3,358	600	1,241	469	2,086	2,800	2,982	438	1,264
Centralia, WA Micro Area	8,366	6,141	3,020	3,944	1,579	2,407	502	862	1,126	1,561	1,531	2,304	504	1,302
Chambersburg-Waynesboro, PA Metro Area	14,897	12,108	3,052	5,544	1,021	2,192	545	780	522	1,813	1,810	3,350	630	1,467

Table H-4: Metropolitan/Micropolitan Statistical Areas—Disability Status and Type of Disability—*Continued*

	Total Population		With a Disability		With a Hearing Disability		With a Vision Disability		With a Cognitive Disability		With an Ambulatory Disability		With a Self-Care Disability	
	65 to 74 Years	75 Years and Over	65 to 74 Years	75 Years and Over	65 to 74 Years	75 Years and Over	65 to 74 Years	75 Years and Over	65 to 74 Years	75 Years and Over	65 to 74 Years	75 Years and Over	65 to 74 Years	75 Years and Over
Champaign-Urbana, IL Metro Area......................	14,534	12,658	3,472	5,456	1,302	2,257	503	929	500	1,517	2,016	3,613	646	1,303
Charleston, WV Metro Area.................................	22,540	16,604	9,369	9,468	4,410	4,185	1,819	2,467	2,321	2,664	5,419	6,342	1,823	2,783
Charleston-Mattoon, IL Micro Area.....................	5,030	3,959	1,124	2,348	326	1,157	91	453	126	512	773	1,737	236	595
Charleston-North Charleston, SC Metro Area........	60,370	35,315	16,234	17,468	5,360	8,102	2,701	3,733	3,979	5,497	10,279	10,980	3,010	5,323
Charlotte-Concord-Gastonia, NC-SC Metro Area...	179,177	109,122	46,783	55,017	16,881	25,898	7,653	9,949	10,393	16,438	28,713	35,081	7,638	16,277
Charlottesville, VA Metro Area............................	18,807	14,373	3,494	7,151	900	3,547	580	1,305	435	1,930	2,359	4,078	348	1,500
Chattanooga, TN-GA Metro Area.........................	49,818	35,832	12,205	17,084	5,272	8,129	1,398	3,632	2,890	5,129	7,767	10,471	1,404	4,347
Cheyenne, WY Metro Area.................................	8,255	5,323	2,232	2,770	848	1,244	229	323	608	1,053	1,432	1,757	432	734
Chicago-Naperville-Elgin, IL-IN-WI Metro Area.....	686,923	495,028	159,382	249,687	44,500	100,430	26,916	49,983	32,110	68,399	107,609	172,687	29,567	74,247
Chico, CA Metro Area.......................................	21,032	15,990	6,896	8,034	2,265	3,976	1,189	993	1,516	2,425	5,063	5,375	1,319	1,789
Chillicothe, OH Micro Area................................	6,458	4,497	2,043	3,032	900	1,482	647	386	506	775	1,129	1,960	514	667
Cincinnati, OH-KY-IN Metro Area........................	164,740	118,364	41,121	56,441	15,494	24,213	7,946	10,466	7,970	14,276	24,699	36,288	6,832	14,295
Claremont-Lebanon, NH-VT Micro Area...............	24,119	15,497	6,265	7,880	2,587	4,199	981	1,314	1,270	1,580	3,734	4,615	735	1,573
Clarksburg, WV Micro Area...............................	9,765	6,203	3,473	3,286	1,447	1,877	619	796	858	972	2,444	1,846	915	949
Clarksville, TN-KY Metro Area...........................	16,897	10,043	6,475	4,520	1,976	1,884	1,450	469	939	1,055	4,678	3,501	1,554	1,308
Clearlake, CA Micro Area..................................	7,662	4,925	2,806	2,414	1,014	1,190	319	544	1,278	869	1,509	1,485	795	757
Cleveland, TN Metro Area.................................	11,428	7,944	3,955	4,177	1,829	2,380	1,041	594	562	1,275	2,267	2,399	395	695
Cleveland-Elyria, OH Metro Area........................	183,924	144,981	46,238	70,089	14,200	29,631	6,557	13,739	9,121	20,126	30,093	46,369	9,775	20,267
Coeur d'Alene, ID Metro Area............................	14,826	10,084	3,897	4,714	2,039	3,557	514	1,158	1,052	1,734	1,928	2,296	874	868
College Station-Bryan, TX Metro Area..................	13,755	9,814	3,879	5,243	1,131	1,788	605	912	983	1,136	2,719	3,580	747	1,385
Colorado Springs, CO Metro Area.......................	48,160	31,114	10,773	14,791	4,903	7,577	1,502	2,609	1,858	4,508	6,173	9,543	984	3,549
Columbia, MO Metro Area.................................	10,958	6,746	2,367	3,281	877	1,351	161	293	265	939	1,330	2,170	318	649
Columbia, SC Metro Area.................................	64,253	37,971	18,060	19,709	6,359	8,968	3,026	4,914	4,246	4,848	11,351	12,848	3,363	5,776
Columbus, GA-AL Metro Area............................	22,260	15,289	7,848	8,756	2,248	3,635	1,315	1,786	2,023	3,211	5,770	6,606	1,463	3,499
Columbus, IN Metro Area..................................	6,738	4,661	2,704	1,998	925	787	305	336	694	580	1,562	1,318	375	526
Columbus, OH Metro Area.................................	139,079	92,685	33,914	45,297	9,947	18,713	4,717	8,504	6,988	13,402	22,452	28,741	6,648	11,158
Concord, NH Micro Area...................................	13,365	9,035	2,780	5,243	1,149	1,837	325	882	578	1,279	1,353	3,510	593	1,372
Cookeville, TN Micro Area................................	10,758	7,593	2,733	3,741	1,001	1,872	518	903	914	831	1,965	2,545	1,017	952
Coos Bay, OR Micro Area..................................	8,701	6,238	3,465	4,124	668	2,061	229	704	915	1,429	2,904	2,890	1,098	1,233
Corning, NY Micro Area....................................	9,450	7,126	2,673	3,742	896	1,736	510	1,154	449	810	1,859	2,445	376	961
Corpus Christi, TX Metro Area...........................	36,677	23,803	13,099	13,324	5,083	5,704	3,409	3,444	2,015	3,671	7,560	8,688	2,363	3,046
Corvallis, OR Metro Area..................................	7,089	5,182	1,211	2,590	665	1,127	142	336	169	614	605	1,662	151	579
Crestview-Fort Walton Beach-Destin, FL Metro Area..	23,653	16,771	5,802	8,790	2,673	3,715	1,010	1,506	787	3,259	3,325	5,516	495	1,902
Cullman, AL Micro Area...................................	8,344	5,539	3,236	3,083	1,394	2,130	567	889	652	1,099	1,615	1,627	779	868
Cumberland, MD-WV Metro Area.......................	10,455	7,690	3,289	4,058	1,264	2,240	624	1,072	700	1,403	1,929	2,290	587	975
Dallas-Fort Worth-Arlington, TX Metro Area........	431,414	263,822	111,255	133,259	36,820	57,580	20,630	26,928	22,405	38,934	73,286	90,134	21,556	34,685
Dalton, GA Metro Area.....................................	10,478	7,269	2,848	3,917	1,370	1,560	514	395	987	1,316	1,635	2,669	318	1,903
Danville, IL Metro Area....................................	7,855	5,708	1,950	3,091	662	1,405	596	480	596	687	1,330	2,108	734	545
Danville, VA Micro Area....................................	11,087	9,025	3,563	4,601	1,018	2,015	484	447	856	1,397	2,715	3,300	537	1,404
Daphne-Fairhope-Foley, AL Metro Area...............	22,261	14,992	5,127	8,011	2,340	3,375	290	1,097	539	1,908	3,298	5,560	878	1,458
Davenport-Moline-Rock Island, IA-IL Metro Area .	34,774	25,944	8,595	11,883	3,232	5,271	1,073	1,997	1,541	2,935	5,232	7,960	1,412	2,845
Dayton, OH Metro Area.....................................	71,992	55,195	19,636	25,266	7,299	11,060	3,484	5,362	3,985	6,438	12,632	16,679	3,498	5,831
Decatur, AL Metro Area....................................	13,742	9,235	4,972	6,279	1,906	3,298	961	1,680	1,270	1,977	2,784	4,357	731	1,681
Decatur, IL Metro Area.....................................	10,039	8,268	2,294	4,421	574	2,353	446	1,115	339	1,472	1,554	2,763	352	1,233
Deltona-Daytona Beach-Ormond Beach, FL Metro Area..	80,298	63,966	18,170	29,568	6,544	12,907	2,080	5,103	3,650	8,174	11,183	20,431	2,693	9,171
Denver-Aurora-Lakewood, CO Metro Area...........	194,466	120,464	42,804	60,950	18,002	30,716	6,397	11,198	7,761	15,938	23,673	35,549	5,971	13,321
Des Moines-West Des Moines, IA Metro Area	41,984	29,531	9,146	12,601	3,847	6,528	1,075	2,272	2,395	3,034	5,375	8,167	1,392	3,105
Detroit-Warren-Dearborn, MI Metro Area............	356,018	262,293	98,328	135,582	32,172	55,551	16,666	28,362	21,383	36,886	65,146	90,752	20,231	38,633
Dothan, AL Metro Area.....................................	14,789	10,036	5,706	5,822	2,213	2,631	994	1,247	910	1,789	3,576	4,192	673	1,359
Dover, DE Metro Area.......................................	15,869	10,121	4,443	4,568	1,610	1,727	464	440	882	1,395	3,147	3,029	947	1,365
DuBois, PA Micro Area......................................	8,168	6,456	2,961	3,090	1,090	1,343	610	919	532	533	1,580	2,029	385	741
Dubuque, IA Metro Area....................................	7,964	6,799	1,544	2,501	512	1,202	168	333	458	724	795	1,663	210	428
Duluth, MN-WI Metro Area................................	25,982	19,370	5,416	9,651	2,629	4,819	804	1,831	1,139	2,219	2,578	6,193	678	2,388
Dunn, NC Micro Area..	8,402	4,794	2,557	2,117	1,071	1,001	403	480	778	693	1,563	1,605	250	809
Durham-Chapel Hill, NC Metro Area...................	41,398	27,185	9,285	13,461	3,284	6,908	1,307	2,441	1,980	3,564	5,607	8,049	1,764	2,577
East Stroudsburg, PA Metro Area	15,062	10,039	3,917	6,551	1,456	3,545	381	2,129	803	1,976	2,710	3,738	857	1,287
Eau Claire, WI Metro Area................................	13,432	10,233	3,057	4,831	1,322	2,813	405	778	662	1,518	1,572	3,192	454	1,232
El Centro, CA Metro Area..................................	11,601	9,835	4,671	5,664	1,564	2,596	1,215	1,055	608	2,105	2,616	3,692	596	2,256
El Paso, TX Metro Area.....................................	51,498	41,082	17,844	25,213	7,211	10,886	5,488	6,638	4,829	8,845	11,030	17,507	3,342	9,432
Elizabeth City, NC Micro Area............................	6,309	4,136	2,192	1,753	637	502	288	450	301	562	1,487	1,082	726	455
Elizabethtown-Fort Knox, KY Metro Area.............	11,675	7,357	3,891	4,865	1,242	2,142	1,196	754	933	1,373	2,559	3,925	406	1,358
Elkhart-Goshen, IN Metro Area	13,812	11,159	4,022	5,548	1,675	2,793	550	1,224	646	1,703	2,275	3,462	655	1,353
Elmira, NY Metro Area......................................	8,118	6,012	2,297	2,484	730	1,004	553	415	591	639	1,432	1,773	244	757
Erie, PA Metro Area..	23,659	18,613	5,211	9,375	2,691	4,194	549	1,410	731	3,024	2,617	5,370	672	1,994
Eugene, OR Metro Area.....................................	36,615	24,888	10,006	14,159	3,595	7,070	1,461	2,582	2,472	3,593	6,032	8,666	1,732	3,198
Eureka-Arcata-Fortuna, CA Micro Area................	12,402	7,725	3,695	3,779	2,093	1,722	633	754	712	1,361	1,999	2,401	500	840
Evansville, IN-KY Metro Area.............................	26,746	20,018	7,840	9,385	2,737	4,779	1,492	2,209	1,086	3,247	5,266	5,785	1,125	2,066
Fairbanks, AK Metro Area.................................	5,193	2,657	1,916	1,690	1,220	606	657	393	318	376	743	1,246	283	978
Fargo, ND-MN Metro Area.................................	13,301	11,337	3,951	6,013	1,549	3,318	761	515	925	1,767	1,930	3,691	488	1,212
Faribault-Northfield, MN Micro Area...................	4,738	4,046	834	1,492	439	569	281	175	181	295	145	743	39	699
Farmington, MO Micro Area..............................	5,555	3,961	1,940	2,611	656	712	606	675	99	704	1,201	1,955	286	560
Farmington, NM Metro Area..............................	8,830	6,533	2,794	3,569	1,173	2,148	325	501	658	1,186	1,747	2,222	304	734
Fayetteville, NC Metro Area..............................	23,250	15,473	8,161	9,523	3,072	4,241	1,726	2,296	1,943	3,006	5,592	6,574	2,005	3,018
Fayetteville-Springdale-Rogers, AR-MO Metro Area..	36,036	23,943	9,788	11,349	4,016	5,966	1,485	2,827	2,079	2,955	5,851	6,930	1,665	2,587

Table H-4: Metropolitan/Micropolitan Statistical Areas—Disability Status and Type of Disability—*Continued*

	Total Population		With a Disability		With a Hearing Disability		With a Vision Disability		With a Cognitive Disability		With an Ambulatory Disability		With a Self-Care Disability	
	65 to 74 Years	75 Years and Over	65 to 74 Years	75 Years and Over	65 to 74 Years	75 Years and Over	65 to 74 Years	75 Years and Over	65 to 74 Years	75 Years and Over	65 to 74 Years	75 Years and Over	65 to 74 Years	75 Years and Over
Findlay, OH Micro Area	6,508	4,860	1,757	2,490	598	962	254	274	120	444	1,277	1,419	528	438
Flagstaff, AZ Metro Area	9,962	5,412	2,647	2,868	1,186	1,794	521	654	312	957	1,579	2,011	376	757
Flint, MI Metro Area	36,404	27,510	9,350	14,141	3,011	6,579	1,346	2,534	1,951	4,205	5,882	9,668	1,178	3,827
Florence, SC Metro Area	19,144	11,537	5,547	6,759	1,661	3,340	1,478	1,825	2,900	2,763	3,550	4,650	921	1,598
Florence-Muscle Shoals, AL Metro Area	15,465	11,161	4,514	6,269	1,225	3,308	666	1,043	1,412	2,214	2,758	3,898	1,081	1,883
Fond du Lac, WI Metro Area	9,097	7,215	2,023	3,525	840	1,922	305	405	277	1,012	1,214	2,219	276	1,134
Forest City, NC Micro Area	7,492	5,179	2,026	2,939	851	1,545	154	736	266	1,056	1,395	1,477	483	469
Fort Collins, CO Metro Area	26,875	17,392	5,073	7,677	2,397	4,325	531	826	1,177	1,387	2,224	4,230	512	2,064
Fort Smith, AR-OK Metro Area	25,029	16,528	9,704	9,442	3,929	5,319	1,912	2,538	2,054	3,221	6,302	6,357	1,787	2,583
Fort Wayne, IN Metro Area	32,669	23,077	7,655	11,030	2,561	5,024	786	1,907	2,086	2,504	4,763	7,180	1,135	2,733
Frankfort, KY Micro Area	6,382	4,243	2,524	2,193	736	1,096	526	495	462	534	1,868	1,388	111	686
Fresno, CA Metro Area	61,200	44,776	18,288	25,893	6,285	12,791	3,047	5,367	4,329	8,096	11,927	18,394	3,856	8,086
Gadsden, AL Metro Area	10,533	6,846	3,623	4,468	911	1,905	682	1,156	1,281	1,360	2,691	3,356	964	1,537
Gainesville, FL Metro Area	20,537	13,742	5,893	6,457	2,329	3,664	824	1,161	806	1,649	3,158	4,235	711	1,335
Gainesville, GA Metro Area	15,306	10,386	3,905	5,149	1,607	2,118	504	1,043	783	1,816	2,276	3,124	512	860
Gallup, NM Micro Area	4,215	3,186	2,419	2,318	1,097	1,160	591	639	586	870	1,344	1,830	291	713
Gettysburg, PA Metro Area	9,951	7,503	1,956	3,258	962	1,573	215	460	445	793	949	1,981	254	661
Glens Falls, NY Metro Area	13,486	9,336	2,600	4,885	1,021	2,597	196	890	582	1,011	1,708	2,640	526	712
Glenwood Springs, CO Micro Area	5,307	3,105	1,250	1,092	555	523	161	211	83	216	638	700	80	286
Goldsboro, NC Metro Area	10,280	7,339	2,604	4,543	693	2,198	628	575	670	1,257	2,202	3,143	261	1,242
Grand Forks, ND-MN Metro Area	6,885	5,587	1,986	3,035	859	1,247	256	405	304	487	1,132	1,976	390	623
Grand Island, NE Metro Area	6,774	6,039	2,438	2,596	1,165	1,310	379	487	337	403	1,090	1,539	76	230
Grand Junction, CO Metro Area	13,998	10,226	3,430	5,003	1,422	2,730	376	1,596	519	1,197	2,117	3,003	610	707
Grand Rapids-Wyoming, MI Metro Area	74,631	54,734	17,638	26,711	7,333	11,832	2,303	4,091	3,411	6,477	9,696	16,447	2,523	5,404
Grants Pass, OR Metro Area	12,197	8,232	2,717	4,356	1,400	2,362	539	855	399	1,068	1,357	2,672	225	811
Great Falls, MT Metro Area	7,545	5,922	2,592	2,954	1,088	1,491	218	568	278	703	1,223	1,555	563	512
Greeley, CO Metro Area	18,723	11,759	4,102	6,245	2,016	4,269	833	1,655	1,345	1,235	2,391	3,592	609	1,688
Green Bay, WI Metro Area	25,062	18,089	4,872	8,813	1,868	4,291	476	1,340	791	2,330	2,839	5,682	640	1,820
Greeneville, TN Micro Area	8,241	4,929	2,955	3,233	762	1,855	1,226	844	585	689	1,963	2,113	535	1,093
Greenfield Town, MA Micro Area	7,791	4,681	1,389	2,177	529	1,362	262	365	165	861	873	1,399	177	925
Greensboro-High Point, NC Metro Area	63,396	43,671	15,829	21,548	5,363	9,030	3,168	3,646	3,015	6,772	10,093	15,101	2,932	7,042
Greenville, NC Metro Area	11,930	7,376	3,228	4,596	704	2,205	615	1,463	530	1,323	2,143	3,286	1,018	1,556
Greenville-Anderson-Mauldin, SC Metro Area	77,807	49,936	20,769	26,227	6,354	11,367	2,582	5,312	4,986	8,442	13,161	18,647	3,408	7,420
Greenwood, SC Micro Area	9,330	6,623	2,582	3,766	1,110	1,953	335	907	206	1,255	1,700	2,668	252	1,167
Gulfport-Biloxi-Pascagoula, MS Metro Area	32,266	21,381	10,116	12,774	3,798	6,447	1,463	3,731	2,017	5,084	7,615	8,832	2,097	4,768
Hagerstown-Martinsburg, MD-WV Metro Area	21,653	14,728	6,298	7,403	2,343	3,692	1,033	1,241	1,242	1,681	3,874	4,468	591	1,670
Hammond, LA Metro Area	10,345	5,554	4,286	3,678	1,373	754	673	420	997	1,880	3,209	2,058	1,622	1,213
Hanford-Corcoran, CA Metro Area	7,604	5,435	2,929	3,344	1,748	1,375	504	330	773	1,491	1,754	2,265	337	792
Harrisburg-Carlisle, PA Metro Area	49,026	36,957	11,529	18,078	3,260	7,463	2,006	3,134	1,618	4,415	6,875	12,659	1,137	4,649
Harrisonburg, VA Metro Area	9,836	7,942	2,132	4,063	844	1,949	276	1,266	540	1,174	1,373	2,501	762	1,083
Hartford-West Hartford-East Hartford, CT Metro Area	102,329	80,053	22,619	37,899	8,526	16,293	3,020	6,560	5,857	8,482	13,518	24,329	4,097	12,645
Hattiesburg, MS Metro Area	10,744	6,867	4,684	3,570	2,055	1,680	679	647	1,527	1,511	3,150	2,686	1,106	1,266
Helena, MT Micro Area	8,183	4,507	1,609	2,431	1,011	1,214	260	249	450	520	882	1,429	377	685
Hermiston-Pendleton, OR Micro Area	7,125	5,425	2,736	3,241	1,385	1,572	421	1,253	884	1,784	1,829	2,448	922	1,840
Hickory-Lenoir-Morganton, NC Metro Area	36,734	24,218	11,012	13,650	3,089	5,543	1,501	2,714	2,251	4,372	7,863	9,543	1,417	3,750
Hilo, HI Micro Area	21,588	12,225	4,728	6,749	1,889	4,846	842	1,817	622	3,211	2,161	4,491	388	2,865
Hilton Head Island-Bluffton-Beaufort, SC Metro Area	29,799	17,082	4,749	6,136	1,898	3,013	527	1,297	825	1,710	2,810	3,221	312	1,634
Hinesville, GA Metro Area	4,255	1,890	1,829	1,452	408	786	920	332	225	670	1,181	1,048	610	584
Hobbs, NM Micro Area	3,742	3,460	1,441	2,076	408	1,359	336	731	305	635	867	1,247	200	770
Holland, MI Micro Area	10,362	6,315	2,224	3,064	915	1,704	147	711	262	991	1,180	1,937	265	1,007
Homosassa Springs, FL Metro Area	26,335	22,032	6,493	10,711	2,074	5,947	631	3,040	1,224	3,605	4,192	6,875	546	3,804
Hot Springs, AR Metro Area	11,482	9,047	2,845	4,423	1,308	2,375	222	809	610	1,184	1,448	2,425	399	973
Houma-Thibodaux, LA Metro Area	15,346	10,922	4,405	6,360	1,310	3,220	1,209	1,038	493	2,393	3,043	4,184	964	1,720
Houston-The Woodlands-Sugar Land, TX Metro Area	395,726	232,804	108,655	122,608	37,604	50,381	19,515	24,045	22,515	36,531	68,303	84,094	19,087	37,324
Huntington-Ashland, WV-KY-OH Metro Area	36,716	25,860	14,195	15,731	5,538	7,999	3,355	3,999	2,589	4,497	8,878	11,140	2,042	3,907
Huntsville, AL Metro Area	33,937	25,286	10,891	12,467	4,708	5,640	1,510	2,723	2,676	2,900	6,364	6,739	1,825	2,781
Huntsville, TX Micro Area	5,906	4,947	1,423	2,665	515	1,333	228	688	243	612	1,123	1,855	495	478
Hutchinson, KS Micro Area	5,927	5,227	1,766	2,621	536	1,267	779	349	640	364	1,275	1,374	837	532
Idaho Falls, ID Metro Area	9,422	6,781	3,039	3,749	1,299	2,467	310	797	424	1,479	1,625	2,101	250	552
Indiana, PA Micro Area	8,121	6,276	1,943	3,128	1,183	1,620	484	486	402	1,046	850	1,908	169	795
Indianapolis-Carmel-Anderson, IN Metro Area	138,600	97,079	37,073	52,431	14,056	24,591	5,551	11,599	8,693	16,048	23,617	36,229	7,164	15,184
Iowa City, IA Metro Area	9,995	7,514	1,352	2,853	635	1,108	150	553	194	518	687	1,837	115	652
Ithaca, NY Metro Area	7,039	4,996	1,166	1,993	543	1,521	36	167	147	107	512	936	313	536
Jackson, MI Metro Area	14,388	10,678	3,598	5,614	1,374	2,063	185	1,136	677	1,912	2,076	3,629	436	1,363
Jackson, MS Metro Area	40,893	29,545	12,257	16,325	2,998	6,488	1,573	3,427	1,984	5,563	8,022	12,046	1,656	6,560
Jackson, TN Metro Area	11,355	7,909	3,251	5,121	1,264	2,282	788	1,913	554	1,464	1,851	3,371	595	2,191
Jacksonville, FL Metro Area	121,090	76,355	34,559	39,026	10,956	18,190	5,674	8,713	7,207	10,876	21,612	25,740	7,140	10,817
Jacksonville, NC Metro Area	9,634	6,104	4,076	3,831	1,472	2,629	527	1,005	864	654	3,040	1,936	612	801
Jamestown-Dunkirk-Fredonia, NY Micro Area	12,533	10,024	3,061	4,566	1,159	2,431	566	833	309	1,390	2,123	3,016	441	1,141
Janesville-Beloit, WI Metro Area	13,255	10,105	3,497	4,954	1,620	1,883	438	904	302	1,207	1,883	3,348	558	1,357
Jefferson City, MO Metro Area	13,086	7,907	4,187	3,656	1,745	2,090	1,415	700	602	1,134	3,155	2,410	414	980
Johnson City, TN Metro Area	20,997	13,835	9,131	7,842	3,848	3,937	1,797	2,210	2,037	2,147	6,328	5,587	2,271	1,896
Johnstown, PA Metro Area	14,503	12,543	3,690	7,320	1,337	2,906	628	1,876	774	1,950	2,266	4,478	746	1,098

Table H-4: Metropolitan/Micropolitan Statistical Areas—Disability Status and Type of Disability—*Continued*

	Total Population		With a Disability		With a Hearing Disability		With a Vision Disability		With a Cognitive Disability		With an Ambulatory Disability		With a Self-Care Disability	
	65 to 74 Years	75 Years and Over	65 to 74 Years	75 Years and Over	65 to 74 Years	75 Years and Over	65 to 74 Years	75 Years and Over	65 to 74 Years	75 Years and Over	65 to 74 Years	75 Years and Over	65 to 74 Years	75 Years and Over
Jonesboro, AR Metro Area	9,876	7,263	3,460	3,754	993	1,241	1,372	607	621	1,312	2,571	2,997	1,028	1,324
Joplin, MO Metro Area	14,609	10,570	4,442	5,063	1,990	2,830	699	1,383	665	640	3,266	3,168	531	831
Kahului-Wailuku-Lahaina, HI Metro Area	14,700	9,503	3,681	5,331	1,566	2,430	379	917	791	2,212	1,731	3,049	282	1,363
Kalamazoo-Portage, MI Metro Area	26,250	19,464	6,101	9,800	2,535	4,289	825	1,442	1,171	2,199	3,012	6,432	530	2,020
Kalispell, MT Micro Area	9,892	6,341	1,275	1,925	616	928	0	189	121	297	574	963	192	389
Kankakee, IL Metro Area	8,904	6,416	2,919	2,911	964	1,326	451	501	792	329	1,958	2,256	627	267
Kansas City, MO-KS Metro Area	155,248	110,430	37,829	55,970	14,464	25,258	5,597	9,038	6,467	13,980	22,030	35,860	5,229	12,663
Kapaa, HI Micro Area	7,138	4,943	1,934	3,040	662	1,768	159	479	423	1,720	1,275	2,012	346	1,314
Keene, NH Micro Area	7,482	5,034	2,479	2,761	1,130	1,665	217	352	157	462	1,444	1,476	379	645
Kennewick-Richland, WA Metro Area	19,056	12,546	5,210	6,703	2,599	3,173	549	1,570	797	2,209	3,037	4,761	841	1,943
Key West, FL Micro Area	9,992	5,754	2,302	2,029	821	1,082	474	517	99	673	1,206	669	238	484
Killeen-Temple, TX Metro Area	25,088	15,777	9,067	9,334	3,178	4,454	2,050	1,786	1,378	2,252	6,127	6,769	1,618	2,435
Kingsport-Bristol-Bristol, TN-VA Metro Area	35,370	25,218	11,131	14,366	3,795	7,355	2,049	3,265	2,729	3,717	7,675	9,196	2,014	3,918
Kingston, NY Metro Area	18,217	12,305	4,351	6,079	1,187	3,096	497	785	1,044	1,735	3,128	3,768	958	1,375
Klamath Falls, OR Micro Area	7,455	4,676	2,373	2,603	1,070	1,692	288	611	349	655	1,458	1,578	514	818
Knoxville, TN Metro Area	85,103	55,894	24,312	31,142	9,391	14,829	4,307	5,555	5,846	9,910	14,207	20,067	4,235	8,671
Kokomo, IN Metro Area	8,152	6,303	2,509	3,137	798	1,753	355	537	471	673	1,380	1,791	264	327
La Crosse-Onalaska, WI-MN Metro Area	11,120	8,697	2,580	3,235	1,055	1,489	394	462	387	614	1,358	2,112	395	815
Lafayette, LA Metro Area	34,435	23,072	10,654	12,205	3,742	3,896	2,164	2,345	2,397	4,236	6,443	7,737	1,962	3,382
Lafayette-West Lafayette, IN Metro Area	13,907	10,517	4,111	5,292	1,290	2,370	516	757	676	1,290	2,913	2,949	635	1,111
LaGrange, GA Micro Area	5,246	4,029	2,320	2,088	1,060	660	664	588	658	737	1,151	1,637	162	684
Lake Charles, LA Metro Area	16,548	11,021	4,874	5,636	1,811	2,786	936	1,209	722	1,618	3,099	3,730	1,026	1,235
Lake City, FL Micro Area	6,885	4,483	2,633	2,694	924	1,757	233	793	447	1,250	1,923	1,959	226	356
Lake Havasu City-Kingman, AZ Metro Area	32,061	22,488	10,808	11,022	5,290	6,312	1,461	2,235	1,868	2,933	6,295	5,979	1,643	2,531
Lakeland-Winter Haven, FL Metro Area	69,955	52,266	16,382	23,395	6,115	11,676	2,273	4,362	3,074	6,742	10,212	16,350	2,293	5,672
Lancaster, PA Metro Area	45,428	38,145	9,225	16,825	4,893	8,184	1,039	2,515	1,168	3,047	4,995	8,504	880	3,026
Lansing-East Lansing, MI Metro Area	37,578	24,756	9,333	12,059	3,771	6,022	1,675	2,215	2,103	3,605	5,271	6,983	1,601	2,713
Laredo, TX Metro Area	13,215	8,878	5,758	6,251	1,711	2,355	1,384	1,622	1,812	2,294	3,828	4,583	1,553	2,775
Las Cruces, NM Metro Area	17,066	12,450	5,205	7,042	1,913	2,724	633	1,641	642	1,754	3,093	5,189	790	1,909
Las Vegas-Henderson-Paradise, NV Metro Area	170,882	101,562	47,951	51,872	16,380	24,500	10,136	10,880	11,110	14,832	32,582	35,366	8,723	13,430
Laurel, MS Micro Area	8,258	5,470	2,675	3,073	1,104	1,587	376	566	427	871	1,679	2,169	602	634
Lawrence, KS Metro Area	6,850	4,985	1,177	2,159	414	1,172	197	209	42	523	755	1,338	211	605
Lawton, OK Metro Area	8,187	6,266	3,124	3,238	1,052	1,461	1,056	915	430	1,089	2,180	2,222	578	777
Lebanon, PA Metro Area	12,861	10,665	3,004	4,693	1,090	1,779	187	1,131	618	1,528	1,798	2,985	179	1,018
Lewiston, ID-WA Metro Area	6,365	5,172	2,658	2,932	1,107	1,243	532	506	919	807	1,335	1,879	507	331
Lewiston-Auburn, ME Metro Area	9,907	6,843	2,244	3,486	474	1,503	237	430	296	520	1,429	2,070	318	709
Lexington-Fayette, KY Metro Area	36,790	23,356	10,564	12,392	4,042	5,331	1,508	2,106	1,863	3,489	7,214	7,999	2,469	3,252
Lima, OH Metro Area	8,884	7,123	1,688	3,644	541	1,932	254	844	294	1,105	1,284	1,996	138	540
Lincoln, NE Metro Area	22,431	16,081	5,746	7,667	2,942	3,948	641	1,037	518	1,993	2,867	4,681	736	1,643
Little Rock-North Little Rock-Conway, AR Metro Area	57,508	37,834	18,585	20,537	6,936	9,176	3,360	3,788	5,290	4,589	11,916	14,501	3,716	4,978
Logan, UT-ID Metro Area	6,602	5,017	1,490	2,056	604	1,271	163	336	245	435	860	952	93	504
London, KY Micro Area	12,043	6,995	4,535	3,397	1,398	1,160	707	768	1,303	856	3,051	2,578	830	1,171
Longview, TX Metro Area	17,712	12,853	5,590	7,188	2,055	2,974	679	1,637	1,036	1,815	3,829	5,069	1,496	2,283
Longview, WA Metro Area	10,828	7,094	4,562	3,764	2,249	1,813	358	766	1,005	937	2,541	1,982	549	998
Los Angeles-Long Beach-Anaheim, CA Metro Area	911,759	702,055	209,278	357,327	57,925	147,311	38,793	70,801	49,480	121,937	133,258	246,917	50,779	133,393
Louisville/Jefferson County, KY-IN Metro Area	106,065	70,208	30,514	37,337	10,535	15,544	4,495	6,874	6,010	9,344	20,050	24,423	5,138	10,097
Lubbock, TX Metro Area	20,497	15,568	6,631	8,222	3,052	4,061	928	2,327	1,229	2,301	4,338	5,188	1,237	1,935
Lufkin, TX Micro Area	7,207	5,609	2,875	3,319	988	1,617	273	907	300	1,488	1,918	2,207	403	1,419
Lumberton, NC Micro Area	10,634	6,073	5,342	3,612	1,754	1,510	1,288	1,212	1,618	1,462	3,704	2,818	610	1,666
Lynchburg, VA Metro Area	25,474	18,623	7,164	8,586	2,592	3,953	1,209	1,927	1,657	1,856	4,024	5,144	830	2,333
Macon, GA Metro Area	19,868	12,507	6,899	6,804	1,858	3,067	1,233	1,171	2,271	1,962	4,712	4,606	1,756	1,426
Madera, CA Metro Area	11,258	7,834	4,351	4,470	1,909	2,842	1,688	1,784	837	1,505	3,205	3,086	1,044	1,623
Madison, WI Metro Area	46,646	31,687	9,230	14,459	3,787	5,918	1,029	2,632	1,553	3,173	4,343	8,106	1,148	2,949
Manchester-Nashua, NH Metro Area	32,137	21,583	6,082	10,813	2,800	4,908	1,018	1,814	987	2,998	4,041	6,565	1,394	3,080
Manhattan, KS Metro Area	4,632	4,142	831	1,617	259	766	90	157	45	382	553	916	59	521
Manitowoc, WI Micro Area	7,999	6,593	923	3,131	449	1,804	104	736	96	472	560	1,859	201	1,004
Mankato-North Mankato, MN Metro Area	6,833	5,538	1,164	2,661	280	1,532	204	362	328	696	831	1,625	338	787
Mansfield, OH Metro Area	11,868	9,508	2,979	4,392	904	1,988	659	622	590	1,187	1,960	2,950	438	1,095
Marinette, WI-MI Micro Area	7,639	5,842	1,891	2,636	1,069	1,249	141	381	287	615	1,003	1,424	258	673
Marion, IN Micro Area	6,720	4,871	2,236	2,364	1,073	1,233	475	240	694	581	1,542	1,848	637	646
Marion, OH Micro Area	5,918	4,777	1,428	2,845	758	1,854	129	520	212	507	1,083	1,695	194	624
Marquette, MI Micro Area	6,112	4,520	1,712	2,037	746	1,001	194	511	301	769	810	1,239	239	828
Marshall, TX Micro Area	5,767	4,074	1,602	1,966	360	1,021	76	632	473	359	956	1,302	281	535
Martinsville, VA Micro Area	7,971	5,945	2,601	3,551	955	2,121	475	817	784	1,142	1,417	2,272	595	1,144
McAllen-Edinburg-Mission, TX Metro Area	48,330	36,031	22,264	22,338	7,592	11,109	7,799	6,332	5,152	7,665	13,964	15,664	7,127	9,578
Meadville, PA Micro Area	9,255	6,371	2,723	2,863	1,397	1,711	514	426	510	348	1,275	1,388	120	579
Medford, OR Metro Area	24,721	17,123	6,839	9,013	3,398	4,636	744	2,102	1,472	2,417	3,691	5,504	843	1,459
Memphis, TN-MS-AR Metro Area	96,852	61,752	27,644	32,763	8,078	10,969	5,175	6,457	6,430	10,328	18,274	23,064	5,669	10,410
Merced, CA Metro Area	16,204	11,786	6,853	6,816	2,182	3,882	2,083	2,206	1,943	1,966	4,520	4,205	1,114	2,177
Meridian, MS Micro Area	8,814	6,975	3,968	4,267	1,802	1,758	1,028	1,045	1,333	1,669	2,714	2,470	710	1,086
Miami-Fort Lauderdale-West Palm Beach, FL Metro Area	520,352	473,386	112,668	223,340	31,060	85,212	22,798	43,602	26,449	72,925	70,418	148,634	19,319	72,964
Michigan City-La Porte, IN Metro Area	10,262	6,568	2,751	2,798	1,106	1,118	421	426	465	468	1,413	2,047	537	435
Midland, MI Metro Area	7,504	6,021	2,130	2,645	928	1,184	228	275	590	507	1,227	1,458	266	534
Midland, TX Metro Area	8,514	6,938	2,381	2,968	1,136	1,159	820	438	344	924	1,220	2,092	240	1,136

Table H-4: Metropolitan/Micropolitan Statistical Areas—Disability Status and Type of Disability—*Continued*

	Total Population		With a Disability		With a Hearing Disability		With a Vision Disability		With a Cognitive Disability		With an Ambulatory Disability		With a Self-Care Disability	
	65 to 74 Years	75 Years and Over	65 to 74 Years	75 Years and Over	65 to 74 Years	75 Years and Over	65 to 74 Years	75 Years and Over	65 to 74 Years	75 Years and Over	65 to 74 Years	75 Years and Over	65 to 74 Years	75 Years and Over
Milwaukee-Waukesha-West Allis, WI Metro Area..	116,737	94,610	24,858	45,060	9,401	19,780	3,401	8,380	4,440	10,658	15,112	30,444	4,370	11,737
Minneapolis-St. Paul-Bloomington, MN-WI Metro Area	243,830	171,150	50,345	79,084	21,899	35,657	6,754	13,411	10,295	21,153	25,607	48,940	8,463	19,817
Minot, ND Micro Area	4,636	4,229	873	2,081	587	952	57	18	43	148	297	1,182	75	158
Missoula, MT Metro Area	9,235	5,571	2,330	3,459	1,363	2,168	153	1,289	241	920	1,101	2,452	109	762
Mobile, AL Metro Area	34,746	23,799	9,526	13,058	3,468	4,773	1,355	2,463	2,331	4,378	6,113	9,705	1,251	4,822
Modesto, CA Metro Area	36,565	26,014	11,722	15,667	4,468	7,878	2,781	2,670	2,913	4,530	6,938	10,776	1,324	5,147
Monroe, LA Metro Area	13,667	9,986	3,549	4,824	994	2,114	492	747	648	1,177	2,245	3,565	502	1,752
Monroe, MI Metro Area	13,508	9,547	2,492	4,338	946	2,196	464	964	515	934	1,574	2,897	312	1,127
Montgomery, AL Metro Area	28,520	20,837	9,224	10,667	2,997	4,421	1,111	2,533	1,882	3,264	5,793	8,353	1,513	3,449
Morehead City, NC Micro Area	9,206	5,765	2,800	2,901	985	1,335	148	982	374	537	1,833	1,924	492	493
Morgantown, WV Metro Area	9,636	6,753	2,759	3,601	1,230	1,741	455	672	782	1,044	2,052	2,434	570	914
Morristown, TN Metro Area	12,809	7,720	4,084	3,977	1,279	1,571	666	600	695	825	2,671	2,628	532	809
Moses Lake, WA Micro Area	6,920	4,518	1,673	2,763	547	1,377	98	444	327	793	831	1,743	214	578
Mount Airy, NC Micro Area	7,643	5,570	2,785	2,732	1,017	1,196	690	474	542	943	2,031	2,032	400	935
Mount Pleasant, MI Micro Area	4,309	2,959	1,171	1,849	771	1,079	43	293	511	345	479	1,138	132	492
Mount Vernon-Anacortes, WA Metro Area	13,349	9,036	3,240	4,452	1,545	2,259	627	559	944	1,599	1,749	2,849	610	981
Muncie, IN Metro Area	10,350	7,523	2,450	4,372	1,254	2,724	689	836	463	1,738	1,446	2,548	660	1,085
Muskegon, MI Metro Area	14,540	10,585	3,568	5,349	1,013	2,376	323	904	893	930	2,359	3,041	518	946
Muskogee, OK Metro Area	6,066	4,379	2,244	2,575	984	1,079	350	495	435	490	1,405	2,036	489	988
Myrtle Beach-Conway-North Myrtle Beach, SC-NC Metro Area	61,181	30,817	17,055	16,051	6,737	8,185	2,899	2,960	3,747	4,082	10,743	10,728	3,599	4,778
Nacogdoches, TX Micro Area	4,421	3,633	1,502	1,948	528	645	169	502	361	626	1,161	1,347	309	614
Napa, CA Metro Area	14,295	9,433	2,310	5,279	930	3,039	218	710	297	1,145	1,389	3,230	258	1,255
Naples-Immokalee-Marco Island, FL Metro Area ..	53,154	48,118	8,132	16,107	2,985	8,061	1,377	1,917	1,058	3,918	4,303	8,659	610	2,870
Nashville-Davidson–Murfreesboro–Franklin, TN Metro Area	131,257	82,015	33,955	42,126	13,502	18,902	6,278	8,251	7,800	12,834	21,288	29,374	5,524	11,377
New Bern, NC Metro Area	13,467	9,827	4,600	5,464	2,219	2,416	693	588	534	1,550	2,631	3,688	478	1,351
New Castle, PA Micro Area	8,889	7,945	2,091	3,596	1,101	1,993	253	479	239	584	1,053	2,315	195	1,063
New Haven-Milford, CT Metro Area	72,282	56,291	15,537	26,930	5,582	11,612	1,905	4,804	3,638	6,040	9,375	17,558	3,836	7,757
New Orleans-Metairie, LA Metro Area	101,782	66,566	27,224	33,623	8,876	11,996	4,750	7,537	5,447	9,959	16,252	23,707	4,922	10,564
New Philadelphia-Dover, OH Micro Area	8,735	7,240	2,263	3,430	1,052	2,015	499	811	451	635	1,131	2,189	603	490
New York-Newark-Jersey City, NY-NJ-PA Metro Area	1,545,534	1,197,768	337,174	589,995	90,313	226,292	62,913	122,768	72,592	176,944	224,477	417,589	62,492	201,572
Niles-Benton Harbor, MI Metro Area	14,994	11,590	3,299	5,236	1,559	2,198	472	758	694	1,269	1,520	3,278	391	893
North Port-Sarasota-Bradenton, FL Metro Area	117,976	103,432	22,206	42,794	8,770	22,498	2,608	5,688	3,686	10,591	13,233	25,853	2,408	11,554
North Wilkesboro, NC Micro Area	7,942	5,359	2,070	3,095	738	1,334	501	603	459	893	1,458	2,425	412	1,237
Norwich-New London, CT Metro Area	24,393	18,052	4,585	8,698	1,738	3,884	821	1,262	952	2,078	3,198	6,109	1,152	2,729
Oak Harbor, WA Micro Area	11,059	6,858	2,313	3,484	1,160	1,914	426	539	493	871	1,437	2,143	465	955
Ocala, FL Metro Area	52,703	40,301	13,718	17,409	4,206	8,775	1,622	4,209	2,400	5,073	9,865	12,405	2,062	4,091
Ocean City, NJ Metro Area	12,859	9,354	2,410	4,721	778	1,845	411	722	674	1,020	1,540	3,195	660	1,020
Odessa, TX Metro Area	8,175	6,234	2,916	3,574	880	1,859	932	673	495	1,102	1,683	2,125	181	867
Ogden-Clearfield, UT Metro Area	36,751	26,463	8,104	13,436	3,669	7,035	1,369	2,842	1,361	2,722	4,165	8,682	1,107	3,354
Ogdensburg-Massena, NY Micro Area	9,694	6,345	3,736	3,380	1,418	1,959	712	1,013	756	928	2,470	1,835	446	1,024
Oklahoma City, OK Metro Area	97,560	67,509	30,260	36,334	12,022	16,972	4,161	7,553	5,180	11,235	19,338	26,357	4,064	10,812
Olean, NY Micro Area	7,487	5,373	2,161	2,804	721	1,630	198	461	546	825	1,452	1,275	334	334
Olympia-Tumwater, WA Metro Area	24,010	15,525	5,657	8,164	2,616	4,342	577	2,039	620	2,960	3,141	5,332	547	2,361
Omaha-Council Bluffs, NE-IA Metro Area	62,117	44,626	13,821	22,559	5,927	11,453	2,241	4,327	2,473	6,280	8,247	12,713	2,129	5,497
Opelousas, LA Micro Area	6,875	4,822	1,791	2,583	549	708	214	631	326	815	890	1,862	334	1,233
Orangeburg, SC Micro Area	8,971	5,953	3,548	3,951	1,124	1,256	1,286	892	1,056	1,559	2,619	3,193	1,078	1,638
Orlando-Kissimmee-Sanford, FL Metro Area	185,289	130,148	45,512	63,388	13,679	27,095	9,695	13,179	10,861	20,419	27,080	45,249	5,682	16,750
Oshkosh-Neenah, WI Metro Area	13,225	11,074	3,630	4,861	1,442	2,183	822	1,007	853	1,506	1,878	3,091	382	970
Ottawa-Peru, IL Micro Area	14,362	11,829	3,842	5,315	1,399	2,389	332	812	849	1,094	2,258	2,969	528	1,314
Owensboro, KY Metro Area	10,654	7,779	3,022	4,171	756	1,832	367	569	1,029	1,243	2,042	3,288	478	1,178
Owosso, MI Micro Area	6,482	4,909	1,655	2,451	627	1,121	276	600	135	667	1,073	1,421	168	782
Oxnard-Thousand Oaks-Ventura, CA Metro Area ..	65,271	48,253	14,759	24,848	5,182	11,678	1,896	4,232	3,726	7,085	8,630	17,002	2,801	8,392
Paducah, KY-IL Micro Area	10,188	7,085	3,370	3,834	1,753	1,908	700	486	618	686	1,962	2,487	188	913
Palatka, FL Micro Area	8,515	6,075	2,171	2,896	980	1,109	304	673	651	811	1,471	1,568	719	708
Palm Bay-Melbourne-Titusville, FL Metro Area	66,810	57,233	16,515	26,676	6,499	12,982	1,813	4,626	3,540	6,555	9,084	17,241	2,646	6,485
Panama City, FL Metro Area	18,095	12,864	7,046	8,671	2,441	4,460	1,236	1,867	2,089	2,885	5,391	6,240	2,163	2,460
Parkersburg-Vienna, WV Metro Area	9,928	7,050	2,240	4,048	1,057	1,749	263	446	304	1,271	1,424	2,289	550	721
Pensacola-Ferry Pass-Brent, FL Metro Area	41,724	29,046	10,628	16,276	4,271	7,301	1,185	3,091	3,054	4,539	6,276	11,823	2,123	4,439
Peoria, IL Metro Area	32,467	25,292	7,042	11,971	2,802	5,655	1,204	1,909	1,549	2,137	4,311	7,542	1,303	1,990
Philadelphia-Camden-Wilmington, PA-NJ-DE-MD Metro Area	478,816	369,819	112,758	174,028	34,133	72,901	20,213	30,254	23,760	49,372	72,651	116,427	20,122	44,333
Phoenix-Mesa-Scottsdale, AZ Metro Area	370,234	260,110	88,661	123,705	36,749	62,792	15,743	28,154	17,406	35,612	52,796	80,937	13,189	32,497
Pine Bluff, AR Metro Area	7,988	5,811	3,313	3,873	1,285	2,191	717	568	483	871	2,062	2,685	283	857
Pinehurst-Southern Pines, NC Micro Area	12,001	9,451	2,135	3,261	988	1,623	229	213	357	408	1,115	1,934	695	907
Pittsburgh, PA Metro Area	224,973	194,447	50,292	93,680	18,981	44,456	5,082	16,545	10,399	24,696	30,436	58,273	7,692	21,897
Pittsfield, MA Metro Area	14,310	10,887	2,594	4,483	1,180	1,888	514	826	602	827	1,377	3,133	453	1,494
Plattsburgh, NY Micro Area	6,876	4,929	1,917	2,126	863	874	398	591	199	656	1,011	1,207	296	730
Pocatello, ID Metro Area	6,222	4,246	1,625	2,186	902	1,467	206	432	565	552	650	1,104	66	526
Port Angeles, WA Micro Area	10,929	8,132	2,982	4,263	1,154	2,024	127	1,248	215	1,316	1,987	2,828	160	712
Port St. Lucie, FL Metro Area	57,121	51,474	13,487	24,224	4,465	12,629	2,786	3,184	3,501	4,606	8,567	15,522	2,221	6,334
Portland-South Portland, ME Metro Area	51,183	36,242	10,761	18,009	4,358	8,654	1,219	4,072	1,865	4,455	6,192	11,844	2,067	4,026
Portland-Vancouver-Hillsboro, OR-WA Metro Area	186,555	119,811	47,489	62,729	20,108	33,703	6,767	13,291	10,165	19,328	27,588	40,548	7,199	16,885

Table H-4: Metropolitan/Micropolitan Statistical Areas—Disability Status and Type of Disability—Continued

	Total Population		With a Disability		With a Hearing Disability		With a Vision Disability		With a Cognitive Disability		With an Ambulatory Disability		With a Self-Care Disability	
	65 to 74 Years	75 Years and Over	65 to 74 Years	75 Years and Over	65 to 74 Years	75 Years and Over	65 to 74 Years	75 Years and Over	65 to 74 Years	75 Years and Over	65 to 74 Years	75 Years and Over	65 to 74 Years	75 Years and Over
Portsmouth, OH Micro Area	6,839	5,158	2,559	3,160	1,123	2,231	286	682	358	992	1,377	1,887	346	1,151
Pottsville, PA Micro Area	14,739	12,189	4,483	6,184	1,830	2,791	758	1,134	694	1,652	2,621	3,709	339	1,750
Prescott, AZ Metro Area	36,601	24,362	7,511	11,473	2,866	5,571	1,567	2,672	2,503	2,608	4,314	7,362	1,024	1,914
Providence-Warwick, RI-MA Metro Area	136,531	106,319	33,495	54,092	11,381	24,262	6,036	9,866	7,294	13,967	20,590	35,973	5,969	14,529
Provo-Orem, UT Metro Area	24,027	16,881	5,978	7,281	3,180	3,647	1,153	1,646	1,436	1,929	3,739	4,315	1,032	1,624
Pueblo, CO Metro Area	15,107	11,332	5,191	5,584	1,922	3,381	1,163	1,175	1,313	1,599	3,112	3,547	951	1,230
Punta Gorda, FL Metro Area	33,584	28,446	7,099	13,477	2,705	7,449	1,249	1,380	1,213	4,264	3,970	7,082	953	2,222
Quincy, IL-MO Micro Area	7,212	5,819	1,352	2,719	533	896	184	500	297	247	1,046	1,578	348	399
Racine, WI Metro Area	16,348	12,651	4,143	5,470	2,032	2,127	171	776	441	1,088	2,216	3,145	592	1,433
Raleigh, NC Metro Area	81,162	47,449	19,684	23,882	6,200	10,785	3,919	4,699	3,801	6,866	12,221	15,703	3,506	6,987
Rapid City, SD Metro Area	12,238	8,773	3,059	4,155	1,109	2,132	79	580	604	888	2,127	3,051	547	699
Reading, PA Metro Area	35,492	28,417	7,849	13,079	2,319	6,101	884	2,375	1,087	3,746	4,654	8,318	942	3,092
Redding, CA Metro Area	20,036	14,021	6,272	7,794	2,606	4,560	888	2,421	1,793	2,528	3,664	5,197	1,360	2,181
Reno, NV Metro Area	40,870	24,162	10,031	11,808	3,931	5,923	1,516	2,446	2,457	2,689	6,033	6,934	1,018	1,945
Richmond, IN Micro Area	6,619	5,172	1,858	2,741	910	1,167	379	701	625	638	1,083	2,062	173	658
Richmond, VA Metro Area	101,708	66,676	21,904	31,194	6,003	12,026	2,678	6,669	3,342	7,951	14,086	22,885	3,426	9,587
Richmond-Berea, KY Micro Area	8,499	5,068	2,690	3,063	1,261	1,584	644	732	603	954	1,405	2,000	262	930
Riverside-San Bernardino-Ontario, CA Metro Area	301,973	215,678	79,769	110,603	28,559	50,300	14,049	23,028	18,651	31,857	50,971	73,890	17,369	35,035
Roanoke Rapids, NC Micro Area	7,460	6,074	2,608	3,750	512	1,223	111	527	470	808	2,180	2,320	679	697
Roanoke, VA Metro Area	32,299	23,715	8,718	11,596	2,846	5,847	1,144	2,411	1,192	3,305	4,735	7,103	1,435	2,122
Rochester, MN Metro Area	16,436	13,924	3,480	5,777	1,231	3,043	393	1,086	604	1,110	2,068	3,122	516	1,043
Rochester, NY Metro Area	95,890	71,167	23,353	34,876	9,985	14,751	3,647	4,878	4,555	9,816	13,707	23,143	3,182	7,432
Rockford, IL Metro Area	30,292	21,023	8,948	11,820	3,297	5,084	1,598	2,298	1,396	2,798	5,690	7,567	1,695	2,831
Rocky Mount, NC Metro Area	14,382	9,613	4,614	5,683	1,414	2,450	507	752	1,273	1,747	2,966	4,284	547	1,581
Rome, GA Metro Area	7,827	6,350	2,863	3,576	1,432	1,409	844	360	485	949	1,644	2,700	386	1,353
Roseburg, OR Micro Area	13,949	10,914	3,561	6,442	1,503	3,342	285	1,057	1,179	1,679	1,944	3,830	731	993
Roswell, NM Micro Area	5,559	4,092	2,620	2,201	912	1,152	295	821	966	756	1,799	1,052	417	489
Russellville, AR Micro Area	7,222	5,375	2,059	3,285	1,425	1,895	572	1,296	756	855	1,310	1,924	612	701
Sacramento–Roseville–Arden-Arcade, CA Metro Area	178,031	130,047	42,646	70,393	15,904	35,373	6,803	13,196	10,027	21,698	23,841	44,906	7,410	21,045
Saginaw, MI Metro Area	18,096	14,139	5,097	6,605	2,413	2,841	1,026	1,310	1,104	2,273	3,141	4,337	899	1,567
Salem, OH Micro Area	10,628	7,600	2,706	3,596	1,152	2,184	579	819	531	649	1,463	1,987	207	836
Salem, OR Metro Area	35,230	24,443	8,570	13,805	3,053	7,014	987	2,616	1,784	4,870	5,213	8,371	1,364	3,935
Salinas, CA Metro Area	28,351	21,486	5,907	12,461	1,876	5,675	1,002	2,124	1,397	4,794	3,840	8,375	895	4,233
Salisbury, MD-DE Metro Area	49,501	29,994	9,509	13,843	3,927	6,716	1,265	2,845	2,148	3,662	5,077	9,233	1,139	3,029
Salt Lake City, UT Metro Area	64,644	43,909	15,417	22,154	6,930	11,485	2,007	3,773	2,692	5,589	8,198	13,924	2,001	5,507
San Angelo, TX Metro Area	8,886	8,094	2,633	5,104	1,183	2,304	648	1,318	452	1,282	1,468	3,836	353	1,626
San Antonio-New Braunfels, TX Metro Area	162,224	111,574	50,760	63,657	20,628	28,533	7,463	14,322	11,976	18,837	31,591	40,615	9,485	17,875
San Diego-Carlsbad, CA Metro Area	229,799	178,670	53,272	91,864	16,140	41,786	10,275	18,555	15,792	29,963	31,431	60,462	10,909	27,799
San Francisco-Oakland-Hayward, CA Metro Area	361,688	269,542	70,420	133,816	23,082	56,965	13,581	24,330	15,477	41,727	42,458	88,912	13,227	44,090
San Jose-Sunnyvale-Santa Clara, CA Metro Area	132,581	100,698	26,705	51,852	8,263	21,585	3,567	9,308	6,366	15,067	14,873	34,739	5,663	17,950
San Luis Obispo-Paso Robles-Arroyo Grande, CA Metro Area	28,506	19,858	6,063	10,267	2,871	5,531	748	1,683	1,384	3,010	3,732	6,228	1,426	2,298
Sandusky, OH Micro Area	8,216	5,836	1,970	2,832	894	1,057	482	673	192	688	981	1,458	69	770
Santa Cruz-Watsonville, CA Metro Area	22,519	13,273	3,997	5,092	1,487	2,337	449	830	782	1,242	2,184	3,397	496	1,002
Santa Fe, NM Metro Area	18,667	10,198	4,213	4,667	2,261	2,449	634	1,286	1,178	1,013	1,883	2,494	656	665
Santa Maria-Santa Barbara, CA Metro Area	31,781	28,290	6,434	14,368	2,516	7,555	728	3,528	1,408	4,214	3,763	7,899	785	3,435
Santa Rosa, CA Metro Area	49,600	31,352	10,168	15,849	3,707	8,234	1,226	2,849	2,062	3,871	5,788	10,465	1,995	3,982
Savannah, GA Metro Area	28,560	17,871	7,871	10,714	2,709	4,099	1,206	1,879	1,060	3,272	5,571	7,561	1,930	3,201
Scranton–Wilkes-Barre–Hazleton, PA Metro Area	54,830	46,003	13,975	25,654	5,339	11,920	1,833	5,325	2,349	6,045	8,647	16,872	2,160	6,862
Searcy, AR Micro Area	6,547	5,018	2,379	2,647	843	1,483	508	392	635	811	1,463	1,799	574	670
Seattle-Tacoma-Bellevue, WA Metro Area	263,469	176,357	64,767	90,584	25,968	44,029	11,054	16,594	16,427	28,146	37,213	57,551	10,474	27,576
Sebastian-Vero Beach, FL Metro Area	21,964	21,445	4,379	8,650	1,910	4,069	605	1,664	797	2,378	2,207	4,791	707	2,039
Sebring, FL Metro Area	16,690	15,910	4,624	7,302	1,120	3,775	678	953	1,042	1,763	2,830	4,520	392	1,315
Seneca, SC Micro Area	9,788	6,029	3,296	3,665	1,609	1,310	502	596	585	1,230	1,946	2,129	318	883
Sevierville, TN Micro Area	10,732	5,959	3,116	2,750	862	1,465	356	733	271	576	2,298	1,406	758	725
Shawnee, OK Micro Area	6,368	4,661	2,868	2,997	1,503	1,356	317	325	431	507	1,636	1,924	508	407
Sheboygan, WI Metro Area	9,723	8,047	1,533	2,899	662	1,255	343	528	301	566	859	1,633	212	558
Shelby, NC Micro Area	9,822	6,830	3,801	3,545	1,777	1,882	1,478	881	466	1,117	2,342	2,438	1,199	1,279
Sherman-Denison, TX Metro Area	12,009	8,026	3,363	4,096	1,623	2,567	832	654	1,094	1,071	2,069	2,462	703	838
Show Low, AZ Micro Area	10,768	6,118	3,893	3,783	1,791	2,432	1,340	1,180	847	1,504	2,368	2,434	534	970
Shreveport-Bossier City, LA Metro Area	36,698	25,537	11,710	12,886	4,032	5,387	2,903	2,122	3,132	3,967	7,801	9,136	2,274	4,627
Sierra Vista-Douglas, AZ Metro Area	14,323	10,482	4,469	5,652	2,189	3,441	1,107	1,561	1,162	2,216	2,584	3,164	1,009	1,770
Sioux City, IA-NE-SD Metro Area	13,668	10,359	3,152	5,151	1,281	2,601	319	651	691	765	1,859	3,071	599	955
Sioux Falls, SD Metro Area	17,039	12,154	3,430	5,598	1,239	2,750	244	1,055	579	2,170	2,050	3,549	907	1,453
Somerset, PA Micro Area	8,172	6,630	2,154	2,957	1,012	1,437	269	501	445	565	1,087	1,777	180	605
South Bend-Mishawaka, IN-MI Metro Area	26,065	20,894	6,782	10,467	2,546	5,272	861	1,516	934	2,142	3,998	7,068	696	2,445
Spartanburg, SC Metro Area	29,196	18,949	8,810	10,872	3,118	4,883	1,035	2,125	2,070	2,173	5,796	6,400	713	2,737
Spokane-Spokane Valley, WA Metro Area	49,848	32,371	13,980	18,253	6,998	9,703	1,965	3,737	2,961	6,420	7,662	11,420	1,758	5,908
Springfield, IL Metro Area	18,227	14,583	4,703	6,992	1,836	2,940	719	1,484	658	1,316	2,909	4,573	906	1,112
Springfield, MA Metro Area	52,002	39,069	12,449	20,081	4,583	8,206	1,894	3,043	2,336	6,216	6,929	12,584	2,570	6,271
Springfield, MO Metro Area	37,973	29,372	10,743	13,579	4,458	6,040	1,503	2,247	1,563	4,468	5,642	8,901	1,096	3,329
Springfield, OH Metro Area	13,645	9,361	3,483	4,129	1,697	2,334	880	821	855	1,408	2,011	3,147	659	1,025
St. Cloud, MN Metro Area	13,252	11,036	2,271	4,852	1,281	2,295	311	1,014	608	811	1,357	2,598	392	778
St. George, UT Metro Area	16,266	13,456	4,652	7,107	2,287	3,251	1,011	1,542	1,019	1,770	2,438	4,713	492	1,431

Table H-4: Metropolitan/Micropolitan Statistical Areas—Disability Status and Type of Disability—*Continued*

	Total Population		With a Disability		With a Hearing Disability		With a Vision Disability		With a Cognitive Disability		With an Ambulatory Disability		With a Self-Care Disability	
	65 to 74 Years	75 Years and Over	65 to 74 Years	75 Years and Over	65 to 74 Years	75 Years and Over	65 to 74 Years	75 Years and Over	65 to 74 Years	75 Years and Over	65 to 74 Years	75 Years and Over	65 to 74 Years	75 Years and Over
St. Joseph, MO-KS Metro Area	10,368	8,023	2,734	3,732	1,131	1,747	736	573	288	545	1,426	2,332	135	753
St. Louis, MO-IL Metro Area	229,016	172,081	56,080	80,870	20,947	32,684	9,644	16,182	10,719	21,876	33,962	51,114	8,337	19,409
State College, PA Metro Area	10,721	8,446	2,626	4,200	987	1,922	236	838	490	1,256	1,414	2,670	419	1,359
Statesboro, GA Micro Area	4,455	2,786	1,477	1,280	412	623	377	278	513	463	863	1,011	284	394
Staunton-Waynesboro, VA Metro Area	13,374	8,936	3,070	3,481	1,223	1,300	614	710	250	603	1,792	2,528	215	1,015
Stevens Point, WI Micro Area	5,763	4,301	785	1,841	369	1,051	62	185	67	434	448	913	83	307
Stillwater, OK Micro Area	4,995	3,671	949	2,450	211	1,107	304	634	101	371	677	1,681	18	669
Stockton-Lodi, CA Metro Area	48,091	33,253	12,940	18,702	4,437	8,523	1,535	3,282	3,309	4,801	8,957	11,522	2,673	5,243
Sumter, SC Metro Area	8,764	6,195	3,803	3,568	1,407	1,539	893	1,041	1,428	1,365	2,356	2,323	919	1,372
Sunbury, PA Micro Area	9,738	7,943	1,790	4,692	758	2,271	328	1,240	150	915	832	2,848	73	1,250
Syracuse, NY Metro Area	54,709	42,046	12,400	19,578	4,715	9,750	2,299	4,126	2,184	5,336	6,756	12,584	2,098	5,406
Talladega-Sylacauga, AL Micro Area	9,487	5,309	3,615	3,028	1,226	1,224	705	745	407	905	2,803	1,797	734	804
Tallahassee, FL Metro Area	27,112	17,328	7,708	9,984	2,980	4,711	1,451	1,940	2,034	3,085	4,926	6,451	1,374	2,269
Tampa-St. Petersburg-Clearwater, FL Metro Area	297,112	236,045	70,390	111,825	26,231	51,081	9,606	20,211	14,252	31,283	43,871	74,597	13,025	30,005
Terre Haute, IN Metro Area	14,735	10,036	4,676	6,245	1,628	2,973	1,034	970	944	1,100	2,925	3,751	1,087	972
Texarkana, TX-AR Metro Area	13,096	8,992	3,692	5,363	1,731	2,071	773	926	917	2,075	2,008	4,064	904	1,775
The Villages, FL Metro Area	38,317	21,276	5,651	10,340	3,315	6,154	1,262	1,094	942	772	2,015	4,579	583	908
Toledo, OH Metro Area	48,699	36,325	12,853	18,134	5,228	8,851	2,122	2,949	2,615	3,888	7,926	11,307	3,035	4,545
Topeka, KS Metro Area	20,609	16,075	6,218	7,363	2,688	3,713	770	1,131	1,189	1,805	3,210	4,582	936	2,117
Torrington, CT Micro Area	19,469	13,602	3,080	5,121	951	2,775	133	884	416	1,634	1,781	2,594	433	1,362
Traverse City, MI Micro Area	16,578	11,928	3,015	5,010	1,403	2,390	232	596	485	897	1,500	3,196	539	1,035
Trenton, NJ Metro Area	28,054	21,527	5,284	9,972	1,153	3,625	770	1,601	1,459	2,514	3,343	6,604	898	3,127
Truckee-Grass Valley, CA Micro Area	13,697	9,047	3,233	3,544	1,780	1,728	388	607	544	886	1,517	2,634	588	1,425
Tucson, AZ Metro Area	99,643	75,661	27,713	35,477	11,846	17,988	4,770	6,354	5,710	8,635	14,296	23,969	4,171	9,532
Tullahoma-Manchester, TN Micro Area	10,877	7,014	3,741	4,439	1,600	2,014	764	602	804	1,428	2,721	2,238	449	1,033
Tulsa, OK Metro Area	78,587	54,773	22,859	29,275	9,300	15,684	4,132	5,092	4,740	6,708	13,197	19,301	3,810	6,951
Tupelo, MS Micro Area	11,349	8,000	4,462	4,873	1,375	2,746	970	1,426	1,160	1,609	2,582	3,666	744	1,308
Tuscaloosa, AL Metro Area	17,046	11,986	5,679	6,623	1,798	2,551	729	1,398	990	2,499	4,344	4,843	693	2,225
Twin Falls, ID Micro Area	8,735	6,245	2,179	3,296	715	1,606	538	785	355	1,122	1,002	2,142	276	1,030
Tyler, TX Metro Area	18,908	14,074	4,755	7,243	1,201	3,112	989	989	1,126	1,533	2,709	4,771	750	2,051
Ukiah, CA Micro Area	10,701	5,949	3,845	3,176	1,680	1,935	811	699	853	1,413	2,094	2,034	937	924
Urban Honolulu, HI Metro Area	82,586	71,000	17,034	38,023	5,319	18,225	2,310	4,878	4,615	13,610	10,939	25,488	3,393	10,803
Utica-Rome, NY Metro Area	27,948	21,347	8,339	11,609	2,663	4,980	1,630	2,145	2,231	2,835	5,599	6,947	1,677	2,638
Valdosta, GA Metro Area	10,830	6,118	3,910	3,130	1,065	1,845	969	463	547	1,144	2,969	2,325	549	639
Vallejo-Fairfield, CA Metro Area	34,155	23,187	8,011	10,692	2,857	4,847	666	1,930	1,710	3,290	5,372	6,384	1,246	3,211
Victoria, TX Metro Area	8,138	6,065	2,726	3,536	1,286	2,285	433	728	775	899	1,724	1,946	597	743
Vineland-Bridgeton, NJ Metro Area	11,839	8,471	3,117	4,326	710	1,995	379	534	373	846	2,379	2,792	579	1,274
Virginia Beach-Norfolk-Newport News, VA-NC Metro Area	129,763	87,579	30,605	44,382	8,288	17,776	3,914	7,463	5,880	12,899	19,940	29,892	5,520	11,191
Visalia-Porterville, CA Metro Area	26,920	18,842	7,695	9,691	2,221	4,280	680	1,592	2,251	2,362	5,615	6,801	1,358	2,579
Waco, TX Metro Area	19,074	14,555	5,548	7,705	2,493	3,769	1,215	1,742	754	2,082	3,796	5,115	1,260	1,865
Walla Walla, WA Metro Area	5,299	4,550	1,579	2,249	894	1,172	381	398	314	290	973	1,310	471	267
Warner Robins, GA Metro Area	12,567	9,152	2,999	4,421	1,213	1,947	428	898	491	1,207	2,029	2,967	295	920
Warsaw, IN Micro Area	6,851	4,678	1,801	1,999	844	584	221	389	265	497	879	1,307	122	499
Washington-Arlington-Alexandria, DC-VA-MD-WV Metro Area	410,618	262,777	82,073	123,277	24,232	49,024	11,905	23,465	15,186	35,961	52,468	80,864	13,599	33,983
Waterloo-Cedar Falls, IA Metro Area	13,544	11,964	3,219	4,604	1,366	1,808	434	866	345	611	1,919	3,123	376	1,115
Watertown-Fort Atkinson, WI Micro Area	7,137	5,044	1,287	1,788	560	734	0	126	191	77	758	1,218	180	410
Watertown-Fort Drum, NY Metro Area	8,315	5,998	2,206	3,016	1,062	1,320	670	461	511	497	1,500	1,637	632	683
Wausau, WI Metro Area	11,414	9,286	2,307	4,331	1,262	2,319	431	542	156	834	1,077	3,116	206	1,311
Weirton-Steubenville, WV-OH Metro Area	12,465	10,729	4,073	5,652	2,096	3,007	466	1,864	316	1,697	2,656	3,790	607	1,048
Wenatchee, WA Metro Area	11,100	8,004	2,684	3,934	1,170	2,557	617	1,135	563	1,732	1,466	2,540	367	1,148
Wheeling, WV-OH Metro Area	14,779	11,698	4,553	4,840	1,799	2,680	954	1,188	674	800	3,000	2,410	630	1,046
Whitewater-Elkhorn, WI Micro Area	8,858	6,239	1,833	2,912	1,179	1,755	119	323	208	1,081	862	1,949	88	730
Wichita Falls, TX Metro Area	11,108	9,635	3,397	5,362	1,056	2,780	751	1,357	420	1,842	2,622	3,989	764	1,238
Wichita, KS Metro Area	46,824	36,491	12,250	15,773	4,658	7,134	1,739	3,107	2,611	5,086	7,784	9,706	2,278	4,031
Williamsport, PA Metro Area	11,027	8,518	3,190	4,895	1,499	2,180	293	852	615	939	1,568	2,995	491	1,097
Wilmington, NC Metro Area	25,667	16,623	5,996	8,157	2,432	4,712	1,023	2,197	1,166	2,927	3,723	4,924	1,145	2,799
Wilson, NC Micro Area	7,623	5,072	2,096	2,809	617	1,354	194	414	603	641	1,499	1,404	759	586
Winchester, VA-WV Metro Area	12,457	8,819	3,046	4,457	838	2,221	160	1,598	646	1,832	2,012	3,460	554	1,573
Winston-Salem, NC Metro Area	58,419	41,390	14,246	19,780	4,340	8,874	2,668	3,175	2,664	4,981	8,771	12,269	1,897	4,872
Wisconsin Rapids-Marshfield, WI Micro Area	7,198	6,546	1,201	2,660	554	1,130	69	456	224	553	472	1,884	180	932
Wooster, OH Micro Area	10,188	7,341	2,229	2,911	867	1,242	370	494	487	565	1,193	1,401	188	413
Worcester, MA-CT Metro Area	72,697	53,337	15,087	27,550	5,532	13,350	2,055	5,074	3,361	7,174	8,956	16,663	3,123	7,531
Yakima, WA Metro Area	17,924	12,721	5,882	7,405	1,910	3,700	236	1,439	1,279	1,963	4,020	4,982	1,283	1,886
York-Hanover, PA Metro Area	39,976	28,343	10,108	12,121	4,804	5,311	1,122	1,895	1,966	2,432	6,560	7,860	1,701	2,960
Youngstown-Warren-Boardman, OH-PA Metro Area	55,785	46,510	13,250	22,984	5,031	10,572	2,011	4,310	2,518	6,198	7,692	15,792	1,548	6,530
Yuba City, CA Metro Area	12,848	9,541	4,106	4,811	1,804	2,179	718	984	1,297	1,258	2,308	3,129	919	1,552
Yuma, AZ Metro Area	18,552	17,185	5,682	7,745	1,664	4,022	712	1,436	939	1,856	3,844	4,903	1,217	1,397
Zanesville, OH Micro Area	7,809	6,071	2,816	3,706	878	2,185	766	943	745	847	1,454	2,660	681	1,436

Table H-5: 114th Congressional Districts—Disability Status and Type of Disability

	Total Population		With a Disability		With a Hearing Disability		With a Vision Disability		With a Cognitive Disability		With an Ambulatory Disability		With a Self-Care Disability	
	65 to 74 Years	75 Years and Over	65 to 74 Years	75 Years and Over	65 to 74 Years	75 Years and Over	65 to 74 Years	75 Years and Over	65 to 74 Years	75 Years and Over	65 to 74 Years	75 Years and Over	65 to 74 Years	75 Years and Over
Alabama														
Congressional District 1.......	65,784	44,909	17,618	24,552	6,641	9,597	2,047	4,638	3,424	7,308	11,642	17,876	2,888	7,618
Congressional District 2.......	59,610	42,421	20,896	23,882	8,065	10,638	3,142	5,684	4,978	7,310	12,939	17,174	3,233	6,668
Congressional District 3.......	63,166	40,006	20,477	21,547	7,091	9,807	3,669	5,200	4,774	5,603	13,777	15,389	3,661	6,338
Congressional District 4.......	67,899	45,646	25,840	29,050	9,616	14,024	4,736	6,330	6,986	8,954	16,508	19,674	4,833	8,780
Congressional District 5.......	60,085	42,952	19,300	23,479	7,602	11,248	2,780	5,301	5,142	6,039	11,362	14,113	3,656	6,034
Congressional District 6.......	61,987	41,971	14,685	21,948	4,694	8,873	1,848	3,667	3,438	7,039	8,392	15,439	2,608	7,286
Congressional District 7.......	51,732	37,001	19,479	20,693	6,353	7,017	4,164	4,920	4,575	7,374	14,742	15,181	3,535	7,434
Alaska														
Congressional District (at Large)...........................	46,028	22,990	15,155	13,206	8,119	6,812	2,663	3,417	2,491	4,318	7,992	8,153	2,527	5,276
Arizona														
Congressional District 1.......	74,773	45,214	20,061	21,742	9,134	12,336	4,834	5,025	4,151	7,319	12,353	13,088	3,571	5,347
Congressional District 2.......	77,786	59,265	19,942	28,523	9,389	15,283	3,176	5,739	3,944	7,409	9,215	18,745	3,092	8,117
Congressional District 3.......	48,681	31,524	18,096	16,455	5,960	7,808	3,630	3,230	5,037	4,662	12,406	11,011	3,300	3,932
Congressional District 4.......	110,321	78,964	28,338	36,558	12,294	19,319	4,416	8,031	6,212	9,515	16,975	22,132	4,698	7,691
Congressional District 5.......	67,230	52,929	16,640	24,756	7,555	14,049	2,433	4,829	2,025	6,845	8,856	15,171	1,176	6,612
Congressional District 6.......	73,736	47,950	13,513	23,612	5,131	11,467	2,861	5,834	2,628	6,723	7,261	16,102	2,261	6,094
Congressional District 7.......	34,374	18,043	11,534	9,441	4,009	4,350	2,909	2,245	2,840	3,165	7,746	6,313	1,931	2,692
Congressional District 8.......	83,590	69,139	19,513	29,271	8,814	15,292	2,525	5,788	3,833	6,973	10,640	19,032	2,351	6,409
Congressional District 9.......	47,542	36,945	12,107	20,164	4,813	9,542	2,391	5,351	2,637	6,302	8,128	14,515	3,052	6,479
Arkansas														
Congressional District 1.......	70,747	49,703	25,847	28,539	10,734	12,876	5,666	6,065	6,106	7,715	16,968	19,444	4,139	7,494
Congressional District 2.......	61,486	42,205	19,576	22,604	7,345	10,004	3,185	4,005	5,525	5,388	12,660	16,195	4,231	5,711
Congressional District 3.......	59,728	41,358	16,450	20,745	6,343	10,999	2,781	5,088	3,123	5,678	10,340	13,300	3,399	5,023
Congressional District 4.......	72,375	50,728	26,163	31,059	12,151	15,675	4,731	6,197	5,326	8,506	15,611	21,466	4,599	7,693
California														
Congressional District 1.......	79,941	56,979	23,264	29,001	9,783	15,942	3,324	6,098	5,205	8,308	14,591	18,881	5,299	7,303
Congressional District 2.......	78,762	48,614	17,273	23,127	8,289	10,816	3,230	3,773	3,220	6,283	8,769	14,995	3,284	5,462
Congressional District 3.......	53,080	38,628	13,785	18,952	5,857	9,225	1,755	3,585	3,907	5,757	8,814	11,993	2,809	5,471
Congressional District 4.......	81,660	54,814	18,969	27,559	8,043	15,702	2,836	5,691	3,940	7,439	10,300	16,035	2,907	5,751
Congressional District 5.......	67,934	44,809	15,702	22,569	4,714	11,795	1,568	4,261	3,972	6,443	9,328	14,050	2,789	6,674
Congressional District 6.......	47,611	34,259	12,839	19,893	3,750	8,377	2,434	3,723	3,449	7,396	8,323	14,120	2,950	7,125
Congressional District 7.......	57,690	44,776	15,589	24,978	5,948	12,360	2,456	4,813	3,717	7,100	8,019	16,100	2,409	8,514
Congressional District 8.......	54,825	35,612	16,929	19,366	6,856	9,485	2,905	4,333	3,958	6,045	10,558	12,892	4,320	5,932
Congressional District 9.......	51,906	36,783	14,361	20,703	4,680	8,928	1,394	4,287	3,188	5,923	9,850	13,314	2,987	6,432
Congressional District 10......	47,856	33,059	14,302	19,324	5,519	9,829	3,235	3,034	3,517	5,115	8,746	12,645	1,722	5,681
Congressional District 11......	63,910	45,538	12,696	23,644	4,819	11,860	2,873	3,722	2,850	7,709	6,625	16,580	1,645	7,729
Congressional District 12......	55,526	49,006	12,476	24,533	4,427	8,970	2,900	6,893	3,492	8,905	7,623	15,953	2,165	8,358
Congressional District 13......	54,020	37,181	13,125	19,902	3,488	8,736	2,278	3,422	2,702	6,450	8,684	12,997	2,485	6,965
Congressional District 14......	60,908	46,614	9,739	23,593	2,576	9,102	1,690	3,141	1,720	6,563	6,468	15,106	2,114	7,568
Congressional District 15......	54,346	38,109	9,477	17,797	2,946	8,089	1,693	3,057	1,802	4,781	5,889	11,930	2,142	5,206
Congressional District 16......	41,963	29,528	16,938	18,615	5,849	9,909	4,990	5,113	4,613	5,731	11,777	12,694	4,232	6,502
Congressional District 17......	49,065	36,122	8,446	17,774	2,279	7,582	1,662	3,087	2,396	4,755	4,460	11,761	1,924	6,427
Congressional District 18......	56,497	46,625	9,297	21,804	3,891	9,093	548	3,283	2,046	6,059	4,077	13,364	1,737	6,401
Congressional District 19......	50,345	35,729	12,302	20,152	3,685	8,243	2,063	3,672	2,818	6,845	7,971	14,689	2,624	8,036
Congressional District 20......	49,181	35,155	10,089	18,132	3,076	8,485	1,470	3,315	2,425	6,392	6,185	12,019	1,704	5,547
Congressional District 21......	32,461	22,501	11,102	11,983	4,661	5,110	1,759	2,388	2,349	3,769	7,450	8,586	2,344	3,122
Congressional District 22......	49,396	34,686	13,157	18,483	4,163	9,044	1,180	4,064	2,987	5,715	8,964	12,380	1,922	5,760
Congressional District 23......	48,695	35,929	12,878	18,527	4,290	7,740	2,035	4,111	3,297	4,993	8,683	12,660	2,166	5,675
Congressional District 24......	60,886	48,343	12,690	24,762	5,387	13,157	1,476	5,321	2,902	7,263	7,624	14,254	2,294	5,750
Congressional District 25......	46,903	28,563	12,248	13,913	4,567	6,792	2,197	3,247	2,665	4,702	7,998	9,370	3,000	4,523
Congressional District 26......	54,278	42,905	12,346	22,363	4,322	10,488	1,581	3,651	3,145	5,981	7,231	15,045	2,606	7,519
Congressional District 27......	62,580	50,555	12,072	24,224	3,486	10,058	1,544	3,900	2,680	7,744	7,670	17,134	2,601	9,676
Congressional District 28......	57,389	43,977	14,248	25,718	3,330	8,695	2,109	4,994	4,315	10,623	8,039	17,769	5,386	12,802
Congressional District 29......	41,280	28,753	12,998	17,431	2,974	7,098	3,008	5,086	3,600	6,188	9,291	12,833	3,453	5,930
Congressional District 30......	58,182	49,271	12,108	25,135	3,848	10,351	929	5,167	3,019	8,679	8,061	18,310	3,185	11,098
Congressional District 31......	43,484	26,688	12,021	15,150	3,754	6,467	1,482	3,248	2,934	4,358	7,943	10,335	2,359	4,460
Congressional District 32......	55,084	38,076	12,774	21,579	3,253	8,346	2,586	4,380	2,652	6,871	7,757	15,584	3,174	8,215
Congressional District 33......	62,868	54,572	9,893	24,738	3,366	10,194	1,626	3,867	1,931	7,641	5,316	16,054	2,442	8,683
Congressional District 34......	42,076	34,047	12,651	19,075	2,723	7,234	3,351	4,951	2,913	7,910	9,201	14,434	2,162	6,573
Congressional District 35......	34,367	23,761	10,306	12,617	3,093	4,963	1,923	2,559	3,141	4,360	6,733	8,855	2,326	4,684
Congressional District 36......	77,865	66,404	18,363	32,054	7,393	15,912	3,520	6,781	3,523	8,250	11,443	19,456	3,591	8,346
Congressional District 37......	48,584	38,886	12,806	22,016	2,264	8,368	2,687	5,501	2,147	7,763	9,339	15,967	3,359	8,410
Congressional District 38......	51,531	42,945	13,946	21,068	4,206	8,653	2,658	3,579	2,491	7,628	8,480	14,884	2,639	7,446
Congressional District 39......	51,448	43,864	10,410	21,007	3,156	9,463	1,541	3,499	1,911	6,175	6,409	14,123	1,702	6,637
Congressional District 40......	31,755	22,927	9,211	12,473	1,765	5,180	1,337	2,686	3,000	4,872	6,189	9,851	2,726	5,167
Congressional District 41......	40,166	25,322	10,743	13,578	3,090	5,273	2,290	2,609	2,574	4,397	7,766	10,203	2,838	6,307
Congressional District 42......	49,637	35,731	12,018	17,637	4,137	7,669	2,326	3,020	2,681	4,685	6,882	11,699	2,234	5,273
Congressional District 43......	46,314	34,042	12,110	15,934	3,358	7,678	3,354	3,671	4,085	5,350	8,277	10,170	3,332	6,207
Congressional District 44......	35,518	24,906	10,875	14,117	2,757	5,391	2,145	2,509	2,950	5,480	7,469	9,585	2,956	5,385
Congressional District 45......	55,971	45,431	8,271	19,247	3,077	8,878	1,634	2,177	1,341	4,305	4,648	12,104	1,391	6,689
Congressional District 46......	37,206	24,479	9,340	12,069	2,687	4,326	2,557	2,300	2,927	4,134	5,723	7,095	3,315	3,012
Congressional District 47......	49,692	37,560	12,479	18,475	3,598	7,774	1,645	3,180	2,739	6,807	7,886	12,904	2,620	7,013
Congressional District 48......	67,179	47,644	9,452	23,267	3,297	10,285	1,413	5,185	1,623	7,336	4,665	16,870	697	7,476
Congressional District 49......	56,737	46,098	9,684	22,922	3,102	11,480	1,812	4,317	2,328	7,307	4,784	12,322	1,124	5,975
Congressional District 50......	59,838	41,544	14,952	22,020	5,507	10,937	2,429	5,718	4,537	7,653	8,645	14,653	3,353	7,057

Table H-5: 114th Congressional Districts—Disability Status and Type of Disability—*Continued*

	Total Population		With a Disability		With a Hearing Disability		With a Vision Disability		With a Cognitive Disability		With an Ambulatory Disability		With a Self-Care Disability	
	65 to 74 Years	75 Years and Over	65 to 74 Years	75 Years and Over	65 to 74 Years	75 Years and Over	65 to 74 Years	75 Years and Over	65 to 74 Years	75 Years and Over	65 to 74 Years	75 Years and Over	65 to 74 Years	75 Years and Over
California—Cont.														
Congressional District 51......	42,193	33,133	14,286	18,237	3,566	7,287	3,567	4,677	3,845	5,939	9,729	12,830	3,048	6,472
Congressional District 52......	53,668	41,604	9,272	19,471	3,571	8,460	1,552	3,689	2,135	5,582	4,720	12,720	1,841	5,423
Congressional District 53......	49,905	42,566	12,355	22,351	3,161	9,976	2,458	2,801	4,122	7,776	7,422	15,422	2,441	7,869
Colorado														
Congressional District 1........	51,187	34,271	11,196	18,693	3,900	8,734	2,362	3,933	2,598	4,670	6,886	11,510	1,690	4,936
Congressional District 2........	64,626	34,515	11,138	15,141	4,819	7,757	1,565	2,005	2,321	2,616	5,213	8,548	1,778	2,817
Congressional District 3........	68,625	44,029	17,186	22,002	7,533	12,625	2,731	5,084	3,753	5,946	9,670	13,741	2,580	4,495
Congressional District 4........	57,042	36,691	12,941	20,447	6,083	12,694	1,642	5,308	2,653	6,059	7,023	11,924	1,834	4,956
Congressional District 5........	57,754	36,752	13,573	17,090	6,559	8,597	1,955	2,925	2,154	5,008	7,198	11,054	1,319	4,068
Congressional District 6........	51,857	31,586	10,176	14,596	3,531	7,923	861	2,580	1,344	3,772	6,381	8,010	1,603	3,093
Congressional District 7........	55,387	39,958	14,866	21,120	7,297	10,263	2,596	3,835	2,973	5,897	7,969	12,753	2,478	4,056
Connecticut														
Congressional District 1........	60,402	49,234	13,824	24,381	5,201	9,966	2,470	3,932	4,231	5,514	8,190	16,395	2,615	8,832
Congressional District 2........	64,661	45,747	12,525	20,291	5,269	9,631	1,561	3,141	2,025	4,593	7,588	12,407	2,142	5,162
Congressional District 3........	59,821	48,576	13,253	22,828	4,539	9,546	1,261	3,978	3,415	5,137	7,872	15,172	3,085	7,273
Congressional District 4........	53,958	44,905	9,441	19,832	2,909	7,584	1,824	3,307	2,465	5,025	5,905	13,481	1,670	5,679
Congressional District 5........	61,165	45,056	12,557	21,081	4,282	9,418	1,028	3,783	2,109	5,963	7,702	11,987	2,975	6,176
Delaware														
Congressional District (at Large)	90,743	58,983	20,915	24,662	7,646	11,141	3,282	4,097	4,771	6,638	12,241	16,951	3,531	6,817
District of Columbia														
Delegate District (at Large) ...	40,997	30,983	10,513	15,807	2,349	4,081	2,678	3,543	2,831	5,260	7,990	10,892	2,931	5,505
Florida														
Congressional District 1........	66,539	46,856	17,033	25,964	7,129	11,670	2,520	4,932	3,928	7,967	9,897	17,693	2,835	6,511
Congressional District 2........	59,970	39,573	20,135	23,838	7,836	11,260	3,767	5,288	5,482	7,001	13,311	16,255	4,499	6,433
Congressional District 3........	71,803	46,600	23,189	23,163	8,862	12,104	3,039	4,750	5,067	8,205	14,100	16,390	4,293	6,386
Congressional District 4........	60,839	38,597	18,239	20,157	6,264	9,663	3,078	4,746	3,510	5,289	11,805	13,023	3,759	5,091
Congressional District 5........	47,329	35,805	15,183	18,717	2,827	6,852	2,883	2,999	4,022	6,344	10,760	13,516	2,486	4,917
Congressional District 6........	96,809	74,294	20,375	34,675	7,623	15,395	3,020	7,138	3,853	9,115	11,523	22,410	2,953	10,540
Congressional District 7........	59,440	41,773	12,371	18,822	3,739	7,939	1,594	4,310	3,232	6,415	7,728	13,711	2,252	5,283
Congressional District 8........	89,780	79,106	21,086	35,754	8,409	17,375	2,478	6,290	4,397	9,049	11,423	22,252	3,416	8,640
Congressional District 9........	52,744	33,835	13,904	18,042	4,040	6,715	4,044	3,079	2,677	6,589	8,054	13,259	1,468	4,916
Congressional District 10......	85,398	56,696	20,434	25,814	7,371	12,980	3,647	4,897	4,750	7,219	11,731	17,847	2,194	6,210
Congressional District 11......	135,010	101,003	30,690	45,148	11,748	25,026	3,887	9,572	5,042	10,010	19,302	28,162	3,347	9,606
Congressional District 12......	83,256	70,906	19,465	33,987	7,209	16,789	1,912	5,435	4,561	9,076	11,303	21,932	3,863	8,571
Congressional District 13......	89,140	72,929	19,797	31,441	8,140	14,272	2,440	5,479	4,228	8,963	12,026	21,545	3,437	8,340
Congressional District 14......	54,108	40,101	14,273	21,451	3,357	8,502	2,907	5,184	2,433	7,173	10,270	14,609	3,024	7,118
Congressional District 15......	61,298	42,028	13,676	20,950	5,710	9,528	2,263	4,420	2,236	5,672	7,906	14,261	2,152	5,273
Congressional District 16......	116,963	103,148	22,049	42,566	8,770	22,498	2,608	5,688	3,686	10,591	13,076	25,625	2,408	11,554
Congressional District 17......	102,081	88,258	23,552	40,232	9,331	20,605	3,395	6,186	4,548	10,990	13,369	24,214	3,417	7,821
Congressional District 18......	90,905	84,451	18,676	36,479	6,362	17,775	3,779	4,917	4,283	7,403	11,387	23,341	3,507	10,159
Congressional District 19......	122,046	95,770	21,791	39,133	10,526	21,383	3,607	5,448	3,531	10,851	10,355	23,010	2,768	7,611
Congressional District 20......	54,748	46,511	16,749	25,950	4,483	8,730	3,940	5,047	4,637	7,755	11,521	16,570	3,571	7,387
Congressional District 21......	80,284	91,226	15,196	40,212	5,030	17,819	2,932	7,610	2,784	9,289	9,138	26,022	2,052	11,322
Congressional District 22......	80,136	73,113	16,660	31,975	5,325	16,396	2,757	5,891	3,836	9,080	10,020	19,574	2,548	9,230
Congressional District 23......	63,190	54,569	14,130	26,609	3,763	10,697	3,705	6,368	2,029	7,367	8,996	17,830	2,337	8,547
Congressional District 24......	51,308	35,473	11,350	19,811	2,110	6,168	2,119	4,948	3,130	8,363	8,302	13,566	1,918	6,986
Congressional District 25......	62,430	53,726	11,337	22,094	2,970	8,047	1,976	4,348	2,772	9,154	6,777	14,931	1,826	7,346
Congressional District 26......	64,108	53,216	14,145	25,129	3,706	8,731	2,937	5,153	2,701	10,887	8,630	16,926	1,756	10,205
Congressional District 27......	63,797	58,477	14,275	28,726	3,969	7,733	2,373	3,946	4,123	11,067	7,760	20,203	2,610	10,520
Georgia														
Congressional District 1........	57,329	35,480	18,701	20,086	5,545	8,538	4,181	3,817	4,257	6,555	13,265	13,789	4,531	6,535
Congressional District 2........	55,749	35,531	20,165	19,476	5,861	7,695	4,102	3,680	5,092	5,885	13,781	13,198	3,899	5,492
Congressional District 3........	60,823	35,764	16,854	19,428	7,052	8,672	2,768	3,438	4,126	6,640	9,587	13,400	2,803	6,222
Congressional District 4........	48,570	24,047	11,797	11,977	2,856	5,095	1,754	2,814	2,756	4,400	7,154	8,393	2,101	3,353
Congressional District 5........	47,744	26,981	15,480	15,027	2,746	4,625	3,528	3,893	3,189	4,275	10,538	11,574	2,540	4,906
Congressional District 6........	46,794	32,192	7,378	14,051	2,869	6,377	786	1,841	2,077	4,468	3,060	9,461	567	4,316
Congressional District 7........	43,047	22,897	9,471	11,311	3,603	4,326	1,612	1,814	1,866	3,483	5,383	8,174	1,553	3,312
Congressional District 8........	59,345	37,927	18,906	20,420	5,520	9,103	4,936	4,788	4,416	6,589	12,351	13,407	3,724	5,357
Congressional District 9........	75,768	45,978	20,113	23,526	9,803	11,416	4,623	7,013	4,616	8,154	11,984	15,367	3,989	7,111
Congressional District 10......	59,979	36,740	18,163	19,312	6,180	7,820	2,740	4,139	3,729	5,751	10,185	12,597	2,292	4,876
Congressional District 11......	50,737	27,204	12,431	13,976	5,015	6,872	1,853	2,690	2,348	3,165	8,171	8,242	1,876	3,347
Congressional District 12......	54,371	34,968	19,361	19,005	6,186	7,896	4,280	4,567	5,860	5,879	12,174	13,507	3,593	5,372
Congressional District 13......	43,960	25,701	12,939	15,272	4,117	6,306	2,520	3,555	3,508	3,733	8,989	10,678	3,579	2,673
Congressional District 14......	56,210	36,150	16,981	18,897	8,035	7,919	2,629	2,887	3,743	5,183	10,027	12,268	1,827	5,994
Hawaii														
Congressional District 1........	62,922	55,431	12,085	29,262	3,735	14,237	1,491	3,927	3,412	11,029	7,802	20,236	2,494	8,490
Congressional District 2........	63,090	42,240	15,292	23,881	5,701	13,032	2,199	4,164	3,039	9,724	8,304	14,804	1,915	7,855
Idaho														
Congressional District 1........	79,878	47,927	22,534	24,588	11,087	15,443	3,235	5,369	5,339	7,117	12,266	13,789	3,354	5,003
Congressional District 2........	60,045	43,483	15,354	23,509	6,444	13,003	2,319	5,385	3,488	6,834	8,181	14,583	1,551	5,702

Table H-5: 114th Congressional Districts—Disability Status and Type of Disability—*Continued*

	Total Population		With a Disability		With a Hearing Disability		With a Vision Disability		With a Cognitive Disability		With an Ambulatory Disability		With a Self-Care Disability	
	65 to 74 Years	75 Years and Over	65 to 74 Years	75 Years and Over	65 to 74 Years	75 Years and Over	65 to 74 Years	75 Years and Over	65 to 74 Years	75 Years and Over	65 to 74 Years	75 Years and Over	65 to 74 Years	75 Years and Over
Illinois														
Congressional District 1	57,631	44,985	16,206	23,897	4,003	8,148	2,873	5,203	3,272	6,610	11,649	17,215	2,651	8,588
Congressional District 2	55,134	39,376	15,048	19,084	3,773	6,849	3,100	3,816	3,621	5,519	11,174	13,897	3,345	6,212
Congressional District 3	56,528	40,516	13,651	22,412	3,448	10,494	3,051	4,636	3,066	5,692	8,794	15,578	2,848	5,406
Congressional District 4	35,603	27,407	10,319	14,669	2,792	5,695	1,638	3,699	2,607	4,507	7,222	10,006	1,741	4,890
Congressional District 5	43,886	38,156	9,067	18,941	3,372	7,227	1,593	3,260	1,668	5,467	5,703	13,511	1,819	5,786
Congressional District 6	60,548	38,738	10,310	16,715	3,869	6,645	1,256	2,394	1,938	4,254	6,295	11,001	1,856	4,419
Congressional District 7	49,832	32,091	12,569	19,015	2,488	5,931	3,436	5,059	3,405	6,288	8,939	14,212	2,280	5,468
Congressional District 8	51,853	33,429	11,740	16,796	3,290	8,225	1,816	3,015	1,425	4,472	6,676	10,894	1,015	4,917
Congressional District 9	56,500	50,052	11,544	24,819	2,430	10,031	1,194	5,448	1,745	6,047	8,540	17,030	3,056	7,447
Congressional District 10	50,675	39,471	9,131	19,315	2,709	8,143	720	2,766	1,631	5,095	6,278	14,218	2,623	6,761
Congressional District 11	39,957	26,605	9,432	12,506	2,775	4,920	2,477	2,239	2,431	2,575	6,348	8,269	1,832	2,772
Congressional District 12	58,878	45,545	16,720	21,464	6,330	8,739	2,432	4,048	3,517	5,544	11,466	14,526	2,883	6,052
Congressional District 13	57,168	45,473	15,683	22,592	4,426	10,108	2,992	4,210	2,598	6,233	10,388	14,140	2,530	4,502
Congressional District 14	56,646	32,848	12,327	15,067	4,406	7,106	1,524	3,476	1,790	4,104	8,371	9,753	1,897	4,327
Congressional District 15	64,245	52,598	17,921	26,757	7,438	13,746	2,697	4,702	3,460	6,064	10,798	17,345	3,221	6,153
Congressional District 16	63,460	47,081	16,130	23,546	6,857	10,843	2,241	3,597	2,449	5,632	9,237	14,231	2,437	5,338
Congressional District 17	66,372	50,007	17,608	23,483	5,732	10,234	2,327	4,515	3,434	4,457	11,202	15,509	2,841	4,889
Congressional District 18	63,344	50,484	13,839	25,247	5,499	11,959	2,071	4,372	2,157	4,047	7,699	15,710	1,918	4,132
Indiana														
Congressional District 1	59,116	42,882	16,593	22,048	4,647	8,506	2,360	4,576	3,797	6,343	10,598	14,906	3,243	5,711
Congressional District 2	57,763	44,828	15,938	22,175	6,253	10,511	2,507	4,803	3,007	4,930	9,404	14,208	2,359	4,328
Congressional District 3	58,725	41,611	14,584	20,928	5,437	9,395	1,898	3,520	3,545	4,731	8,479	12,861	1,980	4,815
Congressional District 4	58,769	43,345	14,947	22,732	5,084	12,220	1,774	4,023	2,916	5,810	9,734	13,968	2,654	4,607
Congressional District 5	55,818	40,789	13,097	20,601	5,987	9,901	1,866	3,964	3,061	6,655	8,071	13,886	2,498	5,948
Congressional District 6	66,079	45,781	17,795	24,198	7,405	12,290	3,272	5,244	3,872	6,672	10,364	16,255	2,510	5,414
Congressional District 7	45,377	32,373	15,806	18,090	5,247	7,747	3,378	4,872	4,251	6,015	10,799	13,359	3,128	6,342
Congressional District 8	63,784	45,643	18,722	23,574	7,345	11,472	3,467	5,192	3,623	6,556	12,070	14,852	3,149	5,398
Congressional District 9	62,415	40,442	16,585	21,385	6,960	10,065	2,143	3,957	2,516	4,838	10,147	13,664	2,328	4,286
Iowa														
Congressional District 1	65,029	55,762	14,246	23,293	5,690	11,140	1,693	3,939	2,098	5,389	8,399	13,633	1,649	4,864
Congressional District 2	66,306	51,216	16,226	22,442	7,115	9,661	1,904	3,872	2,727	4,989	9,035	14,042	2,555	5,039
Congressional District 3	59,607	44,386	13,728	20,251	5,941	10,744	1,978	3,621	3,292	4,845	7,882	12,574	2,418	4,732
Congressional District 4	64,487	60,615	12,638	25,626	6,189	12,305	1,155	3,421	1,701	4,533	6,344	15,625	1,677	4,324
Kansas														
Congressional District 1	56,017	48,905	13,709	24,129	5,381	12,329	2,905	4,405	2,640	4,782	8,369	15,179	2,877	5,248
Congressional District 2	60,655	45,771	17,694	23,101	7,275	10,818	2,758	3,618	3,067	5,033	10,325	14,662	2,798	6,178
Congressional District 3	52,334	37,527	11,938	18,781	4,855	7,967	1,605	3,180	2,021	4,662	7,557	12,329	1,853	5,010
Congressional District 4	54,434	43,699	14,162	19,385	5,396	8,763	2,047	4,066	2,925	5,736	8,894	11,932	2,472	4,615
Kentucky														
Congressional District 1	68,490	47,650	21,894	26,167	9,710	12,428	4,581	4,735	4,060	7,170	13,314	17,246	2,860	5,771
Congressional District 2	62,813	41,177	21,280	23,579	8,936	9,852	4,319	3,975	5,622	6,611	14,080	17,712	3,666	6,357
Congressional District 3	59,233	44,320	16,472	24,088	5,409	9,362	2,449	4,131	3,793	6,384	10,718	16,335	3,153	6,926
Congressional District 4	61,568	38,447	20,027	21,088	7,568	10,714	3,504	5,854	4,337	5,661	12,223	13,366	3,346	6,163
Congressional District 5	69,468	42,600	32,308	26,890	12,277	13,056	7,383	7,186	8,611	8,315	21,442	18,947	5,303	7,754
Congressional District 6	58,570	36,747	18,010	20,235	7,048	9,370	3,615	3,593	3,992	5,560	12,005	12,871	3,711	5,593
Louisiana														
Congressional District 1	66,766	44,673	17,670	21,973	6,397	9,333	2,918	4,604	3,375	6,726	10,201	15,162	3,345	7,867
Congressional District 2	56,699	35,530	18,299	20,090	4,468	5,987	3,665	4,221	4,114	6,214	12,107	14,818	3,848	5,415
Congressional District 3	58,479	39,116	18,133	20,670	6,084	7,940	3,910	4,326	3,759	6,924	11,319	13,775	3,805	5,626
Congressional District 4	63,145	43,255	20,493	22,225	7,420	9,564	4,551	4,994	5,426	6,642	13,567	15,452	4,708	7,322
Congressional District 5	62,929	43,630	21,520	24,665	7,736	10,449	3,453	5,227	5,290	7,706	14,558	16,940	5,443	8,432
Congressional District 6	58,664	37,416	19,359	20,727	5,994	9,491	3,423	4,069	3,798	7,054	13,654	14,365	3,517	6,030
Maine														
Congressional District 1	69,117	48,563	13,813	22,716	5,665	11,100	1,508	4,852	2,344	5,434	7,736	14,564	2,416	5,176
Congressional District 2	70,188	47,909	17,778	24,566	7,886	12,238	2,280	4,238	3,975	4,879	9,985	14,329	3,239	5,557
Maryland														
Congressional District 1	73,988	48,123	15,581	22,111	6,781	10,590	2,110	3,896	3,377	5,966	8,431	13,872	2,747	4,434
Congressional District 2	53,306	36,710	11,977	19,205	4,958	8,210	1,998	4,110	2,347	5,915	7,748	13,019	2,130	5,659
Congressional District 3	58,751	45,606	11,643	22,188	2,855	8,435	1,419	4,240	2,184	5,871	7,625	15,621	1,935	6,741
Congressional District 4	53,385	34,644	11,883	15,094	2,766	5,189	1,724	2,576	1,656	4,436	7,880	10,295	1,527	4,713
Congressional District 5	57,104	31,869	12,918	16,026	3,421	7,004	1,321	3,444	2,941	4,394	8,092	10,864	1,988	4,345
Congressional District 6	56,057	38,417	11,950	18,706	4,084	8,328	1,671	3,511	2,167	5,559	7,384	11,735	1,524	4,636
Congressional District 7	57,425	41,130	13,818	20,985	2,829	6,754	2,005	4,395	3,590	6,260	9,538	14,530	3,049	6,162
Congressional District 8	62,582	49,549	9,938	21,469	3,489	9,173	1,351	3,950	1,964	6,334	5,700	13,630	1,161	5,371
Massachusetts														
Congressional District 1	66,723	48,757	15,113	23,838	5,860	10,260	2,353	3,856	3,115	6,329	8,183	15,044	3,084	7,443
Congressional District 2	57,263	42,686	11,421	21,665	3,806	9,928	1,669	3,932	2,426	6,518	7,235	14,536	2,462	6,898
Congressional District 3	58,860	38,788	12,188	18,584	4,437	9,748	2,047	4,024	2,776	5,282	6,432	10,606	1,920	4,284
Congressional District 4	60,911	42,873	10,883	19,776	4,024	9,957	1,977	3,723	2,432	6,218	6,298	11,958	2,385	5,466
Congressional District 5	59,458	49,131	9,155	22,635	3,174	11,005	889	4,420	2,265	5,865	5,228	14,115	1,804	5,752
Congressional District 6	65,019	53,591	13,586	26,033	5,576	12,661	1,797	4,937	2,282	6,750	7,667	16,154	1,370	6,876
Congressional District 7	41,904	30,818	12,202	17,623	3,255	6,642	3,616	4,800	4,360	6,667	7,730	12,269	2,900	5,765
Congressional District 8	65,415	50,490	14,921	24,135	5,694	12,482	1,570	4,893	3,676	5,839	8,986	15,668	2,058	7,000
Congressional District 9	81,437	62,905	16,089	28,605	6,176	14,035	2,786	4,434	3,887	6,915	8,688	18,727	2,673	8,598

Table H-5: 114th Congressional Districts—Disability Status and Type of Disability—*Continued*

	Total Population		With a Disability		With a Hearing Disability		With a Vision Disability		With a Cognitive Disability		With an Ambulatory Disability		With a Self-Care Disability	
	65 to 74 Years	75 Years and Over	65 to 74 Years	75 Years and Over	65 to 74 Years	75 Years and Over	65 to 74 Years	75 Years and Over	65 to 74 Years	75 Years and Over	65 to 74 Years	75 Years and Over	65 to 74 Years	75 Years and Over
Michigan														
Congressional District 1........	82,678	60,889	19,634	29,205	9,068	14,837	2,620	5,103	3,948	7,265	10,404	17,796	3,283	7,561
Congressional District 2........	57,534	41,959	13,940	20,169	5,358	8,878	1,280	3,688	3,509	4,549	8,382	12,988	2,508	3,988
Congressional District 3........	55,890	39,675	14,219	19,574	5,375	9,213	2,005	2,990	2,679	4,716	8,138	10,747	2,321	4,440
Congressional District 4........	69,641	48,911	18,758	24,352	8,666	12,286	2,920	4,136	3,812	6,266	10,815	14,915	2,554	5,445
Congressional District 5........	64,807	49,044	16,631	25,952	6,092	11,875	2,492	4,511	3,756	7,061	10,453	17,706	2,432	6,977
Congressional District 6........	63,510	44,836	14,800	21,403	6,277	9,775	1,947	3,378	2,479	5,134	7,280	13,937	1,492	4,866
Congressional District 7........	66,144	45,046	16,205	21,564	6,840	9,857	2,506	4,166	3,200	6,559	9,690	13,406	2,030	4,965
Congressional District 8........	57,617	34,473	13,092	16,325	4,958	7,565	1,860	3,503	2,962	5,251	7,163	10,329	2,063	4,304
Congressional District 9........	60,199	49,446	16,978	25,335	6,070	10,572	2,940	5,308	4,066	6,235	11,476	16,797	3,283	6,725
Congressional District 10......	68,453	46,328	19,063	25,066	7,085	10,905	3,023	4,372	3,401	5,809	11,819	16,384	3,029	6,398
Congressional District 11......	58,162	42,848	12,213	20,432	4,522	8,484	1,536	3,713	2,089	6,239	7,667	12,291	1,785	5,653
Congressional District 12......	52,527	40,330	13,682	20,789	5,612	9,885	2,764	3,383	2,560	5,080	8,455	12,620	2,235	5,273
Congressional District 13......	48,966	37,176	18,114	21,189	4,266	8,449	3,724	5,375	4,550	6,303	13,386	15,610	5,412	6,864
Congressional District 14......	59,189	45,137	16,930	22,777	4,045	7,751	2,781	5,162	4,233	6,908	11,585	16,558	4,270	7,074
Minnesota														
Congressional District 1........	53,817	48,230	10,704	21,585	4,528	10,624	1,319	3,724	2,180	4,784	5,528	13,169	1,529	5,233
Congressional District 2........	48,506	33,029	10,643	13,899	4,985	5,828	1,487	2,031	1,873	3,376	5,381	8,671	1,417	4,057
Congressional District 3........	54,524	40,516	7,803	18,289	3,685	8,018	908	2,912	1,445	4,924	3,563	10,455	946	4,090
Congressional District 4........	50,139	37,355	11,033	19,781	4,635	8,128	1,923	3,883	2,229	5,680	5,806	12,440	2,217	5,115
Congressional District 5........	42,323	31,981	11,396	13,654	3,784	7,062	1,915	2,493	3,017	3,169	6,353	9,218	2,410	3,331
Congressional District 6........	44,657	27,319	8,702	12,025	4,523	5,696	568	2,245	1,711	2,757	4,180	6,558	1,243	2,526
Congressional District 7........	61,571	54,182	13,955	24,100	6,275	11,596	1,624	4,207	2,200	5,751	7,936	13,861	2,033	5,887
Congressional District 8........	69,518	49,741	16,116	24,070	7,670	13,270	1,878	4,365	2,657	5,705	8,313	14,324	1,695	5,647
Mississippi														
Congressional District 1........	64,447	44,514	23,070	25,029	8,355	10,938	4,423	6,060	6,793	8,346	15,001	18,072	4,966	7,621
Congressional District 2........	54,469	39,106	17,169	21,272	4,351	8,009	3,191	4,341	3,310	7,932	11,733	15,809	2,910	6,543
Congressional District 3........	62,296	45,696	23,488	26,882	8,244	10,869	4,709	6,141	5,545	8,442	14,799	18,483	3,106	7,343
Congressional District 4........	62,986	41,628	22,429	25,208	8,792	11,902	3,761	7,298	4,649	9,908	15,894	18,063	4,870	9,275
Missouri														
Congressional District 1........	51,346	37,130	14,978	19,098	4,309	6,683	2,424	4,487	3,003	5,757	10,441	12,614	3,075	5,249
Congressional District 2........	69,059	56,631	12,038	25,568	4,846	11,052	1,853	5,356	1,617	5,894	6,443	16,064	1,553	5,758
Congressional District 3........	66,040	42,482	17,918	19,832	7,376	10,100	4,299	3,569	3,271	5,252	10,704	12,730	2,027	4,428
Congressional District 4........	66,933	44,476	19,783	22,879	8,364	12,239	1,998	5,236	3,188	5,574	11,593	14,559	2,374	4,620
Congressional District 5........	57,842	45,607	14,976	22,259	4,911	9,401	2,821	3,781	3,252	7,033	8,413	14,826	2,405	5,026
Congressional District 6........	64,757	44,389	16,325	22,566	6,515	11,732	2,116	3,536	2,738	4,995	9,401	13,509	2,111	4,332
Congressional District 7........	69,753	50,874	20,241	24,675	8,390	11,503	3,136	5,168	3,536	6,391	12,493	16,278	2,989	5,278
Congressional District 8........	74,390	51,897	26,708	27,995	10,984	11,618	5,044	5,702	5,778	7,608	16,430	18,256	5,535	6,137
Montana														
Congressional District (at Large)	98,311	67,203	24,581	31,476	11,923	15,832	3,016	5,699	4,778	6,803	12,905	19,205	3,631	6,285
Nebraska														
Congressional District 1	48,557	36,513	12,494	16,942	5,989	8,563	1,863	2,234	1,656	4,104	6,863	9,540	1,841	3,258
Congressional District 2........	40,115	28,990	8,595	14,522	3,371	7,283	1,151	3,147	1,807	4,308	5,324	8,298	1,186	3,906
Congressional District 3........	54,609	50,507	14,560	23,767	7,038	12,457	2,095	5,140	2,294	4,775	7,648	12,921	1,874	3,463
Nevada														
Congressional District 1........	53,484	34,075	17,704	17,606	6,206	7,945	3,854	4,112	3,415	5,598	12,923	12,003	2,961	4,330
Congressional District 2........	67,572	38,944	19,011	18,927	7,372	9,617	2,865	3,617	3,913	4,405	11,686	11,531	2,314	3,547
Congressional District 3........	65,138	39,869	13,678	19,503	4,765	10,078	2,440	3,878	3,021	4,648	8,702	12,421	2,279	5,212
Congressional District 4........	62,372	34,561	20,870	18,190	7,381	8,287	4,211	3,293	5,644	5,293	14,042	12,952	4,137	4,430
New Hampshire														
Congressional District 1........	60,318	38,855	13,339	18,981	5,346	9,250	1,892	3,208	2,082	4,554	8,371	12,364	1,756	3,187
Congressional District 2........	61,455	40,916	12,606	20,623	5,796	10,179	1,951	3,489	2,037	5,094	7,087	11,893	2,435	5,086
New Jersey														
Congressional District 1........	59,224	43,818	16,007	22,754	4,795	10,194	4,097	3,953	3,679	6,299	10,635	15,260	3,130	5,156
Congressional District 2........	70,016	48,044	17,024	23,230	5,124	10,087	2,254	4,137	3,231	5,449	12,294	13,980	2,966	5,280
Congressional District 3........	71,390	59,209	14,952	29,377	5,226	13,182	2,057	5,202	2,814	8,074	8,384	19,677	1,726	6,080
Congressional District 4........	68,826	59,858	13,315	29,906	3,749	11,957	1,578	5,453	2,231	8,098	8,281	19,267	1,253	8,202
Congressional District 5........	65,836	46,761	12,945	20,859	3,994	8,728	1,728	2,043	2,411	5,164	7,681	13,495	1,406	6,034
Congressional District 6........	54,322	36,435	11,778	15,547	2,853	7,052	1,808	3,139	2,067	4,047	8,020	10,597	1,723	3,795
Congressional District 7........	61,552	43,936	11,279	21,523	4,005	9,037	714	4,406	2,329	7,078	7,166	14,628	2,023	7,092
Congressional District 8........	42,804	31,807	12,838	15,792	2,649	5,655	3,048	3,982	3,310	5,330	9,098	12,460	2,284	6,436
Congressional District 9........	56,469	46,280	10,357	20,382	2,506	7,422	1,670	3,823	1,902	5,582	6,948	15,090	1,897	8,223
Congressional District 10......	47,301	32,690	12,319	17,497	1,944	5,983	2,483	3,964	2,452	4,545	8,747	13,327	2,242	5,529
Congressional District 11......	66,307	55,048	11,440	26,898	3,214	12,267	1,709	5,114	1,847	6,335	7,507	16,805	1,732	8,780
Congressional District 12......	56,834	47,342	10,078	22,875	2,608	9,418	1,554	4,760	2,345	7,188	6,535	15,647	1,961	7,148
New Mexico														
Congressional District 1........	59,932	42,482	16,869	22,616	6,395	10,790	3,867	4,544	5,125	8,214	10,091	15,199	4,193	5,909
Congressional District 2........	63,286	44,271	22,162	24,167	8,937	12,510	3,723	6,234	5,016	6,163	13,308	15,212	3,150	5,750
Congressional District 3........	61,123	42,069	17,302	24,332	8,766	13,211	2,804	6,123	4,051	8,280	9,279	15,628	2,569	6,438
New York														
Congressional District 1........	68,320	46,679	14,589	19,603	4,496	8,788	1,462	3,028	2,189	4,427	9,774	12,620	2,747	5,104
Congressional District 2........	54,578	41,527	11,448	18,515	3,584	8,175	2,010	3,272	1,550	4,408	6,799	11,511	1,247	5,354

Table H-5: 114th Congressional Districts—Disability Status and Type of Disability—*Continued*

	Total Population		With a Disability		With a Hearing Disability		With a Vision Disability		With a Cognitive Disability		With an Ambulatory Disability		With a Self-Care Disability	
	65 to 74 Years	75 Years and Over	65 to 74 Years	75 Years and Over	65 to 74 Years	75 Years and Over	65 to 74 Years	75 Years and Over	65 to 74 Years	75 Years and Over	65 to 74 Years	75 Years and Over	65 to 74 Years	75 Years and Over
New York—Cont.														
Congressional District 3.......	64,895	62,474	8,681	25,432	2,634	10,588	1,272	4,328	1,310	5,065	4,720	16,972	1,116	7,279
Congressional District 4.......	59,836	50,461	9,860	21,963	3,083	7,679	1,526	4,275	1,891	7,229	5,716	14,226	1,677	7,602
Congressional District 5.......	56,434	39,580	14,925	20,908	3,234	6,072	3,295	5,701	3,413	7,149	11,011	15,517	3,368	7,816
Congressional District 6.......	62,124	50,788	12,166	24,953	2,884	8,122	2,623	3,985	2,476	7,259	7,746	18,636	1,849	8,042
Congressional District 7.......	37,323	31,990	11,367	18,755	3,402	5,670	3,615	4,218	3,504	6,323	8,438	14,267	3,006	7,735
Congressional District 8.......	57,318	43,256	16,383	27,124	3,360	8,486	4,670	7,455	4,522	9,846	12,345	22,583	4,079	13,917
Congressional District 9.......	55,354	40,652	11,791	20,900	2,394	6,301	2,684	5,752	2,568	7,309	8,085	16,956	2,126	8,150
Congressional District 10......	60,402	40,148	11,503	22,629	2,846	9,341	1,892	4,677	1,977	7,013	7,346	16,848	2,192	9,347
Congressional District 11......	59,451	45,687	13,511	23,234	3,386	8,497	2,084	4,979	3,648	7,754	9,488	17,886	2,947	9,102
Congressional District 12......	55,369	46,322	9,621	20,634	2,625	6,558	2,268	3,040	2,796	6,226	6,300	15,791	1,576	8,377
Congressional District 13......	45,925	35,106	17,097	21,306	3,831	6,910	3,443	4,962	4,327	9,552	13,431	17,122	3,349	9,540
Congressional District 14......	49,331	37,034	12,121	18,457	2,621	7,057	2,633	3,920	2,578	6,665	8,440	12,528	2,274	5,456
Congressional District 15......	41,150	26,956	15,042	17,388	3,431	6,084	3,586	5,005	5,198	6,040	11,420	14,175	4,606	7,335
Congressional District 16......	56,960	50,857	13,326	25,823	4,329	8,991	3,270	5,944	3,585	8,337	8,293	16,278	2,755	7,516
Congressional District 17......	60,438	47,734	10,941	21,218	3,164	9,873	1,668	3,923	1,978	5,412	6,517	13,351	2,526	5,911
Congressional District 18......	58,290	40,587	11,907	19,380	4,702	9,279	2,030	4,667	1,898	4,800	6,579	12,267	1,995	5,881
Congressional District 19......	73,948	49,214	17,882	25,489	6,619	12,364	2,021	4,488	3,162	5,870	11,697	15,776	3,734	5,964
Congressional District 20......	61,464	44,659	13,338	19,363	4,295	8,014	1,716	2,652	2,120	4,194	8,288	14,074	1,497	5,623
Congressional District 21......	64,153	46,586	17,315	24,182	7,322	11,998	3,429	4,426	2,979	5,727	10,719	13,464	3,020	5,753
Congressional District 22......	64,881	50,156	19,030	26,771	6,652	12,372	3,498	4,054	4,625	6,724	11,817	15,591	3,270	6,851
Congressional District 23......	65,766	49,238	17,304	24,199	6,625	12,494	2,457	4,354	3,082	6,051	11,150	15,288	2,678	6,376
Congressional District 24......	60,110	46,490	12,888	22,616	5,391	10,714	2,141	4,577	2,185	6,332	6,774	14,683	2,308	6,180
Congressional District 25......	60,847	47,255	15,436	22,581	6,282	8,669	2,722	3,119	3,013	6,512	9,844	15,308	2,132	4,801
Congressional District 26......	61,991	54,183	15,732	28,384	4,352	11,303	2,440	4,266	2,752	7,235	11,407	18,665	2,234	6,586
Congressional District 27......	65,786	48,737	12,407	21,209	4,939	9,889	1,425	3,345	1,754	5,153	6,379	12,810	2,086	4,579
North Carolina														
Congressional District 1........	64,021	44,716	22,595	28,577	5,453	11,521	3,318	6,565	5,565	8,823	16,624	20,283	4,931	7,908
Congressional District 2........	62,044	39,018	17,573	18,219	6,766	8,572	3,212	3,930	3,760	5,566	10,779	12,305	3,065	5,398
Congressional District 3........	65,047	43,146	20,599	22,712	7,116	11,706	3,096	4,380	3,438	6,295	13,539	14,027	4,124	5,204
Congressional District 4........	49,106	32,882	11,120	15,906	3,373	6,999	2,568	2,797	2,218	3,688	6,519	10,581	1,721	3,847
Congressional District 5........	69,716	48,854	16,349	23,463	5,430	10,149	3,222	4,704	3,412	6,831	10,506	16,188	2,784	6,872
Congressional District 6........	70,487	51,460	16,461	25,651	6,131	11,404	2,407	3,966	2,961	8,088	10,661	17,424	2,786	8,003
Congressional District 7........	82,898	46,622	25,059	25,870	9,855	11,843	5,587	5,881	5,410	6,925	15,517	16,717	4,648	7,868
Congressional District 8........	66,811	41,338	21,122	22,291	7,215	9,832	4,144	3,561	5,426	6,304	14,106	15,460	4,497	8,294
Congressional District 9........	58,964	36,321	12,900	16,856	4,741	8,292	2,186	3,900	2,820	4,881	7,067	10,388	1,710	4,438
Congressional District 10......	74,113	49,386	22,058	26,740	9,288	12,015	3,194	5,419	4,185	7,780	13,058	17,359	4,053	7,446
Congressional District 11......	91,598	62,801	22,851	31,739	8,376	16,736	4,551	6,580	3,954	8,703	14,019	19,721	4,172	8,345
Congressional District 12......	44,467	26,865	14,154	15,045	4,309	5,731	2,616	2,118	2,524	4,633	9,528	9,151	2,910	4,275
Congressional District 13......	61,007	36,587	12,935	18,066	4,950	9,069	2,234	3,015	2,062	5,592	8,284	11,548	3,020	5,216
North Dakota														
Congressional District (at Large)	53,675	45,217	12,409	21,273	5,569	10,461	1,562	2,949	2,299	4,257	5,889	13,256	1,302	3,145
Ohio														
Congressional District 1........	52,128	40,665	13,127	18,928	4,346	7,408	2,846	3,233	2,381	4,393	7,831	12,242	2,037	3,986
Congressional District 2........	61,796	44,790	15,217	21,800	5,345	10,184	3,143	3,491	3,220	6,198	9,511	14,434	2,543	6,018
Congressional District 3........	42,369	27,843	12,334	14,768	2,998	5,713	1,955	2,633	3,152	5,282	8,788	10,069	3,000	4,831
Congressional District 4........	62,139	49,842	15,968	26,160	5,801	13,101	2,321	5,199	3,079	5,773	10,480	15,900	2,835	5,520
Congressional District 5........	64,656	46,344	15,155	21,918	5,421	10,236	2,204	3,596	2,116	4,501	9,249	13,619	2,873	4,884
Congressional District 6........	72,169	50,779	21,528	27,835	9,088	13,992	3,468	7,512	4,744	7,408	13,141	17,578	3,752	7,261
Congressional District 7........	69,796	50,118	17,632	23,540	6,279	11,130	2,530	4,309	3,116	5,872	10,955	15,668	3,196	5,511
Congressional District 8........	62,788	43,921	15,755	21,113	7,049	9,871	3,139	4,035	3,836	5,431	9,999	13,231	3,077	4,329
Congressional District 9........	54,978	44,495	16,351	24,414	5,379	11,355	2,615	4,126	3,403	5,478	11,077	14,386	3,306	6,679
Congressional District 10......	64,031	49,353	17,374	22,794	6,094	9,996	3,076	4,970	3,235	6,107	11,021	14,893	3,197	5,608
Congressional District 11......	55,077	45,903	16,264	23,697	3,421	7,661	3,391	4,573	4,223	8,097	11,666	17,098	4,305	8,349
Congressional District 12......	58,799	39,453	13,452	19,553	4,446	8,621	1,872	3,750	1,936	5,238	8,057	12,282	2,049	4,080
Congressional District 13......	65,861	54,857	16,467	25,772	5,656	11,763	2,855	4,752	3,126	6,492	9,859	17,565	2,885	6,917
Congressional District 14......	71,742	54,599	14,450	24,057	6,108	10,483	1,645	5,585	2,490	5,933	7,705	15,342	2,436	6,329
Congressional District 15......	60,649	42,126	16,942	18,916	5,621	8,102	3,035	3,436	3,402	4,771	11,178	11,554	3,542	4,428
Congressional District 16......	70,884	53,241	14,966	22,955	5,846	10,850	1,404	4,707	2,631	5,478	8,863	14,159	2,564	5,409
Oklahoma														
Congressional District 1........	59,183	43,403	16,642	22,609	6,555	11,958	3,080	4,416	4,020	6,098	9,967	14,675	3,201	5,742
Congressional District 2........	76,948	50,741	30,166	29,862	13,192	16,301	7,312	6,821	5,918	8,530	18,694	21,417	5,369	8,704
Congressional District 3........	64,275	47,476	20,171	26,268	9,041	12,836	3,342	5,525	3,184	5,630	12,505	17,715	2,554	5,953
Congressional District 4........	58,861	42,295	19,657	22,979	7,421	11,347	3,754	4,889	3,166	6,861	13,046	16,060	3,227	5,520
Congressional District 5........	58,431	41,186	18,860	22,800	7,754	10,884	2,625	4,548	3,582	6,789	11,549	16,524	2,728	7,081
Oregon														
Congressional District 1........	63,005	40,927	15,549	21,574	7,380	11,849	2,288	4,806	2,361	7,059	8,879	13,761	2,287	6,198
Congressional District 2........	86,266	60,909	25,540	30,727	13,238	16,212	3,278	6,527	5,539	8,793	13,670	18,779	4,042	7,521
Congressional District 3........	60,423	39,210	18,036	22,375	6,909	12,588	3,383	5,353	3,950	7,110	10,075	14,487	3,098	5,586
Congressional District 4........	87,856	59,416	24,313	34,473	8,983	17,723	3,094	5,730	6,517	9,866	14,944	21,227	4,930	7,426
Congressional District 5........	75,213	51,370	17,255	27,351	7,351	14,096	1,849	4,716	3,329	8,477	9,854	17,005	2,340	8,015
Pennsylvania														
Congressional District 1........	46,604	34,262	12,153	18,999	3,403	6,866	2,239	3,325	3,209	5,268	8,307	13,010	2,428	5,426
Congressional District 2........	52,164	39,291	14,322	18,509	2,911	5,967	3,371	3,367	3,401	6,117	10,044	13,641	2,126	4,962

Table H-5: 114th Congressional Districts—Disability Status and Type of Disability—*Continued*

	Total Population		With a Disability		With a Hearing Disability		With a Vision Disability		With a Cognitive Disability		With an Ambulatory Disability		With a Self-Care Disability	
	65 to 74 Years	75 Years and Over	65 to 74 Years	75 Years and Over	65 to 74 Years	75 Years and Over	65 to 74 Years	75 Years and Over	65 to 74 Years	75 Years and Over	65 to 74 Years	75 Years and Over	65 to 74 Years	75 Years and Over
Pennsylvania—Cont.														
Congressional District 3........	65,389	55,180	15,921	27,406	7,180	13,093	1,854	5,174	2,940	6,041	8,456	16,354	1,746	6,226
Congressional District 4........	63,631	47,839	15,127	21,798	6,479	9,208	1,975	3,397	2,647	4,793	9,398	14,395	2,223	5,357
Congressional District 5........	66,232	50,342	17,906	23,669	8,117	11,665	2,722	4,541	3,142	5,965	9,140	13,934	2,244	5,398
Congressional District 6........	58,393	48,877	11,789	19,275	3,810	9,794	1,450	2,942	1,553	5,972	7,233	11,404	1,553	4,194
Congressional District 7........	62,380	53,649	10,352	24,151	3,703	10,893	1,429	3,681	1,677	7,659	6,190	15,503	1,496	5,871
Congressional District 8........	64,962	50,705	13,154	23,782	4,391	10,134	1,959	4,476	2,076	6,200	7,932	15,835	1,750	6,376
Congressional District 9........	70,830	57,503	17,187	30,029	7,039	13,062	2,205	5,122	2,863	9,012	9,429	19,932	2,664	8,216
Congressional District 10......	70,790	52,960	17,215	27,547	7,293	13,244	2,624	5,746	2,772	5,767	9,243	16,451	2,663	6,494
Congressional District 11......	68,582	51,663	16,873	26,597	6,439	12,117	2,512	5,470	2,085	6,470	9,923	17,625	2,209	6,884
Congressional District 12......	74,043	63,340	15,594	30,599	6,465	15,589	2,001	5,680	2,956	7,789	8,302	18,265	1,736	6,034
Congressional District 13......	56,923	47,882	15,879	23,551	4,219	9,068	2,341	3,557	3,543	5,566	10,618	16,053	3,801	6,333
Congressional District 14......	55,826	54,477	15,100	27,271	4,172	11,894	1,559	4,704	3,713	7,025	10,489	17,454	3,102	6,103
Congressional District 15......	63,876	50,203	14,015	22,923	5,027	9,298	1,351	4,194	3,266	7,136	8,170	13,560	2,361	5,247
Congressional District 16......	57,334	47,168	12,603	21,325	5,544	9,876	1,328	3,872	1,776	4,081	7,359	11,466	1,356	4,021
Congressional District 17......	67,953	54,554	18,296	30,115	6,761	13,576	2,061	6,103	4,276	8,108	11,428	18,781	2,720	7,189
Congressional District 18......	72,368	57,707	14,754	26,345	6,428	12,699	1,415	4,954	2,866	7,351	9,262	16,172	2,308	7,367
Rhode Island														
Congressional District 1........	41,290	34,809	9,113	17,055	2,652	7,273	1,800	2,711	1,585	4,250	5,771	12,368	1,191	4,058
Congressional District 2........	47,523	36,341	12,819	19,092	4,767	8,813	1,874	4,275	2,858	3,905	7,741	11,700	2,162	4,245
South Carolina														
Congressional District 1........	74,507	43,222	15,840	18,245	5,557	9,215	2,632	3,837	3,702	5,427	9,399	10,589	2,244	5,107
Congressional District 2........	58,299	36,662	16,816	19,242	6,774	8,844	3,321	4,340	3,014	4,840	10,225	12,932	2,850	5,327
Congressional District 3........	69,181	42,638	20,855	23,138	7,465	9,682	2,866	4,625	4,871	7,941	13,134	15,842	2,763	6,707
Congressional District 4........	60,333	40,327	15,703	21,623	5,055	9,399	1,882	4,932	3,063	5,875	9,990	14,224	2,201	6,085
Congressional District 5........	65,152	38,327	20,198	20,081	7,935	10,960	3,584	3,461	5,398	6,029	13,367	12,073	4,184	6,200
Congressional District 6........	57,379	34,466	18,597	20,214	5,789	7,517	3,889	5,436	5,689	6,606	11,957	14,507	4,057	7,109
Congressional District 7........	79,723	44,111	23,016	23,734	7,662	11,367	4,754	5,046	6,139	7,506	15,285	16,175	4,190	6,312
South Dakota														
Congressional District (at Large)	68,243	54,412	16,257	26,041	7,134	13,838	1,503	5,774	2,914	7,105	9,850	16,759	2,690	4,939
Tennessee														
Congressional District 1........	79,212	51,556	28,412	29,087	10,029	14,766	6,392	7,129	6,146	7,485	19,579	19,183	5,612	7,462
Congressional District 2........	71,384	46,048	18,663	25,398	7,371	11,798	3,166	3,711	4,198	7,756	10,992	16,451	2,777	6,815
Congressional District 3........	70,355	47,920	21,673	24,105	8,739	11,117	4,420	6,077	5,545	8,016	13,667	15,740	4,980	7,685
Congressional District 4........	64,064	39,464	19,201	20,224	7,151	10,198	3,686	3,979	4,848	6,432	13,409	13,726	3,337	5,004
Congressional District 5........	49,473	34,012	12,819	17,954	3,537	6,939	1,701	3,036	2,039	4,730	8,774	12,617	1,459	3,905
Congressional District 6........	76,768	46,330	24,001	25,699	10,926	12,495	3,689	5,726	5,525	7,231	14,760	16,622	4,590	7,343
Congressional District 7........	61,843	38,290	18,378	20,085	6,431	9,187	4,345	3,651	4,745	6,848	11,331	12,726	3,841	5,587
Congressional District 8........	65,829	42,503	17,754	24,154	6,171	10,205	3,524	6,208	3,432	6,369	11,442	16,782	3,448	7,657
Congressional District 9........	43,653	29,376	13,304	16,278	3,365	4,984	2,459	2,768	2,660	5,371	8,817	11,481	2,709	5,306
Texas														
Congressional District 1........	62,601	46,821	19,386	24,551	6,789	11,482	2,589	4,890	3,543	6,061	12,359	16,375	3,664	7,214
Congressional District 2........	46,845	25,438	11,685	12,744	4,325	4,687	1,897	2,014	2,483	4,255	6,900	8,367	1,839	3,246
Congressional District 3........	49,877	26,142	9,529	12,459	3,441	5,689	1,533	2,207	1,323	2,938	5,887	7,373	1,652	2,991
Congressional District 4........	65,674	44,925	19,646	24,216	8,202	10,309	4,355	5,194	4,930	7,207	12,683	16,449	4,401	7,100
Congressional District 5........	54,734	35,812	15,447	17,329	4,893	7,835	3,106	3,545	2,944	4,034	10,121	10,386	3,357	3,389
Congressional District 6........	46,337	27,943	12,289	14,775	5,714	6,619	2,198	1,669	2,509	3,935	7,334	10,126	2,469	3,252
Congressional District 7........	42,193	31,425	6,897	15,227	1,984	6,396	705	2,986	1,820	4,401	4,409	10,217	650	4,258
Congressional District 8........	58,451	36,062	17,720	19,873	7,999	10,093	3,665	3,881	2,430	4,779	10,343	12,944	3,014	4,995
Congressional District 9........	43,532	22,925	12,064	11,963	3,601	4,576	2,640	2,197	2,527	3,858	7,282	9,313	2,696	5,027
Congressional District 10......	54,591	31,324	13,095	17,171	4,286	6,611	2,883	4,412	2,659	4,796	7,688	11,084	2,151	4,810
Congressional District 11......	61,321	49,008	17,167	25,425	6,263	12,764	4,205	5,328	2,914	7,422	10,041	16,995	2,440	6,954
Congressional District 12......	53,856	36,388	14,248	19,551	4,619	8,981	3,037	4,085	2,716	6,318	9,273	14,003	2,347	5,610
Congressional District 13......	54,910	42,480	17,379	22,184	6,860	10,553	3,391	4,593	3,079	6,013	11,707	15,623	3,201	5,022
Congressional District 14......	54,009	37,168	17,719	18,990	6,943	8,534	2,301	3,188	3,599	5,619	12,141	12,904	3,275	5,086
Congressional District 15......	47,165	32,093	19,594	18,113	7,240	9,178	6,153	4,868	4,174	6,586	11,044	12,982	5,540	8,116
Congressional District 16......	44,237	37,799	14,277	22,517	5,780	9,894	3,114	5,147	3,079	7,663	8,753	16,080	2,580	8,499
Congressional District 17......	47,495	32,977	14,394	17,626	5,327	7,410	2,646	3,622	2,844	4,084	9,784	11,979	3,027	4,058
Congressional District 18......	39,241	25,962	14,598	14,604	4,040	5,253	3,534	3,738	3,886	5,240	9,442	10,905	2,693	5,315
Congressional District 19......	51,342	40,307	18,939	21,757	8,472	10,681	3,119	5,069	4,078	6,473	12,290	14,068	2,330	6,176
Congressional District 20......	44,223	32,761	14,959	20,282	5,248	9,144	2,216	5,212	3,907	5,671	9,553	12,870	2,985	5,697
Congressional District 21......	67,486	46,298	16,716	21,875	6,656	11,125	1,865	4,030	2,543	5,455	10,487	13,754	2,400	5,452
Congressional District 22......	49,402	28,802	10,550	14,101	2,929	5,250	1,227	2,734	2,150	3,589	6,879	10,572	2,045	3,958
Congressional District 23......	55,338	34,450	20,199	20,895	8,898	9,634	5,211	6,443	5,031	7,289	13,135	12,385	3,895	6,300
Congressional District 24......	46,496	28,523	9,312	13,284	3,415	6,098	1,533	2,244	1,895	4,074	5,478	9,028	1,309	3,442
Congressional District 25......	55,842	34,317	12,571	18,183	5,369	8,637	2,089	4,430	1,712	4,533	7,653	12,093	1,802	3,742
Congressional District 26......	47,195	22,723	11,069	11,780	4,299	4,162	1,530	1,307	1,767	3,298	7,390	8,269	1,828	2,589
Congressional District 27......	59,406	41,045	20,287	23,259	8,422	10,983	4,454	6,093	3,255	6,085	11,336	14,444	3,431	5,024
Congressional District 28......	44,982	30,957	18,460	20,104	6,279	8,523	3,929	4,764	6,331	6,174	12,268	13,127	4,612	7,314
Congressional District 29......	35,502	21,653	10,909	13,570	2,598	5,596	2,485	2,760	2,431	3,995	7,731	9,102	2,188	4,549
Congressional District 30......	40,374	25,752	13,664	12,873	3,109	4,898	1,917	4,158	3,214	4,635	9,597	9,894	3,500	4,542
Congressional District 31......	51,474	31,664	13,534	17,928	4,878	8,516	2,384	3,457	2,006	5,414	8,753	12,086	2,170	4,824
Congressional District 32......	51,432	34,928	12,434	17,509	3,635	7,667	2,540	3,761	2,897	5,032	8,305	10,523	2,568	4,613
Congressional District 33......	32,824	22,337	11,343	11,217	3,090	4,301	2,693	3,504	2,462	3,870	7,478	8,064	2,057	3,480
Congressional District 34......	50,675	41,434	21,532	24,666	8,981	10,826	5,596	6,753	5,082	7,217	13,866	17,712	5,529	9,008

Table H-5: 114th Congressional Districts—Disability Status and Type of Disability—*Continued*

	Total Population		With a Disability		With a Hearing Disability		With a Vision Disability		With a Cognitive Disability		With an Ambulatory Disability		With a Self-Care Disability	
	65 to 74 Years	75 Years and Over	65 to 74 Years	75 Years and Over	65 to 74 Years	75 Years and Over	65 to 74 Years	75 Years and Over	65 to 74 Years	75 Years and Over	65 to 74 Years	75 Years and Over	65 to 74 Years	75 Years and Over
Texas—Cont.														
Congressional District 35......	38,576	26,266	13,538	16,334	4,950	7,651	3,345	4,161	3,492	5,474	9,022	10,724	2,933	4,695
Congressional District 36......	60,926	34,644	20,021	20,971	7,642	11,053	5,252	5,010	5,561	6,239	12,873	13,689	2,653	4,957
Utah														
Congressional District 1........	42,037	29,683	9,384	14,245	4,321	7,812	1,480	3,077	1,680	3,038	4,907	8,960	1,083	3,856
Congressional District 2........	49,728	34,200	13,013	17,209	5,560	8,923	2,486	3,540	2,920	3,798	7,256	11,362	1,484	3,253
Congressional District 3........	39,296	28,605	8,581	12,562	4,747	7,036	1,446	2,563	2,062	4,133	4,586	7,639	1,194	3,118
Congressional District 4........	39,781	27,847	9,686	14,988	4,550	7,169	1,115	2,687	1,615	3,572	5,169	8,758	1,437	3,806
Vermont														
Congressional District (at Large)...............	61,836	41,295	15,048	20,504	6,251	10,686	2,315	3,832	3,582	5,251	8,603	13,212	2,308	5,043
Virginia														
Congressional District 1........	62,896	41,072	13,547	20,797	4,896	9,711	1,605	2,677	2,937	6,949	7,798	13,041	2,622	5,276
Congressional District 2........	53,924	37,623	11,810	17,631	3,082	6,742	1,787	3,522	1,384	4,980	7,030	11,401	1,925	3,806
Congressional District 3........	49,988	37,670	13,673	19,757	3,213	7,274	1,739	3,598	2,748	5,752	10,171	14,234	2,622	6,820
Congressional District 4........	60,928	34,036	14,155	16,938	3,998	6,347	1,450	3,947	2,380	4,338	9,438	11,960	1,699	4,627
Congressional District 5........	77,982	53,974	19,865	26,933	6,725	13,571	2,594	4,967	3,858	8,119	12,173	16,550	2,670	6,949
Congressional District 6........	70,688	53,374	18,446	26,514	6,296	13,064	3,206	6,476	3,569	6,429	10,791	16,673	3,291	6,706
Congressional District 7........	67,673	44,451	13,273	20,251	4,502	8,332	1,461	3,836	2,383	5,101	7,381	14,357	2,403	5,974
Congressional District 8........	48,326	29,766	9,214	14,539	2,684	6,804	1,118	2,466	1,011	3,941	5,429	9,200	1,178	3,609
Congressional District 9........	75,711	53,573	27,340	29,896	10,279	15,696	4,891	6,678	5,748	8,479	17,429	19,259	5,197	8,541
Congressional District 10......	56,510	30,769	10,479	14,153	3,496	6,171	1,016	4,135	2,000	4,526	5,966	9,152	1,371	3,753
Congressional District 11......	48,918	30,646	9,391	13,721	2,915	5,399	1,370	1,541	1,586	2,958	6,265	9,188	1,189	3,093
Washington														
Congressional District 1........	54,790	31,139	12,210	15,088	5,656	6,733	1,574	2,232	3,184	4,932	6,927	8,905	2,095	3,825
Congressional District 2........	63,117	41,225	15,232	21,291	6,387	10,394	3,154	3,942	3,662	6,486	9,267	13,183	3,141	5,743
Congressional District 3........	67,819	42,287	20,161	21,224	9,497	10,821	2,036	4,339	5,471	6,823	12,094	13,276	2,879	6,115
Congressional District 4........	53,881	34,638	16,879	19,861	6,799	9,711	1,413	4,071	3,351	5,908	10,447	13,822	2,932	5,152
Congressional District 5........	62,097	42,043	18,141	23,681	8,715	12,485	2,859	4,694	4,157	7,543	10,023	14,302	2,564	6,907
Congressional District 6........	73,306	45,690	20,245	22,981	9,115	12,264	2,824	5,578	3,808	6,548	12,467	14,028	2,575	5,720
Congressional District 7........	54,676	36,901	11,697	18,968	4,187	8,352	1,101	3,296	2,752	6,189	6,536	12,799	1,478	6,032
Congressional District 8........	50,567	32,836	11,030	16,084	5,219	9,106	1,652	3,209	2,227	5,698	6,132	9,726	1,946	4,775
Congressional District 9........	50,602	40,337	12,957	19,992	4,720	10,727	2,879	4,135	4,107	6,630	7,235	13,036	2,347	7,056
Congressional District 10......	55,806	37,557	16,550	20,810	6,604	10,801	2,272	4,513	3,312	6,240	9,787	13,147	1,748	5,764
West Virginia														
Congressional District 1........	61,104	43,274	18,520	22,923	8,190	11,506	3,294	5,030	3,727	6,555	11,931	13,774	3,949	5,257
Congressional District 2........	63,127	43,194	20,672	21,313	8,484	10,260	3,376	4,529	4,708	4,856	12,182	13,919	3,701	5,662
Congressional District 3........	64,679	44,555	29,229	29,150	13,100	16,602	6,802	9,513	6,385	9,371	19,015	20,097	3,794	9,029
Wisconsin														
Congressional District 1........	58,847	43,702	13,347	19,835	5,878	9,705	805	3,207	1,986	5,446	7,806	12,753	1,658	5,631
Congressional District 2........	56,062	38,917	11,306	18,817	5,026	7,522	1,574	3,486	1,740	4,219	5,127	10,593	1,201	4,107
Congressional District 3........	63,284	48,215	13,103	20,683	5,170	10,555	1,634	3,455	2,286	4,907	7,213	12,738	1,835	5,217
Congressional District 4........	42,113	33,687	11,600	17,699	3,930	7,059	2,143	3,609	2,341	5,148	7,974	12,007	3,032	5,427
Congressional District 5........	61,623	51,675	11,413	21,985	5,097	9,554	1,137	2,960	1,670	3,892	5,978	15,145	1,342	4,418
Congressional District 6........	63,356	51,019	12,991	22,609	5,049	11,428	2,165	3,744	2,248	5,207	7,419	14,066	1,810	5,188
Congressional District 7........	72,512	54,280	16,142	24,105	8,259	13,009	2,330	4,579	2,187	4,917	7,566	14,925	1,861	5,353
Congressional District 8........	61,942	45,227	11,980	19,653	5,312	9,359	1,368	3,262	2,090	5,358	6,509	12,571	1,728	4,182
Wyoming														
Congressional District (at Large).............................	48,444	29,596	12,878	14,446	6,019	6,746	2,239	2,717	2,522	3,762	6,793	8,377	2,218	2,507

PART I

HEALTH INSURANCE COVERAGE AND TYPE OF INSURANCE

HEALTH INSURANCE COVERAGE AND TYPE OF INSURANCE

At age 65, most Americans become eligible and obtain health insurance coverage through the national Medicare program. Of the 46.2 million population age 65 and over, 93.4 percent are insured by Medicare. Some have earlier eligibility and 9.5 percent of the population age 55 to 64 have coverage through Medicare. The District of Columbia has the lowest Medicare coverage rate at 86.0 percent while Idaho has the highest coverage level at 95.8. Eight other states are above 95 percent, including Arizona, Michigan, Mississippi, Montana, North Carolina, Oregon, South Carolina and West Virginia. Among the 55 to 64 population, Medicare coverage is highest in West Virginia at 16.6 percent and lowest in Alaska at 5.8 percent.

However, the categories reported in the ACS are not mutually exclusive. People can obtain coverage through multiple plans depending on their individual and family situations and the benefits offered by different plans. This is seen in the ACS data on insurance coverage where the percentage by coverage type far exceeds 100 percent. For example, while 96.5 percent of the 65 and over population is covered by Medicare, 33.1 percent hold employer based coverage, 30.6 percent are in direct pay plans, and 13.4 percent obtain Medicaid.

Private employer based coverage is most important for the 55 to 64 population as 61.1 percent are covered by such plans. Coverage is highest in New Hampshire at 70 percent but even the lowest level of coverage (Mississippi) is over 50 percent. Employer based plans cover only 33.1 percent of the 65 and over population where the District of Columbia is highest at 51.8 percent and South Dakota is lowest at 20.4 percent.

Montana has the highest percentage of the 55 to 64 population covered by direct purchase plans with 17.7 percent. Among the 65 and over group, 53.1 percent of North Dakota's population has direct purchase plans.

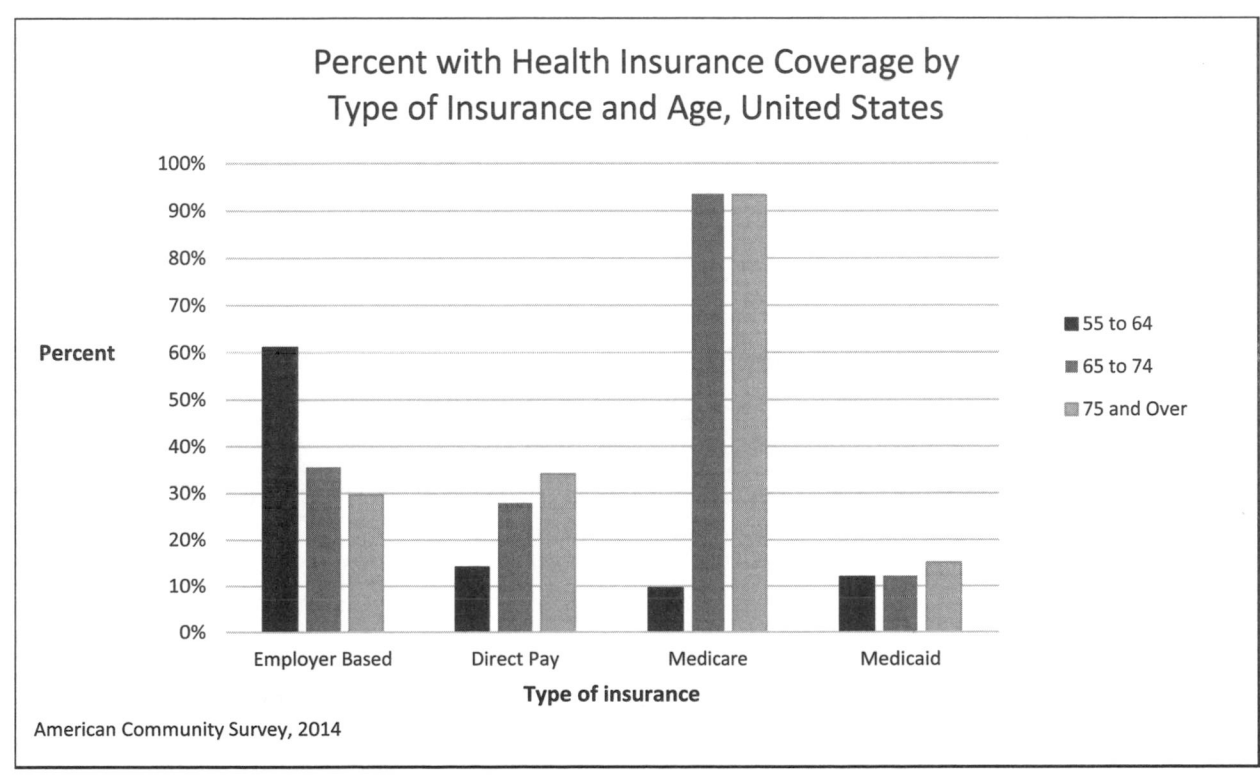

American Community Survey, 2014

Alaska is lowest at 11.7 percent. Thirty-five states have at least 30 percent of the 65 and over population covered by direct purchase plans. For the 55 to 64 population, in all but six states, direct purchase covers between 10 and 20 percent of the population.

The national Medicare program covers only 9.5 percent of the 55 to 64 population and this is mainly for persons with eligible disabilities. By contrast, 93.4 percent of the 65 and over population has Medicare coverage and even in the District of Columbia (the lowest), 86.0 percent have Medicare. Medicaid coverage is more evenly distributed between the 55 to 64 and 65 and over populations. Nationwide, 12.0 percent of the 55 to 64 population has Medicaid compared to 13.4 percent of the 65 and over. The District of Columbia has the highest Medicaid coverage rate for both age categories at 29.7 percent (55 to 64) and 23.5 percent for the 65 and over. New Hampshire has the lowest Medicaid coverage among the 55 to 64 group at 4.7 and is also for the 65 and over population at 6.9 percent.

County coverage of the 55 to 64 population through employer based plans varied from a low of 25.5 percent in McKinley County, New Mexico to a high of 83.5 percent in Hunterdon County, New Jersey. There isn't as wide a range among the 65 and over population starting at the low of 10.2 percent in Miami-Dade County, Florida to the highest coverage of 61.5 percent in Genesee County, Michigan. Direct purchase plans are more prevalent among the 65 and over than then the 55 to 64 population. The county with the highest percent of direct purchase for the 55 to 64 is Kendall County, Illinois at 32.7 percent while Wood County, Wisconsin is highest among the 65 and over population at 61.2 percent.

Coverage through Medicare shows a narrow range for the 65 and over population where 98.8 percent of the

population in Lake County, California is the highest, while the lowest coverage is 84.5 percent in Loudon County, Virginia. Among the 55 to 64 population only a little more than one-third of the population (36.7 percent) is covered in Pike County, Kentucky, the highest coverage level. Medicaid covers more than half of the 65 and over population (50.6 percent) in Imperial County, California but only 38.8 percent in the highest county (Bronx, New York) for the 55 to 64 population.

Employer based plans cover 66.7 percent of the 65 and over population in Davis, California but only 3.6 percent in Hialeah, Florida. Among the 55 to 64 population, 85.6 percent coverage is the highest in O'Fallon, Missouri and lowest (23.5 percent) in Linwood, California. For direct pay coverage, Fargo, North Dakota has the highest rate for the 65 and over population at 61.2 percent. More than 95 percent of the 65 and over is covered by Medicare in 80 counties with Layton, Utah being the highest at a reported 100 percent. The Medicaid program covers 55.2 percent of the 65 and over population in Hialeah, Florida but less than 1 percent in O'Fallon, Missouri.

Employer based plans for the 55 to 64 population cover at least 50 percent in 450 metropolitan and micropolitan areas. In comparison to the 65 and over population, only 21 metro and micro areas have coverage rates over 50 percent. The California-Lexington Park, Maryland metropolitan area has the highest coverage for the 55 to 64 population (78.2 percent) while the Flint, Michigan metro is highest among the 65 and over population at 61.5 percent. Direct purchase plans are more prevalent among the 65 and over than the 55 to 64 population. The coverage range for the 65 and over population is from a low of 12.0 percent in the Anchorage, Alaska metro area to a high of 61.2 percent in the Wisconsin Rapids-Marshfield micropolitan area. For the 55 to 64 population, the Bozeman, Montana micro area is the highest at

Highest and Lowest Metropolitan and Micropolitan Area Percent of Coverage for the Population 65 Years and Over by Health Insurance Type

Employer Based	Direct Pay	Medicare	Medicaid
Highest Percentage			
Congressional District 5 - 59.4%	Congressional District 7, MN - 54.9%	Congressional District 40, CA - 90.0%	Congressional District 15, NY - 59.7%
Congressional District 5 - 56.8%	Congressional District (at Large), ND - 53.1%	Congressional District 12, NJ - 89.9%	Congressional District 13, NY - 47.6%
Congressional District 8 - 56.0%	Congressional District 1, MN - 51.6%	Congressional District 8, MA - 89.9%	Congressional District 7, NY - 46.6%
Congressional District 4 - 55.1%	Congressional District 3, MN - 51.5%	Congressional District 24, FL - 89.6%	Congressional District 40, CA - 44.4%
Congressional District 1 - 54.5%	Congressional District 4, IA - 51.2%	Congressional District 41, CA - 89.6%	Congressional District 34, CA - 43.0%
Lowest Percentage			
Congressional District 40, CA - 14.9%	Congressional District 44, CA - 9.5%	Congressional District 5, NY - 87.5%	Congressional District 6, IL - 5.9%
Congressional District 34, CA - 13.6%	Congressional District 13, NY - 9.2%	Congressional District 9, TX - 87.0%	Congressional District 7, VA - 5.7%
Congressional District 24, FL - 13.2%	Congressional District 35, CA - 9.1%	Congressional District 46, CA - 87.0%	Congressional District 3, MN - 5.4%
Congressional District 26, FL - 11.7%	Congressional District 40, CA - 7.8%	Congressional District 11, VA - 86.6%	Congressional District 2, CO - 5.1%
Congressional District 27, FL - 9.6%	Congressional District 34, CA - 7.2%	Delegate District (at Large), DC - 86.0%	Congressional District 2, MO - 4.0%

25.6 percent and the lowest is 3.9 percent in the Gallup, New Mexico micropolitan area. Nearly 100 percent (98.8 percent) of the 65 and over population in the Clearlake, California micropolitan area is covered by Medicare and 166 areas have over 95 percent coverage. The Alexandria, Louisiana metro area has the lowest percent of Medicare coverage at 85.4 percent.

Among congressional districts, only 24 districts have Medicare coverage rates under 90 percent for the 65 and over population with the District of Columbia's Delegate District lowest at 86.0 percent. Medicaid coverage for the 65 and over population is highest in New York's 15th Congressional District at 59.7 percent. In 147 congressional districts more than one-third of the 65 and over population carries direct pay coverage as do 207 districts for employer based coverage. Michigan's 5th Congressional District has the highest coverage rate for employer based plans at 59.4 percent. Minnesota's 7th District is highest at 54.9 percent for direct pay coverage.

COVERAGE OPTIONS DEFINED

Health insurance coverage in the ACS defines coverage to include plans and programs that provide comprehensive health coverage. Plans that provide insurance for specific conditions or situations such as cancer and long-term care policies are not considered comprehensive coverage. The types of coverage are derived from a series of questions asked of all respondents by their "yes" or "no" response for each type. The types of coverage are further identified as either private or public insurance coverage. While the question is asked of all respondents, the data is reported for only the civilian non-institutional population.

Private Insurance Coverage

Employer Based – Insurance through a current or former employer or union (of this person or another family member).

Direct Purchase – Insurance purchased directly from an insurance company (by this person or another family member).

Public Insurance Coverage

Medicare – Insurance coverage by Medicare for people 65 and over, or people with certain disabilities.

Medicaid – Insurance coverage by Medicaid, Medical Assistance, or any kind of government-assistance plan for those with low incomes or a disability.

Percent of the Population 65 Years and Over With Direct Pay Health Insurance Coverage

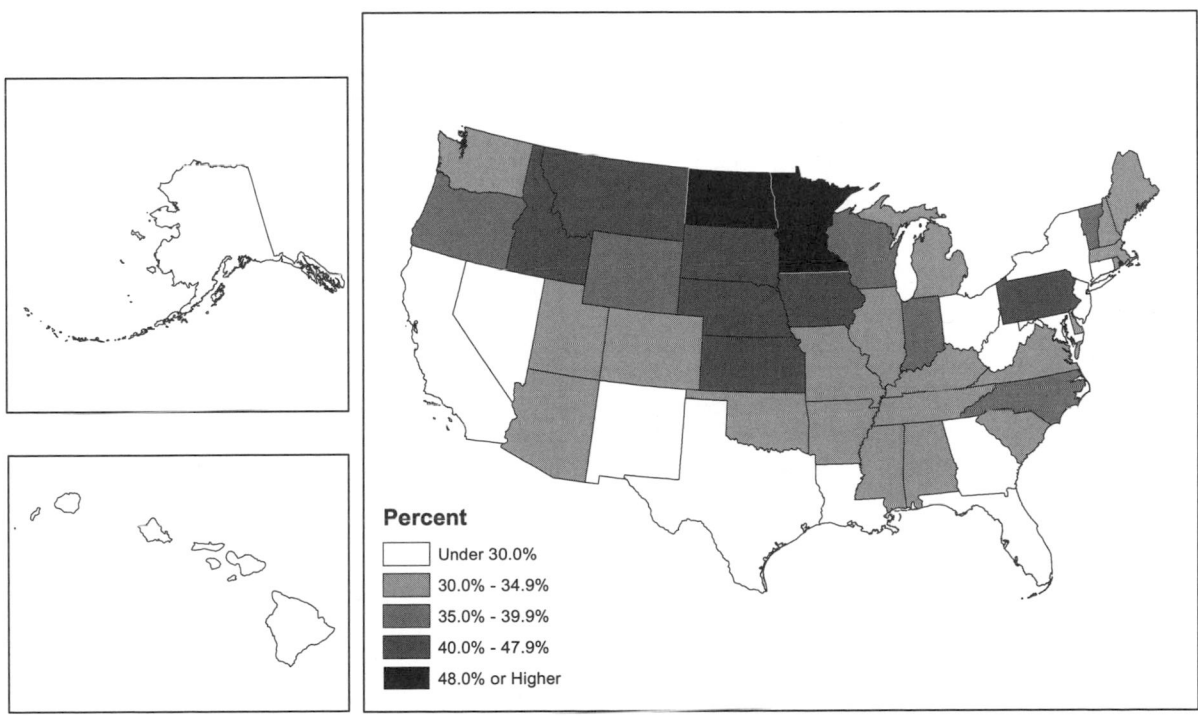

Percent
- Under 30.0%
- 30.0% - 34.9%
- 35.0% - 39.9%
- 40.0% - 47.9%
- 48.0% or Higher

Table I-1: States—Persons With Health Insurance by Source of Insurance

| | Private Health Insurance Coverage | | | | | | Public Health Insurance Coverage | | | | | |
| | Employer Based | | | Direct Purchase | | | Medicare | | | Medicaid/CHIP | | |
	55 to 64 Years	65 to 74 Years	75 Years and Over	55 to 64 Years	65 to 74 Years	75 Years and Over	55 to 64 Years	65 to 74 Years	75 Years and Over	55 to 64 Years	65 to 74 Years	75 Years and Over
United States	24,497,562	9,396,781	5,878,447	5,634,936	7,371,100	6,749,270	3,827,590	24,703,732	18,470,696	4,793,684	3,203,854	2,968,670
Alabama	374,725	159,488	96,748	92,988	123,490	101,208	96,472	415,686	291,938	69,453	56,433	50,199
Alaska	58,612	22,246	9,568	9,797	4,968	3,180	5,337	40,917	22,385	8,079	6,629	6,054
Arizona	431,095	170,069	117,006	118,417	174,199	150,000	74,120	586,519	431,561	112,131	69,427	55,214
Arkansas	203,038	70,836	43,793	55,228	84,328	74,291	56,912	256,941	181,830	53,321	33,143	31,076
California	2,536,891	961,474	593,281	659,406	587,070	531,988	352,806	2,586,237	2,028,440	752,502	491,751	493,631
Colorado	405,117	132,966	78,243	115,679	111,683	99,401	47,020	379,341	251,928	71,154	36,813	33,820
Connecticut	334,212	131,603	82,596	65,928	75,572	83,901	34,427	276,805	230,265	54,009	33,451	36,542
Delaware	85,031	45,707	25,152	12,444	24,337	22,523	11,197	86,992	58,182	15,260	7,937	7,078
District of Columbia	38,462	23,812	14,769	7,692	8,093	8,806	7,000	35,010	29,034	20,462	9,186	8,278
Florida	1,318,889	560,549	412,569	436,606	515,331	511,472	253,523	1,952,847	1,623,093	260,752	259,786	267,572
Georgia	689,002	269,304	137,728	151,720	178,281	142,574	133,495	725,888	449,285	116,295	106,107	82,408
Hawaii	125,708	69,999	44,254	23,267	26,754	29,835	11,337	114,930	94,903	19,565	13,125	13,269
Idaho	112,001	37,415	22,256	41,277	52,279	43,683	17,858	134,301	90,824	15,795	12,599	10,079
Illinois	1,048,494	368,863	233,819	217,770	308,491	298,967	130,172	928,494	721,357	169,626	102,703	92,868
Indiana	544,033	187,757	121,726	111,934	180,480	165,880	87,697	508,365	374,507	73,165	44,447	37,263
Iowa	275,451	76,320	51,733	69,842	114,020	117,446	30,422	247,701	210,419	40,900	24,965	25,961
Kansas	237,530	65,608	42,403	59,466	91,657	93,360	32,508	213,439	174,666	24,850	20,800	21,298
Kentucky	336,636	143,590	87,644	74,075	116,728	96,552	91,875	369,079	248,390	101,486	51,741	40,547
Louisiana	324,856	131,646	74,528	80,220	88,754	74,082	75,813	347,203	238,848	76,701	55,363	47,281
Maine	122,159	44,400	27,043	31,827	41,548	38,998	21,066	134,614	94,980	25,796	19,849	18,740
Maryland	533,765	254,623	147,411	98,827	119,737	113,816	55,990	433,615	318,503	78,194	45,240	47,083
Massachusetts	611,842	246,628	155,712	90,550	154,992	156,576	69,405	515,227	413,397	173,928	82,602	76,212
Michigan	898,472	426,341	304,759	185,401	266,505	240,272	160,107	837,816	620,393	182,577	97,810	82,576
Minnesota	473,662	127,469	79,802	120,707	204,776	182,742	49,673	407,192	319,562	77,063	32,839	32,154
Mississippi	190,805	61,819	34,869	49,736	73,361	60,473	60,956	237,293	169,776	60,894	48,252	37,272
Missouri	486,261	164,279	108,331	116,186	163,737	146,352	96,989	501,845	370,086	71,467	45,635	37,459
Montana	82,369	27,484	16,941	30,139	35,979	32,328	13,951	95,547	66,625	11,718	9,207	7,249
Nebraska	155,533	43,124	24,519	41,341	56,783	61,114	18,712	136,651	115,233	16,148	11,900	13,483
Nevada	205,263	80,209	38,477	41,833	51,039	39,197	29,072	233,759	143,215	39,589	29,835	19,296
New Hampshire	138,558	50,146	29,228	27,019	38,726	33,773	16,241	115,851	78,788	9,317	8,215	6,211
New Jersey	795,824	328,968	191,717	128,196	175,915	191,593	81,462	665,676	540,855	106,196	72,330	79,332
New Mexico	142,228	63,596	42,968	39,083	41,873	32,470	29,191	174,345	125,233	41,512	26,499	18,342
New York	1,610,974	690,252	423,398	274,728	326,287	356,233	213,811	1,477,639	1,194,207	444,279	272,316	269,417
North Carolina	716,704	287,265	162,246	206,616	285,690	226,253	146,062	834,338	553,991	121,955	95,817	84,867
North Dakota	63,870	17,833	9,462	16,507	26,385	29,182	6,027	51,775	44,669	5,203	4,749	5,131
Ohio	1,051,578	399,656	294,656	177,600	274,428	259,251	152,544	944,605	727,061	170,225	93,756	75,170
Oklahoma	271,765	111,263	66,491	66,878	92,681	84,314	55,293	304,480	222,415	38,980	30,698	25,600
Oregon	314,455	110,477	74,305	85,379	129,598	109,380	48,967	357,061	249,339	85,152	44,475	35,938
Pennsylvania	1,194,406	417,610	288,861	262,467	420,967	432,465	161,653	1,088,645	908,095	178,193	119,014	122,479
Rhode Island	91,635	32,081	20,166	17,915	23,931	30,038	14,655	83,440	70,085	22,142	11,261	13,223
South Carolina	361,357	159,826	87,678	89,256	139,855	101,078	83,912	451,397	277,077	71,334	52,426	38,348
South Dakota	69,981	16,499	9,840	22,121	27,720	29,374	7,588	65,443	53,884	7,658	7,409	7,123
Tennessee	487,809	179,572	104,852	123,183	190,577	149,802	108,121	562,739	371,021	98,101	73,795	57,058
Texas	1,716,102	604,968	345,340	390,840	434,425	354,141	263,544	1,684,997	1,171,253	268,600	224,962	203,832
Utah	186,030	62,890	43,785	40,612	50,433	43,320	19,470	161,366	118,645	17,203	13,119	11,947
Vermont	59,469	21,670	11,684	13,291	20,952	18,693	9,914	59,825	41,268	17,564	7,937	7,271
Virginia	675,641	277,842	151,455	153,514	206,780	168,240	89,184	631,503	436,225	56,374	52,160	52,536
Washington	565,125	205,188	121,710	136,004	187,730	154,374	79,483	555,161	379,183	110,665	61,683	53,404
West Virginia	164,192	85,186	58,373	25,443	47,290	37,489	44,667	184,346	130,275	46,351	20,914	15,144
Wisconsin	528,223	153,686	105,538	114,511	177,289	172,615	65,158	463,526	364,169	77,673	46,146	49,971
Wyoming	51,722	14,679	7,014	13,470	16,596	14,175	4,731	45,320	29,333	6,127	4,598	4,364

Table I-2: Counties—Persons With Health Insurance by Source of Insurance

| | Private Health Insurance Coverage | | | | | | Public Health Insurance Coverage | | | | | |
| | Employer Based | | | Direct Purchase | | | Medicare | | | Medicaid/CHIP | | |
	55 to 64 Years	65 to 74 Years	75 Years and Over	55 to 64 Years	65 to 74 Years	75 Years and Over	55 to 64 Years	65 to 74 Years	75 Years and Over	55 to 64 Years	65 to 74 Years	75 Years and Over
Alabama												
Baldwin County	17,707	8,136	4,449	4,065	5,728	5,592	3,548	21,405	14,977	1,968	1,674	1,472
Calhoun County	9,847	5,298	3,136	2,248	3,492	2,432	3,285	10,625	7,051	1,576	1,821	1,519
Cullman County	6,811	1,922	1,868	1,051	2,114	1,603	2,085	8,344	5,539	1,220	1,236	685
DeKalb County	3,453	1,511	519	1,906	1,992	1,474	2,569	6,728	3,863	1,414	1,766	1,683
Elmore County	7,292	3,094	1,858	1,052	1,930	1,368	1,116	6,349	4,295	1,038	428	553
Etowah County	8,243	4,088	3,149	1,508	3,304	2,092	2,838	10,419	6,779	2,393	2,224	1,572
Houston County	7,749	2,850	1,462	2,039	2,943	2,404	2,000	9,425	6,812	1,745	1,068	894
Jefferson County	53,047	20,855	13,732	14,407	13,334	12,690	10,988	49,709	39,425	11,666	6,397	5,550
Lauderdale County	8,514	3,566	2,219	1,898	3,045	3,001	1,841	9,458	6,872	951	887	764
Lee County	8,608	4,302	2,793	2,607	2,523	2,180	2,294	9,214	5,599	1,444	797	698
Limestone County	6,375	2,813	2,218	1,558	2,490	1,669	1,298	7,214	4,726	1,250	952	490
Madison County	30,483	12,675	8,415	6,208	7,519	7,673	3,146	24,881	20,138	2,594	2,647	2,636
Marshall County	5,834	2,248	1,350	2,117	2,696	2,338	2,588	8,688	5,934	899	1,760	699
Mobile County	31,247	11,276	6,384	7,310	11,148	7,813	8,019	33,082	23,115	5,362	4,628	4,053
Montgomery County	16,393	7,837	4,400	4,512	3,364	3,507	3,764	16,194	12,305	3,090	2,745	2,620
Morgan County	9,526	3,778	2,042	2,115	4,287	2,897	2,345	10,351	7,096	1,692	1,056	1,305
Shelby County	18,319	7,442	3,688	4,515	5,017	4,055	2,291	16,374	9,748	1,130	1,294	1,365
St. Clair County	6,964	3,358	1,689	1,260	1,408	1,387	2,150	7,838	5,106	1,692	1,493	492
Talladega County	6,767	2,396	1,489	1,611	2,529	1,628	2,075	7,525	4,719	1,648	1,795	931
Tuscaloosa County	15,285	5,816	4,017	3,557	3,896	2,752	4,480	13,428	9,349	2,517	1,592	1,797
Walker County	5,118	2,728	2,532	1,268	1,724	1,409	2,069	6,747	4,629	1,242	1,124	512
Alaska												
Anchorage Municipality	23,602	8,194	3,866	4,080	1,895	1,056	2,400	14,730	9,645	2,892	2,325	2,914
Fairbanks North Star Borough	7,981	2,782	1,357	1,032	1,002	285	507	4,586	2,582	831	603	687
Matanuska-Susitna Borough	7,301	2,496	966	1,282	865	565	858	5,893	2,567	1,141	959	575
Arizona												
Apache County	3,556	875	294	404	966	404	908	5,246	3,444	2,043	1,874	1,587
Cochise County	8,132	3,990	4,077	3,246	4,436	4,271	1,520	13,344	10,158	3,011	2,687	1,842
Coconino County	9,726	3,546	933	2,743	1,806	2,143	1,350	9,518	5,282	2,086	1,160	1,214
Maricopa County	258,670	91,552	61,342	67,488	89,162	80,403	38,506	306,014	228,972	55,076	34,612	28,019
Mohave County	10,905	7,254	5,559	4,571	10,921	7,943	4,326	31,601	22,264	6,903	2,073	2,523
Navajo County	5,954	1,967	896	1,505	3,377	1,958	1,753	10,223	5,987	2,983	1,587	1,495
Pima County	69,030	26,018	21,547	17,513	23,564	21,459	11,094	95,951	74,742	20,303	10,932	10,021
Pinal County	28,648	12,424	8,050	5,791	14,457	8,236	6,498	42,958	25,437	5,862	4,098	2,141
Yavapai County	17,413	12,126	7,024	9,365	12,694	10,411	4,106	35,744	24,069	5,089	3,948	1,804
Yuma County	8,991	4,552	3,096	2,462	5,645	7,060	1,661	16,692	16,757	3,893	3,361	2,597
Arkansas												
Benton County	16,442	4,382	2,424	3,362	5,903	5,299	1,836	17,106	12,404	2,433	1,305	1,807
Craighead County	5,546	2,097	992	2,181	2,484	3,052	984	7,245	5,382	1,452	799	1,151
Faulkner County	7,375	2,287	1,006	1,986	2,588	2,134	1,225	7,626	4,978	938	376	1,086
Garland County	7,082	4,429	3,014	2,220	3,365	3,894	2,532	11,482	8,932	3,183	972	886
Jefferson County	5,268	1,947	963	1,398	1,228	1,836	1,437	5,818	4,102	1,831	1,128	743
Lonoke County	4,760	1,688	587	1,091	1,433	1,069	1,315	5,416	3,113	442	596	215
Pulaski County	31,357	10,905	7,380	6,627	9,247	8,219	6,264	28,544	21,011	7,080	4,206	3,624
Saline County	8,245	3,702	2,379	1,850	3,943	2,277	2,525	11,720	6,780	1,454	930	1,021
Sebastian County	9,667	2,585	2,336	2,115	3,218	2,920	1,681	9,953	7,009	2,591	1,567	1,268
Washington County	13,919	4,246	2,199	2,113	2,973	3,253	2,496	12,538	8,931	1,953	1,629	1,382
White County	4,693	1,704	1,040	779	1,635	2,457	1,812	6,402	5,018	1,762	510	648
California												
Alameda County	119,549	44,423	25,585	26,826	25,288	22,369	15,567	103,302	79,086	32,893	18,119	18,733
Butte County	14,177	7,513	6,642	4,155	6,808	4,316	4,062	20,186	15,832	6,351	2,375	2,976
Contra Costa County	92,347	40,974	27,069	22,135	27,352	21,388	9,090	84,596	63,335	16,357	9,596	11,817
El Dorado County	17,280	9,522	5,049	5,968	5,321	3,898	3,671	19,507	12,168	4,994	2,201	1,739
Fresno County	52,290	20,105	14,229	13,048	14,315	12,818	8,643	57,342	43,574	20,974	13,442	11,834
Humboldt County	7,414	3,667	2,194	2,857	4,960	3,420	2,826	12,049	7,705	5,587	1,290	457
Imperial County	7,191	2,396	1,434	1,904	1,626	1,409	2,296	10,777	9,476	4,152	5,819	5,151
Kern County	45,697	16,615	8,304	9,880	9,255	8,115	9,166	47,991	32,673	16,917	8,439	6,804
Kings County	5,502	2,415	861	1,434	869	1,796	2,452	7,278	5,316	2,625	1,273	1,259
Lake County	4,279	2,391	1,431	1,454	2,110	1,776	2,362	7,651	4,898	3,194	1,394	596
Los Angeles County	586,319	207,955	123,135	159,417	90,525	92,736	79,774	616,939	508,057	225,338	158,592	171,467
Madera County	8,343	4,327	2,103	2,313	2,849	2,009	1,189	10,759	7,834	3,289	2,281	2,296
Marin County	25,754	12,932	9,365	10,097	9,124	6,826	2,258	26,825	19,002	2,960	2,827	2,250
Mendocino County	6,418	2,532	1,246	2,498	2,822	1,985	1,718	10,359	5,786	3,389	1,784	1,085
Merced County	11,918	3,773	2,101	3,292	4,886	3,065	2,679	14,603	10,943	6,069	3,611	4,289
Monterey County	26,142	9,170	5,178	7,076	7,173	6,370	3,556	26,824	20,965	7,654	5,323	5,986
Napa County	12,115	6,949	4,224	3,550	4,407	3,269	1,308	13,285	9,135	1,930	1,215	1,074
Nevada County	10,735	4,782	3,992	3,093	4,934	2,807	1,883	13,180	8,986	2,075	1,079	835
Orange County	218,276	73,125	44,391	64,975	45,115	39,740	21,687	209,723	173,112	48,181	32,104	33,187
Placer County	33,215	20,042	11,828	8,347	12,160	10,270	3,910	36,058	28,041	4,429	2,853	2,506
Riverside County	129,696	50,081	33,890	31,772	32,950	30,065	20,451	160,366	127,440	43,691	26,620	22,632
Sacramento County	108,650	50,646	32,850	18,026	21,802	20,271	16,562	99,052	76,306	32,033	19,042	18,228
San Bernardino County	120,359	36,125	18,499	22,363	17,458	16,451	19,551	118,082	82,106	44,532	23,649	20,461
San Diego County	215,792	72,328	43,655	58,697	49,526	45,066	23,047	210,065	173,046	45,498	34,377	35,676
San Francisco County	58,739	23,384	18,064	14,877	12,194	12,001	8,358	57,807	54,119	21,466	15,523	19,461
San Joaquin County	42,973	17,113	8,907	8,151	11,985	12,118	7,700	45,464	32,798	15,787	11,246	7,601
San Luis Obispo County	25,240	10,494	9,045	6,709	9,010	8,507	3,259	26,863	19,111	4,231	3,211	1,774

Table I-2: Counties—Persons With Health Insurance by Source of Insurance—*Continued*

| | Private Health Insurance Coverage | | | | | | Public Health Insurance Coverage | | | | | |
| | Employer Based | | | Direct Purchase | | | Medicare | | | Medicaid/CHIP | | |
	55 to 64 Years	65 to 74 Years	75 Years and Over	55 to 64 Years	65 to 74 Years	75 Years and Over	55 to 64 Years	65 to 74 Years	75 Years and Over	55 to 64 Years	65 to 74 Years	75 Years and Over
California—Cont.												
San Mateo County	64,429	28,011	19,173	16,307	17,349	16,221	6,143	55,919	47,290	12,053	6,870	8,861
Santa Barbara County	28,714	11,667	8,655	8,937	10,936	11,296	3,418	30,226	28,042	5,351	3,931	4,363
Santa Clara County	137,315	45,437	28,638	35,804	29,203	28,407	11,270	115,272	95,650	29,383	24,460	26,414
Santa Cruz County	22,503	7,562	3,674	8,398	7,116	5,547	2,152	21,148	13,086	4,846	2,589	2,224
Shasta County	14,073	6,428	3,930	4,167	5,574	5,146	3,877	19,599	13,883	4,632	3,494	2,308
Solano County	35,223	16,185	8,059	6,651	6,736	6,518	5,341	31,306	22,585	7,544	4,096	3,386
Sonoma County	42,763	20,710	11,177	14,050	15,739	14,497	7,948	46,426	30,598	9,653	4,771	4,747
Stanislaus County	31,131	10,642	5,731	8,056	10,924	8,145	6,897	34,215	25,806	12,203	6,680	7,257
Sutter County	5,882	1,895	1,649	953	1,801	2,310	1,141	7,285	5,907	1,650	2,395	1,231
Tulare County	21,961	7,360	4,580	5,294	5,272	5,333	6,153	24,466	18,450	8,501	6,769	4,128
Ventura County	64,928	22,262	14,761	17,833	17,711	15,389	8,109	60,411	47,038	12,740	6,418	9,102
Yolo County	14,221	6,127	4,357	3,021	2,796	3,080	1,335	13,043	9,463	2,897	2,570	1,489
Yuba County	4,040	1,399	1,185	1,287	1,596	841	692	4,922	3,109	1,259	874	686
Colorado												
Adams County	31,344	11,568	4,746	5,936	5,870	7,444	4,443	25,278	16,828	6,178	4,092	2,684
Arapahoe County	49,454	13,841	9,692	11,441	10,589	10,291	5,826	40,645	26,211	6,807	3,490	3,044
Boulder County	25,489	8,374	4,583	8,721	6,320	6,181	1,841	21,147	14,358	3,426	1,548	1,910
Denver County	37,515	14,102	8,909	10,236	9,560	9,964	6,182	38,642	28,069	12,418	6,553	6,384
Douglas County	27,204	8,678	3,716	6,147	5,775	3,731	939	19,584	10,140	1,195	628	234
El Paso County	41,428	11,352	6,593	9,676	11,626	11,680	5,148	42,939	28,921	9,884	3,834	3,324
Jefferson County	55,331	19,306	11,332	15,760	11,744	11,111	4,452	44,398	30,920	4,982	3,721	4,206
Larimer County	27,191	9,351	6,216	8,607	7,630	6,018	2,590	25,594	17,265	3,710	1,199	826
Mesa County	10,954	3,764	2,275	3,283	4,584	4,942	1,451	13,439	9,992	2,384	1,203	790
Pueblo County	12,849	4,814	5,079	3,775	4,597	4,147	2,669	14,276	10,957	2,703	2,532	1,610
Weld County	20,164	4,489	3,176	4,838	6,543	4,982	1,936	17,839	11,526	3,635	1,808	1,425
Connecticut												
Fairfield County	80,754	31,694	19,121	20,773	17,235	22,504	6,299	65,730	57,998	10,513	7,224	6,696
Hartford County	83,265	31,599	22,137	15,120	19,929	20,635	10,020	67,438	59,818	13,728	9,179	10,891
Litchfield County	21,163	8,738	4,722	4,067	5,262	5,225	2,304	18,178	13,466	3,811	1,744	1,917
Middlesex County	18,201	8,479	5,109	2,553	3,900	3,832	1,675	15,017	11,328	2,790	1,226	1,443
New Haven County	78,281	28,831	19,257	14,534	19,219	20,886	9,120	66,959	55,690	15,090	9,182	10,346
New London County	25,734	11,715	6,972	4,850	5,424	5,531	2,308	22,705	17,754	4,321	2,878	2,886
Tolland County	15,929	6,529	3,176	2,634	2,541	2,747	1,055	11,422	7,883	1,009	1,056	1,039
Windham County	10,885	4,018	2,102	1,397	2,062	2,541	1,646	9,356	6,328	2,747	962	1,324
Delaware												
Kent County	12,012	7,591	4,103	2,082	3,528	4,400	2,499	15,630	10,121	2,993	1,961	1,221
New Castle County	50,811	21,378	13,008	6,442	11,371	11,469	5,500	40,314	30,155	8,532	4,193	4,212
Sussex County	22,208	16,738	8,041	3,920	9,438	6,654	3,198	31,048	17,906	3,735	1,783	1,645
Florida												
Alachua County	16,974	7,936	3,893	5,271	5,629	4,036	2,305	17,102	11,921	2,110	1,379	1,628
Bay County	10,653	5,169	3,814	2,681	4,280	3,841	1,979	16,327	11,649	3,363	1,822	2,037
Brevard County	45,945	20,775	17,868	13,119	16,057	18,743	9,598	65,196	56,289	10,520	6,259	6,509
Broward County	121,192	38,706	23,932	48,196	31,875	31,184	15,806	140,641	122,741	21,124	20,222	20,599
Charlotte County	14,679	11,356	8,756	5,820	11,162	11,010	5,291	32,425	28,143	2,172	1,681	2,194
Citrus County	9,970	8,561	7,833	3,632	8,325	7,506	4,703	25,962	21,818	3,618	2,133	1,843
Clay County	13,796	6,059	3,203	2,997	4,602	2,993	3,198	17,556	10,292	2,732	2,066	1,348
Collier County	22,880	15,492	15,539	12,473	18,886	19,309	2,451	50,402	47,248	1,245	2,878	3,904
Columbia County	4,912	1,354	985	1,774	2,070	1,530	1,458	6,811	4,483	645	855	373
Duval County	61,977	18,874	11,331	13,378	17,007	14,503	12,781	64,871	43,195	13,872	9,225	5,164
Escambia County	22,605	6,734	4,615	6,023	9,521	6,960	4,469	26,540	20,296	3,814	2,403	2,249
Flagler County	9,757	5,370	3,491	1,995	4,419	3,121	2,692	16,613	12,123	2,007	3,501	2,630
Hernando County	12,578	6,345	5,283	3,235	8,281	6,687	4,543	25,655	21,086	2,562	2,655	2,590
Highlands County	5,544	4,954	6,305	2,397	4,961	5,869	2,315	16,161	15,718	1,313	1,769	1,922
Hillsborough County	82,923	26,175	17,099	21,846	18,726	18,880	15,790	93,974	69,193	17,618	15,483	13,288
Indian River County	9,775	6,698	6,198	3,699	7,777	8,701	2,847	20,853	21,201	2,148	1,750	2,086
Lake County	24,327	11,829	9,837	5,466	15,859	12,868	4,260	44,484	35,685	3,436	3,712	3,194
Lee County	51,474	34,943	23,026	16,298	29,283	28,509	10,039	94,901	73,037	7,990	5,919	8,964
Leon County	22,269	9,928	6,216	3,606	5,340	3,478	2,299	18,124	11,847	2,066	2,034	1,367
Manatee County	26,023	14,951	14,038	10,506	17,854	15,050	5,554	46,855	39,147	3,863	3,681	3,395
Marion County	23,528	16,674	11,280	8,904	14,410	12,611	6,397	50,449	39,799	4,929	3,878	4,288
Martin County	13,224	6,288	8,571	5,721	7,582	8,906	1,637	21,679	21,518	1,179	1,726	2,462
Miami-Dade County	129,952	28,059	13,174	53,551	22,859	22,372	21,982	193,884	178,989	35,442	67,176	82,655
Monroe County	6,247	2,610	976	3,448	2,857	910	483	9,267	5,427	112	679	742
Nassau County	6,244	2,187	1,563	2,786	2,821	2,315	1,384	9,172	5,545	1,142	420	630
Okaloosa County	10,331	4,093	4,541	3,682	3,374	2,901	2,288	16,319	12,350	1,941	1,331	878
Orange County	77,803	21,503	12,770	16,661	17,573	14,801	11,357	72,342	52,157	13,589	12,407	10,128
Osceola County	15,487	5,349	2,589	4,900	3,849	3,211	4,388	21,255	14,879	4,058	4,874	3,675
Palm Beach County	92,068	38,401	34,483	35,193	39,560	64,266	11,644	141,954	156,659	13,872	16,855	18,293
Pasco County	31,378	15,208	12,767	9,637	13,001	15,224	8,231	57,283	46,575	8,878	7,954	6,315
Pinellas County	78,055	29,423	23,148	21,936	27,411	27,097	14,410	105,204	94,454	13,366	9,655	9,508
Polk County	38,424	19,028	13,284	11,562	14,941	14,591	10,731	66,835	51,125	10,732	8,074	7,814
Putnam County	4,604	2,070	1,361	2,063	1,965	2,100	1,947	8,268	5,815	1,828	1,547	1,139
Santa Rosa County	10,143	5,195	1,725	3,463	4,104	3,158	1,683	14,187	8,537	1,961	661	783
Sarasota County	32,325	20,608	22,565	13,140	22,937	28,943	5,157	65,427	62,905	4,842	3,958	4,055
Seminole County	34,491	9,133	4,115	10,448	9,140	6,569	3,794	35,044	24,795	4,653	2,986	3,648

Table I-2: Counties—Persons With Health Insurance by Source of Insurance—*Continued*

| | Private Health Insurance Coverage | | | | | | Public Health Insurance Coverage | | | | | |
| | Employer Based | | | Direct Purchase | | | Medicare | | | Medicaid/CHIP | | |
	55 to 64 Years	65 to 74 Years	75 Years and Over	55 to 64 Years	65 to 74 Years	75 Years and Over	55 to 64 Years	65 to 74 Years	75 Years and Over	55 to 64 Years	65 to 74 Years	75 Years and Over
Florida—Cont.												
St. Johns County	19,094	7,638	4,758	5,926	8,050	4,472	1,820	23,306	15,158	1,350	1,034	1,307
St. Lucie County	18,283	11,416	11,336	7,394	7,471	8,355	4,677	33,539	29,531	5,041	2,893	4,747
Sumter County	10,232	13,216	6,912	3,715	11,451	9,779	2,345	37,606	21,065	1,642	1,789	993
Volusia County	35,756	19,030	14,942	14,112	18,362	16,988	8,967	60,961	51,267	8,558	7,471	6,660
Georgia												
Barrow County	3,778	1,636	825	604	1,187	643	859	5,132	3,123	1,072	808	792
Bartow County	6,860	2,458	816	1,578	2,162	1,255	1,315	7,760	4,328	1,255	539	675
Bibb County	10,585	3,782	3,824	1,906	2,629	3,222	2,959	11,717	8,153	2,787	2,175	1,103
Bulloch County	3,433	1,327	1,103	1,635	1,389	542	1,199	4,284	2,786	914	299	460
Carroll County	8,715	2,966	1,935	1,248	2,038	1,486	1,018	8,038	5,347	1,121	675	804
Catoosa County	5,276	1,985	942	1,084	2,086	2,206	857	5,864	4,083	141	247	447
Chatham County	19,794	7,350	3,640	4,178	5,991	4,416	3,406	21,315	15,136	2,020	2,905	3,123
Cherokee County	18,357	7,437	3,591	3,988	4,240	2,399	1,741	17,831	8,454	1,339	826	671
Clarke County	5,838	4,109	1,946	1,277	1,868	1,705	1,306	6,766	4,298	831	974	843
Clayton County	14,879	5,473	2,004	3,414	3,401	1,869	3,188	14,601	6,743	2,699	2,223	1,657
Cobb County	58,871	18,683	8,177	11,499	13,119	9,277	3,668	45,857	26,760	4,825	3,840	2,510
Columbia County	11,028	3,734	1,241	2,594	2,442	1,564	1,329	8,582	6,318	376	580	940
Coweta County	10,991	4,655	2,999	2,185	2,671	2,047	1,603	10,062	5,895	820	702	884
DeKalb County	45,498	18,144	9,157	14,050	7,776	7,876	7,864	42,380	25,733	7,759	6,550	4,470
Dougherty County	6,157	2,174	1,272	1,239	1,359	1,628	1,179	7,085	4,990	1,420	1,951	1,242
Douglas County	9,479	3,324	1,090	2,095	2,234	979	2,513	8,404	4,593	978	1,750	1,243
Fayette County	11,686	4,254	1,833	2,453	3,065	2,316	1,078	10,352	6,695	433	1,173	627
Floyd County	7,580	2,406	2,934	879	2,138	2,307	1,429	7,753	6,350	1,889	951	872
Forsyth County	14,460	4,764	2,517	3,162	4,585	2,163	1,143	13,233	7,771	548	1,055	1,784
Fulton County	68,451	22,561	13,929	14,602	12,673	10,914	11,125	56,177	39,922	10,616	8,975	8,035
Glynn County	6,486	3,055	1,952	2,037	1,861	1,048	1,520	8,067	5,577	959	1,394	1,087
Gwinnett County	60,013	21,178	7,782	12,613	8,282	6,815	6,743	44,111	24,476	6,573	5,107	5,729
Hall County	13,815	5,766	3,604	2,861	4,176	3,840	1,802	14,846	10,227	1,103	1,536	1,323
Henry County	12,472	6,656	2,450	3,986	3,443	2,568	3,367	14,457	6,805	2,946	2,483	203
Houston County	8,952	5,192	2,593	1,588	2,018	1,467	2,016	9,582	6,470	1,850	1,365	455
Liberty County	2,237	389	211	774	650	455	704	3,295	1,362	721	595	806
Lowndes County	5,953	1,643	934	918	2,218	1,299	1,273	7,563	4,377	1,797	1,326	682
Muscogee County	10,511	4,275	2,246	2,438	3,091	3,210	2,750	13,062	9,664	3,610	2,310	1,837
Newton County	5,520	2,624	1,232	1,532	2,292	1,502	2,452	7,760	3,858	1,259	1,197	251
Paulding County	10,353	2,803	1,517	2,108	1,221	2,669	1,435	8,758	4,201	962	1,266	256
Richmond County	11,586	4,028	2,455	3,521	2,847	3,190	3,563	13,415	9,679	4,171	3,105	2,764
Rockdale County	7,542	3,051	1,357	1,015	1,493	1,134	1,291	7,154	3,096	665	1,752	796
Troup County	4,836	1,728	791	1,121	1,875	1,624	1,319	5,205	4,029	1,085	794	774
Walker County	5,134	1,706	1,195	962	1,390	1,882	2,439	7,038	4,045	1,319	1,066	1,038
Walton County	6,917	3,224	1,817	1,072	1,857	1,260	900	7,365	4,642	1,044	1,214	1,215
Whitfield County	6,418	1,582	711	1,567	2,298	2,498	1,082	6,551	5,542	1,200	582	854
Hawaii												
Hawaii County	18,992	9,713	3,782	4,384	4,102	4,189	2,632	20,376	12,225	4,230	2,977	1,192
Honolulu County	83,444	50,785	35,778	14,569	17,239	21,188	6,035	75,026	68,833	11,825	8,631	10,093
Kauai County	8,253	3,314	1,791	653	2,110	1,270	625	6,211	4,786	1,241	683	1,048
Maui County	15,019	6,187	2,903	3,661	3,303	3,188	2,045	13,317	9,059	2,269	834	936
Idaho												
Ada County	32,856	9,525	5,309	8,235	10,920	9,530	4,422	30,817	20,977	3,350	2,141	1,994
Bannock County	6,230	1,994	1,503	1,805	2,413	2,261	1,160	6,063	4,168	1,006	292	555
Bonneville County	7,255	1,847	1,669	2,912	3,790	2,872	968	7,133	5,369	967	536	526
Canyon County	10,035	3,277	1,554	3,399	3,903	3,769	2,614	14,738	9,226	2,211	1,187	1,772
Kootenai County	10,521	4,225	2,719	5,643	5,519	4,879	1,487	14,373	10,020	1,335	1,697	821
Twin Falls County	6,046	1,800	1,125	1,339	3,401	2,298	905	6,686	4,971	706	549	779
Illinois												
Adams County	5,777	2,473	1,346	1,731	2,198	3,100	742	6,349	5,166	938	357	605
Champaign County	15,097	6,388	5,247	2,480	3,596	3,364	2,628	10,878	9,896	2,068	892	705
Cook County	369,936	128,730	76,686	80,638	96,544	99,943	50,090	340,075	277,601	88,345	51,434	45,049
DeKalb County	7,188	3,506	2,029	1,423	1,483	2,106	697	5,845	4,805	775	345	547
DuPage County	93,104	29,607	16,355	20,276	26,359	22,454	6,397	65,976	48,402	4,908	5,414	4,656
Kane County	42,562	12,228	7,080	8,273	12,169	9,741	2,876	35,059	23,283	4,868	3,214	1,711
Kankakee County	10,100	3,267	1,858	1,740	3,016	3,315	1,251	8,485	6,400	940	1,191	697
Kendall County	9,166	3,188	1,983	3,355	2,747	1,827	1,535	6,270	3,557	798	106	92
Lake County	63,280	17,548	9,711	12,842	15,895	14,122	5,684	45,537	33,406	4,949	3,056	3,839
LaSalle County	11,066	4,771	3,561	2,542	2,882	3,091	1,663	9,716	8,270	1,389	577	1,069
Macon County	10,481	3,813	3,108	1,045	3,975	3,911	1,853	9,501	8,078	1,822	994	1,086
Madison County	25,324	10,480	6,597	3,447	7,970	7,996	3,405	21,761	18,127	2,732	2,130	1,531
McHenry County	30,144	7,937	4,099	6,062	7,516	5,409	2,152	22,469	13,158	2,672	1,959	1,450
McLean County	14,349	5,698	3,670	2,689	3,690	3,586	1,014	10,364	8,228	1,487	394	633
Peoria County	15,639	5,983	4,745	3,477	5,900	5,201	2,564	14,601	11,466	2,509	1,302	878
Rock Island County	13,347	6,104	5,480	2,590	4,400	3,574	1,963	13,434	10,465	1,650	886	1,254
Sangamon County	19,888	8,794	7,258	3,102	4,525	4,331	2,410	16,508	13,052	2,346	1,998	1,293
St. Clair County	20,355	7,870	4,823	3,573	3,515	4,537	3,443	19,370	14,844	3,546	1,347	1,467
Tazewell County	14,036	4,559	4,265	2,405	6,173	4,871	1,002	11,779	9,544	977	702	1,314
Vermilion County	7,089	2,957	1,922	763	2,966	2,638	1,261	7,697	5,684	1,136	991	609

Table I-2: Counties—Persons With Health Insurance by Source of Insurance—*Continued*

| | Private Health Insurance Coverage | | | | | | Public Health Insurance Coverage | | | | | |
| | Employer Based | | | Direct Purchase | | | Medicare | | | Medicaid/CHIP | | |
	55 to 64 Years	65 to 74 Years	75 Years and Over	55 to 64 Years	65 to 74 Years	75 Years and Over	55 to 64 Years	65 to 74 Years	75 Years and Over	55 to 64 Years	65 to 74 Years	75 Years and Over
Illinois—Cont.												
Will County	60,786	19,444	10,896	8,209	13,907	10,772	3,978	43,750	27,864	4,157	3,389	3,434
Williamson County	5,772	2,537	1,778	969	2,657	1,742	633	6,184	4,636	1,441	632	390
Winnebago County	24,039	7,199	5,057	5,380	9,886	9,365	4,070	25,027	18,255	5,148	2,216	2,224
Indiana												
Allen County	28,298	7,717	6,493	6,213	8,931	8,426	3,875	26,025	19,028	2,972	2,020	1,755
Bartholomew County	6,648	2,287	1,532	1,954	2,952	2,417	1,420	6,337	4,661	942	704	155
Clark County	9,883	3,335	1,580	1,535	3,306	3,147	2,214	9,248	6,040	1,771	1,091	653
Delaware County	8,140	4,722	3,362	1,532	2,762	2,487	1,744	10,043	7,523	1,346	782	597
Elkhart County	13,719	2,051	1,709	2,320	4,992	5,474	2,007	13,174	11,159	2,004	947	444
Floyd County	8,173	2,171	1,417	843	2,298	2,111	1,403	5,994	3,887	1,077	506	352
Grant County	5,754	3,276	1,641	1,564	2,085	2,088	1,074	6,412	4,786	736	797	596
Hamilton County	25,328	8,575	3,109	4,737	7,285	6,032	1,106	18,169	11,420	1,015	982	470
Hancock County	6,389	3,666	2,054	2,195	2,141	1,174	673	6,204	4,019	489	664	63
Hendricks County	12,923	4,508	3,209	2,597	3,385	3,206	989	10,603	7,226	840	718	532
Howard County	8,026	4,556	4,002	1,280	1,485	1,364	1,601	8,048	6,221	1,014	307	444
Johnson County	11,251	4,835	2,670	1,960	5,029	4,058	1,446	11,625	7,369	1,367	176	379
Kosciusko County	6,625	2,136	1,704	1,859	2,033	2,053	1,420	6,506	4,678	1,045	412	257
Lake County	43,602	17,681	12,974	7,555	10,944	10,861	5,950	37,679	29,065	8,084	4,036	3,241
LaPorte County	10,586	3,487	1,666	1,558	3,410	3,482	1,545	10,095	6,568	1,090	705	392
Madison County	10,786	6,029	4,047	1,996	3,862	3,479	1,786	12,023	9,098	1,855	952	1,242
Marion County	63,768	19,000	14,198	13,623	16,464	16,984	13,690	54,947	44,013	14,129	7,527	6,503
Monroe County	9,472	3,574	2,000	2,330	3,468	3,217	733	8,258	6,503	579	531	356
Morgan County	7,105	2,432	1,229	917	1,530	1,700	775	6,034	3,921	1,264	368	383
Porter County	17,612	5,151	2,946	1,839	5,540	3,321	2,592	13,290	9,457	1,169	587	620
St. Joseph County	23,675	6,653	4,450	4,195	6,622	7,249	3,959	19,048	16,745	2,670	1,281	1,591
Tippecanoe County	11,439	4,515	2,784	3,034	3,696	3,863	1,558	10,398	7,846	1,023	1,285	288
Vanderburgh County	15,747	4,032	3,244	4,065	5,282	4,898	2,217	13,923	11,898	2,239	1,237	1,446
Vigo County	7,275	2,362	2,056	1,699	3,524	3,189	2,255	8,675	6,029	1,329	849	959
Wayne County	5,270	2,605	1,758	1,151	2,466	2,751	1,219	6,448	5,172	736	675	471
Iowa												
Black Hawk County	12,693	4,589	2,899	1,705	3,598	4,464	1,660	9,642	8,925	1,708	1,417	1,045
Dallas County	5,853	2,081	1,143	1,142	1,744	1,905	365	4,490	3,334	492	203	352
Dubuque County	9,476	3,274	2,546	1,742	3,070	2,301	798	7,850	6,799	1,128	791	889
Johnson County	11,280	4,116	2,191	2,540	2,466	2,377	505	7,242	5,459	961	217	354
Linn County	19,762	4,515	3,142	3,301	8,649	8,019	2,086	15,962	13,230	2,761	1,280	1,423
Polk County	37,296	9,989	7,802	7,372	11,875	10,301	3,789	29,696	21,256	6,749	3,081	2,769
Pottawattamie County	9,224	2,282	1,988	1,446	2,810	2,828	1,247	7,735	6,165	1,391	477	774
Scott County	15,914	5,354	3,902	1,993	5,984	4,811	1,506	13,010	9,856	2,828	1,310	791
Story County	6,815	2,413	2,180	1,593	1,952	1,924	444	5,311	4,262	498	378	402
Woodbury County	8,407	1,160	788	1,608	3,326	3,451	1,368	7,542	5,638	1,616	1,017	510
Kansas												
Butler County	6,133	1,243	847	1,210	2,257	2,397	449	4,632	4,153	514	264	542
Douglas County	7,185	2,572	2,167	2,727	3,028	2,424	643	6,449	4,935	589	479	460
Johnson County	52,818	14,202	8,942	12,091	15,300	13,842	3,238	37,862	29,686	2,073	1,744	2,820
Leavenworth County	5,797	2,664	1,684	1,088	2,027	1,692	1,635	5,161	3,978	875	313	615
Riley County	4,003	1,204	955	616	695	1,717	501	2,953	2,906	451	474	255
Sedgwick County	39,534	9,709	5,147	9,395	14,313	13,655	5,338	35,013	27,036	4,579	4,238	4,488
Shawnee County	15,911	6,070	4,925	3,350	6,335	6,504	3,257	14,588	11,928	1,844	2,134	1,306
Wyandotte County	9,561	3,324	1,527	1,691	3,843	3,490	3,096	10,048	6,847	2,734	1,014	1,010
Kentucky												
Boone County	12,053	4,020	2,484	1,625	2,948	2,258	1,001	8,415	5,253	1,267	932	742
Bullitt County	7,694	3,570	1,551	1,244	1,937	1,598	880	6,816	3,542	1,040	803	578
Campbell County	9,145	2,684	2,012	1,451	2,382	1,719	987	6,670	4,988	975	900	632
Christian County	3,394	1,218	988	527	1,168	1,117	1,266	3,990	3,424	899	384	640
Daviess County	6,993	3,677	2,600	2,284	3,024	2,838	2,609	8,170	6,395	1,657	1,497	764
Fayette County	22,367	8,170	6,708	5,746	7,192	6,200	3,014	20,174	13,806	4,402	2,478	1,853
Hardin County	6,301	3,431	1,462	2,124	2,076	1,953	2,107	7,305	5,119	1,508	856	365
Jefferson County	64,463	28,067	17,280	12,638	19,857	19,923	11,018	58,583	45,049	16,932	6,210	5,230
Kenton County	13,000	5,013	2,129	2,636	3,702	2,983	2,246	11,321	7,963	3,379	1,280	1,220
Madison County	6,792	2,199	1,706	798	1,135	1,277	1,326	6,107	4,076	1,482	1,414	984
McCracken County	5,542	2,108	1,635	1,274	2,471	1,860	1,961	6,541	4,791	1,583	1,019	831
Pike County	4,779	2,284	1,382	801	2,044	1,415	3,398	6,154	3,641	1,877	994	819
Warren County	8,935	2,989	1,582	1,605	2,628	2,675	1,865	8,174	5,529	1,687	467	674
Louisiana												
Ascension Parish	9,307	2,552	1,820	1,898	797	729	785	7,002	4,107	936	986	733
Bossier Parish	8,973	3,026	2,216	942	2,998	1,592	1,165	8,817	5,971	1,417	1,008	826
Caddo Parish	16,032	8,481	4,759	3,662	5,626	5,493	4,513	19,783	14,843	5,488	2,874	2,775
Calcasieu Parish	14,384	6,307	4,331	3,162	4,371	3,757	4,549	14,909	10,362	3,347	2,274	1,675
East Baton Rouge Parish	34,041	13,873	7,957	6,361	5,773	5,379	4,049	30,085	20,790	4,599	4,504	3,063
Iberia Parish	5,403	2,472	999	1,104	1,076	1,738	1,594	4,893	3,852	1,659	695	768
Jefferson Parish	35,353	12,178	6,363	9,052	7,372	7,562	6,252	35,534	26,348	6,570	5,878	5,097
Lafayette Parish	16,467	6,255	3,467	4,941	3,568	3,503	3,524	13,949	10,068	2,394	1,709	1,543
Lafourche Parish	8,359	2,442	1,945	1,489	2,707	2,138	1,303	7,159	5,143	1,105	642	1,146
Livingston Parish	11,635	3,322	1,401	1,243	2,519	1,917	2,019	9,466	5,134	1,561	1,347	429

Table I-2: Counties—Persons With Health Insurance by Source of Insurance—*Continued*

| | Private Health Insurance Coverage | | | | | | Public Health Insurance Coverage | | | | | |
| | Employer Based | | | Direct Purchase | | | Medicare | | | Medicaid/CHIP | | |
	55 to 64 Years	65 to 74 Years	75 Years and Over	55 to 64 Years	65 to 74 Years	75 Years and Over	55 to 64 Years	65 to 74 Years	75 Years and Over	55 to 64 Years	65 to 74 Years	75 Years and Over
Louisiana—Cont.												
Orleans Parish	23,598	7,174	4,170	7,610	5,393	4,067	7,122	25,268	18,377	10,599	6,814	4,685
Ouachita Parish	10,984	3,951	2,624	2,660	3,202	2,413	2,419	10,763	8,501	1,771	1,170	1,299
Rapides Parish	8,563	4,479	3,028	1,606	3,095	2,149	2,249	9,980	6,939	3,205	1,932	1,279
St. Landry Parish	4,887	1,750	786	1,147	818	1,468	2,475	6,619	4,697	1,635	1,393	767
St. Tammany Parish	21,015	9,475	4,314	7,081	4,675	4,369	2,812	22,218	13,171	2,322	1,619	2,617
Tangipahoa Parish	8,638	4,408	1,649	1,494	2,847	1,041	2,521	9,921	5,540	1,985	1,755	1,605
Terrebonne Parish	7,314	3,041	1,689	2,087	2,587	2,281	1,716	7,221	5,498	1,909	247	1,146
Maine												
Androscoggin County	8,641	3,386	1,265	2,111	2,692	3,041	1,677	9,539	6,542	2,030	1,566	1,754
Aroostook County	5,346	2,295	1,007	1,925	2,594	2,381	1,971	7,810	5,798	2,067	1,931	1,708
Cumberland County	29,125	9,244	7,107	6,828	6,756	7,369	2,140	25,119	18,818	2,825	3,135	2,438
Kennebec County	11,598	4,861	3,470	2,801	4,387	2,906	2,475	11,821	8,431	2,478	1,339	1,181
Penobscot County	12,005	3,821	2,943	2,858	4,478	3,715	2,826	13,726	10,252	3,571	2,951	2,988
York County	21,418	7,288	3,772	4,447	5,592	6,078	2,657	19,809	13,999	2,619	2,217	1,942
Maryland												
Allegany County	6,259	2,952	2,330	712	2,364	2,846	970	7,094	5,552	1,528	1,083	1,092
Anne Arundel County	51,858	26,169	15,897	8,847	12,372	10,786	4,609	41,858	28,237	5,730	2,257	2,755
Baltimore County	75,491	35,461	25,637	16,670	18,063	22,173	8,570	63,276	56,465	12,639	6,892	8,595
Calvert County	8,828	3,953	2,082	1,232	1,954	1,571	861	6,797	4,311	1,454	351	751
Carroll County	17,497	7,603	4,124	2,674	5,231	4,268	871	14,073	9,999	1,608	778	666
Cecil County	10,919	4,366	1,677	1,556	1,688	1,713	1,251	8,566	4,667	1,087	506	581
Charles County	12,673	6,809	3,670	2,257	1,866	1,412	910	9,648	6,571	1,651	921	937
Frederick County	23,696	9,459	5,004	3,717	6,044	4,214	1,633	17,512	11,992	1,512	1,641	1,738
Harford County	25,036	13,578	6,670	4,686	6,164	6,156	3,127	20,549	13,558	2,622	2,219	1,760
Howard County	31,599	14,517	7,071	4,481	7,071	3,522	995	20,783	13,131	1,135	1,657	1,816
Montgomery County	96,610	43,543	27,833	18,662	16,822	18,529	4,110	67,641	56,220	7,954	5,859	9,436
Prince George's County	75,900	37,886	18,206	13,294	12,528	10,021	7,019	55,968	35,513	11,137	6,376	6,517
St. Mary's County	9,908	4,286	2,057	1,332	2,136	1,024	731	7,648	4,235	600	1,142	405
Washington County	12,301	5,888	3,429	3,178	3,644	4,113	2,193	12,152	9,310	1,901	1,420	1,331
Wicomico County	8,368	4,528	1,775	1,539	2,161	2,638	1,310	8,293	5,436	1,909	482	834
Massachusetts												
Barnstable County	24,557	15,052	11,908	4,998	10,902	9,533	2,735	31,003	25,943	6,133	2,283	2,232
Berkshire County	12,847	6,344	5,188	2,488	4,240	4,620	2,163	13,573	10,810	5,302	1,510	1,279
Bristol County	48,547	18,030	12,295	6,926	16,111	13,314	6,933	46,265	35,090	16,070	7,576	8,197
Essex County	72,182	28,366	19,611	9,867	17,254	17,347	8,618	60,722	49,061	22,713	10,729	11,064
Franklin County	8,244	3,923	2,114	895	2,408	1,803	999	7,045	4,625	3,107	646	596
Hampden County	39,576	15,437	8,680	5,052	10,711	10,552	8,337	36,005	29,426	16,448	7,177	5,746
Hampshire County	14,811	6,492	4,125	1,792	4,174	3,735	1,234	12,890	9,139	4,395	1,875	1,343
Middlesex County	146,430	54,165	35,365	21,938	33,933	37,547	12,239	108,718	91,254	27,531	14,626	11,627
Norfolk County	69,933	30,260	19,243	10,066	15,463	18,685	5,586	51,104	45,697	12,477	7,824	7,302
Plymouth County	50,852	22,570	12,039	7,180	13,002	12,046	4,661	44,669	31,174	12,792	5,948	5,676
Suffolk County	42,766	16,843	8,425	7,404	8,006	7,965	8,923	41,635	33,804	26,340	12,504	11,891
Worcester County	78,659	28,301	16,053	10,381	17,952	18,838	6,853	58,935	45,682	20,321	9,606	9,048
Michigan												
Allegan County	10,493	3,392	2,292	1,893	3,075	2,576	1,263	10,316	6,257	1,639	686	952
Bay County	10,840	7,270	4,505	1,739	2,661	2,919	2,874	10,366	8,155	2,601	855	1,567
Berrien County	15,055	5,503	4,270	2,956	6,525	5,401	1,885	14,531	11,487	1,864	1,764	1,082
Calhoun County	11,065	5,120	4,796	2,162	3,547	2,788	2,465	11,917	8,808	2,672	1,277	1,304
Clinton County	8,413	4,253	2,582	1,271	1,917	1,814	790	6,565	4,506	651	193	451
Eaton County	12,159	6,566	3,578	1,406	3,045	3,222	1,329	10,321	7,348	1,202	1,017	773
Genesee County	38,551	23,125	16,822	6,563	8,351	9,730	8,261	35,890	27,417	10,664	4,370	2,964
Grand Traverse County	8,145	4,599	2,896	2,225	2,934	3,167	1,785	8,263	6,215	1,510	197	699
Ingham County	22,710	11,568	7,792	4,159	4,788	3,859	4,330	19,692	12,591	4,981	2,814	1,380
Isabella County	5,059	2,589	1,732	736	964	1,132	856	4,118	2,959	1,092	366	332
Jackson County	14,106	7,984	5,346	2,109	4,089	3,742	3,616	13,985	10,629	3,220	1,541	1,050
Kalamazoo County	21,114	10,713	7,686	3,935	5,106	5,485	3,955	18,465	14,534	4,273	1,997	1,242
Kent County	52,351	16,393	11,627	10,174	13,851	12,949	7,591	40,509	31,981	8,633	4,307	4,408
Lapeer County	8,745	5,270	2,930	2,415	2,586	1,822	1,184	8,486	5,171	1,320	1,070	750
Lenawee County	9,915	4,347	2,869	1,772	4,167	2,913	1,348	9,397	6,402	1,745	483	693
Livingston County	22,229	8,092	5,364	3,342	5,732	4,154	1,773	16,680	9,683	1,624	915	519
Macomb County	80,096	37,227	28,632	15,480	23,571	23,215	13,485	70,651	56,962	14,038	9,410	6,898
Marquette County	5,708	3,907	2,698	1,512	1,217	1,114	1,093	6,012	4,494	1,377	935	778
Midland County	8,017	3,758	4,483	2,186	2,635	2,139	849	7,474	5,997	1,309	497	338
Monroe County	16,844	7,287	5,840	2,585	3,793	3,696	1,956	13,280	9,547	2,700	1,403	972
Muskegon County	12,943	5,752	4,944	3,154	4,324	3,923	4,035	13,878	10,541	4,500	2,007	2,055
Oakland County	128,502	52,394	32,928	28,845	36,082	31,030	12,891	101,661	75,028	11,788	8,901	9,462
Ottawa County	24,002	7,074	5,530	4,458	7,304	5,905	1,888	20,483	14,538	2,624	2,058	1,404
Saginaw County	19,569	10,684	7,862	2,922	5,544	5,819	3,857	17,744	14,127	4,138	1,890	1,848
Shiawassee County	7,334	4,271	2,757	1,255	1,785	2,000	1,594	6,331	4,909	1,258	301	442
St. Clair County	14,850	7,107	5,606	3,332	5,631	5,464	3,439	15,008	10,808	3,770	2,241	2,017
Van Buren County	6,885	3,205	2,138	1,854	1,893	1,846	1,593	7,066	4,733	1,244	898	894
Washtenaw County	31,283	15,220	8,594	5,229	6,425	6,656	3,781	24,683	15,894	3,333	2,952	1,904
Wayne County	136,303	65,815	51,321	26,212	36,142	33,131	34,144	128,696	101,297	51,633	23,565	18,822

Table I-2: Counties—Persons With Health Insurance by Source of Insurance—*Continued*

| | Private Health Insurance Coverage | | | | | | Public Health Insurance Coverage | | | | | |
| | Employer Based | | | Direct Purchase | | | Medicare | | | Medicaid/CHIP | | |
	55 to 64 Years	65 to 74 Years	75 Years and Over	55 to 64 Years	65 to 74 Years	75 Years and Over	55 to 64 Years	65 to 74 Years	75 Years and Over	55 to 64 Years	65 to 74 Years	75 Years and Over
Minnesota												
Anoka County	32,349	8,995	3,985	6,210	11,668	8,060	2,359	23,437	14,797	4,450	1,384	1,542
Blue Earth County	5,293	1,065	613	798	2,355	2,411	482	4,339	3,607	1,019	371	528
Carver County	8,189	1,582	568	2,290	2,397	2,754	260	5,239	3,746	541	320	82
Dakota County	37,606	10,042	6,518	7,822	12,545	10,954	2,672	27,914	20,017	3,514	1,508	1,562
Hennepin County	101,177	26,271	15,073	25,812	39,092	33,475	11,238	78,377	61,717	17,300	7,032	6,181
Olmsted County	14,476	5,722	4,437	2,462	3,949	4,845	1,272	9,950	9,132	1,745	851	533
Ramsey County	44,013	13,546	9,472	7,486	15,470	15,454	4,900	34,822	29,163	10,073	3,771	3,936
Rice County	5,376	890	809	1,738	2,274	2,697	259	4,638	4,004	294	301	148
Scott County	10,450	2,601	937	2,747	3,191	2,823	753	6,983	4,651	951	594	615
Sherburne County	6,508	1,478	785	2,656	2,830	2,384	395	5,370	3,230	532	451	145
St. Louis County	20,408	7,501	4,937	4,258	8,650	7,132	3,767	18,402	14,204	4,150	1,913	1,011
Stearns County	11,537	3,048	1,998	3,245	5,505	5,189	1,486	9,951	8,809	2,365	844	1,190
Washington County	24,281	7,075	4,452	5,492	9,454	5,285	1,996	17,807	11,223	2,231	669	728
Wright County	8,879	2,844	1,435	2,023	3,855	2,600	1,186	8,498	5,340	2,496	623	226
Mississippi												
DeSoto County	12,934	2,800	1,699	1,735	5,857	3,945	1,494	12,318	7,561	1,309	1,498	1,065
Forrest County	2,864	1,667	1,330	884	1,238	1,177	2,083	5,508	3,441	2,098	1,636	492
Harrison County	11,634	5,152	2,876	1,463	3,843	2,922	4,198	14,682	10,420	3,844	1,364	1,457
Hinds County	13,956	5,733	2,210	6,047	4,374	4,362	3,361	15,912	11,913	6,182	3,963	2,564
Jackson County	12,127	3,149	1,683	1,763	3,444	2,434	2,413	11,862	7,569	1,501	811	467
Jones County	5,038	1,562	1,002	968	2,579	1,710	1,152	5,987	4,035	1,353	793	380
Lauderdale County	4,822	1,258	1,217	1,193	986	1,567	1,572	6,215	5,180	1,902	1,831	1,021
Lee County	6,293	1,719	1,110	1,250	2,761	2,312	1,212	6,965	4,508	1,320	1,070	763
Madison County	7,856	3,191	841	2,225	2,205	2,144	1,674	7,240	4,478	1,100	545	663
Rankin County	12,070	2,494	2,542	2,436	3,084	2,866	1,856	10,520	8,026	1,423	1,676	1,305
Missouri												
Boone County	12,637	5,366	2,990	2,084	3,239	2,970	1,360	10,606	6,746	1,112	1,472	902
Buchanan County	6,644	2,543	1,784	1,480	2,994	2,896	1,259	6,715	5,518	1,209	532	749
Cape Girardeau County	6,370	2,373	1,224	1,319	1,706	2,342	1,346	6,000	4,897	927	397	505
Cass County	8,990	2,519	1,449	1,730	3,313	2,541	1,678	8,486	5,936	1,063	623	391
Christian County	6,038	1,443	1,073	2,098	2,381	1,677	1,348	7,095	4,559	697	486	224
Clay County	21,561	6,235	3,770	4,248	6,605	5,327	2,794	16,765	11,604	1,583	586	648
Cole County	6,143	2,240	1,870	2,057	1,990	1,512	1,110	5,932	4,173	761	276	156
Franklin County	8,771	2,589	2,055	3,024	1,947	1,677	1,521	8,810	6,279	326	953	331
Greene County	20,754	6,010	3,486	5,569	7,034	6,890	4,270	22,264	18,710	2,987	1,864	1,133
Jackson County	52,867	19,369	13,440	11,257	15,170	13,113	9,456	48,117	37,881	9,824	3,723	4,216
Jasper County	7,622	2,067	1,501	2,325	3,961	3,440	2,354	8,522	6,408	2,006	606	1,086
Jefferson County	21,944	5,924	4,139	2,965	4,719	2,453	3,348	18,446	10,344	1,384	1,184	729
Platte County	9,840	2,514	1,746	1,640	2,917	2,258	905	6,843	3,955	357	482	300
St. Charles County	37,309	11,783	7,868	6,315	8,384	7,542	2,568	28,310	19,881	1,592	1,547	722
St. Francois County	4,897	1,742	1,041	724	2,005	1,831	1,840	5,545	3,961	743	636	145
St. Louis County	96,757	33,903	23,576	21,666	25,024	25,951	12,193	82,483	69,034	8,738	5,231	4,878
Montana												
Cascade County	5,537	1,886	1,316	2,075	2,878	2,530	1,220	7,422	5,699	491	649	374
Flathead County	9,048	4,051	1,758	2,155	3,140	2,434	961	9,589	6,261	1,016	634	522
Gallatin County	5,869	2,539	1,499	2,737	1,500	2,072	278	6,330	4,011	607	452	226
Lewis and Clark County	6,793	1,607	1,278	1,094	1,985	2,158	1,025	6,268	4,071	861	689	807
Missoula County	8,305	2,620	2,356	2,457	3,736	1,726	1,291	9,191	5,571	1,057	1,060	566
Yellowstone County	13,057	3,803	2,171	4,223	4,749	5,453	2,118	11,976	10,099	2,232	1,066	1,028
Nebraska												
Douglas County	43,142	12,035	7,142	7,852	10,677	9,661	5,233	32,757	25,774	5,630	3,009	3,696
Lancaster County	24,690	7,593	4,256	4,968	8,710	8,292	3,175	19,175	14,971	2,015	1,366	1,301
Sarpy County	12,775	4,372	1,539	2,103	3,712	2,606	1,141	10,101	6,387	972	735	607
Nevada												
Clark County	141,209	54,895	25,600	29,648	32,114	24,896	20,304	159,427	98,262	28,457	21,002	14,536
Washoe County	35,903	13,317	7,313	7,464	9,513	7,417	4,840	38,281	23,113	6,337	3,920	2,166
New Hampshire												
Cheshire County	8,126	2,086	1,815	1,565	2,746	2,023	844	7,238	4,933	766	870	585
Grafton County	9,276	3,597	2,983	1,396	2,709	2,109	995	9,078	6,031	1,304	821	565
Hillsborough County	40,585	13,328	7,466	7,686	9,039	8,834	3,534	29,995	21,113	1,953	1,930	2,014
Merrimack County	17,183	5,037	3,069	2,070	4,359	3,682	1,920	12,948	8,978	1,246	576	610
Rockingham County	33,755	12,629	7,503	6,722	9,164	7,044	2,771	26,427	16,891	1,196	1,683	1,043
Strafford County	10,795	4,544	2,591	1,960	2,038	2,548	2,147	9,178	6,852	770	780	508
New Jersey												
Atlantic County	25,167	11,342	6,407	4,327	6,180	6,804	2,634	23,725	16,664	3,878	3,764	3,139
Bergen County	85,466	30,994	19,737	18,473	18,337	21,083	6,592	73,928	64,465	8,735	6,040	8,386
Burlington County	45,559	20,623	11,724	6,784	11,116	13,672	4,515	36,079	29,730	4,013	2,622	3,014
Camden County	43,238	17,286	10,215	6,453	11,590	11,683	4,573	37,583	30,012	7,188	4,670	4,836
Cape May County	10,081	5,137	3,819	2,240	4,825	4,130	1,165	12,324	9,230	985	862	702
Cumberland County	10,977	4,867	2,792	1,318	2,740	3,337	2,785	10,999	8,396	4,527	1,691	1,356
Essex County	56,275	20,040	12,111	9,040	8,192	10,390	7,502	48,433	39,816	12,973	8,420	9,681
Gloucester County	28,841	12,622	6,286	4,733	5,949	5,860	3,453	22,924	15,750	2,968	1,192	1,380
Hudson County	36,827	13,312	6,998	6,832	6,877	7,342	6,748	36,033	28,237	11,037	7,493	8,352
Hunterdon County	17,002	6,143	2,586	2,552	3,473	3,633	1,137	11,080	7,220	855	627	579

Table I-2: Counties—Persons With Health Insurance by Source of Insurance—*Continued*

	Private Health Insurance Coverage						Public Health Insurance Coverage					
	Employer Based			Direct Purchase			Medicare			Medicaid/CHIP		
	55 to 64 Years	65 to 74 Years	75 Years and Over	55 to 64 Years	65 to 74 Years	75 Years and Over	55 to 64 Years	65 to 74 Years	75 Years and Over	55 to 64 Years	65 to 74 Years	75 Years and Over
New Jersey—Cont.												
Mercer County	33,899	16,669	10,565	3,768	6,036	6,192	3,228	25,820	21,278	4,540	3,089	3,755
Middlesex County	75,298	30,194	15,689	10,696	12,068	14,713	6,428	54,528	45,383	8,458	6,526	7,024
Monmouth County	69,145	27,214	15,211	12,240	15,432	15,161	6,025	52,923	40,208	5,406	4,115	3,698
Morris County	52,912	20,974	13,055	8,311	11,985	11,989	2,943	38,929	31,741	2,033	2,436	3,239
Ocean County	50,747	33,634	24,131	9,485	21,309	25,602	7,175	64,107	58,868	7,312	4,745	5,207
Passaic County	36,471	13,522	6,075	4,723	7,494	6,960	4,363	33,826	26,579	8,603	6,008	5,196
Salem County	6,702	2,480	1,692	649	2,139	1,820	983	5,937	4,411	1,051	629	724
Somerset County	36,811	13,665	7,177	5,704	6,093	6,900	1,563	20,483	19,390	2,178	1,984	2,939
Sussex County	16,456	6,284	3,185	3,164	3,271	2,949	1,543	11,862	7,487	1,134	1,012	1,253
Union County	46,517	17,571	9,310	4,994	7,516	8,543	4,887	34,537	29,453	6,920	3,766	4,369
Warren County	11,433	4,395	2,952	1,710	3,293	2,830	1,220	9,616	6,537	1,322	639	503
New Mexico												
Bernalillo County	48,197	18,853	13,594	12,206	9,907	7,914	7,308	52,091	38,946	13,358	6,543	5,029
Chaves County	3,900	2,165	1,393	987	1,045	1,308	1,086	5,325	4,092	1,474	1,013	725
Doña Ana County	10,814	6,188	5,163	3,244	4,213	3,331	2,740	15,777	12,090	4,108	3,040	2,463
Lea County	4,169	1,379	1,372	650	1,082	845	732	3,447	3,304	956	158	743
McKinley County	2,049	617	541	295	491	424	1,062	3,737	2,961	2,177	1,782	1,222
Otero County	2,976	1,618	1,566	1,149	1,648	978	823	5,967	3,933	940	1,048	433
San Juan County	8,644	2,258	1,600	1,833	2,224	1,812	1,580	8,181	5,906	2,324	1,371	1,592
Sandoval County	12,053	4,988	3,004	2,195	3,253	1,836	1,461	12,438	7,189	1,722	1,502	629
Santa Fe County	12,944	7,350	3,568	5,700	4,828	4,141	1,820	17,365	9,962	2,560	1,388	731
Valencia County	5,284	2,847	1,710	1,693	1,244	1,051	1,853	6,810	4,433	1,417	1,057	517
New York												
Albany County	30,381	16,012	10,313	3,589	4,031	6,303	2,145	24,399	18,902	3,794	2,823	2,257
Bronx County	66,323	26,728	17,223	12,209	11,694	11,381	14,757	81,635	62,765	58,169	37,748	27,306
Broome County	18,566	7,988	7,350	2,294	4,673	5,637	3,566	16,752	15,269	5,072	2,059	1,911
Cattaraugus County	7,769	2,916	1,892	1,267	2,674	2,456	1,204	7,304	5,287	1,816	1,314	652
Cayuga County	8,074	3,706	2,562	968	1,563	1,613	1,804	6,621	5,859	1,422	396	441
Chautauqua County	13,095	4,533	3,280	1,898	4,006	4,517	2,299	12,186	10,024	2,792	1,412	1,601
Chemung County	9,164	3,503	2,773	822	2,922	2,370	1,513	7,877	5,941	1,334	1,170	710
Clinton County	7,649	3,540	2,089	841	1,971	2,289	1,196	6,766	4,640	1,262	1,232	635
Dutchess County	30,422	12,002	8,047	6,350	5,543	6,512	2,964	24,344	18,148	4,382	3,121	2,477
Erie County	90,685	35,440	23,940	14,109	21,224	28,065	12,605	77,758	66,621	16,644	9,138	10,300
Jefferson County	7,314	3,278	2,656	1,133	2,630	2,471	1,224	8,218	5,978	1,987	731	607
Kings County	150,463	58,554	26,187	26,708	20,858	18,400	25,167	155,514	134,098	84,384	55,042	63,091
Livingston County	6,546	2,526	1,437	577	1,642	2,326	945	5,573	4,434	716	241	719
Madison County	6,373	2,247	1,711	1,360	1,622	1,572	916	6,443	4,392	1,515	1,083	260
Monroe County	70,170	23,615	18,055	11,343	19,421	21,785	8,586	61,723	48,088	13,460	5,084	7,243
Nassau County	139,468	60,285	39,552	24,509	28,797	35,241	10,122	106,949	98,864	15,312	9,527	14,039
New York County	99,378	49,597	25,849	26,753	23,924	23,711	16,491	118,316	99,007	48,434	29,801	33,446
Niagara County	23,571	10,650	6,569	3,197	5,254	4,934	3,643	18,804	15,716	3,980	4,096	3,799
Oneida County	20,899	8,985	6,581	3,141	5,600	5,660	3,949	20,689	16,238	6,169	3,213	1,961
Onondaga County	46,074	18,794	15,338	6,610	8,263	9,781	6,000	36,516	30,689	7,485	4,098	4,415
Ontario County	11,855	4,870	3,170	1,961	3,048	3,525	1,183	11,027	7,857	1,528	1,278	1,183
Orange County	35,211	14,509	9,219	4,466	4,585	4,442	3,597	25,385	18,264	4,562	3,678	3,148
Oswego County	10,456	3,731	1,913	1,884	2,806	2,515	1,826	10,180	6,673	2,517	1,136	860
Putnam County	10,810	4,914	2,551	2,815	1,539	2,642	745	8,225	5,307	611	448	757
Queens County	157,268	60,597	34,532	22,602	21,038	22,783	20,828	154,206	129,054	65,327	38,912	39,333
Rensselaer County	16,433	8,917	4,425	1,744	3,077	2,616	1,903	13,278	9,125	2,158	1,490	974
Richmond County	46,340	18,210	9,286	6,429	5,359	5,080	6,026	37,697	25,981	8,866	5,178	4,310
Rockland County	28,875	14,449	7,947	4,948	4,799	6,366	2,544	24,713	19,341	3,464	2,573	3,745
Saratoga County	24,505	12,738	6,914	3,155	5,398	5,733	1,749	19,928	13,295	2,082	1,546	1,848
Schenectady County	15,353	6,345	5,227	1,564	2,897	3,195	1,607	11,341	10,802	2,892	1,494	1,401
St. Lawrence County	9,546	4,707	3,332	1,676	2,384	2,018	2,154	9,673	6,312	2,395	1,921	1,209
Steuben County	9,153	4,024	3,308	2,327	3,048	3,012	2,375	9,191	7,126	2,232	1,354	1,323
Suffolk County	143,491	66,233	37,968	27,113	29,058	32,977	14,758	118,709	92,369	19,912	11,212	8,798
Sullivan County	7,078	4,104	1,832	772	1,782	1,443	1,554	7,960	4,200	1,719	1,130	442
Tompkins County	8,633	4,056	3,048	1,236	924	1,702	529	6,485	4,996	1,214	972	308
Ulster County	17,966	8,174	5,398	3,685	5,654	3,379	2,988	17,212	12,305	3,045	2,180	1,145
Warren County	6,209	3,785	2,229	1,973	2,334	2,451	1,422	7,042	5,177	2,006	720	746
Wayne County	9,380	2,919	2,526	1,629	2,164	2,622	1,183	8,779	5,788	1,685	638	524
Westchester County	93,276	40,928	26,859	14,296	16,108	21,422	7,354	72,149	65,467	12,781	8,981	8,515
North Carolina												
Alamance County	11,464	4,018	2,685	2,743	4,572	4,483	2,811	13,749	10,057	2,452	1,576	1,258
Brunswick County	11,803	9,015	3,291	3,364	8,311	4,291	2,017	21,440	9,472	2,177	1,275	1,388
Buncombe County	19,884	8,130	5,059	7,174	7,366	7,299	2,961	24,775	17,746	2,522	2,442	1,380
Burke County	7,007	3,272	1,703	1,515	2,765	1,936	1,732	9,217	6,221	2,658	1,245	825
Cabarrus County	14,392	3,840	2,206	4,070	5,406	4,663	2,266	13,768	9,306	2,143	1,566	1,614
Caldwell County	6,100	1,625	1,374	1,610	3,430	1,964	2,487	8,421	5,432	1,281	1,061	689
Carteret County	5,818	3,523	1,915	2,492	3,064	2,118	1,272	9,090	5,765	881	603	676
Catawba County	12,609	3,813	1,671	3,972	5,204	4,666	2,341	13,978	9,262	1,597	991	1,517
Chatham County	6,551	4,397	3,389	1,834	2,843	3,361	584	9,028	6,511	352	1,179	535
Cleveland County	7,210	2,942	988	1,960	2,755	2,901	2,751	9,682	6,697	1,276	1,689	1,496
Craven County	6,764	4,131	3,000	2,510	2,683	2,765	1,019	9,931	7,323	944	1,764	1,075
Cumberland County	15,946	7,084	3,809	4,404	5,129	3,287	4,109	19,543	13,400	2,371	2,808	2,311
Davidson County	12,172	3,995	2,859	2,524	6,108	5,151	2,969	15,354	10,314	2,001	1,987	1,586

Table I-2: Counties—Persons With Health Insurance by Source of Insurance—*Continued*

| | Private Health Insurance Coverage | | | | | | Public Health Insurance Coverage | | | | | |
| | Employer Based | | | Direct Purchase | | | Medicare | | | Medicaid/CHIP | | |
	55 to 64 Years	65 to 74 Years	75 Years and Over	55 to 64 Years	65 to 74 Years	75 Years and Over	55 to 64 Years	65 to 74 Years	75 Years and Over	55 to 64 Years	65 to 74 Years	75 Years and Over
North Carolina—Cont.												
Durham County	21,832	9,983	4,924	4,384	5,544	5,181	3,252	17,443	12,291	2,951	2,026	2,058
Forsyth County	29,542	9,217	7,010	7,032	11,293	10,043	3,550	28,042	21,624	3,497	2,645	3,041
Gaston County	15,095	5,211	3,244	4,651	7,611	4,575	4,001	18,528	11,360	3,387	2,468	1,607
Guilford County	38,725	12,119	7,343	10,657	11,506	9,318	5,259	38,096	28,203	5,761	4,542	3,538
Harnett County	6,405	2,555	1,352	2,393	2,519	1,829	2,143	8,288	4,733	1,228	1,447	878
Henderson County	9,030	6,176	4,165	2,952	5,809	5,331	1,535	15,278	11,781	1,369	644	1,015
Iredell County	13,334	4,508	2,777	4,835	5,418	3,406	1,655	14,075	8,867	1,169	1,220	1,240
Johnston County	13,272	4,790	2,696	2,439	2,751	2,042	2,186	13,917	7,516	1,678	1,089	811
Lincoln County	6,379	2,037	1,019	1,823	2,553	1,956	1,307	7,910	4,447	1,089	952	398
Mecklenburg County	66,831	21,134	11,184	16,991	18,836	16,110	9,694	58,210	37,986	8,828	6,848	5,616
Moore County	6,357	2,931	2,175	2,458	4,178	5,082	799	11,927	9,451	1,338	1,019	395
Nash County	8,113	2,737	1,297	1,568	3,348	2,352	1,874	8,703	6,130	1,340	1,208	1,125
New Hanover County	17,861	9,562	4,960	5,433	6,267	4,815	2,436	19,248	13,008	2,295	1,232	1,520
Onslow County	7,325	3,489	1,769	1,708	1,638	2,005	1,834	9,308	6,104	2,097	1,488	1,051
Orange County	11,624	5,780	3,011	4,122	2,105	1,706	853	8,933	5,796	864	535	686
Pitt County	12,094	4,389	2,723	2,911	4,262	2,579	1,809	11,106	7,104	1,811	1,481	1,564
Randolph County	9,809	3,100	1,354	4,128	4,855	3,369	3,226	13,628	8,622	1,201	1,425	1,236
Robeson County	7,217	2,154	1,061	2,403	2,244	2,007	3,480	10,382	6,073	3,239	2,225	1,913
Rockingham County	8,409	2,495	1,976	1,858	4,034	3,442	2,452	9,293	6,592	1,511	514	951
Rowan County	12,158	4,484	2,169	2,198	3,636	3,906	2,496	12,323	8,974	1,359	1,267	1,369
Rutherford County	4,485	1,489	1,766	1,800	3,499	2,261	2,011	7,469	5,063	1,898	1,293	634
Surry County	4,961	1,652	1,481	1,443	2,252	2,219	1,521	7,493	5,363	1,555	1,067	1,014
Union County	13,672	5,329	2,630	4,052	6,886	3,308	2,038	15,795	8,035	1,711	1,583	1,276
Wake County	71,042	26,918	14,647	19,296	21,627	13,898	7,627	57,607	35,529	6,019	5,093	5,371
Wayne County	7,297	3,651	2,187	2,060	2,960	2,652	2,517	10,236	7,339	2,517	1,367	1,183
Wilkes County	4,190	1,944	1,117	1,489	3,548	2,164	1,367	7,707	5,231	1,764	1,432	1,588
Wilson County	6,273	2,646	979	1,604	2,153	1,824	1,534	7,623	5,062	1,039	726	622
North Dakota												
Burleigh County	8,680	3,279	1,869	1,421	3,335	3,049	842	6,843	5,420	520	449	779
Cass County	13,645	4,124	2,421	2,159	4,285	6,053	1,165	9,034	7,690	1,335	1,065	492
Grand Forks County	5,325	1,507	713	769	1,917	2,316	525	4,075	3,218	327	289	369
Ward County	5,022	1,689	928	1,338	1,788	1,715	331	3,873	3,549	220	266	379
Ohio												
Allen County	9,558	3,765	3,622	1,708	2,615	2,491	1,168	8,604	7,080	1,666	862	811
Ashtabula County	8,278	3,345	2,521	2,245	2,810	1,799	2,235	9,388	6,079	1,414	1,651	783
Belmont County	6,577	2,616	2,231	1,000	2,308	1,924	997	6,933	5,331	1,774	376	190
Butler County	35,200	11,394	8,665	3,962	7,941	6,432	4,457	26,710	19,109	4,588	2,080	974
Clark County	11,578	6,442	4,671	1,623	2,645	1,959	2,203	13,165	9,261	3,108	1,076	530
Clermont County	19,010	5,293	4,214	2,991	4,069	3,500	2,102	16,601	10,356	1,911	1,608	1,265
Columbiana County	9,373	4,367	1,659	1,431	2,381	2,006	2,243	10,051	7,522	2,721	1,165	1,301
Cuyahoga County	112,857	44,602	37,371	18,073	28,653	29,054	16,589	101,396	90,449	26,965	14,029	12,978
Delaware County	18,573	6,052	3,491	2,332	3,886	3,648	564	12,377	7,745	585	739	432
Erie County	8,501	4,025	2,444	1,650	2,688	2,755	515	8,104	5,558	1,486	867	548
Fairfield County	12,951	5,397	2,480	1,849	3,688	2,050	1,844	11,820	8,454	2,259	935	936
Franklin County	92,586	29,479	18,921	15,091	17,192	16,740	10,926	71,261	51,882	14,131	8,026	5,569
Geauga County	10,984	5,053	2,434	2,570	3,053	2,684	1,023	8,805	6,276	560	603	361
Greene County	15,318	5,645	3,798	1,899	3,122	3,126	881	13,965	10,214	856	922	435
Hamilton County	68,205	23,685	16,117	14,504	16,559	17,200	11,080	56,417	47,690	11,974	5,197	4,368
Hancock County	7,661	2,716	2,288	1,080	2,562	1,424	1,334	6,431	4,648	358	513	87
Jefferson County	6,358	3,059	2,726	896	1,747	2,026	1,541	6,647	5,578	1,410	892	550
Lake County	25,533	9,323	6,939	3,880	6,977	6,695	2,971	21,959	16,401	1,922	334	912
Licking County	16,373	6,774	4,545	1,969	2,963	2,912	2,293	14,544	9,832	1,660	849	823
Lorain County	30,403	13,517	9,144	5,925	8,866	7,868	3,909	26,471	19,962	3,733	2,807	2,353
Lucas County	39,813	15,092	12,171	6,279	9,928	10,337	5,512	32,708	26,112	7,048	4,483	3,147
Mahoning County	23,340	8,851	7,918	3,939	5,775	6,110	4,226	21,590	19,613	4,732	2,996	2,645
Marion County	4,778	1,513	2,519	1,793	2,234	1,641	1,022	5,814	4,721	915	934	586
Medina County	18,339	6,423	4,759	2,987	5,246	2,965	1,537	15,589	10,037	1,419	1,066	571
Miami County	10,630	4,187	2,555	1,484	2,629	2,496	1,135	9,890	7,056	797	437	644
Montgomery County	45,085	18,071	14,393	7,355	12,517	12,825	7,742	45,205	37,016	8,983	4,112	4,388
Muskingum County	7,294	2,661	1,955	1,332	2,516	2,206	1,726	7,757	6,071	1,316	1,031	716
Portage County	15,860	6,154	4,228	2,231	3,971	2,520	1,219	13,411	9,983	1,433	1,711	1,377
Richland County	10,810	4,749	4,038	2,150	4,186	3,674	1,872	11,611	9,482	1,604	1,254	928
Ross County	6,197	2,485	1,657	968	1,841	1,770	1,424	6,273	4,402	1,635	851	410
Scioto County	6,555	2,543	1,889	949	2,257	1,937	2,170	6,476	5,124	1,782	992	710
Stark County	38,175	15,023	11,917	6,531	9,709	9,816	4,777	34,901	26,444	6,292	3,569	2,713
Summit County	53,537	17,609	14,576	8,605	12,114	13,378	7,972	45,834	36,200	7,717	4,058	3,747
Trumbull County	19,664	7,999	5,327	3,414	5,369	5,177	2,381	21,261	16,275	3,450	1,268	1,548
Tuscarawas County	8,605	2,980	1,853	1,932	2,588	3,090	1,141	8,466	6,918	1,663	1,322	496
Warren County	20,409	7,147	4,668	3,329	3,904	4,620	1,920	14,580	11,552	638	1,153	581
Wayne County	10,337	3,626	2,931	2,163	3,505	3,063	1,140	9,770	7,157	1,156	396	598
Wood County	11,675	5,224	3,718	1,919	3,015	2,365	1,971	9,402	6,941	695	946	470
Oklahoma												
Canadian County	11,063	4,043	1,862	1,762	2,700	2,277	874	9,025	5,927	441	770	581
Cleveland County	20,112	9,298	4,322	4,107	4,430	4,382	2,719	17,906	12,092	2,005	600	1,314
Comanche County	5,922	2,941	1,841	1,744	1,844	1,682	1,029	7,389	5,464	1,070	1,188	579

Table I-2: Counties—Persons With Health Insurance by Source of Insurance—*Continued*

	Private Health Insurance Coverage						Public Health Insurance Coverage					
	Employer Based			Direct Purchase			Medicare			Medicaid/CHIP		
	55 to 64 Years	65 to 74 Years	75 Years and Over	55 to 64 Years	65 to 74 Years	75 Years and Over	55 to 64 Years	65 to 74 Years	75 Years and Over	55 to 64 Years	65 to 74 Years	75 Years and Over
Oklahoma—Cont.												
Creek County	4,735	1,352	1,035	1,648	2,113	1,647	1,437	6,510	4,509	650	631	283
Muskogee County	4,944	1,644	1,524	461	1,803	1,781	1,419	5,851	4,347	833	857	483
Oklahoma County	53,597	22,357	14,780	13,100	14,680	12,827	8,831	51,681	38,413	6,044	5,117	3,488
Payne County	5,033	2,068	796	1,144	1,683	1,228	1,061	4,879	3,512	540	266	472
Pottawatomie County	5,019	2,632	1,565	1,162	1,371	1,044	1,409	6,259	4,560	793	813	578
Rogers County	7,565	2,649	1,454	1,502	2,972	2,788	720	7,691	5,163	686	426	514
Tulsa County	46,676	15,023	10,387	10,381	15,075	13,664	6,225	43,144	33,462	5,114	3,646	3,114
Wagoner County	6,213	2,451	1,152	1,702	2,234	1,608	987	6,875	3,833	784	415	359
Oregon												
Benton County	8,082	2,425	2,026	1,767	2,225	1,232	555	6,866	5,128	985	363	807
Clackamas County	39,511	15,285	9,270	8,549	13,211	11,431	3,433	35,804	24,783	5,615	3,098	2,502
Deschutes County	14,399	3,924	3,329	4,034	7,697	5,261	2,137	18,433	11,328	4,655	1,613	1,523
Douglas County	9,187	3,114	2,638	2,917	3,675	3,865	2,489	13,895	10,877	2,879	1,741	967
Jackson County	15,013	7,026	5,314	6,003	8,742	7,727	4,260	23,723	16,979	6,153	2,712	2,775
Josephine County	4,437	3,142	1,586	3,109	3,381	4,456	2,280	11,754	8,232	3,589	1,305	1,123
Klamath County	4,878	2,089	1,522	2,148	2,883	1,667	838	7,377	4,676	1,800	604	403
Lane County	28,904	9,181	7,229	7,201	15,668	12,012	4,875	35,595	24,646	8,905	4,101	3,348
Linn County	9,393	3,440	1,915	3,058	4,783	3,882	1,865	11,994	8,129	3,011	1,698	1,045
Marion County	25,693	8,722	6,029	4,993	9,318	7,692	2,904	25,609	18,657	5,585	2,954	2,367
Multnomah County	54,811	16,975	10,804	15,624	15,910	13,283	7,734	51,995	35,233	18,469	9,879	6,719
Polk County	6,048	2,550	2,328	955	2,669	1,644	818	7,898	5,382	1,168	1,186	905
Umatilla County	5,512	1,679	564	977	2,084	2,215	732	5,278	5,051	1,193	1,079	934
Washington County	44,409	12,887	7,863	8,701	14,264	11,438	4,055	37,125	25,789	6,657	3,466	2,873
Yamhill County	7,532	2,769	1,700	1,669	3,038	3,442	1,415	8,063	6,375	1,641	479	1,162
Pennsylvania												
Adams County	10,068	3,610	2,276	2,286	4,191	4,215	1,173	9,793	7,445	716	798	280
Allegheny County	124,394	44,135	33,878	26,843	41,572	47,891	13,617	103,886	96,839	17,193	12,095	14,817
Armstrong County	7,449	3,168	2,109	1,578	2,933	3,352	951	7,275	6,080	1,196	802	773
Beaver County	18,564	6,110	5,362	3,196	6,814	8,110	2,153	16,484	15,572	3,114	1,726	2,231
Berks County	37,894	11,657	9,021	6,861	13,531	13,822	5,302	34,416	28,332	5,321	3,086	3,939
Blair County	12,753	4,181	3,313	2,867	5,213	5,066	2,538	12,099	10,384	1,557	1,422	998
Bucks County	71,741	25,447	13,777	14,298	20,020	22,776	5,818	53,810	44,075	3,877	4,059	5,122
Butler County	19,638	6,750	5,550	3,821	6,689	6,505	2,430	16,214	13,768	1,846	822	1,098
Cambria County	14,898	5,544	4,156	3,142	5,179	7,008	2,381	13,869	12,454	2,247	2,017	1,968
Carbon County	6,509	1,883	1,869	1,793	3,939	2,564	1,414	7,047	5,100	886	442	390
Centre County	12,472	5,290	3,790	1,905	4,193	3,440	1,302	10,051	8,429	1,120	605	1,208
Chester County	53,846	18,185	10,579	11,246	14,432	13,758	2,993	38,715	29,759	2,752	2,515	2,684
Clearfield County	6,275	1,937	1,226	1,877	3,919	3,420	1,582	7,933	6,345	1,714	763	891
Columbia County	6,949	2,189	1,372	1,419	2,605	2,702	866	6,125	4,691	947	710	1,022
Crawford County	7,519	2,454	1,448	2,131	3,520	3,296	1,745	8,903	6,273	1,377	1,152	477
Cumberland County	24,731	9,992	6,196	4,222	7,743	7,742	1,866	21,485	17,232	1,823	1,804	1,410
Dauphin County	26,460	9,916	6,828	5,692	7,061	7,718	3,911	21,171	16,710	3,778	2,363	1,310
Delaware County	53,149	17,234	12,552	12,243	14,847	16,686	5,125	40,985	37,616	7,363	3,766	4,546
Erie County	25,931	7,652	4,546	5,534	9,216	8,265	4,066	23,165	18,386	4,781	2,778	2,681
Fayette County	11,398	5,118	3,631	3,022	5,424	4,835	2,644	13,128	11,226	3,798	1,987	1,643
Franklin County	13,555	4,843	5,284	3,289	6,253	3,690	1,478	14,577	11,850	1,324	1,387	672
Indiana County	8,497	3,222	2,272	1,795	3,620	2,953	1,206	7,820	6,215	1,220	627	825
Lackawanna County	19,216	7,441	4,592	3,968	9,035	9,342	3,884	20,097	17,209	3,853	2,505	2,343
Lancaster County	47,274	15,451	11,291	9,096	14,791	16,811	4,908	41,596	37,142	5,381	4,349	4,282
Lawrence County	8,972	2,144	2,190	2,011	3,593	3,455	1,876	8,722	7,805	1,642	1,515	1,629
Lebanon County	12,779	4,910	4,307	2,977	4,917	3,921	1,140	12,609	10,598	1,147	1,466	1,421
Lehigh County	31,723	9,373	7,329	6,324	11,506	10,894	3,772	28,290	24,312	3,725	2,752	3,250
Luzerne County	27,625	10,988	8,351	6,604	12,153	14,771	5,673	30,166	26,581	5,384	3,671	3,921
Lycoming County	11,335	3,394	2,385	2,267	4,377	4,527	1,686	10,549	8,470	1,763	1,151	1,254
Mercer County	11,323	3,151	1,696	2,828	4,031	5,197	1,488	11,532	9,901	1,802	751	889
Monroe County	15,965	6,105	2,816	3,933	3,964	3,014	1,577	14,878	10,039	1,831	1,052	1,353
Montgomery County	83,214	26,536	19,528	18,067	27,336	29,425	6,477	65,336	58,129	5,463	4,664	5,704
Northampton County	29,710	10,093	6,405	6,411	10,139	10,914	3,858	25,742	22,500	3,677	2,077	3,024
Northumberland County	8,286	3,268	2,282	1,764	3,893	3,568	2,103	9,455	7,904	2,067	821	1,295
Philadelphia County	91,125	34,579	22,004	24,128	28,257	30,279	23,681	101,831	81,247	40,539	23,014	18,592
Schuylkill County	13,627	4,801	3,306	2,823	6,154	6,202	3,052	14,299	12,082	2,412	1,870	2,202
Somerset County	6,764	2,352	1,901	2,136	3,838	3,731	1,203	8,049	6,546	962	788	692
Washington County	21,952	8,225	7,118	5,373	8,310	6,847	3,318	20,535	16,694	2,866	2,649	1,927
Westmoreland County	40,917	15,347	10,914	9,214	16,012	17,925	4,432	38,118	32,599	4,707	3,090	3,581
York County	44,782	14,322	7,280	8,611	13,992	14,477	5,326	38,016	28,149	4,426	3,357	4,126
Rhode Island												
Kent County	17,134	6,428	4,103	3,102	5,340	5,443	2,096	14,658	12,236	3,838	1,460	2,316
Newport County	8,647	4,547	2,266	1,511	2,294	2,507	1,494	8,647	6,271	1,470	637	342
Providence County	47,394	14,583	9,834	9,348	10,913	15,386	8,968	43,527	38,076	14,814	8,025	9,094
Washington County	12,980	4,323	2,883	2,940	4,125	4,978	1,527	12,362	9,508	1,557	887	931
South Carolina												
Aiken County	14,375	6,109	4,260	3,485	5,982	3,884	2,581	16,717	10,837	2,575	1,299	921
Anderson County	13,960	5,284	3,439	2,715	6,853	5,494	4,337	18,634	12,459	3,396	1,688	2,521
Beaufort County	14,720	9,266	5,147	4,435	10,149	8,073	1,928	25,095	15,825	1,206	1,207	783
Berkeley County	13,911	6,276	3,129	3,212	4,421	1,848	2,952	15,792	8,000	1,882	1,787	1,255

Table I-2: Counties—Persons With Health Insurance by Source of Insurance—*Continued*

	Private Health Insurance Coverage						Public Health Insurance Coverage					
	Employer Based			Direct Purchase			Medicare			Medicaid/CHIP		
	55 to 64 Years	65 to 74 Years	75 Years and Over	55 to 64 Years	65 to 74 Years	75 Years and Over	55 to 64 Years	65 to 74 Years	75 Years and Over	55 to 64 Years	65 to 74 Years	75 Years and Over
South Carolina—Cont.												
Charleston County	29,336	13,934	8,269	7,968	9,468	6,971	4,210	31,870	20,529	4,772	3,054	2,173
Darlington County	5,697	1,704	1,654	1,009	1,410	807	1,088	6,509	4,224	1,136	971	392
Dorchester County	9,865	4,418	2,518	2,454	2,485	1,789	1,764	10,917	6,343	1,657	1,244	862
Florence County	10,757	4,581	1,714	2,430	3,093	2,522	3,018	12,183	7,251	2,898	1,309	1,676
Greenville County	37,140	11,328	7,517	8,213	14,266	11,075	6,394	39,467	26,288	5,436	4,411	2,810
Greenwood County	4,566	1,571	1,497	1,874	2,168	1,890	967	6,317	4,816	752	823	317
Horry County	22,081	14,340	7,768	8,568	14,629	7,945	6,583	38,607	20,844	5,677	2,767	2,175
Lancaster County	5,785	3,711	1,892	1,653	2,727	1,413	2,189	9,145	5,687	1,089	589	468
Laurens County	5,173	2,265	985	544	2,022	1,939	1,760	6,197	3,908	1,395	753	320
Lexington County	24,088	9,531	4,355	4,667	7,503	5,616	2,828	23,243	14,200	2,490	2,133	1,581
Oconee County	6,126	3,236	2,010	2,710	3,416	2,491	2,313	9,737	5,988	1,320	1,101	935
Orangeburg County	5,648	2,563	1,352	1,911	2,120	1,062	1,727	8,386	5,899	2,167	2,425	2,166
Pickens County	8,158	3,511	1,650	1,683	3,476	2,606	2,740	11,028	6,758	1,668	1,070	515
Richland County	28,279	12,022	7,303	4,730	5,320	6,044	4,558	25,938	16,677	4,309	2,870	2,465
Spartanburg County	22,156	8,939	4,015	4,168	8,521	6,775	6,513	25,112	16,750	5,344	2,968	2,531
Sumter County	5,579	2,324	1,296	1,686	1,736	1,950	2,407	8,709	6,101	1,749	2,027	1,308
York County	20,221	6,605	3,531	4,048	6,163	4,724	2,316	19,606	11,791	1,928	1,578	1,106
South Dakota												
Minnehaha County	15,663	3,856	1,531	2,155	4,284	5,089	1,683	11,820	8,859	1,875	1,525	1,178
Pennington County	8,600	2,624	2,280	2,611	4,321	4,059	1,381	8,659	6,492	1,567	694	945
Tennessee												
Anderson County	7,817	3,392	2,171	1,375	2,161	2,643	1,152	7,635	5,765	905	924	749
Blount County	12,087	4,500	2,559	2,177	4,730	3,666	1,909	13,868	8,896	1,945	1,325	1,340
Bradley County	7,132	2,444	1,222	1,882	3,380	2,062	1,941	9,476	6,406	1,753	647	1,335
Davidson County	45,312	16,075	9,863	11,738	10,991	10,353	7,093	39,658	29,723	8,531	5,885	3,687
Greene County	5,112	1,804	1,220	1,026	2,903	1,620	1,537	7,964	4,929	907	1,189	1,213
Hamilton County	29,464	11,247	7,258	6,265	12,548	10,309	6,932	30,395	22,958	5,003	3,825	3,438
Knox County	33,946	12,292	7,204	8,192	13,556	10,853	6,530	35,390	25,487	6,002	3,858	3,627
Madison County	8,216	2,745	1,176	2,080	2,821	2,496	1,431	7,948	5,682	1,808	568	578
Maury County	7,072	2,895	1,339	1,704	4,073	2,551	1,261	7,483	4,678	960	763	769
Montgomery County	8,881	3,121	1,154	2,056	2,314	2,254	1,737	9,669	5,852	1,175	1,760	832
Putnam County	4,461	2,395	859	1,125	1,857	1,723	1,479	6,437	4,614	1,918	1,477	707
Robertson County	4,148	1,583	1,216	1,733	1,432	1,420	797	5,332	3,250	729	888	310
Rutherford County	19,305	6,296	3,506	4,264	5,710	2,766	2,818	16,756	9,755	2,025	1,136	1,757
Sevier County	6,496	2,375	648	2,109	3,234	2,624	1,523	10,606	5,910	2,094	1,178	933
Shelby County	69,329	24,724	15,748	13,177	17,914	15,909	13,070	59,784	41,508	15,716	7,730	7,895
Sullivan County	13,894	5,474	3,875	3,669	6,725	5,992	2,888	17,763	13,155	2,062	1,955	1,831
Sumner County	14,173	4,300	3,007	2,758	3,288	2,710	1,360	15,300	9,298	968	686	1,047
Washington County	7,980	2,647	1,976	3,553	4,570	3,591	2,117	11,848	8,124	1,632	1,598	1,536
Williamson County	18,109	5,127	3,245	6,303	4,231	2,905	1,201	13,092	8,785	594	642	662
Wilson County	11,713	3,812	1,772	3,106	3,622	1,876	1,548	10,597	6,119	902	733	675
Texas												
Angelina County	4,498	1,562	2,044	1,494	1,883	2,119	1,268	7,133	5,272	813	1,050	760
Bastrop County	7,237	3,269	1,258	1,380	968	552	1,600	5,856	3,251	458	384	481
Bell County	14,672	7,522	3,167	4,205	5,192	3,360	3,908	18,398	11,418	2,235	2,680	2,445
Bexar County	101,587	39,108	21,121	26,450	23,234	19,216	23,767	112,555	81,894	23,727	17,255	15,862
Bowie County	6,606	3,265	2,070	1,387	2,279	1,656	1,693	7,935	5,384	1,247	1,039	628
Brazoria County	27,192	7,266	4,948	4,847	5,322	3,154	2,533	20,019	12,661	2,684	1,228	1,355
Brazos County	11,323	4,832	3,367	2,672	3,223	2,301	1,221	9,247	6,528	1,132	588	666
Cameron County	14,015	4,858	3,668	4,661	4,341	4,857	4,499	25,963	21,528	5,192	8,330	8,180
Collin County	69,816	20,572	8,745	13,571	15,585	9,659	3,592	50,502	27,941	2,010	3,190	2,462
Comal County	10,260	4,866	3,944	3,664	2,953	2,364	1,717	12,115	7,989	1,424	842	801
Coryell County	2,247	1,842	734	677	1,109	940	563	3,599	2,337	267	326	325
Dallas County	145,333	46,211	23,708	37,880	33,371	29,005	23,256	129,259	92,800	29,404	17,967	16,471
Denton County	52,139	17,867	6,333	10,859	11,184	6,510	4,867	41,161	20,770	3,123	3,172	2,188
Ector County	9,943	2,918	2,407	1,636	1,670	1,876	1,701	7,877	5,824	2,124	1,380	571
El Paso County	33,342	10,034	5,370	10,289	6,430	6,830	9,374	46,764	38,454	10,496	14,475	13,508
Ellis County	11,955	4,088	2,088	3,103	3,073	2,632	1,665	11,534	6,397	892	553	591
Fort Bend County	58,675	18,496	7,006	11,881	6,820	4,949	3,318	36,653	21,252	3,264	4,094	3,971
Galveston County	24,253	11,104	6,495	5,246	6,366	5,576	2,674	22,716	15,035	3,036	2,065	1,349
Grayson County	9,774	4,210	2,799	1,961	3,224	2,138	2,143	11,700	7,896	779	810	349
Gregg County	8,630	3,701	2,580	2,185	2,317	2,064	2,119	8,652	7,272	1,217	1,167	1,142
Guadalupe County	10,149	4,550	2,488	2,515	1,992	1,452	1,523	10,415	7,060	614	1,398	1,114
Harris County	282,013	85,907	40,292	50,870	49,025	40,498	34,661	226,942	146,981	52,923	32,047	30,393
Harrison County	4,450	1,800	1,200	963	1,633	1,418	367	5,452	4,074	773	511	528
Hays County	11,967	4,697	2,889	3,597	3,154	2,068	850	11,492	6,083	557	502	537
Henderson County	5,021	3,298	2,320	1,214	3,560	2,957	1,821	9,436	6,523	1,114	704	557
Hidalgo County	23,940	8,976	5,571	9,663	7,811	8,858	6,001	42,735	33,611	7,498	17,757	13,209
Hunt County	6,760	2,108	1,866	866	1,917	1,120	1,826	7,253	5,728	1,103	988	778
Jefferson County	16,346	3,963	4,662	3,145	4,285	5,715	3,995	16,378	14,783	4,453	1,985	1,925
Johnson County	12,754	4,120	2,152	1,705	3,120	2,060	1,371	11,390	7,048	1,075	785	556
Kaufman County	7,338	1,741	1,061	1,255	1,903	1,821	1,078	7,807	3,949	1,177	405	486
Liberty County	5,207	994	778	737	1,653	1,287	1,335	5,465	3,585	1,107	726	347
Lubbock County	16,552	6,752	4,779	4,844	5,178	4,940	3,649	18,034	14,564	2,685	1,661	1,478
McLennan County	16,353	7,394	4,288	3,152	5,146	5,000	2,623	17,046	13,553	2,605	2,199	1,977

Table I-2: Counties—Persons With Health Insurance by Source of Insurance—*Continued*

| | Private Health Insurance Coverage | | | | | | Public Health Insurance Coverage | | | | | |
| | Employer Based | | | Direct Purchase | | | Medicare | | | Medicaid/CHIP | | |
	55 to 64 Years	65 to 74 Years	75 Years and Over	55 to 64 Years	65 to 74 Years	75 Years and Over	55 to 64 Years	65 to 74 Years	75 Years and Over	55 to 64 Years	65 to 74 Years	75 Years and Over
Texas—Cont.												
Midland County	12,401	3,446	2,264	1,142	1,723	2,923	1,142	7,194	6,606	1,120	501	733
Montgomery County	43,750	13,345	7,598	8,271	10,168	7,169	4,368	37,080	21,066	3,766	2,647	1,801
Nacogdoches County	3,779	1,929	849	1,184	1,316	1,146	869	4,249	3,623	679	387	549
Nueces County	24,342	7,168	5,057	4,632	5,874	4,885	4,891	24,879	18,464	5,308	5,030	3,857
Orange County	6,593	1,698	1,170	1,009	2,003	1,815	1,444	6,953	4,545	1,133	771	526
Parker County	11,352	4,851	1,738	2,248	2,383	2,343	834	10,748	6,787	766	818	480
Potter County	6,218	1,774	1,601	879	1,882	2,055	891	7,361	5,940	1,313	878	1,060
Randall County	11,651	3,610	2,305	2,389	3,377	3,249	957	9,488	7,318	787	680	1,068
Rockwall County	7,419	2,388	1,185	1,307	1,427	1,359	525	5,722	3,697	116	226	597
San Patricio County	5,248	1,789	394	782	2,128	1,423	355	5,842	3,058	434	335	400
Smith County	14,708	6,536	4,851	3,882	5,786	4,680	3,071	17,448	13,829	2,147	1,576	1,168
Tarrant County	129,561	38,880	26,120	28,148	23,579	20,764	15,789	109,816	73,824	17,875	12,242	9,536
Taylor County	8,330	4,563	3,103	1,988	1,720	2,203	1,214	9,030	7,805	1,893	1,038	956
Tom Green County	7,112	3,350	2,343	1,856	2,909	1,950	1,088	8,530	7,831	1,502	1,032	1,218
Travis County	77,008	25,567	15,027	17,061	15,336	11,110	7,376	54,322	35,170	9,738	4,953	5,375
Victoria County	7,387	2,263	1,217	1,957	2,243	1,637	654	7,040	5,196	592	1,003	816
Walker County	3,631	1,705	1,351	440	1,138	386	782	3,801	2,979	494	639	304
Webb County	8,518	2,548	1,245	2,234	2,323	1,316	2,338	12,103	8,290	3,138	3,403	4,546
Wichita County	9,038	3,062	2,726	1,965	2,650	2,589	1,681	8,868	7,982	1,721	1,533	1,421
Williamson County	35,366	13,940	7,061	7,461	9,663	5,537	3,962	30,826	19,099	3,753	1,919	2,852
Utah												
Cache County	6,538	1,699	1,250	2,101	1,617	2,156	521	5,049	4,286	275	410	374
Davis County	21,293	8,122	6,013	4,068	6,074	4,248	2,079	16,908	12,197	1,556	1,124	1,276
Salt Lake County	78,254	22,172	13,313	13,340	16,562	14,598	6,979	58,150	41,502	7,537	5,237	4,895
Utah County	25,692	8,427	6,883	6,214	6,846	6,303	2,257	21,294	16,514	1,806	1,721	1,651
Washington County	8,344	4,164	5,597	3,500	5,631	4,556	1,971	15,961	13,212	650	575	666
Weber County	16,058	6,194	3,638	3,260	3,210	3,742	1,819	13,972	10,599	1,470	1,151	559
Vermont												
Chittenden County	15,171	5,542	3,363	2,272	4,267	3,881	1,989	11,474	8,369	3,550	1,313	739
Virginia												
Albemarle County	8,552	4,757	2,142	2,375	3,368	2,939	828	8,652	6,712	425	278	295
Arlington County	18,336	7,315	4,447	4,855	2,472	1,921	1,019	10,725	7,473	670	661	676
Augusta County	6,416	2,578	1,896	2,056	3,686	2,682	1,238	7,914	5,143	479	523	299
Bedford County	7,675	2,524	1,598	2,920	3,737	2,881	1,223	8,645	5,538	456	456	284
Chesterfield County	32,968	13,531	6,470	5,972	9,074	5,170	2,400	25,436	14,696	1,778	1,390	1,179
Fairfax County	103,001	45,903	21,797	21,900	16,459	11,643	2,979	69,676	44,950	2,681	5,004	6,293
Fauquier County	6,137	2,843	1,245	2,070	2,218	1,466	445	6,436	3,753	290	439	509
Frederick County	6,730	2,215	2,056	1,636	3,098	2,088	690	6,918	4,920	222	519	334
Hanover County	11,047	3,885	1,947	2,225	3,043	2,628	768	9,048	6,254	325	235	312
Henrico County	28,714	11,153	6,936	5,722	9,331	7,329	3,509	23,664	18,266	2,208	1,724	1,389
James City County	6,200	3,838	2,682	1,976	3,297	2,209	886	9,008	6,780	265	164	304
Loudoun County	26,959	8,991	3,996	4,842	4,125	3,798	1,002	14,523	9,739	539	951	1,368
Montgomery County	6,656	2,525	1,367	665	2,703	2,802	1,487	6,079	4,375	1,381	563	355
Prince William County	30,508	12,854	5,770	6,094	5,336	2,765	2,171	20,951	11,663	1,599	1,762	1,226
Roanoke County	10,171	3,486	1,931	2,876	3,977	3,452	1,249	9,855	7,216	423	790	666
Rockingham County	7,013	2,225	1,955	1,989	2,912	2,664	1,065	7,351	6,033	313	266	505
Spotsylvania County	10,062	5,133	2,664	2,219	2,551	2,407	1,249	9,168	5,568	465	656	778
Stafford County	10,211	4,591	1,473	1,936	1,267	1,535	727	7,311	4,571	397	193	416
York County	4,494	2,867	1,605	1,004	1,632	1,137	264	5,691	3,741	266	163	412
Washington												
Benton County	16,025	5,585	3,996	2,719	5,908	4,187	1,952	13,547	10,320	2,375	1,375	1,966
Chelan County	6,018	2,811	2,425	2,132	3,334	2,449	794	7,063	5,414	1,390	1,435	258
Clallam County	6,498	3,698	2,893	2,090	3,740	3,603	1,302	10,522	8,132	1,041	536	881
Clark County	37,808	13,666	7,096	8,366	13,277	8,944	4,805	36,832	22,333	6,250	3,787	3,374
Cowlitz County	8,016	3,229	3,047	2,272	4,458	3,302	2,184	10,471	7,094	2,689	1,407	1,097
Franklin County	4,941	1,142	505	963	1,162	712	571	3,882	2,185	914	306	457
Grant County	5,823	1,940	1,113	1,647	2,071	1,462	706	6,852	4,399	1,546	861	682
Grays Harbor County	5,289	2,568	1,026	2,039	3,251	2,523	2,284	7,798	4,954	1,284	958	546
Island County	7,400	4,574	2,919	1,192	3,048	2,509	785	10,702	6,858	980	550	968
King County	168,763	54,567	31,538	36,771	43,793	38,720	16,554	134,004	98,525	27,324	16,731	15,796
Kitsap County	23,155	10,899	6,942	4,484	7,518	6,414	2,961	23,600	14,001	4,708	2,036	1,049
Lewis County	6,226	2,871	2,186	1,596	2,624	3,151	1,423	8,137	6,054	1,558	1,025	860
Pierce County	57,579	19,847	11,507	15,255	16,692	15,937	11,579	59,019	40,303	15,181	7,756	6,392
Skagit County	9,639	4,593	2,866	3,285	5,664	4,041	1,653	12,993	8,967	2,125	965	903
Snohomish County	66,814	16,899	9,640	14,154	16,938	13,132	6,498	52,341	34,014	10,259	6,784	6,168
Spokane County	36,784	15,360	8,151	9,303	11,619	11,221	6,753	40,375	28,344	9,936	4,741	3,169
Thurston County	24,335	11,069	5,840	4,460	6,907	5,378	3,277	23,399	15,184	2,879	1,337	1,939
Whatcom County	16,291	5,350	3,556	6,374	8,529	5,600	2,010	18,731	11,582	3,356	1,759	1,429
Yakima County	15,420	4,541	2,295	3,410	6,638	5,137	2,760	17,147	12,682	3,823	2,125	1,925
West Virginia												
Berkeley County	8,438	4,965	2,443	1,595	2,478	2,355	1,364	8,698	5,292	1,500	1,021	687
Cabell County	7,578	5,020	2,420	1,401	1,954	1,471	2,471	8,959	6,990	1,731	1,082	1,172
Harrison County	6,560	3,328	2,078	1,460	2,181	958	858	6,777	4,862	1,386	718	800
Kanawha County	18,924	9,243	8,132	3,135	5,406	4,056	4,041	18,954	14,120	5,663	1,250	812

Table I-2: Counties—Persons With Health Insurance by Source of Insurance—*Continued*

| | Private Health Insurance Coverage | | | | | | Public Health Insurance Coverage | | | | | |
| | Employer Based | | | Direct Purchase | | | Medicare | | | Medicaid/CHIP | | |
	55 to 64 Years	65 to 74 Years	75 Years and Over	55 to 64 Years	65 to 74 Years	75 Years and Over	55 to 64 Years	65 to 74 Years	75 Years and Over	55 to 64 Years	65 to 74 Years	75 Years and Over
West Virginia—Cont.												
Monongalia County	7,580	3,653	2,142	844	874	1,630	1,150	5,891	4,477	1,537	987	362
Raleigh County	6,301	3,469	1,857	1,234	2,231	1,304	2,111	7,836	5,812	2,294	1,027	422
Wood County	7,113	4,185	2,833	1,255	2,830	2,527	2,502	9,025	6,586	1,950	400	941
Wisconsin												
Brown County	21,800	4,202	3,142	4,788	6,497	7,315	2,621	18,002	13,597	3,021	1,436	1,618
Dane County	46,950	18,302	9,982	7,930	11,877	10,795	3,199	34,031	23,764	4,588	2,683	2,803
Dodge County	9,083	2,401	1,243	2,445	2,547	3,077	1,090	6,853	5,925	1,143	671	997
Eau Claire County	7,535	2,481	1,951	1,839	3,090	2,676	1,682	7,732	5,854	1,321	1,515	1,323
Fond du Lac County	10,246	1,724	1,365	1,861	3,946	3,928	1,110	8,879	7,203	1,784	888	830
Jefferson County	8,079	3,103	1,786	1,809	2,270	2,309	1,142	6,905	5,044	907	541	806
Kenosha County	13,613	5,128	3,436	2,669	4,258	3,783	2,929	11,777	8,587	2,740	1,759	1,396
La Crosse County	10,371	2,614	1,504	1,914	3,438	2,993	1,355	8,831	7,068	1,502	1,269	1,244
Manitowoc County	8,122	2,019	1,099	2,227	3,351	3,495	1,174	7,880	6,533	1,011	547	790
Marathon County	12,942	3,031	1,737	2,651	4,549	4,647	1,235	11,205	9,252	1,822	788	1,346
Milwaukee County	67,458	23,147	19,156	11,464	14,510	16,657	12,807	57,767	50,935	19,936	9,162	8,859
Outagamie County	17,131	2,228	2,591	2,955	4,610	5,274	1,822	12,602	9,640	2,238	606	917
Ozaukee County	10,064	3,479	2,471	2,198	3,416	3,379	251	8,204	6,284	526	997	441
Portage County	6,256	2,007	966	1,390	2,702	2,702	649	5,655	4,301	866	376	429
Racine County	17,411	6,618	5,269	3,067	4,475	4,235	2,580	15,543	12,439	2,849	1,736	1,499
Rock County	15,342	5,124	2,959	3,176	5,776	5,350	1,987	12,999	10,015	2,873	1,524	1,664
Sheboygan County	11,419	2,997	1,997	2,664	3,839	3,683	750	9,489	8,047	1,147	1,010	1,064
St. Croix County	8,830	1,529	695	1,738	2,609	1,681	595	6,060	3,984	554	434	567
Walworth County	10,065	3,203	1,793	1,807	3,530	2,980	926	8,518	6,126	1,169	661	601
Washington County	14,491	4,222	2,349	3,021	3,799	3,403	953	11,572	8,539	914	671	968
Waukesha County	45,736	14,241	9,227	9,165	10,719	12,649	4,209	34,057	28,037	2,140	1,667	2,115
Winnebago County	15,928	3,581	2,965	2,660	4,821	5,315	1,671	12,955	10,904	1,380	584	992
Wood County	6,970	1,408	1,088	2,115	4,115	4,346	694	7,130	6,443	902	567	1,024
Wyoming												
Laramie County	8,707	2,713	1,878	1,726	2,210	2,406	889	7,731	5,323	438	534	687
Natrona County	6,150	1,585	1,129	1,617	1,286	1,890	971	5,255	4,129	2,057	859	765

Table I-3: Places—Persons With Health Insurance by Source of Insurance

| | Private Health Insurance Coverage | | | | | | Public Health Insurance Coverage | | | | | |
| | Employer Based | | | Direct Purchase | | | Medicare | | | Medicaid/CHIP | | |
	55 to 64 Years	65 to 74 Years	75 Years and Over	55 to 64 Years	65 to 74 Years	75 Years and Over	55 to 64 Years	65 to 74 Years	75 Years and Over	55 to 64 Years	65 to 74 Years	75 Years and Over
Alabama												
Birmingham city	14,084	5,653	2,647	3,843	2,585	3,420	5,154	13,837	11,014	6,083	3,028	1,868
Dothan city	5,246	2,148	1,159	1,141	1,718	1,472	1,417	6,037	4,616	1,532	811	587
Hoover city	8,531	2,517	2,029	961	3,130	2,918	213	8,101	6,277	243	205	706
Huntsville city	16,370	6,281	6,281	3,391	3,778	4,976	1,415	12,657	14,342	1,740	1,250	1,891
Mobile city	13,936	5,640	3,026	2,965	4,879	4,451	3,870	14,809	11,617	2,984	2,337	2,178
Montgomery city	14,206	6,451	3,852	3,498	2,936	2,904	3,165	13,813	10,488	2,874	2,240	2,145
Tuscaloosa city	6,188	2,831	1,897	1,091	2,098	1,517	1,504	6,426	4,820	1,008	777	1,099
Alaska												
Anchorage municipality	23,602	8,194	3,866	4,080	1,895	1,056	2,400	14,730	9,645	2,892	2,325	2,914
Arizona												
Avondale city	3,925	817	456	785	652	163	626	3,789	1,748	1,112	773	541
Chandler city	18,445	5,145	2,346	2,869	5,253	2,816	1,509	14,551	9,247	3,266	1,378	1,024
Flagstaff city	4,500	1,401	421	1,279	995	1,076	688	4,084	2,161	675	303	339
Glendale city	15,153	4,424	1,791	3,167	3,243	2,383	2,052	14,595	9,190	4,003	2,443	1,297
Goodyear city	5,857	2,874	1,302	1,660	1,229	1,237	799	5,854	3,611	1,059	354	358
Mesa city	29,204	11,141	10,338	7,813	11,515	11,287	5,595	36,467	31,994	5,350	4,326	3,782
Peoria city	13,131	4,100	1,722	2,559	4,139	4,974	2,699	14,165	11,500	2,170	659	1,458
Phoenix city	83,159	22,212	12,806	18,738	21,837	17,015	13,509	85,858	54,673	23,341	13,619	10,004
Scottsdale city	22,387	7,455	5,434	9,050	9,859	9,410	1,413	25,873	22,047	1,079	1,175	2,251
Surprise city	7,565	5,720	3,031	2,276	4,223	4,004	1,619	14,436	10,234	2,014	1,032	1,230
Tempe city	10,119	3,054	2,502	1,871	3,020	2,343	1,354	10,064	7,063	1,550	1,078	509
Tucson city	28,071	8,602	8,523	6,923	7,074	7,386	6,518	36,393	30,048	13,471	7,035	5,920
Yuma city	4,442	1,647	796	1,270	2,249	2,794	711	6,059	6,073	1,832	890	1,123
Arkansas												
Fayetteville city	5,030	1,048	1,258	716	629	1,091	327	2,683	3,432	116	391	578
Fort Smith city	5,720	1,762	1,670	1,201	1,455	1,720	1,079	5,268	4,919	1,306	1,125	808
Jonesboro city	3,936	1,560	992	965	1,728	2,570	656	4,804	4,191	1,127	519	743
Little Rock city	16,112	6,293	4,536	3,019	4,679	4,558	3,209	13,927	10,678	4,024	1,821	1,129
North Little Rock city	4,328	1,905	747	1,142	975	990	773	4,883	2,836	1,316	763	1,252
Springdale city	3,363	891	505	540	1,054	870	1,312	3,351	2,416	1,072	372	567
California												
Alameda city	6,658	2,808	809	1,547	1,329	847	954	5,483	3,120	1,088	893	502
Alhambra city	5,574	1,646	823	2,027	656	476	699	6,108	5,087	3,260	1,743	1,740
Anaheim city	21,134	5,345	3,572	5,199	2,687	2,068	2,855	17,759	13,179	7,730	3,947	2,977
Antioch city	8,869	2,154	1,872	1,444	2,463	1,291	1,120	6,618	4,993	2,389	606	1,497
Bakersfield city	21,504	6,317	3,709	5,166	4,070	3,306	4,009	17,387	13,472	6,817	3,330	2,337
Baldwin Park city	4,101	607	309	804	276	433	667	4,514	2,980	2,422	1,605	1,694
Bellflower city	5,073	667	477	1,351	764	134	939	4,681	2,824	1,773	952	726
Berkeley city	7,425	4,398	2,708	1,795	1,779	2,176	1,918	8,069	5,311	938	1,009	495
Buena Park city	3,674	1,052	1,379	1,511	824	661	998	4,553	4,096	2,883	1,211	1,008
Burbank city	6,508	3,159	2,509	1,435	1,560	1,064	562	6,955	7,397	2,001	1,208	2,791
Camarillo city	5,774	2,804	2,112	1,483	2,427	2,275	608	6,395	5,293	748	382	596
Carlsbad city	11,175	3,116	1,810	3,793	2,388	1,953	320	9,134	6,774	313	1,071	1,330
Carson city	8,044	2,914	1,675	880	914	867	519	5,977	5,176	1,231	1,390	1,396
Chico city	4,966	2,047	2,552	1,168	1,923	1,157	887	5,242	4,341	1,446	595	575
Chino city	3,380	971	564	1,012	471	253	409	3,525	2,033	722	609	720
Chino Hills city	7,666	952	594	1,281	581	276	344	2,749	3,129	548	393	926
Chula Vista city	13,694	5,096	3,540	3,136	2,988	1,487	518	16,578	13,352	2,624	4,575	5,648
Citrus Heights city	6,563	3,852	2,107	1,428	1,423	1,839	578	6,929	6,369	1,124	1,111	1,082
Clovis city	6,753	2,265	1,954	1,185	1,307	1,759	545	5,666	4,309	1,157	907	473
Compton city	3,305	731	1,029	679	161	595	1,106	3,220	3,036	2,727	909	640
Concord city	9,398	4,756	2,283	2,743	3,178	2,035	1,203	9,962	5,836	1,820	914	792
Corona city	11,658	3,868	1,371	2,118	1,490	818	1,149	8,317	5,076	2,755	1,252	1,374
Costa Mesa city	5,940	1,659	1,305	1,459	1,361	679	640	5,454	4,405	1,722	775	766
Daly City city	7,792	4,403	2,089	945	1,730	2,230	1,101	9,163	7,487	2,153	2,761	1,990
Davis city	4,516	2,110	2,178	1,041	647	764	208	3,043	2,931	112	258	215
Downey city	7,067	2,125	1,194	2,292	393	863	1,004	5,927	5,576	2,668	2,466	1,623
El Cajon city	3,965	2,046	1,144	982	1,317	741	643	6,843	4,096	3,603	2,402	1,292
El Monte city	3,637	907	654	889	518	73	494	6,747	6,180	3,734	1,966	2,208
Elk Grove city	13,800	5,262	2,455	1,505	2,011	1,106	1,222	9,833	7,019	2,164	1,626	3,618
Escondido city	8,071	2,196	1,721	2,316	2,468	1,706	1,159	7,449	7,754	3,032	842	1,165
Fairfield city	7,401	3,248	1,453	1,203	1,005	1,351	1,447	6,634	5,476	2,277	1,077	1,386
Folsom city	6,997	2,977	2,216	860	1,385	1,526	975	4,769	4,580	685	407	1,193
Fontana city	9,913	2,184	884	1,364	779	613	1,226	8,896	5,226	3,375	2,785	1,585
Fremont city	15,700	4,920	3,099	3,804	2,752	2,464	1,088	13,363	9,816	3,802	2,156	2,174
Fresno city	27,390	9,794	7,133	6,347	6,829	6,253	4,506	29,579	21,448	12,499	7,263	7,277
Fullerton city	7,511	2,098	2,343	2,528	1,884	1,800	714	6,664	7,823	1,664	1,029	1,398
Garden Grove city	9,802	2,867	1,142	2,158	1,564	1,410	1,580	11,089	9,729	5,348	3,653	4,253
Glendale city	11,275	4,717	1,901	5,027	2,020	1,575	1,447	16,036	14,155	7,623	7,943	8,452
Hawthorne city	3,665	1,935	837	325	619	394	372	3,426	4,002	2,124	986	1,860
Hayward city	9,814	3,578	2,129	2,488	1,339	2,342	1,079	8,120	7,350	3,551	1,884	2,005
Hemet city	3,576	1,831	2,014	926	874	1,476	1,636	9,181	9,786	2,457	1,275	1,635
Hesperia city	6,431	1,221	741	524	1,005	464	1,133	4,909	3,135	2,043	637	810
Huntington Beach city	15,628	7,357	4,469	4,296	4,375	3,663	952	16,741	12,594	1,995	1,206	1,203

Table I-3: Places—Persons With Health Insurance by Source of Insurance—*Continued*

| | Private Health Insurance Coverage | | | | | | Public Health Insurance Coverage | | | | | |
| | Employer Based | | | Direct Purchase | | | Medicare | | | Medicaid/CHIP | | |
	55 to 64 Years	65 to 74 Years	75 Years and Over	55 to 64 Years	65 to 74 Years	75 Years and Over	55 to 64 Years	65 to 74 Years	75 Years and Over	55 to 64 Years	65 to 74 Years	75 Years and Over
California—Cont.												
Indio city	3,947	2,307	948	680	2,027	967	617	7,584	3,879	938	1,263	981
Inglewood city	6,283	2,887	1,399	983	710	784	925	6,417	3,956	2,316	2,275	1,537
Irvine city	14,072	4,982	2,518	3,697	2,544	1,564	1,474	14,216	9,779	2,147	2,088	2,457
Jurupa Valley city	5,448	1,122	868	451	1,119	630	1,004	4,887	2,745	2,033	734	977
Laguna Niguel city	8,775	3,019	858	3,420	1,515	712	571	6,404	3,136	1,248	377	243
Lake Forest city	6,205	1,663	669	1,413	875	684	606	4,245	3,169	1,055	299	608
Lakewood city	7,185	2,943	1,302	1,030	871	690	998	5,709	3,776	1,010	489	837
Lancaster city	9,578	3,204	1,331	777	1,211	685	1,220	9,104	5,866	3,205	1,368	1,812
Livermore city	9,961	2,836	1,477	1,389	2,262	1,240	338	6,371	3,988	774	726	603
Long Beach city	26,970	7,880	5,083	5,344	3,959	3,990	3,668	26,193	16,723	10,490	5,599	4,769
Los Angeles city	192,450	70,806	45,915	64,439	35,512	37,673	30,442	224,508	188,988	90,471	67,408	71,758
Lynwood city	1,619	334	268	202	179	157	469	2,377	2,331	2,747	1,518	1,292
Manteca city	4,714	2,417	1,296	1,058	1,686	1,171	891	5,705	2,839	1,086	908	537
Menifee city	5,391	1,871	2,075	1,560	1,080	1,287	487	7,810	8,216	1,507	791	939
Merced city	3,768	1,277	838	1,025	1,475	847	1,095	4,959	3,485	1,836	1,746	1,802
Milpitas city	7,532	1,350	846	1,269	691	732	788	3,617	3,145	1,597	623	985
Mission Viejo city	9,321	2,559	1,790	2,766	2,279	2,568	660	7,578	7,550	780	681	1,166
Modesto city	14,259	4,199	3,172	4,092	4,715	3,934	3,236	14,478	12,243	6,040	2,213	3,541
Moreno Valley city	9,956	2,978	1,443	1,033	1,546	1,025	1,295	10,144	5,554	4,421	3,235	1,344
Mountain View city	4,866	1,230	1,138	1,488	1,601	1,339	317	4,623	3,289	720	844	913
Murrieta city	6,033	1,684	1,286	2,435	1,016	1,846	364	4,690	5,501	804	509	852
Napa city	6,506	3,714	1,915	2,025	1,785	1,549	957	5,548	4,300	1,456	387	366
Newport Beach city	6,859	4,062	1,275	4,813	3,891	3,096	82	10,325	7,236	605	505	390
Norwalk city	6,698	1,309	1,006	971	527	542	1,602	5,546	4,770	2,081	1,573	1,909
Oakland city	26,860	10,819	5,594	6,706	5,565	4,605	5,309	25,773	19,158	12,852	6,656	6,552
Oceanside city	12,720	3,723	2,799	2,272	2,793	2,792	1,739	12,835	13,953	2,757	1,602	2,488
Ontario city	8,388	1,981	771	1,657	479	702	1,161	7,278	5,199	2,789	1,823	2,140
Orange city	9,345	2,756	1,410	2,630	1,718	1,081	1,152	7,797	5,856	720	1,165	1,157
Oxnard city	10,453	3,119	1,417	2,055	1,541	1,488	1,709	10,339	7,254	3,456	2,406	3,153
Palmdale city	9,791	2,729	875	1,480	1,041	498	1,930	6,686	4,671	4,310	1,498	1,468
Palo Alto city	5,143	2,972	1,606	2,004	2,111	2,017	189	5,320	5,286	451	537	837
Pasadena city	8,485	4,126	2,065	2,030	1,646	1,631	912	9,288	8,090	3,169	2,257	2,484
Perris city	2,597	697	157	451	179	230	481	2,835	1,065	2,517	1,462	374
Pittsburg city	5,010	1,846	738	1,118	1,178	909	574	4,448	2,867	1,281	1,101	986
Pleasanton city	7,403	2,542	865	1,191	2,124	1,489	239	5,147	4,428	408	494	599
Pomona city	7,423	1,884	1,537	907	530	623	1,430	6,398	6,140	3,395	1,838	2,317
Rancho Cordova city	4,875	1,994	1,280	615	1,077	730	528	4,827	3,191	943	1,095	589
Rancho Cucamonga city	14,319	3,831	1,134	2,680	2,201	1,012	2,022	10,356	5,799	2,584	1,229	1,042
Redding city	6,202	2,901	2,550	1,844	2,175	2,764	1,732	8,522	7,290	1,941	1,663	1,471
Redlands city	5,673	1,296	1,293	837	963	1,577	197	4,381	3,474	724	728	712
Redondo Beach city	4,994	1,912	600	1,600	582	1,077	717	4,052	2,767	900	199	411
Redwood City city	5,861	2,919	1,260	1,280	1,722	1,020	1,123	5,755	3,707	1,249	272	717
Rialto city	4,083	1,640	903	570	585	471	1,145	4,955	3,137	2,848	1,557	1,064
Richmond city	7,799	3,312	1,804	1,393	1,136	872	1,143	6,139	4,842	2,086	975	1,510
Riverside city	19,315	5,128	4,526	2,860	2,169	1,683	2,550	14,811	12,452	5,414	2,477	2,318
Roseville city	9,920	5,847	4,372	2,061	3,486	2,907	225	11,021	9,054	1,089	884	1,062
Sacramento city	29,116	14,802	10,349	5,308	6,552	6,236	5,683	28,874	22,283	11,657	7,791	5,264
Salinas city	8,000	2,215	784	1,927	1,610	1,125	1,330	5,945	5,189	3,267	2,122	2,362
San Bernardino city	8,625	2,523	1,423	1,269	1,411	1,087	1,596	9,737	5,946	6,286	3,105	1,926
San Buenaventura (Ventura) city	9,395	2,494	2,982	3,343	2,270	2,682	1,428	8,169	8,550	2,102	1,059	1,016
San Clemente city	5,800	2,597	1,777	2,108	2,049	1,404	123	6,167	5,635	192	294	707
San Diego city	88,342	26,756	15,285	23,954	18,804	17,516	9,688	79,155	66,114	18,308	13,928	14,066
San Francisco city	58,739	23,384	18,064	14,877	12,194	12,001	8,358	57,807	54,119	21,466	15,523	19,461
San Jose city	67,824	24,062	12,400	15,491	13,392	11,821	6,929	61,462	46,798	20,510	16,490	16,665
San Leandro city	6,782	2,549	1,919	1,618	1,316	1,889	1,211	5,788	5,658	1,458	978	1,140
San Marcos city	4,776	1,962	658	1,812	2,114	1,869	532	6,285	4,429	556	509	406
San Mateo city	8,974	3,677	3,335	1,913	2,538	2,888	812	7,871	7,712	1,896	621	904
San Ramon city	3,785	1,935	593	783	930	1,086	386	4,311	3,043	209	587	850
Santa Ana city	13,788	3,552	1,065	3,152	1,285	1,910	2,908	13,647	10,158	6,228	4,035	3,739
Santa Barbara city	5,626	3,576	2,422	2,435	2,928	2,856	577	7,681	6,540	680	852	1,547
Santa Clara city	6,842	1,924	2,475	2,355	1,502	1,550	1,037	7,233	6,263	1,464	1,423	1,525
Santa Clarita city	14,439	5,257	2,559	2,715	1,893	1,792	1,770	11,276	8,120	1,911	1,063	1,138
Santa Maria city	3,838	1,420	779	1,040	1,153	1,592	690	4,687	4,119	1,721	1,532	1,086
Santa Monica city	6,139	2,768	1,497	3,347	1,703	1,146	674	7,957	6,920	1,635	1,575	1,323
Santa Rosa city	12,453	5,669	2,913	3,594	5,553	4,779	3,176	14,348	9,523	3,553	2,237	1,809
Simi Valley city	10,958	3,790	2,216	3,002	2,843	2,124	1,100	9,585	6,389	1,734	653	1,411
South Gate city	3,494	1,190	154	491	146	0	623	4,571	2,566	3,605	1,396	1,679
South San Francisco city	6,217	2,071	1,871	2,352	1,257	1,406	923	4,550	4,689	974	1,043	1,098
Stockton city	16,248	5,464	2,925	2,239	4,630	4,513	4,169	18,255	13,356	9,372	5,867	3,894
Sunnyvale city	9,294	3,366	2,091	1,534	2,384	1,800	381	7,689	6,625	1,370	1,108	1,910
Temecula city	6,042	3,001	1,564	2,494	1,894	1,087	389	6,643	4,753	858	894	599
Thousand Oaks city	13,490	4,924	3,130	3,094	4,197	3,365	632	11,626	8,902	935	725	475
Torrance city	13,992	5,351	4,333	3,703	1,559	2,208	1,067	11,621	12,030	1,563	1,225	2,384
Tracy city	5,914	826	683	1,053	826	468	433	3,207	2,292	1,320	770	429
Turlock city	3,955	1,811	418	686	1,320	1,324	641	4,607	3,715	1,218	1,145	1,163
Tustin city	4,583	1,501	642	753	1,245	947	1,129	3,788	3,189	1,125	444	462

Table I-3: Places—Persons With Health Insurance by Source of Insurance—*Continued*

	Private Health Insurance Coverage						Public Health Insurance Coverage					
	Employer Based			Direct Purchase			Medicare			Medicaid/CHIP		
	55 to 64 Years	65 to 74 Years	75 Years and Over	55 to 64 Years	65 to 74 Years	75 Years and Over	55 to 64 Years	65 to 74 Years	75 Years and Over	55 to 64 Years	65 to 74 Years	75 Years and Over
California—Cont.												
Union City city	5,546	1,978	631	880	837	722	458	6,163	4,642	1,560	1,074	1,006
Upland city	6,084	2,601	1,314	890	737	1,136	724	5,497	5,041	1,290	784	788
Vacaville city	7,703	2,956	1,549	1,325	1,290	1,184	1,365	5,389	4,627	1,188	407	413
Vallejo city	11,294	4,728	2,854	2,164	1,432	1,641	1,514	9,359	6,242	2,783	1,338	1,043
Victorville city	5,061	1,811	668	1,149	820	498	1,415	6,218	2,831	2,115	1,251	518
Visalia city	7,838	3,457	2,060	2,103	2,152	2,187	1,313	8,348	6,363	2,361	1,938	1,448
Vista city	5,161	1,040	816	1,616	848	763	598	3,969	3,189	1,012	716	342
Walnut Creek city	5,661	3,863	5,660	1,113	3,456	3,623	324	8,290	10,205	496	562	947
West Covina city	9,600	3,117	1,215	1,294	659	748	1,156	8,621	5,416	2,266	2,616	2,028
Westminster city	5,428	1,512	987	2,299	733	1,141	874	8,465	7,184	3,930	3,722	3,421
Whittier city	4,757	1,860	631	521	867	924	363	5,333	4,526	1,305	818	788
Yorba Linda city	7,157	2,946	1,077	1,296	1,144	1,021	155	6,056	3,217	195	192	359
Yuba City city	3,697	945	1,116	495	1,094	1,328	899	4,428	3,551	1,065	1,633	668
Colorado												
Arvada city	11,985	3,816	2,719	2,726	1,852	2,576	1,355	8,016	7,161	821	999	1,279
Aurora city	22,752	6,516	4,181	4,904	4,571	4,402	3,821	20,504	12,428	4,303	2,083	1,337
Boulder city	6,527	2,860	1,482	2,505	1,684	1,565	423	6,147	3,649	690	134	431
Centennial city	11,670	3,608	2,606	2,442	2,952	2,594	434	9,631	5,547	572	469	518
Colorado Springs city	28,625	8,971	5,364	6,315	7,744	9,100	2,872	30,267	22,660	7,088	2,698	2,481
Denver city	37,515	14,102	8,909	10,236	9,560	9,964	6,182	38,642	28,069	12,418	6,553	6,384
Fort Collins city	10,515	3,286	2,039	3,383	2,360	1,948	751	7,799	5,459	835	277	197
Greeley city	5,771	1,753	1,839	1,188	2,055	2,706	886	6,170	5,795	1,240	985	1,045
Lakewood city	12,298	3,662	3,877	3,786	3,138	3,795	1,428	11,124	10,251	1,741	1,442	1,569
Longmont city	6,321	1,644	1,229	1,302	1,849	2,173	762	6,161	4,972	998	782	872
Loveland city	6,396	2,716	2,948	1,702	2,120	2,217	619	7,334	6,515	782	52	444
Pueblo city	7,712	2,742	3,731	2,098	2,327	2,814	2,064	8,364	7,307	2,276	1,728	1,159
Thornton city	8,575	2,872	826	1,272	1,330	2,247	758	6,496	3,657	1,149	873	312
Westminster city	8,730	3,778	1,406	2,831	2,120	1,436	1,117	8,882	4,508	1,246	1,317	593
Connecticut												
Bridgeport city	8,134	3,233	1,627	1,124	1,013	1,217	1,796	7,391	5,961	3,907	1,872	1,875
Danbury city	6,695	2,840	749	1,320	1,431	1,011	390	5,692	3,896	877	787	564
Hartford city	5,541	1,412	993	1,044	449	823	1,501	5,417	4,807	3,773	2,518	2,480
New Britain city	4,339	1,676	1,090	339	829	1,194	1,567	3,206	3,810	1,666	754	1,205
New Haven city	7,053	3,114	1,239	1,759	1,783	1,773	1,158	7,386	4,610	3,311	1,524	1,520
Norwalk city	6,508	2,120	2,440	1,876	1,398	2,275	731	5,971	5,751	962	390	477
Stamford city	10,693	3,652	2,707	3,067	1,829	2,619	122	7,701	7,195	1,237	1,815	713
Waterbury city	6,428	3,111	1,546	1,735	2,075	1,483	1,995	7,323	4,511	3,231	2,048	1,650
Delaware												
Wilmington city	4,061	2,264	879	853	779	1,201	1,134	4,516	3,665	2,452	1,272	974
District of Columbia												
Washington city	38,462	23,812	14,769	7,692	8,093	8,806	7,000	35,010	29,034	20,462	9,186	8,278
Florida												
Boca Raton city	9,402	2,929	1,508	3,931	2,190	3,317	169	9,174	7,279	263	431	473
Boynton Beach city	4,694	1,155	1,714	1,095	1,678	2,798	924	5,546	7,663	1,058	1,393	1,385
Cape Coral city	12,770	7,698	4,394	4,515	5,592	4,511	3,475	20,019	14,714	2,754	768	2,429
Clearwater city	7,233	2,581	2,370	2,993	2,758	3,317	1,993	11,670	9,697	1,007	1,138	1,792
Coral Springs city	11,869	2,293	1,019	3,168	1,917	1,258	843	8,663	3,982	510	1,762	340
Deerfield Beach city	3,720	1,628	1,612	2,100	1,919	3,015	1,487	6,515	7,831	846	897	1,412
Delray Beach city	3,296	1,653	1,938	2,032	1,673	3,257	576	7,978	7,323	1,139	1,058	1,104
Deltona city	5,867	2,173	886	1,031	1,604	1,025	2,021	7,230	3,905	1,048	445	791
Fort Lauderdale city	10,901	4,051	2,100	6,353	4,224	3,370	1,425	17,377	11,861	2,978	2,486	1,926
Fort Myers city	3,713	1,896	1,193	1,096	2,501	1,454	1,239	7,059	4,053	903	317	623
Gainesville city	6,540	3,914	2,068	1,669	1,900	1,801	801	6,285	5,372	1,119	697	1,272
Hialeah city	6,831	1,042	493	2,893	567	703	1,593	19,145	21,763	4,827	10,625	13,082
Hollywood city	8,221	2,596	1,845	3,917	2,698	1,770	1,771	11,845	10,241	1,291	2,312	2,383
Homestead city	2,392	374	0	657	270	112	1,107	3,661	1,537	1,348	2,022	987
Jacksonville city	56,866	17,723	10,539	12,275	15,549	13,684	12,256	61,178	40,191	13,442	9,059	4,911
Kissimmee city	2,132	1,098	103	594	663	419	1,112	3,632	2,292	1,059	326	593
Lakeland city	5,033	3,270	2,494	1,457	2,300	2,960	2,287	9,631	9,813	2,326	1,207	2,015
Largo city	6,521	2,935	2,820	1,416	2,865	3,290	1,470	9,925	8,865	1,141	1,303	701
Lauderhill city	3,298	2,177	1,121	1,200	898	1,541	1,021	5,814	4,789	1,897	1,354	1,050
Melbourne city	5,037	2,262	3,071	1,952	2,606	2,231	1,433	9,026	7,500	1,346	1,280	1,429
Miami Beach city	3,917	1,730	1,004	2,509	1,643	1,711	453	6,959	7,246	1,368	1,681	3,078
Miami city	13,440	3,246	1,096	9,809	2,746	3,013	5,130	35,179	27,881	8,478	16,928	15,324
Miami Gardens city	5,777	1,819	968	1,344	738	992	1,308	7,822	5,700	1,713	2,489	2,716
Miramar city	7,679	2,296	519	2,195	714	314	370	6,904	5,177	628	692	2,158
Orlando city	13,133	4,515	2,554	2,884	2,912	2,610	1,028	13,708	9,912	2,822	3,114	2,439
Palm Bay city	9,281	2,475	2,483	2,256	1,807	1,882	2,403	9,789	7,107	3,395	1,311	1,199
Palm Coast city	7,225	4,616	2,824	1,587	3,660	2,354	1,778	13,559	9,638	1,588	3,106	2,233
Pembroke Pines city	12,036	3,169	2,181	2,570	2,245	2,128	1,127	12,909	12,446	1,312	2,220	2,264
Plantation city	6,976	2,052	1,114	2,045	1,402	1,336	773	6,743	4,797	807	526	537
Pompano Beach city	5,788	2,610	2,866	3,252	3,016	4,003	1,133	8,012	12,047	1,291	1,021	899

Table I-3: Places—Persons With Health Insurance by Source of Insurance—*Continued*

| | Private Health Insurance Coverage | | | | | | Public Health Insurance Coverage | | | | | |
| | Employer Based | | | Direct Purchase | | | Medicare | | | Medicaid/CHIP | | |
	55 to 64 Years	65 to 74 Years	75 Years and Over	55 to 64 Years	65 to 74 Years	75 Years and Over	55 to 64 Years	65 to 74 Years	75 Years and Over	55 to 64 Years	65 to 74 Years	75 Years and Over
Florida—Cont.												
Port St. Lucie city	11,433	6,197	7,301	4,189	2,153	4,194	2,765	17,487	16,812	2,414	1,432	3,283
St. Petersburg city	18,422	5,600	2,685	4,807	5,888	4,065	4,367	23,701	15,550	4,403	2,502	1,423
Sunrise city	6,999	1,585	536	1,921	804	1,229	666	6,533	6,005	1,496	907	1,196
Tallahassee city	11,310	4,917	3,491	1,450	2,568	2,057	885	9,069	6,615	1,146	1,257	788
Tampa city	19,850	5,255	4,616	5,777	4,178	4,813	5,304	22,815	18,993	6,037	5,501	4,859
West Palm Beach city	5,697	1,909	1,232	2,615	1,995	1,098	881	9,860	6,407	1,466	1,726	1,222
Weston city	5,373	1,258	627	2,770	868	1,365	280	2,833	3,402	710	164	405
Georgia												
Albany city	4,504	1,379	1,060	995	1,038	1,517	592	4,889	4,175	1,254	1,537	1,103
Athens-Clarke County unified govt (bal)	5,667	4,032	1,930	1,201	1,841	1,689	1,306	6,661	4,282	792	959	827
Atlanta city	24,965	12,150	5,871	5,967	5,187	4,526	5,299	29,852	18,299	6,499	6,426	4,410
Augusta-Richmond County consolidated govt (bal)	11,234	3,916	2,376	3,380	2,828	2,995	3,519	12,933	9,405	4,049	3,049	2,756
Columbus city	10,511	4,275	2,246	2,438	3,091	3,210	2,750	13,062	9,664	3,610	2,310	1,837
Johns Creek city	8,383	1,414	851	1,743	734	712	751	3,766	2,208	608	108	779
Macon-Bibb County	10,543	3,782	3,824	1,906	2,629	3,222	2,954	11,717	8,153	2,762	2,175	1,103
Roswell city	7,556	2,544	2,233	1,306	1,283	1,567	753	4,895	4,336	370	387	993
Sandy Springs city	6,826	2,821	1,628	2,306	2,625	1,884	634	7,657	4,851	41	1,015	305
Savannah city	7,754	3,067	2,123	2,085	1,683	2,002	1,968	9,585	8,624	1,635	2,009	1,944
Warner Robins city	3,097	2,183	1,385	550	805	864	1,047	3,628	3,162	1,016	324	268
Hawaii												
Urban Honolulu CDP	30,813	18,570	16,309	6,145	6,359	9,040	2,050	28,724	30,792	4,223	4,604	5,117
Idaho												
Boise City city	15,511	3,559	2,697	4,177	5,873	5,907	2,158	14,686	11,432	2,154	1,266	1,655
Meridian city	7,022	3,206	565	1,613	2,447	735	975	6,625	2,457	255	163	0
Nampa city	4,315	862	614	1,743	1,607	1,738	1,101	5,017	4,484	873	567	1,039
Illinois												
Aurora city	13,576	3,457	1,053	1,454	2,410	2,462	1,153	9,591	4,673	2,229	1,362	232
Bloomington city	6,151	2,405	1,562	1,280	1,512	1,690	547	4,485	4,065	1,035	181	342
Champaign city	5,054	2,452	1,861	663	1,170	986	954	3,433	3,492	821	151	467
Chicago city	143,004	53,220	32,242	31,328	34,277	31,356	25,649	157,013	123,615	57,857	32,241	26,457
Decatur city	5,837	2,301	1,758	332	2,582	2,478	1,545	6,274	4,996	1,668	706	633
Elgin city	7,833	2,789	865	1,674	2,139	1,180	957	7,997	4,970	1,453	1,296	255
Evanston city	5,018	2,398	1,445	2,518	1,635	2,027	1,028	4,434	3,751	1,012	371	319
Joliet city	9,047	2,149	1,784	1,177	2,419	1,996	897	6,824	4,751	991	1,306	554
Naperville city	16,511	4,039	2,246	3,386	2,496	1,746	310	7,658	5,252	503	511	428
Peoria city	9,193	3,307	2,192	1,827	2,632	3,133	1,774	8,032	6,650	1,735	835	582
Rockford city	10,510	3,100	2,443	2,885	3,996	4,990	2,229	11,274	9,624	3,218	1,554	1,550
Springfield city	11,135	5,084	4,472	1,536	2,421	2,544	1,887	9,512	8,011	1,903	1,346	1,038
Waukegan city	4,620	1,562	683	883	1,264	934	1,369	3,916	3,071	1,571	450	536
Indiana												
Bloomington city	3,098	1,073	1,068	783	1,097	1,506	379	2,577	2,747	534	193	187
Carmel city	8,718	4,003	1,036	2,015	2,757	2,915	260	7,239	5,069	359	206	224
Evansville city	8,489	2,671	2,177	1,950	3,451	3,460	1,852	8,954	8,269	2,140	968	1,302
Fort Wayne city	17,044	5,141	3,843	3,980	5,546	4,966	2,841	17,800	12,278	2,719	1,546	1,199
Gary city	4,578	2,892	1,775	1,162	1,317	1,604	1,381	6,387	4,783	2,700	1,036	1,225
Hammond city	6,017	2,205	1,629	885	1,237	879	1,326	4,566	3,213	1,251	487	369
Indianapolis city (bal)	57,030	16,717	12,695	12,233	14,550	15,480	12,894	48,682	39,704	12,913	6,916	5,992
Lafayette city	3,573	1,472	1,074	691	2,019	1,562	896	4,833	3,428	558	541	158
Muncie city	3,474	2,756	1,581	994	1,561	1,852	1,177	5,525	4,416	818	574	509
South Bend city	7,080	2,047	1,646	1,204	1,459	2,073	1,873	6,259	5,818	1,616	519	519
Iowa												
Cedar Rapids city	10,812	2,214	1,746	1,755	4,788	4,056	1,261	8,743	7,614	2,199	805	1,039
Davenport city	7,476	2,420	1,675	1,071	2,873	2,548	884	6,063	5,405	2,150	870	509
Des Moines city	13,955	3,557	3,399	2,276	4,594	3,969	2,839	12,500	9,847	4,973	1,821	1,715
Iowa City city	5,328	1,330	1,376	991	885	998	313	2,639	3,189	409	112	0
Sioux City city	6,290	987	662	1,053	2,487	2,869	1,133	6,079	4,557	1,375	929	441
Waterloo city	6,200	2,502	1,711	1,043	1,961	1,829	754	4,896	4,541	1,064	930	684
Kansas												
Kansas City city	9,077	3,157	1,390	1,628	3,526	3,215	2,955	9,309	6,327	2,594	938	1,010
Lawrence city	4,843	1,418	1,890	2,158	2,061	2,080	374	4,084	3,877	475	253	340
Olathe city	9,681	2,783	1,245	954	3,566	1,554	601	7,428	3,564	419	315	607
Overland Park city	17,671	4,448	2,888	4,568	5,407	6,163	1,073	12,605	12,279	963	731	1,312
Topeka city	9,678	3,208	3,467	2,600	3,988	4,513	2,665	9,473	7,961	1,681	1,806	812
Wichita city	28,486	6,932	4,092	6,126	10,073	10,449	4,452	26,014	21,484	4,230	3,429	3,803
Kentucky												
Lexington-Fayette urban county	22,367	8,170	6,708	5,746	7,192	6,200	3,014	20,174	13,806	4,402	2,478	1,853
Louisville/Jefferson County metro govt (bal)	48,953	21,046	12,227	9,587	14,175	14,456	9,430	43,980	33,197	15,521	5,055	4,451
Louisiana												
Baton Rouge city	15,383	5,945	4,909	2,751	2,697	2,969	1,946	14,096	12,856	3,485	2,650	2,392
Bossier City city	4,330	1,545	1,010	474	1,659	1,153	559	4,804	3,381	1,029	828	427

Table I-3: Places—Persons With Health Insurance by Source of Insurance—*Continued*

| | Private Health Insurance Coverage | | | | | | Public Health Insurance Coverage | | | | | |
| | Employer Based | | | Direct Purchase | | | Medicare | | | Medicaid/CHIP | | |
	55 to 64 Years	65 to 74 Years	75 Years and Over	55 to 64 Years	65 to 74 Years	75 Years and Over	55 to 64 Years	65 to 74 Years	75 Years and Over	55 to 64 Years	65 to 74 Years	75 Years and Over
Louisiana—Cont.												
Kenner city	5,331	2,190	563	1,495	1,846	1,245	660	7,408	3,896	862	1,055	322
Lafayette city	9,907	3,862	1,645	3,558	2,349	2,023	1,696	8,199	5,092	1,203	1,195	812
Lake Charles city	4,202	2,291	2,596	1,481	2,192	2,154	1,277	6,174	5,541	1,200	672	1,037
New Orleans city	23,598	7,174	4,170	7,610	5,393	4,067	7,122	25,268	18,377	10,599	6,814	4,685
Shreveport city	10,754	6,685	3,774	1,671	4,255	4,745	3,270	15,044	12,157	5,172	2,183	2,320
Maine												
Portland city	5,252	1,758	1,395	1,165	326	713	266	3,889	3,197	794	718	460
Maryland												
Baltimore city	40,106	17,825	10,340	8,402	9,794	9,888	13,711	40,617	30,695	18,851	9,192	5,587
Frederick city	4,663	1,637	1,032	888	1,499	836	422	4,439	2,266	578	429	241
Gaithersburg city	4,859	1,905	785	896	966	1,032	135	3,329	2,888	326	208	591
Rockville city	6,021	2,608	2,489	1,396	1,410	1,438	185	4,329	4,744	408	364	1,114
Massachusetts												
Boston city	36,100	13,275	6,494	6,816	6,196	6,584	8,055	32,910	27,301	21,923	10,704	9,818
Brockton city	6,850	2,362	1,041	949	1,603	1,280	1,583	6,524	4,146	4,446	2,186	1,641
Cambridge city	5,981	3,451	1,634	1,211	1,460	856	1,161	5,461	3,916	1,478	471	834
Fall River city	4,848	2,293	1,808	431	2,026	1,889	1,634	7,424	5,896	3,987	1,920	2,117
Lawrence city	1,703	1,167	462	280	688	296	477	4,001	2,104	4,064	2,027	1,402
Lowell city	5,588	1,917	1,020	845	1,074	1,669	1,921	5,367	4,625	4,761	1,589	921
Lynn city	7,094	1,723	1,238	662	651	1,094	1,240	5,072	4,712	3,717	2,308	2,229
New Bedford city	6,708	1,593	1,116	1,088	1,418	1,930	1,758	5,531	5,477	3,446	1,844	2,030
Newton city	8,992	5,365	2,622	1,813	2,579	2,493	305	7,709	7,152	548	1,112	1,270
Quincy city	7,405	3,095	2,225	1,539	1,761	2,281	924	6,728	6,151	3,465	1,710	1,694
Somerville city	4,094	1,674	766	817	899	1,380	631	3,967	3,282	1,697	833	922
Springfield city	8,985	3,287	1,950	747	2,299	2,300	3,243	8,273	7,256	7,207	2,399	2,045
Worcester city	11,168	4,215	3,278	2,011	1,583	3,201	1,651	8,233	9,043	6,859	2,326	2,405
Michigan												
Ann Arbor city	7,959	3,751	3,390	1,905	1,233	2,309	720	5,993	5,559	539	933	434
Dearborn city	6,070	3,340	3,487	1,505	1,810	1,532	1,234	6,510	5,485	1,959	911	1,126
Detroit city	38,012	22,712	16,768	7,274	7,691	7,390	17,668	46,420	33,928	32,102	13,408	10,068
Farmington Hills city	9,273	4,636	2,880	2,042	3,401	2,922	458	9,546	7,491	456	990	540
Flint city	6,223	3,932	3,562	1,242	995	1,233	2,294	6,291	5,210	4,133	1,152	954
Grand Rapids city	10,407	4,104	4,336	1,603	3,001	4,006	1,935	9,787	9,944	3,178	1,970	1,741
Kalamazoo city	3,760	1,452	1,576	839	844	1,479	1,485	3,350	3,320	1,892	731	388
Lansing city	6,734	4,191	2,898	992	1,588	1,037	2,429	8,118	4,543	2,772	1,578	496
Livonia city	12,577	4,794	3,226	2,036	3,332	3,533	1,311	8,556	7,503	954	676	540
Rochester Hills city	7,633	3,110	2,078	1,911	2,003	1,561	470	6,162	5,110	801	246	613
Southfield city	8,717	5,747	2,634	1,703	1,799	1,201	1,355	7,796	4,911	1,595	826	785
Sterling Heights city	11,614	5,235	6,085	3,045	3,618	3,343	1,316	10,048	10,795	1,827	1,849	1,699
Troy city	8,833	2,840	2,271	1,466	2,257	2,521	896	6,768	5,640	674	269	955
Warren city	10,106	4,519	4,316	2,082	2,985	3,282	2,344	9,090	9,077	2,798	1,474	1,172
Westland city	6,490	4,312	3,468	1,201	2,008	2,427	1,644	7,162	6,527	1,693	989	1,015
Wyoming city	5,629	1,315	1,769	1,078	862	829	1,298	3,809	3,570	1,375	540	514
Minnesota												
Bloomington city	9,442	2,617	1,832	2,770	4,499	4,683	711	7,806	8,357	1,069	279	1,003
Brooklyn Park city	4,743	1,168	811	1,058	2,370	1,242	521	4,373	2,573	1,051	379	52
Duluth city	7,077	2,439	2,312	1,257	3,315	2,813	1,674	6,342	5,655	2,311	813	158
Eagan city	5,527	1,457	1,103	1,124	2,385	1,763	97	4,429	3,083	504	229	250
Maple Grove city	8,064	2,285	654	1,305	1,999	1,214	524	5,460	1,965	810	149	140
Minneapolis city	23,671	6,501	3,440	5,918	7,875	4,601	4,170	19,606	10,231	7,455	3,035	1,666
Plymouth city	6,823	2,710	962	1,556	4,617	2,021	227	6,970	3,889	349	161	169
Rochester city	9,609	3,881	4,025	1,336	2,735	3,925	1,007	7,074	7,637	1,452	687	437
St. Cloud city	4,356	1,995	921	1,783	2,287	1,300	541	4,207	2,387	1,376	251	256
St. Paul city	19,876	5,039	2,675	2,748	4,994	4,730	2,847	13,969	10,237	7,726	2,304	1,958
Woodbury city	6,814	2,205	1,084	779	2,273	1,280	201	4,544	2,396	642	343	111
Mississippi												
Gulfport city	4,209	1,314	747	621	1,269	961	1,956	4,978	4,394	1,820	708	315
Jackson city	9,265	3,658	1,131	3,689	3,161	2,954	2,843	10,772	7,740	5,162	3,140	2,077
Missouri												
Columbia city	7,335	3,389	1,574	1,056	2,539	1,550	473	6,753	3,334	668	841	403
Independence city	11,155	4,438	3,549	1,760	3,115	2,167	2,133	10,941	8,522	2,542	902	571
Kansas City city	32,069	11,046	8,111	8,046	9,934	10,253	7,115	29,331	23,168	6,781	2,826	2,977
Lee's Summit city	9,701	2,527	1,733	1,639	3,141	1,536	576	7,354	4,944	379	37	355
O'Fallon city	7,633	1,688	2,379	966	1,878	1,490	304	4,290	3,844	233	47	12
Springfield city	8,843	2,891	2,615	2,140	3,795	4,196	2,626	11,748	12,007	2,405	1,623	978
St. Charles city	6,469	1,920	1,610	1,479	1,744	1,715	1,045	4,994	4,490	436	33	391
St. Joseph city	5,373	2,081	1,662	1,042	1,984	2,426	1,077	5,078	4,883	1,164	438	749
St. Louis city	20,202	4,471	3,735	5,598	3,824	3,945	7,466	18,969	14,837	7,700	2,917	3,076
Montana												
Billings city	8,375	2,278	1,805	2,325	3,272	4,445	1,427	7,202	7,745	1,748	350	692
Missoula city	4,462	1,714	1,723	1,867	1,526	864	1,117	4,160	3,911	898	726	384

Table I-3: Places—Persons With Health Insurance by Source of Insurance—*Continued*

| | Private Health Insurance Coverage | | | | | | Public Health Insurance Coverage | | | | | |
| | Employer Based | | | Direct Purchase | | | Medicare | | | Medicaid/CHIP | | |
	55 to 64 Years	65 to 74 Years	75 Years and Over	55 to 64 Years	65 to 74 Years	75 Years and Over	55 to 64 Years	65 to 74 Years	75 Years and Over	55 to 64 Years	65 to 74 Years	75 Years and Over
Nebraska												
Lincoln city	21,190	6,631	3,917	3,886	7,413	7,395	2,987	16,648	13,401	1,903	1,297	1,266
Omaha city	35,634	10,366	5,909	6,115	8,942	7,969	4,490	27,540	22,051	5,100	2,828	3,675
Nevada												
Henderson city	24,098	10,813	4,859	5,444	6,147	4,216	2,697	28,534	18,757	3,302	2,429	1,868
Las Vegas city	39,446	15,292	6,931	8,545	9,274	8,237	5,194	45,247	29,023	9,310	7,093	4,286
North Las Vegas city	12,708	5,947	2,622	2,055	1,796	1,282	3,293	16,045	7,353	2,955	3,060	1,593
Reno city	16,967	5,671	4,148	3,387	4,275	3,997	1,943	17,182	12,528	3,526	2,238	1,436
Sparks city	7,691	3,569	1,360	677	2,669	1,565	895	8,612	4,722	1,649	648	489
New Hampshire												
Manchester city	9,771	2,484	1,326	2,159	1,931	2,601	1,254	7,366	5,181	1,063	1,001	676
Nashua city	9,858	2,831	2,312	1,945	1,935	1,843	1,153	5,789	4,620	633	158	691
New Jersey												
Bayonne city	5,133	1,370	787	796	1,110	950	950	4,378	3,220	1,209	302	590
Camden city	2,435	1,485	422	75	480	430	1,016	4,233	2,481	2,459	1,590	1,165
Clifton city	7,080	1,845	1,341	493	1,211	1,476	275	5,020	3,947	1,526	415	259
East Orange city	4,336	2,164	712	563	767	491	1,179	4,389	3,006	2,039	763	1,277
Elizabeth city	5,791	1,223	498	533	841	551	1,022	5,846	4,233	1,702	1,146	1,514
Jersey City city	14,230	5,158	2,617	2,025	2,000	1,973	2,223	13,295	8,747	4,884	2,735	1,855
Newark city	11,538	3,131	1,648	1,426	1,628	1,323	3,742	13,114	8,144	6,901	4,659	3,403
Passaic city	2,305	592	102	189	289	286	524	3,422	2,184	1,880	1,304	1,279
Paterson city	5,208	1,646	534	509	864	878	2,206	7,404	7,270	3,340	2,864	1,895
Trenton city	3,435	1,642	1,529	505	590	599	1,566	4,547	3,407	2,879	1,334	711
Union City city	2,391	564	459	1,081	195	1,270	362	3,162	3,479	1,404	1,623	1,442
New Mexico												
Albuquerque city	38,420	14,851	11,421	9,420	7,319	6,596	6,290	39,930	30,873	10,655	5,180	3,677
Las Cruces city	6,524	3,823	2,998	2,213	2,165	1,942	1,548	7,395	6,538	1,790	1,038	909
Rio Rancho city	8,503	3,120	1,831	1,353	1,586	1,107	973	6,830	4,095	1,102	576	99
Santa Fe city	5,417	4,216	2,281	2,361	2,189	2,098	406	8,191	5,095	1,629	926	494
New York												
Albany city	6,791	3,851	2,417	878	967	1,176	1,099	6,450	4,156	2,465	1,064	805
Buffalo city	16,577	5,999	4,402	2,624	3,581	3,748	4,780	16,607	14,360	8,535	4,052	4,271
Mount Vernon city	5,284	2,022	1,341	819	1,382	1,511	976	4,837	3,938	1,236	685	801
New Rochelle city	6,449	2,418	1,737	970	885	1,892	737	4,393	4,976	2,187	657	988
New York city	519,772	213,686	113,077	94,701	82,873	81,355	83,269	547,368	450,905	265,180	166,681	167,486
Rochester city	10,453	3,597	1,904	2,073	2,506	2,048	3,570	13,913	6,762	7,395	2,288	2,101
Schenectady city	4,839	1,828	1,982	1,117	1,133	1,196	1,178	3,878	4,370	1,981	863	1,067
Syracuse city	7,217	3,796	2,958	1,015	1,497	1,952	2,277	8,692	7,553	3,736	2,078	2,383
Yonkers city	14,759	8,756	4,821	2,287	3,152	3,883	2,589	16,763	13,419	3,760	3,796	2,733
North Carolina												
Asheville city	6,078	2,071	2,467	2,451	2,638	3,075	1,417	7,615	6,793	1,083	906	723
Charlotte city	49,644	15,886	8,509	13,026	13,375	11,836	8,230	42,652	28,970	8,177	5,646	5,031
Concord city	5,373	1,651	1,056	1,495	2,613	1,909	931	5,687	3,653	693	734	577
Durham city	17,238	7,841	3,926	3,742	4,383	4,369	2,921	14,412	10,456	2,806	1,848	1,887
Fayetteville city	10,731	4,473	2,941	2,697	3,020	2,107	2,068	12,568	9,647	1,455	1,922	1,641
Gastonia city	4,530	2,352	1,268	1,940	2,615	1,753	1,406	6,336	4,048	1,822	774	636
Greensboro city	18,269	6,068	4,364	5,319	4,985	4,421	3,047	19,076	13,587	2,733	2,150	1,611
Greenville city	4,602	2,290	1,546	1,005	2,073	1,044	553	4,964	3,583	859	386	1,078
High Point city	6,771	2,130	1,365	2,095	2,308	1,900	917	7,232	5,204	1,919	1,109	664
Jacksonville city	2,765	897	784	312	226	503	391	2,281	1,614	901	490	407
Raleigh city	25,054	11,495	6,292	8,028	7,913	6,397	2,842	22,082	15,737	2,645	2,697	2,767
Wilmington city	7,803	3,165	1,684	2,743	2,667	2,324	1,702	7,777	6,880	1,537	950	976
Winston-Salem city	15,166	5,590	4,510	4,174	6,365	6,202	2,051	15,980	14,268	2,861	1,639	2,408
North Dakota												
Bismarck city	5,914	2,562	1,686	811	2,917	2,597	722	5,401	4,674	454	334	779
Fargo city	8,834	2,271	1,691	926	2,709	4,600	644	5,076	5,920	1,269	284	384
Ohio												
Akron city	18,312	4,853	4,292	2,304	3,951	3,664	3,776	14,298	10,717	4,286	2,511	1,573
Canton city	5,627	1,453	2,263	983	1,145	1,113	1,061	4,134	4,435	2,189	854	520
Cincinnati city	18,323	6,639	4,068	4,169	4,032	4,812	5,859	16,995	14,226	8,032	3,189	2,124
Cleveland city	21,587	7,979	8,042	3,625	5,675	5,023	8,580	24,266	19,154	15,427	6,836	4,818
Columbus city	53,074	14,810	10,587	8,625	8,705	9,826	8,448	38,989	30,525	11,713	5,596	3,628
Dayton city	8,836	3,210	2,654	757	2,297	1,797	3,177	8,656	6,316	4,443	1,401	1,894
Lorain city	4,822	2,474	1,728	753	1,436	1,269	1,147	5,375	3,807	1,355	833	454
Parma city	7,808	3,348	2,667	1,085	2,162	2,669	531	6,443	6,857	562	770	532
Toledo city	21,122	8,391	7,672	3,052	4,757	6,490	4,395	19,113	16,521	5,917	3,444	2,845
Youngstown city	3,343	1,414	1,595	1,153	977	1,610	1,752	4,365	5,355	2,711	988	1,160
Oklahoma												
Broken Arrow city	9,689	2,845	1,278	1,341	2,484	1,174	586	6,796	3,877	370	431	510
Edmond city	9,220	3,076	1,942	2,468	2,298	1,274	269	6,200	4,266	200	191	400
Lawton city	4,128	1,873	1,367	1,381	1,270	1,396	928	5,391	3,826	980	1,078	390
Norman city	8,711	3,697	1,724	1,289	1,859	2,057	683	7,158	5,407	919	336	719
Oklahoma City city	40,777	17,783	10,065	10,166	11,856	9,602	7,681	42,681	28,457	5,394	4,289	3,155
Tulsa city	27,827	9,216	6,621	6,784	8,856	9,884	4,757	27,395	22,710	4,553	2,799	1,886

Table I-3: Places—Persons With Health Insurance by Source of Insurance—*Continued*

	Private Health Insurance Coverage						Public Health Insurance Coverage					
	Employer Based			Direct Purchase			Medicare			Medicaid/CHIP		
	55 to 64 Years	65 to 74 Years	75 Years and Over	55 to 64 Years	65 to 74 Years	75 Years and Over	55 to 64 Years	65 to 74 Years	75 Years and Over	55 to 64 Years	65 to 74 Years	75 Years and Over
Oregon												
Beaverton city	8,490	1,806	1,245	2,027	2,762	1,264	680	6,324	3,327	1,165	1,143	343
Bend city	6,627	1,759	1,656	1,383	2,563	2,745	607	6,509	5,344	2,000	815	934
Eugene city	11,764	2,999	3,400	2,055	5,004	3,953	1,511	11,792	9,105	3,005	1,195	906
Gresham city	7,008	2,694	1,849	2,472	2,918	2,930	1,229	8,078	5,521	1,943	1,012	897
Hillsboro city	7,076	1,922	1,266	860	2,174	1,405	957	6,071	3,494	1,584	403	440
Medford city	4,440	2,075	1,741	1,059	2,322	3,032	1,447	7,491	6,157	2,158	797	858
Portland city	42,933	12,536	8,673	11,731	11,791	9,792	5,828	39,540	27,795	15,568	8,450	5,674
Salem city	12,858	3,773	3,362	1,052	4,868	3,212	1,549	12,195	8,953	3,204	1,872	1,435
Pennsylvania												
Allentown city	5,432	2,290	1,609	1,074	1,810	3,305	1,863	6,964	6,168	2,507	1,448	1,110
Bethlehem city	5,808	1,650	1,450	1,327	2,214	2,215	1,315	5,623	5,402	1,332	789	889
Erie city	7,034	2,240	1,366	1,601	2,292	2,606	2,014	6,218	6,694	2,502	1,045	1,668
Philadelphia city	91,125	34,579	22,004	24,128	28,257	30,279	23,681	101,831	81,247	40,539	23,014	18,592
Pittsburgh city	21,451	7,644	4,914	5,339	7,583	9,691	4,227	18,925	18,849	5,767	3,849	3,306
Reading city	2,896	1,205	986	545	1,047	1,327	1,678	4,937	4,044	2,253	1,851	1,657
Scranton city	5,308	2,348	1,320	849	2,257	2,955	1,285	5,972	6,079	1,911	1,386	1,155
Rhode Island												
Cranston city	7,564	2,757	1,552	1,861	1,518	2,736	1,266	6,752	6,992	1,733	1,428	1,501
Pawtucket city	3,854	964	735	729	676	1,145	944	3,960	3,082	1,773	566	788
Providence city	6,982	2,063	1,718	1,163	1,439	1,756	2,221	7,176	7,273	4,474	2,357	2,642
Warwick city	9,280	4,086	2,127	1,145	2,524	3,339	1,050	7,527	7,008	2,399	829	1,145
South Carolina												
Charleston city	8,987	4,183	2,115	2,953	2,990	2,177	1,322	10,114	6,036	1,054	650	659
Columbia city	7,045	2,877	1,901	1,124	1,517	1,123	936	6,340	4,412	1,296	922	822
North Charleston city	5,143	2,345	1,105	926	1,898	1,283	1,304	6,508	3,617	1,599	660	431
Rock Hill city	3,489	1,411	739	660	1,355	1,449	577	4,999	4,085	621	787	413
South Dakota												
Rapid City city	5,173	1,549	2,047	1,305	2,504	3,436	965	5,110	5,255	1,127	416	726
Sioux Falls city	14,922	4,034	1,900	1,953	3,895	3,871	1,616	11,097	7,890	1,765	1,546	1,008
Tennessee												
Chattanooga city	11,934	4,809	3,487	3,478	4,699	4,480	4,658	13,318	11,509	3,538	2,159	2,470
Clarksville city	5,517	1,943	874	1,502	1,512	1,680	1,259	6,782	4,322	693	1,388	716
Franklin city	5,486	1,802	1,435	1,638	1,125	1,282	234	3,758	3,347	157	177	239
Jackson city	5,393	1,447	826	1,611	1,512	1,046	1,129	4,157	3,391	1,577	322	476
Johnson City city	3,144	1,449	1,239	1,669	2,212	1,747	1,194	5,668	4,560	910	925	691
Knoxville city	7,570	4,240	2,806	2,535	4,369	3,672	3,967	13,436	9,930	4,573	2,213	1,815
Memphis city	41,979	13,854	10,612	8,546	10,566	10,108	10,797	38,858	29,216	14,183	6,837	6,387
Murfreesboro city	7,314	2,165	1,823	1,534	2,114	1,526	627	6,613	3,996	402	642	560
Nashville-Davidson metropolitan govt (bal)	43,098	14,980	9,633	10,595	10,270	9,974	7,019	36,979	28,394	8,323	5,725	3,618
Texas												
Abilene city	6,829	3,697	2,747	1,620	1,465	1,874	1,094	7,485	6,914	1,738	884	798
Allen city	7,900	1,300	881	907	1,271	367	432	3,197	1,886	397	508	616
Amarillo city	12,809	4,973	3,184	2,792	4,212	4,403	1,555	13,623	10,388	1,647	1,511	1,893
Arlington city	26,704	7,161	4,700	7,117	4,740	3,133	3,429	21,829	12,202	4,258	2,088	1,195
Austin city	55,604	19,557	10,411	12,862	10,541	7,982	5,812	40,669	26,070	8,461	3,795	4,207
Baytown city	4,584	2,727	1,015	767	905	1,083	789	5,396	3,766	903	442	389
Beaumont city	6,983	1,593	1,783	1,745	1,190	2,015	2,419	7,659	6,523	1,846	782	980
Brownsville city	4,092	1,347	910	1,458	1,306	1,247	1,831	10,178	8,447	2,679	3,573	3,742
Bryan city	4,682	2,048	1,117	725	1,506	474	375	4,312	2,433	483	462	376
Carrollton city	10,087	2,678	876	1,886	1,516	1,228	828	6,373	3,995	747	712	818
College Station city	3,950	1,815	1,604	1,597	1,145	1,195	586	3,213	2,699	558	55	257
Conroe city	3,901	825	1,312	453	736	937	466	2,973	3,145	433	220	286
Corpus Christi city	21,474	6,446	4,754	4,086	4,982	4,436	4,479	22,004	16,181	4,749	4,042	3,139
Dallas city	61,417	20,862	11,507	18,085	15,394	14,739	13,507	63,508	47,218	16,963	10,701	9,334
Denton city	6,527	3,905	1,588	1,442	2,170	1,034	689	8,110	3,318	693	304	449
Edinburg city	2,626	913	571	554	401	780	661	3,098	2,676	861	1,152	1,268
El Paso city	29,452	9,186	5,120	8,891	5,979	6,206	7,986	40,451	34,942	8,303	11,423	11,788
Fort Worth city	42,345	12,357	9,966	8,567	7,195	7,683	7,543	38,666	28,867	9,210	6,840	5,249
Frisco city	7,960	2,609	971	1,661	1,351	948	140	6,954	2,292	144	308	0
Garland city	16,171	6,025	1,981	4,923	4,541	2,128	2,636	15,621	9,376	3,271	2,783	2,030
Grand Prairie city	11,068	3,530	1,508	1,548	1,834	1,349	1,642	7,974	4,664	1,891	522	376
Harlingen city	2,914	1,120	926	379	720	992	520	4,592	3,995	496	1,063	1,411
Houston city	114,992	41,490	22,268	23,987	25,291	24,380	19,302	114,268	85,131	33,274	20,216	19,747
Irving city	9,643	3,961	1,067	3,022	2,779	2,215	1,115	9,233	6,348	2,134	1,146	968
Killeen city	4,618	1,155	624	1,418	1,137	598	1,464	4,084	2,610	421	643	635
Laredo city	7,875	2,426	1,213	2,097	2,224	1,210	2,263	11,587	7,691	2,852	3,275	4,205
League City city	6,862	2,517	2,098	1,007	986	1,437	569	4,633	3,130	268	85	271
Lewisville city	6,884	2,112	779	1,208	1,130	1,066	562	4,990	3,649	559	468	377
Longview city	4,458	1,833	1,917	1,367	1,404	1,966	946	5,373	5,607	874	809	908
Lubbock city	13,243	5,538	4,364	3,703	4,191	4,139	2,914	14,165	12,661	2,139	1,243	1,378
McAllen city	5,249	1,749	1,099	3,728	1,945	860	751	7,536	4,274	677	2,691	1,272
McKinney city	8,079	3,626	1,267	1,120	1,415	2,331	563	7,715	5,266	457	99	288

Table I-3: Places—Persons With Health Insurance by Source of Insurance—*Continued*

| | Private Health Insurance Coverage | | | | | | Public Health Insurance Coverage | | | | | |
| | Employer Based | | | Direct Purchase | | | Medicare | | | Medicaid/CHIP | | |
	55 to 64 Years	65 to 74 Years	75 Years and Over	55 to 64 Years	65 to 74 Years	75 Years and Over	55 to 64 Years	65 to 74 Years	75 Years and Over	55 to 64 Years	65 to 74 Years	75 Years and Over
Texas—Cont.												
Mesquite city	11,920	2,279	1,891	2,099	1,376	1,749	889	7,176	5,524	1,465	475	589
Midland city	9,897	2,678	2,118	977	1,183	2,836	627	5,654	6,076	872	501	733
Mission city	2,442	807	699	146	1,264	2,056	928	5,096	3,678	867	1,580	1,333
Missouri City city	9,708	1,707	1,080	1,200	1,351	294	403	4,727	2,039	187	598	765
New Braunfels city	4,193	1,495	1,019	1,204	951	974	1,144	4,287	3,229	1,049	716	429
North Richland Hills city	5,842	2,336	1,502	1,084	1,303	1,274	422	4,914	3,938	162	199	231
Odessa city	7,795	2,620	2,013	1,292	1,695	1,576	1,270	6,563	4,712	1,423	1,185	511
Pasadena city	12,799	3,102	1,597	1,428	2,029	1,670	1,491	8,083	5,749	2,091	1,449	1,062
Pearland city	8,615	2,302	1,776	1,425	1,775	1,304	388	4,808	4,297	767	454	633
Pharr city	1,577	1,291	592	1,128	898	472	456	4,017	3,831	456	2,014	1,758
Plano city	24,334	8,189	3,196	6,585	7,030	3,708	1,031	18,931	10,749	366	1,550	845
Richardson city	10,458	2,654	2,481	1,116	2,440	2,079	131	7,892	5,978	336	259	559
Round Rock city	7,699	2,825	1,230	1,632	1,255	457	812	4,989	2,778	706	290	686
San Angelo city	5,370	2,746	2,018	1,289	1,956	1,485	952	6,949	6,652	1,383	943	1,091
San Antonio city	78,189	31,457	17,307	21,165	17,348	15,344	20,323	87,767	66,738	20,097	14,225	13,872
Sugar Land city	8,882	3,582	1,444	2,376	1,083	969	465	6,282	3,897	348	753	411
Temple city	4,044	2,770	1,615	1,327	2,172	1,272	841	6,638	3,640	1,028	1,103	358
Tyler city	6,075	3,089	2,690	1,708	2,329	2,019	1,429	7,231	6,712	1,051	485	606
Victoria city	4,485	1,476	1,089	1,259	1,639	1,471	338	5,099	3,833	483	926	816
Waco city	6,086	2,408	1,895	1,162	2,057	2,388	1,016	7,394	6,381	1,441	1,331	1,015
Wichita Falls city	6,696	2,368	1,846	1,202	1,888	1,714	1,023	5,852	5,616	1,418	1,093	991
Utah												
Layton city	5,460	2,066	1,101	718	1,624	635	422	3,805	2,599	267	194	306
Ogden city	4,235	1,574	1,094	696	1,081	891	999	4,146	3,428	1,090	590	111
Orem city	4,667	1,574	1,737	1,174	1,048	1,233	337	3,633	3,091	88	100	139
Provo city	4,098	1,979	1,423	1,212	1,048	1,561	591	3,530	3,372	833	332	606
Salt Lake City city	11,267	4,414	1,711	2,536	2,391	2,550	2,047	10,496	6,524	1,954	1,726	1,196
Sandy city	9,255	1,922	788	1,666	2,027	1,128	612	5,843	2,647	406	284	129
St. George city	4,186	2,232	3,389	1,137	2,538	3,259	1,397	7,864	8,641	434	245	444
West Jordan city	7,160	2,088	753	1,184	797	654	584	3,911	2,208	752	260	181
West Valley City city	6,960	1,863	929	628	792	865	1,005	5,430	2,915	1,191	1,197	468
Virginia												
Alexandria city	11,471	5,559	2,828	2,197	2,087	2,106	456	8,353	5,220	395	360	1,236
Chesapeake city	18,616	6,136	3,456	3,116	4,196	2,495	2,661	16,433	9,447	1,100	827	918
Hampton city	10,287	3,970	2,573	2,302	3,111	2,687	2,184	10,293	7,797	735	1,177	1,393
Lynchburg city	4,986	1,153	1,390	1,061	2,263	2,972	1,024	5,193	5,299	626	693	844
Newport News city	11,940	4,623	3,408	2,339	2,622	2,727	1,773	10,833	8,697	1,045	1,295	589
Norfolk city	13,469	4,629	2,470	2,183	2,862	3,419	3,188	12,717	9,873	2,514	3,012	1,880
Portsmouth city	6,222	2,929	1,996	1,180	1,686	2,579	818	6,818	5,555	1,131	803	538
Richmond city	14,338	4,752	3,131	4,182	5,398	4,403	2,771	12,835	10,436	2,219	1,767	1,474
Roanoke city	7,251	2,475	1,544	946	2,470	3,364	1,488	7,554	6,756	1,338	1,523	1,115
Suffolk city	7,038	2,992	1,596	1,407	1,556	1,570	904	6,541	4,172	814	590	672
Virginia Beach city	32,067	11,790	7,479	7,124	9,897	7,080	3,201	30,992	21,767	2,203	1,582	1,694
Washington												
Auburn city	6,025	1,660	1,046	1,393	1,502	1,544	560	3,725	4,165	759	214	321
Bellevue city	11,273	3,212	3,143	2,160	3,627	4,865	549	8,784	9,876	1,317	270	981
Bellingham city	5,480	1,601	1,021	1,532	2,025	2,306	608	6,284	4,362	1,125	730	603
Everett city	6,282	1,192	1,284	1,524	1,554	1,656	1,812	4,823	4,120	2,639	876	1,065
Federal Way city	7,600	2,674	783	1,548	2,312	2,286	991	6,527	4,745	1,038	683	571
Kennewick city	6,127	1,548	1,362	1,270	2,048	1,718	843	4,820	4,436	1,223	770	908
Kent city	10,607	2,444	779	1,665	1,202	1,440	1,852	6,704	4,265	1,508	1,270	1,060
Kirkland city	8,284	2,528	1,201	2,651	2,155	1,877	399	6,121	4,318	921	642	359
Marysville city	5,232	1,350	785	1,065	1,446	1,912	615	5,485	3,723	904	961	908
Pasco city	4,147	882	367	760	369	193	468	2,391	1,292	822	214	457
Renton city	6,881	1,671	1,536	1,447	1,268	1,370	854	3,846	4,534	1,087	855	813
Seattle city	46,195	19,430	10,487	11,139	12,104	10,367	5,398	44,100	29,992	10,380	6,470	6,150
Spokane city	14,721	5,849	3,198	3,138	4,477	4,306	4,007	16,807	11,578	5,940	2,303	1,572
Spokane Valley city	6,722	2,175	1,333	1,707	2,343	2,690	1,353	7,322	5,928	2,106	926	560
Tacoma city	13,836	4,950	2,840	2,917	3,343	3,491	2,618	13,871	9,470	4,754	3,677	2,894
Vancouver city	12,741	4,871	3,177	3,012	3,967	3,422	1,729	12,689	9,292	2,474	2,035	1,457
Yakima city	4,488	1,490	878	933	2,556	2,715	1,321	6,370	5,987	1,994	838	870
Wisconsin												
Appleton city	7,319	1,221	1,299	888	1,678	1,974	866	3,545	3,592	1,337	79	381
Eau Claire city	4,069	1,761	1,229	1,063	1,694	1,688	791	4,784	3,478	836	1,196	958
Green Bay city	7,988	1,845	1,298	1,265	2,052	3,185	1,681	6,107	5,536	2,086	816	652
Kenosha city	7,173	2,878	1,962	1,439	2,565	2,269	1,814	6,880	4,751	2,143	1,158	1,063
Madison city	19,690	8,060	4,395	3,043	5,329	4,648	1,838	15,063	10,213	2,300	1,107	1,667
Milwaukee city	31,340	11,011	8,929	5,850	6,831	6,556	8,360	31,388	25,396	15,091	6,846	5,469
Oshkosh city	4,258	893	1,190	914	1,750	2,556	921	3,735	4,815	700	98	239
Racine city	4,785	1,667	1,650	736	1,021	963	1,549	4,271	4,265	1,626	840	654
Waukesha city	6,153	1,737	549	1,536	1,365	1,551	1,113	3,945	3,254	551	144	483

Table I-4: Metropolitan/Micropolitan Statistical Areas—Persons With Health Insurance by Source of Insurance

	Private Health Insurance Coverage						Public Health Insurance Coverage					
	Employer Based			Direct Purchase			Medicare			Medicaid/CHIP		
	55 to 64 Years	65 to 74 Years	75 Years and Over	55 to 64 Years	65 to 74 Years	75 Years and Over	55 to 64 Years	65 to 74 Years	75 Years and Over	55 to 64 Years	65 to 74 Years	75 Years and Over
Aberdeen, WA Micro Area	5,289	2,568	1,026	2,039	3,251	2,523	2,284	7,798	4,954	1,284	958	546
Abilene, TX Metro Area	10,373	5,627	3,704	2,814	2,915	2,743	1,567	11,970	10,063	2,299	1,538	1,159
Adrian, MI Micro Area	9,915	4,347	2,869	1,772	4,167	2,913	1,348	9,397	6,402	1,745	483	693
Akron, OH Metro Area	69,397	23,763	18,804	10,836	16,085	15,898	9,191	59,245	46,183	9,150	5,769	5,124
Alamogordo, NM Micro Area	2,976	1,618	1,566	1,149	1,648	978	823	5,967	3,933	940	1,048	433
Albany, GA Metro Area	11,038	4,146	1,893	1,863	2,488	2,552	1,752	12,599	7,915	2,029	2,958	1,652
Albany, OR Metro Area	9,393	3,440	1,915	3,058	4,783	3,882	1,865	11,994	8,129	3,011	1,698	1,045
Albany-Schenectady-Troy, NY Metro Area	90,183	45,525	28,003	10,687	16,323	18,649	7,825	72,246	54,474	11,364	7,982	6,724
Albertville, AL Micro Area	5,834	2,248	1,350	2,117	2,696	2,338	2,588	8,688	5,934	899	1,760	699
Albuquerque, NM Metro Area	66,939	27,417	18,421	16,580	15,001	11,193	10,909	72,689	52,046	17,279	9,148	6,472
Alexandria, LA Metro Area	10,152	5,191	3,348	2,024	3,466	2,394	2,751	11,532	7,982	3,369	2,375	1,647
Allentown-Bethlehem-Easton, PA-NJ Metro Area	79,375	25,744	18,555	16,238	28,877	27,202	10,264	70,695	58,449	9,610	5,910	7,167
Altoona, PA Metro Area	12,753	4,181	3,313	2,867	5,213	5,066	2,538	12,099	10,384	1,557	1,422	998
Amarillo, TX Metro Area	18,725	5,673	4,021	3,402	5,690	5,651	1,963	17,841	13,920	2,184	1,602	2,272
Ames, IA Metro Area	6,815	2,413	2,180	1,593	1,952	1,924	444	5,311	4,262	498	378	402
Anchorage, AK Metro Area	30,903	10,690	4,832	5,362	2,760	1,621	3,258	20,623	12,212	4,033	3,284	3,489
Ann Arbor, MI Metro Area	31,283	15,220	8,594	5,229	6,425	6,656	3,781	24,683	15,894	3,333	2,952	1,904
Anniston-Oxford-Jacksonville, AL Metro Area	9,847	5,298	3,136	2,248	3,492	2,432	3,285	10,625	7,051	1,576	1,821	1,519
Appleton, WI Metro Area	22,273	2,842	3,126	3,543	6,470	6,519	2,213	16,179	12,315	2,772	795	1,137
Asheville, NC Metro Area	35,922	17,931	11,499	12,343	16,503	15,688	5,306	50,252	37,073	4,991	3,795	3,202
Ashtabula, OH Micro Area	8,278	3,345	2,521	2,245	2,810	1,799	2,235	9,388	6,079	1,414	1,651	783
Athens, TX Micro Area	5,021	3,298	2,320	1,214	3,560	2,957	1,821	9,436	6,523	1,114	704	557
Athens-Clarke County, GA Metro Area	13,829	7,421	3,142	3,022	4,324	2,949	2,371	13,750	8,211	1,580	1,310	1,387
Atlanta-Sandy Springs-Roswell, GA Metro Area	395,011	144,909	70,136	87,270	85,859	64,338	58,615	356,965	208,335	51,506	45,560	35,740
Atlantic City-Hammonton, NJ Metro Area	25,167	11,342	6,407	4,327	6,180	6,804	2,634	23,725	16,664	3,878	3,764	3,139
Auburn, NY Micro Area	8,074	3,706	2,562	968	1,563	1,613	1,804	6,621	5,859	1,422	396	441
Auburn-Opelika, AL Metro Area	8,608	4,302	2,793	2,607	2,523	2,180	2,294	9,214	5,599	1,444	797	698
Augusta-Richmond County, GA-SC Metro Area	41,990	15,492	9,132	11,378	13,324	10,262	8,004	46,880	31,890	8,025	6,585	6,217
Augusta-Waterville, ME Micro Area	11,598	4,861	3,470	2,801	4,387	2,906	2,475	11,821	8,431	2,478	1,339	1,181
Austin-Round Rock, TX Metro Area	135,011	48,560	26,644	30,011	29,601	19,955	14,127	105,106	65,386	15,048	8,412	9,808
Bakersfield, CA Metro Area	45,697	16,615	8,304	9,880	9,255	8,115	9,166	47,991	32,673	16,917	8,439	6,804
Baltimore-Columbia-Towson, MD Metro Area	247,489	118,135	71,432	46,665	59,893	57,757	32,240	205,827	154,996	43,072	23,172	21,391
Bangor, ME Metro Area	12,005	3,821	2,943	2,858	4,478	3,715	2,826	13,726	10,252	3,571	2,951	2,988
Barnstable Town, MA Metro Area	24,557	15,052	11,908	4,998	10,902	9,533	2,735	31,003	25,943	6,133	2,283	2,232
Baton Rouge, LA Metro Area	64,602	22,973	12,992	11,887	11,564	9,571	8,712	56,243	36,975	8,585	8,578	5,753
Battle Creek, MI Metro Area	11,065	5,120	4,796	2,162	3,547	2,788	2,465	11,917	8,808	2,672	1,277	1,304
Bay City, MI Metro Area	10,840	7,270	4,505	1,739	2,661	2,919	2,874	10,366	8,155	2,601	855	1,567
Beaumont-Port Arthur, TX Metro Area	28,714	8,007	7,161	5,809	10,235	9,229	6,278	31,497	23,481	5,800	3,135	2,903
Beaver Dam, WI Micro Area	9,083	2,401	1,243	2,445	2,547	3,077	1,090	6,853	5,925	1,143	671	997
Beckley, WV Metro Area	10,711	5,921	3,542	1,908	2,871	1,659	3,342	12,502	9,045	3,452	1,372	929
Bellingham, WA Metro Area	16,291	5,350	3,556	6,374	8,529	5,600	2,010	18,731	11,582	3,356	1,759	1,429
Bend-Redmond, OR Metro Area	14,399	3,924	3,329	4,034	7,697	5,261	2,137	18,433	11,328	4,655	1,613	1,523
Billings, MT Metro Area	14,111	4,145	2,343	4,880	5,403	5,874	2,260	13,511	10,966	2,338	1,132	1,062
Binghamton, NY Metro Area	23,977	10,462	8,659	3,147	6,247	7,775	4,031	21,712	18,986	6,281	2,350	2,324
Birmingham-Hoover, AL Metro Area	93,536	39,211	24,276	23,397	24,433	22,325	19,753	93,002	66,715	17,329	11,565	9,600
Bismarck, ND Metro Area	12,259	3,938	2,379	2,184	4,306	4,528	1,089	9,648	7,612	991	920	982
Blacksburg-Christiansburg-Radford, VA Metro Area	12,291	4,587	2,609	1,970	5,410	5,167	3,316	15,189	9,853	3,032	1,310	1,496
Bloomington, IL Metro Area	15,996	6,287	3,998	3,269	4,562	4,170	1,343	11,972	9,408	1,803	427	704
Bloomington, IN Metro Area	11,000	4,361	2,438	3,220	3,945	3,464	990	10,531	7,455	765	667	511
Bloomsburg-Berwick, PA Metro Area	8,834	2,766	2,121	1,719	3,473	3,493	1,183	7,717	6,287	1,311	839	1,272
Bluefield, WV-VA Micro Area	8,546	4,424	3,358	1,652	2,776	3,106	3,609	11,173	8,726	3,398	1,706	995
Boise City, ID Metro Area	45,004	14,172	7,379	12,494	16,568	14,744	7,744	49,903	32,947	6,256	4,328	3,950
Boston-Cambridge-Newton, MA-NH Metro Area	426,713	169,377	104,777	65,137	98,860	103,182	44,945	342,453	274,733	103,819	54,094	49,111
Boulder, CO Metro Area	25,489	8,374	4,583	8,721	6,320	6,181	1,841	21,147	14,358	3,426	1,548	1,910
Bowling Green, KY Metro Area	12,844	4,261	2,284	2,169	4,352	3,352	3,175	12,500	8,119	2,445	901	1,199
Bozeman, MT Micro Area	5,869	2,539	1,499	2,737	1,500	2,072	278	6,330	4,011	607	452	226
Brainerd, MN Micro Area	8,085	2,327	1,854	2,971	6,409	5,014	1,286	11,434	7,912	1,459	594	717
Branson, MO Micro Area	4,874	2,360	1,429	2,720	4,932	2,749	2,060	11,289	7,216	1,702	772	789
Bremerton-Silverdale, WA Metro Area	23,155	10,899	6,942	4,484	7,518	6,414	2,961	23,600	14,001	4,708	2,036	1,049
Bridgeport-Stamford-Norwalk, CT Metro Area	80,754	31,694	19,121	20,773	17,235	22,504	6,299	65,730	57,998	10,513	7,224	6,696
Brownsville-Harlingen, TX Metro Area	14,015	4,858	3,668	4,661	4,341	4,857	4,499	25,963	21,528	5,192	8,330	8,180
Brunswick, GA Metro Area	8,424	3,815	2,545	2,595	2,819	1,492	2,179	11,412	7,621	2,314	2,353	1,494
Buffalo-Cheektowaga-Niagara Falls, NY Metro Area	114,256	46,090	30,509	17,306	26,478	32,999	16,248	96,562	82,337	20,624	13,234	14,099
Burlington, NC Metro Area	11,464	4,018	2,685	2,743	4,572	4,483	2,811	13,749	10,057	2,452	1,576	1,258
Burlington-South Burlington, VT Metro Area	20,427	6,631	4,184	3,349	6,164	5,276	2,816	15,744	11,296	5,087	1,897	1,215
California-Lexington Park, MD Metro Area	9,908	4,286	2,057	1,332	2,136	1,024	731	7,648	4,235	600	1,142	405
Canton-Massillon, OH Metro Area	41,590	15,927	12,833	7,268	10,479	10,443	5,161	37,908	28,566	6,570	3,950	2,764
Cape Coral-Fort Myers, FL Metro Area	51,474	34,943	23,026	16,298	29,283	28,509	10,039	94,901	73,037	7,990	5,919	8,964
Cape Girardeau, MO-IL Metro Area	7,611	3,083	1,492	1,790	2,631	3,034	2,118	8,758	6,233	1,638	502	748
Carbondale-Marion, IL Metro Area	9,198	4,399	3,185	2,520	3,675	2,629	1,238	10,319	7,619	2,332	1,005	545
Carson City, NV Metro Area	4,498	1,510	895	602	1,875	1,907	844	5,311	4,076	916	1,002	780
Casper, WY Metro Area	6,150	1,585	1,129	1,617	1,286	1,890	971	5,255	4,129	2,057	859	765
Cedar Rapids, IA Metro Area	24,144	5,962	3,630	4,434	10,677	10,000	2,618	19,967	16,709	3,310	1,478	2,137
Centralia, WA Micro Area	6,226	2,871	2,186	1,596	2,624	3,151	1,423	8,137	6,054	1,558	1,025	860
Chambersburg-Waynesboro, PA Metro Area	13,555	4,843	5,284	3,289	6,253	3,690	1,478	14,577	11,850	1,324	1,387	672

Table I-4: Metropolitan/Micropolitan Statistical Areas—Persons With Health Insurance by Source of Insurance—*Continued*

| | Private Health Insurance Coverage | | | | | | Public Health Insurance Coverage | | | | | |
| | Employer Based | | | Direct Purchase | | | Medicare | | | Medicaid/CHIP | | |
	55 to 64 Years	65 to 74 Years	75 Years and Over	55 to 64 Years	65 to 74 Years	75 Years and Over	55 to 64 Years	65 to 74 Years	75 Years and Over	55 to 64 Years	65 to 74 Years	75 Years and Over
Champaign-Urbana, IL Metro Area	17,927	7,409	6,088	3,209	4,567	4,728	2,814	13,741	12,232	2,529	1,022	905
Charleston, WV Metro Area	22,043	10,339	9,174	3,361	5,956	4,141	5,808	21,976	16,604	6,870	1,970	1,306
Charleston-Mattoon, IL Micro Area	4,545	1,646	1,744	1,628	1,580	1,423	1,254	4,833	3,874	1,298	616	159
Charleston-North Charleston, SC Metro Area	53,112	24,628	13,916	13,634	16,374	10,608	8,926	58,579	34,872	8,311	6,085	4,290
Charlotte-Concord-Gastonia, NC-SC Metro Area	170,239	57,635	31,216	44,638	60,414	44,582	28,614	172,508	108,339	23,701	18,672	14,889
Charlottesville, VA Metro Area	19,410	8,302	4,208	5,345	7,004	6,022	2,979	17,541	14,246	1,426	995	1,433
Chattanooga, TN-GA Metro Area	44,777	16,227	10,500	9,411	17,868	16,048	11,179	48,548	35,591	7,339	6,186	5,589
Cheyenne, WY Metro Area	8,707	2,713	1,878	1,726	2,210	2,406	889	7,731	5,323	438	534	687
Chicago-Naperville-Elgin, IL-IN-WI Metro Area	759,522	253,070	149,883	154,771	201,123	187,162	86,077	635,806	484,667	123,890	75,524	66,622
Chico, CA Metro Area	14,177	7,513	6,642	4,155	6,808	4,316	4,062	20,186	15,832	6,351	2,375	2,976
Chillicothe, OH Micro Area	6,197	2,485	1,657	968	1,841	1,770	1,424	6,273	4,402	1,635	851	410
Cincinnati, OH-KY-IN Metro Area	192,467	65,431	43,764	33,077	46,561	42,620	26,328	155,008	116,170	26,888	14,574	11,026
Claremont-Lebanon, NH-VT Micro Area	22,370	9,334	5,552	5,588	7,396	6,984	3,358	22,954	15,374	4,349	2,155	1,596
Clarksburg, WV Micro Area	8,675	4,473	2,629	1,592	3,276	1,359	1,490	9,684	6,132	2,081	1,226	977
Clarksville, TN-KY Metro Area	13,463	4,857	2,297	2,703	4,306	3,749	3,164	16,085	10,043	2,298	2,144	1,472
Clearlake, CA Micro Area	4,279	2,391	1,431	1,454	2,110	1,776	2,362	7,651	4,898	3,194	1,394	596
Cleveland, TN Metro Area	8,420	3,014	1,283	2,280	4,515	2,364	2,501	11,272	7,807	2,290	948	1,529
Cleveland-Elyria, OH Metro Area	198,116	78,918	60,647	33,435	52,795	49,266	26,029	174,220	143,125	34,599	18,839	17,175
Coeur d'Alene, ID Metro Area	10,521	4,225	2,719	5,643	5,519	4,879	1,487	14,373	10,020	1,335	1,697	821
College Station-Bryan, TX Metro Area	13,699	5,993	4,488	3,135	4,515	3,816	1,380	12,792	9,623	1,460	1,020	1,028
Colorado Springs, CO Metro Area	43,826	12,252	7,055	9,786	13,023	11,766	5,479	46,015	30,352	10,675	3,896	3,324
Columbia, MO Metro Area	12,637	5,366	2,990	2,084	3,239	2,970	1,360	10,606	6,746	1,112	1,472	902
Columbia, SC Metro Area	61,137	26,183	13,723	12,370	15,736	13,297	10,434	62,508	37,587	9,216	7,602	4,848
Columbus, GA-AL Metro Area	17,275	8,419	3,640	4,822	4,729	4,314	4,464	21,623	14,955	4,888	3,294	3,069
Columbus, IN Metro Area	6,648	2,287	1,532	1,954	2,952	2,417	1,420	6,337	4,661	942	704	155
Columbus, OH Metro Area	161,939	54,401	35,321	24,619	35,257	29,981	19,043	130,515	91,313	21,499	12,953	8,839
Concord, NH Micro Area	17,183	5,037	3,069	2,070	4,359	3,682	1,920	12,948	8,978	1,246	576	610
Cookeville, TN Micro Area	7,305	3,517	1,790	2,062	4,083	2,458	2,301	10,508	7,323	2,885	1,850	1,216
Coos Bay, OR Micro Area	5,640	1,772	1,491	2,332	2,647	2,506	1,799	8,504	6,238	2,199	2,441	1,183
Corning, NY Micro Area	9,153	4,024	3,308	2,327	3,048	3,012	2,375	9,191	7,126	2,232	1,354	1,323
Corpus Christi, TX Metro Area	31,417	9,292	5,641	6,183	9,154	7,221	6,066	35,148	23,592	5,742	5,713	4,748
Corvallis, OR Metro Area	8,082	2,425	2,026	1,767	2,225	1,232	555	6,866	5,128	985	363	807
Crestview-Fort Walton Beach-Destin, FL Metro Area	13,975	6,240	6,267	5,527	5,479	4,282	3,284	23,093	16,413	3,488	2,015	1,166
Cullman, AL Micro Area	6,811	1,922	1,868	1,051	2,114	1,603	2,085	8,344	5,539	1,220	1,236	685
Cumberland, MD-WV Metro Area	8,862	4,015	2,930	1,157	2,821	3,609	1,453	10,189	7,690	2,149	1,474	1,425
Dallas-Fort Worth-Arlington, TX Metro Area	465,272	147,392	77,564	103,804	102,989	80,886	56,198	398,126	257,299	58,568	41,224	34,635
Dalton, GA Metro Area	8,840	2,183	766	1,790	3,262	3,103	2,482	9,768	7,256	2,583	1,511	1,367
Danville, IL Metro Area	7,089	2,957	1,922	763	2,966	2,638	1,261	7,697	5,684	1,136	991	609
Danville, VA Metro Area	9,706	3,414	1,498	1,910	4,584	4,360	2,599	10,766	8,975	1,397	1,211	1,243
Daphne-Fairhope-Foley, AL Metro Area	17,707	8,136	4,449	4,065	5,728	5,592	3,548	21,405	14,977	1,968	1,674	1,472
Davenport-Moline-Rock Island, IA-IL Metro Area	35,720	14,697	11,391	5,712	12,745	10,969	4,183	33,155	25,528	5,328	2,675	2,714
Dayton, OH Metro Area	71,033	27,903	20,746	10,738	18,268	18,447	9,758	69,060	54,286	10,636	5,471	5,467
Decatur, AL Metro Area	12,519	4,761	2,572	3,213	5,495	3,865	2,970	13,402	9,235	2,409	1,290	1,666
Decatur, IL Metro Area	10,481	3,813	3,108	1,045	3,975	3,911	1,853	9,501	8,078	1,822	994	1,086
Deltona-Daytona Beach-Ormond Beach, FL Metro Area	45,513	24,400	18,433	16,107	22,781	20,109	11,659	77,574	63,390	10,565	10,972	9,290
Denver-Aurora-Lakewood, CO Metro Area	213,532	71,804	40,041	53,697	46,523	44,812	22,779	178,868	116,821	32,801	19,019	16,991
Des Moines-West Des Moines, IA Metro Area	50,091	13,924	10,164	10,396	16,899	14,956	4,779	40,515	29,455	8,080	3,550	3,449
Detroit-Warren-Dearborn, MI Metro Area	390,725	175,905	126,781	79,626	109,744	98,816	66,916	341,182	258,949	84,173	46,102	38,468
Dothan, AL Metro Area	11,332	4,410	1,865	2,741	4,513	3,598	2,681	14,401	9,986	2,553	1,536	1,567
Dover, DE Metro Area	12,012	7,591	4,103	2,082	3,528	4,400	2,499	15,630	10,121	2,993	1,961	1,221
DuBois, PA Micro Area	6,275	1,937	1,226	1,877	3,919	3,420	1,582	7,933	6,345	1,714	763	891
Dubuque, IA Metro Area	9,476	3,274	2,546	1,742	3,070	2,301	798	7,850	6,799	1,128	791	889
Duluth, MN-WI Metro Area	27,743	9,627	6,029	5,762	12,041	9,391	4,720	25,415	19,228	5,139	2,613	1,700
Dunn, NC Micro Area	6,405	2,555	1,352	2,393	2,519	1,829	2,143	8,288	4,733	1,228	1,447	878
Durham-Chapel Hill, NC Metro Area	43,933	20,739	11,810	10,980	12,029	11,240	5,737	39,384	27,006	4,871	4,033	3,989
East Stroudsburg, PA Metro Area	15,965	6,105	2,816	3,933	3,964	3,014	1,577	14,878	10,039	1,831	1,052	1,353
Eau Claire, WI Metro Area	13,579	4,323	3,104	3,646	5,488	4,534	2,081	13,194	10,233	2,043	2,213	2,071
El Centro, CA Metro Area	7,191	2,396	1,434	1,904	1,626	1,409	2,296	10,777	9,476	4,152	5,819	5,151
El Paso, TX Metro Area	33,491	10,078	5,370	10,308	6,430	6,830	9,419	47,060	38,583	10,527	14,578	13,508
Elizabeth City, NC Micro Area	3,716	2,124	1,190	1,447	2,271	1,316	746	6,241	4,066	1,184	1,220	1,022
Elizabethtown-Fort Knox, KY Metro Area	9,345	4,825	2,078	2,555	3,299	2,831	3,040	11,083	7,241	2,839	1,312	826
Elkhart-Goshen, IN Metro Area	13,719	2,051	1,709	2,320	4,992	5,474	2,007	13,174	11,159	2,004	947	444
Elmira, NY Metro Area	9,164	3,503	2,773	822	2,922	2,370	1,513	7,877	5,941	1,334	1,170	710
Erie, PA Metro Area	25,931	7,652	4,546	5,534	9,216	8,265	4,066	23,165	18,386	4,781	2,778	2,681
Eugene, OR Metro Area	28,904	9,181	7,229	7,201	15,668	12,012	4,875	35,595	24,646	8,905	4,101	3,348
Eureka-Arcata-Fortuna, CA Micro Area	7,414	3,667	2,194	2,857	4,960	3,420	2,826	12,049	7,705	5,587	1,290	457
Evansville, IN-KY Metro Area	27,867	8,613	6,139	7,262	9,430	9,936	4,442	25,989	19,939	4,656	2,656	2,723
Fairbanks, AK Metro Area	7,981	2,782	1,357	1,032	1,002	285	507	4,586	2,582	831	603	687
Fargo, ND-MN Metro Area	18,130	5,080	2,988	3,297	5,995	8,397	1,434	12,897	11,220	2,030	1,411	657
Faribault-Northfield, MN Micro Area	5,376	890	809	1,738	2,274	2,697	259	4,638	4,004	294	301	148
Farmington, MO Micro Area	4,897	1,742	1,041	724	2,005	1,831	1,840	5,545	3,961	743	636	145
Farmington, NM Metro Area	8,644	2,258	1,600	1,833	2,224	1,812	1,580	8,181	5,906	2,324	1,371	1,592
Fayetteville, NC Metro Area	17,776	7,879	4,337	5,546	5,488	3,778	4,886	21,867	15,283	3,532	3,492	2,763
Fayetteville-Springdale-Rogers, AR-MO Metro Area	33,062	9,170	4,950	6,097	10,026	9,390	5,315	33,570	23,430	4,720	3,503	3,534

Table I-4: Metropolitan/Micropolitan Statistical Areas—Persons With Health Insurance by Source of Insurance—*Continued*

	Private Health Insurance Coverage						Public Health Insurance Coverage					
	Employer Based			Direct Purchase			Medicare			Medicaid/CHIP		
	55 to 64 Years	65 to 74 Years	75 Years and Over	55 to 64 Years	65 to 74 Years	75 Years and Over	55 to 64 Years	65 to 74 Years	75 Years and Over	55 to 64 Years	65 to 74 Years	75 Years and Over
Findlay, OH Micro Area	7,661	2,716	2,288	1,080	2,562	1,424	1,334	6,431	4,648	358	513	87
Flagstaff, AZ Metro Area	9,726	3,546	933	2,743	1,806	2,143	1,350	9,518	5,282	2,086	1,160	1,214
Flint, MI Metro Area	38,551	23,125	16,822	6,563	8,351	9,730	8,261	35,890	27,417	10,664	4,370	2,964
Florence, SC Metro Area	16,454	6,285	3,368	3,439	4,503	3,329	4,106	18,692	11,475	4,034	2,280	2,068
Florence-Muscle Shoals, AL Metro Area	13,211	6,577	3,887	3,149	4,282	4,590	3,494	14,891	11,152	1,595	1,219	1,594
Fond du Lac, WI Metro Area	10,246	1,724	1,365	1,861	3,946	3,928	1,110	8,879	7,203	1,784	888	830
Forest City, NC Micro Area	4,485	1,489	1,766	1,800	3,499	2,261	2,011	7,469	5,063	1,898	1,293	634
Fort Collins, CO Metro Area	27,191	9,351	6,216	8,607	7,630	6,018	2,590	25,594	17,265	3,710	1,199	826
Fort Smith, AR-OK Metro Area	18,325	5,483	3,565	4,754	7,420	6,071	5,641	24,501	16,237	5,189	3,733	2,411
Fort Wayne, IN Metro Area	34,628	9,267	7,292	7,471	11,406	9,922	4,801	31,785	22,976	3,368	2,455	1,879
Frankfort, KY Micro Area	7,203	3,843	2,275	1,176	1,898	1,545	801	6,229	4,243	559	309	317
Fresno, CA Metro Area	52,290	20,105	14,229	13,048	14,315	12,818	8,643	57,342	43,574	20,974	13,442	11,834
Gadsden, AL Metro Area	8,243	4,088	3,149	1,508	3,304	2,092	2,838	10,419	6,779	2,393	2,224	1,572
Gainesville, FL Metro Area	18,087	8,340	4,039	5,349	6,114	4,624	2,709	19,022	13,221	2,398	1,730	1,739
Gainesville, GA Metro Area	13,815	5,766	3,604	2,861	4,176	3,840	1,802	14,846	10,227	1,103	1,536	1,323
Gallup, NM Micro Area	2,049	617	541	295	491	424	1,062	3,737	2,961	2,177	1,782	1,222
Gettysburg, PA Metro Area	10,068	3,610	2,276	2,286	4,191	4,215	1,173	9,793	7,445	716	798	280
Glens Falls, NY Metro Area	11,753	6,998	3,647	3,161	4,318	4,319	2,449	13,073	9,336	3,939	1,057	1,197
Glenwood Springs, CO Micro Area	5,930	1,729	648	1,907	1,761	1,293	506	4,723	3,105	1,103	668	608
Goldsboro, NC Metro Area	7,297	3,651	2,187	2,060	2,960	2,652	2,517	10,236	7,339	2,517	1,367	1,183
Grand Forks, ND-MN Metro Area	7,821	1,900	984	1,951	3,084	3,454	982	6,708	5,529	914	732	579
Grand Island, NE Metro Area	6,365	1,754	1,035	2,248	2,687	3,104	1,191	6,338	5,888	1,249	429	658
Grand Junction, CO Metro Area	10,954	3,764	2,275	3,283	4,584	4,942	1,451	13,439	9,992	2,384	1,203	790
Grand Rapids-Wyoming, MI Metro Area	87,075	29,027	21,488	17,752	24,976	21,825	11,282	72,435	54,466	13,098	7,200	6,595
Grants Pass, OR Metro Area	4,437	3,142	1,586	3,109	3,381	4,456	2,280	11,754	8,232	3,589	1,305	1,123
Great Falls, MT Metro Area	5,537	1,886	1,316	2,075	2,878	2,530	1,220	7,422	5,699	491	649	374
Greeley, CO Metro Area	20,164	4,489	3,176	4,838	6,543	4,982	1,936	17,839	11,526	3,635	1,808	1,425
Green Bay, WI Metro Area	27,775	5,314	4,213	6,488	8,774	9,690	3,455	23,947	18,061	3,931	2,140	2,412
Greenville, TN Micro Area	5,112	1,804	1,220	1,026	2,903	1,620	1,537	7,964	4,929	907	1,189	1,213
Greenfield Town, MA Micro Area	8,244	3,923	2,114	895	2,408	1,803	999	7,045	4,625	3,107	646	596
Greensboro-High Point, NC Metro Area	56,943	17,714	10,673	16,643	20,395	16,129	10,937	61,017	43,417	8,473	6,481	5,725
Greenville, NC Metro Area	12,094	4,389	2,723	2,911	4,262	2,579	1,809	11,106	7,104	1,811	1,481	1,564
Greenville-Anderson-Mauldin, SC Metro Area	64,431	22,388	13,591	13,155	26,617	21,114	15,231	75,326	49,413	11,895	7,922	6,166
Greenwood, SC Micro Area	6,336	2,352	2,250	2,072	2,928	2,196	1,996	9,037	6,572	1,336	1,174	753
Gulfport-Biloxi-Pascagoula, MS Metro Area	27,476	10,272	5,145	4,283	8,274	6,687	7,311	31,073	21,235	6,260	2,956	2,321
Hagerstown-Martinsburg, MD-WV Metro Area	20,739	10,853	5,872	4,773	6,122	6,468	3,557	20,850	14,602	3,401	2,441	2,018
Hammond, LA Metro Area	8,638	4,408	1,649	1,494	2,847	1,041	2,521	9,921	5,540	1,985	1,755	1,605
Hanford-Corcoran, CA Metro Area	5,502	2,415	861	1,434	869	1,796	2,452	7,278	5,316	2,625	1,273	1,259
Harrisburg-Carlisle, PA Metro Area	56,435	21,555	13,922	10,844	16,861	16,807	6,515	46,899	36,403	5,961	4,412	3,014
Harrisonburg, VA Metro Area	9,611	2,680	2,257	2,443	3,403	3,544	1,508	9,027	7,802	688	483	617
Hartford-West Hartford-East Hartford, CT Metro Area	117,395	46,607	30,422	20,307	26,370	27,214	12,750	93,877	79,029	17,527	11,461	13,373
Hattiesburg, MS Metro Area	5,976	3,033	2,197	2,409	2,611	2,456	3,408	10,647	6,746	3,101	2,761	1,027
Helena, MT Micro Area	8,305	1,864	1,408	1,633	3,014	2,437	1,085	8,045	4,483	889	712	818
Hermiston-Pendleton, OR Micro Area	6,620	2,063	564	1,146	2,516	2,413	830	6,495	5,425	1,391	1,229	934
Hickory-Lenoir-Morganton, NC Metro Area	27,310	9,576	5,127	8,390	13,642	10,381	7,501	35,661	23,598	6,548	3,603	3,194
Hilo, HI Micro Area	18,992	9,713	3,782	4,384	4,102	4,189	2,632	20,376	12,225	4,230	2,977	1,192
Hilton Head Island-Bluffton-Beaufort, SC Metro Area	16,546	10,602	5,339	4,713	10,791	8,401	2,597	28,603	17,017	1,855	1,929	1,069
Hinesville, GA Metro Area	2,730	438	345	1,050	796	528	747	4,183	1,849	972	1,085	987
Hobbs, NM Micro Area	4,169	1,379	1,372	650	1,082	845	732	3,447	3,304	956	158	743
Holland, MI Micro Area	10,493	3,392	2,292	1,893	3,075	2,576	1,263	10,316	6,257	1,639	686	952
Homosassa Springs, FL Metro Area	9,970	8,561	7,833	3,632	8,325	7,506	4,703	25,962	21,818	3,618	2,133	1,843
Hot Springs, AR Metro Area	7,082	4,429	3,014	2,220	3,365	3,894	2,532	11,482	8,932	3,183	972	886
Houma-Thibodaux, LA Metro Area	15,673	5,483	3,634	3,576	5,294	4,419	3,019	14,380	10,641	3,014	889	2,292
Houston-The Woodlands-Sugar Land, TX Metro Area	449,544	141,016	69,140	83,729	82,291	64,575	50,118	358,766	225,387	67,733	43,579	39,575
Huntington-Ashland, WV-KY-OH Metro Area	30,149	17,702	11,427	4,312	9,361	5,888	10,260	36,138	25,735	7,459	4,481	3,678
Huntsville, AL Metro Area	36,858	15,488	10,633	7,766	10,009	9,342	4,444	32,095	24,864	3,844	3,599	3,126
Huntsville, TX Micro Area	4,266	2,496	2,039	458	1,849	894	1,093	5,886	4,869	607	708	395
Hutchinson, KS Micro Area	5,155	1,244	1,036	1,558	2,509	2,751	853	5,775	5,098	829	724	606
Idaho Falls, ID Metro Area	9,432	2,098	1,873	3,964	4,649	3,717	1,033	9,208	6,781	1,099	818	742
Indiana, PA Micro Area	8,497	3,222	2,272	1,795	3,620	2,953	1,206	7,820	6,215	1,220	627	825
Indianapolis-Carmel-Anderson, IN Metro Area	151,950	53,529	33,545	31,298	44,700	40,993	22,828	132,815	96,504	22,393	12,332	10,234
Iowa City, IA Metro Area	13,267	4,686	2,856	3,128	3,422	3,454	839	9,281	7,283	1,135	303	429
Ithaca, NY Metro Area	8,633	4,056	3,048	1,236	924	1,702	529	6,485	4,996	1,214	972	308
Jackson, MI Metro Area	14,106	7,984	5,346	2,109	4,089	3,742	3,616	13,985	10,629	3,220	1,541	1,050
Jackson, MS Metro Area	37,457	12,792	6,556	11,863	11,018	10,719	8,252	38,817	29,455	10,728	6,939	6,158
Jackson, TN Metro Area	10,237	2,858	1,430	2,807	4,023	3,800	2,047	10,755	7,886	2,412	1,216	978
Jacksonville, FL Metro Area	102,527	35,645	21,186	25,087	32,765	24,593	19,269	116,904	75,195	19,139	12,935	8,619
Jacksonville, NC Metro Area	7,325	3,489	1,769	1,708	1,638	2,005	1,834	9,308	6,104	2,097	1,488	1,051
Jamestown-Dunkirk-Fredonia, NY Micro Area	13,095	4,533	3,280	1,898	4,006	4,517	2,299	12,186	10,024	2,792	1,412	1,601
Janesville-Beloit, WI Metro Area	15,342	5,124	2,959	3,176	5,776	5,350	1,987	12,999	10,015	2,873	1,524	1,664
Jefferson City, MO Metro Area	13,141	4,358	2,680	3,018	3,684	2,990	2,525	12,633	7,907	1,115	1,153	947
Johnson City, TN Metro Area	13,946	5,251	3,282	5,070	6,703	5,982	4,314	20,497	13,702	3,165	2,579	2,160
Johnstown, PA Metro Area	14,898	5,544	4,156	3,142	5,179	7,008	2,381	13,869	12,454	2,247	2,017	1,968

Table I-4: Metropolitan/Micropolitan Statistical Areas—Persons With Health Insurance by Source of Insurance—*Continued*

	Private Health Insurance Coverage						Public Health Insurance Coverage					
	Employer Based			Direct Purchase			Medicare			Medicaid/CHIP		
	55 to 64 Years	65 to 74 Years	75 Years and Over	55 to 64 Years	65 to 74 Years	75 Years and Over	55 to 64 Years	65 to 74 Years	75 Years and Over	55 to 64 Years	65 to 74 Years	75 Years and Over
Jonesboro, AR Metro Area	6,969	2,196	1,116	2,534	3,300	3,923	1,318	9,766	6,924	1,926	1,433	1,317
Joplin, MO Metro Area	12,660	2,808	2,205	3,734	6,443	5,818	2,987	14,198	10,495	2,322	1,105	1,296
Kahului-Wailuku-Lahaina, HI Metro Area	15,019	6,187	2,903	3,661	3,303	3,188	2,045	13,317	9,059	2,269	834	936
Kalamazoo-Portage, MI Metro Area	27,999	13,918	9,824	5,789	6,999	7,331	5,548	25,531	19,267	5,517	2,895	2,136
Kalispell, MT Micro Area	9,048	4,051	1,758	2,155	3,140	2,434	961	9,589	6,261	1,016	634	522
Kankakee, IL Metro Area	10,100	3,267	1,858	1,740	3,016	3,315	1,251	8,485	6,400	940	1,191	697
Kansas City, MO-KS Metro Area	175,464	55,630	36,007	37,003	54,007	46,453	25,251	146,932	109,214	20,105	9,172	10,637
Kapaa, HI Micro Area	8,253	3,314	1,791	653	2,110	1,270	625	6,211	4,786	1,241	683	1,048
Keene, NH Micro Area	8,126	2,086	1,815	1,565	2,746	2,023	844	7,238	4,933	766	870	585
Kennewick-Richland, WA Metro Area	20,966	6,727	4,501	3,682	7,070	4,899	2,523	17,429	12,505	3,289	1,681	2,423
Key West, FL Micro Area	6,247	2,610	976	3,448	2,857	910	483	9,267	5,427	112	679	742
Killeen-Temple, TX Metro Area	18,298	10,133	4,493	5,123	6,972	4,959	4,617	24,038	15,243	2,551	3,197	2,940
Kingsport-Bristol-Bristol, TN-VA Metro Area	26,513	11,256	7,332	7,135	12,287	11,829	7,869	34,723	24,727	4,169	4,089	3,442
Kingston, NY Metro Area	17,966	8,174	5,398	3,685	5,654	3,379	2,988	17,212	12,305	3,045	2,180	1,145
Klamath Falls, OR Micro Area	4,878	2,089	1,522	2,148	2,883	1,667	838	7,377	4,676	1,800	604	403
Knoxville, TN Metro Area	70,309	27,626	16,281	17,370	29,852	23,094	15,099	82,000	55,237	13,119	10,284	8,114
Kokomo, IN Metro Area	8,026	4,556	4,002	1,280	1,485	1,364	1,601	8,048	6,221	1,014	307	444
La Crosse-Onalaska, WI-MN Metro Area	12,542	2,986	1,755	2,316	4,391	3,749	1,525	10,659	8,585	1,853	1,465	1,507
Lafayette, LA Metro Area	31,546	13,263	6,154	9,995	10,039	8,756	9,758	32,773	22,722	7,813	3,996	4,166
Lafayette-West Lafayette, IN Metro Area	14,687	5,111	3,258	3,576	4,999	5,341	2,099	12,976	10,411	1,388	1,475	514
LaGrange, GA Micro Area	4,836	1,728	791	1,121	1,875	1,624	1,319	5,205	4,029	1,085	794	774
Lake Charles, LA Metro Area	15,126	6,603	4,625	3,391	4,672	3,757	4,661	15,587	10,827	3,534	2,274	1,737
Lake City, FL Micro Area	4,912	1,354	985	1,774	2,070	1,530	1,458	6,811	4,483	645	855	373
Lake Havasu City-Kingman, AZ Metro Area	10,905	7,254	5,559	4,571	10,921	7,943	4,326	31,601	22,264	6,903	2,073	2,523
Lakeland-Winter Haven, FL Metro Area	38,424	19,028	13,284	11,562	14,941	14,591	10,731	66,835	51,125	10,732	8,074	7,814
Lancaster, PA Metro Area	47,274	15,451	11,291	9,096	14,791	16,811	4,908	41,596	37,142	5,381	4,349	4,282
Lansing-East Lansing, MI Metro Area	43,282	22,387	13,952	6,836	9,750	8,895	6,449	36,578	24,445	6,834	4,024	2,604
Laredo, TX Metro Area	8,518	2,548	1,245	2,234	2,323	1,316	2,338	12,103	8,290	3,138	3,403	4,546
Las Cruces, NM Metro Area	10,814	6,188	5,163	3,244	4,213	3,331	2,740	15,777	12,090	4,108	3,040	2,463
Las Vegas-Henderson-Paradise, NV Metro Area	141,209	54,895	25,600	29,648	32,114	24,896	20,304	159,427	98,262	28,457	21,002	14,536
Laurel, MS Micro Area	6,684	1,796	1,085	1,217	2,937	2,108	1,631	8,086	5,470	1,569	1,164	537
Lawrence, KS Metro Area	7,185	2,572	2,167	2,727	3,028	2,424	643	6,449	4,935	589	479	460
Lawton, OK Metro Area	6,354	3,085	1,930	1,882	1,978	1,782	1,029	8,021	6,116	1,131	1,206	708
Lebanon, PA Metro Area	12,779	4,910	4,307	2,977	4,917	3,921	1,140	12,609	10,598	1,147	1,466	1,421
Lewiston, ID-WA Metro Area	4,694	2,191	1,716	1,859	2,804	2,890	1,208	6,254	5,157	972	1,022	468
Lewiston-Auburn, ME Metro Area	8,641	3,386	1,265	2,111	2,692	3,041	1,677	9,539	6,542	2,030	1,566	1,754
Lexington-Fayette, KY Metro Area	38,280	13,902	10,116	8,783	12,131	10,358	5,978	35,496	23,067	7,289	3,955	2,725
Lima, OH Metro Area	9,558	3,765	3,622	1,708	2,615	2,491	1,168	8,604	7,080	1,666	862	811
Lincoln, NE Metro Area	26,144	8,073	4,436	5,576	9,482	9,005	3,310	20,922	16,003	2,138	1,558	1,462
Little Rock-North Little Rock-Conway, AR Metro Area	53,608	19,486	11,961	12,294	17,896	14,672	12,193	55,681	37,615	10,363	6,382	6,213
Logan, UT-ID Metro Area	7,434	2,326	1,446	2,260	2,106	2,478	521	6,101	4,976	282	423	389
London, KY Micro Area	7,039	4,482	1,967	2,060	2,833	1,974	4,146	11,735	6,995	5,969	2,017	1,446
Longview, TX Metro Area	16,059	6,359	3,808	3,541	4,531	4,299	3,639	16,550	12,765	2,368	1,897	1,878
Longview, WA Metro Area	8,016	3,229	3,047	2,272	4,458	3,302	2,184	10,471	7,094	2,689	1,407	1,097
Los Angeles-Long Beach-Anaheim, CA Metro Area	804,595	281,080	167,526	224,392	135,640	132,476	101,461	826,662	681,169	273,519	190,696	204,654
Louisville/Jefferson County, KY-IN Metro Area	111,111	46,357	24,700	19,702	35,949	31,927	19,460	102,156	69,763	23,788	10,318	8,316
Lubbock, TX Metro Area	17,146	7,170	5,043	5,193	5,577	5,197	3,835	19,236	15,447	2,842	1,734	1,589
Lufkin, TX Micro Area	4,498	1,562	2,044	1,494	1,883	2,119	1,268	7,133	5,272	813	1,050	760
Lumberton, NC Micro Area	7,217	2,154	1,061	2,403	2,244	2,007	3,480	10,382	6,073	3,239	2,225	1,913
Lynchburg, VA Metro Area	21,125	6,786	5,407	6,373	10,811	9,642	4,215	24,684	18,501	2,016	2,188	1,869
Macon, GA Metro Area	17,148	6,533	5,016	3,209	4,336	4,713	4,908	19,273	11,908	4,088	3,362	1,534
Madera, CA Metro Area	8,343	4,327	2,103	2,313	2,849	2,009	1,189	10,759	7,834	3,289	2,281	2,296
Madison, WI Metro Area	59,121	21,867	12,428	10,895	16,385	15,178	4,149	44,115	31,476	5,764	3,609	3,596
Manchester-Nashua, NH Metro Area	40,585	13,328	7,466	7,686	9,039	8,834	3,534	29,995	21,113	1,953	1,930	2,014
Manhattan, KS Metro Area	5,783	1,721	1,370	805	1,451	2,645	716	4,462	4,142	720	613	516
Manitowoc, WI Micro Area	8,122	2,019	1,099	2,227	3,351	3,495	1,174	7,880	6,533	1,011	547	790
Mankato-North Mankato, MN Metro Area	8,577	1,998	1,027	1,527	3,499	3,364	571	6,789	5,530	1,147	692	634
Mansfield, OH Metro Area	10,810	4,749	4,038	2,150	4,186	3,674	1,872	11,611	9,482	1,604	1,254	928
Marinette, WI-MI Micro Area	6,273	2,026	1,308	1,780	2,912	3,260	1,114	7,362	5,790	1,224	669	703
Marion, IN Micro Area	5,754	3,276	1,641	1,564	2,085	2,088	1,074	6,412	4,786	736	797	596
Marion, OH Micro Area	4,778	1,513	2,519	1,793	2,234	1,641	1,022	5,814	4,721	915	934	586
Marquette, MI Micro Area	5,708	3,907	2,698	1,512	1,217	1,114	1,093	6,012	4,494	1,377	935	778
Marshall, TX Micro Area	4,450	1,800	1,200	963	1,633	1,418	367	5,452	4,074	773	511	528
Martinsville, VA Micro Area	5,699	1,537	851	2,068	3,434	3,120	1,798	7,822	5,945	1,281	1,090	786
McAllen-Edinburg-Mission, TX Metro Area	23,940	8,976	5,571	9,663	7,811	8,858	6,001	42,735	33,611	7,498	17,757	13,209
Meadville, PA Micro Area	7,519	2,454	1,448	2,131	3,520	3,296	1,745	8,903	6,273	1,377	1,152	477
Medford, OR Metro Area	15,013	7,026	5,314	6,003	8,742	7,727	4,260	23,723	16,979	6,153	2,712	2,775
Memphis, TN-MS-AR Metro Area	98,953	32,016	20,494	19,387	29,574	24,143	19,096	91,871	60,738	20,263	13,015	11,673
Merced, CA Metro Area	11,918	3,773	2,101	3,292	4,886	3,065	2,679	14,603	10,943	6,069	3,611	4,289
Meridian, MS Micro Area	6,968	1,768	1,575	1,542	1,860	2,006	2,318	8,713	6,704	2,802	2,666	1,364
Miami-Fort Lauderdale-West Palm Beach, FL Metro Area	343,212	105,166	71,589	136,940	94,294	117,822	49,432	476,479	458,389	70,438	104,253	121,547
Michigan City-La Porte, IN Metro Area	10,586	3,487	1,666	1,558	3,410	3,482	1,545	10,095	6,568	1,090	705	392
Midland, MI Metro Area	8,017	3,758	4,483	2,186	2,635	2,139	849	7,474	5,997	1,309	497	338
Midland, TX Metro Area	12,963	3,624	2,358	1,229	1,733	2,923	1,142	7,727	6,700	1,120	535	733

Table I-4: Metropolitan/Micropolitan Statistical Areas—Persons With Health Insurance by Source of Insurance—Continued

	Private Health Insurance Coverage						Public Health Insurance Coverage					
	Employer Based			Direct Purchase			Medicare			Medicaid/CHIP		
	55 to 64 Years	65 to 74 Years	75 Years and Over	55 to 64 Years	65 to 74 Years	75 Years and Over	55 to 64 Years	65 to 74 Years	75 Years and Over	55 to 64 Years	65 to 74 Years	75 Years and Over
Milwaukee-Waukesha-West Allis, WI Metro Area..	137,749	45,089	33,203	25,848	32,444	36,088	18,220	111,600	93,795	23,516	12,497	12,383
Minneapolis-St. Paul-Bloomington, MN-WI Metro Area	301,461	80,013	45,858	68,257	111,809	92,592	28,134	231,233	169,520	45,049	17,962	16,944
Minot, ND Micro Area	5,538	1,779	952	1,698	2,199	2,283	406	4,556	4,229	268	313	413
Missoula, MT Metro Area	8,305	2,620	2,356	2,457	3,736	1,726	1,291	9,191	5,571	1,057	1,060	566
Mobile, AL Metro Area	31,247	11,276	6,384	7,310	11,148	7,813	8,019	33,082	23,115	5,362	4,628	4,053
Modesto, CA Metro Area	31,131	10,642	5,731	8,056	10,924	8,145	6,897	34,215	25,806	12,203	6,680	7,257
Monroe, LA Metro Area	12,728	4,865	3,077	3,276	4,065	3,049	2,953	13,141	9,835	2,026	1,417	1,667
Monroe, MI Metro Area	16,844	7,287	5,840	2,585	3,793	3,696	1,956	13,280	9,547	2,700	1,403	972
Montgomery, AL Metro Area	27,718	12,206	8,224	6,351	7,474	5,558	5,367	27,659	20,373	4,728	3,798	3,517
Morehead City, NC Micro Area	5,818	3,523	1,915	2,492	3,064	2,118	1,272	9,090	5,765	881	603	676
Morgantown, WV Metro Area	10,464	4,808	3,189	1,390	2,048	2,339	1,883	9,313	6,731	2,392	1,620	592
Morristown, TN Metro Area	8,278	4,226	1,289	2,076	4,022	3,464	3,146	12,485	7,619	2,975	1,474	906
Moses Lake, WA Micro Area	5,823	1,940	1,113	1,647	2,071	1,462	706	6,852	4,399	1,546	861	682
Mount Airy, NC Micro Area	4,961	1,652	1,481	1,443	2,252	2,219	1,521	7,493	5,363	1,555	1,067	1,014
Mount Pleasant, MI Micro Area	5,059	2,589	1,732	736	964	1,132	856	4,118	2,959	1,092	366	332
Mount Vernon-Anacortes, WA Metro Area	9,639	4,593	2,866	3,285	5,664	4,041	1,653	12,939	8,967	2,125	965	903
Muncie, IN Metro Area	8,140	4,722	3,362	1,532	2,762	2,487	1,744	10,043	7,523	1,346	782	597
Muskegon, MI Metro Area	12,943	5,752	4,944	3,154	4,324	3,923	4,035	13,878	10,541	4,500	2,007	2,055
Muskogee, OK Micro Area	4,944	1,644	1,524	461	1,803	1,781	1,419	5,851	4,347	833	857	483
Myrtle Beach-Conway-North Myrtle Beach, SC-NC Metro Area	33,884	23,355	11,059	11,932	22,940	12,236	8,600	60,047	30,316	7,854	4,042	3,563
Nacogdoches, TX Micro Area	3,779	1,929	849	1,184	1,316	1,146	869	4,249	3,623	679	387	549
Napa, CA Metro Area	12,115	6,949	4,224	3,550	4,407	3,269	1,308	13,285	9,135	1,930	1,215	1,074
Naples-Immokalee-Marco Island, FL Metro Area ..	22,880	15,492	15,539	12,473	18,886	19,309	2,451	50,402	47,248	1,245	2,878	3,904
Nashville-Davidson–Murfreesboro–Franklin, TN Metro Area	132,378	44,094	26,040	35,045	38,542	28,042	20,095	125,488	80,978	18,523	13,655	10,859
New Bern, NC Metro Area	8,769	5,410	3,953	3,208	3,928	3,665	1,748	13,285	9,730	1,329	2,453	1,334
New Castle, PA Micro Area	8,972	2,144	2,190	2,011	3,593	3,455	1,876	8,722	7,805	1,642	1,515	1,629
New Haven-Milford, CT Metro Area	78,281	28,831	19,257	14,534	19,219	20,886	9,120	66,959	55,690	15,090	9,182	10,346
New Orleans-Metairie, LA Metro Area	92,942	33,379	16,829	27,389	20,485	18,034	18,521	96,591	65,102	22,347	16,338	13,664
New Philadelphia-Dover, OH Micro Area	8,605	2,980	1,853	1,932	2,588	3,090	1,141	8,466	6,918	1,663	1,322	496
New York-Newark-Jersey City, NY-NJ-PA Metro Area	1,586,486	663,610	381,452	277,110	298,007	328,513	183,030	1,414,901	1,171,681	403,390	259,832	269,226
Niles-Benton Harbor, MI Metro Area	15,055	5,503	4,270	2,956	6,525	5,401	1,885	14,537	11,487	1,864	1,764	1,082
North Port-Sarasota-Bradenton, FL Metro Area	58,348	35,559	36,603	23,646	40,791	43,993	10,711	112,282	102,052	8,705	7,639	7,450
North Wilkesboro, NC Micro Area	4,190	1,944	1,117	1,489	3,548	2,164	1,367	7,707	5,231	1,764	1,432	1,588
Norwich-New London, CT Metro Area	25,734	11,715	6,972	4,850	5,424	5,531	2,308	22,705	17,754	4,321	2,878	2,886
Oak Harbor, WA Micro Area	7,400	4,574	2,919	1,192	3,048	2,509	785	10,702	6,858	980	550	968
Ocala, FL Metro Area	23,528	16,674	11,280	8,904	14,410	12,611	6,397	50,449	39,799	4,929	3,878	4,288
Ocean City, NJ Metro Area	10,081	5,137	3,819	2,240	4,825	4,130	1,165	12,324	9,230	985	862	702
Odessa, TX Metro Area	9,943	2,918	2,407	1,636	1,670	1,876	1,701	7,877	5,824	2,124	1,380	571
Ogden-Clearfield, UT Metro Area	41,581	15,859	10,719	8,626	10,399	9,019	4,512	34,669	25,911	3,358	2,581	2,082
Ogdensburg-Massena, NY Micro Area	9,546	4,707	3,332	1,676	2,304	2,018	2,154	9,673	6,312	2,395	1,921	1,209
Oklahoma City, OK Metro Area	98,444	41,688	23,223	22,440	25,820	23,276	15,298	93,051	66,702	10,315	7,952	7,163
Olean, NY Micro Area	7,769	2,916	1,892	1,267	2,674	2,456	1,204	7,304	5,287	1,816	1,314	652
Olympia-Tumwater, WA Metro Area	24,335	11,069	5,840	4,460	6,907	5,378	3,277	23,399	15,184	2,879	1,337	1,939
Omaha-Council Bluffs, NE-IA Metro Area	74,305	21,169	11,709	14,246	20,642	18,717	8,652	59,350	44,548	8,882	4,938	5,409
Opelousas, LA Micro Area	4,887	1,750	786	1,147	818	1,468	2,475	6,619	4,697	1,635	1,393	767
Orangeburg, SC Micro Area	5,648	2,563	1,352	1,911	2,120	1,062	1,727	8,386	5,899	2,167	2,425	2,166
Orlando-Kissimmee-Sanford, FL Metro Area	152,108	47,814	29,311	37,475	46,421	37,449	23,799	173,125	127,516	25,736	23,979	20,645
Oshkosh-Neenah, WI Metro Area	15,928	3,581	2,965	2,660	4,821	5,315	1,671	12,955	10,904	1,380	584	992
Ottawa-Peru, IL Micro Area	15,173	6,263	4,575	3,580	5,200	5,385	2,335	14,106	11,829	1,944	682	1,414
Owensboro, KY Metro Area	8,445	4,329	2,947	2,656	4,203	3,283	2,936	10,366	7,742	2,063	1,596	936
Owosso, MI Micro Area	7,334	4,271	2,757	1,255	1,785	2,000	1,594	6,331	4,909	1,258	301	442
Oxnard-Thousand Oaks-Ventura, CA Metro Area ..	64,928	22,262	14,761	17,833	17,711	15,389	8,109	60,411	47,038	12,740	6,418	9,102
Paducah, KY-IL Micro Area	8,772	3,120	2,223	1,786	3,672	2,563	2,621	9,980	7,085	2,159	1,596	1,223
Palatka, FL Micro Area	4,604	2,070	1,361	2,063	1,965	2,100	1,947	8,268	5,815	1,828	1,547	1,139
Palm Bay-Melbourne-Titusville, FL Metro Area	45,945	20,775	17,868	13,119	16,057	18,743	9,598	65,196	56,289	10,520	6,259	6,509
Panama City, FL Metro Area	12,240	5,865	3,952	3,101	4,840	4,348	2,228	17,638	12,837	3,524	1,870	2,219
Parkersburg-Vienna, WV Metro Area	7,347	4,264	3,136	1,292	3,311	2,576	2,629	9,780	7,050	2,082	515	1,027
Pensacola-Ferry Pass-Brent, FL Metro Area	32,748	11,929	6,340	9,486	13,625	10,118	6,152	40,727	28,833	5,775	3,064	3,032
Peoria, IL Metro Area	35,185	12,563	10,145	7,309	14,105	12,451	4,271	31,487	25,006	4,050	2,186	2,527
Philadelphia-Camden-Wilmington, PA-NJ-DE-MD Metro Area	539,145	200,736	123,042	106,599	148,745	159,091	64,369	452,080	365,551	64,033	51,830	51,395
Phoenix-Mesa-Scottsdale, AZ Metro Area	287,318	103,976	69,392	73,279	103,619	88,639	45,004	348,972	254,409	60,938	38,710	30,160
Pine Bluff, AR Metro Area	6,466	2,354	1,356	2,158	2,161	2,278	1,882	7,768	5,727	2,164	1,429	1,196
Pinehurst-Southern Pines, NC Micro Area	6,357	2,931	2,175	2,458	4,178	5,082	799	11,927	9,451	1,338	1,019	395
Pittsburgh, PA Metro Area	244,312	88,853	68,562	53,047	87,754	95,465	29,545	215,640	192,778	34,720	23,171	26,070
Pittsfield, MA Metro Area	12,847	6,344	5,188	2,488	4,240	4,620	2,163	13,573	10,810	5,302	1,510	1,279
Plattsburgh, NY Micro Area	7,649	3,540	2,089	841	1,971	2,289	1,196	6,766	4,640	1,262	1,232	635
Pocatello, ID Metro Area	6,230	1,994	1,503	1,805	2,413	2,261	1,160	6,063	4,168	1,006	292	555
Port Angeles, WA Micro Area	6,498	3,698	2,893	2,090	3,740	3,603	1,302	10,522	8,132	1,041	536	881
Port St. Lucie, FL Metro Area	31,507	17,704	19,907	13,115	15,053	17,261	6,314	55,218	51,049	6,220	4,619	7,209
Portland-South Portland, ME Metro Area	54,255	17,944	11,751	11,501	13,211	14,457	5,482	48,737	35,596	6,142	5,592	4,739
Portland-Vancouver-Hillsboro, OR-WA Metro Area	189,630	63,401	38,020	44,488	61,507	50,487	22,371	176,063	118,110	39,795	21,189	16,860

Table I-4: Metropolitan/Micropolitan Statistical Areas—Persons With Health Insurance by Source of Insurance—*Continued*

| | Private Health Insurance Coverage | | | | | | Public Health Insurance Coverage | | | | | |
| | Employer Based | | | Direct Purchase | | | Medicare | | | Medicaid/CHIP | | |
	55 to 64 Years	65 to 74 Years	75 Years and Over	55 to 64 Years	65 to 74 Years	75 Years and Over	55 to 64 Years	65 to 74 Years	75 Years and Over	55 to 64 Years	65 to 74 Years	75 Years and Over
Portsmouth, OH Micro Area	6,555	2,543	1,889	949	2,257	1,937	2,170	6,476	5,124	1,782	992	710
Pottsville, PA Micro Area	13,627	4,801	3,306	2,823	6,154	6,202	3,052	14,299	12,082	2,412	1,870	2,202
Prescott, AZ Metro Area	17,413	12,126	7,024	9,365	12,694	10,411	4,106	35,744	24,069	5,089	3,948	1,804
Providence-Warwick, RI-MA Metro Area	140,182	50,111	32,461	24,841	40,042	43,352	21,588	129,705	105,175	38,212	18,837	21,420
Provo-Orem, UT Metro Area	26,454	8,776	6,949	6,336	7,067	6,357	2,257	22,035	16,672	1,841	1,748	1,651
Pueblo, CO Metro Area	12,849	4,814	5,079	3,775	4,597	4,147	2,669	14,276	10,957	2,703	2,532	1,610
Punta Gorda, FL Metro Area	14,679	11,356	8,756	5,820	11,162	11,010	5,291	32,425	28,143	2,172	1,681	2,194
Quincy, IL-MO Micro Area	6,670	2,635	1,484	1,899	2,478	3,458	926	7,164	5,819	1,022	573	629
Racine, WI Metro Area	17,411	6,618	5,269	3,067	4,475	4,235	2,580	15,543	12,439	2,849	1,736	1,499
Raleigh, NC Metro Area	89,895	33,383	18,010	22,955	25,887	17,640	10,726	77,797	46,437	8,350	6,639	7,167
Rapid City, SD Metro Area	12,063	3,263	2,778	3,629	6,262	5,137	1,821	11,797	8,683	1,749	1,239	1,066
Reading, PA Metro Area	37,894	11,657	9,021	6,861	13,531	13,822	5,302	34,416	28,332	5,321	3,086	3,939
Redding, CA Metro Area	14,073	6,428	3,930	4,167	5,574	5,146	3,877	19,599	13,883	4,632	3,494	2,308
Reno, NV Metro Area	36,391	13,496	7,453	7,523	9,752	7,799	4,840	38,916	23,730	6,337	3,976	2,308
Richmond, IN Micro Area	5,270	2,605	1,758	1,151	2,466	2,751	1,219	6,448	5,172	736	675	471
Richmond, VA Metro Area	114,129	44,379	24,394	22,761	34,630	26,060	13,423	96,112	65,577	9,434	7,282	6,008
Richmond-Berea, KY Micro Area	7,659	2,574	1,973	1,200	2,048	1,595	1,727	8,083	5,068	2,414	1,736	1,104
Riverside-San Bernardino-Ontario, CA Metro Area	250,055	86,206	52,389	54,135	50,408	46,516	40,002	278,448	209,546	88,223	50,269	43,093
Roanoke Rapids, NC Micro Area	4,176	2,231	1,308	1,906	2,400	2,343	2,456	7,271	6,074	2,471	1,467	1,201
Roanoke, VA Metro Area	29,933	10,409	6,301	7,271	11,347	10,967	4,237	31,527	22,981	2,410	3,119	2,604
Rochester, MN Metro Area	20,423	7,642	5,512	4,248	6,738	7,514	1,918	15,608	13,642	2,428	1,401	1,246
Rochester, NY Metro Area	103,762	36,512	26,777	17,168	28,778	32,422	12,644	93,452	70,746	18,811	8,058	10,109
Rockford, IL Metro Area	28,388	9,727	6,548	5,992	10,896	10,781	4,525	29,974	20,913	5,715	2,709	2,800
Rocky Mount, NC Metro Area	12,018	4,470	2,277	2,425	4,617	4,191	2,879	14,099	9,613	2,987	2,475	1,721
Rome, GA Metro Area	7,580	2,406	2,934	879	2,138	2,307	1,429	7,753	6,350	1,889	951	872
Roseburg, OR Micro Area	9,187	3,114	2,638	2,917	3,675	3,865	2,489	13,895	10,877	2,879	1,741	967
Roswell, NM Micro Area	3,900	2,165	1,393	987	1,045	1,308	1,086	5,325	4,092	1,474	1,013	725
Russellville, AR Micro Area	5,403	2,351	725	1,062	1,705	2,299	1,954	7,153	5,321	1,724	1,152	740
Sacramento–Roseville–Arden-Arcade, CA Metro Area	173,366	86,337	54,084	35,362	42,079	37,519	25,478	167,660	125,978	44,353	26,666	23,962
Saginaw, MI Metro Area	19,569	10,684	7,862	2,922	5,544	5,819	3,857	17,744	14,127	4,138	1,890	1,848
Salem, OH Micro Area	9,373	4,367	1,659	1,431	2,381	2,006	2,243	10,051	7,522	2,721	1,165	1,301
Salem, OR Metro Area	31,741	11,272	8,357	5,948	11,987	9,336	3,722	33,507	24,039	6,753	4,140	3,272
Salinas, CA Metro Area	26,142	9,170	5,178	7,076	7,173	6,370	3,556	26,824	20,965	7,654	5,323	5,986
Salisbury, MD-DE Metro Area	36,296	26,210	12,637	7,121	14,067	11,847	5,300	48,000	29,638	7,240	3,013	3,080
Salt Lake City, UT Metro Area	82,427	23,748	14,082	13,746	17,243	15,406	7,266	61,211	43,420	8,042	5,454	5,526
San Angelo, TX Metro Area	7,277	3,372	2,390	1,932	2,931	2,054	1,116	8,644	8,020	1,502	1,032	1,218
San Antonio-New Braunfels, TX Metro Area	137,822	54,509	31,397	35,823	34,020	27,036	30,200	152,602	108,875	28,134	21,077	20,102
San Diego-Carlsbad, CA Metro Area	215,792	72,328	43,655	58,697	49,526	45,066	23,047	210,065	173,046	45,498	34,377	35,676
San Francisco-Oakland-Hayward, CA Metro Area	360,788	149,724	99,256	90,242	91,307	78,805	41,416	328,449	262,832	85,729	52,935	61,122
San Jose-Sunnyvale-Santa Clara, CA Metro Area	141,982	47,069	29,421	36,852	29,997	29,147	11,988	119,048	97,624	30,247	25,089	26,461
San Luis Obispo-Paso Robles-Arroyo Grande, CA Metro Area	25,240	10,494	9,045	6,709	9,010	8,507	3,259	26,863	19,111	4,231	3,211	1,774
Sandusky, OH Micro Area	8,501	4,025	2,444	1,650	2,688	2,755	515	8,104	5,558	1,486	867	548
Santa Cruz-Watsonville, CA Metro Area	22,503	7,562	3,674	8,398	7,116	5,547	2,152	21,148	13,086	4,846	2,589	2,224
Santa Fe, NM Metro Area	12,944	7,350	3,568	5,700	4,828	4,141	1,820	17,365	9,962	2,560	1,388	731
Santa Maria-Santa Barbara, CA Metro Area	28,714	11,667	8,655	8,937	10,936	11,296	3,418	30,226	28,042	5,351	3,931	4,363
Santa Rosa, CA Metro Area	42,763	20,710	11,177	14,050	15,739	14,497	7,948	46,426	30,598	9,653	4,771	4,747
Savannah, GA Metro Area	26,674	10,226	4,315	4,977	7,517	5,414	4,782	27,541	17,628	3,068	3,210	3,496
Scranton–Wilkes-Barre–Hazleton, PA Metro Area	49,579	19,738	13,456	11,484	22,365	25,216	10,119	53,343	45,618	9,508	6,391	6,360
Searcy, AR Micro Area	4,693	1,704	1,040	779	1,635	2,457	1,812	6,402	5,018	1,762	510	648
Seattle-Tacoma-Bellevue, WA Metro Area	293,156	91,313	52,685	66,180	77,423	67,789	34,631	245,364	172,842	52,764	31,271	28,356
Sebastian-Vero Beach, FL Metro Area	9,775	6,698	6,198	3,699	7,777	8,701	2,847	20,853	21,201	2,148	1,750	2,086
Sebring, FL Metro Area	5,544	4,954	6,305	2,397	4,961	5,869	2,315	16,161	15,718	1,313	1,769	1,922
Seneca, SC Micro Area	6,126	3,236	2,010	2,710	3,416	2,491	2,313	9,737	5,988	1,320	1,101	935
Sevierville, TN Micro Area	6,496	2,375	648	2,109	3,234	2,624	1,523	10,606	5,910	2,094	1,178	933
Shawnee, OK Micro Area	5,019	2,632	1,565	1,162	1,371	1,044	1,409	6,259	4,560	793	813	578
Sheboygan, WI Metro Area	11,419	2,997	1,997	2,664	3,839	3,683	750	9,489	8,047	1,147	1,010	1,064
Shelby, NC Micro Area	7,210	2,942	988	1,960	2,755	2,901	2,751	9,682	6,697	1,276	1,689	1,496
Sherman-Denison, TX Metro Area	9,774	4,210	2,799	1,961	3,224	2,138	2,143	11,700	7,896	779	810	349
Show Low, AZ Micro Area	5,954	1,967	896	1,505	3,377	1,958	1,753	10,223	5,987	2,983	1,587	1,495
Shreveport-Bossier City, LA Metro Area	29,170	13,578	8,375	5,570	11,516	8,991	7,046	35,087	25,152	8,609	4,987	4,671
Sierra Vista-Douglas, AZ Metro Area	8,132	3,990	4,077	3,246	4,436	4,271	1,520	13,344	10,158	3,011	2,687	1,842
Sioux City, IA-NE-SD Metro Area	15,434	2,764	1,274	3,472	5,669	6,265	1,745	13,446	10,153	1,819	1,351	1,444
Sioux Falls, SD Metro Area	21,597	4,982	2,507	3,663	6,082	6,356	2,179	16,109	12,015	2,104	1,830	1,615
Somerset, PA Micro Area	6,764	2,352	1,901	2,136	3,838	3,731	1,203	8,049	6,546	962	788	692
South Bend-Mishawaka, IN-MI Metro Area	28,711	8,700	5,657	5,525	9,269	8,810	4,369	25,129	20,463	3,174	1,742	1,966
Spartanburg, SC Metro Area	24,588	9,932	4,443	4,648	9,329	7,482	7,136	27,867	18,806	5,469	3,275	2,971
Spokane-Spokane Valley, WA Metro Area	41,595	17,172	8,836	10,684	13,968	12,778	8,120	47,661	32,253	11,680	5,629	3,848
Springfield, IL Metro Area	21,657	9,377	7,739	3,162	5,119	4,918	2,555	17,798	14,218	2,535	2,173	1,521
Springfield, MA Metro Area	54,387	21,929	12,805	6,844	14,885	14,287	9,571	48,895	38,565	20,843	9,052	7,089
Springfield, MO Metro Area	31,428	9,379	6,152	9,412	11,667	10,895	7,253	36,855	29,049	5,262	2,941	1,962
Springfield, OH Metro Area	11,578	6,442	4,671	1,623	2,645	1,959	2,203	13,165	9,261	3,108	1,076	530
St. Cloud, MN Metro Area	14,132	3,362	2,169	4,274	7,002	6,395	1,868	12,608	10,924	3,030	966	1,599
St. George, UT Metro Area	8,344	4,164	5,597	3,500	5,631	4,556	1,971	15,961	13,212	650	575	666

Table I-4: Metropolitan/Micropolitan Statistical Areas—Persons With Health Insurance by Source of Insurance—*Continued*

| | Private Health Insurance Coverage | | | | | | Public Health Insurance Coverage | | | | | |
| | Employer Based | | | Direct Purchase | | | Medicare | | | Medicaid/CHIP | | |
	55 to 64 Years	65 to 74 Years	75 Years and Over	55 to 64 Years	65 to 74 Years	75 Years and Over	55 to 64 Years	65 to 74 Years	75 Years and Over	55 to 64 Years	65 to 74 Years	75 Years and Over
St. Joseph, MO-KS Metro Area	9,751	3,565	2,042	1,942	4,701	4,136	1,721	10,054	7,951	1,444	832	967
St. Louis, MO-IL Metro Area	253,620	84,112	58,119	51,703	63,785	61,645	37,865	219,188	169,918	28,772	17,216	14,321
State College, PA Metro Area	12,472	5,290	3,790	1,905	4,193	3,440	1,302	10,051	8,429	1,120	605	1,208
Statesboro, GA Micro Area	3,433	1,327	1,103	1,635	1,389	542	1,199	4,284	2,786	914	299	460
Staunton-Waynesboro, VA Metro Area	10,422	4,000	2,492	3,046	5,727	3,840	1,506	12,895	8,578	1,001	1,180	755
Stevens Point, WI Micro Area	6,256	2,007	966	1,390	2,702	2,702	649	5,655	4,301	866	376	429
Stillwater, OK Micro Area	5,033	2,068	796	1,144	1,683	1,228	1,061	4,879	3,512	540	266	472
Stockton-Lodi, CA Metro Area	42,973	17,113	8,907	8,151	11,985	12,118	7,700	45,464	32,798	15,787	11,246	7,601
Sumter, SC Metro Area	5,579	2,324	1,296	1,686	1,736	1,950	2,407	8,709	6,101	1,749	2,027	1,308
Sunbury, PA Micro Area	8,286	3,268	2,282	1,764	3,893	3,568	2,103	9,455	7,904	2,067	821	1,295
Syracuse, NY Metro Area	62,903	24,772	18,962	9,854	12,691	13,868	8,742	53,139	41,754	11,517	6,317	5,535
Talladega-Sylacauga, AL Micro Area	7,794	2,691	1,524	2,074	3,024	1,833	2,370	9,226	5,309	1,712	1,973	1,151
Tallahassee, FL Metro Area	29,478	13,595	7,855	5,118	7,277	5,022	4,292	26,347	16,974	3,640	3,261	2,882
Tampa-St. Petersburg-Clearwater, FL Metro Area	204,934	77,151	58,297	56,654	67,419	67,888	42,974	282,116	231,308	42,424	35,747	31,701
Terre Haute, IN Metro Area	12,241	5,074	3,282	2,956	5,278	4,719	3,467	14,374	9,989	2,683	1,233	1,662
Texarkana, TX-AR Metro Area	9,823	4,819	2,713	3,135	4,185	3,174	3,282	13,005	8,921	2,163	1,383	1,155
The Villages, FL Metro Area	10,232	13,216	6,912	3,715	11,451	9,779	2,345	37,606	21,065	1,642	1,789	993
Toledo, OH Metro Area	55,962	21,225	17,220	9,358	14,960	14,214	8,004	45,862	35,733	7,936	5,611	3,686
Topeka, KS Metro Area	21,375	7,783	5,840	4,273	8,796	8,470	4,233	19,766	16,038	2,487	2,486	1,724
Torrington, CT Micro Area	21,163	8,738	4,722	4,067	5,262	5,225	2,304	18,178	13,466	3,811	1,744	1,917
Traverse City, MI Micro Area	14,086	8,068	5,721	4,101	5,839	5,029	2,792	16,000	11,735	2,646	989	1,274
Trenton, NJ Metro Area	33,899	16,669	10,565	3,768	6,036	6,192	3,228	25,820	21,278	4,540	3,089	3,755
Truckee-Grass Valley, CA Micro Area	10,735	4,782	3,992	3,093	4,934	2,807	1,883	13,180	8,986	2,075	1,079	835
Tucson, AZ Metro Area	69,030	26,018	21,547	17,513	23,564	21,459	11,094	95,951	74,742	20,303	10,932	10,021
Tullahoma-Manchester, TN Micro Area	7,725	3,194	1,756	1,816	3,724	4,398	1,831	10,691	6,968	1,168	1,044	1,185
Tulsa, OK Metro Area	72,841	25,020	15,510	16,956	25,548	23,004	11,765	74,686	53,898	9,002	6,264	5,034
Tupelo, MS Micro Area	9,705	2,821	1,715	1,992	3,433	3,852	2,226	11,211	7,965	2,227	2,474	2,068
Tuscaloosa, AL Metro Area	18,279	6,756	4,527	4,212	5,002	3,251	6,144	16,680	11,900	3,364	2,179	2,909
Twin Falls, ID Micro Area	7,345	2,324	1,329	2,187	3,795	3,174	1,300	8,379	6,233	1,006	914	1,004
Tyler, TX Metro Area	14,708	6,536	4,851	3,882	5,786	4,680	3,071	17,448	13,829	2,147	1,576	1,168
Ukiah, CA Micro Area	6,418	2,532	1,246	2,498	2,822	1,985	1,718	10,359	5,786	3,389	1,784	1,085
Urban Honolulu, HI Metro Area	83,444	50,785	35,778	14,569	17,239	21,188	6,035	75,026	68,833	11,825	8,631	10,093
Utica-Rome, NY Metro Area	26,654	11,734	8,048	4,362	7,346	7,927	4,998	27,083	21,171	8,202	3,973	2,502
Valdosta, GA Metro Area	7,765	2,388	1,233	1,419	2,394	1,570	1,952	10,563	6,092	2,400	2,240	1,131
Vallejo-Fairfield, CA Metro Area	35,223	16,185	8,059	6,651	6,736	6,518	5,341	31,306	22,585	7,544	4,096	3,386
Victoria, TX Metro Area	7,756	2,895	1,591	2,112	2,509	1,916	667	8,018	6,025	592	1,052	816
Vineland-Bridgeton, NJ Metro Area	10,977	4,867	2,792	1,318	2,740	3,337	2,785	10,999	8,396	4,527	1,691	1,356
Virginia Beach-Norfolk-Newport News, VA-NC Metro Area	125,211	50,053	30,092	25,665	35,322	28,976	17,998	123,973	86,391	10,977	10,331	9,230
Visalia-Porterville, CA Metro Area	21,961	7,360	4,580	5,294	5,272	5,333	6,153	24,466	18,450	8,501	6,769	4,128
Waco, TX Metro Area	17,063	7,670	4,694	3,507	5,553	5,432	3,073	18,319	14,394	3,193	2,357	2,049
Walla Walla, WA Metro Area	5,051	1,670	2,524	1,047	2,242	1,982	1,035	5,114	4,550	1,103	536	374
Warner Robins, GA Metro Area	11,327	6,239	3,644	2,085	3,048	2,317	2,241	12,391	9,034	2,171	1,655	989
Warsaw, IN Micro Area	6,625	2,136	1,704	1,859	2,033	2,053	1,420	6,506	4,678	1,045	412	257
Washington-Arlington-Alexandria, DC-VA-MD-WV Metro Area	499,208	230,340	120,774	97,268	90,836	76,667	34,204	362,197	249,968	53,591	35,867	41,635
Waterloo-Cedar Falls, IA Metro Area	16,374	5,299	3,473	2,376	5,424	6,226	1,749	13,145	11,964	1,877	1,601	1,414
Watertown-Fort Atkinson, WI Micro Area	8,079	3,103	1,786	1,809	2,270	2,309	1,142	6,905	5,044	907	541	806
Watertown-Fort Drum, NY Metro Area	7,314	3,278	2,656	1,133	2,630	2,471	1,224	8,218	5,978	1,987	731	607
Wausau, WI Metro Area	12,942	3,031	1,737	2,651	4,549	4,647	1,235	11,205	9,252	1,822	788	1,346
Weirton-Steubenville, WV-OH Metro Area	11,994	4,936	4,706	2,195	3,215	4,239	2,196	12,084	10,559	2,337	1,378	941
Wenatchee, WA Metro Area	9,430	4,321	2,997	2,418	4,184	3,503	1,110	10,805	8,004	2,042	1,530	566
Wheeling, WV-OH Metro Area	14,198	6,174	5,498	2,537	4,469	4,278	2,783	14,457	11,614	3,664	878	710
Whitewater-Elkhorn, WI Micro Area	10,065	3,203	1,793	1,807	3,530	2,980	926	8,518	6,126	1,169	661	601
Wichita Falls, TX Metro Area	10,714	3,692	3,164	2,722	3,315	3,522	1,860	10,864	9,593	1,949	1,571	1,552
Wichita, KS Metro Area	51,012	12,219	6,659	12,104	19,527	19,085	6,576	45,608	36,310	6,002	4,767	5,642
Williamsport, PA Metro Area	11,335	3,394	2,385	2,267	4,377	4,527	1,686	10,549	8,470	1,763	1,151	1,254
Wilmington, NC Metro Area	22,387	11,258	5,895	6,501	7,978	6,101	3,732	24,877	16,392	3,196	1,831	2,051
Wilson, NC Micro Area	6,273	2,646	979	1,604	2,153	1,824	1,534	7,623	5,062	1,039	726	622
Winchester, VA-WV Metro Area	11,329	3,817	2,871	2,807	4,455	3,259	1,151	11,606	8,819	1,567	872	759
Winston-Salem, NC Metro Area	51,969	16,011	11,891	13,052	22,403	19,613	9,461	56,666	41,137	6,839	6,306	6,576
Wisconsin Rapids-Marshfield, WI Micro Area	6,970	1,408	1,088	2,115	4,115	4,346	694	7,130	6,443	902	567	1,024
Wooster, OH Micro Area	10,337	3,626	2,931	2,163	3,505	3,063	1,140	9,770	7,157	1,156	396	598
Worcester, MA-CT Metro Area	89,544	32,319	18,155	11,778	20,014	21,379	8,499	68,291	52,010	23,068	10,568	10,372
Yakima, WA Metro Area	15,420	4,541	2,295	3,410	6,638	5,137	2,760	17,147	12,682	3,823	2,125	1,925
York-Hanover, PA Metro Area	44,782	14,322	7,280	8,611	13,992	14,477	5,326	38,016	28,149	4,426	3,357	4,126
Youngstown-Warren-Boardman, OH-PA Metro Area	54,327	20,001	14,941	10,181	15,175	16,484	8,095	54,383	45,789	9,984	5,015	5,082
Yuba City, CA Metro Area	9,922	3,294	2,834	2,240	3,397	3,151	1,833	12,207	9,016	2,909	3,269	1,917
Yuma, AZ Metro Area	8,991	4,552	3,096	2,462	5,645	7,060	1,661	16,692	16,757	3,893	3,361	2,597
Zanesville, OH Micro Area	7,294	2,661	1,955	1,332	2,516	2,206	1,726	7,757	6,071	1,316	1,031	716

Table I-5: 114th Congressional Districts—Persons With Health Insurance by Source of Insurance

| | Private Health Insurance Coverage | | | | | | Public Health Insurance Coverage | | | | | |
| | Employer Based | | | Direct Purchase | | | Medicare | | | Medicaid/CHIP | | |
	55 to 64 Years	65 to 74 Years	75 Years and Over	55 to 64 Years	65 to 74 Years	75 Years and Over	55 to 64 Years	65 to 74 Years	75 Years and Over	55 to 64 Years	65 to 74 Years	75 Years and Over
Alabama												
Congressional District 1	55,035	21,973	12,653	12,374	19,354	14,933	13,867	63,096	44,175	8,180	7,578	6,485
Congressional District 2	48,976	21,175	13,246	13,023	16,577	13,116	12,853	57,822	42,126	10,105	7,637	7,815
Congressional District 3	51,857	25,575	13,803	13,674	17,032	13,347	15,768	61,064	39,698	10,895	9,710	6,685
Congressional District 4	51,104	23,146	15,634	14,115	20,105	16,801	18,609	66,844	45,516	11,014	10,806	8,529
Congressional District 5	59,672	24,368	15,550	12,395	19,319	17,197	9,892	57,493	42,521	7,449	6,392	6,205
Congressional District 6	61,241	25,663	15,176	16,408	17,970	15,313	8,835	59,483	41,573	7,169	5,117	6,094
Congressional District 7	46,840	17,588	10,686	10,999	13,133	10,501	16,648	49,884	36,329	14,641	9,193	8,386
Alaska												
Congressional District (at Large)	58,612	22,246	9,568	9,797	4,968	3,180	5,337	40,917	22,385	8,079	6,629	6,054
Arizona												
Congressional District 1	51,794	20,675	11,634	12,795	21,568	14,621	10,443	71,760	44,346	14,359	9,424	7,402
Congressional District 2	51,412	21,350	18,343	15,236	20,146	18,668	8,663	74,386	58,459	14,183	8,048	6,690
Congressional District 3	34,977	10,746	6,158	8,000	8,980	8,422	6,482	45,543	30,953	17,264	10,942	8,407
Congressional District 4	49,787	31,468	21,504	18,712	37,856	30,248	12,531	105,696	78,119	15,959	9,497	6,414
Congressional District 5	52,564	21,083	17,378	13,999	20,458	17,982	6,502	62,821	51,467	6,913	6,445	5,338
Congressional District 6	60,865	21,622	11,052	18,792	23,087	18,603	5,027	69,428	46,896	9,492	5,424	5,190
Congressional District 7	25,306	5,614	4,190	5,797	4,413	3,967	8,752	31,842	17,702	13,663	9,028	4,542
Congressional District 8	56,469	25,596	17,740	14,635	23,832	25,822	8,856	80,301	68,015	11,154	5,230	6,794
Congressional District 9	47,921	11,915	9,007	10,451	13,859	11,667	6,864	44,742	35,604	9,144	5,389	4,437
Arkansas												
Congressional District 1	44,140	15,782	9,526	15,044	23,502	20,433	16,775	69,535	49,036	14,528	10,145	9,440
Congressional District 2	55,381	19,922	12,463	11,907	19,367	16,663	13,165	59,514	42,014	12,262	6,572	7,197
Congressional District 3	52,484	15,225	9,653	11,372	17,971	16,480	11,100	56,835	40,485	10,894	6,509	5,883
Congressional District 4	51,033	19,907	12,151	16,905	23,488	20,715	15,872	71,057	50,295	15,637	9,917	8,556
California												
Congressional District 1	57,054	27,224	19,655	17,685	25,663	19,569	14,646	77,287	56,447	18,751	9,112	8,999
Congressional District 2	61,961	30,068	18,267	23,354	23,519	18,040	10,389	73,600	47,633	17,795	8,244	6,346
Congressional District 3	50,093	21,973	12,410	10,693	12,393	12,043	8,536	50,342	37,453	12,341	8,211	5,839
Congressional District 4	67,072	38,191	23,185	19,039	25,616	19,677	9,704	78,273	53,949	13,191	7,830	5,792
Congressional District 5	59,225	30,360	18,005	16,984	19,980	17,241	10,100	63,997	43,878	13,948	7,869	6,803
Congressional District 6	43,079	21,442	14,216	7,572	8,931	8,324	9,501	43,656	32,983	20,549	12,021	8,345
Congressional District 7	64,386	28,178	18,649	10,035	11,961	11,855	6,928	54,184	42,898	11,805	7,912	9,665
Congressional District 8	43,487	15,889	7,895	9,072	9,289	8,765	8,681	51,710	35,241	17,799	8,802	7,152
Congressional District 9	48,166	19,617	9,769	8,474	14,037	13,228	8,404	49,525	36,421	16,449	10,920	9,085
Congressional District 10	45,065	14,679	8,093	10,722	14,058	10,528	8,703	44,846	32,650	14,745	8,403	8,401
Congressional District 11	62,749	28,496	20,523	16,449	19,447	15,735	5,912	58,787	44,639	11,632	6,445	7,154
Congressional District 12	48,108	19,403	15,393	12,841	10,470	9,947	7,160	50,301	47,316	19,236	13,806	17,463
Congressional District 13	51,442	21,988	12,156	12,857	11,007	10,057	9,580	48,413	35,897	16,544	9,688	8,977
Congressional District 14	63,897	27,834	17,840	14,981	15,370	14,977	6,107	54,691	45,767	12,493	8,249	9,907
Congressional District 15	60,152	20,352	11,754	12,105	12,898	11,078	5,377	48,606	37,210	12,073	7,368	8,068
Congressional District 16	27,242	9,719	6,928	8,517	9,450	6,644	6,850	39,098	28,490	19,440	11,586	11,728
Congressional District 17	52,167	15,368	10,685	12,566	10,219	8,575	4,069	43,890	34,716	11,380	9,218	10,413
Congressional District 18	62,258	23,337	16,374	19,120	17,186	17,312	3,860	51,552	45,221	8,831	4,538	7,315
Congressional District 19	49,957	17,343	8,343	12,353	9,850	8,872	5,755	45,321	34,912	15,957	12,732	12,077
Congressional District 20	49,868	16,011	9,266	14,296	13,375	12,077	6,333	45,981	34,503	12,854	8,501	8,406
Congressional District 21	24,195	7,264	2,391	5,063	4,842	5,960	7,780	30,472	22,012	14,827	8,943	6,980
Congressional District 22	47,769	17,816	12,248	11,158	11,812	11,277	7,558	45,356	33,751	12,195	9,518	6,942
Congressional District 23	47,970	18,344	10,051	9,900	9,687	8,215	8,659	45,610	34,350	13,025	5,939	5,651
Congressional District 24	54,935	22,299	17,700	15,938	20,143	19,942	6,823	57,688	47,348	9,791	7,335	6,176
Congressional District 25	54,760	17,633	8,154	10,450	8,192	5,754	6,413	42,459	27,437	12,736	6,393	5,476
Congressional District 26	53,600	18,617	12,828	14,948	14,604	13,654	7,073	50,815	41,925	11,160	5,679	7,860
Congressional District 27	50,434	19,598	11,906	15,746	8,125	8,316	4,854	58,162	49,490	18,707	12,275	15,510
Congressional District 28	39,819	18,009	8,914	15,173	8,371	7,001	5,329	51,923	42,882	19,221	17,026	19,229
Congressional District 29	32,655	11,626	5,125	7,694	3,569	3,382	5,859	35,948	28,064	18,448	13,625	14,284
Congressional District 30	54,310	20,499	14,724	20,422	12,276	13,137	5,171	52,878	48,184	12,834	10,294	14,001
Congressional District 31	43,343	12,849	6,647	6,691	5,814	5,067	6,326	38,412	25,674	15,299	8,370	7,062
Congressional District 32	45,254	14,337	6,617	6,883	4,957	4,737	6,913	50,938	37,386	17,298	14,364	13,562
Congressional District 33	55,295	24,531	16,791	23,593	16,628	18,056	3,480	56,816	53,245	5,824	5,680	6,711
Congressional District 34	23,934	6,225	4,399	7,219	3,101	2,518	7,088	38,595	32,879	21,316	16,189	17,486
Congressional District 35	32,522	8,579	4,391	6,247	2,657	2,830	5,596	31,609	22,496	14,312	8,146	7,871
Congressional District 36	38,416	21,955	16,525	12,984	18,454	17,942	9,177	73,501	64,934	16,207	10,547	10,648
Congressional District 37	41,146	15,470	10,868	14,270	6,493	8,461	5,909	43,397	37,402	16,598	11,443	12,987
Congressional District 38	46,871	16,043	9,509	7,974	6,511	6,368	6,896	46,106	41,302	11,925	8,154	11,741
Congressional District 39	55,598	17,834	11,808	16,588	8,329	6,738	4,130	46,645	41,803	9,434	5,534	10,003
Congressional District 40	24,112	5,296	3,052	6,502	2,093	2,267	5,171	28,200	22,134	20,436	13,542	11,283
Congressional District 41	38,952	10,965	7,191	5,450	5,330	3,858	5,853	35,882	24,043	15,948	8,570	5,501
Congressional District 42	46,941	14,509	8,746	11,338	7,785	7,234	5,032	46,021	34,905	10,678	7,067	6,185
Congressional District 43	42,458	16,304	9,539	8,301	4,493	5,568	5,555	41,964	32,796	16,405	11,188	10,067
Congressional District 44	31,821	9,671	6,175	5,020	2,699	3,195	5,431	31,726	23,487	18,710	10,619	8,228
Congressional District 45	61,605	18,711	11,253	16,908	12,004	11,362	5,160	51,228	44,408	7,058	5,332	7,540
Congressional District 46	32,429	8,087	4,677	7,397	3,615	3,774	6,418	32,490	23,571	14,113	9,121	6,923
Congressional District 47	46,796	14,955	9,263	11,161	7,589	7,758	5,578	45,428	36,535	16,397	10,939	10,464
Congressional District 48	58,238	23,571	11,672	21,280	14,925	12,258	4,537	61,685	47,027	12,033	6,843	7,277
Congressional District 49	53,309	17,329	12,310	17,742	15,205	11,936	3,909	53,652	45,367	6,275	5,304	6,162
Congressional District 50	53,597	21,297	10,887	14,862	14,759	12,282	6,084	54,276	40,780	12,583	6,657	6,269

Table I-5: 114th Congressional Districts—Persons With Health Insurance by Source of Insurance—*Continued*

| | Private Health Insurance Coverage | | | | | | Public Health Insurance Coverage | | | | | |
| | Employer Based | | | Direct Purchase | | | Medicare | | | Medicaid/CHIP | | |
	55 to 64 Years	65 to 74 Years	75 Years and Over	55 to 64 Years	65 to 74 Years	75 Years and Over	55 to 64 Years	65 to 74 Years	75 Years and Over	55 to 64 Years	65 to 74 Years	75 Years and Over
California—Cont.												
Congressional District 51	30,873	8,358	5,842	5,444	4,570	4,039	8,237	38,859	31,518	13,686	15,328	12,859
Congressional District 52	58,714	19,409	11,018	17,435	13,174	12,640	2,734	48,051	40,795	6,811	5,152	6,389
Congressional District 53	46,792	16,012	10,654	11,910	9,545	9,918	5,478	45,385	40,286	12,399	9,180	10,369
Colorado												
Congressional District 1	49,400	17,588	11,244	13,536	12,217	12,088	7,068	47,638	33,524	14,143	7,286	6,906
Congressional District 2	71,596	24,046	12,090	23,862	17,677	13,210	5,274	60,203	33,869	7,354	2,825	2,313
Congressional District 3	55,790	19,733	13,020	21,322	23,113	18,189	8,523	64,471	43,256	12,294	6,784	6,294
Congressional District 4	57,126	16,943	9,386	16,913	17,901	14,558	6,564	53,960	35,987	9,292	4,938	4,768
Congressional District 5	49,799	14,998	8,820	12,681	16,022	14,156	6,576	55,042	35,940	11,816	4,424	4,079
Congressional District 6	59,565	18,172	10,863	12,339	12,099	11,797	5,857	47,436	30,288	6,743	3,837	3,414
Congressional District 7	61,841	21,486	12,820	15,026	12,654	15,403	7,158	50,591	39,064	9,512	6,719	6,046
Connecticut												
Congressional District 1	67,612	26,166	17,801	12,476	15,839	16,688	7,721	55,181	48,286	11,898	7,713	8,211
Congressional District 2	70,671	30,448	17,704	12,335	15,789	16,028	6,016	60,542	45,335	9,843	6,004	7,167
Congressional District 3	67,295	25,952	16,916	11,604	15,398	17,933	7,814	55,400	48,000	12,116	6,942	7,606
Congressional District 4	61,921	22,877	15,277	16,715	12,742	18,548	4,788	49,045	44,039	8,434	5,602	5,267
Congressional District 5	66,713	26,160	14,898	12,798	15,804	14,704	8,088	56,637	44,605	11,718	7,190	8,291
Delaware												
Congressional District (at Large)	85,031	45,707	25,152	12,444	24,337	22,523	11,197	86,992	58,182	15,260	7,937	7,078
District of Columbia												
Delegate District (at Large)	38,462	23,812	14,769	7,692	8,093	8,806	7,000	35,010	29,034	20,462	9,186	8,278
Florida												
Congressional District 1	47,247	18,449	12,986	15,229	19,308	14,648	9,755	64,982	46,285	9,593	5,323	4,477
Congressional District 2	50,528	24,006	14,317	11,398	15,962	12,931	9,021	58,284	38,945	9,734	8,438	6,689
Congressional District 3	45,193	22,308	11,260	14,136	21,677	18,316	12,215	70,138	46,159	9,488	7,981	6,297
Congressional District 4	51,981	17,273	10,272	12,831	16,827	14,354	7,723	58,412	37,846	7,328	5,091	3,420
Congressional District 5	45,738	12,025	7,474	9,518	8,803	7,894	11,826	43,732	35,033	15,496	9,492	7,388
Congressional District 6	58,595	30,441	22,248	20,591	29,088	23,943	12,226	94,036	73,733	11,357	11,549	9,952
Congressional District 7	54,706	14,562	7,833	14,669	14,376	11,652	7,482	56,156	41,104	7,327	4,872	5,963
Congressional District 8	57,427	28,022	24,325	17,225	23,966	27,625	12,762	86,938	77,918	13,237	8,192	8,595
Congressional District 9	41,358	12,639	6,601	11,049	9,603	8,176	8,453	48,797	32,637	7,471	9,635	7,172
Congressional District 10	51,441	23,297	16,972	13,219	25,562	19,278	8,900	80,721	55,440	8,459	10,636	7,466
Congressional District 11	53,995	42,623	30,992	18,676	39,156	33,931	16,598	131,139	99,783	11,901	9,749	9,000
Congressional District 12	51,820	22,606	18,150	16,413	18,325	19,934	10,153	79,662	70,172	10,626	9,375	9,046
Congressional District 13	59,919	23,444	18,708	16,301	22,733	21,718	10,600	83,607	70,819	9,932	7,638	6,727
Congressional District 14	41,630	11,207	7,398	12,572	8,958	10,399	12,270	51,295	38,859	13,560	12,120	9,224
Congressional District 15	50,053	17,877	10,098	11,959	13,392	12,320	9,282	58,000	41,221	10,419	7,244	6,682
Congressional District 16	57,896	35,412	36,503	23,345	40,329	43,839	10,684	111,269	101,768	8,550	7,639	7,420
Congressional District 17	47,666	32,640	27,756	15,745	28,952	29,305	15,407	97,580	87,337	11,307	7,255	10,418
Congressional District 18	55,549	27,167	25,212	22,428	24,424	29,671	8,889	86,671	83,293	8,064	6,717	9,685
Congressional District 19	58,387	39,814	30,035	23,659	38,616	38,748	9,812	115,232	93,420	7,258	6,122	8,526
Congressional District 20	36,323	10,892	6,397	14,509	10,257	9,965	7,965	48,832	44,507	13,887	9,303	10,144
Congressional District 21	51,347	22,474	23,524	19,435	23,136	38,814	4,657	74,928	88,945	4,814	9,345	9,139
Congressional District 22	53,438	19,905	16,014	22,207	18,736	26,384	6,698	74,587	70,781	7,221	7,864	8,205
Congressional District 23	44,239	14,265	9,036	20,199	13,827	12,426	5,600	56,933	53,211	7,967	10,050	10,540
Congressional District 24	29,525	8,114	3,684	11,272	5,061	4,418	7,472	46,494	33,367	10,750	16,048	16,537
Congressional District 25	36,440	10,804	7,262	13,861	9,845	8,985	5,002	57,820	51,813	6,385	15,795	20,169
Congressional District 26	53,376	9,681	4,127	16,045	8,863	5,453	4,835	58,027	51,445	5,960	15,315	21,192
Congressional District 27	33,072	8,602	3,385	18,115	5,549	6,345	7,236	58,575	57,252	12,661	20,998	27,499
Georgia												
Congressional District 1	46,475	18,787	8,508	9,885	14,764	10,788	10,398	55,747	34,928	9,007	8,348	6,935
Congressional District 2	38,917	17,073	10,533	10,387	11,732	11,287	11,712	53,757	34,906	14,409	12,038	7,299
Congressional District 3	53,653	23,889	11,429	9,394	15,683	11,528	9,969	59,387	35,316	7,482	6,597	5,676
Congressional District 4	52,389	20,955	8,629	11,662	8,426	6,703	9,530	44,043	23,549	8,160	7,678	4,857
Congressional District 5	41,358	17,318	8,346	10,318	8,146	6,764	9,777	44,818	26,027	10,885	8,941	5,985
Congressional District 6	58,308	18,137	11,768	13,974	12,933	10,451	3,709	43,034	31,043	2,948	3,142	4,112
Congressional District 7	50,824	16,664	6,760	11,431	8,788	6,430	5,642	38,924	22,043	4,276	5,135	5,119
Congressional District 8	45,617	19,378	11,056	7,982	13,625	10,961	12,203	57,847	37,291	9,978	10,602	5,333
Congressional District 9	54,223	23,594	13,314	13,355	19,775	16,449	10,352	74,189	45,550	7,399	9,209	7,857
Congressional District 10	50,023	23,735	12,617	9,642	15,774	10,767	10,379	58,325	36,415	8,326	8,613	8,490
Congressional District 11	55,907	18,764	8,772	11,750	13,236	8,455	5,082	49,028	26,934	5,252	2,499	2,874
Congressional District 12	43,836	18,105	8,456	11,213	11,998	9,674	12,254	51,338	34,646	10,965	8,764	8,893
Congressional District 13	49,396	16,539	7,019	11,126	9,381	7,144	10,090	40,915	25,409	7,718	7,585	3,890
Congressional District 14	48,076	16,366	10,521	9,601	14,020	15,173	12,398	54,536	35,228	9,490	6,956	5,088
Hawaii												
Congressional District 1	62,322	38,808	27,257	11,057	13,371	17,017	3,930	57,042	53,627	8,039	6,747	8,214
Congressional District 2	63,386	31,191	16,997	12,210	13,383	12,818	7,407	57,888	41,276	11,526	6,378	5,055
Idaho												
Congressional District 1	57,720	22,227	11,596	22,008	26,993	21,345	10,639	75,857	47,653	9,097	7,509	4,884
Congressional District 2	54,281	15,188	10,660	19,269	25,286	22,338	7,219	58,444	43,171	6,698	5,090	5,195

Table I-5: 114th Congressional Districts—Persons With Health Insurance by Source of Insurance—*Continued*

	Private Health Insurance Coverage						Public Health Insurance Coverage					
	Employer Based			Direct Purchase			Medicare			Medicaid/CHIP		
	55 to 64 Years	65 to 74 Years	75 Years and Over	55 to 64 Years	65 to 74 Years	75 Years and Over	55 to 64 Years	65 to 74 Years	75 Years and Over	55 to 64 Years	65 to 74 Years	75 Years and Over
Illinois												
Congressional District 1	56,519	20,544	14,675	10,774	15,348	14,080	8,395	54,757	44,292	15,261	8,472	8,186
Congressional District 2	57,968	21,504	13,194	9,946	13,626	13,834	9,658	50,159	38,158	16,782	6,480	6,185
Congressional District 3	61,112	19,891	12,182	10,532	15,996	17,567	6,866	52,283	39,518	8,463	6,276	4,843
Congressional District 4	31,825	9,077	5,206	7,186	6,352	6,736	5,793	30,750	25,783	11,472	6,530	5,270
Congressional District 5	47,113	16,821	9,585	10,343	13,552	13,508	4,544	40,155	37,146	7,816	5,269	5,083
Congressional District 6	76,815	24,730	14,055	18,366	21,769	17,039	3,243	56,152	37,756	3,375	3,293	2,765
Congressional District 7	41,125	16,019	8,040	9,780	9,225	6,716	8,410	45,568	31,483	15,694	8,044	6,818
Congressional District 8	60,794	18,681	8,386	12,305	16,724	14,437	5,803	47,432	32,763	6,145	5,382	4,559
Congressional District 9	55,823	19,102	13,711	15,606	17,663	21,533	5,904	51,259	48,986	10,606	7,240	5,907
Congressional District 10	61,344	17,911	9,614	12,220	15,492	16,743	5,660	46,127	39,184	4,854	4,429	4,813
Congressional District 11	58,475	15,146	9,074	10,713	13,187	12,075	4,674	38,009	26,372	6,033	4,285	2,728
Congressional District 12	55,717	23,819	16,276	10,348	16,066	16,833	9,562	56,665	44,484	11,950	5,799	4,446
Congressional District 13	58,303	24,532	17,713	10,872	19,767	18,825	10,593	54,296	44,785	9,941	5,940	5,422
Congressional District 14	70,163	22,063	10,482	13,986	18,857	13,604	4,923	54,156	32,670	5,102	3,976	3,587
Congressional District 15	62,092	22,517	16,536	12,798	23,362	24,397	10,714	63,080	52,005	10,571	7,570	6,154
Congressional District 16	64,575	25,372	16,305	13,094	23,868	23,730	8,818	61,756	46,854	8,329	3,776	5,497
Congressional District 17	59,653	23,658	18,159	13,677	25,034	22,964	10,007	64,763	49,347	10,617	6,101	5,981
Congressional District 18	69,078	27,476	20,626	15,224	22,603	24,346	6,605	61,127	49,771	6,615	3,841	4,624
Indiana												
Congressional District 1	66,094	24,406	17,159	10,116	18,353	16,143	9,382	56,726	42,262	10,029	5,234	4,041
Congressional District 2	60,428	15,997	10,197	12,193	21,646	20,768	9,267	55,163	44,245	7,262	4,257	3,470
Congressional District 3	59,194	16,012	12,143	13,446	20,308	17,830	9,459	56,557	41,227	6,601	4,361	3,849
Congressional District 4	61,419	21,265	15,644	13,619	20,663	20,423	8,742	56,766	42,900	5,612	4,837	3,414
Congressional District 5	63,071	23,434	14,651	14,576	19,602	17,165	6,598	53,190	40,558	5,283	3,604	4,059
Congressional District 6	61,073	26,707	16,281	14,283	22,616	19,823	11,708	63,968	45,670	7,552	5,984	3,462
Congressional District 7	48,029	15,147	9,666	8,599	12,271	12,775	11,543	43,519	32,012	12,670	6,840	5,082
Congressional District 8	62,602	21,287	13,714	14,541	22,880	21,188	10,715	62,279	45,333	9,265	5,020	5,990
Congressional District 9	62,123	23,502	12,271	10,561	22,141	19,765	10,283	60,197	40,300	8,891	4,310	3,896
Iowa												
Congressional District 1	72,314	21,192	13,775	16,914	29,697	30,747	7,616	63,267	55,480	9,188	6,600	6,828
Congressional District 2	68,448	22,023	13,962	16,206	28,009	27,706	7,965	63,662	50,542	11,846	6,922	6,019
Congressional District 3	66,916	18,682	13,243	15,557	24,290	22,937	7,396	57,717	44,203	11,286	5,020	5,319
Congressional District 4	67,773	14,423	10,753	21,165	32,024	36,056	7,445	63,055	60,194	8,580	6,423	7,795
Kansas												
Congressional District 1	55,970	13,438	9,054	16,943	23,673	29,019	7,604	53,343	48,500	5,764	5,865	5,782
Congressional District 2	59,754	19,947	14,445	13,978	25,273	22,842	10,985	58,180	45,426	7,369	6,832	5,324
Congressional District 3	63,551	17,886	10,706	14,106	19,286	17,671	6,334	48,748	37,222	4,857	2,782	3,830
Congressional District 4	58,255	14,337	8,198	14,439	23,425	23,828	7,585	53,168	43,518	6,860	5,321	6,362
Kentucky												
Congressional District 1	52,815	22,888	15,579	14,475	19,928	17,529	16,759	66,641	47,298	17,032	8,343	8,165
Congressional District 2	56,509	24,918	13,004	12,522	20,902	17,544	13,745	61,686	40,789	12,796	7,843	6,045
Congressional District 3	62,181	27,136	16,801	12,392	19,389	19,308	10,865	57,024	43,982	16,478	6,170	5,190
Congressional District 4	63,366	26,065	14,395	11,242	20,790	14,134	12,707	58,825	37,688	13,576	7,908	6,313
Congressional District 5	41,589	20,567	12,108	11,018	17,187	12,813	26,527	68,381	42,284	29,111	13,411	9,698
Congressional District 6	60,176	22,016	15,757	12,426	18,532	15,224	11,272	56,522	36,349	12,493	8,066	5,136
Louisiana												
Congressional District 1	63,901	24,222	13,041	19,209	15,500	14,571	9,177	63,336	43,474	8,396	6,897	7,442
Congressional District 2	49,144	15,608	7,365	12,458	11,234	8,233	13,947	53,844	35,009	18,821	13,701	9,919
Congressional District 3	52,644	22,363	12,115	14,751	16,544	14,216	15,988	55,569	38,506	13,061	8,085	6,736
Congressional District 4	46,240	22,850	13,219	10,710	18,470	15,040	13,503	60,380	42,430	14,211	8,976	8,242
Congressional District 5	48,305	22,504	15,125	10,438	14,854	12,160	13,900	59,032	42,472	14,547	11,247	10,480
Congressional District 6	64,622	24,099	13,663	12,654	12,152	9,862	9,298	55,042	36,957	7,665	6,457	4,462
Maine												
Congressional District 1	67,221	24,883	15,459	16,120	19,701	20,065	7,252	66,076	47,808	9,414	7,459	6,639
Congressional District 2	54,938	19,517	11,584	15,707	21,847	18,933	13,814	68,538	47,172	16,382	12,390	12,101
Maryland												
Congressional District 1	75,135	40,623	20,908	13,366	20,272	20,029	6,554	70,694	47,780	8,750	5,731	5,618
Congressional District 2	56,608	25,539	16,194	11,062	13,702	14,552	10,912	49,311	36,029	15,132	6,492	5,799
Congressional District 3	69,604	32,276	20,967	15,177	14,667	17,044	5,426	52,798	44,711	6,669	5,522	6,303
Congressional District 4	62,056	31,673	17,761	11,144	11,813	10,706	5,101	47,291	33,848	9,017	4,215	5,142
Congressional District 5	70,842	34,656	17,019	10,924	12,114	8,267	5,870	53,159	31,048	8,128	5,290	4,692
Congressional District 6	64,840	26,364	15,341	12,468	16,029	14,339	5,885	52,073	37,135	7,716	5,596	7,069
Congressional District 7	59,543	28,703	16,271	11,462	15,042	12,556	12,265	53,044	40,255	15,864	7,910	6,179
Congressional District 8	75,137	34,789	22,950	13,224	16,098	16,323	3,977	55,245	47,697	6,918	4,484	6,281
Massachusetts												
Congressional District 1	67,132	27,352	16,586	8,928	19,436	19,574	12,231	63,010	48,353	25,849	10,265	8,367
Congressional District 2	72,235	27,212	16,116	9,071	16,280	15,738	6,132	53,016	41,324	18,580	9,030	8,126
Congressional District 3	67,858	24,723	14,683	8,442	15,290	14,109	7,360	54,110	38,460	20,114	9,094	6,353
Congressional District 4	76,827	31,443	18,056	11,858	17,872	16,784	5,766	55,562	42,494	12,407	5,665	6,999
Congressional District 5	66,783	26,934	18,594	11,657	17,546	19,215	5,614	54,435	47,904	14,030	7,367	6,553
Congressional District 6	80,588	28,612	20,669	10,662	18,694	20,737	7,671	60,899	52,636	18,743	8,307	9,402
Congressional District 7	40,444	15,444	8,056	6,218	7,196	7,833	9,417	37,088	29,979	25,589	10,971	11,143
Congressional District 8	66,797	30,612	18,337	10,095	16,265	19,620	7,302	59,357	49,843	19,280	12,244	9,538
Congressional District 9	73,178	34,296	24,615	13,619	26,413	22,966	7,912	77,750	62,404	19,336	9,659	9,731

Table I-5: 114th Congressional Districts—Persons With Health Insurance by Source of Insurance—*Continued*

| | Private Health Insurance Coverage | | | | | | Public Health Insurance Coverage | | | | | |
| | Employer Based | | | Direct Purchase | | | Medicare | | | Medicaid/CHIP | | |
	55 to 64 Years	65 to 74 Years	75 Years and Over	55 to 64 Years	65 to 74 Years	75 Years and Over	55 to 64 Years	65 to 74 Years	75 Years and Over	55 to 64 Years	65 to 74 Years	75 Years and Over
Michigan												
Congressional District 1	66,008	38,605	28,343	20,139	26,793	24,402	14,808	81,152	60,278	14,590	7,519	8,583
Congressional District 2	60,399	21,419	17,143	13,232	18,418	15,631	10,249	56,012	41,665	12,315	6,306	5,791
Congressional District 3	61,189	23,644	16,993	12,672	17,861	15,633	9,681	54,260	39,589	10,255	5,563	4,842
Congressional District 4	66,239	37,272	27,561	13,420	22,929	18,185	11,836	67,740	48,552	11,549	5,744	4,971
Congressional District 5	64,833	40,406	28,693	11,369	15,604	18,032	15,816	63,524	48,951	18,110	7,646	6,333
Congressional District 6	63,656	27,662	19,026	13,522	20,843	18,323	9,926	62,030	44,478	10,322	6,382	4,800
Congressional District 7	73,036	34,613	22,278	10,833	21,440	18,431	11,250	64,795	44,963	10,962	6,278	5,031
Congressional District 8	71,605	29,768	18,514	13,517	17,093	12,629	8,663	55,283	33,985	8,453	4,785	3,162
Congressional District 9	64,065	29,690	23,545	14,359	19,975	21,258	11,280	57,772	48,783	12,692	8,748	5,735
Congressional District 10	69,654	34,402	23,243	15,204	23,183	19,646	12,300	66,647	45,946	11,967	7,628	6,511
Congressional District 11	79,671	26,812	17,974	15,055	22,164	18,937	6,027	55,454	42,293	4,874	3,612	4,761
Congressional District 12	60,133	28,396	21,810	11,216	15,504	14,821	9,748	49,769	39,499	11,907	5,884	5,162
Congressional District 13	43,167	22,457	18,789	7,798	10,390	10,094	15,331	47,098	36,660	24,963	11,198	8,288
Congressional District 14	54,817	31,195	20,847	13,065	14,308	14,250	13,192	56,280	44,751	19,618	10,517	8,606
Minnesota												
Congressional District 1	61,496	16,153	11,963	15,142	26,831	28,436	5,708	52,158	47,759	8,270	4,272	4,390
Congressional District 2	61,167	16,271	9,784	13,989	21,287	18,738	4,418	45,842	32,880	5,462	2,891	3,315
Congressional District 3	71,673	18,587	9,216	16,319	26,815	22,878	4,782	51,231	40,057	6,219	2,205	3,015
Congressional District 4	60,174	19,335	12,433	10,612	21,862	18,946	5,748	47,341	36,778	11,485	4,265	4,376
Congressional District 5	46,203	13,011	8,286	12,794	17,894	16,037	7,919	39,354	31,605	13,432	5,639	4,255
Congressional District 6	54,787	12,959	7,034	14,626	22,167	15,792	5,078	43,247	27,175	9,016	2,829	2,400
Congressional District 7	54,840	12,190	6,825	20,954	32,969	34,149	6,318	59,660	53,866	10,588	5,257	6,107
Congressional District 8	63,322	18,963	14,261	16,271	34,951	27,766	9,702	68,359	49,442	12,591	5,461	4,296
Mississippi												
Congressional District 1	49,383	13,991	7,973	12,313	22,490	18,355	14,247	63,205	44,374	11,923	12,838	10,211
Congressional District 2	40,585	13,843	6,576	13,914	15,922	12,897	15,739	52,563	38,837	19,883	13,929	10,690
Congressional District 3	53,405	15,123	10,359	12,453	17,619	15,552	16,092	60,620	45,204	14,837	11,759	10,155
Congressional District 4	47,432	18,862	9,961	11,056	17,330	13,669	14,878	60,905	41,361	14,251	9,726	6,216
Missouri												
Congressional District 1	56,913	17,803	11,837	11,124	11,417	10,824	14,472	48,259	36,731	12,764	6,302	5,307
Congressional District 2	79,955	25,596	19,741	18,524	22,291	22,417	6,089	66,722	56,114	4,439	2,409	2,830
Congressional District 3	67,303	22,857	14,446	15,195	18,692	13,902	10,386	63,638	41,928	4,500	5,014	3,006
Congressional District 4	51,653	20,696	12,081	14,531	21,010	18,787	12,934	65,514	44,036	8,650	6,727	4,830
Congressional District 5	59,649	21,299	15,217	11,965	18,175	16,999	11,651	55,196	45,201	11,508	4,230	4,666
Congressional District 6	65,886	20,400	12,269	14,749	26,408	23,025	10,499	62,283	44,155	7,003	4,632	4,511
Congressional District 7	51,454	15,393	10,749	17,279	25,342	21,144	13,523	67,788	50,387	9,841	5,792	4,214
Congressional District 8	53,448	20,235	11,991	12,819	20,402	19,254	17,435	72,445	51,534	12,762	10,529	8,095
Montana												
Congressional District (at Large)	82,369	27,484	16,941	30,139	35,979	32,328	13,951	95,547	66,625	11,718	9,207	7,249
Nebraska												
Congressional District 1	53,074	15,465	7,852	12,415	19,992	20,944	6,151	46,190	36,394	4,525	3,910	3,446
Congressional District 2	51,304	14,317	8,058	9,461	12,802	10,865	5,573	37,711	28,961	5,980	3,149	3,865
Congressional District 3	51,155	13,342	8,609	19,465	23,989	29,305	6,988	52,750	49,878	5,643	4,841	6,172
Nevada												
Congressional District 1	42,814	13,706	6,861	7,584	8,725	6,811	7,780	48,441	32,568	12,522	8,560	6,325
Congressional District 2	58,291	22,311	11,288	10,823	17,278	12,699	7,414	64,456	38,114	9,403	7,250	3,753
Congressional District 3	57,547	23,206	10,857	13,186	13,318	9,744	5,403	61,696	38,575	7,997	5,075	4,576
Congressional District 4	46,611	20,986	9,471	10,240	11,718	9,943	8,475	59,166	33,958	9,667	8,950	4,642
New Hampshire												
Congressional District 1	68,546	26,029	13,169	14,375	19,246	17,793	8,648	56,862	38,518	3,909	4,690	2,818
Congressional District 2	70,012	24,117	16,059	12,644	19,480	15,980	7,593	58,989	40,270	5,408	3,525	3,393
New Jersey												
Congressional District 1	65,759	26,672	15,286	10,318	17,326	16,678	7,671	55,642	43,587	9,118	5,699	5,924
Congressional District 2	66,647	31,645	19,132	10,753	19,572	19,784	8,973	66,511	47,515	12,289	7,701	6,790
Congressional District 3	74,864	38,416	23,857	11,902	22,206	26,359	8,434	68,293	58,851	7,159	4,563	6,003
Congressional District 4	73,798	34,274	23,287	12,875	20,007	23,072	6,734	66,379	59,090	7,585	4,537	5,064
Congressional District 5	77,545	29,722	15,318	14,954	18,069	18,190	5,462	60,978	45,744	6,787	5,003	5,101
Congressional District 6	63,635	26,012	12,827	9,804	11,203	11,830	6,000	50,054	34,932	7,446	6,490	5,096
Congressional District 7	83,689	31,225	15,982	11,837	15,463	17,119	4,776	55,276	43,204	4,447	4,061	4,512
Congressional District 8	38,429	12,697	6,054	6,328	5,962	6,823	6,932	37,867	30,046	11,560	9,002	10,414
Congressional District 9	51,394	17,310	11,399	9,656	10,371	10,882	6,707	52,709	45,313	11,543	7,409	8,816
Congressional District 10	51,086	17,945	10,762	7,252	7,122	6,611	9,335	41,561	31,990	15,892	8,267	8,764
Congressional District 11	76,580	31,650	20,678	13,131	16,563	19,451	4,023	60,144	54,354	3,657	3,501	5,479
Congressional District 12	72,398	31,400	17,135	9,386	12,051	14,794	6,415	50,262	46,229	8,713	6,097	7,369
New Mexico												
Congressional District 1	50,827	20,412	13,959	12,814	11,784	8,587	8,149	56,964	41,622	14,175	7,572	5,432
Congressional District 2	42,209	21,467	16,291	11,351	14,258	11,185	10,757	60,157	43,501	14,224	11,061	6,756
Congressional District 3	49,192	21,717	12,718	14,918	15,831	12,698	10,285	57,224	40,110	13,113	7,866	6,154
New York												
Congressional District 1	72,594	36,357	18,671	16,006	17,087	17,630	7,267	64,716	46,322	10,521	6,293	4,372

Table I-5: 114th Congressional Districts—Persons With Health Insurance by Source of Insurance—*Continued*

	Private Health Insurance Coverage						Public Health Insurance Coverage					
	Employer Based			Direct Purchase			Medicare			Medicaid/CHIP		
	55 to 64 Years	65 to 74 Years	75 Years and Over	55 to 64 Years	65 to 74 Years	75 Years and Over	55 to 64 Years	65 to 74 Years	75 Years and Over	55 to 64 Years	65 to 74 Years	75 Years and Over
New York—Cont.												
Congressional District 2	69,637	27,701	16,877	9,084	11,703	12,869	7,624	50,218	40,898	9,187	4,783	4,896
Congressional District 3	75,173	32,562	23,748	16,240	16,669	23,811	5,918	60,369	61,353	6,508	4,694	6,099
Congressional District 4	69,973	31,212	20,252	11,920	14,154	15,497	4,729	55,458	49,347	8,945	4,691	7,978
Congressional District 5	58,833	24,074	12,694	6,984	6,028	6,389	6,836	49,489	38,109	19,844	12,191	11,311
Congressional District 6	53,738	20,770	12,363	7,780	7,204	9,376	7,445	55,623	49,243	22,491	12,591	14,140
Congressional District 7	31,435	8,787	5,407	8,209	3,554	4,405	6,564	33,521	31,291	27,384	16,337	16,615
Congressional District 8	50,013	20,890	8,252	6,786	6,551	4,407	9,335	50,420	42,241	25,043	17,329	21,029
Congressional District 9	49,268	19,303	8,794	6,457	7,546	4,879	6,823	48,782	39,817	20,406	15,562	16,931
Congressional District 10	43,526	24,231	11,482	12,878	10,736	10,491	5,434	55,248	39,471	17,708	9,938	12,343
Congressional District 11	65,487	25,716	13,066	9,710	7,030	7,712	8,972	56,456	45,101	17,519	10,127	12,857
Congressional District 12	47,062	25,436	12,154	12,598	13,480	15,035	6,218	49,505	45,290	13,720	8,462	8,887
Congressional District 13	34,503	10,153	6,904	6,966	4,152	3,694	8,336	43,076	34,687	37,194	21,852	18,880
Congressional District 14	40,965	15,815	8,456	6,801	6,507	6,360	6,149	44,616	35,647	22,218	14,529	12,864
Congressional District 15	21,911	7,039	3,992	4,975	5,004	4,011	8,008	38,158	26,353	34,583	24,667	16,836
Congressional District 16	59,122	28,692	19,778	9,272	10,473	13,189	7,285	51,597	50,151	15,407	8,813	9,681
Congressional District 17	73,041	32,028	19,816	11,340	12,298	15,821	4,838	55,269	45,901	7,791	5,678	6,722
Congressional District 18	71,268	30,027	18,928	12,645	10,370	12,389	6,465	55,102	39,605	8,428	6,716	5,687
Congressional District 19	73,006	37,090	20,737	12,518	19,526	16,661	10,178	71,228	49,176	11,862	7,731	5,390
Congressional District 20	73,950	36,640	23,485	8,291	12,574	14,197	6,477	58,386	44,112	10,445	7,314	5,412
Congressional District 21	62,296	31,555	20,084	12,082	18,436	18,798	11,357	62,738	46,104	14,307	7,659	6,903
Congressional District 22	63,760	27,910	20,265	10,460	17,183	18,844	12,534	62,675	49,729	18,249	8,300	6,064
Congressional District 23	67,584	28,557	20,411	11,666	20,569	20,536	10,834	63,612	48,973	13,972	9,078	7,151
Congressional District 24	70,163	27,500	21,466	10,270	13,558	15,510	10,196	58,115	46,291	12,221	6,015	6,001
Congressional District 25	66,870	22,435	17,527	10,812	18,444	21,102	8,179	59,120	46,915	13,100	4,804	7,059
Congressional District 26	65,309	27,675	19,012	9,320	15,771	21,417	10,808	60,394	53,566	16,782	9,631	9,256
Congressional District 27	80,487	30,097	18,777	12,658	19,680	21,203	9,002	63,748	48,514	8,444	6,531	8,053
North Carolina												
Congressional District 1	46,127	21,976	12,014	14,395	16,189	15,872	14,749	61,788	44,462	17,087	12,312	12,818
Congressional District 2	47,372	19,250	9,338	16,707	20,138	15,791	11,108	60,123	38,629	8,353	7,586	4,856
Congressional District 3	49,994	23,702	13,841	16,543	20,828	16,099	10,684	63,261	42,444	7,874	8,091	5,426
Congressional District 4	47,489	22,435	13,347	11,440	12,898	11,914	6,928	45,684	32,456	5,949	6,020	5,012
Congressional District 5	59,021	21,032	13,545	18,765	27,851	24,330	10,706	67,706	48,473	7,701	6,921	7,057
Congressional District 6	70,095	21,197	14,018	18,520	23,333	20,233	11,661	68,793	50,974	8,972	5,881	7,064
Congressional District 7	62,160	30,996	14,450	16,454	25,842	18,905	12,694	81,450	46,384	11,247	7,242	6,168
Congressional District 8	50,519	18,372	9,487	13,400	22,594	17,454	13,717	65,149	41,154	11,434	8,878	7,429
Congressional District 9	64,104	20,262	12,148	16,617	21,598	14,709	6,724	56,624	36,092	3,868	4,028	4,036
Congressional District 10	57,312	20,489	11,904	17,925	26,475	21,455	14,318	72,723	47,972	10,586	8,448	6,565
Congressional District 11	60,212	30,033	17,918	17,918	33,275	24,318	12,785	89,935	62,383	11,039	9,006	7,836
Congressional District 12	39,556	13,269	7,173	11,143	11,380	9,800	10,855	41,668	26,577	12,131	7,848	5,938
Congressional District 13	62,743	24,252	13,063	16,789	23,289	15,373	9,133	59,434	35,991	5,714	3,556	4,662
North Dakota												
Congressional District (at Large)	63,870	17,833	9,462	16,507	26,385	29,182	6,027	51,775	44,669	5,203	4,749	5,131
Ohio												
Congressional District 1	59,232	20,181	14,148	11,670	13,031	14,482	10,048	48,099	39,952	9,087	4,685	3,372
Congressional District 2	66,072	23,316	15,653	12,025	15,705	15,793	10,824	58,738	44,024	11,259	5,607	4,426
Congressional District 3	47,190	13,452	9,028	6,458	8,434	8,114	7,794	38,957	27,115	11,333	5,751	3,771
Congressional District 4	67,793	24,365	21,573	12,169	21,849	20,675	10,085	60,268	49,416	10,656	4,864	5,625
Congressional District 5	74,297	29,731	22,311	13,957	22,221	18,363	10,237	62,155	45,740	6,939	5,131	3,069
Congressional District 6	68,485	30,258	19,353	10,648	19,015	17,643	13,941	69,506	50,319	14,488	8,076	5,643
Congressional District 7	68,300	29,745	21,213	13,294	20,430	19,464	8,787	66,543	49,058	11,190	6,408	4,384
Congressional District 8	67,179	25,756	18,864	9,843	16,777	14,522	9,408	60,016	43,473	10,059	4,320	3,393
Congressional District 9	58,492	24,365	18,244	8,790	14,552	16,661	9,560	52,737	43,613	14,382	7,877	5,677
Congressional District 10	62,682	24,469	18,578	9,557	16,455	16,439	8,915	61,391	48,487	10,273	5,176	5,008
Congressional District 11	55,013	21,612	18,287	9,126	13,475	13,840	12,657	52,066	45,356	20,570	9,601	8,626
Congressional District 12	71,267	24,892	16,748	11,058	16,125	13,931	6,638	55,882	39,211	6,319	4,186	3,640
Congressional District 13	65,300	24,995	20,960	9,829	16,825	17,708	10,490	63,760	53,905	12,589	8,259	6,611
Congressional District 14	77,210	30,386	22,083	14,143	20,182	18,962	8,227	68,224	53,652	5,841	3,866	4,856
Congressional District 15	61,976	24,618	15,599	11,162	17,482	13,913	8,949	58,042	41,370	9,076	5,970	3,319
Congressional District 16	81,090	27,515	22,014	13,871	21,870	18,741	5,984	68,221	52,370	6,164	3,979	3,750
Oklahoma												
Congressional District 1	59,981	20,175	13,197	13,351	19,085	17,378	8,334	55,761	42,465	6,447	4,303	3,697
Congressional District 2	45,760	22,072	13,305	12,935	22,490	19,328	16,368	74,454	50,395	11,707	9,463	7,306
Congressional District 3	56,549	21,428	12,318	14,846	19,918	19,952	11,016	61,781	47,070	6,754	6,733	5,558
Congressional District 4	55,355	23,772	13,199	11,669	14,891	14,284	9,527	56,386	41,852	7,155	4,268	4,888
Congressional District 5	54,120	23,816	14,472	14,077	16,297	13,372	10,048	56,098	40,633	6,917	5,931	4,151
Oregon												
Congressional District 1	65,427	19,576	11,994	14,511	22,819	18,593	6,827	59,058	40,169	11,086	5,408	5,501
Congressional District 2	57,296	22,767	16,306	19,699	32,223	27,849	13,018	83,600	60,567	20,774	9,959	9,130
Congressional District 3	58,576	18,658	13,263	16,439	17,608	14,974	8,498	57,624	38,863	18,914	10,390	6,725
Congressional District 4	63,647	23,022	15,665	19,545	31,332	26,081	13,123	85,840	58,981	20,759	11,226	8,037
Congressional District 5	69,509	26,454	17,077	15,185	25,616	21,883	7,501	70,939	50,759	13,619	7,492	6,545
Pennsylvania												
Congressional District 1	41,553	14,497	8,459	11,907	13,195	11,210	10,430	44,162	33,653	18,067	9,278	6,820

Table I-5: 114th Congressional Districts—Persons With Health Insurance by Source of Insurance—Continued

| | Private Health Insurance Coverage | | | | | | Public Health Insurance Coverage | | | | | |
| | Employer Based | | | Direct Purchase | | | Medicare | | | Medicaid/CHIP | | |
	55 to 64 Years	65 to 74 Years	75 Years and Over	55 to 64 Years	65 to 74 Years	75 Years and Over	55 to 64 Years	65 to 74 Years	75 Years and Over	55 to 64 Years	65 to 74 Years	75 Years and Over
Pennsylvania—Cont.												
Congressional District 2	45,591	18,298	12,864	11,424	15,007	14,802	9,896	49,896	38,551	19,039	10,733	8,714
Congressional District 3	67,858	20,989	14,815	15,155	25,852	26,668	10,935	63,912	54,500	11,032	6,819	7,102
Congressional District 4	71,315	24,678	13,908	13,629	22,886	24,972	8,215	60,922	47,438	7,789	5,594	5,598
Congressional District 5	63,874	22,326	15,672	15,273	27,093	23,232	9,318	64,596	49,933	9,504	6,664	6,926
Congressional District 6	73,158	22,617	17,733	14,086	23,330	22,888	5,545	55,572	48,644	5,061	4,167	5,001
Congressional District 7	75,165	23,984	18,310	16,512	22,724	24,886	4,304	58,427	53,045	5,172	4,019	4,732
Congressional District 8	81,307	28,018	15,349	16,218	23,544	26,035	6,663	60,879	50,262	4,196	4,915	6,015
Congressional District 9	65,326	25,532	20,746	15,066	28,445	24,046	11,363	68,359	56,994	11,243	7,597	6,931
Congressional District 10	66,134	24,318	15,383	15,362	28,739	27,000	11,136	68,464	52,487	10,913	5,521	6,319
Congressional District 11	69,813	25,544	17,633	14,953	26,705	24,916	10,835	67,011	51,348	8,318	7,165	6,460
Congressional District 12	79,373	28,030	20,978	16,254	29,340	34,469	7,403	70,799	62,907	8,748	6,649	8,558
Congressional District 13	59,836	20,867	13,139	14,786	17,411	22,798	9,625	53,830	47,389	10,498	6,612	7,384
Congressional District 14	64,136	21,232	17,909	13,860	20,200	25,272	10,588	53,800	53,976	14,051	9,237	9,611
Congressional District 15	70,770	22,903	15,562	14,338	23,504	22,929	8,037	60,092	49,750	7,187	5,036	5,896
Congressional District 16	60,029	20,168	13,986	10,771	18,046	20,427	7,914	53,351	46,213	8,836	6,543	6,714
Congressional District 17	61,259	24,444	15,095	14,443	25,591	27,335	11,369	65,628	54,012	11,791	6,535	7,945
Congressional District 18	77,909	29,165	21,320	18,430	29,355	28,580	8,077	68,945	56,993	6,748	5,930	5,753
Rhode Island												
Congressional District 1	43,066	14,925	9,618	8,806	10,429	14,062	8,581	38,550	34,124	12,113	5,559	6,125
Congressional District 2	48,569	17,156	10,548	9,109	13,502	15,976	6,074	44,890	35,961	10,029	5,702	7,098
South Carolina												
Congressional District 1	57,043	30,044	16,205	15,585	22,962	16,460	7,055	72,160	42,990	6,130	5,295	3,619
Congressional District 2	58,776	24,260	12,673	11,479	17,188	13,664	8,678	56,771	36,288	7,662	4,747	4,002
Congressional District 3	49,450	19,853	11,756	12,013	23,211	17,601	16,154	67,765	42,546	10,225	7,009	6,111
Congressional District 4	53,886	18,420	10,870	11,406	19,649	16,236	11,130	57,636	39,661	10,417	6,923	4,863
Congressional District 5	48,760	21,169	10,457	12,061	18,226	13,174	13,819	63,753	38,065	10,764	9,665	4,911
Congressional District 6	42,625	19,295	11,541	10,940	14,113	9,211	12,223	55,277	33,855	12,278	10,160	8,559
Congressional District 7	50,817	26,785	14,176	15,772	24,506	14,732	14,853	78,035	43,672	13,858	8,627	6,283
South Dakota												
Congressional District (at Large)	69,981	16,499	9,840	22,121	27,720	29,374	7,588	65,443	53,884	7,658	7,409	7,123
Tennessee												
Congressional District 1	53,533	20,152	12,018	15,468	27,224	21,413	15,843	77,714	50,824	12,623	10,762	7,934
Congressional District 2	57,650	22,564	12,563	14,636	25,053	19,056	12,615	69,015	45,602	10,988	7,389	6,288
Congressional District 3	60,274	22,761	13,684	14,337	27,003	20,603	15,780	68,390	47,552	11,799	9,644	7,969
Congressional District 4	53,274	19,159	10,395	12,581	23,280	16,183	11,528	62,577	38,899	10,554	8,125	7,108
Congressional District 5	51,538	18,017	10,656	13,392	12,616	11,798	8,275	46,638	33,528	10,493	7,400	4,573
Congressional District 6	54,687	22,093	12,610	15,158	24,562	16,855	12,498	74,826	45,852	10,019	8,761	5,968
Congressional District 7	50,876	18,414	9,843	14,131	18,644	14,514	10,043	59,723	38,059	9,188	8,358	5,050
Congressional District 8	60,382	21,489	12,487	15,172	20,980	19,278	10,183	63,133	41,940	7,600	6,231	5,611
Congressional District 9	45,595	14,923	10,596	8,308	11,215	10,102	11,356	40,723	28,765	14,837	7,125	6,557
Texas												
Congressional District 1	45,351	20,316	14,391	12,755	19,840	17,064	10,609	59,049	45,917	6,936	6,454	5,581
Congressional District 2	62,047	18,298	7,917	10,780	8,858	6,333	4,485	43,352	25,153	5,579	2,972	3,535
Congressional District 3	63,158	19,344	7,865	12,107	13,796	8,909	3,200	44,865	24,973	1,693	2,942	2,277
Congressional District 4	55,871	21,346	13,194	12,577	19,401	13,048	11,560	63,571	44,508	7,063	6,423	5,415
Congressional District 5	45,282	16,253	11,146	11,085	15,072	12,950	9,489	52,646	35,177	7,880	5,322	3,819
Congressional District 6	56,827	17,077	10,529	12,145	10,823	8,256	5,059	43,962	27,257	5,320	3,377	1,811
Congressional District 7	62,424	17,649	9,138	11,840	11,883	11,674	3,683	36,755	30,473	3,892	3,235	3,054
Congressional District 8	58,416	20,409	12,047	11,172	15,328	10,075	6,982	55,401	34,719	6,195	4,796	3,588
Congressional District 9	41,461	14,102	5,617	8,367	6,423	5,580	6,519	36,978	21,888	12,071	9,512	7,329
Congressional District 10	59,513	22,313	12,113	13,939	14,273	11,184	5,962	50,867	30,665	4,773	3,310	3,631
Congressional District 11	52,228	22,347	16,204	13,600	17,391	17,311	7,372	58,468	47,433	7,440	6,183	5,664
Congressional District 12	53,427	18,994	12,449	10,392	10,831	10,775	6,278	50,560	35,998	5,826	4,717	4,045
Congressional District 13	52,133	17,727	12,783	11,448	18,171	17,094	7,334	52,698	42,235	7,081	5,316	5,481
Congressional District 14	53,680	19,216	13,807	10,745	12,845	12,767	8,256	50,052	36,705	8,861	4,820	3,803
Congressional District 15	27,018	11,388	6,053	11,368	7,956	6,483	5,541	42,952	30,602	5,847	15,414	11,299
Congressional District 16	30,117	9,358	5,264	9,041	6,044	6,201	7,954	40,134	35,727	8,493	10,890	12,145
Congressional District 17	47,107	18,091	12,627	10,903	14,861	13,128	6,697	45,067	32,548	6,506	5,233	4,466
Congressional District 18	34,798	10,065	6,145	6,372	6,170	5,883	8,035	36,665	25,374	13,358	7,104	6,520
Congressional District 19	43,340	18,684	12,120	12,196	12,807	13,517	7,111	48,711	40,051	6,319	5,565	5,536
Congressional District 20	36,928	14,335	8,059	10,880	7,123	6,946	9,294	41,233	31,141	9,924	7,065	7,060
Congressional District 21	61,841	28,151	18,631	16,707	19,879	14,261	7,405	63,217	46,025	5,271	3,087	4,569
Congressional District 22	66,983	21,105	9,716	13,309	10,090	7,374	4,424	43,911	27,582	4,380	3,784	4,715
Congressional District 23	37,252	14,848	6,833	9,485	10,078	6,329	8,091	51,968	32,994	8,514	12,098	8,666
Congressional District 24	56,846	16,977	7,523	12,784	11,825	10,314	3,672	41,322	28,157	3,419	2,436	2,895
Congressional District 25	55,720	23,355	12,430	13,693	16,000	12,251	7,442	53,058	34,090	5,605	3,235	4,137
Congressional District 26	53,546	18,411	7,246	11,514	12,267	6,465	5,205	44,789	22,344	3,739	4,119	2,422
Congressional District 27	53,583	17,552	11,240	10,857	15,319	12,624	9,497	57,120	40,794	8,557	9,115	7,411
Congressional District 28	29,322	9,438	5,835	6,531	9,092	8,059	9,116	41,535	29,591	9,330	9,335	10,341
Congressional District 29	29,258	6,958	3,185	4,672	5,770	3,954	6,390	31,971	20,977	12,749	7,223	7,839
Congressional District 30	37,750	13,074	6,217	9,567	6,995	5,846	11,181	37,054	25,210	13,362	6,773	6,883
Congressional District 31	48,820	21,322	10,141	11,398	14,855	8,897	7,532	48,839	30,404	5,818	4,599	5,297
Congressional District 32	55,042	17,781	9,902	14,847	14,021	12,267	5,782	46,755	33,853	6,007	4,576	4,171
Congressional District 33	25,748	6,805	3,798	6,377	5,587	5,068	7,606	29,837	21,344	11,327	7,223	5,917

Table I-5: 114th Congressional Districts—Persons With Health Insurance by Source of Insurance—*Continued*

	Private Health Insurance Coverage						Public Health Insurance Coverage					
	Employer Based			Direct Purchase			Medicare			Medicaid/CHIP		
	55 to 64 Years	65 to 74 Years	75 Years and Over	55 to 64 Years	65 to 74 Years	75 Years and Over	55 to 64 Years	65 to 74 Years	75 Years and Over	55 to 64 Years	65 to 74 Years	75 Years and Over
Texas—Cont.												
Congressional District 34	27,600	10,855	7,336	6,971	10,102	8,934	8,028	46,695	39,710	8,962	14,246	12,811
Congressional District 35	36,437	11,279	6,065	8,194	5,747	5,524	10,542	36,454	25,916	12,101	7,689	6,213
Congressional District 36	59,228	19,745	9,774	10,222	16,902	10,796	10,211	56,486	33,718	8,402	4,774	3,486
Utah												
Congressional District 1	47,476	16,995	10,898	10,821	11,532	10,725	5,143	39,346	29,151	3,648	2,798	2,412
Congressional District 2	42,718	17,119	12,987	11,669	15,550	12,427	6,884	47,640	33,723	5,613	5,055	3,647
Congressional District 3	49,095	13,597	10,281	9,980	11,462	10,720	2,956	36,606	28,332	3,151	2,415	2,926
Congressional District 4	46,741	15,179	9,619	8,142	11,889	9,448	4,487	37,774	27,439	4,791	2,851	2,962
Vermont												
Congressional District (at Large)	59,469	21,670	11,684	13,291	20,952	18,693	9,914	59,825	41,268	17,564	7,937	7,271
Virginia												
Congressional District 1	61,486	28,131	15,680	12,617	17,582	14,398	6,276	59,813	40,062	3,514	3,601	3,903
Congressional District 2	51,261	21,592	12,474	12,070	15,738	12,642	7,199	51,766	36,844	3,862	4,140	3,312
Congressional District 3	49,180	16,524	10,367	10,437	14,196	13,875	9,957	48,246	36,908	8,439	7,105	5,903
Congressional District 4	62,646	25,065	12,308	11,678	17,591	12,110	8,555	58,168	33,339	5,772	4,110	4,119
Congressional District 5	62,656	25,478	13,010	18,792	30,471	23,953	12,974	74,610	53,268	6,760	6,344	8,006
Congressional District 6	63,291	21,494	14,333	16,286	28,159	23,780	8,690	67,789	52,431	6,160	6,045	5,899
Congressional District 7	74,276	32,870	18,650	15,012	22,621	16,733	7,534	63,429	44,022	3,392	3,456	3,041
Congressional District 8	62,627	29,059	15,950	13,593	9,912	7,658	2,757	42,743	28,649	2,405	3,232	3,902
Congressional District 9	54,276	22,909	13,813	15,248	25,725	25,169	20,011	74,354	53,126	12,485	8,061	7,115
Congressional District 10	68,608	27,360	11,338	15,444	13,884	10,016	2,319	49,044	29,106	1,271	3,050	3,157
Congressional District 11	65,334	27,360	13,532	12,337	10,901	7,906	2,912	41,541	28,470	2,314	3,016	4,179
Washington												
Congressional District 1	63,357	19,671	9,686	17,438	20,347	12,526	5,399	51,211	30,369	7,978	4,942	4,111
Congressional District 2	57,971	19,117	12,576	14,577	19,739	17,044	6,707	60,976	40,727	10,391	6,821	6,098
Congressional District 3	57,366	22,351	13,983	14,340	24,420	18,062	10,179	65,094	41,582	12,211	6,730	5,951
Congressional District 4	48,394	16,252	9,032	10,325	18,655	13,368	7,150	50,961	34,439	11,008	5,675	5,578
Congressional District 5	52,658	21,611	12,876	14,101	18,659	16,913	10,402	59,331	41,910	13,914	6,673	4,752
Congressional District 6	59,849	27,484	16,166	15,996	23,963	20,429	10,545	69,696	45,218	12,614	7,342	5,683
Congressional District 7	58,359	21,941	13,218	13,888	16,933	15,083	6,305	50,484	36,079	10,903	4,750	5,378
Congressional District 8	64,676	19,697	11,230	12,405	16,783	13,627	6,412	47,718	32,523	7,916	4,637	3,877
Congressional District 9	51,806	16,518	10,583	11,152	13,416	14,084	6,331	45,821	39,339	10,983	8,152	7,173
Congressional District 10	50,689	20,546	12,360	11,782	14,815	13,238	10,053	53,869	36,997	12,747	5,961	4,803
West Virginia												
Congressional District 1	56,476	26,882	19,232	9,557	16,148	14,616	11,570	59,944	42,963	12,642	6,257	4,875
Congressional District 2	56,934	28,579	20,435	8,752	15,918	13,198	12,276	60,869	42,888	15,862	5,022	4,647
Congressional District 3	50,782	29,725	18,706	7,134	15,224	9,675	20,821	63,533	44,424	17,847	9,635	5,622
Wisconsin												
Congressional District 1	69,501	24,255	17,589	12,892	20,460	17,667	9,263	56,767	43,132	8,737	5,820	5,340
Congressional District 2	69,294	23,830	13,832	13,409	20,655	18,253	5,896	53,767	38,632	8,484	4,542	4,809
Congressional District 3	63,045	17,657	12,334	15,393	28,116	25,476	7,703	61,778	47,877	8,905	7,652	8,218
Congressional District 4	43,662	15,403	12,162	8,087	9,198	9,493	9,668	39,599	33,416	16,785	7,518	6,645
Congressional District 5	74,413	23,948	15,744	14,465	17,801	22,952	7,940	59,376	51,155	6,363	4,014	5,698
Congressional District 6	71,507	18,432	12,591	15,593	24,959	26,448	7,103	61,309	50,709	8,324	5,572	5,574
Congressional District 7	69,019	17,851	10,694	19,897	32,274	28,492	9,314	70,971	54,127	11,044	6,712	8,010
Congressional District 8	67,782	12,310	10,592	14,775	23,826	23,834	8,271	59,959	45,121	9,031	4,316	5,677
Wyoming												
Congressional District (at Large)	51,722	14,679	7,014	13,470	16,596	14,175	4,731	45,320	29,333	6,127	4,598	4,364

PART J
HOUSING SUMMARY

HOUSING SUMMARY

As the Baby Boom entered its household formation years in the late 1960's and 1970's, housing development grew to accommodate the growing adult population and their children. The Baby Boomers are now between the ages of 52 and 70 and their housing needs are changing. Senior residences take a number of forms from independent living apartments to full nursing care, often right within the same residential complex. Virtually every community has seen the development of some type of senior living arrangement. This generation grew up in an era of homeownership and many have the resources for seasonal and second homes. As they age, there will be changes in the market forces affecting housing markets both for primary residences and second homes. A challenge in the market will be location. Will the growing inventory of homes for sale be in the same locations as the demand from younger generations?

Nationwide, 78.2 percent of householders 65 and over are home owners while 21.8 percent are renters. Of the home owners, 32.5 percent are still paying on a mortgage. Home ownership is highest in West Virginia where 85.7 percent are owners but only one in four (24.6 percent) are still paying on a mortgage. In 43 states the percentage of home owners among householders 65 and over is greater than 75 percent. The District of Columbia has the lowest ownership rate at 64.3 percent and therefore the highest rental rate at 35.7 percent. They also have the highest percent of owners with a mortgage (49.2 percent). North Dakota has the lowest percentage of mortgage holders at 17.7 percent.

The American Community Survey also obtains data on whether meals are included in the rent for rental occupied units. This is often used as a measurement of congregate housing within the housing inventory. Renters in continuing care or life facilities are included here if their contracts cover meal services. Nationwide, 11.2 percent

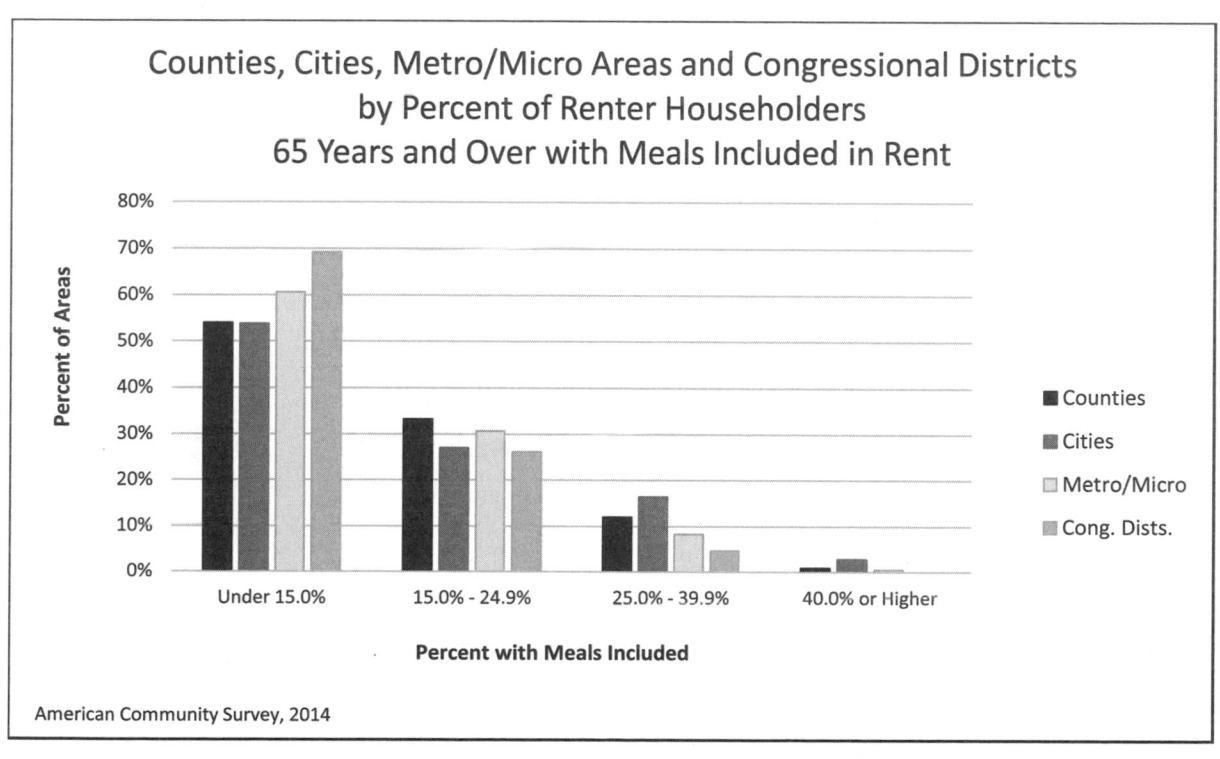

Counties, Cities, Metro/Micro Areas and Congressional Districts by Percent of Renter Householders 65 Years and Over with Meals Included in Rent

American Community Survey, 2014

of renter households have meals included in their rent. This varies from a low of 3.6 percent in New York to a high of 24.8 percent in Oregon.

The nation's Consumer Expenditure Survey shows that housing accounts for about 33 percent of consumer units (roughly households) total expenditures and only slightly higher (33.9 percent) for households age 65 and over. Housing becomes a larger share of expenditures for the 75 and over who spend 36.5 percent.[1] The Census obtains data on owner and renter affordability of housing based on a measure of owner or renter costs as a percentage of income. When a household spends more than 35 percent of its income on housing costs it is considered a housing cost burden. Using this basis, 27.0 percent of owner householders 65 and over pay more than 35 percent on housing costs and would be considered to have a cost burden. For renters, 55.1 percent pay more than 35 percent of their income for rental costs nationwide. New Jersey has the highest owner cost burden at 41.6 percent while California has the highest percentage of householders with renter cost burden at 62.8 percent. West Virginia ranks lowest on both owner and renter costs at 15.5 percent and 33.7 percent, respectively.

---

1. U.S. Bureau of Labor Statistics, Consumer Expenditures, 2014, www.bls.gov/cex/2014/combined/age.pdf.

Coryell County, Texas has the highest percentage of owner occupied units at 95.4 percent. At 27.7 percent, Bronx County, New York has the lowest percent of home owners among the 65 and over population. Almost 86.1 percent of counties represented here have home ownership rates over 75 percent. Prince George's County, Maryland has the highest percentage of home owners who still have a mortgage at 63.8 percent. Lafourche Parish, Louisiana is lowest at 11.0 percent. Polk County, Oregon has the highest percentage of householders 65 and over with meals included in their rent at 70.5 percent. This is often an indicator of large senior community residences. In six counties the percent of renters with meals included is less than 1 percent: Kings, Niagara, and Queens County, New York; Davidson County, North Carolina; Angelina and Hidalgo County, Texas. More than half (52.6 percent) of owners in Hudson County, New Jersey pay 35 percent or more of income on housing costs while McKinley County, New Mexico is lowest at 7.4 percent. For renters, Umatilla County, Oregon has the highest percentage of cost burden households at 88.2 percent while Blount County, Tennessee is lowest at 16.0 percent.

Missouri, Texas is the city with the highest percentage (97.9 percent) of householders 65 and over who are home owners. At 72.1 percent, Union City, New Jersey has the highest percentage of renter householders. New York City by far has the largest absolute number of renter

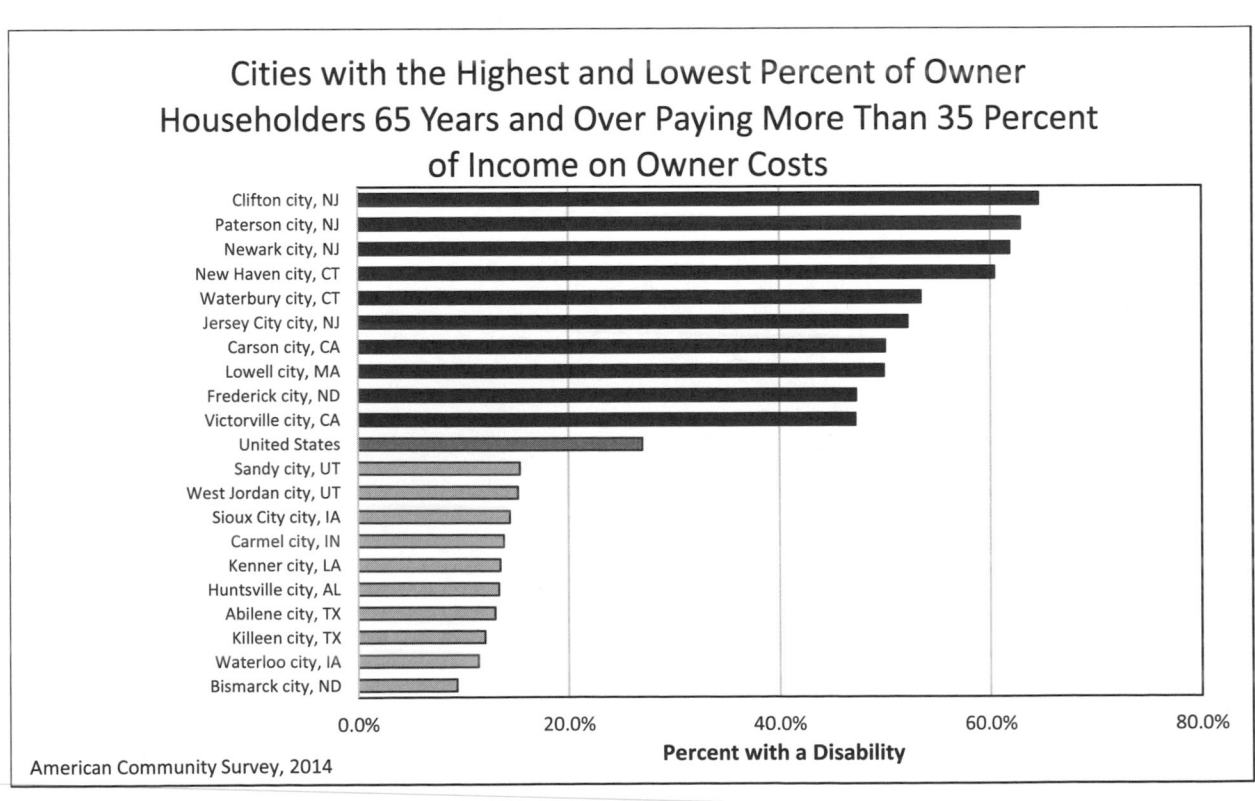

Cities with the Highest and Lowest Percent of Owner Householders 65 Years and Over Paying More Than 35 Percent of Income on Owner Costs

American Community Survey, 2014

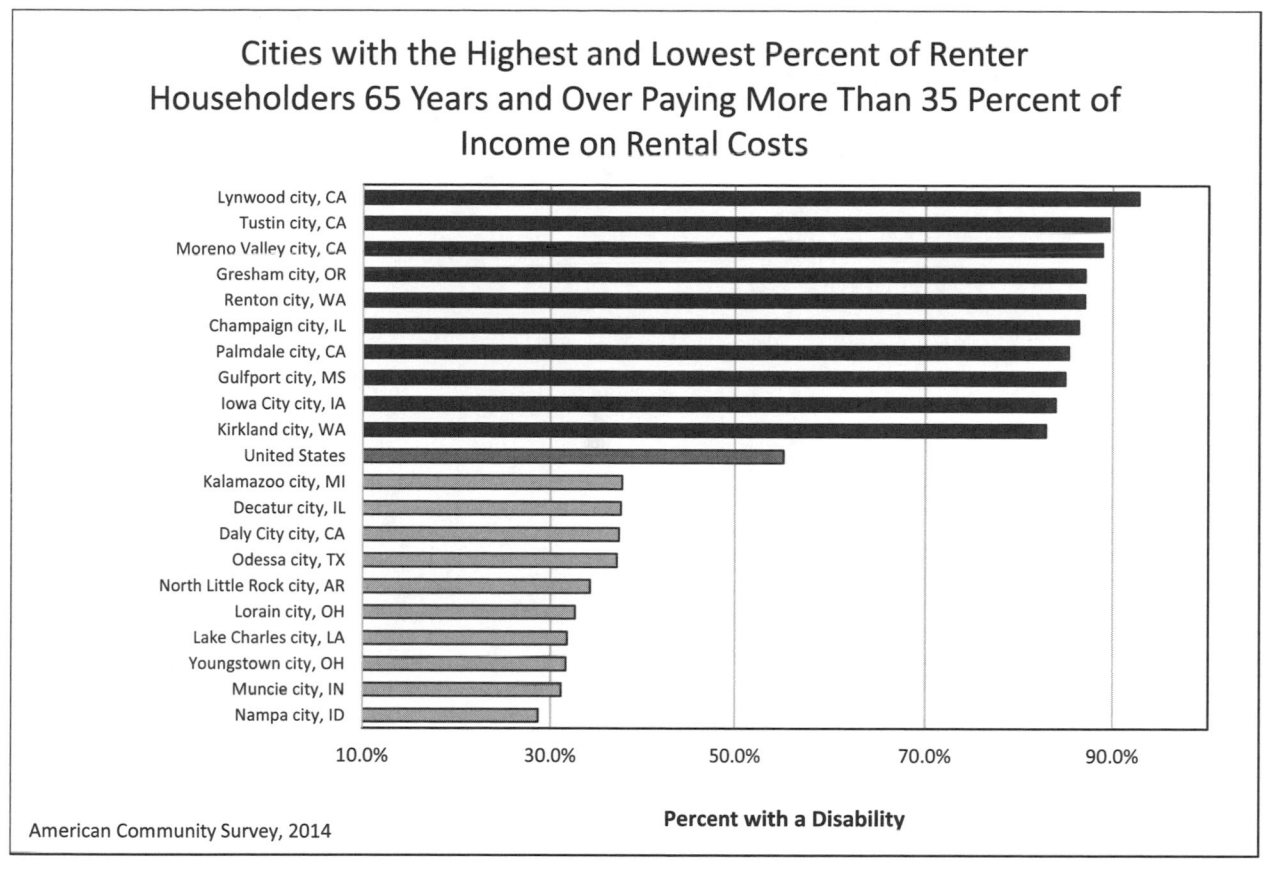

Cities with the Highest and Lowest Percent of Renter Householders 65 Years and Over Paying More Than 35 Percent of Income on Rental Costs

American Community Survey, 2014

Percent with a Disability

householders with 392,500 and more than three times the next largest (Los Angeles) at 113,000. Only 19 cities have fewer than 50 percent owner occupied householders over 65. In Parris, California 77.6 percent of owner occupied households have a mortgage and in 112 cities, more than 50 percent of homeowners still pay on a mortgage. Medford, Oregon is the city with the highest percentage (57.5 percent) of rental households with meals included in the rent. Clifton, New Jersey is the city with the highest percent (64.6 percent) of homeowners paying more than 35 percent of their incomes for housing costs. Newark and Paterson, New Jersey also have more than 60 percent of homeowners in that category and these New Jersey cities are the only ones above 60 percent. In Lynwood, California more than 92.7 percent of rental householders pay more than 35 percent of their income on rental costs.

The range between the highest and lowest homeownership rate at the metropolitan level is less than that for counties and cities. The lowest rate is 55 percent found in the El Centro, California metropolitan area while the highest, at 94.0 percent, is in The Villages, Florida metro area. Seventy-eight metropolitan and micropolitan areas have ownership rates over 85 percent.

In the Vallejo-Fairfield, California metropolitan area, 57.6 percent of owner householders still pay on their mortgage while only 12.4 percent still hold mortgages in the Lufkin, Texas micropolitan area. In the Atlantic City-Hammonton, New Jersey metropolitan area, 46.1 percent of owner householders pay more than 35 percent of their incomes on housing costs. In the Gallup, New Mexico micro area only 7.4 percent have that cost burden. For renters, the Burlington, North Carolina metro is highest at 76.7 percent and in 280 metro and micro areas, more than 50 percent of renters are burdened by rental costs.

Florida's 11th Congressional District has the highest home ownership rate at 89.7 percent among householders 65 and over though more than one-third (37 percent) are currently paying on a mortgage. In New York's 13th Congressional District renters dominate with only 9.2 percent of older householders owning their home. Of those that do own, 32.4 percent still hold a mortgage. The homeownership rate for householders over 65 exceeds 75 percent in 328 congressional districts. In 28 districts more than 50 percent of the owner householders have a mortgage to pay and 19 of them are in California. In 55 congressional districts, more than 20 percent of all renter householders have meals included in their rent payment. More than half of all congressional districts (260) have more than 25 percent of older householders experiencing an owner cost burden in relation to their income. It's highest in New Jersey's 8th Congressional District at 56.1 percent and lowest in West Virginia's 1st District at 14.6 percent. The rental cost burden is highest in the 19th Congressional District of California where nearly three-quarters (72.7 percent) of rental householders pay more than 35 percent of their income in rental costs.

Percent of Owner Householders 65 Years and Over Paying 35 Percent or More of Income on Owner Costs

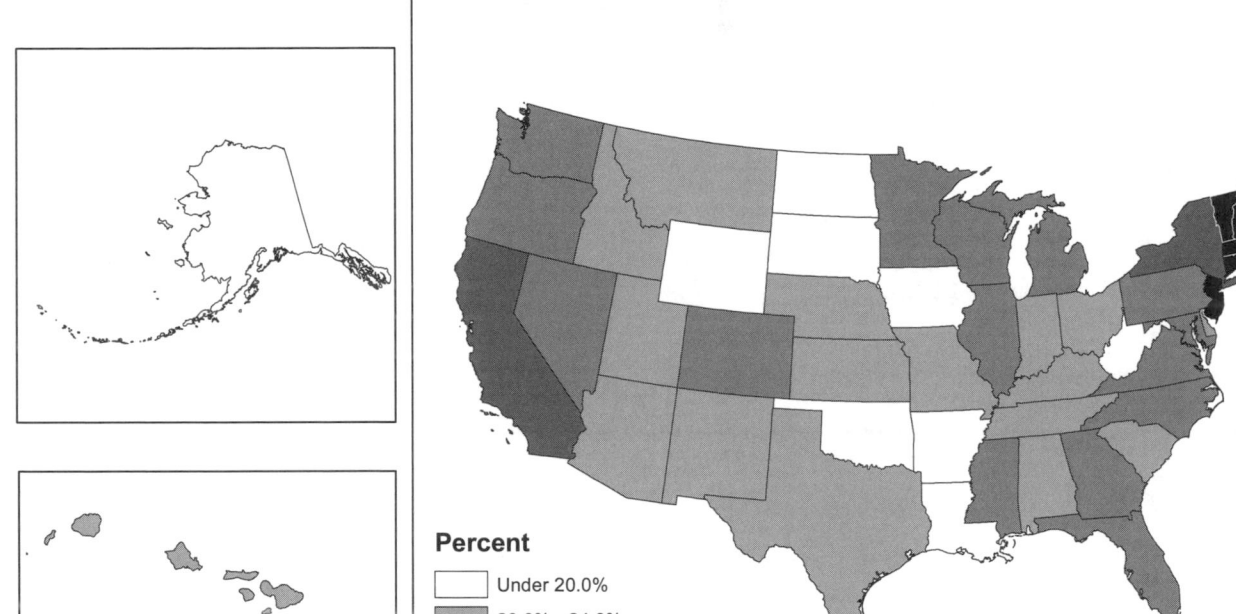

Percent
- Under 20.0%
- 20.0% - 24.9%
- 25.0% - 29.9%
- 30.0% - 34.9%
- 35.0% or Higher

Table J-1: States—Summary of Housing and Householder Characteristics

| | | | | Householders 65 Years and Over | | | | |
| | | | | Owner Householders | | | | |
	Total Housing Units	Total Households	Owner Occupied	Renter Occupied	With a Mortgage	Without a Mortgage	Renter Households With Meals Included in Rent	Percent of Owner Householders Who Pay 35% or More of income for Housing Costs	Percent of Renter Households Who Pay 35% or More of Income for Rental Costs
United States	133,962,970	28,146,157	22,000,455	6,145,702	8,003,888	13,996,567	689,296	27.0%	55.1%
Alabama	2,208,030	472,668	393,705	78,963	128,097	265,608	6,931	22.7%	47.3%
Alaska	308,571	40,996	33,825	7,171	12,610	21,215	316	18.0%	49.1%
Arizona	2,909,336	647,612	523,426	124,186	221,463	301,963	18,233	24.1%	54.5%
Arkansas	1,341,081	289,802	238,953	50,849	69,174	169,779	3,662	19.7%	42.5%
California	13,901,594	2,830,348	2,062,710	767,638	985,985	1,076,725	73,883	32.3%	62.8%
Colorado	2,276,280	418,629	333,729	84,900	145,883	187,846	15,427	26.1%	58.9%
Connecticut	1,493,632	339,658	258,586	81,072	101,794	156,792	9,629	38.4%	54.4%
Delaware	417,413	92,377	78,399	13,978	33,752	44,647	1,514	24.8%	57.5%
District of Columbia	306,184	50,463	32,424	18,039	15,941	16,483	1,701	26.6%	54.3%
Florida	9,144,650	2,223,738	1,825,060	398,678	655,123	1,169,937	48,549	28.2%	59.3%
Georgia	4,151,387	750,454	597,577	152,877	237,958	359,619	14,439	25.8%	53.7%
Hawaii	530,118	122,744	93,653	29,091	42,757	50,896	2,275	26.4%	52.8%
Idaho	685,098	144,224	119,797	24,427	46,046	73,751	5,000	21.9%	51.2%
Illinois	5,307,508	1,105,546	873,826	231,720	296,235	577,591	30,189	29.1%	54.4%
Indiana	2,829,630	585,693	481,204	104,489	189,991	291,213	12,271	21.2%	50.8%
Iowa	1,362,034	310,729	251,378	59,351	64,327	187,051	10,901	19.5%	48.1%
Kansas	1,248,861	260,361	207,737	52,624	60,554	147,183	10,307	21.2%	52.3%
Kentucky	1,950,504	413,817	337,113	76,704	108,498	228,615	6,037	22.1%	48.4%
Louisiana	2,011,037	395,166	323,141	72,025	81,560	241,581	4,262	19.8%	49.4%
Maine	727,693	151,281	121,998	29,283	40,590	81,408	2,093	28.4%	51.4%
Maryland	2,422,317	495,982	386,302	109,680	177,542	208,760	13,210	29.1%	56.4%
Massachusetts	2,828,592	624,797	452,333	172,464	173,734	278,599	16,233	35.1%	53.9%
Michigan	4,540,088	969,176	794,640	174,536	280,282	514,358	21,976	25.6%	54.7%
Minnesota	2,385,261	486,149	382,770	103,379	131,479	251,291	21,180	25.6%	56.7%
Mississippi	1,294,738	273,148	228,869	44,279	62,896	165,973	3,130	25.2%	44.7%
Missouri	2,735,803	584,979	472,369	112,610	162,718	309,651	13,175	24.2%	48.1%
Montana	491,515	106,654	86,510	20,144	24,492	62,018	3,663	23.0%	49.1%
Nebraska	814,957	173,986	136,297	37,689	38,112	98,185	8,513	21.7%	47.0%
Nevada	1,198,969	235,135	171,990	63,145	84,518	87,472	4,196	28.6%	58.3%
New Hampshire	619,865	123,515	97,293	26,222	34,176	63,117	2,515	35.3%	54.8%
New Jersey	3,591,847	783,199	585,541	197,658	227,383	358,158	15,953	41.6%	57.5%
New Mexico	912,910	199,105	164,711	34,394	58,720	105,991	2,718	23.0%	52.5%
New York	8,191,528	1,776,118	1,146,511	629,607	384,353	762,158	22,650	34.4%	58.0%
North Carolina	4,452,464	908,096	734,015	174,081	285,055	448,960	18,590	25.3%	49.8%
North Dakota	350,534	67,092	49,706	17,386	8,782	40,924	2,892	16.0%	49.3%
Ohio	5,147,282	1,142,958	908,129	234,829	338,507	569,622	27,571	24.2%	52.0%
Oklahoma	1,699,556	351,005	289,154	61,851	82,321	206,833	7,805	19.3%	46.3%
Oregon	1,700,611	392,764	298,784	93,980	122,098	176,686	23,297	28.6%	61.3%
Pennsylvania	5,590,712	1,321,941	1,021,956	299,985	310,366	711,590	38,851	27.6%	52.8%
Rhode Island	462,630	102,237	71,248	30,989	29,469	41,779	2,017	32.7%	51.7%
South Carolina	2,188,258	475,305	403,875	71,430	146,193	257,682	9,411	23.9%	47.8%
South Dakota	376,347	82,186	62,590	19,596	13,547	49,043	3,037	19.5%	41.6%
Tennessee	2,869,419	613,436	506,859	106,577	161,363	345,496	10,691	22.3%	46.6%
Texas	10,426,760	1,843,597	1,470,592	373,005	428,037	1,042,555	43,074	22.8%	55.1%
Utah	1,022,593	175,745	147,730	28,015	56,442	91,288	5,570	21.3%	53.0%
Vermont	325,774	67,260	52,680	14,580	18,377	34,303	2,001	36.8%	52.9%
Virginia	3,446,585	702,308	570,833	131,475	235,320	335,513	19,995	25.0%	54.4%
Washington	2,963,293	605,828	468,132	137,696	191,677	276,455	26,959	26.8%	59.8%
West Virginia	884,574	211,788	181,500	30,288	44,596	136,904	1,154	15.5%	33.7%
Wisconsin	2,648,342	552,831	425,585	127,246	140,339	285,246	18,552	28.5%	56.4%
Wyoming	268,205	51,531	42,710	8,821	12,656	30,054	1,081	18.4%	40.2%

Table J-2: Counties—Summary of Housing and Householder Characteristics

| | | | | | Householders 65 Years and Over | | | | |
| | | | | | Owner Householders | | | | |
	Total Housing Units	Total Households	Owner Occupied	Renter Occupied	With a Mortgage	Without a Mortgage	Renter Households With Meals Included in Rent	Percent of Owner Householders Who Pay 35% or More of income for Housing Costs	Percent of Renter Households Who Pay 35% or More of Income for Rental Costs
Alabama									
Baldwin County	107,384	23,509	19,870	3,639	7,827	12,043	605	26.0%	48.6%
Calhoun County	53,287	11,702	10,107	1,595	3,130	6,977	86	25.5%	40.1%
Cullman County	37,144	8,705	7,417	1,288	2,438	4,979	232	28.7%	na
DeKalb County	31,044	7,047	5,686	1,361	1,463	4,223	na	na	na
Elmore County	33,320	7,218	6,286	932	2,714	3,572	na	19.4%	na
Etowah County	47,502	11,562	9,586	1,976	2,673	6,913	216	na	39.3%
Houston County	46,455	10,400	8,779	1,621	2,566	6,213	99	19.6%	45.4%
Jefferson County	305,055	62,053	51,125	10,928	20,894	30,231	2,026	27.6%	58.6%
Lauderdale County	44,348	11,076	8,944	2,132	2,156	6,788	na	16.0%	33.5%
Lee County	65,570	10,631	8,331	2,300	2,588	5,743	230	13.1%	67.3%
Limestone County	35,451	7,272	6,669	603	1,683	4,986	na	16.1%	na
Madison County	154,464	30,351	25,459	4,892	9,374	16,085	718	17.6%	63.6%
Marshall County	40,333	8,968	7,408	1,560	1,387	6,021	na	20.6%	49.8%
Mobile County	181,618	37,513	30,242	7,271	11,029	19,213	431	25.6%	50.9%
Montgomery County	103,434	20,165	16,498	3,667	7,677	8,821	257	24.0%	53.1%
Morgan County	51,500	11,989	9,018	2,971	2,401	6,617	612	13.9%	48.0%
Shelby County	83,495	16,635	14,577	2,058	6,788	7,789	477	27.9%	51.2%
St. Clair County	35,850	8,466	7,327	1,139	2,438	4,889	na	28.5%	na
Talladega County	37,175	7,759	6,641	1,118	1,798	4,843	na	26.5%	52.1%
Tuscaloosa County	87,795	14,352	11,764	2,588	4,259	7,505	299	19.7%	40.7%
Walker County	30,673	7,720	6,600	1,120	1,553	5,047	na	na	na
Alaska									
Anchorage Municipality	114,320	14,870	12,684	2,186	5,440	7,244	na	16.1%	56.7%
Fairbanks North Star Borough	41,690	5,189	4,431	758	1,851	2,580	na	15.6%	57.7%
Matanuska-Susitna Borough	41,311	5,232	4,236	996	1,644	2,592	na	24.8%	48.1%
Arizona									
Apache County	32,657	5,612	5,135	477	986	4,149	na	10.1%	na
Cochise County	60,506	15,100	12,419	2,681	5,157	7,262	na	26.0%	43.5%
Coconino County	64,215	9,700	8,444	1,256	2,986	5,458	107	24.4%	41.6%
Maricopa County	1,680,184	337,926	266,546	71,380	120,389	146,157	12,269	25.4%	56.5%
Mohave County	112,307	32,387	27,871	4,516	11,960	15,911	228	23.4%	50.2%
Navajo County	57,407	10,706	9,218	1,488	2,345	6,873	na	19.5%	42.9%
Pima County	448,835	112,162	88,024	24,138	38,183	49,841	4,151	22.1%	53.8%
Pinal County	165,714	41,068	36,018	5,050	15,400	20,618	210	25.2%	38.8%
Yavapai County	112,534	38,908	32,271	6,637	13,198	19,073	704	25.6%	62.5%
Yuma County	89,909	22,044	18,589	3,455	5,458	13,131	276	19.6%	43.0%
Arkansas									
Benton County	97,543	18,489	15,582	2,907	5,561	10,021	258	23.4%	40.4%
Craighead County	43,308	8,000	6,282	1,718	2,691	3,591	na	13.3%	30.7%
Faulkner County	48,848	7,644	6,517	1,127	1,956	4,561	na	12.4%	32.6%
Garland County	50,555	13,006	10,599	2,407	3,075	7,524	485	16.3%	63.0%
Jefferson County	33,235	6,951	5,863	1,088	1,998	3,865	na	28.8%	31.8%
Lonoke County	28,627	5,881	4,513	1,368	2,056	2,457	na	na	31.4%
Pulaski County	181,434	33,031	25,089	7,942	9,626	15,463	737	19.5%	52.1%
Saline County	46,697	11,194	9,592	1,602	3,085	6,507	na	15.5%	na
Sebastian County	56,039	12,077	10,049	2,028	2,501	7,548	186	23.8%	40.3%
Washington County	89,767	15,798	12,223	3,575	3,898	8,325	393	28.6%	55.0%
White County	33,198	7,197	6,193	1,004	1,567	4,626	na	na	33.6%
California									
Alameda County	592,393	115,959	81,271	34,688	40,398	40,873	3,078	30.3%	62.0%
Butte County	97,491	22,765	18,796	3,969	6,880	11,916	411	21.4%	65.5%
Contra Costa County	406,792	90,887	72,265	18,622	35,810	36,455	3,017	29.8%	63.6%
El Dorado County	88,871	19,247	17,442	1,805	9,611	7,831	289	36.9%	36.6%
Fresno County	324,158	61,609	45,048	16,561	20,265	24,783	1,208	29.6%	59.7%
Humboldt County	62,329	12,469	9,681	2,788	3,287	6,394	192	24.9%	32.1%
Imperial County	56,963	10,308	5,667	4,641	2,476	3,191	142	24.7%	47.0%
Kern County	291,469	49,947	37,090	12,857	16,013	21,077	592	26.0%	63.0%
Kings County	44,872	7,781	6,261	1,520	2,361	3,900	na	18.7%	69.9%
Lake County	35,659	8,588	7,481	1,107	2,223	5,258	na	na	na
Los Angeles County	3,482,681	676,487	438,945	237,542	219,598	219,347	13,256	35.0%	65.4%
Madera County	49,893	10,815	9,013	1,802	4,320	4,693	na	35.3%	32.5%
Marin County	112,308	32,293	24,372	7,921	12,827	11,545	1,537	31.1%	65.7%
Mendocino County	40,719	10,713	7,619	3,094	3,153	4,466	560	35.7%	48.7%
Merced County	84,180	16,007	11,547	4,460	5,223	6,324	233	32.8%	45.1%
Monterey County	140,143	30,238	23,049	7,189	10,806	12,243	689	30.8%	58.1%
Napa County	55,322	14,395	11,888	2,507	5,586	6,302	526	31.3%	53.1%
Nevada County	53,083	13,350	11,967	1,383	5,984	5,983	368	31.6%	61.0%
Orange County	1,072,078	233,783	179,872	53,911	89,336	90,536	6,690	33.4%	66.2%
Placer County	157,477	39,994	32,442	7,552	16,384	16,058	1,826	31.9%	65.1%
Riverside County	820,011	171,808	137,607	34,201	64,500	73,107	3,290	33.7%	64.5%
Sacramento County	561,905	111,627	81,060	30,567	39,841	41,219	4,147	30.3%	60.4%
San Bernardino County	708,364	116,634	88,824	27,810	44,141	44,683	2,280	35.1%	61.7%
San Diego County	1,187,693	234,218	173,630	60,588	83,094	90,536	7,746	33.8%	64.2%

Table J-2: Counties—Summary of Housing and Householder Characteristics—*Continued*

	Total Housing Units	Total Households	Owner Occupied	Renter Occupied	Householders 65 Years and Over		Renter Households With Meals Included in Rent	Percent of Owner Householders Who Pay 35% or More of income for Housing Costs	Percent of Renter Households Who Pay 35% or More of Income for Rental Costs
					Owner Householders				
					With a Mortgage	Without a Mortgage			
California—Cont.									
San Francisco County	386,610	73,562	39,294	34,268	16,438	22,856	1,836	28.4%	55.5%
San Joaquin County	237,547	44,199	32,376	11,823	14,765	17,611	1,675	30.9%	61.7%
San Luis Obispo County	119,138	29,273	23,642	5,631	12,561	11,081	593	30.5%	55.0%
San Mateo County	273,582	62,142	46,189	15,953	20,658	25,531	2,237	29.7%	64.7%
Santa Barbara County	154,414	37,459	28,123	9,336	13,347	14,776	1,700	32.6%	68.4%
Santa Clara County	651,171	123,457	90,327	33,130	39,934	50,393	4,490	30.0%	68.9%
Santa Cruz County	105,251	22,945	18,000	4,945	7,500	10,500	412	31.2%	74.0%
Shasta County	77,916	21,110	16,689	4,421	6,745	9,944	695	29.5%	66.3%
Solano County	154,997	33,203	25,817	7,386	14,862	10,955	656	32.4%	62.1%
Sonoma County	207,220	51,802	38,279	13,523	18,093	20,186	2,432	34.4%	55.9%
Stanislaus County	180,297	37,075	26,376	10,699	11,818	14,558	663	28.6%	63.8%
Sutter County	34,105	8,132	6,366	1,766	2,878	3,488	na	20.0%	45.5%
Tulare County	145,500	25,327	20,005	5,322	7,910	12,095	467	29.4%	43.8%
Ventura County	284,527	68,153	52,691	15,462	27,053	25,638	1,848	32.5%	55.2%
Yolo County	76,736	14,516	10,741	3,775	5,064	5,677	715	29.2%	61.3%
Yuba County	28,009	5,227	4,162	1,065	1,462	2,700	na	na	64.5%
Colorado									
Adams County	166,286	27,741	21,794	5,947	10,714	11,080	943	25.4%	56.5%
Arapahoe County	243,734	43,824	35,096	8,728	17,943	17,153	1,632	24.9%	60.9%
Boulder County	130,924	23,881	18,879	5,002	8,168	10,711	1,637	27.2%	56.3%
Denver County	298,880	47,806	32,515	15,291	14,074	18,441	1,874	26.8%	59.0%
Douglas County	113,806	18,561	15,502	3,059	7,822	7,680	935	29.7%	58.4%
El Paso County	262,160	46,007	38,088	7,919	17,056	21,032	2,545	25.5%	70.1%
Jefferson County	233,294	50,496	41,228	9,268	18,268	22,960	1,956	27.1%	61.8%
Larimer County	138,540	27,063	21,081	5,982	9,135	11,946	1,291	23.4%	61.5%
Mesa County	63,791	15,207	12,375	2,032	5,529	6,846	173	22.9%	63.1%
Pueblo County	70,071	17,236	13,665	3,571	6,275	7,390	189	32.1%	57.9%
Weld County	100,064	19,316	15,238	4,078	6,667	8,571	654	25.4%	61.6%
Connecticut									
Fairfield County	364,966	84,643	65,662	18,981	27,318	38,344	2,709	42.5%	55.3%
Hartford County	374,723	86,024	62,181	23,843	23,797	38,384	2,760	37.4%	56.0%
Litchfield County	87,413	20,304	16,750	3,554	6,326	10,424	188	32.7%	54.9%
Middlesex County	75,276	17,518	14,690	2,828	6,267	8,423	428	34.6%	49.1%
New Haven County	362,307	82,837	59,569	23,268	23,099	36,470	2,868	43.5%	52.8%
New London County	121,263	26,286	21,231	5,055	9,467	11,764	561	30.0%	58.0%
Tolland County	58,526	12,396	10,311	2,085	2,952	7,359	na	28.8%	39.7%
Windham County	49,158	9,650	8,192	1,458	2,568	5,624	na	28.9%	59.5%
Delaware									
Kent County	67,862	15,895	13,665	2,230	5,879	7,786	na	22.7%	63.1%
New Castle County	220,103	45,586	37,425	8,161	16,301	21,124	1,128	25.8%	57.1%
Sussex County	129,448	30,896	27,309	3,587	11,572	15,737	340	24.4%	54.8%
Florida									
Alachua County	114,059	19,828	15,610	4,218	4,294	11,316	572	22.9%	46.5%
Bay County	100,341	16,999	13,812	3,187	4,168	9,644	254	27.9%	57.0%
Brevard County	272,283	76,243	64,788	11,455	23,009	41,779	1,156	23.8%	61.6%
Broward County	817,309	168,076	136,468	31,608	51,769	84,699	4,064	38.1%	62.3%
Charlotte County	101,363	38,266	33,068	5,198	13,300	19,768	1,013	24.5%	52.6%
Citrus County	77,717	29,294	26,394	2,900	10,446	15,948	883	23.8%	49.1%
Clay County	77,433	16,153	13,795	2,358	6,072	7,723	436	23.8%	63.4%
Collier County	203,099	59,575	50,207	9,368	16,384	33,823	1,702	25.8%	53.9%
Columbia County	28,298	7,095	6,132	963	2,109	4,023	na	14.0%	na
Duval County	395,891	72,122	56,120	16,002	23,623	32,497	1,906	29.7%	60.5%
Escambia County	138,619	30,783	22,742	8,041	8,012	14,730	736	18.6%	51.4%
Flagler County	49,574	15,366	13,535	1,831	6,125	7,410	510	na	na
Hernando County	84,618	30,147	26,126	4,021	10,850	15,276	854	25.3%	64.1%
Highlands County	54,894	19,624	16,791	2,833	3,961	12,830	324	na	40.2%
Hillsborough County	554,082	102,060	80,109	21,951	29,130	50,979	3,630	25.1%	65.6%
Indian River County	77,342	26,256	22,200	4,056	7,752	14,448	1,001	30.4%	51.1%
Lake County	146,708	46,585	39,433	7,152	13,031	26,402	990	19.3%	59.7%
Lee County	375,688	102,374	87,705	14,669	30,295	57,410	1,532	27.9%	60.0%
Leon County	126,736	20,891	16,889	4,002	7,137	9,752	748	23.9%	55.4%
Manatee County	179,050	53,715	45,408	8,307	14,843	30,565	1,310	25.4%	54.8%
Marion County	163,560	57,018	50,954	6,064	16,769	34,185	723	22.1%	44.1%
Martin County	78,949	27,796	25,213	2,583	8,468	16,745	604	26.8%	50.1%
Miami-Dade County	1,004,378	202,456	138,519	63,937	55,335	83,184	1,710	39.8%	63.9%
Monroe County	52,927	8,836	6,991	1,845	1,929	5,062	na	na	52.5%
Nassau County	35,983	9,257	7,671	1,586	2,453	5,218	na	na	na
Okaloosa County	95,058	19,161	16,311	2,850	5,733	10,578	167	18.1%	47.4%
Orange County	508,097	75,328	59,388	15,940	26,525	32,863	1,470	30.4%	54.5%
Osceola County	133,989	18,816	15,153	3,663	6,718	8,435	301	35.1%	65.5%
Palm Beach County	674,880	196,495	163,130	33,365	57,441	105,689	4,622	33.3%	65.0%
Pasco County	232,385	65,438	55,604	9,834	17,769	37,835	1,197	21.8%	62.1%

Table J-2: Counties—Summary of Housing and Householder Characteristics—*Continued*

| | | | | Householders 65 Years and Over | | | | |
| | | | | Owner Householders | | | Percent of Owner Householders Who Pay 35% or More of income for Housing Costs | Percent of Renter Households Who Pay 35% or More of Income for Rental Costs |
	Total Housing Units	Total Households	Owner Occupied	Renter Occupied	With a Mortgage	Without a Mortgage	Renter Households With Meals Included in Rent		
Florida—Cont.									
Pinellas County	504,695	134,967	107,499	27,468	35,542	71,957	5,234	30.4%	58.7%
Polk County	282,748	74,155	62,630	11,525	18,787	43,843	873	23.1%	61.7%
Putnam County	36,664	10,067	8,750	1,317	2,557	6,193	na	17.5%	na
Santa Rosa County	67,601	14,143	12,466	1,677	4,995	7,471	na	25.0%	37.0%
Sarasota County	230,981	82,974	68,007	14,967	19,434	48,573	3,711	24.5%	53.5%
Seminole County	185,900	33,408	27,964	5,444	15,847	12,117	701	35.1%	63.1%
St. Johns County	96,909	23,395	19,008	4,387	8,687	10,321	281	28.9%	61.2%
St. Lucie County	137,349	39,460	34,142	5,318	12,256	21,886	817	23.7%	56.1%
Sumter County	64,503	34,307	32,253	2,054	11,307	20,946	157	na	na
Volusia County	256,104	70,258	60,003	10,255	20,913	39,090	1,894	26.4%	63.4%
Georgia									
Barrow County	26,828	4,604	3,733	871	1,802	1,931	na	31.9%	na
Bartow County	39,822	6,989	6,251	738	2,423	3,828	na	25.2%	na
Bibb County	70,302	13,579	8,712	4,867	3,287	5,425	539	23.6%	46.5%
Bulloch County	29,766	4,989	4,055	934	1,889	2,166	na	na	57.6%
Carroll County	44,758	8,925	6,492	2,433	2,188	4,304	441	na	59.8%
Catoosa County	26,804	6,525	5,904	621	2,089	3,815	na	na	na
Chatham County	122,611	23,779	17,859	5,920	7,303	10,556	444	23.9%	49.9%
Cherokee County	85,503	16,062	13,699	2,363	7,161	6,538	na	27.5%	52.5%
Clarke County	51,787	7,604	5,159	2,445	2,038	3,121	523	na	42.4%
Clayton County	104,550	12,424	9,550	2,874	5,360	4,190	206	26.4%	73.8%
Cobb County	292,887	45,973	38,630	7,343	19,112	19,518	1,035	21.1%	65.1%
Columbia County	53,374	7,910	7,101	809	3,509	3,592	na	21.8%	na
Coweta County	52,004	9,871	9,207	664	5,131	4,076	na	30.4%	44.3%
DeKalb County	306,967	45,984	35,934	10,050	16,646	19,288	804	30.7%	66.2%
Dougherty County	40,700	8,532	5,858	2,674	1,840	4,018	115	na	84.2%
Douglas County	51,856	8,231	6,645	1,586	3,334	3,311	na	23.5%	67.9%
Fayette County	41,344	10,184	8,618	1,566	4,278	4,340	391	na	na
Floyd County	40,423	9,055	6,902	2,153	2,482	4,420	363	25.1%	52.7%
Forsyth County	71,039	12,083	10,890	1,193	5,376	5,514	na	26.6%	47.9%
Fulton County	448,924	65,170	42,490	22,680	19,368	23,122	4,178	33.1%	55.5%
Glynn County	41,719	8,667	6,885	1,782	2,662	4,223	na	na	23.8%
Gwinnett County	298,624	38,128	30,949	7,179	15,731	15,218	1,149	25.1%	60.1%
Hall County	69,491	15,730	13,058	2,672	4,908	8,150	793	25.4%	51.3%
Henry County	77,537	12,818	11,265	1,553	6,438	4,827	na	27.2%	74.1%
Houston County	60,556	10,261	8,252	2,009	3,607	4,645	na	26.7%	57.2%
Liberty County	27,193	2,672	2,101	571	725	1,376	na	35.9%	36.8%
Lowndes County	45,662	7,928	6,290	1,638	2,670	3,620	na	21.3%	69.2%
Muscogee County	83,872	15,599	11,257	4,342	5,074	6,183	560	20.9%	51.5%
Newton County	38,361	7,833	6,606	1,227	3,466	3,140	na	na	na
Paulding County	53,110	8,128	6,458	1,670	3,305	3,153	na	30.3%	na
Richmond County	87,067	14,911	10,820	4,091	4,253	6,567	235	26.2%	65.6%
Rockdale County	33,290	5,825	5,175	650	2,848	2,327	na	na	na
Troup County	28,246	6,242	4,762	1,480	1,419	3,343	na	na	50.8%
Walker County	30,100	7,319	6,058	1,261	1,571	4,487	na	na	na
Walton County	32,547	7,324	5,428	1,896	1,600	3,828	270	na	na
Whitfield County	39,648	7,666	6,729	937	1,818	4,911	na	na	75.5%
Hawaii									
Hawaii County	85,173	19,257	15,801	3,456	6,386	9,415	na	17.6%	40.9%
Honolulu County	343,031	83,122	62,524	20,598	29,346	33,178	2,111	27.5%	57.0%
Kauai County	30,350	6,749	4,950	1,799	1,715	3,235	na	na	38.6%
Maui County	71,469	13,616	10,378	3,238	5,310	5,068	146	31.4%	46.7%
Idaho									
Ada County	167,223	32,075	25,867	6,208	11,794	14,073	1,837	22.2%	65.4%
Bannock County	33,369	6,874	6,082	792	2,315	3,767	231	26.6%	58.0%
Bonneville County	40,710	8,348	7,591	757	2,281	5,310	na	20.5%	63.4%
Canyon County	71,325	14,309	11,932	2,377	5,698	6,234	367	22.7%	34.5%
Kootenai County	66,122	15,029	12,437	2,592	5,130	7,307	1,263	21.6%	36.1%
Twin Falls County	31,776	7,574	5,801	1,773	1,702	4,099	116	20.4%	50.7%
Illinois									
Adams County	29,970	8,049	6,374	1,675	1,183	5,191	na	15.4%	60.3%
Champaign County	89,209	14,942	12,718	2,224	4,758	7,960	477	20.4%	73.8%
Cook County	2,175,163	420,247	308,388	111,859	116,851	191,537	10,682	37.0%	58.7%
DeKalb County	40,999	7,023	5,725	1,298	1,554	4,171	195	24.7%	48.7%
DuPage County	357,477	74,062	61,630	12,432	23,173	38,457	3,420	33.5%	53.4%
Kane County	184,048	37,775	31,058	6,717	13,908	17,150	971	35.8%	63.5%
Kankakee County	45,153	9,376	8,032	1,344	2,926	5,106	231	24.3%	69.9%
Kendall County	41,188	6,322	5,715	607	2,202	3,513	na	26.6%	na
Lake County	261,390	49,803	41,472	8,331	16,261	25,211	1,901	34.1%	63.5%
LaSalle County	49,867	11,879	10,023	1,856	1,752	8,271	152	17.8%	33.6%
Macon County	50,355	12,440	10,887	1,553	2,747	8,140	198	15.5%	39.0%
Madison County	118,190	28,067	22,079	5,988	7,040	15,039	556	23.1%	50.2%

Table J-2: Counties—Summary of Housing and Householder Characteristics—*Continued*

| | | | | Householders 65 Years and Over | | | | | |
| | | | | Owner Householders | | | | Percent of Owner Householders Who Pay 35% or More of income for Housing Costs | Percent of Renter Households Who Pay 35% or More of Income for Rental Costs |
	Total Housing Units	Total Households	Owner Occupied	Renter Occupied	With a Mortgage	Without a Mortgage	Renter Households With Meals Included in Rent		
Illinois—Cont.									
McHenry County	117,070	21,959	18,590	3,369	7,521	11,069	805	36.9%	56.2%
McLean County	71,435	12,445	9,822	2,623	3,572	6,250	713	21.3%	55.6%
Peoria County	83,571	18,183	14,156	4,027	4,604	9,552	544	23.8%	44.9%
Rock Island County	65,766	17,268	13,671	3,597	3,717	9,954	592	27.8%	67.1%
Sangamon County	90,529	20,192	15,848	4,344	5,054	10,794	661	18.3%	51.9%
St. Clair County	118,327	24,017	19,188	4,829	6,891	12,297	812	22.6%	36.6%
Tazewell County	58,064	14,198	11,658	2,540	3,281	8,377	576	14.5%	44.8%
Vermilion County	36,010	8,761	6,984	1,777	1,727	5,257	220	14.4%	42.5%
Will County	239,857	43,516	37,292	6,224	14,089	23,203	746	31.5%	65.8%
Williamson County	30,806	6,946	5,731	1,215	1,694	4,037	183	20.6%	39.1%
Winnebago County	125,548	28,626	22,106	6,520	7,688	14,418	919	29.0%	47.5%
Indiana									
Allen County	154,494	30,075	25,183	4,892	9,788	15,395	594	17.0%	47.2%
Bartholomew County	33,547	7,952	6,684	1,268	2,770	3,914	217	22.3%	45.5%
Clark County	48,992	10,542	8,402	2,140	3,627	4,775	390	24.0%	41.6%
Delaware County	52,517	11,571	10,224	1,347	3,953	6,271	na	18.6%	40.9%
Elkhart County	77,937	16,374	12,932	3,442	4,579	8,353	242	13.0%	55.1%
Floyd County	32,305	6,805	5,798	1,007	2,026	3,772	na	24.3%	52.1%
Grant County	30,287	8,091	6,540	1,551	2,687	3,853	na	20.6%	na
Hamilton County	116,292	19,298	15,854	3,444	7,939	7,915	744	20.2%	54.0%
Hancock County	28,893	6,836	6,046	790	2,339	3,707	na	na	na
Hendricks County	58,327	11,731	9,157	2,574	3,749	5,408	291	20.4%	49.8%
Howard County	38,689	9,929	8,309	1,620	3,584	4,725	213	16.4%	43.0%
Johnson County	58,739	11,811	9,342	2,469	4,647	4,695	513	23.0%	na
Kosciusko County	37,562	7,172	6,235	937	2,073	4,162	na	15.1%	47.1%
Lake County	210,385	43,006	35,456	7,550	14,785	20,671	771	26.2%	57.6%
LaPorte County	48,758	11,239	9,017	2,222	3,455	5,562	344	20.9%	59.6%
Madison County	58,793	14,579	12,414	2,165	5,473	6,941	133	20.8%	52.9%
Marion County	419,369	66,134	48,207	17,927	23,370	24,837	2,308	25.5%	53.8%
Monroe County	60,116	9,958	8,600	1,358	4,071	4,529	na	15.3%	42.7%
Morgan County	27,950	6,023	5,244	779	2,092	3,152	na	na	42.2%
Porter County	67,052	14,662	12,905	1,757	5,368	7,537	138	21.2%	74.6%
St. Joseph County	115,597	24,329	20,141	4,188	7,867	12,274	547	19.2%	51.2%
Tippecanoe County	73,905	11,272	9,429	1,843	3,270	6,159	464	16.1%	59.0%
Vanderburgh County	83,390	17,998	13,416	4,582	5,581	7,835	667	20.8%	53.8%
Vigo County	46,442	10,262	7,576	2,686	3,177	4,399	433	19.0%	49.0%
Wayne County	31,148	7,721	6,764	957	2,622	4,142	na	22.8%	45.5%
Iowa									
Black Hawk County	56,883	12,981	10,771	2,210	2,481	8,290	833	14.8%	54.7%
Dallas County	29,888	5,192	3,992	1,200	1,621	2,371	192	21.2%	na
Dubuque County	40,349	9,597	7,340	2,257	1,528	5,812	445	15.1%	69.4%
Johnson County	58,778	8,573	7,072	1,501	2,368	4,704	362	17.3%	74.3%
Linn County	94,654	20,002	17,397	2,605	6,021	11,376	837	18.5%	42.4%
Polk County	192,985	34,468	27,048	7,420	9,613	17,435	1,603	31.2%	53.8%
Pottawattamie County	39,573	9,357	7,130	2,227	1,983	5,147	703	21.5%	67.8%
Scott County	73,037	15,479	12,296	3,183	4,329	7,967	525	16.8%	40.3%
Story County	38,114	6,087	5,202	885	1,533	3,669	111	9.8%	33.2%
Woodbury County	41,508	8,423	6,474	1,949	1,468	5,006	392	16.7%	71.1%
Kansas									
Butler County	26,397	6,286	5,247	1,039	2,201	3,046	185	25.3%	61.0%
Douglas County	48,278	7,496	5,410	2,086	2,435	2,975	426	20.1%	58.9%
Johnson County	233,179	45,448	34,443	11,005	12,772	21,671	4,187	23.5%	62.4%
Leavenworth County	29,099	5,373	4,918	455	1,880	3,038	na	17.8%	na
Riley County	29,711	3,835	3,288	547	861	2,427	na	na	36.9%
Sedgwick County	214,423	41,124	31,867	9,257	9,847	22,020	1,983	20.4%	54.0%
Shawnee County	79,477	18,107	14,141	3,966	4,773	9,368	805	18.1%	67.8%
Wyandotte County	67,349	11,729	9,126	2,603	3,368	5,758	169	30.6%	55.5%
Kentucky									
Boone County	47,952	8,586	6,551	2,035	3,205	3,346	364	31.6%	na
Bullitt County	30,457	6,786	6,016	770	1,904	4,112	na	18.9%	na
Campbell County	39,812	7,975	6,246	1,729	2,840	3,406	156	29.2%	29.1%
Christian County	29,748	5,274	3,846	1,428	943	2,903	na	na	57.6%
Daviess County	42,546	9,745	7,588	2,157	2,141	5,447	307	16.0%	48.2%
Fayette County	138,832	22,793	17,442	5,351	7,133	10,309	825	25.4%	44.3%
Hardin County	45,740	8,860	7,156	1,704	3,026	4,130	282	20.9%	47.3%
Jefferson County	341,499	71,392	56,091	15,301	21,091	35,000	1,961	23.7%	58.8%
Kenton County	69,555	13,193	9,928	3,265	4,403	5,525	365	27.3%	42.6%
Madison County	35,821	7,004	5,427	1,577	1,906	3,521	175	na	54.9%
McCracken County	31,388	7,522	5,885	1,637	1,533	4,352	na	na	53.9%
Pike County	30,311	6,768	6,136	632	1,269	4,867	na	27.3%	na
Warren County	49,799	9,565	7,475	2,090	2,515	4,960	na	2na	66.4%

Table J-2: Counties—Summary of Housing and Householder Characteristics—*Continued*

| | | | | Householders 65 Years and Over | | | | |
| | | | | Owner Householders | | | | |
	Total Housing Units	Total Households	Owner Occupied	Renter Occupied	With a Mortgage	Without a Mortgage	Renter Households With Meals Included in Rent	Percent of Owner Householders Who Pay 35% or More of income for Housing Costs	Percent of Renter Households Who Pay 35% or More of Income for Rental Costs
Louisiana									
Ascension Parish	44,108	6,832	5,925	907	1,160	4,765	na	17.0%	na
Bossier Parish	54,048	9,661	7,799	1,862	2,524	5,275	401	20.7%	38.2%
Caddo Parish	112,721	23,269	19,164	4,105	5,052	14,112	200	19.6%	45.3%
Calcasieu Parish	85,733	16,874	14,133	2,741	3,697	10,436	123	18.4%	40.2%
East Baton Rouge Parish	191,218	34,864	27,221	7,643	9,298	17,923	1,197	24.5%	67.9%
Iberia Parish	30,092	6,093	5,197	896	689	4,508	na	na	na
Jefferson Parish	189,064	42,086	33,413	8,673	9,534	23,879	319	20.1%	54.0%
Lafayette Parish	97,494	16,922	13,612	3,310	4,059	9,553	470	17.7%	47.2%
Lafourche Parish	39,637	7,759	7,073	686	776	6,297	na	8.1%	na
Livingston Parish	53,710	9,362	8,332	1,030	1,667	6,665	na	13.9%	na
Orleans Parish	192,472	30,343	21,710	8,633	6,361	15,349	345	33.0%	61.0%
Ouachita Parish	66,297	13,274	10,533	2,741	2,488	8,045	na	18.4%	50.6%
Rapides Parish	57,088	12,179	10,245	1,934	2,488	7,757	na	20.9%	49.6%
St. Landry Parish	36,154	7,856	6,355	1,501	865	5,490	na	21.5%	na
St. Tammany Parish	98,804	21,728	18,685	3,043	7,461	11,224	459	23.6%	58.2%
Tangipahoa Parish	52,556	9,280	7,934	1,346	2,356	5,578	na	26.7%	53.2%
Terrebonne Parish	44,603	8,103	7,011	1,092	1,013	5,998	na	na	24.5%
Maine									
Androscoggin County	49,142	11,311	8,594	2,717	2,726	5,868	131	28.0%	52.4%
Aroostook County	39,483	9,323	6,902	2,421	1,879	5,023	na	23.8%	42.8%
Cumberland County	140,285	29,244	22,448	6,796	9,427	13,021	1,020	35.1%	62.1%
Kennebec County	61,503	13,203	11,111	2,092	3,342	7,769	na	29.0%	54.2%
Penobscot County	74,275	16,041	12,700	3,341	4,791	7,909	412	26.8%	38.9%
York County	107,281	22,173	17,603	4,570	5,925	11,678	212	26.8%	62.7%
Maryland									
Allegany County	33,220	8,621	7,115	1,506	1,885	5,230	na	17.4%	37.1%
Anne Arundel County	218,910	46,746	39,444	7,302	20,593	18,851	404	29.0%	50.3%
Baltimore County	337,023	80,304	60,836	19,468	22,835	38,001	3,879	26.9%	58.3%
Calvert County	34,600	7,333	6,180	1,153	3,475	2,705	263	30.8%	na
Carroll County	63,156	15,953	12,773	3,180	5,289	7,484	824	24.6%	66.5%
Cecil County	42,375	8,804	7,073	1,731	2,453	4,620	na	29.3%	42.7%
Charles County	58,159	10,298	8,440	1,858	4,777	3,663	na	33.9%	67.8%
Frederick County	93,592	18,569	15,221	3,348	7,184	8,037	597	33.9%	54.4%
Harford County	98,230	20,953	17,095	3,858	6,694	10,401	947	30.9%	57.5%
Howard County	115,318	19,963	16,645	3,318	7,503	9,142	617	27.1%	66.3%
Montgomery County	385,713	81,009	62,523	18,486	30,371	32,152	3,742	26.6%	60.7%
Prince George's County	330,514	59,365	45,976	13,389	29,330	16,646	473	34.9%	61.5%
St. Mary's County	43,267	7,889	6,483	1,406	3,068	3,415	na	24.4%	55.5%
Washington County	61,211	14,529	10,365	4,164	3,344	7,021	79	26.0%	60.5%
Wicomico County	42,155	8,973	6,994	1,979	2,562	4,432	343	26.0%	51.8%
Massachusetts									
Barnstable County	161,721	38,887	33,414	5,473	14,451	18,963	419	34.3%	59.2%
Berkshire County	68,333	17,764	13,718	4,046	5,179	8,539	142	27.7%	42.0%
Bristol County	231,285	53,030	36,682	16,348	13,468	23,214	1,212	36.3%	51.5%
Essex County	307,806	72,038	50,884	21,154	18,940	31,944	2,146	35.8%	50.9%
Franklin County	33,670	8,174	6,501	1,673	1,949	4,552	114	32.8%	50.4%
Hampden County	191,788	44,605	33,336	11,269	12,237	21,099	976	33.3%	51.9%
Hampshire County	62,885	15,614	12,270	3,344	4,430	7,840	400	33.1%	42.2%
Middlesex County	618,976	135,519	101,756	33,763	37,405	64,351	4,310	36.2%	58.1%
Norfolk County	272,917	65,417	48,469	16,948	19,518	28,951	2,166	34.1%	53.7%
Plymouth County	202,493	47,601	38,267	9,334	16,137	22,130	1,375	33.1%	43.0%
Suffolk County	318,318	54,064	25,965	28,099	11,421	14,544	1,275	39.7%	59.4%
Worcester County	329,081	69,289	48,731	20,558	17,703	31,028	1,698	35.0%	53.2%
Michigan									
Allegan County	49,759	10,476	9,378	1,098	2,449	6,929	na	19.2%	na
Bay County	48,020	12,621	11,048	1,573	3,112	7,936	na	18.2%	66.1%
Berrien County	76,737	17,528	14,278	3,250	4,861	9,417	442	23.2%	52.4%
Calhoun County	60,685	13,899	11,321	2,578	3,237	8,084	332	24.3%	48.5%
Clinton County	30,871	6,754	5,932	822	2,230	3,702	na	19.3%	33.2%
Eaton County	47,061	11,184	9,316	1,868	2,953	6,363	312	18.5%	45.0%
Genesee County	190,905	42,588	35,638	6,950	12,370	23,268	481	27.2%	57.3%
Grand Traverse County	42,329	10,196	8,937	1,259	3,709	5,228	214	36.5%	na
Ingham County	122,077	21,687	16,604	5,083	6,939	9,665	583	27.1%	52.5%
Isabella County	28,690	4,940	4,067	873	1,184	2,883	61	20.1%	58.8%
Jackson County	69,070	16,640	14,000	2,640	5,246	8,754	499	29.5%	63.5%
Kalamazoo County	110,308	21,548	17,695	3,853	6,261	11,434	478	20.5%	49.7%
Kent County	248,730	47,846	38,061	9,785	12,641	25,420	1,571	26.0%	49.5%
Lapeer County	36,198	8,529	7,339	1,190	2,780	4,559	71	28.2%	59.1%
Lenawee County	43,454	10,605	9,767	838	3,794	5,973	na	23.9%	40.6%
Livingston County	74,200	16,676	15,116	1,560	6,537	8,579	529	29.3%	63.7%
Macomb County	361,278	84,860	67,516	17,344	24,578	42,938	2,754	24.2%	55.1%

Table J-2: Counties—Summary of Housing and Householder Characteristics—*Continued*

| | | | | Householders 65 Years and Over | | | | |
| | | | | Owner Householders | | | Percent of Owner Householders Who Pay 35% or More of income for Housing Costs | Percent of Renter Households Who Pay 35% or More of Income for Rental Costs |
	Total Housing Units	Total Households	Owner Occupied	Renter Occupied	With a Mortgage	Without a Mortgage	Renter Households With Meals Included in Rent		
Michigan—Cont.									
Marquette County	34,497	6,904	5,208	1,696	1,349	3,859	na	22.4%	51.3%
Midland County	36,273	8,858	7,511	1,347	2,086	5,425	268	19.3%	56.2%
Monroe County	63,513	13,962	11,795	2,167	4,741	7,054	na	24.0%	64.0%
Muskegon County	73,328	17,066	14,150	2,916	4,163	9,987	547	13.2%	60.2%
Oakland County	533,071	119,199	91,635	27,564	40,212	51,423	4,592	28.4%	58.2%
Ottawa County	104,387	22,645	18,703	3,942	5,901	12,802	1,323	22.5%	69.6%
Saginaw County	86,792	21,226	18,303	2,923	6,382	11,921	577	22.3%	54.2%
Shiawassee County	30,063	6,935	5,916	1,019	1,894	4,022	79	19.1%	39.6%
St. Clair County	71,766	17,313	14,374	2,939	4,998	9,376	322	23.2%	61.0%
Van Buren County	36,643	7,044	6,128	916	2,312	3,816	na	31.0%	42.6%
Washtenaw County	148,496	27,312	22,412	4,900	9,717	12,695	769	25.3%	49.7%
Wayne County	814,470	159,506	120,948	38,558	42,933	78,015	2,982	29.8%	56.6%
Minnesota									
Anoka County	129,583	23,879	20,295	3,584	8,785	11,510	544	24.0%	51.8%
Blue Earth County	27,139	5,028	3,673	1,355	1,000	2,673	386	23.0%	57.3%
Carver County	36,342	6,245	4,674	1,571	1,548	3,126	368	30.4%	na
Dakota County	162,879	31,239	24,341	6,898	10,652	13,689	1,588	29.0%	71.9%
Hennepin County	522,907	97,368	73,093	24,275	30,084	43,009	3,842	30.8%	58.8%
Olmsted County	61,768	12,547	10,740	1,807	3,646	7,094	694	18.7%	55.5%
Ramsey County	218,192	44,594	32,177	12,417	12,937	19,240	2,882	26.3%	60.6%
Rice County	24,570	6,214	4,492	1,722	1,719	2,773	433	29.5%	na
Scott County	49,175	7,874	6,532	1,342	2,388	4,144	209	27.1%	63.3%
Sherburne County	32,872	5,370	4,500	870	1,884	2,616	na	23.2%	na
St. Louis County	103,222	22,900	17,661	5,239	4,117	13,544	1,595	16.0%	55.3%
Stearns County	62,905	12,262	10,026	2,236	2,960	7,066	291	25.3%	56.3%
Washington County	95,671	18,287	15,491	2,796	6,024	9,467	925	21.5%	70.5%
Wright County	49,896	8,544	7,337	1,207	2,711	4,626	na	26.3%	na
Mississippi									
DeSoto County	63,930	12,206	10,447	1,759	5,013	5,434	252	27.5%	37.9%
Forrest County	32,599	5,532	3,993	1,539	1,004	2,989	na	na	42.9%
Harrison County	89,743	18,357	14,650	3,707	5,428	9,222	496	22.3%	72.8%
Hinds County	104,091	19,283	15,341	3,942	5,068	10,273	300	22.3%	52.4%
Jackson County	61,130	11,759	10,369	1,390	3,074	7,295	na	16.5%	52.8%
Jones County	28,636	6,516	5,971	545	1,723	4,248	na	na	na
Lauderdale County	34,945	7,202	5,351	1,851	846	4,505	122	na	39.6%
Lee County	36,211	6,963	5,783	1,180	2,074	3,709	146	22.2%	34.3%
Madison County	41,143	7,871	6,731	1,140	3,062	3,669	470	39.7%	67.2%
Rankin County	58,213	11,985	10,781	1,204	3,749	7,032	na	20.8%	40.4%
Missouri									
Boone County	73,173	11,871	9,485	2,386	3,993	5,492	na	18.5%	35.1%
Buchanan County	38,450	8,952	6,966	1,986	1,824	5,142	331	18.2%	41.0%
Cape Girardeau County	33,037	7,147	5,650	1,497	1,631	4,019	414	21.2%	29.0%
Cass County	40,485	9,240	7,086	2,154	2,876	4,210	531	21.8%	na
Christian County	32,620	7,253	5,805	1,448	2,342	3,463	na	20.2%	na
Clay County	94,978	19,267	15,181	4,086	5,422	9,759	na	20.4%	43.5%
Cole County	32,802	6,748	5,656	1,092	1,862	3,794	na	20.3%	34.6%
Franklin County	43,895	9,697	8,194	1,503	2,823	5,371	479	22.5%	na
Greene County	129,163	28,854	21,935	6,919	8,302	13,633	598	25.7%	55.1%
Jackson County	314,695	59,505	44,856	14,649	17,359	27,497	1,699	28.2%	51.4%
Jasper County	51,311	9,867	7,893	1,974	2,408	5,485	na	16.0%	45.7%
Jefferson County	88,800	17,812	15,396	2,416	5,205	10,191	na	21.0%	35.0%
Platte County	40,151	7,048	5,457	1,591	1,831	3,626	566	17.4%	74.2%
St. Charles County	147,195	31,721	26,909	4,812	12,521	14,388	848	25.0%	60.7%
St. Francois County	29,363	6,200	5,070	1,130	1,242	3,828	320	29.8%	na
St. Louis County	438,116	105,403	87,531	17,872	34,341	53,190	5,006	26.3%	53.3%
Montana									
Cascade County	37,560	9,011	7,441	1,570	2,129	5,312	na	15.5%	46.8%
Flathead County	47,355	9,898	8,564	1,334	2,133	6,431	na	22.3%	66.6%
Gallatin County	44,857	6,915	5,342	1,573	1,317	4,025	331	20.8%	60.2%
Lewis and Clark County	30,593	6,192	4,600	1,592	1,422	3,178	377	15.6%	65.5%
Missoula County	51,415	10,170	7,859	2,311	2,590	5,269	660	28.7%	52.3%
Yellowstone County	67,067	14,746	11,774	2,972	4,001	7,773	736	27.9%	41.3%
Nebraska									
Douglas County	226,907	41,021	30,456	10,565	11,441	19,015	2,980	24.5%	59.6%
Lancaster County	124,818	23,688	18,057	5,631	6,043	12,014	1,400	19.1%	44.5%
Sarpy County	65,934	10,850	8,536	2,314	3,834	4,702	774	22.2%	49.3%
Nevada									
Clark County	863,073	156,767	112,351	44,416	57,640	54,711	2,506	28.6%	61.8%
Washoe County	187,153	40,668	29,483	11,185	15,185	14,298	960	33.4%	55.5%

Table J-2: Counties—Summary of Housing and Householder Characteristics—*Continued*

| | | | | Householders 65 Years and Over | | | | |
| | | | | Owner Householders | | | | |
	Total Housing Units	Total Households	Owner Occupied	Renter Occupied	With a Mortgage	Without a Mortgage	Renter Households With Meals Included in Rent	Percent of Owner Householders Who Pay 35% or More of income for Housing Costs	Percent of Renter Households Who Pay 35% or More of Income for Rental Costs
New Hampshire									
Cheshire County	34,820	8,186	6,380	1,806	2,435	3,945	na	41.8%	39.7%
Grafton County	51,637	9,339	7,814	1,525	2,366	5,448	222	30.9%	43.1%
Hillsborough County	167,428	31,803	24,219	7,584	10,352	13,867	1,026	36.3%	57.6%
Merrimack County	63,629	13,787	10,762	3,025	3,369	7,393	277	40.4%	65.4%
Rockingham County	128,442	27,957	21,890	6,067	8,470	13,420	869	38.1%	58.4%
Strafford County	52,411	9,910	7,832	2,078	1,379	6,453	na	29.7%	58.3%
New Jersey									
Atlantic County	127,386	26,503	20,457	6,046	8,643	11,814	259	46.1%	49.4%
Bergen County	356,367	84,279	63,138	21,141	21,599	41,539	1,275	43.7%	55.1%
Burlington County	177,671	43,499	36,078	7,421	16,148	19,930	770	39.8%	69.9%
Camden County	206,640	47,093	35,106	11,987	12,461	22,645	1,241	39.8%	56.1%
Cape May County	98,928	14,468	12,288	2,180	5,173	7,115	239	40.0%	67.2%
Cumberland County	56,363	13,024	9,712	3,312	3,348	6,364	176	37.6%	47.4%
Essex County	314,545	61,017	33,628	27,389	14,548	19,080	1,571	48.3%	56.8%
Gloucester County	112,272	25,692	20,758	4,934	7,203	13,555	916	35.0%	69.2%
Hudson County	277,172	43,207	19,041	24,166	7,555	11,486	377	52.6%	58.7%
Hunterdon County	49,736	11,952	9,963	1,989	4,698	5,265	na	42.3%	52.7%
Mercer County	144,999	30,427	22,274	8,153	9,774	12,500	1,210	37.2%	57.5%
Middlesex County	299,506	63,356	48,872	14,484	17,553	31,319	949	39.2%	54.7%
Monmouth County	260,754	59,863	46,060	13,803	18,562	27,498	2,342	39.4%	56.1%
Morris County	191,482	45,402	35,400	10,002	14,424	20,976	1,136	42.5%	56.8%
Ocean County	278,634	81,638	74,597	7,041	27,200	47,397	1,251	36.4%	43.4%
Passaic County	176,724	35,641	24,173	11,468	9,246	14,927	357	52.3%	64.5%
Salem County	27,563	7,136	5,473	1,663	1,751	3,722	149	35.9%	na
Somerset County	126,037	24,819	20,617	4,202	7,751	12,866	641	43.0%	67.4%
Sussex County	62,201	12,312	10,452	1,860	4,684	5,768	114	40.1%	47.3%
Union County	201,601	41,557	29,742	11,815	11,935	17,807	638	45.0%	60.1%
Warren County	45,266	10,314	7,712	2,602	3,127	4,585	207	39.4%	52.2%
New Mexico									
Bernalillo County	288,413	59,692	46,930	12,762	21,497	25,433	1,061	28.3%	54.6%
Chaves County	26,692	6,495	5,071	1,424	1,349	3,722	na	na	na
Doña Ana County	84,225	17,799	14,319	3,480	4,902	9,417	737	13.6%	50.6%
Lea County	25,092	4,381	3,868	513	738	3,130	na	na	na
McKinley County	25,779	4,880	3,890	990	568	3,322	na	7.4%	28.0%
Otero County	30,969	6,074	5,477	597	2,123	3,354	na	21.1%	na
San Juan County	49,613	9,919	8,326	1,593	2,777	5,549	179	22.8%	60.2%
Sandoval County	54,493	13,613	11,730	1,883	5,378	6,352	na	26.4%	63.0%
Santa Fe County	71,726	18,581	15,605	2,976	6,280	9,325	312	26.2%	54.2%
Valencia County	30,190	7,783	7,085	698	2,874	4,211	na	28.9%	na
New York									
Albany County	138,229	29,822	20,044	9,778	6,408	13,636	775	24.4%	47.5%
Bronx County	522,161	98,671	27,298	71,373	9,793	17,505	855	38.2%	61.2%
Broome County	89,811	21,537	16,829	4,708	5,218	11,611	690	24.1%	54.3%
Cattaraugus County	40,957	8,548	6,557	1,991	1,230	5,327	55	23.2%	54.7%
Cayuga County	36,394	8,338	6,461	1,877	1,723	4,738	343	22.6%	48.5%
Chautauqua County	66,661	14,768	11,905	2,863	3,561	8,344	292	20.4%	59.5%
Chemung County	38,380	8,995	7,220	1,775	2,025	5,195	270	20.5%	44.8%
Clinton County	35,939	7,776	6,318	1,458	1,743	4,575	121	19.6%	na
Dutchess County	119,108	25,920	19,796	6,124	8,243	11,553	399	39.2%	55.9%
Erie County	421,172	101,398	77,984	23,414	25,255	52,729	2,266	25.5%	51.7%
Jefferson County	58,780	8,616	6,664	1,952	1,694	4,970	na	23.3%	20.5%
Kings County	1,022,569	196,991	77,000	119,991	28,587	48,413	1,121	43.0%	61.3%
Livingston County	27,309	7,095	5,528	1,567	1,621	3,907	273	28.5%	na
Madison County	31,770	6,308	5,043	1,265	1,391	3,652	na	26.4%	39.2%
Monroe County	323,252	74,052	53,465	20,587	19,462	34,003	1,842	28.7%	59.5%
Nassau County	466,973	126,595	107,524	19,071	35,945	71,579	1,851	44.6%	59.5%
New York County	867,643	167,700	53,165	114,535	13,984	39,181	1,831	28.2%	55.8%
Niagara County	99,197	24,133	19,402	4,731	5,240	14,162	0	25.3%	51.8%
Oneida County	103,967	24,683	18,060	6,623	5,883	12,177	417	23.6%	43.4%
Onondaga County	204,458	45,806	35,254	10,552	11,592	23,662	1,034	20.0%	54.0%
Ontario County	49,614	12,487	9,911	2,576	3,526	6,385	378	26.1%	49.0%
Orange County	139,651	27,498	21,865	5,633	7,607	14,258	204	36.3%	64.2%
Oswego County	53,702	10,409	8,103	2,306	2,987	5,116	na	27.5%	29.2%
Putnam County	38,319	8,294	7,034	1,260	2,795	4,239	na	45.4%	na
Queens County	847,773	176,063	98,846	77,217	31,851	66,995	681	40.1%	62.5%
Rensselaer County	71,818	15,633	12,067	3,566	4,891	7,176	499	24.0%	51.7%
Richmond County	178,596	38,825	29,389	9,436	11,785	17,604	104	39.6%	58.5%
Rockland County	104,524	25,950	20,126	5,824	7,490	12,636	561	39.3%	58.6%
Saratoga County	101,832	22,418	17,415	5,003	6,954	10,461	395	23.5%	54.0%
Schenectady County	68,126	14,354	10,776	3,578	3,551	7,225	646	25.8%	68.4%
St. Lawrence County	52,240	9,894	7,761	2,133	2,014	5,747	na	24.3%	47.2%
Steuben County	48,839	11,088	8,607	2,481	2,212	6,395	192	28.0%	52.6%
Suffolk County	570,465	135,519	113,309	22,210	43,921	69,388	1,100	46.1%	60.6%

Table J-2: Counties—Summary of Housing and Householder Characteristics—*Continued*

| | | | | Householders 65 Years and Over | | | | | |
| | | | | Owner Householders | | | | Percent of Owner Householders Who Pay 35% or More of income for Housing Costs | Percent of Renter Households Who Pay 35% or More of Income for Rental Costs |
	Total Housing Units	Total Households	Owner Occupied	Renter Occupied	With a Mortgage	Without a Mortgage	Renter Households With Meals Included in Rent		
New York—Cont.									
Sullivan County	49,627	7,204	5,787	1,417	1,644	4,143	na	36.2%	na
Tompkins County	42,087	7,857	5,807	2,050	1,981	3,826	403	18.8%	53.5%
Ulster County	83,713	21,122	17,035	4,087	5,386	11,649	86	39.8%	58.5%
Warren County	38,999	7,527	5,801	1,726	2,631	3,170	120	32.2%	43.8%
Wayne County	41,342	9,442	7,527	1,915	2,305	5,222	na	25.4%	34.2%
Westchester County	369,881	91,882	64,529	27,353	22,256	42,273	1,541	40.1%	60.8%
North Carolina									
Alamance County	68,101	16,058	13,380	2,678	4,650	8,730	362	24.6%	76.7%
Brunswick County	81,427	18,313	16,049	2,264	8,155	7,894	na	29.1%	70.5%
Buncombe County	115,683	27,853	22,407	5,446	7,511	14,896	1,226	19.5%	48.4%
Burke County	40,651	9,454	7,864	1,590	2,398	5,466	na	23.0%	na
Cabarrus County	75,519	15,055	13,026	2,029	5,854	7,172	224	29.9%	47.8%
Caldwell County	37,594	9,454	7,577	1,877	2,281	5,296	na	na	na
Carteret County	48,897	9,697	8,566	1,131	3,366	5,200	59	25.7%	43.2%
Catawba County	67,766	14,624	11,921	2,703	4,539	7,382	136	19.6%	41.6%
Chatham County	29,967	10,205	8,280	1,925	3,110	5,170	683	22.1%	na
Cleveland County	43,263	11,438	9,368	2,070	2,649	6,719	na	24.1%	72.6%
Craven County	45,922	11,320	9,556	1,764	4,218	5,338	347	28.0%	65.0%
Cumberland County	143,893	22,057	17,486	4,571	8,814	8,672	170	25.4%	55.1%
Davidson County	73,006	17,710	15,116	2,594	4,615	10,501	0	22.8%	52.0%
Durham County	128,821	20,075	15,377	4,698	7,591	7,786	487	25.1%	47.5%
Forsyth County	160,648	33,763	25,700	8,063	10,990	14,710	802	18.9%	50.7%
Gaston County	89,925	18,971	15,715	3,256	6,049	9,666	438	24.7%	59.8%
Guilford County	223,182	44,306	32,652	11,654	14,504	18,148	1,975	26.4%	54.7%
Harnett County	49,321	8,883	7,078	1,805	2,426	4,652	142	22.2%	56.5%
Henderson County	55,476	16,786	14,063	2,723	4,713	9,350	870	18.6%	73.9%
Iredell County	70,280	13,802	12,114	1,688	5,094	7,020	na	24.6%	49.5%
Johnston County	70,094	13,892	10,975	2,917	3,897	7,078	na	24.2%	36.4%
Lincoln County	33,986	7,702	6,321	1,381	2,225	4,096	na	19.5%	na
Mecklenburg County	419,150	62,064	46,239	15,825	22,692	23,547	2,780	29.3%	56.2%
Moore County	45,235	13,871	11,752	2,119	5,018	6,734	699	28.8%	62.7%
Nash County	42,389	10,013	7,257	2,756	2,463	4,794	na	27.3%	49.1%
New Hanover County	105,549	21,442	17,101	4,341	9,282	7,819	388	31.3%	51.6%
Onslow County	76,061	9,938	8,371	1,567	3,576	4,795	na	31.9%	47.4%
Orange County	56,508	9,772	8,007	1,765	4,323	3,684	399	27.4%	36.1%
Pitt County	76,615	12,463	9,072	3,391	3,157	5,915	607	19.4%	51.2%
Randolph County	61,248	15,552	12,938	2,614	4,076	8,862	93	21.2%	47.2%
Robeson County	52,284	11,080	8,777	2,303	1,731	7,046	25	29.3%	54.2%
Rockingham County	43,604	10,672	8,732	1,940	3,016	5,716	na	18.4%	30.5%
Rowan County	60,164	14,616	11,840	2,776	4,653	7,187	195	21.8%	26.9%
Rutherford County	33,878	8,116	7,183	933	2,407	4,776	246	na	na
Surry County	33,568	8,171	6,380	1,791	2,040	4,340	169	23.9%	37.0%
Union County	76,512	14,167	12,211	1,956	6,000	6,211	116	31.1%	46.6%
Wake County	402,030	59,068	46,202	12,866	23,679	22,523	1,746	21.6%	57.9%
Wayne County	53,203	11,015	8,691	2,324	3,576	5,115	383	24.0%	63.0%
Wilkes County	33,031	8,517	6,987	1,530	2,058	4,929	88	na	na
Wilson County	35,662	8,299	6,483	1,816	2,490	3,993	na	na	44.7%
North Dakota									
Burleigh County	39,997	8,176	6,231	1,945	1,246	4,985	489	10.4%	50.2%
Cass County	75,131	11,545	7,384	4,161	2,276	5,108	1,179	18.1%	60.2%
Grand Forks County	31,336	5,261	3,783	1,478	930	2,853	na	16.7%	59.3%
Ward County	31,723	5,001	4,243	758	929	3,314	na	10.2%	56.1%
Ohio									
Allen County	44,847	10,595	8,567	2,028	3,097	5,470	530	24.0%	39.9%
Ashtabula County	45,851	10,195	8,082	2,113	2,811	5,271	70	31.4%	46.8%
Belmont County	32,161	7,957	6,700	1,257	1,318	5,382	na	13.6%	48.4%
Butler County	149,282	29,611	24,099	5,512	9,819	14,280	719	24.1%	48.2%
Clark County	61,182	15,290	12,165	3,125	4,214	7,951	866	21.5%	64.8%
Clermont County	82,046	17,922	14,885	3,037	6,770	8,115	428	20.5%	43.3%
Columbiana County	46,674	12,009	10,043	1,966	2,916	7,127	na	19.0%	43.6%
Cuyahoga County	618,853	136,488	99,738	36,750	39,828	59,910	3,508	29.1%	57.6%
Delaware County	69,689	12,304	10,751	1,553	5,316	5,435	448	26.3%	48.7%
Erie County	37,714	9,653	7,891	1,762	2,978	4,913	na	20.2%	na
Fairfield County	59,688	13,321	10,997	2,324	4,125	6,872	295	24.9%	61.9%
Franklin County	541,108	83,709	60,487	23,222	27,319	33,168	2,797	29.2%	55.6%
Geauga County	36,742	9,686	8,723	963	3,211	5,512	na	19.8%	na
Greene County	69,173	15,735	12,864	2,871	5,600	7,264	389	23.9%	47.3%
Hamilton County	376,943	76,287	56,656	19,631	23,828	32,828	2,784	28.8%	58.1%
Hancock County	33,272	7,754	5,759	1,995	2,439	3,320	742	22.9%	36.5%
Jefferson County	32,523	8,680	7,062	1,618	2,159	4,903	na	na	33.3%
Lake County	101,728	26,291	22,171	4,120	8,227	13,944	602	20.4%	59.2%
Licking County	69,948	16,224	12,977	3,247	5,669	7,308	na	18.0%	41.8%
Lorain County	128,739	31,749	25,443	6,306	9,269	16,174	1,120	29.4%	49.4%

Table J-2: Counties—Summary of Housing and Householder Characteristics—*Continued*

| | | | | | Householders 65 Years and Over | | | | |
| | | | | | Owner Householders | | | | |
	Total Housing Units	Total Households	Owner Occupied	Renter Occupied	With a Mortgage	Without a Mortgage	Renter Households With Meals Included in Rent	Percent of Owner Householders Who Pay 35% or More of income for Housing Costs	Percent of Renter Households Who Pay 35% or More of Income for Rental Costs
Ohio—Cont.									
Lucas County	202,129	41,777	32,606	9,171	13,452	19,154	863	25.2%	52.0%
Mahoning County	111,351	29,231	23,570	5,661	7,466	16,104	443	20.4%	48.6%
Marion County	27,776	7,518	6,058	1,460	2,034	4,024	203	12.8%	na
Medina County	70,626	16,367	13,834	2,533	5,333	8,501	498	24.6%	59.5%
Miami County	44,270	11,088	9,394	1,694	3,525	5,869	432	21.6%	46.8%
Montgomery County	254,413	57,759	44,369	13,390	17,324	27,045	1,036	27.3%	52.1%
Muskingum County	37,778	9,403	7,426	1,977	2,723	4,703	324	26.1%	49.2%
Portage County	68,061	15,282	12,744	2,538	4,799	7,945	398	25.9%	47.1%
Richland County	54,262	15,369	12,272	3,097	4,033	8,239	148	21.9%	60.2%
Ross County	31,787	7,322	5,594	1,728	1,343	4,251	na	na	49.4%
Scioto County	34,095	7,877	6,232	1,645	1,362	4,870	na	26.0%	42.4%
Stark County	165,561	41,136	33,050	8,086	11,655	21,395	829	18.8%	48.7%
Summit County	245,180	56,247	44,360	11,887	17,805	26,555	2,325	23.8%	61.9%
Trumbull County	95,477	25,474	21,308	4,166	6,602	14,706	352	18.2%	36.1%
Tuscarawas County	39,988	10,625	9,024	1,601	2,528	6,496	466	24.4%	54.9%
Warren County	83,588	16,994	14,319	2,675	6,267	8,052	464	26.6%	46.5%
Wayne County	46,011	10,626	9,085	1,541	2,844	6,241	77	20.9%	33.8%
Wood County	53,829	11,081	9,454	1,627	3,685	5,769	157	23.0%	46.3%
Oklahoma									
Canadian County	47,133	9,226	7,624	1,602	2,776	4,848	na	17.6%	48.1%
Cleveland County	110,387	19,193	16,117	3,076	5,719	10,398	550	22.5%	47.1%
Comanche County	51,659	8,367	6,987	1,380	2,197	4,790	191	22.4%	47.6%
Creek County	30,020	7,083	6,311	772	1,499	4,812	107	20.3%	45.6%
Muskogee County	30,916	6,952	5,373	1,579	1,321	4,052	151	20.8%	35.1%
Oklahoma County	330,154	60,997	48,220	12,777	16,135	32,085	2,371	18.1%	54.2%
Payne County	35,208	5,632	4,341	1,291	1,564	2,777	260	28.1%	72.0%
Pottawatomie County	29,633	6,475	5,417	1,058	1,194	4,223	na	14.9%	39.0%
Rogers County	36,378	8,787	7,730	1,057	2,570	5,160	93	20.3%	54.5%
Tulsa County	277,044	51,474	40,069	11,405	14,881	25,188	2,265	22.1%	55.5%
Wagoner County	30,773	6,775	6,136	639	2,448	3,688	na	18.5%	19.1%
Oregon									
Benton County	37,115	7,923	6,390	1,533	2,407	3,983	545	na	66.7%
Clackamas County	160,778	38,693	30,194	8,499	12,878	17,316	2,666	27.7%	55.9%
Deschutes County	82,420	18,070	14,679	3,391	7,375	7,304	446	34.1%	57.1%
Douglas County	48,933	15,674	11,969	3,705	4,262	7,707	1,019	22.7%	57.4%
Jackson County	91,919	26,718	20,319	6,399	8,163	12,156	2,311	32.4%	56.1%
Josephine County	38,023	12,767	10,553	2,214	3,993	6,560	152	na	na
Klamath County	32,756	8,131	7,108	1,023	2,590	4,518	na	21.6%	51.1%
Lane County	157,908	39,122	30,981	8,141	12,976	18,005	1,791	27.8%	59.5%
Linn County	49,304	12,694	10,146	2,548	4,106	6,040	175	23.5%	59.9%
Marion County	122,448	30,083	22,179	7,904	8,762	13,417	2,532	29.5%	59.5%
Multnomah County	330,804	57,511	38,642	18,869	17,762	20,880	4,342	36.9%	64.7%
Polk County	30,601	8,211	6,714	1,497	3,260	3,454	1,055	31.0%	88.2%
Umatilla County	29,699	5,823	4,245	1,578	1,089	3,156	360	19.2%	60.8%
Washington County	218,885	41,521	30,094	11,427	13,485	16,609	3,247	28.7%	69.7%
Yamhill County	37,524	9,461	7,153	2,308	2,879	4,274	497	23.1%	78.2%
Pennsylvania									
Adams County	41,290	10,910	9,050	1,860	2,996	6,054	na	20.1%	38.1%
Allegheny County	589,772	142,538	105,127	37,411	32,481	72,646	5,451	24.4%	54.4%
Armstrong County	32,382	9,063	7,491	1,572	1,384	6,107	74	19.0%	39.1%
Beaver County	78,383	21,820	17,409	4,411	5,339	12,070	356	24.8%	46.3%
Berks County	164,846	40,172	32,165	8,007	10,340	21,825	799	32.2%	48.6%
Blair County	56,067	14,864	11,660	3,204	2,605	9,055	164	22.1%	41.8%
Bucks County	246,850	61,999	47,856	14,143	16,919	30,937	4,151	35.6%	65.0%
Butler County	80,358	20,090	15,086	5,004	3,887	11,199	805	21.1%	47.4%
Cambria County	65,262	18,477	14,631	3,846	3,075	11,556	649	26.2%	27.9%
Carbon County	34,395	7,877	6,412	1,465	2,215	4,197	na	32.2%	na
Centre County	65,105	12,199	9,682	2,517	3,092	6,590	391	21.3%	45.2%
Chester County	195,657	44,264	35,784	8,480	14,009	21,775	2,265	29.6%	62.0%
Clearfield County	38,573	9,947	8,304	1,643	1,602	6,702	209	27.2%	42.1%
Columbia County	29,587	7,303	6,047	1,256	1,275	4,772	35	19.7%	41.9%
Crawford County	44,390	10,082	7,904	2,178	2,101	5,803	na	17.9%	36.5%
Cumberland County	102,906	26,592	20,538	6,054	7,415	13,123	1,035	20.5%	64.7%
Dauphin County	121,799	25,789	19,581	6,208	7,300	12,281	1,029	25.8%	63.3%
Delaware County	221,950	52,263	40,372	11,891	14,785	25,587	2,433	33.8%	59.5%
Erie County	119,824	27,024	21,142	5,882	5,478	15,664	912	19.0%	50.9%
Fayette County	62,858	15,564	12,166	3,398	2,632	9,534	127	20.0%	34.6%
Franklin County	64,125	16,463	13,798	2,665	4,399	9,399	305	20.7%	42.0%
Indiana County	38,612	9,335	7,766	1,569	1,962	5,804	234	17.2%	33.7%
Lackawanna County	96,646	24,720	18,480	6,240	4,611	13,869	322	31.8%	47.8%
Lancaster County	206,431	50,614	36,564	14,050	9,869	26,695	2,587	24.4%	59.7%
Lawrence County	40,729	11,449	9,149	2,300	2,169	6,980	421	21.4%	49.8%
Lebanon County	56,207	14,125	10,360	3,765	2,557	7,803	213	25.9%	43.7%

Table J-2: Counties—Summary of Housing and Householder Characteristics—*Continued*

| | | | | | Householders 65 Years and Over | | | | |
| | | | | | Owner Householders | | | Percent of Owner Householders Who Pay 35% or More of income for Housing Costs | Percent of Renter Households Who Pay 35% or More of Income for Rental Costs |
	Total Housing Units	Total Households	Owner Occupied	Renter Occupied	With a Mortgage	Without a Mortgage	Renter Households With Meals Included in Rent		
Pennsylvania—Cont.									
Lehigh County	143,379	34,260	25,625	8,635	8,171	17,454	699	30.6%	65.3%
Luzerne County	148,231	36,645	29,300	7,345	8,361	20,939	551	32.3%	41.2%
Lycoming County	52,639	12,944	9,739	3,205	2,703	7,036	345	21.9%	58.0%
Mercer County	51,606	14,146	11,032	3,114	3,093	7,939	276	20.4%	38.1%
Monroe County	80,699	12,922	11,043	1,879	4,770	6,273	na	42.0%	54.1%
Montgomery County	327,459	81,685	61,258	20,427	21,867	39,391	4,790	34.1%	59.1%
Northampton County	121,141	30,546	23,368	7,178	7,975	15,393	1,399	36.4%	55.4%
Northumberland County	44,949	11,777	8,648	3,129	1,980	6,668	645	22.0%	45.6%
Philadelphia County	670,445	124,800	85,064	39,736	26,560	58,504	1,980	34.6%	58.4%
Schuylkill County	69,064	17,799	14,747	3,052	3,064	11,683	265	28.0%	34.1%
Somerset County	37,961	9,658	7,673	1,985	1,838	5,835	59	26.0%	35.9%
Washington County	93,925	24,643	19,825	4,818	6,031	13,794	411	20.6%	39.8%
Westmoreland County	168,282	47,595	39,529	8,066	10,669	28,860	944	24.4%	45.7%
York County	180,662	41,712	35,206	6,506	11,388	23,818	648	29.8%	65.9%
Rhode Island									
Kent County	73,594	18,266	13,387	4,879	5,637	7,750	387	32.0%	55.8%
Newport County	41,858	10,345	8,328	2,017	4,004	4,324	308	27.3%	58.7%
Providence County	263,487	54,243	34,523	19,720	13,723	20,800	868	33.1%	49.8%
Washington County	62,898	13,918	10,836	3,082	4,506	6,330	277	32.8%	47.4%
South Carolina									
Aiken County	74,034	17,610	15,488	2,122	5,551	9,937	323	20.4%	56.1%
Anderson County	85,464	20,200	17,004	3,196	5,747	11,257	440	18.4%	64.5%
Beaufort County	94,299	25,981	22,980	3,001	11,288	11,692	459	32.8%	57.3%
Berkeley County	77,294	13,756	11,293	2,463	4,736	6,557	150	31.8%	29.4%
Charleston County	178,052	34,760	28,405	6,355	10,896	17,509	1,165	26.9%	58.9%
Darlington County	30,213	7,554	6,476	1,078	1,602	4,874	na	18.0%	na
Dorchester County	57,681	10,319	9,683	636	3,502	6,181	69	29.6%	53.5%
Florence County	59,089	12,482	9,933	2,549	2,689	7,244	559	24.5%	53.3%
Greenville County	200,854	42,834	35,405	7,429	12,796	22,609	1,551	17.9%	61.8%
Greenwood County	31,124	7,829	6,636	1,193	2,285	4,351	534	23.5%	na
Horry County	193,101	38,767	33,864	4,903	14,039	19,825	394	26.7%	56.0%
Lancaster County	34,097	9,146	7,562	1,584	3,143	4,419	na	na	na
Laurens County	30,614	7,067	6,308	759	2,137	4,171	na	20.9%	na
Lexington County	118,633	25,022	21,919	3,103	7,773	14,146	1,126	23.1%	57.0%
Oconee County	39,125	9,788	9,192	596	2,882	6,310	na	21.9%	na
Orangeburg County	42,190	9,240	7,519	1,721	2,014	5,505	na	32.0%	37.9%
Pickens County	52,112	11,532	10,145	1,387	3,479	6,666	na	29.8%	40.1%
Richland County	167,017	29,698	24,808	4,890	11,248	13,560	404	23.9%	43.1%
Spartanburg County	124,522	27,831	21,582	6,249	7,625	13,957	768	20.2%	38.3%
Sumter County	47,021	9,981	8,203	1,778	2,791	5,412	196	na	44.3%
York County	98,863	19,598	16,358	3,240	7,152	9,206	231	21.7%	44.4%
South Dakota									
Minnehaha County	76,139	14,087	10,095	3,992	3,431	6,664	690	18.1%	47.7%
Pennington County	46,810	10,370	7,708	2,662	1,874	5,834	476	20.0%	48.2%
Tennessee									
Anderson County	34,759	8,798	7,521	1,277	2,247	5,274	46	22.8%	na
Blount County	55,881	13,469	12,016	1,453	3,828	8,188	na	21.8%	16.0%
Bradley County	42,421	10,286	8,085	2,201	2,438	5,647	na	22.0%	35.2%
Davidson County	292,930	47,229	35,456	11,773	14,159	21,297	1,698	22.7%	61.6%
Greene County	32,158	7,564	5,734	1,830	1,511	4,223	na	na	19.7%
Hamilton County	154,639	35,090	27,567	7,523	8,764	18,803	970	18.9%	50.3%
Knox County	198,925	41,265	33,928	7,337	11,875	22,053	840	22.7%	60.0%
Madison County	42,678	9,190	7,967	1,223	2,539	5,428	343	25.5%	64.8%
Maury County	35,953	7,418	6,011	1,407	1,651	4,360	na	20.7%	33.0%
Montgomery County	76,989	9,301	7,631	1,670	2,923	4,708	na	17.1%	39.0%
Putnam County	32,826	8,106	6,429	1,677	1,740	4,689	na	32.1%	50.6%
Robertson County	26,458	5,423	5,131	292	1,646	3,485	na	25.7%	na
Rutherford County	109,539	16,979	13,201	3,778	4,599	8,602	356	25.0%	45.6%
Sevier County	56,268	10,950	8,848	2,102	2,007	6,841	94	na	30.5%
Shelby County	403,395	67,957	53,919	14,038	22,462	31,457	1,861	29.8%	55.9%
Sullivan County	74,118	20,462	17,793	2,669	4,833	12,960	54	16.5%	52.2%
Sumner County	68,068	14,283	12,118	2,165	4,637	7,481	519	19.8%	53.9%
Washington County	58,886	13,840	11,538	2,302	3,180	8,358	133	14.0%	37.7%
Williamson County	73,799	13,046	11,680	1,366	4,948	6,732	544	24.1%	67.7%
Wilson County	48,770	10,626	8,741	1,885	3,655	5,086	302	24.3%	51.0%
Texas									
Angelina County	36,196	7,889	6,676	1,213	831	5,845	0	19.3%	50.2%
Bastrop County	29,586	5,639	4,675	964	1,833	2,842	na	22.0%	na
Bell County	133,804	19,437	14,644	4,793	3,861	10,783	906	22.4%	50.2%
Bexar County	678,225	124,741	97,625	27,116	33,748	63,877	4,340	22.3%	57.0%
Bowie County	39,133	8,827	7,066	1,761	1,468	5,598	na	18.5%	58.1%
Brazoria County	126,259	20,884	17,230	3,654	5,571	11,659	na	22.5%	48.7%

Table J-2: Counties—Summary of Housing and Householder Characteristics—*Continued*

| | | Householders 65 Years and Over | | | | | | | |
| | | | | | Owner Householders | | | Percent of Owner Households Who Pay 35% or More of income for Housing Costs | Percent of Renter Households Who Pay 35% or More of Income for Rental Costs |
	Total Housing Units	Total Households	Owner Occupied	Renter Occupied	With a Mortgage	Without a Mortgage	Renter Households With Meals Included in Rent		
Texas—Cont.									
Brazos County	83,493	11,057	8,916	2,141	2,847	6,069	412	24.5%	42.2%
Cameron County	146,207	30,043	24,191	5,852	4,742	19,449	64	24.4%	43.0%
Collin County	327,582	48,511	36,926	11,585	16,261	20,665	1,791	23.8%	62.1%
Comal County	51,426	13,048	11,367	1,681	3,153	8,214	358	19.9%	49.3%
Coryell County	26,033	4,034	3,849	185	958	2,891	na	na	21.1%
Dallas County	974,522	146,790	111,463	35,327	39,843	71,620	6,195	26.3%	61.5%
Denton County	280,431	37,253	28,776	8,477	13,005	15,771	643	27.4%	66.4%
Ector County	56,510	9,158	7,216	1,942	1,067	6,149	na	20.4%	42.5%
El Paso County	286,672	52,580	40,529	12,051	11,694	28,835	439	23.1%	38.6%
Ellis County	57,061	11,745	9,361	2,384	3,106	6,255	304	26.2%	50.2%
Fort Bend County	223,989	33,770	29,609	4,161	13,276	16,333	678	26.9%	61.5%
Galveston County	139,627	25,568	19,619	5,949	6,258	13,361	517	18.0%	59.5%
Grayson County	54,398	12,404	9,795	2,609	2,322	7,473	266	22.0%	50.3%
Gregg County	51,422	10,987	8,290	2,697	1,911	6,379	555	14.5%	54.7%
Guadalupe County	53,983	11,530	9,854	1,676	3,046	6,808	258	14.2%	60.0%
Harris County	1,683,039	244,310	183,570	60,740	58,023	125,547	6,082	24.8%	61.3%
Harrison County	28,017	7,012	6,362	650	1,480	4,882	na	21.6%	na
Hays County	70,729	10,742	8,724	2,018	4,054	4,670	225	26.5%	74.0%
Henderson County	39,975	10,304	8,668	1,636	2,499	6,169	165	24.1%	na
Hidalgo County	261,199	44,905	37,142	7,763	5,333	31,809	68	19.5%	57.3%
Hunt County	36,919	7,898	6,679	1,219	1,747	4,932	na	22.3%	na
Jefferson County	107,249	22,367	16,986	5,381	2,763	14,223	301	20.9%	45.3%
Johnson County	59,031	12,410	11,176	1,234	2,744	8,432	na	23.5%	38.4%
Kaufman County	39,196	7,131	5,829	1,302	1,969	3,860	na	24.7%	54.7%
Liberty County	29,505	5,944	4,407	1,537	673	3,734	na	na	na
Lubbock County	121,114	23,469	17,575	5,894	4,572	13,003	964	21.0%	56.5%
McLennan County	97,273	21,145	16,343	4,802	4,724	11,619	523	20.0%	49.9%
Midland County	58,012	9,061	7,619	1,442	1,332	6,287	234	20.1%	70.8%
Montgomery County	195,373	38,397	30,620	7,777	11,416	19,204	1,764	22.8%	54.7%
Nacogdoches County	27,951	5,704	4,341	1,363	964	3,377	na	na	27.9%
Nueces County	145,677	28,983	21,982	7,001	5,271	16,711	735	20.5%	56.5%
Orange County	36,077	7,803	6,817	986	1,125	5,692	na	na	na
Parker County	47,804	11,109	9,135	1,974	3,212	5,923	na	28.9%	40.6%
Potter County	49,046	9,261	7,011	2,250	1,536	5,475	280	19.6%	55.2%
Randall County	53,504	11,006	9,464	1,542	3,083	6,381	181	21.5%	44.8%
Rockwall County	30,629	5,014	4,478	536	1,632	2,846	na	28.4%	na
San Patricio County	27,008	6,278	4,758	1,520	1,297	3,461	na	na	na
Smith County	88,447	20,300	16,183	4,117	5,337	10,846	513	24.4%	63.3%
Tarrant County	739,400	119,389	91,061	28,328	33,746	57,315	4,610	25.1%	58.9%
Taylor County	56,708	10,911	9,104	1,807	2,024	7,080	331	12.7%	66.5%
Tom Green County	47,702	10,470	7,208	3,262	1,864	5,344	na	14.5%	48.8%
Travis County	474,957	58,269	46,096	12,173	18,068	28,028	2,233	29.4%	59.8%
Victoria County	36,045	7,916	6,899	1,017	1,401	5,498	na	16.0%	72.5%
Walker County	24,936	4,737	3,797	940	1,041	2,756	na	na	na
Webb County	78,050	12,074	9,323	2,751	1,844	7,479	na	27.9%	54.7%
Wichita County	56,035	11,817	9,420	2,397	2,273	7,147	659	24.4%	48.1%
Williamson County	175,673	28,309	23,110	5,199	10,204	12,906	1,192	23.8%	68.8%
Utah									
Cache County	39,375	6,400	5,378	1,022	1,709	3,669	355	18.8%	57.8%
Davis County	103,633	17,527	15,432	2,095	5,780	9,652	749	24.7%	60.1%
Salt Lake County	376,486	64,084	51,186	12,898	21,836	29,350	2,502	22.1%	49.5%
Utah County	157,461	21,905	18,930	2,975	7,317	11,613	941	18.8%	51.2%
Washington County	62,439	17,020	14,152	2,868	5,315	8,837	366	20.1%	59.3%
Weber County	87,851	15,863	12,927	2,936	4,398	8,529	493	21.2%	67.8%
Vermont									
Chittenden County	67,255	13,660	10,478	3,182	3,978	6,500	921	39.3%	61.5%
Virginia									
Albemarle County	43,919	9,918	7,945	1,973	3,099	4,846	621	24.9%	65.7%
Arlington County	110,597	13,054	9,413	3,641	4,507	4,906	218	29.2%	59.4%
Augusta County	31,800	8,167	7,523	644	3,137	4,386	na	22.1%	na
Bedford County	35,783	8,680	7,729	951	2,761	4,968	na	19.3%	na
Chesterfield County	126,429	25,786	21,914	3,872	11,914	10,000	1,454	20.7%	69.5%
Fairfax County	410,280	74,927	62,597	12,330	32,006	30,591	3,093	23.3%	54.4%
Fauquier County	26,225	5,663	4,909	754	2,514	2,395	na	18.9%	na
Frederick County	32,402	6,926	5,840	1,086	2,493	3,347	521	23.6%	na
Hanover County	39,873	10,084	8,556	1,528	2,452	6,104	102	16.3%	23.6%
Henrico County	135,030	26,909	19,751	7,158	8,894	10,857	1,951	24.1%	58.5%
James City County	31,747	10,401	8,533	1,868	3,693	4,840	na	na	na
Loudoun County	123,150	13,846	10,726	3,120	5,606	5,120	1,023	28.2%	62.1%
Montgomery County	39,222	6,191	5,017	1,174	1,519	3,498	na	19.6%	34.6%
Prince William County	144,785	19,265	16,699	2,566	9,877	6,822	380	26.7%	62.3%

Table J-2: Counties—Summary of Housing and Householder Characteristics—*Continued*

| | | | | Householders 65 Years and Over | | | | | |
| | | | | Owner Householders | | | | | |
	Total Housing Units	Total Households	Owner Occupied	Renter Occupied	With a Mortgage	Without a Mortgage	Renter Households With Meals Included in Rent	Percent of Owner Householders Who Pay 35% or More of income for Housing Costs	Percent of Renter Households Who Pay 35% or More of Income for Rental Costs
Virginia—Cont.									
Roanoke County	40,575	12,015	9,944	2,071	3,292	6,652	na	13.6%	na
Rockingham County	34,537	8,823	6,844	1,979	2,407	4,437	347	19.1%	52.9%
Spotsylvania County	46,246	9,065	7,133	1,932	3,963	3,170	367	23.4%	61.1%
Stafford County	46,529	6,419	5,805	614	3,281	2,524	237	28.9%	74.1%
York County	27,268	6,077	5,776	301	2,985	2,791	na	na	na
Washington									
Benton County	72,336	15,174	12,155	3,019	4,149	8,006	1,123	19.3%	67.7%
Chelan County	36,244	7,680	6,425	1,255	2,241	4,184	na	na	na
Clallam County	35,811	12,052	10,138	1,914	3,358	6,780	416	na	56.1%
Clark County	172,778	37,639	28,692	8,947	13,246	15,446	1,322	24.6%	59.6%
Cowlitz County	43,506	11,975	9,095	2,880	2,953	6,142	947	22.4%	59.3%
Franklin County	26,451	3,904	3,260	644	1,186	2,074	na	na	na
Grant County	35,521	7,129	5,667	1,462	1,623	4,044	235	na	52.7%
Grays Harbor County	35,248	8,568	7,096	1,472	3,450	3,646	na	28.8%	37.5%
Island County	40,676	10,375	8,328	2,047	3,723	4,605	240	na	66.0%
King County	880,488	154,794	113,031	41,763	49,663	63,368	9,856	29.6%	62.6%
Kitsap County	109,329	25,250	20,311	4,939	9,329	10,982	982	28.1%	58.9%
Lewis County	34,081	9,400	7,592	1,808	2,628	4,964	242	21.0%	71.0%
Pierce County	332,742	63,751	49,567	14,184	22,732	26,835	2,190	28.2%	66.9%
Skagit County	51,885	13,628	10,645	2,983	4,318	6,327	734	30.5%	55.6%
Snohomish County	297,751	53,519	40,614	12,905	16,194	24,420	2,256	29.5%	59.7%
Spokane County	206,106	45,346	33,876	11,470	12,851	21,025	2,230	24.0%	59.5%
Thurston County	111,797	24,728	18,600	6,128	7,215	11,385	664	23.0%	57.7%
Whatcom County	92,462	20,850	16,428	4,422	6,341	10,087	1,079	30.7%	73.8%
Yakima County	86,370	18,654	14,563	4,091	5,069	9,494	514	31.8%	37.1%
West Virginia									
Berkeley County	46,210	8,312	7,075	1,237	3,361	3,714	na	23.1%	na
Cabell County	46,462	10,872	9,024	1,848	2,933	6,091	509	20.2%	42.2%
Harrison County	31,544	8,001	6,719	1,282	1,977	4,742	na	17.1%	32.6%
Kanawha County	92,421	23,441	20,373	3,068	5,442	14,931	239	15.3%	37.7%
Monongalia County	44,499	6,989	5,755	1,234	1,158	4,597	na	15.5%	23.7%
Raleigh County	36,015	9,425	8,397	1,028	2,917	5,480	na	na	na
Wood County	40,251	11,022	9,179	1,843	2,326	6,853	184	18.1%	39.4%
Wisconsin									
Brown County	107,319	21,159	15,706	5,453	5,719	9,987	714	24.1%	48.5%
Dane County	222,390	38,868	28,833	10,035	10,861	17,972	1,500	29.2%	63.6%
Dodge County	37,385	8,850	6,983	1,867	2,174	4,809	258	28.9%	61.6%
Eau Claire County	43,047	8,825	6,372	2,453	2,626	3,746	308	27.7%	52.1%
Fond du Lac County	44,488	10,414	8,249	2,165	2,188	6,061	456	27.5%	62.6%
Jefferson County	35,296	7,994	6,418	1,576	2,510	3,908	259	34.5%	49.4%
Kenosha County	69,606	14,242	10,979	3,263	4,208	6,771	216	30.4%	71.3%
La Crosse County	49,313	10,519	8,212	2,307	2,740	5,472	495	23.3%	67.8%
Manitowoc County	37,182	9,744	7,816	1,928	2,247	5,569	319	19.8%	58.0%
Marathon County	58,379	13,355	10,953	2,402	2,662	8,291	157	26.6%	45.3%
Milwaukee County	417,115	74,007	47,872	26,135	17,181	30,691	3,907	33.1%	63.9%
Outagamie County	75,125	14,650	11,578	3,072	3,679	7,899	255	23.6%	42.1%
Ozaukee County	36,728	10,031	7,432	2,599	2,774	4,658	884	24.7%	59.2%
Portage County	30,363	6,738	5,554	1,184	1,578	3,976	86	27.0%	53.2%
Racine County	82,283	19,041	14,782	4,259	4,800	9,982	201	33.8%	53.8%
Rock County	68,309	15,033	11,581	3,452	3,528	8,053	588	19.8%	50.3%
Sheboygan County	50,611	11,782	9,097	2,685	3,124	5,973	436	25.0%	52.9%
St. Croix County	34,694	5,858	4,475	1,383	1,888	2,587	507	23.7%	68.6%
Walworth County	51,709	9,925	7,740	2,185	2,795	4,945	372	30.9%	54.1%
Washington County	55,512	13,671	10,889	2,782	4,462	6,427	680	34.7%	68.4%
Waukesha County	162,595	40,660	32,381	8,279	12,529	19,852	1,312	28.3%	66.1%
Winnebago County	74,207	16,060	11,961	4,099	4,685	7,276	687	33.8%	64.5%
Wood County	34,394	9,251	6,989	2,262	1,933	5,056	534	19.1%	68.6%
Wyoming									
Laramie County	41,651	8,768	7,793	975	3,084	4,709	na	26.1%	27.5%
Natrona County	35,822	7,213	5,506	1,707	1,417	4,089	541	9.6%	45.3%

Table J-3: Places—Summary of Housing and Householder Characteristics

				Householders 65 Years and Over					
				Owner Householders				Percent of Owner Householders Who Pay 35% or More of income for Housing Costs	Percent of Renter Households Who Pay 35% or More of Income for Rental Costs
	Total Housing Units	Total Households	Owner Occupied	Renter Occupied	With a Mortgage	Without a Mortgage	Renter Households With Meals Included in Rent		
Alabama									
Birmingham city	109,659	18,584	13,942	4,642	6,368	7,574	54	33.1%	55.5%
Dothan city	30,388	6,879	5,489	1,390	1,802	3,687	89	21.6%	54.3%
Hoover city	38,749	9,713	7,236	2,477	4,191	3,045	822	36.1%	na
Huntsville city	89,231	18,606	14,551	4,055	4,109	10,442	601	13.3%	62.7%
Mobile city	90,778	18,539	13,213	5,326	4,882	8,331	431	28.9%	56.9%
Montgomery city	91,689	17,248	13,941	3,307	6,477	7,464	257	22.3%	50.1%
Tuscaloosa city	47,469	7,595	5,582	2,013	1,803	3,779	235	17.4%	50.6%
Alaska									
Anchorage municipality	114,320	14,870	12,684	2,186	5,440	7,244	na	16.1%	56.7%
Arizona									
Avondale city	26,914	2,820	2,222	598	1,616	606	na	21.6%	68.4%
Chandler city	94,060	13,500	10,679	2,821	5,935	4,744	374	20.3%	56.6%
Flagstaff city	24,997	3,897	3,085	812	1,358	1,727	107	28.2%	48.8%
Glendale city	87,296	14,813	9,430	5,383	5,083	4,347	633	33.4%	62.1%
Goodyear city	29,114	6,045	5,081	964	2,765	2,316	na	na	na
Mesa city	202,534	43,735	35,572	8,163	12,976	22,596	2,378	22.6%	72.1%
Peoria city	70,168	15,825	11,530	4,295	5,715	5,815	1,225	25.0%	63.5%
Phoenix city	603,500	90,321	66,430	23,891	30,689	35,741	2,589	26.3%	54.9%
Scottsdale city	127,711	31,511	24,907	6,604	12,825	12,082	1,774	32.1%	53.6%
Surprise city	54,247	15,018	13,381	1,637	5,972	7,409	294	22.5%	68.1%
Tempe city	72,913	11,278	8,205	3,073	4,298	3,907	646	23.6%	48.5%
Tucson city	232,004	46,294	32,286	14,008	13,204	19,082	1,925	23.1%	52.9%
Yuma city	40,005	8,707	6,651	2,056	2,139	4,512	276	20.6%	44.7%
Arkansas									
Fayetteville city	36,384	5,021	3,385	1,636	903	2,482	232	na	52.6%
Fort Smith city	39,978	7,690	5,952	1,738	1,347	4,605	186	26.4%	42.9%
Jonesboro city	30,797	5,829	4,676	1,153	2,246	2,430	na	na	40.2%
Little Rock city	95,025	16,457	13,169	3,288	5,131	8,038	701	20.2%	63.0%
North Little Rock city	31,581	5,156	3,385	1,771	1,477	1,908	0	28.7%	34.3%
Springdale city	27,237	4,332	2,966	1,366	826	2,140	na	na	na
California									
Alameda city	32,061	6,453	4,069	2,384	2,080	1,989	188	na	72.5%
Alhambra city	29,625	6,209	3,510	2,699	1,417	2,093	81	na	65.2%
Anaheim city	103,304	18,062	11,375	6,687	6,755	4,620	758	30.8%	63.7%
Antioch city	36,473	6,234	4,484	1,750	2,221	2,263	na	22.6%	na
Bakersfield city	122,393	19,005	13,218	5,787	5,950	7,268	592	28.1%	65.3%
Baldwin Park city	20,675	3,402	2,483	919	817	1,666	na	na	50.7%
Bellflower city	26,073	4,540	2,600	1,940	1,243	1,357	164	na	59.4%
Berkeley city	46,445	9,722	6,959	2,763	3,585	3,374	92	20.9%	54.2%
Buena Park city	24,722	4,647	3,656	991	1,476	2,180	na	na	na
Burbank city	45,250	8,929	5,531	3,398	2,606	2,925	64	na	70.1%
Camarillo city	24,059	7,459	6,142	1,317	3,153	2,989	188	33.5%	na
Carlsbad city	46,381	10,215	8,051	2,164	4,404	3,647	1,133	na	na
Carson city	26,343	6,846	5,813	1,033	3,816	1,997	na	50.0%	na
Chico city	39,449	6,668	5,115	1,553	1,563	3,552	201	19.8%	71.5%
Chino city	18,978	2,674	2,093	581	1,271	822	na	26.5%	na
Chino Hills city	22,853	3,086	2,435	651	1,598	837	na	na	na
Chula Vista city	85,213	17,558	13,027	4,531	5,746	7,281	83	26.4%	64.4%
Citrus Heights city	35,950	9,454	6,828	2,626	3,346	3,482	205	35.5%	54.1%
Clovis city	35,946	6,658	5,110	1,548	2,338	2,772	146	34.5%	68.2%
Compton city	24,990	4,086	3,031	1,055	1,656	1,375	0	36.6%	6na
Concord city	46,524	10,031	7,985	2,046	4,104	3,881	457	30.6%	67.8%
Corona city	51,935	8,019	6,279	1,740	3,456	2,823	462	37.9%	70.6%
Costa Mesa city	40,533	6,368	4,421	1,947	2,537	1,884	335	33.9%	57.0%
Daly City city	31,068	7,380	4,613	2,767	1,883	2,730	na	27.1%	37.4%
Davis city	26,596	4,224	3,022	1,202	773	2,249	389	na	38.4%
Downey city	35,966	6,453	4,715	1,738	2,434	2,281	0	na	na
El Cajon city	32,002	5,369	3,353	2,016	1,033	2,320	106	na	65.1%
El Monte city	33,196	5,961	3,200	2,761	1,028	2,172	0	na	64.5%
Elk Grove city	52,225	7,958	5,664	2,294	3,230	2,434	298	36.8%	70.7%
Escondido city	46,644	9,541	6,319	3,222	3,391	2,928	625	36.4%	66.2%
Fairfield city	37,311	6,986	5,623	1,363	2,809	2,814	222	28.4%	59.3%
Folsom city	26,452	5,957	4,787	1,170	2,559	2,228	568	35.5%	na
Fontana city	53,700	5,801	4,344	1,457	2,458	1,886	na	36.3%	56.1%
Fremont city	76,883	12,648	9,945	2,703	4,359	5,586	641	24.9%	64.4%
Fresno city	178,577	31,243	20,538	10,705	10,062	10,476	979	28.6%	62.9%
Fullerton city	46,796	8,868	6,219	2,649	2,582	3,637	561	32.3%	64.3%
Garden Grove city	48,193	10,083	6,374	3,709	2,661	3,713	na	25.9%	73.3%
Glendale city	75,764	17,427	7,554	9,873	4,092	3,462	381	46.1%	72.6%
Hawthorne city	33,300	4,333	1,829	2,504	1,165	664	na	na	65.9%
Hayward city	50,216	9,324	6,502	2,822	2,888	3,614	469	30.6%	60.9%

Table J-3: Places—Summary of Housing and Householder Characteristics—*Continued*

| | | | | | Householders 65 Years and Over | | | | |
| | | | | | Owner Householders | | | Percent of Owner Householders Who Pay 35% or More of income for Housing Costs | Percent of Renter Households Who Pay 35% or More of Income for Rental Costs |
	Total Housing Units	Total Households	Owner Occupied	Renter Occupied	With a Mortgage	Without a Mortgage	Renter Households With Meals Included in Rent		
California—Cont.									
Hemet city	36,551	13,288	9,319	3,969	3,432	5,887	616	na	na
Hesperia city	29,234	5,155	3,994	1,161	2,132	1,862	na	36.4%	na
Huntington Beach city	82,155	19,057	15,847	3,210	7,140	8,707	346	29.4%	68.4%
Indio city	32,406	7,007	5,496	1,511	2,418	3,078	na	37.9%	76.7%
Inglewood city	37,683	6,571	3,783	2,788	2,112	1,671	40	na	70.4%
Irvine city	94,979	13,548	9,676	3,872	5,366	4,310	499	28.8%	68.6%
Jurupa Valley city	25,704	4,127	3,030	1,097	1,435	1,595	140	29.6%	na
Laguna Niguel city	27,134	6,069	5,462	607	3,986	1,476	na	na	na
Lake Forest city	26,113	4,433	3,890	543	2,343	1,547	na	42.0%	na
Lakewood city	27,981	5,521	4,593	928	2,549	2,044	na	31.1%	na
Lancaster city	54,180	8,632	6,385	2,247	3,991	2,394	na	46.2%	68.1%
Livermore city	31,509	6,443	4,944	1,499	2,883	2,061	na	25.7%	na
Long Beach city	170,977	27,282	17,622	9,660	8,520	9,102	769	29.3%	65.4%
Los Angeles city	1,433,123	261,218	147,775	113,443	76,875	70,900	6,270	37.9%	64.8%
Lynwood city	15,852	1,698	1,079	619	633	446	na	na	92.7%
Manteca city	25,154	5,354	4,164	1,190	2,234	1,930	na	32.0%	na
Menifee city	29,014	9,373	7,485	1,888	3,388	4,097	193	38.1%	na
Merced city	28,344	5,246	3,172	2,074	1,910	1,262	233	na	45.0%
Milpitas city	21,992	3,546	2,900	646	1,301	1,599	87	na	na
Mission Viejo city	33,719	9,116	8,024	1,092	4,378	3,646	474	26.2%	na
Modesto city	76,710	17,326	12,387	4,939	5,402	6,985	259	25.5%	66.7%
Moreno Valley city	53,737	7,677	5,611	2,066	3,887	1,724	na	40.5%	88.9%
Mountain View city	36,266	5,265	3,198	2,067	836	2,362	na	na	64.3%
Murrieta city	33,847	5,796	4,722	1,074	2,536	2,186	na	30.7%	na
Napa city	30,242	7,078	5,613	1,465	2,743	2,870	343	33.7%	56.8%
Newport Beach city	46,072	12,641	9,463	3,178	5,290	4,173	544	na	62.4%
Norwalk city	27,899	5,729	4,202	1,527	2,030	2,172	0	28.2%	52.8%
Oakland city	167,945	31,156	17,950	13,206	9,906	8,044	666	35.7%	60.9%
Oceanside city	67,445	16,383	12,414	3,969	5,722	6,692	208	36.0%	60.9%
Ontario city	50,676	6,587	4,317	2,270	1,731	2,586	na	33.4%	60.2%
Orange city	43,438	7,669	5,967	1,702	2,884	3,083	na	29.7%	60.9%
Oxnard city	55,666	9,871	7,974	1,897	4,212	3,762	na	29.6%	63.5%
Palmdale city	47,428	6,429	5,074	1,355	3,273	1,801	251	32.4%	85.3%
Palo Alto city	27,963	7,784	5,463	2,321	1,935	3,528	744	na	60.3%
Pasadena city	57,728	11,297	7,096	4,201	3,635	3,461	394	31.6%	65.9%
Perris city	18,106	1,826	1,383	443	1,073	310	na	na	na
Pittsburg city	21,688	3,844	2,800	1,044	1,432	1,368	na	24.7%	na
Pleasanton city	27,313	5,929	4,442	1,487	2,275	2,167	na	na	na
Pomona city	41,589	6,313	4,578	1,735	1,953	2,625	na	31.1%	57.2%
Rancho Cordova city	26,103	4,927	3,813	1,114	1,687	2,126	na	29.3%	51.2%
Rancho Cucamonga city	60,846	8,841	6,102	2,739	3,357	2,745	318	32.2%	78.6%
Redding city	37,365	10,201	7,109	3,092	3,145	3,964	695	32.7%	71.5%
Redlands city	24,371	4,848	3,117	1,731	1,471	1,646	132	na	51.0%
Redondo Beach city	27,575	4,948	2,935	2,013	1,481	1,454	na	37.5%	51.6%
Redwood City city	30,158	5,999	4,353	1,646	1,959	2,394	237	na	57.8%
Rialto city	26,822	4,629	3,551	1,078	1,933	1,618	na	27.9%	46.2%
Richmond city	42,271	7,086	4,804	2,282	2,621	2,183	na	27.3%	57.3%
Riverside city	97,175	15,524	11,860	3,664	5,926	5,934	628	26.3%	66.5%
Roseville city	50,395	13,779	9,903	3,876	5,099	4,804	1,108	30.2%	63.5%
Sacramento city	193,062	35,122	23,376	11,746	11,458	11,918	1,150	27.8%	58.1%
Salinas city	41,083	6,480	4,222	2,258	1,875	2,347	261	28.4%	55.8%
San Bernardino city	59,698	9,306	6,786	2,520	3,188	3,598	34	28.8%	53.5%
San Buenaventura (Ventura) city	45,041	11,652	8,987	2,665	3,829	5,158	304	na	62.9%
San Clemente city	27,104	7,847	6,812	1,035	3,301	3,511	386	na	na
San Diego city	530,490	89,228	62,581	26,647	29,443	33,138	2,133	32.0%	65.1%
San Francisco city	386,610	73,562	39,294	34,268	16,438	22,856	1,836	28.4%	55.5%
San Jose city	323,195	59,611	42,628	16,983	21,104	21,524	1,526	31.7%	72.3%
San Leandro city	34,625	7,478	5,321	2,157	2,173	3,148	208	27.9%	79.0%
San Marcos city	29,691	6,690	5,026	1,664	1,999	3,027	228	na	48.4%
San Mateo city	42,578	10,570	7,359	3,211	2,891	4,468	791	25.9%	82.5%
San Ramon city	25,046	3,454	2,765	689	1,680	1,085	na	4na	na
Santa Ana city	79,902	12,454	9,159	3,295	4,415	4,744	139	29.5%	63.9%
Santa Barbara city	38,806	9,968	5,691	4,277	2,733	2,958	1,001	na	66.5%
Santa Clara city	46,705	7,717	4,504	3,213	1,453	3,051	290	18.4%	72.7%
Santa Clarita city	59,991	11,788	9,575	2,213	5,128	4,447	na	34.3%	52.2%
Santa Maria city	28,634	5,153	3,661	1,492	1,454	2,207	130	33.8%	63.1%
Santa Monica city	50,563	10,231	4,482	5,749	2,464	2,018	292	na	68.0%
Santa Rosa city	68,112	16,477	11,401	5,076	5,245	6,156	1,370	37.1%	58.5%
Simi Valley city	43,815	10,587	7,664	2,923	3,765	3,899	na	31.2%	42.5%
South Gate city	23,784	3,870	2,095	1,775	1,256	839	0	na	68.6%
South San Francisco city	24,314	5,175	3,746	1,429	1,658	2,088	na	na	na
Stockton city	103,663	17,432	11,736	5,696	6,023	5,713	582	30.1%	67.4%
Sunnyvale city	57,768	9,250	7,065	2,185	2,369	4,696	194	24.8%	69.8%

Table J-3: Places—Summary of Housing and Householder Characteristics—*Continued*

| | | | | | Householders 65 Years and Over | | | | |
| | | | | | Owner Householders | | | | |
	Total Housing Units	Total Households	Owner Occupied	Renter Occupied	With a Mortgage	Without a Mortgage	Renter Households With Meals Included in Rent	Percent of Owner Householders Who Pay 35% or More of income for Housing Costs	Percent of Renter Households Who Pay 35% or More of Income for Rental Costs
California—Cont.									
Temecula city	36,119	6,339	4,766	1,573	3,163	1,603	na	44.3%	na
Thousand Oaks city	46,952	13,740	10,624	3,116	6,277	4,347	947	38.4%	51.4%
Torrance city	57,841	15,122	11,718	3,404	4,530	7,188	402	na	60.8%
Tracy city	24,351	2,481	1,847	634	969	878	na	na	81.5%
Turlock city	26,250	5,810	3,270	2,540	1,328	1,942	175	na	69.8%
Tustin city	27,233	4,296	3,172	1,124	1,966	1,206	79	na	89.6%
Union City city	21,319	4,994	3,874	1,120	2,024	1,850	136	na	na
Upland city	30,039	6,692	5,063	1,629	2,783	2,280	na	na	57.3%
Vacaville city	33,188	7,162	5,546	1,616	3,405	2,141	291	36.1%	69.9%
Vallejo city	47,201	9,711	6,764	2,947	3,997	2,767	143	na	73.5%
Victorville city	35,301	4,916	3,637	1,279	2,334	1,303	na	47.1%	62.7%
Visalia city	45,165	8,783	7,078	1,705	2,771	4,307	290	31.0%	45.0%
Vista city	30,685	4,268	3,181	1,087	1,656	1,525	na	45.4%	72.1%
Walnut Creek city	32,767	13,048	9,700	3,348	3,167	6,533	957	33.5%	61.9%
West Covina city	32,429	7,108	5,677	1,431	3,171	2,506	60	30.9%	68.1%
Westminster city	29,069	8,163	4,636	3,527	2,160	2,476	157	na	77.4%
Whittier city	27,307	6,065	4,637	1,428	2,592	2,045	na	na	66.7%
Yorba Linda city	21,663	5,981	4,925	1,056	2,891	2,034	na	30.0%	na
Yuba City city	23,694	4,994	3,838	1,156	1,803	2,035	na	18.0%	41.7%
Colorado									
Arvada city	44,486	10,289	7,947	2,342	3,702	4,245	438	25.5%	69.6%
Aurora city	133,434	21,898	17,399	4,499	9,270	8,129	891	24.5%	71.3%
Boulder city	46,668	7,086	5,295	1,791	1,952	3,343	617	34.3%	63.1%
Centennial city	40,452	9,307	8,845	462	4,381	4,464	na	24.7%	66.7%
Colorado Springs city	187,010	34,450	27,523	6,927	12,840	14,683	2,545	25.6%	75.5%
Denver city	298,880	47,806	32,515	15,291	14,074	18,441	1,874	26.8%	59.0%
Fort Collins city	59,857	8,830	6,441	2,389	2,989	3,452	476	18.2%	68.3%
Greeley city	35,382	8,073	5,916	2,157	2,555	3,361	567	23.9%	75.8%
Lakewood city	67,611	14,660	11,144	3,516	4,345	6,799	1,125	27.7%	68.1%
Longmont city	33,975	7,205	5,451	1,754	2,518	2,933	569	na	62.0%
Loveland city	33,571	9,494	6,315	3,179	2,325	3,990	766	22.2%	59.1%
Pueblo city	47,562	11,571	8,523	3,048	3,910	4,613	189	31.6%	57.6%
Thornton city	44,766	6,686	5,442	1,244	2,521	2,921	na	22.3%	38.6%
Westminster city	46,195	9,185	7,017	2,168	4,046	2,971	713	24.7%	60.0%
Connecticut									
Bridgeport city	56,738	9,660	5,885	3,775	2,525	3,360	29	45.6%	55.4%
Danbury city	31,423	6,217	4,513	1,704	1,764	2,749	292	na	56.0%
Hartford city	53,116	7,453	2,302	5,151	1,147	1,155	502	na	57.7%
New Britain city	30,887	4,729	3,030	1,699	996	2,034	128	37.1%	51.7%
New Haven city	55,809	9,275	3,960	5,315	2,412	1,548	170	60.4%	42.4%
Norwalk city	35,194	7,780	6,228	1,552	2,972	3,256	na	46.7%	51.7%
Stamford city	53,491	11,163	7,946	3,217	3,869	4,077	473	41.6%	49.2%
Waterbury city	46,327	8,338	5,277	3,061	2,326	2,951	0	53.4%	57.2%
Delaware									
Wilmington city	35,713	6,632	3,623	3,009	1,941	1,682	329	na	67.4%
District of Columbia									
Washington city	306,184	50,463	32,424	18,039	15,941	16,483	1,701	26.6%	54.3%
Florida									
Boca Raton city	47,386	11,644	9,099	2,545	3,158	5,941	683	31.6%	72.5%
Boynton Beach city	35,114	8,263	6,895	1,368	2,356	4,539	333	na	62.0%
Cape Coral city	83,580	21,305	17,767	3,538	8,160	9,607	286	34.7%	79.1%
Clearwater city	59,229	15,507	11,289	4,218	4,224	7,065	998	na	62.5%
Coral Springs city	43,317	6,081	4,834	1,247	2,532	2,302	na	43.5%	39.5%
Deerfield Beach city	40,532	10,628	8,660	1,968	2,599	6,061	708	39.0%	71.5%
Delray Beach city	33,713	11,781	8,080	3,701	3,536	4,544	561	41.6%	78.9%
Deltona city	32,223	6,813	6,002	811	3,222	2,780	na	41.9%	na
Fort Lauderdale city	99,462	20,346	14,904	5,442	5,106	9,798	0	35.9%	68.6%
Fort Myers city	35,420	6,835	4,857	1,978	2,219	2,638	324	28.5%	51.3%
Gainesville city	58,617	8,820	7,167	1,653	1,972	5,195	140	22.5%	40.0%
Hialeah city	72,417	20,395	11,025	9,370	4,654	6,371	260	46.3%	65.8%
Hollywood city	71,633	14,733	11,375	3,358	4,117	7,258	492	34.8%	65.0%
Homestead city	22,130	2,201	1,060	1,141	581	479	na	na	na
Jacksonville city	371,254	67,188	52,478	14,710	22,105	30,373	1,612	29.3%	62.1%
Kissimmee city	25,737	2,939	2,205	734	1,373	832	na	na	na
Lakeland city	46,626	12,712	9,342	3,370	2,657	6,685	272	23.3%	68.4%
Largo city	45,889	13,624	9,596	4,028	2,285	7,311	1,143	25.9%	73.8%
Lauderhill city	27,687	6,029	5,010	1,019	2,455	2,555	na	na	na
Melbourne city	40,450	11,725	8,035	3,690	2,882	5,153	506	na	64.0%
Miami Beach city	68,766	9,107	5,266	3,841	1,351	3,915	na	36.4%	58.5%
Miami city	191,653	37,894	17,622	20,272	5,920	11,702	286	37.5%	63.0%

Table J-3: Places—Summary of Housing and Householder Characteristics—*Continued*

| | | | | | Householders 65 Years and Over | | | | |
| | | | | | Owner Householders | | | | |
	Total Housing Units	Total Households	Owner Occupied	Renter Occupied	With a Mortgage	Without a Mortgage	Renter Households With Meals Included in Rent	Percent of Owner Householders Who Pay 35% or More of income for Housing Costs	Percent of Renter Households Who Pay 35% or More of Income for Rental Costs
Florida—Cont.									
Miami Gardens city	34,830	8,286	6,754	1,532	3,136	3,618	na	36.5%	na
Miramar city	42,678	4,054	3,934	120	2,205	1,729	na	na	na
Orlando city	127,324	16,912	9,855	7,057	4,096	5,759	646	31.2%	55.3%
Palm Bay city	43,731	9,804	7,864	1,940	3,223	4,641	na	20.0%	na
Palm Coast city	35,858	11,851	10,177	1,674	4,757	5,420	510	na	na
Pembroke Pines city	61,944	15,395	13,821	1,574	5,674	8,147	na	45.7%	na
Plantation city	38,918	7,511	6,676	835	2,798	3,878	na	36.4%	75.7%
Pompano Beach city	57,395	14,641	9,841	4,800	2,501	7,340	1,593	27.1%	64.7%
Port St. Lucie city	73,342	21,129	18,077	3,052	7,503	10,574	639	27.3%	na
St. Petersburg city	126,883	25,780	19,479	6,301	7,494	11,985	618	30.3%	54.6%
Sunrise city	38,128	8,022	6,706	1,316	2,875	3,831	na	46.2%	62.8%
Tallahassee city	85,959	12,043	8,974	3,069	3,995	4,979	642	21.9%	57.0%
Tampa city	161,455	26,403	18,932	7,471	5,891	13,041	604	21.7%	62.5%
West Palm Beach city	54,853	11,322	7,531	3,791	3,899	3,632	459	43.8%	65.4%
Weston city	25,971	4,270	3,222	1,048	1,607	1,615	na	na	na
Georgia									
Albany city	32,562	6,494	4,032	2,462	1,130	2,902	na	na	82.9%
Athens-Clarke County unified govt (bal)	51,256	7,501	5,084	2,417	1,994	3,090	523	na	42.3%
Atlanta city	235,865	35,365	20,491	14,874	8,034	12,457	1,925	32.7%	53.4%
Augusta-Richmond County consolidated govt (bal)	85,200	14,469	10,467	4,002	4,199	6,268	235	27.0%	66.8%
Columbus city	83,872	15,599	11,257	4,342	5,074	6,183	560	20.9%	51.5%
Johns Creek city	28,874	3,735	3,078	657	1,724	1,354	na	na	na
Macon-Bibb County	70,213	13,579	8,712	4,867	3,287	5,425	530	23.6%	46.5%
Roswell city	36,304	5,898	4,829	1,069	2,887	1,942	na	na	na
Sandy Springs city	50,197	8,023	5,706	2,317	2,086	3,620	1,151	28.5%	62.1%
Savannah city	64,389	12,670	8,273	4,397	3,275	4,998	359	24.0%	57.6%
Warner Robins city	31,388	5,042	3,462	1,580	1,586	1,876	na	na	na
Hawaii									
Urban Honolulu CDP	147,186	37,927	24,562	13,365	9,272	15,290	1,195	27.4%	58.4%
Idaho									
Boise City city	90,449	17,197	12,497	4,700	5,122	7,375	1,632	20.6%	68.9%
Meridian city	32,185	6,095	5,646	449	3,570	2,076	na	na	na
Nampa city	31,039	6,283	4,575	1,708	2,210	2,365	na	na	28.6%
Illinois									
Aurora city	65,376	8,469	6,440	2,029	3,014	3,426	217	33.1%	55.6%
Bloomington city	33,677	5,832	3,920	1,912	1,556	2,364	527	23.0%	61.8%
Champaign city	36,905	5,174	4,710	464	1,986	2,724	na	na	86.4%
Chicago city	1,192,346	196,065	121,453	74,612	48,416	73,037	3,917	37.3%	59.5%
Decatur city	35,380	8,194	6,819	1,375	1,857	4,962	198	19.1%	37.6%
Elgin city	40,447	7,503	5,810	1,693	3,129	2,681	na	36.0%	62.7%
Evanston city	31,770	6,153	4,767	1,386	2,250	2,517	250	na	68.3%
Joliet city	51,042	7,714	5,992	1,722	2,275	3,717	119	29.2%	63.2%
Naperville city	53,362	8,329	6,952	1,377	3,300	3,652	411	32.2%	57.5%
Peoria city	53,607	10,416	7,038	3,378	2,488	4,550	544	26.0%	43.8%
Rockford city	67,984	14,526	9,867	4,659	3,211	6,656	860	30.8%	49.5%
Springfield city	55,835	12,632	8,852	3,780	2,962	5,890	661	17.6%	50.7%
Waukegan city	30,912	4,373	3,307	1,066	1,219	2,088	na	na	49.6%
Indiana									
Bloomington city	33,659	3,598	2,771	827	991	1,780	na	na	49.1%
Carmel city	34,310	8,080	6,697	1,383	2,972	3,725	570	13.8%	na
Evansville city	58,998	12,499	9,179	3,320	4,093	5,086	367	20.9%	58.2%
Fort Wayne city	114,194	21,156	17,285	3,871	7,124	10,161	331	15.9%	50.9%
Gary city	41,659	7,700	5,717	1,983	2,330	3,387	na	na	61.0%
Hammond city	32,529	5,055	4,038	1,017	1,654	2,384	43	19.1%	42.1%
Indianapolis city (bal)	382,494	59,437	43,744	15,693	21,115	22,629	1,837	26.4%	53.0%
Lafayette city	31,279	4,974	3,947	1,027	1,702	2,245	na	na	62.3%
Muncie city	32,253	6,377	5,497	880	2,049	3,448	na	na	31.1%
South Bend city	48,002	8,925	7,213	1,712	2,710	4,503	287	17.4%	40.3%
Iowa									
Cedar Rapids city	58,754	11,580	9,608	1,972	3,374	6,234	754	20.2%	46.5%
Davenport city	44,544	8,170	6,170	2,000	2,145	4,025	305	17.4%	38.5%
Des Moines city	90,683	15,788	11,341	4,447	4,048	7,293	754	32.2%	58.4%
Iowa City city	31,200	4,080	3,203	877	881	2,322	na	na	83.9%
Sioux City city	33,149	6,786	5,012	1,774	1,171	3,841	392	14.3%	75.4%
Waterloo city	31,407	6,873	5,522	1,351	1,063	4,459	471	11.4%	43.7%
Kansas									
Kansas City city	62,692	10,753	8,431	2,322	3,082	5,349	169	31.0%	54.9%
Lawrence city	38,776	5,439	3,691	1,748	1,651	2,040	426	na	61.7%
Olathe city	46,951	7,151	5,111	2,040	2,062	3,049	704	19.8%	71.8%

Table J-3: Places—Summary of Housing and Householder Characteristics—*Continued*

					Householders 65 Years and Over				
					Owner Householders			Percent of Owner Householders Who Pay 35% or More of income for Housing Costs	Percent of Renter Households Who Pay 35% or More of Income for Rental Costs
	Total Housing Units	Total Households	Owner Occupied	Renter Occupied	With a Mortgage	Without a Mortgage	Renter Households With Meals Included in Rent		
Kansas—Cont.									
Overland Park city	80,293	16,657	12,439	4,218	4,773	7,666	2,122	25.6%	57.0%
Topeka city	59,220	11,974	8,721	3,253	2,664	6,057	703	15.3%	72.7%
Wichita city	169,594	31,417	23,574	7,843	7,308	16,266	1,815	21.8%	50.4%
Kentucky									
Lexington-Fayette urban county	138,832	22,793	17,442	5,351	7,133	10,309	825	25.4%	44.3%
Louisville/Jefferson County metro govt (bal)	274,774	53,042	41,401	11,641	15,096	26,305	1,173	24.3%	58.2%
Louisiana									
Baton Rouge city	102,842	19,560	14,281	5,279	4,546	9,735	895	23.5%	67.1%
Bossier City city	28,285	5,211	3,545	1,666	1,517	2,028	na	na	40.8%
Kenner city	28,751	7,390	5,482	1,908	1,595	3,887	295	13.4%	na
Lafayette city	55,846	10,215	7,742	2,473	2,475	5,267	393	na	56.0%
Lake Charles city	36,524	8,354	6,451	1,903	1,656	4,795	na	na	31.8%
New Orleans city	192,472	30,343	21,710	8,633	6,361	15,349	345	33.0%	61.0%
Shreveport city	88,685	18,496	14,735	3,761	3,472	11,263	200	22.0%	45.1%
Maine									
Portland city	33,258	5,751	3,505	2,246	1,703	1,802	505	46.4%	66.2%
Maryland									
Baltimore city	297,027	52,216	33,495	18,721	14,612	18,883	619	34.5%	49.9%
Frederick city	29,249	4,645	3,437	1,208	2,180	1,257	251	47.2%	na
Gaithersburg city	24,965	3,665	2,232	1,433	1,200	1,032	504	na	74.0%
Rockville city	26,795	6,438	4,227	2,211	1,952	2,275	370	31.0%	68.6%
Massachusetts									
Boston city	274,459	43,696	20,570	23,126	9,030	11,540	992	40.5%	58.6%
Brockton city	35,367	7,102	4,197	2,905	1,923	2,274	176	39.1%	44.9%
Cambridge city	48,231	7,644	4,311	3,333	2,029	2,282	119	34.8%	47.5%
Fall River city	43,819	9,414	4,534	4,880	1,817	2,717	369	41.2%	53.6%
Lawrence city	26,683	4,104	1,480	2,624	564	916	42	na	54.2%
Lowell city	41,153	7,275	4,624	2,651	1,657	2,967	224	49.9%	53.5%
Lynn city	33,871	6,378	3,192	3,186	1,252	1,940	160	36.4%	50.1%
New Bedford city	41,887	7,776	4,052	3,724	1,465	2,587	151	42.9%	52.3%
Newton city	33,006	10,070	7,584	2,486	2,363	5,221	907	na	72.0%
Quincy city	42,305	9,321	4,788	4,533	1,874	2,914	797	na	57.9%
Somerville city	33,085	5,097	2,863	2,234	1,140	1,723	128	na	54.7%
Springfield city	62,231	11,472	8,283	3,189	3,131	5,152	147	32.6%	49.0%
Worcester city	71,164	12,197	6,963	5,234	2,608	4,355	403	37.1%	50.9%
Michigan									
Ann Arbor city	50,041	8,228	6,452	1,776	2,483	3,969	277	21.4%	43.7%
Dearborn city	34,851	7,987	6,145	1,842	1,770	4,375	196	29.0%	37.9%
Detroit city	367,958	59,257	40,232	19,025	14,523	25,709	234	32.8%	59.4%
Farmington Hills city	37,519	11,077	7,432	3,645	3,094	4,338	598	na	49.6%
Flint city	51,819	8,369	6,874	1,495	2,400	4,474	0	24.7%	37.9%
Grand Rapids city	79,838	14,506	9,686	4,820	3,415	6,271	1,032	29.7%	51.5%
Kalamazoo city	33,552	4,700	3,238	1,462	1,363	1,875	138	21.6%	37.8%
Lansing city	54,970	8,827	6,655	2,172	2,478	4,177	116	29.8%	64.0%
Livonia city	37,779	10,299	8,584	1,715	3,182	5,402	379	27.0%	na
Rochester Hills city	28,957	7,676	5,905	1,771	2,590	3,315	621	na	na
Southfield city	37,626	9,558	5,561	3,997	2,766	2,795	633	na	69.5%
Sterling Heights city	51,915	13,641	10,700	2,941	3,721	6,979	905	18.9%	61.1%
Troy city	32,824	7,929	6,312	1,617	2,467	3,845	282	na	na
Warren city	59,498	12,733	10,142	2,591	3,448	6,694	na	18.3%	56.8%
Westland city	36,825	9,447	6,316	3,131	2,191	4,125	642	28.1%	46.0%
Wyoming city	29,073	4,965	4,146	819	1,501	2,645	na	25.9%	72.9%
Minnesota									
Bloomington city	39,079	10,509	8,958	1,551	3,231	5,727	123	21.1%	60.7%
Brooklyn Park city	28,770	4,945	3,931	1,014	1,987	1,944	na	36.5%	na
Duluth city	39,020	8,747	6,025	2,722	1,513	4,512	857	15.4%	70.9%
Eagan city	28,006	4,723	3,904	819	1,751	2,153	301	34.5%	na
Maple Grove city	28,340	4,932	4,016	916	2,259	1,757	232	27.1%	na
Minneapolis city	182,617	23,005	15,374	7,631	6,433	8,941	299	32.8%	54.2%
Plymouth city	30,870	7,280	6,042	1,238	2,558	3,484	na	28.6%	54.4%
Rochester city	47,161	9,817	8,275	1,542	2,840	5,435	595	18.7%	56.3%
St. Cloud city	27,094	4,491	3,657	834	1,060	2,597	na	20.6%	51.3%
St. Paul city	117,391	17,553	10,701	6,852	4,214	6,487	1,367	25.5%	57.6%
Woodbury city	27,027	4,388	3,920	468	1,473	2,447	na	na	na
Mississippi									
Gulfport city	35,050	7,242	5,500	1,742	2,055	3,445	348	na	85.0%
Jackson city	75,710	12,952	9,776	3,176	3,370	6,406	na	26.1%	55.0%

Table J-3: Places—Summary of Housing and Householder Characteristics—*Continued*

| | | | | | Householders 65 Years and Over | | | | |
| | | | | | Owner Householders | | | Percent of Owner Households Who Pay 35% or More of income for Housing Costs | Percent of Renter Households Who Pay 35% or More of Income for Rental Costs |
	Total Housing Units	Total Households	Owner Occupied	Renter Occupied	With a Mortgage	Without a Mortgage	Renter Households With Meals Included in Rent		
Missouri									
Columbia city	49,842	7,080	4,976	2,104	2,384	2,592	na	16.2%	39.1%
Independence city	53,744	12,769	10,485	2,284	3,691	6,794	na	25.1%	46.9%
Kansas City city	226,206	37,862	27,119	10,743	10,323	16,796	1,346	27.1%	48.2%
Lee's Summit city	37,542	7,931	5,879	2,052	3,001	2,878	713	33.3%	na
O'Fallon city	30,857	5,357	3,997	1,360	2,334	1,663	398	27.8%	na
Springfield city	77,828	17,249	12,057	5,192	4,640	7,417	598	24.7%	51.4%
St. Charles city	28,210	6,498	5,266	1,232	1,961	3,305	177	15.8%	46.3%
St. Joseph city	33,280	7,418	5,437	1,981	1,445	3,992	331	20.3%	41.1%
St. Louis city	175,369	24,010	15,032	8,978	5,381	9,651	128	34.4%	49.8%
Montana									
Billings city	47,018	10,379	7,816	2,563	2,896	4,920	736	28.3%	40.9%
Missoula city	32,625	5,797	3,643	2,154	1,237	2,406	660	33.9%	56.1%
Nebraska									
Lincoln city	114,052	21,278	15,770	5,508	5,433	10,337	1,381	18.5%	44.4%
Omaha city	189,952	35,064	25,812	9,252	9,409	16,403	2,365	24.4%	57.8%
Nevada									
Henderson city	119,423	28,217	22,694	5,523	12,261	10,433	371	31.8%	55.2%
Las Vegas city	247,144	46,224	32,904	13,320	17,055	15,849	541	27.0%	58.4%
North Las Vegas city	81,361	12,277	9,062	3,215	5,440	3,622	na	27.8%	82.2%
Reno city	103,322	21,629	13,631	7,998	6,372	7,259	592	33.3%	53.5%
Sparks city	38,619	8,455	6,084	2,371	3,345	2,739	300	36.0%	67.5%
New Hampshire									
Manchester city	48,885	8,171	5,192	2,979	2,177	3,015	517	37.3%	59.9%
Nashua city	37,524	6,403	4,773	1,630	1,902	2,871	283	35.1%	68.5%
New Jersey									
Bayonne city	26,125	4,357	2,451	1,906	825	1,626	na	na	70.1%
Camden city	32,683	6,042	3,658	2,384	901	2,757	na	na	59.8%
Clifton city	32,822	5,859	4,726	1,133	1,307	3,419	na	64.6%	64.4%
East Orange city	30,730	5,998	2,289	3,709	972	1,317	0	na	49.8%
Elizabeth city	45,128	6,042	3,047	2,995	1,242	1,805	36	na	54.1%
Jersey City city	110,896	15,824	6,867	8,957	3,570	3,297	259	52.2%	60.5%
Newark city	106,616	15,434	5,454	9,980	2,814	2,640	179	61.9%	56.8%
Passaic city	21,861	3,548	1,220	2,328	430	790	118	na	77.4%
Paterson city	47,410	8,388	2,970	5,418	1,364	1,606	25	62.9%	60.8%
Trenton city	35,242	5,591	2,946	2,645	995	1,951	43	na	55.4%
Union City city	27,350	4,553	1,271	3,282	373	898	na	na	55.7%
New Mexico									
Albuquerque city	240,461	48,418	36,458	11,960	17,265	19,193	1,061	29.0%	54.2%
Las Cruces city	44,762	9,355	7,180	2,175	2,518	4,662	326	na	56.6%
Rio Rancho city	35,408	7,725	6,279	1,446	3,474	2,805	na	33.8%	na
Santa Fe city	37,051	10,284	7,905	2,379	3,175	4,730	312	na	53.6%
New York									
Albany city	48,460	7,767	4,286	3,481	1,678	2,608	428	25.5%	44.4%
Buffalo city	131,604	23,277	14,481	8,796	5,578	8,903	503	29.0%	46.3%
Mount Vernon city	26,664	5,949	3,812	2,137	1,769	2,043	129	na	78.1%
New Rochelle city	29,274	7,137	4,065	3,072	1,697	2,368	215	na	67.4%
New York city	3,438,742	678,250	285,698	392,552	96,000	189,698	4,592	38.4%	59.8%
Rochester city	96,285	15,228	7,503	7,725	2,707	4,796	159	28.7%	62.7%
Schenectady city	32,723	5,189	3,089	2,100	1,114	1,975	465	na	80.3%
Syracuse city	65,264	11,056	6,614	4,442	1,981	4,633	182	21.7%	50.2%
Yonkers city	81,682	20,776	12,467	8,309	3,969	8,498	138	38.4%	54.4%
North Carolina									
Asheville city	43,621	9,967	7,292	2,675	2,650	4,642	607	22.4%	44.4%
Charlotte city	334,471	47,756	34,345	13,411	16,444	17,901	2,088	30.6%	53.0%
Concord city	32,882	6,519	5,190	1,329	2,134	3,056	110	29.8%	na
Durham city	114,191	17,276	12,578	4,698	6,466	6,112	487	26.1%	47.5%
Fayetteville city	94,304	14,543	11,391	3,152	5,973	5,418	170	26.9%	57.4%
Gastonia city	32,581	6,574	5,123	1,451	2,535	2,588	420	27.9%	70.2%
Greensboro city	127,413	23,393	16,309	7,084	7,724	8,585	1,629	26.8%	57.7%
Greenville city	42,592	5,777	3,956	1,821	1,497	2,459	607	21.5%	61.0%
High Point city	44,868	8,256	5,567	2,689	3,150	2,417	287	31.5%	65.9%
Jacksonville city	23,821	2,312	1,620	692	795	825	na	na	44.7%
Raleigh city	192,504	26,544	17,973	8,571	9,288	8,685	877	22.4%	55.0%
Wilmington city	56,326	10,603	7,420	3,183	3,889	3,531	195	34.9%	48.1%
Winston-Salem city	105,647	21,394	15,449	5,945	6,512	8,937	499	18.6%	51.4%
North Dakota									
Bismarck city	31,543	6,789	4,896	1,893	870	4,026	489	9.3%	50.0%
Fargo city	54,338	8,362	5,085	3,277	1,945	3,140	1,082	17.7%	64.3%

Table J-3: Places—Summary of Housing and Householder Characteristics—*Continued*

| | | | | | Householders 65 Years and Over | | | | |
| | | | | | Owner Householders | | | | |
	Total Housing Units	Total Households	Owner Occupied	Renter Occupied	With a Mortgage	Without a Mortgage	Renter Households With Meals Included in Rent	Percent of Owner Householders Who Pay 35% or More of income for Housing Costs	Percent of Renter Households Who Pay 35% or More of Income for Rental Costs
Ohio									
Akron city	97,486	18,210	13,415	4,795	5,346	8,069	274	27.9%	59.5%
Canton city	35,297	6,344	4,702	1,642	2,265	2,437	234	na	44.1%
Cincinnati city	163,103	25,463	15,338	10,125	7,119	8,219	1,225	33.7%	57.6%
Cleveland city	209,848	33,681	20,480	13,201	8,267	12,213	273	30.0%	53.2%
Columbus city	381,780	50,131	32,550	17,581	15,340	17,210	2,280	30.2%	57.7%
Dayton city	72,665	11,354	7,461	3,893	3,168	4,293	43	27.3%	55.9%
Lorain city	28,713	6,090	4,536	1,554	1,316	3,220	na	na	32.6%
Parma city	36,563	9,382	7,778	1,604	2,129	5,649	na	24.2%	na
Toledo city	138,203	26,214	19,326	6,888	7,961	11,365	663	25.8%	52.4%
Youngstown city	34,112	7,604	5,613	1,991	1,727	3,886	391	na	31.6%
Oklahoma									
Broken Arrow city	39,356	6,656	5,465	1,191	2,515	2,950	294	19.3%	45.0%
Edmond city	34,828	6,752	5,161	1,591	2,122	3,039	820	18.2%	49.8%
Lawton city	40,706	6,211	4,898	1,313	1,649	3,249	191	23.6%	50.0%
Norman city	51,789	8,245	7,029	1,216	2,520	4,509	0	19.1%	55.8%
Oklahoma City city	266,902	46,993	37,053	9,940	12,496	24,557	1,532	18.4%	54.2%
Tulsa city	188,306	34,775	25,892	8,883	8,883	17,009	1,750	22.8%	54.6%
Oregon									
Beaverton city	41,022	6,292	3,997	2,295	1,651	2,346	593	25.0%	77.2%
Bend city	36,990	7,517	5,574	1,943	2,187	3,387	366	32.9%	na
Eugene city	69,146	14,864	10,072	4,792	4,555	5,517	1,598	28.9%	71.1%
Gresham city	41,342	9,217	6,242	2,975	2,928	3,314	540	31.8%	87.1%
Hillsboro city	38,475	6,631	4,340	2,291	2,551	1,789	975	38.4%	61.3%
Medford city	32,923	8,593	6,036	2,557	2,244	3,792	1,471	na	59.7%
Portland city	270,527	44,071	29,109	14,962	13,125	15,984	3,802	38.5%	60.4%
Salem city	63,266	14,193	8,920	5,273	3,979	4,941	1,743	22.0%	59.8%
Pennsylvania									
Allentown city	44,629	8,774	5,417	3,357	1,634	3,783	64	23.8%	56.7%
Bethlehem city	32,288	7,843	4,589	3,254	1,225	3,364	71	na	49.5%
Erie city	45,629	9,063	6,209	2,854	2,175	4,034	363	23.6%	53.9%
Philadelphia city	670,445	124,800	85,064	39,736	26,560	58,504	1,980	34.6%	58.4%
Pittsburgh city	153,098	28,274	19,164	9,110	5,570	13,594	841	26.4%	50.2%
Reading city	35,706	6,525	3,793	2,732	1,634	2,159	na	na	65.7%
Scranton city	33,180	8,401	5,225	3,176	1,532	3,693	107	na	53.1%
Rhode Island									
Cranston city	33,090	8,849	6,421	2,428	2,774	3,647	na	35.5%	45.1%
Pawtucket city	29,368	5,034	3,303	1,731	1,528	1,775	na	45.8%	51.1%
Providence city	71,807	10,316	5,048	5,268	2,383	2,665	202	39.1%	52.3%
Warwick city	37,052	9,995	7,397	2,598	3,420	3,977	327	31.0%	66.7%
South Carolina									
Charleston city	60,089	10,952	7,762	3,190	3,357	4,405	457	29.6%	59.2%
Columbia city	51,812	7,894	5,367	2,527	2,206	3,161	125	22.5%	51.7%
North Charleston city	45,413	6,844	5,279	1,565	2,471	2,808	na	28.9%	55.8%
Rock Hill city	29,626	5,886	3,888	1,998	1,563	2,325	231	27.1%	48.5%
South Dakota									
Rapid City city	30,634	7,146	4,834	2,312	1,146	3,688	476	22.1%	51.4%
Sioux Falls city	71,713	12,944	9,182	3,762	3,179	6,003	858	17.0%	47.9%
Tennessee									
Chattanooga city	82,641	17,375	12,352	5,023	5,070	7,282	631	25.7%	51.9%
Clarksville city	61,451	7,033	5,684	1,349	2,398	3,286	na	17.1%	48.3%
Franklin city	27,044	4,514	3,445	1,069	1,532	1,913	na	na	na
Jackson city	29,366	5,098	4,075	1,023	1,344	2,731	343	30.3%	na
Johnson City city	31,922	7,325	5,834	1,491	1,743	4,091	133	na	40.9%
Knoxville city	88,304	16,720	11,955	4,765	4,685	7,270	728	27.2%	59.4%
Memphis city	300,637	48,707	36,329	12,378	14,391	21,938	1,332	32.8%	55.0%
Murfreesboro city	49,290	7,449	5,476	1,973	1,799	3,677	na	31.6%	56.2%
Nashville-Davidson metropolitan govt (bal)	282,620	44,768	33,176	11,592	13,248	19,928	1,698	22.8%	61.7%
Texas									
Abilene city	47,610	9,239	7,446	1,793	1,567	5,879	331	12.9%	67.0%
Allen city	31,274	3,027	2,082	945	960	1,122	na	na	na
Amarillo city	83,800	16,390	12,996	3,394	3,790	9,206	461	18.5%	48.6%
Arlington city	148,731	21,203	16,585	4,618	6,461	10,124	994	28.2%	68.9%
Austin city	392,184	44,806	34,679	10,127	11,741	22,938	1,707	26.6%	63.7%
Baytown city	31,372	5,810	4,902	908	1,416	3,486	na	na	na
Beaumont city	51,580	10,045	7,299	2,746	1,328	5,971	na	21.3%	48.9%
Brownsville city	55,540	10,856	7,920	2,936	1,616	6,304	64	28.7%	47.2%
Bryan city	32,190	5,373	3,941	1,432	1,387	2,554	326	43.9%	43.9%
Carrollton city	47,471	6,565	5,150	1,415	1,884	3,266	434	16.3%	64.6%
College Station city	41,336	3,785	3,243	542	1,015	2,228	na	16.7%	44.6%
Conroe city	25,619	3,691	2,459	1,232	733	1,726	396	na	na

Table J-3: Places—Summary of Housing and Householder Characteristics—*Continued*

| | | | | Householders 65 Years and Over | | | | |
| | | | | Owner Householders | | | | |
	Total Housing Units	Total Households	Owner Occupied	Renter Occupied	With a Mortgage	Without a Mortgage	Renter Households With Meals Included in Rent	Percent of Owner Householders Who Pay 35% or More of income for Housing Costs	Percent of Renter Households Who Pay 35% or More of Income for Rental Costs
Texas—Cont.									
Corpus Christi city	129,241	25,209	18,947	6,262	4,702	14,245	735	21.3%	55.8%
Dallas city	540,447	76,474	55,909	20,565	19,677	36,232	3,370	27.5%	59.3%
Denton city	49,109	7,434	5,435	1,999	2,662	2,773	na	33.9%	81.8%
Edinburg city	26,222	3,625	2,779	846	682	2,097	na	na	na
El Paso city	244,766	46,798	35,419	11,379	10,303	25,116	439	21.9%	38.7%
Fort Worth city	309,326	45,983	33,423	12,560	11,546	21,877	1,914	24.5%	57.9%
Frisco city	50,407	5,359	4,650	709	2,445	2,205	na	34.6%	67.1%
Garland city	80,814	15,697	11,940	3,757	4,287	7,653	796	20.8%	72.2%
Grand Prairie city	61,908	7,664	6,378	1,286	2,530	3,848	na	29.0%	57.3%
Harlingen city	23,938	5,593	4,549	1,044	735	3,814	na	na	na
Houston city	931,083	137,392	96,418	40,974	25,227	71,191	4,208	23.7%	59.7%
Irving city	90,708	10,332	7,848	2,484	2,401	5,447	262	27.3%	48.8%
Killeen city	57,695	4,504	3,446	1,058	1,362	2,084	na	12.0%	52.4%
Laredo city	72,972	11,300	8,670	2,630	1,720	6,950	na	26.3%	57.2%
League City city	33,530	4,608	3,909	699	1,724	2,185	na	na	na
Lewisville city	42,261	5,954	3,491	2,463	1,704	1,787	448	na	73.2%
Longview city	34,068	7,631	5,597	2,034	1,543	4,054	555	na	57.4%
Lubbock city	103,366	19,168	13,714	5,454	3,403	10,311	964	21.6%	59.0%
McAllen city	47,882	6,779	4,942	1,837	1,508	3,434	na	na	61.7%
McKinney city	56,104	7,938	5,464	2,474	2,476	2,988	398	25.0%	62.0%
Mesquite city	51,941	8,169	6,442	1,727	2,227	4,215	483	20.1%	69.0%
Midland city	46,380	7,439	5,997	1,442	1,102	4,895	234	22.8%	70.8%
Mission city	27,962	4,875	4,246	629	454	3,792	na	na	na
Missouri City city	23,457	3,521	3,448	73	1,820	1,628	na	na	na
New Braunfels city	23,812	5,151	4,054	1,097	1,156	2,898	238	16.0%	55.1%
North Richland Hills city	26,297	5,809	4,409	1,480	1,476	2,933	614	na	na
Odessa city	44,978	7,892	6,114	1,778	569	5,545	na	16.2%	37.2%
Pasadena city	55,379	8,727	6,559	2,168	2,104	4,455	na	16.9%	58.0%
Pearland city	36,225	5,052	3,930	1,122	1,912	2,018	na	na	na
Pharr city	23,242	4,146	3,349	797	291	3,058	na	na	na
Plano city	108,910	18,614	13,196	5,418	5,673	7,523	865	23.7%	59.9%
Richardson city	46,162	9,583	7,434	2,149	2,256	5,178	518	23.8%	76.1%
Round Rock city	37,918	4,471	2,996	1,475	1,416	1,580	520	na	80.7%
San Angelo city	40,582	8,818	5,868	2,950	1,527	4,341	na	16.4%	54.0%
San Antonio city	535,546	100,110	77,125	22,985	26,184	50,941	3,478	22.9%	57.5%
Sugar Land city	29,848	6,371	5,613	758	2,199	3,414	na	27.5%	na
Temple city	29,367	6,643	4,247	2,396	862	3,385	643	na	64.9%
Tyler city	41,114	9,397	6,402	2,995	1,874	4,528	513	22.7%	72.2%
Victoria city	26,985	5,640	4,623	1,017	955	3,668	na	na	72.5%
Waco city	52,403	10,158	6,555	3,603	1,972	4,583	523	25.9%	53.6%
Wichita Falls city	41,610	8,025	6,096	1,929	1,541	4,555	659	20.7%	42.8%
Utah									
Layton city	23,762	4,170	3,692	478	1,740	1,952	na	na	na
Ogden city	33,160	5,607	3,868	1,739	1,219	2,649	202	20.8%	67.1%
Orem city	26,754	4,276	3,499	777	1,018	2,481	153	16.3%	38.5%
Provo city	34,864	4,063	3,469	594	1,399	2,070	na	18.4%	77.8%
Salt Lake City city	81,715	13,227	8,512	4,715	3,273	5,239	503	23.5%	53.4%
Sandy city	28,882	4,911	3,941	970	1,870	2,071	339	15.3%	na
St. George city	34,272	9,483	7,840	1,643	2,905	4,935	366	na	63.5%
West Jordan city	33,305	3,460	3,035	425	1,412	1,623	na	15.1%	na
West Valley City city	36,924	5,200	4,443	757	2,202	2,241	na	16.2%	na
Virginia									
Alexandria city	75,334	9,620	6,419	3,201	3,325	3,094	461	30.6%	55.6%
Chesapeake city	88,116	16,451	14,207	2,244	5,609	8,598	na	30.6%	64.2%
Hampton city	60,347	11,850	9,015	2,835	4,077	4,938	70	30.4%	63.3%
Lynchburg city	32,349	7,509	5,103	2,406	1,846	3,257	496	na	70.0%
Newport News city	77,396	12,876	9,428	3,448	3,987	5,441	686	28.9%	59.7%
Norfolk city	96,690	15,883	10,905	4,978	5,213	5,692	685	33.5%	61.9%
Portsmouth city	41,056	8,758	6,419	2,339	2,811	3,608	na	30.9%	63.4%
Richmond city	100,108	17,129	10,203	6,926	4,314	5,889	372	34.4%	68.3%
Roanoke city	47,384	10,367	7,483	2,884	2,975	4,508	418	26.1%	47.6%
Suffolk city	35,201	7,248	5,533	1,715	2,584	2,949	282	32.1%	69.6%
Virginia Beach city	182,152	34,442	28,694	5,748	14,688	14,006	1,427	33.4%	75.9%
Washington									
Auburn city	29,774	4,890	3,610	1,280	1,483	2,127	131	27.2%	54.6%
Bellevue city	59,317	12,331	9,669	2,662	4,174	5,495	1,029	32.9%	66.7%
Bellingham city	37,482	7,944	4,944	3,000	2,182	2,762	846	39.0%	74.4%
Everett city	43,767	6,673	3,861	2,812	1,428	2,433	446	37.7%	63.3%
Federal Way city	36,864	7,765	5,430	2,335	2,557	2,873	681	31.3%	71.3%
Kennewick city	29,428	5,914	4,264	1,650	1,877	2,387	661	19.3%	72.3%
Kent city	45,137	6,863	4,625	2,238	2,121	2,504	429	29.6%	63.0%
Kirkland city	36,470	6,571	4,795	1,776	2,673	2,122	349	31.1%	82.9%
Marysville city	25,679	5,333	4,145	1,188	1,459	2,686	127	24.8%	na

Table J-3: Places—Summary of Housing and Householder Characteristics—*Continued*

| | | | | | Householders 65 Years and Over | | | | |
| | | | | | Owner Householders | | | | |
	Total Housing Units	Total Households	Owner Occupied	Renter Occupied	With a Mortgage	Without a Mortgage	Renter Households With Meals Included in Rent	Percent of Owner Householders Who Pay 35% or More of income for Housing Costs	Percent of Renter Households Who Pay 35% or More of Income for Rental Costs
Washington—Cont.									
Pasco city	20,958	2,613	1,969	644	759	1,210	na	na	na
Renton city	39,530	5,388	4,035	1,353	2,065	1,970	440	33.2%	87.1%
Seattle city	324,490	52,142	34,288	17,854	13,846	20,442	3,754	26.4%	59.8%
Spokane city	95,947	19,774	13,421	6,353	5,113	8,308	1,163	26.7%	54.6%
Spokane Valley city	38,957	9,147	6,345	2,802	2,061	4,284	640	21.8%	76.3%
Tacoma city	86,224	16,417	10,171	6,246	5,210	4,961	1,225	24.5%	60.4%
Vancouver city	70,901	14,948	9,816	5,132	3,992	5,824	745	20.5%	62.1%
Yakima city	35,453	8,154	5,714	2,440	1,760	3,954	514	31.9%	46.2%
Wisconsin									
Appleton city	30,075	4,767	3,778	989	1,023	2,755	323	23.4%	54.2%
Eau Claire city	28,433	5,565	3,940	1,625	1,634	2,306	308	27.7%	59.6%
Green Bay city	45,356	8,151	5,821	2,330	1,566	4,255	184	19.8%	64.4%
Kenosha city	40,712	8,318	5,813	2,505	2,386	3,427	151	26.4%	66.8%
Madison city	110,222	17,553	12,261	5,292	4,685	7,576	671	31.7%	56.9%
Milwaukee city	259,404	38,497	24,567	13,930	9,690	14,877	1,094	35.0%	62.1%
Oshkosh city	28,883	6,269	4,141	2,128	1,247	2,894	309	34.4%	67.7%
Racine city	33,581	6,207	4,335	1,872	1,327	3,008	na	37.6%	61.2%
Waukesha city	29,067	4,989	3,207	1,782	1,291	1,916	na	31.6%	62.0%

Table J-4: Metropolitan/Micropolitan Statistical Areas—Summary of Housing and Householder Characteristics

					Householders 65 Years and Over				
					Owner Householders		Renter Households With Meals Included in Rent	Percent of Owner Householders Who Pay 35% or More of income for Housing Costs	Percent of Renter Households Who Pay 35% or More of Income for Rental Costs
	Total Housing Units	Total Households	Owner Occupied	Renter Occupied	With a Mortgage	Without a Mortgage			
Aberdeen, WA Micro Area	35,248	8,568	7,096	1,472	3,450	3,646	na	28.8%	37.5%
Abilene, TX Metro Area	70,507	14,504	12,368	2,136	2,596	9,772	331	17.1%	59.8%
Adrian, MI Micro Area	43,454	10,605	9,767	838	3,794	5,973	na	23.9%	40.6%
Akron, OH Metro Area	313,241	71,529	57,104	14,425	22,604	34,500	2,723	24.3%	59.3%
Alamogordo, NM Micro Area	30,969	6,074	5,477	597	2,123	3,354	na	21.1%	na
Albany, GA Metro Area	66,262	14,031	10,752	3,279	3,328	7,424	115	19.4%	76.2%
Albany, OR Metro Area	49,304	12,694	10,146	2,548	4,106	6,040	175	23.5%	59.9%
Albany-Schenectady-Troy, NY Metro Area	397,239	86,243	63,160	23,083	22,845	40,315	2,315	24.8%	53.4%
Albertville, AL Micro Area	40,333	8,968	7,408	1,560	1,387	6,021	na	20.6%	49.8%
Albuquerque, NM Metro Area	380,455	82,564	66,944	15,620	30,578	36,366	1,061	28.1%	53.8%
Alexandria, LA Metro Area	66,123	14,007	11,775	2,232	2,721	9,054	na	21.1%	44.3%
Allentown-Bethlehem-Easton, PA-NJ Metro Area	344,181	82,997	63,117	19,880	21,488	41,629	2,403	34.0%	58.8%
Altoona, PA Metro Area	56,067	14,864	11,660	3,204	2,605	9,055	164	22.1%	41.8%
Amarillo, TX Metro Area	107,463	21,264	17,440	3,824	4,733	12,707	461	19.8%	50.6%
Ames, IA Metro Area	38,114	6,087	5,202	885	1,533	3,669	111	9.8%	33.2%
Anchorage, AK Metro Area	155,631	20,102	16,920	3,182	7,084	9,836	11	18.2%	54.0%
Ann Arbor, MI Metro Area	148,496	27,312	22,412	4,900	9,717	12,695	769	25.3%	49.7%
Anniston-Oxford-Jacksonville, AL Metro Area	53,287	11,702	10,107	1,595	3,130	6,977	86	25.5%	40.1%
Appleton, WI Metro Area	95,106	18,685	15,099	3,586	4,799	10,300	383	25.3%	42.2%
Asheville, NC Metro Area	216,863	55,387	45,722	9,665	15,444	30,278	2,120	20.1%	52.5%
Ashtabula, OH Micro Area	45,851	10,195	8,082	2,113	2,811	5,271	70	31.4%	46.8%
Athens, TX Micro Area	39,975	10,304	8,668	1,636	2,499	6,169	165	24.1%	na
Athens-Clarke County, GA Metro Area	83,470	14,195	11,088	3,107	3,718	7,370	568	16.7%	41.3%
Atlanta-Sandy Springs-Roswell, GA Metro Area	2,214,354	353,875	280,674	73,201	133,337	147,337	9,260	27.3%	58.8%
Atlantic City-Hammonton, NJ Metro Area	127,386	26,503	20,457	6,046	8,643	11,814	259	46.1%	49.4%
Auburn, NY Micro Area	36,394	8,330	6,461	1,877	1,723	4,738	343	22.6%	48.5%
Auburn-Opelika, AL Metro Area	65,570	10,631	8,331	2,300	2,588	5,743	230	13.1%	67.3%
Augusta-Richmond County, GA-SC Metro Area	248,805	49,028	40,452	8,576	15,430	25,022	609	23.0%	57.9%
Augusta-Waterville, ME Micro Area	61,503	13,203	11,111	2,092	3,342	7,769	na	29.0%	54.2%
Austin-Round Rock, TX Metro Area	764,778	105,797	84,920	20,877	34,713	50,207	3,720	27.2%	62.7%
Bakersfield, CA Metro Area	291,469	49,947	37,090	12,857	16,013	21,077	592	26.0%	63.0%
Baltimore-Columbia-Towson, MD Metro Area	1,150,424	240,780	184,460	56,320	79,348	105,112	7,290	29.1%	55.2%
Bangor, ME Metro Area	74,275	16,041	12,700	3,341	4,791	7,909	412	26.8%	38.9%
Barnstable Town, MA Metro Area	161,721	38,887	33,414	5,473	14,451	18,963	419	34.3%	59.2%
Baton Rouge, LA Metro Area	341,968	61,930	50,362	11,568	14,287	36,075	1,197	21.6%	56.0%
Battle Creek, MI Metro Area	60,685	13,899	11,321	2,578	3,237	8,084	332	24.3%	48.5%
Bay City, MI Metro Area	48,020	12,621	11,048	1,573	3,112	7,936	na	18.2%	66.1%
Beaumont-Port Arthur, TX Metro Area	174,712	37,765	30,449	7,316	4,352	26,097	301	18.5%	44.2%
Beaver Dam, WI Micro Area	37,385	8,850	6,983	1,867	2,174	4,809	258	28.9%	61.6%
Beckley, WV Metro Area	57,532	14,622	13,042	1,580	3,862	9,180	na	14.8%	21.3%
Bellingham, WA Metro Area	92,462	20,850	16,428	4,422	6,341	10,087	1,079	30.7%	73.8%
Bend-Redmond, OR Metro Area	82,420	18,070	14,679	3,391	7,375	7,304	446	34.1%	57.1%
Billings, MT Metro Area	74,215	16,291	13,131	3,160	4,507	8,624	736	28.5%	42.8%
Binghamton, NY Metro Area	112,006	27,324	21,918	5,406	6,491	15,427	728	23.4%	51.5%
Birmingham-Hoover, AL Metro Area	507,800	107,765	90,315	17,450	34,540	55,775	2,503	26.2%	52.2%
Bismarck, ND Metro Area	56,389	11,754	8,866	2,888	1,751	7,115	489	14.6%	60.8%
Blacksburg-Christiansburg-Radford, VA Metro Area	78,992	15,631	12,572	3,059	3,404	9,168	363	20.9%	34.9%
Bloomington, IL Metro Area	78,513	14,146	11,261	2,885	3,994	7,267	713	19.4%	54.2%
Bloomington, IN Metro Area	69,527	11,974	10,401	1,573	4,728	5,673	224	16.5%	39.9%
Bloomsburg-Berwick, PA Metro Area	37,627	9,142	7,685	1,457	1,556	6,129	35	20.6%	45.3%
Bluefield, WV-VA Micro Area	50,498	13,568	11,835	1,733	2,794	9,041	na	18.2%	71.7%
Boise City, ID Metro Area	256,178	51,350	42,121	9,229	19,571	22,550	2,204	22.7%	54.4%
Boston-Cambridge-Newton, MA-NH Metro Area	1,901,363	412,506	295,063	117,443	113,270	181,793	12,191	35.6%	55.3%
Boulder, CO Metro Area	130,924	23,881	18,879	5,002	8,168	10,711	1,637	27.2%	56.3%
Bowling Green, KY Metro Area	71,018	14,024	11,156	2,868	3,463	7,693	na	21.1%	62.9%
Bozeman, MT Micro Area	44,857	6,915	5,342	1,573	1,317	4,025	331	20.8%	60.2%
Brainerd, MN Micro Area	66,214	12,583	10,655	1,928	4,039	6,616	186	29.8%	57.1%
Branson, MO Micro Area	50,659	12,253	10,508	1,745	4,353	6,155	na	27.7%	56.6%
Bremerton-Silverdale, WA Metro Area	109,329	25,250	20,311	4,939	9,329	10,982	982	28.1%	58.9%
Bridgeport-Stamford-Norwalk, CT Metro Area	364,966	84,643	65,662	18,981	27,318	38,344	2,709	42.5%	55.3%
Brownsville-Harlingen, TX Metro Area	146,207	30,043	24,191	5,852	4,742	19,449	64	24.4%	43.0%
Brunswick, GA Metro Area	58,235	12,140	9,927	2,213	3,367	6,560	na	na	29.2%
Buffalo-Cheektowaga-Niagara Falls, NY Metro Area	520,369	125,531	97,386	28,145	30,495	66,891	2,266	25.5%	51.7%
Burlington, NC Metro Area	68,101	16,058	13,380	2,678	4,650	8,730	362	24.6%	76.7%
Burlington-South Burlington, VT Metro Area	94,393	18,342	14,167	4,175	4,916	9,251	921	38.9%	57.3%
California-Lexington Park, MD Metro Area	43,267	7,889	6,483	1,406	3,068	3,415	na	24.4%	55.5%
Canton-Massillon, OH Metro Area	179,159	44,574	35,917	8,657	12,756	23,161	829	18.5%	47.3%
Cape Coral-Fort Myers, FL Metro Area	375,688	102,374	87,705	14,669	30,295	57,410	1,532	27.9%	60.0%
Cape Girardeau, MO-IL Metro Area	42,901	9,954	8,126	1,828	1,967	6,159	414	20.7%	27.4%
Carbondale-Marion, IL Metro Area	59,413	11,887	9,824	2,063	2,719	7,105	476	18.8%	40.3%
Carson City, NV Metro Area	23,461	6,651	4,676	1,975	1,503	3,173	532	na	57.7%
Casper, WY Metro Area	35,822	7,213	5,506	1,707	1,417	4,089	541	9.6%	45.3%

Table J-4: Metropolitan/Micropolitan Statistical Areas—Summary of Housing and Householder Characteristics—*Continued*

| | Total Housing Units | Householders 65 Years and Over | | | | | | | Percent of Owner Households Who Pay 35% or More of income for Housing Costs | Percent of Renter Households Who Pay 35% or More of Income for Rental Costs |
| | | Total Households | Owner Householders | | | | Renter Households With Meals Included in Rent | | | |
			Owner Occupied	Renter Occupied	With a Mortgage	Without a Mortgage				
Cedar Rapids, IA Metro Area	114,637	25,107	21,449	3,658	6,704	14,745	1,084	18.3%	45.1%
Centralia, WA Micro Area	34,081	9,400	7,592	1,808	2,628	4,964	242	21.0%	71.0%
Chambersburg-Waynesboro, PA Metro Area	64,125	16,463	13,798	2,665	4,399	9,399	305	20.7%	42.0%
Champaign-Urbana, IL Metro Area	103,311	18,635	15,804	2,831	5,590	10,214	486	19.7%	68.7%
Charleston, WV Metro Area	107,528	27,136	23,661	3,475	5,819	17,842	239	14.7%	34.8%
Charleston-Mattoon, IL Micro Area	28,067	6,127	4,949	1,178	1,169	3,780	138	14.0%	38.3%
Charleston-North Charleston, SC Metro Area	313,027	58,835	49,381	9,454	19,134	30,247	1,384	28.6%	50.9%
Charlotte-Concord-Gastonia, NC-SC Metro Area	973,099	178,503	144,427	34,076	63,695	80,732	4,053	26.1%	49.4%
Charlottesville, VA Metro Area	99,207	20,925	17,111	3,814	6,319	10,792	727	24.3%	65.3%
Chattanooga, TN-GA Metro Area	237,911	56,504	46,125	10,379	14,344	31,781	1,006	19.1%	47.9%
Cheyenne, WY Metro Area	41,651	8,768	7,793	975	3,084	4,709	na	26.1%	27.5%
Chicago-Naperville-Elgin, IL-IN-WI Metro Area	3,803,831	741,292	577,180	164,112	223,281	353,899	19,891	34.5%	59.2%
Chico, CA Metro Area	97,491	22,765	18,796	3,969	6,880	11,916	411	21.4%	65.5%
Chillicothe, OH Micro Area	31,787	7,322	5,594	1,728	1,343	4,251	na	na	49.4%
Cincinnati, OH-KY-IN Metro Area	918,989	185,564	145,439	40,125	62,253	83,186	5,338	26.7%	51.7%
Claremont-Lebanon, NH-VT Micro Area	123,044	24,525	20,423	4,102	7,092	13,331	366	36.2%	47.4%
Clarksburg, WV Micro Area	42,370	10,942	9,181	1,761	2,331	6,850	na	15.5%	35.4%
Clarksville, TN-KY Metro Area	114,809	16,860	13,596	3,264	4,562	9,034	na	16.9%	45.2%
Clearlake, CA Micro Area	35,659	8,588	7,481	1,107	2,223	5,258	na	na	na
Cleveland, TN Metro Area	51,095	12,406	9,985	2,421	2,769	7,216	285	21.2%	34.9%
Cleveland-Elyria, OH Metro Area	956,688	220,581	169,909	50,672	65,868	104,041	5,889	27.1%	56.8%
Coeur d'Alene, ID Metro Area	66,122	15,029	12,437	2,592	5,130	7,307	1,263	21.6%	36.1%
College Station-Bryan, TX Metro Area	100,093	15,260	12,443	2,817	3,477	8,966	412	21.2%	45.7%
Colorado Springs, CO Metro Area	275,214	48,830	40,642	8,188	17,713	22,929	2,545	25.5%	69.9%
Columbia, MO Metro Area	73,173	11,871	9,485	2,386	3,993	5,492	na	18.5%	35.1%
Columbia, SC Metro Area	341,066	67,284	58,206	9,078	22,823	35,383	1,530	23.0%	47.0%
Columbus, GA-AL Metro Area	132,216	23,640	18,409	5,231	7,701	10,708	560	24.1%	49.5%
Columbus, IN Metro Area	33,547	7,952	6,684	1,268	2,770	3,914	217	22.3%	45.5%
Columbus, OH Metro Area	840,063	147,766	113,234	34,532	48,957	64,277	3,621	26.1%	53.1%
Concord, NH Micro Area	63,629	13,787	10,762	3,025	3,369	7,393	277	40.4%	65.4%
Cookeville, TN Micro Area	48,907	12,176	9,667	2,509	2,594	7,073	na	27.4%	44.5%
Coos Bay, OR Micro Area	30,397	9,135	7,370	1,765	2,738	4,632	167	na	44.9%
Corning, NY Micro Area	48,839	11,088	8,607	2,481	2,212	6,395	192	28.0%	52.6%
Corpus Christi, TX Metro Area	187,486	38,942	30,081	8,861	7,097	22,984	769	18.7%	55.2%
Corvallis, OR Metro Area	37,115	7,923	6,390	1,533	2,407	3,983	545	na	66.7%
Crestview-Fort Walton Beach-Destin, FL Metro Area	142,870	26,949	22,585	4,364	7,836	14,749	167	22.5%	41.8%
Cullman, AL Micro Area	37,144	8,705	7,417	1,288	2,438	4,979	232	28.7%	na
Cumberland, MD-WV Metro Area	46,324	11,770	8,933	2,837	2,264	6,669	na	17.8%	27.5%
Dallas-Fort Worth-Arlington, TX Metro Area	2,645,453	420,736	326,563	94,173	120,288	206,275	14,570	25.6%	60.0%
Dalton, GA Metro Area	55,420	10,758	9,202	1,556	2,472	6,730	na	17.0%	58.5%
Danville, IL Metro Area	36,010	8,761	6,984	1,777	1,727	5,257	220	14.4%	42.5%
Danville, VA Micro Area	53,770	13,851	11,843	2,008	3,305	8,538	na	25.7%	53.5%
Daphne-Fairhope-Foley, AL Metro Area	107,384	23,509	19,870	3,639	7,827	12,043	605	26.0%	48.6%
Davenport-Moline-Rock Island, IA-IL Metro Area	167,892	40,792	32,504	8,288	9,659	22,845	1,195	21.4%	52.5%
Dayton, OH Metro Area	367,856	84,582	66,627	17,955	26,449	40,178	1,857	25.8%	50.9%
Decatur, AL Metro Area	66,672	15,624	12,194	3,430	3,010	9,184	612	13.2%	44.1%
Decatur, IL Metro Area	50,355	12,440	10,887	1,553	2,747	8,140	198	15.5%	39.0%
Deltona-Daytona Beach-Ormond Beach, FL Metro Area	305,678	85,624	73,538	12,086	27,038	46,500	2,404	26.7%	60.6%
Denver-Aurora-Lakewood, CO Metro Area	1,114,105	198,278	154,513	43,765	73,198	81,315	7,817	26.9%	59.4%
Des Moines-West Des Moines, IA Metro Area	254,484	47,347	36,876	10,471	13,091	23,785	2,094	28.6%	49.3%
Detroit-Warren-Dearborn, MI Metro Area	1,890,983	406,083	316,928	89,155	122,038	194,890	11,250	27.9%	57.1%
Dothan, AL Metro Area	68,053	15,885	13,651	2,234	4,341	9,310	99	20.6%	40.0%
Dover, DE Metro Area	67,862	15,895	13,665	2,230	5,879	7,786	na	22.7%	63.1%
DuBois, PA Micro Area	38,573	9,947	8,304	1,643	1,602	6,702	209	27.2%	42.1%
Dubuque, IA Metro Area	40,349	9,597	7,340	2,257	1,528	5,812	445	15.1%	69.4%
Duluth, MN-WI Metro Area	141,916	30,770	23,907	6,863	6,103	17,804	1,778	18.4%	55.0%
Dunn, NC Micro Area	49,321	8,883	7,078	1,805	2,426	4,652	142	22.2%	56.5%
Durham-Chapel Hill, NC Metro Area	233,471	43,911	34,486	9,425	15,590	18,896	1,755	24.4%	44.7%
East Stroudsburg, PA Metro Area	80,699	12,922	11,043	1,879	4,770	6,273	na	42.0%	54.1%
Eau Claire, WI Metro Area	70,716	15,310	11,592	3,718	4,202	7,390	468	25.6%	49.9%
El Centro, CA Metro Area	56,963	10,308	5,667	4,641	2,476	3,191	142	24.7%	47.0%
El Paso, TX Metro Area	288,141	52,864	40,768	12,096	11,694	29,074	439	23.3%	38.6%
Elizabeth City, NC Micro Area	27,061	6,264	5,029	1,235	2,028	3,001	na	25.6%	na
Elizabethtown-Fort Knox, KY Metro Area	63,379	13,028	10,798	2,230	4,118	6,680	282	20.6%	48.1%
Elkhart-Goshen, IN Metro Area	77,937	16,374	12,932	3,442	4,579	8,353	242	13.0%	55.1%
Elmira, NY Metro Area	38,380	8,995	7,220	1,775	2,025	5,195	270	20.5%	44.8%
Erie, PA Metro Area	119,824	27,024	21,142	5,882	5,478	15,664	912	19.0%	50.9%
Eugene, OR Metro Area	157,908	39,122	30,981	8,141	12,976	18,005	1,791	27.8%	59.5%
Eureka-Arcata-Fortuna, CA Micro Area	62,329	12,469	9,681	2,788	3,287	6,394	192	24.9%	32.1%
Evansville, IN-KY Metro Area	140,124	30,371	23,233	7,138	8,585	14,648	899	20.8%	58.8%
Fairbanks, AK Metro Area	41,690	5,189	4,431	758	1,851	2,580	na	15.6%	57.7%
Fargo, ND-MN Metro Area	100,080	16,843	11,312	5,531	3,662	7,650	1,432	22.3%	63.9%

Table J-4: Metropolitan/Micropolitan Statistical Areas—Summary of Housing and Householder Characteristics—*Continued*

				Householders 65 Years and Over					
				Owner Householders			Percent of Owner Householders Who Pay 35% or More of income for Housing Costs	Percent of Renter Households Who Pay 35% or More of Income for Rental Costs
	Total Housing Units	Total Households	Owner Occupied	Renter Occupied	With a Mortgage	Without a Mortgage	Renter Households With Meals Included in Rent		
Faribault-Northfield, MN Micro Area	24,570	6,214	4,492	1,722	1,719	2,773	433	29.5%	na
Farmington, MO Micro Area	29,363	6,200	5,070	1,130	1,242	3,828	320	29.8%	na
Farmington, NM Metro Area	49,613	9,919	8,326	1,593	2,777	5,549	179	22.8%	60.2%
Fayetteville, NC Metro Area	163,907	24,426	19,430	4,996	9,367	10,063	170	25.5%	53.5%
Fayetteville-Springdale-Rogers, AR-MO Metro Area	205,553	38,246	30,918	7,328	10,737	20,181	651	26.2%	49.8%
Findlay, OH Micro Area	33,272	7,754	5,759	1,995	2,439	3,320	742	22.9%	36.5%
Flagstaff, AZ Metro Area	64,215	9,700	8,444	1,256	2,986	5,458	107	24.4%	41.6%
Flint, MI Metro Area	190,905	42,588	35,638	6,950	12,370	23,268	481	27.2%	57.3%
Florence, SC Metro Area	89,302	20,036	16,409	3,627	4,291	12,118	609	21.9%	52.3%
Florence-Muscle Shoals, AL Metro Area	70,551	17,403	13,966	3,437	3,644	10,322	111	19.4%	31.9%
Fond du Lac, WI Metro Area	44,488	10,414	8,249	2,165	2,188	6,061	456	27.5%	62.6%
Forest City, NC Micro Area	33,878	8,116	7,183	933	2,407	4,776	246	na	na
Fort Collins, CO Metro Area	138,540	27,063	21,081	5,982	9,135	11,946	1,291	23.4%	61.5%
Fort Smith, AR-OK Metro Area	123,026	28,526	23,832	4,694	5,823	18,009	530	21.4%	44.2%
Fort Wayne, IN Metro Area	180,658	36,659	30,796	5,863	11,753	19,043	695	18.4%	48.1%
Frankfort, KY Micro Area	32,820	6,903	5,950	953	2,016	3,934	na	13.6%	na
Fresno, CA Metro Area	324,158	61,609	45,048	16,561	20,265	24,783	1,208	29.6%	59.7%
Gadsden, AL Metro Area	47,502	11,562	9,586	1,976	2,673	6,913	216	na	39.3%
Gainesville, FL Metro Area	121,217	22,119	17,818	4,301	5,068	12,750	572	22.6%	47.1%
Gainesville, GA Metro Area	69,491	15,730	13,058	2,672	4,908	8,150	793	25.4%	51.3%
Gallup, NM Micro Area	25,779	4,880	3,890	990	568	3,322	na	7.4%	28.0%
Gettysburg, PA Metro Area	41,290	10,910	9,050	1,860	2,996	6,054	na	20.1%	38.1%
Glens Falls, NY Metro Area	68,026	13,564	11,069	2,495	4,063	7,006	145	29.4%	48.4%
Glenwood Springs, CO Micro Area	34,304	5,544	4,483	1,061	2,326	2,157	na	31.3%	na
Goldsboro, NC Metro Area	53,203	11,015	8,691	2,324	3,576	5,115	383	24.0%	63.0%
Grand Forks, ND-MN Metro Area	46,034	8,567	6,140	2,427	1,371	4,769	283	17.8%	56.2%
Grand Island, NE Metro Area	34,818	8,353	6,491	1,862	2,058	4,433	273	26.1%	46.4%
Grand Junction, CO Metro Area	63,791	15,207	12,375	2,832	5,529	6,846	173	22.9%	63.1%
Grand Rapids-Wyoming, MI Metro Area	408,258	82,744	66,988	15,756	21,362	45,626	3,303	24.4%	53.8%
Grants Pass, OR Metro Area	38,023	12,767	10,553	2,214	3,993	6,560	152	na	na
Great Falls, MT Metro Area	37,560	9,011	7,441	1,570	2,129	5,312	na	15.5%	46.8%
Greeley, CO Metro Area	100,064	19,316	15,238	4,078	6,667	8,571	654	25.4%	61.6%
Green Bay, WI Metro Area	140,377	27,801	21,348	6,453	7,162	14,186	759	25.6%	47.5%
Greeneville, TN Micro Area	32,158	7,564	5,734	1,830	1,511	4,223	na	na	19.7%
Greenfield Town, MA Micro Area	33,670	8,174	6,501	1,673	1,949	4,552	114	32.8%	50.4%
Greensboro-High Point, NC Metro Area	328,034	70,530	54,322	16,208	21,596	32,726	2,106	23.9%	50.6%
Greenville, NC Metro Area	76,615	12,463	9,072	3,391	3,157	5,915	607	19.4%	51.2%
Greenville-Anderson-Mauldin, SC Metro Area	369,044	81,633	68,862	12,771	24,159	44,703	2,645	20.1%	58.2%
Greenwood, SC Micro Area	42,954	10,887	9,507	1,380	3,108	6,399	541	20.4%	50.1%
Gulfport-Biloxi-Pascagoula, MS Metro Area	174,472	35,579	29,786	5,793	9,953	19,833	496	19.9%	62.2%
Hagerstown-Martinsburg, MD-WV Metro Area	107,421	22,841	17,440	5,401	6,705	10,735	79	24.8%	58.7%
Hammond, LA Metro Area	52,556	9,280	7,934	1,346	2,356	5,578	na	26.7%	53.2%
Hanford-Corcoran, CA Metro Area	44,872	7,781	6,261	1,520	2,361	3,900	na	18.7%	69.9%
Harrisburg-Carlisle, PA Metro Area	245,202	56,876	43,735	13,141	15,738	27,997	2,064	23.1%	63.3%
Harrisonburg, VA Metro Area	52,600	11,181	8,311	2,870	3,055	5,256	440	20.2%	52.1%
Hartford-West Hartford-East Hartford, CT Metro Area	508,525	115,938	87,182	28,756	33,016	54,166	3,257	35.9%	54.2%
Hattiesburg, MS Metro Area	62,505	11,282	9,392	1,890	2,806	6,586	na	23.5%	39.0%
Helena, MT Micro Area	35,929	7,564	5,746	1,818	1,804	3,942	377	16.3%	59.8%
Hermiston-Pendleton, OR Micro Area	34,326	7,109	4,990	2,119	1,319	3,671	416	20.3%	53.4%
Hickory-Lenoir-Morganton, NC Metro Area	162,183	38,170	31,440	6,730	10,101	21,339	209	19.8%	44.9%
Hilo, HI Micro Area	85,173	19,257	15,801	3,456	6,386	9,415	na	17.6%	40.9%
Hilton Head Island-Bluffton-Beaufort, SC Metro Area	104,719	28,322	25,122	3,200	11,722	13,400	459	31.2%	6na
Hinesville, GA Metro Area	33,779	3,679	3,013	666	984	2,029	na	32.3%	31.5%
Hobbs, NM Micro Area	25,092	4,381	3,868	513	738	3,130	na	na	na
Holland, MI Micro Area	49,759	10,476	9,378	1,098	2,449	6,929	na	19.2%	na
Homosassa Springs, FL Metro Area	77,717	29,294	26,394	2,900	10,446	15,948	883	23.8%	49.1%
Hot Springs, AR Metro Area	50,555	13,006	10,599	2,407	3,075	7,524	485	16.3%	63.0%
Houma-Thibodaux, LA Metro Area	84,240	15,862	14,084	1,778	1,789	12,295	51	11.8%	31.2%
Houston-The Woodlands-Sugar Land, TX Metro Area	2,441,230	377,793	292,752	85,041	97,648	195,104	9,041	24.1%	59.6%
Huntington-Ashland, WV-KY-OH Metro Area	165,632	41,916	35,218	6,698	10,005	25,213	570	15.8%	47.4%
Huntsville, AL Metro Area	189,915	37,623	32,128	5,495	11,057	21,071	767	17.3%	63.4%
Huntsville, TX Micro Area	33,091	7,210	6,094	1,116	1,257	4,837	328	na	na
Hutchinson, KS Micro Area	28,323	7,134	6,227	907	1,315	4,912	na	21.5%	27.2%
Idaho Falls, ID Metro Area	50,977	10,672	9,848	824	2,931	6,917	131	19.3%	62.1%
Indiana, PA Micro Area	38,612	9,335	7,766	1,569	1,962	5,804	234	17.2%	33.7%
Indianapolis-Carmel-Anderson, IN Metro Area	835,923	150,796	118,734	32,062	55,005	63,729	4,238	22.7%	51.6%
Iowa City, IA Metro Area	68,318	11,302	9,331	1,971	2,958	6,373	362	14.8%	64.0%
Ithaca, NY Metro Area	42,087	7,857	5,807	2,050	1,981	3,826	403	18.8%	53.5%
Jackson, MI Metro Area	69,070	16,640	14,000	2,640	5,246	8,754	499	29.5%	63.5%
Jackson, MS Metro Area	236,776	46,494	39,217	7,277	12,851	26,366	770	24.8%	51.3%

Table J-4: Metropolitan/Micropolitan Statistical Areas—Summary of Housing and Householder Characteristics—*Continued*

				Householders 65 Years and Over				
				Owner Householders			Percent of Owner Householders Who Pay 35% or More of income for Housing Costs	Percent of Renter Households Who Pay 35% or More of Income for Rental Costs
	Total Housing Units	Total Households	Owner Occupied	Renter Occupied	With a Mortgage	Without a Mortgage	Renter Households With Meals Included in Rent		
Jackson, TN Metro Area	56,098	12,029	10,488	1,541	3,021	7,467	479	23.6%	65.2%
Jacksonville, FL Metro Area	615,239	122,887	98,478	24,409	41,555	56,923	2,699	27.7%	62.0%
Jacksonville, NC Metro Area	76,061	9,938	8,371	1,567	3,576	4,795	na	31.9%	47.4%
Jamestown-Dunkirk-Fredonia, NY Micro Area	66,661	14,768	11,905	2,863	3,561	8,344	292	20.4%	59.5%
Janesville-Beloit, WI Metro Area	68,309	15,033	11,581	3,452	3,528	8,053	588	19.8%	50.3%
Jefferson City, MO Metro Area	63,966	13,240	10,939	2,301	3,126	7,813	290	18.1%	42.7%
Johnson City, TN Metro Area	95,846	23,000	19,350	3,650	5,268	14,082	133	17.4%	33.9%
Johnstown, PA Metro Area	65,262	18,477	14,631	3,846	3,075	11,556	649	26.2%	27.9%
Jonesboro, AR Metro Area	54,241	10,678	8,297	2,381	3,124	5,173	362	12.3%	34.1%
Joplin, MO Metro Area	75,641	16,199	13,442	2,757	3,780	9,662	72	19.8%	47.0%
Kahului-Wailuku-Lahaina, HI Metro Area	71,564	13,616	10,378	3,238	5,310	5,068	146	31.4%	46.7%
Kalamazoo-Portage, MI Metro Area	146,951	28,592	23,823	4,769	8,573	15,250	478	23.2%	48.3%
Kalispell, MT Micro Area	47,355	9,898	8,564	1,334	2,133	6,431	na	22.3%	66.6%
Kankakee, IL Metro Area	45,153	9,376	8,032	1,344	2,926	5,106	231	24.3%	69.9%
Kansas City, MO-KS Metro Area	884,387	172,768	133,546	39,222	48,916	84,630	7,487	24.4%	54.8%
Kapaa, HI Micro Area	30,350	6,749	4,950	1,799	1,715	3,235	na	na	38.6%
Keene, NH Micro Area	34,820	8,186	6,380	1,806	2,435	3,945	na	41.8%	39.7%
Kennewick-Richland, WA Metro Area	98,787	19,078	15,415	3,663	5,335	10,080	1,578	21.1%	69.6%
Key West, FL Micro Area	52,927	8,836	6,991	1,845	1,929	5,062	na	na	52.5%
Killeen-Temple, TX Metro Area	169,053	25,887	20,740	5,147	5,082	15,658	906	19.2%	48.2%
Kingsport-Bristol-Bristol, TN-VA Metro Area	147,346	40,278	34,105	6,173	8,829	25,276	407	18.2%	49.0%
Kingston, NY Metro Area	83,713	21,122	17,035	4,087	5,386	11,649	86	39.8%	58.5%
Klamath Falls, OR Micro Area	32,756	8,131	7,108	1,023	2,590	4,518	na	21.6%	51.1%
Knoxville, TN Metro Area	386,341	89,830	76,839	12,991	23,994	52,845	1,412	23.0%	47.1%
Kokomo, IN Metro Area	38,689	9,929	8,309	1,620	3,584	4,725	213	16.4%	43.0%
La Crosse-Onalaska, WI-MN Metro Area	57,949	12,824	10,178	2,646	3,184	6,994	528	22.7%	65.3%
Lafayette, LA Metro Area	201,867	38,161	31,492	6,669	6,355	25,137	510	15.1%	46.9%
Lafayette-West Lafayette, IN Metro Area	87,861	14,598	12,352	2,246	4,240	8,112	464	17.8%	54.9%
LaGrange, GA Micro Area	28,246	6,242	4,762	1,480	1,419	3,343	na	na	50.8%
Lake Charles, LA Metro Area	89,211	17,517	14,776	2,741	3,839	10,937	123	18.2%	40.2%
Lake City, FL Micro Area	28,298	7,095	6,132	963	2,109	4,023	na	14.0%	na
Lake Havasu City-Kingman, AZ Metro Area	112,307	32,387	27,871	4,516	11,960	15,911	228	23.4%	50.2%
Lakeland-Winter Haven, FL Metro Area	282,748	74,155	62,630	11,525	18,787	43,843	873	23.1%	61.7%
Lancaster, PA Metro Area	206,431	50,614	36,564	14,050	9,869	26,695	2,587	24.4%	59.7%
Lansing-East Lansing, MI Metro Area	200,009	39,625	31,852	7,773	12,122	19,730	895	23.1%	48.7%
Laredo, TX Metro Area	78,050	12,074	9,323	2,751	1,844	7,479	na	27.9%	54.7%
Las Cruces, NM Metro Area	84,225	17,799	14,319	3,480	4,902	9,417	737	13.6%	50.6%
Las Vegas-Henderson-Paradise, NV Metro Area	863,073	156,767	112,351	44,416	57,640	54,711	2,506	28.6%	61.8%
Laurel, MS Micro Area	37,482	8,738	8,090	648	2,206	5,884	na	28.1%	na
Lawrence, KS Metro Area	48,278	7,496	5,410	2,086	2,435	2,975	426	20.1%	58.9%
Lawton, OK Metro Area	54,613	9,147	7,699	1,448	2,384	5,315	191	22.3%	45.4%
Lebanon, PA Metro Area	56,207	14,125	10,360	3,765	2,557	7,803	213	25.9%	43.7%
Lewiston, ID-WA Metro Area	27,246	8,152	6,757	1,395	2,016	4,741	255	18.5%	42.2%
Lewiston-Auburn, ME Metro Area	49,142	11,311	8,594	2,717	2,726	5,868	131	28.0%	52.4%
Lexington-Fayette, KY Metro Area	214,924	39,175	30,159	9,016	12,438	17,721	1,142	23.0%	41.5%
Lima, OH Metro Area	44,847	10,595	8,567	2,028	3,097	5,470	530	24.0%	39.9%
Lincoln, NE Metro Area	131,847	25,476	19,582	5,894	6,667	12,915	1,468	19.1%	44.2%
Little Rock-North Little Rock-Conway, AR Metro Area	318,614	60,596	48,244	12,352	17,124	31,120	930	18.1%	46.9%
Logan, UT-ID Metro Area	43,905	7,340	6,192	1,148	1,861	4,331	355	16.9%	53.9%
London, KY Micro Area	55,066	12,112	9,585	2,527	2,642	6,943	na	23.8%	39.1%
Longview, TX Metro Area	89,542	19,425	15,935	3,490	3,295	12,640	555	16.1%	51.4%
Longview, WA Metro Area	43,506	11,975	9,095	2,880	2,953	6,142	947	22.4%	59.3%
Los Angeles-Long Beach-Anaheim, CA Metro Area	4,554,759	910,270	618,817	291,453	308,934	309,883	19,946	34.5%	65.5%
Louisville/Jefferson County, KY-IN Metro Area	547,269	115,701	93,942	21,759	35,776	58,166	2,718	23.3%	55.6%
Lubbock, TX Metro Area	126,878	24,877	18,800	6,077	4,808	13,992	995	20.8%	56.3%
Lufkin, TX Micro Area	36,196	7,889	6,676	1,213	831	5,845	0	19.3%	50.2%
Lumberton, NC Micro Area	52,284	11,080	8,777	2,303	1,731	7,046	25	29.3%	54.2%
Lynchburg, VA Metro Area	114,612	28,161	22,992	5,169	7,857	15,135	562	20.3%	48.0%
Macon, GA Metro Area	103,088	20,490	15,071	5,419	5,713	9,358	539	22.9%	48.2%
Madera, CA Metro Area	49,893	10,815	9,013	1,802	4,320	4,693	na	35.3%	32.5%
Madison, WI Metro Area	275,149	50,608	38,204	12,404	13,955	24,249	1,575	29.9%	59.3%
Manchester-Nashua, NH Metro Area	167,428	31,803	24,219	7,584	10,352	13,867	1,026	36.3%	57.6%
Manhattan, KS Metro Area	38,749	5,683	4,910	773	999	3,911	na	16.2%	40.1%
Manitowoc, WI Micro Area	37,182	9,744	7,816	1,928	2,247	5,569	319	19.8%	58.0%
Mankato-North Mankato, MN Metro Area	40,334	7,626	5,808	1,818	1,638	4,170	609	22.1%	58.5%
Mansfield, OH Metro Area	54,262	15,369	12,272	3,097	4,033	8,239	148	21.9%	60.2%
Marinette, WI-MI Micro Area	44,554	8,992	7,569	1,423	1,854	5,715	247	25.4%	55.4%
Marion, IN Micro Area	30,287	8,091	6,540	1,551	2,687	3,853	na	20.6%	na
Marion, OH Micro Area	27,776	7,518	6,058	1,460	2,034	4,024	203	12.8%	na
Marquette, MI Micro Area	34,497	6,904	5,208	1,696	1,349	3,859	na	22.4%	51.3%
Marshall, TX Micro Area	28,017	7,012	6,362	650	1,480	4,882	na	21.6%	na
Martinsville, VA Micro Area	33,535	9,167	7,681	1,486	2,286	5,395	na	na	na

Table J-4: Metropolitan/Micropolitan Statistical Areas—Summary of Housing and Householder Characteristics—*Continued*

| | | | | Householders 65 Years and Over | | | | |
| | | | | Owner Householders | | | Percent of Owner Households Who Pay 35% or More of income for Housing Costs | Percent of Renter Households Who Pay 35% or More of Income for Rental Costs |
	Total Housing Units	Total Households	Owner Occupied	Renter Occupied	With a Mortgage	Without a Mortgage	Renter Households With Meals Included in Rent		
McAllen-Edinburg-Mission, TX Metro Area	261,199	44,905	37,142	7,763	5,333	31,809	68	19.5%	57.3%
Meadville, PA Micro Area	44,390	10,082	7,904	2,178	2,101	5,803	na	17.9%	36.5%
Medford, OR Metro Area	91,919	26,718	20,319	6,399	8,163	12,156	2,311	32.4%	56.1%
Memphis, TN-MS-AR Metro Area	564,280	100,887	81,552	19,335	33,183	48,369	2,431	28.6%	53.4%
Merced, CA Metro Area	84,180	16,007	11,547	4,460	5,223	6,324	233	32.8%	45.1%
Meridian, MS Micro Area	47,749	10,037	7,737	2,300	1,386	6,351	122	27.6%	39.7%
Miami-Fort Lauderdale-West Palm Beach, FL Metro Area	2,496,567	567,027	438,117	128,910	164,545	273,572	10,396	36.8%	63.8%
Michigan City-La Porte, IN Metro Area	48,758	11,239	9,017	2,222	3,455	5,562	344	20.9%	59.6%
Midland, MI Metro Area	36,273	8,858	7,511	1,347	2,086	5,425	268	19.3%	56.2%
Midland, TX Metro Area	60,209	9,395	7,916	1,479	1,363	6,553	234	19.7%	69.0%
Milwaukee-Waukesha-West Allis, WI Metro Area	671,950	138,369	98,574	39,795	36,946	61,628	6,783	31.1%	64.4%
Minneapolis-St. Paul-Bloomington, MN-WI Metro Area	1,416,988	267,566	208,027	59,539	84,000	124,027	11,886	27.7%	61.6%
Minot, ND Micro Area	36,404	5,950	5,050	900	956	4,094	na	12.4%	49.8%
Missoula, MT Metro Area	51,415	10,170	7,859	2,311	2,590	5,269	660	28.7%	52.3%
Mobile, AL Metro Area	181,618	37,513	30,242	7,271	11,029	19,213	431	25.6%	50.9%
Modesto, CA Metro Area	180,297	37,075	26,376	10,699	11,818	14,558	663	28.6%	63.8%
Monroe, LA Metro Area	77,316	15,804	12,877	2,927	2,879	9,998	na	15.5%	49.3%
Monroe, MI Metro Area	63,513	13,962	11,795	2,167	4,741	7,054	na	24.0%	64.0%
Montgomery, AL Metro Area	164,416	32,901	27,578	5,323	12,214	15,364	257	21.9%	50.3%
Morehead City, NC Micro Area	48,897	9,697	8,566	1,131	3,366	5,200	59	25.7%	43.2%
Morgantown, WV Metro Area	59,543	10,484	8,969	1,515	2,190	6,779	na	16.7%	21.8%
Morristown, TN Metro Area	50,662	12,957	10,869	2,088	3,114	7,755	na	na	40.2%
Moses Lake, WA Micro Area	35,521	7,129	5,667	1,462	1,623	4,044	235	na	52.7%
Mount Airy, NC Micro Area	33,568	8,171	6,380	1,791	2,040	4,340	169	23.9%	37.0%
Mount Pleasant, MI Micro Area	28,690	4,940	4,067	873	1,184	2,883	61	20.1%	58.8%
Mount Vernon-Anacortes, WA Metro Area	51,885	13,628	10,645	2,983	4,318	6,327	734	30.5%	55.6%
Muncie, IN Metro Area	52,517	11,571	10,224	1,347	3,953	6,271	na	18.6%	40.9%
Muskegon, MI Metro Area	73,328	17,066	14,150	2,916	4,163	9,987	547	13.2%	60.2%
Muskogee, OK Micro Area	30,916	6,952	5,373	1,579	1,321	4,052	151	20.8%	35.1%
Myrtle Beach-Conway-North Myrtle Beach, SC-NC Metro Area	274,528	57,080	49,913	7,167	22,194	27,719	457	27.4%	60.6%
Nacogdoches, TX Micro Area	27,951	5,704	4,341	1,363	964	3,377	na	na	27.9%
Napa, CA Metro Area	55,322	14,395	11,888	2,507	5,586	6,302	526	31.3%	53.1%
Naples-Immokalee-Marco Island, FL Metro Area	203,099	59,575	50,207	9,368	16,384	33,823	1,702	25.8%	53.9%
Nashville-Davidson–Murfreesboro–Franklin, TN Metro Area	730,825	132,276	106,343	25,933	39,843	66,500	3,548	22.7%	55.7%
New Bern, NC Metro Area	57,975	15,137	12,859	2,278	5,463	7,396	347	30.8%	56.8%
New Castle, PA Micro Area	40,729	11,449	9,149	2,300	2,169	6,980	421	21.4%	49.8%
New Haven-Milford, CT Metro Area	362,307	82,837	59,569	23,268	23,099	36,470	2,868	43.5%	52.8%
New Orleans-Metairie, LA Metro Area	553,396	107,714	86,076	21,638	27,012	59,064	1,123	23.4%	56.6%
New Philadelphia-Dover, OH Micro Area	39,988	10,625	9,024	1,601	2,528	6,496	466	24.4%	54.9%
New York-Newark-Jersey City, NY-NJ-PA Metro Area	7,880,970	1,691,688	1,061,772	629,916	386,510	675,262	21,145	41.5%	59.2%
Niles-Benton Harbor, MI Metro Area	76,737	17,520	14,278	3,250	4,861	9,417	442	23.2%	52.4%
North Port-Sarasota-Bradenton, FL Metro Area	410,031	136,689	113,415	23,274	34,277	79,138	5,021	24.9%	53.9%
North Wilkesboro, NC Micro Area	33,031	8,517	6,987	1,530	2,058	4,929	88	na	na
Norwich-New London, CT Metro Area	121,263	26,286	21,231	5,055	9,467	11,764	561	30.0%	58.0%
Oak Harbor, WA Micro Area	40,676	10,375	8,328	2,047	3,723	4,605	240	na	66.0%
Ocala, FL Metro Area	163,560	57,018	50,954	6,064	16,769	34,185	723	22.1%	44.1%
Ocean City, NJ Metro Area	98,928	14,468	12,288	2,180	5,173	7,115	239	40.0%	67.2%
Odessa, TX Metro Area	56,510	9,158	7,216	1,942	1,067	6,149	na	20.4%	42.5%
Ogden-Clearfield, UT Metro Area	212,268	37,737	32,193	5,544	11,442	20,751	1,274	23.0%	60.6%
Ogdensburg-Massena, NY Micro Area	52,240	9,894	7,761	2,133	2,014	5,747	na	24.3%	47.2%
Oklahoma City, OK Metro Area	557,408	105,072	85,764	19,308	28,011	57,753	3,127	18.8%	50.0%
Olean, NY Micro Area	40,957	8,548	6,557	1,991	1,230	5,327	55	23.2%	54.7%
Olympia-Tumwater, WA Metro Area	111,797	24,728	18,600	6,128	7,215	11,385	664	23.0%	57.7%
Omaha-Council Bluffs, NE-IA Metro Area	374,241	71,113	54,338	16,775	19,521	34,817	4,804	23.2%	58.2%
Opelousas, LA Micro Area	36,154	7,856	6,355	1,501	865	5,490	na	21.5%	na
Orangeburg, SC Micro Area	42,190	9,240	7,519	1,721	2,014	5,505	na	32.0%	37.9%
Orlando-Kissimmee-Sanford, FL Metro Area	974,694	174,137	141,938	32,199	62,121	79,817	3,462	28.8%	58.4%
Oshkosh-Neenah, WI Metro Area	74,207	16,060	11,961	4,099	4,685	7,276	687	33.8%	64.5%
Ottawa-Peru, IL Micro Area	68,804	17,048	14,219	2,829	2,688	11,531	152	18.7%	26.3%
Owensboro, KY Metro Area	50,396	12,013	9,704	2,309	2,928	6,776	307	16.1%	46.1%
Owosso, MI Micro Area	30,063	6,935	5,916	1,019	1,894	4,022	79	19.1%	39.6%
Oxnard-Thousand Oaks-Ventura, CA Metro Area	284,527	68,153	52,691	15,462	27,053	25,638	1,848	32.5%	55.2%
Paducah, KY-IL Micro Area	46,214	10,957	8,646	2,311	2,324	6,322	na	19.2%	50.2%
Palatka, FL Micro Area	36,664	10,067	8,750	1,317	2,557	6,193	na	17.5%	na
Palm Bay-Melbourne-Titusville, FL Metro Area	272,283	76,243	64,788	11,455	23,009	41,779	1,156	23.8%	61.6%
Panama City, FL Metro Area	109,797	18,635	15,389	3,246	4,546	10,843	254	27.5%	57.7%
Parkersburg-Vienna, WV Metro Area	43,301	11,881	9,899	1,982	2,396	7,503	184	17.0%	38.2%
Pensacola-Ferry Pass-Brent, FL Metro Area	206,220	44,926	35,200	9,718	13,007	22,201	1,029	20.9%	48.9%
Peoria, IL Metro Area	165,392	38,761	31,034	7,727	8,763	22,271	1,188	19.0%	43.1%

Table J-4: Metropolitan/Micropolitan Statistical Areas—Summary of Housing and Householder Characteristics—*Continued*

| | | Householders 65 Years and Over | | | | | | | |
| | | | | | Owner Householders | | | | |
	Total Housing Units	Total Households	Owner Occupied	Renter Occupied	With a Mortgage	Without a Mortgage	Renter Households With Meals Included in Rent	Percent of Owner Householders Who Pay 35% or More of income for Housing Costs	Percent of Renter Households Who Pay 35% or More of Income for Rental Costs
Philadelphia-Camden-Wilmington, PA-NJ-DE-MD Metro Area	2,448,985	542,821	412,247	130,574	150,457	261,790	19,881	34.2%	60.3%
Phoenix-Mesa-Scottsdale, AZ Metro Area	1,845,898	378,994	302,564	76,430	135,789	166,775	12,479	25.4%	55.3%
Pine Bluff, AR Metro Area	42,570	9,236	7,890	1,346	2,279	5,611	na	25.2%	29.2%
Pinehurst-Southern Pines, NC Micro Area	45,235	13,871	11,752	2,119	5,018	6,734	699	28.8%	62.7%
Pittsburgh, PA Metro Area	1,105,960	281,313	216,633	64,680	62,423	154,210	8,168	23.4%	49.7%
Pittsfield, MA Metro Area	68,333	17,764	13,718	4,046	5,179	8,539	142	27.7%	42.0%
Plattsburgh, NY Micro Area	35,939	7,776	6,318	1,458	1,743	4,575	121	19.6%	na
Pocatello, ID Metro Area	33,369	6,874	6,082	792	2,315	3,767	231	26.6%	58.0%
Port Angeles, WA Micro Area	35,811	12,052	10,138	1,914	3,358	6,780	416	na	56.1%
Port St. Lucie, FL Metro Area	216,298	67,256	59,355	7,901	20,724	38,631	1,421	25.0%	54.1%
Portland-South Portland, ME Metro Area	265,977	56,005	44,051	11,954	16,818	27,233	1,300	30.1%	62.7%
Portland-Vancouver-Hillsboro, OR-WA Metro Area	946,580	190,816	139,469	51,347	61,827	77,642	12,278	29.6%	63.6%
Portsmouth, OH Micro Area	34,095	7,877	6,232	1,645	1,362	4,870	na	26.0%	42.4%
Pottsville, PA Micro Area	69,064	17,799	14,747	3,052	3,064	11,683	265	28.0%	34.1%
Prescott, AZ Metro Area	112,534	38,908	32,271	6,637	13,198	19,073	704	25.6%	62.5%
Providence-Warwick, RI-MA Metro Area	693,915	155,267	107,930	47,337	42,937	64,993	3,229	33.9%	51.6%
Provo-Orem, UT Metro Area	161,303	22,346	19,349	2,997	7,516	11,833	963	19.4%	51.6%
Pueblo, CO Metro Area	70,071	17,236	13,665	3,571	6,275	7,390	189	32.1%	57.9%
Punta Gorda, FL Metro Area	101,363	38,266	33,068	5,198	13,300	19,768	1,013	24.5%	52.6%
Quincy, IL-MO Micro Area	34,711	9,020	7,148	1,872	1,279	5,869	150	16.7%	56.4%
Racine, WI Metro Area	82,283	19,041	14,782	4,259	4,800	9,982	201	33.8%	53.8%
Raleigh, NC Metro Area	499,039	79,654	62,274	17,380	29,404	32,870	1,789	22.9%	52.8%
Rapid City, SD Metro Area	62,996	13,423	10,473	2,950	2,397	8,076	476	22.4%	46.6%
Reading, PA Metro Area	164,846	40,172	32,165	8,007	10,340	21,825	799	32.2%	48.6%
Redding, CA Metro Area	77,916	21,110	16,689	4,421	6,745	9,944	695	29.5%	66.3%
Reno, NV Metro Area	189,622	41,425	30,240	11,185	15,359	14,881	960	33.3%	55.5%
Richmond, IN Micro Area	31,148	7,721	6,764	957	2,622	4,142	na	22.8%	45.5%
Richmond, VA Metro Area	518,539	107,795	84,287	23,508	37,321	46,966	4,042	22.7%	57.5%
Richmond-Berea, KY Micro Area	43,498	8,709	6,906	1,803	2,369	4,537	175	17.5%	50.2%
Riverside-San Bernardino-Ontario, CA Metro Area	1,528,375	288,442	226,431	62,011	108,641	117,790	5,570	34.3%	63.3%
Roanoke Rapids, NC Micro Area	36,557	9,066	7,005	2,061	2,344	4,661	na	na	46.6%
Roanoke, VA Metro Area	145,272	36,891	30,743	6,148	10,434	20,309	753	21.1%	50.2%
Rochester, MN Metro Area	89,676	19,359	16,385	2,974	5,261	11,124	968	18.5%	53.5%
Rochester, NY Metro Area	473,694	110,552	82,893	27,659	28,423	54,470	2,760	28.0%	57.3%
Rockford, IL Metro Area	145,523	33,441	26,242	7,199	9,071	17,171	919	29.5%	46.0%
Rocky Mount, NC Metro Area	67,063	16,555	11,669	4,886	3,978	7,691	122	31.6%	51.9%
Rome, GA Metro Area	40,423	9,055	6,902	2,153	2,482	4,420	363	25.1%	52.7%
Roseburg, OR Micro Area	48,933	15,674	11,969	3,705	4,262	7,707	1,019	22.7%	57.4%
Roswell, NM Micro Area	26,692	6,495	5,071	1,424	1,349	3,722	na	na	na
Russellville, AR Micro Area	35,959	7,902	6,250	1,652	1,589	4,661	na	na	26.8%
Sacramento-Roseville-Arden-Arcade, CA Metro Area	884,989	185,384	141,685	43,699	70,900	70,785	6,977	31.4%	60.3%
Saginaw, MI Metro Area	86,792	21,226	18,303	2,923	6,382	11,921	577	22.3%	54.2%
Salem, OH Micro Area	46,674	12,009	10,043	1,966	2,916	7,127	na	19.0%	43.6%
Salem, OR Metro Area	153,049	38,294	28,893	9,401	12,022	16,871	3,587	29.8%	64.0%
Salinas, CA Metro Area	140,143	30,238	23,049	7,189	10,806	12,243	689	30.8%	58.1%
Salisbury, MD-DE Metro Area	237,372	49,882	42,971	6,911	17,181	25,790	683	24.9%	54.3%
Salt Lake City, UT Metro Area	396,858	67,200	53,881	13,319	22,468	31,413	2,502	21.8%	49.3%
San Angelo, TX Metro Area	48,584	10,610	7,322	3,288	1,864	5,458	na	14.2%	48.4%
San Antonio-New Braunfels, TX Metro Area	862,036	166,825	133,303	33,522	44,663	88,640	5,003	21.5%	56.0%
San Diego-Carlsbad, CA Metro Area	1,187,693	234,218	173,630	60,588	83,094	90,536	7,746	33.8%	64.2%
San Francisco-Oakland-Hayward, CA Metro Area	1,771,685	374,843	263,391	111,452	126,131	137,260	11,705	29.8%	60.9%
San Jose-Sunnyvale-Santa Clara, CA Metro Area	669,279	127,012	93,232	33,780	41,722	51,510	4,490	30.2%	68.8%
San Luis Obispo-Paso Robles-Arroyo Grande, CA Metro Area	119,138	29,273	23,642	5,631	12,561	11,081	593	30.5%	55.0%
Sandusky, OH Micro Area	37,714	9,653	7,891	1,762	2,978	4,913	na	20.2%	na
Santa Cruz-Watsonville, CA Metro Area	105,251	22,945	18,000	4,945	7,500	10,500	412	31.2%	74.0%
Santa Fe, NM Metro Area	71,726	18,581	15,605	2,976	6,280	9,325	312	26.2%	54.2%
Santa Maria-Santa Barbara, CA Metro Area	154,414	37,459	28,123	9,336	13,347	14,776	1,700	32.6%	68.4%
Santa Rosa, CA Metro Area	207,220	51,802	38,279	13,523	18,093	20,186	2,432	34.4%	55.9%
Savannah, GA Metro Area	156,071	28,809	21,985	6,824	8,644	13,341	507	24.1%	49.8%
Scranton-Wilkes-Barre-Hazleton, PA Metro Area	258,192	64,628	50,484	14,144	13,834	36,650	873	31.8%	44.5%
Searcy, AR Micro Area	33,198	7,197	6,193	1,004	1,567	4,626	na	na	33.6%
Seattle-Tacoma-Bellevue, WA Metro Area	1,510,981	272,064	203,212	68,852	88,589	114,623	14,302	29.3%	63.0%
Sebastian-Vero Beach, FL Metro Area	77,342	26,256	22,200	4,056	7,752	14,448	1,001	30.4%	51.1%
Sebring, FL Metro Area	54,894	19,624	16,791	2,833	3,961	12,830	324	na	40.2%
Seneca, SC Micro Area	39,125	9,788	9,192	596	2,882	6,310	na	21.9%	na
Sevierville, TN Micro Area	56,268	10,950	8,848	2,102	2,007	6,841	94	na	30.5%
Shawnee, OK Micro Area	29,633	6,475	5,417	1,058	1,194	4,223	na	14.9%	39.0%
Sheboygan, WI Metro Area	50,611	11,782	9,097	2,685	3,124	5,973	436	25.0%	52.9%
Shelby, NC Micro Area	43,263	11,438	9,368	2,070	2,649	6,719	na	24.1%	72.6%

Table J-4: Metropolitan/Micropolitan Statistical Areas—Summary of Housing and Householder Characteristics—*Continued*

					Householders 65 Years and Over				
					Owner Householders			Percent of Owner Householders Who Pay 35% or More of income for Housing Costs	Percent of Renter Households Who Pay 35% or More of Income for Rental Costs
	Total Housing Units	Total Households	Owner Occupied	Renter Occupied	With a Mortgage	Without a Mortgage	Renter Households With Meals Included in Rent		
Sherman-Denison, TX Metro Area	54,398	12,404	9,795	2,609	2,322	7,473	266	22.0%	50.3%
Show Low, AZ Micro Area	57,407	10,706	9,218	1,488	2,345	6,873	na	19.5%	42.9%
Shreveport-Bossier City, LA Metro Area	198,597	40,247	33,226	7,021	8,849	24,377	648	20.5%	43.9%
Sierra Vista-Douglas, AZ Metro Area	60,506	15,100	12,419	2,681	5,157	7,262	na	26.0%	43.5%
Sioux City, IA-NE-SD Metro Area	69,002	15,558	12,098	3,460	2,635	9,463	434	17.0%	57.7%
Sioux Falls, SD Metro Area	101,462	18,872	14,041	4,831	4,262	9,779	1,086	17.4%	47.7%
Somerset, PA Micro Area	37,961	9,658	7,673	1,985	1,838	5,835	59	26.0%	35.9%
South Bend-Mishawaka, IN-MI Metro Area	141,495	30,275	25,765	4,510	9,540	16,225	547	19.9%	50.2%
Spartanburg, SC Metro Area	138,533	31,274	24,703	6,571	8,569	16,134	863	20.3%	38.9%
Spokane-Spokane Valley, WA Metro Area	233,958	52,153	39,551	12,602	14,896	24,655	2,370	24.0%	57.8%
Springfield, IL Metro Area	96,311	21,883	17,175	4,708	5,405	11,770	710	18.3%	52.6%
Springfield, MA Metro Area	254,673	60,219	45,606	14,613	16,667	28,939	1,376	33.2%	49.7%
Springfield, MO Metro Area	197,091	44,305	34,294	10,011	12,437	21,857	703	22.3%	55.9%
Springfield, OH Metro Area	61,182	15,290	12,165	3,125	4,214	7,951	866	21.5%	64.8%
St. Cloud, MN Metro Area	79,387	15,334	12,186	3,148	3,528	8,658	507	27.0%	51.7%
St. George, UT Metro Area	62,439	17,020	14,152	2,868	5,315	8,837	366	20.1%	59.3%
St. Joseph, MO-KS Metro Area	53,905	12,920	10,099	2,821	2,619	7,480	331	20.9%	39.1%
St. Louis, MO-IL Metro Area	1,236,725	265,178	214,933	50,245	80,012	134,921	8,632	25.1%	51.2%
State College, PA Metro Area	65,105	12,199	9,682	2,517	3,092	6,590	391	21.3%	45.2%
Statesboro, GA Metro Area	29,766	4,989	4,055	934	1,889	2,166	na	na	57.6%
Staunton-Waynesboro, VA Metro Area	54,325	14,271	11,948	2,323	4,653	7,295	171	21.2%	53.3%
Stevens Point, WI Micro Area	30,363	6,738	5,554	1,184	1,578	3,976	86	27.0%	53.2%
Stillwater, OK Micro Area	35,208	5,632	4,341	1,291	1,564	2,777	260	28.1%	72.0%
Stockton-Lodi, CA Metro Area	237,547	44,199	32,376	11,823	14,765	17,611	1,675	30.9%	61.7%
Sumter, SC Metro Area	47,021	9,981	8,203	1,778	2,791	5,412	196	na	44.3%
Sunbury, PA Micro Area	44,949	11,777	8,648	3,129	1,980	6,668	645	22.0%	45.6%
Syracuse, NY Metro Area	289,930	62,523	48,400	14,123	15,970	32,430	1,100	21.9%	48.6%
Talladega-Sylacauga, AL Micro Area	43,102	9,339	7,898	1,441	2,066	5,832	na	23.8%	40.4%
Tallahassee, FL Metro Area	163,609	30,156	25,167	4,989	9,686	15,481	748	26.7%	48.5%
Tampa-St. Petersburg-Clearwater, FL Metro Area	1,375,780	332,612	269,338	63,274	93,291	176,047	10,915	26.6%	61.9%
Terre Haute, IN Metro Area	73,919	16,481	13,108	3,373	5,392	7,716	547	20.7%	50.2%
Texarkana, TX-AR Metro Area	64,576	14,570	12,009	2,561	2,487	9,522	na	20.0%	53.5%
The Villages, FL Metro Area	64,503	34,307	32,253	2,054	11,307	20,946	157	na	na
Toledo, OH Metro Area	273,328	56,992	45,644	11,348	17,934	27,710	1,068	23.8%	50.7%
Topeka, KS Metro Area	104,225	24,175	19,541	4,634	6,042	13,499	815	17.8%	61.9%
Torrington, CT Micro Area	87,413	20,304	16,750	3,554	6,326	10,424	188	32.7%	54.9%
Traverse City, MI Micro Area	81,968	18,300	16,491	1,809	6,447	10,044	214	31.5%	53.8%
Trenton, NJ Metro Area	144,999	30,427	22,274	8,153	9,774	12,500	1,210	37.2%	57.5%
Truckee-Grass Valley, CA Micro Area	53,083	13,350	11,967	1,383	5,984	5,983	368	31.6%	61.0%
Tucson, AZ Metro Area	448,835	112,162	88,024	24,138	38,183	49,841	4,151	22.1%	53.8%
Tullahoma-Manchester, TN Micro Area	45,775	12,022	10,443	1,579	2,286	8,157	269	19.2%	39.1%
Tulsa, OK Metro Area	421,147	85,626	70,005	15,621	23,658	46,347	2,618	21.1%	51.6%
Tupelo, MS Micro Area	58,747	12,350	10,118	2,232	2,931	7,187	188	22.9%	35.5%
Tuscaloosa, AL Metro Area	104,442	18,044	14,812	3,232	4,791	10,021	299	22.6%	44.8%
Twin Falls, ID Micro Area	40,577	9,351	7,125	2,226	2,433	4,692	202	20.1%	43.0%
Tyler, TX Metro Area	88,447	20,300	16,183	4,117	5,337	10,846	513	24.4%	63.3%
Ukiah, CA Micro Area	40,719	10,713	7,619	3,094	3,153	4,466	560	35.7%	48.7%
Urban Honolulu, HI Metro Area	343,031	83,122	62,524	20,598	29,346	33,178	2,111	27.5%	57.0%
Utica-Rome, NY Metro Area	137,324	31,917	23,858	8,059	6,972	16,886	417	24.1%	46.7%
Valdosta, GA Metro Area	58,587	11,392	9,004	2,388	3,881	5,123	na	27.2%	56.2%
Vallejo-Fairfield, CA Metro Area	154,997	33,203	25,817	7,386	14,862	10,955	656	32.4%	62.1%
Victoria, TX Metro Area	39,717	9,079	8,062	1,017	1,489	6,573	na	15.3%	72.5%
Vineland-Bridgeton, NJ Metro Area	56,363	13,024	9,712	3,312	3,348	6,364	176	37.6%	47.4%
Virginia Beach-Norfolk-Newport News, VA-NC Metro Area	708,273	139,331	111,697	27,634	50,431	61,266	4,871	29.6%	63.2%
Visalia-Porterville, CA Metro Area	145,500	25,327	20,005	5,322	7,910	12,095	467	29.4%	43.8%
Waco, TX Metro Area	105,853	22,603	17,688	4,915	4,819	12,869	523	20.2%	49.0%
Walla Walla, WA Metro Area	25,876	6,214	5,352	862	1,500	3,852	na	na	na
Warner Robins, GA Metro Area	77,387	13,927	11,430	2,497	4,776	6,654	na	27.7%	57.5%
Warsaw, IN Micro Area	37,562	7,172	6,235	937	2,073	4,162	na	15.1%	47.1%
Washington-Arlington-Alexandria, DC-VA-MD-WV Metro Area	2,304,073	402,152	313,782	88,370	165,466	148,316	12,673	28.0%	58.0%
Waterloo-Cedar Falls, IA Metro Area	72,567	17,443	14,390	3,053	3,357	11,033	1,045	16.2%	53.4%
Watertown-Fort Atkinson, WI Micro Area	35,296	7,994	6,418	1,576	2,510	3,908	259	34.5%	49.4%
Watertown-Fort Drum, NY Metro Area	58,780	8,616	6,664	1,952	1,694	4,970	na	23.3%	20.5%
Wausau, WI Metro Area	58,379	13,355	10,953	2,402	2,662	8,291	157	26.6%	45.3%
Weirton-Steubenville, WV-OH Metro Area	58,343	15,436	12,311	3,125	3,771	8,540	68	14.0%	40.6%
Wenatchee, WA Metro Area	52,473	11,579	9,577	2,002	3,962	5,615	425	26.6%	48.7%
Wheeling, WV-OH Metro Area	69,055	17,770	14,754	3,016	2,996	11,758	75	14.2%	46.4%
Whitewater-Elkhorn, WI Micro Area	51,709	9,925	7,740	2,185	2,795	4,945	372	30.9%	54.1%
Wichita Falls, TX Metro Area	65,310	14,242	11,495	2,747	2,516	8,979	659	22.3%	44.8%
Wichita, KS Metro Area	270,272	54,312	43,167	11,145	13,745	29,422	2,189	20.0%	52.2%
Williamsport, PA Metro Area	52,639	12,944	9,739	3,205	2,703	7,036	345	21.9%	58.0%
Wilmington, NC Metro Area	132,764	26,961	22,372	4,589	11,440	10,932	388	29.7%	50.6%

Table J-4: Metropolitan/Micropolitan Statistical Areas—Summary of Housing and Householder Characteristics—*Continued*

	Total Housing Units				Householders 65 Years and Over				
		Total Households	Owner Occupied	Renter Occupied	Owner Householders		Renter Households With Meals Included in Rent	Percent of Owner Householders Who Pay 35% or More of income for Housing Costs	Percent of Renter Households Who Pay 35% or More of Income for Rental Costs
					With a Mortgage	Without a Mortgage			
Wilson, NC Micro Area..............................	35,662	8,299	6,483	1,816	2,490	3,993	na	na	44.7%
Winchester, VA-WV Metro Area	58,711	13,121	10,489	2,632	3,542	6,947	521	24.3%	33.5%
Winston-Salem, NC Metro Area	290,878	66,793	54,484	12,309	19,812	34,672	802	20.9%	49.8%
Wisconsin Rapids-Marshfield, WI Micro Area.......	34,394	9,251	6,989	2,262	1,933	5,056	534	19.1%	68.6%
Wooster, OH Micro Area...........................	46,011	10,626	9,085	1,541	2,844	6,241	77	20.9%	33.8%
Worcester, MA-CT Metro Area	378,239	78,939	56,923	22,016	20,271	36,652	1,744	34.2%	53.6%
Yakima, WA Metro Area............................	86,370	18,654	14,563	4,091	5,069	9,494	514	31.8%	37.1%
York-Hanover, PA Metro Area..................	180,662	41,712	35,206	6,506	11,388	23,818	648	29.8%	65.9%
Youngstown-Warren-Boardman, OH-PA Metro Area	258,434	68,851	55,910	12,941	17,161	38,749	1,071	19.6%	42.0%
Yuba City, CA Metro Area........................	62,114	13,359	10,528	2,831	4,340	6,188	142	21.1%	52.7%
Yuma, AZ Metro Area...............................	89,909	22,044	18,589	3,455	5,458	13,131	276	19.6%	43.0%
Zanesville, OH Micro Area........................	37,778	9,403	7,426	1,977	2,723	4,703	324	26.1%	49.2%

Table J-5: 114th Congressional Districts—Summary of Housing and Householder Characteristics

| | | | | Householders 65 Years and Over | | | | | |
| | | | | Owner Householders | | | | | |
	Total Housing Units	Total Households	Owner Occupied	Renter Occupied	With a Mortgage	Without a Mortgage	Renter Households With Meals Included in Rent	Percent of Owner Householders Who Pay 35% or More of income for Housing Costs	Percent of Renter Households Who Pay 35% or More of Income for Rental Costs
Alabama									
Congressional District 1	328,532	71,277	58,816	12,461	20,636	38,180	1,036	25.6%	51.4%
Congressional District 2	309,169	67,200	56,348	10,852	18,786	37,562	316	19.3%	44.8%
Congressional District 3	324,122	67,169	56,592	10,577	17,713	38,879	459	23.0%	48.7%
Congressional District 4	311,200	73,422	61,600	11,822	15,670	45,930	814	20.9%	36.0%
Congressional District 5	310,432	66,956	55,138	11,818	16,370	38,768	1,406	16.4%	50.7%
Congressional District 6	298,431	66,627	57,013	9,614	21,711	35,302	2,411	24.8%	52.0%
Congressional District 7	326,144	60,017	48,198	11,819	17,211	30,987	489	29.7%	48.2%
Alaska									
Congressional District (at Large)	308,571	40,996	33,825	7,171	12,610	21,215	316	18.0%	49.1%
Arizona									
Congressional District 1	331,747	75,218	65,493	9,725	24,891	40,602	714	21.7%	42.2%
Congressional District 2	345,434	89,098	68,638	20,460	28,988	39,650	3,857	22.3%	55.5%
Congressional District 3	269,999	46,538	36,863	9,675	15,218	21,645	254	26.0%	47.7%
Congressional District 4	384,567	113,071	98,195	14,876	37,792	60,403	1,139	23.0%	55.0%
Congressional District 5	310,218	70,872	59,869	11,003	23,936	35,933	1,667	24.5%	55.6%
Congressional District 6	350,948	76,013	61,130	14,883	30,117	31,013	2,508	28.3%	48.0%
Congressional District 7	261,283	30,263	20,486	9,777	9,035	11,451	223	30.9%	60.0%
Congressional District 8	326,564	94,086	76,243	17,843	34,338	41,905	4,188	22.1%	58.2%
Congressional District 9	328,576	52,453	36,509	15,944	17,148	19,361	3,683	24.8%	61.8%
Arkansas									
Congressional District 1	338,438	79,867	64,925	14,942	18,940	45,985	848	19.3%	38.8%
Congressional District 2	335,178	65,456	52,719	12,737	17,462	35,257	996	18.5%	46.6%
Congressional District 3	324,420	65,607	54,042	11,565	17,025	37,017	1,076	22.9%	44.9%
Congressional District 4	343,045	78,872	67,267	11,605	15,747	51,520	742	18.3%	40.5%
California									
Congressional District 1	324,834	84,018	69,993	14,025	28,399	41,594	1,989	27.9%	59.5%
Congressional District 2	320,423	81,683	62,317	19,366	29,221	33,096	2,934	31.0%	53.6%
Congressional District 3	264,765	55,847	45,494	10,353	21,597	23,897	1,336	29.6%	53.8%
Congressional District 4	353,558	84,023	71,015	13,008	34,699	36,316	2,507	33.2%	58.9%
Congressional District 5	287,407	69,937	53,391	16,546	25,605	27,786	2,515	33.0%	61.3%
Congressional District 6	286,820	50,970	34,432	16,538	17,442	16,990	1,572	30.4%	60.8%
Congressional District 7	274,333	59,781	44,994	14,787	21,508	23,486	2,609	29.5%	60.9%
Congressional District 8	308,186	54,549	43,669	10,880	20,356	23,313	1,139	38.3%	60.4%
Congressional District 9	246,207	47,782	36,170	11,612	17,803	18,367	1,749	31.2%	60.9%
Congressional District 10	243,718	47,092	34,155	12,937	15,529	18,626	963	29.6%	63.1%
Congressional District 11	281,591	66,857	51,776	15,081	24,239	27,537	2,561	28.9%	64.1%
Congressional District 12	350,084	65,252	33,134	32,118	13,724	19,410	1,681	27.8%	54.2%
Congressional District 13	300,263	59,551	37,925	21,626	19,710	18,215	1,501	31.1%	62.5%
Congressional District 14	265,184	59,497	43,153	16,344	19,247	23,906	2,130	29.0%	66.4%
Congressional District 15	254,808	49,013	37,567	11,446	18,574	18,993	1,033	30.0%	62.2%
Congressional District 16	226,066	40,628	27,381	13,247	13,051	14,330	398	32.2%	55.0%
Congressional District 17	260,541	43,857	32,767	11,090	13,200	19,567	1,770	27.4%	63.4%
Congressional District 18	285,121	61,855	48,173	13,682	19,953	28,220	2,274	29.7%	67.3%
Congressional District 19	229,697	44,725	31,692	13,033	16,647	15,045	1,283	34.5%	72.7%
Congressional District 20	247,741	52,030	39,857	12,173	18,535	21,322	1,101	31.4%	64.2%
Congressional District 21	195,325	30,001	22,650	7,351	8,478	14,172	83	25.7%	58.6%
Congressional District 22	251,110	48,857	39,057	9,800	17,462	21,595	1,333	30.7%	54.1%
Congressional District 23	270,707	50,468	37,236	13,232	16,489	20,747	769	27.3%	61.2%
Congressional District 24	277,637	67,270	52,053	15,217	26,012	26,041	2,293	31.5%	63.2%
Congressional District 25	235,325	40,984	32,285	8,699	18,276	14,009	422	35.8%	57.8%
Congressional District 26	241,663	58,450	45,940	12,510	23,616	22,324	1,810	32.4%	57.2%
Congressional District 27	257,231	60,320	42,600	17,720	18,950	23,650	1,549	31.6%	65.1%
Congressional District 28	318,123	58,539	30,209	28,330	15,502	14,707	791	40.4%	69.8%
Congressional District 29	209,616	35,620	21,513	14,107	10,928	10,585	417	39.0%	63.3%
Congressional District 30	290,214	63,729	43,862	19,867	22,364	21,498	2,291	37.0%	61.5%
Congressional District 31	233,311	36,874	25,925	10,949	12,899	13,026	892	31.0%	61.5%
Congressional District 32	209,870	45,765	32,900	12,865	15,017	17,883	1,520	28.6%	69.8%
Congressional District 33	328,288	75,283	52,786	22,497	26,742	26,044	2,460	31.5%	59.9%
Congressional District 34	257,743	43,055	15,108	27,947	7,648	7,460	958	36.5%	62.7%
Congressional District 35	195,747	27,614	20,066	7,548	9,719	10,347	205	31.2%	59.4%
Congressional District 36	349,892	90,719	73,610	17,109	29,833	43,777	1,319	32.6%	64.3%
Congressional District 37	289,749	56,344	31,808	24,536	16,187	15,621	1,183	37.4%	70.8%
Congressional District 38	214,707	51,026	38,855	12,171	18,203	20,652	559	29.5%	63.3%
Congressional District 39	228,508	51,356	41,480	9,876	22,360	19,120	1,518	35.9%	68.5%
Congressional District 40	188,054	26,284	15,213	11,071	7,674	7,539	93	36.9%	65.9%
Congressional District 41	207,336	32,241	24,266	7,975	13,305	10,961	1,017	31.2%	71.8%
Congressional District 42	233,095	44,085	35,734	8,351	18,735	16,999	954	36.1%	58.1%
Congressional District 43	254,377	47,677	31,922	15,755	15,740	16,182	81	37.3%	67.2%
Congressional District 44	193,694	32,690	21,895	10,795	12,051	9,844	199	41.4%	65.1%
Congressional District 45	277,017	58,224	46,852	11,372	24,044	22,808	1,877	33.9%	70.2%
Congressional District 46	193,810	30,943	19,540	11,403	10,530	9,010	800	30.9%	60.9%
Congressional District 47	255,020	49,151	33,213	15,938	14,764	18,449	1,121	30.0%	63.3%

Table J-5: 114th Congressional Districts—Summary of Housing and Householder Characteristics—*Continued*

| | | | | Householders 65 Years and Over | | | | | |
| | | | | Owner Householders | | | | Percent of Owner Householders Who Pay 35% or More of income for Housing Costs | Percent of Renter Households Who Pay 35% or More of Income for Rental Costs |
	Total Housing Units	Total Households	Owner Occupied	Renter Occupied	With a Mortgage	Without a Mortgage	Renter Households With Meals Included in Rent		
California—Cont.									
Congressional District 48	289,122	70,006	55,652	14,354	26,883	28,769	1,633	34.2%	69.1%
Congressional District 49	275,385	62,730	50,982	11,748	26,121	24,861	2,950	36.1%	67.2%
Congressional District 50	258,043	58,738	46,633	12,105	22,798	23,835	2,100	40.3%	62.5%
Congressional District 51	220,996	39,205	23,242	15,963	10,007	13,235	569	28.0%	58.0%
Congressional District 52	303,518	55,711	40,836	14,875	19,662	21,174	1,711	31.1%	67.0%
Congressional District 53	286,014	51,442	37,732	13,710	17,947	19,785	1,361	30.6%	62.4%
Colorado									
Congressional District 1	351,177	56,915	40,050	16,865	17,611	22,439	1,994	26.1%	59.2%
Congressional District 2	368,687	61,254	49,585	11,669	21,486	28,099	2,836	26.1%	56.9%
Congressional District 3	357,512	71,846	59,225	12,621	24,473	34,752	697	27.7%	52.0%
Congressional District 4	293,140	58,798	47,593	11,205	20,106	27,487	2,347	26.7%	59.6%
Congressional District 5	314,604	58,669	49,361	9,308	20,463	28,898	2,545	24.6%	66.3%
Congressional District 6	290,406	50,915	41,086	9,829	20,968	20,118	2,149	25.4%	60.9%
Congressional District 7	300,754	60,232	46,829	13,403	20,776	26,053	2,859	25.8%	59.8%
Connecticut									
Congressional District 1	303,974	71,138	50,732	20,406	19,473	31,259	2,304	37.6%	57.4%
Congressional District 2	301,250	67,409	56,464	10,945	21,861	34,603	874	32.0%	49.6%
Congressional District 3	302,123	69,849	51,352	18,497	20,712	30,640	2,627	45.8%	55.4%
Congressional District 4	283,579	63,660	48,714	14,946	20,609	28,105	1,819	41.8%	54.2%
Congressional District 5	302,706	67,602	51,324	16,278	19,139	32,185	2,005	35.7%	53.0%
Delaware									
Congressional District (at Large)	417,413	92,377	78,399	13,978	33,752	44,647	1,514	24.8%	57.5%
District of Columbia									
Delegate District (at Large)	306,184	50,463	32,424	18,039	15,941	16,483	1,701	26.6%	54.3%
Florida									
Congressional District 1	354,090	73,410	59,171	14,239	21,309	37,862	1,196	21.3%	47.3%
Congressional District 2	340,451	64,479	54,364	10,115	17,886	36,478	1,077	27.2%	50.4%
Congressional District 3	309,080	72,526	62,823	9,703	20,597	42,226	952	22.2%	44.0%
Congressional District 4	313,316	62,922	50,859	12,063	20,598	30,261	1,982	26.4%	65.9%
Congressional District 5	315,342	52,304	38,615	13,689	16,327	22,288	276	30.2%	53.1%
Congressional District 6	372,846	102,474	87,529	14,945	32,412	55,117	1,854	25.8%	59.5%
Congressional District 7	301,228	58,004	48,861	9,143	23,622	25,239	1,987	32.9%	62.2%
Congressional District 8	355,549	103,216	87,645	15,571	31,284	56,361	2,157	25.8%	59.0%
Congressional District 9	316,665	44,691	36,037	8,654	17,272	18,765	383	35.0%	66.3%
Congressional District 10	346,066	80,880	66,462	14,418	22,423	44,039	2,242	21.2%	58.5%
Congressional District 11	369,455	142,838	128,066	14,772	47,345	80,721	2,500	22.2%	57.0%
Congressional District 12	342,946	92,508	77,364	15,144	26,820	50,544	2,791	24.8%	62.7%
Congressional District 13	391,351	107,006	85,957	21,049	26,544	59,413	4,080	29.6%	60.8%
Congressional District 14	335,762	57,456	41,279	16,177	14,891	26,388	1,862	27.1%	60.5%
Congressional District 15	294,163	62,657	52,760	9,897	17,815	34,945	752	22.9%	64.9%
Congressional District 16	407,974	136,033	112,759	23,274	34,188	78,571	5,021	25.0%	53.9%
Congressional District 17	360,575	114,554	99,991	14,563	32,205	67,786	2,364	22.7%	46.1%
Congressional District 18	366,911	110,320	96,039	14,281	34,326	61,713	2,522	29.1%	59.3%
Congressional District 19	455,732	128,026	109,164	18,862	36,968	72,196	3,159	27.9%	61.0%
Congressional District 20	295,695	59,018	44,701	14,317	17,583	27,118	1,566	35.1%	64.2%
Congressional District 21	332,001	103,633	90,489	13,144	31,353	59,136	2,278	33.4%	56.6%
Congressional District 22	405,133	100,876	79,937	20,939	26,626	53,311	3,249	34.6%	68.5%
Congressional District 23	379,265	71,549	56,659	14,890	20,834	35,825	899	40.8%	61.3%
Congressional District 24	277,982	48,511	31,094	17,417	13,328	17,766	209	40.4%	58.2%
Congressional District 25	264,980	57,967	43,522	14,445	17,505	26,017	437	33.5%	63.5%
Congressional District 26	259,096	54,237	44,415	9,822	18,964	25,451	282	38.6%	62.5%
Congressional District 27	280,996	61,643	38,498	23,145	14,098	24,400	472	36.3%	65.9%
Georgia									
Congressional District 1	314,752	57,508	45,365	12,143	15,683	29,682	674	22.6%	42.3%
Congressional District 2	298,934	60,723	46,236	14,487	14,965	31,271	271	24.7%	56.7%
Congressional District 3	286,599	60,882	48,923	11,959	20,815	28,108	1,570	26.4%	58.3%
Congressional District 4	280,930	43,299	34,681	8,618	19,652	15,029	822	32.8%	59.6%
Congressional District 5	354,402	50,505	32,214	18,291	13,609	18,605	1,915	33.8%	56.8%
Congressional District 6	298,471	46,602	37,979	8,623	16,431	21,548	2,572	24.0%	57.2%
Congressional District 7	259,690	34,875	28,480	6,395	14,181	14,299	829	26.5%	59.5%
Congressional District 8	299,346	62,890	49,279	13,611	16,978	32,301	868	26.0%	52.9%
Congressional District 9	320,370	74,286	62,851	11,435	21,553	41,298	1,022	25.5%	43.2%
Congressional District 10	292,764	57,195	47,289	9,906	17,211	30,078	838	26.0%	39.3%
Congressional District 11	289,679	47,502	39,705	7,797	19,484	20,221	612	24.1%	64.6%
Congressional District 12	294,385	56,063	44,759	11,304	14,855	29,904	692	24.6%	50.3%
Congressional District 13	280,844	40,043	31,875	8,168	16,923	14,952	1,140	24.6%	68.8%
Congressional District 14	280,221	58,081	47,941	10,140	15,618	32,323	614	23.5%	51.1%
Hawaii									
Congressional District 1	258,008	63,780	46,856	16,924	20,913	25,943	1,655	27.5%	57.5%

Table J-5: 114th Congressional Districts—Summary of Housing and Householder Characteristics—*Continued*

| | | | | | Householders 65 Years and Over | | | | |
| | | | | | Owner Householders | | | | |
	Total Housing Units	Total Households	Owner Occupied	Renter Occupied	With a Mortgage	Without a Mortgage	Renter Households With Meals Included in Rent	Percent of Owner Householders Who Pay 35% or More of income for Housing Costs	Percent of Renter Households Who Pay 35% or More of Income for Rental Costs
Hawaii—Cont.									
Congressional District 2..................	272,110	58,964	46,797	12,167	21,844	24,953	620	25.2%	46.2%
Idaho									
Congressional District 1...................	353,223	77,362	65,200	12,162	27,596	37,604	2,411	23.0%	47.4%
Congressional District 2...................	331,875	66,862	54,597	12,265	18,450	36,147	2,589	20.7%	54.9%
Illinois									
Congressional District 1...................	304,253	68,981	50,577	18,404	22,038	28,539	735	37.9%	60.6%
Congressional District 2...................	303,071	61,057	48,307	12,750	20,222	28,085	1,533	33.2%	61.3%
Congressional District 3...................	264,675	59,770	50,622	9,148	16,620	34,002	1,133	36.8%	49.7%
Congressional District 4...................	251,320	34,683	23,456	11,227	8,417	15,039	744	40.9%	66.6%
Congressional District 5...................	318,333	53,721	39,104	14,617	12,762	26,342	1,276	37.0%	54.8%
Congressional District 6...................	279,793	60,986	51,285	9,701	19,510	31,775	3,145	34.1%	51.3%
Congressional District 7...................	339,562	56,109	31,755	24,354	14,519	17,236	1,076	37.0%	60.5%
Congressional District 8...................	268,662	49,012	41,286	7,726	16,417	24,869	1,173	34.5%	53.5%
Congressional District 9...................	310,715	68,205	50,766	17,439	17,454	33,312	2,845	36.6%	62.6%
Congressional District 10.................	265,247	54,782	43,949	10,833	15,605	28,344	2,806	33.2%	57.3%
Congressional District 11.................	252,741	40,276	33,158	7,118	12,234	20,924	760	28.8%	64.5%
Congressional District 12.................	319,289	70,647	56,318	14,329	16,093	40,225	2,258	19.4%	43.8%
Congressional District 13.................	319,169	69,702	57,128	12,574	17,428	39,700	2,202	18.3%	54.7%
Congressional District 14.................	266,222	54,959	47,755	7,204	20,739	27,016	1,626	37.4%	62.0%
Congressional District 15.................	315,465	76,931	64,130	12,801	15,103	49,027	1,647	17.3%	40.5%
Congressional District 16.................	297,404	72,216	60,287	11,929	17,650	42,637	1,272	23.9%	40.4%
Congressional District 17.................	321,126	78,897	62,091	16,806	17,482	44,609	1,640	22.7%	43.2%
Congressional District 18.................	310,461	74,612	61,852	12,760	15,942	45,910	2,318	17.7%	51.4%
Indiana									
Congressional District 1...................	303,811	63,780	53,561	10,219	22,285	31,276	960	25.0%	59.7%
Congressional District 2...................	306,940	66,436	54,660	11,776	20,394	34,266	1,541	18.3%	56.1%
Congressional District 3...................	314,418	65,510	54,753	10,757	19,407	35,266	1,370	19.2%	48.6%
Congressional District 4...................	309,346	65,949	54,898	11,051	20,878	34,020	1,125	20.7%	48.0%
Congressional District 5...................	317,665	63,514	51,566	11,948	23,099	28,467	2,295	21.4%	46.4%
Congressional District 6...................	312,312	73,490	62,716	10,774	23,082	39,634	864	19.9%	51.0%
Congressional District 7...................	333,640	49,583	35,936	13,647	17,871	18,065	1,057	26.1%	54.9%
Congressional District 8...................	317,760	72,470	59,050	13,420	20,143	38,907	1,639	20.3%	49.0%
Congressional District 9...................	313,738	64,961	54,064	10,897	22,752	31,312	1,420	22.0%	43.5%
Iowa									
Congressional District 1...................	337,117	80,762	66,062	14,700	15,861	50,201	3,199	17.4%	51.6%
Congressional District 2...................	338,446	77,746	62,930	14,816	17,010	45,920	1,910	19.1%	45.2%
Congressional District 3...................	339,874	69,055	53,975	15,080	16,865	37,110	3,231	25.6%	51.4%
Congressional District 4...................	346,597	83,166	68,411	14,755	14,591	53,820	2,561	17.0%	44.2%
Kansas									
Congressional District 1...................	317,108	68,107	55,698	12,409	11,719	43,979	1,403	19.5%	44.3%
Congressional District 2...................	315,760	69,590	55,974	13,616	17,360	38,614	2,158	20.8%	51.8%
Congressional District 3...................	305,290	58,168	44,243	13,925	16,313	27,930	4,392	24.7%	61.2%
Congressional District 4...................	310,703	64,496	51,822	12,674	15,162	36,660	2,354	20.4%	50.9%
Kentucky									
Congressional District 1...................	332,284	77,242	64,044	13,198	17,145	46,899	233	21.4%	44.8%
Congressional District 2...................	318,253	67,302	55,795	11,507	18,262	37,533	1,233	20.1%	55.3%
Congressional District 3...................	333,978	70,239	54,938	15,301	20,606	34,332	1,961	23.9%	58.8%
Congressional District 4...................	306,845	62,197	49,991	12,206	20,537	29,454	1,037	24.8%	48.2%
Congressional District 5...................	329,516	74,642	63,453	11,189	13,855	49,598	163	21.0%	38.1%
Congressional District 6...................	329,628	62,195	48,892	13,303	18,093	30,799	1,410	22.2%	42.6%
Louisiana									
Congressional District 1...................	332,907	68,554	57,020	11,534	16,323	40,697	883	19.6%	51.9%
Congressional District 2...................	350,321	62,129	46,744	15,385	13,627	33,117	319	26.2%	57.0%
Congressional District 3...................	329,317	64,299	53,028	11,271	11,296	41,732	679	15.9%	44.3%
Congressional District 4...................	340,258	68,931	57,730	11,201	13,489	44,241	761	18.3%	40.4%
Congressional District 5...................	329,546	71,150	57,439	13,711	12,965	44,474	372	19.8%	45.8%
Congressional District 6...................	328,688	60,103	51,180	8,923	13,860	37,320	1,248	20.0%	56.3%
Maine									
Congressional District 1...................	351,630	75,384	60,781	14,603	21,965	38,816	1,377	29.6%	58.9%
Congressional District 2...................	376,063	75,897	61,217	14,680	18,625	42,592	716	27.1%	44.0%
Maryland									
Congressional District 1...................	338,413	75,955	64,512	11,443	24,764	39,748	1,539	28.6%	52.4%
Congressional District 2...................	302,093	56,987	43,218	13,769	17,194	26,024	1,006	29.1%	56.9%
Congressional District 3...................	315,879	65,092	47,991	17,101	20,975	27,016	3,016	28.9%	59.2%
Congressional District 4...................	284,673	54,092	42,068	12,024	25,802	16,266	665	34.3%	62.7%
Congressional District 5...................	274,055	53,079	45,145	7,934	25,461	19,684	501	29.5%	58.9%
Congressional District 6...................	297,669	56,961	45,006	11,955	18,895	26,111	1,268	26.2%	57.9%
Congressional District 7...................	319,108	63,904	44,948	18,956	20,429	24,519	2,351	30.2%	49.5%
Congressional District 8...................	290,427	69,912	53,414	16,498	24,022	29,392	2,864	26.9%	56.7%

Table J-5: 114th Congressional Districts—Summary of Housing and Householder Characteristics—*Continued*

| | | | | | Householders 65 Years and Over | | | | |
| | | | | Owner Householders | | | | | |
	Total Housing Units	Total Households	Owner Occupied	Renter Occupied	With a Mortgage	Without a Mortgage	Renter Households With Meals Included in Rent	Percent of Owner Householders Who Pay 35% or More of income for Housing Costs	Percent of Renter Households Who Pay 35% or More of Income for Rental Costs
Massachusetts									
Congressional District 1	319,385	77,027	58,702	18,325	21,409	37,293	1,287	32.3%	48.1%
Congressional District 2	297,227	63,503	44,831	18,672	15,748	29,083	1,701	33.2%	52.6%
Congressional District 3	291,341	61,551	44,606	16,945	16,670	27,936	1,731	36.2%	54.2%
Congressional District 4	290,181	64,533	48,806	15,727	19,684	29,122	2,005	33.3%	56.6%
Congressional District 5	308,341	70,670	51,517	19,153	19,765	31,752	1,750	35.8%	60.8%
Congressional District 6	303,080	73,451	55,090	18,361	19,595	35,495	2,460	36.1%	51.6%
Congressional District 7	303,572	48,348	22,004	26,344	9,522	12,482	916	40.7%	53.6%
Congressional District 8	314,300	73,309	52,964	20,345	21,465	31,499	2,651	37.4%	57.4%
Congressional District 9	401,165	92,405	73,813	18,592	29,876	43,937	1,732	34.3%	49.6%
Michigan									
Congressional District 1	443,848	92,775	81,361	11,414	25,388	55,973	846	26.1%	50.3%
Congressional District 2	313,719	64,455	53,085	11,370	16,897	36,188	2,019	22.2%	60.3%
Congressional District 3	295,974	61,839	50,361	11,478	15,928	34,433	2,262	25.4%	48.1%
Congressional District 4	344,608	75,303	65,235	10,068	20,088	45,147	1,324	23.1%	46.4%
Congressional District 5	329,603	75,937	65,226	10,711	21,915	43,311	562	24.1%	56.7%
Congressional District 6	325,708	68,168	58,032	10,136	18,966	39,066	1,072	21.9%	49.4%
Congressional District 7	304,753	70,855	60,892	9,963	22,693	38,199	1,476	24.9%	56.1%
Congressional District 8	295,594	58,139	47,821	10,318	20,901	26,920	2,060	27.2%	57.7%
Congressional District 9	322,836	75,302	58,219	17,083	21,133	37,086	1,875	25.0%	53.6%
Congressional District 10	305,706	71,246	60,910	10,336	21,523	39,387	1,564	24.5%	57.3%
Congressional District 11	292,518	64,684	53,261	11,423	21,336	31,925	2,760	27.1%	60.6%
Congressional District 12	290,736	60,740	48,732	12,008	17,465	31,267	1,424	26.5%	51.2%
Congressional District 13	339,393	59,444	42,040	17,404	14,295	27,745	866	30.6%	57.0%
Congressional District 14	335,092	70,289	49,465	20,824	21,754	27,711	1,866	33.6%	57.4%
Minnesota									
Congressional District 1	285,084	66,836	53,953	12,883	14,849	39,104	3,673	20.6%	55.0%
Congressional District 2	266,439	51,713	40,847	10,866	16,262	24,585	2,170	27.9%	63.9%
Congressional District 3	281,573	60,336	48,857	11,479	21,283	27,574	2,340	29.0%	61.8%
Congressional District 4	281,445	57,315	42,960	14,355	17,201	25,759	3,551	24.5%	62.1%
Congressional District 5	313,138	51,551	35,706	15,845	13,630	22,076	2,085	31.3%	57.1%
Congressional District 6	260,310	44,534	37,480	7,054	13,721	23,759	1,116	24.9%	56.1%
Congressional District 7	327,413	76,384	59,749	16,635	15,048	44,701	3,367	25.1%	49.4%
Congressional District 8	369,859	77,480	63,218	14,262	19,485	43,733	2,878	24.4%	51.2%
Mississippi									
Congressional District 1	323,162	70,107	59,213	10,894	16,940	42,273	1,237	23.2%	39.7%
Congressional District 2	310,126	63,779	50,725	13,054	13,543	37,182	467	26.9%	42.8%
Congressional District 3	329,850	72,252	61,648	10,604	15,378	46,270	875	26.3%	42.1%
Congressional District 4	331,600	67,010	57,283	9,727	17,035	40,248	559	24.6%	55.8%
Missouri									
Congressional District 1	370,871	60,997	44,276	16,721	17,909	26,367	862	28.5%	51.9%
Congressional District 2	315,314	83,030	70,584	12,446	27,618	42,966	4,928	26.2%	53.7%
Congressional District 3	335,146	67,252	57,684	9,568	20,998	36,686	1,032	23.5%	52.5%
Congressional District 4	344,251	71,976	59,786	12,190	19,557	40,229	1,312	23.0%	49.2%
Congressional District 5	354,606	70,105	52,342	17,763	19,354	32,988	1,904	27.4%	49.1%
Congressional District 6	327,132	71,255	58,137	13,118	16,005	42,132	1,057	18.3%	40.6%
Congressional District 7	348,845	78,366	63,112	15,254	23,205	39,907	929	24.0%	56.8%
Congressional District 8	339,638	81,998	66,448	15,550	18,072	48,376	1,151	23.5%	32.6%
Montana									
Congressional District (at Large)	491,515	106,654	86,510	20,144	24,492	62,018	3,663	23.0%	49.1%
Nebraska									
Congressional District 1	268,041	56,407	44,036	12,371	13,188	30,848	2,917	21.2%	43.8%
Congressional District 2	262,055	46,308	34,748	11,560	13,440	21,308	3,122	23.8%	60.1%
Congressional District 3	284,861	71,271	57,513	13,758	11,484	46,029	2,474	20.8%	38.8%
Nevada									
Congressional District 1	301,626	54,073	32,852	21,221	15,050	17,802	918	28.2%	59.4%
Congressional District 2	299,015	67,849	51,080	16,769	23,543	27,537	1,690	28.8%	53.4%
Congressional District 3	317,951	59,400	45,180	14,220	23,580	21,600	1,303	30.7%	60.5%
Congressional District 4	280,377	53,813	42,878	10,935	22,345	20,533	285	26.4%	60.8%
New Hampshire									
Congressional District 1	316,142	62,176	48,251	13,925	16,550	31,701	1,466	32.2%	56.0%
Congressional District 2	303,723	61,339	49,042	12,297	17,626	31,416	1,049	38.3%	53.4%
New Jersey									
Congressional District 1	297,501	68,271	51,788	16,483	18,673	33,115	1,979	38.2%	60.7%
Congressional District 2	384,623	75,481	60,640	14,841	23,250	37,390	1,001	40.9%	55.4%
Congressional District 3	312,039	82,952	73,084	9,868	29,897	43,187	1,178	37.8%	56.2%
Congressional District 4	299,770	82,620	67,945	14,675	25,794	42,151	3,287	37.8%	58.7%
Congressional District 5	283,618	65,224	52,638	12,586	21,049	31,589	1,209	41.9%	46.2%
Congressional District 6	273,497	54,830	41,226	13,604	15,875	25,351	458	40.6%	56.5%
Congressional District 7	281,504	62,766	49,552	13,214	19,663	29,889	991	43.1%	56.2%
Congressional District 8	304,819	44,930	19,236	25,694	7,400	11,836	268	56.1%	57.7%

Table J-5: 114th Congressional Districts—Summary of Housing and Householder Characteristics—*Continued*

| | Total Housing Units | Total Households | Owner Occupied | Renter Occupied | Householders 65 Years and Over | | Renter Households With Meals Included in Rent | Percent of Owner Householders Who Pay 35% or More of income for Housing Costs | Percent of Renter Households Who Pay 35% or More of Income for Rental Costs |
| | | | | | Owner Householders | | | | |
					With a Mortgage	Without a Mortgage			
New Jersey—Cont.									
Congressional District 9	283,719	59,278	37,910	21,368	11,815	26,095	572	49.1%	64.7%
Congressional District 10	302,278	54,385	27,664	26,721	13,703	13,961	1,041	54.1%	57.6%
Congressional District 11	279,324	71,126	56,743	14,383	22,096	34,647	2,165	40.5%	60.7%
Congressional District 12	289,155	61,336	47,115	14,221	18,168	28,947	1,804	38.7%	53.2%
New Mexico									
Congressional District 1	301,123	64,389	50,900	13,489	23,339	27,561	1,061	27.5%	53.8%
Congressional District 2	304,327	68,238	57,353	10,885	17,155	40,198	1,105	18.6%	53.9%
Congressional District 3	307,460	66,478	56,458	10,020	18,226	38,232	552	23.3%	49.0%
New York									
Congressional District 1	308,215	72,206	60,721	11,485	23,158	37,563	274	46.2%	59.7%
Congressional District 2	241,254	58,967	49,033	9,934	19,157	29,876	620	48.2%	61.4%
Congressional District 3	264,312	73,784	63,065	10,719	19,101	43,964	1,210	41.2%	57.5%
Congressional District 4	246,424	65,338	55,220	10,118	19,438	35,782	847	45.1%	61.9%
Congressional District 5	244,124	53,390	34,005	19,385	14,849	19,156	0	43.4%	62.6%
Congressional District 6	289,505	66,597	36,132	30,465	9,327	26,805	634	36.9%	63.1%
Congressional District 7	274,845	43,626	12,467	31,159	4,325	8,142	407	44.8%	53.3%
Congressional District 8	311,229	64,981	26,343	38,638	11,662	14,681	392	46.5%	56.4%
Congressional District 9	300,391	61,570	24,050	37,520	10,113	13,937	196	39.2%	64.8%
Congressional District 10	358,347	67,272	28,103	39,169	7,750	20,353	1,076	33.3%	59.0%
Congressional District 11	281,155	63,069	40,620	22,449	14,597	26,023	104	40.0%	63.4%
Congressional District 12	420,598	74,429	32,976	41,453	7,869	25,107	243	28.8%	53.6%
Congressional District 13	311,203	55,969	5,158	50,811	1,671	3,487	1,017	na	61.7%
Congressional District 14	267,535	49,001	21,699	27,302	6,350	15,349	75	41.2%	62.3%
Congressional District 15	261,761	46,280	6,243	40,037	2,206	4,037	244	42.3%	64.6%
Congressional District 16	284,688	70,132	40,388	29,744	14,340	26,048	1,133	38.5%	55.7%
Congressional District 17	258,232	63,796	47,837	15,959	16,788	31,049	1,173	40.5%	59.6%
Congressional District 18	273,831	58,508	46,959	11,549	17,819	29,140	558	38.7%	58.5%
Congressional District 19	362,881	79,439	65,376	14,063	21,953	43,423	505	33.5%	55.1%
Congressional District 20	325,554	69,952	49,351	20,601	17,146	32,205	2,047	24.3%	54.6%
Congressional District 21	368,555	69,707	55,693	14,014	17,119	38,574	663	27.5%	43.1%
Congressional District 22	320,683	73,982	57,615	16,367	17,210	40,405	1,292	24.7%	49.3%
Congressional District 23	340,391	75,608	59,991	15,617	16,180	43,811	1,641	22.3%	52.5%
Congressional District 24	313,716	69,822	53,617	16,205	17,248	36,369	1,642	21.0%	47.1%
Congressional District 25	312,169	71,712	51,467	20,245	18,802	32,665	1,800	28.9%	60.2%
Congressional District 26	344,704	81,837	60,207	21,630	18,815	41,392	1,816	25.2%	53.6%
Congressional District 27	305,226	75,144	62,175	12,969	19,360	42,815	1,041	27.0%	49.8%
North Carolina									
Congressional District 1	336,393	74,055	52,125	21,930	19,601	32,524	2,118	33.1%	48.6%
Congressional District 2	322,074	64,947	54,179	10,768	22,318	31,861	1,211	23.4%	58.3%
Congressional District 3	377,057	69,395	59,088	10,307	23,554	35,534	318	27.4%	43.2%
Congressional District 4	342,252	53,434	38,798	14,636	18,687	20,111	1,633	24.8%	50.6%
Congressional District 5	352,324	77,817	65,233	12,584	21,522	43,711	1,300	19.3%	46.8%
Congressional District 6	334,901	77,737	63,631	14,106	23,943	39,688	2,240	23.2%	47.9%
Congressional District 7	369,467	82,751	68,875	13,876	27,745	41,130	815	28.4%	49.1%
Congressional District 8	313,858	71,074	59,800	11,274	20,405	39,395	658	28.2%	46.0%
Congressional District 9	326,055	56,843	47,090	9,753	23,073	24,017	2,033	29.6%	50.2%
Congressional District 10	336,118	78,257	64,664	13,593	23,359	41,305	1,189	22.9%	47.5%
Congressional District 11	395,432	94,233	79,796	14,437	24,248	55,548	2,080	20.4%	45.2%
Congressional District 12	328,293	48,212	30,427	17,785	14,641	15,786	1,432	27.9%	56.9%
Congressional District 13	318,240	59,341	50,309	9,032	21,959	28,350	1,563	25.2%	58.9%
North Dakota									
Congressional District (at Large)	350,534	67,092	49,706	17,386	8,782	40,924	2,892	16.0%	49.3%
Ohio									
Congressional District 1	318,883	62,140	48,025	14,115	20,321	27,704	1,510	28.9%	53.6%
Congressional District 2	325,455	72,544	56,462	16,082	23,158	33,304	2,476	25.3%	52.7%
Congressional District 3	338,665	46,478	30,437	16,041	13,652	16,785	754	30.7%	58.3%
Congressional District 4	308,515	76,550	62,874	13,676	19,191	43,683	1,736	23.7%	46.2%
Congressional District 5	310,674	73,459	60,650	12,809	21,665	38,985	2,143	21.4%	46.2%
Congressional District 6	322,005	79,648	66,262	13,386	18,450	47,812	532	19.2%	41.4%
Congressional District 7	305,686	77,403	65,465	11,938	23,306	42,159	1,885	24.0%	49.3%
Congressional District 8	301,411	68,145	55,618	12,527	20,076	35,542	2,362	22.3%	56.0%
Congressional District 9	351,035	69,370	52,188	17,182	19,609	32,579	1,165	23.9%	53.1%
Congressional District 10	334,060	75,909	59,271	16,638	23,428	35,843	1,425	26.1%	50.9%
Congressional District 11	365,350	71,354	48,584	22,770	22,368	26,216	1,700	31.1%	57.1%
Congressional District 12	307,084	63,629	51,452	12,177	22,829	28,623	1,934	23.9%	47.3%
Congressional District 13	336,217	81,590	65,254	16,336	22,295	42,959	1,499	20.6%	48.0%
Congressional District 14	309,442	81,678	67,275	14,403	25,446	41,829	2,497	25.4%	59.0%
Congressional District 15	307,857	64,398	52,679	11,719	19,890	32,789	1,405	24.5%	50.0%
Congressional District 16	304,943	78,663	65,633	13,030	22,823	42,810	2,548	23.0%	58.2%

Table J-5: 114th Congressional Districts—Summary of Housing and Householder Characteristics—*Continued*

| | | | | | Householders 65 Years and Over | | | | |
| | | | | | Owner Householders | | | | |
	Total Housing Units	Total Households	Owner Occupied	Renter Occupied	With a Mortgage	Without a Mortgage	Renter Households With Meals Included in Rent	Percent of Owner Householders Who Pay 35% or More of income for Housing Costs	Percent of Renter Households Who Pay 35% or More of Income for Rental Costs
Oklahoma									
Congressional District 1	340,569	65,940	52,612	13,328	19,406	33,206	2,631	21.6%	55.2%
Congressional District 2	352,474	84,298	70,400	13,898	15,769	54,631	631	18.4%	39.5%
Congressional District 3	334,939	71,857	60,308	11,549	14,891	45,417	998	18.8%	37.7%
Congressional District 4	326,343	64,333	54,606	9,727	15,845	38,761	1,342	20.3%	45.7%
Congressional District 5	345,231	64,577	51,228	13,349	16,410	34,818	2,203	17.7%	52.5%
Oregon									
Congressional District 1	328,332	65,156	47,257	17,899	19,836	27,421	4,611	27.9%	67.9%
Congressional District 2	356,040	91,423	71,727	19,696	27,829	43,898	4,294	27.5%	55.3%
Congressional District 3	336,887	62,500	43,847	18,653	19,786	24,061	4,269	36.4%	63.3%
Congressional District 4	347,465	93,134	74,425	18,709	29,262	45,163	3,697	25.7%	59.0%
Congressional District 5	331,887	80,551	61,528	19,023	25,385	36,143	6,426	28.5%	61.5%
Pennsylvania									
Congressional District 1	305,016	52,194	37,470	14,724	12,397	25,073	492	32.1%	59.7%
Congressional District 2	324,153	64,690	43,772	20,918	13,720	30,052	944	34.9%	56.7%
Congressional District 3	318,291	79,461	61,082	18,379	15,829	45,253	2,293	20.1%	44.2%
Congressional District 4	300,921	70,561	56,885	13,676	19,190	37,695	1,762	27.2%	61.6%
Congressional District 5	340,403	76,241	62,157	14,084	15,071	47,086	976	20.7%	42.2%
Congressional District 6	280,285	66,895	53,421	13,474	18,362	35,059	2,734	30.0%	57.3%
Congressional District 7	271,756	72,192	58,175	14,017	19,701	38,474	4,147	33.4%	61.8%
Congressional District 8	279,237	69,837	53,723	16,114	18,835	34,888	4,842	34.8%	64.4%
Congressional District 9	319,108	82,081	66,626	15,455	16,880	49,746	921	20.6%	37.3%
Congressional District 10	343,734	78,768	64,757	14,011	18,052	46,705	1,301	26.4%	45.7%
Congressional District 11	322,060	77,826	62,339	15,487	19,644	42,695	1,437	25.2%	49.7%
Congressional District 12	320,084	91,695	73,947	17,748	20,810	53,137	2,631	25.5%	43.1%
Congressional District 13	289,911	65,577	46,063	19,514	16,715	29,348	2,830	35.7%	56.9%
Congressional District 14	359,588	78,109	55,135	22,974	17,438	37,697	2,227	27.0%	51.7%
Congressional District 15	290,299	71,594	54,256	17,338	17,067	37,189	1,552	30.8%	53.7%
Congressional District 16	284,556	64,185	46,144	18,041	14,063	32,081	2,862	27.0%	60.9%
Congressional District 17	322,319	75,051	58,764	16,287	17,086	41,678	1,933	34.3%	49.5%
Congressional District 18	318,991	84,984	67,240	17,744	19,506	47,734	2,967	21.0%	54.0%
Rhode Island									
Congressional District 1	229,718	48,914	33,076	15,838	13,012	20,064	1,118	34.2%	54.1%
Congressional District 2	232,912	53,323	38,172	15,151	16,457	21,715	899	31.5%	49.2%
South Carolina									
Congressional District 1	335,444	71,036	61,180	9,856	26,707	34,473	1,843	29.1%	51.7%
Congressional District 2	296,386	61,668	54,370	7,298	20,639	33,731	1,587	21.9%	52.0%
Congressional District 3	300,902	72,226	63,311	8,915	21,214	42,097	1,702	22.1%	47.5%
Congressional District 4	295,072	64,297	51,088	13,209	18,146	32,942	2,319	19.0%	50.4%
Congressional District 5	294,163	66,373	56,031	10,342	20,203	35,828	558	21.1%	37.1%
Congressional District 6	294,791	60,294	49,622	10,672	14,904	34,718	341	28.1%	43.9%
Congressional District 7	371,500	79,411	68,273	11,138	24,380	43,893	1,061	25.4%	52.4%
South Dakota									
Congressional District (at Large)	376,347	82,186	62,590	19,596	13,547	49,043	3,037	19.5%	41.6%
Tennessee									
Congressional District 1	347,048	84,988	71,215	13,773	18,092	53,123	515	17.8%	38.3%
Congressional District 2	325,031	73,990	62,860	11,130	20,690	42,170	1,276	21.5%	46.9%
Congressional District 3	323,216	76,832	63,530	13,302	18,052	45,478	1,106	22.3%	47.5%
Congressional District 4	307,659	66,528	53,884	12,644	16,272	37,612	783	20.7%	38.3%
Congressional District 5	326,334	53,893	40,621	13,272	16,274	24,347	1,698	23.0%	61.8%
Congressional District 6	313,797	78,575	66,453	12,122	21,512	44,941	1,411	22.2%	43.1%
Congressional District 7	312,592	61,094	52,966	8,128	15,917	37,049	966	21.2%	42.1%
Congressional District 8	298,101	68,914	58,919	9,995	19,940	38,979	1,835	24.9%	46.5%
Congressional District 9	315,641	48,622	36,411	12,211	14,614	21,797	1,101	31.8%	53.7%
Texas									
Congressional District 1	305,038	69,577	58,441	11,136	13,051	45,390	1,191	19.3%	52.7%
Congressional District 2	288,898	43,804	34,755	9,049	11,346	23,409	1,768	25.4%	67.0%
Congressional District 3	297,549	43,498	32,483	11,015	14,108	18,375	1,791	23.5%	61.1%
Congressional District 4	302,255	68,369	57,839	10,530	13,431	44,408	672	21.2%	52.0%
Congressional District 5	286,691	56,327	46,957	9,370	13,893	33,064	1,109	23.8%	53.9%
Congressional District 6	276,650	44,972	36,493	8,479	13,213	23,280	1,643	25.4%	61.6%
Congressional District 7	319,976	45,707	33,458	12,249	10,750	22,708	2,601	27.0%	65.0%
Congressional District 8	295,237	60,442	49,738	10,704	15,505	34,233	2,127	20.9%	56.5%
Congressional District 9	287,117	38,572	26,317	12,255	9,536	16,781	765	22.9%	57.3%
Congressional District 10	305,006	51,065	43,031	8,034	15,262	27,769	1,020	27.6%	58.2%
Congressional District 11	325,575	69,340	56,655	12,685	10,974	45,681	1,237	22.8%	46.2%
Congressional District 12	298,938	55,966	43,221	12,745	15,326	27,895	2,258	26.4%	56.4%
Congressional District 13	303,657	63,080	52,626	10,454	11,223	41,403	1,350	19.8%	43.5%
Congressional District 14	309,903	60,139	47,201	12,938	11,795	35,406	818	19.9%	53.5%
Congressional District 15	249,713	44,688	36,784	7,904	7,511	29,273	326	19.8%	50.5%
Congressional District 16	258,285	47,385	35,813	11,572	10,333	25,480	439	22.8%	39.1%
Congressional District 17	310,017	52,613	41,339	11,274	12,086	29,253	1,445	21.9%	50.7%

Table J-5: 114th Congressional Districts—Summary of Housing and Householder Characteristics—*Continued*

| | | | | | Householders 65 Years and Over | | | | |
| | | | | | Owner Householders | | | | |
	Total Housing Units	Total Households	Owner Occupied	Renter Occupied	With a Mortgage	Without a Mortgage	Renter Households With Meals Included in Rent	Percent of Owner Householders Who Pay 35% or More of income for Housing Costs	Percent of Renter Households Who Pay 35% or More of Income for Rental Costs
Texas—Cont.									
Congressional District 18	292,735	42,364	30,743	11,621	8,308	22,435	273	25.2%	60.9%
Congressional District 19	296,216	59,989	47,236	12,753	10,105	37,131	1,798	18.3%	49.2%
Congressional District 20	270,784	45,644	37,031	8,613	13,171	23,860	1,141	23.7%	57.1%
Congressional District 21	341,995	73,292	57,964	15,328	20,542	37,422	3,690	21.9%	62.0%
Congressional District 22	277,521	42,330	35,432	6,898	15,132	20,300	767	24.9%	61.6%
Congressional District 23	261,100	51,174	42,286	8,888	10,085	32,201	670	22.2%	37.8%
Congressional District 24	322,952	45,655	34,125	11,530	13,791	20,334	2,125	26.3%	55.9%
Congressional District 25	302,058	55,791	49,247	6,544	14,854	34,393	438	23.5%	47.9%
Congressional District 26	279,494	40,455	31,022	9,433	13,992	17,030	681	28.5%	66.7%
Congressional District 27	309,361	64,415	51,883	12,532	10,721	41,162	1,320	18.6%	56.1%
Congressional District 28	238,252	42,688	35,580	7,108	7,055	28,525	59	18.7%	54.6%
Congressional District 29	246,164	32,967	24,970	7,997	6,385	18,585	0	25.2%	55.2%
Congressional District 30	274,649	40,286	31,216	9,070	11,438	19,778	439	28.2%	61.9%
Congressional District 31	296,027	47,520	37,594	9,926	13,979	23,615	2,098	23.3%	60.3%
Congressional District 32	312,995	52,931	40,019	12,912	15,113	24,906	3,311	26.1%	61.0%
Congressional District 33	246,860	35,769	26,224	9,545	7,360	18,864	555	22.8%	60.2%
Congressional District 34	256,405	55,273	45,281	9,992	7,701	37,580	64	22.5%	50.8%
Congressional District 35	280,250	41,117	30,149	10,968	8,556	21,593	637	24.2%	50.3%
Congressional District 36	300,437	58,393	49,439	8,954	10,406	39,033	448	18.2%	46.2%
Utah									
Congressional District 1	269,093	43,547	37,568	5,979	13,321	24,247	1,338	22.2%	56.9%
Congressional District 2	275,514	52,140	42,180	9,960	15,388	26,792	1,078	20.8%	56.2%
Congressional District 3	233,515	39,088	34,084	5,004	12,200	21,884	1,594	19.1%	52.7%
Congressional District 4	244,471	40,970	33,898	7,072	15,533	18,365	1,569	23.3%	45.4%
Vermont									
Congressional District (at Large)	325,774	67,260	52,680	14,580	18,377	34,303	2,001	36.8%	52.9%
Virginia									
Congressional District 1	304,779	61,991	53,818	8,173	23,978	29,840	2,308	24.5%	53.3%
Congressional District 2	308,304	59,210	49,242	9,968	22,784	26,458	2,266	30.3%	63.1%
Congressional District 3	322,684	57,552	38,324	19,228	17,354	20,970	896	33.5%	65.5%
Congressional District 4	290,795	60,850	51,195	9,655	21,716	29,479	864	25.7%	63.1%
Congressional District 5	346,726	84,852	72,736	12,116	24,507	48,229	969	25.7%	45.9%
Congressional District 6	330,414	81,215	64,160	17,055	23,825	40,335	2,429	22.4%	49.7%
Congressional District 7	310,783	69,449	56,352	13,097	25,624	30,728	3,750	20.3%	54.2%
Congressional District 8	333,194	49,403	36,720	12,683	17,977	18,743	1,783	26.1%	57.6%
Congressional District 9	342,477	85,129	70,205	14,924	16,773	53,432	838	21.1%	38.5%
Congressional District 10	277,560	46,709	39,663	7,046	20,631	19,032	1,817	27.3%	60.6%
Congressional District 11	278,869	45,948	38,418	7,530	20,151	18,267	2,075	23.2%	49.1%
Washington									
Congressional District 1	284,841	51,723	42,196	9,527	18,567	23,629	2,297	30.6%	62.2%
Congressional District 2	307,937	65,104	48,600	16,504	20,392	28,208	3,424	30.5%	63.4%
Congressional District 3	291,304	69,054	54,192	14,862	22,148	32,044	2,621	23.9%	60.0%
Congressional District 4	260,944	54,375	44,085	10,290	14,751	29,334	2,422	24.4%	51.5%
Congressional District 5	299,216	66,503	51,307	15,196	18,924	32,383	2,632	23.4%	55.0%
Congressional District 6	315,203	75,550	60,937	14,613	27,142	33,795	2,523	27.4%	53.9%
Congressional District 7	349,848	59,863	41,893	17,970	15,849	26,044	4,011	26.9%	62.1%
Congressional District 8	280,491	50,179	41,849	8,330	18,914	22,935	1,476	28.3%	52.4%
Congressional District 9	287,342	55,278	39,386	15,892	17,500	21,886	3,701	29.6%	65.4%
Congressional District 10	286,167	58,199	43,687	14,512	17,490	26,197	1,852	24.4%	66.0%
West Virginia									
Congressional District 1	289,575	69,426	57,936	11,490	13,271	44,665	359	14.6%	35.4%
Congressional District 2	295,466	69,289	60,425	8,864	15,942	44,483	286	16.8%	35.3%
Congressional District 3	299,533	73,073	63,139	9,934	15,383	47,756	509	15.0%	30.3%
Wisconsin									
Congressional District 1	302,906	67,267	52,321	14,946	18,998	33,323	2,137	29.3%	61.5%
Congressional District 2	323,122	61,641	46,950	14,691	15,911	31,039	1,920	29.0%	58.7%
Congressional District 3	321,123	72,525	57,209	15,316	16,560	40,649	2,305	24.8%	51.7%
Congressional District 4	311,611	49,461	32,365	17,096	11,857	20,508	1,758	33.3%	64.0%
Congressional District 5	307,379	74,606	55,547	19,059	20,702	34,845	3,585	31.7%	63.0%
Congressional District 6	322,862	75,390	58,676	16,714	19,368	39,308	3,319	27.8%	57.9%
Congressional District 7	416,006	82,287	66,878	15,409	19,138	47,740	1,013	27.6%	44.7%
Congressional District 8	343,333	69,654	55,639	14,015	17,805	37,834	1,915	26.8%	46.8%
Wyoming									
Congressional District (at Large)	268,205	51,531	42,710	8,821	12,656	30,054	1,081	18.4%	40.2%

APPENDIXES

Core Based Statistical Areas (Metropolitan and Micropolitan), Metropolitan Divisions, and Components (as defined February 2013)

Core based statistical area	State/ County FIPS code	Title and Geographic Components	2010 Census Population	2014 Estimated Population
10100		Aberdeen, SD Micro area	40,602	42,391
	46013	Brown County, SD	36,531	38,408
	46045	Edmunds County, SD	4,071	3,983
10140		Aberdeen, WA Micro area	72,797	70,818
	53027	Grays Harbor County, WA	72,797	70,818
10180		Abilene, TX Metro area	165,252	168,592
	48059	Callahan County, TX	13,544	13,513
	48253	Jones County, TX	20,202	19,936
	48441	Taylor County, TX	131,506	135,143
10220		Ada, OK Micro area	37,492	38,005
	40123	Pontotoc County, OK	37,492	38,005
10300		Adrian, MI Micro area	99,892	99,047
	26091	Lenawee County, MI	99,892	99,047
10420		Akron, OH Metro area	703,200	703,825
	39133	Portage County, OH	161,419	161,882
	39153	Summit County, OH	541,781	541,943
10460		Alamogordo, NM Micro area	63,797	65,082
	35035	Otero County, NM	63,797	65,082
10500		Albany, GA Metro area	157,308	154,925
	13007	Baker County, GA	3,451	3,255
	13095	Dougherty County, GA	94,565	92,407
	13177	Lee County, GA	28,298	29,191
	13273	Terrell County, GA	9,315	9,132
	13321	Worth County, GA	21,679	20,940
10540		Albany, OR Metro area	116,672	119,356
	41043	Linn County, OR	116,672	119,356
10580		Albany-Schenectady-Troy, NY Metro area	870,716	880,167
	36001	Albany County, NY	304,204	308,171
	36083	Rensselaer County, NY	159,429	159,774
	36091	Saratoga County, NY	219,607	224,921
	36093	Schenectady County, NY	154,727	155,735
	36095	Schoharie County, NY	32,749	31,566
10620		Albemarle, NC Micro area	60,585	60,600
	37167	Stanly County, NC	60,585	60,600
10660		Albert Lea, MN Micro area	31,255	30,840
	27047	Freeborn County, MN	31,255	30,840
10700		Albertville, AL Micro area	93,019	94,636
	01095	Marshall County, AL	93,019	94,636
10740		Albuquerque, NM Metro area	887,077	904,587
	35001	Bernalillo County, NM	662,564	675,551
	35043	Sandoval County, NM	131,561	137,608
	35057	Torrance County, NM	16,383	15,611
	35061	Valencia County, NM	76,569	75,817
10780		Alexandria, LA Metro area	153,922	154,872
	22043	Grant Parish, LA	22,309	22,384
	22079	Rapides Parish, LA	131,613	132,488
10820		Alexandria, MN Micro area	36,009	36,790
	27041	Douglas County, MN	36,009	36,790
10860		Alice, TX Micro area	40,838	41,353
	48249	Jim Wells County, TX	40,838	41,353
10900		Allentown-Bethlehem-Easton, PA-NJ Metro area	821,173	829,835
	34041	Warren County, NJ	108,692	106,917
	42025	Carbon County, PA	65,249	64,441
	42077	Lehigh County, PA	349,497	357,823
	42095	Northampton County, PA	297,735	300,654
10940		Alma, MI Micro area	42,476	41,665
	26057	Gratiot County, MI	42,476	41,665
10980		Alpena, MI Micro area	29,598	28,988
	26007	Alpena County, MI	29,598	28,988
11020		Altoona, PA Metro area	127,089	125,955
	42013	Blair County, PA	127,089	125,955
11060		Altus, OK Micro area	26,446	25,998
	40065	Jackson County, OK	26,446	25,998
11100		Amarillo, TX Metro area	251,933	259,885
	48011	Armstrong County, TX	1,901	1,955
	48065	Carson County, TX	6,182	6,013
	48359	Oldham County, TX	2,052	2,070
	48375	Potter County, TX	121,073	121,627
	48381	Randall County, TX	120,725	128,220
11140		Americus, GA Micro area	37,829	36,395
	13249	Schley County, GA	5,010	5,163

Core Based Statistical Areas (Metropolitan and Micropolitan), Metropolitan Divisions, and Components (as defined February 2013)

Core based statistical area	State/ County FIPS code	Title and Geographic Components	2010 Census Population	2014 Estimated Population
	13261	Sumter County, GA	32,819	31,232
11180		Ames, IA Metro area	89,542	94,073
	19169	Story County, IA	89,542	94,073
11220		Amsterdam, NY Micro area	50,219	49,779
	36057	Montgomery County, NY	50,219	49,779
11260		Anchorage, AK Metro area	380,821	398,892
	02020	Anchorage Municipality, AK	291,826	301,010
	02170	Matanuska-Susitna Borough, AK	88,995	97,882
11380		Andrews, TX Micro area	14,786	17,477
	48003	Andrews County, TX	14,786	17,477
11420		Angola, IN Micro area	34,185	34,308
	18151	Steuben County, IN	34,185	34,308
11460		Ann Arbor, MI Metro area	344,791	356,874
	26161	Washtenaw County, MI	344,791	356,874
11500		Anniston-Oxford-Jacksonville, AL Metro area	118,572	115,916
	01015	Calhoun County, AL	118,572	115,916
11540		Appleton, WI Metro area	225,666	231,497
	55015	Calumet County, WI	48,971	49,491
	55087	Outagamie County, WI	176,695	182,006
11580		Arcadia, FL Micro area	34,862	35,012
	12027	DeSoto County, FL	34,862	35,012
11620		Ardmore, OK Micro area	47,557	48,821
	40019	Carter County, OK	47,557	48,821
11660		Arkadelphia, AR Micro area	22,995	22,576
	05019	Clark County, AR	22,995	22,576
11680		Arkansas City-Winfield, KS Micro area	36,311	35,963
	20035	Cowley County, KS	36,311	35,963
11700		Asheville, NC Metro area	424,858	442,316
	37021	Buncombe County, NC	238,318	250,539
	37087	Haywood County, NC	59,036	59,471
	37089	Henderson County, NC	106,740	111,149
	37115	Madison County, NC	20,764	21,157
11740		Ashland, OH Micro area	53,139	53,035
	39005	Ashland County, OH	53,139	53,035
11780		Ashtabula, OH Micro area	101,497	99,175
	39007	Ashtabula County, OH	101,497	99,175
11820		Astoria, OR Micro area	37,039	37,474
	41007	Clatsop County, OR	37,039	37,474
11860		Atchison, KS Micro area	16,924	16,513
	20005	Atchison County, KS	16,924	16,513
11900		Athens, OH Micro area	64,757	64,713
	39009	Athens County, OH	64,757	64,713
11940		Athens, TN Micro area	52,266	52,626
	47107	McMinn County, TN	52,266	52,626
11980		Athens, TX Micro area	78,532	79,290
	48213	Henderson County, TX	78,532	79,290
12020		Athens-Clarke County, GA Metro area	192,541	199,016
	13059	Clarke County, GA	116,714	120,938
	13195	Madison County, GA	28,120	28,312
	13219	Oconee County, GA	32,808	35,093
	13221	Oglethorpe County, GA	14,899	14,673
12060		Atlanta-Sandy Springs-Roswell, GA Metro area	5,286,728	5,614,323
	13013	Barrow County, GA	69,367	73,240
	13015	Bartow County, GA	100,157	101,736
	13035	Butts County, GA	23,655	23,368
	13045	Carroll County, GA	110,527	114,093
	13057	Cherokee County, GA	214,346	230,985
	13063	Clayton County, GA	259,424	267,542
	13067	Cobb County, GA	688,078	730,981
	13077	Coweta County, GA	127,317	135,571
	13085	Dawson County, GA	22,330	22,957
	13089	DeKalb County, GA	691,893	722,161
	13097	Douglas County, GA	132,403	138,776
	13113	Fayette County, GA	106,567	109,664
	13117	Forsyth County, GA	175,511	204,302
	13121	Fulton County, GA	920,581	996,319
	13135	Gwinnett County, GA	805,321	877,922
	13143	Haralson County, GA	28,780	28,641
	13149	Heard County, GA	11,834	11,603
	13151	Henry County, GA	203,922	213,869

Core Based Statistical Areas (Metropolitan and Micropolitan), Metropolitan Divisions, and Components (as defined February 2013)

Core based statistical area	State/County FIPS code	Title and Geographic Components	2010 Census Population	2014 Estimated Population
	13159	Jasper County, GA	13,900	13,432
	13171	Lamar County, GA	18,317	18,207
	13199	Meriwether County, GA	21,992	21,198
	13211	Morgan County, GA	17,868	17,956
	13217	Newton County, GA	99,958	103,675
	13223	Paulding County, GA	142,324	148,987
	13227	Pickens County, GA	29,431	29,997
	13231	Pike County, GA	17,869	17,784
	13247	Rockdale County, GA	85,215	87,754
	13255	Spalding County, GA	64,073	63,988
	13297	Walton County, GA	83,768	87,615
12100		Atlantic City-Hammonton, NJ Metro area	274,549	275,209
	34001	Atlantic County, NJ	274,549	275,209
12140		Auburn, IN Micro area	42,223	42,383
	18033	DeKalb County, IN	42,223	42,383
12180		Auburn, NY Micro area	80,026	78,823
	36011	Cayuga County, NY	80,026	78,823
12220		Auburn-Opelika, AL Metro area	140,247	154,255
	01081	Lee County, AL	140,247	154,255
12260		Augusta-Richmond County, GA-SC Metro area	564,873	583,632
	13033	Burke County, GA	23,316	22,709
	13073	Columbia County, GA	124,053	139,257
	13181	Lincoln County, GA	7,996	7,622
	13189	McDuffie County, GA	21,875	21,370
	13245	Richmond County, GA	200,549	201,368
	45003	Aiken County, SC	160,099	164,753
	45037	Edgefield County, SC	26,985	26,553
12300		Augusta-Waterville, ME Micro area	122,151	121,112
	23011	Kennebec County, ME	122,151	121,112
12380		Austin, MN Micro area	39,163	39,323
	27099	Mower County, MN	39,163	39,323
12420		Austin-Round Rock, TX Metro area	1,716,289	1,943,299
	48021	Bastrop County, TX	74,171	78,069
	48055	Caldwell County, TX	38,066	39,810
	48209	Hays County, TX	157,107	185,025
	48453	Travis County, TX	1,024,266	1,151,145
	48491	Williamson County, TX	422,679	489,250
12460		Bainbridge, GA Micro area	27,842	27,220
	13087	Decatur County, GA	27,842	27,220
12540		Bakersfield, CA Metro area	839,631	874,589
	06029	Kern County, CA	839,631	874,589
12580		Baltimore-Columbia-Towson, MD Metro area	2,710,489	2,785,874
	24003	Anne Arundel County, MD	537,656	560,133
	24005	Baltimore County, MD	805,029	826,925
	24013	Carroll County, MD	167,134	167,830
	24025	Harford County, MD	244,826	250,105
	24027	Howard County, MD	287,085	309,284
	24035	Queen Anne's County, MD	47,798	48,804
	24510	Baltimore city, MD	620,961	622,793
12620		Bangor, ME Metro area	153,923	153,414
	23019	Penobscot County, ME	153,923	153,414
12660		Baraboo, WI Micro area	61,976	63,379
	55111	Sauk County, WI	61,976	63,379
12680		Bardstown, KY Micro area	43,437	44,812
	21179	Nelson County, KY	43,437	44,812
12700		Barnstable Town, MA Metro area	215,888	214,914
	25001	Barnstable County, MA	215,888	214,914
12740		Barre, VT Micro area	59,534	58,998
	50023	Washington County, VT	59,534	58,998
12780		Bartlesville, OK Micro area	50,976	51,937
	40147	Washington County, OK	50,976	51,937
12820		Bastrop, LA Micro area	27,979	26,760
	22067	Morehouse Parish, LA	27,979	26,760
12860		Batavia, NY Micro area	60,079	59,162
	36037	Genesee County, NY	60,079	59,162
12900		Batesville, AR Micro area	36,647	36,959
	05063	Independence County, AR	36,647	36,959
12940		Baton Rouge, LA Metro area	802,484	825,478
	22005	Ascension Parish, LA	107,215	117,029
	22033	East Baton Rouge Parish, LA	440,171	446,042
	22037	East Feliciana Parish, LA	20,267	19,813
	22047	Iberville Parish, LA	33,387	33,327
	22063	Livingston Parish, LA	128,026	135,751
	22077	Pointe Coupee Parish, LA	22,802	22,406
	22091	St. Helena Parish, LA	11,203	10,619
	22121	West Baton Rouge Parish, LA	23,788	25,085
	22125	West Feliciana Parish, LA	15,625	15,406
12980		Battle Creek, MI Metro area	136,146	134,878
	26025	Calhoun County, MI	136,146	134,878
13020		Bay City, MI Metro area	107,771	106,179
	26017	Bay County, MI	107,771	106,179
13060		Bay City, TX Micro area	36,702	36,519
	48321	Matagorda County, TX	36,702	36,519
13100		Beatrice, NE Micro area	22,311	21,663
	31067	Gage County, NE Micro area	22,311	21,663
13140		Beaumont-Port Arthur, TX Metro area	403,190	405,427
	48199	Hardin County, TX	54,635	55,621
	48245	Jefferson County, TX	252,273	252,235
	48351	Newton County, TX	14,445	14,138
	48361	Orange County, TX	81,837	83,433
13180		Beaver Dam, WI Micro area	88,759	88,574
	55027	Dodge County, WI	88,759	88,574
13220		Beckley, WV Metro area	124,898	123,373
	54019	Fayette County, WV	46,039	45,132
	54081	Raleigh County, WV	78,859	78,241
13260		Bedford, IN Micro area	46,134	45,704
	18093	Lawrence County, IN	46,134	45,704
13300		Beeville, TX Micro area	31,861	32,863
	48025	Bee County, TX	31,861	32,863
13340		Bellefontaine, OH Micro area	45,858	45,507
	39091	Logan County, OH	45,858	45,507
13380		Bellingham, WA Metro area	201,140	208,351
	53073	Whatcom County, WA	201,140	208,351
13420		Bemidji, MN Micro area	44,442	45,664
	27007	Beltrami County, MN	44,442	45,664
13460		Bend-Redmond, OR Metro area	157,733	170,388
	41017	Deschutes County, OR	157,733	170,388
13500		Bennettsville, SC Micro area	28,933	27,924
	45069	Marlboro County, SC	28,933	27,924
13540		Bennington, VT Micro area	37,125	36,445
	50003	Bennington County, VT	37,125	36,445
13620		Berlin, NH-VT Micro area	39,361	37,778
	33007	Coos County, NH	33,055	31,653
	50009	Essex County, VT	6,306	6,125
13660		Big Rapids, MI Micro area	42,798	43,186
	26107	Mecosta County, MI	42,798	43,186
13700		Big Spring, TX Micro area	36,238	37,942
	48173	Glasscock County, TX	1,226	1,291
	48227	Howard County, TX	35,012	36,651
13720		Big Stone Gap, VA Micro area	61,313	59,274
	51051	Dickenson County, VA	15,903	15,308
	51195	Wise County, VA	41,452	39,935
	51720	Norton city, VA	3,958	4,031
13740		Billings, MT Metro area	158,934	166,885
	30009	Carbon County, MT	10,078	10,399
	30037	Golden Valley County, MT	884	852
	30111	Yellowstone County, MT	147,972	155,634
13780		Binghamton, NY Metro area	251,725	247,219
	36007	Broome County, NY	200,600	197,349
	36107	Tioga County, NY	51,125	49,870
13820		Birmingham-Hoover, AL Metro area	1,128,047	1,143,772
	01007	Bibb County, AL	22,915	22,506
	01009	Blount County, AL	57,322	57,719
	01021	Chilton County, AL	43,643	43,931
	01073	Jefferson County, AL	658,466	660,793
	01115	St. Clair County, AL	83,593	86,697
	01117	Shelby County, AL	195,085	206,655
	01127	Walker County, AL	67,023	65,471
13900		Bismarck, ND Metro area	114,778	126,597
	38015	Burleigh County, ND	81,308	90,503
	38059	Morton County, ND	27,471	29,822
	38065	Oliver County, ND	1,846	1,850
	38085	Sioux County, ND	4,153	4,422
13940		Blackfoot, ID Micro area	45,607	45,269
	16011	Bingham County, ID	45,607	45,269
13980		Blacksburg-Christiansburg-Radford, VA Metro area	178,237	181,605
	51063	Floyd County, VA	15,279	15,578
	51071	Giles County, VA	17,286	16,815
	51121	Montgomery County, VA	94,392	97,244
	51155	Pulaski County, VA	34,872	34,322
	51750	Radford city, VA	16,408	17,646
14010		Bloomington, IL Metro area	186,133	190,345
	17039	De Witt County, IL	16,561	16,284
	17113	McLean County, IL	169,572	174,061
14020		Bloomington, IN Metro area	159,549	164,308
	18105	Monroe County, IN	137,974	143,339
	18119	Owen County, IN	21,575	20,969
14100		Bloomsburg-Berwick, PA Metro area	85,562	85,763
	42037	Columbia County, PA	67,295	67,122
	42093	Montour County, PA	18,267	18,641
14140		Bluefield, WV-VA Micro area	107,342	105,237
	51185	Tazewell County, VA	45,078	43,452
	54055	Mercer County, WV	62,264	61,785
14180		Blytheville, AR Micro area	46,480	44,235
	05093	Mississippi County, AR	46,480	44,235
14220		Bogalusa, LA Micro area	47,168	46,286
	22117	Washington Parish, LA	47,168	46,286

Core Based Statistical Areas (Metropolitan and Micropolitan), Metropolitan Divisions, and Components (as defined February 2013)

Core based statistical area	State/ County FIPS code	Title and Geographic Components	2010 Census Population	2014 Estimated Population
14260		Boise City, ID Metro area	616,561	664,422
	16001	Ada County, ID	392,365	426,236
	16015	Boise County, ID	7,028	6,824
	16027	Canyon County, ID	188,923	203,143
	16045	Gem County, ID	16,719	16,866
	16073	Owyhee County, ID	11,526	11,353
14340		Boone, IA Micro area	26,306	26,433
	19015	Boone County, IA	26,306	26,433
14380		Boone, NC Micro area	51,079	52,560
	37189	Watauga County, NC	51,079	52,560
14420		Borger, TX Micro area	22,150	21,773
	48233	Hutchinson County, TX	22,150	21,773
14460		Boston-Cambridge Newton, MA-NH Metro area	4,552,402	4,732,161
14460		Boston, MA Metro Div 14454	1,887,792	1,966,530
	25021	Norfolk County, MA	670,850	692,254
	25023	Plymouth County, MA	494,919	507,022
	25025	Suffolk County, MA	722,023	767,254
14460		Cambridge-Newton-Framingham, MA Metro Div 15764	2,246,244	2,339,406
	25009	Essex County, MA	743,159	769,091
	25017	Middlesex County, MA	1,503,085	1,570,315
14460		Rockingham County-Strafford County-NH Metro Div 40484	418,366	426,225
	33015	Rockingham County, NH	295,223	300,621
	33017	Strafford County, NH	123,143	125,604
14500		Boulder, CO Metro area	294,567	313,333
	08013	Boulder County, CO	294,567	313,333
14540		Bowling Green, KY Metro area	158,599	165,732
	21003	Allen County, KY	19,956	20,384
	21031	Butler County, KY	12,690	12,875
	21061	Edmonson County, KY	12,161	12,013
	21227	Warren County, KY	113,792	120,460
14580		Bozeman, MT Micro area	89,513	97,308
	30031	Gallatin County, MT	89,513	97,308
14620		Bradford, PA Micro area	43,450	42,554
	42083	McKean County, PA	43,450	42,554
14660		Brainerd, MN Micro area	91,067	91,824
	27021	Cass County, MN	28,567	28,559
	27035	Crow Wing County, MN	62,500	63,265
14700		Branson, MO Micro area	83,877	85,334
	29209	Stone County, MO Micro area	32,202	31,104
	29213	Taney County, MO Micro area	51,675	54,230
14720		Breckenridge, CO Metro area	27,994	29,404
	08117	Summit County, CO	27,994	29,404
14740		Bremerton-Silverdale, WA Metro area	251,133	254,183
	53035	Kitsap County, WA	251,133	254,183
14780		Brenham, TX Micro area	33,718	34,438
	48477	Washington County, TX	33,718	34,438
14820		Brevard, NC Micro area	33,090	33,045
	37175	Transylvania County, NC	33,090	33,045
14860		Bridgeport-Stamford-Norwalk, CT Metro area	916,829	945,438
	09001	Fairfield County, CT	916,829	945,438
15020		Brookhaven, MS Micro area	34,869	34,775
	28085	Lincoln County, MS	34,869	34,775
15060		Brookings, OR Micro area	22,364	22,335
	41015	Curry County, OR	22,364	22,335
15100		Brookings, SD Micro area	31,965	33,314
	46011	Brookings County, SD	31,965	33,314
15180		Brownsville-Harlingen, TX Metro area	406,220	420,392
	48061	Cameron County, TX	406,220	420,392
15220		Brownwood, TX Micro area	38,106	37,653
	48049	Brown County, TX	38,106	37,653
15260		Brunswick, GA Metro area	112,370	114,806
	13025	Brantley County, GA	18,411	18,417
	13127	Glynn County, GA	79,626	82,175
	13191	McIntosh County, GA	14,333	14,214
15340		Bucyrus, OH Micro area	43,784	42,480
	39033	Crawford County, OH	43,784	42,480
15380		Buffalo-Cheektowaga-Niagara Falls, NY Metro area	1,135,509	1,136,360
	36029	Erie County, NY	919,040	922,835
	36063	Niagara County, NY	216,469	213,525
15420		Burley, ID Micro area	43,021	43,863
	16031	Cassia County, ID	22,952	23,540
	16067	Minidoka County, ID	20,069	20,323
15460		Burlington, IA-IL Micro area	47,656	47,171
	17071	Henderson County, IL	7,331	6,916
	19057	Des Moines County, IA	40,325	40,255
15500		Burlington, NC Metro area	151,131	155,792
	37001	Alamance County, NC	151,131	155,792
15540		Burlington-South Burlington, VT Metro area	211,261	216,167
	50007	Chittenden County, VT	156,545	160,531
	50011	Franklin County, VT	47,746	48,642

Core Based Statistical Areas (Metropolitan and Micropolitan), Metropolitan Divisions, and Components (as defined February 2013)

Core based statistical area	State/ County FIPS code	Title and Geographic Components	2010 Census Population	2014 Estimated Population
	50013	Grand Isle County, VT	6,970	6,994
15580		Butte-Silver Bow, MT Micro area	34,200	34,680
	30093	Silver Bow County, MT	34,200	34,680
15620		Cadillac, MI Micro area	47,584	47,923
	26113	Missaukee County, MI	14,849	15,037
	26165	Wexford County, MI	32,735	32,886
15660		Calhoun, GA Micro area	55,186	56,047
	13129	Gordon County, GA	55,186	56,047
15680		California-Lexington Park, MD Metro area	105,151	110,382
	24037	St. Mary's County, MD	105,151	110,382
15700		Cambridge, MD Micro area	32,618	32,578
	24019	Dorchester County, MD	32,618	32,578
15740		Cambridge, OH Micro area	40,087	39,590
	39059	Guernsey County, OH	40,087	39,590
15780		Camden, AR Micro area	31,488	30,030
	05013	Calhoun County, AR	5,368	5,202
	05103	Ouachita County, AR	26,120	24,828
15820		Campbellsville, KY Micro area	24,512	25,257
	21217	Taylor County, KY	24,512	25,257
15860		Cañon City, CO Micro area	46,824	46,502
	08043	Fremont County, CO	46,824	46,502
15900		Canton, IL Micro area	37,069	36,007
	17057	Fulton County, IL	37,069	36,007
15940		Canton-Massillon, OH Metro area	404,422	403,923
	39019	Carroll County, OH	28,836	28,187
	39151	Stark County, OH	375,586	375,736
15980		Cape Coral-Fort Myers, FL Metro area	618,754	679,513
	12071	Lee County, FL	618,754	679,513
16020		Cape Girardeau, MO-IL Metro area	96,275	97,929
	17003	Alexander County, IL	8,238	7,492
	29017	Bollinger County, MO	12,363	12,394
	29031	Cape Girardeau County, MO	75,674	78,043
16060		Carbondale-Marion, IL Metro area	126,575	126,685
	17077	Jackson County, IL	60,218	59,677
	17199	Williamson County, IL	66,357	67,008
16100		Carlsbad-Artesia, NM Micro area	53,829	56,395
	35015	Eddy County, NM	53,829	56,395
16180		Carson City, NV Metro area	55,274	54,522
	32510	Carson City, NV Metro area	55,274	54,522
16220		Casper, WY Metro area	75,450	81,624
	56025	Natrona County, WY	75,450	81,624
16260		Cedar City, UT Micro area	46,163	47,269
	49021	Iron County, UT	46,163	47,269
16300		Cedar Rapids, IA Metro area	257,940	263,885
	19011	Benton County, IA	26,076	25,680
	19105	Jones County, IA	20,638	20,454
	19113	Linn County, IA	211,226	217,751
16340		Cedartown, GA Micro area	41,475	41,133
	13233	Polk County, GA	41,475	41,133
16380		Celina, OH Micro area	40,814	40,831
	39107	Mercer County, OH	40,814	40,831
16460		Centralia, IL Micro area	39,437	38,571
	17121	Marion County, IL	39,437	38,571
16500		Centralia, WA Micro area	75,455	75,128
	53041	Lewis County, WA	75,455	75,128
16540		Chambersburg-Waynesboro, PA Metro area	149,618	152,892
	42055	Franklin County, PA	149,618	152,892
16580		Champaign-Urbana, IL Metro area	231,891	237,252
	17019	Champaign County, IL	201,081	207,133
	17053	Ford County, IL	14,081	13,688
	17147	Piatt County, IL	16,729	16,431
16620		Charleston, WV Metro area	227,078	222,878
	54005	Boone County, WV	24,629	23,714
	54015	Clay County, WV	9,386	8,941
	54039	Kanawha County, WV	193,063	190,223
16660		Charleston-Mattoon, IL Micro area	64,921	64,153
	17029	Coles County, IL	53,873	53,320
	17035	Cumberland County, IL	11,048	10,833
16700		Charleston-North Charleston, SC Metro area	664,607	727,689
	45015	Berkeley County, SC	177,843	198,205
	45019	Charleston County, SC	350,209	381,015
	45035	Dorchester County, SC	136,555	148,469
16740		Charlotte-Concord-Gastonia, NC-SC Metro area	2,217,012	2,380,314
	37025	Cabarrus County, NC	178,011	192,103
	37071	Gaston County, NC	206,086	211,127
	37097	Iredell County, NC	159,437	166,675
	37109	Lincoln County, NC	78,265	79,829
	37119	Mecklenburg County, NC	919,628	1,012,539
	37159	Rowan County, NC	138,428	138,630
	37179	Union County, NC	201,292	218,568
	45023	Chester County, SC	33,140	32,337
	45057	Lancaster County, SC	76,652	83,160
	45091	York County, SC	226,073	245,346
16820		Charlottesville, VA Metro area	218,705	226,968

Core Based Statistical Areas (Metropolitan and Micropolitan), Metropolitan Divisions, and Components (as defined February 2013)

Core based statistical area	State/County FIPS code	Title and Geographic Components	2010 Census Population	2014 Estimated Population
	51003	Albemarle County, VA	98,970	104,489
	51029	Buckingham County, VA	17,146	16,913
	51065	Fluvanna County, VA	25,691	26,092
	51079	Greene County, VA	18,403	19,031
	51125	Nelson County, VA	15,020	14,850
	51540	Charlottesville city, VA	43,475	45,593
16860		Chattanooga, TN-GA Metro area	528,143	544,559
	13047	Catoosa County, GA	63,942	65,621
	13083	Dade County, GA	16,633	16,389
	13295	Walker County, GA	68,756	68,218
	47065	Hamilton County, TN	336,463	351,220
	47115	Marion County, TN	28,237	28,407
	47153	Sequatchie County, TN	14,112	14,704
16940		Cheyenne, WY Metro area	91,738	96,389
	56021	Laramie County, WY	91,738	96,389
16980		Chicago-Naperville-Elgin, IL-IN-WI Metro area	9,461,105	9,554,598
16980		Chicago-Naperville-Arlington Heights, IL Metro Div 16974	7,262,718	7,343,641
	17031	Cook County, IL	5,194,675	5,246,456
	17043	DuPage County, IL	916,924	932,708
	17063	Grundy County, IL	50,063	50,425
	17093	Kendall County, IL	114,736	121,350
	17111	McHenry County, IL	308,760	307,283
	17197	Will County, IL	677,560	685,419
16980		Elgin, IL Metro Div 20994	620,429	632,768
	17037	DeKalb County, IL	105,160	105,462
	17089	Kane County, IL	515,269	527,306
16980		Gary, IN Metro Div 23844	708,070	704,935
	18073	Jasper County, IN	33,478	33,475
	18089	Lake County, IN	496,005	490,228
	18111	Newton County, IN	14,244	14,156
	18127	Porter County, IN	164,343	167,076
16980		Lake County-Kenosha County, IL-WI Metro Div 29404	869,888	873,254
	17097	Lake County, IL	703,462	705,186
	55059	Kenosha County, WI	166,426	168,068
17020		Chico, CA Metro area	220,000	224,241
	06007	Butte County, CA	220,000	224,241
17060		Chillicothe, OH Micro area	78,064	77,159
	39141	Ross County, OH	78,064	77,159
17140		Cincinnati, OH-KY-IN Metro area	2,114,580	2,149,449
	18029	Dearborn County, IN	50,047	49,506
	18115	Ohio County, IN	6,128	6,035
	18161	Union County, IN	7,516	7,246
	21015	Boone County, KY	118,811	126,413
	21023	Bracken County, KY	8,488	8,406
	21037	Campbell County, KY	90,336	91,833
	21077	Gallatin County, KY	8,589	8,589
	21081	Grant County, KY	24,662	24,875
	21117	Kenton County, KY	159,720	163,929
	21191	Pendleton County, KY	14,877	14,493
	39015	Brown County, OH	44,846	44,116
	39017	Butler County, OH	368,130	374,158
	39025	Clermont County, OH	197,363	201,560
	39061	Hamilton County, OH	802,374	806,631
	39165	Warren County, OH	212,693	221,659
17200		Claremont-Lebanon, NH-VT Micro area	218,466	217,634
	33009	Grafton County, NH	89,118	89,658
	33019	Sullivan County, NH	43,742	43,103
	50017	Orange County, VT	28,936	28,859
	50027	Windsor County, VT	56,670	56,014
17220		Clarksburg, WV Micro area	94,196	94,221
	54017	Doddridge County, WV	8,202	8,391
	54033	Harrison County, WV	69,099	68,761
	54091	Taylor County, WV	16,895	17,069
17260		Clarksdale, MS Micro area	26,151	24,807
	28027	Coahoma County, MS	26,151	24,807
17300		Clarksville, TN-KY Metro area	260,625	278,353
	21047	Christian County, KY	73,955	74,250
	21221	Trigg County, KY	14,339	14,142
	47125	Montgomery County, TN	172,331	189,961
17340		Clearlake, CA Micro area	64,665	64,184
	06033	Lake County, CA	64,665	64,184
17380		Cleveland, MS Micro area	34,145	33,768
	28011	Bolivar County, MS	34,145	33,768
17420		Cleveland, TN Metro area	115,788	119,705
	47011	Bradley County, TN	98,963	102,975
	47139	Polk County, TN	16,825	16,730
17460		Cleveland-Elyria, OH Metro area	2,077,240	2,063,598
	39035	Cuyahoga County, OH	1,280,122	1,259,828
	39055	Geauga County, OH	93,389	94,295
	39085	Lake County, OH	230,041	229,230
	39093	Lorain County, OH	301,356	304,216
	39103	Medina County, OH	172,332	176,029
17500		Clewiston, FL Micro area	39,140	38,505
	12051	Hendry County, FL	39,140	38,505
17540		Clinton, IA Micro area	49,116	48,051
	19045	Clinton County, IA	49,116	48,051
17580		Clovis, NM Micro area	48,376	50,969
	35009	Curry County, NM	48,376	50,969
17660		Coeur d'Alene, ID Metro area	138,494	147,326
	16055	Kootenai County, ID	138,494	147,326
17700		Coffeyville, KS Micro area	35,471	34,065
	20125	Montgomery County, KS	35,471	34,065
17740		Coldwater, MI Micro area	45,248	43,545
	26023	Branch County, MI	45,248	43,545
17780		College Station-Bryan, TX Metro area	228,660	242,905
	48041	Brazos County, TX	194,851	209,152
	48051	Burleson County, TX	17,187	17,253
	48395	Robertson County, TX	16,622	16,500
17820		Colorado Springs, CO Metro area	645,613	686,908
	08041	El Paso County, CO	622,263	663,519
	08119	Teller County, CO	23,350	23,389
17860		Columbia, MO Metro area	162,642	172,717
	29019	Boone County, MO	162,642	172,717
17900		Columbia, SC Metro area	767,598	800,495
	45017	Calhoun County, SC	15,175	14,878
	45039	Fairfield County, SC	23,956	22,976
	45055	Kershaw County, SC	61,697	63,161
	45063	Lexington County, SC	262,391	277,888
	45079	Richland County, SC	384,504	401,566
	45081	Saluda County, SC	19,875	20,026
17980		Columbus, GA-AL Metro area	294,865	314,005
	01113	Russell County, AL	52,947	59,608
	13053	Chattahoochee County, GA	11,267	11,837
	13145	Harris County, GA	32,024	32,876
	13197	Marion County, GA	8,742	8,797
	13215	Muscogee County, GA	189,885	200,887
18020		Columbus, IN Metro area	76,794	80,217
	18005	Bartholomew County, IN	76,794	80,217
18060		Columbus, MS Micro area	59,779	59,730
	28087	Lowndes County, MS	59,779	59,730
18100		Columbus, NE Micro area	32,237	32,666
	31141	Platte County, NE	32,237	32,666
18140		Columbus, OH Metro area	1,901,974	1,994,536
	39041	Delaware County, OH	174,214	189,113
	39045	Fairfield County, OH	146,156	150,381
	39049	Franklin County, OH	1,163,414	1,231,393
	39073	Hocking County, OH	29,380	28,725
	39089	Licking County, OH	166,492	169,390
	39097	Madison County, OH	43,435	43,918
	39117	Morrow County, OH	34,827	35,152
	39127	Perry County, OH	36,058	35,812
	39129	Pickaway County, OH	55,698	56,876
	39159	Union County, OH	52,300	53,776
18180		Concord, NH Micro area	146,445	147,171
	33013	Merrimack County, NH	146,445	147,171
18220		Connersville, IN Micro area	24,277	23,468
	18041	Fayette County, IN	24,277	23,468
18260		Cookeville, TN Micro area	106,042	107,761
	47087	Jackson County, TN	11,638	11,568
	47133	Overton County, TN	22,083	22,028
	47141	Putnam County, TN	72,321	74,165
18300		Coos Bay, OR Micro area	63,043	62,475
	41011	Coos County, OR	63,043	62,475
18380		Cordele, GA Micro area	23,439	22,934
	13081	Crisp County, GA	23,439	22,934
18420		Corinth, MS Micro area	37,057	37,380
	28003	Alcorn County, MS	37,057	37,380
18460		Cornelia, GA Micro area	43,041	43,752
	13137	Habersham County, GA	43,041	43,752
18500		Corning, NY Micro area	98,990	98,394
	36101	Steuben County, NY	98,990	98,394
18580		Corpus Christi, TX Metro area	428,185	448,108
	48007	Aransas County, TX	23,158	24,972
	48355	Nueces County, TX	340,223	356,221
	48409	San Patricio County, TX	64,804	66,915
18620		Corsicana, TX Micro area	47,735	48,195
	48349	Navarro County, TX	47,735	48,195
18660		Cortland, NY Micro area	49,336	49,024
	36023	Cortland County, NY	49,336	49,024
18700		Corvallis, OR Metro area	85,579	86,316
	41003	Benton County, OR	85,579	86,316
18740		Coshocton, OH Micro area	36,901	36,516
	39031	Coshocton County, OH	36,901	36,516
18780		Craig, CO Micro area	13,795	12,928
	08081	Moffat County, CO	13,795	12,928
18820		Crawfordsville, IN Micro area	38,124	38,146
	18107	Montgomery County, IN	38,124	38,146

Core Based Statistical Areas (Metropolitan and Micropolitan), Metropolitan Divisions, and Components (as defined February 2013)

Core based statistical area	State/County FIPS code	Title and Geographic Components	2010 Census Population	2014 Estimated Population
18860		Crescent City, CA Micro area	28,610	27,212
	06015	Del Norte County, CA	28,610	27,212
18880		Crestview-Fort Walton Beach-Destin, FL Metro area	235,865	258,042
	12091	Okaloosa County, FL	180,822	196,512
	12131	Walton County, FL	55,043	61,530
18900		Crossville, TN Micro area	56,053	57,985
	47035	Cumberland County, TN	56,053	57,985
18980		Cullman, AL Micro area	80,406	81,289
	01043	Cullman County, AL	80,406	81,289
19000		Cullowhee, NC Micro area	40,271	40,981
	37099	Jackson County, NC	40,271	40,981
19060		Cumberland, MD-WV Metro area	103,299	100,530
	24001	Allegany County, MD	75,087	72,952
	54057	Mineral County, WV	28,212	27,578
19100		Dallas-Fort Worth-Arlington, TX Metro area	6,426,214	6,954,330
19100		Dallas-Plano-Irving, TX Metro Div 19124	4,230,520	4,604,097
	48085	Collin County, TX	782,341	885,241
	48113	Dallas County, TX	2,368,139	2,518,638
	48121	Denton County, TX	662,614	753,363
	48139	Ellis County, TX	149,610	159,317
	48231	Hunt County, TX	86,129	88,493
	48257	Kaufman County, TX	103,350	111,236
	48397	Rockwall County, TX	78,337	87,809
19100		Fort Worth-Arlington, TX Metro Div 23104	2,195,694	2,350,233
	48221	Hood County, TX	51,182	53,921
	48251	Johnson County, TX	150,934	157,456
	48367	Parker County, TX	116,927	123,164
	48425	Somervell County, TX	8,490	8,694
	48439	Tarrant County, TX	1,809,034	1,945,360
	48497	Wise County, TX	59,127	61,638
19140		Dalton, GA Metro area	142,227	142,952
	13213	Murray County, GA	39,628	39,410
	13313	Whitfield County, GA	102,599	103,542
19180		Danville, IL Metro area	81,625	79,728
	17183	Vermilion County, IL	81,625	79,728
19220		Danville, KY Micro area	53,174	54,151
	21021	Boyle County, KY	28,432	29,706
	21137	Lincoln County, KY	24,742	24,445
19260		Danville, VA Micro area	106,561	104,827
	51143	Pittsylvania County, VA	63,506	62,383
	51590	Danville city, VA	43,055	42,444
19300		Daphne-Fairhope-Foley, AL Metro area	182,265	200,111
	01003	Baldwin County, AL	182,265	200,111
19340		Davenport-Moline-Rock Island, IA-IL Metro area	379,690	383,030
	17073	Henry County, IL	50,486	49,635
	17131	Mercer County, IL	16,434	15,945
	17161	Rock Island County, IL	147,546	146,063
	19163	Scott County, IA	165,224	171,387
19380		Dayton, OH Metro area	799,232	800,836
	39057	Greene County, OH	161,573	163,820
	39109	Miami County, OH	102,506	103,900
	39113	Montgomery County, OH	535,153	533,116
19420		Dayton, TN Micro area	31,809	32,641
	47143	Rhea County, TN	31,809	32,641
19460		Decatur, AL Metro area	153,829	153,084
	01079	Lawrence County, AL	34,339	33,477
	01103	Morgan County, AL	119,490	119,607
19500		Decatur, IL Metro area	110,768	108,350
	17115	Macon County, IL	110,768	108,350
19540		Decatur, IN Micro area	34,387	34,791
	18001	Adams County, IN	34,387	34,791
19580		Defiance, OH Micro area	39,037	38,510
	39039	Defiance County, OH	39,037	38,510
19620		Del Rio, TX Micro area	48,879	48,974
	48465	Val Verde County, TX	48,879	48,974
19660		Deltona-Daytona Beach-Ormond Beach, FL Metro area	590,289	609,939
	12035	Flagler County, FL	95,696	102,408
	12127	Volusia County, FL	494,593	507,531
19700		Deming, NM Micro area	25,095	24,673
	35029	Luna County, NM	25,095	24,673
19740		Denver-Aurora-Lakewood, CO Metro area	2,543,482	2,754,258
	08001	Adams County, CO	441,603	480,718
	08005	Arapahoe County, CO	572,003	618,821
	08014	Broomfield County, CO	55,889	62,138
	08019	Clear Creek County, CO	9,088	9,187
	08031	Denver County, CO	600,158	663,862
	08035	Douglas County, CO	285,465	314,638
	08039	Elbert County, CO	23,086	24,195
	08047	Gilpin County, CO	5,441	5,851
	08059	Jefferson County, CO	534,543	558,503
	08093	Park County, CO	16,206	16,345
19760		DeRidder, LA Micro area	35,654	36,198

Core Based Statistical Areas (Metropolitan and Micropolitan), Metropolitan Divisions, and Components (as defined February 2013)

Core based statistical area	State/County FIPS code	Title and Geographic Components	2010 Census Population	2014 Estimated Population
	22011	Beauregard Parish, LA	35,654	36,198
19780		Des Moines-West Des Moines, IA Metro area	569,633	611,549
	19049	Dallas County, IA	66,135	77,400
	19077	Guthrie County, IA	10,954	10,722
	19121	Madison County, IA	15,679	15,609
	19153	Polk County, IA	430,640	459,862
	19181	Warren County, IA	46,225	47,956
19820		Detroit-Warren-Dearborn, MI Metro area	4,296,250	4,296,611
19820		Detroit-Dearborn-Livonia, MI Metro Div 19804	1,820,584	1,764,804
	26163	Wayne County, MI	1,820,584	1,764,804
19820		Warren-Troy-Farmington Hills, MI Metro Div 47664	2,475,666	2,531,807
	26087	Lapeer County, MI	88,319	88,153
	26093	Livingston County, MI	180,967	185,596
	26099	Macomb County, MI	840,978	860,112
	26125	Oakland County, MI	1,202,362	1,237,868
	26147	St. Clair County, MI	163,040	160,078
19860		Dickinson, ND Micro area	24,199	30,372
	38089	Stark County, ND	24,199	30,372
19940		Dixon, IL Micro area	36,031	34,735
	17103	Lee County, IL	36,031	34,735
19980		Dodge City, KS Micro area	33,848	34,795
	20057	Ford County, KS	33,848	34,795
20020		Dothan, AL Metro area	145,639	148,095
	01061	Geneva County, AL	26,790	26,712
	01067	Henry County, AL	17,302	17,190
	01069	Houston County, AL	101,547	104,193
20060		Douglas, GA Micro area	42,356	42,811
	13069	Coffee County, GA	42,356	42,811
20100		Dover, DE Metro area	162,310	171,987
	10001	Kent County, Delaware	162,310	171,987
20140		Dublin, GA Micro area	58,414	57,552
	13167	Johnson County, GA	9,980	9,701
	13175	Laurens County, GA	48,434	47,851
20180		DuBois, PA Micro area	81,642	81,191
	42033	Clearfield County, PA	81,642	81,191
20220		Dubuque, IA Metro area	93,653	96,370
	19061	Dubuque County, IA	93,653	96,370
20260		Duluth, MN-WI Metro area	279,771	280,218
	27017	Carlton County, MN	35,386	35,571
	27137	St. Louis County, MN	200,226	200,949
	55031	Douglas County, WI	44,159	43,698
20300		Dumas, TX Micro area	21,904	22,148
	48341	Moore County, TX	21,904	22,148
20340		Duncan, OK Micro area	45,048	44,493
	40137	Stephens County, OK	45,048	44,493
20380		Dunn, NC Micro area	114,678	126,666
	37085	Harnett County, NC	114,678	126,666
20420		Durango, CO Micro area	51,334	53,989
	08067	La Plata County, CO	51,334	53,989
20460		Durant, OK Micro area	42,416	44,486
	40013	Bryan County, OK	42,416	44,486
20500		Durham-Chapel Hill, NC Metro area	504,357	542,710
	37037	Chatham County, NC	63,505	68,698
	37063	Durham County, NC	267,587	294,460
	37135	Orange County, NC	133,801	140,420
	37145	Person County, NC	39,464	39,132
20540		Dyersburg, TN Micro area	38,335	37,935
	47045	Dyer County, TN	38,335	37,935
20580		Eagle Pass, TX Micro area	54,258	57,023
	48323	Maverick County, TX	54,258	57,023
20660		Easton, MD Micro area	37,782	37,643
	24041	Talbot County, MD	37,782	37,643
20700		East Stroudsburg, PA Metro area	169,842	166,314
	42089	Monroe County, PA	169,842	166,314
20740		Eau Claire, WI Metro area	161,151	165,024
	55017	Chippewa County, WI	62,415	63,460
	55035	Eau Claire County, WI	98,736	101,564
20780		Edwards, CO Micro area	52,197	52,921
	08037	Eagle County, CO	52,197	52,921
20820		Effingham, IL Micro area	34,242	34,320
	17049	Effingham County, IL	34,242	34,320
20900		El Campo, TX Micro area	41,280	41,168
	48481	Wharton County, TX	41,280	41,168
20940		El Centro, CA Metro area	174,528	179,091
	06025	Imperial County, CA	174,528	179,091
20980		El Dorado, AR Micro area	41,639	40,227
	05139	Union County, AR	41,639	40,227
21020		Elizabeth City, NC Micro area	64,094	63,584
	37029	Camden County, NC	9,980	10,331
	37139	Pasquotank County, NC	40,661	39,787
	37143	Perquimans County, NC	13,453	13,466
21060		Elizabethtown-Fort Knox, KY Metro area	148,338	151,585

Core Based Statistical Areas (Metropolitan and Micropolitan), Metropolitan Divisions, and Components (as defined February 2013)

Core based statistical area	State/County FIPS code	Title and Geographic Components	2010 Census Population	2014 Estimated Population
	21093	Hardin County, KY	105,543	108,266
	21123	Larue County, KY	14,193	14,180
	21163	Meade County, KY	28,602	29,139
21120		Elk City, OK Micro area	22,119	23,691
	40009	Beckham County, OK	22,119	23,691
21140		Elkhart-Goshen, IN Metro area	197,559	201,971
	18039	Elkhart County, IN	197,559	201,971
21180		Elkins, WV Micro area	29,405	29,429
	54083	Randolph County, WV	29,405	29,429
21220		Elko, NV Micro area	50,805	54,784
	32007	Elko County, NV	48,818	52,766
	32011	Eureka County, NV	1,987	2,018
21260		Ellensburg, WA Micro area	40,915	42,522
	53037	Kittitas County, WA	40,915	42,522
21300		Elmira, NY Metro area	88,830	87,770
	36015	Chemung County, NY	88,830	87,770
21340		El Paso, TX Metro area	804,123	836,698
	48141	El Paso County, TX	800,647	833,487
	48229	Hudspeth County, TX	3,476	3,211
21380		Emporia, KS Micro area	33,690	33,212
	20111	Lyon County, KS	33,690	33,212
21420		Enid, OK Micro area	60,580	63,091
	40047	Garfield County, OK	60,580	63,091
21460		Enterprise, AL Micro area	49,948	50,909
	01031	Coffee County, AL	49,948	50,909
21500		Erie, PA Metro area	280,566	278,443
	42049	Erie County, PA	280,566	278,443
21540		Escanaba, MI Micro area	37,069	36,559
	26041	Delta County, MI	37,069	36,559
21580		Española, NM Micro area	40,246	39,777
	35039	Rio Arriba County, NM	40,246	39,777
21660		Eugene, OR Metro area	351,715	358,337
	41039	Lane County, OR	351,715	358,337
21700		Eureka-Arcata-Fortuna, CA Micro area	134,623	134,809
	06023	Humboldt County, CA	134,623	134,809
21740		Evanston, WY Micro area	21,118	20,904
	56041	Uinta County, WY	21,118	20,904
21780		Evansville, IN-KY Metro area	311,552	315,162
	18129	Posey County, IN	25,910	25,540
	18163	Vanderburgh County, IN	179,703	182,006
	18173	Warrick County, IN	59,689	61,149
	21101	Henderson County, KY	46,250	46,467
21820		Fairbanks, AK Metro area	97,581	99,357
	02090	Fairbanks North Star Borough, AK	97,581	99,357
21840		Fairfield, IA Micro area	16,843	17,325
	19101	Jefferson County, IA	16,843	17,325
21900		Fairmont, WV Micro area	56,418	56,803
	54049	Marion County, WV	56,418	56,803
21980		Fallon, NV Micro area	24,877	23,989
	32001	Churchill County, NV	24,877	23,989
22020		Fargo, ND-MN Metro area	208,777	228,291
	27027	Clay County, MN	58,999	61,286
	38017	Cass County, ND	149,778	167,005
22060		Faribault-Northfield, MN Micro area	64,142	65,151
	27131	Rice County, MN	64,142	65,151
22100		Farmington, MO Micro area	65,359	65,960
	29187	St. Francois County, MO	65,359	65,960
22140		Farmington, NM Metro area	130,044	123,785
	35045	San Juan County, NM	130,044	123,785
22180		Fayetteville, NC Metro area	366,383	377,939
	37051	Cumberland County, NC	319,431	326,328
	37093	Hoke County, NC	46,952	51,611
22220		Fayetteville-Springdale-Rogers, AR-MO Metro area	463,204	501,653
	05007	Benton County, AR	221,339	242,321
	05087	Madison County, AR	15,717	15,740
	05143	Washington County, AR	203,065	220,792
	29119	McDonald County, MO	23,083	22,800
22260		Fergus Falls, MN Micro area	57,303	57,635
	27111	Otter Tail County, MN	57,303	57,635
22280		Fernley, NV Micro area	51,980	51,789
	32019	Lyon County, NV	51,980	51,789
22300		Findlay, OH Micro area	74,782	75,337
	39063	Hancock County, OH	74,782	75,337
22340		Fitzgerald, GA Micro area	17,634	17,464
	13017	Ben Hill County, GA	17,634	17,464
22380		Flagstaff, AZ Metro area	134,421	137,682
	04005	Coconino County, AZ	134,421	137,682
22420		Flint, MI Metro area	425,790	412,895
	26049	Genesee County, MI	425,790	412,895
22500		Florence, SC Metro area	205,566	207,030
	45031	Darlington County, SC	68,681	67,799
	45041	Florence County, SC	136,885	139,231
22520		Florence-Muscle Shoals, AL Metro area	147,137	147,639
	01033	Colbert County, AL	54,428	54,543
	01077	Lauderdale County, AL	92,709	93,096
22540		Fond du Lac, WI Metro area	101,633	101,759
	55039	Fond du Lac County, WI	101,633	101,759
22580		Forest City, NC Micro area	67,810	66,600
	37161	Rutherford County, NC	67,810	66,600
22620		Forrest City, AR Micro area	28,258	26,899
	05123	St. Francis County, AR	28,258	26,899
22660		Fort Collins, CO Metro area	299,630	324,122
	08069	Larimer County, CO	299,630	324,122
22700		Fort Dodge, IA Micro area	38,013	36,955
	19187	Webster County, IA	38,013	36,955
22780		Fort Leonard Wood, MO Micro area	52,274	53,436
	29169	Pulaski County, MO	52,274	53,436
22800		Fort Madison-Keokuk, IA-IL-MO Micro area	62,105	60,767
	17067	Hancock County, IL	19,104	18,564
	19111	Lee County, IA	35,862	35,286
	29045	Clark County, MO	7,139	6,917
22820		Fort Morgan, CO Micro area	28,159	28,328
	08087	Morgan County, CO	28,159	28,328
22860		Fort Polk South, LA Micro area	52,334	52,132
	22115	Vernon Parish, LA	52,334	52,132
22900		Fort Smith, AR-OK Metro area	280,467	279,592
	05033	Crawford County, AR	61,948	61,697
	05131	Sebastian County, AR	125,744	126,776
	40079	Le Flore County, OK	50,384	49,761
	40135	Sequoyah County, OK	42,391	41,358
23060		Fort Wayne, IN Metro area	416,257	427,183
	18003	Allen County, IN	355,329	365,918
	18179	Wells County, IN	27,636	27,862
	18183	Whitley County, IN	33,292	33,403
23140		Frankfort, IN Micro area	33,224	32,776
	18023	Clinton County, IN	33,224	32,776
23180		Frankfort, KY Micro area	70,706	71,768
	21005	Anderson County, KY	21,421	21,888
	21073	Franklin County, KY	49,285	49,880
23240		Fredericksburg, TX Micro area	24,837	25,520
	48171	Gillespie County, TX	24,837	25,520
23300		Freeport, IL Micro area	47,711	46,435
	17177	Stephenson County, IL	47,711	46,435
23340		Fremont, NE Micro area	36,691	36,744
	31053	Dodge County, NE	36,691	36,744
23380		Fremont, OH Micro area	60,944	60,179
	39143	Sandusky County, OH	60,944	60,179
23420		Fresno, CA Metro area	930,450	965,974
	06019	Fresno County, CA	930,450	965,974
23460		Gadsden, AL Metro area	104,430	103,531
	01055	Etowah County, AL	104,430	103,531
23500		Gaffney, SC Micro area	55,342	56,024
	45021	Cherokee County, SC	55,342	56,024
23540		Gainesville, FL Metro area	264,275	273,377
	12001	Alachua County, FL	247,336	256,380
	12041	Gilchrist County, FL	16,939	16,997
23580		Gainesville, GA Metro area	179,684	190,761
	13139	Hall County, GA	179,684	190,761
23620		Gainesville, TX Micro area	38,437	38,761
	48097	Cooke County, TX	38,437	38,761
23660		Galesburg, IL Micro area	52,919	52,069
	17095	Knox County, IL	52,919	52,069
23700		Gallup, NM Micro area	71,492	74,098
	35031	McKinley County, NM	71,492	74,098
23780		Garden City, KS Micro area	40,753	41,099
	20055	Finney County, KS	36,776	37,184
	20093	Kearny County, KS	3,977	3,915
23820		Gardnerville Ranchos, NV Micro area	46,997	47,536
	32005	Douglas County, NV	46,997	47,536
23860		Georgetown, SC Micro area	60,158	60,773
	45043	Georgetown County, SC	60,158	60,773
23900		Gettysburg, PA Metro area	101,407	101,714
	42001	Adams County, PA	101,407	101,714
23940		Gillette, WY Micro area	46,133	48,320
	56005	Campbell County, WY	46,133	48,320
23980		Glasgow, KY Micro area	52,272	53,138
	21009	Barren County, KY	42,173	43,148
	21169	Metcalfe County, KY	10,099	9,990
24020		Glens Falls, NY Metro area	128,923	127,345
	36113	Warren County, NY	65,707	64,973
	36115	Washington County, NY	63,216	62,372
24060		Glenwood Springs, CO Micro area	73,537	75,087
	08045	Garfield County, CO	56,389	57,461
	08097	Pitkin County, CO	17,148	17,626
24100		Gloversville, NY Micro area	55,531	54,105
	36035	Fulton County, NY	55,531	54,105
24140		Goldsboro, NC Metro area	122,623	124,456
	37191	Wayne County, NC	122,623	124,456
24220		Grand Forks, ND-MN Metro area	98,461	101,842

Core Based Statistical Areas (Metropolitan and Micropolitan), Metropolitan Divisions, and Components (as defined February 2013)

Core based statistical area	State/County FIPS code	Title and Geographic Components	2010 Census Population	2014 Estimated Population
	27119	Polk County, MN	31,600	31,704
	38035	Grand Forks County, ND	66,861	70,138
24260		Grand Island, NE Metro area	81,850	84,755
	31079	Hall County, NE	58,607	61,492
	31081	Hamilton County, NE	9,124	9,135
	31093	Howard County, NE	6,274	6,362
	31121	Merrick County, NE	7,845	7,766
24300		Grand Junction, CO Metro area	146,723	148,255
	08077	Mesa County, CO	146,723	148,255
24340		Grand Rapids-Wyoming, MI Metro area	988,938	1,027,703
	26015	Barry County, MI	59,173	59,281
	26081	Kent County, MI	602,622	629,237
	26117	Montcalm County, MI	63,342	62,893
	26139	Ottawa County, MI	263,801	276,292
24380		Grants, NM Micro area	27,213	27,349
	35006	Cibola County, NM	27,213	27,349
24420		Grants Pass, OR Metro area	82,713	83,599
	41033	Josephine County, OR	82,713	83,599
24460		Great Bend, KS Micro area	27,674	27,385
	20009	Barton County, KS	27,674	27,385
24500		Great Falls, MT Metro area	81,327	82,344
	30013	Cascade County, MT	81,327	82,344
24540		Greeley, CO Metro area	252,825	277,670
	08123	Weld County, CO	252,825	277,670
24580		Green Bay, WI Metro area	306,241	314,531
	55009	Brown County, WI	248,007	256,670
	55061	Kewaunee County, WI	20,574	20,444
	55083	Oconto County, WI	37,660	37,417
24620		Greeneville, TN Micro area	68,831	68,335
	47059	Greene County, TN	68,831	68,335
24640		Greenfield Town, MA Micro area	71,372	70,862
	25011	Franklin County, MA	71,372	70,862
24660		Greensboro-High Point, NC Metro area	723,801	746,593
	37081	Guilford County, NC	488,406	512,119
	37151	Randolph County, NC	141,752	142,778
	37157	Rockingham County, NC	93,643	91,696
24700		Greensburg, IN Micro area	25,740	26,524
	18031	Decatur County, IN	25,740	26,524
24740		Greenville, MS Micro area	51,137	48,958
	28151	Washington County, MS	51,137	48,958
24780		Greenville, NC Metro area	168,148	175,354
	37147	Pitt County, NC	168,148	175,354
24820		Greenville, OH Micro area	52,959	52,196
	39037	Darke County, OH	52,959	52,196
24860		Greenville-Anderson-Mauldin, SC Metro area	824,112	862,463
	45007	Anderson County, SC	187,126	192,810
	45045	Greenville County, SC	451,225	482,752
	45059	Laurens County, SC	66,537	66,533
	45077	Pickens County, SC	119,224	120,368
24900		Greenwood, MS Micro area	42,914	41,676
	28015	Carroll County, MS	10,597	10,254
	28083	Leflore County, MS	32,317	31,422
24940		Greenwood, SC Micro area	95,078	94,485
	45001	Abbeville County, SC	25,417	24,965
	45047	Greenwood County, SC	69,661	69,520
24980		Grenada, MS Micro area	21,906	21,666
	28043	Grenada County, MS	21,906	21,666
25060		Gulfport-Biloxi-Pascagoula, MS Metro area	370,702	386,144
	28045	Hancock County, MS	43,929	45,949
	28047	Harrison County, MS	187,105	199,058
	28059	Jackson County, MS	139,668	141,137
25100		Guymon, OK Micro area	20,640	21,853
	40139	Texas County, OK	20,640	21,853
25180		Hagerstown-Martinsburg, MD-WV Metro area	251,599	260,070
	24043	Washington County, MD	147,430	149,573
	54003	Berkeley County, WV	104,169	110,497
25200		Hailey, ID Micro area	27,701	27,837
	16013	Blaine County, ID	21,376	21,482
	16025	Camas County, ID	1,117	1,039
	16063	Lincoln County, ID	5,208	5,316
25220		Hammond, LA Metro area	121,097	127,049
	22105	Tangipahoa Parish, LA	121,097	127,049
25260		Hanford-Corcoran, CA Metro area	152,982	150,269
	06031	Kings County, CA	152,982	150,269
25300		Hannibal, MO Micro area	38,948	39,175
	29127	Marion County, MO	28,781	28,920
	29173	Ralls County, MO	10,167	10,255
25420		Harrisburg-Carlisle, PA Metro area	549,475	560,849
	42041	Cumberland County, PA	235,406	243,762
	42043	Dauphin County, PA	268,100	271,453
	42099	Perry County, PA	45,969	45,634
25460		Harrison, AR Micro area	45,233	45,100
	05009	Boone County, AR	36,903	37,196
	05101	Newton County, AR	8,330	7,904
25500		Harrisonburg, VA Metro area	125,228	130,649
	51165	Rockingham County, VA	76,314	78,171
	51660	Harrisonburg city, VA	48,914	52,478
25540		Hartford-West Hartford-East Hartford, CT Metro area	1,212,381	1,214,295
	09003	Hartford County, CT	894,014	897,985
	09007	Middlesex County, CT	165,676	164,943
	09013	Tolland County, CT	152,691	151,367
25580		Hastings, NE Micro area	31,364	31,457
	31001	Adams County, NE	31,364	31,457
25620		Hattiesburg, MS Metro area	142,842	148,656
	28035	Forrest County, MS	74,934	76,330
	28073	Lamar County, MS	55,658	60,099
	28111	Perry County, MS	12,250	12,227
25700		Hays, KS Micro area	28,452	29,013
	20051	Ellis County, KS	28,452	29,013
25720		Heber, UT Micro area	23,530	27,714
	49051	Wasatch County, UT	23,530	27,714
25740		Helena, MT Micro area	74,801	77,414
	30043	Jefferson County, MT	11,406	11,558
	30049	Lewis and Clark County, MT	63,395	65,856
25760		Helena-West Helena, AR Micro area	21,757	19,930
	05107	Phillips County, AR	21,757	19,930
25780		Henderson, NC Micro area	45,422	44,614
	37181	Vance County, NC	45,422	44,614
25820		Hereford, TX Micro area	19,372	19,195
	48117	Deaf Smith County, TX	19,372	19,195
25840		Hermiston-Pendleton, OR Micro area	87,062	87,892
	41049	Morrow County, OR	11,173	11,187
	41059	Umatilla County, OR	75,889	76,705
25860		Hickory-Lenoir-Morganton, NC Metro area	365,497	362,896
	37003	Alexander County, NC	37,198	37,392
	37023	Burke County, NC	90,912	89,486
	37027	Caldwell County, NC	83,029	81,484
	37035	Catawba County, NC	154,358	154,534
25880		Hillsdale, MI Micro area	46,688	45,830
	26059	Hillsdale County, MI	46,688	45,830
25900		Hilo, HI Micro area	185,079	194,190
	15001	Hawaii County, HI	185,079	194,190
25940		Hilton Head Island-Bluffton-Beaufort, SC Metro area	187,010	203,022
	45013	Beaufort County, SC	162,233	175,852
	45053	Jasper County, SC	24,777	27,170
25980		Hinesville, GA Metro area	77,917	82,311
	13179	Liberty County, GA	63,453	65,198
	13183	Long County, GA	14,464	17,113
26020		Hobbs, NM Micro area	64,727	69,999
	35025	Lea County, NM	64,727	69,999
26090		Holland, MI Micro area	111,408	113,847
	26005	Allegan County, MI	111,408	113,847
26140		Homosassa Springs, FL Metro area	141,236	139,377
	12017	Citrus County, FL	141,236	139,377
26220		Hood River, OR Micro area	22,346	22,885
	41027	Hood River County, OR	22,346	22,885
26300		Hot Springs, AR Metro area	96,024	97,322
	05051	Garland County, AR	96,024	97,322
26340		Houghton, MI Micro area	38,784	38,712
	26061	Houghton County, MI	36,628	36,495
	26083	Keweenaw County, MI	2,156	2,217
26380		Houma-Thibodaux, LA Metro area	208,178	211,348
	22057	Lafourche Parish, LA	96,318	98,020
	22109	Terrebonne Parish, LA	111,860	113,328
26420		Houston-The Woodlands-Sugar Land, TX Metro area	5,920,416	6,490,180
	48015	Austin County, TX	28,417	29,114
	48039	Brazoria County, TX	313,166	338,124
	48071	Chambers County, TX	35,096	38,145
	48157	Fort Bend County, TX	585,375	685,345
	48167	Galveston County, TX	291,309	314,198
	48201	Harris County, TX	4,092,459	4,441,370
	48291	Liberty County, TX	75,643	78,117
	48339	Montgomery County, TX	455,746	518,947
	48473	Waller County, TX	43,205	46,820
26460		Hudson, NY Micro area	63,096	62,122
	36021	Columbia County, NY	63,096	62,122
26500		Huntingdon, PA Micro area	45,913	45,750
	42061	Huntingdon County, PA	45,913	45,750
26540		Huntington, IN Micro area	37,124	36,706
	18069	Huntington County, IN	37,124	36,706
26580		Huntington-Ashland, WV-KY-OH Metro area	364,908	363,325
	21019	Boyd County, KY	49,542	48,832
	21089	Greenup County, KY	36,910	36,308
	39087	Lawrence County, OH	62,450	61,623
	54011	Cabell County, WV	96,319	97,109

Core Based Statistical Areas (Metropolitan and Micropolitan), Metropolitan Divisions, and Components (as defined February 2013)

Core based statistical area	State/ County FIPS code	Title and Geographic Components	2010 Census Population	2014 Estimated Population
	54043	Lincoln County, WV	21,720	21,561
	54079	Putnam County, WV	55,486	56,770
	54099	Wayne County, WV	42,481	41,122
26620		Huntsville, AL Metro area	417,593	441,086
	01083	Limestone County, AL	82,782	90,787
	01089	Madison County, AL	334,811	350,299
26660		Huntsville, TX Micro area	82,446	84,013
	48455	Trinity County, TX	14,585	14,224
	48471	Walker County, TX	67,861	69,789
26700		Huron, SD Micro area	17,398	18,169
	46005	Beadle County, SD	17,398	18,169
26740		Hutchinson, KS Micro area	64,511	63,794
	20155	Reno County, KS	64,511	63,794
26780		Hutchinson, MN Micro area	36,651	35,882
	27085	McLeod County, MN	36,651	35,882
26820		Idaho Falls, ID Metro area	133,265	138,266
	16019	Bonneville County, ID	104,234	108,623
	16023	Butte County, ID	2,891	2,622
	16051	Jefferson County, ID	26,140	27,021
26860		Indiana, PA Micro area	88,880	87,706
	42063	Indiana County, PA	88,880	87,706
26900		Indianapolis-Carmel-Anderson, IN Metro area	1,887,877	1,971,274
	18011	Boone County, IN	56,640	61,915
	18013	Brown County, IN	15,242	14,962
	18057	Hamilton County, IN	274,569	302,623
	18059	Hancock County, IN	70,002	71,978
	18063	Hendricks County, IN	145,448	156,056
	18081	Johnson County, IN	139,654	147,538
	18095	Madison County, IN	131,636	130,069
	18097	Marion County, IN	903,393	934,243
	18109	Morgan County, IN	68,894	69,693
	18133	Putnam County, IN	37,963	37,618
	18145	Shelby County, IN	44,436	44,579
26940		Indianola, MS Micro area	29,450	27,496
	28133	Sunflower County, MS	29,450	27,496
26960		Ionia, MI Micro area	63,905	64,294
	26067	Ionia County, MI	63,905	64,294
26980		Iowa City, IA Metro area	152,586	164,357
	19103	Johnson County, IA	130,882	142,287
	19183	Washington County, IA	21,704	22,070
27020		Iron Mountain, MI-WI Micro area	30,591	30,438
	26043	Dickinson County, MI	26,168	25,957
	55037	Florence County, WI	4,423	4,481
27060		Ithaca, NY Metro area	101,564	104,691
	36109	Tompkins County, NY	101,564	104,691
27100		Jackson, MI Metro area	160,248	159,741
	26075	Jackson County, MI	160,248	159,741
27140		Jackson, MS Metro area	567,122	577,564
	28029	Copiah County, MS	29,449	28,797
	28049	Hinds County, MS	245,285	243,729
	28089	Madison County, MS	95,203	101,688
	28121	Rankin County, MS	141,617	148,070
	28127	Simpson County, MS	27,503	27,463
	28163	Yazoo County, MS	28,065	27,817
27160		Jackson, OH Micro area	33,225	32,748
	39079	Jackson County, OH	33,225	32,748
27180		Jackson, TN Metro area	130,011	130,225
	47023	Chester County, TN	17,131	17,379
	47033	Crockett County, TN	14,586	14,668
	47113	Madison County, TN	98,294	98,178
27220		Jackson, WY-ID Micro area	31,464	33,271
	16081	Teton County, ID	10,170	10,341
	56039	Teton County, WY	21,294	22,930
27260		Jacksonville, FL Metro area	1,345,596	1,419,127
	12003	Baker County, FL	27,115	27,093
	12019	Clay County, FL	190,865	199,798
	12031	Duval County, FL	864,263	897,698
	12089	Nassau County, FL	73,314	76,619
	12109	St. Johns County, FL	190,039	217,919
27300		Jacksonville, IL Micro area	40,902	40,133
	17137	Morgan County, IL	35,547	34,929
	17171	Scott County, IL	5,355	5,204
27340		Jacksonville, NC Metro area	177,772	187,589
	37133	Onslow County, NC	177,772	187,589
27380		Jacksonville, TX Micro area	50,845	50,902
	48073	Cherokee County, TX	50,845	50,902
27420		Jamestown, ND Micro area	21,100	21,129
	38093	Stutsman County, ND	21,100	21,129
27460		Jamestown-Dunkirk-Fredonia, NY Micro area	134,905	132,053
	36013	Chautauqua County, NY	134,905	132,053
27500		Janesville-Beloit, WI Metro area	160,331	161,188
	55105	Rock County, WI	160,331	161,188
27540		Jasper, IN Micro area	54,734	54,969

Core Based Statistical Areas (Metropolitan and Micropolitan), Metropolitan Divisions, and Components (as defined February 2013)

Core based statistical area	State/ County FIPS code	Title and Geographic Components	2010 Census Population	2014 Estimated Population
	18037	Dubois County, IN	41,889	42,345
	18125	Pike County, IN	12,845	12,624
27600		Jefferson, GA Micro area	60,485	61,870
	13157	Jackson County, GA	60,485	61,870
27620		Jefferson City, MO Metro area	149,807	150,866
	29027	Callaway County, MO	44,332	44,750
	29051	Cole County, MO	75,990	76,557
	29135	Moniteau County, MO	15,607	15,856
	29151	Osage County, MO	13,878	13,703
27700		Jesup, GA Micro area	30,099	29,949
	13305	Wayne County, GA	30,099	29,949
27740		Johnson City, TN Metro area	198,716	201,091
	47019	Carter County, TN	57,424	56,886
	47171	Unicoi County, TN	18,313	17,963
	47179	Washington County, TN	122,979	126,242
27780		Johnstown, PA Metro area	143,679	137,732
	42021	Cambria County, PA	143,679	137,732
27860		Jonesboro, AR Metro area	121,026	126,764
	05031	Craighead County, AR	96,443	102,518
	05111	Poinsett County, AR	24,583	24,246
27900		Joplin, MO Metro area	175,518	176,141
	29097	Jasper County, MO	117,404	117,543
	29145	Newton County, MO	58,114	58,598
27920		Junction City, KS Micro area	34,362	36,713
	20061	Geary County, KS	34,362	36,713
27940		Juneau, AK Micro area	31,275	32,406
	02110	Juneau City and Borough, AK	31,275	32,406
27980		Kahului-Wailuku-Lahaina, HI Metro area	154,924	163,108
	15005	Kalawao County, HI	90	89
	15009	Maui County, HI	154,834	163,019
28020		Kalamazoo-Portage, MI Metro area	326,589	334,017
	26077	Kalamazoo County, MI	250,331	258,818
	26159	Van Buren County, MI	76,258	75,199
28060		Kalispell, MT Micro area	90,928	94,924
	30029	Flathead County, MT	90,928	94,924
28100		Kankakee, IL Metro area	113,449	111,375
	17091	Kankakee County, IL	113,449	111,375
28140		Kansas City, MO-KS Metro area	2,009,342	2,071,133
	20091	Johnson County, KS	544,179	574,272
	20103	Leavenworth County, KS	76,227	78,797
	20107	Linn County, KS	9,656	9,502
	20121	Miami County, KS	32,787	32,822
	20209	Wyandotte County, KS	157,505	161,636
	29013	Bates County, MO	17,049	16,584
	29025	Caldwell County, MO	9,424	9,034
	29037	Cass County, MO	99,478	100,889
	29047	Clay County, MO	221,939	233,682
	29049	Clinton County, MO	20,743	20,299
	29095	Jackson County, MO	674,158	683,191
	29107	Lafayette County, MO	33,381	32,688
	29165	Platte County, MO	89,322	94,788
	29177	Ray County, MO	23,494	22,949
28180		Kapaa, HI Micro area	67,091	70,475
	15007	Kauai County, HI	67,091	70,475
28260		Kearney, NE Micro area	52,591	54,868
	31019	Buffalo County, NE	46,102	48,224
	31099	Kearney County, NE	6,489	6,644
28300		Keene, NH Micro area	77,117	76,115
	33005	Cheshire County, NH	77,117	76,115
28340		Kendallville, IN Micro area	47,536	47,618
	18113	Noble County, IN	47,536	47,618
28380		Kennett, MO Micro area	31,953	31,344
	29069	Dunklin County, MO	31,953	31,344
28420		Kennewick-Richland, WA Metro area	253,340	274,295
	53005	Benton County, WA	175,177	186,486
	53021	Franklin County, WA	78,163	87,809
28500		Kerrville, TX Micro area	49,625	50,562
	48265	Kerr County, TX	49,625	50,562
28540		Ketchikan, AK Micro area	13,477	13,787
	02130	Ketchikan Gateway Borough, AK	13,477	13,787
28580		Key West, FL Micro area	73,090	77,136
	12087	Monroe County, FL	73,090	77,136
28620		Kill Devil Hills, NC Micro area	38,327	39,219
	37055	Dare County, NC	33,920	35,104
	37177	Tyrrell County, NC	4,407	4,115
28660		Killeen-Temple, TX Metro area	405,300	424,858
	48027	Bell County, TX	310,235	329,140
	48099	Coryell County, TX	75,388	75,562
	48281	Lampasas County, TX	19,677	20,156
28700		Kingsport-Bristol-Bristol, TN-VA Metro area	309,544	308,079
	47073	Hawkins County, TN	56,833	56,735
	47163	Sullivan County, TN	156,823	157,047
	51169	Scott County, VA	23,177	22,384
	51191	Washington County, VA	54,876	54,729
	51520	Bristol city, VA	17,835	17,184

Core based statistical area	State/ County FIPS code	Title and Geographic Components	2010 Census Population	2014 Estimated Population
28740		Kingston, NY Metro area	182,493	180,445
	36111	Ulster County, NY	182,493	180,445
28780		Kingsville, TX Micro area	32,477	32,590
	48261	Kenedy County, TX	416	400
	48273	Kleberg County, TX	32,061	32,190
28820		Kinston, NC Micro area	59,495	58,485
	37107	Lenoir County, NC	59,495	58,485
28860		Kirksville, MO Micro area	30,038	29,972
	29001	Adair County, MO	25,607	25,602
	29197	Schuyler County, MO	4,431	4,370
28900		Klamath Falls, OR Micro area	66,380	65,455
	41035	Klamath County, OR	66,380	65,455
28940		Knoxville, TN Metro area	837,571	857,585
	47001	Anderson County, TN	75,129	75,528
	47009	Blount County, TN	123,010	126,339
	47013	Campbell County, TN	40,716	39,918
	47057	Grainger County, TN	22,657	22,864
	47093	Knox County, TN	432,226	448,644
	47105	Loudon County, TN	48,556	50,771
	47129	Morgan County, TN	21,987	21,660
	47145	Roane County, TN	54,181	52,748
	47173	Union County, TN	19,109	19,113
29020		Kokomo, IN Metro area	82,752	82,982
	18067	Howard County, IN	82,752	82,982
29060		Laconia, NH Micro area	60,088	60,305
	33001	Belknap County, NH	60,088	60,305
29100		La Crosse-Onalaska, WI-MN Metro area	133,665	136,749
	27055	Houston County, MN	19,027	18,738
	55063	La Crosse County, WI	114,638	118,011
29180		Lafayette, LA Metro area	466,750	484,974
	22001	Acadia Parish, LA	61,773	62,486
	22045	Iberia Parish, LA	73,240	73,913
	22055	Lafayette Parish, LA	221,578	235,644
	22099	St. Martin Parish, LA	52,160	53,315
	22113	Vermilion Parish, LA	57,999	59,616
29200		Lafayette-West Lafayette, IN Metro area	201,789	211,697
	18007	Benton County, IN	8,854	8,700
	18015	Carroll County, IN	20,155	19,923
	18157	Tippecanoe County, IN	172,780	183,074
29260		La Grande, OR Micro area	25,748	25,691
	41061	Union County, OR	25,748	25,691
29300		LaGrange, GA Micro area	67,044	69,469
	13285	Troup County, GA	67,044	69,469
29340		Lake Charles, LA Metro area	199,607	203,883
	22019	Calcasieu Parish, LA	192,768	197,204
	22023	Cameron Parish, LA	6,839	6,679
29380		Lake City, FL Micro area	67,531	67,857
	12023	Columbia County, FL	67,531	67,857
29420		Lake Havasu City-Kingman, AZ Metro area	200,186	203,361
	04015	Mohave County, AZ	200,186	203,361
29460		Lakeland-Winter Haven, FL Metro area	602,095	634,638
	12105	Polk County, FL	602,095	634,638
29500		Lamesa, TX Micro area	13,833	13,372
	48115	Dawson County, TX	13,833	13,372
29540		Lancaster, PA Metro area	519,445	533,320
	42071	Lancaster County, PA	519,445	533,320
29620		Lansing-East Lansing, MI Metro area	464,036	470,458
	26037	Clinton County, MI	75,382	77,297
	26045	Eaton County, MI	107,759	108,579
	26065	Ingham County, MI	280,895	284,582
29660		Laramie, WY Micro area	36,299	37,811
	56001	Albany County, WY	36,299	37,811
29700		Laredo, TX Metro area	250,304	266,673
	48479	Webb County, TX	250,304	266,673
29740		Las Cruces, NM Metro area	209,233	213,676
	35013	Doña Ana County, NM	209,233	213,676
29780		Las Vegas, NM Micro area	29,393	28,239
	35047	San Miguel County, NM	29,393	28,239
		Las Vegas-Henderson-Paradise,		
29820		NV Metro area	1,951,269	2,069,681
	32003	Clark County, NV	1,951,269	2,069,681
29860		Laurel, MS Micro area	84,823	84,891
	28061	Jasper County, MS	17,062	16,601
	28067	Jones County, MS	67,761	68,290
29900		Laurinburg, NC Micro area	36,157	35,576
	37165	Scotland County, NC	36,157	35,576
29940		Lawrence, KS Metro area	110,826	116,585
	20045	Douglas County, KS	110,826	116,585
29980		Lawrenceburg, TN Micro area	41,869	42,274
	47099	Lawrence County, TN	41,869	42,274
30020		Lawton, OK Metro area	130,291	131,183
	40031	Comanche County, OK	124,098	125,033
	40033	Cotton County, OK	6,193	6,150
30060		Lebanon, MO Micro area	35,571	35,439
	29105	Laclede County, MO	35,571	35,439

Core based statistical area	State/ County FIPS code	Title and Geographic Components	2010 Census Population	2014 Estimated Population
30140		Lebanon, PA Metro area	133,568	136,359
	42075	Lebanon County, PA	133,568	136,359
30220		Levelland, TX Micro area	22,935	23,577
	48219	Hockley County, TX	22,935	23,577
30260		Lewisburg, PA Micro area	44,947	44,874
	42119	Union County, PA	44,947	44,874
30280		Lewisburg, TN Micro area	30,617	31,269
	47117	Marshall County, TN	30,617	31,269
30300		Lewiston, ID-WA Metro area	60,888	62,196
	16069	Nez Perce County, ID	39,265	40,007
	53003	Asotin County, WA	21,623	22,189
30340		Lewiston-Auburn, ME Metro area	107,702	107,440
	23001	Androscoggin County, ME	107,702	107,440
30380		Lewistown, PA Micro area	46,682	46,552
	42087	Mifflin County, PA	46,682	46,552
30420		Lexington, NE Micro area	26,370	26,066
	31047	Dawson County, NE	24,326	24,096
	31073	Gosper County, NE	2,044	1,970
30460		Lexington-Fayette, KY Metro area	472,099	494,189
	21017	Bourbon County, KY	19,985	19,972
	21049	Clark County, KY	35,613	35,758
	21067	Fayette County, KY	295,803	310,797
	21113	Jessamine County, KY	48,586	50,815
	21209	Scott County, KY	47,173	51,284
	21239	Woodford County, KY	24,939	25,563
30580		Liberal, KS Micro area	22,952	23,465
	20175	Seward County, KS	22,952	23,465
30620		Lima, OH Metro area	106,331	105,040
	39003	Allen County, OH	106,331	105,040
30660		Lincoln, IL Micro area	30,305	29,746
	17107	Logan County, IL	30,305	29,746
30700		Lincoln, NE Metro area	302,157	318,945
	31109	Lancaster County, NE	285,407	301,795
	31159	Seward County, NE	16,750	17,150
		Little Rock-North Little Rock-		
30780		Conway, AR Metro area	699,757	729,135
	05045	Faulkner County, AR	113,237	120,768
	05053	Grant County, AR	17,853	18,144
	05085	Lonoke County, AR	68,356	71,557
	05105	Perry County, AR	10,445	10,245
	05119	Pulaski County, AR	382,748	392,702
	05125	Saline County, AR	107,118	115,719
30820		Lock Haven, PA Micro area	39,238	39,745
	42035	Clinton County, PA	39,238	39,745
30860		Logan, UT-ID Metro area	125,442	131,364
	16041	Franklin County, ID	12,786	13,021
	49005	Cache County, UT	112,656	118,343
30880		Logan, WV Micro area	36,743	35,348
	54045	Logan County, WV	36,743	35,348
30900		Logansport, IN Micro area	38,966	38,438
	18017	Cass County, IN	38,966	38,438
30940		London, KY Micro area	126,369	127,316
	21121	Knox County, KY	31,883	31,798
	21125	Laurel County, KY	58,849	60,015
	21235	Whitley County, KY	35,637	35,503
30980		Longview, TX Metro area	214,369	217,481
	48183	Gregg County, TX	121,730	123,204
	48401	Rusk County, TX	53,330	53,923
	48459	Upshur County, TX	39,309	40,354
31020		Longview, WA Metro area	102,410	102,133
	53015	Cowlitz County, WA	102,410	102,133
31060		Los Alamos, NM Micro area	17,950	17,682
	35028	Los Alamos County, NM	17,950	17,682
		Los Angeles-Long Beach-		
31080		Anaheim, CA Metro area	12,828,837	13,262,220
		Anaheim-Santa Ana-Irvine, CA		
31080		Metro Div 11244	3,010,232	3,145,515
	06059	Orange County, CA	3,010,232	3,145,515
		Los Angeles-Long Beach-Glendale,		
31080		CA Metro Div 31084	9,818,605	10,116,705
	06037	Los Angeles County, CA	9,818,605	10,116,705
		Louisville/Jefferson County,		
31140		KY-IN Metro area	1,235,708	1,269,702
	18019	Clark County, IN	110,232	114,262
	18043	Floyd County, IN	74,578	76,179
	18061	Harrison County, IN	39,364	39,299
	18143	Scott County, IN	24,181	23,712
	18175	Washington County, IN	28,262	27,878
	21029	Bullitt County, KY	74,319	77,955
	21103	Henry County, KY	15,416	15,572
	21111	Jefferson County, KY	741,096	760,026
	21185	Oldham County, KY	60,316	63,490
	21211	Shelby County, KY	42,074	44,875
	21215	Spencer County, KY	17,061	17,668
	21223	Trimble County, KY	8,809	8,786

Core Based Statistical Areas (Metropolitan and Micropolitan), Metropolitan Divisions, and Components (as defined February 2013)

Core based statistical area	State/County FIPS code	Title and Geographic Components	2010 Census Population	2014 Estimated Population
31180		Lubbock, TX Metro area	290,805	305,644
	48107	Crosby County, TX	6,059	5,899
	48303	Lubbock County, TX	278,831	293,974
	48305	Lynn County, TX	5,915	5,771
31220		Ludington, MI Micro area	28,705	28,824
	26105	Mason County, MI	28,705	28,824
31260		Lufkin, TX Micro area	86,771	87,750
	48005	Angelina County, TX	86,771	87,750
31300		Lumberton, NC Micro area	134,168	134,760
	37155	Robeson County, NC	134,168	134,760
31340		Lynchburg, VA Metro area	252,634	257,835
	51009	Amherst County, VA	32,353	32,041
	51011	Appomattox County, VA	14,973	15,279
	51019	Bedford County, VA	74,866	76,583
	51031	Campbell County, VA	54,842	54,885
	51680	Lynchburg city, VA	75,568	79,047
31380		Macomb, IL Micro area	32,612	31,880
	17109	McDonough County, IL	32,612	31,880
31420		Macon, GA Metro area	232,293	230,450
	13021	Bibb County, GA	155,547	153,905
	13079	Crawford County, GA	12,630	12,387
	13169	Jones County, GA	28,669	28,787
	13207	Monroe County, GA	26,424	27,051
	13289	Twiggs County, GA	9,023	8,320
31460		Madera, CA Metro area	150,865	154,548
	06039	Madera County, CA	150,865	154,548
31500		Madison, IN Micro area	32,428	32,494
	18077	Jefferson County, IN	32,428	32,494
31540		Madison, WI Metro area	605,435	633,787
	55021	Columbia County, WI	56,833	56,615
	55025	Dane County, WI	488,073	516,284
	55045	Green County, WI	36,842	37,063
	55049	Iowa County, WI	23,687	23,825
31580		Madisonville, KY Micro area	46,920	46,376
	21107	Hopkins County, KY	46,920	46,376
31620		Magnolia, AR Micro area	24,552	23,933
	05027	Columbia County, AR	24,552	23,933
31660		Malone, NY Micro area	51,599	51,262
	36033	Franklin County, NY	51,599	51,262
31680		Malvern, AR Micro area	32,923	33,368
	05059	Hot Spring County, AR	32,923	33,368
31700		Manchester-Nashua, NH Metro area	400,721	405,184
	33011	Hillsborough County, NH	400,721	405,184
31740		Manhattan, KS Metro area	92,719	98,091
	20149	Pottawatomie County, KS	21,604	22,897
	20161	Riley County, KS	71,115	75,194
31820		Manitowoc, WI Micro area	81,442	80,160
	55071	Manitowoc County, WI	81,442	80,160
31860		Mankato-North Mankato, MN Metro area	96,740	98,478
	27013	Blue Earth County, MN	64,013	65,385
	27103	Nicollet County, MN	32,727	33,093
31900		Mansfield, OH Metro area	124,475	121,942
	39139	Richland County, OH	124,475	121,942
31930		Marietta, OH Micro area	61,778	61,213
	39167	Washington County, OH	61,778	61,213
31940		Marinette, WI-MI Micro area	65,778	65,012
	26109	Menominee County, MI	24,029	23,714
	55075	Marinette County, WI	41,749	41,298
31980		Marion, IN Micro area	70,061	68,569
	18053	Grant County, IN	70,061	68,569
32000		Marion, NC Micro area	44,996	44,965
	37111	McDowell County, NC	44,996	44,965
32020		Marion, OH Micro area	66,501	65,720
	39101	Marion County, OH	66,501	65,720
32100		Marquette, MI Micro area	67,077	67,676
	26103	Marquette County, MI	67,077	67,676
32140		Marshall, MN Micro area	25,857	25,665
	27083	Lyon County, MN	25,857	25,665
32180		Marshall, MO Micro area	23,370	23,347
	29195	Saline County, MO	23,370	23,347
32220		Marshall, TX Micro area	65,631	67,336
	48203	Harrison County, TX	65,631	67,336
32260		Marshalltown, IA Micro area	40,648	40,866
	19127	Marshall County, IA	40,648	40,866
32280		Martin, TN Micro area	35,021	34,373
	47183	Weakley County, TN	35,021	34,373
32300		Martinsville, VA Micro area	67,972	65,792
	51089	Henry County, VA	54,151	52,081
	51690	Martinsville city, VA	13,821	13,711
32340		Maryville, MO Micro area	23,370	23,081
	29147	Nodaway County, MO	23,370	23,081
32380		Mason City, IA Micro area	51,749	50,878
	19033	Cerro Gordo County, IA	44,151	43,254
	19195	Worth County, IA	7,598	7,624
32460		Mayfield, KY Micro area	37,121	37,618
	21083	Graves County, KY	37,121	37,618
32500		Maysville, KY Micro area	17,490	17,166
	21161	Mason County, KY	17,490	17,166
32540		McAlester, OK Micro area	45,837	44,626
	40121	Pittsburg County, OK	45,837	44,626
32580		McAllen-Edinburg-Mission, TX Metro area	774,769	831,073
	48215	Hidalgo County, TX	774,769	831,073
32620		McComb, MS Micro area	53,535	52,687
	28005	Amite County, MS	13,131	12,629
	28113	Pike County, MS	40,404	40,058
32660		McMinnville, TN Micro area	39,839	39,969
	47177	Warren County, TN	39,839	39,969
32700		McPherson, KS Micro area	29,180	29,241
	20113	McPherson County, KS	29,180	29,241
32740		Meadville, PA Micro area	88,765	87,175
	42039	Crawford County, PA	88,765	87,175
32780		Medford, OR Metro area	203,206	210,287
	41029	Jackson County, OR	203,206	210,287
32820		Memphis, TN-MS-AR Metro area	1,324,829	1,343,230
	05035	Crittenden County, AR	50,902	49,548
	28009	Benton County, MS	8,729	8,296
	28033	DeSoto County, MS	161,252	170,913
	28093	Marshall County, MS	37,144	36,234
	28137	Tate County, MS	28,886	28,204
	28143	Tunica County, MS	10,778	10,598
	47047	Fayette County, TN	38,413	39,011
	47157	Shelby County, TN	927,644	938,803
	47167	Tipton County, TN	61,081	61,623
32860		Menomonie, WI Micro area	43,857	44,305
	55033	Dunn County, WI	43,857	44,305
32900		Merced, CA Metro area	255,793	266,353
	06047	Merced County, CA	255,793	266,353
32940		Meridian, MS Micro area	107,449	106,201
	28023	Clarke County, MS	16,732	16,299
	28069	Kemper County, MS	10,456	10,163
	28075	Lauderdale County, MS	80,261	79,739
32980		Merrill, WI Micro area	28,743	28,493
	55069	Lincoln County, WI	28,743	28,493
33020		Mexico, MO Micro area	25,529	25,887
	29007	Audrain County, MO	25,529	25,887
33060		Miami, OK Micro area	31,848	32,105
	40115	Ottawa County, OK	31,848	32,105
33100		Miami-Fort Lauderdale-West Palm Beach, FL Metro area	5,564,635	5,929,819
33100		Fort Lauderdale-Pompano Beach-Deerfield Beach, FL Metro Div 22744	1,748,066	1,869,235
	12011	Broward County, FL	1,748,066	1,869,235
33100		Miami-Miami Beach-Kendall, FL Metro Div 33124	2,496,435	2,662,874
	12086	Miami-Dade County, FL	2,496,435	2,662,874
33100		West Palm Beach-Boca Raton-Delray Beach, FL Metro Div 48424	1,320,134	1,397,710
	12099	Palm Beach County, FL	1,320,134	1,397,710
33140		Michigan City-La Porte, IN Metro area	111,467	111,444
	18091	LaPorte County, IN	111,467	111,444
33180		Middlesborough, KY Micro area	28,691	27,778
	21013	Bell County, KY	28,691	27,778
33220		Midland, MI Metro area	83,629	83,427
	26111	Midland County, MI	83,629	83,427
33260		Midland, TX Metro area	141,671	161,290
	48317	Martin County, TX	4,799	5,460
	48329	Midland County, TX	136,872	155,830
33300		Milledgeville, GA Micro area	55,149	54,418
	13009	Baldwin County, GA	45,720	45,909
	13141	Hancock County, GA	9,429	8,509
33340		Milwaukee-Waukesha-West Allis, WI Metro area	1,555,908	1,572,245
	55079	Milwaukee County, WI	947,735	956,406
	55089	Ozaukee County, WI	86,395	87,470
	55131	Washington County, WI	131,887	133,251
	55133	Waukesha County, WI	389,891	395,118
33420		Mineral Wells, TX Micro area	28,111	28,096
	48363	Palo Pinto County, TX	28,111	28,096
33460		Minneapolis-St. Paul-Bloomington, MN Metro area	3,348,859	3,495,176
	27003	Anoka County, MN	330,844	341,864
	27019	Carver County, MN	91,042	97,338
	27025	Chisago County, MN	53,887	54,025
	27037	Dakota County, MN	398,552	412,529
	27053	Hennepin County, MN	1,152,425	1,212,064
	27059	Isanti County, MN	37,816	38,413
	27079	Le Sueur County, MN	27,703	27,770
	27095	Mille Lacs County, MN	26,097	25,884
	27123	Ramsey County, MN	508,640	532,655
	27139	Scott County, MN	129,928	139,672

Core Based Statistical Areas (Metropolitan and Micropolitan), Metropolitan Divisions, and Components (as defined February 2013)

Core Based Statistical Areas (Metropolitan and Micropolitan), Metropolitan Divisions, and Components (as defined February 2013)

Core based statistical area	State/County FIPS code	Title and Geographic Components	2010 Census Population	2014 Estimated Population
	27141	Sherburne County, MN	88,499	91,126
	27143	Sibley County, MN	15,226	14,918
	27163	Washington County, MN	238,136	249,283
	27171	Wright County, MN	124,700	129,918
	55093	Pierce County, WI	41,019	40,958
	55109	St. Croix County, WI	84,345	86,759
33500		Minot, ND Micro area	69,540	77,959
	38049	McHenry County, ND	5,395	5,988
	38075	Renville County, ND	2,470	2,587
	38101	Ward County, ND	61,675	69,384
33540		Missoula, MT Metro area	109,299	112,684
	30063	Missoula County, MT	109,299	112,684
33580		Mitchell, SD Micro area	22,835	23,304
	46035	Davison County, SD	19,504	19,885
	46061	Hanson County, SD	3,331	3,419
33620		Moberly, MO Micro area	25,414	25,072
	29175	Randolph County, MO	25,414	25,072
33660		Mobile, AL Metro area	412,992	415,123
	01097	Mobile County, AL	412,992	415,123
33700		Modesto, CA Metro area	514,453	531,997
	06099	Stanislaus County, CA	514,453	531,997
33740		Monroe, LA Metro area	176,441	178,864
	22073	Ouachita Parish, LA	153,720	156,325
	22111	Union Parish, LA	22,721	22,539
33780		Monroe, MI Metro area	152,021	149,824
	26115	Monroe County, MI	152,021	149,824
33860		Montgomery, AL Metro area	374,536	373,141
	01001	Autauga County, AL	54,571	55,395
	01051	Elmore County, AL	79,303	80,977
	01085	Lowndes County, AL	11,299	10,580
	01101	Montgomery County, AL	229,363	226,189
33940		Montrose, CO Micro area	41,276	40,873
	08085	Montrose County, CO	41,276	40,873
33980		Morehead City, NC Micro area	66,469	68,811
	37031	Carteret County, NC	66,469	68,811
34020		Morgan City, LA Micro area	54,650	53,162
	22101	St. Mary Parish, LA	54,650	53,162
34060		Morgantown, WV Metro area	129,709	137,251
	54061	Monongalia County, WV	96,189	103,463
	54077	Preston County, WV	33,520	33,788
34100		Morristown, TN Metro area	113,951	115,713
	47063	Hamblen County, TN	62,544	63,036
	47089	Jefferson County, TN	51,407	52,677
34140		Moscow, ID Micro area	37,244	38,411
	16057	Latah County, ID	37,244	38,411
34180		Moses Lake, WA Micro area	89,120	93,147
	53025	Grant County, WA	89,120	93,147
34220		Moultrie, GA Micro area	45,498	46,102
	13071	Colquitt County, GA	45,498	46,102
34260		Mountain Home, AR Micro area	41,513	40,857
	05005	Baxter County, AR	41,513	40,857
34300		Mountain Home, ID Micro area	27,038	26,094
	16039	Elmore County, ID	27,038	26,094
34340		Mount Airy, NC Micro area	73,673	72,968
	37171	Surry County, NC	73,673	72,968
34380		Mount Pleasant, MI Micro area	70,311	70,616
	26073	Isabella County, MI	70,311	70,616
34420		Mount Pleasant, TX Micro area	32,334	32,506
	48449	Titus County, TX	32,334	32,506
34460		Mount Sterling, KY Micro area	44,396	45,967
	21011	Bath County, KY	11,591	12,206
	21165	Menifee County, KY	6,306	6,287
	21173	Montgomery County, KY	26,499	27,474
34500		Mount Vernon, IL Micro area	38,827	38,534
	17081	Jefferson County, IL	38,827	38,534
34540		Mount Vernon, OH Micro area	60,921	61,167
	39083	Knox County, OH	60,921	61,167
34580		Mount Vernon-Anacortes, WA Metro area	116,901	120,365
	53057	Skagit County, WA	116,901	120,365
34620		Muncie, IN Metro area	117,671	117,074
	18035	Delaware County, IN	117,671	117,074
34660		Murray, KY Micro area	37,191	38,282
	21035	Calloway County, KY	37,191	38,282
34700		Muscatine, IA Micro area	42,745	42,903
	19139	Muscatine County, IA	42,745	42,903
34740		Muskegon, MI Metro area	172,188	172,344
	26121	Muskegon County, MI	172,188	172,344
34780		Muskogee, OK Micro area	70,990	69,966
	40101	Muskogee County, OK	70,990	69,966
34820		Myrtle Beach-Conway-North Myrtle Beach, NC-SC Metro area	376,722	417,668
	37019	Brunswick County, NC	107,431	118,836
	45051	Horry County, SC	269,291	298,832
34860		Nacogdoches, TX Micro area	64,524	65,301
	48347	Nacogdoches County, TX	64,524	65,301
34900		Napa, CA Metro area	136,484	141,667
	06055	Napa County, CA	136,484	141,667
34940		Naples-Immokalee-Marco Island, FL Metro area	321,520	348,777
	12021	Collier County, FL	321,520	348,777
34980		Nashville-Davidson–Murfreesboro–Franklin, TN Metro area	1,670,890	1,792,649
	47015	Cannon County, TN	13,801	13,757
	47021	Cheatham County, TN	39,105	39,764
	47037	Davidson County, TN	626,681	668,347
	47043	Dickson County, TN	49,666	50,575
	47081	Hickman County, TN	24,690	24,384
	47111	Macon County, TN	22,248	23,003
	47119	Maury County, TN	80,956	85,515
	47147	Robertson County, TN	66,283	68,079
	47149	Rutherford County, TN	262,604	288,906
	47159	Smith County, TN	19,166	19,009
	47165	Sumner County, TN	160,645	172,706
	47169	Trousdale County, TN	7,870	8,002
	47187	Williamson County, TN	183,182	205,226
	47189	Wilson County, TN	113,993	125,376
35020		Natchez, MS-LA Micro area	53,119	52,203
	22029	Concordia Parish, LA	20,822	20,466
	28001	Adams County, MS	32,297	31,737
35060		Natchitoches, LA Micro area	39,566	39,166
	22069	Natchitoches Parish, LA	39,566	39,166
35100		New Bern, NC Metro area	126,802	127,534
	37049	Craven County, NC	103,505	104,510
	37103	Jones County, NC	10,153	10,076
	37137	Pamlico County, NC	13,144	12,948
35140		Newberry, SC Micro area	37,508	37,783
	45071	Newberry County, SC	37,508	37,783
35220		New Castle, IN Micro area	49,462	48,995
	18065	Henry County, IN	49,462	48,995
35260		New Castle, PA Micro area	91,108	88,771
	42073	Lawrence County, PA	91,108	88,771
35300		New Haven-Milford, CT Metro area	862,477	861,277
	09009	New Haven County, CT	862,477	861,277
35380		New Orleans-Metairie, LA Metro area	1,189,866	1,251,849
	22051	Jefferson Parish, LA	432,552	435,716
	22071	Orleans Parish, LA	343,829	384,320
	22075	Plaquemines Parish, LA	23,042	23,447
	22087	St. Bernard Parish, LA	35,897	44,409
	22089	St. Charles Parish, LA	52,780	52,745
	22093	St. James Parish, LA	22,102	21,638
	22095	St. John the Baptist Parish, LA	45,924	43,745
	22103	St. Tammany Parish, LA	233,740	245,829
35420		New Philadelphia-Dover, OH Micro area	92,582	92,788
	39157	Tuscarawas County, OH	92,582	92,788
35440		Newport, OR Micro area	46,034	46,406
	41041	Lincoln County, OR	46,034	46,406
35460		Newport, TN Micro area	35,662	35,374
	47029	Cocke County, TN	35,662	35,374
35500		Newton, IA Micro area	36,842	36,872
	19099	Jasper County, IA	36,842	36,872
35580		New Ulm, MN Micro area	25,893	25,292
	27015	Brown County, MN	25,893	25,292
35620		New York-Newark-Jersey City, NY-NJ-PA Metro area	19,567,410	20,092,883
35620		Dutchess County-Putnam County, NY Metro Div 20524	397,198	396,066
35620	36027	Dutchess County, NY	297,488	296,579
	36079	Putnam County, NY	99,710	99,487
35620		Nassau County-Suffolk County, NY Metro Div 35004	2,832,882	2,861,595
	36059	Nassau County, NY	1,339,532	1,358,627
	36103	Suffolk County, NY	1,493,350	1,502,968
35620		Newark, NJ-PA Metro Div 35084	2,471,171	2,508,124
	34013	Essex County, NJ	783,969	795,723
	34019	Hunterdon County, NJ	128,349	126,067
	34027	Morris County, NJ	492,276	499,727
	34035	Somerset County, NJ	323,444	332,568
	34037	Sussex County, NJ	149,265	144,909
	34039	Union County, NJ	536,499	552,939
	42103	Pike County, PA	57,369	56,191
35620		New York-Jersey City-White Plains, NY-NJ Metro Div 35614	13,866,159	14,327,098
	34003	Bergen County, NJ	905,116	933,572
	34017	Hudson County, NJ	634,266	669,115
	34023	Middlesex County, NJ	809,858	836,297
	34025	Monmouth County, NJ	630,380	629,279
	34029	Ocean County, NJ	576,567	586,301
	34031	Passaic County, NJ	501,226	508,856
	36005	Bronx County, NY	1,385,108	1,438,159
	36047	Kings County, NY	2,504,700	2,621,793

Core Based Statistical Areas (Metropolitan and Micropolitan), Metropolitan Divisions, and Components (as defined February 2013)

Core based statistical area	State/County FIPS code	Title and Geographic Components	2010 Census Population	2014 Estimated Population
	36061	New York County, NY	1,585,873	1,636,268
	36071	Orange County, NY	372,813	376,099
	36081	Queens County, NY	2,230,722	2,321,580
	36085	Richmond County, NY	468,730	473,279
	36087	Rockland County, NY	311,687	323,866
	36119	Westchester County, NY	949,113	972,634
35660		Niles-Benton Harbor, MI Metro area	156,813	155,233
	26021	Berrien County, MI	156,813	155,233
35700		Nogales, AZ Micro area	47,420	46,695
	04023	Santa Cruz County, AZ	47,420	46,695
35740		Norfolk, NE Micro area	48,271	48,445
	31119	Madison County, NE	34,876	35,174
	31139	Pierce County, NE	7,266	7,202
	31167	Stanton County, NE	6,129	6,069
35820		North Platte, NE Micro area	37,590	37,063
	31111	Lincoln County, NE	36,288	35,815
	31113	Logan County, NE	763	750
	31117	McPherson County, NE	539	498
35840		North Port-Sarasota-Bradenton, FL Metro area	702,281	748,708
	12081	Manatee County, FL	322,833	351,746
	12115	Sarasota County, FL	379,448	396,962
35860		North Vernon, IN Micro area	28,525	28,000
	18079	Jennings County, IN	28,525	28,000
35900		North Wilkesboro, NC Micro area	69,340	68,838
	37193	Wilkes County, NC	69,340	68,838
35940		Norwalk, OH Micro area	59,626	58,714
	39077	Huron County, OH	59,626	58,714
35980		Norwich-New London, CT Metro area	274,055	273,676
	09011	New London County, CT	274,055	273,676
36020		Oak Harbor, WA Micro area	78,506	79,275
	53029	Island County, WA	78,506	79,275
36100		Ocala, FL Metro area	331,298	339,167
	12083	Marion County, FL	331,298	339,167
36140		Ocean City, NJ Metro area	97,265	95,344
	34009	Cape May County, NJ	97,265	95,344
36220		Odessa, TX Metro area	137,130	153,904
	48135	Ector County, TX	137,130	153,904
36260		Ogden-Clearfield, UT Metro area	597,159	632,293
	49003	Box Elder County, UT	49,975	51,518
	49011	Davis County, UT	306,479	329,692
	49029	Morgan County, UT	9,469	10,608
	49057	Weber County, UT	231,236	240,475
36300		Ogdensburg-Massena, NY Micro area	111,944	111,400
	36089	St. Lawrence County, NY	111,944	111,400
36340		Oil City, PA Micro area	54,984	53,529
	42121	Venango County, PA	54,984	53,529
36380		Okeechobee, FL Micro area	39,996	39,149
	12093	Okeechobee County, FL	39,996	39,149
36420		Oklahoma City, OK Metro area	1,252,987	1,336,767
	40017	Canadian County, OK	115,541	129,582
	40027	Cleveland County, OK	255,755	269,908
	40051	Grady County, OK	52,431	53,854
	40081	Lincoln County, OK	34,273	34,619
	40083	Logan County, OK	41,848	45,276
	40087	McClain County, OK	34,506	37,313
	40109	Oklahoma County, OK	718,633	766,215
36460		Olean, NY Micro area	80,317	78,600
	36009	Cattaraugus County, NY	80,317	78,600
36500		Olympia-Tumwater, WA Metro area	252,264	265,851
	53067	Thurston County, WA	252,264	265,851
36540		Omaha-Council Bluffs, NE-IA Metro area	865,350	904,421
	19085	Harrison County, IA	14,928	14,324
	19129	Mills County, IA	15,059	14,831
	19155	Pottawattamie County, IA	93,158	93,128
	31025	Cass County, NE	25,241	25,524
	31055	Douglas County, NE	517,110	543,244
	31153	Sarpy County, NE	158,840	172,193
	31155	Saunders County, NE	20,780	20,919
	31177	Washington County, NE	20,234	20,258
36580		Oneonta, NY Micro area	62,259	61,128
	36077	Otsego County, NY	62,259	61,128
36620		Ontario, OR-ID Micro area	53,936	53,195
	16075	Payette County, ID	22,623	22,836
	41045	Malheur County, OR	31,313	30,359
36660		Opelousas, LA Micro area	83,384	83,709
	22097	St. Landry Parish, LA	83,384	83,709
36700		Orangeburg, SC Micro area	92,501	90,090
	45075	Orangeburg County, SC	92,501	90,090
36740		Orlando-Kissimmee-Sanford, FL Metro	2,134,411	2,321,418
	12069	Lake County, FL	297,052	315,690
	12095	Orange County, FL	1,145,956	1,253,001
	12097	Osceola County, FL	268,685	310,211
	12117	Seminole County, FL	422,718	442,516
36780		Oshkosh-Neenah, WI Metro area	166,994	169,511
	55139	Winnebago County, WI	166,994	169,511
36820		Oskaloosa, IA Micro area	22,381	22,370
	19123	Mahaska County, IA	22,381	22,370
36830		Othello, WA Micro area	18,728	19,179
	53001	Adams County, WA	18,728	19,179
36840		Ottawa, KS Micro area	25,992	25,611
	20059	Franklin County, KS	25,992	25,611
36860		Ottawa-Peru, IL Micro area	154,908	150,895
	17011	Bureau County, IL	34,978	33,840
	17099	LaSalle County, IL	113,924	111,241
	17155	Putnam County, IL	6,006	5,814
36900		Ottumwa, IA Micro area	44,378	43,993
	19051	Davis County, IA	8,753	8,781
	19179	Wapello County, IA	35,625	35,212
36940		Owatonna, MN Micro area	36,576	36,573
	27147	Steele County, MN	36,576	36,573
36980		Owensboro, KY Metro area	114,752	116,506
	21059	Daviess County, KY	96,656	98,275
	21091	Hancock County, KY	8,565	8,753
	21149	McLean County, KY	9,531	9,478
37020		Owosso, MI Micro area	70,648	68,933
	26155	Shiawassee County, MI	70,648	68,933
37060		Oxford, MS Micro area	47,351	52,930
	28071	Lafayette County, MS	47,351	52,930
37080		Oxford, NC Micro area	59,916	58,500
	37077	Granville County, NC	59,916	58,500
37100		Oxnard-Thousand Oaks-Ventura, CA Metro area	823,318	846,178
	06111	Ventura County, CA	823,318	846,178
37120		Ozark, AL Micro area	50,251	49,484
	01045	Dale County, AL	50,251	49,484
37140		Paducah, KY-IL Micro area	98,762	97,820
	17127	Massac County, IL	15,429	14,905
	21007	Ballard County, KY	8,249	8,240
	21139	Livingston County, KY	9,519	9,359
	21145	McCracken County, KY	65,565	65,316
37220		Pahrump, NV Micro area	43,946	42,282
	32023	Nye County, NV	43,946	42,282
37260		Palatka, FL Micro area	74,364	72,143
	12107	Putnam County, FL	74,364	72,143
37300		Palestine, TX Micro area	58,458	57,627
	48001	Anderson County, TX	58,458	57,627
37340		Palm Bay-Melbourne-Titusville, FL Metro area	543,376	556,885
	12009	Brevard County, FL	543,376	556,885
37420		Pampa, TX Micro area	22,535	23,044
	48179	Gray County, TX	22,535	23,044
37460		Panama City, FL Metro area	184,715	194,929
	12005	Bay County, FL	168,852	178,985
	12045	Gulf County, FL	15,863	15,944
37500		Paragould, AR Micro area	42,090	43,694
	05055	Greene County, AR	42,090	43,694
37540		Paris, TN Micro area	32,330	32,204
	47079	Henry County, TN	32,330	32,204
37580		Paris, TX Micro area	49,793	49,523
	48277	Lamar County, TX	49,793	49,523
37620		Parkersburg-Vienna, WV Metro area	92,673	92,082
	54105	Wirt County, WV	5,717	5,845
	54107	Wood County, WV	86,956	86,237
37660		Parsons, KS Micro area	21,607	20,960
	20099	Labette County, KS	21,607	20,960
37740		Payson, AZ Micro area	53,597	53,119
	04007	Gila County, AZ	53,597	53,119
37780		Pecos, TX Micro area	13,783	14,349
	48389	Reeves County, TX	13,783	14,349
37860		Pensacola-Ferry Pass-Brent, FL Metro area	448,991	474,081
	12033	Escambia County, FL	297,619	310,659
	12113	Santa Rosa County, FL	151,372	163,422
37900		Peoria, IL Metro area	379,186	380,040
	17123	Marshall County, IL	12,640	12,014
	17143	Peoria County, IL	186,494	187,319
	17175	Stark County, IL	5,994	5,813
	17179	Tazewell County, IL	135,394	135,707
	17203	Woodford County, IL	38,664	39,187
37940		Peru, IN Micro area	36,903	35,954
	18103	Miami County, IN	36,903	35,954
37980		Philadelphia-Camden-Wilmington, PA-NJ-DE-MD Metro area	5,965,343	6,051,170
37980		Camden, NJ Metro Div 15804	1,250,679	1,251,711
	34005	Burlington County, NJ	448,734	449,722
	34007	Camden County, NJ	513,657	511,038
	34015	Gloucester County, NJ	288,288	290,951
37980		Montgomery County-Bucks County-Chester County, PA Metro Div 33874	1,924,009	1,956,326
	42017	Bucks County, PA	625,249	626,685

Core Based Statistical Areas (Metropolitan and Micropolitan), Metropolitan Divisions, and Components (as defined February 2013)

Core based statistical area	State/County FIPS code	Title and Geographic Components	2010 Census Population	2014 Estimated Population
	42029	Chester County, PA	498,886	512,784
	42091	Montgomery County, PA	799,874	816,857
37980		Philadelphia, PA Metro Div 37964	2,084,985	2,123,257
	42045	Delaware County, PA	558,979	562,960
	42101	Philadelphia County, PA	1,526,006	1,560,297
37980		Wilmington, DE-MD-NJ Metro Div 48864	705,670	719,876
	10003	New Castle County, Delaware	538,479	552,778
	24015	Cecil County, MD	101,108	102,383
	34033	Salem County, NJ	66,083	64,715
38060		Phoenix-Mesa-Scottsdale, AZ Metro area	4,192,887	4,489,109
	04013	Maricopa County, AZ	3,817,117	4,087,191
	04021	Pinal County, AZ	375,770	401,918
38100		Picayune, MS Micro area	55,834	55,224
	28109	Pearl River County, MS	55,834	55,224
38180		Pierre, SD Micro area	21,361	22,063
	46065	Hughes County, SD	17,022	17,642
	46117	Stanley County, SD	2,966	2,983
	46119	Sully County, SD	1,373	1,438
38220		Pine Bluff, AR Metro area	100,258	94,716
	05025	Cleveland County, AR	8,689	8,449
	05069	Jefferson County, AR	77,435	72,297
	05079	Lincoln County, AR	14,134	13,970
38240		Pinehurst-Southern Pines, NC Micro area	88,247	93,077
	37125	Moore County, NC	88,247	93,077
38260		Pittsburg, KS Micro area	39,134	39,290
	20037	Crawford County, KS	39,134	39,290
38300		Pittsburgh, PA Metro area	2,356,285	2,355,968
	42003	Allegheny County, PA	1,223,348	1,231,255
	42005	Armstrong County, PA	68,941	67,785
	42007	Beaver County, PA	170,539	169,392
	42019	Butler County, PA	183,862	185,943
	42051	Fayette County, PA	136,606	134,086
	42125	Washington County, PA	207,820	208,187
	42129	Westmoreland County, PA	365,169	359,320
38340		Pittsfield, MA Metro area	131,219	128,715
	25003	Berkshire County, MA	131,219	128,715
38380		Plainview, TX Micro area	36,273	34,720
	48189	Hale County, TX	36,273	34,720
38420		Platteville, WI Micro area	51,208	51,829
	55043	Grant County, WI	51,208	51,829
38460		Plattsburgh, NY Micro area	82,128	81,632
	36019	Clinton County, NY	82,128	81,632
38500		Plymouth, IN Micro area	47,051	47,107
	18099	Marshall County, IN	47,051	47,107
38540		Pocatello, ID Metro area	82,839	83,347
	16005	Bannock County, ID	82,839	83,347
38580		Point Pleasant, WV-OH Micro area	58,258	57,413
	39053	Gallia County, OH	30,934	30,397
	54053	Mason County, WV	27,324	27,016
38620		Ponca City, OK Micro area	46,562	45,478
	40071	Kay County, OK	46,562	45,478
38700		Pontiac, IL Micro area	38,950	37,903
	17105	Livingston County, IL	38,950	37,903
38740		Poplar Bluff, MO Micro area	42,794	42,972
	29023	Butler County, MO	42,794	42,972
38780		Portales, NM Micro area	19,846	19,536
	35041	Roosevelt County, NM	19,846	19,536
38820		Port Angeles, WA Micro area	71,404	72,715
	53009	Clallam County, WA	71,404	72,715
38840		Port Clinton, OH Micro area	41,428	41,154
	39123	Ottawa County, OH	41,428	41,154
38860		Portland-South Portland, ME Metro area	514,098	523,552
	23005	Cumberland County, ME	281,674	287,797
	23023	Sagadahoc County, ME	35,293	35,045
	23031	York County, ME	197,131	200,710
38900		Portland-Vancouver-Hillsboro, OR-WA Metro area	2,226,009	2,348,247
	41005	Clackamas County, OR	375,992	394,972
	41009	Columbia County, OR	49,351	49,459
	41051	Multnomah County, OR	735,334	776,712
	41067	Washington County, OR	529,710	562,998
	41071	Yamhill County, OR	99,193	101,758
	53011	Clark County, WA	425,363	451,008
	53059	Skamania County, WA	11,066	11,340
38920		Port Lavaca, TX Micro area	21,381	21,797
	48057	Calhoun County, TX	21,381	21,797
38940		Port St. Lucie, FL Metro area	424,107	444,420
	12085	Martin County, FL	146,318	153,392
	12111	St. Lucie County, FL	277,789	291,028
39020		Portsmouth, OH Micro area	79,499	77,258
	39145	Scioto County, OH	79,499	77,258
39060		Pottsville, PA Micro area	148,289	145,797
	42107	Schuylkill County, PA	148,289	145,797
39140		Prescott, AZ Metro area	211,033	218,844
	04025	Yavapai County, AZ	211,033	218,844

Core Based Statistical Areas (Metropolitan and Micropolitan), Metropolitan Divisions, and Components (as defined February 2013)

Core based statistical area	State/County FIPS code	Title and Geographic Components	2010 Census Population	2014 Estimated Population
39220		Price, UT Micro area	21,403	20,660
	49007	Carbon County, UT	21,403	20,660
39260		Prineville, OR Micro area	20,978	20,998
	41013	Crook County, OR	20,978	20,998
39300		Providence-Warwick, RI-MA Metro area	1,600,852	1,609,367
	25005	Bristol County, MA	548,285	554,194
	44001	Bristol County, RI	49,875	49,060
	44003	Kent County, RI	166,158	165,128
	44005	Newport County, RI	82,888	82,358
	44007	Providence County, RI	626,667	631,974
	44009	Washington County, RI	126,979	126,653
39340		Provo-Orem, UT Metro area	526,810	571,460
	49023	Juab County, UT	10,246	10,486
	49049	Utah County, UT	516,564	560,974
39380		Pueblo, CO Metro area	159,063	161,875
	08101	Pueblo County, CO	159,063	161,875
39420		Pullman, WA Micro area	44,776	46,827
	53075	Whitman County, WA	44,776	46,827
39460		Punta Gorda, FL Metro area	159,978	168,474
	12015	Charlotte County, FL	159,978	168,474
39500		Quincy, IL-MO Micro area	77,314	77,126
	17001	Adams County, IL	67,103	66,988
	29111	Lewis County, MO	10,211	10,138
39540		Racine, WI Metro area	195,408	195,163
	55101	Racine County, WI	195,408	195,163
39580		Raleigh, NC Metro area	1,130,490	1,242,974
	37069	Franklin County, NC	60,619	62,860
	37101	Johnston County, NC	168,878	181,423
	37183	Wake County, NC	900,993	998,691
39660		Rapid City, SD Metro area	134,598	143,638
	46033	Custer County, SD	8,216	8,445
	46093	Meade County, SD	25,434	26,951
	46103	Pennington County, SD	100,948	108,242
39700		Raymondville, TX Micro area	22,134	21,903
	48489	Willacy County, TX	22,134	21,903
39740		Reading, PA Metro area	411,442	413,691
	42011	Berks County, PA	411,442	413,691
39780		Red Bluff, CA Micro area	63,463	63,067
	06103	Tehama County, CA	63,463	63,067
39820		Redding, CA Metro area	177,223	179,804
	06089	Shasta County, CA	177,223	179,804
39860		Red Wing, MN Micro area	46,183	46,423
	27049	Goodhue County, MN	46,183	46,423
39900		Reno, NV Metro area	425,417	443,990
	32029	Storey County, NV	4,010	3,912
	32031	Washoe County, NV	421,407	440,078
39940		Rexburg, ID Metro area	50,778	50,905
	16043	Fremont County, ID	13,242	12,867
	16065	Madison County, ID	37,536	38,038
39980		Richmond, IN Micro area	68,917	67,671
	18177	Wayne County, IN	68,917	67,671
40060		Richmond, VA Metro area	1,208,101	1,260,029
	51007	Amelia County, VA	12,690	12,855
	51033	Caroline County, VA	28,545	29,778
	51036	Charles City County, VA	7,256	7,023
	51041	Chesterfield County, VA	316,236	332,499
	51053	Dinwiddie County, VA	28,001	27,859
	51075	Goochland County, VA	21,717	21,936
	51085	Hanover County, VA	99,863	101,918
	51087	Henrico County, VA	306,935	321,924
	51101	King William County, VA	15,935	16,186
	51127	New Kent County, VA	18,429	20,021
	51145	Powhatan County, VA	28,046	28,449
	51149	Prince George County, VA	35,725	37,333
	51183	Sussex County, VA	12,087	11,767
	51570	Colonial Heights city, VA	17,411	17,731
	51670	Hopewell city, VA	22,591	22,196
	51730	Petersburg city, VA	32,420	32,701
	51760	Richmond city, VA	204,214	217,853
40080		Richmond-Berea, KY Micro area	99,972	104,166
	21151	Madison County, KY	82,916	87,340
	21203	Rockcastle County, KY	17,056	16,826
40100		Rio Grande City, TX Micro area	60,968	62,955
	48427	Starr County, TX	60,968	62,955
40140		Riverside-San Bernardino-Ontario, CA	4,224,851	4,441,890
	06065	Riverside County, CA	2,189,641	2,329,271
	06071	San Bernardino County, CA	2,035,210	2,112,619
40180		Riverton, WY Micro area	40,123	40,703
	56013	Fremont County, WY	40,123	40,703
40220		Roanoke, VA Metro area	308,707	313,388
	51023	Botetourt County, VA	33,148	33,100
	51045	Craig County, VA	5,190	5,234
	51067	Franklin County, VA	56,159	56,358
	51161	Roanoke County, VA	92,376	93,785
	51770	Roanoke city, VA	97,032	99,428

Core Based Statistical Areas (Metropolitan and Micropolitan), Metropolitan Divisions, and Components (as defined February 2013)

Core based statistical area	State/County FIPS code	Title and Geographic Components	2010 Census Population	2014 Estimated Population
	51775	Salem city, VA	24,802	25,483
40260		Roanoke Rapids, NC Micro area	76,790	73,433
	37083	Halifax County, NC	54,691	52,970
	37131	Northampton County, NC	22,099	20,463
40300		Rochelle, IL Micro area	53,497	52,085
	17141	Ogle County, IL	53,497	52,085
40340		Rochester, MN Metro area	206,877	212,778
	27039	Dodge County, MN	20,087	20,353
	27045	Fillmore County, MN	20,866	20,776
	27109	Olmsted County, MN	144,248	150,287
	27157	Wabasha County, MN	21,676	21,362
40380		Rochester, NY Metro area	1,079,671	1,083,393
	36051	Livingston County, NY	65,393	64,586
	36055	Monroe County, NY	744,344	749,857
	36069	Ontario County, NY	107,931	109,707
	36073	Orleans County, NY	42,883	41,984
	36117	Wayne County, NY	93,772	92,051
	36123	Yates County, NY	25,348	25,208
40420		Rockford, IL Metro area	349,431	342,411
	17007	Boone County, IL	54,165	53,869
	17201	Winnebago County, IL	295,266	288,542
40460		Rockingham, NC Micro area	46,639	45,733
	37153	Richmond County, NC	46,639	45,733
40540		Rock Springs, WY Micro area	43,806	45,010
	56037	Sweetwater County, WY	43,806	45,010
40580		Rocky Mount, NC Metro area	152,392	149,290
	37065	Edgecombe County, NC	56,552	54,933
	37127	Nash County, NC	95,840	94,357
40620		Rolla, MO Micro area	45,156	44,847
	29161	Phelps County, MO	45,156	44,847
40660		Rome, GA Metro area	96,317	96,063
	13115	Floyd County, GA	96,317	96,063
40700		Roseburg, OR Micro area	107,667	106,972
	41019	Douglas County, OR	107,667	106,972
40740		Roswell, NM Micro area	65,645	65,878
	35005	Chaves County, NM	65,645	65,878
40780		Russellville, AR Micro area	83,939	85,152
	05115	Pope County, AR	61,754	63,201
	05149	Yell County, AR	22,185	21,951
40820		Ruston, LA Micro area	46,735	47,617
	22061	Lincoln Parish, LA	46,735	47,617
40860		Rutland, VT Micro area	61,642	60,086
	50021	Rutland County, VT	61,642	60,086
40900		Sacramento–Roseville–Arden-Arcade, CA Metro area	2,149,127	2,244,397
	06017	El Dorado County, CA	181,058	183,087
	06061	Placer County, CA	348,432	371,694
	06067	Sacramento County, CA	1,418,788	1,482,026
	06113	Yolo County, CA	200,849	207,590
40940		Safford, AZ Micro area	37,220	37,957
	04009	Graham County, AZ	37,220	37,957
40980		Saginaw, MI Metro area	200,169	195,012
	26145	Saginaw County, MI	200,169	195,012
41060		St. Cloud, MN Metro area	189,093	192,418
	27009	Benton County, MN	38,451	39,506
	27145	Stearns County, MN	150,642	152,912
41100		St. George, UT Metro area	138,115	151,948
	49053	Washington County, UT	138,115	151,948
41140		St. Joseph, MO-KS Metro area	127,329	127,431
	20043	Doniphan County, KS	7,945	7,874
	29003	Andrew County, MO	17,291	17,379
	29021	Buchanan County, MO	89,201	89,486
	29063	DeKalb County, MO	12,892	12,692
41180		St. Louis, MO-IL Metro area	2,787,701	2,806,207
	17005	Bond County, IL	17,768	17,269
	17013	Calhoun County, IL	5,089	4,956
	17027	Clinton County, IL	37,762	37,857
	17083	Jersey County, IL	22,985	22,571
	17117	Macoupin County, IL	47,765	46,453
	17119	Madison County, IL	269,282	266,560
	17133	Monroe County, IL	32,957	33,722
	17163	St. Clair County, IL	270,056	265,729
	29071	Franklin County, MO	101,492	102,084
	29099	Jefferson County, MO	218,733	222,716
	29113	Lincoln County, MO	52,566	54,249
	29183	St. Charles County, MO	360,485	379,493
	29189	St. Louis County, MO	998,954	1,001,876
	29219	Warren County, MO	32,513	33,253
	29510	St. Louis city, MO	319,294	317,419
41220		St. Marys, GA Micro area	50,513	52,027
	13039	Camden County, GA	50,513	52,027
41400		Salem, OH Micro area	107,841	105,686
	39029	Columbiana County, OH	107,841	105,686
41420		Salem, OR Metro area	390,738	404,026
	41047	Marion County, OR	315,335	326,110
	41053	Polk County, OR	75,403	77,916
41460		Salina, KS Micro area	61,697	61,820
	20143	Ottawa County, KS	6,091	6,065
	20169	Saline County, KS	55,606	55,755
41500		Salinas, CA Metro area	415,057	431,344
	06053	Monterey County, CA	415,057	431,344
41540		Salisbury, MD-DE Metro area	373,802	389,922
	10005	Sussex County, DE	197,145	210,849
	24039	Somerset County, MD	26,470	25,859
	24045	Wicomico County, MD	98,733	101,539
	24047	Worcester County, MD	51,454	51,675
41620		Salt Lake City, UT Metro area	1,087,873	1,153,340
	49035	Salt Lake County, UT	1,029,655	1,091,742
	49045	Tooele County, UT	58,218	61,598
41660		San Angelo, TX Metro area	111,823	118,182
	48235	Irion County, TX	1,599	1,574
	48451	Tom Green County, TX	110,224	116,608
41700		San Antonio-New Braunfels, TX Metro	2,142,508	2,328,652
	48013	Atascosa County, TX	44,911	47,774
	48019	Bandera County, TX	20,485	20,892
	48029	Bexar County, TX	1,714,773	1,855,866
	48091	Comal County, TX	108,472	123,694
	48187	Guadalupe County, TX	131,533	147,250
	48259	Kendall County, TX	33,410	38,880
	48325	Medina County, TX	46,006	47,894
	48493	Wilson County, TX	42,918	46,402
41740		San Diego-Carlsbad, CA Metro area	3,095,313	3,263,431
	06073	San Diego County, CA	3,095,313	3,263,431
41760		Sandpoint, ID Micro area	40,877	41,585
	16017	Bonner County, ID	40,877	41,585
41780		Sandusky, OH Micro area	77,079	75,828
	39043	Erie County, OH	77,079	75,828
41820		Sanford, NC Micro area	57,866	59,662
	37105	Lee County, NC	57,866	59,662
41860		San Francisco-Oakland-Hayward, CA Metro area	4,335,391	4,594,060
41860		Oakland-Hayward-Berkeley, CA Metro Div 36084	2,559,296	2,722,260
	06001	Alameda County, CA	1,510,271	1,610,921
	06013	Contra Costa County, CA	1,049,025	1,111,339
41860		San Francisco-Redwood City-South San Francisco, CA Metro Div 41884	1,523,686	1,611,050
	06075	San Francisco County, CA	805,235	852,469
	06081	San Mateo County, CA	718,451	758,581
41860		San Rafael, CA Metropolitan Div 42034	252,409	260,750
	06041	Marin County, CA	252,409	260,750
41940		San Jose-Sunnyvale-Santa Clara, CA Metro area	1,836,911	1,952,872
	06069	San Benito County, CA	55,269	58,267
	06085	Santa Clara County, CA	1,781,642	1,894,605
42020		San Luis Obispo-Paso Robles-Arroyo Grande, CA Metro area	269,637	279,083
	06079	San Luis Obispo County, CA	269,637	279,083
42100		Santa Cruz-Watsonville, CA Metro area	262,382	271,804
	06087	Santa Cruz County, CA	262,382	271,804
42140		Santa Fe, NM Metro area	144,170	148,164
	35049	Santa Fe County, NM	144,170	148,164
42200		Santa Maria-Santa Barbara, CA Metro	423,895	440,668
	06083	Santa Barbara County, CA	423,895	440,668
42220		Santa Rosa, CA Metro area	483,878	500,292
	06097	Sonoma County, CA	483,878	500,292
42300		Sault Ste. Marie, MI Micro area	38,520	38,321
	26033	Chippewa County, MI	38,520	38,321
42340		Savannah, GA Metro area	347,611	372,708
	13029	Bryan County, GA	30,233	33,906
	13051	Chatham County, GA	265,128	283,379
	13103	Effingham County, GA	52,250	55,423
42380		Sayre, PA Micro area	62,622	61,784
	42015	Bradford County, PA	62,622	61,784
42420		Scottsbluff, NE Micro area	38,971	38,532
	31007	Banner County, NE	690	764
	31157	Scotts Bluff County, NE	36,970	36,465
	31165	Sioux County, NE	1,311	1,303
42460		Scottsboro, AL Micro area	53,227	52,665
	01071	Jackson County, AL	53,227	52,665
42540		Scranton—Wilkes-Barre—Hazleton, PA Metro area	563,631	559,679
	42069	Lackawanna County, PA	214,437	212,719
	42079	Luzerne County, PA	320,918	318,829
	42131	Wyoming County, PA	28,276	28,131
42620		Searcy, AR Micro area	77,076	78,592
	05145	White County, AR	77,076	78,592
42660		Seattle-Tacoma-Bellevue, WA Metro area	3,439,809	3,671,478
42660		Seattle-Bellevue-Everett, WA Metro Div 42644	2,644,584	2,839,550

Core based statistical area	State/County FIPS code	Title and Geographic Components	2010 Census Population	2014 Estimated Population
	53033	King County, WA	1,931,249	2,079,967
	53061	Snohomish County, WA	713,335	759,583
42660		Tacoma-Lakewood, WA Metro Div 45104	795,225	831,928
	53053	Pierce County, WA	795,225	831,928
42680		Sebastian-Vero Beach, FL Metro area	138,028	144,755
	12061	Indian River County, FL	138,028	144,755
42700		Sebring, FL Metro area	98,786	98,236
	12055	Highlands County, FL	98,786	98,236
42740		Sedalia, MO Micro area	42,201	42,225
	29159	Pettis County, MO	42,201	42,225
42780		Selinsgrove, PA Micro area	39,702	40,323
	42109	Snyder County, PA	39,702	40,323
42820		Selma, AL Micro area	43,820	41,711
	01047	Dallas County, AL	43,820	41,711
42860		Seneca, SC Micro area	74,273	75,192
	45073	Oconee County, SC	74,273	75,192
42900		Seneca Falls, NY Micro area	35,251	34,884
	36099	Seneca County, NY	35,251	34,884
42940		Sevierville, TN Micro area	89,889	95,110
	47155	Sevier County, TN	89,889	95,110
42980		Seymour, IN Micro area	42,376	43,705
	18071	Jackson County, IN	42,376	43,705
43020		Shawano, WI Micro area	46,181	46,101
	55078	Menominee County, WI	4,232	4,522
	55115	Shawano County, WI	41,949	41,579
43060		Shawnee, OK Micro area	69,442	71,811
	40125	Pottawatomie County, OK	69,442	71,811
43100		Sheboygan, WI Metro area	115,507	115,290
	55117	Sheboygan County, WI	115,507	115,290
43140		Shelby, NC Micro area	98,078	97,076
	37045	Cleveland County, NC	98,078	97,076
43180		Shelbyville, TN Micro area	45,058	46,627
	47003	Bedford County, TN	45,058	46,627
43220		Shelton, WA Micro area	60,699	60,711
	53045	Mason County, WA	60,699	60,711
43260		Sheridan, WY Micro area	29,116	30,032
	56033	Sheridan County, WY	29,116	30,032
43300		Sherman-Denison, TX Metro area	120,877	123,534
	48181	Grayson County, TX	120,877	123,534
43320		Show Low, AZ Micro area	107,449	108,101
	04017	Navajo County, AZ	107,449	108,101
43340		Shreveport-Bossier City, LA Metro area	439,811	445,142
	22015	Bossier Parish, LA	116,979	125,064
	22017	Caddo Parish, LA	254,969	252,603
	22031	De Soto Parish, LA	26,656	27,142
	22119	Webster Parish, LA	41,207	40,333
43380		Sidney, OH Micro area	49,423	48,951
	39149	Shelby County, OH	49,423	48,951
43420		Sierra Vista-Douglas, AZ Metro area	131,346	127,448
	04003	Cochise County, AZ	131,346	127,448
43460		Sikeston, MO Micro area	39,191	38,903
	29201	Scott County, MO	39,191	38,903
43500		Silver City, NM Micro area	29,514	29,096
	35017	Grant County, NM	29,514	29,096
43580		Sioux City, IA-NE-SD Metro area	168,563	168,806
	19149	Plymouth County, IA	24,986	24,874
	19193	Woodbury County, IA	102,172	102,271
	31043	Dakota County, NE	21,006	20,850
	31051	Dixon County, NE	6,000	5,782
	46127	Union County, SD	14,399	15,029
43620		Sioux Falls, SD Metro area	228,261	248,351
	46083	Lincoln County, SD	44,828	51,548
	46087	McCook County, SD	5,618	5,649
	46099	Minnehaha County, SD	169,468	182,882
	46125	Turner County, SD	8,347	8,272
43660		Snyder, TX Micro area	16,921	17,328
	48415	Scurry County, TX	16,921	17,328
43700		Somerset, KY Micro area	63,063	63,825
	21199	Pulaski County, KY	63,063	63,825
43740		Somerset, PA Micro area	77,742	76,218
	42111	Somerset County, PA	77,742	76,218
43760		Sonora, CA Micro area	55,365	53,831
	06109	Tuolumne County, CA	55,365	53,831
43780		South Bend-Mishawaka, IN-MI Metro area	319,224	319,226
	18141	St. Joseph County, IN	266,931	267,618
	26027	Cass County, MI	52,293	51,608
43900		Spartanburg, SC Metro area	313,268	321,418
	45083	Spartanburg County, SC	284,307	293,542
	45087	Union County, SC	28,961	27,876
43940		Spearfish, SD Micro area	24,097	24,657
	46081	Lawrence County, SD	24,097	24,657
43980		Spencer, IA Micro area	16,667	16,515
	19041	Clay County, IA	16,667	16,515
44020		Spirit Lake, IA Micro area	16,667	16,935
	19059	Dickinson County, IA	16,667	16,935

Core based statistical area	State/County FIPS code	Title and Geographic Components	2010 Census Population	2014 Estimated Population
44060		Spokane-Spokane Valley, WA Metro area	527,753	540,953
	53051	Pend Oreille County, WA	13,001	12,985
	53063	Spokane County, WA	471,221	484,318
	53065	Stevens County, WA	43,531	43,650
44100		Springfield, IL Metro area	210,170	211,567
	17129	Menard County, IL	12,705	12,570
	17167	Sangamon County, IL	197,465	198,997
44140		Springfield, MA Metro area	621,570	629,100
	25013	Hampden County, MA	463,490	468,161
	25015	Hampshire County, MA	158,080	160,939
44180		Springfield, MO Metro area	436,712	452,297
	29043	Christian County, MO	77,422	82,101
	29059	Dallas County, MO	16,777	16,389
	29077	Greene County, MO	275,174	285,865
	29167	Polk County, MO	31,137	31,054
	29225	Webster County, MO	36,202	36,888
44220		Springfield, OH Metro area	138,333	136,554
	39023	Clark County, OH	138,333	136,554
44260		Starkville, MS Micro area	47,671	49,414
	28105	Oktibbeha County, MS	47,671	49,414
44300		State College, PA Metro area	153,990	158,742
	42027	Centre County, PA	153,990	158,742
44340		Statesboro, GA Micro area	70,217	72,087
	13031	Bulloch County, GA	70,217	72,087
44420		Staunton-Waynesboro, VA Metro area	118,502	119,766
	51015	Augusta County, VA	73,750	73,862
	51790	Staunton city, VA	23,746	24,538
	51820	Waynesboro city, VA	21,006	21,366
44460		Steamboat Springs, CO Micro area	23,509	23,865
	08107	Routt County, CO	23,509	23,865
44500		Stephenville, TX Micro area	37,890	40,147
	48143	Erath County, TX	37,890	40,147
44540		Sterling, CO Micro area	22,709	22,524
	08075	Logan County, CO	22,709	22,524
44580		Sterling, IL Micro area	58,498	56,876
	17195	Whiteside County, IL	58,498	56,876
44620		Stevens Point, WI Micro area	70,019	70,482
	55097	Portage County, WI	70,019	70,482
44660		Stillwater, OK Micro area	77,350	80,264
	40119	Payne County, OK	77,350	80,264
44700		Stockton-Lodi, CA Metro area	685,306	715,597
	06077	San Joaquin County, CA	685,306	715,597
44740		Storm Lake, IA Micro area	20,260	20,578
	19021	Buena Vista County, IA	20,260	20,578
44780		Sturgis, MI Micro area	61,295	60,946
	26149	St. Joseph County, MI	61,295	60,946
44860		Sulphur Springs, TX Micro area	35,161	35,921
	48223	Hopkins County, TX	35,161	35,921
44900		Summerville, GA Micro area	26,015	24,939
	13055	Chattooga County, GA	26,015	24,939
44920		Summit Park, UT Micro area	36,324	39,105
	49043	Summit County, UT	36,324	39,105
44940		Sumter, SC Metro area	107,456	107,919
	45085	Sumter County, SC	107,456	107,919
44980		Sunbury, PA Micro area	94,528	93,944
	42097	Northumberland County, PA	94,528	93,944
45000		Susanville, CA Micro area	34,895	31,749
	06035	Lassen County, CA	34,895	31,749
45020		Sweetwater, TX Micro area	15,216	15,093
	48353	Nolan County, TX	15,216	15,093
45060		Syracuse, NY Metro area	662,577	661,478
	36053	Madison County, NY	73,442	72,369
	36067	Onondaga County, NY	467,026	468,196
	36075	Oswego County, NY	122,109	120,913
45140		Tahlequah, OK Micro area	46,987	48,341
	40021	Cherokee County, OK	46,987	48,341
45180		Talladega-Sylacauga, AL Micro area	93,830	92,208
	01037	Coosa County, AL	11,539	10,886
	01121	Talladega County, AL	82,291	81,322
45220		Tallahassee, FL Metro area	367,413	375,751
	12039	Gadsden County, FL	46,389	46,281
	12065	Jefferson County, FL	14,761	14,050
	12073	Leon County, FL	275,487	283,988
	12129	Wakulla County, FL	30,776	31,432
45300		Tampa-St. Petersburg-Clearwater, FL Metro area	2,783,243	2,915,582
	12053	Hernando County, FL	172,778	175,855
	12057	Hillsborough County, FL	1,229,226	1,316,298
	12101	Pasco County, FL	464,697	485,331
	12103	Pinellas County, FL	916,542	938,098
45340		Taos, NM Micro area	32,937	33,084
	35055	Taos County, NM	32,937	33,084
45380		Taylorville, IL Micro area	34,800	33,892
	17021	Christian County, IL	34,800	33,892
45460		Terre Haute, IN Metro area	172,425	171,480

Core Based Statistical Areas (Metropolitan and Micropolitan), Metropolitan Divisions, and Components (as defined February 2013)

Core based statistical area	State/County FIPS code	Title and Geographic Components	2010 Census Population	2014 Estimated Population
	18021	Clay County, IN	26,890	26,562
	18153	Sullivan County, IN	21,475	21,050
	18165	Vermillion County, IN	16,212	15,693
	18167	Vigo County, IN	107,848	108,175
45500		Texarkana, TX-AR Metro area	149,198	149,235
	05081	Little River County, AR	13,171	12,532
	05091	Miller County, AR	43,462	43,428
	48037	Bowie County, TX	92,565	93,275
45520		The Dalles, OR Micro area	25,213	25,515
	41065	Wasco County, OR	25,213	25,515
45540		The Villages, FL Metro area	93,420	114,350
	12119	Sumter County, FL	93,420	114,350
45580		Thomaston, GA Micro area	27,153	26,256
	13293	Upson County, GA	27,153	26,256
45620		Thomasville, GA Micro area	44,720	44,959
	13275	Thomas County, GA	44,720	44,959
45660		Tiffin, OH Micro area	56,745	55,669
	39147	Seneca County, OH	56,745	55,669
45700		Tifton, GA Micro area	40,118	40,704
	13277	Tift County, GA	40,118	40,704
45740		Toccoa, GA Micro area	26,175	25,480
	13257	Stephens County, GA	26,175	25,480
45780		Toledo, OH Metro area	610,001	607,456
	39051	Fulton County, OH	42,698	42,580
	39095	Lucas County, OH	441,815	435,286
	39173	Wood County, OH	125,488	129,590
45820		Topeka, KS Metro area	233,870	233,758
	20085	Jackson County, KS	13,462	13,539
	20087	Jefferson County, KS	19,126	18,855
	20139	Osage County, KS	16,295	15,936
	20177	Shawnee County, KS	177,934	178,406
	20197	Wabaunsee County, KS	7,053	7,022
45860		Torrington, CT Micro area	189,927	184,993
	09005	Litchfield County, CT	189,927	184,993
45900		Traverse City, MI Micro area	143,372	147,610
	26019	Benzie County, MI	17,525	17,519
	26055	Grand Traverse County, MI	86,986	90,782
	26079	Kalkaska County, MI	17,153	17,394
	26089	Leelanau County, MI	21,708	21,915
45940		Trenton, NJ Metro area	366,513	371,537
	34021	Mercer County, NJ	366,513	371,537
45980		Troy, AL Micro area	32,899	33,389
	01109	Pike County, AL	32,899	33,389
46020		Truckee-Grass Valley, CA Micro area	98,764	98,893
	06057	Nevada County, CA	98,764	98,893
46060		Tucson, AZ Metro area	980,263	1,004,516
	04019	Pima County, AZ	980,263	1,004,516
46100		Tullahoma-Manchester, TN Micro area	100,210	101,344
	47031	Coffee County, TN	52,796	53,623
	47051	Franklin County, TN	41,052	41,402
	47127	Moore County, TN	6,362	6,319
46140		Tulsa, OK Metro area	937,478	969,224
	40037	Creek County, OK	69,967	70,632
	40111	Okmulgee County, OK	40,069	39,095
	40113	Osage County, OK	47,472	47,981
	40117	Pawnee County, OK	16,577	16,401
	40131	Rogers County, OK	86,905	89,815
	40143	Tulsa County, OK	603,403	629,598
	40145	Wagoner County, OK	73,085	75,702
46180		Tupelo, MS Micro area	136,268	139,723
	28057	Itawamba County, MS	23,401	23,527
	28081	Lee County, MS	82,910	85,246
	28115	Pontotoc County, MS	29,957	30,950
46220		Tuscaloosa, AL Metro area	230,162	237,761
	01065	Hale County, AL	15,760	15,184
	01107	Pickens County, AL	19,746	20,365
	01125	Tuscaloosa County, AL	194,656	202,212
46300		Twin Falls, ID Micro area	99,604	103,732
	16053	Jerome County, ID	22,374	22,818
	16083	Twin Falls County, ID	77,230	80,914
46340		Tyler, TX Metro area	209,714	218,842
	48423	Smith County, TX	209,714	218,842
46380		Ukiah, CA Micro area	87,841	87,869
	06045	Mendocino County, CA	87,841	87,869
46460		Union City, TN-KY Micro area	38,620	37,206
	21075	Fulton County, KY	6,813	6,265
	47131	Obion County, TN	31,807	30,941
46500		Urbana, OH Micro area	40,097	39,128
	39021	Champaign County, OH	40,097	39,128
46520		Urban Honolulu, HI Metro area	953,207	991,788
	15003	Honolulu County, HI	953,207	991,788
46540		Utica-Rome, NY Metro area	299,397	296,615
	36043	Herkimer County, NY	64,519	63,744
	36065	Oneida County, NY	234,878	232,871
46620		Uvalde, TX Micro area	26,405	27,117
	48463	Uvalde County, TX	26,405	27,117
46660		Valdosta, GA Metro area	139,588	143,317
	13027	Brooks County, GA	16,243	15,418
	13101	Echols County, GA	4,034	4,003
	13173	Lanier County, GA	10,078	10,373
	13185	Lowndes County, GA	109,233	113,523
46700		Vallejo-Fairfield, CA Metro area	413,344	431,131
	06095	Solano County, CA	413,344	431,131
46740		Valley, AL Micro area	34,215	34,076
	01017	Chambers County, AL	34,215	34,076
46780		Van Wert, OH Micro area	28,744	28,462
	39161	Van Wert County, OH	28,744	28,462
46820		Vermillion, SD Micro area	13,864	13,932
	46027	Clay County, SD	13,864	13,932
46860		Vernal, UT Micro area	32,588	36,867
	49047	Uintah County, UT	32,588	36,867
46900		Vernon, TX Micro area	13,535	12,973
	48487	Wilbarger County, TX	13,535	12,973
46980		Vicksburg, MS Micro area	58,377	57,063
	28021	Claiborne County, MS	9,604	9,080
	28149	Warren County, MS	48,773	47,983
47020		Victoria, TX Metro area	94,003	98,630
	48175	Goliad County, TX	7,210	7,549
	48469	Victoria County, TX	86,793	91,081
47080		Vidalia, GA Micro area	36,346	36,273
	13209	Montgomery County, GA	9,123	8,991
	13279	Toombs County, GA	27,223	27,282
47180		Vincennes, IN Micro area	38,440	37,938
	18083	Knox County, IN	38,440	37,938
47220		Vineland-Bridgeton, NJ Metro area	156,898	157,389
	34011	Cumberland County, NJ	156,898	157,389
47240		Vineyard Haven, MA Micro area	16,535	17,356
	25007	Dukes County, MA	16,535	17,356
47260		Virginia Beach-Norfolk-Newport News, VA-NC Metro area	1,676,822	1,716,624
	37053	Currituck County, NC	23,547	24,976
	37073	Gates County, NC	12,197	11,567
	51073	Gloucester County, VA	36,858	37,141
	51093	Isle of Wight County, VA	35,270	36,007
	51095	James City County, VA	67,009	72,583
	51115	Mathews County, VA	8,978	8,836
	51199	York County, VA	65,464	66,342
	51550	Chesapeake city, VA	222,209	233,371
	51650	Hampton city, VA	137,436	136,879
	51700	Newport News city, VA	180,719	182,965
	51710	Norfolk city, VA	242,803	245,428
	51735	Poquoson city, VA	12,150	12,048
	51740	Portsmouth city, VA	95,535	96,004
	51800	Suffolk city, VA	84,585	86,806
	51810	Virginia Beach city, VA	437,994	450,980
	51830	Williamsburg city, VA	14,068	14,691
47300		Visalia-Porterville, CA Metro area	442,179	458,198
	06107	Tulare County, CA	442,179	458,198
47340		Wabash, IN Micro area	32,888	32,252
	18169	Wabash County, IN	32,888	32,252
47380		Waco, TX Metro area	252,772	260,430
	48145	Falls County, TX	17,866	16,989
	48309	McLennan County, TX	234,906	243,441
47420		Wahpeton, ND-MN Micro area	22,897	22,927
	27167	Wilkin County, MN	6,576	6,495
	38077	Richland County, ND	16,321	16,432
47460		Walla Walla, WA Metro area	62,859	63,829
	53013	Columbia County, WA	4,078	3,985
	53071	Walla Walla County, WA	58,781	59,844
47540		Wapakoneta, OH Micro area	45,949	45,841
	39011	Auglaize County, OH	45,949	45,841
47580		Warner Robins, GA Metro area	179,605	187,516
	13153	Houston County, GA	139,900	149,111
	13225	Peach County, GA	27,695	26,922
	13235	Pulaski County, GA	12,010	11,483
47620		Warren, PA Micro area	41,815	40,703
	42123	Warren County, PA	41,815	40,703
47660		Warrensburg, MO Micro area	52,595	54,362
	29101	Johnson County, MO	52,595	54,362
47700		Warsaw, IN Micro area	77,358	78,564
	18085	Kosciusko County, IN	77,358	78,564
47780		Washington, IN Micro area	31,648	32,729
	18027	Daviess County, IN	31,648	32,729
47820		Washington, NC Micro area	47,759	47,585
	37013	Beaufort County, NC	47,759	47,585
		Washington-Arlington-Alexandria, DC-VA-MD-WV Metro area	5,636,232	6,033,737
47900		Silver Spring-Frederick-Rockville, MD Metro Div 43524	1,205,162	1,274,122
	24021	Frederick County, MD	233,385	243,675

Core Based Statistical Areas (Metropolitan and Micropolitan), Metropolitan Divisions, and Components (as defined February 2013)

Core based statistical area	State/ County FIPS code	Title and Geographic Components	2010 Census Population	2014 Estimated Population
	24031	Montgomery County, MD	971,777	1,030,447
47900		Washington-Arlington-Alexandria, DC-VA-MD-WV Metro Div 47894	4,431,070	4,759,615
	11001	District of Columbia, DC	601,723	658,893
	24009	Calvert County, MD	88,737	90,613
	24017	Charles County, MD	146,551	154,747
	24033	Prince George's County, MD	863,420	904,430
	51013	Arlington County, VA	207,627	226,908
	51043	Clarke County, VA	14,034	14,423
	51047	Culpeper County, VA	46,689	49,166
	51059	Fairfax County, VA	1,081,726	1,137,538
	51061	Fauquier County, VA	65,203	68,248
	51107	Loudoun County, VA	312,311	363,050
	51153	Prince William County, VA	402,002	446,094
	51157	Rappahannock County, VA	7,373	7,361
	51177	Spotsylvania County, VA	122,397	129,188
	51179	Stafford County, VA	128,961	139,992
	51187	Warren County, VA	37,575	38,987
	51510	Alexandria city, VA	139,966	150,575
	51600	Fairfax city, VA	22,565	24,483
	51610	Falls Church city, VA	12,332	13,601
	51630	Fredericksburg city, VA	24,286	28,350
	51683	Manassas city, VA	37,821	42,081
	51685	Manassas Park city, VA	14,273	15,174
	54037	Jefferson County, WV	53,498	55,713
47920		Washington Court House, OH Micro area	29,030	28,800
	39047	Fayette County, OH	29,030	28,800
47940		Waterloo-Cedar Falls, IA Metro area	167,819	169,993
	19013	Black Hawk County, IA	131,090	132,897
	19017	Bremer County, IA	24,276	24,721
	19075	Grundy County, IA	12,453	12,375
47980		Watertown, SD Micro area	27,227	27,938
	46029	Codington County, SD	27,227	27,938
48020		Watertown-Fort Atkinson, WI Micro area	83,686	84,395
	55055	Jefferson County, WI	83,686	84,395
48060		Watertown-Fort Drum, NY Metro area	116,229	119,103
	36045	Jefferson County, NY	116,229	119,103
48100		Wauchula, FL Micro area	27,731	27,469
	12049	Hardee County, FL	27,731	27,469
48140		Wausau, WI Metro area	134,063	135,780
	55073	Marathon County, WI	134,063	135,780
48180		Waycross, GA Micro area	55,070	54,506
	13229	Pierce County, GA	18,758	18,991
	13299	Ware County, GA	36,312	35,515
48220		Weatherford, OK Micro area	27,469	29,500
	40039	Custer County, OK	27,469	29,500
48260		Weirton-Steubenville, WV-OH Metro area	124,454	121,336
	39081	Jefferson County, OH	69,709	67,694
	54009	Brooke County, WV	24,069	23,530
	54029	Hancock County, WV	30,676	30,112
48300		Wenatchee, WA Metro area	110,884	114,392
	53007	Chelan County, WA	72,453	74,588
	53017	Douglas County, WA	38,431	39,804
48460		West Plains, MO Micro area	40,400	40,173
	29091	Howell County, MO	40,400	40,173
48540		Wheeling, WV-OH Metro area	147,950	145,205
	39013	Belmont County, OH	70,400	69,461
	54051	Marshall County, WV	33,107	32,416
	54069	Ohio County, WV	44,443	43,328
48580		Whitewater-Elkhorn, WI Micro area	102,228	103,527
	55127	Walworth County, WI	102,228	103,527
48620		Wichita, KS Metro area	630,919	641,076
	20015	Butler County, KS	65,880	66,227
	20079	Harvey County, KS	34,684	34,820
	20095	Kingman County, KS	7,858	7,698

Core Based Statistical Areas (Metropolitan and Micropolitan), Metropolitan Divisions, and Components (as defined February 2013)

Core based statistical area	State/ County FIPS code	Title and Geographic Components	2010 Census Population	2014 Estimated Population
	20173	Sedgwick County, KS	498,365	508,803
	20191	Sumner County, KS	24,132	23,528
48660		Wichita Falls, TX Metro area	151,306	151,536
	48009	Archer County, TX	9,054	8,811
	48077	Clay County, TX	10,752	10,370
	48485	Wichita County, TX	131,500	132,355
48700		Williamsport, PA Metro area	116,111	116,508
	42081	Lycoming County, PA	116,111	116,508
48780		Williston, ND Micro area	22,398	32,130
	38105	Williams County, ND	22,398	32,130
48820		Willmar, MN Micro area	42,239	42,285
	27067	Kandiyohi County, MN	42,239	42,285
48900		Wilmington, NC Metro area	254,884	272,548
	37129	New Hanover County, NC	202,667	216,298
	37141	Pender County, NC	52,217	56,250
48940		Wilmington, OH Micro area	42,040	41,835
	39027	Clinton County, OH	42,040	41,835
48980		Wilson, NC Micro area	81,234	81,401
	37195	Wilson County, NC	81,234	81,401
49020		Winchester, VA-WV Metro area	128,472	133,403
	51069	Frederick County, VA	78,305	82,377
	51840	Winchester city, VA	26,203	27,543
	54027	Hampshire County, WV	23,964	23,483
49080		Winnemucca, NV Micro area	16,528	17,279
	32013	Humboldt County, NV	16,528	17,279
49100		Winona, MN Micro area	51,461	51,097
	27169	Winona County, MN	51,461	51,097
49180		Winston-Salem, NC Metro area	640,595	655,015
	37057	Davidson County, NC	162,878	164,072
	37059	Davie County, NC	41,240	41,434
	37067	Forsyth County, NC	350,670	365,298
	37169	Stokes County, NC	47,401	46,419
	37197	Yadkin County, NC	38,406	37,792
49220		Wisconsin Rapids-Marshfield, WI Micro area	74,749	73,608
	55141	Wood County, WI	74,749	73,608
49260		Woodward, OK Micro area	20,081	21,529
	40153	Woodward County, OK	20,081	21,529
49300		Wooster, OH Micro area	114,520	115,537
	39169	Wayne County, OH	114,520	115,537
49340		Worcester, MA-CT Metro area	916,980	930,473
	09015	Windham County, CT	118,428	116,998
	25027	Worcester County, MA	798,552	813,475
49380		Worthington, MN Micro area	21,378	21,590
	27105	Nobles County, MN	21,378	21,590
49420		Yakima, WA Metro area	243,231	247,687
	53077	Yakima County, WA	243,231	247,687
49460		Yankton, SD Micro area	22,438	22,684
	46135	Yankton County, SD	22,438	22,684
49620		York-Hanover, PA Metro area	434,972	440,755
	42133	York County, PA	434,972	440,755
49660		Youngstown-Warren-Boardman, OH-PA Metro area	565,773	553,263
	39099	Mahoning County, OH	238,823	233,204
	39155	Trumbull County, OH	210,312	205,175
	42085	Mercer County, PA	116,638	114,884
49700		Yuba City, CA Metro area	166,892	169,813
	06101	Sutter County, CA	94,737	95,847
	06115	Yuba County, CA	72,155	73,966
49740		Yuma, AZ Metro area	195,751	203,247
	04027	Yuma County, AZ	195,751	203,247
49780		Zanesville, OH Micro area	86,074	85,818
	39119	Muskingum County, OH	86,074	85,818
49820		Zapata, TX Micro area	14,018	14,319
	48505	Zapata County, TX	14,018	14,319

APPENDIX B. CITIES BY COUNTY

The following table is arranged alphabetically by state. Under each state heading are listed all cities with a 2010 census population of 25,000 or more, along with their component counties and the population in each component.

State code	Place code	County code	Geographic Area Name	2010 census population
01			**ALABAMA**	4,779,736
01		00820	Alabaster city	30,352
01	117	00820	Shelby County	30,352
01		03076	Auburn city	53,380
01	081	03076	Lee County	53,380
01		05980	Bessemer city	27,456
01	073	05980	Jefferson County	27,456
01		07000	Birmingham city	212,237
01	073	07000	Jefferson County	210,609
01	117	07000	Shelby County	1,628
01		20104	Decatur city	55,683
01	083	20104	Limestone County	84
01	103	20104	Morgan County	55,599
01		21184	Dothan city	65,496
01	045	21184	Dale County	887
01	067	21184	Henry County	5
01	069	21184	Houston County	64,604
01		24184	Enterprise city	26,562
01	031	24184	Coffee County	26,139
01	045	24184	Dale County	423
01		26896	Florence city	39,319
01	077	26896	Lauderdale County	39,319
01		28696	Gadsden city	36,856
01	055	28696	Etowah County	36,856
01		35800	Homewood city	25,167
01	073	35800	Jefferson County	25,167
01		35896	Hoover city	81,619
01	073	35896	Jefferson County	58,582
01	117	35896	Shelby County	23,037
01		37000	Huntsville city	180,105
01	083	37000	Limestone County	1,521
01	089	37000	Madison County	178,584
01		45784	Madison city	42,938
01	083	45784	Limestone County	3,453
01	089	45784	Madison County	39,485
01		50000	Mobile city	195,111
01	097	50000	Mobile County	195,111
01		51000	Montgomery city	205,764
01	101	51000	Montgomery County	205,764
01		57048	Opelika city	26,477
01	081	57048	Lee County	26,477
01		59472	Phenix City city	32,822
01	081	59472	Lee County	4,153
01	113	59472	Russell County	28,669
01		62328	Prattville city	33,960
01	001	62328	Autauga County	32,168
01	051	62328	Elmore County	1,792
01		77256	Tuscaloosa city	90,468
01	125	77256	Tuscaloosa County	90,468
01		78552	Vestavia Hills city	34,033
01	073	78552	Jefferson County	34,019

State code	Place code	County code	Geographic Area Name	2010 census population
01	117	78552	Shelby County	14
02			**ALASKA**	710,231
02		03000	Anchorage municipality	291,826
02	020	03000	Anchorage Municipality	291,826
02		24230	Fairbanks city	31,535
02	090	24230	Fairbanks North Star Borough	31,535
02		36400	Juneau city and borough	31,275
02	110	36400	Juneau City and Borough	31,275
04			**ARIZONA**	6,392,017
04		02830	Apache Junction city	35,840
04	013	02830	Maricopa County	294
04	021	02830	Pinal County	35,546
04		04720	Avondale city	76,238
04	013	04720	Maricopa County	76,238
04		07940	Buckeye town	50,876
04	013	07940	Maricopa County	50,876
04		08220	Bullhead City city	39,540
04	015	08220	Mohave County	39,540
04		10530	Casa Grande city	48,571
04	021	10530	Pinal County	48,571
04		12000	Chandler city	236,123
04	013	12000	Maricopa County	236,123
04		22220	El Mirage city	31,797
04	013	22220	Maricopa County	31,797
04		23620	Flagstaff city	65,870
04	005	23620	Coconino County	65,870
04		23760	Florence town	25,536
04	021	23760	Pinal County	25,536
04		27400	Gilbert town	208,453
04	013	27400	Maricopa County	208,453
04		27820	Glendale city	226,721
04	013	27820	Maricopa County	226,721
04		28380	Goodyear city	65,275
04	013	28380	Maricopa County	65,275
04		37620	Kingman city	28,068
04	015	37620	Mohave County	28,068
04		39370	Lake Havasu City city	52,527
04	015	39370	Mohave County	52,527
04		44270	Marana town	34,961
04	019	44270	Pima County	34,961
04	021	44270	Pinal County	0
04		44410	Maricopa city	43,482
04	021	44410	Pinal County	43,482
04		46000	Mesa city	439,041
04	013	46000	Maricopa County	439,041
04		51600	Oro Valley town	41,011
04	019	51600	Pima County	41,011
04		54050	Peoria city	154,065

State code	Place code	County code	Geographic Area Name	2010 census population
04	013	54050	Maricopa County	154,058
04	025	54050	Yavapai County	7
04		55000	Phoenix city	1,445,632
04	013	55000	Maricopa County	1,445,632
04		57380	Prescott city	39,843
04	025	57380	Yavapai County	39,843
04		57450	Prescott Valley town	38,822
04	025	57450	Yavapai County	38,822
04		58150	Queen Creek town	26,361
04	013	58150	Maricopa County	25,912
04	021	58150	Pinal County	449
04		62140	Sahuarita town	25,259
04	019	62140	Pima County	25,259
04		63470	San Luis city	25,505
04	027	63470	Yuma County	25,505
04		65000	Scottsdale city	217,385
04	013	65000	Maricopa County	217,385
04		66820	Sierra Vista city	43,888
04	003	66820	Cochise County	43,888
04		71510	Surprise city	117,517
04	013	71510	Maricopa County	117,517
04		73000	Tempe city	161,719
04	013	73000	Maricopa County	161,719
04		77000	Tucson city	520,116
04	019	77000	Pima County	520,116
04		85540	Yuma city	93,064
04	027	85540	Yuma County	93,064
05			**ARKANSAS**	2,915,918
05		04840	Bella Vista town	26,461
05	007	04840	Benton County	26,461
05		05290	Benton city	30,681
05	125	05290	Saline County	30,681
05		05320	Bentonville city	35,301
05	007	05320	Benton County	35,301
05		15190	Conway city	58,908
05	045	15190	Faulkner County	58,908
05		23290	Fayetteville city	73,580
05	143	23290	Washington County	73,580
05		24550	Fort Smith city	86,209
05	131	24550	Sebastian County	86,209
05		33400	Hot Springs city	35,193
05	051	33400	Garland County	35,193
05		34750	Jacksonville city	28,364
05	119	34750	Pulaski County	28,364
05		35710	Jonesboro city	67,263
05	031	35710	Craighead County	67,263
05		41000	Little Rock city	193,524
05	119	41000	Pulaski County	193,524
05		50450	North Little Rock city	62,304
05	119	50450	Pulaski County	62,304
05		53390	Paragould city	26,113
05	055	53390	Greene County	26,113
05		55310	Pine Bluff city	49,083
05	069	55310	Jefferson County	49,083
05		60410	Rogers city	55,964
05	007	60410	Benton County	55,964
05		61670	Russellville city	27,920
05	115	61670	Pope County	27,920
05		63800	Sherwood city	29,523
05	119	63800	Pulaski County	29,523

State code	Place code	County code	Geographic Area Name	2010 census population
05		66080	Springdale city	69,797
05	007	66080	Benton County	6,054
05	143	66080	Washington County	63,743
05		68810	Texarkana city	29,919
05	091	68810	Miller County	29,919
05		74540	West Memphis city	26,245
05	035	74540	Crittenden County	26,245
06			**CALIFORNIA**	37,253,956
06		00296	Adelanto city	31,765
06	071	00296	San Bernardino County	31,765
06		00562	Alameda city	73,812
06	001	00562	Alameda County	73,812
06		00884	Alhambra city	83,089
06	037	00884	Los Angeles County	83,089
06		00947	Aliso Viejo city	47,823
06	059	00947	Orange County	47,823
06		02000	Anaheim city	336,265
06	059	02000	Orange County	336,265
06		02252	Antioch city	102,372
06	013	02252	Contra Costa County	102,372
06		02364	Apple Valley town	69,135
06	071	02364	San Bernardino County	69,135
06		02462	Arcadia city	56,364
06	037	02462	Los Angeles County	56,364
06		03064	Atascadero city	28,310
06	079	03064	San Luis Obispo County	28,310
06		03162	Atwater city	28,168
06	047	03162	Merced County	28,168
06		03386	Azusa city	46,361
06	037	03386	Los Angeles County	46,361
06		03526	Bakersfield city	347,483
06	029	03526	Kern County	347,483
06		03666	Baldwin Park city	75,390
06	037	03666	Los Angeles County	75,390
06		03820	Banning city	29,603
06	065	03820	Riverside County	29,603
06		04758	Beaumont city	36,877
06	065	04758	Riverside County	36,877
06		04870	Bell city	35,477
06	037	04870	Los Angeles County	35,477
06		04982	Bellflower city	76,616
06	037	04982	Los Angeles County	76,616
06		04996	Bell Gardens city	42,072
06	037	04996	Los Angeles County	42,072
06		05108	Belmont city	25,835
06	081	05108	San Mateo County	25,835
06		05290	Benicia city	26,997
06	095	05290	Solano County	26,997
06		06000	Berkeley city	112,580
06	001	06000	Alameda County	112,580
06		06308	Beverly Hills city	34,109
06	037	06308	Los Angeles County	34,109
06		08100	Brea city	39,282
06	059	08100	Orange County	39,282
06		08142	Brentwood city	51,481
06	013	08142	Contra Costa County	51,481
06		08786	Buena Park city	80,530
06	059	08786	Orange County	80,530
06		08954	Burbank city	103,340

State code	Place code	County code	Geographic Area Name	2010 census population
06	037	08954	Los Angeles County	103,340
06		09066	Burlingame city	28,806
06	081	09066	San Mateo County	28,806
06		09710	Calexico city	38,572
06	025	09710	Imperial County	38,572
06		10046	Camarillo city	65,201
06	111	10046	Ventura County	65,201
06		10345	Campbell city	39,349
06	085	10345	Santa Clara County	39,349
06		11194	Carlsbad city	105,328
06	073	11194	San Diego County	105,328
06		11530	Carson city	91,714
06	037	11530	Los Angeles County	91,714
06		12048	Cathedral City city	51,200
06	065	12048	Riverside County	51,200
06		12524	Ceres city	45,417
06	099	12524	Stanislaus County	45,417
06		12552	Cerritos city	49,041
06	037	12552	Los Angeles County	49,041
06		13014	Chico city	86,187
06	007	13014	Butte County	86,187
06		13210	Chino city	77,983
06	071	13210	San Bernardino County	77,983
06		13214	Chino Hills city	74,799
06	071	13214	San Bernardino County	74,799
06		13392	Chula Vista city	243,916
06	073	13392	San Diego County	243,916
06		13588	Citrus Heights city	83,301
06	067	13588	Sacramento County	83,301
06		13756	Claremont city	34,926
06	037	13756	Los Angeles County	34,926
06		14218	Clovis city	95,631
06	019	14218	Fresno County	95,631
06		14260	Coachella city	40,704
06	065	14260	Riverside County	40,704
06		14890	Colton city	52,154
06	071	14890	San Bernardino County	52,154
06		15044	Compton city	96,455
06	037	15044	Los Angeles County	96,455
06		16000	Concord city	122,067
06	013	16000	Contra Costa County	122,067
06		16350	Corona city	152,374
06	065	16350	Riverside County	152,374
06		16532	Costa Mesa city	109,960
06	059	16532	Orange County	109,960
06		16742	Covina city	47,796
06	037	16742	Los Angeles County	47,796
06		17568	Culver City city	38,883
06	037	17568	Los Angeles County	38,883
06		17610	Cupertino city	58,302
06	085	17610	Santa Clara County	58,302
06		17750	Cypress city	47,802
06	059	17750	Orange County	47,802
06		17918	Daly City city	101,123
06	081	17918	San Mateo County	101,123
06		17946	Dana Point city	33,351
06	059	17946	Orange County	33,351
06		17988	Danville town	42,039
06	013	17988	Contra Costa County	42,039

State code	Place code	County code	Geographic Area Name	2010 census population
06		18100	Davis city	65,622
06	113	18100	Yolo County	65,622
06		18394	Delano city	53,041
06	029	18394	Kern County	53,041
06		18996	Desert Hot Springs city	25,938
06	065	18996	Riverside County	25,938
06		19192	Diamond Bar city	55,544
06	037	19192	Los Angeles County	55,544
06		19766	Downey city	111,772
06	037	19766	Los Angeles County	111,772
06		20018	Dublin city	46,036
06	001	20018	Alameda County	46,036
06		20956	East Palo Alto city	28,155
06	081	20956	San Mateo County	28,155
06		21712	El Cajon city	99,478
06	073	21712	San Diego County	99,478
06		21782	El Centro city	42,598
06	025	21782	Imperial County	42,598
06		22020	Elk Grove city	153,015
06	067	22020	Sacramento County	153,015
06		22230	El Monte city	113,475
06	037	22230	Los Angeles County	113,475
06		22300	El Paso de Robles (Paso Robles)	29,793
06	079	22300	San Luis Obispo County	29,793
06		22678	Encinitas city	59,518
06	073	22678	San Diego County	59,518
06		22804	Escondido city	143,911
06	073	22804	San Diego County	143,911
06		23042	Eureka city	27,191
06	023	23042	Humboldt County	27,191
06		23182	Fairfield city	105,321
06	095	23182	Solano County	105,321
06		24638	Folsom city	72,203
06	067	24638	Sacramento County	72,203
06		24680	Fontana city	196,069
06	071	24680	San Bernardino County	196,069
06		25338	Foster City city	30,567
06	081	25338	San Mateo County	30,567
06		25380	Fountain Valley city	55,313
06	059	25380	Orange County	55,313
06		26000	Fremont city	214,089
06	001	26000	Alameda County	214,089
06		27000	Fresno city	494,665
06	019	27000	Fresno County	494,665
06		28000	Fullerton city	135,161
06	059	28000	Orange County	135,161
06		28168	Gardena city	58,829
06	037	28168	Los Angeles County	58,829
06		29000	Garden Grove city	170,883
06	059	29000	Orange County	170,883
06		29504	Gilroy city	48,821
06	085	29504	Santa Clara County	48,821
06		30000	Glendale city	191,719
06	037	30000	Los Angeles County	191,719
06		30014	Glendora city	50,073
06	037	30014	Los Angeles County	50,073
06		30378	Goleta city	29,888
06	083	30378	Santa Barbara County	29,888
06		31960	Hanford city	53,967
06	031	31960	Kings County	53,967

State code	Place code	County code	Geographic Area Name	2010 census population
06		32548	Hawthorne city	84,293
06	037	32548	Los Angeles County	84,293
06		33000	Hayward city	144,186
06	001	33000	Alameda County	144,186
06		33182	Hemet city	78,657
06	065	33182	Riverside County	78,657
06		33434	Hesperia city	90,173
06	071	33434	San Bernardino County	90,173
06		33588	Highland city	53,104
06	071	33588	San Bernardino County	53,104
06		34120	Hollister city	34,928
06	069	34120	San Benito County	34,928
06		36000	Huntington Beach city	189,992
06	059	36000	Orange County	189,992
06		36056	Huntington Park city	58,114
06	037	36056	Los Angeles County	58,114
06		36294	Imperial Beach city	26,324
06	073	36294	San Diego County	26,324
06		36448	Indio city	76,036
06	065	36448	Riverside County	76,036
06		36546	Inglewood city	109,673
06	037	36546	Los Angeles County	109,673
06		36770	Irvine city	212,375
06	059	36770	Orange County	212,375
06		39220	Laguna Hills city	30,344
06	059	39220	Orange County	30,344
06		39248	Laguna Niguel city	62,979
06	059	39248	Orange County	62,979
06		39290	La Habra city	60,239
06	059	39290	Orange County	60,239
06		39486	Lake Elsinore city	51,821
06	065	39486	Riverside County	51,821
06		39496	Lake Forest city	77,264
06	059	39496	Orange County	77,264
06		39892	Lakewood city	80,048
06	037	39892	Los Angeles County	80,048
06		40004	La Mesa city	57,065
06	073	40004	San Diego County	57,065
06		40032	La Mirada city	48,527
06	037	40032	Los Angeles County	48,527
06		40130	Lancaster city	156,633
06	037	40130	Los Angeles County	156,633
06		40340	La Puente city	39,816
06	037	40340	Los Angeles County	39,816
06		40354	La Quinta city	37,467
06	065	40354	Riverside County	37,467
06		40830	La Verne city	31,063
06	037	40830	Los Angeles County	31,063
06		40886	Lawndale city	32,769
06	037	40886	Los Angeles County	32,769
06		41124	Lemon Grove city	25,320
06	073	41124	San Diego County	25,320
06		41474	Lincoln city	42,819
06	061	41474	Placer County	42,819
06		41992	Livermore city	80,968
06	001	41992	Alameda County	80,968
06		42202	Lodi city	62,134
06	077	42202	San Joaquin County	62,134
06		42524	Lompoc city	42,434
06	083	42524	Santa Barbara County	42,434
06		43000	Long Beach city	462,257
06	037	43000	Los Angeles County	462,257
06		43280	Los Altos city	28,976
06	085	43280	Santa Clara County	28,976
06		44000	Los Angeles city	3,792,621
06	037	44000	Los Angeles County	3,792,621
06		44028	Los Banos city	35,972
06	047	44028	Merced County	35,972
06		44112	Los Gatos town	29,413
06	085	44112	Santa Clara County	29,413
06		44574	Lynwood city	69,772
06	037	44574	Los Angeles County	69,772
06		45022	Madera city	61,416
06	039	45022	Madera County	61,416
06		45400	Manhattan Beach city	35,135
06	037	45400	Los Angeles County	35,135
06		45484	Manteca city	67,096
06	077	45484	San Joaquin County	67,096
06		46114	Martinez city	35,824
06	013	46114	Contra Costa County	35,824
06		46492	Maywood city	27,395
06	037	46492	Los Angeles County	27,395
06		46842	Menifee city	77,519
06	065	46842	Riverside County	77,519
06		46870	Menlo Park city	32,026
06	081	46870	San Mateo County	32,026
06		46898	Merced city	78,958
06	047	46898	Merced County	78,958
06		47766	Milpitas city	66,790
06	085	47766	Santa Clara County	66,790
06		48256	Mission Viejo city	93,305
06	059	48256	Orange County	93,305
06		48354	Modesto city	201,165
06	099	48354	Stanislaus County	201,165
06		48648	Monrovia city	36,590
06	037	48648	Los Angeles County	36,590
06		48788	Montclair city	36,664
06	071	48788	San Bernardino County	36,664
06		48816	Montebello city	62,500
06	037	48816	Los Angeles County	62,500
06		48872	Monterey city	27,810
06	053	48872	Monterey County	27,810
06		48914	Monterey Park city	60,269
06	037	48914	Los Angeles County	60,269
06		49138	Moorpark city	34,421
06	111	49138	Ventura County	34,421
06		49270	Moreno Valley city	193,365
06	065	49270	Riverside County	193,365
06		49278	Morgan Hill city	37,882
06	085	49278	Santa Clara County	37,882
06		49670	Mountain View city	74,066
06	085	49670	Santa Clara County	74,066
06		50076	Murrieta city	103,466
06	065	50076	Riverside County	103,466
06		50258	Napa city	76,915
06	055	50258	Napa County	76,915
06		50398	National City city	58,582
06	073	50398	San Diego County	58,582

State code	Place code	County code	Geographic Area Name	2010 census population	State code	Place code	County code	Geographic Area Name	2010 census population
06		50916	Newark city	42,573	06		59451	Rancho Cucamonga city	165,269
06	001	50916	Alameda County	42,573	06	071	59451	San Bernardino County	165,269
06		51182	Newport Beach city	85,186	06		59514	Rancho Palos Verdes city	41,643
06	059	51182	Orange County	85,186	06	037	59514	Los Angeles County	41,643
06		51560	Norco city	27,063	06		59587	Rancho Santa Margarita city	47,853
06	065	51560	Riverside County	27,063	06	059	59587	Orange County	47,853
06		52526	Norwalk city	105,549	06		59920	Redding city	89,861
06	037	52526	Los Angeles County	105,549	06	089	59920	Shasta County	89,861
06		52582	Novato city	51,904	06		59962	Redlands city	68,747
06	041	52582	Marin County	51,904	06	071	59962	San Bernardino County	68,747
06		53000	Oakland city	390,724	06		60018	Redondo Beach city	66,748
06	001	53000	Alameda County	390,724	06	037	60018	Los Angeles County	66,748
06		53070	Oakley city	35,432	06		60102	Redwood City city	76,815
06	013	53070	Contra Costa County	35,432	06	081	60102	San Mateo County	76,815
06		53322	Oceanside city	167,086	06		60466	Rialto city	99,171
06	073	53322	San Diego County	167,086	06	071	60466	San Bernardino County	99,171
06		53896	Ontario city	163,924	06		60620	Richmond city	103,701
06	071	53896	San Bernardino County	163,924	06	013	60620	Contra Costa County	103,701
06		53980	Orange city	136,416	06		60704	Ridgecrest city	27,616
06	059	53980	Orange County	136,416	06	029	60704	Kern County	27,616
06		54652	Oxnard city	197,899	06		62000	Riverside city	303,871
06	111	54652	Ventura County	197,899	06	065	62000	Riverside County	303,871
06		54806	Pacifica city	37,234	06		62364	Rocklin city	56,974
06	081	54806	San Mateo County	37,234	06	061	62364	Placer County	56,974
06		55156	Palmdale city	152,750	06		62546	Rohnert Park city	40,971
06	037	55156	Los Angeles County	152,750	06	097	62546	Sonoma County	40,971
06		55184	Palm Desert city	48,445	06		62896	Rosemead city	53,764
06	065	55184	Riverside County	48,445	06	037	62896	Los Angeles County	53,764
06		55254	Palm Springs city	44,552	06		62938	Roseville city	118,788
06	065	55254	Riverside County	44,552	06	061	62938	Placer County	118,788
06		55282	Palo Alto city	64,403	06		64000	Sacramento city	466,488
06	085	55282	Santa Clara County	64,403	06	067	64000	Sacramento County	466,488
06		55520	Paradise town	26,218	06		64224	Salinas city	150,441
06	007	55520	Butte County	26,218	06	053	64224	Monterey County	150,441
06		55618	Paramount city	54,098	06		65000	San Bernardino city	209,924
06	037	55618	Los Angeles County	54,098	06	071	65000	San Bernardino County	209,924
06		56000	Pasadena city	137,122	06		65028	San Bruno city	41,114
06	037	56000	Los Angeles County	137,122	06	081	65028	San Mateo County	41,114
06		56700	Perris city	68,386	06		65042	San Buenaventura (Ventura)	106,433
06	065	56700	Riverside County	68,386	06	111	65042	Ventura County	106,433
06		56784	Petaluma city	57,941	06		65070	San Carlos city	28,406
06	097	56784	Sonoma County	57,941	06	081	65070	San Mateo County	28,406
06		56924	Pico Rivera city	62,942	06		65084	San Clemente city	63,522
06	037	56924	Los Angeles County	62,942	06	059	65084	Orange County	63,522
06		57456	Pittsburg city	63,264	06		66000	San Diego city	1,307,402
06	013	57456	Contra Costa County	63,264	06	073	66000	San Diego County	1,307,402
06		57526	Placentia city	50,533	06		66070	San Dimas city	33,371
06	059	57526	Orange County	50,533	06	037	66070	Los Angeles County	33,371
06		57764	Pleasant Hill city	33,152	06		67000	San Francisco city	805,235
06	013	57764	Contra Costa County	33,152	06	075	67000	San Francisco County	805,235
06		57792	Pleasanton city	70,285	06		67042	San Gabriel city	39,718
06	001	57792	Alameda County	70,285	06	037	67042	Los Angeles County	39,718
06		58072	Pomona city	149,058	06		67112	San Jacinto city	44,199
06	037	58072	Los Angeles County	149,058	06	065	67112	Riverside County	44,199
06		58240	Porterville city	54,165	06		68000	San Jose city	945,942
06	107	58240	Tulare County	54,165	06	085	68000	Santa Clara County	945,942
06		58520	Poway city	47,811	06		68028	San Juan Capistrano city	34,593
06	073	58520	San Diego County	47,811	06	059	68028	Orange County	34,593
06		59444	Rancho Cordova city	64,776	06		68084	San Leandro city	84,950
06	067	59444	Sacramento County	64,776	06	001	68084	Alameda County	84,950

State code	Place code	County code	Geographic Area Name	2010 census population
06		68154	San Luis Obispo city	45,119
06	079	68154	San Luis Obispo County	45,119
06		68196	San Marcos city	83,781
06	073	68196	San Diego County	83,781
06		68252	San Mateo city	97,207
06	081	68252	San Mateo County	97,207
06		68294	San Pablo city	29,139
06	013	68294	Contra Costa County	29,139
06		68364	San Rafael city	57,713
06	041	68364	Marin County	57,713
06		68378	San Ramon city	72,148
06	013	68378	Contra Costa County	72,148
06		69000	Santa Ana city	324,528
06	059	69000	Orange County	324,528
06		69070	Santa Barbara city	88,410
06	083	69070	Santa Barbara County	88,410
06		69084	Santa Clara city	116,468
06	085	69084	Santa Clara County	116,468
06		69088	Santa Clarita city	176,320
06	037	69088	Los Angeles County	176,320
06		69112	Santa Cruz city	59,946
06	087	69112	Santa Cruz County	59,946
06		69196	Santa Maria city	99,553
06	083	69196	Santa Barbara County	99,553
06		70000	Santa Monica city	89,736
06	037	70000	Los Angeles County	89,736
06		70042	Santa Paula city	29,321
06	111	70042	Ventura County	29,321
06		70098	Santa Rosa city	167,815
06	097	70098	Sonoma County	167,815
06		70224	Santee city	53,413
06	073	70224	San Diego County	53,413
06		70280	Saratoga city	29,926
06	085	70280	Santa Clara County	29,926
06		70742	Seaside city	33,025
06	053	70742	Monterey County	33,025
06		72016	Simi Valley city	124,237
06	111	72016	Ventura County	124,237
06		72520	Soledad city	25,738
06	053	72520	Monterey County	25,738
06		73080	South Gate city	94,396
06	037	73080	Los Angeles County	94,396
06		73220	South Pasadena city	25,619
06	037	73220	Los Angeles County	25,619
06		73262	South San Francisco city	63,632
06	081	73262	San Mateo County	63,632
06		73962	Stanton city	38,186
06	059	73962	Orange County	38,186
06		75000	Stockton city	291,707
06	077	75000	San Joaquin County	291,707
06		75630	Suisun City city	28,111
06	095	75630	Solano County	28,111
06		77000	Sunnyvale city	140,081
06	085	77000	Santa Clara County	140,081
06		78120	Temecula city	100,097
06	065	78120	Riverside County	100,097
06		78148	Temple City city	35,558
06	037	78148	Los Angeles County	35,558
06		78582	Thousand Oaks city	126,683
06	111	78582	Ventura County	126,683
06		80000	Torrance city	145,438
06	037	80000	Los Angeles County	145,438
06		80238	Tracy city	82,922
06	077	80238	San Joaquin County	82,922
06		80644	Tulare city	59,278
06	107	80644	Tulare County	59,278
06		80812	Turlock city	68,549
06	099	80812	Stanislaus County	68,549
06		80854	Tustin city	75,540
06	059	80854	Orange County	75,540
06		80994	Twentynine Palms city	25,048
06	071	80994	San Bernardino County	25,048
06		81204	Union City city	69,516
06	001	81204	Alameda County	69,516
06		81344	Upland city	73,732
06	071	81344	San Bernardino County	73,732
06		81554	Vacaville city	92,428
06	095	81554	Solano County	92,428
06		81666	Vallejo city	115,942
06	095	81666	Solano County	115,942
06		82590	Victorville city	115,903
06	071	82590	San Bernardino County	115,903
06		82954	Visalia city	124,442
06	107	82954	Tulare County	124,442
06		82996	Vista city	93,834
06	073	82996	San Diego County	93,834
06		83332	Walnut city	29,172
06	037	83332	Los Angeles County	29,172
06		83346	Walnut Creek city	64,173
06	013	83346	Contra Costa County	64,173
06		83542	Wasco city	25,545
06	029	83542	Kern County	25,545
06		83668	Watsonville city	51,199
06	087	83668	Santa Cruz County	51,199
06		84200	West Covina city	106,098
06	037	84200	Los Angeles County	106,098
06		84410	West Hollywood city	34,399
06	037	84410	Los Angeles County	34,399
06		84550	Westminster city	89,701
06	059	84550	Orange County	89,701
06		84816	West Sacramento city	48,744
06	113	84816	Yolo County	48,744
06		85292	Whittier city	85,331
06	037	85292	Los Angeles County	85,331
06		85446	Wildomar city	32,176
06	065	85446	Riverside County	32,176
06		85922	Windsor town	26,801
06	097	85922	Sonoma County	26,801
06		86328	Woodland city	55,468
06	113	86328	Yolo County	55,468
06		86832	Yorba Linda city	64,234
06	059	86832	Orange County	64,234
06		86972	Yuba City city	64,925
06	101	86972	Sutter County	64,925
06		87042	Yucaipa city	51,367
06	071	87042	San Bernardino County	51,367
08			**COLORADO**	5,029,196
08	03455		Arvada city	106,433

State code	Place code	County code	Geographic Area Name	2010 census population
08	001	03455	Adams County	2,849
08	059	03455	Jefferson County	103,584
08		04000	Aurora city	325,078
08	001	04000	Adams County	39,871
08	005	04000	Arapahoe County	285,090
08	035	04000	Douglas County	117
08		07850	Boulder city	97,385
08	013	07850	Boulder County	97,385
08		08675	Brighton city	33,352
08	001	08675	Adams County	33,009
08	123	08675	Weld County	343
08		09280	Broomfield city	55,889
08	014	09280	Broomfield County	55,889
08		12415	Castle Rock town	48,231
08	035	12415	Douglas County	48,231
08		12815	Centennial city	100,377
08	005	12815	Arapahoe County	100,377
08		16000	Colorado Springs city	416,427
08	041	16000	El Paso County	416,427
08		16495	Commerce City city	45,913
08	001	16495	Adams County	45,913
08		20000	Denver city	600,158
08	031	20000	Denver County	600,158
08		24785	Englewood city	30,255
08	005	24785	Arapahoe County	30,255
08		27425	Fort Collins city	143,986
08	069	27425	Larimer County	143,986
08		27865	Fountain city	25,846
08	041	27865	El Paso County	25,846
08		31660	Grand Junction city	58,566
08	077	31660	Mesa County	58,566
08		32155	Greeley city	92,889
08	123	32155	Weld County	92,889
08		43000	Lakewood city	142,980
08	059	43000	Jefferson County	142,980
08		45255	Littleton city	41,737
08	005	45255	Arapahoe County	39,328
08	035	45255	Douglas County	28
08	059	45255	Jefferson County	2,381
08		45970	Longmont city	86,270
08	013	45970	Boulder County	86,240
08	123	45970	Weld County	30
08		46465	Loveland city	66,859
08	069	46465	Larimer County	66,859
08		54330	Northglenn city	35,789
08	001	54330	Adams County	35,777
08	123	54330	Weld County	12
08		57630	Parker town	45,297
08	035	57630	Douglas County	45,297
08		62000	Pueblo city	106,595
08	101	62000	Pueblo County	106,595
08		77290	Thornton city	118,772
08	001	77290	Adams County	118,772
08	123	77290	Weld County	0
08		83835	Westminster city	106,114
08	001	83835	Adams County	63,696
08	059	83835	Jefferson County	42,418
08		84440	Wheat Ridge city	30,166
08	059	84440	Jefferson County	30,166
09			**CONNECTICUT**	3,574,097
09		08000	Bridgeport city	144,229
09	001	08000	Fairfield County	144,229
09		08420	Bristol city	60,477
09	003	08420	Hartford County	60,477
09		18430	Danbury city	80,893
09	001	18430	Fairfield County	80,893
09		37000	Hartford city	124,775
09	003	37000	Hartford County	124,775
09		46450	Meriden city	60,868
09	009	46450	New Haven County	60,868
09		47290	Middletown city	47,648
09	007	47290	Middlesex County	47,648
09		49880	Naugatuck borough	31,862
09	009	49880	New Haven County	31,862
09		50370	New Britain city	73,206
09	003	50370	Hartford County	73,206
09		52000	New Haven city	129,779
09	009	52000	New Haven County	129,779
09		52280	New London city	27,620
09	011	52280	New London County	27,620
09		55990	Norwalk city	85,603
09	001	55990	Fairfield County	85,603
09		56200	Norwich city	40,493
09	011	56200	New London County	40,493
09		68100	Shelton city	39,559
09	001	68100	Fairfield County	39,559
09		73000	Stamford city	122,643
09	001	73000	Fairfield County	122,643
09		76500	Torrington city	36,383
09	005	76500	Litchfield County	36,383
09		80000	Waterbury city	110,366
09	009	80000	New Haven County	110,366
09		82800	West Haven city	55,564
09	009	82800	New Haven County	55,564
10			**DELAWARE**	897,934
10		21200	Dover city	36,047
10	001	21200	Kent County	36,047
10		50670	Newark city	31,454
10	003	50670	New Castle County	31,454
10		77580	Wilmington city	70,851
10	003	77580	New Castle County	70,851
11			**DISTRICT OF COLUMBIA**	601,723
11		50000	Washington city	601,723
11	001	50000	District of Columbia	601,723
12			**FLORIDA**	18,801,310
12		00950	Altamonte Springs city	41,496
12	117	00950	Seminole County	41,496
12		01700	Apopka city	41,542
12	095	01700	Orange County	41,542
12		02681	Aventura city	35,762
12	086	02681	Miami-Dade County	35,762
12		07300	Boca Raton city	84,392
12	099	07300	Palm Beach County	84,392
12		07525	Bonita Springs city	43,914
12	071	07525	Lee County	43,914
12		07875	Boynton Beach city	68,217
12	099	07875	Palm Beach County	68,217
12		07950	Bradenton city	49,546
12	081	07950	Manatee County	49,546
12		10275	Cape Coral city	154,305
12	071	10275	Lee County	154,305

State code	Place code	County code	Geographic Area Name	2010 census population
12		11050	Casselberry city	26,241
12	117	11050	Seminole County	26,241
12		12875	Clearwater city	107,685
12	103	12875	Pinellas County	107,685
12		12925	Clermont city	28,742
12	069	12925	Lake County	28,742
12		13275	Coconut Creek city	52,909
12	011	13275	Broward County	52,909
12		14125	Cooper City city	28,547
12	011	14125	Broward County	28,547
12		14250	Coral Gables city	46,780
12	086	14250	Miami-Dade County	46,780
12		14400	Coral Springs city	121,096
12	011	14400	Broward County	121,096
12		15968	Cutler Bay town	40,286
12	086	15968	Miami-Dade County	40,286
12		16335	Dania Beach city	29,639
12	011	16335	Broward County	29,639
12		16475	Davie town	91,992
12	011	16475	Broward County	91,992
12		16525	Daytona Beach city	61,005
12	127	16525	Volusia County	61,005
12		16725	Deerfield Beach city	75,018
12	011	16725	Broward County	75,018
12		16875	DeLand city	27,031
12	127	16875	Volusia County	27,031
12		17100	Delray Beach city	60,522
12	099	17100	Palm Beach County	60,522
12		17200	Deltona city	85,182
12	127	17200	Volusia County	85,182
12		17935	Doral city	45,704
12	086	17935	Miami-Dade County	45,704
12		18575	Dunedin city	35,321
12	103	18575	Pinellas County	35,321
12		24000	Fort Lauderdale city	165,521
12	011	24000	Broward County	165,521
12		24125	Fort Myers city	62,298
12	071	24125	Lee County	62,298
12		24300	Fort Pierce city	41,590
12	111	24300	St. Lucie County	41,590
12		25175	Gainesville city	124,354
12	001	25175	Alachua County	124,354
12		27322	Greenacres city	37,573
12	099	27322	Palm Beach County	37,573
12		28452	Hallandale Beach city	37,113
12	011	28452	Broward County	37,113
12		30000	Hialeah city	224,669
12	086	30000	Miami-Dade County	224,669
12		32000	Hollywood city	140,768
12	011	32000	Broward County	140,768
12		32275	Homestead city	60,512
12	086	32275	Miami-Dade County	60,512
12		35000	Jacksonville city	821,784
12	031	35000	Duval County	821,784
12		35875	Jupiter town	55,156
12	099	35875	Palm Beach County	55,156
12		36950	Kissimmee city	59,682
12	097	36950	Osceola County	59,682
12		38250	Lakeland city	97,422

State code	Place code	County code	Geographic Area Name	2010 census population
12	105	38250	Polk County	97,422
12		39075	Lake Worth city	34,910
12	099	39075	Palm Beach County	34,910
12		39425	Largo city	77,648
12	103	39425	Pinellas County	77,648
12		39525	Lauderdale Lakes city	32,593
12	011	39525	Broward County	32,593
12		39550	Lauderhill city	66,887
12	011	39550	Broward County	66,887
12		43125	Margate city	53,284
12	011	43125	Broward County	53,284
12		43975	Melbourne city	76,068
12	009	43975	Brevard County	76,068
12		45000	Miami city	399,457
12	086	45000	Miami-Dade County	399,457
12		45025	Miami Beach city	87,779
12	086	45025	Miami-Dade County	87,779
12		45060	Miami Gardens city	107,167
12	086	45060	Miami-Dade County	107,167
12		45100	Miami Lakes town	29,361
12	086	45100	Miami-Dade County	29,361
12		45975	Miramar city	122,041
12	011	45975	Broward County	122,041
12		49425	North Lauderdale city	41,023
12	011	49425	Broward County	41,023
12		49450	North Miami city	58,786
12	086	49450	Miami-Dade County	58,786
12		49475	North Miami Beach city	41,523
12	086	49475	Miami-Dade County	41,523
12		49675	North Port city	57,357
12	115	49675	Sarasota County	57,357
12		50575	Oakland Park city	41,363
12	011	50575	Broward County	41,363
12		50750	Ocala city	56,315
12	083	50750	Marion County	56,315
12		51075	Ocoee city	35,579
12	095	51075	Orange County	35,579
12		53000	Orlando city	238,300
12	095	53000	Orange County	238,300
12		53150	Ormond Beach city	38,137
12	127	53150	Volusia County	38,137
12		53575	Oviedo city	33,342
12	117	53575	Seminole County	33,342
12		54000	Palm Bay city	103,190
12	009	54000	Brevard County	103,190
12		54075	Palm Beach Gardens city	48,452
12	099	54075	Palm Beach County	48,452
12		54200	Palm Coast city	75,180
12	035	54200	Flagler County	75,180
12		54700	Panama City city	36,484
12	005	54700	Bay County	36,484
12		55775	Pembroke Pines city	154,750
12	011	55775	Broward County	154,750
12		55925	Pensacola city	51,923
12	033	55925	Escambia County	51,923
12		56975	Pinellas Park city	49,079
12	103	56975	Pinellas County	49,079
12		57425	Plantation city	84,955
12	011	57425	Broward County	84,955

State code	Place code	County code	Geographic Area Name	2010 census population
12		57550	Plant City city	34,721
12	057	57550	Hillsborough County	34,721
12		58050	Pompano Beach city	99,845
12	011	58050	Broward County	99,845
12		58575	Port Orange city	56,048
12	127	58575	Volusia County	56,048
12		58715	Port St. Lucie city	164,603
12	111	58715	St. Lucie County	164,603
12		60975	Riviera Beach city	32,488
12	099	60975	Palm Beach County	32,488
12		62100	Royal Palm Beach village	34,140
12	099	62100	Palm Beach County	34,140
12		62625	St. Cloud city	35,183
12	097	62625	Osceola County	35,183
12		63000	St. Petersburg city	244,769
12	103	63000	Pinellas County	244,769
12		63650	Sanford city	53,570
12	117	63650	Seminole County	53,570
12		64175	Sarasota city	51,917
12	115	64175	Sarasota County	51,917
12		69700	Sunrise city	84,439
12	011	69700	Broward County	84,439
12		70600	Tallahassee city	181,376
12	073	70600	Leon County	181,376
12		70675	Tamarac city	60,427
12	011	70675	Broward County	60,427
12		71000	Tampa city	335,709
12	057	71000	Hillsborough County	335,709
12		71900	Titusville city	43,761
12	009	71900	Brevard County	43,761
12		75812	Wellington village	56,508
12	099	75812	Palm Beach County	56,508
12		76582	Weston city	65,333
12	011	76582	Broward County	65,333
12		76600	West Palm Beach city	99,919
12	099	76600	Palm Beach County	99,919
12		78250	Winter Garden city	34,568
12	095	78250	Orange County	34,568
12		78275	Winter Haven city	33,874
12	105	78275	Polk County	33,874
12		78300	Winter Park city	27,852
12	095	78300	Orange County	27,852
12		78325	Winter Springs city	33,282
12	117	78325	Seminole County	33,282
13			**GEORGIA**	9,687,653
13		01052	Albany city	77,434
13	095	01052	Dougherty County	77,434
13		01696	Alpharetta city	57,551
13	121	01696	Fulton County	57,551
13		04000	Atlanta city	420,003
13	089	04000	DeKalb County	28,292
13	121	04000	Fulton County	391,711
13		19000	Columbus city	189,885
13	215	19000	Muscogee County	189,885
13		21380	Dalton city	33,128
13	313	21380	Whitfield County	33,128
13		23900	Douglasville city	30,961
13	097	23900	Douglas County	30,961
13		24600	Duluth city	26,600
13	135	24600	Gwinnett County	26,600
13		24768	Dunwoody city	46,267
13	089	24768	DeKalb County	46,267
13		25720	East Point city	33,712
13	121	25720	Fulton County	33,712
13		31908	Gainesville city	33,804
13	139	31908	Hall County	33,804
13		38964	Hinesville city	33,437
13	179	38964	Liberty County	33,437
13		42425	Johns Creek city	76,728
13	121	42425	Fulton County	76,728
13		43192	Kennesaw city	29,783
13	067	43192	Cobb County	29,783
13		44340	LaGrange city	29,588
13	285	44340	Troup County	29,588
13		45488	Lawrenceville city	28,546
13	135	45488	Gwinnett County	28,546
13		49000	Macon city	91,351
13	021	49000	Bibb County	90,885
13	169	49000	Jones County	466
13		49756	Marietta city	56,579
13	067	49756	Cobb County	56,579
13		51670	Milton city	32,661
13	121	51670	Fulton County	32,661
13		55020	Newnan city	33,039
13	077	55020	Coweta County	33,039
13		59724	Peachtree City city	34,364
13	113	59724	Fayette County	34,364
13		66668	Rome city	36,303
13	115	66668	Floyd County	36,303
13		67284	Roswell city	88,346
13	121	67284	Fulton County	88,346
13		68516	Sandy Springs city	93,853
13	121	68516	Fulton County	93,853
13		69000	Savannah city	136,286
13	051	69000	Chatham County	136,286
13		71492	Smyrna city	51,271
13	067	71492	Cobb County	51,271
13		73256	Statesboro city	28,422
13	031	73256	Bulloch County	28,422
13		73704	Stockbridge city	25,636
13	151	73704	Henry County	25,636
13		78800	Valdosta city	54,518
13	185	78800	Lowndes County	54,518
13		80508	Warner Robins city	66,588
13	153	80508	Houston County	66,224
13	225	80508	Peach County	364
15			**HAWAII**	1,360,301
15		06290	East Honolulu CDP	49,914
15	003	06290	Honolulu County	49,914
15		14650	Hilo CDP	43,263
15	001	14650	Hawaii County	43,263
15		22700	Kahului CDP	26,337
15	009	22700	Maui County	26,337
15		23150	Kailua CDP	38,635
15	003	23150	Honolulu County	38,635
15		28250	Kaneohe CDP	34,597
15	003	28250	Honolulu County	34,597
15		51050	Mililani Town CDP	27,629
15	003	51050	Honolulu County	27,629

State code	Place code	County code	Geographic Area Name	2010 census population
15		62600	Pearl City CDP	47,698
15	003	62600	Honolulu County	47,698
15		71550	Urban Honolulu CDP	337,256
15	003	71550	Honolulu County	337,256
15		79700	Waipahu CDP	38,216
15	003	79700	Honolulu County	38,216
16			**IDAHO**	1,567,582
16		08830	Boise City city	205,671
16	001	08830	Ada County	205,671
16		12250	Caldwell city	46,237
16	027	12250	Canyon County	46,237
16		16750	Coeur d'Alene city	44,137
16	055	16750	Kootenai County	44,137
16		39700	Idaho Falls city	56,813
16	019	39700	Bonneville County	56,813
16		46540	Lewiston city	31,894
16	069	46540	Nez Perce County	31,894
16		52120	Meridian city	75,092
16	001	52120	Ada County	75,092
16		56260	Nampa city	81,557
16	027	56260	Canyon County	81,557
16		64090	Pocatello city	54,255
16	005	64090	Bannock County	54,239
16	077	64090	Power County	16
16		64810	Post Falls city	27,574
16	055	64810	Kootenai County	27,574
16		67420	Rexburg city	25,484
16	065	67420	Madison County	25,484
16		82810	Twin Falls city	44,125
16	083	82810	Twin Falls County	44,125
17			**ILLINOIS**	12,830,632
17		00243	Addison village	36,942
17	043	00243	DuPage County	36,942
17		00685	Algonquin village	30,046
17	089	00685	Kane County	8,433
17	111	00685	McHenry County	21,613
17		01114	Alton city	27,865
17	119	01114	Madison County	27,865
17		02154	Arlington Heights village	75,101
17	031	02154	Cook County	75,101
17	097	02154	Lake County	0
17		03012	Aurora city	197,899
17	043	03012	DuPage County	49,433
17	089	03012	Kane County	130,976
17	093	03012	Kendall County	6,019
17	197	03012	Will County	11,471
17		04013	Bartlett village	41,208
17	031	04013	Cook County	16,797
17	043	04013	DuPage County	24,411
17	089	04013	Kane County	0
17		04078	Batavia city	26,045
17	043	04078	DuPage County	0
17	089	04078	Kane County	26,045
17		04845	Belleville city	44,478
17	163	04845	St. Clair County	44,478
17		05092	Belvidere city	25,585
17	007	05092	Boone County	25,585
17		05573	Berwyn city	56,657
17	031	05573	Cook County	56,657
17		06613	Bloomington city	76,610
17	113	06613	McLean County	76,610
17		07133	Bolingbrook village	73,366
17	043	07133	DuPage County	1,571
17	197	07133	Will County	71,795
17		09447	Buffalo Grove village	41,496
17	031	09447	Cook County	13,644
17	097	09447	Lake County	27,852
17		09642	Burbank city	28,925
17	031	09642	Cook County	28,925
17		10487	Calumet City city	37,042
17	031	10487	Cook County	37,042
17		11163	Carbondale city	25,902
17	077	11163	Jackson County	25,902
17	199	11163	Williamson County	0
17		11332	Carol Stream village	39,711
17	043	11332	DuPage County	39,711
17		11358	Carpentersville village	37,691
17	089	11358	Kane County	37,691
17		12385	Champaign city	81,055
17	019	12385	Champaign County	81,055
17		14000	Chicago city	2,695,598
17	031	14000	Cook County	2,695,598
17	043	14000	DuPage County	0
17		14026	Chicago Heights city	30,276
17	031	14026	Cook County	30,276
17		14351	Cicero town	83,891
17	031	14351	Cook County	83,891
17		15599	Collinsville city	25,579
17	119	15599	Madison County	22,573
17	163	15599	St. Clair County	3,006
17		17887	Crystal Lake city	40,743
17	111	17887	McHenry County	40,743
17		18563	Danville city	33,027
17	183	18563	Vermilion County	33,027
17		18823	Decatur city	76,122
17	115	18823	Macon County	76,122
17		19161	DeKalb city	43,862
17	037	19161	DeKalb County	43,862
17		19642	Des Plaines city	58,364
17	031	19642	Cook County	58,364
17		20591	Downers Grove village	47,833
17	043	20591	DuPage County	47,833
17		22255	East St. Louis city	27,006
17	163	22255	St. Clair County	27,006
17		23074	Elgin city	108,188
17	031	23074	Cook County	24,032
17	089	23074	Kane County	84,156
17		23256	Elk Grove Village village	33,127
17	031	23256	Cook County	33,127
17	043	23256	DuPage County	0
17		23620	Elmhurst city	44,121
17	031	23620	Cook County	0
17	043	23620	DuPage County	44,121
17		24582	Evanston city	74,486
17	031	24582	Cook County	74,486
17		27884	Freeport city	25,638
17	177	27884	Stephenson County	25,638
17		28326	Galesburg city	32,195
17	095	28326	Knox County	32,195
17		29730	Glendale Heights village	34,208
17	043	29730	DuPage County	34,208
17		29756	Glen Ellyn village	27,450
17	043	29756	DuPage County	27,450
17		29938	Glenview village	44,692

State code	Place code	County code	Geographic Area Name	2010 census population
17	031	29938	Cook County	44,692
17		30926	Granite City city	29,849
17	119	30926	Madison County	29,849
17		32018	Gurnee village	31,295
17	097	32018	Lake County	31,295
17		32746	Hanover Park village	37,973
17	031	32746	Cook County	20,636
17	043	32746	DuPage County	17,337
17		33383	Harvey city	25,282
17	031	33383	Cook County	25,282
17		34722	Highland Park city	29,763
17	097	34722	Lake County	29,763
17		35411	Hoffman Estates village	51,895
17	031	35411	Cook County	51,895
17	089	35411	Kane County	0
17		38570	Joliet city	147,433
17	093	38570	Kendall County	9,749
17	197	38570	Will County	137,684
17		38934	Kankakee city	27,537
17	091	38934	Kankakee County	27,537
17		41183	Lake in the Hills village	28,965
17	111	41183	McHenry County	28,965
17		42028	Lansing village	28,331
17	031	42028	Cook County	28,331
17		44407	Lombard village	43,165
17	043	44407	DuPage County	43,165
17		45694	McHenry city	26,992
17	111	45694	McHenry County	26,992
17		48242	Melrose Park village	25,411
17	031	48242	Cook County	25,411
17		49867	Moline city	43,483
17	161	49867	Rock Island County	43,483
17		51089	Mount Prospect village	54,167
17	031	51089	Cook County	54,167
17		51349	Mundelein village	31,064
17	097	51349	Lake County	31,064
17		51622	Naperville city	141,853
17	043	51622	DuPage County	94,533
17	197	51622	Will County	47,320
17		53000	Niles village	29,803
17	031	53000	Cook County	29,803
17		53234	Normal town	52,497
17	113	53234	McLean County	52,497
17		53481	Northbrook village	33,170
17	031	53481	Cook County	33,170
17		53559	North Chicago city	32,574
17	097	53559	Lake County	32,574
17		54638	Oak Forest city	27,962
17	031	54638	Cook County	27,962
17		54820	Oak Lawn village	56,690
17	031	54820	Cook County	56,690
17		54885	Oak Park village	51,878
17	031	54885	Cook County	51,878
17		55249	O'Fallon city	28,281
17	163	55249	St. Clair County	28,281
17		56640	Orland Park village	56,767
17	031	56640	Cook County	56,583
17	197	56640	Will County	184
17		56887	Oswego village	30,355
17	093	56887	Kendall County	30,355
17		57225	Palatine village	68,557

State code	Place code	County code	Geographic Area Name	2010 census population
17	031	57225	Cook County	68,557
17	097	57225	Lake County	0
17		57875	Park Ridge city	37,480
17	031	57875	Cook County	37,480
17		58447	Pekin city	34,094
17	143	58447	Peoria County	0
17	179	58447	Tazewell County	34,094
17		59000	Peoria city	115,007
17	143	59000	Peoria County	115,007
17		60287	Plainfield village	39,581
17	093	60287	Kendall County	2,079
17	197	60287	Will County	37,502
17		62367	Quincy city	40,633
17	001	62367	Adams County	40,633
17		65000	Rockford city	152,871
17	201	65000	Winnebago County	152,871
17		65078	Rock Island city	39,018
17	161	65078	Rock Island County	39,018
17		65442	Romeoville village	39,680
17	197	65442	Will County	39,680
17		66040	Round Lake Beach village	28,175
17	097	66040	Lake County	28,175
17		66703	St. Charles city	32,974
17	043	66703	DuPage County	543
17	089	66703	Kane County	32,431
17		68003	Schaumburg village	74,227
17	031	68003	Cook County	74,227
17	043	68003	DuPage County	0
17		70122	Skokie village	64,784
17	031	70122	Cook County	64,784
17		72000	Springfield city	116,250
17	167	72000	Sangamon County	116,250
17		73157	Streamwood village	39,858
17	031	73157	Cook County	39,858
17		75484	Tinley Park village	56,703
17	031	75484	Cook County	49,236
17	197	75484	Will County	7,467
17		77005	Urbana city	41,250
17	019	77005	Champaign County	41,250
17		77694	Vernon Hills village	25,113
17	097	77694	Lake County	25,113
17		79293	Waukegan city	89,078
17	097	79293	Lake County	89,078
17		80060	West Chicago city	27,086
17	043	80060	DuPage County	27,086
17		81048	Wheaton city	52,894
17	043	81048	DuPage County	52,894
17		81087	Wheeling village	37,648
17	031	81087	Cook County	37,642
17	097	81087	Lake County	6
17		82075	Wilmette village	27,087
17	031	82075	Cook County	27,087
17		83245	Woodridge village	32,971
17	031	83245	Cook County	0
17	043	83245	DuPage County	32,949
17	197	83245	Will County	22
18			**INDIANA**	6,483,802
18		01468	Anderson city	56,129
18	095	01468	Madison County	56,129
18		05860	Bloomington city	80,405
18	105	05860	Monroe County	80,405
18		10342	Carmel city	79,191

State code	Place code	County code	Geographic Area Name	2010 census population
18	057	10342	Hamilton County	79,191
18		14734	Columbus city	44,061
18	005	14734	Bartholomew County	44,061
18		16138	Crown Point city	27,317
18	089	16138	Lake County	27,317
18		19486	East Chicago city	29,698
18	089	19486	Lake County	29,698
18		20728	Elkhart city	50,949
18	039	20728	Elkhart County	50,949
18		22000	Evansville city	117,429
18	163	22000	Vanderburgh County	117,429
18		23278	Fishers town	76,794
18	057	23278	Hamilton County	76,794
18		25000	Fort Wayne city	253,691
18	003	25000	Allen County	253,691
18		27000	Gary city	80,294
18	089	27000	Lake County	80,294
18		28386	Goshen city	31,719
18	039	28386	Elkhart County	31,719
18		29898	Greenwood city	49,791
18	081	29898	Johnson County	49,791
18		31000	Hammond city	80,830
18	089	31000	Lake County	80,830
18		34114	Hobart city	29,059
18	089	34114	Lake County	29,059
18		38358	Jeffersonville city	44,953
18	019	38358	Clark County	44,953
18		40392	Kokomo city	45,468
18	067	40392	Howard County	45,468
18		40788	Lafayette city	67,140
18	157	40788	Tippecanoe County	67,140
18		42426	Lawrence city	46,001
18	097	42426	Marion County	46,001
18		46908	Marion city	29,948
18	053	46908	Grant County	29,948
18		48528	Merrillville town	35,246
18	089	48528	Lake County	35,246
18		48798	Michigan City city	31,479
18	091	48798	LaPorte County	31,479
18		49932	Mishawaka city	48,252
18	141	49932	St. Joseph County	48,252
18		51876	Muncie city	70,085
18	035	51876	Delaware County	70,085
18		52326	New Albany city	36,372
18	043	52326	Floyd County	36,372
18		54180	Noblesville city	51,969
18	057	54180	Hamilton County	51,969
18		60246	Plainfield town	27,631
18	063	60246	Hendricks County	27,631
18		61092	Portage city	36,828
18	127	61092	Porter County	36,828
18		64260	Richmond city	36,812
18	177	64260	Wayne County	36,812
18		68220	Schererville town	29,243
18	089	68220	Lake County	29,243
18		71000	South Bend city	101,168
18	141	71000	St. Joseph County	101,168
18		75428	Terre Haute city	60,785
18	167	75428	Vigo County	60,785

State code	Place code	County code	Geographic Area Name	2010 census population
18		78326	Valparaiso city	31,730
18	127	78326	Porter County	31,730
18		82700	Westfield town	30,068
18	057	82700	Hamilton County	30,068
18		82862	West Lafayette city	29,596
18	157	82862	Tippecanoe County	29,596
19			**IOWA**	3,046,355
19		01855	Ames city	58,965
19	169	01855	Story County	58,965
19		02305	Ankeny city	45,582
19	153	02305	Polk County	45,582
19		06355	Bettendorf city	33,217
19	163	06355	Scott County	33,217
19		09550	Burlington city	25,663
19	057	09550	Des Moines County	25,663
19		11755	Cedar Falls city	39,260
19	013	11755	Black Hawk County	39,260
19		12000	Cedar Rapids city	126,326
19	113	12000	Linn County	126,326
19		14430	Clinton city	26,885
19	045	14430	Clinton County	26,885
19		16860	Council Bluffs city	62,230
19	155	16860	Pottawattamie County	62,230
19		19000	Davenport city	99,685
19	163	19000	Scott County	99,685
19		21000	Des Moines city	203,433
19	153	21000	Polk County	203,419
19	181	21000	Warren County	14
19		22395	Dubuque city	57,637
19	061	22395	Dubuque County	57,637
19		28515	Fort Dodge city	25,206
19	187	28515	Webster County	25,206
19		38595	Iowa City city	67,862
19	103	38595	Johnson County	67,862
19		49485	Marion city	34,768
19	113	49485	Linn County	34,768
19		49755	Marshalltown city	27,552
19	127	49755	Marshall County	27,552
19		50160	Mason City city	28,079
19	033	50160	Cerro Gordo County	28,079
19		60465	Ottumwa city	25,023
19	179	60465	Wapello County	25,023
19		73335	Sioux City city	82,684
19	149	73335	Plymouth County	6
19	193	73335	Woodbury County	82,678
19		79950	Urbandale city	39,463
19	049	79950	Dallas County	6,337
19	153	79950	Polk County	33,126
19		82425	Waterloo city	68,406
19	013	82425	Black Hawk County	68,406
19		83910	West Des Moines city	56,609
19	049	83910	Dallas County	11,569
19	153	83910	Polk County	44,999
19	181	83910	Warren County	41
20			**KANSAS**	2,853,118
20		18250	Dodge City city	27,340
20	057	18250	Ford County	27,340
20		25325	Garden City city	26,658
20	055	25325	Finney County	26,658
20		33625	Hutchinson city	42,080
20	155	33625	Reno County	42,080

State code	Place code	County code	Geographic Area Name	2010 census population
20		36000	Kansas City city	145,786
20	209	36000	Wyandotte County	145,786
20		38900	Lawrence city	87,643
20	045	38900	Douglas County	87,643
20		39000	Leavenworth city	35,251
20	103	39000	Leavenworth County	35,251
20		39075	Leawood city	31,867
20	091	39075	Johnson County	31,867
20		39350	Lenexa city	48,190
20	091	39350	Johnson County	48,190
20		44250	Manhattan city	52,281
20	149	44250	Pottawatomie County	146
20	161	44250	Riley County	52,135
20		52575	Olathe city	125,872
20	091	52575	Johnson County	125,872
20		53775	Overland Park city	173,372
20	091	53775	Johnson County	173,372
20		62700	Salina city	47,707
20	169	62700	Saline County	47,707
20		64500	Shawnee city	62,209
20	091	64500	Johnson County	62,209
20		71000	Topeka city	127,473
20	177	71000	Shawnee County	127,473
20		79000	Wichita city	382,368
20	173	79000	Sedgwick County	382,368
21			**KENTUCKY**	4,339,367
21		08902	Bowling Green city	58,067
21	227	08902	Warren County	58,067
21		17848	Covington city	40,640
21	117	17848	Kenton County	40,640
21		24274	Elizabethtown city	28,531
21	093	24274	Hardin County	28,531
21		27982	Florence city	29,951
21	015	27982	Boone County	29,951
21		28900	Frankfort city	25,527
21	073	28900	Franklin County	25,527
21		30700	Georgetown city	29,098
21	209	30700	Scott County	29,098
21		35866	Henderson city	28,757
21	101	35866	Henderson County	28,757
21		37918	Hopkinsville city	31,577
21	047	37918	Christian County	31,577
21		40222	Jeffersontown city	26,595
21	111	40222	Jefferson County	26,595
21		46027	Lexington-Fayette urban county	295,803
21	067	46027	Fayette County	295,803
21		56136	Nicholasville city	28,015
21	113	56136	Jessamine County	28,015
21		58620	Owensboro city	57,265
21	059	58620	Daviess County	57,265
21		58836	Paducah city	25,024
21	145	58836	McCracken County	25,024
21		65226	Richmond city	31,364
21	151	65226	Madison County	31,364
22			**LOUISIANA**	4,533,372
22		00975	Alexandria city	47,723
22	079	00975	Rapides Parish	47,723
22		05000	Baton Rouge city	229,493
22	033	05000	East Baton Rouge Parish	229,493
22		08920	Bossier City city	61,315
22	015	08920	Bossier Parish	61,315
22		13960	Central city	26,864
22	033	13960	East Baton Rouge Parish	26,864
22		36255	Houma city	33,727
22	109	36255	Terrebonne Parish	33,727
22		39475	Kenner city	66,702
22	051	39475	Jefferson Parish	66,702
22		40735	Lafayette city	120,623
22	055	40735	Lafayette Parish	120,623
22		41155	Lake Charles city	71,993
22	019	41155	Calcasieu Parish	71,993
22		51410	Monroe city	48,815
22	073	51410	Ouachita Parish	48,815
22		54035	New Iberia city	30,617
22	045	54035	Iberia Parish	30,617
22		55000	New Orleans city	343,829
22	071	55000	Orleans Parish	343,829
22		70000	Shreveport city	199,311
22	015	70000	Bossier Parish	2,702
22	017	70000	Caddo Parish	196,609
22		70805	Slidell city	27,068
22	103	70805	St. Tammany Parish	27,068
23			**MAINE**	1,328,361
23		02795	Bangor city	33,039
23	019	02795	Penobscot County	33,039
23		38740	Lewiston city	36,592
23	001	38740	Androscoggin County	36,592
23		60545	Portland city	66,194
23	005	60545	Cumberland County	66,194
23		71990	South Portland city	25,002
23	005	71990	Cumberland County	25,002
24			**MARYLAND**	5,773,552
24		01600	Annapolis city	38,394
24	003	01600	Anne Arundel County	38,394
24		04000	Baltimore city	620,961
24	510	04000	Baltimore city	620,961
24		08775	Bowie city	54,727
24	033	08775	Prince George's County	54,727
24		18750	College Park city	30,413
24	033	18750	Prince George's County	30,413
24		30325	Frederick city	65,239
24	021	30325	Frederick County	65,239
24		31175	Gaithersburg city	59,933
24	031	31175	Montgomery County	59,933
24		36075	Hagerstown city	39,662
24	043	36075	Washington County	39,662
24		45900	Laurel city	25,115
24	033	45900	Prince George's County	25,115
24		67675	Rockville city	61,209
24	031	67675	Montgomery County	61,209
24		69925	Salisbury city	30,343
24	045	69925	Wicomico County	30,343
25			**MASSACHUSETTS**	6,547,629
25		00840	Agawam Town city	28,438
25	013	00840	Hampden County	28,438
25		02690	Attleboro city	43,593
25	005	02690	Bristol County	43,593

State code	Place code	County code	Geographic Area Name	2010 census population
25		03690	Barnstable Town city	45,193
25	001	03690	Barnstable County	45,193
25		05595	Beverly city	39,502
25	009	05595	Essex County	39,502
25		07000	Boston city	617,594
25	025	07000	Suffolk County	617,594
25		07740	Braintree Town city	35,744
25	021	07740	Norfolk County	35,744
25		09000	Brockton city	93,810
25	023	09000	Plymouth County	93,810
25		11000	Cambridge city	105,162
25	017	11000	Middlesex County	105,162
25		13205	Chelsea city	35,177
25	025	13205	Suffolk County	35,177
25		13660	Chicopee city	55,298
25	013	13660	Hampden County	55,298
25		21990	Everett city	41,667
25	017	21990	Middlesex County	41,667
25		23000	Fall River city	88,857
25	005	23000	Bristol County	88,857
25		23875	Fitchburg city	40,318
25	027	23875	Worcester County	40,318
25		25172	Franklin Town city	31,635
25	021	25172	Norfolk County	31,635
25		26150	Gloucester city	28,789
25	009	26150	Essex County	28,789
25		29405	Haverhill city	60,879
25	009	29405	Essex County	60,879
25		30840	Holyoke city	39,880
25	013	30840	Hampden County	39,880
25		34550	Lawrence city	76,377
25	009	34550	Essex County	76,377
25		35075	Leominster city	40,759
25	027	35075	Worcester County	40,759
25		37000	Lowell city	106,519
25	017	37000	Middlesex County	106,519
25		37490	Lynn city	90,329
25	009	37490	Essex County	90,329
25		37875	Malden city	59,450
25	017	37875	Middlesex County	59,450
25		38715	Marlborough city	38,499
25	017	38715	Middlesex County	38,499
25		39835	Medford city	56,173
25	017	39835	Middlesex County	56,173
25		40115	Melrose city	26,983
25	017	40115	Middlesex County	26,983
25		40710	Methuen Town city	47,255
25	009	40710	Essex County	47,255
25		45000	New Bedford city	95,072
25	005	45000	Bristol County	95,072
25		45560	Newton city	85,146
25	017	45560	Middlesex County	85,146
25		46330	Northampton city	28,549
25	015	46330	Hampshire County	28,549
25		52490	Peabody city	51,251
25	009	52490	Essex County	51,251
25		53960	Pittsfield city	44,737
25	003	53960	Berkshire County	44,737
25		55745	Quincy city	92,271
25	021	55745	Norfolk County	92,271

State code	Place code	County code	Geographic Area Name	2010 census population
25		56585	Revere city	51,755
25	025	56585	Suffolk County	51,755
25		59105	Salem city	41,340
25	009	59105	Essex County	41,340
25		62535	Somerville city	75,754
25	017	62535	Middlesex County	75,754
25		67000	Springfield city	153,060
25	013	67000	Hampden County	153,060
25		69170	Taunton city	55,874
25	005	69170	Bristol County	55,874
25		72600	Waltham city	60,632
25	017	72600	Middlesex County	60,632
25		73440	Watertown Town city	31,915
25	017	73440	Middlesex County	31,915
25		76030	Westfield city	41,094
25	013	76030	Hampden County	41,094
25		77890	West Springfield Town city	28,391
25	013	77890	Hampden County	28,391
25		78972	Weymouth Town city	53,743
25	021	78972	Norfolk County	53,743
25		81035	Woburn city	38,120
25	017	81035	Middlesex County	38,120
25		82000	Worcester city	181,045
25	027	82000	Worcester County	181,045
26			**MICHIGAN**	9,883,640
26		01380	Allen Park city	28,210
26	163	01380	Wayne County	28,210
26		03000	Ann Arbor city	113,934
26	161	03000	Washtenaw County	113,934
26		05920	Battle Creek city	52,347
26	025	05920	Calhoun County	52,347
26		06020	Bay City city	34,932
26	017	06020	Bay County	34,932
26		12060	Burton city	29,999
26	049	12060	Genesee County	29,999
26		21000	Dearborn city	98,153
26	163	21000	Wayne County	98,153
26		21020	Dearborn Heights city	57,774
26	163	21020	Wayne County	57,774
26		22000	Detroit city	713,777
26	163	22000	Wayne County	713,777
26		24120	East Lansing city	48,579
26	037	24120	Clinton County	1,969
26	065	24120	Ingham County	46,610
26		24290	Eastpointe city	32,442
26	099	24290	Macomb County	32,442
26		27440	Farmington Hills city	79,740
26	125	27440	Oakland County	79,740
26		29000	Flint city	102,434
26	049	29000	Genesee County	102,434
26		31420	Garden City city	27,692
26	163	31420	Wayne County	27,692
26		34000	Grand Rapids city	188,040
26	081	34000	Kent County	188,040
26		38640	Holland city	33,051
26	005	38640	Allegan County	7,016
26	139	38640	Ottawa County	26,035
26		40680	Inkster city	25,369
26	163	40680	Wayne County	25,369

State code	Place code	County code	Geographic Area Name	2010 census population
26		41420	Jackson city	33,534
26	075	41420	Jackson County	33,534
26		42160	Kalamazoo city	74,262
26	077	42160	Kalamazoo County	74,262
26		42820	Kentwood city	48,707
26	081	42820	Kent County	48,707
26		46000	Lansing city	114,297
26	045	46000	Eaton County	4,734
26	065	46000	Ingham County	109,563
26		47800	Lincoln Park city	38,144
26	163	47800	Wayne County	38,144
26		49000	Livonia city	96,942
26	163	49000	Wayne County	96,942
26		50560	Madison Heights city	29,694
26	125	50560	Oakland County	29,694
26		53780	Midland city	41,863
26	017	53780	Bay County	157
26	111	53780	Midland County	41,706
26		56020	Mount Pleasant city	26,016
26	073	56020	Isabella County	26,016
26		56320	Muskegon city	38,401
26	121	56320	Muskegon County	38,401
26		59440	Novi city	55,224
26	125	59440	Oakland County	55,224
26		59920	Oak Park city	29,319
26	125	59920	Oakland County	29,319
26		65440	Pontiac city	59,515
26	125	65440	Oakland County	59,515
26		65560	Portage city	46,292
26	077	65560	Kalamazoo County	46,292
26		65820	Port Huron city	30,184
26	147	65820	St. Clair County	30,184
26		69035	Rochester Hills city	70,995
26	125	69035	Oakland County	70,995
26		69800	Roseville city	47,299
26	099	69800	Macomb County	47,299
26		70040	Royal Oak city	57,236
26	125	70040	Oakland County	57,236
26		70520	Saginaw city	51,508
26	145	70520	Saginaw County	51,508
26		70760	St. Clair Shores city	59,715
26	099	70760	Macomb County	59,715
26		74900	Southfield city	71,739
26	125	74900	Oakland County	71,739
26		74960	Southgate city	30,047
26	163	74960	Wayne County	30,047
26		76460	Sterling Heights city	129,699
26	099	76460	Macomb County	129,699
26		79000	Taylor city	63,131
26	163	79000	Wayne County	63,131
26		80700	Troy city	80,980
26	125	80700	Oakland County	80,980
26		84000	Warren city	134,056
26	099	84000	Macomb County	134,056
26		86000	Westland city	84,094
26	163	86000	Wayne County	84,094
26		88900	Wyandotte city	25,883
26	163	88900	Wayne County	25,883
26		88940	Wyoming city	72,125
26	081	88940	Kent County	72,125
27			**MINNESOTA**	5,303,925
27		01486	Andover city	30,598
27	003	01486	Anoka County	30,598
27		01900	Apple Valley city	49,084
27	037	01900	Dakota County	49,084
27		06382	Blaine city	57,186
27	003	06382	Anoka County	57,186
27	123	06382	Ramsey County	0
27		06616	Bloomington city	82,893
27	053	06616	Hennepin County	82,893
27		07948	Brooklyn Center city	30,104
27	053	07948	Hennepin County	30,104
27		07966	Brooklyn Park city	75,781
27	053	07966	Hennepin County	75,781
27		08794	Burnsville city	60,306
27	037	08794	Dakota County	60,306
27		13114	Coon Rapids city	61,476
27	003	13114	Anoka County	61,476
27		13456	Cottage Grove city	34,589
27	163	13456	Washington County	34,589
27		17000	Duluth city	86,265
27	137	17000	St. Louis County	86,265
27		17288	Eagan city	64,206
27	037	17288	Dakota County	64,206
27		18116	Eden Prairie city	60,797
27	053	18116	Hennepin County	60,797
27		18188	Edina city	47,941
27	053	18188	Hennepin County	47,941
27		22814	Fridley city	27,208
27	003	22814	Anoka County	27,208
27		31076	Inver Grove Heights city	33,880
27	037	31076	Dakota County	33,880
27		35180	Lakeville city	55,954
27	037	35180	Dakota County	55,954
27		39878	Mankato city	39,309
27	013	39878	Blue Earth County	39,305
27	079	39878	Le Sueur County	4
27	103	39878	Nicollet County	0
27		40166	Maple Grove city	61,567
27	053	40166	Hennepin County	61,567
27		40382	Maplewood city	38,018
27	123	40382	Ramsey County	38,018
27		43000	Minneapolis city	382,578
27	053	43000	Hennepin County	382,578
27		43252	Minnetonka city	49,734
27	053	43252	Hennepin County	49,734
27		43864	Moorhead city	38,065
27	027	43864	Clay County	38,065
27		47680	Oakdale city	27,378
27	163	47680	Washington County	27,378
27		49300	Owatonna city	25,599
27	147	49300	Steele County	25,599
27		51730	Plymouth city	70,576
27	053	51730	Hennepin County	70,576
27		54214	Richfield city	35,228
27	053	54214	Hennepin County	35,228
27		54880	Rochester city	106,769
27	109	54880	Olmsted County	106,769
27		55852	Roseville city	33,660
27	123	55852	Ramsey County	33,660

State code	Place code	County code	Geographic Area Name	2010 census population
27		56896	St. Cloud city	65,842
27	009	56896	Benton County	6,396
27	141	56896	Sherburne County	6,785
27	145	56896	Stearns County	52,661
27		57220	St. Louis Park city	45,250
27	053	57220	Hennepin County	45,250
27		58000	St. Paul city	285,068
27	123	58000	Ramsey County	285,068
27		58738	Savage city	26,911
27	139	58738	Scott County	26,911
27		59350	Shakopee city	37,076
27	139	59350	Scott County	37,076
27		59998	Shoreview city	25,043
27	123	59998	Ramsey County	25,043
27		71032	Winona city	27,592
27	169	71032	Winona County	27,592
27		71428	Woodbury city	61,961
27	163	71428	Washington County	61,961
28			**MISSISSIPPI**	2,967,297
28		06220	Biloxi city	44,054
28	047	06220	Harrison County	44,054
28		14420	Clinton city	25,216
28	049	14420	Hinds County	25,216
28		29180	Greenville city	34,400
28	151	29180	Washington County	34,400
28		29700	Gulfport city	67,793
28	047	29700	Harrison County	67,793
28		31020	Hattiesburg city	45,989
28	035	31020	Forrest County	41,000
28	073	31020	Lamar County	4,989
28		33700	Horn Lake city	26,066
28	033	33700	DeSoto County	26,066
28		36000	Jackson city	173,514
28	049	36000	Hinds County	172,891
28	089	36000	Madison County	622
28	121	36000	Rankin County	1
28		46640	Meridian city	41,148
28	075	46640	Lauderdale County	41,148
28		54040	Olive Branch city	33,484
28	033	54040	DeSoto County	33,484
28		55760	Pearl city	25,092
28	121	55760	Rankin County	25,092
28		69280	Southaven city	48,982
28	033	69280	DeSoto County	48,982
28		74840	Tupelo city	34,546
28	081	74840	Lee County	34,546
29			**MISSOURI**	5,988,927
29		03160	Ballwin city	30,404
29	189	03160	St. Louis County	30,404
29		06652	Blue Springs city	52,575
29	095	06652	Jackson County	52,575
29		11242	Cape Girardeau city	37,941
29	031	11242	Cape Girardeau County	37,941
29	201	11242	Scott County	0
29		13600	Chesterfield city	47,484
29	189	13600	St. Louis County	47,484
29		15670	Columbia city	108,500
29	019	15670	Boone County	108,500
29		24778	Florissant city	52,158
29	189	24778	St. Louis County	52,158
29		27190	Gladstone city	25,410
29	047	27190	Clay County	25,410
29		31276	Hazelwood city	25,703
29	189	31276	St. Louis County	25,703
29		35000	Independence city	116,830
29	047	35000	Clay County	0
29	095	35000	Jackson County	116,830
29		37000	Jefferson City city	43,079
29	027	37000	Callaway County	22
29	051	37000	Cole County	43,057
29		37592	Joplin city	50,150
29	097	37592	Jasper County	43,955
29	145	37592	Newton County	6,195
29		38000	Kansas City city	459,787
29	037	38000	Cass County	197
29	047	38000	Clay County	113,415
29	095	38000	Jackson County	302,499
29	165	38000	Platte County	43,676
29		39044	Kirkwood city	27,540
29	189	39044	St. Louis County	27,540
29		41348	Lee's Summit city	91,364
29	037	41348	Cass County	1,917
29	095	41348	Jackson County	89,447
29		42032	Liberty city	29,149
29	047	42032	Clay County	29,149
29		46586	Maryland Heights city	27,472
29	189	46586	St. Louis County	27,472
29		54074	O'Fallon city	79,329
29	183	54074	St. Charles County	79,329
29		60788	Raytown city	29,526
29	095	60788	Jackson County	29,526
29		64082	St. Charles city	65,794
29	183	64082	St. Charles County	65,794
29		64550	St. Joseph city	76,780
29	021	64550	Buchanan County	76,780
29		65000	St. Louis city	319,294
29	510	65000	St. Louis city	319,294
29		65126	St. Peters city	52,575
29	183	65126	St. Charles County	52,575
29		70000	Springfield city	159,498
29	043	70000	Christian County	2
29	077	70000	Greene County	159,496
29		75220	University City city	35,371
29	189	75220	St. Louis County	35,371
29		78442	Wentzville city	29,070
29	183	78442	St. Charles County	29,070
29		79820	Wildwood city	35,517
29	189	79820	St. Louis County	35,517
30			**MONTANA**	989,415
30		06550	Billings city	104,170
30	111	06550	Yellowstone County	104,170
30		08950	Bozeman city	37,280
30	031	08950	Gallatin County	37,280
30		32800	Great Falls city	58,505
30	013	32800	Cascade County	58,505
30		35600	Helena city	28,190
30	049	35600	Lewis and Clark County	28,190
30		50200	Missoula city	66,788
30	063	50200	Missoula County	66,788
31			**NEBRASKA**	1,826,341
31		03950	Bellevue city	50,137
31	153	03950	Sarpy County	50,137

State code	Place code	County code	Geographic Area Name	2010 census population
31		17670	Fremont city	26,397
31	053	17670	Dodge County	26,397
31		19595	Grand Island city	48,520
31	079	19595	Hall County	48,520
31		25055	Kearney city	30,787
31	019	25055	Buffalo County	30,787
31		28000	Lincoln city	258,379
31	109	28000	Lancaster County	258,379
31		37000	Omaha city	408,958
31	055	37000	Douglas County	408,958
32			**NEVADA**	2,700,551
32		09700	Carson City	55,274
32	510	09700	Carson City	55,274
32		31900	Henderson city	257,729
32	003	31900	Clark County	257,729
32		40000	Las Vegas city	583,756
32	003	40000	Clark County	583,756
32		51800	North Las Vegas city	216,961
32	003	51800	Clark County	216,961
32		60600	Reno city	225,221
32	031	60600	Washoe County	225,221
32		68400	Sparks city	90,264
32	031	68400	Washoe County	90,264
33			**NEW HAMPSHIRE**	1,316,470
33		14200	Concord city	42,695
33	013	14200	Merrimack County	42,695
33		18820	Dover city	29,987
33	017	18820	Strafford County	29,987
33		45140	Manchester city	109,565
33	011	45140	Hillsborough County	109,565
33		50260	Nashua city	86,494
33	011	50260	Hillsborough County	86,494
33		65140	Rochester city	29,752
33	017	65140	Strafford County	29,752
34			**NEW JERSEY**	8,791,894
34		02080	Atlantic City city	39,558
34	001	02080	Atlantic County	39,558
34		03580	Bayonne city	63,024
34	017	03580	Hudson County	63,024
34		05170	Bergenfield borough	26,764
34	003	05170	Bergen County	26,764
34		07600	Bridgeton city	25,349
34	011	07600	Cumberland County	25,349
34		10000	Camden city	77,344
34	007	10000	Camden County	77,344
34		13690	Clifton city	84,136
34	031	13690	Passaic County	84,136
34		19390	East Orange city	64,270
34	013	19390	Essex County	64,270
34		21000	Elizabeth city	124,969
34	039	21000	Union County	124,969
34		21480	Englewood city	27,147
34	003	21480	Bergen County	27,147
34		22470	Fair Lawn borough	32,457
34	003	22470	Bergen County	32,457
34		24420	Fort Lee borough	35,345
34	003	24420	Bergen County	35,345
34		25770	Garfield city	30,487
34	003	25770	Bergen County	30,487
34		28680	Hackensack city	43,010
34	003	28680	Bergen County	43,010
34		32250	Hoboken city	50,005
34	017	32250	Hudson County	50,005
34		36000	Jersey City city	247,597
34	017	36000	Hudson County	247,597
34		36510	Kearny town	40,684
34	017	36510	Hudson County	40,684
34		40350	Linden city	40,499
34	039	40350	Union County	40,499
34		41310	Long Branch city	30,719
34	025	41310	Monmouth County	30,719
34		46680	Millville city	28,400
34	011	46680	Cumberland County	28,400
34		51000	Newark city	277,140
34	013	51000	Essex County	277,140
34		51210	New Brunswick city	55,181
34	023	51210	Middlesex County	55,181
34		55950	Paramus borough	26,342
34	003	55950	Bergen County	26,342
34		56550	Passaic city	69,781
34	031	56550	Passaic County	69,781
34		57000	Paterson city	146,199
34	031	57000	Passaic County	146,199
34		58200	Perth Amboy city	50,814
34	023	58200	Middlesex County	50,814
34		59190	Plainfield city	49,808
34	039	59190	Union County	49,808
34		61530	Rahway city	27,346
34	039	61530	Union County	27,346
34		65790	Sayreville borough	42,704
34	023	65790	Middlesex County	42,704
34		74000	Trenton city	84,913
34	021	74000	Mercer County	84,913
34		74630	Union City city	66,455
34	017	74630	Hudson County	66,455
34		76070	Vineland city	60,724
34	011	76070	Cumberland County	60,724
34		79040	Westfield town	30,316
34	039	79040	Union County	30,316
34		79610	West New York town	49,708
34	017	79610	Hudson County	49,708
35			**NEW MEXICO**	2,059,179
35		01780	Alamogordo city	30,403
35	035	01780	Otero County	30,403
35		02000	Albuquerque city	545,852
35	001	02000	Bernalillo County	545,852
35		12150	Carlsbad city	26,138
35	015	12150	Eddy County	26,138
35		16420	Clovis city	37,775
35	009	16420	Curry County	37,775
35		25800	Farmington city	45,877
35	045	25800	San Juan County	45,877
35		32520	Hobbs city	34,122
35	025	32520	Lea County	34,122
35		39380	Las Cruces city	97,618
35	013	39380	Doña Ana County	97,618
35		63460	Rio Rancho city	87,521
35	001	63460	Bernalillo County	130

State code	Place code	County code	Geographic Area Name	2010 census population
35	043	63460	Sandoval County	87,391
35		64930	Roswell city	48,366
35	005	64930	Chaves County	48,366
35		70500	Santa Fe city	67,947
35	049	70500	Santa Fe County	67,947
36			**NEW YORK**	19,378,102
36		01000	Albany city	97,856
36	001	01000	Albany County	97,856
36		03078	Auburn city	27,687
36	011	03078	Cayuga County	27,687
36		06607	Binghamton city	47,376
36	007	06607	Broome County	47,376
36		11000	Buffalo city	261,310
36	029	11000	Erie County	261,310
36		24229	Elmira city	29,200
36	015	24229	Chemung County	29,200
36		27485	Freeport village	42,860
36	059	27485	Nassau County	42,860
36		29113	Glen Cove city	26,964
36	059	29113	Nassau County	26,964
36		32402	Harrison village	27,472
36	119	32402	Westchester County	27,472
36		33139	Hempstead village	53,891
36	059	33139	Nassau County	53,891
36		38077	Ithaca city	30,014
36	109	38077	Tompkins County	30,014
36		38264	Jamestown city	31,146
36	013	38264	Chautauqua County	31,146
36		42554	Lindenhurst village	27,253
36	103	42554	Suffolk County	27,253
36		43335	Long Beach city	33,275
36	059	43335	Nassau County	33,275
36		47042	Middletown city	28,086
36	071	47042	Orange County	28,086
36		49121	Mount Vernon city	67,292
36	119	49121	Westchester County	67,292
36		50034	Newburgh city	28,866
36	071	50034	Orange County	28,866
36		50617	New Rochelle city	77,062
36	119	50617	Westchester County	77,062
36		51000	New York city	8,175,133
36	005	51000	Bronx County	1,385,108
36	047	51000	Kings County	2,504,700
36	061	51000	New York County	1,585,873
36	081	51000	Queens County	2,230,722
36	085	51000	Richmond County	468,730
36		51055	Niagara Falls city	50,193
36	063	51055	Niagara County	50,193
36		53682	North Tonawanda city	31,568
36	063	53682	Niagara County	31,568
36		55530	Ossining village	25,060
36	119	55530	Westchester County	25,060
36		59223	Port Chester village	28,967
36	119	59223	Westchester County	28,967
36		59641	Poughkeepsie city	32,736
36	027	59641	Dutchess County	32,736
36		63000	Rochester city	210,565
36	055	63000	Monroe County	210,565
36		63418	Rome city	33,725
36	065	63418	Oneida County	33,725
36		65255	Saratoga Springs city	26,586
36	091	65255	Saratoga County	26,586
36		65508	Schenectady city	66,135
36	093	65508	Schenectady County	66,135
36		70420	Spring Valley village	31,347
36	087	70420	Rockland County	31,347
36		73000	Syracuse city	145,170
36	067	73000	Onondaga County	145,170
36		75484	Troy city	50,129
36	083	75484	Rensselaer County	50,129
36		76540	Utica city	62,235
36	065	76540	Oneida County	62,235
36		76705	Valley Stream village	37,511
36	059	76705	Nassau County	37,511
36		78608	Watertown city	27,023
36	045	78608	Jefferson County	27,023
36		81677	White Plains city	56,853
36	119	81677	Westchester County	56,853
37			**NORTH CAROLINA**	9,535,483
37		01520	Apex town	37,476
37	183	01520	Wake County	37,476
37		02080	Asheboro city	25,012
37	151	02080	Randolph County	25,012
37		02140	Asheville city	83,393
37	021	02140	Buncombe County	83,393
37		09060	Burlington city	49,963
37	001	09060	Alamance County	49,308
37	081	09060	Guilford County	655
37		10740	Cary town	135,234
37	037	10740	Chatham County	1,422
37	183	10740	Wake County	133,812
37		11800	Chapel Hill town	57,233
37	063	11800	Durham County	2,836
37	135	11800	Orange County	54,397
37		12000	Charlotte city	731,424
37	119	12000	Mecklenburg County	731,424
37		14100	Concord city	79,066
37	025	14100	Cabarrus County	79,066
37		19000	Durham city	228,330
37	063	19000	Durham County	228,300
37	135	19000	Orange County	30
37	183	19000	Wake County	0
37		22920	Fayetteville city	200,564
37	051	22920	Cumberland County	200,564
37		25480	Garner town	25,745
37	183	25480	Wake County	25,745
37		25580	Gastonia city	71,741
37	071	25580	Gaston County	71,741
37		26880	Goldsboro city	36,437
37	191	26880	Wayne County	36,437
37		28000	Greensboro city	269,666
37	081	28000	Guilford County	269,666
37		28080	Greenville city	84,554
37	147	28080	Pitt County	84,554
37		31060	Hickory city	40,010
37	023	31060	Burke County	66
37	027	31060	Caldwell County	18
37	035	31060	Catawba County	39,926
37		31400	High Point city	104,371
37	057	31400	Davidson County	5,310
37	067	31400	Forsyth County	8
37	081	31400	Guilford County	99,042
37	151	31400	Randolph County	11

State code	Place code	County code	Geographic Area Name	2010 census population
37		33120	Huntersville town	46,773
37	119	33120	Mecklenburg County	46,773
37		33560	Indian Trail town	33,518
37	179	33560	Union County	33,518
37		34200	Jacksonville city	70,145
37	133	34200	Onslow County	70,145
37		35200	Kannapolis city	42,625
37	025	35200	Cabarrus County	33,194
37	159	35200	Rowan County	9,431
37		41960	Matthews town	27,198
37	119	41960	Mecklenburg County	27,198
37		43920	Monroe city	32,797
37	179	43920	Union County	32,797
37		44220	Mooresville town	32,711
37	097	44220	Iredell County	32,711
37		46340	New Bern city	29,524
37	049	46340	Craven County	29,524
37		55000	Raleigh city	403,892
37	063	55000	Durham County	1,067
37	183	55000	Wake County	402,825
37		57500	Rocky Mount city	57,477
37	065	57500	Edgecombe County	17,524
37	127	57500	Nash County	39,953
37		58860	Salisbury city	33,662
37	159	58860	Rowan County	33,662
37		59280	Sanford city	28,094
37	105	59280	Lee County	28,094
37		67420	Thomasville city	26,757
37	057	67420	Davidson County	26,493
37	151	67420	Randolph County	264
37		70540	Wake Forest town	30,117
37	069	70540	Franklin County	899
37	183	70540	Wake County	29,218
37		74440	Wilmington city	106,476
37	129	74440	New Hanover County	106,476
37		74540	Wilson city	49,167
37	195	74540	Wilson County	49,167
37		75000	Winston-Salem city	229,617
37	067	75000	Forsyth County	229,617
38			**NORTH DAKOTA**	672,591
38		07200	Bismarck city	61,272
38	015	07200	Burleigh County	61,272
38		25700	Fargo city	105,549
38	017	25700	Cass County	105,549
38		32060	Grand Forks city	52,838
38	035	32060	Grand Forks County	52,838
38		53380	Minot city	40,888
38	101	53380	Ward County	40,888
38		84780	West Fargo city	25,830
38	017	84780	Cass County	25,830
39			**OHIO**	11,536,504
39		01000	Akron city	199,110
39	153	01000	Summit County	199,110
39		03828	Barberton city	26,550
39	153	03828	Summit County	26,550
39		04720	Beavercreek city	45,193
39	057	04720	Greene County	45,193
39		07972	Bowling Green city	30,028
39	173	07972	Wood County	30,028
39		09680	Brunswick city	34,255
39	103	09680	Medina County	34,255
39		12000	Canton city	73,007
39	151	12000	Stark County	73,007
39		15000	Cincinnati city	296,943
39	061	15000	Hamilton County	296,943
39		16000	Cleveland city	396,815
39	035	16000	Cuyahoga County	396,815
39		16014	Cleveland Heights city	46,121
39	035	16014	Cuyahoga County	46,121
39		18000	Columbus city	787,033
39	041	18000	Delaware County	7,245
39	045	18000	Fairfield County	9,666
39	049	18000	Franklin County	770,122
39		19778	Cuyahoga Falls city	49,652
39	153	19778	Summit County	49,652
39		21000	Dayton city	141,527
39	113	21000	Montgomery County	141,527
39		21434	Delaware city	34,753
39	041	21434	Delaware County	34,753
39		22694	Dublin city	41,751
39	041	22694	Delaware County	4,018
39	049	22694	Franklin County	35,367
39	159	22694	Union County	2,366
39		25256	Elyria city	54,533
39	093	25256	Lorain County	54,533
39		25704	Euclid city	48,920
39	035	25704	Cuyahoga County	48,920
39		25914	Fairborn city	32,352
39	057	25914	Greene County	32,352
39		25970	Fairfield city	42,510
39	017	25970	Butler County	42,510
39	061	25970	Hamilton County	0
39		27048	Findlay city	41,202
39	063	27048	Hancock County	41,202
39		29106	Gahanna city	33,248
39	049	29106	Franklin County	33,248
39		29428	Garfield Heights city	28,849
39	035	29428	Cuyahoga County	28,849
39		31860	Green city	25,699
39	153	31860	Summit County	25,699
39		32592	Grove City city	35,575
39	049	32592	Franklin County	35,575
39		33012	Hamilton city	62,477
39	017	33012	Butler County	62,477
39		35476	Hilliard city	28,435
39	049	35476	Franklin County	28,435
39		36610	Huber Heights city	38,101
39	057	36610	Greene County	0
39	109	36610	Miami County	959
39	113	36610	Montgomery County	37,142
39		39872	Kent city	28,904
39	133	39872	Portage County	28,904
39		40040	Kettering city	56,163
39	057	40040	Greene County	467
39	113	40040	Montgomery County	55,696
39		41664	Lakewood city	52,131
39	035	41664	Cuyahoga County	52,131
39		41720	Lancaster city	38,780
39	045	41720	Fairfield County	38,780
39		43554	Lima city	38,771
39	003	43554	Allen County	38,771
39		44856	Lorain city	64,097

State code	Place code	County code	Geographic Area Name	2010 census population
39	093	44856	Lorain County	64,097
39		47138	Mansfield city	47,821
39	139	47138	Richland County	47,821
39		47754	Marion city	36,837
39	101	47754	Marion County	36,837
39		48188	Mason city	30,712
39	165	48188	Warren County	30,712
39		48244	Massillon city	32,149
39	151	48244	Stark County	32,149
39		48790	Medina city	26,678
39	103	48790	Medina County	26,678
39		49056	Mentor city	47,159
39	085	49056	Lake County	47,159
39		49840	Middletown city	48,694
39	017	49840	Butler County	45,994
39	165	49840	Warren County	2,700
39		54040	Newark city	47,573
39	089	54040	Licking County	47,573
39		56882	North Olmsted city	32,718
39	035	56882	Cuyahoga County	32,718
39		56966	North Ridgeville city	29,465
39	093	56966	Lorain County	29,465
39		57008	North Royalton city	30,444
39	035	57008	Cuyahoga County	30,444
39		61000	Parma city	81,601
39	035	61000	Cuyahoga County	81,601
39		66390	Reynoldsburg city	35,893
39	045	66390	Fairfield County	910
39	049	66390	Franklin County	26,157
39	089	66390	Licking County	8,826
39		67468	Riverside city	25,201
39	113	67468	Montgomery County	25,201
39		70380	Sandusky city	25,793
39	043	70380	Erie County	25,793
39		71682	Shaker Heights city	28,448
39	035	71682	Cuyahoga County	28,448
39		74118	Springfield city	60,608
39	023	74118	Clark County	60,608
39		74944	Stow city	34,837
39	153	74944	Summit County	34,837
39		75098	Strongsville city	44,750
39	035	75098	Cuyahoga County	44,750
39		77000	Toledo city	287,208
39	095	77000	Lucas County	287,208
39		77588	Troy city	25,058
39	109	77588	Miami County	25,058
39		79002	Upper Arlington city	33,771
39	049	79002	Franklin County	33,771
39		80892	Warren city	41,557
39	155	80892	Trumbull County	41,557
39		83342	Westerville city	36,120
39	041	83342	Delaware County	7,792
39	049	83342	Franklin County	28,328
39		83622	Westlake city	32,729
39	035	83622	Cuyahoga County	32,729
39		86548	Wooster city	26,119
39	169	86548	Wayne County	26,119
39		86772	Xenia city	25,719
39	057	86772	Greene County	25,719
39		88000	Youngstown city	66,982
39	099	88000	Mahoning County	66,971
39	155	88000	Trumbull County	11
39		88084	Zanesville city	25,487
39	119	88084	Muskingum County	25,487
40			**OKLAHOMA**	3,751,351
40		04450	Bartlesville city	35,750
40	113	04450	Osage County	3
40	147	04450	Washington County	35,747
40		09050	Broken Arrow city	98,850
40	143	09050	Tulsa County	80,634
40	145	09050	Wagoner County	18,216
40		23200	Edmond city	81,405
40	109	23200	Oklahoma County	81,405
40		23950	Enid city	49,379
40	047	23950	Garfield County	49,379
40		41850	Lawton city	96,867
40	031	41850	Comanche County	96,867
40		48350	Midwest City city	54,371
40	109	48350	Oklahoma County	54,371
40		49200	Moore city	55,081
40	027	49200	Cleveland County	55,081
40		50050	Muskogee city	39,223
40	101	50050	Muskogee County	39,223
40		52500	Norman city	110,925
40	027	52500	Cleveland County	110,925
40		55000	Oklahoma City city	579,999
40	017	55000	Canadian County	44,541
40	027	55000	Cleveland County	63,723
40	109	55000	Oklahoma County	471,671
40	125	55000	Pottawatomie County	64
40		56650	Owasso city	28,915
40	131	56650	Rogers County	2,614
40	143	56650	Tulsa County	26,301
40		59850	Ponca City city	25,387
40	071	59850	Kay County	25,387
40		66800	Shawnee city	29,857
40	125	66800	Pottawatomie County	29,857
40		70300	Stillwater city	45,688
40	119	70300	Payne County	45,688
40		75000	Tulsa city	391,906
40	113	75000	Osage County	6,136
40	131	75000	Rogers County	0
40	143	75000	Tulsa County	385,613
40	145	75000	Wagoner County	157
41			**OREGON**	3,831,074
41		01000	Albany city	50,158
41	003	01000	Benton County	6,463
41	043	01000	Linn County	43,695
41		05350	Beaverton city	89,803
41	067	05350	Washington County	89,803
41		05800	Bend city	76,639
41	017	05800	Deschutes County	76,639
41		15800	Corvallis city	54,462
41	003	15800	Benton County	54,462
41		23850	Eugene city	156,185
41	039	23850	Lane County	156,185
41		30550	Grants Pass city	34,533
41	033	30550	Josephine County	34,533
41		31250	Gresham city	105,594
41	051	31250	Multnomah County	105,594
41		34100	Hillsboro city	91,611
41	067	34100	Washington County	91,611
41		38500	Keizer city	36,478

State code	Place code	County code	Geographic Area Name	2010 census population	State code	Place code	County code	Geographic Area Name	2010 census population
41	047	38500	Marion County	36,478	42		61536	Plum borough	27,126
					42	003	61536	Allegheny County	27,126
41		40550	Lake Oswego city	36,619					
41	005	40550	Clackamas County	34,066	42		63624	Reading city	88,082
41	051	40550	Multnomah County	2,544	42	011	63624	Berks County	88,082
41	067	40550	Washington County	9					
					42		69000	Scranton city	76,089
41		45000	McMinnville city	32,187	42	069	69000	Lackawanna County	76,089
41	071	45000	Yamhill County	32,187					
					42		73808	State College borough	42,034
41		47000	Medford city	74,907	42	027	73808	Centre County	42,034
41	029	47000	Jackson County	74,907					
					42		85152	Wilkes-Barre city	41,498
41		55200	Oregon City city	31,859	42	079	85152	Luzerne County	41,498
41	005	55200	Clackamas County	31,859					
					42		85312	Williamsport city	29,381
41		59000	Portland city	583,776	42	081	85312	Lycoming County	29,381
41	005	59000	Clackamas County	744					
41	051	59000	Multnomah County	581,485	42		87048	York city	43,718
41	067	59000	Washington County	1,547	42	133	87048	York County	43,718
41		61200	Redmond city	26,215	44			**RHODE ISLAND**	1,052,567
41	017	61200	Deschutes County	26,215					
					44		19180	Cranston city	80,387
41		64900	Salem city	154,637	44	007	19180	Providence County	80,387
41	047	64900	Marion County	130,398					
41	053	64900	Polk County	24,239	44		22960	East Providence city	47,037
					44	007	22960	Providence County	47,037
41		69600	Springfield city	59,403					
41	039	69600	Lane County	59,403	44		54640	Pawtucket city	71,148
					44	007	54640	Providence County	71,148
41		73650	Tigard city	48,035					
41	067	73650	Washington County	48,035	44		59000	Providence city	178,042
					44	007	59000	Providence County	178,042
41		74950	Tualatin city	26,054					
41	005	74950	Clackamas County	2,862	44		74300	Warwick city	82,672
41	067	74950	Washington County	23,192	44	003	74300	Kent County	82,672
41		80150	West Linn city	25,109	44		80780	Woonsocket city	41,186
41	005	80150	Clackamas County	25,109	44	007	80780	Providence County	41,186
42			**PENNSYLVANIA**	12,702,379	45			**SOUTH CAROLINA**	4,625,364
42		02000	Allentown city	118,032	45		00550	Aiken city	29,524
42	077	02000	Lehigh County	118,032	45	003	00550	Aiken County	29,524
42		02184	Altoona city	46,320	45		01360	Anderson city	26,686
42	013	02184	Blair County	46,320	45	007	01360	Anderson County	26,686
42		06064	Bethel Park municipality	32,313	45		13330	Charleston city	120,083
42	003	06064	Allegheny County	32,313	45	015	13330	Berkeley County	8,095
					45	019	13330	Charleston County	111,988
42		06088	Bethlehem city	74,982					
42	077	06088	Lehigh County	19,343	45		16000	Columbia city	129,272
42	095	06088	Northampton County	55,639	45	063	16000	Lexington County	559
					45	079	16000	Richland County	128,713
42		13208	Chester city	33,972					
42	045	13208	Delaware County	33,972	45		25810	Florence city	37,056
					45	041	25810	Florence County	37,056
42		21648	Easton city	26,800					
42	095	21648	Northampton County	26,800	45		29815	Goose Creek city	35,938
					45	015	29815	Berkeley County	35,933
42		24000	Erie city	101,786	45	019	29815	Charleston County	5
42	049	24000	Erie County	101,786					
					45		30850	Greenville city	58,409
42		32800	Harrisburg city	49,528	45	045	30850	Greenville County	58,409
42	043	32800	Dauphin County	49,528					
					45		30985	Greer city	25,515
42		33408	Hazleton city	25,340	45	045	30985	Greenville County	18,635
42	079	33408	Luzerne County	25,340	45	083	30985	Spartanburg County	6,880
42		41216	Lancaster city	59,322	45		34045	Hilton Head Island town	37,099
42	071	41216	Lancaster County	59,322	45	013	34045	Beaufort County	37,099
42		42168	Lebanon city	25,477	45		48535	Mount Pleasant town	67,843
42	075	42168	Lebanon County	25,477	45	019	48535	Charleston County	67,843
42		50528	Monroeville municipality	28,386	45		49075	Myrtle Beach city	27,109
42	003	50528	Allegheny County	28,386	45	051	49075	Horry County	27,109
42		54656	Norristown borough	34,324	45		50875	North Charleston city	97,471
42	091	54656	Montgomery County	34,324	45	015	50875	Berkeley County	0
					45	019	50875	Charleston County	78,393
42		60000	Philadelphia city	1,526,006	45	035	50875	Dorchester County	19,078
42	101	60000	Philadelphia County	1,526,006					
					45		61405	Rock Hill city	66,154
42		61000	Pittsburgh city	305,704	45	091	61405	York County	66,154
42	003	61000	Allegheny County	305,704					
					45		68290	Spartanburg city	37,013

State code	Place code	County code	Geographic Area Name	2010 census population
45	083	68290	Spartanburg County	37,013
45		70270	Summerville town	43,392
45	015	70270	Berkeley County	3,643
45	019	70270	Charleston County	1,010
45	035	70270	Dorchester County	38,739
45		70405	Sumter city	40,524
45	085	70405	Sumter County	40,524
46			**SOUTH DAKOTA**	814,180
46		00100	Aberdeen city	26,091
46	013	00100	Brown County	26,091
46		52980	Rapid City city	67,956
46	103	52980	Pennington County	67,956
46		59020	Sioux Falls city	153,888
46	083	59020	Lincoln County	21,095
46	099	59020	Minnehaha County	132,793
47			**TENNESSEE**	6,346,105
47		03440	Bartlett city	54,613
47	157	03440	Shelby County	54,613
47		08280	Brentwood city	37,060
47	187	08280	Williamson County	37,060
47		08540	Bristol city	26,702
47	163	08540	Sullivan County	26,702
47		14000	Chattanooga city	167,674
47	065	14000	Hamilton County	167,674
47		15160	Clarksville city	132,929
47	125	15160	Montgomery County	132,929
47		15400	Cleveland city	41,285
47	011	15400	Bradley County	41,285
47		16420	Collierville town	43,965
47	047	16420	Fayette County	0
47	157	16420	Shelby County	43,965
47		16540	Columbia city	34,681
47	119	16540	Maury County	34,681
47		16920	Cookeville city	30,435
47	141	16920	Putnam County	30,435
47		27740	Franklin city	62,487
47	187	27740	Williamson County	62,487
47		28540	Gallatin city	30,278
47	165	28540	Sumner County	30,278
47		28960	Germantown city	38,844
47	157	28960	Shelby County	38,844
47		33280	Hendersonville city	51,372
47	165	33280	Sumner County	51,372
47		37640	Jackson city	65,211
47	113	37640	Madison County	65,211
47		38320	Johnson City city	63,152
47	019	38320	Carter County	1,252
47	163	38320	Sullivan County	367
47	179	38320	Washington County	61,533
47		39560	Kingsport city	48,205
47	073	39560	Hawkins County	2,854
47	163	39560	Sullivan County	45,351
47		40000	Knoxville city	178,874
47	093	40000	Knox County	178,874
47		41200	La Vergne city	32,588
47	149	41200	Rutherford County	32,588
47		41520	Lebanon city	26,190
47	189	41520	Wilson County	26,190
47		46380	Maryville city	27,465
47	009	46380	Blount County	27,465
47		48000	Memphis city	646,889

State code	Place code	County code	Geographic Area Name	2010 census population
47	157	48000	Shelby County	646,889
47		50280	Morristown city	29,137
47	063	50280	Hamblen County	29,131
47	089	50280	Jefferson County	6
47		51560	Murfreesboro city	108,755
47	149	51560	Rutherford County	108,755
47		55120	Oak Ridge city	29,330
47	001	55120	Anderson County	26,271
47	145	55120	Roane County	3,059
47		69420	Smyrna town	39,974
47	149	69420	Rutherford County	39,974
47		70580	Spring Hill city	29,036
47	119	70580	Maury County	7,023
47	187	70580	Williamson County	22,013
48			**TEXAS**	25,145,561
48		01000	Abilene city	117,063
48	253	01000	Jones County	5,145
48	441	01000	Taylor County	111,918
48		01924	Allen city	84,246
48	085	01924	Collin County	84,246
48		03000	Amarillo city	190,695
48	375	03000	Potter County	105,486
48	381	03000	Randall County	85,209
48		04000	Arlington city	365,438
48	439	04000	Tarrant County	365,438
48		05000	Austin city	790,390
48	209	05000	Hays County	2
48	453	05000	Travis County	754,691
48	491	05000	Williamson County	35,697
48		06128	Baytown city	71,802
48	071	06128	Chambers County	4,116
48	201	06128	Harris County	67,686
48		07000	Beaumont city	118,296
48	245	07000	Jefferson County	118,296
48		07132	Bedford city	46,979
48	439	07132	Tarrant County	46,979
48		08236	Big Spring city	27,282
48	227	08236	Howard County	27,282
48		10768	Brownsville city	175,023
48	061	10768	Cameron County	175,023
48		10912	Bryan city	76,201
48	041	10912	Brazos County	76,201
48		11428	Burleson city	36,690
48	251	11428	Johnson County	29,111
48	439	11428	Tarrant County	7,579
48		13024	Carrollton city	119,097
48	085	13024	Collin County	2
48	113	13024	Dallas County	49,352
48	121	13024	Denton County	69,743
48		13492	Cedar Hill city	45,028
48	113	13492	Dallas County	44,477
48	139	13492	Ellis County	551
48		13552	Cedar Park city	48,937
48	453	13552	Travis County	489
48	491	13552	Williamson County	48,448
48		15364	Cleburne city	29,337
48	251	15364	Johnson County	29,337
48		15976	College Station city	93,857
48	041	15976	Brazos County	93,857
48		16432	Conroe city	56,207
48	339	16432	Montgomery County	56,207
48		16612	Coppell city	38,659
48	113	16612	Dallas County	37,905
48	121	16612	Denton County	754

State code	Place code	County code	Geographic Area Name	2010 census population
48		16624	Copperas Cove city	32,032
48	027	16624	Bell County	0
48	099	16624	Coryell County	31,457
48	281	16624	Lampasas County	575
48		17000	Corpus Christi city	305,215
48	007	17000	Aransas County	0
48	273	17000	Kleberg County	0
48	355	17000	Nueces County	305,215
48	409	17000	San Patricio County	0
48		19000	Dallas city	1,197,816
48	085	19000	Collin County	46,885
48	113	19000	Dallas County	1,124,296
48	121	19000	Denton County	26,579
48	257	19000	Kaufman County	0
48	397	19000	Rockwall County	56
48		19624	Deer Park city	32,010
48	201	19624	Harris County	32,010
48		19792	Del Rio city	35,591
48	465	19792	Val Verde County	35,591
48		19972	Denton city	113,383
48	121	19972	Denton County	113,383
48		20092	DeSoto city	49,047
48	113	20092	Dallas County	49,047
48		21628	Duncanville city	38,524
48	113	21628	Dallas County	38,524
48		21892	Eagle Pass city	26,248
48	323	21892	Maverick County	26,248
48		22660	Edinburg city	77,100
48	215	22660	Hidalgo County	77,100
48		24000	El Paso city	649,121
48	141	24000	El Paso County	649,121
48		24768	Euless city	51,277
48	439	24768	Tarrant County	51,277
48		25452	Farmers Branch city	28,616
48	113	25452	Dallas County	28,616
48		26232	Flower Mound town	64,669
48	121	26232	Denton County	64,457
48	439	26232	Tarrant County	212
48		27000	Fort Worth city	741,206
48	121	27000	Denton County	7,813
48	367	27000	Parker County	7
48	439	27000	Tarrant County	733,386
48	497	27000	Wise County	0
48		27648	Friendswood city	35,805
48	167	27648	Galveston County	25,510
48	201	27648	Harris County	10,295
48		27684	Frisco city	116,989
48	085	27684	Collin County	72,489
48	121	27684	Denton County	44,500
48		28068	Galveston city	47,743
48	167	28068	Galveston County	47,743
48		29000	Garland city	226,876
48	085	29000	Collin County	266
48	113	29000	Dallas County	226,608
48	397	29000	Rockwall County	2
48		29336	Georgetown city	47,400
48	491	29336	Williamson County	47,400
48		30464	Grand Prairie city	175,396
48	113	30464	Dallas County	123,487
48	139	30464	Ellis County	45
48	439	30464	Tarrant County	51,864
48		30644	Grapevine city	46,334
48	113	30644	Dallas County	0
48	121	30644	Denton County	0
48	439	30644	Tarrant County	46,334
48		30920	Greenville city	25,557

State code	Place code	County code	Geographic Area Name	2010 census population
48	231	30920	Hunt County	25,557
48		31928	Haltom City city	42,409
48	439	31928	Tarrant County	42,409
48		32312	Harker Heights city	26,700
48	027	32312	Bell County	26,700
48		32372	Harlingen city	64,849
48	061	32372	Cameron County	64,849
48		35000	Houston city	2,099,451
48	157	35000	Fort Bend County	38,124
48	201	35000	Harris County	2,057,280
48	339	35000	Montgomery County	4,047
48		35528	Huntsville city	38,548
48	471	35528	Walker County	38,548
48		35576	Hurst city	37,337
48	439	35576	Tarrant County	37,337
48		37000	Irving city	216,290
48	113	37000	Dallas County	216,290
48		38632	Keller city	39,627
48	439	38632	Tarrant County	39,627
48		39148	Killeen city	127,921
48	027	39148	Bell County	127,921
48		39352	Kingsville city	26,213
48	273	39352	Kleberg County	26,213
48		39952	Kyle city	28,016
48	209	39952	Hays County	28,016
48		40588	Lake Jackson city	26,849
48	039	40588	Brazoria County	26,849
48		41212	Lancaster city	36,361
48	113	41212	Dallas County	36,361
48		41440	La Porte city	33,800
48	201	41440	Harris County	33,800
48		41464	Laredo city	236,091
48	479	41464	Webb County	236,091
48		41980	League City city	83,560
48	167	41980	Galveston County	81,998
48	201	41980	Harris County	1,562
48		42016	Leander city	26,521
48	453	42016	Travis County	1,077
48	491	42016	Williamson County	25,444
48		42508	Lewisville city	95,290
48	113	42508	Dallas County	841
48	121	42508	Denton County	94,449
48		43012	Little Elm city	25,898
48	121	43012	Denton County	25,898
48		43888	Longview city	80,455
48	183	43888	Gregg County	78,585
48	203	43888	Harrison County	1,870
48		45000	Lubbock city	229,573
48	303	45000	Lubbock County	229,573
48		45072	Lufkin city	35,067
48	005	45072	Angelina County	35,067
48		45384	McAllen city	129,877
48	215	45384	Hidalgo County	129,877
48		45744	McKinney city	131,117
48	085	45744	Collin County	131,117
48		46452	Mansfield city	56,368
48	139	46452	Ellis County	95
48	251	46452	Johnson County	1,652
48	439	46452	Tarrant County	54,621
48		47892	Mesquite city	139,824
48	113	47892	Dallas County	139,731
48	257	47892	Kaufman County	93

State code	Place code	County code	Geographic Area Name	2010 census population
48		48072	Midland city	111,147
48	317	48072	Martin County	0
48	329	48072	Midland County	111,147
48		48768	Mission city	77,058
48	215	48768	Hidalgo County	77,058
48		48804	Missouri City city	67,358
48	157	48804	Fort Bend County	61,755
48	201	48804	Harris County	5,603
48		50256	Nacogdoches city	32,996
48	347	50256	Nacogdoches County	32,996
48		50820	New Braunfels city	57,740
48	091	50820	Comal County	47,586
48	187	50820	Guadalupe County	10,154
48		52356	North Richland Hills city	63,343
48	439	52356	Tarrant County	63,343
48		53388	Odessa city	99,940
48	135	53388	Ector County	98,270
48	329	53388	Midland County	1,670
48		55080	Paris city	25,171
48	277	55080	Lamar County	25,171
48		56000	Pasadena city	149,043
48	201	56000	Harris County	149,043
48		56348	Pearland city	91,252
48	039	56348	Brazoria County	86,706
48	157	56348	Fort Bend County	721
48	201	56348	Harris County	3,825
48		57176	Pflugerville city	46,936
48	453	57176	Travis County	46,636
48	491	57176	Williamson County	300
48		57200	Pharr city	70,400
48	215	57200	Hidalgo County	70,400
48		58016	Plano city	259,841
48	085	58016	Collin County	254,525
48	121	58016	Denton County	5,316
48		58820	Port Arthur city	53,818
48	245	58820	Jefferson County	53,814
48	361	58820	Orange County	4
48		61796	Richardson city	99,223
48	085	61796	Collin County	28,569
48	113	61796	Dallas County	70,654
48		62828	Rockwall city	37,490
48	397	62828	Rockwall County	37,490
48		63284	Rosenberg city	30,618
48	157	63284	Fort Bend County	30,618
48		63500	Round Rock city	99,887
48	453	63500	Travis County	1,362
48	491	63500	Williamson County	98,525
48		63572	Rowlett city	56,199
48	113	63572	Dallas County	49,188
48	397	63572	Rockwall County	7,011
48		64472	San Angelo city	93,200
48	451	64472	Tom Green County	93,200
48		65000	San Antonio city	1,327,407
48	029	65000	Bexar County	1,327,381
48	091	65000	Comal County	0
48	325	65000	Medina County	26
48		65516	San Juan city	33,856
48	215	65516	Hidalgo County	33,856
48		65600	San Marcos city	44,894
48	055	65600	Caldwell County	3
48	187	65600	Guadalupe County	0
48	209	65600	Hays County	44,891
48		66128	Schertz city	31,465
48	029	66128	Bexar County	1,157
48	091	66128	Comal County	845
48	187	66128	Guadalupe County	29,463
48		66644	Seguin city	25,175
48	187	66644	Guadalupe County	25,175
48		67496	Sherman city	38,521
48	181	67496	Grayson County	38,521
48		68636	Socorro city	32,013
48	141	68636	El Paso County	32,013
48		69032	Southlake city	26,575
48	121	69032	Denton County	773
48	439	69032	Tarrant County	25,802
48		70808	Sugar Land city	78,817
48	157	70808	Fort Bend County	78,817
48		72176	Temple city	66,102
48	027	72176	Bell County	66,102
48		72368	Texarkana city	36,411
48	037	72368	Bowie County	36,411
48		72392	Texas City city	45,099
48	071	72392	Chambers County	0
48	167	72392	Galveston County	45,099
48		72530	The Colony city	36,328
48	121	72530	Denton County	36,328
48		74144	Tyler city	96,900
48	423	74144	Smith County	96,900
48		75428	Victoria city	62,592
48	469	75428	Victoria County	62,592
48		76000	Waco city	124,805
48	309	76000	McLennan County	124,805
48		76816	Waxahachie city	29,621
48	139	76816	Ellis County	29,621
48		76864	Weatherford city	25,250
48	367	76864	Parker County	25,250
48		77272	Weslaco city	35,670
48	215	77272	Hidalgo County	35,670
48		79000	Wichita Falls city	104,553
48	485	79000	Wichita County	104,553
48		80356	Wylie city	41,427
48	085	80356	Collin County	39,957
48	113	80356	Dallas County	415
48	397	80356	Rockwall County	1,055
49			**UTAH**	2,763,885
49		01310	American Fork city	26,263
49	049	01310	Utah County	26,263
49		07690	Bountiful city	42,552
49	011	07690	Davis County	42,552
49		11320	Cedar City city	28,857
49	021	11320	Iron County	28,857
49		13850	Clearfield city	30,112
49	011	13850	Davis County	30,112
49		16270	Cottonwood Heights city	33,433
49	035	16270	Salt Lake County	33,433
49		20120	Draper city	42,274
49	035	20120	Salt Lake County	40,532
49	049	20120	Utah County	1,742
49		36070	Holladay city	26,472
49	035	36070	Salt Lake County	26,472
49		40360	Kaysville city	27,300
49	011	40360	Davis County	27,300
49		43660	Layton city	67,311
49	011	43660	Davis County	67,311
49		44320	Lehi city	47,407
49	049	44320	Utah County	47,407

State code	Place code	County code	Geographic Area Name	2010 census population
49		45860	Logan city	48,174
49	005	45860	Cache County	48,174
49		49710	Midvale city	27,964
49	035	49710	Salt Lake County	27,964
49		53230	Murray city	46,746
49	035	53230	Salt Lake County	46,746
49		55980	Ogden city	82,825
49	057	55980	Weber County	82,825
49		57300	Orem city	88,328
49	049	57300	Utah County	88,328
49		60930	Pleasant Grove city	33,509
49	049	60930	Utah County	33,509
49		62470	Provo city	112,488
49	049	62470	Utah County	112,488
49		64340	Riverton city	38,753
49	035	64340	Salt Lake County	38,753
49		65110	Roy city	36,884
49	057	65110	Weber County	36,884
49		65330	St. George city	72,897
49	053	65330	Washington County	72,897
49		67000	Salt Lake City city	186,440
49	035	67000	Salt Lake County	186,440
49		67440	Sandy city	87,461
49	035	67440	Salt Lake County	87,461
49		70850	South Jordan city	50,418
49	035	70850	Salt Lake County	50,418
49		71290	Spanish Fork city	34,691
49	049	71290	Utah County	34,691
49		72280	Springville city	29,466
49	049	72280	Utah County	29,466
49		75360	Taylorsville city	58,652
49	035	75360	Salt Lake County	58,652
49		76680	Tooele city	31,605
49	045	76680	Tooele County	31,605
49		82950	West Jordan city	103,712
49	035	82950	Salt Lake County	103,712
49		83470	West Valley City city	129,480
49	035	83470	Salt Lake County	129,480
50			**VERMONT**	625,741
50		10675	Burlington city	42,417
50	007	10675	Chittenden County	42,417
51			**VIRGINIA**	8,001,024
51		01000	Alexandria city	139,966
51	510	01000	Alexandria city	139,966
51		07784	Blacksburg town	42,620
51	121	07784	Montgomery County	42,620
51		14968	Charlottesville city	43,475
51	540	14968	Charlottesville city	43,475
51		16000	Chesapeake city	222,209
51	550	16000	Chesapeake city	222,209
51		21344	Danville city	43,055
51	590	21344	Danville city	43,055
51		35000	Hampton city	137,436
51	650	35000	Hampton city	137,436
51		35624	Harrisonburg city	48,914
51	660	35624	Harrisonburg city	48,914
51		44984	Leesburg town	42,616
51	107	44984	Loudoun County	42,616
51		47672	Lynchburg city	75,568
51	680	47672	Lynchburg city	75,568
51		48952	Manassas city	37,821
51	683	48952	Manassas city	37,821
51		56000	Newport News city	180,719
51	700	56000	Newport News city	180,719
51		57000	Norfolk city	242,803
51	710	57000	Norfolk city	242,803
51		61832	Petersburg city	32,420
51	730	61832	Petersburg city	32,420
51		64000	Portsmouth city	95,535
51	740	64000	Portsmouth city	95,535
51		67000	Richmond city	204,214
51	760	67000	Richmond city	204,214
51		68000	Roanoke city	97,032
51	770	68000	Roanoke city	97,032
51		76432	Suffolk city	84,585
51	800	76432	Suffolk city	84,585
51		82000	Virginia Beach city	437,994
51	810	82000	Virginia Beach city	437,994
51		86720	Winchester city	26,203
51	840	86720	Winchester city	26,203
53			**WASHINGTON**	6,724,540
53		03180	Auburn city	70,180
53	033	03180	King County	62,761
53	053	03180	Pierce County	7,419
53		05210	Bellevue city	122,363
53	033	05210	King County	122,363
53		05280	Bellingham city	80,885
53	073	05280	Whatcom County	80,885
53		07380	Bothell city	33,505
53	033	07380	King County	17,090
53	061	07380	Snohomish County	16,415
53		07695	Bremerton city	37,729
53	035	07695	Kitsap County	37,729
53		08850	Burien city	33,313
53	033	08850	King County	33,313
53		17635	Des Moines city	29,673
53	033	17635	King County	29,673
53		20750	Edmonds city	39,709
53	061	20750	Snohomish County	39,709
53		22640	Everett city	103,019
53	061	22640	Snohomish County	103,019
53		23515	Federal Way city	89,306
53	033	23515	King County	89,306
53		33805	Issaquah city	30,434
53	033	33805	King County	30,434
53		35275	Kennewick city	73,917
53	005	35275	Benton County	73,917
53		35415	Kent city	92,411
53	033	35415	King County	92,411
53		35940	Kirkland city	48,787
53	033	35940	King County	48,787
53		36745	Lacey city	42,393
53	067	36745	Thurston County	42,393
53		37900	Lake Stevens city	28,069
53	061	37900	Snohomish County	28,069
53		38038	Lakewood city	58,163
53	053	38038	Pierce County	58,163
53		40245	Longview city	36,648
53	015	40245	Cowlitz County	36,648

State code	Place code	County code	Geographic Area Name	2010 census population
53		40840	Lynnwood city	35,836
53	061	40840	Snohomish County	35,836
53		43955	Marysville city	60,020
53	061	43955	Snohomish County	60,020
53		47560	Mount Vernon city	31,743
53	057	47560	Skagit County	31,743
53		51300	Olympia city	46,478
53	067	51300	Thurston County	46,478
53		53545	Pasco city	59,781
53	021	53545	Franklin County	59,781
53		56625	Pullman city	29,799
53	075	56625	Whitman County	29,799
53		56695	Puyallup city	37,022
53	053	56695	Pierce County	37,022
53		57535	Redmond city	54,144
53	033	57535	King County	54,144
53		57745	Renton city	90,927
53	033	57745	King County	90,927
53		58235	Richland city	48,058
53	005	58235	Benton County	48,058
53		61115	Sammamish city	45,780
53	033	61115	King County	45,780
53		62288	SeaTac city	26,909
53	033	62288	King County	26,909
53		63000	Seattle city	608,660
53	033	63000	King County	608,660
53		63960	Shoreline city	53,007
53	033	63960	King County	53,007
53		67000	Spokane city	208,916
53	063	67000	Spokane County	208,916
53		67167	Spokane Valley city	89,755
53	063	67167	Spokane County	89,755
53		70000	Tacoma city	198,397
53	053	70000	Pierce County	198,397
53		73465	University Place city	31,144
53	053	73465	Pierce County	31,144
53		74060	Vancouver city	161,791
53	011	74060	Clark County	161,791
53		75775	Walla Walla city	31,731
53	071	75775	Walla Walla County	31,731
53		77105	Wenatchee city	31,925
53	007	77105	Chelan County	31,925
53		80010	Yakima city	91,067
53	077	80010	Yakima County	91,067
54			**WEST VIRGINIA**	1,852,994
54		14600	Charleston city	51,400
54	039	14600	Kanawha County	51,400
54		39460	Huntington city	49,138
54	011	39460	Cabell County	45,214
54	099	39460	Wayne County	3,924
54		55756	Morgantown city	29,660
54	061	55756	Monongalia County	29,660
54		62140	Parkersburg city	31,492
54	107	62140	Wood County	31,492
54		86452	Wheeling city	28,486
54	051	86452	Marshall County	276
54	069	86452	Ohio County	28,210
55			**WISCONSIN**	5,686,986
55		02375	Appleton city	72,623
55	015	02375	Calumet County	11,088
55	087	02375	Outagamie County	60,045
55	139	02375	Winnebago County	1,490
55		06500	Beloit city	36,966
55	105	06500	Rock County	36,966
55		10025	Brookfield city	37,920
55	133	10025	Waukesha County	37,920
55		22300	Eau Claire city	65,883
55	017	22300	Chippewa County	1,981
55	035	22300	Eau Claire County	63,902
55		25950	Fitchburg city	25,260
55	025	25950	Dane County	25,260
55		26275	Fond du Lac city	43,021
55	039	26275	Fond du Lac County	43,021
55		27300	Franklin city	35,451
55	079	27300	Milwaukee County	35,451
55		31000	Green Bay city	104,057
55	009	31000	Brown County	104,057
55		31175	Greenfield city	36,720
55	079	31175	Milwaukee County	36,720
55		37825	Janesville city	63,575
55	105	37825	Rock County	63,575
55		39225	Kenosha city	99,218
55	059	39225	Kenosha County	99,218
55		40775	La Crosse city	51,320
55	063	40775	La Crosse County	51,320
55		48000	Madison city	233,209
55	025	48000	Dane County	233,209
55		48500	Manitowoc city	33,736
55	071	48500	Manitowoc County	33,736
55		51000	Menomonee Falls village	35,626
55	133	51000	Waukesha County	35,626
55		53000	Milwaukee city	594,833
55	079	53000	Milwaukee County	594,833
55	131	53000	Washington County	0
55	133	53000	Waukesha County	0
55		54875	Mount Pleasant village	26,197
55	101	54875	Racine County	26,197
55		55750	Neenah city	25,501
55	139	55750	Winnebago County	25,501
55		56375	New Berlin city	39,584
55	133	56375	Waukesha County	39,584
55		58800	Oak Creek city	34,451
55	079	58800	Milwaukee County	34,451
55		60500	Oshkosh city	66,083
55	139	60500	Winnebago County	66,083
55		66000	Racine city	78,860
55	101	66000	Racine County	78,860
55		72975	Sheboygan city	49,288
55	117	72975	Sheboygan County	49,288
55		77200	Stevens Point city	26,717
55	097	77200	Portage County	26,717
55		78600	Sun Prairie city	29,364
55	025	78600	Dane County	29,364
55		78650	Superior city	27,244
55	031	78650	Douglas County	27,244
55		84250	Waukesha city	70,718
55	133	84250	Waukesha County	70,718
55		84475	Wausau city	39,106
55	073	84475	Marathon County	39,106
55		84675	Wauwatosa city	46,396

State code	Place code	County code	Geographic Area Name	2010 census population
55	079	84675	Milwaukee County	46,396
55		85300	West Allis city	60,411
55	079	85300	Milwaukee County	60,411
55		85350	West Bend city	31,078
55	131	85350	Washington County	31,078
56			WYOMING	563,626
56		13150	Casper city	55,316

State code	Place code	County code	Geographic Area Name	2010 census population
56	025	13150	Natrona County	55,316
56		13900	Cheyenne city	59,466
56	021	13900	Laramie County	59,466
56		31855	Gillette city	29,087
56	005	31855	Campbell County	29,087
56		45050	Laramie city	30,816
56	001	45050	Albany County	30,816

INDEX

INDEX

LOS ALAMOS COUNTY LIBRARY
MESA PUBLIC LIBRARY
2400 CENTRAL AVENUE
LOS ALAMOS, NM 87544

WITHDRAWN

FOR REFERENCE
Not to be taken
from this room